Scholastic

DICTIONARY

of

American English

(Original title: Basic Dictionary of American English*)*

SCHOLASTIC BOOK SERVICES

NEW YORK · TORONTO · LONDON · AUCKLAND · SYDNEY · TOKYO

Table of Contents

30 29 28 27 26 25 24 23 22 21   8 9/7 01/8

Pronunciation Key

Accent Marks

A word that has only one syllable has no accent mark:

mast

When a word has two or more syllables, one syllable is usually pronounced louder than the others, that is, it is accented. The accented syllable is marked with a heavy accent mark ′:

mas′ter

Many words have both a strong accent and a weaker one. The weaker accent is marked with a lighter accent mark ′:

mas′ter piece′

Vowels

ā	as in fate, age	ī	as in bite, ice	ou	as in out, loud
ă	as in fat, map	ĭ	as in bit, if	o͞o	as in too, rule
â	as in fare, air	ō	as in note, go	o͝o	as in took, put
ä	as in father, art	ŏ	as in hot, box	ū	as in fuse, use
ē	as in be, even	ô	as in nor, order	ŭ	as in fun, up
ĕ	as in bet, ebb	oi	as in oil, boy	û	as in fur, term

Schwa (ə)

ə may stand for any vowel sounds in syllables that are not accented. It is called a schwa (shwä). When vowels are not accented, they are usually slurred over instead of being clearly pronounced. Most of them tend to have the same sound (ə), something like a short u, as in nut, but said less clearly. Notice in the following table how all the different vowels in the syllables that are not accented sound alike.

ə stands for:

- **a** as in ago [ə gō] china [chĭ′nə], senator [sĕn′ə tər]
- **e** as in open [ō′pən], opener [ō′pən ər]
- **i** as in peril [pĕr′əl], notify [nō′tə fī′]
- **o** as in lemon [lĕm′ən], lemonade [lĕm′ən ād′]
- **u** as in minus [mī′nəs], insulate [ĭn′sə lāt′]
- **ou** as in famous [fā′məs]
- **ai** as in mountain [moun′tən]
- **oi** as in tortoise [tôr′təs]

Consonants

b as in bed [bĕd].

ch as in chill [chĭl], catch [kăch].

d as in deed [dēd].

f as in fate [fāt].

g as in get [gĕt], leg [lĕg].

h as in hop [hŏp].

j as in jam [jăm], job [jŏb].

     also for g as in gem [jĕm].

k as in kin [kĭn], smoke [smōk];

     also for c as in coal [kōl], pack [păk].

l as in let [lĕt], bell [bĕl].

m as in men [mĕn], him [hĭm].

n as in not [nŏt], ran [răn].

ng as in song [sông], think [thĭngk].

p as in pup [pŭp].

r as in ride [rīd], store [stôr].

s as in sod [sŏd], must [mŭst];

     also for c as in cent [sĕnt], price [prīs].

sh as in she [shē], rush [rŭsh].

t as in tea [tē], hot [hŏt].

th as in thin [thĭn], bath [băth], breath [brĕth].

~~th~~ as in then [~~th~~ĕn], bathe [bā~~th~~], breathe [brē~~th~~].

v as in vat [văt], of [ŏv].

w as in we [wē].

y as in yet [yĕt].

z as in zero [zē′rō], buzz [bŭz].

     also for s as in wise [wīz].

hw for wh as in what [hwŏt], wheel [hwēl].

zh for s as in usual [ū′zho͞o əl], vision [vĭzh′ən];

     also for some g's as in mirage [mĭ räzh′]

(The English letters c, q, and x are not used in the pronunciation key. This is because c is pronounced like either k or s: cat [kăt], cent [sĕnt]. q is usually pronounced like k (as kw for qu): quick [kwĭk]. x is usually pronounced like ks or gz, or z at the beginning of a syllable: expand [ĕks pănd′]; exact [ĕg zăkt′]; xylophone [zī′le fōn′].)

EDITORIAL POLICY COMMITTEE

Professor Alvina Treut Burrows

Professor Sarah Lou Hammond

Professor Samuel I. Hayakawa

Professor Robert E. Krebs

Professor Wanda Robertson

Professor S. Stephenson Smith

SPECIAL EDITORS

Professor Irving Lorge	WORD LISTS
Professor Felix B. Giovanelli	DEFINITIONS AND ETYMOLOGIES
Ralph Weiman, Ph.D.	PRONUNCIATIONS
Mrs. Elizabeth Vazquez, B.S., MA.,	YOU AND YOUR DICTIONARY

Principal, Garden City Public Schools

EDITORIAL STAFF

EDITORIAL DIRECTOR: Morgan L. Walters

MANAGING EDITOR: William T. Atwood

SENIOR EDITORS:
Elizabeth C. Bigelow; John Darden; John Farrelly.

STAFF EDITORS AND ASSISTANTS:
Gerry Bothmer; Eden Force; Jack Freed; E. D. Gross; Dora Thea Hettwer; Gwendolyn H. Hicks; Ann Karry; David Lougée; Sofia Obolensky; Lilija Austrin Rinder; Elia Esther Sanchez; Charlotte Schenck.

ILLUSTRATIONS: Alan Young

DESIGN: Ernst Reichl Associates

You and Your Dictionary

Many people think of a dictionary as a book to be used occasionally to find out how to spell words or what a new word means. Your dictionary is a great deal more than that. You might even call it a treasure chest of our language, American English.

Try to imagine getting along without any language for a week, a day, or even an hour. Imagine not speaking, not hearing, not reading or writing, and not even thinking your language. You will quickly see that we can't get along without language.

On page 403 of this dictionary you will find the word **language.** Following it are numbered groups of words that tell the meanings of the word **language.** All together they tell that language includes all the ways people tell each other their ideas and feelings. But the most important part of language is described by the first numbered group of words:

> **lan·guage** (lăng′wĭj) **1** speech sounds and
> the way they are put together to tell some-
> thing: *Thoughts, feelings, and ideas are*
> *expressed in a* language.

This tells us that language is more than the spoken sounds we call words. Language consists of words carefully chosen and put together for a purpose. Think of a pile of bricks, a stack of boards, some sand, and some bags of cement. One can hardly tell one brick from another. However, when put together, the bricks, boards, sand, and cement may be a house. It may be small or large, beautiful or ugly, comfortable or uncomfortable. It may be any kind of a house, depending on the purpose and skill of the builder. In the same way, most words standing alone have little meaning; they need other words with them to give them the meaning and force we want them to have.

Words are only building materials of a language. To have a useful language, we must choose the right words and the right combinations of words to express our ideas or serve some other purpose. A "Please, may I" rather than a direct "I want" says the same thing but may get far different results. It may even mean the difference between a "Yes" or a "No."

If we want to excite someone's imagination, we may choose mysterious and romantic words. If you saw two books, "The Ghost of Blue Dragon Hill" and "The Haunted House on the Hill," which one would you pick up first?

On the other hand, we may choose the very simplest words and arrange them to express our feelings about something and to cause someone else to share our feelings. If we are describing a storm, we might say, "There is thunder and lightning." But notice how a poet, by her choice and arrangement of words, makes us feel the violence of the storm:

> Thunder crumples the sky,
> Lightning tears at it.

From "The Squall," by Leonora Speyer.
A Canopic Jar, E.P. Dutton and Co., 1921

Many books have been called treasure chests of language. Your dictionary, however, is a specially valuable one. It has been carefully arranged and written to help you learn more about words, the building materials of your language. It will help you to choose words and put them together to do what you want them to do. It will help you most if you learn how to use it quickly, what things it has to tell you, and how it tells them to you.

What Your Dictionary Does For You

On page 220 is the *entry* for the word **dictionary**. A dictionary entry is a word and all the information about that word that is given with it. Since **dictionary** is the first entry we will study, it is also given here:

8

dic·tion·ar·y (dĭk'shə nĕr'ĭ) **1** a book that lists words of a language in alphabetical order and explains them in the same language. A dictionary tells what words mean, how to pronounce them, and how to spell them. A dictionary may also show how words are used and where they come from. **2** book that lists words of one language and explains them in another language.

From this entry we can get six main ideas about what we find in dictionaries, as follows:

1. How to Find Words: a dictionary lists words in alphabetical order.
2. Word Meanings: a dictionary tells what words mean (in the various ways they can be used).
3. Pronunciation: a dictionary tells how to pronounce words.
4. Spelling: a dictionary tells how to spell words.
5. How to Use Words: a dictionary may show how to use words (in the right combinations and order to say what we want them to say).
6. Word Histories: a dictionary may tell us where words come from.

From here to page 45, you will find a great deal of information about these ideas that will help you get the most out of your dictionary. Some of this information you already know, but you need practice in using it. Other information may be new to you. All the information is valuable, but you need not try to learn it all at once. You should read it carefully and remember what you can. Then, as you need parts of it, you can come back to them and study them more carefully. You will find them listed in the Table of Contents.

How to Find Words

When you want to look up a word in your dictionary for some reason, you don't want to spend three minutes finding it. You already, of course, know the alphabet from **A** to **Z** and can say it rapidly, possibly in six seconds. You could find the first word in your dictionary that begins with **d** if you opened the book near the beginning and started turning pages. However, you would waste a lot of time finding words this way. This dictionary has two kinds of signposts to help you find a word quickly. They are:

1. Four dark blocks on the edges of the pages to help you open the book near the word you want.
2. Two *guide words* at the top of every page.

DIVIDING THE DICTIONARY INTO FOURTHS

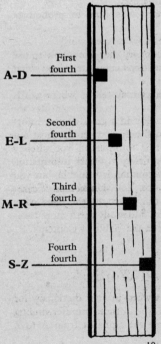

In the *Dictionary of American English*, four dark blocks have been placed on the edges of the pages to help you reach quickly the letter you need. These blocks divide your dictionary into four parts. The first dark block shows the location of all words beginning with **A, B, C,** or **D** (**A-D**), which make up about the first fourth of all of the words in the dictionary.

The letters **E, F, G, H, I, J, K,** and **L** (**E-L**) finish the first half, ending near the middle.

The letters **M, N, O, P, Q,** and **R** (**M-R**) begin near the middle and complete the third fourth.

The letters **S, T, U, V, W, X, Y,** and **Z** (**S-Z**) are in the last fourth.

You will save yourself much time if you remember which letters each of the dark blocks stands for. Suppose the word you are trying to find begins with **c.** If you open the book near the middle of the first dark block, you will be near the page where the **c**'s begin. If you want a word beginning with **m,** you open the book near the beginning of the third dark block.

On page 14 is a practice exercise that will help you use the dark blocks quickly. You might also want to spend a few minutes testing yourself. You think of a word and the letter it begins with. Then, using the dark blocks, you open your dictionary where you think you will find words beginning with the same letter. If you are wrong, close the book and try again, or use another word.

ALPHABETIZING AFTER THE FIRST LETTER

You know of course that you need to use more than the first letter to find a word in the dictionary. In this dictionary there are nearly 70 pages of words beginning with **c.** There are nearly 13 pages beginning with **ca.** There are over 3 pages beginning with **car.** Thus you may need to use the fourth, fifth, sixth, or even more letters of the beginning of a word.

If you look in your dictionary among the **d**'s on page 220 you will find the entry **dictionary.** The **d**'s come after the **a**'s, **b**'s, and **c**'s and before the **e**'s. **Di** comes after the **da**'s, **de**'s and before the **do**'s. **Dic** comes after the **dia**'s. **Dicti** comes after the **dicta**'s.

It is very important to be able to tell quickly whether one word comes before another. Sometimes, we need to use the seventh, or even the eleventh letter for alphabetizing words. For the following two words we need to use the tenth letter (the letter after the second **t**):

1 2 3 4 5 6 7 8 9 10 11 12
in·tro·duc·t i o n
in·tro·duc·to·ry

USING THE GUIDE WORDS

To help you quickly find a word in your dictionary, a *guide word* is printed in *bold* (very black) type at the top of each column of words. Thus, in turning pages you should look first at the guide words.

Suppose you want to find the word **aroma**. You open your dictionary in the first black block **(A-D)**. Now suppose you happen to open the book to page 85. The top of the page looks like this:

autocrat

au·to·crat (ô′tə krăt′) **1** ruler with un-limited power. **2** person who demands complete obedience to his will: *The father was the* autocrat *of the household.*

au·to·graph (ô′tə grăf′) **1** person's own signature or handwriting. **2** to write one's name on or in: *to* autograph *one's picture.*

au·to·mat·ic (ô′tə măt′ĭk) **1** self-operating; self-acting; capable of being run or worked

avid

av·a·rice (ăv′ə rĭs) greed for money: *Wealth beyond the dreams of* avarice.

av·a·ri·cious (ăv′ə rĭsh′əs) greedy; stingy; worshipping money. **av·a·ri·cious·ly.**

Ave. avenue.

a·venge (ə vĕnj′) to take revenge for: *The savage* avenged *his brother's death by tracking down the murderer.*

avenge oneself to get even; to get satis-

The word **autocrat** on the left tells the first word on the page. The word **avid** on the right tells the last word on the page. Since **aroma** should come before **autocrat** (**r** comes before **u**), you turn the pages on the left until you find a left-hand guide word that **aroma** follows:

arithmetic

a·rith·me·tic (ə rĭth′mə tĭk′) science of numbers; the art of using numbers to add, subtract, multiply, divide, etc.

Ariz. Arizona.

Ar·i·zo·na (ăr′ə zō′nə) State in the south-western part of the United States.

ark (ärk) **1** in the Bible, the ship that Noah built as a shelter from the Flood for him-self, his family, and a pair of each kind of animal. **2 Ark of the Covenant** the chest in which the ancient Hebrews kept the stone tablets containing the Ten Com-mandments. (Homonym: arc)

Ark. Arkansas.

Ar·kan·sas (är′kən sô) State in the south central part of the United States.

¹arm (ärm) **1** the part of the body between

arrange

ar·mor (är′mər) **1** a covering to protect the body while fighting: *Battle* armor *used to be made of metal or leather.* **2** the steel plating of a warship. **3** any protective cov-ering: *the* armor *of a turtle.* **4** to provide with a protective cov-ering.

armored (är′mərd) **1** covered with steel plates: *an* armored *truck.* **2** wearing ar-mor: *a knight* armored *in chain mail.*

ar·mor·y (är′mə rĭ) **1** a place where arms are stored. **2** large building containing

Chain and plate armor

Your word **aroma** should come between **arithmetic** and **arrange** (**o** comes between **i** and **r**), and therefore you will find it on that page. Check page 77 and see if **aroma** is there.

When you open your dictionary, you may find that your word should come after the guide word on the right (which tells the last word on the page). If so, turn the pages on the right, looking only at the guide words at the top of each page. When you find the two guide words which your word should fall between, you have found the page for your word.

To be able to find words quickly in your dictionary, you should:

1. Know what letters begin in each fourth of the book, as shown by the dark blocks.
2. Know how to alphabetize backwards and forwards with several letters in words.
3. Look first at the guide words and use them correctly.

If you are weak in any of these skills, your teacher may want you to practice with some of the following exercises.

PRACTICE EXERCISES

1. Copy the following letters in the order they are given here. Then fill the blanks with the letter that comes before in the alphabet and the letter that comes after. The first is done for you.

_c_ d _e_	__ h __	__ g __	__ k __	__ c __	__ j __
__ f __	__ o __	__ s __	__ m __	__ r __	__ n __
__ v __	__ b __	__ w __	__ x __	__ q __	__ l __
__ y __	__ i __	__ p __	__ t __	__ e __	__ u __

With a friend, read the list to each other to see if you can quickly give the letters that come before and after.

2. Here are groups of five words each. The words in each group begin with the same letter. Copy the words in each group in alphabetical order, using the second letter to arrange them.

apart	four	danger	several	people	mountain
about	flag	drop	strange	pleasant	many
among	front	dinner	shutter	pirate	muster
around	family	deck	slush	pride	merry
ashen	fixed	dove	skim	phone	mind

3. To practice using the fourth, fifth, or even the eleventh letter for alphabetizing words, copy each of the following groups in alphabetical order. Check yourself by finding them in the dictionary.

accommodating	extensive	judgment	perception
accommodate	extension	judicious	perceptible
accommodation	extend	judicial	percentage

4. This exercise will help you learn the letters that come in each fourth of this dictionary, as shown by the dark blocks. Make four headings on a sheet of paper as follows:

| *First fourth* | *Second fourth* | *Third fourth* | *Fourth fourth* |
| *A to D* | *E to L* | *M to R* | *S to Z* |

Now copy each word in the following list under its proper heading.

aghast	pincers	hyphen	scramble	blast
changeable	rampart	icicle	lengthways	knowledge
magnify	courage	evaporate	tyrant	author
novice	unfamiliar	quotient	banner	outrage
justice	yeast	warning	zoology	diagram
ghost	daughter	fortune	X-ray	vicious

5. Try to open your dictionary to words beginning with:
   y m d g p v j q b w r o c n t l a f s e u k
   You should practice this exercise until you can quickly open the dictionary near the letter you are looking for.

6. Copy these four pairs of guide words to make four column headings on a sheet of paper:
   airy — alibi   **alien — alligator**
   allot — aloud   **alpaca — am**
   Now write each word in the following list under the correct pair of guide words.

although	alert	allow	alike	altar
aisle	alphabet	alliance	algebra	alley
allude	alabaster	already	aluminum	allure
allay	aloof	allergy	alloy	alternate
album	alfalfa	alone	alight	alder
alongside	align	alcove	almanac	alluvial
alkali	akin	ally	allegiance	alto

Now rewrite the words in each of your new columns, this time putting them in alphabetical order. Check yourself by looking in your dictionary.

14

Word Meanings

One of the main purposes of a dictionary is to tell the meaning of words. Suppose you see in a book, "The aimless boy worried his parents," and suppose you have never before seen or heard the word "aimless." From the sentence you would know only that something was wrong with this boy. To find out exactly why the boy worried his parents, you would need to look in your dictionary for the *definition* of the word **aimless.** A definition is a word or group of words that tells a meaning of a word.

> **aim·less** (ām′lĭs) having no particular goal or purpose. **aim·less·ly.**

After reading the definition, you have a better understanding of what kind of boy he was—and even why he worried his parents.

LOOKING FOR THE RIGHT MEANINGS

Some words in our language have many meanings. When a word has more than one meaning, your dictionary numbers each definition: **1, 2, 3,** etc. The meaning most often used for a word is given in the number **1** definition. When a word has many meanings, the definitions are numbered according to how often people use the word with each meaning. When you are looking for a meaning of a word, you should skim quickly through all the definitions listed. For example:

> **log** (lŏg or lôg) **1** a length of wood from a tree trunk or branch as it comes from the tree. **2** to cut trees into logs and move them from the forest. **3** a float on the end of a long line, used for measuring the speed of a ship. **4** a book in which the speed and position of a ship, the weather, and daily happenings are recorded. **5** to enter (facts) in a ship's record book. **logged, log·ging.**

If you see the word "log" in a book about lumbering, it is likely to have meaning **1** or **2**. If you see the word in a sea story, however, you may have to decide from the sense of the sentence which of these meanings is the right one. Suppose you read, "We recorded our position in the log." If you don't know this meaning, you will have to read down to the fourth definition before the sentence makes sense. Or, suppose you read, "We put into port and took on a cargo of logs." You would probably decide that the first meaning is the right one, even in a sea story, because an entire shipload of single books or small instruments does not seem reasonable.

READING THE EXAMPLES

Often a definition alone is enough to tell the meaning of a word. Some words, however, are hard to understand from the definitions alone. Others have several similar meanings, and it may be hard to tell them apart. Still others have different meanings when they do different things to the other words in sentences.

Wherever an exact meaning of a word is not clear from the definition, your dictionary gives you an example of how the word is used in a sentence or a small part of a sentence (*phrase*). These examples are printed in *italics:*

> **i·tal·ic** (ĭ tăl′ĭk) **1** having to do with a type in which the letters slant to the right. **2** the style of type: *Most of this sentence is printed in* italic. **3 italics** letters in slanting type. In this book we use italics for all the words in an example except the word being explained. This is done so the reader can easily tell the example from the definition, and the word itself from the other words in the example.

After you have found the definition you think is right, look at the example to see if it is like the phrase or sentence in which you just found the word. They may be somewhat similar, and you will know you have the right meaning. For instance, you read in a newspaper article: "In my opinion, gambling leads to all sorts of license." You turn to the dictionary and read:

li·cense or **li·cence** (lī səns) **1** legal written permission (to do something): *a* license *to drive a taxi; a fishing* license. **2** to give a legal written permission (to do something): *In most states doctors must be* licensed *to practice.* **3** freedom or right (to ignore rules): *No one has* license *to damage public property.* **4** abuse of freedom; immoral action: *The soldiers showed unbelievable* license *when they entered the captured city.* **li·censed** or **li·cenced, li·cens·ing** or **li·cenc·ing.**

Definition **4** seems to be closest to the meaning of the writer. The example given is similar also, because both suggest bad behavior in general.

SUBSTITUTING A DEFINITION FOR A WORD

You may find that no example is given with the definition, or you may not be sure which definition and example give the best meaning for the sentence you have read. You can then try *substituting* a definition (the one you think is right) for the word in your sentence. Even when you think you have the right meaning, you can check yourself by substituting. Thus, in the sentence given above, "Gambling leads to all sorts of license," you could substitute either "abuse of freedom" or "immoral action" for "license." Either one will make sense in the sentence. Try it.

USING THE PICTURES

Your dictionary uses many pictures, as well as definitions and examples, to give the meanings of words:

right angle an angle like each of the four angles of a cross; a 90° angle.

Right angle

Right angles are studied in geometry, and are found almost everywhere. (Look at the corner of a book, a sheet of paper, or a flat wall.) This picture shows two right angles, while the definition tells you how many degrees are in a right angle.

gy·ro·scope (ji′rō-skōp′) wheel with a heavy rim and an axle mounted so that the axle is free to turn in any direction. When the wheel is spinning, the axle will stay pointing in the same direction, no matter how the outside frame is turned.

Gyroscope

Here the definition tells you what a gyroscope is, while the picture shows you how it is put together.

These two examples show that you need both pictures and definitions to understand the meanings of some words. It will help you to look at both the pictures and the definitions in your dictionary.

FINDING THE RIGHT MEANING FOR THE SUBJECT

Your dictionary *defines*, or explains the meanings of, words for any subject you wish to study. Words used in science, history, geography, mathematics, music, health, recreation, and art are carefully defined for their use in each particular subject. Sometimes the same word is defined for several subjects. Its right use or meaning depends on the subject wanted. For example, here is the entry **teeth,** as found on page 738:

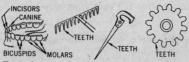
Teeth of a man, of a rake, of a saw, and of a gear

teeth (tēth) **1** the hard, white, bony parts of the jaw with which a person or animal bites or chews. A child about 10 years old has 28 teeth. **2** any toothlike part or thing: *the* teeth *of a saw;* teeth *of a cogwheel;* teeth *of a rake or comb.*

The pictures, the definitions, and the examples together give the meaning of "teeth" when used in different subjects:
Teeth, subject of nature study, health, and growth.
Teeth, subject of gardening.
Teeth, subject of woodworking.
Teeth, subject of mechanics.

KNOWING PREFIXES AND SUFFIXES

In our language we can form many new words from one *root word* (base word). We simply add certain beginning syllables, or *prefixes*, and ending syllables, or *suffixes*, to change the word and its meaning. Starting with the word "help," we can add the suffix **-ful** to get "help**ful**." Or we can add the suffix **-less** to get "help**less**." We can even add a second suffix to "helpful" to get "helpful**ness**." We can add the prefix **un-** (meaning "not") to either "helpful" or "helpfulness" to get "**un**helpful" or "**un**helpfulness."

You know that the suffix **-ly** is added to many *descriptive* words, such as "careful," to make them describe a way of doing something. In the phrase, *a* careful *man*, the word "careful" describes the man. In the sentence, "*The man drives* carefully," the word "carefully" describes the way the man is driving. In this dictionary most of these **-ly** words are given at the end of the entry for the root word:

> **cau·tious** (kô′shəs) careful to avoid danger or trouble: *a* cautious *driver*. **cau·tious·ly.**

There are a number of words that have a much greater change in meaning when an **-ly** is added to them. Still others have many meanings for the root word and only one for the **-ly** word. For all these words, the **-ly** word is listed and defined separately in its proper alphabetical position:

> **late** (lāt) **1** after the usual or expected time: *Spring came* late *this year*. **2** tardy: *He was* late *for work today*. **3** toward the end of a period of time: *The leaves began to fall* late *in autumn*. **4** of recent time or date; happening not long ago: *the* late *floods; his* late *illness*. **5** no longer living: *the* late *Mr. Barns*. **lat·er, lat·est** or **last.**

late·ly (lāt′lĭ) recently: *His work was poor, but it has improved* lately.

When you know the meaning of the prefix or suffix in a new word, you can often tell the meaning of the word. You think of the meaning of the root word and add the meaning of the prefix or suffix. Here are some examples:

dis- (dĭs) prefix meaning "not" or "the opposite of," such as: dis·like, dis·obey, dis·honest, dis·agree.

fore- (fôr) prefix meaning "before," such as: fore·noon, fore·see, fore·cast, fore·tell.

-ful (fəl) suffix meaning "full of" or "showing the quality of," such as: power·ful, thought·ful, thank·ful, help·ful.

Suppose we replace the suffix **-ful** by **-less** (lĭs), which is a suffix meaning "without" or "having no." Now each of the new words becomes the opposite of the word listed above under **-ful:** power·less, thought·less, thank·less, help·less.

Your dictionary gives you the meaning of prefixes and suffixes under their own entries. Here is the entry for **-ness:**

> **-ness** (nĭs) suffix used to change a descriptive word to a name word. It means "the condition or quality of being (what the descriptive word says)." The condition of being "hard" (descriptive word) is "hardness" (name word). The quality of being "good" (descriptive word) is "goodness" (name word): *a good man known for his* goodness.

Examples are: homesick·ness, near·ness, rough·ness and kind·ness.

Here is a list of the prefixes and suffixes that have entries in this dictionary:

20

Prefixes

ante-	in-	out-	tri-
anti-	inter-	post-	ultra-
bi-	mid-	pre-	un-
dis-	mis-	re-	under-
down-	non-	semi-	up-
fore-	over-	sub-	

Suffixes

-en	-ing	-ly	-ship
-er or -or	-ish	-ment	-some
-ful	-less	-ness	-ward
-hood	-like	-or	-y

Sometimes we are not sure of the meaning of a new word, even though we know the meaning of the root word, the prefix, and the suffix. The word may have taken on a special meaning in the many years it has been used. If you are not perfectly sure of the meaning of such a word, you should not trust your knowledge of its parts but should look it up in the dictionary. For example, **incorrect** means "not correct," but **intense** does not mean "not tense."

CHECKING ON WORDS YOU MISUSE

In our language we frequently confuse the meanings of certain pairs of words and how each should be used. Sometimes we do this because the words sound somewhat alike, though not exactly. Sometimes we have failed to look up a new word because the meaning seemed obvious in the sentence where we found it. Suppose you want to describe a flower. You say, "It has a large (pistol or pistil?) in its center." Which word would you use? They are defined on page 536.

Some words frequently confused are:

affect *and* effect	zinc *and* sink
learn *and* teach	color *and* collar
famous *and* infamous	accept *and* except
proceed *and* precede	through *and* thorough

21

Perhaps there are other words that are confusing to you. To be able to say exactly what you mean, be sure to look up any word you are not sure about. You may have to look up some words several times as you want to use them, before you will be really sure of them.

To help you understand the meanings of words, your dictionary:

1. Numbers the definitions according to how often people use the word with each meaning.
2. Uses a phrase or sentence in italics to make the meaning clear.
3. Uses pictures to help define the word and clarify meanings.
4. Gives -ly words as separate entries where the meaning is not quickly clear from the meaning of the root word.
5. Defines prefixes and suffixes.

To find the right meaning for a word you have read or heard, you should:

1. Skim through all numbered definitions in the entry.
2. Choose the definition that seems to give the meaning you are looking for.
3. Compare the phrase or sentence in italics with your own phrase or sentence where you found the word or want to use it.
4. Try substituting the dictionary definition in your own phrase or sentence.
5. Study the picture with the entry, if there is one.

PRACTICE EXERCISES

1. Some words have several meanings. Copy from this dictionary two definitions for each of the following words. Write a new sentence to illustrate each meaning.

loud	clear	due	empty	freeze
heave	jam	reserve	support	wide

22

2. Find the entry **check** in this dictionary. Read the different meanings listed and the examples given after each. Then copy the following sentences containing the word **check**. Read them carefully and note down the number of the definition that gives the meaning of **check** in each sentence. If a sentence is given as an example, copy it, and compare the two sentences.

    a. I must hurry to the bank to cash my check.
       Definition No. _____ *Example* _____
    b. Poor man, he has lost his coat check.
       Definition No. _____ *Example* _____
    c. Remember to check your subtraction problems by adding.
       Definition No. _____ *Example* _____
    d. The blue and white check of your dress is very becoming.
       Definition No. _____ *Example* _____

Now write sentence **d,** substituting the proper numbered definition for the word **check.**

3. On page 21 are eight pairs of words that are often confused and misused. Look up their meanings and write sentences using one of each pair of words.

4. Copy the following root words and add either a prefix or a suffix to each to make a new word. Use your dictionary to check on the meaning. (See the list of prefixes and suffixes, page 21.)

| real | enter | hope | equal | hurt |
| proper | faith | dark | fold | witch |

5. Find in your dictionary the underlined words in the following paragraph. Read the different meanings silently. Find the definition that clearly gives the meaning of the word as used in this paragraph. Write the number of the definition above the word. Be prepared to read the definition aloud and to discuss why you chose it.

Food is the prime attraction for birds. Planting of berry-bearing trees and shrubs will provide natural food during the summer. Artificial feeding is usually necessary beginning late in October. No elaborate feeding devices need be built; dried bread or birdseed can be thrown on the lawn. Some birds prefer ground feeding. To protect the food from snow or animals, an elevated feeding station is helpful.

Pronunciation

You don't have to be told how to pronounce "road," "sky," "mother," or many other words. You already pronounce them the way your parents and teachers and most of the people in your community pronounce them. You do have to learn to pronounce new words that you see in print or want to use in speaking. Your dictionary tells you how to pronounce new words as they are pronounced by the educated people in your community.

In almost all of the entries in your dictionary, after each word is printed in bold type, it is written again and enclosed in *parentheses* (two curved lines). This second printing of the word is to show how to pronounce the word.

> **dic·tion·ar·y** (dĭk′shə nĕr′ĭ)
> **i·tal·ic** (ĭ tăl′ĭk)
> **check** (chĕk)

In the parentheses the word is written in symbols that tell you the sounds you hear rather than the letters you spell. To learn to *read sounds*, you should say the word aloud as you look at the sound symbols. Some of the sound symbols are the same as the letters in the word. This is true of most of the consonants.

Say dĭk′shə nĕr′ĭ, ĭ tăl′ĭk, chĕk. What sounds do you hear? Why was the first syllable **dic** changed to dĭk? The **tion** becomes shə and the **n** is added to the next sound syllable. You know the sound of **sh,** but the ə may be new to you. The ə stands for any vowel sounds that are slurred over. The nĕr replaces the **ar,** and the **y** becomes ĭ. Thus the sound symbols tell us to say dĭk′shə nĕr′ĭ. The first syllable has a heavy (black) *accent mark*. The third syllable has a lighter accent mark. In the word **italic,** the second syllable has the accent (ĭ tăl′ĭk).

ACCENT MARKS

A heavy accent mark (′) is used to show which syllable receives the strongest stress. A lighter mark (′) indicates a lighter stress. Words of one syllable have no accent marks: **ran** (răn); **mast** (măst); **check** (chĕk).

24

When a word has two or more syllables, one syllable is pronounced with greater force than the others, that is, it is accented. The accented syllable is marked with a heavy accent mark: **mas′ter, self″ish, wood″en.**

Many words of three or more syllables have both a strong accent and a weaker one. The weaker accent is marked with a lighter accent mark. **dic′tion ar′y, mas′ter piece′, war′like′.**

Some words have two strongly accented syllables such as: **hard″heart′ed, clear″cut′.**

In some English words the accent changes with the particular meaning such as:

> **pres′ent** *and* **pre sent′**
> **con′duct** *and* **con duct′**

In some words, a letter of the word may change in sound with different uses of the word:

> **abuse** (ə būz′) and **abuse** (ə būs′)

In this dictionary, to help you pronounce the word for the meaning you want, these words are listed separately:

> ¹**a·buse** (ə būz′) **1** to treat badly or harshly:
> *The boy* abuses *the dog by twisting his tail.*
> **2** to make wrong use of: *The manager*
> abused *his authority. He* abused *his host's*
> *hospitality.* **3** to use insulting language to
> or about: *The candidates* abused *each other*
> *during the campaign.* **a·bused, a·bus·ing.**
> ²**a·buse** (ə būs′) **1** wrong or harsh treat-
> ment. **2** wrong use; misuse: *the abuse of*
> *our power.* **3** corrupt custom or practice:
> *Such* abuses *as bribery or graft are punish-*
> *able by law.* **4** insulting language.

You already know many of the sound symbols in your dictionary, but a few of them may be new to you. They are all printed as part of the Pronunciation Key in the front of the book. Many of them are also printed at the bottom of every right-hand page of entries:

---

fāte, făt, fâre, fär; bē, bĕt; bīte, bĭt; nō, nŏt, nôr; fūse, fŭn, fûr; tōō, tŏŏk; foil; foul; thin; ~~then~~;
hw for wh as in *wh*at; zh for s as in u*s*ual; ə for a, e, i, o, u, as in *a*go, lin*e*n, per*i*l, at*o*m, min*u*s

This list contains all the sound symbols except those consonants which have only one pronunciation.

THE VOWEL SOUNDS

The five vowels A, E, I, O, U of our English language have many different sounds. We use the sound symbols to tell which sound is needed. This dictionary has a different symbol for each vowel sound.

First, there are *six* long vowel sounds:

ā as in fate, age, great	ō as in note, go, boat
ē as in be, even, seen	ū as in fuse, use
ī as in bite, ice, height	o͞o as in too, rule, threw

Second, there are *six* short vowel sounds:

ă as in fat, map	ŏ as in hot, box
ĕ as in bet, ebb	ŭ as in fun, up
ĭ as in bit, if	o͝o as in took, put

Third, there are *three* vowel sounds that fall between the short and the long. Perhaps you could remember that with two of these vowels we start out to make them long but change them to say **r** following them: hâre, môre. (If you try to say them with the long sound you will see how preparing to say the **r** changes the vowel.) With the other vowel sound we start out with a short sound and change the vowel to say the **r**: fûr. Practice with someone and say fate, fat, fare; no, not, nor; fuse, fun, fur. Practice speaking and listening for the change in the vowel sound.

The **a** vowel has still another sound, neither short, long, nor in between. It is something like a short **o** (ŏ) but heavier. It too is represented by a sound symbol: ä as in father, far.

Two other vowel sounds you know are those of the **oi** as in oil, boy; and the **ou,** as in out, loud, how.

Finally, as you have seen, there is one sound symbol that is not an ordinary letter or a letter plus a mark. It is the symbol ə, called a schwa (shwä). The ə may stand for any vowel sounds in syllables that are not accented. When vowels are not accented, they are usually slurred over instead of being pronounced. Most of them tend to have the same sound (ə), something like a short **u,** as in nut, but said less clearly. Say the words in the following list. Notice how the vowels that are not accented tend to sound alike:

> ə stands for:
> a as in ago [ə gō′], china [chī′nə], senator [sĕn′ə tər]
> e as in open [ō′pən], opener [ō′pən ər]
> i as in peril [pĕr′əl], notify [nō′tə fī′]
> o as in lemon [lĕm′ən], lemonade [lĕm′ən ād′]
> u as in minus [mī′nəs], insulate [ĭn′sə lāt′]
> ou as in famous [fā′məs]
> ai as in mountain [moun′tən]
> oi as in tortoise [tôr′təs]

The vowel sounds to practice are six long (ā, ē, ī, ō, ū, o͞o), six short (ă, ĕ, ĭ, ŏ, ŭ, o͝o), three in between (â, ô, û), a heavier short vowel sound (ä), the oi and ou, and the ə (schwa). The exercises at the end of this section will suggest ways of practicing the vowel sounds.

THE CONSONANT SOUNDS

In the pronunciation key for the twenty-one consonants, the letters, **c, q,** and **x** are not used. This is because **c** is either pronounced like **k** or **s: cat** (kăt), **cent** (sĕnt); **q** is usually pronounced like **k,** or **kw** for **qu** as **quick** (kwĭk). **X** is usually pronounced like **ks** or **gz,** or **z** at the beginning of a syllable: **expand** (ĕks pănd′), **exact** (ĕg zăkt′), **xylophone** (zī′lə fōn′).

For other consonants, the letter stands for the sound symbol with only two exceptions: 1. **zh** is used as a symbol for the **s** as in **usual** (ū′zho͞o əl) or **vision** (vĭzh′ən), and also for some **g**'s as in **mirage** (mĭ räzh′); 2. **hw** is used for **wh** as in **what** (hwŏt), **wheel** (hwēl). (Notice that when you say the **wh** in **what,** you are really saying **hw.**)

It takes practice to use the pronunciation key of your dictionary quickly. You should practice the symbols you know as well as those that are new to you. If the word has two pronunciations in all its meanings, they are shown thus:

27

en·dure (ĕn dŏŏr′ or ĕn dyŏŏr′) **1** to bear bravely; suffer: *The pioneers* endured *many hardships.* **2** to bear; put up with; tolerate: *She cannot* endure *cold weather.* **3** to continue to exist; last: *Lincoln's name will* endure *forever.* **en·dured, en·dur·ing.**

To be able to use your dictionary effectively for pronunciations, you should:

1. Always look at the sound symbols in the parentheses to see if you know the pronunciation.
2. Learn the sound symbols and the sounds they stand for. They are given in the pronunciation key in the front of your dictionary.
3. Use the short key at the bottom of the right-hand pages for a quick reminder.
4. Practice saying the sound symbols in words or syllables.

PRACTICE EXERCISES

1. The following words have two or more syllables. Copy them, breaking them into syllables. Place the accent marks where they belong. Practice saying each word as you write it in syllables. Did you place the accent on the right syllable?

murmur	human	cedar	notion	forest	transom
doctor	parent	special	flavor	elephant	skipper
column	crickets	dwelling	lumber	famous	standing

2. Extend the pronunciation key given in the front of your dictionary by finding words of more than one syllable to illustrate each vowel sound. Here is an example:

   ā *as in* fate, age, *and in* station, celebrate, estimation.

3. In the list of words in Exercise 1, the first vowel is either short, long, or in between because of the r. On your copy, put the right mark (˘, ¯, *or* ^) on the first vowel.

4. Some of the words in Exercise 1 have vowels that are pronounced with a schwa. Draw a line through those vowels on your copy. Look up the words to see if all your vowel marks are right. Correct your copy.

5. Here is a list of words that have a vowel pronounced o͟u. Look them up and check the pronunciations:

28

cow	allow	rout	tower
thou	aloud	towel	sour

Some words that are spelled with **ou** are not pronounced <u>ou</u>.
Write five such words. Check your choices in the dictionary.

6. The consonant blend of **th** is sometimes *voiced* (sounded in the throat) as in **then, bathe, breathe**. (Say these words aloud and notice the sound in your throat as you begin them.) In many other words the **th** is not voiced: **thin, both, breath**. Use your dictionary and first look up **then, bathe, breathe**. How is the **th** marked? Then look up **thin, both, breath**.
Read through the words beginning with **th** on pages 744-746 and compare your own pronunciation with the sound symbols as written. In which of the following words is the **th** voiced?

theater	the	thou	theory
than	thanksgiving	there	thigh

7. Turn to page 817 and notice the many words beginning with **wh** (**whack, whale,** etc.). Study the pronunciation symbol for **wh**. In very early English this sound was written **hw** (or **hu**) instead of **wh**. No one is sure why the spelling was changed to **wh**. Look at some of the entries beginning with **wh**. What happens when the **wh** is followed by the vowel **o**?

8. In the pronunciation key, the **g** is used only for the hard **g** sound, as in **get**. Copy the words in the following list that have this sound.

guess	sugar	gush	gems	hug
sag	just	cage	grace	huge
sage	genius	usual	goes	ghost

9. In the pronunciation key, the s̱ is used only for the hissing **s** sound as in **soon, geese, cent, price**. From the list of words in exercise 8, copy the words that have this sound.

10. Here are four pairs of words that are pronounced differently when they are used differently in sentences:

> [1]**contest** *and* [2]**contest**　　　　[1]**conflict** *and* [2]**conflict**
> [1]**suspect** *and* [2]**suspect**　　　　[1]**excuse** *and* [2]**excuse**

Look up these words and notice the pronunciation and the meanings of each. Write four sentences using one word from each pair. Then copy the proper pronunciation of the word at the end of its sentence.

Spelling

In our language, many words are not spelled as they are pronounced. Your dictionary will help you to check when you are not sure of the spelling of a word and to study the spelling of new words.

DIVIDING WORDS INTO SYLLABLES

One way your dictionary helps you in spelling is by dividing words into syllables for you. You have learned three general rules that usually work for breaking words into syllables:

1. When one consonant stands between two vowels, the consonant usually begins the second syllable. Example: **ca·noe.**
2. When two consonants stand between two vowels, the first consonant usually ends the first syllable. Example: **bet·ter.**
3. When a word ends in *le*, the consonant before *le* begins the last syllable: Example: **am·ble.**

Sometimes rules 1 and 2 do not apply:

> **hon·or   loos·en   co·bra   ca·price**

If you are not sure of the syllables in a word, your dictionary will tell you. Each word with more than one syllable is given first with small dots to separate the syllables.

> **dis·cour·age   sat·is·fac·to·ry**

Words with one syllable are printed solid.

> **check   gay   break**

Seeing words divided into syllables helps us to include all the letters when we write and spell the words. It also helps us to read words that are partly on one line and partly on the next. When, in your writing, you have to break a long word at the end of a line, look in your dictionary to see how to do it.

WORDS WITH MORE THAN ONE SPELLING

Many words have more than one spelling. If two spellings are commonly used, your dictionary gives both. The first spelling is the one more often used:

> **en·roll·ment** or **en·rol·ment** (ĕn rōl′mənt)

If a word has two spellings but one is not often used, it may be listed at the end of the definition after the words, "Also spelled":

> **gai·e·ty** (gā′ə tï) **1** merriment; cheerfulness; glee: *New Year's is a time of* gaiety **2** showiness; finery: *the* gaiety *of the Christmas decorations.* **gai·e·ties.** Also spelled **gay·e·ty.**

FORMING PLURALS

As you have seen, we can form a number of different words from one root word by adding prefixes and suffixes. We also add endings to many words for the following reasons:

1. With nouns (name words), to change the number: hat, hats (**s**)
2. With adjectives or adverbs, to mean more or most: fast, faster, fastest (**er, est**)
3. With verbs (action words), to change the time: look, looked, looking (**ed, ing**)

When we add an **s** to a noun to change the number of things it means (book, books), we are forming a *plural:*

> **plu·ral** (plŏŏr′əl) **1** indicating more than one. **2** form of a word showing that more than one is meant. The plural of "cat" is "cats," of "child" is "children."

To form some plurals, we must add **es**: ax, axes. Often we have to change the spelling of the root word before we add **es**: thief, thieves; story, stories.

Sometimes to form a plural we have to change the spelling and pronunciation of the root word: man, men; goose, geese.

To help you with spelling, your dictionary gives the plurals of all words that change the spelling of the root word; the plural form is given near the end of the entry:

> **tap·es·try** (tăp′ĭs trï) fabric that is woven with pictures or designs and usually hung on walls. **tap·es·tries.**
>
> **thief** (thēf) one who steals, especially one who steals secretly rather than by force **thieves.**

For some words, the plural is exactly the same as the root word:

bi·son (bī′sən) oxlike animal of North America also known as the buffalo. It has a shaggy mane and a large hump. pl. **bi·son.**

At the end of this entry, we see: pl. **bi·son.** This means that we always use "bison" whether we are speaking of only one bison or several bison.

CHANGING ADJECTIVES AND ADVERBS

To change or give additional meaning to certain adjectives and adverbs, **er** or **est** is added to the root word: fast, fast**er**, fast**est.** When we add **er** to the root word fast (fast**er**), the new word means "more fast." When we add **est** (fast**est**), the new word means the most fast. Sometimes we need to change the spelling of the root word to add **er** or **est.** Your dictionary gives the complete spelling of the "more" and "most" forms where there is a change in the root word:

taw·ny (tô′nĭ) of a brownish-yellow color:
a tawny *lion* **taw·ni·er, taw·ni·est.**

CHANGING THE TIME OF VERBS

To change verbs to mean a different time, we may add **ed** or **ing** to the root word: ask, ask**ed,** ask**ing.** Often we have to add a letter to the root word or drop a letter. For these words your dictionary spells the different time forms at the end of the entry:

drip (drĭp) **1** to fall or let fall in drops:
Water drips *from the trees. The spigot* drips
2 a falling in drops: *a steady* drip *from the
roof.* **dripped, drip·ping.**
tel·e·vise (tĕl′ə vīz′) to send a still or moving picture over a distance by television:
The boxing match will be televised. **tel·e·
vised, tel·e·vis·ing.**

32

For some verbs, we have to change the root word to change the time: sing, sang, sung, singing; go, went, gone, going. These are also spelled at the end of the entry:

> **strive** (striv) **1** to try hard; make an effort: *You must* strive *for better marks.* **2** to struggle; battle: *The sailboat* strove *against the heavy wind.* **strove, striv·en, striv·ing.**

Often a word is an adjective or adverb and also a verb, and can use the **–er** and **–est** endings as well as the **–ed, –ing** and even the **–ly**:

> **bus·y** (biz′ĭ) **1** at work; not idle; active. **2** crowded with activity: *a* busy *day; a* busy *street.* **3** to make or keep busy: *Tim* busied *himself with the puzzle until it was time to go.* **bus·i·er, bus·i·est; bus·ied, bus·y·ing; bus·i·ly.**

Sometimes we refer to these various forms of a word as *inflected forms.* The endings are added to fit the use we wish to make of the word in a sentence.

FINDING HOMONYMS

In the English language we have a group of words that are pronounced the same but are not spelled alike and have very different meanings. These words are called *homonyms:*

> **hom·o·nym** (hŏm′ə nim) word that sounds the same as another but has a different spelling and meaning. "Deer" and "dear" are homonyms.

If you look up **rain, reign,** and **rein** in your dictionary, you will find they are all pronounced alike (rān). When we come across these words in sentences, we usually know exactly what they mean. When we hear them used with other words, we can usually tell which (rān) is meant. But when we want to write them, we sometimes forget which spelling goes with the meaning we want. Worse still, when we don't know how to spell them, we even have trouble finding them in the dictionary. This dictionary, however, tells you how to find the spelling you want. Look at these three entries from pages 582 and 596, and notice that they are pronounced alike:

rain (rān) **1** moisture condensed from the air and falling in drops. **2** to fall in drops of condensed moisture from the air. **3** a fall or shower of moisture in drops: *The heavy* rains *flooded the land.* **4** shower of anything: *a* rain *of blessings.* **5** to shower upon; give or offer abundantly: *Their friends* rained *presents on the bride and groom.* (Homonyms: reign, rein)

reign (rān) **1** period of rule, as of a king: *The American Revolution was fought during the* reign *of George III.* **2** to rule as a monarch. **3** to prevail: *Happiness* reigned *in every heart at the news of victory.* (Homonyms: rain, rein)

rein (rān) **1** one of the two long straps attached to the bit of a horse to guide and control it. **2** control; something that holds in check: *Keep a tight* rein *on your temper.* **3** to check; to control. (Homonyms: rain, reign)

Now suppose you want to use the word "reign" in a story about a kingdom, but you can't remember how to spell it. You do know how to spell "rain," and you know the two words sound alike. All you need to do is look up the word you know (**rain**) and then look at the last line of the entry, (Homonyms: reign, rein). When two homonyms are listed, you will usually recognize the one you want. However, if you don't know whether **reign** or **rein** is the spelling you want, you can look them up to check the meaning.

Most people like puns if they are witty and clever. The best puns are made on homonyms, groups of words that sound exactly alike, rather than words that are intentionally pronounced wrongly to make them sound alike.

Most people also like tongue twisters. Perhaps you would like to call them spelling teasers. Here are two examples:

1.

The playwright writes right about the rites of holidays.

2.

The barefoot ape,
Ran from the barefoot bear,
He stepped in the trap,
Set for the barefoot hare.
The trap caught the hair,

Of the ape's foot bare,
Instead of the hair,
Of the barefoot bear
Or the hair,
Of the barefoot hare.

When you hear, "Ted saw a bear," you should immediately know that he means "bear" and not "bare." Also, a trap set for a "hare" is not for a "hair." Perhaps you can think of some other spelling teasers or tongue twisters using homonyms.

One of the best ways to improve your spelling is to use your dictionary to check your own mistakes. To help you with spelling, your dictionary:

1. Divides words into syllables.
2. Shows the plurals of nouns.
3. Shows the "more" and "most" forms of adjectives and adverbs.
4. Shows the time forms of nouns.
5. Tells you how to find the spelling of homonyms.

To use your dictionary quickly and effectively for spelling, you should:

1. Look for alternate spellings and decide which ones are right for you.
2. Look at the ends of the entries for spelling changes of plurals, adjectives or adverbs, and verbs.
3. Watch out for homonyms at the end of an entry.

PRACTICE EXERCISES

1. Here is a rough draft of the beginning of John's adventure story. He has spelled some words incorrectly, and should use his dictionary to correct them. Copy the story, spelling the words correctly.

   The mornin brok clear and cold as I roled over in my sleeping bag. "Time to raise and built the fire," shouted my parner. "Letuce be up! The bares wil not wayt."

How to Use Words

It takes a long time to learn to use our language well. It also takes practice and very frequent use of the dictionary. To use words well, we must:

1. Be sure to select the words that mean exactly what we want to say.
2. Pronounce the words correctly when we are speaking.
3. Spell the words correctly when we write.
4. Put the words together in the right order.

In the last three sections you have studied word meanings, pronunciation, and spelling, and how your dictionary can help you with them. This section will tell you how your dictionary can help you put words together in the right order to say what you want to say.

On page 16 we saw how the examples in italics help us to know the meanings of words. These examples also show how words are put together in sentences and phrases to say what we want them to say. Look at the entry **telegraph**:

> **tel·e·graph** (tĕl′ə grăf′) **1** electric or radio device for sending and receiving messages. **2** to send (a message) by such a device: *Please* telegraph *the news to me, as soon as you can. Please* telegraph *me as soon as you can. Please* telegraph.

Three examples are given for definition **2.** They show that telegraph means to send a message about something to someone, or simply to send a message to someone. The last example makes sense because you know that it means "telegraph me."

Now look up the word **bring** on page 120. Notice that one can bring something to someone at some place. But if we say only "Please bring," we would not express anything. We use "telegraph" without saying what message we are sending, but we can't use "bring" without saying what we are bringing. When we use "bring," we must add other words to tell what is meant.

Your dictionary uses examples in italics to show how different words are used differently. The examples also show how the different forms of verbs are used. Look at the definition of the word write:

> **write** (rit) **1** to make letters or words with a pen, pencil, chalk or the like: *Lucy could write when she was five.* **2** to express in words or symbols with a pen, pencil, etc.: *The teacher is* writing *the answers on the blackboard.* **3** to tell in a letter: *Susan has* written *twice that she is having a wonderful time.* **4** to produce stories or compose music: *Grimm* wrote *fairy tales. Beethoven* wrote *nine symphonies.* **5** to show by leaving marks, traces, or signs: *Tim's guilt was* written *all over his face.*
> **write down** to put into writing: *Don't try to remember it;* write *it* down.
> **write out** to write in full: *The reporter* wrote out *his notes of the meeting.*
> **write up** to describe in detail by writing: *For homework, you are to* write up *the experiment you saw today.*
> **wrote, writ·ten, writ·ing.** (Homonyms: right, rite, wright)

Notice that there are examples using **write, wrote, writing,** and **written** to show how they are used to mean different times.

If you read the examples in italics every time you look up words, you will find other ways they help you to use words. As you read the examples, you will get a better idea of sentence patterns in English. The examples will also show you how to use words such as **for, like, through, since, however,** etc., that are used in many different ways.

IDIOMS

American English has hundreds of thousands of words. Most people, however, cannot learn more than a small portion of these well enough to use them accurately. Yet the ideas that people wish to express are countless, going far beyond all the words in our treasure chest of language.

We can understand, then, that people, instead of learning more and more words, use combinations of simple words to express their ideas. Over a long period of time, people use the same combinations of words often because they are very useful. They mean things that people often want to say. These combinations of words are called *idioms:*

> **id·i·om** (ĭd′ĭ əm) **1** a group of words whose meaning must be known as a whole, for it cannot be learned from the meaning of these same words used separately. "To go back on," for example, doesn't mean "to move backward onto" but "to betray or fail." **2** the language used by the people of a certain region, group, class, etc.: *the American* idiom; *the* idiom *of sailors.* **3** a particular person's way of using words: *Shakespeare's* idiom.

Many idioms mean what the separate words in them say, but with special meaning. For example, the words "at home" mean "at (my, your, someone's) home." They can also mean "ready to receive callers." People just learning the English language may not understand you if you use the words "at home" for the second meaning.

A good dictionary not only has to explain words; it should also explain idioms. Otherwise people who understand only the words would never find the meaning of the special word combinations. Your dictionary gives you many idioms. They are listed with the entry of the key word. Each idiom is clearly defined. Then, if there are special reasons for using one idiom rather than another, examples are given in italics to show which idiom you should use for your purpose.

Look back at the entry **write** (page 37). Near the end of the entry, three idioms are given:

> **write down** to put into writing: *Don't try to remember it;* write *it* down.
> **write out** to write in full: *The reporter* wrote out *his notes of the meeting.*
> **write up** to describe in detail by writing: *For homework, you are to* write up *the experiment you saw today.*

For all these definitions and examples, the word "write" would be enough if the reader or listener knew the intention of the speaker or writer. However, the addition of the extra words makes the exact meaning clearer than the word "write" alone.

Idioms that begin with action words are listed in black type at the end of the entry for the beginning word. Each idiom has a separate paragraph so that it can easily be seen in alphabetical order (**write, write down, write out, write up**).

Other kinds of idioms are given in black type but are numbered along with the other meanings of the key word. Look up the entry **time**. Read all the definitions from 1 to 11. Near the end of the entry you will find the following idioms:

> **12 for the time being** for now; for the present: *We will stay here* for the time being. **13 in time** (**1**) early enough: *Will you be home* in time *for dinner?* (**2**) eventually: In time, *I hope to learn Spanish.* **14 on time** not late: *He usually arrives* on time. **15 lose time** to go at too slow a rate: *The train* lost time *between Chicago and St. Louis.* **16 gain time** (**1**) to go at too fast a rate: *Our kitchen clock* gains time. (**2**) to take less time: *to* gain time *by a short cut.* **17 behind the times** not up-to-date on current events, ideas, etc.; old-fashioned: *He was* behind the times *in his scientific views.* **18 time out of mind** longer than anyone can remember. **19 take time out** to set aside a period of time for some special purpose: *Let's* take time out *for lunch.* **timed, tim·ing.** (Homonym: thyme)

Most of these idioms would not mean very much if we read them word by word. How can one "gain time" when time is always passing? Nevertheless, the idiom "gain time" expresses two ideas that would otherwise need many more words.

The idioms in your dictionary show you how to use word combinations so that you will be quickly understood by all listeners. Take time to look at the idioms when you look up a word. One of them may be necessary for the exact meaning you are looking for.

SYNONYMS

Often we repeat the same words when other words would be better for our particular purpose. For example, we are likely to say "northern lights" instead of "aurora borealis":

> **au·ror·a bor·e·al·is** (ô rôr′ə bôr′ĭ ăl′ĭs)
> glowing or flickering streamers of light
> seen at night in the northern sky; the
> northern lights.

The two can be interchanged, one in place of the other, with the same meaning. However, if we were asked to write a science report about the lights of the north, we would use "aurora borealis." When two words can be interchanged with about the same meaning, they are called *synonyms:*

The people who wrote your dictionary have tried to write all of the definitions in simple words that all can understand. Often, after the simple definition, the dictionary will give another word, or synonym, that means about the same thing. As we learn to use more of the synonyms, we are able to vary our speech and writing so that they are more interesting. For example, if you saw the following paragraph in a story, you might want to throw the book away:

> "Hold the ladder. Do you think it will
> hold me? I hold that it will. Please! hold
> still! I'll hold back until you stop holding
> forth."

If you look up the entry **hold,** you will find other words for most of these meanings. Some are given near the beginning of a numbered definition; others at the end. Try rewriting the paragraph with words you find in the entry **hold.**

Your dictionary gives many synonyms to help you make your speech and writing more interesting.

ADDING TO YOUR VOCABULARY

We often use the dictionary to look up words we find in our reading and do not understand. The headlines of the newspaper state "Crew Abandons Ship." We may need to look up the word "abandon."

> **a·ban·don** (ə băn'dən) **1** to give up completely: *to* abandon *all hope.* **2** to leave (a place) for good: *They* abandoned *ship.* **3** to desert; to leave in a heartless way: *to* abandon *one's family.* **4** a letting oneself go: *She danced with* abandon.
> **abandon oneself to** to give oneself over completely to: *He* abandoned himself to *despair.*

Why did the headlines read "Crew Abandons Ship"? Why not "Crew Leaves Ship"? "Abandon" is a stronger word in feeling. It means "leave for good." You might want to make some sentences of your own, spoken or written, showing the various meanings of "abandon." In this way you may add the word to your speaking vocabulary.

To help you use words to say what you want to say, your dictionary:

1. Gives examples in italics.
2. Shows how to use connecting words.
3. Gives many idioms with meanings and examples.
4. Gives many synonyms.

Your dictionary will help you most if you:

1. Read the examples as well as the definitions when you look up a word. This is especially important for many of the simple connecting words.
2. Look for the idioms in the entries, and notice how they are used in examples.
3. Look for synonyms instead of using the same word too often.

41

1. The following entries include useful idioms for much of your speaking and writing. Look them up and use some of the idioms in sentences that are clear and sensible.

carry	make	short	clear	better
step	under	take	turn	come

Compare your sentences with those given in the examples in italics. Select some of your sentences and read each to a friend, along with the example given in the dictionary. Ask your friend to decide which one you found in the dictionary.

2. Look up the ten words given below if you are not sure of their meaning. Choose three of them, and write a paragraph using each.

unicorn	prism	catapult	silhouette	rosette
sorceress	tiara	ricochet	trellis	pinafore

Word Histories

Our American English includes words that come from many different languages, but its true beginnings can be traced back to a language we call *Old English* or *Anglo-Saxon*.

About fourteen hundred years ago, three tribes from North Germany invaded England. Two of these were called *Angles* and *Saxons*. They spoke slightly different varieties of an old Germanic language. During the next six hundred years, they developed a common language (Old English). During that time, Viking invaders from Norway and Denmark conquered most of England, bringing with them words and forms of words of their *Old Norse*. Thus, by the year 1000 A.D., Old English was a mixture of the original tongue of the Angles and Saxons, with borrowings from Old Norse and, to a lesser extent, from *Latin*. Latin was the language of the Romans, who conquered England two thousand years ago.

After the Battle of Hastings (1066) the Normans, from what is now western France, took full control of England. The Normans spoke a language that we call *Old French* and established it as the official language of the court. The better-educated Normans also spoke Latin. However, they did not interfere with the Old English of the common people. In fact, the new rulers eventually began learning English. The common people, in turn, borrowed new words from Old French and Latin.

In 1363 when English became the official language in English law courts, it was already a very rich language. We now call it Middle English. From then on, English continued to borrow from Latin, French, Spanish, Italian, German, Arabic, etc.

After English was brought to America by the first English settlers, it borrowed words from the languages of the American Indians, and more words from Spanish and French. Today our American English might be said to come from every major language in the world, including Eskimo (**igloo**). It is still growing and changing as people learn new things and invent new ways to express themselves.

College dictionaries and the very large dictionaries tell where each word in American English comes from, if the origin is known. This is a great help to people who are studying our language, a foreign language, or how languages in general develop. It also helps us to understand and remember the various meanings of words, especially words that are spelled alike but mean entirely different things.

HOMOGRAPHS

Your dictionary cannot tell you where all the words listed come from. If it did, it would have to be much larger than you could handle comfortably. However, it does give the word histories, called *etymologies*, of certain groups of words to show you how words develop and to help you understand their meanings. Your dictionary gives etymologies of groups of words that are spelled alike but have very different meanings because they came into English from different sources. Such groups of words are called *homographs*:

> **hom·o·graph** (hŏm′ə grăf′) word that is spelled the same as another but has a different meaning. This book gives the origins of all homographs listed in it.

43

Here are entries for five words spelled **b a y.** Each has a small number above and to the left of it. You have already learned on page 25 that words spelled alike but pronounced differently have such numbers to help tell them apart. We also use such numbers to identify words that are homographs.

[1]**bay** (bā) large inlet formed by a deep recess or curve in the shore of a lake or ocean. [[1]**bay** is from a French word (baie).]

[2]**bay** (bā) **1** part of a room extending beyond the main outside wall, often having several windows in it. **2** compartment in the body of an airplane. **3** the forward part of a ship between decks. [[2]**bay** is from an Old French word (baee) meaning "opening."]

[3]**bay** (bā) the laurel tree, a small evergreen with shiny leaves. [[3]**bay** is from an Old French word (baie) which goes back to a Latin word (bacca) meaning "berry."]

[4]**bay** (bā) **1** long, deep howling bark made by a dog: *The hunters heard the* bay *of the dogs that had seen the fox.* **2** to bark with a long, deep tone: *The hound* bayed *at the moon.* **3 at bay** (1) in a position ready to fight off pursuers: *The bear stood* at bay *as the dogs attacked from all sides.* (2) in a position from which attack or escape is impossible: *The boy held the thief* at bay. [[1]**bay** is from an Old French word (abaier) meaning "to bark."]

[5]**bay** (bā) **1** having a reddish-brown color: *a* bay *horse.* **2** reddish-brown horse. [[5]**bay** is from an Old French word (bai) which goes back to a Latin word (badius) meaning "chestnut brown."]

The etymologies are given between brackets—[ ]—near or at the end of each entry. You may be interested to notice that these five words came from French, Old French, and Latin.

Look up the homographs [1]**race** and [2]**race.** They came from Old Norse and from Italian through French. If you look up the homographs [1]**yen** and [2]**yen,** you will find that they both came from Chinese, but [1]**yen** was first borrowed and changed by the Japanese before we learned it.

It will probably surprise you that the word "quarry," meaning "a hunted animal," came from a word meaning "skin." Look up ²**quarry** and you will understand how this happened. This etymology might help you remember ²**quarry** (the hunted animal) so that you won't confuse it with a stone **quarry** when you come across it.

All homographs are spelled alike, and when we read them we have to tell by the rest of the sentence which one is meant. With your dictionary, you can decide quickly by reading the first definition of each entry with a small number above it. Many homographs (such as the five **bays**) are pronounced alike. If you hear one of them, you may need to use your dictionary to find out which one is meant.

You should not try to remember all the etymologies in your dictionary. We hope you will find them fun to read. You may remember some of the specially interesting ones, and these will help you to remember meanings. You should, however, be sure to notice the small numbers above words. These numbers tell you that there is more than one entry for the particular spelling. They tell you that you may have to look farther for the meaning or pronunciation you want.

PRACTICE EXERCISES

1. Here is a list of words that have several homographs:

race	row	light	bit
ring	rest	jerk	batter
root	match	jet	bark
tear	loaf	date	arch
tender	mark	calf	sow
stake	ball	brake	bore

Look up each in your dictionary and arrange them on a paper in the following columns:

Homograph	Pronunciation	Etymology
¹**race**	(rās)	Old Norse
²**race**	(rās)	Italian through French

How many sets of homographs are there in which all are pronounced alike? How many sets include homographs that are pronounced differently? How many old or modern languages did we borrow from in order to get this list?

45

Exploration and Discussion

If you have studied the information on the pages between page 7 and this page, you know the chief ways a dictionary can help you and how to use it quickly and accurately. However, to get the most out of your dictionary you should try exploring—reading it on your own. You will learn much about words and the ideas they convey when they are used.

Not many people ever write dictionaries, but almost everyone enjoys watching for new words or old words used with different meanings. As we view TV, listen to the radio, and read current publications, we hear or read new words frequently. Some words are so new that they cannot be found in a dictionary. Some new words are used for a short time and then forgotten because most people do not need them. Others are so useful that they soon become a permanent part of our language. If you see a word that you can't find in this or a larger dictionary, it may be very new. You might keep these words in a notebook to help you remember them when you see them again. You should be sure to write down the meaning and pronunciation as well as the date.

You may be interested in animals, electricity, music, sports, or some other special subject. Your dictionary can give you much information about your special interest. Simply look up the words you know, and they will lead you to other words on the same subject.

Almost everyone has played word games at one time or another. There are many dictionary games that are fun to play. Also, we learn a great deal while we play them. You can make up your own games, but here are some suggestions:

QUESTIONS AND ANSWERS

In the tables at the end of your dictionary the following information is listed:

The Nations of the World
The States of the United States
The Provinces and Territories of Canada
The Presidents of the United States
Sixty Indian Tribes of North America
Domestic Weights and Measures
The Metric System Simplified

Using one of these tables as your authority, write up three questions for your friends to answer. Check the time and ask your three questions. After they have been answered correctly, record the time it took to answer your questions. The member of your group who keeps the others searching the longest, wins the game.

STORY GAME

Here is a list of words that takes up a whole column on one page in your dictionary. These words are found in the first column on page 187. Turn to the page and read the definitions. Could you write a story and use every word in this column? Try putting the words in groupings that will help you with the plot of your story:

countrywoman		
county		
coupe		
couple		
coupling		
coupon		
courage	courageous	courage
courageous	courier	countrywoman
courier	coupe	county
course	coupling	couple
	course	coupon

Read your story to some friends to see how they like it. Then read it slowly again while they try to find the right page in the dictionary. The one who first discovers the page wins.

A

¹**A, a** (ā) the first letter of the English alphabet.

²**a** (ə; when stressed, ā) **1** one; any: *Not a creature was stirring.* **2** each; every: *two dollars a yard; three meals a day.* [²**a** is a form of an Old English word (ān) that means "one."]

a·back (ə băk′) **take aback** to surprise or upset: *I was taken aback by his rudeness.*

ab·a·cus (ăb′ə kəs) a frame with sliding beads or counters strung on wires, used in doing arithmetic. It is especially used by the Chinese. **ab·a·cus·es** or **ab·a·ci** (ăb′ə sī).

Abacus

a·ban·don (ə băn′dən) **1** to give up completely: *to abandon all hope.* **2** to leave (a place) for good: *They abandoned ship.* **3** to desert; to leave in a heartless way: *to abandon one's family.* **4** a letting oneself go: *She danced with abandon.*

abandon oneself to to give oneself over to: *He abandoned himself to despair. He abandoned himself to his work.*

a·bashed (ə băsht′) overcome with shame; confused; embarrassed: *She was abashed when her lie was discovered.*

a·bate (ə bāt′) **1** to become less: *After the storm the wind abated.* **2** to lessen; reduce: *The tax was abated.* **3** in law, to put an end to: *to abate a nuisance.* **a·bat·ed, a·bat·ing.**

ab·bess (ăb′is) head of a religious community of women.

ab·bey (ăb′ĭ) **1** one or more buildings used as a monastery or convent, governed by an abbot or abbess. **2** church that was once part of a monastery: *Westminster Abbey.*

ab·bot (ăb′ət) head of a religious community of men.

ab·bre·vi·ate (ə brē′vĭ āt′) to make shorter: *The word "foot" is abbreviated "ft."* **ab·bre·vi·at·ed, ab·bre·vi·at·ing.**

ab·bre·vi·a·tion (ə brē′vĭ ā′shən) a shortened form: *The accepted abbreviation for "inch" is "in."*

ab·di·cate (ăb′də kāt′) to give up (a position of power, a throne, or a serious responsibility); renounce; resign: *Edward VIII abdicated the British throne in 1936.* **ab·di·cat·ed, ab·di·cat·ing.**

ab·do·men (ăb′də mən or ăb dō′mən) **1** the part of the human body containing the stomach, intestines, etc.; belly. **2** the rear section of the body of an insect.

ab·dom·i·nal (ăb dŏm′ə-nəl) having to do with the abdomen: *an abdominal pain; an abdominal operation.* **ab·dom·i·nal·ly.**

ab·hor (ăb hôr′) to shrink from with disgust; detest; loathe: *A gentleman abhors vulgarity.* **ab·horred, ab·hor·ring.**

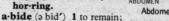
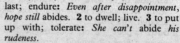

Abdomen

a·bide (ə bīd′) **1** to remain; last; endure: *Even after disappointment, hope still abides.* **2** to dwell; live. **3** to put up with; tolerate: *She can't abide his rudeness.*

abide by 1 to accept: *The players must abide by the umpire's decision.* **2** to remain faithful to: *I shall abide by the contract.* **a·bode** or **a·bid·ed, a·bid·ing.**

a·bid·ing (ə bī′dĭng) never-ending; lasting: *an abiding devotion to his country; abiding faith.*

---

fāte, făt, fâre, fär; bē, bĕt; bite, bĭt; nō, nŏt, nôr; fūse, fŭn, fûr; tōō, tŏŏk; foil; foul; thin; ~~then~~;
hw for wh as in what; zh for s as in usual; ə for a, e, i, o, u, as in ago, linen, peril, atom, minus

49

a·bil·i·ty (ə bil′ə ti) **1** power (to do something); strength: *the* ability *to walk.* **2** talent; skill; aptitude: *The young man showed* ability *in painting.* **3 to the best of one's ability** as well as one can. **a·bil·i·ties.**

a·blaze (ə blāz′) **1** on fire; burning: *logs* ablaze *in the fireplace.* **2** shining brightly; flashing: *a house* ablaze *with lights; a face* ablaze *with anger.*

a·ble (ā′bəl) **1** capable (through power, skill, or money); with the ability or means (to): *When I'm not tired I'm* able *to work faster. The President is* able *to declare war.* **2** talented; skillful: *The lawyer was a very* able *man.* **3** showing skill: *an* able *speech.* **a·bler, a·blest; a·bly.**

ab·nor·mal (ăb nôr′məl) not normal; different from the ordinary; unusual: *It is* abnormal *to have the heart on the right side.* **ab·nor·mal·ly.**

a·board (ə bôrd′) into or on a ship, bus, train, or airplane; on board.

a·bode (ə bōd′) **1** home; dwelling: *a pleasant* abode. **2** See **abide.** *"Three days and three nights he there* abode.*"*

a·bol·ish (ə bŏl′ish) to do away with; put an end to: *How can we* abolish *war?*

ab·o·li·tion (ăb ə lish′ən) a doing away with; a putting an end to: *the* abolition *of poverty.*

ab·o·li·tion·ist (ăb′ə lish′ən ist) one who favored the doing away with slavery.

A-bomb (ā′bŏm′) atom bomb.

a·bom·i·na·ble (ə bŏm′ə nə bəl) **1** very hateful: *the* abominable *cruelties of Nero.* **2** very bad or unpleasant: *an* abominable *winter.* **a·bom·i·na·bly.**

a·bound (ə bound′) to be in great plenty; be numerous: *In these lakes trout* abound.
abound in or **with** to overflow or teem with: *He* abounds *in courage. These lakes* abound *with trout.*

a·bout (ə bout′) **1** of; concerning: *a story* about *a bear.* **2** around; here and there: *He walked* about *aimlessly.* **3** almost; in the neighborhood of: *I weigh* about *100 pounds.* **4** in the opposite direction: *to turn* about. **5 about to** just going to: *Something is* about *to happen.*

a·bove (ə bŭv′) **1** over; higher than: *one brick* above *another;* above *the clouds.* **2** overhead: *the sky* above. **3** beyond: *We drove to the mountain tower* above *the tree line.* **4** more than: *children* above *ten years*

---

of age. **5** too good for; superior to: *She thinks herself* above *housework.* **6** before; earlier: *See the reference* above.

a·breast (ə brĕst′) **1** side by side: *The soldiers marched three* abreast. **2 keep abreast of** to keep up with: *to* keep abreast of *the news.*

a·bridge (ə brij′) **1** to use fewer words while keeping the sense; to shorten: *to* abridge *a long book for magazine publication.* **2** to cut off; lessen: *to* abridge *one's liberty.* **a·bridged, a·bridg·ing.**

a·broad (ə brôd′) **1** in or to a foreign country: *to live* abroad; *to travel* abroad. **2** widely: *Spread the good news* abroad. **3** outside the house: *to be* abroad *early.*

a·brupt (ə brŭpt′) **1** sudden; unexpected: *an* abrupt *stop.* **2** steep: *an* abrupt *incline.* **3** curt in speech; short and blunt: *Although she spoke kindly to him, he answered in an* abrupt *manner.* **a·brupt·ly.**

ab·scess (ăb′sĕs) **1** a mass of pus in some part of the body. **2** a cavity or swelling containing pus: *an* abscess *on a tooth.*

ab·sence (ăb′səns) **1** a being away: *His* absence *was immediately noted.* **2** a being without; lack: *an utter* absence *of humor.*

¹ab·sent (ăb′sənt) **1** not present; away; missing. **2** lost in thought; not paying attention: *She was daydreaming, and answered in an* absent *manner.* **ab·sent·ly.**

²ab·sent (ăb sĕnt′) to take (oneself) or keep away: *to* absent *oneself from class.*

ab·sen·tee (ăb′sən tē′) one who is absent: *an* absentee *voter; an* absentee *from work.*

ab·so·lute (ăb′sə lōōt′ or ăb′sə lūt′) **1** complete; perfect: *the* absolute *truth.* **2** not limited or restricted in any way: *Very few rulers nowadays have* absolute *power.* **3** real; positive: *to have* absolute *proof.*

ab·so·lute·ly (ăb′sə lōōt′li or ăb′sə lūt′li) **1** wholly; completely: *You're* absolutely *right.* **2** certainly.

ab·solve (ăb sŏlv′) **1** to clear of guilt or blame: *The jury* absolved *him of all the charges.* **2** to free (from a promise, etc.): *He* absolved *me from the promise I made.* **ab·solved, ab·solv·ing.**

ab·sorb (ăb sôrb′) **1** to take in; soak up: *A towel* absorbs *water. A bright child* absorbs *knowledge easily.* **2** to occupy all one's attention; interest very much: *The little girl was* absorbed *in play.*

ab·sorb·ent (ăb sôr′bənt) **1** capable of taking up moisture: *an absorbent cotton.* **2** a substance that absorbs: *Cotton is an absorbent.*

ab·sorb·ing (ăb sôr′bĭng) taking up all one's attention; very interesting: *to tell an absorbing tale.*

ab·sorp·tion (ăb sôrp′shən) **1** a soaking up; a swallowing up: *the* absorption *of ink by a blotter.* **2** a being intensely interested or occupied: *His* absorption *in his book was such that he didn't hear me.*

ab·stain (ăb stān′) to do without; refrain (from); hold oneself back: *Vegetarians always* abstain *from eating meat.*

ab·sti·nence (ăb′stĭ nəns) **1** a refraining from something; a giving up of certain foods, alcoholic drinks, etc. **2 total abstinence** a complete giving up of alcoholic drinks.

¹**ab·stract** (ăb′străkt or ăb străkt′) **1** thought of apart from any concrete objects or real things: *The word "beauty" is an* abstract *word.* **2** hard to understand; difficult: *an* abstract *subject like philosophy.* **3** (ăb′-străkt) short account of the main points in a book, speech, etc. **ab·stract·ly.**

²**ab·stract** (ăb străkt′) **1** to take out or away, often dishonestly: *George slyly* abstracted *marbles from the bag.* **2** to separate: *to* abstract *gold from ore.* **3** to make a summary of: *to* abstract *a book.*

ab·surd (ăb sûrd′) ridiculous; silly; contrary to reason or sense. **ab·surd·ly.**

ab·surd·i·ty (ăb sûr′də tĭ) **1** foolishness; a being absurd: *It would be sheer* absurdity *to make a speech while standing on your hands.* **2** something absurd: *He said a number of* absurdities. **ab·surd·i·ties.**

a·bun·dance (ə bŭn′dəns) **1** great plenty; number or amount that is more than enough: *an* abundance *of food.* **2 live in abundance** to have plenty of the things that make life enjoyable.

a·bun·dant (ə bŭn′dənt) plenty of; more than enough: *The settlers found* abundant *game in the forests.* **a·bun·dant·ly.**

¹**a·buse** (ə būz′) **1** to treat badly or harshly. **2** to make wrong use of: *The manager* abused *his authority. He* abused *his host's*

hospitality. **3** to use insulting language to or about: *The candidates* abused *each other during the campaign.* **a·bused, a·bus·ing.**

²**a·buse** (ə būs′) **1** wrong or harsh treatment. **2** wrong use; misuse: *the* abuse *of our power.* **3** corrupt custom or practice: *Such* abuses *as bribery or graft are punishable by law.* **4** insulting language.

a·byss (ə bĭs′) **1** deep hole in the earth; chasm. **2** anything of limitless depth.

A.C. alternating current.

ac·a·dem·ic (ăk′ə dĕm′ĭk) **1** of an academy, school, or college: *an academic degree;* academic *studies.* **2** having to do with theory rather than practice; without practical effect; idle: *Whether to have a monarchy or a democracy in this country is now a purely* academic *question.*

a·cad·e·my (ə kăd′ə mĭ) **1** private high school. **2** school for special study: *a military academy.* **3** a society of learned men organized to encourage arts, letters, or sciences. **a·cad·e·mies.**

ac·cel·er·ate (ăk sĕl′ə rāt′) **1** to increase the speed of: *to accelerate the motor by stepping on the pedal.* **2** to bring about sooner; hasten: *The dictator's harsh measures* accelerated *his fall.* **ac·cel·e·rat·ed, ac·cel·e·rat·ing.**

ac·cel·e·ra·tion (ăk sĕl ə rā′shən) increase of speed; a hastening: *an* acceleration *in the pulse rate of a runner.*

ac·cel·er·a·tor (ăk sĕl′ə rā′tər) anything, as a pedal, a muscle, or substance, that increases the speed of motion, reaction, or development: *to step on the* accelerator.

ac·cent (ăk′sĕnt) **1** a stress upon a syllable of a word or a note of music. **2** to stress: *She* accented *her words so that we would hear her clearly. The judge* accented *his request with a rap of the gavel.* **3** to mark with an accent. **4** special or unusual way of pronouncing: *a foreign* accent. **5** accent mark.

accent mark 1 mark (′) placed after a syllable in a word to show that it is stressed, that is, pronounced with greater force than the other syllables. In the word "re la′tion" the accent mark is on the syllable "la." **2** in foreign languages or words borrowed from foreign languages, a

---

fāte, făt, fâre, fär; bē, bĕt; bīte, bĭt; nō, nŏt, nôr; fūse, fŭn, fûr; tōō, tŏŏk; foil; foul; thin; ~~then~~; hw for wh as in *what*; zh for s as in u*su*al; ə for a, e, i, o, u, as in *ago*, linen, peril, atom, min*u*s

mark used to indicate that a letter is pronounced in a particular way. In the Spanish word "señor" the mark (~) shows that the "ñ" is pronounced like "ny."

ac·cept (ăk sĕpt′) **1** to take what is offered: *to* accept *a gift.* **2** to answer yes to: *to* accept *an invitation.* **3** to agree to: *to* accept *a proposal.* **4** to recognize as true: *The jury* accepted *his story.* **5** to receive into a group; include: *The children immediately* accepted *their new classmate.*

ac·cept·a·ble (ăk sĕpt′ə bəl) **1** worth accepting; welcome: *The plan was* acceptable *to everyone.* **2** fitting or satisfactory: *quite* acceptable *behavior.* **ac·cept·a·bly.**

ac·cept·ance (ăk sĕp′təns) **1** a taking or willingness to receive (something offered or given): *the* acceptance *of responsibilities; the* acceptance *of a gift.* **2** approval: *The invention found widespread* acceptance.

ac·cept·ed (ăk sĕp′tĭd) approved or believed by nearly everyone: *Once it was an* accepted *belief that the world is flat.*

ac·cess (ăk′sĕs) **1** right of admittance or approach to a person or place: *He had* access *to the records.* **2** a way or means of approach: *The avalanche cut off the* access *to the mountain village.*

ac·ces·si·ble (ăk sĕs′ə bəl) easy to get at or reach: *Only the books on the lower shelves are* accessible. **ac·ces·si·bly.**

ac·ces·so·ry (ăk sĕs′ə rĭ) **1** something which, though not essential, adds to the usefulness of machines and the like: *to buy automobile* accessories. **2** article that adds to the appearance of a costume: *gloves, handbags, and other* accessories. **3** person who, though not present at the scene of a crime, aids a criminal before or after the crime. **4** added: *an* accessory *item.* **ac·ces·so·ries.**

ac·ci·dent (ăk′sə dənt) **1** unexpected, unplanned, or unforeseen happening, often unfortunate: *Our flat tire was an unlucky* accident. **2 by accident** by chance: *to be discovered by* accident.

ac·ci·den·tal (ăk′sə dĕn′təl) happening unexpectedly or by chance: *an* accidental *discovery of oil.* **ac·ci·den·tal·ly.**

ac·claim (ə klām′) **1** to praise; shout approval; pay tribute to: *All the newspapers* acclaimed *the explorers for their bravery.* **2** applause; show of approval or praise: *They greeted the winner with loud* acclaim.

ac·cla·ma·tion (ăk′lə mā′shən) **1** a shout or other demonstration of approval. **2 by acclamation** by loud shouts and without taking a vote: *elected by* acclamation.

ac·com·mo·date (ə kŏm′ə dāt′) **1** to have room for: *The hotel room will* accommodate *two guests.* **2** to oblige; help out: *He will* accommodate *me with the use of his car.* **3** to adjust or become adjusted: *The pupil of the eye* accommodates *itself to light. He* accommodated *himself to his circumstances.* **ac·com·mo·dat·ed, ac·com·mo·dat·ing.**

ac·com·mo·dat·ing (ə kŏm′ə dā′tĭng) obliging; courteous: *An* accommodating *host sees to the needs of his guests.* **ac·com·mo·da·ting·ly.**

ac·com·mo·da·tion (ə kŏm′ə dā′shən) **1** convenience: *The hotel has a restaurant for the* accommodation *of its guests.* **2** a fitting or adjusting of something to something else: *the* accommodation *of the eye to light; the* accommodation *of one's plans to those of another.* **3** something done or given in order to oblige: *That $10.00 loan was an* accommodation. **4 accommodations** lodging, or food and lodging: *They finally found* accommodations *at a motel.*

ac·com·pa·ni·ment (ə kŭm′pə nĭ mənt) **1** something that naturally goes with something else: *Usually an* accompaniment *of measles is fever.* **2** music to support instruments, voice, or dance: *a drum* accompaniment *to a dance.*

ac·com·pa·ny (ə kŭm′pə nĭ) **1** to go along with; escort: *Father will* accompany *us to the concert.* **2** to be or to happen together with: *Wind* accompanied *the rain.* **3** to play or sing an accompaniment to another. **ac·com·pa·nied, ac·com·pa·ny·ing.**

ac·com·plice (ə kŏm′plĭs) a person who aids another in a crime or wrongdoing.

ac·com·plish (ə kŏm′plĭsh) to carry out; complete; finish: *to* accomplish *a task.*

ac·com·plished (ə kŏm′plĭsht) **1** completed; carried out: *an* accomplished *task.* **2** perfected by training; expert: *He is an* accomplished *musician.*

ac·com·plish·ment (ə kŏm′plĭsh mənt) **1** a carrying into effect or completion; doing: *the* accomplishment *of a purpose.* **2** a skill or excellence, especially one acquired by training: *Singing and dancing were among the many* accomplishments *of the actress.*

3 achievement; something carried out with skill and knowledge: *Building a model ship is an accomplishment for a young boy.*

ac·cord (ə kôrd′) **1** to agree or harmonize: *He gets along with the group, because his ideas accord with theirs.* **2** to grant: *We accord praise to those who deserve it.* **3 in accord** in agreement or harmony: *His account of the matter is not in accord with the facts. The costumes in the play were in accord with the setting.* **4 of one's own accord** without being asked.

ac·cord·ance (ə kôr′dəns) agreement: *carried out in accordance with instructions.*

ac·cord·ing (ə kôr′ding) agreeing; harmonizing: *several according decisions.*

according to 1 in agreement with: *We play according to the rules.* **2** on the authority of: *John is an excellent student, according to his teacher.*

ac·cord·ing·ly (ə kôr′ding lï) **1** in agreement (with what has been laid down): *The students were given new instructions and told to act accordingly.* **2** therefore; as a result.

ac·cor·di·on (ə kôr′dï ən) portable musical instrument having a keyboard, bellows, and metal reeds. The bellows are stretched and squeezed to force air through reeds selected by pressing the right keys.

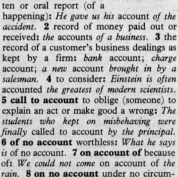

Accordion

ac·count (ə kount′) **1** written or oral report (of a happening): *He gave us his account of the accident.* **2** record of money paid out or received: *the accounts of a business.* **3** the record of a customer's business dealings as kept by a firm: *bank account; charge account; a new account brought in by a salesman.* **4** to consider: *Einstein is often accounted the greatest of modern scientists.* **5 call to account** to oblige (someone) to explain an act or make good a wrong: *The students who kept on misbehaving were finally called to account by the principal.* **6 of no account** worthless: *What he says is of no account.* **7 on account of** because of: *We could not come on account of the rain.* **8 on no account** under no circum-

stances; never. **9 take into account** to consider; give attention to.

account for 1 to explain and justify; to answer for: *You must account for every penny spent.* **2** to explain: *How do you account for your tardiness?* **3** to be the reason for: *A dry spell accounted for the poor crops.*

ac·count·ant (ə koun′tənt) person who keeps or inspects the records of money spent and received by a business to see that they are correct.

ac·cu·mu·late (ə kū′mū lāt′) **1** to pile up; collect; gather: *Boys accumulate many things in their pockets.* **2** to become greater in amount; increase: *Dust accumulated in every corner.* **ac·cu·mu·lat·ed, ac·cu·mu·lat·ing.**

ac·cu·mu·la·tion (ə kū′mū lā′shən) **1** a growing by repeated additions: *the steady accumulation of interest.* **2** a collected mass: *an accumulation of odds and ends in the attic.*

ac·cu·ra·cy (ăk′yŏŏ rə sï) freedom from error or mistake; exactness: *I trust the accuracy of his story.* **ac·cu·ra·cies.**

ac·cu·rate (ăk′yŏŏ rĭt) correct; exact: *an accurate report.* **ac·cu·rate·ly.**

ac·cu·sa·tion (ăk′yŏŏ zā′shən) a charge of wrongdoing.

ac·cuse (ə kūz′) to blame for wrongdoing or crime; bring a charge against. **ac·cused, ac·cus·ing.**

ac·cus·tom (ə kŭs′təm) to get used to; make familiar with: *The new boys soon accustom themselves to the school.*

ac·cus·tomed (ə kŭs′təmd) **1** habitual; usual: *People prefer to keep to their accustomed ways.* **2 accustomed to** used to: *We are accustomed to three meals a day.*

ace (ās) **1** card or one of a pair of dice with a single spot. **2** flyer in the armed forces who has brought down at least five enemy planes. **3** an expert. **4** first-class: *an ace athlete.*

Ace

ache (āk) **1** steady pain. **2** to be in pain: *The fever caused her body to ache.* **3** in popular language, to wish very strongly: *I am aching to see the new car.* **ached, ach·ing.**

---

fāte, făt, fâre, fär; bē, bĕt; bīte, bĭt; nō, nŏt, nôr; fūse, fŭn, fûr; tōō, tŏŏk; foil; foul; thin; ~~then~~;
hw for wh as in *wh*at; zh for s as in u*s*ual; ə for a, e, i, o, u, as in *a*go, lin*e*n, per*i*l, at*o*m, min*u*s

a·chieve (ə chēv′) to bring about; accomplish; gain: *to* achieve *success.* **a·chieved, a·chiev·ing.**

a·chieve·ment (ə chēv′mənt) **1** something accomplished, especially by great effort or superior ability; feat: *The Hoover Dam is an engineering* achievement. **2** an attaining: *The* achievement *of skill takes practice.*

ac·id (ăs′ĭd) **1** sour: *the* acid *taste of green apples.* **2** biting; sarcastic: *Helen made* acid *remarks about the amateur production.* **3** sour substance. **4** in chemistry, a substance that will combine with a base to form a salt, and turns litmus paper red.

ac·knowl·edge (ăk nŏl′ĭj) **1** to admit (that something is true): *to* acknowledge *a mistake or a fault.* **2** to recognize (as): *He is* acknowledged *as the leader of his party.* **3** to say one has received (something): *A letter was written to* acknowledge *the gift.* **ac·knowl·edged, ac·knowl·edg·ing.**

ac·knowl·edg·ment (ăk nŏl′ĭj mənt) **1** admission that something is true: *He made an* acknowledgment *of his error.* **2** recognition: *a medal given in* acknowledgment *of long service.* **3** statement that something has been received: *a letter of* acknowledgment.

ac·ne (ăk′nĭ) pimples caused by swollen and infected oil glands under the skin.

Acorn

a·corn (ā′kôrn) the nut of the oak tree.

ac·quaint (ə kwānt′) **1** to make familiar: *I* acquainted *the new clerk with his duties.* **2 be acquainted with** to have personal knowledge of; be familiar with.

ac·quaint·ance (ə kwān′təns) **1** person known slightly: *He is only an* acquaintance, *not a close friend.* **2** knowledge from experience or contact: *The lawyer had a close* acquaintance *with the facts of the case.*

ac·qui·esce (ăk′wĭ ĕs′) to give consent by remaining silent: *He* acquiesced *in our plans.* **ac·qui·esced, ac·qui·esc·ing.**

ac·quire (ə kwīr′) to get; gain: *to* acquire *land; to* acquire *skill in running.* **ac·quired, ac·quir·ing.**

ac·qui·si·tion (ăk′wə zĭsh′ən) **1** a getting or gaining as one's own: *the* acquisition *of knowledge.* **2** something gained: *His newest* acquisition *was a toy fire engine.*

ac·quit (ə kwĭt′) **1** to set free from a charge of crime; declare (someone) not guilty: *The*

jury acquitted *the man.* **2** to behave or conduct (oneself); to do one's part: *The new player* acquitted *himself well in the football game.* **ac·quit·ted, ac·quit·ting.**

a·cre (ā′kər) a unit used in measuring land. An acre is about the area of a square field 208 feet on each side.

a·cre·age (ā′kər ĭj) land measured in acres.

ac·rid (ăk′rĭd) bitter; biting: *the* acrid *smoke of gasoline;* acrid *remarks.* **ac·rid·ly.**

ac·ro·bat (ăk′rə băt) person who does daring and skillful exercises or stunts, such as walking along a tightrope.

a·cro·po·lis (ə krŏp′ə lĭs) **1** highest part of an old Greek city, used as a fortress; citadel. **2 the Acropolis** the citadel of Athens.

a·cross (ə krôs′) **1** from one side to the other side of: *We walked* across *the park. The park is a mile* across. **2** on the other side of: *They live* across *the railroad tracks.* **3 come** or **run across** to discover or find: *On your field trip you will* come across *many fossils.*

act (ăkt) **1** a thing done; deed: *Helping the blind man was an* act *of kindness.* **2** one of the main parts into which a play is divided. **3** law; decree: *an* Act *of Congress.* **4** to do something: *He* acted *so quickly that he put out the fire almost before it started.* **5** to play (the part of); to perform: *Would you like to* act *the part of the king?* **6** to pretend: *He's just* acting. **7** to behave: *He* acts *as if he were sick.* **8 Acts** or **Acts of the Apostles** the fifth book of the New Testament.

act as to do the work of: *to* act as *interpreter.*

act for 1 to take someone's place. **2** to do (someone) a service.

act on 1 to follow; obey: *They* acted on *my suggestion.* **2** to have effect: *The acid* acted on *the metal.*

ac·tion (ăk′shən) **1** an act; deed: *People say that* actions *speak louder than words.* **2** energetic motion or activity: *The adventure story was packed with* action. **3** effect: *The* action *of the rain washed away the soil.* **4** manner of working or functioning: *the* action *of the heart; the graceful* action *of that horse.* **5 in** or **into action** in or into battle. **6 take action** to begin to act.

ac·tive (ăk′tĭv) **1** lively; vigorous: *an* active *mind.* **2** energetic; moving about a good deal: *Children are more* active *in the morning* *than at night.* **3** acting or capable of acting: *an active volcano.* **4** in present use: *an active file.* **5** taking full part in: *an active member of an organization.* **ac·tive·ly.**

ac·tiv·i·ty (ăk tĭv′ə tĭ) **1** movement; action: *physical activity; mental activity.* **2** liveliness: *There is much activity at the zoo at feeding time.* **3** thing to do: *the classroom activities; church activities.* **ac·tiv·i·ties.**

ac·tor (ăk′tər) person who performs or takes the part of a character in a stage play, motion picture, or broadcast.

ac·tress (ăk′trĭs) girl or woman who performs or takes the part of a character in a stage play, motion picture, or broadcast.

ac·tu·al (ăk′chōō əl) real; not imaginary: *Davy Crockett was an actual person.*

ac·tu·al·ly (ăk′chōō ə lĭ) really; in fact: *Did you actually build this model airplane?*

a·cute (ə kūt′) **1** keen; alert; sharp: *Dogs have an acute sense of hearing. Being an acute observer, the chief of police found several clues the detective had missed.* **2** very serious; severe: *an acute attack of appendicitis.* **3 acute angle** an angle smaller than a right angle. For picture, see **angle.** **a·cute·ly.**

A.D. letters used before dates to show the number of years after the beginning of the Christian era. The letters come from the Latin words, "Anno Domini," meaning "in the year of our Lord": *in A.D. 1066.*

ad·a·mant (ăd′ə mănt′) hard; unyielding: *Once he had made his decision, he was adamant and would not change his mind.* **ad·a·mant·ly.**

a·dapt (ə dăpt′) **1** to change and make suitable (for new conditions); adjust: *to adapt oneself to new circumstances.* **2** to change so as to be suitable for another use: *to adapt a novel for the movies; to adapt a garage for use as a workshop.*

a·dapt·a·ble (ə dăp′tə bəl) **1** easily changed to fit new situations: *an adaptable schedule.* **2** capable of changing easily to meet new situations; flexible: *an adaptable person.*

ad·ap·ta·tion (ăd′əp tā′shən) **1** a changing to fit different conditions: *He found adaptation to the hot climate difficult. The change of an arctic fox's fur from brown in*

summer to white in winter is a good example of adaptation *in nature.* **2** something produced by a process of changing and arranging: *The play was a successful* adaptation *of the novel.*

add (ăd) **1** to join or unite into a whole; combine numbers to form a sum. **2** to say or write further: *She added another sentence to the letter.*

add to 1 to cause an increase of: *to add books to the library.* **2** to put with: *to add sugar to coffee.* **3** to make greater: *to add to our joy.*

add up to 1 to reach a total of. **2** to mean: *What do his remarks add up to?*

ad·dend (ăd′ĕnd) a number added to another number. In the example $2 + 5 = 7$, 5 is the addend.

ad·der (ăd′ər) **1** any of several harmless American snakes. **2** the poisonous viper of Europe. **3** a large, poisonous, African snake.

ad·dict (ăd′ĭkt) person completely given over to (a habit): *a drug addict.*

ad·dict·ed to (ə dĭkt′ĭd) **1** given to: *to be addicted to gossip.* **2** enslaved by: *to be addicted to drugs.*

ad·di·tion (ə dĭsh′ən) **1** the adding of two or more numbers together in order to figure out their sum: $5 + 7 = 12$ *is an example of* addition. *Can you do* addition *quickly?* **2** something that is added or joined: *an addition to a house.* **3** the adding or joining of one thing to another: *the addition of a gymnasium to the school.* **4 in addition to** as well as; besides: *He works* in addition to *going to school.*

ad·di·tion·al (ə dĭsh′ən əl) extra; more: *He took a job on Saturdays because he needed additional income.* **ad·di·tion·al·ly.**

¹ad·dress (ăd′rĕs or ə drĕs′) **1** the place where one lives or to which one's mail is directed. **2** the direction written on mail.

²ad·dress (ə drĕs′) **1** to speak or write to: *She addressed the stranger politely.* **2** to direct for delivery: *to address a letter.* **3** a speech: *The mayor gave an address at the club meeting.* **4** skill and tact: *the address of an experienced diplomat.*

address oneself to to apply oneself to: *He addressed himself to other tasks.*

---

fāte, făt, fâre, fär; bē, bĕt; bīte, bĭt; nō, nŏt, nôr; fūse, fŭn, fûr; tōō, tŏŏk; foil; foul; thin; ~~then~~; hw for wh as in *wh*at; zh for s as in u*s*ual; ə for a, e, i, o, u, as in *a*go, lin*e*n, per*i*l, at*o*m, min*u*s

ad·e·noids (ăd′ə noidz′) spongy growths in the passage leading from the nose to the throat. When infected and enlarged, adenoids cause difficulty in breathing.

Adenoids

a·dept (ə dĕpt′) highly skilled; expert: *John is adept at repairing things about the house.* **a·dept·ly.**

ad·e·quate (ăd′ə kwit) **1** as much as is needed; sufficient: *His skill was adequate for the job.* **2** competent enough: *an adequate speaker.* **ad·e·quate·ly.**

ad·here (ăd hir′) **1** to stick fast, as if glued: *Gum adheres to your fingers.* **2** to be attached or give steady support (to): *to adhere to an idea.* **ad·hered, ad·her·ing.**

ad·he·sive (ăd hē′siv) **1** sticking fast or causing to stick: *an adhesive tape.* **2** sticky substance used to hold things together: *Paste, glue, and sealing wax are adhesives.*

ad·ja·cent (ə jā′sənt) next to; near: *a house adjacent to the church.* **ad·ja·cent·ly.**

ad·jec·tive (ăj′ĭk tiv) a word that describes a person, place, or thing. "Funny," "favorite," "ugly," "strange," "young," "red," and "old" are adjectives in these sentences:
The funny clowns are in the circus.
Jane is my favorite friend.
This is ugly.
It has a strange taste.
He is very young.
Some red apples hung on the old tree.

ad·join (ə join′) to be so near as to touch; be next to: *Canada adjoins the United States.*

ad·journ (ə jûrn′) **1** to break off a meeting or session until another time: *The judge adjourned the court until the following day.* **2** to bring or come to a close: *Congress adjourned when all business was finished.*

ad·just (ə jŭst′) **1** to make mechanical changes so that parts fit or work together properly; regulate: *The mechanic adjusted the fuel pump in the engine.* **2** to make or become suitable; fit: *to adjust the length of a coat.* **3** to adapt: *to adjust oneself to new circumstances.* **4** to settle: *to adjust differences in a quarrel; to adjust a claim.*

ad·just·ment (ə jŭst′mənt) **1** an adjusting. **2** arrangement; settlement: *the adjustment of my insurance claim.*

ad·min·is·ter (ăd mĭn′əs tər) **1** to manage; look after: *The President administers the affairs of our country.* **2** to put into effect: *to administer the laws.* **3** to present (to someone) to take: *The bailiff administered the oath to the witness.*

ad·min·is·tra·tion (ăd mĭn′ə strā′shən) **1** act of administering. **2** direction; management: *His administration of the government was honest.* **3** that part of the government which directs the business of a nation, state, or city. **4** the term of office of one Administration. **5 the Administration** the President of the United States, the members of his cabinet, and the departments they run.

ad·mi·ra·ble (ăd′mə rə bəl) **1** worth admiring: *That soldier showed admirable courage in battle.* **2** good; excellent: *to show admirable punctuality.* **ad·mi·ra·bly.**

ad·mi·ral (ăd′mə rəl) naval officer of the highest rank.

ad·mi·ra·tion (ăd′mə rā′shən) **1** feeling of strong approval, pleasure, and respect: *We noticed the boy's admiration of the trapeze performers.* **2** that which is admired: *The team was the admiration of all the school.*

ad·mire (ăd mir′) to look at with pleasure and wonder: *We admired the beautiful picture.* **2** to have a high opinion of: *Miss Perry admired Jane's handling of the younger children.* **ad·mired, ad·mir·ing.**

ad·mir·er (ăd mir′ər) person who regards (someone or something) with approval, delight, or affection: *She has many admirers.*

ad·mis·sion (ăd mĭsh′ən) **1** permission to enter: *Free admission is limited to certain days.* **2** price paid in order to enter. **3** a saying that something is true; acknowledgment: *He signed an admission of his guilt.*

ad·mit (ăd mĭt′) **1** to allow to enter: *This ticket will admit you to the concert. The child was admitted to school.* **2** to accept as true: *I admit that you are right.*
admit of to leave room for: *The emergency admits of no delay.*
ad·mit·ted, ad·mit·ting.

ad·mon·ish (ăd mŏn′ish) **1** to take to task; to reprove mildly: *The boys were admonished for their misbehavior.* **2** to warn; caution: *Ben admonished us not to sail far.*

ad·mo·ni·tion (ăd mə nĭsh′ən) an admonishing; warning.

a·do (ə dōō′) fuss; bustle: *There was much* ado *over the new baby.*

a·do·be (ə dō′bĭ) **1** brick made of earth or clay and baked in the sun. It is used in the southwestern United States, Mexico, and other countries having little rainfall. **2** made of sun-dried brick: *an* adobe *house.*

Adobe house

a·dopt (ə dŏpt′) **1** to take by choice as one's own: *to* adopt *a child; to* adopt *a name.* **2** to approve; accept: *The committee* adopted *the chairman's plan.*

a·dop·tion (ə dŏp′shən) **1** a taking as one's own: *the* adoption *of the child.* **2** approval; acceptance: *the* adoption *of a law.*

a·dor·a·ble (ə dôr′ə bəl) **1** worthy of deep love or worship. **2** lovely; charming: *an* adorable *baby.* **a·dor·a·bly.**

ad·o·ra·tion (ăd′ə rā′shən) **1** worship of God or of a person or thing regarded as holy. **2** devoted love.

a·dore (ə dôr′) **1** to love and worship. **2** to regard with deep affection and respect: *She* adored *her father.* **3** to like very much: *I* adore *swimming.* **a·dored, a·dor·ing.**

a·dorn (ə dôrn′) to add beauty to; decorate: *The hat was* adorned *with roses.*

a·dorn·ment (ə dôrn′mənt) **1** something that adds beauty; decoration: *A jeweled pin was the only* adornment *on the dress.* **2** a decorating: *to be busy with the* adornment *of the room the day before the party.*

a·drift (ə drĭft′) floating about at random: *The boat was set* adrift *by the storm.*

a·droit (ə droit′) clever; skillful: *We admired the lawyer's* adroit *questioning of the witness.* **a·droit·ly.**

a·dult (ə dŭlt′ or ăd′ŭlt) **1** a grown-up person: *Children are looked after by* adults. **2** mature; grown-up; full grown in size, strength, etc. **3** full-grown animal or plant.

a·dul·ter·a·ted (ə dŭl′tə rā′tĭd) made inferior by being mixed with something else: *Milk* adulterated *with water is not as good as whole milk.*

ad·vance (ăd văns′) **1** to go forward: *The army* advanced. **2** a moving forward;

progress: *the* advance *of science.* **3** to go up in rank, price, etc.: *He* advanced *to the presidency of the firm.* **4** to promote: *He was* advanced *to the next grade.* **5** a rise in rank or price: *There has been another* advance *in gasoline taxes.* **6** to progress: *His work* advanced *rapidly.* **7** to give beforehand: *My father* advanced *me my next week's allowance.* **8** approach made to form an acquaintance, settle a quarrel, etc.: *When the family moved to the new house, their neighbors made the first* advances. **9 in advance** ahead of time: *to pay rent* in advance. **ad·vanced, ad·vanc·ing.**

ad·vanced (ăd vănst′) **1** ahead; out in front: *an* advanced *observation post.* **2** ahead of the average: *a class for* advanced *students.* **3** far along in years: *a man of* advanced *age.*

ad·vance·ment (ăd văns′mənt) **1** a moving forward. **2** promotion in rank or standing: *to have hopes of* advancement.

ad·van·tage (ăd văn′tĭj) **1** anything helpful, favorable, or beneficial: *He had the* advantage *of good training.* **2 take advantage of** (1) to make the best use of (something). (2) to impose upon or treat (someone) unfairly: *Don't let him take* advantage *of you.*

ad·van·ta·geous (ăd′vən tā′jəs) favorable; useful; profitable: *an* advantageous *position.* **ad·van·ta·geous·ly.**

ad·vent (ăd′věnt) **1** a coming into place or being; arrival: *the* advent *of spring.* **2 Advent** the coming of Jesus Christ into the world; also the season (including four Sundays) of preparation for Christmas.

ad·ven·ture (ăd věn′chər) **1** bold and difficult undertaking in which risks are run: *The climbing of Mt. Everest is one of the boldest* adventures *of man.* **2** an exciting or unexpected experience.

ad·ven·tur·er (ăd věn′chər ər) **1** person who seeks or has adventures. **2** one who lives by dishonest schemes: *The* adventurer *swindled the old lady out of her savings.*

ad·ven·tur·ous (ăd věn′chər əs) **1** inclined to seek exciting experiences. **2** risky and requiring courage: *an* adventurous *undertaking.* **ad·ven·tur·ous·ly.**

fāte, făt, fâre, fär; bē, bĕt; bīte, bĭt; nō, nŏt, nôr; fūse, fŭn, fûr; tōō, tŏŏk; foil; foul; thin; ~~then~~;
hw for wh as in *wh*at; zh for s as in u*s*ual; ə for a, e, i, o, u, as in *a*go, lin*e*n, per*i*l, at*o*m, min*u*s

57

ad·verb (ăd′vûrb) a word that asks or answers the questions "when?" "where?" "how?" or "how much?" "Tomorrow," "away," "badly," "fast," and "very" are adverbs in these sentences:
I'm leaving tomorrow.
He went away.
He writes badly.
She runs fast.
She is very *pretty.*

ad·ver·sar·y (ăd′vər sĕr′ĭ) **1** enemy. **2** opponent; rival: *He shook hands with his adversary before the match.* **ad·ver·sar·ies.**

ad·verse (ăd′vûrs or ăd vûrs′) **1** unfavorable: *The judge gave an* adverse *decision. He struggled against* adverse *circumstances.* **2** in a contrary direction: *An* adverse *wind delayed the boat.* **3** unfriendly; opposing; hostile: *There were* adverse *forces at work to prevent his nomination.* **ad·verse·ly.**

ad·ver·si·ty (ăd vûr′sə tĭ) great trouble or trial; misfortune; hardship: *He knew many days of* adversity. **ad·ver·si·ties.**

ad·ver·tise (ăd′vər tīz′) **1** to give public notice of; announce publicly: *to* advertise *a change of schedule.* **2** to call attention to in print, over the radio, on television, etc. in order to arouse a desire to buy: *The store manager* advertised *a sale of shoes.* **advertise for** to ask for by public notice: *to* advertise for *a lost article.* **ad·ver·tised, ad·ver·tis·ing.**

ad·ver·tise·ment (ăd′vər tīz′mənt or ăd-vûr′tĭz mənt) public notice about things that are sold, needed, lost, or found.

ad·vice (ăd vīs′) **1** opinion about what ought to be done; counsel; guidance. **2 piece of advice** advice about one thing.

ad·vis·a·ble (ăd vī′zə bəl) worth taking as good advice; sensible; wise: *It is advisable to cross streets only at corners.* **ad·vis·a·bly.**

ad·vise (ăd vīz′) **1** to give an opinion as to what should be done; give advice to: *I would* advise *you to save your money.* **2** to tell; notify: *The campers were* advised *about the danger of touching poison ivy.* **ad·vised, ad·vis·ing.**

ad·vis·er or **ad·vi·sor** (ăd vī′zər) person who gives advice or counsel.

¹ad·vo·cate (ăd′və kāt′) to recommend publicly; favor: *The senator* advocates *careful spending of our country's money.* **ad·vo·cat·ed, ad·vo·cat·ing.**

²ad·vo·cate (ăd′və kĭt) person who speaks in favor of; supporter: *Our teacher is an* advocate *of summer reading programs.*

adz or **adze** (ădz) cutting tool for shaping and finishing timber.

Adz

aer·i·al (âr′ĭ əl) **1** antenna wires, or rods for sending or receiving radio and television waves. **2** (also ə ir′ĭ əl) having to do with, or taking place in, the air: *an* aerial *stunt;* aerial *currents.* **aer·i·al·ly.**

aer·o·nau·tics (âr′ə nô′tĭks) study of flying: *The boy found* aeronautics *fascinating because he wanted to be a pilot.*

aer·o·plane (âr′ə plān) airplane.

a·far (ə fär′) far away; far off; from a distance.

af·fa·ble (ăf′ə bəl) easy to talk to; friendly and polite: *Grandfather is a pleasant and* affable *gentleman.* **af·fa·bly.**

af·fair (ə fâr′) **1** event; happening: *The birthday party, a gay* affair, *became more lively when the monkeys arrived.* **2** thing to do; job; business: *an* affair *of state; to mind one's own* affairs.

¹af·fect (ə fĕkt′) **1** to influence; have a result on: *Horror movies* affected *her dreams.* **2** to move the feelings of; stir the emotions of: *Your story* affects *me deeply.* [**¹affect** comes from a Latin word (affectus) meaning "influence."]

²af·fect (ə fĕkt′) **1** to pretend to do or to have: *He* affected *a sorrow he did not feel.* **2** to like to use: *He* affects *loud neckties.* [**²affect** comes through a French word (affecter) which comes from a Latin word (affectare) meaning "to aim at."]

¹af·fect·ed (ə fĕk′tĭd) **1** influenced: *The climate* affected *our health.* **2** moved; stirred: *He looked much* affected *after hearing the news.* [**¹affected** is from **¹affect.**]

²af·fect·ed (ə fĕk′tĭd) not natural; artificial; pretended: *an* affected *accent.* **af·fect·ed·ly.** [**²affected** is from **²affect.**]

af·fec·tion (ə fĕk′shən) **1** fondness; love: *Although he teased her sometimes, the boy had a great* affection *for his little sister.* **2** in medicine, a disease or complaint: *an* affection *of the right lung.*

af·fec·tion·ate (ə fĕk′shən ĭt) tender; showing affection; loving: *Jane is gentle and* affectionate *toward her younger sister.* **af·fec·tion·ate·ly.**

af·firm (ə fûrm′) to say for certain; declare positively: *He* affirmed *his innocence.*

af·firm·a·tive (ə fûr′mə tĭv) **1** saying yes: Some affirmative expressions are *"O.K.,"* *"all right,"* and *"certainly."* **2** the side arguing that a statement is true: *He was a member of the* affirmative *in the debate.* **3 in the affirmative** in favor: *The majority of the class voted* in the affirmative *when asked if they wanted to study rockets.* **af·firm·a·tive·ly.**

af·flict (ə flĭkt′) to cause great pain or trouble to; make miserable; distress: *A swarm of locusts* afflicted *the countryside.*

af·flic·tion (ə flĭk′shən) **1** distress; misfortune; pain: *Friends sympathized with Jane in her* affliction. **2** something causing suffering or grief: *Heart disease remains one of man's worst* afflictions.

af·flu·ent (ăf′lōō ənt) wealthy; rich: *an* affluent *nation or man.* **af·flu·ent·ly.**

af·ford (ə fôrd′) **1** to give; furnish: *Swimming* affords *enjoyment and muscular training.* **2 can afford** to bear the expense of; spare: *I* can't afford *a car. Can you* afford *the time?*

af·front (ə frŭnt′) **1** to insult openly and on purpose: *He* affronted *me by walking out in the middle of my speech.* **2** open insult: *That speech was an* affront *to the audience.*

a·field (ə fēld′) **1** in or to the field. **2** to, or at, a distance; away: *The traveler wandered far* afield. **3** away from the subject: *To discuss that topic takes us too far* afield.

a·fire (ə fīr′) on fire: *A spark set the forest* afire.

a·flame (ə flām′) **1** on fire; flaming. **2** as if on fire: *to be* aflame *with anger.*

a·float (ə flōt′) **1** carried on water; floating. **2** on board ship: *The old sailor had spent thirty years* afloat. **3** flooded: *The ship's deck was* afloat *during the storm.* **4** in circulation: *There were many rumors* afloat.

a·foot (ə fŏŏt′) **1** on foot; walking. **2** taking place; about to happen; astir: *The guard heard the prisoners whispering, and he knew trouble was* afoot.

a·fraid (ə frād′) full of fear; frightened.

a·fresh (ə frĕsh′) again; anew: *He had to start* afresh *because of his mistakes.*

Af·ri·ca (ăf′rĭ kə) the second largest continent, located south of Europe.

Af·ri·can (ăf′rĭ kən) **1** of Africa or its people. **2** native of Africa.

aft (ăft) at or toward the back of a ship.

FORE or BOW / PORT / STARBOARD / AFT or STERN / Aft

af·ter (ăf′tər) **1** following: *B comes after A. We talked after dinner.* **2** later than: *Come sometime after three o'clock.* **3** following the time that: *We played after we had done our homework.* **4** later; behind: *to go ten days after; to come trailing after.* **5** in search of; in pursuit of: *The police were after the robber, but he escaped.* **6** in spite of; even with the help of: *She still can't sing, even after all those lessons.* **7** because of: *Nobody trusts him after that lie.* **8 look after** to take care of. **9 run after** to try to catch. **10 take after** to be like: *He takes after his grandfather.*

af·ter·noon (ăf′tər nōōn′) **1** the time from noon until evening. **2** held or happening in the afternoon: *an* afternoon *nap.*

af·ter·ward (ăf′tər wərd′) or **af·ter·wards** (ăf′tər wərdz′) at a later time.

a·gain (ə gĕn′) once more; another time: *It snowed* again *this evening. Come* again *soon.*

a·gainst (ə gĕnst′) **1** in an opposite direction to: *They tried to row* against *the tide.* **2** upon; in contact with; touching: *He leaned* against *the fence.* **3** in contrast with: *black* against *the gold.* **4** in opposition to: *There were twenty votes* against *the increase in club dues.* **5** in preparation for: *to save money* against *a rainy day.*

a·gar (ăg′ər or ăg′ər) product from various seaweeds, used in laboratories to grow bacteria.

ag·ate (ăg′ĭt) **1** a kind of quartz with colored bands or cloudy spots, used in jewelry. **2** child's playing marble made to look like this material.

Agate

age (āj) **1** time of life: *at the* age *of ten.* **2** length of life: *Methuselah reached a great* age. **3** period in history: *the*

fāte, făt, fâre, fär; bē, bĕt; bīte, bĭt; nō, nŏt, nôr; fūse, fŭn, fûr; tōō, tŏŏk; foil; foul; thin; ~~then~~; hw for wh as in *what*; zh for s as in *usual*; ə for a, e, i, o, u, as in *ago*, *linen*, *peril*, *atom*, *minus*

59

age *of space travel.* **4** old age. **5** to grow old: *After the shock, he* aged *overnight.* **6** to make old: *Fear and worry* aged *him.* **7** to improve by allowing to stand for a time: *to* age *cheese or wine.* **8** of age 21 years old or over. **aged, ag·ing.**

¹**aged** (ājd) of the age of: *a boy* aged *five.*

²**ag·ed** (ā′jid) old: *an* aged *man.*

a·gen·cy (ā′jən sĭ) **1** business or office of an agent, whether that agent is a person, company, or the government: *employment* agency. **2** action; operation; means: *Through the* agency *of spies the general learned the enemy's plans.* **a·gen·cies.**

a·gent (ā′jənt) **1** person or company that acts for another; representative: *a real estate* agent. **2** power or cause that produces an effect: *Soap is a cleansing* agent.

ag·gra·vate (ăg′rə vāt′) **1** to make worse: *Scratching a mosquito bite* aggravates *it.* **2** in popular language, to irritate: *He* aggravated *his parents by staying out late at night.* **ag·gra·vat·ed, ag·gra·vat·ing.**

ag·gra·va·tion (ăg′rə vā′shən) **1** something that aggravates or makes worse. **2** in popular language, irritation; exasperation.

¹**ag·gre·gate** (ăg′rə gāt′) to add up to; amount to: *Last year's sales* aggregated *$100,000.* **ag·gre·gat·ed, ag·gre·gat·ing.**

²**ag·gre·gate** (ăg′rə git) **1** the total: *The* aggregate *of all his debts was $100.* **2 in the aggregate** taken all together.

ag·gres·sion (ə grĕsh′ən) **1** the starting of an attack or assault. **2** the making of an attack on the rights or territory of another without just cause.

ag·gres·sive (ə grĕs′ĭv) **1** first to attack; quick to pick a quarrel: *an* aggressive *boy.* **2** energetic; enterprising: *an* aggressive *salesman.* **ag·gres·sive·ly.**

ag·gres·sor (ə grĕs′ər) person or country that attacks first.

ag·grieved (ə grēvd′) having a grievance; wronged; hurt in one's feeling: *The old man felt* aggrieved *when his pay was cut.*

a·ghast (ə găst′) struck with sudden horror and showing it; shocked: *We stood* aghast *as we watched the ship strike the reef.*

ag·ile (ăj′əl) quick and light in movement; nimble: *Dancers must be* agile. *An* agile *mind solves problems quickly.* **ag·ile·ly.**

a·gil·i·ty (ə jĭl′ə tĭ) ability to move quickly and gracefully.

ag·i·tate (ăj′ə tāt′) **1** to disturb; excite: *The bad news* agitated *him.* **2** to stir up violently: *The wind* agitated *the lake.* **3** to stir up public opinion: *The paper* agitated *for better housing.* **ag·i·tat·ed, ag·i·tat·ing.**

ag·i·ta·tion (ăj′ə tā′shən) **1** anxiety; worry: *to show* agitation *over a friend's safety.* **2** excited discussion; energetic activity (to promote a cause): *There was general* agitation *for lower taxes.* **3** a moving to and fro: *an* agitation *of the air.*

a·go (ə gō′) **1** past; back; gone by: *two days* ago. **2** in the past: *It happened long* ago.

ag·o·niz·ing (ăg′ə nīz′ĭng) causing great suffering of mind or body: *The day without water in the desert was an* agonizing *experience.* **ag·o·niz·ing·ly.**

ag·o·ny (ăg′ə nĭ) extreme pain of body or mind. **ag·o·nies.**

a·gree (ə grē′) **1** to consent: *They* agreed *to go to the show.* **2** to be of the same opinion: *I* agree *with you about his stinginess.* **3** to be in harmony: *His story* agrees *with mine.* **4** to go well (with one's digestion or health): *Rich foods do not* agree *with me.* **5** to decide together; settle: *We* agreed *on a plan.* **a·greed, a·gree·ing.**

a·gree·a·ble (ə grē′ə bəl) **1** pleasant: *A good dinner and* agreeable *talk go together.* **2** willing to agree: *Are you* agreeable *to this plan?* **a·gree·a·bly.**

a·gree·ment (ə grē′mənt) **1** a being of the same opinion; an understanding: *The two countries came to* agreement *on the terms of the treaty.* **2** harmony; accord: *There was complete* agreement *between the stories of the two witnesses.* **3** a contract; an understanding: *an* agreement *to buy.*

ag·ri·cul·tur·al (ăg′rə kŭl′chər əl) having to do with farming. **ag·ri·cul·tur·al·ly.**

ag·ri·cul·ture (ăg′rə kŭl′chər) farming; the raising of crops and animals.

a·ground (ə ground′) on or onto the bottom in shallow water: *The boat ran* aground.

ah (ä) exclamation of pity, surprise, joy, etc.

a·head (ə hĕd′) **1** forward; onward: *I went* ahead *on the path.* **2** straight in front: *There is a big mud hole* ahead *in the road.* **3 ahead of** in advance of: *Tim was* ahead *of the others in arithmetic.* **4 be ahead** (**1**) to be in front. (**2**) to be to the good: *I am five dollars* ahead. **5 get ahead** to succeed. **6 get ahead of** to pass; excel.

a·hoy (ə hoi′) call used by sailors to hail a ship: *Ship*, *ahoy!*

aid (ād) **1** to help or assist. **2** person or thing that helps or assists: *Books are an aid to learning.* **3** help: *with the aid of a doctor.* (Homonym: aide)

aide (ād) **1** helper; assistant: *a nurse's aide.* **2** officer who is an assistant to a superior: *General Clark's aides.* (Homonym: aid)

ail (āl) **1** to cause pain or discomfort to; be the matter with; trouble: *What ails the man?* **2** to feel sick; be ill. (Homonym: ale)

ai·ler·on (ā′lə rŏn) hinged part on the rear edge of each wing of an airplane to steady it in flight. For picture, see **airplane.**

ail·ment (āl′mənt) sickness; illness.

aim (ām) **1** to point (a gun, arrow, etc.). **2** the pointing of a weapon, etc.: *to take aim.* **3** to send; direct: *The boxer aimed his blows at the chin. Those insults were aimed at you.* **4** to intend; try: *We aim to please.* **5** purpose; goal: *an aim in life.*

aim·less (ām′lis) having no particular goal or purpose. **aim·less·ly.**

ain't (ānt) **1** am not; are not. **2** have not; has not. Careful speakers avoid using ain't.

air (âr) **1** mixture of gases, mostly oxygen and nitrogen, surrounding the earth; the atmosphere. **2** space above the earth; sky: *The air was full of kites.* **3** light breeze. **4** a tune or melody: *He sang many airs his grandmother taught him.* **5** to expose to the air; ventilate: *Let us open the window and air the room.* **6** to make known; display: *Sullen Susie airs her grievances to everyone.* **7** appearance; look: *an air of dignity.* **8 airs** manners or appearance (put on to impress people); affected attitude: *Her city airs annoy her friends at home.* **9 in the air** (**1**) in circulation: *Reports of defeat were in the air.* (**2**) not yet settled; vague: *Our plans are still in the air.* **10 on the air** being broadcast by radio or *television; broadcasting. (Homonyms: e'er, ere, heir)

air base landing field and buildings where military aircraft are kept and repaired.

air·con·di·tion (âr′kən dĭsh′ən) to bring air to the desired temperature, humidity, and state of purity, in a room, building, bus, railroad car, or the like.

air conditioning a means of making the air pure and of controlling its temperature and humidity in a room, building, etc.

air·craft (âr′krăft′) airplane, airship, or balloon. pl. **aircraft.**

air·drome (âr′drōm′) airport.

Aire·dale (âr′dāl′) large terrier with a rough coat of brown or tan with black markings.

air·field (âr′fēld′) level field with runways where airplanes may take off or land.

air gun rifle or pistol operated by compressed air instead of gunpowder.

air line company that owns and operates airplanes to carry passengers and freight.

air liner a large passenger airship.

air mail **1** mail carried by aircraft. **2** system for carrying mail by aircraft.

air·plane (âr′plān′) aircraft supported by fixed wings and driven by one or more engines.

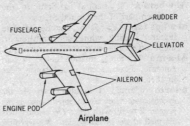

Airplane

air·port (âr′pôrt′) a place for the taking off, landing, loading, fueling, or repairing of aircraft.

air pressure **1** pressure caused by the weight of air in the atmosphere (about 15 pounds per square inch at sea level). **2** pressure of compressed air: *the air pressure in an automobile tire.*

air rifle a rifle operated by compressed air instead of gunpowder.

air·ship (âr′ship′) **1** aircraft that is lighter than air and is driven by one or more engines; a dirigible balloon. **2** an airplane.

air·tight (âr′tīt′) closed or sealed so that no air can get in or out.

air·way (âr′wā′) route for aircraft.

fāte, făt, fâre, fär; bē, bĕt; bīte, bĭt; nō, nŏt, nôr; fūse, fŭn, fûr; tōō, tŏŏk; foil; foul; thin; then; hw for wh as in what; zh for s as in usual; ə for a, e, i, o, u, as in ago, linen, peril, atom, minus

61

air·y (âr′ĭ) **1** in or of the air; high up. **2** with air moving freely; breezy: *an* airy *room.* **3** light-hearted; graceful; gay: *an* airy *manner;* airy *laughter.* **air·i·er, air·i·est; air·i·ly.**

aisle (īl) **1** passageway between seats in a church, theater, or the like. **2** passageway between counters in a store. (Homonyms: I'll, isle)

a·jar (ə jär′) partly opened: *He leaves the door* ajar *so the cat can come in.*

a·kim·bo (ə kĭm′bō) with hands resting on hips and the elbows bent outward.

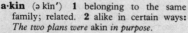

Akimbo

a·kin (ə kĭn′) **1** belonging to the same family; related. **2** alike in certain ways: *The two plans were* akin *in purpose.*

Ala. Alabama.

Al·a·bam·a (ăl′ə băm′ə) a State in the southern part of the United States.

al·a·bas·ter (ăl′ə băs′tər) stone of fine texture, usually white and translucent, often carved into vases or other ornaments.

Al·a·mo (ăl′ə mō′) mission house in San Antonio, Texas, scene of a historic siege in 1836.

a·larm (ə lärm′) **1** sudden fear: *As the enemy came near,* alarm *spread among the people.* **2** to fill with fear: *The country was* alarmed *at the threat of war.* **3** a warning of danger: *Paul Revere gave the* alarm *to the people of Concord.* **4** to give or send an alarm. **5** a sounding device to call attention or warn: *a burglar* alarm; *a fire* alarm.

a·lar·um (ə lăr′əm) in old or poetic language, alarm.

a·las (ə lăs′) exclamation showing sorrow, pity, or regret.

A·las·ka (ə lăs′kə) the 49th State of the United States, located in northwestern North America and admitted in 1959.

al·be·it (ôl bē′ĭt) although; even though.

al·bi·no (ăl bī′nō) **1** person with white or very light skin and hair, and pink eyes. **2** any animal or plant that lacks the color usual for its kind. **al·bi·nos.**

al·bum (ăl′bəm) **1** book with blank pages in which to keep photographs, stamps, autographs, etc. **2** holder, in the form of a book, for phonograph records.

al·co·hol (ăl′kə hôl′ or ăl′kə hŏl′) colorless liquid made from fermented grains, fruit juices, sugars, or starches. Alcohol is the intoxicating substance in beer, wine, whiskey, etc. It is also used in medicines, in manufacturing, and as a fuel.

al·co·hol·ic (ăl′kə hôl′ĭk or ăl′kə hŏl′ĭk) **1** containing alcohol: *Whiskey is an* alcoholic *drink.* **2** of alcohol: *an* alcoholic *vapor.* **3** person addicted to the use of liquor.

al·cove (ăl′kōv) small room opening out of a larger room; nook.

al·der (ôl′dər) any of several shrubs or trees related to the birch, usually growing in moist ground. Alder bark is used in dyeing and tanning.

Alcove

al·der·man (ôl′dər mən) member of the governing body of a ward, district, or city. **al·der·men.**

ale (āl) a fermented drink made from malt and hops. Ale is like beer but is darker, heavier, and contains more alcohol. (Homonym: ail)

a·lert (ə lûrt′) **1** mentally quick in perception and action: *an* alert *mind.* **2** attentive; wide-awake; watchful; bright: *an* alert *student.* **3** to warn of coming danger: *The troops were* alerted *before the enemy attack.* **4** a warning of coming danger: *an air* alert. **5 on the alert** on the lookout; watchful. **a·lert·ly.**

al·fal·fa (ăl făl′fə) deep-rooted plant with cloverlike leaves and purple flowers. It is used as food for cattle and horses.

al·gae (ăl′jē) large group of simple plants that contain chlorophyll but have no flowers. Algae live in water or damp places, and each plant may have only one cell (pond scum) or many cells (seaweed).

al·ge·bra (ăl′jə brə) branch of mathematics that uses letters as well as numbers to show relationships.

a·li·bi (ăl′ə bī′) **1** claim made by a person accused of a crime or wrongdoing, that he was somewhere else when the crime was committed: *The* alibi *of the accused was that he was making a speech in another town at the time of the crime.* **2** in loose language, an excuse: *Tom has a ready* alibi *for everything.*

al·ien (ā′lĭ ən or āl′yən) **1** foreigner; person who is not a citizen of the country in which he is living. **2** foreign: *an* alien *language; an* alien *land.* **3 alien to** strange to; not characteristic of: *Dishonesty is* alien *to him.*

¹a·light (ə lit′) **1** kindled or burning: *The fire is* alight *on the hearth.* **2** bright: *The bride's face was* alight *with happiness.* [**¹alight** is a combination of an Old English word (an) meaning "on" and ¹**light**.]

²a·light (ə lit′) **1** to come down (from): *to* alight *from a train.* **2** to come down and settle: *The bird* alighted *on the top branch.* [²**alight** is a form of an Old English word (ālihtan).]

a·lign (ə lin′) **1** to put into line: *The mechanic* aligned *the front and rear wheels.* **2** to be in line: *The wheels* align.

a·like (ə lik′) **1** similar: *The two brothers look* alike, *but they are not twins.* **2** similarly; in the same way: *The two sisters dress* alike.

al·i·men·ta·ry ca·nal (ăl′ə mĕn′tə rĭ kə-năl′) the tube that passes food through the body, and in which food is digested. It is made up of the esophagus, stomach, and intestines.

a·line (ə lin′) align. **a·lined, a·lin·ing.**

a·live (ə liv′) **1** living; existent: *He is* alive. *He is keeping his claim* alive. **2** lively; full of spirit. **3 alive to** aware of; sensitive to: *An ambitious man is* alive *to his chances.* **4 alive with** filled with (living things): *a stream* alive *with fish.*

al·ka·li (ăl′kə lĭ) **1** bitter, burning substance found in soil and water of many deserts. **2** in chemistry, a base that can be dissolved in water. **al·ka·lis** or **al·ka·lies.**

al·ka·line (ăl′kə lĭn′ or ăl′kə lĭn) **1** containing alkali. **2** capable of combining with an acid to form a salt.

all (ôl) **1** the whole of: *The story is known by* all *the world.* **2** every one of: *The boys ate* all *the apples.* **3** everyone (as a group): *They are* all *going to the party.* **4** completely; wholly; entirely: *The work is* all *done.* **5** everything: *He gave* all *he had to charity.* **6** nothing but: *This is* all *work and no play.* **7 all but** almost: *He* all *but collapsed.* **8 at all** in any way; to any

extent: *His singing is not* at all *bad. Do you mind helping me? Not* at all! **9 in all** altogether: *That's five* in all. (Homonym: awl)

Al·lah (ăl′ə or äl′ə) name of God in the Moslem religion.

al·lay (ə lā′) to quiet; calm; make less or reduce: *The doctor* allayed *his fears.*

al·lege (ə lĕj′) **1** to claim or assert without proving: *He* alleged *that the money had been stolen.* **2** to offer as an excuse: *to* allege *illness as a reason for being absent.* **al·leged, al·leg·ing.**

al·le·gi·ance (ə lē′jəns) **1** loyalty and duty owed to or shown toward one's country, ruler, or leader. **2** faithfulness; devotion: *his* allegiance *to his family.*

al·ler·gic (ə lûr′jĭk) having an allergy (to): *Mae is* allergic *to pork.*

al·ler·gy (ăl′ər jĭ) condition of being sensitive to certain plants, foods, cloths, etc., with harmful effects: *an* allergy *to golden-rod.* **al·ler·gies.**

al·ley (ăl′ĭ) **1** a narrow back street. **2** in bowling, a long narrow enclosure with a smooth wooden floor. **3 blind alley (1)** a path or an alley that leads nowhere. **(2)** an idea or activity that leads to nothing.

al·li·ance (ə li′əns) union or joining together by agreement of two or more persons, families, groups, or nations: *an* alliance *by marriage; an* alliance *for war.*

al·lied (ăl′ĭd or ə lid′) **1** joined together by agreement or treaty: *the* allied *powers.* **2** related: *Reading and writing are closely* allied *subjects.*

Alligator, 10 to 12 ft. long.

al·li·ga·tor (ăl′ə gā′tər) a large lizardlike animal with four short legs, a thick skin, a broad snout, and a long tail. Alligators live in swamps in the warm parts of America.

---

fāte, făt, fâre, fär; bē, bĕt; bīte, bĭt; nō, nŏt, nôr; fūse, fŭn, fûr; tōō, tŏŏk; foil; foul; thin; ~~then~~; hw for wh as in *w*hat; zh for s as in u*s*ual; ə for a, e, i, o, u, as in ag*o*, lin*e*n, per*i*l, at*o*m, min*u*s

al·lot (ə lŏt′) **1** to give (each one) his share; distribute: *The prize money was* allotted *to the various winners.* **2** to assign: *Phillip* allots *two hours of the day for homework.* **al·lot·ted, al·lot·ting.**

al·low (ə lou′) **1** to permit: *The hospital* allows *no visitors.* **2** to let have; give: *The class was* allowed *one hour to finish the test.* **3** to accept as true: *His claim was* allowed. **allow for** to take into consideration (something which might cause a change): *Because of the icy streets,* allow for *extra time to travel.*

al·low·a·ble (ə lou′ə bəl) permissible; allowed; not forbidden: *Two mistakes are* allowable *in this game.*

al·low·ance (ə lou′əns) **1** definite amount given for a purpose: *an* allowance *of pocket money; a travel* allowance. **2** an amount added on or subtracted: *an* allowance *for wear and tear.* **3 make allowance for** to take into consideration (anything which might cause a change): *He left early to* make allowance for *bad road conditions.*

¹al·loy (ăl′oi or ə loi′) a mixture of two or more metals: *Bronze is an* alloy *of copper and tin.*

²al·loy (ə loi′) to melt two or more metals together.

all right 1 correct; satisfactory: *If your work is quite* all right, *start something new.* **2** neither hurt nor sick; safe: *I had measles last month, but I'm* all right *now.* **3** yes; certainly: *Oh,* all right, *you may go.*

al·lude (ə lōōd′ or ə lūd′) to refer to; mention: *In his book the professor* alluded *to his earlier essay on the subject.* **al·lud·ed, al·lud·ing.**

al·lure (ə lōōr′) **1** to win over; attract; entice: *to* allure *by the promise of pleasure.* **2** something which attracts: *the* allure *of adventure.* **al·lured, al·lur·ing.**

al·lu·sion (ə lōō′zhən or ə lū′zhən) passing reference (usually to somebody or something familiar) to make a comparison or to make something clear: *The circus poster about the strong man made an* allusion *to Hercules.*

al·lu·vi·al (ə lōō′vi əl or ə lū′vi əl) made up of mud, sand, and clay deposited by running water or by flood waters: *Much land along the Mississippi River has* alluvial *soil, good for farming.*

¹al·ly (ə li′) to join (oneself or another) with someone for a particular purpose: *The United States* allied *itself with Western Europe in NATO.* **al·lied, al·ly·ing.**

²al·ly (ăl′i) person or group of persons, especially a nation, united with another for a common purpose: *They were natural* allies *and agreed perfectly.* **al·lies.**

al·ma·nac (ôl′mə năk′) calendar of the days, weeks, and months of the year, that gives information about the weather, sunrise, and sunset, important anniversaries, etc. during that period.

al·might·y (ôl mi′ti) **1** all-powerful. **2 the Almighty** God.

al·mond (ä′mənd or ăm′ənd) **1** nut or seed of the fruit of a tree somewhat like the peach or plum tree. **2** the tree itself. **3** pale tan color.

Almond, shell and kernel

al·most (ôl′mōst or ôl mōst′) nearly.

alms (ämz) money given to the poor; charity: *to give* alms *to a beggar.*

a·loft (ə lôft′) **1** far above the earth; high up: *The planes were* aloft *at the time of the air raid.* **2** high above the deck of a ship in the upper rigging: *The sailor nimbly climbed* aloft.

a·lo·ha (ə lō′ə or ä lō′hä) Hawaiian greeting meaning both "hello" and "good-by."

a·lone (ə lōn′) **1** by oneself: *He's going* alone. **2** only: *He* alone *has the answer.*

a·long (ə lông′) **1** over the length of: *We picked up shells* along *the beach.* **2** beside the length of; at the border of: *There were flowers planted* along *the garden walk.* **3** onward: *The policeman asked the crowd to move* along. **4** together; with one: *He came* along. *They brought him* along. **5 all along** all the while: *He knew it* all along. **6 along with** together with.

a·long·side (ə lông′sid′) **1** to or at the side (usually of a ship, dock, or pier): *The pirates brought their small boat* alongside *and then boarded the ship.* **2** next to: *He parked his car* alongside *the building.*

a·loof (ə lōōf′) apart or away from other people; not wanting to associate with others: *The boy stood* aloof *and did not join the crowd.* **a·loof·ly.**

a·loud (ə loud′) out loud: *He read the story* aloud *to the class.*

al·pac·a (ăl păk′ə) **1** kind of South American llama having long woolly hair. **2** cloth made from the hair of this animal.

al·pen·stock (ăl′pən stŏk′) strong staff with a pointed metal tip on one end, used by mountain climbers.

al·pha·bet (ăl′fə bĕt′) the letters used in spelling or writing the words of a language, arranged in a certain order. The 26 letters of the English alphabet are A, B, C, D, E, F, G, H, I, J, K, L, M, N, O, P, Q, R, S, T, U, V, W, X, Y, Z.

al·pha·bet·i·cal (ăl′fə bĕt′ə kəl) in the order of the letters of the alphabet: *The names were arranged in* alphabetical *order.* **al·pha·bet·i·cal·ly.**

al·pha·bet·ize (ăl′fə bə tīz′) to arrange in the order of the letters of the alphabet: *Please* alphabetize *this list of names for me.* **al·pha·bet·ized, al·pha·bet·iz·ing.**

Alps (ălps) range of mountains, extending through France, Germany, Switzerland, Italy, Austria, and Yugoslavia.

al·read·y (ôl rĕd′ĭ) by this (or that) time; before now (or then): *We had* already *eaten when he arrived.*

al·so (ôl′sō) too; in addition: *She is clever and also pretty.*

al·tar (ôl′tər) **1** raised place or structure on which religious sacrifices are offered, or at which religious ceremonies are performed. **2** in many Christian churches, the communion table. (Homonym: alter)

al·ter (ôl′tər) to change; make or become different: *The tailor altered the suit to fit the boy. My opinion altered when I learned all the facts.* (Homonym: altar)

al·ter·a·tion (ôl′tə rā′shən) a change: *Simple alterations improved the airplane.*

¹al·ter·nate (ôl′tər nĭt) **1** every second one (of a series): *The boys and girls used the gymnasium on* alternate *days of the week.* **2** first one and then the other; by turns: *The cake had* alternate *layers of vanilla and chocolate.* **3** a substitute: *When the juror fell ill, an* alternate *took his place.* **al·ter·nate·ly.**

²al·ter·nate (ôl′tər nāt′) **1** to take turns: *My sister and I* alternate *in cleaning our room.* **2** to take place or appear by turns:* White tiles alternated *with black.* **3** to cause to take place or appear by turns: *We* alternated *the colors as we laid the tiles.* **al·ter·nat·ed, al·ter·nat·ing.**

alternating current (ôl′tər nāt′ĭng kûr′ənt) electric current that flows first in one direction and then in the other. The alternating current used in the home usually reverses direction 120 times per second.

al·ter·na·tive (ôl tûr′nə tĭv) **1** choice (usually between two things): *Since it was raining, we had no* alternative *but to play indoors.* **2** one of two or more things to choose from: *Planes are* alternatives *for trains.* **3** offering or giving a choice: *an* alternative *plan.* **al·ter·na·tive·ly.**

al·though (ôl thō′) even though; in spite of the fact that: *I don't really know him very well* although *he lives next door.* Also spelled **altho.**

al·tim·e·ter (ăl tĭm′ə tər or ăl′tə mē′tər) instrument for measuring altitude, as in an aircraft to show how high it is flying.

al·ti·tude (ăl′tə tōōd′ or ăl′tə tūd′) **1** height above the earth's surface: *the altitude of an airplane.* **2** height on the earth's surface above sea level: *the altitude of a city or mountain.* **3** a place far above sea level: *In high altitudes people find it hard to breathe.*

al·to (ăl′tō) **1** in music, the lowest female voice; contralto. **2** a singer having an alto voice. **3** having a range like that of the alto voice: *an alto saxophone.* **4** part for such a voice or instrument. **al·tos.**

al·to·geth·er (ôl′tə gĕth′ər) **1** entirely; wholly; completely: *The boy took careful aim but he missed the target* altogether. *His composition was not* altogether *bad.* **2** all told: *There were ten absentees* altogether.

al·um (ăl′əm) transparent, whitish mineral substance, used to stop bleeding from slight cuts, and in dyeing fabrics.

a·lu·mi·num (ə lōō′mə nəm or ə lū′mə nəm) silver-white, very light metal element that does not rust easily.

al·ways (ôl′wāz) at all times; on all occasions; without exception: *My father is always generous. I always shop on Monday.*

am (ăm) a form of **be** that is used with *I*: *"I am here," she said. "I am coming."*

---

fāte, făt, fâre, fär; bē, bĕt; bīte, bĭt; nō, nŏt, nôr; fūse, fŭn, fûr; tōō, tŏŏk; foil; foul; thin; ~~then~~; hw for wh as in *wh*at; zh for s as in u*s*ual; ə for a, e, i, o, u, as in *a*go, lin*e*n, per*i*l, at*o*m, min*u*s

AM (ā′ĕm′) amplitude modulation.

A.M. or **a.m.** before noon; the time between midnight and noon.

a·mass (ə măs′) to collect; gather; pile up; accumulate: *to amass a fortune.*

am·a·teur (ăm′ə chŏŏr′, ăm′ə chər, or ăm′-ə tər) **1** person who takes part in a sport or engages in some art or hobby for pleasure and not for money: *The players on a school team are* amateurs. **2** person whose work is not very skillful: *The rough edges on the carving showed that an* amateur *had done the job.* **3** of or like an amateur; done by amateurs: *an* amateur *tennis player; an* amateur *performance.*

a·maze (ə māz′) to surprise greatly; overwhelm with astonishment: *They were so amazed by the magician's tricks that they forgot to applaud.* **a·mazed, a·maz·ing.**

a·maze·ment (ə māz′mənt) great surprise; sudden wonder: *The savages were filled with amazement at the eclipse of the sun.*

a·maz·ing (ə mā′zing) causing amazement; wonderful; very surprising. **a·maz·ing·ly.**

am·bas·sa·dor (ăm băs′ə dər) **1** a representative of the highest rank sent by one government or ruler to another. **2** any representative with a special mission; messenger; agent.

am·ber (ăm′bər) **1** a hard, yellow or yellow-brown gum that can be polished and made into beads, jewelry, and pipe stems. Amber is actually fossil resin. **2** made of amber. **3** yellow or yellowish-brown.

am·bi·tion (ăm bĭsh′ən) **1** strong desire for power, fame, or position: *Napoleon's excessive* ambition *led him into war.* **2** the thing strongly desired: *He attained his* ambition *to become a reporter.*

am·bi·tious (ăm bĭsh′əs) **1** determined to succeed. **2** strongly desiring; eager: *to be* ambitious *for knowledge.* **3** showing great ambition: *Timmy has an* ambitious *plan to walk across the country.* **am·bi·tious·ly.**

am·ble (ăm′bəl) **1** gait of a horse, in which both legs on the same side are lifted at once, followed by a similar movement on the other side. **2** of a horse, etc., to walk in this way. **3** to walk at a slow, easy pace. **4** slow, easy way of walking. **am·bled, am·bling.**

am·bu·lance (ăm′byə ləns) automobile or other vehicle equipped for carrying the sick or wounded.

am·bush (ăm′bŏŏsh) **1** hiding place from which to make a surprise attack. **2** troops hidden so that they can make a surprise attack. **3** sudden surprise attack from a hidden place. **4** to stage a surprise attack from a hidden position: *The bandits* ambushed *the stagecoach.*

a·me·ba (ə mē′bə) amoeba.

a·men (ā′mĕn′ or ä′mĕn′) a word used at the end of a prayer. It means "Let it be so" or "So be it."

a·mend (ə mĕnd′) **1** to change formally: *to* amend *a law.* **2** to change for the better; correct: *to* amend *bad habits.*

a·mend·ment (ə mĕnd′mənt) **1** formal change, as in a legal document: *There are over twenty* amendments *to the Constitution of the United States.* **2** a change of one's ways for the better: *I'm hoping to see some* amendment *in him.*

a·mends (ə mĕndz′) something that makes up for harm done; compensation; reparation: *The boy made* amends *for his rudeness by writing a letter of apology.*

A·mer·i·ca (ə mĕr′ə kə) **1** North and South America. **2** North America. **3** the United States of America.

A·mer·i·can (ə mĕr′ə kən) **1** of the United States: *The* American *flag has 50 stars.* **2** a citizen of the United States. **3** of or having to do with North or South America or both: *Corn, potatoes, and tobacco are all New World, or* American, *plants.* **4** an inhabitant of North or South America.

American Revolution war from 1775-1783 in which the American colonies won their independence from Great Britain.

am·e·thyst (ăm′ə thĭst) **1** a purple or violet quartz used in jewelry. **2** purple; violet.

a·mi·a·ble (ā′mĭ ə bəl) friendly; pleasant; good-natured: *She is jolly and* amiable *and never loses her temper.* **a·mi·a·bly.**

a·mid (ə mĭd′) in the middle of; among: *Only one column stood* amid *the ruins.*

a·mid·ships (ə mĭd′shĭps) in or toward the middle of a ship.

a·midst (ə mĭdst′) amid.

a·miss (ə mĭs′) **1** wrong; out of order: *The night watchman checked the building to be sure that nothing was* amiss. **2 take amiss** to have one's feelings hurt: *Don't take it* amiss *if I criticize your work.*

am·mo·ni·a (ə mōn′yə) **1** a colorless gas with a strong, sharp smell. **2** a solution of ammonia gas in water, used for cleaning. Ammonia is used in fertilizers, cleaning fluid, and in the manufacture of ice.

am·mu·ni·tion (ăm′yōō nish′ən) powder, bullets, shells, or other missile for firing at game, a target, or in warfare.

a·moe·ba (ə mē′bə) a tiny water animal having only one cell. It can be seen only with the aid of a microscope. Also spelled **ameba. a·moe·bae** (ə mē′bē) or **a·moe·bas.**

Amoeba, magnified 100 times

a·mong (ə mŭng′) **1** in the midst of; surrounded by: *When he went back to school he was* among *friends.* **2** by the joint action of: *They solved the problem among themselves.* **3** in the time of: *Automobiles were unknown* among *the ancient Romans.* **4** in shares to each of: *The books were divided* among *the students.* **5** in the class of: *He said that* among *American presidents, three or four stood out.*

a·mongst (ə mŭngst′) amid; among.

a·mount (ə mount′) **1** sum; quantity: *This purchase requires a small* amount *of money.* **2** total sum: *The* amount *for cleaning and polishing is $7.*

amount to to add up to; be equal to: *The bills* amount *to $10. This* amounts *to disobedience.*

am·pere (ăm′pir) unit for measuring the amount of electricity flowing through a circuit each second.

am·phib·i·an (ăm fib′i ən) **1** plant or animal that can live both on land and in water: *Frogs are* amphibians. **2** an airplane that can take off and land on either land or water. **3** tank, or other vehicle, that can be used on land and water.

am·phib·i·ous (ăm fib′i əs) able to live or to operate both on land and in water. **am·phib·i·ous·ly.**

am·phi·the·a·ter (ăm′fə thē′ə tər) circular or oval building, open or enclosed, with rows of seats sloping upward from a central space or arena.

am·ple (ăm′pəl) **1** of large size or amount: *The* ample *rooms held all of the furniture.* **2** enough: *He has* ample *money to live comfortably.* **3** abundant; more than enough: *We have* ample *food for the trip and can share it with you.* **am·ply.**

am·pli·fi·er (ăm′plə fī′ər) device used in radios, phonographs, etc., to increase the strength of electrical impulses.

am·pli·fy (ăm′plə fī′) **1** to add fuller details to; enlarge on: *Will you* amplify *that statement so that I can understand it?* **2** to enlarge in volume or amount, as sound on a radio. **am·pli·fied, am·pli·fy·ing.**

am·pli·tude (ăm′plətōōd′ or ăm′plə tūd′) **1** breadth; width; sufficiency. **2** the greatest distance from the upper or lower curve of a sound wave or the like to a midpoint in the curve. **3 amplitude modulation** way of radio broadcasting in which the amplitude of the radio wave is changed according to the sound being broadcast. Also called **AM.**

Amplitude

am·u·let (ăm′yōō lit) a charm or token worn by superstitious people as a protection against evil or harm.

a·muse (ə mūz′) to entertain; divert; to cause to smile or laugh: *The story* amused *the children.* **a·mused, a·mus·ing.**

a·muse·ment (ə mūz′mənt) entertainment; pleasure: *to seek* amusement *at the park.*

an (ăn when stressed; ən when unstressed) **1** any; one: *Give her* an *apple.* **2** each; every: *two dollars* an *hour.* **An** is used instead of **a** before words beginning with **a, e, i, o,** or **u** sounds.

an·a·con·da (ăn′ə kon′də) a very large snake of tropical South America that coils around and crushes its prey.

an·a·lyse (ăn′ə līz′) analyze. **an·a·lysed, an·a·lys·ing.**

a·nal·y·sis (ə năl′ə sis) **1** separation of a thing into its parts or elements to find out what it is made of: *An* analysis *of water shows that it contains oxygen and hydrogen.* **2** careful examination: *an* analysis *of a plan.* **a·nal·y·ses** (ə năl′ə sēz′).

---

fāte, făt, fâre, fär; bē, bĕt; bīte, bĭt; nō, nŏt, nôr; fūse, fŭn, fûr; tōō, tŏŏk; foil; foul; thin; ~~then~~; hw for wh as in *wh*at; zh for s as in u*s*ual; ə for a, e, i, o, u, as in *a*go, lin*e*n, per*i*l, at*o*m, min*u*s

an·a·lyze (ăn'ə līz') **1** to separate into parts: *The chemist* analyzes *many compounds.* **2** to examine; study carefully: *A judge must* analyze *all of the evidence.* **an·a·lyzed, an·a·lyzing.** Also spelled **analyse.**

an·ar·chy (ăn'ər kĭ) **1** absence of law and government. **2** confusion; disorder: *After the chairman lost control of the meeting there was complete* anarchy *in the hall.*

a·nat·o·my (ə năt'ə mĭ) **1** the physical structure of animals or plants: *The* anatomy *of a snake is quite different from that of a rabbit.* **2** the scientific study of the structure of animals and plants. **a·nat·o·mies.**

an·ces·tor (ăn'sĕs tər) a person from whom one is directly descended.

an·ces·tral (ăn sĕs'trəl) belonging to, or inherited from, ancestors: *an* ancestral *home.*

an·chor (ăng'kər) **1** a heavy iron or steel implement lowered from a ship to the bottom of the sea or of a river to hold the ship fast. **2** any similar device for holding fast or checking motion: *a balloon* anchor. **3** to hold in place by an anchor: *It was hard to anchor the ship in the current.* **4** to drop anchor: *The ship* anchored *at noon.* **5** anything that makes one feel safe and secure: *He relied on the* anchor *of his faith.*

Ship's anchor

an·chor·age (ăng'kər ĭj) a place where ships are anchored or moored.

an·cient (ān'shənt) **1** belonging to times long past, especially to the times of the Greeks and the Romans: *an* ancient *coin bearing the profile of Alexander.* **2** very old: *an* ancient *tree.* **3** a very old person. **4 the ancients** (1) the civilized nations of old, especially Greece and Rome. (2) the classical writers (of Greece and Rome). **an·cient·ly.**

and (ănd) **1** with; along with; added to: *pencil and paper; pork and beans.* **2** also: *They set up camp and went fishing. This tea is good and strong.*

Andirons

and·i·ron (ănd'ī'ərn) one of a pair of stands, usually made of iron or brass, used to support firewood burned in an open fireplace.

an·ec·dote (ăn'ĭk dōt') brief story about an interesting incident or person.

an·e·mom·e·ter (ăn'ə mŏm'ə tər) instrument for measuring the speed of the wind.

a·nem·o·ne (ə něm'ə nē') a plant with a slender stem and white flowers that grows in the woods in the early spring.

a·new (ə nōō' or ə nū') once more; again; afresh: *He decided to start the work* anew.

an·gel (ān'jəl) **1** a spiritual being that is an attendant or messenger of God. **2** a drawing, painting, or sculpture of such a spiritual being in human form with wings. **3** a good, kindly, loving person.

an·gel·ic (ăn jĕl'ĭk) **1** of an angel or angels: *the* angelic *choir.* **2** like an angel: *an* angelic *smile.*

An·ge·lus (ăn'jə ləs) **1** in the Roman Catholic Church, a certain prayer said at morning, noon, and evening. **2** bell that announces the time for this prayer.

an·ger (ăng'gər) **1** strong, hostile feeling stirred up by wrong or injury to oneself or others; emotion that makes a person want to quarrel or fight. **2** to make angry: *The nasty remark* angered *her.*

¹an·gle (ăng'gəl) **1** to fish with a hook and line. **2** to try to get as if by fishing: *She* angled *for a compliment by mentioning her new dress several times.* **an·gled, an·gling.** [¹**angle** is a form of an Old English word (angul) meaning "fishhook."]

²an·gle (ăng'gəl) **1** space between two lines or surfaces that meet at a point or that cross each other: *the* angle *formed by two neighboring walls.* **2** a corner: *in the chimney* angle. **3** point of view: *What was the reporter's* angle *in that story?* [²**angle** comes through French (angle) from a Latin word (angulus).]

ACUTE RIGHT OBTUSE

Angles

an·gler (ăng'glər) fisherman, especially one who fishes for pleasure.

an·gle·worm (ăng'gəl wûrm') earthworm used as bait by anglers.

An·glo-Sax·on (ăng'glō săk'sən) **1** a member of the German tribes who invaded England in the fifth and sixth centuries. **2** a person chiefly of English descent. **3** the language used before 1100 in Britain; Old English. **4** having to do with the Anglo-Saxons or their language.

an·go·ra (ăng gôr′ə) **1** a domestic cat with long, soft hair. **2** a domestic goat with long, silky hair. **3** the wool of this goat.

an·gry (ăng′grĭ) feeling or showing anger. **an·gri·er, an·gri·est; an·gri·ly.**

an·guish (ăng′gwĭsh) acute suffering or pain, either of body or of mind.

an·gu·lar (ăng′gyŏŏ lər) **1** having angles or sharp corners. **2** bony; gaunt. **an·gu·lar·ly.**

an·i·mal (ăn′ə məl) **1** a living thing that can feel and move by itself; any living thing except a plant. All nature is divided into three kingdoms: animal, vegetable, and mineral. **2** any animal other than man. **3** a four-legged animal. **4** of or like an animal: *This* animal *cracker is shaped like a bear.*

¹an·i·mate (ăn′ə māt′) **1** to make lively, gay, or energetic: *Joy* animated *his face.* **2** to be a reason or motive for; inspire: *In all his achievements he was* animated *by love of country.* **an·i·mat·ed, an·i·mat·ing.**

²an·i·mate (ăn′ə mĭt) **1** alive. **2 animate nature** all living things.

an·i·mat·ed (ăn′ə māt′ĭd) **1** full of life; lively. **2** made to seem alive and moving: *an* animated *cartoon.* **an·i·mat·ed·ly.**

an·i·ma·tion (ăn′ə mā′shən) **1** liveliness; spirit; life. **2** the process of preparing drawings to be filmed as animated cartoons.

an·i·mos·i·ty (ăn′ə mŏs′ə tĭ) feeling of dislike or hatred: *The misdeeds of the ruler aroused* animosity. **an·i·mos·i·ties.**

an·kle (ăng′kəl) **1** the joint connecting the foot with the leg. **2** slender part of the leg just above this joint.

an·klet (ăng′klĭt) **1** a sock which reaches just above the ankle. **2** a bracelet worn around the ankle.

¹an·nex (ə nĕks′) to add or join (something smaller) to a larger thing: *The company* annexed *two smaller stores to its national chain.*

²an·nex (ăn′ĕks) an addition to a building.

an·nex·a·tion (ăn′ĭk sā′shən) the act of joining a smaller to a larger thing, especially a country, territory, or city to a larger one: *The* annexation *of Brooklyn to New York took place in 1898.*

an·ni·hi·late (ə nī′ə lāt′) to destroy completely: *This bomb can* annihilate *a city.* **an·ni·hi·lat·ed, an·ni·hi·lat·ing.**

an·ni·hi·la·tion (ə nī′ə lā′shən) complete destruction; a wiping out: *The bomb threatened the* annihilation *of the whole city.*

an·ni·ver·sa·ry (ăn′ə vûr′sə rĭ) **1** yearly return of the date on which something happened: *a wedding* anniversary. **2** having to do with such a date: *an* anniversary *gift.* **an·ni·ver·sa·ries.**

an·nounce (ə nouns′) to give formal notice of; make known: *to* announce *an engagement.* **an·nounced, an·nounc·ing,**

an·nounce·ment (ə nouns′mənt) **1** act of making known: *the* announcement *of a marriage.* **2** something made known; public notice: *an* announcement *in a newspaper.*

an·nounc·er (ə noun′sər) person or thing that announces: *a train* announcer; *a radio* announcer.

an·noy (ə noi′) to bother; pester; vex.

an·noy·ance (ə noi′əns) **1** feeling of being bothered or vexed: *to express* annoyance *because of noise.* **2** thing that annoys: *The buzzing of the mosquito is an* annoyance. **3** act of bothering or vexing: *The annoyance of mosquitoes kept me awake.*

an·nu·al (ăn′yŏŏ əl) **1** yearly; once a year: *an* annual *picnic;* annual *tests.* **2** during a year; in a year; for a year: *an* annual *subscription rate of $4.* **3** living one year or season: *an* annual *plant.* **4** plant that lives but one year or season. **an·nu·al·ly.**

a·noint (ə noint′) **1** to rub with oil; put ointment on: *to* anoint *a burn.* **2** to put oil on (a person) in a religious ceremony.

a·non (ə nŏn′) **1** soon; in a little while. **2** at another time; again: *About that, more* anon.

anon. anonymous.

a·non·y·mous (ə nŏn′ə məs) **1** with the name not known or given: *an* anonymous *author; an* anonymous *gift.* **2** not signed: *an* anonymous *letter.* **a·non·y·mous·ly.**

an·oth·er (ə nŭth′ər) **1** one more: *He took another sip.* **2** a different: *Ask me another time.* **3** someone or something else; a different one; an additional one: *I have one hat but I need* another.

ans. answer.

---

fāte, făt, fâre, fär; bē, bĕt; bīte, bĭt; nō, nŏt, nôr; fūse, fŭn, fûr; tōō, tŏŏk; foil; foul; thin; ~~then~~;
hw for wh as in *wh*at; zh for s as in u*s*ual; ə for a, e, i, o, u, as in a*g*o, lin*e*n, per*i*l, at*o*m, min*u*s

answer
an·swer (ăn′sər) **1** solution: *Do you know the answer to this problem?* **2** a reply: *an answer to a letter.* **3** to write, speak, or act in reply to: *to answer a question; to answer a note; to answer a telephone ring.* **4** to be enough for; fulfill satisfactorily: *This apartment answers all our needs at present.* **answer back** to be rude or impudent.
answer for 1 to be responsible for: *I'll answer for his safety if he goes with us.* **2** to suffer because of: *You will have to answer for your dishonesty.*
answer the door to see who is at the door.
answer to a description to be as described: *He doesn't answer to your description.*

ant (ănt) small insect that lives in tunnels dug in the ground or in wood. Ants live in colonies. (Homonym: aunt)

Ant

an·tag·o·nism (ăn tăg′ə niz əm) active opposition; hostility; hatred.
an·tag·o·nist (ăn tăg′ə nist) person who struggles, competes, or fights against another; opponent.
an·tag·o·nis·tic (ăn tăg′ə nis′tĭk) **1** opposed to; unfriendly: *an antagonistic attitude.* **2** conflicting; opposed: *The two friends had antagonistic views in politics.*
an·tag·o·nize (ăn tăg′ə nīz′) to make hostile or unfriendly: *His sarcasm antagonized people.* **an·tag·o·nized, an·tag·o·niz·ing.**
ant·arc·tic or **Ant·arc·tic** (ănt ärk′tĭk) **1** in or of the South Polar regions: *Penguins are antarctic birds.* **2** the region around the South Pole. **3 Antarctic Circle** northern boundary of the South Polar region. On maps and globes it is represented by a line parallel to the equator at 23 degrees and 30 minutes (23° 30′) north of the South Pole.
Ant·arc·ti·ca (ănt ärk′tĭ kə) continent around the South Pole.

Antelope, about 2½ft. high at shoulder

an·te- prefix meaning "before" in space or time: ante*room.*
an·te·lope (ăn′tə lōp′) any one of a group of animals somewhat resembling deer.

anticipate
an·ten·na (ăn tĕn′ə) **1** aerial; wires or rods used in sending or receiving radio or television waves. The broadcasting antenna is a high tower. The receiving antenna may be mounted on a set, or outdoors on the roof of a building, or on a tall pole. **2** one of the feelers on the heads of lobsters, insects, etc. **an·ten·nas** (definition 1), **an·ten·nae** (ăn tĕn′ē) (definition 2).

1 Television antenna
2 Antennae of insect

an·te·room (ăn′tĭ rōōm′) **1** room leading to another room. **2** a waiting room.
an·them (ăn′thəm) **1** a piece of sacred music, usually set to words taken from the Bible. **2 national anthem** the song or hymn of a country: *"The Star-Spangled Banner" is our* national anthem.
an·ther (ăn′thər) in a flower, the part of the stamen which produces the pollen.
ant hill pile of earth heaped up by ants in digging their tunnels.

Anther

an·thol·o·gy (ăn thŏl′ə jĭ) collection of poems or prose passages from the writings of a number of authors. **an·thol·o·gies.**
an·thra·cite (ăn′thrə sīt′) hard coal that burns with little smoke or flame.
an·thro·pol·o·gy (ăn′thrə pŏl′ə jĭ) the story or study of man, his body structure and ways of living, now and in the past. Anthropology is concerned with both early and modern men, their different races, languages, customs, beliefs, etc.
an·ti- prefix meaning "against" or "opposed to": anti*freeze;* anti*toxin.*
an·ti-air·craft (ăn′tĭ âr′krăft′) used in defense against attack by enemy aircraft: *an anti-aircraft gun.*
an·ti·bi·ot·ic (ăn′tĭ bī ŏ′tĭk) a chemical substance, taken from a mold or fungus, which kills germs.
an·ti·bod·y (ăn′tĭ bŏd′ĭ) a substance in a person's blood which acts against germs and other poisons. **an·ti·bod·ies.**
an·tic·i·pate (ăn tĭs′ə pāt′) **1** to look forward to: *We anticipated a good time on the picnic.* **2** to guess correctly; foresee: *I*

anticipated *his question and had an answer ready.* **3** to be ahead of someone in some attempt: *Some people say that the Vikings* anticipated *Columbus in the discovery of America.* **an·tic·i·pat·ed, an·tic·i·pat·ing.**

an·tic·i·pa·tion (ăn tĭs′ə pā′shən) expectation; a looking forward with pleasure: *The children waited with eager* anticipation *for Christmas.*

an·tics (ăn′tĭks) playful and grotesque actions and gestures: *We laughed at the antics of the clowns.*

an·ti·dote (ăn′tĭ dōt′) **1** medicine that works against the effects of a poison. **2** remedy for anything harmful: *Education is an antidote for ignorance.*

an·ti·freeze (ăn′tĭ frēz′) liquid that is poured into the radiator of an automobile to keep the water that cools the engine from freezing.

an·ti·mo·ny (ăn′tə mō′nĭ) silvery-white, brittle metal element that is combined with tin and lead to produce harder alloys. Antimony is also used in medicines and paints.

an·ti·quat·ed (ăn′tə kwā′tĭd) out-of-date; old-fashioned: *The business failed because of its* antiquated *methods.*

an·tique (ăn tēk′) **1** belonging to a bygone period: *There are* antique *statues in the museum.* **2** an object made in a time long past: *This old clock is an* antique.

an·tiq·ui·ty (ăn tĭk′wə tĭ) **1** oldness; great age. **2** the time before the Middle Ages; ancient times: *Greece has many monuments of* antiquity. **3** **antiquities** ruins, works of art, and other things coming down from people who lived long ago: *We enjoy studying Roman* antiquities *at the museum.* **an·tiq·ui·ties.**

an·ti·sep·tic (ăn′tə sĕp′tĭk) **1** having the ability to kill germs that cause disease and decay: *Iodine and alcohol are* antiseptic. **2** a substance that kills germs: *Iodine is an* antiseptic.

an·ti·tox·in (ăn′tĭ tŏk′sĭn) **1** substance produced by the body to resist a poison (toxin) from a germ disease. **2** similar substance made from the blood of animals that have been injected with germ poison.

ant·ler (ănt′lər) a horn of a deer or one of the branches of such a horn.

an·to·nym (ăn′tə nĭm′) word that means the opposite of another word. The antonym of "hard" is "soft."

an·vil (ăn′vĭl) block of iron or steel on which heated metals are hammered into shape.

Antlers

anx·i·e·ty (ăng zī′ə tĭ) **1** feeling of uncertainty or uneasiness about the future; worry: *The* anxiety *of the sailors increased as the wind rose.* **2** something that causes anxiety: *His illness is one of my* anxieties. **3** strong desire: *an* anxiety *to win.* **anx·i·e·ties.**

anx·ious (ăngk′shəs or ăng′shəs) **1** worried; deeply troubled: *to be* anxious *about money.* **2** eager; wishing very strongly: *He is* anxious *to help.* **anx·ious·ly.**

an·y (ĕn′ĭ) **1** one of several, but no particular one: *Take* any *card.* **2** one: *I haven't* any. **3** every: *Yes,* any *man can do it.* **4** some: *If you have* any, *I'll take a cracker.* **5** one bit; at all: *Don't go* any *further.* **6** at **any rate** at least. **7** in **any case** whatever happens: *I'm going in* any *case.*

an·y·bod·y (ĕn′ĭ bŏd′ĭ) any person; anyone.

an·y·how (ĕn′ĭ hou′) **1** in any manner or way: *This is a poor mark* anyhow *you look at it.* **2** in any case: *She is not invited but wants to go* anyhow. **3** carelessly: *One dresses* anyhow *when in a hurry.*

an·y·one (ĕn′ĭ wŭn′ or ĕn′ĭ wən) any person; anybody.

an·y·thing (ĕn′ĭ thĭng′) **1** a thing of any sort. **2** in any way; at all: *Is this* anything *like yours?*

an·y·way (ĕn′ĭ wā′) nevertheless; in any case: *I know I shouldn't spend that money, but I'll do it* anyway.

an·y·where (ĕn′ĭ hwâr′) in, at, or to any place.

a·or·ta (ā ôr′tə) main artery that carries all blood leaving the heart except that which goes to the lungs.

a·pace (ə pās′) at a good pace; rapidly; speedily: *Time passed, and the work went on* apace.

---

fāte, făt, fâre, fär; bē, bĕt; bite, bĭt; nō, nŏt, nôr; fūse, fŭn, fûr; tōō, tŏŏk; foil; foul; thin; ~~then~~;
hw for wh as in *wh*at; zh for s as in u*s*ual; ə for a, e, i, o, u, as in *a*go, lin*e*n, per*i*l, at*o*m, min*u*s

a·part (ə pärt′) **1** in or into pieces: *It fell apart.* **2** separated: *The two towns were many miles* apart. **3 know apart** to be able to tell the difference between. **4 live apart** to live separately or far away from others. **5 apart from** except for: *It was a good house,* apart from *its drab color.*

a·part·ment (ə pärt′mənt) room or group of rooms for a single household and generally located in a large building.

ap·a·thy (ăp′ə thĭ) lack of feeling or interest; indifference: *The lecture failed to rouse Felix from his* apathy. **ap·a·thies.**

ape (āp) **1** long-armed tailless monkey such as the chimpanzee, gibbon, gorilla, or orangutang. **2** person who mimics or imitates. **3** to mimic or imitate: *The boys* aped *the circus clown's actions.* **aped, ap·ing.**

ap·er·ture (ăp′ər chər) hole; gap; any small opening: *The* aperture *in the wall was too small for the boy to get through easily.*

a·pex (ā′pĕks) peak or summit: *the* apex *of his ambition; the* apex *of a triangle.* **a·pex·es** or **a·pi·ces.** (ā′pə sēz′ or ăp′ə sēz′)

a·phid (ā′fĭd or ăf′ĭd) very small insect that sucks the juice of plants; plant louse.

a·piece (ə pēs′) for each one; each: *There is an orange* apiece *for the children. The pears are 15 cents* apiece.

Aphid on edge of elm leaf

a·pol·o·get·ic (ə pŏl′ə jĕt′ĭk) **1** admitting or excusing a fault or failure: *The tardy boy was* apologetic *for keeping us waiting.* **2** in a manner which indicates that one is unsure of oneself: *He answered in an* apologetic *tone of voice.*

a·pol·o·gize (ə pŏl′ə jīz′) **1** to express regret for something; say one is sorry: *I* apologize *for troubling you.* **2** to offer an excuse: *There's no need to* apologize *for a hearty appetite.* **a·pol·o·gized, a·pol·o·giz·ing.**

a·pol·o·gy (ə pŏl′ə jĭ) **1** words of regret for a fault, failure, or shortcoming; explanation asking forgiveness: *The noisy boy made an* apology *for disturbing the class.* **2** poor substitute: *A chocolate bar is only an* apology *for a lunch.* **a·pol·o·gies.**

a·pos·tle (ə pŏs′əl) **1** any early Christian leader or missionary. **2 Apostle** one of the twelve men chosen by Jesus Christ to preach the Gospel to the world.

a·pos·tro·phe (ə pŏs′trə fē) sign (') used to show (**1**) that one or more letters have been left out: *I don't* know. (**2**) that something belongs to someone or something: *the* boy's *hat; the* dog's *tail.* (**3**) certain plurals: *There are six* 0's *in a million. There are two* a's *in* always.

a·poth·e·car·y (ə pŏth′ə kĕr′ĭ) person who prepares and sells medicines and drugs; druggist; pharmacist. **a·poth·e·car·ies.**

Ap·pa·lach·i·an Moun·tains (ăp′ə lăch′- ĭ ən or ăp′ə lăch′ĭ ən mount′ənz) mountain chain near and parallel to the eastern coast of North America.

ap·pall or **ap·pal** (ə pôl′ or ə păl′) to fill with horror; shock: *The town was* appalled *by the number of traffic accidents.*

ap·pa·ra·tus (ăp′ə rā′təs or ăp′ə răt′əs) **1** equipment, instruments, etc., put together for a special purpose: *laboratory* apparatus; *gymnasium* apparatus. **2** group of bodily organs: *our digestive* apparatus. **ap·pa·ra·tus** or **ap·pa·ra·tus·es.**

ap·par·el (ə păr′əl) clothing; dress.

ap·par·ent (ə păr′ənt or ə pâr′ənt) **1** easily seen; plain; clear; easily understood: *From the burst of laughter it was* apparent *that they were having a good time.* **2** seeming rather than actual: *His* apparent *anger was only a means of getting his way.*

ap·par·ent·ly (ə păr′ənt lĭ or ə pâr′ənt lĭ) seemingly; to all appearances: *There is* apparently *no way out.*

ap·pa·ri·tion (ăp′ə rish′ən) **1** ghost or phantom: *He does not believe in* apparitions. **2** something (startling or unusual) that (suddenly) appears: *the* apparition *of the black vessel as the fog parted.*

ap·peal (ə pēl′) **1** a request for help or mercy: *An* appeal *went out from the flooded town.* **2** interest; attraction: *The picture has a wide* appeal *because of its soft colors.* **3** to make a plea for; request: *The committee* appealed *for funds.* **4** request to have a case tried again before a higher court or judge. **5** to make such a request.

appeal to to be interesting or attractive: *The idea* appeals *to me.*

ap·pear (ə pir′) **1** to come into sight: *The first flowers* appeared *above the snow.* **2** to seem: *The book* appears *to have been used many times.* **3** to come before the public: *That actor* appeared *in a new play.*

ap·pear·ance (ə pîr′əns) **1** a coming into view; appearing: *Wild ducks made a sudden* appearance *on the marsh.* **2** outward look; bearing: *The girl's excellent* appearance *will help her get the job.* **3** outward show: *After he lost his job he tried to keep up* appearances. **4** a coming before the people: *the* appearance *of an actor in a play.*

ap·pease (ə pēz′) **1** to make calm or peaceful; quiet: *The angry crowd was* appeased *by his gentle words.* **2** to satisfy: *to* appease *hunger; to* appease *curiosity.* **ap·peased, ap·peas·ing.**

ap·pend (ə pĕnd′) to add to; attach: *to* append *a signature; to* append *a seal.*

ap·pend·age (ə pĕn′dĭj) something attached that may or may not be essential: *A mouse's tail is a mere* appendage.

ap·pen·di·ci·tis (ə pĕn′də sī′tĭs) inflammation of the appendix, caused by bacteria.

ap·pen·dix (ə pĕn′dĭks) **1** narrow tube, three or four inches long, closed at one end and attached at the other end to the large intestine. **2** section added at the end of a book or document to give further information. **ap·pen·dix·es** or **ap·pen·di·ces** (ə-pĕn′də sēz′).

ap·pe·tite (ăp′ə tīt′) **1** desire for food. **2** strong and active liking or desire: *an* appetite *for reading.*

ap·plaud (ə plôd′) **1** to show approval or enjoyment, especially by clapping the hands: *The audience* applauded *the pianist's performance.* **2** to admire: *I* applaud *your courage.*

ap·plause (ə plôz′) **1** a clapping of the hands to show approval or appreciation. **2** admiration: *courage worthy of* applause.

ap·ple (ăp′əl) **1** red, yellow, or green fruit that grows on a tree in temperate climates and is used as food. It has small brown seeds. **2** The tree that bears this fruit.

ap·ple·sauce (ăp′əl sôs′) apples stewed to a pulp. **Apple**

ap·pli·ance (ə plī′əns) device for a particular purpose, usually electrically operated. Irons, toasters, radios, television sets, washing machines, and vacuum cleaners are household appliances.

ap·pli·cant (ăp′lə kənt) person who applies for or requests something.

ap·pli·ca·tion (ăp′lə kā′shən) **1** request made personally or in writing: *an* application *for a job; a letter of* application. **2** a putting something to use: *the* application *of astronomy to navigation.* **3** what something has to do with something else; bearing: *This testimony has no* application *to the case.* **4** a putting on: *The* application *of bandages will protect his wound.* **5** things put on or applied: *This* application *will relieve the itching.* **6** close attention or effort: *The student's* application *to his studies should result in higher grades.*

ap·ply (ə plī′) **1** to ask; to make a request: *to* apply *for a job.* **2** to put on; put into contact with: *We must* apply *ice to relieve the swelling on his legs.* **3** to be suitable to; fit; have reference to: *The new rules do not* apply *to this case.* **4** to put into use or practice: *to* apply *money towards a purchase; to* apply *a grammatical rule.*

apply oneself to to concentrate on: *Please* apply *yourself to your studies.*

ap·plied, ap·ply·ing.

ap·point (ə point′) **1** to name or choose for an office or position: *He was* appointed *captain of the basketball team.* **2** to fix by agreement; decide on: *Tuesday was* appointed *as the day the trial would be held.*

ap·point·ment (ə point′mənt) **1** a naming for an office; a choosing: *The* appointment *of a city manager was delayed.* **2** office or position. **3** agreement to be at a certain place or to meet someone; engagement: *an* appointment *with the dentist at 5 o'clock.*

ap·pre·ci·a·ble (ə prē′shə bəl) large enough to be seen or felt; noticeable: *an* appreciable *improvement.* **ap·pre·ci·a·bly.**

ap·pre·ci·ate (ə prē′shĭ āt′) **1** to value properly: *A hungry man* appreciates *a good dinner.* **2** to be grateful for: *We* appreciate *your help.* **3** to judge the worth of; enjoy intelligently: *to* appreciate *music or poetry.* **4** to be aware of; judge rightly: *H-bombs have made us* appreciate *the full horror of war.* **5** to rise in value: *These stocks have* appreciated *twofold over the last ten years.* **ap·pre·ci·at·ed, ap·pre·ci·at·ing.**

---

fāte, făt, fâre, fär; bē, bĕt; bīte, bĭt; nō, nŏt, nôr; fūse, fŭn, fûr; tōō, tŏŏk; foil; foul; thin; ~~then~~; hw for wh as in *wh*at; zh for s as in u*s*ual; ə for a, e, i, o, u, as in *a*go, lin*e*n, per*i*l, at*o*m, min*u*s

ap·pre·ci·a·tion (ə prē′shĭ ā′shən) **1** an understanding and enjoyment; a valuing: Appreciation *of art is an important part of education.* **2** gratitude; thanks: *a letter expressing* appreciation. **3** increase in value: *the amount of* appreciation *of this property.*

ap·pre·ci·a·tive (ă prē′shə tĭv or ə prē′shĭ·ā′tĭv) feeling appreciation or gratitude: *The girl was appreciative of all that was being done to help her brother.* **ap·pre·ci·a·tive·ly.**

ap·pre·hend (ăp′rĭ hĕnd′) **1** to arrest; seize. **2** to grasp with the mind; understand thoroughly: *He fully apprehended what he read.* **3** to forsee with fear: *Mother apprehended the danger of driving on icy roads.*

ap·pre·hen·sion (ăp′rĭ hĕn′shən) **1** fear of what may happen: *We had no apprehension about spending the night in the woods.* **2** power to understand: *a pupil of slow apprehension.* **3** an arrest or capture: *The apprehension of the robbers put an end to the holdups.*

ap·pre·hen·sive (ăp′rĭ hĕn′sĭv) fearful; worried; uneasy about an outcome, a person's safety, etc.: *Jerry was apprehensive about his test marks.* **ap·pre·hen·sive·ly.**

ap·pren·tice (ə prĕn′tĭs) **1** person who works for another to learn a trade. **2** to put (someone) under the supervision of an employer to learn a trade: *Benjamin Franklin was apprenticed to a printer.* **ap·pren·ticed, ap·pren·tic·ing.**

ap·pren·tice·ship (ə prĕn′tĭs shĭp′) **1** time during which a person is serving as an apprentice. **2** a serving as an apprentice.

ap·proach (ə prōch′) **1** come near; move towards: *We are approaching the city. Winter is approaching.* **2** to come close to; approximate: *to approach perfection.* **3** to speak to: *When is the best time to approach him?* **4** a coming near; a moving towards: *They fled at our approach. We started for home at the approach of night.* **5** the way or road by which a place is reached: *the approaches to the city.* **6** a way of beginning something: *a new approach to the study of language.*

ap·proach·a·ble (ə prō′chə bəl) **1** that can be approached; *a mountain peak approachable from the north side.* **2** easy to approach: *a friendly approachable person.*

¹ap·pro·pri·ate (ə prō′prĭ ĭt) fitting; suitable: *That dress is not* appropriate *for a formal dance.* **ap·pro·pri·ate·ly.**

²ap·pro·pri·ate (ə prō′prĭ āt′) **1** to set aside for a particular use: *The government appropriated money for road improvement.* **2** to take and use for oneself: *The escaped convicts appropriated the farmer's car.* **ap·pro·pri·at·ed, ap·pro·pri·at·ing.**

ap·pro·pri·a·tion (ə prō′prĭ ā′shən) **1** money set aside for a particular purpose: *The* appropriation *was for the improvement of the subway system.* **2** the taking over of something as one's own or for use by a governmental body: *The* appropriation *of land for the new highway was met with mixed feelings.*

ap·prov·al (ə prōō′vəl) **1** acceptance or agreement: *The extra holiday was hailed with hearty approval.* **2** official consent: *The governor gave his approval to the bill.* **3 on approval** on trial: *We bought the machine* on approval *and got our money back when it proved unsatisfactory.*

ap·prove (ə prōōv′) **1** to speak or think well (of): *His mother approves of his new friends.* **2** to show approval: *Mother approved.* **3** to consent to: *The candidate did not approve the plans for the campaign.* **ap·proved, ap·prov·ing.**

¹ap·prox·i·mate (ə prŏk′sə mĭt) not exact but nearly so; almost correct: *The approximate weight of a pint of milk is one pound.* **ap·prox·i·mate·ly.**

²ap·prox·i·mate (ə prŏk′sə māt′) to come near to; approach: *The translation approximates the original.* **ap·prox·i·mat·ed, ap·prox·i·mat·ing.**

ap·prox·i·ma·tion (ə prŏk′sə mā′shən) something more or less exact or true: *an* approximation *to the true story.*

Apr. April.

a·pri·cot (ā′prə kŏt′ or ăp′rə kŏt′) **1** small, round, orange-colored fruit with downy skin somewhat like a peach. **2** tree which bears this fruit. **3** pale orange-yellow.

A·pril (ā′prəl) fourth month of the year. April has 30 days.

a·pron (ā′prən) **1** piece of wearing apparel, made of cloth, rubber, or leather, etc., worn over the front of the body to protect clothing. **2** the area that lies in front: *the apron of a hangar; the apron of the stage.*

apt (ăpt) **1** suitable; appropriate: *The "space age" is an* apt *name for the period we are living in.* **2** quick to learn: *He is an* apt *student of arithmetic.* **3** likely: *When in a hurry, anyone is* apt *to be careless.* **apt·ly.**

apt. apartment.

ap·ti·tude (ăp′tə tōōd′ or ăp′tə tūd′) **1** talent; fitness; ability: *an aptitude for mechanical inventions.* **2 aptitude test** a test designed to find out what a person is best suited for.

a·quar·i·um (ə kwâr′ĭ əm) **1** bowl, pond, or tank for fish, other water animals, and water plants. **2** building where fish, other water animals, and water plants are cared for and displayed.

a·quat·ic (ə kwăt′ĭk) **1** in or on water: *Swimming and skin diving are* aquatic *sports.* **2** living in water: *The porpoise is an* aquatic *animal.*

aq·ue·duct (ăk′wə dŭkt′) **1** bridgelike structure built across a valley or stream to support channels or large pipes which carry flowing water. **2** pipe or artificial channel for conducting water from a distance.

Roman aqueduct

Ar·ab (ăr′əb) **1** member of a race of people found especially in Arabia, in some other parts of the Middle East, and in North Africa. **2** having to do with Arabs or Arabia. **3** horse noted for its graceful proportions, speed, and fiery spirit.

A·ra·bi·a (ə rā′bĭ ə) large peninsula in southwest Asia.

A·ra·bi·an (ə rā′bĭ ən) **1** having to do with the Arabs or Arabia. **2** an Arab.

Ar·a·bic (ăr′ə bĭk′) **1** language of the Arabs. **2** originating in Arabia or with the Arabs.

1234567890
Arabic numerals

Arabic numerals the figures 1, 2, 3, 4, 5, 6, 7, 8, 9, 0.

ar·a·ble (ăr′ə bəl) suitable for plowing: *Hilly, rocky country has little* arable *land.*

ar·bi·trar·y (ăr′bə trĕr′ĭ) based on whim, not on reason or rules; using power without regard for laws: *The umpire's decision seemed* arbitrary *until we checked the rules and found he was right.* **ar·bi·trar·i·ly.**

ar·bi·trate (ăr′bə trāt′) to act as judge in deciding a dispute: *A three-man board is* arbitrating *the strike.* **ar·bi·trat·ed, ar·bi·trat·ing.**

ar·bi·tra·tion (ăr′bə trā′shən) way of settling a dispute in which the two sides submit their arguments to a third person or group for decision: *The steel workers agreed to try* arbitration *instead of striking.*

ar·bor (ăr′bər) **1** frame or lattice for vines. **2** place shaded by trees or shrubs.

ar·bu·tus (ăr bū′təs) **1** any of several evergreen shrubs having scarlet or red berries. **2** a creeping plant which has fragrant pink or white flowers in the early spring.

arc (ărk) **1** part of a circle. **2** part of a curved line or path. **3** band of light or sparks produced by an electric current jumping from one conductor to another. **4 arc** Arc **light** (1) lamp in which a brilliant light is created by causing electricity to pass across a space between two carbon rods. (2) the light from such a lamp. (Homonym: ark)

ar·cade (ăr kăd′) **1** arched passageway around or through a building, especially one with shops. **2** rows of arches. Arcade

¹arch (ărch) **1** curved structure used to hold up the material above it. Arches are seen at the tops of windows or doors and under bridges. **2** archway: *An* arch *covered the church entrance.* **3** monument shaped like an arch. **4** an instep: *A flat-footed person has fallen* arches. **5** to curve like an arch: *The cat* arches *his back.* [¹**arch** comes through Old French from a Latin word (arcus) meaning "a bow." It is related to **arc.**]

Arch

fāte, făt, fâre, fär; bē, bĕt; bite, bĭt; nō, nŏt, nôr; fūse, fŭn, fûr; tōō, tŏŏk; foil; foul; thin; then; hw for wh as in what; zh for s as in usual; ə for a, e, i, o, u, as in ago, linen, peril, atom, minus

75

²**arch** (ärch) **1** principal; chief; first: *an* arch *villain.* **2** showing a wish for mischief; looking very coy: *her* arch *look.* **arch·ly.** [²**arch** comes through a Latin form (arch-) meaning "chief." The meaning "mischievous" arose from words like "archknave" or "archrogue."]

ar·chae·ol·o·gy or **ar·che·ol·o·gy** (är′kiŏl′ə jı) the study of the life and culture of ancient peoples. We learn about them by digging up what they left behind, such as old cities, graves, pottery, coins, ornaments, arrowheads, etc.

arch·bish·op (ärch′bish′əp) a chief bishop.

arch·er (är′chər) person who shoots with a bow.

arch·er·y (är′chə rĭ) use of bow and arrows, especially as a sport.

ar·chi·pel·a·go (är′kə pĕl′ə gō′) **1** sea with many islands. **2** group of islands in a sea. **ar·chi·pel·a·gos** or **ar·chi·pel·a·goes.**

Archer

ar·chi·tect (är′kə tĕkt) person who plans buildings and directs their construction.

ar·chi·tec·ture (är′kə tĕk′chər) **1** art of planning buildings. **2** particular style of building: *colonial* architecture.

arch·way (ärch′wā′) **1** passageway under an arch or curved roof. **2** entrance with an arch above it.

arc·tic or **Arc·tic** (ärk′tĭk) **1** having to do with the north polar regions: *white* arctic *animals; cold* arctic *winds.* **2** the north polar region. **3 Arctic Circle** imaginary boundary of the north polar region. On maps and globes it is shown as a line parallel to the equator at 23 degrees and 30 minutes (23°30′) south of the North Pole.

Arctic Ocean ocean lying north of Europe, Asia, North America, and the Arctic Circle.

ar·dent (är′dənt) eager; enthusiastic; warm: *As an* ardent *lover of music, he attended all the concerts.* **ar·dent·ly.**

ar·dor (är′dər) great eagerness; passion; strong warmth of feeling: *In his* ardor *for knowledge he would read half the night.*

ar·du·ous (är′jŏŏ əs) difficult; hard to do; strenuous: *an* arduous *task.* **ar·du·ous·ly.**

are (är) a form of **be** used with *you* (one person or more than one), and with *we,*

they, and other plural subjects: *You* are *very lucky. We* are *about to leave. Jack and Lucy* are *late.*

ar·e·a (âr′ĭ ə) **1** surface, space, or size of a space: *ground* area; *floor* area; *the* area *of a country.* **2** region; tract; district: *an industrial* area; *a mountainous* area.

a·re·na (ə rē′nə) **1** central space in a stadium, circus, or amphitheater where contests or shows are held. **2** any area where men compete: *the* arena *of politics.*

aren't (ärnt or är′ənt) are not.

Ar·gen·ti·na (är′jən tē′nə) a country in southern South America.

ar·gue (är′gū) **1** to give reasons for or against something: *In the debate, one team* argued *for disarmament, the other team* argued *against it.* **2** to dispute: *He* argued *with his brother over whose turn it was to do the chores.* **3** to persuade by giving reasons: *You've* argued *me into going.* **ar·gued, ar·gu·ing.**

ar·gu·ment (är′gyŏŏ mənt) **1** discussion in which reasons are given for or against something; debate: *the* argument *over whether the movies should be censored or not.* **2** a dispute: *an* argument *about money.* **3** a reason: *The best* argument *for this plan is that it will save money.*

ar·id (ăr′ĭd) **1** dry; parched; having little or no rain: *the* arid *regions in the western United States.* **2** uninteresting: *an* arid *subject; an* arid *personality.* **ar·id·ly.**

a·right (ə rit′) correctly; rightly.

a·rise (ə riz′) **1** to rise; get up: *The spectators* arose *when the judge entered the courtroom.* **2** to move upward: *Clouds of smoke* arise *from a forest fire.* **3** to begin; start up: *If an argument should* arise, *try to keep your temper.* **a·rose, a·ris·en, a·ris·ing.**

a·ris·en (ə riz′ən) See **arise.**

ar·is·toc·ra·cy (är′ĭs tŏk′rə sĭ) **1** class of persons of high rank or noble birth; the nobility. **2** class of persons superior in ability, culture, or wealth. **3** government in which the nobles rule. **4** a state so governed. **ar·is·toc·ra·cies.**

a·ris·to·crat (ə rĭs′tə krăt′) **1** person of high rank, birth, or title. **2** person superior in ability, intellect, or culture.

a·ris·to·crat·ic (ə rĭs′tə krăt′ĭk) **1** belonging to a person of high rank or noble birth. **2** of or like an aristocrat.

a·rith·me·tic (ə rith′mə tĭk′) science of numbers; the art of using numbers to add, subtract, multiply, divide, etc.

Ariz. Arizona.

Ar·i·zo·na (ăr′ə zō′nə) State in the southwestern part of the United States.

ark (ärk) **1** in the Bible, the ship that Noah built as a shelter from the Flood for himself, his family, and a pair of each kind of animal. **2 Ark of the Covenant** the chest in which the ancient Hebrews kept the stone tablets containing the Ten Commandments. (Homonym: arc)

Ark. Arkansas.

Ar·kan·sas (är′kən sô) State in the south central part of the United States.

¹arm (ärm) **1** the part of the body between the hand and the shoulder. **2** anything shaped like an arm: *the* arm *of a chair; an* arm *of the sea.* [¹**arm** is the unchanged form of an Old English word.]

²arm (ärm) **1** weapon: *such* arms *as swords and guns.* **2** branch of the armed services. **3** to equip with weapons: *The explorer* armed *his followers.* **4** to prepare for war. **5 arms** military service; warfare: *a call to* arms; *a comrade in* arms. [²**arm** is the singular of **arms**, which is from a Latin word (arma) meaning "weapons."]

ar·ma·da (är mä′də) **1** fleet of armed ships. **2** fleet of airplanes.

ar·ma·dil·lo (är′mə dĭl′ō) small burrowing animal found in South America and parts of North America. Its head and body have a hard bony covering. **ar·ma·dil·los.**

Armadillo, 2 ft. long, including tail

ar·ma·ment (är′mə mənt) **1** military force of a nation: *The peace conference urged a* reduction in armament. **2** preparations for war: *the* armament *of a country against attack.*

arm·chair (ärm′châr′) chair with arms.

arm·ful (ärm′fŏŏl′) as much as can be held in one or both arms.

ar·mi·stice (är′mə stĭs′) agreement between two opposing armies to suspend fighting; a truce.

ar·mor (är′mər) **1** a covering to protect the body while fighting: *Battle* armor *used to be made of metal or leather.* **2** the steel plating of a warship. **3** any protective covering: *the* armor *of a turtle.* **4** to provide with a protective covering.

Chain and plate armor

armored (är′mərd) **1** covered with steel plates: *an* armored *truck.* **2** wearing armor: *a knight* armored *in chain mail.*

ar·mor·y (är′mə rĭ) **1** a place where arms are stored. **2** large building containing drill halls and offices where soldiers assemble. **3** a place where arms are manufactured. **ar·mor·ies.**

arm·pit (ärm′pĭt′) the hollow beneath the arm where it meets the shoulder.

ar·my (är′mĭ) **1** large body of men trained, equipped, and organized for war. **2** a great number: *an army of officials.* **ar·mies.**

a·ro·ma (ə rō′mə) pleasant odor; fragrance.

ar·o·mat·ic (ăr′ə măt′ĭk) having a pleasant, spicy odor.

a·rose (ə rōz′) See **arise.** *New questions* arose *daily.*

a·round (ə round′) **1** in a circle about; surrounding: *The bug crawled* around *the rim of the plate.* **2** on every side of: *The police were stationed* around *the house.* **3** here and there; about: *They traveled* around *the country. I was looking* around. **4** about; approximately: *I'll be there* around *noon.* **5** in the neighborhood: *No one was* around, *so I came home.* **6** by: *They came* around *to see us.* **7** out of the way of; roundabout: *He stepped* around *the rock.* **8 around the clock** all day and all night: *That plant works* around *the clock.*

a·rouse (ə rouz′) **1** to awaken: *The singing of the birds* aroused *her early this morning.* **2** to stir up; excite: *His troubles* aroused *our sympathy.* **a·roused, a·rous·ing.**

ar·range (ə rānj′) **1** to put in order: *The librarian* arranged *the books on the shelf.* **2** to come to an agreement about: *I am sure*

fāte, făt, fâre, fär; bē, bĕt; bite, bĭt; nō, nŏt, nôr; fūse, fŭn, fûr; tōō, tŏŏk; foil; foul; thin; ~~then~~; hw for wh as in *wh*at; zh for s as in u*s*ual; ə for a, e, i, o, u, as in *a*go, lin*e*n, per*i*l, at*o*m, min*u*s

77

we can arrange *a compromise.* **3** to make plans and preparations: *I will* arrange *to meet you at the train.* **4** to fit; adapt: *to* arrange *a tune for a dance band.* **ar·ranged, ar·rang·ing.**

ar·range·ment (ə rānj′mənt) **1** a putting in order: *an* arrangement *of books by subject.* **2** order in which things are put: *We changed the* arrangement *of furniture in the room.* **3** an agreement. **4** adaptation (of music): *a jazz* arrangement *of an old tune.* **5 arrangements** plans and preparations: *The* arrangements *for the picnic.*

ar·ray (ə rā′) **1** to place in order: *The troops were* arrayed *in long ranks.* **2** a particular order or arrangement: *in battle* array. **3** to clothe elaborately; dress up: *The dancers were* arrayed *in costumes from foreign lands.* **4** elaborate dress; fine clothes: *in bridal* array. **5** a display: *an* array *of armor in the museum.*

ar·rest (ə rĕst′) **1** to seize or hold a person by authority of the law: *He was* arrested *for stealing horses.* **2** seizure or holding by authority of the law. **3** to stop; bring to a stop: *The flow of water must be* arrested *or the land will be flooded.*

ar·riv·al (ə rī′vəl) **1** a coming to a place; a reaching a destination: *His* arrival *was delayed because of bad weather.* **2** person or thing coming to a place: *Late* arrivals *will not be seated.*

ar·rive (ə rīv′) **1** to come to a place. **2** to come: *The day of the picnic has finally* arrived.
  arrive at to come to; reach: *After studying the problem he* arrived at *a solution.* **ar·rived, ar·riv·ing.**

ar·ro·gance (ăr′ə gəns) a show of extreme pride in oneself and disrespect for others; haughtiness.

ar·ro·gant (ăr′ə gənt) overly proud; haughty in manner. **ar·ro·gant·ly.**

ar·row (ăr′ō) **1** slender stick or shaft made to be shot from a bow, usually pointed at one end, and having feathers at the other end to guide it. **2** mark shaped like an arrow, to indicate directions.

ar·row·head (ăr′ō hĕd′) piercing end of an arrow or a tip for this end.

ar·se·nal (är′sə nəl) public building where guns and ammunition are made, stored, owned, or repaired.

ar·se·nic (är′sə nĭk′) grayish-white solid element. Its compounds are very poisonous, and are used to kill insects.

¹art (ärt) **1** painting, drawing, or sculpture. **2** study or creation of beautiful or unusual things that give pleasure to the mind when they are seen or heard. The arts include painting, drawing, sculpture, architecture, music, literature, drama, and the dance. For **fine arts,** see **fine. 3** principles, methods, and skills needed for some special kind of work: *the* art *of war; the* art *of healing; the household* arts *of cooking and sewing.* **4** literature, languages, and history, as studied in college or university. **5** human work or skill: *Her complexion owes more to* art *than to nature.* **6** skilled craftsmanship: *a design carried out with exquisite* art. **7** cunning; trickery; wiles: *The witch doctor used strange* arts *in casting a spell.* [**¹art** comes from a form of the Latin word (ars) meaning "skill."]

²art (ärt) an old form of **are** used with *thou:* *"Wherefore* art *thou Romeo?"* [**²art** is a form of an Old English word (aron) from which we also get **are.**]

ar·ter·y (är′tə rĭ) **1** any of the tubes in the body that carry blood from the heart to any part of the body. **2** any main road or important channel: *The new highway is the main* artery *of travel across the state.* **ar·ter·ies.**

ar·te·sian well (är tē′zhən wĕl) a well from which the water gushes without being pumped.

art·ful (ärt′fəl) **1** cunning; tricky: *an artful excuse to avoid work.* **2** skillful; clever: *an artful arrangement of flowers.* **art·ful·ly.**

ar·ti·choke (är′tə chōk′) **1** tall plant, the flowering head of which is used as a vegetable. **2** the vegetable itself.

ar·ti·cle (är′tə kəl) **1** literary composition on a specific topic, complete in itself, in a book, newspaper, magazine, etc. **2** individual thing; particular object: *A blouse is an* article *of clothing.* **3** single section of a written document.

Artichoke

¹ar·tic·u·late (är tĭk′yōō lāt′) **1** to utter syllables; to enunciate. **2** to speak or enunciate precisely and distinctly. **ar·tic·u·lat·ed, ar·tic·u·lat·ing.**

²**ar·tic·u·late** (är tĭk′yŏŏ lĭt) **1** said in syllables or words: *She is old enough for* articulate *speech.* **2** able to speak well; able to express one's thoughts effectively: *a very* articulate *man.* **ar·tic·u·late·ly.**

ar·ti·fice (är′tə fĭs′) **1** clever scheme or method; cunning trick. **2** ingenious device; clever contrivance.

ar·ti·fi·cial (är′tə fĭsh′əl) **1** made by man; not occurring naturally: *a bouquet of* artificial *flowers;* artificial *pearls.* **2** not natural; affected: *an artificial way of speaking.* **ar·ti·fi·cial·ly.**

ar·til·ler·y (är tĭl′ə rĭ) **1** mounted guns, together with their ammunition. **2** the branch of an army using these guns.

ar·ti·san (är′tə zən) person skilled in an industrial art or trade; craftsman. Carpenters and jewelers are artisans.

art·ist (är′tĭst) **1** person who practices one of the fine arts, especially a painter or sculptor. **2** person who shows creative power and skill in his work.

ar·tis·tic (är tĭs′tĭk) **1** having to do with art or artists. **2** appreciative of beauty: *an* artistic *nature.* **3** showing skill: *an* artistic *design.*

art·less (ärt′lĭs) natural; sincere; without guile: *her* artless *words.* **art·less·ly.**

as (ăz) **1** equally; to the same extent: *This yellow paper will do* as *well.* **2** for instance: *long rivers,* as *the Nile.* **3** in the manner of: *He came dressed* as *a pirate.* **4** because: *He sat down,* as *he was tired.* **5** while; when: *They ran* as *we approached.* **6** in the same way that: *Go to bed* as *your brother does.* **7** though: *Dark* as *it was, we could still see the sign.* **8 as for** speaking of; concerning: *Well,* as for *him, he doesn't count.* **9 as to** concerning; about: *Nothing was done* as to *our request.*

as·bes·tos (ăs bĕs′təs) fiberlike mineral substance that does not burn. Asbestos is used in mats under hot dishes, in fireproof curtains, in welders' gloves, etc.

as·cend (ə sĕnd′) **1** to climb or go up; rise: *They* ascended *a hill. Warm air* ascends.

as·cent (ə sĕnt′) **1** a climbing: *the* ascent *of a mountain.* **2** a going up; a rising: *the* ascent *of a balloon.* (Homonym: assent)

as·cer·tain (ăs′ər tān′) to find out for certain: *I want to* ascertain *the truth.*

as·cribe (ə skrīb′) to say that (something) is caused by; attribute (to): *The forest ranger* ascribed *his health to exercise and good food.* **as·cribed, as·crib·ing.**

¹**ash** (ăsh) **1** common shade tree. **2** hard tough wood of this tree. [¹**ash** is a form of the Old English name (æsc) of this tree.]

²**ash** (ăsh) substance that is left after something is burned: *the* ash *of a volcano.* [²**ash** is a form of an Old English word (æsce).]

a·shamed (ə shāmd′) **1** feeling uncomfortable because knowing one has done wrong; feeling uncomfortable because of the fear of being laughed at, turned down, or looked down upon: *After getting a black eye, he was* ashamed *to show his face.* **2** unwilling (to act) because of such a feeling: *He was* ashamed *to ask for a third helping.* **3** ashamed of feeling shame and guilt over: *He was* ashamed *of his conduct.*

a·shore (ə shôr′) on the shore; to the shore: *to go* ashore *at Naples.*

A·sia (ā′zhə) the largest continent. It is east of Europe and west of the Pacific Ocean. China and India are both in Asia.

A·sian (ā′zhən) **1** having to do with Asia or its people. **2** person born or living in Asia.

A·si·at·ic (ā′zhĭ ăt′ĭk) **1** having to do with Asia or its people: *to buy* Asiatic *figs.* **2** person born or living in Asia; Asian.

a·side (ə sīd′) **1** to one side: *Pull the curtain* aside. **2** apart; away: *Put* aside *your problems.* **3** on the stage, a remark spoken to the audience which the other players are not supposed to hear.

ask (ăsk) **1** to put a question to; seek an answer from; try to find out from: *Dora* asked *him. Dora* asked *him how old he was.* **2** to put a question: *Dora* asked. *I am* asking. **3** to request: *I want to* ask *a favor.* **4** to invite: *You must* ask *her to your party.* **5** to demand: *What price do you* ask *for this?*

a·skance (ə skăns′) **1** sidelong; to one side. **2 look askance (at)** to look at with disapproval, distrust, or suspicion.

a·skew (ə skū′) crooked; out of line; awry: *Janet was in such a hurry that she put her hat on* askew.

---

fāte, făt, fâre, fär; bē, bĕt; bīte, bĭt; nō, nŏt, nôr; fūse, fŭn, fûr; tōō, tŏŏk; foil; foul; thin; then;
hw for wh as in what; zh for s as in usual; ə for a, e, i, o, u, as in ago, linen, peril, atom, minus

a·sleep (ə slēp′) **1** sleeping. **2** into a sleeping state: *Tim fell* asleep *in the movies.* **3** numb: *His foot was* asleep *too.*

as·par·a·gus (ə spăr′ə gəs) **1** plant whose tender young stalks are used as a vegetable. **2** the vegetable itself.

as·pect (ăs′pĕkt) **1** side or view (of a subject): *Look at all* aspects *of the problem before you try to solve it.* **2** look; expression: *The fierce* aspect *of the stranger frightened the children.* **3** appearance: *We were charmed by the pleasant* aspect *of the countryside.* **4** a side or part facing a given direction: *a northern* aspect.

Asparagus stalks

as·pen (ăs′pən) kind of poplar tree with leaves that rustle in the slightest breeze.

as·phalt (ăs′fôlt) black tarry mineral substance used in paving, roofing, and making tiles. It is obtained from petroleum and is mixed with sand or crushed rock.

as·pir·ant (ə spir′ənt or ăs′pə rənt) person ambitious for high honor or position: *Some students were* aspirants *for the honor roll.*

as·pi·ra·tion (ăs′pə rā′shən) strong desire; ambition: *He has* aspirations *to be a doctor.*

as·pire (ə spīr′) to desire eagerly; be filled with ambition for a particular thing: *Many politicians* aspire *to be president.* **as·pired, as·pir·ing.**

as·pi·rin (ăs′pə rĭn) a medicine for easing the pain of colds, headaches, etc.

ass (ăs) **1** donkey. **2** a fool; stupid or silly person.

as·sail (ə sāl′) to attack violently: *The enemy* assailed *the castle.*

as·sail·ant (ə sāl′ənt) person who attacks.

as·sas·sin (ə săs′ĭn) person who commits a sudden and treacherous murder, usually for political reasons.

as·sas·si·nate (ə săs′ə nāt′) to murder by a sudden and treacherous attack, usually for political reasons. **as·sas·si·nat·ed, as·sas·si·nat·ing.**

as·sas·si·na·tion (ə săs′ə nā′shən) a sudden or treacherous murder, usually for political reasons.

as·sault (ə sôlt′) **1** violent attack: *an* assault *with intent to rob; a vicious* assault *on an opponent's character.* **2** to attack violently; assail.

as·say (ə sā′) **1** to test an ore or alloy to determine the quantity of different metals in it. **2** examination; testing. **3** (also ăs′ā) test so made.

as·sem·blage (ə sĕm′blĭj) group of persons or things gathered together; an assembly.

as·sem·ble (ə sĕm′bəl) **1** to bring together: *to* assemble *members of the party.* **2** to come together; meet: *The students* assembled *in the auditorium.* **3** to put together the parts of: *to* assemble *a motor.* **as·sem·bled, as·sem·bling.**

as·sem·bly (ə sĕm′blĭ) **1** company of people gathered together for a common purpose: *a student* assembly. **2** a legislative body: *the United Nations* Assembly. **3** a putting together of parts: *the* assembly *of a model airplane.* **as·sem·blies.**

as·sent (ə sĕnt′) **1** agreement; an accepting: *The governor's* assent *is needed before the bill becomes law.* **2** to agree. (Homonym: ascent)

as·sert (ə sûrt′) **1** to declare; state positively: *The lawyer* asserted *that his client was innocent of the crime.* **2** to insist upon: *By revolting, the colonies* asserted *their right to govern themselves.* **3** to put in force; enforce: *The tyrant* asserted *his authority over most of Europe.*

assert oneself to insist on one's rights; to make demands.

as·ser·tion (ə sûr′shən) positive statement.

as·set (ăs′ĕt) **1** anything of value that belongs to a person or business: *A good reputation is an* asset. *A stock of goods is an* asset. **2 assets** all the property of a person, business, or estate that may be changed into cash.

as·sign (ə sĭn′) **1** to give out; allot; distribute as a part or share: *The host* assigned *rooms to the visiting delegates.* **2** to appoint: *He was* assigned *to the position of treasurer of the club.*

as·sign·ment (ə sĭn′mənt) **1** thing assigned: *an* assignment *in arithmetic.* **2** a giving out or assigning: *the* assignment *of seats in a classroom.*

as·sim·i·late (ə sĭm′ə lāt′) to take in and make a part of oneself; digest; absorb: *He* assimilated *the customs of his new country. Plants* assimilate *nourishment through their roots.* **as·sim·i·lat·ed, as·sim·i·lat·ing.**

as·sist (ə sĭst′) to help.

as·sist·ance (ə sĭs′təns) help; aid.

as·sist·ant (ə sĭs′tənt) **1** helper. **2** acting under another person: *an* assistant *manager.*

¹**as·so·ci·ate** (ə sō′sē at, ə sō′shat) **1** to connect in thought: *He* associates *wooden houses with his childhood.* **2** to join as a partner; unite: *They* associated *in publishing the book.* **3** to keep company: *He* associates *chiefly with people in his own profession.* **as·so·ci·at·ed, as·so·ci·at·ing.**

²**as·so·ci·ate** (ə sō′shĭ ĭt) **1** having membership but not all the rights and privileges: *The* associate *members of the club cannot vote for officers.* **2** a partner; a friend.

as·so·ci·a·tion (ə sō′sĭ ā′shən or ə sō′shĭ ā′shən) **1** group of persons organized for a common purpose: *a trade* association. **2** a joining together; an associating: *an* association *with congenial people.* **3** connection in the mind: *an* association *of ideas.* **4** an idea connected with another idea: *What are the* associations *of the word "beautiful"?* **5** companionship.

as·sort·ed (ə sôr′tĭd) **1** of different kinds: *a box of* assorted *crackers.* **2** arranged by kinds: *shirts* assorted *by size.*

as·sort·ment (ə sôrt′mənt) a collection of different kinds: *an* assortment *of candy.*

as·suage (ə swāj′) to make easier; relieve; to make less; calm: *Comforting words* assuaged *the child's grief.* **as·suaged, as·suag·ing.**

as·sume (ə sōōm′ or ə sūm′) **1** to take for granted: *We* assume *that you will be home for dinner.* **2** to take upon oneself; undertake: *He* assumed *the president's duties during his chief's absence.* **3** to pretend; put on: *He* assumed *an air of friendship toward his rival.* **as·sumed, as·sum·ing.**

as·sump·tion (ə sŭmp′shən) **1** a taking for granted; an assuming. **2** something taken for granted: *Columbus acted on the* assumption *that he could reach Asia by sailing west.* **3** a taking upon oneself; a seizing: *an* assumption *of authority.*

as·sur·ance (ə shŏŏr′əns) **1** a statement to inspire confidence or certainty: *We had his* assurance *that he would take care of the matter.* **2** certainty; confidence: *We had every* assurance *our team would win.* **3** self-

confidence: *The actor played the part with complete* assurance.

as·sure (ə shŏŏr′) **1** to say positively: *They* assured *us that there would be no delay.* **2** to make (something or someone) sure; make certain: *Practice can* assure *a better batting average.* **3** to make (someone) confident: *The doctor* assured *me that I was out of danger.* **as·sured, as·sur·ing.**

as·sured (ə shŏŏrd′) confident: *The speaker had an* assured *manner.*

as·sur·ed·ly (ə shŏŏr′ĭd li) **1** certainly; surely; unquestionably. **2** with confidence; with assurance.

as·ter (ăs′tər) **1** any of various plants related to the daisy. **2** the white, pink, blue, or purple flowers of this plant.

Aster

a·stern (ə stûrn′) **1** toward the rear end of a ship. **2** behind a ship: *A shark dived close* astern.

as·ter·oid (ăs′tə roid) one of a number of small heavenly bodies that revolve around the sun, mostly between the orbits of Jupiter and Mars; planetoid.

asth·ma (ăz′mə) a disease marked by wheezing, coughing, and short breath.

a·stir (ə stûr′) in a state of activity; on the move: *The campers were* astir *before dawn.*

as·ton·ish (ə stŏn′ĭsh) to surprise greatly; amaze: *We were* astonished *at his boldness.*

as·ton·ish·ing (ə stŏn′ĭsh ĭng) very surprising; amazing: *The acrobat performed* astonishing *feats.* **as·ton·ish·ing·ly.**

as·ton·ish·ment (ə stŏn′ĭsh mənt) extreme surprise; amazement: *Imagine our* astonishment *when the weaker team won the game.*

as·tound (ə stound′) to strike with amazement; astonish greatly: *The achievements of modern science* astound *us.*

a·stray (ə strā′) in the wrong direction; to the wrong place: *The letter went* astray.

a·stride (ə strid′) with one leg on each side; straddling: *He sat* astride *the log.*

as·trol·o·gy (ə strŏl′ə ji) a study of the stars and their movements in order to foretell how they influence a person's life and what events will happen. Astronomy grew out of this false science.

---

fāte, făt, fâre, fär; bē, bĕt; bite, bĭt; nō, nŏt, nôr; fūse, fŭn, fûr; tōō, tŏŏk; foil; foul; thin; ~~then~~;
hw for wh as in *wh*at; zh for s as in u*s*ual; ə for a, e, i, o, u, as in *a*go, lin*e*n, per*i*l, at*o*m, min*u*s

as·tro·naut (ăs'trə nôt) a traveler in outer space.

as·tron·o·mer (ə strŏn'ə mər) person who makes a scientific study of the sun, moon, planets, and stars.

as·tron·o·my (ə strŏn'ə mĭ) the scientific study of the sun, moon, planets, stars, and other heavenly bodies.

a·sun·der (ə sŭn'dər) in or into two or more parts; apart: *The tree was split asunder by lightning. They were driven asunder by the war.*

a·sy·lum (ə sī'ləm) **1** institution or hospital for the care of the helpless or the insane. **2** refuge: *The rebel leader found asylum in a neighboring country.*

at (ăt) **1** in; in the exact position of: *to wait at the corner;* at *home.* **2** near; in the vicinity of: *the car at the door.* **3** on: *to be at the bottom of the tank.* **4** with an interval of: *a station at a mile's distance.* **5** present in: *to be at the dance.* **6** over: *to shudder at the thought.* **7** dependent on: *to be at his mercy.* **8** according to: *Come at your convenience.* **9** on the coming of; during the time of: *to wake at noon; at sunrise.* **10** busy with; occupied in: *to be at work; at dinner.* **11** in the manner of: *to go at a fast pace; at a run.* **12** in the state of: *to be at ease; at peace.* **13** in the direction of; toward: *They shot at the target.* **14** to the extent of; in the amount of: *apples at five cents each; going at 60 miles an hour.*

ate (āt) See **eat**. *They ate fish.* (Homonym: eight)

a·the·ist (ā'thĭ ĭst) person who does not believe in the existence of any god.

Ath·ens (ăth'ĭnz) capital of Greece, in the southeast part of the country. Athens was the center of ancient Greek civilization.

a·thirst (ə thûrst') **1** thirsty. **2** having a keen desire: *to be* athirst *for knowledge.*

ath·lete (ăth'lēt) person good at sports and exercises requiring strength, speed, skill, and endurance.

ath·let·ic (ăth lĕt'ĭk) **1** active and strong. **2** of or like an athlete: *an* athletic *build.* **3** of or for athletics: *to buy* athletic *equipment.*

ath·let·ics (ăth lĕt'ĭks) games and sports requiring strength, agility, and stamina.

a·thwart (ə thwôrt') across: *The pirates fired a shot* athwart *the bow of the ship.*

At·lan·tic (ăt lăn'tĭk) **1** the ocean lying between Europe and Africa on the one side and the American continents on the other. **2** of, on, or near the Atlantic: *the* Atlantic *coastline; the* Atlantic *States.*

at·las (ăt'ləs) collection of maps bound into a book.

at·mos·phere (ăt'məs fîr) **1** the air that surrounds the earth. **2** air in a particular place: *the damp* atmosphere *of the cellar.* **3** surrounding influence: *the quiet* atmosphere *in the library.*

at·mos·pher·ic (ăt'məs fĕr'ĭk) **1** having to do with the atmosphere: *The* atmospheric *conditions today are poor for flying.* **2** **atmospheric pressure** pressure caused by the weight of the atmosphere (about 15 pounds per square inch at sea level).

at·om (ăt'əm) **1** the smallest particle of a chemical element that can exist and still be that element. Atoms are made up of protons, electrons, and (except for ordinary hydrogen) neutrons. Atoms are so small that 250 million hydrogen atoms side by side would measure less than an inch. **2** a tiny bit: *not an* atom *of sense.*

atom bomb bomb that gets its enormous power from the splitting of atoms.

a·tom·ic (ə tŏm'ĭk) having to do with atoms or run by energy from the splitting of atoms: *an* atomic *submarine.*

atomic power power generated from the heat given off by atoms splitting at a slower rate than needed to produce an explosion.

atomic reactor large tank in which controlled nuclear fission takes place; reactor.

a·tone (ə tōn') to make amends for an offense or crime: *To* atone *for his rudeness, Tom brought his teacher a bouquet of flowers.* **a·toned, a·ton·ing.**

a·tone·ment (ə tōn'mənt) **1** amends or satisfaction for a wrong that has been done. **2** **the Atonement** the sufferings and death of Jesus Christ to save mankind from sin. **3** **Day of Atonement** Yom Kippur.

a·top (ə tŏp') **1** at or to the top: *The sailors swarmed* atop. **2** on top of.

a·tro·cious (ə trō'shəs) extremely cruel or wicked: *an* atrocious *crime.* **a·tro·cious·ly.**

a·troc·i·ty (ə trŏs'ə tĭ) **1** wicked or cruel act or thing: *wartime* atrocities. **2** something ridiculously ugly or poorly made: *Her hat is an* atrocity. **a·troc·i·ties.**

at·tach (ə tăch′) **1** to fasten to or upon something; join: *The written directions are* attached *to the tool.* **2** to assign to a military company: *Corporal Smith is* attached *to Company G.* **3** to assign: *He* attaches *great importance to his new work.* **4** to take property by a court order: *His salary was* attached *by his creditors.* **5** to belong: *Certain duties* attach *to this position.*

at·tach·ment (ə tăch′mənt) **1** something fastened to or upon something else: *Several* attachments *came with the vacuum cleaner.* **2** something which ties or fastens one thing to another. **3** affection or regard: *The two had a strong* attachment *for each other.*

at·tack (ə tăk′) **1** to begin to fight; set upon forcefully: *The enemy* attacked *us from the rear.* **2** to make an attack: *The enemy* attacked. **3** an attacking; an onset: *an enemy* attack; *an* attack *of flu.* **4** to criticize; find fault with: *The newspapers* attacked *the senator's speech.* **5** to have a harmful effect upon: *Some insects* attack *our gardens.* **6** to begin on: *to* attack *a job with vigor.*

at·tain (ə tān′) **1** to achieve or gain by effort: *He* attained *his goal by hard work.* **2** to reach; arrive at: *Grandfather* attained *the age of ninety.*

at·tain·ment (ə tān′mənt) **1** an achieving; a gaining: *His chief goal was* attainment *of the prize.* **2** accomplishment; skill: *His* attainments *included skill in painting.*

at·tempt (ə tĕmpt′) **1** to make an effort; try: *The pilot* attempted *to land the crippled plane.* **2** effort; trial: *His second* attempt *at skating was successful.*

at·tend (ə tĕnd′) **1** to be present at: *to* attend *school; to* attend *church.* **2** to look after; apply oneself to; work at: *The store owner* attended *to his business.* **3** to go with; accompany: *A company of nobles* attended *the king.* **4** to serve or wait upon: *The maid* attends *her mistress.*

at·tend·ance (ə tĕn′dəns) **1** an attending; presence: *Her* attendance *was necessary.* **2** the number of persons present: *The* attendance *at the game was very small.*

at·tend·ant (ə tĕn′dənt) **1** person who is with another for service or company. **2** serving or helping another: *an* attendant

nurse. **3** going along with; accompanying: *certain* attendant *circumstances.*

at·ten·tion (ə tĕn′shən) **1** a looking, listening, or thinking carefully and steadily: *The students gave their full* attention *to the experiment.* **2** care; consideration: *Give* attention *to this request.* **3** a command to stand straight with the eyes front and arms down at the sides. **4** stand at attention to stand straight and still on command.

at·ten·tive (ə tĕn′tĭv) **1** observant; heedful: *The* attentive *student learns his lessons well.* **2** eager to offer service; courteous: *a waiter* attentive *to patrons.* **at·ten·tive·ly.**

at·test (ə tĕst′) to testify to: *His good conduct was* attested *by many witnesses.*

at·tic (ăt′ĭk) space in a house directly under the roof; garret.

at·tire (ə tīr′) **1** to dress or adorn, especially for formal occasions: *The queen was* attired *in her coronation robe.* **2** clothes or apparel: *formal* attire. **at·tired, at·tir·ing.**

at·ti·tude (ăt′ə tōōd′ or ăt′ə tūd′) **1** way of thinking, feeling, or acting: *What accounts for his hostile* attitude *towards us?* **2** position of the body to show feeling, mood, or purpose.

at·tor·ney (ə tûr′nĭ) **1** lawyer. **2** person who has the legal power to act for another.

at·tract (ə trăkt′) to draw to oneself or to itself: *A magnet* attracts *iron. He shouted to* attract *attention. A courteous man* attracts *friends easily.*

at·trac·tion (ə trăk′shən) **1** a drawing toward; attracting: *the* attraction *of gravity.* **2** power of attracting: *Adventure stories have great* attraction *for me.* **3** thing that attracts: *The clowns were the main* attraction *at the circus.*

at·trac·tive (ə trăk′tĭv) **1** appealing; charming; pleasing. **2** having the power to attract: *the* attractive *force of a magnet.* **at·trac·tive·ly.**

¹at·trib·ute (ə trĭb′ūt) **1** to consider as belonging to: *This play is* attributed *by some to Shakespeare.* **2** to consider a thing as caused by: *He* attributes *his success to hard work.* **at·trib·ut·ed, at·trib·ut·ing.**

²at·trib·ute (ăt′rə būt′) something considered as belonging to a person or thing;

---

fāte, făt, fâre, fär; bē, bĕt; bīte, bĭt; nō, nŏt, nôr; fūse, fŭn, fûr; tōō, tŏŏk; foil; foul; thin; ~~then~~; hw for wh as in *what*; zh for s as in *usual*; ə for a, e, i, o, u, as in *ago, linen, peril, atom, minus*

83

a characteristic: *His chief* attributes *are honesty and courage.*

au·burn (ô′bərn) reddish brown.

auc·tion (ôk′shən) **1** public sale at which property or goods are sold to the highest bidder. **2** to sell at an auction: *The sofa was auctioned off to the highest bidder.*

au·da·cious (ô dā′shəs) bold; daring. **au·da·cious·ly.**

au·dac·i·ty (ô dăs′ə tĭ) **1** boldness. **2** impudence; insolent boldness: *He had the audacity to ask me to do his work for him.*

au·di·ble (ô′də bəl) loud enough to be heard: *a barely audible whisper.* **au·di·bly.**

au·di·ence (ô′dĭ əns) **1** a group of people gathered to hear or see something. **2** people within hearing range; listeners: *The television audience heard his speech.* **3** interview with a person of high rank: *an audience with the king.*

au·di·tor (ô′də tər) **1** hearer; listener. **2** person who examines and checks on accounts and records.

au·di·tor·i·um (ô′də tôr′ĭ əm) **1** building or large room used for public gatherings. **2** the part of a church, theater, etc., where the audience sits.

au·di·tor·y (ô′də tôr′ĭ) **1** having to do with hearing. **2 auditory nerve** one of the two special nerves of hearing.

Aug. August.

au·ger (ô′gər) a tool for boring holes.

aug·ment (ôg mĕnt′) to make larger; increase: *He augmented his income by taking an additional job.*

Auger

au·gust (ô gŭst′) having great dignity; majestic; inspiring great respect: *an august personage.*

August (ô′gəst) the eighth month of the year. August has 31 days.

auk (ôk) arctic sea bird with a heavy body, short wings, and webbed feet.

aunt (ănt) **1** the sister of one's father or one's mother. **2** the wife of one's uncle. (Homonym: ant)

Auk, 16 in. long

au·ror·a bor·e·al·is (ô rôr′ə bôr′ĭ ăl′ĭs) glowing or flickering streamers of light seen at night in the northern sky; the northern lights.

aus·pic·es (ôs′pə sĭz) **1** a sponsoring; patronage: *He traveled abroad under government auspices.* **2** omens or signs: *The ancient Romans studied the flight of birds for auspices to guide their actions.*

aus·pi·cious (ô spĭsh′əs) favorable; promising success: *Our team made an auspicious beginning by winning the first game of the season.* **aus·pi·cious·ly.**

aus·tere (ô stîr′) **1** severe and stern in manner or appearance: *the austere look on the old judge's face.* **2** strict and severely simple in manner of living or behaving: *the austere life of the first pioneers.* **3** plain; without ornament: *The castle hall looked dark and austere.* **aus·tere·ly.**

Aus·tral·ia (ô strāl′yə) island continent southeast of Asia.

au·then·tic (ô thĕn′tĭk) **1** genuine; not falsified: *an authentic signature.* **2** true; trustworthy: *Do you think this is an authentic account of what happened?*

au·thor (ô′thər) **1** person who writes a book, story, article, etc. **2** person who begins or originates anything: *the author of an ingenious scheme.*

au·thor·i·ta·tive (ə thôr′ə tā′tĭv or ə thôr′ə tā′tĭv) **1** having the weight of authority; worthy of belief: *The news came from an authoritative source.* **2** commanding: *The officer spoke to the crew in an authoritative tone.* **au·thor·i·ta·tive·ly.**

au·thor·i·ty (ə thôr′ə tĭ or ə thôr′ə tĭ) **1** power or right (to command, direct, or act): *The general had authority to start the attack.* **2** accepted source of expert information or advice, such as a writing or a person: *The doctor was an authority on tropical diseases.* **3 authorities** government officials: *The authorities stopped all traffic.* **au·thor·i·ties.**

au·thor·ize (ô′thə rīz′) **1** to give the power or right to do something: *He was authorized to buy the supplies for the office.* **2** to allow by law; approve: *The legislature authorized funds for roads.* **3** to justify; give sanction for: *Halloween pranks are authorized by tradition.* **au·thor·ized, au·thor·iz·ing.**

au·to (ô′tō) automobile. **au·tos.**

au·to·bi·og·ra·phy (ô′tə bī ŏg′rə fĭ) story of a person's life, written or told by himself. **au·to·bi·og·ra·phies.**

au·to·crat (ô′tə krăt′) **1** ruler with unlimited power. **2** person who demands complete obedience to his will: *The father was the autocrat of the household.*

au·to·graph (ô′tə grăf′) **1** person's own signature or handwriting. **2** to write one's name on or in: *to autograph one's picture.*

au·to·mat·ic (ô′tə măt′ĭk) **1** self-operating; self-acting; capable of being run or worked without an operator: *an automatic elevator; an automatic washing machine.* **2** done unconsciously or from habit: *Breathing is automatic.* **3** firearm that continues to fire so long as the trigger is held and the ammunition lasts.

au·to·mat·i·cal·ly (ô′tə măt′ĭk ə lĭ) in an automatic way.

au·to·ma·tion (ô′tə mā′shən) **1** the use of machines that, once started, run themselves according to directions that have been fed into a control apparatus. Human workers are needed to watch the dials and signal lights that show whether the machines are operating according to plan. **2** the installing of automatic machinery.

au·to·mo·bile (ô′tə mə bēl′ or ô′tə mō′bēl or ô′tə mə bēl′) vehicle that carries its own engine and is used on streets and highways.

au·tumn (ô′təm) **1** third season of the year, between summer and winter; fall. **2** belonging to this season: *red autumn leaves.*

aux·il·ia·ry (ôg zĭl′yə rĭ) **1** helper, especially a foreign soldier serving with another nation at war. **2** helping; serving to take the place of: *an auxiliary power station.* **aux·il·ia·ries.**

a·vail (ə vāl′) **1** to be of use or value to: *Our best efforts availed us little.* **2** a benefit; value: *Forts are of no avail against bombs.*
avail oneself of to take advantage of: *He availed himself of this opportunity.*

a·vail·a·ble (ə vā′lə bəl) **1** that can be obtained; handy: *The car is not available tonight because Father has it.* **2** usable; capable of being put to service: *other available men for the team.* **a·vail·a·bly.**

av·a·lanche (ăv′ə lănch) large mass of snow, ice, or earth suddenly sliding or falling down a mountain.

av·a·rice (ăv′ə rĭs) greed for money: *Wealth beyond the dreams of avarice.*

av·a·ri·cious (ăv′ə rĭsh′əs) greedy; stingy; worshipping money. **av·a·ri·cious·ly.**

Ave. avenue.

a·venge (ə vĕnj′) to take revenge for: *The savage avenged his brother's death by tracking down the murderer.*
avenge oneself to get even; to get satisfaction for a wrong done to oneself.
a·venged, a·veng·ing.

a·veng·er (ə vĕn′jər) person who takes revenge by punishing the wrongdoer.

av·e·nue (ăv′ə nŏŏ′ or ăv′ə nū′) **1** wide street. **2** road with trees on each side. **3** way of reaching; approach: *The teacher prescribed hard work as the surest avenue to success.*

av·er·age (ăv′ər ĭj) **1** result obtained by adding two or more quantities and dividing the total by the number of quantities: *The average of 3, 7, and 8 is 6.* **2** to find the average of. **3** obtained by averaging: *an average price.* **4** to have or be as an average: *The boys in the class average four feet in height. He averages three dollars an hour.* **5** ordinary; usual: *The average American likes baseball.* **6 on an average** approximately: *We read, on an average, two books a week last year.* **av·er·aged, av·er·ag·ing.**

a·verse (ə vûrs′) opposed; not inclined: *Tom Sawyer was averse to hard work.* **a·verse·ly.**

a·ver·sion (ə vûr′zhən) **1** dislike; disgust: *She has an aversion to snakes.* **2** thing or person disliked: *One of her pet aversions was mosquitoes.*

a·vert (ə vûrt′) **1** to turn away: *He averted his eyes from the sight of the accident.* **2** to avoid: *to avert danger by quick thinking.*

a·vi·ar·y (ā′vĭ ĕr′ĭ) place for keeping birds. **a·vi·ar·ies.**

a·vi·a·tion (ā′vĭ ā′shən or ăv′ĭ ā′shən) the science and practice of flying aircraft.

a·vi·a·tor (ā′vĭ ā′tər or ăv′ĭ ā′tər) person who flies an airplane; airplane pilot.

av·id (ăv′ĭd) **1** eager: *Tom is an avid reader.* **2** desirous of, greedy for: *to be avid for praise.* **av·id·ly.**

---

fāte, făt, fâre, fär; bē, bĕt; bīte, bĭt; nō, nŏt, nôr; fūse, fŭn, fûr; tōō, tŏŏk; foil; foul; thin; then; hw for wh as in what; zh for s as in usual; ə for a, e, i, o, u, as in ago, linen, peril, atom, minus

85

av·o·ca·do (ăv′ə kä′dō) **1** pear-shaped tropical American fruit, green to black in color, with a very large, hard pit. **2** the tree that it grows on. **av·o·ca·dos.**

av·o·ca·tion (ăv′ə kā′shən) an interest or occupation outside one's regular work: *The lawyer's* avocation *was painting.*

Avocado

a·void (ə void′) to keep away from: *Always* avoid *poison ivy.*

a·void·a·ble (ə voi′də bəl) that can be kept away or avoided: *an* avoidable *accident.*

a·void·ance (ə void′əns) a keeping away from: *The surest way of keeping slim is* avoidance *of fattening food.*

av·oir·du·pois (ăv′ər də poiz′) **1** common system of weighing, based on 16 ounces to the pound. **2** a person's weight; heaviness.

a·vow (ə vou′) to admit; confess; declare openly: *He* avowed *his intention to finish the job.*

a·vow·al (ə vou′əl) a free and open statement, declaration, or admission: *The boy made an open* avowal *of his part in the prank.*

a·wait (ə wāt′) **1** to wait for: *Children eagerly* await *Christmas.* **2** to be ready for; be in store for: *A warm welcome* awaits *you.*

a·wake (ə wāk′) **1** to wake up; arouse: *The campers* awoke *at dawn. He* awoke *the campers.* **2** not asleep: *Are you* awake? **3** awake to aware of: *They are still not* awake *to the danger of their position.* **a·woke** or **a·waked, a·wak·ing.**

a·wak·en (ə wā′kən) to wake up; rouse from sleep; stir up.

a·wak·en·ing (ə wā′kən ĭng) **1** a waking up. **2** sudden awareness: *an* awakening *to danger.*

a·ward (ə wôrd′) **1** to give after careful consideration: *A medal was* awarded *to the best athlete.* **2** something granted after careful deliberation; a prize: *Her cat received the* award *of a blue ribbon.*

a·ware (ə wâr′) realizing; knowing; being conscious of: *to be* aware *of danger.*

a·way (ə wā′) **1** from a place; off: *to go* away. **2** aside: *to look* away. **3** at a distance; distant: *ten miles* away. **4** absent: *to be* away *from home.* **5** out of one's possession: *to give money* away. **6** out of existence: *The echo died* away. **7** on and on; without stopping: *to work* away *at a job.*

awe (ô) **1** great wonder combined with fear or reverence: *He stood in* awe *of the judge.* **2** to fill with awe: *He was* awed *by the ocean's vastness.* **awed, aw·ing.**

aw·ful (ô′fəl) **1** dreadful; inspiring awe: *the* awful *power of a lightning bolt.* **2** very bad; very ugly: *His handwriting is* awful.

aw·ful·ly (ô′flĭ) **1** terribly; frightfully. **2** very: *It's* awfully *hot today.*

a·while (ə hwīl′) for a short time.

awk·ward (ôk′wərd) **1** clumsy: *an* awkward *skater.* **2** embarrassing: *A hostess is in an* awkward *situation if the food runs short at a party.* **3** not handy; not designed for easy use: *This is an* awkward *door to open.* **4** hard to manage: *an* awkward *turn in the road.* **awk·ward·ly.**

awl (ôl) a pointed tool for making small holes in leather or wood. (Homonym: all)

Awl

awn·ing (ô′nĭng) a rooflike covering that overhangs a door or window as a protection from sun or rain.

a·woke (ə wōk′) See awake. *I* awoke *early.*

a·wry (ə rī′) **1** to one side; askew: *The wind blew her hat* awry. **2** go awry to go wrong; go amiss: *Our plans went* awry.

ax or **axe** (ăks) a tool for chopping wood. **ax·es.**

Ax

ax·is (ăk′sĭs) line around which an object turns. *The earth's* axis *is an imaginary line that runs through the center of the earth between the North and South Poles.* **ax·es** (ăk′sēz).

ax·le (ăk′səl) **1** the bar on which a wheel turns. **2** the center rod of a wheel which revolves as the wheel turns; the rod that joins two wheels.

Axle

¹ay or **aye** (ā) always; ever: *forever and* ay. [**¹ay, aye** comes from an Old Norse word (ei) meaning "ever" or "always."]

²ay or **aye** (ī) **1** yes. **2** a vote in favor of something: *The* ayes *have it.* [**²ay, aye** is a word of unknown origin.] (Homonyms: eye, I)

a·zal·ea (ə zāl′yə) **1** a bush of the heath family with white, pink, or brilliant red flowers. **2** the flower of this plant.

Az·tec (ăz′tĕk) **1** one of a group of Indians of advanced civilization in central Mexico, conquered by the Spanish under Cortes in 1521. **2** having to do with these Indians, their language, or their culture.

az·ure (ăzh′ər) sky blue.

B

B, b (bē) second letter of the English alphabet.

baa (bă or bä) **1** sound made by a sheep or lamb; bleat. **2** to make this sound.

bab·ble (băb′əl) **1** to make sounds that have no meaning; talk like a baby. **2** to talk in a hurried, excited way without making sense. **3** to chatter idly: *The silly girl babbled on and on about her boy friends.* **4** idle chatter; foolish talk. **5** confused, indistinct sound (of voices): *When the door opened, a loud babble of voices was heard.* **6** murmuring sound: *the babble of a brook.* **bab·bled, bab·bling.**

babe (bāb) very young child or baby.

ba·boon (bă boon′) type of ape that has a doglike face and a short tail and lives on the ground. Baboons are very intelligent, have fierce tempers, and live in highly organized herds.

Baboon, body 2 ft. long, tail 18 in.

ba·by (bā′bĭ) **1** young child or infant. **2** youngest member of a family. **3 baby sitter** person who cares for small children while their parents are absent. **ba·bies.**

bach·e·lor (băch′ə lər) **1** man who has never married. **2** person who has taken the first or lowest degree at a college or university: *a bachelor of arts or science.*

back (băk) **1** in man and animals having a backbone, the rear or upper part of the body from the neck to the end of the spine; in other animals, the upper part of the body. **2** opposite of front; rear: *the back of the house.* **3** in the rear: *the back seat of a car.* **4** to or toward the rear: *Move back in the bus and make room for others.* **5** away: *The police held the crowd back from the fire.* **6** to a person or place from which something came: *He paid back the money he had borrowed.* **7** to a former state or condition: *Ice turns back into water as it melts.* **8** to cause to move backward: *to back a car.* **9** to support: *to back a plan.*

back down to give up an argument, claim, opinion, etc.: *He claimed he could juggle, but he backed down when asked to.*

back out to withdraw: *At first he said he would go, but then he backed out.*

back·ache (băk′āk′) a pain or ache in the spine or back.

back·bone (băk′bōn′) **1** the spine. **2** courage; firmness: *It took backbone to stand up to such a big man.*

back·ground (băk′ground′) **1** back part of a scene or landscape: *There were mountains in the background of the picture.* **2** surface on which patterns or designs are drawn: *The stars of the flag are drawn on a blue background.* **3** past education, experience, or the like: *The new boy had a French background.* **4 in the background** out of sight or notice.

back·hand (băk′hănd′) **1** writing in which the letters slant back or to the left. **2** stroke in tennis, badminton, etc., with the arm drawn across the body and the back of the hand moving toward the net.

back·ward (băk′wərd) **1** toward the rear: *A backward step landed him in the pond.* **2** toward the past: *The old man spent the days looking backward to his youth.* **3** not developed; behind the times: *Some backward nations do not have modern farm machinery.* **4** shy; timid: *The child was too backward to speak.* **5** dull; slow in learning: *a backward student.* **back·ward·ly.**

back·wards (băk′wərdz) **1** in reverse of the usual or right way: *He put his shirt on backwards in the excitement.* **2** with the back first: *to walk backwards.*

---

fāte, făt, fâre, fär; bē, bĕt; bīte, bĭt; nō, nŏt, nôr; fūse, fŭn, fûr; tōo, tŏŏk; foil; foul; thin; ~~then;~~ hw for wh as in *wh*at; zh for s as in u*s*ual; ə for a, e, i, o, u, as in *a*go, lin*e*n, per*i*l, at*o*m, min*u*s

back·wa·ter (băk′wô′tər or băk′wŏ′tər)
1 water held back by a dam, or a current
turned backward by an obstruction: *The
boat was caught in the* backwater *of the mill
pond.* **2** not active; stagnant: *Oldville is a*
backwater *town where nothing changes.*

back·woods (băk′woŏdz′) thinly settled
woodland far from towns and cities: *Abraham Lincoln was born in the* backwoods *of
Kentucky.*

back·woods·man (băk′woŏdz′mən) **1** man
of the backwoods: *Daniel Boone was a
famous* backwoodsman. **2** a crude, awkward person. **back·woods·men.**

back·yard (băk′yärd′) yard at the back of
a house or other building.

ba·con (bā′kən) salted and
smoked meat from the back
and sides of a hog.

bac·te·ri·a (băk tĭr′ĭ ə) tiny
plants of one cell that can
be seen only through
a microscope. Some are
harmful, causing disease,
and others are useful.

Bacteria,
magnified
1000 times

bac·te·ri·ol·o·gy (băk tĭr′ĭ ŏl′ə jĭ) study of
bacteria and their effects.

bad (băd) **1** not good; not right; not as it
should be: *a bad habit.* **2** evil; wicked: *It
is bad to lie. He is a bad man.* **3** incorrect;
faulty: *His English is very bad.* **4** of poor
quality: *There is bad housing in the slums.*
5 rotten; spoiled: *a barrel of bad apples.*
6 unpleasant: *a bad taste.* **7** severe;
serious: *a bad accident.* **8** sick: *to feel bad.*
worse, worst. (Homonym: bade)

bade (băd) See **bid.** *Washington* bade *the
army farewell.* (Homonym: bad)

badge (băj) a mark, token, or something
worn to show membership, authority, or
achievement: *a policeman's* badge; *a badge
for perfect attendance.*

badg·er (băj′ər) **1**
hairy, burrowing ani-
mal, about two feet
long, that eats flesh.
2 its fur. **3** to tease;
worry; pester: *The
child* badgered *his
mother all day with questions.*

Badger, about
2 ft. long

bad·ly (băd′lĭ) **1** in an imperfect way; not
well; poorly: *The house is* badly *heated. The
project turned out* badly. **2** in a way causing

pain, danger, or harm: *The prisoners were
badly treated.* **3** very much: *very badly
damaged.*

bad·min·ton (băd′mĭn tən) a game, somewhat like tennis, played with light rackets
on a court divided into halves by a high net.

bad-tem·pered (băd′tĕm′pərd) often in a
bad humor; quarrelsome and disagreeable.
bad-tem·pered·ly.

baf·fle (băf′əl) to frustrate or balk by confusing or puzzling: *The fox* baffled *the
hounds. This arithmetic problem* baffles *me.*
baf·fled, baf·fling.

bag (băg) **1** sack for holding anything; container made of paper, cloth, etc., that can
be closed at the top. **2** purse; handbag.
3 suitcase; traveling bag. **4** to put into a
bag. **5** to capture or kill while hunting:
The hunter bagged *two deer.* **6** game killed
on a hunting trip: *The day's* bag *was eight
ducks.* **7** to bulge; hang loosely: *The jacket*
bagged *at the elbow.* **bagged, bag·ging.**

ba·gel (bā′gəl) doughnut-shaped roll made
of unsalted yeast dough. The bagel is simmered in water before it is baked.

bag·gage (băg′ĭj) bags,
trunks, suitcases, and
boxes a person takes
on a trip; luggage.

bag·pipe (băg′pīp′)
musical instrument
with a tube, an air
bag, and reed pipes,
now played chiefly in
Scotland.

Man playing bagpipe

¹**bail** (bāl) to scoop
water out of a boat
with a dipper, bucket,
or the like.

bail out to jump from an airplane by
parachute. [¹**bail** is really another meaning of ³**bail** which once meant a type of
bucket used on shipboard to scoop out
water.] (Homonym: bale)

²**bail** (bāl) **1** to obtain release (of a person)
from arrest by depositing a guarantee that
the accused will appear for trial when
wanted: *His friend* bailed *him out of jail.*
2 the money, etc. so deposited: *Mr. Smith
gave* bail *for his accused friend.* **3** the person
or persons making such a guarantee. [²**bail**
comes from an Old French word (bail)
meaning "custody."] (Homonym: bale)

bail

³bail (bāl) curved handle of a kettle or bucket. [³**bail** comes from a French word (baille) meaning "bucket."] (Homonym: bale)

bail·iff (bā′lif) **1** a deputy sheriff. **2** an officer who guards prisoners and watches over jurors in a courtroom.

bairn (bârn) a Scottish word for child; a son or daughter.

bait (bāt) **1** anything, especially food, used to attract or catch fish or other animals. **2** to put food or other objects on a fishhook or in a trap to catch animals: *He baited his hook with minnows.*

bake (bāk) **1** to cook in an oven: *Susan baked her own birthday cake.* **2** to dry or harden by heat: *The sun baked the muddy river banks.* **baked, bak·ing.**

bak·er (bāk′ər) **1** one who makes bread, cakes, and the like. **2 baker's dozen** thirteen.

bak·er·y (bā′kə rĭ) place where bread, cakes, and pastries are made; store where baked goods are sold. **bak·er·ies.**

bak·ing (bā′kĭng) **1** cooking in an oven. **2** amount baked at one time.

baking powder powder used to make cake or biscuit rise and become light. Baking powder contains baking soda.

baking soda a white powder used to make cake rise and as a medicine.

bal·ance (băl′əns) **1** an instrument for weighing. **2** to weigh up; compare: *to balance the chances of the two groups.* **3** equality or proportion in weight, amount, or importance: *Be sure to keep a balance between meats and vege-tables in your diet.* **4** to keep equal or in proper proportion: *to balance a budget.* **5** steady or firm position; steadiness; equilibrium: *The tightrope walker lost his balance.* **6** control of the feelings; mental steadiness. **7** to keep (an object) steady: *The seal balanced a ball on his nose.* **8** the rest; part left over: *to play the balance of the afternoon.* **bal·anced, bal·anc·ing.**

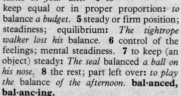
Balance

ballad

bal·co·ny (băl′kə nĭ) platform, with a railing, built out from the wall of a building. A balcony may be outside or inside a building. **bal·co·nies.**

Balcony

bald (bôld) **1** without hair on the head. **2** without natural covering: *a bald tree; a bald mountain.* ▸ **3** bare; plain: *the bald truth.* **4** of birds, having white on the top of the head: *the bald eagle.*

bale (bāl) **1** large package or bundle of goods held together for storing or shipping: *a bale of cotton.* **2** to make into bales: *Modern farm machines bale hay.* **baled, bal·ing.** (Homonym: bail)

bale·ful (bāl′fəl) full of spite and ill will; evil: *The old witch cast a baleful look at Hansel and Gretel.* **bale·ful·ly.**

balk (bôk) **1** to stop short and refuse to budge: *The horse balked at the high jump.* **2** to hinder; check: *The barricade balked the enemy's advance.*

balk·y (bô′ki) unwilling to budge; stubbornly refusing to move: *a balky mule.* **balk·i·er, balk·i·est.**

¹ball (bôl) **1** any round body; sphere: *the flaming ball of the sun.* **2** round, or nearly round, object used in a game: *a golf ball; a croquet ball; a tennis ball.* **3** game using a ball, especially baseball: *to play ball.* **4** in baseball, a pitch of a ball too high, or too low, or not over the home plate, and not struck at by the batter; not a strike. **5** solid bullet or shot for a firearm: *musket ball.* **6** rounded part at the base of the thumb or great toe. [¹**ball** is from a French word (balle) also meaning "ball."] (Homonym: bawl)

²ball (bôl) a large formal dance: *Cinderella rode to the ball in a pumpkin coach.* [²**ball** is from a French word (bal) which goes back to a Latin word (ballare) meaning "to dance."] (Homonym: bawl)

bal·lad (băl′əd) **1** simple song, especially one with several verses sung to the same melody. **2** poem that tells a story.

---

fāte, făt, fâre, fär; bē, bět; bīte, bĭt; nō, nŏt, nôr; fūse, fŭn, fûr; tōō, tŏŏk; foil; foul; thin; then; hw for wh as in what; zh for s as in usual; ə for a, e, i, o, u, as in ago, linen, peril, atom, minus

ballast

bal·last (băl′əst) **1** anything heavy used in the absence of cargo to steady a ship or submarine. **2** anything heavy that can be dropped to lighten a balloon or dirigible. Sand bags are often used for ballast.

ball bearing 1 grooved ring holding small metal balls on which some moving part of a machine turns. **2** any of the metal balls of a ball bearing.

bal·let (băl′ā or bă lā′) **1** story or idea acted out in dance form; also the music for it. **2** a company of ballet dancers.

bal·lis·tic (bə lis′tĭk) of missiles, intended to be shot, hurled, or thrown. A rocket or a bullet is a ballistic missile.

bal·loon (bə lōōn′) **1** an airtight bag which rises and floats in the air when it is filled with a gas that is lighter than air. **2** a child's toy, which consists of a rubber sack that can be blown up. **3** to go up or ride in a balloon. **4** to swell up like a balloon.

bal·lot (băl′ət) **1** secret voting by marking a printed or written form, or by using a voting machine. **2** a written or printed form used in secret voting. **3** to vote by ballot. **4** the total votes cast.

Balloon

ball·room (bôl′rōōm′) a large room with a polished floor for dancing.

balm (bäm) **1** an oil or gummy substance from certain plants and trees, used as a healing salve; balsam. **2** anything that heals or soothes: *His kind words were a balm to her hurt feelings.*

balm·y (bä′mĭ) **1** soft and gentle; soothing: *After the storm, we welcomed the balmy weather.* **2** having a sweet smell; fragrant. **balm·i·er, balm·i·est; balm·i·ly.**

bal·sa (bôl′sə or băl′sə) **1** tropical American tree with strong wood lighter than cork. **2** the wood of this tree, used in making life preservers, life rafts, etc.

bal·sam (bôl′səm) **1** an oily, fragrant substance obtained from certain shrubs and trees and used as a healing medicine; balm. **2** a shrub or tree of the fir family from which this substance is taken.

bam·boo (băm bōō′) **1** a woody, treelike, tropical plant of the grass family. **2** its

bang

hollow, jointed stems, used in building in tropical climates, and in making furniture, fishing poles, canes, etc. **3** made of bamboo. **bam·boos.**

ban (băn) **1** to prohibit; forbid: *Our town bans fireworks.* **2** an order that something must not be done or said: *a ban on the sale of fireworks.* **banned, ban·ning.**

ba·nan·a (bə năn′ə) **1** a pulpy, long fruit with a yellow, red or green rind and sweet flesh, that grows in bunches. **2** the tropical plant that bears this fruit.

Bamboo

band (bănd) **1** a group of persons united for a purpose: *a band of thieves.* **2** a group of musicians who play together: *dance band.* **3** to unite or join in a group: *The states banded together to form a union.* **4** a thin, flat strip of material or rubber for binding, trimming, or holding together. **5** a stripe. **6** in radio, a particular range of wave lengths.

Banana plant

band·age (băn′dĭj) **1** a strip of cloth used for binding injuries. **2** to bind or cover (injuries) with a strip of cloth. **band·aged, band·ag·ing.**

ban·dan·na or **ban·dan·a** (băn dăn′ə) large colored handkerchief.

band·box (bănd′bŏks′) box made of light wood or pasteboard, used to hold hats, collars, or the like.

ban·dit (băn′dĭt) outlaw or robber.

ban·dy (băn′dĭ) **1** to throw or knock to and fro: *They bandied the tennis ball about the court.* **2** to give and take; exchange: *to bandy words.* **ban·died, ban·dy·ing.**

ban·dy-leg·ged (băn′dĭ lĕg′ĭd or băn′dĭ-lĕgd′) having legs bent outward at the knees; bow-legged.

bane (băn) something that causes destruction, ruin, or trouble.

¹bang (băng) **1** a loud, sudden noise. **2** a heavy, noisy blow. **3** to strike or beat

90

noisily: *They* banged *the dishes with their spoons.* **4** to make a loud, sudden noise: *The guns* banged *in the distance.* **5** to shut noisily: *He* banged *the door on his way out.* [¹**bang** is probably an imitation of a noise, though some think it is from an Old Norse word (banga) meaning "to hammer."]

²**bang** (băng) a fringe of short hair over the forehead. [²**bang** is of unknown origin.]

ban·ish (băn′ĭsh) **1** to condemn to leave; send from a country by legal decree; expel: *The former dictator was* banished *from the country.* **2** to drive out; send away: *The doctor's talk* banished *his fears of illness.*

ban·ish·ment (băn′ĭsh mənt) expulsion from a country; exile.

ban·is·ter (băn′ĭs tər) handrail and upright supports along the edge of a staircase, bridge, balcony, etc.

Banjo

ban·jo (băn′jō) stringed musical instrument played with the fingers or with a small piece of wood or metal. **ban·jos.**

¹**bank** (băngk) **1** a pile or heap: *a bank of snow.* **2** slope or ridge of earth bordering a river, stream, etc. **3** submerged mass of earth in the sea or at the mouth of a river over which the water is shallow; shoal: *a sand* bank. **4** to form into a pile: *Let's* bank *up the earth against this wall.* **5** to cover (a fire) with ashes or fuel to make it burn slowly. **6** in road building, to make the inner edge of a curve lower than the outer edge, for ease in driving. **7** to tilt (an airplane) in making a turn. [¹**bank** is a form of an older English word (banke).]

²**bank** (băngk) **1** arrangement of objects in a line. **2** a row of keys in an organ. **3** a bench for rowers in a galley. **4** a row or tier of oars. [²**bank** is actually ¹**bank** in later meanings.]

³**bank** (băngk) **1** place of business which receives money for safekeeping, and which exchanges and lends money. **2** to put in a bank; deposit. **3** to have an account at a

bank: *We* bank *downtown.* **4** any reserve supply: *blood* bank; *eye* bank; *soil* bank. [³**bank** is from an Italian word (banca) meaning "bench" or "table." The meaning arose, of course, from the giving and taking of money across a table.]

bank·er (băngk′ər) person who manages or works for a bank.

bank·ing (băngk′ĭng) the business of investing, lending, and guarding money.

bank·rupt (băngk′rŭpt) **1** unable to pay one's debts. **2** person who is legally declared unable to pay his debts and whose property is divided among the people to whom he owes money. **3** to make bankrupt: *His extravagant life* bankrupted *him.*

ban·ner (băn′ər) **1** flag. **2** piece of cloth with a design, picture, or writing on it. **3** outstanding, exceptional: *a banner year.*

ban·quet (băng′kwĭt) a feast; formal dinner at which speeches are made.

ban·ter (băn′tər) **1** good-natured teasing talk. **2** to tease in a friendly, joking way. **3** to exchange joking remarks.

bap·tism (băp′tĭz əm) **1** practice of sprinkling a person or dipping him in water, as a sign of washing away sin and of admission into the Christian church. **2** first experience; initiation; trial: *The recruit had his* baptism *of gunfire.*

bap·tize (băp′tīz or băp tīz′) **1** to pour or sprinkle water on a person or dip a person in water, as a sign of admission into a Christian church. **2** to give a name at the time of baptism; christen: *The boy was* baptized *John.* **bap·tized, bap·tiz·ing.**

bar (bär) **1** piece of some solid substance of even shape, and longer than it is wide or thick: *a bar of iron.* **2** to fasten with a bar: *I locked and* barred *the door.* **3** to supply with bars to prevent extrance or escape: *We* barred *the first floor windows.* **4** something that blocks the way; a barrier: *Poor reading is a* bar *to success in school work.* **5** to block; close off; obstruct: *Snow* barred *the way through the pass.* **6** underwater bank of sand or gravel which obstructs the passage of ships: *a harbor* bar. **7** place set off by a rail in a courtroom where prisoners stand for trial or sentence:

---

fāte, făt, fâre, fär; bē, bĕt; bīte, bĭt; nō, nŏt, nôr; fūse, fŭn, fûr; tōō, tŏŏk; foil; foul; thin; ~~then~~;
hw for wh as in *wh*at; zh for s as in usual; ə for a, e, i, o, u, as in a*go*, lin*e*n, per*i*l, at*o*m, min*u*s

the prisoner at the bar. **8** profession of law: *He was admitted to the* bar. **9** counter or place where food and drinks are sold. **10** excepting; excluding: *Everyone is welcome,* bar *none.* **11** one of the upright lines drawn through a staff of written music to divide it into equal measures of time; a measure of music. **barred, barring.**

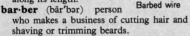

BAR   DOUBLE BAR

BAR BAR BAR
Bar of music

barb (bärb) sharp hook or point extending backward, as on the tip of a fishhook, arrow, etc.

Barb

bar·bar·i·an (bär bâr´ĭ ən) **1** uncivilized person. **2** not civilized; crude; nearly savage.

bar·bar·ic (bär bãr´ĭk) **1** uncivilized; primitive: *The music was* barbaric *and wild.* **2** savage: *their* barbaric *cruelty.*

bar·ba·rous (bär´bə rəs) **1** uncivilized; crude; outlandish: *his* barbarous *manners.* **2** cruel; inhuman: *The* barbarous *treatment of prisoners included torture and starvation.* **bar·ba·rous·ly.**

bar·be·cue (bär´bə kū´) **1** a picnic at which an animal, such as an ox, is roasted whole. **2** meat roasted on a revolving spit or cooked over an outdoor grill. **3** to cook meat in this way. **4** a grill or outdoor fireplace over which meat is roasted. **5** a party around an outdoor grill. **bar·be·cued, bar·be·cu·ing.**

barbed (bärbd) having sharp points as some fence wires, or barbs as some fishhooks.

barbed wire a twisted wire with sharp points spaced along its length.

Barbed wire

bar·ber (bär´bər) person who makes a business of cutting hair and shaving or trimming beards.

bard (bärd) **1** a poet and singer in olden times. **2** poet.

bare (bâr) **1** not covered; naked: *on bare feet.* **2** without a covering: *a bare floor; to have one's head* bare. **3** empty: *The house was quite* bare. **4** scanty; mere: *a bare majority; the* bare *necessities of life; on the* bare *chance.* **5** to uncover; reveal; expose: *He* bared *his sword. The dog* bared *his teeth.* **bar·er, bar·est; bared, bar·ing.** (Homonym: bear)

bare·back (bâr´băk´) without a saddle; on the bare back of a horse: *to ride* bareback.

bare·foot (bâr´fo͝ot´) with bare feet: *the* barefoot *boy; to walk* barefoot.

bare·head·ed (bâr´hĕd´ĭd) with nothing on the head; without a hat.

bare·ly (bâr´lĭ) **1** hardly; scarcely: *We* barely *had time to escape the flood.* **2** in a bare way; poorly; scantily: *a barely furnished room.*

bar·gain (bär´gĭn) **1** agreement on the terms of a deal: *He made a* bargain *to deliver the coal weekly.* **2** to make a trade or deal. **3** something bought cheap or offered for sale at a low price. **4** to argue over a price; haggle: *I* bargained *with the rug dealer for an hour, and got him down to half his asking price.*

bargain for to expect: *His staying all night was more than I* bargained for.

barge (bärj) boat with a flat bottom, used in inland and coastal waters for carrying freight.

Barge

bar·i·um (bär´ĭ əm or bâr´ĭ əm) a chemical element. It is a soft, heavy metal which is used in alloys, luminous paints, etc.

¹bark (bärk) **1** outer covering of trees and other woody plants. **2** to strip bark or skin from: *He* barked *his shins on a chair.* [¹**bark** is from a Scandinavian word.] (Homonym: barque)

²bark (bärk) **1** sharp, explosive sound made by a dog or fox. **2** to make this sound: *The dog* barked *gleefully.* **3** to speak in a sharp or gruff way: *The captain* barked *his orders.* [²**bark** is a form of an old English word (beorcan).] (Homonym: barque)

³bark (bärk) a kind of ship with three masts. Also spelled **barque.** [³**bark** is from an Italian word (barca) meaning "vessel."]

bar·ley (bär´lĭ) **1** grasslike cereal plant. **2** its grain used as a food.

Bark

bar mitz·vah (bär mĭts´vä) **1** ceremony held for a Jewish boy at his thirteenth year to mark his adulthood in his religion. **2** Jewish boy for whom this ceremony has been held.

barn (bärn) farm building used for storing grain, hay, etc., and for housing livestock.

bar·na·cle (bär'nə kəl) small sea animal with a thin shell which attaches itself to the bottoms of ships, to rocks, wharves, etc.

barn·yard (bärn'yärd') a plot of ground around a barn.

ba·rom·e·ter (bə-rŏm'ə tər) an instrument for measuring the pressure of the air, used in showing height above sea level and in forecasting weather.

Barometer

bar·on (băr'ən) **1** in Great Britain, the title of the lowest rank of nobility. **2** a person holding this title. **3** in the Middle Ages, a person who held an estate directly from the king. (Homonym: barren)

bar·on·et (băr'ən ĭt or băr'ə nĕt) **1** in Great Britain, a rank between baron and knight. **2** the title that shows this rank.

barque (bärk) ³bark. (Homonym: bark)

bar·racks (băr'əks) a large building or group of buildings for housing soldiers. pl. **bar·racks.**

bar·rel (băr'əl) **1** round, bulging cask greater in length than in width, usually of wood, with flat ends. **2** quantity which such a cask contains: *The new oil well produces 600 barrels of oil a day.* **3** to put or pack in a barrel. **4** part or case of something in the shape of a tube: *a gun* barrel.

Barrel

bar·ren (băr'ən) **1** not fertile or productive: *There is much* barren *land in the West.* **2** unable to bear young: *a* barren *mare.* **3** not bearing fruit: *a* barren *pear tree.* (Homonym: baron)

bar·ri·cade (băr'ə kād' or băr'ə kād') **1** crude wall or barrier, especially one hastily put in place to keep back an enemy. **2** to put a makeshift wall or barrier into position: *They* barricaded *the road to the fort with logs.* **bar·ri·cad·ed, bar·ri·cad·ing.**

bar·ri·er (băr'ĭ ər) **1** something built to bar or prevent passage: *The Great Wall of China was a* barrier *against invasion.* **2** anything that prevents progress or creates difficulty: *a language* barrier; *a* barrier *to trade; a* barrier *to success.*

¹**bar·row** (băr'ō) a wheelbarrow, or a flat wooden frame with handles at the ends, on which things may be carried. [¹**barrow** is from an Old English word (beran) meaning "bear."]

²**bar·row** (băr'ō) an ancient artificial mound of earth or stones over a grave: *Indian* barrows *were found near the town.* [²**barrow** is from an Old English word (beorg).]

bar·ter (bär'tər) **1** to exchange or trade one thing for another without the use of money: *Indians used to* barter *their furs for guns.* **2** to engage in trade or exchange: *Eskimos* barter *at the trading post every spring.* **3** an exchanging or trading without money.

¹**base** (bās) **1** the bottom part of a thing, on which it stands or rests: *a lamp* base. **2** the main part of a mixture; foundation: *Beef stock is the* base *of many soups.* **3** starting place for an operation; headquarters: *the* base *of an exploring party; a naval* base. **4** a station or goal in some games, such as baseball. **5** to establish firmly; found: *a business* based *on honesty; a story* based *on facts.* **6** in chemistry, a substance that will combine with an acid to form a salt and which turns litmus paper blue. **based, bas·ing.** [¹**base** is from the same Greek word (basis) that gives us the word "basis."] (Homonym: ²bass)

²**base** (bās) **1** of little value; comparatively inferior: *iron is a* base *metal.* **2** morally bad; mean; vile: *Kidnapping is a* base *crime.* **bas·er, bas·est; base·ly.** [²**base** is from a Late Latin word (bassus) meaning "short," "low."] (Homonym: ²bass)

base·ball (bās'bôl') **1** game played with a ball and bat by teams of nine players on a side. The game is played on a field with four bases at the corners of a square called a diamond. **2** ball used in this game.

base·man (bās'mən) in baseball, a man guarding first, second, or third base. **base·men.**

---

fāte, făt, fâre, fär; bē, bĕt; bite, bĭt; nō, nŏt, nôr; fūse, fŭn, fûr; tōō, tŏŏk; foil; foul; thin; ~~then~~;
hw for wh as in *w*hat; zh for s as in u*s*ual; ə for a, e, i, o, u, as in *a*go, lin*e*n, per*i*l, at*o*m, min*u*s

base·ment (bās′mənt) story of a building, partly or completely underground.

bash·ful (băsh′fəl) very shy or timid. **bash·ful·ly.**

ba·sic (bā′sĭk) **1** main or fundamental; forming a basis or foundation: *A basic ingredient in a cake is flour.* **2** primary; beginning: *the basic training of recruits.*

ba·si·cal·ly (bā′sĭ kə lĭ) in the main part; primarily; fundamentally: *The house is basically sound. He is basically honest.*

ba·sin (bā′sən) **1** wide, shallow vessel, usually round or oval, for holding water or other liquids; a bowl. **2** the quantity held by such a vessel. **3** hollow or enclosed area containing water: *a yacht basin.* **4** all the land drained by a river and its tributaries: *the basin of the Columbia River.*

Basin

ba·sis (bā′sĭs) **1** part on which anything rests or depends; foundation: *Common interests form a good basis for friendship.* **2** fundamental facts or reasons: *What basis do you have for that statement?* **3** fundamental part or ingredient: *The basis of a cake is flour and eggs.* **ba·ses** (bā′sēz).

bask (băsk) to lie in comfortable warmth; warm oneself pleasantly: *to bask in the sun.*

bas·ket (băs′kĭt) **1** container made of thin strips of wood, straw, twigs, reeds, etc., woven together: *Easter* basket; *clothes* basket. **2** amount a basket will hold; basketful. **3** hoop with a bottomless net through which a basketball player must toss the ball to score points. **4** a toss of the ball through this hoop, counted as a score.

bas·ket·ball (băs′kĭt bôl′) **1** a game in which the opposing teams score points by tossing a ball through baskets at either end of the court. **2** ball used in this game.

¹bass (băs) a food fish of several kinds, found both in fresh water and in the ocean. pl. **bass,** rarely, **bass·es.** [**¹bass** is the changed form of a dialect word (barse) meaning "perch."]

²bass (bās) **1** low and deep in tone. **2** lowest part sung by a male voice. **3** any instrument or singer that plays or sings the lowest part. [**²bass** is a word growing out of **²base.** Its spelling was influenced by an Italian word (basso) meaning "a singer with a low voice."] (Homonym: base)

bas·soon (bă sōōn′) musical wood-wind instrument with a deep tone. It has a long double wooden tube for a body and a curved metal mouthpiece.

bass viol (bās vī′əl) the largest and lowest-toned musical instrument of the violin group. The player stands and holds the viol like a cello while playing.

¹baste (bāst) to sew with long stitches to hold cloth pieces in place temporarily. **bast·ed, bast·ing.** [**¹baste** is from an Old French word (bastir) also meaning "to sew loosely."]

²baste (bāst) to moisten with fat, gravy, or other liquid while roasting: *She basted the turkey with melted butter.* **bast·ed, bast·ing.** [**²baste** is from an Old French word (basser) meaning "to soak."]

¹bat (băt) **1** wooden club or stick, especially one used in a game: *baseball* bat. **2** a turn at batting: *Who's at bat?* **3** to hit or strike with a bat. **bat·ted, bat·ting.** [**¹bat** is the slightly changed form of an Old English word (batt).]

²bat (băt) any of a group of furry animals with large wings of thin, hairless skin. Most bats fly at night. [**²bat** is the greatly changed form of an earlier English word (bakke).]

Brown bat, about 3½ in. long

batch (băch) **1** amount baked at one time; a baking: *a batch of cookies.* **2** quantity of material to be used or made at one time: *a batch of cement.* **3** group of similar things: *a batch of letters.*

bath (băth) **1** a cleaning or washing of all the body. **2** water for bathing: *to draw a bath.* **3** room or building for bathing: *the public baths of Rome.*

bathe (bāth) **1** to clean; wash. **2** to give a bath to: *to bathe a baby.* **3** to go into the sea, a river, lake, etc. for enjoyment. **4** to apply water or other liquid to: *You should bathe your sore foot in hot water.* **5** to surround or cover as water does: *The stage was bathed in light.* **bathed, bath·ing.**

bath·robe (băth′rōb′) a long coat worn to and from the bath, for lounging, or the like.

bath·room (băth′rōōm′) a room with a bathtub and basin, usually containing a toilet.

bath·tub (băth′tŭb′) tub, now usually equipped with faucets and drain, used for taking a bath.

ba·ton (bă tŏn′) **1** stick used by an orchestra conductor to beat time. **2** rod carried by a drum major. **3** stick passed from one runner to the next in a relay race.

bat·tal·ion (bə tăl′yən) an army unit of two of more companies that forms part of a regiment.

¹bat·ter (băt′ər) **1** to beat or strike with repeated blows; pound: *The rescue squad* battered *down the door.* **2** to damage by use or misuse: *The boys soon* battered *all the new furniture.* [**¹batter** is at least in part from a French word (battre) meaning "to beat."]

²bat·ter (băt′ər) thin mixture of flour, liquid, and other ingredients: *pancake* batter. [**²batter** is **¹batter** in a later and special use.]

³bat·ter (băt′ər) the player who is batting or whose turn it is to bat. [**³batter** is a word growing out of **¹bat.**]

bat·tered (băt′ərd) damaged by pounding, use, or misuse: *a* battered *old ship; the* battered *face.*

bat·ter·y (băt′ə rĭ) **1** a device that uses chemicals to produce electricity: *flashlight* battery; *automobile* battery. **2** group of similar articles or machines; set: *a battery of cameras.* **3** two or more big guns: *The admiral fired the main* battery. **4** the pitcher and catcher in baseball. **bat·ter·ies.**

bat·tle (băt′əl) **1** fight between opposing armies, fleets, or air forces. **2** any fight or struggle: *a battle between the two gangs; a* battle *against the jungle.* **3** to fight; struggle: *to* battle *a hurricane; to* battle *for freedom.* **bat·tled, bat·tling.**

bat·tle-ax or **bat·tle-axe** (băt′əl ăks′) ax once used as a weapon. **bat·tle-axes.**

Battle-ax

bat·tle·field (băt′əl fēld′) ground or place where a battle is fought or was fought.

bat·tle·ment (băt′əl mənt) wall at the top of a building or tower, constructed with gaps or openings through which, in olden times, men shot at their enemies.

bat·tle·ship (băt′əl shĭp′) a large warship with heavy armor and very powerful guns.

bau·ble (bô′bəl) cheap ornament; a thing that is showy, but of little value: *Her jewels were only* baubles, *but glittered impressively.*

baux·ite (bôk′sĭt or bō′zĭt) a claylike mineral from which aluminum is obtained.

bawl (bôl) **1** to cry loudly; howl: *The child* bawled *in anger.* **2** to shout; call out loudly: *The sergeant* bawled *his orders.* (Homonym: ball)

¹bay (bā) large inlet formed by a deep recess or curve in the shore of a lake or ocean. [**¹bay** is from a French word (baie).]

²bay (bā) **1** part of a room extending beyond the main outside wall, often having several windows in it. **2** compartment in the body of an airplane. **3** the forward part of a ship between decks. [**²bay** is from an Old French word (baee) meaning "opening."]

³bay (bā) the laurel tree, a small evergreen with shiny leaves. [**³bay** is from an Old French word (baie) which goes back to a Latin word (bacca) meaning "berry."]

⁴bay (bā) **1** long, deep howling bark made by a dog: *The hunters heard the* bay *of the dogs that had seen the fox.* **2** to bark with a long, deep tone: *The hound* bayed *at the moon.* **3 at bay (1)** in a position ready to fight off pursuers: *The bear stood at* bay *as the dogs attacked from all sides.* **(2)** in a position from which attack or escape is impossible: *The boy held the thief at* bay. [**⁴bay** is from an Old French word (abaier) meaning "to bark."]

⁵bay (bā) **1** having a reddish-brown color: *a* bay *horse.* **2** reddish-brown horse. [**⁵bay** is from an Old French word (bai) which goes back to a Latin word (badius) meaning "chestnut brown."]

bay·o·net (bā′ə nĕt′) **1** dagger that can be attached to the muzzle of a rifle, and used for stabbing or slashing. **2** to stab with a bayonet. **bay·o·net·ed, bay·o·net·ing.**

Bayonet on rifle

bay·ou (bī′ōō) sluggish stream, flowing through marshy land, into or out of a river, lake, or the like, especially in Louisiana and its neighborhood.

---

fāte, făt, fâre, fär; bē, bĕt; bīte, bĭt; nō, nŏt, nôr; fūse, fŭn, fûr; tōō, tŏŏk; foil; foul; thin; then; hw for wh as in *wh*at; zh for s as in u*s*ual; ə for a, e, i, o, u, as in *a*go, lin*e*n, per*i*l, at*o*m, min*u*s

ba·zaar (bə zär′) **1** sale of various kinds of articles for some special purpose: *a charity bazaar.* **2** place for the sale of a variety of goods. **3** in Oriental countries, a market place or street lined with shops. Also spelled **bazar.**

bbl. barrel.

B.C. before Christ. These letters are used with dates to show the number of years before the Christian Era. A.D. is used with dates from the beginning of the Christian Era: *Augustus Caesar ruled Rome 46 years, from 31 B.C. to A.D. 14.*

be (bē) **1** to exist: *Can these things be?* **2** to occur: *There will be a fight.* **3** to belong to the class of: *to be a doctor.* **4** to have as a quality: *to be beautiful.* **5** to remain: *to be at peace.* **6** to equal or stand for: *Let x be ten.* **7** (a helping word with action words when we mean that something is acted upon): *It is to be praised. She was praised. They were praised. She has been praised.* **8 be to,** (**am to, is to, are to**) will: *They are to appear.* **was, were, been, be·ing.** See also **am, are, is.** (Homonym: bee)

beach (bēch) **1** sandy or pebbly part of a river, lake, or ocean shore washed by waves or tides. **2** to bring (a boat) up out of the water onto the shore. (Homonym: beech)

beach·head (bēch′hĕd′) part of an enemy shore first captured by an invading army and used as a base for further operations.

bea·con (bē′kən) **1** fire, light, or radio signal used for guiding or warning. Beacon lights and radio signals are used especially in the navigation of ships and airplanes. **2** tower or framework on which a signal light is mounted.

bead (bēd) **1** small ball or piece of wood, glass, stone, or the like, pierced through to be strung together with others for ornament or in a rosary. **2** any small, round body: *a bead of dew; a bead of sweat.* **3** small metal knob at the muzzle end of a gun barrel, used in taking aim. **4** to decorate with beads. **5 beads** a rosary.

bea·gle (bē′gəl) a small hunting dog having short legs and drooping ears.

beak (bēk) **1** the bill of a bird. **2** anything pointed or shaped like the bill of a bird, such as the lip of a pitcher or the prow of some ancient warships.

beak·er (bē′kər) **1** cup or glass with a pouring lip, used in laboratories. **2** large cup.

beam (bēm) **1** long, heavy piece of wood or metal, used in the framework of buildings. **2** supporting bar of wood or metal: *the beam of a plow; the beam of a balance.* **3** in the framework of a ship, a main support running from one side to the other. **4** widest part of a ship or boat. **5** ray (of light): *a beam of sunlight.* **6** to shine: *The sun beamed.* **7** a smile: *A beam of joy lighted his face.* **8** to smile: *She beamed with happiness.* **9** a radio signal sent in a certain direction, especially used to guide ships or airplanes. **10** to send a radio signal in a certain direction: *A broadcast was beamed to Europe from the United States.*

Laboratory beaker

bean (bēn) **1** bushy or vinelike plant which bears pods containing seeds which are used for food, such as the string bean. **2** the pod or seed of the bean plant. **3** a seed that is like a bean, such as the coffee bean.

bean·bag (bēn′băg′) a small cloth bag filled with beans, used in some games.

bean·stalk (bēn′stôk′) the stem or stalk of a bean plant.

¹bear (bâr) **1** large animal with long, shaggy hair, and a very short tail. **2** rough, surly person. [**¹bear** is a form of an Old English word (bera).] (Homonym: bare)

Black bear, about 5 ft. long

²bear (bâr) **1** to support; carry: *The donkey can bear a heavy load.* **2** to endure; stand: *She can't bear to look at a snake.* **3** to have; show: *to bear the name of his grandfather; to bear scars.* **4** to press: *You must not bear down so hard on the crayon.* **5** to bring forth; produce: *to bear fruit.* **6** to give birth to: *to bear children.*

bear on to refer to; have to do with.

bear to or **toward** to go toward.

bore, borne, bear·ing. [**²bear** is a form of an Old English word (beran).] (Homonym: bare)

bear·a·ble (bâr′ə bəl) that can be endured or borne: *a bearable ache.*

beard (bîrd) **1** hair that grows on the chin and cheeks of a man. **2** long hair on the

chin of some animals, such as the goat.
3 growths like hairs on the heads of some
grains, such as wheat or barley.

bear·ing (bâr′ing) **1** way of carrying oneself
in standing, walking, etc.; manner: *The
leader had a proud* bearing. **2** a part of a
machine in or on which another part turns
or moves: *A bicycle wheel turns on ball*
bearings. **3** meaning; relation: *The question
has no* bearing *on the subject.* **4 bearings**
direction or position in relation to other
things: *The boy lost his* bearings *in the forest.*

beast (bēst) **1** any four-footed animal, especially a large or ferocious animal. **2** a
coarse or brutal person.

beast·ly (bēst′lĭ) **1** savage; brutal; disgusting: *a beastly crime;* beastly *manners.* **2** unpleasant; annoying: *a* beastly *nuisance.*
beast·li·er, beast·li·est.

beat (bēt) **1** to strike or hit repeatedly: *to*
beat *a drum; to* beat *a donkey.* **2** to throb:
The heart beats. **3** sound repeated in a
steady rhythm: *the* beat *of marching feet.*
4 to flap repeatedly: *A bird* beats *its wings.*
5 to stir vigorously: *to* beat *eggs.* **6** to indicate rhythm or accent in music by tapping
or waving: *to* beat *time.* **7** the rhythm or
accent in music. **8** to defeat; conquer: *We
can* beat *their team if the field isn't muddy.*
9 a route or course that is gone over repeatedly: *A policeman walks his* beat. **beat·en**
or **beat, beat·ing.** (Homonym: beet)

beat·en (bē′tən) **1** hammered; shaped by
hammering: *an Indian rice bowl made of*
beaten *brass.* **2** worn by use; packed hard
by repeated footsteps: *a* beaten *path.* **3** See
beat. *Our team is not* beaten *yet.*

beat·ing (bē′ting) **1** whipping, as punishment. **2** a severe defeat: *The team took a*
beating. **3** a pulsating; throbbing: *the
beating of the heart.*

beau (bō) **1** a man who escorts a lady; ad-
mirer; lover. **2** dude; dandy. **beaux** or
beaus. (Homonym: ¹bow)

beau·te·ous (bū′tĭ əs) beautiful.

beau·ti·ful (bū′tə fəl) delighting the ear,
eye, or mind; lovely. **beau·ti·ful·ly.**

beau·ti·fy (bū′tə fī′) to make beautiful;
adorn: *to* beautify *a yard with flowers.*
beau·ti·fied, beau·ti·fy·ing.

beau·ty (bū′tĭ) **1** the qualities of a person
or a thing that give pleasure to the eye or
ear; a quality that delights the mind; loveliness: *The girl's* beauty *in the portrait was
far beyond mere prettiness.* **2** lovely woman:
She was a great beauty. **beau·ties.**

¹**bea·ver** (bē′vər)
1 small, furry animal
with strong teeth,
webbed hind feet, and
a broad, flat tail.
Beavers live both in
water and on land.
They are able to cut
down trees with their
sharp teeth and to use
the trees to build dams. **2** the fur of this
animal. [¹**beaver** is a form of an Old English word (beofor).]

Beaver, about
2ft. long

²**bea·ver** (bē′vər) the movable part of a
knight's metal helmet that protected the
mouth and chin. [²**beaver** is from an Old
French word (baviere) meaning "a bib to
catch saliva."]

be·came (bĭ kām′) See **become.** *He became angry and started to shout.*

be·cause (bĭ kôz′) **1** for the reason that;
since; for: *We didn't stay outside long because it was too cold.* **2 because of** on account of: *I couldn't sleep* because of *the
heat.*

beck (běk) **1** a nod or gesture as a signal of
summoning or command. **2 at (one's)
beck and call** at one's service.

beck·on (běk′ən) to signal (someone) with
a movement of the head or hand.

be·come (bĭ kŭm′ or bē kŭm′) **1** to come
or grow to be: *A lamb* becomes *a sheep.*
2 to suit; be suitable to; look well on: *That
new pink dress* becomes *her.* **be·came,
be·come, be·com·ing.**

be·com·ing (bĭ kŭm′ing) going well with
the appearance or character; suitable; appropriate: *a* becoming *dress; conduct that
is not* becoming *to a lady.* **be·com·ing·ly.**

bed (běd) **1** article of furniture designed for
resting or sleeping. **2** any place a person
or animal might sleep: *The cat's* bed *was a
cardboard box.* **3** plot of earth in which
plants are set: *a* bed *of tulips.* **4** bottom or

---

fāte, făt, fâre, fär; bē, bĕt; bīte, bĭt; nō, nŏt, nôr; fūse, fŭn, fûr; tōō, tŏŏk; foil; foul; thin; then;
hw for wh as in *what*; zh for s as in u*s*ual; ə for a, e, i, o, u, as in ago, linen, peril, atom, minus

base: *a bed of gravel; a lake* bed. **5** to put to bed; arrange sleeping quarters for: *They bedded the horses in the barn.* **6** to plant: *We bedded the iris in rich, black soil.* **bed·ded, bed·ding.**

bed·bug (bĕd′bŭg′) small biting insect with an unpleasant odor, sometimes found in bedding, upholstered furniture, etc.

bed·clothes (bĕd′klōz′ or bĕd′klōᵺz′) coverings for a bed; sheets, blankets, quilts, etc.

bed·ding (bĕd′ĭng) **1** bedclothes and mattress. **2** materials for a bed: *Straw is used as bedding for horses.*

bed·lam (bĕd′ləm) scene of confusion and noisy disorder: *The auditorium was a complete bedlam when the rally got out of hand.*

Bed·ou·in (bĕd′ōō in) a wandering Arab of the desert. Bedouins live in tents and raise flocks and herds, especially camels.

be·drag·gled (bi drăg′əld) wet, limp, and dirty: *Water was streaming down her face, and her dress was torn and bedraggled.*

bed·room (bĕd′rōōm′) a room with a bed in it; a sleeping room.

bed·side (bĕd′sīd′) **1** the space beside a bed: *The doctor sat at the patient's bedside.* **2** beside a bed: *a bedside lamp.*

bed·spread (bĕd′sprĕd′) covering, often decorative, spread over other bedclothes when the bed is not in use.

bed·stead (bĕd′stĕd′) the wood or metal framework of a bed that holds the springs and mattress.

bed·time (bĕd′tīm′) the time when a person should go, or usually goes, to bed.

bee (bē) **1** a small winged insect with sucking and stinging organs that lives with many other bees in a hive where it stores pollen and honey. **2** a social gathering for work, competition, or amusement: *a quilting bee; a spelling bee.* (Homonym: be)

beech (bēch) **1** a wide-spreading tree, with smooth gray bark and dark green leaves. It bears nuts that can be eaten. **2** the wood of this tree. (Homonym: beach)

beef (bēf) **1** flesh of an ox, bull, cow, or steer used for food. **2** a fully-grown ox, bull, steer, or cow that is raised for its meat. **beeves.**

beef·steak (bēf′stāk′) a slice of meat from a steer, cow, or bull, suitable for broiling or frying.

bee·hive (bē′hīv′) box made to house a swarm of bees and to store their honey.

been (bĭn) See **be.** *It has been cold all week. Have you been to Florida?* (Homonym: bin)

Beehive

beer (bîr) **1** an alcoholic beverage usually made from malted barley and flavored with hops. **2** drink made from roots or plants: *root beer; ginger beer.* (Homonym: bier)

bees·wax (bēz′wăks′) the wax from which the bees make their honeycomb. It is used to stiffen thread, for candles, etc.

beet (bēt) **1** plant grown for its root which is used as a vegetable. One variety of beet has a pinkish white root from which sugar is extracted. **2** root of this plant used as a vegetable. (Homonym: beat)

bee·tle (bē′təl) a kind of insect with four wings, the outer pair of which are hard and shiny and serve to protect the inner pair.

be·fall (bi fôl′) to happen to: *Whatever luck befalls them, they are ready to meet it.* **be·fell, be·fall·en, be·fall·ing.**

Beetle

be·fell (bi fĕl′) See **befall.**

be·fit (bi fĭt′) to be suited to; be suitable or appropriate for: *The room was decorated with roses to befit the occasion.* **be·fit·ted, be·fit·ting.**

be·fore (bi fôr′) **1** in front of: *the scene before us.* **2** ahead of: *There are still many good times before us.* **3** earlier than: *That happened before the war.* **4** previously; at an earlier time: *I thought I had seen that movie before.* **5** in sight or presence of: *The children performed before their parents.* **6** rather than: *I'd walk before I'd ride in that uncomfortable wagon.*

be·fore·hand (bi fôr′hănd′) ahead of time; in advance: *All the preparations for the party were made beforehand.*

be·friend (bi frĕnd′) to act as a friend toward; help: *The rich old man befriended the little waif.*

beg (bĕg) **1** to ask for as charity: *to beg for food; to beg for money.* **2** to ask for as a favor: *He begged his mother to let him go to the circus.* **3** to make a living by asking charity or alms: *He begs on the streets.*

beg off to obtain release from; to make an excuse for not doing something.

beg pardon to ask to be pardoned: *I beg your pardon for interrupting you.*

begged, beg·ging.

be·gan (bĭ găn′) See **begin.** *It all began long ago.*

beg·gar (bĕg′ər) **1** one who begs. **2** a person who lives by asking for alms. **3** a very poor, penniless person.

be·gin (bĭ gĭn′) **1** to start; take the first step: *When did you begin school?* **2** to arise; come into being: *The brook begins in the hills.* **be·gan, be·gun, be·gin·ning.**

be·gin·ner (bĭ gĭn′ər) person who is just starting something; one who has had no training or experience.

be·gin·ning (bĭ gĭn′ĭng) **1** a start: *the beginning of a race.* **2** time or place of origin; source: *The Nile River has its beginning in the mountains of Africa.* **3** first part: *the beginning of the story.*

be·gone (bĭ gôn′ or bĭ gŏn′) go away: *The princess cried to the dwarf, "Begone!"*

be·go·ni·a (bĭ gōn′yə) a house plant with glossy leaves and waxlike red, pink, or white flowers.

be·guile (bĭ gīl′) **1** to deceive: *They beguiled the enemy into an ambush.* **2** to amuse; charm; delight: *He beguiled us with stories.* **3** to pass pleasantly: *to beguile the time.* **be·guiled, be·guil·ing.**

be·gun (bĭ gŭn′) See **begin.** *Finish the work you have begun.*

be·half (bĭ hăf′) **1** interest; support; favor. **2 in behalf of** for; in the interest of: *The lawyer spoke in behalf of his client.*

be·have (bĭ hāv′) **1** to act; conduct oneself: *He behaved like a fool.* **2** to act properly; do what is right: *Please let me go and I'll behave.* **be·haved, be·hav·ing.**

be·hav·ior (bĭ hāv′yər) way of acting; conduct; actions: *a prize for good behavior.*

be·head (bĭ hĕd′) to cut off the head of: *Charles I of England was beheaded in 1649.*

be·held (bĭ hĕld′) See **behold.** *He beheld a strange sight.*

be·hind (bĭ hīnd′) **1** back of; following: *They marched behind the band.* **2** inferior to; below the level of: *He was behind the class in arithmetic.* **3** in support of: *The mayor is behind the plan.* **4** in the rear of in direction or time: *We were left behind. He left confusion behind him.* **5** to the rear; backward: *Look behind.* **6** not up to date: *She is behind in her payments.*

be·hold (bĭ hōld′) to look at; gaze upon; see: *The garden was a joy to behold.* **be·held, be·hold·ing.**

be·hold·er (bĭ hōl′dər) person who looks at something; spectator: *Beauty is in the eye of the beholder.*

be·ing (bē′ĭng) **1** living creature: *a human being.* **2** existence: *The airplane did not come into being until gasoline engines were invented.* **3** that which makes a thing or person what it is; essence: *His very being rebelled at the suggestion.* **4 The Supreme Being** God.

be·lab·or (bĭ lā′bər) **1** to beat with hard blows: *The farmer belabored his mule.* **2** to keep after; assail: *They belabored the teacher with questions.*

be·lat·ed (bĭ lā′tĭd or bē lā′tĭd) delayed; too late: *His belated arrival made him miss his dinner.* **be·lat·ed·ly.**

belch (bĕlch) **1** to discharge gas from the stomach through the mouth. **2** to throw out with force: *The volcano belched molten rock and ashes.* **3** the act of belching.

bel·fry (bĕl′frĭ) a bell tower; the part of a tower or cupola where the bell is hung. **bel·fries.**

be·lie (bĭ lī′) **1** to give a false or contrary impression of: *His black hair and brisk walk* belie *his great age.* **2** to fail to come up to; contradict: *Her neglect of her brother belies her claim to devotion.* **be·lied, be·ly·ing.**

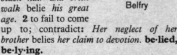

Belfry

be·lief (bĭ lēf′) **1** acceptance of something as existing or true; faith; trust: *Nothing will shake my* belief *in his honesty.* **2** creed; religious faith. **3** opinion.

be·lieve (bĭ lēv′) **1** to accept as true: *We* believe *some of her stories.* **2** to trust the word of; have confidence in: *I* believe *him.* **3** to think: *Do you* believe *it will rain to-morrow?* **be·lieved, be·liev·ing.**

be·liev·er (bĭ lē′vər) **1** person who believes: *a* believer *in ghosts.* **2** person who has religious faith: *a true* believer.

be·lit·tle (bĭ lĭt′əl or bē lĭt′əl) to make little of; speak scornfully of: *He* belittles *our city in his book.* **be·lit·tled, be·lit·tling.**

bell (bĕl) **1** hollow metal device, usually cup-shaped, which makes a ringing sound when struck with a clapper or hammer. **2** anything shaped like a bell: *the* bell *of a horn; a diving* bell. **3** stroke sounded on a ship's bell, each stroke meaning a half-hour of time. **4** to put a bell on: *The mice decided to* bell *the cat.* (Homonym: belle)

Bells

belle (bĕl) **1** beautiful woman or girl. **2** the most popular girl or woman: *the* belle *of the ball.* (Homonym: bell)

bel·lig·er·ent (bə lĭj′ər ənt) **1** warlike; quarrelsome: *to speak* belligerent *words; a* belligerent *attitude.* **2** engaged in war: *The* belligerent *nations continued fighting.* **3** a nation at war, or member of the military force of such a nation: *Both* belligerents *suffered great losses.* **bel·lig·er·ent·ly.**

bel·low (bĕl′ō) **1** the loud, deep cry of a bull. **2** to make this sound: *The bulls* bel-lowed *when they saw each other.* **3** a loud, deep cry. **4** to cry out in a loud, deep voice; roar; bawl: *The movie director* bellowed *his orders over the loudspeaker.*

bel·lows (bĕl′ōz) apparatus for blowing air into a fire, the pipes of an organ, etc.

bel·ly (bĕl′ĭ) **1** the front part of the body of man between the chest and the thighs, containing the stomach, bowels, etc.; the abdomen. **2** the underpart of the body of a four-footed

Bellows for fire

animal. **3** the inside, front, or under surface of anything: *The* belly *of the ship was damaged.* **4** the bulging part of anything: *The intense cold cracked the* belly *of the laboratory flask.* **5** to swell out; bulge: *The sails* bellied *in the wind.* **bel·lies; bel·lied, bel·ly·ing.**

be·long (bĭ lông′ or bĭ lŏng′) to have one's or its proper place: *This tool* belongs *in the drawer.*

belong to 1 to be the property of: *This book* belongs *to the library.* **2** to be a member or part of: *He* belongs *to the club.*

be·long·ings (bĭ lông′ĭngz or bĭ lŏng′ĭngz) possessions; things that are one's own.

be·lov·ed (bĭ lŭv′ĭd or bĭ lŭvd′) **1** greatly loved. **2** person who is greatly loved.

be·low (bĭ lō′ or bē lō′) **1** lower down than: *He was bruised* below *the knee.* **2** in a lower rank than: *The secretary is* below *the presi-dent.* **3** in or to a lower place: *The sailor went* below *on the captain's orders.*

belt (bĕlt) **1** band of leather, cloth, or other material worn around the waist as an ornament or as a support for a garment or weapon. **2** a wide strip or band: *a* belt *of trees around a town.* **3** a region having certain distinctive characteristics: *the Cotton* Belt. **4** a band running around two or more wheels or pulleys to pass mo-tion from one to the other. **5** to encircle with, or as with, a

Machine belt

belt: *The equator* belts *the earth.* **6** to fasten on with a belt: *The knight* belted *on his sword.* **7** to beat with a belt, strap, etc.: *The cruel guard* belted *the prisoner.*

bench (bĕnch) **1** a long seat. **2** the seat judges sit on in court. **3** position of judge: *He was chosen for the* bench *by the Presi-dent.* **4** judges as a group. **5** a strong work table at which craftsmen work.

bend (bĕnd) **1** to force into a curved shape: *The blacksmith* bent *the piece of metal.* **2** to turn: *The road* bends *slightly to the left.* **3** something curved: *a* bend *in the road.* **4** to become crooked or curved: *The tree* bent *in the wind.* **5** to stoop; crouch: *Sarah* bent *down to pick up the papers.*

6 to direct to a certain goal: *Let's bend our energies toward solving this problem.* **7** to submit; yield: *I bend to your wishes.* **8** to force to submit or give in: *The tyrant bent everyone to his will.* **bent, bend·ing.**

be·neath (bĭ nēth′) **1** in a lower place; below. **2** under: *Don't sweep the dirt beneath the rug.* **3** lower in rank or position: *A private is beneath a sergeant.* **4** unworthy of: *He feels it is beneath him to apologize.*

ben·e·dic·tion (bĕn′ə dik′shən) a blessing, such as the one pronounced at the end of a church service.

ben·e·fac·tor (bĕn′ə făk′tər or bĕn′ə făk′-tər) a person who helps another, either with service or with money; a patron.

be·nef·i·cent (bə nĕf′ə sənt) doing or causing good. **be·nef·i·cent·ly.**

ben·e·fi·cial (bĕn′ə fĭsh′əl) helpful; producing good results: *Food and sleep are beneficial to health.* **ben·e·fi·cial·ly.**

ben·e·fit (bĕn′ə fĭt) **1** anything that is of help; advantage. **2** act of kindness. **3** public entertainment to raise money for a worthy cause. **4** to do good to; help: *The rest benefited his health.* **5** to get good (from); receive help; profit: *He benefited from his past experience.*

be·nev·o·lence (bə nĕv′ə ləns) **1** desire to do good for others; good will: *His benevolence led him to work for a charitable organization.* **2** an act of kindness.

be·nev·o·lent (bə nĕv′ə lənt) kind and helpful; doing good; generous. **be·nev·o·lent·ly.**

bent (bĕnt) **1** curved; crooked: *The hose was bent and curled like a snake.* **2** determined; set: *He is bent on becoming a doctor.* **3** a natural ability, interest, or inclination: *He has a bent for painting.* **4** See **bend.**

be·numb (bĭ nŭm′) **1** to make numb; deprive of feeling: *The cold benumbed our fingers.* **2** to make inactive or insensible: *Fear benumbed his mind.*

ben·zene (bĕn′zēn or bĕn zēn′) a colorless, inflammable liquid prepared from coal tar. It is used in medicine, in perfumes, in liquid fuels, and as a solvent. It is sometimes confused with **benzine.**

ben·zine (bĕn′zēn or bĕn zēn′) a colorless,

inflammable liquid prepared from petroleum. It is used as a fuel and a solvent. Also, incorrectly, spelled **benzene.**

be·queath (bĭ kwēth′ or bĭ kwēth′) **1** to give or leave by will: *He bequeathed his money to his sons.* **2** to hand down: *Our forefathers bequeathed us a love of liberty.*

be·rate (bĭ rāt′) to scold; upbraid. **be·rat·ed, be·rat·ing.**

be·reave (bĭ rēv′) to deprive; leave desolate: *to be bereaved by the death of a friend or relative.* **bereaved** or **be·reft, be·reav·ing.**

be·reft (bĭ rĕft′) See **bereave.**

be·ret (bə rā′) a round, close-fitting cap, of wool or other soft material, without a brim.

Ber·lin (bûr lĭn′) largest city in Germany, in the central part of the country; formerly the capital. Berlin is now divided into East Berlin and West Berlin.

Man wearing beret

ber·ry (bĕr′ĭ) **1** a small juicy fruit with many seeds. Gooseberries, blueberries, and cranberries are examples of berries. **2** the dry seed or kernel of certain plants: *the wheat berry.* **3** fruit of the coffee tree. **ber·ries; ber·ried, ber·ry·ing.** (Homonym: bury)

ber·ry·ing (bĕr′ĭ ĭng) picking or gathering berries: *We went berrying in July.*

berth (bûrth) **1** bed, in a train, ship, or plane, which is built like a large shelf; a bunk. **2** place where a ship ties up or lies at anchor. (Homonym: birth)

Railroad car berths

be·seech (bĭ sēch′) **1** to implore; entreat: *We beseech you, O King, to hear our plea.* **2** to beg for: *We beseech your mercy.* **be·sought, be·seech·ing.**

be·set (bĭ sĕt′ or bē sĕt′) **1** to attack from all sides; assail: *Many doubts beset him.* **2** to surround; hem in: *Dangers beset his path.* **be·set, be·set·ting.**

---

fāte, făt, fâre, fär; bē, bĕt; bīte, bĭt; nō, nŏt, nôr; fūse, fŭn, fûr; tōō, tŏŏk; foil; foul; thin; ~~then~~;
hw for wh as in *wh*at; zh for s as in u*s*ual; ə for a, e, i, o, u, as in ag*o*, lin*e*n, per*i*l, at*o*m, min*u*s

be·set·ting (bǐ sĕt'ǐng or bē sĕt'ǐng) constantly attacking; habitually tempting: *Greed is the miser's besetting sin.*

be·side (bǐ sīd') **1** at or by the side of; nearby: *He stood beside me.* **2** in comparison with: *My foot is small beside yours.* **3** away from: *a case beside the point.* **4 be beside oneself** to be very excited; to be out of one's senses, as from anger, fear, etc.: *He was beside himself with rage.*

be·sides (bǐ sīdz') **1** also; as well; moreover: *There will be hunting, fishing, and hiking, and swimming besides.* **2** in addition to; over and above: *The book club is giving a record album besides its book dividend.*

be·siege (bǐ sēj' or bē sēj') **1** to lay siege to; to surround in order to capture: *For nine weeks the enemy besieged the castle.* **2** to pester or harass: *They besieged the actor for autographs.* **be·sieged, be·sieg·ing.**

be·sought (bǐ sôt') See **beseech.** *The prophet besought the help of Heaven.*

be·speak (bǐ spēk') to give evidence of; show: *His good manners bespeak a fine upbringing.* **be·spoke, be·spo·ken** or **be·spoke, be·speak·ing.**

be·spoke (bǐ spōk') See **bespeak.**

best (bĕst) **1** good in the highest degree; most excellent; finest: *Jane's work is good, but Ralph's is better, and Stan's is best.* **2** largest: *The job took the best part of a week to finish.* **3** the finest: *You deserve the best.* **4** height of excellence: *I am at my best early in the morning.* **5** in the most successful way: *I can write best after a good night's sleep.* **6 make the best of** to do as well as possible: *We must make the best of a bad bargain.* **7 get the best of** to defeat. **8 at best** at most; under the most favorable circumstances: *The book, at best, may sell 1000 copies.*

be·stow (bǐ stō' or bē stō') to give; confer; put: *The king bestowed a title on the general. He bestowed much thought upon his plan.*

bet (bĕt) **1** to agree to give (money or something of value) to another person if his guess is right and yours is wrong: *I'll bet you a soda it will rain before morning.* **2** the bargain agreed to: *All right, it's a bet!* **3** the amount agreed upon: *My bet was a soda.* **4** an event or thing on which a bet is placed: *That horse was a poor bet.* **bet** or **bet·ted, bet·ting.**

be·think (bǐ thǐngk') to think about; call to mind; consider.
    bethink oneself to remember: *He bethought himself of all that remained to be done.*
be·thought, be·think·ing.

be·thought (bǐ thôt') See **bethink.**

be·tide (bǐ tīd' or bē tīd') **1** in old-fashioned language, to happen. **2 woe betide you** may misfortune overtake you. **be·tid·ed, be·tid·ing.**

be·tray (bǐ trā' or bē trā') **1** to give into the hands of an enemy by deceit: *A disloyal soldier betrayed the army.* **2** to be disloyal to: *Would you betray a friend?* **3** to show; disclose; reveal: *His confusion betrayed his nervousness.*

be·tray·al (bǐ trā'əl or bē trā'əl) the act of betraying: *the betrayal of a trust.*

be·troth (bǐ trōth' or bǐ trôth') to promise to give in marriage: *The king betrothed his daughter to a prince.*

be·troth·al (bǐ trō'thəl or bǐ trô'thəl) engagement; promise to marry: *The parents announced their daughter's betrothal.*

be·trothed (bǐ trōthd' or bǐ trôtht') **1** engaged to be married. **2** person engaged to be married.

bet·ter (bĕt'ər) **1** good in a higher degree; more excellent: *Apples are better in the fall. He /quit to take a better job.* **2** improved: *His work is getting better.* **3** more effective: *His swimming stroke is better than mine.* **4** improved in health: *The patient is feeling better today.* **5** larger; greater: *The walk to town takes the better part of an hour.* **6** in a finer or more excellent way: *He played better than I and beat me easily.* **7** more: *I like him better than I used to.* **8** to improve: *He took some courses to better himself.* **9 better off** in better conditions or circumstances. **10 get the better of** win an advantage over: *He got the better of his opponent.* **11 had better** would be safer to or wiser to: *You had better go before it rains.*

bet·ter·ment (bĕt'ər mənt) improvement.

be·tween (bǐ twēn') **1** in the space which separates (two objects or things): *There is a narrow lane between the two houses.* **2** in the time which separates (one thing from another): *The accident happened between dusk and dark.* **3** more than one thing and

betwixt

less than another: *It is between 5 and 6 feet long.* **4** from one to another of: *Not a word passed between them.* **5** connecting: *There is a bridge between the two cities.* **6** by joint action of: *We shall finish this job between us.* **7** one or the other of: *Choose between the two vases.*

be·twixt (bǐ twǐkst′) **1** between: *That dream came betwixt waking and sleeping.* **2 betwixt and between** in a middle position; neither the one nor the other.

bev·el (běv′əl) **1** a sloping or slanting edge. **2** to give a sloping or slanting edge to something: *The edge of the table has been beveled.*

Bevel

bev·er·age (běv′ər ij) something to drink.

bev·y (běv′ĭ) **1** a group, especially of women or girls. **2** a flock of birds, especially of quail or larks. **bev·ies.**

be·wail (bǐ wāl′) to lament; mourn for: *They bewailed the death of their leader.*

be·ware (bǐ wâr′ or bē wâr′) to be careful (of); watch out: *One should beware of strange dogs.*

be·wil·der (bǐ wǐl′dər or bē wǐl′dər) to confuse; puzzle: *The noise and crowds of the city bewildered them.*

be·wil·der·ment (bǐ wǐl′dər mənt or bē·wǐl′dər mənt) confusion; a being puzzled.

be·witch (bǐ wǐch′ or bē wǐch′) **1** to cast a spell on by magic: *The bad fairy bewitched Sleeping Beauty.* **2** to charm; delight: *Her beauty bewitched the prince.*

be·yond (bǐ yŏnd′) **1** on the farther side of: *My house is beyond the hill.* **2** farther than a given point; past: *The runner dashed beyond the finish line.* **3** later than: *We stayed beyond the time limit.* **4** too much for; too difficult for: *That kind of arithmetic is beyond him.*

bi- prefix meaning "every two," "two," "twice," or "doubly": b*imonthly;* b*icycle.*

bi·as (bī′əs) **1** to make a person feel or think a certain way; to influence, usually unfairly: *Loyalty to the team biased us against the umpire.* **2** a prejudice: *That article shows a bias against the other political party.* **3** slanting: *a bias seam or joint.* **4** a

bide

slanting line; the diagonal direction of a cut, seam, or stitching made to slant across the threads of material: *to cut a skirt on the bias.*

bi·ased (bī′əst) willing to see only one side; prejudiced: *This newspaper is biased in favor of one political party.*

bib (bĭb) a covering like a small apron worn under the chin to keep food off the clothing.

Bias joint on belt

Bi·ble (bī′bəl) **1** sacred writings of the Old and the New Testaments. **2** sacred writings of any religion.

bib·li·cal (bĭb′lə kəl) having to do with the Bible or with times, persons, and events connected with the Bible: *the biblical wars; biblical scholars; biblical geography.*

bick·er (bĭk′ər) to quarrel; squabble: *The girls bickered over which TV program to turn on.*

bi·cus·pid (bī kŭs′pĭd) one of the eight teeth having two points: *Man has eight bicuspids. For picture, see* **teeth.**

bi·cy·cle (bī′sĭk əl or bī′sə kəl) **1** light vehicle with a metal frame, two wheels, one behind the other, and a saddlelike seat. The rider moves it by pushing alternately on two pedals and steers it by means of handlebars. **2** to ride a bicycle. **bi·cy·cled, bi·cy·cling.**

bid (bĭd) **1** to command; order; request: *The captain bade his company to halt.* **2** to invite: *The host bade us make ourselves at home.* **3** to say as a greeting or farewell: *Let's bid them good-by.* **4** to offer as a price: *I bid five dollars for the bicycle.* **5** the amount offered for something: *The bid was five dollars.* **6** an attempt to get: *a bid for fame.* **bade** or **bid, bid·den** or **bid, bid·ding.**

bid·den (bĭd′ən) See **bid.** *All the peasants were bidden to the feast.*

bid·ding (bĭd′ing) **1** an offering of prices on something: *The bidding at the auction was brisk.* **2** request: *What is your bidding?* **3** command; order: *He came and went at his master's bidding.*

bide (bīd) to wait. **bide one's time** to wait for the right time. **bode** or **bid·ed, bid·ing.**

---

fāte, fǎt, fâre, fär; bē, bět; bīte, bǐt; nō, nŏt, nôr; fūse, fŭn, fûr; tōō, tŏŏk; foil; foul; thin; ~~then~~; hw for wh as in *wh*at; zh for s as in u*s*ual; ə for a, e, i, o, u, as in ago, linen, peril, atom, minus

bi·en·ni·al (bī ĕn′ĭ əl) **1** happening every two years: *a biennial* election. **2** an event which occurs every two years. **3** lasting two years: *a biennial* plant. **4** plant that produces seeds and fruit the second year, then dies: *Carrots and beets are* biennials. **bi·en·ni·al·ly.**

bier (bĭr) the frame on which a dead person or a coffin containing a dead person is placed or carried. (Homonym: beer)

big (bĭg) **1** great in size or amount; large: *a* big *horse; a* big *load.* **2** important: *a* big *issue.* **3** grown-up. **big·ger, big·gest.**

big·horn (bĭg′hôrn′) wild sheep of the Rocky Mountains.

big·ness (bĭg′nĭs) a being big.

bike (bīk) bicycle.

bile (bīl) the bitter yellow or greenish fluid produced by the liver to aid in digestion.

bil·ious (bĭl′yəs) **1** suffering from a liver ailment. **2** caused by this ailment. **3** cross; fretful; peevish: *Mr. Miller takes a* bilious *view of life.* **bil·ious·ly.**

¹**bill** (bĭl) **1** a listing of things, such as services given, goods sold, or work done, for which money is owed. **2** in North America, a piece of paper money: *a dollar* bill. **3** to charge; send a list of charges: *The store will* bill *me for these things later.* **4** a printed advertisement; poster: *The* bill *says that the circus comes in August.* **5** to advertise by posters: *The actor is* billed *to appear next week.* **6** a form or plan of a new law to be presented to a law-making body. **7** program; entertainment: *There is a good* bill *at the theater tonight.* [¹**bill** is from a Late Latin word (billa) meaning "seal" or "document," which in turn goes back to an earlier Latin form (bulla) meaning a "blob" or "bubble" of wax or lead used to seal documents.]

²**bill** (bĭl) the beak of a bird. [²**bill** is a form of an Old English word (bile).]

Bill of hummingbird

bill·board (bĭl′bôrd′) a board, usually set up outdoors to display public notices or advertising.

bil·liards (bĭl′yərdz) a game played by two or more players, on an oblong table having raised, cushioned sides. Each player has a long stick, called a cue, which he uses to drive balls against each other.

bil·lion (bĭl′yən) in the United States, a thousand million (1,000,000,000); in Great Britain, a million million (1,000,000,000,-000).

bill of fare list of foods served at a restaurant or hotel; menu.

bil·low (bĭl′ō) **1** a great wave of the sea. **2** to rise and roll in large waves. **3** to swell out; bulge: *The sails* billow *in the breeze.*

bin (bĭn) box or enclosed place used for storing things: *a coal* bin; *a grain* bin. (Homonym: been)

bind (bīnd) **1** to tie up with a cord or band. **2** to hold together: *Cement* binds *bricks together in the walls of buildings.* **3** to hold by bonds of affection or loyalty: *Friendship* binds *them together.* **4** to finish or protect with a band or border: *The dressmaker* binds *the seams of suits.* **5** to bandage: *to* bind *up a wound.* **6** of a book, to fasten the pages into a cover. **bound, bind·ing.**

bind·er (bīn′dər) **1** person or thing that binds. **2** machine that cuts and binds grain into bundles.

bind·ing (bīn′dĭng) **1** the act of a person or thing that binds. **2** something that covers or binds, as a bandage. **3** the covers of a book. **4** having the force to hold one to an agreement, promise, etc.: *A contract is not* binding *if it is not signed.* **bind·ing·ly.**

bin·oc·u·lars (bə nŏk′yə lərz or bī nŏk′-yə lərz) field glasses or opera glasses with two tubes, one for each eye.

bi·og·ra·phy (bī ŏg′rə fĭ) **1** the story of a person's life. **2** the branch of literature dealing with the lives of people. **bi·og·ra·phies.**

bi·ol·o·gy (bī ŏl′ə jĭ) study of living things.

Binoculars

birch (bûrch) **1** tree with close-grained wood and a smooth outer bark. **2** the wood of this tree.

birch bark (bûrch′bärk′) thin, papery bark of some kinds of birch tree.

bird (bûrd) a two-legged, egg-laying animal having wings and feathers.

birth (bûrth) **1** a coming into life. **2** beginning: *The* birth *of a nation.* **3** descent; ancestry: *of French* birth. **4 give birth to** to bring forth: *to give birth to a son; to give birth to an idea.* (Homonym: berth)

birth·day (bûrth′dā′) **1** day on which a person is born. **2** yearly celebration of that day.

birth·place (bûrth′plās′) **1** place where a person is born. **2** place of beginning or origin: *Philadelphia was the* birthplace *of the Constitution of the United States.*

birth·right (bûrth′rīt′) **1** rights belonging to the eldest son in a family: *Esau sold his* birthright *to his brother, Jacob.* **2** a right held by a person because of his family or country of birth: *Freedom is the* birthright *of every American.*

bis·cuit (bis′kit) **1** kind of bread baked in small, flat cakes. **2** cracker or cooky.

bish·op (bish′əp) **1** clergyman of high rank, in charge of a large church district. **2** piece used in the game of chess.

bi·son (bī′sən) oxlike animal of North America also known as the buffalo. It has a shaggy mane and a large hump. pl. **bi·son.**

Bison, 5½ to 6 ft. high at shoulder

¹bit (bit) **1** See **bite.** *He* bit *into the apple.* **2** small piece of anything; a little: *a bit of bread; just a bit of sugar.* **3** a little while: *Please wait a bit.* [¹**bit** is a form of an Old English word (bita).]

²bit (bit) **1** tool for boring holes. **2** metal piece of a bridle that goes into the mouth of an animal. [²**bit** is a form of an Old English word (bitan) meaning "to bite."]

Carpenter's bit

Bit for horse

bite (bit) **1** to cut into or cut off with the teeth. **2** a piece bitten off; morsel: *Have a* bite *to eat.* **3** to seize or grasp with the teeth; wound with the teeth: *The police dog* bit *the thief.* **4** to pierce the skin for food as do certain blood-sucking insects: *A mosquito* bites. **5** wound made by biting: *a flea* bite; *a snake* bite; *a dog* bite. **6** to cause pain to: *The icy wind was* biting *my face.* **7** to take the bait: *Fish are* biting *today.* **bit, bit·ten** or **bit, bit·ing.**

bit·ing (bī′ting) **1** sharp: *the* biting *taste of vinegar.* **2** sarcastic; sneering: *to give a* biting *answer; to make a* biting *remark.* **3** stinging; sharp; bitter: *a* biting *wind.* **bit·ing·ly.**

bit·ten (bit′ən) See **bite.** *This piece of candy has been* bitten *into.*

bit·ter (bit′ər) **1** sharp and unpleasant to the taste. **2** sharp; painful; stinging: *in the* bitter *cold.* **3** hard to bear or receive: *their* bitter *sorrow; a* bitter *lesson.* **4** severe; harsh: *the passing of* bitter *words.* **5** unforgiving; unyielding: *to remain* bitter *enemies; out of* bitter *hatred.* **bit·ter·ly.**

bit·ter·ness (bit′ər nis) the taste of anything bitter; a being bitter.

bit·ter·root (bit′ər rōōt′) a plant of the Rocky Mountains, with fleshy root and pink flowers. The bitterroot is the State flower of Montana.

bi·tu·mi·nous (bi tōō′mə nəs or bi tū′mə-nəs) **1** containing tar, especially asphalt or coal tar. **2 bituminous coal** soft coal.

biv·ou·ac (biv′ōō ăk or biv′wăk) **1** temporary camp in the open air. **2** to encamp, as for the night, in the open air. **biv·ou·acked, biv·ou·ack·ing.**

black (blăk) **1** the color of coal; opposite of white. **2** a dye or stain of this color. **3** almost without light; very dark: *a black pit.* **4** gloomy; threatening: *a black outlook.* **5** without moral goodness; evil: *a black deed; a soul black as night.* **6** dark-skinned; Negro. **7** to polish with a black dressing: *to black shoes.*

black·ber·ry (blăk′-bĕr′ĭ) **1** a vine or bush bearing berries which turn bluish black when ripe. **2** the small fruit of this bush. **black·ber·ries.**

Blackberry leaves and fruit

black·bird (blăk′-bûrd′) any one of a number of birds the male of which is almost entirely black.

black·board (blăk′bôrd′) dark, smooth surface, often of slate, for writing or drawing on with chalk.

---

fāte; făt; fâre; fär; bē, bĕt; bīte, bĭt; nō, nŏt, nôr; fūse, fŭn, fûr; tōō, tŏŏk; foil; foul; thin; ~~then~~;
hw for wh as in *wh*at; zh for s as in u*s*ual; ə for a, e, i, o, u, as in *a*go, lin*e*n, per*i*l, at*o*m, min*u*s

105

blacken

black·en (blăk′ən) **1** to make black; darken: *Soot* blackens *kettles.* **2** to grow dark or threatening: *The sky* blackened. **3** to injure.

black-eyed Susan (blăk′īd′ sōō′zən) flower resembling a daisy with a dark center and yellow petals. It is the State flower of Maryland.

black·guard (blăg′ərd or blăk′gärd′) shameless rascal; scoundrel.

black·mail (blăk′māl′) **1** an attempt to get money from a person by threatening to say something bad about him. **2** the money thus collected. **3** to make, or try to make, a person pay in this way.

black·ness (blăk′nĭs) dark or black color; darkness.

black·out (blăk′out′) **1** a putting out or covering of all lights at night that would be visible to an enemy plane. **2** a sudden loss of consciousness.

black·smith (blăk′smĭth′) person who shoes horses, and does work in iron.

blad·der (blăd′ər) **1** a small bag or sac in the body which receives and temporarily holds waste fluids from the kidneys. **2** any similar inside bag or sac: *a football* bladder; *the air* bladder *of a fish.*

blade (blād) **1** cutting part of a knife, sword, tool, instrument, or machine. **2** a leaf of grass, especially one that is long and narrow. **3** broad flat object or part: *shoulder* blade; blade *of an oar.* **4** a sword.

Paddle blade

blame (blām) **1** to hold responsible (for); attribute guilt to: *The truck driver* blamed *the bus driver for the accident.* **2** to find fault with: *I don't* blame *you.* **3** responsibility (for some fault or wrong): *She must take the* blame *for her children's bad manners.* **4 be to blame** to be at fault; deserve the blame: *Who is to* blame *for the mistake?* **blamed, blam·ing.**

blame·less (blām′lĭs) free from fault or guilt. **blame·less·ly.**

blanch (blănch) **1** to whiten by taking out color. **2** to put in boiling water and then into cold water to remove skins: *to* blanch *almonds.* **3** to turn pale from shame or fear.

bland (blănd) **1** gentle; agreeable; mild: *a* bland *tone of voice.* **2** not irritating: *a* bland *diet.* **bland·ly.**

blaze

blank (blăngk) **1** not written or printed on: *a* blank *paper.* **2** an empty space: *Leave a* blank *for the question you didn't answer.* **3** printed form with empty spaces to be filled in: *an order* blank. **4** without expression: *a* blank *look.* **5** without any clear idea: *My mind was* blank *and I couldn't remember a thing.* **6** not decorated; unbroken by an opening: *a* blank *wall.* **blank·ly.**

blan·ket (blăng′kĭt) **1** covering of soft cloth, such as wool, cotton, etc., used to keep people or animals warm. **2** any covering like a blanket: *a* blanket *of fog.* **3** to cover with, or as with, a blanket: *Snow* blanketed *the earth.*

blare (blâr) **1** to give forth a loud sound like that of a trumpet: *The radio* blared *when I turned up the volume.* **2** a loud sound as of a trumpet. **blared, blar·ing.**

blas·phe·my (blăs′fə mĭ) words or actions that show contempt for God or sacred things. **blas·phe·mies.**

blast (blăst) **1** strong, sudden rush of wind or air. **2** a sudden loud sound from a horn or trumpet. **3** an explosion: *a* blast *of dynamite.* **4** to shatter by an explosion: *to* blast *rocks in a quarry.* **5** to wither or kill; ruin: *The cherry blossoms were* blasted *by frost.* **6 blast furnace** furnace for separating a metal from an ore. The great heat needed is built up by a blast of hot air forced in at the bottom of the furnace.

blast off to take off with explosive power (said of a rocket).

¹blaze (blāz) **1** to burn with a bright flame. **2** to explode; burst into flame; flare up: *The signal fires suddenly* blazed *along the hills.* **3** a bright flame; fire. **4** strong direct light; glare: *the* blaze *of headlights.* **5** to glow or shine like a flame: *Lights* blazed *out from all the windows.* **6** brilliant display: *a* blaze *of color from the sunset.* **7** sudden outburst: *He reached the finish line in a* blaze *of energy.* **blazed, blaz·ing.** [¹blaze is a form of an Old English word (blæse) meaning "a torch."]

²blaze (blāz) **1** mark made on a tree, by removing a patch of bark, to mark a trail. **2** to mark trees or trample undergrowth in order to make a trail. **3** a white patch on the forehead of an animal. **blazed, blaz·ing.** [²blaze is probably of Germanic origin.]

bleach (blēch) **1** to remove color or whiten by exposure to the sun or by a chemical process. **2** a substance that whitens or removes color.

bleach·ers (blē'chərz) uncovered plank seats for spectators at an outdoor event.

bleak (blēk) **1** unsheltered; exposed to wind and cold: *a bleak mountain top.* **2** dismal; cold: *The weather was bleak and snow was expected.* **3** cheerless; gloomy: *to have a bleak outlook on life.* **bleak·ly.**

bleat (blēt) **1** the cry of a sheep, goat, or calf, or a sound like it. **2** to make this sound.

bled (blĕd) See **bleed.**

bleed (blēd) **1** to lose blood: *His finger bled from the cut.* **2** to shed one's blood: *During the late war men bled and died for their country.* **3** to lose sap or juice from a cut surface: *The tree is bleeding where the branch was cut off.* **4** to be filled with sympathy or pity: *My heart fairly bled for the poor man.* **bled, bleed·ing.**

blem·ish (blĕm'ish) **1** a mark that spoils the appearance; a flaw. **2** to put a bad mark on; mar; stain: *One bad mistake can blemish a man's reputation.*

blend (blĕnd) **1** to mix so thoroughly that the ingredients can no longer be separated or told apart. **2** to shade into each óther; go together: *The colors in the sunset blend so well that there is no telling where one ends and another begins.* **3** a mixture of colors or flavors: *a blend of blue and gray; a blend of coffee.*

bless (blĕs) **1** to make holy: *to bless an altar.* **2** to call down the favor of God upon a person, thing, or event. **3** to favor (with a blessing, happiness, success, etc.): *Fortune blessed him with a good disposition.* **4** to praise; honor: *to bless the Lord.* **blessed** or **blest, bless·ing.**

bless·ed (blĕs'id or blĕst) **1** holy: *the blessed saints.* **2** extremely happy: *What a blessed bit of news.* **3** fortunate; favored: *to be blessed with good health.* **bless·ed·ly.**

bless·ing (blĕs'ing) **1** prayer asking for the favor of God: *The pastor gave the travelers his blessing.* **2** prayer of thanks at a meal; a grace. **3** something that makes for happiness, health, or good fortune: *Peace of mind is a great blessing.*

blest (blĕst) See **bless.**

blew (blo̅o̅) See **blow.** *The wind blew and the rain fell.* (Homonym: blue)

blight (blīt) **1** any disease that makes plants wither and decay. **2** anything that destroys good fortune and shatters hope. **3** to cause to decay; wither: *Frost blighted that garden.*

blimp (blĭmp) small dirigible that is not rigid; motor-driven balloon.

blind (blīnd) **1** sightless. **2** unable or unwilling to understand: *He was blind to his own weakness.* **3** unthinking; heedless; rash: *in blind haste.* **4** without reason: *blind panic.* **5** hidden: *a blind curve.* **6** with no outlet: *a blind alley.* **7** something to obstruct vision or keep out light: *a window blind.* **8** something meant to mislead: *His fishing trips were a blind for smuggling operations.* **9** to take away the power to see; to make blind: *The driver was blinded by the sun and lost control of the car.* **10** to deprive of judgment: *Anger blinded him so he couldn't think straight.*

blind·fold (blīnd'fōld') **1** something used to cover the eyes. **2** to cover the eyes. **3** with the eyes covered.

blind·ly (blīnd'lĭ) **1** without seeing. **2** without looking or thinking beforehand: *Don't rush blindly into this dangerous situation.*

blink (blĭngk) **1** to open and shut the eyes rapidly; wink. **2** turn (lights) off and on rapidly: *The truck blinked its lights in greeting.* **3** to shine as if going on and off: *The stars were blinking in the clear sky.*

bliss (blĭs) great happiness; perfect joy; ecstasy.

bliss·ful (blĭs'fəl) very happy; joyful. **bliss·ful·ly.**

blis·ter (blĭs'tər) **1** a little pocket of watery liquid under the surface of the skin which causes swelling: *A burn will cause blisters.* **2** a bubble formed beneath the surface of a layer of paint or within a slab of glass. **3** to raise blisters on: *The sunburn blistered my back and arms.* **4** to become covered with blisters: *The paint blistered in the hot sun.*

---

fāte, făt, fâre, fär; bē, bĕt; bīte, bĭt; nō, nŏt, nôr; fūse, fŭn, fûr; to̅o̅, to͝ok; foil; foul; thin; ~~then~~;
hw for wh as in *wh*at; zh for s as in u*s*ual; ə for a, e, i, o, u, as in a*go*, lin*e*n, per*i*l, at*o*m, min*u*s

blithe

blithe (blith or blith) gay; glad; cheerful:
He whistled a blithe *little tune.* **blithe·ly.**

bliz·zard (bliz′ərd) a storm with snow,
strong winds, and bitter cold.

bloat (blōt) to cause to swell up: *Too much
liquid* bloats *the stomach.*

blob (blŏb) a small formless mass, as of a
sticky or creamy substance.

bloc (blŏk) political group, often of different
parties, who unite for a time in order to
promote some particular purpose: *the farm*
bloc. (Homonym: block)

block (blŏk) **1** solid piece of
wood, stone, metal, etc.: *Cement
blocks are used for building.*
2 part of a city, often square,
bounded by four streets: *The
building occupied a whole city
block.* **3** the length of one side
of such a square: *Walk two
blocks west.* **4** to get in the way
of; hinder: *The stalled car
blocked traffic.* **5** something
that hinders or stops; an ob-
stacle: *The police set up a road* block. **6** a
pulley made of a frame holding one or
more wheels on which ropes move, used
for lifting, hauling, etc. (Homonym: bloc)

Block of
a pulley

block·ade (blŏ kād′) **1** the shutting off of a
place, especially a port, by ships or troops
to keep anything or anybody from coming
in or going out. **2** to set up or carry out
such a blockade. **3** any barrier or obstruction: *The barrels piled at the entrance
made an effective* blockade. **4** to block up;
obstruct. **block·ad·ed, block·ad·ing.**

block·head (blŏk′hĕd′) a stupid person;
dunce.

block·house (blŏk′-
hous′) **1** a fortified
building with loop-
holes in the walls
through which to
shoot at the enemy.
2 at one time, a fort
built of logs or heavy timber, with a projecting upper story.

Blockhouse

blond (blŏnd) **1** having light skin and
hair: *Many Swedish people are* blond.
2 person with skin and hair of light color.
When referring to a girl, the word is
written "blonde." **3** light in color: *The
house is furnished with* blond *furniture.*

blot

blood (blŭd) **1** a red fluid which circulates
through the bodies of men and animals. It
carries food and oxygen to all parts of the
body and takes away the waste. **2** kinship:
related by blood. **3 bad blood** hatred;
dislike: *There is* bad blood *between the
feuding families.* **4 in cold blood** on purpose; cruelly; ruthlessly.

blood bank 1 a supply of different types of
blood for blood transfusions. **2** the place
where such a supply is kept.

blood·cur·dling (blŭd′kûrd′ling) terrifying; horrible as if congealing the blood
through fear and horror: *a* bloodcurdling
movie.

blood·hound (blŭd′hound′) a large black
and tan dog with a wrinkled face and an
excellent sense of smell. Bloodhounds are
often used for tracking criminals or people
who are lost.

blood·less (blŭd′lĭs) **1** without shedding
blood: *a* bloodless *victory.* **2** very pale: *her*
bloodless *cheeks.* **blood·less·ly.**

blood·shed (blŭd′shĕd′) destruction of
life; killing: *The city was swiftly encircled
and captured without* bloodshed.

blood·thirst·y (blŭd′thûrs′tĭ) eager to
shed blood; brutal; intent upon killing.
blood·thirst·i·ly.

blood vessel one of many tubes through
which blood circulates in the body.

blood·y (blŭd′ĭ) **1** stained with blood: *The
bandage has become* bloody. **2** bleeding: *a
bloody nose; a* bloody *wound.* **3** with much
shedding of blood: *a* bloody *war.* **blood·i·
er, blood·i·est, blood·i·ly.**

bloom (blōōm) **1** the flower of a plant:
The violet has a delicate bloom. **2** to
produce flowers: *The lilac* blooms *every
spring.* **3** a time of flowering. **4** time when
one is at the peak of health, beauty, etc.;
prime: *the* bloom *of youth.* **5** a fine white
coating as on some fruit or leaves: *the*
bloom *on a grape.*

blos·som (blŏs′əm) **1** the flower of a plant,
especially a plant which bears fruit: *apple*
blossom; *peach* blossom. **2** to produce or
yield flowers: *The cherry trees are about to*
blossom. **3** time of bearing flowers: *The
trees are in* blossom.

blot (blŏt) **1** a spot or stain: *The ink left a*
blot *on the paper.* **2** something against a
person's reputation or character: *His bad*

marks left a blot *on his record.* **3** to make a spot or stain on. **4** to dry or soak up with a blotter.

blot out 1 to hide completely: *The eclipse* blotted out *the sun.* **2** to destroy wholly: *The eruption of a volcano can* blot out *a town.*

blot·ted, blot·ting.

blotch (blŏch) **1** a large spot: *There is a bad* blotch *of ink on the curtain.* **2** an ugly spot or mark on the skin: *He had a large* blotch *on his neck from poison ivy.* **3** to mark with blotches.

blot·ter (blŏt′ər) a piece of spongy paper used to absorb ink.

blouse (blous) **1** a kind of shirt worn by women and children. **2** coat or jacket of some military uniforms.

¹**blow** (blō) **1** to be in motion, as a strong current of air. **2** to cause to move or move along by the motion of air: *The wind is* blowing *the papers all over the lawn.* **3** to force air (on or into): *Leslie* blew *on his burned finger.* **4** to puff up by blowing air into: *to* blow *a soap bubble.* **5** to cause to sound by forcing air through: *to* blow *a trumpet; to* blow *a whistle.*

blow over to pass: *The storm* blew over.

blow up 1 to inflate; expand: *to* blow up *a balloon; to* blow up *a tire.* **2** to explode: *The boiler* blew up *because of too much steam pressure.* **3** to enlarge (a photograph). **4** to begin; come up: *A bad storm* blew up *over the mountain.*

blew, blown, blow·ing. [¹**blow** is a form of an Old English word (blāwan) with the same meaning.]

²**blow** (blō) **1** a hard hit with the hand, fist, or a weapon. **2** a sudden shock or upset: *The bad news was quite a* blow. [²**blow** is a form of an earlier English word (blaw). It is probably related to ¹**blow**.]

blow·er (blō′ər) a device for forcing air through a building, furnace, machine, mine, etc.

blown (blōn) See **blow.** *The wind has* blown *the clouds away.*

blow·out (blō′out′) explosive escape of air from a punctured automobile tire or any other inflated object.

blow·torch (blō′tôrch′) torch which shoots out a very hot flame from a small tank of gasoline or other fuel under pressure. It is used by plumbers, painters, etc.

blub·ber (blŭb′ər) the fat of whales, seals, and walruses, used as a source of oil.

bludg·eon (blŭj′ən) **1** short club with a heavy head. **2** to beat with a club.

blue (blōo) **1** the color of the clear sky. **2** having this color or some shade of it: *a* blue *dress.* **3** of a bluish tinge: *My nose was* blue *with cold.* **4** a dye or powder that colors blue. **5** to treat with such a dye. **6** sad; gloomy; dismal: *He was lonely and* blue. **7 blues** a gloomy mood, or music expressing this mood. **8 out of the blue** completely unexpected. **blu·er, blu·est; blued, blu·ing** or **blue·ing; blue·ly.** (Homonym: blew)

blue·bell (blōo′běl′) **1** any of various plants that bear a bell-shaped flower. **2** the blue flower of such a plant.

blue·ber·ry (blōo′běr′ĭ) **1** a round, blue, berry that is good to eat. **2** the shrub that bears it. **blue·ber·ries.**

blue·bird (blōo′bûrd′) a songbird of the thrush family. The male has a blue back.

blue·bon·net (blōo′bŏn′ĭt) a plant with blue, white, pink, or purple flowers. The bluebonnet is the State flower of Texas.

blue·fish (blōo′fĭsh′) **1** a much favored food fish of the Atlantic coast of North America, silvery blue in color. **2** any variety of other fishes bluish in color. pl. **blue·fish,** rarely, **blue·fish·es.**

blue·grass (blōo′grăs′) a pasture grass with bluish-green stems.

blue·jack·et (blōo′jăk′ĭt) a sailor in the Navy.

Bluejay, about 11 in. long

blue·jay (blōo′jā′) a bird found in eastern North America, with bright blue plumage and a crest of blue and gray. It is known for its noisy screaming.

---

fāte, făt, fâre, fär; bē, bĕt; bīte, bĭt; nō, nŏt, nôr; fūse, fŭn, fûr; tōo, tŏŏk; foil; foul; thin; then; hw for wh as in *wh*at; zh for s as in u*s*ual; ə for a, e, i, o, u, as in *a*go, lin*e*n, per*i*l, at*o*m, min*u*s

blueprint

blue·print (bloo'prĭnt') a photographic print, white on blue paper, used as a plan in building operations, etc.

¹bluff (blŭf) **1** a high, steep bank or cliff. **2** rising steeply: *the bluff headlands that rose along the shore.* **3** rough but hearty and full of good humor: *a bluff greeting.* **bluff·ly.** [**¹bluff** is probably from an early German word (blaf) meaning "flat."]

²bluff (blŭf) **1** to put on a bold front or pretense in order to hide weakness or shortcomings: *That card player was only bluffing, but won anyway.* **2** a pretense or show of confidence meant to cover up weakness or lack: *We knew his brave words were only a bluff.* **3** to deceive by pretense: *to bluff one's way through a lesson.* [**²bluff** is probably from a Dutch word (verbluffen) meaning "to baffle," "mislead."]

blu·ing or **blue·ing** (bloo'ĭng) a blue coloring substance used to whiten clothes.

blun·der (blŭn'dər) **1** stupid or careless mistake. **2** to make a mistake from stupidity, ignorance, or lack of attention. **3** to move clumsily; stumble: *The boy blundered around the dark room.*

blun·der·buss (blŭn'dər bŭs') an old-time gun with a bell-shaped muzzle that spread a quantity of shot at close range.

Blunderbuss

blunt (blŭnt) **1** without a sharp edge or point; not sharp; dull: *a blunt knife.* **2** to make less sharp or keen: *to blunt a knife on a stone.* **3** frank and plain-spoken; abrupt: *a blunt answer.* **blunt·ly.**

blur (blûr) **1** to make or become indistinct or dim: *Sheets of rain blurred the outline of the hills. His eyes blurred with tears.* **2** an indistinct shape or spot: *a blur in a picture.* **blurred, blur·ring.**

blurt (blûrt) to speak suddenly and without thinking: *He rushed in and blurted out the bad news.*

blush (blŭsh) **1** to become red in the face from shame or embarrassment. **2** to feel shame or embarrassment: *I blush for your mistake.* **3** a reddening of the face from shame or embarrassment. **4** rosy color: *the first blush of dawn.*

blus·ter (blŭs'tər) **1** to talk in a noisy, excited manner: *He blustered about all the fights he had won.* **2** noisy talk; empty

bob

threats. **3** to blow in noisy gusts: *The wind howled and blustered around the house.*

boar (bôr) **1** a male pig or hog. **2** a wild pig. (Homonym: bore)

Wild boar, about 4 ft. long

board (bôrd) **1** flat piece of sawed timber, longer or wider than it is thick. **2** to cover (up) with such pieces of wood: *to board up windows.* **3** flat piece of wood or other material prepared for a definite use: *a surf board; a bread board.* **4** a group of persons with power to advise, manage, or direct: *a board of health.* **5** to provide meals, and sometimes lodging: *to board students.* **6** to eat or live at a house where paying guests are accepted. **7** meals provided regularly for pay: *to pay for board by the week.* **8** to go on (a ship, train, or plane). **9 on board** on a ship, train, etc.

board·er (bôr'dər) a person who regularly gets meals, or meals and lodging, at a fixed charge. (Homonym: border)

board·ing (bôr'dĭng) **1** boards. **2** something made of boards.

boarding school a school where students live during the school year.

boast (bōst) **1** to brag; praise loudly and rashly oneself and one's belongings or actions. **2** bragging speech: *It was his proud boast that he had always paid his way.* **3** to pride oneself on: *The city boasted a fifteen-story hotel.* **4** something to be proud of: *The new hospital was the boast of the town.*

boast·ful (bōst'fəl) speaking too highly about oneself; full of self-praise: *Alec was boastful about his strength.* **boast·ful·ly.**

boat (bōt) **1** any kind of small open vessel, as a rowboat, sailboat, or motorboat. **2** a ship, such as a steamboat. **3** to travel or go by boat.

boat·house (bōt'hous') a building, at the water's edge, in which boats are stored.

boat·man (bōt'mən) man who rows, sails, or rents boats. **boat·men.**

boat·swain (bō'sən) ship's officer who is in charge of cables, rigging, anchor, etc.

bob (bŏb) **1** quick jerking movement up and down or to and fro. **2** weight attached to the end of a line: *a pendulum bob.* **3** a float

110

on a fish line. **4** short haircut for girls or women. **5** to cut a girl's or woman's hair short. **6** to move rapidly or jerkily up and down or to and fro: *The little boat* bobbed *on the rough sea.* **bobbed, bob·bing.**

bob·o·link (bŏb′ə lĭngk′) a common North American songbird.

bob·sled (bŏb′slĕd′) **1** a long sled made of two short sleds joined by a plank. **2** either of the two short sleds.

bob·white (bŏb′hwīt′) an American game bird, known also as quail or partridge, named from its call.

bode (bōd) to be a sign of; foretell: *His laziness* boded *ill for his future at school.* **bod·ed, bod·ing.**

bod·i·ly (bŏd′ə li) **1** having to do with the body: *a bodily ill.* **2** by physical force: *He was dragged away* bodily. **3** as one mass or body; in a group.

bod·y (bŏd′ĭ) **1** the physical form of a person or animal, living or dead. **2** the main portion of a person or animal, not including the head, arms, or legs. **3** a person: *The hermit is a harmless old* body. **4** the greater part of anything: *the body of a letter.* **5** a group of persons or things: *a body of facts; a body of men.* **6** a mass of matter: *a heavenly* body. **7** thickness; substance: *This soup has no* body. **bod·ies.**

bod·y·guard (bŏd′ĭ gärd′) a man or group of men who guards and protects a person.

bog (bŏg) **1** wet, spongy ground made up of partly decayed plants; marsh; swamp. **2** to sink and stick fast in wet ground: *The wagon* bogged *down in the mud.* **bogged, bog·ging.**

bo·gy or **bo·gey** (bō′gĭ) **1** goblin; terrifying spirit. **2** something feared or dreaded.

bo·gus (bō′gəs) fake; counterfeit; not genuine: *to pass* bogus *money.*

¹boil (boil) **1** of a liquid, to give off vapor so fast that the surface bubbles. **2** to cause a liquid to boil by heating it: *to boil* milk. **3** to cook by boiling: *to boil an egg.* **4** to be stirred up as if boiling: *The water* boiled *through the canyon.* **5** to be very angry: *He* boiled *with rage.* **6** the boiling point: *Bring the syrup to a* boil. **7 boiling point:** the lowest point at which a liquid will boil.

boil down 1 to reduce the amount (of something) by boiling so as to eliminate some of the liquid in it. **2** to shorten (a report, etc.) by leaving out material that is not strictly necessary. [**¹boil** is from an Old French word (boillir) which is from a Latin word (bulla) meaning "bubble."]

²boil (boil) a painful swelling of the skin, containing pus and a hard core. [**²boil** is a form of an Old English word (bȳle).]

boil·er (boi′lər) **1** large metal vessel in which steam is produced for heating buildings and driving engines. **2** tank for storing hot water. **3** vessel in which things are boiled: *a wash* boiler.

bois·ter·ous (boi′stər əs) **1** noisy and not restrained: *the boys'* boisterous *laughter.* **2** stormy; violent; rough: *a* boisterous *wind.* **bois·ter·ous·ly.**

bold (bōld) **1** courageous; fearless: *a bold knight.* **2** clear; striking: *a bold handwriting.* **3** impudent; rude: *a bold remark, a bold manner.* **4** daring: *to have bold ideas.* **bold·ly.**

bold·ness (bōld′nĭs) **1** courage; daring; fearlessness. **2** impudence; rudeness: *The boldness of his stare annoyed them.* **3** vigor; clearness: *the boldness of a drawing.*

bo·le·ro (bō lâr′ō) **1** lively Spanish dance. **2** music for this dance. **3** short jacket with or without sleeves, not quite reaching to the waist. **bo·le·ros.**

Bo·liv·i·a (bō lĭv′ĭ ə) a country in western South America.

boll (bōl) the seed pod of a plant such as cotton or flax. (Homonym: bowl)

Boll weevil, ¼ in. long

boll weevil a grayish beetle which lays its eggs in cotton bolls. As the eggs develop, the cotton is damaged.

bol·ster (bōl′stər) **1** long pillow that extends across a bed. **2** cushioned pad or support. **3** to support; brace: *The song* bolstered *our courage.*

Door bolt and machine bolt

bolt (bōlt) **1** a sliding catch for a door or gate. **2** part of a lock which is drawn back

fāte, făt, fâre, fär; bē, bĕt; bīte, bĭt; nō, nŏt, nôr; fūse, fŭn, fûr; tōō, tŏŏk; foil; foul; thin; then; hw for wh as in *wh*at; zh for s as in u*s*ual; ə for a, e, i, o, u, as in *a*go, lin*e*n, per*i*l, at*o*m, min*u*s

111

bomb

by the key. **3** metal pin or rod with a threaded end on which a nut fits, used for fastening together parts of machinery, furniture, etc. **4** to fasten with a sliding catch: *to* bolt *the door*. **5** to fasten with bolts: *to* bolt *metal plates together*. **6** a sudden dashing away: *the* bolt *of a horse*. **7** to dash away; break away. **8** to swallow food rapidly: *I'll have to* bolt *my lunch to catch the train*. **9.** anything that strikes suddenly: *a* bolt *of lightning*. **10** a roll of cloth. **11 bolt upright** stiffly upright.

bomb (bŏm) **1** hollow shell filled with an explosive, which may be set off by a time fuse, or by the force with which it strikes. **2** to attack with bombs; drop bombs on.

bom·bard (bŏm bärd′) **1** to attack with bombs or artillery: *The city was* bombarded *from land and air*. **2** to hit repeatedly (with things thrown); pelt: *The boys* bombarded *the roof with pebbles*. **3** to press; assail; beset: *The scientist was* bombarded *with questions after his lecture.*

bom·bard·ment (bŏm bärd′mənt) attack consisting of continued cannon fire or repeated bombing.

bomb·er (bŏm′ər) airplane from which bombs may be dropped.

bomb·proof (bŏm′prōōf′) providing safety from bombs: *a* bombproof *shelter*.

bon·bon (bŏn′bŏn′) a candy made from a thick, creamy, sugar paste.

bond (bŏnd) **1** something that binds, ties, or unites: *a* bond *of friendship*. **2** a written agreement to pay out a certain amount of money if the person covered by the agreement fails to carry out his duties properly. **3** to put (a person) under such an agreement; cover with a bond: *The firm* bonds *its employees to protect itself against theft*. **4** certificate, issued by a corporation or government, promising to pay back with interest the money borrowed from the purchaser of the certificate.

bond·age (bŏn′dij) slavery; servitude: *The Jews were held in* bondage *in Egypt*.

bone (bōn) **1** the hard, white material composing the skeleton. **2** one of the separate pieces of the skeleton. **3** made of bone: *a* bone *carving*. **4** to remove bones: *to* bone *a chicken*. **boned, bon·ing.**

bon·fire (bŏn′fīr′) fire built out of doors, as for burning leaves, a celebration, etc.

boom

bon·net (bŏn′ĭt) **1** head covering for women and children, with ribbons or strings which tie under the chin. **2** cap worn by men and boys in Scotland. **3** headdress of feathers worn by American Indians.

bon·ny or **bon·nie** (bŏn′ĭ) handsome or pretty: *a* bonny *lass*. **bon·ni·er, bon·ni·est; bon·ni·ly.**

Bonnet

bo·nus (bō′nəs) something extra; a sum paid in addition to what is usual or due: *a Christmas* bonus; *a soldier's* bonus.

bon·y (bō′nĭ) **1** made of bone. **2** full of bones: *a* bony *fish*. **3** having prominent bones; gaunt. **bon·i·er, bon·i·est.**

boo·by (bōō′bĭ) a stupid person. **boo·bies.**

book (bŏŏk) **1** sheets of paper bound together in a cover. **2** volume containing one long written work or a number of short pieces. **3** a section of a literary work: *a* book *of the Bible*. **4** to reserve; engage: *to* book *a seat on an airplane*. **5** to record: *to* book *an order*.

book·case (bŏŏk′kās′) cabinet or set of shelves to hold books.

book·keep·er (bŏŏk′kē′pər) person who keeps business accounts.

book·keep·ing (bŏŏk′kē′pĭng) the work of keeping business accounts.

book·let (bŏŏk′lĭt) small book, often with a paper binding; pamphlet.

book·mo·bile (bŏŏk′mə bēl′) a truck fitted out like a library, used as an extension, or substitute, for library service.

book·shelf (bŏŏk′shĕlf′) shelf for books. **book·shelves.**

book·store (bŏŏk′stôr′) store where books are sold.

book·worm (bŏŏk′wûrm′) **1** person who is very fond, sometimes too fond, of reading and studying books. **2** insect larva that eats book bindings and pages.

¹boom (bōōm) **1** deep, rumbling sound: *the* boom *of a cannon*. **2** to make or utter such a sound: *His voice* boomed *out in the empty room*. **3** to increase or develop swiftly: *Business* boomed. **4** a great increase (of): *the business* boom. [**¹boom** is from a Germanic word which was probably the imitation of a sound.]

²boom (boom) **1** a long pole or beam attached to a ship's mast to hold out the

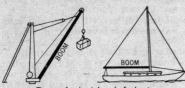

Boom of a derrick and of a boat

bottom edge of a sail. **2** the lifting arm of a derrick. [**²boom** is the unchanged form of a Dutch word meaning "tree," "pole."]

boom·e·rang (boo'mə răng') **1** bent, flat piece of wood used as a throwing weapon by the original inhabitants of Australia. Some boomerangs can be thrown so that they return to the thrower. **2** to come back and harm the doer or user: *His practical joke* boomeranged *when his trick cigar blew up in his own face.*

¹boon (boon) a favor, gift, or blessing: *Grant me a* boon, *O King.* [**¹boon** is a form of an Old English word (bēn) meaning "prayer" or "petition."]

²boon (boon) cheerful and congenial; jovial: *a* boon *companion.* [**²boon** is from a Latin word (bonus) meaning "good."]

boor (boor) crude person with bad manners.

boost (boost) **1** to lift by pushing up from underneath: *If you* boost *me I can climb that tree.* **2** a push or shove that helps someone or something to rise or advance.

boot (boot) **1** outer covering of leather or rubber for the foot and part of the leg. **2** to put boots on. **3** to kick: *He booted the football over the goal posts.*

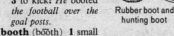

Rubber boot and hunting boot

booth (booth) **1** small compartment: *a telephone* booth; *a toll* booth; *a voting* booth. **2** restaurant compartment containing facing benches with a table between them. **3** stall at a fair or bazaar, or in a market.

boo·ty (boo'tĭ) **1** plunder taken by robbers, bandits, pirates, etc. **2** supplies, arms, or treasure taken from an enemy in time of war; loot. **3** rich prize or gain. **boo·ties.**

bor·der (bôr'dər) **1** edge: *reeds along the* border *of a stream.* **2** narrow strip along or around something: *a* border *of flowers along a walk.* **3** to make a border around: *to* border *a path with flowers.* **4** frontier of a country; boundary: *to patrol the* border. **5** to be next to; adjoin; touch: *His plot* borders *mine.*

border on to come near to being: *His excuse* bordered on *the ridiculous.* (Homonym: boarder)

¹bore (bôr) **1** to make a circular hole by twisting a screwlike tool with a cutting edge: *The oil drill* bores *into the ground.* **2** to make (a tunnel, hole, etc.) by, or as by, drilling: *They plan to* bore *a tunnel through a mountain.* **3** the distance across the inside of a hollow tube such as a pipe or gun barrel. **4** the hole inside a gun barrel or pipe. **bored, bor·ing.** [**¹bore** is a form of an Old English word (borian).] (Homonym: boar)

²bore (bôr) **1** to make weary: *His old jokes* bore *us.* **2** tiresome person or thing: *That tune is a* bore *when it is played over and over.* **bored, bor·ing.** [**²bore** is probably **¹bore** in a later and different meaning.] (Homonym: boar)

³bore (bôr) See **²bear.** *She* bore *three children.* [**³bore** is a form of **²bear.**] (Homonym: boar)

bo·ric ac·id (bôr'ĭk ăs'ĭd) a mild antiseptic, often used to bathe the eyes.

born (bôrn) **1** brought into life. *George Washington was* born *in 1732.* **2** natural: *He is a* born *leader.* (Homonym: borne)

borne (bôrn) See **²bear.** *The tree has* borne *good fruit.* (Homonym: born)

bo·ron (bôr'ŏn' or bō'rŏn) a chemical element. It appears as a yellowish-brown crystal. It is used in preparing boric acid, in hardening steel, etc.

bor·ough (bûr'ō) **1** in some Eastern States, an incorporated town smaller than a city. **2** one of the five political divisions of New York City. (Homonyms: burrow, burro)

fāte, făt, fâre, fär; bē, bět; bīte, bĭt; nō, nŏt, nôr; fūse, fŭn, fûr; too, took; foil; foul; thin; then; hw for wh as in what; zh for s as in usual; ə for a, e, i, o, u, as in ago, linen, peril, atom, minus

bor·row (bŏr′ō or bôr′ō) **1** to get something to use for a while with the understanding that it must be returned: *You are allowed to borrow two books a week from the library.* **2** to copy; adopt: *Many English words are borrowed from the French.*

bos·om (bŏŏz′əm) **1** the breast of a human being. **2** part of the clothing which covers the breast. **3** something likened to the human breast: *the earth's bosom.* **4** personal; special; close: *a bosom friend.*

boss (bôs or bŏs) **1** person with others working under him; foreman; employer. **2** to give orders to: *He bosses his little sister.*

bo·tan·i·cal (bə tăn′ə kəl) of or having to do with botany: *a botanical garden.*

bot·a·nist (bŏt′ən ĭst) scientist skilled in botany.

bot·a·ny (bŏt′ə nĭ) the study of plant life.

botch (bŏch) **1** to spoil by poor work; bungle: *He botched the letter.* **2** bungled or poor piece of work; clumsy job.

both (bōth) **1** the two: *I know both girls. Are both present?* **2** alike; equally: *Girls and boys are both included.*

both·er (bŏth′ər) **1** to give trouble to; worry; pester: *The ringing telephone bothers the busy doctor.* **2** to take trouble: *Don't bother to do that now.* **3** source of worry; nuisance: *This broken zipper is a bother.*

both·er·some (bŏth′ər səm) annoying; troublesome: *a bothersome cold.*

bot·tle (bŏt′əl) **1** hollow container, with a narrow neck or mouth, usually made of glass. **2** contents of such a container: *a bottle of milk.* **3** to put into bottles: *Milk is bottled by machines.*

Bottle

bottle up to shut in or hold back: *She bottled up her feelings and didn't complain.* **bot·tled, bot·tling.**

bot·tom (bŏt′əm) **1** lowest part of anything: *the bottom of the hill.* **2** underside: *the bottom of a plate.* **3** the ground under water: *the bottom of the lake.* **4** low land bordering a stream: *the Mississippi River bottoms.* **5** part of a ship below the water line. **6** important part; foundation: *Let's get to the bottom of the matter.*

bot·tom·less (bŏt′əm lĭs) **1** without a bottom. **2** extremely deep: *in the bottomless pit of a volcano.*

bough (bou) limb or branch of a tree. (Homonyms: ²bow, ³bow)

bought (bôt) See **buy.** *He bought a racing car.*

boul·der (bōl′dər) a large piece of loose rock rounded or worn smooth by water or weather.

boul·e·vard (bŏŏl′ə värd) wide street.

bounce (bouns) **1** to spring back up when thrown down: *How far did the ball bounce?* **2** such an upward or backward spring: *He caught the ball on the first bounce.* **3** to cause (something) to bounce: *to bounce a ball against a wall.* **4** springiness: *The ball has no bounce.* **5** to bound; leap up suddenly: *He bounced out of the chair.* **bounced, bounc·ing.**

¹**bound** (bound) **1** to leap or spring lightly; jump: *The dancer bounded onto the stage.* **2** to spring back: *The ball bounded off the fence.* **3** a leap or jump: *With one bound he made the distance from boat to shore.* [¹ **bound** is from a French word (bondir) meaning "rebound."]

²**bound** (bound) **1** See **bind.** *The packages were bound with heavy twine.* **2** obliged; required: *You are bound to obey.* **3** certain; sure: *You're bound to be tired if you hike all day.* [²**bound** is a form of **bind.**]

³**bound** (bound) **1** to form the boundary of: *Canada bounds the United States on the north.* **2** limiting line; boundary: *out of bounds.* [³**bound** is from an Old French word (bodne, bonde) of the same meaning.]

⁴**bound** (bound) ready to start; on the way; going: *The plane is bound for New York.* [⁴**bound** is a form of an older English word (boun) meaning "ready."]

bound·a·ry (boun′də rĭ) **1** anything that limits or marks a limit: *The Rio Grande is part of the boundary of Texas.* **2** a dividing line: *The boundary between the United States and Canada was fixed by treaty.* **bound·a·ries.**

bound·less (bound′lĭs) unlimited; vast: *the boundless ocean; a man of boundless energy.*

boun·te·ous (boun′tĭ əs) **1** generous. **2** plentiful; abundant: *a bounteous harvest.* **boun·te·ous·ly.**

boun·ti·ful (boun′tĭ fəl) **1** generous: *a bountiful person.* **2** plentiful; bounteous: *a bountiful harvest.* **boun·ti·ful·ly.**

boun·ty (boun'tĭ) **1** generosity; generous gifts: *The library was built by the* bounty *of one man.* **2** money offered or paid by a government as a reward for killing harmful animals. **boun·ties.**

bou·quet (bōō kā') **1** (also bō kā') bunch of flowers. **2** sweet smell; pleasant odor: *That perfume has a delicate* bouquet.

bout (bout) **1** a contest; test of strength or skill: *a wrestling* bout; *a boxing* bout. **2** period (of time); spell: *a long* bout *of fever.*

¹bow (bō) **1** weapon for shooting arrows. It is usually a strip of wood bent by a cord tightly stretched between its two ends. **2** slender stick strung with horsehairs for playing the violin or other stringed instruments. **3** a knot with loops: *a* bow *of ribbon.* [**¹bow** is a form of an Old English word (boga). It is related to **²bow.**] (Homonym: beau)

²bow (bou) **1** bend of the head, body, or knee expressing greeting, farewell, thanks, or respect. **2** to make this motion: *The singer* bowed *in response to the applause.* **3** to give in; yield: *I* bow *to your wishes.* [**²bow** is a form of an Old English word (būgan) meaning "bend."] (Homonym: bough)

³bow (bou) front end of a boat, ship, or aircraft. [**³bow** is from a Germanic or Scandinavian word.] (Homonym: bough)

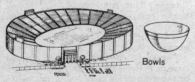

Bow of a boat

bow·el (bou'əl or boul) **1** intestine. **2** innermost, hidden part of anything: *the* bowels *of the earth.*

bow·er (bou'ər) shelter of tree branches or vines; arbor.

Bowls

¹bowl (bōl) **1** hollow, rounded dish. **2** contents of such a dish; bowlful: *She ate a* bowl

of pudding. **3** rounded, hollow part of something: *the* bowl *of a spoon;* *the* bowl *of a pipe.* **4** bowl-shaped stadium. [**¹bowl** is a form of an Old English word (bolla).] (Homonym: boll)

²bowl (bōl) **1** round ball used in some games. **2** to play the game of bowling. **3** to move rapidly and smoothly as if rolling: *The huge truck* bowled *down the mountain road.*

bowl over 1 to knock over: *He was* bowled *over by a motorcycle rounding the corner.* **2** to confuse; stagger: *to be* bowled *over by bad news.* [**²bowl** is from a French word (boule) which goes back to a Latin word (bulla) meaning "bubble."] (Homonym: boll)

bow·leg·ged (bō'lĕg'ĭd or bō'lĕgd') having legs that curve outward at the knees.

bowl·ing (bō'ling) **1** game in which a heavy ball is rolled over a smooth floor at ten bottle-shaped pins, with the object of knocking them down; also, a game in which a ball is rolled over turf at a stationary ball. **2** the act of playing this game.

bow·man (bō'mən) person who shoots with a bow and arrow; archer. **bow·men.**

Bowman

bow·sprit (bou'sprĭt or bō'sprĭt') long pole jutting forward from the bow of a ship.

bow·string (bō'string') cord stretched between the two ends of a bow.

BOWSPRIT
BOW
Bowsprit

¹box (bŏks) **1** to fight with fists as a sport, usually with gloves. **2** a light slap on the face; a cuff on the ear. [**¹box** is of unknown origin.]

²box (bŏks) **1** case or container, usually with a lid. **2** contents of a box: *a* box *of crackers.* **3** enclosure for one or more persons: *a jury* box; *a theater* box; *a sentry* box. **4** place where the batter or pitcher stands in baseball. **5** to put in a box: *The candy was* boxed *attractively.* [**²box** is the un-

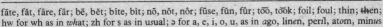

fāte, făt, fâre, fär; bē, bĕt; bite, bĭt; nō, nŏt, nôr; fūse, fŭn, fûr; tōō, tŏŏk; foil; foul; thin; ~~then~~; hw for wh as in *wh*at; zh for s as in u*s*ual; ə for a, e, i, o, u, as in ago, linen, peril, atom, minus

115

changed form of an Old English word that goes back to a Latin word (buxus) also meaning "box."]

³**box** (bŏks) any of a variety of small evergreen trees or shrubs. [³**box** is ²**box** in a special use. Originally, boxes were commonly made of this wood.]

box·car (bŏks′kär′) enclosed freight car.

box·er (bŏk′sər) **1** person who fights with his fists as a sport, usually wearing padded gloves. **2** sturdy short-haired dog either fawn-colored or streaked gray.

box·ing (bŏk′sĭng) the art or sport of fighting with the fists. The object is to deliver blows and avoid those of an opponent rather than to inflict injury.

boxing gloves heavily padded gloves used for boxing.

boy (boi) **1** male child from the time he is a baby until he is a young man; lad. **2** lad who does errands: *office* boy. (Homonym: buoy)

boy·hood (boi′hŏŏd′) time of being a boy.

boy·ish (boi′ish) like a boy; suitable for a boy; youthful: *a* boyish *trick.* **boy·ish·ly.**

Boy Scouts 1 organization for training boys in physical fitness, good citizenship, and helpfulness to others. **2 boy scout** member of the Boy Scouts, or one who observes the aims of Boy Scouts.

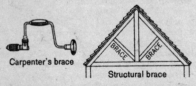

Carpenter's brace

Structural brace

brace (brās) **1** something that holds parts together or in place; something that supports or steadies, as in the framework of a building or machine or a device to support or straighten a part of the body. **2** to steady or support: *We braced the wall so that it could withstand the wind. Sit down and brace yourself for a shock.* **3** to strengthen; invigorate: *The mountain air braced our exhausted spirits.* **4** a pair: *a brace of ducks.* **5** a frame for turning and holding a boring tool. **braced, brac·ing.**

brace·let (brās′lĭt) ornamental band for the wrist or arm.

brack·et (brăk′ĭt) **1** a wooden, stone, or metal support, shaped like a triangle, placed under a shelf and attached to a wall. **2** to support with a bracket: *We must* bracket *this shelf more strongly or it will fall.* **3** either of two marks ([ ]) used to enclose a word or separate a certain part of the text from the rest. **4** to enclose within brackets: *to* bracket *a paragraph in a composition.*

Brackets supporting a shelf

brag (brăg) **1** to boast. **2** boastful talk. **bragged, brag·ging.**

braid (brād) **1** a woven length of three or more strands of hair. **2** a narrow band of ornamental or protective material used as trimming for garments, etc.: *gold* braid *on the captain's cap.* **3** to weave together three or more strands of hair or material. **4** to make out of braids or by braiding: *to* braid *a rug.*

Braid in mat making

braille or **Braille** (brāl) **1** system of printing for the blind, in which raised dots on a surface represent letters and punctuation. These dots are read by the fingers. **2** the raised dots used in this system.

brain (brān) **1** the soft mass of gray nerve tissue in the skull; the center of thought and feeling. For picture, see **nerve.** **2** mind; intelligence: *He has a fine* brain. *Use your* brain. **3 brains** intelligence.

¹**brake** (brāk) **1** device for slowing or stopping the motion of a wheel, vehicle, etc. **2** to slow down or stop by applying a brake. **braked, brak·ing.** [¹**brake** is of unknown origin.] (Homonym: break)

²**brake** (brāk) place overgrown with bushes, shrubs, etc.; thicket. [²**brake** is probably of Germanic origin.] (Homonym: break)

³**brake** (brāk) a kind of large, coarse fern. [³**brake** is probably of Scandinavian origin.] (Homonym: break)

brake·man (brāk′mən) on a railroad, a trainman who operates the brakes and assists the conductor. **brake·men.**

bram·ble (brăm′bəl) a rough prickly shrub.

bran (brăn) outer coat or husk of ground grain, separated from flour by sifting.

branch (brănch) **1** limb of a tree that grows out of the trunk or out of another limb. **2** anything like a branch; a part or division of a main body: *a branch of the family; the three branches of government.* **3** to divide into separate parts: *The road branches in three directions.* **4** coming out of or connected to the main body: *the branch lines of a railroad; the branch offices of a business.*

brand (brănd) **1** particular kind or make of product. **2** a mark, name, or label given a product by the company that makes it. **3** an identifying mark made by burning: *The rancher put his brand on the cattle.* **4** the mark on a branding iron or stamp. **5** to mark by burning the skin. **6** to point out (a person) as deserving disgrace: *They branded him as a spy.* **7** a piece of burning wood.

bran·dish (brăn'dĭsh) to wave about or shake as a threat: *As the mob approached, the guards brandished their weapons.*

brand-new (brănd'nōō' or brănd'nū') very new; unused.

bran·dy (brăn'dĭ) a strong alcoholic beverage distilled from wine or other fermented fruit juice. **bran·dies.**

brass (brăs) **1** yellow metal made by melting copper and zinc together. **2** made of brass: *a brass doorknob.* **3** musical instrument made of brass, such as the trumpet or horn. **4** bold impudence: *He had the brass to tell me he wouldn't pay.*

brat (brăt) spoiled or naughty child.

brave (brāv) **1** having or showing courage: *The brave soldiers attacked their enemies.* **2** North American Indian warrior. **3** to meet or face with courage: *to brave the storm.* **brav·er, brav·est; braved, brav·ing; brave·ly.**

brav·er·y (brā'və rĭ) courage, fearlessness.

brawl (brôl) **1** a noisy quarrel or fight. **2** to quarrel or fight in a noisy manner: *The rowdies brawled in the street.*

brawn (brôn) **1** firm, strong muscles. **2** muscular strength: *The boxer had more brawn than skill.*

brawn·y (brô'nĭ) muscular; strong: *his brawny arms.* **brawn·i·er, brawn·i·est.**

bray (brā) **1** a harsh, loud cry made by a donkey. **2** any sound like it. **3** to utter a loud, harsh sound.

bra·zen (brā'zən) **1** made of brass; like brass. **2** bold and shameless: *a brazen lie.*
brazen out to put on a bold and shameless front to get out of a bad situation: *When he was caught stealing, he tried to brazen it out.*
bra·zen·ly.

bra·zier (brā'zhər) open pan for holding burning charcoal or live coals.

Bra·zil (brə zĭl') a country in northeastern South America.

breach (brēch) **1** an opening made by breaking through; a gap: *a breach in a wall.* **2** to make a break, opening, or gap in. **3** the action of breaking (a law, a promise, etc.); violation: *a breach of contract; a breach of duty; a breach of friendship.*

bread (brĕd) **1** article of food made from flour or meal which is moistened, raised, kneaded, and baked. **2** livelihood: *He earns his bread by hard work.* **3** to cover with bread crumbs before cooking: *to bread a veal chop.* (Homonym: bred)

bread·fruit (brĕd'frōōt') **1** a large, round fruit which grows on a tree in the islands of the South Pacific. When roasted, it resembles bread. **2** the tree this fruit grows on.

Breadfruit

breadth (brĕdth) the measure of a thing from side to side; width.

break (brāk) **1** to cause to come to pieces by a blow or a strain: *to break a dish.* **2** to come into pieces from a blow or a strain; shatter: *The glass broke.* **3** a broken place: *a break in a water pipe.* **4** interruption: *a break in the conversation.* **5** to interrupt: *to break an electric circuit.* **6** a gap; rift; opening: *a break in the clouds; a break in the skin.* **7** to force an opening in; pierce: *The prisoners broke through the wall.* **8** to change tone: *His voice broke when he told about the lost dog.* **9** to burst forth suddenly: *The storm broke with great fury.*

---

fāte, făt, fâre, fär; bē, bĕt; bīte, bĭt; nō, nŏt, nôr; fūse, fŭn, fûr; tōō, tŏŏk; foil; foul; thin; then; hw for wh as in what; zh for s as in usual; ə for a, e, i, o, u, as in ago, linen, peril, atom, minus

10 the beginning: *at* break *of day.* **11** to weaken the force of; lessen: *The firemen's net will* break *your fall.* **12** to fail to keep; violate: *to* break *the law; to* break *a promise.* **13** to tame; curb the spirit of: *to* break *a bronco.* **14** to make bankrupt: *Every shopping trip nearly* breaks *me.* **15** to go beyond; surpass: *to* break *a swimming record.* **16** to make known; tell: *to* break *the news.*

break down 1 to fail; cease to work properly: *My car* broke down *this morning.* **2** to give way under pressure: *The prisoner* broke down *and told the truth.* **3** to cause to give way by blows or pressure: *to* break down *a door; to* break down *the enemy's resistance.*

break in 1 to train; get ready for work or use: *The sergeant* broke in *the new recruits. A new car has to be* broken in. **2** to enter by forcing.

break into to begin suddenly: *The horse* broke into *a gallop.*

break in on 1 to interrupt: *to* break in on *a conversation.* **2** to intrude on.

break off 1 to put an end to; discontinue: *to* break off *relations with another country.* **2** to stop suddenly; cease abruptly: *He* broke off *in the middle of his speech.*

break out 1 to force a way out: *to* break out *of prison.* **2** to have a rash: *to* break out *with measles.* **3** to start suddenly: *A fire* broke out *during the night.*

break up 1 to stop: *to* break up *a fight.* **2** to separate; scatter: *The crowd* broke up.

break with to stop being friendly with; stop relations with: *They had been chums, but they* broke with *each other.*

broke, bro·ken, break·ing. (Homonym: brake)

break·a·ble (brā′kə bəl) that can be broken; fragile: *Plastic cups are not* breakable.

break·down (brāk′doun′) **1** mental or physical collapse. **2** a failure to work properly: *A* breakdown *of machinery stopped production.*

break·er (brā′kər) **1** wave which hits the rocks or the shore and breaks into foam. **2** person or thing that breaks.

break·fast (brĕk′fəst) **1** first meal of the day. **2** to eat breakfast.

break·neck (brāk′nĕk′) reckless; rash; dangerous: *Wallace rode his bicycle at* breakneck *speed.*

break·through (brāk′thrōō′) movement or advance through and beyond a barrier: *The troops made a* breakthrough *and attacked the enemy from the rear.*

break·wa·ter (brāk′wô′tər or brāk′wŏt′ər) wall or barrier built to break the force of waves.

breast (brĕst) **1** the upper front part of the body between the neck and the abdomen; the chest. **2** either of the milk glands on the chest. **3** the heart; the feelings. **4** to oppose; struggle with: *to* breast *the waves; to* breast *a storm of abuse.* **5 make a clean breast of** to confess fully.

breast·plate (brĕst′plāt′) a piece of armor to protect the chest.

breast·work (brĕst′wûrk′) hastily constructed wall for defense, usually chest high.

Breastplate

breath (brĕth) **1** air drawn into and forced out of the lungs. **2** a drawing in or forcing out of air: *Take a deep* breath. **3** the power to breathe easily: *Wait until I get my* breath. **4** slight stirring (of air): *There's not a* breath *of air in the room.* **5 under one's breath** in a whisper: *to mutter* under one's breath.

breathe (brēth) **1** to draw air into the lungs and force it out. **2** to whisper: *Don't* breathe *a word of this.* **3** to inspire: *The quarterback* breathed *new life into the team by his touchdown.* **4** to stop to rest after action or strain: *The worst is over, we can* breathe *again.* **breathed, breath·ing.**

breath·less (brĕth′lis) **1** out of breath: *The climb left him* breathless. **2** holding the breath; tense: *The spectators were* breathless *with excitement.* **breath·less·ly.**

breath·tak·ing (brĕth′tā′king) taking away the breath; very exciting: *a* breathtaking *ride on the roller coaster; a* breathtaking *view from a mountain peak.* **breath·tak·ing·ly.**

bred (brĕd) See **breed.** (Homonym: bread)

breech·es (brich′iz) short trousers fastened below the knee.

breed (brēd) **1** to produce young; bear offspring: *Guinea pigs* breed *rapidly.* **2** to mate and raise: *The ranch owner* breeds *cattle and sheep for the market.* **3** to be the cause of; bring about: *Slums* breed *crime.*

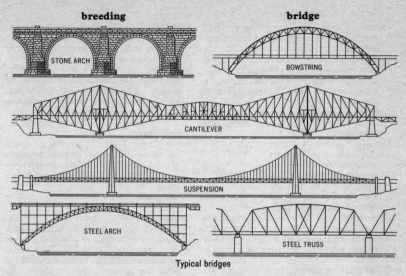

STONE ARCH

BOWSTRING

CANTILEVER

SUSPENSION

STEEL ARCH

STEEL TRUSS

Typical bridges

4 to train; rear: *The prince was* bred *to be a king.* **5** a variety or strain (of a species of plant or animal): *The Saint Bernard is a breed of large dog.* **bred, breed·ing.**

breed·ing (brē′dĭng) **1** upbringing; training: *His manners show good* breeding. **2** good manners and behavior: *A man of breeding is considerate of others.* **3** producing plants and animals to get better kinds: *the* breeding *of livestock.*

breeze (brēz) a gentle wind.

breez·y (brē′zĭ) **1** fanned by light winds: *a large, breezy porch.* **2** lively; jolly; gay and cheerful: *a breezy manner.* **breez·i·er, breez·i·est; breez·i·ly.**

breth·ren (brĕth′rĭn) in religious language, brothers.

brev·i·ty (brĕv′ə tĭ) shortness; briefness.

brew (broo) **1** to make by steeping, boiling, and fermenting: *Beer is* brewed. **2** to make by steeping: *Will you please* brew *the tea?* **3** to plan; plot; concoct: *to* brew *mischief.* **4** to grow in force; gather: *A storm is* brewing *in the east.* **5** a drink made by brewing.

bri·ar or **bri·er** (brī′ər) a thorny plant or bush: *a patch of* briars.

bribe (brīb) **1** gift made or promised to a person to influence him to decide or act dishonestly: *The man tried to give the policeman a* bribe *to let him go.* **2** to offer or give a bribe. **bribed, brib·ing.**

brib·er·y (brī′bə rĭ) the giving or taking of bribes. **brib·er·ies.**

brick (brĭk) **1** oblong block of clay hardened by baking in the sun or in an oven. **2** brick material; bricks: *a house built of* brick. **3** made of such blocks: *a brick wall; a brick house.* **4** anything shaped like such a block: *a brick of ice cream.* **5** to build, pave, or close with bricks.

brick·yard (brĭk′yärd′) place where bricks are made.

bri·dal (brī′dəl) having to do with a bride or a wedding. (Homonym: bridle)

bride (brīd) a woman newly married or about to be married.

bride·groom (brīd′groom′) a man newly married or about to be married.

brides·maid (brīdz′mād′) one of the women who attend a bride at her wedding.

¹bridge (brĭj) **1** structure built for passage across a river or valley. **2** to put a bridge

fāte, făt, fâre, fär; bē, bĕt; bīte, bĭt; nō, nŏt, nôr; fūse, fŭn, fûr; tōō, tŏŏk; foil; foul; thin; then; hw for wh as in *wh*at; zh for s as in u*s*ual; ə for a, e, i, o, u, as in *a*go, lin*e*n, per*i*l, at*o*m, min*u*s

119

over. **3** to get over (something that hinders): *to* bridge *a difficulty*. **4** arched support for the strings on a violin, cello, etc. **5** the upper bony part of the nose. **6** platform above the deck of a ship for the officer in charge. **bridged, bridg·ing.** [¹**bridge** is a form of an Old English word (brycg) of the same meaning.]

²**bridge** (brij) a card game. [²**bridge** is from the Russian name (biritch) of an old card game similar to bridge.]

bri·dle (brī'dəl) **1** leather straps placed on the head of a horse or other animal to guide and control it. It includes the bit and the reins. **2** to put a bit and reins on: *Saddle and* bridle *the horses*. **3** to hold; check; control: *You must learn to* bridle *your temper*. **4** a check; restraint: *Put a* bridle *on your tongue*. **bri·dled, bri·dling.** (Homonym: bridal)

Bridle

brief (brēf) **1** not long in time; short: *The train made a* brief *stop. The speech was* brief *and to the point*. **2** a summary, especially a lawyer's outline of a case. **3** to give a detailed summary of instructions to: *The captain* briefed *the officers before the battle*. **brief·ly.**

brig (brig) **1** sailing ship with two masts and a square rigging. **2** prison on a warship.

bri·gade (brĭ gād') **1** body of military troops, usually two or more regiments. **2** body of men organized for a special purpose: *a fire* brigade.

Brig

brig·and (brig'ənd) member of a gang of robbers; bandit.

bright (brīt) **1** giving or reflecting light; shining: *The sun is* bright. *Rub the silver to a* bright *polish*. **2** vivid; intense: *to wear* bright *colors*. **3** cheerful; happy: *They tried to be* bright *and gay*. **4** clever: *a* bright *idea; a* bright *student*. **5** favorable; hopeful: *The future looks* bright. **bright·ly.**

bright·en (brī'tən) **1** to grow clearer or lighter: *The day* brightens. **2** to make more pleasant or cheerful: *Flowers* brighten *a room*.

bril·liance (bril'yəns) **1** great brightness; splendor: *the* brilliance *of the stars*. **2** outstanding ability: *Einstein was a scientist of great* brilliance.

bril·liant (brĭl'yənt) **1** shining brightly; sparkling: *The lake looked* brilliant *in the sunlight*. **2** splendid; magnificent: *a* brilliant *celebration*. **3** having outstanding ability: *a* brilliant *scholar*. **4** a diamond or other precious stone cut to sparkle brightly. **bril·liant·ly.**

brim (brim) **1** edge or rim: *the* brim *of a cup*. **2** edge that stands out from the crown of a hat. **3** to be full to the very edge: *Her eyes* brimmed *with tears*. **brimmed, brim·ming.**

brim·stone (brim'stōn') sulfur.

brine (brīn) very salty water.

bring (bring) **1** to cause (a person or thing) to come along; fetch: *to* bring *home a friend; to* bring *lunch to school*. **2** to cause to come; draw: *That speaker always* brings *out a big crowd*. **3** to be accompanied by; result in: *Springtime* brings *flowers. Age* brings *white hair*. **4** to sell for: *Your jewelry will* bring *a good price*. **5** to persuade: *I cannot* bring *myself to tell him*.

bring about to cause to happen.

bring forth to produce; give birth to.

bring to to restore to consciousness: *She was* brought to *by a dash of cold water*.

bring up 1 to rear; educate. **2** to mention: *Don't* bring up *that subject now*. **brought, bring·ing.**

brink (bringk) **1** edge or top of a steep place: *the* brink *of a pit*. **2** verge: *the* brink *of disaster*.

brin·y (brī'nĭ) very salty.

brisk (brisk) **1** active; lively; swift; nimble: *a* brisk *walker*. **2** keen; bracing: *a* brisk *wind*. **brisk·ly.**

bris·tle (bris'əl) **1** a short, stiff, coarse hair. **2** to stand up in a stiff, prickly way: *The cat's hair* bristled *when the dog barked*. **3** to show signs of anger or defiance: *The witness* bristled *at the rude question*.

bristle with to be thick with, or as with, bristles: *a battlefield* bristling *with bayonets. A subject* bristling *with difficulties*.

bris·tled, bris·tling.

Brit·ain (brit'ən) the island on which England, Scotland, and Wales are located; Great Britain.

Brit·ish (brĭt′ĭsh) **1** of Great Britain or its people. **2 the British** the people of Great Britain.

brit·tle (brĭt′əl) easily broken; apt to break: *a brittle glass; an old man's brittle bones.*

broach (brōch) **1** to begin to talk about; introduce: *How do you broach an unpleasant subject?* **2** to pierce or tap: *to broach a keg of cider.*

broad (brôd) **1** wide from side to side. **2** spacious; large: *a broad stretch of land.* **3** tolerant; liberal; without prejudice: *a broad view; a broad outlook.* **4** clear: *in broad daylight.* **5** plain; obvious; evident: *a broad hint.* **broad·ly.**

broad·cast (brôd′kăst′) **1** to send out over radio or television. **2** a radio or television program. **3** to spread around: *Don't broadcast the secret I just told you.* **4** to scatter: *The seed was broadcast over the entire five acres.* **5** so as to scatter widely: *to sow broadcast.* **broad·cast** or **broad·cast·ed, broad·cast·ing.**

broad·cloth (brôd′klôth′ or brôd′klŏth′) **1** a fine grade of cotton or silk cloth used for shirts, skirts, dresses, blouses, etc. **2** fine woolen cloth with a smooth surface.

broad·en (brôd′ən) to make or grow wide or wider: *The river broadens into a bay. Reading broadened his mind.*

broad·side (brôd′sīd′) **1** entire side of a ship that shows above the water. **2** a firing of all the guns on one side of a ship. **3** with the widest side turned toward (an object): *The barge bore down broadside upon the tug.*

broad·sword (brôd′sôrd′) sword with a broad, flat blade.

bro·cade (brō kād′) rich cloth with raised designs woven into it.

broc·co·li (brŏk′ə li) a plant somewhat like cauliflower, the stalks and tops of which are cooked as a vegetable.

Broccoli

broil (broil) **1** to cook or be cooked by direct exposure to the fire. **2** to be or make very hot.

broil·er (broil′ər) **1** rack, pan, or part of a stove for broiling. **2** young chicken suitable for broiling.

broke (brōk) See **break.** *He broke a bone.*

bro·ken (brō′kən) **1** not whole; in pieces: *a broken cup.* **2** fractured: *a broken bone.* **3** not kept; violated: *a broken promise.* **4** weakened: *in broken health.* **5** imperfectly spoken: *to speak broken English.* **6** trained to obedience: *a broken horse.* **7** incomplete: *a broken set of chessmen.* **8** crushed; subdued: *a broken spirit.* **9** See **break:** *I have broken an egg.* **bro·ken·ly.**

bro·ker (brō′kər) person who buys or sells for another person as his agent: *a cotton broker; a real estate broker.*

bron·chi·al tubes (brŏng′ki əl tōōbz or tūbz) the larger air tubes of the lungs.

bron·chi·tis (brŏng ki′tĭs) inflammation inside the bronchial tubes.

bron·co or **bron·cho** (brŏng′kō) a small wild or half-tamed horse of western North America. **bron·cos; bron·chos.**

bronze (brŏnz) **1** metal made by melting copper and tin together. **2** a statue, ornament, medal, etc., made of this metal. **3** made of bronze: *a bronze coin.* **4** the color of bronze, a reddish brown or yellowish brown. **5** to make the color of bronze; to tan: *His face was bronzed by the sun.* **bronzed, bronz·ing.**

brooch (brōch or brōōch) ornamental pin fastened with a clasp.

Brooch

brood (brōōd) **1** all the young hatched by a bird at one time: *a brood of chickens.* **2** all the children of one mother: *Our neighbors had a brood of ten children.* **3** to sit on eggs: *A hen is brooding in the coop.* **4** to think long and moodily.

brood on or **over** to think about something long and moodily; worry over: *to brood over one's misfortunes.*

¹brook (brōōk) small, natural stream of water. [**¹brook** is a form of an Old English word (broc) and is related to **break.**] ·

²brook (brōōk) to bear; tolerate: *I will brook no interference with my plans.* [**²brook** is a form of an Old English word (brucan) meaning "enjoy."]

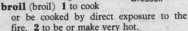

fāte, făt, fâre, fär; bē, bĕt; bīte, bĭt; nō, nŏt, nôr; fūse, fŭn, fûr; tōō, tŏŏk; foil; foul; thin; ~~t~~hen; hw for wh as in *wh*at; zh for s as in u*s*ual; ə for a, e, i, o, u, as in *a*go, lin*e*n, per*i*l, at*o*m, min*u*s

brook·let (brŏŏk′lĭt) little brook.

broom (brŏŏm) **1** brush with a long handle, for sweeping. **2** a wild shrub with long, slender branches and yellow flowers.

broom·stick (brŏŏm′stik′) the long handle of a broom.

broth (brôth or brŏth) thin soup made by boiling meat in water.

broth·er (brŭth′ər) **1** boy or man with the same parents as another person. **2** man of the same race or nationality as another; fellow man. **3** fellow member of same profession, union, church, or other association.

broth·er·hood (brŭth′ər hŏŏd′) **1** group of men with common interests; fraternal organization. **2** fellowship; kinship: *the brotherhood of man.*

broth·er·in·law (brŭth′ər in lô′) **1** the brother of one's husband or wife. **2** the husband of one's sister. **broth·ers·in·law.**

broth·er·ly (brŭth′ər lĭ) **1** of or like a brother; kindly. **2** friendly: *There was a brotherly feeling among the boys in the class.*

brought (brôt) See **bring.** *I brought my lunch from home today.*

brow (brou) **1** the forehead. **2** arch of hair over an eye; eyebrow. **3** the edge of a steep place: *the brow of a hill.*

brown (broun) **1** the color of coffee or chocolate. **2** of this color: *The dead leaves were brown.* **3** to make or become brown: *The cook browned the chicken on both sides.*

brown·ie (broun′ĭ) **1** in stories, a good elf or fairy who does useful household tasks by night. **2** a small, sweet, rich, flat chocolate cake containing nuts. **3 Brownie** member of the junior division of the Girl Scouts.

Brownie

browse (brouz) **1** to nibble on grass or twigs; graze: *Deer like to browse on young willow twigs.* **2** to glance here and there in books, a library, etc. **browsed, brows·ing.**

bru·in (brŏŏ′ən) a bear.

bruise (brŏŏz) **1** an injury, caused by a blow or fall, which does not break the skin but sometimes discolors it. **2** an injury to the outside of a fruit, vegetable, or plant. **3** to injure the outside of; produce a bruise in: *I fell and bruised my leg.* **4** to become bruised: *Tomatoes bruise easily.* **5** to hurt (the feelings). **bruised, bruis·ing.**

bru·net (brŏŏ nĕt′) **1** having dark hair and eyes. **2** person with dark hair and eyes. When referring to a woman, the word is written "brunette."

brunt (brŭnt) heaviest part of a shock or strain: *The infantry bore the brunt of the battle.*

¹brush (brŭsh) **1** an implement made of bristles, hair, or wire, set in a stiff back or fastened to a handle, and used for scrubbing, cleaning, painting, smoothing, etc. **2** to sweep, clean, paint, or smooth with a brush. **3** to remove by brushing: *to brush the dirt away.* **4** short, quick fight or skirmish: *The troops had a brush with the enemy.* **5** to touch lightly in passing: *He brushed my shoulder on the way out.* **6** the bushy tail of an animal, especially of a fox. [**brush** is from an Old French word (broisse).]

²brush (brŭsh) **1** a dense growth of bushes; thicket. **2** branches broken from trees; brushwood. [**²brush** is from an Old French word (broche).]

brush·wood (brŭsh′wŏŏd′) **1** branches broken or cut from trees. **2** dense thicket of shrubs and small trees.

brusque (brŭsk) rough or abrupt in speech or manner: *Bruce gave a brusque reply to the friendly question.* **brusque·ly.**

Brus·sels sprouts (brŭs′əlz sprouts) **1** plant which bears on its stalk closely rolled leaf balls that look like little cabbages. **2** these heads used as food.

bru·tal (brŏŏ′təl) cruel; savage. **bru·tal·ly.**

bru·tal·i·ty (brŏŏ tăl′ə tĭ) **1** cruelty. **2** inhuman act. **bru·tal·i·ties.**

brute (brŏŏt) **1** a beast; an animal without reasoning power. **2** like an animal: *his brute strength.* **3** a cruel, inhuman person. **4** without intelligence or feeling: *Hurricanes and floods show the brute forces of nature.*

bu. bushel.

bub·ble (bŭb′əl) **1** a thin globelike film of liquid filled with air or gas: *a soap bubble.* **2** a small globelike ball of air or gas rising to the surface of water or other liquid, or held within a solid such as ice or glass. **3** to foam; gurgle: *The spring bubbled up out of the moss.* **4** to make bubbles and gurgle: *The pot boiled and bubbled on the stove.* **bub·bled, bub·bling.**

buc·ca·neer (bŭk′ə nîr′) a pirate; a sea robber.

buck (bŭk) **1** the male of the deer, rabbit, and certain other kinds of animals. **2** a sudden jump upward, as of an unruly horse. **3** to jump upward with the back arched, as a horse does to throw off a rider.

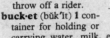

Bucking horse

buck·et (bŭk′it) **1** container for holding or carrying water, milk, etc.; a pail. **2** the amount a bucket holds; a bucketful.

buck·eye (bŭk′ī′) **1** any of several trees related to the horse chestnut tree. **2** the nut of such a tree.

buck·le (bŭk′əl) **1** a clasp for holding together the ends of a strap. **2** a clasp-like ornament for hats, dresses, shoes, etc. **3** to fasten with such a clasp: *Your seat belt must be buckled before the plane takes off.* **4** to bend or become twisted from heat or strain: *The bridge buckled when the armored tanks were halfway across it.*
buckle down to to work hard at: *to buckle down to the job.*
buck·led, buck·ling.

buck·ler (bŭk′lər) small, round shield.

buck·shot (bŭk′shŏt′) heavy lead shot used to shoot deer and other big game.

buck·skin (bŭk′skĭn′) **1** a soft yellowish or grayish leather made from the skin of a deer or sheep. **2** made of buckskin: *a buckskin jacket.*

buck·wheat (bŭk′hwēt′) **1** cereal plant with black, triangular seeds which are ground into flour. **2** the flour itself.

bud (bŭd) **1** a flower or leaf that is not yet open: *a rose bud.* **2** to put forth new shoots; sprout: *The trees are budding early this year.* **3 in bud** in the first stage of growth of a branch, leaf, or flower: *The trees were in bud.* **bud·ded, bud·ding.**

Bud·dha (bōōd′ə) "The Enlightened One," the title of Gautama, holy man of India who lived from 563? to 483? B.C. and founded Buddhism.

Bud·dhism (bōōd′ĭz əm) great Asiatic religion founded by Gautama Buddha in the 6th century, B.C. It teaches the "Eight-fold Path" of "right belief, right resolve, right word, right act, right life, right effort, right thinking, and right meditation."

budge (bŭj) to move slightly: *The mule wouldn't budge. The box was so heavy that no one could budge it.* **budged, budg·ing.**

bud·get (bŭj′ĭt) **1** a listing or plan that shows how much money is available and how it is to be divided up and spent for various purposes: *a family budget; a government budget.* **2** to plan how to spend (money, time, etc.) by making a budget; allot: *I try to budget my time so that I have Sundays free.*

buff (bŭf) **1** dull yellowish tan color. **2** soft, yellowish leather formerly made from the skin of a buffalo and now from that of an ox. **3** to polish with a leather-covered wheel.

buf·fa·lo (bŭf′ə lō′) **1** any of several kinds of oxen, such as the tame water buffalo of East Asia or the African Cape buffalo. **2** in America, the bison, a wild ox with a large shaggy head, a

African buffalo, about 5 ft. high at shoulder

hump over the shoulders, and powerful front legs. For picture, see **bison. buf·fa·loes, buf·fa·los,** or **buf·fa·lo.**

¹buf·fet (bŭf′ĭt) **1** a blow struck by the hand or fist. **2** a knock or stroke. **3** to strike with the hand or fist. **4** to beat; knock about: *The waves buffeted the boat.* [**¹buffet** is from an Old French word (buffe) also meaning "a blow."]

²buf·fet (bə fā′ or bŏŏ fā′) **1** sideboard or piece of furniture for a dining room, used to hold dishes, silver, and table linen. Dishes of food are sometimes placed on the buffet, so that guests can help themselves. **2** refreshment counter, or restaurant with such a counter. **3** served from a buffet: *a buffet supper.* **4** a meal so served. [**²buffet** is from a French word (buffet) with the same meaning.]

---

fāte, făt, fâre, fär; bē, bĕt; bite, bĭt; nō, nŏt, nôr; fūse, fŭn, fûr; tōō, tŏŏk; foil; foul; thin; ~~then~~;
hw for wh as in *wh*at; zh for s as in u*s*ual; ə for a, e, i, o, u, as in *a*go, lin*e*n, per*i*l, at*o*m, min*u*s

bug (bŭg) **1** any crawling insect. **2** a flattened insect with a sucking mouth, with or without wings: *a water bug.*

bug·a·boo (bŭg′ə bōō′) **1** an imaginary monster used to frighten children into obedience. **2** anything real or imaginary that causes fear. **bug·a·boos.**

bug·bear (bŭg′bâr′) something feared without reason; bugaboo.

Buggy

bug·gy (bŭg′ĭ) a light carriage with a single seat and with or without a top. **bug·gies.**

bu·gle (bū′gəl) a trumpetlike, brass, wind instrument for sounding military calls.

bu·gler (bū′glər) person who plays a bugle.

Bugle

build (bĭld) **1** to make by putting materials or parts together; construct: *Men build houses and ships. Birds build nests.* **2** way, form or shape in which the body is put together: *That wrestler has a heavy build.* **build up** to make steadily larger or better: *to* build up *a business; to* build up *your health.* **built, build·ing.**

build·er (bĭl′dər) **1** person whose business is the construction of buildings. **2** person who makes or develops something: *The writers of the Constitution were* builders *of a new nation.*

build·ing (bĭl′dĭng) **1** the constructing of houses, churches, factories, bridges, ships, etc. **2** thing constructed; a structure such as a house, school, barn, factory, etc.: *the Empire State* Building.

built (bĭlt) See **build.** *Who built this house?*

bulb (bŭlb) **1** round, underground bud of some plants, from which the plant grows. The lily, onion, tulip, and narcissus all grow from bulbs.

Electric bulb
Onion bulb

2 anything shaped like a bulb: *the bulb of a thermometer.* **3** small glass globe which has a fine wire in it that gives off light when electricity passes through it: *light* bulb.

bulb·ous (bŭl′bəs) **1** having a bulb or bulbs: *Lilies are* bulbous *plants.* **2** like a bulb; somewhat round; swollen: *The circus clown had a* bulbous *red nose.*

bulge (bŭlj) **1** rounded part which stands out; hump: *What is that bulge in your pocket?* **2** to swell or bend outwards: *The bags are so full they* bulge. **bulged, bulg·ing.**

Bulge

bulk (bŭlk) **1** size; mass; great size: *In spite of its bulk, the elephant can move quickly.* **2 the bulk of** the greater part of: *I've paid the bulk of the debt. Oceans form the bulk of the earth's surface.*

bulk·head (bŭlk′hĕd′) a wall in a ship, separating watertight compartments.

BULKHEAD
Bulkhead of a ship

bulk·y (bŭl′kĭ) massive; big; hard to handle. **bulk·i·er, bulk·i·est; bulk·i·ly.**

bull (bŏŏl) **1** the male of any animal of the ox family. **2** any of several other large male animals, such as the whale or elephant.

bull·dog (bŏŏl′dôg′ or bŏŏl′dŏg′) a dog of medium size with a large head, short hair, and a jaw that sticks out. It is known for its courage and strong grip.

Bulldog, about 15 in. high

bull·doz·er (bŏŏl′dō′zər) a powerful motor vehicle that moves earth, trees, stumps, and rocks by ·pushing them with a wide blade.

bul·let (bŏŏl′ĭt) a small piece of metal shaped to be fired from a rifle, pistol, machine gun, etc.

Bulldozer

bul·le·tin (bŏŏl′ə tən) **1** a brief report on some matter of public interest: *The doctor released a* bulletin *on his famous patient's condition.* **2** a notice: *Put a* bulletin *on the board.* **3** a magazine published regularly, containing the reports of a club or society.

bull·fight (bŏŏl′fīt′) a combat between men and a bull, held in an arena.

bull·finch (bŏŏl′fĭnch′) a sparrowlike European songbird with a short, strong bill and bright plumage.

bull·frog (bŏŏl′frŏg′ or bŏŏl′frôg′) a large frog with a very deep croaking voice.

bull·head·ed (bŏŏl′hĕd′ĭd) stupidly obstinate or stubborn: *He was bullheaded in arguing after he was proved wrong.*

bul·lion (bŏŏl′yən) uncoined gold or silver in a mass, lumps, or bars.

bull·ock (bŏŏl′ək) ox; steer.

bul·ly (bŏŏl′ĭ) 1 a quarrelsome person who teases, threatens, or torments a smaller or weaker person. 2 to frighten by loud threats or by tormenting actions: *The big boy* bullies *everybody on the playground.* **bul·lies; bul·lied, bul·ly·ing.**

bul·rush (bŏŏl′rŭsh′) tall plant with slender stalks that grows in wet places.

bul·wark (bŏŏl′wərk) 1 a barrier or wall built for defense or protection. Earthworks, ramparts, and breakwaters are bulwarks. 2 anything that protects: *The Bill of Rights is a bulwark of our freedom.* 3 the solid part of a ship's side above the level of the deck.

Bulwark of a ship

bum·ble·bee (bŭm′bəl bē′) a large, hairy bee that makes a loud, humming sound as it flies.

Bumblebee, about life size

bump (bŭmp) 1 to hit or strike (against something) with a jolt; knock against or with: *The baby* bumped *his head when he fell. The truck* bumped *into a small car.* 2 to knock together: *We* bumped *our heads as we leaned over.* 3 a heavy blow or knock; a jolt: *The plane landed with a* bump. 4 a swelling due to a blow or knock; a lump. 5 a small place raised above the level of the area around it: *a* bump *in the road.* 6 to move with bumps; jolt: *The wagon* bumped *along the road.*

bump·er (bŭm′pər) 1 a bar across the front or back of a car to protect it against bumps. 2 very large; abundant: *a* bumper *crop.*

bun (bŭn) a bread roll, usually sweetened.

bunch (bŭnch) 1 a number of things growing together; a cluster: *a bunch of grapes.* 2 a collection of similar things fastened or grouped together: *a bunch of flowers; a* bunch *of keys.* 3 to gather into a bunch.

bun·dle (bŭn′dəl) 1 a number of things bound or tied together: *a bundle of rags.* 2 a package. 3 to tie or wrap: *Will you please* bundle *these shirts together?*
bundle off to send away in a hurry.
bundle up to dress warmly.
bun·dled, bun·dling.

bung (bŭng) 1 stopper of wood or cork for the hole of a cask. 2 hole for filling or emptying a cask.

bun·ga·low (bŭng′gə lō′) small house, usually of one story.

bun·gle (bŭng′gəl) 1 to do something in a clumsy and unsuccessful way; spoil: *to* bungle *a job.* 2 clumsy or botched job.
bun·gled, bun·gling.

Bungalow

bunk (bŭngk) 1 a bed built as a shelf on a wall or built into a recess in a wall. 2 a narrow bed or cot. 3 to sleep in a bunk. 4 to sleep in a makeshift bed: *You can* bunk *on the sofa.*

bun·ny (bŭn′ĭ) in children's language, a rabbit. **bun·nies.**

bunt (bŭnt) 1 the tapping of a baseball with a loosely held bat so that the ball goes only a short distance within the infield. 2 to make such a hit in baseball. 3 to butt or push with head or horns: *The goat* bunted *my leg.* 4 a push with head or horns.

¹bun·ting (bŭn′tĭng) a kind of small, thick-billed bird about the size of a sparrow. [**¹bunting** is a form of an earlier English word (bountyng).]

²bun·ting (bŭn′tĭng) 1 coarse cotton material used for flags. 2 long pieces of this material with flaglike patterns, used for decoration on holidays. [**²bunting** is of uncertain origin.]

---

fāte, făt, fâre, fär; bē, bĕt; bīte, bĭt; nō, nŏt, nôr; fūse, fŭn, fûr; tōō, tŏŏk; foil; foul; thin; ~~then~~; hw for wh as in *w*hat; zh for s as in u*s*ual; ə for a, e, i, o, u, as in *a*go, lin*e*n, per*i*l, at*o*m, min*u*s

buoy   burr

buoy (boi or boॅo̅′ĭ) **1** a float carrying a light, whistle, bell, or marker, anchored to show the position of rocks, shoals, or a channel or anchorage. **2** device to keep a person afloat: *a life buoy.* **3** to act as a buoy; keep buoyant. (Homonym: boy)

Conical and spar buoys

buoy·an·cy (boi′ən sĭ) **1** power to float in water or other liquid; lightness: *A cork has buoyancy.* **2** upward force of a liquid on an object floating in it. **3** cheerfulness: *his buoyancy of spirit.*

buoy·ant (boi′ənt) **1** able to float in liquid. **2** capable of keeping an object afloat. **3** light-hearted; gay: *in buoyant spirits.* **4** springy; light: *a buoyant stride.*

bur·den (bûr′dən) **1** something carried; a load. **2** weight or load on the mind or spirit: *a burden of grief, sorrow, or care.* **3** to weary; put too much upon: *I will not burden you with my troubles.* **4 beast of burden** an animal used to carry loads.

bur·den·some (bûr′dən səm) heavy; troublesome; wearying: *a burdensome task.*

bur·dock (bûr′dŏk) coarse weed with broad leaves and prickly burrs that stick to the clothing and to the coats of animals.

bu·reau (byॅoo̅r′ō) **1** chest of drawers for holding clothing, often with a mirror. **2** office for some special business: *a travel bureau.* **3** government office or department: *Federal Bureau of Investigation.*

bur·gess (bûr′jĭs) **1** an inhabitant, especially one entitled to vote, of a town, borough, etc. **2** in some localities, a town official. **3 House of Burgesses** before the American Revolution, the legislative body of certain American colonies.

burgh·er (bûr′gər) in former times, a citizen of a borough or town.

bur·glar (bûr′glər) person who breaks into a building to steal.

bur·glar·y (bûr′glə rĭ) crime of breaking into a building to steal. **bur·glar·ies.**

bur·go·mas·ter (bûr′gə măs′tər) the mayor of a town in Germany, Austria, the Netherlands, and parts of Belgium.

bur·i·al (bĕr′ĭ əl) **1** the placing of a body in a grave. **2** having to do with a burial.

bur·ied (bĕr′ĭd) See **bury.** *The dog buried his bone. They found buried treasure.*

bur·lap (bûr′lăp) coarse cloth of hemp or other fiber, used mostly in making bags and wrappings.

bur·ly (bûr′lĭ) big and strong; muscular. **bur·li·er, bur·li·est.**

burn (bûrn) **1** to destroy, damage, or injure by fire or heat: *The match burned my fingers.* **2** to be on fire: *A log burned in the fireplace.* **3** to use fuel or electricity for heat or light: *This furnace burns coal.* **4** to destroy, damage, or injure by the action of chemicals, friction, electricity, the sun's rays, wind, etc.: *The sun burned and blistered her back.* **5** to be destroyed, damaged, or injured by burning: *Don't let the roast burn.* **6** to make by burning: *to burn a hole in a dress.* **7** injury or damage caused by burning: *a bad burn on the hand.* **8** to give light; glow: *The lights burned all night.* **9** to be filled with strong feelings of: *to burn with indignation.* **10** to feel warm; redden: *Her face burned with embarrassment.*

burn down to destroy (a building) by fire; to be destroyed by fire.

burn out to make or become useless by long burning or overwork: *The motor burned out. We burned out the motor.*

burn up to destroy or be completely destroyed by fire.

burned or **burnt, burn·ing.**

burn·er (bûr′nər) part of a lamp, stove, or furnace from which the flame or heat comes.

bur·nish (bûr′nĭsh) to polish by rubbing; give a shiny finish to: *Mother burnished the copper pots until they gleamed.*

bur·noose or **bur·nous** (bər-noॅo̅s′ or bûr′noॅo̅s) cloak with a hood worn by Arabs.

burn·out (bûrn′out′) time when the fuel in a rocket is burned out.

Burnoose

burnt (bûrnt) See **burn.**

burr or **bur** (bûr) **1** seedcase or pod with sharp points or prickles, such as those of the chestnut and burdock. A burr will cling to people's clothes and to the hair of animals. **2** a plant that bears such a seedcase.

126

burro

bur·ro (bûr′ō or bŏŏr′ō) small donkey.
bur·ros. (Homonyms: borough, burrow)

bur·row (bûr′ō) **1** hole
in the ground dug by
an animal such as a
rabbit or a fox; such a
hole used as a home.
2 to dig a hole: *The
mole* burrowed *under
the lawn.* **3** to dig or
search: *Alec* burrowed
*through the basket
of clothes.* (Homonym: borough)

Burro, 3 to 3½
ft. high

burst (bûrst) **1** to break open violently;
explode: *Bombs* burst *in the air.* **2** outbreak: *a burst of laughter.* **3** a spurt; rush:
a burst of energy. **4** to come or go, begin,
or do something suddenly: *The boy* burst
into the room. The storm burst. **5** to start or
break out (into some action or expression
of feeling): *The birds* burst *into song. She*
burst *into tears.* **6** to be full to overflowing: *The paper bag was* bursting *with
apples.* burst, burst·ing.

bur·y (bĕr′ĭ) **1** to put in a grave or a tomb.
2 to cover; hide: *to bury treasure in the
ground.* bur·ied, bur·y·ing. (Homonym:
berry)

bus (bŭs) large automobile with rows of
seats: *school* bus. bus·es or bus·ses.

bush (bŏŏsh) **1** a plant, smaller than a
tree, with many branches growing out near
the ground; shrub. **2** land with many
bushes and trees; land that is not cleared.

bush·el (bŏŏsh′əl) **1** measure used for
grains, fruits, vegetables, or other dry
products. A bushel is equal to four pecks
or eight gallons. **2** capable of holding a
bushel: *a bushel basket.*

bush·y (bŏŏsh′ĭ) **1** thick and spreading:
bushy eyebrows. **2** overgrown with shrubs:
a bushy vacant lot. bush·i·er, bush·i·est.

busi·ness (bĭz′nĭs) **1** a buying and selling
of goods; trade: *My father is in the clothing
business.* **2** work; occupation: *What
business are you in?* **3** affairs or concerns:
He minds his own business. **4** commercial
enterprise: *The business was handed down
from father to son.* **5** having to do with
business: *a business agreement.*

butt

busi·ness·like (bĭz′nĭs lĭk′) orderly; efficient: *a businesslike manner.*

busi·ness·man (bĭz′nĭs măn′) man who engages in business. busi·ness·men.

bust (bŭst) **1** breast, especially of a woman.
2 piece of sculpture showing the head,
neck, and shoulders of a person.

bus·tle (bŭs′əl) **1** to hurry in a noisy or
fussy way: *He* bustled *about the room trying
to look busy.* **2** noisy flurry of activity: *the
hustle and* bustle *of the holiday season.* bus·
tled, bus·tling.

bus·y (bĭz′ĭ) **1** at work; not idle; active.
2 crowded with activity: *a busy day; a busy
street.* **3** to make or keep busy: *Tim*
busied *himself with the puzzle until it was
time to go.* bus·i·er, bus·i·est; bus·ied,
bus·y·ing; bus·i·ly.

bus·y·bod·y (bĭz′ĭ bŏd′ĭ) a meddling person; person who interferes in other people's affairs. bus·y·bod·ies.

but (bŭt) **1** yet; still: *I planted the seed,* but
it never sprouted. **2** only: *There is* but *one
way to do this right.* **3** except: *everyone* but
you. **4** that: *I do not doubt* but *he will go.*
(Homonym: butt)

butch·er (bŏŏch′ər) **1** person whose job is
killing animals and preparing their meat
for food. **2** person who cuts and sells
meat. **3** person who kills (men or animals)
needlessly. **4** to slaughter. **5** to spoil;
ruin: *Don't* butcher *our play by mumbling
your lines.*

butch·er·y (bŏŏch′ə rĭ) brutal killing; unnecessary slaughter. butch·er·ies.

but·ler (bŭt′lər) the chief male servant of
a household.

¹butt (bŭt) **1** to strike with the lowered
head: *A goat* butts *people who annoy him.*
2 a blow or push with the head: *The calf
gave a playful* butt. [¹**butt** is from an Old
French word (buter) meaning "to thrust
against."] (Homonym: but)

²butt (bŭt) **1** the thicker, heavier, or lower
part of a thing: *the butt of a rifle.* **2** what
is left of something after most of it has
been cut away or used up; stub: *a ham*
butt; *a cigarette* butt. [²**butt** is probably
from an Old English word (butte) meaning
"thick end."] (Homonym: but)

---

fāte, făt, fâre, fär; bē, bĕt; bīte, bĭt; nō, nŏt, nôr; fūse, fŭn, fûr; tōō, tŏŏk; foil; foul; thin; ~~then~~;
hw for wh as in *wh*at; zh for s as in u*s*ual; ə for a, e, i, o, u, as in *a*go, lin*e*n, per*i*l, at*o*m, min*u*s

butt

³butt (bŭt) **1** a target. **2** a person who is the target for ridicule, jokes, criticism, etc. [³**butt** is from a French word (but) meaning "goal."] (Homonym: but)

butte (būt) a steep, flat-topped hill standing alone.

Butte

but·ter (bŭt'ər) **1** yellow, fatty substance obtained from milk or cream by churning. **2** a substance that spreads like butter: *peanut* butter. **3** to spread butter on.

but·ter·cup (bŭt'ər cŭp') **1** common meadow plant with glossy, cup-shaped, yellow flowers. **2** its flower.

but·ter·fly (bŭt'ər flī') an insect with a slender body and four broad wings, usually brightly colored. A long, slender tube serves as a mouth, and it has two knobbed feelers. **but·ter·flies.**

Butterfly

but·ter·milk (bŭt'ər milk') liquid left after butter has been removed from churned milk.

but·ter·nut (bŭt'ər nŭt') **1** the oily nut of the American white walnut tree. **2** the tree that bears this nut.

but·ter·scotch (bŭt'ər skŏch') **1** a kind of hard, sticky candy made of melted butter, brown sugar, vanilla, etc. **2** having the flavor of this candy: *a* butterscotch *sauce.*

but·ton (bŭt'ən) **1** a small disk or knob of bone, wood, glass, plastic, etc. which fastens by being slipped through a slit. It may also be used for decoration. **2** to fasten with such a disk or knob. **3** a disk that is pushed to operate an electric switch.

but·ton·hole (bŭt'ən hōl') **1** a stitched slit for a button to pass through. **2** to make such openings in. **3** to force (a person) to listen as if by taking hold of him by the buttonhole. **but·ton·holed, but·ton·hol·ing.**

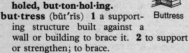
Buttress

but·tress (bŭt'rĭs) **1** a supporting structure built against a wall or building to brace it. **2** to support or strengthen; to brace.

by-path

bux·om (bŭk'səm) plump; healthy.

buy (bī) **1** to get by paying a price; purchase. **2** a bargain: *We got a good* buy *on the furniture.* **bought, buy·ing.** (Homonym: by)

buy·er (bī'ər) **1** person who buys. **2** person whose work is buying for a store.

buzz (bŭz) **1** a steady humming sound; a prolonged sound of "z": *the* buzz *of flies; a* buzz *of conversation.* **2** to make this sound. **3** to fly a plane very low over: *The pilot* buzzed *the signal tower.*

buz·zard (bŭz'ərd) a kind of vulture; the American turkey buzzard.

buz·zer (bŭz'ər) an electrical device that signals by buzzing.

by (bī) **1** beside or near to: *a lamp* by *the bed.* **2** alongside: *a road* by *the river.* **3** during: *to travel* by *night.* **4** past and beyond: *to go* by *a house.* **5** according to: *I can tell* by *his accent that he is French.* **6** not any later than: *Finish* by *tomorrow noon.* **7** through the means of: *I'll let you know* by *phone.* **8** through the action of: *a speech* by *the President.* **9** in the amount of; to the number of: *younger* by *three years; eggs* by *the dozen.* **10** with regard to: *They have done well* by *us.* **11** in the manner of: *to meet* by *chance.* **12** aside; in reserve: *to put* by *some money.* **13** at: *Stop* by *my house for dinner.* **14 by and by** after a while; later on; before long. **15 by the by** or **by the way** incidentally. **16 by and large** on the whole; in general. (Homonym: buy)

Turkey buzzard, about 30 in. long

by·gone (bī'gôn' or bī'gŏn') **1** past; gone by: *in* bygone *days.* **2** a thing of the past: *Let* bygones *be bygones.*

by·law (bī'lô') a rule or law made by an organization to govern its own activities.

by·line (bī'līn') line under the title of an article in a newspaper or magazine, giving the name of the author.

by·pass (bī'păs') **1** a road, path, or channel that can be used as a substitute or alternate for the main route. **2** to go around: *We* by-passed *Pittsburgh on our trip.*

by·path (bī'păth') a side path.

128

by-prod·uct (bī′prŏd′əkt) something that is produced in a manufacturing process, other than the main product, and that has a value of its own.

by-road (bī′rōd′) a side road.

by-stand·er (bī′stăn′dər) a person who looks on, but does not take part.

by·way (bī′wā′) road which is not well known or much used.

by·word (bī′wûrd′) **1** familiar saying or proverb. **2** person or thing that becomes widely known in an unfavorable way; object of scorn or mocking: *His mischievous pranks made him a* byword *in the town.*

C

C, c (sē) **1** third letter of the English alphabet. **2** Roman numeral for 100.

cab (kăb) **1** automobile in which passengers pay a fare; taxi. **2** covered part of a locomotive or truck where the engineer or driver sits. **3** carriage for hire, pulled by one horse.

Cab

cab·bage (kăb′ij) vegetable with thick, curved leaves forming a round, firm head.

cab·in (kăb′in) **1** small hut or house. **2** room on a ship, used as quarters for officers or passengers. **3** enclosed part of an airplane occupied by the passengers.

Cabbage

cab·i·net (kăb′ə nit) **1** piece of furniture with shelves or drawers in which articles are stored or displayed: *a medicine* cabinet; *a kitchen* cabinet. **2** group of advisors chosen by the head of a nation to help him manage the country's affairs.

Cabin

ca·ble (kā′bəl) **1** thick, heavy rope of hemp or wire, used for supporting suspension bridges, towing automobiles, mooring ships, etc. **2** insulated, waterproof rope of wires to carry electric current. **3** message sent by telegraph wires laid under the sea. **4** to send a cable to: *Please* cable *your*

office *that you will sail next week.* **ca·bled, ca·bling.**

cable·gram (kā′bəl-gram′) message sent underwater by cable.

Cable

ca·boose (kə bōōs′) **1** small car, usually at the end of a train, in which railroad workers can rest or sleep. **2** kitchen on the deck of a ship.

ca·ca·o (kə kā′ō or kə kä′ō) **1** seeds of a small, evergreen tree of tropical America, from which cocoa and chocolate are made. **2** the tree itself.

cache (kăsh) **1** hiding place for treasure or supplies. **2** what has been hidden in such a place: *a* cache *of food.* **3** to hide: *He* cached *the treasure at the back of the cave.* **cached, cach·ing.** (Homonym: cash)

cack·le (kăk′əl) **1** sharp, broken sound that a hen or goose makes after laying an egg. **2** to make such a sound. **3** to chatter noisily. **cack·led, cack·ling.**

cac·tus (kăk′təs) leafless, desert plant with sharp spines or prickles along a fleshy stem and branches. **cac·tus·es** or **cac·ti.** (kăk′tī)

Fishhook cactus

cad·die or **cad·dy** (kăd′ī) **1** person hired by a golf player to carry his clubs, hunt for balls, etc. **2** to work in this way. **cad·dies; cad·died, cad·dy·ing.**

ca·dence (kād′əns) **1** rhythm; beat. **2** rhythmic rise and fall of the voice in singing or speaking. **3** closing notes of a musical passage.

---

fāte, făt, fâre, fär; bē, bĕt; bīte, bĭt; nō, nŏt, nôr; fūse, fŭn, fûr; tōō, tŏŏk; foil; foul; thin; ~~then~~;
hw for wh as in *wh*at; zh for s as in u*s*ual; ə for a, e, i, o, u, as in *a*go, lin*e*n, per*i*l, at*o*m, min*u*s

ca·det (kə dĕt′) student in a naval or military academy.

cad·mi·um (kăd′mĭ əm) a chemical element. It is a white metal which is used in alloys for automobile bearings, etc.

ca·fé (kă fā′) restaurant.

caf·e·te·ri·a (kăf′ə tir′ĭ ə) restaurant where people serve themselves.

caf·feine or **caf·fein** (kăf′ēn′) drug found in coffee and tea and used in many medicines.

cage (kāj) **1** boxlike container, usually made of wire or bars, for birds or other animals. **2** anything like a cage in form or purpose. **3** to pen up; shut up. **caged, cag·ing.**

cais·son (kā′sən or kā′sŏn) **1** ammunition wagon. **2** watertight box in which men work under water when building bridges, dams, tunnels, etc. **3** a float used to raise sunken vessels.

COMPRESSION CHAMBER
LOCK · LOCK
WORKING CHAMBER
Construction caisson

cake (kāk) **1** mixture of flour, milk, sugar, eggs, etc., usually baked as a loaf or in layers, often covered with frosting. **2** small portion of thin batter or of ground meat, fish, potatoes, etc., cooked on a griddle. **3** any small mass pressed together or flattened: *a cake of soap.* **4** to form or harden into a hard mass. **caked, cak·ing.**

ca·lam·i·ty (kə lăm′ə tĭ) **1** event that causes destruction far and wide, such as a hurricane, flood, or earthquake. **2** great personal misfortune. **ca·lam·i·ties.**

cal·ci·um (kăl′sĭ əm) metal element found in lime, marble, bone, etc. It is a necessary element in bones, teeth, blood, etc.

cal·cu·late (kăl′kyŏŏ lāt′) **1** to add, subtract, multiply, or divide to obtain a result; figure out by arithmetic. **2** to figure out in advance; estimate: *to calculate how many miles one can travel in a day.* **ca·cu·lat·ed, ca·cu·lat·ing.**

cal·cu·la·tion (kăl′kyŏŏ lā′shən) **1** the use of numbers and arithmetic in solving a problem. **2** the result of figuring: *The engineer's calculations show that the rocket is off its course.* **3** careful planning or thought: *after long calculation.*

cal·cu·la·tor (kăl′kyŏŏ lā′tər) person or machine that makes a calculation.

cal·dron (kôl′drən) large kettle or boiler.

cal·en·dar (kăl′ən dər) **1** way of dividing up time into days, weeks, months, and years. **2** table showing the arrangement of days, weeks, and months of a year. **3** a list or schedule of things to be done or that happen at certain times: *a church calendar of festivals.*

JUNE						
SUN	MON	TUE	WED	THU	FRI	SAT
			1	2	3	4
5	6	7	8	9	10	11
12	13	14	15	16	17	18
19	20	21	22	23	24	25
26	27	28	29	30		

Calendar

¹calf (kăf) **1** baby cow or bull. **2** young whale, elephant, moose, walrus, seal, etc. **3** leather made from the skin of a calf. **calves.** [¹**calf** is a form of an Old English word (cealf) with the same meaning.]

²calf (kăf) the thick part at the back of the leg between the knee and ankle. **calves.** [²**calf** is probably from an Old Norse word (kālfi), related to ¹**calf.**]

Calf

cal·i·ber or **cal·i·bre** (kăl′ə bər) **1** diameter of the bore of a gun, or of a bullet: *a* .22-caliber *pistol.* **2** mental or physical ability: *a person of high* caliber.

cal·i·co (kăl′ə kō′) **1** cheap cotton cloth, usually printed with flower or other designs. **2** made of this material. **3** like calico; spotted. **cal·i·coes** or **cal·i·cos.**

Calif. California.

Cal·i·for·nia (kăl′ə fôrn′yə) western State of the United States, on the Pacific coast.

ca·liph or **ca·lif** (kā′lif or kăl′if) former title of the head of a Moslem state.

call (kôl) **1** to cry out in a loud voice: *Mother* called, *but I didn't hear.* **2** a shout. **3** to send for; summon: *The principal* called *me to his office.* **4** tune or signal used as an announcement; summons: *Reveille is a bugle* call *to waken soldiers.* **5** to telephone. **6** to arouse from sleep: *Please call me at 6 A.M.* **7** to make a brief visit. **8** short visit: *We paid a* call *on our new neighbors.* **9** to name: *Let's* call *the pup Blackie.* **10** to declare: *to* call *a foul; to* call *a halt.* **11** the cry or note of a bird or animal: *The bluejay has a harsh* call. **12** to utter such a cry or note. **13** to estimate: *I'd* call *the pond about ten feet deep.* **14** a need: *You have no* call *to complain.*

call for 1 to go and get; fetch: *Mother will* call for *you at two*. 2 to require; demand: *Boxing* calls for *quick reactions*.

call off to cancel; postpone: *The game was* called off *because of rain*.

call·er (kôl′ər) 1 person who calls. 2 person who pays a brief, formal call; visitor.

call·ing (kôl′ing) profession; occupation; vocation: *It is important to find the right* calling.

cal·lous (kăl′əs) 1 to harden: *Rough work will* callous *your hands*. 2 unfeeling; not sensitive: *Cruel people are* callous *to the suffering of others*. **cal·lous·ly**. (Homonym: callus)

cal·lus (kăl′əs) a hardened place on the skin. (Homonym: callous)

calm (käm) 1 quiet; peaceful; undisturbed: *The lake was* calm *until the breeze sprang up*. 2 period of quiet and stillness: *The sailboat was motionless during the* calm. 3 to make calm: *The trainer* calmed *the angry lion*.

calm down to make or become quiet or peaceful: *The wild colt* calmed down.

calm·ly.

cal·or·ie or **cal·or·y** (kăl′ə rĭ) 1 unit used for measuring the amount of heat (in something). 2 **great calorie** (equal to 1,000 calories) unit for measuring the energy the body gets from foods. One egg has about 75 great calories. **cal·or·ies**.

calves (kăvz) more than one calf.

ca·lyx (kāl′ĭks or kăl′ĭks) the outside covering, usually green, of a flower bud, which splits open as the petals grow.

Calyx

cam·bi·um (kăm′bĭ əm) layer of soft tissue between the bark and the wood of trees and plants, which develops into new wood and new bark.

came (kām) See **come**. *The dog* came *when we called him*.

cam·el (kăm′əl) large, four-footed animal with one or two humps. Camels are used to carry riders and burdens in the desert areas of Africa and Asia. See picture in opposite column.

cam·er·a (kăm′ər ə) 1 apparatus in which film is exposed for taking still photographs or motion pictures. 2 device that changes pictures into electrical impulses for television broadcast.

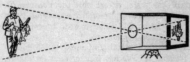

Camera, showing upside-down image on film

cam·er·a·man (kăm′ər ə măn′) man who operates a camera, especially a motion-picture camera. **cam·er·a·men**.

cam·ou·flage (kăm′ə fläzh′) 1 art of concealing or disguising guns, ships, fortifications, etc. to deceive an enemy. 2 concealment; disguise; pretense: *Barney's joking and laughing was only* camouflage *to cover his uneasiness*. 3 to hide or disguise: *The tanks were* camouflaged *with painted canvas*. **cam·ou·flaged, cam·ou·flag·ing**.

camp (kămp) 1 group of people living in temporary shelters in the country for recreation, health, etc.: *activities of a summer* camp. 2 group of tents, huts, or temporary living quarters: *The Red Cross set up* camps *for flood victims*. 3 to make, or stay in, a camp: *We* camped *overnight*. 4 group of people who agree on a subject, support a cause, etc.: *Lillian prefers popular to classical music, but I belong to the opposite* camp.

cam·paign (kăm pān′) 1 series of military operations carried on for a particular purpose: *The general planned a* campaign *to capture the city*. 2 organized activity for a particular purpose: *a political* campaign. 3 to carry on or take part in a campaign: *She* campaigned *for the fund*.

Camel, 7½ ft. high

camp·fire (kămp′fīr′) 1 a fire in a camp for warmth or cooking. 2 social gathering around such a fire.

---

fāte, făt, fâre, fär; bē, bĕt; bīte, bĭt; nō, nŏt, nôr; fūse, fŭn, fûr; tōō, tŏŏk; foil; foul; thin; then; hw for wh as in what; zh for s as in usual; ə for a, e, i, o, u, as in ago, linen, peril, atom, minus

131

cam·phor (kăm'fər) white substance obtained chiefly from the camphor tree of Asia, used in mothballs, medicines, etc.

cam·pus (kăm'pəs) grounds of a school or college.

¹**can** (kăn) am, is, are able to: *You* can *lift ten pounds easily. I* can *see your point.* [¹**can** is from an Old English word meaning "to know" or "be able to."]

²**can** (kăn) **1** metal container. **2** contents of a can: *We ate two* cans *of beets for dinner.* **3** to preserve food by putting it into airtight metal or glass containers: *She* canned *her own pears.* **canned, can·ning.** [²**can** is a form of an Old English word (canne) meaning "cup."]

Can·a·da (kăn'ə də) the northernmost country of North America.

Ca·na·di·an (kə nā'dĭ ən) **1** of Canada or its people. **2** citizen of Canada or person of Canadian descent.

ca·nal (kə năl') **1** waterway dug for boats or ships or to carry water for irrigation. **2** tubelike part in a body or plant for liquids, air, or food.

ca·nar·y (kə nâr'ĭ) **1** small yellow songbird. **2** light yellow. **ca·nar·ies.**

can·cel (kăn'səl) **1** to cross out by drawing a line or lines through; mark so as to take away the value of: *to* cancel *a stamp.* **2** to take back; withdraw: *The magazine order was* canceled *hers and the result was a tie.* **3** to offset; balance: *My vote* canceled *hers and the result was a tie.*

can·cer (kăn'sər) **1** dangerous growth in the body; a malignant disease. **2** something that destroys by growing and is difficult to check: *Growing crime is a* cancer *on society.*

can·did (kăn'dĭd) outspoken; frank; sincere: *a* candid *opinion.* **can·did·ly.**

can·di·date (kăn'də dāt') person who offers himself, or who is put up by others, as a contestant for an office or honor.

can·dle (kăn'dəl) **1** stick of tallow or wax with a wick inside it that is burned to give light. **2 not worth the candle** not worth the trouble or the expense.

can·dle·light (kăn'dəl lĭt') **1** the light of a candle. **2** time when candles are lighted; twilight.

candle power unit for measuring the brightness of a source of light such as an electric bulb.

can·dle·stick (kăn'dəl stĭk') holder for a candle.

can·dor (kăn'dər) frankness; honesty: *The child said in* candor *what the others were unwilling to say.*

can·dy (kăn'dĭ) **1** something to eat, made chiefly of sugar, often with the addition of flavoring, fruits, nuts, etc.; sweets. **2** one piece of such a sweet. **3** to turn into sugar: *Syrup was cooked until it* candied. **4** to coat or preserve with sugar: *to* candy *fruit.* **can·dies; can·died, can·dy·ing.**

Candlestick

cane (kān) **1** stick carried as an aid in walking; walking stick. **2** to beat with a cane. **3** a long, hollow, jointed, woody stem of certain plants, such as bamboo. **4** any plant having such a stem, such as sugar cane. **5** to use strips of wicker to make or repair a chair. **caned, can·ing.**

ca·nine (kā'nīn') **1** of or like a dog. **2** a dog. **3** any of the four pointed teeth next to the front teeth. For picture see **teeth.**

can·ker (kăng'kər) **1** white sore in the mouth. **2** anything that causes decay or rot by a steady eating away.

can·ner·y (kăn'ə rĭ) a place where meat, vegetables, etc. are canned. **can·ner·ies.**

can·ni·bal (kăn'ə bəl) **1** human being who eats human flesh. **2** any animal that eats its own kind.

can·non (kăn'ən) a large mounted gun. (Homonym: canon)

can·non·ade (kăn'ən ād') **1** a continuous firing of cannon. **2** to attack with cannon; bombard: *The fort was* cannonaded *and captured.* **can·non·ad·ed, can·non·ad·ing.**

Cannon

can·not (kăn'ŏt or kă nŏt') am, is, are unable to: *I* cannot *meet you today.*

can·ny (kăn'ĭ) shrewd; cautious: *A* canny *man knows when to speak and when to be silent.* **can·ni·er, can·ni·est; can·ni·ly.**

ca·noe (kə nōō') **1** a light, narrow boat that is moved by a paddle or paddles rather than by oars. **2** to ride in or paddle a canoe. **ca·noed, ca·noe·ing.**

Canoe

can·on (kăn'ən) **1** rule or code of a church, especially the Roman Catholic Church. **2** principle or standard by which things are judged: *the canons of good conduct.* **3** the books of the Bible accepted by the Christian Church as genuine. (Homonym: cannon)

ca·ñon (kăn'yən) canyon.

can·o·py (kăn'ə pĭ) **1** cloth covering fixed above a bed or a throne, or held up on poles above an important personage. **2** any overhanging covering at an entrance; awning. **can·o·pies.**

Canopy

canst (kănst) an old form of **can**, used with *thou*: "Thou canst *not say I did it.*"

can't (kănt) cannot: *I can't go.*

can·ta·loupe or **can·ta·loup** (kăn'tə lōp') melon with a hard, rough rind and sweet, juicy, orange-colored flesh.

can·tan·ker·ous (kăn tăng'kər əs) hard to get along with; fault-finding; cranky: *a cantankerous person.* **can·tan·ker·ous·ly.**

can·ta·ta (kən tä'tə) a musical composition telling a story. Cantatas are sung without acting by a chorus and soloists.

can·teen (kăn tēn') **1** small container used for carrying drinking water. **2** small store or booth in a factory, office, or camp, for the sale of food, tobacco, etc. **3** a place for recreation where refreshments are served to soldiers and sailors.

can·ter (kăn'tər) **1** slow gallop: *The horse had an easy canter.* **2** to ride or go at a slow gallop.

can·ti·le·ver (kăn'tə lĕv'ər or kăn'tə lē'vər) **1** projecting beam or brace, supported only at one end, such as that used to hold up a balcony. **2 cantilever bridge** a bridge with the span made of two joining parts that are projected toward each other from opposite banks. For picture, see **bridge.**

can·ton (kăn'tŏn) small, political division of a country or territory, especially Switzerland.

can·tor (kăn'tôr) **1** choir leader in a church. **2** soloist in the Jewish religious service.

can·vas (kăn'vəs) **1** coarse heavy cloth of cotton, hemp, or flax, used for tents, sails, awnings, tennis shoes, etc., and as a material on which to paint in oil. **2** an oil painting. (Homonym: canvass)

can·vass (kăn'vəs) **1** to examine or look over thoroughly; discuss in detail: *We* canvassed *the local papers for a house to rent.* **2** to seek or solicit votes, subscriptions, orders, etc.: *The boys* canvassed *the neighborhood for magazine subscriptions.* **3** a survey of public opinion: *a canvass of television viewers.* (Homonym: canvas)

can·yon (kăn'yən) deep valley with steep sides, usually with a stream flowing through it; a gorge.

cap (kăp) **1** a small covering for the head: *a baseball* cap; *a nurse's* cap. **2** anything shaped or used like a cap: *a mushroom* cap; *a bottle* cap. **3** to cover with a cap or as a cap does: *I forgot to* cap *the bottle. Snow* caps *the mountain top.* **4** to match and do better than: *Can you* cap *this story?* **5** small explosive charge in a wrapper, especially one used in a toy pistol. **capped, cap·ping.**

ca·pa·bil·i·ty (kā'pə bĭl'ə tĭ) ability; power of doing things. **ca·pa·bil·i·ties.**

ca·pa·ble (kā'pə bəl) **1** having skill or ability; able; competent: *A capable typist does quick, accurate work.* **2 capable of** (1) having the necessary nature or qualities for: *John's achievement tests show that he is* capable *of college work.* (2) open to; permitting: *This situation is* capable *of improvement.* **ca·pa·bly.**

ca·pa·cious (kə pā'shəs) able to hold much; roomy: *a capacious handbag.*

ca·pac·i·ty (kə păs'ə tĭ) **1** power to receive or hold; amount or number that can be held: *a capacity of a million gallons.* **2** mental ability: *a student of great capacity.* **3** position; place: *a teacher who serves in the capacity of. coach.* **ca·pac·i·ties.**

Policeman wearing cape

¹cape (kāp) outer garment without sleeves, worn over the shoulders. [**¹cape** is from a Spanish word (capa) meaning "hood" which is from a Latin word (caput) meaning "head."]

fāte, făt, fâre, fär; bē, bĕt; bīte, bĭt; nō, nŏt, nôr; fūse, fŭn, fûr; tōō, tŏŏk; foil; foul; thin; ~~then~~; hw for wh as in *wh*at; zh for s as in u*s*ual; ə for a, e, i, o, u, as in *a*go, lin*e*n, per*i*l, at*o*m, min*u*s

²**cape** (kāp) point of land jutting out into a body of water; a headland. [²**cape** is from a French word (cap) with the same meaning. It comes from the same Latin word as ¹**cape**. A cape is a "headland."]

ca·per (kā′pər) **1** to skip about or leap playfully: *Clowns* capered *about the circus tent.* **2** playful leap or jump. **3** a prank.

cap·il·lar·y (kăp′ə lĕr′ĭ) slender, hairlike tube, especially one of the very small blood vessels in the body. **cap·il·lar·ies.**

cap·i·tal (kăp′ə təl) **1** city which is the seat of government of a country or State: *Washington, D.C. is the* capital *of the United States.* **2** kind of letter used at the beginning of a sentence, a person's name, etc.: *THIS IS PRINTED IN CAPITALS.* **3** punishable by death: *Murder is a* capital *crime.* **4** wealth and property that can be used in business and industry to make more money. **5** first-rate; excellent: *a* capital *idea.* **6** the broad, ornamental top part of a column. (Homonym: capitol)

Corinthian
capital

cap·i·tal·ism (kăp′ə tə lĭz′əm) system of living in which private individuals or companies own, control, and develop the land, public utilities, business, etc.

cap·i·tal·ist (kăp′ə tə lĭst′) **1** person who believes in or practices capitalism. **2** a very wealthy person.

cap·i·tal·i·za·tion (kăp′ə təl ə zā′shən) **1** the act of writing or printing a letter or letters as a capital or capitals. **2** the money invested in a business: *This firm has a* capitalization *of $60,000,000.*

cap·i·tal·ize (kăp′ə tə līz′) **1** to print or write with a capital letter. **2** to take advantage of: *She* capitalized *on her good looks and became a fashion model.* **3** to fix or set the capital at a certain amount: *This company was* capitalized *at $200,000.* **cap·i·tal·ized, cap·i·tal·i·zing.**

cap·i·tol (kăp′ə təl) **1** the building in which a State legislature meets. **2** **Capitol** the building in Washington, D.C., in which Congress meets. (Homonym: capital)

ca·pit·u·late (kə pĭch′ə lāt′) to surrender to an enemy, usually on terms agreed upon. **ca·pit·u·lat·ed, ca·pit·u·lat·ing.**

ca·pon (kā′pŏn) rooster unable to father baby chicks, and raised for the table.

ca·price (kə prēs′) sudden change of mind or behavior without reason; whim: *Her decision was based on* caprice, *not thought.*

ca·pri·cious (kə prĭsh′əs) changing without reason; given to whims; unpredictable: *That girl is so* capricious *that you never know what she'll do next.* **ca·pri·cious·ly.**

cap·size (kăp sīz′ or kăp′sīz) to overturn; upset: *A sudden wind* capsized *the little sailboat.* **cap·sized, cap·siz·ing.**

cap·stan (kăp′stən) large, upright, spool-shaped machine which raises or lowers heavy weights as the cable around it is wound or unwound. Capstans are used for raising and lowering ships' anchors.

Capstan

cap·sule (kăp′səl) **1** small case of gelatin containing a dose of medicine. **2** seedcase that bursts when ripe. **3** enclosure in a rocket to hold instruments or a passenger.

Capsule
1 seed
2 medical

cap·tain (kăp′tĭn) **1** army officer ranking above a lieutenant and below a major. **2** officer in the navy ranking above a commander and below a rear admiral. **3** master of a merchant ship. **4** person in authority over others in a group; leader: *the* captain *of a baseball team.*

cap·tion (kăp′shən) **1** title or explanation of a picture. **2** brief title for an article, chapter, etc., set above it in large type. **3** a heading or headline.

cap·ti·vate (kăp′tə vāt′) to attract; charm; fascinate: *She* captivated *her audience with her songs.* **cap·ti·vat·ed, cap·ti·vat·ing.**

cap·tive (kăp′tĭv) **1** person or animal taken into captivity; prisoner. **2** not free; captured: *a* captive *deer; the* captive *nations.*

cap·tiv·i·ty (kăp tĭv′ə tĭ) a being held captive or in prison: *They endured* captivity *all during the war.*

cap·tor (kăp′tər) person who seizes another as a prisoner.

cap·ture (kăp′chər) **1** to take or seize by force, skill, surprise, trickery, or other means: *to* capture *a thief; to* capture *the attention of an audience.* **2** person or thing seized: *Our first* capture *was a lion.* **3** a seizing or being seized: *The* capture *of a criminal.* **cap·tured, cap·tur·ing.**

car (kär) **1** automobile. **2** vehicle running on rails: *a trolley* car; *a railway* car. **3** the part of an elevator that carries passengers or freight.

ca·ra·ba·o (kär′ə bä′ō) water buffalo of the Philippine Islands. **ca·ra·ba·os.**

car·a·mel (kär′ə məl or kär′məl) **1** a kind of candy made of burnt sugar. **2** burnt sugar used for coloring and flavoring.

car·at (kăr′ət) **1** unit of weight for precious stones. **2** a measure of the purity of gold. In commercial use, 24 carats is pure gold. (Homonym: carrot)

car·a·van (kăr′ə văn) **1** company of persons traveling together for safety, as across a desert or through dangerous country. **2** a train of pack animals or vehicles. **3** large covered vehicle that is lived in.

car·a·way (kăr′ə wā′) a plant whose seed is used to flavor small cakes, rye bread, etc.

car·bine (kär′bīn) a short, light rifle.

car·bo·hy·drate (kär′bō hī′drāt′) a compound of carbon, hydrogen, and oxygen. Sugars and starches are carbohydrates.

car·bol·ic ac·id (kär bŏl′ik ăs′ĭd) poisonous acid made from coal tar and used in water as an antiseptic and disinfectant.

car·bon (kär′bən) a chemical element found in its pure state as diamond and graphite. Carbon is a necessary element in all living matter, and is the chief element in coal.

car·bon di·ox·ide (kär′bən dī ŏk′sīd) a colorless, odorless gas found in the air and made up of one part carbon and two parts oxygen. Carbon dioxide is breathed out by animals. Plants absorb carbon dioxide from the air and use it to make food.

car·bon mon·ox·ide (kär′bən mə nŏk′sīd) a colorless, odorless, poisonous gas made up of one part carbon and one part oxygen. Exhaust fumes from automobiles contain large amounts of carbon monoxide.

car·cass (kär′kəs) body of a dead animal.

card (kärd) **1** piece of pasteboard, usually rectangular in shape: *a post* card; *a playing* card. **2 cards** any game played with playing cards. One game of cards is bridge.

card·board (kärd′bôrd′) thin, stiff pasteboard used in making posters, boxes, etc.

car·di·nal (kär′də nəl) **1** of first importance; chief: *Honesty is the* cardinal *quality of his character.* **2** of a rich red color. **3** high official in the Roman Catholic Church. **4** an American songbird. The male cardinal has bright red plumage. **5** a cardinal number.

Cardinal, about 10 in. long

cardinal number one of the numbers, such as 1, 2, 3, etc., spoken or written out as one, two, three, etc. The ordinal numbers are 1st, 2nd, 3rd, etc., spoken or written out as first, second, third, etc.

care (kâr) **1** anxiety; worry; trouble; concern: *I haven't a* care *in the world.* **2** to feel interest, anxiety, or worry; be concerned: *I doubt if you* care *how the game comes out.* **3** close attention: *work done with painstaking* care. **4** supervision; charge: *under a doctor's* care. **5** to wish; want: *He does not* care *to go.* **6 take care** to watch out. **7 take care of** to look after.

care for 1 to like: *Do you* care *for jazz?* **2** to look after: *Her neighbor will* care for *the children while she's away.*

cared, car·ing.

ca·reer (kə rîr′) **1** occupation or profession: *Many young men wish to make a* career *of science.* **2** course of action throughout life: *The* careers *of Jefferson and Lincoln still influence our history.*

care·free (kâr′frē′) without worry.

care·ful (kâr′fəl) **1** watchful; cautious: *He is* careful *to stay on the sidewalk.* **2** done or made with care: *a careful piece of work.* **3** mindful: *to be* careful *of the rights of others.* **care·ful·ly.**

care·less (kâr′lĭs) **1** not paying enough attention: *Some people are* careless *when they cross the street.* **2** inaccurate; not exact: *messy, careless work.* **3** not thoughtful of others: *a careless remark.* **care·less·ly.**

ca·ress (kə rĕs′) **1** a touch showing affection; a kiss; embrace. **2** to touch or stroke lovingly: *The little girl* caressed *her kitten.*

---

fāte, făt, fâre, fär; bē, bĕt; bīte, bĭt; nō, nŏt, nôr; fūse, fŭn, fûr; tōō, tŏŏk; foil; foul; thin; ~~then~~;
hw for wh as in *wh*at; zh for s as in u*s*ual; ə for a, e, i, o, u, as in *a*go, lin*e*n, per*i*l, at*o*m, min*u*s

care·tak·er (kâr′tā′kər) person who looks after a place, thing, or person for another: *the* caretaker *of the chapel.*

car·go (kär′gō) the load of goods carried by a ship; freight. **car·goes** or **car·gos.**

Car·ib·be·an Sea (kăr′ə bē′ən sē or kə rĭb′ĭ ən sē) a sea between Central America, South America, and the West Indies.

car·i·bou (kăr′ə bōō′) a North American reindeer.

car·il·lon (kăr′ə lŏn′) **1** set of tuned bells on which music may be played. **2** melody played on such bells.

car·load (kär′lōd′) the amount that a car, especially a freight car, can carry.

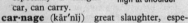
Mountain caribou, 4 ft. high at shoulder

car·nage (kär′nĭj) great slaughter, especially in a battle.

car·na·tion (kär nā′shən) a fragrant red, white, or pink flower that is grown in gardens and greenhouses.

car·nau·ba (kär nou′bə) **1** a Brazilian palm tree that yields wax. **2** this wax used for making candles, polish, varnish, etc.

Carnation

car·ni·val (kär′nə vəl) **1** a public amusement show, often with booths, Ferris wheel, merry-go-round, games, side shows, etc. **2** noisy merry-making; a revel: *the Mardi Gras carnival.*

car·niv·o·rous (kär nĭv′ə rəs) flesh-eating: *Dogs and cats are* carnivorous *animals.* **car·niv·o·rous·ly.**

car·ol (kăr′əl) **1** song of joy or praise: *Christmas* carols. **2** to sing joyfully; praise in song.

¹carp (kärp) to find fault; complain. [**¹carp** seems to be from two words, one an Old Norse word (karpa) meaning "to boast," and the other a Latin word (carpere) meaning "to pluck."]

²carp (kärp) a bony fresh-water fish that lives in ponds. pl. Carp

carp, rarely, **carps.** [**²carp** is from a Latin word (carpa) of the same meaning.]

car·pen·ter (kär′pən tər) person who works in wood and builds or repairs the woodwork of houses, ships, etc.

car·pet (kär′pĭt) **1** heavy fabric for covering floors. **2** to cover with a carpet: *to carpet a room.* **3** any covering like a carpet: *a carpet of pine needles.*

car·pet·bag·ger (kär′pĭt băg′ər) adventurer or politician who went from the Northern to the Southern States after the Civil War seeking political or other advantages made possible by the unsettled conditions at that time. A carpetbagger usually traveled with all his property in an old-fashioned valise made of carpet.

car·riage (kăr′ĭj) **1** wheeled vehicle for carrying people, usually drawn by horses.

Carriages: baby carriage, Concord buggy

2 light, often folding, vehicle for a baby, pushed by a person on foot. **3** a carrying or transporting of goods. **4** moving part of a machine which supports another part: *a typewriter* carriage. **5** wheeled support: *the* carriage *for a cannon.* **6** manner of holding one's body: *The old general still has an erect* carriage.

car·ri·er (kăr′ĭ ər) **1** person or thing that carries: *The mail* carriers *were rushed with Christmas deliveries.* **2** person, animal, or thing that carries disease germs and may pass them on to others.

car·ri·on (kăr′ĭ ən) dead and decaying flesh.

car·rot (kăr′ət) **1** plant of the celery family with a long, orange-yellow root. **2** its root used as a vegetable. (Homonym: carat)

car·ry (kăr′ĭ) **1** to take (something or someone) from one place to another: *That ship* carries *cargo from New York to London. Who will* carry *the groceries home?* **2** to hold up; support: *Beams* carry *the weight of the roof.* **3** to have power to reach a distance: *That actor's voice* carries *all the way to the gallery.* **4** to keep on hand for sale: *Drugstores* carry *toothpaste.* **5** to win:

136

Which party will carry *the election?* **6** to hold (the body, head, etc.) in a certain posture: *He* carries *himself like a soldier.*

carry away to enchant; move to ecstasy: *I was* carried away *by the music.*

carry on 1 to keep on; continue: *He will* carry on *the work started by his grandfather.* **2** to manage; conduct: *to* carry on *a correspondence.*

carry out to finish; accomplish: *The plans were* carried out *to the last detail.*

car·ried, car·ry·ing.

cart (kärt) **1** two-wheeled vehicle for carrying heavy goods. **2** light delivery wagon used by tradesmen and often moved by hand. **3** a light two-wheeled carriage for pleasure. **4** to carry in a cart: *Please* cart *this baggage out to the plane.*

Cart

cart·er (kär'tər) person who drives a cart.

car·ti·lage (kär'tə lij) tough, elastic white or yellowish body tissue that makes up part of the skeleton; gristle.

car·ton (kär'tən) cardboard box.

car·toon (kär tōōn') **1** a drawing, especially in a newspaper or magazine, that deals with well-known people or public events in a humorous or critical way. **2** motion picture made of drawings that seem to move and be alive. **3** comic strip.

car·toon·ist (kär tōō'nist) artist who draws cartoons.

car·tridge (kär'trij) **1** case made of metal or cardboard, containing powder and a bullet or shot for a firearm. **2** container shaped like this case: *Some fountain pens can be filled with* cartridges *of ink.*

RIFLE
SHOTGUN
Cartridges

cart·wheel or **cart wheel** (kärt'hwēl') **1** wheel of a cart. **2** sidewise handspring.

carve (kärv) **1** to cut up (meat) into pieces: *to* carve *a roast or a chicken.* **2** to make by cutting: *to* carve *a statue from wood or marble; to* carve *initials on a tree.* **3** to

decorate by cutting designs or figures: *to* carve *a chest.* **carved, carv·ing.**

carv·er (kär'vər) **1** person who carves. **2** knife used for carving.

carv·ing (kär'ving) **1** design or figure made by cutting: *an ivory* carving *of an elephant.* **2** the work or art of one who carves: *The* carving *of ship models.*

cas·cade (kas kād') **1** small waterfall, or a series of small waterfalls. **2** anything that resembles a waterfall: *a cascade of ruffles.* **3** to fall in torrents: *The rain* cascaded *from the eaves.* **cas·cad·ed, cas·cad·ing.**

Cascade

¹**case** (kās) **1** state of affairs: *If that is the case you will have to pay.* **2** set of facts, conditions, or circumstances having to do with a particular person or thing: *to investigate the* case *of a missing person.* **3** thing that has happened; example; occurrence: *a case of bad temper; a case of careless work.* **4** instance or occurrence of a disease or injury: *a case of mumps.* **5** person having a disease; patient: *The doctor saw ten* cases *today.* **6** lawsuit or question to be decided in a court: *Which lawyer will try that* case? **7** facts or arguments for or against a person: *He stated his* case. *He had no* case. **8 in case of** if there is: *Call a doctor in case of accident.* **9 in any case** regardless of what happens; anyhow. [¹**case** is from a Latin word (casum) meaning "that which has happened."]

²**case** (kās) **1** container or covering: *a clock case; a camera case.* **2** glass box for exhibiting goods; a showcase. **3** amount a box or other container holds: *a case of soft drinks.* [²**case** is from an Old French word (casse) which goes back to a Latin word (capsa) meaning "chest." It is related to **capsule.**]

Casement

case·ment (kās'mənt) window which opens out on hinges like a door.

---

fāte, făt, fâre, fär; bē, bĕt; bīte, bĭt; nō, nŏt, nôr; fūse, fŭn, fûr; tōō, tŏŏk; foil; foul; thin; ~~then~~; hw for wh as in *what*; zh for s as in u*s*ual; ə for a, e, i, o, u, as in *a*go, lin*e*n, per*i*l, at*o*m, min*u*s

cash

cash (kăsh) **1** money in the form of coins or bills. **2** money paid at the time something is bought: *to pay* cash. **3** to exchange for money in coins or bills: *to* cash *a check.* (Homonym: cache)

cash·ew (kăsh′oō) **1** the kidney-shaped nut of a tropical evergreen. **2** the tree itself.

cash·ier (kă shir′) person in charge of. receiving and paying out money in a bank, business, etc.

cask (kăsk) **1** barrel-shaped wooden container for liquids; keg. **2** amount such a container holds: *a* cask *of vinegar.*

cask·et (kăs′kĭt) **1** a coffin. **2** small chest or box for holding jewels or other valuable things.

Cask

cas·sa·va (kə sä′və) **1** tropical plant with a starchy root from which tapioca is made. **2** starch obtained from this plant.

cas·se·role (kăs′ə rōl′) **1** deep, covered baking dish. **2** food, usually a mixture, baked and served in such a dish.

cast (kăst) **1** to throw; hurl: *to* cast *stones.* **2** a throw: *The fisherman made a* cast *of forty feet.* **3** to put off; shed: *A snake* casts *its skin.* **4** to send or turn in a certain direction: *to* cast *a glance; to* cast *a shadow.* **5** to shape by pouring (hot liquid metal, etc.) into a mold so that it will harden into a certain shape: *to* cast *a bronze statue.* **6** something formed by molding or being poured into a mold: *a plaster* cast *on the arm.* **7** appearance: *the sad* cast *of his countenance.* **8** to assign a part in a play: *Let us* cast *him as the hero.* **9** all the actors in a play. **10** a tinge or hue: *rosy* cast.

cast a ballot to vote.

cast about (for) to look about for; try to find: *He* cast about for *a solution to his problem.*

cast down to make sad or discouraged: *She was* cast down *after the scolding.*

cast off to leave shore (in a boat or ship): *We waited until high tide to* cast off.

cast, cast·ing. (Homonym: caste)

caste (kăst) **1** any fixed system of social divisions based on birth, wealth, and rank. **2** any of the hereditary social classes of the Hindus, among whom a person born into a certain caste cannot rise above it.

lose caste to lose one's standing or good name. (Homonym: cast)

catapult

cast iron hard, brittle iron shaped in a mold. Cast iron is not as strong as steel.

cas·tle (kăs′əl) **1** large building or group of buildings with high walls, towers, and often a moat as defense against attack. **2** large castlelike house.

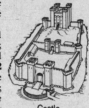

Castle

cas·u·al (kăzh′oō əl) **1** happening by chance; accidental: *a* casual *meeting on the street.* **2** without any definite purpose; not planned; offhand: *He gave the book a* casual *glance but did not study it.* **3** indifferent; vague: *a* casual *attitude in one's studies.* **cas·u·al·ly.**

cas·u·al·ty (kăzh′oō əl tĭ) **1** unfortunate accident, especially of a serious physical nature: *Traffic was tied up by the* casualty *at the crossroads.* **2** person killed, wounded, or lost in war, disaster, or accident: *the* casualties *in a battle.* **cas·u·al·ties.**

cat (kăt) **1** small fur-covered animal often kept as a household pet or to catch rats and mice. **2** any member of the cat family. Lions, tigers, leopards, pumas, etc. are cats. **3** let the

Siamese and Persian cats

cat out of the bag to give away a secret. **4** rain cats and dogs to rain very hard.

cat·a·logue or **cat·a·log** (kăt′ə lôg′ or kăt′ə lôg′) **1** a list of names, books, things, places, etc., usually arranged alphabetically. **2** to make an orderly list; enter in a list: *to* catalogue *books in a library.* **cat·a·logued** or **cat·a·loged, cat·a·logu·ing** or **cat·a·log·ing.**

ca·tal·pa (kə tăl′pə) a tree with large heart-shaped leaves, white flowers speckled with brown, and long, narrow seed pods.

Catapult

cat·a·pult (kăt′ə pŭlt′) **1** ancient military weapon somewhat like a crossbow, for shooting arrows, javelins, etc. **2** device for launching an airplane from the deck of a ship. **3** to hurl some-

thing from a catapult. **4** to rush headlong; hurtle: *He* catapulted *downstairs.*

cat·a·ract (kăt′ə răkt′)
1 large waterfall. **2** a
rush of water; rapids.
3 disease of the eye in
which the lens be-
comes cloudy, caus-
ing partial or total
blindness.

Cataract

ca·tarrh (kə tär′) inflammation of the
membranes of the nose and throat.

ca·tas·tro·phe (kə tăs′trə fĭ) a sudden ca-
lamity or widespread disaster, such as an
earthquake or a great fire.

cat·bird (kăt′bûrd′) American songbird,
slate-gray in color, that has a cry resembling
the mewing of a cat.

catch (kăch) **1** to get hold of; capture: *The
police will* catch *the thief.* **2** thing or things
caught: *The fisherman made a good* catch.
3 to stop the motion of and seize: *to* catch
a ball. **4** to reach in time: *I* caught *the bus
home and* caught *the plumber before he left.*
5 to deceive; fool: *He* caught *all of us on the
riddle.* **6** to be infected with; receive by
contact: *to* catch *a cold; to* catch *fire; to*
catch *the spirit of the crowd.* **7** to come upon
suddenly; discover: *I* caught *him trying to
sneak out of the room.* **8** to understand;
grasp: *I don't* catch *your meaning.* **9** to
become entangled: *The kite* caught *in the
tree.* **10** to take and keep hold: *The lock
finally* caught. **11** a fastening, hook, door
latch, etc. **12** something to trick, puzzle,
or trap: *a* catch *in a contract.*

catch sight or **a glimpse of** to see for a
moment.

catch up to stop being behind: *I have
neglected my work for so long that I'll
never* catch up.

catch up with to overtake.

caught, catch·ing.

catch·er (kăch′ər) **1** person or thing that
catches or seizes. **2** player on a baseball
team who stands behind the batter to catch
the ball thrown by the pitcher.

catch·ing (kăch′ĭng) carried from one person to another; contagious; infectious:
Measles is a catching *disease.*

cat·e·chism (kăt′ə kĭz′əm) **1** list of questions with answers for instruction in a
religion. **2** any similar list used in teaching.

ca·ter (kā′tər) **1** to supply and serve food:
to cater *for a party.* **2** to supply what is
wanted: *This town* caters *to tourists.*

cat·er·pil·lar (kăt′ər pĭl′ər) the
wormlike form that hatches
from the eggs of such insects
as the moth or butterfly; larva.
The caterpillar spins a cocoon
or chrysalis from which it
comes out as a fully developed
insect with wings.

cat·fish (kăt′fĭsh′) any one of
several kinds of fish, usually
without scales, having feelers
about the mouth that resemble
a cat's whiskers.

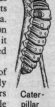

Cater-
pillar

cat·gut (kăt′gŭt′) a dried and twisted cord
made from intestines of sheep or other animals, used for strings
of tennis rackets, mu-
sical instruments, etc.

ca·the·dral (kə thē′-
drəl) **1** resident
church of a bishop,
and chief church of
a diocese. **2** any
large and important
church.

cath·o·lic (kăth′ə lĭk)
1 general; universal:
He has catholic *tastes
and reads all kinds
of books.* **2 Catholic** **(1)** belonging to the
original Christian church,
or a church that claims
to have inherited the au-
thority of the original Christian church. **(2)** member
of such a church. **3 Ro-
man Catholic (1)** belonging to the church of which
the Pope in Rome is the
head. **(2)** member of this
church.

Cathedral

Catkin of birch

cat·kin (kăt′kĭn) a slender, hanging cluster
of tiny, scalelike flowers as on birch or
willow trees.

---

fāte, făt, fâre, fär; bē, bĕt; bīte, bĭt; nō, nŏt, nôr; fūse, fŭn, fûr; tōō, tŏŏk; foil; foul; thin; ~~then~~;
hw for wh as in *wh*at; zh for s as in u*s*ual; ə for a, e, i, o, u, as in *a*go, lin*e*n, per*i*l, at*o*m, min*u*s

cat·nip (kăt′nĭp) a common plant of the mint family with fragrant leaves which cats like.

cat·sup (kăt′səp or kĕch′əp) ketchup.

cat·tail (kăt′tāl′) a swamp plant with a closely packed spike of tiny brown flowers at the end of a long stalk. The flower spike looks like a cat's furry tail.

cat·tle (kăt′əl) **1** cows, bulls, or oxen. **2** farm animals; livestock.

cat·tle·man (kăt′əl mən) man who raises or deals in cattle. **cat·tle·men.**

cat·walk (kăt′wôk′) narrow footpath on a bridge, airship, or other structure, or on a large machine.

caught (kôt) See **catch.** *I* caught *a fish.*

cau·li·flow·er (kô′lə flou′-ər) **1** a plant of the cabbage family with a white, solid head. **2** the head of this plant used as a vegetable.

Cauliflower

cause (kôz) **1** person or thing that makes something happen or brings about a result: *The sudden storm was the* cause *of the shipwreck.* **2** to make (something happen); bring about: *Speeding* causes *many accidents on the highway.* **3** a subject in which many people are interested and to which they give support: *We should all work for the* cause *of peace.* **caused, caus·ing.**

cause·way (kôz′wā′) a raised path or road over low or marshy ground.

cau·tion (kô′shən) **1** to warn (against danger, wrongdoing, etc.): *The boys were cautioned not to be late.* **2** a warning (against danger, wrongdoing, etc.): *I heeded his* caution *against driving in icy weather.* **3** care in avoiding danger: *You should use* caution *before crossing busy streets.*

cau·tious (kô′shəs) careful to avoid danger or trouble: *a* cautious *driver; a* cautious *suggestion.* **cau·tious·ly.**

cav·al·cade (kăv′əl kād′) procession of people riding horseback or in carriages.

cav·a·lier (kăv′ə lîr′) **1** horseman; knight. **2** a courteous, chivalrous man. **3** offhand; gay; free and easy: *the* cavalier *manner with which he treated my objection.* **cav·a·lier·ly.**

cav·al·ry (kăv′əl rĭ) soldiers who fight on horseback; mounted troops. **cav·al·ries.**

cave (kāv) a hollow space underground, especially one formed by nature.

cave in to fall in; collapse: *The street* caved in *when the water main broke.* **caved, cav·ing.**

cave-in (kāv′ĭn′) a falling in of the walls of a mine, tunnel, etc.; also, the site of this.

cave man 1 primitive man who lived in caves. **2** man who behaves in a rough or crude manner, especially towards women.

cav·ern (kăv′ərn) a large cave.

cav·ern·ous (kăv′ər nəs) **1** containing caves: *a* cavernous *mountain.* **2** hollow like a cave; large and empty: *his* cavernous *mouth.*

cav·i·ty (kăv′ə tĭ) hollow place; hole: *a* cavity *in a tooth.* **cav·i·ties.**

ca·vort (kə vôrt′) to prance or leap about: *The colts* cavorted *in the meadow.*

caw (kô) **1** the cry of a crow or raven. **2** to make this sound.

cease (sēs) to come to an end or bring to an end; stop: *The rain* ceased. *The boys* ceased *quarreling.* **ceased, ceas·ing.**

cease·less (sēs′lĭs) without end or pause: *the brook's* ceaseless *murmur.* **cease·less·ly.**

ce·dar (sē′dər) an evergreen tree of the pine family with durable and fragrant wood.

cede (sēd) to give up; surrender to another: *to cede land; to cede a point in an argument.* **ced·ed, ced·ing.** (Homonym: seed)

ceil·ing (sē′lĭng) **1** inner overhead covering of a room. **2** the greatest height an airplane can reach under certain conditions. **3** distance of the lowest clouds from the earth: *Because of fog there is a low* ceiling *today.*

cel·e·brate (sĕl′ə brāt′) **1** to observe (a special occasion) with ceremonies and festivals: *to celebrate the hero's return; to celebrate the Fourth of July.* **2** to perform (a religious ceremony): *to celebrate a Mass.* **3** to make merry: *Let's celebrate.* **cel·e·brat·ed, cel·e·brat·ing.**

cel·e·brat·ed (sĕl′ə brā′tĭd) famous; well-known: *Mark Twain is a* celebrated *author.*

cel·e·bra·tion (sĕl′ə brā′shən) the observing of a day or special occasion with ceremonies: *a birthday* celebration; *a Labor Day* celebration; *the* celebration *of a religious holiday.*

ce·leb·ri·ty (sə lĕb′rə tĭ) **1** famous or well-known person: *The author became a* celebrity *in his home town.* **2** fame. **ce·leb·ri·ties.**

ce·ler·i·ty (sə lĕr′ə tĭ) swiftness; speed.

cel·er·y (cĕl′ə rĭ) garden plant with crisp stalks that are good to eat either raw or cooked.

ce·les·ti·al (sə lĕs′chəl) **1** of or in the sky or heavens: *The stars are called* celestial *bodies.* **2** heavenly; divine: *Angels are* celestial *beings.* **ce·les·ti·al·ly.**

cell (sĕl) **1** small room in a prison, monastery, or convent. **2** smallest unit of living matter of which all animals and plants are made. **3** small, enclosed space: *a honeycomb* cell. **4** container holding chemical substances that act on each other to generate electric current: *an electric* cell. (Homonym: sell)

cel·lar (sĕl′ər) underground room or group of rooms, generally under a building and often used for storage. (Homonym: seller)

cel·list or **'cel·list** (chĕl′ĭst) person who plays the cello.

cel·lo or **'cel·lo** (chĕl′ō) a stringed musical instrument, larger and deeper in tone than the violin. It is rested upright on the floor and held between the player's knees. **cel·los.** Also called **violoncello.**

Man playing cello

cel·lo·phane (sĕl′ə fān′) a transparent material that keeps out moisture. It is used for wrapping food, and other things.

cel·lu·lose (sĕl′yŏŏ lōs′) the fibrous substance that forms the woody parts of trees and other plants. Cellulose is used in making paper, plastics, etc.

Cel·tic (sĕl′tĭk) group of languages spoken in parts of Britain, Ireland, and northwestern France.

ce·ment (sĭ mĕnt′) **1** substance made by burning clay and limestone. It is mixed with sand, gravel, and water to form a paste that becomes hard like stone. Cement is used in making walls, floors, sidewalks, etc. **2** anything that causes things to stick together. **3** to fasten with cement: *to cement linoleum to the floor.* **4** to cover or pave with cement.

cem·e·ter·y (sĕm′ə tĕr′ĭ) burial ground; graveyard. **cem·e·ter·ies.**

cen·ser (sĕn′sər) container in which incense is burned. (Homonym: censor)

cen·sor (sĕn′sər) **1** official who examines books, motion pictures, etc. to keep out anything that is thought wrong or undesirable. **2** official who in time of war, examines letters and printed matter to keep out anything that might help the enemy. **3** to examine books, plays, messages, etc., and remove parts that are thought to be wrong or undesirable. (Homonym: censer)

Censer

cen·sure (sĕn′shər) **1** disapproval; blame: *A man in public office often receives much* censure *from all sides.* **2** to find fault with; disapprove of: *to* censure *careless work.* **cen·sured, cen·sur·ing.**

cen·sus (sĕn′səs) an official count of the population, including information about age, sex, employment, etc.: *A* census *of the United States is made every ten years.*

cent (sĕnt) **1** the 100th part of a dollar. **2** coin of this value; penny: *Father will put three* cents *in the parking meter.* (Homonyms: scent, sent)

cen·taur (sĕn′tôr) in Greek myths, a creature that is half man and half horse.

cen·ten·ni·al (sĕn tĕn′ĭ əl) **1** relating to a period of 100 years: *a* centennial *celebration.* **2** the 100th anniversary of an event: *The year 1961 marked the* centennial *of the fall of Fort Sumter.*

Centaur

cen·ter (sĕn′tər) **1** middle point of a circle or sphere. **2** point about which something turns: *the* center *of a wheel.* **3** place where people gather for a particular purpose: *a shopping* center. **4** principal object: *She is the* center *of attention.* **5** the middle: *the* center *of the road.* **6** to place at the same distance from both sides: *We* centered *the picture over the sofa.* **7** to fix upon; focus: *The crowd's attention was* centered *on the fire engine.* Also spelled **centre.**

---

fāte, făt, fâre, fär; bē, bĕt; bīte, bĭt; nō, nŏt, nôr; fūse, fŭn, fûr; tōō, tŏŏk; foil; foul; thin; ~~then~~; hw for wh as in *wh*at; zh for s as in u*s*ual; ə for a, e, i, o, u, as in *a*go, lin*e*n, per*i*l, at*o*m, min*u*s

cen·ti·grade (sĕn′tə grād′) **1** having 100 equal degrees. **2 centigrade thermometer** thermometer on which 0 degrees is the freezing point of water and 100 degrees is the boiling point. For picture, see **thermometer.**

cen·ti·me·ter or **cen·ti·me·tre** (sĕn′tə mē′tər) a measure of length equal to the 100th part of a meter, or 0.3937 inch.

cen·ti·pede (sĕn′tə pēd′) a small wormlike animal with a long, flattened body made up of many sections. Each section has a pair of legs.

Centipede

cen·tral (sĕn′trəl) **1** in, at, or near the middle: *the central part of the city.* **2** main; leading: *the central idea of the book.* **3** telephone exchange. **4** telephone operator. **cen·tral·ly.**

Central America the countries between Mexico and South America.

cen·tral·i·za·tion (sĕn′trə lə zā′shən) a centralizing; a bringing to a central point or under one control, as in government.

cen·tral·ize (sĕn′trə līz′) to bring to the center; concentrate at a single point; bring into one system or under one control: *Considerable power has been centralized in Washington.* **cen·tral·ized, cen·tral·iz·ing.**

cen·tre (sĕn′tər) center.

cen·tu·ry (sĕn′chə rĭ) **1** a period of 100 years. **2** each group of 100 years before or after some fixed date, such as the birth of Christ. Most people living today were born in the 20th century A.D. **cen·tu·ries.**

ce·ram·ics (sə răm′ĭks) the art of making articles of baked clay.

ce·re·al (sîr′ĭ əl) **1** a grass that yields grain or seed used for food, such as barley, rice, oats, wheat, rye, etc. **2** any of these grains. **3** food made from grain. **4** having to do with grain or foods made from it. (Homonym: serial)

cer·e·mo·ni·al (sĕr′ə mō′nĭ əl) **1** formal; with ceremony: *a ceremonial dinner.* **2** system of rites or formalities observed on a particular occasion: *the ceremonial of a christening.* **3** used in a ceremony: *a ceremonial outfit.* **cer·e·mo·ni·al·ly.**

cer·e·mo·ni·ous (sĕr′ĭ mō′nĭ əs) **1** formally polite: *a ceremonious bow.* **2** with rites or formalities; formal: *a ceremonious reception.* **cer·e·mo·ni·ous·ly.**

cer·e·mo·ny (sĕr′ə mō′nĭ) **1** set, formal manner of conducting a religious or important public occasion: *the wedding* ceremony; *an inauguration* ceremony. **2** very polite behavior; formality: *She serves tea with a great deal of* ceremony. **3 stand on ceremony** to be very formal or polite. **cer·e·mo·nies.**

ce·rise (sə rēs′ or sə rēz′) a bright, light red color.

cer·tain (sûr′tən) **1** beyond question; sure: *It is* certain *that the sun sets each night.* **2** sure to happen: *to face* certain *death.* **3** definite but not named; some: *Our plan doesn't please* certain *persons.*

cer·tain·ly (sûr′tən lĭ) **1** definitely; without doubt: *They will* certainly *come.* **2** yes! of course!: Certainly, *you may come on the trip!*

cer·tain·ty (sûr′tən tĭ) **1** freedom from doubt; a being certain: *a feeling of* certainty. **2** something that is sure: *It is a* certainty *that the sun will rise tomorrow.* **cer·tain·ties.**

cer·tif·i·cate (sər tĭf′ə kĭt) written statement, signed by a public official or qualified person, that may be used as proof of something: *a birth* certificate; *a health* certificate; *a teacher's* certificate.

cer·ti·fied (sûr′tə fīd′) guaranteed to meet certain standards: *a bottle of* certified *milk.*

cer·ti·fy (sûr′tə fī′) to say something is true, usually in writing: *The doctor* certified *that the man had been absent from work because of illness.* **cer·ti·fied, cer·ti·fy·ing.**

ces·sa·tion (sĕ sā′shən) a pause; stop: *a cessation of warfare.*

chafe (chāf) **1** to warm by rubbing: *to chafe cold hands.* **2** to make sore by rubbing: *The collar* chafed *his neck.* **3** to annoy or be annoyed or irritated: *to chafe at the slightest delay.* **chafed, chaf·ing.**

¹chaff (chăf) **1** husks separated from the grain. **2** anything worthless; trash. [¹**chaff** is a form of an Old English word (ceaf).]

²chaff (chăf) **1** a joking; teasing: *She was good natured and didn't mind the* chaff *about her new haircut.* **2** to tease: *Boys like to* chaff *each other about girl friends.* [²**chaff** is of unknown origin.]

cha·grin (shə grĭn′) **1** feeling of annoyance because of failure, disappointment, or embarrassment. **2** to cause to feel chagrin: *He was* chagrined *when he lost the race.*

chain (chān) **1** number of links or rings joined together. **2** anything that binds or restrains. **3** series of connected things: *a chain of mountains; a chain of ideas; a chain of stores.* **4** to fasten with a chain: *to chain a dog to a fence.*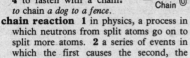

Chain

chain reaction 1 in physics, a process in which neutrons from split atoms go on to split more atoms. **2** a series of events in which the first causes the second, the second causes the third, and so on.

chain store one of a number of stores operated by the same company.

chair (châr) **1** seat for one person. A chair usually has four legs, a back, and may have arms. **2** an official position, especially of a professor: *the chair of history at the university.* **3** chairman: *Address your questions to the chair during the meeting.*

chair·man (châr′mən) person in charge of a meeting or a committee; presiding officer. **chair·men.**

chal·ice (chăl′ĭs) **1** cup or goblet. **2** cup to hold the wine used in the Communion service.

chalk (chôk) **1** soft limestone made mostly of tiny sea shells. **2** material like chalk, used to make white or colored crayons for writing or drawing on blackboards. **3** to mark, draw, or write with chalk: *to chalk a line on the sidewalk.* **4** made with chalk: *a chalk drawing.*
  chalk up 1 to score. **2** to record.

chalk·y (chôk′ĭ) of chalk; like chalk: *The medicine had a* chalky *taste.* **chalk·i·er, chalk·i·est.**

chal·lenge (chăl′ĭnj) **1** to refuse to accept without proof; dispute: *to* challenge *a hasty remark.* **2** a demand for proof or a statement of disagreement. **3** to invite to a contest: *I* challenge *anyone to race me.* **4** a call to prove one's courage, skill, etc. **5** to demand an identification card or a password from: *The sentry* challenged *him at the gate.* **6** a demand for identification. **chal·lenged, chal·leng·ing.**

chal·leng·er (chăl′ĭn jər) person who challenges, such as one who calls on another to fight, join in a contest, or take a dare.

cham·ber (chām′bər) **1** room in a house, especially a bedroom. **2** a meeting hall. **3** group of people organized to make laws: *The Congress has two* chambers, *the Senate and the House of Representatives.* **4** group of people organized for a business purpose: *the* Chamber *of Commerce.* **5** enclosed space: *The bullet is fired from the* chamber *in a gun.*

cham·ber·lain (chām′bər lĭn) person in charge of the household of a king or nobleman.

cha·me·le·on (kə mē′lĭ ən) lizard that can change the color of its skin.

Chameleon, 6 or 7 in. long

cham·ois (shăm′ĭ) **1** antelope, about the size of a goat, that lives in the mountains of Europe and Asia. **2** soft leather made from the hide of a chamois, sheep, or deer. It is used as a polishing cloth, and in gloves, coats, etc. pl. **cham·ois.**

champ (chămp) to bite noisily or impatiently: *The horse was* champing *at the bit.*

Chamois, 30 in. high at shoulder

cham·pi·on (chăm′pĭ ən) **1** person recognized as the best in a sport or competition: *a spelling* champion; *a boxing* champion. **2** holding first place in a sport or competition: *a* champion *swimmer; a* champion *pig; a* champion *photograph.* **3** person who speaks for another or fights for a cause; defender. **4** to defend; support: *The speaker* championed *the right of every man to choose his own job.*

cham·pi·on·ship (chăm′pĭ ən shĭp) **1** position of champion: *He tried for the diving championship.* **2** the defense of a person or cause.

chance (chăns) **1** luck; fate; fortune: *Your future should not be decided by* chance *but by choice.* **2** to happen: *It* chanced *that I was away the day you dropped by.* **3** opportunity: *Give me another* chance *to show*

---

fāte, făt, fâre, fär; bē, bĕt; bite, bĭt; nō, nŏt, nôr; fūse, fŭn, fûr; tōo, tŏŏk; foil; foul; thin; ~~then~~; hw for wh as in *w*hat; zh for s as in u*s*ual; ə for a, e, i, o, u, as in *a*go, lin*e*n, per*i*l, at*o*m, min*u*s

143

chancellor

I can work hard. **4** possibility: *There is not much* chance *of rain today.* **5** a risk: *Good drivers don't take* chances. **6** accidental; unforeseen: *It was a* chance *meeting.*

chance upon to come upon by chance: *I* chanced upon *the exact gift that I wanted.* **chanced, chanc·ing.**

chan·cel·lor (chăn′sə lər) title given to a high official in some governments, courts, or universities.

chan·de·lier (shăn′də lîr′) fixture that hangs from the ceiling, with branches for holding lights.

Chandelier

change (chānj) **1** to put or take one thing in place of another; to substitute: *to* change *one's coat or tie.* **2** to vary; to make different: *Leaves* change *their colors in the fall. The ring can be* changed *to fit your finger.* **3** to become different: *He has* changed *for the better.* **4** to exchange: *They* changed *places with each other.* **5** a becoming different: *a* change *of mind; a* change *of scene.* **6** a making different: *their* change *of tactics.* **7** the thing changed: *a* change *in the program.* **8** to give or get smaller units of money that equal a larger unit: *He* changed *the five dollar bill to five one-dollar bills.* **9** smaller units of money: *Five nickels are* change *for a quarter.* **10** coins: *His* change *jingled in his pocket.* **11** money equal to the difference between the cost and the amount paid: *He got 25¢* change *from a dollar bill after buying a 75¢ ticket.* **changed, chang·ing.**

change·a·ble (chān′jə bəl) likely to change; often changing; variable: *This* changeable *weather.* **change·a·bly.**

chan·nel (chăn′əl) **1** bed of a stream. **2** deepest part of a river, bay, etc. **3** narrow body of water separating two bodies of land: *The English* Channel. **4** long groove. **5** way by which anything passes and is carried: *a news* channel. **6** to direct through a channel: *to* channel *all the work through one office.* **7** range of wave frequencies used by a radio or television station.

chant (chănt) **1** to sing. **2** song, especially one in which several words or syllables are sung in the same tone. **3** to sing in this way. **4** psalm, prayer, etc. to be chanted. **5** to

character

talk or tell over and over again: *They* chanted *his praises.*

chan·ti·cleer (chăn′tə klîr′) rooster.

cha·os (kā′ŏs) great confusion; complete disorder: *the* chaos *after the hurricane.*

cha·ot·ic (kā ŏt′ĭk) highly confused; in great disorder: *After the hurricane, the city was left in a* chaotic *condition.*

¹chap (chăp) **1** to cause the skin to crack or become rough. **2** to become cracked or rough: *His lips* chap *easily.* **chapped, chap·ping.** [**¹chap** is a form of an earlier English word (chappen). It is related to **¹chop** and **chip.**]

²chap (chăp) a fellow; man or boy: *a* chap *who can be trusted.* [**²chap,** which once meant "one who buys," is a short form of an older English word (chapman) meaning "one who buys or sells."]

chap·el (chăp′əl) **1** a building for religious worship, usually not as large as a church. **2** place for religious worship in a building: *a school* chapel. **3** a religious service in such a place.

chap·er·on or **chap·er·one** (shăp′ə rōn′) **1** an older person, usually a woman, who supervises young people's social activities. **2** to act as a chaperon: *Parents* chaperoned *the dance.* **chap·er·oned, chap·er·on·ing.**

chap·lain (chăp′lĭn) clergyman who serves with the armed forces, or in a family chapel, school, hospital, prison, etc.

chaps (shăps or chăps) protective leg coverings, usually leather, worn by cowboys.

chap·ter (chăp′tər) **1** one of the parts into which a book is divided. **2** group that is a part of a larger organization: *a Red Cross* chapter.

char (chär) **1** to change wood into charcoal. **2** to burn slightly or partly. **charred, char·ring.**

Chaps

char·ac·ter (kăr′ĭk tər) **1** qualities that make a thing what it is; individuality; nature: *The* character *of the country changed as we flew south.* **2** moral strength or weakness: *A person's* character *is usually formed in childhood.* **3** person who is markedly different from others because he is odd or unusual. **4** person in a story, play, etc.: *The hero is the main* character *in a book.* **5** symbol used in a system of writing, such as a letter of the alphabet.

144

char·ac·ter·is·tic (kăr´ĭk tər ĭs´tĭk) **1** belonging to a person or thing as part of its nature; typical: *the* characteristic *smell of burning rubber.* **2** special mark or quality: *One* characteristic *of a greyhound is speed.*

char·ac·ter·ize (kăr´ĭk tə rīz´) **1** to describe a person in such a way as to classify him: *The author* characterizes *the hero as a generous man.* **2** to mark or distinguish: *Stubbornness* characterizes *the donkey.* **char·ac·ter·ized, char·ac·ter·iz·ing.**

char·coal (chär´kōl´) black substance made by the airless burning of wood. Charcoal is used as fuel and as drawing crayon.

charge (chärj) **1** to ask as a price or payment: *He* charged *a dime for the candy.* **2** a price; required payment: *The* charge *for parking is a quarter.* **3** to put off payment to a later date: *You may* charge *all your purchases here.* **4** an accusation: *a* charge *of murder.* **5** to accuse; blame: *The general* charged *the runaway with cowardice.* **6** safekeeping; care: *Her child is in my* charge *for the afternoon.* **7** person or thing entrusted to someone's care: *the nurse-maid's young* charges. **8** responsibility; duty: *The nurse has the* charge *of watching the children.* **9** instructions; order: *the judge's* charge *to the jury.* **10** to order; instruct: *The judge* charged *the jury to weigh all the evidence.* **11** a rushing attack: *The Indians made a* charge *on the fort.* **12** to make such an attack (on): *The cavalry* charged *the marching column.* **13** amount of explosive to be set off: *the* charge *in a gun.* **14** amount of electricity: *a* charge *of six volts.* **15** to fill or load: *to* charge *a gun; to* charge *a battery.* **16 in charge** in the position of responsibility: *Who is in* charge *here?* **17 in charge of** having the responsibility or control of: *Claude is in* charge *of the family business.* **charged, charg·ing.**

¹charg·er (chär´jər) **1** person or thing that charges. **2** horse ridden in war. [**¹charger** is formed from **charge.**]

²charg·er (chär´jər) a large platter: *meat served on a silver* charger. [**²charger** is from an Old French word (chargeoir) meaning "dish for carrying things."]

char·i·ot (chär´ĭ ət) vehicle with two wheels, drawn by horses, and used in ancient times for war, racing, etc.

Chariot

char·i·ta·ble (chär´ə- tə bəl) **1** generous in helping people who are in need. **2** providing for the poor: *a* charitable *institution.* **3** forgiving; kindly: *It was indeed* charitable *of you to overlook my mistakes.* **char·i·ta·bly.**

char·i·ty (chär´ə tĭ) **1** assistance given freely to people who are poor, sick, or otherwise in trouble. **2** an organization formed to give assistance to needy people. **3** brotherly love; good will: *with malice toward none, with* charity *for all.* **4** kindness and tolerance in judging people's faults. **char·i·ties.**

charm (chärm) **1** power to attract and please: *Paris has great* charm *for tourists.* **2** to please very much; delight; attract strongly: *Her friendly manner* charmed *the children.* **3** words or a song supposed to have magic power. **4** to act on by, or as if by magic: *Her smile* charmed *away his anger.* **5** anything, such as a piece of jewelry or carving, supposed to have magic power or bring good luck: *He carried a rabbit's foot as a* charm.

charm·ing (chär´mĭng) pleasing; delightful. **charm·ing·ly.**

chart (chärt) **1** a map for seamen, showing the outlines of coasts, depths of water, currents, etc. **2** information given in the form of diagrams, pictures, tables, etc. to show a change in some condition: *a weather* chart; *a fever* chart. **3** to make a chart of: *to* chart *a course.*

char·ter (chär´tər) **1** official paper giving certain rights and privileges: *William Penn was given a* charter *to form the colony of Pennsylvania.* **2** declaration giving the aims or principles of a group or organization: *the* charter *of the United Nations.* **3** to grant or give a charter to. **4** to hire or lease for private use: *to* charter *a bus.*

fāte, făt, fâre, fär; bē, bĕt; bīte, bĭt; nō, nŏt, nôr; fūse, fŭn, fûr; tōo, tŏŏk; foil; foul; thin; ~~then~~; hw for wh as in *wh*at; zh for s as in u*s*ual; ə for a, e, i, o, u, as in ago, linen, peril, atom, minus

145

chase

chase (chās) **1** to drive away: *The farmer chased the boys from his watermelon patch.* **2** to follow with the purpose of capturing or killing; to hunt. **3** a pursuit: *After a long chase, the fox escaped the hunters.* **chased, chas·ing.**

chasm (kăz′əm) a deep opening in the earth; gorge; gap.

chas·sis (chăs′ĭ or shăs′ĭ) the frame that supports the body of an automobile or airplane.

Chassis of an automobile

chaste (chāst) **1** morally pure; innocent. **2** simple in taste or style. **chaste·ly.**

chas·ten (chā′sən) **1** to punish for the purpose of correcting; to discipline. **2** to restrain; subdue: *to be chastened by experience.*

chas·tise (chăs′tīz′) to punish severely in order to correct. **chas·tised, chas·tis·ing.**

chat (chăt) **1** to talk in an easy, friendly way. **2** an informal talk. **chat·ted, chat·ting.**

cha·teau (shă·tō′) **1** French castle. **2** a large country house in France, or one built in imitation of such a house. **cha·teaux.**

chat·ter (chăt′ər) **1** to talk fast and foolishly; jabber. **2** foolish talk. **3** to make short, rapid sounds the way monkeys and some birds do. **4** the sounds made by monkeys and some birds. **5** to make a steady, rattling noise: *my teeth chattered from cold.*

chat·ty (chăt′ĭ) fond of chat; talkative. **chat·ti·er, chat·ti·est; chat·ti·ly.**

chauf·feur (shō′fər or shō fûr′) person whose work is to drive an automobile.

cheap (chēp) **1** low in price; not expensive. **2** not very good; of poor quality: *He wasted his time reading cheap novels.* **3** at a low cost: *to buy cheap and sell dear.* **4** charging low prices: *a cheap store.* **5** not worthy of respect; common: *their cheap behavior.* **cheap·ly.** (Homonym: cheep)

cheap·en (chē′pən) to make cheap; lower the price or value of.

cheat (chēt) **1** to act dishonestly; use trickery to gain an advantage: *to cheat on a test.* **2** person who acts dishonestly or gets his own way by tricking others.

check (chĕk) **1** to look over or test for accuracy: *Did you check your paper before you handed it in?* **2** a mark (✓) used to

cheer

show that something has been checked. **3** to put this mark on something. **4** a bill in a restaurant. **5** to keep back; curb; stop: *He started to speak, but then he checked himself.* **6** restraint: *a check on one's tongue.* **7** to leave for safekeeping: *to check a coat.* **8** ticket or metal disk to reclaim something that has been checked: *a check for coats and hats.* **9** pattern of squares of different colors: *a gingham check of red and blue.* **10** written order on a bank to pay money from the account of the signer of the order: *to write a check for $10.*

check in to register or sign in at a hotel, on the job, etc.

check off to make a mark, showing that something has been checked.

check out to pay one's bill and leave a hotel.

check·book (chĕk′bŏok′) blank checks bound together in a cover, issued to a depositor by a bank.

check·er·board (chĕk′-ər bôrd′) a board marked off into 64 squares of two alternating colors on which the games of chess and checkers are played.

Checkerboard

check·ered (chĕk′ərd) **1** varied: *a checkered career.* **2** marked with blocks of color: *a checkered pattern.*

check·ers (chĕk′ərz) game played by two people, each having 12 disks that are moved about on a checkerboard.

check·up or **check-up** (chĕk′ŭp′) **1** a careful examination: *Mother makes a daily checkup on the tidiness of the girls' rooms.* **2** physical examination.

cheek (chēk) **1** either side of the face below the eyes and above the level of the mouth. **2** impudence: *the cheek of the boys in contradicting the teacher.*

cheep (chēp) **1** a shrill faint noise, such as that of a baby bird or chick; a peep. **2** to make such a noise. (Homonym: cheap)

cheer (chîr) **1** a shout of joy, approval, or encouragement: *to give a cheer for our team.* **2** to shout to show enthusiasm, approval, joy, etc.; urge on: *The crowds cheered the winning runner.* **3** to comfort;

146

gladden; encourage: *The boy tried to* cheer
his sad friend. **4** encouragement; comfort:
Cards and letters were a cheer *to Genevieve
when she was in the hospital.* **5** good spirits;
gaiety and gladness: *Christmas* cheer.

cheer up to make or become hopeful or
glad.

cheer·ful (chir′fəl) **1** full of good spirits;
good-humored: *I'm glad to have a* cheerful
person with me on this trip. **2** bright and
pleasant; causing happiness: *a* cheerful
room. **cheer·ful·ly.**

cheer·lead·er (chēr′lē′dər) person who
leads the cheering.

cheer·less (chēr′lis) without cheer; gloomy:
a cold, cheerless *day.* **cheer·less·ly.**

cheer·y (chir′ĭ) **1** lively and merry; gay and
bright: *a* cheery *smile.* **2** causing cheer: *a
room painted in* cheery *colors.* **cheer·i·er,
cheer·i·est; cheer·i·ly.**

cheese (chēz) solid food made from curds
of milk.

chef (shĕf) **1** a head cook: *Jules was the* chef
of the hotel. **2** any cook: *Her husband is a
very good* chef.

chem·i·cal (kĕm′ə kəl) **1** having to do with
chemistry: *a* chemical *laboratory; a* chemical *experiment.* **2** substance made by or
used in chemistry: *Alcohol, soda, and salt
are common* chemicals. **chem·i·cal·ly.**

chem·ist (kĕm′ĭst) **1** person trained in
chemistry and engaged in it as a profession.
2 druggist.

chem·is·try (kĕm′ĭs trĭ) the scientific study
of the elements, how they combine to form
compounds, and how elements and compounds act under various conditions.

cher·ish (chĕr′ĭsh) **1** to love; care for tenderly: *A mother* cherishes *her children.* **2** to
hold dear; keep in mind; treasure: *Grandmother* cherished *her childhood memories.*

Cher·o·kee rose (chĕr′ə kē′ rōz) a white
rose of southern United States, coming
originally from China. The Cherokee rose
is the State flower of Georgia.

cher·ry (chĕr′ĭ) **1** small, red, purple, or
yellow fruit with a stone in the center.
2 tree this fruit grows on. **3** wood of this
tree. **4** of the color of ripe red cherries.
cher·ries.

cher·ub (chĕr′əb) **1** an angel, shown in pictures as a beautiful child with wings. **2** a
beautiful child.

chess (chĕs) a game played by two persons,
each having 16 pieces which are called
chessmen. The
pieces are moved
about on a **chess-
board** of 64 squares.

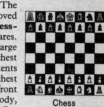

chest (chĕst) **1** large
box with a lid: *a chest
for linen.* **2** contents
of such a box: *a chest
of tea.* **3** upper front
part of a human body,
enclosed by the ribs,

Chess

containing the heart and lungs. **4** a fund
for a chosen purpose: *a community* chest.

chest·nut (chĕs′nŭt′)
1 an edible nut which
grows inside a prickly
bur. **2** the tree on
which this nut grows.
3 the wood of this
tree. **4** reddish-brown.
5 an old joke or story.

Chestnut bur and nuts

chew (choo) **1** to crush and grind with the
teeth: *It is hard to* chew *tough meat.*
2 piece of something to be chewed.

chewing gum flavored and sweetened gum
for chewing.

chick (chĭk) **1** baby chicken. **2** baby bird.
3 young child.

chick·a·dee (chĭk′ə dē′) a small bird with
black, white, and gray coloring.

chick·en (chĭk′ən) **1** hen or rooster, especially a young one. **2** any young bird.
3 the flesh of hen or rooster, used as food:
a chicken *for dinner.*

chick·en·coop (chĭk′ən koop′) a cage or
pen in which chickens are kept.

chick·en·heart·ed (chĭk′ən här′tĭd) cowardly; fearful.

chicken pox (chĭk′ən pŏks) mild contagious disease, causing red spots on the skin.

chic·le (chĭk′əl) a gum obtained from certain Central American trees, used in
making chewing gum.

chid (chĭd) See **chide.**

chid·den (chĭd′ən) See **chide.**

---

fāte, făt, fâre, fär; bē, bĕt; bīte, bĭt; nō, nŏt, nôr; fūse, fŭn, fûr; tōo, tŏŏk; foil; foul; thin; ~~then~~;
hw for wh as in *wh*at; zh for s as in u*s*ual; ə for a, e, i, o, u, as in *a*go, lin*e*n, per*i*l, at*o*m, min*u*s

chide

chide (chīd) to scold; rebuke: *The teacher chided him for being tardy.* **chid·ed** or **chid, chid·ed** or **chid** or **chid·den, chid·ing.**

chief (chēf) **1** head or leader of a tribe or other group of people: *an Indian* chief. **2** most important; principal; leading: *the* chief *crop grown in a state.*

chief·ly (chēf'lĭ) principally; for the most part: *Candy is made* chiefly *of sugar.*

chief·tain (chēf'tən) leader of a tribe, clan, etc.; chief: *a robber* chieftain.

chig·ger (chĭg'ər) wormlike young of the mite, which burrows under the skin, causing intense itching. For picture, see **mite.**

child (chīld) **1** baby. **2** young boy or girl. **3** son or daughter. **4 child's play** something very easy. **children.**

child·hood (chīld'hŏŏd') the time when a person is a child.

child·ish (chīl'dĭsh) **1** of or like a child: *a* childish *way of talking.* **2** not grown-up: *It is* childish *to want your own way all the time.* **child·ish·ly.**

chil·dren (chĭl'drən) more than one child.

Chi·le (chĭl'ī) a country on the Pacific coast of South America. (Homonyms: chili, chilly)

chil·i (chĭl'ī) **1** the pod of a kind of red pepper. When ripe, it is dried and powdered to make a seasoning. **2** a highly spiced dish of meat and beans seasoned with chili. **chil·ies.** (Homonyms: Chile, chilly)

chill (chĭl) **1** coldness: *an autumn* chill *in the air.* **2** sudden cold feeling in the body, accompanied by shivering. **3** very cool: *In the evening, a* chill *breeze blew across the lake.* **4** to make cold: *Please* chill *the fruit juice.* **5** to become or feel cold: *Do you* chill *easily?* **6** not warm or friendly; discouraging: *He got a* chill *answer to his offer to pay a visit.*

chill·y (chĭl'ī) **1** very cool; rather cold: *a* chilly *day.* **2** without warmth; unfriendly: *a* chilly *welcome.* **chill·i·er, chill·i·est; chill·i·ly.** (Homonyms: Chile, chili)

chime (chīm) **1** a set of bells or other apparatus tuned to sound musically when struck. **2** the sound of these bells. **3** to make a musical sound by striking such bells. **4** to ring: *The bells* chimed *at noon.* **chime in** to join in (a conversation). **chimed, chim·ing.**

chip

chim·ney (chĭm'nĭ) **1** an outlet for smoke from a fireplace, furnace, etc., especially one on the roof of a house. **2** the glass tube shielding the flame of a lamp or lantern.

chimney sweep person whose work is to clean chimneys.

chim·pan·zee (chĭm-'păn'zē or chĭm'păn-zē') a dark brown, highly intelligent ape of Africa that lives in trees and on the ground. It is easily trained.

Chimpanzee, 4½ to 5 ft. tall

chin (chĭn) **1** the part of the face under the lower lip. **2** to pull oneself up by the hands on a horizontal bar until the chin is on a level with it. **chinned, chin·ning.**

chi·na (chī'nə) **1** fine porcelain with a white background, made of clay baked in a special way, originally produced in China. **2** made of porcelain. **3** plates, cups, saucers, vases, and other things made of this material.

Chi·na (chī'nə) a large country in eastern Asia.

Chi·nese (chī nēz') **1** of China, its people, or its language. **2** citizen of China or person of Chinese descent. **3** language of the Chinese people. pl. **Chi·nese.**

¹chink (chĭngk) **1** a narrow crack or opening. **2** to fill the cracks of: *The walls of the log cabin were* chinked *with earth.* [¹chink is perhaps a form of an Old English word (cinu) also meaning "crack."]

²chink (chĭngk) ringing or tinkling sound like that made by small pieces of metal or glass striking together. [²chink is a word imitating a sound.]

chi·nook (chĭ nŏŏk') **1** warm, moist sea wind blowing onto the coasts of Oregon and Washington. **2** warm dry wind blowing down the eastern slopes of the Rocky Mountains.

chip (chĭp) **1** small bit or piece cut or broken off wood, stone, or china. **2** gap left when a small piece is broken from something. **3** to cut or break small bits or pieces from: *to* chip *ice.* **4** to become chipped: *The dish* chipped *when I dropped it.* **chipped, chip·ping.**

chip·munk (chĭp′mŭngk′) a small, striped, burrowing American squirrel.

chirp (chûrp) **1** short, sharp sound made by birds and insects. **2** to make such a sound: *Crickets* chirp.

chis·el (chĭz′əl) **1** a tool with a steel edge for cutting and shaping wood, stone, or metal. **2** to cut or shape with such a tool: *to chisel out a keyhole.*

Chipmunk, about 10 in. long

chiv·al·rous (shĭv′əl rəs) brave, courteous, honorable, kind, etc., as knights were supposed to be. **chiv·al·rous·ly.**

Wood chisel

Stone chisel

chiv·al·ry (shĭv′əl rĭ) **1** the ideal qualities of a knight, such as courage, honor, and courtesy. **2** the system of knighthood.

chlo·rin·ate (klôr′ə nāt′) to add chlorine to, especially to water to make it safe to drink or bathe in: *The city* chlorinates *the water in the pool.* **chlo·rin·ated, chlo·rin·at·ing.**

chlo·rine (klô′rēn′) a chemical element. It is a strong-smelling, greenish-yellow gas at ordinary temperatures.

chlo·ro·form (klôr′ə fôrm′) **1** colorless liquid that evaporates quickly at room temperature and has a sweetish odor. It is sometimes used in medicine to produce unconsciousness. **2** to make unconscious by giving chloroform.

chlo·ro·phyll or **chlo·ro·phyl** (klôr′ə fĭl) the green coloring matter of plants.

choc·o·late (chŏk′ə lĭt or chôk′ə lĭt) **1** food substance made by roasting and grinding cacao beans. **2** piece of candy made from this substance. **3** drink made of chocolate, and hot milk or water. **4** made or flavored with chocolate. **5** of the color of chocolate.

choice (chois) **1** a choosing; selection: *I will leave the choice of a movie to you.* **2** power to choose: *We had a choice between the mountains and the seashore for our vacation.* **3** the thing or person chosen: *My choice in flavors is peppermint.* **4** large selection from which to choose: *There is a choice of*

colors among these hats. **5** of fine quality: *It is hard to find choice tomatoes at this season.* **6** carefully chosen; appropriate: *a* choice *remark.* **choic·er, choic·est.**

choir (kwīr) **1** a group of trained singers, usually in a church. **2** the part of a church in which the choir sings.

choke (chōk) **1** to stop the breath by squeezing or blocking the windpipe; stifle: *The smoke* choked *the firemen.* **2** to be unable to breathe: *The boy* choked *after taking a big swallow of water.* **3** to block up; clog: *Mud and leaves* choked *the drain.* **4** to stop the growth of: *Weeds* choked *the flowers.* **5** act or sound of choking. **6** valve in an automobile, etc., to regulate the air intake.

choke back to hold back; suppress: *He* choked back *his anger.*

choked, chok·ing.

chol·er·a (kŏl′ər ə) **1** disease of the stomach and intestines, marked by severe pains and vomiting. It is not contagious. **2** dangerous contagious disease of the stomach and intestines. It is found mostly in the tropics.

choose (chōōz) **1** to select from a number; pick out: *to choose a special kind of candy.* **2** to prefer; see fit: *He* chooses *not to answer.* **chose, chos·en, choos·ing.**

¹**chop** (chŏp) **1** to cut by blows with an ax or similar tool: *to chop down a tree.* **2** to cut into small pieces: *to chop vegetables.* **3** short, cutting blow: *the chop of the woodman's ax.* **4** small cut of meat containing a rib or section of bone. **5** short, rough movement of waves. **chopped, chop·ping.** [¹**chop** is a form of an earlier English word (choppen) with the same meaning.]

²**chop** (chŏp) **1** jaw. **2 chops** jaw or fleshy parts about the mouth: *The dog licked his chops when he smelled the meat.* [²**chop** is a form of another English word (chap) meaning "jaw of an animal".]

Chopsticks in use

chop·sticks (chŏp′stĭks) two small sticks of wood or ivory used by the Chinese and Japanese to carry food to the mouth.

fāte, făt, fâre, fär; bē, bĕt; bīte, bĭt; nō, nŏt, nôr; fūse, fŭn, fûr; tōō, tŏŏk; foil; foul; thin; ~~then~~; hw for wh as in *wh*at; zh for s as in u*s*ual; ə for a, e, i, o, u, as in *a*go, lin*e*n, per*i*l, at*o*m, min*u*s

¹chord (kôrd) a straight line joining any two points on a circle or an arc. [¹**chord** comes from a Latin word (chorda) meaning "string," which in turn is from a Greek word (chordē) meaning "gut" or "string of a musical instrument." This word is related to **cord.**] (Homonym: cord)

²chord (kôrd) three or more musical notes sounded together in harmony. [²**chord** is actually a form of **accord,** but influenced in the spelling by ¹**chord.**] (Homonym: cord)

chore (chôr) odd job; task: *I have a few chores to do.*

cho·rus (kôr′əs) **1** group of people singing together. **2** piece of music arranged for a number of voices. **3** part of a song that is sung again at the end of each verse. **4** to sing or say something together. **5** something said or called out by a number of people at one time: *There was a chorus of "ayes" when the chairman called for a vote.* **6 in chorus** all together.

chose (chōz) See **choose.** *She chose the brown puppy.*

cho·sen (chō′zən) See **choose.** *He was chosen to be leader.*

chow (chou) a medium-sized dog of a breed originating in China. It has a black tongue, thick black or red-brown coat, and a short tail that curves over the back.

chow·der (chou′dər) thick soup made of clams or fish and vegetables.

Christ (krīst) a title given to Jesus, meaning "the Anointed."

christ·en (krīs′ən) **1** to baptize; give a name to at baptism: *The baby was christened "John."* **2** to give a name to: *They christened the first atomic submarine, "Nautilus."*

Chris·ten·dom (krīs′ən dəm) all Christian people and countries.

chris·ten·ing (krīs′ən ĭng) ceremony at which a baby is christened.

Chris·tian (krīs′chən) **1** person who believes in the teachings of Jesus Christ. **2** believing in or belonging to the religion of Christ: *all Christian nations.* **3** having to do with Christ or the religion that bears His name. **4** showing the qualities taught by Christ, such as gentleness, patience, generosity, and humility: *to forgive one's enemies in a Christian spirit.*

Chris·ti·an·i·ty (krĭs′chĭ ăn′ə tĭ) the Christian religion.

Christ·mas (krĭs′məs) the yearly celebration, on December 25, of the birth of Christ.

chrom·i·um (krō′mĭ əm) a very hard silver-colored metal element used for plating other metals and in alloys.

chro·mo·some (krō′mə sōm′) very tiny threadlike body in the germ cells of animals or plants. Chromosomes contain the genes that determine what qualities are passed from one generation to another.

chron·ic (krŏn′ĭk) **1** lasting over a long period of time: *He has a chronic cough.* **2** habitual: *She is a chronic complainer.*

chron·i·cle (krŏn′ə kəl) **1** record of events in the order in which they happened; a history: *a chronicle of the early kings of England.* **2** to record. **3 Chronicles** the thirteenth and fourteenth books of the Old Testament. **chron·i·cled, chron·i·cling.**

chrys·a·lis (krĭs′ə lĭs) **1** the resting stage (pupa) of a butterfly between the larva and the adult insect. When the insect comes out of the chrysalis stage, it is a fully grown butterfly with wings. **2** hard shell of a pupa.

Butterfly chrysalis

chry·san·the·mum (krĭ săn′thə məm) **1** a plant with showy flowers that blooms late in the fall. **2** the flower of this plant.

chub·by (chŭb′ĭ) plump; round: *a chubby face.* **chub·bi·er, chub·bi·est.**

chuck (chŭk) **1** light stroke; tap: *a chuck under the chin.* **2** to stroke or tap: *to chuck a baby under the chin.* **3** to toss; throw: *He chucked the letter into the wastebasket.*

Chrysanthemums

chuck·le (chŭk′əl) **1** to laugh quietly, expressing satisfaction: *He chuckled when he looked at the funny cartoon.* **2** low, quiet laugh. **chuck·led, chuck·ling.**

chum (chŭm) close friend; pal. **chum with** or **together** to be very intimate with. **chummed, chum·ming.**

chunk (chŭngk) short, thick, solid piece: *a chunk of bread; a chunk of wood.*

chunk·y (chŭng′kĭ) **1** stocky; solidly and compactly built: *a chunky lad.* **2** in a chunk or chunks; thick: *meat cut in* chunky *pieces.* **chunk·i·er, chunk·i·est.**

church (chûrch) **1** building for public worship, especially one for Christian worship. **2** religious service: *to go to* church. **3** organized group of people with the same religious beliefs. **4** having to do with a church: *Do you like* church *music?* **5 the Church** (1) all Christians. (2) the clergy as a profession: *to enter* the Church.

church·man (chûrch′mən) **1** minister; priest. **2** man who is a member of a church. **church·men.**

church·yard (chûrch′yärd′) ground around a church. Sometimes part of the churchyard is used as a graveyard.

churl (chûrl) rude person; a boor.

churn (chûrn) **1** vessel or machine in which cream is shaken or beaten to make butter. **2** to shake or stir in a churn. **3** to shake or stir violently: *The injured whale* churned *the water.*

chute (shōōt) **1** slanting slide or shaft: *a coal* chute; *a laundry* chute; *a letter* chute. **3** waterfall or rapid in a river. **4** parachute. **5** toboggan slide. (Homonym: shoot)

ci·ca·da (sĭ kā′də) large insect with transparent wings; locust. The male cicada makes a shrill sound.

ci·der (sī′dər) apple juice, whether fermented or unfermented.

ci·gar (sĭ gär′) roll of tobacco leaves for smoking.

cig·a·rette (sĭg′ə rĕt′) shredded tobacco rolled in a thin paper for smoking.

cinch (sĭnch) **1** strap for holding a saddle or a pack on a horse; girth. **2** to tighten with a girth; tie firmly. For picture see next column.

cin·der (sĭn′dər) **1** small piece of partly burned coal or wood that is not yet ash. **2** a piece of ash.

Churn

Cicada, 1¼ in. long

cin·e·ma (sĭn′ə mə) **1** motion picture. **2** motion-picture theater.

cin·na·mon (sĭn′ə mən) **1** spice that comes from the inner bark of a cinnamon tree. **2** the tree itself. **3** spiced with cinnamon: *a bag of* cinnamon *buns.* **4** the color of cinnamon; reddish brown.

ci·pher (sī′fər) **1** in mathematics, zero; naught. **2** person or thing of no importance. **3** a code; secret writing: *A map in* cipher *showed where the treasure was buried.* **4** written key explaining a code. **5** to write in code. **6** to do arithmetic; to work with figures.

cir·cle (sûr′kəl) **1** a closed curve, every point of which is the same distance from the center. A line drawn around the edge of a coin is a circle. **2** the space enclosed by such a line. The whole face of a coin is a circle. **3** complete series; cycle: *A year is made up of a* circle *of twelve months.* **4** a ring: *The children made a* circle *for their May Day folk dance.* **5** group of people held together by common interests: *a* circle *of friends; family* circle. **6** to move in a circle around: *The airplane* circled *the landing field.* **7** to surround: *Guards* circled *the prison.* **8** to draw a circle around: *Please* circle *the right answers.* **cir·cled, cir·cling.**

Circle and circumference

cir·cuit (sûr′kĭt) **1** a going around; revolution: *Every year the earth completes its* circuit *of the sun.* **2** route regularly traveled by a judge who holds court in different towns, or by a preacher who serves a number of widely scattered churches. **3** boundary line around an area. **4** distance around any space or area; circumference. **5** complete path of an electric current.

Cinch on a saddle

cir·cu·i·tous (sər kū′ə təs) roundabout; not direct: *We took a* circuitous *route to town to avoid the flood waters.* **cir·cu·i·tous·ly.**

fāte, făt, fâre, fär; bē, bĕt; bīte, bĭt; nō, nŏt, nôr; fūse, fŭn, fûr; tōō, tōŏk; foil; foul; thin; then;
hw for wh as in *wh*at; zh for s as in u*s*ual; ə for a, e, i, o, u, as in *a*go, lin*e*n, per*i*l, at*o*m, min*u*s

151

cir·cu·lar (sûr′kyŏŏ lər) **1** round: *a circular table.* **2** moving in a circle; revolving: *The turning of a phonograph record is a circular motion.* **3** printed letter or notice for circulation among the public: *a circular advertising the country fair.* **cir·cu·lar·ly.**

cir·cu·late (sûr′kyŏŏ lāt′) **1** to travel over a course and back to the starting place: *Hot water* circulates *in a heating system. Blood* circulates *in the body.* **2** to go or send from place to place or person to person: *Money* circulates. *The post cards were* circulated *around the classroom.* **cir·cu·lat·ed, cir·cu·lat·ing.**

cir·cu·la·tion (sûr′kyŏŏ lā′shən) **1** passage of anything from place to place, person to person, etc.: *the* circulation *of news.* **2** a moving in a circle or in a course that leads back to the starting place: *the* circulation *of the blood.* **3** the number of copies distributed of each issue of a magazine or newspaper: *a magazine of large* circulation.

cir·cu·la·to·ry (sûr′kyŏŏ lə tôr′ĭ) having to do with circulation or a round trip over a continuous path: *The arteries and veins form the* circulatory *system of the body.*

cir·cum·fer·ence (sər kŭm′fər əns) **1** the line that bounds a circle. **2** the distance around a circle. For picture, see **circle.**

cir·cum·nav·i·gate (sûr′kəm năv′ə gāt′) to sail completely around, especially around the earth. **cir·cum·nav·i·gat·ed, cir·cum·nav·i·gat·ing.**

cir·cum·stance (sûr′kəm stăns′) **1** fact or detail in a group or sequence of events: *the happy* circumstance *of his arrival.* **2** **circumstances** **(1)** facts or events surrounding and influencing an action or event: *to know all the* circumstances. **(2)** financial condition: *poor* circumstances.

cir·cum·vent (sûr′kəm vĕnt′) to block or hinder by better strategy; outwit: *The colonel* circumvented *the plan of the enemy to blow up the bridge.*

cir·cus (sûr′kəs) **1** a traveling show of performers, horses, wild animals, etc. **2** the performance by such a company. **3** a large level space surrounded by seats, in tiers, usually within a tent, for putting on shows of acrobatics, wild animals, etc. **4** having to do with a circus.

cis·tern (sĭs′tərn) tank or man-made reservoir for storing water, often underground.

cit·a·del (sĭt′ə dəl) **1** fortress above a city. **2** any last stronghold.

ci·ta·tion (sī tā′shən) **1** direct reference or quotation: *A* citation *from Scripture is usual in sermons.* **2** honorable mention of a soldier or military unit for bravery.

cite (sīt) **1** to quote: *He* cited *a page in the science book to prove his point.* **2** to mention for praise or as an example. **cit·ed, cit·ing.** (Homonyms: sight, site)

cit·i·zen (sĭt′ə zən) **1** member of a nation, having political rights in it and owing loyalty to it. One may be born a citizen, or citizenship may be granted by a country. **2** a resident of a town or city.

cit·i·zen·ry (sĭt′ə zən rĭ) all the citizens of a particular place.

cit·i·zen·ship (sĭt′ə zən ship′) possession of the rights and duties of a citizen.

cit·ric ac·id (sĭt′rĭk as′ĭd) acid found in oranges, lemons, limes, and similar fruit

cit·ron (sĭt′rən) **1** fruit which looks like a lemon but is larger and not so acid. **2** thick rind of this fruit, cooked in sugar and used in pudding and fruit cakes.

cit·rus fruit (sĭt′rəs frŏŏt) a lemon, lime, orange, grapefruit, or citron.

cit·y (sĭt′ĭ) **1** large or important town. **2** the whole population of a city: *All the* city *turned out to see the parade.* **3** great city a city which, with its suburbs, has more than a million inhabitants. **cit·ies.**

civ·ic (sĭv′ĭk) having to do with a city, citizens, or citizenship: *We feel* civic *pride in the new museum.*

civ·ics (sĭv′ĭks) the study or science of community government and of the rights and duties of a citizen.

civ·il (sĭv′əl) **1** having to do with citizens: *our* civil *rights.* **2** not connected with the church or military: *a civil marriage; to return to* civil *life.* **3** in law, having to do with private, not public rights: *a civil, not a criminal case.* **4** courteous; polite: *to show* civil *behavior in company.*

ci·vil·ian (sĭ vĭl′yən) any person not a member of the armed services: *The mayor was the only* civilian *in the military parade.*

ci·vil·i·ty (sĭ vĭl′ə tĭ) politeness; courtesy. **ci·vil·i·ties.**

civ·i·li·za·tion (sĭv′ə lə zā′shən) **1** way of life far advanced beyond a savage level in government, manners, arts, sciences, etc.;

state of being civilized. **2** the culture of a particular race, country, etc.: *Our museums displayed works of art from many* civilizations. **3** act of civilizing: *The civilization of man has been a long, hard struggle.* **4** all civilized countries and people: *All* civilization *is shocked when a country employs slave labor.*

civ·i·lize (sĭv′ə līz′) to bring out of a primitive way of life; educate in the arts, sciences, government, etc. **civ·i·lized, civ·i·liz·ing.**

civil service government work or service outside of the armed forces, and not connected with courts or legislatures. The post office is a branch of the civil service. States and cities also have civil service.

civil war a war between different areas or groups of the same nation.

Civil War the war that took place in the United States between the Northern and Southern States from 1861 to 1865; War Between the States.

clack (klăk) **1** a sudden, sharp sound: *the* clack *of typewriter keys.* **2** to make this sound.

clad (klăd) See **clothe.** *She was* clad *in blue from head to toe.*

claim (klām) **1** to demand or ask for as one's own or as one's due: *She* claimed *her purse at the lost-and-found desk.* **2** a demand for something as a right or because it is due: *a* claim *for damages.* **3** to call for; require; deserve: *Important matters* claimed *his attention.* **4** to assert as a fact; maintain: *The customer* claimed *that he had already paid.* **5** the asserting of something as a fact: *the* claims *of a company about its product.* **6** piece of land to which someone has filed the rights: *a mining* claim. **7 have a claim on** to have a right to demand something from. **8 lay claim** to assert one's right to obtain. **9 put in a claim** to try to establish a right to obtain.

clair·voy·ance (klâr voi′əns) **1** power, claimed by some people, of knowing about things that are not actually present to the senses: *Through a kind of* clairvoyance *she knew of the accident before she heard the news.* **2** unusual insight.

clam (klăm) **1** shellfish with a hinged double shell, living partly or wholly buried in sand or mud, and used as food. **2** to gather or dig for clams. **clammed, clam·ming.**

clam·bake (klăm′bāk′) a shore picnic at which clams, lobsters, corn, etc. are cooked on hot stones covered with seaweed.

Clam

clam·ber (klăm′bər) to climb using both hands and feet; climb with difficulty: *The boy scouts* clambered *up a rocky slope.*

clam·my (klăm′ĭ) cold and damp: *a* clammy *hand.* **clam·mi·er, clam·mi·est.**

clam·or (klăm′ər) **1** loud and continued outcry or demand; uproar. **2** to make a loud and continued demand; raise an uproar: *They* clamored *for an encore.*

clam·or·ous (klăm′ər əs) loud and noisy: *the* clamorous *applause.*

clamp (klămp) **1** a brace, band, clasp, or other device for holding things tightly together. **2** to put in a clamp; fasten with a clamp; strengthen with clamps.

Clamp

clan (klăn) **1** group of families, especially in the Scottish Highlands, united under one leader and claiming descent from a common ancestor: *Each Scottish* clan *has its own tartan.* **2** any group of people united by a common interest.

clang (klăng) **1** loud, harsh, ringing sound like metal being struck. **2** to make a loud, harsh, ringing sound.

clank (klăngk) **1** a sound like that of heavy chains rattling together. **2** to make or cause to make this sound.

clap (klăp) **1** to strike the hands together in applause, to gain attention, etc.: *The audience* clapped *with enthusiasm. The teacher* clapped *for attention.* **2** to strike or slap, usually in a friendly way: *to* clap *one on the back.* **3** a slap. **4** a short, sharp, loud sound: *a* clap *of thunder.* **clap eyes on** to catch sight of. **clapped, clap·ping.**

Clapper

clap·per (klăp′ər) tongue of a bell.

---

fāte, făt, fâre, fär; bē, bĕt; bīte, bĭt; nō, nŏt, nôr; fūse, fŭn, fûr; tōō, tŏŏk; foil; foul; thin; then; hw for wh as in *wh*at; zh for s as in u*s*ual; ə for a, e, i, o, u, as in ag*o*, lin*e*n, per*i*l, at*o*m, min*u*s

153

clar·i·fy (klăr′ə fī′) to make clear: *Roger clarified his statement by an explanation. Elda clarified the bacon fat by straining it.* **clar·i·fied, clar·i·fy·ing.**

clar·i·net (klăr′ə nĕt′) musical wind instrument shaped like a straight tube.

clar·i·on (klăr′ĭ ən) **1** clear; loud: *The clarion call of the bugle awoke us.* **2** a kind of small trumpet.

Clarinet

clar·i·ty (klăr′ə tĭ) clearness: *his clarity of speech; the clarity of water in a stream.*

clash (klăsh) **1** to make a loud, harsh noise by striking together: *The cymbals clashed.* **2** loud noise made by striking together: *a clash of swords.* **3** to be opposed; come into conflict: *to clash in a debate.* **4** sharp disagreement: *a clash of opinions.*

clasp (klăsp) **1** fastening device that grips or closes to hold two parts or things together: *a bracelet clasp; a tie clasp.* **2** to fasten with a clasp: *Will you please clasp these pearls for me?* **3** a firm hold; a grasp; an embrace. **4** to hold close in the arms: *The mother clasped her infant to her breast.* **5** to grasp firmly: *He clasped his friend's hand.*

Tie clasp

class (klăs) **1** group of students taught by the same teacher. **2** the meeting of such a group: *History class starts at nine.* **3** group of students in the same year at school or graduating together. **4** persons grouped according to profession, social position, wealth, etc.: *the middle class of society.* **5** large group of plants or animals that are alike in certain ways: *Birds and reptiles are two classes of animals with backbones.* **6** kind; sort: *That store carries a good class of products.* **7** to group or place together persons or things in a certain way; classify: *Do you class a bat as a bird?* **8 in a class by itself** unique; outstanding.

clas·sic (klăs′ĭk) **1** a book or work of art of such high quality that it is generally recognized as a permanent model or standard. **2** any person whose works are so regarded: *Shakespeare and Dickens are classics among English authors.* **3** of the highest quality; serving as a model or standard of its kind: *a classic remark.* **4** of or like the art or

culture of ancient Greece or Rome: *a classic design.* **5 the classics** the literature of ancient Greece and Rome.

clas·si·cal (klăs′ə kəl) **1** of the first rank; classic; *a classical piece of early American furniture.* **2** having to do with the literature, art, or civilization of ancient Greece or Rome. **clas·si·cal·ly.**

clas·si·fi·ca·tion (klăs′ə fə kā′shən) **1** an arranging or grouping according to class or kind. **2** the arrangement so made: *the classification of animals in a zoo.*

clas·si·fied (klăs′ə fīd′) **1** grouped according to class. **2** kept secret except to certain people: *a classified report on rocket research.*

clas·si·fy (klăs′ə fī′) to arrange or group according to class or kind: *You can classify a collection of shells according to shape, color, or size.* **clas·si·fied, clas·si·fy·ing.**

class·mate (klăs′māt′) a member of the same class at school.

class·room (klăs′rōōm′) a room in a school where classes are held.

clat·ter (klăt′ər) **1** a rattling noise. **2** to make or cause to make a rattling sound: *The knives clattered when he shook the box that held them.* **3** noisy or idle talk. **4** to talk noisily and idly.

clause (klôz) **1** a group of words that express a single thought in a sentence: *The sentence "I will stay while you go." has two clauses.* **2** a separate part of a written agreement, contract, or treaty: *There is a clause in my contract which allows a month's vacation a year.*

claw (klô) **1** a sharp, hooked nail on the foot of some animals and birds. **2** a foot with such nails: *The eagle on the coin holds an arrow in its claw.* **3** the pincers of a lobster or a crab. **4** something like a claw in shape or use: *the claw of a hammer.* **5** to get hold of with the claws; tear or scratch with the claws or fingernails: *The man clawed at the earth with both hands.*

Bird's claw

clay (klā) soft, sticky earth which may be molded when moist, and which becomes hard when baked. Bricks and earthenware are made of clay.

clean (klēn) **1** not dirty; pure: *with clean hands.* **2** free from litter or things that get in the way: *a clean path.* **3** to make free from dirt, litter, or impurities: *Be sure to* clean *your shoes.* **4** complete: *Our team made a* clean *sweep of all events in the track meet.* **5** wholly; entirely: *The knife cut* clean *through to the bone.* **6** straight; not glancing; accurate: *a* clean *hit.* **7** simple; clearcut: *a car with* clean *lines.*

clean up 1 to tidy up; put in order: *When are you going to* clean up *your desk?* **2** to finish: *to* clean up *our homework.*

clean·er (klē'nər) person or thing that removes dirt, stains, or impurities.

clean·li·ness (klĕn'lĭ nĭs) habit or practice of being clean.

¹clean·ly (klĕn'lĭ) careful to keep clean: *A* cleanly *cook washes her hands before preparing food.* **clean·li·er, clean·li·est.** [¹**cleanly** is a form of an Old English word (clænlice) meaning "pure."]

²clean·ly (klēn'lĭ) in a clean way or manner: *The diver cut the water* cleanly, *without a splash.* [²**cleanly** is a form of **clean.**]

cleanse (klĕnz) to make clean or pure. **cleansed, cleans·ing.**

cleans·er (klĕnz'ər) substance used for cleaning.

clear (klĭr) **1** easy to see through; not clouded: *The air and the water were* clear. **2** to make or become free of muddiness, cloudiness, or anything else that obscures: *The wind* cleared *the landing field of fog. The sky* cleared. **3** to make or become free of obstruction or of anything unwanted: *They* cleared *the field of stumps. The channel* cleared *when the ice melted.* **4** free from anything that obscures or obstructs: *a* clear *view; a* clear *path.* **5** distinct; not fuzzy or blurred; readily taken in by the eye, ear, or mind: *a* clear *photograph; a* clear *voice; a* clear *explanation.* **6** free from any feeling of guilt; untroubled: *a* clear *conscience.* **7** not confused: *a* clear *head.* **8** to pass or jump over (something) without striking or catching: *The runner* cleared *the hurdle.* **9** to make as profit: *The school* cleared *fifty dollars on the fair.*

clear of 1 free from: *No matter how hard he works, the poor man can't get* clear of *debt.* **2** to free from (a charge of wrongdoing): *The prisoner was* cleared of *a charge of murder.*

clear out 1 to clean out; empty: *The teacher* cleared out *her desk.* **2** to go away; leave: *The gang* cleared out *fast.*

clear up 1 to make or become clear. **2** to solve and explain: *The detective* cleared up *the mystery.*

clear-cut (klĭr'kŭt') **1** having a distinct outline: *a* clear-cut *profile.* **2** clear; definite: *a* clear-cut *statement.*

clear·ing (klĭr'ĭng) piece of land from which trees and underbrush have been removed.

clear·ly (klĭr'lĭ) plainly; distinctly: *I hear you quite* clearly.

cleat (klēt) **1** one of the blocks or spikes put on the soles of some athletic shoes to prevent slipping. **2** strip of wood or metal fastened across a board to give support, hold something in place, prevent slipping, etc.   **Cleat** **3** a kind of hook used for temporary fastening of ropes, particularly on ships.

cleav·age (klē'vĭj) **1** a split. **2** act of splitting or dividing.

¹cleave (klēv) **1** to split or cut open. **2** to cut a way through: *The destroyer* cleaved *the water.* **3** to come or split apart, especially along a crack or line of weakness: *Dry wood* cleaves *easily.* **cleft** or **cleaved** or **clove, cleft** or **cleaved** or **clo·ven, cleav·ing.** [¹**cleave** is a form of an Old English word (clēofan) meaning "to split."]

²cleave (klēv) to cling; hold fast or be faithful: *to* cleave *to one's principles.* **cleaved, cleav·ing.** [²**cleave** is a form of an Old English word (clifian, cleofian) meaning "to stick."]

cleav·er (klē'vər) heavy knife with a broad, square blade. It is used by cooks and butchers for chopping bones, etc.

clef (klĕf) in music, a sign showing the range of pitch of the notes on the staff.

cleft (klĕft) **1** a crack; crevice; fissure: *water trickled from a* cleft *in the rock.* **2** partly divided; appearing to be split: *a* cleft *chin.* **3** See ¹**cleave.** *The lightning* cleft *the tree.*

clem·en·cy (klĕm'ən sĭ) **1** mercy; compassion: *The court showed* clemency *toward the young prisoner.* **2** mildness, as of the weather or climate.

---

fāte, făt, fâre, fär; bē, bĕt; bīte, bĭt; nō, nŏt, nôr; fūse, fŭn, fûr; tōō, tŏŏk; foil; foul; thin; ~~then~~; hw for wh as in *w*hat; zh for s as in u*s*ual; ə for a, ҽ, i, o, u, as in ago, linen, peril, atom, minus

clench (klĕnch) **1** to press closely together: *He* clenched *his teeth.* **2** to grasp firmly: *He* clenched *the sword in his hand.*

cler·gy (klûr′jĭ) all persons ordained for religious work, such as ministers, priests, rabbis, etc.: *member of the* clergy. **cler·gies.**

cler·gy·man (klûr′jĭ mən) a minister, rabbi, priest, etc. **cler·gy·men.**

cler·ic (klĕr′ĭk) clergyman.

cler·i·cal (klĕr′ə kəl) **1** having to do with the clergy: *a* clerical *collar.* **2** connected with the work of a clerk, typist, or bookkeeper, etc.: *Filing is a* clerical *task.*

clerk (klûrk) **1** salesman or saleswoman in a store. **2** person who does the routine work of an office, especially keeping records: *a file* clerk. **3** public official who keeps records and does routine business: *a town* clerk. **4** to work as a clerk.

clev·er (klĕv′ər) **1** mentally quick or alert: *A* clever *fox can escape the hounds.* **2** skillfull: *I wish I were* clever *enough to make my own clothes.* **3** showing skill or mental quickness: *a* clever *scheme.* **clev·er·ly.**

clev·er·ness (klĕv′ər nĭs) **1** skill; talent. **2** quickness in learning and understanding.

clew (klōō) clue.

click (klĭk) **1** slight, sharp sound: *The key made a* click *in the lock.* **2** to make such a sound: *Her high heels* clicked *on the pavement.*

cli·ent (klī′ənt) person for whom a professional service is performed: *a lawyer's* client.

cliff (klĭf) high, steep face of rock or earth; precipice.

cli·mate (klī′mĭt) the weather conditions of a place over a period of time: *the warm* climate *of Florida in the winter.*

cli·max (klī′măks) the highest point of interest or excitement: *The* climax *of the story is when Baby Bear finds Goldilocks.*

climb (klīm) **1** to go up; mount: *to* climb *the steps.* **2** to go up or down (something) using both hands and feet: *to* climb *a tree; to* climb *down a ladder.* **3** to go up by twining: *Ivy* climbs *the wall.* **4** to rise by effort: *to* climb *to fame.* **5** a place to be climbed: *That high hill is a steep* climb. (Homonym: clime)

clime (klīm) climate or region. (Homonym: climb)

clinch (klĭnch) **1** to fasten tightly, especially by bending the end of a nail over. **2** to settle a matter: *to* clinch *a deal.* **3** to grasp and hold tightly: *The boxer* clinched *his opponent around the shoulders.* **4** a struggle at close grips: *The fighters are in a desperate* clinch.

cling (klĭng) to hold fast or stick to someone or something: *He* clung *to his father in the crowd. Ivy* clings *to the walls.* **clung, cling·ing.**

clin·ic (klĭn′ĭk) a place where diseases or problems of a particular type are studied and treated, sometimes free of charge: *eye* clinic; *speech* clinic.

clink (klĭngk) **1** to make or cause to make a slight tinkling or ringing sound: *The glasses* clinked *when the shelf was bumped. He* clinked *the ice in the glass.* **2** a light tinkling or ringing sound: *the* clink *of coins dropping into Santa's kettle on the street corner.*

clink·er (klĭng′kər) partly melted stony mass left after burning coal in a stove or furnace.

¹clip (klĭp) **1** to hold tightly together with a clasp. **2** a clasp, especially for holding papers: *a paper* clip. **3** a pin which is held by a clasp: *She wore a diamond* clip. **clipped, clip·ping.** [¹clip is a form of an Old English word (clyppan) meaning "to embrace, fondle."]
Clip

²clip (klĭp) **1** to cut or trim with shears: *Wool is* clipped *from sheep.* **2** a cut or a snip: *With a* clip *of the shears, the barber finished the haircut.* **3** amount of wool cut from a sheep at one time. **4** pace; rapid rate: *at a good* clip. **5** to cut short: *He* clips *his words when he talks fast.* **clipped, clip·ping.** [²clip is a form of an earlier English word (clippen) that goes back to an Old Norse word (klippa).]

clip·per (klĭp′ər) **1** any of various tools for trimming hair, finger nails, hedges, etc. **2** a sailing vessel built for speed: *China* clipper.
HAIR
NAIL
HEDGE
Clippers

clip·ping (klĭp′ĭng) a piece cut out of a newspaper or magazine.

clique (klēk) small set of persons who cling closely together.

156

cloak

cloak (klōk) **1** loose outer garment. **2** a covering or disguise: *His sweet words were a cloak for his treachery.* **3** to conceal; cover: *Fog cloaks the city buildings.*

cloak·room (klōk'room') room where jackets, coats, and hats are left temporarily.

Man in cloak

¹**clock** (klŏk) **1** device for measuring and indicating time, especially one larger than a watch, with a pair of pointers, or hands, that move around a dial marked for hours and minutes. **2** to time (somebody or something) with a clock, watch, etc.: *to clock a race.* [¹**clock** is a form of an earlier English word (clokke) which in turn goes back to an Old English word (clugga) meaning "bell."]

²**clock** (klŏk) a woven or embroidered design on the ankle of a sock or stocking. [²**clock** is of unknown origin.]

clock·wise (klŏk'wīz') in the direction in which the hands of a clock turn.

clock·work (klŏk'wûrk') **1** the machinery of a clock. **2** any machinery like that of a clock. **3** like clockwork smoothly; with regularity and exactness.

clod (klŏd) **1** lump of earth or clay. **2** stupid person.

clog (klŏg) **1** to obstruct; stop up; block: *Leaves clogged the drain.* **2** to become obstructed or stopped up: *The fountain pen clogged and wouldn't write.* **3** to hinder the movement of by blocking or obstructing: *Grease clogged the gears of the machine.* **4** a shoe with a wooden sole. **clogged, clog·ging.**

Bath clog

clois·ter (klois'tər) **1** a covered walk with open arches on one side, usually built around a courtyard. **2** a monastery or convent. **3** to confine, as in a monastery or convent; seclude.

Cloister

clothespin

¹**close** (klōz) **1** to shut: *Please close the window. The suitcase won't close.* **2** to stop up; obstruct: *Fallen rocks had closed the old mine opening.* **3** to come or bring to an end; conclude: *The meeting closed at five o'clock.* **4** an end: *at the close of day.* **5** to bring or come together: *The soldiers closed ranks. The curtains closed at the end of the play.* **closed, clos·ing.** [¹**close** is from an Old French word (clos) meaning "closed," which in turn goes back to a Latin word form (clausum) also meaning "closed."]

²**close** (klōs) **1** near: *He parked close to the curb.* **2** with very little space between; not widely separated: *a close weave.* **3** stuffy: *With the windows shut, it was very close in the room.* **4** strict; careful: *The prisoner was under close guard.* **5** stingy: *The miser was close with his money.* **6** almost equal: *a close race.* **7 close quarters** crowded space: *They lived in close quarters at the barracks.* **close·ly.** [²**close** is probably a later meaning of ¹**close**.]

close·ness (klōs'nis) **1** nearness. **2** narrowness. **3** stuffiness: *The stifling closeness of the room.* **4** stinginess.

clos·et (klŏz'it) **1** small room or cupboard for storing things. **2** small, private room especially one for prayer or study. **3** to shut up in a private place: *The two leaders closeted themselves to discuss their plans.*

clot (klŏt) **1** to thicken into a soft, sticky mass; coagulate: *Blood clots easily when exposed to air.* **2** soft lump of something that has clotted: *a blood clot.* **clot·ted, clot·ting.**

cloth (klôth) **1** fabric made from wool, cotton, silk, linen, etc. **2** piece of fabric used for a special purpose: *a dust cloth.*

clothe (klōth) **1** to dress; put clothes on. **2** to provide clothing for: *The poor man could not feed and clothe his family properly.* **3** to cover: *In spring the trees are clothed with leaves.* **clothed** or **clad, cloth·ing.**

clothes (klōz or klōthz) garments; clothing.

clothes·line (klōz'līn' or klōthz'līn') a line on which clothes are hung to dry.

clothes·pin (klōz'pin' or klōthz'pin') forked piece of wood, or a clamp, used to fasten clothes to a line.

---

fāte, făt, fâre, fär; bē, bĕt; bīte, bĭt; nō, nŏt, nôr; fūse, fŭn, fûr; tōō, tŏŏk; foil; foul; thin; then; hw for wh as in *wh*at; zh for s as in u*s*ual; ə for a, e, i, o, u, as in *a*go, lin*e*n, per*i*l, at*o*m, min*u*s

cloth·ing (klō′ᵗhing) garments of any sort; clothes.

cloud (kloud) **1** mass of tiny water drops floating above the earth. **2** thick mass of smoke, sand, or dust moving through the air. **3** mass of things moving together: *a cloud of gnats.* **4** to cover with a mist or cloud: *Smoke* clouded *the air.* **5** to grow cloudy; become covered (with clouds): *Toward noon the sky* clouded *over.* **6** to make or become gloomy, troubled, etc.: *Grief* clouded *his mind.* **7** anything that troubles, causes gloom, etc.: *a cloud of hate or suspicion.*

cloud·burst (kloud′bûrst′) sudden heavy downpour of rain.

cloud·less (kloud′lĭs) free from clouds; clear: *a cloudless sky.* **cloud·less·ly.**

cloud·y (klou′dĭ) **1** covered with clouds; overcast: *a cloudy sky.* **2** not transparent: *a cloudy liquid.* **3** not clear; obscure: *his cloudy notions.* **cloud·i·er, cloud·i·est; cloud·i·ly.**

clout (klout) **1** a blow: *a clout on the head.* **2** to hit. **3** a rag; a patch.

¹clove (klōv) the dried flower bud of a tropical evergreen tree, used as spice or in medicine. [**¹clove** is a form of an Old English word (clufu).]

²clove (klōv) See **¹cleave.** *He* clove *the log with an ax.* [**²clove** is a form of **¹cleave.**]

clo·ven (klō′vən) **1** divided; split: *a cloven hoof.* **2** See **cleave.** *The oak tree was* cloven *by the lightning.*

clo·ver (klō′vər) **1** plant growing close to the ground, which has three leaflets in each leaf cluster, and round, sweet-smelling flower heads of red, white, and purple. **2 in clover** prosperous; having everything: *When Jason comes into his inheritance, he will be* in clover.

Red clover

clown (kloun) **1** person who performs amusing acts in the circus, on the stage, on television, etc. **2** to act like a clown; be amusing: *The boy was only* clowning *when he imitated his sister.* **3** rude, clumsy, bad-mannered man.

cloy (kloi) to make weary by too much of anything pleasant: *It is easy to* cloy *your appetite with too much candy.*

club (klŭb) **1** heavy stick, thick at one end, especially one used as a weapon. **2** to beat with a heavy stick. **3** any of certain sticks or bats for hitting a ball: *a golf* club. **4** group of people united for some common purpose: *a garden* club. **5** building or room occupied by such a group. **6** any one of a suit of playing cards marked with a black design resembling a clover leaf.

club together to join together for a common purpose: *The boys* clubbed together *to buy a basketball.*

clubbed, club·bing.

cluck (klŭk) **1** sound made by a hen calling her chickens. **2** to make such a sound.

clue (klōō) something that helps solve a problem or a mystery: *The footprints were a* clue *to the identity of the criminal.* Also spelled **clew.**

clump (klŭmp) **1** a cluster or group: *a clump of bushes.* **2** to tread heavily: *The horses* clumped *along the road.*

clum·sy (klŭm′zĭ) **1** awkward; lacking in ease or grace. **2** hard to handle; awkwardly made; unwieldy: *The rake was* clumsy *to use.* **clum·si·er, clum·si·est; clum·si·ly.**

clung (klŭng) See **cling.** *The vines* clung *to the trellis.*

clus·ter (klŭs′tər) **1** group of things of the same kind, growing or collected together; a bunch: *a cluster of grapes.* **2** to group or bunch together: *Students* clustered *around the band leader.* **3** group of persons or things close together.

clutch (klŭch) **1** a tight hold; grasp. **2** to grasp or hold tightly: *The hawk* clutched *the chicken in its claws.* **3** a grasping claw, hand, etc.: *He felt a* clutch *on his shoulder.* **4** part of a machine that puts it in or out of gear by connecting or disconnecting the motor from the parts it moves: *an automobile* clutch. **5** a brood of chickens.

clutch at to try to snatch or seize: *He* clutched at *the rope, but couldn't quite reach it.*

clut·ter (klŭt′ər) **1** a disorderly heap. **2** to make untidy; litter: *The untidy girl* cluttered *the floor with her clothes.*

Co. company.

coach (kōch) **1** large enclosed carriage with four wheels. **2** enclosed automobile with two doors. **3** railroad passenger car. **4** person who trains athletes. **5** to train athletes.

6 tutor who prepares a student for an examination. **7** to give special teaching

Stagecoach

outside of class; to tutor: *The boy was coached until he could pass his examination.*

coach·man (kōch′mən) person who drives a coach or carriage for a living. **coach·men.**

co·ag·u·late (kō ăg′yŏŏ lāt′) **1** to become clotted; to change from a liquid to a pasty solid: *When the blood from a cut coagulates, the bleeding stops.* **2** to cause such a change. **co·ag·u·lat·ed, co·ag·u·lat·ing.**

coal (kōl) **1** a black, hard mineral formed from buried vegetable matter by heat and the pressure of the earth above it. **2** to furnish with or take in coal: *to coal a vessel.* **3** a piece of charred wood or other material that is still glowing; ember.

co·a·li·tion (kō′ə lĭsh′ən) a temporary alliance of persons or countries for a special purpose.

coal tar a thick, black, sticky substance obtained from coal by heating without air, used in chemicals, dyes, etc.

coarse (kôrs) **1** crude; vulgar; lacking in refinement: *a coarse manner; to use* coarse *language.* **2** not of fine texture: *a coat of* coarse *cloth.* **3** thick and heavy: *a coarse thread; a man with* coarse *features.* **4** made of large particles: *the coarse gravel.* **5** of poor or inferior quality; not refined: *The prisoners had a diet of* coarse *bread and water.* **coars·er, coars·est; coarse·ly.** (Homonym: course)

coars·en (kôr′sən) to make or become coarse: *He coarsened with age.*

coarse·ness (kôrs′nĭs) a being coarse.

coast (kōst) **1** the land and region next to the sea; seashore. **2** to sail along a coast, or from port to port. **3** to ride down a hill without the use of power. **4** to slide down hill, as on a sled.

coast·al (kōs′təl) of or on a coast: *a coastal city; a coastal plain.*

coast guard 1 a sea-going force organized to guard a coast, enforce shipping regulations, and carry out rescue operations. **2** member of such a force.

coat (kōt) **1** an outer garment with sleeves. **2** the hair or fur of an animal. **3** any outer layer that covers: *Put another coat of paint on the wall.* **4** to cover with a layer: *to coat furniture with shellac.* (Homonym: cote)

coat·ing (kō′tĭng) layer; covering.

coat of arms 1 a group of emblems showing rank or achievement, originally granted to a knight or person of distinction and later used by his descendants. **2** a shield marked with such emblems.

coax (kōks) **1** to persuade by using soft words and by being gentle and pleasing; wheedle: *to* coax *a baby to eat.* **2** to get by coaxing: *to* coax *a smile from the baby.*

co·ax·i·al ca·ble (kō ăk′sī əl kā′bəl) cable made up of an insulated wire covered by an insulated copper tube. It is used for sending telephone and telegraph messages and television broadcasts.

cob (kŏb) **1** corncob. **2** strong horse with short legs.

co·balt (kō′bôlt) **1** hard gray metal element used in very hard alloys. **2** a blue coloring matter obtained from this metal.

cob·bler (kŏb′lər) **1** person whose job is mending shoes. **2** fruit pie baked in a deep pan. **3** clumsy workman.

cob·ble·stone (kŏb′əl-stōn′) a naturally rounded stone, once much used for paving streets.

Cobblestones in a brook bed

co·bra (kō′brə) poisonous snake living in Asia and Africa. When excited the cobra spreads out its neck like a hood.

cob·web (kŏb′wĕb′) **1** web or net spun by a spider. A cobweb looks flimsy but it snares many insects. **2** something flimsy or entangling like a spider's web.

---

fāte, făt, fâre, fär; bē, bĕt; bite, bĭt; nō, nŏt, nôr; fūse, fŭn, fûr; tōo, tŏŏk; foil; foul; thin; ~~then~~; hw for wh as in *wh*at; zh for s as in u*s*ual; ə for a, e, i, o, u, as in *a*go, lin*e*n, per*i*l, at*o*m, min*u*s

¹**cock** (kŏk) **1** male chicken; rooster. **2** any male bird. **3** faucet to turn on or off a flow of liquid or gas. **4** hammer of a gun. **5** position of the hammer (of a gun) when it is drawn back: *The gun is at half* cock. **6** to pull back the hammer of a gun to firing position. **7 cock of the walk** one who dominates in a group of boys or men. [¹**cock** is a form of an Old English word (cocc). This word is probably an imitation of a rooster's cry.]

²**cock** (kŏk) to tilt or turn up: *The turkey cocked his eye at me and strutted. The boy cocked his hat at a jaunty angle.* [²**cock** is a later meaning of ¹**cock** (definition 6).]

³**cock** (kŏk) **1** small pile of hay. **2** to stack in such piles. [³**cock** is probably from a Scandinavian word.]

cock·a·too (kŏk′ə tōō′) large Australian parrot, often brightly colored and with a crest. **cock·a·toos.**

cock·le (kŏk′əl) **1** shellfish with a soft body and a hard, hinged shell. **2** small, shallow boat. **3 warm the cockles of one's heart** to cheer one; to make one happy.

cock·pit (kŏk′pĭt′) **1** space for the pilot and copilot in some airplanes. **2** a small, enclosed space used in cock fighting.

cock·roach (kŏk′rōch′) an insect pest found in kitchens and around water pipes. Cockroaches run about chiefly at night.

cock·y (kŏk′ĭ) overbearing; insolent; smug; too sure of oneself: *Merton was very* cocky *about his chances of winning.* **cock·i·er, cock·i·est; cock·i·ly.**

Cockroach

co·co (kō′kō) **1** the coconut. **2** the coconut palm tree. **co·cos.**

co·coa (kō′kō) **1** dark brown powder made from the seeds of the cacao tree. **2** drink made of cocoa, sugar, and milk or water.

co·co·nut or **co·coa·nut** (kō′kə nŭt) fruit of the coco palm tree. The coconut has a hard brown shell containing a milky liquid and coated inside with a layer of white substance that is good to eat. Coconut meat is used in cakes and pies and in candy making.

SHELL   MEAT
HUSK
Coconut

co·coon (kə kōōn′) silk case spun by a caterpillar as a protection while it is changing into a butterfly or moth.

cod (kŏd) large fish used for food. Cod are caught in the cold northern waters of the Atlantic Ocean. **pl. cod;** rarely, **cods.**

C.O.D. cash on delivery; collect on delivery: *He paid the mailman for the clock he had ordered* C.O.D.

Cod, 12 to 25 pounds

cod·dle (kŏd′əl) **1** to treat tenderly; pamper: *to* coddle *a sick person.* **2** to cook gently in hot water below the boiling point: *to* coddle *eggs.* **cod·dled, cod·dling.**

code (kōd) **1** system of symbols, letters, words, numbers, etc. used to stand for the letters and words of messages. Codes are used for secret messages or for brevity. **2** system, especially an alphabet, of dots and dashes, signs, etc. used for sending messages by telegraph, wigwag, and so forth. **3** a collection of laws or rules arranged in a clear and orderly fashion: *a building* code. **4** principles and rules of conduct generally accepted by a group of people: *the social* code; *the code of honor.* **5** to write in or put into code: *to* code *a message.* **cod·ed, cod·ing.**

cod·fish (kŏd′fĭsh′) the cod or its flesh, especially when cured and salted.

cod·ger (kŏj′ər) an odd, quaint, or eccentric man: *a lovable old* codger.

co·erce (kō ûrs′) to force; compel: *He was* coerced *into signing the contract.* **co·erced, co·erc·ing.**

cof·fee (kôf′ĭ) **1** drink made from the seeds, roasted and ground, of a tropical shrub. **2** prepared seeds used to make this drink. **3** the shrub itself. **4** flavored with coffee: *a dish of* coffee *ice cream.*

cof·fee·pot (kôf′ĭ pŏt′) pot in which coffee is made.

cof·fer (kôf′ər) money box; treasure chest.

cof·fin (kôf′ĭn) a case or box in which a dead person is buried; casket.

cog (kŏg) one of a series of teeth on the rim of a wheel that mesh with teeth on another wheel to transmit or receive motion.

COG
Cogwheel and cog

cog·wheel (kŏg′hwēl′) a wheel with teeth or cogs in its rim for transmitting or receiving motion.

coil (koil) **1** anything wound in a series of circles or spirals: *a coil of rope*. **2** one of the circles of a spiral, or a series of circles. **3** length of pipe wound in spirals for carrying water, etc. **4** a length of electric wire wound in spirals. **5** to wind in circles: *The snake coiled around the tree limb*.

Coil of rope

coin (koin) **1** piece of metal, stamped by a government, used for money. **2** metal money: *Change the dollar bill for coin*. **3** any stamped piece of metal: *Souvenir coins were given away to advertise the new store*. **4** to make metal into coins. **5** to invent or make up: *Who coined the word "astronaut"?*

coin·age (koi′nĭj) **1** method of stamping pieces of money. **2** coins. **3** system of metal money used in a country. **4** invention or making up: *a coinage of new words*.

co·in·cide (kō′ĭn sīd′) **1** to happen or occur at the same time: *They wanted their vacations to coincide so they could go somewhere together*. **2** to occupy the same space: *This highway has two different numbers for the stretch where two roads coincide*. **3** to agree; be alike: *our ideas coincide*. **co·in·cid·ed, co·in·cid·ing**.

co·in·ci·dence (kō ĭn′sə dəns) **1** a remarkable occurrence of events, ideas, etc., at the same time by mere chance: *By coincidence the dress my cousin wore was exactly like mine*. **2** a coinciding; a happening at the same time or occupying the same space: *the coincidence of the State and Federal routes*.

coke (kōk) coal from which the tars have been removed by heating without air.

col·an·der (kŏl′ən dər or kŭl′ən dər) a strainer; vessel with holes in the sides and bottom, used to drain water from vegetables, etc.

Colander

cold (kōld) **1** not warm; low in temperature; chilly: *The night is cold and stormy. I feel*

cold *in this room*. **2** lack of heat; lowness of temperature: *I mind the cold less than the heat*. **3** indifferent; not cordial or friendly: *He was cold to our appeal for money*. **4** a common illness, marked by a stuffy or running nose, cough, and sometimes a sore throat. **5** not fresh; faint: *The scent of the fox was so cold that the hounds lost the trail*. **cold·ly**.

cold-blood·ed (kōld′blŭd′ĭd) **1** unfeeling; cruel; without pity: *a cold-blooded criminal*. **2** having blood that stays at about the temperature of surrounding air or water. Fish, frogs, snakes, lizards, and turtles are cold-blooded animals. **cold·blood·ed·ly**.

cold cream an oily substance used to soften and cleanse the skin.

cold frame glass-covered, boxlike structure to protect young plants and seedlings.

cole·slaw (kōl′slô′) a salad made of shredded cabbage with a dressing.

col·ic (kŏl′ĭk) severe pains in the abdomen or bowels.

col·lage (kō läzh′) **1** design made by pasting scraps of paper, cloth, metal, string, etc. on a background. **2** art of making such designs.

col·lapse (kə lăps′) **1** to fall down or in: *The roof collapsed under the weight of the unusually heavy snow*. **2** to shrink or cause to shrink together: *The rubber life raft collapses for storage*. **3** to fold together: *Some card tables and chairs can be collapsed*. **4** to fail suddenly; break down: *The truce talks collapsed before a settlement was reached*. **5** a falling down or in; shrinking or folding together; sudden failure or breakdown: *the sudden collapse of a bridge; the collapse of a punctured rubber ball; a nervous collapse*. **col·lapsed, col·laps·ing**.

SHAFT

BRACKET COLLAR

Collars, shirt and machine

col·lar (kŏl′ər) **1** the part of a shirt, dress, or coat that fits around the neck. **2** an ornamental band of cloth, lace, or jewels worn around the neck. **3** a band of leather or metal for the neck of an animal.

---

fāte, făt, fâre, fär; bē, bĕt; bīte, bĭt; nō, nŏt, nôr; fūse, fŭn, fûr; tōō, tŏŏk; foil; foul; thin; ~~then~~; hw for wh as in *what*; zh for s as in u*s*ual; ə for a, e, i, o, u, as in ag*o*, lin*e*n, per*i*l, at*o*m, min*u*s

161

4 the part of a harness that fits over the neck of a horse. **5** metal ring on a machine shaft that keeps it in place. **6** to seize by the collar; lay hold of; capture: *The police* collared *the thief.* **7** to put a collar on: *to* collar *a dog.*

col·league (kŏl′ēg) a fellow worker; someone of the same profession.

col·lect (kə lĕkt′) **1** to gather up: *Jane will* collect *the papers from the class.* **2** to make a hobby of collecting: *to* collect *stamps.* **3** to ask and receive payment for: *to* collect *rent.* **4** to meet; assemble: *A crowd* collected *at the corner.* **5** to mount up; accumulate: *Water* collects *in ditches.*

col·lect·ed (kə lĕk′tĭd) under control; calm; undisturbed. **col·lect·ed·ly.**

col·lec·tion (kə lĕk′shən) **1** a gathering or coming together; collecting: *The hospital organized the* collection *of old clothes.* **2** something gathered together: *a* collection *of dust in the corner.* **3** things of some special kind brought together for display or study: *a* stamp collection. **4** the taking in of money as a payment or donation: *the* collection *of taxes; a church* collection. **5** a sum of money taken in: *The class took up a* collection *of ten dollars.*

col·lec·tive (kə lĕk′tĭv) having to do with a group: *to accomplish something by* collective *action; the* collective *wisdom of mankind.* **col·lec·tive·ly.**

col·lec·tor (kə lĕk′tər) **1** person whose work is to collect: *a tax* collector. **2** person who gathers together things of some special kind: *an art or stamp* collector.

col·lege (kŏl′ĭj) **1** school following high school which gives degrees to students when they have finished their courses. **2** buildings and grounds of such a school. **3** school in which a special subject is taught: *a business* college.

col·lide (kə lid′) **1** to meet and strike together with force; crash: *Cars are likely to* collide *on that turn.* **2** to clash; conflict. **col·lid·ed, col·lid·ing.**

col·lie (kŏl′ĭ) a large intelligent dog with a shaggy coat and bushy tail. Collies are especially used for herding sheep.

col·li·sion (kə lizh′ən) **1** a meeting and striking together with force; a crashing, as of trains. **2** a clash of interests, ideas, etc.

Colo. Colorado.

co·logne (kə lōn′) a light perfume.

Co·lom·bi·a (kə lŭm′bĭ ə) a country in the northwest of South America.

¹co·lon (kō′lən) a mark (:) of punctuation used to introduce a list or series, and to show that something is coming which is closely related to what has just been said. It sometimes follows the greeting in a letter. In this dictionary a colon is used to introduce examples. [**¹colon** comes from a Greek word (kōlon) meaning "limb," "part."]

²co·lon (kō′lən) the large intestine which, in the human body, is about six feet long. [**²colon** is from a Greek word (kōlon) also meaning "the large intestine."]

colo·nel (kûr′nəl) the rank next below that of general in the army. (Homonym: kernel)

co·lo·ni·al (kə lō′nĭ əl) **1** having to do with the thirteen British colonies which united to form the United States of America. **2** having to do with any colony or colonies. **3** inhabitant of a colony. **co·lo·ni·al·ly.**

col·o·nist (kŏl′ə nist) **1** person who goes to settle in a colony. **2** person who lives in a colony.

col·o·ni·za·tion (kŏl′ə nĭ zā′shən) a colonizing; a founding of a colony or sending settlers to a colony.

col·o·nize (kŏl′ə niz′) **1** to found a colony or colonies in: *People from Spain* colonized *Mexico and Florida.* **2** to send colonists to: *France and England* colonized *Canada.* **col·o·nized, col·o·niz·ing.**

col·on·nade (kŏl′ə nād′) a row of columns evenly spaced along or around a building.

col·o·ny (kŏl′ə nĭ) **1** body of people who leave their country to settle in another land, but remain subject to their mother country: *A* colony *of Puritans settled in Massachusetts.* **2** place or area settled in this way: *The first English* colonies *were on the Atlantic coast.* **3** territory at a distance from a country but governed by it: *European countries once governed African* colonies. **4** a group of people drawn together by nationality, common interest, or the like: *the French* colony *in New York; a* colony *of artists.* **5** a group of plants or animals living together: *a* colony *of ants.* **6** the **Colonies** the thirteen British Colonies that became the first states of the United States. **col·o·nies.**

col·or (kŭl′ər) **1** red, yellow, and blue are colors. All other colors are combinations of these. **2** hue or tint of the complexion: *His fine color showed he was in good health.* **3** a paint; dye; pigment. **4** to give color to; paint; dye. **5** to misrepresent or exaggerate; slant: *Newspapers sometimes color a story to make it more exciting than the actual happening.* **6** to blush; flush: *He colored when he was caught in a lie.* **7 show one's true colors** to show what one really is. **8 the colors** the flag: *a salute to the colors.*

Col·o·ra·do (kŏl′ə rä′dō or kŏl′ə răd′ō) a western State of the United States.

col·ored (kŭl′ərd) **1** having color; not black or white. **2** belonging or relating to a race other than the white, especially to the Negro race.

col·or·ful (kŭl′ər fəl) **1** rich with color. **2** interesting; fascinating; exciting the imagination: *The opening up of the West was a colorful period in our history.* **col·or·ful·ly.**

col·or·ing (kŭl′ər ing) **1** appearance as to color: *His coloring was pale after his illness.* **2** substance used to give color to something: *She put pink coloring in the cake icing.*

col·or·less (kŭl′ər lĭs) **1** without color. **2** not vivid; not striking: *His colorless story made everyone yawn.* **col·or·less·ly.**

co·los·sal (kə lŏs′əl) huge; immense. **co·los·sal·ly.**

colt (kōlt) a young horse, or any young of the horse family.

col·um·bine (kŏl′əm bĭn′) **1** a plant with three-part notched leaves and drooping blossoms having long spurs. **2** the red yellow, blue, and sometimes white flowers of different kinds of this plant.

col·umn (kŏl′əm) **1** an upright pillar serving as a support or ornament for a building, or standing alone as a monument. **2** anything that resembles such a pillar in shape or use: *the spinal column; a column of smoke.* **3** one of two or more vertical divisions of type on a printed page: *There are two columns on this page.*

Column

4 a piece of writing contributed regularly to a newspaper by one person, and consisting of his comments or observations on a particular subject: *a society column.* **5** a line of figures, letters, or words arranged one above the others: *Add up that column.* **6** a line of troops or ships following one after the other.

col·um·nist (kŏl′əm nĭst) person who writes a column in a newspaper: *a sports columnist.*

comb (kōm) **1** a thin piece of hard rubber, plastic, metal, or the like, made with projections called teeth, and used to smooth, arrange, or hold the hair. **2** to smooth or arrange the hair with a comb. **3** an implement used for grooming horses. **4** toothed metal device for separating and cleaning the fibers of flax or wool, etc. **5** the fleshy, red growth on the head of a hen, rooster, or other fowl; crest. **6** honeycomb. **7** to search through: *They combed the woods for the missing child.*

COMB

Comb of rooster

com·bat (kŏm′băt) **1** a struggle; fight. **2** to fight; oppose: *Vaccines help combat disease.* **3 single combat** a fight between two persons. **com·bat·ed** or **com·bat·ted, com·bat·ing** or **com·bat·ting.**

¹**com·bat·ant** (kŏm′bə tənt) fighter, especially a member of the armed forces who takes part in battle.

²**com·bat·ant** (kəm băt′ənt) ready and willing to fight.

com·bi·na·tion (kŏm′bə nā′shən) **1** a combining; joining together; mixing: *New substances can be made by the combination of various chemical elements.* **2** thing made by joining together or mixing two or more things: *The color green is a combination of blue and yellow.*

¹**com·bine** (kəm bīn′) **1** to unite; join: *The two boys combined their efforts to solve the problem. Oxygen combines with iron to form rust.* **2** to mix: *to combine ingredients to make a cake.* **com·bined, com·bin·ing.**

²**com·bine** (kŏm′bīn) a machine that harvests and threshes grain.

---

fāte, făt, fâre, fär; bē, bĕt; bīte, bĭt; nō, nŏt, nôr; fūse, fŭn, fûr; tōō, tŏŏk; foil; foul; thin; then; hw for wh as in *wh*at; zh for s as in u*s*ual; ə for a, e, i, o, u, as in *a*go, lin*e*n, per*i*l, at*o*m, min*u*s

com·bus·ti·ble (kəm bŭs′tə bəl) capable of catching fire and burning: *Dry wood is combustible.*

com·bus·tion (kəm bŭs′chən) a chemical action in which one or more substances combine with oxygen to produce heat; a burning: *the combustion of logs in the fireplace; the combustion of food in the body.*

come (kŭm) **1** to draw near; approach: *Cold weather is coming.* **2** to arrive: *He will come tomorrow.* **3** to reach (to a certain point): *Her hair comes to her shoulders.* **4** to happen: *How did you come to know that?* **5** to occur to the mind: *A new idea came to me.* **6** to happen as a result: *This accident comes of your carelessness.* **7** to become: *The knot came untied.* **8** to derive; descend: *to come from a famous family.*

come about to happen; occur.

come across to meet with or find by chance: *I came across an old friend today.*

come back to return, especially to the mind: *His name will come back to me soon.*

come by to get; acquire: *He comes by his wealth honestly.*

come down 1 to lose rank or standing: *He came down in the world after the loss of his business.* **2** to be handed down through tradition: *This custom comes down from our ancestors.*

come in 1 to enter. **2** to arrive. **3** to begin; be brought into use: *Law and order came in with the new sheriff.*

come into 1 to enter. **2** to inherit: *When her uncle died, she came into a fortune.*

come off to turn out to be: *The play came off better than we had hoped.*

come on 1 to meet or find by chance: *He came on the cabin while wandering through the woods.* **2** to progress: *How are you coming on at your new job?* **3** to come on stage; enter: *The actress came on dressed as a queen.*

come out 1 to be shown; to become evident: *It came out that they had friends in common.* **2** to be published or released: *Many books and movies come out every year.* **3** to turn out: *Did everything come out as planned?*

come out with 1 to say frankly: *If anything bothers you, you come out with it.* **2** to bring out: *The automobile company came out with a new model.*

come to 1 to amount to: *The bill came to five dollars.* **2** to become conscious again: *He came to after we threw cold water in his face.*

come up to arise: *The question came up at the meeting.*

came, com·ing.

co·me·di·an (kə mē′dĭ ən) **1** actor who plays in comedies. **2** person who acts a comic sketch, tells jokes, does funny stunts, and the like; a clown.

com·e·dy (kŏm′ə dĭ) **1** an amusing play, movie, or the like, with a happy ending. **2** any humorous event. **com·e·dies.**

come·li·ness (kŭm′lĭ nĭs) pleasing appearance; fairness.

come·ly (kŭm′lĭ) of pleasing appearance; fair: *a comely woman.*

com·et (kŏm′ĭt) a heavenly body that moves about the sun in a long oval orbit. It usually has a bright center and a long, shining tail.

Comet

com·fort (kŭm′fərt) **1** to soothe or console (a person) in grief, pain, or trouble: *A letter from home comforted the wounded soldier.* **2** person or thing that relieves distress or makes trouble easier to bear: *Sympathy from friends is a real comfort to anyone in trouble.* **3** relief from grief, pain, or trouble: *Ointment on a burn gives some comfort.* **4** ease and satisfaction at being free from hunger, thirst, cold, or the like: *An open fire gives a feeling of comfort.* **5** thing that produces ease: *The pioneers had few of the comforts of life.*

com·fort·a·ble (kŭm′fər tə bəl) **1** free from any distress; at ease: *to feel comfortable in new shoes.* **2** giving ease or comfort: *a comfortable chair.* **com·fort·a·bly.**

com·fort·er (kŭm′fər tər) **1** person who soothes or consoles another in grief, pain, or trouble. **2** a quilted bed covering.

com·ic (kŏm′ĭk) **1** funny; humorous: *a comic song.* **2** a comedian. **3** of or having to do with comedy: *a comic writer; a comic situation.* **4 comics** comic strips.

com·i·cal (kŏm′ə kəl) funny; causing laughter or amusement: *Dressed in his sister's clothes, he was a comical sight.* **com·i·cal·ly.**

comic strip series of drawings telling an adventure or funny story: *Jeffrey's favorite comic strips are in the evening paper.*

com·ing (kŭm'ĭng) **1** arrival; approach: *the* coming *of spring.* **2** approaching: *the* coming *storm; this* coming *week.*

com·ma (kŏm'ə) a mark (,) of punctuation used to show a slight interruption in thought, to separate words and ideas in a series, and to set off some grammatical constructions. In reading aloud, there should be a slight pause for each comma.

com·mand (kə mănd') **1** to give orders to with authority: *The general commanded the troops to march forward.* **2** to have authority and control over: *A captain commands his ship and men.* **3** the right to give orders; authority: *The general had his command taken away because he disobeyed orders. A new general is now in* command. **4** an order: *He gave the* command *to stand at attention.* **5** body of men under an officer; troops: *The officer will inspect his* command. **6** to be in a position that controls; overlook: *The fort commands the entrance to the harbor.* **7** control; mastery: *a good* command *of English; to have* command *of one's temper.* **8** to deserve and get: *to* command *respect; to* command *a high price.*

com·mand·er (kə măn'dər) **1** person in authority who orders or directs other people. **2** military leader or chief. **3** officer in the navy ranking next below captain.

com·mand·ment (kə mănd'mənt) **1** an order; a command. **2** a law, especially one of the Ten Commandments in the Bible.

com·man·do (kə măn'dō) **1** member of an army force trained to make surprise attacks on enemy territory. **2** of or by such a force: *a commando raid.* **com·man·dos** or **com·man·does.**

com·mem·o·rate (kə mĕm'ə rāt') to honor or keep alive the memory of: *The names of many cities* commemorate *men who were important in building our country.* **com·mem·o·rat·ed, com·mem·o·rat·ing.**

com·mence (kə mĕns') to begin; start. **com·menced, com·menc·ing.**

com·mence·ment (kə mĕns'mənt) **1** a beginning; origin. **2** ceremony in which students are given their diplomas; graduation exercises.

com·mend (kə mĕnd') **1** to praise: *I want to* commend *you for being on time every day.* **2** to recommend as worthy of attention: *My friend* commended *this book to me.* **3** to give into the care of another; entrust: *to* commend *one's soul to God.*

com·men·da·tion (kŏm'ən dā'shən) **1** praise; approval: *His teacher's* commendation *encouraged the student.* **2** official recognition and praise: *The soldier received a* commendation *for bravery.*

com·ment (kŏm'ĕnt) **1** written or spoken remark: *The teacher put a short* comment *on each paper.* **2** talk; gossip: *There was much* comment *about the plans for a new gymnasium.* **3** to give views and opinions: *Everyone* commented *on the good food.*

com·merce (kŏm'ərs) buying and selling large amounts of goods; trade; business transactions.

com·mer·cial (kə mûr'shəl) **1** having to do with trade or business: *a commercial enterprise; the* commercial *interests of the town.* **2** advertising message on a radio or television program. **com·mer·cial·ly.**

com·mis·sion (kə mĭsh'ən) **1** to appoint or authorize (someone to do a thing): *President Jefferson* commissioned *Lewis and Clark to explore the western lands.* **2** matter entrusted (to someone to perform): *Explorers went out with a* commission *to find and claim new lands.* **3** group of persons given authority to perform certain duties: *A* commission *will investigate the traffic problem.* **4** a doing or performing (usually a wrong act): *a* commission *of a serious crime.* **5** certificate giving rank to an officer in the army or navy. **6** to confer rank upon. **7** to put into service: *to* commission *a ship to carry troops and supplies.* **8** fee (money) paid to an agent for selling something: *The salesman got a $50* commission *for every car he sold.* **9** *in commission* working properly; ready for use. **10** *out of commission* not working properly; not ready for use.

com·mis·sion·er (kə mĭsh'ən ər) person given authority to do or perform certain duties: *a road* commissioner; *a game* commissioner.

---

fāte, făt, fâre, fär; bē, bĕt; bīte, bĭt; nō, nŏt, nôr; fūse, fŭn, fûr; tōō, tŏŏk; foil; foul; thin; then; hw for wh as in *wh*at; zh for s as in u*s*ual; ə for a, e, i, o, u, as in *a*go, lin*e*n, per*i*l, at*o*m, min*u*s

165

com·mit (kə mĭt′) **1** to do or perform, especially something wrong: *to* commit *a blunder; to* commit *a crime.* **2** to give over for care or safekeeping: *The patient was* committed *to a hospital. The thief was* committed *to prison.* **3** to pledge; promise: *I am* committing *myself to help at the cookie sale.* **commit to memory** to learn by heart. **commit to writing** to write (a thing) down.
com·mit·ted, com·mit·ting.

com·mit·tee (kə mĭt′ĭ) group of persons appointed or elected for a special purpose: *a* committee *to arrange the party.*

com·mo·di·ous (kə mō′dĭ əs) roomy; spacious: *a* commodious *house.*

com·mod·i·ty (kə mŏd′ə tĭ) anything that is bought and sold: *Wheat, gold, and clothes are* commodities. **com·mod·i·ties.**

com·mon (kŏm′ən) **1** usual; frequently met with; widespread: *It is a* common *thing for families to have a television set. Violets are a* common *wild flower.* **2** general: *It is* common *knowledge that sneezing spreads colds.* **3** shared; belonging to a group or more than one: *National parks are* common *property of all the people.* **4** land shared by all the people of a community: *Early New England towns had* commons *which everyone could use.* **5** coarse; vulgar: *She has such* common *manners that no one will associate with her.* **6 in common** shared by two or more: *The two have hobbies in* common.

com·mon·ly (kŏm′ən lĭ) usually; generally: *Boys* commonly *enjoy sports.*

com·mon·place (kŏm′ən plās′) **1** ordinary; not striking or new. **2** everyday thing or event: *Jet flight has become a* commonplace. **3** remark or saying that everybody already knows: *It is a* commonplace *that haste makes waste.*

com·mon sense practical, good sense.

com·mon·wealth (kŏm′ən wĕlth′) **1** free democratic nation; republic. **2** all the people in a state or nation. **3** group of states or nations joined together: *The British* Commonwealth *includes Canada, Australia, New Zealand, etc.* **4** official name used in the title of several States, such as Pennsylvania, Massachusetts, Virginia, and Kentucky.

com·mo·tion (kə mō′shən) noisy disturbance; confusion; tumult.

¹com·mune (kə mūn′) **1** to talk intimately; come to a close and sympathetic relationship; feel at one (with): *Audubon, the famous bird painter,* communed *with nature.* **2** to take Holy Communion. **com·muned, com·mun·ing.** [**commune** comes through Old French from a Latin word (communicare) meaning "to communicate."]

²com·mune (kŏm′ūn) a group of people organized to live and work together who hold all property in common. [**²commune** is a word adopted from French and comes from a Latin word (communia) meaning "common property."]

com·mu·ni·ca·ble (kə mū′nə kə bəl) capable of being passed on from person to person. **com·mu·ni·ca·bly.**

com·mu·ni·cate (kə mū′nə kāt′) **1** to exchange information or ideas: *They* communicate *with each other often by mail.* **2** to pass on; convey: *Measles can be* communicated *by contact.* **3** to get in touch: *The salesman* communicates *regularly with his home office.* **4** to be connected: *The bedroom* communicates *with the bathroom.* **5** to take Holy Communion. **com·mu·ni·cat·ed, com·mu·ni·cat·ing.**

com·mu·ni·ca·tion (kə mū′nə kā′shən) **1** exchange of information, ideas, etc.: *People speaking different languages often find* communication *difficult.* **2** a passing on; a transmitting: *the* communication *of news by radio.* **3** message; something communicated: *What was in that* communication *from headquarters?* **4** way or means of communicating: *Telephone* communication *was cut off by the flood.* **5 communications** telephone, telegraph, radio, and television: *The Federal* Communications *Commission supervises the* communications *industries.*

com·mun·ion (kə mūn′yən) **1** sharing of experience; fellowship: *close* communion *between friends.* **2** group of persons sharing the same religious beliefs. **3 Communion** or **Holy Communion** sacrament that commemorates Christ's last meeting and supper with the Apostles.

com·mu·nism (kŏm′yə nĭz′əm) **1** political idea that the community as a whole should own all property, and run all business and industry. **2 Communism** system of government which claims to put this idea into operation, as in the Soviet Union.

com·mu·nist (kŏm′yə nĭst) **1** person who believes in common ownership of property. **2** of or having to do with communism or communists. **3 Communist** person who belongs to a political party that believes in Communism, especially as found in the Soviet Union, the People's Republic of China, and countries under their influence.

com·mu·ni·ty (kə mū′nə tĭ) **1** all the people who live in one place; the citizens of a town or city: *Everyone should do his bit for the good of the* community. **2** group of people who live together: *a community of nuns.* **3** a holding in common; a sharing together: *a community of interests; a community of ideas.* **4** held in common; of a community: *A park is* community *property.* **com·mun·i·ties.**

com·mute (kə mūt′) **1** to travel regularly back and forth over a distance, usually from one's home in the suburbs to work in the city. **2** to make a punishment less harsh: *The Governor* commuted *the prisoner's sentence from fifteen years to ten.* **com·mut·ed, com·mut·ing.**

com·mut·er (kə mū′tər) person who travels regularly back and forth from his home in the suburbs to his work in the city.

¹com·pact (kəm păkt′) **1** closely or firmly set together; compressed: *We tied all the little packages together in one* compact *bundle. He expressed all of his ideas in a few* compact *sentences.* **2** (kom′păkt) a small case holding face powder and often rouge. **com·pact·ly.** [¹**compact** is from a form (compactus) meaning "joined," of a Latin word (compingere) meaning "to join."]

²com·pact (kŏm′păkt) an agreement. [²**compact** is from a form (compactum) of a Latin word (compacisci) meaning "to make an agreement with."]

com·pan·ion (kəm păn′yən) **1** person who regularly shares the work, play, interests, etc., of another; comrade: *He was my close* companion *all through school.* **2** person who accompanies another or others: *He found that his* companion *in the next seat was also going to Canada.* **3** thing that matches another; one of a pair: *I broke the* companion *to that vase.*

com·pan·ion·a·ble (kəm păn′yən ə bəl) sociable; agreeable; pleasant to be with. **com·pan·ion·a·bly.**

com·pan·ion·ship (kəm păn′yən shĭp′) fellowship; agreeable association.

com·pan·ion·way (kəm păn′yən wā′) stairway leading below from the deck of a ship.

com·pa·ny (kŭm′pə nĭ) **1** companionship; society: *The trapper lived alone and had little* company. **2** companions; associates: *He keeps bad* company. **3** guest or guests: *My* company *came for dinner.* **4** group of people gathered together: *She addressed the assembled* company. **5** business or commercial firm. **6** troupe of actors. **7** body of soldiers; military unit made up of three or four platoons. **com·pa·nies.**

com·pa·ra·ble (kŏm′pə rə bəl) **1** capable of being compared: *An airplane and a bird are* comparable *because both have wings and both can fly.* **2** worthy or fit to be compared: *Jewelry made of glass is not* comparable *to diamonds.* **com·pa·ra·bly.**

com·par·a·tive (kəm păr′ə tĭv) **1** making a comparison; done by comparing: *a comparative study of the weights of boys and girls.* **2** measured by comparison with something else; relative: *Although we are not rich, we live in* comparative *comfort.* **3** a form of an adjective or adverb used in comparisons: *The* comparatives *of "pretty" and "well" are "prettier" and "better."* **com·par·a·tive·ly.**

com·pare (kəm pâr′) **1** to examine in order to find out, or show, likeness or difference in: *Before buying, she* compared *the two watches.* **2** to describe as similar; liken: *The writer* compared *the sound of guns to thunder.* **3** to be worthy of comparison: *His house* compares *with the best in town.* **com·pared, com·par·ing.**

com·par·i·son (kəm păr′ə sən) **1** examination to find out likenesses or differences: *a* comparison *of natural resources in two countries; a* comparison *of one car with another.* **2** a likening: *a* comparison *of a pretty girl to a melody.* **3** statement that one thing is like another in some way: *"Time is like a flowing stream," is a* comparison *often heard.* **4 no comparison** no basis

---

fāte, făt, fâre, fär; bē, bĕt; bīte, bĭt; nō, nŏt, nôr; fūse, fŭn, fûr; tōō, tŏŏk; foil; foul; thin; ~~then~~; hw for wh as in *wh*at; zh for s as in u*s*ual; ə for a, e, i, o, u, as in *a*go, lin*e*n, per*i*l, at*o*m, min*u*s

compartment

for comparison; very little likeness: *There is* no comparison *between a hi-fi and an ordinary phonograph.*

com·part·ment (kəm pärt′mənt) a separate part, division, or section of an enclosed space: *a compartment on a Pullman car; a watertight* compartment *in the hull of a ship.*

com·pass (kŭm′pəs or kŏm′pəs) **1** an instrument for determining direction, either a free-swinging magnetic needle that always points to the north magnetic pole or a gyrocompass that always points to the true north. **2** an instrument (also called **compasses**) for drawing or dividing circles, etc. **3** range; extent: *the compass of a singing voice.* **4** bounds; boundary: *The old lady stayed within the compass of her house.* **5** to encircle; surround; go around: *The high mountains* compass *the little valley.* **6** to accomplish; achieve: *to* compass *a goal after a hard struggle.* **7** to grasp mentally: *It will take study to* compass *this problem.*

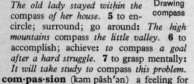

Magnetic compass

Drawing compass

com·pas·sion (kəm păsh′ən) a feeling for the sorrow or suffering of others; sympathy.

com·pas·sion·ate (kəm păsh′ən ĭt) feeling or showing compassion; merciful. **com·pas·sion·ate·ly.**

com·pat·i·ble (kəm păt′ə bəl) able to get along together; harmonious: *The two cousins are* compatible. **com·pat·i·bly.**

com·pel (kəm pĕl′) **1** to force: *The bandit's conscience* compelled *him to return the money.* **2** to get or secure by force: *to* compel *obedience.* **com·pelled, com·pel·ling.**

com·pen·sate (kŏm′pən sāt′) **1** to pay: *The firm will* compensate *them for working overtime.* **2** to make up (for): *Glasses* compensate *for weaknesses of the eyes.* **com·pen·sat·ed, com·pen·sat·ing.**

com·pen·sa·tion (kŏm′pən sā′shən) **1** something that makes up for a lack or loss: *One* compensation *for my illness was the many new books I had time to enjoy.* **2** pay: *Workers receive* compensation *for time lost because of injuries.*

com·pete (kəm pēt′) to enter into a contest; contend: *Three runners will* compete *for the prize.* **com·pet·ed, com·pet·ing.**

completion

com·pe·tent (kŏm′pə tənt) having skill or ability; capable: *A* competent *worker makes few mistakes.* **com·pe·tent·ly.**

com·pe·ti·tion (kŏm′pə tĭsh′ən) **1** a contest: *Many fine athletes are entered in the* competition. **2** rivalry: *There is sharp* competition *between the two stores.*

com·pet·i·tive (kəm pĕt′ə tĭv) involving competition or a contest: *a* competitive *sport.* **com·pet·i·tive·ly.**

com·pet·i·tor (kəm pĕt′ə tər) a rival or contestant: *The two automobile companies are* competitors.

com·pile (kəm pīl′) to put together (facts, stories, etc.) from various sources into a collection: *to* compile *a history of a town.* **com·piled, com·pil·ing.**

com·pla·cen·cy (kəm plā′sən sĭ) being pleased with oneself; self-satisfaction.

com·pla·cent (kəm plā′sənt) pleased with oneself; self-satisfied: *a* complacent *smile.* **com·pla·cent·ly.**

com·plain (kəm plān′) **1** to grumble; express pain, sorrow, discontent, etc.: *to* complain *about poor health.* **2** to report a wrong or injury: *to* complain *to the police.*

com·plaint (kəm plānt′) **1** expression of unhappiness, grief, dissatisfaction, etc.; grumbling. **2** something causing pain or discomfort: *He went to the doctor with a stomach* complaint. **3** a formal charge against a person: *The tenant swore out a* complaint *against his landlord.*

com·ple·ment (kŏm′plə mənt) **1** something added that makes a thing complete: *In a race horse, stamina is the* complement *to speed.* **2** the required number or amount: *The office now has its full* complement *of workers.* (Homonym: ¹compliment)

com·plete (kəm plēt′) **1** to bring to an end; finish: *When you* complete *your work you may go outdoors.* **2** finished; ended; concluded: *The report will be* complete *in a few days.* **3** to make whole or entire: *I need several stamps to* complete *my collection.* **4** whole; full: *a* complete *set of china.* **5** absolute: *a* complete *surprise.* **com·plet·ed, com·plet·ing; com·plete·ly.**

com·ple·tion (kəm plē′shən) **1** a finishing: *Diplomas are given upon* completion *of the course.* **2** a making whole; putting in all the parts: *We all worked toward the* completion *of the puzzle.*

com·plex (kŏm′plĕks or kəm plĕks′) **1** made up of many parts: *a complex piece of machinery.* **2** hard to understand or explain: *a complex argument.* **com·plex·ly.**

com·plex·ion (kəm plĕk′shən) **1** the color, texture, and general appearance of the skin, especially of the face. **2** general character; nature: *The new evidence changes the complexion of the case.*

com·plex·i·ty (kəm plĕk′sə tĭ) **1** a being complex or complicated: *We lost our way because of the complexity of your directions.* **2** a difficulty; thing that complicates or puzzles: *The game of chess has many complexities.* **com·plex·i·ties.**

com·pli·cate (kŏm′plə kāt′) to make difficult, confusing, or hard: *Unexpected guests complicate her plans for dinner.* **com·pli·cat·ed, com·pli·cat·ing.**

com·pli·cat·ed (kŏm′plə kā′tĭd) **1** hard to explain, take apart, or understand: *His directions were very complicated because of the many details.* **2** with many parts; not simple: *The typewriter is a complicated machine.* **com·pli·cat·ed·ly.**

com·pli·ca·tion (kŏm′plə kā′shən) **1** thing that complicates; thing that increases difficulty or confusion: *There were so many complications in the rules that we couldn't understand the game.* **2** a tangle or confusion (of a state of affairs, events, etc.): *His life was a complication of worries.* **3** illness developing out of another sickness.

¹**com·pli·ment** (kŏm′plə mənt) an expression of praise or pleasure: *The guests paid the hostess many compliments on her cooking.* (Homonym: complement)

²**com·pli·ment** (kŏm′plə mĕnt′) to praise or express approval.

com·pli·men·ta·ry (kŏm′plə mĕn′tə rĭ) **1** giving approval or praise: *Her remarks on the new house were complimentary.* **2** given free: *I have complimentary tickets to the play.* **com·pli·men·ta·ri·ly.**

com·ply (kəm plī′) to act as requested or ordered: *He asked us to be quiet and we complied.*

comply with to obey: *A good soldier must comply with orders he receives.* **com·plied, com·ply·ing.**

com·pose (kəm pōz′) **1** to make by combining: *Paste is composed of flour and water.* **2** to construct or put together: *to compose a piece of music, a speech, an essay, letter, etc.* **3** to settle (a quarrel or dispute): *The coach composed the quarrel between the two players.* **4** to calm (oneself): *The girl composed herself before she spoke.* **com·posed, com·pos·ing.**

com·posed (kəm pōzd′) calm; quiet; tranquil; serene. **com·pos·ed·ly.**

com·pos·er (kəm pō′zər) person who composes, especially one who writes music.

com·pos·ite (kəm pŏz′ĭt) **1** made up of various parts: *a composite song of old folk melodies.* **2** a compound: *The paste was a composite of flour and water.*

com·po·si·tion (kŏm′pə zĭsh′ən) **1** piece of writing such as an essay, story, etc.: *His English composition was an account of a fishing trip.* **2** the creating of a piece of music or writing. **3** a piece of music. **4** parts of a thing or the way they are put together: *That drawing is a fine composition of light and shadow.* **5** combination of elements to make up something; a mixture: *soil of a rich composition.* **6** the setting up of type for printing.

com·po·sure (kəm pō′zhər) calmness: *The man kept his composure during the storm.*

¹**com·pound** (kŏm′pound) **1** substance formed by the chemical combination of two or more elements. Salt is a compound of sodium and chlorine. **2** a mixture of substances, ideas, characteristics, etc.: *His reaction was a compound of joy and surprise.* **3** composed of two or more parts, ingredients, etc.: *The words "horseback" and "battleship" are compound words.*

²**com·pound** (kəm pound′) to prepare by mixing various ingredients: *The druggist compounds a medicine for the doctor.*

com·pre·hend (kŏm′prĭ hĕnd′) **1** to understand: *I heard his speech but did not comprehend his meaning.* **2** to include; take in: *Science comprehends the study of chemistry, physics, and biology.*

com·pre·hen·sion (kŏm′prĭ hĕn′shən) understanding; the ability to understand: *The lecture was beyond our comprehension.*

---

fāte, făt, fâre, fär; bē, bĕt; bīte, bĭt; nō, nŏt, nôr; fūse, fŭn, fûr; tōō, tŏŏk; foil; foul; thin; ~~then~~; hw for wh as in *w*hat; zh for s as in u*s*ual; ə for a, e, i, o, u, as in *a*go, lin*e*n, per*i*l, at*o*m, min*u*s

comprehensive

com·pre·hen·sive (kŏm′prĭ hĕn′sĭv) full; complete; including much: *a comprehensive description.* **com·pre·hen·sive·ly.**

¹**com·press** (kəm prĕs′) to squeeze or press together: *to compress cotton into bales; to compress gas into a tank.*

²**com·press** (kŏm′prĕs) a pad applied hot or cold to a part of the body to reduce soreness or swelling.

compressed air air forced into much less space than it usually occupies. When it is released, it expands with enough energy to operate drills, brakes, etc.

com·pres·sor (kəm prĕs′ər) someone or something that compresses, especially a machine for compressing gas or air, as in an electric refrigerator, etc.

com·prise or **com·prize** (kəm prīz′) to include; consist of: *These two books comprise all the best poems by that author.* **com·prised** or **com·prized, com·pris·ing** or **com·priz·ing.**

com·pro·mise (kŏm′prə mīz′) **1** settlement of differences in which each side yields something: *The strike was settled by a compromise.* **2** to settle differences by such yielding: *The family compromised and divided their vacation between the seashore and the mountains.* **3** to lay open to suspicion; endanger: *to compromise one's good name.* **com·pro·mised, com·pro·mis·ing.**

com·pul·sion (kəm pŭl′shən) use of force; a forcing or compelling: *the compulsion used by a dictator to stay in power.*

com·pul·so·ry (kəm pŭl′sə rĭ) required: *Attendance at school is compulsory.*

com·pu·ta·tion (kŏm′pyŏŏ tā′shən) the process of finding an answer by arithmetic; calculation: *to predict an eclipse by computation.*

com·pute (kəm pūt′) to find out by arithmetic; calculate: *Scientists have computed the distance from the earth to the sun.* **com·put·ed, com·put·ing.**

com·put·er (kəm pū′tər) an electronic device used for quickly solving problems in mathematics, and for storing, sorting, and comparing different information.

com·rade (kŏm′răd) friend; companion.

¹**con** (kŏn) to study carefully; learn by heart. **conned, con·ning.** [¹**con** is the unchanged form of an Old English word. It is related to ¹**can.**]

concentration

²**con** (kŏn) argument against (as used in the phrase **pro and con,** meaning "for and against"): *He weighed all the pros and cons before going on the expedition.* [²**con** is the short form of a Latin word (contra) meaning "against."]

con·cave (kŏn′kāv′) curved inward like the inside of a saucer. **con·cave·ly.**

Concave

con·ceal (kən sēl′) to hide; keep secret: *She concealed the book where nobody would find it.*

con·ceal·ment (kən sēl′mənt) **1** a hiding or being hidden: *The concealment of facts by a witness is a criminal offense.* **2** a place of hiding: *The scout remained in concealment until the Indians passed.*

con·cede (kən sēd′) **1** to admit (the truth of); acknowledge; yield: *to concede a point in a debate.* **2** to grant as a right or privilege: *to concede a rise in wages.* **con·ced·ed, con·ced·ing.**

con·ceit (kən sēt′) too much pride in oneself; vanity: *The star athlete was puffed up with conceit.*

con·ceit·ed (kən sēt′ĭd) very pleased with oneself. **con·ceit·ed·ly.**

con·ceiv·a·ble (kən sē′və bəl) thought of or imagined as possible: *It is conceivable that man will some day reach Mars.* **con·ceiv·a·bly.**

con·ceive (kən sēv′) **1** to think (of); imagine: *Can you conceive of such a situation?* **2** to form (a plan, idea, purpose, etc.) in the mind: *They conceived a plot to assassinate the king.* **con·ceived, con·ceiv·ing.**

con·cen·trate (kŏn′sən trāt′) **1** to fix the whole attention upon: *to concentrate on a problem.* **2** to bring or come together at one point: *The general concentrated his troops on one side of the hill.* **3** to increase (a solution) in strength: *The orange juice was concentrated by removing the excess water.* **4** solution that has been made stronger: *Frozen orange juice is a concentrate.* **con·cen·trat·ed, con·cen·trat·ing.**

con·cen·tra·tion (kŏn′sən trā′shən) **1** a fixed attention on one object: *It requires concentration to study during a thunderstorm.* **2** a group or mass brought together in one place: *a concentration of enemy troops in a valley; a concentration of vitamins in a tablet.*

con·cept (kŏn′sĕpt) a mental image or general idea (of something): *a concept of the solar system; a* concept *of a word's meaning.*

con·cep·tion (kən sĕp′shən) **1** a forming of ideas and images in the mind. **2** idea; notion: *I have no* conception *of what he meant by that strange remark.*

con·cern (kən sûrn′) **1** to relate to; to have to do with; affect: *This problem doesn't* concern *you.* **2** something that is related to one's interests; business: *This is no* concern *of yours.* **3** anxious interest; anxiety: *My chief* concern *is his refusal to study.* **4** a business firm.

concern oneself with to interest or engage oneself in: *Don't* concern *yourself with lunch; we'll buy it.*

con·cerned (kən sûrnd′) **1** busy; interested: *to be* concerned *in a new project.* **2** worried; troubled: *I'm* concerned *about him.*

con·cern·ing (kən sûr′nĭng) relating to; regarding; about.

con·cert (kŏn′sərt) **1** musical performance by singers, or players, or both. **2 in concert** in agreement; together: *The two armies* acted *in concert.*

con·cer·to (kŏn chĕr′tō) musical composition for one or more solo instruments accompanied by an orchestra. **con·cer·tos.**

con·ces·sion (kən sĕsh′ən) **1** a yielding or conceding: *Without* concession *by both sides, an agreement will never be reached.* **2** the thing yielded: *Giving up his plan was a great* concession *for him.* **3** right granted to conduct a business: *The candy* concession *in the park was given to a big company.*

conch (kŏngk or kŏnch) large, spiral sea shell. For picture, see **shell.**

con·cil·i·ate (kən sĭl′ĭ āt′) to gain the good will of; overcome the hostility of: *The boy's apology* conciliated *his angry father.* **con·cil·i·at·ed, con·cil·i·a·ting.**

con·cise (kən sīs′) expressing much in few words; short and to the point: *a* concise *and witty remark.* **con·cise·ly.**

con·clude (kən klōōd′) **1** to end; finish: *As he* concluded *his speech, there was loud applause.* **2** to settle; arrange after discussion or argument: *A trade agreement was*

concluded *between the two countries.* **3** to arrive at an opinion by reasoning: *After study, I* concluded *that Russian is a difficult language.* **con·clud·ed, con·clud·ing.**

con·clu·sion (kən klōō′zhən) **1** opinion arrived at by reasoning: *What* conclusion *did you reach in your discussion?* **2** final part; end: *Graduation comes at the* conclusion *of the term.* **3** a concluding; final settlement: *the* conclusion *of a treaty.*

con·clu·sive (kən klōō′sĭv) decisive; final. **con·clu·sive·ly.**

con·coct (kŏn kŏkt′) **1** to make out of various parts or things: *Wanda* concocted *a salad of fruit and nuts.* **2** to make up; invent: *Gus* concocted *an unbelievable story.*

con·cord (kŏn′kôrd) agreement; harmony.

con·course (kŏn′kôrs) **1** a running, flowing, or coming together: *St. Louis is located at the* concourse *of the Mississippi and Missouri.* **2** a crowd or assembly. **3** open place where crowds gather or roads meet.

¹con·crete (kŏn′krēt) a hardened mixture of cement, sand, gravel, and water, used in building and paving.

²con·crete (kŏn krēt′ or kŏn′krēt) actual; real; specific; not abstract: *I'll give you a* concrete *example.*

con·cur (kən kûr′) **1** to agree: *All the judges* concurred *in the decision.* **2** to happen or work together: *Careful planning and good luck* concurred *to give them the victory.* **con·curred, con·cur·ring.**

con·cus·sion (kən kŭsh′ən) **1** a violent jarring; shock: *the* concussion *of an explosion.* **2** brain injury due to a blow or fall.

con·demn (kən dĕm′) **1** to disapprove of strongly; censure: *to* condemn *an act or the person who did it.* **2** to declare guilty in court and sentence: *The judge* condemned *him to ten years of prison at hard labor.* **3** to declare unfit for use: *The road was* condemned *and closed to travel.* **4** to take property for public use: *to* condemn *land for a road.*

con·dem·na·tion (kŏn′dĕm nā′shən) **1** strong disapproval. **2** a sentencing for crime. **3** official statement that a thing is unfit for use. **4** government seizure of property for public use.

---

fāte, făt, fâre, fär; bē, bĕt; bīte, bĭt; nō, nŏt, nôr; fūse, fŭn, fûr; tōō, tŏŏk; foil; foul; thin; ~~then~~;
hw for wh as in *wh*at; zh for s as in u*s*ual; ə for a, e, i, o, u, as in *a*go, lin*e*n, per*i*l, at*o*m, min*u*s

con·den·sa·tion (kŏn′dĕn sā′shən) **1** the change from vapor into a liquid: *Rain is formed by the* condensation *of water vapor in the air.* **2** something reduced in size, bulk, length, etc.: *the* condensation *of a report; the* condensation *of orange juice.*

con·dense (kən dĕns′) **1** to change from a gas or vapor to a liquid: *to* condense *steam to water.* **2** to reduce the volume of (a liquid) by removing water; to concentrate: *to* condense *milk or orange juice.* **3** to express in fewer words: *The newspaper* condensed *the long speech to a paragraph.* **con·densed, con·dens·ing.**

condensed milk sweetened milk from which part of the water has been removed.

con·dens·er (kən dĕn′sər) **1** device for holding and storing a charge of electricity. **2** device to change gases into liquid.

con·de·scend (kŏn′dĭ sĕnd′) **1** to stoop or come down willingly to the level of one's inferiors: *The king* condescended *to eat with the people.* **2** to do a favor with a superior air: *Though she thought it beneath her, she finally* condescended *to clean the house.*

con·de·scend·ing (kŏn′dĭ sĕn′dĭng) having a superior air: *a* condescending *smile.* **con·de·scend·ing·ly.**

con·di·tion (kən dĭsh′ən) **1** thing that must be if something else is to be or take place: *Mother made it a* condition *that we finish our homework before we could watch television.* **2** state in which a person or thing is: *This car is in running* condition. *He is in healthy* condition. **3** to put in better shape or state: *to* condition *a race horse.* **4** rank in society: *Medieval serfs were of low* condition. **5 on condition that** provided that: *I will go* on condition that *you go also.*

con·di·tion·al (kən dĭsh′ən əl) depending on a condition or certain terms: *Parole of a prisoner is a* conditional *freedom.* **con·di·tion·al·ly.**

con·dor (kŏn′dər) very large vulture with dull black feathers and a white neck ruff. Condors live in the mountains of California and South America.

Condor, 4 ft. long

¹con·duct (kən dŭkt′) **1** to lead; guide: *The guide* conducted *us through the museum.* **2** to manage; direct: *to* conduct *an orchestra.* **3** to carry; transmit: *Gutters* conduct *rain water. Wires* conduct *electricity.* **conduct oneself** to behave.

²con·duct (kŏn′dŭkt) way of acting; behavior (usually thought of as good or bad): *Her* conduct *was better than I expected.*

con·duc·tor (kən dŭk′tər) **1** guide; leader: *the* conductor *of an orchestra.* **2** person in charge of passengers on a train, bus, or street car. **3** in science, a material that transmits heat, sound, electricity, etc.

cone (kōn) **1** solid body that is flat and round at one end and narrows evenly to a point at the other end. **2** anything shaped like a cone: *ice cream* cone; *nose* cone *of a rocket.* **3** seed case of pine trees, fir trees, and some other evergreens.

Cones

con·fec·tion (kən fĕk′shən) sweet food, as candy, pastry, or the like.

con·fec·tion·er (kən fĕk′shən ər) **1** person who makes or sells candy, cakes, and other sweet things. **2 confectioners′ sugar** finely ground sugar; powdered sugar.

con·fec·tion·er·y (kən fĕk′shə nĕr′ĭ) business or shop that makes and sells confections. **con·fec·tion·er·ies.**

con·fed·er·a·cy (kən fĕd′ər ə sĭ) **1** states or countries that have joined together; union; league; alliance. **2 the Confederacy** the Confederate States of America, the 11 Southern States that seceded from the United States in 1860 and 1861. The end of the War Between the States in 1865 brought this league back into the United States. **con·fed·er·a·cies.**

¹con·fed·er·ate (kən fĕd′ər it) **1** an ally; accomplice: *The bank robber and his* confederates *escaped.* **2 Confederate** of or having to do with the Confederacy: *a* Confederate *flag.*

²con·fed·er·ate (kən fĕd′ə rāt′) to join together in a league. **con·fed·er·at·ed, con·fed·er·at·ing.**

con·fed·er·a·tion (kən fĕd′ə rā′shən) **1** league; confederacy. **2** joining together; confederating: *The 13 colonies first tried* confederation, *and later formed a closer union.*

con·fer (kən fûr′) **1** to consult; have a conference: *Mother conferred with the teacher about my stuttering.* **2** to bestow: *to confer a medal.* **con·ferred, con·fer·ring.**

con·fer·ence (kŏn′fər əns) meeting for discussing and exchanging ideas: *The citizens had a conference about building a new school.*

con·fess (kən fĕs′) **1** to admit; acknowledge: *He confessed that he broke the vase. I confess that you won that argument.* **2** to tell one's mistakes and sins, especially to a priest.

con·fes·sion (kən fĕsh′ən) **1** an admission of something: *a confession of one's true feelings.* **2** thing acknowledged or admitted, especially a statement admitting a crime or fault: *The prisoner signed a confession.* **3** in certain churches, the telling of one's sins to a priest.

con·fide (kən fīd′) **1** to tell as a secret: *She confided her problems to her mother.* **2** to entrust; commit: *We confided the children to their grandmother's care.*

confide in **1** to tell secrets to: *The safest way to keep a secret is to confide in no one.* **2** to have trust in: *to confide in God.* **con·fid·ed, con·fid·ing.**

con·fi·dence (kŏn′fə dəns) **1** trust; belief: *I have confidence in your ability to pass the test.* **2** belief in oneself; self-assurance: *His confidence makes him a fine actor.* **3** a secret: *The girl and her best friend exchanged confidences.* **4 in confidence** as a secret: *That story was told to me in confidence, so I can't give it away.*

con·fi·dent (kŏn′fə dənt) **1** assured; self-reliant; bold: *The boxer had a jaunty, confident air.* **2** sure; convinced: *We are confident of victory.* **con·fi·dent·ly.**

con·fi·den·tial (kŏn′fə dĕn′shəl) **1** secret; private: *The agent turned in a confidential report.* **2** trusted with secret matters: *A confidential secretary must have good judgment.* **con·fi·den·tial·ly.**

con·fine (kən fīn′) to keep or hold (within limits): *A cold confined her to her bed.* **con·fined, con·fin·ing.**

con·fines (kŏn′fīnz) limits; boundaries: *the confines of a park.*

con·fine·ment (kən fīn′mənt) **1** imprisonment: *His confinement lasted two years.* **2** a staying indoors or in bed because of illness.

con·firm (kən fûrm′) **1** to assure the truth of; verify: *The doctor confirmed the reports about the polio vaccine.* **2** to approve legally: *The Senate confirmed his appointment as a judge.* **3** in some churches, to admit to full membership by a special rite.

con·fir·ma·tion (kŏn′fər mā′shən) **1** act of making sure or establishing. **2** proof; evidence; a making more sure: *Is there any confirmation of that report?* **3** in some churches, a ceremony that admits a newly baptized person to full church membership. **4** in some churches, a rite confirming and strengthening a person in the Christian faith.

con·firmed (kən fûrmd′) settled; chronic: *a confirmed bachelor; a confirmed invalid.*

con·fis·cate (kŏn′fĭs kāt′) **1** to seize with authority: *The teacher confiscated all the comic books.* **2** to take over (private property) by public authority without payment: *The shore patrol confiscated the smuggler's boat.* **con·fis·cat·ed, con·fis·cat·ing.**

con·fla·gra·tion (kŏn′flə grā′shən) a large and destructive fire.

¹con·flict (kŏn′flĭkt) **1** a battle; fight; struggle. **2** a clash; failure to be in agreement or harmony: *a conflict between the two accounts of the accident.*

²con·flict (kən flĭkt′) to be in opposition; clash: *One account of the accident conflicts with the other.*

con·form (kən fôrm′) **1** to act or be in agreement (with) a standard pattern: *We conform to the rule of law.* **2** to make similar; be identical: *He conformed his plans to ours. His plans conform with ours.*

con·form·i·ty (kən fôr′mə tĭ) **1** agreement; accord: *a conformity of opinion.* **2** action or behavior that agrees (with some standard): *to live in conformity with the law; their conformity to fashion.*

con·found (kən found′) to throw into disorder; confuse: *The little boy confounded the experts by solving hard problems.*

---

fāte, făt, fâre, fär; bē, bĕt; bite, bit; nō, nŏt, nôr; fūse, fŭn, fûr; tōō, tŏŏk; foil; foul; thin; ~~then~~; hw for wh as in *wh*at; zh for s as in u*s*ual; ə for a, e, i, o, u, as in *a*go, lin*e*n, per*i*l, at*o*m, min*u*s

con·front (kən frŭnt') **1** to bring face to face: *to* confront *a prisoner with his accusers.* **2** to face up to; stand up to: *He* confronted *the enemy boldly.*

Con·fu·cian·ism (kən fū'shən ĭz'əm) moral teachings of the Chinese philosopher Confucius and his followers.

con·fuse (kən fūz') **1** to throw into disorder; bewilder; perplex: *Don't let all those questions* confuse *you.* **2** to mix up in the mind; mistake one thing for another: *The announcer* confused *the dates of the two events.* **con·fused, con·fus·ing.**

con·fu·sion (kən fū'zhən) **1** disorder: *The papers lay about in utter* confusion. **2** embarrassment: *I was unable to hide my* confusion. **3** a mistaking or mixing up: *the* confusion *of the sounds of "m" and "n" over the telephone.*

con·geal (kən jēl') to change from a liquid to a solid by freezing; stiffen from cold.

con·gen·ial (kən jēn'yəl) **1** having the same tastes and interests: *a congenial roommate.* **2** suited to one's taste and nature: *This work is* congenial *to me.* **con·gen·ial·ly.**

con·gest·ed (kən jĕs'tĭd) filled too full; overcrowded: *streets* congested *with traffic.*

con·grat·u·late (kən grăch'yōō lāt') **1** to express one's pleasure to (someone) on some happy occasion: *to* congratulate *a student on his graduation.* **con·grat·u·lat·ed, con·grat·u·lat·ing.**

con·grat·u·la·tion (kən grăch'yōō lā'shən) an expression of pleasure to a person about his success or good fortune.

con·gre·gate (kŏng'grə gāt') to come together; assemble: *People* congregate *to watch a parade.* **con·gre·gat·ed, con·gre·gat·ing.**

con·gre·ga·tion (kŏng'grə gā'shən) group of people meeting for religious worship or instruction.

con·gress (kŏng'grĭs) **1** a meeting of representatives to discuss a particular thing; a conference. **2** the chief lawmaking body of some republics. **3 Congress** the national lawmaking body of the United States, made up of the Senate and the House of Representatives.

con·gress·man (kŏng'grĭs mən) a member of Congress, especially of the House of Representatives. **con·gress·men.**

con·i·cal (kŏn'ə kəl) shaped like a cone.

con·i·fer (kŏn'ə fər) a kind of tree that bears cones, such as the pine, fir, and spruce.

con·jec·ture (kən jĕk'chər) **1** a guess. **2** to make a guess; form an opinion without definite proof: *Can you* conjecture *what life will be like in A.D. 2000?* **con·jec·tured, con·jec·tur·ing.**

con·junc·tion (kən jŭngk'shən) **1** a joining together; union. **2** a word such as *and, but, or, if, when,* etc., that connects two other words or groups of words. Conjunctions also show the intended relationships between parts of a sentence.

con·jure (kŭn'jər or kŏn'jər) **1** to make appear or disappear as if by magic: *The magician* conjured *a rabbit out of a hat.* **2** (kŭn jŏŏr') to appeal to; implore: *His mother* conjured *him to come home.*

conjure up to call up; bring into existence: *The old sailor's story* conjured up *scenes of pirate raids and buried treasure.* **con·jured, con·jur·ing.**

Conn. Connecticut.

con·nect (kə nĕkt') **1** to join or fasten together; unite: *A bus line* connects *the two towns.* **2** to put together in the mind; associate: *You should always* connect *names with faces.*

Con·nect·i·cut (kə nĕt'ĭ kət) a New England State of the United States.

con·nec·tion (kə nĕk'shən) **1** a joining or being joined: *When you hang up the telephone, the* connection *is broken.* **2** thing or part that joins other things together: *a broken* connection *in a pipe.* **3** relation: *What is the* connection *between those two ideas?* **4** a relative, especially by marriage: *a* connection *on my mother's side of the family.* **5** relationship or contact because of common interest or occupation: *a good business* connection. **6** meeting of one system of transportation with another that enables passengers to transfer without great delay: *There was a poor bus* connection *with the afternoon train.*

conn·ing tow·er (kŏn'ĭng tou'ər) low tower on the deck of a submarine, used for observation and as entrance to the interior.

con·quer (kŏng'kər) **1** to subdue by war: *to* conquer *a country.* **2** to overcome by effort or will; gain the victory over: *She must* conquer *her temper.* **3** to be victorious.

con·quer·or (kŏng′kər ər) a person who conquers, especially one who subdues a country by war.

con·quest (kŏng′kwĕst) **1** a winning or conquering, especially by war: *the* conquest *of Mexico by the Spanish.* **2** that which is conquered.

con·qui·sta·dor (kŏn kwĭs′tə dôr′) a conqueror, especially one of the Spanish conquerors of parts of North and South America in the 16th century.

con·science (kŏn′shəns) inward sense that tells a person to choose right and avoid wrong.

con·sci·en·tious (kŏn′shĭ ĕn′shəs) **1** acting according to one's sense of right: *a* conscientious *and painstaking student.* **2** done according to a sense of right; honestly and carefully done: *his* conscientious *work.* **con·sci·en·tious·ly.**

con·scious (kŏn′shəs) **1** mentally awake; in possession of one's senses: *The patient was* conscious *for the first time since the accident.* **2** aware: *I was not* conscious *that I had hurt my friend.* **3** that one is aware of: *Breathing does not require* conscious *effort.* **con·scious·ly.**

con·scious·ness (kŏn′shəs nĭs) **1** a being mentally awake; possession of one's senses: *A person who faints loses* consciousness. **2** a person's thoughts and feelings at a given moment: *A new idea entered his* consciousness.

con·se·crate (kŏn′sə krāt′) **1** to set apart or dedicate as sacred: *to* consecrate *a. chapel.* **2** to devote to some worthy purpose: *She* consecrated *her life to the care of the sick.* **con·se·crat·ed, con·se·crat·ing.**

con·sec·u·tive (kən sĕk′yōō tĭv) following without a break; coming in order: *Four, five, and six are* consecutive *numbers.* **con·sec·u·tive·ly.**

con·sent (kən sĕnt′) **1** to agree; express willingness: *He* consented *to be a candidate.* **2** permission; approval; agreement: *He got his sister's* consent *to use her book.*

con·se·quence (kŏn′sə kwĕns′) **1** result; outcome: *You must suffer the* consequences *of your carelessness.* **2** importance: *The banker was a person of* consequence.

con·se·quent (kŏn′sə kwĕnt) resulting: *The storm and* consequent *flood caused great damage.* **con·se·quent·ly.**

con·ser·va·tion (kŏn′sûr vā′shən) careful use and protection, especially of natural resources such as soil, forest, and game; preservation.

con·serv·a·tive (kən sûr′və tĭv) **1** inclined to keep things as they are; opposed to sudden or extreme changes. **2** cautious about taking risks: *The weather man was* conservative *about making forecasts.* **3** figured low on purpose: *a* conservative *estimate.* **4** a person who opposes sudden or extreme changes. **con·serv·a·tive·ly.**

¹**con·serve** (kən sûrv′) to keep from decay, destruction, loss, or waste; preserve: *Scientific farming* conserves *the soil.* **con·served, con·serv·ing.**

²**con·serve** (kŏn′sûrv) fruit or berries preserved in sugar; jam (usually in plural): *She made dozens of jars of plum* conserves.

con·sid·er (kən sĭd′ər) **1** to think over carefully: *to* consider *the risk before going ahead.* **2** to be thoughtful of: *The selfish boy never* considered *his brother's feelings.* **3** to regard (someone or something) as: *I* consider *him our best player.*

con·sid·er·a·ble (kən sĭd′ər ə bəl) worth taking note of; of some importance: *a* considerable *difference between his price and yours.* **con·sid·er·a·bly.**

con·sid·er·ate (kən sĭd′ər ĭt) thoughtful of others; kindly. **con·sid·er·ate·ly.**

con·sid·er·a·tion (kən sĭd′ə rā′shən) **1** careful thought; deliberation: *After much* consideration, *he decided which car to buy.* **2** thoughtfulness (for others): *He turned down the radio out of* consideration *for his neighbors.* **3** something taken, or worth taking, into account: *Her welfare is my first* consideration. **4** reason for an action or opinion: *to weigh all* considerations. **5** fee or payment in reward; compensation.

con·sid·er·ing (kən sĭd′ər ing) taking into account; allowing for; in view of: *He did well* considering *his lack of preparation.*

con·sign (kən sīn′) **1** to hand over; deliver formally: *They* consigned *the thief to jail.* **2** to send (usually merchandise).

---

fāte, făt, fâre, fär; bē, bĕt; bīte, bĭt; nō, nŏt, nôr; fūse, fŭn, fûr; tōō, tŏŏk; foil; foul; thin; ~~then;~~ hw for wh as in *what*; zh for s as in u*s*ual; ə for a, e, i, o, u, as in *a*go, lin*e*n, per*i*l, at*o*m, min*u*s

consist

con·sist (kən sist′) to be made up or composed (of): *Water* consists *of hydrogen and oxygen.*

con·sist·en·cy (kən sis′tən sĭ) **1** degree of thickness: *The thick oil had the* consistency *of molasses.* **2** a being always the same in thought or action: *a person of moral consistency.* **3** agreement; harmony: *a consistency between words and actions.* **con·sist·en·cies.**

con·sist·ent (kən sis′tənt) **1** continuing without change; constant: *a consistent friend; a consistent winner.* **2** in agreement; in accord (with something): *His last report was not consistent with his usual good work.* **con·sist·ent·ly.**

con·so·la·tion (kŏn′sə lā′shən) **1** comfort in time of distress: *The hurt child received* consolation *from his mother.* **2** a person who or thing that consoles: *She was his consolation.*

¹con·sole (kən sōl′) to comfort; cheer up. **con·soled, con·sol·ing.** [¹console is indirectly from a Latin word (consolari) meaning "to comfort greatly."]

²con·sole (kŏn′sōl) **1** a radio or television cabinet that rests on the floor. **2** a table designed to stand against the wall. **3** the part of a pipe organ at which the organist sits, containing the keyboard and pedals. [²console is from a French word of the same spelling, meaning a "support," "bracket," especially in architecture.]

Console

con·sol·i·date (kən sŏl′ə dāt′) to unite; combine: *The two companies* consolidated *into one organization.* **con·sol·i·dat·ed, con·sol·i·dat·ing.**

con·so·nant (kŏn′sə nənt) **1** speech sound made by stopping, or partly stopping, the breath. Most consonants cannot be pronounced without a vowel sound before or after them. **2** a letter that stands for such a sound. The letters b, d, and g are consonants.

¹con·sort (kŏn′sôrt) a husband or wife.

²con·sort (kən sôrt′) to keep company; associate: *Artists usually* consort *with artists.*

con·spic·u·ous (kən spĭk′yŏŏ əs) **1** easily seen. **2** attracting attention; striking: *Her*

constitution

beauty was conspicuous *even in a crowd.* **con·spic·u·ous·ly.**

con·spir·a·cy (kən spîr′ə sĭ) secret agreement to do something unlawful or evil; a plot: *a conspiracy to overthrow the government.* **con·spir·a·cies.**

con·spir·a·tor (kən spîr′ə tər) person who takes part in a secret plot: *The conspirators planned to betray the king.*

con·spire (kən spîr′) **1** to plan together to do something unlawful or evil; plot. **2** to act or work together: *All things* conspired *for a happy day.* **con·spired, con·spir·ing**

con·sta·ble (kŏn′stə bəl or kŭn′stə bəl) policeman.

con·stan·cy (kŏn′stən sĭ) faithfulness to a person or a cause; firmness of purpose: *Washington's* constancy *through defeats and disappointments was his strength.*

con·stant (kŏn′stənt) **1** firm in belief or affection; faithful: *a constant friend.* **2** always present; regular; continual: *the constant noise of the street traffic.* **con·stant·ly.**

con·stel·la·tion (kŏn′stə lā′shən) a group of stars with a name. The Big Dipper is a constellation.

Constellation

con·ster·na·tion (kŏn′stər nā′shən) bewilderment; frightened astonishment; dismay: *To my* consternation *my wallet had disappeared.*

con·stit·u·ent (kən stĭch′ŏŏ ənt) **1** needed in the make-up of something: *Hydrogen and oxygen are* constituent *elements in water.* **2** a necessary ingredient or part. **3** a voter in a political district.

con·sti·tute (kŏn′stə tŏŏt′ or kŏn′stə tūt′) **1** to make up or form: *Twelve things* constitute *a dozen.* **2** to appoint; set up: *The will* constituted *him guardian of the estate.* **con·sti·tut·ed, con·sti·tut·ing.**

con·sti·tu·tion (kŏn′stə tŏŏ′shən or kŏn′stə tū′shən) **1** the way in which a thing is made up: *Astronomers study the* constitution *of the stars.* **2** way in which the body is made up and functions as to health, energy, strength, etc.: *a robust* constitution. **3** the basic law and principles of a nation, state, or other organized body. **4 the Constitution** written document setting forth the basic law and principles of the United States.

con·sti·tu·tion·al (kŏn′stə tōō′shən əl or kŏn′stə tū′shən əl) **1** inherent in a person's physical make-up: *a constitutional weakness.* **2** of or having to do with the constitution of a nation, state, etc.: *a constitutional amendment.* **3** a walk taken for one's health. **con·sti·tu·tion·al·ly.**

con·straint (kən strānt′) **1** force; compulsion: *to keep silent under constraint.* **2** a keeping back of natural feeling or behavior: *The boys were usually noisy, but they showed constraint when visitors came.*

con·struct (kən strŭkt′) to build; put together: *to construct a house.*

con·struc·tion (kən strŭk′shən) **1** a putting together: *the construction of a bridge.* **2** way of building: *fireproof construction required by law.* **3** thing built: *The department store is a huge construction of steel and glass.* **4** explanation; interpretation: *He puts a wrong construction on my words.*

con·struc·tive (kən strŭk′tĭv) building up rather than destroying; creative: *a constructive suggestion.* **con·struc·tive·ly.**

con·strue (kən strōō′) to explain (the meaning of); interpret: *His failure to answer was construed as fear.* **con·strued, con·stru·ing.**

con·sul (kŏn′səl) **1** an official appointed by a government to live in a foreign country, look after trade, and help any citizens of his own country who live or travel there. **2** either of two chief officials of the ancient Roman republic.

con·sult (kən sŭlt′) **1** to seek advice or information from: *to consult a lawyer; to consult a dictionary.* **2** to have regard for: *I always try to consult my mother's wishes.* **3** to take counsel together; confer: *The doctors consulted before operating.*

con·sume (kən sōōm′) **1** to use up: *She consumes most of the day on the telephone.* **2** to eat or drink up. **3** to destroy: *Fire consumed the old barn.* **con·sumed, con·sum·ing.**

con·sum·er (kən sōō′mər) **1** person who buys and uses food, clothing, services, etc. **2** person or thing that uses up or consumes: *Television is often a time consumer.*

con·sump·tion (kən sŭmp′shən) **1** a using up; a consuming: *We store food when production is greater than consumption.* **2** amount used (in a given time or by a given number); rate of using up: *The ship's consumption of oil is five tons per hour.* **3** old name for some types of tuberculosis.

con·tact (kŏn′tăkt) **1** a touching: *The contact of two wires.* **2** connection: *The Coast Guard made contact with the sinking ship.* **3** to get in touch with: *Please contact me next week.*

con·ta·gion (kən tā′jən) **1** a spreading of a disease by contact. **2** a disease that can spread from one person or animal to another. **3** a spreading of a feeling or influence: *the contagion of fear.*

con·ta·gious (kən tā′jəs) **1** spreading by contact; catching: *Mumps is a contagious disease.* **2** easily spreading: *Laughter is often contagious.* **con·ta·gious·ly.**

con·tain (kən tān′) **1** to hold in it: *That Thermos bottle contains a pint.* **2** to include as a part: *Some paints contain lead.* **3** to hold back; restrain: *The crowd could scarcely contain their excitement.* **4** to be equal to: *A quart contains two pints.*

con·tain·er (kən tā′nər) box, carton, crate, can, etc., that may contain something.

con·tam·i·nate (kən tăm′ə nāt′) to make bad; pollute; infect: *Germs contaminate water.* **con·tam·i·nat·ed, con·tam·i·nat·ing.**

con·tem·plate (kŏn′təm plāt′) **1** to look at or think about long and carefully: *The painter contemplated the beauty of the desert scene.* **2** to intend: *I do not contemplate making a trip.* **3** to look forward to; expect: *Do you contemplate any difficulty because of bad weather?* **con·tem·plat·ed, con·tem·plat·ing.**

con·tem·pla·tion (kŏn′təm plā′shən) **1** a looking at or thinking about something long and seriously. **2** expectation: *to lay in food in contemplation of a blizzard.*

con·tem·po·rar·y (kən tĕm′pə rĕr′ĭ) **1** living or occurring during the same period of time. **2** person who lives at the same time as another: *Washington and Franklin were contemporaries.* **con·tem·po·rar·ies.**

fāte, făt, fâre, fär; bē, bĕt; bīte, bĭt; nō, nŏt, nôr; fūse, fŭn, fûr; tōō, tŏŏk; foil; foul; thin; ~~then~~; hw for wh as in *wh*at; zh for s as in u*s*ual; ə for a, e, i, o, u, as in *a*go, lin*e*n, per*i*l, at*o*m, min*u*s

177

con·tempt (kən těmpt′) **1** a feeling that a person or act is mean or vile; scorn: *We have only* contempt *for a liar.* **2** condition of being despised: *Anyone who tattles is held in* contempt.

con·tempt·i·ble (kən těmp′tə bəl) mean; low; deserving contempt: *his* contemptible *conduct.* **con·tempt·i·bly.**

con·temp·tu·ous (kən těmp′chōō əs) scornful; sneering: *a* contemptuous *smile.* **con·temp·tu·ous·ly.**

con·tend (kən těnd′) **1** to compete; struggle: *Builders of the Panama Canal had to* contend *with insects and hot weather.* **2** to argue; maintain: *Louis Pasteur* contended *that germs can be destroyed by heat.*

¹con·tent (kŏn′tĕnt) **1** thought, ideas, and subject matter in speech or writing: *The speech was well delivered, but had very little* content. **2 contents** all that is inside; what is contained (in something): *the* contents *of a bottle; the table of* contents *of a book.* [**¹content** is from the form (con-tentum) of a Latin word (continere) that means "contain."]

²con·tent (kən těnt′) **1** to satisfy: *It was a dull job and did not* content *him.* **2** satisfied: *He was* content *to bask in the sun.* **3** satisfaction: *The dog lolled by the fire in sleepy* content. [**²content** is from the form (con-tentum) meaning "satisfied" of a Latin word (continere) meaning "contain," "be bounded in one's desire."]

con·tent·ed (kən těn′tĭd) satisfied: *A* contented *person does not worry or feel restless.* **con·tent·ed·ly.**

con·ten·tion (kən těn′shən) **1** a quarreling; disputing: *constant* contention *in a family.* **2** idea a person believes in or argues for: *the* contention *that poverty causes crime.*

con·tent·ment (kən těnt′mənt) peace of mind; satisfaction.

¹con·test (kŏn′tĕst) competition; a struggle: *Games, debates, and lawsuits are* contests.

²con·test (kən tĕst′) **1** to dispute; challenge: *to* contest *an election; to* contest *a will.* **2** to fight for: *Troops* contested *every foot of the battlefield.*

con·test·ant (kən tĕs′tənt) person who takes part in a contest.

con·ti·nent (kŏn′tə nənt) **1** one of the seven large divisions of land on the earth. North America, South America, Europe,

Asia, Africa, Australia, and Antarctica are the continents. **2 the Continent** the mainland of Europe.

con·ti·nen·tal (kŏn′tə něn′təl) **1** of or belonging to a continent. **2 Continental** (1) having to do with the American side in the American Revolution: *the* Continental *Army; the* Continental *Congress.* (2) having to do with the mainland of Europe: *a* Continental *tour.* **3 continental shelf** shore of a continent under shallow water. **4 continental slope** steep submerged edge of a continent that inclines to the ocean floor.

Continental Divide high ground in western North America that separates streams flowing to the Pacific Ocean from those flowing to the Atlantic Ocean, the Arctic Ocean, or the Gulf of Mexico. Also called the Great Divide.

con·tin·u·al (kən tĭn′yōō əl) **1** going on without stopping; ceaseless: *There is a* continual *buzzing of saws in the sawmill.* **2** frequent; repeated: *The little boy makes* continual *trips to the cookie jar.* **con·tin·u·al·ly.**

con·tin·u·ance (kən tĭn′yōō əns) a keeping on, lasting, or continuing; going on with; maintaining: *a* continuance *of stormy weather.*

con·tin·u·a·tion (kən tĭn′yōō ā′shən) **1** a carrying on without a break; going on: *Commuters asked for a* continuation *of regular train service during the summer.* **2** a taking up again after an interruption: *a* continuation *of the story in next month's magazine.*

con·tin·ue (kən tĭn′ū) **1** to keep up or keep on without a break: *The rain* continued *all day.* **2** to take up again after an interruption: *We will* continue *the game after dinner.* **3** to remain or stay (in a place or condition): *He* continued *calm during the trouble.* **con·tin·ued, con·tin·u·ing.**

con·ti·nu·i·ty (kŏn′tə nū′ə tĭ) unbroken series; smooth succession; continuation without interruption: *the* continuity *of warm spring days.*

con·tin·u·ous (kən tĭn′yōō əs) unbroken; going on without interruption: *There is one* continuous *line of traffic on Main Street.* **con·tin·u·ous·ly.**

con·tor·tion (kən tôr′shən) a twisting or bending out of shape; distortion.

178

con·tour (kŏn'tŏor) **1** the outline of a figure, object, coast, mountain, etc. **2** an outline drawing.

con·tra·band (kŏn'trə-bănd') **1** anything forbidden to be brought into or sent out of a country, especially in time of war; smuggled goods. **2** prohibited; forbidden: *a shipment of contraband weapons to the rebels.* **3** a bringing in or out of such goods; smuggling.

Contour

¹con·tract (kŏn'trăkt) **1** agreement between two or more persons, groups, etc. to do something. Contracts are private agreements but are enforced by the courts. **2** the written record of such an agreement.

²con·tract (kən trăkt') **1** to make a legal agreement: *to contract to rent a house.* **2** to draw closer together; shorten and thicken: *A rubber band contracts after it has been stretched.* **3** to become infected with; catch: *to contract a disease.*

con·trac·tion (kən trăk'shən) **1** a drawing together; shrinking; shortening: *the contraction of a muscle; a contraction of the eyebrows.* **2** an entering into; incurring: *the contraction of a debt.* **3** a catching; getting: *the contraction of a disease.*

con·trac·tor (kŏn'trăk tər) person who agrees to supply something or do work for a certain price.

con·tra·dict (kŏn'trə dĭkt') **1** to state or tell the opposite of: *He contradicted his brother's story.* **2** to deny the words of: *The little girl contradicted her friend.*

con·tra·dic·tion (kŏn'trə dĭk'shən) **1** a saying the opposite; denial. **2** opposition; being inconsistent: *a contradiction between words and actions.*

con·tra·dic·to·ry (kŏn'trə dĭk'tə rĭ) opposing; inconsistent: *The witnesses gave contradictory evidence at the trial.*

con·tral·to (kən trăl'tō) **1** the lowest singing voice of a woman: *Elaine sings contralto in the quartet.* **2** a singer with such a voice. **3** indicating or having to do with this voice range: *Everyone enjoyed the contralto song.* **con·tral·tos.**

con·tra·ry (kŏn'trĕr ĭ) **1** opposed; conflicting: *They held contrary opinions.* **2** opposite in direction; adverse: *the contrary tides.* **3** always saying or doing the opposite; cranky and obstinate: *The contrary man argued with everyone.* **con·tra·ri·ly.**

¹con·trast (kən trăst') **1** to compare to show unlikeness or difference of: *The buyer contrasted the price of the two lamps.* **2** to be very different by comparison: *Her black hair contrasts with her milky white skin.*

²con·trast (kŏn'trăst) a striking difference: *There is quite a contrast between the sound of the violin and that of the trumpet.*

con·trib·ute (kən trĭb'ūt) **1** to give to some fund or cause: *to contribute to the blood bank.* **2** to help or aid; be of use: *Sunshine contributes to the health of the body.* **con·trib·ut·ed, con·trib·ut·ing.**

con·trib·u·tor (kən trĭb'yə tər) **1** person who gives to a cause: *a contributor to a building fund.* **2** person who writes an article for a newspaper or magazine.

con·tri·bu·tion (kŏn'trə bū'shən) **1** the giving of something to a fund or cause: *a contribution to the church.* **2** the thing given.

con·trite (kən trīt' or kŏn'trīt) repentant: *Oliver was always very contrite after he lost his temper.* **con·trite·ly.**

con·tri·tion (kən trĭsh'ən) sorrow for sins; sincere repentance: *He felt great contrition and hoped for forgiveness.*

con·triv·ance (kən trī'vəns) **1** an invention; a device, especially a mechanical one: *The electric eye is a contrivance for opening the door automatically.* **2** a contriving; a scheming: *a plan of his own contrivance.* **3** a plan or scheme: *What contrivance was used to get Alice to her surprise party?*

con·trive (kən trĭv') **1** to plan; devise; plot with cleverness: *The boys contrived a scheme to get out of work.* **2** to invent. **con·trived, con·triv·ing.**

con·trol (kən trōl') **1** to direct; command; take charge of: *The coach controls the health habits of the football team.* **2** command; power (over): *police control of traffic.* **3** to hold in check; hold back: *to control one's temper.* **4** a method or means

fāte, făt, fâre, fär; bē, bĕt; bīte, bĭt; nō, nŏt, nôr; fūse, fŭn, fûr; tōō, tŏŏk; foil; foul; thin; ~~then~~; hw for wh as in *what*; zh for s as in u*s*ual; ə for a, e, i, o, u, as in *a*go, lin*e*n, per*i*l, at*o*m, min*u*s

179

of holding back; a check: *price* control.
5 a device for regulating and guiding a
machine: *the* controls *of an airplane.* **con·
trolled, con·trol·ling.**

con·tro·ver·sial (kŏn'trə vûr'shəl) likely
to cause disagreement or discussion: *a
controversial issue.* **con·tro·ver·sial·ly.**

con·tro·ver·sy (kŏn'trə vûr'sĭ) argument;
dispute; disagreement: *There was a con-
troversy over the umpire's decision.* **con·
tro·ver·sies.**

co·nun·drum (kə nŭn'drəm) a riddle; puzzling question. "What has four wheels and
flies?" is a conundrum. (The answer is "a
garbage truck.")

con·va·lesce (kŏn'və lĕs') to get better
after sickness; to recover strength and
health: *He is in Florida to* convalesce. **con·
va·lesced, con·va·lesc·ing.**

con·va·les·cent (kŏn'və lĕs'ənt) **1** getting
better after sickness; recovering: *He is
convalescent, but still in the hospital.* **2** having to do with recovery from illness: *a
convalescent diet.* **3** person who is getting
well.

con·vene (kən vēn') **1** to come together; to
assemble (for a meeting): *The legislature
convened for the fall session.* **2** to call together: *The mayor convened the city
council.* **con·vened, con·ven·ing.**

con·ven·ience (kən vēn'yəns) **1** a being
easy to use; a being suitable for a purpose:
*the convenience of the automobile as com-
pared with the horse and buggy.* **2** a saving
of time and trouble; advantage: *It would be
a convenience if the library would stay open
longer.* **3** a handy device; a useful appliance: *The telephone is a convenience in
most homes.* **4 at one's convenience** at a
time suitable to a person.

con·ven·ient (kən vēn'yənt) **1** easy to use
or reach; handy: *Everything is convenient
in this modern kitchen.* **2** suitable; causing
no trouble or difficulty: *to meet at a convenient time and place.* **3 convenient to**
near to; within easy access of: *My house is
convenient to the school.* **con·ven·ient·ly.**

con·vent (kŏn'vĕnt) **1** a society of women
who live together and devote themselves to
a religious life. **2** the building or buildings
occupied by such a society.

con·ven·tion (kən vĕn'shən) **1** a meeting
for some special purpose: *a convention of*

doctors. **2** a generally accepted practice;
custom: *It is a convention for men to shake
hands when introduced.* **3** an agreement
between nations, persons, etc.: *the conven-
tions for proper treatment of prisoners of war.*

con·ven·tion·al (kən vĕn'shən əl) **1** following accepted practices and customs; customary: *"How do you do?" is a* conventional *greeting.* **2** not new or original;
commonplace: *The furnishings in the room
were* conventional. **con·ven·tion·al·ly.**

con·ver·sa·tion (kŏn'vər sā'shən) informal
talk between two or more people.

con·verse (kən vûrs') to talk together. **con·
versed, con·vers·ing.**

con·ver·sion (kən vûr'zhən) **1** a changing
(from one form or use to another): *the
conversion of a vacant lot into a playground.*
2 a change by which a person accepts a
religion or shifts from one religion to another.

¹**con·vert** (kən vûrt') **1** to change (from one
form, use, or purpose to another): *A boiler
converts water into steam.* **2** to cause (a
person) to believe in a religion, a point of
view, etc.: *Missionaries converted everyone
in the village.*

²**con·vert** (kŏn'vûrt) person who becomes a
believer in a religion or is led to accept
someone else's opinions, ideas, etc.

con·vert·i·ble (kən vûr'tə bəl) **1** capable of
change or adaptation: *This stool is* con-
vertible *to a stepladder.* **2** an automobile
with a top that can be lowered. **con·
vert·i·bly.**

con·vex (kŏn'vĕks') curved outward like the outside of a ball
or arch. **con·vex·ly.**

con·vey (kən vā') **1** to carry
from one place to another;
transport: *A truck will* convey
the equipment to the boat. **2** to make known:
Her expression conveyed *her disappointment.*
3 to transfer (property) from one person
to another.

Convex

con·vey·ance (kən vā'əns) **1** the carrying
(of something) from one place to another:
Trucks and trains are used for the con-
veyance *of goods from factories to stores.*
2 a vehicle; thing used for carrying.

con·vey·or belt (kən vā'ər bĕlt) a moving
belt used to transport things from one place
to another.

¹con·vict (kən vĭkt′) to prove or declare to be guilty: *He was* convicted *of theft.*

²con·vict (kŏn′vĭkt) a person sentenced to prison for a crime.

con·vic·tion (kən vĭk′shən) **1** a declaring or proving that someone is guilty: *The trial ended in the* conviction *and imprisonment of the thief.* **2** a being found guilty: *The thief's* conviction *sent him to prison.* **3** firm belief; definite opinion: *We had a strong* conviction *that we would win.*

con·vince (kən vĭns′) to make (someone) certain; cause (someone) to believe: *I* convinced *him that he was wrong.* **con·vinced, con·vinc·ing.**

con·vinc·ing (kən vĭn′sĭng) causing (one) to believe; persuading by proofs: *He made a* convincing *speech.* **con·vinc·ing·ly.**

con·voy (kŏn′voi) **1** (also kən voi′) to accompany (ships, vehicles, etc.) in order to protect or guide them; to escort: *Two destroyers* convoyed *the supply ships.* **2** a group of ships, vehicles, etc., led or guarded by an escort. **3** a ship, etc., that acts as an escort. **4** act of escorting and protecting: *The* convoy *of merchant ships is necessary in time of war.*

con·vulse (kən vŭls′) **1** to shake or affect with spasms of laughter, pain, or emotion: *The audience was* convulsed *by the funny show.* **2** to agitate or disturb violently; shake: *The earthquake* convulsed *a huge area.* **con·vulsed, con·vuls·ing.**

con·vul·sion (kən vŭl′shən) **1** violent jerking or contortion caused by tightening of certain muscles; a fit. **2** violent disturbance: *Earthquakes and eruptions of volcanoes are* convulsions *of the earth.*

con·vul·sive (kən vŭl′sĭv) like a convulsion; causing or showing violent disturbance: *The comedian's jokes threw her into* convulsive *laughter.* **con·vul·sive·ly.**

coo (kōō) **1** soft, murmuring sound like that made by doves and pigeons. **2** to make such a sound. **coos.**

cook (kŏŏk) **1** to prepare food by the use of heat. Boiling, frying, and baking are ways of cooking food. **2** to be prepared by heating: *The ham* cooked *for an hour.* **3** a person who cooks.

cook·er·y (kŏŏk′ə ri) art or work of preparing food to be eaten.

cook·ie (kŏŏk′ĭ) small, flat, sweet cake. Also spelled **cooky. cook·ies.**

cool (kōōl) **1** not warm; slightly cold: *There is a* cool *breeze blowing off the lake.* **2** to make slightly cold; chill: *Please* cool *the dessert in the refrigerator before serving.* **3** to become slightly cold: *The pies* cooled *on the window sill.* **4** not letting in or keeping in heat: *a* cool *summer suit.* **5** not excited; calm: *He alone remained* cool *in the confusion that followed the explosion.* **6** lacking in warmth and friendliness; not cordial: *He was given a* cool *reception.* **7** time that is moderately cold or not warm: *the* cool *of the evening.* **8** place that is cool: *Let's sit in the* cool *of the shade tree.* **cool·ly.**

cool·er (kōō′lər) device for keeping foods or liquids cool: *a water* cooler.

coo·lie (kōō′lĭ) in the Orient, an unskilled laborer. (Homonym: coulee)

cool·ness (kōōl′nĭs) **1** a feeling of mild cold. **2** aloofness; unfriendliness.

coon (kōōn) raccoon.

coop (kōōp) a cage or enclosure for fowls, rabbits, etc.; a pen. (Homonym: coupe) **coop up** to shut up; confine.

coop·er (kōō′pər) person who makes or mends barrels, casks, etc.

co-op·er·ate or **co·op·er·ate** or **co·öp′er·ate** (kō ŏp′ə rāt′) to work or act together for a particular purpose or end: *If everyone* co-operates, *the job will be finished sooner.* **co-op·er·at·ed** or **co·op·er·at·ed** or **co·öp·er·at·ed, co-op·er·at·ing** or **co·op·er·at·ing** or **co·öp·er·at·ing.**

co-op·er·a·tion or **co·op·er·a·tion** or **co·öp·er·a·tion** (kō ŏp′ə rā′shən) a working together for the same purpose or end: *The play requires everyone's* co-operation.

co-op·er·a·tive or **co·op·er·a·tive,** or **co·öp·er·a·tive** (kō ŏp′ər ə tĭv or kō ŏp′ə-rā′tĭv) **1** working or willing to work with others for the same ends: *The project was successful because everyone working on it was* co-operative. **2** of or having to do with co-operation: *A* co-operative *effort will get this job done quickly.* **co-op·er·a·tive·ly** or **co·op·er·a·tive·ly** or **co·öp·er·a·tive·ly.**

---

fāte, făt, fâre, fär; bē, bĕt; bīte, bĭt; nō, nŏt, nôr; fūse, fŭn, fûr; tōō, tŏŏk; foil; foul; thin; then; hw for wh as in *what;* zh for s as in u*su*al; ə for a, e, i, o, u, as in ago, linen, peril, atom, minus

co·or·di·nate or **co·or·di·nate** or **co·or·di·nate** (kō ôr′də nāt′) **1** to harmonize; fit together; to work in a smooth and efficient manner: *to* co-ordinate *the departments of a business.* **2** to work in harmony: *An athlete's muscles must* co-ordinate *well.* **3** (also kō ôr′də nĭt) of equal importance: *Mercy and justice are* co-ordinate *virtues.* **co·or·di·nat·ed** or **co·or·di·nat·ed** or **co·or·di·nat·ed, co·or·di·nat·ing** or **co·or·di·nat·ing** or **co·or·di·nat·ing.**

¹cope (kōp) to contend; struggle successfully: *There were so many customers that one clerk could not* cope *with all their demands.* **coped, cop·ing.** [¹cope is from a French word (couper) meaning "to strike."]

²cope (kōp) a long cloak or mantle worn by priests on certain occasions. [²cope is from a medieval Latin word (capa or cappa) which goes back to an earlier Latin word (caput) meaning "head." It is related to ¹cape.]

co·pi·lot (kō′pī′lət) the second pilot in an aircraft who assists the pilot in operating the plane.

co·pi·ous (kō′pī əs) large; plentiful; ample; abundant: *There were* copious *showers that spring.* **co·pi·ous·ly.**

cop·per (kŏp′ər) **1** a common, reddish metal element, easily worked, and an excellent conductor of heat and electricity. **2** made of this metal: *a* copper *pot.* **3** reddish brown: *She has* copper-*colored hair.*

cop·per·head (kŏp′ər hĕd′) **1** poisonous snake with a copper-colored head, found in the United States. **2 Copperhead** person from the North who sympathized with the South during the Civil War.

cop·per·smith (kŏp′ər smith′) one who works in copper.

co·pra (kōp′rə) the dried meat of the coconut, which furnishes coconut oil.

copse (kŏps) a thick grove of bushes and small trees; a thicket.

cop·y (kŏp′ī) **1** to make or do something to look or be like something else: *to* copy *a report; to* copy *the movements of a dancer.* **2** something made to be or look like something else; a reproduction; an imitation: *a* copy *of a picture.* **3** a single one of a number of things made to be alike, such as books, magazines, etc.: *We ordered several* copies *of that new book.* **4** typed or written material ready to be sent to the printer. **cop·ies; cop·ied, cop·y·ing.**

cop·y·right (kŏp′ī rīt′) **1** the right granted by law for a term of years to an author, composer, or artist, and to him alone, to publish and sell an original literary, musical, or artistic work. **2** to secure such a right: *to* copyright *a book.*

cor·a·cle (kôr′ə kəl) short, wide fishing boat made of waterproof cloth or hide stretched over a frame.

cor·al (kôr′əl or kŏr′əl) **1** a substance, somewhat like limestone, built up of the skeletons of great numbers of tiny sea animals called polyps. Coral may be white, red, pink, or black, and is often used for making jewelry. **2** one of these tiny animals. **3** orange-red.

Coral

cord (kôrd) **1** a string or small rope. **2** wires bound together and insulated to make a small, flexible cable for electrical fixtures: *a lamp* cord. **3** in the body, anything like a cord: *vocal* cords; *spinal* cord. **4** a measure of cut wood equal to a pile 4 feet high, 4 feet wide, and 8 feet long. **5** to bind with string or rope. (Homonym: chord)

cor·dial (kôr′jəl) hearty; sincere; warm; friendly: *a* cordial *welcome.* **cor·dial·ly.**

cor·dial·i·ty (kôr jăl′ə tī) good will; heartiness; friendliness; warmth: *They were moved by the* cordiality *of the welcome.*

cor·du·roy (kôr′də roi′) **1** a cotton cloth with a surface of velvety ridges. **2 corduroys** trousers made of corduroy.

core (kôr) **1** central part that contains the seeds of certain fleshy fruits. Apples and pears have cores. **2** to remove the core from: *She* cored *the apples before baking them.* **3** central or essential part: *the* core *of an argument.* **cored, cor·ing.** (Homonym: corps)

cork (kôrk) **1** the light outer bark of a certain kind of oak tree. Cork is used to make such things as bottle stoppers, life preservers, and floor coverings. **2** a stopper, especially one made of cork, for a bottle or container. **3** to put a cork or other stopper in (a bottle).

cork·screw (kôrk'skrōō') **1** a spiral-shaped pointed metal tool for pulling corks from bottles. **2** shaped like a corkscrew; spiral.

cor·mo·rant (kôr'mə-rənt) a large sea bird with a long neck and an elastic throat for holding fish.

¹corn (kôrn) **1** an American cereal plant which produces large ears of grain on tall stalks. It is also called Indian corn ör maize. **2** the kernels or seeds of this plant, used for food. [¹**corn** is the unchanged form of an Old English word meaning "wheat," "grain."]

Cormorant, about 2½ ft. long

²corn (kôrn) a horny thickening of the skin, usually on the toe or foot. [²**corn** is from a Latin word (cornu) meaning "horn." ²**Corn** and **horn** have a common origin.]

corn bread bread made of corn meal baked in a shallow pan.

corn·cob (kôrn'kŏb') the woody center of an ear of corn, on which the kernels grow.

Ear of corn

cor·ne·a (kôr'nĭ ə) the transparent membrane that covers the iris and pupil at the front of the eyeball. For picture, see **eye.**

corned (kôrnd) preserved with salt: *A dinner of* corned *beef and cabbage.*

cor·ner (kôr'nər) **1** the place where two lines, sides, or edges meet: *The flag stood in a corner of the classroom. There are four corners where two streets cross.* **2** nook; hidden or secluded place: *Let's find a quiet corner where we can talk.* **3** faraway place: *He has stamps from every corner of the earth.* **4** place or situation from which escape is difficult: *The lawyer's question put the witness in a corner.* **5** to drive (someone or something) into a corner: *The cat cornered the mouse.* **6** on or at a corner: *a corner house or lot.* **7** piece to strengthen, fasten, or ornament a corner.

cor·net (kôr nĕt') a brass musical instrument similar to a trumpet.

corn·field (kôrn'fēld') a field in which corn is grown.

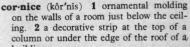
Cornet

corn·husk (kôrn'hŭsk') the covering of flat green leaves that surround an ear of corn. Also called **corn shuck.**

cor·nice (kôr'nĭs) **1** ornamental molding on the walls of a room just below the ceiling. **2** a decorative strip at the top of a column or under the edge of the roof of a building.

corn meal coarse flour made of ground kernels of corn, used in making corn bread, muffins, etc.

corn·stalk (kôrn'stôk') the stem of the plant on which corn grows.

corn·starch (kôrn'stärch') a kind of flour made from corn, used in making puddings and as a thickening for foods.

cor·nu·co·pi·a (kôr'nyōō-kō'pĭ ə) **1** the horn of plenty, shown overflowing with fruit and flowers. **2** horn-shaped ornament or container, often used on Christmas trees.

Cornucopia

co·rol·la (kə rŏl'ə) all the petals of a flower.

co·ro·na (kə rō'nə) **1** outer atmosphere of the sun, made up of hot gases. It is seen as a circle of light beyond the moon during an eclipse of the sun. **2** bright ring or crown.

cor·o·na·tion (kôr'ə nā'shən or kôr'ə nā'shən) **1** the crowning of a king, queen, or other ruler. **2** having to do with a coronation: *a coronation procession.*

cor·o·ner (kôr'ə nər or kŏr'ə nər) public officer who investigates the cause of any unnatural or violent death.

cor·o·net (kôr'ə nĕt' or kŏr'-ə nĕt') **1** a small crown worn by nobles below kings and queens in rank. **2** a band of jewels, flowers, gold, etc., worn as a head ornament by women.

Coronet

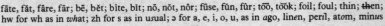

fāte, făt, fâre, fär; bē, bĕt; bīte, bĭt; nō, nŏt, nôr; fūse, fŭn, fûr; tōō, tŏŏk; foil; foul; thin; ~~then~~; hw for wh as in *wh*at; zh for s as in u*s*ual; ə for a, e, i, o, u, as in *a*go, lin*e*n, per*i*l, at*o*m, min*u*s

corporal

¹cor·po·ral (kôr′pə rəl) of the body; physical: *harsh* corporal *punishment.* **cor·po·ral·ly.** [¹**corporal** is from a form (corporalis) of a Latin word (corpus) meaning "body." From this Latin word we also get **corpse** and **corps.**]

²cor·po·ral (kôr′pə rəl) a soldier in the army above the rank of private first class and below a sergeant. [²**corporal** is from an Italian word (caporale) that goes back to a Latin word (caput) meaning "head." ²**corporal** has no connection whatever with ¹**corporal.**]

cor·po·ra·tion (kôr′pə rā′shən) a group of persons permitted by law to act as one person in carrying on a business.

corps (kôr) **1** a large unit of an army, made up of two or more divisions. **2** body of troops trained for special duties: *the medical* corps. **3** body of persons associated in a common work: *the diplomatic* corps. (Homonym: core)

corpse (kôrps) a dead human body.

cor·pu·lent (kôr′pyŏŏ lənt) heavy and fat.

cor·pus·cle (kôr′pəs əl) one of the tiny red or white cells of the blood.

Corral

cor·ral (kə răl′) **1** pen or enclosure for horses, cattle, or other livestock. **2** to drive into or shut up in such a pen: *The cowboy* corralled *the cattle.* **3** a circle of wagons drawn up for defense. **4** to arrange wagons in such a circle. **cor·ralled, cor·al·ling.**

cor·rect (kə rĕkt′) **1** right; exact; accurate: *Is 20 to 13 the* correct *score?* **2** right according to a standard of manners, taste, etc.: *the* correct *way to make an introduction.* **3** to remove errors from; make (something) right: *to* correct *a watch by a radio time signal.* **4** to mark errors in; point out mistakes: *to* correct *a test.* **5** to point out (someone's) faults and scold or punish: *The parents* corrected *the child for lying.* **cor·rect·ly.**

corsage

cor·rec·tion (kə rĕk′shən) **1** the pointing out or removing of mistakes; a changing something wrong to make it right: *The* correction *of papers is part of a teacher's job.* **2** something put in place of a mistake or error: *The editor made a* correction *before printing the story.* **3** punishment: *An unruly child needs* correction.

cor·re·spond (kŏr′ə spŏnd′ or kôr′ə spŏnd′) **1** to agree; match: *My answer* corresponds *with yours.* **2** to be like or similar to in position, use, character, or amount: *The wings of a bird* correspond *to the arms of a man.* **3** to exchange letters: *Do you* correspond *with her?*

cor·re·spond·ence (kŏr′ə spŏn′dəns or kôr′ə spŏn′dəns) **1** agreement; likeness: *close* correspondence *in height.* **2** letter writing: *the* correspondence *of a business firm.* **3** letters: *Put the* correspondence *on the desk top.*

cor·re·spond·ent (kŏr′ə spŏn′dənt or kôr′ə spŏn′dənt) **1** person with whom one exchanges letters. **2** person who writes news from a certain place for a newspaper or magazine: *a foreign* correspondent.

cor·re·spond·ing (kŏr′ə spŏn′dĭng or kôr′ə spŏn′dĭng) similar; agreeing in some way: *statements* corresponding *in every detail.* **cor·re·spond·ing·ly.**

cor·ri·dor (kŏr′ə dôr′ or kôr′ə dôr′) a long passage into which rooms open: *a school* corridor.

cor·rob·o·rate (kə rŏb′ə rāt′) to confirm; make more certain: *We* corroborated *the driver's story of the accident.* **cor·rob·o·rat·ed, cor·rob·o·rat·ing.**

cor·ru·gate (kŏr′ə gāt′ or kôr′ə gāt′) to bend or shape into wavelike folds. **cor·ru·gat·ed, cor·ru·gat·ing.**

cor·rupt (kə rŭpt′) **1** dishonest; influenced by bribery: *a corrupt government.* **2** to cause to be dishonest; influence by bribery: *to* corrupt *a judge or government official.* **3** morally bad; evil: *a corrupt life.* **4** to cause to be evil or morally bad: *Bad companions* corrupted *his morals.* **cor·rupt·ly.**

cor·rup·tion (kə rŭp′shən) **1** a making or becoming evil; a corrupting. **2** dishonesty, especially because of bribery. **3** a rotting away; decay.

cor·sage (kôr säzh′) flowers worn by a woman as a decoration.

184

cor·set (kôr′sĭt) tight-fitting undergarment worn to support the back or to shape the waist and hips.

cos·met·ic (kŏz mĕt′ĭk) preparation used to beautify the skin or hair. Hand lotion, powder, and lipstick are cosmetics.

cos·mic (kŏz′mĭk) **1** having to do with the whole universe: *a* cosmic *philosophy*. **2** immense or vast like the universe.

cosmic rays atomic particles of great speed and energy that reach the earth from outer space.

cos·mos (kŏz′məs) **1** the universe. **2** a garden plant with feathery leaves and daisylike pink and white flowers.

cost (kŏst or kôst) **1** price charged: *What is the* cost *of these shoes?* **2** to be priced at; require the payment of (money, time, etc.): *The book* costs *one dollar.* **3** loss; sacrifice: *He got rich at the* cost *of his health.* **4** to cause the loss of: *The forest fire* cost *the lives of many animals.* **5 at all costs** no matter what the cost may be. **cost, cost·ing.**

Cos·ta Ri·ca (kŏs′tə rē′kə) a country in Central America.

cost·ly (kŏst′lĭ or kôst′lĭ) expensive in terms of money, time, etc.: *a* costly *mistake; a* costly *string of pearls.* **cost·li·er, cost·li·est.**

cos·tume (kŏs′tūm) **1** clothes: *a winter* costume; *traveling* costume. **2** clothes of a certain country or period of time: *Mexican* costume; *colonial* costume. **3** to dress in or provide with a costume. **cos·tumed, cos·tum·ing.**

co·sy (kō′zĭ) cozy. **co·si·er, co·si·est; co·si·ly.**

¹**cot** (kŏt) narrow bed, especially one made of canvas stretched over a frame. [¹cot is from a word (khat) used in India.]

Cot

²**cot** (kŏt) **1** cottage. **2** shelter for small animals; cote. [²cot is the unchanged form of an Old English word.]

cote (kōt) coop, shed, or pen for birds or other small animals: *a dove* cote (Homonym: coat)

cot·tage (kŏt′ĭj) **1** small house. **2** house at a vacation resort.

cot·ton (kŏt′ən) **1** a plant with soft white fibers attached to its seeds. **2** the fibers of this plant. **3** thread made of cotton fibers. **4** cloth spun from cotton thread. **5** made of cotton: *a* cotton *shirt; a* cotton *dress.*

Cotton flower and boll

cot·ton·tail (kŏt′ən-tāl′) a small wild American rabbit with a fluffy tuftlike white tail.

cot·ton·wood (kŏt′ən wŏŏd′) **1** a kind of poplar tree with cottonlike hairs on the seeds. **2** the wood of this tree.

couch (kouch) **1** long upholstered seat; sofa. **2** to put into words: *The diplomat* couched *his request in formal language.*

cou·gar (kŏŏ′gər) yellow-brown American animal of the cat family; puma; mountain lion.

cough (kôf or kŏf) **1** to force air from the lungs with a sharp or wheezing noise. **2** act or sound of coughing. **3** coughing as a habit or illness: *a bad* cough.

could (kŏŏd) was able to; were able to.

could·n't (kŏŏd′ənt) could not: *They* couldn't *go.*

couldst (kŏŏdst) old form of **could** used only with *thou.*

cou·lee (kŏŏ′lĭ) deep gulch with sloping sides, usually the valley of a stream that is dry in summer. (Homonym: coolie)

coun·cil (koun′səl) **1** group of people called together to discuss and settle problems, give advice, etc.: *A student* council *met to discuss the school dance.* **2** a meeting of a selected group for discussion of problems, planning, etc.: *The Indian chiefs held a war* council. (Homonym: counsel)

coun·ci·lor or **coun·cil·lor** (koun′sə lər) member of a group called together to discuss, make plans, govern, etc. (Homonym: counselor)

coun·sel (koun′səl) **1** advice; instruction: *the* counsel *of an experienced person.* **2** to advise: *The lawyer* counseled *his client about making his will.* **3** lawyer or lawyers:

---

fāte, făt, fâre, fär; bē, bĕt; bīte, bĭt; nō, nŏt, nôr; fūse, fŭn, fûr; tōō, tŏŏk; foil; foul; thin; ~~then~~; hw for wh as in *wh*at; zh for s as in usual; ə for a, e, i, o, u, as in *a*go, linen, peril, atom, minus

counselor

the counsel *for the defense.* **4 take counsel**
to confer; consult and exchange ideas: *The
generals* took counsel *before attacking.*
(Homonym: council)

coun·se·lor or **coun·sel·lor** (koun'sə lər)
1 adviser. **2** person who instructs or supervises activities at a camp. **3** lawyer. (Homonym: councilor)

¹count (kount) **1** to say numbers in order: *to
count from 1 to 100.* **2** to find a total by
numbering: *He* counted *the marbles in
the box.* **3** a counting: *A* count *showed
that one boy was missing.* **4** the total reached
by counting: *The final* count *was fifty
dollars.* **5** to consider: *You can* count *me
one of the party on the trip.* **6** to be of
value; have effect: *Every penny* counts *in
raising money for the city hospital.* **7** to
include; take into account: *If we* count
those in the other room there are ten of us.
count on to rely on: *I'm* counting *on you.*
[**¹count** is from a Latin word (com-
putare). **Compute** also comes from this
Latin word.]

²count (kount) title of nobility in several
European countries, or a man holding the
title. [**²count** is from a French word
(comte) that comes from a form of a Latin
word (comes) meaning "companion."]

count·down (kount'doun') a counting
backward from some number to zero to indicate the time remaining before firing a
rocket, guided missile, etc.

coun·te·nance (koun'tə nəns) **1** the face: *a
countenance of even features.* **2** expression
of the face showing feeling or character: *a
happy* countenance. **3** approval; encouragement: *I won't give any aid or* countenance
to such a crooked scheme. **4** to give approval to; support: *He would not* countenance *dishonesty.* **coun·te·nanced, coun·
te·nanc·ing.**

¹coun·ter (koun'tər) **1** narrow table or flat
surface at which goods are sold and money
is handled. **2** person or thing that counts:
The electric traffic counter *showed that
2,000 cars passed it in an hour.* **3** small disk
or other object used in games for keeping
score. [**¹counter** is from **¹count**. A table
where counting was done quite naturally
became a **counter.**]

²count·er (koun'tər) **1** in the contrary or
opposite way: *The soldier was punished for*

countryside

going counter *to orders.* **2** opposing; contrary: *to make a* counter *proposal.* **3** to
oppose: *The boxer* countered *the blow with a
left jab.* [**²counter** is from a French word
(contre) that comes from a Latin word
(contra).]

coun·ter·act (koun'tər ăkt') to act against;
offset the effect of: *A piece of sugar* coun-
teracted *the bitterness of the medicine.*

coun·ter·clock·wise (koun'tər klŏk'wīz')
in the opposite direction from that in
which the hands of a clock move.

coun·ter·feit (koun'tər fĭt) **1** made in
exact imitation of something genuine in
order to deceive; not genuine: *a* counterfeit
dollar bill. **2** a copy or imitation of something made to pass as genuine: *The spy's
passport was a* counterfeit. **3** to copy or
imitate exactly in order to deceive. **4** to
make a pretense of: *to* counterfeit *grief.*

coun·ter·part (koun'tər pärt') person or
thing that matches or corresponds closely
to another: *An admiral in the navy is the
counterpart in rank of a general in the army.*

coun·ter·sign (koun'tər sīn') **1** password
or secret signal: *If you give the* countersign
tonight the guard will admit you. **2** to add a
signature to a document already signed to
make it of value: *The bank may ask you to
have someone else* countersign *the check.*

count·ess (koun'tĭs) **1** wife or widow of a
count or earl. **2** woman with a rank equal
to that of a count or earl.

count·less (kount'lĭs) too many to be
counted; innumerable: *the* countless *stars.*

coun·try (kŭn'trĭ) **1** territory occupied by
a nation: *The* country *of Switzerland is
small.* **2** nation; a state with its own
government: *an independent* country. **3** the
place where one was born or of which one is
a citizen. **4** the people of a nation: *The*
country *will vote for a new president.*
5 land; region: *The* country *near the river
was fertile.* **6 the country** rural region;
area outside of cities or towns. **coun·tries.**

coun·try·man (kŭn'trĭ mən) **1** man who
is of another's country. **2** person who lives
in the country. **coun·try·men.**

coun·try·side (kŭn'trĭ sīd') **1** rural region
or landscape: *The* countryside *glowed with
color in the fall.* **2** people living in a rural
district: *The whole* countryside *turned out
for the celebration.*

186

coun·try·wom·an (kŭn′trĭ wŏŏm′ən) **1** woman who is of another's country. **2** woman who lives in the country. **coun·try·wom·en.**

coun·ty (koun′tĭ) **1** part or division of a state. A county usually has its own government for local affairs. **2** of or belonging to a county: *a county road.* **coun·ties.**

coupe (kōōp) or **cou·pé** (kōō pā′) closed two-door automobile, usually seating two or three persons. (Homonym: coop)

cou·ple (kŭp′əl) **1** two things of the same kind; pair. **2** a man and woman together: *a married* couple. **3** to join in pairs: *to* couple *dogs to pull a sled.* **4** to join; connect: *to* couple *railroad cars.* **cou·pled, cou·pling.**

cou·pling (kŭp′lĭng) **1** a joining; a connection. **2** device that joins things together: *A* coupling *holds railroad cars together.*

Car coupling

cou·pon (kū′pŏn or kōō′pŏn) **1** small part of a bond that can be cut off or detached and given in to collect interest that is due. **2** a ticket or part of a printed advertisement that can be exchanged for prizes, samples, or the like.

cour·age (kûr′ĭj) strength of mind and spirit that enables one to control fear when facing difficulties and dangers; bravery.

cou·ra·geous (kə rā′jəs) having courage; brave. **cou·ra·geous·ly.**

cour·i·er (kōōr′ĭ ər or kûr′ĭ ər) **1** messenger, usually carrying important letters or documents to be delivered with great speed. **2** person who accompanies a party of travelers to take care of tickets, hotel reservations, and the like; guide.

course (kôrs) **1** onward motion; progress: *the* course *of history.* **2** direction; path: *the* course *of a ship; the* course *of a river.* **3** way of proceeding: *Your only proper* course *is to write the paper over.* **4** set of things in a series: *a* course *of X-ray treatments.* **5** lessons and classes in a certain subject: *a three-year* course *in nursing.* **6** piece of land laid out for a sport: *a golf* course*; a racing* course. **7** part of a meal served at one time: *The last* course *was dessert.* **8** to run; flow: *The falling water* coursed *swiftly over the rapids.* **9** of course naturally; certainly. **coursed, cours·ing.** (Homonym: coarse)

cours·er (kôr′sər) a swift horse.

court (kôrt) **1** open place enclosed by buildings or walls; courtyard: *We saw a* court *from the apartment window.* **2** place marked for a game: *a tennis* court. **3** residence of a king or other sovereign; royal palace. **4** people attending a king or other sovereign; royal attendants. **5** a sovereign and his followers. **6** official meeting of a sovereign and his advisers. **7** place for administering justice, or holding trials, etc: *The witness was brought to* court. **8** judge or judges and officials who administer justice, hold trials, etc.: *The* court *sentenced the guilty man.* **9** assembly for legal trial: *The case will be heard at the next* court. **10** to seek the favor of. **11** to woo; try to win in marriage. **12** to try to get; seek; invite: *to* court *fame.*

cour·te·ous (kûr′tĭ əs) polite: *a courteous reply.* **cour·te·ous·ly.**

cour·te·sy (kûr′tə sĭ) **1** politeness. **2** act of politeness or respect. **3** kindness or generosity: *Ice cream was given for the school picnic through the* courtesy *of the dairy.* **cour·te·sies.**

court·house (kôrt′hous′) building where courts of law are held. Many courthouses have offices for county officials.

court·ti·er (kôr′tĭ ər) attendant at a royal court.

court·ly (kôrt′lĭ) very courteous and dignified. **court·li·er, court·li·est.**

court·room (kôrt′rōōm′) room where law cases are tried.

court·ship (kôrt′shĭp′) a courting; wooing.

court·yard (kôrt′yärd′) an open place enclosed by buildings or walls; a court.

cous·in (kŭz′ən) son or daughter of an aunt or uncle.

cove (kōv) small bay; inlet of the sea; mouth of a creek.

cov·e·nant (kŭv′ə nənt) **1** a solemn agreement; contract. **2** to make a solemn agreement.

---

fāte, făt, fâre, fär; bē, bĕt; bīte, bĭt; nō, nŏt, nôr; fūse, fŭn, fûr; tōō, tŏŏk; foil; foul; thin; ~~then~~;
hw for wh as in *wh*at; zh for s as in u*s*ual; ə for a, e, i, o, u, as in ago, linen, peril, atom, minus

187

cov·er (kŭv'ər) **1** to put or lay over: *Use this cloth to* cover *the table.* **2** to spread over: *Water slowly* covered *the basement floor.* **3** to lie or be placed over: *A lid* covers *a box.* **4** to hide: *to* cover *a mistake.* **5** anything that hides or protects: *Under the* cover *of fog, the smuggler's boat slipped off to sea.* **6** to include: *That book* covers *the geography of America.* **7** to go or travel over: *We* covered *seven miles on our bicycles.*

cov·er·all (kŭv'ər ôl') a one-piece garment combining shirt and trousers, worn like overalls.

covered wagon large wagon with a canvas top, used by pioneers traveling to the central and western parts of the United States.

Covered wagon

cov·er·ing (kŭv'ər ing) anything that covers.

cov·er·let (kŭv'ər lĭt) bedspread.

cov·ert (kŭv'ərt) **1** secret; hidden: *The girl stole a* covert *glance at the note when no one was looking.* **2** protected place; shelter. **3** underbrush, thicket, etc. where animals hide. **cov·ert·ly.**

cov·et (kŭv'ĭt) to desire eagerly (especially, something that belongs to somebody else): *He* covets *his big brother's bicycle.*

cov·et·ous (kŭv'ə təs) desiring too greatly something that belongs to another: *He gave the bicycle a* covetous *glance.* **cov·et·ous·ly.**

cov·ey (kŭv'ĭ) a brood or flock of game birds: *a* covey *of quail;* covey *of grouse.*

¹cow (kou) **1** full-grown female domestic animal that gives milk. **2** female moose, elephant, whale, etc. [**¹cow** is a form of an Old English word (cu).]

Cow, about 5 ft. high

²cow (kou) to make afraid; frighten. [**²cow** is from an Old Norse word and has no connection whatever with **¹cow.**]

cow·ard (kou'ərd) person who lacks courage; one who is shamefully timid.

cow·ard·ice (kou'ər dĭs) lack of courage; shameful timidity.

cow·ard·ly (kou'ərd lĭ) showing lack of courage; shamefully timid; contemptible: *a* cowardly *retreat.*

cow·bell (kou'bĕl') small, four-sided bell with a dull, tinkling sound, usually hung about a cow's neck.

cow·bird (kou'bûrd') a small blackbird with a brown head, often seen near cattle.

cow·boy (kou'boi') man who looks after cattle on a ranch, usually on horseback.

cow·catch·er (kou'căch'ər) framework on the front of a locomotive for removing obstacles from the track.

cow·er (kou'ər) to crouch down in fear, shame, or misery: *The frightened puppy* cowered *in a corner.*

cow·girl (kou'gûrl') a girl who helps herd and care for cattle on a ranch.

cow hand man who herds or cares for cattle; cowboy.

cow·hide (kou'hid') **1** the skin of a cow. **2** leather made by preparing such skin.

cowl (koul) **1** monk's long robe with a hood. **2** the hood itself.

cow·pox (kou'pŏks') contagious disease of cows. Cowpox germs are used in vaccinating people against smallpox.

Monk wearing cowl

cow·punch·er (kou'pŭn'chər) cowboy.

cow·slip (kou'slĭp') a wild plant with yellow flowers that grows in damp places.

cox·swain (kŏk'sən or kŏk'swăn') man who steers a boat, especially a racing shell.

coy (koi) **1** bashful; shy. **2** pretending to be shy. **coy·ly.**

coy·ote (ki'ōt' or ki-ō'ti) small prairie wolf of western North America.

Coyote, about 3½ ft. long

co·zy (kō'zi) snug; warm and comfortable: *The cat likes her* cozy *corner by the fire.* **co·zi·er, co·zi·est; co·zi·ly.** Also spelled **cosy.**

crab (krăb) any of various broad, flat shellfish with eight legs and two claws. Many kinds of crabs are good to eat.

Crab

crab apple 1 a kind of small, sour apple much used in jelly making. **2** tree that bears this fruit.

crab·bed (krăb′ĭd) surly; cranky; cross.

crack (krăk) **1** line of division or narrow gap without a complete separation of parts: *a long* crack *in the ceiling.* **2** to break or split without complete separation of parts: *A dish fell and* cracked. *I* cracked *the cup.* **3** long, narrow opening between boards, etc.; crevice. **4** sharp, snapping sound: *the* crack *of a pistol.* **5** to make or cause to make such a sound: *The whip* cracked. **6** to break abruptly: *The singer's voice* cracked *on a high note.* **7** to tell or make (a joke). **8** sharp blow: *a* crack *on the head.*

crack·er (krăk′ər) thin, crisp biscuit.

crack·le (krăk′əl) **1** to make sharp, rapidly repeated snapping noises: *The fire* crackled *on the hearth.* **2** sharp, rapidly repeated snapping noise: *the* crackle *of gravel under the wheels.* **3** glaze or surface of fine, irregular cracks on pottery, paintings, etc. **crack·led, crack·ling.**

crack-up (krăk′ŭp′) **1** a crash; smash. **2** mental or physical breakdown.

cra·dle (krā′dəl) **1** small bed for a baby or doll, usually on rockers. **2** place of origin; birthplace: *the* cradle *of liberty.* **3** period of infancy: *insurance from the* cradle *to the grave.* **4** to hold (something) as in a cradle: *The girl* cradled *the doll in her arms.* **5** to place or rock in a cradle: *The mother* cradled *the baby until it fell asleep.* **6** to shelter or care for in infancy: *The prince was* cradled *in luxury.* **7** a frame attached to a scythe for mowing grain. **8** a frame for holding something, as a ship, during building or repair. **cra·dled, cra·dling.**

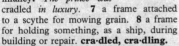

BABY'S

MOWER'S

Cradles

craft (krăft) **1** skill, especially in making things by hand: *The wooden figure had been carved with great* craft. **2** clever deceit; cunning: *The general used* craft *to mislead the enemy.* **3** art or trade requiring artistic skill: *Making pottery and weaving by hand are* crafts. **4** boat, ship, or aircraft: *Ten naval* craft *were anchored in the harbor and a strange* craft *was circling overhead.*

crafts·man (krăfts′mən) skilled workman; artisan. **crafts·men.**

craft·y (krăf′tĭ) skillful at carrying out underhanded schemes; cunning; wily; tricky. **craft·i·er, craft·i·est; craft·i·ly.**

crag (krăg) a steep, rugged rock.

cram (krăm) to fill something by force with more than it has room for; stuff: *to* cram *one's mouth with food; to* cram *a suitcase.* **crammed, cram·ming.**

cramp (krămp) **1** a sudden, sharp, painful tightening of the muscles, caused by chill, strain, etc. **2** to affect with cramp. **3** to hem in tightly; restrict or confine (movement or growth): *to* cramp *initiative.*

cran·ber·ry (krăn′bĕr′ĭ) **1** a small, tart, red berry that grows on a shrub in bogs. **2** the shrub itself. **cran·ber·ries.**

Hoisting crane

Whooping crane, 5 ft. tall

crane (krān) **1** a wading bird with very long legs, a long straight bill, and a long neck. **2** a machine for raising and moving heavy weights. **3** a mechanical arm or support that swings on a pivot. **4** to stretch (the neck) to see better. **craned, cran·ing.**

cra·ni·um (krā′nĭ əm) the skull, especially the part that encloses the brain.

crank (krăngk) **1** an arm or handle that is turned to work a machine. Most pencil sharpeners work with a crank. **2** to move or work with a crank. **3** grouchy or cross person. **4** person who has odd ideas or one fixed idea.

Crank

crank·y (krăng′kĭ) having a bad temper; easily annoyed; irritable. **crank·i·er, crank·i·est; crank·i·ly.**

---

fāte, făt, fâre, fär; bē, bĕt; bīte, bĭt; nō, nŏt, nôr; fūse, fŭn, fûr; too, took; foil; foul; thin; ~~then~~;
hw for wh as in *wh*at; zh for s as in u*s*ual; ə for a, e, i, o, u, as in *a*go, lin*e*n, per*i*l, at*o*m, min*u*s

cranny

cran·ny (krăn´ĭ) a small opening in a wall, rock, etc.; a crack. **cran·nies.**

crape (krāp) crepe.

crash (krăsh) **1** a loud noise like that made by things falling and breaking: *a crash of thunder*. **2** to make such a noise. **3** to break or force a way noisily: *The searching party crashed through the underbrush*. **4** to fall against or bump into noisily: *He crashed into a chair in the dark*. **5** to collide: *Two cars crashed on that curve*. **6** a violent collision: *an automobile crash*. **7** to make a bad or forced landing, causing great damage, injury, etc.: *The airplane crashed*. **8** a falling to earth or forced landing with great destruction (to the plane): *an airplane crash*. **9** failure or collapse of business.

crate (krāt) **1** box or case made of wooden slats, used for shipping goods. **2** to pack in such a box. **crat·ed, crat·ing.**

Orange crate

cra·ter (krā´tər) **1** mouth or opening of a volcano. **2** a hole in the ground caused by an explosion, as of a shell or bomb.

cra·vat (krə văt´) necktie.

crave (krāv) **1** to want badly; long for: *to crave company; to crave food*. **2** to ask or beg for: *to crave a favor*. **craved, crav·ing.**

cra·ven (krā´vən) **1** cowardly: *a craven fear*. **2** a contemptible coward. **cra·ven·ly.**

crav·ing (krā´vĭng) a longing (for); strong desire: *a craving for food or knowledge.*

craw·fish (krô´fĭsh´) crayfish.

crawl (krôl) **1** to move slowly on hands and knees or by dragging the body along the ground. **2** to move or do something very slowly: *The long line of cars crawled up the crowded street*. **3** to be or feel as if covered with creeping things: *The house crawls with spiders. Her flesh crawled as she gazed at the centipede*. **4** slow movement along the ground. **5** a swimming stroke.

Crayfish

cray·fish (krā´fĭsh´) a shellfish found in fresh water. It looks somewhat like a lob-

ster, but is much smaller. Also called **crawfish.**

cray·on (krā´ŏn) **1** a stick of wax material, colored chalk, or charcoal, shaped like a pencil and used for drawing. **2** to draw with crayon. **3** a drawing made with crayon.

craze (krāz) **1** strong but passing interest; fad: *Large hats are the craze this year*. **2** to make insane: *He was crazed by money troubles*. **crazed, craz·ing.**

cra·zy (krā´zĭ) **1** insane; mad: *The men on the desert island went crazy from heat and thirst*. **2** shaky; unsound. **3** wildly enthusiastic. **cra·zi·er, cra·zi·est; cra·zi·ly.**

creak (krēk) **1** to make a sharp squeaking or grating sound: *That old gate creaks in the wind*. **2** a harsh, squeaky sound. (Homonym: creek)

creak·y (krē´kĭ) creaking; squeaky: *The door was no longer creaky after the hinges were oiled*. **creak·i·er, creak·i·est.**

cream (krēm) **1** the rich, fatty part of milk that rises to the top. **2** to take or skim the cream from milk. **3** dessert or food made of cream or like cream: *ice cream; butter creams*. **4** to cook with a cream sauce or cream: *to cream carrots*. **5** to mix together to the thickness of heavy cream: *to cream sugar and butter*. **6** a light yellow color. **7** oily, creamlike lotion for the skin: *hand cream; cold cream*. **8 the cream of** the best part of: the cream of *the crop.*

cream·er·y (krē´mə rĭ) **1** a place where cream is separated from milk, and butter and cheese are made. **2** place where milk, butter, and cheese are bought and sold. **cream·er·ies.**

cream·y (krē´mĭ) of, like, or full of cream. **cream·i·er, cream·i·est.**

crease (krēs) **1** mark or line left by folding; a fold; ridge: *a crease in trousers*. **2** to make a fold or wrinkle in: *to crease trousers with an iron; to crease a dress by sitting on it*. **3** to become folded or wrinkled: *The dress creased in the suitcase*. **creased, creas·ing.**

cre·ate (krē āt´) **1** to bring into being; cause to come into existence: *A painter creates pictures*. **2** to cause; bring about: *to create trouble*. **cre·at·ed, cre·at·ing.**

cre·a·tion (krē ā´shən) **1** a creating; an originating: *The creation of a great poem requires inspiration and hard work*. **2** anything created or brought into being:

Shakespeare's plays are great creations. **3** the universe, the world, and its creatures; all created things and beings: *On a beautiful morning, all* creation *seems to rejoice.* **4 the Creation** the beginning of the world, as described in the first book of the Bible.

cre·a·tive (krē ā′tiv) having or showing the power to create: *a* creative *writer; the* creative *arts.* **cre·a·tive·ly.**

cre·a·tor (krē ā′tər) **1** person who originates something: *Stephen Foster was the* creator *of many songs.* **2 the Creator** God.

crea·ture (krē′chər) any living animal or human being.

cred·it (krĕd′it) **1** belief; trust; confidence: *I place* credit *in her statement as being true.* **2** to give belief to; put confidence in; to trust: *Who would* credit *that ridiculous story?* **3** honor; good reputation: *It is to his* credit *that he told the truth about the broken window.* **4** recognition: *The Wright brothers are given* credit *for the invention of the airplane.* **5** reputation for paying debts; financial standing: *Your* credit *must be good to open a charge account.* **6** amount of money deposited or remaining in a bank account. **7** amount paid on a debt and entered on a business account. **8** to enter a record in favor of; give credit to: *to* credit *one for returned goods.*

cred·it·a·ble (krĕd′it ə bəl) bringing honor; praiseworthy: *That boy had a* creditable *record in school.* **cred·it·a·bly.**

cred·i·tor (krĕd′i tər) person to whom money is owed.

cred·u·lous (krĕj′ə ləs) ready to believe anything: *a* credulous *man.* **cred·u·lous·ly.**

creed (krēd) **1** a set of principles or beliefs on any subject: *a boy scout's* creed. **2** a brief statement of the main points of Christian belief. One of these is the Apostles' Creed.

creek (krēk or krik) **1** a small natural stream of water, larger than a brook. **2** a very narrow bay. (Homonym: creak.)

Creel

creel (krēl) **1** a wicker basket used for carrying fish. **2** a wicker trap used for catching fish.

creep (krēp) **1** to move with the body close to the ground; crawl. **2** to move slowly or carefully: *We will* creep *up on them from behind and surprise them.* **3** to feel as if something were crawling on one's skin: *That horror story makes my flesh* creep. **4** to grow along the ground or a surface by putting forth clinging tendrils: *The ivy* creeps *over the ground and up the wall.* **crept, creep·ing.**

creep·y (krē′pi) having or causing a sensation as if something were crawling on the skin: *Do ghost stories give you a* creepy *feeling?* **creep·i·er, creep·i·est; creep·i·ly.**

crepe or **crêpe** (krāp) **1** a soft, light fabric of silk, wool, cotton, or rayon, with a crinkled or wavy surface. **2** a similar fabric used as a veil, an arm band, etc., usually black, to show mourning. Also spelled **crape.**

crept (krĕpt) See **creep.** *The baby* crept *over the floor.*

cres·cent (krĕs′ənt) **1** the figure of the moon in its first or last quarter or anything shaped like it. **2** shaped like the new moon. **3** increasing; growing: *the* crescent *moon.*

Crescent

cress (krĕs) water cress.

crest (krĕst) **1** a tuft or other growth on the top of an animal's head. **2** a plume or other decoration on the top of a helmet. **3** the ridge or top; summit: *the* crest *of a wave; the* crest *of a hill.* **4** the figure at the top of a coat of arms or the figure itself used as a decoration or seal. **5** to crown or top: *Green woods* crest *the hills.*

Crest of peacock

crest·ed (krĕs′tid) having a crest: *a* crested *bird; the duke's* crested *note paper.*

crest·fall·en (krĕst′fô′lən) dejected; discouraged: *Tommy was* crestfallen *over his failure to make the football team.* **crest·fall·en·ly.**

Crete (krēt) an island south of Greece that was the site of an ancient Mediterranean civilization.

cre·vasse (krə văs′) deep crack or crevice in a glacier.

---

fāte, făt, fâre, fär; bē, bĕt; bīte, bĭt; nō, nŏt, nôr; fūse, fŭn, fûr; tōō, tŏŏk; foil; foul; thin; then; hw for wh as in *w*hat; zh for s as in u*s*ual; ə for a, e, i, o, u, as in *a*go, lin*e*n, per*i*l, at*o*m, min*u*s

crev·ice (krĕv′ĭs) a narrow crack or split: *She hid a note in a* crevice *in the wall.*

¹crew (krōō) 1 all the persons manning a ship or aircraft, rowing a boat, etc. 2 all the men, except officers, manning a ship or aircraft: *Both officers and* crew *of the submarine were experienced.* 3 group or gang of people who work together: *a gun* crew *on a ship.* [**¹crew** is from an Old French word (accreue) meaning "reinforcement," "increase."]

²crew (krōō) See **²crow.** *The cock* crew *an hour ago.* [**²crew** is a form of **²crow.**]

crib (krĭb) 1 small bed with enclosed sides for a child or doll. 2 rack or trough for feeding animals. 3 shed or bin with slatted sides for storing unshelled corn.

Baby's crib

¹crick·et (krĭk′ĭt) British outdoor game played with bats, balls, and wickets. There are eleven players on each side. [**¹cricket** is from an Old French word (criquet) meaning "a bat used in a ball game."]

Corn crib

²crick·et (krĭk′ĭt) small, black or green, hopping insect. The male makes a shrill, chirping sound by rubbing its wings together. [**²cricket** is from an Old French word (criquet) which was probably an imitation of the insect's sound.]

Cricket, about 1 in. long

cried (krīd) See **cry.** *The baby* cried *until it was fed.*

cries (krīz) See **cry.** *She* cries *often. We heard his* cries *of terror.*

crime (krīm) 1 very wrong act that is against the law. Murder, robbery, and kidnaping are crimes. 2 wrongdoing in general. 3 a foolish or useless action: *It's a* crime *to waste so much money on a car.*

crim·i·nal (krĭm′ə nəl) 1 person guilty of crime. 2 involving guilt for crime: *a* criminal *record; a* criminal *act.* 3 having to do with crime; of crime: *the study of* criminal *law.* **crim·i·nal·ly.**

crim·son (krĭm′zən) 1 deep red. 2 to turn deep red in color: *Her face* crimsoned *with embarrassment.*

cringe (krĭnj) 1 to crouch down or shrink back in fear: *The terrier* cringed *when he heard his master shout "Down!"* 2 to act in a humble, timid manner; abase oneself. **cringed, cring·ing.**

crin·kle (krĭng′kəl) 1 to wrinkle or crumple: *Chocolate candies are often wrapped in little* crinkled *papers.* 2 to rustle: *Paper* crinkles *when crumpled.* **crin·kled, crin·kling.**

crip·ple (krĭp′əl) 1 person unable to use his body properly because of injury, deformity, or loss of a part; lame person. 2 to lame; maim; make a cripple of: *He was* crippled *by a fall.* 3 to disable; damage: *The strike* crippled *the steel industry.* **crip·pled, crip·pling.**

cri·sis (krī′sĭs) 1 turning point toward life or death in an illness. 2 event that is a turning point in history: *Lincoln's election was a* crisis *in the struggle over slavery.* 3 time of unusual difficulty or danger. **cri·ses** (krī′sēz).

crisp (krĭsp) 1 stiff, dry, and brittle: *a sandwich of* crisp *bacon and toast.* 2 fresh and firm: *a salad of* crisp *vegetables.* 3 brisk: *the* crisp *October air; a* crisp *manner of speaking.* 4 stiff and tight: *the child's* crisp *curls.* **crisp·ly.**

criss·cross (krĭs′krôs′ or krĭs′krŏs′) 1 crossed like the lines of an ×: *Eileen covered the paper with* crisscross *lines as she talked.* 2 something composed of crisscross lines or objects: *A lattice is a* crisscross *of narrow slats.* 3 to mark with crossing lines, as to blot out: *Mildred* crisscrossed *over the misspelled word.*

crit·ic (krĭt′ĭk) 1 person who is a good judge of the worth of plays, art, music, etc. 2 person who finds fault or judges harshly.

crit·i·cal (krĭt′ĭ kəl) 1 inclined to find fault or judge harshly: *Why are you so* critical *of everyone?* 2 of a critic or critics: *The book did not sell well, but received* critical *praise.* 3 important as a turning point; decisive: *a* critical *battle; a* critical *step in the experiment.* **crit·i·cal·ly.**

crit·i·cism (krĭt′ə sĭz′əm) 1 the making of judgments, favorable or unfavorable, especially on books, plays, acting, art, music, etc.; the work of a critic. 2 a finding fault;

blame; disapproval: *The President's speech met with bitter* criticism *in the press.* **3** an opinion, spoken or written, on what is good or bad about a book, play, concert, action, etc.; a critical review or comment: *a flattering* criticism *of a play.*

crit·i·cize (krit′ə sīz′) **1** to make judgments on; point out the good and bad features of (something): *It is helpful for a music student to have an expert* criticize *his playing.* **2** to find fault with: *The candidate* criticized *his opponent.* **crit·i·cized, crit·i·ciz·ing.**

croak (krōk) **1** low, harsh sound made by a frog, crow, or raven. **2** to utter such sounds. **3** to speak in a rasping voice.

cro·chet (krō shā′) **1** to make a piece of needlework by looping thread with a single hooked needle. **2** needlework made in this way.

Crochet

crock (krŏk) earthenware pot or jar.

crock·er·y (krŏk′ə rĭ) earthenware, especially kitchen bowls, dishes, etc.

croc·o·dile (krŏk′ə dīl′) large, fresh-water reptile with tough skin and long rows of teeth. Crocodiles resemble alligators.

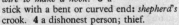
Nile crocodile, 16 ft. or more long

cro·cus (krō′kəs) small, colorful, early spring flower of the iris family.

crone (krōn) a withered or ugly old woman.

cro·ny (krō′nĭ) a close friend or companion; chum. **cro·nies.**

crook (krŏok) **1** the bent, curved, or hooked part of anything: *the* crook *of the elbow.* **2** to bend or curve: *to* crook *a finger; to* crook *wire to make a hook.* **3** a stick with a bent or curved end: *shepherd's* crook. **4** a dishonest person; thief.

Crooks

crook·ed (krŏok′ĭd) **1** not straight; bent; curved: *a* crooked *road; a* crooked *back.* **2** not honest: *a* crooked *business.* **crook·ed·ly.**

croon (krōōn) to sing or hum gently and softly.

crop (krŏp) **1** amount of produce grown or gathered: *We had a big* crop *of potatoes this year.* **2** a lot of people or things thought of together as if they were harvested: *There is a large* crop *of new books this year.* **3** to cut short: *to* crop *hair, tail, ears, etc.* **4** short haircut: *The barber gave him a close* crop. **5** to bite off: *The goat* cropped *the grass.* **6** a pouch in some birds' gullets where food is made ready to be digested. **7** a short riding whip.

crop up to appear unexpectedly. **cropped, crop·ping.**

crop rotation system of planting first one type of crop and then another, to prevent minerals in the soil from becoming used up.

Croquet ground. Dotted lines and arrows show route.

cro·quet (krō kā′) a lawn game in which wooden balls are driven by mallets from a starting stake through a number of low wire arches to a turning stake, and back again to the starting point.

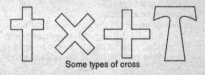
Some types of cross

cross (krôs or krŏs) **1** two posts fixed together to form a shape something like a plus sign. Such crosses were used by the ancient Romans as instruments of torture and for execution. **2 the Cross** the cross upon which Jesus Christ was crucified. **3** a model or picture of the Cross upon

fāte, făt, fâre, fär; bē, bět; bīte, bĭt; nō, nŏt, nôr; fūse, fŭn, fûr; tōō, tŏŏk; foil; foul; thin; ~~then~~;
hw for wh as in *wh*at; zh for s as in u*s*ual; ə for a, e, i, o, u, as in *a*go, lin*e*n, per*i*l, at*o*m, min*u*s

which Jesus Christ was crucified, used as a sacred symbol of Christianity. **4** to make the sign of the Cross, usually by touching the hand to the forehead, chest, and both shoulders. **5** a suffering or trouble to be borne. **6** a mark (×, +) made by drawing one straight line across another. **7** to draw a line across: *to* cross *a "t."* **8** to go from one side to the other of: *A bridge* crosses *the river. Let's* cross *the street.* **9** to place or lay across: *He* crossed *his legs.* **10** to meet and pass while going in different directions: *Our letters* crossed *in the mail.* **11** to go against; oppose: *Don't* cross *him when he is angry.* **12** ill-tempered; fretful: *What makes the baby so* cross? **13** to mix breeds of plants or animals. **14** a mixture of breeds: *The mule is a* cross *between a horse and a donkey.*

   cross out to mark out or mark over.

   cross·ly.

cross·bar (krôs′bär′ or krŏs′bär′) a bar, line, or stripe going crosswise: *a* crossbar *on a hurdle.*

cross·bones (krôs′bōnz′ or krŏs′bōnz′) thigh bones crossed in the form of a ×, usually beneath a skull. The skull and crossbones on a black flag were used by pirates. Sometimes they appear as a warning on poison labels.

cross·bow (krôs′bō′ or krŏs′bō′) a weapon of the Middle Ages consisting of a bow across a wooden stock with a groove to guide a stone or an arrow.

Crossbow

cross·coun·try (krôs′kŭn′trĭ or krŏs′kŭn′trĭ) across fields, through woods, and over obstacles, without regard to roads or fences: *John came in last in the* cross-country *race.*

cross·cut (krôs′kŭt′ or krŏs′kŭt′) **1** a short diagonal route across a field or the like; short cut. **2** of a saw, suitable for cutting across the grain.

cross-ex·am·ine (krôs′ĕg zăm′ĭn) **1** to question closely after a previous questioning. **2** to examine a witness who has testified for the opposing side: *The lawyer for the defense* cross-examined *the witness for the prosecution.* **cross-ex·am·ined, cross-ex·am·in·ing.**

cross-eyed (krôs′īd′ or krŏs′īd′) with one or both eyes turned toward the nose.

cross·ing (krôs′ĭng or krŏs′ĭng) **1** a place where two streets or railroads cross one another or where a street crosses a railroad. **2** a place where a street, river, or railroad may be crossed. **3** a trip across a body of water, especially an ocean. **4** a mixing of breeds or, sometimes, species: *the* crossing *of a donkey and a horse.*

cross·piece (krôs′pēs′ or krŏs′pēs′) a piece of any material placed across something; a crossbar: *a* crosspiece *on a kite.*

cross·road (krôs′rōd′ or krŏs′rōd′) **1** a road that crosses a main road, or runs from one main road to another. **2 crossroads** the place where two or more roads cross each other.

cross section **1** a slice made by cutting through something crosswise: *A slice of bread is a* cross section *of the loaf.* **2** a group of people or things chosen as typical of a larger group.

Cross section

cross·ways (krôs′wāz′ or krŏs′wāz′) **1** crosswise. **2** a crossing of paths: *Traffic lights are placed at busy* crossways *for safety.*

cross·wise (krôs′wīz′ or krŏs′wīz′) **1** from side to side; across. **2** one crossing another: *The logs of a cabin are laid* crosswise *at the corners.*

cross·word puz·zle (krôs′wûrd′ pŭz′əl) a puzzle in which clues are given for words to be written in a diagram of small numbered squares. Some of the words read up and down, and others read across. In this way, the same letter and square may be used in two different words.

crotch (krŏch) point of separation into parts, branches, or legs; fork: *the* crotch *of a tree; the* crotch *of a pair of pants.*

Crotch

crouch (krouch) **1** to stoop or bend low; bend close to the ground. **2** to shrink or bend down in fear; cringe. **3** a crouching. **4** a crouching position.

croup (krōōp) a children's disease marked by a harsh cough.

¹crow (krō) **1** large black bird with a harsh voice. **2** a rook, raven, or other bird closely related to the crow. [**¹crow** is a form of an Old English word (crāwe).]

²crow (krō) **1** to make a shrill sound like that of a rooster. **2** the sound made by a rooster. **3** to boast; brag: *The winning player* crowed *over his success.* **4** the joyful sound made by a baby. **5** to make this sound. **crowed** or (for **1**) **crew, crow·ing.** [**²crow** is a form of an Old English word (crāwan) meaning "to crow like a cock." The word probably started as an imitation of the sound.]

crow·bar (krō′bär′) a long, straight iron bar, pointed or wedge-shaped at the working end, and used as a lever.

crowd (kroud) **1** a number of persons or things collected closely together. **2** to fill too full; pack: *People* crowd *the beaches.* **3** to press (people or things) closely together; cram: *The cattle were* crowded *into a cattle car.* **4** to force; shove, push: *He* crowded *into the elevator.* **5** people in general; the masses or the common people: *The politician's speech was aimed at the* crowd. **6** group; set: *the college* crowd.

crown (kroun) **1** a head-dress, often of gold and jewels, worn by kings and queens on ceremonial occasions. **2** to put a crown upon the head of. **3** the monarch himself, or his power. **4** the top: *the* crown *of a hill, hat, tooth, the head, etc.* **5** to occupy the top part; complete: *A statue* crowns *the dome.* **6** completion; perfection: *This work is the* crown *of his achievements.* **7** to honor; reward: *His efforts were* crowned *with success.* **8 crown prince** the first male heir to a throne. **9 crown princess** a woman or girl who would be next in line for the throne, or the wife of a crown prince.

Crown

crown a tooth to put an artificial top on a tooth.

crow's-nest (krōz′něst′) a partly enclosed box or platform on the masthead of a ship, used as a shelter for the lookout man.

cru·cial (krōō′shəl) important because it marks a turning point; decisive: *a* crucial *battle.* **cru·cial·ly.**

cru·ci·ble (krōō′sə bəl) a pot or vessel, usually of earthenware, to which great heat can be applied, used in melting metal, ore, etc.

cru·ci·fix (krōō′sə fĭks) a model or image of Christ on the cross.

cru·ci·fix·ion (krōō′sə fĭk′-shən) **1** a crucifying or being crucified. **2 the Cruci-fixion** the execution of Christ on the cross; a picture or statue of Christ on the cross.

Crucible

cru·ci·fy (krōō′sə fī′) **1** to put (a person) to death by nailing or binding the hands and feet to a cross: *Many early Christians were* crucified. **2** to torture; torment. **cru·ci·fied, cru·ci·fy·ing.**

crude (krōōd) **1** in its natural state; unrefined: *the* crude *oil from a well.* **2** lacking finish or refinement; rough; rude: *a* crude *hut; such* crude *ideas; his* crude *manners.* **crud·er, crud·est; crude·ly.**

cru·el (krōō′əl) **1** willing or inclined to cause suffering and pain to others; merciless: *a* cruel *tyrant.* **2** causing suffering; painful: *a* cruel *death.* **cru·el·ly.**

cru·el·ty (krōō′əl tĭ) **1** willingness or inclination to cause pain and suffering: *a streak of* cruelty *in his nature.* **2** cruel act or acts: *Torture is a* cruelty. **cru·el·ties.**

cru·et (krōō′ət) small glass bottle for vinegar, oil, etc., used at the dining table.

cruise (krōōz) **1** to make a long boat trip for pleasure or without special destination: *The yacht* cruised *along the coast. Destroyers* cruise *in search of submarines.* **2** any sea voyage, especially a pleasure trip with numerous stops: *a two-month* cruise *around Europe.* **3** to move or drive about with no special destination: *The police car* cruised *slowly through the park.* **cruised, cruis·ing.**

Cruet

cruis·er (krōō′zər) a fast warship, smaller and with less armor than a battleship.

crul·ler (krŭl′ər) a doughnut; especially, a twisted doughnut.

---

fāte, făt, fâre, fär; bē, bĕt; bīte, bĭt; nō, nŏt, nôr; fūse, fŭn, fûr; tōō, tŏŏk; foil; foul; thin; then; hw for wh as in *wh*at; zh for s as in usual; ə for a, e, i, o, u, as in a*go*, lin*e*n, per*i*l, at*o*m, min*u*s

crumb (krŭm) **1** tiny piece broken from something, especially bread, cake, etc. **2** small amount; scrap: *mere* crumbs *of knowledge.*

crum·ble (krŭm′bəl) **1** to break into small pieces: *He* crumbled *bread to feed to the birds.* **2** to fall to pieces: *The general's hopes* crumbled *as his soldiers retreated.* **crum·bled, crum·bling.**

crum·ple (krŭm′pəl) **1** to press or crush (something) so as to make irregular creases or wrinkles in it. **2** to become wrinkled, or creased. **crum·pled, crum·pling.**

crunch (krŭnch) **1** to chew with a sharp, crushing sound: *to* crunch *celery.* **2** a noisy chewing or grinding, or the sound it produces: *the* crunch *of crackers.* **3** to make a crushing or grinding noise: *The gravel* crunched *under our feet.*

cru·sade (krōō sād′) **1** any one of the holy wars or expeditions undertaken by Christians during the Middle Ages to recover the Holy Land from the Moslems. **2** any campaign for reform or improvement: *a* crusade *against cancer; a* crusade *against crime.* **3** to go on or take part in a crusade: *He* crusaded *for fire prevention.* **cru·sad·ed, cru·sad·ing.**

cru·sad·er (krōō sā′dər) person who takes part in a crusade.

crush (krŭsh) **1** to press together so as to crumple or injure; squash: *The hat was* crushed *when he sat on it.* **2** to break into small pieces: *to* crush *ice.* **3** to destroy; overwhelm: *The government* crushed *the rebellion.* **4** dense crowd: *a great* crush *of people.* **5** great pressure or squeezing: *The* crush *of the holiday shoppers left her breathless.*

crust (krŭst) **1** hard outer layer of bread. **2** a piece of this or of stale bread. **3** the pastry forming the outside of a pie. **4** any similar hard outer layer: *an icy* crust *on the snow; the* crust *of the earth.* **5** to cover with a hard outside coating: *Freezing rain* crusted *the snow.*

crus·ta·cean (krŭs tā′shən) any of a class of animals, such as crabs and lobsters, which have hard outer shells. Most crustaceans live in water.

crutch (krŭch) **1** a staff with a crosspiece to go under the arm, used to help a lame person in walking. **2** any device, mechan-

ical or moral, used as a support: *Copying another's work is a poor* crutch *for a student.*

cry (krī) **1** to weep; shed tears. **2** to shout or call loudly: *The wounded man* cried *out with pain.* "*Help!*" cried *the frightened girl.* **3** sound of pain, surprise, etc.: *He heard a low* cry *behind him.* **4** a shout or call: *a* cry *for help; the* cry *of battle.* **5** call or sound made by some birds and animals. **6** to sell or announce by calling: *to* cry *one's wares; to* cry *the news.* **7** such a call: *the* cry *of the peddler.* **8** slogan or watchword: *the* cry *of "Go West!"* **cries; cries, cried, cry·ing.**

Crutches

crys·tal (krĭs′təl) **1** solid object with flat sides, formed naturally from a liquid or a material dissolved in a liquid. **2** clear, transparent type of quartz that looks like ice. **3** piece of such quartz, or piece of fine glass cut into the shape of a crystal, for use as an ornament: *beads of* crystal. **4** bowls, goblets, etc., made of fine glass: *The table was set with sparkling silver and* crystal. **5** made of quartz or fine glass: *a* crystal *ball.* **6** like crystal: *the* crystal *clear water.* **7** glass or transparent cover over a watch dial.

SNOW

SUGAR

QUARTZ

Crystals

crys·tal·line (krĭs′tə lin or krĭs′tə lin′) **1** in the form of crystals: *Marble, diamonds, and amethysts have* crystalline *structure.* **2** clear and brilliant as crystal.

crys·tal·lize (krĭs′tə līz′) **1** to form into crystals: *The syrup* crystallized *into sugar.* **2** to take definite form: *His suspicions* crystallized *into certainty.* **crys·tal·lized, crys·tal·liz·ing.**

cub (kŭb) **1** young of the fox, bear, lion, etc. **2 cub scout** member of the junior division of the Boy Scouts.

Cu·ba (kū′bə) an island country in the West Indies.

Cu·ban (kū′bən) **1** of Cuba or its people. **2** citizen of Cuba or a person of Cuban descent.

cub·by·hole (kŭb′i hōl′) small enclosed space.

cube (kūb) **1** solid body with six equal sides. **2** any block having six sides: *ice* cube;

sugar cube. **3** to form or cut into blocks: *Potatoes and beets are sometimes cubed instead of being sliced for cooking.* **4** the product that results when a number is multiplied by itself twice. Twenty-seven is the cube. of 3, for 3 × 3 × 3 = 27. **cubed, cub·ing.**

Cube

cu·bic (kū′bĭk) **1** cube-shaped: *the* cubic *alphabet blocks.* **2** having length, width, and depth. A cubic foot is equal to the amount of space inside a cube whose every side is one foot square.

cu·bit (kū′bĭt) ancient measure of length varying from 17 to 21 inches.

cuck·oo (kŏŏk′kŏŏ′ or kŏŏk′ŏŏ′) **1** a bird, the call of which sounds like the word "cuckoo." The European cuckoo lays its eggs in the nests of other birds and leaves them to be hatched. The American cuckoo hatches its own eggs. **2** call of the cuckoo. **cuck·oos.**

Cuckoo, about 12 in. long

cu·cum·ber (kū′kŭm bər) **1** a long, fleshy vegetable with a green rind, used in salads and for making pickles. **2** vine it grows on.

cud (kŭd) wad of grass or other food swallowed by certain animals, then brought back to the mouth to be chewed again. Cows and goats are cud-chewing animals.

cud·dle (kŭd′əl) **1** to hold closely and tenderly: *to cuddle a baby.* **2** to lie snug; nestle: *The kittens cuddled together in the cold.* **cud·dled, cud·dling.**

cudg·el (kŭj′əl) **1** a short thick stick used as a weapon; club. **2** to hit with a club. **cudgel one's brains** to think hard.

¹cue (kū) **1** signal; hint: *Give me a cue when you're ready to leave the party.* **2** on the stage, a word or an action that indicates the time for the next actor to speak, act or enter. [**¹cue** is probably the spelling of the letter "q", which is the first letter of a Latin word (quando) meaning "when." This Latin word was often used in stage directions.] (Homonym: queue)

²cue (kū) long stick used to strike the ball in playing pool or billiards. [**²cue** is from a French word (queue) meaning "tail," which goes back to a Latin word (cauda) also meaning "tail."] (Homonym: queue)

¹cuff (kŭf) band or fold of cloth on the bottom edge of a sleeve or trouser leg. [**¹cuff** is from an earlier English word (coffe) meaning "glove."]

²cuff (kŭf) **1** to hit with the open hand; slap. **2** a slap. [**²cuff** is probably of Scandinavian origin.]

cull (kŭl) **1** to pick; select: *She culled the prettiest flowers from the garden to make a bouquet.* **2** something picked out as inferior: *The farmer kept the best cattle for himself and sold the culls from the herd.*

cul·mi·nate (kŭl′mə nāt′) to reach the highest point; come to a climax: *The party culminated in a display of fireworks.* **cul·mi·nat·ed, cul·mi·nat·ing.**

cul·pa·ble (kŭl′pə bəl) deserving blame: *Hiding a criminal is a* culpable *offense.* **cul·pa·bly.**

cul·prit (kŭl′prĭt) **1** a guilty person; an offender. **2** someone accused: *He said an old offender was the culprit.*

cul·ti·vate (kŭl′tə vāt′) **1** to prepare (the soil) for the planting and care of crops. **2** to raise (plants): *to cultivate roses.* **3** to loosen the soil around (plants). **4** to improve; develop: *to cultivate the mind by study.* **5** to try to win the friendship of (someone): *That snobbish woman cultivates only rich and important people.* **cul·ti·vat·ed, cul·ti·vat·ing.**

cul·ti·vat·ed (kŭl′tə vā′tĭd) **1** prepared for growing crops: *an acre of* cultivated *land.* **2** cultured; refined: *a* cultivated *man.* **3 cultivated taste** taste (especially for certain foods) that has been acquired.

cul·ti·va·tion (kŭl′tə vā′shən) **1** a growing (of plants): *We depend upon the* cultivation *of crops for food.* **2** a tilling (of the land); a plowing and breaking up of the soil (around growing plants). **3** improvement or development of the mind or body. **4** culture; refinement. **5** a seeking the friendship of (someone): *the* cultivation *of interesting people.*

---

fāte, făt, fâre, fär; bē, bĕt; bīte, bĭt; nō, nŏt, nôr; fūse, fŭn, fûr; tōō, tŏŏk; foil; foul; thin; ~~then~~; hw for wh as in *wh*at; zh for s as in usual; ə for a, e, i, o, u, as in *a*go, lin*e*n, per*i*l, at*o*m, min*u*s

cul·ti·va·tor (kŭl′tə vā′tər) **1** person or thing that cultivates. **2** a farm tool used to loosen the soil and dig up weeds around growing plants.

Cultivator

cul·tur·al (kŭl′chər əl) having to do with culture, especially cultivation of the mind: *Good breeding, taste, and learning are marks of* cultural *accomplishment.* **cul·tur·al·ly.**

cul·ture (kŭl′chər) **1** result of improving the mind, tastes, and manners; refinement. **2** a training and developing of the mind or body: *a class in physical* culture. **3** knowledge, customs, and arts of a people or group at a certain time: *the* culture *of ancient Greece.* **4** cultivation of land. **5** care and breeding (of bees, fish, silkworms, etc.). **6** a growth of bacteria in a special laboratory preparation.

cul·tured (kŭl′chərd) cultivated; refined; well-bred; educated.

cul·vert (kŭl′vərt) a drain or passage for water under a road or railroad.

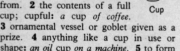

Culvert

cum·ber·some (kŭm′bər səm) burdensome; heavy and clumsy: *a cumbersome package.* **cum·ber·some·ly.**

cu·ne·i·form (kū nē′ə fôrm′ or kū′nĭ ə-fôrm′) **1** shaped like a wedge, as the marks' in the writing of the ancient Persians, Babylonians, etc. **2** such a mark.

cun·ning (kŭn′ĭng) **1** clever at deceiving; crafty; sly: *as* cunning *as a fox.* **2** cleverness at deceiving; craft: *He used* cunning *to avoid capture.* **3** appealing; charming: *What a* cunning *baby!* **cun·ning·ly.**

cup (kŭp) **1** small, usually bowl-shaped container used to drink from. **2** the contents of a full cup; cupful: *a cup of coffee.*

Cup

3 ornamental vessel or goblet given as a prize. **4** anything like a cup in use or shape: *an oil* cup *on a machine.* **5** to form (something) in the shape of a cup: *He* cupped *his hands to drink from the stream.* **cupped, cup·ping.**

cup·board (kŭb′ərd) closet or enclosed storage space with shelves for dishes, food, etc.; any small closet.

cup·ful (kŭp′fəl) amount a cup will contain; half a pint: *a cupful of blueberries.*

Cu·pid (kū′pĭd) **1** in Roman mythology, the god of love. **2** **cupid** a picture or statue of Cupid as a pretty, winged boy with bow and arrow.

Cupola

cu·po·la (kū′pə lə) a small dome on a building; a small tower raised above a roof.

cur (kûr) a mongrel dog.

cu·rate (kyoor′ĭt) a clergyman who assists a pastor or vicar.

cu·ra·tor (kyoo rā′tər) person in charge of a museum, art gallery, etc.

curb (kûrb) **1** to keep within bounds; restrain: *to curb one's temper.* **2** protecting rim of cement, stone, etc., along the edge of a street or walk: *Cars are parked along the* curb. **3** something which holds back, checks, or restrains: *Her parents should put a curb on her wild spending.* **4** a chain or strap on a bit, used to control a horse.

curd (kûrd) soft, thick substance that separates from the whey when milk turns sour. It is used in making cheese.

cur·dle (kûr′dəl) to thicken into curds: *The milk* curdled *in the sun.* **cur·dled, cur·dling.**

cure (kyoor) **1** method of treatment or medicine used to restore health; remedy: *a cure for a cold.* **2** restoration to health; healing: *a complete* cure *after a long illness.* **3** to bring back to health; heal: *This medicine* cured *me.* **4** to get rid of (something bad); overcome: *We must* cure *his laziness.* **5** to preserve by salting, drying, etc.: *to* cure *meat, leather, etc.* **cured, cur·ing.**

cur·few (kûr′fū) **1** a signal at a certain time in the evening that persons, usually children, must be off the streets. **2** the time set for this.

cu·ri·o (kyoor′ĭ ō) an article which is valued because it is unusual, odd, or rare; a curiosity. Old shoe buckles, snuff boxes, and quill pens are curios. **cu·ri·os.**

cu·ri·os·i·ty (kyoor′ĭ ŏs′ə ti) **1** eager desire to know or learn: *The explorer had great* curiosity *about Africa.* **2** something unusual or rare; a curio: *A wooden plow is a curiosity in this country.* **cu·ri·os·i·ties.**

cu·ri·ous (kyŏŏr′ĭ əs) **1** eager to know: *A curious child asks many questions.* **2** odd; strange; unusual: *a curious old costume.* **cu·ri·ous·ly.**

curl (kûrl) **1** to twist into spirals or ringlets: *She curled her hair for the party.* **2** a coil or spiral of hair; a ringlet. **3** something in a curl or like a curl: *a heap of curls of wood shavings.* **4** to form into a curve or spiral: *Smoke curled from the chimney.*

curl·y (kûr′lĭ) **1** having curls: *a curly head.* **2** in the shape of a curl: *a pig's curly tail.* **curl·i·er, curl·i·est.**

cur·rant (kûr′ənt) **1** small, seedless raisin used in pudding, cake, etc. **2** small, sour, edible berry that grows in clusters. It is used to make jelly. **3** bush on which this berry grows. (Homonym: current)

cur·ren·cy (kûr′ən sĭ) **1** money in present use in a country. **2** circulation; a passing from one person to another: *Clever jokes quickly gain currency among friends.* **3** general use or acceptance: *That custom has little currency today.* **cur·ren·cies.**

cur·rent (kûr′ənt) **1** a flow; stream: *the current of a river or of air.* **2** a flow of electricity through a wire, etc. **3** course; direction; trend: *the current of public opinion.* **4** of the present time; contemporary; latest: *a current fashion; the current issue of a magazine.* **5** passing from person to person; circulating: *Many rumors were current about the new teacher.* **cur·rent·ly.** (Homonym: currant)

¹cur·ry (kûr′ĭ) to rub down or clean (an animal) with a brush or comb: *to curry a horse.*

curry favor to try to win favor by flattery, etc.: *He curried favor with the cook by praising the food.*

cur·ried, cur·ry·ing. [¹**curry** seems to be from an Old French word (correier, conreder) meaning "prepare," "make ready."]

²cur·ry (kûr′ĭ) **1** highly spiced powder from Asia, or sauce made from it. **2** a dish of meat, rice, etc., flavored with curry. **cur·ries.** [²**curry** is from a word used in India (kari) meaning "sauce."]

curse (kûrs) **1** to call down evil or harm on: *The witch cursed her tormentors.* **2** word or words used in calling down evil or harm. **3** to use bad language; swear: *The sailor's parrot cursed loudly when it was angry.* **4** word or words used in such swearing. **5** thing that causes evil or harm: *Mosquitoes are a curse in the tropics.* **6** to afflict: *He was cursed with a bad temper.* **cursed, curs·ing.**

curt (kûrt) abrupt in a rude way; short: *a curt answer to a question.* **curt·ly.**

cur·tail (kər tāl′) to make shorter or less than planned; cut short: *The speaker curtailed his talk in order to catch a plane home.*

cur·tain (kûr′tən) **1** a drapery of cloth or other material used to cover, protect, separate one place from another, or decorate: *the curtains at the window.* **2** to hang or provide with curtains: *The windows were curtained with silk.* **3** anything like a curtain: *a curtain of fog.*

curt·sy (kûrt′sĭ) **1** a respectful bow which girls and women make by bending the knees and lowering the body. **2** to make a curtsy. Also spelled **curtsey. curt·sies; curt·sied, curt·sy·ing.**

curve (kûrv) **1** a line no part of which is straight. **2** a bending without angles: *a curve in the road.* **3** to bend. **4** in baseball, a ball pitched so it swerves from a straight course. **5** to cause to bend or turn from a straight line. **curved, curv·ing.**

Curves

cush·ion (kŏŏsh′ən) **1** pillow or soft pad to sit, lie, or rest on. **2** anything resembling such a pillow or pad: *a cushion of leaves.* **3** to supply or furnish with a pillow, soft pad, or the like: *He fell from the roof but a pile of hay cushioned his fall.*

cus·pid (kŭs′pĭd) tooth with only one point; canine tooth. For picture, see **teeth.**

cus·tard (kŭs′tərd) a cooked mixture of eggs, milk, and sugar.

cus·to·di·an (kŭs tō′dĭ ən) **1** person in charge (of something): *A county clerk is the custodian of public records.* **2** person who takes care of a building; janitor.

---

fāte, făt, fâre, fär; bē, bĕt; bīte, bĭt; nō, nŏt, nôr; fūse, fŭn, fûr; tōō, tŏŏk; foil; foul; thin; ~~then~~;
hw for wh as in *wh*at; zh for s as in usual; ə for a, e, i, o, u, as in ago, linen, peril, atom, minus

cus·to·dy (kŭs′tə dǐ) **1** care; keeping: *The orphan was in the* custody *of his uncle.* **2 take into custody** to arrest and put under guard.

cus·tom (kŭs′təm) **1** habit or generally accepted way of doing things: *It is a Chinese* custom *to eat with chopsticks. It is her* custom *to get up at seven.* **2** made to order: *a* custom *suit.* **3** doing only work made to order: *a* custom *tailor.* **4** regular trade given to a store or business: *He gives most of his* custom *to one store.* **5 customs** (1) taxes or duties on goods brought into a country. (2) government agency that collects these taxes.

cus·tom·ar·y (kŭs′tə mĕr′ĭ) according to custom; usual: *It is* customary *to shake hands when introduced.* **cus·tom·ar·i·ly.**

cus·tom·er (kŭs′təm ər) person who buys, especially a regular purchaser.

cus·tom·house (kŭs′təm hous′) government building where taxes or duties are collected on imported and exported goods.

cut (kŭt) **1** to divide, separate, or make an opening in with a knife or sharp tool: *She* cut *the ribbon in two.* **2** a division, separation, or opening made by something sharp: *The lumberman made a deep* cut *in the tree.* **3** to wound (with something sharp); to gash: *He* cut *himself with a knife.* **4** a slight wound; a gash: *a* cut *on the finger.* **5** to hurt (someone's feelings) as if by a cut: *Her vicious remark* cut *me deeply.* **6** to shorten by taking off a part with a sharp tool: *to* cut *the grass.* **7** to make (something) with a sharp tool: *to* cut *initials in a tree; to* cut *firewood; to* cut *a hole in the fence.* **8** to direct a sharp blow or stroke with a weapon, ax, whip, etc.: *The sailor* cut *at the pirate with his sword.* **9** a blow or stroke of a weapon, ax, whip, etc.: *a cut of his whip.* **10** to reduce or make less: *to* cut *prices, expenses, quality, etc.* **11** a reduction: *a* cut *in price.* **12** to take out; eliminate: *Since the show was long, two songs were* cut. **13** to interrupt: *The storm* cut *all telephone service.* **14** to cross; pass through or across: *The letter "X" consists of one line* cut *by another.* **15** to permit being divided, sliced, etc., by a sharp instrument: *This frozen meat won't* cut. **16** piece (of meat) cut off: *a steak is a* cut *of beef.* **17** shape or style (of clothes): *I like the* cut *of this coat.* **18** to go by a short route: *Don't* cut *across the flower bed.* **19** to change direction suddenly: *A reckless driver* cut *in front of the bus.* **20** to loosen or dissolve: *This soap will* cut *the grease.*

cut down to bring down by means of a sharp tool; chop down: *to* cut down *a tree.*

cut a tooth to have a tooth grow through the gum.

cut up 1 to cut into pieces: *Please* cut up *the meat for the baby.* **2** to act in a noisy, disturbing way.

cut, cut·ting.

cute (kūt) **1** pleasing in a pretty or dainty way: *a* cute *kitten.* **2** clever; shrewd: *a* cute *retort.* **cut·er, cut·est; cute·ly.**

cu·ti·cle (kū′tə kəl) outer layer of skin, especially that around the base of fingernails or toenails.

cut·lass (kŭt′ləs) a short, heavy sword with a broad, curving blade.

Cutlass

cut·ler·y (kŭt′lə rĭ) cutting instruments such as knives and scissors, especially implements used in cutting or serving food.

cut·ter (kŭt′ər) **1** person or thing that cuts: *a* cutter *in a clothing factory.* **2** small, fast boat used by the Coast Guard. **3** small boat used by ships of war for trips to and from the shore. **4** type of small sailboat with one mast. **5** sleigh for two persons.

cut·ting (kŭt′ĭng) **1** able to cut, carve, etc.: *A chisel has a narrow* cutting *edge.* **2** a shoot or branch cut from a plant for rooting or grafting. **3** sharp; piercing: *a* cutting *wind.* **4** meant to sting or hurt; sarcastic: *a* cutting *remark.* **cut·ting·ly.**

cy·cle (sī′kəl) **1** a series of events or actions that takes place regularly over and over again. The cycle of the seasons is the regular change from one season to the next in the same order every year. **2** the period of time in which such a series of events or actions takes place. **3** a long period of time; an age. **4** a series of poems or stories about some central event or person. **5** a bicycle, motorcycle, or tricycle. **6** to ride a bicycle, tricycle, or motorcycle. **cy·cled, cy·cling.**

cy·clone (sī′klōn) **1** weather condition in which winds whirl around a center of low air pressure. **2** loosely, a tornado or hurricane.

cy·clo·tron (sī′klə trŏn) an atom-smashing machine in which electrically charged particles are made to move at very high speed in a spiral direction.

cyl·in·der (sĭl′ĭn dər) **1** a body shaped like a piece of pipe with the ends cut flat and even. Cylinders may be solid or hollow. **2** a space, shaped like a cylinder, in which a piston moves in some kinds of engines.

Cylinder

cy·lin·dri·cal (sĭ lĭn′drə kəl) shaped like a cylinder. **cy·lin·dri·cal·ly.**

cym·bal (sĭm′bəl) either one of a pair of circular metal plates which are struck together to make a clashing sound in music. (Homonym: symbol)

cyn·ic (sĭn′ĭk) person who doubts the goodness of human nature; one who believes that people act wholly out of self-interest.

Cymbals

cyn·i·cal (sĭn′ə kəl) **1** pertaining to a cynic; distrustful of human nature. **cyn·i·cal·ly.**

cy·press (sī′prəs) **1** an evergreen tree that bears cones and small, sharp, scalelike overlapping leaves. **2** wood of this tree.

czar (zär) title of the former emperors of Russia.

D

D, d (dē) **1** the fourth letter of the English alphabet. **2** Roman numeral for 500.

dab (dăb) **1** to touch lightly; tap or pat gently: *Sally dabbed her face with a sponge.* **2** a light tap or pat: *to give some dabs with a wet sponge.* **3** to put on in light, rapid strokes: *to dab paint on a picture.* **4** a small bit: *a dab of this and a dab of that.* **5** a small, soft or moist lump: *a dab of butter.* **dabbed, dab·bing.**

dab·ble (dăb′əl) to dip (the hands or feet) in and out or to splash about: *Ned dabbled his feet in the pond.*

dabble in 1 to deal in something part of the time: *The auto dealer also dabbled in real estate.* **2** to work at something in an amateur way: *She dabbles in art.* **dab·bled, dab·bling.**

dachs·hund (dăks′-hŏont′ or dăks′-hŏond′) small hound with very short legs, long body, pointed nose, and drooping ears.

Dachshund, about 18 in. long

Da·cron (dā′krŏn) the trademark name of a strong artificial yarn from which a cloth is made that withstands wrinkling and stretching.

dad (dăd) fond word for "father."

dad·dy (dăd′ĭ) fond word for "father." **dad·dies.**

dad·dy long·legs (dăd′ĭ lông′lĕgz′) a spiderlike creature with very long legs and a small, round body. It does not bite and is quite harmless. pl. **dad·dy long·legs.**

daf·fo·dil (dăf′ə dĭl′) **1** a plant with long, narrow leaves and long yellow or white, single or double, flowers. It is grown from a bulb and blooms in the spring. **2** the flower of this plant.

daft (dăft) weakminded, simple; foolish; crazy. **daft·ly.**

dag·ger (dăg′ər) **1** short, pointed, double-edged sword or knife, used to stab. **2** printing reference mark (†).

Dagger

dahl·ia (dăl′yə or däl′yə) **1** a tall plant that grows from a bulb and blooms in the early autumn with large, brightly colored flowers. **2** the flower of this plant.

dai·ly (dā′lĭ) **1** occurring, appearing, or done every day: *a daily nap; a daily visitor.* **2** every day; day by day. **3** a newspaper published every day. **dai·lies.**

dain·ty (dān′tĭ) **1** pretty in a delicate way: *The bridesmaid wore a thin, dainty dress of pink.* **2** showing taste; delicate; fastidious: *She has very dainty eating habits for such a*

---

fāte, făt, fâre, fär; bē, bĕt; bīte, bĭt; nō, nŏt, nôr; fūse, fŭn, fûr; tōō, tŏŏk; foil; foul; thin; ~~then~~; hw for wh as in *what*; zh for s as in u*s*ual; ə for a, e, i, o, u, as in *a*go, lin*e*n, per*i*l, at*o*m, min*u*s

young child. **3** choice bit of food; something delicious: *a box of* dainties *from the bakery.* **4** delicious: *a* dainty *morsel.* **dainties; dain·ti·er, dain·ti·est.**

dair·y (dâr′ĭ) **1** building or room in which milk and cream are kept and made into butter and cheese. **2** having to do with milk production: *the* dairy *cattle;* dairy *farm.* **3** a shop or company that sells milk and dairy products. **dair·ies.**

dair·y·maid (dâr′ĭ mād′) girl or woman employed in a dairy; milkmaid.

dair·y·man (dâr′ĭ-
mən) **1** man who
owns or manages a
dairy. **2** man who is
employed in a dairy.
dair·y·men.

da·is (dā′ĭs) slightly
raised platform to
hold a throne, speak-
er's desk, or the like.

Dais

dai·sy (dā′zĭ) **1** one of several varieties of common plants the flowers of which have a brown or yellow center surrounded by white, yellow, or pink petals. **2** the flower of one of these plants. **dai·sies.**

dale (dāl) low ground between hills; a valley.

dal·ly (dăl′ĭ) **1** to toy (with): *to* dally *with the idea of going to college.* **2** to waste time; loiter: *He* dallied *all the way home, stopping at every store window.* **dal·lied, dal·ly·ing.**

¹**dam** (dăm) **1** barrier
of earth, wood, or
masonry to hold back
water. **2** the water
thus held back. **3** to
hold back with a dam;
check the flow of:
Beavers dammed *the
river.*

dam up to hold
back; control.

Dam

dammed, dam·ming. [¹**dam** comes from a Germanic word (dam) with the same meaning.] (Homonym: damn)

²**dam** (dăm) female parent of any four-footed animal, such as a horse, a sheep, or a deer. [²**dam** is a variation of the word **dame.**] (Homonym: damn)

dam·age (dăm′ĭj) **1** injury or harm: *Was there much* damage *caused by the fire?* **2** to injure; harm; hurt: *The shipment of fruit was* damaged *by frost.* **3** damages amount claimed or allowed in court for harm or injury. **dam·aged, dam·ag·ing.**

dam·ask (dăm′əsk) **1** a reversible fabric of linen, silk, etc., woven with patterns. **2** made of such a fabric: *heavy* damask *curtains.* **3** a deep pink.

dame (dām) **1** formerly, the mistress of a household; lady. **2** an old woman. **3 Dame** title given to a knight's or baronet's wife, or to a woman who has been honored by such rank.

damn (dăm) **1** to condemn; judge as bad or as a failure. **2** to doom to eternal punishment. **3** to curse; swear at; call down a curse on. (Homonym: dam)

damp (dămp) **1** moist; somewhat wet: *a* damp *cloth.* **2** to moisten. **3** moisture: *He could feel the cold and* damp *penetrating his bones.* **4** poisonous vapor or gas: *Coal* damp *exploded in the mine.* **5** to discourage; depress: *The gloomy surroundings* damped *his spirits.* **6** to check; stifle; put out: *to* damp *a fire.* **damp·ly.**

damp·en (dăm′pən) **1** to make or become moist. **2** to lessen; deaden. **3** to depress; discourage.

damp·er (dăm′pər) **1** a metal plate in the tube or shaft of a stove or furnace, which can be moved to control the draft. **2** something that depresses or discourages: *The gloomy news over the radio put a* damper *on everyone's gaiety.*

dam·sel (dăm′zəl) an old word for "young girl," "maiden."

dance (dăns) **1** to move the body and feet in time to music. **2** the motion of body and feet in time to music. **3** a particular series of steps used in dancing. **4** to perform (a dance): *to* dance *a jig.* **5** to cause to dance: *He* danced *his partner across the floor.* **6** a dancing party. **7** a round of dancing: *The next* dance *is reserved for you.* **8** to move about lightly: *Raindrops* danced *on the pavement.* **9** for dancing: *a* dance *band;* dance *music.* **danced, danc·ing.**

danc·er (dăn′sər) **1** person who dances. **2** person who makes his living by dancing.

dan·de·li·on (dăn′də lī′ən) **1** a common weed with yellow flowers and a rosette of jagged leaves that can be eaten. **2** the flower of this plant.

dan·dle (dăn'dəl) to move (a baby) up and down on the knee, or in the arms. **dan· dled, dan·dling.**

dan·druff (dăn'drəf) tiny scales of dead skin that flake off the scalp.

dan·dy (dăn'dĭ) a man who gives too much attention to his clothes and appearance. **dan·dies.**

Dane (dān) **1** citizen of Denmark; person who comes from Denmark. **2** person of Danish descent. (Homonym: deign)

dan·ger (dān'jər) **1** chance of harm; risk; peril: *A fireman faces* danger *every day.* **2** possible cause of loss, injury, or death; hazard: *Icebergs are a* danger *to all ships.*

dan·ger·ous (dān'jər əs) **1** unsafe; risky; perilous: *Handling explosives is a* dangerous *occupation.* **2** likely to do harm: *A mad dog is* dangerous. **dan·ger·ous·ly.**

dan·gle (dăng'gəl) to hang or swing loosely: *The puppet* dangled *on a string. The boy* dangled *his legs over the edge of the pool.* **dan·gled, dan·gling.**

Dan·ish (dā'nĭsh) **1** of Denmark, its people or language. **2** the language of the Danes.

dank (dăngk) wet; unpleasantly damp; sodden: *a dark,* dank *cellar.* **dank·ly.**

dap·per (dăp'ər) **1** neat and smart in appearance: *The new coach was very* dapper. **2** small and active: *a* dapper *jockey.*

dap·ple (dăp'əl) **1** dappled. **2** to make a spotted or mottled pattern on: *Sunlight* dappled *the grass.* **dap·pled, dap·pling.**

dap·pled (dăp'əld) spotted; mottled: *a* dappled *mare.*

dare (dâr) **1** to have courage; be bold or adventurous enough: *Who would* dare *to try that jump?* **2** to have courage for; meet boldly: *Columbus* dared *the peril of the sea.* **3** to challenge: *His older brother* dared *him to climb the cliff.* **4** a challenge: *Jimmy was too sensible to take his brother's* dare. **dared, dar·ing.**

dare·dev·il (dâr'dĕv'əl) **1** person who takes great risks recklessly: *The racing-car driver is a* daredevil. **2** reckless; daring: *a* daredevil *act on a high trapeze.*

dar·ing (dâr'ĭng) **1** bravery; boldness. **2** fearless; bold: *a* daring *aviator.* **dar· ing·ly.**

dark (därk) **1** having little or no light: *a* dark *room.* **2** absence of light: *the* dark *of the night.* **3** nearer black than white; not light in color: *a* dark *shade of blue.* **4** having a brunet complexion: *a tall* dark *man.* **5** gloomy: *a* dark *mood.* **6** mysterious: *a deep,* dark *secret.* **7** evil: *a* dark *deed.* **8** nightfall: *after* dark. **9 in the dark** in ignorance: *They kept us* in the dark *about their plan.* **dark·ly.**

dark·en (där'kən) **1** to make dark; make gloomy. **2** to become dark or gloomy: *The sky* darkened *as the clouds rolled in.*

dar·ling (där'lĭng) **1** a much loved person; object of deep affection: *the* darling *of her father's heart.* **2** tenderly loved; very dear.

darn (därn) **1** to mend by weaving thread or yarn back and forth across a hole. **2** a place thus mended.

dart (därt) **1** to move in a quick, sudden way: *The dog* darted *after the rabbit.* **2** a sudden movement: *Aunt Maggie made a* dart *at the trespassing hens.* **3** to shoot out suddenly: *She* darted *a glance at me.* **4** a light, spearlike missile thrown with the hand or shot from a blow gun. **5** a needlelike point on a feathered handle, thrown at a mark in certain games. **6 darts** game in which darts are tossed at a target.

Dart

dash (dăsh) **1** to rush with violence: *He* dashed *outside.* **2** a sudden rush: *a* dash *for freedom.* **3** a short race: *a hundred yard* dash. **4** a little bit: *a* dash *of pepper.* **5** to splash; splatter: *They* dashed *him with water.* **6** to throw violently: *to* dash *a cup to the floor.* **7** to ruin; destroy: *She* dashed *all my hopes.* **8** a mark (—) used in writing or printing to mark a pause or break.

dash off to do hastily: *to* dash off *a letter.*

dash·board (dăsh'bôrd') **1** instrument panel of an automobile. **2** a screen of wood, leather, or metal at the front of a carriage, boat, etc., used as protection against splashing.

dash·ing (dăsh'ĭng) **1** lively; bold: *a* dashing *knight.* **2** showy; bright: *a* dashing *costume.*

da·ta (dā'tə or dăt'ə) facts and figures; information: *The* data *for a report.*

---

fāte, făt, fâre, fär; bē, bĕt; bīte, bĭt; nō, nŏt, nôr; fūse, fŭn, fûr; tōō, tŏŏk; foil; foul; thin; ~~then~~; hw for wh as in *wh*at; zh for s as in u*s*ual; ə for a, e, i, o, u, as in *a*go, lin*e*n, per*i*l, at*o*m, min*u*s

¹**date** (dāt) **1** a particular point of time when something happens, is done, or is made. Dates are usually expressed in a statement telling the day of the month and the year: *The* date *on this letter is May 20, 1962. The* date *is engraved on coins.* **2** to mark with a date: *We* date *letters in the heading.* **3** the period of time to which anything belongs: *It was at an early* date *that the wheel was invented.* **4** to find or fix the time of: *Historians now* date *events as before or after the birth of Jesus Christ.* **5** an appointment to meet a person at a certain time and place. **6 out of date** no longer in use or style. **7 up to date** (**1**) in fashion. (**2**) up to now.

date from to belong to the time of; have origin in: *These costumes* date from *the Revolutionary period.*

dat·ed, dat·ing. [¹**date** is from a Latin word (data) meaning "things given."]

²**date** (dāt) **1** a kind of palm tree which bears clusters of oblong, one-seeded fruit. **2** the sweet fruit, usually dried, of this tree. [²**date** goes back by way of a number of languages to a Greek word (daktylos) meaning "finger." It was probably thought that the fruit looked like a finger.]

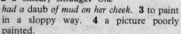
Date palm

daub (dôb) **1** to cover or coat with mud, plaster, etc. **2** a smear; smudge: *She had a* daub *of mud on her cheek.* **3** to paint in a sloppy way. **4** a picture poorly painted.

daugh·ter (dô′tər) **1** a female child; a girl or woman, when thought of in relation to her parents. **2** girl or woman who belongs to a particular group, comes from some particular place, etc.: *Many of the sons and* daughters *of Ireland came to settle in America.*

daugh·ter-in-law (dô′tər ĭn lô′) a son's wife. **daugh·ters-in-law.**

daunt (dônt) frighten; dishearten; make less courageous: *Even the risk of death did not* daunt *the brave knight.*

daunt·less (dônt′lĭs) fearless; brave: *a* dauntless *explorer;* dauntless *courage.* **daunt·less·ly.**

dav·en·port (dăv′ən pôrt′) a large sofa.

daw·dle (dô′dəl) to loiter; waste time: *He* dawdled *through his breakfast.* **daw·dled, daw·dling.**

dawn (dôn) **1** the coming of daylight in the morning. **2** to begin to grow light in the morning: *The day* dawns *in the east.* **3** earliest appearance; beginning: *The invention of the airplane marked the* dawn *of a new age.* **4** to begin to appear or develop: *A new age* dawned. **5** to begin to make a mental impression: *The answer finally* dawned *on me.*

day (dā) **1** the period of light between sunrise and sunset. **2** a period of 24 hours. **3** a particular age or period: *in the* days *of hoop skirts.* **4** a particular day on which some special event takes place: *Thanksgiving* Day. **5** the number of hours given to work or school: *the eight-hour* day.

day·break (dā′brāk′) the first appearance of light in the morning; dawn.

day·dream (dā′drēm′) **1** to think about something in a dreamy, time-wasting way. **2** what one thinks about in this way.

day·light (dā′līt′) **1** the light of day. **2** the time between dawn and dusk when the sun gives light; daytime. **3** daybreak: *Before* daylight *the milkman starts out on his route.*

daylight saving time system of keeping time in the summer. Clocks are set one hour ahead of standard time so that people will go to work an hour earlier in the morning. This gives them an extra hour of daylight in the evening for recreation, etc.

day·time (dā′tīm′) the time between sunrise and sunset.

daze (dāz) **1** to cause to feel stupid or out of one's senses; stun; confuse: *to be* dazed *by a shock or blow.* **2 in a daze** in a state of confusion or shock. **dazed, daz·ing.**

daz·zle (dăz′əl) **1** to overcome or confuse by very bright light. **2** to cause great admiration (by brilliant appearance or performance): *The fine performance of the opera* dazzled *us.* **3** brightness; glitter: *the* dazzle *of tinsel.* **daz·zled, daz·zling.**

daz·zling (dăz′lĭng) **1** so bright as to prevent clear vision: *a* dazzling *light.* **2** overwhelming: *a* dazzling *wit.* **daz·zling·ly.**

D.C. 1 District of Columbia. **2** direct current.

DDT (dē dē tē′) a powerful insect-killer.

dea·con (dē′kən) **1** a church officer who does not preach but assists in certain ceremonies, in caring for the poor, etc. **2** in some churches, an ordained member of the clergy next below a priest in rank.

dead (děd) **1** no longer living: *a dead plant or animal.* **2** person who has died; persons who have died. **3** without life: *Outer space has much dead matter in it, especially cosmic dust.* **4** inactive; without force, motion, etc.: *a dead tennis ball;* dead *air.* **5** the time of the greatest quietness: *the dead of night.* **6** no longer used: *a dead language.* **7** complete; entire: *a dead silence; a dead loss.* **8** exact: *at dead center.* **9** entirely: *to be dead right.* **10** straight: *Steer dead ahead.* **11** not bright or shiny: *a dead color.*

dead·en (děd′ən) to make less alive; dull; weaken: *to* deaden *sound;* deaden *pain.*

dead·line (děd′līn′) the latest time set for something to be finished; a time limit.

dead·lock (děd′lŏk′) **1** situation in which opposing sides are even in strength and neither will give in; standstill. **2** to cause or bring about a deadlock.

dead·ly (děd′lĭ) **1** causing or tending to cause death: *the deadly bite of the cobra.* **2** very hostile; aiming to kill or destroy: *a deadly enemy.* **3** in a manner resembling death; like death: *She is deadly pale.* **dead·li·er, dead·li·est.**

Dead Sea a salt-water lake between Israel and Jordan.

deaf (děf) **1** unable to hear. **2** partly unable to hear; hard of hearing. **3 deaf to** unwilling to listen: *She was deaf to his pleas.*

deaf·en (děf′ən) **1** to make unable to hear. **2** to overpower or stun with noise: *to be* deafened *by a shrieking whistle.*

deal (dēl) **1** to be concerned; have to do: *History* deals *with the past.* **2** to act; take action: *He* deals *fairly with his partner.* **3** to trade; do business: *That jewelry store* deals *mainly in watches. We* deal *at the neighborhood market.* **4** business transaction; bargain: *They got a good* deal *on their new car.* **5** to give out; distribute: *Please* deal *the cards.* **6** giving out; distribution: *a new* deal. **7** to give; deliver: *The soldier* dealt *a blow to his enemy.* **8 great deal**

great amount: *A great deal of silver was found in the hills.* **dealt, deal·ing.**

deal·er (dē′lər) **1** person who buys and sells goods; trader; merchant: *a diamond dealer.* **2** a card player who deals the cards.

deal·ing (dē′lĭng) **1** act of one who deals. **2 dealings** business relations; transactions: *his dealings with the Eskimos.*

dealt (dělt) See **deal.** *The fighter dealt his opponent a hard blow.*

dean (dēn) **1** head of a college or school faculty. **2** person in charge of the discipline and counseling of students at a school: *a dean of men; a dean of women.* **3** the member of a group or organization who has served the longest: *the dean of the diplomatic corps.* **4** clergyman in charge of a cathedral.

dear (dĭr) **1** loved; precious: *a dear friend.* **2** darling; loved one: *Yes, dear, I'm home.* **3** expensive; costly: *We pay a dear price for repairs.* **4** highly valued (used in letters as a polite form of address). **5** dearly: *That will cost you dear, my friend.* (Homonym: deer)

dear·ly (dĭr′lĭ) **1** very much: *She loved her grandfather dearly.* **2** at a high price; expensively: *to pay dearly for a mistake.*

dearth (dûrth) want; lack; scarcity: *There is a dearth of food in many parts of Asia.*

death (děth) **1** the ending of life. **2** the ending of anything: *the death of hope; the death of the local mining industry.* **3** the fact or condition of being dead: *In death he looked serene.* **4** a cause of dying; something that kills: *That dangerous ladder will be the death of you yet.* **5 at death's door** near death. **6 put to death** to kill. **7 to death** very much; to the last degree: *I'm worried to death over this.*

death·less (děth′lĭs) never dying; immortal: *Shakespeare's deathless words.*

death·ly (děth′lĭ) **1** deadly; threatening death. **2** like that of death: *a deathly quiet.* **3** in a manner like that of death: *His skin felt deathly cold.* **4** extremely; utterly: *She is deathly afraid of fire.*

death's-head (děths′hěd′) a human skull, or a picture of it, taken as a symbol of death.

---

fāte, făt, fâre, fär; bē, bĕt; bīte, bĭt; nō, nŏt, nôr; fūse, fŭn, fûr; tōō, tŏŏk; foil; foul; thin; ~~then~~;
hw for wh as in *wh*at; zh for s as in u*s*ual; ə for a, e, i, o, u, as in *a*go, lin*e*n, per*i*l, atom, min*u*s.

de·base (dĭ bās′) to make lower in value or in quality: *to debase gold by mixing it with copper; to debase oneself by cheating.* **de·based, de·bas·ing.**

de·bat·a·ble (dĭ bā′tə bəl) open to debate; not yet decided: *a debatable question.*

de·bate (dĭ bāt′) **1** to think about; consider: *I debated whether to buy a new coat now or later.* **2** to discuss by giving reasons for and against: *We debated the question of where we would stop for the night.* **3** argument; discussion: *After much debate we finally chose a new car.* **4** a formal argument, according to rules, in which each side of a question is presented before an audience. **5** to take part in such an argument. **de·bat·ed, de·bat·ing.**

de·bris or **dé·bris** (də brē′ or dā′brē) shattered, broken pieces; rubbish: *to clear away the debris.*

debt (dĕt) **1** money or an obligation one person owes another; payment owed. **2 in debt** owing money; under an obligation.

debt·or (dĕt′ər) person who owes a debt.

Dec. December.

dec·ade (dĕk′ād) a period of ten years.

de·cay (dĭ kā′) **1** to rot: *Plants that have died decay and make the soil rich.* **2** to lose strength and quality gradually; fail; waste away: *Many civilizations have prospered, then decayed later.* **3** loss of strength or quality by degrees; gradual failure; decline: *the decay of a business.*

de·cease (dĭ sēs′) **1** death. **2** to die. **de·ceased, de·ceas·ing.**

de·ceased (dĭ sēst′) **1** dead; especially dead only a short time: *The names of many deceased voters were still on the voting list.* **2 the deceased** dead person or persons.

de·ceit (dĭ sēt′) **1** habit or practice of deceiving, lying, or misleading. **2** dishonest action or trick.

de·ceit·ful (dĭ sēt′fəl) given to trickery, lying, or cheating; dishonest: *a deceitful person.* **de·ceit·ful·ly.**

de·ceive (dĭ sēv′) to mislead; cause (a person) to believe what is untrue: *to deceive people in order to get one's own way.* **de·ceived, de·ceiv·ing.**

De·cem·ber (dĭ sĕm′bər) the twelfth month of the year. December has 31 days.

de·cen·cy (dē′sən sĭ) **1** quality of being decent; observance of proper standards of

behavior, speech, dress, etc.: *He said that decency requires us to speak courteously.* **2 the decencies** the requirements for a decent and proper life: *Common courtesy and cleanliness are among the decencies.* **de·cen·cies.**

de·cent (dē′sənt) **1** proper for a particular time or place: *to have decent clothes to wear.* **2** worthy of respect: *the decent people of a community.* **3** not causing people to feel shame; modest: *That is not a very decent story.* **4** good enough; fair: *a decent salary.* **5** kind; understanding: *He was very decent about my tardiness.* **de·cent·ly.**

de·cen·tral·i·za·tion (dē sĕn′trə lə zā′-shən) a breaking up or spreading (of authority, activities, etc.) from one center to many branches: *the decentralization of industries into the suburbs.*

de·cen·tral·ize (dē sĕn′trə līz′) to transfer from a central point to outlying points, especially in government or industry. **de·cen·tral·ized, de·cen·tral·iz·ing.**

de·cep·tion (dĭ sĕp′shən) **1** act of deceiving. **2** a piece of trickery; something that fools or cheats.

de·cep·tive (dĭ sĕp′tĭv) deceiving; giving a false appearance or impression: *a deceptive calm before the storm.* **de·cep·tive·ly.**

dec·i·bel (dĕs′ə bĕl′) a unit for measuring the loudness of sounds.

de·cide (dĭ sīd′) **1** to settle (a question, dispute, doubt, etc.): *to decide what movie to see.* **2** to make up one's mind; come to a conclusion or decision on: *We've decided to sell our farm.* **3** to give a judgment or decision: *The judge decided in my favor.* **de·cid·ed, de·cid·ing.**

de·cid·ed (dĭ sī′dĭd) **1** definite; clear; unmistakable: *a decided improvement.* **2** not showing hesitation; determined: *He has very decided opinions.* **de·cid·ed·ly.**

de·cid·u·ous (dĭ sĭj′ōō əs) shedding leaves or foliage yearly: *a deciduous shrub.*

dec·i·mal (dĕs′ə məl) **1** a fraction like .6, which is the same as $\frac{6}{10}$, or .32, which is the same as $\frac{32}{100}$. **2** based on tens or tenths: *the decimal system of United States money.*

decimal point the dot before a decimal fraction or between a whole number and a decimal, such as .25 or 3.7.

de·ci·pher (dĭ sī′fər) **1** to make out or interpret the meaning of something that is not plain or clear: *The handwriting was so bad we could hardly* decipher *it.* **2** to change from a code or cipher to ordinary words: *You need a key to* decipher *a coded message.*

de·ci·sion (dĭ sĭzh'ən) **1** act of deciding or making up one's mind; judgment. **2** the judgment or conclusion decided on: *The court's* decision *is final.* **3** firmness; determination: *a man of* decision.

de·ci·sive (dĭ sī'sĭv) **1** settling something once and for all; conclusive: *A* decisive *battle ended the war.* **2** showing decision; positive; firm: *A leader must be* decisive *in a crisis.* **de·ci·sive·ly.**

deck (dĕk) **1** any of the floors of a ship. **2** any flat surface like the deck of a ship: *sun* deck; *an observation* deck *of a train or plane.* **3** pack of playing cards. **4** to decorate; array; adorn: *to* deck *the halls with holly; to* deck *oneself in a new uniform.*

dec·la·ra·tion (dĕk'lə rā'shən) **1** a statement. **2** public statement; proclamation: *a* declaration *of war.* **3** a list of goods liable to tax or duty: *a customs* declaration.

Declaration of Independence document of July 4, 1776, by which the 13 American colonies declared themselves to be free and independent of Great Britain.

de·clare (dĭ klâr') **1** to make known; announce; make a positive statement: *The company* declared *a new dividend. The witness* declared *that he hadn't seen the accident.* **2** to list goods on which duty is to be paid. **declare oneself 1** to call oneself: *He* declared *himself a friend.* **2** to take a stand: *He* declared *himself in favor of athletics.* **de·clared, de·clar·ing.**

de·cline (dĭ klīn') **1** to refuse: *When he was asked to help he* declined. **2** to refuse courteously: *to* decline *an invitation to dinner, etc.* **3** to go down; become less: *After the record sales, business* declined. **4** a gradual lessening; a going down: *The safety campaign brought about a* decline *in accidents.* **de·clined, de·clin·ing.**

de·cliv·i·ty (dĭ klĭv'ə tĭ) downward slope.

de·com·pose (dē'kəm pōz') **1** to decay; rot: *Dead plants gradually* decompose *and enrich the soil.* **2** to separate into basic parts. **de·com·posed, de·com·pos·ing.**

de·com·po·si·tion (dē'kŏm pə zĭsh'ən) **1** a decaying; a rotting; a disintegrating. **2** a breaking down into basic parts: *The* decomposition *of water yields hydrogen and oxygen.*

dec·o·rate (dĕk'ə rāt') **1** to put ornaments on; adorn: *We* decorated *our Christmas tree.* **2** to paint or paper a room. **3** to give (someone) a mark of distinction, such as a medal or badge: *The general* decorated *the hero.* **dec·o·rat·ed, dec·o·rat·ing.**

dec·o·ra·tion (dĕk'ə rā'shən) **1** the adding of ornaments; adornment: *the* decoration *of the room for the party.* **2** something to add beauty; ornament: *the* decorations *for the fall dance.* **3** medal; honorary ribbon or pin: *a* decoration *for bravery.*

Decoration Day Memorial Day.

dec·o·ra·tive (dĕk'ə rā'tĭv *or* dĕk'rə tĭv) serving to beautify or adorn; ornamental. **dec·o·ra·tive·ly.**

de·co·rum (dĭ kôr'əm) what is proper and fitting in behavior and language; propriety and good taste: *People with a sense of* decorum *do not laugh or talk during church service.*

de·coy (dĭ koi') **1** to attract by trickery; lure; entice. **2** (also dē'koi) someone or something designed to entice or trap, especially a live or a painted wooden duck used to attract wild ducks into shooting range.

Decoy

¹de·crease (dĭ krēs') **1** to grow less; become smaller; diminish: *Speed* decreased *as the engine went up a steep grade.* **2** to make less; cause to grow less: *One can* decrease *friction by oiling the wheels.* **de·creased, de·creas·ing.**

²de·crease (dē'krēs) a lessening; decline: *a* decrease *in the number of accidents.*

de·cree (dĭ krē') **1** order put forth by a ruler or public authority, and having the force of law: *The premier ruled by* decree. **2** to put forth a decree. **de·creed, de·cree·ing.**

ded·i·cate (dĕd'ə kāt') **1** to set apart for a purpose, often by a ceremony: *The bishop will* dedicate *the new church.* **2** to give up or devote (to some cause or purpose): *He*

---

fāte, făt, fâre, fär; bē, bĕt; bīte, bĭt; nō, nŏt, nôr; fūse, fŭn, fûr; tōō, tŏŏk; foil; foul; thin; ~~then~~; hw for wh as in *w*hat; zh for s as in u*s*ual; ə for a, e, i, o, u, as in ago, linen, peril, atom, min*u*s

dedicated *his life to medical work among the poor.* **3** to inscribe or address (a book or other artistic work) to a patron or friend. **ded·i·cat·ed, ded·i·cat·ing.**

ded·i·ca·tion (dĕd′ə kā′shən) **1** a devoting to a religious or other special purpose: *The dedication of the new school took place today.* **2** an inscription of gratitude or affection for someone, often placed at the beginning of a book, piece of music, etc.

de·duce (di dōōs′ or di dūs′) to reach a conclusion from facts that are known; infer: *I deduce from your remarks that you don't agree with me.* **de·duced, de·duc·ing.**

de·duct (di dŭkt′) to take away (an amount or part); subtract: *Income taxes are deducted from most employee's salaries.*

de·duc·tion (di dŭk′shən) **1** act of taking away: *the deduction of taxes from a salary.* **2** amount taken away: *After the deductions there was not much left in my salary.* **3** conclusion drawn from information: *The deduction from these statistics is that most people watch television.*

deed (dēd) **1** that which is done; an act or action: *a kind deed.* **2** an achievement; an act of bravery, skill, etc. **3** a legal writing or record which shows that property or rights belong to a certain person or persons: *He could not find the deed to his farm.* **4** to make over or transfer: *He deeded the farm to his son.*

deem (dēm) to think; believe: *The Pilgrims deemed it fitting to have a day of thanksgiving.*

deep (dēp) **1** going far down, inward, or far back: *a deep well; a deep drawer; a deep cave.* **2** far into; in the middle of: *lost deep in the woods.* **3** having a certain depth downward, back, etc.: *a pool nine feet deep; a lot 150 feet deep.* **4** hard to understand: *a deep subject.* **5** penetrating: *a deep insight.* **6** attentive or interested: *to be deep in study.* **7** heavy: *a deep sleep.* **8** heartfelt: *to feel deep sympathy or deep love.* **9** dark; rich in color: *a deep purple.* **10** low in pitch: *a deep voice.* **11** tricky; cunning: *She's a deep one.* **12 the deep** the sea. **deep·ly.**

deep·en (dē′pən) **1** to make (something) go farther down, back, or in: *The men will deepen the trench tomorrow.* **2** to become darker: *The shadows deepened.*

deer (dir) any of several hoofed, cudchewing animals, the males of which have branching horns, or antlers. Deer are admired for their swift and graceful movements. pl. **deer.** (Homonym: dear)

White-tail deer, 3½ ft. high at shoulder

deer·skin (dir′skin′) **1** the skin of a deer. **2** leather made from this. **3** made of this leather: *a pair of deerskin leggings.*

def. definition.

de·face (di fās′) to spoil the appearance of (by marking or damaging); disfigure: *to deface a wall with crayon marks.* **de·faced, de·fac·ing.**

de·feat (di fēt′) **1** to overcome; beat; win a victory over: *to defeat an enemy.* **2** an overthrow: *the defeat of an army.* **3** to bring to nothing; frustrate: *to defeat a plan.* **4** a coming to naught: *the defeat of his hopes.*

de·fect (dē′fĕkt or di fĕkt′) **1** fault; flaw: *A defect in construction weakened the bridge.* **2** mental or physical imperfection: *A defect in speech can often be overcome.*

de·fec·tive (di fĕk′tiv) **1** not made, formed, or functioning correctly; faulty; imperfect: *defective speech; defective wiring.* **2** person who is not normal in intelligence or mental capacities. **de·fec·tive·ly.**

de·fence (di fĕns′) defense.

de·fence·less (di fĕns′lĭs) defenseless. **de·fence·less·ly.**

de·fend (di fĕnd′) **1** to protect from harm or danger; guard. **2** to uphold or keep to; maintain: *to defend an idea; to defend a righteous cause.* **3** to state a case for; to act for: *to engage a lawyer to defend the accused.*

de·fend·er (di fĕn′dər) a person who protects; a protector.

de·fense (di fĕns′) **1** a defending; resistance to attack. **2** person or thing that protects; protector; protection: *Cleanliness is one defense against disease.* **3** reply of a person to a lawsuit brought against him: *What defense did the accused man offer?* **4** the defending side in a contest or battle. **5** the side for the accused person in a lawsuit: *Who is the lawyer for the defense?* Also spelled **defence.**

de·fense·less (dǐ fěns′lǐs) helpless; without protection: *a defenseless babe.* Also spelled **defenceless. de·fense·less·ly.**

de·fen·sive (dǐ fěn′sǐv) **1** meant or made to resist attack: *a defensive weapon;* defensive *warfare.* **2 on the defensive** (**1**) ready to resist attack. (**2**) in the position of having to defend or justify oneself. **de·fen·sive·ly.**

¹de·fer (dǐ fûr′) to put off until later; postpone: *to defer a visit; to defer a payment on a loan.* **de·ferred, de·fer·ring.** [¹**defer** is from an Old French word (differer) that goes back to a Latin word (differre) meaning "put off."]

²de·fer (dǐ fûr′) to give respect (to); to yield; submit (to): *We gladly defer to the opinions of a man who has proved his wisdom and skill.* **de·ferred, de·fer·ring.** [²**defer** is from a French word (déférer) that comes from a Latin word (deferre) meaning "hand over."]

def·er·ence (děf′ər əns) **1** a giving in to or yielding to the wishes or beliefs of someone else. **2** respect; regard: *The boy showed* deference *for his grandmother.*

de·fi·ance (dǐ fī′əns) **1** a going against; open resistance; open refusal to obey or respect: *In* defiance *of all common sense, the boys went swimming right after eating.* **2** hostile challenge: *The angry prisoner shouted his* defiance *at the guard.*

de·fi·ant (dǐ fī′ənt) **1** openly refusing to obey or respect; boldly disobedient. **2** challenging; expressing bold opposition. **de·fi·ant·ly.**

de·fi·cien·cy (dǐ fǐsh′ən sǐ) **1** a shortage; lack: *a vitamin* deficiency. **2** amount or sum by which something falls short: *There's a* deficiency *of $10 in our club funds.* **de·fi·cien·cies.**

de·fi·cient (dǐ fǐsh′ənt) lacking; not having enough of; below standard: *a diet* deficient *in milk.* **de·fi·cient·ly.**

¹de·file (dǐ fīl′) **1** to make foul or impure; to make dirty; pollute: *to defile the air with smog; to defile a river with refuse.* **2** to put to an unworthy use; spoil the purity of (something noble or sacred): *to defile a church or temple.* **3** to bring dishonor upon: *The report* defiled *his good reputation.*

de·filed, de·fil·ing. [¹**defile** is a changed form of an obsolete word (befile) which was a form of an Old English word (befýlan) meaning "to soil."]

²de·file (dǐ fīl′ or dē′fīl′) **1** narrow pass or passage between cliffs or mountains. **2** to march in single file: *The marching column of soldiers* defiled *to the barracks.* **de·fil·ed, de·fil·ing.** [²**defile** is from a French word (défilé) which was taken from another French word (défiler) meaning "to march in a file," "to unroll thread."]

de·fine (dǐ fīn′) **1** to give the exact meaning and explain the use of: *This dictionary* defines *each word.* **2** to describe in an exact manner by showing the limits of: *to define their duties.* **3** to fix or give the limits of: *The treaty* defined *the borders of the two countries.* **4** to show clearly in outline: *The jagged line of hills was sharply* defined *against the sky.* **de·fined, de·fin·ing.**

def·i·nite (děf′ə nǐt) **1** exact; precise; having specific limits: *The buyer made a* definite *offer of ten dollars.* **2** clear; not doubtful: *Frayed wire is a* definite *fire hazard. He gave a* definite *answer.* **def·i·nite·ly.**

def·i·ni·tion (děf′ə nǐsh′ən) **1** the explaining of a thing or idea; the making clear of the meaning of a word or group of words; a defining. **2** an explanation of the meaning of a word: *How many meanings does the complete* definition *of "jet" have in your dictionary?* **3** sharpness or clearness of outline.

de·flate (dǐ flāt′) **1** to let air or gas out of: *to deflate a rubber raft.* **2** to make smaller; to reduce the amount of: *to deflate prices.* **de·flat·ed, de·flat·ing.**

de·flect (dǐ flěkt′) to turn aside; change from a straight course: *The ball was* deflected *by a tree.*

de·form (dǐ fôrm′) to change the form of; disfigure; mar: *Tight shoes* deform *the feet.*

de·form·i·ty (dǐ fôr′mə tǐ) **1** part of a human or animal body not properly shaped. **2** condition of being disfigured. **3** moral defect or ugliness. **de·form·i·ties.**

de·fraud (dǐ frôd′) to cheat; trick dishonestly; swindle: *To make a false tax return is to* defraud *the government.*

---

fāte, fǎt, fâre, fär; bē, bět; bīte, bǐt; nō, nǒt, nôr; fūse, fǔn, fûr; tōō, tŏŏk; foil; foul; thin; then; hw for wh as in *wh*at; zh for s as in u*s*ual; ə for a, e, i, o, u, as in *a*go, lin*e*n, per*i*l, at*o*m, min*u*s

de·frost (dē frôst') to cause to thaw; remove frost from: *to defrost a refrigerator.*

deft (dĕft) skillful; clever; nimble: *The dressmaker was deft with her needle.* **deft·ly.**

de·fy (dĭ fī') **1** to challenge or dare: *This store defies all others to beat its prices.* **2** to treat as of no account or with contempt: *to defy the law; to defy a parent's wishes.* **3** to resist successfully: *The window defies every attempt to open it.* **de·fied, de·fy·ing.**

deg·ra·da·tion (dĕg'rə dā'shən) a degrading or being degraded.

de·grade (dĭ grād') **1** to lower the character of; debase: *Anyone who cheats degrades himself.* **2** to lower in social standing or rank; deprive of honors or dignity: *Cinderella's sisters tried to degrade her by making her do the chores. The cowardly officer was degraded.* **de·grad·ed, de·grad·ing.**

de·gree (dĭ grē') **1** unit used in measuring temperature: *Water boils at 212 degrees (212°) Fahrenheit.* **2** unit used in measuring angles and parts of circles: *A right angle or one-fourth of a circle has 90 degrees (90°). A complete circle has 360 degrees (360°).* **3** title given by a college or university for passing

Degrees

a certain course of study or as a mark of honor. **4** a step or stage in progress: *You should climb a steep hill by easy degrees.* **5** amount; extent: *a high degree of skill in dancing.* **6** social rank: *lords and ladies of high degree.*

de·hy·drate (dē hī'drāt') to remove the water from; dry out: *Many foods are dehydrated to preserve them.* **de·hy·drat·ed, de·hy·drat·ing.**

de·hy·dra·tion (dē'hī drā'shən) **1** the condition of being without water or moisture. **2** the removing of water from a substance by heat or chemical means.

deign (dān) **1** to think it fitting; condescend: *The governor deigned to grant us an audience.* **2** to give; grant: *He did not deign an answer to our request.* (Homonym: Dane)

de·i·ty (dē'ə tĭ) **1** a god or goddess: *Many ancient peoples worshipped the sun as a deity.* **2 the Deity** God. **de·i·ties.**

de·ject·ed (dĭ jĕk'tĭd) depressed; low-spirited; downcast: *The coach was dejected after the defeat.* **de·ject·ed·ly.**

Del. Delaware.

Del·a·ware (dĕl'ə wâr') a Middle Atlantic State of the United States.

de·lay (dĭ lā') **1** to put off until later: *Rain delayed the game twenty minutes.* **2** a putting off of something; a wait: *The accident caused a short delay.*

del·e·gate (dĕl'ə gāt) **1** (also dĕl'ə gĭt) person chosen to act for a group; representative: *One delegate from each State attended the conference.* **2** to select (someone) as an agent or representative: *The class delegated their best speaker to represent them at the assembly program.* **3** to entrust; hand over: *The sheriff delegated certain duties to a deputy.* **del·e·gat·ed, del·e·gat·ing.**

del·e·ga·tion (dĕl'ə gā'shən) **1** a delegating: *The delegation of duties to others is part of an executive's job.* **2** group of representatives: *The school sent a delegation of five students to the convention.*

de·lete (dĭ lēt') to strike out; eliminate: *The editor deleted the story from the paper.* **de·let·ed, de·let·ing.**

¹de·lib·er·ate (dĭ lĭb'ər ĭt) **1** thought out beforehand; intentional: *He told a deliberate lie.* **2** leisurely in action; unhurried: *a deliberate pace.* **3** careful; cautious: *a deliberate judgment.* **de·lib·er·ate·ly.**

²de·lib·er·ate (dĭ lĭb'ə rāt') to consider carefully; think and talk over: *The jury deliberated all day before giving a verdict.* **de·lib·er·at·ed, de·lib·er·at·ing.**

de·lib·er·a·tion (dĭ lĭb'ə rā'shən) **1** calm, careful thought: *The judge gave his decision after long deliberation.* **2** slowness and care: *The chess player moved with the utmost deliberation.* **3** discussion or weighing up of reasons for and against action: *The deliberations over the bill lasted for weeks.*

del·i·ca·cy (dĕl'ə kə sĭ) **1** something pleasing to the taste; delicious food. **2** fineness of quality, texture, etc.; daintiness: *the delicacy of lace.* **3** fineness of skill or touch: *the delicacy of an artist's brush strokes.* **4** fineness of feeling as to what is proper, fitting, or nice; regard for the feelings of others: *Natural delicacy kept him from asking personal questions.* **5** physical weakness; lack of vigor. **del·i·ca·cies.**

del·i·cate (dĕl′ə kĭt) **1** fine; dainty in quality, form, texture, or to the taste: *a delicate flavor*. **2** of a soft, pale tint: *a delicate pink*. **3** frail: *in delicate health*. **4** easily broken; fragile: *a delicate cup*. **5** finely sensitive: *a delicate touch; a delicate instrument*. **6** requiring skill; difficult to handle: *a delicate operation; a delicate diplomatic mission*. **del·i·cate·ly.**

de·li·cious (dĭ lĭsh′əs) pleasing; delightful, especially to taste and smell. **de·li·cious·ly.**

de·light (dĭ līt′) **1** to please greatly; give enjoyment and pleasure to: *Toys delight a child*. **2** a great amount of pleasure; joy: *It was a delight to the boys to go fishing with their father*. **3** something that causes pleasure: *A bright sunny day is a delight*. **delight in** to take great pleasure in.

de·light·ful (dĭ līt′fəl) giving enjoyment; pleasing; charming: *a delightful evening*. **de·light·ful·ly.**

de·lin·quent (dĭ lĭng′kwənt) **1** failing in duty or responsibility: *a delinquent parent*. **2** past due: *a delinquent bill*. **3** person who does not observe his duties and responsibilities; person who breaks the law repeatedly or habitually. **de·lin·quent·ly.**

de·lir·i·ous (dĭ lĭr′ĭ əs) **1** raving; wandering in the mind: *to be delirious from fever*. **2** wild with excitement: *to be delirious with joy*. **de·lir·i·ous·ly.**

de·lir·i·um (dĭ lĭr′ĭ əm) **1** a wandering and confused state of mind in which a person does not know where he is or what he is saying or doing. Delirium is usually temporary and often caused by fever, nervous shock, etc. **2** wild excitement: *A delirium of joy followed the winning of the prize*.

de·liv·er (dĭ lĭv′ər) **1** to hand over; give to another person; take to a certain person or place: *to deliver mail*. **2** to set free; save from danger, trouble, etc.: *to deliver from captivity*. **3** to give forth in words: *to deliver a speech*. **4** to launch; aim: *to deliver a blow*.

de·liv·er·ance (dĭ lĭv′ər əns) a rescue; release; a setting free: *to pray for deliverance from pain and trouble*.

de·liv·er·er (dĭ lĭv′ər ər) person who rescues or frees another.

de·liv·er·y (dĭ lĭv′ə rĭ) **1** distribution; a handing over: *mail delivery; the delivery of the ransom money*. **2** what is delivered: *the suspension of further deliveries*. **3** releasing; a setting free: *the delivery of prisoners from jail*. **4** manner of speaking: *His forceful delivery made the speech effective*. **5** way of pitching a ball: *The pitcher used a tricky delivery*. **6** a giving birth to a child. **de·liv·er·ies.**

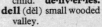

dell (dĕl) small wooded valley.

del·ta (dĕl′tə) more or less triangular accumulation of earth and sand at the mouth of a river.

Delta

de·lude (dĭ lōōd′ or dĭ lūd′) to mislead; deceive: *A boaster usually deludes nobody but himself*. **de·lud·ed, de·lud·ing.**

del·uge (dĕl′ūj) **1** a heavy downpour; an overflowing of water; a flood. **2** anything that overwhelms like a flood: *a deluge of fan letters; a deluge of visitors*. **3** to overflow; flood. **4** to overwhelm: *The chairman was deluged with questions*. **del·uged, del·ug·ing.**

de·lu·sion (dĭ lōō′zhən or dĭ lū′zhən) an idea or belief that is contrary to facts or reason: *An insane person may have a delusion that he is a famous person*.

delve (dĕlv) **1** to search carefully for information: *to delve in a library*. **2** to dig with a spade. **delved, delv·ing.**

de·mand (dĭ mănd′) **1** to ask for with authority; claim as a right: *Father demands obedience from his children*. **2** to ask for urgently: *to demand to be paid; demand to be told*. **3** a strong request: *a demand for an answer*. **4** to have need for; require: *His business demanded his full time*. **5** a requirement or claim: *the many demands of his business*. **6** a desire to have or get; call: *There is a great demand for houses in the new area*.

de·mean·or (dĭ mē′nər) conduct; behavior; manner: *The speaker kept an even and composed demeanor in spite of the outcries*.

---

fāte, făt, fâre, fär; bē, bĕt; bīte, bĭt; nō, nŏt, nôr; fūse, fŭn, fûr; tōō, tŏŏk; foil; foul; thin; ~~then~~; hw for wh as in *w*hat; zh for s as in usual; ə for a, e, i, o, u, as in ago, linen, peril, atom, minus

de·ment·ed (dǐ měn′tǐd) out of one's mind;
insane; mad; crazed. **de·ment·ed·ly.**

de·mer·it (dē měr′ǐt) **1** something that calls
for blame; a fault; a wrong act. **2** a mark
against one for failure or bad conduct.

de·mo·bi·lize (dē mō′bə liz′) to disband or
dismiss: *to* demobilize *troops.* **de·mo·bi·**
lized, de·mo·bi·liz·ing.

de·moc·ra·cy (dǐ mŏk′rə sǐ) **1** a form of
government in which the people rule directly by assembling in meetings in order
to vote on issues, or indirectly by going to
the polls in order to elect representatives
who will so act for them. **2** a nation or
state so governed. The United States is a
democracy. **3** the treating of others as
equals: *A snob does not practice* democracy.
de·moc·ra·cies.

dem·o·crat (děm′ə krăt) **1** a person who
believes that all should have an equal voice
in government. **2** person who believes and
acts on the belief that all others are his
equals. **3 Democrat** a member of the
Democratic Party in the United States.

dem·o·crat·ic (děm′ə krăt′ĭk) **1** of democracy; like democracy. **2** treating people as
one's equals: *The Prince had a* democratic
manner that put everybody he met at ease.
3 the Democratic Party one of the two
chief political parties in the United States.

dem·o·crat·i·cal·ly (děm′ə krăt′ə kəl ǐ) in
a democratic way.

de·mol·ish (dǐ mŏl′ĭsh) to tear down; pull
down; destroy: *Old buildings were* demol-
ished *to make room for new houses.*

de·mon (dē′mən) **1** evil spirit; devil; fiend.
2 very cruel and wicked person. **3** a person
with exceptional energy: *a* demon *for work.*

dem·on·strate (děm′ən strāt′) **1** to teach or
explain by showing examples, pictures, and
the like: *Mary will* demonstrate *how to
solve the problem by working it on the board.*
2 to prove: *An experiment will* demonstrate
that wood cannot burn without oxygen. **3** to
exhibit and explain the good points of (a
product or machine): *The salesman* demon-
strated *the sewing machine by making different kinds of stitches.* **4** to hold a meeting,
parade, or the like to show public feelings.
dem·on·strat·ed, dem·on·strat·ing.

dem·on·stra·tion (děm′ən strā′shən) **1** explanation by showing examples, pictures,
etc.: *Our teacher gave a* demonstration *of*
the new dance step. **2** proof: *The experiment
was clear* demonstration *that a fire needs
oxygen to burn.* **3** an outward expression
of feeling: *Crying is a* demonstration *of
grief. A kiss is a* demonstration *of affection.*
4 a public showing of the good points of a
product or working of a machine. **5** a
meeting, parade, or the like, to show public
feelings: *A noisy* demonstration *greeted the
returning hero.*

de·mor·al·ize (dǐ mŏr′ə liz′ or dǐ môr′ə-
liz′) **1** to weaken the morals of; corrupt:
He was demoralized *by the kind of friends
he associated with.* **2** to weaken the morale,
spirit, or self-discipline of: *An attack on
the rear guard* demoralized *the army.* **de-**
mor·al·ized, de·mor·al·iz·ing.

de·mote (dǐ mōt′) to reduce to a lower rank,
grade, or the like: *to* demote *an army officer.*
de·mot·ed, de·mot·ing.

de·mure (dǐ myŏŏr′) **1** quiet and modest:
In her demure *way she was delighted also.*
2 pretending to be shy; coy: *She gave a*
demure *smile.* **de·mure·ly.**

den (děn) **1** home of a wild animal. **2** small,
dirty room. **3** a haunt for criminals: *a den
of thieves.* **4** cozy private room where one
can study or work undisturbed: *Father's*
den *is filled with books.*

de·ni·al (dǐ ni′əl) **1** a saying "no" to; refusal:
a denial *of my request to borrow money.*
2 refusal to admit: *a* denial *of guilt by an
accused person; the mayor's* denial.

den·im (děn′əm) coarse, twilled cotton used
for overalls, work jackets, etc.

Den·mark (děn′märk) a country in northern Europe, north of Germany.

de·nom·i·na·tion (dǐ nŏm′ə nā′shən) **1**
name, especially a general name: *Music,
literature, and painting come under the* denomination *of fine arts.* **2** a religious
group; a sect: *a church of the Presbyterian*
denomination. **3** a unit of value or measure: *He was paid with three bills of the same*
denomination.

de·nom·i·na·tor (dǐ nŏm′ə nā′tər) number
below the line in a fraction. A denominator
shows how many equal parts a whole thing
or unit is divided into. In the fraction ⅘,
5 is the denominator and 4 the numerator.

de·note (dǐ nōt′) to show; be a sign of;
mean: *A flag flown upside down* denotes
distress. **de·not·ed, de·not·ing.**

de·nounce (dĭ nouns′) **1** to speak against publicly; condemn: *The minister denounced gambling.* **2** to accuse; inform against: *One of the bandits denounced the rest of his gang to the police.* **de·nounced, de·nounc·ing.**

dense (dĕns) **1** crowded; thick; heavy: *a dense forest; a dense fog.* **2** dull; stupid: *Maybe I'm a little dense, but I don't understand that joke.* **dens·er, dens·est; dense·ly.**

den·si·ty (dĕn′sə tĭ) **1** thickness; closeness. **2** weight of something in proportion to its size; heaviness: *The density of iron is greater than that of wood.* **3** stupidity. **den·si·ties.**

dent (dĕnt) **1** sunken place or hollow in a surface caused by a blow or by pressure: *We hit a tree and made a dent in the car fender.* **2** to make a dent in: *to dent a fender.* **3** to become dented: *A tin can dents easily.*

den·tal (dĕn′təl) **1** having to do with the teeth. **2** having to do with the work of a dentist.

den·ti·frice (dĕn′tə frĭs) a powder, paste, or liquid for cleaning the teeth.

den·tine (dĕn′tēn) the hard substance that forms most of a tooth. It is beneath the enamel and around the pulp.

den·tist (dĕn′tĭst) doctor who treats teeth. A dentist cleans teeth, straightens them, and fills cavities. When necessary he pulls teeth and replaces them by artificial teeth.

de·nun·ci·a·tion (dĭ nŭn′sĭ ā′shən) public accusation or condemnation: *the candidate's denunciation of his opponent.*

de·ny (dĭ nī′) **1** to say "no" to; refuse to grant: *Father denied my request for a larger allowance.* **2** to refuse to admit; say that a thing is not true: *to deny an accusation.* **3** to refuse to recognize; disown: *to deny one's son.* **de·nied, de·ny·ing.**

de·part (dĭ pärt′) **1** to go away; leave: *The bus departs at 10 o'clock.* **2** to change; turn aside: *The builders departed from the original plan and put in more windows.*

de·part·ment (dĭ pärt′mənt) **1** a division or branch of a government, business, or other organization: *the police department of the city government; the shipping depart-*ment *of a business.* **2 department store** a large store selling different kinds of goods in separate departments.

de·par·ture (dĭ pär′chər) **1** a going away; leaving: *This timetable records the arrival and departure of every train.* **2** a changing; turning away from old ways or methods: *The use of automobiles instead of horses marked a new departure in transportation.*

de·pend (dĭ pĕnd′) **1** in old-fashioned language, to hang down. **2 it depends** it is impossible to say with certainty (until other things are known).

depend on or **upon 1** to trust and count on: *I depend on you to be on time.* **2** to rely on (for help and support): *to depend on relatives; to* depend *on what one earns.* **3** to be governed or controlled (by something else): *The yield of the crop* depends *on the weather.*

de·pen·da·ble (dĭ pĕn′də bəl) reliable; trustworthy: *a dependable friend.*

de·pen·dence (dĭ pĕn′dəns) **1** the state of having to rely on for aid or support: *The dependence of children on their parents.* **2** trust; reliance: *You can't put much dependence on the weather.* **3** a being controlled, governed, or determined (by something else): *the dependence of strength on health.* **4** that on which one relies: *Her son was her only dependence.*

de·pen·dent (dĭ pĕn′dənt) **1** person who relies on another for support. **2** relying on another for support: *a dependent relative.* **3** determined, controlled, or governed (by something else): *Winning the scholarship is dependent on your hard work and study.* **4** hanging down.

de·pict (dĭ pĭkt′) to present a picture of; show or describe; portray: *The book depicted life on a farm.*

de·plore (dĭ plôr′) to be very sorry about; lament; express regret over: *The civic leader deplored the rise of crime.* **de·plored, de·plor·ing.**

de·port (dĭ pôrt′) **1** to send (a person) out of a country as a punishment or because he has no right to be there: *to deport an alien criminal.* **2** to behave or conduct (oneself) in a particular way.

---

fāte, făt, fâre, fär; bē, bĕt; bīte, bĭt; nō, nŏt, nôr; fūse, fŭn, fûr; tōō, tŏŏk; foil; foul; thin; ~~then~~;
hw for wh as in *w*hat; zh for s as in u*s*ual; ə for a, e, i, o, u, as in ag*o*, lin*e*n, per*i*l, at*o*m, min*u*s

de·port·ment (dĭ pôrt′mənt) **1** behavior; conduct: *His report card showed a low grade for* deportment. **2** the way one holds oneself in standing and walking; carriage of the body; bearing: *Balancing a book on top of the head is part of our* deportment *training.*

de·pose (dĭ pōz′) **1** to remove from a throne or high office: *to* depose *a king.* **2** to say under oath. **de·posed, de·pos·ing.**

de·pos·it (dĭ pŏz′ĭt) **1** to put or set down; place: *The postman* deposited *the package on the doorstep.* **2** to put (money or valuable things) in a bank or safe place: *I* deposited *two dollars in the bank.* **3** sum of money placed in a bank: *Two dollars is a small* deposit. **4** part payment in advance: *He made a ten dollar* deposit *on the bicycle.* **5** a natural mass or accumulation of mineral ore, oil, etc.: *a* deposit *of coal.* **6** solid matter that settles out from a liquid or from the air: *A delta is a* deposit *of mud at the mouth of a river. The dust storm left a de-*posit *of sand covering everything.* **7** to leave a layer or coating of: *Rivers* deposit *mud on the land when they flood.*

de·pos·i·tor (dĭ pŏz′ə tər) a person who places money in a bank.

¹de·pot (dē′pō) a railroad station.

²de·pot (dĕp′ō) **1** place where military supplies are stored. **2** place where troops are assembled before being assigned to various military units.

de·pre·ci·ate (dĭ prē′shĭ āt′) **1** to lower (the value or price of). **2** to be diminished in value. **de·pre·ci·at·ed, de·pre·ci·at·ing.**

de·press (dĭ prĕs′) **1** to push or press down: *We* depress *the keys of a typewriter or piano to make them work.* **2** to make gloomy or sad; discourage: *Bad news* depresses *most people.* **3** to make less active; to weaken; to lower in vigor or activity: *This medicine* depresses *the action of the heart. Trading was* depressed *by rumors.*

de·pres·sion (dĭ prĕsh′ən) **1** sunken place; hollow: *Oceans and lakes fill many of the* depressions *in the earth's surface.* **2** a pushing or pressing down: *It is the depression of the accelerator that makes a car go faster.* **3** low spirits; melancholy: *After his failure he was in a state of* depression. **4** period in which business is not active; a lessening of activity in buying, selling, and producing goods.

de·prive (dĭ prīv′) to keep from using, having, or enjoying; take away from: *to* deprive *of sleep, pleasure, wealth, etc.* **de·prived, de·priv·ing.**

depth (dĕpth) **1** distance from the top to the bottom: *The* depth *of the pool was ten feet.* **2** distance below the surface: *The sunken ship lies at a* depth *of 50 feet.* **3** distance from front to back: *You must measure the height, width, and* depth *of a box to tell its size.* **4** deepness of thought, tone, color, etc.: *The grand piano had great* depth *of tone.* **5** inmost, deepest, or central part: *in the* depths *of the forest; from the* depths *of one's heart.*

dep·u·ty (dĕp′yoō tĭ) **1** a person who is appointed to act for, or in the place of, another: *A policeman is a* deputy *of the law.* **2** acting as a deputy. **dep·u·ties.**

de·rail (dē rāl′) to force off a rail or rails: *A stone on the track* derailed *the train.*

de·range (dĭ rānj′) **1** to upset; confuse; put into disorder: *All our plans were* deranged *by having to move.* **2** to make insane. **de·ranged, de·rang·ing.**

der·by (dûr′bĭ) **1** man's hat of stiffened felt, having a narrow rolled brim and a rounded crown. **2 Derby** a championship race for three-year-old horses. **der·bies.**

Man wearing derby

de·ride (dĭ rīd′) to make fun of; laugh at; jeer at: *Many people* derided *the first automobiles.* **de·rid·ed, de·rid·ing.**

de·ri·sion (dĭ rĭzh′ən) ridicule; scorn; mockery: *He became an object of general* derision.

de·ri·sive (dĭ rī′sĭv) expressing ridicule; jeering: *The boys gave a shout of* derisive *laughter when the big dog was chased by the kitten.* **de·ri·sive·ly.**

der·i·va·tion (dĕr′ə vā′shən) **1** a deriving or being derived: *an American family of Irish* derivation. **2** source or original form, especially of a word: *Many English words have Latin* derivations. **3** a recording or tracing of the development of a word from its original form and first meaning; etymology: *This dictionary gives the* derivations *of many words.*

derive

de·rive (dĭ rīv′) to get or obtain (from some source): *We* derive *much pleasure from having good friends.*

  derive from to come from; have its origin in: *The word "canal" derives from a Latin word (canalis) meaning "channel."* **de·rived, de·riv·ing.**

de·rog·a·to·ry (dĭ rŏg′ə tôr′ĭ) tending to take away from (someone's) credit or reputation; belittling; unfavorable: *to make* derogatory *remarks.*

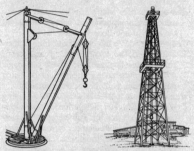

Hoisting derrick and oil-well derrick

der·rick (dĕr′ĭk) 1 lifting machine consisting of a tall mast and hinged boom on the end of which weights are lifted and moved by means of pulleys. 2 framework above an oil well to hold drilling or hoisting machinery.

de·scend (dĭ sĕnd′) 1 to go or come down; move or fall downwards: *We* descended *two flights of stairs. The elevator* descended *to the basement.* 2 to slope downward: *The hill gradually* descends *to the lake.* 3 to pass by inheritance: *The estate* descends *from father to son.*

  descend from to have as ancestors: *He* descended *from a long line of soldiers.*

  descend on or upon 1 to attack suddenly; fall upon in force: *The fleet* descended on *the island, bombarding it fiercely.* 2 to visit suddenly or in force: *Twenty guests* descended upon *us Saturday afternoon.*

de·scend·ant (dĭ sĕn′dənt) one having a certain ancestor or family line: *He was a* descendant *of the founder of the town.*

desert

de·scent (dĭ sĕnt′) 1 a going or coming down; movement to a lower level: *After the climb up the mountain, the* descent *seemed easy.* 2 downward slope: *That hill has a sharp* descent *that is good for sledding.* 3 sudden attack or visit: *a* descent *by the hordes of locusts; a* descent *of week-end guests.* 4 ancestry: *She was of Spanish* descent. (Homonym: dissent)

de·scribe (dĭ skrīb′) 1 to give an account or picture of in words; tell what a person or thing is like: *She* described *her coat so well that I found it right away.* 2 to draw or trace the outline of: *He* described *a circle in the air.* **de·scribed, de·scrib·ing.**

de·scrip·tion (dĭ skrĭp′shən) 1 a telling in words of what something or somebody is like; word picture: *His description of the dinner party was hilarious.* 2 sort; class; variety: *I like food of every* description.

de·scrip·tive (dĭ skrĭp′tĭv) giving a picture in words; telling what someone or something is like: *a* descriptive *booklet about a cruise.* **de·scrip·tive·ly.**

de·seg·re·gate (dē sĕg′rə gāt′) to put an end to the forced separation of races in public schools, theaters, public vehicles, etc. **de·seg·re·gat·ed, de·seg·re·gat·ing.**

de·seg·re·ga·tion (dē sĕg′rə gā′shən) the act or policy of ending the forced separation of races in schools and public facilities.

¹**de·sert** (dĭ zûrt′) 1 to leave someone or something when there is a duty to remain; forsake; abandon: *He did not* desert *his friends in their hour of need.* 2 to leave (a naval or military post or duty) without permission or authority and with the intention of staying away permanently. [¹desert comes through French from a form of a Latin word (deserere). This Latin word is based on two other Latin forms, one (de-) meaning "dis-, from," and the other (serere) meaning "to join, unite."] (Homonym: dessert)

²**des·ert** (dĕz′ərt) 1 dry, sandy region, sometimes without plants. 2 uninhabited and uncultivated: *a* desert *island.* [²desert comes through Old French from a Latin word (desertum) meaning "a solitary place."]

---

fāte, făt, fâre, fär; bē, bĕt; bite, bĭt; nō, nŏt, nôr; fūse, fŭn, fûr; tōō, tŏŏk; foil; foul; thin; then; hw for wh as in *wh*at; zh for s as in u*s*ual; ə for a, e, i, o, u, as in *a*go, lin*e*n, per*i*l, at*o*m, min*u*s

de·sert·er (dĭ zûr′tər) person who deserts, especially from the armed services.

de·ser·tion (dĭ zûr′shən) act of deserting or leaving, especially leaving without permission: *a desertion from the army.*

de·serts (dĭ zûrts′) what is deserved, whether a reward or punishment: *The bully met with his just deserts.*

de·serve (dĭ zûrv′) to be worthy of; merit: *Such good work deserves praise.* **de·served, de·serv·ing.**

de·sign (dĭ zin′) **1** to draw a plan for some work to be done; plan in detail: *to design a building.* **2** an outline, sketch, or plan of something to be made or constructed: *a dress design; an airplane design.* **3** to devise or form in the mind: *She designed a plan for getting the housework done in less time.* **4** a plan; a project; a scheme: *a design for saving money.* **5** decoration; pattern: *a flower design.*

des·ig·nate (dĕz′ĭg nāt′) **1** to point out; show; mark: *The cross on the map designates where the troops landed.* **2** to name; choose; select: *She designated three bridesmaids to attend her.* **3** to call by a name: *Trees, moss, and ferns are designated plants.* **des·ig·nat·ed, des·ig·nat·ing.**

de·sign·ing (dĭ zi′ning) **1** the art of originating or planning designs. **2** plotting; scheming; artful: *a designing person, not to be trusted.*

de·sir·a·bil·i·ty (dĭ zir′ə bĭl′ə tĭ) ability to cause desire: *The desirability of the apartment was increased by its being next to a park.*

de·sir·a·ble (dĭ zir′ə bəl) such as to arouse desire; pleasing; worth having: *a desirable friend.* **de·sir·a·bly.**

de·sire (dĭ zir′) **1** to wish for; crave: *to desire happiness.* **2** a strong longing for; a wish. **3** to express a wish for; ask for: *They desire us to leave.* **4** thing wanted or wished for: *We do not always get our desires.* **de·sired, de·sir·ing.**

de·sir·ous (dĭ zir′əs) desiring; eager (to have or do): *He was desirous of learning. He was desirous to learn.*

de·sist (dĭ zĭst′) to stop: *You had better desist.*

    desist from to cease; bring a halt to: *The company was ordered by the court to desist from making false claims.*

desk (dĕsk) **1** a piece of furniture with a flat top on which to write, and drawers and compartments to hold writing materials. **2** a cabinet or stand with a sloping top to hold a book for a reader. **3** a desk or department reserved for some special work: *These orders came from the city editor's desk.*

Desk

¹**des·o·late** (dĕs′ə lāt′) to lay waste; make unfit for inhabitants: *A cyclone desolated the area.* **des·o·lat·ed, des·o·lat·ing.**

²**des·o·late** (dĕs′ə lĭt) **1** without inhabitants; abandoned; in a condition of neglect or ruin: *a desolate ghost town.* **2** overcome with sorrow; having the feeling of being without friends or hope. **des·o·late·ly.**

des·o·la·tion (dĕs′ə lā′shən) **1** a laying waste: *widespread desolation by an earthquake.* **2** wasted or ruined state; dreary barrenness: *the desolation of a cold desert.* **3** friendlessness; loneliness: *a feeling of desolation on returning to an empty house.*

de·spair (dĭ spâr′) **1** loss of hope; hopelessness: *As the ship passed out of sight, despair came upon the men on the life raft.* **2** to lose all hope: *He despaired of ever seeing his lost dog again.* **3** that which causes hopelessness or that for which there is no hope: *That son of mine is the despair of my life.*

des·patch (dĭ spăch′) dispatch.

des·per·ate (dĕs′pər ĭt) **1** without regard to danger; reckless; frantic: *a desperate criminal.* **2** beyond hope; hopeless: *a desperate sickness.* **3** past caring because of despair: *He was so desperate he wished for death.* **des·per·ate·ly.**

des·per·a·tion (dĕs′pə rā′shən) recklessness of despair: *In desperation he decided to sell all he owned and move away.*

de·spise (dĭ spiz′) to look down upon; regard as worthless; scorn: *to despise traitors; to despise a weakling.* **de·spised, de·spis·ing.**

de·spite (dĭ spit′) in spite of; heedless of: *The fishermen went out on the lake despite the storm warnings.*

de·spoil (dĭ spoil′) to rob; strip; take away all belongings from: *The plunderers despoiled the city.*

de·spond·ent (dĭ spŏn′dənt) in low spirits; having lost hope and courage: *He was despondent over his wife's death.* **de·spond·ent·ly.**

des·pot (dĕs′pət or dĕs′pŏt) ruler who has complete power and uses it as he pleases; tyrant: *a country ruled by a line of despots.*

des·pot·ic (dĕs pŏt′ĭk) **1** behaving like a despot: *the despotic Napoleon.* **2** having to do with tyranny.

des·sert (dĭ zûrt′) a serving of fruits, pastry, pudding, ice cream, etc., at the end of a meal. (Homonym: ¹*desert*.)

des·ti·na·tion (dĕs′tə nā′shən) the place to which a person or thing is going: *the destination of a traveler or a package.*

des·tine (dĕs′tĭn) **1** to set apart for a special purpose: *to destine a son for the ministry.* **2 destined** caused by fate or destiny: *We were destined never to meet again.* **3 destined for** (1) bound for: *a train destined for New York.* (2) intended for: *to be destined for better things.* **des·tined, des·tin·ing.**

des·ti·ny (dĕs′tə ni) **1** final lot or fortune of a person, country, or thing: *Death in a foreign land was his destiny.* **2** the power that controls events; fate: *to try to rebel against destiny.* **des·ti·nies.**

des·ti·tute (dĕs′tə tōōt′ or dĕs′tə tūt′) **1** not having what is necessary to live on; needy; penniless: *Many families were left destitute by the fire.* **2 destitute of** lacking in: *a person destitute of honor.*

de·stroy (dĭ stroi′) **1** to lay waste; ruin; make useless: *The flood destroyed the village.* **2** to kill; put an end to: *After the horse broke its leg, it was destroyed.*

de·stroy·er (dĭ stroi′ər) **1** a person or thing that destroys. **2** a swift, light, heavily-armed warship.

de·struc·tion (dĭ strŭk′shən) **1** a destroying or being destroyed: *The hurricane caused destruction of many homes on the coast.* **2** cause of ruin or downfall: *Love of gambling will be his destruction.*

de·struc·tive (dĭ strŭk′tĭv) **1** harmful; causing destruction or ruin: *The farmer told us how to stop destructive locusts.* **2** likely to do damage: *Puppies and children

are naturally destructive and like to pull things apart.*

de·tach (dĭ tăch′) **1** to unfasten and remove; disconnect: *to detach the buttons before having a coat cleaned.* **2** to send (troops or ships) away for a special duty: *Soldiers were detached to guard the visiting official.*

de·tach·ment (dĭ tăch′mənt) **1** separation: *the detachment of a key from a key chain.* **2** a being without interest; aloofness: *He had an air of detachment throughout the whole dinner and speeches.* **3** a group of troops or ships sent away to do some special task.

de·tail (dĭ tāl′ or dē′tāl) **1** a single item or fact; one small part of a whole: *The picture is perfect except for one detail.* **2** a small, unimportant thing or occurrence: *a mere detail.* **3** to relate fully; explain item by item: *The judge detailed the reasons for his decision.* **4** a small group of troops assigned to special duty: *The kitchen detail was put to work peeling potatoes.* **5** to appoint for special duty: *Several men were detailed to guard the visiting royalty.* **6 in detail** item by item: *He answered the question in detail.*

de·tain (dĭ tān′) **1** to delay; hold back: *The doctor was detained after office hours by a tardy patient.* **2** to keep in custody: *The police detained him.*

de·tect (dĭ tĕkt′) **1** to find out; discern: *to detect a person's lie.* **2** to sense the existence of: *to detect a difference in color; to detect a new sound.*

de·tec·tive (dĭ tĕk′tĭv) **1** a person (usually a police officer) who investigates and obtains information about crimes. **2** having to do with detecting: *a detective agency.*

de·ter (dĭ tûr′) to prevent (by discouraging); hinder (by fear or doubt): *Neither difficulties nor dangers deter men from attempting space flight.* **de·terred, de·ter·ring.**

de·ter·gent (dĭ tûr′jənt) substance used for cleansing, either alone or with soap: *Many people wash their dishes in detergent.*

de·ter·mi·na·tion (dĭ tûr′mə nā′shən) **1** great firmness of mind; resolution: *a show of determination.* **2** the act of deciding or settling upon: *The determination of a new name for the club was left to the next meeting.*

---

fāte, făt, fâre, fär; bē, bĕt; bīte, bĭt; nō, nŏt, nôr; fūse, fŭn, fûr; tōō, tŏŏk; foil; foul; thin; ~~then~~; hw for wh as in *what*; zh for s as in u*su*al; ə for a, e, i, o, u, as in *a*go, lin*e*n, per*i*l, at*o*m, min*u*s

de·ter·mine (dĭ tûr′mĭn) **1** to decide firmly: *to* determine *to go to college.* **2** to cause to decide: *The accident* determined *her to be more careful.* **3** to decide beforehand: *to* determine *the date for a trip.* **4** to find out exactly: *to* determine *the exact meaning of the damage.* **5** to be the cause or reason for: *The pull of the moon* determines *the tides on the earth.* **de·ter·mined, de·ter·min·ing.**

de·ter·mined (dĭ tûr′mĭnd) firm; resolute: *a* determined *man.* **de·ter·mined·ly.**

de·ter·min·er (dĭ tûr′mə nər) a word that comes before a noun in a phrase and helps to determine the exact meaning of the phrase. "The," "some," "our," and "whichever" are determiners in the following sentences:

The *boy is happy.*
Some *cats are black.*
I *saw* our *old house.*
Take whichever *cake you wish.*

de·test (dĭ tĕst′) to hate; dislike violently; loathe: *I* detest *people who cheat.*

de·test·a·ble (dĭ tĕs′tə bəl) deserving to be detested; hateful. **de·test·a·bly.**

de·throne (dē thrōn′) to remove from a throne or position of authority: *to* dethrone *a king.* **de·throned, de·thron·ing.**

de·tour (dē′tŏŏr or dĭ tŏŏr′) **1** a roundabout way temporarily replacing a main route: *Take this* detour. **2** a turning aside from the main road. **3** to use a detour.

deuce (dŏŏs or dūs) **1** a playing card having two spots: *the* deuce *of hearts.* **2** in tennis, **(1)** a tie score of 40. **(2)** five games each.

dev·as·tate (dĕv′ə stāt′) to lay waste; make desolate: *War* devastated *the country.* **dev·as·tat·ed, dev·as·tat·ing.**

de·vel·op (dĭ vĕl′əp) **1** to cause to grow and mature: *Water, sunlight, and air help to* develop *plants.* **2** to grow and mature: *Buds* develop *into blossoms. The mind* develops *from year to year.* **3** to bring into being: *You should try to* develop *the reading habit.* **4** to work out in detail: *The candidate* developed *his plan of campaign.* **5** to put to use: *to* develop *a country's natural resources.* **6** to bring out an image on exposed photographic film or paper.

de·vel·op·ment (dĭ vĕl′əp mənt) **1** a growing and maturing: *the* development *of a bud into a flower.* **2** a bringing to light, a bringing into being: *the* development *of new*

habits. **3** an improving: *the* development *of a person's talents or mind.* **4** a putting to use: *the* development *of water power.* **5** treatment of exposed photographic films or paper to show the image. **6** a working out; a taking or giving shape: *the* development *of a plan.* **7** areas where improvements, especially new buildings, have been made: *a housing* development.

de·vice (dĭ vīs′) **1** a tool or machine designed for a special use: *a* device *for cutting paper; a* device *for opening jars.* **2** trick; scheme: *The fox knows clever* devices *to throw the hounds off his trail.* **3** sign or symbol, especially a coat of arms: *a banner with a strange* device. **4 leave to one's own devices** to leave to one's own wishes, with no help or advice.

dev·il (dĕv′əl) **1** an evil spirit. **2** a wicked person. **3** a pitiful person: *The poor* devil *was cold and hungry.* **4 the Devil** Satan.

dev·il·ish (dĕv′əl ĭsh) **1** naughty; implike: *a* devilish *gleam in his eye.* **2** very wicked; evil; fiendish. **dev·il·ish·ly.**

de·vise (dĭ vīz′) to think up; contrive; invent: *to* devise *new ways of extracting coal.* **de·vised, de·vis·ing.**

de·void of (dĭ void′əv) completely without; empty of: *She is* devoid *of good sense.*

de·vote (dĭ vōt′) **1** to set apart for a special reason: *They agreed to* devote *part of the park to a playground.* **2** to give (oneself) up to completely: *She* devoted *herself to the study of dancing.* **de·vot·ed, de·vot·ing.**

de·vot·ed (dĭ vō′tĭd) wholly given up to (some object, cause, or person); loyal; dedicated: *a* devoted *nurse.* **de·vot·ed·ly.**

de·vo·tion (dĭ vō′shən) **1** strong love or loyalty: *a mother's* devotion *to her children.* **2** a giving of oneself (to a person or a cause): *his* devotion *to his work.* **3 devotions** prayers: *the monks at their* devotions.

de·vour (dĭ vour′) **1** to eat up greedily: *The lion* devoured *its prey.* **2** to destroy or lay waste: *Fire* devoured *the building.* **3** to take in eagerly with the eyes, ears, or mind: *to* devour *an adventure story.* **4 be devoured by** to be a prey to; be absorbed completely by: *He was* devoured *by anxiety.*

de·vout (dĭ vout′) **1** devoted to religious thoughts and practices; very pious: *the* devout *life of a saint.* **2** sincere; earnest: *a* devout *wish for success.* **de·vout·ly.**

dew (dōō or dū) **1** moisture from the air formed in small drops on cool surfaces at night: *morning* dew *on the flowers.* **2** freshness; youthful glow: *the* dew *of sleep; the* dew *of youth.* **3** to wet with or as with dew; moisten. (Homonyms: do, due)

dew·drop (dōō′drŏp′ or dū′drŏp′) a drop of dew.

dew point air temperature at which dew forms.

dew·y (dōō′ĭ or dū′ĭ) **1** moist with dew. **2** moist as if with dew; glowing: *her* dewy *eyes.* **dew·i·er, dew·i·est.**

dex·ter·i·ty (dĕks tĕr′ə tĭ) **1** ease and skill in using the hands and other parts of the body: *It takes a great deal of* dexterity *to play ice hockey.* **2** cleverness; skill in using one's mind: *The detective showed* dexterity *in solving the robbery.*

dex·ter·ous or **dex·trous** (dĕks′trəs) **1** skilled in using the hands: *a* dexterous *juggler.* **2** having mental skill or agility; clever: *He was* dexterous *in adding long columns of figures.* **dex·ter·ous·ly.**

di·a·be·tes (dī′ə bē′tĭs or dī′ə bē′tēz) disease in which the body fails to absorb a normal amount of sugar.

di·a·bol·ic·al (dī′ə bŏl′ĭk əl) devilish; cruel. **di·a·bol·ic·al·ly.**

di·a·crit·i·cal mark (dī′ə krĭt′ə kəl) a mark or character to show the sound of a letter.

di·a·dem (dī′ə dəm) a kind of crown.

di·ag·nose (dī′əg nōs′ or dī′əg nōz′) to find out or identify by examining; discover from symptoms: *to* diagnose *a disease; to* diagnose *a pupil's emotional troubles; to* diagnose *business conditions.* **di·ag·nosed, di·ag·nos·ing.**

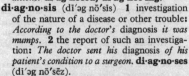
Diadem

di·ag·no·sis (dī′əg nō′sĭs) **1** investigation of the nature of a disease or other trouble: *According to the doctor's* diagnosis *it was mumps.* **2** the report of such an investigation: *The doctor sent his* diagnosis *of his patient's condition to a surgeon.* **di·ag·no·ses** (dī′əg nō′sēz).

di·ag·o·nal (dī ăg′ə nəl) **1** in a figure of four or more sides, a slanting straight line between any two corners that are not next to each other. **2** slanting; oblique: *Jay took a* diagonal *course across the field.* **di·ag·o·nal·ly.**

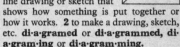
DIAGONAL

di·a·gram (dī′ə grăm′) **1** line drawing or sketch that shows how something is put together or how it works. **2** to make a drawing, sketch, etc. **di·a·gramed** or **di·a·grammed, di·a·gram·ing** or **di·a·gram·ming.**

di·al (dī′əl) **1** a round surface which is marked into units and has a moving pointer that measures something. The face of a clock, watch, or compass is a dial. **2** lettered or numbered plate on an automatic telephone that is rotated when making a call. **3** to make connections on an automatic telephone: *to* dial *a number.* **4** device on a radio or television set for tuning in different stations, etc.

CLOCK

TELEPHONE
Dials

di·a·lect (dī′ə lĕkt) a form of speech peculiar to a locality, region, or group.

di·a·logue (dī′ə lŏg′ or dī′ə lôg′) **1** conversation. **2** conversation in a story, play, etc.

di·am·e·ter (dī ăm′ə tər) **1** straight line through the center of a circle, which cuts the circle in half. **2** length of a straight line through the center of something circular; thickness: *The* diameter *of this branch is six inches.*

DIAMETER

di·a·mond (dī′ə mənd) **1** brilliant precious stone formed of pure crystallized carbon. **2** flat figure which is shaped like a part of a cut diamond. **3** in baseball, the part of the playing field having the four bases as its corners. **4** any one of a suit of playing cards marked with a red diamond-shaped figure.

Diamond

---

fāte, făt, fâre, fär; bē, bĕt; bīte, bĭt; nō, nŏt, nôr; fūse, fŭn, fûr; tōō, tŏŏk; foil; foul; thin; ~~then~~; hw for wh as in *what*; zh for s as in u*s*ual; ə for a, e, i, o, u, as in *a*go, lin*e*n, per*i*l, at*o*m, min*u*s

219

diaper

di·a·per (dī′ə pər) **1** piece of cloth usually folded several times and wrapped and fastened about the lower part of a baby's body as an undergarment. **2** to put a diaper on (a baby). **3** cloth woven in a geometric pattern repeated over and over.

di·a·phragm (dī′ə frăm′) **1** the muscular membrane inside the body that separates the chest from the abdomen. **2** in a telephone, loudspeaker, or the like, the vibrating disk or cone that produces sound waves. **3** a device for regulating the size of the lens opening in a camera.

Diaphragm

di·a·ry (dī′ə rĭ) **1** a record written down from day to day of the events in a person's life and what he thinks of them. **2** a book in which such a record is kept. **di·a·ries.**

di·a·tom (dī′ə tŏm′) one of a large group of very tiny, one-celled algae, living in water and having beautifully marked, glasslike shells.

dice (dīs) **1** small cubes of bone, plastic, etc., having sides marked with from one to six spots, used in playing certain games. **2** to play with dice; gamble. **3** to cut into small cubes: *Alice diced the potatoes.* **diced, dic·ing.**

Dice

dic·tate (dĭk′tāt) **1** to say with authority; order or command: *An absolute ruler dictates what his people are to do.* **2** to say something for someone to write down: *The executive dictated a letter to his secretary.* **3** direction or order that should be obeyed: *the dictates of a ruler, of fashion, or of conscience.* **dic·tat·ed, dic·tat·ing.**

dic·ta·tion (dĭk tā′shən) **1** the speaking of words to be written down: *a dictation too rapid for the secretary to follow.* **2** the words which are written down: *The stenographer read the dictation back to him.* **3** a telling someone what to do; commanding: *As she was earning her own living she found her father's dictation hard to bear.*

dic·ta·tor (dĭk′tā tər) **1** a ruler who has unlimited power; the absolute head of a government: *Caesar made himself dictator.* **2** a person whose authority is accepted in some special field: *a dictator of fashion.*

diet

dic·tion·ar·y (dĭk′shə nĕr′ĭ) **1** book that lists words of a language in alphabetical order and explains them in the same language. A dictionary tells what words mean, how to pronounce them, and how to spell them. A dictionary may also show how words are used and where they come from. **2** book that lists words of one language and explains them in another language: *a French-English dictionary.* **dic·tion·ar·ies.**

did (dĭd) See ¹**do.** *He did all his homework.*

did·n't (dĭd′ənt) did not: *They didn't know.*

¹**die** (dī) **1** to stop living; pass out of existence: *John Adams and Thomas Jefferson both died on July 4, 1825.* **2** to fade; disappear; lose strength: *The breeze died toward evening. His fame died soon after him.* **3** to wish or feel strongly: *She was dying to find out who was behind the mask.* **died, dy·ing.** [¹**die** is a form of an earlier English word (dēyen) that probably comes from an Old Norse word (deyja).] (Homonym: dye)

²**die** (dī) **1** a device for stamping designs on coins, making raised patterns on paper, cutting shapes in leather, sheet metal, etc. **2** a tool for cutting threads on bolts, pipes, etc. **3** one of a pair of dice. **4 The die is cast.** The decision is made and there is no turning back from it. **dies** (definitions 1 and 2), **dice** (definition 3). [²**die** is a form of an earlier English word (dē) that came through Old French (de) from a Latin word form (datum) meaning "given" or "thrown."] (Homonym: dye)

Die for stamping cent

Die·sel en·gine (dē′zəl ĕn′jən) engine that burns oil in cylinders. The oil is exploded by the heat of air compressed in the cylinders, instead of by a spark as in the gasoline engine.

di·et (dī′ət) **1** one's usual food and drink: *The prisoner's diet was coarse and dry.* **2** a special choice of food, eaten to gain or lose weight, etc.: *a reducing diet.* **3** to eat only certain foods (for a purpose).

di·e·ti·tian (dī′ə tish′ən) a person who knows the effect of different foods upon the body and plans meals to meet a person's needs.

dif·fer (dĭf′ər) 1 to be unlike: *Wrens and buzzards* differ *greatly in size.* 2 to be of opposite opinion; disagree.

dif·fer·ence (dĭf′ər əns) 1 way in which things are unlike; lack of similarity: *What is the* difference *between living and nonliving substances?* 2 the amount or extent by which one thing differs from another: *The* difference *between 10 and 8 is 2.* 3 disagreement: *a serious* difference *of opinion.*

dif·fer·ent (dĭf′ər ənt) 1 unlike; not alike: *boys of* different *ages; a coat* different *from mine.* 2 separate; distinct; not the same: *The boy had the same excuse for being late on three* different *occasions.* 3 not the same as others; unusual: *She has a very* different *way of dressing.* **dif·fer·ent·ly.**

dif·fer·en·ti·ate (dĭf′ə rĕn′shĭ āt′) 1 to contrast; mark off; single out as unlike: *Aging* differentiates *a really good cheese from an ordinary one.* 2 to observe an unlikeness or difference between; distinguish between: *to* differentiate *the warbles of various birds.* **dif·fer·en·ti·at·ed, dif·fer·en·ti·at·ing.**

dif·fi·cult (dĭf′ə kŭlt′) 1 not easy; hard to do or understand: *a* difficult *problem; a* difficult *language.* 2 hard to get along with; not easily managed: *a* difficult *child; a* difficult *situation.* **dif·fi·cult·ly.**

dif·fi·cul·ty (dĭf′ə kŭl′tĭ) 1 hard work: *to read with* difficulty. 2 something that is difficult; obstacle: *the* difficulties *of the German language.* 3 a situation that is difficult; trouble: *to be in* difficulty. 4 **difficulties** disagreement; friction; quarrels. 5 **be in difficulties** to be short of money. 6 **make difficulties** to raise objections; cause trouble. **dif·fi·cul·ties.**

¹dif·fuse (dĭ fūz′) to spread out in every direction; send out: *Newspapers* diffuse *the news throughout the country.* **dif·fused, dif·fus·ing.**

²dif·fuse (dĭ fūs′) 1 long and wordy: *a* diffuse *speech.* 2 spread out: *in the* diffuse *light of the grove.* **dif·fuse·ly.**

dif·fu·sion (dĭ fū′zhən) 1 a spreading: *the* diffusion *of knowledge by means of lowpriced books; the* diffusion *of pollen by wind and insects.* 2 in science, a natural spreading of one substance through another.

dig (dĭg) 1 to break or turn up soil with a spade or other instrument: *The ground is* dug *every spring before planting.* 2 to make a hole, excavation, etc., by removing earth: *He* dug *a well in the garden.* 3 to get something out by turning up the ground: *to* dig *potatoes; to* dig *worms; to* dig *for gold.* 4 to make a way (through): *He* dug *through the pile of old letters.* 5 to seek; search for: *to* dig *for information; to* dig *out the truth.* 6 to poke or prod: *He* dug *the horse with his spurs.* 7 a thrust; a prod: *a* dig *in the ribs.* 8 a biting remark. **dug, dig·ging.**

¹di·gest (dĭ jĕst′ or dī jĕst′) 1 to change (food) into a form that can be used by the body: *You can* digest *some foods more easily than others.* 2 to undergo change for use in the body: *Some fats do not* digest *easily.* 3 to absorb in the mind; think over; understand: *He* digested *his father's advice.*

²di·gest (dī′jĕst) a shortened but complete account; a summary: *a book* digest; *a news* digest.

di·gest·i·ble (dĭ jĕs′tə bəl) that can be digested or easily digested: *Lamb is more* digestible *than pork.* **di·gest·i·bly.**

di·ges·tion (dĭ jĕs′chən) 1 the digesting (of food): *A short rest after a meal aids* digestion. 2 the ability to digest food: *A nervous person often has poor* digestion.

di·ges·tive (dĭ jĕs′tĭv) having to do with digesting food: *the* digestive *system; to prescribe* digestive *aids.* **di·ges·tive·ly.**

dig·ger (dĭg′ər) 1 person or animal that digs. 2 tool or machine that digs.

dig·it (dĭj′ĭt) 1 finger or toe. 2 any of the figures 0, 1, 2, 3, 4, 5, 6, 7, 8, 9.

dig·ni·fied (dĭg′nə fīd′) calm and serious in manner; stately; noble in bearing; inspiring respect: *The governor had a* dignified *air.*

dig·ni·fy (dĭg′nə fī′) 1 to make worthy or noble; show honor to: *By his achievements, the president* dignified *his office.* 2 to raise in rank; confer honor upon: *Do not*

---

fāte, făt, fâre, fär; bē, bĕt; bīte, bĭt; nō, nŏt, nôr; fūse, fŭn, fûr; tōō, tŏŏk; foil; foul; thin; ~~then~~;
hw for wh as in *what*; zh for s as in *usual*; ə for a, e, i, o, u, as in *ago*, linen, peril, atom, minus

dignify *the job by calling it a position.*
dig·ni·fied, dig·ni·fy·ing.

dig·ni·tar·y (dĭg′nə tĕr′ĭ) a person of rank, position, or standing, especially in the church. **dig·ni·tar·ies.**

dig·ni·ty (dĭg′nə tĭ) **1** worthiness; nobleness: *the* dignity *of honest labor.* **2** poise; nobility of bearing; calm and serious manner: *to keep one's* dignity *through thick and thin.* **3** a high office; honorable rank: *the* dignity *of the Presidency.* **dig·ni·ties.**

dike (dīk) **1** a bank to keep out water: *In Holland* dikes *hold back the sea.* **2** a ditch. **3** to protect with banks of earth: *Along a river farmers* dike *their fields.* **4** to drain by means of ditches. **diked, dik·ing.**

Dike

di·lap·i·dat·ed (dĭ lăp′ə dā′tĭd) run-down from neglect or hard use; fallen into ruin: *a* dilapidated *house; a* dilapidated *car.*

di·late (dī lāt′) **1** to make larger or wider: *The doctor* dilated *the pupil of the eye to examine it.* **2** to become larger or wider: *A cat's eyes* dilate *in the dark.* **3** to speak or write at length: *The speaker* dilated *on his favorite subject.* **di·lat·ed, di·lat·ing.**

dil·i·gence (dĭl′ə jəns) constant, earnest effort; care; zeal: *to exercise* diligence *in the performance of a task.*

dil·i·gent (dĭl′ə jənt) hard-working; painstaking; steady and careful: *Are you a* diligent *student?* **dil·i·gent·ly.**

dill (dĭl) **1** spicy seeds which are used to season foods, especially pickles. **2** the plant that bears these seeds.

dil·ly·dal·ly (dĭl′ĭ dăl′ĭ) to waste time; to take too much time: *to* dillydally *over a job.* **dil·ly·dal·lied, dil·ly·dal·ly·ing.**

di·lute (dī lo͞ot′ or dī lūt′) **1** to weaken or make thinner by adding water or another liquid: *Lemon juice is* diluted *before it is drunk.* **2** to weaken the force or strength of (by adding something unnecessary): *He* diluted *his argument with silly comparisons.* **di·lut·ed, di·lut·ing.**

dim (dĭm) **1** not bright or clear: *in* dim *candlelight.* **2** to make or become less bright: *to* dim *the lights of a car.* **3** not seeing or understanding clearly: *eyes* dim *with tears.* **4** hazy; not clearly seen: *The*

hard pencil makes a dim *mark.* **dim·mer, dim·mest; dimmed, dim·ming; dim·ly.**

dime (dīm) a United States or Canadian coin worth ten cents.

di·men·sion (dĭ mĕn′shən) **1** measurement of length, breadth, or thickness of something. **2 dimensions** size; importance: *a plan of vast* dimensions.

di·min·ish (dĭ mĭn′ĭsh) to make or become smaller; lessen: *Rain* diminishes *the danger of forest fires.*

di·min·u·tive (dĭ mĭn′yə tĭv) small; little; tiny: *a* diminutive *child.* **di·min·u·tive·ly.**

dim·ple (dĭm′pəl) **1** a small hollow or dent in the surface of anything: *a dimple in the cheek.* **2** to show dimples; become dimpled: *Her cheek* dimpled *as she smiled.* **dim·pled, dim·pling.**

din (dĭn) **1** loud, continued noise; confused uproar: *the* din *of horns in city traffic.* **2** to repeat over and over: *Father* dinned *into our minds the need for safe driving.* **3** to make a noise: *Music from the party above us was* dinning *in our ears all night.* **dinned, din·ning.**

dine (dīn) **1** to eat dinner. **2** to give a dinner for; feed. **dined, din·ing.**

din·er (dī′nər) **1** person eating dinner. **2** railroad car in which meals are served. **3** small restaurant; especially, one built to look somewhat like such a car.

di·nette (dī nĕt′) small dining room.

ding-dong (dĭng′dŏng′ or dĭng′dông′) **1** the sound of the repeated strokes of a bell. **2** with the lead changing back and forth: *a* ding-dong *battle; a* ding-dong *race.*

din·ghy (dĭng′gĭ) **1** a small rowboat. **2** a small sailboat. **3** a small boat carried on a warship. **din·ghies.**

din·gy (dĭn′jĭ) dark; dull; dirty; not fresh or bright: *a* dingy *house; a* dingy *neighborhood.* **din·gi·er, din·gi·est; din·gi·ly.**

dining room a room in which meals are usually served, either in a home, hotel, or public place.

din·ner (dĭn′ər) **1** the main meal of the day. **2** a formal meal given in honor of some person or occasion: *The evening before his wedding a bachelor* dinner *was given by Philip.*

di·no·saur (dī′nə sôr′) any of several kinds of reptiles that lived millions of years ago,

dint

especially certain giant reptiles which were the largest land animals that ever lived.

Dinosaur, over 80 ft. long

dint (dint) **1** force; strength: *The project was finished by* dint *of much effort.* **2** a dent. **3** to make a dent in.

di·o·cese (dī′ə sĭs or dī′ə sēs) the district under the authority of a bishop.

dip (dĭp) **1** to put quickly into liquid and take out again: *to dip a garment in dye.* **2** to go into water and come out quickly: *to dip in the ocean.* **3** a dipping of any kind, especially a plunge into water: *a morning dip.* **4** to scoop up with a ladle, spoon, etc.: *to dip water from a bucket.* **5** a liquid in which to dip something: *a vat of sheep dip.* **6** to slope downward: *The street dips.* **7** a downward slope: *a dip in the road.* **8** to make (a candle) by repeatedly putting a wick in wax. **9** to lower and raise again: *to dip the flag in salutation.* **10** to reach into and take out: *to dip into the cookie barrel.* **dip into** to read or study slightly. **dipped, dip·ping.**

diph·the·ri·a (dĭf thĭr′ĭ ə) a dangerous and contagious disease of the throat.

diph·thong (dĭf′thŏng or dĭf′thông) two vowel sounds said together as one continuous sound, such as "oi" in "coil," or "ou" in "doubt."

di·plo·ma (dĭ plō′mə) an official document to show that some honor or degree has been given, especially when a student has been graduated from a school or college.

dip·lo·mat (dĭp′lə măt′) **1** a person who handles problems and relations between nations. **2** a person who is persuasive and tactful.

dip·lo·mat·ic (dĭp′lə măt′ĭk) **1** having to do with the management of affairs between nations: *Officials in embassies and consu-*

direction

lates are in the diplomatic *service.* **2** skillful in saying and doing the right thing; having ability to deal with others; tactful: *a diplomatic sales-man; a diplomatic refusal.*

dip·per (dĭp′ər) **1** round vessel with a straight handle; a ladle. **2** Big Dipper and Little Dipper two groups of seven stars each in the northern sky, suggesting the outline of dippers.

Dipper

Big Dipper

dire (dīr) **1** dreadful; awful; extreme: *a dire accident; under* dire *circumstances.* **dir·er, dir·est; dire·ly.**

di·rect (dĭ rĕkt′ or dī rĕkt′) **1** to control; manage; guide: *A teacher directs pupils. Policemen direct traffic. A conductor directs an orchestra.* **2** to order; command: *to direct the troops to retreat.* **3** to aim; point: *You should direct your energy to worthwhile projects.* **4** to tell or show (a person) the way: *Can you direct me to the post office?* **5** straight; not roundabout: *Take the direct road to town.* **6** frank; honest: *Give me a direct answer.* **7** in an unbroken line, from grandfather, to father, to child, etc.: *He is the fifth direct heir to that land.* **8** directly; without stopping: *Some airplanes fly direct to large cities.* **9** to address a letter or package.

direct current an electric current that flows continuously in the same direction. Direct current is used in automobiles, electric locomotives, and some industries.

di·rec·tion (dĭ rĕk′shən or dī rĕk′shən) **1** point toward which a person or thing faces, points, or moves: *a direction to the north; in the direction of my house; to scatter in all directions.* **2** course taken by a moving object, such as a bullet; path along which movement takes place. **3** line of action or development; tendency: *improvement in the direction of simplicity; progress in many directions.* **4** guidance; management: *Teachers work under the direction of a principal.* **5** order; instruction: *Read the directions before you begin*

---

fāte, făt, fâre, fär; bē, bĕt; bīte, bĭt; nō, nŏt, nôr; fūse, fŭn, fûr; tōō, tŏŏk; foil; foul; thin; ~~then~~; hw for wh as in *wh*at; zh for s as in u*s*ual; ə for a, e, i, o, u, as in *a*go, lin*e*n, per*i*l, at*o*m, min*u*s

223

the test. We'll leave directions *so that he can follow us.* **6** address on a letter or package.

di·rect·ly (di rĕkt′li or di rĕkt′lĭ) **1** in a direct line or manner; straight: *Travel directly north.* **2** at once: *Return home directly.*

di·rec·tor (di rĕk′tər or di rĕk′tôr) **1** person who directs or manages: *He's a director of plays, films, and television shows.* **2** person who directs the affairs of a business.

di·rec·to·ry (di rĕk′tə ri or di rĕk′tə rĭ) list of names, addresses, etc.: *a telephone directory.* **di·rec·to·ries.**

dirge (dûrj) funeral hymn; mourning song.

dir·i·gi·ble (dîr′ə jə-bəl or də rij′ə bəl) a more or less cigar-shaped balloon with motors and rudders to drive and guide it.

Dirigible

dirk (dûrk) a short dagger.

dirt (dûrt) **1** dust, mud, or anything that makes something unclean; filth: *to wash the* dirt *from one's hands.* **2** loose earth or soil: *They covered the front lot with new* dirt. **3** any unclean action, writing, or talk.

dirt·i·ness (dûr′ti nĭs) condition of being dirty.

dirt·y (dûr′ti) **1** not clean; soiled: *a dirty coat.* **2** mean; unfair: *a dirty trick.* **3** not decent: *his dirty talk.* **4** not clear in color: *a dirty green.* **5** stormy; foul: *the dirty weather.* **6** to soil: *They* dirtied *their socks by walking about without shoes.* **dirt·i·er, dirt·i·est; dirt·ied, dirt·y·ing; dirt·i·ly.**

dis- prefix meaning (**1**) "not"; "the opposite of": dis*obedient;* dis*honest.* (**2**) "fail to"; "cease to"; "refuse to": dis*satisfy;* dis*agree.* (**3**) "lack of": dis*union.*

dis·a·bil·i·ty (dĭs′ə bĭl′ə tĭ) **1** loss or lack of physical or mental powers: *That insurance policy covers death or* disability. **2** something that disables: *His lack of training proved a great* disability. **dis·a·bil·i·ties.**

dis·a·ble (dĭs ā′bəl) to cripple; take away power or ability: *Grandma was* disabled *by her stroke.* **dis·a·bled, dis·a·bling.**

dis·ad·van·tage (dĭs′əd văn′tij) **1** thing that holds back or obstructs; handicap: *Fear of water is a* disadvantage *in learning to swim.* **2** loss; harm: *Rumors were spread to his* disadvantage.

dis·a·gree (dĭs′ə grē′) **1** to fail to agree; be unlike; conflict: *Your statements about John Smith* disagree *with those in my history book.* **2** to differ in opinion; quarrel: *I* disagree *with you.* **3** to have bad effects; to be unsuitable: *Sea food* disagrees *with him.* **dis·a·greed, dis·a·gree·ing.**

dis·a·gree·a·ble (dĭs′ə grē′ə bəl) **1** unpleasant: *The market place had* disagreeable *odors.* **2** bad-tempered; quarrelsome; not affable: *Father gets* disagreeable *if dinner is too late.* **dis·a·gree·a·bly.**

dis·a·gree·ment (dĭs′ə grē′mənt) **1** difference: *a* disagreement *between the two word lists.* **2** difference of opinion; failure to agree: *a* disagreement *among members of the jury.* **3** quarrel; argument.

dis·ap·pear (dĭs′ə pir′) **1** to go out of sight: *A ship* disappears *as it sails around the curve of the earth.* **2** to vanish; cease to be: *Many old customs have* disappeared.

dis·ap·pear·ance (dĭs′ə pir′əns) a passing from sight; a vanishing.

dis·ap·point (dĭs′ə point′) **1** to fail to satisfy the wish or hope of: *I was* disappointed *by the play.* **2** to fail to keep a promise to: *Please don't* disappoint *me again.*

dis·ap·point·ment (dĭs′ə point′mənt) **1** a disappointing: *his* disappointment *of his parents' hopes.* **2** a feeling of being disappointed: *They couldn't hide their* disappointment. **3** person who or thing that disappoints: *He is a* disappointment *to them.*

dis·ap·prov·al (dĭs′ə prōō′vəl) the act of disapproving; dislike; unfavorable feeling: *She viewed the dirty streets with* disapproval.

dis·ap·prove (dĭs′ə prōōv′) to fail to approve; to refuse permission; be against; have a bad opinion of: *She wanted to go out but her mother* disapproved. *His father* disapproved *of his choice of clothes.* **dis·ap·proved, dis·ap·prov·ing.**

dis·arm (dĭs ärm′) **1** to take a weapon or weapons from: *He tried to* disarm *the gunman.* **2** to do away with or reduce arms, armies, or the like: *Before the countries would* disarm *they had to agree on an inspection system.* **3** to cause to become friendly: *He* disarmed *me with his smile.*

dis·ar·ma·ment (dĭs är′mə mənt) **1** a putting aside of weapons. **2** the reduction of weapons and men in the armed forces.

dis·ar·range (dĭs′ə rānj′) to put out of order. **dis·ar·ranged, dis·ar·rang·ing.**

dis·as·ter (dĭ zăs′tər) something that causes great trouble or suffering; a great misfortune.

dis·as·trous (dĭ zăs′trəs) causing suffering, loss, or misery: *a disastrous fire; a disastrous flood.* **dis·as·trous·ly.**

dis·band (dĭs bănd′) to break up; disperse: *The regiment was disbanded at the end of the year. The marchers disbanded after the parade.*

disc (dĭsk) disk.

¹dis·card (dĭs kärd′) to throw away as useless; get rid of: *to discard old clothes.*

²dis·card (dĭs′kärd) **1** anything that is thrown away: *The three of hearts was a discard.* **2** act of throwing aside as useless: *His discard of the coat proved a mistake.* **3 the discard** any place where unwanted things are put: *old files thrown into the discard.*

dis·cern (dĭ zûrn′ or dĭ sûrn′) **1** to make out clearly; perceive: *I discerned his plan. We can discern stars in the sky.* **2** to distinguish: *Sometimes it is hard to discern the true from the false.*

¹dis·charge (dĭs chärj′) **1** to let go; release; dismiss: *to discharge a worker; to discharge a soldier at the end of service.* **2** to remove; unload: *The ship discharged its cargo at the wharf.* **3** to let escape; carry off: *The overflow pipe discharged water from the tank.* **4** to fire a gun, arrow, or other weapon. **5** to carry out; complete: *Wilbur faithfully discharged his duty.* **6** to settle; pay: *to discharge a debt.* **dis·charged, dis·charg·ing.**

²dis·charge (dĭs′chärj) **1** the act of dismissing; statement proving dismissal: *Clement received an honorable discharge from the army.* **2** an unloading: *the discharge of cotton bales.* **3** something discharged: *a continuous discharge from the wound.* **4** a carrying out; performance: *He was hurt in the discharge of his duty.*

dis·ci·ple (dĭ sī′pəl) **1** person who accepts the teachings of a leader and helps to spread them; follower. **2** one of the early followers of Jesus.

dis·ci·pline (dĭs′ə plĭn) **1** strict training of mind and body to carry out duties, obey orders, etc.: *military discipline.* **2** to train in self-control and obedience. **3** the self-control and order thus gained: *The pupils showed their discipline in the fire drill.* **4** to punish in order to train: *to discipline an unruly prisoner; to be disciplined for disobedience.* **5** punishment thus given. **dis·ci·plined, dis·ci·plin·ing.**

dis·claim (dĭs klām′) to deny; disown: *He disclaimed the statement reprinted in the newspapers.*

dis·close (dĭs klōz′) to uncover; reveal: *The explorer's excavation disclosed a secret door. He will disclose his plan.* **dis·closed, dis·clos·ing.**

dis·col·or (dĭs kŭl′ər) **1** to stain: *Rust marks discolored the shirt.* **2** to change color: *This cloth is guaranteed not to discolor in sunlight.*

dis·com·fort (dĭs kŭm′fərt) lack of comfort; mild pain; uneasiness: *The bad air caused much discomfort in the audience.*

dis·con·cert (dĭs′kən sûrt′) to upset; disorder; disturb (a person's) calm: *I was disconcerted by her change of attitude.*

dis·con·nect (dĭs′kə někt′) to break or undo the connection of: *to disconnect an electric iron.*

dis·con·tent (dĭs′kən tĕnt′) a feeling of not being satisfied; discomfort: *Her discontent arose from her slow progress.*

dis·con·tent·ed (dĭs′kən tĕn′tĭd) not happy or content; not satisfied: *He was discontented with his small salary.* **dis·con·tent·ed·ly.**

dis·con·tin·ue (dĭs′kən tĭn′ū) to put an end to; stop; cease: *He had to discontinue work on the project because of illness.* **dis·con·tin·ued, dis·con·tin·u·ing.**

dis·cord (dĭs′kôrd) **1** argument; disagreement; strife: *The group was too full of discord to work together.* **2** in music, lack of harmony: *The discord in modern music startles many people.*

dis·cord·ant (dĭs kôr′dənt) not agreeing; clashing; out of harmony: *a discordant meeting; a discordant musical chord.* **dis·cord·ant·ly.**

---

fāte, făt, fâre, fär; bē, bĕt; bīte, bĭt; nō, nŏt, nôr; fūse, fŭn, fûr; tōō, tŏŏk; foil; foul; thin; ~~then~~; hw for wh as in *wh*at; zh for s as in u*s*ual; ə for a, e, i, o, u, as in ag*o*, lin*e*n, per*i*l, at*o*m, min*u*s

225

dis·count (dĭs′kount) **1** an allowance for cash payment, dealer's rate, etc.: *All catalog prices are subject to a 25% discount.* **2** to give such a price reduction. **3** (also dĭs·kount′) to take (something) as not entirely true; allow for exaggeration in: *We must discount any political speech.*

dis·cour·age (dĭs·kûr′ĭj) **1** to take away confidence or hope: *The teacher's criticism should not discourage the pupil.* **2** to make (something) seem wrong or not worth the effort: *Highway patrols discourage speeding.* **dis·cour·aged, dis·cour·ag·ing.**

dis·cour·age·ment (dĭs·kûr′ĭj mənt) **1** act of discouraging: *He tried to make friends with her but met with discouragement.* **2** a feeling of being discouraged: *In his discouragement he gave up.* **3** something that discourages.

dis·course (dĭs·kôrs′) **1** to talk at length on a subject: *They discoursed for hours on the subject of politics.* **2** (also dĭs′kôrs) treatment of some subject, whether spoken or written: *a discourse hard to follow.*

dis·cour·te·ous (dĭs·kûr′tĭ əs) rude; impolite: *It is discourteous to interrupt when someone else is talking.* **dis·cour·te·ous·ly.**

dis·cour·te·sy (dĭs·kûr′tə sĭ) lack of politeness; a show of bad manners; an insult: *It would be a discourtesy to ignore his question.* **dis·cour·te·sies.**

dis·cov·er (dĭs·kŭv′ər) **1** to find or come upon anything for the first time: *The explorer discovered the source of the stream.* **2** to find out: *She discovered she was late.*

dis·cov·er·er (dĭs·kŭv′ər ər) one who discovers: *the discoverer of America.*

dis·cov·er·y (dĭs·kŭv′ə rĭ) **1** a finding out about (something) or coming upon (something) for the first time: *the discovery of gold.* **2** the thing found, or found out: *Penicillin was a great discovery.* **dis·cov·er·ies.**

dis·cred·it (dĭs·krĕd′ĭt) **1** to throw doubt on; to destroy (belief in): *to discredit the belief that toads cause warts.* **2** to refuse to believe: *I discredit all those stories.* **3** loss of good name or reputation: *to bring discredit on the whole family.* **4** person who causes loss of reputation: *He was a discredit to the family.*

dis·creet (dĭs·krēt′) tactful; careful in what one says or does; prudent: *He told his secret to a discreet friend.* **dis·creet·ly.**

dis·cre·tion (dĭs·krĕsh′ən) **1** ability to choose wisely or to judge for oneself; good judgment: *to act with discretion in buying a house.* **2** ability to keep certain things to oneself; quality of being discreet: *She showed great discretion about the secret.*

dis·crim·i·nate (dĭs·krĭm′ə nāt′) **1** to note fine differences between; distinguish: *Careful reading helps us to discriminate between good writers and bad writers.* **2** to treat differently because of race, religion, etc.: *to discriminate against the poor.* **dis·crim·i·nat·ed, dis·crim·i·nat·ing.**

dis·crim·i·na·tion (dĭs·krĭm′ə nā′shən) **1** a noting of fine differences: *to buy without discrimination.* **2** ability to discriminate. **3** difference in treatment or attitude: *without discrimination as to creed or color.*

dis·cuss (dĭs·kŭs′) to talk over thoughtfully; consider: *He will discuss the problem.*

dis·cus·sion (dĭs·kŭsh′ən) **1** exchange of ideas between two or more persons: *Their discussion was based on an article in a scientific magazine.* **2** a handling or presentation of a subject, as in a lecture: *His discussion was illustrated by charts.*

dis·dain (dĭs dān′) **1** to show contempt for; look down upon: *She disdained everyone outside her set.* **2** a looking down upon; contempt; scorn: *to treat with disdain.*

dis·dain·ful (dĭs dān′fəl) showing disdain; haughty: *His disdainful attitude made many enemies.* **dis·dain·ful·ly.**

dis·ease (dĭ zēz′) **1** sickness; illness. **2** any particular kind of sickness: *Measles and mumps are diseases.*

dis·eased (dĭ zēzd′) **1** suffering from a disease. **2** showing the effects of a disease: *to remove the diseased branches.*

dis·em·bark (dĭs′ĕm bärk′) **1** to leave a ship or aircraft; land: *Madeline disembarked at New York.* **2** to put ashore; land: *We shall disembark the passengers at Pier 23.*

dis·fa·vor (dĭs fā′vər) **1** dislike; hostility; disapproval: *to view with disfavor.* **2** a state of being out of favor: *Edgar was in disfavor because of his practical joke.*

dis·fig·ure (dĭs fĭg′yər) to mar or spoil the form or appearance: *Billboards disfigure the highways.* **dis·fig·ured, dis·fig·ur·ing.**

dis·grace (dĭs grās′) **1** shame; loss of honor or good name. **2** cause of shame or discredit: *These dirty streets are a* disgrace *to the city.* **3** to bring shame upon; to dishonor: *He disgraced his mother by being rude to her guests.* **4 in disgrace** out of favor or honor: *The mischievous puppy was in disgrace.* **dis·graced, dis·grac·ing.**

dis·grace·ful (dĭs grās′fəl) shameful; unworthy: *their disgraceful behavior; his disgraceful performance.* **dis·grace·ful·ly.**

dis·guise (dĭs gīz′) **1** to change the appearance in order to hide the identity: *The soldier disguised himself before entering the enemy camp.* **2** to mask; cover up: *He disguised his anger with a smile.* **3** an unusual manner or dress, put on to hide the identity: *In spite of his disguise, he was quickly recognized.* **4** the hiding of the real under a false appearance: *Her calm manner was merely a disguise.* **dis·guised, dis·guis·ing.**

dis·gust (dĭs gŭst′) **1** very strong distaste; sickening dislike; loathing: *They turned away in disgust.* **2** to cause strong distaste or loathing in; sicken: *His table manners disgusted us.*

dis·gust·ed (dĭs gŭs′tĭd) filled with disgust or violent dislike. **dis·gust·ed·ly.**

dish (dĭsh) **1** a plate or shallow bowl, generally used for holding food. **2** a particular food: *His favorite dish was chicken and biscuits.* **3** amount served: *He ate two dishes of ice cream.*

dish up to put into a dish and serve.

dis·heart·en (dĭs här′tən) to discourage; cause to lose hope: *They were disheartened by their many failures.*

di·shev·eled (dĭ shĕv′əld) thrown into disorder; untidy; mussed: *her disheveled hair.*

dis·hon·est (dĭs ŏn′ĭst) not honest. **dis·hon·est·ly.**

dis·hon·es·ty (dĭs ŏn′ĭs tĭ) **1** lack of honesty. **2** a dishonest act or saying. **dis·hon·es·ties.**

dis·hon·or (dĭs ŏn′ər) **1** disgrace or shame; loss of good name: *to prefer death to dishonor.* **2** a cause of shame or disgrace: *Signing the unfair treaty was a dishonor to the country.* **3** to bring reproach or shame upon; show disrespect to: *By living an evil life he dishonored the family name.*

dis·hon·or·a·ble (dĭs ŏn′ər ə bəl) not honorable. **dis·hon·or·a·bly.**

dis·in·fect (dĭs′ĭn fĕkt′) to make free from harmful germs: *City water is often disinfected with chlorine.*

dis·in·fec·tant (dĭs′ĭn fĕk′tənt) **1** a substance that kills disease germs. **2** able to kill disease germs: *a disinfectant powder.*

dis·in·te·grate (dĭs ĭn′tə grāt′) to break into small parts or pieces; crumble: *The quilt disintegrated in the washing machine. Rocks disintegrate into sand.* **dis·in·te·grat·ed, dis·in·te·grat·ing.**

dis·in·ter·est·ed (dĭs ĭn′tə rĕs′tĭd) having no personal interest in an affair; free from bias; impartial: *The referee at a prize fight must be disinterested.* **dis·in·ter·est·ed·ly.**

disk (dĭsk) **1** a flat, circular plate of metal, plastic, etc. A phonograph record is a disk. **2** anything that looks like this: *The sun's disk sank slowly in the west.* **3 disk jockey** person who broadcasts a program of music from records. Also spelled **disc.**

Disk

dis·like (dĭs līk′) **1** to have a feeling against; not like: *She dislikes visiting the dentist.* **2** a feeling against someone or something; distaste: *He has a dislike of rising early.* **dis·liked, dis·lik·ing.**

dis·lo·cate (dĭs′lō kāt′) **1** to force out of place: *to dislocate one's shoulder.* **2** to upset; throw into confusion: *Plans for a new shopping center were dislocated by a building law.* **dis·lo·cat·ed, dis·lo·cat·ing.**

dis·lodge (dĭs lŏj′) to move or force out of position: *Several large stones were dislodged in the quarry.* **dis·lodged, dis·lodg·ing.**

dis·loy·al (dĭs loi′əl) not loyal: *to be disloyal to one's friends.* **dis·loy·al·ly.**

dis·loy·al·ty (dĭs loi′əl tĭ) lack of loyalty: *their disloyalty to the country.*

dis·mal (dĭz′məl) **1** gloomy; dreary; cheerless: *a dismal swamp.* **2** depressed; sad: *a dismal mood.* **dis·mal·ly.**

dis·man·tle (dĭs măn′təl) **1** to strip of furniture, equipment, etc.: *to dismantle a house.* **2** to take apart: *to dismantle a machine.* **dis·man·tled, dis·man·tling.**

---

fāte, făt, fâre, fär; bē, bĕt; bite, bĭt; nō, nŏt, nôr; fūse, fŭn, fûr; tōō, tŏŏk; foil; foul; thin; ~~then~~;
hw for wh as in *wh*at; zh for s as in u*s*ual; ə for a, e, i, o, u, as in *a*go, lin*e*n, per*i*l, at*o*m, min*u*s

dis·may (dĭs mā′) 1 to take away courage; frighten; dishearten: *The surprise attack dismayed them.* 2 sudden loss of courage; frightened amazement: *the dismay of the swimmers when they found their clothes gone.*

dis·miss (dĭs mĭs′) 1 to send away; direct or allow to leave: *to dismiss a class.* 2 to discharge; remove from office or employment: *to dismiss a clerk.* 3 to refuse to consider further: *The judge dismissed the case.*

dis·miss·al (dĭs mĭs′əl) a dismissing: *the dismissal of the class; a dismissal from employment; the judge's dismissal of the case.*

dis·mount (dĭs mount′) 1 to get off or down from: *to dismount from a horse, bicycle, etc.* 2 to put (a rider) off a horse by force. 3 to remove (something) from its setting, mounting, support, etc.: *to dismount a cannon.* 4 to take apart: *to dismount a watch.*

dis·o·be·di·ence (dĭs′ə bē′dĭ əns) refusal to obey; failure to follow a rule or command: *an attitude of disobedience; a disobedience of the school rules.*

dis·o·be·di·ent (dĭs′ə bē′dĭ ənt) not obedient: *a disobedient child.* **dis·o·be·di·ent·ly.**

dis·o·bey (dĭs′ə bā′) to refuse or fail to obey: *to disobey parents; to disobey school rules.*

dis·or·der (dĭs ôr′dər) 1 without order: *a room in disorder.* 2 to put out of order; disarrange. 3 a public disturbance; commotion: *the disorder in the streets during the strike.* 4 a mental or physical ailment: *a disorder of the heart.*

dis·or·der·ly (dĭs ôr′dər lĭ) 1 not orderly; untidy: *a disorderly desk.* 2 lawless; unruly: *the disorderly mob.*

dis·or·gan·ize (dĭs ôr′gə nīz′) to throw into confusion or disorder: *Fog disorganized the airplane schedule.* **dis·or·gan·ized, dis·or·gan·iz·ing.**

dis·own (dĭs ōn′) to refuse to recognize as one's own; reject: *to disown a leader; to disown one's flag; to disown a child.*

dis·patch (dĭs păch′) 1 to send off quickly: *to dispatch a message.* 2 a message, especially an official one: *a dispatch from the President.* 3 to finish quickly; settle: *to dispatch a business deal.* 4 quick action (upon): *He handled their applications with dispatch.* 5 to put to death; kill. 6 a news report: *a dispatch from New York.*

dis·pel (dĭs pĕl′) to drive away; scatter; cause to disappear: *The sun dispelled the gloom.* **dis·pelled, dis·pel·ling.**

dis·pense (dĭs pĕns′) 1 to deal out in portions; distribute: *They dispensed clothing to the needy.* 2 to prepare and distribute: *The druggist dispenses medicine.* **dispense with** to do without; get rid of: *We can dispense with his services.* **dis·pensed, dis·pens·ing.**

dis·perse (dĭs pûrs′) 1 to send in different directions; scatter: *The police dispersed the mob.* 2 to go off in different directions; separate: *The crowd dispersed after the meeting.* **dis·persed, dis·pers·ing.**

dis·place (dĭs plās′) 1 to take the place of; replace: *The jet plane is displacing the propeller-driven plane.* 2 to put out of the usual place: *Don't displace anything on my desk.* **dis·placed, dis·plac·ing.**

dis·play (dĭs plā′) 1 to show; exhibit; reveal: *to display talent; to display fear.* 2 a showing or an exhibition: *a display of automobiles; a display of fear.* 3 a showing off because of vanity or for some secret purpose: *a display of wealth.*

dis·please (dĭs plēz′) to offend; annoy; make angry: *His bad manners displease his friends.* **dis·pleased, dis·pleas·ing.**

dis·pleas·ure (dĭs plĕzh′ər) displeased feeling; disapproval; annoyance: *father's displeasure over our tardiness.*

dis·pos·al (dĭs pō′zəl) 1 a getting rid of: *the disposal of garbage.* 2 a getting rid of by sale or transfer: *the disposal of the estate; his disposal of the car.* 3 settlement; conclusion: *their final disposal of the matter.* 4 a placing in a particular order; arrangement: *the disposal of objects in a window display.* 5 **at one's disposal** available for use at any time as one pleases: *Dick had his friend's boat at his disposal.*

dis·pose (dĭs pōz′) 1 to put in a certain position; arrange: *The shrubs were attractively disposed about the garden.* 2 **disposed to** subject to; inclined to: *He is disposed to colds. I am disposed to hear your request.*
dispose of 1 to get rid of (by throwing away, selling, etc.): *to dispose of rubbish.* 2 to finish with; settle: *to dispose of a quarrel.* **dis·posed, dis·pos·ing.**

disposition

dis·po·si·tion (dĭs'pə zĭsh'ən) **1** a person's natural attitude or habit of mind; temperament: *a generous* disposition; *a jealous* disposition. **2** a liking; preference: *a disposition for quiet places.* **3** putting in position; arrangement; distribution: *the disposition of furniture in a room.* **4** power to dispose or use as one wishes: *He has a fortune at his* disposition.

dis·pos·sess (dĭs'pə zĕs') to put out of possession by legal action: *to dispossess a family of an apartment.*

dis·prove (dĭs prōōv') to prove to be false or wrong: *to disprove a story with the facts.* **dis·proved, dis·prov·ing.**

dis·pute (dĭs pūt') **1** to argue; debate; quarrel in words: *They disputed over politics for hours.* **2** argument; debate; difference of opinion. **3** a quarrel: *a violent dispute between neighbors over a boundary.* **4** to say something is wrong, false, or unlikely; question the truth of: *People once disputed the idea that the Earth goes around the sun.* **5** to fight for; contest: *The Marines disputed every inch of the beach when enemy boats landed.* **dis·put·ed, dis·put·ing.**

dis·qual·i·fy (dĭs kwŏl'ə fī') **1** to make unfit or unable: *His deafness disqualified him for military service.* **2** to declare unfit or not eligible: *to be disqualified for office.* **dis·qual·i·fied, dis·qual·i·fy·ing.**

dis·qui·et (dĭs kwī'ət) **1** to make uneasy or restless; disturb: *The sudden silence disquieted him.* **2** uneasiness; anxiety: *A feeling of disquiet spread through the waiting crowd.*

dis·re·gard (dĭs'rĭ gärd') **1** to pay no attention to; to ignore: *He disregarded the warnings not to swim in the deep water.* **2** refusal to pay attention: *his disregard for traffic lights.* **3** lack of respect: *his disregard for my feelings.*

dis·rep·u·ta·ble (dĭs rĕp'yə tə bəl) **1** of bad reputation; shady: *Not all disreputable people are in jail.* **2** not respectable: *a disreputable old coat.* **dis·rep·u·ta·bly.**

dis·re·spect (dĭs'rĭ spĕkt') lack of respect; rudeness: *to treat with disrespect.*

dis·re·spect·ful (dĭs'rĭ spĕkt'fəl) rude; lacking in respect. **dis·re·spect·ful·ly.**

dissuade

dis·rupt (dĭs rŭpt') to break apart; break up: *to disrupt a meeting by starting a fight.*

dis·sat·is·fac·tion (dĭs'săt ĭs făk'shən) discontent; lack of satisfaction: *The tenants felt much dissatisfaction with the house.*

dis·sat·is·fied (dĭs săt'ĭs fīd') not pleased; discontented: *The soldiers were dissatisfied with the food.* **dis·sat·is·fied·ly.**

dis·sect (dĭ sĕkt') **1** to cut in pieces (an animal or plant) in order to study or examine the inner parts: *The biology class dissected frogs last week.* **2** to study or analyze part by part: *The teacher dissected my report.*

dis·sen·sion (dĭ sĕn'shən) quarreling; angry disagreement because of difference of opinion: *There was dissension among the pirates over the division of the booty.*

dis·sent (dĭ sĕnt') **1** to disagree; to have a different opinion: *Only one person dissented when swimming was suggested.* **2** difference in opinion: *a dissent from the majority.* (Homonym: descent)

dis·sim·i·lar (dĭ sĭm'ə lər) different; unlike: *two brothers with dissimilar tastes.* **dis·sim·i·lar·ly.**

dis·si·pate (dĭs'ə pāt) **1** to break up; drive away: *The sun rose and dissipated the fog.* **2** to spend foolishly; waste: *The prodigal son dissipated his money in almost no time.* **dis·si·pat·ed, dis·si·pat·ing.**

dis·solve (dĭ zŏlv') **1** to become liquid: *The snow man dissolved into a puddle of water.* **2** to mix evenly (through a fluid) so as to disappear from sight: *Salt dissolves in water. We can dissolve salt in water.* **3** to take up a substance so that it disappears from sight: *Gasoline dissolves wax.* **4** to break up; put an end to; dismiss: *to dissolve a friendship; to dissolve a company.* **5** to disappear: *The coach's dreams of success dissolved when the team lost the fourth game.* **dis·solved, dis·solv·ing.**

dis·so·nant (dĭs'ə nənt) not harmonious: *the dissonant sounds from my brother's battered trumpet; the dissonant views of otherwise good friends.* **dis·so·nant·ly.**

dis·suade (dĭ swād') to talk (someone) out of doing something; advise against: *His father dissuaded him from flying during the snow storm.* **dis·suad·ed, dis·suad·ing.**

fāte, făt, fâre, fär; bē, bĕt; bīte, bĭt; nō, nŏt, nôr; fūse, fŭn, fûr; tōō, tŏŏk; foil; foul; thin; then; hw for wh as in *what*; zh for s as in u*s*ual; ə for a, e, i, o, u, as in *a*go, lin*e*n, per*i*l, at*o*m, min*u*s

229

dis·tance (dĭs′təns) **1** a being distant. **2** amount of space between two points, objects, places, or the like: *The distance between the two cities is 300 miles.* **3 in the distance** far away (from here): *We saw the smoke from a ship* in the distance.

dis·tant (dĭs′tənt) **1** far away: *The sun is* distant *from the earth.* **2** long ago: *Dinosaurs lived in the* distant *past.* **3** not close in relationship: *Third cousins are* distant *relatives.* **4** away: *two blocks* distant. **5** not friendly: *Jane has been very* distant *since our argument.* **dis·tant·ly.**

dis·taste (dĭs tāst′) a dislike: *a distaste for chocolate; a* distaste *for hard work.*

dis·taste·ful (dĭs tāst′fəl) disagreeable; unpleasant: *a distasteful medicine; a* distasteful *conversation.* **dis·taste·ful·ly.**

dis·tem·per (dĭs tĕm′pər) a disease, especially an infection in dogs and other animals, in which there is fever, coughing, loss of appetite, and loss of strength.

dis·tend (dĭs tĕnd′) to swell out or cause to swell out: *The horse's nostrils* distended *in fear. The horse's belly was* distended *by colic.*

dis·till or **dis·til** (dĭs tĭl′) **1** to make a liquid pure by heating it until it becomes a vapor and then cooling the vapor so that it changes back again into a liquid: *Sea water can be* distilled *to remove the salt.* **2** to make by this process: *to* distill *alcohol from grain.* **3** to trickle down; fall or let fall in drops. **4** to draw out the pure spirit or essence of: *to* distill *wisdom from experience.* **dis·tilled, dis·till·ing.**

dis·til·la·tion (dĭs′tə lā′shən) **1** a distilling. **2** the product of a distilling: *Gasoline is a* distillation *from petroleum.*

dis·tinct (dĭs tĭngkt′) **1** different; separate: *two* distinct *kinds of animals.* **2** clear; plain: *a* distinct *pronunciation.* **3** very definite; unmistakable: *a* distinct *improvement.*

dis·tinc·tion (dĭs tĭngk′shən) **1** the making of a difference: *to treat everybody alike without* distinction *as to race or creed.* **2** difference; point of difference: *to note the* distinction *between mice and rats.* **3** excellence; superiority: *a writer of* distinction. **4** mark of favor or honor: *to win many* distinctions *for bravery.*

dis·tinc·tive (dĭs tĭngk′tĭv) marking a difference from others: *They wore* distinctive *uniforms.* **dis·tinc·tive·ly.**

dis·tinct·ly (dĭs tĭngkt′lĭ) **1** clearly; exactly: *Speak* distinctly *and he will understand you.* **2** without doubt; definitely: *It is* distinctly *warmer today than yesterday.*

dis·tin·guish (dĭs tĭng′gwĭsh) **1** to mark as different; to set apart: *Their uniforms* distinguish *soldiers, sailors, and marines from each other.* **2** to see clearly the difference between (two things): *He could not* distinguish *right from wrong.* **3** to perceive; recognize: *The captain could* distinguish *a lighthouse through the fog.* **4** to do credit to (oneself); make (oneself) well-known: *He* distinguished *himself by his courage on the battlefield.*

dis·tin·guished (dĭs tĭng′gwĭsht) **1** famous (because of achievement): *a* distinguished *statesman.* **2** showing distinction: *a record of* distinguished *service.*

dis·tort (dĭs tôrt′) **1** to change the shape of; twist: *Pain* distorted *his face.* **2** to change the original meaning of: *Several newspapers* distorted *the politician's speech.*

dis·tract (dĭs trăkt′) **1** to draw away the mind or attention of; divert: *Music* distracts *her from her troubles. The noise of the parade* distracted *me from my work.* **2** to confuse or bewilder to the point that thought is impossible: *All my directions serve only to* distract *him.* **3** to craze; drive mad: *That constant noise must stop before it* distracts *me entirely.*

dis·trac·tion (dĭs trăk′shən) **1** that which turns the attention from something: *Television is a* distraction *when you are trying to read.* **2** amusement; diversion: *Alice needed some* distraction *after her examinations.* **3** confusion; perplexity: *In his* distraction *after the accident, my father let the other car escape.* **4** madness; frenzy: *That noise drives me to* distraction.

dis·tress (dĭs trĕs′) **1** misery; sorrow; pain: *She is in great* distress *over the illness of her son.* **2** to cause grief or suffering: *News of the accident* distressed *her.* **3** poverty; misery; lack of necessities: *The floods this year have caused great* distress *in several states.* **4** danger; difficulty: *a ship in* distress.

dis·trib·ute (dĭs trĭb′ūt) **1** to hand out or send out: *Pamphlets were* distributed *among the crowd.* **2** to spread out; scatter; strew: *The wind* distributed *leaves over the countryside.* **3** to arrange; sort; put into groups

or classes: *Mail is* distributed *each morning.*
dis·trib·ut·ed, dis·trib·ut·ing.

dis·tri·bu·tion (dĭs′trə bū′shən) **1** a giving
or dealing out: *the* distribution *of food and
clothing to the flood victims.* **2** the way
something is spread out or distributed: *the*
distribution *of animal life in this region.*

dis·trict (dĭs′trĭkt) **1** a region or area: *a
slum* district *in the older part of the city.*
2 a part of a country, state, or county
marked out for a special purpose: *a school*
district; *a voting* district.

District of Columbia (dĭs′trĭkt əv kə-
lŭm′bĭ ə) Federal district between Maryland and Virginia, covering the same area
as Washington, the national capital.

dis·trust (dĭs trŭst′) **1** lack of confidence;
suspicion: *He looked at the friendly stranger
with* distrust. **2** to have no faith in; suspect: *They* distrusted *his answers.*

dis·turb (dĭs tûrb′) **1** to break in upon;
bother; interrupt: *The noise will* disturb
my work. **2** to put into disorder: *Don't* disturb *the books on that shelf.* **3** to upset;
worry; make uneasy: *Rumors of the airplane
crash* disturbed *her greatly.*

dis·turb·ance (dĭs tûr′bəns) **1** a disturbing; interruption: *their* disturbance *of her
privacy.* **2** something that disturbs: *The
radio can be a great* disturbance. **3** result
of disturbing; disorder: *a* disturbance *in
the crowd.* **4** result of disturbing the mind;
worry: *Her* disturbance *was plain to see.*

ditch (dĭch) **1** long, narrow trench dug in
the earth. **2** to dig a trench in or around: *to*
ditch *a garden for drainage.* **3** to throw into
a ditch: *to* ditch *a car.*

dit·ty (dĭt′ĭ) a short, light song. **dit·ties.**

di·van (dī′văn or dĭ văn′) long, low, cushioned seat, usually having no back or ends.

dive (dīv) **1** to plunge headfirst: *She* dived
from the prow of the boat into the waves.
2 to go under water and search for something: *to* dive *for pearls;* dive *for coins.* **3** to
go quickly and deeply into something: *to*
dive *into one's pocket; to* dive *into a book;
to* dive *into a hallway.* **4** a sudden downward plunge; the act of diving: *The bombing
plane made a* dive *at its target.* **dived** or
dove, div·ing.

div·er (dī′vər) **1** person or animal that
dives into water. **2** person who makes a
living by gathering sponges,
pearl oysters, etc., from the
sea bottom. **3** person who works
under water, either in a special
suit and helmet connected with
the surface by an air hose or
with air tanks on his back.

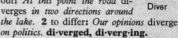
Diver

di·verge (dĭ vûrj′ or dī vûrj′)
1 to go out from a point; branch
out: *At this point the road* di-
verges *in two directions around
the lake.* **2** to differ: *Our opinions* diverge
on politics. **di·verged, di·verg·ing.**

di·vers (dī′vərz) several; various: *He has
lived in* divers *places in the world.*

di·verse (dĭ vûrs′ or dī vûrs′ or dī′vûrs)
clearly different: *to have* diverse *views.*

di·ver·si·fy (dĭ vûr′sə fī or dī vûr′sə fī) to
give variety to; vary: *to* diversify *one's reading.* **di·ver·si·fied, di·ver·si·fy·ing.**

di·ver·sion (dĭ vûr′zhən or dī vûr′zhən) **1**
pastime; recreation; amusement: *Her favorite* diversion *was dancing.* **2** a turning
something aside or in a different direction:
the diversion *of a stream from its original
course.* **3** a turning of attention in a different direction; distracting movement: *A* diversion *was created by a surprise attack from
another point.*

di·ver·si·ty (dĭ vûr′sə tĭ or dī vûr′sə tĭ) variety; difference: *a* diversity *of opinion; a*
diversity *of color.* **di·ver·si·ties.**

di·vert (dĭ vûrt′ or dī vûrt′) **1** to turn aside,
or in a different direction: *Traffic was* diverted *until the highway was repaired. The
band* diverted *our attention from the game.*
2 to amuse; entertain: *We were* diverted *by
the puppet show.*

di·vide (dĭ vīd′) **1** to separate; keep apart:
A high fence divides *their farm from ours.*
2 to separate into parts; share: *The money
was* divided *equally among the boys.* **3** to
separate by feeling or ideas: *They were*
divided *on the question of borrowing money.*
4 to arrange in groups; classify: *The books
were* divided *according to subjects.* **5** a
line of high land between two river systems.

fāte, făt, fâre, fär; bē, bĕt; bīte, bĭt; nō, nŏt, nôr; fūse, fŭn, fûr; tōō, tŏŏk; foil; foul; thin; then;
hw for wh as in what; zh for s as in usual; ə for a, e, i, o, u, as in ago, linen, peril, atom, minus

231

divide by 1 to find the size of the equal groups that can be in another group a given number of times. When we divide forty by four, we find that the size of each of the four groups is ten. 2 to find out how many groups of a given size are contained in another group. When we divide forty by four, we find that there are ten groups of four in forty. **di·vid·ed, di·vid·ing.**

div·i·dend (dĭv′ə dĕnd) 1 a number to be divided. In 238 ÷ 2, 238 is the dividend. 2 money divided from time to time among people who own stock in a company or corporation as their share of the profits. 3 a share of anything divided.

di·vid·er (dĭ vī′dər) 1 person or thing that divides. 2 **dividers** compasses with two sharp points, used for dividing lines, measuring distances, etc.

di·vine (dĭ vīn′) 1 having to do with or coming from God: *a divine prophecy.* 2 godlike; seemingly more than human; extraordinary: *He was a painter born with a divine gift.* 3 a priest or clergyman. 4 to guess; detect: *He divined their reason for coming.* **di·vined, di·vin·ing; di·vine·ly.**

di·vin·i·ty (dĭ vĭn′ə tĭ) 1 divine nature; godlike nature: *Christians believe in the divinity of Christ. Many kings have believed in their own divinity.* 2 a god; a divine being, 3 the study of religion; theology: *He has a degree of Doctor of Divinity.* 4 **the Divinity** God. **di·vin·i·ties.**

di·vis·i·ble (dĭ vĭz′ə bəl) capable of being divided. **di·vis·i·bly.**

di·vi·sion (dĭ vĭzh′ən) 1 the process of dividing; separation of a whole thing into parts: *the division of a house into rooms; the division of a play into acts.* 2 portion or part; department: *sales division of a company; divisions of a book.* 3 partition; separation; separating wall. 4 difference of opinion; lack of agreement: *There was a division among the members on the choice of a name for the club.* 5 a unit in the army under the command of a major general.

di·vi·sor (dĭ vī′zər) a number by which another number is divided. In 36 ÷ 3, 3 is the divisor.

di·vorce (dĭ vôrs′) 1 legal ending of a marriage: *to sue for divorce.* 2 to win release

from the marriage agreement or contract. 3 to separate: *We will divorce the two subjects entirely.* 4 separation: *a divorce between intentions and acts.* **di·vorced, di·vorc·ing.**

di·vulge (dĭ vŭlj′) to make known; reveal; disclose: *to divulge a secret.* **di·vulged, di·vulg·ing.**

diz·zi·ness (dĭz′ĭ nĭs) feeling of being dizzy

diz·zy (dĭz′ĭ) 1 feeling as if one were whirling or turning and falling; giddy; unsteady. 2 causing giddiness or unsteadiness: *a dizzy whirling.* 3 to make dizzy. **diz·zi·er, diz·zi·est; diz·zied, diz·zy·ing; diz·zi·ly.**

¹**do** (do͞o) 1 to perform; carry out; complete; produce: *to do a job; to do a play; to do a painting.* 2 to give; grant: *to do a favor; to do justice.* 3 to be the cause of; bring about: *to do good; to do harm.* 4 to work on; set in order; arrange: *to do one's hair.* 5 to be satisfactory; be good enough: *Those shoes won't do for walking.* 6 to reach; cover: *to do 60 miles an hour; to do 300 miles in a day.* 7 to fare: *to do well in business.* 8 a helping word that is used (1) to make what one says stronger: *I do know how to sew.* (2) with *not* to show that something is not happening or not true: *He does not drive.* (3) to take the place of an action word which has been mentioned: *Who runs this machine? I do.*

do away with to put an end to: *to do away with a department in a store.*

do up to wrap or tie up: *We must do up these things for the hospital.*

do without to get on without.

does, did, done, do·ing. [¹**do** is a form of an Old English word (don).] (Homonyms: dew, due)

²**do** (dō) the first note of a musical scale. [²**do** is a syllable that was made up, perhaps by an Italian musician.]

doc·ile (dŏs′əl) easily trained or handled: *a docile horse.* **doc·ile·ly.**

Dock

¹**dock** (dŏk) 1 a waterway between piers, where ships may tie up to load and unload; a slip. 2 less correctly, a pier. 3 to bring into or arrive at a dock: *The cap-*

tain docked *his boat beside Pier 36.* **4** to bring together and connect two space ships: *They will* dock *the two ships 500 miles above the Earth.* [**¹dock** seems to be from an early Dutch word (docke) meaning "channel."]

²dock (dŏk) **1** the stump of an animal's tail. **2** to cut off the end of: *to* dock *a puppy's tail.* **3** to take part off: *His pay was* docked *for time off work.* [**²dock** is probably from an Old Norse word (dockr) meaning "a short, thick tail."]

³dock (dŏk) the place in a courtroom where a prisoner is placed during a trial. [**³dock** is from a Flemish word (docke, dok) meaning "a pen" or "a cage."]

⁴dock (dŏk) a long-rooted, coarse weed with red-veined leaves and seeds in reddish husks. [**⁴dock** is a form of an Old English word (docce).]

doc·tor (dŏk′tər) **1** person who is licensed to practice medicine or surgery. **2** person who holds the highest degree given by a university. **3** to try to cure: *to* doctor *a cold.* **4** to tamper with: *to* doctor *an account.*

doc·trine (dŏk′trĭn) something taught as the deeply held belief or principles (of a church, political party, or other group of persons): *the* doctrine *of states' rights.*

doc·u·ment (dŏk′yə mənt) an official paper that gives information or proof of something; a record, such as a birth certificate.

dodge (dŏj) **1** to move aside quickly (to avoid something): *to* dodge *through traffic; to* dodge *a blow.* **2** a sudden move aside. **3** to avoid by cunning: *to* dodge *an issue.* **4** a trick: *I know that old* dodge. **dodged, dodg·ing.**

dodge·ball (dŏj′bôl′) game in which a group of players, in a circle, square, or two lines, throw a large ball at another group in the center who try to avoid being hit by it.

do·do (dō′dō) a large bird with very short legs, small wings, and a large hooked beak. Dodoes could not fly. No dodoes are alive today. **do·does** or **do·dos.**

Dodo

doe (dō) the female of the deer, antelope, goat, rabbit, and some other animals. (Homonym: dough)

does (dŭz) See **¹do.** *He* does *what he likes.*

does·n't (dŭz′ənt) does not.

doff (dŏf) take off (a hat, clothing): *Mr. Jones* doffed *his hat in greeting.*

dog (dôg or dŏg) **1** a four-footed, domesticated animal used as a pet, for hunting, tracking, guiding, guarding, and work. **2** a male of the dog, fox, wolf, etc. **3** to follow closely; trail: *to* dog *someone's footsteps.* **dogged, dog·ging.**

dog days a stretch of hot, sultry weather in the summer.

dog-eared (dôg′ird′ or dŏg′ird′) having the corners of the pages turned down or crumpled: *a* dog-eared *book.*

dog·ged (dôg′id or dŏg′id) stubborn; steady; persistent: *The settlers pushed westward with* dogged *courage.* **dog·ged·ly.**

dog·trot (dôg′trŏt′ or dŏg′trŏt′) a slow, gentle trot.

dog·wood (dôg′wŏŏd′ or dŏg′wŏŏd′) shrub or small tree with heavily veined leaves and a "flower" that consists of four white or pink modified leaves surrounding a group of small true flowers which turn into red berries.

Dogwood

doi·ly (doi′lĭ) a small mat of linen, lace, paper, etc., often placed under a vase or the like, on a table, dresser, etc.: *Grandma likes to crochet* doilies. **doi·lies.**

do·ings (dōō′ĭngz) **1** things done; acts. **2** activities; events.

dol·drums (dōl′drəmz or dŏl′drəmz) **1** part of the ocean near the equator with very little wind. **2** gloomy feeling; low spirits.

dole (dōl) **1** to give out in small amounts, often grudgingly. **2** something given in this way. **3** the giving of a portion of money, food, etc., for charity. **doled, dol·ing.**

dole·ful (dōl′fəl) mournful: *a* doleful *wail.* **dole·ful·ly.**

fāte, făt, fâre, fär; bē, bĕt; bite, bĭt; nō, nŏt, nôr; fūse, fŭn, fûr; tōō, tŏŏk; foil; foul; thin; ~~then;~~ hw for wh as in *wh*at; zh for s as in u*s*ual; ə for a, e, i, o, u, as in ag*o*, lin*e*n, per*i*l, at*o*m, min*u*s.

233

doll (dŏl) toy shaped like a baby, child, or grown person.

dol·lar (dŏl'ər) **1** the unit of money in the United States and some other countries. **2** paper note or silver coin equal to 100 cents.

dol·or·ous (dō'lər əs or dŏl'ər əs) sorrowful; mournful; sad: *the* dolorous *news of the lost battle.* **dol·or·ous·ly.**

dol·phin (dŏl'fĭn) a small, toothed whale with a long snout and a hook-shaped fin on its back. Dolphins gather in groups called schools.

Dolphin, 6 to 8 ft. long

do·main (dō mān') **1** lands owned by one person or family; estate. **2** lands under the control of one ruler or government; realm. **3** field or sphere of thought or action: *the* domain *of natural science.*

dome (dōm) **1** a roof or ceiling shaped like an upside-down bowl. **2** a dome-shaped object: *the* dome *of the sky.*

Dome

do·mes·tic (də mĕs'tĭk) **1** having to do with home or household: *a* domestic *chore;* domestic *cares.* **2** of one's own country; native: *Our postal system carries both* domestic *and foreign mail.* **3** tame; not wild: *The dog is a* domestic *animal.* **4** fond of household affairs and family life: *a* domestic *sort of woman.* **5** a household servant.

do·mes·ti·cate (də mĕs'tə kāt') to train (animal or plant) to live under the care of man; tame; cultivate. **do·mes·ti·cat·ed, do·mes·ti·cat·ing.**

dom·i·nant (dŏm'ə nənt) most important; ruling; controlling: *The* dominant *reason for going to school is to learn.* **dom·i·nant·ly.**

dom·i·nate (dŏm'ə nāt') **1** to rule or control by will or strength: *He* dominated *his younger brother.* **2** to rise higher than; to tower over: *The mountain* dominates *the valley.* **dom·i·nat·ed, dom·i·nat·ing.**

dom·i·na·tion (dŏm'ə nā'shən) mastery; rule; control: *the* domination *of a weak country by a strong one.*

Do·min·i·can Re·pub·lic (də mĭn'ə kən rĭ pŭb'lĭk) a country in the West Indies. It occupies the eastern part of the same island as Haiti.

do·min·ion (də mĭn'yən) **1** highest authority; power to govern; rule. **2** territory under a ruler: *the Queen's* dominions.

dom·i·no (dŏm'ə nō') **1** a thin block of wood, bone, or the like, marked with two groups of spots, used in playing a game called dominoes. **2** a loose cloak and a mask covering the upper part of the face, worn at masquerades. **dom·i·noes** or **dom·i·nos.**

Dominoes

¹don (dŏn) to put on; dress in: *The judge* donned *his robe.* **donned, don·ning.** [**¹don** is a contraction of "do on."]

²don (dŏn) **1** Spanish lord or gentleman. **2 Don** Spanish title meaning Sir or Mr. [**²don** is the unchanged form of a Spanish word that goes back to a Latin word (dominus) meaning "master."]

do·nate (dō'nāt) to give; contribute: *to* donate *money to charity.* **do·nat·ed, do·nat·ing.**

do·na·tion (dō nā'shən) a charitable gift; grant; contribution.

done (dŭn) **1** See **¹do.** *Have you* done *your French lesson?* **2** cooked enough: *Is the roast* done *yet?* (Homonym: dun)

don·key (dŭng'kĭ or dŏng'kĭ) **1** animal somewhat like a horse but smaller and having long ears and a tufted tail; an ass. **2** a stupid or stubborn person.

Donkey, 4 to 5 ft. high

do·nor (dō'nər) giver; person who donates: *a blood* donor.

don't (dōnt) do not: *They* don't *know.*

doom (dōōm) **1** terrible fate; ruin; death: *He met his* doom *at the gallows.* **2** to destine: *to be* doomed *to disappointment.* **3** to pronounce sentence against; condemn: *The criminal* doomed *himself by his crime.*

door (dôr) **1** a movable barrier, swinging on hinges or sliding, at the entrance of a house, room, etc. **2** a means of entrance or a way out; a doorway.

door·bell (dôr′bĕl′) bell inside a house or apartment rung by pressing a button or pulling a handle at an outer door to announce a caller.

door·knob (dôr′nŏb′) a handle or knob for opening a door.

door·step (dôr′stĕp′) step or steps leading up to an outside door.

door·way (dôr′wā′) the opening or entrance into a building, house, room, etc., in which a door may be placed.

door·yard (dôr′yärd′) a yard at the entrance of a house: *Lilacs bloomed in the dooryard.*

dope (dōp) **1** narcotic drug. **2** to give such a drug. **3** substance used to airproof or waterproof cloth parts of aircraft. **4** to apply this substance. **doped, dop·ing.**

dor·mant (dôr′mənt) inactive; asleep, or as if asleep: *Some plants lie dormant in the wintertime.*

dor·mer (dôr′mər) **1** an upright window in a sloping roof. **2** structure that contains such a window

Dormer with dormer window

dor·mi·to·ry (dôr′mə-tôr′ĭ) **1** a building containing a number of sleeping rooms. **2** a sleeping room containing a number of beds, especially in schools and institutions. **dor·mi·to·ries.**

dor·mouse (dôr′mous′) a small, hibernating squirrel-like animal of Europe, Asia, and Africa. **dor·mice.**

do·ry (dôr′ĭ) a fishing boat with a narrow, flat bottom and high ends and sides that curve upward and outward. **do·ries.**

dose (dōs) **1** amount of medicine to be taken at one time. **2** to give medicine to. **dosed, dos·ing.**

dost (dŭst) old form of **do,** used with *thou:* "*What* dost *thou here, Elijah?*" (Homonym: dust)

dot (dŏt) **1** a very small rounded spot or speck; a point. **2** to mark with such small spots or points: *Be sure to* dot *your i's.* **3** to be scattered here and there on: *The field was* dotted *with dogwood trees.* **dot·ted, dot·ting.**

dote (dōt) to be weak-minded and foolish from old age.

dote on or **upon** to show a great or excessive love or fondness for: *Grandmother* doted on *all her grandchildren.* **dot·ed, dot·ing.**

doth (dŭth) old form of **does.**

dou·ble (dŭb′əl) **1** twice as much, heavy, strong, etc.: *a* double *portion;* double *work.* **2** twice as much: *Bread costs* double *what it used to.* **3** to make twice as great: *to* double *a sum.* **4** to become twice as great: *The investment* doubled *in value in ten years.* **5** to fold over: *to* double *a paper or blanket.* **6** for two things, people, or purposes: *a* double *bed.* **7** in pairs; of two identical parts: *with* double *doors.* **8** combining two different things, kinds, etc.: *His remark had a* double *meaning.* **9** a thing or person that matches or looks like another: *He's your* double. **10** to be a substitute; take the place (of): *Jane* doubled *for her sister waiting on customers.* **11** by twos; in a pair: *to sit* double *on a seat.* **12** a two-base hit in baseball. **13** having more than a single row of petals: *a* double *nasturtium.* **14** doubles in tennis, a game with two players on each side.

double back to turn and retrace a course.

double up 1 to bend over (in laughter or pain). **2** to share a room, a desk, or the like with someone.

dou·bled, dou·bling; dou·bly.

dou·blet (dŭb′lĭt) a fitted jacket worn by men from about 1400 to about 1650.

dou·bloon (dŭb loon′) a Spanish gold coin of former times, worth about $5.

dou·bly (dŭb′lĭ) in twice the quantity or degree; in a twofold manner: *to be* doubly *pleased.*

Doublet

doubt (dout) **1** to be uncertain (in opinion) or undecided: *I* doubt *whether they will come.* **2** a state of uncertainty; difficulty of believing: *grave* doubts *as to our safety.* **3** to question; distrust: *I* doubt *his honesty.* **4 no doubt** or **without doubt** certainly; without question.

---

fāte, făt, fâre, fär; bē, bĕt; bīte, bĭt; nō, nŏt, nôr; fūse, fŭn, fûr; tōō, tŏŏk; foil; foul; thin; ~~then~~;
hw for wh as in *wh*at; zh for s as in u*s*ual; ə for a, e, i, o, u, as in *a*go, lin*e*n, per*i*l, at*o*m, min*u*s

doubtful

doubt·ful (dout′fəl) **1** of uncertain meaning, character, truth, etc.; questionable: *a doubtful act; a doubtful statement.* **2** full of doubt; feeling doubt; uncertain: *The driver was doubtful as to which turn to take.* **doubt·ful·ly.**

doubt·less (dout′lis) certainly; assuredly: *He will doubtless be late.* **doubt·less·ly.**

dough (dō) thick mixture of flour, water or milk, and other ingredients for baking into bread, cake, etc. (Homonym: doe)

dough·nut (dō′nŭt′) a small cake of sweetened dough, often in the shape of a ring, fried in deep fat.

douse (dous) **1** to plunge into water or other liquid; soak; wet completely. **2** to throw water over; drench: *Father doused the children with the hose.* **doused, dous·ing.**

¹dove (dŭv) bird of the pigeon family. [¹**dove** seems to be from an Old Norse word (dufa).]

²dove (dōv) See dive. *He dove into the water.* [²**dove** is a form of **dive.**]

dow·dy (dou′dĭ) shabby; without style; badly dressed: *a dowdy woman.* **dow·di·er, dow·di·est; dow·di·ly.**

dow·el (dou′əl) a pin or rod used to join two pieces of material by fitting into holes in each piece.

Dowel

¹down (doun) **1** in, at, to, or into a lower place, state, or condition: *to fall down; to slow down; to calm down; to be down.* **2** from a higher to a lower point on: *to row down the stream.* **3** from an earlier to a later time: *The name John was handed down in the Green family.* **4** from a larger to a smaller quantity: *to boil down the jelly.* **5** ill; inactive: *The boy was down with the mumps.* **6** upon paper: *to put down a telephone number.* **7** to defeat; subdue: *to down an enemy.* **8** in a serious way: *to get down to work.* **9** in cash; at once: *The price is $12 down, the rest in weekly payments.* **10 down and out** of a person, penniless and friendless. **11 down on** bearing a grudge against: *Why are you down on Eric?* [¹**down** is from an Old English word (adūne) meaning "from the hill." It is related to ³**down** and **dune.**]

²down (doun) **1** the first feathers of young birds. **2** the soft under feathers of birds:

dowry

a pillow of down. **3** soft fuzz or hair: *the down of a peach.* [²**down** is a form of an earlier English word (doun) that goes back to an Old Norse word (dūnn).]

³down (doun) open, grassy, rolling country. [³**down**, from an Old English word (dūn) meaning "hill," is related to **dune.**]

down- prefix meaning "down."

down·cast (doun′kăst′) **1** sad; discouraged: *The team was downcast over the loss of the game.* **2** directed toward the ground or downward: *with downcast eyes.*

down·fall (doun′fôl′) **1** a fall from rank, reputation, or prosperity; ruin; disgrace: *His downfall was caused by his dishonesty.* **2** a fall: *a downfall of rain.*

down·heart·ed (doun′här′tĭd) sad; unhappy; downcast: *He was downhearted over his failure.* **down·heart·ed·ly.**

down·hill (doun′hĭl′) **1** down a slope; downward: *He went downhill on his sled.* **2** going downward; descending: *a downhill ride.*

down·pour (doun′pôr′) heavy rain.

down·right (doun′rīt′) **1** complete; thorough: *a downright shame; a downright lie.* **2** straightforward; plain: *a downright manner.* **3** completely: *He is downright mean.*

down·stairs (doun′stârz′) **1** to or on a lower floor; below stairs: *She's going downstairs to the kitchen.* **2** on a lower floor: *a downstairs room.* **3** lower floor or floors.

down·stream (doun′strēm′) in the direction of the current or flow of the stream: *We waded downstream.*

down·town (doun′toun′) in or toward the business center or lower part of a city: *Father's office is downtown.*

down·ward (doun′wərd) **1** toward a lower place: *the downward flight of a bird; to fly downward.* **2** from an earlier time: *to come downward through the ages.* **3** declining; tending towards a lower condition or state: *a downward career.*

down·wards (doun′wərdz) downward: *The bird flew downwards.*

down·y (dou′nĭ) **1** made of or covered with soft feathers, hair, wool, down, etc.: *a downy baby bird.* **2** soft; fluffy. **down·i·er, down·i·est.**

dow·ry (dou′rĭ) the money or property a woman brings to her husband at marriage. **dow·ries.**

dox·ol·o·gy (dŏks ŏl′ə jĭ) any of certain hymns in praise of God. One doxology begins with the line: "Praise God from whom all blessings flow." **dox·ol·o·gies.**

doz. dozen.

doze (dōz) **1** to sleep lightly: *Father dozed in his chair.* **2** a light sleep; a nap. **dozed, doz·ing.**

doz·en (dŭz′ən) 12; group of 12.

Dr. Doctor.

drab (drăb) **1** dull; uninteresting: *a drab existence.* **2** a dull grayish-brown color. **drab·ber, drab·best; drab·ly.**

draft or **draught** (drăft) **1** a drawing, plan, or design: *a draft for an engine.* **2** to draw the outlines or plan of. **3** first form or outline: *He made several drafts of his speech before he had it ready.* **4** a current of air: *a draft from an open window.* **5** a device for controlling the air that comes into a stove, furnace, etc. **6** a written order for payment or drawing out of money: *a bank* draft. **7** a method for taking men for military service. **8** to select men for some special service: *The army drafts young men.* **9** the pulling of a load (by beasts): *Oxen are used for* draft. **10** used for pulling loads: *fine* draft *horses.* **11** a drink: *a draft of water.* **12** drawn from a container such as a keg: *cold draft beer.* **13** a catch of fish. **14** the depth of water needed to float a boat.

drag (drăg) **1** to draw or pull along with force; haul: *The woodsmen dragged the heavy log by a chain.* **2** to search the bottom of (a river or lake) for sunken objects: *They will drag the lake today.* **3** a device for searching the bottom of a river or lake. **4** to move or go slowly: *The time dragged on. Tommy dragged behind the big boys.* **5** to trail on the ground: *Her skirt dragged.* **6** anything that hinders or slows down: *Geoffrey is lazy and a drag on the job.* **dragged, drag·ging.**

drag·gle (drăg′əl) **1** to become wet or soiled by trailing in the mud or along the damp ground. **2** to follow slowly: *They draggled at the end of the procession.* **drag·gled, drag·gling.**

drag·net (drăg′nĕt′) **1** a net for drawing along the bottom of a river, pond, etc.

2 a police hunt into which every resource is brought into play.

drag·on (drăg′ən) a large, imaginary, fire-breathing, winged reptile.

drag·on·fly (drăg′ən-fli′) slender insect with four gauzy wings and a long, green, blue, or brown body, usually found near water. **drag·on·flies.**

Dragon

dra·goon (drə gōōn′) **1** heavily armed mounted soldier; cavalryman. **2** to force (someone into doing something): *The enemy dragooned the peasant into doing slave labor.*

Dragonfly

drain (drān) **1** to draw off gradually: *They drained the water from the river.* **2** to draw off liquid from: *to drain a swamp; to drain a wound.* **3** pipe, ditch, sewer, etc., for carrying away unwanted liquids: *a street* drain; *a kitchen* drain. **4** to become dry or empty: *She left the dishes to drain.* **5** to discharge water: *The street drains into the sewer.* **6** to drink to the last drop; to empty: *to drain a pint of cider; to drain one's last glass.* **7** to use up; exhaust: *The country was drained by the war.* **8** something that uses up slowly: *Holding two jobs is a drain on his strength.*

drain·age (drā′nĭj) **1** a drawing off or flowing off of water or waste: *the drainage of a piece of land.* **2** system of pipes for drawing off water. **3** material that drains away.

drake (drāk) male duck.

dra·ma (drăm′ə or dräm′ə) **1** story written in conversation form, to be acted on a stage; a play. **2** events that have the interest and excitement of a play. **3 the drama** the art of writing or producing plays.

dra·mat·ic (drə măt′ĭk) **1** having to do with plays or the study of plays. **2** having the exciting quality of a play: *the dramatic events of the Civil War.* **3 dramatics** the art of performing or producing plays.

---

fāte, făt, fâre, fär; bē, bĕt; bīte, bĭt; nō, nŏt, nôr; fūse, fŭn, fûr; tōō, tŏŏk; foil; foul; thin; then; hw for wh as in *wh*at; zh for s as in u*s*ual; ə for a, e, i, o, u, as in *a*go, lin*e*n, per*i*l, at*o*m, min*u*s

dra·mat·i·cal·ly (drə măt′ĭk ə lĭ) in a dramatic way.

dram·a·tist (drăm′ə tĭst) person who writes plays; playwright.

dram·a·ti·za·tion (dră′mə tĭ zā′shən) **1** the turning (of a story) into a play or movie: *the* dramatization *of "Moby Dick."* **2** play or movie made from a story: *That movie is the* dramatization *of a novel of the same name.*

dram·a·tize (drăm′ə tīz′) **1** to make into a play: *to* dramatize *a novel.* **2** to make dramatic, vivid, or spectacular: *The newspaper* dramatized *the wedding.* **dram·a·tized, dram·a·tiz·ing.**

drank (drăngk) See **drink.** *Alice in Wonderland* drank *the contents of the bottle.*

drape (drāp) **1** to cover with cloth: *She* draped *the painting so it would not get dusty.* **2** to arrange or hang (cloth) in folds: *She* draped *her coat around her.* **3** curtain; hanging cloth: *There are* drapes *on the living room windows.* **draped, drap·ing.**

dra·per·y (drā′pə rĭ) **1** artistic arrangement of a fabric or garment so that it falls in loose, graceful folds. **2** the fabric so used. **drap·er·ies.**

dras·tic (drăs′tĭk) very forceful; having a powerful effect: *to take* drastic *measures; a* drastic *remedy.*

draught (drăft) draft.

draw (drô) **1** to pull or drag: *Horses* draw *carts.* **2** to pull out; haul up: *to* draw *water from a well.* **3** to move: *to* draw *near; to* draw *away.* **4** to attract; cause to come toward: *Flowers* draw *bees.* **5** to be moved: *The wagon* draws *easily.* **6** to form a picture, likeness, or diagram with pen or pencil, chalk, etc. **7** to extract; bring out: *to* draw *a cork; to* draw *a gun.* **8** to take out: *to* draw *money from the bank; to* draw *a card.* **9** to get; receive: *to* draw *a salary; to* draw *interest; to* draw *facts from a book.* **10** to write out: *to* draw *a check.* **11** to close: *to* draw *the curtains.* **12** to require a certain depth in which to float: *The boat* draws *fifteen feet.* **13** to make a current of air pass: *The furnace* draws *well.* **14** a tie; game in which neither side wins. **15** to breathe in; inhale: *to* draw *a deep breath.* **16** to bring forth: *to* draw *applause or tears.*
draw out 1 to make (a person) talk: *to* draw out *the shy girl.* **2** to extend; prolong: *to* draw out *a speech.*

draw up 1 to write in legal form: *to* draw up *a will.* **2** to stop: *The carriage* drew up *at the gate.*
drew, drawn, draw·ing.

draw·back (drô′băk′) disadvantage; hindrance: *It is a* drawback *not to have binoculars at the races.*

draw·bridge (drô′brĭj′) a bridge that can be raised or turned to prevent someone from crossing it (as in old castles) or to permit boats to pass (as on a river).

Medieval drawbridge

¹draw·er (drô′ər) person who draws: *a* drawer *of water.*

²draw·er (drôr) **1** box (with handles) that slides in and out of a bureau, table, etc. **2 drawers** an undergarment for the lower part of the body.

draw·ing (drô′ĭng) **1** a dragging, pulling, etc. (of something): *the* drawing *of a load; the* drawing *of a gun.* **2** picture or sketch made with pen, pencil, chalk, etc. **3** the art of making such a picture.

drawing room room for receiving and entertaining guests; living room or parlor.

drawl (drôl) **1** to speak in a lazy, drawn-out way. **2** a lazy, slow manner of speaking.

drawn (drôn) **1** left undecided: *Even though the game was* drawn, *they did not continue to play.* **2** twisted out of shape; haggard: *a face* drawn *with pain; to look* drawn *after an illness.* **3** See **draw.** *The horses had* drawn *the heavy load all day.*

dray (drā) low, strong cart without sides, for carrying heavy loads.

dread (drĕd) **1** to look forward to with fear: *He* dreads *going to the dentist.* **2** fear, especially of harm to come: *his* dread *of storms.* **3** causing fear, terror, or awe: *a* dread *ruler;* dread *omens.*

dread·ful (drĕd′fəl) **1** terrible; causing fear or awe: *a* dreadful *hurricane.* **2** very bad; unpleasant: *a* dreadful *mistake.*

dread·ful·ly (drĕd′fə lĭ) **1** in a dreadful manner. **2** very; extremely: *I am* dreadfully *sorry.*

dream (drēm) **1** something felt, thought, or seen during sleep. **2** to think, feel, or see during sleep; have dreams. **3** something pleasant imagined when awake; daydream: *his* dreams *of untold wealth.* **4** to imagine or hope for: *to* dream *of a better day.* **5** to suppose; think of (a thing) as possible: *He never dreamed he would win first prize.* **dreamed** or **dreamt, dream·ing.**

dream·er (drē′mər) **1** person who has dreams. **2** person who plans and thinks about things that are impractical.

dreamt (drĕmt) See **dream.** *She* dreamt *that she was a movie star.*

dream·y (drē′mĭ) **1** like a dream; dim; vague: *a* dreamy *recollection.* **2** likely to daydream often; impractical: *a* dreamy *person.* **dream·i·er, dream·i·est; dream·i·ly.**

drear (drĭr) a poetic word for **dreary.**

drear·y (drĭr′ĭ) gloomy; cheerless; causing low spirits: *a* dreary *day.* **drear·i·er, drear·i·est; drear·i·ly.**

dredge (drĕj) **1** a boat equipped with machinery to deepen ship channels, clean harbors, etc. **2** to dig out; deepen: *The government will* dredge *the river.* **3** device with a net, used for gathering shellfish. **4** to scoop up or gather with a dredge. **dredged, dredg·ing.**

Dredge

dregs (drĕgz) **1** what is found at the bottom of a liquid after it has been standing: *the* dregs *of coffee.* **2** worthless part of anything: *the* dregs *of society.*

drench (drĕnch) to soak; to wet thoroughly: *We were* drenched *to the skin in the storm last night.*

dress (drĕs) **1** outer garment worn by a woman, girl, or child. **2** clothes; attire. **3** to put clothes on. **4** to put on formal clothes: *Do we have to* dress *for the reception?* **5** to wear clothes: *He* dresses *well.* **6** any outer covering: *birds in winter* dress. **7** to treat; prepare: *to* dress *a wound; to* dress *meat.* **8** to arrange; straighten: *to* dress *hair.* **9** to decorate; deck out: *to* dress *a store window; to* dress *a ship with flags.* **dress down** to scold severely.

dress up to put on one's best clothes.

¹dress·er (drĕs′ər) chest of drawers, often with a mirror. [**¹dresser** is from an Old French word (dresseur) which was formed from another French word (dresser) meaning "make straight," "arrange."]

²dress·er (drĕs′ər) **1** person who assists another to dress; a valet: *He is a* dresser *in a theater.* **2** person who dresses something: *a* dresser *of leather; a* dresser *of wounds; a window* dresser. **3** person who dresses (in a certain way): *He is a flashy* dresser. [**²dresser** is formed from **dress.**]

dress·ing (drĕs′ĭng) **1** a sauce for salads. **2** stuffing for a roast fowl. **3** bandage and medicine for a wound.

dress·mak·er (drĕs′mā′kər) person whose work is making clothes for women and children.

dress·y (drĕs′ĭ) **1** wearing showy, elaborate clothes. **2** smart; fashionable: *a* dressy *social event.* **dress·i·er, dress·i·est.**

drew (drōō) See **draw.** *She* drew *a picture.*

drib·ble (drĭb′əl) **1** to fall or let fall in drops; trickle: *Water is* dribbling *from the leaky faucet.* **2** to drip saliva from the mouth; to drool: *A baby* dribbles *when it's teething.* **3** a dripping; trickle. **4** a light rain; drizzle. **5** to move by rapid bouncing along a floor: *to* dribble *a basketball.* **6** to move by slight kicks or shoves: *to* dribble *a soccer ball.* **drib·bled, drib·bling.**

drib·let (drĭb′lĭt) small amount; bit: *He repaid his debts in* driblets.

dried (drĭd) **1** See **dry.** *She* dried *the dishes.* **2** with the moisture removed: *sweet* dried *prunes.*

dri·er or **dry·er** (drī′ər) **1** person or thing that removes moisture. **2** machine that removes water by the use of heat or air: *a clothes* drier. **3** substance added to paint or varnish to make it dry more quickly.

dries (drīz) See **dry.** *This shirt* dries *fast.*

drift (drĭft) **1** to be carried along by wind or water: *The log* drifted *downstream.* **2** to drive into heaps: *Strong winds* drifted *the snow.* **3** heap of snow, sand, leaves, etc., piled up by the wind or water: *buried in* drifts *of sand.* **4** slow movement caused by air or water currents: *the* drift *of floating matter.* **5** direction of drift: *the easterly*

fāte, făt, fâre, fär; bē, bĕt; bite, bĭt; nō, nŏt, nôr; fūse, fŭn, fûr; tōō, tŏŏk; foil; foul; thin; ~~then~~; hw for wh as in *wh*at; zh for s as in u*s*ual; ə for a, e, i, o, u, as in *a*go, lin*e*n, per*i*l, at*o*m, min*u*s

239

drift *of the abandoned ship.* **6** to be carried aimlessly along by circumstances: *Some people* drift *through life.* **7** meaning; tendency; *I couldn't get the* drift *of his speech.*

drift·wood (drift'wo͞od') wood washed ashore by the tide.

drill (drĭl) **1** a boring tool for making holes in wood, metal, or other hard substances. **2** to bore holes. **3** to teach or improve by repeated exercise or practice: *The sergeant* drills *soldiers. The teacher* drills *her pupils in spelling.* **4** to undergo training: *They* drilled *in the hot sun.* **5** training; practice; exercise: *We have spelling* drill.

Drill

drink (drĭngk) **1** to swallow a liquid. **2** any liquid to be swallowed; beverage: *a cold* drink. **3** to drink alcoholic liquor: *A man who* drinks *should not drive a car.* **4** to suck in; absorb: *Plants* drink *water.* **5** the quantity of liquid swallowed: *a* drink *of iced coffee.*

  drink in to receive through the senses: *to* drink in *beautiful scenery.*

  drank, drunk, drink·ing.

drip (drĭp) **1** to fall or let fall in drops: *Water* drips *from the trees. The spigot* drips. **2** a falling in drops: *a steady* drip *from the roof.* **dripped, drip·ping.**

drive (drīv) **1** to put in motion and guide; steer: *to* drive *a car;* drive *a train.* **2** to make move: *to* drive *a herd of cattle.* **3** to move by hitting: *to* drive *a golf ball; to* drive *a nail.* **4** a swift hard blow or hit: *a* drive *to left field.* **5** trip in an automobile or carriage: *a* drive *in the country.* **6** to go or carry in a driven vehicle: *We* drove *home. My brother will* drive *me to the station.* **7** a road for vehicles: *a winding* drive *from the gates to the house.* **8** to urge forward or along by force; overwork: *to* drive *a person to do a task.* **9** to carry through forcefully; conclude: *to* drive *a bargain.* **10** effort to carry out some purpose; campaign: *a clothing* drive. **11** forceful effort; energy: *a man of* drive *and ambition.* **12** to force into a particular state or action: *This incessant noise* drives *me mad. Ambition* drove *him to success.*

  drive at to mean; intend: *He* dropped *hints, but I don't know what he's* driving *at.*

  drove, driv·en, driv·ing.

driv·en (drĭv'ən) See **drive.** *He has* driven *a car for ten years.*

driv·er (drī'vər) **1** person who drives a vehicle or animal. **2** person who overworks people who are under him: *a slave* driver. **3** a golf club with a wooden head.

drive·way (drīv'wā') path for automobiles, leading from a garage or house to the street.

driz·zle (drĭz'əl) **1** to rain slightly. **2** a fine, misty rain. **driz·zled, driz·zling.**

droll (drōl) amusing and strange; quaint; odd: *The children were amused by the old man's* droll *stories.* **drol·ly.**

drom·e·dar·y (drŏm'ə dĕr'ĭ) a swift, one-humped camel used for riding rather than for burden-bearing. **drom·e·dar·ies.**

Dromedary, 7 ft. high

drone (drōn) **1** to make a dull, monotonous sound; hum: *The airplanes* droned *overhead.* **2** monotonous tone; humming: *the* drone *of mosquitoes.* **3** to speak or read in a monotonous tone: *A few people fell asleep as the speaker* droned *on.* **4** the male of the honeybee, which produces no honey and does no work. **5** a lazy person who does not do his share of the work; idler. **6** an airplane without a pilot. It is controlled from the ground and is used for target practice or to dump explosives on the enemy. **droned, dron·ing.**

drool (dro͞ol) **1** to let saliva run from the mouth. **2** saliva.

droop (dro͞op) **1** to sink, bend, or hang down: *The flowers are* drooping *with the heat. The child's head* drooped *drowsily.* **2** to weaken; languish: *His spirits* drooped. **3** a hanging down; a drooping: *a* droop *in a hem; a* droop *of the head.*

drop (drŏp) **1** to fall or let fall: *The apple* dropped *to the ground. I* dropped *a glass.* **2** sudden fall or descent: *a* drop *in prices.* **3** distance of a fall or descent: *There is a 60-foot* drop *off the cliff.* **4** small, rounded mass of liquid or something shaped like it: *a* drop *of water; a chocolate* drop. **5** to fall or let fall in drops: *Tears* dropped *from her eyes. He* dropped *his medicine in his eyes.* **6** a small quantity: *There's not a* drop *of*

truth in the story. **7** to knock down (with a blow or shot): *The hunter* dropped *two geese with one shot.* **8** to have no more to do with; end: *to drop a discussion; to drop an acquaintance.* **9** opening through which something may fall: *a letter* drop. **10** to send: *to drop a note to someone.* **11** to express casually: *to drop a hint or suggestion.* **12** to make or become lower: *She* dropped *her voice to a whisper. The temperature* dropped *overnight.* **13** to set down from a vehicle; leave: *Where shall we* drop *you?* **14 a drop in the bucket** tiny portion of what is needed: *The amount we have collected is just* a drop in the bucket. **15 let (something) drop** to let slip, as a secret.
drop behind to fall behind: *Jesse* dropped behind *on the hike when he became too tired to keep up.*
drop in, over, or **by** to visit informally: *Do* drop in *for tea on Sunday.*
drop off to fall asleep: *Timmy* dropped off *right away.*
drop through to come to nothing.
dropped, drop·ping.

drought or **drouth** (drout or drouth) **1** long period of dry weather. **2** absence of moisture; dryness.

¹drove (drōv) See **drive.** *We* drove *home late.* [**¹drove** is a form of **drive.**]

²drove (drōv) **1** a herd of animals driven in a group: *a* drove *of oxen.* **2** a crowd of people: *Visitors came to the fair in* droves. [**²drove** is a form of an Old English word (drāf) also meaning "herd."]

dro·ver (drō′vər) **1** a person who drives cattle, sheep, etc., to market. **2** a cattle dealer.

drown (droun) **1** to die from having the breath cut off while in water or other liquid. **2** to kill by keeping under water. **3** to overpower: *Their chatter* drowned *the music.*

drowse (drouz) to be half asleep: *He* drowsed *while at his studies.* **drowsed, drows·ing.**

drow·sy (drou′zĭ) **1** sleepy; inclined to sleep: *Everyone felt* drowsy *after the feast.* **2** making one sleepy: *the* drowsy *sound of rain.* **drow·si·er, drow·si·est; drow·si·ly.**

drudge (drŭj) **1** a person who does hard, tiresome, uninteresting work; a slave. **2** to work hard at disagreeable tasks; slave away. **drudged, drudg·ing.**

drudg·er·y (drŭj′ə rĭ) hard, disagreeable, uninteresting work: *a life spent in* drudgery. **drudg·er·ies.**

drug (drŭg) **1** a medicine, or substance used in making medicine. **2** a substance used to lessen pain or cause sleep. **3** to make dull or sleepy with such a substance: *to* drug *a patient before an operation.* **4** a habit-forming substance. **5** to put drugs in (in order to stupefy or poison): *to* drug *a person's tea.* **drugged, drug·ging.**

drug·gist (drŭg′ĭst) **1** a person who prepares and sells drugs; pharmacist. **2** one who owns a drugstore.

drug·store (drŭg′stôr′) store where medicines are sold. It often sells cosmetics, magazines, and other items as well.

drum (drŭm) **1** a musical instrument consisting of a hollow cylinder, etc., with skin stretched tightly over one or both ends. **2** to play upon a drum. **3** to tap monotonously with the fingers or feet: *Lester* drummed *idly on his desk.* **4** a drum-shaped container: *an oil* drum. **5** the inner part of the ear or the membrane in it. **6** to make a hollow noise by flapping the wings rapidly. **7** to force into by repetition: *Father finally* drummed *the idea into my head.* **drummed, drum·ming.**

Kettle drum

Snare drum

drum·mer (drŭm′ər) **1** person who plays the drum. **2** a traveling salesman.

drum·stick (drŭm′stĭk′) **1** stick for beating a drum. **2** the lower part of the leg of a cooked fowl.

drunk (drŭngk) **1** overcome by alcohol; intoxicated. **2** overcome; excited beyond reason: *to be* drunk *with power;* drunk *with joy.* **3** a person who is under the effects of alcohol. **4** See **drink.** *The camels had* drunk *enough water to last the trip.*

drunk·ard (drŭngk′ərd) person who has the habit of getting drunk.

fāte, făt, fâre, fär; bē, bĕt; bīte, bĭt; nō, nŏt, nôr; fūse, fŭn, fûr; tōō, tŏŏk; foil; foul; thin; then; hw for wh as in *wh*at; zh for s as in u*s*ual; ə for a, e, i, o, u, as in *a*go, linen, peril, atom, minus

241

drunk·en (drŭngk'ən) **1** overcome by alcohol: *a drunken man.* **2** caused by drink: *a drunken rage;* drunken *sleep.* **drunk·en·ly.**

dry (drī) **1** not wet or moist: *the dry air;* dry *eyes.* **2** having little or no rainfall: *India has a dry season and a rainy season.* **3** not under or in water: *They pulled the boat onto dry land.* **4** empty of its water supply; drained away: *a dry river; a dry well.* **5** thirsty: *He felt dry after working in the sun.* **6** to make or become dry: *They dried the puppy with a large towel. The road dried rapidly.* **7** quiet, but shrewd: *The joke was made funnier by the dry manner in which he told it.* **8** unsweetened: *a dry wine.* **9** harsh: *He has a dry cough.* **10** uninteresting; dull: *a dry book.* **11** of solid, rather than liquid, substances: *a dry measure.* **dri·er, dri·est; dries, dried, dry·ing.**

dry cell a sealed electric cell in which the opposite poles (negative and positive) are separated by a paste rather than a liquid.

dry·er (drī'ər) a drier.

dry goods cloth, laces, ribbons, etc.

dry·ly (drī'lī) quietly but shrewdly.

dry measure a system for measuring dry things, in which two pints equal a quart, eight quarts equal a peck, and four pecks equal a bushel.

dry·ness (drī'nĭs) a being dry.

du·al (dōō'əl or dū'əl) double; having two parts: *under* dual *ownership; a* dual *purpose.* **du·al·ly.** (Homonym: duel)

dub (dŭb) **1** to make a man a knight by touching the shoulder with a sword. **2** to give a title or nickname to: *The lion has been dubbed "King of Beasts."* **dubbed, dub·bing.**

du·bi·ous (dōō'bĭ əs or dū'bĭ əs) **1** doubtful: *a dubious venture;* dubious *compliment* **2** of questionable character: *a dubious friend.* **du·bi·ous·ly.**

duch·ess (dŭch'ĭs) **1** wife or widow of a duke. **2** a woman who rules a duchy.

duch·y (dŭch'ĭ) lands governed by a duke or duchess. **duch·ies.**

Mallard duck, about 2 ft. long

¹duck (dŭk) **1** any of several wild and tame waterfowl smaller than a goose and having a shorter neck.

2 female duck. **3** flesh of the duck, used as food. [**¹duck** is a form of an Old English word (dūce) meaning "a bird that dives."]

²duck (dŭk) **1** to dive under water and come up quickly. **2** to plunge a person's head in water: *The bathers laughingly* ducked *one another.* **3** to lower the head or bend the body suddenly: *to duck under low branches.* **4** to avoid: *to duck a question.* **5** a ducking. [**²duck** is a form of an earlier Old English word (douke).]

³duck (dŭk) **1** coarse linen or cotton cloth used for outer clothing, tents, sails, and awnings. **2** ducks trousers made of duck. [**³duck** is from a Dutch word (doek) meaning "cloth."]

duck·bill (dŭk'bĭl') Australian egg-laying, water-loving, furry animal with webbed feet and a bill like that of a duck. Also called **platypus.**

Duckbill, about 20 in. long

duck·ling (dŭk'lĭng) young duck.

duct (dŭkt) **1** a tube or canal for carrying a gas or a liquid. **2** a pipe through which wires or cables are led.

dude (dōōd or dūd) **1** a man who is too concerned with his clothing or appearance. **2** in western United States, a tourist, especially one from the East, who visits a ranch.

due (dōō or dū) **1** owed; payable: *a fine is due on the library book.* **2** proper or fit; appropriate: *They showed due respect to the distinguished visitor.* **3** required or expected to arrive: *The plane is due in ten minutes.* **4** directly; exactly: *The ship traveled due north.* **5** that which is owed; that which must be given to another: *Pay the man his due.* **6** dues a fee or charge, as for membership in a club. **7** due to owing to; caused by: *The poor harvest was due to the lack of rainfall.* **8** fall due to become payable. **9** in due course in good time; at the proper time. (Homonyms: do, dew)

du·el (dōō'əl or dū'əl) **1** a private fight arranged according to rules between two persons, with swords or pistols, in the presence of witnesses called **seconds.** **2** any contest between two opponents: *The rival politicians had a duel of words.* **3** to fight a duel. (Homonym: dual)

du·et (dōō ĕt′ or dū ĕt′) musical composition for two voices or instruments.

dug (dŭg) See **dig**. *He dug a hole.*

dug·out (dŭg′out′) **1** hole dug out of a hillside or in the ground and roofed over with logs, sod, etc., to form a shelter. **2** canoe or boat made by hollowing out a tree trunk.

duke (dōōk or dūk) **1** ruler of a duchy. **2** in Great Britain, a nobleman who ranks next below a prince.

duke·dom (dōōk′dəm or dūk′dəm) the territory ruled by a duke.

dull (dŭl) **1** not sharp or pointed: *a dull pencil; a dull razor; a dull pain.* **2** stupid; slow to learn or understand: *a dull boy; a dull student.* **3** not interesting: *a dull book.* **4** not clear or bright; vague: *a dull yellow; a dull suit; a dull sound.* **5** not lively: *a dull party; a dull look.* **6** not active: *Business is dull this summer.* **7** to make dull: *to dull the pain; to dull the blade; to be dulled by sorrow.* **dul·ly.**

dull·ard (dŭl′ərd) stupid or slow-witted person.

dull·ness (dŭl′nĭs) a being dull.

du·ly (dōō′lĭ or dū′lĭ) in a suitable and proper way: *The new officers were duly sworn in.*

dumb (dŭm) **1** unable to speak: *a deaf and dumb person.* **2** not having the gift of speech: *our dumb animal friends.* **3** not speaking; silent: *He remained dumb.* **4** stupid. **dumb·ly.**

dumb·bell (dŭm′bĕl′) an exercising device consisting of two wood or metal balls connected by a bar.   **Dumbbell**

dumb·found or **dum·found** (dŭm found′) to make speechless with surprise or fear; amaze.

dum·my (dŭm′ĭ) **1** a person who seems to lack the power of speech. **2** a stupid or thick-witted person. **3** an object that looks like and takes the place of a real one: *The soldiers trained with wooden dummies instead of rifles.* **4** sham; make-believe: *a dummy board of directors; a dummy door on the stage.* **5** in bridge, a person whose cards are laid on the table and played by his partner. **dum·mies.**

dump (dŭmp) **1** to let fall in a mass; unload: *to dump sand from a truck.* **2** a place where trash may be thrown out: *the city dump.* **3** a place where military supplies are kept: *an ammunition dump.*

dump·ling (dŭmp′lĭng) **1** dough boiled or steamed and served with meat: *stew with dumplings.* **2** a shell of dough wrapped around a piece of fruit which is then boiled or baked: *apple dumplings.*

¹dun (dŭn) dull grayish-brown. [**¹dun** is a form of the Old English word (dunn).] (Homonym: done)

²dun (dŭn) **1** a demand for the payment of a debt. **2** person who continually demands the payment of a debt. **3** to bother by repeated demands for payment: *The restaurant dunned him for the whole banquet bill.* **dunned, dun·ning.** [**²dun** is in all likelihood a dialect form of **din**.] (Homonym: done)

dunce (dŭns) **1** stupid person. **2** backward pupil.

dune (dōōn or dūn) low sand hill formed by the wind, especially near a shore.   **Dunes**

dun·ga·ree (dŭng′gə rē′) **1** a coarse, cotton material. **2 dungarees** trousers or work clothes made from this material.

dun·geon (dŭn′jən) dark, underground prison.

dupe (dōōp or dūp) **1** person who is easily tricked or believes everything he is told. **2** to deceive by tricking. **duped, dup·ing.**

¹du·pli·cate (dōō′plə kāt′ or dū′plə kāt′) to make an exact or nearly exact copy of: *She duplicated the dress she had admired at the fashion show.* **du·pli·cat·ed, du·pli·cat·ing.**

²du·pli·cate (dōō′plə kĭt or dū′plə kĭt) **1** exactly like another: *a duplicate key.* **2** something that is exactly like another: *This print is a duplicate of the original.* **3** in **duplicate** double; in another copy: *Type this in duplicate.*

du·ra·ble (dōōr′ə bəl or dyōōr′ə bəl) lasting; not wearing out easily: *a durable pair of shoes; a durable friendship.* **du·ra·bly.**

---

fāte, făt, fâre, fär; bē, bĕt, bīte, bit; nō, nŏt, nôr; fūse, fŭn, fûr; tōō, tŏŏk; foil; foul; thin; then;
hw for wh as in *wh*at; zh for s as in u*s*ual; ə for a, e, i, o, u, as in *a*go, lin*e*n, per*i*l, at*o*m, min*u*s

du·ra·tion (dŏŏ rā'shən or dyŏŏ rā'shən) amount of time during which anything lasts: *a storm of short* duration.

dur·ing (dŏŏr'ĭng or dyŏŏr'ĭng) **1** throughout the time of: *We do not go to school* during *the summer.* **2** at some point of time in: *He will telephone me sometime* during *the evening.*

durst (dûrst) old word for **dare.**

dusk (dŭsk) **1** the time of evening between daylight and dark; twilight. **2** darkness; gloom: *in the* dusk *of the forest.*

dusk·y (dŭs'kĭ) **1** somewhat dark in color. **2** lacking light; shadowy. **dus·ki·er, dusk·i·est; dusk·i·ly.**

dust (dŭst) **1** fine, dry particles of earth or other powderlike material: *a cloud of* dust. **2** to brush away or remove dust from: *Susie* dusted *the furniture and then polished it.* **3** to cover or sprinkle (with powder): *She* dusted *the cake with sugar.* **4 bite the dust** to fall in battle; be defeated. **5 throw dust in (someone's) eyes** to mislead; to fool. (Homonym: dost)

dust bowl region from which the top soil blows away in periods of drought.

dust·proof (dŭst'prŏŏf') capable of keeping dust away; protecting from dust.

dust·y (dŭs'tĭ) **1** covered with dust: *a* dusty *attic.* **2** like dust in appearance; powdery. **dust·i·er, dust·i·est.**

Dutch (dŭch) **1** of the Netherlands, its people, or language. **2** the language of the Dutch people. **3 the Dutch** the people of the Netherlands.

du·ti·ful (dŏŏ'tĭ fəl or dū'tĭ fəl) doing one's duty; obedient to parents or superiors. **du·ti·ful·ly.**

du·ty (dŏŏ'tĭ or dū'tĭ) **1** what one ought to do; obligation to do what is right: *a sense of* duty; *a man's* duty *to his country.* **2** service required by one's work or position: *the* duties *of a secretary.* **3** a tax, especially on goods brought into a country: *a* duty *on perfume.* **du·ties.**

dwarf (dwôrf) **1** person, animal, or plant greatly below normal size, often deformed in some way. **2** in fairy tales, a tiny person with unusual powers. **3** to prevent from growing to natural size: *The lack of rain* dwarfed *the flowers.* **4** to make look small by comparison: *The giant redwood* dwarfs *the oak.*

dwell (dwĕl) to live in a place; reside: *The princess* dwells *in yonder castle.*

dwell on to think, speak, or write about at length: *His mind* dwells *on unhappy memories.*

dwelled or **dwelt, dwell·ing.**

dwell·er (dwĕl'ər) person who lives in and makes his home in (some place): *a city* dweller; *a tree* dweller.

dwell·ing (dwĕl'ĭng) house; place of residence.

dwelt (dwĕlt) See **dwell.** *They* dwelt *in a mountain village.*

dwin·dle (dwĭn'dəl) to become smaller or less; to shrink: *The water supply* dwindled *from lack of rain.* **dwin·dled, dwin·dling.**

dye (dī) **1** to give color to material, usually by dipping it into a liquid containing coloring matter: *She* dyed *her dress blue.* **2** a coloring matter. **3** color produced by dyeing. **dyed, dye·ing.** (Homonym: die)

dye·stuff (dī'stŭf') any coloring matter used in dyeing; dye.

dy·ing (dī'ĭng) **1** passing from life: *the last wish of the* dying *man.* **2** said or done at the time of death: *a* dying *wish.* **3** See **die.** *The wounded man was* dying.

dyke (dīk) dike.

dy·nam·ic (dī năm'ĭk) **1** full of energy; forceful: *Brian's success is due to his* dynamic *personality.* **2** having to do with the energy of motion.

dy·na·mite (dī'nə mīt') **1** a mixture of explosives, made up in sticks, for blasting rock, hard earth, etc. **2** to move or break up with dynamite. **dy·na·mit·ed, dy·na·mit·ing.**

dy·na·mo (dī'nə mō') **1** a machine for producing an electric current. **2** a very active person. **dy·na·mos.**

Dynamo

dy·nas·ty (dī'nəs tĭ) a line of kings or rulers who belong to the same family: *Elizabeth I of England belonged to the Tudor* dynasty. **dy·nas·ties.**

dy·sen·ter·y (dĭs'ən tĕr'ĭ) painful disease of the bowels with severe inflammation in which mucus and blood are discharged. Some forms are very contagious.

E

E, e (ē) fifth letter of the English alphabet.

E. **1** east. **2** eastern.

each (ēch) **1** every (individual of two or more considered apart from the rest): *He had* each *student take his turn.* **2** every individual: *He had* each *take his turn.* **3** all (considered one by one): *They* each *took turns.* **4** apiece: *These books are two dollars* each. **5** **each other** each the other.

ea·ger (ē′gər) full of keen desire: *He was* eager *to play football.* **ea·ger·ly.**

ea·gle (ē′gəl) any of several large, sharp-sighted birds of prey. The eagle, because of its power and alertness, is a symbol of the United States.

Bald eagle, about 3 ft. long

¹ear (ir) **1** the part of the body with which animals and men hear. **2** the outside part of the ear, which we can see: *A dachshund has long, drooping ears. A cat has pointed ears that stand up.* **3** attention: *Give* ear *to good advice.* **4** musical sense: *He has no* ear. **5** **be all ears** to listen with all one's attention. [¹ear is a form of an Old English word (ēare) with the same meaning.]

²ear (ir) the seed-bearing head or spike of grain: *an* ear *of wheat; an* ear *of corn.* [²ear is the unchanged form of an Old English word (ear) with the same meaning.]

Ear of corn

ear·ache (ir′āk′) pain in the ear.

ear·drum (ir′drum′) the thin membrane between the outer and middle ear that vibrates when sound waves strike it.

earl (ûrl) British nobleman, below a marquis and above a viscount in rank.

ear·ly (ûr′li) **1** at or near the beginning of: *Snow fell* early *this winter.* **2** before the usual time: *He arrived at school* early.

3 coming or occurring before or near the beginning of the usual time: *Crocuses are* early *spring flowers.* **ear·li·er, ear·li·est.**

earn (ûrn) **1** to receive as payment for service, labor, etc.: *He* earns *a lot of money.* **2** to gain through effort: *He* earned *the office the hard way.* **3** to deserve: *You have* earned *our gratitude.* (Homonym: urn)

ear·nest (ûr′nist) **1** eager and serious; sincere: *He is* earnest *about his studies.* **2** **in earnest** (1) seriously; resolutely: *He set about his task in* earnest. (2) serious: *His plea was in* earnest. **ear·nest·ly.**

earn·ings (ûr′ningz) payment received for services or labor; wages; profits.

ear·phone (ir′fōn′) a telephone or radio receiver held to the ear by a band over the head.

ear·ring (ir′ring′) an ornament worn in or on the lobe of the ear.

ear·shot (ir′shot′) range within which the voice can be heard; hearing distance: *They didn't speak until he was out of* earshot.

earth (ûrth) **1** our planet, third in order of distance from the sun. **2** the world we inhabit: *Peace on* earth, *good will to men.* **3** the people who inhabit it: *All the* earth *rejoices.* **4** the solid matter that composes it; the land: *"The waters covered the face of the* earth." **5** soil; ground: *Some pine trees grow best in sandy* earth. **6** **down to earth** sensible; practical.

earth·en (ûr′thən) **1** made of earth: *an* earthen *rampart.* **2** made of clay hardened by fire: *an* earthen *flower pot.*

earth·en·ware (ûr′thən wâr′) dishes and containers made of clay hardened by fire.

earth·ly (ûrth′li) **1** having to do with this world; not heavenly or spiritual: *our* earthly *goods.* **2** possible; imaginable: *Her idea is of no* earthly *use.* **earth·li·er, earth·li·est.**

earth·quake (ûrth′kwāk′) sudden trembling of the ground, caused by a shifting of rock layers under the earth's surface.

earth·work (ûrth′wûrk′) a wall or hill of earth, piled up for defense.

fāte, făt, fâre, fär; bē, bĕt; bīte, bĭt; nō, nŏt, nôr; fūse, fŭn, fûr; tōō, tŏŏk; foil; foul; thin; then; hw for wh as in *wh*at; zh for s as in u*s*ual; ə for a, e, i, o, u, as in *a*go, lin*e*n, per*i*l, at*o*m, min*u*s

earth·worm (ûrth′wûrm′) a worm that burrows in the soil; an angleworm.

ease (ēz) **1** freedom from pain, toil, or trouble; comfort: *a life of ease.* **2** freedom from difficulty: *The* ease *with which he answered the questions surprised us.* **3** to relieve; lighten: *to ease pain.* **4** to loosen; make less tight: *to ease a dress at the side seams.* **5** to move slowly and carefully: *He* eased *the car into the garage.* **eased, eas·ing.**

ea·sel (ē′zəl) a stand or frame, often with a movable prop at the back, used to hold a picture, or the like, in an upright position.

Easel

eas·i·ly (ē′zə lǐ) **1** without difficulty. **2** comfortably: *to rest* easily. **3** without doubt: *He is* easily *the tallest man here.*

east (ēst) **1** the direction halfway between north and south and generally toward the rising sun; also, the point of the compass indicating this direction; opposite of west. **2** the region or part of a country or continent in this direction: *the* east *of England.* **3 the East** (1) Asia; the Orient. (2) the eastern part of the United States, especially the area from Maine through Maryland. **4** in or to the east: *the* east *side of town.* **5** of winds, from the east. **6** toward the east: *He faced* east. **7 Down East** New England, especially Maine.

East→

East·er (ēs′tər) yearly festival of the Christian Church to celebrate the rising from the dead of Jesus Christ, observed on the first Sunday after the first full moon of spring.

eas·ter·ly (ēs′tər lǐ) **1** eastward. **2** of winds, coming from the east.

east·ern (ēs′tərn) **1** in or toward the east: *an* eastern *port; an* eastern *view.* **2** from the east: *an* eastern *storm.* **3 Eastern** (1) of or in the eastern part of the United States. (2) of or in Asia.

East In·dies (ēst ĭn′dēz) **1** chain of islands between the mainland of Asia and Australia; Malay Archipelago. **2** central and southeastern Asia (India, Burma, Thailand, Cambodia, and the Malay Archipelago).

east·ward (ēst′wərd) to or toward the east.

eas·y (ē′zǐ) **1** not difficult: *This story is* easy *to read.* **2** at peace; free from care or pain: *to be* easy *in one's mind; to rest* easy. **3** comfortable; loose: *The coat was an* easy *fit.* **4** smooth and pleasant: *an* easy *manner.* **5** not strict or demanding: *very* easy *parents; an* easy *teacher.* **eas·i·er, eas·i·est.**

eas·y·go·ing (ē′zǐ gō′ǐng) having a calm temper; not easily excited or annoyed: *an* easygoing *manner.*

eat (ēt) **1** to take into the mouth and swallow, as food. **2** to take meals; dine: *I ate there several times.* **3** to wear or waste (away): *A stream* eats *away land along its bank.* **4** to make a way (into) by wearing away or corroding: *The acid* ate *into the metal.* **ate, eat·en, eat·ing.**

eat·a·ble (ēt′ə bəl) **1** something suitable for food. **2** fit or safe to be eaten; edible.

eat·en (ēt′ən) See **eat**. *Dinner was* eaten *in silence.*

eaves (ēvz) the overhanging edge of a sloping roof.

eaves·drop·per (ēvz′drŏp′-ər) a person who listens unseen to the conversation of others.

Eaves

ebb (ĕb) **1** the flowing back, or fall, of the tide. **2** to flow back; recede: *The tide* ebbed, *leaving the beach covered with shells.* **3** a falling off from a high to a low state; a decline: *the* ebb *of market values.* **4** to weaken; decline: *The wounded soldier's strength* ebbed *day by day.*

eb·on·y (ĕb′ən ǐ) **1** a hard, heavy, black wood. **2** made of ebony. **3** black: *the* ebony *keys of a piano.* **eb·on·ies.**

ec·cen·tric (ĕk sĕn′trĭk) **1** having odd or peculiar habits and manners. **2** an odd or peculiar person. **3** not having the same center, as two circles that partly overlap. **4** turning on an axis that is not at the center, as does a wheel-like part in certain machines. **5** such a part.

ec·cle·si·as·tic (ĭ klē′zǐ ăs′tĭk) **1** clergyman; priest. **2** ecclesiastical.

ec·cle·si·as·ti·cal (ĭ klē′zǐ ăs′tǐ kəl) of or having to do with the church or clergy; clerical: *the bishop's* ecclesiastical *vestments.* **ec·cle·si·as·ti·cal·ly.**

ech·o (ĕk′ō) **1** a repetition of sound, caused by the throwing back of sound waves. **2** to give back or repeat sound; resound: *The hills* echoed *his shouts.* **3** to repeat as an echo: *The shouts* echo. **4** to repeat or imitate the words or actions of another: *He* echoed *his father's opinion.* **echoes; echoed, echo·ing.**

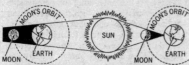

Eclipse of the moon.   Eclipse of the sun.
The eclipse of the sun is seen where
the moon's shadow touches the earth.

e·clipse (ĭ klĭps′) **1** a complete or partial darkening of the sun by the passage of the moon between it and the earth: *an* eclipse *of the sun; a solar* eclipse. **2** a complete or partial darkening of the moon by the shadow of the earth: *an* eclipse *of the moon; a lunar* eclipse. **3** to throw into the shade; outshine: *Alan's latest performance* eclipsed *all his others.* **e·clipsed, e·clips·ing.**

e·co·nom·ic (ē′kə nŏm′ĭk or ĕk′ə nŏm′ĭk) having to do with the production, distribution, and use of wealth: *the* economic *history of the country.*

e·co·nom·i·cal (ē′kə nŏm′ə kəl or ĕk′ə-nŏm′ə kəl) wise in the spending of money and in the use of goods; thrifty. **e·co·nom·i·cal·ly.**

e·co·nom·ics (ē′kə nŏm′ĭks or ĕk′ə nŏm′-ĭks) the science of the production, distribution, and use of wealth.

e·con·o·mize (ĭ kŏn′ə mīz′) **1** to use to the greatest advantage; be thrifty: *We* economized *on gas by putting several things in the oven at the same time.* **2** to cut down expenses: *While her father was out of work, Emily* economized *by buying fewer new dresses.* **e·con·o·mized, e·con·o·miz·ing.**

e·con·o·my (ĭ kŏn′ə mĭ) **1** thrifty use of money, goods, etc. **2** the whole system of producing, distributing, and consuming goods and services of a country: *the national* economy. **e·con·o·mies.**

ec·sta·sy (ĕk′stə sĭ) extreme joy; rapture; bliss. **ec·sta·sies.**

ec·stat·ic (ĕk stăt′ĭk) **1** rapturous; overwhelmed with joy: *The baby was* ecstatic *over Santa Claus.* **2** causing ecstasy.

Ec·ua·dor (ĕk′wə dôr′) a country on the Pacific coast of South America.

-ed 1 suffix meaning "having" or "characterized by": *a bead*ed *bag; lin*ed *paper.* **2** a word ending that shows that an action has taken place: *wash*ed; *tapp*ed.

ed·dy (ĕd′ĭ) **1** current of air or water that runs against the main current, making a circular motion; small whirlwind or whirlpool. **2** to move with a circular motion: *The wind whipped up an* eddy *of dust.* **ed·dies; ed·died, ed·dy·ing.**

edge (ĕj) **1** sharp, cutting side of a blade. **2** rim; border; margin: *the* edge *of a table; the* edge *of a river.* **3** to put a border on: *to* edge *a tablecloth with lace.* **4** to move carefully, little by little: *to* edge *into the water.* **5 on edge** very nervous; impatient. **edged, edg·ing.**

ed·i·ble (ĕd′ə bəl) fit or safe to be used for food: *Some kinds of mushrooms are* edible.

e·dict (ē′dĭkt) command from an official authority that has the strength of a law; a decree.

ed·i·fice (ĕd′ə fĭs) a building, especially one that is large and impressive.

ed·it (ĕd′ĭt) **1** to correct, check, and put into proper style and good English a manuscript offered for publication. **2** to be in charge of the contents of a magazine or a newspaper: *Jonathan Stubbs* edits *our hometown paper.*

e·di·tion (ĭ dĭsh′ən) **1** published form of a written work: *the Oxford* edition *of Shakespeare; an illustrated* edition. **2** all the copies of a book, magazine, or newspaper produced at one printing: *first* edition.

ed·i·tor (ĕd′ĭ tər) **1** person or one of the persons in charge of the contents of a newspaper or magazine. **2** person who selects and prepares literary work for publication.

ed·i·tor·i·al (ĕd′ə tôr′ĭ əl) **1** an article in a newspaper or magazine or a comment on a radio or TV station that gives the views and opinion of the publisher or owner on a public question. **2** having to do with an editor or editing. **ed·i·tor·i·al·ly.**

---

fāte, făt, fâre, fär; bē, bĕt; bīte, bĭt; nō, nŏt, nôr; fūse, fŭn, fûr; tōō, tŏŏk; foil; foul; thin; ~~then~~;
hw for wh as in *wh*at; zh for s as in u*s*ual; ə for a, e, i, o, u, as in *a*go, lin*e*n, per*i*l, at*o*m, min*u*s

ed·u·cate (ĕj′ə kāt′) **1** to teach (a person) or train (the mind). **2** to send to school. **ed·u·cat·ed, ed·u·cat·ing.**

ed·u·ca·tion (ĕj′ə kā′shən) **1** teaching; training; schooling. **2** knowledge and skill gained from training: *His education in the field of science is remarkable.* **3** study of the methods of teaching and learning: *a school of* education.

ed·u·ca·tion·al (ĕj′ə kā′shən əl) **1** having to do with teaching or learning. **2** offering information or knowledge; instructive: *Visiting a museum is very* educational. **ed·u·ca·tion·al·ly.**

eel (ēl) snakelike fish with a smooth, slippery skin.

Eel, 2 to 3 ft. long

e′en (ēn) a poetic word for **even.**

e′er (âr) a poetic word for **ever.** (Homonyms: air; ere; heir)

ee·rie or **ee·ry** (ir′ĭ) causing fear; weird: *the* eerie *sound of the midnight wind.* **ee·ri·er, ee·ri·est; ee·ri·ly.**

ef·face (ĭ fās′) to erase; wipe out; destroy: *Time has effaced the ancient city.*
efface oneself to keep oneself out of sight or in the background.
ef·faced, ef·fac·ing.

ef·fect (ĭ fĕkt′) **1** what happens when something acts on something else: *the effect of a magnet on steel.* **2** to cause; bring about; accomplish: *He tried to effect an end to the quarrel.* **3** impression produced, as by a work of art: *The music created the effect of a wild thunderstorm.* **4 effects** personal possessions; movable goods: *The household effects were sold at auction.* **5 for effect** for show; for the sake of impressing: *to talk for effect.* **6 give effect to** to put into action. **7 take effect** to begin to act or have force. **8 in effect** (1) in actual fact; really: *The fence which was intended to prevent accident,* in effect *increased it.* (2) in force or action.

ef·fec·tive (ĭ fĕk′tĭv) **1** having the power to produce a result, especially a desired result: *an* effective *medicine; an* effective *argument.* **2** in force: *The law is* effective *starting next week.* **ef·fec·tive·ly.**

ef·fec·tu·al (ĭ fĕk′chŏŏ əl) producing or able to produce a desired result. **ef·fec·tu·al·ly.**

ef·fi·ca·cy (ĕf′ə kə sĭ) the power to produce results, especially desired results: *Quinine has real* efficacy *in treating fever.*

ef·fi·cien·cy (ĭ fish′ən sĭ) ability to produce desired results with the least amount of time, expense, and labor.

ef·fi·cient (ĭ fish′ənt) able; competent; able to get desired results with the least output of time, expense, and labor. **ef·fi·cient·ly.**

ef·fort (ĕf′ərt) **1** a putting forth of power (of mind or body); exertion: *With great effort, he held back an angry reply.* **2** a try; an attempt: *The dog made an effort to get through the opening.*

¹egg (ĕg) **1** the oval or round body produced by the females of many animals, from which the young develop. Birds, insects, fish, and most reptiles hatch from eggs. **2 egg cell** living cell produced by female animals and many plants, from which young may develop. [¹egg is from an Old Norse word of the same spelling.]

²egg (ĕg) to urge (on); goad; provoke: *The boys egged him on to fight.* [²egg is from an Old Norse word (eggja) meaning "to give edge."]

egg·plant (ĕg′plănt′) **1** plant that bears a large, oval, purple-skinned fruit. **2** the fruit of this plant eaten as a vegetable.

Eggplant

egg·shell (ĕg′shĕl′) **1** the shell of an egg. **2** very thin and fragile: *a piece of* eggshell *china.* **3** a very light tan color.

e·go (ē′gō or ĕg′ō) **1** one's self. **2** high regard for oneself; conceit: *That actor is known for his ego.* **e·gos.**

e·go·tism (ē′gə tĭz′əm or ĕg′ə tĭz′əm) frequent use of the word "I"; the habit of thinking, talking, or writing too much about oneself; conceit; selfishness: *Such was his* egotism *that he kept steering the discussion to himself.*

e·go·tis·ti·cal (ē′gə tĭs′tĭ kəl or ĕg′ə tĭs′tə kəl) concerned with oneself; conceited. **e·go·tis·ti·cal·ly.**

e·gret (ē′grĭt) a large wading bird of the heron family. During the breeding season it has long, white plumes drooping over the tail.

E·gypt (ē′jĭpt) a country in northeast Africa.

E·gyp·tian (ĭ jĭp′shən) **1** of Egypt, its people, or language. **2** a citizen of Egypt or person of Egyptian descent.

ei·der (ī′dər) large, northern sea duck having soft downy breast feathers.

eider down soft breast feathers of eider ducks, used to stuff pillows, quilts, etc.

eight (āt) amount or quantity that is one greater than seven; 8. (Homonym: ate)

eight·een (ā′tēn′) amount or quantity that is one greater than 17; 18.

eight·eenth (ā′tēnth′) **1** next after 17th; 18th. **2** one of 18 equal parts.

eighth (ātth) **1** next after seventh; 8th. **2** one of eight equal parts.

eight·i·eth (ā′tĭ ith) **1** next after 79th; 80th. **2** one of 80 equal parts.

eight·y (ā′tĭ) amount or quantity that is one greater than 79; 80. **eight·ies.**

ei·ther (ē′thər or ī′thər) **1** one or the other (of two): *They will leave* either *today or tomorrow. You may take* either *seat. He looked at two cars but didn't buy* either. **2** each of two: *Trees were planted on* either *side of the street.* **3** also: *I didn't go, and he didn't go,* either.

e·jac·u·late (ĭ jăk′yŏŏ lāt′) to exclaim; blurt out. **e·jac·u·lat·ed, e·jac·u·lat·ing.**

e·ject (ĭ jĕkt′) to throw out; turn out; force out: *The pilot was* ejected *from the burning plane. The noisy boys were* ejected *from the theater.*

eke out (ēk out) **1** to add to; supplement: *Mother* eked out *the soup with vegetables when she ran out of meat.* **2** to barely make or gain (a living). **eked out, ek·ing out.**

¹**e·lab·o·rate** (ĭ lăb′ə rĭt) carefully worked out in great detail; complicated: *We made* elaborate *decorations for a costume party.* **e·lab·o·rate·ly.**

²**e·lab·o·rate** (ĭ lăb′ə rāt′) to work out with great care and detail: *The general* elaborated *his plan for the campaign.* **elaborate on** to give more details about. **e·lab·o·rat·ed, e·lab·o·rat·ing.**

e·lapse (ĭ lăps′) to go by; pass: *Many days* elapsed *before they returned.* **e·lapsed, e·laps·ing.**

e·las·tic (ĭ lăs′tĭk) **1** capable of springing back to its normal size, shape, or position after being stretched or pressed together. **2** able to recover quickly from depression: *a very* elastic *spirit.* **3** easily stretched; flexible; adaptable. **4** band of cloth made stretchable by rubber threads woven into it. **5** a rubber band.

e·las·tic·i·ty (ĭ lăs′tĭs′ə tĭ or ē′lăs tĭs′ə tĭ) ability to return to former shape, after squeezing or bending, as rubber and some metals do.

e·lat·ed (ĭ lā′tĭd) very happy; overjoyed: *to be* elated *by victory.* **e·lat·ed·ly.**

el·bow (ĕl′bō) **1** the joint in the arm between wrist and shoulder; also, the outer part of the arm at this point: *Eva bumped her* elbow *on the desk.* **2** something bent at an angle, such as a curved section of pipe. **3** to nudge, jostle, or push with the elbow: *The woman* elbowed *the shoppers aside.*

Pipe elbow

eld·er (ĕl′dər) **1** older: *Which is the* elder *sister?* **2** an older or more experienced person: *Young Indians respected the* elders *of the tribe.* **3** an officer of certain churches.

eld·er·ly (ĕl′dər lĭ) somewhat old.

eld·est (ĕl′dĭst) oldest; first born: *the* eldest *child.*

e·lect (ĭ lĕkt′) **1** to choose or select by vote: *The club* elects *officers in May.* **2** to decide; prefer: *Tom* elected *to stay at home last night while his sister went to the movies.* **3** chosen for an office but not yet serving: *the governor-*elect.

e·lec·tion (ĭ lĕk′shən) a choosing or selecting, especially by vote.

e·lec·tor·al (ĭ lĕk′tər əl) **1** having to do with electors or an election. **2 electoral college** in the United States, a group of citizens chosen by the people of each state to elect a President and Vice-president. **3 electoral vote** the vote cast by the members of the electoral college.

e·lec·tric (ĭ lĕk′trĭk) **1** having to do with electricity: *an* electric *current; an* electric *shock; an* electric *train.* **2** thrilling; exciting: *An* electric *quiver ran through the crowd when the band struck up.* **3 electric**

---

fāte, făt, fâre, fär; bē, bĕt; bīte, bĭt; nō, nŏt, nôr; fūse, fŭn, fûr; tōō, tŏŏk; foil; foul; thin; then; hw for wh as in *what*; zh for s as in u*s*ual; ə for a, e, i, o, u, as in *a*go, lin*e*n, per*i*l, at*o*m, min*u*s

charge more or fewer electrons than are usually present on or in a substance.

e·lec·tri·cal (i lĕk′trə kəl) **1** operated by electricity: *new* electrical *appliances.* **2** having to do with electricity: *an* electrical *engineer.* **e·lec·tri·cal·ly.**

electric eye photoelectric cell used to turn switches on and off in order to open doors, start fans, etc.

electric field space around an electric charge in which the charge can exert a force on another charge.

e·lec·tri·cian (i lĕk′trish′ən) a person who installs, repairs, or works with electrical wiring or appliances.

e·lec·tric·i·ty (i lĕk′tris′ə tĭ) transfer of energy in a flow of electrons from one place to another. For example, energy in falling water drives a generator which drives electrons through a wire. The electrons in turn drive motors in homes and factories.

e·lec·tri·fy (i lĕk′trə fī′) **1** to equip for the use of electricity. **2** to apply electricity to. **3** to thrill: *His speech* electrified *the audience.* **e·lec·tri·fied, e·lec·tri·fy·ing.**

e·lec·tro·mag·net (i lĕk′trō măg′nĭt) a magnet made by sending an electric current through a wire coiled around a soft iron core.

Electromagnet

e·lec·tron (i lĕk′trŏn) tiny particle of matter having one unit of negative charge. Electrons move around the nucleus of the atom, which has a positive charge. They also move in a stream from one atom to another as an electric current.

e·lec·tron·ic (i lĕk′trŏn′ik) having to do with electrons and equipment that operates by the motion of electrons: *Television sets and computers are* electronic *equipment.*

electron microscope extremely high-powered microscope in which beams of electrons instead of light are used to produce an enlarged image.

e·lec·tro·scope (i lĕk′trə skōp′) an instrument that can detect very small electric charges and show whether they are positive or negative.

el·e·gance (ĕl′ə gəns) good taste; polish; correctness: *The writer is noted for the* elegance *of his style.*

el·e·gant (ĕl′ə gənt) marked by good taste; refined: *the* elegant *manners of the eighteenth-century French court.* **el·e·gant·ly.**

el·e·ment (ĕl′ə mənt) **1** one of the main principles or steps of a subject: *the* elements *of arithmetic.* **2** substance that cannot be broken down into other substances by chemical means. Gold, iron, hydrogen, and oxygen are elements. There are about 102 elements known. Also called **chemical element.** **3** necessary part (of a whole); ingredient: *Honesty is one of the* elements *of a good character.* **4 the elements** the forces of nature, such as rain, wind, and the like.

el·e·men·ta·ry (ĕl′ə mĕn′tə rĭ) dealing with the first steps; beginning: *an* elementary *education.*

elementary school the first six or eight grades of school.

el·e·phant (ĕl′ə fənt) African or Asian animal with a thick, gray, wrinkled hide, stout legs, long tusks, and a long, flexible snout called a trunk, which it uses somewhat like a hand. The elephant is the largest living land animal.

Asiatic elephant, 8 to 10 ft. high

el·e·vate (ĕl′ə vāt′) to raise to a higher level; lift up: *Dennis's new stilts* elevated *him two feet.* **el·e·vat·ed, el·e·vat·ing.**

el·e·va·tion (ĕl′ə vā′shən) **1** raised place: *The house sits on a slight* elevation *overlooking the valley.* **2** a raising: *an* elevation *of prices.* **3** height above sea level: *The* elevation *of this land is 1,603 feet.*

el·e·va·tor (ĕl′ə vā′tər) **1** anything that lifts up. **2** cage that can be raised or lowered in a shaft, to carry people or goods from one level to another. **3** a building for storing grain.

e·lev·en (i lĕv′ən) **1** amount or quantity that is one greater than ten; 11. **2** a football team.

e·lev·enth (i lĕv′ənth) **1** next after tenth; 11th. **2** one of 11 equal parts.

elf (ĕlf) a kind of fairy, described in folk tales as sometimes mischievous, sometimes helpful. **elves.**

Elf

el·i·gi·ble (ĕl′ə jə bəl) fit or proper to be chosen; qualified: *Only fifth-grade pupils are eligible for next week's spelling contest.* **el·i·gi·bly.**

e·lim·i·nate (ĭ lĭm′ə nāt′) to get rid of; remove: *The trees were sprayed to eliminate the insects in them.* **e·lim·i·nat·ed, e·lim·i·nat·ing.**

e·lim·i·na·tion (ĭ lĭm′ə nā′shən) **1** a taking out or getting rid (of): *a committee for the elimination of slums.* **2** an expelling (getting rid) of waste matter: *Poor elimination is harmful to a person's health.*

elk (ĕlk) **1** large European deer related to the American moose. **2** large American deer with spreading antlers, related to the red deer of Europe. pl. **elk**; rarely, **elks.**

American elk, about 5 ft. high at shoulder

ell (ĕl) **1** addition to a building, often L-shaped. **2** old measure of length based originally on the length of an arm. It varies from 27 to 45 inches.

el·lipse (ĭ lĭps′) a closed curve or oval with both ends equal in size. For picture, see **oval.**

el·lip·tic (ĭ lĭp′tĭk) or **el·lip·ti·cal** (ĭ lĭp′-tĭ kəl) having the shape of an ellipse or part of an ellipse. **el·lip·ti·cal·ly.**

elm (ĕlm) **1** a tall, graceful shade tree. **2** the hard, tough wood of this tree.

e·lon·gate (ĭ lông′gāt′) to lengthen; extend: *Machines can elongate bars of hot steel.* **e·lon·gat·ed, e·lon·gat·ing.**

e·lope (ĭ lōp′) to go or run away secretly, especially to run away to be married. – **e·loped, e·lop·ing.**

el·o·quence (ĕl′ə kwəns) **1** speech or writing that has force, ease, and clearness: *The speaker's eloquence brought applause from his hearers.* **2** ability to speak or write with force, ease, and clearness.

el·o·quent (ĕl′ə kwənt) **1** telling one's thoughts with force, ease, and clearness: *an*

eloquent *speaker.* **2** meaningful; expressive: *an* eloquent *gesture.* **el·o·quent·ly.**

El Sal·va·dor (ĕl săl′və dôr′) a country in northwestern Central America.

else (ĕls) **1** besides; in addition: *Who else would like to speak?* **2** instead: *What else could I do?* **3** otherwise; if not: *Run, or else you will be tardy.*

else·where (ĕls′hwâr′) in, at, or to some other place; somewhere else.

e·lude (ĭ lōōd′ or ĭ lūd′) to escape by being quick or clever; evade: *The wild horse eluded the cowboy.* **e·lud·ed, e·lud·ing.**

e·lu·sive (ĭ lōō′sĭv or ĭ lū′sĭv) **1** hard to catch or retain; evasive: *an elusive bandit.* **2** hard to understand, remember, or express: *an elusive idea.* **e·lu·sive·ly.**

elves (ĕlvz) more than one **elf.**

e·ma·ci·at·ed (ĭ mā′shĭ ā′tĭd) wasted away; made thin: *He was emaciated from lack of food.*

e·man·ci·pate (ĭ măn′sə pāt′) to set free from slavery or strict control; liberate. **e·man·ci·pat·ed, e·man·ci·pat·ing.**

e·man·ci·pa·tion (ĭ măn′sə pā′shən) a setting free from, or freedom from, slavery or other oppressive condition: *the* emancipation *of the slaves by Lincoln; the* emancipation *of women by household machines.*

Emancipation Proclamation a proclamation made by President Lincoln, effective January 1, 1863, giving freedom to slaves living in those states then in active rebellion against the United States.

em·balm (ĕm bäm′) to preserve (a dead body) with spices, chemicals, etc.

em·bank·ment (ĕm-băngk′mənt) **1** a mound of earth or gravel piled up to support a highway, etc. **2** a raised bank along a river to hold back water.

Embankment

em·bark (ĕm bärk′) **1** to go on board ship as a passenger: *to embark for France.* **2** to put on board ship: *to embark cargo.*

embark on to begin: *to embark on a law career.*

---

fāte, făt, fâre, fär; bē, bĕt; bīte, bĭt; nō, nŏt, nôr; fūse, fŭn, fûr; tōō, tŏŏk; foil; foul; thin; then; hw for wh as in what; zh for s as in usual; ə for a, e, i, o, u, as in ago, linen, peril, atom, minus

em·bar·rass (ĕm băr′əs) **1** to cause (a person) to feel self-conscious; fluster: *His teacher's praise* embarrassed *the shy boy.* **2** to worry; hinder: *Lack of money* embarrassed *him.*

em·bar·rass·ment (ĕm băr′əs mənt) **1** ruffled state of mind: *To my embarrassment I spilled the coffee on the guest's lap.* **2** something that impedes or hinders.

em·bas·sy (ĕm′bə sĭ) **1** residence or office of an ambassador. **2** an ambassador and his assistants. **em·bas·sies.**

em·bat·tled (ĕm băt′əld) **1** drawn up in battle order; armed and ready to fight. **2** fortified: *an* embattled *frontier.*

em·ber (ĕm′bər) **1** a glowing piece of wood or coal in the ashes of a fire. **2** embers smoldering ashes.

em·bez·zle (ĕm bĕz′əl) to steal money entrusted to one: *The cashier* embezzled *a large sum of money from the bank.* **em·bez·zled, em·bez·zling.**

em·bit·ter (ĕm bĭt′ər) to make bitter, morose, or resentful; sour: *The death of her only son* embittered *the woman.*

em·blem (ĕm′bləm) something that represents an idea; symbol that can be seen: *The dove is an* emblem *of peace.*

em·bod·y (ĕm bŏd′ĭ) **1** to put into a form that can be touched or seen: *to* embody *an idea in marble.* **2** to collect into a united whole: *The bylaws are* embodied *in this pamphlet.* **3** to introduce into: *The new law will be* embodied *in the present code.* **em·bod·ied, em·bod·y·ing.**

em·boss (ĕm bôs′) **1** to raise above a surface by pressure of a die: *to* emboss *a border on a paper napkin.* **2** to decorate with raised figures: *The printer* embossed *the paper with my monogram.*

em·brace (ĕm brās′) **1** to grasp in the arms; hug: *Mitzi ran down the path and* embraced *her father.* **2** to take up; adopt: *The class gladly* embraced *the museum's offer of a tour.* **3** to include: *The vegetable kingdom.* embraces *flowers, bushes, and trees.* **4** a hug. **em·braced, em·brac·ing.**

em·broi·der (ĕm broi′dər) **1** to decorate by sewing colored threads into a design: *to* embroider *a scarf.* **2** to add imaginary details to; exaggerate: *to* embroider *a story.*

em·broi·der·y (ĕm broi′də rĭ) ornamental needlework. **em·broi·der·ies.**

em·bry·o (ĕm′brĭ ō′) **1** an unborn or unhatched animal. **2** an unsprouted plant germ in a seed. **3** an early stage of growth or development: *A frontier fort was the* embryo *of the city of Pittsburgh.* **em·bry·os.**

Embryo of fish

em·er·ald (ĕm′ər əld) **1** a precious stone of a clear, deep green color. **2** the color of this stone: *an* emerald *sweater.*

e·merge (ĭ mûrj′) **1** to come forth into view: *The sun* emerged *from a bank of clouds.* **2** to become known; appear: *The facts about the crime* emerged *after a long investigation.* **e·merged, e·merg·ing.**

e·mer·gen·cy (ĭ mûr′jən sĭ) **1** sudden or unexpected happening that makes quick action necessary. **2** for use at such a time: *an* emergency *exit; an* emergency *light.* **e·mer·gen·cies.**

em·er·y (ĕm′ə rĭ) a very hard mineral substance used in powdered form for grinding or polishing.

em·i·grant (ĕm′ə grənt) a person who leaves his country to settle in another: *Many* emigrants *settled in Virginia.*

em·i·grate (ĕm′ə grāt′) to leave one's own country to settle in another: *Many Spaniards* emigrated *to Mexico in the 16th century.* **em·i·grat·ed, em·i·grat·ing.**

em·i·gra·tion (ĕm′ə grā′shən) a moving from a person's native country to another country: *an* emigration *because of famine.*

em·i·nence (ĕm′ə nəns) **1** high standing; great distinction: *He has achieved great* eminence *in the medical profession.* **2** high ground; an elevation.

em·i·nent (ĕm′ə nənt) outstanding; distinguished: *Washington was* eminent *both as soldier and as statesman.* **em·i·nent·ly.**

em·is·sar·y (ĕm′ə sĕr′ĭ) person sent on a mission or errand, especially one of a confidential nature: *The President sent an* emissary *to the capitals of the new African states.* **em·is·sar·ies.**

e·mit (ĭ mĭt′) to send forth; discharge: *A volcano* emits *lava.* **e·mit·ted, e·mit·ting.**

e·mo·tion (ĭ mō′shən) **1** strong feeling: *to speak with* emotion. **2** any particular feeling, such as joy, fear, etc.: *to appeal to the* emotions *rather than to the mind.*

e·mo·tion·al (ĭ mō′shən əl) **1** having to do with the emotions; based on feeling: *a silly,* emotional *quarrel.* **2** stirring the emotion: *His talk on loyalty was full of* emotional *appeal for the audience.* **3** easily stirred; excitable: *an* emotional *person.* **e·mo·tion·al·ly.**

em·per·or (ĕm′pər ər) ruler of an empire.

em·pha·sis (ĕm′fə sĭs) **1** attention or stress (given to something because of its importance): *an* emphasis *on correct spelling.* **2** stress of the voice, given to one or more words or syllables: *We noticed the* emphasis *he placed on the word "duty."* **em·pha·ses** (ĕm′fə sēz).

em·pha·size (ĕm′fə sīz′) to stress; to place special value or importance on: *The speaker* emphasized *the need for quick action.* **em·pha·sized, em·pha·siz·ing.**

em·phat·ic (ĕm făt′ĭk) **1** said or done with special force or emphasis: *an* emphatic *reply.* **2** striking; forceful; definite: *the* emphatic *contrast between black and white.*

em·phat·i·cal·ly (ĕm făt′ĭ kəl ĭ) forcefully; positively: *He spoke most* emphatically *on the dangers of careless driving.*

em·pire (ĕm′pīr) **1** group of countries under the control of one ruler. **2** a country of which the ruler bears the title of emperor. **3** absolute power or authority. **4** power; sovereignty: *the responsibilities of* empire.

em·ploy (ĕm ploi′) **1** to give work to (a person); hire: *We hope to* employ *a new secretary tomorrow.* **2** to make use of: *He* employed *his spare time to good advantage.* **3** to occupy; take up: *Driving* employs *much of a salesman's time.* **4** service: *That boy is in my father's* employ.

em·ploy·ee (ĕm ploi′ē) person who works for another for pay.

em·ploy·er (ĕm ploi′ər) person who hires another.

em·ploy·ment (ĕm ploi′mənt) **1** the act of hiring: *He was busy with the* employment *of new help.* **2** a being employed; having work: *Full* employment *keeps a country prosperous.* **3** a use: *the* employment *of harsh measures.* **4** work; occupation: *His regular* employment *is welding.*

em·pow·er (ĕm pou′ər) to give power or authority to: *The sheriff* empowered *the posse to arrest the outlaws.*

em·press (ĕm′prĭs) the wife of an emperor, or a woman ruling an empire.

emp·ti·ness (ĕmp′tĭ nĭs) lack of contents; lack of meaning; lack of sincerity: *the* emptiness *of the deserted house; the* emptiness *of her life; the* emptiness *of his promises; the* emptiness *of that play.*

emp·ty (ĕmp′tĭ) **1** containing nothing; unoccupied: *an* empty *closet; an* empty *house.* **2** to remove the contents from: *She* emptied *her desk.* **3** to drain: *They* emptied *the water from the tank. The river* empties *into the ocean.* **4** to become vacant: *The room* emptied *when the bell rang for lunch.* **5** without meaning: *an* empty *promise.* **emp·ti·er, emp·ti·est; emp·tied, emp·ty·ing; emp·ti·ly.**

em·u·late (ĕm′yŏŏ lāt′) to strive to equal or surpass (someone): *We* emulate *people we admire.* **em·u·lat·ed, em·u·lat·ing.**

e·mul·sion (ĭ mŭl′shən) liquid mixture in which very fine drops of one liquid are scattered through another.

-en 1 suffix meaning **(1)** "to make" or "to become": *hard*en; *straight*en. **(2)** "to cause to have more" or "to acquire more": *length*en; *strength*en. **(3)** "made of" or "resembling": *gold*en; *wheat*en. **2** word ending sometimes used **(1)** instead of "-ed" to show that an action has happened: *giv*en; *tak*en. **(2)** instead of "-s" or "-es" to show more than one: *ox*en.

en·a·ble (ĭn ā′bəl) to give (one or something) power or ability (to do something): *The scholarship* enabled *her to go to college.* **en·a·bled, en·a·bling.**

en·act (ĭn ăkt′) to make into law: *Congress* enacted *a bill to lower tariffs.*

e·nam·el (ĭ năm′əl) **1** a substance used in coating the surface of metal, glass, or pottery for protection and decoration. After the enamel has been melted and applied, it cools to form a hard glossy surface. **2** paint that dries with a glossy surface. **3** to cover with enamel for the purpose of protection or decoration. **4** hard, white outer surface of the teeth.

---

fāte, făt, fâre, fär; bē, bĕt; bīte, bĭt; nō, nŏt, nôr; fūse, fŭn, fûr; tōō, tŏŏk; foil; foul; thin; ~~then~~;
hw for wh as in *w*hat; zh for s as in u*s*ual; ə for a, e, i, o, u, as in *a*go, lin*e*n, per*i*l, at*o*m, min*u*s

en·camp (ĕn kămp´) to make a camp; settle in a camp: *The hikers encamped in the forest. The guide encamped the boys near a stream.*

en·camp·ment (ĕn kămp´mənt) **1** the making of a camp; settling in a camp. **2** a camp: *The encampment was in the woods.*

en·chant (ĕn chănt´) **1** to bewitch; overcome by magic: *Merlin enchanted the knight's sword.* **2** to delight greatly: *She enchanted him with her smile.*

en·chant·ing (ĕn chănt´ĭng) so charming that it bewitches; causing great delight. **en·chant·ing·ly.**

en·chant·ment (ĕn chănt´mənt) **1** great delight: *a child's enchantment when he sees a Christmas tree.* **2** magic spell: *The witch's enchantment turned the prince into a frog.*

en·chant·ress (ĕn chănt´rĭs) **1** woman who uses charms or spells; a witch. **2** very charming or fascinating woman.

en·cir·cle (ĕn sûr´kəl) **1** to make a circle around; surround: *The crowd encircled the winning team.* **2** to go completely around: *A jet airplane can encircle the earth very quickly.* **en·cir·cled, en·cir·cling.**

en·close (ĕn klōz´) **1** to close in on all sides: *We enclosed the baby's crib with mosquito netting.* **2** to surround with a fence or wall: *We enclosed the lot with a wire fence.* **3** to place inside (something); insert: *He enclosed a check with the letter.* **en·closed, en·clos·ing.** Also spelled **in·close.**

en·clo·sure (ĕn klō´zhər) **1** the closing or shutting in of (something): *The enclosure of the porch with glass was done quickly.* **2** something that closes in; fence; wall. **3** place that is closed in by a fence, wall, etc.: *The elephants at the zoo walked about in their large enclosure.* **4** something that is put in with something else: *an enclosure in a letter.*

en·com·pass (ĕn kŭm´pəs or ĕn kŭm´pəs) to surround; encircle: *Enemy forces encompassed the camp.*

en·core (äng´kôr) **1** again! once more! (a cry to a performer for a repetition or for something additional). **2** a response to such a request: *As an encore, the pianist played Brahms' "Lullaby."*

en·coun·ter (ĕn koun´tər) **1** to meet unexpectedly: *We encountered bad weather on our trip.* **2** chance or unexpected meeting: *Our encounter with a movie star was very exciting.* **3** to meet in conflict; fight. **4** a fight or battle: *There was a frightening encounter between the two gangs.*

en·cour·age (ĕn kûr´ĭj) **1** to give hope, confidence, or courage to: *The girl's parents encouraged her to study music.* **2** to aid; foster: *to encourage learning.* **en·cour·aged, en·cour·ag·ing.**

en·cour·age·ment (ĕn kûr´ĭj mənt) **1** the giving of hope or courage: *The doctor's constant encouragement helped the crippled child to learn to walk again.* **2** something that gives courage or hope: *Talking to the successful violinist was an encouragement to the music student.* **3** a fostering: *money for the encouragement of research.*

en·croach (ĕn krōch´) **1** to make free with another's rights or property: *The salesman encroached upon my time.* **2** to go beyond the normal limits: *The flooding river had encroached upon the land along its banks.*

en·cum·ber (ĕn kŭm´bər) or **in·cum·ber** (ĭn kŭm´bər) **1** to get in the way of; hinder: *The girl's tight skirt encumbered her when she tried to climb a tree.* **2** to crowd or fill: *The attic was encumbered with old furniture.* **3** to weigh down; burden: *to be encumbered with debts.*

en·cum·brance (ĕn kŭm´brəns) something that hinders or holds back; a burden: *Too much luggage is an encumbrance.*

en·cy·clo·pe·di·a or **en·cy·clo·pae·di·a** (ĕn sī´klə pē´dĭ ə) a book or set of books containing articles, usually arranged in alphabetical order, on all branches of knowledge, or on some special subject.

end (ĕnd) **1** the point or part at which something begins or leaves off: *both ends of the stick.* **2** the farthest or last part of anything: *the end of the road; the end of a rope.* **3** the point at which something ceases to exist; final limit: *I'm at the end of my patience. His life came to an end.* **4** aim; purpose; object: *His family's happiness was the end for which he worked.* **5** to come to an end: *The music ended.* **6** to bring to an end: *He ended the music.* **7** to form the end of: *That scene ended the play.* **8 at the end** at last. **9 end to end** lengthwise. **10 in the end** finally, ultimately. **11 on end** (1) in an upright position. (2) one after another: *to stand for hours on end.*

end in smoke to come to nothing.

end up to arrive or become in time: *He'll end up in jail. He'll end up a prisoner.*

en·dan·ger (ĕn dān′jər) to put in danger: *He endangered his life by careless driving.*

en·dear (ĕn dĭr′) to make dear: *His thoughtfulness endeared him to his friends.*

en·deav·or (ĕn dĕv′ər) **1** to attempt; strive; try hard: *He will endeavor to swim across the channel.* **2** effort; attempt: *He made every endeavor to win her friendship.*

end·ing (ĕnd′ĭng) conclusion; last part: *The movie had a happy ending.*

end·less (ĕnd′lĭs) **1** lasting forever; having no end. **2** joined at the ends; continuous: *an endless chain.* **end·less·ly.**

en·dorse (ĕn dôrs′) or **in·dorse** (ĭn dôrs′) **1** to write one's name on the back of (a check or document). **2** to approve; support: *The governor endorsed Mr. Miller for mayor.* **en·dorsed, en·dors·ing.**

en·dow (ĕn dou′) **1** to provide with a permanent fund or source of income: *His father endowed the college with a large sum of money.* **2** to equip; furnish: *He was endowed with a wonderful sense of humor.*

en·dow·ment (ĕn dou′mənt) **1** money or other property given an institution for its support: *The college received a large endowment from Mr. Jones.* **2** the act of making such a gift: *On the occasion of his endowment he was given an honorary degree.* **3** a person's abilities or talents: *Good looks were not his only endowment.*

en·dur·ance (ĕn dŏŏr′əns or ĕn dyŏŏr′əns) **1** power of bearing up under strain, suffering, fatigue, or hardship: *A long-distance swimmer needs great endurance.* **2** ability to withstand hard wear or use: *to test the endurance of a car.*

en·dure (ĕn dŏŏr′ or ĕn dyŏŏr′) **1** to bear bravely; suffer: *The pioneers endured many hardships.* **2** to bear; put up with; tolerate: *She cannot endure cold weather.* **3** to continue to exist; last: *Lincoln's name will endure forever.* **en·dured, en·dur·ing.**

end·ways (ĕnd′wāz′) **1** on end: *Pile these boxes endways.* **2** with the end forward: *The long pipe was carried in endways.*

end·wise (ĕnd′wīz′) endways.

en·e·my (ĕn′ə mĭ) **1** unfriendly opponent; foe. **2** an opposing military force: *Our regiment attacked the enemy at dawn.* **3** a hostile nation. **4** anything that harms or injures: *Polio is an enemy of humanity.* **5** belonging to a foe: *a fleet of enemy warships.* **en·e·mies.**

en·er·get·ic (ĕn′ər jĕt′ĭk) full of purpose; active; vigorous: *He was more energetic on the baseball field than in the classroom.*

en·er·get·i·cal·ly (ĕn′ər jĕt′ĭk ə lĭ) vigorously; actively; forcefully.

en·er·gy (ĕn′ər jĭ) **1** material power of the universe; ability to do work: *Einstein studied the relation of energy to matter.* **2** ability to put forth muscular effort; vigor: *He needed all his energy to win the race.* **3** mental or physical force: *He spoke with energy and enthusiasm.* **en·er·gies.**

en·fold (ĕn fōld′) **1** to wrap up; enclose: *The petals of a rosebud enfold its stamen.* **2** to clasp; embrace: *She enfolded the child in her arms.*

en·force (ĕn fôrs′) **1** to compel obedience to: *The police enforce the law.* **2** to impose by force: *to enforce silence.* **en·forced, en·forc·ing.**

en·force·ment (ĕn fôrs′mənt) an enforcing: *Law enforcement is necessary to keep order.*

en·fran·chise (ĕn frăn′chĭz′) **1** to give the right to vote: *American women have been enfranchised since 1919.* **2** to free, as from slavery. **en·fran·chised, en·fran·chis·ing.**

en·gage (ĕn gāj′) **1** to occupy (the time or attention of): *Tennis and golf engaged most of his time.* **2** to promise: *He engaged to make payments for his house.* **3** to get the right to occupy or use; reserve: *They engaged three balcony seats at the theater.* **4** to hire; to employ: *Mr. Smith engaged Pete as a gardener for the summer.* **5** to attract; hold: *The sports page engaged Mr. Whale's attention.* **6** to enter into battle or conflict with; attack: *We engage the enemy at dawn.* **7** to interlock, as the teeth of a gear. **engage in** to be busy with: *He engaged in gardening.* **en·gaged, en·gag·ing.**

en·gaged (ĕn gājd′) **1** bound by a promise to marry; betrothed. **2** busy; occupied.

fāte, făt, fâre, fär; bē, bĕt; bīte, bĭt; nō, nŏt, nôr; fūse, fŭn, fûr; tōō, tŏŏk; foil; foul; thin; then; hw for wh as in what; zh for s as in usual; ə for a, e, i, o, u, as in ago, linen, peril, atom, minus

255

en·gage·ment (ĕn gāj′mənt) **1** a promise to
marry; betrothal. **2** appointment; promise
to meet someone somewhere at a fixed
time: *I have a three o'clock engagement
with my lawyer.* **3** employment: *The
actress had a six weeks' engagement in a
summer theater.* **4** battle; conflict.

en·gag·ing (ĕn gā′jĭng) winning; attractive;
pleasing: *an engaging pastime;* engaging
manners. **en·gag·ing·ly.**

en·gen·der (ĕn jĕn′dər) to give birth to;
create: *Truthfulness engenders confidence.*

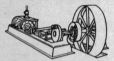

Steam and internal combustion (gasoline) engines

en·gine (ĕn′jən) **1** a machine that develops
power to run other machines. An engine
uses steam pressure, gas explosions, etc., to
do work, as in a locomotive or automobile;
a motor. **2** any machine or instrument:
Cannons and bombs are engines *of destruction.* **3** a locomotive.

en·gi·neer (ĕn′jə nĭr′) **1** a person who designs and builds machines, ships, docks,
bridges, roads, forts, etc.: *a mechanical
engineer.* **2** to plan or direct the building
of: *to* engineer *a road.* **3** a person who
drives a locomotive. **4** a person who is in
charge of engines. **5** to plan; direct; bring
about: *He engineered the entire project.*

en·gi·neer·ing (ĕn′jə nĭr′ĭng) the designing and building (of machinery, roads,
bridges, etc.): *The engineering of the
Hoover Dam took many years.*

Eng·land (ĭng′glənd) the largest part of
the island of Great Britain.

Eng·lish (ĭng′glĭsh) **1** of or having to do
with England, its people, or its language.
2 the people of England. **3** the language of
England, the United States, Canada,
Australia, and some other places.

English horn a wood-wind musical instrument somewhat like a large oboe.

en·grave (ĕn grāv′) **1** to cut letters or designs into the surface of a stone, wood, or
metal object: *to* engrave *a silver cup.* **2** to
cut (letters, figures, designs, etc.) on stone,
wood, or a metal plate for printing on

paper. **3** to print from such a block or
plate. **4** to fix (in the mind or memory):
The happening was engraved upon his mind.
en·graved, en·grav·ing.

en·grav·ing (ĕn grā′vĭng) **1** a cutting of
designs into stone, hard wood, or metal.
2 a design cut in this way. **3** a print made
from a block or plate cut in this way.

en·gross (ĕn grōs′) to occupy wholly; fill
the mind or time of: *She was engrossed in
her task.*

en·gulf (ĕn gŭlf′) to swallow up: *High
waves* engulfed *the swimmers.*

en·hance (ĕn häns′) to add to; increase:
Flowering bushes enhanced *the beauty of the
garden.* **en·hanced, en·hanc·ing.**

e·nig·ma (ĭ nĭg′mə) person or thing not
easily understood; puzzle: *His intentions
remained an enigma.*

e·nig·mat·ic (ĕn′ĭg mătĭk) or **e·nig·mat·
i·cal** (ĕn′ĭg mătĭk əl) like an enigma;
puzzling; difficult to understand: *an* enigmatic *remark; an* enigmatic *smile that could
be read in a number of ways.*

en·join (ĕn join′) **1** to direct; order; command: *The safety officer* enjoined *students
to obey bicycle rules.* **2** to impose; decree:
to enjoin *silence.*

en·joy (ĕn joi′) **1** to take pleasure or delight
in: *We* enjoyed *the picnic.* **2** to possess;
have the use of: *I* enjoy *good health.*

enjoy oneself to have a good time.

en·joy·a·ble (ĕn joi′ə bəl) pleasing; delightful. **en·joy·a·bly.**

en·joy·ment (ĕn joi′mənt) **1** pleasure:
Many people find enjoyment *in reading.*
2 possession or use: *We had the* enjoyment *of their house when they were away.*

en·large (ĕn lärj′) to make or become
larger; increase: *We* enlarged *our house.
The population* enlarges *each year.*

enlarge on or **upon** to say or write more
about: *The teacher* enlarged *upon the idea
of courage by giving examples.*

en·larged, en·larg·ing.

en·large·ment (ĕn lärj′mənt) **1** an increasing; a making larger: *An* enlargement
of duties followed John's promotion. **2** a
thing that is added: *The new wing is an*
enlargement *to our house.* **3** something
made larger, as a photograph.

en·light·en (ĕn li′tən) to furnish with
knowledge; free from ignorance; instruct;

inform: *Teachers were sent to the backward countries to* enlighten *the natives. Let me* enlighten *you as to your duties.*

en·list (ĕn list′) **1** to join an armed service voluntarily: *to enlist in the army, navy, etc.* **2** to make a member of the armed forces: *The Navy* enlisted *many new recruits.* **3** to get the help or support of: *The president* enlisted *a committee to plan the program.*

en·list·ment (ĕn list′mənt) an enlisting or being enlisted, especially for service in the armed forces for a certain period of time.

en·liv·en (ĕn li′vən) to put life into; brighten: *The host's tricks of magic* enlivened *the party.*

en·mi·ty (ĕn′mĭ tĭ) hatred; ill will: *a choice between friendship and* enmity. **en·mi·ties.**

e·nor·mous (ĭ nôr′məs) very large; huge. **e·nor·mous·ly.**

e·nough (ĭ nŭf′) **1** as much or as many as necessary or desirable: *He drinks* enough *milk. He has had* enough. *She has practiced her piano lesson* enough *for today.* **2** fully; quite: *I was glad* enough *to go.* **3** well enough fairly well: *He writes* well enough *for a beginner.*

en·quire (ĕn kwîr′) inquire. **en·quired, en·quir·ing.**

en·rage (ĕn rāj′) to make very angry; infuriate: *Teasing* enraged *the dog.* **en·raged, en·rag·ing.**

en·rich (ĕn rĭch′) to make rich or richer: *The oil industry has* enriched *Texas. The farmer* enriched *the soil with fertilizer. Reading good books* enriches *the mind.*

en·roll or **en·rol** (ĕn rōl′) **1** to put (the name of a person) on a list or register: *The club* enrolled *him as a member.* **2** to make a member: *The club* enrolled *him.* **3** to become a member: *He* enrolled *yesterday.* **4** to enlist: *He* enrolled *in the army.* **en·rolled, en·roll·ing.**

en·roll·ment or **en·rol·ment** (ĕn rōl′mənt) **1** number of persons admitted to a group: *The* enrollment *of the fourth grade is 35.* **2** admission to membership: *Frieda's* enrollment *in the Scouts comes next week.*

en route (än rōōt′) on the way: *The plane is* en route *to London.*

en·shrine (ĕn shrin′) to place in a shrine, or think of as in a shrine; hold in reverence: *George Washington was* enshrined *in the hearts of his countrymen.* **en·shrined, en·shrin·ing.**

en·sign (ĕn′sin) **1** a flag. **2** pennant showing office, rank, or authority: *The general's* ensign *flew from the car.* **3** (ĕn′sən) a commissioned officer of the lowest grade in the United States Navy.

Norway ensign

en·slave (ĕn slāv′) **1** to make a slave of; place in bondage. **2** to dominate completely: *He was* enslaved *by a fear of poverty.* **en·slaved, en·slav·ing.**

en·sue (ĕn sōō′ or ĕn sū′) to follow as a result: *When one boy bumped another, an argument* ensued. *After the storm, warm weather* ensued. **en·sued, en·su·ing.**

en·sure (ĕn shōōr′) insure. **en·sured, en·sur·ing.**

en·tail (ĕn tāl′) to make necessary; require: *Writing a book* entails *a great deal of work.*

en·tan·gle (ĕn tăng′gəl) **1** to catch or trap in a tangle: *The kitten's paws were* entangled *in the yarn.* **2** to involve (in difficulties): *to become* entangled *in debts.* **en·tan·gled, en·tan·gling.**

en·tan·gle·ment (ĕn tăng′gəl mənt) **1** an entangling. **2** a being caught in or as in a snare or a snarl: *Early political* entanglements *proved his undoing.* **3** a tangle; a snarl: *barbed-wire* entanglements *in warfare.*

en·ter (ĕn′tər) **1** to come or go into or in: *They* entered *the house. Will you* enter? **2** to enroll (someone): *to* enter *a child in school.* **3** to join; become a member of: *He* entered *the club two years ago.* **4** to record: *His secretary* enters *expenses in the account book.* **5** to begin; start upon: *He* entered *life with many advantages.*

enter on or **upon** to begin: *We have* entered *upon a new period of history.*

enter into to go into; to take part in: *to* enter into *details; to* enter into *a talk.*

en·ter·prise (ĕn′tər prĭz′) **1** an undertaking; a project: *a difficult* enterprise. **2** willingness or energy to start new projects: *a spirit of* enterprise; *a man of no* enterprise.

fāte, făt, fâre, fär; bē, bĕt; bīte, bĭt; nō, nŏt, nôr; fūse, fŭn, fûr; tōō, tŏŏk; foil; foul; thin; ~~then~~;
hw for wh as in *what*; zh for s as in *usual*; ə for a, e, i, o, u, as in *ago, linen, peril, atom, minus*

257

en·ter·pris·ing (ĕn′tər prī′zĭng) willing to start new and untried projects; venturesome: *The Wright brothers were enterprising young men.* **en·ter·pris·ing·ly.**

en·ter·tain (ĕn′tər tān′) **1** to receive as a guest; give food and drink to: *They will entertain two friends at dinner tonight.* **2** to amuse; divert; interest: *That magician has entertained many audiences.* **3** to consider; keep in mind: *He is entertaining the offer of a new job.*

en·ter·tain·ment (ĕn′tər tān′mənt) **1** an entertaining or being entertained: *the entertainment of guests.* **2** something that amuses, interests, diverts, etc., such as a play or a circus.

en·thrall or **en·thral** (ĕn thrôl′) to hold under a spell; charm; captivate: *The new singer enthralled his audience.* **en·thralled, en·thrall·ing.**

en·throne (ĕn thrōn′) to place on a throne or in a position of power, glory, or reverence: *The idea of liberty is enthroned in our hearts.* **en·throned, en·thron·ing.**

en·thu·si·asm (ĕn thōō′zĭ ăz′əm or ĕn thū′zĭ ăz′əm) strong feeling or show of warm admiration: *no enthusiasm for work; to receive someone with enthusiasm.*

en·thu·si·ast (ĕn thōō′zĭ ăst′ or ĕn thū′zĭ ăst′) person with keen interest in or feeling for something; a fan: *a tennis enthusiast.*

en·thu·si·as·tic (ĕn thōō′zĭ ăs′tĭk or ĕnthū′zĭ ăs′tĭk) full of enthusiasm; keenly interested: *an enthusiastic baseball fan.*

en·thu·si·as·ti·cal·ly (ĕn thōō′zĭ ăs′tĭk ə lĭ or ĕn thū′zĭ ăs′tĭk ə lĭ) with enthusiasm.

en·tice (ĕn tīs′) to lead on by arousing hope or desire; lure: *He enticed the dog into the house with a bone.* **en·ticed, en·tic·ing.**

en·tire (ĕn tīr′) whole; complete: *the entire family; an entire day; an entire set of teeth; our entire attention.* **en·tire·ly.**

en·tire·ty (ĕn tīr′tĭ) **1** the whole; the total: *The entirety of his estate was left to the Seamen's Home.* **2 in its entirety** as a whole; completely: *The report in its entirety was accepted by the delegates.*

en·ti·tle (ĕn tī′təl) **1** to give a right to: *The law entitles every person accused of a crime to a trial.* **2** to give a title to: *Mark Twain entitled his book "The Adventures of Tom Sawyer."* **en·ti·tled, en·ti·tling.**

¹en·trance (ĕn′trəns) **1** door or passage through which one enters: *the entrance to a tunnel.* **2** an entering: *The actress makes a dramatic entrance wherever she goes.* **3** permission to enter: *He gained entrance to the palace* [¹**entrance** is from an Old French word formed from another Old French word (entrer) meaning "to enter."]

²en·trance (ĕn trăns′) **1** to put under a spell. **2** to fill with delight: *She was entranced by the ballet.* **en·tranced, en·tranc·ing.** [²**entrance** is formed from two elements, one (en-) meaning "in" and the other (trance) meaning "a spell."]

en·treat (ĕn trēt′) to ask earnestly; beg: *He entreated his father's permission to go.*

en·treat·y (ĕn trē′tĭ) earnest request; prayer: *He was deaf to her entreaties.* **en·treat·ies.**

en·trench (ĕn trĕnch′) **1** to surround or protect by digging deep ditches: *The soldiers entrenched themselves near the enemy lines.* **2** to establish firmly: *He strongly entrenched himself in the firm.*

en·trench·ment (ĕn trĕnch′mənt) a system of trenches and earthworks, used for protection and defense: *The entrenchment extended along the riverbank.*

en·trust (ĕn trŭst′) **1** to give into the care of; turn over for safekeeping: *He entrusted his money to the bank.* **2** to give as a charge or duty: *I will entrust you with mailing this letter.*

en·try (ĕn′trĭ) **1** a going into; entering: *Their entry into the country was illegal.* **2** place through which one goes or comes in; a vestibule, or the like. **3** item recorded in a list, diary, etc.: *He made an entry in the ship's log.* **4** person or thing entered in a contest: *There were only four entries in the horse race.* **en·tries.**

en·twine (ĕn twīn′) to wind around; twist together: *The girls entwined their arms as they walked.* **en·twined, en·twin·ing.**

e·nu·mer·ate (ĭ nōō′mə rāt′ or ĭ nū′mə rāt′) to count or name one by one: *The class enumerated the states of the Union.* **e·nu·mer·at·ed, e·nu·mer·at·ing.**

e·nun·ci·ate (ĭ nŭn′sĭ āt′) **1** to pronounce (words): *He does not enunciate with care.* **2** to proclaim; announce: *to enunciate a decree; to enunciate a scientific theory.* **e·nun·ci·at·ed, e·nun·ci·at·ing.**

e·nun·ci·a·tion (ĭ nŭn′sĭ ā′shən) **1** manner of pronouncing words: *We heard everything she said because of her clear* enunciation. **2** statement; announcement: *an* enunciation *of new policies.*

en·vel·op (ĕn vĕl′əp) to cover; wrap up or in; hide: *Fog enveloped the city.*

en·ve·lope (ĕn′və lōp′ or ăn′və lōp′) a covering, especially a paper covering for a letter.

en·vi·a·ble (ĕn′vĭ ə bəl) arousing a desire to have as one's own; desirable: *Their new house is an* enviable *possession.* **en·vi·a·bly.**

en·vi·ous (ĕn′vĭ əs) **1** full of desire for something possessed by another: *He is* envious *of his friend's boat.* **2** jealous: *Judy was* envious *of her classmate.* **en·vi·ous·ly.**

en·vi·ron·ment (ĕn vī′rən mənt) **1** surroundings: *He is a very different person in the* environment *of his home.* **2** surroundings, conditions, and influences which may affect physical development or growth of character: *a healthy* environment.

en·voy (ĕn′voi or ăn′voi) **1** messenger. **2** government official sent on a mission to another government.

en·vy (ĕn′vĭ) **1** feeling of discontent aroused by the advantages or possessions of another; resentful jealousy: *The sick child was filled with* envy *of his healthy friend.* **2** to feel envy toward or because of: *He* envies *anyone who is happy. He* envies *anyone's happiness.* **3** person who or thing that is envied: *Pretty clothes make her the* envy *of all her friends.* **en·vied, en·vy·ing.**

ep·ic (ĕp′ĭk) **1** long poem written in a dignified style, telling the story of a hero or heroes: *The Odyssey is an* epic *about the adventures of Ulysses.* **2** noble; like an epic: *an* epic *journey to the South Pole.*

ep·i·dem·ic (ĕp′ə dĕm′ĭk) **1** attacking many people at the same time and spreading from person to person: *Influenza is an* epidemic *disease.* **2** general attack of a disease in a particular area: *The town had an* epidemic *of measles.* **3** a widespread occurrence of anything: *an* epidemic *of rumors.*

ep·i·lep·sy (ĕp′ə lĕp′sĭ) disease of the nervous system marked by fainting and a jerking of the muscles.

e·pis·co·pal (ĭ pĭs′kə pəl) **1** having to do with a bishop or bishops: *an* episcopal *letter to be read in all the churches.* **2** governed by bishops: *an* episcopal *church.* **e·pis·co·pal·ly.**

ep·i·sode (ĕp′ə sōd′) **1** an outstanding incident in a person's life, in history, or in a story: *the* episode *of Washington crossing the Delaware.* **2** an installment of a story or play published or performed serially: *The first* episode *of Gulliver's Travels will be shown on WXY at 8:30.*

e·pis·tle (ĭ pĭs′əl) **1** a letter, especially a formal one. **2 Epistle** one of the letters or collections of letters written by the Apostles and forming part of the New Testament.

ep·och (ĕp′ək) **1** period of time in which unusual or important events take place: *The* epoch *of space exploration began with the launching of the first earth satellite.* **2** the beginning of such a period: *an* epoch *in space exploration.*

e·qual (ē′kwəl) **1** to be the same as in size, rank, value, etc.; match: *Sixteen ounces* equal *one pound.* **2** to make or do (something) the same as: *He first* equaled *my batting average and then surpassed it.* **3** person or thing having the same rank, value, ability, etc., as another: *The fox has few* equals *in cunning.* **4** of the same number, size, amount, or value: *The two boys are of* equal *strength. We divided the candy bar into three* equal *parts.* **5 equal to** (1) the same as: *Four plus four is* equal to *eight.* (2) able or strong enough for: *He is* equal to *climbing the mountain.* **e·qualed** or **e·qualled, e·qual·ing** or **e·qual·ling; e·qual·ly.**

e·qual·i·ty (ĭ kwŏl′ə tĭ) sameness of rank, value, etc.: *The Constitution speaks of the* equality *of all men before the law.* **e·qual·i·ties.**

e·qual·ize (ē′kwə līz′) to make equal or even: *Mrs. Ryan* equalized *the house chores among her children.* **e·qual·ized, e·qual·iz·ing.**

e·qua·tion (ĭ kwā′zhən) a statement that two quantities are equal: $3 + 3 = 6$ *is an* equation.

---

fāte, făt, fâre, fär; bē, bĕt; bīte, bĭt; nō, nŏt, nôr; fūse, fŭn, fûr; tōō, tŏŏk; foil; foul; thin; ~~then~~; hw for wh as in *wh*at; zh for s as in u*s*ual; ə for a, e, i, o, u, as in a*g*o, lin*e*n, per*i*l, at*o*m, min*u*s

e·qua·tor (ĭ kwā′tər) an imaginary circle around the earth halfway between the North Pole and the South Pole. For picture, see **latitude**.

e·qua·to·ri·al (ē′kwə tôr′ĭ əl or ĕk′wə tôr′-ĭ əl) **1** of or near the earth's equator. **2** like conditions near the earth's equator: *a week of* equatorial *heat*. **e·qua·to·ri·al·ly**.

e·qui·lib·ri·um (ē′kwə lĭb′rĭ əm) balance: *A tightrope walker keeps his* equilibrium *with a pole*.

e·qui·nox (ē′kwə nŏks′) the two days each year (about March 21 and September 22) on which the sun is directly above the equator. On these days, day and night are of equal length everywhere on earth.

e·quip (ĭ kwĭp′) to supply with something needed; fit out: *to equip a polar expedition*. **e·quipped, e·quip·ping**.

e·quip·ment (ĭ kwĭp′mənt) **1** things needed for a particular purpose: *Camping equipment includes tents and sleeping bags*. **2** a fitting out; equipping: *The law requires the equipment of all bicycles with lights*.

eq·ui·ta·ble (ĕk′wə tə bəl) just; fair; impartial: *The judge made an equitable decision*. **eq·ui·ta·bly**.

eq·ui·ty (ĕk′wə tĭ) fairness; justice: *No one questions the equity of this transaction*.

e·quiv·a·lent (ĭ kwĭv′ə lənt) **1** equal in value, amount, meaning, etc.: *Cheating is equivalent to lying*. **2** something that is equivalent: *Two nickels are the equivalent of a dime*. **e·quiv·a·lent·ly**.

-er suffix meaning (1) "person or thing that": *danc*er; *roll*er. (2) "more": *pal*er. (3) "one who lives in or comes from": *New English*er. (4) person having to do with: *philosoph*er; *astronom*er.

e·ra (ē′rə) **1** period of time measured from a particular event: *The Christian* Era *dates from the birth of Christ*. **2** period of history characterized by certain events, men, etc.: *the* era *of Napoleon; the jazz* era; *an era of prosperity*.

e·rad·i·cate (ĭ răd′ə kāt′) to destroy completely; wipe out: *Vaccination has practically* eradicated *smallpox*. **e·rad·i·cat·ed, e·rad·i·cat·ing**.

e·rase (ĭ rās′) **1** to rub out: *to erase a problem from the blackboard*. **2** to remove all marks of; obliterate: *to erase a thought from the mind*. **e·rased, e·ras·ing**.

e·ras·er (ĭ rā′sər) anything used for rubbing out written marks: *an eraser for the blackboard; an eraser on a pencil*.

ere (âr) poetic word meaning "before." (Homonyms: air, e'er, heir)

e·rect (ĭ rĕkt′) **1** upright in posture or position: *Stand erect, please!* **2** to construct or build: *They will erect a new building*. **e·rect·ly**.

e·rec·tion (ĭ rĕk′shən) **1** a raising; a building; setting up: *The erection of a new school will be expensive*. **2** something that is erected; building: *The new school is a handsome erection*.

er·mine (ûr′mĭn) **1** a kind of weasel, the fur of which, except the tail tip, turns white in winter. **2** the winter fur of this animal.

Ermine, about 14 in. long

e·rode (ĭ rōd′) to wear away, as by rubbing; eat away: *Rain eroded deep gullies in the hillside. The wiring was eroded by acid*. **e·rod·ed, e·rod·ing**.

e·ro·sion (ĭ rō′zhən) gradual wearing or eating away: *the erosion of rocks by running water; the erosion of freedom by unjust laws*.

err (ûr) to make a mistake; do wrong; be incorrect: *To err is human*.

er·rand (ĕr′ənd) **1** trip for a special purpose: *an errand of mercy*. **2** thing to be done on such a trip: *I've finished my errands*.

er·rant (ĕr′ənt) **1** roving in search of adventure: *an errant minstrel; an errant knight*. **2** mistaken; wrong: *his errant behavior*.

er·rat·ic (ĭ răt′ĭk) **1** wandering; irregular: *an erratic imagination*. **2** odd; eccentric: *her erratic behavior*.

er·ro·ne·ous (ə rō′nē əs) incorrect; mistaken: *an erroneous belief*. **er·ro·ne·ous·ly**.

er·ror (ĕr′ər) **1** mistake: *an error in spelling*. **2** wrongness of conduct: *At last he saw the error of his ways*. **3 in error** in a mistaken or erroneous state of mind.

e·rupt (ĭ rŭpt′) **1** to burst forth: *The volcano erupted. The meeting erupted into a din of angry voices*. **2** to hurl out: *The volcano erupts lava*.

e·rup·tion (ĭ rŭp′shən) **1** a bursting out or forth; outbreak: *the eruption of a volcano; an eruption of violence*. **2** a rash on the skin.

es·ca·la·tor (ĕs′kə lā′tər) a moving stairway (to convey passengers from floor to floor of a building, subway, etc.).

es·cape (ĕs kāp′) **1** to break loose; get free; get away: *The criminals escaped from prison.* **2** to keep free or safe from; avoid: *He was lucky to escape the storm.* **3** to flow out: *Some gas escaped from the stove.* **4** a getting free from or away from: *The prisoner's escape was successful.* **5** a means of escape: *a fire escape.* **es·caped, es·cap·ing.**

escape velocity velocity to which a space craft must be accelerated before the power is cut off, in order to overcome the force of gravity. The escape velocity from Earth is about 25,000 m.p.h.

¹**es·cort** (ĕs′kôrt) **1** a group or body of persons, ships, or planes that accompanies and safeguards another: *An escort of destroyers accompanied the aircraft carrier. An armed guard formed an escort for the President.* **2** a person who attends or accompanies another.

²**es·cort** (ĕs kôrt′) to attend or accompany: *Jet fighters escorted the bombers.*

Es·ki·mo (ĕs′kə mō′) member of the race that lives mainly in the arctic regions of North America. **Es·ki·mos** or **Es·ki·mo.**

Eskimos

Eskimo dog a powerful, wolflike dog with a heavy gray coat, used by Eskimos to draw sleds. Also called **Husky.**

e·soph·a·gus (ē sŏf′ə gəs) the tube through which food passes from the mouth to the stomach.

es·pe·cial (ĕs pĕsh′əl) special. **es·pe·cial·ly.**

es·pi·o·nage (ĕs′pĭ ə nĭj or ĕs′pĭ ə näzh′) **1** spying; the work of a government spy. **2** the systematic use of spies: *the use of espionage to discover military secrets.*

¹**es·say** (ĕs′ā) **1** a short piece of writing on some chosen subject, generally giving the personal views of the author. **2** (also ĕ sā′) an attempt; an experiment.

²**es·say** (ĕ sā′) to try: *Tom essayed the high jump.*

es·sence (ĕs′əns) **1** that which makes a thing what it is; true inward nature: *A friendly attitude is the very essence of peace.* **2** concentrated extract that is dissolved in alcohol: *the essence of peppermint.* **3** a perfume.

es·sen·tial (ə sĕn′shəl) **1** necessary; not to be done without; basic: *Food is essential for life.* **2** necessary part: *Free speech and the right to vote are essentials of a democracy.* **3** basic thing or idea: *Teach the essentials of reading and writing.*

es·sen·tial·ly (ə sĕn′shə lĭ) for the most part; basically; fundamentally: *Most dogs have essentially the same habits.*

-est a suffix meaning "most." It is used when three or more things are being compared: *cold*est; *prettiest.*

es·tab·lish (ĕs tăb′lĭsh) **1** to found: *to establish a school.* **2** to settle; place firmly: *He established his son in business.* **3** to cause to be accepted: *to establish a rule; to establish a custom.* **4** to prove legally or beyond any doubt: *to establish a claim.*

es·tab·lish·ment (ĕs tăb′lĭsh mənt) **1** an establishing or being established: *the establishment of a new town.* **2** a thing established, such as a business, household, etc.: *That clothing establishment has been on Maple Street for 60 years.*

es·tate (ĕs tāt′) **1** large house and lands: *an estate in the country.* **2** everything owned by a person; property: *His estate was divided among his children.* **3** position or stage in life: *He reached man's estate at the age of 21.*

es·teem (ĕs tēm′) **1** to think highly of; regard as valuable: *The staff officers esteem the general.* **2** to consider; look upon as: *I shall esteem it an honor to attend the governor's dinner.* **3** high opinion; respect: *"Treasure Island" has enjoyed the esteem of generations of readers.*

¹**es·ti·mate** (ĕs′tə māt′) to form an opinion or judgment about (value, amount, size, etc.): *to estimate a man's character; to estimate the size of a room.* **es·ti·mat·ed, es·ti·mat·ing.**

---

fāte, făt, fâre, fär; bē, bĕt; bīte, bĭt; nō, nŏt, nôr; fūse, fŭn, fûr; tōō, tŏŏk; foil; foul; thin; ~~then~~;
hw for wh as in *wh*at; zh for s as in u*s*ual; ə for a, e, i, o, u, as in *a*go, lin*e*n, per*i*l, at*o*m, min*u*s

²es·ti·mate (ĕs′tə mĭt) **1** calculation of cost or value: *The carpenter gave an* estimate *of $45 for the job.* **2** a written statement of such a calculation.

es·ti·ma·tion (ĕs′tə mā′shən) **1** judgment; opinion: *In my* estimation *this book is very well written.* **2** regard; esteem; respect: *a man held in high* estimation *by all.*

es·tu·ar·y (ĕs′chōō ĕr′ĭ) wide mouth of a river where it joins the sea or ocean and into which the tide flows. **es·tu·ar·ies.**

etc. et cetera.

et cet·er·a (ĕt sĕt′ər ə) and others; and so forth; and so on.

etch (ĕch) **1** to make designs on metal, glass, etc., by causing acid to eat into the surface: *to* etch *a flower on a tumbler.* **2** to practice this art.

etch·ing (ĕch′ĭng) **1** the making of a design or picture on metal, glass, etc., by the use of acid or a sharp tool. **2** picture printed from a metal plate etched by acid or by a pointed tool: *a collection of* etchings.

e·ter·nal (ĭ tûr′nəl) **1** without beginning or end; everlasting; timeless: *the promise of* eternal *life.* **2** never ceasing: *their* eternal *chatter; her* eternal *complaints.* **e·ter·nal·ly.**

e·ter·ni·ty (ĭ tûr′nə tĭ) **1** time without beginning or end; everlasting. time. **2** time that seems endless: *I feel as if I've waited an* eternity *for an answer.* **3** life after death: *He hovered between life and* eternity. **e·ter·ni·ties.**

e·ther (ē′thər) **1** a liquid whose fumes cause unconsciousness. **2** an imaginary substance thought of as filling up space.

e·the·re·al (ĭ thĭr′ĭ əl) **1** light; airy; delicate: *What* ethereal *music!* **2** heavenly; unearthly: *Angels are* ethereal *beings.* **e·the·re·al·ly.**

eth·i·cal (ĕth′ĭ kəl) **1** having to do with ethics or morality: *an* ethical *basis for action.* **2** in keeping with moral standards: *It was not the* ethical *thing to do.* **3** according to the standards of proper action in a particular profession: *It is not* ethical *for a lawyer to reveal information about his clients.* **eth·i·cal·ly.**

eth·ics (ĕth′ĭks) **1** standards of right conduct; morals: *I won't go into the* ethics *of his dealings.* **2** standards of proper action within a particular profession: *legal* ethics; *medical* ethics. **3** the branch of philosophy

that deals with the principles of right and wrong action.

et·i·quette (ĕt′ə kĕt′) rules of behavior used by polite people.

eu·ca·lyp·tus (ū′kə lĭp′təs) a tall Australian tree, valuable for its timber, fragrant gum, and medicinal oil. **eu·ca·lyp·ti** (ū′kə lĭp′tī) or **eu·ca·lyp·tus·es.**

Eu·cha·rist (ū′kə rĭst) **1** the sacrament of the Lord's Supper; Holy Communion. **2** consecrated bread and wine used in this sacrament.

Eu·rope (yŏŏr′əp) a continent west of Asia and east of the Atlantic Ocean.

Eu·ro·pe·an (yŏŏr′ə pē′ən) **1** of the countries in Europe or their people. **2** a citizen of a country in Europe, or person who comes from a country in Europe, or person of European descent.

e·vac·u·ate (ĭ văk′yŏŏ āt′) **1** to empty out. **2** to leave empty; withdraw people from: *The threatening floods made it necessary to* evacuate *the town.* **e·vac·u·at·ed, e·vac·u·at·ing.**

e·vade (ĭ vād′) to dodge; go or get around; slyly avoid meeting or getting in the way of: *The platoon* evaded *the Indians ahead by turning off to the west. He found ways to* evade *the law.* **e·vad·ed, e·vad·ing.**

e·van·ge·list (ĭ văn′jə lĭst) **1** a traveling preacher, especially one who holds revival meetings. **2** anyone who preaches the Gospel. **3** any one of the four writers of the Gospel: Matthew, Mark, Luke, or John.

e·vap·o·rate (ĭ văp′ə rāt′) **1** to change from solid or liquid into vapor: *Water* evaporates. **2** to remove moisture from by heating or drying: *to* evaporate *milk.* **3** to disappear like vapor; fade: *Their hopes for a pleasant day* evaporated *when the rain began to fall.* **e·vap·o·rat·ed, e·vap·o·rat·ing.**

evaporated milk canned milk that is thickened by evaporation of some of its water.

e·vap·o·ra·tion (ĭ văp′ə rā′shən) **1** a changing or being changed into vapor. **2** removal of moisture by heating or drying.

e·va·sive (ĭ vā′sĭv) seeking to avoid or escape; not straightforward: *When his mother asked him where he had been, Tom gave an* evasive *answer.* **e·va·sive·ly.**

eve (ēv) **1** poetic form of **evening. 2** time just before: *the* eve *of a battle.* **3 Eve** the evening or day before a holiday: *Christmas* Eve.

e·ven (ē'vən) **1** flat; smooth: *The land is* even, *without hills.* **2** at the same level: *He hung the picture* even *with his eye.* **3** equal: *These two horses were* even *at the finish.* **4** steady; regular: *A healthy person has an* even *pulse.* **5** to make level: *Our neighbor* evened *his hedge.* **6** to make equal: *The last home run* evened *the score.* **7** so much as: *He didn't* even *apologize when he was late.* **8** exact; precise: *An* even *quart has two pints.* **9** still: *You can do* even *better.* **10** just; at the same time as: *We were wondering about the time* even *as the clock struck.* **11** no matter: *I'll go for a walk* even *if it rains.* **12** as well: *Their weather is warm* even *in winter.* **13** even *number* number that can be divided by 2 without leaving a remainder. Some even numbers are 2, 4, 6, and 10. **e·ven·ly.**

eve·ning (ēv'ning) time between sunset and bedtime; late hours of daylight and early hours of darkness.

e·vent (ĭ vĕnt') **1** happening: *to read about current* events. **2** result; outcome: *On the* event *of the game depends our chance for the championship.* **3** item in a program, especially a sports program: *He was third in the javelin* event. **4 at all events** or **in any event** whatever happens; in any case.

e·vent·ful (ĭ vĕnt'fəl) **1** full of happenings: *an eventful day.* **2** important; outstanding: *an eventful choice.* **e·vent·ful·ly.**

e·ven·tide (ē'vən tĭd') old word for "evening."

e·ven·tu·al (ĭ vĕn'chōō əl) happening at the end; final: *His eventual success is certain.* **e·ven·tu·al·ly.**

ev·er (ĕv'ər) **1** at any time: *Did you* ever *ride a horse?* **2** at all times: *The Minute Men were* ever *ready for battle.* **3** in any way; at all: *How* ever *did you finish the book so quickly?* **4 ever so** very: *I am* ever *so pleased that you enjoyed the book.*

Ev·er·glades (ĕv'ər glādz') a swampy region in southern Florida largely covered by forest.

ev·er·green (ĕv'ər grēn') **1** remaining green throughout the year: *We planted* evergreen *shrubs.* **2** a plant, shrub, or tree that remains green throughout the year: *Holly is an* evergreen *popular at Christmas.*

Evergreens

ev·er·last·ing (ĕv'ər-lăs'tĭng) **1** lasting forever. **2** kept up too long; seemingly endless: *that everlasting racket from the radio next door.* **ev·er·last·ing·ly.**

ev·er·more (ĕv'ər môr') always; forever.

eve·ry (ĕv'rĭ) **1** all in an entire group; each: *He colored* every *picture in the book. He comes* every *day.* **2** all possible: *I have* every *confidence in his ability.* **3 every now and then** from time to time. **4 every other** each second (person or thing).

eve·ry·bod·y (ĕv'rĭ bŏd'ĭ) every person; everyone: *Is* everybody *here?*

eve·ry·day (ĕv'rĭ dā') **1** daily; characteristic of all days: *Watching television is an* everyday *event in most households.* **2** for ordinary days: *Wear* everyday *clothes to school.* **3** ordinary; commonplace: *He talked about* everyday *matters like food and the weather.*

eve·ry·one (ĕv'rĭ wŭn') each person; everybody: *We hear that* everyone *will be asked.*

eve·ry·thing (ĕv'rĭ thĭng') all things: *Tell me* everything *about your birthday party.*

eve·ry·where (ĕv'rĭ hwâr') in every place; in all places or parts: *We looked* everywhere *in the neighborhood for my lost cat.*

ev·i·dence (ĕv'ə dəns) **1** facts; proof; indication: *What* evidence *do you have that he robbed the bank?* **2** to show; prove: *His pleasant tone* evidenced *his good will.* **3 in evidence** (plainly) to be seen: *He is nowhere* in evidence. **ev·i·denced, ev·i·denc·ing.**

ev·i·dent (ĕv'ə dənt) clear; plain; easy to see or understand; obvious: *The facts made his guilt* evident *to all.* **ev·i·dent·ly.**

e·vil (ē'vəl) **1** bad; wrong; harmful: *the* evil *effects of a flood.* **2** sin; wrongdoing. **3** anything that takes away happiness and well-being. **e·vil·ly.**

---

e·voke (ĭ vōk′) to call forth; call up; produce: *His letter* evoked *a nasty response.* **e·voked, e·vok·ing.**

ev·o·lu·tion (ĕv′ə lōō′shən or ĕv ə lū′shən) **1** growth; development: *the* evolution *of an oak from an acorn.* **2** theory that plants and animals which are now living have developed from lower and simpler forms of life.

e·volve (ĭ vŏlv′) to unfold; develop by degrees: *An oak tree* evolves *from a tiny acorn. The doctor* evolved *a new cure.* **e·volved, e·volv·ing.**

ewe (ū) female sheep. (Homonyms: yew, you)

ex·act (ĕg zăkt′) **1** correct; precise; accurate: *He made an* exact *copy of the painting.* **2** to require; insist upon: *The bank* exacted *6% interest on the loan.*

ex·act·ing (ĕg zăk′tĭng) making great demands; trying; severe: *Engineering is very* exacting *work. He is an* exacting *teacher.* **ex·act·ing·ly.**

ex·act·ly (ĕg zăkt′lĭ) **1** without error; precisely: *to follow instructions* exactly. **2** yes, indeed; quite so: *He answered,* "Exactly!"

ex·ag·ger·ate (ĕg zăj′ə rāt′) to speak of or show (something) as greater than it is: *The boy* exaggerated *the size of the fish he caught.* **ex·ag·ger·ated, ex·ag·ger·at·ing.**

ex·ag·ger·a·tion (ĕg zăj′ə rā′shən) **1** a speaking of or showing (something) as larger or greater than it is: *an* exaggeration *of the truth.* **2** something described or shown in a way that goes beyond the facts: *a story full of* exaggerations.

ex·alt (ĕg zôlt′) **1** to raise in rank and dignity: *The people* exalted *him to the office of President.* **2** to praise highly; glorify: *They* exalted *God in their hymns.*

ex·am·i·na·tion (ĕg zăm′ə nā′shən) **1** a careful check in order to find out facts; inspection; investigation: *He went to the dentist for an* examination *of his teeth.* **2** a test of knowledge or skill: *The teacher gave us an* examination *in spelling and reading.* **3** a questioning of a witness in court.

ex·am·ine (ĕg zăm′ən) **1** to look at carefully in order to find out the facts; inspect; investigate: *He* examined *the flower under the microscope.* **2** to question in order to find out the knowledge of: *to* examine *a class; to* examine *a witness in court.* **ex·am·ined, ex·am·in·ing.**

ex·am·ple (ĕg zăm′pəl) **1** one part of a group which is used to show what the whole is like; sample: *This embroidery is an* example *of her best work.* **2** an illustration of a rule, process, or procedure: *The teacher wrote some* examples *in addition on the blackboard.* **3** person, thing, or act that is fit to be copied; model: *The boy is an* example *for all of us.* **4** case or instance set aside as warning: *Let this be an* example *to you!* **5 set an example** to be or give an example.

ex·as·per·ate (ĕg zăs′pə rāt′) to make intensely angry; annoy keenly; irritate greatly: *The child's insolence* exasperated *his mother.* **ex·as·per·at·ed, ex·as·per·at·ing.**

ex·as·per·a·tion (ĕg zăs′pə rā′shən) keen annoyance; great irritation; great vexation: *She gave up in* exasperation.

ex·ca·vate (ĕks′kə vāt′) **1** to dig or hollow out: *to* excavate *a cave in a hillside.* **2** to uncover by digging: *The men* excavated *the ruins of the ancient city.* **ex·ca·vat·ed, ex·ca·vat·ing.**

ex·ca·va·tion (ĕks′kə vā′shən) **1** the digging or hollowing out of something: *The* excavation *of the street for new pipes will take a long time.* **2** hole formed by digging: *an* excavation *for water pipes.*

ex·ceed (ĕk sēd′) **1** to go beyond (the limit of): *Her baggage* exceeded *the weight limit on the plane.* **2** to be greater than; surpass: *Edison's genius* exceeded *that of the other inventors of his time.*

ex·ceed·ing (ĕk sē′dĭng) more than usual; extraordinary. **ex·ceed·ing·ly.**

ex·cel (ĕk sĕl′) to be superior to others in ability or quality; to stand out: *He* excels *in sports.* **ex·celled, ex·cel·ling.**

ex·cel·lence (ĕk′sə ləns) superior quality; outstanding goodness or worth.

ex·cel·len·cy (ĕk′sə lən sĭ) **1** excellence. **2 Excellency** title of honor for certain high officials. **ex·cel·len·cies.**

ex·cel·lent (ĕk′sə lənt) extremely good; unusually high in quality. **ex·cel·lent·ly.**

ex·cept (ĕk sĕpt′) **1** outside of; but; apart from: *Everyone was here* except *me.* **2** to leave out; omit: *They were* excepted *from the list of guests to be invited.*

ex·cept·ing (ĕk sĕp′tĭng) except; not including: *The whole class* excepting *Judy passed the test.*

ex·cep·tion (ĕk sĕp'shən) **1** a leaving out of a person or thing; omission: *Every boy without exception must be there by noon.* **2** something that differs from others of the same class or group: *This is an exception to the rule.* **3 take exception to** to object to; protest against: *I took exception to his views on civil rights.*

ex·cep·tion·al (ĕk sĕp'shən əl) uncommon; unusual; extraordinary: *She was a singer of exceptional talent.* **ex·cep·tion·al·ly.**

ex·cess (ĕk'sĕs or ĕk sĕs') **1** more than enough; abundance: *He has an excess of energy.* **2** the amount by which one thing is more than another: *The baggage weighed sixty pounds, an excess of sixteen pounds over the limit.* **3** extra: *our excess baggage; to pay excess postage.* **4 to excess** too much: *He eats to excess and puts on weight.*

ex·ces·sive (ĕk sĕs'ĭv) too much; extreme: *his excessive demands.* **ex·ces·sive·ly.**

ex·change (ĕks chānj') **1** to give something for something else; barter: *to exchange a knife for a top.* **2** to give and receive: *to exchange ideas.* **3** a giving of one thing for another: *an exchange of ten marbles for a whistle.* **4** a giving and receiving: *an exchange of greetings.* **5** substitution: *We found the exchange of city life for a country vacation very restful.* **6** a place where trading is carried on: *The stock exchange is next door.* **7** a central office of a telephone system. **ex·changed, ex·chang·ing.**

ex·cit·a·ble (ĕk sī'tə bəl) easily stirred up; easily roused: *He is too excitable to be trusted in dangerous work.* **ex·cit·a·bly.**

ex·cite (ĕk sīt') **1** to stir the mind or emotions: *The first day of school excited us.* **2** to stir up; arouse; set in motion: *to excite pity.* **3** to stir to action; impel: *to excite troops to an assault.* **ex·cit·ed, ex·cit·ing.**

ex·cit·ed (ĕk sī'tĭd) aroused; stirred up; emotionally moved; stimulated. **ex·cit·ed·ly.**

ex·cite·ment (ĕk sīt'mənt) **1** an excited or stirred up state; ado; commotion: *The news of victory aroused excitement everywhere.* **2** something that excites.

ex·claim (ĕks klām') to speak or cry out suddenly in surprise, anger, pleasure, etc.:

"Hurrah!" he exclaimed, *when he saw his new bicycle.*

ex·cla·ma·tion (ĕks'klə mā'shən) sudden outcry as an expression of feeling, such as *Watch out! Stop! Ouch! Hurrah!*

exclamation point or **mark** a mark in writing or printing (!) indicating surprise, sorrow, or other strong feeling.

ex·clam·a·to·ry (ĕks klăm'ə tôr'ĭ) using, expressing, or containing an exclamation: *an exclamatory sentence.*

ex·clude (ĕks klōōd') to shut or keep out; prevent from entering: *He was excluded from the club because of his age. Thick walls exclude sound.* **ex·clud·ed, ex·clud·ing.**

ex·clud·ing (ĕks klōō'dĭng) with the exception of; not including: *Everybody in the class, excluding Sally, has brown eyes.*

ex·clu·sion (ĕks klōō'zhən) **1** a shutting out or excluding: *The exclusion of women from certain jobs.* **2** the condition of being excluded: *John's exclusion from the team.*

ex·clu·sive (ĕks klōō'sĭv) **1** not easy to join; excluding most: *an exclusive club.* **2** sole; not shared: *his exclusive control of the company.* **3 exclusive of** not including: *This car costs $2000.00 exclusive of extras.* **4 mutually exclusive** not capable of existing together or at the same time: *"Dictatorship" and "liberty" are* mutually exclusive *terms.* **ex·clu·sive·ly.**

ex·com·mu·ni·cate (ĕks'kə mū'nə kāt') to cut off from membership in a church. **ex·com·mu·ni·cat·ed, ex·com·mu·ni·cat·ing.**

ex·cur·sion (ĕks kûr'zhən) **1** a short trip generally made by a group of people for a special purpose or for pleasure: *The class went on an excursion to the museum.* **2** a special round trip at a reduced fare.

¹ex·cuse (ĕks kūz') **1** to pardon; forgive: *He excused his brother's mistake.* **2** to free from duty or obligation: *He was excused from school. He excused himself from attending.* **3** to make an apology or explanation for: *Shyness excuses her awkwardness.* **ex·cused, ex·cus·ing.**

²ex·cuse (ĕks kūs') **1** reason given as an explanation: *an excuse for being late.* **2** a release (from a duty, promise, etc.).

---

fāte, făt, fâre, fär; bē, bĕt; bīte, bĭt; nō, nŏt, nôr; fūse, fŭn, fûr; tōō, tŏŏk; foil; foul; thin; ~~then~~; hw for wh as in *wh*at; zh for s as in u*s*ual; ə for a, e, i, o, u, as in *a*go, lin*e*n, per*i*l, at*o*m, min*u*s

ex·e·cute (ĕk′sə kūt′) **1** to carry out; complete: *The contractor executed the architect's plan.* **2** to put to death according to law: *The murderer was executed for his crime.* **3** to perform: *The player executed the piano solo perfectly.* **ex·e·cut·ed, ex·e·cut·ing.**

ex·e·cu·tion (ĕk′sə kū′shən) **1** a carrying out (of a piece of work); completion: *The proper execution of a plan.* **2** manner or style (in which a thing is done); skill: *the violinist's fine execution.* **3** punishment by death.

ex·e·cu·tion·er (ĕk′sə kū′shən ər) person who puts a condemned person to death.

ex·ec·u·tive (ĕg zĕk′yōō tĭv′) **1** a person who is in charge of the affairs of an organization: *A good executive is expert in supervising the work of others.* **2** person, body, or branch of government that puts laws into effect: *The President is the chief executive of this country.* **3** having to do with the managing of a company or the governing of a country: *at the executive level; an executive order.*

ex·em·pli·fy (ĕg zĕm′plə fī′) to show or serve as an example of; illustrate; demonstrate: *This picture exemplifies the artist's skill.* **ex·em·pli·fied, ex·em·pli·fy·ing.**

ex·empt (ĕg zĕmpt′) **1** free (from a tax, etc.): *Common foods are generally exempt from direct tax.* **2** to make free (from a duty, etc.); excuse: *That injury will exempt him from military service.*

ex·er·cise (ĕk′sər sīz′) **1** to put into action; use: *to exercise authority, care, or self-control.* **2** to use in order to train or develop: *to exercise the muscles or the mind.* **3** physical or mental activity that improves the body or mind: *Swimming is good exercise.* **4** to take exercise: *to exercise every day.* **5** lesson for practice: *arithmetic exercises in addition.* **6** formal program; ceremony: *Opening exercises are held each morning.* **ex·er·cised, ex·er·cis·ing.**

ex·ert (ĕg zûrt′) to use; put into use: *to exert all one's strength.*

exert oneself to make an effort: *He didn't exert himself to win the prize.*

ex·er·tion (ĕg zûr′shən) **1** use of strength or force; effort: *Football requires a great deal of exertion. Their exertions were in vain.* **2** active use: *by exertion of his will.*

ex·hale (ĕks hāl′) **1** to breathe out; give off: *to exhale breath.* **2** to give off in form of vapor: *A plant exhales oxygen in the sunlight.* **ex·haled, ex·hal·ing.**

ex·haust (ĕg zôst′) **1** to empty; drain; use up: *He had exhausted our supply of water long before we reached the spring.* **2** to tire (oneself) out completely: *He exhausted himself playing tennis.* **3** to discuss or treat thoroughly: *They exhausted the subject of politics.* **4** discharge of used steam or gas fumes from an engine after each stroke of a piston: *The air was black from the exhaust of the car.* **5** the pipe through which discharged steam or gas fumes escape. **6** discharged steam or gas fumes.

ex·haust·ed (ĕg zôs′tĭd) **1** worn out; tired out completely. **2** used up: *My funds were exhausted by the trip.* **ex·haust·ed·ly.**

ex·haus·tion (ĕg zôs′chən) **1** the draining or using up (of something): *The exhaustion of the water supply came as a shock to everyone.* **2** condition of being worn out; extreme fatigue: *the exhaustion that follows long exercise.*

ex·hib·it (ĕg zĭb′ĭt) **1** to show: *He exhibited all the symptoms of a cold.* **2** to show publicly; display: *to exhibit paintings; to exhibit courage.* **3** object or collection of objects offered for public view: *We went to an exhibit at the art museum.*

ex·hi·bi·tion (ĕk′sə bĭsh′ən) public showing; display: *an exhibition at the art gallery; an exhibition of strength.*

ex·hil·a·rate (ĕg zĭl′ə rāt′) to make merry or joyous; enliven: *Their walk in the snow exhilarated them.* **ex·hil·a·rat·ed, ex·hil·a·rat·ing.**

ex·hort (ĕg zôrt′) to advise strongly; urge earnestly: *The politician exhorted his hearers to vote for him.*

ex·ile (ĕg′zĭl or ĕk′sĭl) **1** to send away from home or country; banish: *They exiled the prisoner.* **2** banishment: *The man lived in exile on an island.* **3** person who is banished or goes away from his country for a long time: *The exile returned after ten years.* **ex·iled, ex·il·ing.**

ex·ist (ĕg zĭst′) **1** to be; be real: *He believes that goblins and elves exist.* **2** to live; continue to go on living: *Plants cannot exist without water.* **3** to be found; occur: *Does life exist on the other planets?*

ex·ist·ence (ĕg zĭs′təns) **1** the condition of being real: *Do you believe in the existence of ghosts?* **2** life: *Man's existence depends on oxygen.* **3** way of life: *He leads a peaceful existence in the country.*

ex·it (ĕg′zĭt or ĕk′sĭt) **1** a going out or away; departure: *The actor made his exit as the curtain fell.* **2** way or passage out: *They left the theater through the exit at the rear.*

ex·o·dus (ĕk′sə dəs) **1** a going away; a mass departure: *There is usually an exodus from cities on summer weekends.* **2 Exodus** second book of the Bible, which tells of the mass departure of the Jews from Egypt.

ex·or·bi·tant (ĕg zôr′bə tənt) much too high; excessive; out of all reason: *an exorbitant demand; an exorbitant price.* **ex·or·bi·tant·ly.**

ex·ot·ic (ĕg zŏt′ĭk) **1** from another part of the world; not native; strange: *an exotic plant.* **2** having the charm of strangeness: *an exotic Spanish dance.*

ex·pand (ĕks pănd′) **1** to spread out; become larger; increase: *Air expands as it rises. Metals expand when heated.* **2** to add more details to; enlarge; develop: *The author expanded his short story into a novel.*

ex·panse (ĕks păns′) wide, open space or area: *There is a great expanse of desert in the western United States.*

ex·pan·sion (ĕks păn′shən) **1** a spreading out; increasing: *the expansion of metals under heat.* **2** something that is spread out: *The book is the expansion of a short story.*

ex·pect (ĕks pĕkt′) **1** to look forward to as something that will probably happen: *I expect to go on a trip.* **2** to wait for or feel sure of the coming or arrival of: *I was expecting you. He expected a storm.* **3** to require: *You are expected to do a good job.*

ex·pect·ant (ĕks pĕk′tənt) looking forward to; thinking something will come or happen: *The children around the Christmas tree had an expectant look.* **ex·pect·ant·ly.**

ex·pec·ta·tion (ĕks′pĕk tā′shən) **1** a looking forward to something; anticipation: *After weeks of expectation the big day came.* **2** good reason for looking forward to something; prospect: *He has expectations of inheriting valuable property.*

ex·pec·to·rate (ĕks pĕk′tə rāt′) to spit. **ex·pec·to·rat·ed, ex·pec·to·rat·ing.**

ex·pe·di·ent (ĕks pē′dĭ ənt) **1** useful; suitable for accomplishing a certain purpose: *He found it expedient to take the plane rather than spend the night on a train.* **2** means of getting or accomplishing something; device: *Buying on credit is an expedient when you do not have the cash.* **ex·pe·di·ent·ly.**

ex·pe·di·tion (ĕks′pə dĭsh′ən) **1** trip for a special purpose: *a hunting expedition; a fishing expedition to Squam Lake.* **2** a group of people making a trip: *The expedition went to the South Pole.* **3** promptness: *The firemen showed great expedition in answering the call.*

ex·pel (ĕks pĕl′) to drive or force out: *He was expelled from school. The car expelled black fumes.* **ex·pelled, ex·pel·ling.**

ex·pend (ĕks pĕnd′) to use up; spend: *to expend strength, time, and money.*

ex·pen·di·ture (ĕks pĕn′də chər) **1** a spending (of money, time, labor, etc.). **2** something spent; outlay: *heavy expenditures for military preparation.*

ex·pense (ĕks pĕns′) **1** a spending of money, time, labor, etc.: *He was educated at considerable expense.* **2** cost: *the expense of an education.* **3** cause of spending: *Food, rent, and clothing are our chief expenses.* **4 at the expense of** with the loss of: *He succeeded, but at the expense of his health.*

ex·pen·sive (ĕks pĕn′sĭv) costly; high-priced. **ex·pen·sive·ly.**

ex·pe·ri·ence (ĕks pē′rĭ əns) **1** knowledge or skill gained by doing or seeing things: *Do you have the necessary experience for the job?* **2** a seeing, living through, or feeling something: *By experience we learn.* **3** to feel; live through: *The designers experienced a thrill at the first successful launching of their rocket.* **4** something felt, lived through, or enjoyed: *childhood experiences; frightening experiences in dreams.* **ex·pe·ri·enced, ex·pe·ri·enc·ing.**

ex·pe·ri·enced (ĕks pē′rĭ ənst) having skill or knowledge gained through doing and seeing things; expert; skilled: *an experienced doctor; an experienced traveler.*

---

fāte, făt, fâre, fär; bē, bĕt; bīte, bĭt; nō, nŏt, nôr; fūse, fŭn, fûr; tōō, tŏŏk; foil; foul; thin; ~~then~~;
hw for wh as in *what*; zh for s as in u*s*ual; ə for a, e, i, o, u, as in a*g*o, lin*e*n, per*i*l, at*o*m, min*u*s

experiment

ex·per·i·ment (ĕks pĕr′ə mənt) **1** trial or test to discover something new or whether something is true: *a science* experiment. **2** to make tests to find out something: *Pasteur experimented with bacteria.*

ex·per·i·men·tal (ĕks pĕr′ə mĕn′təl) having to do with experiments; trial: *an experimental engine.* **ex·per·i·men·tal·ly.**

ex·pert (ĕks′pûrt) **1** a person who has special skill or knowledge: *a science* expert; *a music* expert. **2** (also ĕks pûrt′) having special skill or knowledge; trained by practice; skillful: *an expert swimmer; an* expert *mechanic.* **ex·pert·ly.**

ex·pi·ra·tion (ĕk′spə rā′shən) **1** a coming to an end or close; completion; ending: *We shall renew our lease at its* expiration *next month.* **2** the act of breathing out.

ex·pire (ĕk spīr′) **1** to come to an end: *My driver's license* expires *next month.* **2** to die. **ex·pired, ex·pir·ing.**

ex·plain (ĕks plān′) **1** to make plain or clear; tell the meaning of: *An arithmetic book* explains *subtraction. Will you please* explain *these directions?* **2** to account for; give the reason or cause of: *How do you* explain *your mistake?*

ex·pla·na·tion (ĕks′plə nā′shən) **1** a making clear or plain: *This lesson requires a great deal of* explanation *to be understood.* **2** statement or fact which makes plain or accounts for something: *Did you hear his* explanation *of the accident?*

ex·plan·a·to·ry (ĕks plăn′ə tôr′ĭ) making clear: *an* explanatory *footnote.*

ex·plic·it (ĕks plĭs′ĭt) clearly stated so as to be unmistakable: *The directions were brief but* explicit. **ex·plic·it·ly.**

ex·plode (ĕks plōd′) **1** to burst forth with sudden loud noise: *The boiler* exploded. **2** to cause to burst suddenly with a loud noise: *Too much pressure* exploded *the boiler.* **3** to break forth: *The children* exploded *with laughter.* **4** to show to be false: *to* explode *a popular notion.* **ex·plod·ed, ex·plod·ing.**

ex·ploit (ĕks ploit′) **1** to put to use; develop; work: *The United States has many natural resources to be* exploited *in the future.* **2** to use selfishly for one's own purpose; make unfair use of: *to* exploit *one's friends.* **3** (also ĕks′ploit) bold, adventurous act; heroic deed.

expound

ex·plo·ra·tion (ĕks′plə rā′shən) **1** a searching out of unknown things or places: *an* exploration *of the ocean floor.* **2** investigation: *an* exploration *of the facts.*

ex·plore (ĕks plôr′) **1** to travel over or into (a region) to learn more about it: *Scientists from many countries have* explored *Antarctica.* **2** to examine closely: *Let us* explore *the subject of weather.* **ex·plored, ex·plor·ing.**

ex·plor·er (ĕks plôr′ər) a person who travels in unknown or far places to find out about them.

ex·plo·sion (ĕks plō′zhən) **1** sudden, violent bursting with a loud noise: *the* explosion *of an oil tank.* **2** sudden outburst: *an* explosion *of anger.*

ex·plo·sive (ĕks plō′sĭv) **1** likely to explode: *an* explosive *substance.* **2** material that explodes; gunpowder. **3** like an explosion: *an* explosive *burst of laughter.* **ex·plo·sive·ly.**

ex·port (ĕks′pôrt) **1** (also ĕks pôrt′) to send or carry out (goods) to another country for sale: *The United States* exports *cotton to Britain.* **2** goods sold and sent to a foreign country: *Sheep and sheep products are important* exports *of Australia.* **3** having to do with the sending of goods abroad to be sold: *My uncle is in the* export *trade.*

ex·pose (ĕks pōz′) **1** to lay open to view; uncover; make known: *to* expose *a crime; to* expose *a secret.* **2** to leave unprotected; deprive of protection: *to* expose *to cold, danger, etc.; to* expose *a friend to blame.* **3** to uncover; bare: *She* exposed *her back to the sun.* **4** to allow light to reach (a photographic film). **ex·posed, ex·pos·ing.**

ex·po·si·tion (ĕks′pə zĭsh′ən) **1** large exhibition or showing (of products, art, etc.): *an* exposition *of modern art.* **2** written or spoken explanation.

ex·po·sure (ĕks pō′zhər) **1** a making known; revealing: *the* exposure *of a plot.* **2** a being open or subject (to): *their* exposure *to disease;* exposure *to cold; her* exposure *to gossip.* **3** outlook: *the western* exposure *of a house.* **4** a letting light reach photographic film. **5** the length of time the film is subjected to light.

ex·pound (ĕks pound′) to set forth in detail; explain: *The pastor* expounded *the Book of Jonah.*

ex·press (ĕks prĕs′) **1** to show or make known (a meaning, idea, or feeling): *He expressed his thanks with a beaming smile. She expressed her deep feeling in a beautiful poem.* **2** plainly stated; definite: *It was Grandfather's express wish that George should receive his gold watch.* **3** in transportation, speedy; making few stops: *an* express *elevator.* **4** a train, plane, elevator, etc., that makes such trips: *The* express *leaves at 5:21.* **5** to send by speedy carrier: *to* express *a package to Chicago.* **6** a means of speedy transportation: *Send this package by* express *to Boston.*

ex·pres·sion (ĕks prĕsh′ən) **1** an expressing; a setting forth: *He was free in the expression of his opinions.* **2** a look on the face that shows feeling or thought: *a sad expression.* **3** a saying: *"Sick as a dog" is an old* expression.

ex·pres·sive (ĕks prĕs′ĭv) **1** full of expression; showing hidden meaning: *an* expressive *look.* **2** **expressive of** expressing. **ex·pres·sive·ly.**

ex·press·ly (ĕks prĕs′lĭ) **1** on purpose; specially: *He did it* expressly *to annoy me. This dress looks as if it were made expressly for you.* **2** clearly; plainly: *Mother told us* expressly *to come home at six o'clock.*

ex·pul·sion (ĕks pŭl′shən) a forcing or driving out: *the* expulsion *of air from the lungs; the* expulsion *of an enemy.*

ex·qui·site (ĕks′kwĭ zĭt) **1** delicately beautiful: *Many ferns are* exquisite *plants.* **2** excellent; refined: *her* exquisite *manners.* **3** keenly felt; intense: *an* exquisite *joy or pain.* **ex·qui·site·ly.**

ex·tend (ĕks tĕnd′) **1** to lengthen: *to extend a road; to extend a visit.* **2** to stretch out; spread out: *These plains* extend *for many miles.* **3** to enlarge; increase. **4** to give; offer: *to* extend *a warm welcome; to extend credit.*

ex·ten·sion (ĕks tĕn′shən) **1** a making longer or larger. **2** a stretching or reaching out. **3** an addition; enlargement.

ex·ten·sive (ĕks tĕn′sĭv) wide; far-reaching. **ex·ten·sive·ly.**

ex·tent (ĕks tĕnt′) size, space, amount, or degree to which a thing is extended;

length; limit: *the* extent *of his knowledge; to agree with someone to a certain* extent.

ex·te·ri·or (ĕks tē′rĭ ər) **1** outer part; outside: *The* exterior *of the house is white.* **2** outward or visible appearance: *He has a gruff* exterior *but he is really very kind.* **3** outer; external.

ex·ter·mi·nate (ĕks tûr′mə nāt′) to get rid of; destroy wholly: *This spray will* terminate *termites.* **ex·ter·mi·nat·ed, ex·ter·mi·nat·ing.**

ex·ter·nal (ĕks tûr′nəl) outside; exterior. **ex·ter·nal·ly.**

ex·tinct (ĕks tĭngkt′) **1** no longer existing; having died out: *The dinosaur is an* extinct *animal.* **2** no longer active: *an* extinct *volcano.*

ex·tinc·tion (ĕks tĭngk′shən) **1** a putting out: *the* extinction *of a fire.* **2** a wiping out; a destroying: *Naturalists are trying to prevent the* extinction *of rare birds.*

ex·tin·guish (ĕks tĭng′gwĭsh) **1** to put out: *to* extinguish *a light.* **2** to put an end to; destroy: *to* extinguish *hope.*

ex·tol (ĕks tōl′) to praise highly: *The guest of honor was* extolled *by the speakers at the banquet.* **ex·tolled, ex·tol·ling.**

ex·tra (ĕks′trə) **1** more than what is usual or expected: *I need* extra *time to finish this test.* **2** something added: *Use your allowance for* extras, *such as toys and books.* **3** especially: *an* extra *good meal.* **4** special edition of a newspaper.

¹ex·tract (ĕks trăkt′) **1** to pull out; draw out with effort: *to* extract *a tooth.* **2** to obtain by pressing, cooking, or some other special process: *to* extract *oil from olives; to* extract *gold from ore.* **3** to get; take out: *to* extract *a letter from a file; to* extract *information.*

²ex·tract (ĕks′trăkt) something taken out or obtained: *to use vanilla* extract; *an* extract *from a book.*

ex·traor·di·nar·y (ĕks trôr′də nĕr′ĭ) unusual; very special: *an* extraordinary *height; an* extraordinary *appearance.* **ex·traor·di·nar·i·ly.**

ex·trav·a·gance (ĕks trăv′ə·gəns) **1** a going beyond the bounds of reason or common sense: *Don't listen to his* extravagance. **2** careless or foolish spending of money.

---

fāte, făt, fâre, fär; bē, bĕt; bīte, bĭt; nō, nŏt, nôr; fūse, fŭn, fûr; tōō, tŏŏk; foil; foul; thin; ~~then~~; hw for wh as in *wh*at; zh for s as in u*s*ual; ə for a, e, i, o, u, as in ag*o*, lin*e*n, per*i*l, at*o*m, min*u*s

269

ex·trav·a·gant (ĕks trăv′ə gənt) **1** spending too much; wasteful. **2** going beyond reasonable limits: *an* extravagant *liar*. **ex·trav·a·gant·ly.**

ex·treme (ĕks trēm′) **1** highest; greatest; utmost: *with* extreme *joy; in* extreme *danger.* **2** farthest from what is usual: *today's* extreme *fashions.* **3** farthest: *the* extreme *end of the landing strip.* **4** the greatest possible degree: *I didn't know he'd go to that* extreme. **5 extremes** things as different as possible: *Freezing and boiling are* extremes *of temperature.* **6 go to ex·tremes** to do or say more than is usual or desirable. **ex·treme·ly.**

ex·trem·i·ty (ĕks trĕm′ə tĭ) **1** very end; last point or stage; tip: *the farthest* extremity *of Greenland.* **2** greatest or highest degree: *the* extremity *of misery.* **3** an extreme measure or action: *The starving explorers were forced to the* extremity *of eating their horses.* **4 extremities** hands and feet. **ex·trem·i·ties.**

ex·tri·cate (ĕks′trə kāt′) to release or set free (from danger or difficulty): *The woodsman* extricated *the deer from the quicksand.* **ex·tri·cat·ed, ex·tri·cat·ing.**

ex·ult (ĕg zŭlt′) to feel great joy or triumph; rejoice: *The football players* exulted *at winning the championship.*

ex·ult·ant (ĕg zŭl′tənt) showing or feeling great joy; triumphant. **ex·ult·ant·ly.**

ex·ul·ta·tion (ĕg′zŭl tā′shən) great joy; triumphant rejoicing: *The crowd cheered in* exultation *at the news.*

eye (ī) **1** the bodily organ with which a person sees. **2** a gaze; a look: *Archie cast a longing* eye *at the cake.* **3** close watch: *Keep an* eye *on the baby.* **4** something thought to resemble an eye, such as the hole where a needle is threaded or the bud of a potato. **5** to look at; gaze at: *The policeman* eyed *the gang on the corner.*

6 catch one's eye to capture (a person's) attention. **7 eyes** judgment; opinion: *Bert's work had little worth in the* eyes *of his teacher.* **8 have an eye for** to be able to notice with appreciation: *to have an* eye for *beauty; to* have an eye for *a bargain.*

Eye

9 make eyes at to flirt with. **10 see eye to eye** to agree perfectly. **11 set eyes on** to see. **eyed, ey·ing** or **eye·ing.** (Homonyms: ²ay or ²aye, I)

eye·ball (ī′bôl′) all of the eye, without the lids and the socket. For picture, see **eye.**

eye·brow (ī′brou′) **1** the ridge above the eye. **2** the hair that grows on this ridge.

eye dropper small glass tube with a rubber bulb used to apply drops of medicine to the eye.

eye·glass (ī′glăs′) **1** the lens through which a person looks in a telescope or microscope. **2 eyeglasses** a pair of glass lenses used to improve poor eyesight.

eye·lash (ī′lăsh′) **1** a protective fringe of hair that grows on the eyelid. **2** single hair of this fringe.

eye·let (ī′lĭt) **1** small hole in leather or cloth for a lace or cord. **2** metal ring to strengthen the hole. (Homonym: islet)

eye·lid (ī′lĭd′) upper or lower cover of skin that opens or closes the eye.

eye·piece (ī′pēs′) in a telescope, microscope, etc., the lens nearest the eye of the user.

eye·sight (ī′sīt′) **1** power to see. **2** range of sight: *The house is within* eyesight.

eye strain tired or strained condition of the eyes caused by poor eyesight, reading in bad light, etc.

eye·tooth (ī′tooth′) either of the two pointed or canine teeth in the upper jaw. **eye·teeth.**

F

F, f (ĕf) sixth letter of the English alphabet.

fa (fä) fourth note in the musical scale.

fa·ble (fā′bəl) **1** story that teaches a moral or lesson, especially one in which animals talk and act like people. **2** a statement or

tale that is not true: *His story of having helped put out the fire is a* fable.

fab·ric (făb′rĭk) woven or knitted cloth.

fab·u·lous (făb′yə ləs) **1** hard or impossible to believe; amazing: *to win a* fabulous fortune. **2** found in fables; imaginary: *the fabulous monsters in fairy tales.* **fab·u·lous·ly.**

fa·çade (fə säd′) **1** entire outer side of a building, especially the main front or the side facing the street. **2** an appearance put on in order to deceive others: *A facade of calmness hid her terror.*

face (fās) **1** the front of the head. The eyes, nose, and mouth are parts of the face. **2** a surface; the side of an object that is more important or has a special purpose: *the face of a clock, coin, playing card, etc.* **3** to turn toward; be opposite to: *She faced her partner in the square dance.* **4** to stand bravely against; confront: *to face an enemy; to face danger, ruin, or disgrace.* **5** to cover (with something): *to face a house with brick.* **6 face to face** with faces turned toward one another: *They stood face to face.* **7 face to face with** in the presence of: *He came face to face with his enemy.* **8 in the face of** in the presence of: *He showed courage in the face of danger.* **9 to one's face** openly; in one's presence: *He didn't dare say it to my face.* **10 lose face** to suffer a loss of reputation; be humiliated. **11 make a face** to twist the features to show disgust, disapproval, etc. **12 save one's face** to escape disgrace or loss of reputation. **faced, fac·ing.**

fac·et (făs′ĭt) any of the small, flat surfaces on a cut gem.

fa·cial (fā′shəl) **1** of or for the face: *a facial expression.* **2** a treatment of the face by massage, rubbing in of lotions, etc.: *She asked the girl in the beauty shop for a facial.* **fa·cial·ly.**

Facets of a gem

fa·cil·i·tate (fə sĭl′ə tāt′) to make easy or easier: *Airplanes facilitate travel.* **fa·cil·i·tat·ed, fa·cil·i·tat·ing.**

fa·cil·i·ty (fə sĭl′ə tĭ) **1** ease; skill: *She has a facility for learning languages.* **2** device or means which makes something easier: *Good kitchen facilities are a help in cooking.* **fa·cil·i·ties.**

fact (făkt) **1** something real; a proved and accepted truth: *That fire burns is a fact.* **2** an actual event, experience, or deed: *The Battle of Bunker Hill is a historic fact.* **3** reality; the quality of being real: *to be able to tell fact from fiction.* **4** statement of something established as true: *to check the facts in a report.*

fac·tor (făk′tər) **1** something that helps to bring about a result: *Diet and exercise are important factors in healthy living.* **2** in arithmetic, any number which can be multiplied by another number to get a given product: *The factors of 10 are 2 and 5.*

fac·to·ry (făk′tə rĭ) building, group of buildings, or part of a building where goods are manufactured. **fac·to·ries.**

fac·tu·al (făk′chŏŏ əl) having to do with facts; based on facts; consisting of facts; not theoretical; real. **fac·tu·al·ly.**

fac·ul·ty (făk′əl tĭ) **1** ability to do something; talent: *She has a faculty for saying the right thing.* **2** a power of the mind or body: *the faculty of sight.* **3** staff of teachers in a school or university. **fac·ul·ties.**

fad (făd) fashion or craze; something everyone does for a time.

fade (fād) **1** to grow dim or faint: *Some colors fade easily. The sound of drums faded away.* **2** to cause to lose color: *The sun faded the dress.* **3** to wither: *The flowers fade in autumn.* **fad·ed, fad·ing.**

fag (făg) to work, or cause to work, until completely tired out: *We were fagged by the long climb.* **fagged, fag·ging.**

fa·got or **fag·got** (făg′ət) bundle of sticks tied together and used for firewood.

Fahr·en·heit (făr′ən hīt′) a temperature scale on which 32 degrees is the freezing point and 212 degrees is the boiling point of water. It is used in cooking, weather forecasts, etc.

fail (fāl) **1** to be unsuccessful (in): *to fail a test.* **2** to fall short of what is expected or desired: *The town's water supply failed again.* **3** to lose strength; become weaker: *His hearing has failed in the last year.* **4** not to carry out; to neglect: *He has failed to keep his promise.* **5** to become bankrupt: *The bank failed last year.* **6** to neglect to help or support: *to fail a friend.* **7 without fail** certainly; surely.

---

fāte, făt, fâre, fär; bē, bĕt; bīte, bĭt; nō, nŏt, nôr; fūse, fŭn, fûr; tōō, tŏŏk; foil; foul; thin; ~~then;~~
hw for wh as in *what*; zh for s as in u*s*ual; ə for a, e, i, o, u, as in *a*go, lin*e*n, per*i*l, at*o*m, min*u*s

fail·ing (fā'ling) weakness; fault: *Habitual tardiness was one of his chief* failings.

fail·ure (fāl'yər) **1** lack of success; unsuccessful effort: *a failure in a history examination.* **2** a falling short of something expected, desired, or needed: *the failure of this year's crops; the* failure *of his health.* **3** a ceasing to perform: *the failure of electric power.* **4** an unsuccessful person or thing: *He was a failure in business.*

fain (fān) an old word meaning "willingly"; "gladly": *He would* fain *go.* (Homonym: feign)

faint (fānt) **1** weak; exhausted: *The travelers were faint from hunger.* **2** indistinct; dim: *a faint noise; a faint light.* **3** feeble; half-hearted: *Joe made a faint attempt at mending the book.* **4** to lose consciousness briefly. **5** a brief loss of consciousness. **faint·ly.** (Homonym: feint)

¹fair (fār) **1** honest; just; according to the rules: *a fair decision;* fair *play.* **2** light in color; blond: *to have fair skin;* fair *hair.* **3** clear; not rainy or stormy; favorable: *in fair weather.* **4** average; reasonably satisfactory: *His spelling is only fair. He has a fair chance of success.* **5** pleasing to the sight; lovely: *this land so green and fair.* **6** straight in an honest and direct way. [¹**fair** is a form of an Old English word (faeger) meaning "bountiful."] (Homonym: fare)

²fair (fār) **1** a gathering, usually of country people, at a fixed time and place for the display and sale of goods. **2** a display and sale of useful and fancy goods; a bazaar. **3** a large exhibition of products, commercial goods, etc: *a trade fair.* [²**fair** is from an Old French word (feire) that goes back to a Latin word (feriae) meaning "holidays."] (Homonym: fare)

fair·ground (fār'ground') place where fairs are held.

fair·ly (fār'lĭ) **1** justly; in an honest manner: *The games were judged fairly. They treated us* fairly. **2** somewhat; moderately; rather: *Jane plays the piano fairly well.*

fair·y (fār'ĭ) **1** an imaginary being of tiny, human shape, often with wings, and usually having magical powers. **2** light; dainty: *to walk with fairy footsteps.* **fair·ies.**

fair·y·land (fār'ĭ lănd') **1** the country of the fairies. **2** a beautiful, enchanting place.

fairy tale 1 a story about fairies, witches, or unreal beings, as "Puss-in-Boots." **2** story that isn't true; lie: *He told a fairy tale about having been a captain in the army.*

faith (fāth) **1** trust; confidence: *Do you have faith in his word?* **2** belief in God. **3** system of religious belief: *the Christian faith; the Jewish faith.* **4** promise of loyalty: *to keep or break faith.* **5 good faith** honesty; sincerity. **6 bad faith** dishonesty; insincerity.

faith·ful (fāth'fəl) **1** loyal; trustworthy: *a faithful dog; a faithful friend.* **2** without mistakes; accurate: *a faithful copy of a picture.* **faith·ful·ly.**

faith·less (fāth'lĭs) disloyal; false: *He proved to be a faithless friend.* **faith·less·ly.**

fake (fāk) **1** to imitate (in order to deceive); pretend: *to fake blindness.* **2** false; counterfeit: *a fake dollar bill.* **3** something or someone that is not as represented: *The dealer sold a fake as a painting by Rembrandt.* **faked, fak·ing.**

fal·con (fôl'kən or făl'kən) any of several small, swift hawks trained to hunt birds and small game.

Falcon, about 18 in. long

fall (fôl) **1** to come down; drop from a higher to lower place: *Rain falls from clouds.* **2** a coming down; descent: *a fall of rain.* **3** the amount that drops down: *a heavy fall of snow.* **4** to tumble: *to fall downstairs.* **5** to give up; surrender: *The beseiged city finally fell.* **6** the ruin; destruction: *the fall of the Roman Empire.* **7** to die: *Many people fell in the diphtheria epidemic.* **8** to give way (to sin or error): *to fall into bad habits.* **9** loss of grace or favor: *the fall of Adam.* **10** to become or pass into a certain state or condition: *to fall sick; to fall asleep.* **11** autumn. **12 falls** a waterfall.

fall back to withdraw; move back or away: *The enemy fell back from the city.*

fall back on to go back to: *We fell back on the old ice chest when the refrigerator was out of order.*

fall behind to be unable to keep up.

fall flat to fail to have the intended effect: *The best joke can fall flat.*

fall in 1 to take the proper place in a line: *The soldiers fell in for inspection.* **2** to meet or join by chance. **3** to agree: *We fell in with his plan.*

fall on or **upon 1** to come or descend upon: *A hush fell on the audience.* **2** to attack; injure: *They fell on the foe.*

fall out 1 to quarrel; disagree: *They fell out over the price.* **2** to drop out of line.

fall short 1 to be not enough: *Our supplies fell short.* **2** to fail to reach the place aimed at or the standard required: *The arrow fell short. His work falls short.*

fall through to fail; come to nothing: *Our plans fell through.*

fall to 1 to begin an attack. **2** to begin to eat: *They fell to with good appetites.*

fell, fall·en, fall·ing.

fal·la·cy (făl′ə sĭ) mistaken idea, opinion, or belief; unsound or false reasoning: *the fallacy that wealth always means happiness.* **fal·la·cies.**

fall·en (fô′lən) **1** dropped: *a fallen leaf.* **2** ruined; overthrown: *a fallen nation.* **3** killed in battle: *a fallen soldier.* **4** See **fall.** *Snow had fallen during the night.*

fall line boundary between a coastal plain and higher, usually hilly, land. Many waterfalls occur along this boundary, and they block boats from going farther up the rivers.

fall·out or **fall-out** (fôl′out′) the harmful particles and dust that fall to earth after an atomic explosion.

fal·low (făl′ō) plowed up, but left unseeded or without crops for a season: *the fallow land.*

false (fôls) **1** untrue or incorrect; wrong: *He had a false idea of her character.* **2** misleading; deceitful: *a false promise.* **3** not natural; artificial: *to wear false teeth.* **fals·er, fals·est; false·ly.**

false·hood (fôls′hŏod) a lie; an untrue statement.

false·ness (fôls′nĭs) a being false.

fal·si·ty (fôl′sə tĭ) **1** a not being true or honorable; falseness. **2** an error. **fal·si·ties.**

fal·ter (fôl′tər) **1** to move or act in an uncertain or unsteady way; waver; hesitate: *He faltered at the door, wondering if he should go in.* **2** to speak with hesitation; stammer: *He faltered as he tried to find the right words to show his gratitude.*

fame (fām) **1** a being well known: *His fame was based on his enormous wealth.* **2** fine reputation; renown: *Edison gained fame as an inventor.*

famed (fāmd) famous; well-known; celebrated.

fa·mil·iar (fə mĭl′yər) **1** well-known; often seen or heard: *I recognized the familiar voice on the telephone.* **2** well-acquainted: *Are you familiar with the facts in the case?* **3** having close acquaintance; personally close; intimate: *He has few familiar friends.* **4** easy; informal: *to write in a familiar style; in familiar language.* **5** forward; bold; taking liberties: *He has much too familiar a manner with people he meets for the first time.* **fa·mil·iar·ly.**

fa·mil·i·ar·i·ty (fə mĭl′ĭ ăr′ə tĭ) **1** close acquaintance (with): *His familiarity with their customs made him liked by the natives.* **2** freedom from formality: *to be on terms of familiarity with someone.* **3** forwardness (in speech or manner). **fa·mil·i·ar·i·ties.**

fam·i·ly (făm′ə lĭ) **1** parents and their children: *The Brown family lives next door.* **2** the children of a married couple: *Mr. and Mrs. Brown have a large family.* **3** persons closely related by birth; all people descended from the same ancestor: *The Nelson family has been in New York for 250 years.* **4** group of related plants or animals: *Lions and tigers belong to the same genus (long-tailed cats) of the cat family.* **5** of or having to do with a family: *a family resemblance; family Bible.* **fam·i·lies.**

fam·ine (făm′ĭn) **1** extreme scarcity of food; starvation. **2** shortage of some one thing, especially a crop: *a wheat famine.*

fam·ish (făm′ĭsh) to be very hungry; suffer great hunger.

fa·mous (fā′məs) widely known; renowned: *Admiral Byrd was a famous explorer.*

fāte, făt, fâre, fär; bē, bĕt; bite, bĭt; nō, nŏt, nôr; fūse, fŭn, fûr; tōō, tŏŏk; foil; foul; thin; ~~then~~;
hw for wh as in *wh*at; zh for s as in u*s*ual; ə for a, e, i, o, u, as in ago, linen, peril, atom, minus

¹**fan** (făn) **1** anything used to move air around. **2** a set of revolving blades, driven by a motor and used to bring air in or out of a room, machinery, etc. **3** a light, often folding tool of paper, cloth, etc., moved back and forth in the hand to make a breeze. **4** to wave something to cast a breeze on: *to fan oneself; to fan a fire.* **5** to stir up; excite; rouse: *The speaker fanned the crowd's enthusiasm.* **6** in baseball, to strike out. **fanned, fanning.** [¹**fan** is a form of an Old English word (fann) that goes back to a Latin word (vannus), "a fan for winnowing grain."]

Fans

²**fan** (făn) an enthusiastic supporter: *a baseball* fan; *a movie* fan. [²**fan** is short for **fanatic.**]

fa·nat·ic (fə năt′ĭk) a person having unduly strong and unreasonable beliefs about something: *a fresh-air* fanatic.

fan·ci·ful (făn′sĭ fəl) **1** imaginary; not real: *Her story was about goblins, dragons, and other* fanciful *creatures.* **2** having or showing imagination: *a* fanciful *writer.* **3** showing fancy; strangely designed. **fan·ci·ful·ly.**

fan·cy (făn′sĭ) **1** imagination: *Such strange tales show a lively* fancy. **2** to suppose; imagine: *I can't* fancy *his doing such a thing.* **3** to like; have a liking for: *Which of the toys do you* fancy *most?* **4** extravagant: *a* fancy *price;* fancy *ideas.* **5** not plain; ornamental: *a* fancy *costume.*

fancy oneself to regard oneself (as): *He* fancies himself *an expert locksmith.* **fan·cies; fan·cied, fan·cy·ing; fan·ci·er, fan·ci·est; fan·ci·ly.**

fang (făng) a long, sharp tooth.

fan·tas·tic (făn tăs′tĭk) **1** imaginative; unreal: *He told some* fantastic *story about riding a subway in the desert.* **2** odd; queer; grotesque: *the* fantastic *shapes of many insects.*

FANGS
Fangs of a tiger

fan·ta·sy (făn′tə sĭ or făn′tə zĭ) **1** imagination. **2** thing imagined or not real; day-dream; fanciful idea: *The report of treasure in the cave proved a* fantasy. **3** poem, play, or story showing much imagination or having fanciful ideas: *"Peter Pan" is a* fantasy. **fan·ta·sies.**

far (fär) **1** not near; distant: *a* far *country.* **2** to or at a definite distance: *You cannot go* far *before you come to a wall.* **3** by a great deal; very much: *This new road is* far *better than the old one.* **4** more distant: *the* far *side of the street.* **5** **far and away** very much: *His idea is* far and away *better than mine.* **6** **go far** to be successful. **7** **How far . . . ?** at what distance? **8** **so far** up to now: *We have had no trouble with the car so far.* **far·ther, far·thest.**

far·a·way (fär′ə wā′) **1** distant; remote: *He wants to travel to all the* faraway *places.* **2** dreamy: *a* faraway *look.*

farce (färs) **1** a play in which there are many exaggerated happenings intended to cause laughter. **2** an absurd or useless proceeding: *The election was a* farce.

fare (fâr) **1** money paid for a trip: *bus* fare; *train* fare. **2** to get along: *How did you* fare *on your visit?* **3** to happen; turn out: *All will* fare *well if he tells the truth.* **4** food and drink: *How is the* fare *at the lodge?* **fared, far·ing.** (Homonym: fair)

Far East the part of Asia that includes China, India, Japan, etc.

fare·well (fâr′wĕl′) **1** good-by. **2** parting: *a* farewell *dinner.*

farm (färm) **1** land used for growing crops or raising animals: *a dairy* farm; *a wheat* farm. **2** such land and the buildings on it: *Peter lived on a* farm. **3** to work or use land for crops or livestock: *Some of the pioneers* farmed, *while others hunted or traded for a living.* **4** to cultivate (land): *We* farm *300 acres and use the rest for pasture.*

farm out to lease; to let: *The baseball players were* farmed out *to another team.*

farm·er (fär′mər) person who owns or rents and operates a farm.

farm·house (färm′hous′) dwelling house on a farm.

farm·ing (fär′mĭng) **1** the running of a farm. **2** having to do with farms: *sturdy* farming *tools.*

farm·yard (färm′yärd′) area around farm buildings.

far-off (fär′ôf′) far away; distant.

far·reach·ing (fär′rē′chĭng) **1** influencing or affecting many people: *a far-reaching plan.* **2** extending a great distance.

far·see·ing (fär′sē′ĭng) using good judgment in planning for the future; wise.

far·sight·ed (fär′sīt′ĭd) **1** able to see distant objects. **2** well-planned; showing good judgment: *a far-sighted policy; a far-sighted statesman.* **far·sight·ed·ly.**

far·ther (fär′thər) **1** at or to a greater distance: *Those mountains are much farther away than you think.* **2** more distant: *the farther end of the field.*

far·thest (fär′thĭst) **1** to or at the greatest distance: *Let's see who can run farthest.* **2** most distant: *the farthest planet.*

far·thing (fär′thĭng) a former British coin worth one fourth of a British penny, or about a half cent in United States money.

fas·ci·nate (făs′ə nāt′) to attract and hold the attention of; enchant or charm: *Space travel fascinates us.* **fas·ci·nat·ed, fas·ci·nat·ing.**

fas·ci·na·tion (făs′ə nā′shən) **1** a being fascinated; charmed condition: *He stared at her in* fascination. **2** strong attraction; charm: *an actress of great* fascination.

fash·ion (făsh′ən) **1** way; manner: *to behave in a strange fashion.* **2** to make; form; shape: *He fashioned a boat from a piece of wood.* **3** style, habit, or custom of a time: *the fashions of the colonial period.*

fash·ion·a·ble (făsh′ən ə bəl) following the fashion; stylish. **fash·ion·a·bly.**

¹fast (făst) **1** rapid; swift: *a fast runner.* **2** rapidly: *Don't talk so fast.* **3** firm; steady: *Those boys are fast friends. The stake is fast in the ground.* **4** fixed; nonfading: *The color is fast and will not fade.* **5** firmly: *Hold fast to the sled as we go downhill.* **6** ahead of the correct time: *The clock is fast.* **7** wild; too gay: *to lead a fast life.* **8 fast asleep** in a deep sleep. [**fast** is a form of an Old English word (fæst) meaning "firmly." The meaning "rapidly" is an outcome of phrases like "follow fast (firmly) upon a person's tracks."]

²fast (făst) **1** to eat little or no food: *He fasted half a day before the blood test.* **2** to go without food or without certain foods

as a religious duty: *Many Christians fast on Fridays.* **3** a period of going without food: *He ended his fast with a light diet.* [**²fast** is a form of an Old English word (fæstan) meaning "to abstain from food."]

fas·ten (făs′ən) **1** to join; attach: *to fasten a shelf to a wall.* **2** to fix firmly; make fast; lock: *Did you fasten all the doors?* **3** to fix; direct: *The children fastened their attention on the magician.*

fas·ten·ing (făs′ən ĭng) something that fastens or holds things together. A lock, bolt, clasp, or chain is a fastening.

fas·tid·i·ous (făs tĭd′i əs) hard to please; very critical or particular: *to be fastidious about food or dress.* **fas·tid·i·ous·ly.**

fast·ness (făst′nĭs) **1** swiftness. **2** stronghold: *a mountain* fastness.

fat (făt) **1** an oily yellow or white substance found in animals and plants. **2** having much fat: *This meat is fat.* **3** plump; heavy with flesh: *She is fat, but her sister is thin.* **4** well-filled: *a fat pocketbook.* **5** to make or become fat. **6 the fat of the land** the best of everything. **fat·ter, fat·test; fat·ted, fat·ting.**

fa·tal (fā′təl) **1** causing death: *a fatal accident.* **2** causing great harm or ruin: *a fatal mistake.* **fa·tal·ly.**

fate (fāt) **1** a power that is believed to control and decide what will happen; destiny: *I was going on a trip but fate stepped in and changed my plans.* **2** what happens to someone; one's lot: *We wondered about the fate of the missing pilot.* **3 the Fates** three Greek goddesses said to control fate.

fat·ed (fā′tĭd) fixed or controlled by fate; destined: *one's fated lot in life.*

fate·ful (fāt′fəl) **1** important; decisive: *a fateful day.* **2** foretelling the future; prophetic: *a fateful speech.* **3** deadly; bringing death: *a fateful arrow.*

fa·ther (fä′thər) **1** male parent. **2** to be the male parent of. **3** founder or important leader: *the Pilgrim Fathers.* **4** to make; create: *Thomas Edison fathered many inventions.* **5** form of address for a priest. **6 Our Father** God.

fa·ther-in-law (fä′thər ĭn lô′) father of a person's wife or husband. **fa·thers-in-law.**

---

fāte, făt, fâre, fär; bē, bĕt; bīte, bĭt; nō, nŏt, nôr; fūse, fŭn, fûr; tōō, tŏŏk; foil; foul; thin; ~~then~~;
hw for wh as in *wh*at; zh for s as in u*s*ual; ə for a, e, i, o, u, as in *a*go, linen, peril, atom, minus

fa·ther·land (fä′thər lănd′) country of a person's birth.

fa·ther·ly (fä′thər lĭ) of or like a father: *He was given some* fatherly *advice.*

fath·om (făth′əm) **1** a measure equal to six feet, used mostly in measuring the depth of water. **2** to find the depth of. **3** to get to the bottom of; understand: *I can't* fathom *his meaning.*

fath·om·less (făth′əm lĭs) **1** too deep to measure. **2** impossible to understand. **fath·om·less·ly.**

fa·tigue (fə tēg′) **1** weariness; tiredness; exhaustion of body or mind: *Too much work and too little sleep cause* fatigue. **2** to tire; weary: *Running can* fatigue *a person.* **fa·tigued, fa·ti·guing.**

fat·ten (făt′ən) to make or become fat.

fat·ty (făt′ĭ) rich; oily; greasy: *too many fatty foods.* **fat·ti·er, fat·ti·est.**

fau·cet (fô′sĭt) device for turning on or off the flow of liquids from a pipe or container; a tap; a cock.

fault (fôlt) **1** mistake: *a fault in grammar.* **2** weakness; shortcoming: *Carelessness is a fault.* **3** blame; responsibility: *The accident was your* fault. **4** a defect: *We found a fault in the electric system.* **5** ball in tennis that fails to land in the proper section of the opponent's court. **6 find fault with** to object; criticize: *She is always finding fault with our work.*

fault·less (fôlt′lĭs) without flaw or defect; perfect: *The actor gave a* faultless *performance.* **fault·less·ly.**

fault·y (fôl′tĭ) imperfect; defective; having faults. **fault·i·er, fault·i·est; fault·i·ly.**

faun (fôn) a Roman minor woodland god, often pictured as having a goat's horns and hind legs and pointed ears. (Homonym: fawn)

Faun

fa·vor (fā′vər) **1** kindness: *Will you do me a* favor? **2** to like; approve: *I* favor *that idea.* **3** approval: *The singer won the* favor *of the audience.* **4** small gift or souvenir: *party* favor. **5** to oblige: *Will you* favor *me with a reply?* **6** to look like: *I* favor *my mother.* **7** to give unfair advantage to; prefer: *A coach should not* favor *one*

player over another on his team. **8 in favor of** on the side of; in support of.

fa·vor·a·ble (fā′vər ə bəl) **1** approving: *a* favorable *answer.* **2** helpful; advantageous: *a* favorable *breeze.* **fa·vor·a·bly.**

fa·vor·ite (fā′vər ĭt) **1** best liked: *My* favorite *book is "Tom Sawyer."* **2** person given the preference; the one best liked: *Nancy is her uncle's* favorite. **3** contestant thought most likely to win.

¹fawn (fôn) **1** a young or baby deer. **2** a light tan color. [**¹fawn** is from an Old French word (faon) that goes back to a Latin word (fetus) meaning "offspring."] (Homonym: faun)

Fawn

²fawn (fôn) **1** to show fondness or submission as by wagging the tail, whining etc.: *A dog often* fawns *on his master.* **2** to try to win favor by flattery or by cringing: *A person will often* fawn *on a rich relative.* [**²fawn** is a form of an Old English word (fahnian) meaning "to welcome, to rejoice."] (Homonym: faun)

fear (fîr) **1** feeling of fright or alarm; dread; terror: *The threat of a storm caused* fear *among the ship's passengers.* **2** awe; reverence: *a* fear *of God.* **3** anxiety: *We all felt* fear *for the missing airman.* **4** to be afraid of; be alarmed by; be frightened by: *Cats* fear *water.*

fear·ful (fîr′fəl) **1** causing alarm or fright; awful; terrible: *That was a* fearful *accident.* **2** afraid; scared: *The plane passengers were* fearful *of an accident.* **fear·ful·ly.**

fear·less (fîr′lĭs) unafraid; courageous; completely without fear. **fear·less·ly.**

fea·si·ble (fē′zə bəl) possible; capable of being done; within reach: *In spite of the cost, your plan is* feasible. **fea·si·bly.**

feast (fēst) **1** rich meal with fine foods and many courses. **2** to eat such a meal. **3** to honor or entertain with a rich meal: *Next week we will* feast *a British war hero.* **4** day in honor of; festival in memory of: *the* feast *of St. John.* **5** to give pleasure to; delight: *to* feast *one's eyes.*

feat (fēt) great achievement; accomplishment: *Hitting three home runs in one game was quite a* feat. (Homonym: feet)

feath·er (fĕth′ər) **1** one of the outgrowths on a bird's skin that form its coat and flying equipment. **2** to provide or cover with feathers: *The Indian* feathered *the arrow.* **3** to turn (an oar or propeller blade) so that the edge cuts water. **4 feather in one's cap** an achievement to be proud of.

Feather

feather one's nest to make oneself rich.

feath·er·bed (fĕth′ər bĕd′) a mattress filled with feathers.

feath·er·y (fĕth′ə rĭ) **1** filled or covered with feathers. **2** fluffy; light; soft: *A* feathery *blanket of snow covered the ground.* **3** like a feather: *delicate,* feathery *ferns.*

fea·ture (fē′chər) **1** something distinct or noticeable about a thing: *The tower clock is a* feature *of the new school building.* **2** chief or special attraction: *The ballet was a* feature *of the show.* **3** main attraction of a movie show: *The* feature *began at 7:30.* **4** part of the face. The eyes, ears, nose, mouth, chin, and forehead are features. **5** to give special attention to; emphasize: *Today's newspaper* features *a story on our mayor.* **fea·tured, fea·tur·ing.**

Feb. February.

Feb·ru·ar·y (fĕb′rŏŏ ĕr′ĭ) second month of the year. February has 28 days except in leap year when it has 29 days.

fed (fĕd) See **feed.** *He* fed *his chickens.*

fed·er·al (fĕd′ər əl) of or belonging to a nation formed by the union of smaller states. The United States has a federal government.

fee (fē) charge or payment for service by a professional man or for a right to do something: *a doctor's* fee; *an admission* fee.

fee·ble (fē′bəl) **1** weak; frail: *a* feeble *old woman; a* feeble *cry.* **2** without force or vigor; half-hearted: *a* feeble *attempt.* **fee·bler, fee·blest; fee·bly.**

feed (fēd) **1** to give food to: *It's time to* feed *the baby.* **2** to give as food: *We* feed *lettuce to our rabbit.* **3** food for animals: *chicken* feed. **4** to supply with something:

The lake is fed *by mountain springs.* **fed, feed·ing.**

feel (fēl) **1** to touch with the hand: *to* feel *someone's pulse; to* feel *the edge of a knife.* **2** quality one is aware of by touch; feeling: *Babies like the* feel *of soft toys.* **3** to try to find by touching; grope: *He had to* feel *for the light switch in the dark.* **4** to be aware of by the sense of touch: *to* feel *whether the water is hot.* **5** to have a sense of; be moved by: *to* feel *sorrow; to* feel *remorse; to* feel *anger.* **6** to be sensitive to: *He doesn't seem to* feel *the cold at all.* **7** to be sure; consider; believe: *I* feel *it is my duty to warn you.* **8** to sense that one is (happy, hungry, angry, ill, etc.): *to* feel *dizzy; to* feel *angry.*

feel like 1 to have a desire for: *I* feel like *taking a walk.* **2** to seem to the touch: *This material* feels like *silk.*

felt, feel·ing.

feel·er (fē′lər) **1** a part of an animal that gives it information by touch, such as a cat's whisker or one of the threadlike projections on an insect's head. **2** something said or done to find out the opinions or purposes of others: *The politician's* feeler *met with no response.*

Feelers of an ant

feel·ing (fē′lǐng) **1** the sense of touch by which a person tells hot from cold, rough from smooth, etc. **2** sensation: *a* feeling *of pain; a* feeling *of hunger.* **3** emotion: *a* feeling *of anger; a* feeling *of joy.* **4** sympathy; pity: *Has he any* feeling *for the suffering of others?* **5** effect made on mind or emotions: *a* feeling *of achievement.* **6** opinion; impression: *We all share the* feeling *that the story is too long.* **7** emotional excitement: *There was a great deal of* feeling *over the town elections.* **8 feelings** sensitive part of one's nature: *He hurt her* feelings *by his unkind remarks.* **feel·ing·ly.**

feet (fēt) more than one **foot.** (Homonym: feat)

feign (fān) to pretend; put on an appearance of: *to* feign *friendship; to* feign *illness.* (Homonym: fain)

---

fāte, făt, fâre, fär; bē, bĕt; bīte, bĭt; nō, nŏt, nôr; fūse, fŭn, fûr; tōō, tŏŏk; foil; foul; thin; ~~then~~; hw for wh as in *what*; zh for s as in u*s*ual; ə for a, e, i, o, u, as in *a*go, lin*e*n, per*i*l, at*o*m, min*u*s

feint (fānt) **1** pretense: *Tim made a* feint *at reading but was really listening to a jazz record.* **2** pretense in fencing, war, or boxing, of attacking at one point or place while really intending to attack at another. **3** to make a feint: *to feint with the left hand and strike with the right hand.* (Homonym: faint)

¹fell (fĕl) See **fall.** *The little boy* fell *down the steps.* [¹**fell** is a form of **fall.**]

²fell (fĕl) to cause to fall; shoot, knock, or cut down: *to fell a deer; to fell an opponent with a blow; to fell a tree.* [²**fell** is a form of an Old English word (fellan) meaning "to cause to fall."]

³fell (fĕl) **1** fierce; cruel: *a fell blow.* **2** deadly: *a fell disease.* [³**fell** is from an Old French word (fel). It is related to ¹**felon.**]

fel·low (fĕl'ō) **1** man or boy: *He's a fine fellow.* **2** companion; associate: *a fellow in suffering.* **3** belonging to the same class or group; sharing the same interests, experiences, etc.: *a fellow worker; a fellow student.*

fel·low·ship (fĕl'ō ship') **1** friendliness; companionship: *We enjoyed a warm fellowship during our time together.* **2** group of persons having similar beliefs, interests, or tastes. **3** membership in such a group: *He was admitted into the fellowship of the church.* **4** a sum of money and a rank given to a person to further his studies or training: *With the help of a fellowship, the young scientist completed his research.*

¹fel·on (fĕl'ən) person who has committed a serious crime. [¹**felon** is from an Old French word of the same spelling.]

²fel·on (fĕl'ən) a red, painful swelling on a finger or toe, usually near or under the nail. [²**felon** is probably ¹**felon** in a special use. The pain from one may have been thought of as wicked or treacherous.]

fel·o·ny (fĕl'ə nĭ) a major crime such as murder and burglary. **fel·o·nies.**

¹felt (fĕlt) See **feel.** *He felt the water to see if it was cold.* [¹**felt** is a form of **feel.**]

²felt (fĕlt) **1** a kind of cloth made of wool, hair, or fur pressed together instead of woven. **2** made of this material: *a felt hat.* [²**felt** is the unchanged form of an Old English word.]

fe·male (fē'māl') **1** a person or animal that may at some time give birth to young.

2 belonging to or describing such persons or animals.

fem·i·nine (fĕm'ə nĭn) having to do with women; suitable for women: *a feminine fashion; a feminine voice.* **fem·i·nine·ly.**

fen (fĕn) low, marshy land.

fence (fĕns) **1** a barrier or boundary of stone, wood, wire, etc., around or along a field, yard, etc.: *a pasture fence.* **2** to enclose with such a boundary: *We fenced in our yard.* **3** to fight with swords or foils, especially as a sport. **fenced, fenc·ing.**

fenc·er (fĕn'sər) a person who fences.

fenc·ing (fĕn'sĭng) **1** the art of fighting with a sword. **2** a sport consisting of fighting with slender, blunted swords called foils. **3** material for a fence. **4** an enclosing fence.

Fencing

fend·er (fĕn'dər) **1** metal piece over an automobile or bicycle wheel. **2** metal guard in front of an open fireplace. **3** a device on the front of a locomotive or streetcar to catch or push aside anything hit.

fen·nel (fĕn'əl) a plant with a sweet smell, the seeds of which are used in cooking and in medicine.

¹fer·ment (fər mĕnt') **1** to go through a chemical change because of the action of tiny living plants such as yeasts, certain bacteria, etc. **2** to stir up; agitate.

²fer·ment (fûr'mĕnt) **1** the yeasts, molds, bacteria, etc., that cause a chemical change, such as the curdling of milk. **2** a state of unrest, agitation, or excitement: *The whole nation was in a ferment over the election.*

fer·men·ta·tion (fûr'mĕn tā'shən) **1** chemical change brought about by the action of yeasts, certain bacteria, etc. **2** the action of fermenting.

fern (fûrn) any of several kinds of plants having feathery leaves but no flowers.

fe·ro·cious (fə rō'shəs) fierce; savage; cruel: *a ferocious lion.* **fe·ro·cious·ly.**

fe·roc·i·ty (fə rŏs'ə tĭ) fierceness; savage cruelty: *The wolves attacked the sheep with ferocity.* **fe·roc·i·ties.**

Fern

fer·ret (fĕr′ĭt) **1** a fierce, slender weasel with a long body, sometimes used to destroy rats and mice or to hunt rabbits. **2** to hunt down; pursue without rest: *Detectives* ferreted *out the criminals.*

Ferret, about 18 in. long

Fer·ris wheel (fĕr′ĭs hwēl) an amusement park attraction consisting of a huge wheel with passenger cars hanging freely on rods between twin rims.

fer·ry (fĕr′ĭ) **1** a boat that carries vehicles, goods, and passengers across a narrow body of water. **2** to cross a body of water on such a boat: *We* ferried *over to the island.* **3** to carry on such a boat: *to* ferry *troops across a river.* **4** to deliver (aircraft) by flying to the destination. **5** a place where things are ferried. **fer·ries; fer·ried, fer·ry·ing.**

fer·tile (fûr′təl) **1** producing a great amount: *our* fertile *land.* **2** able to bear seeds, fruit, or young: *a* fertile *plant.* **3** able to grow into a plant or animal: *a* fertile *seed; a* fertile *egg.* **fer·tile·ly.**

fer·til·i·ty (fər tĭl′ə tĭ) **1** ability to grow; a being fertile. **2** ability (of soil) to help plants grow: *Prairie soil is valued for its* fertility. **3** ability to bear children. **4** of animals, ability to produce many offspring: *the* fertility *of rabbits.*

fer·ti·li·za·tion (fûr′tə lə zā′shən) **1** the adding of manure or other fertilizers to soil to make it richer. **2** change that takes place in an egg or a seed before it can begin to grow.

fer·ti·lize (fûr′tə līz′) **1** to add substances to soil to make it richer and more productive. **2** to give an egg cell power to grow by combining it with a male cell. **fer·ti·lized, fer·ti·liz·ing.**

fer·ti·liz·er (fûr′tə lī′zər) material used to make soil more productive.

fer·vent (fûr′vənt) strong or warm in feeling; intense; earnest: *a* fervent *prayer.* **fer·vent·ly.**

fer·vid (fûr′vĭd) burning; glowing; impassioned: *a* fervid *loyalty;* fervid *oratory.* **fer·vid·ly.**

fer·vor (fûr′vər) warmth and earnestness of feeling: *to speak with* fervor.

fes·ti·val (fĕs′tə vəl) time of rejoicing and feasting, usually in memory of some special event: *the* festival *of Thanksgiving.*

fes·tive (fĕs′tĭv) having to do with a feast or festival; gay; joyous; merry: *a* festive *occasion; a* festive *scene.* **fes·tive·ly.**

fes·tiv·i·ty (fĕs tĭv′ə tĭ) merrymaking; rejoicing; celebration. **fes·tiv·i·ties.**

fes·toon (fĕs tōōn′) **1** a rope of leaves, flowers, etc., draped in curves, or a sculptured copy of such a rope. **2** to decorate with festoons: *Workmen* festooned *City Hall with garlands and streamers.*

Festoon

fetch (fĕch) to bring; go and get: *Please* fetch *me the book from my desk.*

fetch·ing (fĕch′ĭng) charming; pretty: *What a* fetching *girl!* **fetch·ing·ly.**

fete or **fête** (fāt) **1** festival; celebration. **2** to entertain or honor with a celebration: *The famous writer was* feted *in every town that he visited.* **fet·ed** or **fêt·ed, fet·ing** or **fêt·ing.** (Homonym: fate)

fet·ter (fĕt′ər) **1** ankle rings connected by a short chain: *Prisoners are sometimes placed in* fetters. **2** anything that limits, checks, or holds back. **3** to chain the feet of. **4** to restrain or hinder.

feud (fūd) **1** a bitter quarrel or hatred which has gone on for a long time, especially between families or clans. **2** to carry on such a quarrel or hatred.

feu·dal (fū′dəl) of or having to do with feudalism. **feu·dal·ly.**

feu·dal·ism (fū′də liz′əm) the social, political, and economic system in Europe during the Middle Ages. Under the feudal system a person who held land (called a vassal) had to perform certain military and other services for the lord from whom he held the land.

fe·ver (fē′vər) **1** a condition in which the body temperature is higher than usual. **2** disease in which there is this condition: *scarlet* fever; *typhoid* fever. **3** nervous excitement: *to be in a* fever *of activity.*

---

fāte, făt, fâre, fär; bē, bĕt; bīte, bĭt; nō, nŏt, nôr; fūse, fŭn, fûr; tōō, tŏŏk; foil; foul; thin; ~~then~~;
hw for wh as in *wh*at; zh for s as in usual; ə for a, e, i, o, u, as in *a*go, lin*e*n, per*i*l, at*o*m, min*u*s

fe·vered (fē'vərd) **1** affected by fever; hot. **2** excited: *a* fevered *imagination*.

fe·ver·ish (fē'vər ish) **1** having a fever: *He was* feverish *from his cold*. **2** caused by a fever: *wild*, feverish *dreams*. **3** excited; restless: *in* feverish *haste*. **fe·ver·ish·ly.**

few (fū) **1** not many: *Very few people showed up for the meeting. He was a man of few words.* **2** a small number: *I want only a few.*

fez (fĕz) a high, red cap with no brim, a flat top, and a black tassel.

fib (fib) **1** a lie, especially about something unimportant. **2** to tell such a lie: *Amos* fibbed *about washing his ears, but he couldn't fool his mother.* **fibbed, fib·bing.**

Fez

fi·ber (fī'bər) **1** one of many thin threadlike strands that form certain plant and animal substances: *muscle* fibers; *wood* fibers. **2** substance containing such strands: *cotton* fiber; *wool* fiber; *hemp* fiber. **3** nature; quality; character: *the moral* fiber *of a nation.* Also spelled **fibre.**

fi·brous (fī'brəs) having, made of, or like fibers: *the fibrous trunk of a coconut palm.*

fick·le (fik'əl) uncertain; changeable; unsteady: *He is too* fickle *to be relied upon.*

fic·tion (fik'shən) **1** writings, such as novels and short stories, which tell of imaginary happenings and characters: *The story of Peter Rabbit is* fiction. **2** anything made up or imagined; not real or true: *I think his explanation for being late was pure* fiction.

fid·dle (fid'əl) **1** violin. **2** to play on the violin: *to* fiddle *a tune.* **3** to waste time; do useless things; make aimless movements: *He* fiddled *with his watch. He* fiddled *the day away.* **fid·dled, fid·dling.**

fid·dler (fid'lər) person who plays a fiddle.

fi·del·i·ty (fə dĕl'ə ti or fī dĕl'ə ti) **1** faithfulness; loyalty; devotion: *a dog's* fidelity *to his master.* **2** accuracy; exactness: *He reported the news with* fidelity *and without adding to it.* **fi·del·i·ties.**

fid·get (fij'it) **1** to move about restlessly; make nervous movements; be uneasy: *We all began to* fidget *as the speaker talked on and on.* **2 the fidgets** restlessness; uneasiness: *a case of* the fidgets.

fie (fī) Shame!: *Oh,* fie *on you for lying!*

field (fēld) **1** piece of open land used for planting, pasture, etc.: *a corn*field. **2** piece of land which has a special use: *a football* field. **3** region or section of land from which some natural product is obtained: *coal* fields; *oil* fields. **4** large area (covered by something): *a* field *of ice; a* field *of tents.* **5** place of military operations or battle: *battle*field. **6** area or sphere of special interest or activity: *Tom decided to go into the* field *of medicine.* **7** background against which something is seen: *His coat of arms has a lion on a* field *of blue.* **8** people taking part in a contest or sport: *He led the* field *at the hunt.* **9** side not at bat in baseball. **10** to catch or stop and return a ball from the field in baseball.

field glasses a pair of small telescopes mounted side by side for use of both eyes.

field house a building on an athletic field, with lockers, showers, etc., for the players.

fiend (fēnd) **1** devil; demon; evil spirit. **2** extremely wicked or cruel person.

fiend·ish (fēn'dish) devilish; savage; cruel: *a* fiendish *crime.* **fiend·ish·ly.**

fierce (firs) **1** violent and angry; savage and cruel: *a* fierce *dog.* **2** intense: *the* fierce *heat.* **fierc·er, fierc·est; fierce·ly.**

fier·y (fī'ə ri) **1** flaming; burning. **2** resembling a fire: *a* fiery *sunset.* **3** spirited; passionate; ardent: *a* fiery *speech.* **4** easily aroused: *a* fiery *temper.* **fier·i·er, fier·i·est.**

fi·es·ta (fi ĕs'tə) **1** religious holiday or festival. **2** a lively celebration.

fife (fif) shrill musical wind instrument of the flute class.

Boy playing fife

fif·teen (fif'tēn') amount or quantity that is one greater than 14; 15.

fif·teenth (fif'tēnth') **1** next after 14th; 15th. **2** one of 15 equal parts.

fifth (fifth) **1** next after fourth; 5th. **2** one of five equal parts.

fif·ti·eth (fif'ti ith) **1** next after 49th; 50th. **2** one of 50 equal parts.

fif·ty (fif'ti) amount or quantity that is one greater than 49; 50. **fif·ties.**

fig (fig) **1** sweet, pear-shaped fruit with many small seeds, usually eaten dried or preserved. **2** tree which bears this fruit.

fight (fīt) **1** a struggle with fists or weapons: *The quarrel led to a fight.* **2** any struggle: *the fight against disease; the fight for liberty.* **3** to take part in a struggle: *He fought long and hard. The army fought another battle.* **4** to struggle against: *Doctors fight disease.* **5** spirit of struggle: *He was still full of fight after the tenth round.*

Fig

fight off to overcome an attack.
fought, fight·ing.

fight·er (fī′tər) **1** person who engages in physical conflict with another. **2** person who struggles or battles for a cause: *Patrick Henry was a fighter for liberty.*

fig·ure (fig′yər) **1** a shape; outline: *He saw the figure of a man in the dark.* **2** a drawing or diagram: *The teacher drew figures, such as squares and triangles, on the blackboard.* **3** a design or pattern in cloth. **4** pattern made by movement in skating or dancing. **5** symbol for a number: *1, 2, and 5 are figures.* **6** a price: *He bought the car at a low figure.* **7** to appear; play a part; be prominent: *to figure in the news; to figure in history.* **8** to imagine; think; consider: *He figures himself a hero.* **9 figures** numbers; arithmetic: *Are you good at figures?* **10 figure of speech** fanciful expression, using words in a way outside their ordinary meaning in order to say something in a more striking or forceful manner.

figure out 1 to get a result by using figures: *Can you figure out this arithmetic problem?* **2** to understand: *I can't figure out his purpose.*
fig·ured, fig·ur·ing.

fig·ured (fig′yərd) having a design or pattern: *a figured cloth.*

fig·ure·head (fig′yər hĕd′) **1** person in a position of authority who has no real

power: *Most European kings are figureheads.* **2** ornamental statue or carving on the bow of a ship.

fil·a·ment (fil′ə mənt) **1** hairlike strand of material; very slender, delicate fiber. **2** fine wire in an electric bulb. **3** slender stem of a flower stamen.

Filament
1 of thread
2 of stamen

filch (filch) to steal, especially something of small value; pilfer.

¹file (fīl) **1** steel bar or a tapering rod with a raised, uneven surface used for smoothing, wearing down, or cutting hard surfaces. **2** flat metal strip with a rough surface used for trimming one's nails. **3** to use a file. **filed, fil·ing.** [¹file is a form of an Old English word (fēol).]

File

²file (fīl) **1** case or folder in which papers are kept in order. **2** papers arranged in order. **3** row of people or objects one behind the other: *The soldiers marched in double file.* **4** to arrange (papers) in order: *Please file these in alphabetical order.* **5** to hand in for consideration or record: *to file an application.* **6** to march in line, one behind the other: *They filed out of school.* **filed, fil·ing.** [²file is from a French word (fil) that goes back to a Latin word (filum) meaning "thread."]

Card file

fi·let (fi lā′ or fil′ā) **1** slice of meat or fish, without bone: *a filet of sole.* **2** to make free from bones. Also spelled **fil·let.**

fil·i·al (fil′ī əl) of a son or daughter; suitable to or due from a child to his parents: *his filial love; filial respect.* **fil·i·al·ly.**

fil·ings (fī′lingz) fragments rubbed off by a file.

Fil·i·pi·no (fil′ə pē′nō) **1** of or pertaining to the Philippine Islands. **2** citizen of the Philippine Islands; descendant of Filipinos. **Fil·i·pi·nos.**

fill (fil) **1** to make full: *Mother filled the jar with cookies.* **2** to become full: *The tank filled with water.* **3** to stop up holes or openings (in something): *The dentist filled*

fāte, făt, fâre, fär; bē, bĕt; bīte, bĭt; nō, nŏt, nôr; fūse, fŭn, fûr; tōō, tŏŏk; foil; foul; thin; then; hw for wh as in *what;* zh for s as in u*s*ual; ə for a, e, i, o, u, as in *a*go, lin*e*n, per*i*l, at*o*m, min*u*s

281

my tooth. **4** anything put in to stop up a hole or an opening, or fill up a hollow: *a* fill *of earth and rocks.* **5** enough to satisfy: *to eat and drink one's* fill. **6** to spread throughout: *The sound of singing* filled *the air.* **7** to supply (what is needed): *The grocer will* fill *the order.* **8** to hold (a position) and do all the duties of: *He* fills *the position of president.* **9** to put a person into: *They* filled *the job yesterday.*

fil·let (fil′ĭt) **1** ribbon or band worn around the head. **2** narrow, flat molding between two other moldings. **3** filet.

fill·ing (fil′ĭng) material used to fill something.

fil·ly (fil′ĭ) young female horse. **fil·lies.**

film (film) **1** thin layer or coating: *a* film *of dust on a shelf.* **2** to cover with a thin coating: *Ice* filmed *the window.* **3** thin strip or roll prepared for taking photographs. **4** motion picture. **5** to make a motion picture of: *They* filmed *the story in Africa.*

film·y (fil′mĭ) **1** very thin; sheer: *a* filmy *scarf; a* filmy *cloud.* **2** covered with a thin layer of something: *These windows are* filmy *from the steam.* **film·i·er, film·i·est; film·i·ly.**

fil·ter (fil′tər) **1** material such as sand, cloth, paper, etc., or a device containing such materials, used to strain solid matter from liquid: *Sand is often used as a* filter *for water that we drink.* **2** to cause to pass through a filter: *Automobile oil is* filtered *to keep it clean.* **3** to move slowly (through something): *The police* filtered *through the crowd.* **4** a special camera lens that shuts out certain kinds of light.

filth (filth) offensive dirt: *The floods had left the streets covered with* filth *and rubbish.*

filth·y (fil′thĭ) disgustingly dirty. **filth·i·er, filth·i·est; filth·i·ly.**

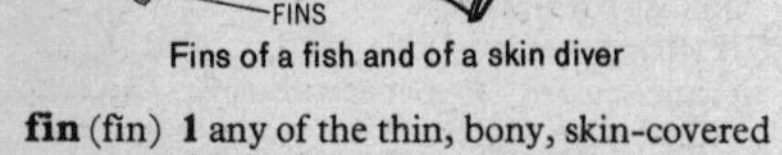

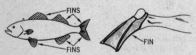

Fins of a fish and of a skin diver

fin (fin) **1** any of the thin, bony, skin-covered parts of a fish's body by which it balances, steers, and drives itself through the water. **2** something shaped like or used like a fin: *an airplane* fin.

fi·nal (fī′nəl) **1** coming at the end; last: *the* final *act of a play.* **2** settling the matter; deciding: *the* final *word on the subject.*

fi·na·le (fĭ nä′lĭ) **1** final part of a long piece of music. **2** closing scene of an opera or play.

fi·nal·ly (fī′nə lĭ) **1** in or at the end; lastly: *I wish,* finally, *to express my thanks.* **2** at last: *The job is* finally *done.*

fi·nance (fĭ năns′ or fī′năns) **1** management of money affairs: *A banker is skilled in* finance. **2** to provide money for: *Who is going to* finance *the trip?* **3 finances** money; funds: *Our* finances *are low this month.* **fi·nanced, fi·nanc·ing.**

fi·nan·cial (fĭ năn′shəl or fī năn′shəl) having to do with money matters: *Many students need* financial *help to get through college.* **fi·nan·cial·ly.**

fin·an·cier (fin′ən sĭr′ or fī′nən sĭr′) **1** person skilled in money management. **2** person who makes investment his business.

finch (finch) any of several small songbirds. Buntings, canaries, and sparrows are finches.

find (find) **1** to look for and get back (something lost): *Did you* find *your umbrella? He* found *his little son safe in the woods.* **2** to come upon by chance: *to* find *a quarter in the street.* **3** to learn or discover: *to* find *the answer.* **4** to reach; get to: *The bullet* found *its mark.* **5** to determine; declare: *The jury* found *him guilty.* **6** valuable or pleasing discovery: *The ancient manuscript was quite a* find.

find oneself to discover one's abilities.
find out to discover.
found, find·ing.

find·er (fin′dər) **1** person or thing that finds. **2** small lens on a camera or telescope that is used to locate the area to be photographed or observed.

[1]**fine** (fin) **1** of high or superior grade or quality; excellent: *a* fine *silk; a* fine *voice.* **2** bright; clear; pleasant: *a* fine *day.* **3** refined: *He has* fine *manners.* **4** thin; not coarse: *This needle is too* fine *to use with heavy thread.* **5 fine arts** arts mainly concerned with the creation of beauty, as painting and music. **fin·er, fin·est; fine·ly.** [[1]**fine** is from a French word (fin) that goes back to a form of a Latin word (finire) meaning "to finish."]

fine   fireman

²fine (fin) **1** money paid as a penalty for breaking a law or rule. **2** to punish by making a person pay money: *The judge fined him $15 for speeding.* **fined, fin·ing.** [²fine is from an Old French word (fin) meaning "end," "settlement" that goes back to a Latin word (fines) meaning "end," "boundary."]

fin·er·y (fī'nə rī) showy dress or ornaments: *The girls came to the party in their best finery.* **fin·er·ies.**

fin·ger (fing'gər) **1** one of the five separate parts of the end of the hand, especially one of the four besides the thumb. **2** part of a glove made to hold a finger. **3** to touch or handle with the fingers: *She fingered the material to feel its weight.*

fin·ger·nail (fing'gər nāl') hard, protective, hornlike covering at the end of a finger.

finger painting 1 the making of pictures on a specially prepared paper by applying a thick paint with the fingers and palms. **2** picture created in this way.

fin·ger·print (fing'gər print') **1** an impression of the lines on the end of the finger left on something: *Police examined the gun for* fingerprints. **2** to cause a person to make inked fingerprints so that he may be identified: *The police fingerprinted the prisoner.*

Fingerprint

fin·ish (fin'ish) **1** to bring to an end; complete; conclude: *You must finish your work before you go out to play.* **2** end; completion: *He stayed to the finish of the game.* **3** to treat the surface of: *to finish wood with varnish.* **4** surface or texture: *The table has a glossy finish.*

Fin·land (fin'lənd) a country in northern Europe, east of Sweden.

fiord (fyôrd) a long, narrow arm of the sea between high cliffs, as on the coast of Norway. Also spelled **fjord.**

fir (fûr) **1** an evergreen tree with cones and needlelike leaves, resembling a pine. **2** wood of this tree. (Homonym: fur)

fire (fir) **1** heat and light produced by burning: *We watched the* fire *from a mile away.* **2** burning fuel: *Put more coal on the fire before it goes out.* **3** to set on fire: *Enemy*

troops fired *the fields.* **4** to add fuel to: *to fire a furnace.* **5** a destructive burning: *a forest* fire. **6** to discharge (a weapon): *to fire a gun.* **7** a discharging of weapons: *The attack was met by heavy* fire. **8** strong feeling; spirit: *His patriotic stories were full of* fire. **9** to excite; stir up: *His speech fired the hearers to action.* **10** to apply intense heat to: *to fire bricks.* **11** to dismiss from a job: *Mr. Walsh fired his secretary after only one week.* **12** on fire burning: *His house was on fire.* **13** under fire under attack. **fired, fir·ing.**

fire·arm (fir'ärm') a gun, revolver, or rifle small enough to be carried by a man.

fire·boat or **fire boat** (fir'bōt') steamboat equipped with apparatus for fighting fires.

fire·brand (fir'brănd') **1** piece of burning wood. **2** person who stirs up trouble and discontent.

fire·crack·er (fir'krăk'ər) small roll of paper which contains gunpowder and a fuse. Firecrackers explode with a loud noise and are often used in celebrations.

Fire engine

fire engine a truck equipped to fight fires.

fire escape a device, such as a ladder, stairway, or chute, to provide escape from a burning building.

fire extinguisher any device for putting out small fires, such as a small tank holding chemicals to squirt on the blaze.

fire·fly (fir'fli') small flying beetle which gives off a glowing light in the dark. **fire·flies.**

fire·house (fir'hous') a building in which firemen and equipment for fighting fires are housed.

fire·light (fir'līt') light from the flames of a fire.

fire·man (fir'mən) **1** man whose work is to prevent and put out fires. **2** man who tends the fire in a furnace, an engine, etc. **fire·men.**

---

fāte, făt, fâre, fär; bē, bĕt; bite, bĭt; nō, nŏt, nôr; fūse, fŭn, fûr; tōō, tŏŏk; foil; foul; thin; ~~then~~;
hw for wh as in *wh*at; zh for s as in usual; ə for a, e, i, o, u, as in *a*go, lin*e*n, per*i*l, at*o*m, min*u*s

fire·place (fīr′plās′) **1** any place where a fire may be built, as a barbeque pit: *Father built a fireplace in the backyard.* **2** an opening in a chimney to hold an open fire; a hearth.

fire·proof (fīr′prōōf′) **1** made of material which does not burn or does not burn easily: *a fireproof building.* **2** to treat with a substance or furnish with a material which does not burn easily: *to fireproof a stage curtain.*

Fireplace

fire·side (fīr′sīd′) the place near the fire; hearth: *We all sat around the fireside.*

fire·wood (fīr′wŏŏd′) wood for use as fuel.

fire·works (fīr′wûrks′) devices which burn or explode, used in celebrations to make loud noises or bright displays of light.

¹firm (fûrm) **1** solid; not yielding easily to the touch: *a firm muscle.* **2** fixed in place; not easily moved: *The tall building was placed on a firm foundation.* **3** not easily changed; steadfast: *a firm faith; a firm belief.* **4** not shaking; steady: *a firm voice; to walk with a firm step.* **firm·ly.** [¹**firm** is from an Old French word (ferme) which comes from the Latin (firmus).]

²firm (fûrm) group of persons who have joined in a business: *a law firm.* [²**firm** is from an Italian word (firma) meaning "signature," "firm name" that goes back to a Latin word (firmare) meaning "to sign, confirm."]

fir·ma·ment (fûr′mə mənt) the sky; the heavens.

first (fûrst) **1** coming before any other in time, place, or order: *the first day of this month; the first snow of the winter.* **2** most important in quality, time, etc.: *to send mail first class.* **3** ahead of any other person or thing: *Which runner came in first?* **4** sooner; rather: "*Eat that food! I'd starve first!*" **5 at first** in the beginning: *She did not wish to go at first but changed her mind.*

first aid treatment or help given a sick or hurt person before regular medical treatment from a doctor is obtained.

first-class (fûrst′klăs′) of the highest quality: *a first-class hotel.*

first-hand (fûrst′hănd′) obtained directly from a source; direct: *a firsthand account.*

first-rate (fûrst′rāt′) excellent; very good: *a first-rate book.*

firth (fûrth) a narrow arm of the sea; mouth of a river, especially in Scotland.

fish (fish) **1** a cold-blooded water animal with a backbone, which has fins and breathes through gills. It usually has a scaly body. **2** the flesh of fish used for food: *I like fried fish.* **3** to catch or try to catch fish: *Donald fishes for recreation.* **4** to try to catch fish in: *He fishes all the streams around this valley.* **5** to search (inside something): *He fished in his pocket for a dime.* **6** to pull or draw out: *We fished him from the water.* **7** to try indirectly to get something: *to fish for an invitation; to fish for a compliment.* pl. **fish** (of the same kind), **fish·es** (of different kinds).

fish·er (fish′ər) **1** fisherman. **2** an animal of the weasel family. (Homonym: fissure)

fish·er·man (fish′ər mən) person who fishes for sport or for a living. **fish·er·men.**

fish·er·y (fish′ə rĭ) **1** the business of catching fish: *Sardine fisheries are an important Maine industry.* **2** place where fish are caught: *Salmon are taken in large numbers at Pacific fisheries.* **fish·er·ies.**

fish·hook (fish′hŏŏk′) a barbed hook, to be attached to a line and baited, for catching fish.

Fishhook

fish·pond (fish′pŏnd′) a pond in which fish are kept.

fis·sion (fish′ən) a splitting into parts: *atomic fission; the growth of new bacteria by fission.*

fis·sure (fish′ər) narrow opening; crack; cleft: *a fissure in the earth.* (Homonym: fisher)

fist (fist) closed hand with the fingers tightly bent.

¹fit (fit) **1** suitable; proper: *This jewel is fit for a crown.* **2** to make suitable; adapt: *The man fitted himself for his new job.* **3** in good physical condition: *He is again fit after a long illness.* **4** something that is right in size and shape: *The jacket is a perfect fit.* **5** to be or make right in size or shape: *The dress fits. He had his new coat fitted.*

fit in to have a suitable place or position: *Some pieces of the puzzle do not fit in.*

fit out supply with what is suitable for a purpose: *He was* fitted out *with warm clothes for his trip to Alaska.*

fit·ter, fit·test; fit·ted, fit·ting. [¹**fit** is a form of an earlier English word (fyt) of doubtful origin.]

²**fit** (fĭt) **1** sudden attack or outburst: *a fit of coughing; a* fit *of laughter.* **2 by fits and starts** in efforts that start and stop irregularly: *He does his homework* by fits and starts. [²**fit** is a form of an Old English word (fitt) meaning "struggle."]

fit·ful (fĭt′fəl) **1** not regular; stopping for a short time and then starting again: *The baby's* fitful *crying woke his mother many times.* **2** restless: *a fitful sleep.* **fit·ful·ly.**

fit·ness (fĭt′nĭs) **1** good condition: *Physical fitness depends on exercise, plus good sleeping and eating habits.* **2** suitability: *Tests showed the boy's fitness to go to college.*

fit·ting (fĭt′ĭng) **1** suitable; proper: *The hymn "America the Beautiful" is a fitting tribute to our country.* **2** adjustment of a garment being made or altered to make sure it fits correctly: *He went to the tailor for a* fitting *of his suit.* **3 fittings** fixtures; furniture; necessary equipment for a house, factory, etc. **fit·ting·ly.**

five (fīv) amount or quantity that is one greater than four; 5.

fix (fĭks) **1** to make firm; fasten: *The sailors* fixed *a new mast on the boat.* **2** to set definitely; establish: *He* fixed *a time and place for our meeting.* **3** to repair: *A plumber* fixed *the leaky pipe.* **4** to arrange; prepare: *Mother* fixed *lunch.* **5 in a fix** in a bad situation; in a predicament: *We will be in a fix if we miss the train.*

fix·ture (fĭks′chər) something permanently fastened in place: *an electric light fixture.*

fizz (fĭz) **1** a hissing sound. **2** to make a hissing sound. **3** a bubbling drink: *a lime fizz.*

fiz·zle (fĭz′əl) **1** to make a hissing sound: *Wet firecrackers fizzle.* **2** a person or attempt that comes to nothing.
fizzle out to fail; come to nothing.
fiz·zled, fiz·zling.

fjord (fyôrd) fiord.

Fla. Florida.

¹**flag** (flăg) **1** piece of cloth bearing marks or patterns that give it a certain meaning: *a signal* flag; *a club* flag. **2** to signal with, or as with, a flag: *Jo* flagged *the train with his coat.* **flagged, flag·ging.** [¹**flag** is probably an obsolete word (flack) meaning "to flutter" in a later sense of "something that flutters in the wind."]

United States flag

²**flag** (flăg) to lose strength; to grow weak or tired: *Our energy* flagged. *The children's interest with the new toy* flagged *after a while.* **flagged, flag·ging.** [²**flag** is supposed by some to come from both an Old French word (flaquir) meaning "to droop" and the obsolete word (flack) of ¹**flag**.]

³**flag** (flăg) **1** a plant with long, sword-shaped leaves and large flowers; an iris. **2** the flower of this plant. [³**flag** is probably a form of ¹**flag**, the plant having been taken as "that which flutters in the wind."]

flag·on (flăg′ən) a metal or earthenware vessel for holding liquids. It has a spout, handle, and often a lid.

Flagon

flag·pole (flăg′pōl′) a mast or staff from which a flag is flown.

flail (flāl) **1** two sticks, one of which is a handle, joined by a thong or link, used to beat ripe grain from the stalks. **2** to beat with, or as with, a flail: *to flail the air with one's arms.*

Flail

flair (flâr) **1** natural ability to see or make use of what is good, useful, or distinctive: *to have a flair for bargains; to have a flair for poetry.* **2** air of distinction; stylish manner: *Models must be able to wear fashionable clothes with a flair.* (Homonym: flare)

flake (flāk) **1** small, fine particle of something: *a flake of soap; a flake of snow.* **2** to break or chip off in small pieces: *The paint has flaked off.* **flaked, flak·ing.**

---

fāte, făt, fâre, fär; bē, bĕt; bīte, bĭt; nō, nŏt, nôr; fūse, fŭn, fûr; tōō, tŏŏk; foil; foul; thin; ~~then~~; hw for wh as in *wh*at; zh for s as in u*s*ual; ə for a, e, i, o, u, as in *a*go, lin*e*n, per*i*l, at*o*m, min*u*s

flam·boy·ant (flăm boi′ənt) **1** as brilliant as a flame: *The* flamboyant *colors of the sunset.* **2** showy; ornate: *a* flamboyant *piece of jewelry.* **flam·boy·ant·ly.**

flame (flām) **1** burning gas or vapor coming up from a fire: *The* flames *from the kitchen damaged the whole house.* **2** strong feeling: *a* flame *of rage.* **3** to burn with or like a flame; burst into fire. **flamed, flam·ing.**

fla·min·go (flə ming′gō) a pink or red bird with long legs and neck, found in warm climates. **fla·min·gos** or **fla·min·goes.**

Flamingo, about 5 ft. tall

flam·ma·ble (flăm′ə-bəl) easily set afire; likely to catch fire; inflammable: *Gasoline is highly* flammable.

flank (flăngk) **1** fleshy part of an animal between the hip and ribs. **2** side of anything: *the* flank *of a building; the* flank *of a mountain.* **3** right or left side of a fleet or army. **4** to be located by the side of: *Trees* flanked *the road.* **5** to attack or go around the side of enemy troops.

flan·nel (flăn′əl) **1** soft, finely woven cloth, usually made of wool. **2** made of flannel: *a* flannel *nightgown.*

flap (flăp) **1** anything broad and flat that is attached on one side with the rest hanging loose: *the* flap *of an envelope; a tent* flap. **2** a light blow from, or a movement made by, something broad and flat: *the* flap *of a window shade; the* flap *of wings.* **3** to move, or cause to move, lightly up and down or to and fro: *The bird was* flapping *its wings. The laundry on the clothes line* flapped *in the breeze.* **flapped, flap·ping.**

flare (flâr) **1** bright, unsteady flame or light. **2** to burn brightly with a large or unsteady flame or light: *The candle* flared *in the dark room.* **3** fire or blaze used as a signal: *The* flare *on the road showed danger.* **4** sudden outburst: *a* flare *of hatred.* **5** to burst out suddenly: *She* flared *into a rage.* **6** to spread out: *The skirt* flares *from the waist.* **flared, flar·ing.** (Homonym: flair)

flash (flăsh) **1** sudden burst of light: *a flash of lightning.* **2** to shine suddenly for just a moment: *A light* flashed *on the dark shore.* **3** sudden outburst: *a flash of anger.* **4** to gleam; glitter: *The angry woman's eyes* flashed *with rage.* **5** to pass (by) quickly; appear for an instant: *The train* flashed *by.* **6** to send out (a signal) in short bursts of light. **7 in a flash** in a very short time: *He solved the puzzle* in a flash.

flash·light (flăsh′līt′) **1** a small electric torch. **2** a flash of light used to make a photograph.

flash·y (flăsh′ī) showy but cheap-looking; gaudy: *to wear* flashy *clothes or jewelry.* **flash·i·er, flash·i·est; flash·i·ly.**

flask (flăsk) **1** a flat glass or metal bottle that fits into a pocket. **2** a bottle with a narrow neck used in laboratories, etc.

Flask

¹flat (flăt) **1** level; even: *Beaches are* flat. *A good floor is* flat. **2** evenly spread out: *Lay the paper* flat *on the floor.* **3** not deep; not thick: *a* flat *pan; a* flat *coin.* **4** dull; with little flavor: *This drink tastes* flat. **5** not changing: *They pay a* flat *rate.* **6** downright; absolute: *a* flat *refusal.* **7** the wide part: *the* flat *of the hand.* **8** level land; plain; swamp: *a mud* flat; *river* flats. **9** to make or become flat. **10** below the true pitch: *to sing* flat. **11** the tone a half step below the natural tone: *B* flat. **12** a sign (♭) meaning a note is to be lowered a half step. **flat·ter, flat·test; flat·ted, flat·ting; flat·ly.** [¹flat is probably from an Old Norse word (flatr).]

²flat (flăt) an apartment, all the rooms of which are on the same floor. [²flat is a form of an Old English word (flet) meaning "floor." It was probably influenced in its spelling by ¹flat.]

flat·boat (flăt′bōt′) a large boat with a flat bottom, used especially to float goods down a river or in shallow waters.

flat·car (flăt′kär′) railroad car without roof or sides, for carrying freight.

Flatfish

flat·fish (flăt′fish′) any of a number of flat broad fishes with eyes on the upper side, such as the sole or the flounder. pl. **flat·fish;** rarely, **flat·fish·es.**

flat·i·ron (flăt′ī′ərn) a heavy iron with a flat surface used for pressing clothes, etc.

flat·ten (flăt′ən) to make or become flat.

flat·ter (flăt′ər) **1** to exaggerate (a person's) good points. **2** to try to win by insincere praise. **3** to compliment; cause to feel pleased: *I am flattered that you asked me.*

flat·ter·y (flăt′ə rĭ) **1** exaggeration of (a person's) good points. **2** false compliments. **flat·ter·ies.**

flaunt (flônt) to show off: *She flaunts her expensive clothes.*

fla·vor (flā′vər) **1** taste: *The flavor of the soup was spoiled by too much salt.* **2** to give taste to; season: *to flavor gum with mint.*

fla·vor·ing (flā′vər ĭng) something used to give a special taste to food or drink: *chocolate flavoring.*

flaw (flô) crack; defect; fault: *a flaw in a glass; a flaw in someone's character.*

flaw·less (flô′lĭs) without a defect; perfect: *a flawless diamond.* **flaw·less·ly.**

flax (flăks) **1** a slender plant grown for its fibers and seeds. The fibers are spun into threads and then woven into linen. The seeds yield linseed oil. Flax has narrow leaves and blue flowers. **2** the threadlike fibers from the stem of this plant.

flax·en (flăk′sən) **1** like flax or made of flax. **2** the color of flax; pale yellow: *May's flaxen hair.*

flay (flā) **1** to strip off the skin. **2** to scold severely.

flea (flē) a small insect that sucks blood from animals and is noted for its ability to make long jumps. (Homonym: flee)

Flea

fleck (flĕk) **1** a spot; a mark: *A freckle is a fleck in the skin.* **2** to mark; to spot: *Clouds flecked the sky.*

fled (flĕd) See **flee.** *The enemy fled.*

fledg·ling (flĕj′lĭng) **1** a young bird just able to fly. **2** an inexperienced person.

flee (flē) to hurry away; run away: *The bandits fled, but the police caught them.* **fled, flee·ing.** (Homonym: flea)

fleece (flēs) **1** the woolly coat that covers a sheep. **2** all the wool shorn or cut off a sheep at one time. **3** to cut wool off a sheep. **4** to strip of money or property; rob; cheat. **fleeced, fleec·ing.**

fleec·y (flē′sĭ) soft and light, like a fleece: *the fleecy clouds.* **fleec·i·er, fleec·i·est.**

¹fleet (flēt) **1** a group of warships under one command. **2** a group of boats, airplanes, cars, or other vehicles, moving or working together. [**¹fleet** is a form of an Old English word (flēot) meaning "ship."]

²fleet (flēt) fast; swift: *a fleet horse.* **fleet·ly.** [**²fleet** is from an Old English word (flēotan) "to float." Something that glided away like a stream might well have been taken as moving swiftly.]

fleet·ing (flē′tĭng) passing quickly; lasting a short time; brief: *a fleeting glimpse.* **fleet·ing·ly.**

Flem·ish (flĕm′ĭsh) **1** of or having to do with the part of Belgium called Flanders. **2** the language of this district.

flesh (flĕsh) **1** the soft parts of the body between the skin and bones, chiefly muscle and fat. **2** the meat of animals, birds, or fish used as food. **3** soft pulp of fruits and vegetables used as food. **4** the body, but not the mind and soul: *The spirit is willing, but the flesh is weak.* **5 flesh and blood** kin: *Your brothers and sisters are your own flesh and blood.*

flesh·y (flĕsh′ĭ) plump, fat. **flesh·i·er, flesh·i·est.**

flew (flōō) See **¹fly.** *The birds flew away.* (Homonyms: flu, flue)

flex (flĕks) **1** to bend or curve: *to flex the finger.* **2** to draw up (a muscle) tightly: *to flex a muscle.*

flex·i·ble (flĕk′sə bəl) **1** easily bent: *a flexible fishing rod.* **2** capable of fitting to new conditions; adaptable: *Our present plans are flexible.* **flex·i·bly.**

flick (flĭk) **1** light, quick stroke: *He gave his horse a flick with the whip.* **2** to remove something with such a stroke: *She flicked the dust from the chair with her handkerchief.* **3** to whip or strike lightly: *He flicked the horse with a whip.* **4** short quick movement: *a flick of the wrist.*

¹flick·er (flĭk′ər) **1** to shine or burn unsteadily; waver: *A candle flickers in the breeze.* **2** to move back and forth; tremble; quiver: *The shadows flickered in the firelight.* **3** unsteady flame: *The fire gave one last flicker*

fāte, făt, fâre, fär; bē, bĕt; bite, bit; nō, nŏt, nôr; fūse, fŭn, fûr; tōō, tōŏk; foil; foul; thin; ~~then~~; hw for wh as in *what;* zh for s as in *usual;* ə for a, e, i, o, u, as in *ago, linen, peril, atom, minus*

287

and died. **4** slight movement: *the flicker of an eyelid.* [¹**flicker** is from an Old English word (flicorian) meaning "to flutter."]

²**flick·er** (flĭk′ər) kind of North American woodpecker with a bright red mark at the neck and yellow under the wings and tail. [²**flicker** is probably an imitation of one of its notes.]

fli·er (flī′ər) **1** an aviator: *He is a flier in the Air Force.* **2** anything that flies. **3** an express train or bus.

flies (flīz) **1** See ¹**fly:** *That airplane flies across the ocean.* **2** See ²**fly:** *a swarm of buzzing flies.*

¹**flight** (flīt) **1** a flying or way of flying: *A bat has a zigzag flight.* **2** the distance flown: *a long airplane flight.* **3** swift passage: *the flight of time.* **4** a flying group: *a flight of geese; a flight of arrows.* **5** a group or series of stairs: *The artist lived three flights up.* **6** a passing beyond the usual: *a flight of the imagination.* [¹**flight** is a form of an Old English word (fliht) meaning "a flying."]

Flight of steps

²**flight** (flīt) a hasty departure: *The thief took flight when the policeman saw him.* [²**flight** is a form of an earlier English word (fluht) meaning "a fleeing."]

flim·sy (flĭm′zĭ) **1** fragile; not solid; poorly made: *The flimsy boat was crushed like an eggshell.* **2** weak; not convincing: *a flimsy excuse.* **flim·si·er, flim·si·est; flim·si·ly.**

flinch (flĭnch) to draw back or away in fear, pain, etc.: *He flinches at the sight of blood. She never flinched from her duty, however unpleasant.*

fling (flĭng) **1** to throw or cast with force: *to fling stones at a scarecrow.* **2** a throw or toss: *He gave his hat a fling in the air.* **3** to move a part of the body rapidly, violently, or impulsively: *to fling one's arms around a person's neck.* **4** a lively dance from Scotland: *the Highland fling.* **5 in full fling** at its height: *The party was in full fling.* **6 have a fling at** to have a try at. **flung, fling·ing.**

flint (flĭnt) very hard quartz, usually gray, that produces sparks when struck against steel, once generally used for lighting fires.

flint·lock (flĭnt′lŏk′) an old-fashioned gun fired by a spark from a flint and steel attached to the barrel.

Flintlock

flint·y (flĭn′tĭ) **1** made of or like flint: *The horse's hoofs struck sparks on the flinty rocks.* **2** hard; unyielding: *a flinty look.* **flint·i·er, flint·i·est.**

flip (flĭp) **1** to strike with the fingers; tap; hit lightly: *to flip the ash from a cigarette.* **2** light stroke or tap with the fingers: *Mary gave the bug a flip to remove it from the rose.* **3** short, quick turn: *She gave the pancake a flip.* **4** to turn rapidly: *to flip the pages of a book.* **5** to toss with a quick motion of a finger and thumb: *to flip a coin.* **flipped, flip·ping.**

flip·pant (flĭp′ənt) not showing proper seriousness: *He was annoyed by her flippant answer to such an important question.* **flip·pant·ly.**

flip·per (flĭp′ər) fin-like limb of a seal, sea turtle, etc.

Flippers

flirt (flûrt) **1** to give special attention to the opposite sex in a playful romantic way: *He flirted with all the girls by telling them how sweet they were.* **2** a person who flirts: *No boys take Alice seriously because they know she is a flirt.* **3** to toy: *to flirt with an idea.* **4** to toss to and fro quickly: *The dancer flirted her skirts as she whirled about.*

flit (flĭt) **1** to move lightly and quickly; fly; dart: *The bird flitted from branch to branch.* **2** to pass quickly: *Time flits by.* **flit·ted, flit·ting.**

float (flōt) **1** to be held up by liquid or air: *Wood floats on water. A balloon floats in the air.* **2** to move or drift freely: *A cloud floated across the sky. The boat floated about with the tide.* **3** to cause to rest or move on the surface of a liquid: *to float a raft.* **4** something that floats or helps something else to float: *a float on a fishline.* **5** an exhibit on a platform with wheels, used in a parade.

flock (flŏk) **1** a group of animals or birds of one kind which travel or feed together: *a* flock *of sheep; a* flock *of geese.* **2** large number (of people) together; crowd: *There were* flocks *of people at the beach.* **3** group of people under a pastor; congregation; group; band: *A minister visits the sick of his* flock. **4** to gather or move together in numbers: *People* flocked *to the exhibit.*

floe (flō) a large sheet or mass of drifting ice on the sea. (Homonym: flow)

flog (flŏg) to beat hard with a stick or whip. **flogged, flog·ging.**

flood (flŭd) **1** a great quantity or flow of water (over land that is usually dry): *The long period of rain brought* floods *to the valley.* **2** to cover or cause to be covered with water: *The basements in the storm area were all* flooded. **3** a great outpouring or abundance: *a* flood *of tears; a* flood *of letters.* **4** to supply in large quantity: *His admirers* flooded *him with letters.* **5 the Flood** in the Bible, the water that covered the earth in Noah's time.

flood·light (flŭd'līt') **1** broad beam of light covering a large area. **2** a lamp that gives such a light. **3** to light by such means: *to* floodlight *a football field.*

floor (flôr) **1** the part of a room that one walks on: *a wooden* floor. **2** to put a floor in: *to* floor *a house.* **3** story of a building: *We live on the second* floor. **4** bottom: *the* floor *of a cave; ocean* floor. **5** to knock down: *The boxer* floored *his opponent.*

flop (flŏp) **1** to drop or fall heavily or clumsily: *She* flopped *onto the bed.* **2** to fall or flap awkwardly: *The wounded bird* flopped *about in the brush.* **3** the act or sound of flopping: *He fell into the puddle with a* flop. **flopped, flop·ping.**

flo·ral (flôr'əl) of or like flowers: *a* floral *arrangement; a* floral *print.* **flo·ral·ly.**

Flor·i·da (flŏr'ə də or flôr'ə də) the most southeastern State of the United States.

flo·rist (flŏr'ist or flôr'ist) a person who grows or sells flowers as a business.

floss (flŏs or flôs) **1** strands of silk used in embroidering, crocheting, etc. **2** waxed thread used to clean between the teeth. **3** soft, silky fibers in certain plant pods.

flot·sam (flŏt'səm) the wreckage of a ship or its cargo found floating in the sea.

¹**floun·der** (floun'dər) **1** to make violent and usually vain efforts: *The horses* floundered *in the deep mud.* **2** to hesitate and make mistakes: *He* floundered *through the speech he tried to give in French.* [¹**flounder** is probably a changed form of ²**founder.**]

²**floun·der** (floun'dər) small fish with a flat body, used as food. [²**flounder** comes through an Old French word (flondre) from a Scandinavian word.]

flour (flour or flou'ər) **1** fine meal of ground wheat or other grain. **2** to sprinkle with flour: *The cook* floured *the fish before he fried it.* (Homonym: flower)

flour·ish (flûr'ish) **1** to grow; prosper; thrive; be successful: *Citrus fruits* flourish *in warm climates. Business* flourished *last year.* **2** to wave or swing about in the air: *She ran about* flourishing *the blue ribbon her team had won.* **3** showy waving: *a* flourish *of flags, hats, etc.* **4** decoration added to handwriting: *He signed his name with a* flourish. **5** a showy passage of music, often played by trumpets, bugles, etc.

flout (flout) to mock; scoff at; treat with scorn: *The girl* flouted *her teacher's advice.*

flow (flō) **1** to move or run along in a stream: *Rivers* flow. *Blood* flows *through the body.* **2** a moving or running in a stream: *a constant* flow *of water from a spring.* **3** a coming in of the tide: *There is a steady ebb and* flow *of the ocean.* **4** to spread, as if flowing: *The old man's beard* flowed *over his vest.* **5** a pouring out: *a* flow *of blood.* (Homonym: floe)

flow·er (flou'ər) **1** the part of a plant in which its seeds are produced; a bloom; a blossom. **2** a plant grown for its blossoms: *We shall plant these* flowers *in our garden.* **3** the best part: *the* flower *of one's youth.* **4** to blossom; bloom: *Cherry trees* flower *in early spring.* (Homonym: flour)

STAMEN   PISTIL

PETAL   SEPAL

Parts of a flower

---

fāte, făt, fâre, fär; bē, bĕt; bīte, bĭt; nō, nŏt, nôr; fūse, fŭn, fûr; tōō, tŏŏk; foil; foul; thin; then; hw for wh as in *wh*at; zh for s as in u*s*ual; ə for a, e, i, o, u, as in *a*go, linen, peril, atom, minus

flow·er·y (flou′ə rī) **1** covered with flowers: *a flowery meadow*. **2** full of fine words and phrases: *a flowery speech*. **flow·er·i·er, flow·er·i·est.**

flown (flōn) See ¹**fly**. *The geese have flown south*.

flu (flōō) influenza. (Homonyms: flew, flue)

flue (flōō) a pipe or tube for carrying away smoke or gases. (Homonyms: flew, flu)

fluff (flŭf) **1** soft, light, downy materials, such as feathers, fur, hair, wool, etc.: *The kitten was a little ball of gray fluff*. **2** to shake or puff out into a soft mass: *The bird fluffed its feathers*.

fluff·y (flŭf′ī) like or covered with fluff: *a fluffy cloud; a fluffy dog*. **fluff·i·er, fluff·i·est.**

flu·id (flōō′ĭd) **1** a substance that will flow. Water, mercury, and air are fluids. **2** able to flow; not solid; liquid: *Molten steel is steel in a fluid form*.

flung (flŭng) See **fling**. *The boy flung a pebble into the pond*.

flu·o·res·cent (flōō′ə rĕs′ənt) **1** able to light up when acted upon by invisible rays, such as ultraviolet rays and X rays. **2 fluorescent lamp** an electric lamp consisting of a gas-filled tube coated on the inside with a fluorescent substance.

flu·o·ri·date (flōō′ə rə dāt′) to treat with fluorides: *to fluoridate water to reduce tooth decay*. **flu·o·ri·dat·ed, flu·o·ri·dat·ing.**

flu·o·ri·da·tion (flōō′ə rə dā′shen) the addition of a very small amount of fluorides to the water supply to reduce tooth decay.

flu·o·ride (flōō′ə rid′) one of a group of chemical compounds containing fluorine.

flu·o·rine (flōō′ə rin or flōō′ə rēn′) a chemical element. It is a yellowish-green gas at ordinary temperature.

flur·ry (flŭr′ī) **1** state of confusion or excitement: *She was in a flurry, trying to get packed before train time*. **2** to excite; confuse: *Mother was flurried with the many preparations for her guests*. **3** a light fall of rain or snow. **4** a sudden gust of wind. **flur·ries; flur·ried, flur·ry·ing.**

flush (flŭsh) **1** to redden; blush: *The girl flushed when the young man complimented her*. **2** a blush; a glow: *A flush colored her cheeks*. **3** to excite; elate: *The team was flushed with victory*. **4** to cleanse or flood

with a flow of water: *to flush out a pipe*. **5** even or level: *doors flush with the walls*.

flus·ter (flŭs′tər) **1** to confuse; flurry; upset: *Mrs. Whipple was flustered when she mislaid her key*. **2** flurry; confusion; nervousness.

Man playing a flute

flute (flōōt) **1** a pipe-like musical instrument with finger holes, played by blowing across a mouthpiece near one end. **2** a shallow groove, as in a column. **3** to play on, or make a sound like, a flute. **4** to form grooves or folds in. **flut·ed, flut·ing.**

flut·ist (flōō′tist) a flute player.

flut·ter (flŭt′ər) **1** to move wings quickly without flying: *The bird fluttered its wings*. **2** quick, irregular movement: *the flutter of wings*. **3** to move quickly without a set pattern: *Leaves flutter in the breeze*. **4** to move about excitedly without getting anything done. **5** state of nervous excitement: *We were in a flutter over the party*.

¹**fly** (flī) **1** to move through the air with wings, as a bird or butterfly does. **2** to move through or in the air: *The bullet flew toward the target. The flag flew in the breeze*. **3** to move swiftly; speed. **4** to make or cause to fly: *to fly a kite*. **5** in baseball, a ball batted high in the air. **6** an extra roof for a tent or the flap which forms the door. **7** a strip of cloth on a garment to cover buttons, zippers, etc., on trousers. **flies; flies, flew, flown, fly·ing.** [¹**fly** is from an Old English word (flēogan) meaning "to move through the air with wings."]

²**fly** (flī) **1** any of various insects with a single pair of gauzy wings, especially the common housefly. **2** a fishhook fitted with feathers to look like an insect. **flies.** [²**fly** is from an Old English word (flēoge, flyge). It is of course from ¹**fly**.]

Housefly

fly·catch·er (flī′kăch′ər) any of several kinds of birds that catch insects in flight.

fly·er (flī′ər) flier.

flying fish any of several tropical fishes with long, winglike fins, that can make long, gliding leaps over the surface of the water.

flying saucer any one of various disk-shaped objects which people say they have seen flying in the sky at great speeds.

fly·wheel (flī′hwēl′) a wheel with a heavy rim used on a machine to keep its speed even.

Flying fish, 8 to 18 in. long

FM (ĕf ĕm) frequency modulation.

foal (fōl) **1** young horse or donkey. **2** to give birth to a young horse or donkey.

foam (fōm) **1** white mixture of many tiny bubbles formed on liquids by shaking or fermentation, or in the mouths of some animals; froth: *We watched the sea foam made by the waves breaking on the shore.* **2** to form or produce a mixture of tiny white bubbles; to froth: *The mad dog foamed at the mouth.*

fo·cus (fō′kəs) **1** point at which waves of light, heat, or sound meet after being bent by a lens, curved mirror, sound reflector, etc. **2** distance from a lens or curved mirror to the point where the rays from it come together. **3** adjustment of eyes, camera lens, etc., to give clear sight or images: *to bring into focus.* **4** to adjust eyes, camera lens, etc., for clear sight or images: *He focused the camera on the dog.* **5** central point; center of interest. **6** to center; concentrate: *She focused her attention on dancing.* **fo·cus·es** or **fo·ci** (fō′sī).

fod·der (fŏd′ər) coarse food, such as hay for horses, cattle, and sheep.

foe (fō) enemy; adversary.

fog (fŏg or fôg) **1** cloud of water drops near the surface of the sea or land; thick mist. **2** to cover or be covered with thick mist. **3** cloudiness in the air. **4** confused state: *Susan was in a fog and couldn't decide what to do.* **fogged, fog·ging.**

fog·gy (fŏg′ī or fôg′ī) **1** not clear; misty: *London is known for its foggy weather.* **2** dim; blurred; muddled: *a foggy notion.* **fog·gi·er, fog·gi·est; fog·gi·ly.**

fog·horn (fŏg′hôrn′ or fôg′hôrn′) siren or horn that sends warning signals to ships in a fog.

¹foil (foil) **1** metal rolled into a paperlike sheet. **2** something that sets off another thing by contrast: *Her simple dress was a perfect* foil *for her diamond necklace.* [**¹foil** comes (through French) from a Latin word (folium) meaning "a leaf."]

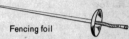

Fencing foil

²foil (foil) slender sword with a blunt point, used in fencing. [**²foil** is of unknown origin.]

³foil (foil) to keep from carrying out or from being carried out; defeat; outwit: *The prisoner's attempt to escape was foiled by his guards.* [**³foil** probably comes from an Old French word (fuler) meaning "to trample." It was supposed that an animal's trampling would spoil its trail and thwart the hunter.]

¹fold (fōld) **1** to double or bend something in sections: *He folded his newspaper.* **2** part doubled or bent over in sections; crease made by folding: *a fold in a blanket.* **3** to clasp together: *The child quietly folded her hands in her lap.* **4** to bend close to the body: *The bird folded its wings and went to sleep.* **5** to embrace: *She folded the puppy in her arms.* [**fold** is from an Old English word (faldan) meaning "to fold"; "double over."]

²fold (fōld) pen for sheep. [**²fold** is from an Old English word (fāld) with the same meaning.]

fold·er (fōl′dər) **1** a small book of pages which are not stitched together. **2** a stiff outer cover for holding loose papers.

fo·li·age (fō′li ij) all the leaves of a plant.

folk (fōk) **1** people: *It's hard to satisfy some folk. Country folk lead different lives from city folk.* **2** of or existing among the people: *a folk saying.* **3** folks one's relatives.

folk dance 1 a dance that is handed down from generation to generation among a people. **2** music for this kind of dance.

---

fāte, făt, fâre, fär; bē, bĕt; bite, bit; nō, nŏt, nôr; fūse, fŭn, fûr; tōō, tŏŏk; foil; foul; thin; ~~th~~en; hw for wh as in *wh*at; zh for s as in u*s*ual; ə for a, e, i, o, u, as in *a*go, lin*e*n, per*i*l, at*o*m, min*u*s.

folk music music that is handed down from generation to generation among a people.

folk song song that is handed down from generation to generation among a people.

folk tale a story, often about a local hero or superstition, handed down from generation to generation among the common people of a race or region. The stories of Robin Hood and Paul Bunyan are folk tales.

fol·low (fŏl′ō) **1** to come after; go after: *Please* follow *me. Monday* follows *Sunday.* **2** to go along: *If you* follow *this road, you will see it.* **3** to accept as a guide; obey: *You should* follow *her advice. When you bake a cake, it is important to* follow *directions.* **4** to keep the eyes on: *to* follow *an eclipse of the moon.* **5** to pay attention to; be interested in: *to* follow *the news.* **6** to understand: *The speaker was hard to* follow *because he talked so fast.* **7** to result from: *Thunder* follows *lightning.* **8** to make a living from: *to* follow *a trade.*

follow through to carry through to the end, especially of a stroke after hitting a ball, as in golf.

follow up to pursue steadily: *to* follow up *someone's work.*

fol·low·er (fŏl′ō ər) person who follows and supports the beliefs of another person; a disciple.

fol·low·ing (fŏl′ō ing) **1** coming after; next: *the* following *day.* **2** group of followers.

fol·ly (fŏl′ĭ) **1** foolishness; lack of sense. **2** foolish idea or behavior. **fol·lies.**

fond (fŏnd) **1** loving; affectionate: *a fond mother; a fond look.* **2** doting; foolishly affectionate. **3 to be fond of** to like; love: *She is fond of children.* **fond·ly.**

fon·dle (fŏn′dəl) to touch lovingly; pet; caress. **fon·dled, fon·dling.**

fond·ness (fŏnd′nĭs) liking; affection.

font (fŏnt) **1** a basin or other vessel holding holy water or water for baptizing. **2** a spring; source: *a font of information.*

food (fōōd) **1** anything that people or animals eat or drink, or that plants use to make them live and grow. **2** things to eat: *Eat your food slowly.*

Font

fool (fōōl) **1** person who lacks sense. **2** to act like a fool; play or joke in a silly way. **3** to trick; deceive. **4** in olden times, a clown; jester.

fool·har·dy (fōōl′här′dĭ) taking foolish risks; heedless of danger; rash; reckless. **fool·har·di·er, fool·har·di·est; fool·har·di·ly.**

fool·ish (fōō′lĭsh) **1** without sense; unwise. **2** silly; ridiculous. **fool·ish·ly.**

fool·proof (fōōl′prōōf′) **1** made in such a way that anyone, even a fool, can use it safely: *a foolproof machine.* **2** so simple and certain that nothing can go wrong: *a foolproof plan.*

foot (fŏŏt) **1** part of a leg on which a person or animal walks. **2** end of the leg of a piece of furniture, base of a vase, etc. **3** lowest part of a thing: *the foot of a column; the foot of the stairs.* **4** lowest place in rank or order; the bottom: *the foot of the list.* **5** end of a bed where the feet of a sleeper lie. **6** part of a shoe or stocking to fit the foot. **7** measure of length; 12 inches. **8** to add: *to foot a column of figures.* **9** a division of a line of poetry. **10** to pay: *to foot a bill.* **11 put one's foot down** to be firm; assert oneself. **12 put one's foot in it** to make an embarrassing mistake. **feet.**

FOOT

Foot of a goblet

foot·ball (fŏŏt′bôl′) **1** a leather, air-filled ball used in certain games in which it is, or may be, advanced by kicking. **2** a game played with a football; especially, in the United States, a game played by two teams of 11 men each on a field with a crossbar goal at each end. The object is to carry the ball across the opponent's goal line or kick it over his goal.

foot·fall (fŏŏt′fôl′) sound of footsteps.

foot·hill (fŏŏt′hĭl′) low hill at the base of a mountain or mountain range.

foot·hold (fŏŏt′hōld′) **1** place for a foot; footing: *The mountain climbers chopped footholds in the cliff.* **2** secure position; firm footing.

foot·ing (fŏŏt′ing) **1** firm placing of the feet: *He lost his footing and fell down on the ice.* **2** place or support for the feet. **3** position; relationship: *to get a footing in society.*

foot·man (foŏt'mən) a male servant, usually in uniform, who answers the doorbell, waits on the table, opens carriage or car doors, etc. **foot·men.**

foot·path (foŏt'păth') trail or path for people who are walking.

foot·pound (foŏt'pound') **1** the work done when a weight of one pound is lifted one foot. **2** work done when a force of one pound acts through a distance of one foot.

foot·print (foŏt'print') mark made by a foot.

foot·sore (foŏt'sôr') having sore feet: *Marching in the parade left us* footsore.

foot·step (foŏt'stĕp') **1** a step or pace. **2** sound of a step. **3** footprint; mark of a step: *There were* footsteps *in the sand.* **4** a foothold in a steep incline.

foot·stool (foŏt'stoŏl') low stool on which to rest the feet when sitting down.

foot·wear (foŏt'wâr') slippers, shoes, boots, etc.

for (fôr or fər) **1** suited to; fitting the need, use, or purpose of: *a book of stories* for *children; a knife* for *cutting meat.* **2** meant to belong to; directed to: *a gift* for *you; a letter* for *Mary.* **3** to have or to do: *It is time* for *tea. He was hired* for *the job.* **4** during: *It has been raining* for *the last two hours. He was gone* for *three days.* **5** with the purpose of: *to go* for *a walk.* **6** with the intention of reaching, getting, doing, etc.: *to leave* for *New York; to go* for *the groceries.* **7** because of: *to shout* for *joy; to weep* for *sorrow.* **8** in place of; instead of: *Use this table* for *a desk.* **9** in favor of; in support of: *to vote* for *a larger budget.* **10** as or at the price of: *to pay a dollar* for *a book.* **11** to the amount of: *a check* for *seven dollars.* **12** intended to be used by: *This swimming pool is* for *everybody.* **13** on account of; in the interest of: *I'll do it* for *a friend.* (Homonyms: fore, four)

for·age (fôr'ij or fŏr'ij) **1** food for horses and cattle. **2** a search for food or provisions: *The soldiers went on a* forage *through the farmyards.* **3** to search for something, especially food: *to* forage *in the refrigerator.* **for·aged, for·ag·ing.**

for·ay (fôr'ā) a raid for the purpose of taking supplies: *an enemy* foray *on a town.*

for·bade or **for·bad** (fôr băd') See **forbid.** *Father* forbade *us to go out after dark.*

for·bear (fôr bâr') **1** to keep oneself (from); refrain: *I will* forbear *from asking a question.* **2** to be patient: *You will have to* forbear *a while longer.* **for·bore, for·borne, for·bear·ing.**

for·bear·ance (fôr bâr'əns) gentleness and mercy toward offenders; patient endurance; indulgence: *Uncle Ned looked on our pranks with* forbearance.

for·bid (fôr bid') to command (a person) not to do something; to rule against; not to allow; to prohibit: *The doctor has* forbidden *him to eat candy.* **for·bade** or **for·bad, for·bid·den, for·bid·ding.**

for·bid·den (fôr bid'ən) **1** not allowed; prohibited: *a* forbidden *pleasure.* **2** See **forbid.**

for·bid·ding (fôr bid'ing) **1** stern; disagreeable: *His manner was so* forbidding *that the children shrank back.* **2** threatening; looking dangerous: *The black clouds had a* forbidding *look.* **for·bid·ding·ly.**

for·bore (fôr bôr') See **forbear.** *He* forbore *to take revenge on his enemies.*

for·borne (fôr bôrn') See **forbear.** *We have* forborne *long enough, and now we must speak.*

force (fôrs) **1** push or pull (on an object): *The* force *of the wind nearly caved in the house.* **2** strength: *The wind lost its* force *after the storm.* **3** strength or power used against a person or thing: *The police used* force *to break up the fight.* **4** power to influence or persuade: *the* force *of evidence.* **5** to make to do something; compel: *The thief* forced *his victim to open the safe.* **6** to break open: *to* force *a lock.* **7** to bring about, as by force: *to* force *a smile.* **8** group of persons organized to work together: *an office* force; *a police* force. **9** body of persons in military service: *ground* forces; *armed* forces. **10** to cause to grow more quickly: *He* forced *the plants by bringing them into the warm house.* **11 in force** in use or operation: *The new traffic law is now* in force. **forced, forc·ing.**

---

fāte, făt, fâre, fär; bē, bĕt; bite, bit; nō, nŏt, nôr; fūse, fŭn, fûr; toō, toŏk; foil; foul; thin; ~~then~~; hw for wh as in *wh*at; zh for s as in u*s*ual; ə for a, e, i, o, u, as in *a*go, lin*e*n, per*i*l, at*o*m, min*u*s

293

force·ful (fôrs′fəl) strong; powerful; convincing: *a* forceful *argument*. **force·ful·ly.**

for·ceps (fôr′səps) a kind of pincers with specially shaped jaws used in dentistry, surgery, etc. pl. **forceps.**

for·ci·ble (fôr′sə bəl) **1** done by force or violence: *The police made a* forcible *entry into the thief's hiding place.* **2** energetic; powerful; effective: *to take* forcible *measures; to be a* forcible *speaker.* **for·ci·bly.**

Surgical and dental forceps

ford (fôrd) **1** shallow part of a stream which can be crossed by walking or driving through the water. **2** to cross (a stream) by walking or driving through the shallow water.

fore (fôr) **1** at or toward the front. **2** the front part of a ship. For picture, see **aft. 3** a shout used on a golf course to warn players who are in danger of being hit by the ball. **4 to the fore** to a prominent position: *After his book was published, he came* to the fore *as an author.* (Homonyms: for, four)

fore- prefix meaning **(1)** "before": *the* fore*noon;* fore*tell;* fore*see.* **(2)** "front part of": fore*arm;* fore*ground;* fore*head.*

fore-and-aft (fôr′ənd äft′) in the direction of a ship's length: *The schooner has* fore-and-aft *sails.*

¹fore·arm (fôr′ärm′) the part of the arm between the elbow and the wrist. [**¹fore-arm** is a word that is made up of **fore** and **¹arm.**]

²fore·arm (fôr ärm′) to arm beforehand. [**²forearm** is a word that is made up of **fore** and **²arm.**]

fore·bear (fôr′bâr) an ancestor; forefather (usually used in the plural): *This is a portrait of one of my* forebears. Also spelled **forbear.**

fore·bod·ing (fôr bō′ding) a feeling that something bad is going to happen: *He had a* foreboding *of disaster.*

fore·cast (fôr′kăst′) **1** to tell ahead of time; predict. **2** a foretelling; a prediction: *a weather* forecast; *a forecast of a Presidential election.* **fore·cast** or **fore·cast·ed, fore·cast·ing.**

fore·cas·tle (fōk′səl or fôr′kăs′əl) **1** the part of a ship's upper deck in front of the forward mast. **2** the crew's quarters in the fore part of a ship.

fore·father (fôr′fä-thər) ancestor.

fore·fin·ger (fôr′-fing′gər) the finger next to the thumb; the index finger.

Forecastle

fore·foot (fôr′fŏŏt′) one of the front feet of an animal with four legs. **fore·feet.**

fore·go·ing (fôr gō′ing) coming just before; immediately preceding: *The* foregoing *quotation was from the Bible.*

Forefinger

fore·gone (fôr gôn′ or fôr gŏn′) decided ahead of time; determined in advance: *His promotion was a* foregone *conclusion.*

fore·ground (fôr′ground′) part of a scene, landscape, or picture that is or seems nearest to the observer.

fore·head (fôr′ĭd or fôr′hĕd′) the part of the face above the eyes; brow.

for·eign (fôr′in or fôr′in) **1** belonging to or coming from another country or nation: *She speaks a* foreign *language.* **2** having to do with other nations or countries: *Our class had a discussion on* foreign *affairs.* **3** not related or not belonging: *Dishonesty is* foreign *to his nature. A* foreign *body in the eye, such as a cinder, can be painful.*

for·eign·er (fôr′in ər or fôr′in ər) person from or native of another country.

fore·leg (fôr′lĕg′) one of the front legs of an animal with four feet.

fore·man (fôr′mən) **1** person in charge of a group of workers. **2** speaker; spokesman: *the* foreman *of a jury.* **fore·men.**

fore·mast (fôr′măst′ or fôr′məst) mast nearest to the front of a ship.

fore·most (fôr′mōst′) chief; most important: *He was the* foremost *singer of his day.*

fore·noon (fôr′nŏŏn′) time between sunrise and midday.

fore·saw (fôr sô′) See **foresee.**

fore·see (fôr sē′) to see ahead; anticipate; realize beforehand: *They did not* foresee *the trouble that would come from one small mistake.* **fore·saw, fore·seen, for·see·ing.**

fore·seen (fôr sēn′) See **foresee.**

fore·sight (fôr′sīt′) careful planning; a seeing beforehand; prudence: *She had foresight and saved money for the trip.*

for·est (fôr′ist or fŏr′ist) **1** a growth of trees covering a large tract of land; large woods. **2** to cover with trees or forest.

for·est·er (fôr′is tər or fŏr′is tər) **1** a person in charge of the care of a forest, guarding the trees and wildlife in it. **2** a forest dweller.

for·est·ry (fôr′is tri or fŏr′is tri) science of planting and caring for trees, proper lumbering, etc.

fore·tell (fôr těl′) to tell in advance; predict: *Who can foretell what will happen next week?* **fore·told, fore·tell·ing.**

fore·told (fôr tōld′) See **foretell.**

for·ev·er (fôr ěv′ər) **1** eternally; without ever ending. **2** continually; always: *He is forever watching television.*

for·ev·er·more (fôr ěv′ər môr′) from now on; forever.

for·feit (fôr′fit) **1** to lose or give up because of neglect or fault: *The team failed to show up and forfeited the game.* **2** something lost as the result of neglect, fault, etc.

for·fei·ture (fôr′fi chər) the losing of something as a punishment or because of neglect or wrongdoing: *He paid for careless driving with the forfeiture of his license.*

for·gave (fôr gāv′) See **forgive.** *He forgave me when I apologized for my rudeness.*

¹forge (fôrj) **1** place for heating metals. **2** blacksmith shop; smithy. **3** to shape heat-softened metal with a hammer: *The blacksmith forges horseshoes.* **4** to write or copy (a document or another's name) with intent to deceive; counterfeit: *to forge a signature; to forge a check.* **forged, forg·ing.** [**¹forge** comes through French from a Latin word (fabrica) meaning "workshop."]

Forge

²forge (fôrj) to move forward steadily, but with difficulty: *to forge ahead; to forge through a crowd.* **forged, forg·ing.** [**²forge** is a word of unknown origin.]

for·get (fôr gět′) **1** to be unable to remember: *I forgot the book's name.* **2** to cease to think of: *I will try to forget the mean remark he made.* **3** to neglect or fail to remember: *When he is playing, he sometimes forgets his lessons.* **for·got, for·got·ten, for·get·ting.**

for·get·ful (fôr gět′fəl) in the habit of forgetting; having a poor memory: *Some people must write things down because they're so forgetful.* **for·get·ful·ly.**

for·get-me-not (fôr gět′mi nŏt′) **1** a small plant with tiny blue or white flowers. **2** the flower of this plant.

for·give (fôr giv′) to pardon; excuse: *Please forgive me for hurting you. The king forgave the man and set him free.* **for·gave, for·given, for·giv·ing.**

for·giv·en (fôr giv′ən) See **forgive.**

for·give·ness (fôr giv′nis) **1** pardon: *He asked forgiveness for his rudeness.* **2** act of forgiving or pardoning.

for·go (fôr gō′) to give up; do without: *Ann decided to forgo candy to lose weight.* **for·went, for·gone, for·go·ing.**

for·gone (fôr gôn′ or fôr gŏn′) See **forgo.**

for·got (fôr gŏt′) See **forget.** *I forgot to send him a birthday card.*

for·got·ten (fôr gŏt′ən) **1** See **forget.** *I have forgotten the poem.* **2** no longer remembered: *a forgotten book.*

fork (fôrk) **1** instrument with two or more long points, such as a table fork, a pitchfork, a tuning fork. **2** a branching; a point of separation, such as a fork of a tree or a fork in the road. **3** one of the branches in such a separation: *the fork to the left.* **4** to pitch or lift with, or as with, a fork: *Ted forked the hay onto the wagon.* **5** to divide; separate: *The road to Devon forks to the left. The tree branch forks again and again.*

Table fork | Tuning fork | Pitchfork

for·lorn (fôr lôrn′) **1** pitiful; lonely; wretched: *The child felt forlorn at the death of his pet dog.* **2** neglected; deserted: *The old house looked dark and forlorn.* **for·lorn·ly.**

---

fāte, făt, fâre, fär; bē, bět; bīte, bĭt; nō, nŏt, nôr; fūse, fŭn, fûr; tōō, tŏŏk; foil; foul; thin; ~~then~~;
hw for wh as in *wh*at; zh for s as in u*s*ual; ə for a, e, i, o, u, as in *a*go, lin*e*n, per*i*l, at*o*m, min*u*s

form

form (fôrm) **1** outward appearance; shape: *The enchanted prince appeared in the* form *of a bear. The arena is in the* form *of a U.* **2** to give shape to; make: *She formed a small bowl from the clay.* **3** something that gives shape; a mold: *a* form *for making bricks; a cake* form. **4** to take shape; to become: *Ice formed on the lake.* **5** to mold; develop: *to* form *good habits.* **6** accepted manner of doing something; custom: *It is good* form *to greet guests at the door.* **7** typewritten or printed paper with spaces to be filled in: *a tax* form; *an order* form. **8** to serve to make up; to compose: *Four students* form *the committee.* **9** kind; variety: *The lemon is a* form *of citrus fruit.* **10** any of the ways in which a word is written or pronounced to show its meaning: *"Cactuses" and "cacti" are* forms *of "cactus."* **11** to add an ending or make some other change in a word: *"Goes" is* formed *from* go." *"Men" is* formed *from* "man."

for·mal (fôr′məl) **1** according to strict rules, customs, or usage: *a formal dinner.* **2** authoritative; official: *to give formal permission.* **for·mal·ly.**

for·mal·i·ty (fôr mǎl′ə tǐ) **1** attention to forms, rules, and customs: *All the guests were greeted with formality at the reception.* **2** something required by custom, rule, or social practice: *legal formalities; the formalities of a wedding.* **for·mal·i·ties.**

for·ma·tion (fôr mā′shən) **1** a shaping; molding: *the formation of good habits.* **2** an originating; starting: *the formation of a business.* **3** way in which a thing is formed in the arrangement of its parts, etc.: *We studied the formation of a tooth in class.* **4** arrangement: *troops in marching formation.* **5** certain natural pattern or arrangement: *a rock formation; a land formation.*

for·mer (fôr′mər) **1** coming before in time or order; past; earlier: *The old captain spun many yarns about the sailing ships of former days.* **2 the former** the first (of two) mentioned: *The farmer raises horses and cows, the former for riding and the latter for milk.*

for·mer·ly (fôr′mər lǐ) in past time; once: *People formerly traveled in carriages.*

for·mi·da·ble (fôr′mǐ də bəl) causing fear, dread, or difficulty: *a formidable army; a formidable obstacle.* **for·mi·da·bly.**

fortitude

for·mu·la (fôr′myo̅o̅ lə) **1** a set of rules; detailed instructions; recipe. **2** in chemistry, a statement that tells the contents of something: *H_2O is the formula for water.* **3** in mathematics, a statement of a rule or process: *$A = lw$ is the formula for finding the area of a rectangle (area equals length multiplied by width).* **for·mu·las** or, in scientific writing, **for·mu·lae** (fôr′myə lē).

for·mu·late (fôr′myo̅o̅ lāt′) to put into definite form; state in an orderly way: *to formulate plans.* **for·mu·lat·ed, for·mu·lat·ing.**

for·sake (fôr sāk′) to give up; leave; abandon: *We should not forsake our friends when they are in trouble.* **for·sook, for·sak·en, for·sak·ing.**

for·sak·en (fôr sā′kən) See **forsake.**

for·sook (fôr so̅o̅k′) See **forsake.**

for·sooth (fôr so̅o̅th′) an old word meaning "indeed," "in truth," "truly."

fort (fôrt) a place or building made strong for defense against enemies.

forth (fôrth) **1** onward; forward (in time, place, or order): *The soldiers went forth to battle.* **2** out, as from hiding or concealment: *The plants put forth tender new shoots.* (Homonym: fourth)

forth·com·ing (fôrth′kŭm′ĭng) **1** about to happen; approaching: *We put notices of forthcoming activities on the bulletin board.* **2** available; at hand: *Money for the project will be forthcoming when needed.*

forth·with (fôrth′wĭth′ or fôrth′wĭth′) at once; directly; immediately.

for·ti·eth (fôr′tĭ ĭth) **1** next after 39th; 40th. **2** one of 40 equal parts.

for·ti·fi·ca·tion (fôr′tə fə kā′shən) **1** a making strong; preparation against attack: *The fortification of the canal went forward rapidly. Proper diet, rest, and exercise are fortification against sickness.* **2** a protective wall, mound of earth, or other structure, sometimes temporary, as on a battlefield. **3** a fort or system of forts.

for·ti·fy (fôr′tə fī′) **1** to strengthen against attack by building forts, walls, etc.: *to fortify a city.* **2** to make strong: *Vitamins help to fortify us against colds.* **for·ti·fied, for·ti·fy·ing.**

for·ti·tude (fôr′tə to̅o̅d′ or fôr′tə tūd′) courage or firmness in meeting pain, danger, or trouble: *to face illness with fortitude.*

fort·night (fôrt′nīt′) two weeks.

for·tress (fôr′trĭs) a fortified place; place of safety; fort.

for·tu·nate (fôr′chə nĭt) favored; lucky: *You are* fortunate *to be so healthy.* **for·tu·nate·ly.**

for·tune (fôr′chən) **1** what happens (good or bad) to a person; chance; luck: *He had the bad* fortune *to lose his bicycle.* **2** destiny; fate: *The gypsy said she could tell my* fortune. **3** wealth; riches: *He made a* fortune *in the steel business.*

for·ty (fôr′tĭ) the amount or quantity that is one greater than 39; 40. **for·ties.**

for·ty-nin·er (fôr′tĭ nī′nər) person who went to California to seek gold in 1849.

fo·rum (fôr′əm) **1** in ancient Rome, the place where public meetings and assemblies were held. **2** any place where matters are discussed publicly: *The country store became a political* forum *for the local farmers.* **3** a discussion open to the public: *The citizens held a* forum *to discuss the school situation.*

for·ward (fôr′wərd) **1** to or toward the front; onward: *Let us move* forward *in the bus. Forward march!* **2** placed in the front: *a* forward *line in a football formation.* **3** help; to advance: *Clara Barton* forwarded *the profession of nursing.* **4** toward the future: *from this time* forward. **5** to send ahead to a new address: *to* forward *letters.* **6** bold; impudent: *a* forward *manner.* **7** a player stationed in a scoring position in certain games, as hockey, basketball, and some types of football.

for·wards (fôr′wərdz) to or toward the front; onward: *to move* forwards.

for·went (fôr wĕnt′) See **forgo.** *We* forwent *dinner to see the play.*

fos·sil (fŏs′əl) remains of ancient animals and plants found buried in the earth or imbedded in rock, as fossil ferns in coal, fossil shells in mountain shale, dinosaur footprints in mud that has turned to rock.

fos·ter (fôs′tər or fŏs′tər) **1** to advance; promote; encourage: *The children's concerts* foster *an appreciation of music.* **2** to nourish; bring up; care for: *to* foster *a child.* **3** belonging to a family though not related by blood: *a* foster *child or parent.*

fought (fôt) See **fight.** *He* fought *a hard battle.*

foul (foul) **1** offensive; disgusting: *a* foul *smell; a* foul *taste.* **2** to make impure or dirty: *The smoke from many factories* fouls *the air.* **3** to tangle: *The sailors* fouled *the ropes.* **4** evil; wicked; vile: *a* foul *deed;* foul *talk.* **5** stormy; bad: *some* foul *weather.* **6** unfair: *She would have her way by fair means or* foul. **7** a play or act which breaks the rules in some sports. **8 foul ball** a baseball hit that goes outside the base line.
foul up to mix up; confuse: *Our plans were* fouled up *by the strike.* (Homonym: fowl)

¹**found** (found) See **find.** *Have you* found *your lost umbrella?* [¹**found** is a form of **find.**]

²**found** (found) to begin; establish; set up: *to* found *a colony in a new country; to* found *a new business.* [²**found** is a word that comes through Old French (funder) from a Latin word (fundare) meaning "to lay the bottom (funda) of."]

foun·da·tion (foun dā′shən) **1** the part of a building, usually underground, on which the walls rest. **2** basis for an idea or belief: *There is no* foundation *for the story that Washington chopped down a cherry tree.* **3** beginning; setting up; establishing: *The* foundation *of Jamestown was in 1607.* **4** an institution which has been endowed with a fund for its support. **5** such a fund.

¹**found·er** (foun′dər) person who establishes or founds: *The Pilgrims were the* founders *of Plymouth Colony.* [¹**founder** is a form of ²**found.**] ———

²**found·er** (foun′dər) **1** to become filled with water and sink: *Our boat shipped water and began to* founder. **2** of a horse, to become lame. [²**founder** is from an Old French word (fondrer) meaning "go to the bottom." This last is formed from another French word (fond) meaning "bottom."]

found·ling (found′lĭng) baby or child that is found deserted.

found·ry (foun′drĭ) place where metal is molded into tools, machine parts, etc. **found·ries.**

fount (fount) **1** fountain. **2** source.

---

fāte, făt, fâre, fär; bē, bĕt; bite, bĭt; nō, nŏt, nôr; fūse, fŭn, fûr; tōō, tŏŏk; foil; foul; thin; then; hw for wh as in *wh*at; zh for s as in u*s*ual; ə for a, e, i, o, u, as in *a*go, lin*e*n, per*i*l, at*o*m, min*u*s

foun·tain (foun'tən) **1** a spring of water. **2** a place or machine where water or other drinks may be had: *a drinking* fountain; *a soda* fountain. **3** a jet or jets of water: *The fountain rose in tall, feathery plumes of water.* **4** the structure, often ornamental, from which these jets come: *This* fountain *is made of bronze.* **5** a source or reservoir: *A library is a fountain of knowledge.*

Fountain

fountain pen a pen which feeds ink automatically to the writing point from a reservoir in the barrel.

four (fôr) the amount or quantity that is one greater than three; 4. (Homonyms: for, fore)

four·fold (fôr'fōld') **1** four times as many or as much. **2** having four parts.

four·score (fôr'skôr') four times 20; 80.

four·teen (fôr'tēn') amount or quantity that is one greater than 13; 14.

four·teenth (fôr'tēnth') **1** next after 13th; 14th. **2** one of 14 equal parts.

fourth (fôrth) **1** next after third; 4th. **2** one of 4 equal parts. (Homonym: forth)

Fourth of July Independence Day; the anniversary of the signing of the Declaration of Independence.

fowl (foul) **1** bird. **2** barnyard bird kept for flesh or eggs to be used as food. Chickens, geese, ducks, turkeys, and guinea hens are all fowl. (Homonym: foul)

fox (fŏks) **1** wild animal, somewhat like a dog, with a pointed muzzle, sharp ears, and a long bushy tail. It is known for its cunning, and in stories it is shown as outwitting other animals. **2** the fur of this animal. **3** a sly person.

Red fox, about 3½ ft. long

fox·glove (fŏks'glŭv') **1** plant which has a long stalk with purple and white bell-shaped flowers. **2** the flower of this plant.

fox·hound (fŏks'hound') a special kind of dog with a keen sense of smell. Foxhounds are bred and trained to hunt foxes.

fox·y (fŏk'sĭ) like a fox; sly. **fox·i·er, fox·i·est; fox·i·ly.**

frac·tion (frăk'shən) **1** part or fragment: *You haven't handed in even a fraction of your work.* **2** in mathematics, any number written so as to show that it is the quotient of two numbers; a ratio. ¾ is a fraction and is the quotient of 3 divided by 4. **3 proper fraction** fraction with the numerator smaller than the denominator. **4 improper fraction** fraction with the numerator equal to or greater than the denominator.

frac·ture (frăk'chər) **1** a breaking or cracking. **2** a break or crack. **3** a break or crack in a bone: *The X ray showed a bad fracture of her arm.* **4** to break or crack: *The bones of old people* fracture *easily.* **frac·tured, frac·tur·ing.**

frag·ile (frăj'əl) delicate; easily broken: *a fragile vase.* **frag·ile·ly.**

frag·ment (frăg'mənt) part broken off from a whole; portion; piece: *The fragments of the broken bowl were glued together.*

fra·grance (frā'grəns) pleasant odor; sweet smell: *the fragrance of roses.*

fra·grant (frā'grənt) pleasing in odor; sweet-smelling. **fra·grant·ly.**

frail (frāl) **1** physically weak: *a frail child.* **2** delicate; fragile; easily broken; unsubstantial. **frail·ly.**

frame (frām) **1** the supporting or shaping part of a structure: *The skeleton is the frame of the body.* **2** a surrounding part or

Frame of a boat

border: *a picture frame; a door frame.* **3** the body structure: *a girl of slender frame.* **4** general structure; system: *The Constitution established a frame of government to fit the needs of all the people.* **5** mental state: *Patricia was in a happy frame of mind.* **6** to put together; construct; assemble: *John framed his reply carefully.* **7** to surround with a frame; enclose in a border: *to frame a picture.* **framed, fram·ing.**

frame·work (frām'wûrk') the structure that gives shape to and holds together: *the framework of a building.*

franc (frăngk) the unit of money used in France, Belgium, and Switzerland. (Homonym: frank)

France (frăns) a country in southwestern Europe.

frank (frăngk) showing thoughts or feelings openly and honestly: *a frank look; a frank confession.* **frank·ly.** (Homonym: franc)

frank·furt·er (frăngk'fər tər) a spiced sausage of beef or beef and pork.

frank·in·cense (frăngk'ĭn sĕns') sweet, spicy resin from certain African and Asiatic trees, burned as incense.

fran·tic (frăn'tĭk) wildly excited: *The lost boy was frantic with fear.*

fran·ti·cal·ly (frăn'tĭk ə lĭ) in a wildly excited manner.

fra·ter·nal (frə tûr'nəl) of or like a brother or brothers: *The boys have a* fraternal *affection for one another.* **fra·ter·nal·ly.**

fra·ter·ni·ty (frə tûr'nə tĭ) a society or group of men or boys joined by a common interest, especially such an organization in high schools and colleges. **fra·ter·ni·ties.**

fraud (frôd) **1** deceitfulness; trickery; dishonesty: *Having failed to earn the money honestly, he used* fraud *to get it.* **2** person or thing which is not what it pretends to be; a cheat.

fraught (frôt) filled: *a voyage* fraught *with dangers.*

¹fray (frā) battle; brawl; rough-and-tumble fight. [**¹fray** is short for "affray" meaning "a public brawl."]

²fray (frā) to ravel; wear to shreds: *The sweater was* frayed *at the wrists.* [**²fray** comes through French (frayer) from a Latin word (fricare) meaning "to rub."]

freak (frēk) **1** thing or person that is unnatural or abnormal: *A calf with two heads is a* freak *of nature.* **2** very unusual or queer: *a* freak *accident; a* freak *storm.*

freck·le (frĕk'əl) **1** tan or brown spot on the skin. **2** to mark or become marked with freckles: *Being in the sun causes her to freckle.* **freck·led, freck·ling.**

free (frē) **1** having personal and political liberty; not controlled by others: *a free citizen; a* free *country.* **2** to let go; to set at liberty; release: *to* free *a man from prison; to* free *a man from slavery.* **3** to relieve (from some burden or trouble): *to free from debt; to* free *a person of fear.* **4** not in prison or captivity; able to go wherever one wishes or do what one wants

to; at liberty: *The prisoners were* free *at last.* **5** not attached or fastened; loose: *the free end of the reins.* **6** given without cost or payment: *Admission is* free. **7 free from** or **of** without; not having: *to be* free *from pain; free of debt; free of prejudice.*

free·boot·er (frē'bōō'tər) pirate.

freed·man (frēd'mən) a man freed from slavery.

free·dom (frē'dəm) **1** the state of being free; liberty: *He had* freedom *to travel where he wished. The colonies fought for* freedom. **2** free or complete use: *He was given the* freedom *of the city.* **3** familiarity: *Jimmy asked the guests personal questions with too much* freedom. **4** ease: *She has much* freedom *of motion for a beginning skater.* **5 freedom from** a being free from; exemption from; safety from.

free·hand (frē'hănd') drawn by hand without the aid of a ruler or some other instrument.

free·man (frē'mən) person who is not a slave. **free·men.**

freeze (frēz) **1** to change into ice: *Water freezes at 32 degrees Fahrenheit.* **2** to make or become hard or solid with cold: *Mother froze the meat in the refrigerator.* **3** to be or become very cold: *I froze out in that wind.* **4** a frost; a condition of extreme coldness: *There was a sudden* freeze *last night.* **5** to chill, damage, or kill with frost or cold: *Late frosts sometimes* freeze *the apple blossoms.* **6** to be killed by frost or cold: *The plants froze in last night's cold.* **7** to become closed or clogged by ice: *The pipes froze.* **8** to become motionless: *Ellen froze in terror at the frightful sight.* **froze, froz·en, freez·ing.** (Homonym: frieze)

freez·er (frē'zər) **1** a cabinet in which things, especially foods, are kept frozen to preserve them. **2** a machine for freezing liquids: *an ice cream* freezer.

Home freezer

freight (frāt) **1** the carrying or transporting of goods by trucks, trains, ships, or airplanes: *We sent the refrigerator by* freight. **2** goods that are

---

fāte, făt, fâre, fär; bē, bĕt; bite, bĭt; nō, nŏt, nôr; fūse, fŭn, fûr; tōō, tŏŏk; foil; foul; thin; ~~then~~; hw for wh as in *wh*at; zh for s as in usual; ə for a, e, i, o, u, as in *a*go, lin*e*n, per*i*l, at*o*m, min*u*s

transported; cargo: *The ship carried a large amount of freight.* **3** to load with freight. **4** to send as freight. **5** the amount paid for transporting: *How much was the freight on the books?* **6** a train carrying freight.

freight·er (frā'tər) a cargo vessel; a ship that carries goods rather than passengers.

French (frĕnch) **1** of France, its people, or its language. **2** the language of France. **3 the French** the people of France.

French horn a brass wind instrument with a long, coiled tube and flaring end. It produces a mellow tone.

French horn

fren·zied (frĕn'zĭd) wildly excited; frantic: *The chained dog made a* frenzied *attempt to get loose.*

fren·zy (frĕn'zĭ) **1** rage; fury: *The miser is in a* frenzy *over being robbed.* **2** wild excitement; enthusiasm: *The children are in a* frenzy *over going to the circus.* **fren·zies.**

fre·quen·cy (frē'kwən sĭ) **1** an occurring over and over within a short period of time: *The frequency of bad weather made it hard to have baseball practice.* **2** number of times that a certain action happens in a given time: *Her pulse has a frequency of eighty beats to the minute.* **3** in science, the rate of vibration. **fre·quen·cies.**

frequency modulation type of radio broadcasting that is free from static. The frequency of radio wave changes according to the pitch of the signal. Also called **FM.**

¹**fre·quent** (frē'kwənt) happening often: *His trips to Europe are* frequent. **fre·quent·ly.**

²**fre·quent** (frē kwĕnt') to go to often; be found in: *He* frequents *the museum.*

fresh (frĕsh) **1** newly gathered or made: *The hostess put* fresh *flowers in the vase.* **2** new; not used before: *a* fresh *cake of soap.* **3** not stale: *We bought* fresh *bread at the store.* **4** pure: *The air was* fresh *and cool.* **5** new; recent: *Is there any* fresh *news?* **6** not spoiled: *Is the meat* fresh? **7** not tired; lively: *I feel* fresh *after a nap.* **8** not experienced: *a* fresh *recruit.* **9** not salty: *a stream of* fresh *water.* **fresh·ly.**

fresh·en (frĕsh'ən) **1** to make new, lively, pure, or bright. **2** to become brisk or strong: *The breeze* freshened.

fresh·et (frĕsh'ĭt) stream swollen by melting snow or heavy rain.

fresh·man (frĕsh'mən) a student in the first year of high school or college. **fresh·men.**

fresh·ness (frĕsh'nĭs) a being fresh.

fresh-wa·ter (frĕsh'wô'tər) of or living in water that is not salty: *a fresh-water fish.*

¹**fret** (frĕt) **1** to make or be worried or irritated: *What's* fretting *you? She* frets *over little things.* **2** to wear away by rubbing, chafing, etc.: *Water* fretted *a channel through the rock.* **3** annoyance; irritation: *the* frets *and cares of life.* **fret·ted, fret·ting.** [¹**fret** comes from an Old English word (fretan) meaning "to eat up."]

²**fret** (frĕt) ornamental design made of short straight lines. [²**fret** comes from an Old French word (frete) meaning "interlaced design."]

Fret

³**fret** (frĕt) one of the ridges on the neck of certain stringed instruments. [³**fret** is from a French word (frette) meaning "band" or "ring."]

fret·ful (frĕt'fəl) irritable; peevish: *the* fretful *child.* **fret·ful·ly.**

Fri. Friday.

fri·ar (frī'ər) member of any one of several religious orders; a monk.

fric·tion (frĭk'shən) **1** the rubbing of one object against another: *the* friction *of a towel on the skin.* **2** resistance of one object to the motion of another object that touches it: *We wax our skis to reduce the* friction *of the snow.* **3** disagreement or irritation between two or more people.

Fri·day (frī'dā or frī'dĭ) sixth day of the week.

fried (frīd) See ¹**fry.** *We* fried *some fish.*

friend (frĕnd) **1** person one knows and likes. **2** ally. **3** person who gives support (to someone or something): *a friend to many charities.*

friend·less (frĕnd'lĭs) without any friends.

friend·li·ness (frĕnd'lĭ nĭs) good will; cordiality.

friend·ly (frĕnd'lĭ) **1** like a friend; kind. **2** not hostile: *Many of the Indian tribes were* friendly. **3** favorable: *a* friendly *wind.* **friend·li·er, friend·li·est; friend·li·ly.**

friend·ship (frĕnd′shĭp) feeling between people which grows out of their liking and respect for each other; friendly relationship.

fries (friz) See ¹**fry**. *He* fries *eggs.*

frieze (frēz) **1** a decorative band around the walls of a room. **2** a band below the cornice of a building, often decorated. (Homonym: freeze)

Frieze

frig·ate (frĭg′ĭt) an old-fashioned warship with three masts.

fright (frit) violent and sudden fear; alarm: *He felt great* fright *when he saw the wolves.*

fright·en (fri′tən) to fill with terror; alarm suddenly: *The strange noises* frightened *her.*

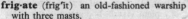

Frigate

fright·ful (frit′fəl) **1** horrible; causing fear: *a* frightful *disaster.* **2** unpleasant; disagreeable; ugly: *a* frightful *noise.* **fright·ful·ly.**

frig·id (frij′ĭd) **1** freezing; very cold: *a* frigid *climate.* **2** cool; icy; very unfriendly: *The crowd greeted the unpopular speaker with a* frigid *silence.* **3 Frigid Zone** old name for the parts of the earth north of the Arctic Circle and south of the Antarctic Circle. **frig·id·ly.**

frill (fril) **1** narrow strip of decorative trimming; ruffle: *a* frill *on a dress.* **2 frills** useless or excessive ornaments:

fringe (frĭnj) **1** an ornamental border on a cloth with loose threads, either plain or knotted. **2** an outer edge: *a court with a* fringe *of cottages.* **3** to put a fringe on; serve as a fringe: *Trees* fringed *the road.* **fringed, fring·ing.**

frisk (frisk) to run, dance, or skip; be lively or playful; frolic: *The squirrels* frisked *about the park.*

Fringe

frisk·y (frĭs′kĭ) lively; playful; frolicsome: *The* frisky *kittens ran and wrestled.* **frisk·i·er, frisk·i·est; frisk·i·ly.**

friv·o·lous (frĭv′ə ləs) **1** foolish; not serious; giddy: *Joan is a* frivolous *girl who never does her work and is always going to parties.* **2** unimportant; trivial; insignificant: *Do not waste study time on* frivolous *reading.* **friv·o·lous·ly.**

fro (frō) **1** back; backward. **2 to and fro** back and forth.

frock (frŏk) **1** a dress; gown. **2** long robe worn by a monk or by various clergymen.

frog (frŏg or frôg) **1** small animal with smooth skin and webbed feet. It lives in and around the water and is noted for its long leaps and swimming ability. **2 frog in the throat** hoarseness caused by soreness in the throat.

Leopard frog, 2 to 4 in. long

frol·ic (frŏl′ĭk) **1** outburst of fun; lighthearted play; gaiety: *The children were delighted and had a* frolic *when the new swings arrived.* **2** to have fun; romp; make merry: *We can hear the laughter of the children as they* frolic *on the beach.* **frol·icked, frol·ick·ing.**

from (frŏm) **1** beginning with; starting at: *We will read stories* from *now until three o'clock. It is 40 feet* from *the bottom of the flagpole to the top.* **2** having as a source or place of origin: *Much of our tin is* from *South America. I have a letter* from *my cousin.* **3** out of: *Great oaks* from *little acorns grow. We make steel* from *iron.* **4** out of reach of; out of the possession of: *Take the candy away* from *the baby.* **5** as being unlike: *I don't know one musical instrument* from *another.* **6** because of: *weak* from *hunger.*

frond (frŏnd) the long, fringed leaf of a fern or palm tree.

front (frŭnt) **1** first or foremost part of any thing or place: *The* front *of the bus was empty.* **2** land which faces a body of water: *The cottage was on the lake* front. **3** actual scene of fighting during a war: *The captain was at the* front *during the North African campaign.* **4** appearance: *to put up a bold* front. **5** located at the foremost part: *The*

---

fāte, făt, fâre, fär; bē, bĕt; bite, bit; nō, nŏt, nôr; fūse, fŭn, fûr; tōō, tŏŏk; foil; foul; thin; ~~then~~; hw for wh as in *wh*at; zh for s as in u*s*ual; ə for a, e, i, o, u, as in *a*go, lin*e*n, per*i*l, at*o*m, min*u*s

front *wall needs paint.* **6** to stand opposite: *Your home* fronts *the Browns'*. **7** to have the front facing in a certain direction: *The hotel* fronts *the ocean.* **8** in meteorology, a line where cold and warm air masses come together. **9 cold front** the forward edge of a mass of cold air coming into a warmer area. **10 warm front** the forward edge of a mass of warm air coming into a colder area.

fron·tier (frŭn tēr′) **1** the most remote settled area of a country beyond which lies wild, unsettled territory: *The frontier of America moved slowly west in the early days of her history.* **2** boundary; border. **3** of or on a frontier: *a frontier town.*

fron·tiers·man (frŭn tērz′mən) man who lives on a frontier. **fron·tiers·men.**

frost (frôst or frŏst) **1** small white crystals formed from water vapor or dew. **2** freezing weather; freezing temperature: *The first* frost *came in early November.* **3** to cover with something which looks like frost: *Light bulbs are* frosted *at the factory.* **4** to cover (a cake) with a sugar mixture.

frost·bite (frôst′bīt′ or frŏst′bīt′) a frozen or partially frozen condition of some part of the body.

frost·bit·ten (frôst′bĭt′ən or frŏst′bĭt′ən) suffering from frostbite.

frost·ing (frôs′tĭng or frŏs′tĭng) **1** mixture of sugar, egg whites, and liquid used for covering cakes or pastry. **2** dull finish on glass or metal that looks like frost.

frost·y (frôs′tĭ or frŏs′tĭ) **1** cold with frost: *a frosty morning.* **2** covered with frost: *the frosty grass.* **3** cold and unfriendly: *a frosty smile; a frosty stare.* **frost·i·er, frost·i·est; frost·i·ly.**

froth (frôth or frŏth) **1** mass of small bubbles found on top of some liquids after they have been shaken or poured: *the foaming froth on a glass of root beer.* **2** idle talk; shallow, worthless ideas: *His conversation was usually more froth than sense.* **3** to foam; to give off froth: *Mad dogs often froth at the mouth.*

frown (froun) **1** a drawing together of the brows when one is displeased or in thought; stern look: *The child's lateness brought a frown to the teacher's face.* **2** to draw the brows together when in anger, uncertainty, or thought: *Mr. Miller frowned when he*

saw the low grades on his son's report card.

frown on to disapprove of: *Many States frown on gambling.*

froze (frōz) See **freeze**. *The pond froze overnight.*

fro·zen (frō′zən) See **freeze**. *The milk was frozen from standing outside.*

fru·gal (frōō′gəl) **1** not wasteful; thrifty; economical: *A frugal housewife saves food that is left over.* **2** not plentiful and not expensive: *a frugal supper.* **fru·gal·ly.**

fru·gal·i·ty (frōō găl′ə tĭ) thriftiness; care in avoiding waste. **fru·gal·i·ties.**

fruit (frōōt) **1** the seed or seed-bearing part of a plant. Acorns and grains of wheat are fruits. **2** the part of a plant which contains the seeds and is good to eat. Apples, oranges, and grapes are fruits. **3** product or result: *This book is the* fruit *of years of hard work.*

fruit·ful (frōōt′fəl) **1** producing fruit: *a* fruitful *tree.* **2** yielding results; productive: *a fruitful discussion.* **fruit·ful·ly.**

fruit·less (frōōt′lĭs) **1** without result; unsuccessful: *We made a* fruitless *search for the lost money.* **2** bearing no fruit. **fruit·less·ly.**

fruit·y (frōō′tĭ) having the taste or smell of fruit. **fruit·i·er, fruit·i·est.**

frus·trate (frŭs′trāt′) to foil; baffle; defeat: *The wet wood* frustrated *his attempts to build a fire.* **frus·trat·ed, frus·trat·ing.**

¹**fry** (frī) to cook in hot fat: *We fried eggs and bacon for breakfast.* **fries, fried, fry·ing.** [¹**fry** comes through Old French (frire) from a Latin word (frigere) meaning "to fry."]

²**fry** (frī) **1** young fish or fishes. **2 small fry** (1) small children. (2) unimportant persons or things. [²**fry** is from two words, one Old Norse (frio) meaning "offspring," and the other Old French (froi) meaning "fish eggs."]

ft. **1** foot. **2** feet.

fudge (fŭj) a kind of candy made by boiling or mixing sugar, milk, and butter, sometimes with chocolate, until the mixture starts to thicken. When it cools or sets it is cut into squares.

fuel (fū′əl) **1** anything burned to give heat or to operate an engine. Coal, wood, and oil are fuels. **2** to supply with fuel: *The airplane was* fueled *and ready to go.* **3** anything that stirs up or keeps alive anger, resentment, or the like: *The girl's saucy reply added* fuel *to her father's anger.*

fu·gi·tive (fū′jə tiv) **1** a runaway: *An escaped convict is a fugitive from justice.* **2** running away: *a fugitive slave.*

-ful suffix meaning (1) "full of" or "showing the quality of": *hopeful; wonderful.* (2) "likely to" or "able to": *forgetful; helpful.* (3) "amount that will fill": *hatful.*

ful·crum (fŭl′krəm) the point on which a lever turns when it is used. **ful·crums.**

ful·fill or **ful·fil** (fŏŏl-fil′) **1** to do; accomplish; carry out: *to fulfill a requirement; to fulfill a promise.* **2** to satisfy: *to fulfill a wish.* **ful·filled, ful·fill·ing.**

ful·fill·ment or **ful·fil·ment** (fŏŏl fil′-mənt) a carrying out; satisfying; completing: *a fulfillment of all promises.*

full (fŏŏl) **1** holding all that it can or should hold: *Drink a full glass of milk. The cup was so full that it overflowed.* **2** having plenty: *purse full of money; full of ideas.* **3** complete; whole: *to sail a ship full speed ahead; a full moon.* **4** not tightly fitted: *a full sleeve.* **5** completely: *Fill the basket full.*

full-grown (fŏŏl′grōn′) having reached full size; mature.

full·ness or **ful·ness** (fŏŏl′nis) state of being full.

ful·ly (fŏŏl′i) **1** completely; entirely: *Carlos was fully dressed long before train time.* **2** abundantly: *The citizens were fully warned of the danger.*

fum·ble (fŭm′bəl) **1** to grope about awkwardly: *He fumbled about in the dark for the light switch.* **2** to handle clumsily; drop instead of catching and holding: *to fumble a ball.* **3** a fumbling. **fum·bled, fum·bling.**

fume (fūm) **1** vapor; smoke: *strong fumes from ammonia; tobacco fumes.* **2** to give off smoke or vapor: *The damp wood fumed.* **3** to show anger by complaining: *He was fuming because the bus was late.* **fumed, fum·ing.**

fu·mi·gate (fū′mə gāt′) to disinfect (a place) with fumes in order to destroy disease germs or vermin: *to fumigate a sick room.* **fu·mi·gat·ed, fu·mi·gat·ing.**

fun (fŭn) **1** amusement; sport; pleasure: *We had great fun at the picnic.* **2** **make fun of** to ridicule. **3** **for** or **in fun** not seriously; for amusement; as a joke.

func·tion (fŭngk′shən) **1** proper or natural work; purpose: *The function of the heart is to pump blood.* **2** to work; operate: *Does this typewriter function properly?* **3** a social gathering or official ceremony.

fund (fŭnd) **1** money set aside for a special use: *a fund for library books.* **2** supply; stock: *a fund of information.* **3** **funds** money: *Lack of funds halted the work.*

fun·da·men·tal (fŭn′də men′təl) **1** an essential or basic part: *Learning to recognize letters is a fundamental of reading.* **2** basic; essential: *Government by the people is a fundamental belief of democracy.* **fun·da·men·tal·ly.**

fu·ner·al (fū′nər əl) **1** burial service for a dead person. **2** of or for a funeral: *a funeral march.*

fun·gus (fŭng′gəs) **1** one of a group of plants, without leaves or green color, which feed upon plants or animal matter. Bacteria, molds, mushrooms, toadstools, and mildews are kinds of fungus. **2** having to do with a fungus; like a fungus: *a fungus disease; a fungus growth.* **fun·gi** (fŭn′ji) or **fun·gus·es.**

Fungi

fun·nel (fŭn′əl) **1** cone-shaped vessel ending in a tube. It is used for filling bottles, etc. **2** a steamship's smokestack or chimney.

fun·ny (fŭn′i) **1** amusing; comical: *a funny clown; a funny joke.* **2** strange; peculiar: *He gave me a funny look.* **fun·ni·er, fun·ni·est; fun·ni·ly.**

Funnels

---

fāte, făt, fâre, fär; bē, bĕt; bīte, bĭt; nō, nŏt, nôr; fūse, fŭn, fûr; tōō, tŏŏk; foil; foul; thin; then;
hw for wh as in what; zh for s as in usual; ə for a, e, i, o, u, as in ago, linen, peril, atom, minus

fur (fûr) **1** thick, soft hair that covers certain animals. **2** the skin of an animal with the fur on it. **3** a garment made of fur: *We put our furs in storage for the summer.* **4** made of fur: *a fur coat.* (Homonym: fir)

fu·ri·ous (fûr′ĭ əs) **1** very angry: *He was furious at the insult.* **2** violent: *a furious storm.* **fu·ri·ous·ly.**

furl (fûrl) to roll up and fasten to a mast, pole, etc.: *The captain ordered the crew to furl the sails of the ship.*

fur·long (fûr′lông or fûr′lŏng) one eighth of a mile; 220 yards.

fur·lough (fûr′lō) leave of absence, especially from a military service.

fur·nace (fûr′nĭs) **1** central heating device for buildings, especially one that circulates warm air. **2** any heating device for separating metal from ore, producing coke, hardening pottery, etc.

fur·nish (fûr′nĭsh) **1** to supply; provide: *Jane will furnish cookies for the party.* **2** to equip with furniture: *to furnish a house.*

fur·ni·ture (fûr′nə chər) articles such as tables, desks, chairs, beds, etc.

furred (fûrd) covered, lined, or trimmed with fur: *a furred jacket.*

fur·row (fûr′ō) **1** a ditch in which to plant seed; the trench made by a plow. **2** a crease; a wrinkle: *Deep furrows lined the old man's forehead.* **3** to make furrows in.

Furrows

fur·ry (fûr′ĭ) **1** covered with fur: *a furry animal.* **2** like fur or made of fur: *a furry toy bear.* **fur·ri·er, fur·ri·est.**

fur·ther (fûr′thər) **1** to or at a greater distance; farther: *Their house is a mile further down the road.* **2** besides; also; in addition: *And, further, I'd like to say another thing.* **3** more; extra; additional: *We wrote again for further information.* **4** to advance; to help on: *money to further his education.*

fur·ther·more (fûr′thər môr′) besides; in addition; also.

fur·ther·most (fûr′thər mōst′) most distant; furthest.

fur·thest (fûr′thĭst) most distant in time or space: *to run furthest; the furthest point.*

fur·tive (fûr′tĭv) sly; stealthy: *a furtive glance;* furtive *behavior.* **fur·tive·ly.**

fu·ry (fyōōr′ĭ) **1** great anger; rage: *He stalked off the field in a fury over the umpire's decision.* **2** violence; fierceness: *the fury of a storm.* **fur·ies.**

¹fuse (fūz) **1** piece of metal which fills a gap in an electric circuit. The metal melts and breaks the circuit when the current is too strong for safety. **2** tube filled with gunpowder or similar material, or a cord covered with inflammable material, used to set off an explosive. [**¹fuse** comes through Italian (fuso) from a Latin word (fusus) meaning "spindle."]

Fuses

²fuse (fūz) **1** to blend or combine by melting: *Copper is fused with tin in the making of bronze.* **2** to melt; become fluid: *Tin fuses at 450° Fahrenheit.* **3** to blend or unite, as if by melting. **fused, fus·ing.** [**²fuse** is from a Latin word form (fusus) meaning "melted," "fused."]

fu·se·lage (fū′sə läzh′ or fū′sə lĭj) the body of an airplane, which holds the crew, passengers, and cargo and to which the wings, rudders, etc., are attached. For picture, see **airplane.**

fu·sion (fū′zhən) **1** a melting as a result of heat: *the fusion of iron in a furnace.* **2** a mixing or blending by melting: *Bronze is made by the fusion of copper and tin.* **3** a blending or union of separate things into one: *There was a fusion of two political parties during the campaign.*

fuss (fŭs) **1** needless activity; unnecessary stir: *She made a lot of fuss about preparing dinner.* **2** to worry or get nervous: *She fussed and fumed over preparations for the party.* **3** complaint, especially about something unimportant: *She made a loud fuss over the leaky faucet.* **4** to quarrel. **5** a quarrel.

fuss·y (fŭs′ĭ) **1** painstaking in a nervous way; fastidious: *Nancy is so fussy she can't stand to see a speck of dust on the table.* **2** requiring delicate and patient work; exacting: *Watch repairing is a fussy job.* **3** petulant; irritable: *a fussy baby.* **fuss·i·er, fuss·i·est; fuss·i·ly.**

fu·tile (fū′təl) useless and hopeless; not getting anywhere: *The sailors made a futile attempt to save the ship.* **fu·tile·ly.**

fu·ture (fū′chər) **1** time that is to come:
*We cannot tell what will happen in the
future.* **2** yet to happen; coming: *The
future activities are listed in the bulletin.*

fuzz (fŭz) fine, light particles of hair, down,
etc.: *the fuzz on a cheek or a caterpillar.*

fuzz·y (fŭz′ĭ) **1** covered with or like fuzz or
down: *a fuzzy chick.* **2** vague; clouded and
hazy: *We could see only the fuzzy outline of
the hills through the fog. The writing on the
rain-soaked letter was fuzzy.* **fuzz·i·er,
fuzz·i·est; fuzz·i·ly.**

G

G, g (jē) seventh letter of the English
alphabet.

Ga. Georgia.

gab·ar·dine or **gab·er·dine** (găb′ər dēn′
or găb′ər dēn′) a kind of woolen, cotton,
or rayon cloth, used for suits, coats, etc.

gab·ble (găb′əl) **1** to talk fast without meaning or about unimportant things; jabber.
2 quick, meaningless sounds: *the gabble of
geese.* **gab·bled, gab·
bling.**

ga·ble (gā′bəl) part of an
outside wall in the shape of
a triangle between sloping
roofs.

Gable

ga·bled (gā′bəld) in the form of a gable or
having a gable: *a gabled house.*

gad (găd) to go restlessly from place to place
without purpose; ramble: *to gad about
town.* **gad·ded, gad·ding.**

gad·fly (găd′flī′) **1** a kind of fly that stings
horses and cattle. **2** person who is a pest
or acts as a goad. **gad·flies.**

gadg·et (găj′ĭt) tool or instrument, usually
small, which has a very special use: *This
gadget opens bottles and cracks nuts.*

gag (găg) **1** something put into or on a person's mouth to keep him from speaking or
to keep it open, as, for example, while a
dentist is working. **2** to stop up the mouth:
The burglar bound and gagged his victim.
3 to choke; strain with nausea: *The baby
gagged on a piece of candy in his throat.*
gagged, gag·ging.

¹gage (gāj) **1** an old word meaning "something given as a pledge or guarantee."
2 a challenge, especially a glove, or the like,
thrown down in challenge. [¹**gage** is from
an Old French word (gage) of German

origin. It is closely related to **wage**.]
(Homonym: gauge)

²gage (gāj) gauge. **gaged, gag·ing.** [²**gage**
is from an Old French word (gauger)
meaning "to measure."]

gai·e·ty (gā′ə tĭ) **1** merriment; cheerfulness;
gay spirits: *a time of* gaiety. **2** gay, bright
appearance: *the* gaiety *of Chistmas decorations.* **gai·e·ties.** Also spelled **gay·e·ty.**

gai·ly (gā′lĭ) **1** merrily; happily: *Her voice
rang out* gaily. **2** brightly; strikingly: *the*
gaily *painted walls.* Also spelled **gay·ly.**

gain (gān) **1** to get; acquire; win: *to gain
experience; to gain a prize.* **2** a profit; advantage: *his gains from his business.* **3** an
increase; advance; improvement: *a gain
in weight; a gain in knowledge.* **4** to improve or increase: *He has gained in wisdom
with age.* **5** to arrive at: *We gained the
shore after long, hard rowing.*

gain on to draw nearer to; overtake:
The last runner gained on the others.

gain·ful (gān′fəl) profitable; paid: *His
mother told him to stop daydreaming and
find some gainful occupation.* **gain·ful·ly.**

gain·said (gān′sĕd′) See **gainsay.**

gain·say (gān′sā′) to deny; say the opposite of: *There is no gainsaying his humor.*
gainsaid, gain·say·ing.

gait (gāt) **1** way a person
or animal walks or runs.
2 any of the several foot
movements of a horse,
such as a walk, trot, canter,
etc. (Homonym: gate)

Gaiter

gai·ter (gā′tər) **1** fitted cloth or leather
covering for the foot and ankle or foot
and lower leg. **2** a shoe with an elastic
strip on each side.

---

fāte, făt, fâre, fär; bē, bĕt; bīte, bĭt; nō, nŏt, nôr; fūse, fŭn, fûr; tōō, tŏŏk; foil; foul; thin; ~~then~~;
hw for wh as in *wh*at; zh for s as in usual; ə for a, e, i, o, u, as in ag*o*, lin*e*n, per*i*l, at*o*m, min*u*s

gal.

gal. **1** gallon. **2** gallons.

ga·la (gā′lə or găl′ə) **1** festive; showy: *The party was a gala affair.* **2** a festival; celebration.

gal·ax·y (găl′ək sĭ) **1** huge group of stars in space: *The Milky Way is a galaxy.* **2** any brilliant group: *a galaxy of movie stars.* **gal·ax·ies.**

gale (gāl) **1** strong wind. **2** outburst: *The comedian was rewarded by a gale of laughter from the audience.*

¹gall (gôl) **1** bitter substance made by the liver and stored in a sac in the body called the **gall bladder. 2** rudeness; impudence: *The salesman had the gall to walk in without knocking.* [**¹gall** is from an Old English word (galla) meaning "bitter substance"; "bile."]

²gall (gôl) **1** sore on the skin caused by chafing, especially on a horse. **2** to make sore by chafing. **3** to annoy; vex; irritate: *He galled me by his constant criticism.* [**²gall** is probably a form of **¹gall.**]

³gall (gôl) a swelling or growth on a leaf or stem, caused by the attack of certain insects, bacteria, or fungi. [**³gall** comes through the French (galle) from a Latin word (galla) meaning "a gall of the oak tree, shaped like a nut."]

Galls on oak leaf

gal·lant (găl′ənt) **1** brave; high-spirited; daring: *Sir Galahad was a gallant knight.* **2** (also gə länt′) showing courtesy and attention to women. **3** (also gə länt′) man very polite and attentive to women: *She was surrounded by the gallants of the town.* **gal·lant·ly.**

gal·lant·ry (găl′ən trĭ) **1** bravery; chivalry and courage: *Knights of old were known for their gallantry.* **2** brave and daring action: *The soldier was decorated for gallantry.* **3** chivalrous attention to women: *His gallantries were not gladly received.* **gal·lant·ries.**

Galleon

gal·le·on (găl′ĭ ən) a large sailing vessel, used mainly by the Spanish in the 15th

gamble

and 16th centuries. It had several decks, and its high stern was often armed.

gal·ler·y (găl′ə rĭ) **1** highest balcony of a theater, assembly hall, etc.: *a spectator's gallery.* **2** audience that sits in the gallery of a theater. **3** building or room for exhibiting works of art. **4** long, narrow passage or hall, often with windows on one side only. **gal·ler·ies.**

gal·ley (găl′ĭ) **1** ship driven by both oars and sails, used in ancient times and in the Middle Ages. **2** a ship's kitchen. **3** a tray for holding metal type set up in words, sentences, etc.; also a proof printed from such type.

Roman galley

gal·lon (găl′ən) unit of measure for liquids; four quarts.

gal·lop (găl′əp) **1** fastest gait of a horse, in which all four feet are off the ground at one time in each stride. **2** to ride a horse at this gait: *They galloped across the field.* **3** a ride on a galloping horse: *Shall we go for a gallop?* **4** to move at a gallop: *The horse galloped down the lane.* **5** to cause to move at a gallop: *They galloped the horses.* **6** to hurry; race; go very quickly: *He galloped through his homework.*

gal·lows (găl′ōz) **1** framework with a crossbar holding a suspended noose from which criminals are hanged. **2** death by hanging: *The judge sentenced the pirate to the* gallows. pl. **gal·lows.**

Gallows

ga·losh·es (gə lŏsh′əs) protective overshoes, usually made of rubber or plastic.

gal·va·nize (găl′və nīz′) **1** to coat (iron or steel) with zinc to prevent rusting. **2** to stir up; arouse, as if by an electric shock: *The hunting dog was galvanized into action by the gunshot.* **gal·va·nized, gal·va·niz·ing.**

gam·ble (găm′bəl) **1** to play games of chance for money or some other prize: *He gambled at cards, and usually lost.* **2** to risk (something) or take risks for the sake of uncertain gain: *to gamble one's reputation; to gamble with one's life.* **3** any risk or act that does not have a sure result.

306

gamble away to lose by gambling: *He gambled away his savings.*
gam·bled, gam·bling. (Homonym: gambol)

gam·bler (găm′blər) person who gambles or is fond of gambling.

gam·bol (găm′bəl) **1** to dance or skip about playfully; frolic: *to gambol in the lane.* **2** a frolicking. (Homonym: gamble)

game (gām) **1** form of play, especially a contest, played according to rules: *The game of football is a popular sport.* **2** a single contest played according to rules: *We won our game today.* **3** materials or equipment making a game: *The store sold games.* **4** a unit or division of a match: *In tennis, at least six games are needed for a set.* **5** amusement; joke; playful trick. **6** a plan; scheme: *I can see through your clever game.* **7** definite number of points needed to win a single game: *Twenty-one points make a game in handball.* **8** wild animals, fish, or birds that are hunted for sport. **9** the flesh of these animals, used for food. **10** having to do with animals that are hunted: *Wardens enforce game laws.* **11** plucky; courageous: *a game fighter.* **12 make game of** to make fun of; ridicule.

game·cock (gām′kŏk′) rooster trained to fight other roosters as a sport.

gam·ma rays (gă′mə) very strong rays with a shorter wave length than X rays and with a greater power to go through matter.

gan·der (găn′dər) male goose.

gang (găng) **1** group of persons working or doing something together: *a gang of workmen.* **2** group of criminals acting together: *a gang of thieves.*

  gang together to go around in a group because of habit, interest, etc.

  gang up to form a group for a common purpose: *to gang up around a cheerleader.*

gang·plank (găng′plăngk′) movable platform by which to enter or leave a ship.

gang·ster (găng′stər) one of a gang of criminals.

gang·way (găng′wā′) **1** movable platform or bridge between a ship and the shore; gangplank. **2** passageway; aisle. **3 Gangway!** Stand aside and make room.

gaol (jāl) in British spelling, **jail.**

gap (găp) **1** opening or space: *a gap in a fence.* **2** mountain pass. **3** space or period of time that is not filled; a blank: *a gap in the conversation.*

gape (gāp) **1** to open the mouth wide, from sleepiness, wonder, etc.; yawn. **2** to stare with open mouth in amazement: *The country boy gaped at the big stores in the city.* **3** a yawn or an open-mouthed stare. **4** to open or spread apart: *The jacket was so tight that it gaped at the seams.* **gaped, gap·ing.**

ga·rage (gə räj′ or gə räzh′) building or shed in which automobiles are sheltered, stored, or repaired.

garb (gärb) **1** clothing, especially of a distinct style: *the garb of a nurse.* **2** to dress; clothe: *He garbed himself as a cowboy for the costume party.*

gar·bage (gär′bĭj) waste material, usually food, thrown out from a kitchen, market, etc.

gar·den (gär′dən) **1** piece of ground set aside for growing flowers, fruits, vegetables, etc. **2** place where plants or animals are displayed to the public: *botanical garden; zoological garden.* **3** to work in or grow a garden: *My father likes to garden.*

gar·den·er (gär′dən ər) **1** person who works in a garden. **2** person hired to care for a garden.

gar·gle (gär′gəl) **1** to rinse the throat with a (healing) liquid that is kept in motion by forcing the breath out through it. **2** a liquid used for this purpose. **gar·gled, gar·gling.**

gar·goyle (gär′goil) a jutting spout to carry off water, often in the shape of a grotesque human being or animal.

Gargoyle

gar·ish (gâr′ĭsh or găr′ĭsh) showy; too bright or glaring; gaudy: *The beautiful road was spoiled by a string of garish billboards.* **gar·ish·ly.**

gar·land (gär′lənd) **1** a wreath of leaves or flowers to be worn on the head. **2** to decorate with a wreath.

---

fāte, făt, fâre, fär; bē, bĕt; bīte, bĭt; nō, nŏt, nôr; fūse, fŭn, fûr; tōō, tŏŏk; foil; foul; thin; ~~then~~;
hw for wh as in *wh*at; zh for s as in u*s*ual; ə for a, e, i, o, u, as in *a*go, lin*e*n, per*i*l, at*o*m, min*u*s

gar·lic (gär'lik) **1** plant of the lily family with a strong, biting taste and a sharp odor. **2** the dried bulb of this plant, used to flavor food.

gar·ment (gär'mənt) any article of clothing.

gar·ner (gär'nər) to gather in; store away: *to garner sayings from a book.*

gar·net (gär'nit) **1** a deep-red, semiprecious stone, used in jewelry. **2** deepred color.

gar·nish (gär'nish) **1** to decorate a dish of food: *The steak was garnished with parsley.* **2** decoration, especially of food.

gar·ret (gar'it) attic; space directly under the roof of a house.

gar·ri·son (gar'ə sən) **1** group of soldiers stationed in a fort or in a town for defense. **2** fort or town where soldiers are stationed for defense. **3** to station soldiers in (a fort or town) for defense: *to garrison a town.*

gar·ter (gär'tər) band or strap, usually elastic, used to hold up a sock or stocking.

garter snake small, harmless snake with yellow stripes.

gas (gas) **1** one of the three main forms of matter (solid, liquid, gas); vapor. A gas will expand to fill a much larger space or can be compressed into a much smaller space. Air is a mixture of gases. **2** any mixture of gases that will burn and can be used for heating and cooking. **3** one of several kinds of gas used in medicine to make patients unconscious during an operation. **4** a gas used as a weapon: *tear gas; poison gas.* **5** to injure or poison with gas. **6** gasoline. **gassed, gas·sing.**

gas·e·ous (gas'ĭ əs or gash'əs) **1** in the form of gas: *Steam is water in its gaseous state.* **2** of or like gas; a gaseous mixture.

gash (gash) **1** to make a deep cut in: *He gashed his arm on a piece of metal.* **2** long, deep cut.

gas·o·line or **gas·o·lene** (gas'ə lēn') liquid, made from petroleum, that turns to vapor easily and burns violently. It is used chiefly as fuel for automobile and aircraft engines.

gasp (gasp) **1** to struggle for breath: *The fish in the boat were gasping.* **2** short, sudden breath: *He gave a gasp when he saw the tiger.* **3** to speak breathlessly: "*The dam has broken,*" gasped *the runner.*

gas·tric (gas'trik) **1** having to do with the stomach: *a gastric pain.* **2 gastric juices** the acid fluid produced by glands in the stomach lining to aid in digestion.

gate (gāt) **1** opening in a fence or wall. **2** movable part or framework that closes this opening. **3** valve or door for controlling the flow of water in a canal, irrigation ditch, pipe, etc. (Homonym: gait)

gate·post (gāt'pōst') either of the two posts between which a gate swings.

gate·way (gāt'wā') **1** opening fitted with a gate. **2** way of entering: *The St. Lawrence River is a gateway to the Great Lakes. Observing and listening are gateways to knowledge.*

gath·er (gath'ər) **1** to bring together; come together: *He gathered a crowd about him. Storm clouds are gathering.* **2** to pick and collect: *to gather sea shells; to gather a harvest.* **3** to gain slowly; pick up: *to gather speed; to gather strength.* **4** to conclude; understand: *By the look of your hands I gather you washed quickly.* **5** to draw together in small folds: *to gather a skirt at the waist.* **6** one such small fold.

gath·er·ing (gath'ər ing) a coming together of people; a meeting in a group.

gau·cho (gou'chō) South American cowboy, usually of Spanish and Indian origin. **gau·chos.**

gaud·y (gô'dĭ) bright or gay in a vulgar way; showy: *a gaudy orange and purple necktie.* **gaud·i·er, gaud·i·est; gaud·i·ly.**

gauge (gāj) **1** a standard measurement: *The gauge between railroad rails on standard track is four feet eight and a half inches. Wire comes in various gauges.* **2** an instrument for measuring and recording the quantity of rainfall, force of the wind, etc. **3** an instrument for measuring the size, diameter, etc., of

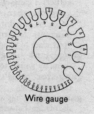

Wire gauge

tools, wire, etc. **4** to measure with a gauge: *to gauge the diameter of a wire.* **5** to estimate; judge: *to gauge one's speed; to gauge a person's character.* **gauged, gaug·ing.** Also spelled **gage.** (Homonym: gage)

gaunt (gônt) **1** very thin; bony; emaciated: *After his long illness, the man was weak and gaunt.* **2** barren and desolate; grim: *the gaunt rocky desert.* **gaunt·ly.**

gaunt·let (gônt′lĭt) **1** in the Middle Ages, a mailed glove to protect wrists and hands from wounds. **2** a glove with a flaring cuff, especially a canvas or leather working glove with a deep, stiff cuff to protect the wrist. **3** the cuff itself. **4 throw down the gauntlet** to challenge. **5 run the gauntlet** (1) to run as a punishment through a double line of men who strike out as one passes them. (2) to be exposed to severe criticism.

MODERN　　EARLY
Gauntlets

gauze (gôz) thin cloth, easily through.

gave (gāv) See **give.** *She gave it to me.*

gav·el (găv′əl) small mallet used by presiding officers, judges, etc., to call a group to order.

Gavel

gay (gā) **1** merry; lighthearted; lively: *a gay party; the gay music.* **2** bright and cheerful: *a gay red color.* **gai·ly** or **gay·ly.**

gay·e·ty (gā′ə tĭ) gaiety. **gay·e·ties.**

gaze (gāz) **1** to look long and steadily: *Janet gazed at the scenery as the train sped on.* **2** a long, steady look. **gazed, gaz·ing.**

ga·zelle (gə zĕl′) small, graceful kind of antelope, known for its speed and large, beautiful eyes.

Gazelle, about 3 ft. high at shoulder

gear (gĭr) **1** a set of toothed wheels working together in a machine. The teeth of one wheel fit into the teeth of a second wheel. If the wheels are of different sizes, they turn at different speeds. The engine of a car or truck is connected to the wheels by means of a set of gears. **2** any wheel of a set of gears. It is also called a **gear wheel. 3** any arrangement of parts used for a special purpose: *the steering gear of a ship; the landing gear of an airplane.* **4** equipment in general: *hunting gear.* **5** to adjust; fit: *We have geared our organization to this type of work.* **6 in gear** having the gear wheels connected with the engine. **7 out of gear** (1) having the gear wheels disconnected from the engine: (2) not working smoothly: *Our lawnmower got out of gear and had to be fixed.* **8 high gear** gear arrangement for high speed. **9 low gear** gear arrangement for low speed but great power.

Gear

GEAR WHEEL

PINION

geese (gēs) more than one **goose.**

Gei·ger count·er (gī′gər koun′tər) instrument used to detect and measure radioactivity.

gel·a·tin (jĕl′ə tĭn) clear, jellylike substance made from the bones, hoofs, and skin of animals or from some vegetables. It is sold in the form of a powder and used in making jellies, marshmallows, and ice cream, as well as in glue, medicine, etc.

gem (jĕm) **1** precious stone. **2** anything of great value or beauty: *This is the gem of my record collection.*

gen·darme (zhän′därm) in France, Belgium, etc., a policeman.

gene (jēn) tiny unit in a cell that causes a particular trait to be passed from parent to child. The color of a child's hair is determined by the genes of its parents. (Homonym: jean)

gen·e·ra (jĕn′ə rə) more than one **genus.**

gen·er·al (jĕn′ər əl) **1** military officer of high rank, usually in command of an army or main division of an army. **2** having to do with all or nearly all: *a general panic.* **3** widespread; common: *Afternoon tea is a general custom in England.* **4** not limited to one thing, class, or region: *the general public; a physician with a general practice.* **5** not definite; not in detail: *I have a general*

---

fāte, făt, fâre, fär; bē, bĕt; bīte, bĭt; nō, nŏt, nôr; fūse, fŭn, fûr; tōō, tŏŏk; foil; foul; thin; ~~then~~; hw for wh as in *wh*at; zh for s as in u*s*ual; ə for a, e, i, o, u, as in a*g*o, lin*e*n, per*i*l, at*o*m, min*u*s

309

idea *of how rockets work.* **6** chief or head: *postmaster* general. **7 in general** usually; for the most part: *Children in general enjoy being read to.*

gen·er·al·i·ty (jĕn'ə răl'ə tĭ) **1** general statement that may be too broad to be useful: *Please stop talking in generalities and come to the point.* **2** the large part of; the mass: *The* generality *of citizens in the United States eat well.* **gen·er·al·i·ties.**

gen·er·al·i·za·tion (jĕn'ər ə lə zā'shən) **1** the act of generalizing, or drawing a general conclusion from a number of particular cases. **2** a statement or conclusion formed in this way (which may not be true in all cases): *It is a* generalization *to say that cats are afraid of dogs.*

gen·er·al·ize (jĕn'ər ə līz') **1** to treat as a whole rather than in parts; treat in a vague, superficial, or casual way by emphasizing the general aspect: *The politician* generalized *on the need for better housing but neglected to offer any program.* **2** to make a general rule from known facts. **gen·er·al·ized, gen·er·al·iz·ing.**

gen·er·al·ly (jĕn'ər ə lĭ) **1** most of the time; usually: *We* generally *have dinner at six o'clock.* **2** in most places or by most people; widely: *The new styles have been* generally *accepted.* **3** without being definite about particular things or persons: *They were speaking* generally, *not in particular.*

gen·er·ate (jĕn'ə rāt') to produce; bring into existence: *Electricity is often* generated *by water power.* **gen·er·at·ed, gen·er·at·ing.**

gen·er·a·tion (jĕn'ə rā'shən) **1** all the people who are born at about the same time: *Our* generation *is producing many scientists.* **2** one step in the line of family descent. Grandparents, their children, and grandchildren make up three generations. **3** period of time, about 30 years, between the birth of one generation and the next. **4** a producing: *the* generation *of power.*

gen·er·a·tor (jĕn'ə rā'tər) machine that produces electricity when. driven by an engine or a water wheel.

gen·er·os·i·ty (jĕn'ə rŏs'ə tĭ) **1** willingness to share or give; unselfishness. **2** freedom from spitefulness or meanness; nobility: *He showed* generosity *in praising his opponent.* **3** a generous act. **gen·er·os·i·ties.**

gen·er·ous (jĕn'ər əs) **1** unselfish; free in giving or sharing: *Mrs. Brown is always* generous *to people in need.* **2** noble; not mean or spiteful: *a* generous *nature.* **3** large; plentiful: *Each student was given a* generous *supply of paper.* **gen·er·ous·ly.**

gen·e·sis (jĕn'ə sĭs) **1** a beginning; the coming into being of anything: *We can see the* genesis *of this novel in an early short story of his.* **2 Genesis** the first book of the Bible. It includes the story of God's creation of the world. **gen·e·ses** (jĕn'ə sēz).

gen·ial (jĕn'yəl) **1** smilingly pleasant; warmly friendly: *a genial meeting.* **2** favorable to comfort and growth; warm or mild: *a genial climate.* **gen·ial·ly.**

ge·nie (jē'nĭ) in Arabian tales, a powerful spirit, good or bad, who could influence people's lives: *Aladdin's* genie *brought him many treasures.*

gen·ius (jĕn'yəs) **1** outstanding ability to think, create, or invent: *Mozart showed* genius *in music almost from infancy.* **2** person who has this ability: *Einstein was a mathematical* genius. **3** natural ability or fitness (for a special thing): *He has a* genius *for making up excuses.*

gen·tian (jĕn'shən) tall plant with deep-blue flowers.

gen·tile or **Gen·tile** (jĕn'tīl) **1** person who is not a Jew. **2** having to do with that which is not Jewish.

gen·til·i·ty (jĕn tĭl'ə tĭ) good manners; refinement. **gen·til·i·ties.**

gen·tle (jĕn'təl) **1** mild in manner; kind: *The doctor is* gentle *with his patients.* **2** light; not rough; soft: *a gentle breeze; a* gentle *touch.* **3** having a mild or good temper: *a gentle dog.* **4** gradual; not extreme: *The driveway has a* gentle *slope.* **5** coming from a good family; wellborn: *Lancelot was of* gentle *birth.* **gen·tler, gen·tlest; gen·tly.**

gen·tle·man (jĕn'təl mən) **1** a well-bred, considerate man. **2** man of good family. **3** in very polite language, a man: *There is a* gentleman *to see you.* **gen·tle·men.**

gen·tle·man·ly (jĕn'təl mən lĭ) like or of a gentleman; polite: *He was* gentlemanly *enough to give up his seat.*

gen·tle·ness (jĕn'təl nĭs) tenderness; kindliness; a being gentle in touch or manner: *the* gentleness *of the doctor's touch.*

gen·tle·wom·an (jĕn′tĕl wŏŏm′ən) woman of good birth or breeding; a lady. **gen·tle·wom·en.**

gen·try (jĕn′trĭ) people of good birth and social position.

gen·u·ine (jĕn′yŏŏ in) **1** real; not false; true: *a* genuine *leather belt; a* genuine *pearl.* **2** frank; sincere: *to show* genuine *affection.* **gen·u·ine·ly.**

ge·nus (jē′nəs) group (of plants or animals) that are related but are different in important respects. A genus is made up of one or more species: *The lion and tiger are different species of the same genus.* **gen·er·a** (jĕn′ər ə) or **ge·nus·es.**

ge·o·graph·ic (jē′ə grăf′ĭk) geographical.

ge·o·graph·i·cal (jē′ə grăf′ə kəl) having to do with geography. **ge·o·graph·i·cal·ly.**

ge·og·ra·phy (jĭ ŏg′rə fĭ) **1** study of the earth and the living things on the earth. Geography deals with such things as continents, countries, oceans, rivers, kinds of land, people, animals, plants, climate, industries, and ways of making a living. **2** features of the earth's surface, such as mountains, plains, and rivers.

ge·o·log·i·cal (jē′ə lŏj′ə kəl) having to do with geology. **ge·o·log·i·cal·ly.**

ge·ol·o·gist (jĭ ŏl′ə jĭst) person trained in geology and engaged in it as a profession.

ge·ol·o·gy (jĭ ŏl′ə jĭ) study of the earth's crust and its changes. Geology deals with such things as layers of rocks, fossils, and the finding of useful minerals.

ge·o·met·ric (jē′ə mĕt′rĭk) **1** of geometry. **2** following the patterns of geometry: *a* geometric *design of circles and triangles.*

ge·om·e·try (jĭ ŏm′ə trĭ) the branch of mathematics that deals with the shapes and sizes of things. In geometry we study circles, cubes, spheres, etc.

ge·o·phys·i·cal (jē′ō fĭz′ə kəl) having to do with the study of the physical make-up of the earth and the forces in space that affect the earth and its inhabitants. In the International Geophysical Year (July 1, 1957 to December 31, 1959) scientists made many measurements to find the exact size and shape of the earth. They also studied the earth's magnetic field, atmosphere, etc.

Geor·gia (jôr′jə) a southern State on the Atlantic coast of the United States.

ge·ra·ni·um (jĭ rā′nĭ əm) **1** a roadside plant with deeply cut leaves and a delicate lavender blossom. **2** the flower of this plant. **3** any of several garden plants, some with fragrant leaves, with clusters of red, white, or pink blooms. **4** the flower of any such plant.

Wild geranium

germ (jûrm) **1** a tiny animal or plant that may cause disease. Germs are too small to be seen without a microscope. **2** tiny mass of living matter that may develop into an animal or plant: *Wheat* germ *is the living part of the wheat grain.* **3** something small that may grow, as a seed grows into a plant: *the* germ *of war; the* germ *of an idea.*

Ger·man (jûr′mən) **1** of Germany, its people, or its language. **2** citizen of Germany or person of German descent. **3** language of the German people.

Ger·man·ic (jər măn′ĭk) **1** having to do with a family of languages in northern and central Europe that are related to German. **2** of Germany.

Ger·ma·ny (jûr′mə nĭ) a country in central Europe.

ger·mi·cide (jûr′mə sĭd′) anything used to kill germs, especially germs causing disease.

ger·mi·nate (jûr′mə nāt′) **1** to sprout; start to grow. **2** to cause to grow: *Fertile soil* germinates *seeds.* **ger·mi·nat·ed, ger·mi·nat·ing.**

ger·min·a·tion (jûr′mə nā′shən) a beginning of growth; a sprouting; start: *the* germination *of a seed.*

ges·ture (jĕs′chər) **1** movement of the body, arms, hands, or face to express an idea or feeling, or to stress what is being said: *A skillful actor uses gestures.* **2** to make a gesture. **3** something said or done to impress other people, or as a courtesy: *Inviting new neighbors to visit is a friendly* gesture. **ges·tured, ges·tur·ing.**

---

fāte, făt, fâre, fär; bē, bĕt; bīte, bĭt; nō, nŏt, nôr; fūse, fŭn, fûr; tōō, tŏŏk; foil; foul; thin; then;
hw for wh as in *wh*at; zh for s as in u*s*ual; ə for a, e, i, o, u, as in *a*go, lin*e*n, per*i*l, at*o*m, min*u*s

get

get (gĕt) **1** to gain or obtain possession of; acquire: *First you will háve to go and* get *permission from Mother.* **2** to receive: *Did you* get *my letter?* **3** to become: *to get sleepy.* **4** to understand: *to get the meaning of a story; to get the point of a joke.* **5** to cause to do, be, or become: *Please get your hair cut. Please get him to go with us.* **6** to reach; arrive at: *Did he* get *here?*

get across to make or be understood: *He got his meaning across.*

get along 1 to be on good terms. **2** to succeed enough: *He's not wealthy but he gets along.* **3** to move on.

get around 1 to move around and observe: *We ought to listen to him because he gets around.* **2** of news, to spread about. **3** to bypass (a difficulty). **4** to win (someone) over: *I can always* get *around Mother.*

get away 1 to go away: *to get away from the city.* **2** to escape: *One of the captured men tried to* get *away.*

get away with 1 to escape with. **2** to escape punishment for: *He didn't* get *away with his rudeness.*

get by 1 to manage or live well enough. **2** to barely manage: *I just got by on the test.*

get down to 1 to begin. **2** to find and consider: *to get down to facts.*

get even to get revenge; to strike back; to pay back in kind.

get in 1 to go inside: *Father told me to* get *in the car.* **2** to arrive: *Did the train get in ón time?* **3** to put in: *to get in a word.*

get off 1 to get down from: *to get off a bicycle.* **2** to start: *to get off early from school.* **3** to escape: *He got off with only a scratch from the accident.*

get on 1 to go up on: *to get on a bus.* **2** to continue; move along: *Let's get on with this lesson.* **3** to succeed or manage: *He is getting on in the company.* **4** to put on (clothing). **5** to be on good terms: *They get on very well.* **6** to grow older.

get out 1 to go; leave: *The door was locked and we couldn't* get *out.* **2** to become known: *Sometimes a secret gets out.*

get out of to escape; avoid: *I can't get out of going.*

get over to recover from.

get through to finish.

gifted

get together 1 to come together; meet: *Let's get together Tuesday.* **2** to collect: *Please get your books together.*

get up 1 to get out of bed. **2** to stand up.

got, got or **got·ten, get·ting.**

gey·ser (gī′zər) a hot spring that throws a jet of hot water into the air, often at regular intervals.

ghast·ly (găst′lĭ) **1** horrible; shocking: *Four men were killed in the* ghastly *accident.* **2** like a ghost; deathly pale: *The sick man's face looked* ghastly. **3** very bad: *a* ghastly *mistake.* **ghast·li·er, ghast·li·est.**

ghost (gōst) **1** the spirit of a dead person, thought of as appearing or making its presence known to the living: *The old castle was haunted by a* ghost *that rattled chains.* **2 Holy Ghost** the spirit of God.

Geyser

ghost·ly (gōst′lĭ) like a ghost: *Moving in the shadows he presented a* ghostly *appearance.* **ghost·li·er, ghost·li·est.**

gi·ant (jī′ənt) **1** in fable and myth, man of huge size and great strength. **2** man who is much larger than ordinary. **3** huge; gigantic: *a* giant *cabbage.*

gib·bet (jĭb′ĭt) a kind of gallows.

gib·bon (gĭb′ən) a small ape of Southeast Asia, tailless and with very long arms.

gibe (jīb) **1** a remark expressing scorn or contempt. **2** to jeer; make fun of: *to* gibe *at someone's mistakes* **gibed, gib·ing.**

gid·dy (gĭd′ĭ) **1** dizzy; light-headed; having the feeling of spinning about: *Riding on a merry-go-round makes her* giddy. **2** causing dizziness: *We looked down from the* giddy *height.* **3** not serious; frivolous: *a* giddy *young girl.* **gid·di·er, gid·di·est; gid·di·ly.**

Gibbon, about 3 ft. tall

gift (gĭft) **1** a present; a thing given: *The two girls exchanged Christmas* gifts. **2** natural ability; talent: *a* gift *for singing.*

gift·ed (gĭf′tĭd) having great natural ability; talented.

312

gig (gĭg) **1** an open, two-wheeled carriage pulled by a horse. **2** a ship's small boat used by the captain.

gi·gan·tic (jī găn′tĭk) like a giant in size; very large; huge.

gig·gle (gĭg′əl) **1** to laugh in a nervous, mischievous, or silly way. **2** a light, silly, or mischievous laugh. **gig·gled, gig·gling.**

gild (gĭld) **1** to cover with gold or with any gold-colored substance: *to gild a picture frame.* **2** to make bright or attractive: *The sun gilded the sky.* **gild·ed, gild·ing.** (Homonym: guild)

¹**gill** (gĭl) part of a fish's body that is used for breathing under water. Fish have gills instead of lungs. [¹**gill** is a form of an earlier English word (gile) that probably comes from a Scandinavian word.]

²**gill** (jĭl) unit of liquid measure; a quarter of a pint. Four gills equal one pint. [²**gill** is from an Old French word (gelle) meaning a "wine measure."]

gilt (gĭlt) **1** covered with gold; gilded: *a gilt statue; a gilt-edged book.* **2** thin layer of gold or a gold-colored substance. (Homonym: guilt)

gim·let (gĭm′lĭt) a tool with a screw point for making small holes.

Gimlet

¹**gin** (jĭn) **1** machine for removing seeds from cotton: *a cotton gin.* **2** to remove seeds from (cotton). **ginned, gin·ning.** [¹**gin** is short for **engine.**]

²**gin** (jĭn) a clear, distilled alcoholic drink. [²**gin** is short for "geneva" meaning "Holland gin." It comes from a Dutch word (genever) that goes back to an Old French word (genevre) based in turn upon a Latin word (juniperus) meaning "juniper," "juniper berry."]

gin·ger (jĭn′jər) **1** a spice made from the powdered root of a tropical plant. **2** the root of this plant, sometimes dried and coated with sugar to make a candy. **3** the plant itself.

ginger ale soft drink flavored with ginger root.

gin·ger·bread (jĭn′jər brĕd′) cake or cookie flavored with ginger and molasses.

ging·ham (gĭng′əm) a cotton cloth, usually with a woven design of checks or stripes.

gip·sy (jĭp′sĭ) gypsy. **gip·sies.**

gi·raffe (jə răf′) African animal with long legs and a long neck that enables it to feed on the leaves of tall trees. It has short horns covered with skin and chews a cud.

Giraffe, about 18 ft. high

gird (gûrd) **1** to fasten with a belt or cord: *to gird on a sword.* **2** to surround; encircle: *Mountains* girded *the valley.* **3** to make ready; prepare: *to gird oneself for battle.* **gird·ed** or **girt, gird·ing.**

gird·er (gûr′dər) a strong, horizontal beam, often of steel, which supports the floor of a building or bridge.

Girder

gir·dle (gûr′dəl) **1** elastic undergarment worn to flatten the abdomen. **2** wide belt or sash. **3** something that encircles as a girdle. **4** to gird or encircle: *Wide fields* girdle *the village.* **gir·dled, gir·dling.**

girl (gûrl) female child or young woman.

girl·hood (gûrl′hŏŏd) the time of being a girl.

girl·ish (gûr′lĭsh) like a girl; of a girl: *a girlish giggle.* **girl·ish·ly.**

Girl Scouts 1 organization for training girls in physical fitness, good citizenship, and helpfulness to others. **2 girl scout** member of the Girl Scouts.

girt (gûrt) See **gird.** *The warriors girt themselves for battle.*

girth (gûrth) **1** distance around: *a man's girth at the waist; the girth of a tree trunk.* **2** a strap fastened around an animal to hold a saddle, blanket, etc., in place.

give (gĭv) **1** to hand over (to another) freely or as a present: *I will give you a pencil.* **2** to let have; grant: *Just give the dog a bone and he'll be your friend. The school gave us a holiday.* **3** to pass on to: *Please*

---

fāte, făt, fâre, fär; bē, bĕt; bīte, bĭt; nō, nŏt, nôr; fūse, fŭn, fûr; tōō, tŏŏk; foil; foul; thin; then; hw for wh as in what; zh for s as in usual; ə for a, e, i, o, u, as in ago, linen, peril, atom, minus

give *your mother my message. He* gave *me the measles.* **4** to pay: *We can* give *you a hundred dollars for this ring.* **5** to present: *Our class is giving a play. This book* gives *a table of measures.* **6** to provide; be a source of: *The sun* gives *light. Her baby* gave *her much pleasure.* **7** to furnish as entertainment: *to* give *a party.* **8** to utter: *to* give *a speech; to* give *a shout.* **9** to yield: *The floor of the old house* gave *under my feet.* **10** a yielding because of pressure: *An airplane wing must have a certain amount of* give.

give in **1** to surrender; yield; to stop struggling or arguing: *Our opponents were finally forced to* give in. **2** to hand in; pass in: *Please* give in *your cards now.*

give out **1** to become tired out; become exhausted: *The horses* gave out *yesterday.* **2** to become used up: *The food began to* give out. **3** to pass out: *The teacher* gave out *the papers.* **4** to make known; make public.

give rise to to be the cause of.

give up **1** to stop trying: *The puzzle was too hard for me, so I* gave up. **2** to do without; abstain from: *to* give up *candy.* **3** to surrender: *The bandit* gave *himself* up.

give way **1** to fail to hold up; collapse. **2** to surrender oneself to: *He* gave way *to despair.* **3** to be replaced by: *Her sorrow* gave way *to happiness.*

gave, giv·en, giv·ing.

giv·en (giv′ən) **1** agreed upon; fixed: *We agreed to meet at a* given *time.* **2** See **give.** **3 given to** in the habit of; inclined to: *He is* given *to bragging.*

giv·er (giv′ər) person who gives; donor.

giz·zard (giz′ərd) muscular stomach of a bird in which food is crushed and ground; a bird's second stomach.

gla·cial (glā′shəl) **1** of ice; icy: *this* glacial *weather; a* glacial *look.* **2** having to do with the ice age or with glaciers: *the* glacial *period.* **gla·cial·ly.**

gla·cier (glā′shər) a mass of ice, formed from snow in high cold mountains, that moves very slowly down a valley. A glacier melts gradually at the advancing edge, or breaks off at the sea to form icebergs.

glad (glăd) **1** joyous; cheerful: *Easter is a* glad *season.* **2** happy; pleased: *I am* glad *that you could come.* **3** causing, bringing,

or showing joy: *This is* glad *news.* **glad·der, glad·dest; glad·ly.**

glad·den (glăd′ən) to make or become happy: *She was* gladdened *by the good news.*

glade (glād) small open space in a forest.

glad·i·a·tor (glăd′ĭ ā′tər) man who was trained to fight with a sword or other weapon to entertain the people in the public arenas of ancient Rome.

glad·i·o·lus (glăd′ĭ ō′ləs) **1** garden plant bearing rushlike leaves and spikes of red, white, or pink flowers. **2** the flower of this plant. **glad·i·o·li** (glăd′ĭ ō′lī) or **glad·i·o·lus·es.**

Gladiolus

glam·or·ous (glăm′ər əs) enchanting; fascinating; filled with magical charm: *a* glamorous *actress.* **glam·or·ous·ly.**

glam·our or **glam·or** (glăm′ər) enchantment; mysterious charm; fascination: *The stories told of the* glamour *of tropical islands.*

glance (glăns) **1** to take a quick look: *He* glanced *at the passing car.* **2** a quick look: *to take a* glance *at the newspaper; to see a problem at a* glance. **3** to strike at a slant and fly (off): *The bullet* glanced *off the target.* **4** to gleam; flash: *His sword* glanced *in the sun.* **5** a gleam; glint. **glanced, glanc·ing.**

gland (glănd) organ that removes substances from the blood to be given off from the body, or manufactures substances to be used in the body. Two glands of our bodies are the liver and kidneys.

glare (glâr) **1** very bright or blinding light: *the* glare *on the windshield from the lights of the other car.* **2** to shine with a strong, bright light: *The hot desert sun* glared *down on us all day.* **3** to stare angrily or fiercely: *The librarian* glared *at the noisy, chattering girls.* **4** angry or fierce look: *The noisy girls noticed the librarian's* glare. **glared, glar·ing.**

glar·ing (glâr′ing) **1** brilliant; unpleasantly bright: *the* glaring *headlights of a car.* **2** of colors, gaudy; too bright. **3** very easily seen: *a* glaring *mistake.* **glar·ing·ly.**

glass (glăs) **1** hard, easily broken substance used to make windows, etc. **2** object made of glass, such as a mirror, a drinking vessel, or a telescope: *Look at your face in the glass. The sailor sighted land through his glass.* **3** glassful. **4** made of glass.

glass·ful (glăs′fŏŏl) amount a glass will hold: *a glassful of milk.*

glass·ware (glăs′wâr′) table glasses, glass pitchers, dishes, etc.

glass·y (glăs′ĭ) **1** smooth; like glass: *The sea was glassy in the calm before the storm.* **2** lifeless; without expression: *The dazed boy looked at his rescuers with a glassy stare.* **glass·i·er, glass·i·est; glass·i·ly.**

glaze (glāz) **1** to furnish (a window) with glass or (a building) with windows. **2** a coating of a smooth glasslike material: *a glaze on china.* **3** to cover with this substance: *to glaze a china bowl.* **4** any other coating that is shiny, transparent, or smooth: *a sugar and water glaze on fruit; a glaze on an oil painting; a glaze of ice on the streets.* **5** to cover with a shiny, transparent, or smooth coating: *to glaze fruit; to glaze an oil painting.* **6** to become lifeless or glassy: *His eyes glazed with fear.* **glazed, glaz·ing.**

gleam (glēm) **1** flash or beam of light: *There was a gleam in the dark alley from the open doorway.* **2** to send out rays of light; shine: *The stars gleamed.* **3** brief flash or glint: *a gleam of hope; a gleam of sanity.*

glean (glēn) **1** to pick or gather what the reapers have left in a field: *to glean corn.* **2** to gather bit by bit or slowly: *He gleaned his facts by careful reading.*

glee (glē) gaiety; joy; merriment.

glee·ful (glē′fəl) merry; gay. **glee·ful·ly.**

glen (glĕn) narrow valley.

glib (glĭb) quick and ready; smooth; without much thought or sincerity: *a glib excuse; a glib talker.* **glib·ber, glib·best; glib·ly.**

glide (glīd) **1** to move smoothly and easily, without apparent effort: *Skaters glided on the ice.* **2** smooth, sliding movement. **glid·ed, glid·ing.**

Glider

glid·er (glī′dər) **1** motorless airplane that floats on air currents. **2** person or thing that glides.

glim·mer (glĭm′ər) **1** faint, flickering light: *the glimmer of a dying fire.* **2** to shine in this way: *The lights glimmered in the fog.* **3** a hint or faint glimpse: *a glimmer of hope.*

glimpse (glĭmps) **1** short look; quick view: *I had a glimpse of the thief as he turned the corner.* **2** to get a quick view of: *The group glimpsed a bird in the tree.* **glimpsed, glimps·ing.**

glint (glĭnt) **1** a gleam; sparkle: *the glint of silver; a merry glint in his eye.* **2** to gleam.

glis·ten (glĭs′ən) to sparkle; shine: *The dewdrops glistened in the sunshine.*

glit·ter (glĭt′ər) **1** to sparkle coldly; shine with bright, flashing light: *Her diamonds glittered.* **2** bright, sparkling light: *the glitter of Christmas tree decorations.*

gloat (glōt) to watch or think about with malicious or greedy joy: *He is gloating because we were scolded. The miser gloats over his money.*

globe (glōb) **1** a body shaped like a ball; a sphere. **2** a sphere representing the earth, with a map of the world upon it, or a sphere representing the sky, showing the heavenly bodies in their relative positions. **3** the earth: *A submarine circled the globe without coming to the surface.*

Globe

glob·ule (glŏb′ūl) a small globe; a drop: *the globules of fat in the soup.*

gloom (glŏŏm) **1** dimness; darkness: *in the evening gloom.* **2** sadness; low spirits: *the gloom of the fans when the team lost.*

gloom·y (glŏŏ′mĭ) **1** dim; dull: *a gloomy cave; a gloomy day.* **2** sad; low in spirits; not cheerful: *to feel gloomy.* **gloom·i·er, gloom·i·est; gloom·i·ly.**

glo·ri·fy (glôr′ə fī′) **1** to give honor and glory to: *to glorify a war hero.* **2** to praise and worship: *to glorify God.* **3** to make (something) appear better, grander, or more beautiful: *Moonlight glorified the dingy village.* **glo·ri·fied, glo·ri·fy·ing.**

---

fāte, făt, fâre, fär; bē, bĕt; bīte, bĭt; nō, nŏt, nôr; fūse, fŭn, fûr; tōō, tŏŏk; foil; foul; thin; ~~then~~;
hw for wh as in *wh*at; zh for s as in u*s*ual; ə for a, e, i, o, u, as in *a*go, linen, peril, at*o*m, min*u*s

glorious · **go**

glo·ri·ous (glôr′ĭ əs) **1** splendid; having great beauty: *a glorious show of fireworks.* **2** having or bringing honor and glory; worthy of praise: *a glorious victory.* **3** delightful: *We had a glorious time at the party.* **glo·ri·ous·ly.**

glo·ry (glôr′ĭ) **1** fame and honor: *to dream of wealth and glory.* **2** praise; credit: *I did most of the work, but he got the glory.* **3** reason for pride: *Great works of art are among the glories of Italy.* **4** praise or worship: *a hymn to God's glory.* **5** great beauty; splendor: *the glory of the sunset.* **glory in** to rejoice in; be proud of. **glo·ries; glo·ried, glo·ry·ing.**

gloss (glôs) smooth, shining surface; luster: *the gloss of satin.* **gloss over** to cover up or excuse a mistake or wrong act.

glos·sa·ry (glŏs′ə rĭ or glôs′ə rĭ) a list of the unusual words in a book, and their meanings, in alphabetical order at the end of the text. **glos·sa·ries.**

gloss·y (glôs′ĭ) smooth and shiny: *a paint that dries a glossy red.* **gloss·i·er, gloss·i·est.**

glove (glŭv) **1** covering for the hand with a separate sheath for each finger and the thumb. **2** padded covering to protect the hand: *a catcher's glove.*

glow (glō) **1** to give off light and heat without flame: *Hot coals glowed after the fire died.* **2** to give off light but not heat: *The hands and numbers of this clock glow in the dark.* **3** to shine with strong color: *The trees glow with autumn shades.* **4** brightness; light: *the glow of a firefly; a red glow at sunset.* **5** to be warm and flushed: *to glow from embarrassment.* **6** rosy color: *the glow of good health.* **7** to have a shining or eager look: *to glow at good news; to glow with pride.* **8** such a look: *the glow of happiness.*

glow·er (glou′ər) **1** to stare in an angry way; scowl: *The robber glowered at the bank clerk.* **2** an angry or sullen stare.

glue (glōō) **1** sticky liquid that hardens and holds things together. **2** to stick with glue: *to glue a map to a piece of paper.* **3** to fasten as if with glue; fix firmly: *He sat glued to his chair.* **glued, glu·ing.**

glum (glŭm) silent and gloomy: *a glum look.* **glum·mer, glum·mest; glum·ly.**

glut·ton (glŭt′ən) **1** person who eats too much; greedy person. **2 glutton for work** or **punishment** one who can stand an unusual amount of work or punishment.

gnarl (närl) a knot on a tree or in wood.

gnarled (närld) twisted; knotty: *The old man's hands were brown and gnarled.*

gnash (năsh) to grind or strike (the teeth) together: *The wolf gnashed his teeth in a snarl.*

gnat (năt) any of several tiny flies, some of which have an itch-causing bite, while others produce lumps on plants by laying eggs in the stems and leaves.

Gnat

gnaw (nô) **1** to bite and wear away: *A dog gnaws a bone.* **2** to torment as if by gnawing: *The lie he told gnawed his conscience.*

gnome (nōm) in fable and myth, dwarf that lives underground to guard treasures of gold, silver, and jewels.

go (gō) **1** to pass from one place to another; move; travel: *Will you go to the store? Did you go by train?* **2** to move away; leave: *Are you coming or going? The bus had already gone.* **3** to pass: *An hour goes quickly.* **4** to be used up; be spent: *My money is going fast.* **5** to extend; reach: *A bridge goes across a river.* **6** to work; run: *Can you make this watch go?* **7** to pass from one condition to another: *to go to sleep.* **8** to make its special sound: *A cat goes "Mew, mew."* **9** to become: *to go deaf.* **10** to fit; belong: *This shoe goes on the left foot.* **11** to be given: *First prize went to my friend.* **12 on the go** active and busy.

go ahead to go on (with something one is doing or intends to do); proceed: *Go ahead and ask her.*

go along with 1 to accompany. **2** to agree with.

go around or **go round 1** to be enough: *The ice cream will just go around.* **2** to make a detour. **3** to pay a visit (to): *I will go around to his house today.*

go at to begin on; attack: *to go at one's work with enthusiasm.*

go back on 1 to betray or fail: *to go back on a friend.* **2** to fail to carry out: *to go back on one's promise.*

go beyond to exceed: *You must not go beyond the speed limit.*

316

go by 1 to pass: *as time* goes by. 2 to be guided by: *He* goes by *the rules.* 3 to be called by (the name of).

go in for to take up (as one's work, hobby, etc.): *to* go in for *tennis.*

go in with 1 to join: *He plans to* go in with *a new business firm.* 2 to share expenses; contribute.

go off 1 to explode: *I jumped when the firecracker* went off. 2 to happen: *The play* went off *well.* 3 to cease; depart: *The lights* went off.

go on 1 to continue: *He* goes on *working.* 2 to take place; proceed: *The show must* go on. 3 to start; begin: *The lights* go on.

go out 1 to stop burning: *The campfire* went out. 2 to go to parties, meetings, etc.: *She* goes out *a lot.* 3 to be published or broadcasted: *The news* went out *that the strike was over.* 4 to be given (of love, sympathy, etc.). 5 of labor, or trade union, to strike.

go through 1 to review or rehearse: *to* go through *one's work; to* go through *one's part in a play.* 2 to experience or endure: *to* go through *an illness.* 3 to search: *to* go through *a desk to find a paper.* 4 to spend completely; exhaust: *to* go through *a fortune.*

go through with to complete; endure to the end.

go together 1 to match. 2 to accompany.

go without to be or do without.

goes, went, gone, go·ing.

goad (gōd) 1 sharp-pointed stick used to drive cattle. 2 anything that drives or urges a person to do something: *a* goad *to his ambition.* 3 to drive or urge on: *Taunts from the rebels* goaded *the soldiers to fire.*

goal (gōl) 1 the place at either end of a field or court where the score is made in such games as football and basketball. 2 a score: *Our team made a* goal. 3 line or mark at the end of a race: *The winner will be the first person to cross the* goal. 4 thing a person plans to do or get; aim; purpose: *What is your* goal *in life?*

goat (gōt) active, inquisitive, cud-chewing animal about the size of a sheep, with short horns and a beard. It is valued for its flesh, its milk, and, in some of its varieties, for its hair.

goat·herd (gōt′hûrd′) one who tends goats, especially while at pasture.

Goat, about 3 ft. long

goat·skin (gōt′skin′) 1 the skin of a goat. 2 made of the skin of a goat.

¹**gob·ble** (gŏb′əl) to eat fast and greedily: *The little boy* gobbled *his food and hurried out to play.* **gob·bled, gob·bling.** [¹**gobble** is from an Old French word (gober) meaning "to swallow."]

²**gob·ble** (gŏb′əl) 1 noise made by a male turkey. 2 to make this noise. **gob·bled, gob·bling.** [²**gobble** is a changed form of ¹**gobble.**]

gob·bler (gŏb′lər) male turkey.

go-be·tween (gō′bə twēn′) person who makes peace, does business, or settles difficulties between two persons or groups who do not meet during the arrangements.

Goblet

gob·let (gŏb′lit) drinking glass with a slender stem and a flat base.

gob·lin (gŏb′lin) in fable or myth, evil or mischievous spirit having the form of an ugly, grotesque dwarf.

God (gŏd) the Creator and ruler of the universe.

god (gŏd) 1 a being who is thought of and worshiped as having greater than human powers over nature and human affairs. 2 thing or person that takes all of a person's time, interest, or devotion: *He has made a* god *of money.*

god·dess (gŏd′is) 1 female god. Among the goddesses of ancient Rome were Venus, goddess of love, and Diana, goddess of the hunt. 2 woman with the majestic beauty shown in Greek statues of goddesses.

god·fa·ther (gŏd′fä′thər) man who promises, at the baptism of someone else's child, to help in its religious training.

god·like (gŏd′lik′) like, or suitable to, a god; divine.

---

fāte, făt, fâre, fär; bē, bĕt; bīte, bĭt; nō, nŏt, nôr; fūse, fŭn, fûr; tōō, tŏŏk; foil; foul; thin; ~~then~~;
hw for wh as in *what*; zh for s as in u*s*ual; ə for a, e, i, o, u, as in *a*go, lin*e*n, per*i*l, at*o*m, min*u*s

god·ly (gŏd′lĭ) **1** obeying and loving God. **2** like a god in appearance or nature. **god·li·er, god·li·est.**

god·moth·er (gŏd′mŭ~~th~~′ər) woman who promises, at the baptism of someone else's child, to bring up in its religious training.

goes (gōz) See **go**. *He often goes to the movies.*

go·ing (gō′ĭng) **1** a moving away; departure: *His going was regretted by all.* **2** condition of a road or path: *The going is very bad on that dirt road.* **3** working successfully: *a going concern.* **4 be going to** to be intending to; will or shall: *He is going to let the dog out.*

goi·ter (goi′tər) **1** disease of the thyroid gland that causes swelling in the front of the neck. **2** the swelling caused by this disease.

gold (gōld) **1** heavy, precious metal element of bright yellow color in its pure state, used for making coins and jewelry. **2** made of gold: *a gold watch.* **3** money; wealth. **4** the color of gold: *The autumn trees were ablaze with scarlet and gold.* **5** the highest or best in quality; like gold: *a heart of gold.*

gold·en (gōl′dən) **1** made of gold: *a golden ring.* **2** bright and shining like gold: *her golden hair; a golden dawn.* **3** beautiful; superb: *She had a golden voice.* **4** ideal; best: *The golden age of boxing is over.*

gold·en·rod (gōl′dən rŏd′) tall plant with many clusters of tiny yellow flowers.

gold·finch (gōld′fĭnch′) **1** American songbird with a yellow body and black crown, wings, and tail. **2** European songbird with a crimson head and wings marked with yellow.

gold·fish (gōld′fĭsh′) small yellow- or orange-colored fresh-water fish native to China. It is kept and raised for its beauty. pl. **gold·fish;** rarely, **gold·fish·es.**

gold·smith (gōld′smĭth′) person who makes things of gold.

golf (gŏlf) **1** outdoor game in which a small, hard ball is driven with one of a set of clubs, and in the fewest possible strokes, from hole to hole over a 9- or 18-hole course. **2** to play this game.

Gondola

gon·do·la (gŏn′də lə) **1** a narrow, sharp-pointed boat, with high, ornamental ends,

rowed with a single oar by a standing boatman. It is used for transportation in Venice. **2** freight car with low sides and no top. **3** the cabin of a dirigible.

gone (gôn or gŏn) See **go**. *My pen is gone.*

gong (gŏng or gông) saucer-shaped metal disk which makes a loud noise when struck.

good (gŏod) **1** excellent; of high quality: *This is a good book. Dr. Howard is a good surgeon.* **2** suited (to its purpose): *This knife is good for cutting meat.* **3** well-behaved; making no trouble: *The children were good all afternoon.* **4** upright; honest; moral: *He tried to live a good life.* **5** act or thing that is helpful, beneficial, etc.: *He did more harm than good.* **6** merit; worth: *There is some good in everyone.* **7** profit; advantage; benefit: *The disobedient child was punished for his own good.* **8** fresh; not spoiled: *You can tell if an egg is good by its smell.* **9** enjoyable; pleasant: *We all had a good time at the picnic.* **10** thorough; complete: *He got a good spanking for being naughty.* **11** real; not false: *Can you tell the difference between counterfeit and good money?* **12 as good as** almost; practically: *The job is as good as done.* **13 for good** forever: *He says he's leaving town for good.* **14 make good** (1) to repay or replace. (2) to succeed. **bet·ter, best.**

good-by or **good-bye** (gŏod′bī′) farewell.

good-look·ing (gŏod′lŏok′ĭng) attractive; handsome in appearance.

good·ly (gŏod′lĭ) **1** large; abundant: *a goodly harvest.* **2** beautiful; pleasing to see: *a goodly land.* **3** considerable: *a goodly amount of money.* **good·li·er, good·li·est.**

good-na·tured (gŏod′nā′chərd) easy to get along with; having an even temper. **good-na·tured·ly.**

good·ness (gŏod′nĭs) a being good.

goods (gŏodz) **1** things that are bought and sold; merchandise. **2** things owned; possessions, especially things that can be moved: *household goods.*

good-sized (gŏod′sīzd′) large; of considerable size.

good-tem·pered (gŏod′tĕm′pərd) with an even temper; not easily made angry; having a pleasant disposition. **good-tem·pered·ly.**

good will 1 kind feeling; friendly understanding. **2** the extra value that a business has because of its good reputation.

good·y (gŏŏd′ĭ) candy or cake. **good·ies.**

goose (gōōs) **1** any of several water birds, larger than a duck, with webbed feet, stout bodies, and a long neck. **2** female goose as distinguished from the male, or **gander. 3** the flesh of the goose as food. **4** a silly person. **geese.**

Wild goose, 2 to 3 ft. long

goose·ber·ry (gōōs′bĕr′ĭ) **1** small berry used for pies and jams. **2** bush it grows on. **goose·ber·ries.**

go·pher (gō′fər) **1** burrowing animal with large, fur-lined cheek pouches and powerful, long-clawed forefeet. **2** striped ground squirrel of western North America.

Pocket gopher, about 9 in. long

¹**gore** (gôr) thick, sticky blood coming from a cut or wound. [¹**gore** is from an Old English word (gor) meaning "mud," "filth."]

²**gore** (gôr) to pierce with a horn or tusk. **gored, gor·ing.** [²**gore** is from an Old English word (gār) meaning "a spear."]

³**gore** (gôr) wedge-shaped piece of cloth. Gores are sewn together to make umbrellas and skirts. [³**gore** is a form of an Old English word (gāra) meaning "a triangular piece of land."]

gorge (gôrj) **1** deep, steep-sided valley; ravine. **2** to stuff with food: *The hungry boy gorged himself with three helpings of chicken pie.* **gorged, gorg·ing.**

gor·geous (gôr′jəs) rich in color; splendid: *a very gorgeous sunset.* **gor·geous·ly.**

go·ril·la (gə rĭl′ə) the largest of the manlike apes. Its home is in Africa.

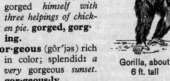

Gorilla, about 6 ft. tall

gor·y (gôr′ĭ) bloody. **gor·i·er, gor·i·est; gor·i·ly.**

gos·ling (gŏz′lĭng) young goose.

gos·pel (gŏs′pəl) **1** teachings of Jesus and the Apostles. **2 Gospel (1)** any of the first four books of the New Testament: *The story of Christmas is told mainly in the Gospel of St. Luke.* (**2**) any part of these books, read at a religious service: *People in church stand up at the reading of the Gospel.* **3** anything believed as absolutely true: *She took his word as gospel.*

gos·sa·mer (gŏs′ə mər) **1** fine, silky thread or web made by a spider. **2** thin, filmy fabric: *a scarf of gossamer.* **3** light and thin: *a gossamer cloud.*

gos·sip (gŏs′əp) **1** idle talk about people and happenings, often unfriendly. **2** to chat; talk in an idle, often unfriendly, way about people and their affairs. **3** person fond of gossiping.

got (gŏt) See **get.** *I got a new hat today.*

got·ten (gŏt′ən) See **get.** *The weather has gotten colder.*

gouge (gouj) **1** kind of chisel for cutting rounded or V-shaped grooves in wood. **2** a cut of such shape; a deep scratch: *The sharp stick left a long gouge in Bert's leg.* **3** to cut or scoop with, or as with, a gouge: *Penny gouged out the melon with a spoon.* **gouged, goug·ing.**

Gouge

gourd (gôrd or gōōrd) **1** bulb- or bottle-shaped fruit of various plants of the melon family. When dried, gourds have hard shells and seeds which rattle. They are used as bowls, dippers, rattles, etc. **2** plant that bears a gourd.

Gourds

gour·met (gōōr mā′) person who is fond of and can appreciate fine foods and drinks.

gov·ern (gŭv′ərn) to control; manage; direct: *The mayor and town council govern a town. Learn to govern your temper.*

fāte, făt, fâre, fär; bē, bĕt; bīte, bĭt; nō, nŏt, nôr; fūse, fŭn, fûr; tōō, tŏŏk; foil; foul; thin; ~~then~~; hw for wh as in *what*; zh for s as in u*s*ual; ə for a, e, i, o, u, as in *a*go, lin*e*n, per*i*l, at*o*m, min*u*s

gov·ern·ess (gŭv′ər nĭs) woman who teaches someone else's children in their own home.

gov·ern·ment (gŭv′ərn mənt) **1** control; direction; management: *the* government *of a country, state, or city.* **2** person or group of persons who govern. **3** system of governing: *Republican* governments *have gradually replaced monarchies.*

gov·er·nor (gŭv′ər nər) **1** person elected head of a State in the United States. **2** man appointed to be the head of government of a colony, province, etc. **3** device attached to an engine or machine to keep it going at an even speed.

gown (goun) **1** a dress, especially a long one. **2** informal garment, such as a nightgown or a dressing gown. **3** loose outer garment worn by upper classmen, graduating students, clergymen, judges, etc.

College gown

grab (grăb) **1** to take hold of suddenly; snatch: *Alvin* grabbed *the ball and threw it to first base. The thief was caught* grabbing *a lady's purse.* **2** quick, snatching movement: *He made a* grab *for the ball.* **grabbed, grab·bing.**

grace (grās) **1** easy, flowing manner; beautiful movement: *the* grace *of a dancer.* **2** charming quality; pleasing manner: *a young lady with many* graces. **3** sense of right: *He had the* grace *to say he was sorry.* **4** to favor or honor: *The table was* graced *by the great singer's presence.* **5** mercy; favor: *By God's* grace *the ship landed safely.* **6** extra time given to pay a debt: *You have five days'* grace *to settle this note.* **7** short prayer of thanks before or after a meal. **8 be in a person's good graces** to enjoy a person's favor; be liked by him. **graced, grac·ing.**

grace·ful (grās′fəl) showing or having charm and elegance of movement, posture, form, or expression: *The ballet is a* graceful *dance. She wrote a* graceful *letter of thanks.* **grace·ful·ly.**

gra·cious (grā′shəs) **1** full of grace and charm; pleasant: *A* gracious *hostess welcomes her guests and makes them feel at home.* **2** courteous and kindly (to people of lower social position): *the* gracious *smile of the king.* **gra·cious·ly.**

grack·le (grăk′əl) black bird about the size of a starling. Its shiny feathers look purple in certain lights.

grade (grād) **1** class or year in school: *the fourth* grade. **2** letter or number showing how well one has done school work; mark. **3** to give a mark to: *The teacher is* grading *papers.* **4** to sort into grades; place in classes: *These eggs are* graded *by size.* **5** degree of quality or rank: *a high* grade *of meat.* **6** rate at which a road slopes: *a steep* grade. **7** to make level or more even: *A bulldozer* graded *the road.* **8 the grades** elementary school. **grad·ed, grad·ing.**

grade school elementary school.

grad·u·al (grăj′ōō əl) taking place little by little; moving or progressing by degrees; slow: *He noticed a* gradual *improvement.* **grad·u·al·ly.**

¹**grad·u·ate** (grăj′ōō ĭt′) person who has finished a course of study in a school and has received a diploma.

²**grad·u·ate** (grăj′ōō āt′) **1** to give a degree or diploma for finishing work at a school or college: *Our high school* graduated *200 students last year. These students were* graduated *last year.* **2** to receive a degree or diploma: *My sister* graduated *from high school last week.* **3** to mark off in equal spaces or amounts: *That thermometer is* graduated *in Fahrenheit degrees.* **grad·u·at·ed, grad·u·at·ing.**

grad·u·a·tion (grăj′ōō ā′shən) **1** ceremony at which diplomas are given to students of a school; commencement exercises. **2** a mark showing equal spaces or amounts: *the* graduations *on a ruler, thermometer, or measuring cup.*

graft (grăft) **1** twig or branch of one plant set into another of which it will become a living part. **2** body tissue transplanted in like manner. **3** to make such a transfer: *The surgeon* grafted *skin from the patient's leg to his burned face.* **4** dishonest using of a position, especially by a public official, to gain money.

Graft

gra·ham (grā′əm) made of coarse wholewheat (flour): *a box of* graham *crackers;* graham *bread.*

grain (grān) **1** seed of wheat, rice, oats, corn, and other cereal plants. **2** plant or plants bearing such seeds: *a field of* grain. **3** tiny, hard particle of sugar, salt, sand, etc. **4** any tiny bit: *There isn't a grain of truth in her story.* **5** very small unit of weight. One pound is equal to 7,000 grains. **6** lines and patterns in wood or stone caused by the way the fibers or layers are arranged. **7 go against the grain** to be distasteful or unpleasant: *It goes against his grain to do a sloppy job.*

gram (grăm) unit of weight in the metric system. One ounce is equal to about 28 grams.

gram·mar (grăm'ər) **1** study of the forms of words and their uses in sentences. **2** rules about the forms and uses of words. **3** book containing such rules.

grammar school 1 in the United States, an elementary school. **2** in England, a school preparing for college.

gram·mat·i·cal (grə măt'ə kəl) according to the rules of grammar: *"She and me" is not* grammatical. **gram·mat·i·cal·ly.**

gran·a·ry (grăn'ə rī) storehouse for grain. **gran·a·ries.**

grand (grănd) **1** stately; dignified; showing high social standing: *a* grand *manner; a* grand *lady.* **2** great in size or general effect; impressive: *a* grand *spectacle.* **3** most important; main: *the* grand *ballroom.* **4** including everything; complete: *a* grand *total.* **5** very good; very satisfying: *a* grand *time; a* grand *person.* **6 grand piano** piano with strings lying flat. **grand·ly.**

Grand Canyon a deep gorge cut by the Colorado River through northwestern Arizona.

grand·child (grănd'chīld') child of one's son or daughter. **grand·chil·dren.**

grand·dad or **gran·dad** (grănd'dăd') in everyday language, grandfather: *We called one grandfather* granddad.

grand·daugh·ter (grănd'dô'tər) daughter of one's son or daughter.

gran·deur (grăn'jər) greatness; splendor: *the* grandeur *of mountain scenery.*

grand·fa·ther (grănd'fä'thər) father's father; mother's father.

grand·ma (grănd'mä') in everyday language, grandmother.

grand·moth·er (grănd'mŭth'ər) father's mother; mother's mother.

grand·pa (grănd'pä') in everyday language, grandfather: *We called the other grandfather* grandpa.

grand·par·ent (grănd'pâr'ənt) either parent of one's father or mother; grandfather or grandmother.

grand·son (grănd'sŭn') son of one's son or daughter.

grand·stand (grănd'stănd') main rows of seats, often roofed, at an athletic field, race course, along a parade route, etc.

grange (grānj) **1** a farm and its buildings. **2 Grange** organization of farmers.

gran·ite (grăn'it) hard rock, usually gray, used for buildings and monuments.

gran·ny (grăn'ī) in everyday language, grandmother. **gran·nies.**

grant (grănt) **1** to give (something asked for); permit: *The principal granted us permission to print and sell a newspaper.* **2** to admit; agree: *I grant that you are right.* **3** something given or allowed: *a grant of money; a grant of land.* **4 take for granted** to suppose to be true; assume: *We took it for granted that you would want to come so we bought an extra ticket.*

gran·u·late (grăn'yōō lāt') **1** to make into or become grains: *Wind and rain granulate rock into sand.* **2 granulated sugar** sugar that has been taken from beets or cane, refined, and crystallized into small grains. **gran·u·lat·ed, gran·u·lat·ing.**

grape (grāp) juicy fruit growing in clusters on a vine. The juice of grapes is used to make wine. Raisins are certain kinds of dried grapes.

grape·fruit (grāp'frōōt') **1** pale yellow citrus fruit with a pleasantly sour taste. A grapefruit is larger than an orange. **2** the tree that bears it.

grape·shot (grāp'shŏt') small iron balls that scatter when fired from a cannon.

grape·vine (grāp'vīn') **1** vine that bears grapes. **2** network of rumor and hearsay: *I heard by the* grapevine *that Lois is getting married.*

---

fāte, făt, fâre, fär; bē, bĕt; bīte, bĭt; nō, nŏt, nôr; fūse, fŭn, fûr; tōō, tŏŏk; foil; foul; thin; then; hw for wh as in *wh*at; zh for s as in u*s*ual; ə for a, e, i, o, u, as in *a*go, lin*e*n, per*i*l, at*o*m, min*u*s

graph

graph (grăf) drawing that shows by lines, bars, or divisions the course of change in a thing, the relation of one thing to others, or the relation of a part to a whole.

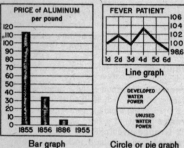

PRICE of ALUMINUM per pound

120 110 100 90 80 70 60 50 40 30 20 10 0

1855 1856 1886 1955

Bar graph

FEVER PATIENT

106 104 102 100 98.6

1d 2d 3d 4d 5d 6d

Line graph

DEVELOPED WATER POWER

UNUSED WATER POWER

Circle or pie graph

graph·ic (grăf'ĭk) **1** having to do with graphs, diagrams, or the use of charts and pictures instead of words. **2** vivid; lifelike: *This book gives a* graphic *description of a roundup.* **3** having to do with drawing, painting, etc.: *the* graphic *arts.*

graph·ite (grăf'īt) black, soft form of carbon. Graphite is used in lead pencils.

grap·ple (grăp'əl) **1** to fasten closely: *to* grapple *it with hoops of steel.* **2** to wrestle; struggle: *Wrestlers* grapple *with each other. Hubert* grappled *with his arithmetic lesson.* **3** light anchor with more than two arms, often used in dragging for things under water. **grap·pled, grap·pling.**

Grapple

grasp (grăsp) **1** to hold firmly in the hand: *to* grasp *a baseball bat.* **2** firm hold: *Get a* grasp *on the rope.* **3** to hold in the mind; understand: *to* grasp *a problem.* **4** understanding: *to have a firm* grasp *of subtraction.*

grasp·ing (grăs'pĭng) greedy; eager to get all one can. **grasp·ing·ly.**

grass (grăs) **1** cultivated or wild green plants growing on lawns and in pastures. **2** any of a group of plants with jointed stems and narrow leaves called blades. Wheat, corn, bamboo, and sugar cane are all grasses.

grass·hop·per (grăs'hŏp'ər) leaping insect of the locust family, with wings and long, powerful hind legs. For picture, see next column.

grating

grass·land (grăs'lănd') land, usually without trees, on which grass grows abundantly: *The prairies of the central States and the pampas of South America are* grasslands.

grass·y (grăs'ĭ) **1** covered with grass. **2** of or like grass. **grass·i·er, grass·i·est.**

¹grate (grāt) **1** to make into bits or powder by rubbing on a rough surface: *Mother* grated *carrots for a salad.* **2** to make a harsh, scraping sound: *The chalk* grated *on the blackboard.* **3** to irritate; vex: *Her shrill voice* grates *on my nerves.* **grat·ed, grat·ing.** [¹**grate** is from an Old French word (grater) meaning "to scratch."] (Homonym: great)

²grate (grāt) **1** frame of metal bars to hold fuel in a fireplace, or a frame that can be rocked to dislodge ashes in a stove. **2** frame of crossed or parallel bars, as at a window to prevent escape or entrance; a grating. **3** to furnish with iron bars: *The windows of prison cells are* grated. **grat·ed, grat·ing.** [²**grate** goes back to a Latin word (crātis) meaning "a hurdle" or "a harrow."] (Homonym: great)

Grate

grate·ful (grāt'fəl) thankful; showing thanks: *I am* grateful *to you for all your help.* **grate·ful·ly.**

grat·i·fi·ca·tion (grăt'ə fə kā'shən) **1** satisfaction; a being pleased: *The painter looked upon his completed work with* gratification. **2** a giving satisfaction to; humoring: *He studied law to his father's great* gratification.

grat·i·fy (grăt'ə fī') **1** to please; give pleasure to: *He was* gratified *by his son's success.* **2** to give satisfaction to; indulge; humor: *to* gratify *someone's thirst for knowledge.* **grat·i·fied, grat·i·fy·ing.**

¹grat·ing (grā'tĭng) **1** harsh (in sound); scraping: *The rusty door opened with a* grating *sound.* **2** getting on one's nerves; irritating: *a* grating *habit.* **grat·ing·ly.** [¹**grating** is a form of ¹**grate.**]

Grasshopper, about 1¼ in. long

322

²**grat·ing** (grā′tĭng) framework of bars side by side or crossed, used to cover an opening without shutting out light and air. [²**grating** is a form of ²**grate**.]

grat·i·tude (grăt′ə-tōōd′ or grăt′ə tūd′) thankfulness for help, kindness, or good fortune.

Grating

¹**grave** (grāv) **1** hole in the ground in which a dead body is placed. **2** any place of burial: *a grave in the ocean.* **3** death: *The brave do not fear the* grave. **4** to shape or cut with a chisel or pointed instrument. **graved, grav·en, grav·ing.** [¹**grave** is a form of an Old English word (græf) meaning "a place dug out"; "a grave." The Old English word was formed from another Old English word (grafan) meaning "to dig"; "engrave." Hence, ¹**grave** and **en·grave** are related.]

²**grave** (grāv) **1** serious; solemn; thoughtful: *Everyone was grave at the inauguration.* **2** needing serious thought; important: *The President has grave responsibilities.* **grav·er, grav·est; grave·ly.** [²**grave** comes through French from a Latin word (gravis) meaning "heavy."]

grav·el (grăv′əl) **1** mixture of small stones and pebbles. **2** to cover with gravel: *to gravel a road.*

grave·yard (grāv′yärd′) place where the dead are buried; cemetery.

grav·i·tate (grăv′ə tāt′) **1** to be drawn toward the center of the earth or to another body by a natural force called gravity; sink; settle: *Mud carried by a river gravitates to the bottom in still water.* **2** to be drawn toward anything: *During the summer people gravitate to the seashore.* **grav·i·tat·ed, grav·i·tat·ing.**

grav·i·ta·tion (grăv′ə tā′shən) **1** the force that draws all bodies in the universe toward one another. Gravitation draws everything on the surface of the earth toward its center, keeps the planets revolving around the sun, etc. **2** the act of being drawn towards: *the gravitation of people to the seashore during the summer.*

grav·i·ty (grăv′ə tĭ) **1** seriousness; solemnity; importance: *The child quickly sensed the gravity of the occasion.* **2** the pull of the earth that draws all objects in or near the earth toward its center. **3** force of gravitation of a heavenly body. **4 center of gravity** point inside an object on which it will exactly balance in every direction; center of equilibrium. **grav·i·ties.**

gra·vy (grā′vĭ) **1** fat and juices that come from cooking meat. **2** sauce made from meat juices. **gra·vies.**

gray (grā) **1** any shade that is a mixture of black and white. **2** of this color: *She wore a gray dress.* **3** dull; cheerless: *a gray day.* **gray·ly.** Also spelled **grey.**

¹**graze** (grāz) **1** to eat growing grass, like sheep in a pasture. **2** to put into a pasture or on a range to feed: *to graze cattle.* **grazed, graz·ing.** [¹**graze** is a form of an Old English word (grasian) that comes from another Old English word (græs) meaning "grass."]

²**graze** (grāz) **1** to touch, rub, or scrape lightly against: *A bullet grazed his temple.* **2** slight rub or scrape. **grazed, graz·ing.** [²**graze** is probably from ¹**graze**, in a possible early sense of "coming close to the grass."]

grease (grēs) **1** melted animal fat. **2** to cover with fat: *to grease a baking dish.* **3** any thick, oily substance. **4** to oil or lubricate: *to grease a car.* **greased, greas·ing.** (Homonym: Greece)

greas·y (grē′sĭ) covered with or having too much grease: *His hands were greasy. The food was greasy.* **greas·i·er, greas·i·est; greas·i·ly.**

great (grāt) **1** large in size; vast: *The forest was ruined by a great fire.* **2** large in number: *A great crowd attended the game.* **3** extreme; more than usual: *a great danger; a great pain.* **4** distinguished; famous; of unusual skill: *Admiral Byrd was a great explorer.* **5** important; weighty: *Generals must make great decisions.* (Homonym: grate)

Great Britain island in northwestern Europe, containing England, Scotland, and Wales.

---

fāte, făt, fâre, fär; bē, bĕt; bīte, bĭt; nō, nŏt, nôr; fūse, fŭn, fûr; tōō, tŏŏk; foil; foul; thin; ~~then~~;
hw for wh as in *wh*at; zh for s as in u*s*ual; ə for a, e, i, o, u, as in *a*go, lin*e*n, per*i*l, at*o*m, min*u*s

323

great-grand·fath·er (grāt′grănd′fā′thər) father of one's grandfather or grandmother.

great-grand·moth·er (grāt′grănd′mŭth′-ər) mother of one's grandfather or grandmother.

great·ly (grāt′lĭ) much; highly: *He was greatly pleased at the success of the project.*

great·ness (grāt′nĭs) **1** hugeness; vastness: *The greatness of the Grand Canyon is overwhelming.* **2** fame; distinction; outstanding position: *He achieved greatness as an artist.* **3** natural dignity or nobility (of mind, character, etc.): *He showed true greatness by his generosity to his enemies.*

Greece (grēs) small country in southeastern Europe. In ancient times it was called Hellas. (Homonym: grease)

greed (grēd) intense, selfish craving; desire for more than one's share: *the miser's greed for money.*

greed·i·ness (grēd′ĭ nĭs) a being greedy.

greed·y (grē′dĭ) **1** having or showing an extremely keen desire for food and drink: *The dog has had enough to eat; he is just greedy.* **2** wanting more than one's share; desiring or wanting too much: *to be greedy for gold; to be greedy for power.* **greed·i·er; greed·i·est; greed·i·ly.**

Greek (grēk) **1** of Greece, its people, or language. **2** citizen of Greece or person of Greek descent. **3** language of the modern Greeks. **4** language of the ancient Greeks.

green (grēn) **1** color of growing plants and grass. **2** having this color. **3** closely cut plot of grass. **4** unripe: *Those green apples are not ready to be eaten.* **5** untrained; inexperienced: *The young man's mistakes proved that he was still green at his job.* **6** not dried; unseasoned: *The green lumber didn't burn well.* **7 greens** (**1**) wreaths, garlands, etc., used as decoration: *Christmas greens.* (**2**) leafy vegetables, used for food: *beet greens; dandelion greens.* **8 green with envy** envious to an extreme.

green·horn (grēn′hôrn′) **1** inexperienced person; newcomer. **2** person easily fooled.

green·house (grēn′hous′) a building with glass sides and a glass roof, heated for growing plants; hothouse.

Green·wich time (grĕn′ĭj tĭm) time measured by the sun at Greenwich, England. Greenwich time is used as a basis for standard time around the world.

green·wood (grēn′wŏŏd′) forest or wood when the leaves are green.

greet (grēt) **1** to address a person by saying, "Hello," "Good morning," etc. **2** to welcome; hail: *A large crowd will greet the President.* **3** to appear before: *A surprising sight greeted us.*

greet·ing (grē′tĭng) written or spoken expression of friendship; a welcome.

gre·nade (grə nād′) small bomb thrown by hand or fired from a rifle.

gren·a·dier (grĕn′ə dĭr′) **1** originally, a foot soldier who threw grenades. **2** member of a special British Army regiment.

grew (grōō) See **grow.** *Harry grew taller this summer.*

grey (grā) gray.

grey·hound (grā′hound′) sharp-faced, slender-bodied, long-legged dog, famous for its grace and speed, used in racing and sometimes in hunting.

Greyhound, about 2 ft. high at shoulder

grid (grĭd) **1** a grating of parallel iron bars; gridiron. **2** in electricity, a wire mesh that controls the flow of electrons in a vacuum tube.

grid·dle (grĭd′əl) flat, heavy, metal plate used for cooking pancakes and the like.

grid·i·ron (grĭd′ī′ərn) **1** rack of parallel bars on which to broil meat, etc. **2** something that looks like a gridiron, especially a football field.

Gridiron

grief (grēf) **1** deep sorrow; great sadness. **2** cause or source of sorrow. **3 come to grief** to meet with disaster; fail: *The ship came to grief on a reef.*

griev·ance (grē′vəns) real or imagined wrong; cause of annoyance or resentment: *The leaking roof was the tenant's chief grievance.*

grieve (grēv) **1** to feel sorrow: *I grieve over your misfortune.* **2** to cause sorrow to; distress: *Your misfortune grieves me.* **grieved, griev·ing.**

griev·ous (grē′vəs) **1** causing physical or mental suffering; severe: *a grievous wrong.* **2** outrageous; glaring: *a grievous mistake.* **griev·ous·ly.**

grill (gril) **1** gridiron. **2** to cook on a gridiron. **3** dish of food cooked over a gridiron: *We had a mixed* grill *for dinner.* **4** restaurant that specializes in food cooked on a grill. **5** to put to severe questioning: *The detectives* grilled *the prisoner until he told the whole story.*

grim (grim) **1** cruel; fierce: *a grim battle.* **2** unyielding: *a grim determination.* **3** forbidding; threatening: *Gray grim cliffs towered above us.* **4** frightening; horrible: *a grim tale of murder.* **grim·mer, grim·mest; grim·ly.**

gri·mace (gri mās′) **1** an ugly expression of the face; a twisting of features to show disgust or disapproval: *to make a grimace.* **2** a twisting of facial features caused by pain. **3** to make a face: *He grimaced when I said I'd be late.* **gri·maced, gri·mac·ing.**

grime (grīm) **1** dirt that is hard to get off: *The old stove was covered with* grime. **2** to make dirty; soil.

grim·y (grī′mi) covered with grime; dirty: *The plumber's hands were* grimy. **grim·i·er, grim·i·est; grim·i·ly.**

grin (grin) **1** to draw back the lips or show teeth in a smile, or as though in a smile. **2** this action or expression. **grinned, grin·ning.**

grind (grīnd) **1** to make into a powder; crush into small pieces: *to grind wheat; to grind coffee beans.* **2** to make or produce by grinding: *to grind flour.* **3** to grate; rub harshly: *to grind one's teeth.* **4** to smooth or sharpen by rubbing against a rough surface: *to grind an ax.* **5** to oppress; crush: *The tyrant ground down the people.* **6** to operate by turning a crank: *to grind a hand organ.* **7** long, continuing, monotonous activity: *the daily grind at the office.* **ground, grind·ing.**

grind·stone (grīnd′stōn′) disk of fine-grained stone, turned by a crank or treadle. On its revolving edge, cutting tools are ground sharp.

Grindstone

grip (grip) **1** to grasp tightly: *If you grip the side of the cart you won't fall out.* **2** tight grasp; strong hold. **3** to appeal strongly to; interest very much: *a story that grips the imagination.* **4** valise; handbag. **gripped, grip·ping.** (Homonym: grippe)

grippe (grip) influenza. (Homonym: grip)

grist (grist) **1** grain to be ground. **2** flour or meal made by grinding. **3 grist to (one's) mill** something that can be turned to good use.

gris·tle (gris′əl) tough, white substance found in the body tissue of animals; cartilage.

grit (grit) **1** small, hard particles of sand or the like. **2** ability to endure hardships; firm spirit: *It took grit to start a farm in Alaska.* **3** to press or grind together: *to grit one's teeth.* **grit·ted, grit·ting.**

griz·zled (griz′əld) streaked with gray; gray-haired: *a grizzled beard; a grizzled old man.*

griz·zly (griz′li) **1** gray. **2** grizzly bear. **griz·zlies; griz·zli·er, griz·zli·est.**

grizzly bear North American animal, largest and fiercest of all bears. It is named for its silver-tipped brown hair.

Grizzly bear, 8 to 10 ft. long

groan (grōn) **1** low, sad throat sound; a moan: *a groan of pain.* **2** to make a low, sad sound: *He groaned when Mother said he couldn't go.* **3** to make a sound like a groan: *The old house groaned and creaked during the storm.* (Homonym: grown)

gro·cer (grō′sər) person who sells food and household supplies.

gro·cer·y (grō′sə ri) **1** food store. **2 gro·cer·ies** foods, such as flour, sugar, spices, butter, etc. **gro·cer·ies.**

groom (grōōm) **1** man about to be married or one just married; a bridegroom. **2** man or boy who takes care of horses. **3** to clean and feed horses. **4** to make neat in appearance: *Sally was carefully* groomed *for the wedding.*

---

fāte, făt, fâre, fär; bē, bĕt; bīte, bĭt; nō, nŏt, nôr; fūse, fŭn, fûr; tōō, tŏŏk; foil; foul; thin; ~~then~~;
hw for wh as in *wh*at; zh for s as in u*s*ual; ə for a, e, i, o, u, as in *a*go, lin*e*n, per*i*l, at*o*m, min*u*s

groove (grōōv) **1** narrow track or channel; a furrow or rut: *A window slides up and down in* grooves. *Running water made a* groove *in the rock.* **2** to make a groove in. **3** unchanging way of thinking or of doing things: *to get into a* groove. **grooved, groov·ing.**

grope (grōp) **1** to feel about uncertainly with the hands: *He* groped *for the doorknob in the dark.* **2** to search about in the mind: *to* grope *for an idea.* **groped, grop·ing.**

gross (grōs) **1** including everything; total: *the* gross *profits of a business.* **2** 12 dozen; 144. **3** thick; heavy: *the* gross *body of a hippopotamus.* **4** very bad and easily seen; glaring: *a* gross *mistake.* **5** coarse; vulgar: *Her* gross *manners offended her companions.* **gross·ly. pl. gross.**

gro·tesque (grō tĕsk´) distorted; odd; fantastic: *the* grotesque *face of a monster.* **gro·tesque·ly.**

grot·to (grŏt´ō) picturesque man-made or natural cave. **grot·toes** or **grot·tos.**

grouch (grouch) **1** an ill-tempered, complaining person. **2** a fit of ill-temper; a complaining mood. **3** to complain; to be ill-tempered.

grouch·y (grouch´ĭ) having a bad temper; sullen; irritable. **grouch·i·er, grouch·i·est; grouch·i·ly.**

¹ground (ground) **1** surface of the earth: *from* ground *to sky.* **2** soil; earth; land: *fertile* ground; *frozen* ground. **3** land for a particular use: *hunting* ground; *fishing* ground. **4** land under water: *The ship hit* ground. **5** to cause to hit bottom; to run aground: *to* ground *a boat.* **6** to force (an airplane) to land or to stay on land: *Planes were* grounded *by the fog.* **7** to connect with the ground: *Lightning rods must be* grounded. **8** of or on the ground: *the* ground *floor of a house.* **9 gain ground** to move forward; make progress; advance. **10 give ground** to move back; retreat; give up some of one's hopes or demands. **11 lose ground** to be forced back; fail; lose what has been gained. **12 grounds** (1) land around a house. (2) basis; reasons: *Tell me your* grounds *for believing he is smart.* **13 stand one's ground** to refuse to give in. **14 common ground** point of contact; point of agreement. [**¹ground** is a form of an Old English word (grŭnd).]

²ground (ground) **1** See **grind.** *The butcher* ground *the meat in a machine.* **2 coffee grounds** ground coffee left after brewing. [**²ground** is a form of **grind.**]

ground·hog (ground´hŏg´ or ground´hôg´) woodchuck. According to tradition, on the second of February, Groundhog Day, the groundhog comes out of his hole; if he sees his shadow, he goes back in and winter continues for six more weeks.

group (grōōp) **1** number of persons or things clustered together or considered as a whole: *a* group *of people on a street corner; the modern art* group. **2** to gather together: *The people* grouped *around the tables.* **3** to arrange or place together: *Please* group *the chairs into two circles.*

grouse (grous) any of several game birds related to domestic fowl, such as the partridge. **pl. grouse.**

Ruffed grouse, about 18 in. long

grove (grōv) **1** group of trees standing together. **2** group of cultivated fruit trees; orchard.

grov·el (grŏv´əl or grŭv´əl) **1** to lie flat or crawl on the ground, as if begging for mercy: *to* grovel *in the dust at the feet of a conqueror.* **2** to humble oneself: *to* grovel *before a king.*

grow (grō) **1** to become bigger by natural development: *I do believe this boy is* growing *an inch a day!* **2** to spring up naturally; come from seed: *Daisies* grow *in meadows.* **3** to plant and care for: *He* grows *tomatoes in his garden.* **4** to increase: *The volume of their shouts* grew *to a roar.* **5** to become: *The sky began to* grow *dark. The sick boy is* growing *stronger each day.*

grow on or **upon** to become gradually more attractive to: *You may not like this book at first but it* grows *on you.*

grow out of 1 to be a result of: *Most prejudices* grow *out of ignorance.* **2** to get too big for: *to* grow *out of one's clothes.* **3** to cease to practice; abandon: *He has* grown *out of his bad habits.*

grow up to pass from childhood to the stage of being an adult.

grew, grown, grow·ing.

growl (groul) **1** low, threatening throat sound: *The dog gave a growl as the stranger approached.* **2** to make such a sound; snarl: *The bear growled at the hunter.* **3** to say in an angry, muttering voice: *He growled an answer to his roommate.* **4** angry complaint: *Whenever Jack has work to do, all I hear are growls and mutterings.*

grown (grōn) See **grow**. (Homonym: groan)

grown-up (grōn'ŭp') an adult: *All the grownups sat at the large table.*

grown-up (grōn'ŭp') of an adult; suitable for an adult: *He has grown-up manners.*

growth (grōth) **1** natural development: *He has reached his full growth. This plant has had a slow growth.* **2** increase in quantity, number, size, etc.: *There has been a large growth in population this past year.* **3** something growing or that has grown: *a day's growth of beard; a season's growth of wheat.* **4** an abnormal lump on a body or plant.

grub (grŭb) **1** to dig in the ground: *Pigs grub in the forest for food.* **2** to dig up by the roots: *to grub a stump from the ground.* **3** to toil; do hard labor. **4** insect in its wormlike stage. **grubbed, grub·bing.**

grudge (grŭj) **1** feeling of envy, spite, or ill will: *He has a grudge against me because I voted against his plan.* **2** to begrudge. **grudged, grudg·ing.**

grudg·ing·ly (grŭj'ing li) unwillingly: *His father grudgingly gave him the car keys.*

gru·el (grōō'əl) thin porridge, made by boiling cereal in milk or water.

grue·some (grōō'səm) horrible and repulsive: *a gruesome auto wreck.*

gruff (grŭf) **1** harsh; hoarse: *a gruff voice.* **2** rough; showing impatience: *He had a good heart but a gruff manner.* **gruff·ly.**

grum·ble (grŭm'bəl) **1** to mutter complaints; find fault: *He was always grumbling about the weather.* **2** bad-tempered complaining: *a grumble of discontent.* **3** to make a rumbling sound like thunder. **grum·bled, grum·bling.**

grump·y (grŭm'pi) easily annoyed; ill-tempered; grouchy: *a grumpy old man.* **grump·i·er, grump·i·est; grump·i·ly.**

grunt (grŭnt) **1** gruff, deep sound, especially of hogs. **2** to make such a sound:

The plumber grunted with each tug on the wrench. **3** to speak in jerky growls: *He was so tired he could only grunt his answers.*

gua·no (gwä'nō) the waste matter dropped by sea birds, especially that found on islands near Peru.

guar·an·tee (găr'ən tē') **1** statement or promise that something is what it is said to be, or that it will be repaired or replaced if not satisfactory: *I received a guarantee with my watch.* **2** to make such a promise or statement: *The company guaranteed the watch for one year.* **3** pledge; assurance: *Paying a high price for something is not always a guarantee that it is good.* **4** to make sure: *He thought that a good education would guarantee success.* **5** to say with certainty: *I guarantee you'll have a good time.* **guar·an·teed, guar·an·tee·ing.**

guard (gärd) **1** to protect; keep from harm; defend: *The faithful dog guarded his sleeping master.* **2** person who protects or keeps watch: *A guard is stationed at the bank door.* **3** protection; defense: *Iodine is a guard against infection.* **4** to watch over; control: *to guard a prisoner.* **5** man or group of men employed for control: *prison guards.* **6** soldier or group of soldiers who watch against danger, protect a place from disturbance, entry, etc.; sentry. **7** device to protect against injury: *a guard on an electric saw.* **8** either of two football players on each side of the center of a forward line. **9** one of the defensive players in basketball. **10 keep guard** to watch over. **11 on guard** prepared against attack or danger; watchful: *Be on guard against burglars.* **12 off guard** unprepared: *The teacher caught him off guard with a question about the lesson.* **13 stand guard** to act as a sentry.

guard against to prevent by being careful and watchful: *to guard against disease; to guard against mistakes.*

guard·i·an (gärd'i ən) **1** person or thing that protects: *Congress is the guardian of our liberties.* **2** person who, by law, has the care of another person or his property or both: *The judge appointed a guardian for the orphan.*

Gua·te·ma·la (gwä′tə mä′lə) a country in Central America.

guess (gĕs) **1** notion or opinion formed without specific knowledge: *My* guess *is that it will rain tomorrow.* **2** to form an opinion without certain knowledge: *I'm not sure, but I* guess *this button starts the machine.* **3** to form an estimate or judgment about the cost, size, or value; estimate: *He* guessed *that the cost of the book would be about three dollars.* **4** an estimate: *Make a* guess *as to how wide this box is.* **5** to make a correct answer without having any information: *He* guessed *the riddle.* **6** to think; suppose: *I* guess *I'll stay here.*

guest (gĕst) **1** person who is at another's house for a meal or for a visit; a visitor. **2** person staying at a hotel.

guid·ance (gī′dəns) leadership; direction: *The class is under the* guidance *of an excellent teacher.*

guide (gīd) **1** person or thing that shows the way or directs: *My cousin was my* guide *around the city. This book is a good* guide *in studying birds.* **2** to lead; steer: *Henry* guided *us through the woods. The helmsman* guided *the ship toward the port.* **3** to direct; instruct: *The book* guided *us in the art of making jewelry.* **4** guidebook. **guid·ed, guid·ing.**

guide·book (gīd′bŏŏk′) book of directions and information for travelers.

guided missile an explosive missile that guides itself automatically or is guided from a distance by radioed electric signals. A guided missile has explosives, electronic tubes, and an engine.

guild (gĭld) **1** in the Middle Ages, an organization of men in the same trade whose aim was to keep their standards high and protect their interests. **2** organization of people for a common purpose. (Homonym: gild)

guile (gīl) sly tricks; deceitful ways: *He used* guile *to get his own way.*

guil·lo·tine (gĭl′ə tēn′) **1** heavy knife with a slanting blade that slides up and down in two grooved posts. It was invented during the French Revolution to behead people.

2 (also gĭl′ə tēn′) to cut off a person's head with a guillotine. **guil·lo·tined, guil·lo·tin·ing.**

guilt (gĭlt) **1** the state or fact of having done wrong, sinned, broken a law: *The prosecuting attorney tried to establish the* guilt *of the accused man.* **2** wrong action; crime; sin: *a life of* guilt *and shame.* (Homonym: gilt)

guilt·less (gĭlt′lĭs) free from guilt; innocent. **guilt·less·ly.**

guilt·y (gĭl′tĭ) **1** having done wrong and deserving blame; responsible for a crime and deserving punishment: *Who is* guilty *of telling the secret? The jury declared him* guilty *of robbery.* **2** showing guilt; having to do with guilt: *a* guilty *look; a* guilty *feeling.* **guilt·i·er, guilt·i·est; guilt·i·ly.**

guin·ea fowl (gĭn′ĭ foul) **1** gray-and-white speckled domestic fowl having a small featherless head with a bright red comb. **2** flesh of this fowl as food. Also called **guinea hen.**

Guinea hen, about 18 in. long

guin·ea pig (gĭn′ĭ pĭg) small, plump, gentle animal of the rat family with short legs and short ears. The guinea pig is kept as a pet or for experiments.

Guinea pig, about 9 in. long

guise (gīz) **1** appearance; dress: *This movie is an old story in a new* guise. **2** pretense; false appearance: *The spy hid his intentions under the* guise *of friendship.*

Guitar

Guillotine

gui·tar (gĭ tär′) musical instrument having six strings and shaped somewhat like a violin. It is played by plucking the strings with the fingers or a pick.

gulch (gŭlch) water-worn valley or ravine with steep sides; gorge.

gulf (gŭlf) **1** large bay or arm of a sea or ocean, partly enclosed by land. **2** deep hollow in the earth; abyss. **3** wide separation: *The disagreement left a gulf between the neighbors.*

Gulf of Mexico a curved arm of the Atlantic Ocean, bordered on three sides by Florida, Alabama, Mississippi, Louisiana, Texas, and Mexico.

Gulf Stream warm ocean current, about fifty miles wide, which flows from the Gulf of Mexico north along the coast of the United States and then northeast toward the British Isles.

¹**gull** (gŭl) a large, light-colored sea bird of graceful, often hovering, flight, found everywhere near the coast. It is a valuable scavenger and is protected by law in many places. [¹**gull** is from a Celtic word.]

Herring gull, about 2 ft. long

²**gull** (gŭl) **1** to cheat; outwit. **2** person easily cheated or deceived. [²**gull** is based on one or both of two obsolete words, one (gull) meaning "to guzzle, swallow," the other (gull) meaning "fledgling," "inexperienced bird."]

gul·li·ble (gŭl′ə bəl) easily fooled or deceived. **gul·li·bly.**

gul·ly (gŭl′ĭ) **1** ditch or channel worn by water. **2** to wear channels in: *Heavy rains gullied the hillside.* **gul·lies; gul·lied, gul·ly·ing.**

gulp (gŭlp) **1** to swallow quickly or greedily: *The thirsty boy gulped the water.* **2** big swallow: *to empty a glass in one gulp.* **3** to hold back as if by swallowing; choke back: *to gulp down a sob.*

¹**gum** (gŭm) firm, pink flesh around the teeth. [¹**gum** is a form of an Old English word (gōma) meaning "palate."]

²**gum** (gŭm) **1** a sticky substance obtained from trees. It dissolves in water but hardens in the air. It is used in making glue, drugs, and other products. **2** gum specially prepared in some way, as chewing gum. **3** to stick with mucilage or glue: *to*

gum *down the flap of an envelope.* **gummed, gum·ming.** [²**gum** is from an Old French word (gomme) coming from a Latin word (gummi), which in turn is taken from a Greek word (kommi).]

gum·drop (gŭm′drŏp′) jellylike candy drop covered with sugar crystals.

gun (gŭn) **1** weapon that fires a shot; firearm. A pistol, rifle, or cannon is a gun. **2** tool similar to a gun: *a grease* gun. **3** a shooting of a gun as a salute or signal: *a salute of twenty-one* guns; *a starting* gun. **4 stick to one's guns** to be firm; not yield or retreat.

gun for 1 to hunt with a gun. **2** to look for in order to shoot. **gunned, gun·ning.**

gun·boat (gŭn′bōt′) small warship for use on rivers and coastal waters.

gun·fire (gŭn′fīr′) a shooting off of guns; firing.

gun·lock (gŭn′lŏk′) mechanism of a gun that controls the hammer and fires the charge, especially in old types of guns such as the flintlock.

gun·ner (gŭn′ər) **1** man who fires a gun, especially on a military ship or airplane. **2** hunter who uses a gun.

gun·pow·der (gŭn′pou′dər) explosive powder used in guns, fireworks, blasting, etc.

gun·wale (gŭn′əl) upper edge of the side of a boat.

Gunwale

gup·py (gŭp′ĭ) tiny fresh-water fish often kept in aquariums. **gup·pies.**

gur·gle (gûr′gəl) **1** to make the sound of liquid being poured from a bottle: *The river gently gurgled over the stones.* **2** a bubbling sound: *the gurgles of the happy baby.* **gur·gled, gur·gling.**

gush (gŭsh) **1** to burst out violently; pour forth suddenly: *Oil gushed from the well.* **2** sudden heavy flow: *a gush of lava from a volcano.* **3** to speak with too much enthusiasm, admiration, etc.: "*What a perfectly gorgeous baby,*" gushed *the caller.* **4** such speech: *She speaks with schoolgirl gush.*

fāte, făt, fâre, fär; bē, bĕt; bīte, bĭt; nō, nŏt, nôr; fūse, fŭn, fûr; tōō, tŏŏk; foil; foul; thin; ~~then~~; hw for wh as in *wh*at; zh for s as in u*s*ual; ə for a, e, i, o, u, as in *a*go, lin*e*n, per*i*l, at*o*m, min*us*

329

gush·er (gŭsh′ər) oil well with a strong, natural flow that makes pumping unnecessary.

gust (gŭst) **1** sudden rush of wind. **2** outburst (of feeling): *The comedian was greeted by gusts of laughter.*

gut·ter (gŭt′ər) **1** trough or ditch to carry off water, as a trough along the eaves of a building to catch water from the roof, a ditch along a road, or the part of a roadway close to the curb. **2** to wear a channel in: *Heavy rains guttered the hillside.* **3** of a candle, to melt rapidly and let the wax run down the sides in channels: *As the wind blew its flame, the candle guttered and went out.*

Gutter

guy (gī) **1** wire or rope used to keep something steady: *the guys of a tent pole.* **2** to steady with a guy.

gym (jĭm) gymnasium.

gym·na·si·um (jĭm nā′zĭ əm) large room or building equipped for exercising and indoor sports.

gym·nas·tics (jĭm năs′tĭks) physical exercises such as tumbling, rope climbing, etc., for developing the body.

gyp·sy (jĭp′sĭ) **1** a member of a dark-skinned race of people often traveling and camping in family bands for purposes of trading, fortune-telling, etc. **2** a person who looks or lives like a gypsy. **3** belonging to or like a gypsy; carefree; unconventional: *to live a gypsy life.* **gyp·sies.** Also spelled **gipsy.**

gy·ro·com·pass (jī′rō kŭm′pəs or jī′rō-kŏm′pəs) a compass that is kept pointing north by a gyroscope instead of a magnetic needle.

gy·ro·scope (jī′rō-skōp′) wheel with a heavy rim and an axle mounted so that the axle is free to turn in any direction. When the wheel is spinning, the axle will stay pointing in the same direction, no matter how the outside frame is turned.

Gyroscope

H

H, h (āch) eighth letter of the English alphabet.

hab·it (hăb′ĭt) **1** action repeated so often that one does it either without thought or from a need for it. **2** usual or characteristic way of doing something: *Bats have the habit of sleeping hanging head down.* **3** type of dress worn for a certain activity or by members of a religious group, or the like.

NUN'S   RIDING
Habits

hab·it·a·ble (hăb′ə tə bəl) fit or suitable for living in: *a habitable house.*

hab·i·tat (hăb′ə tăt′) **1** natural home of a plant or animal: *The polar region is the habitat of the polar bear.* **2** dwelling place.

hab·i·ta·tion (hăb′ə tā′shən) **1** act of occupying or inhabiting: *a shack not fit for the habitation of human beings.* **2** place to live in: *There were many kinds of habitation in the new mining town.*

ha·bit·u·al (hə bĭch′ōō əl) **1** acting by force of habit: *a habitual late sleeper; a habitual coffee drinker.* **2** resulting from habit; usual: *her habitual smile.* **ha·bit·u·al·ly.**

ha·ci·en·da (hä′sĭ ĕn′də) house and land of a ranch, estate, or plantation in parts of Latin America settled by Spaniards.

¹hack (hăk) **1** to cut roughly; chop: *He hacked at the tree with a dull ax.* **2** a cut; a gash. **3** to give dry, harsh coughs. **4** a dry, harsh cough. [**¹hack** is a form of an Old English word (haccian).]

²hack (hăk) **1** coach, carriage, or taxi for hire. **2** horse for hire. **3** all-purpose horse. **4** one who does dull work for hire: *a literary hack.* **5** done merely for money; hired: *The artist did hack work to support his children.* [**²hack** is short for "hackney," that is, "a horse for driving or riding."]

had (hăd) See **have.** *She had a cold.*

had·dock (hăd′ək) North Atlantic food fish related to the cod. pl. **had·dock;** rarely, **had·docks.**

had·n't (hăd′ənt) had not.

hadst (hădst) old form of **had** used with *thou.*

haft (hăft) handle of a knife, sword, etc.

hag (hăg) **1** ugly old woman. **2** witch.

hag·gard (hăg′ərd) having a worn and worried look; tired: *the old man's haggard eyes; a haggard expression.* **hag·gard·ly.**

hag·gle (hăg′əl) to argue or dispute, especially over prices. **hag·gled, hag·gling.**

¹hail (hāl) **1** rounded bits of ice, usually small, that fall in showers like rain; hailstones. **2** to rain hailstones. **3** anything that falls like hail: *a hail of rocks; a hail of curses.* [**¹hail** is a form of an Old English word (haegel) with the same meaning.] (Homonym: hale)

²hail (hāl) **1** to call out to: *to hail a taxi.* **2** to greet: *Cheerful voices hailed me at the front door.* **3** a greeting. [**²hail** is from an Old Norse word (heilla). It is related to **¹hale** meaning "healthy." Ancient greetings often started as wishes for good health.] (Homonym: hale)

hail·stone (hāl′stōn′) ball of ice, usually small, that is formed in thunder clouds and sometimes falls to the earth.

hair (hâr) **1** mass of threadlike growths forming the coat or fur of an animal, or such natural growth on a person's skin. **2** any one of these threadlike growths. **3** thickness of a hair; very small distance. **4 not turn a hair** to remain absolutely calm. **5 split hairs** to make tiny or unimportant distinctions in argument: *Stop splitting hairs over minor matters.* (Homonym: hare)

hair·cut (hâr′kŭt′) a cutting of, or a style of cutting, the hair.

hair·dress·er (hâr′drĕs′ər) **1** a barber. **2** a person who cuts or arranges ladies' hair.

hair·pin (hâr′pĭn′) **1** metal or plastic pin with two prongs, used to hold the hair in place. **2 hairpin curve** a U-shaped turn in the road.

hair-rais·ing (hâr′rā′zĭng) terrifying.

hair·y (hâr′ĭ) **1** covered with hair: *The ape is a hairy animal.* **2** of or like hair: *the hairy husk of coconuts.* **hair·i·er, hair·i·est.**

Hai·ti (hā′tĭ) a country in the West Indies, occupying the western part of the same island as the Dominican Republic.

¹hale (hāl) strong; healthy; robust. [**¹hale** is a form of an Old English word (hāl) and is related to **whole.**] (Homonym: hail)

²hale (hāl) to pull or drag by, or as by, force: *He was haled into court.* **haled, hal·ing.** [**²hale** is a variation of **haul.**] (Homonym: hail)

half (hăf) **1** one of two equal parts: *a half of a cake.* **2** forming one of two equal parts (of something): *a half pound.* **3** partly: *These rolls are only half baked.* **4 do something by halves** to do something badly or in an incomplete way. **5 not half bad** rather good. **halves.**

half-breed (hăf′brēd′) person whose parents are of different races.

half brother brother related through one parent only.

half·heart·ed (hăf′här′tĭd) uninterested; not enthusiastic: *He gave only half-hearted attention.* **half·heart·ed·ly.**

half-mast (hăf′măst′) of a flag, flying at some distance below the top of its staff. A flag at half-mast is a sign of mourning.

half-moon (hăf′mōōn′) moon when only half the side we see is lit by the sun.

half sister sister related through one parent only.

half·way (hăf′wā′) **1** at a point that is half the distance (between); midway: *They met halfway between the two towns.* **2** located half the distance between two places: *the halfway mark.* **3** partial; not enough: *the mayor's halfway measures.* **4** partially: *He halfway consented to go.*

hal·i·but (hăl′ə bət) the largest of the flatfish, used as food. pl. **hal·i·but;** rarely, **hal·i·buts.**

hall (hôl) **1** passageway leading to rooms in a building. **2** large room for public gatherings: *the great dining hall.* **3** public building: *a town hall.* **4** a stately home: manor house: *Bracebridge Hall.* **5** a school or college building. (Homonym: haul)

---

fāte, făt, fâre, fär; bē, bĕt; bīte, bĭt; nō, nŏt, nôr; fūse, fŭn, fûr; tōō, tŏŏk; foil; foul; thin; ~~then~~; hw for wh as in *wh*at; zh for s as in u*s*ual; ə for a, e, i, o, u, as in *a*go, lin*e*n, per*i*l, at*o*m, min*u*s

hal·le·lu·jah or **hal·le·lu·iah** (hăl´ə lōō´-yə) **1** cry or song of praise to God. **2** exclamation meaning "Praise be to God."

hal·loo (hə lōō´) a shout to get attention.

hal·low (hăl´ō) to make sacred; set apart or honor as holy: *The ancient battlefield is* hallowed *by the patriots buried there.*

Hal·low·een or **Hal·low·e'en** (hăl´ō ēn´) evening of October 31; eve of All Saints' Day.

hall·way (hôl´wā´) entrance hall or passageway in a building.

ha·lo (hā´lō) **1** in pictures, a ring, disk, or burst of light, surrounding or above the heads of holy persons. **2** ring of light sometimes seen around the sun or moon. **3** glory or splendor that surrounds, as a halo does. **ha·los** or **ha·loes.**

Halo

¹**halt** (hôlt) **1** a stop or pause: *After a short* halt *the parade moved forward.* **2** to come to a stop: *The train* halted *at the crossroads.* **3** to bring to a stop: *The driver* halted *the prancing team of horses.* [¹**halt** comes through French from a form of a German word (halten) meaning "to stop."]

²**halt** (hôlt) **1** to hesitate: *to* halt *in speaking.* **2** lame; crippled. **3 the halt** those who are lame. [²**halt** is a form of an Old English word (healt) meaning "halt in gait."]

hal·ter (hôl´tər) **1** a rope or strap by which an animal is led or tied. **2** noose for hanging criminals. **3** backless blouse that ties around the neck, worn by girls and women.

Halter

halve (hăv) **1** to divide in equal parts: *to* halve *the melon.* **2** to lessen by half: *This machine* halves *the work.* **halved, halv·ing.** (Homonym: have)

halves (hăvz) more than one **half:** *Two* halves *make a whole.*

hal·yard (hăl´yərd) a rope or tackle on a ship for hoisting or lowering a sail, yard, or flag.

ham (hăm) thigh of a hog, especially this part smoked and salted, used as food.

ham·burg·er (hăm´bûr´gər) **1** finely ground beef: *Ann bought two pounds of*

hamburger *for a meat loaf.* **2** small pat of such meat, especially one inserted in a sliced roll or bun.

ham·let (hăm´lĭt) small village: *They lived in a tiny* hamlet *in the Alps.*

ham·mer (hăm´ər) **1** a tool consisting of a wood or metal head across the end of a handle. It is used for driving nails, beating metals, etc. **2** to pound or beat with such a tool: *to* hammer *a sheet of copper into a bowl.*

Hammers

3 to drive into place by pounding: *to* hammer *a nail into a wall.* **4** to strike heavy blows: *He* hammered *on the table with his fist.* **5** to work hard, as if pounding out with a hammer: *to* hammer *away at a problem.* **6** anything like a hammer, as a hammer in a gun or a piano.

ham·mock (hăm´ək) swinging bed or couch made of cloth or a network of cords and suspended by cords at both ends.

Hammock

¹**ham·per** (hăm´pər) large basket with a cover, usually made of wicker: *a picnic* hamper; *a clothes* hamper. [¹**hamper** is from an Old French word (hanapier) meaning "a case to hold a cup."]

²**ham·per** (hăm´pər) to obstruct; hinder: *Her tight skirt* hampered *her walking.* [²**hamper** comes from an Old English word (hampren) with the same meaning.]

ham·ster (hăm´stər) small rodent with a short tail and cheek pouches for carrying food. Hamsters are somewhat larger than mice and are very playful.

hand (hănd) **1** part of the arm below the wrist, consisting of thumb, fingers, palm, etc. **2** carried, operated, or done by the hand: *a* hand *fire extinguisher; a* hand *drill;* hand*work.* **3** to lead or assist with the hand: *He* handed *her into the car.* **4** deftness; skill: *The wall paintings showed the hand of an artist.* **5** person who is skilled at or used to doing something: *an old hand at diplomacy.* **6** assistance: *Give me a hand at opening the window.* **7** active part; influence: *He had a hand in making the rules* *of the club.* **8** workman; employee: *a hired* hand *on the farm.* **9** to pass (something to someone): *Please* hand *me my hat.* **10** handwriting: *I knew his* hand *on the envelope.* **11** a round of a card game, or the cards one player holds. **12** pointer on a dial: *the* hands *of a clock.* **13** a measure of four inches, used chiefly in measuring the height of horses. **14** a pledge; promise: *He gave me his* hand *on the bargain.* **15 hands** (1) possession; control: *The club left the selection of prizes in Jane's* hands. (2) care; supervision: *Make sure you leave the children in good* hands *before you go out.* **16 at hand** very near (in distance or time). **17 on hand** near-by; ready for use. **18 try (one's) hand** to make an attempt. **19 ask for (someone's) hand** to propose marriage. **20 from hand to hand** from one person to the next. **21 hand to mouth** with nothing saved for the future: *to live* hand to mouth.

hand down to bequeath; transmit: *This old sword was* handed down *by my ancestors.*

hand·bag (hănd′băg′) **1** small suitcase or traveling bag. **2** woman's purse to hold change, handkerchief, make-up, etc.

hand·ball (hănd′bôl′) **1** game in which the players bat a ball against a wall, using their hands as rackets. **2** ball used in this game.

hand·book (hănd′bŏŏk′) small, handy guidebook or manual.

hand·cuff (hănd′kŭf′) **1** one of a pair of hinged metal bracelets, joined by a short chain, that locks when clasped around the wrist. Used to control prisoners. **2** to restrain with handcuffs.

Handcuffs

hand·ful (hănd′fŏŏl′) **1** amount one hand can hold: *a handful of clay; a handful of nails.* **2** very small number or amount: *Only a handful of people came.*

hand·i·cap (hăn′dĭ kăp′) **1** disadvantage; hindrance: *the handicap of a sprained ankle.* **2** disadvantage placed on a better contestant or an advantage granted to a poorer contestant in order to give both

a fair chance in a race, contest, or game. **3** game or contest in which handicaps are given. **4** to hinder: *The ball player was* handicapped *by a sore finger.* **hand·i·capped, hand·i·cap·ping.**

hand·i·craft (hăn′dĭ krăft′) **1** skillful use of the hands: *Excellent* handicraft *is shown in these carved dolls.* **2** any art requiring the use of hands: *One of the earliest* handicrafts *is pottery.* **3** article made by hand: *This store sells Mexican* handicrafts.

hand·i·work (hăn′dĭ wûrk′) **1** work done by the hands; manual craftsmanship. **2** one's personal work: *This garden is Mary's* handiwork.

hand·ker·chief (hăng′kər chĭf) **1** square piece of cloth for wiping the face, nose, or eyes. **2** kerchief worn around the neck.

han·dle (hăn′dəl) **1** part of a tool, vessel, etc., grasped in the hand. **2** to hold or touch with the hands: *Don't offer a biscuit if you have* handled *it.* **3** to operate; control: *I am too sleepy to* handle *a car.* **4** to manage; treat: *How do you* handle *a crying baby?* **5** to buy and sell; deal in: *A grocer* handles *foods, soaps, brooms, etc.* **han·dled, han·dling.**

handle bar curved steering bar of a bicycle.

hand·maid·en (hănd′mād′ən) female servant or attendant. Also called **handmaid.**

hand·rail (hănd′rāl′) a rail at the side of a stairway, platform, or the like.

hand·some (hăn′səm) **1** of pleasing appearance; good-looking. **2** ample; generous: *The finder of the watch received a handsome reward.* **hand·some·ly.**

hand·spring (hănd′spring′) a somersault in which only one's outstretched palms touch the ground as one whirls and lands on one's feet.

hand·writ·ing (hănd′rī′tĭng) **1** way a person writes: *The old man's* handwriting *was clear and bold in spite of his age.* **2** writing done by hand, not typed or printed: *The secretary made corrections in* handwriting *in the typed letter.*

hand·y (hăn′dĭ) **1** skillful; deft: *He is* handy *with tools.* **2** convenient: *a* handy *basket for carrying groceries.* **hand·i·er, hand·i·est; hand·i·ly.**

---

fāte, făt, fâre, fär; bē, bĕt; bite, bĭt; nō, nŏt, nôr; fūse, fŭn, fûr; tōo, tŏŏk; foil; foul; thin; ~~then~~; hw for wh as in *wh*at; zh for s as in u*s*ual; ə for a, e, i, o, u, as in *a*go, lin*e*n, per*i*l, at*o*m, min*u*s

333

hang (hăng) **1** to swing free from overhead;
dangle: *A lamp* hung *from the ceiling.* **2** to
float in the upper air: *Dark clouds* hung
over the city. **3** to suspend from a nail, hook,
or the like: *to* hang *a picture; to* hang *up a
coat.* **4** to execute on the gallows: *The
murderer was* hanged *at eight o'clock.* **5** to
cling to; seek support from: *The baby* hung
on its mother's skirt. **6** to droop: *The leaves*
hang *wilted in the sun.* **7** to cause or allow
to droop: *John* hung *his head in shame.*
8 way a thing hangs: *It took a long time
to get the right* hang *to the draperies.* **9** to
fall or drape in a certain way: *This curtain*
hangs *in graceful folds.* **10** attach by
hinges or the like: *to* hang *a door.* **11** to
depend: *War or peace* hangs *on the dictator's
actions.* **12** to threaten: *Disaster* hung *over
the mountain village.* **13** knack: *to get the*
hang *of riding a bicycle.* **hung** (for definition 4, **hanged**), **hang·ing.**

hang·ar (hăng'ər) shed for housing airplanes and other aircraft.

hang·er (hăng'ər) **1** a device upon which
something may be hung: *a coat* hanger.
2 person who hangs (something): *a paper-
hanger.*

hang·ing (hăng'ing) **1** execution in which
a person is suspended by the neck until
dead. **2 hangings** drapery for walls,
windows, etc.

hang·nail (hăng'nāl') shred of loose skin
close to the fingernail.

hank (hăngk) skein, especially of yarn.

Ha·nuk·kah or **Cha·nuk·kah** (hä'nŏŏ kä)
Feast of the Dedication (of the Temple at
Jerusalem, 165 B.C.), a Jewish festival last-
ing eight days, usually in December.

hap (hăp) **1** chance; fortune. **2** to happen;
befall. **happed, hap·ping.**

hap·haz·ard (hăp'hăz'ərd) **1** happening by
chance; not planned: *a* haphazard *conversation.* **2** by chance; at random: *books piled*
haphazard *on the table.* **hap·haz·ard·ly.**

hap·less (hăp'lĭs) unlucky. **hap·less·ly.**

hap·ly (hăp'lĭ) perhaps; by chance.

hap·pen (hăp'ən) **1** to take place; occur:
What happened *when the lion escaped?* **2** to
come about by chance: *It* happened *that
we were indoors when the storm came.*

happen on or **upon** to find by chance;
meet with: *The farmer* happened *upon
buried treasure while plowing his fields.*

happen to 1 to come by chance: *He* happened *to walk in at that moment.* **2** to
become of: *The author speculated as to
what* happened *to the lion when he was
caught.*

hap·pen·ing (hăp'ən ing) something that
takes place; event; occurrence.

hap·pi·ness (hăp'ĭ nĭs) **1** condition of being glad or contented. **2** good fortune.

hap·py (hăp'ĭ) **1** having or expressing gladness or pleasure: *a* happy *person; a* happy
smile. **2** lucky; fortunate: *It was a* happy
day when he got the job. **hap·pi·er, hap-
pi·est; hap·pi·ly.**

har·ass (hăr'əs or hə răs') **1** to annoy or
worry constantly: *All that summer at the
seashore, the family was* harassed *by bad
weather.* **2** to trouble by raids or pillage:
Outlaw bands harassed *the villagers, burning their huts and driving off their cattle.*

har·bor (här'bər) **1** protected part of a
sea, lake, or river which serves as a shelter
for ships; a port. **2** any place of shelter or
safety. **3** to shelter or lodge: *He was forced
to* harbor *an escaped convict.* **4** to keep in
one's mind: *to* harbor *a grudge.*

hard (härd) **1** solid; firm; rigid: *Is the ice*
hard *enough to skate on?* **2** harsh; stern;
exacting: *The colonel was* hard *in his discipline.* **3** not easy; difficult: *a* hard
problem. **4** with difficulty: *He was breathing* hard *after a long run.* **5** strong; forceful; vigorous: *a* hard *blow on the chin.*
6 with energy or effort: *He studied* hard
for the test. **7** heavy; severe: *a* hard *rain;
a* hard *winter.* **8** of the letters **c** and **g,** pronounced as in "cat" and "go." **9 hard
coal** kind of coal that burns with comparatively little soot and smoke; anthracite.
10 hard water water that contains certain
minerals, such as lime, and does not readily
form lather with soap. **11 hard of hearing**
somewhat deaf. **12 hard times** needy
period: *War brings* hard times *to everyone.*

hard-boiled (härd'boild') **1** of an egg,
boiled until white and yolk become solid.
2 unfeeling; hardened by experience;
tough: *a* hard-boiled *judge.*

hard·en (här'dən) to make or become
hard: *We* harden *clay by baking it. He*
hardened *his body by exercise. The ground*
hardened *in the winter.* **2** to make pitiless:
to harden *one's heart.*

hard·head·ed (härd′hĕd′ĭd) not easily swayed by feeling; practical; shrewd: *a* hardheaded *businessman.*

hard·heart·ed (härd′här′tĭd) not showing pity or sympathy. **hard·heart·ed·ly.**

har·di·hood (här′dĭ hŏŏd′) boldness; daring.

hard·ly (härd′lĭ) **1** barely; scarcely: *There is* hardly *enough food for all of us.* **2** severely: *Gwen was treated* hardly *by her stepmother.* **3** with difficulty: *Frank's success was won very* hardly.

hard·ness (härd′nĭs) condition of being unyielding or hard: *The* hardness *of the diamond is such that it can cut glass.*

hard·ship (härd′shĭp) something that is hard to endure, such as hunger, privation, cold, etc.: *The explorers suffered great* hardships *when their food and fuel ran short.*

hard·ware (härd′wâr′) articles made from metal. Pots, pans, tools, locks, nails, etc., are hardware.

hard·wood (härd′wŏŏd′) **1** strong, heavy wood from certain broad-leafed trees such as the maple or oak. **2** made of such wood: *a* hardwood *floor.* **3** tree that yields hardwood.

har·dy (här′dĭ) **1** strong; able to bear suffering or hardship: *Soldiers must be* hardy *and fit to stand forced marches.* **2** daring; bold: *Testing rocket planes calls for a* hardy *spirit.* **har·di·er, har·di·est; har·di·ly.**

hare (hâr) member of the rabbit family that jumps rather than runs. It has longer ears and more powerful legs than the rabbit and does not burrow. Some hares are called rabbits, such as the jack rabbit. (Homonym: hair)

Varying hare, about 18 in. long

hare·bell (hâr′bĕl′) **1** a plant with a slender stalk and blue flowers shaped like bells. **2** flower of this plant.

hark (härk) to listen; listen closely, used especially as an exclamation.

hark back to to go back to or refer to:

This superstition harks back to *the Middle Ages.*

hark·en (här′kən) to listen closely; pay attention to. Also spelled **hearken.**

harm (härm) **1** injury; hurt; damage. **2** to hurt; injure; damage: *Be careful not to* harm *the plants.* **3** wrong; evil: *I meant no* harm *in daring him to climb the tree.*

harm·ful (härm′fəl) hurtful; causing damage; injurious: *Reading in a dim light can be* harmful *to the eyes.* **harm·ful·ly.**

harm·less (härm′lĭs) not doing, wanting to do, or able to do any harm: *It's just a* harmless *little garter snake.* **harm·less·ly.**

har·mon·i·ca (här mŏn′ə kə) small musical instrument with metal reeds, sounded by blowing and sucking air through a set of holes; mouth organ.

har·mo·ni·ous (här mō′nĭ əs) **1** free from quarreling; agreeable; peaceable: *Family life that is* harmonious *can make a home an enjoyable place.* **2** combining to form a pleasing and agreeable whole: *The* harmonious *colors gave the room a restful air.* **3** having a sweet or pleasant sound; melodious: *The voices in the boys' choir were* harmonious. **har·mo·ni·ous·ly.**

har·mo·nize (här′mə nīz′) **1** to bring into agreement or accord: *The father tried to* harmonize *the different wishes of his sons.* **2** to combine musical tones to make chords. **3** to engage in part singing. **4** to put colors together in a pleasing way. **har·mo·nized, har·mo·niz·ing.**

har·mo·ny (här′mə nĭ) **1** a getting on well together; agreement: *the* harmony *between the different groups.* **2** a going well together; a pleasing combination: *There was* harmony *of color and design in the room's decoration.* **3** pleasing combination of musical sounds. **4** arrangement of musical tones to form chords. **har·mo·nies.**

har·ness (här′nĭs) **1** arrangement of straps by which an animal is driven and hitched to a vehicle. **2** to put a harness on; attach by means of a harness:

Harness

---

fāte, făt, fâre, fär; bē, bĕt; bīte, bĭt; nō, nŏt, nôr; fūse, fŭn, fûr; tōō, tŏŏk; foil; foul; thin; then; hw for wh as in what; zh for s as in usual; ə for a, e, i, o, u, as in ago, linen, peril, atom, minus

Joel harnessed *the horses.* **3** to make useful or ready for use: *By building dams we* harness *water power.*

harp (härp) **1** large triangular musical instrument with many strings, played by plucking the strings with the fingers. **2** to play a harp.

harp on to repeat or talk about at great length: *Amos* harped on *his troubles from morning till night.*

Woman playing harp

harp·ist (här'pĭst) person who plays a harp.

Harpoons

har·poon (här pōōn') **1** barbed spear with a rope attached, either shot from a gun or thrown, used to catch whales and large fish. **2** to strike or kill with a harpoon: *The sailor* harpooned *a huge whale.*

harp·si·chord (härp'sĭ kôrd') musical instrument, developed before the piano, with a keyboard and wire strings that are plucked by quill or leather points.

har·row (hăr'ō) **1** farm implement with sharp iron teeth, or sharp steel disks. It is drawn by a horse or tractor over plowed land to break up the soil or cover up seed. **2** to draw a harrow over: *The farmer* harrowed *his fields after the plowing.* **3** to distress or trouble; disturb painfully: *The thought of her ill mother* harrowed *Mimi.*

har·ry (hăr'ĭ) **1** to torment; annoy: *He* harried *the leader with many questions.* **2** to keep raiding; plunder: *The pirates* harried *the coasts of Spain.* **har·ried, har·ry·ing.**

harsh (härsh) **1** unkind; hard; severe: *She was wounded by his* harsh *words.* **2** rough; coarse: *That material is too* harsh *to put next to the baby's skin.* **3** unpleasant; disagreeable: *a* harsh *sound.* **harsh·ly.**

harsh·ness (härsh'nĭs) quality or condition of being harsh: *the* harshness *of his voice.*

hart (härt) male of the red deer over five years old; stag. The female is called a **hind.** (Homonym: heart)

har·vest (här'vĭst) **1** a crop: *There was a large* harvest *of apples this year.* **2** the gathering of a crop of grain, fruit, etc.: *The farmer hired men for the wheat* harvest. **3** to gather in; reap: *The boys are* harvesting *corn in the fields.* **4** time for gathering of a crop, usually late summer or early fall. **5** a result or reward: *His good grades are the* harvest *of hard work.*

har·vest·er (här'vĭs tər) **1** person who gathers a crop; reaper. **2** machine for gathering crops.

harvest moon full moon in late September when it often appears unusually large and bright.

has (hăz) form of **have** used with *he, she, it,* or a name word: *Mary* has *a very pretty little pony.*

hash (hăsh) **1** mixture of meat and vegetables chopped into small pieces and fried together. **2** to chop into small pieces. **3 make a hash of** to make a mess of: *He made a hash of his part in the play.*

has·n't (hăz'ənt) has not: *Joe* hasn't *gone.*

haste (hāst) **1** a hurry; rush: *The travelers left in great* haste *to catch their train.* **2 make haste** to hurry: *Please* make haste; *we are already late.* **hast·ed, hast·ing.**

has·ten (hā'sən) **1** to hurry; move with speed: *He* hastened *to the bank before closing time.* **2** to cause to move faster or be done more quickly: *Everyone worked hard to* hasten *the work.*

hast·y (hās'tĭ) **1** quick; hurried; speedy: *a short,* hasty *visit.* **2** carelessly said or done; rash: *His* hasty *remarks made many enemies.* **3** quick-tempered; fiery. **hast·i·er, hast·i·est; hast·i·ly.**

hat (hăt) type of head covering. A man's hat usually has a crown and brim; women's hats are of fanciful shapes.

¹hatch (hăch) **1** an opening in a deck, floor, or the like. **2** the cover for such an opening; a trap door.

Hatch

[**¹hatch** is a form of an Old English word (hæcc) meaning "a grating."]

hatch — Hawaiian

²hatch (hăch) **1** to cause (eggs) to produce young: *The hen* hatched *all the eggs.* **2** to produce from eggs: *The incubator* hatched *a fine brood of chickens.* **3** to yield young: *All the eggs* hatched. **4** to come out of the shell: *These chicks* hatched *yesterday.* **5** a brood: *a hatch of chicks.* **6** to plot: *The rebels* hatched *a scheme to get arms.* [²hatch is a word of unknown origin.]

hatch·er·y (hăch'ə rĭ) place where eggs, especially those of fish or poultry, are hatched. **hatch·er·ies.**

hatch·et (hăch'ĭt) **1** small, light ax with a short handle. A hatchet is used with one hand. **2 bury the hatchet** to make peace; agree to end a quarrel.

hate (hāt) **1** to feel a strong dislike for; detest; loathe: *The coach* hates *a poor sport.* **2** extreme or intense dislike: *The soldier felt no* hate *toward the enemy.* **hat·ed, hat·ing.**

hate·ful (hāt'fəl) **1** detestable; loathsome; deserving hate: *Ingratitude is a* hateful *vice.* **2** full of hate: *The woman gave the man a* hateful *look.* **hate·ful·ly.**

hath (hăth) old form of **has.**

ha·tred (hā'trĭd) hate; intense dislike.

haugh·ty (hô'tĭ) too proud and disdainful; arrogant: *The* haughty *actress would not speak to the chorus girls.* **haugh·ti·er, haugh·ti·est; haugh·ti·ly.**

haul (hôl) **1** to pull with force; tug with effort: *The dogs will* haul *the sled.* **2** to move; transport: *The moving van will* haul *the furniture away.* **3** amount of fish taken in one pull of the net. **4** loot; booty; captured cargo: *The pirate had a valuable* haul *in the captured ship.* **5** distance over which a thing is pulled or drawn: *From St. Louis to California was a long* haul *for the wagon train.* **6** a strong pull or tug. **7** to change course, especially of a sailing ship. (Homonym: hall)

haunch (hônch) **1** fleshy part of the hip of a man or animal: *The wolf sat on his* haunches *and glared at me.* **2** leg and loin of animal which is used for food.

haunt (hônt) **1** to visit often or repeatedly; to frequent: *The boys* haunt *the drugstore on weekends.* **2** to trouble or bother con-

stantly: *The memory of the accident will probably* haunt *him for a time.* **3** place frequently visited: *The swimming pool is a favorite summer* haunt.

haunt·ed (hôn'tĭd) **1** frequently visited or inhabited by ghosts: *a* haunted *wood.* **2** continually beset: *a mind* haunted *by sad memories.*

have (hăv) **1** to hold; possess; own: *They* have *a new car.* **2** to possess or show a mental or physical trait: *Claudette* has *tact and charm.* **3** to hold in the mind; to know: *I* have *a plan for raising money.* **4** to put up with; tolerate: *I won't* have *anyone with bad manners at my table!* **5** to accept; take: *Will you* have *a glass of milk?* **6** to experience: *Did you* have *a nice time?* **7** to cause (a person) to do something: *I want to* have *the artist paint my portrait.* **8** to bear the parent or parents of: *Mrs. Green* had *a baby last week. The Greens* have *six children in all.* **9** helping word used to show completion of an action: *I* have *studied my lessons. I shall* have *written three letters when I finish this one. We* have *been here three weeks.*

have to to be obliged or forced to; must: *You* have to *eat to live. We* had to *walk instead of ride.*

had, hav·ing. See also **has.** (Homonym: halve)

ha·ven (hā'vən) **1** a sheltered harbor or port for ships. **2** any place of shelter or safety: *The weary travelers found* haven *at the inn.*

have·n't (hăv'ənt) have not: *We* haven't *seen him all day.*

hav·er·sack (hăv'ər săk') a soldier's or hiker's canvas bag for provisions.

hav·oc (hăv'ək) ruin; destruction: *The hurricane caused* havoc *in the small town.*

Ha·wai·i (hə wī'ē) the 50th State of the United States, made up of a group of islands located in the North Pacific, 2090 miles from the mainland of the United States.

Ha·wai·ian (hə wī'ĭn) **1** of Hawaii, its people, or language. **2** citizen of Hawaii or person of Hawaiian descent. **3** the language of the Hawaiian people.

---

fāte, făt, fâre, fär; bē, bĕt; bīte, bĭt; nō, nŏt, nôr; fūse, fŭn, fûr; tōō, tŏŏk; foil; foul; thin; then; hw for wh as in *wh*at; zh for s as in u*s*ual; ə for a, e, ĭ, o, u, as in *a*go, lin*e*n, per*i*l, at*o*m, min*u*s

337

Hawaiian Islands the group of islands in the North Pacific which make up Hawaii.

Goshawk, about 2 ft. long

¹hawk (hôk) **1** any of several birds of prey, smaller than an eagle, with a curved beak and sharp talons. Some kinds of hawks are trained to hunt other birds and small game. **2** to hunt with a hawk or falcon. [¹**hawk** is a greatly changed form of an Old English word (hafuc).]

²hawk (hôk) to peddle or cry out goods for sale. [²**hawk** is from another English word (hawker) meaning "peddler."]

³hawk (hôk) to clear the throat noisily and forcibly. [³**hawk** probably comes from the sound made when the throat is cleared in this way.]

haw·ser (hô′zər) strong rope used for towing and mooring ships.

haw·thorn (hô′thôrn′) a thorny shrub or tree which has fragrant white, pink, or red blossoms in the spring, and red or orange berries in the fall.

hay (hā) **1** grass, clover, alfalfa, etc., cut and dried for food for cattle, horses, etc. **2** to cut grass, etc., for hay.

hay·cock (hā′kŏk′) small pile of hay shaped like a dome and stacked in a field.

hay fever sneezing, watery eyes, etc., caused by the pollen of certain plants, especially ragweed.

hay·field (hā′fēld′) field set aside for growing hay.

hay·loft (hā′lôft′ or hā′lŏft′) in a barn, the upper part where hay is stored.

hay·mow (hā′mou′) place in a barn where hay is stored.

hay·rick (hā′rĭk′) haystack.

hay·stack (hā′stăk′) large pile of hay stacked in the open air.

haz·ard (hăz′ərd) **1** chance of damage or loss; risk; danger: *It is a hazard to drive fast on the highway.* **2** to leave to chance; take the risk of: *People who are careless with fire hazard their lives.* **3** to offer; venture: *to hazard a guess.*

haz·ard·ous (hăz′ər dəs) dangerous; risky. **haz·ard·ous·ly.**

¹haze (hāz) **1** light fog, mist, or smoke in the air: *Through the haze, we could see the outline of mountains.* **2** confusion of thought; daze: *His mind was in such a haze after the lawyer's questioning that he wasn't sure of his own name.* [¹**haze** is from **hazy,** a word that may be a form of an Old French word (hasu) meaning "gray."]

²haze (hāz) to make (someone) do unpleasant tasks or foolish tricks. **hazed, haz·ing.** [²**haze** is from an Old English word (haser) meaning "to irritate."]

ha·zel (hā′zəl) **1** shrub or small tree that bears nuts that are good to eat. **2** the wood of this tree. **3** light, reddish brown.

ha·zel·nut (hā′zəl nŭt′) the nut of the hazel.

ha·zy (hā′zĭ) **1** misty; smoky: *a hazy view.* **2** vague; confused: *a hazy memory of one's childhood.* **ha·zi·er, ha·zi·est; ha·zi·ly.**

H-bomb (āch′bäm′) hydrogen bomb.

he (hē) **1** boy, man, or male animal that has been named just before: *Where is Charles? He is upstairs.* **2** male: *a he goat.* **3 he who** any person who: *We believe that he who works hard will be rewarded.*

head (hĕd) **1** the part of the body of man and most animals which contains the brain, eyes, ears, nose, and mouth. **2** mind; intelligence: *a good head for figures.* **3** poise; calmness: *Keep your head when an accident happens.* **4** picture or sculpture of a head: *a marble head of Caesar.* **5** round, tight, top part of a plant: *a head of cabbage; a head of cauliflower.* **6** knob on top of a tool, etc.: *the head of a hammer; the head of a nail.* **7** top part; main end: *the head of a staircase; the head of a bed.* **8** front end: *at the head of a parade.* **9** source: *the head of a river.* **10** top position: *at the head of the government.* **11** person in top position: *the head of the firm.* **12** to occupy a top position: *to head the firm.* **13** to be at the front of: *to head a parade.* **14** each; a single one (of persons or animals): *fifty head of cattle.* **15** topic or title: *He arranged his report under three heads.* **16** the main side of a coin, often stamped with a head. **17** main; chief: *a head gardener.* **18** to go toward: *to head south.* **19** coming from the front: *a head wind.* **20** pressure or amount of pressure: *The head of steam is 60 pounds.* **21 bring to a head** to cause a crisis. **22 give a horse his head** to let a horse choose its own pace. **23 go to one's head** or **turn one's**

head to make someone so vain as to affect his judgment. **24 head on** with the front part first: *to collide* head on; *a* head-on *collision.* **25 over one's head** too hard or strange to understand: *That theory is way* over my head.

head off 1 to get in front of and turn aside: *to* head off *the cattle.* **2** to avert: *to* head off *a collision.*

head·ache (hĕd'āk') pain in the head.

head·dress (hĕd'drĕs') something worn on the head, or an arrangement of the hair, designed to improve one's appearance, mark one's station, or provide comfort.

Headdress

head·first (hĕd'fûrst') with the head in front: *dive* headfirst *into a pool.*

head·ing (hĕd'ĭng) **1** title, as of a newspaper story. **2** topic or title at the beginning of a chapter, paragraph, etc.

head·land (hĕd'lənd) point of land jutting into the sea, especially a cliff.

head·light (hĕd'līt') bright light on the front of an automobile, train, or other vehicle to illuminate the road ahead.

head·line (hĕd'līn') **1** title or summary of a news story printed in large type at its beginning. **2** important; worthy of a headline: *a bit of* headline *news.*

head·long (hĕd'lông' or hĕd'lŏng') **1** with the head in front; headfirst: *to fall* headlong; *a* headlong *dive.* **2** without thinking; recklessly: *to dash* headlong *in front of a car.* **3** reckless; rash: *a* headlong *rush.*

head·man (hĕd'mən) leader; chief; highest official: *We met the* headman *of the African village.* **head·men.**

head·quar·ters (hĕd'kwôr'tərz) place from which orders are sent out; center of control; main office: *a police* headquarters.

head·strong (hĕd'strông') determined to have one's own way; stubborn; rash.

head·wa·ters (hĕd'wô'tərz) the small stream or streams that are the source of a river.

head·way (hĕd'wā') **1** forward motion; progress: *He is not making much* headway *with his plans.* **2** clear space overhead, for passing under a bridge, arch, etc.

head wind wind that blows exactly opposite to the direction in which a ship, airplane, etc., is moving.

heal (hēl) **1** to cure; bring back to good health: *A doctor tries to* heal *sick people.* **2** to get well; become healthy: *The cut* healed *quickly.* (Homonym: heel, he'll)

health (hĕlth) **1** a being well; freedom from sickness. **2** condition of the body: *good* health; *bad* health. **3** a health toast to a person's health and happiness.

health·ful (hĕlth'fəl) giving health; good for the health: *Milk is a* healthful *drink. Utah has a* healthful *climate.* **health·ful·ly.**

health·y (hĕl'thĭ) **1** in good health: *a* healthy *child.* **2** showing health: *a* healthy *appetite.* **health·i·er, health·i·est.**

heap (hēp) **1** things lying one on another; pile: *a* heap *of rocks.* **2** to pile; put in a heap: *The dirty clothes were* heaped *in the middle of the floor.* **3** to fill; load: *to* heap *a plate with food.* **4** to give in large amounts: *to* heap *gifts upon someone.*

hear (hîr) **1** to be aware of sound through the ears: *A deaf person can't* hear. *I* hear *a siren.* **2** to listen to; pay attention to: *Please* hear *what I have to say.* **3** to be told; get news: *I* heard *about your new puppy.* **4** to get a message (from): *Did you* hear *from Bill?* **heard, hear·ing.** (Homonym: here)

heard (hûrd) See **hear.** (Homonym: herd)

hear·er (hîr'ər) person who hears; listener.

hear·ing (hîr'ĭng) **1** ability to perceive sound by the ears: *His* hearing *isn't very good.* **2** chance to be heard: *The judge granted him a* hearing. **3** distance over which sound can be heard: *Keep the children within* hearing.

heark·en (här'kən) harken.

hear·say (hîr'sā') **1** rumor; gossip: *We know this only by* hearsay. **2** told to, but not actually known by, the speaker: *It is only* hearsay *evidence.*

hearse (hûrs) automobile or other vehicle for carrying the casket at a funeral.

heart (härt) **1** muscular organ in the chest that pumps blood through the body.

Human heart and its ordinary picture

---

2 center; core: *the* heart *of the city; get to
the* heart *of the matter.* **3** seat of one's deepest feelings and ideals; true nature: *a*
heart *of gold; a* heart *of stone.* **4** sympathy; tenderness: *Verna's* heart *was
touched by the child's loneliness.* **5** courage:
Alfred had the heart *for heroic deeds.* **6** enthusiasm: *Put more* heart *into your work.*
7 design shaped somewhat like a human
heart. **8** any one of a suit of playing cards
marked with red, heart-shaped designs.
9 after one's own heart that suits or
pleases one perfectly: *She is a girl* after my
own heart. **10 at heart** in (one's) inmost
being: *I have your welfare* at heart. **11 by
heart** perfectly; by memory. **12 take
heart** to cheer up; have courage. **13 take
to heart** to think about seriously; be
deeply affected. **14 with all one's heart**
sincerely or very gladly. (Homonym: hart)

heart·bro·ken (härt′brō′kən) very sad;
suffering from grief. **heart·bro·ken·ly.**

heart·en (här′tən) to give courage; cheer:
to be heartened *by good news.*

heart·felt (härt′fĕlt′) deeply felt; sincere:
our heartfelt *thanks.*

hearth (härth) **1** floor,
usually of flat stone,
in front of a fireplace.
2 fireplace as a sym-
bol of home: *The
traveler longed for his own* hearth. Hearth

hearth·stone (härth′stōn′) **1** flat stone
forming a hearth. **2** center of a home.

heart·less (härt′lĭs) without feeling or
affection; cruel. **heart·less·ly.**

heart·y (här′tĭ) **1** cordial; friendly: *a*
hearty *welcome.* **2** healthy: *a hearty old
man.* **3** vigorous; enthusiastic: *a hearty
laugh.* **4** large; heavy: *a hearty meal.*
heart·i·er, heart·i·est; heart·i·ly.

heat (hēt) **1** warmth, especially great
warmth: *the heat of a fire; the* heat *of the
sun.* **2** hot weather: *Does the* heat *bother
you?* **3** intense feeling; excitement: *Jack
said things in the* heat *of the argument that
he later regretted.* **4** to make hot or warm: *A
furnace* heats *the house.* **5** to become hot or
warm: *The water is* heating *on the stove.*
6 single race or contest in a series: *Jim won
the first* heat *and John the second.*

heat up to make or become hot or warm: *I*
heated up *the food. An engine* heats *up.*

heat·er (hē′tər) stove, furnace, radiator,
etc., for warming a room or house, or for
heating water.

heath (hēth) **1** in Great Britain, flat wasteland, often overgrown with shrubs; moor.
2 any one of several low-growing shrubs,
including heather, found on wasteland.

hea·then (hē′thən) **1** a worshiper of false
gods or of no god. **2** having to do with
such worship: *a* heathen *idol.* **3** crude
person; barbarian; savage. **4** barbaric;
rude: *a* heathen *custom.*

heath·er (hĕth′ər) tiny-leaved shrub with
stalks of small, pale-purple blossoms, common in Scotland and England.

heat shield anything that protects something from heat; especially, a part of a
space ship that protects it against the intense heat of re-entry.

heave (hēv) **1** to raise or lift with effort:
The workmen heaved *the last stone to the
top of the wall.* **2** to throw; hurl: *Herbert
can* heave *the shot 30 feet.* **3** distance a
thing is thrown: *That is a long* heave *for a
boy of his age.* **4** effort in lifting or throwing: *With a tremendous* heave, *he put the
bundle on the truck.* **5** to force out with an
effort; utter with exertion: *to* heave *a
great sigh.* **6** to rise and fall rhythmically,
as the chest in heavy breathing. **heaved** or
hove, heav·ing.

heav·en (hĕv′ən) **1** dwelling place of God
and angels, and of the souls of the good
after death. **2** any place or state of great
happiness. **3 the heavens** the sky, where
the sun, moon, and stars appear.

heav·en·ly (hĕv′ən lĭ) **1** of the dwelling
place of God; divine: *the* heavenly *choirs.*
2 beyond compare; very beautiful: *a*
heavenly *day.* **3** of the sky; celestial: *The
sun, moon, and stars are* heavenly *bodies.*

heav·i·ness (hĕv′ĭ nĭs) a being heavy;
weight.

heav·y (hĕv′ĭ) **1** hard to lift or carry;
weighty: *This box is too* heavy *for me to
move.* **2** of great amount or force: *a* heavy
rain; a heavy *blow on the head.* **3** loaded;
weighed down: *The trees are* heavy *with
apples.* **4** grievous; harsh: distressing: *The
punishment was too* heavy *for him to bear.*
5 cast down with sorrow; sad: *Her heart was*
heavy *at parting from her home.* **6** dull;
ponderous: *a* heavy *manner.* **7** powerful;

loud; deep: *He had a very* heavy *bass voice.* **8** thick; dense; coarse: *a heavy black line;* heavy *fog.* **9** overcast; gloomy: *a* heavy *sky.* **10** hard to digest: *rich* heavy *foods.* **heav·i·er, heav·i·est; heav·i·ly.**

He·brew (hē′brōō) **1** one of an ancient people in Palestine. **2** person considered as one of their descendants; a Jew. **3** ancient language of the Jews. **4** the modern form of the language, used in present-day Israel. **5** having to do with the Hebrew language or people.

hec·tic (hĕk′tĭk) **1** wild or exciting: *She spent a* hectic *day rushing from one thing to another.* **2** feverish; flushed and hot.

he'd (hēd) **1** he had: *If he'd wanted to come, he could have.* **2** he would: *He said he'd go when he was ready.* (Homonym: heed)

hedge (hĕj) **1** a thick row of bushes or small trees serving as a fence: *There is a* hawthorn hedge *between the two houses.* **2** to put a fence of bushes or trees around: *We* hedged *the garden with flowering shrubs.* **3** to avoid being frank or direct: *He* hedged *when asked about the missing cookies.* **hedge in** to surround; hem in: *The army* hedged in *the enemy.* **hedged, hedg·ing.**

hedge·hog (hĕj′hŏg′) **1** an insect-eating, small animal, whose back is covered with fur and stiff hairs which harden into spines at the ends. It can defend itself by rolling into a ball. **2** porcupine.

Hedgehog, about 10½ in. long

hedge·row (hĕj′rō′) a row of bushes or small trees forming a hedge.

heed (hēd) **1** to pay attention to: *He* heeded *his friend's advice.* **2** careful attention; notice: *He paid no* heed *to the warning.* (Homonym: he'd)

heed·less (hēd′lĭs) not attentive; careless. **heed·less·ly.**

¹heel (hēl) **1** back part of the human foot. **2** the part of a boot, shoe, or stocking that covers the heel, or the block of leather or rubber beneath it. **3** anything like a heel in position or shape: *a* heel *of bread.* **4** to

put a heel on a shoe or boot. **5** of a pet, to follow closely behind a person. [**¹heel** is a form of an Old English word (hēla) with the same meaning as **1.**] (Homonyms: heal, he'll)

²heel (hēl) to lean to one side; list: *The ship* heeled *over when the cargo shifted.* [**²heel** is a form of an Old English word (hieldan) meaning "to slope."] (Homonyms: heal, he'll)

heif·er (hĕf′ər) a young cow.

height (hīt) **1** distance from the head to the foot, or from the ground to the top: *a man's* height; *the* height *of a tower.* **2** the distance something rises above the earth or sea level; altitude: *The* height *of the mountain is 6,213 feet.* **3** highest point: *The author reached the* height *of his career at the age of 30.*

height·en (hī′tən) **1** to make higher or more intense: *They* heightened *the fence around the house. His words* heightened *the tension.* **2** to become higher or more intense: *The tension in the room* heightened.

heir (âr) **1** person who receives or has the right to receive money, property, title, etc., at the death of the owner. **2 fall heir to** to inherit: *She fell heir to her mother's jewelry.* (Homonyms: air, e'er, ere)

heir·ess (âr′ĭs) woman or girl who inherits money, property, a title, etc.

heir·loom (âr′lōōm′) piece of personal property which has been in a family for generations.

held (hĕld) See **hold.** *She* held *the cat.*

hel·i·cop·ter (hĕl′ə kŏp′tər) a kind of airplane supported and driven by horizontal rotating wings above it. A helicopter can rise and descend straight up or down, and also stay still in the air.

Helicopter

he·li·o·trope (hē′lĭ ə trōp′) **1** a plant with sweet-smelling white or purple flowers. **2** reddish purple.

hel·i·port (hĕl′ə pôrt′) landing place for helicopters.

he·li·um (hē′lĭ əm) a chemical element. It is a light, colorless gas that does not com-

---

fāte, făt, fâre, fär; bē, bĕt; bīte, bĭt; nō, nŏt, nôr; fūse, fŭn, fûr; tōō, tŏŏk; foil; foul; thin; then; hw for wh as in *wh*at; zh for s as in usual; ə for a, e, i, o, u, as in ago, linen, peril, atom, minus

bine with other elements. It is used in weather balloons and in scientific work.

hell (hĕl) **1** in some religions, the place where the wicked are punished forever after death. **2** any place or condition of extreme misery or evil.

he'll (hēl) he will; he shall. (Homonyms: heal, heel)

hel·lo (hĕ lō′) **1** a greeting; salutation: *He gave me a cheerful "Hello" as we passed.* **2** an exclamation of surprise. **hel·los.**

helm (hĕlm) **1** a rudder handle, tiller, or a ship's wheel. **2** the complete steering gear of a ship. **3** the post of control or command: *When Mr. Green took the* helm, *the business prospered.*

Helm

hel·met (hĕl′mĭt) hat or enclosing globe of metal, plastic, or other rigid material, to protect the head from missiles, blows, pressure, or other dangers: *a soldier's helmet; a fireman's helmet.*

ROMAN

MODERN INDUSTRIAL
Helmets

helms·man (hĕlmz′mən) person who steers or guides a ship or boat; pilot. **helms·men.**

help (hĕlp) **1** to aid; assist: *We help Mother by doing the dishes.* **2** to keep from; avoid: *He could not help dropping the glass.* **3** support; aid; assistance: *The Red Cross gives help in time of disaster.* **4** a hired servant or servants: *Father pays the help each week.* **5** a person or thing that aids or assists: *Your favors were a big help at the party.* **6** remedy or solution: *There is no help for her illness.*

help oneself to to serve oneself with: *Please help yourself to more meat.*

help·er (hĕl′pər) person who aids or assists another person.

help·ful (hĕlp′fəl) giving aid; useful: *Jane was helpful around the house.* **help·ful·ly.**

help·ing (hĕl′pĭng) **1** aiding; assisting: *a helping hand.* **2** a portion of food served at table, or the amount of food served: *Eunice asked Father for a second helping of carrots.*

help·less (hĕlp′lĭs) unable to take care of oneself: *a helpless invalid.* **help·less·ly.**

hel·ter-skel·ter (hĕl′tər skĕl′tər) pell-mell; in confused haste.

¹**hem** (hĕm) **1** the folded edge of a garment, which is sewn down so that there is a double thickness. **2** to sew down the folded edge of a piece of cloth. **3** to surround; enclose; encircle: *Indians tried to hem in the soldiers.* **hemmed, hem·ming.** [¹**hem** is the unchanged form of an Old English word whose original meaning was probably "piece of enclosed land."]

²**hem** (hĕm) a sound which resembles a slight clearing of the throat, used to attract attention or express doubt.

hem and haw 1 to speak in a hesitating way. **2** to try to avoid giving an answer. **hemmed, hem·ming.** [²**hem** is the imitation of a sound.]

hem·i·sphere (hĕm′ə sfîr′) **1** half of a sphere or globe. **2** any half of the Earth's surface. The equator divides the Earth into the Northern Hemisphere and Southern Hemisphere. A meridian divides the Earth into the Eastern Hemisphere, which includes Europe, Asia, Africa, and Australia, and the Western Hemisphere, which includes North and South America.

hem·lock (hĕm′lŏk′) **1** an evergreen tree of the pine family. **2** the wood of this tree. **3** a poisonous herb.

he·mo·glo·bin (hē′mə glō′bĭn) red coloring matter of the blood. Hemoglobin carries oxygen from the lungs to the tissues of the body.

hemp (hĕmp) a plant whose fibers are used for making rope and coarse cloth.

hen (hĕn) **1** female of the domestic fowl that lays eggs to be used as food; chicken. The male is called a **rooster** or **cock.** **2** female of other birds.

Hen

hence (hĕns) **1** from this time: *School starts two weeks hence.* **2** from this place: *a mile hence.* **3** therefore; for this reason.

hence·forth (hĕns′fôrth′) from now on.

hence·for·ward (hĕns′fôr′wərd) from this time on; henceforth.

her (hûr) **1** a girl, or woman, or female animal spoken or written about. It is used instead of **she** in the following ways: *I like*

herald   herring

her. *Give* her *the pencil. I wrote* her *a letter. Bring the milk to* her. *I sat beside* her. **2** of or belonging to her: *Sonia wore* her *new dress to the party.* **3** made or done by her: *She showed* her *paintings to me.*

her·ald (hĕr′əld) **1** official who made public announcements or carried messages for a ruler during medieval times. **2** to tell of or announce the coming of: *A fanfare of trumpets* heralded *the opening of the festival.* **3** a person or thing which announces the coming of another person or event.

herb (ûrb or hûrb) **1** a flowering plant with a soft juicy stem, which lives for one season. **2** leaves of such a plant used for medicine, for food, or for flavoring.

herb·age (ûr′bĭj or hûr′bĭj) grass and herbs.

her·biv·or·ous (hûr bĭv′ə rəs) feeding on vegetable matter; plant-eating, as cows.

herd (hûrd) **1** group of animals, especially cattle or sheep, that travel and feed together; flock; drove. **2** to gather or keep (together) or to drive: *He* herded *the cattle toward the gate.* **3** to tend (cattle, sheep, etc.): *He* herded *sheep for a living.* **4** flock or mob of people. (Homonym: heard)

herd·er (hûr′dər) herdsman.

herds·man (hûrdz′mən) herder. **herds·men.**

here (hîr) **1** to or toward this place: *Please come* here. **2** in this place or spot: *The vase is* here. **3** at this point: *Is it* here *that we turn?* **4** in answering a roll call, "Here" means present. (Homonym: hear)

here·a·bout (hîr′ə bout′) or **here·a·bouts** (hîr′ə bouts′) near here; around this place.

here·af·ter (hîr ăf′tər) **1** after this time; in the future. **2 the hereafter** life after death; world to come.

here·by (hîr bī′) by this means: *The mayor announced, "I* hereby *declare a holiday."*

he·red·i·tar·y (hə rĕd′ə tĕr′ĭ) **1** passed from parent to child, or from generation to generation. **2** passed from possessor to heir. **he·red·i·tar·i·ly.**

he·red·i·ty (hə rĕd′ə tĭ) **1** the passing on of physical traits, etc., from parent to child, or from generation to generation. **2** the traits, etc., thus passed. **he·red·i·ties.**

here·in (hîr ĭn′) in here; in this place.

here's (hîrz) here is.

her·e·sy (hĕr′ə sĭ) belief different from accepted belief, especially of a religion. **her·e·sies.**

her·e·tic (hĕr′ə tĭk) person whose beliefs are different from accepted beliefs, especially in religion.

here·to·fore (hîr′tə fôr′) before this time; until now; formerly.

here·up·on (hîr′ə pŏn′ or hîr′ə pôn′) at this point; on this; at once.

here·with (hîr with′ or hîr wĭth′) with this; at this point.

her·it·age (hĕr′ə tĭj) thing which belongs to a person by birth; inheritance; tradition.

her·mit (hûr′mĭt) person who withdraws from society and lives alone, especially to lead a holy life.

her·mit·age (hûr′mə tĭj) home of a hermit.

he·ro (hîr′ō) **1** one who does a courageous or noble deed. **2** man admired for bravery or noble qualities. **3** leading male character in a story, poem, or play. **he·roes.**

he·ro·ic (hĭ rō′ĭk) of or having to do with a hero; fit for or worthy of a hero; courageous; noble.

her·o·ine (hĕr′ō ĭn) **1** brave or noble woman. **2** woman admired for bravery or noble qualities: *Many young girls think of Florence Nightingale as their* heroine. **3** leading female character in a story, poem, or play.

her·o·ism (hĕr′ō ĭz′əm) great courage; heroic conduct.

her·on (hĕr′ən) long-legged, marsh-loving bird with a long, slender neck and long bill. It feeds on frogs and fish.

Great blue heron, about 4 ft. high

her·ring (hĕr′ĭng) **1** small food fish caught in the North Atlantic Ocean and the streams running into it where they go to lay their eggs. Sardines are young or small herring. **2** any of several kinds of fish related to the herring.

---

fāte, făt, fâre, fär; bē, bĕt; bīte, bĭt; nō, nŏt, nôr; fūse, fŭn, fûr; tōō, tŏŏk; foil; foul; thin; ~~then~~;
hw for wh as in *wh*at; zh for s as in u*s*ual; ə for a, e, i, o, u, as in *a*go, lin*e*n, per*i*l, at*o*m, min*u*s

hers (hûrz) **1** of or for her: *She did the work alone, and the credit is all* hers. **2** the one or ones belonging to her: *I have my skates, but she has lost* hers.

her·self (hər sĕlf′) **1** her own self: *She cut herself with the knife. She is ashamed of herself.* **2** her normal self; her true self: *Gwen isn't* herself *today.* **3** used for emphasis: *She* herself *told me about it.* **4 by herself (1)** alone: *She was all by herself in the lonely house.* **(2)** without any help: *She did this all by herself.*

he's (hēz) **1** he is: *Do you know if he's going?* **2** he has: *Yes, he's said so several times.*

hes·i·tant (hĕz′ə tənt) hesitating; uncertain. **hes·i·tant·ly.**

hes·i·tate (hĕz′ə tāt′) **1** to pause or stop because of doubt or inability to decide: *He who hesitates is lost.* **2** to pause or falter in speaking; stammer. **hes·i·tat·ed, hes·i·tat·ing.**

hes·i·ta·tion (hĕz′ə tā′shən) **1** a pausing in uncertainty or doubt; a wavering: *After some hesitation, she bought the blue dress.* **2** a faltering in speech; stammer.

hew (hū) **1** to chop; hack: *The knight hewed right and left with his trusty sword.* **2** to shape by chopping or chipping with, or as with, an ax or adz: *Early settlers hewed beams from logs.* **hewed** or **hewn, hew·ing.** (Homonym: hue)

hewn (hūn) **1** shaped with a broad ax or adz: *The floor was supported by hewn beams.* **2** See **hew.**

hi·ber·nate (hī′bər nāt′) to spend the winter in a sleeplike state. *Bears, woodchucks, and frogs hibernate.* **hi·ber·nat·ed, hi·ber·nat·ing.**

hi·ber·na·tion (hī′bər nā′shən) the act of hibernating.

hi·bis·cus (hī bĭs′kəs or hĭ bĭs′kəs) any of a group of plants, shrubs, or trees with large colorful flowers. The red hibiscus is the state flower of Hawaii.

hic·cup or **hic·cough** (hĭk′ŭp) **1** an involuntary gasp accompanied by a short, sharp sound due to air pressure on the vocal chords. **2** to have hiccups.

hick·o·ry (hĭk′ə rĭ) **1** a nut-bearing hardwood tree of North America. **2** the wood of this tree. **hick·o·ries.**

hid (hĭd) See ¹**hide.** *She hid her money under a mattress.*

hid·den (hĭd′ən) **1** out of sight; concealed: *to dig for* hidden *treasure.* **2** See ¹**hide.**

¹**hide** (hīd) **1** to put or keep out of sight: *She said to hide the candy before the baby saw it.* **2** to keep secret; conceal: *He tried to hide the truth from us.* **3** to conceal oneself; be concealed: *Quick, hide in the closet!* **hid, hid·den** or **hid, hid·ing.** [¹**hide** is a form of an Old English word (hȳdan).]

²**hide** (hīd) the skin of an animal, either raw or made ready for use: *The old trapper traded hides for supplies.* [²**hide** is a form of an Old English word (hȳd).]

hide-and-seek (hīd′ənd sēk′) children's game in which all the players hide, except the one who tries to find them.

hid·e·ous (hĭd′ĭ əs) extremely ugly; horrible; frightful: *Some Halloween masks are hideous to look at. The hideous crime had shocked everyone.* **hid·e·ous·ly.**

hie (hī) to hurry; go in haste: *Quick! Hie thee to the hills!* **hied, hy·ing** or **hie·ing.** (Homonym: high)

hi·er·o·glyph·ic (hī′ər ə glĭf′ĭk) **1** a picture or symbol standing for a word or syllable. **2** having to do with picture writing: *a hieroglyphic inscription.* **3 hieroglyphics** writing (of the ancient Egyptians and others) which used pictures and symbols instead of letters.

Hieroglyphics

hi-fi (hī′fī′) high fidelity.

high (hī) **1** far above the ground or sea level: *a high plateau.* **2** tall: *That is a high tower. It is 300 feet high.* **3** to an elevated point, place, or level; to or at a great altitude: *We will climb high on our expedition.* **4** chief; important; above others: *He is a high government official.* **5** noble; great in character: *He was an honest, trustworthy man with high aims.* **6** great; above the usual; extreme: *a high speed; high temperatures.* **7** above the usual pitch; in the upper range of a voice or instrument: *a high voice; a high note.* **8 leave high and dry** to put in an isolated and helpless condition; maroon: *He deserted me and left me high and dry.* **9 the high seas** the open ocean: *He sailed the high seas.* **10 in high spirits** happy; merry: *Everyone on the pleasure cruise was in high spirits.* **11 high tide** the time (twice a day) at which the water at a given point of a sea or ocean is at its highest level. **12 high time** the latest possible time: *It is* high time *for us to get started.* (Homonym: hie)

high fidelity the reproduction of sound (as by a radio or phonograph) so that it sounds very much like the original.

high·land (hī'lənd) **1** high or mountainous land. **2 the Highlands** mountainous region in northern and western Scotland.

high·ly (hī'lĭ) **1** in a great degree; very much; extremely: *a taste for* highly *seasoned food; a* highly *educated man.* **2** favorably; with approval: *The man's employer spoke* highly *of his work.*

high·ness (hī'nĭs) **1** state or quality of being noble or lofty: *a* highness *of purpose.* **2 Highness** a title given to people of royal families: *His Royal* Highness, *Prince Charles.*

high·road (hī'rōd') main road; highway.

high school a school that is above elementary school and below college.

high-strung (hī'strŭng') tense; sensitive; excitable; nervous.

high·way (hī'wā') **1** main road. **2** any public road.

high·way·man (hī'wā'mən) person who robs travelers on a highway or public road. **high·way·men.**

hike (hīk) **1** long walk or march: *The Boy Scout troop went for a* hike *in the country.* **2** to walk or march a long way. **hiked, hik·ing.**

hi·lar·i·ous (hĭ lâr'ĭ əs) gay and merry in a noisy way. **hi·lar·i·ous·ly.**

hi·lar·i·ty (hĭ lăr'ə tĭ) noisy mirth; gaiety.

hill (hĭl) **1** elevation of the earth that is less than a mountain. **2** heap or mound of earth: *an ant* hill. **3** a heap of earth around a plant, or the heap and plant: *a* hill *of beans.*

hill·ock (hĭl'ək) small hill.

hill·side (hĭl'sīd') side or slope of a hill.

hill·top (hĭl'tŏp') top of a hill.

hill·y (hĭl'ĭ) having many hills; not level: *through* hilly *country.* **hill·i·er, hill·i·est.**

hilt (hĭlt) handle of a dagger or sword. *Hilt*

him (hĭm) boy, man, or male animal spoken or written about: *I see* him. *Pass* him *the bread.* (Homonym: hymn)

him·self (hĭm sĕlf') **1** his own self: *He hid* himself *under the table. He is proud of* himself. **2** a form of **him,** used for emphasis: *I saw the boy* himself. **3** his normal self; his real self: *Relaxing in the country, he was more like* himself. **4 by himself** (**1**) alone: *He stood under the tree* by himself. (**2**) without any help: *He built the scooter* by himself.

¹hind (hīnd) at the back; rear: *the* hind *legs of a dog.* **hind·er, hind·most** or **hind·er·most.** [**¹hind** goes back to an Old English word (hindan) meaning "from behind."]

²hind (hīnd) female of the deer, especially the red deer. The male is a **hart.** [**²hind** is the unchanged form of an Old English word.]

hin·der (hĭn'dər) to get in the way of; put obstacles in the way of; impede; prevent: *Are you going to help or* hinder *while I'm cooking? The sand* hindered *our walking.*

hind·quar·ter (hīnd'kwôr'tər) **1** either side of the hind part of a carcass of beef, veal, lamb, etc. **2 hindquarters** haunches.

hin·drance (hĭn'drəns) **1** person or thing that gets in the way; obstacle. **2** a hindering.

Hin·du (hĭn'dōō) **1** member of a large group of people in India who speak certain languages related to the languages of Europe. **2** followers of Hinduism. **3** having to do with the main religion or racial groups of India.

Hin·du·ism (hĭn'dōō ĭz'əm) a religion and social system practiced in India, which grew out of an ancient religion. Hinduism now includes some practices from Buddhism and other religions.

hinge (hĭnj) **1** jointed pieces of metal on which a gate, door, lid, etc., swings to open and close. **2** a natural movable joint, such as the knee or the joining cartilage of a clamshell. **3** to attach by hinges; furnish with hinges. **4** to swing on a hinge. **hinge on** to hang or depend on: *Good habits* hinge on *self-control.* **hinged, hing·ing.**

---

fāte, făt, fâre, fär; bē, bĕt; bīte, bĭt; nō, nŏt, nôr; fūse, fŭn, fûr; tōō, tŏŏk; foil; foul; thin; ~~then~~; hw for wh as in *wh*at; zh for s as in u*s*ual; ə for a, e, i, o, u, as in *a*go, lin*e*n, per*i*l, at*o*m, min*u*s

hint (hĭnt) **1** roundabout suggestion; indirect or slight indication: *I might guess the riddle if you give me a hint. A hint of spring was in the air.* **2** to suggest or refer to in a roundabout way: *She hinted that I should polish my shoes.*

hip (hĭp) **1** part of the body that curves outward on each side below the waist. **2** joint where the leg joins the body: *Marguerite broke her hip.*

hip·po·pot·a·mus (hĭp´ə pŏt´ə məs) large African river animal with tough, practically hairless hide, a huge mouth, and short legs. **hip·po·pot·a·mus·es** or **hip·po·pot·a·mi.**

Hippopotamus, about 14 ft. long

hire (hīr) **1** to employ for pay: *The manager hired a secretary.* **2** to pay for the use of: *to hire a truck.* **3** money paid as wages or as rent: *That man is not worth his hire.*

hire out 1 to give services for pay. **2** to allow others to use for pay: *He hired out his truck for $10 a day.* **hired, hir·ing.**

his (hĭz) **1** of or belonging to him: *Fortunately his fall wasn't serious.* **2** made or done by him: *When his homework was done, he went out to play.* **3** inhabited by him: *All sorts of odd things filled his room.* **4** the thing or things belonging to him: *My tie is blue, and his is red.*

hiss (hĭs) **1** to make a sound like that of the letter "s": *The steam hissed in the radiator.* **2** hissing sound: *the hiss of a snake.* **3** to show dislike or anger by hissing.

his·to·ri·an (his tôr´ĭ ən) person who writes a history; an expert in history.

his·tor·ic (his tôr´ĭk) **1** having to do with history: *in historic times.* **2** famous because of connection with history: *a historic spot.*

his·tor·i·cal (his tôr´ə kəl) **1** of history: *a historical event.* **2** based on history: *a historical play.* **his·tor·i·cal·ly.**

his·to·ry (hĭs´tə rĭ) **1** record of past facts and events: *We shall read a history of the United States.* **2** past events or facts connected with a thing, person, nation, etc.: *the weird history of that family.* **3** branch of learning which deals with past events: *a class in history.* **his·tor·ies.**

hit (hĭt) **1** to give a blow to; strike: *He hit the bully on the chin.* **2** to strike against; bump: *He hit his head on a rack when he stood up.* **3** to cause suffering to; distress: *The bad news hit him suddenly.* **4** to strike something aimed at: *The arrow hit the target.* **5** stroke that reaches its target: *three hits and two misses.* **6** to find; come or light upon: *After several guesses, he finally hit the right answer.* **7** success: *Everyone liked the song so well that it became a big hit.* **8** in baseball, a ball so struck that the batter can reach base safely. **9 hard hit** affected deeply: *He was hard hit by his father's death.*

hit the mark to achieve exactly what one attempts.

hit, hit·ting.

hitch (hĭch) **1** to attach; tie; fasten: *Please hitch the horse to the wagon.* **2** to pull with a short jerk: *Tom hitched up his trousers.* **3** a short jerk: *Tom gave his trousers a nitch.* **4** obstacle; delay; halt: *There was a sudden hitch in the program.* **5** a kind of knot; especially a temporary knot.

Hitches

hitch·hike (hĭch´hīk´) to travel by asking for rides along the way. **hitch·hiked, hitch·hik·ing.**

hitch·hik·er (hĭch´hī´kər) one who hitchhikes.

hith·er (hĭth´ər) here: *Come hither!*

hith·er·to (hĭth´ər tōō´) up to this time.

hit·ter (hĭt´ər) one who hits.

hive (hīv) **1** box or house for honeybees. **2** swarm of bees living in this place. **3** place where there are crowds of busy people: *The big store was a hive of activity.* **4** to put (bees) into a hive. **5** to enter or live together in a hive. **hived, hiv·ing.**

hives (hīvz) a rash that makes the skin itch. It is often caused by an allergy to something.

hoard (hôrd) **1** to collect and save: *The squirrel hoarded nuts for the winter.* **2** thing collected: *The miser had a hoard of gold coins.* (Homonym: horde)

hoar·frost (hôr´frôst´) white frost; tiny drops of dew frozen on plants, trees, the ground, etc.; rime.

hoarse (hôrs) **1** rough, harsh, or gruff in sound: *A cold had made Jane's voice hoarse.* **2** having a hoarse voice: *Jane was hoarse from a bad cold.* **hoars·er, hoars·est; hoarse·ly.** (Homonym: horse)

hoar·y (hôr′ĭ) **1** white or gray with age. **2** ancient; deserving honor and respect. **hoar·i·er, hoar·i·est.**

Hobble

hob·ble (hŏb′əl) **1** to limp; walk with difficulty. **2** to tie the legs of an animal together with a short rope to keep it from straying. **3** a cord used for this purpose. **4** a limping walk. **hob·bled, hob·bling.**

hob·by (hŏb′ĭ) a favorite interest aside from one's regular occupation: *His favorite hobby is collecting postage stamps.* **hob·bies.**

hob·by·horse (hŏb′ĭ hôrs′) **1** a stick with a horse's head, on which children pretend to ride a real horse. **2** wooden horse on rockers or on a merry-go-round.

hob·gob·lin (hŏb′gŏb′lĭn) **1** troublesome elf. **2** imaginary thing that causes fear; bogey.

hob·nail (hŏb′nāl′) a thick-headed nail, attached to the bottom of a heavy shoe to lessen wear or to prevent slipping.

Hobnails

ho·bo (hō′bō) person without regular work who wanders from place to place; a tramp. **ho·bos** or **ho·boes.**

hock·ey (hŏk′ĭ) **1** an outdoor field game played between two teams of eleven players each. Each player carries a stick with a curve at one end which is used to drive a ball into the opponents' goal. **2 ice hockey** a type of hockey played on ice by two teams of six skaters each. A rubber disk instead of a ball is used.

hod (hŏd) **1** a bucket for carrying coal; coal scuttle. **2** a V-shaped trough on a long handle, for carrying bricks or mortar. For picture, see next column.

hodge·podge (hŏj′pŏj′) a jumble; mixture: *a hodgepodge of toys.*

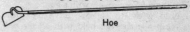

Hoe

hoe (hō) **1** a digging tool with a flat blade on a long handle. **2** to dig with a hoe: *Early in the morning Barney hoed his garden.* **hoed, hoe·ing.**

hog (hŏg) **1** full-grown pig. **2** a greedy or dirty person.

hogs·head (hŏgz′hĕd′) **1** large cask. **2** a liquid measure, equal to 63 gallons.

hoist (hoist) **1** to lift up; raise, especially by means of tackle, cranes, etc.: *to hoist the sails of a ship.* **2** apparatus for raising things: *The elevator is one kind of hoist.* **3** a lift; push: *a hoist over the wall.*

¹hold (hōld) **1** to have or keep in the hand; grasp; grip; clasp: *to hold a bouquet.* **2** a grasp or grip: *He took a good hold on the bat before swinging it.* **3** to keep in a certain pose or manner: *She held her head erect.* **4** to contain: *This jug holds one gallon.* **5** to keep by force; protect; defend: *to hold a fort.* **6** to control; keep back; check: *It is better to hold your temper before you speak out angrily.* **7** to believe; accept: *Most Americans hold the opinion that democracy is desirable.* **8** to carry on; observe; celebrate: *to hold a meeting; to hold a church service.* **9** to occupy; keep: *He held the office of secretary.* **10** to stay the same; be true: *The same rule holds for everyone.*

hold forth to speak at length; to lecture or preach: *He held forth for two hours.*

hold in to check; keep back; restrain.

hold out to last; remain firm; stand: *The pioneers held out against hunger and cold all winter.*

hold over 1 to postpone for later consideration: *We will hold over the new business until the next meeting.* **2** to keep for an additional period: *The movie is being held over another week.*

MASON'S

COAL

Hods

---

fāte, făt, fâre, fär; bē, bĕt; bīte, bĭt; nō, nŏt, nôr; fūse, fŭn, fûr; tōō, tŏŏk; foil; foul; thin; then; hw for wh as in what; zh for s as in usual; ə for a, e, i, o, u, as in ago, linen, peril, atom, minus

hold up 1 to delay; hinder: *He held up our departure because he got up late.* 2 to rob by force, usually with a gun.

hold with to approve of; agree with: *Grandma does not* hold with *all the new cooking methods.*

held, hold·ing. [¹**hold** is a form of an Old English word (hāldan).]

²**hold** (hōld) space for cargo in a ship. [²**hold** is probably from two words, ¹**hold** and a Dutch word (hol).]

hold·er (hōl′dər) 1 person who owns or possesses something: *He was the holder of many awards.* 2 a device for holding on to something or keeping something in: *He used the box as a holder for pencils.*

hold·ing (hōl′ding) something owned; property, especially real estate or stocks: *The company has large holdings in the West.*

hold·up (hōld′ŭp′) 1 armed robbery or attempt to rob. 2 a delay: *a traffic holdup due to an accident.*

hole (hōl) 1 an opening in or through something: *a hole in the tablecloth.* 2 a cavity in a solid body or mass: *a hole in a tooth.* 3 place hollowed in the ground by an animal; burrow: *A woodchuck lives in a hole.* 4 on a golf course, a sunken cup into which a ball is driven. 5 to drive into a hole: *The golfer holed the ball in four strokes.*

hole up to go into seclusion or hiding; hibernate: *He holed up in a mountain cabin. Bears hole up in the winter.* **holed, hol·ing.** (Homonym: whole)

hol·i·day (hŏl′ə dā′) 1 day of freedom from work fixed by law or custom: *Thanksgiving is a holiday.* 2 period of time which a person takes off from work; vacation: *We will spend a month's holiday at the lake.* 3 gay; carefree: *We are in a holiday mood at Christmas.*

ho·li·ness (hō′lĭ nĭs) 1 a being holy or sacred: *The pilgrim felt the holiness of the shrine.* 2 **His Holiness** title given to the Pope.

Hol·land (hŏl′ənd) a country in northwestern Europe; the Netherlands.

hol·low (hŏl′ō) 1 empty inside; not solid: *The squirrel hid in the hollow tree.* 2 sunken: *She had hollow cheeks after her illness.* 3 deep, muffled, and echoing: *We heard hollow sounds from the cave.* 4 unreal; insincere; false: *He spoke hollow words of praise.* 5 an empty space; cavity. 6 a sunken place; valley; space between hills. **hollow out** to make hollow; scoop out: *The children hollowed out the pumpkin.* **hol·low·ly.**

hol·low·ness (hŏl′ō nĭs) 1 the condition of being hollow; emptiness. 2 lack of meaning; lack of sincerity: *The hollowness of his promises was soon evident.*

hol·ly (hŏl′ĭ) 1 a shrub or small tree with stiff, prickly, glossy evergreen leaves and bright red berries. 2 branches of this shrub used as a decoration: *Decorate the halls with holly.* **hol·lies.**

Holly

hol·ly·hock (hŏl′ĭ hŏk′) 1 a tall plant with hairy leaves and large flowers of various colors growing from the main stem. 2 its flower.

hol·ster (hōl′stər) a leather pistol case, attached to belt or saddle.

ho·ly (hō′lĭ) 1 belonging to or having to do with God; sacred: *the Holy Bible; a holy day.* 2 very good; saintly: *a holy man; a holy life.* **ho·li·er, ho·li·est.** (Homonym: wholly)

Holster

Holy Land Palestine.

hom·age (hŏm′ĭj) 1 reverence; respect: *We pay homage to the memory of a great leader.* 2 an act by which a vassal promised faithful service to his lord.

home (hōm) 1 place where a person lives; residence. 2 family group: *He kept his home together though business made moving frequent.* 3 one's native country, state, or town: *His home is Ireland.* 4 place where an animal is commonly found; habitat: *The polar bear's home is the Arctic.* 5 an institution for care or relief: *an orphan home; a home for the aged.* 6 the goal in some games. 7 to the point aimed at; to the heart: *The carpenter drove the nail home. The minister's sermon struck home.* 8 to or at home: *They are home from their travels.* 9 having to do with the home; domestic: *William and John have a happy home life.*

home·less (hōm′lĭs) having no home.

home·ly (hōm'lĭ) **1** homelike; plain; simple: *The speaker used* homely *everyday words*. **2** plain featured: *Lincoln had a* homely *but noble face*. **3** not polished or refined: *the* homely *but hospitable manners of this part of the country*. **home·li·er, home·li·est.**

home·made (hōm'mād') made, or as if made, at home: *to like* homemade *food*.

home run (hōm'rŭn') in baseball, a hit which allows the batter to score a run by rounding all the bases without stopping.

home·sick (hōm'sĭk') longing for home; sad because away from home: *She was* homesick *during her first weeks at college*.

home·spun (hōm'spŭn') **1** cloth made from yarn spun at home; coarse, loosely woven cloth. **2** made of homespun, as a dress. **3** plain; simple; unpolished: *a quiet* homespun *manner*.

home·stead (hōm'stĕd') **1** a house with the land and buildings which are around it. **2** 160-acre tract of public land given to a settler by the government on condition that he live on it and improve it.

home·ward (hōm'wərd) **1** toward home: *We started* homeward. **2** bound for home: *a* homeward *journey*.

home·wards (hōm'wərdz) towards home: *We walked* homewards.

home·work (hōm'wûrk') school lessons to be done at home: *The teacher assigned 12 arithmetic examples for* homework.

hom·i·cide (hŏm'ə sīd') the killing of a person by another, either by intention or by accident.

hom·i·ny (hŏm'ə nĭ) hulled Indian corn, coarsely ground, used as a food.

ho·mo·gen·ized milk (hō mŏj'ə nīzd' mĭlk) milk in which the fat particles are so finely divided and mixed that they do not rise to the top as cream.

hom·o·graph (hŏm'ə grăf') word that is spelled the same as another but has a different meaning. This book gives the origins of all homographs listed in it.

hom·o·nym (hŏm'ə nĭm) word that sounds the same as another but has a different spelling and meaning. "Deer" and "dear" are homonyms.

Hon·du·ras (hŏn dŏŏr'əs or hŏn dyŏŏr'əs) a country in Central America on the Caribbean Sea and the Pacific Ocean.

hon·est (ŏn'ĭst) **1** not in the habit of lying, cheating, or stealing; trustworthy: *An* honest *man will tell the truth even if it hurts*. **2** open; frank: *an* honest *face*. **3** genuine; without fraud: *an* honest *price*. **hon·est·ly.**

hon·es·ty (ŏn'ĭs tĭ) truthfulness; sincerity; uprightness: *One of the rarest kinds of* honesty *is to be able to admit being wrong*.

hon·ey (hŭn'ĭ) sweet, thick, sticky liquid made by bees from the nectar of flowers.

hon·ey·bee (hŭn'ĭ bē') a bee that makes honey. Large colonies are kept in hives to produce honey.

Honeybee, about ¾ in. long

hon·ey·comb (hŭn'ĭ kōm') **1** a framework of six-sided cells with walls of wax built by bees to hold honey and eggs. **2** to pierce with system of holes or tunnels: *The beam was* honeycombed *with ant tunnels*.

Honeycomb

hon·ey·moon (hŭn'ĭ mōōn') **1** holiday taken by a man and woman just after their wedding. **2** to take a honeymoon: *They will* honeymoon *in Canada*.

hon·ey·suck·le (hŭn'ĭ sŭk'əl) vine with dark green leaves and sweet-smelling flowers shaped like trumpets. The flowers are white, yellow, or red.

honk (hŏngk) **1** call of a wild goose. **2** any sound like this call: *the* honk *of an automobile horn*. **3** to make or cause to make such a sound: *We heard the geese* honk. *I* honked *the automobile horn*.

hon·or (ŏn'ər) **1** good name; good repute; nobility: *It is a matter of* honor *to do one's duty*. **2** high esteem; great respect; admiration: *The club paid Joe a great* honor *by re-electing him president*. **3** token of esteem and respect; award: *The returning soldiers were heaped with* honors *by the whole town*. **4** to show great respect;

---

fāte, făt, fâre, fär; bē, bĕt; bīte, bĭt; nō, nŏt, nôr; fūse, fŭn, fûr; tōō, tŏŏk; foil; foul; thin; then; hw for wh as in *wh*at; zh for s as in u*s*ual; ə for a, e, i, o, u, as in *a*go, lin*e*n, per*i*l, at*o*m, min*u*s

esteem: *We* honor *the founders of our country.* **5** to present with tokens of respect: *Lindberg was* honored *with a parade up Broadway.* **6** a cause of respect or esteem: *Sheila is an* honor *to her family.* **7** to show respect for: *to* honor *his mother's wishes.* **8** to accept and pay when due: *to* honor *a check at the bank.* **9 Honor** title of respect for a judge: *your* Honor; *his* Honor. **10 on one's honor** on trust to do something expected or required: *You are* on your honor *not to cheat during the test.*

hon·or·a·ble (ŏn'ər ə bəl) **1** worthy of respect: *His behavior is always* honorable. **2** having and showing regard for truth and high principles: *an* honorable *man.* **3** with merit and good name: *an* honorable *discharge.* **4 Honorable** title of respect for certain officials. **hon·or·a·bly.**

hon·or·ar·y (ŏn'ə rěr'ĭ) bestowed as a courtesy or mark of respect; without the usual duties, fees, or requirements: *an* honorary *member of a club; an* honorary *degree from a college.*

hood (hŏŏd) **1** a head covering that leaves only the face exposed, sometimes attached to a robe or coat. **2** anything like this in looks or use. **3** the cover of an automobile engine. **4** to cover with a hood.

Hood

-hood suffix meaning **(1)** "the condition of being": *mother*hood; *state*hood. **(2)** "the entire class or group": *priest*hood.

hoof (hŏŏf or hŏŏf) the horny covering of the toes of some animals, as the horse or cow; also the whole foot. **hoofs** or **hooves.**

of HORSE

of DEER

Hoof

hoofed (hŏŏft or hŏŏft) having hoofs.

hook (hŏŏk) **1** a curved piece of metal, bone, wood, or the like, designed to catch, hold, or fasten something: *a crochet* hook; *a door* hook. **2** a hooklike curve: *His writing was a scrawl of* hooks *and dashes.* **3** a sharp bend, as in a road or stream. **4** to catch with a hook: *to* hook *a fish.* **5** to make with a hook: *to* hook *a rug.* **6** to fasten with a hook: *to* hook *the door.* **7** to be fastened with a hook: *The door* hooks *on the*

inside. *The dress* hooks *up the back.* **8 by hook or by crook** by fair means or foul.

hook·worm (hŏŏk'wûrm') small worm that attaches itself to the inside of the intestine. Hookworms suck blood and cause weakness.

Hooks

hook·y (hŏŏk'ĭ) **1** absence without permission; truancy. **2 play hooky** to be absent from school without permission.

hoop (hŏŏp or hŏŏp) **1** circle of metal or wood for holding together the staves of a barrel, tub, or the like. **2** similar circle used as a toy by children. **3** circle of whalebone or wire used to expand a woman's skirt.

hoot (hŏŏt) **1** to shout to show dislike or contempt: *The crowd* hooted *and stamped their feet.* **2** to shout sneers at: *to* hoot *an unpopular speaker.* **3** to drive away by jeering: *The audience* hooted *the actor off the stage.* **4** a shout showing dislike or anger. **5** cry of an owl or any sound like it. **6** to make such a cry.

hooves (hŏŏvz or hŏŏvz) more than one **hoof.**

¹hop (hŏp) **1** vine with green flowers shaped like cones. **2 hops** dried flowers of this vine, used to flavor beer and ale. [**¹hop** is from an early Dutch word (hoppe).]

²hop (hŏp) **1** to move by short jumps, using all feet at once: *Frogs and birds* hop. **2** to move by short jumps, using only one leg: *He dropped the stone on his foot and* hopped *about in pain.* **3** to jump over or onto: *to* hop *a fence; to* hop *a train.* **4** a short jump. **hopped, hop·ping.** [**²hop** is a form of an Old English word (hoppian).]

hope (hōp) **1** a desire for something with a feeling that the desire may be fulfilled; restrained expectation: *He has high* hopes *of making money.* **2** the thing desired: *All his* hopes *had failed.* **3** feeling of trust and confidence: *During the storm the pilot lost all* hope *of finding the airport. You must never lose* hope. **4** to expect and desire: *We* hope *to see you soon. We* hope *for the best.* **5** cause of hope: *The oldest son is the* hope *of the family.* **hoped, hop·ing.**

hope·ful (hōp'fəl) **1** having desire and expectation: *We are* hopeful *that the crop next year will be a large one.* **2** full of trust and confidence: *The team was very discouraged at first, but became more* hopeful *after scoring twice.* **3** promising success or a good outcome: *His good appetite is a* hopeful *sign that he is getting well.* **hope·ful·ly.**

hope·less (hōp′lĭs) **1** without hope. **2** with little likelihood of success or of a good outcome: *a* hopeless *task; a* hopeless *search.* **hope·less·ly.**

hop·per (hŏp′ər) **1** something that hops, such as a grasshopper. **2** a container or chute from which something is fed to a machine, bin, or the like: *Madge dropped meat into the* hopper *of the food grinder while I turned the crank.*

Hopper

hop·scotch (hŏp′skŏch′) children's game, in which the players hop from one square to another on a design drawn on the ground, without touching any lines.

horde (hôrd) **1** great number; multitude: *a* horde *of crickets.* **2** wandering tribe of people: *a gypsy* horde. (Homonym: hoard)

ho·ri·zon (hə rī′zən) **1** the line where the earth and sky seem to meet. **2** the limit of one's knowledge or interest: *Reading can broaden our* horizon.

hor·i·zon·tal (hôr′ə zŏn′təl or hôr′ə zŏn′təl) **1** parallel to the horizon level. **2** something that is horizontal: *The surface of water in a pan is always a* horizontal. **hor·i·zon·tal·ly.**

Horizontal

hor·mone (hôr′mōn) a body chemical produced by one organ and carried by the blood to other parts of the body. Hormones regulate growth, action of organs, etc.

horn (hôrn) **1** the hard, often pointed growth on the heads of certain animals, such as the cow or goat. **2** the material of which such growths are made. **3** anything that sticks out like a horn from a creature's head, such as the eye stalk of a snail. **4** a container made of horn: *a powder* horn. **5** anything curved and pointed like a horn, such as the points of the new moon. **6** a musical wind instrument made of horn. **7** any of a group of brass musical wind instruments: *the* horn *section of the orchestra.* **8** a device that makes a loud sound as a warning signal: *an automobile* horn; *a fog* horn.

Horns

horned toad a kind of harmless, flat-bodied lizard. It has a scaly skin with horny spikes on the body and about the head, which give it its name.

hor·net (hôr′nĭt) a large wasp that can give a painful sting.

Hornet, about ¾ in. long

horn·y (hôr′nĭ) of or like a horn; made hard: *His hands were* horny *from hard work.* **horn·i·er, horn·i·est.**

hor·ri·ble (hôr′ə bəl or hôr′ə bəl) causing fear; terrible; dreadful: *a horrible* monster. **hor·ri·bly.**

hor·rid (hôr′ĭd or hŏr′ĭd) frightful; hideous. **hor·rid·ly.**

hor·ri·fy (hôr′ə fī′ or hŏr′ə fī′) to fill with great terror, fear, or alarm: *The whole town was* horrified *by the news of the accident.* **hor·ri·fied, hor·ri·fy·ing.**

hor·ror (hôr′ər or hŏr′ər) **1** strong feeling of terror or dread: *Any story of cruelty fills her with* horror. **2** dislike; aversion: *She has a* horror *of wearing the wrong style.* **3** thing that causes great terror.

horse (hôrs) **1** large, hoofed animal used for drawing vehicles and for riding. **2** movable frame consisting of two pairs of legs joined by a crossbar, used as a support; a trestle. (Homonym: hoarse)

Horse

horse·back (hôrs′băk′) **1** the back of a horse: *He rode the range on* horseback. **2** on the back of a horse: *He rides* horseback.

---

fāte, făt, fâre, fär; bē, bĕt; bīte, bĭt; nō, nŏt, nôr; fūse, fŭn, fûr; tōō, tŏŏk; foil; foul; thin; ~~then~~; hw for wh as in *wh*at; zh for s as in u*s*ual; ə for a, e, i, o, u, as in *a*go, lin*e*n, per*i*l, at*o*m, min*u*s

horse chestnut 1 large spreading tree with clusters of white or pink blossoms and reddish-brown seeds growing in burrs. **2** nut of this tree.

horse·fly (hôrs′flī′) large black fly that bites horses and cattle. **horse·flies.**

horse·hair (hôrs′hâr′) **1** hair of the mane and tail of a horse. **2** smooth, stiff cloth made from this hair.

horse·man (hôrs′mən) **1** rider on horseback. **2** person who is skilled in riding or managing horses. **horse·men.**

horse·play (hôrs′plā′) rough play: *The children tumbled one another about in noisy* horseplay.

horse·pow·er (hôrs′pou′ər) a unit of power. One horsepower is the amount of power required to raise 33,000 pounds one foot in one minute.

horse·shoe (hôrs′shōō′) **1** flat, U-shaped, protective iron plate nailed to the bottom of a horse's hoof. **2** something shaped like a horseshoe.

Horseshoe

hose (hōz) **1** flexible tubing of rubber, plastic, etc., used for carrying liquids: *We need a new* hose *for watering the garden.* **2** to water or wet thoroughly with a hose: *He* hosed *the lawn every day.* **3** stockings. **hosed, hos·ing.**

ho·sier·y (hō′zhə rī) stockings.

hos·pi·ta·ble (hŏs′pĭ tə bəl) generous and friendly in welcoming guests and strangers: *It was* hospitable *of you to have the children for the weekend.* **hos·pi·ta·bly.**

hos·pi·tal (hŏs′pĭ təl) place for treatment and care of the sick.

hos·pi·tal·i·ty (hŏs′pə tăl′ə tī) warm, generous reception and entertainment of guests and strangers. **hos·pi·tal·i·ties.**

hos·pi·tal·ize (hŏs′pə tə līz′) to place in a hospital for treatment. **hos·pi·tal·ized, hos·pi·tal·iz·ing.**

¹host (hōst) **1** person who receives and entertains guests in his home or somewhere else: *Our* host *took us to a restaurant for dinner.* **2** person who provides food and lodging for pay. **3 Host** in certain Christian churches, the consecrated bread. [**¹host** comes through Old French (hoste) from a Latin word (hospes) meaning "guest" or "host." **Hospitality** is related to this word.]

²host (hōst) great number of persons or things; a throng: *a* host *of daffodils.* [**²host** comes through Old French from a Latin word (hostis), from which we also get **hostile.**]

hos·tage (hŏs′tĭj) person given or held as a security or guarantee that certain things asked for will be done: *The bandits asked ransom for their* hostage.

hos·tel (hŏs′təl) inn; lodging place for travelers.

hos·tess (hōs′tĭs) **1** woman who receives and entertains guests in her home or somewhere else. **2** woman in a restaurant who welcomes and seats guests.

hos·tile (hŏs′təl) **1** of or like an enemy; warlike: *The* hostile *army was preparing to attack.* **2** unfriendly; opposed: *People who don't like changes are often* hostile *to new ideas.* **hos·tile·ly.**

hos·til·i·ty (hŏs tĭl′ə tī) **1** unfriendliness; hatred; dislike: *The campaign was marked by* hostility. **2 hostilities** acts of warfare: *to cease* hostilities. **hos·til·i·ties.**

hos·tler (hŏs′lər or ŏs′lər) a man who takes care of horses.

hot (hŏt) **1** of high temperature: *There is* hot *water in the teakettle.* **2** fiery; showing anger; violent: *a* hot *temper.* **3** having a burning effect on the mouth; sharp and biting in taste: *Do you like* hot *pepper?* **4** fresh; strong: *The hounds followed the* hot *scent of the rabbit.* **5** close behind: *to follow* hot *on the trail.* **hot·ter, hot·test; hot·ly.**

ho·tel (hō tĕl′) an establishment that furnishes food and lodging to the public for pay.

hot·head (hŏt′hĕd′) rash, excitable, quick-tempered person.

hot·house (hŏt′hous′) a building with glass sides and a glass roof, heated for growing plants; greenhouse.

hound (hound) **1** any of several breeds of dog used for hunting, especially those that hunt by scent. **2** any dog. **3** to chase with hounds. **4** to pursue; nag: *The bill collectors* hounded *him to pay his debts.*

hour (our) **1** 60 minutes. **2** time of day: *The* hour *is three o'clock.* **3** fixed period of time: *Office* hours *are from 9:00 to 5:00.* **4** particular time: *in the* hour *of danger.* (Homonym: our)

hour·glass (our′glăs′) device for measuring the passage of one hour. Two glass globes are connected by a narrow neck through which sand trickles. The passage of sand from one globe to the other takes one hour.

Hourglass

hour·ly (our′lĭ) **1** every hour: *Trains to Boston run* hourly. **2** happening every hour: *the* hourly *chime of the clock.* **3** for every hour; by the hour: *an* hourly *wage.* **4** very soon: *We expect his answer* hourly.

¹**house** (hous) **1** building made for people to live in; dwelling. **2** building made for a particular purpose: *a* house *of worship; fraternity* house; *opera* house. **3** division of a lawmaking body or group: *the* House *of Representatives; the* House *of Commons.* **4** number of people at a performance: *There was a full* house *to see the show.* **5** family, especially a ruling family: *a prince of the ruling* house.

²**house** (houz) to provide with a house or shelter: *to* house *guests; to* house *furniture.* **housed, hous·ing.**

house·boat (hous′-bōt′) boat fitted as a dwelling.

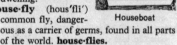

Houseboat

house·fly (hous′flī′) common fly, dangerous as a carrier of germs, found in all parts of the world. **house·flies.**

house·hold (hous′hōld′) **1** all the persons living in a house. **2** having to do with a household; domestic: *All* household *goods are sold on the third floor.*

house·hold·er (hous′hōl′dər) **1** head of a family or household. **2** person who occupies a house, especially an owner.

house·keep·er (hous′kē′pər) woman who performs or directs the work of a house.

house·keep·ing (hous′kē′pĭng) care and management of a household.

house·top (hous′tŏp′) top or roof of a house.

house·wife (hous′wīf′) woman who manages a home for her family. **house·wives.**

house·work (hous′wûrk′) cleaning, ironing, cooking, and other work to be done in a house.

hous·ing (hou′zĭng) **1** the providing of homes for people: *The mayor has promised better* housing *for the city.* **2** having to do with this: *the* housing *problem.* **3** a house or shelter. **4** a protective cover or container for a machine or a machine part.

hove (hōv) See **heave.** *The ship* hove *into sight.*

hov·el (hŏv′əl or hŭv′əl) small, dirty cottage or hut in bad repair.

hov·er (hŏv′ər or hŭv′ər) **1** to stay in the air over one place: *The bird* hovered *over its nest. The helicopter* hovered *over the highway.* **2** to stay or wait near-by: *The children* hovered *around the toy counter.* **3** to waver: *to* hover *between life and death.*

how (hou) **1** in what way or manner; by what means: *But* how *do you do that?* **2** to what extent or degree: *We didn't know* how *serious his injury was.* **3** in what state or condition: *Hello,* how *are you today?* **4** for what reason; why: *Then* how *is it that you are late every day?* **5 how much** what price: *Tell me,* how much *are the oranges?*

how·e′er (hou âr′) however.

how·ev·er (hou ĕv′ər) **1** nevertheless; yet; in spite of that: *Our vacation is short;* however, *we still plan to go on our trip.* **2** no matter how; in whatever way: *Every effort,* however *small, will be a help.*

howl (houl) **1** long, wailing cry of a wolf, dog, or hyena. **2** cry of pain, rage, distress, or contempt. **3** to make a wailing sound: *The wind* howls *through the trees.*

hr. hour.

hub (hŭb) **1** central part of a wheel from which the spokes spread out. **2** center of interest or activity: *Downtown is the* hub *of business in our city.*

Hub

hub·bub (hŭb′ŭb) loud confused noise; uproar: *The* hubbub *of five o'clock traffic was deafening.*

huck·le·ber·ry (hŭk′əl bĕr′ĭ) **1** blue-black berry with hard seeds, sometimes confused

---

fāte, făt, fâre, fär; bē, bĕt; bīte, bĭt; nō, nŏt, nôr; fūse, fŭn, fûr; tōō, tŏŏk; foil; foul; thin; ~~then~~; hw for wh as in *wh*at; zh for s as in u*s*ual; ə for a, e, i, o, u, as in *a*go, lin*e*n, per*i*l, at*o*m, min*u*s

with the blueberry. **2** shrub on which it grows. **huck·le·ber·ries.**

hud·dle (hŭd′əl) **1** to crowd together in a confused way: *The ice skaters* huddled *around the fire.* **2** group of persons or things crowded together: *a* huddle *of cars.* **3** a gathering together of a football team to decide upon the next play. **hud·dled, hud·dling.**

Hud·son Bay (hŭd′sən bā) a branch of the Atlantic Ocean forming an inland sea in northern Canada.

hue (hū) color; tint; shade of color: *flowers of every* hue. (Homonym: hew)

hug (hŭg) **1** to hold tightly in the arms; squeeze. **2** close embrace: *Nancy gave her mother a* hug *and a kiss.* **3** to hold fast to: *to* hug *a belief.* **4** to keep close to: *The swimmers* hugged *the shore just to be safe.* **hugged, hug·ging.**

huge (hūj) very large; enormous: *The elephant is a* huge *animal.* **hug·er, hug·est; huge·ly.**

hu·la-hu·la (hōō′lə hōō′lə) Hawaiian dance which tells a story. The hula-hula is performed by women and girls who move their hands and arms to describe different things and events, and sway their hips in time to the music.

hulk (hŭlk) **1** wreck of an old ship; dismantled hull. **2** heavy, clumsy ship. **3** overgrown, awkward person or thing: *He was such a* hulk *of a man that he had difficulty getting into small spaces.*

hulk·ing (hŭl′kĭng) big and clumsy: *The giant's* hulking *form filled the doorway.*

hull (hŭl) **1** the body of a ship without rigging or deck structures; body of an airship. **2** the covering of certain seeds or the stem of certain berries. **3** to remove such covering or stem: *to* hull *peas; to* hull *strawberries.*

Hull

hum (hŭm) **1** to sing with closed lips: *The boys will* hum *the melody.* **2** to make a continuous droning or low buzzing sound: *Bees* hummed *in the garden.* **3** continuous murmuring or buzzing sound; drone: *a* hum *of voices in the next room; the* hum *of an engine.* **hummed, hum·ming.**

hu·man (hū′mən) **1** of or having the qualities of man or mankind: *It is only* human *to make a mistake now and then. We are all* human *beings.* **2** human being.

hu·mane (hū mān′) showing mercy, kindness, and tenderness for others. **hu·mane·ly.**

hu·man·i·ty (hū măn′ə tĭ) **1** mankind; the race of man: *This is a history of* humanity. **2** human nature. **3** kindness of heart; feeling for others: *He showed* humanity *in his generous treatment of the poor.* **4 humanities** branches of learning having to do with history, literature, and philosophy. **hu·man·i·ties.**

hum·ble (hŭm′bəl or ŭm′bəl) **1** not proud or boastful; meek. **2** not grand or important: *Abraham Lincoln had a* humble *beginning.* **3** to lower in pride or condition; make meek: *He* humbled *himself in true repentance.* **hum·bler, hum·blest; hum·bled, hum·bling; hum·bly.**

hum·ble·ness (hŭm′bəl nĭs) a being humble.

hum·bug (hŭm′bŭg) **1** a sham; fraud. **2** a cheat; impostor. **3** to deceive; cheat. **hum·bugged, hum·bug·ging.**

hu·mid (hū′mĭd) damp; moist: *The air is* humid *before a rain.*

hu·mid·i·ty (hū mĭd′ə tĭ) **1** dampness; moisture. **2** amount of moisture in the air: *Weather reports tell the temperature and* humidity.

hu·mil·i·ate (hū mĭl′ĭ āt′) to put to shame; cause to lose dignity and pride: *Jack was* humiliated *when his little sister outran him.* **hu·mil·i·at·ed, hu·mil·i·at·ing.**

hu·mil·i·a·tion (hū mĭl′ĭ ā′shən) a lowering of pride; a putting or being put to shame: *The child's tantrum caused the mother great* humiliation.

hu·mil·i·ty (hū mĭl′ə tĭ) modest or humble sense of one's own importance; meekness: *He accepted the honors with* humility.

Ruby-throated hummingbird, about 3½ in. long

hum·ming·bird (hŭm′ĭng bûrd′) tiny, bright-colored, long-billed bird that feeds upon the nectar of flowers. The rapid movement of its wings in flight makes a humming sound.

hum·mock (hŭm′ək) small hill or rounded mound: *In the swamp*, hummocks *served as stepping stones.*

hu·mor (hū′mər) **1** funny or amusing feature: *The rescue of the lost guide added* humor *to our trip.* **2** funny quality; amusing treatment: *The* humor *of the story was in the way he told it.* **3** mood; state of mind: *Don't bother him when he is in a bad* humor. **4** to yield to the whims of; indulge: *If we don't* humor *her, she cries and becomes angry.* **5 sense of humor** ability to see the absurd or amusing: *Some people have a sense of* humor *that makes everyday incidents seem funny.*

hu·mor·ist (hū′mər ist) person who writes or says amusing things.

hu·mor·ous (hū′mər əs) funny; amusing; comical: *a* humorous *story; a* humorous *situation.* **hu·mor·ous·ly.**

hump (hŭmp) rounded or bulging lump: *a camel's* hump.

hump·back (hŭmp′băk′) a hunchback.

hump·backed (hŭmp′băkt′) having a hunchback.

hu·mus (hū′məs) rich black or brown substance in the soil formed by the decay of leaves or other vegetable matter.

hunch (hŭnch) **1** a hump. **2** to bend (the back, etc.) to form a hump: *You must* hunch *your back to get under that low door.* **3** a feeling that something will happen: *I've got a* hunch *that I'll pass this test.*

hunch·back (hŭnch′băk′) **1** person whose back is crooked into a hump at the shoulders. **2** crooked back that forms a hump at the shoulders.

hunch·backed (hŭnch′băkt′) humpbacked.

hun·dred (hŭn′drid) amount or quantity that is one greater than 99; 100.

hun·dred·fold (hŭn′drid fōld′) 100 times as much or as many.

hun·dredth (hŭn′dridth) **1** next after 99th. **2** one of 100 equal parts.

hun·dred·weight (hŭn′drid wāt′) unit of weight equal to 100 pounds.

hung (hŭng) See **hang.** *He* hung *his coat on a hook.*

hun·ger (hŭng′gər) **1** a craving or need for food: *She satisfies her* hunger *with a candy bar.* **2** strong or eager desire: *He has a* hunger *for friendship.* **3** to feel hungry: *He* hungered *for a good meal.* **4** to long for; yearn: *He* hungered *for a sight of home.*

hun·gry (hŭng′grĭ) **1** wanting food: *He was* hungry *at lunchtime.* **2** eager; desirous: *That child is* hungry *for attention.* **3** showing or feeling hunger or need: *a lean and* hungry *look.* **hun·gri·er, hun·gri·est; hun·gri·ly.**

hunk (hŭngk) large piece or lump; chunk: *a* hunk *of clay.*

hunt (hŭnt) **1** to pursue (wild animals) for food or sport: *He* hunts *deer.* **2** to look for; search for; try to find: *They* hunted *the lost ball.* **3** pursuit (of wild animals or game): *We went on a duck* hunt. **4** a search: *After a long* hunt, *we found the right house.*

hunt·er (hŭn′tər) **1** person who pursues game; a huntsman: *The* hunter *fired his gun at the rabbit.* **2** horse or hound trained for hunting. **3** one who seeks or looks for something.

hunt·ress (hŭn′trĭs) woman who pursues game or wild animals.

hunts·man (hŭnts′mən) man who pursues game; hunter. **hunts·men.**

hur·dle (hûr′dəl) **1** kind of fence in movable sections. **2** a frame or other barrier over which runners or horses jump in a kind of race. **3** obstacle. **4** to leap over with a running stride. **5** to overcome (an obstacle). **hur·dled, hur·dling.**

Hurdle

hur·dy-gur·dy (hûr′dĭ gûr′dĭ) mechanical musical instrument played by turning a crank. It is often fitted with wheels and pulled through the streets. **hur·dy-gur·dies.**

hurl (hûrl) **1** to throw with force; fling violently: *A rock was* hurled *through the window.* **2** to utter or speak with violence: *The crowd* hurled *insults at the umpire.*

---

fāte, făt, fâre, fär; bē, bĕt; bīte, bĭt; nō, nŏt, nôr; fūse, fŭn, fûr; tōō, tŏŏk; foil; foul; thin; then; hw for wh as in *wh*at; zh for s as in usual; ə for a, e, i, o, u, as in *a*go, linen, peril, atom, minus

355

hur·rah (hə rä′) or **hur·ray** (hə rā′) **1** shout, expressing joy, applause, or triumph: *The team shouted* "Hurrah! *We won!*" **2** to utter such a shout.

hur·ri·cane (hûr′i kān′) vast tropical storm of great violence, consisting of rotating winds and heavy rains.

hur·ried (hûr′īd) showing haste; hasty; done in a hurry: *She sent a* hurried *note to a friend. It was a* hurried *trip.* **hur·ried·ly.**

hur·ry (hûr′ī) **1** to move or act quickly: *I have to* hurry *to work.* **2** impatient or needless haste: *No need for* hurry, *we have all day.* **3** to cause to move or act quickly; rush: *Don't* hurry *me, I like to take my time.* **hur·ried, hur·ry·ing.**

hurt (hûrt) **1** to cause pain to: *The hangnail* hurts *his thumb.* **2** to be painful: *That bump* hurts. **3** injury; wound: *a* hurt *to the pride.* **4** to grieve; offend: *He* hurt *me with his spiteful words.* **5** to damage; harm: *It won't* hurt *this watch to wear it in water.* **hurt, hurt·ing.**

hurt·ful (hûrt′fəl) harmful; causing pain or injury. **hurt·ful·ly.**

hur·tle (hûr′təl) **1** to rush, speed, shoot, or fly wildly: *The jet* hurtled *through the air.* **2** to dash; throw oneself; rush recklessly: *The boys* hurtled *out of the door.* **hur·tled, hur·tling.**

hus·band (hŭz′bənd) **1** man who has a wife. **2** to use carefully; save: *to* husband *one's supplies.*

hus·band·man (hŭz′bənd mən) farmer. **hus·band·men.**

hus·band·ry (hŭz′bən drī) **1** farming; tilling of the soil. **2** careful management: *By good* husbandry *Mr. White had amassed a considerable fortune.*

hush (hŭsh) **1** to make or become quiet: *The mother* hushed *her crying child with soft words. He asked me to* hush *during the music.* **2** silence; stillness: *Not a sound broke the* hush *of the evening.*

husk (hŭsk) **1** outermost covering of certain nuts and grains, such as Indian corn and coconuts. **2** to remove the husk from: *to* husk *corn.* **3** any worthless outer covering.

Butternut husks

husk·i·ness (hŭs′kī nĭs) **1** slight hoarseness or low, dry quality of the voice. **2** state of being big and strong.

husking bee gathering of friends and neighbors to help a farmer husk his corn.

husk·y (hŭs′kī) **1** somewhat hoarse; almost like a whisper: *His voice was* husky *from shouting.* **2** big and strong. **husk·i·er, husk·i·est; husk·i·ly.**

Husk·y or **husk·y** (hŭs′kī) Eskimo dog. **Husk·ies** or **husk·ies.**

hus·tle (hŭs′əl) **1** to push, crowd, or shove roughly; jostle: *The police* hustled *the thieves into the police station.* **2** to hurry; move or act with speed: *We'll have to* hustle *to get there on time.* **3 hustle and bustle** energetic and confusing activity: *the* hustle and bustle *of the city.* **hus·tled, hus·tling.**

hut (hŭt) small, roughly built house.

hy·a·cinth (hī′ə sĭnth) **1** plant of the lily family, grown from a bulb. It has spikes of small, bright flowers of various colors. **2** the flower of this plant.

hy·brid (hī′brĭd) **1** offspring produced by the mating of two different varieties of species of plants or animals: *Some roses are* hybrids. **2** produced by two different species: *The mule is a* hybrid *animal.*

Hyacinth

hy·dran·gea (hī drān′jə) **1** shrub with large, round clusters of white, blue, or pink flowers. **2** the flower of this plant.

hy·drant (hī′drənt) large pipe with a valve and hose connections. From it water may be drawn from a main to fight fires.

hy·drau·lic (hī drô′lĭk) **1** having to do with water or other liquids in motion. **2** operated by the pressure of a liquid or by the force of liquid in motion. **3** hardening under water: *a* hydraulic *cement.* **4 hydraulic brakes** brakes operated by the pressure of liquid in cylinders. **5 hydraulic mining** mining by the direct use of a powerful stream of water.

Hydrant

hy·dro·e·lec·tric (hī′drō ĭ lĕk′trĭk) producing electricity by means of water power: *a* hydroelectric *plant.*

hy·dro·gen (hī′drə jən) the lightest known chemical element. It is a gas without taste, color, or smell. It burns with a very hot flame, and combines with oxygen to form water.

hydrogen bomb bomb of tremendous force, resulting from the fusion of hydrogen atoms. The fusion is triggered by the explosion of an atomic bomb. Also called H-bomb.

hy·dro·pho·bi·a (hī′drə fō′bĭ ə) virus disease, especially of dogs, foxes, etc., marked by fear of water, inability to swallow, frenzy, and convulsions. It may be transmitted to man or other animals by the bite of an infected animal. Also called **rabies.**

Hydroplanes

hy·dro·plane (hī′drə plān′) **1** a light motorboat with a flat bottom on which it skims along the surface of the water at high speed. **2** kind of airplane that can land on or take off from the surface of water; seaplane.

hy·e·na (hī ē′nə) night-prowling, meat-eating animal of Africa and Asia, somewhat like a large dog.

hy·giene (hī′jēn) **1** study of good health practices; principles or rules of good health. **2** practice of good health rules.

hy·grom·e·ter (hī grŏm′ə tər) instrument that measures the amount of moisture in the air.

hy·ing (hī′ĭng) **1** a hurrying; going quickly. **2** See **hie.**

hymn (hĭm) **1** song of praise to God. **2** any song of praise, thanksgiving, or the like. (Homonym: him)

hym·nal (hĭm′nəl) book of hymns.

hy·phen (hī′fən) a mark (-) used to join two words into a single word or to divide a word at the end of a line of writing or printing. The division in the word can be made only between syllables.

hy·phen·ate (hī′fə nāt′) to write or print with a hyphen: *The word "great-grand-*

mother" is hyphenated *twice in this sentence. Oscar's family* hyphenates *its last name Blake-Jones.* **hy·phen·at·ed, hy·phen·at·ing.**

hyp·no·sis (hĭp nō′sĭs) a condition like sleep in which a person loses consciousness but will do and say things at the suggestion of the person who has put him into this condition. **hyp·no·ses** (hĭp nō′sēz).

hyp·no·tism (hĭp′nə tĭz′əm) act or process of hypnotizing a person.

hyp·no·tize (hĭp′nə tīz′) to put a person in a state resembling sleep, in which the mind easily comes under another's influence. **hyp·no·tized, hyp·no·tiz·ing.**

hy·poc·ri·sy (hĭ pŏk′rə sĭ) pretense of being what one is not or feeling what one does not feel, especially a false assumption of goodness: *His sympathy is rank* hypocrisy. **hy·poc·ri·sies.**

hyp·o·crite (hĭp′ə krĭt) person who puts on a false appearance of being good, kind, honest, etc.

hyp·o·crit·i·cal (hĭp′ə krĭt′ĭ kəl) of or like a hypocrite; insincere: *He was a poor loser, and* hypocritical *when he congratulated the winner of the game.*

hy·po·der·mic (hī′pə dûr′mĭk) **1** beneath the skin; having to do with skin puncture: *a hypodermic injection.* **2** short for **hypodermic syringe,** an instrument consisting of a piston attached to a hollow needle for injecting drugs, etc., beneath the skin. **3** an injection by this means.

hy·poth·e·sis (hī pŏth′ə sĭs) assumption that something is true, even though not proved; tentative explanation; unproved theory: *Columbus set sail on the* hypothesis *that the earth is round.* **hy·poth·e·ses** (hī pŏth′ə sēz′).

hys·te·ri·a (hĭs tĭr′ĭ ə or hĭs tĕr′ĭ ə) an extreme nervous disorder marked chiefly by violent fits of laughing and crying.

hys·ter·i·cal (hĭs tĕr′ə kəl) lacking emotional control; violently emotional: *The* hysterical *throngs raced down the street destroying everything in reach.* **hys·ter·i·cal·ly.**

hys·ter·ics (hĭs tĕr′ĭks) nervous fit of uncontrolled emotion.

---

fāte, făt, fâre, fär; bē, bĕt; bīte, bĭt; nō, nŏt, nôr; fūse, fŭn, fûr; tōō, tŏŏk; foil; foul; thin; ~~then~~; hw for wh as in *wh*at; zh for s as in usual; ə for a, e, i, o, u, as in *a*go, lin*e*n, per*i*l, at*o*m, min*u*s

I

¹I, i (ī) **1** ninth letter of the English alphabet. **2** Roman numeral for the number one.

²I (ī) the person speaking or writing: *Shall I cut the grass?* [²I is a form of an Old English word (ic) with the same meaning.] (Homonyms: ²ay or ²aye, eye)

ice (īs) **1** frozen water. **2** of ice: *six ice cubes.* **3** having to do with ice: *an ice skate.* **4** to cool with ice: *to ice drinks.* **5** frozen dessert made with fruit flavoring or juice and water: *Orange ice is good in hot weather.* **6** to cover with frosting or icing: *to ice a cake.* **7** something which looks, feels, or acts like ice: *dry ice.* **iced, ic·ing.**

ice age period of time when a large area of the earth was covered with glaciers.

ice·berg (is′bûrg′) mass of floating ice, often of great size.

PART BELOW WATER

Iceberg

ice·boat (īs′bōt′) a kite-shaped frame resting on two blades or runners at the ends of the crosspiece and a third movable runner controlled by a tiller at the end of the long beam. The boat is equipped with a mast and sail.

ice·box (īs′bŏks′) refrigerator.

ice·break·er (īs′brāk′ər) a strong ship that cuts channels in frozen rivers, lakes, or harbors to permit the passage of ships.

ice·cap (īs′kăp′) a permanent sheet of ice, especially either of those surrounding the North and the South Poles.

ice cream frozen dessert made with milk, cream, sugar, flavoring, and sometimes with gelatin and eggs added.

i·ci·cle (ī′sĭ kəl) hanging spike of ice formed by the freezing of dripping water.

ic·ing (ī′sĭng) sugar-coating for cakes and cookies, etc.; frosting.

i·cy (ī′sĭ) **1** like ice; very cold: *an icy wind.* **2** covered with ice: *an icy road.* **3** of ice: *an icy film around the fence.* **4** cold and unfriendly. **ic·i·er, ic·i·est; i·ci·ly.**

I'd (īd) **1** I had: *I knew I'd seen him somewhere.* **2** I would: *If I could, I'd go.* **3** I should: *I thought I'd get there on time.*

I·da·ho (ī′də hō′) a State in the northwestern part of the United States.

i·de·a (ī dē′ə) **1** a thought; notion; understanding: *Have you any idea what he is talking about?* **2** a plan or scheme: *It would be a good idea to plant some trees in front.* **3** impression or picture formed in the mind: *She found the house quite different from her idea of it.* **4** purpose or meaning of something: *The idea of the game is to get the other players out.*

i·de·al (ī dē′əl) **1** a perfect type; a standard of perfection: *the ideal of liberty.* **2** measuring up to one's highest wish; perfect: *an ideal day for a picnic.* **3** any person or thing looked on as a perfect model: *A small boy's ideal is often his father.* **i·de·al·ly.**

i·den·ti·cal (ī dĕn′tə kəl) **1** the very same: *These are the identical gloves which I lost two months ago.* **2** exactly alike: *The pictures were identical except for one detail.* **i·den·ti·cal·ly.**

i·den·ti·fi·ca·tion (ī dĕn′tə fə kā′shən) **1** a telling or showing what something is: *Dora's identification of a horned toad as a lizard was correct.* **2** recognition of what an object or person is: *Although he was certain of his identification of the man, he said nothing.* **3** proof that someone or something is what is claimed: *He showed his driver's license as identification at the bank.*

i·den·ti·fy (ī dĕn′tə fī′) **1** to recognize or show who a person is or what a thing is: *Can you identify the man by his picture?* **2** to make, treat as, or consider the same: *He identified his interests with ours by joining forces with us.* **3** to associate (oneself with): *He refused to identify himself with their schemes.* **i·den·ti·fied, i·den·ti·fy·ing.**

i·den·ti·ty (ī dĕn′tə tĭ) **1** who a person is; what a thing is: *The bank teller must know the identity of a person before cashing his check.* **2** sameness; likeness: *We quickly noticed the identity of the two plans.* **3** individuality. **i·den·ti·ties.**

id·i·om (id′ī əm) **1** a group of words whose meaning must be known as a whole, for it cannot be learned from the meaning of these same words used separately. "To go back on," for example, doesn't mean "to move backward onto" but "to betray or fail." **2** the language used by the people of a certain region, group, class, etc.: *the American idiom; the* idiom *of sailors.* **3** a particular person's way of using words: *Shakespeare's* idiom.

id·i·ot (id′ī ət) **1** person born with almost no mental powers, and unable to learn. **2** silly or stupid person.

id·i·ot·ic (id′ī ŏt′ĭk) **1** of or like an idiot. **2** senseless; foolish.

i·dle (ī′dəl) **1** not employed; not used; not working: *an* idle *workman;* idle *machinery.* **2** not willing to work; lazy: *He is an idle boy and will not do his chores.* **3** useless; of no importance or worth: *The gossips wasted their days in idle talk.* **4** to run without doing work, as an engine in neutral gear. **5** to waste time; do nothing.
  idle away to pass (time) idly: *We idled away the afternoon by the brook.*
  i·dled, i·dling. (Homonym: idol)

i·dler (ī′dlər) person who is lazy or wastes time in doing nothing.

i·dly (ī′dlī) without any particular aim or purpose: *He sat idly staring into space.*

i·dol (ī′dəl) **1** image of a god used as an object of worship. **2** person or thing greatly loved or admired. (Homonym: idle)

Idol

i·dol·ize (ī′də līz′) **1** to worship; hold in great respect or reverence. **2** to love or admire beyond reason: *Charlotte kept photographs of movie stars whom she idolized.* **i·dol·ized, i·dol·iz·ing.**

if (if) **1** on the condition that: *I'll go to the movies if you'll go with me.* **2** in case that; supposing that: *I'm not going if it rains.* **3** whether: *I wonder if the plane will be on time.* **4** even though: *I'll learn to hit that ball if it's the last thing I ever do.*

ig·loo (ĭg′lōō) Eskimo hut, especially one built in the shape of a dome with blocks of snow. **ig·loos.**

ig·ne·ous (ĭg′nĭ əs) **1** having to do with fire. **2** produced by fire, intense heat, or volcanic action: *an igneous rock.*

Igloo

ig·nite (ĭg nīt′) **1** to set fire to; set on fire: *Boy scouts can ignite wood without matches.* **2** to catch fire; take fire: *Dry leaves may ignite from a spark.* **ig·nit·ed, ig·nit·ing.**

ig·ni·tion (ĭg nĭsh′ən) **1** act of catching fire or lighting a fire. **2** system in a gasoline engine that ignites the fuel.

ig·no·ble (ĭg nō′bəl) **1** of low character; mean; base: *His cheating proved him to be an ignoble man.* **2** shameful; disgraceful: *to suffer an ignoble defeat.* **ig·no·bly.**

ig·no·rance (ĭg′nə rəns) lack of knowledge: *His ignorance of spelling cost him his job.*

ig·no·rant (ĭg′nə rənt) **1** knowing little; not learned; lacking in knowledge: *The early settlers were ignorant of the ways of the Indians.* **2** unaware: *He was ignorant of the fact we were waiting for him.* **3** showing or caused by ignorance: *an ignorant answer to my question.* **ig·no·rant·ly.**

ig·nore (ĭg nôr′) to pay no attention to; refuse to notice: *Anyone who ignores the speed limit may be arrested.* **ig·nored, ig·nor·ing.**

i·gua·na (ĭ gwä′nə) any of several long-tailed lizards, especially a tropical kind with a crest of scales along its back and a throat puffed out like a pouch.

Iguana, different kinds vary from a few inches to 6 ft. long

ill (ĭl) **1** sick; not well: *He is ill with measles.* **2** a sickness: *the ills of mind and body.* **3** harmful; bad; evil: *Your ill advice led him to hurt many people.* **4** a harm; evil: *War is one of the great ills of the world.* **5** badly: *Do not speak ill of anyone.* **worse, worst.**

---

fāte, făt, fâre, fär; bē, bĕt; bīte, bĭt; nō, nŏt, nôr; fūse, fŭn, fûr; tōō, tŏŏk; foil; foul; thin; ~~then~~;
hw for wh as in *wh*at; zh for s as in u*s*ual; ə for a, e, i, o, u, as in *a*go, lin*e*n, per*i*l, at*o*m, min*u*s

Ill. Illinois.

I'll (īl) **1** I shall: *I hope I'll see him today.* **2** I will: *I am sure that I'll never go there again.* (Homonyms: aisle, isle)

il·le·gal (i lē′gəl) not lawful; forbidden by law. **il·le·gal·ly.**

Il·li·nois (il′ə noi′ or il′ə noiz′) a State in the north central part of the United States.

il·lit·er·ate (i lit′ər it) **1** unable to read or write. **2** person who cannot read or write. **3** showing lack of education: *an illiterate letter.*

ill-na·tured (il′nā′chərd) cross; disagreeable; surly. **ill-na·tured·ly.**

ill·ness (il′nis) **1** sickness: *Sudden illness was his excuse for being absent.* **2** disease: *I was troubled by flu and other illnesses.*

il·log·i·cal (i lŏj′ə kəl) not logical; not reasoned out well. **il·log·i·cal·ly.**

ill-tem·pered (il′tĕm′pərd) cross; quarrelsome; irritable: *Here comes ill-tempered Enos, who finds fault with everything and quarrels with everybody.* **ill-tem·pered·ly.**

ill-treat (il′trēt′) to treat badly or cruelly; abuse; mistreat.

il·lu·mi·nate (i lōō′mə nāt′ or i lū′mə nāt′) **1** to furnish with light: *Floodlights illuminated the ball park.* **2** to explain; make clear. **3** to ornament (a capital letter or the border of a page) with gold and colored designs. **il·lu·mi·nat·ed, il·lu·mi·nat·ing.**

il·lu·mi·na·tion (i lōō′mə nā′shən or i lū′mə nā′shən) **1** a lighting or being lighted: *The illumination of the hallway is poor.* **2** light supplied: *One small light bulb does not give enough illumination.* **3** colored and gilded decorations of a page, manuscript, etc.

il·lu·mine (i lōō′mīn or i lū′mīn) to light up; illuminate. **il·lu·mined, i·lu·min·ing.**

il·lu·sion (i lōō′zhən or i lū′zhən) **1** impression that something is something else or looks different from what it is; misleading appearance: *The shadow of the rock on the snowbank created the* illusion *of an animal standing there.* **2** false or mistaken idea: *A flimsy shelter gives an* illusion *of safety in a storm.*

Illusion: crown and brim same length

il·lus·trate (il′ə strāt′ or i lŭs′trāt) **1** to supply with pictures, diagrams, maps, etc., that help to explain or ornament something. **2** to make clear by using examples or comparisons: *to illustrate a spelling rule with an example.* **il·lus·trat·ed, il·lus·trat·ing.**

il·lus·tra·tion (il′ə strā′shən) **1** a picture, diagram, map, etc., used to explain or decorate: *There are many illustrations in your dictionary.* **2** example or comparison: *Washington's conduct at Valley Forge is an illustration of courage.* **3** an explaining by the use of examples or pictures: *The illustration of the use and meaning of a word makes it clearer.*

il·lus·tra·tor (il′əs trā′tər) a person who makes pictures in a book, magazine, etc.

il·lus·tri·ous (i lŭs′trĭ əs) famous for greatness, courage, nobility, etc.; celebrated: *an illustrious statesman; an illustrious deed.* **il·lus·tri·ous·ly.**

ill will unfriendly feeling; hate.

I'm (īm) I am.

im·age (im′ij) **1** object made in the likeness of a person, animal, etc.: *an image carved in stone.* **2** what is seen in a mirror, or through a magnifying glass, camera lens, etc.: *A microscope gives a large image of tiny things.* **3** copy; close likeness: *That boy is the image of his father.* **4** to reflect, as in a mirror: *The low branches of the trees were imaged in the pond.* **5** a picture in the mind: *His dreams were full of vivid images.* **6** to picture in the mind; describe; portray. **im·aged, im·ag·ing.**

im·ag·i·na·ble (i măj′ə nə bəl) capable of being imagined or pictured in the mind; possible: *the greatest joy imaginable.*

im·ag·i·nar·y (i măj′ə nĕr′ĭ) existing only in the mind or imagination; not real.

im·ag·i·na·tion (i măj′ə nā′shən) **1** power to form mental pictures or ideas of things not actually present: *A vivid imagination is necessary for a writer of adventure stories.* **2** act of forming a picture or idea in the mind; fancy: *It was only his imagination when he thought he heard voices.* **3** power to create through mental images new things or new ideas: *Only a great imagination can produce original art.*

im·ag·i·na·tive (i măj′ə nə tĭv) **1** having or using imagination: *an imaginative artist.* **2** coming from the imagination; fanciful: *an imaginative story.* **im·ag·i·na·tive·ly.**

im·ag·ine (ĭ măj′ĭn) **1** to form an idea or mental picture of: *Try to* imagine *yourself living in a pioneer cabin.* **2** to suppose; guess: *I* imagine *it's time to leave.* **im·ag·ined, im·ag·in·ing.**

im·be·cile (ĭm′bə sĭl) **1** person with a weak mind. **2** of weak mind; foolish: *an* imbecile *remark.*

im·i·tate (ĭm′ə tāt′) **1** to do or try to do the same as; follow the example of: *He* imitated *the accents of his language teacher.* **2** to mimic: *She followed the little man,* imitating *his short steps.* **3** to look like; resemble: *Manufactured pearls are made to* imitate *real ones.* **im·i·tat·ed, im·i·tat·ing.**

im·i·ta·tion (ĭm′ə tā′shən) **1** a copying; imitating: *By* imitation *one may learn.* **2** a mimicking: *The comedian did* imitations *of famous people.* **3** made to resemble something real or superior: *an* imitation *flower;* imitation *leather.*

im·mac·u·late (ĭ măk′yə lĭt) **1** spotless; absolutely clean: *Our clothes were* immaculate *as we started for school.* **2** pure; faultless. **im·mac·u·late·ly.**

im·ma·ture (ĭm′ə choor′ or ĭm′ə tyoor′ or ĭm′ə toor′) **1** not fully grown or developed; not ripe: *an* immature *ear of corn.* **2** not grown-up enough: *His behavior is* immature *for his age.* **im·ma·ture·ly.**

im·meas·ur·a·ble (ĭ mĕzh′ər ə bəl) boundless; impossible to measure: *the* immeasurable *depth of the sea.* **im·meas·ur·a·bly.**

im·me·di·ate (ĭ mē′dĭ ĭt) **1** happening or coming at once; without delay: *His answer to the telegram was* immediate. **2** having to do with the present time or moment: *We have no* immediate *plans.* **3** nearest; closest: *One's* immediate *family includes parents, brothers, and sisters.* **4** direct: *The* immediate *cause of his trouble was lack of money.* **im·me·di·ate·ly.**

im·me·mo·ri·al (ĭm′ə môr′ĭ əl) beyond reach of memory or record: *time* immemorial.

im·mense (ĭ mĕns′) very large; huge; vast: *an* immense *building;* an immense *area.* **im·mense·ly.**

im·men·si·ty (ĭ mĕns′ə tĭ) hugeness; vastness. **im·men·si·ties.**

im·merse (ĭ mûrs′) **1** to plunge or dip into a liquid: *to* immerse *a dress in dye.* **2** to baptize by plunging (a person) entirely under water. **3** to engage deeply; absorb: *He was* immersed *in his work.* **im·mersed, im·mers·ing.**

im·mi·grant (ĭm′ə grənt) person who comes into a country to make it his home: *We have special schools for teaching* immigrants *our language and government.*

im·mi·grate (ĭm′ə grāt′) to come into a country to make it one's home. **im·mi·grat·ed, im·mi·grat·ing.**

im·mi·gra·tion (ĭm′ə grā′shən) **1** the coming into another country to make it one's home. **2** the number of those immigrating at a certain time.

im·mi·nent (ĭm′ə nənt) about to happen; close at hand: *an* imminent *storm.* **im·mi·nent·ly.**

im·mor·al (ĭ môr′əl or ĭ mŏr′əl) not moral; against what is right; wicked. **im·mor·al·ly.**

im·mor·tal (ĭ môr′təl) **1** living forever; never dying. **2** person who lives forever; a god. **3** never to be forgotten; lasting forever: *Shakespeare's* immortal *poetry.* **4** person of lasting fame: *the* immortals *of music.* **im·mor·tal·ly.**

im·mor·tal·i·ty (ĭm′ôr tăl′ə tĭ) **1** life that never ends. **2** everlasting fame.

im·mov·a·ble (ĭ moo′və bəl) **1** firmly fixed; impossible to move. **2** firm; unchanging: *Once she decides a thing, she is* immovable. **im·mov·a·bly.**

im·mune (ĭ mūn′) **1** safe (from); protected (against): *Even the President is not* immune *from his critics. The fort was* immune *against attack from the sea.* **2** immune to not affected by; resistant to: *She is* immune *to polio since her shots. He is* immune *to persuasion.*

im·mu·ni·ty (ĭ mū′nə tĭ) **1** a not being affected by something, as a disease: *an* immunity *to smallpox.* **2** freedom (from): *Women may claim* immunity *from jury duty.* **im·mu·ni·ties.**

im·mu·ni·za·tion (ĭm′yə nə zā′shən) a protecting against attack, especially of a disease; an immunizing.

---

fāte, făt, fâre, fär; bē, bĕt; bīte, bĭt; nō, nŏt, nôr; fūse, fŭn, fûr; tōō, tŏŏk; foil; foul; thin; ~~then~~; hw for wh as in *what*; zh for s as in u*s*ual; ə for a, e, i, o, u, as in *ago, linen, peril, atom, minus*

im·mu·nize (ĭm′yə nīz′) **1** to protect from a disease by means of vaccination or inoculation; make immune. **2** to make safe from attack: *The thorn bushes immunized the camp against wild animals.* **im·mu·nized, im·mu·niz·ing.**

imp (ĭmp) **1** small devil; spiteful elf. **2** mischievous child.

im·pact (ĭm′păkt) a striking of one thing against another; collision: *We were jarred by the impact of our boat against the dock.*

Imp

im·pair (ĭm pâr′) to weaken; damage; injure: *Reading in poor light impaired his sight.*

im·part (ĭm pärt′) **1** to give; contribute: *Flowers impart a cheerful air to the room.* **2** to tell; pass on: *Indian fathers imparted wood lore to their sons.*

im·par·tial (ĭm pär′shəl) not favoring either side; not biased; fair: *The referee was completely impartial.* **im·par·tial·ly.**

im·pass·a·ble (ĭm păs′ə bəl) that cannot be crossed or passed over, through, or along; not passable: *an impassable swamp; impassable roads after a heavy snow.* **im·pass·a·bly.**

im·pas·sioned (ĭm păsh′ənd) full of deep feeling; passionate: *an impassioned appeal.*

im·pas·sive (ĭm păs′ĭv) showing or feeling no emotion; unmoved; calm: *His speech left the audience completely impassive.* **im·pas·sive·ly.**

im·pa·tience (ĭm pā′shəns) unwillingness to wait or delay; a lack of patience: *The horse showed its impatience by pawing the ground.*

im·pa·tient (ĭm pā′shənt) **1** unwilling to wait or delay: *We were impatient to start the trip.* **2** not able to endure annoyance: *I was impatient with her complaints.* **3** showing a lack of patience: *an impatient reply.* **im·pa·tient·ly.**

im·peach (ĭm pēch′) **1** to accuse of wrongdoing and bring official charges against (a public official before a court). **2** to cast discredit on; view with suspicion; bring to question: *The man's enemies impeached the motives of his generosity.*

im·pede (ĭm pēd′) to hold back; obstruct; hinder: *Long illness impeded the girl's progress in school.* **im·ped·ed, im·ped·ing.**

im·ped·i·ment (ĭm pĕd′ə mənt) **1** something that holds back or obstructs; a hindrance: *Ignorance is an impediment to progress.* **2** a speech defect.

im·pel (ĭm pĕl′) **1** to drive or push forward: *The current impelled the raft.* **2** to force; urge on: *Fear impelled him to lie.* **im·pelled, im·pel·ling.**

im·pen·e·tra·ble (ĭm pĕn′ə trə bəl) **1** impossible to penetrate, pierce, or pass through: *an impenetrable stone wall.* **2** impossible to understand: *an impenetrable maze of statistics.* **im·pen·e·tra·bly.**

im·per·a·tive (ĭm pĕr′ə tĭv) **1** not to be avoided or disobeyed; commanding: *The policeman's imperative gesture meant "Stop!"* **2** urgent; essential: *It is imperative that you be on time.* **3** a command or order. **im·per·a·tive·ly.**

im·per·cep·ti·ble (ĭm′pər sĕp′tə bəl) too small, slight, or subtle to be easily seen, heard, felt, etc.: *an almost imperceptible sound.* **im·per·cep·ti·bly.**

im·per·fect (ĭm pûr′fĭkt) incomplete; faulty; defective: *Unfortunately, the imperfect wiring made the machine of no use.* **im·per·fect·ly.**

im·per·fec·tion (ĭm′pər fĕk′shən) a defect; fault; incompleteness: *An imperfection in the glass made the lens worthless.*

im·pe·ri·al (ĭm pîr′ī əl) of or suitable to an empire, an emperor, or an empress: *the king's imperial robes; imperial power.* **im·pe·ri·al·ly.**

im·pe·ri·al·ism (ĭm pîr′ī ə lĭz′əm) **1** policy of extending the rule or control of a nation over other countries. **2** desire or will to dominate other nations: *Roman imperialism.*

im·per·il (ĭm pĕr′əl) to put in danger; endanger: *Floods imperiled the lowlands.*

im·pe·ri·ous (ĭm pîr′ē əs) haughty; domineering; masterful: *With an imperious gesture, she ordered us to leave the room.* **im·pe·ri·ous·ly.**

im·per·son·al (ĭm pûr′sən əl) **1** not aimed at or referring to any particular person: *The teacher kept an impersonal tone in reproaching the class.* **2** not prejudiced; not influenced by personal feeling: *an impersonal approach to a subject.* **3** not existing as a person: *the impersonal forces of nature.* **im·per·son·al·ly.**

im·per·ti·nence (ĭm pûr′tə nəns) **1** insolence; impudence. **2** impudent remark or other action: *his rude* impertinences.

im·per·ti·nent (ĭm pûr′tə nənt) **1** saucy; disrespectful: *It is* impertinent *to ask questions that are too personal.* **2** not relating (to the matter at hand); not to the point: *The judge ruled that the facts of the earlier offense were* impertinent *to the present case.* **im·per·ti·nent·ly.**

im·pet·u·ous (ĭm pĕch′ŏŏ əs) **1** inclined to act suddenly without thinking; impulsive; rash: *An* impetuous *person often does things that he regrets later.* **2** moving fast or with violent force: *an* impetuous *wind.* **im·pet·u·ous·ly.**

im·pe·tus (ĭm′pə təs) **1** forward push: *The growth in population has given an* impetus *to the building industry.* **2** force or momentum of a moving body: *The* impetus *of the truck threw the parked car across the sidewalk.*

im·pi·ous (ĭm′pĭ əs) irreverent toward God or sacred things; not pious. **im·pi·ous·ly.**

¹**im·ple·ment** (ĭm′plə mənt) tool or instrument with which work is done: *Hoes and spades are garden* implements.

²**im·ple·ment** (ĭm′plə mĕnt′) to carry out; put into effect: *to* implement *a plan.*

im·plore (ĭm plôr′) to ask earnestly; beg: *to* implore *aid.* **im·plored, im·plor·ing.**

im·ply (ĭm plī′) to suggest indirectly; give an impression; hint: *She didn't tell me my test grade, but she* implied *that it was a good one.* **im·plied, im·ply·ing.**

¹**im·port** (ĭm pôrt′) **1** product brought in from another country: *Coffee is an* import *from Brazil.* **2** the meaning: *the* import *of a speech.* **3** importance: *a speech of no* import.

²**im·port** (ĭm pôrt′) **1** to bring in goods from another country: *The United States* imports *tea from India.* **2** to mean or signify.

im·por·tance (ĭm pôr′təns) a being important; value; significance: *a book of* importance; *the* importance *of good health.*

im·por·tant (ĭm pôr′tənt) **1** filled with meaning; serious; valuable: *an* important

test; *an* important *day in history.* **2** having power or authority: *The governor of a state is an* important *man.* **im·por·tant·ly.**

im·por·ta·tion (ĭm′pôr tā′shən) **1** a bringing in of goods from other countries. **2** product brought in from another country; an import.

im·pose (ĭm pōz′) **1** to put on as a tax, burden, penalty, charge, etc.: *The judge* imposed *a fine.* **2** to force: *He didn't* impose *his advice on me, but I listened to him willingly.*

impose on to take advantage of: *I won't* impose *on you by asking too many favors.* **im·posed, im·pos·ing.**

im·pos·ing (ĭm pō′zĭng) worthy of notice; demanding attention; impressive. **im·pos·ing·ly.**

im·pos·si·bil·i·ty (ĭm pŏs′ə bĭl′ə tĭ) **1** condition of not being possible: *the* impossibility *of knowing what will happen next week.* **2** thing that is not possible: *It is an* impossibility *to live yesterday over.* **im·pos·si·bil·i·ties.**

im·pos·si·ble (ĭm pŏs′ə bəl) **1** not capable of being done or happening; not possible: *It is* impossible *to be in two places at the same time.* **2** not easy or not convenient: *It is* impossible *for me to be there on time.* **3** hard to endure; objectionable: *an* impossible *person.* **im·pos·si·bly.**

im·pos·tor (ĭm pŏs′tər) person who tries to deceive others by pretending to be someone or something else: *He isn't really a senator, but an* impostor.

im·po·tent (ĭm′pə tənt) lacking power; weak; powerless. **im·po·tent·ly.**

im·pov·er·ish (ĭm pŏv′ər ĭsh) **1** to make poor. **2** to exhaust (natural resources, fertility, etc.): *The soil was* impoverished *by bad farming methods.*

im·prac·ti·ca·ble (ĭm prăk′tə kə bəl) not suited to practical use: *His plan was* impracticable *because it required too much expensive equipment.* **im·prac·ti·ca·bly.**

im·prac·ti·cal (ĭm prăk′tə kəl) not practical; not concerned with realities: *an* impractical *scheme; an* impractical *man.* **im·prac·ti·cal·ly.**

im·pre·ca·tion (ĭm′prə kā′shən) a curse.

---

fāte, făt, fâre, fär; bē, bĕt; bīte, bĭt; nō, nŏt, nôr; fūse, fŭn, fûr; tōō, tŏŏk; foil; foul; thin; ~~then~~; hw for wh as in *what*; zh for s as in usual; ə for a, e, i, o, u, as in ago, linen, peril, atom, minus

im·preg·na·ble (ĭm prĕg′nə bəl) secure against attack; not to be overcome or taken by force: *an* impregnable *fortress in the mountains.* **im·preg·na·bly.**

¹**im·press** (ĭm prĕs′) **1** to mark by, or as by, pressing; to stamp: *to impress wax with a seal.* **2** to influence or affect strongly: *I was impressed by his wit.*

²**im·press** (ĭm′prĕs) mark made by, or as by, a stamp; impression.

im·pres·sion (ĭm prĕsh′ən) **1** mark made by pressing: *the* impression *of a seal on wax.* **2** an effect on the mind or feelings: *Her first airplane ride made a strong* impression *on her.* **3** vague idea: *He didn't say so, but I had the* impression *he was in a hurry.*

im·pres·sive (ĭm prĕs′ĭv) strongly affecting the mind, feelings, or actions: *The fireman's* impressive *talk made the boys more careful with matches.* **im·pres·sive·ly.**

¹**im·print** (ĭm prĭnt′) to print; impress: *The king* imprinted *the document with the royal seal.*

²**im·print** (ĭm′prĭnt) a mark; impression: *the* imprint *of a foot in the sand.*

im·pris·on (ĭm prĭz′ən) **1** to put or keep in prison. **2** to keep shut up; confine: *to* imprison *a tiger in a cage.*

im·pris·on·ment (ĭm prĭz′ən mənt) **1** a putting in prison: *The* imprisonment *took place February 2nd.* **2** a stay in prison. **3** any restraint thought of as being in prison: *In summer, he resented his* imprisonment *in the factory.*

im·prob·a·ble (ĭm prŏb′ə bəl) not probable; not likely to happen or be true: *It is* improbable *that you will ever see a purple cow.* **im·prob·a·bly.**

im·prop·er (ĭm prŏp′ər) **1** not proper; not suitable: *to use* improper *tools.* **2** contrary to good taste: *It is* improper *to eat peas with a knife.* **3** wrong; incorrect: *the* improper *use of a word.* **im·prop·er·ly.**

improper fraction any number greater than 1 expressed in the form of a fraction; fraction with a numerator that is larger than the denominator, as ⁴⁄₃. It can also be written 1 ¹⁄₃.

im·prove (ĭm prōōv′) **1** to make better: *Exercise* improves *the posture.* **2** to become better: *Her health* improved *in the milder climate.* **im·proved, im·prov·ing.**

im·prove·ment (ĭm prōōv′mənt) **1** a making or becoming better: *Much* improvement *of roads is necessary.* **2** a change or addition that makes something better: *The farm looks better after all the* improvements.

im·pro·vise (ĭm′prə vīz′) **1** to make up as one goes along: *As he sang, he* improvised *words to fit the music.* **2** to invent or construct to fit an immediate need: *The scouts* improvised *a shelter of pine branches for the night.* **im·pro·vised, im·pro·vis·ing.**

im·pru·dent (ĭm prōō′dənt) not wise or prudent; heedless; rash: *It is* imprudent *to cross against the lights.* **im·pru·dent·ly.**

im·pu·dence (ĭm′pyōō dəns) disrespect; sauciness: *The* impudence *of that child, to disobey and then laugh when corrected!*

im·pu·dent (ĭm′pyōō dənt) disrespectful; rude: *It is* impudent *to turn your back on a speaker.* **im·pu·dent·ly.**

im·pulse (ĭm′pŭls) **1** sudden desire to do something: *Henrietta acts on* impulse, *without stopping to think.* **2** a sudden push or driving force: *The* impulse *of the storm drove waves high up on the shore.*

im·pul·sive (ĭm pŭl′sĭv) **1** coming from some sudden feeling: *an* impulsive *smile.* **2** moved by or likely to act on sudden feeling: *She is so* impulsive *she is always speaking out of turn.* **3** pushing forward: *an* impulsive *force.* **im·pul·sive·ly.**

im·pu·ni·ty (ĭm pū′nə tĭ) freedom from punishment, injury, or loss: *Only stupid people think they can steal with* impunity.

im·pure (ĭm pūr′) **1** unclean; unwholesome; contaminated; dirty: *to purify* impure *water.* **2** mixed with another substance, especially something inferior: *There are laws against* impure *drugs.* **3** bad; corrupt in thought or action.

im·pu·ri·ty (ĭm pūr′ə tĭ) **1** something that makes a substance impure: *the* impurities *in water;* impurities *in metal.* **2** a being impure; being unclean in thought or feeling. **im·pu·ri·ties.**

in (ĭn) **1** inside: *to put clothes in a trunk; to live in a town.* **2** within a condition, situation, etc.: *be in business; in pain; in a hurry.* **3** into: *She just went in the house.* **4** at home, at the office, etc.: *Is the doctor in?* **5** during: *He came in the evening.* **6** after: *Call back in an hour.* **7** at the time of: *It was cold in the morning.* **8** for: *a parade in* honor of the returning heroes. **9** with the use of: *a note scribbled* in *pencil.* (Homonym: inn)

in. **1** inch. **2** inches.

in- prefix meaning (**1**) "in," "within," "to," or "towards": in*born;* in*trust;* in*land.* (**2**) "not" or "without": in*active;* in*experience.*

in·a·bil·i·ty (ĭn′ə bĭl′ə tĭ) a being unable; lack of power or means: *an* inability *to sleep;* inability *to pay a debt.* **in·a·bil·i·ties.**

in·ac·ces·si·ble (ĭn′ək sĕs′ə bəl) impossible or difficult to reach or get to: *a place* inaccessible *by car; an* inaccessible *goal.* **in·ac·ces·si·bly.**

in·ac·cu·ra·cy (ĭn ăk′yə rə sĭ) **1** condition of being not accurate or exact: *Wilbur was given to* inaccuracy *in his figuring.* **2** something not accurate; a mistake or error: *A slight* inaccuracy *in direction may throw an aviator far off his course.* **in·ac·cu·ra·cies.**

in·ac·cu·rate (ĭn ăk′yə rĭt) not correct; not accurate; not exact. **in·ac·cu·rate·ly.**

in·ac·tive (ĭn ăk′tĭv) **1** not moving about; not active: *Sickness made Victor* inactive. **2** not in use or action: *an* inactive *bank account; an* inactive *volcano.* **in·ac·tive·ly.**

in·ad·e·quate (ĭn ăd′ə kwĭt) not sufficient; not enough to meet some need: *The dining space is* inadequate *for our large group.* **in·ad·e·quate·ly.**

in·ad·vis·a·ble (ĭn′əd vī′zə bəl) not wise or sensible: *It is* inadvisable *to skate on thin ice.* **in·ad·vis·a·bly.**

in·al·ien·a·ble (ĭn ăl′yən ə bəl) that cannot be taken away or transferred to another: *Liberty is an* inalienable *right.*

in·ane (ĭn ān′) foolish; silly: *Pay no attention to such* inane *remarks!* **in·ane·ly.**

in·ap·pro·pri·ate (ĭn′ə prō′prĭ ĭt) **1** not suitable or appropriate: *A party dress is* inappropriate *for a hike.* **in·ap·pro·pri·ate·ly.**

in·as·much as (ĭn′əz mŭch′ ăz) since; because.

in·at·ten·tive (ĭn′ə tĕn′tĭv) not paying attention; heedless. **in·at·ten·tive·ly.**

in·aug·u·ral (ĭn ô′gyŏŏ rəl or ĭn ô′gə rəl) **1** having to do with an inauguration: *an* inaugural *parade.* **2** speech made at the beginning of a term of office.

in·au·gu·rate (ĭn ô′gyŏŏ rāt′) **1** to place in office with formal ceremony; install: *to* inaugurate *a president.* **2** to make a formal beginning of; commence: *to* inaugurate *a policy.* **3** to open formally for public use: *to* inaugurate *a new building.* **in·au·gu·rat·ed, in·au·gu·rat·ing.**

in·au·gu·ra·tion (ĭn ô′gyŏŏ rā′shən) an inaugurating, especially a placing in office with formal ceremony: *the impressive Presidential* inauguration.

in·born (ĭn′bôrn′) present in a person at birth; natural: *an* inborn *talent.*

In·ca (ĭng′kə) **1** king or chief of a group of South American Indian tribes that dominated Peru until the Spanish conquest. **2 Incas** modern name for the tribes ruled by the Inca.

in·can·des·cent (ĭn′kən dĕs′ənt) **1** glowing with heat; bright; brilliant. **2 incandescent lamp** lamp that gives light from an electrically heated filament.

in·ca·pa·ble (ĭn kā′pə bəl) **1** lacking necessary power or ability; not capable. **2 incapable of** not open to; not accessible to: *be* incapable *of speech; a situation* incapable *of improvement.*

¹in·cense (ĭn sĕns′) to make angry: *The boy was* incensed *by the man's cruel treatment of his dog.* **in·censed, in·cens·ing.** [¹**incense** comes through Old French (incenser) from the form (incensum) of a Latin word (incendere) meaning "to set on fire," "inflame."]

²in·cense (ĭn′sĕns) **1** substance which produces a sweet odor when burned. **2** perfume or smoke given off by such a substance when burned. **3** any pleasant odor: *the sweet* incense *of blossoms.* [²**incense** comes through Old French (encens) from the same Latin word as ¹**incense.**]

in·cen·tive (ĭn sĕn′tĭv) a cause or reason which arouses to action, effort, etc.; motive: *A desire for wealth was his* incentive.

in·ces·sant (ĭn sĕs′ənt) constant; not stopping; not ceasing; continual: *an* incessant *chirping of insects.* **in·ces·sant·ly.**

---

fāte, făt, fâre, fär; bē, bĕt; bīte, bĭt; nō, nŏt, nôr; fūse, fŭn, fûr; tōō, tŏŏk; foil; foul; thin; ~~then~~;
hw for wh as in *wh*at; zh for s as in u*s*ual; ə for a, e, i. o, u, as in *a*go, lin*e*n, per*i*l, at*o*m, min*u*s
365

inch (ĭnch) **1** measure of length. There are 12 inches in one foot. **2** to proceed slowly; move little by little: *to inch along the icy walk.*

in·ci·dent (ĭn′sə dənt) **1** a happening: *He told us incidents from his childhood.* **2 incident to** likely to happen in connection with (something else): *Risks and danger are incident to the life of a soldier.*

in·ci·den·tal (ĭn′sə dĕn′təl) **1** happening in connection with something more important: *the incidental expenses of a trip.* **2** made or added casually; thrown in: *an incidental remark.* **3 incidentals** small, unimportant items.

in·ci·den·tal·ly (ĭn′sə dĕn′tə lĭ) with less attention or emphasis; as a less important part (of something else); by the way: *He talked about Mexico, but mentioned his work there only incidentally.*

in·cin·er·a·tor (ĭn sĭn′ə rā′tər) furnace or container for burning trash.

in·ci·sor (ĭn sī′zər) cutting tooth; in man one of the four front teeth in either jaw. For picture, see **teeth.**

in·cite (ĭn sīt′) to rouse; stir up: *The sailor was punished for inciting the crew to mutiny.* **in·cit·ed, in·cit·ing.**

in·clem·ent (ĭn klĕm′ənt) harsh; stormy; not mild: *December's inclement weather.*

in·cli·na·tion (ĭn′klə nā′shən) **1** a leaning, sloping, or bending: *He showed his agreement by a slight inclination of the head.* **2** degree of slope: *The inclination of the roof is great enough to allow water to run off.* **3** a liking; choice; preference: *His present inclinations are toward a singing career.*

in·cline (ĭn klīn′) **1** to tilt; slant: *Italic type inclines to the right.* **2** (also ĭn′klīn) a slope; slanting surface: *A gentle incline carried the railroad track up the hillside.* **3** to favor; lean towards: *I am inclined to believe you, now that I've heard your story.* **4** to bow; nod: *He inclined his head in acceptance of the offer.* **in·clined, in·clin·ing.**

Incline

in·clined (ĭn klīnd′) slanting; sloping: *an inclined surface.*

in·close (ĭn klōz′) enclose. **in·closed, in·clos·ing.**

in·clude (ĭn klōōd′) **1** to contain as part of the whole: *Does this price include the tax?* **2** to put in with others; enter: *Please include me on your list.* **in·clud·ed, in·clud·ing.**

in·clud·ing (ĭn klōō′dĭng) taking or counting in as part of a whole: *All of us, including the dog, jumped into the water.*

in·clu·sion (ĭn klōō′zhən) a taking into or being taken into: *The inclusion of Roger in the game was a great mistake.*

in·clu·sive (ĭn klōō′sĭv) including or taking in the first- and last-mentioned things in a group: *The figures zero to nine, inclusive, are called digits.* **in·clu·sive·ly.**

in·come (ĭn′kŭm) amount of money one gets from labor, business, property, etc.

in·com·pa·ra·ble (ĭn kŏm′pə rə bəl) matchless; unequaled: *her incomparable beauty.* **in·com·pa·ra·bly.**

in·com·pe·tent (ĭn kŏm′pə tənt) lacking enough ability, skill, etc.; not competent: *As a carpenter, I am completely incompetent.* **in·com·pe·tent·ly.**

in·com·plete (ĭn′kŭm plēt′) with some part or parts missing; not finished; not complete: *an incomplete deck of cards; an incomplete book report.* **in·com·plete·ly.**

in·com·pre·hen·si·ble (ĭn′kŏm prĭ hĕn′sə bəl) not to be understood; beyond understanding: *His actions are incomprehensible.* **in·com·pre·hen·si·bly.**

in·con·ceiv·a·ble (ĭn′kən sē′və bəl) **1** impossible to imagine: *A square circle is inconceivable.* **2** hard to believe or understand: *Light travels at an inconceivable speed.* **in·con·ceiv·a·bly.**

in·con·sid·er·ate (ĭn′kən sĭd′ə rĭt) thoughtless; without proper regard for others; not considerate. **in·con·sid·er·ate·ly.**

in·con·sist·ent (ĭn′kən sĭs′tənt) **1** not in keeping or agreement: *His actions are inconsistent with his words.* **2** having contradictions within itself: *The man's story was so inconsistent that we didn't believe any of it.* **3** changeable; fickle; not logical: *He's an inconsistent fellow, cheerful one minute and depressed the next.* **in·con·sist·ent·ly.**

in·con·spic·u·ous (ĭn′kən spĭk′yōō əs) not easily seen or noticed; not striking or showy: *an inconspicuous part in a play; inconspicuous hat.* **in·con·spic·u·ous·ly.**

in·con·stant (ĭn kŏn′stənt) likely to change; not dependable: *an* inconstant *friend;* inconstant *winds.* **in·con·stant·ly.**

in·con·ven·ience (ĭn′kən vēn′yəns) **1** a trouble, bother, or annoyance: *A water shortage causes* inconveniences. **2** a cause of trouble, bother, or annoyance: *A water shortage is an* inconvenience. **3** to cause bother or annoyance: *The water shortage* inconvenienced *us.* **in·con·ven·ienced, in·con·ven·ienc·ing.**

in·con·ven·ient (ĭn′kən vēn′yənt) causing bother or annoyance; not convenient: *Would it be* inconvenient *for you to visit me this afternoon at my office?* **in·con·ven·ient·ly.**

in·cor·po·rate (ĭn kôr′pə rāt′) **1** to put (in): *I will* incorporate *your ideas in my report.* **2** to bring together as part of a whole; include: *The new automobile* incorporates *the best features of last year's model.* **3** to form into a corporation, or a body of people acting as a single person: *The business was* incorporated. **in·cor·po·rat·ed, in·cor·po·rat·ing.**

in·cor·rect (ĭn′kə rĕkt′) **1** not according to fact; not true or accurate: *His account of the accident was* incorrect. **2** not in keeping with good usage or standards: *It is* incorrect *to wear one's hat in the house.* **in·cor·rect·ly.**

¹in·crease (ĭn krēs′) to make or become greater; add to or grow: *Trade* increased *the country's wealth. His skill* increased *with practice.* **in·creased, in·creas·ing.**

²in·crease (ĭn′krēs) **1** growth or enlargement: *an* increase *of membership in a club.* **2** amount that is added: *an* increase *of ten dollars in the price.*

in·creas·ing·ly (ĭn krē′sĭng lĭ) more and more: *The path became* increasingly *steep as we neared the top.*

in·cred·i·ble (ĭn krĕd′ə bəl) hard to believe; beyond belief: *He told a tale of* incredible *adventures.* **in·cred·i·bly.**

in·cred·u·lous (ĭn krĕj′ə ləs) **1** doubting; questioning as to truth or accuracy; not willing or able to believe: *to be* incredulous *of the statement.* **2** showing doubt: *an* incredulous *smile.* **in·cred·u·lous·ly.**

in·cu·ba·tor (ĭn′kyōō bā′tər or ĭng′kyōō-bā′tər) **1** heated box for hatching eggs. **2** heated box or cabinet used to help the growth of very small babies.

in·cum·bent (ĭn kŭm′bənt) **1** lying or leaning with its weight on something else. **2** person who holds office. **3** incumbent on resting on as a duty: *It is* incumbent *on you as a citizen to serve on the jury.* **in·cum·bent·ly.**

in·cum·ber (ĭn kŭm′bər) encumber.

in·cur (ĭn kûr′) to fall into; bring upon oneself: *By living beyond his means he* incurred *many debts. His disrespect* incurred *her anger.* **in·curred, in·cur·ring.**

in·cur·a·ble (ĭn kyōōr′ə bəl) **1** not possible to cure: *an* incurable *disease.* **2** person having a disease that cannot be cured. **in·cur·a·bly.**

Ind. Indiana.

in·debt·ed (ĭn dĕt′əd) owing (money, gratitude, or the like); under obligation: *We are* indebted *to you for your help.*

in·de·cent (ĭn dē′sənt) **1** not proper; not suitable: *He is in an* indecent *hurry to get his money back.* **2** not modest; unfit to be seen or heard; not decent. **in·de·cent·ly.**

in·de·ci·sion (ĭn′də sĭzh′ən) lack of decision; inability to make up one's mind: *Her* indecision *about what dress to wear made us late for the party.*

in·deed (ĭn dēd′) in fact; really: *We were* indeed *pleased by his success.*

in·def·i·nite (ĭn dĕf′ə nĭt) **1** having no fixed or exact limit: *Our relatives arrived for an* indefinite *stay.* **2** not clear or certain; vague: *There will be a party, but plans are still* indefinite. **in·def·i·nite·ly.**

in·del·i·ble (ĭn dĕl′ə bəl) impossible to remove or erase; permanent: *an* indelible *ink.* **in·del·i·bly.**

in·dem·ni·ty (ĭn dĕm′nə tĭ) payment to make up for a loss by fire, theft, etc. **in·dem·ni·ties.**

in·dent (ĭn dĕnt′) **1** to notch; zigzag; give a sawlike edge to: *Small coves* indent *the rocky coast.* **2** to impress; make a dent or impression in: *The boy's crutch had* indented *the hard sand.* **3** (also ĭn′dĕnt) a blank space that sets a line in from a

---

fāte, făt, fâre, fär; bē, bĕt; bīte, bĭt; nō, nŏt, nôr; fūse, fŭn, fûr; tōō, tŏŏk; foil; foul; thin; ~~then;~~
hw for wh as in *wh*at; zh for s as in u*s*ual; ə for a, e, i, o, u, as in *a*go, lin*e*n, per*i*l, at*o*m, min*us*

margin, as at the beginning of a paragraph. **4** to begin a line with one or more blank spaces: *Please* indent *each paragraph.*

in·den·tured (ĭn dĕn'chərd) **1** bound by a written contract. **2 indentured servant** servant who is bound by a written agreement to work for the same master for a certain length of time.

in·de·pend·ence (ĭn'dĭ pĕn'dəns) freedom from influence or control by others: *to gain* independence *from another country.*

Independence Day July 4th, celebrated in the United States as the anniversary of the day on which the Declaration of Independence was adopted in 1776.

in·de·pend·ent (ĭn'dĭ pĕn'dənt) **1** not depending on or controlled by others: *an* independent *country; a man of* independent *mind.* **2** not willing to accept help from others: *a poor but* independent *man.* **3** acting or doing separately: *The one-man minority made an* independent *report.* **4** person who thinks for himself, especially in political matters. **in·de·pend·ent·ly.**

in·de·scrib·a·ble (ĭn'dĭs krī'bə bəl) impossible to describe; beyond expression: *an* indescribable *fear of the dark.* **in·de·scrib·a·bly.**

in·de·struct·i·ble (ĭn'dĭ strŭk'tə bəl) not capable of being destroyed.

in·dex (ĭn'dĕks) **1** alphabetical list of the names and topics in a book, with the page on which each is treated. **2** to furnish (a book) with, or enter (a word) into, such a list. **3** something that points out; a sign or indication: *High living standards are an* index *of a country's prosperity.* **in·dex·es** or **in·di·ces** (ĭn'də sēz').

index finger forefinger; finger next to the thumb.

In·di·a (ĭn'dĭ ə) country in southern Asia.

In·di·an (ĭn'dĭ ən) **1** person living in America at the time of its discovery or a descendant of such a person; an American Indian. **2** of the peoples living in America at the time of its discovery, or their descendants: *an* Indian *war dance.* **3** any of the languages of the American Indians. **4** of India or the East Indies, their people, or their languages. **5** citizen of India or person of Indian or East Indian descent.

In·di·an·a (ĭn'dĭ ăn'ə) a north central State of the United States.

Indian Ocean a large ocean south of Asia, east of Africa, and west of Australia.

In·di·an paintbrush 1 one of a group of plants with showy flowers, growing in western United States. **2** the flower of this plant. It is the state flower of Wyoming.

Indian summer period of mild weather following autumn frosts. The days are usually dry, hazy, and windless.

in·di·cate (ĭn'də kāt') **1** to be a sign of; suggest: *Soft teeth* indicate *a lack of proper diet.* **2** to show: *The shortest route is* indicated *on the map.* **3** to make known or state briefly; point out: *Please* indicate *your choice of color and size.* **in·di·cat·ed, in·di·cat·ing.**

in·di·ca·tion (ĭn'də kā'shən) something that serves to point out or show; a sign: *His slow pace was an* indication *of his weariness.*

in·di·ca·tor (ĭn'də kā'tər) **1** someone or something that indicates: *Facial expression is an* indicator *of the feelings.* **2** a needle or pointer on a dial; any device, such as a flashing light, that shows heat, pressure, speed, etc.: *The* indicator *shows an empty gas tank.*

in·dict (ĭn dīt') to charge formally with a crime.

in·dict·ment (ĭn dīt'mənt) **1** an indicting or being indicted. **2** written accusation of a crime, presented to the court by a special jury, called a **grand jury,** after it has considered the evidence.

in·dif·fer·ence (ĭn dĭf'ər əns) **1** lack of interest or feeling: *She did not conceal her* indifference *to our plans.* **2** no importance: *It is a matter of* indifference *whether this work is done today or tomorrow.*

in·dif·fer·ent (ĭn dĭf'ər ənt) **1** not caring or concerned; without any strong feeling one way or the other: *When you see others suffering, can you remain* indifferent? **2** not very good or very bad: *Some movies are good, some bad, some* indifferent. **in·dif·fer·ent·ly.**

in·dig·e·nous (ĭn dĭj'ə nəs) native; growing or produced naturally in certain locations, regions, or climates: *The rubber tree is* indigenous *to the tropics.*

in·di·gest·i·ble (ĭn'də jĕs'tə bəl) impossible to digest or not easily digested; not digestible. **in·di·gest·i·bly.**

in·di·ges·tion (ĭn'də jĕs'chən) difficulty in digesting food; discomfort resulting from such difficulty: *Eating too fast may give you* indigestion.

in·dig·nant (ĭn dĭg'nənt) angry at something considered unfair, mean, or cruel: *It makes me* indignant *to see anyone mistreat an animal.* **in·dig·nant·ly.**

in·dig·na·tion (ĭn'dĭg nā'shən) anger at something considered unfair, mean, or cruel: *His lies aroused my* indignation.

in·dig·ni·ty (ĭn dĭg'nə tĭ) thing that humiliates, lowers the dignity, or wounds the pride: *Jim didn't mind washing dishes but thought it an* indignity *that he had to wear a ruffled apron.* **in·dig·ni·ties.**

in·di·go (ĭn'də gō') **1** blue dye, formerly obtained from the indigo plant, but now made chiefly from coal tar. **2** the plant itself. **3** deep violet-blue color. **in·di·gos** or **in·di·goes.**

in·di·rect (ĭn'də rĕkt') **1** not in a straight line; roundabout: *He was delayed because he went by an* indirect *route.* **2** not closely connected or intended: *an* indirect *cause; an* indirect *result.* **3** not straightforward or to the point: *an* indirect *answer.* **in·di·rect·ly.**

in·dis·creet (ĭn'dĭs krēt') not careful or cautious; unwise; not discreet: *His* indiscreet *remarks got him into trouble.* **in·dis·creet·ly.**

in·dis·cre·tion (ĭn'dĭs krĕsh'ən) **1** lack of caution or prudence: *Our* indiscretions *in diet may lead to illness.* **2** imprudent act or step: *to commit an* indiscretion.

in·dis·pens·a·ble (ĭn'dĭs pĕn'sə bəl) absolutely necessary; essential: *Machinery is* indispensable *in industry.*

in·dis·posed (ĭn'dĭs pōzd') **1** not willing: *We are* indisposed *to accept your offer.* **2** mildly sick: *Mother is* indisposed *with a headache.*

in·dis·tinct (ĭn'dĭs tĭngkt') not clear or distinct; obscure: *All I could hear was an* indistinct *murmur.* **in·dis·tinct·ly.**

in·di·vid·u·al (ĭn'də vĭj'ōō əl) **1** person: *a determined* individual. **2** particular; separate: *He gave* individual *help to each student.* **3** having features that belong to it alone:

an individual *hair style.* **4** belonging to or intended for one person: *an* individual *bed in a dormitory.* **5** a single person, animal, or thing: *The Constitution protects the rights of the* individual.

in·di·vid·u·al·i·ty (ĭn'də vĭj'ōō ăl'ə tĭ) **1** all the characteristics that make a person different from other persons: *His marked* individuality *was reflected in his speech.* **2** condition of being different from all others: *Keep your* individuality. **in·di·vid·u·al·i·ties.**

in·di·vid·u·al·ly (ĭn'də vĭj'ōō ə lĭ) one by one; separately; personally: *He spoke to each person* individually.

in·di·vis·i·ble (ĭn'də vĭz'ə bəl) impossible to divide or separate into parts; not divisible. **in·di·vis·i·bly.**

in·do·lence (ĭn'də ləns) laziness; dislike for work: *His* indolence *cost him his job.*

in·do·lent (ĭn'də lənt) lazy; idle: *He was too* indolent *to learn to play tennis.* **in·do·lent·ly.**

in·dom·i·ta·ble (ĭn dŏm'ə tə bəl) unconquerable; unyielding; steadfast: *He had* indomitable *courage.* **in·dom·i·ta·bly.**

in·door (ĭn'dôr') belonging to or done inside a house or building: *Basketball is usually an* indoor *sport.*

in·doors (ĭn'dôrz') not outdoors; inside a building: *When it rains, we play* indoors.

in·dorse (ĭn dôrs') endorse.

in·duce (ĭn dōōs' or ĭn dūs') **1** to persuade; prevail upon: *We* induced *Father to take us to the movies.* **2** to cause; bring on or about: *His illness was* induced *by extreme weariness.* **in·duced, in·duc·ing.**

in·duce·ment (ĭn dōōs'mənt or ĭn dūs'mənt) something that persuades or influences; incentive: *The prize was an* inducement *to study.*

in·duct (ĭn dŭkt') **1** to place officially in a position: *to* induct *a governor.* **2** to enroll: *The soldiers will be* inducted *at Camp Dix.*

in·dulge (ĭn dŭlj') **1** to humor by giving in to: *The family* indulged *the little girl's every whim.* **2** to yield to; gratify: *to* indulge *a liking for candy.* **3** to please oneself (by doing something): *to* indulge *in daydreaming.* **in·dulged, in·dulg·ing.**

---

fāte, făt, fâre, fär; bē, bĕt; bīte, bĭt; nō, nŏt, nôr; fūse, fŭn, fûr; tōō, tŏŏk; foil; foul; thin; ~~then~~;
hw for wh as in *what*; zh for s as in u*s*ual; ə for a, e, i, o, u, as in ago, linen, peril, atom, minus

in·dul·gence (ĭn dŭl′jəns) **1** the humoring or satisfying of another: *I request your indulgence in this matter.* **2** something taken, done, or given to gratify; a favor: *Smoking is one* indulgence *he allows himself.* **3** a giving way to one's own likings: *Too much* indulgence *in sweets is bad for us.*

in·dul·gent (ĭn dŭl′jənt) yielding easily to whims or desires of others; lenient; not very strict: *Father was* indulgent *toward our pranks.* **in·dul·gent·ly.**

in·dus·tri·al (ĭn dŭs′trĭ əl) having to do with industry, trades, or manufacturing; not agricultural or commercial: *an* industrial *city with many factories; an* industrial *school or course of training.* **in·dus·tri·al·ly.**

in·dus·tri·ous (ĭn dŭs′trĭ əs) working hard and steadily; diligent: *The* industrious *farmer cultivated his land from dawn to dark.* **in·dus·tri·ous·ly.**

in·dus·try (ĭn′dəs trĭ) **1** hard work; diligence. **2** production of goods; manufacturing, mining, etc. **3** certain branch of manufacturing: *the paper* industry. **4** manufacturing, trade, and transportation considered as a single interest: *The people of northeastern United States are supported by* industry. **in·dus·tries.**

in·ed·i·ble (ĭn ĕd′ə bəl) not fit to be eaten; not edible.

in·ef·fec·tu·al (ĭn′ĭ fĕk′chŏŏ əl) not having the effect intended; useless; weak; unsuccessful. **in·ef·fec·tu·al·ly.**

in·ef·fi·cien·cy (ĭn′ə fĭsh′ən sĭ) **1** failure to act or function in an efficient way: *The* inefficiency *of some forms of animal life led to their dying out.* **2** lack of necessary skill or ability: *The employer was hampered by the* inefficiency *of his workmen.*

in·ef·fi·cient (ĭn′ə fĭsh′ənt) **1** unable to get things done quickly and well; not capable or skillful: *Lack of training made him an* inefficient *worker.* **2** requiring unnecessary time and work; not producing the desired effect: *an* inefficient *method of production.* **in·ef·fi·cient·ly.**

in·ept (ĭn ĕpt′) **1** not fit or suited; out of place; inappropriate: *an* inept *choice; inept remarks.* **2** awkward; clumsy: *an* inept *carpenter.* **in·ept·ly.**

in·e·qual·i·ty (ĭn′ĭ kwŏl′ə tĭ) a being unequal; lack of uniformity: *People live and work differently from one another because of* inequality *of talents or opportunity.* **in·e·qual·i·ties.**

in·ert (ĭn ûrt′) **1** having no power to act or move: *an* inert *lump of clay.* **2** slow; sluggish. **in·ert·ly.**

in·er·tia (ĭn ûr′shə) **1** tendency to remain at rest or, if in motion, to continue moving in the same direction, unless acted upon by some outside force. **2** unwillingness to change or act: *A feeling of* inertia *often follows a long illness.*

in·es·ti·ma·ble (ĭn ĕs′tə mə bəl) too great to be measured: *Vaccines have been of* inestimable *value to the nation's health.* **in·es·ti·ma·bly.**

in·ev·i·ta·ble (ĭn ĕv′ə tə bəl) certain; not to be avoided, escaped, or averted; sure to happen: *With our team so far in the lead,* victory seems inevitable. **in·ev·i·ta·bly.**

in·ex·act (ĭn′ĕg zăkt′) not accurate; hot exact; roughly but not absolutely correct: *"Half past six" is* inexact *if the clock reads 6:29½.* **in·ex·act·ly.**

in·ex·cus·a·ble (ĭn′ĕks kū′zə bəl) not to be forgiven, pardoned, or justified; not to be explained away: *That boy's continued carelessness is* inexcusable. **in·ex·cus·a·bly.**

in·ex·haust·i·ble (ĭn′ĕg zôs′tə bəl) without end or limits; impossible to use up: *He uses paper as if the supply were* inexhaustible. **in·ex·haust·i·bly.**

in·ex·o·ra·ble (ĭn ĕk′sə rə bəl) not changed or influenced by pleas; relentless: *an* inexorable *enemy.* **in·ex·o·ra·bly.**

in·ex·pen·sive (ĭn′ĕks pĕn′sĭv) costing little; cheap; not expensive. **in·ex·pen·sive·ly.**

in·ex·pe·ri·ence (ĭn′ĕks pē′rĭ əns) lack of experience.

in·ex·pe·ri·enced (ĭn′ĕks pē′rĭ ənst) without knowledge or skill gained through experience or practice; not used to; not familiar with: *The* inexperienced *worker needs much help.*

in·ex·pli·ca·ble (ĭn ĕks′plə kə bəl) not to be explained; impossible to account for; beyond understanding: *For some* inexplicable *reason the mob suddenly became quiet.* **in·ex·pli·ca·bly.**

in·fal·li·ble (ĭn făl′ə bəl) not capable of making a mistake or of failing; very reliable: *Weather forecasts do not claim to be* infallible. **in·fal·li·bly.**

in·fa·mous (ĭn′fə məs) **1** having a reputation for wickedness: *an infamous pirate.* **2** shameful; disgraceful: *an infamous day in history.* **in·fa·mous·ly.**

in·fa·my (ĭn′fə mĭ) **1** public shame, disgrace, and scorn: *The traitor brought ruin and infamy upon himself.* **2** wickedness; evil: *Blackbeard led a life of infamy.* **in·fa·mies.**

in·fan·cy (ĭn′fən sĭ) **1** babyhood; early childhood. **2** first stages of development: *Fifty years ago the airplane was still in its infancy.* **in·fan·cies.**

in·fant (ĭn′fənt) **1** very young child; baby. **2** in an early stage of development: *an infant industry.*

in·fan·tile (ĭn′fən tīl′) **1** having to do with babies: *an infantile disease.* **2** childish; like a baby: *Sue's infantile behavior.*

infantile paralysis disease which attacks the nervous system, sometimes causing permanent paralysis; poliomyelitis.

in·fan·try (ĭn′fən trĭ) body of soldiers who are armed, equipped, and trained to fight on foot; foot soldiers. **in·fan·tries.**

in·fect (ĭn fĕkt′) **1** to fill with disease germs: *Dirt can infect a cut.* **2** to affect or influence with a mood, feeling, etc.: *Mary's laughter infected the whole class.*

in·fec·tion (ĭn fĕk′shən) **1** a causing of disease by contact with germs or viruses: *We should guard burns against infection.* **2** disease caused by germs or viruses: *His ear infection lasted a week.*

in·fec·tious (ĭn fĕk′shəs) **1** caused or spread by germs or viruses: *an infectious disease.* **2** tending to spread to others: *Enthusiasm is often infectious.* **in·fec·tious·ly.**

in·fer (ĭn fûr′) to figure out; reach a conclusion by reasoning: *From his shabby appearance, I inferred he was poor.* **in·ferred, in·fer·ring.**

in·fer·ence (ĭn′fər əns) **1** conclusion reached by reasoning: *His inferences seem logical, but I question the evidence on which they are based.* **2** the reasoning used in reaching such a conclusion: *By inference we may expect a mild winter.*

in·fe·ri·or (ĭn fîr′ĭ ər) **1** lower in rank, quality, or importance: *Cotton clothing is inferior to wool for cold weather. His small size never made him feel inferior.* **2** of low quality: *Cheap furniture is made of inferior wood.* **3** person of lower rank: *The sergeant always treats his inferiors well.*

in·fe·ri·or·i·ty (ĭn fîr′ĭ ŏr′ə tĭ) the condition of being below others; lower rank, quality, or importance.

in·fer·nal (ĭn fûr′nəl) of or like hell: *the infernal regions; infernal heat.*

in·fer·no (ĭn fûr′nō) **1** hell. **2** any place of terror or misery, especially one of intense heat: *Before the fire department arrived the house was an inferno.* **in·fer·nos.**

in·fest (ĭn fĕst′) to be present in troublesome numbers; overrun or be overrun: *The islands were infested by smugglers. Mosquitoes infested the swamps.*

in·fi·del (ĭn′fə dəl) **1** person who does not believe in any religion. **2** person who does not believe in a certain religion.

in·field (ĭn′fēld′) **1** part of a baseball diamond bounded by the base lines. **2** players of the defending team stationed in this area: the pitcher, catcher, shortstop, and basemen.

in·fi·nite (ĭn′fə nĭt) **1** without limits; endless: *stars scattered through infinite space.* **2** seemingly endless; vast; inexhaustible: *to act with infinite care.* **in·fi·nite·ly.**

in·fin·i·tive (ĭn fĭn′ə tĭv) the simple form of an action word, or verb, not changed for person, number, or time. It is generally preceded by "to." "To go," "stay," "to read" are infinitives in these sentences:
> *It is time to go.*
> *Let them stay.*
> *This book is easy to read.*

in·firm (ĭn fûrm′) weak; not strong or steady; feeble, especially from old age. **in·firm·ly.**

in·fir·mi·ty (ĭn fûr′mə tĭ) **1** state of being weak or sick: *the infirmity of old age.* **2** a weakness: *Ralph's only infirmity is a quick temper.* **in·fir·mi·ties.**

in·flame (ĭn flām′) **1** to stir up; arouse: *His fiery speech inflamed the people.* **2** to make red, swollen, and painful: *Her eyes were inflamed with crying.* **in·flamed, in·flam·ing.**

---

fāte, făt, fâre, fär; bē, bĕt; bīte, bĭt; nō, nŏt, nôr; fūse, fŭn, fûr; tōō, tŏŏk; foil; foul; thin; then;
hw for wh as in what; zh for s as in usual; ə for a, e, i, o, u, as in ago, linen, peril, atom, minus

in·flam·ma·ble (in flăm′ə bəl) 1 easily set on fire; flammable: *Gasoline is highly inflammable.* 2 easily excited or aroused: *an inflammable temper.* **in·flam·ma·bly.**

in·flam·ma·tion (in′flə mā′shən) 1 a diseased condition marked by redness, swelling, and heat of some part of the body. 2 a stirring up or being stirred up: *the inflammation of public feeling.*

in·flate (in flāt′) 1 to swell out with enclosed air or gas, as a balloon. 2 to puff up, as with pride or self-satisfaction: *David's new honors helped to* inflate *his already high opinion of himself.* **in·flat·ed, in·flat·ing.**

in·flex·i·ble (in flĕk′sə bəl) 1 not bending easily; rigid: *an inflexible iron rod.* 2 not to be turned from a set plan or purpose; unyielding: *Once he has made up his mind, he is* inflexible. **in·flex·i·bly.**

in·flict (in flĭkt′) 1 to lay on (a blow, etc.); cause (wounds, pain, etc.): *The angry lion attacked the trainer and* inflicted *many wounds.* 2 to put on or impose (a punishment or something not welcome): *He* inflicts *his troubles on everyone.*

in·flu·ence (in′flōō əns) 1 power to persuade others by suggestion and example: *Use your* influence *to improve your class.* 2 effect produced by such power: *Florence Nightingale had a great* influence *on the development of nursing.* 3 person who or thing that produces such an effect: *Florence Nightingale was a great* influence *in improved medical care.* 4 to have an effect on: *Weather* influences *our lives.* 5 power that comes from wealth, social position, connections, etc.: *Will you use your* influence *to help me?* **in·flu·enced, in·flu·enc·ing.**

in·flu·en·tial (in′flōō ĕn′shəl) having influence; exerting power: *The mayor of our town is an* influential *man.* **in·flu·en·tial·ly.**

in·flu·en·za (in′flōō ĕn′zə) severe contagious disease, accompanied by inflamed nose and throat, fever, nausea, etc.; flu.

in·form (in fôrm′) 1 to tell; make known to; give information to: *Please* inform *me when she arrives.* 2 to give information of unlawful or secret acts or plans: *One convict* informed *against the others who were planning to escape.*

in·for·mal (in fôr′məl) not according to strict rules or set customs: *to write an in-*formal *letter; an* informal *party.* **in·for·mal·ly.**

in·form·ant (in fôr′mənt) person who gives information.

in·for·ma·tion (in′fər mā′shən) 1 an informing: *This booklet is for the* information *of new students.* 2 knowledge; facts: *Do you have any* information *on taxes?*

in·fra·red rays (in′frə rĕd′ rāz) 1 radiant energy that cannot be seen but can usually be felt as heat. These rays have a longer wave length than those of red light, but shorter than radio waves. 2 **infrared** having to do with such rays.

in·fre·quent (in frē′kwənt) not frequent; rare; uncommon: *Since he moved away his visits have become more* infrequent. **in·fre·quent·ly.**

in·fringe (in frinj′) to violate; disregard or fail to keep, as a law, patent, etc. **infringe on** or **upon** to trespass on. **in·fringed, in·fring·ing.**

in·fu·ri·ate (in fū′rĭ āt′) to enrage; make furious; madden. **in·fu·ri·at·ed, in·fu·ri·at·ing.**

in·fuse (in fūz′) 1 to put in; instill: *The coach* infused *enthusiasm into the team.* 2 to inspire: *to* infuse *one's fellows with confidence.* **in·fused, in·fus·ing.**

-ing 1 word ending used to show that an action continues for a time: *I am go*ing. *You are driv*ing. *It is hopp*ing. *He was rac*ing. 2 suffix meaning (1) "the act that results when someone or something does something": *our walk*ing; *its buzz*ing. (2) "what something is used to or for": *Stuff*ing *for a cushion; seat cover*ing. (3) "what is made" (when something is done): *a draw*ing; *a build*ing.

in·gen·ious (in jēn′yəs) 1 clever; inventive; resourceful: *an ingenious mechanic.* 2 skillfully invented, made, or done: *an ingenious machine; an ingenious plan.* **in·gen·ious·ly.**

in·ge·nu·i·ty (in′jə nū′ə tĭ) cleverness or skill in invention or design: *Edison used his ingenuity to invent the electric lamp.* **in·ge·nu·i·ties.**

in·gen·u·ous (in jĕn′yōō əs) simple and natural; without guile: *the* ingenuous *question of a child.* **in·gen·u·ous·ly.**

in·got (ing′gət) a lump or bar of metal cast at a refinery for future manufacture.

in·gra·ti·ate (ĭn grā'shĭ āt') to make one's way into a person's favor; endear oneself to someone: *The friendly pup quickly ingratiated itself to Vernon.* **in·gra·ti·at·ed, in·gra·ti·at·ing.**

in·grat·i·tude (ĭn grăt'ə tōōd' or ĭn grăt'ə tūd') lack of gratitude or appreciation; thankless or ungrateful conduct: *Bessie's ingratitude was rude after all our help.*

in·gre·di·ent (ĭn grē'dĭ ənt) any one of the things that make up a mixture: *Eggs and butter are two ingredients of a cake.*

in·hab·it (ĭn hăb'ĭt) to live in or occupy: *The house was recently inhabited by a French family. Seals inhabit these islands.*

in·hab·it·ant (ĭn hăb'ə tənt) permanent or habitual dweller in a place: *The town has 6,000 inhabitants. Ducks are inhabitants of marshes.*

in·hale (ĭn hāl') to draw into the lungs; breathe in: *He opened the window to inhale fresh air.* **in·haled, in·hal·ing.**

in·her·ent (ĭn hîr'ənt) existing as a natural part of a person or thing: *the inherent hardness of steel.* **in·her·ent·ly.**

in·her·it (ĭn hĕr'ĭt) **1** to come into possession of at the death of a former owner; succeed to: *She inherited a fortune in jewels.* **2** to receive by birth; get from one's ancestors: *He inherited his brown hair from his father.*

in·her·it·ance (ĭn hĕr'ə təns) **1** something inherited: *His inheritance was a million dollars.* **2** an inheriting: *His fortune came to him by inheritance, not by hard work.*

in·hos·pi·ta·ble (ĭn hŏs'pĭt ə bəl) **1** not welcoming visitors or guests: *an inhospitable host.* **2** not providing food, shelter, or other resources; barren: *an inhospitable region.* **in·hos·pi·ta·bly.**

in·hu·man (ĭn hū'mən) not humane; cruel; brutal: *the inhuman treatment of prisoners.* **in·hu·man·ly.**

in·iq·ui·ty (ĭ nĭk'wə tĭ) wickedness; sinfulness. **in·iq·ui·ties.**

i·ni·tial (ĭ nĭsh'əl) **1** first letter of each part of a person's name: *Sam Allen's initials are S.A.* **2** having to do with a beginning or first time: *He had not been there before; this was his initial visit.* **3** to mark or sign with a person's initials: *He initialed the papers after he finished correcting them.* **i·ni·tial·ly.**

i·ni·ti·ate (ĭ nĭsh'ĭ āt') **1** to begin; start: *He will initiate a drive to raise money.* **2** to help or instruct (a person) in something new: *He was initiated into the study of Spanish.* **3** to admit or introduce (a person) to a club, society, etc., with formal ceremonies: *They initiated him into the fraternity.* **4** (also ĭ nĭsh'ĭ ĭt) a person who has been initiated. **i·ni·ti·at·ed, i·ni·ti·at·ing.**

i·ni·ti·a·tion (ĭ nĭsh'ĭ ā'shən) **1** an initiating or being initiated: *the initiation of a new rule.* **2** the ceremonies with which a person is made a member of a group, club, etc.

i·ni·ti·a·tive (ĭ nĭsh'ĭ ə tĭv) **1** first step in an undertaking: *He took the initiative in producing the play.* **2** ability to see and readiness to undertake what must be done, without detailed instructions: *He has plenty of initiative for the job.*

in·ject (ĭn jĕkt') **1** to force (a liquid) into a body cavity with a syringe or into the flesh with a needle: *The doctor injected oil into Alan's sore ear, and typhoid serum into his arm.* **2** to throw in; introduce: *He tried to inject some common sense into the talk.*

in·jec·tion (ĭn jĕk'shən) **1** act of forcing a liquid into some part of the body: *a polio injection.* **2** the material injected. **3** an injecting: *His paper needed the injection of a little humor.*

in·junc·tion (ĭn jŭng'shən) **1** order; command; instruction: *He obeyed his father's injunction to stay home.* **2** a legal order from a court, directing someone to do or not do something.

in·jure (ĭn'jər) to damage; harm: *to injure a plant by stepping on it; to injure one's reputation by gossip.* **in·jured, in·jur·ing.**

in·ju·ri·ous (ĭn jōōr'ĭ əs) harmful; hurtful: *an injurious wound.* **in·ju·ri·ous·ly.**

in·ju·ry (ĭn'jə rĭ) harm; damage: *Reading in a dim light may cause injury to the eyes.* **in·ju·ries.**

in·jus·tice (ĭn jŭs'tĭs) **1** unfairness; lack of justice. **2** unjust act; unfair treatment: *You do him an injustice in not listening to his side of the story.*

---

fāte, făt, fâre, fär; bē, bĕt; bīte, bĭt; nō, nŏt, nôr; fūse, fŭn, fûr; tōō, tŏŏk; foil; foul; thin; ~~then~~;
hw for wh as in *wh*at; zh for s as in u*s*ual; ə for a, e, i, o, u, as in *a*go, lin*e*n, per*i*l, at*o*m, min*u*s

ink (ĭngk) **1** colored fluid used for writing, drawing, and printing. **2** to mark or cover with ink: *to ink in the outline of a map.*

ink·ling (ĭngk′lĭng) slight idea; faint suggestion; hint: *Constance had no inkling of her coming birthday party.*

ink·well (ĭngk′wĕl′) small container for ink, usually on a desk.

ink·y (ĭngk′ĭ) **1** spotted or covered with ink: *Mike's inky fingers.* **2** dark as black ink: *an inky sky.* **ink·i·er, ink·i·est.**

in·laid (ĭn′lād′ or ĭn·lād′) **1** set into the surface as decoration: *an inlaid design of gold in a silver bracelet.* **2** decorated with a design set into the surface: *an inlaid box.*

in·land (ĭn′lənd) **1** having to do with or located in the interior part of a country; away from the sea: *an inland journey; an inland town.* **2** toward the interior; away from the sea: *to travel inland.*

in·let (ĭn′lĕt) **1** small bay; cove; arm of the sea. **2** an entrance: *the inlet of a street water main to a house.*

Inlets on Maine coast

in·mate (ĭn′māt′) one of a group living in the same place, especially in a prison, or other institution.

in·most (ĭn′mōst′) **1** farthest in; deepest: *the inmost part of the jungle.* **2** most personal, private, or intimate: *a person's inmost thoughts; a person's inmost longings.*

inn (ĭn) small hotel, usually in the country: *Stagecoaches used to stop at inns along the way.* (Homonym: in)

in·ner (ĭn′ər) **1** farther in; interior: *to withdraw to an inner room; the inner lining of a coat.* **2** having to do with the mind or soul: *man's inner life.* **3** private; personal; secret: *one's inner feelings.*

in·ner·most (ĭn′ər mōst′) farthest in from the outside; inmost: *the innermost room of a temple.*

in·ning (ĭn′ĭng) period in a baseball game during which each team has a turn at batting while the other plays in the field.

inn·keep·er (ĭn′kē′pər) person who owns or manages an inn.

in·no·cence (ĭn′ə səns) **1** freedom from guilt or blame: *We accept a person's in-*

nocence until he is proved guilty. **2** freedom from evil or sin; purity. **3** freedom from trickery or deceit; simplicity; openness: *the innocence of a child.*

in·no·cent (ĭn′ə sənt) **1** free from guilt or wrongdoing; blameless: *She was innocent of spreading gossip.* **2** harmless in meaning and effect: *an innocent little prank.* **3** knowing no evil: *as innocent as a baby.* **in·no·cent·ly.**

in·noc·u·ous (ĭ nŏk′yōō əs) harmless: *an innocuous remark.* **in·noc·u·ous·ly.**

in·no·vate (ĭn′ə vāt′) to introduce something that is new or that makes a change; make innovations: *Dress designers are always innovating in the field of fashion.* **in·no·vat·ed, in·no·vat·ing.**

in·no·va·tion (ĭn′ə vā′shən) **1** something new or different; a change in customs, ways of doing things, etc.: *The automobile was a great innovation in transportation.* **2** an introducing or bringing in something new: *the innovation of plastics into industry.*

in·nu·mer·a·ble (ĭ nōō′mər ə bəl or ĭ nū′mər ə bəl) too many to be counted; countless: *the innumerable stars.* **in·nu·mer·a·bly.**

in·oc·u·late (ĭn ŏk′yə lāt′) **1** to inject a vaccine or other serum through the skin to prevent or cure a disease; to vaccinate. **2** to introduce germs, molds, etc., into something, usually for a scientific purpose: *to inoculate an egg yolk with germs to study their growth.* **in·oc·u·lat·ed, in·oc·u·lat·ing.**

in·oc·u·la·tion (ĭ nŏk′yə lā′shən) the injecting of vaccine or other serums through the skin (to guard a person or animal against disease); vaccination.

in·of·fen·sive (ĭn′ə fĕn′sĭv) not displeasing or disagreeable; causing no injury or damage; harmless: *an inoffensive remark.* **in·of·fen·sive·ly.**

in·or·gan·ic (ĭn′ôr găn′ĭk) made up of matter that is neither animal nor vegetable. Rocks and metals are inorganic.

in·quire (ĭn kwīr′) **1** to seek information by asking; ask: *I will inquire about train schedules at the station.* **2** to make an investigation: *The committee inquired into the causes of crime.* **in·quired, in·quir·ing.**

in·quir·y (ĭn kwîr′ĭ or ĭn′kwə rĭ) **1** an inquiring: *Details will be given on inquiry.*

2 investigation: *Officials held an* inquiry *into the cause of the accident.* **3** a question: *She made several* inquiries *about the subject.* **in·quir·ies.** Also spelled **en·quir·y.**

in·qui·si·tion (in′kwə zish′ən) thorough inquiring; examination.

in·quis·i·tive (in kwiz′ə tĭv) **1** eager to learn; curious: *an inquisitive* mind. **2** too curious; prying: *an inquisitive* gossip. **in·quis·i·tive·ly.**

in·road (in′rōd′) **1** sudden invasion; entry by force: *an inroad into the enemy's line.* **2** an advance that destroys the thing attacked: *Disease made great* inroads *on his reserve of strength.*

in·sane (in sān′) **1** out of one's mind; not sane; mad; crazy. **2** used by or for the insane: *an insane* ward *in a hospital.* **3** very foolish; senseless: *an insane* idea. **in·sane·ly.**

in·san·i·ty (in săn′ə tĭ) **1** mental illness; madness; inability to think reasonably or to act responsibly. **2** extreme folly or senselessness: *Climbing on the icy cliff is sheer* insanity. **in·san·i·ties.**

in·sa·ti·a·ble (in sā′shĭ ə bəl) not to be satisfied: *The child's insatiable* curiosity *often got him into trouble.* **in·sa·ti·a·bly.**

in·scribe (in skrīb′) to write (on) or engrave: *We inscribed his name on the honor roll. The ring was inscribed with his initials.* **in·scribed, in·scrib·ing.**

in·scrip·tion (in-skrĭp′shən) **1** something written, especially the painted, carved, engraved, or embossed words on a wall, tombstone, ring, coin, or the like. **2** the dedication of a book. **3** the act of inscribing.

Inscription

in·scru·ta·ble (in skrōō′tə bəl) hard to understand; baffling: *His* inscrutable *expression kept us wondering whether he was angry or not.* **in·scru·ta·bly.**

in·sect (in′sĕkt) any of many small creatures, often winged, with six legs, and a body divided into head, thorax, and abdomen.

Flies, grasshoppers, fleas, etc., are insects. For additional picture, see also **ab·domen.**

Parts of an Insect

in·sec·ti·cide (in sĕk′tə sīd′) poisonous preparation for driving away or killing insects.

in·sen·si·ble (in sĕn′sə bəl) **1** senseless; unconscious: *He was knocked* insensible *by a rock.* **2** without feeling; numb: *His arm was* insensible *for an hour after the accident.* **3** indifferent: *He is* insensible *to the beauties of nature.* **4** unaware: *to be* insensible *of danger.* **in·sen·si·bly.**

in·sen·si·tive (in sĕn′sə tĭv) **1** without sensation; numb: *The dentist made Tom's tooth* insensitive *before he filled it.* **2** unmoved by beauty, suffering, etc.; unsympathetic: *The farmer,* insensitive *to the glory of the sunset, saw it only as a promise of fair weather.* **in·sen·si·tive·ly.**

in·sep·a·ra·ble (in sĕp′ə rə bəl) impossible to separate or part: *two* inseparable *friends.* **in·sep·a·ra·bly.**

¹in·sert (in sûrt′) to put in: *to insert a coin in a slot.*

²in·sert (in′sûrt) something put in: *The book's illustrations are six-color inserts.*

in·ser·tion (in sûr′shən) **1** a putting in: *The insertion of advertisements in a newspaper often gets results.* **2** something put in; insert. **3** piece of fabric set in a garment.

Insertion

¹in·side (in′sīd′) within: *Look inside the box.*

²in·side (in′sīd′) **1** inner part; interior: *Clean the inside of the tub.* **2** inner: *the inside pages of a newspaper.* **3** private or secret: *some inside information.*

in·sid·i·ous (in sĭd′ĭ əs) doing harm secretly; treacherous: *an insidious disease;* insidious *gossip.* **in·sid·i·ous·ly.**

in·sight (in′sīt′) ability to see (into) and to understand: *a good teacher's insight into the problems of the students.*

---

fāte, făt, fâre, fär; bē, bĕt; bite, bĭt; nō, nŏt, nôr; fūse, fŭn, fûr; tōō, tŏŏk; foil; foul; thin; ~~then~~;
hw for wh as in *wh*at; zh for s as in u*s*ual; ə for a, e, i, o, u, as in *a*go, lin*e*n, per*i*l, at*o*m, min*u*s

in·sig·ni·a (in sig'ni ə) emblems of rank or honor. The insignia of the armed services include stripes on the sleeve, metal shoulder bars, and the like. The insignia of royalty are scepters, robes, crowns, etc.

Insignia

in·sig·nif·i·cant (in'sig nif'ə kənt) of small or no importance; having little meaning or value: *an insignificant sum; an insignificant person.* **in·sig·nif·i·cant·ly.**

in·sin·cere (in'sin sir') not sincere; not genuine; false. **in·sin·cere·ly.**

in·sin·u·ate (in sin'yōō āt') **1** to hint slyly; imply: *Without saying so outright, the lawyer insinuated that the witness was lying.* **2** to push or get (oneself) in by clever, indirect means: *The courtier insinuated himself into the king's favor.* **in·sin·u·at·ed, in·sin·u·at·ing.**

in·sist (in sist') **1** to make an urgent demand: *I insist that you go.* **2** to take a firm stand and refuse to budge: *He insists that he is right.*

in·sist·ence (in sis'təns) **1** a demanding without let up: *His insistence finally wore down my resistance.* **2** the taking of a firm stand: *Please forgive my insistence on this matter, but I must do what I believe in.*

in·sist·ent (in sis'tənt) **1** demanding: *I did not want to go, but he was insistent.* **2** continuing to demand attention or action; urgent: *the insistent ringing of a bell.* **in·sist·ent·ly.**

in·sole (in'sōl') **1** inner sole of a shoe. **2** extra inner sole, worn for comfort or protection.

in·so·lence (in'sə ləns) rude and contemptuous disrespect: *The gangster showed his insolence by jeering at the policeman.*

in·so·lent (in'sə lənt) not respectful; rude and arrogant: *The witness's insolent replies angered the judge.* **in·so·lent·ly.**

in·sol·u·ble (in sol'yōō bəl) **1** impossible to dissolve: *Grease is insoluble in cold water.* **2** impossible to solve or explain: *an insoluble problem.* **in·sol·u·bly.**

in·som·ni·a (in sŏm'ni ə) inability to sleep; prolonged sleeplessness.

in·spect (in spĕkt') **1** to examine carefully; check for faults, errors, etc.: *Each morning the foreman inspected our work.* **2** to ex-

amine or review (troops, military equipment, etc.) officially: *The general inspected the troops.*

in·spec·tion (in spĕk'shən) **1** an inspecting; careful examination for faults, errors, etc.: *In some States, inspection of automobiles must be made twice a year.* **2** official review or examination (of troops, military equipment, etc.).

in·spec·tor (in spĕk'tər) person who inspects.

in·spi·ra·tion (in'spə rā'shən) **1** a stirring of mind, feelings, or imagination that leads to action or creation: *The artist's inspiration came from his everyday surroundings.* **2** person or thing that inspires: *The music of the band was an inspiration to the marchers.* **3** bright idea; impulse or sudden thought that leads to action or creation. **4** a drawing of air into the lungs.

in·spire (in spir') **1** to stir deeply; breathe life into; arouse to action. **2** to be the cause of; arouse; call forth: *Honesty inspires respect. Her beauty inspired the poem.* **3** to draw air into the lungs. **in·spired, in·spir·ing.**

in·stall (in stôl') **1** to put into place and make ready for use: *The plumber installed a hot water unit.* **2** to put into office with ceremony: *He was installed as president.* **3** to place or settle: *The cat installed itself near the fire.*

in·stall·ment or **in·stal·ment** (in stôl'-mənt) **1** any one of several parts that follow in a series: *The second installment of the story will appear next month.* **2** any one of several partial payments made in settlement of a bill: *The third installment on the car is due Tuesday.*

in·stance (in'stəns) **1** a case; example: *There have been many instances of people failing this test.* **2** for instance as an example.

in·stant (in'stənt) **1** moment; space of time almost too short to measure: *He stopped the car not an instant too soon.* **2** immediate: *A cool breeze brought instant relief after our exhausting game of tennis.*

in·stan·ta·ne·ous (in'stən tā'nĭ əs) happening or following in an instant: *an instantaneous explosion; an instantaneous reply.* **in·stan·ta·ne·ous·ly.**

in·stant·ly (ĭn′stənt lĭ) immediately; at once: *The dog obeyed his master's order instantly.*

in·stead (ĭn stĕd′) **1** as a substitute or alternative: *They didn't come to our house, so we went to theirs instead.* **2 instead of** in place of: *I will go instead of you.*

in·step (ĭn′stĕp′) arched upper side of the foot between the toes and the ankle.

in·still or **in·stil** (ĭn stĭl′) to add little by little; put in gradually; infuse: *to instill respect for the rights of others.* **in·stilled, in·stil·ling.**

in·stinct (ĭn′stĭngkt) **1** urge to do things in a certain way; natural untaught way of acting: *Squirrels gather food for winter by instinct.* **2** talent; natural ability: *He has a happy instinct for saying the right thing.*

in·stinc·tive (ĭn stĭngk′tĭv) inborn; natural; not gained through learning or experience: *Babies have an instinctive fear of loud noises.* **in·stinc·tive·ly.**

in·sti·tute (ĭn′stə tōōt′ or ĭn′stə tūt′) **1** association or organization for a special purpose: *We study mathematics at the institute.* **2** building or group of buildings that houses such an organization or establishment. **3** to begin; start; originate: *We instituted a search for the missing man.* **4** to establish: *The club members instituted several new laws.* **in·sti·tut·ed, in·sti·tut·ing.**

in·sti·tu·tion (ĭn′stə tōō′shən or ĭn′stə tū′-shən) **1** an established custom, law, etc.: *Thanksgiving Day is an American institution.* **2** a setting up; an establishing: *the institution of new traffic regulations.* **3** society or organization for a particular purpose. Some schools and hospitals are called institutions. **4** building used by such a society or organization.

in·struct (ĭn strŭkt′) **1** to teach: *He instructs two classes in swimming.* **2** to direct; order: *We instructed him to report for duty as soon as he heard the siren.*

in·struc·tion (ĭn strŭk′shən) **1** an instructing; education: *Ann got her early instruction at home, but Ralph went to school.* **2** lessons: *Some grade schools give instruction in foreign languages.* **3 instructions**

directions or orders: *We couldn't assemble the toy until we had read the instructions.*

in·struc·tive (ĭn strŭk′tĭv) informative; giving knowledge: *an instructive talk on art.* **in·struc·tive·ly.**

in·struc·tor (ĭn strŭk′tər) teacher.

in·stru·ment (ĭn′strə mənt) **1** tool used for some particular kind of work: *a surgeon's instruments.* **2** means by which something is accomplished: *The army was the dictator's instrument for controlling the country.* **3** person who is someone else's tool: *Jones was merely an instrument of the criminal gang.* **4** device used to measure, control, or examine: *A thermostat is an instrument to control a furnace. The telescope and microscope are scientific instruments.* **5** device by which musical sounds are made, such as the harp, flute, etc.

in·stru·men·tal (ĭn′strə mĕn′təl) **1** helping to bring about; serving as a means: *He was instrumental in our finding a new home.* **2** performed on or written for a musical instrument: *A pianist and violinist supplied the instrumental accompaniment.* **in·stru·men·tal·ly.**

in·suf·fer·a·ble (ĭn sŭf′ər ə bəl) unbearable: *There was no excuse for his insufferable rudeness.* **in·suf·fer·a·bly.**

in·suf·fi·cient (ĭn′sə fĭsh′ənt) not enough; inadequate; not sufficient: *The time allowed for the job was insufficient.* **in·suf·fi·cient·ly.**

in·su·late (ĭn′sə lāt′ or ĭn′syōō lāt′) **1** to separate by a material that will not conduct electricity, heat, or sound: *to insulate a wire; to insulate a roof.* **2** to set apart; isolate: *to insulate patients with infectious diseases.* **in·su·lat·ed, in·su·lat·ing.**

in·su·la·tion (ĭn′sə lā′shən or ĭn′syōō lā′-shən) **1** material used to prevent the passage of heat, sound, electricity, etc. **2** an insulating; insulated condition: *The vacuum in the Thermos bottle supplies* insulation.

Electric insulators

in·su·la·tor (ĭn′sə lā′tər or ĭn′syōō lā′tər) something that separates or keeps apart, especially something that

---

fāte, făt, fâre, fär; bē, bĕt; bīte, bĭt; nō, nŏt, nôr; fūse, fŭn, fûr; tōō, tŏŏk; foil; foul; thin; then; hw for wh as in what; zh for s as in usual; ə for a, e, i, o, u, as in ago, linen, peril, atom, minus

insulin

prevents the passage of heat, electricity, or sound.

in·su·lin (ĭn′sə lĭn) chemical given off by the pancreas which helps the body to use sugar. Insulin made from the pancreas of sheep or cattle is used in the treatment of diabetes.

¹in·sult (ĭn sŭlt′) to treat a person or thing with rudeness or scorn; affront: *She insulted him by calling him a coward.*

²in·sult (ĭn′sŭlt) a rude or scornful action or speech; an affront: *To question a man's honesty is an insult.*

in·sur·ance (ĭn shoor′əns) **1** a system of guarding against loss by the paying of small, regular amounts to a company in exchange for a promise to pay an agreed amount in case of death, accident, theft, etc. **2** the contract by which such an agreement is made. **3** regular amount paid for this service: *John's father pays $35 a month life insurance.* **4** amount for which a person or thing is insured: *The insurance on that burned house helped build a new one.*

in·sure (ĭn shoor′) **1** to guard against loss (of life, property, etc.) by making small, regular payments to a company that promises to pay money in case of death, fire, etc.: *He insured his home against fire damage.* **2** to guarantee: *He hoped a new lock on the door would insure his safety.* **in·sured, in·sur·ing.**

in·sur·gent (ĭn sûr′jənt) **1** rising in revolt; rebellious: *The insurgent troops were defeated.* **2** a rebel: *The insurgents were defeated.*

in·sur·rec·tion (ĭn′sə rĕk′shən) active revolt against authority: *Unjust laws led to insurrection among the people.*

in·tact (ĭn tăkt′) untouched; whole; uninjured: *After the bombing only a few buildings remained intact.*

in·take (ĭn′tāk′) **1** a taking in: *an intake of money; an intake of water.* **2** the amount taken in: *The intake of each boiler is 3,000 gallons an hour.* **3** pipe or channel through which a fluid is brought in, or the opening where a fluid enters: *The intake of one pump is clogged by mud.*

in·tan·gi·ble (ĭn tăn′jə bəl) **1** not capable of being touched. *Time, hope, and darkness are intangible.* **2** vague; hazy; difficult to grasp with the mind: *an intangible fear;*

intend

intangible *suspicions.* **3** something intangible: *Good will is an* intangible. **in·tan·gi·bly.**

in·te·grate (ĭn′tə grāt′) **1** to bring parts together to make a whole: *to integrate studies with athletics in the school day.* **2** to make schools, housing, transportation, etc., open to all races on an equal basis. **in·te·grat·ed, in·te·grat·ing.**

in·te·gra·tion (ĭn′tə grā′shən) an integrating or being integrated: *the integration of parts of an automobile; the integration of races in a school.*

in·teg·ri·ty (ĭn tĕg′rə tĭ) **1** honesty; uprightness; moral soundness: *The integrity of the mayor was not questioned during the scandal.* **2** wholeness; completeness: *The integrity of the United States was preserved by the War between the States.*

in·tel·lect (ĭn′tə lĕkt′) **1** the understanding and reasoning power of the mind: *Man is a creature of* intellect *as well as feeling.* **2** great intelligence: *a man of* intellect.

in·tel·lec·tu·al (ĭn′tə lĕk′choo əl) **1** having to do with the mind and its reasoning powers: *Winning a scholarship is an* intellectual *achievement.* **2** having or showing intellect: *an* intellectual *man; an* intellectual *face.* **3** a scholarly person. **in·tel·lec·tu·al·ly.**

in·tel·li·gence (ĭn tĕl′ə jəns) **1** ability to learn, understand, or know: *He shows high* intelligence *for a boy of his age.* **2** news or information, especially secret information such as gathered by a government in time of war.

in·tel·li·gent (ĭn tĕl′ə jənt) having or showing a keen and able mind: *An* intelligent *child learns quickly.* **in·tel·li·gent·ly.**

in·tel·li·gi·ble (ĭn tĕl′ə jə bəl) capable of being understood; clear: *The baby's talking was barely* intelligible. **in·tel·li·gi·bly.**

in·tem·per·ance (ĭn tĕm′pər əns) **1** lack of moderation; lack of restraint; excess: *The* intemperance *of the excited speaker's remarks was clear to his hearers.* **2** excessive use of alcoholic liquor.

in·tem·per·ate (ĭn tĕm′pə rĭt) **1** not moderate; not restrained; excessive: *his* intemperate *language.* **2** given to excessive use of alcoholic liquors. **in·tem·per·ate·ly.**

in·tend (ĭn tĕnd′) **1** to have as a purpose; mean: *He did not* intend *to go away.* **2** to

378

design for a purpose: *The book on birds is intended for reference.*

in·tense (ĭn tĕns′) **1** extreme; very great: *an intense pain.* **2** having strong feelings: *an intense person.* **in·tense·ly.**

in·ten·si·fi·er (ĭn tĕn′sə fī′ər) word or phrase such as "so," "too," "very," "a little," or "a bit," which modifies an adjective or adverb, as in these sentences:
This wood is too soft.
He works very hard.
Bill is studying a little harder now.

in·ten·si·fy (ĭn tĕn′sə fī′) to make or become more intense: *He intensified his efforts. He took medicine when the pain intensified.* **in·ten·si·fied, in·ten·si·fy·ing.**

in·ten·si·ty (ĭn tĕn′sə tĭ) **1** strength or degree (of heat, sound, etc.): *The sound increased in intensity.* **2** a being intense; great degree, strength, or force: *the intensity of his anger; the intensity of the storm.* **in·ten·si·ties.**

in·ten·sive (ĭn tĕn′sĭv) thorough; concentrated; carried out with the greatest care: *an intensive search.* **in·ten·sive·ly.**

in·tent (ĭn tĕnt′) **1** determined; bent on: *The young doctor was intent on succeeding.* **2** purpose; aim; intention: *He read with an intent to learn.* **in·tent·ly.**

in·ten·tion (ĭn tĕn′shən) that which is intended; purpose; plan: *It is my intention to build a new house next year.*

in·ten·tion·al (ĭn tĕn′shən əl) done deliberately; not accidental: *an intentional rudeness.* **in·ten·tion·al·ly.**

in·ter (ĭn tûr′) to bury. **in·terred, in·ter·ring.**

in·ter- prefix meaning (1) "between" or "among": inter*planetary,* inter*continental.* (2) "together" or "one with the other": inter*weave.*

in·ter·cede (ĭn′tər sēd′) to make a plea (for someone else): *Roy's sister interceded for him.* **in·ter·ced·ed, in·ter·ced·ing.**

in·ter·cept (ĭn′tər sĕpt′) to seize, catch, or stop on the way: *to intercept a message; to intercept a forward pass.*

in·ter·cep·tion (ĭn′tər sĕp′shən) act of catching or heading off before arrival at a destination; an intercepting.

in·ter·change (ĭn′tər chānj′) **1** to put persons or things in the place of each other: *The parts of these machines may be interchanged.* **2** a putting of persons or things in the other's place: *an interchange of notes or goods.* **3** an exchanging: *an interchange of ambassadors.* **4** to exchange. **in·ter·changed, in·ter·chang·ing.**

in·ter·change·a·ble (ĭn′tər chān′jə bəl) capable of being put in place of one another: *Tires on an automobile are interchangeable.* **in·ter·change·a·bly.**

in·ter·con·ti·nen·tal (ĭn′tər kŏn′tə nĕn′təl) traveling or capable of traveling from one continent to another: *an intercontinental flight; an intercontinental missile.*

in·ter·course (ĭn′tər kôrs′) dealings, relations, and communications: *The intercourse between them has been peaceful.*

in·ter·de·pen·dence (ĭn′tər dĭ pĕn′dəns) dependence on each other or one another: *the interdependence of members of a family.*

in·ter·est (ĭn′tər ĭst) **1** desire to take part in, work at, or hear about: *Omar shows an interest in sports.* **2** the cause of such desire; attraction; hobby: *Football is his chief interest.* **3** to cause or arouse desire, enthusiasm, or curiosity: *Can I interest you in joining our club? The story interests me very much.* **4** power to hold attention: *Suspense adds interest to a story.* **5** well-being; welfare: *a club working for the public interest.* **6** money paid by a person for the use of borrowed money. **7** share; investment; part ownership: *Father has an interest in a shoe factory.* **8 interests** a group of people who are concerned with the same kind of activity: *the farming interests; business interests.*

in·ter·est·ed (ĭn′tər ĭs tĭd) **1** attracted; curious; intrigued: *an interested audience.* **2** showing interest: *an interested look.* **3** having a share or part in: *The interested persons were present when the will was read.* **in·ter·est·ed·ly.**

in·ter·est·ing (ĭn′tər ĭs tĭng) holding the attention; arousing interest. **in·ter·est·ing·ly.**

in·ter·fere (ĭn′tər fîr′) **1** to obstruct; hamper; conflict with; clash: *A tight arm band*

---

fāte, făt, fâre, fär; bē, bĕt; bite, bĭt; nō, nŏt, nôr; fūse, fŭn, fûr; tōō, tŏŏk; foil; foul; thin; ~~then~~;
hw for wh as in *what*; zh for s as in usual; ə for a, e, i, o, u, as in *ago*, linen, peril, atom, minus
379

will interfere *with circulation of the blood.*
Absence interferes *with school work.* **2** to
meddle: *This doesn't concern you, so don't*
interfere. **in·ter·fered, in·ter·fer·ing.**

in·ter·fer·ence (ĭn′tər fĭr′əns) **1** a coming
into conflict; clashing. **2** thing that stops or
hampers; a block: *The heavy snowfall was
a serious* interference *to travel.* **3** a meddling.

in·te·ri·or (ĭn tĭr′ĭ ər) **1** on the inside; having to do with the inside: *the* interior *parts
of a telephone; an* interior *decorator.* **2** the
inside: *the* interior *of a building.* **3** inland;
away from the coast or border: *the* interior *cities of a country.* **4** the part away
from the coast or border: *deep in the*
interior *of Africa.*

in·ter·ject (ĭn′tər jĕkt′) to insert; throw
in: *to* interject *a question or argument.*

in·ter·jec·tion (ĭn′tər jĕk′shən) **1** act of
throwing in or interjecting. **2** word used
as an exclamation. *Ah!* and *Ouch!* are
interjections.

in·ter·lace (ĭn′tər lās′) to join by lacing or
weaving together; intermingle: *to* interlace
strips of cloth. **in·ter·laced, in·ter·lac·ing.**

in·ter·lock (ĭn′tər lŏk′) **1** to make or become tightly interlaced: *The branches of the
bushes* interlocked *in a dense hedge.* **2** to
fit closely together: *The parts of a picture
puzzle* interlock.

in·ter·lop·er (ĭn′tər lō′pər) one who thrusts
himself in where he is not wanted; an
intruder; a meddler: *an* interloper *at a
party; an* interloper *in one's affairs.*

in·ter·lude (ĭn′tər lōōd′ or ĭn′tər lūd′) **1**
period of time or event that differs from
those coming before and after it: *an* inter-
lude *of sunshine during a rainy spell.* **2** a
piece of music played between the acts of
a play, the parts of a church service, etc.

in·ter·me·di·ate (ĭn′tər mē′dĭ ĭt) being or
coming between two points, stages, things,
or persons: *The* intermediate *stage of a
frog's growth is a tadpole.*

in·ter·mi·na·ble (ĭn tûr′mə nə bəl) endless or seeming to be endless; very long:
To the restless boy, the stay in bed seemed
interminable. **in·ter·mi·na·bly.**

in·ter·min·gle (ĭn′tər mĭng′gəl) to mix
together: *The visitors soon* intermingled
with the crowd. **in·ter·min·gled, in·ter·
min·gling.**

in·ter·mis·sion (ĭn′tər mĭsh′ən) a break; a
pause; interval between periods of activity:
an intermission *between the acts of a play;
to work all morning without* intermission.

in·ter·mit·tent (ĭn′tər mĭt′ənt) alternately
starting and stopping; repeated at intervals;
coming and going: *an* intermittent *rain.*
in·ter·mit·tent·ly.

in·ter·nal (ĭn tûr′nəl) **1** of or on the inside;
inner: *The heart is an* internal *organ.*
2 within a country; domestic: *One country
should not meddle in the* internal *affairs of
another.* **in·ter·nal·ly.**

internal-combustion engine engine
that produces power by the expansion of
hot gas (from the burning fuel) against a
piston in a cylinder or an enclosed fan.

in·ter·na·tion·al (ĭn′tər năsh′ən əl) having
to do with or going on between two or more
nations: *The United Nations is an* international *organization. Imports and exports
make up our* international *trade.* **in·ter·
na·tion·al·ly.**

in·ter·plan·e·tar·y (ĭn′tər plăn′ə tĕr′ĭ) between the planets of the solar system: *an*
interplanetary *rocket;* interplanetary *travel.*

in·ter·pose (ĭn′tər pōz′) **1** to put in or
introduce (between other things): *At this
point of the story, he* interposed *a comment.*
2 to step in; come between; interfere: *Just
as the argument reached a peak, the father*
interposed. **in·ter·posed, in·ter·pos·ing.**

in·ter·pret (ĭn tûr′prĭt) **1** to translate conversation, speeches, etc., for people who
speak different languages: *He* interpreted
*for the Spanish students visiting in the United
States.* **2** to explain the meaning of: *Can
you* interpret *the poem in your own words?*
3 to bring out the meaning of or give a
special meaning to (in acting or performing): *This actor is noted for* interpreting *the
roles of old men.* **4** to read a meaning into:
He interpreted *my look as one of anger.*

in·ter·pre·ta·tion (ĭn tûr′prə tā′shən) **1**
translation; work done by an interpreter:
An interpretation *of the speech was broadcast at 7:45.* **2** explanation: *Your* interpretation *of the poem made its meaning clear.*
3 a bringing out or giving a special meaning to in acting or performing: *a conductor's*
interpretation *of French music.*

in·ter·pret·er (ĭn tûr′prə tər) **1** person
who translates conversation, speeches, etc.,

for people who speak different languages.
2 one who explains.

in·ter·ro·gate (in tĕr′ə gāt′) to question, especially question closely; examine. **in·ter·ro·gat·ed, in·ter·ro·gat·ing.**

in·ter·ro·ga·tion (in tĕr′ə gā′shən) **1** a question. **2** act of asking a question or questions: *He grew weary under her continuous* interrogation. **3** examination; official questioning: *The prisoner was forced to undergo* interrogation *by the police.*

interrogation mark or **point** question mark (?).

in·ter·rog·a·tive (in′tə rŏg′ə tĭv) **1** containing a question: *an* interrogative *sentence.* **2** questioning: *an* interrogative *look.* **3** word like "why," "where," "who," or "when," used to ask a question. **in·ter·rog·a·tive·ly.**

in·ter·rupt (in′tə rŭpt′) **1** to break in upon: *The ringing of the telephone* interrupted *his sleep.* **2** to make a break in; cut off: *Bad weather* interrupted *air travel for a few days. That house* interrupts *our view of the beautiful lake.*

in·ter·rup·tion (in′tə rŭp′shən) **1** a being broken in upon or a breaking in upon: *There was an* interruption *in the program for a special announcement.* **2** temporary pause or ceasing; interval: *He worked without* interruption *all morning.*

in·ter·sect (in′tər sĕkt′) **1** to cut across: *Elm Street* intersects *Second Avenue.* **2** to cross each other. The lines of a × intersect.

in·ter·sec·tion (in′tər sĕk′shən) **1** a crossing; place where things, streets for example, cross: *There is a traffic light at the* intersection *of Main and Broad streets.* **2** a cutting across: *The* intersection *of three main roads caused traffic jams.*

Intersection

in·ter·sperse (in′tər spûrs′) **1** to scatter; place here and there (among): *to* intersperse *green leaves among the flowers in a bouquet.* **2** to give variety to (by inserting things here and there): *He* interspersed *his lecture with little jokes and comments.* **in·ter·spersed, in·ter·spers·ing.**

in·ter·state (in′tər stāt′) between states: *an* interstate *highway.*

in·ter·twine (in′tər twin′) to twine or twist together; interlace: *Ivy and wisteria vines* intertwined *above the door.* **in·ter·twined, in·ter·twin·ing.**

in·ter·val (in′tər vəl) **1** period of time between events: *After a brief* interval, *the program continued.* **2** space between objects, etc.: *The* interval *between the two lawns was filled with flowers.* **3** difference of pitch between tones of music. **4 at intervals** (1) at regular distances: *He spread out his men* at intervals *of thirty feet.* (2) now and then; here and there: *to wake* at intervals *through the night; campgrounds* at intervals *along the highway.*

in·ter·vene (in′tər vēn′) **1** to come (between): *The years that* intervene *between grade school and college bring many changes.* **2** to get in the way; interfere: *If nothing unexpected* intervenes, *we shall go as planned.* **3** to step in to settle: *The argument continued until Father* intervened. **in·ter·vened, in·ter·ven·ing.**

in·ter·ven·tion (in′tər vĕn′shən) **1** an interfering: *the* intervention *of one country in the affairs of another.* **2** a coming between: *A friend's* intervention *prevented a fight between the two boys.*

in·ter·view (in′tər vū′) **1** personal meeting to discuss something: *the foreman's* interviews *with people seeking work.* **2** to question in order to get information, especially for the press: *The reporter* interviewed *the visiting diplomat.* **3** written account of such information: *Smith's* interview *with the governor was published in the papers.*

in·ter·weave (in′tər wēv′) to twist or weave together; intertwine: *to* interweave *silk with cotton; to* interweave *fact and imagination in a story.* **in·ter·wove, in·ter·wov·en** or **in·ter·wove, in·ter·weav·ing.**

in·ter·wove (in′tər wōv′) See **interweave.**

in·ter·wo·ven (in′tər wō′vən) **1** woven together; mingled: *Many historical movies are* interwoven *fact and fiction.* **2** woven or knitted into: *mittens with an* interwoven *design.* **3** See **interweave.**

---

fāte, făt, fâre, fär; bē, bĕt; bīte, bĭt; nō, nŏt, nôr; fūse, fŭn, fûr; tōō, tŏŏk; foil; foul; thin; ~~then~~; hw for wh as in *what*; zh for s as in *usual*; ə for a, e, i, o, u, as in *ago, linen, peril, atom, minus*

in·tes·ti·nal (in tĕs′tĭn əl) having to do with the intestines: *an intestinal tract.*

in·tes·tine (in tĕs′tĭn) tube from the stomach through which partially digested food passes on its way through the body. It is composed of a long section of smaller tubing, called the **small intestine**, ending in a larger but much shorter section, called the **large intestine**.

STOMACH

Intestines

in·ti·ma·cy (ĭn′tə mə sĭ) close friendship; confidential relationship: *The girls' intimacy allowed them to share their personal problems.* **in·ti·ma·cies.**

¹in·ti·mate (ĭn′tə mĭt) **1** close; confidential: *He told his intimate friend some of his deepest secrets.* **2** innermost; private; personal: *She wrote her intimate thoughts in her diary.* **3** coming from close study and experience: *His years in China gave him an intimate knowledge of the country.* **4** close friend; confidant: *Bess had many acquaintances, but no intimates.* **in·ti·mate·ly.** [¹intimate comes through French (intime) from a Latin word (intimus) meaning "innermost." It was influenced in the spelling by ²intimate.]

²in·ti·mate (ĭn′tə māt′) to make known indirectly; hint: *He intimated that there was more to the story than we knew.* **in·ti·mat·ed, in·ti·mat·ing.** [²intimate is from a form (intimatus) of a Latin word (intimare) meaning "announce"; "make known."]

in·ti·ma·tion (ĭn′tə mā′shən) a hint; indirect suggestion: *He gave no intimation of leaving.*

in·tim·i·date (in tĭm′ə dāt′) to make afraid; fill with fear; to cow. **in·tim·i·dat·ed, in·tim·i·dat·ing.**

in·to (ĭn′tōō) **1** to the inside of: *to fall into a pond; to walk into a building.* **2** to a time in: *He worked all night and into the next day.* **3** to the form or state of: *The bear turned into a prince. The water changed into steam.*

in·tol·er·a·ble (in tŏl′ər ə bəl) very hard to endure; unbearable: *his intolerable manners; the intolerable heat.* **in·tol·er·a·bly.**

in·tol·er·ance (in tŏl′ər əns) **1** unwillingness to allow customs, behavior, opinions, beliefs, etc., not like one's own; lack of

tolerance: *Religious intolerance in their homelands brought many early settlers to America.* **2** inability to endure: *an intolerance to certain drugs.*

in·tol·er·ant (in tŏl′ər ənt) **1** not willing to allow opinions, beliefs, customs, or behavior different from one's own: *He was too intolerant to be a good teacher.* **2** intolerant of not able or willing to endure. **in·tol·er·ant·ly.**

in·tox·i·cate (in tŏk′sə kāt′) **1** to make drunk. **2** to fill with wild excitement; elate: *The warm spring air intoxicated the colt.* **in·tox·i·cat·ed, in·tox·i·cat·ing.**

in·tox·i·ca·tion (in tŏk′sə kā′shən) **1** a being drunk; drunkenness. **2** great excitement: *Who can resist the intoxication of the first spring day?*

in·tra·mu·ral (ĭn′trə mūr′əl) **1** entirely within the walls or limits of a city, university, etc. **2** limited to the members of a school, college, or other organization: *an intramural basketball competition.*

in·trench (in trĕnch′) entrench.

in·trep·id (in trĕp′ĭd) fearless; bold: *The intrepid patrol crept closer to the enemy lines.* **in·trep·id·ly.**

in·tri·cate (ĭn′trə kĭt) involved; complicated: *The plot of the story was too intricate to follow. The box was carved with an intricate design.* **in·tri·cate·ly.**

in·trigue (in trēg′) **1** to plot; to scheme secretly: *The nobles intrigued to overthrow the king.* **2** to make curious; interest; beguile: *His strange accent intrigues us.* **3** (also ĭn′trēg) secret plot and scheme: *His petty intrigues annoyed his friends.* **in·trigued, in·tri·guing.**

in·tro·duce (ĭn′trə dōōs′ or ĭn′trə dūs′) **1** to make known formally: *We were introduced to his family.* **2** to bring in: *New fashions are introduced every year. A new subject was introduced for discussion.* **3** to begin; open: *A short overture introduced the opera.* **in·tro·duced, in·tro·duc·ing.**

in·tro·duc·tion (ĭn′trə dŭk′shən) **1** a making known, often by a formal presenting: *The introduction of guests to each other is the duty of a hostess.* **2** a bringing in: *The introduction of the automobile made the horse and buggy old-fashioned.* **3** a being introduced: *Their introduction led to a lifelong friendship.* **4** beginning section of a book, speech, etc., that prepares the audience for what is to follow. **5** a book that introduces beginners to a subject.

in·tro·duc·to·ry (ĭn′trə dŭk′tə rĭ) serving to introduce: *An introductory paragraph preceded the story.*

in·trude (ĭn trōōd′) **1** to enter without invitation or welcome; break in (on): *A loud crash intruded on the silence of the night.* **2** to force or thrust (into or upon): *He intruded his opinion into the conversation.* **in·trud·ed, in·trud·ing.**

in·trud·er (ĭn trōō′dər) person who comes uninvited and unwelcome; one who forces his way or breaks in: *The noisy intruder was thrown out of the meeting.*

in·tru·sion (ĭn trōō′zhən) **1** an entering without being invited; a forcing or breaking in; trespass: *The law protects our homes from intrusion.* **2** a thrusting of advice, opinion, etc., upon another: *The card players resented his advice as an intrusion.*

in·trust (ĭn trŭst′) entrust.

in·tu·i·tion (ĭn′tōō ĭsh′ən or ĭn′tū ĭsh′ən) **1** power to perceive something immediately without special information or reasoning: *to know someone's troubles by intuition.* **2** something perceived in this way.

in·tu·i·tive (ĭn tōō′ə tĭv or ĭn tū′ə tĭv) **1** perceiving by intuition: *an intuitive judge of character.* **2** perceived by intuition: *an intuitive sense of danger.* **in·tu·i·tive·ly.**

in·un·date (ĭn′ən dāt′) **1** to overflow; flood: *Heavy rains inundated the fields.* **2** to spread over or cover, as by a flood: *On holidays the studio was inundated with visitors.* **in·un·dat·ed, in·un·dat·ing.**

in·un·da·tion (ĭn′ən dā′shən) a flood; an overflow.

in·vade (ĭn vād′) **1** to enter to attack: *An enemy invaded the country and conquered it.* **2** to enter and overrun: *Swarms of children invaded the swimming pool.* **in·vad·ed, in·vad·ing.**

in·vad·er (ĭn vā′dər) person or thing that intrudes or enters to attack: *The invader of our garden was a small brown rabbit. The whole country rose up against the invaders.*

¹in·val·id (ĭn văl′ĭd) of no force; not valid: *He forgot to renew his passport and it be-*

came invalid. [**¹invalid** is from a Latin word (invalidus) meaning "not valid."]

²in·va·lid (ĭn′və lĭd) a sick or weak person; someone constantly ill. [**²invalid** comes through Old French from a Latin word (invalidus) that is in turn based on two other Latin forms, one (in-) meaning "not" and the other (validus) meaning "strong."]

in·val·u·a·ble (ĭn văl′yōō ə bəl) having great worth or value: *an invaluable friend.* **in·val·u·a·bly.**

in·var·i·a·ble (ĭn vâr′ĭ ə bəl) never changing; constant; not variable: *a man of invariable habits.* **in·var·i·a·bly.**

in·va·sion (ĭn vā′zhən) an invading or being invaded: *The invasion of the country amounted to a declaration of war. The old town welcomed its yearly invasion by tourists.*

in·vent (ĭn vĕnt′) **1** to make or devise (something new): *James Watt invented the steam engine.* **2** to make up: *He invented excuses for arriving home so late.*

in·ven·tion (ĭn vĕn′shən) **1** a making or devising something new; inventing: *The invention of automatic machines has created serious labor problems.* **2** thing invented: *The lightning rod is one of Benjamin Franklin's inventions.* **3** something made up or false: *The story of George Washington and the cherry tree is pure invention.* **4** power of inventing: *"Alice in Wonderland" shows both poetic and comic invention.*

in·ven·tive (ĭn vĕn′tĭv) creative; able to invent; original: *He turned his inventive mind to designing new automobiles.* **in·ven·tive·ly.**

in·ven·tor (ĭn vĕn′tər) person who invents; one who finds new ways of doing things or creates new tools, machines, or the like.

in·ven·to·ry (ĭn′vən tôr′ĭ) **1** a list of things, as goods in a store. **2** to make such a list; catalogue. **in·ven·to·ries; in·ven·to·ried, in·ven·to·ry·ing.**

in·vert (ĭn vûrt′) **1** to turn upside down: *If we invert a capital "M" it looks like a "W."* **2** to reverse the order or positions of: *We inverted the order of numbers, and counted from ten to one.*

---

fāte, făt, fâre, fär; bē, bĕt; bīte, bĭt; nō, nŏt, nôr; fūse, fŭn, fûr; tōō, tŏŏk; foil; foul; thin; ~~then~~; hw for wh as in *what*; zh for s as in *usual*; ə for a, e, i, o, u, as in *ago, linen, peril, atom, minus*

in·ver·te·brate (ĭn vûr′tə brāt′ or ĭn vûr′- tə brĭt′) **1** without a backbone. **2** animal without a backbone, as an earthworm, snail, etc.

in·vest (ĭn vĕst′) **1** to put money into (something) in the expectation of profit from dividends or increasing value: *He invested in railroad stock.* **2** to install in office: *The new bishop will be invested tomorrow.* **3** to give power or authority to: *to invest a person with the right to vote.*

in·ves·ti·gate (ĭn vĕs′tə gāt′) to look into thoroughly; probe: *Police investigated the cause of the accident.* **in·ves·ti·gat·ed, in·ves·ti·gat·ing.**

in·ves·ti·ga·tion (ĭn vĕs′tə gā′shən) thorough inquiry: *an investigation of the fire.*

in·ves·ti·ga·tor (ĭn vĕs′tə gā′tər) person who investigates.

in·vest·ment (ĭn vĕst′mənt) **1** an investing: *an investment in oil stocks; an investment of one's time.* **2** amount invested: *The original investment doubled in value.* **3** something in which money is invested: *The new house was a valuable* investment.

in·ves·tor (ĭn vĕs′tər) person who invests money for profit.

in·vig·or·ate (ĭn vĭg′ə rāt′) to give strength or vigor: *The tired man was invigorated by the air.* **in·vig·or·at·ed, in·vig·or·at·ing.**

in·vin·ci·ble (ĭn vĭn′sə bəl) unable to be conquered or overcome; unconquerable: *an invincible enemy.* **in·vin·ci·bly.**

in·vis·i·ble (ĭn vĭz′ə bəl) not able to be seen; not visible. **in·vis·i·bly.**

in·vi·ta·tion (ĭn′və tā′shən) a written or spoken request to attend or take part in: *a wedding* invitation; *admission by* invitation *only.*

in·vite (ĭn vīt′) **1** to ask (a person) to come somewhere or to take part in something: *to invite one to a banquet.* **2** to request; ask for: *The speaker invites your comments following his speech.* **3** to demand; call for: *A good performance* invites *applause.* **in·vit·ed, in·vit·ing.**

in·vit·ing (ĭn vī′tĭng) tempting; attractive: *an inviting offer of a new job.* **in·vit·ing·ly.**

in·vo·ca·tion (ĭn′və kā′shən) opening prayer in a church service or at a formal public meeting.

in·voice (ĭn′vois) **1** itemized list of merchandise sent to a buyer, giving prices, quantity, shipping charges, etc. **2** the merchandise listed. **3** to make an invoice of; enter in an invoice.

in·voke (ĭn vōk′) **1** to call for in prayer; plead for: *to invoke God's blessing.* **2** to ask for earnestly; beg for: *to invoke the protection of the law.* **3** to call forth by magic: *to invoke a genie.* **in·voked, in·vok·ing.**

in·vol·un·tar·y (ĭn vŏl′ən tĕr′ĭ) not done under the control of the will: *Sue gave an involuntary cry when she saw the injured bird.* **in·vol·un·tar·i·ly.**

in·volve (ĭn vŏlv′) **1** to entangle; draw into; mix up with or in: *He suspected that many people were involved in the scandal.* **2** to require; demand; include as a necessary part: *Success always* involves *effort.* **3** to occupy; engage: *I am involved in my work most of the time.* **in·volved, in·volv·ing.**

in·ward (ĭn′wərd) **1** inner; internal: *Her face expressed her* inward *happiness.* **2** towards the inside or center: *The ballet dancer, trained to turn her toes out, pointed her toes* inward *with difficulty.*

in·ward·ly (ĭn′wərd lĭ) secretly; privately: *Although outwardly calm, he was* inwardly *terrified.*

in·wards (ĭn′wərdz) inward: *She pointed her toes* inwards.

i·o·dine or **i·o·din** (ī′ə dīn′) grayish-black solid element that gives off a purple vapor. It is used with alcohol to kill germs in minor cuts and scratches. Its compounds are used in medicine, photography, and many industries.

i·on (ī′ən or ī′ŏn) atom or group of atoms that has an electric charge caused by the gain or loss of electrons.

i·on·o·sphere (ī ŏn′ə sfĭr′) region of electrically charged air that begins about 50 miles above the earth's surface. The ionosphere contains several layers from which radio waves are reflected.

I·o·wa (ī′ə wə) State in the north central part of the United States.

i·rate (ī′rāt or ī rāt′) angry: *The irate man stormed out of the room.* **i·rate·ly.**

ire (īr) anger; wrath: *His* ire *was aroused when he saw the bully pick on the boy.*

Ire·land (īr′lənd) island country west of England.

i·ris (ī′rĭs) **1** colored part of the eye around the pupil. For picture, see **eye.** **2** a plant with large, flaring, loose-petaled flowers and sword-shaped leaves. **3** the flower of this plant.

I·rish (i′rish) **1** of Ireland, its people, or language. **2 the Irish** the people of Ireland or their descendants.

irk·some (ûrk′səm) tiresome; so dull as to cause impatience: *She finds it irksome to do the same tasks day after day.*

i·ron (i′ərn) **1** silver-white metal element. Iron is the main element in steel. **2** tool or appliance made of iron or steel: *a branding* iron; *an electric* iron; *a soldering* iron; *a waffle* iron. **3** to press wrinkles out of something with a hot iron: *Mother is ironing the clothes.* **4** made of iron: *an iron gate; an iron bar.* **5** golf club with a metal head. **6** firm; unyielding; strong: *A man with an iron will is not easily changed.* **7 irons** fetters: *The prisoners were placed in irons.*

Iris

i·ron·i·cal (i rŏn′ə kəl) **1** meaning the opposite of what is expressed: *He was full of ironical remarks like "How bighearted, how touching of you to worry about me."* **2** contrary to what would usually be expected: *He was under the ironical necessity of having to rest from his vacation.* **i·ron·i·cal·ly.**

iron lung steel cylinder fitted with a bellows that applies rhythmic air pressure to the chest of a patient lying inside it. This device causes normal lung expansion and contraction in patients whose chest muscles are temporarily paralyzed.

i·ro·ny (i′rə ni) **1** a humorous or sarcastic way of expressing the direct opposite of what is really meant. To say "That's just wonderful!" when someone has made a mistake is irony. **2** a situation or happening that is the direct opposite of what was intended or expected: *By one of life's ironies, the thief was paid for his stolen goods in counterfeit money.* **i·ro·nies.**

ir·ra·di·ate (i rā′di āt′) **1** to direct light upon or through. **2** to treat with X rays, ultraviolet light, or other radiation: *This*

milk has been irradiated. **ir·ra·di·at·ed, ir·ra·di·at·ing.**

ir·reg·u·lar (i rĕg′yŏŏ lər) **1** not regular or even; not uniform in shape, order, arrangement, etc.: *an irregular coastline; buses running at* irregular *intervals.* **2** not according to rule or custom: *At one time it was highly irregular for a woman to travel without a chaperon.* **ir·reg·u·lar·ly.**

ir·reg·u·lar·i·ty (i rĕg′yŏŏ lăr′ə tĭ) **1** a being irregular: *the irregularity of the coastline.* **2** uneven or irregular part: *an irregularity in a wall.* **3** something contrary to established rules: *an irregularity in the bank's accounts.* **ir·reg·u·lar·i·ties.**

ir·rel·e·vant (i rĕl′ə vənt) having no bearing on or connection with the matter at hand; unrelated; not relevant: *Henry's irrelevant remark showed that he was not listening.* **ir·rel·e·vant·ly.**

ir·re·sist·i·ble (ĭr′ĭ zĭs′tə bəl) too strong to be resisted or withstood: *an irresistible temptation.* **ir·re·sist·i·bly.**

ir·res·o·lute (i rĕz′ə lōōt′ or i rĕz′ə lŭt′) undecided; wavering; hesitating: *An irresolute person is not a good chairman.* **ir·res·o·lute·ly.**

ir·re·spon·si·ble (ĭr′rə spŏn′sĭ bəl) not to be depended upon; not trustworthy. **ir·re·spon·si·bly.**

ir·rev·er·ent (i rĕv′ər ənt) not reverent; showing lack of respect, especially toward sacred things. **ir·rev·er·ent·ly.**

ir·ri·gate (ĭr′ə gāt′) **1** to supply (land) with water from a main source by means of ditches, canals, etc. **2** to wash out with a constant flow of liquid in order to clean or disinfect: *The doctor irrigated an infected ear.* **ir·ri·gat·ed, ir·ri·gat·ing.**

ir·ri·ga·tion (ĭr′ə gā′shən) **1** the science and practice of furnishing water to growing plants by means of ditches, etc. **2** the flushing of wounds, etc., with water.

Sugarbeet irrigation

ir·ri·ta·ble (ĭr′ə tə bəl) **1** easily annoyed or angered; cranky: *A baby becomes* irritable

fāte, făt, fâre, fär; bē, bĕt; bīte, bĭt; nō, nŏt, nôr; fūse, fŭn, fûr; tōō, tŏŏk; foil; foul; thin; then; hw for wh as in *wh*at; zh for s as in u*s*ual; ə for a, e, i, o, u, as in a*g*o, lin*e*n, per*i*l, at*o*m, min*u*s.

385

when he is sleepy. **2** extremely sensitive: *an* irritable *wound.* **ir·ri·ta·bly.**

ir·ri·tate (ir′ə tāt′) **1** to annoy; make impatient or angry: *The child's loud noises* irritated *him.* **2** to make sore; cause redness and pain to: *Strong soap can* irritate *a baby's skin.* **ir·ri·tat·ed, ir·ri·tat·ing.**

ir·ri·ta·tion (ir′ə tā′shən) **1** a being annoyed; annoyance: *He could not hide his* irritation *when we were late.* **2** soreness; unpleasant sensation: *a skin* irritation.

is (iz) a form of **be,** used with *he, she, it,* or the name of a person, place, or thing: *He* is *here, but she* is *not. Who* is *there? Is it* raining? *The work* is *being done.*

-ish suffix meaning **(1)** "somewhat" or "rather": *reddish; sweetish.* **(2)** "resembling" or "having the characteristics of": *hoggish; boyish.*

Is·lam (is läm′) **1** the religion of the Moslems, first taught by the prophet Mohammed in the seventh century, A.D. The Moslems worship one God, Allah, and consider Mohammed as the last of the true prophets. **2** the Moslems as a group, their culture, and their lands.

is·land (ī′lənd) **1** piece of land completely surrounded by water. **2** something that is like an island: *an* island *of ice floating on the water; a safety* island *in the street.*

is·land·er (ī′lən dər) person who was born on or is living on an island.

isle (īl) small island. (Homonyms: aisle, I'll)

is·let (ī′lit) tiny island. (Homonym: eyelet)

is·n't (iz′ənt) is not: *He* isn't *here.*

i·so·bar (ī′sə bär′) a line on a weather map connecting all places having the same atmospheric pressure at a particular time.

i·so·late (ī′sə lāt′) to set apart or to cause to be away from others; separate from others: *It is necessary to* isolate *people with contagious diseases. The shipwrecked party was* isolated *from the outside world.* **i·so·lat·ed, i·so·lat·ing.**

i·so·la·tion (ī′sə lā′shən) a setting or being set apart or away from others; separation.

i·so·tope (ī′sə tōp′) any of certain atoms of an element having a different number of neutrons in the nucleus than other atoms of the same element.

Is·ra·el (iz′rī əl) **1** ancient kingdom in northern Palestine. **2** modern country in Palestine.

Is·rae·li (iz rā′lī) citizen of the modern country of Israel.

is·sue (ish′ū or ish′ōō) **1** something printed and published, usually as a part of a series: *an* issue *of a magazine; an* issue *of a newspaper.* **2** publishing or making public: *to buy stamps on the day of their* issue. **3** to send out; put forth; circulate: *a magazine which is* issued *once a month; to* issue *a decree or proclamation.* **4** to come, flow, or pass out: *Lava* issues *from a volcano.* **5** a coming, flowing, or passing out: *the* issue *of blood from a wound.* **6** thing that comes, flows, or is sent out: *land buried under the* issue *from a volcano.* **7** to distribute or give out officially: *to* issue *clothing to troops.* **8** subject of dispute; point or question for debate: *the political* issues *of a campaign.* **9** outcome; result: *What was the final* issue *of the problem?* **10** offspring; children. **11 take issue** to disagree: *to take* issue *with someone over politics.* **is·sued, is·su·ing.**

isth·mus (is′məs) narrow strip of land connecting two larger bodies of land.

it (it) **1** thing, animal, happening, or idea talked about: *I wanted the book and*

Isthmus of Panama

he handed it *to me. I'll give you a kitten if you'll take care of* it. *It is raining.* It *is a long walk to town.* **2** the person in some games who must do a certain thing: *Let's play tag. You're* it!

I·tal·ian (i tal′yən) **1** of Italy, its people, or language. **2** citizen of Italy, or person of Italian descent. **3** the language of the Italian people.

i·tal·ic (i tal′ik) **1** having to do with a type in which the letters slant to the right. **2** the style of type: *Most of this sentence is printed in* italic. **3 italics** letters in slanting type. In this book we use italics for all the words in an example except the word being explained. This is done so the reader can easily tell the example from the definition, and the word itself from the other words in the example.

i·tal·i·cize (i tal′ə sīz′) **1** to print with letters that slant toward the right. **2** to underline a letter or word in writing. **i·tal·i·cized, i·tal·i·ciz·ing.**

It·a·ly (ĭt′ə lĭ) country in southern Europe.

itch (ĭch) **1** stinging, tingling sensation that makes one want to scratch. **2** to cause such a feeling: *Some insect bites itch.* **3** contagious disease that is characterized by intense itching. **4** restless urge; intense longing: *an itch for popularity.* **5** to feel such an urge: *He was itching to fight.*

i·tem (ī′təm) **1** one thing among several: *What is the first item on the shopping list?* **2** piece of news: *Here's an interesting item from today's paper.* **3** entry in an account book.

i·tem·ize (ī′tə mīz′) to list the parts of; put down separately the items of which something is made up: *to itemize a milk bill.* **i·tem·ized, i·tem·iz·ing.**

its (ĭts) **1** of or belonging to it: *The tree lost its leaves.* **2** made or done by it: *The robin did not return to its nest.* **3** inhabited by it: *The turtle returned to its pond.*

it's (ĭts) **1** it is: *I think it's too cool to swim.* **2** it has: *Well, it's been a long trip.*

it·self (ĭt sĕlf′) **1** its own self: *The cat was licking itself.* **2** word used for emphasis: *The frame itself is worth more than the picture.* **3 by itself** (**1**) alone: *The owl perched by itself on the tree.* (**2**) without any help: *The door opened by itself.*

I've (īv) I have: *Oh, I've seen that movie!*

i·vo·ry (ī′və rĭ) **1** white, bonelike substance which forms the tusks of elephants, walruses, etc., used to make ornaments, piano keys, and the like. **2** color of ivory; creamy white: *The paper had turned ivory with age.* **3** of or made of ivory: *an ivory statue.* **i·vo·ries.**

i·vy (ī′vĭ) **1** any of several climbing or trailing vines with glossy, usually five-pointed, dark leaves. **2** any of several unrelated vines, such as the poison ivy. **i·vies.**

ENGLISH

POISON
Ivy

J

J, j (jā) tenth letter of the English alphabet.

jab (jăb) **1** to stab; poke with something sharp: *He jabbed me with his elbow.* **2** a quick stab; sharp poke. **jabbed, jab·bing.**

jab·ber (jăb′ər) **1** to talk in a rapid and confused manner; babble: *I can't understand you when you jabber like that.* **2** rapid and confused talk; senseless chatter: *the jabber of monkeys.*

jack (jăk) **1** man or fellow; chap: *a jack-of-all-trades.* **2** any playing card with a picture of a young man; knave. It comes between the ten and queen. **3** any of several tools or machines, especially a device used to lift cars and other heavy objects. **4** to lift or raise with a jack: *to jack up a car to replace a tire.* **5** small metal piece

Raising car with jack

used in a child's game called **jacks** or **jack-stones.** **6** small flag flown on a ship to show its nationality: *The ship was flying the British Union Jack.*

jack·al (jăk′əl) wild dog of Asia and Africa, about the size of a fox. It feeds on carrion and small game.

jack·ass (jăk′ăs′) **1** a male donkey. **2** a stupid person.

jack·daw (jăk′dô′) dusky, black, mischievous, European crow. It can learn to imitate human speech.

jack·et (jăk′ĭt) **1** short coatlike outer garment, with or without sleeves. **2** outer covering: *a book jacket.*

jack-in-the-box (jăk′ĭn thə bŏks′) doll that pops out of a box when the lid is released.

Jackdaw, about
14 in. long

---

fāte, făt, fâre, fär; bē, bĕt; bīte, bĭt; nō, nŏt, nôr; fūse, fŭn, fûr; tōō, tŏŏk; foil; foul; thin; ~~then~~;
hw for wh as in *wh*at; zh for s as in u*s*ual; ə for a, e, i, o, u, as in *a*go, lin*e*n, per*i*l, at*o*m, min*u*s

jack-in-the-pul·pit (jăk′ĭn thə po͞ol′pĭt) a North American plant, growing in damp woods, with tiny yellow flowers arched over by a hoodlike leaf.

jack·knife (jăk′nīf′) **1** large pocketknife with blades that can be folded back into the handle. **2** fancy dive in which the diver bends double, then straightens out. **jack·knives.**

jack-of-all-trades (jăk′əv ôl′trādz′) man who can do all kinds of jobs or make all sorts of repairs.

jack-o′-lan·tern (jăk′ə lăn′tərn) hollowed-out pumpkin with a face cut in it, used as a lantern at Halloween.

jack rabbit long-eared western hare whose long hind legs enable it to make 20-foot jumps.

jacks (jăks) child's game played by tossing a small ball while small metal pieces called **jacks** are moved from one position to another. Also called **jackstones.**

¹jade (jād) hard stone, usually green, used in jewelry and other ornaments. [¹**jade** is a shortened form of an older French word (ejade) that is in turn from a Spanish phrase (piedra de ijada) meaning "stone for (curing) the side."]

²jade (jād) **1** worthless or worn-out horse. **2** a worthless woman. **3** to make tired; dull: *to be* jaded *with overwork.* **jad·ed, jad·ing.** [²**jade** seems to be a form of a Scottish dialect word (yaud) that probably goes back to an Old Norse word (jalda) meaning "a mare."]

jag·ged (jăg′ĭd) having ragged edges; sharply notched: *The coast has a* jagged *outline.* **jag·ged·ly.**

jag·uar (jăg′wär) fierce and handsome wildcat of tropical America. It resembles a leopard, but is stockier and more powerful.

Jaguar, about 6½ ft. long

jail (jāl) **1** prison, especially one where people are locked up as punishment for lesser crimes, or to wait for trial. **2** to put or keep in a jail.

jail·er or **jail·or** (jā′lər) person in charge of a jail or of prisoners in a jail.

¹jam (jăm) **1** number of persons or things so tightly crowded together that movement is difficult or impossible: *a traffic* jam. **2** to pack tightly; cram: *She* jammed *all her clothes into one suitcase.* **3** to put or place forcibly; crush down: *He* jammed *his hat on his head.* **4** to make unworkable by sticking or blocking some part: *A stray thread* jammed *the sewing machine.* **5** to become unworkable because of a sticking or blocking of a part: *The rifle* jammed *when he tried to fire it.* **jammed, jam·ming.** [¹**jam** is probably a changed form of "to champ," meaning "to chew noisily." From this, squeezing and crowding might well have come as special meanings.]

²jam (jăm) a preserve made by boiling fruit with sugar until thick. [²**jam** is probably a special use of ¹**jam**, since in making jam a great deal of fruit is packed tightly together.]

jam·bo·ree (jăm′bə rē′) **1** noisy, lively party or spree. **2** large gathering of the Boy Scouts.

Jan. January.

jan·gle (jăng′gəl) **1** to make a noise that is harsh or out of tune: *A cracked bell* jangles. **2** harsh, discordant noise: *the* jangle *of an alarm clock..* **3** to upset; irritate: *That banging on the piano* jangles *my nerves.* **jan·gled, jan·gling.**

jan·i·tor (jăn′ə tər) man whose job it is to clean and take care of a building.

Jan·u·ar·y (jăn′yo͞o ĕr′ĭ) first month of the year. January has 31 days.

Ja·pan (jə păn′) island country off the eastern coast of Asia.

Jap·a·nese (jăp′ə nēz′) **1** of Japan, its people, or language. **2** citizen of Japan, or person of Japanese descent. **3** language of the Japanese people. pl. **Jap·a·nese.**

¹jar (jär) **1** to cause to shake: *Strong winds* jarred *the house.* **2** to cause a shock to: *News of the accident* jarred *him.* **3** sudden shake; shock: *Jumping from the tree gave me a* jar. *The bad news was a* jar *to him.* **4** to make a harsh sound. **5** a harsh sound. **6** to come into or be in conflict: *His ideas* jarred *with mine.*

jar on to have an unpleasant effect on: *His loud laugh* jars *on my ears.*

jarred, jar·ring. [¹**jar** is of uncertain origin.]

²**jar** (jär) **1** wide-mouthed vessel of glass or pottery. Some jars have covers which seal the contents and thus help to preserve them. **2** such a vessel and its contents: *She gave me this* jar *of jelly.* **3** quantity a jar will hold: *This bowl will hold two* jars *of cherries.* [²**jar** is from a French word (jarre) that goes back to an Arabic word (jarrah) meaning "an earthenware water vessel."]

Jar

jas·mine (jăz′mən) a shrub of the olive family, bearing fragrant white, red, or yellow flowers. Also called **jessamine.** The Carolina yellow jessamine is the state flower of South Carolina.

jas·per (jăs′pər) cloudy stone, usually red, brown, or yellow, used for ornamental objects.

jaunt (jônt) short pleasure trip.

jaun·ty (jôn′tĭ) gay and carefree; lighthearted and confident; cheerful: *a jaunty smile.* **jaun·ti·er, jaun·ti·est; jaun·ti·ly.**

jave·lin (jăv′lĭn) light spear used in ancient warfare. Nowadays it is used in sports contests.

jaw (jô) **1** one of the two bones that frame the mouth; jawbone. **2** lower part of the face. **3** anything like a jaw: *the jaws of a vise.*

jaw·bone (jô′bōn′) one of the two bones in which the teeth are set.

jay (jā) any of several chattering, bright-colored birds, especially the bluejay.

jay·walk·er (jā′wôk′ər) person on foot who crosses streets against traffic lights or at places other than marked crossings.

jazz (jăz) kind of American popular music that plays tricks with the melody and uses odd combinations of rhythm. Jazz musicians like to make up their own treatment of tunes and harmonies as they go along.

jeal·ous (jĕl′əs) **1** feeling ill will and envy: *She is* jealous *because I got the part in the play that she wanted.* **2** afraid of losing someone's affection or love: *He's so* jealous *that he won't let her talk to other boys.* **3** careful and watchful: *He is* jealous *of his good reputation in the community.* **jeal·ous·ly.**

jeal·ous·y (jĕl′ə sĭ) **1** ill will and envy. **2** fear of a loss of love. **3** an act or remark showing jealousy: *The party was marred by the petty* jealousies *of the guests.* **jeal·ous·ies.**

jean (jēn) **1** closely woven, heavy cotton cloth. **2 jeans** trousers made of this cloth, usually dark blue. (Homonym: gene)

jeep (jēp) a small, powerful motor car originally made for military use. It is now used where power and ruggedness are required.

Jeep

jeer (jĭr) **1** to sneer at; taunt; make fun of: *Only poor sports* jeer *the losing team.* **2** sneering sound or remark; a taunt: *the* jeers *from the crowd.*

Je·ho·vah (jĭ hō′və) principal name of God in the Old Testament.

jel·ly (jĕl′ĭ) **1** a food made out of fruit juice and sugar, or meat juice, or any similar substance that thickens by itself or that can be thickened by adding gelatin. Jelly holds its shape when cool, but melts easily. **2** to become jelly: *The soup* jellied *as it cooled.* **3** to cause to become like jelly: *The cook* jellied *the soup by cooling it.* **4** substance like jelly: *petroleum* jelly. **jel·lies; jel·lied, jel·ly·ing.**

jel·ly·fish (jĕl′ĭ fĭsh′) boneless sea creature with an umbrella-shaped, partly transparent body that looks like jelly. Some kinds have slender, stinging threads on the underside.

Jellyfish, 1 in. to 12 ft. across

jen·ny (jĕn′ĭ) **1** machine for spinning several threads at the same time. **2** the female of some animals: *the* jenny *wren.* **jen·nies.**

jeop·ard·ize (jĕp′ər dīz′) to put in danger; risk; endanger: *The fireman* jeopardized *his life to save the trapped child from the burning house.* **jeop·ard·ized, jeop·ard·iz·ing.**

jeop·ard·y (jĕp′ər dĭ) danger; peril: *to be in* jeopardy *of one's life.*

---

fāte, făt, fâre, fär; bē, bĕt; bite, bĭt; nō, nŏt, nôr; fūse, fŭn, fûr; tōō, tŏŏk; foil; foul; thin; then; hw for wh as in *wh*at; zh for s as in u*s*ual; ə for a, e, i, o, u, as in *a*go, lin*e*n, per*i*l, at*o*m, min*u*s

¹jerk (jûrk) **1** to pull or twist quickly: *Don't try to* jerk *the tablecloth from under the dishes!* **2** a quick pull; twitch: *Give the rope a* jerk *to tighten the knot.* **3** to move with sudden starts and stops: *The train* jerked *along.* [**¹jerk** is of unknown origin.]

²jerk (jûrk) to cut meat, especially beef, into long, thin strips and dry it in the sun. [**²jerk** is a form of "charqui," meaning "dried beef." This word comes from a Spanish word (charqui) of Indian origin.]

jer·kin (jûr′kĭn) a close-fitting, waist-length jacket without sleeves, often made of leather.

jerk·y (jûr′kĭ) with sudden starts and stops; not smooth: *a* jerky *motion.* **jerk·i·er, jerk·i·est; jerk·i·ly.**

jer·sey (jûr′zĭ) **1** light-weight knitted fabric. **2** shirt, sweater, or other garment made of this material. **3 Jersey** Jersey cow, noted for the richness of its milk.

Jerkin

Je·ru·sa·lem (jĭ rōō′sə ləm) a city, partly in Israel and partly in Jordan, which was the capital of ancient Palestine. It is considered a holy city by Jews, Christians, and Moslems.

jest (jĕst) **1** witty or clever remark; joke; something said or done to cause amusement: *His* jests *made the company laugh.* **2** to speak in a teasing, humorous way; make witty remarks. **3** an object of fun or joking. **4 in jest** in fun; not seriously: *He said that* in jest; *he didn't mean it.*

jest·er (jĕs′tər) **1** person who makes jokes. **2** man kept by a nobleman of the Middle Ages to entertain him and his court with jokes and stories; court clown.

Je·sus (jē′zəs) Jesus Christ, on whose life, death, and teachings the Christian religion is based.

¹jet (jĕt) **1** stream of gas, liquid, etc., gushing or squirting from an opening: *He shot a* jet *of water from his pistol.* **2** spout or nozzle out of which the stream comes: *a gas* jet. **3** jet engine or plane. **4** to shoot, gush, or spout out. **jet·ted, jet·ting.** [**¹jet** is from a French word (jeter) meaning "to throw." The French word goes back to a Latin word (jactare).]

²jet (jĕt) **1** black mineral which can be highly polished and is used for making ornaments. **2** made of jet: *a dress with* jet *buttons;* jet *beads.* **3** a deep, glossy black. **4 jet-black** very black. [**²jet** comes through Old French (jaiet) from a Greek word (gagates). The Greek word is from the name of a town, Gagas, in a part of Asia near Greece.]

jet engine engine in which continuous burning of fuel ejects a high-speed stream of gases from the rear. The escaping gases push the craft forward in the same way that air escaping from an inflated balloon causes it to dart forward when it is released.

jet plane airplane driven by jet engines.

jet-pro·pelled (jĕt′prə pĕld′) driven by a jet engine, as a jet plane.

jet propulsion the propelling of a boat or aircraft by jet engines.

jet·sam (jĕt′səm) **1** cargo thrown overboard to lighten a ship in danger. **2** such cargo washed ashore.

jet·ty (jĕt′ĭ) **1** structure built out into the water to break the force of the waves. **2** landing pier; wharf. **jet·ties.**

Jew (jōō) person who accepts Judaism as his religion, or identifies himself with Judaism because of his family background.

jew·el (jōō′əl) **1** precious stone; gem. Diamonds, rubies, and emeralds are jewels. **2** valuable ornament set with gems. **3** to set or adorn with jewels: *The pin was* jeweled *with diamonds.* **4** piece of precious stone or other hard material used as a bearing in the works of a watch, etc. **5** person or thing that is highly valued: *I have found a dressmaker who is a* jewel.

jew·el·er or **jew·el·ler** (jōō′əl ər) person who makes, repairs, or deals in jewelry.

jew·el·ry or **jew·el·ler·y** (jōō′əl rĭ) ornaments of silver, gold, gems, etc.; jewels.

Jew·ish (jōō′ĭsh) of or having to do with Jews.

jib (jĭb) small three-cornered sail in front of the foremast.

jif·fy (jĭf′ĭ) moment; instant: *I'll be ready in a* jiffy. **jif·fies.**

jig (jĭg) **1** quick, lively dance: *an Irish* jig. **2** music for this dance. **3** to dance a jig. **jigged, jig·ging.**

jig·gle (jĭg′əl) **1** to move with short, quick jerks: *The coins* jiggled *in his pocket.* **2** to cause to move with short, quick jerks: *He jiggled the coins in his pocket.* **3** a light, jerky motion; a slight shake. **jig·gled, jig·gling.**

jig·saw (jĭg′sô′) a saw with a thin blade set in a D-shaped frame, used for cutting along curved or jagged lines.

jigsaw puzzle a puzzle made of a picture which has been cut into many irregular pieces. One must put the pieces together to form the original picture.

jin·gle (jĭng′gəl) **1** light tinkling or ringing sound: *the jingle of sleigh bells.* **2** to make this sound: *The bells jingled.* **3** to cause to make this sound: *He jingled the bells.* **4** simple poem, often using nonsense words, with repeated sounds that make it easy to remember. "Hickory, dickory, dock" is a jingle. **jin·gled, jin·gling.**

jin·rik·i·sha or **jin·rik·sha** (jĭn rĭk′shô or jĭn rĭk′shä) light two-wheeled vehicle drawn by a man, originally used in Japan. Also called **rick·sha** or **rickshaw.**

Jinrikisha

job (jŏb) **1** something a person has to do; duty; responsibility: *It is his job to empty the trash.* **2** employment; work: *What kind of job do you have?* **3** piece of work: *He did a good job of waxing the car.*

jock·ey (jŏk′ĭ) **1** man whose profession is riding race horses. **2** to move or shift about (in order to gain a favorable position or advantage): *The racing cars jockeyed for position at the beginning of the race.*

joc·und (jŏk′ənd) merry; pleasant; cheerful: *His jocund remarks kept us in good spirits.*

¹**jog** (jŏg) **1** to move at a slow, jolting pace or trot: *The old horse jogged along.* **2** slow, jolting pace or trot. **3** to push or shake slightly; jar; nudge: *to jog someone's elbow.* **4** slight shake; nudge. **jogged, jog·ging.** [¹**jog** is a word of unknown origin.]

²**jog** (jŏg) **1** sudden bend in a road, etc.; a part that sticks out. **2** to make such a bend: *The road jogged.* **jogged, jog·ging.** [²**jog** is a form of (jag) meaning "a notch," "a projecting point."]

jog·gle (jŏg′əl) **1** to give a slight shake; nudge: *to joggle someone's elbow.* **2** a slight shake; a jolt. **jog·gled, jog·gling.**

join (join) **1** to put together; unite: *Let's join hands.* **2** to come together; connect: *The roads join here.* **3** to become a member of; become associated with: *to join the Boy Scouts.* **4** to come into the company of: *Will you join us for a swim?* **5** to take part with others; participate.

joint (joint) **1** part of an animal where two bones are joined, usually to allow motion: *the elbow joint.* **2** a connecting part between two things: *a pipe joint.* **3** place where two things are connected: *It is hard to find the joints at the corner of that cabinet.* **4** united; combined: *It took the joint efforts of the team to win.* **5** used, shared, or held by two or more persons: *a joint bank account.* **6** a large piece of meat for a roast.

Elbow joint

joint·ly (joint′lĭ) together; in combination.

joist (joist) one of the beams supporting a floor or ceiling.

FLOOR

Joists

joke (jōk) **1** something funny said or done to cause laughter. **2** to make jokes; jest. **3** object of laughter; something not taken seriously: *He treated the rule as a joke.* **joked, jok·ing.**

jol·li·ty (jŏl′ə tĭ) merriment; fun; gaiety. **jol·li·ties.**

jol·ly (jŏl′ĭ) merry; gay; full of fun or laughter. **jol·li·er, jol·li·est; jol·li·ly.**

jolt (jōlt) **1** to shake with jerky movements; jar: *The rough ride jolted us.* **2** a sudden jerk, bump, shake, or shock.

jon·quil (jŏng′kwĭl or jŏn′kwĭl) **1** plant of the narcissus family with sword-shaped leaves. **2** the fragrant yellow or white flowers of this plant.

jos·tle (jŏs′əl) to push roughly; elbow: *The people jostled one another on the subway.* **jos·tled, jos·tling.**

jot (jŏt) **1** to write down briefly and quickly: *The student jotted down a few notes on the lecture.* **2** tiny bit: *There is not a jot of truth in his story.* **jot·ted, jot·ting.**

---

fāte, făt, fâre, fär; bē, bĕt; bīte, bĭt; nō, nŏt, nôr; fūse, fŭn, fûr; tōō, tŏŏk; foil; foul; thin; ~~then~~; hw for wh as in *wh*at; zh for s as in u*s*ual; ə for a, e, i, o, u, as in *a*go, lin*e*n, per*i*l, at*o*m, min*u*s

jounce (jouns) **1** to shake up and down; jolt; bounce. **2** sudden jerk; jolt. **jounced, jounc·ing.**

jour·nal (jûr′nəl) **1** daily record of news or events; diary. **2** daily record of acts of a legislature or transactions of a business. **3** newspaper or periodical appearing at regular intervals.

jour·nal·ism (jûr′nə liz′əm) the work of publishing, editing, or writing for a newspaper or magazine.

jour·nal·ist (jûr′nəl ist) person who writes for or edits a newspaper or magazine.

jour·ney (jûr′nĭ) **1** a trip, especially a long one, or one taking considerable time. **2** distance traveled in a certain time: *a day's journey.* **3** to make a trip; travel: *He journeyed to Spain.*

jour·ney·man (jûr′nĭ mən) person who has learned a trade or skill and works for another. **jour·ney·men.**

joust (joust or jŭst) **1** a combat, often in sport, between two mounted knights with lances. **2** to take part in such a contest.

Joust

Jove (jōv) name for Jupiter, chief of the gods in Roman mythology.

jo·vi·al (jō′vĭ əl) full of laughter and good spirits; jolly. **jo·vi·al·ly.**

jowl (joul) **1** lower jaw. **2** the cheek.

joy (joi) **1** a feeling of great happiness, gladness, or pleasure. **2** that which causes happiness: *Her thoughtfulness is a joy to her mother.*

joy·ful (joi′fəl) full of gladness; showing or causing joy; happy; joyous. **joy·ful·ly.**

joy·less (joi′lĭs) dull; dismal; cheerless: *a joyless home; a joyless future.* **joy·less·ly.**

joy·ous (joi′əs) happy; glad; joyful. **joy·ous·ly.**

Jr. junior.

ju·bi·lant (jōō′bə lənt) showing great joy; triumphantly joyful; exultant: *The crowd was jubilant.* **ju·bi·lant·ly.**

ju·bi·lee (jōō′bə lē′) **1** anniversary, especially the 50th or 25th. **2** any period or occasion of great and general rejoicing.

Ju·da·ism (jōō′dĭ iz′əm) one of the world's great religions and the religion of the Jews. Judaism was the first religion that taught

a belief in one God, and was the ancestor of Christianity.

judge (jŭj) **1** official who hears cases, makes decisions, passes sentences, etc., in a court of law. **2** to hear cases, make decisions, pass sentences, etc., as a judge in a court of law. **3** to make decisions after careful consideration of (a contest, competition, etc.): *to judge a speech contest.* **4** person who decides (in a contest): *a judge in a dog show.* **5** person who has enough knowledge or experience to decide on the quality, value, or extent of something: *a judge of cattle; a good judge of distance.* **6** to think; consider: *We judged his story to be true.* **7** to criticize and blame: *Don't judge people too harshly.* **8 Judges** the seventh book of the Old Testament. **judged, judg·ing.**

judg·ment (jŭj′mənt) **1** a judging; making a decision after careful consideration: *the judgment of a criminal.* **2** decision made after careful consideration: *The judgment of the court was in his favor.* **3** opinion; estimation: *In his judgment this car is the best buy.* **4** good sense: *a man of excellent judgment.* **5** misfortune considered as a punishment from God: *People often think their troubles are a judgment for their sins.*

ju·di·cial (jōō dĭsh′əl) **1** having to do with a judge or court of law: *the judicial proceedings.* **2** impartial; able to decide wisely: *a judicial mind.* **ju·di·cial·ly.**

ju·di·cious (jōō dĭsh′əs) showing good judgment; wise; sensible: *By judicious actions he avoided war.* **ju·di·cious·ly.**

ju·do (jōō′dō) Japanese sport and form of physical training that uses an opponent's own strength and weight in order to defeat him.

jug (jŭg) **1** glass or earthenware container with a small, short neck and a handle. **2** such a container and its contents: *a jug of cider.* **3** quantity a jug holds.

Jug

jug·gle (jŭg′əl) **1** to perform tricks with, especially to toss objects in the air and catch them in rapid succession: *The clown juggled three oranges and a lemon.* **2** to change (facts or figures) so as to deceive: *He juggled the figures to make the company seem prosperous.* **jug·gled, jug·gling.**

jug·gler (jŭg′lər) person who performs the trick of keeping objects moving rapidly in the air.

jug·u·lar (jŭg′yə lər) having to do with the neck or throat; especially naming either of the large veins, the **jugular veins,** on either side of the neck.

juice (jōōs) liquid part of vegetables, fruits, meats, etc.: *tomato* juice; *apple* juice.

juic·y (jōō′sĭ) full of juice: *a juicy orange.* **juic·i·er, juic·i·est; juic·i·ly.**

Ju·ly (jōō lī′) seventh month of the year. July has 31 days.

jum·ble (jŭm′bəl) **1** to mix in a confused way; put together without order: *He* jumbled *the letters of the word and asked us to guess what they spelled.* **2** confused mass; disorder: *Books and papers were in a* jumble *on the desk.* **jum·bled, jum·bling.**

jum·bo (jŭm′bō) **1** large; huge: *a jumbo ice-cream cone.* **2** large, clumsy person, animal, or thing. **jum·bos.**

jump (jŭmp) **1** a leap, spring, or bound: *a high* jump *off a diving board.* **2** to leap, spring, or bound: *to jump over a puddle.* **3** to cause (something) to leap, spring, or bound: *to jump a horse over a hurdle.* **4** sudden start: *The baby gave a startled* jump *at the loud noise.* **5** to give a sudden start: *Helen* jumped *in fright at the strange sound.* **6** sudden rise: *a jump in temperature.* **7** to rise suddenly: *The price of wheat just* jumped *three cents on the bushel.* **8** to pass or move abruptly (from one thing to another): *The conversation* jumped *from one subject to another.*

¹jump·er (jŭmp′ər) person, animal, or thing that jumps. [**¹jumper** is formed from **jump.**]

²jump·er (jŭmp′ər) sleeveless dress, usually worn with a blouse. [**²jumper** is formed from an earlier dialect word (jump) that comes from a French word (jupe) meaning "skirt."]

jump·y (jŭmp′ĭ) **1** moving in short, quick jumps or jerks. **2** nervous; easily made nervous. **jump·i·er, jump·i·est; jump·i·ly.**

junc·tion (jŭngk′shən) **1** a joining; a being joined: *The Mississippi River is formed by*

the junction *of many smaller rivers.* **2** a place where two or more things meet or cross, especially railroads.

junc·ture (jŭngk′chər) **1** a joining or being joined; junction. **2** point or line at which things join; joint: *a pipe's* juncture. **3** point in time or events: *at this* juncture.

June (jōōn) sixth month of the year. June has 30 days.

jun·gle (jŭng′gəl) land covered with a thick growth of plants, trees, and vines.

jun·ior (jōōn′yər) **1** person who is younger (than another): *He is my* junior *by six years.* **2** of lower standing or position: *the* junior *partner in a business.* **3** of or having to do with the third year of a four-year course in high school or college: *The* junior *dance will be held in May.* **4** member of this class: *Fred is a* junior *in college.* **5 Junior** the younger (used to describe a son named for his father): *James Stone,* Junior.

ju·ni·per (jōō′nə pər) evergreen tree or shrub of the pine family, with berrylike fruits and flat, branched leaves.

¹junk (jŭngk) **1** useless articles; trash: *Let's throw away that old* junk *in the attic.* **2** to discard (a thing) as worthless or useless: *We finally* junked *our old car.* [**¹junk** is from an Old French word (jonc) meaning "a plant with a hollow stem," "a string," "a cord," which goes back to a Latin word (juncus) meaning "a reed." **¹junk** used to mean "cord," then "old or discarded cord," and finally anything old or ready to be thrown away.]

²junk (jŭngk) kind of Chinese sailing vessel with a flat bottom and high stern. [**²junk** comes through Portuguese (junco) from the word of a South Pacific language (jong).]

Chinese junk

Ju·pi·ter (jōō′pə tər) **1** the largest planet in the solar system, fifth in order of distance from the sun. **2** supreme deity of the Romans, who rules all the other gods.

ju·ror (jōōr′ər) member of a jury.

fāte, făt, fâre, fär; bē, bĕt; bīte, bĭt; nō, nŏt, nôr; fūse, fŭn, fûr; tōō, tŏŏk; foil; foul; thin; then; hw for wh as in *wh*at; zh for s as in u*s*ual; ə for a, e, i, o, u, as in *a*go, lin*e*n, per*i*l, at*o*m, min*u*s

393

ju·ry (jŏŏr′ĭ) **1** group of citizens selected under oath in a court of law to listen to testimony and present a fair decision, or verdict therefrom. **2** any group of people who make decisions in a dispute, contest, etc. **ju·ries.**

just (jŭst) **1** not showing favor; fair; honest: *The judge handed down a* just *decision.* **2** having a sound or reasonable basis: *Ellen had a* just *dislike for the people who had mistreated her.* **3** rightly given; deserved; earned: *He received a* just *reward for his work.* **4** exactly: *That is* just *what I wanted.* **5** a moment ago; very recently: *We* just *finished dinner.* **6** barely: *The ball* just *missed us.* **7** right now; at this moment: *He is* just *coming.* **8** only: *Give me* just *one.* **9** quite: *That's* just *wonderful.* **just·ly.**

jus·tice (jŭs′tĭs) **1** fairness; right action: *We should use* justice *even in dealing with our enemies.* **2** a defending, supporting, and carrying out of law; legal administration: *a court of* justice. **3** a judge; judicial officer. **4** justice of the peace officer, of varying duties in different states, who tries minor cases, administers oaths, performs marriages, etc.

jus·ti·fi·a·ble (jŭs′tə fī′ə bəl) capable of being justified: *They argued about whether it was* justifiable *for a starving man to steal bread.* **jus·ti·fi·a·bly.**

jus·ti·fi·ca·tion (jŭs′tə fə kā′shən) **1** a showing (a thing) to be right or just: *In* justification *of the killing, the accused man pleaded self-defense.* **2** good reason; acceptable defense: *Do you have any* justification *for accusing this man of stealing?*

jus·ti·fy (jŭs′tə fī) **1** to show to be right or just; defend with good reason: *How do you* justify *your absence?* **2** to declare frèe from blame: *The verdict* justified *him in the eyes of the law.* **jus·ti·fied, jus·ti·fy·ing.**

jut (jŭt) to stick out; project: *A peninsula* juts *into the sea.* **jut·ted, jut·ting.**

jute (jōōt) **1** fiber of a tropical plant, used to make burlap and rope. **2** the plant itself.

ju·ve·nile (jōō′və nil or jōō′və nil′) **1** young; youthful; childish; immature: *Pouting is a* juvenile *manner of getting your own way.* **2** of or for young people: *a* juvenile *book.* **3** a youth; young person. **4** book for young people. **5** actor who plays youthful parts. **ju·ve·nile·ly.**

K

K, k (kā) 11th letter of the English alphabet.

kale (kāl) **1** vegetable, similar to cabbage, having loose, curly leaves instead of a head. **2** leaves of this plant eaten as a vegetable or as a salad.

ka·lei·do·scope (kə lī′də skōp′) a tube lined with three mirrors and fitted at one end with an eyepiece and at the other end with loose bits of colored glass held between a double glass disk. As the disk or tube is turned, the colored pieces fall into various positions, appearing through the eyepiece as beautiful geometric patterns.

kan·ga·roo (kăng′gə rōō′) animal of Australia that leaps along on its strong hind legs. The female has a pouch for carrying her young. **kan·ga·roos.**

Kans. Kansas.

Kan·sas (kăn′zəs) a State in central United States.

ka·pok (kā′pŏk) mass of silky fibers in the seed pods of a tropical tree called the **kapok tree,** used for stuffing cushions, mattresses, etc.

ka·ty·did (kā′tĭ dĭd′) insect that looks somewhat like a green grasshopper. Most kinds live in trees and make a sound that suggests the name.

Katydid, 1½ to 2 in. long

kay·ak (kī′ăk) **1** single-seated Eskimo canoe with a covered deck, made of waterproof skins stretched over a light frame. **2** similar canoe made of

Kayak

nylon stretched over a frame of aluminum or steel. A kayak is rowed with a double paddle.

keel (kēl) **1** the timber running the length of the bottom of a ship, on which the rest of the frame is built.

2 anything looking like a ship's keel as on an airplane, airship, etc.

keel over to capsize; overturn: *The canoe* keeled over *and we swam to shore.*

keen (kēn) **1** sharp; cutting: *a keen blade.* **2** stinging; bitter: *a keen north wind;* keen *sarcasm.* **3** sensitive; highly developed: *He has keen sight and hearing.* **4** alert; quick; clever: *a keen mind.* **5** eager; enthusiastic: *a keen interest in sports.* **keen·ly.**

keen·ness (kēn′nĭs) a being keen; sharpness; quickness: *the keenness of a razor;* keenness *of smell;* keenness *of mind.*

keep (kēp) **1** to have; own; possess: *You may keep this toy.* **2** to save; store; retain: *Irma gave away her bicycle but kept her dolls. Helen kept the secret all day.* **3** to remain; stay: *You must keep quiet while your father is reading.* **4** to continue: *If you keep trying, you will succeed.* **5** to care for; provide for: *Walter keeps pigeons.* **6** to look after; manage: *to keep house.* **7** to carry out; fulfill: *to keep a promise, an appointment, etc.* **8** to maintain or hold: *to keep one's hair short.* **9** to observe; celebrate: *to keep the Sabbath.* **10** to record; set down: *to keep an account.* **11** to restrain; hold back: *She kept her little brother out of mischief.* **12** to carry in stock: *Mr. Wilson keeps a large assortment of cookies at his store.* **13** to prevent: *The soldiers kept the enemy from advancing.* **14** to remain unspoiled or in good condition: *Milk keeps well in a refrigerator.* **15** to protect; guard: *The museum kept his paintings while he was away.* **16** the strongest part of a castle. **17** board and lodging: *That lazy fellow is not worth his keep.*

Keep of Norman castle

keep in to prevent from leaving; detain.

keep on 1 to continue without change: *to keep on doing the same work; to keep on asking questions.* **2** to let stay; retain: *The maid was very lazy, but we kept her on.*

keep one's temper not to get angry although one has a reason to.

keep time 1 to maintain and show the correct hours, minutes, etc. **2** to maintain the same rhythm.

keep up 1 to go or progress at an equal pace: *Johnny had trouble keeping up with his class.* **2** to continue: *The rain kept up all day.* **3** to maintain: *Can you keep up the house now that you've lost your job?*

kept, keep·ing.

keep·er (kē′pər) person who guards, watches, or takes care of something.

keep·ing (kē′pĭng) **1** care; charge. **2 in keeping with** in agreement with; in harmony with.

keep·sake (kēp′sāk′) something kept in memory of the giver or of an occasion.

keg (kĕg) **1** small cask or barrel. **2** such a container and its contents: *I bought a keg of nails.* **3** amount a keg will hold: *It takes four kegs of water to fill the trough.*

Keg

kelp (kĕlp) **1** a kind of large brown seaweed. **2** ashes of seaweed, from which iodine is made.

ken (kĕn) understanding; comprehension.

ken·nel (kĕn′əl) **1** a place where dogs are bred and raised for sale or looked after. **2** dog house.

Ken·tuck·y (kən tŭk′ĭ) a State in the south central part of the United States.

kept (kĕpt) See **keep.** *What kept you?*

ker·chief (kûr′chĭf) **1** piece of cloth used to cover the head or tie around the neck. **2** handkerchief.

ker·nel (kûr′nəl) **1** meat of a nut. **2** seed of grain, as of corn, etc. **3** central or important part of an argument, plan, or the like. (Homonym: colonel)

Walnut kernel

ker·o·sene (kĕr′ə sēn′) thin, clear oil made from petroleum and used as a fuel.

fāte, făt, fâre, fär; bē, bĕt; bīte, bĭt; nō, nŏt, nôr; fūse, fŭn, fûr; tōō, tŏŏk; foil; foul; thin; ~~then~~; hw for wh as in *wh*at; zh for s as in u*s*ual; ə for a, e, i, o, u, as in *a*go, lin*e*n, per*i*l, at*o*m, min*u*s

ketch (kĕch) small sailboat with two masts. The sails are set lengthwise.

ketch·up (kĕch'əp) a sauce made of tomatoes and spices. Also spelled **catsup.**

ket·tle (kĕt'əl) metal pot used to heat liquids, especially a teakettle, which has a handle and a spout.

ket·tle·drum (kĕt'əl drŭm') bowl-shaped brass or copper drum with parchment stretched over the top.

¹**key** (kē) 1 piece of shaped metal used for turning the bolt in a lock to fasten or open a door, padlock, or the like. 2 anything like this in shape or use: *a key to wind a toy; a key to open a can.* 3 place or position controlling entrance: *New Orleans is the key to the Mississippi.* 4 main clue; means of finding a solution or explanation: *This letter is the key to the whole mystery.* 5 list that explains a map or chart; answers: *a color key to a map; a key to a test.* 6 important; necessary; vital: *Steel is a key industry.* 7 part pressed down by the finger on a piano, typewriter, etc., to make it work. 8 series of musical tones related to one tone called a **keynote:** *the key of F.* 9 tone or pitch: *She sang off key.* 10 to adjust; make appropriate to: *a TV program keyed to the interests of the children.* **key up** to stimulate; excite: *The players were all keyed up before the game.* [¹**key** is a form of an Old English word (cæg).] (Homonym: quay)

²**key** (kē) low island or reef. [²**key** comes through Spanish (cayo) from an American Indian word (taino) meaning "a small island."] (Homonym: quay)

Keyboard of a piano

key·board (kē'bôrd') 1 complete series of black and white keys by means of which a piano or organ is played. 2 arrangement of lettered disks by means of which a typewriter or the like is operated.

key·note (kē'nōt') 1 first note of a musical scale. 2 main idea; chief theme. 3 **keynote speech** in politics, a speech that outlines the policy of a political party.

key·stone (kē'stōn') 1 stone, sometimes ornamented, in the middle of an arch. It holds the other stones in place. 2 something essential upon which other things depend: *Freedom is the keystone of democracy.*

Keystone

khak·i (kăk'ĭ or kä'kĭ) 1 yellowish brown. 2 cloth of a dull yellow-brown color. 3 made of this cloth: *a khaki uniform.*

kick (kĭk) 1 to hit, strike, or thrust out with the foot. 2 a blow or thrust made with the foot. 3 to push or spring back; recoil: *The gun kicked when he fired it.* 4 a backward push or spring: *The kick of the gun knocked him down.*

kid (kĭd) 1 young goat. 2 leather made from the skin of a young goat. 3 made of this leather: *white kid gloves.* 4 child. 5 to tease; fool; joke with. **kid·ded, kid·ding.**

kid·nap (kĭd'năp) to carry off and hold a person by force or by trickery. This is usually done to collect a ransom. **kid·naped** or **kid·napped, kid·nap·ing** or **kid·nap·ping.**

kid·ney (kĭd'nĭ) 1 either of the two bean-shaped organs of the body in the lower back near the spine. They separate watery waste matter from the blood. 2 kidney of an animal used as food.

Kidneys, showing position from back

kill (kĭl) 1 to take life from; deprive of life. 2 act of killing: *We closed in around the tiger for the kill.* 3 to destroy: *The frost killed the crops.* 4 to defeat; reject; discard: *The senators killed the tax bill.* 5 to use up; spend (time) idly: *We killed an hour looking out the window.*

kill·deer (kĭl'dĭr') kind of plover with brown back and wings, orange-brown tail, and white breast crossed by two brown bands. It is named after its call. For picture, see **plover.**

kill·er (kĭl'ər) person, animal, or thing that takes life from another.

kiln (kĭln or kĭl) oven or furnace in which clay articles like bricks and pottery are burned, baked, or dried.

ki·lo (kĭl'ō or kē'lō) 1 kilogram. 2 kilometer. **ki·los.**

kil·o·gram (kĭl′ə grăm′) unit of weight in the metric system equal to 1,000 grams or about 2⅕ pounds.

kil·o·me·ter (kĭl′ə mē′tər or kĭ-lŏm′ə tər) distance equal to 1,000 meters or about 3,281 feet. Also spelled **kil·o·me·tre.**

kil·o·watt (kĭl′ə wŏt′) a unit of electrical power equal to 1,000 watts.

kilt (kĭlt) short, pleated skirt worn by men of the Scottish Highlands.

Kilt

ki·mo·no (kə mō′nə) **1** loose outer garment, bound with a broad sash, worn by men and women in Japan. **2** dressing gown resembling this. **ki·mo·nos.**

kin (kĭn) **1** person's family; relatives. **2** related: *John is kin to me.* **3** next of kin person or persons most closely related.

¹kind (kīnd) **1** gentle and loving: *Be kind to animals.* **2** thoughtful; considerate: *It was kind of you to send flowers.* [**¹kind** is a form of an Old English word (cynde, gecynde) having the same meaning.]

Kimono

²kind (kīnd) sort; class; variety: *What kind of apple is that? It takes all kinds of people to make a world.* [**²kind** is a form of an Old English word (cynd). It is related to **kin.**]

kin·der·gar·ten (kĭn′dər gär′dən or kĭn′dər gär′tən) a school or class for young children that prepares them for elementary school by playing games, reading stories, or the like.

kind·heart·ed (kīnd′härt′ĭd) gentle and thoughtful of others. **kind·heart·ed·ly.**

kin·dle (kĭn′dəl) **1** to set fire to; light: *to kindle a fire.* **2** to catch fire: *The dry wood kindled immediately.* **3** to arouse; stir up: *The insult kindled his anger.* **4** to become aroused or stirred up: *to kindle with enthusiasm.* **5** to become bright and glowing: *Her eyes kindled with excitement as the curtain rose.* **kin·dled, kin·dling.**

kind·li·ness (kīnd′li nis) gentleness and sympathy; thoughtfulness of others.

kin·dling (kĭn′dlĭng) material for starting a fire, such as small pieces of wood.

kind·ly (kīnd′lĭ) **1** gentle and thoughtful of others; kind: *He is a kindly man who will help anyone.* **2** in a kind, friendly way: *He treated me kindly and took care of me.* **3** please; be good enough to: *Will you kindly explain what you mean?* **kind·li·er, kind·li·est.**

kind·ness (kīnd′nĭs) **1** gentleness to and thoughtfulness of others; a being kind: *He showed kindness by helping us.* **2** helpful or thoughtful act; kind act: *He did me a kindness when he got me a job.*

kin·dred (kĭn′drĭd) **1** relatives. **2** of the same kind; related: *Writing and spelling are kindred studies.*

kine (kīn) cows; cattle.

king (kĭng) **1** male ruler or sovereign of a country. Kings usually inherit the crown and hold their position for life. Most modern kings have very limited power. **2** a person or thing that is thought of as being very important or powerful: *The lion is the king of the jungle.* **3** a playing card with the picture of a king. **4** a piece in a checker game which has been moved over to the opponent's last row on the board and can now move backwards or forwards. **5** the principal piece in the game of chess. **6 Kings** the eleventh and twelfth books of the Old Testament. In the Roman Catholic Church, the ninth, tenth, eleventh and twelfth books of the Old Testament.

king·bird (kĭng′bûrd′) any of certain small quarrelsome birds that eat insects.

king·dom (kĭng′dəm)

1 country that has a king or queen. **2** one of the three groups into which all natural things are divided: *the animal, vegetable, and mineral* kingdoms. **3** something thought of as a kingdom; realm: *the kingdom of the mind.*

Kingfisher, about 1 ft. long

king·fish·er (kĭng′fĭsh′ər) a crested bird with a blue back and white breast and

---

fāte, făt, fâre, fär; bē, bĕt; bīte, bĭt; nō, nŏt, nôr; fūse, fŭn, fûr; tōō, tŏŏk; foil; foul; thin; ~~then~~; hw for wh as in what; zh for s as in usual; ə for a, e, i, o, u, as in ago, linen, peril, atom, minus

neckband. It catches fish with its long, black beak as it flies over the surface of the water.

king·ly (kǐng′lǐ) **1** suitable for a king: *a kingly treasure.* **2** of or like a king; royal: *his kingly rights.* **king·li·er, king·li·est.**

kink (kǐngk) **1** a twist, curl, or sharp bend in a rope, wire, hair, etc. **2** to form, or cause to form, twists, curls, or sharp bends: *Don't let that lamp cord kink.* **3** stiffness in some part of the body; cramp: *a kink in the neck.* **4** an odd twist of mind or character; a strange notion.

kins·folk (kǐnz′fōk′) relations.

kin·ship (kǐn′shǐp′) **1** family relationship: *They are bound together by kinship as well as ideas.* **2** relationship arising from common origin, needs, or other factors; similarity: *There is a kinship between checkers and chess.*

kins·man (kǐnz′mən) male relative. **kins·men.**

kirk (kûrk) Scottish word for church: *the wee kirk on the moor.*

kiss (kǐs) **1** to touch or press with the lips as a caress, greeting, or sign of respect. **2** a touching or pressing with the lips as a caress, etc. **3** to touch gently; to caress (used of the wind, waves, etc.).

kit (kǐt) **1** set or collection of tools, materials, etc., for a particular job or purpose: *a kit for building a model boat; a sewing kit; a soldier's kit.* **2** case, box, or bag holding a kit.

kitch·en (kǐch′ən) a room in which food is prepared.

¹**kite** (kǐt) any of several hawks with slender wings, noted for their graceful flight. Some kinds have forked tails. [¹**kite** is a form of an Old English word (cȳta) having the same meaning.]

Swallow-tailed kite, 1½ to 2 ft. long

²**kite** (kǐt) a frame of light wood over which is stretched a silk or paper covering, flown at the end of a long string. [²**kite** is ¹**kite** in a later, special use, from the fact that a kite looks like a bird in the sky.]

Box kite and common kite

kith (kǐth) old word meaning "friends." It is now used only in the phrase **kith and kin,** which means friends and relations.

kit·ten (kǐt′ən) young cat.

kit·ty (kǐt′ǐ) pet name for a cat or kitten. **kit·ties.**

knack (nǎk) a special skill or ability: *It takes practice to get the knack of serving in tennis.*

knap·sack (nǎp′sǎk′) leather or canvas bag for clothing, food, etc., carried on the back by straps fitting over the shoulders.

Knapsack

knave (nāv) **1** dishonest or deceitful person. **2** in card games, a jack. (Homonym: nave)

knav·er·y (nā′və rǐ) cunning; dishonesty; treachery. **knav·er·ies.**

knav·ish (nā′vǐsh) deceitful; cunning in a dishonest way. **knav·ish·ly.**

knead (nēd) **1** to mix and make into a doughlike mass by pressing and stretching, either with the hands or by machine: *Clay should be kneaded before being molded.* **2** to rub and press with the hands or fingers; massage: *He kneaded the muscle which caused the cramp.* (Homonym: need)

knee (nē) **1** joint of a person's leg between the thigh and the lower leg. **2** part of a garment covering this joint: *He tore the knee of his trousers.*

knee·cap (nē′kǎp′) small, flat, movable bone that covers the front of the knee joint.

kneel (nēl) to bend the knees or rest on the knees: *to kneel in prayer.* **knelt or kneeled, kneel·ing.**

knell (něl) the slow sounding of a bell to announce a death or a funeral.

knelt (nělt) See **kneel.** *We knelt to pray.*

knew (nōō or nū) See **know.** *He knew the answer.* (Homonym: new)

knick·er·bock·ers (nǐk′ər bŏk′-ərz) full-cut breeches that gather and reach just below the knee; knickers.

Knicker-bockers

knick·ers (nǐk′ərz) knickerbockers.

knick·knack (nǐk′nǎk′) any small decorative ornament.

398

knife (nīf) 1 a cutting tool of many forms, with a keen, usually single-edged, blade. 2 to cut or stab with a knife. **knives; knifed, knif·ing.**

Carving knife   Table knife   Pocket knife

knight (nīt) 1 during the Middle Ages, a man of noble birth who served his king or lord after having served as a page and squire. 2 today, a man honored by the British sovereign. He ranks below a baronet and is called Sir. 3 to raise a man to knighthood. 4 in chess, the piece having the figure of a horse's head. (Homonym: night)

knight-er·rant (nīt′ĕr′ənt) medieval knight who wandered about in search of adventure. **knights-er·rant.**

knight·hood (nīt′hŏŏd′) 1 character, rank, or dignity of a knight. 2 whole body or class of knights.

knight·ly (nīt′lĭ) chivalrous; brave, courteous, gentle. **knight·li·er, knight·li·est.** (Homonym: nightly)

knit (nĭt) 1 to make a fabric or article of clothing of looped yarn either by hand with long needles or by machine: *Mother* knitted *Don a pair of socks. Suzy's dress was* knitted *by machine.* 2 to wrinkle; draw together: *Chloe* knits *her forehead when she reads.* 3 to grow together; unite: *The broken bone* knitted *quickly.* 4 to put or join together: *The families were* knit *together by common interests. The mystery story plot was closely* knit. 5 made by knitting: *to specialize in* knit *goods.* **knit** or **knit·ted, knit·ting.**

knit·ting (nĭt′ĭng) 1 act of a person making a fabric by looping yarn with two or more needles. 2 what is being knitted: *She laid her* knitting *down when she answered the doorbell.* 3 a joining, as of a broken bone: *The bone was slow in* knitting.

Knitting

knob (nŏb) 1 rounded handle of a door, drawer, umbrella, etc. 2 rounded swelling, lump, or mass on a surface.

knock (nŏk) 1 to strike, hit, or rap with the fist or something hard: *He* knocked *softly on the door.* 2 to collide; bump: *His knees* knocked *together in fright.* 3 noisy banging or pounding of parts of machinery: *a* knock *in the engine.* 4 a rap or blow: *There was a* knock *at the window.*

knock about 1 to wander without purpose: *He had* knocked about *for years.* 2 to toss about: *The small boat was* knocked about *in the rough sea.*

knock down 1 to cause to fall to the ground: *Charles didn't watch where he was going and accidentally* knocked *his brother down.* 2 to reduce or lower the price of: *The cost of the painting was* knocked down *to $5.* 3 to take something apart in order to transport it: *The furniture was* knocked down *before shipment.*

knock out to strike (a person) so that he is no longer conscious: *The boxer* knocked out *his opponent.*

knock together to make or put together quickly: *A doghouse was* knocked together *in no time.*

knock·er (nŏk′ər) 1 one who knocks. 2 ring, knob, or the like, hinged to a metal plate on a door. By tapping the knob against the plate, a visitor announces himself.

Knocker

knoll (nōl) small, round hill.

knot (nŏt) 1 any of many forms of interweaving or tying together a cord or cords.

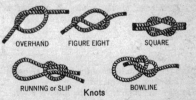

OVERHAND   FIGURE EIGHT   SQUARE

RUNNING or SLIP   Knots   BOWLINE

2 a lump: *The veins in his arm stood out in* knots. 3 hard spot in wood where a branch has grown. 4 a group; gathering: *There was a* knot *of people on the courthouse steps.* 5 unit of measuring speed at sea; nautical

---

fāte, făt, fâre, fär; bē, bĕt; bīte, bĭt; nō, nŏt, nôr; fūse, fŭn, fûr; tōō, tŏŏk; foil; foul; thin; ~~then~~; hw for wh as in *wh*at; zh for s as in u*s*ual; ə for a, e, i, o, u, as in *a*go, lin*e*n, per*i*l, at*o*m, min*u*s

mile traveled in an hour: *The ship has a speed of ten knots.* **6** to make a knot; tie together; bind. **knot·ted, knot·ting.** (Homonym: not)

knot·hole (nŏt′hōl′) round hole in a board where a knot has fallen out.

knot·ty (nŏt′ĭ) **1** full of knots: *a knotty cord;* knotty *wood.* **2** hard to solve or explain; difficult: *a* knotty *problem.* **knot·ti·er, knot·ti·est.**

know (nō) **1** to have in the mind as a result of study or experience: *A good speaker must know his subject.* **2** to be certain: *I know you'll like the show.* **3** to be aware (of); be informed (of): *Everyone knows of the accident. Who knows where they went?* **4** to be familiar with; be acquainted with: *He knows the road. We know all our neighbors.* **5** to recognize: *I wouldn't know her in a crowd. He knows good music when he hears it.* **6** to experience; meet with: *She has known hardship all her life.* **knew, known, know·ing.** (Homonym: no)

know-how (nō′hou′) special ability to do something well; technical skill.

know·ing (nō′ĭng) **1** intelligent. **2** showing special knowledge; shrewd; sly: *When asked who had broken the window, the boys exchanged* knowing *looks.*

know·ing·ly (nō′ĭng lĭ) **1** intentionally: *He would never* knowingly *do anything to harm you.* **2** in a knowing or sly manner.

knowl·edge (nŏl′ĭj) **1** that which one knows, whether through study or experience: *his* knowledge *of chemistry; his* knowledge *of the trails.* **2** all that is known; learning: *the branches of* knowledge.
3 to one's knowledge: as far as one knows: *He hasn't come in yet,* to my knowledge.

known (nōn) **1** familiar to all; widely accepted: *That the world is round is a* known *fact.* **2** See **know.** *I've* known *him for a long time.*

knuck·le (nŭk′əl) **1** a finger joint. **2** the knob formed by it when the finger is bent. **3** knee joint of a four-legged animal when considered as a meat cut.

ko·al·a (kō ä′lə) Australian animal that looks like a teddy bear. It has soft gray fur and large ears, lives in trees, and carries its young in a pouch.

Koala, about 2 ft. long

Ko·ran (kô răn′) the sacred book of the Moslems.

Ko·re·a (kô rē′ə) country on the coast of eastern Asia, divided into two countries since 1945.

Ko·re·an War (kô rē′ən wôr) war between North and South Korea (1950–1953) in which the United Nations supported South Korea. It was the first time that the United Nations took police action in a conflict. Many United States soldiers were involved.

ko·sher (kō′shər) **1** according to Jewish law, especially rules dealing with what foods may be eaten and how they must be prepared and served. **2** serving or dealing in such food: *a* kosher *restaurant.*

Ky. Kentucky.

L

L, l (ĕl) **1** 12th letter of the English alphabet. **2** Roman numeral for 50.

la (lä) the sixth note of the musical scale.

La. Louisiana.

la·bel (lā′bəl) **1** small piece of paper, metal, cloth, etc., attached to an article and giving information about it; a tag: *This store sews its* label *in every coat. Contents of the bottle are listed on the* label. **2** to mark with a label or tag: *She* labeled *all her books.* **3** to describe by a name or phrase; call: *to* label *someone a liar.*

la·bor (lā′bər) **1** to work hard; put forth great effort; toil: *They* labored *night and day on the new bridge. She* labored *over the composition.* **2** hard work, bodily or mental. **3** a task: *the* labors *of Hercules.* **4** working people as a group: *In the United States* labor *enjoys high wages.* **5** to go slowly and with effort: *The little train* labored *up the steep hill.*

lab·o·ra·to·ry (lăb′ə rə tôr′ĭ) a room or building where scientific research and experiments are carried on. **lab·o·ra·to·ries.**

Labor Day a holiday in honor of labor, celebrated on the first Monday of September in most States of the United States.

la·bor·er (lā′bər ər) **1** a worker. **2** person who works chiefly with his hands, or does heavy physical work.

la·bo·ri·ous (lə bôr′ĭ əs) **1** requiring great effort; requiring hard work; difficult: *a laborious task.* **2** showing signs of effort or difficulty: *a laborious handwriting.* **la·bo·ri·ous·ly.**

labor union an organization of workers which protects their rights and tries to get higher wages, shorter working hours, better working conditions, etc.

lab·y·rinth (lăb′ə rĭnth) a complicated system of winding paths in which it is difficult to find one's way; a maze.

lace (lās) **1** a delicate, open-work fabric into which decorative designs are woven. **2** to trim with such fabric. **3** a cord passed through eyelets to fasten parts of a garment, shoe, etc. **4** to fasten with a lace. **laced, lac·ing.**

Needlepoint lace

lac·er·ate (lăs′ə rāt′) **1** to tear badly; mangle: *The glass he held shattered, lacerating his hand.* **2** to distress; wound (in feelings): *Such sharp criticism lacerated his pride.* **lac·er·at·ed, lac·er·at·ing.**

lack (lăk) **1** to be without; not to have: *All the team lacks is a pitcher. Your story lacks imagination.* **2** want; shortage; state of being without: *He couldn't make the trip for lack of money.*

lack·ey (lăk′ĭ) male servant.

lack·ing (lăk′ĭng) **1** not having enough; deficient; wanting: *He is lacking in both talent and ambition. Money is lacking for this project.* **2** without; not having: *We are lacking two members of the class.*

lac·quer (lăk′ər) **1** clear varnish used for giving a shiny protective finish to metal, wood, etc. **2** to cover or coat with lacquer.

lac·y (lā′sĭ) like lace or made of lace: *a lacy pattern of frost on a window.* **lac·i·er, lac·i·est; lac·i·ly.**

lad (lăd) a boy or youth.

lad·der (lăd′ər) **1** a device of parallel bars or ropes with evenly spaced crosspieces between them, used for climbing. **2** stepladder. **3** steep flight of stairs. **4** a means by which one achieves a purpose: *His father's famous name was his ladder to success.*

lad·en (lā′dən) **1** loaded: *trees laden with fruit.* **2** weighed down; oppressed: *one laden with sorrow.*

Ladder

la·dle (lā′dəl) **1** a long-handled, bowl-shaped spoon or dipper. **2** to use such a spoon; dip. **la·dled, la·dling.**

Ladle

la·dy (lā′dĭ) **1** woman: *The nurse is a nice lady.* **2** a woman who is refined and has good manners: *Your daughter acted like a perfect lady at the party.* **3** woman of high social position: *That girl puts on airs as if she were a great lady.* **4 Lady** title in Great Britain held by certain women. **5 lady in waiting** lady who attends a queen or princess. **6 Our Lady** the Virgin Mary. **la·dies.**

la·dy·bird (lā′dĭ bûrd′) a small beetle; ladybug.

la·dy·bug (lā′dĭ bŭg′) a small, round-backed beetle, usually reddish brown with large black spots. It is valuable as a destroyer of harmful insects.

Ladybug

la·dy's slip·per (lā′dĭz slĭp′ər) or **la·dy-slip·per** (lā′dĭ slĭp′ər) any of a group of wild orchids with a flower that resembles a slipper.

lag (lăg) **1** to fail to keep pace; fall back: *The slow runners soon lagged behind the others in the race.* **2** a falling behind: *There was a lag in the work when the machinery broke down.* **lagged, lag·ging.**

lag·gard (lăg′ərd) **1** slow; falling behind: *to be laggard in one's studies.* **2** one who is slow or who falls behind.

la·goon (lə goon′) a shallow bay or lake, usually connected with the sea.

laid (lād) See ¹**lay.** *He laid out the rug.*

laid up forced to stay in bed or be inactive because of illness or injury.

---

fāte, făt, fâre, fär; bē, bĕt; bīte, bĭt; nō, nŏt, nôr; fūse, fŭn, fûr; tōō, tŏŏk; foil; foul; thin; ~~then~~; hw for wh as in *wh*at; zh for s as in usual; ə for a, e, i, o, u, as in *a*go, lin*e*n, per*i*l, at*o*m, min*u*s

lain (lān) See ²**lie.** *He has* lain *in bed for an hour trying to sleep.* (Homonym: lane)

lair (lâr) den or home of a wild animal: *The fox returned to his* lair *at dawn.*

laird (lârd) Scottish name for the owner of an estate.

lake (lāk) large body of water, usually smaller than a sea, surrounded by land; a large pond.

lamb (lăm) **1** a young sheep. **2** flesh of this animal, used as food. **3** a gentle, innocent, or helpless person.

Lamb

lame (lām) **1** crippled or disabled, especially in leg or foot. **2** to cripple: *He is on crutches because he was* lamed *by a bad fall.* **3** stiff or painful: *a* lame *back.* **4** poor; weak: *a* lame *excuse.* **lam·er, lam·est; lamed, lam·ing; lame·ly.**

lame·ness (lām'nĭs) **1** crippled condition: *His* lameness *forced him to use a cane.* **2** stiffness or soreness: *a* lameness *from too much exercise.* **3** weakness: *He himself realized the* lameness *of the story he had made up to explain his lateness.*

la·ment (lə mĕnt') **1** to show or feel great sorrow; mourn: *to* lament *the death of a friend.* **2** to regret; be sorry about: *to* lament *a person's folly; to* lament *a person's absence.* **3** an expression of grief. **4** poem, song, etc., expressing grief: *David's* lament *over Saul and Jonathan.*

lam·en·ta·ble (lăm'ən tə bəl) **1** to be regretted; sorrowful; mournful: *a* lamentable *sight.* **2** inferior; poor: *a* lamentable *performance.* **lam·en·ta·bly.**

lam·en·ta·tion (lăm'ən tā'shən) **1** expression of sorrow; a lament. **2 Lamentations** the twenty-fifth book of the Old Testament.

lamp (lămp) a device for giving artificial light.

lam·prey (lăm'prĭ) a water animal with gills and an eel-like body, but not a true fish. The lamprey has no jaws, but scrapes food into its round mouth with a rasplike tongue.

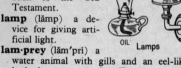

ELECTRIC

OIL Lamps

lance (lăns) **1** a long pole or shaft with a sharp metal point on the end. Lances were

Military lance

used chiefly by soldiers fighting on horseback. **2** to pierce with a lance. **3** to cut open with a sharp instrument: *to* lance *a boil.* **lanced, lanc·ing.**

land (lănd) **1** the solid part of the surface of the earth not covered by water. **2** soil; ground: *fertile* land. **3** country or nation: *We live in the* land *of the free.* **4** region: *a* land *of lakes.* **5** ground held as property. **6** to arrive, as a ship or an airplane. **7** to go ashore; disembark: *The passengers* landed *at noon.* **8** to come to the ground; alight: *The paratroopers* landed *safely.* **9** to bring to the ground: *The pilot* landed *the plane.* **10** to bring to a destination; cause to arrive: *This train will* land *you in New York. Such behavior will* land *you in jail.* **11** to arrive; reach; end up in; be in a certain position or in certain circumstances: *to* land *in a strange city; to* land *in jail; to* land *in great difficulties.* **12** to bring (a fish) to shore: *We* landed *a three-pound trout.*

land·ing (lăn'dĭng) **1** a wide step or platform at the end of, or between flights of, stairs. **2** a wharf or pier at which ships

Stair landing

may discharge passengers or goods. **3** the act of coming to land from, or as from, a ship: *The* landing *of Columbus was on San Salvador.* **4** the setting down of an airplane at the end of a flight.

landing field a field set aside for airplanes to land and take off.

landing gear apparatus on the under part of a plane on which it lands and travels on land or water. Wheels and pontoons are landing gear.

landing strip runway where planes land and take off.

land·la·dy (lănd'lā'dĭ) **1** woman who runs an inn or rents rooms in her house. **2** woman who rents to others land or houses that she owns. **3** wife of a landlord. **land·la·dies.**

land·lord (lănd′lôrd′) **1** man who rents to others land or houses that he owns. **2** man who runs an inn or rents rooms in a house.

land·mark (lănd′märk′) **1** an easily seen and well-known object which serves as a guide to travelers and sailors. **2** event that is a turning point or is very important: *The invention of radio was a* landmark *in history.* **3** object that marks a boundary of a tract of land.

land·own·er (lănd′ō′nər) person who owns land.

land·scape (lănd′skāp′) **1** a stretch of land or land and water seen as one view. **2** a picture of a view or scene from nature. **3** to arrange and make attractive the grounds around a building or in a park, with trees, shrubs, flowers, etc. **land·scaped, land·scap·ing.**

land·slide (lănd′slīd′) **1** a sliding of a mass of earth or rock down a steep slope. **2** a mass of falling earth or rock. **3** victory in an election which one side wins by a great majority.

lane (lān) **1** a narrow path or road, especially one between fences, hedges, or walls: *a green country* lane. **2** a fixed route or course for ships or planes. **3** a section of a road used for one line of traffic. (Homonym: lain)

lan·guage (lăng′gwĭj) **1** speech sounds and the way they are put together to tell something: *Thoughts, feelings, and ideas are expressed in* language. **2** a person's total means of communicating, including expression of the face, gestures, tone of voice, etc. **3** the words and forms of expression used by a group of people or a nation: *the* German language. **4** terms and expressions for a certain field of knowledge: *the* language *of science.* **5** any way or means of communicating: *the* language *of animals.* **6** a form, way, or style of using words: *simple* language; *the* language *of poetry.*

lan·guid (lăng′gwĭd) weak, as if from weariness. **lan·guid·ly.**

lan·guish (lăng′gwĭsh) **1** to lose health or strength; droop: *The roses* languished *in the summer heat.* **2** to pass through a period of discomfort and unhappiness: *to* languish

in prison; to languish *in poverty.* **3** to pine (for); long: *The exiles* languished *for their native land.*

lank (lăngk) **1** tall and lean: *Lincoln had a* lank *figure.* **2** of hair, straight and limp.

lank·y (lăngk′ĭ) tall, slender, and loose-jointed. **lank·i·er, lank·i·est.**

lan·tern (lăn′tərn) **1** a lamp with a handle for carrying it. **2** the top story of a lighthouse.

Electric lantern

¹lap (lăp) the part of a person's body from the waist to the knees when he sits down. [**¹lap** is a form of an Old English word (laepa) meaning "fold or hanging part of a garment."]

²lap (lăp) **1** to lay or fold a thing over something else. **2** to lie partly over something. **3** part of anything that extends over another part: *These shingles have a four-inch* lap. **4** one part of a longer distance: *a* lap *of a journey; the first* lap *of a race.* **lapped, lap·ping.** [**²lap** is **¹lap** in a later and different meaning.]

³lap (lăp) **1** to take up liquid with the tongue as a cat or dog does: *to* lap *up milk.* **2** to splash gently against with a sound resembling this: *The waves* lapped *against the side of the boat.* **3** the sound of lapping. **lapped, lap·ping.** [**³lap** is from a Germanic word.]

la·pel (lə pĕl′) part of a coat formed by a continuation of the collar and turned back on the chest.

Lapel

lapse (lăps) **1** slight error or mistake; slip; momentary forgetfulness: *a* lapse *of the tongue; a* lapse *of memory.* **2** to fall away from what is right or what is good; fall into error: *She has* lapsed *from her former good behavior.* **3** a slipping back; a falling into bad ways: *a* lapse *into crime; a* lapse *into savagery.* **4** to slip or glide away slowly: *His attention* lapsed *during the long speech.* **5** slow gliding or passing away: *after the* lapse *of several hours; after a long* lapse. **6** to end or pass to another because of failure to fulfill certain conditions: *His lease* lapsed *when he didn't pay the rent.* **7** the loss of a right, claim,

---

fāte, făt, fâre, fär; bē, bĕt; bīte, bĭt; nō, nŏt, nôr; fūse, fŭn, fûr; tōō, tŏŏk; foil; foul; thin; ~~then~~;
hw for wh as in *wh*at; zh for s as in u*s*ual; ə for a, e, i, o, u, as in *a*go, lin*e*n, per*i*l, at*o*m, min*u*s

or privilege through failure to use or renew it: *He was notified of the* lapse *of his driver's license after he failed to renew it.* **lapsed, laps·ing.**

lar·board (lär′bôrd′) **1** left side of a ship when one faces towards the front. This word is no longer in active use, having been replaced by **port. 2** on or towards this side of a ship.

lar·cen·y (lär′sə nĭ) the taking of property without the owner's permission; theft. **lar·cen·ies.**

larch (lärch) **1** tree of the pine family with small cones and needlelike leaves that drop in the fall. **2** tough, hard wood of this tree.

lard (lärd) **1** white, greasy substance made from the fat of hogs, used in cooking. **2** to smear with fat or grease.

lard·er (lär′dər) **1** place where meat and other foods are kept. **2** a supply or stock of food.

large (lärj) **1** big; great in size, amount, or number. **2** not little; not petty; broad in understanding and sympathy: *a man of* large *and generous nature.* **3** at large (1) free; out of prison: *An escaped convict is still* at large *in the county.* (2) chosen to represent all the districts of a certain area rather than just one: *He was elected congressman* at large *for his district.* **larg·er, larg·est.**

large·ly (lärj′lĭ) to a great extent; for the most part: *He is* largely *to blame.*

lar·i·at (lär′ĭ ət) long rope with a sliding noose, used to catch horses or cattle; lasso.

¹lark (lärk) **1** any of a group of small, European songbirds, especially the skylark. **2** a similar North American bird, the meadow lark. [**¹lark** is a form of an Old English word (læwerce, lãferce). In Scotland the word "laverock" is still used for "lark."]

²lark (lärk) amusing adventure; frolic; prank. [**²lark** seems to be a special use of **¹lark**, from the fact that the bird's movements seem very playful.]

lark·spur (lärk′spûr′) **1** any of several wild or cultivated plants with finely divided leaves and small white, pink, or, especially, blue flowers growing in spikes. **2** flowers of such plants.

lar·va (lär′və) **1** young insect in the stage, often wormlike, between the egg and the pupa. **2** the young of certain other animals in a similar stage, as the tadpoles of frogs and toads.

lar·vae (lär′vē).

lar·ynx (lär′ingks) cavity that is located at the upper end of the windpipe and contains the vocal cords.

Larva of moth and mosquito

la·ser (lā′zər) device that gives a narrow beam of intense light that does not spread out. The beam can be used to bore holes in metals, carry telephone messages, etc.

lash (lăsh) **1** the part of a whip used for striking: *The rider used a* lash *to make his horse go faster.* **2** to strike with a whip: *It used to be a common punishment to* lash *criminals.* **3** stroke given with a whip. **4** to switch to and fro like a lash: *The caged lion* lashed *its tail.* **5** to beat; strike violently: *The wind* lashed *the trees.* **6** to attack (with words); rebuke or scold severely: *He* lashed *me with a torrent of angry words.* **7** to stir up; arouse: *The speaker* lashed *the crowd into a state of excitement.* **8** to fasten with a cord or rope: *They* lashed *poles together.* **9** eyelash.

lass (lăs) girl; young woman.

las·so (lăs′ō) noosed rope used by cowboys to catch cattle, etc.; lariat. **las·sos** or **las·soes.**

¹last (lăst) **1** coming after others in time, place, order, etc.; final: *The* last *letter of the alphabet is z.* **2** after all others: *The slowest runner comes in* last *in the race.* **3** directly before the present: *the dance* last *night;* last *month.* **4** most recent: *The* last *time I saw him was yesterday.* **5** most recently: *When did you* last *go to the dentist?* **6** the only remaining: *the* last *cookie in the jar.* **7** least likely; least fitted: *He is the* last *man for such a job.* **8** person or thing that is last: *He is the* last *of his family.* **9** end: *to be loyal to the* last. **10** at last finally. [**¹last** is a form of an Old English word (latost) meaning "latest."]

Cowboy twirling lasso

²last (lăst) **1** to go on; continue: *The rain* lasted *three days.* **2** to be enough; hold out:

This much bread ought to last *for two days.*
3 to hold up; endure: *Stone buildings last longer than wooden ones.* [²last is a form of an Old English word (læstan) meaning "follow," "continue," which comes from another Old English word (lāst) meaning "footstep" or "track." ²last is related to ³last.]

³**last** (lăst) a model, the shape of the foot, on which shoes are made or repaired. [³last is a form of an Old English word (læst) meaning "a boot," which in turn comes from another Old English word (lāst) meaning "a footstep."]

last·ing (lăs′tĭng) keeping up or continuing a long time; enduring; permanent: *a* lasting *friendship.* **last·ing·ly.**

last·ly (lăst′lĭ) finally; in conclusion; at the end: *And* lastly, *we shall sum up what we learned from the experiment.*

latch (lăch) **1** locking device consisting of a bar pivoted at one end. The free end may be raised from or lowered into a notch to fasten a door, etc. **2** any of several devices used for a similar purpose: *a window* latch. **3** to fasten; lock: *Please* latch *the screen door before all those flies get in.*

Latch on door

late (lāt) **1** after the usual or expected time: *Spring came* late *this year.* **2** tardy: *He was* late *for work today.* **3** toward the end of a period of time: *The leaves began to fall in* late *autumn.* **4** of recent time or date; happening not long ago: *the* late *floods; his* late *illness.* **5** no longer living: *the* late *Mr. Barns.* **lat·er, lat·est** or **last.**

late·ly (lāt′lĭ) recently: *His work was poor, but it has improved* lately.

la·tent (lā′tənt) hidden; present but not active: *his* latent *strength; a* latent *talent for the theater; a* latent *disease.* **la·tent·ly.**

lat·er·al (lăt′ər əl) of, at, or coming from the side: *a* lateral *pass.* **lat·er·al·ly.**

la·tex (lā′tĕks) any of several milky juices found in various plants and trees, from which various products are made. Rubber is made from the latex of one kind of tropical tree.

lath (lăth) one of the thin, narrow strips of wood fastened to the frame of a building and used to support the plaster of walls and ceilings.

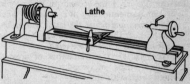

Lathe

lathe (lāth) a machine for holding a piece of wood, metal, etc., and spinning it against a shaping tool.

lath·er (lăth′ər) **1** foam made from soap and water. **2** foamy sweat of a horse. **3** to cover with a froth or foam: *She* lathered *her hair with shampoo.* **4** to make a froth or foam: *Most soap won't* lather *in salt water.*

Lat·in (lăt′ĭn) **1** of or having to do with ancient Rome, its people, or its language. **2** the language of ancient Rome. **3** of or having to do with languages which come from the language of ancient Rome or with the people who speak them, their countries, etc. **4** the people who speak any of these languages. Spanish, French, Portuguese, and Italians are called Latins.

Latin America countries of the Western Hemisphere south of the border of the United States. Their official languages (Spanish, Portuguese, and French) came from Latin.

lat·i·tude (lăt′ə tōōd′ or lăt′ə tūd′) **1** distance north or south of the equator measured in degrees, represented on maps or globes by lines parallel to the equator. **2** freedom of judgment, thought, or action; freedom from restrictions: *The government allowed its people great* latitude *in their religious belief. The diplomat was given wide* latitude *in negotiating the treaty.* **3 low latitudes** region from 0° to 30° from the

Parallels of latitude

fāte, făt, fâre, fär; bē, bĕt; bīte, bĭt; nō, nŏt, nôr; fūse, fŭn, fûr; tōō, tŏŏk; foil; foul; thin; then; hw for wh as in *wh*at; zh for s as in u*s*ual; ə for a, e, i, o, u, as in *a*go, lin*e*n, per*i*l, at*o*m, min*u*s

405

equator. **4 middle latitudes** region between 30° and 60° from the equator. **5 high latitudes** region from 60° to 90° from the equator.

lat·ter (lăt′ər) **1** the second (of two people or things mentioned): *We measured Sam and Henry, and found the* latter *was taller.* **2** later; near the end: *I shall be going shopping the* latter *part of the week.*

lat·tice (lăt′ĭs) **1** a framework of crossed parallel strips of wood, metal, etc., with space between them for air or light. **2** door, gate, window, etc., made of such a framework. **3** to make or furnish with a lattice. **lat·ticed, lat·tic·ing.**

Lattice

laud (lôd) to praise; extol.

laugh (lăf) **1** to make sounds and facial movements to express joy, amusement, scorn, etc.: *Everybody laughed at the joke.* **2** a series of such sounds and facial movements: *a laugh of scorn.* **3** to move or affect (someone) by laughing; cause (something to happen) as a result of laughing: *We laughed him out of his bad mood. Just laugh your troubles away.*

laugh·a·ble (lăf′ə bəl) causing amusement; funny; comical: *The puppy's awkward attempts to catch the fly were laughable.* **laugh·a·bly.**

laugh·ter (lăf′tər) laughing; sound of laughing: *The room was filled with the laughter of happy children.*

¹launch (lônch) **1** to lower or cause to be lowered into the water; set afloat: *The new ship was launched after a colorful ceremony.* **2** to start off; begin: *to launch a new business; to launch an attack.* **3** to hurl; cause to go forth with force: *to launch a glider; to launch a rocket.* [¹**launch** is from an Old French word (lancier) meaning "to lance."]

²launch (lônch) **1** the largest boat carried by a warship. **2** a motor-driven pleasure boat, usually without a deck or partly decked. [²**launch** is from a Spanish word (lancha).]

Launch

launching pad platform from which a rocket or missile is launched.

laun·der (lôn′dər) to wash and iron clothes, linens, etc.

laun·dress (lôn′drĭs) woman who makes a living by washing and ironing clothes.

laun·dry (lôn′drĭ) **1** clothes and linens to be washed. **2** place where clothes and linens are washed. **laun·dries.**

lau·rel (lôr′əl or lŏr′əl) **1** an evergreen shrub of southern Europe, with glossy leaves used by the ancient Greeks and Romans to make crowns for heroes. **2** a flowering shrub similar to the true laurel: *the mountain* laurel. **3 laurels** fame and honor.

la·va (lăv′ə or lä′və) **1** melted rock flowing from a volcano. **2** this rock when hardened.

lav·a·to·ry (lăv′ə tôr′ĭ) **1** a room with a basin or basins for washing the hands and face, and a toilet. **2** a basin with faucets, for washing hands and face. **lav·a·to·ries.**

lav·en·der (lăv′ən dər) **1** pale purple or pale violet color. **2** a plant with pale purple flowers and narrow woolly leaves, cultivated for its oil which is much used for perfume. **3** dried leaves and flowers of this plant, used to scent linens.

lav·ish (lăv′ĭsh) **1** giving freely or too freely: *to be* lavish *with money; to be* lavish *of praise.* **2** to give or spend freely and generously: *to lavish money on the poor; to lavish one's affection on unworthy objects; to lavish care on one's children.* **3** given freely or too freely; very abundant: *a* lavish *gift;* lavish *expenditures;* lavish *hospitality.* **lav·ish·ly.**

law (lô) **1** a rule or regulation set up by a government to be followed by all of the people under its authority. Congress makes laws for the nation. States also make laws. Cities make laws called **ordinances.** **2** the body of laws and regulations set up by a government: *The Constitution is the basic law of the United States.* **3** the study or practice of law: *to choose law as a profession.* **4** the working of the law: *to keep law and order.* **5** any custom, rule, or regulation followed and generally accepted by a group of people. **6** a statement of what happens under certain conditions: *the law of gravity.*

law·a·bid·ing (lô′ə bīd′ĭng) observing laws and the customs of good society: *A law-abiding citizen will not throw litter about.*

406

lawful

law·ful (lô'fəl) **1** allowed or recognized by the law: *a lawful claim.* **2** according to law; right, not wrong: *his lawful acts.* **law·ful·ly.**

law·less (lô'lĭs) **1** without laws: *a lawless country.* **2** not obeying the laws: *a lawless bandit.* **law·less·ly.**

law·less·ness (lô'lĭs nĭs) disregard for law or rule; wild and unrestrained conduct: *the lawlessness of the early mining camps.*

law·mak·er (lô'mā'kər) person who has a part in making laws; legislator.

law·mak·ing (lô'mā'kĭng) **1** that makes laws: *a lawmaking assembly.* **2** the making of laws.

¹lawn (lôn) **1** a stretch of ground covered with grass that is kept closely cut, especially such ground near or around a house. **2** such a stretch of grass used for a game: *a tennis lawn; a croquet lawn.* [¹**lawn** is a changed form of earlier "laund," which is from an Old French word (launde) meaning "wooded ground."]

²lawn (lôn) a thin, fine cloth, usually of cotton or linen. [²**lawn** is a word from an earlier English phrase, "laune lynen," meaning "linen from Laon." Laon is the French town where it was first woven.]

lawn mower a machine used to cut grass.

law·suit (lô'sōōt' or lô'sūt') a question or claim to be decided in a court of law.

law·yer (lô'yər) person trained in the law and engaged in it as a profession; attorney.

lax (lăks) **1** careless; negligent; not strict: *to have lax morals; lax behavior; lax discipline.* **2** not tight or firm; loose; slack: *a lax rope.* **lax·ly.**

lax·a·tive (lăk'sə tĭv) **1** a medicine or remedy used to make the bowels move. **2** causing the bowels to move: *For some people prunes are a laxative food.*

lax·i·ty (lăk'sə tĭ) lack of strictness or carefulness. **lax·i·ties.**

¹lay (lā) **1** to put or place: *to lay a book on the table; to lay one's hand on someone's shoulder.* **2** to put down in a certain position or place: *to lay linoleum; to lay bricks; lay a submarine cable.* **3** of birds, fish, and some other animals, to produce (eggs): *Ants lay eggs. The hens are laying well this year.*

lay

4 to bring or beat down: *One blow laid him low.* **5** to bet: *to lay a wager.* **6** to impose: *to lay a tax.* **7** to set in time or place: *The scene is laid in Colonial America.* **8** to put down or quiet; settle: *to lay the dust by sprinkling; to lay a ghost.* **9 the lay of the land** (1) the way the land lies; the position of hills, woods, streams, etc.: *Before the battle, the officer sent a scouting party to determine the lay of the land.* (2) the general situation: *Before proceeding with our plan, we thought we had better find out the lay of the land.*

lay aside 1 to put down or away: *She laid her book aside when her mother called to her.* **2** to save for future needs: *to lay money aside for future needs.*

lay away 1 to set something aside until paid for: *The department store will lay away Christmas presents.* **2** to save: *to lay away money.*

lay by to save: *to lay by money for a vacation.*

lay in to keep; store: *Some animals lay in food for the winter.*

lay off 1 to put out of work temporarily; discharge: *Workers were laid off while the factory was being rebuilt.* **2** to mark off: *to lay off a badminton court.*

lay on to apply; spread: *to lay the paint on in a thin coat.*

lay oneself out to take pains; make an effort.

lay open to cut open.

lay out 1 to mark off; plot: *to lay out a garden.* **2** to spend: *to lay out money.*

lay up 1 to put aside; store: *to lay up a supply of groceries.* **2** to cause to stay in bed, or be inactive because of illness or injury.

laid, lay·ing. [¹**lay** is a form of an Old English word (lecgan).] (Homonym: lei)

²lay (lā) See ²**lie.** *She lay in the shade of the tree for a long time.* [²**lay** is a form of ²**lie.**] (Homonym: lei)

³lay (lā) **1** having to do with a person who is not a clergyman: *a lay assistant to the minister.* **2** of a person outside any profession: *In legal matters it is better to have expert advice than a lay opinion.* [³**lay** is

fāte, făt, fâre, fär; bē, bĕt; bīte, bĭt; nō, nŏt, nôr; fūse, fŭn, fûr; tōō, tŏŏk; foil; foul; thin; then; hw for wh as in *what;* zh for s as in usual; ə for a, e, i, o, u, as in ago, linen, peril, atom, minus

407

from an Old French word (lai) that goes back to a Latin word (laicus). This Latin word in turn comes from a Greek word (laos) meaning "people."] (Homonym: lei)

⁴lay (lā) a short poem or song. [**⁴lay** is from an Old French word (lai) of Celtic origin.] (Homonym: lei)

lay·er (lā′ər) **1** one thickness of a material spread over a surface: *the outer* layer *of skin; the* layers *of the earth.* **2** someone or something that lays: *a hen that's a good* layer; *a brick*layer.

lay·man (lā′mən) **1** person who is a church member, but not a clergyman. **2** person who is not an expert on a subject: *Even a* layman *can understand this book on rockets.* **lay·men.**

laz·i·ness (lā′zĭ nĭs) being lazy.

la·zy (lā′zĭ) **1** not inclined to work. **2** slow-moving; sluggish: *the* lazy *river.* **3** relaxing: *a* lazy *day.* **la·zi·er, la·zi·est; la·zi·ly.**

lb. pound.

¹lead (lēd) **1** to go before to show the way: *The scout* led *the troops through the valley.* **2** to guide or conduct, by either the hand or some connecting thing: *The boy* led *the horse by the reins.* **3** to go at the head of; be first in: *The color guard* leads *the parade.* **4** the first place; the position ahead: *to take the* lead *in a race.* **5** the amount by which one is ahead: *a ten-foot* lead. **6** to command or direct: *A general* leads *an army. A conductor* leads *an orchestra.* **7** to influence or guide in an opinion or action: *I am easily* led *by my friends.* **8** influence; guidance: *He usually follows his sister's* lead. **9** clue; tip; hint: *The footprints were a* lead *in solving the crime.* **10** to extend: *This road* leads *to the river.* **11** to live; pass; spend: *to* lead *a good life.* **12** chief part in a play; chief actor. **led, lead·ing.** [**¹lead** is a form of an Old English word (lædan) meaning "cause to go."]

²lead (lĕd) **1** a heavy, soft, blue-gray metal element. **2** made of lead. **3** thin rod of black or colored material used in a pencil. **4** a weight attached to a rope, lowered to measure the depth of water at sea. **5** bullets; shot. [**²lead** is a form of an Old English word (lēad).] (Homonym: led)

lead·en (lĕd′ən) **1** made of lead. **2** hard to move; heavy: *His legs were* leaden *from fatigue.* **3** sluggish; dull; depressed: *the*

team's leaden *spirits after defeat.* **4** the color of lead: *a* leaden *sky.*

lead·er (lē′dər) **1** person who guides, conducts, or directs: *an orchestra* leader. **2** person who holds the first place or is fitted to do so: *The boy's energy and skill in baseball made him a* leader *on the playground.* **3** the part of a fishing line that holds the hook.

lead·er·ship (lē′dər shĭp′) **1** ability to lead: *Lincoln showed great* leadership. **2** guidance; leading: *That scout troop had good* leadership. **3** position of a leader.

Types of leaf

leaf (lēf) **1** one of the green, usually flat, parts that grow from the stem or roots of a plant or tree. **2** to put forth leaves: *Our lilac began to* leaf *in April.* **3** a flower petal: *We filled the jar with rose* leaves. **4** a sheet of paper in a book, consisting of a page and its reverse side. **5** to turn, as sheets of paper: *Ella* leafed *through her new book.* **6** a thin sheet of metal: *gold* leaf. **7** any of various flat parts: *a table* leaf. **leaves.**

leaf·less (lēf′lĭs) without leaves.

leaf·let (lēf′lĭt) small printed sheet folded together; pamphlet.

leaf·y (lē′fĭ) **1** covered with or having many leaves. **2** like leaves: *a* leafy *design.* **leaf·i·er, leaf·i·est.**

¹league (lēg) **1** union or group formed by two or more countries, organizations, or persons for a common purpose: *the League of Nations; a baseball* league. **2** to form a league; unite or combine. **3 in league** in close union; in association: *Witches were thought to be in* league *with the devil.* **leagued, lea·guing.** [**¹league** is from an Old French word (ligue) that goes back to a Latin word (ligare) meaning "bind."]

²league (lēg) a measure of distance, about three miles. [**²league** is from an Old French word (legue) of Celtic origin.]

leak (lēk) **1** hole, crack, or opening which lets something pass in or out accidentally: *The roof has a bad* leak. **2** to pass in or out accidentally: *Water is* leaking *from this bucket.* **3** to let (something) pass in or out accidentally: *The boat leaks like a sieve. This pipe leaks gas.* **4** a passing in or out accidentally: *The gas leak is serious.* **5** to let be known or become known when it should be secret: *The news of the jury's verdict leaked out.* (Homonym: leek)

leak·age (lēk′ĭj) **1** the process of leaking in or out: *the* leakage *of gas; the* leakage *of military information.* **2** that which leaks in or out: *Gas* leakage *into the refrigerator spoiled the food.* **3** the quantity that leaks: *The broken faucet had a* leakage *of two gallons an hour.*

leak·y (lēk′ĭ) permitting the accidental entrance or escape of a gas or liquid: *a* leaky *faucet; a* leaky *boat.* **leak·i·er, leak·i·est.**

¹lean (lēn) **1** to slant, slope, or incline from a straight position: *There is a famous tower in Italy that* leans. **2** to bend the upper part of the body: *He* leaned *over the table.* **3** to rest on or against something for support: *Don't* lean *on your desk.* **4** to depend; rely on: *She still* leans *on her mother.* **5** to be inclined to; show a preference: *Her interests* lean *towards sports.* **6** to place something in a slanting position: *The painter* leaned *the ladder against the wall.* [¹lean was formed from a blend of two Old English words, one (hleonian) meaning "to lean" and the other (hlǣnan) meaning "to cause to lean."]

²lean (lēn) **1** thin; without fat: *the* lean *meat.* **2** not productive; scant: *a* lean *year; a* lean *harvest.* **lean·ly.** [²lean is a form of an Old English word (hlaene) meaning "thin."]

lean·ing (lē′nĭng) inclination; tendency; bent: *to have a* lean- *ing towards medicine as a profession.*

lean-to (lēn′tōō′) **1** a small building with a roof sloping toward its free side, built

Camper's lean-to

against another building. **2** a temporary shelter of sloping branches, thatch, etc., built by campers, hunters, etc.

leap (lēp) **1** to jump or spring: *The Indian* leaped *from the cliff. The salmon* leaped *up the falls.* **2** to move quickly, as if with a jump: *He* leaped *to his feet.* **3** to pass over with a jump or bound: *The runner* leaped *the ditch.* **4** a jump; a bound. **5** the distance jumped: *a ten-foot* leap. **leaped** or **leapt, leap·ing.**

leap·frog (lēp′frŏg′) a game in which each player takes turns running and jumping over the bent back of the player in front of him, and then bends over in his turn for the next runner.

leapt (lĕpt) See **leap.** *He* leapt *over the fence.*

leap year a year with 366 days, in which February has 29 instead of 28 days. Years having numbers that can be divided evenly by 4 are leap years, but those years ending centuries are leap years only if they can be divided evenly by 400. Thus the year 2000 will be a leap year, but 1900 was not.

learn (lûrn) **1** to gain knowledge of; gain skill in: *She is* learning *French. The baby has* learned *how to walk.* **2** to become skillful, able, or informed: *She has never cooked, but she can* learn. **3** to find out: *He* learned *where the gold was hidden.* **4** to memorize: *Will you* learn *a poem and recite it for the class?*

learn·ed (lûr′nĭd) having or showing much knowledge; scholarly: *a* learned *man; a* learned *book.* **learn·ed·ly.**

learn·ing (lûr′nĭng) **1** knowledge gained by study: *That history book was written by a man of great* learning. **2** gaining of knowledge, skill, or ability: *Much* learning *takes place outside of school.*

lease (lēs) **1** written agreement for the renting of land or buildings for a certain time: *We signed a two-year* lease *for this house.* **2** to rent (something) according to the terms of an agreement: *He* leased *the land for a year.* **3** the period of time agreed upon in a lease: *How long is your* lease *on that land?* **leased, leas·ing.**

leash (lēsh) **1** a strap, chain, or cord for holding or leading a dog or other animal. **2** to put on a leash; fasten or hold with a leash.

---

fāte, făt, fâre, fär; bē, bĕt; bīte, bĭt; nō, nŏt, nôr; fūse, fŭn, fûr; tōō, tŏŏk; foil; foul; thin; ~~then~~;
hw for wh as in *w*hat; zh for s as in u*s*ual; ə for a, e, i, o, u, as in *a*go, lin*e*n, per*i*l, at*o*m, min*u*s

least (lēst) **1** the smallest: *the* least *of my worries.* **2** smallest amount of: *Who did the* least *work?* **3** to the smallest extent: *the* least *important thing.* **4 at least** at any rate; as a minimum concession: *You could at least talk to him.* **5 least of all** less than any other: *Of the chores he had to do he liked scrubbing* least *of all.*

leath·er (lĕth′ər) skin of an animal tanned and prepared for use.

leath·er·y (lĕth′ə rĭ) like leather: *a* leathery *skin.*

¹leave (lēv) **1** to go away; depart: *All the guests* left *by ten o'clock.* **2** to withdraw from; cease to remain in; abandon; quit: *to* leave *home; to* leave *a job; to* leave *school before graduating.* **3** to let (something or someone) stay or be: *We'll* leave *the cake where it is.* **4** to fail to bring or take from; forget: *I* left *my books upstairs and had to go back for them.* **5** to deliver: *The postman* left *a letter.* **6** to hand over; entrust: *I will* leave *the choice to you.* **7** to have remaining after subtraction: *Two from 5* leaves *3.* **8** to give by will: *When he died he* left *everything to his wife.*

leave alone not to touch or bother: *You should* leave *matches alone.*

leave behind **1** to forget; fail to bring: *I* left *my bathing suit* behind *so I can't go swimming.* **2** to go or draw ahead of: *The fast runner* left *all the others* behind.

leave out to omit: *Don't* leave out *my middle name.*

left, leav·ing. [**¹leave** is a form of an Old English word (lǣfan) meaning "let remain."]

²leave (lēv) **1** permission to be absent from work or duty: *The soldier asked for* leave *to visit his family.* **2** period of time for which such permission is given: *a ten-day* leave. **3** permission. **4 take leave of** to say good-by to. **5 by your leave** with your permission. [**²leave** is a form of an Old English word (lēaf) meaning "permission."]

³leave (lēv) to put out leaves. **leaved, leav·ing.** [**³leave** is a form of **leaf.**]

leav·en (lĕv′ən) **1** yeast or similar substance that causes dough to rise. **2** to cause fermentation in by means of yeast or other leaven; make dough light; make dough rise.

leaves (lēvz) more than one **leaf.**

lec·ture (lĕk′chər) **1** a talk or address before an audience or class: *a series of* lectures *on art.* **2** to give a lecture or course of lectures: *He* lectured *on modern literature.* **3** scolding: *She gave them a* lecture *on their bad manners.* **4** to give a scolding to: *She* lectured *us on our bad manners.* **lec·tured, lec·tur·ing.**

lec·tur·er (lĕk′chər ər) person who gives a lecture or course of lectures.

led (lĕd) See **¹lead.** *A guide* led *us through the cave.* (Homonym: **²lead**)

ledge (lĕj) **1** a narrow shelf along a wall: *a window* ledge. **2** a shelflike ridge of rock: *a* ledge *on the face of a cliff.*

lee (lē) **1** side away from the wind; sheltered side: *the* lee *of a ship.* **2** away from the wind; sheltered: *the* lee *side of an island; the* lee *of the hill.*

leech (lēch) any of certain flat worms which fasten themselves to the skin and suck blood.

leek (lēk) a plant of the onion family, used in seasoning. (Homonym: leak.)

leer (lir) **1** a sly or nasty sidelong look. **2** to give such a look.

lee·ward (lē′wərd) **1** side sheltered or away from the wind: *We anchored the boat to the* leeward *of the island.* **2** away from the wind; sheltered: *It will be warmer on the* leeward *side of the deck.*

¹left (lĕft) See **¹leave.** *I* left *home at nine o'clock.* [**¹left** is a form of **¹leave.**]

²left (lĕft) **1** on the side from which one starts reading a page; opposite of right: *Some people write with the* left *hand, but most people use the right.* **2** direction or side to the left: *Steering wheels of American cars are on the* left. **3** in the direction to the left: *to turn* left. [**²left** is a form of an Old English word (lyft) meaning "weak." The left hand was traditionally regarded as the weaker.]

left-hand (lĕft′hănd′) **1** at or in the direction of one's left hand: *a* left-hand *turn.* **2** counterclockwise: *a screw with a* left-hand *thread.*

left-hand·ed (lĕft′hăn′dĭd) **1** able to use the left hand more naturally and with more skill than the right. **2** designed for use by a left-handed person: *a* left-handed *golf club.* **3** using the left hand: *Can you write* left-handed? **left-hand·ed·ly.**

left·o·ver (lĕft'ō'vər) **1** what remains, especially food remaining unserved at a meal: *Mother made the leftovers into hash.* **2** remaining unused or uneaten: *We had the leftover ham for lunch.*

leg (lĕg) **1** one of the limbs of the body that give it support and by which men and animals walk and run. Human beings have two legs. A dog has four legs. **2** part of a garment which covers the leg: *a trouser leg.* **3** something like a leg in use or appearance: *a table leg.* **4** stage (of a journey or other undertaking): *The travelers are on the last leg of the trip.*

leg·a·cy (lĕg'ə sĭ) **1** property or money left to someone by a will: *The servant received a large legacy from his deceased master.* **2** something handed down from an ancestor or person who has gone before: *The United States Constitution is a legacy from the men who founded our government.* **leg·a·cies.**

le·gal (lē'gəl) **1** of or having to do with the law: *Lawyers and judges deal with legal matters.* **2** permitted or required by the law: *What is the legal age for obtaining a driver's license?* **le·gal·ly.**

leg·end (lĕj'ənd) **1** story handed down from the past. Legends are often based on historical events or people but are not true history: *There are many old Indian legends.* **2** inscription on a coin. **3** title and description under a picture, or a key explaining a map or chart.

le·gen·da·ry (lĕj'ən dĕr'ĭ) **1** based on or told in legends or myths: *a legendary hero.* **2** famous; celebrated: *His deeds became legendary throughout the country.*

leg·gings (lĕg'ĭngz) protective outer garments for the legs, reaching from foot to knee, or above.

leg·i·ble (lĕj'ə bəl) clear and easy to read. **leg·i·bly.**

Leggings

le·gion (lē'jən) **1** large body of soldiers; army. **2** very great number of persons or things: *a legion of angels.*

leg·is·late (lĕj'ĭs lāt') **1** to make laws: *Congress legislates for the United States.* **2** to make into a law; enact: *The State*

Senate will legislate *a new tax bill.* **leg·is·lat·ed, leg·is·lat·ing.**

leg·is·la·tion (lĕj'ĭs lā'shən) **1** making a law or laws; enacting: *The bill has gone to Congress for* legislation. **2** laws made or enacted: *The governor asked for* legislation *to provide for new highways.*

leg·is·la·tive (lĕj'ĭs lā'tĭv) **1** having the power of making laws: *the* legislative *branch of the government.* **2** having to do with making laws: *new* legislative *measures;* legislative *reforms.* **leg·is·la·tive·ly.**

leg·is·la·tor (lĕj'ĭs lā'tər) member of a lawmaking group: *Senators and Representatives are* legislators.

leg·is·la·ture (lĕj'ĭs lā'chər) lawmaking group of a country or state.

le·git·i·mate (lĭ jĭt'ə mĭt) **1** lawful; rightful; according to the rules: *to use tax money for* legitimate *purposes; to be the* legitimate *heir to a throne.* **2** reasonable; justifiable: *a* legitimate *excuse.* **le·git·i·mate·ly.**

leg·ume (lĕg'ūm or lĭ gūm') **1** plant bearing podlike fruit such as beans and peas. **2** fruit of such a plant. **3** legumes the seed of such fruit used as food.

lei (lā'ĭ or lā) Hawaiian wreath or necklace made of flowers. (Homonym: lay)

lei·sure (lē'zhər) **1** free; not occupied by work or duties: *Her* leisure *time was spent in reading and taking walks.* **2** freedom from work or duties; spare time.

lei·sure·ly (lē'zhər lĭ) **1** slow; not hurried: *When we have time, we enjoy a* leisurely *walk.* **2** slowly and without hurrying: *We strolled* leisurely *through the park.*

lem·on (lĕm'ən) **1** small, oval-shaped, yellow fruit with a sour juice used to flavor foods and drinks. **2** the tree which bears this fruit. **3** yellow; the color of lemons: *a* lemon-*colored dress.*

lem·on·ade (lĕm'ə nād') a drink made of lemon juice, sugar, and water.

lend (lĕnd) **1** to allow someone to have or to use a thing with the understanding that it is to be returned: *Can you lend me a book to read?* **2** to provide; give; contribute: *A sparkling lake* lends *beauty to the countryside. He* lent *assistance to the man.*

---

fāte, făt, fâre, fär; bē, bĕt; bīte, bĭt; nō, nŏt, nôr; fūse, fŭn, fûr; tōō, tŏŏk; foil; foul; thin; ~~then~~;
hw for wh as in *wh*at; zh for s as in u*s*ual; ə for a, e, i, o, u, as in *a*go, lin*e*n, per*i*l, at*o*m, min*u*s

lend itself to to be useful for; be suitable for; serve for: *This tool* lends itself to *many uses.*

lend oneself to to stoop to: *Don't lend yourself to* such dishonest schemes.

lent, lend·ing.

length (lĕngkth or lĕngth) **1** the measurement of a thing from end to end: *The* length *of this board is 6 feet.* **2** the longer or longest measurement of a thing: *This rug is 9 feet in width and 12 feet in* length. **3** extent, amount, time, etc., from beginning to end: *What was the* length *of your stay in New York? The* length *of the journey makes it necessary to carry provisions.* **4** piece of something, usually of a certain size, cut from a larger piece: *a* length *of rope.* **5** at length (1) in detail: *The salesman explained* at length *the uses of his product.* (2) finally; at last.

length·en (lĕngk'thən or lĕng'thən) **1** to make longer: *These short trousers will need to be* lengthened. **2** to grow longer: *The shadows* lengthen *as evening comes on.*

length·ways (lĕngkth'wāz' or lĕngth'wāz') in the direction of the greatest length; lengthwise: *to saw a board* lengthways.

length·wise (lĕngkth'wīz' or lĕngth'wīz') in the direction from end to end: *Get the* lengthwise *measurement of the rug.*

length·y (lĕngk'thĭ or lĕng'thĭ) long; drawn out: *The audience grew weary of the* lengthy *speeches.* **length·i·er, length·i·est; length·i·ly.**

le·ni·ent (lē'nĭ ənt) mild; merciful; not severe or harsh: *The judge is more* lenient *toward first offenders.* **le·ni·ent·ly.**

lens (lĕnz) **1** a piece of transparent material, curved on one or both sides, which spreads or brings together (focuses) the rays of light that pass through it. A lens may focus the sun's rays to a point where they cause fire. A reading glass is a lens. Spectacles, cameras, telescopes, motion-picture projectors, etc., have lenses. **2** a part of the eye, shaped somewhat like a reading glass, that focuses light on the back of the eyeball. For picture, see **eye.**

Lens as a burning glass

lent (lĕnt) See **lend.** *Jim* lent *me his bat.*

Lent (lĕnt) a period of 40 weekdays from Ash Wednesday to Easter. Lent is observed in some Christian churches as a period of fasting and penance in memory of Christ's forty days of fasting in the wilderness.

len·til (lĕn'tĭl) **1** a pod-bearing plant. **2** the small seeds of this plant, which are cooked and eaten, like peas and beans.

leop·ard (lĕp'ərd) **1** a large tawny cat with black spots, found in Asia and Africa. **2** made of leopard skin: *Sue has a* leopard *coat.*

Leopard, 7 to 8 ft. long

lep·er (lĕp'ər) a person suffering from leprosy.

lep·ro·sy (lĕp'rə sĭ) a germ disease causing gradual loss of feeling, swellings and sores on the skin, wasting away of the flesh, and deformities.

less (lĕs) **1** smaller: *The area of Mexico is* less *than that of the United States.* **2** fewer: *Ten is* less *than a dozen.* **3** not so much: *Make* less *noise, please!* **4** to a smaller extent or degree: *I was* less *scared than surprised.* **5** shorter: *We'll get home in* less *time if we fly.* **6** a smaller quantity: *I had* less *than a dollar to spend.* **7** minus: *They were in Europe four months* less *five days.* **8 more or less** about: *This will cost $10* more or less. **9 none the less** nevertheless.

-less suffix meaning "without" or "having no": *tree*less; *bone*less.

less·en (lĕs'ən) **1** to reduce; make smaller, fewer, weaker, etc.: *We can't carry the trunk unless we* lessen *its weight.* **2** to become smaller, fewer, weaker, etc.: *The rain* lessened, *but still the wind blew.* (Homonym: lesson)

less·er (lĕs'ər) **1** smaller: *He did the* lesser *part of the work, and left most of it for me.* **2** the one that is smaller: *the* lesser *of two dangers.*

les·son (lĕs'ən) **1** a unit of study to be learned at one time; assignment: *This is the easiest arithmetic* lesson *we've had.* **2** instruction given at one time: *Jane takes her piano* lesson *at three o'clock.* **3** a thing serving as an example of what is right or wrong; what is learned from experience: *That was a* lesson *to us.* **4** a part of the Bible used as teaching: *After the hymn the minister read the* lesson. **5 lessons** school work; studies: *Sports are important, but so are* lessons. (Homonym: lessen)

lest (lĕst) **1** for fear that: *We watched all night* lest *the bandits should return.* **2** that; used after words expressing fear or anxiety: *I was afraid* lest *I should be too late.*

let (lĕt) **1** to permit; allow: *Please* let *me see your watch. The police* let *no one enter the building.* **2** to allow to run out, flow out, or escape: *They* let *some air out of the balloon.* **3** to rent: *She* lets *rooms by the week.*

let alone 1 not to mention; to say nothing of: *He can't juggle two balls,* let alone *six.* **2** not to interfere with; leave undisturbed; not touch or trouble: *Just* let *him* alone *and stop bothering him. Please* let *the record player* alone, *or you'll break it.*

let be to stop bothering or interfering with: *He doesn't need your help;* let *him* be!

let down 1 to lower; cause to descend: *You* let down *the bucket and I'll fill it.* **2** to disappoint; fail: *Your friends needed you, but you* let *them* down. **3** to stop making an effort: *Don't* let down *till the job is finished.*

let go of to release; stop holding on to: *Do* let go of *my coat!*

let in to allow to enter: *Please* let *me* in *the house; it's cold outside.*

let know to tell; inform: *Please* let *me* know *if you can't come.*

let off 1 to allow to escape, flow out, or run out: *The boiler* let off *steam.* **2** to set free: *The judge* let *my brother* off *with a warning not to speed.* **3** to explode; set off: *to* let off *a giant firecracker.*

let on 1 to admit: *Don't* let on *that you see him.* **2** to give the impression; pretend: *He* lets on *he is healthy. Don't* let on *what we're buying Dad for Christmas.*

let out 1 to loosen a garment by opening the seams: *Mother* let *out my old winter coat.* **2** to permit to go out: *Before we go to bed we* let *the cat* out. **3** let escape unintentionally: *to* let out *a secret.*

let up to stop or diminish: *The wind* let up *but the snow still fell.*

let, let·ting.

let's (lĕts) let us: *Turn off the TV and* let's *find a good book instead.*

let·ter (lĕt'ər) **1** one of the characters or symbols of an alphabet. *Our alphabet has 26* letters. *The Russian alphabet has 32* letters. **2** to form letters or mark with letters: *Alfred* lettered *a sign for the school play.* **3** a written message, usually sent by mail: *business* letter; *a* letter *of thanks.* **4** exact, word-for-word meaning: *We must obey the spirit as well as the* letter *of the law.* **5** the initial or initials of a school, worn as an award for skill in sports or other activities: *Harry won his football* letter. **6 letters** literature and learning: *We study the lives of famous men of* letters. **7 letter perfect** without any mistakes: *Jimmy's recitation was* letter perfect. **8 open letter** a letter written on some matter of public interest, supposedly addressed to a certain person or group, but actually meant to be read by everyone: *The morning paper printed our teacher's* open letter *to the mayor.* **9 to the letter** in every detail: *Students are expected to follow examination rules* to the letter.

let·ter·ing (lĕt'ər ĭng) **1** act of drawing letters, as for a sign. **2** letters or words so made: *The* lettering *of the sign was very attractive.*

let·tuce (lĕt'ĭs) a leafy garden vegetable used mainly in salads and as a garnish.

¹lev·ee (lĕv'ĭ) **1** a high bank built along a river to prevent floods: *We sat on the* levee *and watched the boats.* **2** a landing place or quay. [¹levee is from a French word (levée) meaning "something raised." It is related to ²levee.] (Homonym: levy)

²lev·ee (lĕv'ĭ) **1** a morning reception once held by a king or other person of high rank on awakening from sleep. It was considered a great honor to be invited to a levee. **2** in England, an afternoon court assembly at which the king or queen receives only men. **3** any social reception. [²levee comes from a Latin word (levare) meaning "to raise."] (Homonym: levy)

---

fāte, făt, fâre, fär; bē, bĕt; bīte, bĭt; nō, nŏt, nôr; fūse, fŭn, fûr; tōō, tŏŏk; foil; foul; thin; ~~then~~; hw for wh as in *wh*at; zh for s as in u*s*ual; ə for a, e, i, o, u, as in *a*go, lin*e*n, per*i*l, at*o*m, min*u*s

level

lev·el (lĕv′əl) **1** horizontal; parallel to the surface of still water: *A ball rolls when laid on a floor that is not level.* **2** an instrument for finding whether a thing is level. **3** flat; smooth: *a level field.* **4** a place from which something

Level surface of a pond

is measured: *The house is 20 feet above sea* level. **5** of equal height: *The shelf is* level *with my chin.* **6** steady; sensible: *a level head.* **7** grade; standing; rank: *a high* level *of intelligence.* **8** to smooth; make even; make horizontal: *Scrapers* leveled *the road. Carpenters* leveled *the sunken floor.* **9** to tear down; raze: *Workmen* leveled *the building for a parking lot.* **10** to aim: *to level a gun; to* level *criticism.* **level off 1** to make a surface flat or even. **2** to come or bring into a horizontal or level position: *The plane climbed to 7,000 feet and then* leveled off.

lev·er (lĕv′ər or lē′vər) **1** a bar used to pry up or lift a heavy object, as a crowbar. **2** a simple machine based on the fact that when light pressure is applied on the long end of a bar resting on a fixed point, it will lift a heavy weight on the short end. Levers are widely used as parts of machinery.

lev·y (lĕv′ĭ) **1** to impose (a fine or tax); collect money (by taxation): *Congress* levies *taxes for national defense.* **2** the imposing or collection of taxes or fines. **3** forced enlistment of men for military service: *The draft in the Second World War made possible the greatest* levy *of troops in our history.* **4** number or amount collected by levy: *Higher* levies *are made necessary by the increasing costs of government undertakings.* **lev·ies; lev·ied, lev·y·ing.** (Homonym: levee)

lex·i·cog·ra·pher (lĕk′sə kŏg′rə fər) person who makes a dictionary.

li·a·ble (lī′ə bəl) **1** legally responsible: *If the car is damaged, I will consider you* liable. **2 to be liable to (1)** to have the tendency to; be likely to: *If you hurry too much in your work you* are liable to *make mistakes.* **(2)** to be subject to (a tax, punishment, etc.): *If you disobey the law you* are liable *to arrest.* **3 be liable for** to be legally

lice

responsible for: *A husband is* liable for *his wife's debts.*

li·ar (lī′ər) a person who says things that are not true; one who tells lies.

lib·er·al (lĭb′ər əl) **1** tolerant; free from prejudice: *The Bill of Rights encourages a* liberal *attitude toward religious worship.* **2** generous: *He is* liberal *with his time and money.* **3** ample; plentiful: *We all enjoyed* liberal *servings of ham and eggs.* **4** broad; not limited: *a* liberal *education.* **5** favoring social progress and democratic reform: *a* liberal *government.* **6** one who has liberal political views: *The* liberals *in Congress supported the President's recommendations.* **lib·er·al·ly.**

lib·er·al·i·ty (lĭb′ə răl′ə tĭ) **1** generosity: *We owe this new auditorium to the* liberality *of the townspeople.* **2** tolerance; lack of prejudice: *In early days the Rhode Island colony showed its* liberality *by welcoming settlers of different beliefs and religions.* **lib·er·al·i·ties.**

lib·er·ate (lĭb′ə rāt′) to set free: *to* liberate *a slave or a prisoner.* **lib·er·at·ed, lib·er·at·ing.**

lib·er·ty (lĭb′ər tĭ) **1** freedom from foreign rule or harsh, unreasonable government: *The colonies fought to gain their* liberty *from England.* **2** freedom from captivity, prison, slavery, etc.: *The prisoner pleaded for his* liberty. **3** freedom from control: *Freedom of speech is a* liberty *we enjoy in the United States.* **4** freedom of choice; right or power to do as one pleases: *to have a lot of* liberty. **5 at liberty** free: *I'm not at* liberty *to tell you the test grades.* **6 take the liberty of** to assume permission for: *I took the* liberty of *borrowing your book while you were gone.* **lib·er·ties.**

li·brar·i·an (lī brâr′ĭ ən) person in charge of a library.

li·brar·y (lī′brĕr′ĭ) **1** room or building where books are kept to be used or borrowed. **2** room in a private house where books are kept. **3** a collection of books, magazines, phonograph records, etc. **li·brar·ies.**

li·bret·to (lĭ brĕt′ō) **1** the words or text of an opera or other long musical composition. **2** a book containing these words. **li·bret·tos** or **li·bret·ti** (lĭ brĕt′ē).

lice (līs) more than one **louse.**

414

li·cense or **li·cence** (lī′səns) **1** legal written permission to do something: *a license to drive a taxi; a fishing* license. **2** to give legal written permission (to do something): *Doctors must be* licensed *to practice.* **3** freedom or right (to ignore rules): *No one has* license *to damage public property.* **4** abuse of freedom; immoral action: *The soldiers showed unbelievable* license *when they entered the captured city.* **li·censed** or **li·cenced, li·cens·ing** or **li·cenc·ing.**

li·chen (lī′kən) small plant without flowers or true leaves that grows flat on rocks, trees, etc. Some lichens look like crinkly paper, others like dry moss or tiny bushes. (Homonym: liken)

lick (lĭk) **1** to pass the tongue over: *to* lick *a lollipop.* **2** a movement of the tongue (over something): *The cow gave her calf a* lick. **3** to move or pass over lightly: *The flames* licked *the meat on the grill.* **4** a salt lick; a place with a natural deposit of salt where animals go to lick the salt. **5** a small amount; a bit: *You didn't do a* lick *of work all day!* **6** to beat; defeat: *Our team can* lick *yours.* **7** to whip; thrash: *A bully deserves to be* licked. **8** fast stroke or blow: *"Hit him a* lick*!" the boys shouted.*

lic·o·rice (lĭk′ə·ris or lĭk′rĭsh) **1** the dried root of a plant of the pea family, or an extract made from it which is used in medicines and candy. **2** the plant itself. **3** candy flavored with licorice.

lid (lĭd) **1** a movable top or cover to a container, box, etc.: *a pot* lid. **2** an eyelid.

¹lie (lī) **1** untrue statement made in order to deceive; a deliberate untruth: *I trust him because he never tells a* lie. **2** to make an untrue statement in order to deceive: *If you do something wrong, don't* lie *about it.* **lied, ly·ing.** [¹**lie** is a form of an Old English word (lyge) of the same meaning.] (Homonym: lye)

²lie (lī) **1** to be in a flat or resting position: *A pen is* lying *on the desk.* **2** to put oneself in a flat or resting position: *to* lie *on the sofa and rest.* **3** to be situated: *Canada* lies *north of the United States.* **4** to remain in a certain condition: *Don't let your talent* lie

idle. **5** to be; exist: *It* lies *within your power to do good or evil.* **lay, lain, ly·ing.** [²**lie** is a form of an Old English word (licgan) of the same meaning.] (Homonym: lye)

lie de·tect·or (lī dĭ těk′tər) instrument that records the bodily reactions of a person as he is being questioned. From these reactions the truth of his answers can usually be determined: *The prisoner refused to submit to the* lie detector.

liege (lēj) **1** in medieval times, a lord, master, or ruler who had a right to services and loyalty from all of the people under his authority and protection. **2** a person who owed services and loyalty to a lord, master, or ruler in medieval times; a vassal.

lieu·ten·ant (lōō těn′ənt or lū těn′ənt) **1** an army officer ranking next below a captain. **2** a navy officer ranking next below a lieutenant commander. **3** used with the name of a rank or position to indicate the next lower rank: *a* lieutenant *colonel;* lieutenant *governor.*

life (līf) **1** the particular quality which distinguishes animals and plants from rocks, earth, and other objects that do not grow and produce. **2** being alive; existence. **3** a living person: *Two* lives *were lost in the accident.* **4** period of a person's existence, between birth and death: *He was happy all his* life. **5** living beings: *There is animal* life *on earth.* **6** report of a person's existence; biography: *The* life *of the famous hero was published.* **7** energy; vitality: *He's full of* life. **8** way of living: *a* life *of luxury.* **9** cheering influence; moving spirit: *the* life *of the party.* **lives.**

life belt belt filled with cork or light material or inflated to keep a person afloat in the water.

life·boat (līf′bōt′) boat for saving people at sea in case of accident.

life buoy a float, usually a ring filled with light material or air, for keeping a person afloat in the water; life preserver.

life·guard (līf′gärd′) an expert swimmer trained in rescue work, whose job is to look after the safety of bathers at a beach or swimming pool.

fāte, făt, fâre, fär; bē, bĕt; bite, bĭt; nō, nŏt, nôr; fūse, fŭn, fûr; tōō, tŏŏk; foil; foul; thin; ~~then~~;
hw for wh as in *wh*at; zh for s as in u*s*ual; ə for a, e, i, o, u, as in *a*go, lin*e*n, per*i*l, at*o*m, min*u*s
415

life insurance 1 agreement by which a company insures a person's life in return for certain payments. The company agrees to pay a certain sum of money, at his death, to a person named by the purchaser. **2** amount of money to be received according to the terms of a life insurance policy.

life·less (lif′lĭs) **1** dead: *a lifeless body.* **2** never having been alive; without life: *a lifeless statue.* **3** without living things: *a lifeless planet.* **4** not lively; dull.

life·like (lif′līk′) like a real or living thing; natural: *That statue is so lifelike, I thought it would move.*

life line 1 any rope used for lifesaving, especially one shot by rocket to a ship in distress. **2** line attached to a lifeboat or life buoy for saving life. **3** signal rope used by a diver and by which he is lowered or raised from the water. **4** route by which supplies can be sent to a place which cannot be reached in any other way.

life·long (lif′lông′) lasting throughout life: *a lifelong friendship.*

life preserver a ring or jacket filled with material which floats, to be worn under the arms or about the body to prevent sinking in water.

Life preserver

life·sav·ing (lif′sā′vĭng) **1** rescue work, especially saving people from drowning. **2** having to do with rescuing people from drowning, accidents, etc.: *a lifesaving course.*

life·time (lif′tīm′) **1** the length of time that a person lives. **2** lasting the length of a person's life: *This pen has a lifetime guarantee.*

lift (lĭft) **1** to raise to a higher position or condition: *Can you lift the box from the ground? The good news lifted my spirits. Hard work lifted him out of poverty.* **2** raising; rise; elevation: *With a lift of his hand he signaled to his driver.* **3** piece of help; assistance, especially a ride: *He gave me a lift into town.* **4** to seem to rise; disappear: *The fog lifted.* **5** layer that makes the heel of a shoe higher.

lig·a·ment (lĭg′ə mənt) band of tough tissue which connects bones or holds a part of the body in place.

¹light (līt) **1** the kind of radiant energy which affects the eye so that we see: *Please open the blinds and let in the* light. **2** anything which gives light, such as an electric lamp. **3** having light; bright: *a light day; a light, airy room.* **4** to give or provide light: *Electric power lights the town at night.* **5** to show or guide, by making bright and clear: *He lighted the way through the tunnel.* **6** pale in color: *a light red.* **7** way in which something appears or is viewed: *He put me in a bad light.* **8** a flame; a spark: *a light for a pipe.* **9** to take fire: *The match lit as soon as I struck it.* **10** to set on fire; kindle: *to light the fire.* **11 according to one's lights** according to one's beliefs and ideas: *Each acted according to his lights.* **12 in the light of** considering; taking into account: *It seems possible, in the light of recent discoveries, that there is life on many worlds.* **13 cast, throw,** or **shed light on** to help in the understanding of; clarify: *to throw light on a problem.* **14 bring to light** to reveal: *to bring facts to light.*

light up 1 of lights, to come on together or one by one: *At nightfall, the city slowly lighted up.* **2** to brighten: *His face lit up with a smile.*

light·ed or **lit, light·ing.** [**¹light** is from an Old English word (lēoht) meaning "light."]

²light (līt) **1** not heavy; little in weight or amount: *a light snow; light traffic; a light tap on the shoulder.* **2** graceful; nimble: *He was light on his feet.* **3** cheerful; gay: *with a light heart; in a light mood.* **4** not soggy: *a light pastry.* **5** frivolous; thoughtless: *That silly girl treats serious problems in a light and airy way.* **6** easy to do or bear: *a light task; light punishment.* **light·ly.** [**²light** is a form of an Old English word (lighte) meaning "not heavy."]

³light (līt) to settle; come to rest: *The bird lighted on the bush. I happened to light on the right answer.* **light·ed** or **lit, light·ing.** [**³light** is a form of an Old English word (lihtan) meaning "to alight."]

¹light·en (lī′tən) **1** to become light; grow brighter: *The sky lightened as the clouds lifted.* **2** to make light, bright, or clear: *The sun lightened her hair.* **3** to flash lightning: *It lightened and thundered all night.* [**lighten** is a form of **¹light.**]

²**light·en** (līˈtən) **1** to make less heavy: *She lightened his load by carrying some of the packages.* **2** to make more cheerful; enliven: *His jokes always lighten any occasion.* [²**lighten** is a form of ²**light.**]

light·head·ed (lītˈhĕdˈid) **1** dizzy or giddy on account of illness. **2** silly; foolish; thoughtless. **light·head·ed·ly.**

light·heart·ed (lītˈhärˈtid) **1** gay; cheerful. **2** free from worry. **light·heart·ed·ly.**

light·house (lītˈhousˈ) a building, usually a tower, with a powerful light at the top to guide ships. Its position often marks dangerous rocks, shoals, etc.

Lighthouse

¹**light·ness** (lītˈnĭs) **1** brightness. **2** a being light in color. [¹**lightness** comes from ¹**light.**]

²**light·ness** (lītˈnĭs) **1** smallness in amount or weight; lack of heaviness: *The lightness of the trunk made it easy to lift.* **2** lack of harshness or severity; mildness: *We were surprised at the lightness of the judge's sentence.* **3** nimbleness: *the lightness of her step.* [²**lightness** comes from ²**light.**]

light·ning (lītˈnĭng) a flashing of light in the sky caused by electricity passing between clouds or from clouds to earth.

lightning bug a small beetle whose abdomen gives off flashes of light; a firefly.

lightning rod a thin rod of metal reaching above a building and connected to the earth. It serves as a conductor to carry the lightning to the ground so that it will not strike the building.

light-year (lītˈyĭrˈ) the distance light travels in one year, about six million million miles. Astronomers use the light-year to measure distance between the stars.

lig·nite (lĭgˈnīt) a soft, dark-brown coal.

lik·a·ble (līˈkə bəl) pleasing and agreeable; inspiring friendly feelings or liking.

¹**like** (līk) **1** similar; almost or exactly the same: *Those twins are very like.* **2** almost or exactly the same as; equal to: *There is nothing like a good dinner.* **3** inclined to; in the mood for: *I feel like going for a walk.*

4 in the manner of: *Sit there like a good boy.* **5** characteristic of: *It is just like him to give you a nice present.* **6** the equal of a person or thing: *I have never seen its like before.* **7** and the like and others of the same kind. [¹**like** is a form of an Old English word (gelic) meaning "similar"; "equal."]

²**like** (līk) **1** to find agreeable or pleasant; enjoy: *All his classmates like him. Do you like sports?* **2** to prefer; choose: *I will go when I like.* **3 likes** preferences: *What are your likes and dislikes?* **liked, lik·ing.** [²**like** is a form of an Old English word (lician) meaning "to be pleasing to."]

-**like** suffix meaning "resembling" or "similar to": *child*like.

like·li·hood (līkˈli hŏŏdˈ) probability: *With the new dam built, there is less likelihood of flood.*

like·ly (līkˈli) **1** apt (to): *It's likely to snow any minute now.* **2** probable: *Will he come? It's very likely.* **3** promising: *This is a likely place to stop. He's a likely lad.* **4** probably: *More likely than not, it will rain.* **like·li·er, like·li·est.**

lik·en (līkˈən) to say one thing is like another; compare: *The poet likened the airplane to a great bird.* (Homonym: lichen)

like·ness (līkˈnĭs) **1** picture; representation; portrait: *That photograph is a good likeness of you.* **2** appearance; form: *an enemy in the likeness of a friend.* **3** resemblance; similarity: *There is a great likeness between the two sisters.*

like·wise (līkˈwīzˈ) **1** in the same manner: *Go and do likewise.* **2** also; too: *Goliath was of huge size and likewise of great strength.*

lik·ing (līˈkĭng) **1** fondness: *I have a liking for books.* **2** taste: *This food is not to my liking.*

li·lac (līˈlək) **1** a shrub with clusters of white or pinkish-purple blossoms, often fragrant. **2** the blossoms of this shrub. **3** the color of lilacs; pinkish purple.

lilt (lĭlt) **1** lively rhythm: *We heard the lilt of Judith's song as she danced down the garden path.* **2** a gay song. **3** to sing with a gay, light rhythm.

fāte, făt, fâre, fär; bē, bĕt; bīte, bĭt; nō, nŏt, nôr; fūse, fŭn, fûr; tōō, tŏŏk; foil; foul; thin; ~~then~~; hw for wh as in *wh*at; zh for s as in usual; ə for a, e, i, o, u, as in *a*go, lin*e*n, per*i*l, at*o*m, min*u*s

417

lil·y (lĭl′ĭ) **1** a plant grown from a bulb and having a trumpet-shaped blossom. **2** the blossom of such a plant. **lil·ies.**

lily of the valley 1 a low plant with tiny white or pink bell-shaped flowers on a slender stalk. **2** the sweet-smelling flowers of this plant. **lilies of the valley.**

Lily

li·ma bean (lī′mə bēn) **1** a plant with broad pods and creamy blossoms. **2** broad, flat bean of this plant, used as a food.

limb (lĭm) **1** arm or leg of a man or animal or the wing of a bird. **2** one of the main branches of a tree.

lim·ber (lĭm′bər) **1** able to bend and move easily; supple; flexible: *a limber tree branch; a limber body.* **2** to make limber: *Exercise limbers the body.*

limber up to make or become limber by doing exercise, etc.: *The dancers limbered up before the performance.*

¹lime (lĭm) chemical compound of calcium and oxygen made by burning limestone, bones, or shells. It is used for making cement, for making soil less acid, etc. [**¹lime** is a form of an Old English word (lim).]

²lime (lĭm) **1** small yellowish-green citrus fruit, somewhat like a lemon. **2** the tree that bears it. [**²lime** is from an Arabic word (limah). It is related to the word **lemon.**]

³lime (lĭm) the linden tree. [**³lime** is the changed form of an Old English word (lind) meaning "linden."]

lim·er·ick (lĭm′ər ĭk) a humorous poem of five lines. The first, second, and fifth lines rhyme, as do the third and fourth.

There once was an old man of Lyme
Who married three wives at a time.
When asked why a third,
He replied, "One's absurd,
And bigamy, sir, is a crime."

lime·stone (lĭm′stōn′) rock used for building, road making, etc. It gives lime when burned.

lim·it (lĭm′ĭt) **1** furthest point: *I have reached the limit of my patience.* **2** boundary: *outside the city limits.* **3** greatest amount allowed: *a speed limit.* **4** to put a

limit on; restrict: *She limits herself to one piece of candy a day.*

lim·it·ed (lĭm′ĭt ĭd) **1** fixed (in number, time, or amount); restricted: *You may enter the contest only a limited number of times.* **2** making only a few stops, as a bus or train.

¹limp (lĭmp) **1** a lame, halting walk. **2** to walk with a limp: *A thorn in its paw made the dog limp.* [**¹limp** is probably a form of an Old English word (limphealt) meaning "lame."]

²limp (lĭmp) **1** weak; lacking strength: *Once the sick baby was out of danger, its mother felt limp with relief.* **2** not stiff or straight; drooping: *The flowers were limp and lifeless.* **limp·ly.** [**²limp** is a word of Germanic origin.]

lin·den (lĭn′dən) large shade tree with heart-shaped leaves and clusters of cream-colored flowers. Also called **lime.**

¹line (lĭn) **1** long narrow mark made with a pencil, pen, tool, etc.: *Draw a line down the center.* **2** long, strong piece of string, rope, or wire used for a special purpose: *telephone* line; *fishing* line. **3** a wrinkle or crease on the face or palm of the hand. **4** long row or series of persons or things: *a waiting* line; *a line of cars.* **5** row of printed or written words on a page or column: *This article takes ten* lines *in the paper.* **6** boundary; border: *The prisoner escaped across the state* line. **7** plan of thought or action: *Along what* line *will the story be written?* **8** direction; path of travel: *The bird flew in a straight* line *across the sky.* **9** a series of persons following one another, in a family: *He comes from a royal* line. **10** outline; contour: *The* line *of his back was stiff and straight.* **11** business; occupation: *What is his* line? **12** range of items: *The salesman showed his* line *to the shopkeeper.* **13** a series of ships, trains, buses, etc., which give regular service; a transportation company: *Not many bus* lines *run in the country.* **14** to mark with lines: *You must* line *the paper before you start to write.* **15** to form a line along: *Cars* lined *the curb.* **16** lines an actor's words in a play: *He forgot his* lines. **17 all along the line** at every point; everywhere: *He had success all along the* line. **18 in line** **(1)** in a line. **(2)** in agreement or harmony.

19 read between the lines to find a hidden meaning in a letter, speech, etc. **20 hold the line** to stand firm; permit no retreat.

  line up 1 to form a line: *to* line up *for inspection*. **2** to bring into a line; align: *to* line up *the wheels of a car*. **3** to enlist the support of: *to* line up *workers for a cause*. **lined, lin·ing.** [¹line is a form of an Old English word (line) meaning "a cord." It goes back to a Latin word (linea) meaning "linen thread."]

²line (līn) to cover the inside of: *They* lined *the box with paper*. **lined, lin·ing.** [²line is ¹line in a later and special use. It used to mean "to put linen on a thing."]

lin·e·age (lĭn′ĭ ĭj) line of ancestors; descent: *a family of fine* lineage.

lin·en (lĭn′ən) **1** the thread spun from flax fibers. **2** the strong, loosely woven cloth made of this thread. **3** made of linen: *a* linen *dress*. **4 linens** articles once made of linen, but now made of cotton and other materials as well. They include sheets, tablecloths, towels, and sometimes shirts and underwear.

lin·er (lī′nər) **1** large, fast, commercial ship. **2** in baseball, a ball hit straight and low: *a* liner *to third base*. **3** something that makes lines: *a road* liner.

lin·ger (lĭng′gər) to stay on; delay; tarry: *The departing guests* lingered *in the doorway*.

lin·i·ment (lĭn′ə mənt) a liquid for rubbing on the skin to ease aches, sprains, etc.

lin·ing (lī′nĭng) something that covers an inner surface: *a coat with a fur* lining; *the stomach* lining.

link (lĭngk) **1** one of a series of loops or connecting rings: *a* link *in a chain*. **2** something that connects (one thing to another); a tie: *The hermit cut every* link *to the outside world*. **3** to join by a link, or as a link does; connect: *She* linked *the bracelet around her wrist. Gossip* linked *their names.*

links (lĭngks) golf course. pl. **links.** (Homonym: lynx)

lin·net (lĭn′ĭt) small European songbird.

li·no·le·um (lĭ nō′lĭ əm) a floor covering made of compressed cork and linseed oil, or of plastic.

li·no·type (lī′nə tīp′) a machine for setting type. It is operated with keys similar to those of a typewriter. It casts a complete line of type in one bar.

lin·seed (lĭn′sēd′) **1** the seed of the flax plant. **2 linseed oil** oil pressed from the seed of flax. It is used in making paints, linoleum, etc.

lint (lĭnt) **1** short fibers that work loose from some kinds of cloth: *His blue coat was speckled with* lint. **2** fibers scraped from linen cloth and used in bandages for dressing wounds.

Lintel

lin·tel (lĭn′təl) a piece of stone or timber set into a wall above a door or window to support the wall above the opening.

li·on (lī′ən) **1** a large and powerful African or Asian cat, called the King of Beasts because of its great strength and majestic appearance. Adult males have shaggy manes. **2** a man of strength and courage. **3 a social lion** a person prominent in society. **4 the lion's share** the greater or greatest part: *He took* the lion's share *of the watermelon.*

Lion, about 9 ft. long

li·on·ess (lī′ə nĭs) a female lion.

lip (lĭp) **1** either of the fleshy edges of the mouth. **2** the rim or edge of a hollow opening or container: *The heat kept us from exploring the* lip *of the volcano.*

li·que·fy (lĭk′wə fī′) **1** to become liquid; melt: *Ice cream* liquefies *quickly in hot weather*. **2** to change to a liquid: *Great heat is needed to* liquefy *metals*. **li·que·fied, li·que·fy·ing.**

liq·uid (lĭk′wĭd) **1** one of the three main forms of matter (solid, liquid, gas). A liquid flows readily into any shape without being forced, but does not naturally expand as a gas does: *Water is a* liquid *at room temperature*. **2** having the nature of a liquid: *Milk is a* liquid *food*. **3** sounding smooth and clear: *This bell has an unusually*

fāte, făt, fâre, fär; bē, bĕt; bīte, bĭt; nō, nŏt, nôr; fūse, fŭn, fûr; tōō, tŏŏk; foil; foul; thin; ~~then~~; hw for wh as in *wh*at; zh for s as in u*s*ual; ə for a, e, i, o, u, as in a*g*o, lin*e*n, per*i*l, at*o*m, min*u*s

419

liquid *tone.* **4** bright and clear in appearance: *The spaniel watched me with his big liquid eyes.* **5** easily changed into cash: *His only liquid assets were some government bonds.* **liq·uid·ly.**

liquid measure the system of measuring liquids. Four gills make one pint, two pints make one quart, four quarts make one gallon.

liq·uor (lĭk′ər) **1** any alcoholic drink, especially a distilled alcoholic drink such as whiskey or brandy. **2** any liquid, as broth, syrup, brine, etc.

lisp (lĭsp) **1** to pronounce **s** or **z** incorrectly as **th.** A person who lisps would pronounce "sunspot" as "thunthpot," and "zip" as "thip." **2** speech in which **s** and **z** sound like **th:** *She spoke with a lisp.*

¹list (lĭst) **1** a written series of names, items, titles, things, etc.: *shopping* list; *reading* list; *a list of club members.* **2** to write down a series of names, etc.: *Please* list *all the jobs you have held.* [**¹list** is from an Old French word (liste) formed from an early German word (lista).]

²list (lĭst) **1** to lean to one side; used mainly of ships: *A leak in the hull made the ship* list *to starboard.* **2** a leaning to one side: *In the storm the ship developed a bad list.* [**²list** is from an Old English word (lystan) meaning "to desire," "have an inclination." Note that the word "incline" includes both the idea of leaning and that of desiring.]

³list (lĭst) to please; choose: *The wind blows where it* lists. [**³list** comes from the same Old English word as **²list.**]

lis·ten (lĭs′ən) **1** to pay attention in order to hear: *We spent the evening listening to music.* **2** to follow advice or instruction: *You'll never do that job right if you don't* listen.

lis·ten·er (lĭs′ən ər) **1** a person who listens; a member of an audience. **2** one who waits courteously to hear what others have to say: *He's too impatient to talk to be a good listener.*

list·less (lĭst′lĭs) lacking energy or desire to move or act; indifferent; uninterested: *The hot weather makes us all feel* listless. **list·less·ly.**

lists (lĭsts) the field or enclosure in which tournaments were fought by mounted knights in armor: *No one dared to speak as*

the terrible Black Knight rode slowly into the lists *and challenged the king himself.*

¹lit (lĭt) See **¹light.** *The candles were* lit.

²lit (lĭt) See **²light.** *The bird* lit *on a bush.*

lit·a·ny (lĭt′ə nĭ) form of prayer, led by the clergyman with responses from the congregation. **lit·a·nies.**

li·ter (lē′tər) measure of volume in the metric system. One liter equals 1,000 cubic centimeters or about 1 quart.

lit·er·al (lĭt′ər əl) **1** word-for-word: *Here is a* literal *translation of the motto on the United States silver dollar:* "E pluribus unum" *means "From many, one."* **2** following the exact truth; not exaggerated; precise: *the* literal *truth.* **3** inclined to follow the exact words; matter-of-fact: *a* literal *mind.* **lit·er·al·ly.**

lit·er·a·ry (lĭt′ə rĕr′ĭ) **1** of literature or the study of literature: *to enjoy* literary *studies.* **2** having great interest in or knowledge of literature: *a* literary *mind.*

lit·er·ate (lĭt′ər ĭt) **1** able to read and write; educated. **2** a person who can read and write.

lit·er·a·ture (lĭt′ər ə chŏŏr′ or lĭt′ər ə tyŏŏr′) **1** written works, especially such imaginative works as poems, plays, essays, and stories considered valuable for their style, form, and subject matter: *Shakespeare, Blake, and Dickens created different kinds of* literature. **2** any collection or body of imaginative written works from a particular country, period of time, etc.: *American* literature; *modern* literature. **3** everything written on a single subject, considered as a group or whole: *medical* literature; *the* literature *of space travel.* **4** the study or writing of literary works, as a profession or occupation.

lithe (lĭth) able to bend easily; supple; limber. **lithe·ly.**

lith·i·um (lĭth′ĭ əm) soft, silver-white, metal element. It is the lightest metal known. It is used in making porcelain, medicines, etc.

lit·mus (lĭt′məs) **1** a dye made from a plant. It turns red in acid and blue in alkali. **2 litmus paper** a soft paper stained with litmus and used to indicate whether something is acid or alkali.

lit·ter (lĭt′ər) **1** loose rubbish. **2** straw, sawdust, etc., used as bedding for animals.

3 to scatter carelessly: *Ira littered his desk with papers, broken pencils, and crumpled letters.* **4** a stretcher, a movable cot for carrying wounded persons. **5** a covered couch with long poles, used to carry passengers. **6** of some animals, the young in a single birth: *a litter of kittens.*

Roman litter

lit·tle (lit′əl) **1** small in size: *A little dog followed me home.* **2** short in stature: *He is very stout for such a little man.* **3** small in quantity or amount: *a little sugar and a little cream.* **4** short in time or distance: *In a little while we'll take a little trip.* **5** a short time: *Please stay with me a little.* **6** a short distance: *The car jerks forward a little and then stalls.* **7** small quantity or amount (of): *I saw only a little of his work.* **8** hardly anything: *She gives little to charity.* **9** unimportant; trivial: *I've no time to worry about such little things.* **10** narrow; petty: *Your generosity seemed foolish to his little mind.* **11** slightly; hardly any: *We waited little more than an hour.* **12** seldom: *He talks little with other students.* **13 little by little** gradually; by degrees. **14 little or nothing** hardly anything. **15 not a little** very; very much: *The problem has given us not a little trouble.* **less, less·er,** or **lit·tler; least** or **lit·tlest.**

lit·ur·gy (lit′ər jĭ) ritual, ceremonies, and prayers for public worship in any of various Christian churches. **lit·ur·gies.**

¹live (lĭv) **1** to exist; have life: *The dinosaurs lived millions of years ago.* **2** to remain alive; survive: *Fish cannot live out of water.* **3** to reside; dwell: *He lives in Paris.* **4** to conduct one's affairs: *He lives extravagantly.* **5** to gain a livelihood: *While a student he lived by taking odd jobs.* **6** to enjoy life fully: *There's a man who really knows how to live!*

live and let live to be tolerant; mind one's own business.

live down to live in such a way that past mistakes are forgotten: *to live down a shame.*

live off 1 to be supported by: *He lived off his parents and never earned a penny of his own.* **2** to take nourishment from: *Many farmers live off the land they cultivate.*

live on 1 to continue to live: *He lived on for many years after his sons had left him.* **2** to subsist on: *You can't live on candy and ice cream alone.*

live through to survive the experience of: *She has lived through serious illness and poverty, and still she is cheerful.*

live up to to fulfill: *He didn't live up to the hopes of his parents.*

lived, liv·ing. [**¹live** is a form of an Old English word (lifian) meaning "to live."]

²live (līv) **1** alive; having life: *to buy a live chameleon at the circus.* **2** full of life, energy, interest, etc.: *a live issue; a live question.* **3** burning; glowing: *We roasted corn in the live coals.* **4** not exploded: *a live bomb.* **5** charged with electricity: *a live wire.* [**²live** is short for **alive.**]

live·li·hood (līv′li hŏŏd′) food, clothing, and shelter; subsistence: *to earn one's livelihood by teaching music.*

live·li·ness (līv′li nĭs) **1** a being lively. **2** gaiety; brightness. **3** energy; vigor.

live·long (līv′lông′) whole; entire: *the livelong day.*

live·ly (līv′li) **1** full of life; active; vigorous: *That horse is very lively.* **2** quick; gay; spirited: *a lively tune.* **3** exciting; eventful: *We had a lively day.* **4** alert; keen: *a lively interest.* **5** vivid; bright: *a lively color.* **6** bouncing back quickly: *a lively ball.* **live·li·er, live·li·est.**

liv·en (lī′vən) to put life into; wake up; enliven: *Ethel's cheerfulness livens every party.*

liv·er (liv′ər) **1** a large organ in the upper part of the abdomen which produces bile and changes and stores certain substances from the blood. **2** meat of the liver of animals used as food.

Liver, showing position

liv·er·ied (liv′ər ēd′) dressed in livery.

liv·er·y (liv′ə rĭ) **1** the special uniform of male servants in a wealthy household.

---

fāte, făt, fâre, fär; bē, bět; bīte, bĭt; nō, nŏt, nôr; fūse, fŭn, fûr; tōō, tŏŏk; foil; foul; thin; then; hw for wh as in *wh*at; zh for s as in u*s*ual; ə for a, e, i, o, u, as in *a*go, lin*e*n, per*i*l, at*o*m, min*u*s

421

2 livery stable a place where horses are boarded and where horses and carriages may be hired. **liv·er·ies.**

lives (livz) more than one **life.**

live·stock (liv'stŏk') horses, cattle, sheep, pigs, etc., kept or raised on a farm or ranch.

liv·id (liv'id) **1** black and blue from a bruise. **2** grayish blue: *a face* livid *with anger.*

liv·ing (liv'ing) **1** alive; not dead. **2** strong; active: *a living faith.* **3** livelihood: *how to earn a* living. **4** enough to live on: *a living wage.* **5** a way of life: *We are used to plain* living. **6** having to do with the way of life: *good* living *conditions.* **7** real; true to life: *the living image of his father.* **8 the living** all those who are alive.

living room a room where a family spends most of its indoor leisure; a sitting room.

liz·ard (liz'ərd) a reptile usually having a slender body tapering into a long tail, four legs with five-toed feet, a scaly skin, ear holes, and movable eyelids. There are some 2,500 kinds.

Collared lizard, about 1 ft. long

lla·ma (lä'mə) a South American beast of burden related to the camel. It has woolly hair and a long neck but no hump.

lla·no (lä'nō) in Spanish American countries, a treeless, grassy plain. **lla·nos.**

Llama, 4 to 5 ft. high at shoulder

lo (lō) look! see! behold!: *and,* lo! *he was turned into a frog.* (Homonym: low)

load (lōd) **1** something laid or put on a person, beast, or vehicle in order to be carried: *The men put a* load *of wood onto the truck.* **2** the amount carried or that can be carried: *The truck has a full* load *now.* **3** to fill up (something) with a load: *We* loaded *the truck with our things.* **4** to put something to be carried (onto or in): *The men* loaded *the bag onto the truck.* **5** a burden; something hard to bear or endure: *Her good news took a* load *off my mind.* **6** to burden; weigh down: *They* loaded *her with work.* **7** charge, or amount of ammunition, in a gun. **8** to put ammunition in

a gun; to charge: *to* load *a gun.* **9** the amount of electricity a circuit carries. **10** to make heavier on one side: *The gambler* loaded *the dice.* **11** to heap; pile: *The people* loaded *the general with honors.* (Homonym: lode)

load·stone (lōd'stōn') **1** a piece of magnetic iron ore. **2** anything that attracts. Also spelled **lodestone.**

¹loaf (lōf) **1** shaped mass of baked bread or cake. **2** shaped mass of other food that looks like a loaf of bread: *a meat* loaf. **loaves.** [¹**loaf** is a form of an Old English word (hlāf).]

Loaf of bread

²loaf (lōf) to pass the time doing nothing; be lazy. [²**loaf** comes from **loafer.**]

loaf·er (lō'fər) **1** an idler; a lazy person. **2** a kind of sport shoe.

loam (lōm) a rich soil of clay and sand mixed with decayed leaves and plants.

loan (lōn) **1** to lend: *He* loaned *me his pen.* **2** something lent, especially a sum of money: *a government* loan. **3** a lending or being lent: *to ask for the* loan *of something; give someone the* loan *of something; books on* loan. (Homonym: lone)

loath (lōth) loth.

loathe (lōth) to feel extreme dislike or disgust toward (something); detest: *Many people* loathe *spiders.* **loathed, loath·ing.**

loath·ing (lō'thing) great disgust or dislike; aversion.

loath·some (lōth'səm) detestable; disgusting. **loath·some·ly.**

loaves (lōvz) more than one **loaf.**

lob·by (lŏb'i) **1** hall, corridor, or room which is an entrance or a waiting room: *a hotel* lobby. **2** person or group that tries to influence members of a legislature for or against a measure. **3** to try to influence members of a legislature for or against a measure: *Many groups are* lobbying *against an increase in taxes.* **lob·bies; lob·bied, lob·by·ing.**

lobe (lōb) a rounded, more or less separated part of a leaf or animal organ: *the* lobe *of the ear.*

of LEAF   of EAR
Lobes

lob·ster (lŏb'stər) **1** a sea creature with two large, powerful claws and eight legs. Lobsters are enclosed in a thin, tough shell that turns red when cooked. **2** the flesh of this animal used for food.

lo·cal (lō′kəl) **1** having to do with a particular place: *the local news.* **2** limited to a single part of the body: *a local irritation; a local injury.* **3** stopping at all stations: *a local train.* **4** a train, bus, etc., that stops at all stations. **lo·cal·ly.**

lo·cal·i·ty (lō kăl′ə tĭ) particular place or region. **lo·cal·i·ties.**

Lobster, about 1 ft. long

lo·cate (lō′kāt′) **1** to find the place or position of: *We located the leak in the pipe.* **2** to tell or show where (a thing or person) is: *Can you locate Colorado on this map?* **3** to put or place; situate; establish: *That town is located east of the Mississippi.* **4** to settle: *The Joneses would like to locate in the West when they retire.* **lo·cat·ed, lo·cat·ing.**

lo·ca·tion (lō kā′shən) **1** place or position: *a central location for a new post office.* **2** a locating or being located: *the location of a missing person.*

loch (lŏk) Scottish word for a lake or an arm of the sea.

¹lock (lŏk) curl or strand of hair. [¹lock is a form of an Old English word (locc) of the same meaning.]

²lock (lŏk) **1** any device for fastening a door, window, lid, drawer, or the like, especially one operated by a key. **2** a section of a canal or other water- way, with watertight gates at each end, in which boats are raised or lowered to another water level. **3** the firing mechanism of a gun. **4** to fasten securely: *to lock a door.* **5** to fit together securely: *to lock the pieces of a picture puzzle in place.* **6** to link

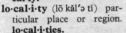
Locks in the Panama Canal

together: *to lock arms.* **7** to shut up; con- fine: *to lock papers in a drawer.* [²lock is a form of an Old English word (loc) meaning "lock," "bolt," "bar."]

lock·er (lŏk′ər) **1** cabinet with a lock, for individual use, usually one of a number in a public building, gymnasium, etc. **2** chest or small trunk: *foot locker.*

lock·et (lŏk′ĭt) a small, thin, ornamental case with a hinged cover for hold- ing a portrait, usually worn on a neck chain.

Locket

lock·jaw (lŏk′jô′) disease in which the jaws become firmly locked; a type of tetanus.

lock·smith (lŏk′smĭth′) a person who makes and repairs locks.

lo·co·mo·tion (lō′kə mō′shən) a moving from place to place. Animals have the power of locomotion. Automobiles, trains, and airplanes are all means of locomotion.

Steam locomotive

lo·co·mo·tive (lō′kə mō′tĭv) an engine that pulls railroad trains.

lo·cust (lō′kəst) **1** a kind of grasshopper which flies in great swarms and is very destructive to plants of all kinds. **2** the cicada. **3** a tree with fernlike leaves and clusters of fragrant pale blossoms. Its seed pods look like bean pods.

Locust, about 2 in. long

lode (lōd) vein or deposit of metal ore. (Homonym: load.)

lode·stone (lōd′stōn′) loadstone.

lodge (lŏj) **1** a country house or cabin, espe- cially one used by hunters. **2** a small house or cottage on the grounds of a large estate. **3** to provide with a temporary shelter or place to sleep: *The flood victims were lodged in the schoolhouse.* **4** to live in rented rooms. **5** the den or shelter of some

fāte, făt, fâre, fär; bē, bĕt; bīte, bit; nō, nŏt, nôr; fūse, fŭn, fûr; tōō, tŏŏk; foil; foul; thin; ~~then~~; hw for wh as in *wh*at; zh for s as in u*s*ual; ə for a, e, i, o, u, as in *a*go, lin*e*n, per*i*l, at*o*m, min*u*s

wild animals: *a beaver* lodge. **6** to get stuck; catch: *A fish bone* lodged *in his throat.* **7** to put or fix in some particular place: *He* lodged *a bullet in the tree.* **8** to place formally before a judge or other official: *to lodge a complaint.* **9** local branch or chapter of certain organizations, or the local chapter's meeting place. **10** an American Indian hut or wigwam, or all those living in such a lodge. **lodged, lodg·ing.**

lodg·er (lŏj′ər) person who rents one or more rooms in another person's house.

lodg·ing (lŏj′ĭng) **1** a temporary place to live or a place to sleep: *a lodging for the night.* **2 lodgings** room or rooms rented as living quarters.

loft (lôft or lŏft) **1** attic; garret. **2** a storage place just below the roof of a barn: *a hay loft.* **3** gallery; balcony: *a choir loft.* **4** an upper floor in a warehouse, factory, etc.

loft·y (lôf′tĭ or lŏf′tĭ) **1** very high: *the lofty mountain peaks.* **2** noble and dignified; elevated: *his lofty ambitions.* **3** proud; haughty: *a lofty manner.* **loft·i·er, loft·i·est; loft·i·ly.**

log (lŏg or lôg) **1** a length of wood cut from the trunk or from a branch of a felled tree. **2** to cut trees into logs and move them from the forest. **3** a float on the end of a long line, used for measuring the speed of a ship. **4** a book in which the speed and position of a ship, the weather, and daily happenings are recorded. **5** to enter (facts) in a ship's record book. **logged, log·ging.**

lo·gan·ber·ry (lō′gən bĕr′ĭ) **1** large, dark red berry of a plant that is a cross between the raspberry and the blackberry. **2** the plant on which it grows. **lo·gan·ber·ries.**

log·ging (lŏg′ĭng or lôg′ĭng) the work of cutting trees, sawing the trunks and branches into logs, and moving the logs from the forest.

log·ic (lŏj′ĭk) **1** sound reasoning; clear thinking: *Be guided by* logic, *not by feelings.* **2** a way or method of reasoning. **3** study of ways and methods of reasoning and clear thinking.

log·i·cal (lŏj′ə kəl) **1** in agreement with sound reasoning; sensible: *It is* logical *to look for a fire if you smell smoke.* **2** having to do with logic. **log·i·cal·ly.**

loin (loin) **1** the lower part of the back of the body between the ribs and the hip bones. **2** a cut of meat from this part of an animal.

loi·ter (loi′tər) **1** to go slowly and stop frequently on the way; linger: *Don't* loiter *on your way home from school.* **2** to sit or stand idly; spend time idly: *No* loitering *is allowed in the courthouse halls.*

loll (lŏl) **1** to sit, lie, or stand in a lazy, very relaxed way: *He was so tired that he just* lolled *on the sofa.* **2** to hang or droop loosely: *The sick dog lay with his tongue* lolling *out of his mouth.*

lol·li·pop (lŏl′ĭ pŏp′) a hard sugar candy on the end of a small stick.

Lon·don (lŭn′dən) capital and largest city of the United Kingdom, in the southeast part of England.

lone (lōn) alone; single; solitary: *one* lone *tree in the middle of a field.* (Homonym: loan)

lone·li·ness (lōn′lĭ nĭs) **1** the sad feeling of not having companions: *At camp I had a few days of* loneliness *until I made some friends.* **2** a being alone; solitude.

lone·ly (lōn′lĭ) **1** unhappy from lack of companionship: *He was* lonely *on his first long trip by himself.* **2** alone; solitary: *We saw a* lonely *traveler on the road.* **3** remote; isolated; seldom visited: *a* lonely *mountain village.* **lone·li·er, lone·li·est.**

lone·some (lōn′səm) lonely: *a* lonesome *widow; a* lonesome *road.* **lone·some·ly.**

¹**long** (lông or lŏng) **1** great in distance or time from beginning to end; not short or brief: *Get a* long *string for the kite. We had a* long *wait for the bus.* **2** great in number from beginning to end: *a* long *list.* **3** for or during a considerable time: *I can't stay* long. **4** in length or in time: *a foot* long; *a week* long. **5** lasting for a considerable time: *a* long, *adventure story.* **6** much time: *That happened* long *ago. It takes too* long *to go that way. Stay as* long *as you like.* **7 as long as** or **so long as** provided that: *You may go so* long as *you come home before ten o'clock.* **8 a long face** a sad or disappointed expression. **9 in the long run** in the end; over a period of time: *An inexpensive second-hand car may prove expensive* in the long run. **10 long vowel** vowel that has the sound of its own

name: *The "a" of "ate" and the "o" in "go" are long vowels.* **11 the long and short of** all there is to say about; a summary of: *That's the long and short of the matter.* [¹**long** is a form of an Old English word (long, lang).]

²**long** (lông or lŏng) to wish very much: *He longs to see his old friends again.* [²**long** is a form of an Old English word (langian) meaning "grow long."]

long·hand (lông′hănd′ or lŏng′hănd′) ordinary handwriting: *People always sign their names in* longhand.

long·horn (lông′hôrn′ or lŏng′hôrn′) a breed of cattle with long horns, formerly common in Mexico and the southwestern United States.

long·ing (lông′ĭng or lŏng′ĭng) **1** strong desire. **2** showing strong desire: *The children cast longing looks at the cake.* **long·ing·ly.**

lon·gi·tude (lŏn′jə-tōōd′ or lŏn′jə tūd′) distance east or west on the earth's surface, measured in degrees. On a map or globe, longitude is shown by lines running between the North and South Poles.

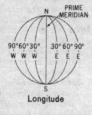

Longitude

lon·gi·tu·di·nal (lŏn′jə tōō′də nəl or lŏn′-jə tū′də nəl) **1** having to do with length or longitude. **2** running lengthwise: *The planks of a boat are* longitudinal. **lon·gi·tu·di·nal·ly.**

look (lŏŏk) **1** to direct the eyes: *to look at the blackboard.* **2** act of looking or examining; a glance: *After one look, I knew I liked this car. Take a look at this book.* **3** to search: *I've been looking everywhere for you.* **4** to notice; pay attention: *Just look what you're doing!* **5** to appear: *She looks happy.* **6** appearance: *He has a sad look lately.* **7** to face; allow a view of: *This window looks out onto the garden.*

look after to take care of: *Please look after the baby.*

look alive to be alert; hurry up.

look at to examine: *The plumber looked at the clogged drain.*

look down on to feel superior to.

look for 1 to search: *Do look for that lost book.* **2** to expect: *I'll look for you about three o'clock.*

look forward to to expect (usually something pleasant): *I look forward to a wonderful party.*

look in to make a short visit: *The doctor will look in again tomorrow.*

look into to investigate: *The school looks into the record of each new student.*

look on 1 to regard; consider: *I look on him as my best friend.* **2** to watch: *You two play and I'll look on.*

look oneself to look normal: *You don't look yourself today!*

look out to watch out: *Do look out for the wet paint.*

look over to examine: *Please look over your papers before you hand them in.*

look to 1 to see to: *You must look to it that you are on time.* **2** to count on: *I look to him for help.*

look up to search for; try to find: *We'll look up the time of the show in the newspaper.*

look up to to respect highly.

looking glass a mirror.

look·out (lŏŏk′out′) **1** a person who watches to guard against attack or to see what is happening: *The bandits posted a lookout on the hill above their secret cave.* **2** a careful watch: *Keep a good lookout and let me know when you see the train coming.* **3** place from which to watch or look out. **4** care; concern; business: *If he gets into trouble, it's his lookout, not mine.* **5 on the lookout** watchful: *Be on the lookout for rattlesnakes while walking in the desert.*

Hand loom

¹**loom** (lōōm) a frame or machine on which cloth is woven. [¹**loom** is a form of an Old English word (gelōma) meaning "tool."]

---

fāte, făt, fâre, fär; bē, bĕt; bīte, bĭt; nō, nŏt, nôr; fūse, fŭn, fûr; tōō, tŏŏk; foil; foul; thin; then; hw for wh as in *what*; zh for s as in usual; ə for a, e, i, o, u, as in *ago, linen, peril, atom, minus*

425

²**loom** (lōōm) to appear in an indistinct way or in a form that seems large and threatening: *The outline of a truck* loomed *out of the mist and seemed to fill the road.* [²**loom** is a word of uncertain origin.]

Loon, 2 to 3 ft. long

¹**loon** (lōōn) a large water bird with a short neck and pointed bill, noted for its uncanny call. The loon dives for fish. [¹**loon** is a word of Scandinavian origin.]

²**loon** (lōōn) a silly or ignorant person. [²**loon** is a form of a Scottish word, "loun."]

loop (lōōp) 1 the shape of a written "l." 2 anything bent, tied, or fastened in this shape. 3 a bend or curve in a stream, road, etc., suggesting a loop. 4 an airplane stunt of flying a vertical circle. 5 to make a loop.

Decorative loops on a uniform

loop·hole (lōōp′hōl′) 1 a small opening in a wall through which a gun may be fired. 2 an omission or lack of clearness in a law, contract, etc., which permits it to be broken or gotten around.

Loophole

¹**loose** (lōōs) 1 not firmly fixed, fastened, or bound: *a* loose *board; a* loose *knot;* loose *papers in a box.* 2 not tied up; not confined; free: *The dog got* loose *and ran away.* 3 not tightly or closely packed: *the* loose *sand.* 4 not tight or close-fitting: *a* loose *collar.* 5 not close or compact: *a* loose *weave.* 6 not sufficiently controlled: *his* loose *talk;* loose *conduct.* 7 not exact or strict: *A* loose *count showed there were more than 50 people.* 8 to unfasten; set free; release. **loosed, loos·ing; loose·ly.**

loos·en (lōō′sən) 1 to make loose or less tight: *to* loosen *a screw;* loosen *one's belt.* 2 to become loose or more loose: *The jar lid may* loosen *if you heat it.* 3 to unfasten; undo: *Just* loosen *the halter and let the horse graze.* 4 to make less dense or compact: *One should* loosen *the soil before planting.*

loot (lōōt) 1 things stolen or taken by force; booty: *The pirates buried their* loot *on an island.* 2 to rob by force; plunder: *The outlaws attacked and* looted *the mail train.* (Homonym: lute)

¹**lop** (lŏp) to cut: *to* lop *off the branches of a tree.* **lopped, lop·ping.** [¹**lop** is a form of an earlier English word (loppen).]

²**lop** (lŏp) 1 to hang or let hang limply; flop. 2 **lop-eared** having ears which flop down: *a* lop-eared *spaniel.* **lopped, lop·ping.** [²**lop** is a word of unknown origin.]

lope (lōp) 1 gait marked by long, smooth strides: *The hunter walks with a* lope. 2 to move with easy, long steps: *The horse* loped *along.* **loped, lop·ing.**

lop·sid·ed (lŏp′sī′dĭd) with one side lower than the other; heavier or larger on one side than on the other. **lop·sid·ed·ly.**

lor·an (lô′rən) navigation system by means of which a ship or an aircraft may figure its position by radio signals received from various ground stations.

lord (lôrd) 1 a ruler; person having power to rule others. 2 in Great Britain, a nobleman. 3 **Lord** (1) God. (2) Jesus Christ. (3) title in Great Britain held by certain noblemen.

lord it over to act in a superior way toward (someone): *Ever since John won the prize he has* lorded it over *his friends.*

lord·ly (lôrd′lĭ) suitable for a lord; grand; magnificent. **lord·li·er, lord·li·est.**

lord·ship (lôrd′shĭp) 1 authority; rule. 2 **Lordship** (with "Your" or "His") in Great Britain, title used in speaking to or speaking of a judge or nobleman.

lore (lôr) 1 traditions, legends, tales, etc., of or about a special group: *Indian* lore; *gypsy* lore. 2 learning or knowledge about a special subject: *bird* lore.

lor·ry (lôr′ĭ or lŏr′ĭ) a British word for truck. **lor·ries.**

lose (lōōz) 1 to have no longer; be unable to find: *I've* lost *my key. We've* lost *the way.* 2 to be deprived of; have taken from one by death, accident, carelessness, etc.: *He* lost *his son in a car accident.* 3 to fail to keep: *Don't* lose *your patience.* 4 to fail to win; be defeated: *My horse* lost *in the second race.* 5 to become worse off; suffer a loss: *We* lost *on that deal.* 6 to cause the loss of: *His mean remarks* lost *him many* *friends*. **7** to waste (time); spend uselessly: *We lost time because of heavy traffic.* **8** to fail to hear, see, or understand: *I lost your last few sentences.* **9** of a clock or watch, to run slow: *My watch loses two minutes a day.*

lose oneself 1 to disappear: *The boy ran away and lost himself in the crowd.* **2** to be absorbed (in something): *He lost himself in his work.*

lost, los·ing.

los·er (lōō′zər) person, animal, or thing that loses: *You'll be the loser if you don't do your work. He was the loser in the race.*

loss (lôs or lŏs) **1** a losing: *the loss of a ship.* **2** person, thing, or amount lost: *His business had a loss this year instead of a profit. The closing of the hospital was a serious loss for the town.* **3** failure to win, keep, or obtain: *the loss of the foot race; loss of the contract.* **4 losses** number of soldiers killed, wounded, or captured in battle: *Both sides suffered heavy losses in the battle.*

lost (lôst or lŏst) **1** See **lose.** *He lost his pet turtle.* **2** missing: *The police found the lost boy.* **3** off the right path; astray: *to be lost in the forest.* **4** unseen; not visible: *to be lost in the distance.* **5** departed; no longer present: *a lost friend; lost hopes.* **6** destroyed; ruined: *Too much rain resulted in a lost harvest.* **7** wasted; useless: *a lost opportunity; lost time.* **8** not won: *the lost foot race.* **9** absorbed: *He didn't hear me calling as he was lost in thought.* **10** hopeless: *a lost cause.* **11 lost to** no longer having any feeling for; insensitive to: *He is lost to any sense of honor.* **12 be lost on** to fail to have any influence; be wasted on: *All my advice was lost on him.*

lot (lŏt) **1** number, piece of wood, straw, etc., used to decide something by chance: *We will draw lots for the prize.* **2** use of lots to decide something by chance: *The class chose their representative by lot.* **3** luck; fate; fortune: *Poverty is his lot.* **4** piece or plot of ground: *an empty lot.* **5** group of things taken together: *A new lot of shoes just arrived in the store.* **6** a great deal of; quite a bit of: *We have a lot of work to do.*

loth (lōth) very unwilling: *I was loth to tell her the truth.* Also spelled **loath.**

lo·tion (lō′shən) liquid preparation used to soothe, treat, or beautify the skin.

lot·ter·y (lŏt′ə rĭ) scheme of distributing prizes by lot. People buy numbered tickets and the person who has a ticket with the same number as the one picked out by chance in the drawing wins a prize. **lot·ter·ies.**

loud (loud) **1** not low or quiet; having a strong and powerful sound: *a loud voice; a loud knocking.* **2** noisy: *a loud group; a loud party.* **3** too bright; too colorful; gaudy: *a loud necktie.* **loud·ly.**

loud·ness (loud′nĭs) a being loud.

loud·speak·er (loud′spē′kər) part of a radio, phonograph, television set, etc., which changes electrical signals into sound.

Lou·is·i·an·a (lōō ē zĭ ăn′ə) a State in southern United States.

lounge (lounj) **1** to move, act, or rest in a lazy manner. **2** comfortable room to relax in; parlor: *We watched TV in the airport lounge.* **3** a couch or sofa. **lounged, loung·ing.**

louse (lous) **1** a small, wingless insect that lives in the hair and on the bodies of men and animals. **2** an insect that sucks the sap of plants; an aphid. **lice.**

Body louse

lout (lout) a stupid, awkward person.

lov·a·ble (lŭv′ə bəl) having qualities that inspire love; deserving of love: *a lovable disposition; a lovable baby.* **lov·a·bly.**

love (lŭv) **1** a strong feeling of affection: *a mother's love; the love between husband and wife; love for a friend.* **2** to have a strong feeling of affection for: *I love my mother.* **3** a strong liking; fondness: *a love for music.* **4** to like (something) very much: *He loves watching the baseball game on TV.* **5** sweetheart; someone dear: *She is my love.* **6 in love** having a feeling of love for someone: *He thinks he's in love.* **loved, lov·ing.**

love·li·ness (lŭv′lĭ nĭs) beauty; charm.

love·ly (lŭv′lĭ) **1** beautiful in appearance or character. **2** charming; delightful: *such lovely music.* **love·li·er, love·li·est.**

---

fāte, făt, fâre, fär; bē, bĕt; bīte, bĭt; nō, nŏt, nôr; fūse, fŭn, fûr; tōō, tŏŏk; foil; foul; thin; ~~then~~; hw for wh as in *what*; zh for s as in u*s*ual; ə for a, e, i, o, u, as in *ago*, lin*e*n, per*i*l, at*o*m, min*u*s

lov·er (lŭv′ər) **1** person who loves another. **2** person who has a fondness or strong liking for something: *a lover of music.*

lov·ing (lŭv′ĭng) showing or feeling love; affectionate: *She has a loving nature.* **lov·ing·ly.**

¹**low** (lō) **1** not high: *a room with a low ceiling.* **2** near the ground, floor, or base of something: *That shelf is too low on the wall.* **3** at, toward, or near the ground, floor, etc.: *to aim low; fly low.* **4** thing that is low; low point or position: *The price of apples reached a new low during harvest season.* **5** soft; not loud: *Speak in a low voice.* **6** quietly; softly: *Speak low so they won't hear us.* **7** deep; not shrill: *the low notes of a tuba.* **8** less than usual: *That is a low price for such a beautiful diamond.* **9** below the usual level: *The river is low.* **10** small: *Name a low number.* **11** feeble; weak: *The patient is very low, but we hope the new drug will help him.* **12** gloomy; depressed: *to be in low spirits.* **13** unfavorable: *I have a low opinion of liars.* **14** mean; not kind: *a low trick.* **15** coarse; vulgar: *to use low talk.* [¹**low** is a form of an earlier word (lah) which comes from an early Norse word (lagr).] (Homonym: lo)

²**low** (lō) **1** a moo; the sound that a cow makes. **2** to moo; make this sound. [²**low** is a form of an Old English word (hlōwan).] (Homonym: lo)

low·er (lō′ər) **1** below (another or others) in place, rank, or the like: *the lower lip; the lower grades in school.* **2** to make less; reduce: *to lower the price of milk.* **3** to make less loud: *Please lower your voice.* **4** to reduce the height or level of: *to lower the light beam of a car; to lower the water in a canal.*

low·land (lō′lənd) low, level country.

low·ly (lō′lĭ) **1** humble: *the lowly dwelling of a shepherd.* **2** low in rank, position, standard, etc.: *The king was kind to even his most lowly servants.* **low·li·er, low·li·est.**

loy·al (loi′əl) faithful; true: *his loyal devotion; to be loyal to a creed.* **loy·al·ly.**

loy·al·ty (loi′əl tĭ) faithfulness; being loyal: *a loyalty to one's country; loyalty to a friend.* **loy·al·ties.**

lu·bri·cant (lōō′brə kənt) oil, grease, or other substance used to make moving parts of machines work smoothly.

lu·bri·cate (lōō′brə kāt′) to apply oil, grease, or other substances to make the parts of a machine work smoothly: *to lubricate a car.* **lu·bri·cat·ed, lu·bri·cat·ing.**

lu·bri·ca·tion (lōō′brə kā′shən) a lubricating or being lubricated.

lu·cid (lōō′sĭd or lū′sĭd) **1** clear; easy to understand: *a lucid explanation.* **2** sane; mentally sound: *An insane person often has lucid moments.* **3** transparent: *the lucid waters of a mountain lake.* **lu·cid·ly.**

luck (lŭk) **1** fortune; chance: *That's his hard luck. Better luck next time.* **2** good fortune: *My luck seems to have run out.*

luck·less (lŭk′lĭs) unfortunate; not lucky. **luck·less·ly.**

luck·y (lŭk′ĭ) **1** fortunate; having good luck: *He is usually lucky in card games.* **2** bringing good fortune; having a fortunate result: *a lucky charm; a lucky guess.* **luck·i·er, luck·i·est; luck·i·ly.**

lu·di·crous (lōō′də krəs or lū′də krəs) ridiculous; causing laughter; comical: *The elephant's attempts at dancing were simply ludicrous.* **lu·di·crous·ly.**

lug (lŭg) to carry or drag by putting forth great effort: *He was trying to lug the television set into the bedroom.* **lugged, lug·ging.**

lug·gage (lŭg′ĭj) bags, suitcases, trunks, and boxes a person takes on a trip; baggage.

luke·warm (lōōk′wôrm′) **1** fairly warm; not hot or cold; tepid: *a lukewarm bath.* **2** showing no enthusiasm; indifferent: *the lukewarm applause.*

lull (lŭl) **1** to quiet; calm: *The sound of the waves lulled me to sleep.* **2** a quiet period; a temporary lessening of noise, activity, etc.: *a lull in the storm; a lull in conversation.*

lul·la·by (lŭl′ə bī′) a song to lull a baby to sleep. **lul·la·bies.**

lum·ba·go (lŭm bā′gō) rheumatism in the lower part of the back; backache.

¹**lum·ber** (lŭm′bər) planks; boards: *Would you buy us some lumber for a tree house?* [¹**lumber** is a word of uncertain origin.]

²**lum·ber** (lŭm′bər) to move in a clumsy, heavy way: *The bear lumbered up to our car.* [²**lumber** is a form of an earlier English word (lomeren) of Old Norse origin.]

lum·ber·jack (lŭm′bər jăk′) man who cuts and prepares forest timber.

lum·ber·man (lŭm′bər mən) 1 man who cuts trees and prepares lumber. 2 man who buys and sells lumber. **lum·ber·men.**

lu·mi·nous (lōō′mə nəs or lū′mə nəs) 1 giving off light; shining; bright: *The stars are luminous.* 2 easy to understand; clear: *a luminous way of writing.* **lu·mi·nous·ly.**

lump (lŭmp) 1 small mass of solid material, usually without any special shape: *a lump of dough; lumps in mashed potatoes.* 2 a bump or swelling: *a lump on the head.* 3 a cube or small square (of sugar). 4 to form into a lump or lumps: *Cooked cereal will lump unless well stirred.* 5 to put (things) together in one amount, mass, or pile: *Let's lump the expenses of the trip and all pay equally.*

lu·nar (lōō′nər or lū′nər) having to do with the moon: *a lunar eclipse.*

lu·na·tic (lōō′nə tĭk or lū′nə tĭk) 1 mad; crazy; very foolish: *a lunatic idea or scheme.* 2 an insane person. 3 for or having to do with insane people: *a lunatic asylum.*

lunch (lŭnch) 1 the light midday meal, eaten between breakfast and dinner: *We eat lunch at school.* 2 to eat the midday meal.

lunch·eon (lŭn′chən) a lunch, especially a formal midday meal to which guests are invited.

lunch·room (lŭnch′rōōm′) 1 place in a school or office where people can eat. 2 restaurant that serves light meals.

lung (lŭng) either of two saclike organs in the chest of man and higher animals, used for breathing.

lunge (lŭnj) 1 a sudden forward movement; a jump or leap forward, usually in order to strike or seize: *He made a lunge for the fumbled football. The fencer made a quick lunge and struck his opponent.* 2 to make such a movement: *The kitten lunged at the spool and caught it.* **lunged, lung·ing.**

lurch (lûrch) 1 a sudden leaning or swaying motion to one side: *The bus gave a lurch as one wheel went into a ditch.* 2 to make a lurch or lurches; stagger or sway: *As the boat pitched, the passengers lurched against the rail.*

lure (lŏŏr or lūr) 1 to attract or draw, by promising profit or pleasure; tempt with promises; entice: *The sound of the circus parade lured the children away from their studies.* 2 thing that attracts by offering pleasure or profit; attraction: *Gold was the lure that started a rush to California in 1849.* 3 an artificial minnow, bait, or other device used to attract and catch fish. **lured, lur·ing.**

lu·rid (lŏŏr′ĭd or lūr′ĭd) 1 shining with a red or fiery glow; glaring in color: *The lurid posters attracted attention.* 2 sensational; striking or shocking: *the lurid career of a criminal.* **lu·rid·ly.**

lurk (lûrk) 1 to hide or remain secretly in or near a place: *The burglar lurked in the bushes until the watchman had passed.* 2 to sneak or slink: *I saw a suspicious man lurking around the building.*

lus·cious (lŭsh′əs) 1 very pleasant and sweet to taste or smell; delicious: *a luscious ripe peach.* 2 pleasing to any of the senses: *the luscious music.* **lus·cious·ly.**

lust (lŭst) 1 strong desire: *a lust for power; a lust for gold.* 2 to have a strong desire: *The pirate chief lusted for treasure.*

lus·ter or **lus·tre** (lŭs′tər) 1 a shine or brilliance of a surface that reflects light; gloss: *New cars have a high luster.* 2 brightness; radiance: *Tinsel and colorful balls gave luster to the Christmas tree.* 3 glory; splendor: *The runner's victory added new luster to his fame.*

lus·trous (lŭs′trəs) shiny; glossy; gleaming: *a lustrous silk gown.* **lus·trous·ly.**

lust·y (lŭs′tĭ) strong and healthy; vigorous: *a lusty boxer; a lusty shout.* **lust·i·er; lust·i·ly.**

lute (lōōt or lūt) an old-time musical instrument with six pairs of strings and a bent neck. It is played like a mandolin. (Homonym: loot)

Lute

lux·u·ri·ant (lŭg zhŏŏr′ĭ ənt or lŭk shŏŏr′ĭ ənt) abundant or thick in growth: *the luxuriant vegetation of the tropics.* **lux·u·ri·ant·ly.**

---

fāte, făt, fâre, fär; bē, bĕt; bīte, bĭt; nō, nŏt, nôr; fūse, fŭn, fûr; tōō, tŏŏk; foil; foul; thin; ~~then~~; hw for wh as in *what*; zh for s as in u*s*ual; ə for a, e, i, o, u, as in *a*go, lin*e*n, per*i*l, at*o*m, min*u*s

lux·u·ri·ous (lŭg zhŏŏr′ĭ əs or lŭk shŏŏr′ĭ-əs) splendid; rich; lavish: *A luxurious banquet was given in honor of the* luxurious *new theater.* **lux·u·ri·ous·ly.**

lux·u·ry (lŭk′shə rĭ) **1** something which is not necessary for life but which can make it more enjoyable or comfortable. Luxuries are often things that are expensive or difficult to get. **2** a way or condition of life in which a person enjoys great comfort and many fine things: *Most Americans live in* luxury *compared to people of very poor countries.* **lux·u·ries.**

-ly suffix meaning (**1**) in a way which is like the word to which "ly" is added: *loving*ly; *quick*ly. (**2**) "once every": *hour*ly; *year*ly. (**3**) "like": *man*ly; *beast*ly.

lye (lī) an alkali obtained from wood ashes and used in making soap. (Homonym: lie)

¹ly·ing (lī′ĭng) **1** the telling of lies: *To deceive others by* lying *is dishonest.* **2** deliberately untruthful: *The* lying *thief accused an innocent man.* **3** See **¹lie.** *Is he* lying *about that?* [**¹lying** is a form of **¹lie.**]

²ly·ing (lī′ĭng) See **²lie.** *That lazy boy is still* lying *in bed, though he should have been up an hour ago.* [**²lying** is a form of **²lie.**]

lymph (lĭmf) a colorless fluid that comes from blood plasma. It bathes and nourishes the body cells and carries their waste matter back to the blood stream.

lynch (lĭnch) to put to death without a legal trial, usually by a mob and by hanging.

lynx (lĭngks) a short-tailed wildcat with tufted ears and a light gray or brown speckled coat. (Homonym: links)

Lynx, about 3 ft. long

lyre (līr) musical instrument like a small harp with three to ten strings. Lyres were used by the ancient Greeks to accompany singing and poetry.

lyr·ic (lĭr′ĭk) **1** like a song; musical. **2** a short poem, usually expressing very personal feelings. **3** of or having to do with such poetry: *a* lyric *poet.* **4 lyrics** words for a song.

lyr·i·cal (lĭr′ĭ kəl) **1** like a song; musical; lyric: *the* lyrical *call of a bird.* **2** showing great emotion; poetical: *She became quite* lyrical *in praising the picture.* **lyr·i·cal·ly.**

M

M, m (ĕm) **1** 13th letter of the English alphabet. **2** Roman numeral for 1,000.

ma'am (măm) madam.

mac·a·ro·ni (măk′ə rō′nĭ) a food made of dried, wheat-flour paste, shaped into long hollow tubes. **mac·a·ro·nis** or **mac·a·ro·nies.**

mac·a·roon (măk′ə rōōn′) a cooky made of sugar, egg whites, and almonds or coconut.

ma·chine (mə shēn′) **1** a device to do work. The wheel and axle, pulley, lever, screw, wedge, etc., are simple machines. **2** an apparatus with moving parts made up of simple machines: *a sewing* machine; *a threshing* machine. **3** automobile.

machine gun a gun that keeps shooting as long as the trigger is held back. Small cartridges are fed to it from a long belt. For picture, see next column.

ma·chin·er·y (mə shē′nə rĭ) **1** machines: *new* machinery *for a factory.* **2** the parts of a machine: *the* machinery *of a clock.* **3** system and organization by which something works: *the* machinery *of government.* **ma·chin·er·ies.**

machine tool a power-driven machine used to make other machines or their parts.

Machine gun

ma·chin·ist (mə shē′nĭst) **1** person who operates a machine. **2** person who makes or repairs machines.

Mach number (măk or mäk nŭm'bər) a number giving the speed of an object in the air as compared with the speed of sound at the same altitude. An aircraft moving at twice the speed of sound would have a Mach number of 2.

mack·er·el (măk'ər əl) a fish growing 12 to 18 inches long, found in the North Atlantic. It has a greenish back with deep-blue stripes. pl. **mack·er·el**; rarely, **mack·er·els.**

mack·i·naw (măk'ə nô') heavy jacket or short coat, often with a plaid pattern.

mack·in·tosh (măk'ĭn tŏsh') raincoat.

mad (măd) **1** out of one's mind; insane. **2** angry: *He was so mad that his face was red.* **3** foolish; rash: *It was mad of him to try to swim in the icy water.* **4** very enthusiastic: *to be mad about baseball.* **5** wild; excited; frantic: *a mad rush toward the exit.* **6** having rabies: *A mad dog is dangerous.* **7** like mad very hard; very fast. **mad·der, mad·dest; mad·ly.**

mad·am (măd'əm) a polite word used in speaking or writing to a woman. **mes·dames** (mě dăm').

mad·ame (măd'əm) French title or form of address for a married woman equivalent to "Mrs." or "Madam." **mes·dames.**

mad·cap (măd'kăp') **1** lively, spirited person who acts on impulse: *You never know what that madcap will do next!* **2** lively or rash: *the children's madcap pranks at Halloween.*

mad·den (măd'ən) **1** to cause to become insane; craze. **2** to cause to become very angry; enrage.

made (mād) See **make.** *I made a kite.* (Homonym: maid)

mad·e·moi·selle (măd'mwə zěl') French title or form of address equal to "Miss." **mes·de·moi·selles** (měd mwä zěl').

mad·house (măd'hous') **1** home for insane people. **2** noisy, disorderly place: *The noise and litter of the children's party made the place a madhouse.*

mad·man (măd'măn') insane person; lunatic. **mad·men.**

mad·ness (măd'nĭs) **1** illness of the mind; insanity. **2** anger. **3** wild or foolish behavior: *It's madness to go out in this weather.*

mag·a·zine (măg'ə zēn' or măg'ə zēn') **1** collection of stories, poems, or other reading matter issued at regular times. **2** a building or compartment used as storage space: *The magazine of a rifle holds cartridges.*

Magazine of rifle

ma·gen·ta (mə jěn'tə) a purple-red color.

mag·got (măg'ət) a worm-like stage in the life of some insects between the egg and the full-grown insect.

mag·ic (măj'ĭk) **1** the art by which people are said to be able to do things that are beyond the normal powers of man. Magic is practiced by the use of spells and with the help of spirits, demons, and the like. Witches and sorcerers in fairy tales have magic powers. **2** mysterious effects produced by tricks, usually as entertainment: *The magician pulled the rabbit out of the hat by* magic. **3** special or mysterious charm or power: *The magic of the music made us feel like dancing.* **4** having magic power; done by magic; used in magic: *a magic wand; a magic spell.*

Fly and maggot

mag·i·cal (măj'ĭ kəl) **1** having to do with magic: *Cinderella's fairy godmother turned a pumpkin into a coach by* magical *power.* **2** like magic; casting a mysterious spell: *the magical effect of moonlight on the lake.* **mag·i·cal·ly.**

ma·gi·cian (mə jĭsh'ən) **1** person who uses magic; sorcerer. **2** person who produces mysterious effects by deft tricks: *The magician pulled a rabbit out of his hat.*

mag·is·trate (măj'ĭs trāt') **1** government official with power to administer and enforce the law. **2** local judge; justice of the peace.

mag·ne·si·um (măg nē'shĭ əm or măg nē'-zhĭ əm) a light, silver-white metal element that burns with a bright, dazzling light. Mixed with other metals, magnesium is used to make light airplane parts, etc.

fāte, făt, fâre, fär; bē, bět; bīte, bĭt; nō, nŏt, nôr; fūse, fŭn, fûr; tōō, tŏŏk; foil; foul; thin; ~~then~~;
hw for wh as in *wh*at; zh for s as in u*s*ual; ə for a, e, i, o, u, as in *a*go, lin*e*n, per*i*l, at*o*m, min*u*s

431

mag·net (măg′nĭt) **1** piece of metal or ore that draws iron toward it. **2** anything that attracts: *John's tree hut was a* magnet *for all his friends.*

Bar magnet (compass needle)

mag·net·ic (măg nĕt′- ĭk) **1** of a magnet; having the qualities of a magnet: *a* magnetic *needle.* **2** having to do with the earth's magnetism: *the North Magnetic Pole.*

Electro-magnet   Horseshoe magnet

3 having the power to charm and attract: *That actor has a* magnetic *personality.*

magnetic field space around a magnetic body, in which magnetic force can be observed.

magnetic pole 1 either pole of a magnet. **2 Magnetic Pole** either of the two points of the earth's surface, in the arctic and the antarctic, to which a magnetic needle points.

mag·net·ism (măg′nə tĭz′əm) **1** the power to act like a magnet; magnetic action. **2** the power of attracting others; personal charm: *He won everybody over by the* magnetism *of his personality.*

mag·ne·tize (măg′nə tīz′) **1** to cause to be magnetic. **2** to attract as with a magnet; to put under a spell: *The orator's voice* magnetized *his audience.* **mag·ne·tized, mag·ne·tiz·ing.**

mag·nif·i·cence (măg nĭf′ə səns) splendor and richness of ornament; grandeur of appearance: *the* magnificence *of a palace.*

mag·nif·i·cent (măg nĭf′ə sənt) **1** grand in appearance; richly ornamented; splendid: *a* magnificent *palace; a* magnificent *procession.* **2** noble; very fine: *a* magnificent *idea; a* magnificent *proposal.* **mag·nif·i·cent·ly.**

mag·ni·fy (măg′nə fī′) **1** to make (something) appear larger: *The microscope* magnified *by 100 times the tiny cells on the slide.* **2** to exaggerate; make seem greater than what is true: *to* magnify *the difficulties of an undertaking as an excuse not to act.* **mag·ni·fied, mag·ni·fy·ing.**

magnifying glass lens that causes objects to appear larger than they actually are.

mag·ni·tude (măg′nə tood′ or măg′nə tūd′) size; largeness: *the* magnitude *of the universe; the* magnitude *of the task.*

mag·no·li·a (măg nō′lĭ ə) **1** a kind of shrub or tree with large pink or white blossoms and dark glossy leaves. Some kinds blossom in early spring before the leaves appear. **2** its flower.

Magnolia

mag·pie (măg′pī′) **1** a large black-and-white bird of the crow family. Magpies gather in chattering flocks. **2** a person who chatters continuously.

ma·hog·a·ny (mə-hŏg′ə nĭ) **1** any of several tropical trees having a hard wood, often used in making furniture. **2** the reddish-brown wood of this tree. **3** reddish brown; the color of mahogany. **ma·hog·a·nies.**

Magpie, about 20 in. long

maid (mād) **1** unmarried woman; maiden. **2** female servant. (Homonym: made)

maid·en (mā′dən) **1** a girl; an unmarried woman; maid. **2** unmarried: *my* maiden *aunt.* **3** of or like a maiden. **4** first: *a* maiden *voyage; a* maiden *effort.*

¹**mail** (māl) **1** letters, packages, magazines, etc., sent through the post office: *There was no* mail *today.* **2** government system of carrying and delivering letters, magazines, etc.: *Send that parcel by* mail. **3** to put into the mail. **4** carrying mail; having to do with mail: *a* mail *train; a* mail *bag.* [¹**mail** is from an Old German word (malha) meaning "wallet." Wallets and traveling bags were once used to carry mail.] (Homonym: male)

CHAIN

SCALE
Mail

²**mail** (māl) armor, especially garments made of or covered with interlocking metal links, metal rings, or overlapping metal scales. [²**mail** comes through Old French (maille) from a Latin word (macula) meaning "a spot," "mesh of a net."] (Homonym: male)

mail·box (māl′bŏks′) **1** box in which mail is placed when delivered. **2** box in which mail is placed to be collected by the post office.

mail·man (māl′măn′) person who collects and delivers mail; postman. **mail·men.**

maim (mām) to deprive (someone) of the use of a part of the body; mutilate; cripple: *A leg wound maimed the soldier for life.*

main (mān) **1** most important; central; principal: *a main street; the main idea.* **2** central pipe, line, or tube: *Water and gas mains usually run under the streets.* **3** wide stretch of sea; the open sea: *Treasure ships sailed across the Spanish Main from South America to Spain.* **4** sheer; unaided: *The boy lifted the weight by main force.* **5 in the main** for the most part: *I agree with you in the main.* **6 might and main** strength: *I pushed the wagon up the hill with all my might and main.* (Homonyms: Maine, mane)

Maine (mān) a New England State in the United States. (Homonyms: main, mane)

main·land (mān′lănd′) continent or broad stretch of land, as distinct from the islands off its coast.

main·ly (mān′lĭ) chiefly; principally; for the most part.

main·mast (mān′măst′ or mān′məst) the chief mast of a ship.

main·sail (mān′sāl′ or mān′səl) the largest sail on the mainmast of a ship.

main·spring (mān′sprĭng′) **1** the spring that makes a watch or clock go. **2** the chief driving force: *Ambition provided the mainspring for his energy.*

main·stay (mān′stā′) **1** strong rope or cable holding in place the mainmast of a sailing ship. **2** main support: *Bread is a mainstay of daily diet.*

main·tain (mān tān′) **1** to keep up: *A good student maintains his grades by regular study.* **2** to keep in good working condition; keep in operation: *To maintain our schools and highways we must spend money.* **3** to preserve; keep in existence: *We must maintain quiet in the library.* **4** to say firmly; insist: *He maintained that he had told the truth.* **5** to defend by argu-

ment: *Paul maintained his innocence when accused of breaking the window.* **6** to support: *George works hard to maintain a large family.*

main·te·nance (mān′tə nəns) **1** a maintaining or being maintained; support; upkeep: *the maintenance of an opinion; the maintenance of quiet; the maintenance of one's health.* **2** food and shelter: *The camp counselors receive maintenance and a small salary.*

maize (māz) **1** Indian corn. **2** a pale yellow; the color of corn. For picture, see **corn.** (Homonym: maze)

ma·jes·tic (mə jĕs′tĭk) dignified and impressive; noble; stately: *He bowed in the majestic presence of the king. The majestic mountains rose high above the plain.*

ma·jes·ti·cal·ly (mə jĕs′tə kə lĭ) in a stately or dignified manner: *The great ship moved majestically into the harbor.*

ma·jes·ty (măj′ĭs tĭ) **1** whatever moves to awe by its size or greatness: *the majesty of the sea.* **2** royal authority: *to offend against majesty.* **3 Majesty** (with "Your," "His," or "Her") used in speaking of or to a king, queen, emperor, or empress: *Her Majesty smiled.* **ma·jes·ties.**

ma·jor (mā′jər) **1** of first importance: *Carelessness is a major cause of highway accidents.* **2** greater; larger: *The major portion of the earth's surface is water.* **3** an army officer ranking below a lieutenant colonel and above a captain. **4** to follow a special course of study in school: *A boy who wants to design rockets should major in physics.* **5** principal subject of study: *He is taking an English major.* **6** student of a special subject: *A science major studies mathematics.* **7** relating to a musical scale or chord having half tones between the third and fourth and seventh and eighth notes.

ma·jor·i·ty (mə jŏr′ə tĭ or mə jôr′ə tĭ) **1** the greater number; larger part; more than half: *The majority of people enjoy watching television.* **2** the number of votes by which one side is elected: *Sue had a majority of eight votes for class president.* **3** legal age for voting, for managing one's own property, etc. **ma·jor·i·ties.**

fāte, făt, fâre, fär; bē, bĕt; bite, bĭt; nō, nŏt, nôr; fūse, fŭn, fûr; tōō, tŏŏk; foil; foul; thin; then; hw for wh as in what; zh for s as in usual; ə for a, e, i, o, u, as in ago, linen, peril, atom, minus

433

make

make (māk) **1** to build; put together; create: *Can you* make *a chocolate cake? Congress* makes *the nation's laws.* **2** brand; kind: *Father always buys the same* make *of car.* **3** to produce; cause: *Gossip always* makes *trouble.* **4** to carry on; conduct: *The United States does not want to* make *war.* **5** to have what is needed for: *He will* make *a good mayor.* **6** to cause to be or become: *A good purpose* makes *hard work a pleasure.* **7** to add up to: *Five and three* make *eight. That* makes *the third robin I've seen today.* **8** to cause to do or act: *Cold weather* makes *me shiver.* **9** to cause to succeed: *Your dance will* make *the show.* **10** to force to; compel to: *Please don't* make *me climb that ladder!* **11** to do or perform a movement: *to* make *a bow and face the class.* **12** to be enough for: *One high note does not* make *a singer.* **13** to reach; get to: *If we hurry we can* make *home by sundown.* **14** to win a position on: *Bob hopes to* make *the track team next spring.* **15** to win; gain; earn: *You can't* make *money by sleeping all day.* **16** to understand: *I can* make *nothing from these scribblings.* **17** to judge; estimate: *I* make *the total weight as ten tons.* **18** to set out upon; undertake: *I must* make *a visit to my dentist.* **19** to proceed; move: *to climb the hill and* make *toward the farm house.*

make away with **1** to kill; destroy: *In this play the villain tries to* make away with *the king.* **2** to consume; finish: *The hungry tiger soon* made away with *all the meat.* **3** to steal: *Someone* made away with *my coat.*

make believe to pretend: *We shall* make believe *we're pirates.*

make for **1** to move toward: *A good swimmer always* makes for *the shore in a storm.* **2** to lead to; produce: *Clear speech* makes for *understanding.*

make good **1** to succeed: *One seldom* makes good *without hard work.* **2** to pay back; restore: *The man who ruined my car must* make good *my loss.*

make off with to steal: *The puppy* made off with *a beefsteak.*

make out **1** to understand: *I can't* make out *what you're saying.* **2** to see clearly; distinguish: *The ship is too far away for me to* make out *her flag.* **3** to succeed:

malaria

How did you make out *in the race?* **4** to fill out; complete: *He* made out *his income tax return.* **5** to write out: *I must* make out *a list of things I need.*

make over **1** to remake; alter: *Sue* made over *her blue dress for the party.* **2** to transfer the ownership of: *Father* made over *the boat to my older brother.*

make up **1** to invent: *Let's* make up *a good story.* **2** to form; compose: *Water* makes up *most of the earth's surface.* **3** to put together; construct: *I* made up *a book from these loose pages.* **4** to complete; fill out: *We need one more player to* make up *the team.* **5** to write out; compile: *The teacher will* make up *the report cards today.* **6** to become friendly again: *They won't* make up *since they quarreled.* **7** to catch up on: *Students should* make up *the work they miss.* **8** to put on make-up: *The actors can* make up *in the dressing room.*

make up for **1** to compensate for; repay: *He must* make up for *the damage he caused.* **2** to regain; recover: *It is hard to* make up for *lost time.*

make up one's mind to decide.

made, mak·ing.

make-be·lieve (māk′bə lēv′) **1** pretended; sham; imagined: *Christopher hunted* make-believe *lions and tigers among the furniture. The* make-believe *flowers looked real at a distance.* **2** something imaginary or pretended: *children playing* make-believe.

mak·er (mā′kər) creator; builder; person who makes.

make·shift (māk′shĭft′) substitute for the real thing: *Until you find a hammer you can use your shoe as a* makeshift.

make-up (māk′ŭp′) **1** way a thing is put together; composition; structure: *Chemists often have to find out the* make-up *of new compounds.* **2** arrangement; layout: *The editor changed the* make-up *of the front page.* **3** disposition; nature: *Unselfishness seems to be part of her basic* make-up. **4** cosmetics: *She wore no* make-up *and was still beautiful.* **5** face paint, powder, false hair, and other things used by an actor to change his appearance.

mal·a·dy (măl′ə dī) sickness; illness; disease. **mal·a·dies.**

ma·lar·i·a (mə lâr′ĭ ə) disease causing chills, fever, and weakness. Malaria germs are

434

carried in the body of a certain kind of mosquito and given to man by the mosquito's bite.

male (māl) **1** person or animal that may at some time become a father. **2** belonging to or describing such persons or animals. **3** made up of men or boys: *A male choir sang at the party.* (Homonym: mail)

mal·ice (măl′ĭs) desire to harm; spite: *Tattling is usually inspired by* malice.

ma·li·cious (mə lĭsh′əs) spiteful; unkind; with evil intent: *That false rumor is a piece of* malicious *gossip.* **ma·li·cious·ly.**

ma·lign (mə līn′) **1** harmful; injurious: *Cancer is a malign growth in the body.* **2** malicious; evil: *Everyone suffers under the malign rule of a tyrant.* **3** to speak evil of; slander: *to malign an innocent person by spreading gossip.* **ma·lign·ly.**

ma·lig·nant (mə lĭg′nənt) **1** wishing or causing harm or evil; filled with great hate or malice: *a malignant plot; his malignant fury.* **2** likely to cause death: *a malignant disease.* **ma·lig·nant·ly.**

mal·lard (măl′ərd) a kind of green-headed wild duck, with a blue wing patch between white stripes.

Mallard, about 2 ft. long

mal·le·a·ble (măl′ĭ ə bəl) capable of being worked or hammered into shape: *to work with* malleable *iron.*

mal·let (măl′ĭt) **1** a hammer with a wooden head. **2** a long-handled wooden hammer used in croquet and polo.

mal·nu·tri·tion (măl′nū trĭsh′ən) a not getting enough of, or a getting the wrong kind of, food.

Mallet

malt (môlt) barley or other grain made to sprout, after which it is roasted and dried for use in brewing beer and in the preparing of a food extract.

mal·treat (măl trēt′) to treat roughly or neglect; misuse: *The poor rider* maltreated *his horse.*

ma·ma or **mam·ma** (mä′mə) word for "mother."

mam·mal (măm′əl) animal that has a backbone and (in the female) milk glands for feeding its young. Most of the common four-footed, furry or hairy animals are mammals. Human beings, bats, and whales are also mammals.

mam·moth (măm′əth) **1** a large, hairy elephant with curved tusks. Mammoths disappeared from earth 10,000 years ago. **2** gigantic; huge.

Mammoth, up to 13 ft. high at shoulder

man (măn) **1** a grown male human being. **2** mankind; the human race: *In the twentieth century,* man *has made rapid progress in science.* **3** person: *Every* man *to his own taste.* **4** soldier or member of a military force: *The major led his* men *into battle.* **5** player on a team: *The best* man *on our junior team was hurt.* **6** male employee; workman: *The electric company sent a* man *to fix our lights.* **7** a boy or man with manly qualities, such as strength and bravery: *We told the boy to stop crying and act like a* man. **8** one of the pieces in checkers, chess, or similar games. **9** to furnish or staff with men: *to* man *a ship.* **10** to take one's place for work or duty at: *One of you* man *the observation post while the others* man *the gun.* **11 man and wife** husband and wife. **men; manned, man·ning.**

man·age (măn′ĭj) **1** to be in charge of: *to* manage *a store; to* manage *a baseball team.* **2** to control: *Nobody could* manage *that wild horse.* **3** to contrive; succeed somehow: *I* managed *to get the cat down from the tree.* **man·aged, man·ag·ing.**

man·age·ment (măn′ĭj mənt) **1** direction, control, or handling; a managing: *By good* management *the new owner doubled the profits of the business.* **2** people who control and direct the affairs of a business: *When labor and* management *cannot agree, sometimes an outsider is asked to consider both sides of their problems.*

man·ag·er (măn′ĭj ər) **1** person who has control or direction; person in charge: *sales* manager; *the* manager *of a team.*

fāte, făt, fâre, fär; bē, bĕt; bite, bĭt; nō, nŏt, nôr; fūse, fŭn, fûr; tōō, tŏŏk; foil; foul; thin; then; hw for wh as in what; zh for s as in usual; ə for a, e, i, o, u, as in ago, linen, peril, atom, minus

435

2 person who conducts household affairs: *My mother is a good* manager.

man·date (măn'dāt) **1** an official order; a command. **2** the will of the people shown by their votes in an election: *to receive a* mandate *in the elections to change foreign policy.*

man·di·ble (măn'də bəl) a jaw or jawlike part, as the beak of a bird or the biting part of an insect's mouth.

man·do·lin (măn'də lĭn') a musical instrument with a rounded tapering sound box and wire strings, played by plucking.

mane (mān) the long hair on or about the neck of a horse, lion, zebra, and some other animals. (Homonyms: main, Maine)

Mandolin

ma·neu·ver (mə nōō'vər) **1** planned movement or change of position of troops, ships, etc.: *The general cut off the enemy army from its supplies by a clever* maneuver. **2** to move (troops, ships, etc.) according to a plan: *The admiral maneuvered his fleet so well that the enemy battleship could not escape.* **3** to perform or carry out planned military movements: *The two ships maneuvered so that they were in a position to attack.* **4** a clever, skillful movement or action: *Our team scored by using an unexpected maneuver.* **5** to move or carry out an action in a clever, skillful way: *The driver maneuvered his car into the narrow parking space.* **6 maneuvers** practice exercises carried out by military forces: *to send new recruits out on* maneuvers.

man·ful (măn'fəl) like a man; manly; determined: *He accepted his assignment in a manful spirit.* **man·ful·ly.**

man·ga·nese (măng'gə nēs' or măn'gə nēz') a hard, brittle, gray metal element, used in making glass, paint, and hard steel.

man·ger (măn'jər) trough or box in a stable or barn, from which cattle and horses eat.

¹man·gle (măng'gəl) **1** to cut or tear; maim; crush: *The raccoon mangled its paw in a trap.* **2** to spoil by making mistakes; botch: *to mangle a piece of music.* **man·gled, man·gling.** [¹**mangle** is from an Old French word (mahaignier) meaning "to maim."]

²man·gle (măng'gəl) **1** machine or electric appliance that presses cloth and clothes by means of rollers. **2** to iron or press in a mangle. **man·gled, man·gling.** [²**mangle** is from a Dutch word (mangel) meaning "a machine for smoothing."]

man·go (măng'gō) **1** an oval or kidney-shaped fruit with a thin tough yellow or reddish skin. **2** the evergreen tropical tree that bears this fruit. **man·goes** or **man·gos.**

Mango

man·grove (măng'grōv or măn'grōv) a tropical tree or shrub that grows in swampy ground. Its wide-spreading branches send down roots, thus forming new branches that twine together and form thickets.

man·hole (măn'hōl') an opening used by workmen who build and repair sewage systems, wiring systems, etc.

man·hood (măn'hŏod) **1** the state or time of being a man: *to arrive at* manhood. **2** manly qualities; manliness: *Courage to stand up for your own beliefs is a sign of* manhood. **3** men as a group: *The manhood of the nation answered the call to arms.*

ma·ni·a (mā'nĭ ə) **1** violent insanity; frenzy. **2** wild enthusiasm: *Mrs. Olds has a mania for antiques.*

ma·ni·ac (mā'nĭ ăk') raving lunatic; madman.

man·i·cure (măn'ə kūr') **1** a treatment of the hands and nails. **2** to give a manicure to. **man·i·cured, man·i·cur·ing.**

man·i·fest (măn'ə fĕst') **1** clear; obvious: *The evidence made it* manifest *that the thief was guilty.* **2** to show; make plain: *Tom* manifested *an interest in chemistry even as a child.* **3** a list of a ship's cargo. **man·i·fest·ly.**

man·i·fes·ta·tion (măn'ə fĕs tā'shən) **1** a showing; making plain or evident. **2** something that makes manifest; a display or proof: *Standing up for a friend in trouble is a* manifestation *of loyalty.*

man·i·fold (măn'ə fōld') **1** many and varied; of many kinds: *his* manifold *duties.* **2** including many parts or forms: *a* manifold *interest in science.* **man·i·fold·ly.**

ma·ni·oc (măn′ĭ ŏk′) **1** a tropical plant with a starchy, edible root; the cassava. **2** the root of this plant from which tapioca is prepared.

ma·nip·u·late (mə nĭp′yŏo lāt′) **1** to handle or operate skillfully, especially with the hands: *Jerry can* manipulate *his puppets so well that they seem to be alive.* **2** to manage or control by the shrewd use of influence, often unfairly: *to* manipulate *public opinion by spreading rumors.* **3** to handle dishonestly; twist to one's own advantage: *The bookkeeper* manipulated *the expense accounts in order to steal from the company that employed him.* **ma·nip·u·lat·ed, ma·nip·u·lat·ing.**

man·kind (măn′kīnd′) the human race; all human beings.

man·li·ness (măn′lĭ nĭs) the qualities of a man; a being manly: *The boy showed a* manliness *beyond his years.*

man·ly (măn′lĭ) having the qualities of a fine man (brave, frank, honorable, strong, etc.): *a* manly *appearance.* **man·li·er, man·li·est.**

man·na (măn′ə) **1** in the Bible, food miraculously supplied to the children of Israel during their wandering in the wilderness. **2** anything much needed that is unexpectedly supplied: *The words of praise were* manna *to the discouraged boy.*

man·ner (măn′ər) **1** person's way of acting or of doing things; individual style: *The announcer had an easy, natural* manner *in reading the news.* **2** way in which a thing is done or happens: *Solve this problem in the usual* manner. **3** kind; sort: *What* manner *of man is he?* **4 manners** (1) ways of behaving toward others: *Good* manners *are based on thoughtfulness for others.* (2) way of life; habits and customs: *This book tells about the* manners *and morals of the ancient Romans.* (Homonym: manor)

man-of-war (măn′əv wôr′) a warship. **men-of-war.**

man·or (măn′ər) large estate with part of the land kept for the use of the owner and the rest rented out and farmed by tenants who pay the owner in produce, services, or money. (Homonym: manner)

man·sion (măn′shən) large house; stately residence: *to dwell in a* mansion.

man·tel (măn′təl) the ornamental frame of a fireplace and the shelf above it. (Homonym: mantle)

Mantel

man·tel·piece (măn′təl pēs′) shelf over a fireplace; a mantel.

man·tle (măn′təl) **1** a long, loose cape. **2** to cover; hide: *Snow* mantled *the ground. Ivy* mantled *the old tower.* **man·tled, man·tling.** (Homonym: mantle)

man·u·al (măn′yŏo əl) **1** handbook that is easy to understand and use and that deals with a certain subject or tells how to do something. **2** guidebook that tells how to use another book. **3** of the hands; done or operated by the hands: *hard* manual *labor; a machine with* manual *controls.* **man·u·al·ly.**

Mantle

manual training training in work that is done with the hands; practice in woodwork and other arts and crafts.

man·u·fac·ture (măn′yŏo făk′chər) **1** to make by hand or in a factory, usually in large numbers: *The plant* manufactures *office furniture.* **2** to make or make up (anything): *to* manufacture *an excuse.* **3** a making; production: *the* manufacture *of household appliances.* **man·u·fac·tured, man·u·fac·tur·ing.**

man·u·fac·tur·er (măn′yŏo făk′chər ər) a person or company whose business is manufacturing.

ma·nure (mə nūr′ or mə nŏor′) **1** animal waste used to make the soil richer; fertilizer. **2** to put manure on or in. **ma·nured, ma·nur·ing.**

man·u·script (măn′yŏo skrĭpt′) **1** book or paper written by hand or on the typewriter, especially an author's copy for the printer. Before the invention of printing, all books were manuscripts. **2** handwriting, as opposed to printing. **3 manuscript writing** handwriting in which each letter is formed like a printed letter.

---

fāte, făt, fâre, fär; bē, bĕt; bīte, bĭt; nō, nŏt, nôr; fūse, fŭn, fûr; tōō, tŏŏk; foil; foul; thin; then; hw for wh as in *what*; zh for s as in u*s*ual; ə for a, e, i, o, u, as in *a*go, lin*e*n, per*i*l, at*o*m, min*u*s

man·y (měn′ĭ) **1** a large number: *In that village*, many *of the houses are white*. **2** a large number of: *There are* many *trees in the park*. **3** a great number of people: *Were there* many *at school the day of the storm?* **4 a good many** a fairly large number. **more, most.**

map (măp) **1** drawing, picture, or model of the surface of the earth or a part of it. **2** chart of the skies, showing the positions of the stars, etc. **3** to draw or make a map. **map out** to plan: *The city* mapped out *a campaign to get rid of slums.* **mapped, map·ping.**

ma·ple (mā′pəl) **1** a tree of several varieties all of which have deeply notched leaves, gray bark, and, usually, symmetrical shape. Some kinds furnish maple sugar; others, fine lumber; and all are valuable shade trees. **2** the wood of this tree. **3** of or made of maple. **4** flavored with maple.

Leaves and seeds of sugar maple

maple sugar sugar made by boiling down the sap of certain maples.

mar (mär) to damage; deface; spoil: *Don't* mar *the table top by leaving a wet glass on it.* **marred, mar·ring.**

Mar. March.

mar·a·thon (măr′ə thŏn′) **1** long-distance foot race. The official length is 26 miles, 385 yards. **2** any endurance contest: *a dance* marathon.

ma·raud·er (mə rôd′ər) one who roves about searching for booty and plunder: *In ancient times people living along the coast feared pirate* marauders.

mar·ble (mär′bəl) **1** a hard limestone, mottled in color, which can be given a smooth finish. Marble is used as building material and for sculpture. **2** made of marble: *the* marble *columns in the church.* **3** small, smooth, colored ball, made of glass or agate, used in playing a child's game. **4 marbles** the child's game played with these little balls.

march (märch) **1** to walk with regular steps, as soldiers do. **2** a regular step or walk, especially of soldiers. **3** a foot journey of a certain distance, usually made by soldiers:

It was a day's march *back to camp.* **4** to move forward at a steady pace: *Time* marches *on.* **5** steady movement forward; progress: *the onward* march *of science.* **6** to lead or cause to move at a regular pace: *The sergeant* marched *his men through the swamp. The boy was* marched *off to bed by his father at ten o'clock.* **7** musical composition to march by.

March (märch) third month of the year. March has 31 days.

Mar·di gras (mär′dĭ grä) the last day before Lent. It is celebrated in New Orleans and some other cities with public merriment and festivities.

mare (mâr) female horse, donkey, zebra, etc.

mar·ga·rine (mär′jə rĭn) a butterlike spread for bread, made from vegetable or animal fats.

mar·gin (mär′jĭn) **1** border around print or writing on a page: *Don't write in the* margin *of the page.* **2** extra amount allowed beyond what is needed: *He gave himself a* margin *of ten minutes to catch the train.* **3** edge; rim: *along the* margin *of the river.*

mar·i·gold (măr′ə gōld′) **1** a garden plant with blossoms of many colors. **2** the flower of this plant.

ma·ri·na (mə rē′nə) section of a harbor where sailboats, motorboats, and yachts are moored and serviced.

ma·rine (mə rēn′) **1** of or having to do with the sea or navigation: *a* marine *plant; to take out* marine *insurance.* **2** one of a body of troops originally trained for sea service and as a landing force, but now serving also on land and in the air; a member of the U.S. Marine Corps.

mar·i·ner (măr′ə nər) a sailor.

mar·i·o·nette (măr′ĭ ə nĕt′) a jointed puppet made to move and gesture by strings or by hand.

mar·i·time (măr′ə tīm′) **1** having to do with the sea, boats, shipping, or navigation: *the study of* maritime *law.* **2** bordering on the sea; coastal: *Boston and San Francisco are* maritime *cities.*

Marionette

¹**mark** (märk) **1** a line, dot, scratch, stain, or spot on a surface: *His muddy shoes left a* mark *on the rug.* **2** to make a line, dot,

scratch, stain, or spot on a surface: *The wet vase* marked *the table with a white ring.* **3** a sign or symbol written or placed to show something: *The* mark *on the boulder showed that they were halfway up the mountain.* **4** to write, make, or place a sign or symbol in order to show something: *The architect* marked *the spot where the living room was to be.* **5** to show something by means of a sign or symbol: *The circle on the map* marks *the place where the treasure is buried.* **6** sign; indication: *An ability to make the right decision in an emergency is a* mark *of intelligence.* **7** to show clearly; indicate; characterize: *His record* marks *him as a promising candidate for class president.* **8** to single out; select: *They* marked *him for early promotion.* **9** to pay attention to; heed: *You* mark *my word.* **10** a grade, in number or letter form, given for schoolwork. **11** to give a grade on or set the value of: *to* mark *a test; to* mark *the price.* **12** something aimed at; a target; a goal: *The arrow hit the* mark. *His work failed to reach the* mark · he *had set for himself.* **13** lasting impression; influence: *A great man leaves his* mark *on the world.* **14 beside the mark** not to the point: *The answers given by the witness were* beside the mark. **15 make one's mark** to achieve success: *to make one's* mark *in the world.*

mark off to separate or divide with lines: *to* mark off *a distance on a map.*

mark out 1 to mark off completely. **2** to set apart.

mark time 1 to move the feet in marching time without going forward. **2** to make no further progress: *We will* mark time *in our sales campaign until the new manager arrives and explains his plans.* [¹**mark** is a form of an Old English word (mearc) meaning "boundary."]

²**mark** (märk) the unit of money in Germany. [²**mark** in this meaning is from a German word of the same spelling.]

marked (märkt) **1** clear; plain; noticeable: *The patient showed a* marked *improvement after being given the new drug.* **2** having a mark or marks: *The lumbermen cut the*

marked *trees.* **3** set apart; watched closely: *a* marked *man.* **mark·ed·ly** (mär′kĭd li).

mar·ket (mär′kĭt) **1** place where goods are bought and sold: *a food* market. **2** to buy in a market: *I* marketed *this morning.* **3** to sell; offer for sale: *The cattle are* marketed *in the fall.* **4** a buying and selling: *The used-car* market *is very active when new models come out.* **5** an area or country where goods may be sold: *a foreign* market *for cars.* **6** demand: *There is a big* market *for warm clothing during the winter.* **7 in the market for** buying or wanting to buy. **8 on the market** up for sale.

mark·ing (mär′kĭng) a mark or marks: *The* markings *on the moon look like a face.*

marks·man (märks′-mən) person who is skilled in shooting. **marks·men.**

mar·ma·lade (mär′-mə lād′) a jellylike preserve made of oranges and other fruit, including their peel.

Marmoset, 18 in. long

mar·mo·set (mär′mə zĕt′) a South American monkey about the size of a squirrel. It has long silky fur.

mar·mot (mär′mət) **1** an animal of the western United States that looks like a woodchuck. **2** a woodchuck; a prairie dog.

¹**ma·roon** (mə rōon′) to leave helpless and alone: *When our boat drifted away, we were* marooned *on the island for two nights.* [¹**maroon** is from a French word (mar-rŏn) meaning "a Negro slave of the West Indies." The French word comes from a Spanish word (cimarron) meaning "wild."]

Marmot, about 27 in. long

²**ma·roon** (mə rōon′) **1** dark-red or reddish-brown color. **2** dark red; reddish brown:

fāte, făt, fâre, fär; bē, bĕt; bīte, bĭt; nō, nŏt, nôr; fūse, fŭn, fûr; tōō, tŏŏk; foil; foul; thin; ~~then~~;
hw for wh as in *what*; zh for s as in u*s*ual; ə for a, e, i, o, u, as in *ago*, lin*e*n, per*i*l, at*o*m, min*u*s

439

The king wore a maroon *cloak trimmed with ermine.* [²**maroon** is from a French word (marron) meaning "chestnut."]

mar·quis (mär′kwis) a nobleman ranking below a duke. Also spelled **marquess.**

mar·riage (mär′ij) **1** the relationship between a husband and wife; married life. **2** a wedding: *There were two* marriages *at our church today.*

mar·ried (mär′īd) **1** of marriage: *a married life.* **2** joined in marriage; wedded: *a married couple; a married woman.*

mar·row (mär′ō) the soft substance that fills the hollow of a bone.

mar·ry (mär′ī) **1** to take for a husband or wife; wed: *John asked Ann to* marry *him.* **2** to enter into a marriage: *Do you think you are old enough to* marry? **3** to join as husband and wife; perform the wedding ceremony: *A minister* married *them.* **4** to give in marriage: *He* married *his youngest daughter to a writer.* **mar·ried, mar·ry·ing.**

Mars (märz) **1** planet fourth in order of distance from the sun. Mars is noted for its red light. **2** the Roman god of war.

marsh (märsh) low wet land; a swamp.

mar·shal (mär′shəl) **1** a federal officer having duties like those of a sheriff. **2** a fire or police chief. **3** official in charge of ceremonies: *the* marshal *of a parade.* **4** officer of highest rank in some armies. **5** to put in order; organize: *to* marshal *ideas for a debate.* (Homonym: martial)

marsh·mal·low (märsh′măl′ō) a soft, spongy, white candy with a vanilla flavor.

marsh·y (mär′shi) of or like a marsh or swamp: *a marshy meadow.* **marsh·i·er, marsh·i·est.**

mart (märt) market; trading place.

mar·ten (mär′tən) **1** a slender-bodied animal of the weasel family, valued for its dark-brown fur. **2** the fur of this animal. (Homonym: martin)

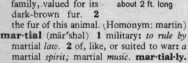

American marten, about 2 ft. long

mar·tial (mär′shəl) **1** military: *to rule by* martial *law.* **2** of, like, or suited to war: *a* martial *spirit;* martial *music.* **mar·tial·ly.** (Homonym: marshal)

mar·tin (mär′tən) any of several birds in the swallow family, one of the most common being the purple martin. (Homonym: marten)

mar·tyr (mär′tər) **1** person who suffers torture or death for the sake of his religion or principles. **2** to torture or put to death for loyalty to a belief. **3** to make suffer greatly; persecute. **4** one who endures great suffering, especially silent suffering. **5 a martyr to** sufferer from: *He's a* martyr *to asthma.*

Purple martin, about 8 in. long

mar·tyr·dom (mär′tər dəm) **1** a suffering of death for the sake of one's principles or one's religion. **2** any long, intense suffering: *to endure the* martyrdom *of arthritis.*

mar·vel (mär′vəl) **1** extraordinary thing; a wonder: *A large dam is a* marvel *of modern engineering.* **2** to be struck with wonder: *We* marveled *at the Grand Canyon.*

mar·vel·ous or **mar·vel·lous** (mär′vəl əs) astonishing; surprising; wonderful. **mar·vel·ous·ly** or **mar·vel·lous·ly.**

Mar·y·land (mer′ə lənd) a State on the eastern coast of the United States.

mas·cot (măs′kŏt) person, animal, or thing that is supposed to bring good luck: *The Navy team's* mascot *is a goat.*

mas·cu·line (măs′kŏŏ lin) **1** of or for boys or men: *John and Peter are* masculine *names.* **2** having the qualities of a man; manly: *a* masculine *handwriting.*

mash (măsh) **1** to squash; crush: *The elephant's heavy feet* mashed *down the grass.* **2** to make into a soft, pulplike mixture: *Mother* mashed *the potatoes.* **3** a soft, pulplike mixture: *The baby ate a* mash *of bananas and water.* **4** warm mixture of bran or meal and water used as food for animals.

AFRICAN

WELDER'S

Mask

mask (măsk) **1** a covering to hide or protect the face: *Each dancer took off his* mask *at midnight.* **2** a false face, often grotesque, worn in fun or drama to make the wearer look like someone else. **3** to disguise; conceal; hide: *Clouds* masked *the moon.* (Homonym: masque)

ma·son (mā′sən) person who works or builds with stone, brick, etc.

ma·son·ry (mā′sən ri) **1** something built of stone or brick. **2** the trade or craft of a mason. **ma·son·ries.**

Brick and stone masonry

masque (măsk) **1** form of entertainment consisting of pantomime and dance, sometimes with words. It was particularly popular in the 17th century. **2** a masquerade; masked ball. (Homonym: mask)

mas·quer·ade (măs′kə rād′) **1** party or dance at which the guests wear masks and costumes. **2** to put on a disguise and costume: *On Halloween the children masquerade.* **3** to wear a disguise: *The spy masqueraded as a reporter.* **4** a disguise: *the masquerade of a prince as a peasant.* **mas·quer·ad·ed, mas·quer·ad·ing.**

¹mass (măs) **1** quantity of matter without regular shape; lump: *The baker shaped the mass of dough into a loaf.* **2** large number or quantity: *a mass of people in the courthouse square; a mass of lava from the volcano.* **3** to bring or come together into one group: *The general massed his troops for an attack. The troops massed for the attack.* **4** size; bulk: *The huge mass of the pyramid amazed me.* **5** main or larger part: *The mass of voters want a new school.* **6** of or having to do with a large number or quantity: *a mass production.* **7** in science, quantity of matter in a body or object. **8 the masses** the general public. [**¹mass** is from the Latin word (massa) meaning "a lump," "a mass."]

²mass or **Mass** (măs) celebration of the Lord's Supper or Holy Eucharist (service of the Catholic Church). [**²mass** is a form of an Old English word (mæsse) which

comes from a Latin phrase uttered by the priest at the end of the service: "Ite, missa est," meaning "Go, you are dismissed."]

Mass. Massachusetts.

Mas·sa·chu·setts (măs′ə choo′sits) a State on the northeast coast of the United States.

mas·sa·cre (măs′ə kər) **1** a killing or slaughter of a large number of people or animals: *The massacre of helpless prisoners is a savage act.* **2** to kill a large number without mercy. **mas·sa·cred, mas·sa·cring.**

mas·sage (mə säzh′) **1** a rubbing, kneading, or vibrating of the muscles and joints to take away stiffness, soreness, or fatigue. **2** to rub, knead, or vibrate the body or some part of it: *to massage the scalp.* **mas·saged, mas·sag·ing.**

mas·sive (măs′ĭv) **1** solid and heavy; bulky: *Our way was blocked by a massive door.* **2** strong and imposing: *his massive features; massive evidence.* **mas·sive·ly.**

mass production manufacture of goods in large quantities, especially by machinery.

mast (măst) **1** upright pole for supporting the sail of a ship or the boom of a derrick. **2** any upright pole, as a flagstaff.

Masts

mas·ter (măs′tər) **1** person who has control of something or rules the actions and behavior of others: *the dog's master; the ship's master.* **2** to get control over; dominate: *The animal trainer mastered the lions and taught them tricks.* **3** to get complete understanding of; become skillful in: *It takes practice to master a foreign language.* **4** person who has great skill or ability: *The teacher is a master at telling stories.* **5** expert; chief: *a master carpenter.* **6** in some schools, a male teacher. **7 old master** (**1**) one of the great artists of the past. (**2**) a painting by such an artist. **8 Master** title used before a young boy's name, instead of Mr. **9 Master of** (**1**) person given an advanced degree by a college or university. (**2**) the advanced degree given.

---

fāte, făt, fâre, fär; bē, bĕt; bīte, bĭt; nō, nŏt, nôr; fūse, fŭn, fûr; tōō, tŏŏk; foil; foul; thin; then; hw for wh as in *wh*at; zh for s as in usual; ə for a, e, i, o, u, as in *a*go, lin*e*n, per*i*l, at*o*m, min*u*s

mas·ter·ful (măs′tər fəl) **1** expert; showing mastery: *The tennis champion had a masterful serve.* **2** inclined to dominate or gain control: *The little girl didn't like her older brother's masterful tone.* **mas·ter·ful·ly.**

mas·ter·ly (măs′tər lǐ) showing mastery: *a masterly touch on the piano.*

mas·ter·piece (măs′tər pēs′) **1** something, especially a work of art, done with great skill; an almost perfect piece of work: *Many consider this statue a* masterpiece. **2** the best thing that a person has written, made, painted, etc.: *"Huckleberry Finn" is considered Mark Twain's* masterpiece.

mas·ter·y (măs′tə rǐ) **1** a control; a rule: *to have complete* mastery *over one's own temper.* **2** skill and knowledge; a command: *a good* mastery *of arithmetic.* **mas·ter·ies.**

mast·head (măst′hěd′) top of a ship's mast, especially of the lower mast, used as a lookout.

mas·tiff (măs′tǐf) kind of large, short-haired dog with heavy jowls. It is usually light brown in color.

Mastiff, about 3½ ft. high at shoulder

mat (măt) **1** flat piece of cloth, plastic, woven straw, etc.: *a door* mat; *a place* mat *on the table.* **2** pad covering the floor for gymnasium exercises or wrestling. **3** anything entangled in a thick mass: *a mat of hair.* **4** to tangle together in a thick mass: *The sea breeze* matted *his hair.* **5** to cover with a mat. **mat·ted, mat·ting.**

mat·a·dor (măt′ə dôr′) man who kills the bull in a bullfight.

¹match (măch) small stick of wood or pasteboard with a tip that bursts into flame when rubbed or scratched. [**¹match** is from an Old French word (*mesche*) meaning "wick."]

²match (măch) **1** thing that is exactly like another: *I am looking for a* match *for this paint.* **2** to be alike: *The two candlesticks* match *each other exactly.* **3** person or thing that is suitable for another: *Tan shoes are a good* match *for a brown dress.* **4** person or animal that can compete with another on equal terms: *She is not yet a* match *for her*

mother in cooking. **5** to meet on equal terms: *As hard as I try, I can't* match *him in tennis.* **6** to put together two things that are alike or go together: *to* match *socks.* **7** marriage. **8** person considered for marriage: *He is a good* match. **9** a contest: *a wrestling* match. **10** to place in a contest with another: *The promoter* matched *the two fighters.* [**²match** is a form of an Old English word (*gemæcca*) meaning "one of a pair."]

match·less (măch′lǐs) not having an equal: *The great pianist played with* matchless *skill.* **match·less·ly.**

mate (māt) **1** the other of a pair: *the* mate *to a shoe.* **2** companion; associate: *He and his* mates *left the school grounds.* **3** husband or wife. **4** to marry. **5** the male or female of a pair of animals. **6** to join as mates: *Birds* mate *in the spring and build their nests.* **7** officer on a merchant ship ranking below the captain. **mat·ed, mat·ing.**

ma·te·ri·al (mə tǐr′ǐ əl) **1** stuff of which something is made. **2** made of matter; physical; not spiritual or mental: *Stones, chairs, and the human body are* material *things.* **3** woven fabric; cloth. **4** one or more persons likely to be useful or good in some particular field: *splendid* material *for the team.* **5** information, such as facts and figures, to be used in a book, composition, report, etc. **6** essential; important: *The man who saw the shooting was held as a* material *witness.* **7 materials** things needed to do something: *to secure building* materials.

ma·te·ri·al·ly (mə tǐr′ǐ ə lǐ) **1** considerably: *The music teacher's ideas helped* materially *in planning the play.* **2** in a physical or material way: *The enemy was strong* materially *but weak in leadership.*

ma·ter·nal (mə tûr′nəl) **1** like or of a mother; motherly: *The old hen took a* maternal *interest in the motherless ducklings.* **2** on the mother's side of the family: *Your mother's father is your* maternal *grandfather.* **ma·ter·nal·ly.**

math·e·mat·i·cal (măth′ə măt′ǐ kəl) **1** having to do with mathematics: *Engineers need* mathematical *training.* **2** exact; carefully calculated: *The parts of a fine watch are made with* mathematical *precision.* **math·e·mat·i·cal·ly.**

math·e·ma·ti·cian (măth′ə mə tĭsh′ən) **1** person trained in mathematics and engaged in it as a profession. **2** person skillful in mathematics.

math·e·mat·ics (măth′ə măt′ĭks) the study that deals with numbers, amounts and quantities, measurements, shapes, sizes, etc. Arithmetic and geometry are branches of mathematics.

mat·i·nee or **mat·i·née** (măt′ə nā′) afternoon performance of a play, movie, etc.

ma·tron (mā′trən) **1** married woman or widow, especially an older one. **2** a woman in charge of household affairs or of a group of people in an institution: *a hospital matron: the matron in a prison.*

mat·ter (măt′ər) **1** everything that takes up space and has weight; material substance: *Some of the matter in an atom bomb is changed to energy.* **2** the content or thought (of something written or spoken): *The matter of the lecture was good, but the delivery was bad.* **3** affair; business: *Burglary is a matter for the police to handle.* **4** to be of importance: *It hardly matters one way or the other.* **5** importance; significance: *an idea of little matter.* **6** printed material: *advertising matter.* **7** pus. **8 as a matter of fact** indeed; to tell the truth: *As a matter of fact, I talked with him this morning.* **9 for that matter** as far as that goes; in regard to that: *Well, for that matter, his schooling does not fit him for the job.* **10 matter of course** thing taken for granted; natural and expected thing: *A late breakfast was with him a matter of course.* **11 no matter** (1) of no importance. (2) in spite of; regardless of: *I will come no matter what happens.*

mat·ter-of-fact (măt′ər əv făkt′) concerned with facts rather than feelings; literal and practical: *We discussed our differences in a matter-of-fact tone.*

mat·tress (măt′rĭs) **1** a cloth-covered pad of springy material for a bed or cot. **2** any soft, springy bed: *The campers made a mattress of pine branches.*

Mattress

ma·ture (mə chŏŏr′ or mə tūr′ or mə tŏŏr′) **1** fully grown: *When a kitten is mature, it is called a cat.* **2** to become fully grown: *Most animals mature faster than human beings.* **3** grown-up; not silly or childish: *a mature mind.* **4** ripe: *A green peach is not mature.* **5** to become ripe. **6** fully developed or completed: *It will be several years before plans for the housing project are mature.* **7** to develop fully or reach completion. **8** to become due for payment: *When your savings bond matures, you can collect its full value.* **ma·tured, ma·tur·ing; ma·ture·ly.**

ma·tu·ri·ty (mə chŏŏr′ə tĭ or mə tūr′ə tĭ or mə tŏŏr′ə tĭ) **1** a being mature, fully grown, or fully developed: *A puppy that has reached maturity is called a dog.* **2** a being grown-up and not silly or childish: *Willingness to take responsibility is a sign of maturity.* **3** a being due for payment: *What is the date of maturity on your savings bond?*

matz·o (măt′sə) thin, flat piece of unleavened bread, resembling a cracker, eaten by Jews during Passover. **matz·os** or **matz·oth** (măt′sōth).

maul (môl) **1** to handle in a rough way; bruise or injure: *The lion mauled the hunter.* **2** large, heavy hammer.

mau·so·le·um (mô′sə lē′əm) large and imposing tomb.

mauve (mōv) **1** pale purple color. **2** of a pale purple color.

maw (mô) **1** mouth and throat of an animal. **2** stomach of an animal. **3** the crop of a bird.

max·im (măk′sĭm) a general truth expressed as a wise saying. "Honesty is the best policy" is a maxim.

max·i·mum (măk′sə məm) **1** the most, highest, or greatest; top: *The maximum temperature today was 80 degrees.* **2** greatest amount: *We will pay a maximum of ten dollars for the present.* **max·i·ma** or **max·i·mums.**

may (mā) **1** will possibly: *If I am sick, I may have to stay in bed. It may rain.* **2** am, is, or are allowed to: *You may come in.* **3** word used to express a wish or a hope: *He said, "May all your days be happy!"* **might.**

---

fāte, făt, fâre, fär; bē, bĕt; bīte, bĭt; nō, nŏt, nôr; fūse, fŭn, fûr; tōō, tŏŏk; foil; foul; thin; ~~then~~; hw for wh as in *wh*at; zh for s as in u*s*ual; ə for a, e, i, o, u, as in *a*go, lin*e*n, per*i*l, at*o*m, min*u*s

May

May (mā) fifth month of the year. May has 31 days.

Ma·ya (mä′yə) a Central American Indian civilization that reached its height between 600 and 900 A.D.

may·be (mā′bē) perhaps; possibly: *Well, maybe I'll do it tomorrow.*

May Day the first day of May, often celebrated as a spring festival with outdoor dances, games, and other activities.

may·on·naise (mā′ə nāz′) thick sauce or dressing made of beaten egg yolks, olive oil, lemon juice or vinegar, and seasoning.

may·or (mā′ər) chief elected official of a city or town.

may·pole (mā′pōl′) tall pole, decorated with ribbons and flowers, around which people dance on May Day.

maze (māz) 1 a crisscrossing of passageways, tunnels, or paths, through which it is hard to find one's way. 2 state of confusion or indecision: *I was in such a maze I couldn't answer.* 3 a tangle; jumble: *The inside of a radio is a maze of wires.* (Homonym: maize)

Md. Maryland.

M.D. Doctor of Medicine.

me (mē) used of the person who is writing or speaking when he is not doing or acting, but is being acted upon or is the object of action: *He saw me. He gave the book to me. He did it for me.*

¹mead (mēd) intoxicating drink made from honey: *After the battle the warriors drank mead in the castle hall.* [¹mead is a form of an Old English word (meodu) of the same meaning.]

²mead (mēd) grassy field; meadow: *The shepherd wandered through the mead.* [²mead is a form of an Old English word (mǣd).]

mead·ow (mĕd′ō) grassy field used for grazing animals or growing hay.

meadow lark a North American songbird with a yellow breast.

mea·ger (mē′gər) 1 scanty; insufficient; unsatisfactory: *The prisoner was fed a meager diet of bread and water.* 2 lean; thin; skinny: *His meager frame hardly cast a shadow.* **mea·ger·ly.**

¹meal (mēl) 1 breakfast, lunch, dinner, or supper; a regular occasion when food is served: *Don't eat too much candy between meals.* 2 food eaten or served at a regular

mean

time: *We eat three meals a day.* [¹meal is a form of an Old English word (mǣl) meaning "mark," "fixed time," "time when food is taken."]

²meal (mēl) coarsely ground grain, especially corn meal. [²meal is a form of an Old English word (melu) meaning "that which is ground."]

meal·y (mē′li) 1 dry and powdery; like meal: *a dish of mealy potatoes.* 2 of or containing meal: *a mealy dough.* **meal·i·er, meal·i·est.**

¹mean (mēn) 1 to express or indicate the idea of; have the sense of: *Your dictionary shows that one word often means several different things.* 2 to have in mind; intend: *Try to say what you mean as clearly as possible.* 3 to be a sign of: *Those black clouds mean rain.* 4 to be certain to cause: *This means war!* 5 to have value or importance: *It means a lot to have good friends when you are in trouble.* **meant, mean·ing.** [¹mean is a form of an Old English word (mǣnan) meaning "tell," "intend."] (Homonym: mien)

²mean (mēn) 1 spiteful; unkind: *They were mean to laugh at his mistakes.* 2 selfish; not generous: *That boy is as mean as a miser.* 3 low; humble: *Many great men have risen from mean beginnings to positions of importance.* 4 shabby; of poor appearance: *This handsome park was once a mean slum area.* 5 inferior; poor: *clothes of mean quality.* **mean·ly.** [²mean is a form of an Old English word (gemǣne) meaning "common," "general."] (Homonym: mien)

³mean (mēn) 1 something that is midway between two things that are opposite: *Our climate is a happy mean between tropical heat and arctic cold.* 2 halfway between two extremes: *The mean temperature for the day was 70°, halfway between the high of 80° and the low of 60°.* 3 the average: *The mean of five plus six plus ten is seven, a result obtained by adding the figures (5 + 6 + 10 = 21) and dividing by three the number of items.* 4 **means** (1) way by which something is accomplished: *The footprint was the means of catching the thief.* (2) wealth: *His family had only modest means.* 5 **by all means** at any cost; without fail: *You should by all means see that exhibit.* 6 **by no means** in no way;

444

not at all: *We are* by no means *satisfied.*
7 by means of by the use of; through: *He won* by means of *clever tricks.* [³**mean** is from an Old French word (meien) that comes from a Latin word (medianus) meaning "in the middle."] (Homonym: mien)

me·an·der (mĭ ăn′dər) **1** to follow a winding course: *The brook* meanders *across the meadow with many twists and turns.* **2** to wander along in an aimless way: *He* meandered *along the boulevard.*

mean·ing (mē′nĭng) **1** way in which a thing can be understood; sense: *The word "ball" has more than one* meaning. **2** way in which a thing is meant; intention: *When I said, "Put it out," he misunderstood my* meaning *and put out the cat instead of the light.* **3** having meaning: *The girl warned her friend with a* meaning *glance not to give away the secret.* **mean·ing·ly.**

mean·ing·less (mē′nĭng lĭs) having no meaning; making no sense.

mean·ness (mēn′nĭs) **1** spite; malice: *He smashed his brother's bicycle out of pure* meanness. **2** stinginess: *his* meanness *in money matters.* **3** shabbiness; squalor: *He was struck by the* meanness *of the neighborhood.*

meant (měnt) See ¹**mean.** *He* meant *well.*

mean·time (mēn′tĭm′) **1** time between occasions: *You can start work tomorrow, and in the* meantime *I'll find you a helper.* **2** present time or time remaining: *The girls laid out the* meantime *lunch. Meantime the boys built a fire for heating the soup. I'll do as I've always done, for the* meantime.

mean·while (mēn′hwīl′) meantime.

mea·sles (mē′zəlz) contagious disease more common among children than grownups, marked by fever and red spots on the skin.

meas·ure (mězh′ər) **1** any unit by which the length, area, contents, weight, or time of a thing may be found, such as a foot, square foot, pint, pound, or minute. **2** a device for using such units, as a foot rule, a pint cup, a pound weight, etc. **3** to find the length, size, contents, weight, or length of time of anything in standard units: *Let us* measure *the length of the*

board *in inches.* **4** to be of a certain size, weight, etc.: *The card table* measures *three feet across.* **5** a basis of judgment or comparison: *Deeds are a better* measure *of character than words.* **6** quality; degree: *A* measure *of success is certain.* **7** legislative bill: *The* measure *before the senate required serious thought.* **8** means; course of action: *The government takes* measures *to prevent floods.* **9** a group of musical notes.

Measure

measure off to mark off; set the boundaries of: *The track coach* measured off *a hundred-yard course.*

measure out to take a portion by measuring: *She* measured out *enough flour for a cake.*

measure up to to meet the standards of: *Some men failed to* measure up to *the Army's physical requirements.*

meas·ured, meas·ur·ing.

meas·ure·ment (mězh′ər mənt) **1** finding of size, dimensions, weight, distance, volume, etc.; measuring: *A yardstick is used in the* measurement *of length.* **2** size, dimensions, volume, weight, etc., found by measuring: *The* measurements *of the room are six feet by eight.*

meat (mēt) **1** flesh of animals used as food: *The main source of* meat *in this country is cattle.* **2** fleshy edible part of fruits and vegetables: *We eat the* meat *of the walnut but not the shell.* **3** the most important part: *the* meat *of the book.* (Homonyms: meet, mete)

Mec·ca (měk′ə) **1** city in Saudi Arabia where Mohammed was born. It is the chief sacred city for Moslems, who turn toward its shrines when they pray and try to visit it at least once in a lifetime. **2 mecca** any place visited by many people: *New York City is a* mecca *for tourists.*

me·chan·ic (mə kăn′ĭk) person who is skilled in building, using, or repairing machinery: *We took the car to a* mechanic *for repairs.*

me·chan·i·cal (mə kăn′ə kəl) **1** by machine: *The automobile is a means of* mechan-

fāte, făt, fâre, fär; bē, bĕt; bīte, bĭt; nō, nŏt, nôr; fūse, fŭn, fûr; tōō, tŏŏk; foil; foul; thin; then; hw for wh as in what; zh for s as in usual; ə for a, e, i, o, u, as in ago, linen, peril, atom, minus

445

ical *transport*. **2** having to do with machines: *The wheel was one of man's earliest mechanical inventions.* **3** of machinery: *A mechanical breakdown delayed the train an hour.* **4** automatic; thoughtless; machine-like: *He recited his lesson with mechanical gestures.* **me·chan·i·cal·ly.**

me·chan·ics (mə kăn'iks) **1** the branch of physics that deals with the effects of forces on physical bodies. **2** the principles of machines and how they work: *the mechanics of automobile repair.*

me·chan·ism (měk'ə nĭz'əm) **1** machine: *A pulley is a simple mechanism.* **2** working parts (of a machine): *Sand in the mechanism will stop a watch.* **3** any system of parts working together: *the mechanism of government.*

med·al (měd'əl) a flat metal badge, often coin-shaped, honoring an important event or given as a reward for a heroic or important act or service. A medal is marked with fitting words and usually hangs from a bit of ribbon. (Homonym: meddle)

Medal

me·dal·lion (mə dǎl'yən) **1** a large medal. **2** a wall decoration consisting of a raised design or figures in a round frame.

med·dle (měd'əl) **1** to interfere (in other people's affairs): *This quarrel is none of your business, so don't meddle.* **2** to touch, handle, or tamper with other people's possessions without permission: *Don't meddle with the things in my desk drawer.* **med·dled, med·dling.** (Homonym: medal)

Medallion

med·dler (měd'lər) person who forces himself into other people's affairs or tampers with their possessions without permission.

med·dle·some (měd'əl səm) in the habit of interfering in other people's affairs or tampering with their possessions. **med·dle·some·ly.**

me·di·a (mē'dĭ ə) more than one **medium**: *The telephone, telegraph, and mail are media of communication.*

me·di·ae·val (mē'dĭ ē'vəl) medieval. **me·di·ae·val·ly.**

me·di·ate (mē'dĭ āt') **1** to act as a go-between to bring about peace or agreement: *The mayor was asked to mediate when the bus company and its employees could not reach an agreement.* **2** to bring about by acting as a go-between: *The mayor mediated a settlement between the bus company and its employees.* **me·di·at·ed, me·di·at·ing.**

med·i·cal (měd'ə kəl) having to do with the study and practice of medicine or the treatment of disease by the use of medicine. **med·i·cal·ly.**

me·dic·i·nal (mə dĭs'ə nəl) **1** having the power to prevent or cure disease, relieve pain, etc.: *The Indians knew many medicinal roots and herbs.* **2** of or like a medicine: *Some mineral water has a medicinal taste.* **me·dic·i·nal·ly.**

med·i·cine (měd'ə sən) **1** drug or other substance used to prevent or cure disease, relieve pain, etc. **2** the scientific study that deals with the prevention, treatment, and cure of disease; the art of healing.

me·di·e·val (mē'dĭ ē'vəl) of or having to do with the Middle Ages, the period in history from about A.D. 500 to about A.D. 1400. Also spelled **mediaeval. me·di·e·val·ly.**

me·di·o·cre (mē'dĭ ō'kər) not outstanding; neither very good nor very bad: *Is his work poor, mediocre, or good?*

med·i·tate (měd'ə tāt') **1** to think deeply; reflect: *to meditate upon the wonders of nature.* **2** to consider; plan: *After our fight I meditated revenge but finally decided to forget the whole thing.* **med·i·tat·ed, med·i·tat·ing.**

med·i·ta·tion (měd'ə tā'shən) deep thought; quiet, serious reflection: *Many churches set aside a room for meditation.*

Med·i·ter·ra·ne·an (měd'ə tə rā'nĭ ən) **1** large inland sea between Europe and Africa. **2** having to do with this sea or the territory bordering it: *the Mediterranean ports of Naples and Algiers.*

me·di·um (mē'dĭ əm) **1** occupying a middle position, condition, or state: *a medium-priced dress; a medium-rare steak.* **2** a middle position: *a happy medium between want and wealth.* **3** means or agent through

medley

or by which something is accomplished: *The telephone is a* medium *of communication.* **4** substance in which a thing exists: *Paint is pigment in an oil* medium. **5** a person assumed to be a messenger between spirits and living persons: *The* medium *gave me a message from my great-grandfather's spirit.* **me·di·ums** or **me·di·a.**

med·ley (mĕd'lĭ) **1** mixture; jumble (of various things): *There was a medley of sounds in the busy street.* **2** musical piece made up of several different songs or pieces.

meek (mēk) **1** very patient, gentle, and mild; humble. **2** easily imposed upon; not inclined to assert oneself. **meek·ly.**

meek·ness (mēk'nĭs) **1** patience, gentleness, and mildness; humbleness. **2** a being easily imposed upon and ready to submit to the will of others.

¹meet (mēt) **1** to come upon; come face to face with; encounter: *I happened to meet her on the stairs. He overcame every obstacle he met.* **2** to come together; come face to face: *I saw them meet in the hall.* **3** to come into contact with; connect with: *His bat met the ball with a crack.* **4** to come into contact; connect: *A capital L consists of two lines that meet at the lower left.* **5** to be introduced to: *I want you to meet my cousin when she comes to visit.* **6** to become acquainted with: *I have met a lot of interesting people while traveling.* **7** to be present at the arrival of: *I'll meet the late bus.* **8** to come together as a group; assemble: *The student council will meet in the library.* **9** to satisfy: *to meet the demand for a product.* **10** to pay: *to meet bills regularly.* **11** to answer or deal with in a satisfactory way: *The director met all the objections to his new plan.* **12** to come or be brought to the attention of; to be seen by; be heard by: *What a sight met her eyes!* **13** a gathering for competition in sports: *a track meet; a swimming meet.*

meet with to experience; encounter: *The expedition met with disaster.*

met, meet·ing. [**¹meet** is a form of an Old English word (mētan) with the same meaning.] (Homonyms: meat, mete)

melody

²meet (mēt) proper; fitting; right: *It is meet to give thanks unto the Lord.* [**²meet** is from an Old English word (gemǣte) with the same meaning.] (Homonyms: meat, mete)

meet·ing (mē'tĭng) **1** a coming together; an encounter: *a chance meeting with a friend on the street.* **2** a coming together of people for discussion or some common purpose; an assembly: *a meeting of the faculty.* **3** the people at a meeting: *The town meeting voted to increase taxes.* **4** place where things come together: *A large fortress was built at the meeting of the two rivers.*

meeting house a building for public worship.

meg·a·phone (mĕg'ə fōn') device, usually a funnel-shaped speaking trumpet, for increasing or directing the sound of the voice. Cheerleaders use megaphones at sports events.

meg·a·ton (mĕg'ə tŭn) explosive power equal to the energy released by one million tons of TNT.

mel·an·chol·y (mĕl'ən kŏl'ĭ) **1** sad; downcast; gloomy: *a melancholy mood.* **2** causing sadness or gloom: *The old abandoned house was a* melancholy *sight.* **3** sad or gloomy state of mind; a sorrowful mood.

mel·low (mĕl'ō) **1** soft, juicy, sweet, and fully ripe: *lucious* mellow *peaches.* **2** of a rich flavor: *a mellow cheese.* **3** full and rich: *the* mellow *sound of a cello.* **4** softened and made gentle by age, experience, etc.: *a mellow old gentleman.* **5** to make or become mature, gentle, or sweet: *Sorrow sometimes mellows people's dispositions.* **mel·low·ly.**

me·lo·di·ous (mə lō'dĭ əs) musical; pleasing to hear: *a melodious voice.* **me·lo·di·ous·ly.**

mel·o·dy (mĕl'ə dĭ) **1** an arrangement of musical sounds making up a tune: *The melody is familiar but I don't know the words to that song.* **2** chief voice part in a song: *You sing the melody and I will harmonize.* **3** any sound considered to be like the sound of music: *A poet uses words that form a beautiful melody.* **mel·o·dies.**

---

fāte, făt, fâre, fär; bē, bĕt; bīte, bĭt; nō, nŏt, nôr; fūse, fŭn, fûr; tōō, tŏŏk; foil; foul; thin; ~~then~~; hw for wh as in *what*; zh for s as in u*s*ual; ə for a, e, i, o, u, as in *a*go, lin*e*n, per*i*l, at*o*m, min*u*s

mel·on (mĕl'ən) the fleshy, juicy, round or oval fruit of any of several vines, such as the watermelon, muskmelon, or cantaloupe.

melt (mĕlt) **1** to change from a solid to a liquid by heating: *A temperature above 32 degrees* melts *ice.* **2** to dissolve: *Sugar* melts *in the mouth.* **3** to soften; make or become tender: *Her heart* melted *at the baby's smile.*

Melons

melt away to disappear: *As the sun grew hotter, the fog* melted *away.*

mem·ber (mĕm'bər) **1** person who belongs to a group, society, etc.: *a club* member; *a class* member. **2** a limb or other part of the body.

mem·ber·ship (mĕm'bər shĭp') **1** a being a member: *a membership in a club.* **2** number of people who belong: *The membership in the art class is limited to 30.* **3** having to do with members: *a membership committee.*

mem·brane (mĕm'brān) **1** thin, flexible sheet or layer of animal or vegetable tissue that serves as a cover or a lining of an organ: *mucous* membrane. **2** flexible sheet of plastic or other material used in various instruments. The top of a drum is a membrane.

mem·o (mĕm'ō) memorandum.

mem·oir (mĕm'wär) **1** record of events written by one who has personal knowledge of them or who has gathered special information about them. **2 memoirs** story of one's life, written by oneself; autobiography.

mem·o·ra·ble (mĕm'ə rə bəl) worth being remembered; unforgettable: *This play has many* memorable *scenes.* **mem·o·ra·bly.**

mem·o·ran·dum (mĕm'ə răn'dəm) **1** brief note written to remind one of something. **2** a brief written report or communication, especially one of a business nature. **mem·o·ran·dums** or **mem·o·ran·da.**

me·mo·ri·al (mə môr'ĭ əl) **1** something that serves as a reminder (of persons or events): *Many towns have erected* memorials *to the men who were killed in war.* **2** in memory or honor of some person or event: *A* memorial *library was dedicated to the founder of the town.*

Memorial Day day set aside to honor soldiers and sailors killed in war. It is May 30 in most States.

mem·o·rize (mĕm'ə rīz') to learn by heart; fix in the memory: *to* memorize *a speech.* **mem·o·rized, mem·o·riz·ing.**

mem·o·ry (mĕm'ə rĭ) **1** power of remembering: *I have a poor* memory *for names. She recited the poem from* memory. **2** a remembering or being remembered: *He never did anything worthy of* memory. **3** person or thing remembered: *The building that once stood here is only a* memory *now.* **4** what is remembered of someone: *We honor the* memory *of the founders of our country.* **5** length of time within which something is remembered: *Never before within the* memory *of man had there been such a storm.* **6 in memory of** in honor or remembrance of: *Christmas is celebrated in* memory *of Christ's birth.* **mem·o·ries.**

men (mĕn) **1** mankind: *For many years* men *thought the world was flat.* **2** more than one **man:** *Two* men *entered the shop.*

men·ace (mĕn'ĭs) **1** threat; danger: *Careless drivers are a* menace *to public safety.* **2** to threaten; endanger: *The rising river* menaced *the town.* **men·aced, men·ac·ing.**

me·nag·er·ie (mə năj'ə rĭ) **1** collection of wild animals in cages, kept for exhibition. **2** place where they are kept.

mend (mĕnd) **1** to repair; fix: *to* mend *a coat.* **2** place that has been mended; a patch: *There was a* mend *in the elbow of the old coat.* **3** to reform; make right: *The thief promised to* mend *his ways if given another chance.* **4** to return to good health: *Under his mother's care the sick child* mended *quickly.* **5 on the mend** getting better.

men·folk (mĕn'fōk') **1** men. **2** the men of a group, family, clan, or the like.

men·ha·den (mĕn hā'dən) a fish of the herring family, much used for fertilizer and making oil.

me·ni·al (mē'nĭ əl) **1** lowly; degrading: *Do you consider scrubbing the floor a* menial *job?* **2** a servant who performs the most lowly tasks. **me·ni·al·ly.**

-ment suffix used to change a verb to a noun. It means (1) "the state of being" (what the verb says). The state of being "disappointed" (verb) is "disappointment" (noun). (2) "the act of" (what the verb says). The act of "enforcing" (verb) is "enforcement" (noun). (3) "the means or instrument of" (what the verb says). The means or instrument of "adorning" (verb) is "adornment" (noun). (4) "the thing produced by" or "the result of" (what the verb says). The thing produced by or the result of "paving" (verb) is "pavement" (noun).

men·tal (měn′təl) **1** of or having to do with the mind: *a mental breakdown;* mental *powers.* **2** done or carried on in the mind: *to take* mental *note of a telephone number.* **men·tal·ly.**

men·tal·i·ty (měn tăl′ə tĭ) amount or quality of mental powers or intellectual ability: *These instructions can be understood by persons of average* mentality. **men·tal·i· ties.**

men·tion (měn′shən) **1** to touch on briefly (in speech or writing); talk about: *Don't* mention *our plans to a soul!* **2** a brief notice: *There was a* mention *of the accident in the newspaper.* **3 make mention of** to refer to; remark on: *He never made* mention *of having met you.* **4 not to men· tion** to say nothing of: *We ate cake and ice cream at the party,* not to mention *peanuts.*

men·u (měn′ū) **1** bill of fare; list of dishes that may be ordered in a restaurant. **2** foods served at a particular meal: *Our luncheon* menu *was chicken salad, biscuits, and ice cream.*

me·ow (mĭ ou′) **1** the mewing sound cats make. **2** to make this sound.

mer·can·tile (mûr′kən tēl′) of or having to do with merchants or trade.

mer·ce·nar·y (mûr′sə něr′ĭ) **1** greedy for money; prompted by love of money: *The boy was so* mercenary *he expected pay even to do a favor for his mother.* **2** soldier hired to serve in a foreign army. **mer·ce·nar·ies; mer·ce·nar·i·ly.**

mer·chan·dise (mûr′chən dīz′ or mûr′- chən dĭs′) goods or articles that are bought and sold: *Department stores carry many kinds of* merchandise.

mer·chant (mûr′chənt) **1** person who buys and sells goods: *a hardware* merchant.

2 of or having to do with trade: *Our* mer- chant *ships sail to all parts of the world.*

merchant marine 1 the ships or vessels of a nation engaged in trade or commerce. **2** the officers and crews of these vessels.

mer·ci·ful (mûr′sĭ fəl) feeling or showing mercy; kindhearted; not cruel. **mer·ci· ful·ly.**

mer·ci·less (mûr′sĭ lĭs) without mercy; cruel; not relenting: *a* merciless *tyrant; the sun's* merciless *heat.* **mer·ci·less·ly.**

mer·cu·ry (mûr′kyə rĭ) heavy metal element that stays liquid at ordinary temperatures. It is used in thermometers and barometers. Also called **quicksilver.**

Mer·cu·ry (mûr′kyə rĭ) **1** the planet nearest to the sun. **2** the swift messenger of the Roman gods.

mer·cy (mûr′sĭ) **1** kindness or goodness shown by a person to someone else: *to show* mercy *to a defeated enemy.* **2** something to be thankful for; a blessing: *It is a* mercy *that no one was hurt.* **3 at the mercy of** completely in the power of: *The dam- aged ship was at the mercy of the sea.* **mer·cies.**

mere (mĭr) nothing more than; only: *a* mere *hint of spring in the air.*

mere·ly (mĭr′lĭ) only; simply; just: *Don't be afraid of the dog* merely *because it barks.*

merge (mûrj) **1** to blend; mingle: *Dawn* merged *into day. He* merged *into the crowd.* **2** to flow together: *Traffic* merges *here. The tributary* merges *with the river.* **3** to join; combine: *Several small trucking companies* merged *and formed one large company.* **merged, merg·ing.**

me·rid·i·an (mə rĭd′ĭ ən) **1** an imaginary half circle on the earth's surface passing between the North and the South poles; line of longitude. For picture, see **longi- tude. 2** the highest point in the sky that the sun or a star reaches. **3** the highest or greatest point, as of happiness, success, etc.: *the* meridian *of his life.*

me·ri·no (mə rē′nō) **1** a breed of sheep with short legs and long, silky wool. **2** fine cloth made from this wool. **me·ri·nos.**

mer·it (měr′ĭt) **1** worth; value: *a man of great* merit. **2** thing that is valuable or deserves praise: *What are the* merits *of your plan?* **3** the fact of having worth or not having worth: *You will be judged on your own* merits. **4** to deserve: *Bad conduct* merits *punishment.* **5** of or having to do with merit: *a* merit *badge.*

mer·maid (mûr′mād′) an imaginary creature having the head and upper body of a woman and the tail of a fish.

Mermaid

mer·man (mûr′măn′) an imaginary creature having the head and upper body of a man and the tail of a fish. **mer·men.**

mer·ri·ment (měr′ĭ mənt) gaiety; mirth.

mer·ry (měr′ĭ) happy and cheerful; full of good spirits; jolly: *a* merry *twinkle in his eye.* **mer·ri·er, mer·ri·est; mer·ri·ly.**

mer·ry-go-round (měr′ĭ gō round′) a revolving circular platform with wooden animals or seats on which people may ride.

Merry-go-round

mer·ry·mak·ing (měr′ĭ mā′kĭng) gaiety; merriment: *a party filled with* merrymaking.

me·sa (mā′sə) flat-topped, steep-sided hill.

mesh (měsh) **1** any one of the open spaces of a network, screen, or the like. **2** having meshes: *a pair of* mesh *stockings.* **3** to fit together; engage; interlock: *The teeth of a zipper* mesh. **4** **meshes** means of tangling or catching: *to be caught in the* meshes *of the law.*

Mesa

mes·quite (měs kēt′ or měs′kēt) a low thorny tree which grows in dry climates. It is common in southwestern United States and Mexico.

mess (měs) **1** state of being dirty or in disorder: *The burglars left the room in a* mess. **2** a bungle; bad job: *You've made a complete* mess *of your painting.* **3** plight; difficult situation: *How did you get into such a* mess? **4** batch; quantity (of food): *a* mess *of fish.* **5** group of people taking their

meals together, especially soldiers or sailors. **6** meal eaten by such a group. **7** to eat as one of such a group: *The four roommates will* mess *together.*

mess up to make dirty or untidy; make a mess of: *Don't* mess up *the living room. The rain* messed up *our plans to camp out.*

mes·sage (měs′ĭj) any news or information sent from one person to another.

mes·sen·ger (měs′ən jər) person who carries messages or does errands.

Mes·si·ah (mə sī′ə) **1** the deliverer of the Jews promised in the Old Testament. **2** Jesus, considered by Christians to be this deliverer. **3** messiah an expected liberator of a people or a nation.

mess·y (měs′ĭ) disorderly; untidy; sloppy. **mess·i·er, mess·i·est; mess·i·ly.**

met (mět) See ¹**meet.** *We* met *on the corner.*

met·al (mět′əl) **1** a chemical element that is shiny when pure or polished and is a good conductor of electricity. Gold, silver, copper, tin, iron, and aluminum are metals. Mercury is a metal in liquid form at normal temperatures. **2** an alloy made by mixing two or more metals. **3** made of metal: *a* metal *tip on an arrow.* (Homonym: mettle)

me·tal·lic (mə tăl′ĭk) of or like metal: *a* metallic *thread; the* metallic *sound of a bell.*

mete (mēt) to give or measure (out); allot: *The judge* meted *punishment to each of the criminals according to his just deserts.* **met·ed, met·ing.** (Homonyms: meat, meet)

me·te·or (mē′tĭ ər) shooting star; piece of matter which falls toward the earth at great speed from outer space. Meteors burn with a bright glow when they hit the air around the earth, and are usually burned up before they reach the ground.

me·te·or·ic (mē′tĭ ôr′ĭk or mē′tĭ ŏr′ĭk) **1** of a meteor or meteors: *a* meteoric *shower.* **2** dazzling; brilliant for a short time: *Some popular singers have* meteoric *careers.*

me·te·or·ite (mē′tĭ ə rīt′) lump of metal or stone that falls to the earth from outer space.

me·te·or·ol·o·gy (mē′tĭ ə rŏl′ə jĭ) science that studies and attempts to foretell changes in the atmosphere, such as heat, cold, storms, winds, and the like; the study of weather and climate.

meter

¹me·ter (mē′tər) **1** instrument which measures and shows a record of the measurement: *an electric* meter; *a parking* meter. **2** a unit of length in the metric system, equal to about 39⅓ inches. [¹**meter** is from a French word (metre) which in turn comes from a Greek word (metron) meaning "a measure."]

²me·ter (mē′tər) **1** particular way syllables are arranged in a line of poetry to have a certain rhythm. **2** time, beat, or rhythm in music. Also spelled **metre.** [²**meter** comes from a Latin word (metrum) which in turn comes from a Greek word (metron) meaning "measure."]

meth·od (mĕth′əd) **1** regular way or system of doing something: *Studying a language by hearing it spoken is a good* method *of learning.* **2** orderly arrangement of ideas, subjects, etc.: *to use* method *in one's studies.*

me·thod·i·cal (mə thŏd′ə kəl) **1** done or arranged in an orderly or systematic way: *a* methodical *outline.* **2** inclined to be orderly or systematic: *a* methodical *person.* **me·thod·i·cal·ly.**

me·tre (mē′tər) ²meter.

met·ric sys·tem (mĕt′rĭk sĭs′təm) system of weights and measures based on the meter for length and the gram for weight.

met·ro·nome (mĕt′rə-nōm′) a machine that beats time in loud ticks for music practice.

Metronome

me·trop·o·lis (mə trŏp′ə lĭs) **1** large city, especially one that is a center for business and culture. **2** the chief city of a country, state, or region.

met·ro·pol·i·tan (mĕt′rə pŏl′ə tən) **1** having to do with or belonging to a large city. **2** a person who lives in and knows the ways of a large city. **3** in the Orthodox Eastern Church, a bishop next in rank below Patriarch. **4 metropolitan area** major city and the surrounding area.

met·tle (mĕt′əl) spirit; courage: *The fight proved his* mettle. (Homonym: metal)

mew (mū) **1** the cry of a cat; meow. **2** to make this sound; to meow.

mid

Mex·i·can (mĕk′sə kən) **1** of Mexico, or its people. **2** citizen of Mexico or person of Mexican descent.

Mexican War war fought between the United States and Mexico (1846-1848) through which the United States acquired large parts of the Southwest.

Mex·i·co (mĕk′sə kō′) a country of North America, south of the United States.

mi (mē) in music, the third note of the scale.

mi. mile.

mi·ca (mī′kə) mineral that is easily separated into thin sheets that look like transparent or cloudy glass. Mica can stand great heat and is a good insulator for electricity.

mice (mīs) more than one **mouse.**

Mich. Michigan.

Mich·i·gan (mĭsh′ə gən) a north central State of the United States.

mi·crobe (mī′krōb) **1** living plant or animal so small that it can be seen only through a microscope. **2** disease germ.

mi·cro·film (mī′krə fĭlm′) narrow film for making very small photographs of printed pages, pictures, and the like, for keeping and for storing in a small space.

mi·cro·phone (mī′krə fōn′) instrument which changes sounds into electrical signals for recording or broadcasting. These signals are strengthened and sent out, through the air or wires, and are changed back into sound.

mi·cro·scope (mī′krə-skōp′) instrument which, by an arrangement of lenses, makes very tiny things look large enough to be seen.

mi·cro·scop·ic (mī′krə-skŏp′ĭk) **1** so small it can be seen only through a microscope: *a microscopic animal or plant.* **2** having to do with a microscope; done with a microscope: *a microscopic examination of a blood sample.*

Microscope

¹mid or **'mid** (mĭd) in the middle of; amid. [¹**mid** is a shortened form of **amid.**]

---

fāte, făt, fâre, fär; bē, bĕt; bīte, bĭt; nō, nŏt, nôr; fūse, fŭn, fûr; tōō, tŏŏk; foil; foul; thin; ~~then~~; hw for wh as in *wh*at; zh for s as in u*s*ual; ə for a, e, i, o, u, as in ag*o*, lin*e*n, per*i*l, at*o*m, min*u*s

²**mid** (mĭd) the middle. [²**mid** is a form of an Old English word (mĭdd) with the same meaning.]

mid- prefix meaning "middle" or "middle part of a": mid*day*; mid*stream*; mid*summer*.

mid·day (mĭd′dā′) **1** the middle of the day; noon. **2** at noon: *the* midday *meal*.

mid·dle (mĭd′əl) **1** point or part halfway between two ends or sides; point or part halfway between the beginning and the end: *The island is directly in the* middle *of the river. The fire bell rang in the* middle *of geography class.* **2** in between (two others): *the* middle *room.*

mid·dle-aged (mĭd′əl ājd′) neither very young nor very old, usually considered to include the ages from about 40 to about 60.

Middle Ages the medieval period of European history, from about A.D. 500 to about A.D. 1400.

middle ear a part of the ear inside the head behind the eardrum. Sounds which strike the eardrum are carried to the nervous system by vibration of three bones inside the middle ear.

Middle East the land from the eastern Mediterranean east to India and including the Arabian Peninsula.

Middle West the Midwest; the region of the United States lying between the Appalachian and Rocky mountains and north of Arkansas and Oklahoma.

mid·dy (mĭd′ĭ) **1** midshipman. **2** loose blouse like a sailor's for women's and children's sportswear. **mid·dies.**

Middy blouse

midge (mĭj) a very small fly, gnat, or similar flying insect.

midg·et (mĭj′ĭt) **1** very small person, perfectly formed but much below the normal size. **2** a thing that is tiny of its kind. **3** tiny; very small: *a* midget *racing car.*

mid·land (mĭd′lənd) **1** interior or central part of a country. **2** in or of the central part of a country; inland: *The* midland *plains of the United States are a great farming district for corn.*

mid·night (mĭd′nĭt) **1** 12 o'clock at night; the middle of the night. **2** at midnight: *a*

midnight *train.* **3** of or resembling midnight: *a* midnight *blue.*

mid·ship·man (mĭd′shĭp′mən) man who is in training at the United States Naval Academy. **mid·ship·men.**

¹**midst** (mĭdst) **1** middle; central part. **2** **in the midst of** (1) in the middle of: *The brave knight was always* in the midst of *the battle.* (2) during: *She left* in the midst of *the party.* **3** **in our, their,** or **your midst** among us, them, or you. [¹**midst** is a form of earlier "middest," "in middest," which is of course based on ²**mid.**]

²**midst** or **'midst** (mĭdst) amidst; among: *A tiny horse stood* midst *the tall trees.* [²**midst** is a short form of **amidst.**]

mid·stream (mĭd′strēm′) the middle of a stream.

mid·sum·mer (mĭd′sŭm′ər) **1** the middle of the summer; time of year halfway between spring and fall. **2** the period about June 21, the day with the longest period of daylight in the year. **3** in or of the middle of the summer: *the* midsummer *heat.*

mid·way (mĭd′wā′) **1** halfway: *the point* midway *in a trip;* midway *through the campaign.* **2** part of a circus, carnival, or fair, where side shows and other amusements are located.

Mid·west (mĭd′wĕst′) Middle West; the region of the United States lying between the Appalachian and Rocky mountains and north of Arkansas and Oklahoma.

mid·win·ter (mĭd′wĭn′tər) **1** the middle of the winter; the time of year halfway between fall and spring. **2** the period about December 21, the day with the shortest period of daylight. **3** in or like the middle of winter: *a* midwinter *vacation; the* midwinter *cold.*

mien (mēn) appearance; manner; bearing: *The young knight had a proud and noble* mien. (Homonym: mean)

¹**might** (mīt) **1** may possibly: *I* might *let you have my bicycle tomorrow.* **2** could possibly: *The money* might *have been here then, but it is gone now.* **3** would be allowed to: *She said I* might *keep the book for a week.* [¹**might** is a form of an Old English word (mihte) meaning "I was able."] (Homonym: mite)

²**might** (mīt) power; strength: *He pushed with all his* might, *but the door wouldn't*

open. [²**might** is a form of an Old English word (miht) meaning "strength."] (Homonym: mite)

might·y (mī'tĭ) **1** powerful; very strong: *a mighty army; a mighty king.* **2** great; huge: *a mighty tree.* **might·i·er, might·i·est; might·i·ly.**

mi·gnon·ette (mĭn'yə nĕt') a garden plant that bears clusters of tiny, fragrant, greenish-white flowers.

mi·grant (mī'grənt) **1** moving from place to place, especially with the changes of season: *The migrant workers move about the country to harvest crops.* **2** a person or animal that migrates.

mi·grate (mī'grāt') **1** to travel from one region to another as the seasons change: *Ducks and geese* migrate *southward in the fall.* **2** to move to a new home in a different region. **mi·grat·ed, mi·grat·ing.**

mi·gra·tion (mī grā'shən) **1** a traveling from one region to another as the seasons change: *The great migrations of birds take place in the spring and fall.* **2** a number of people or animals moving together from one region to another: *We saw a large migration of ducks last fall.* **3** a moving from one region or country to live in another: *Many settlers came to America in migrations from Europe.*

mild (mīld) **1** gentle; kind; calm: *a mild answer.* **2** not extreme, harsh, or severe: *a mild winter.* **3** not sharp, bitter, or harsh in taste: *a mild sauce;* mild *cheese.* **mild·ly.**

mil·dew (mĭl'dōō' or mĭl'dū') **1** any fungus found on plants, decaying matter, leather, paper, etc. Mildew often appears during warm, damp weather as spots of mold or a whitish coating. **2** to cause to be affected with mildew: *The dampness at the seashore* mildewed *some of my books.* **3** to become affected with mildew: *Leather left in a damp cellar will* mildew.

mild·ness (mīld'nĭs) a being mild; gentleness.

mile (mīl) a measure of length or distance. A land mile, called a statute mile, is equal to 5,280 feet. A nautical mile is 6,080 feet.

mile·age (mī'lĭj) **1** total number of miles traveled in one trip or in a certain time:

What was the mileage *of your vacation trip? Our airline has the highest accident-free* mileage *of any.* **2** average number of miles traveled on a unit of fuel: *This car gets a* mileage *of 32 miles a gallon.* **3** money allowed for car expense: *Their salesmen get commission plus* mileage. **4** distance over which something remains usable for travel: *We got rather low* mileage *out of these tires.*

mile·stone (mīl'stōn') **1** roadside stone used to mark distance: *The* milestone *showed we were ten miles from town.* **2** important event: *The Declaration of Independence was a* milestone *in American history.*

mil·i·tant (mĭl'ə tənt) aggressive; warlike; ready to fight: *to be* militant *in the defense of freedom.* **mil·i·tant·ly.**

mil·i·tar·y (mĭl'ə tĕr'ĭ) **1** relating to war or the armed forces: *My brother received* military *training in college.* **2** of, for, or by soldiers: *a* military *band.* **3 the military** soldiers; the army: *to place the government in the hands of the* military. **mil·i·tar·i·ly.**

mi·li·tia (mǐ lĭsh'ə) body of citizens who are trained for defense of their country in emergencies. In the United States the militia is called the National Guard.

milk (mĭlk) **1** white fluid produced by female mammals for feeding their young. The milk of certain domestic animals such as cows and goats is used as human food. **2** to get milk from: *Few city people can* milk *a cow.* **3** juice of some plants or trees: *Coconut* milk *makes a refreshing drink.*

milk·maid (mĭlk'mād') woman or girl who milks cows and works in a dairy.

milk·man (mĭlk'măn') man who sells or delivers milk. **milk·men.**

milk·weed (mĭlk'wēd') tall field plant with oval leaves, clus-

PARTLY
OPEN
POD

Milkweed

tered purple flower heads, and sticky, milklike juice which gives it its name.

fāte, făt, fâre, fär; bē, bĕt; bīte, bĭt; nō, nŏt, nôr; fūse, fŭn, fûr; tōō, tŏŏk; foil; foul; thin; ~~then~~; hw for wh as in *wh*at; zh for s as in usual; ə for a, e, i, o, u, as in *a*go, lin*e*n, per*i*l, at*o*m, min*u*s

453

milk·y (mĭl′kĭ) **1** like milk: *a milky sap.*
2 white: *a milky sky.* **3** containing milk:
a milky sauce. **milk·i·er, milk·i·est.**

Milky Way a band of faint light reaching
across the night sky, composed of stars too
distant and numerous to be seen separately
with the naked eye.

mill (mĭl) **1** a machine
for grinding or pul-
verizing: *a pepper
mill.* **2** a building
containing such ma-
chinery: *A gristmill
stood just below the
dam.* **3** any factory:
a paper mill; *a cotton*

Mill

mill; *a steel* mill. **4** to grind: *to mill flour.*
5 to surge about, like a restless crowd.

mill·er (mĭl′ər) **1** man who owns or runs a
mill for grinding grain into flour or meal:
*The pioneers grew their own wheat and gave
it to the miller to make flour.* **2** any moth
with wings that seem dusted with flour.

mil·let (mĭl′ĭt) a grass grown in Europe and
Asia for its grain. In the United States it
is used mainly as fodder.

mil·li·gram (mĭl′ə grăm′) unit of weight
in the metric system. 1,000 milligrams
equal 1 gram.

mil·li·me·ter or **mil·li·met·re** (mĭl′ə-
mē′tər) unit of length in the metric system
equal to one thousandth of a meter.

mil·li·ner (mĭl′ə nər) maker or seller of
women's hats.

mil·li·ner·y (mĭl′ə nĕr′ĭ) articles sold by
a milliner, especially women's hats, but
including laces, ribbons, and other trimmings.

mil·lion (mĭl′yən) one thousand thousands;
1,000,000.

mil·lion·aire (mĭl′yə nâr′) **1** a person
owning a million dollars or more, or property worth such an amount. **2** any very
wealthy person.

mil·lionth (mĭl′yənth) **1** last in a series of a
million; 1,000,000th.
2 one of a million
equal parts.

Millstone

mill·stone (mĭl′stōn′)
1 either of a pair of
large, grooved, circular stones used to
grind grain. **2** a crushing burden or responsibility.

mim·e·o·graph (mĭm′ĭ ə grăf′) **1** machine
that makes copies of drawings and typewritten or written material. **2** to make
copies on this machine.

mim·ic (mĭm′ĭk) **1** one who copies another's
speech, actions, or looks, usually for fun or
ridicule; imitator: *Some comedians are very
skillful mimics.* **2** to copy in fun or mockery; imitate: *It is not easy to mimic a person
without offending him.* **3** imitative or copying: *the mimic habits of a monkey.* **4** pretended; mock: *a mimic battle.* **mim·icked,
mim·ick·ing.**

min. minute; minutes.

min·a·ret (mĭn′ə rĕt′) slender tower of a
mosque. From its balconies
Moslems are called to prayers.

Twin
minarets

mince (mĭns) **1** to chop or cut
into fine pieces: *The cook* minced
an onion for the soup. **2** to move
or speak in an affected, prim,
and dainty way: *She* minced
across the room. **3** to tell in part
or by degrees; make weaker
or less direct: *I won't* mince
*words; your paper was the poor-
est I read.* **4** made of mincemeat:
a mince pie. **5** mincemeat, or a dish of
finely chopped bits of meat. **minced,
minc·ing.**

mince·meat (mĭns′mēt) a mixture of finely
chopped apples, raisins, currants, lemon
peel, suet, etc., used as a filling for pie.

mind (mīnd) **1** ability to think or reason,
judge, feel, etc.; intellect: *He has a good
mind if he would only use it.* **2** memory;
recollection: *He searched his mind for the
man's name.* **3** person, thought of in terms
of his mental ability: *He was one of the
really great minds of this century.* **4** ideas;
thoughts; opinions: *to speak your mind.*
5 to object to: *Do you* mind *having to stay
here alone?* **6** to obey: *That dog won't* mind
anyone. **7** to watch; take care of: *Who*
minds *the baby when your mother is out?*
8 be of one mind to agree; share a single
opinion: *We are of one mind on the subject.*
9 have a mind to to be inclined to: *I
have a mind to ask her to the dance.* **10
make up one's mind** to reach a decision:
*You must make up your mind to work
harder.* **11 mind's eye** imagination; fancy:
I see the beaches of Hawaii in my mind's eye.

12 on one's mind in one's thoughts: *The test will be* on my mind *till I know I passed it.* **13 put in mind** to remind; make one think: *That puts me in mind of a very funny story.* **14 set one's mind on** to determine to have or get: *Once he sets his mind on something he works tirelessly for it.* **15 to my mind** in my opinion or judgment: *The best vacation, to my mind, is a month at the shore.*

mind·ful (mīnd'fəl) aware of; conscious of; thoughtful: *Father was always mindful of the needs and feelings of his family.* **mind·ful·ly.**

¹**mine** (mīn) **1** tunnel or pit for taking minerals from the earth: *The largest diamond mines are in South Africa.* **2** to get by digging in the ground: *Much coal is mined in West Virginia.* **3** to dig up to find minerals: *The gold prospectors had to mine the entire hillside.* **4** in warfare, explosives placed underground or in the water to delay or destroy enemy troops, vehicles, or ships. **5** to lay mines in warfare: *The defenders of the island mined the surrounding seas and beaches.* **mined, min·ing.** [¹**mine** is from an Old French word (mine) of Celtic origin.]

²**mine** (mīn) **1** of or for me: *I broke the vase, so the blame is* mine. **2** the one or ones belonging to me: *If this is your book, then I have lost* mine. **3** sometimes used instead of "my": *I will raise* mine *eyes to heaven.* [²**mine** is a form of an Old English word (mīn) meaning "my," "of me."]

min·er (mī'nər) person who works in a mine. (Homonym: minor)

min·er·al (mĭn'ər əl) **1** substance that is neither animal nor vegetable, especially a substance taken from the earth by mining. Salt is a common mineral. **2** having to do with or consisting of a mineral or minerals: *Colorado has rich* mineral *deposits.*

min·gle (mĭng'gəl) **1** to mix: *The waters of the Missouri and Mississippi rivers* mingle *near St. Louis.* **2** to associate: *The soldiers were forbidden to* mingle *with their prisoners.* **min·gled, min·gling.**

min·i·a·ture (mĭn'ĭ ə chər or mĭn'ĭ chər) **1** very small in scale or dimension: *to build*

miniature *trains.* **2** small model or reproduction: *We bought a* miniature *of the Liberty Bell.* **3** very small portrait: *She wore a* miniature *of her mother in a locket.*

min·i·mum (mĭn'ə məm) **1** smallest amount possible or allowable: *Practice your music a* minimum *of an hour a day.* **2** least possible or allowed: *a* minimum *wage, rent, etc.* **3** lowest point or degree reached: *a* minimum *of 28° on the thermometer.* **min·i·mums** or **min·i·ma.**

min·ing (mī'nĭng) **1** the work of taking ores, coal, etc., from the earth: *Coal* mining *is the chief industry of several states.* **2** having to do with mines or obtaining minerals from mines: *a* mining *tool; a* mining *engineer.* **3** the laying of explosive mines: *the* mining *of harbors during a war.*

min·ion (mĭn'yən) a fawning servant or follower: *Hoping to gain favor, he was the prince's* minion.

min·is·ter (mĭn'ĭs tər) **1** clergyman. **2** diplomat sent to a foreign country to represent his government. **3** in some countries, the head of a government department. The ministers of the British government have duties similar to those of members of the President's Cabinet in the United States. **4** to give help, attention, or service: *Doctors* minister *to the sick.*

min·is·try (mĭn'ĭs trĭ) **1** the work or profession of a clergyman: *He is studying for the* ministry. **2** in some countries, a government department. The French Foreign Ministry corresponds to our State Department. **3** the service or length of service of a clergyman or officer of state: *During the* ministry *of Mr. Jones we built a new church.* **4** devoted service or help: *the* ministry *of nurses to the sick.* **5** church or government ministers as a group. **min·is·tries.**

mink (mĭngk) **1** a slender, aggressive, water-loving member of the weasel family. **2** the valuable fur of this animal.

American mink, about 20 in. long

Minn. Minnesota.

Min·ne·so·ta (mĭn'ə sō'tə) a State in the north central part of the United States.

---

fāte, făt, fâre, fär; bē, bĕt; bīte, bĭt; nō, nŏt, nôr; fūse, fŭn, fûr; tōō, tŏŏk; foil; foul; thin; ~~then~~; hw for wh as in *what*; zh for s as in usual; ə for a, e, i, o, u, as in *ago*, *linen*, *peril*, *atom*, *minus*

min·now (mĭn′ō) **1** any of several very small fresh-water fishes commonly used as bait. **2** any of several fishes, usually small, of the carp family.

Minnow, commonly 1 to 6 in. long

mi·nor (mī′nər) **1** unimportant: *She had minor cuts and bruises but no major injuries.* **2** lesser; smaller: *Land occupies the minor portion of the earth's surface.* **3** a person not old enough to be entitled to full civil rights. Anyone under 21 years of age is usually considered a minor. **4** a course of study in college that is next in importance to the major course. **5** to follow a course of study next in importance to a major course: *to minor in science.* **6** of or related to the musical scale that has certain tones a half tone lower than the major scale. (Homonym: miner)

min·or·i·ty (mi nôr′ə tǐ or mə nôr′ə tǐ) **1** smaller number or part; less than half: *He received a minority of the votes cast in the election.* **2** time during which a boy or girl is a minor: *While a boy is in his minority, his parents are legally responsible for him.* **3** representing the minority: *a minority opinion.* **4** made up of people in a minority: *a minority group.* **min·or·i·ties.**

min·strel (mĭn′strəl) **1** Negro performer, or one made up as a Negro, in a form of musical show, popular in the United States after about 1850, consisting of songs, dances, jokes, etc. **2** medieval entertainer who sang or recited stories, songs, ballads, etc., to music: *A band of minstrels amused the king and queen.*

¹mint (mint) **1** any of several sweet-smelling herbs used for flavoring, as the peppermint. **2** candy flavored with mint. [**¹mint** comes through French from a Latin word (menta, mentha).]

²mint (mint) **1** place where coins are made by the government. **2** to make coins by stamping out of metal. **3** to make into coins: *No gold is minted nowadays.* **4** vast sum of money; fortune: *He made a mint in the iron and steel industries.* [**²mint** is a form of an Old English word (mynet) meaning "coin." This word comes from a Latin word (moneta) from which we also get the word **money.**]

min·u·end (mĭn′yŏŏ ĕnd′) number from which another number is subtracted. In 4 − 2 = 2, the minuend is 4.

min·u·et (mĭn′yŏŏ ĕt′) **1** a slow, stately dance popular in the 17th and 18th centuries. **2** music for such a dance.

mi·nus (mī′nəs) **1** less; decreased by: *Eight minus three is five.* **2** sign (−) showing that the number following is to be subtracted. **3** without; lacking: *He came home from the hospital minus his tonsils.*

Minuet

¹min·ute (mĭn′ĭt) **1** sixty seconds; 1/60th of an hour. **2** 1/60th of a degree in an angle. **3** moment; very brief time: *I'll be back in a minute.* **4** a specific point of time: *The doctor came the minute we sent for him.* **5** minutes official record of a meeting: *As secretary, Jim will read the minutes of our last meeting.* [**¹minute** comes from a Latin word (minuere) meaning "to make smaller."]

²mi·nute (mī nōōt′ or mī nūt′) **1** extremely small; tiny: *Sand consists mainly of minute particles of rock.* **2** precise; detailed: *a minute description.* **mi·nute·ly.** [**²minute** is from a Latin word (minutus) meaning "small."]

min·ute·man (mĭn′ĭt măn′) in the Revolutionary War, an American colonist ready for military service at a minute's notice. **min·ute·men.**

minx (mĭngks) bold or saucy girl.

mir·a·cle (mĭr′ə kəl) **1** event that cannot be explained by the laws of nature and is therefore believed to be caused by divine power: *The parting of the Red Sea is a miracle recorded in the Bible.* **2** wonder; marvel; highly unusual event: *It is a miracle that we won the game.*

mi·rac·u·lous (mĭ răk′yə ləs) **1** in the nature of a miracle: *We read of the miraculous parting of the Red Sea.* **2** wonderful; marvelous: *Television is one of the miraculous inventions of our time.* **mi·rac·u·lous·ly.**

mire (mīr) **1** deep mud: *We waded through the mire to reach the road.* **2** to stick or sink in mud: *We were delayed when our bus mired on a country road.* **mired, mir·ing.**

mir·ror (mĭr′ər) 1 looking glass; any surface that reflects an image. 2 to reflect: *The pond mirrors the house and garden.* 3 anything that gives a clear picture or likeness: *Old newspapers are a mirror of past times.*

mirth (mûrth) fun; merriment; jollity: *Christmas is a time for generosity and mirth.*

mirth·ful (mûrth′fəl) gay; jolly; merry: *a mirthful laugh.* **mirth·ful·ly.**

mis- prefix meaning (1) "bad" or "wrong": *a misdeed.* (2) "badly" or "wrongly": *to misspell; mistreat.*

mis·ad·ven·ture (mĭs′əd vĕn′chər) 1 bad luck; misfortune. 2 a mishap; piece of bad luck: *We had several misadventures on the trip, such as taking the wrong road.*

mis·be·have (mĭs′bĭ hāv′) to behave badly; be naughty. **mis·be·haved, mis·be·hav·ing.**

mis·cel·la·ne·ous (mĭs′ə lā′nĭ əs) consisting of several kinds mixed together: *The boy had a collection of miscellaneous coins in his pocket.* **mis·cel·la·ne·ous·ly.**

mis·chance (mĭs chăns′) 1 bad luck; misfortune: *By mischance, he slipped and fell.* 2 piece of bad luck; a mishap.

mis·chief (mĭs′chĭf) 1 foolish or thoughtless behavior that could cause harm or injury: *Don't get into mischief while your mother is away.* 2 harm; injury: *People who carry tales about others can do great mischief.* 3 teasing; merry pranks: *She is full of mischief and is the life of every party.* 4 person who causes mischief, plays tricks, etc.: *That child is a little mischief.*

mis·chie·vous (mĭs′chə vəs) 1 playful in an annoying way; teasing: *That mischievous boy tied knots in my socks.* 2 harmful; causing injury: *Don't start mischievous rumors.* **mis·chie·vous·ly.**

¹**mis·con·duct** (mĭs kŏn′dŭkt) wrong behavior: *to punish for misconduct.*

²**mis·con·duct** (mĭs′kən dŭkt′) to manage badly: *to misconduct one's affairs.*

mis·deed (mĭs dēd′) a wrong act; crime: *The pirate was punished for his misdeeds.*

mis·de·mean·or (mĭs′dĭ mē′nər) a wrongdoing; in law, a minor offense punishable by a fine or short jail sentence.

mi·ser (mī′zər) greedy and stingy person who loves money for its own sake. Misers hoard wealth and often live as though they were poor.

mis·er·a·ble (mĭz′ər ə bəl) 1 unhappy; wretched: *The dog gave a miserable howl when we left him alone.* 2 bad; worthless: *a miserable meal of stale bread and burnt meat.* 3 causing unhappiness, trouble, or annoyance: *a miserable headache.* **mis·er·a·bly.**

mis·er·y (mĭz′ə rĭ) 1 great unhappiness, wretchedness, pain, etc.: *He is in misery with a bad toothache.* 2 wretched conditions: *Some people have risen from poverty and misery to fame and fortune.* **mis·er·ies.**

mis·fit (mĭs′fĭt) 1 something that does not fit: *His coat was a misfit and his trousers baggy.* 2 a person who is out of place among his associates: *Ned felt like a misfit in the new school until he became acquainted.*

mis·for·tune (mĭs fôr′chən) 1 bad luck: *In spite of all his misfortune he had a cheerful spirit.* 2 piece of bad luck; unlucky accident: *The hail storm was a misfortune for the farmers.*

mis·giv·ing (mĭs gĭv′ĭng) feeling of doubt, distrust, or worry: *He had misgivings about his ability to give the speech.*

mis·hap (mĭs′hăp) minor accident or piece of bad luck: *The spilling of the gravy was the only mishap at the party.*

mis·judge (mĭs jŭj′) to make an error in judging; make a wrong estimate of: *The baseball player misjudged the ball and struck out.* **mis·judged, mis·judg·ing.**

mis·lay (mĭs lā′) to put in a place and then forget the place; to put in the wrong place: *Dad mislaid the key and can't unlock the trunk.* **mis·laid, mis·lay·ing.**

mis·lead (mĭs lēd′) 1 to deceive: *I was misled by her glowing account of the movie and was disappointed when I saw it.* 2 to lead astray: *Joe was misled by bad companions and got into trouble.* **mis·led, mis·lead·ing.**

mis·lead·ing (mĭs lē′dĭng) deceiving; giving a wrong impression: *Her smile was misleading, for she was really angry.*

mis·led (mĭs lĕd′) See **mislead.**

---

fāte, făt, fâre, fär; bē, bĕt; bīte, bĭt; nō, nŏt, nôr; fūse, fŭn, fûr; tōō, tŏŏk; foil; foul; thin; then; hw for wh as in *wh*at; zh for s as in u*s*ual; ə for a, e, i, o, u, as in *a*go, lin*e*n, per*i*l, at*o*m, min*u*s

mis·no·mer (mĭs nō′mər) wrong name or term; incorrect use of a name: *It would be a misnomer to call a bat a "bird."*

mis·place (mĭs plās′) **1** to put in a place and then forget the place: *I have misplaced the letter with his new address.* **2** to put in the wrong place: *to misplace a comma.* **3** to give (trust, love, etc.) where it is not deserved: *He misplaced his trust when he told secrets to a friend who gossiped.* **mis·placed, mis·plac·ing.**

mis·print (mĭs prĭnt′) **1** to make a mistake in printing. **2** (also mĭs′prĭnt′) a mistake in printing.

mis·pro·nounce (mĭs′prə nouns′) to say with a wrong sound or to accent a wrong syllable: *Clarence* mispronounces *"granted" as "granite."* **mis·pro·nounced, mis·pro·nounc·ing.**

mis·read (mĭs rēd′) **1** to read incorrectly: *to misread directions.* **2** to misunderstand; interpret wrongly: *She sometimes misreads my expression and thinks I am angry.* **mis·read** (mĭs rĕd′), **mis·read·ing.**

¹miss (mĭs) **1** to fail to hit, touch, or reach: *The boxer's punch* missed. **2** failure to hit, touch, or reach: *His first shot was a miss.* **3** to fail to catch or get: *I missed the bus and had to walk.* **4** to fail to attend, hear, or see: *He missed school for a week.* **5** to fail to find or recognize: *You can't miss my house.* **6** to fail to understand or appreciate: *She missed the point of the joke.* **7** to be sad at the absence or loss of: *We miss our friends when they go away.* **8** to realize the absence of: *I missed my purse when I went to buy a ticket.* **9** to fail to perform correctly: *She missed some notes in her song.* **10** to overlook; fail to take care of: *She missed some dust in the corner.* **11** to fail to keep: *He missed his footing on the broken step.* **12** to avoid; escape: *He barely missed getting hurt in the accident.* **13** to fail to take advantage of; let go by: *to miss a chance.* [¹**miss** is a form of an Old English word (missan) meaning "fail to hit (the mark)."]

²miss (mĭs) **1** young unmarried woman; girl: *She's a pretty little miss.* **2 Miss** title used before the name of a girl or unmarried woman: *She was Miss Cole before she married.* [²**miss** is a shortened form of **mistress.**]

Miss. Mississippi.

mis·sal (mĭs′əl) **1** in the Roman Catholic Church, prayers for the Mass of each day of the year. **2** book of prayers and devotions. (Homonym: missile)

mis·shap·en (mĭs shā′pən) poorly shaped; deformed. **mis·shap·en·ly.**

mis·sile (mĭs′əl) an object or weapon that is thrown or shot. (Homonym: missal)

miss·ing (mĭs′ĭng) lost; absent: *A page is missing from this history book that I have been reading for class.*

mis·sion (mĭsh′ən) **1** group of people sent to carry out a special task or assignment: *The United Nations sends missions to help countries with their problems.* **2** special task or assignment: *Sir Walter Raleigh's mission was to establish a colony.* **3** church, school, or building used by missionaries: *The Alamo was a Spanish mission before it was a fort.* **4** person's life work; calling. **5 missions** the establishment of churches and setting up of schools, hospitals, and other services; missionary work.

mis·sion·ar·y (mĭsh′ə nĕr′ĭ) **1** person who works to spread his religion by trying to convert other people. **2** having to do with religious missions or missionaries. **mis·sion·ar·ies.**

Mis·sis·sip·pi (mĭs′ə sĭp′ĭ) **1** a State in the southern part of the United States. **2** the largest river in North America, flowing from northern Minnesota into the Gulf of Mexico.

Mis·sour·i (mĭ zoor′ĭ or mĭ zoor′ə) **1** a State in the central part of the United States. **2** river flowing from Montana into the Mississippi.

mis·spell (mĭs spĕl′) to spell incorrectly. **mis·spelled** or **mis·spelt, mis·spell·ing.**

mist (mĭst) **1** visible water vapor in the air; a fine fog: *A mist hung over the river.* **2** to fall in fine drops; come down in mist: *It's misting, not raining.* **3** anything that blurs or dims sight: *a mist of tears.* **4** to cover or dim, as with a mist: *Tears misted her eyes.*

mis·take (mə stāk′) **1** error: *Your paper has six spelling mistakes. Everyone makes mistakes.* **2** misunderstanding: *We had an argument, but it was all a mistake.* **3** to make an error in; misunderstand; be wrong about: *I mistook her joking and took it seriously.* **4** to take one person or thing

for another: *I* mistook *you for your sister.*
mis·took, mis·tak·en, mis·tak·ing.

mis·tak·en (məs tā′kən) **1** wrong; not correct: *a case of* mistaken *identity.* **2** See
mistake. mis·tak·en·ly.

Mis·ter (mĭs′tər) a title usually written
as "Mr.," used before the name of a man
or the name of his office: *my father,* Mr.
Smith; Mr. *President.*

mis·tle·toe (mĭs′əl-
tō′) an evergreen
plant that grows on
the branches of trees
and bears waxy,
greenish-white ber-
ries.

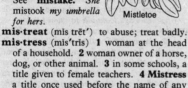

Mistletoe

mis·took (mĭs tŏŏk′)
See **mistake.** *She*
mistook *my umbrella
for hers.*

mis·treat (mĭs trēt′) to abuse; treat badly.

mis·tress (mĭs′trĭs) **1** woman at the head
of a household. **2** woman owner of a horse,
dog, or other animal. **3** in some schools, a
title given to female teachers. **4 Mistress**
a title once used before the name of any
woman.

mis·trust (mĭs trŭst′) **1** to fail to have
trust or confidence in; to doubt: *I* mistrust
*a man who doesn't look you straight in the
eye.* **2** lack of confidence; doubt.

mist·y (mĭs′tĭ) **1** having mist; filled or
covered with mist; slightly foggy: *a* misty
morning. **2** tearful; moist: *She didn't cry
but her eyes were* misty. **3** not clear; vague:
a misty *memory of a dream.* **mist·i·er,
mist·i·est; mist·i·ly.**

mis·un·der·stand (mĭs′ŭn dər stănd′) to
fail to understand; be wrong about the
meaning of: *He* misunderstood *me and put
out my hat instead of my cat.* **mis·un·der·
stood, mis·un·der·stand·ing.**

mis·un·der·stand·ing (mĭs′ŭn dər stăn′-
dĭng) **1** mistake as to meaning or motive:
Their misunderstanding *of the recipe caused
them to make a mess of the cake.* **2** disagreement; quarrel: *Their* misunderstandings
last only a little while.

mis·un·der·stood (mĭs′ŭn dər stŏŏd′) See
misunderstand.

¹mis·use (mĭs ūz′) **1** to use wrongly: *to*
misuse *a word; to* misuse *study time.* **2** to
treat badly; to abuse: *to* misuse *a horse
by making him run too fast.* **mis·used,
mis·us·ing.**

²mis·use (mĭs ūs′) wrong use: *The* misuse
*of privileges sometimes causes them to be
withdrawn.*

mite (mīt) **1** any of several
tiny spiderlike creatures,
as the chigger and cheese
mite, that live on animals,
plants, and stored goods.
2 any very tiny thing.
(Homonym: might)

Mite (chigger
larva)

mitt (mĭt) **1** kind of glove
without fingers or with half fingers.
2 mitten. **3** thick glove with a pad over
the palm, used in baseball.

mit·ten (mĭt′ən) covering for the hand
with one place for the fingers and a smaller
place for the thumb.

mix (mĭks) **1** to put together: *to* mix *flour
with water to make paste.* **2** to become
united or blended: *Oil doesn't* mix *with
water.* **3** to make by putting together different ingredients: *to* mix *concrete.* **4** combination of different ingredients; mixture:
a package of cake mix. **5** to get along in a
friendly way; mingle: *to* mix *with people.*
mix up 1 to mix thoroughly. **2** to confuse: *He always* mixes up *your name and
mine.*

mixed (mĭkst) **1** of different kinds: *a bowl
of* mixed *nuts.* **2** of girls and boys; of
women and men: *a* mixed *chorus.*

mixed number number and a fraction
written together, such as 3 ¼.

mix·er (mĭk′sər) **1** device or machine for
mixing ingredients: *an electric* mixer; *a
cement* mixer. **2 good mixer** person who
gets along well with all kinds of people.

mix·ture (mĭks′chər) **1** something made
by mixing: *Lemonade is a* mixture *of lemon
juice, sugar, and water.* **2** a blending or
mingling; mixing: *From the* mixture *of
copper and zinc we get brass.*

miz·zen·mast (mĭz′ən măst′ or mĭz′ən-
məst) rear mast in a two-masted or three-
masted vessel.

---

fāte, făt, fâre, fär; bē, bĕt; bīte, bĭt; nō, nŏt, nôr; fūse, fŭn, fûr; tōō, tŏŏk; foil; foul; thin; ~~then~~;
hw for wh as in *w*hat; zh for s as in u*s*ual; ə for a, e, i, o, u, as in *a*go, lin*e*n, per*i*l, at*o*m, min*u*s

Mme.

Mme. madame.

mo. month.

Mo. Missouri.

moan (mōn) **1** long, low sound of pain or sorrow: *the moans of a sick person.* **2** to utter this sound; to make moans: *to moan in one's sleep.* **3** any sound like a moan: *the moan of the wind.* **4** to bewail; complain about. (Homonym: mown)

moat (mōt) a ditch, usually water filled, around a building or enclosure to prevent entrance or escape: *Monkey island at the zoo is surrounded by a moat.* (Homonym: mote)

Moat

mob (mŏb) **1** large, disorderly, or violent crowd of people. **2** to crowd around and jostle: *Autograph hunters mobbed the popular singer.* **3** to attack as a mob does: *The angry crowd mobbed the palace.* **4** common or general run of people: *Do you think for yourself, or do you run with the mob?* **5** of a mob: *a mob scene in a movie.* **6** done by a mob: *The police broke up the mob violence.* **mobbed, mob·bing.**

mo·bile (mō′bəl or mō′bēl) **1** movable; easily moved: *Our mobile troops use many airplanes and helicopters.* **2** able to change quickly or easily: *the actor's mobile features.* **3** sculpture or decoration made of bits of colored paper, glass, wood, wire, etc., hung on wire or string and revolving freely.

mo·bil·i·ty (mō bil′ə tĭ) **1** ease of movement: *the mobility of modern armies.* **2** ease of change: *the mobility of her features.*

mo·bil·ize (mō′bə līz′) to assemble and make ready for active use: *to mobilize the country for an emergency.* **mo·bi·lized, mo·bi·liz·ing.**

moc·ca·sin (mŏk′ə sən) **1** a soft-soled, slipperlike Indian shoe. **2** any of certain poisonous snakes of the southern States.

mock (mŏk) **1** to ridicule; imitate to make fun of: *It is cruel to mock anyone who stammers.* **2** to scoff at; jeer at; defy: *Pirates mocked the laws of every nation.* **3** make-believe; imitation; not real: *a mock battle; mock turtle soup.*

Moccasin

moderate

mock·er·y (mŏk′ə rĭ) **1** scornful ridicule; mimicking to make fun of a person or thing: *Anyone who acts self-important simply invites mockery.* **2** a bad imitation; an empty sham: *a mockery of justice.* **mock·er·ies.**

mock·ing·bird (mŏk′ing bûrd) a slate-gray bird of the southern United States, which mimics other bird's songs.

Mockingbird,
10½ in. long

mode (mōd) **1** way; manner: *The actor's mode of speaking was very dramatic. The airplane is a modern mode of transportation.* **2** style or fashion of the time in manners or dress: *Dress that was the mode fifty years ago looks old-fashioned today.*

mod·el (mŏd′əl) **1** guide; pattern; standard: *Use the business letter in the book as a model.* **2** to pattern (oneself) after someone or something: *Ruth modeled herself after her mother.* **3** a person or thing to pattern oneself after: *The young officer chose the famous general as his model.* **4** setting an example: *a model child.* **5** a small exact copy of something larger: *an airplane model.* **6** small, exact representation of something to be built or made: *The architect showed us the model of the school that will soon be built.* **7** style or design of something manufactured, usually changed every year: *That car is the latest model.* **8** to form; shape: *to model a dog out of clay.* **9** person who poses for an artist. **10** to pose for an artist. **11** person who displays or advertises clothes by wearing them: *a fashion model.* **12** to display clothes by wearing them: *to model a dress.*

¹**mod·er·ate** (mŏd′ər it) **1** reasonable; not extreme: *This store sells suits at a moderate price.* **2** not very much or very great; limited: *Mother showed only moderate enthusiasm when Father suggested a fishing trip.* **mod·er·ate·ly.**

²**mod·er·ate** (mŏd′ə rāt′) **1** to calm; make or become quiet, less violent, etc.: *Even though you are angry, try to moderate your voice.* **2** to preside over or direct a public meeting, debate, or discussion. **mod·er·at·ed, mod·er·at·ing.**

mod·er·a·tion (mŏd′ə rā′shən) **1** a moderating; becoming milder or less extreme: *There has been a gradual* moderation *of the climate since the ice age.* **2** a being moderate; self-control; restraint; freedom from extremes, etc.: *to eat with* moderation.

mod·ern (mŏd′ərn) of, or having to do with, the present time; recent: *Television is a* modern *invention.* **mod·ern·ly.**

mod·ern·ize (mŏd′ər nīz′) to make modern or suitable for present needs; to bring up to date: *to* modernize *a house.* **mod·ern·ized, mod·ern·iz·ing.**

mod·est (mŏd′ĭst) **1** not boastful or proud: *The* modest *athlete never brags about all the games he won.* **2** not grand; simple: *Even after they were rich, they lived in a* modest *house.* **3** having, or showing a sense of what is fitting, proper, or suitable; decent. **mod·est·ly.**

mod·es·ty (mŏd′əs tĭ) **1** a lack of vanity; lack of pride or boastfulness: *Being elected class president didn't change Jack's* modesty. **2** decency; sense of what is proper, fitting, and acceptable; propriety: *It was an old-fashioned idea of* modesty *that women should not show their ankles.* **mod·es·ties.**

mod·i·fi·ca·tion (mŏd′ə fə kā′shən) **1** a modifying; changing: *The* modification *of the plans for the new hospital reduced expenses.* **2** a change: *We made a few* modifications *in the school Christmas program.*

mod·i·fi·er (mŏd′ə fī′ər) a word or group of words that limits the meaning of, or describes, another word or group of words. In the sentence "Catch the white kitten." "white" is a modifier of "kitten."

mod·i·fy (mŏd′ə fī′) **1** to change; alter: *Now that you know the facts, will you* modify *your opinion?* **2** to limit the meaning of, or describe, a word or group of words. In the sentence "Watch the red kite." "red" modifies "kite " **mod·i·fied, mod·i·fy·ing.**

mod·u·late (mŏj′ə lāt′) **1** to vary the tone of; tone down: *to* modulate *the voice.* **2** in music, to pass smoothly from one key to another. **mod·u·lat·ed, mod·u·lat·ing.**

mod·u·la·tion (mŏj′ə lā′shən) act of modulating; a change of tone.

mo·hair (mō′hâr′) a woven material made from the hair of the Angora goat.

Mo·ham·med (mō hăm′ĭd) Arabian prophet, founder of the Moslem religion.

Mo·ham·med·an (mō hăm′ə dən) word used by Christians to mean "Moslem," but disliked by the Moslems themselves. See **Moslem.**

moist (moist) damp; slightly wet: *Postage stamps often stick together when the air is* moist. **moist·ly.**

moist·en (mois′ən) **1** to make slightly wet or damp: *to* moisten *an envelope flap with a sponge.* **2** to become full of tears: *Her eyes* moistened *as she read the sad news.*

mois·ture (mois′chər) **1** dampness; slight wetness: *There is still* moisture *in the ground from the spring rains.* **2** water vapor in the air or condensed on a surface: *Beads of* moisture *formed on the outside of the pitcher.*

mo·lar (mō′lər) one of the large, double-rooted teeth in the back of the jaws, used for grinding food. For picture, see **teeth.**

mo·las·ses (mə lăs′ĭz) dark-colored, sticky syrup which is a by-product in sugar making.

¹mold (mōld) **1** a hollow form into which something is poured to be shaped, such as molten metal, gelatin, pudding, etc. **2** to make or form into a definite shape: *to* mold *a clay figure.* **3** shape the character of: *Our earlier experiences sometimes* mold *our lives.* **4** something formed in or by a mold: *a custard* mold. **5** to make in a mold: *to* mold *a candle.* **6** physical shape; form. **7** kind; character: *a man of honest* mold. Also spelled **mould.** [**¹mold** comes through French from a Latin word (modulus) meaning "a small measure."]

²mold (mōld) fine, soft soil, rich in decayed matter such as leaves. Also spelled **mould.** [**²mold** is a form of an Old English word (molde).]

³mold (mōld) **1** a fuzzy fungus growth appearing on the surface of decaying foods, damp leather, wood, etc., and spreading quickly in moist or warm air. **2** to become covered with mold: *Bread* molds *quickly in the summer.* Also spelled **mould.** [**³mold** is a word of unknown origin.]

---

fāte, făt, fâre, fär; bē, bĕt; bīte, bĭt; nō, nŏt, nôr; fūse, fŭn, fûr; tōō, tŏŏk; foil; foul; thin; ~~then~~;
hw for wh as in *wh*at; zh for s as in u*s*ual; ə for a, e, i, o, u, as in ago, linen, peril, atom, minus

mold·er (mōl′dər) to decay; crumble to dust: *The walls of the old fortress moldered beneath the ivy.* Also spelled **moulder.**

mold·ing (mōl′dĭng) **1** act of shaping by or as by a mold. **2** a thing so shaped: *the molding on a cornice.* **3** strip of wood or plaster placed along the upper walls of a room for hanging pictures or for decoration.

mold·y (mōl′dĭ) **1** covered with mold: *the moldy bread.* **2** damp; musty: *a moldy cellar.* Also spelled **mouldy. mold·i·er, mold·i·est.**

¹mole (mōl) a dark-colored spot or growth on the skin. [**¹mole** is a form of an Old English word (māl) of the same meaning.]

²mole (mōl) a small animal with dark-gray velvety fur and tiny, almost sightless, eyes. Its large front feet are suited to digging, and it spends most of its life underground. [**²mole** is a form of an earlier English word (molle).]

Mole, about 6 in. long

³mole (mōl) a solid stone wall or pier built out into the sea to break the force of the waves. [**³mole** comes through French from a Latin word (moles) meaning "mass," "heap."]

mol·e·cule (mŏl′ə kūl′) **1** the tiniest bit into which a substance can be divided and still be the same substance. A molecule of a chemical element may be made up of one or more atoms of that element. A molecule of a chemical compound is made up of atoms of different elements. **2** any tiny part or thing.

mo·lest (mə lĕst′) to interfere with or harm: *You should not molest the animals at the zoo.*

mol·lusk (mŏl′əsk) class of animals with soft bodies usually enclosed in a hard shell. Snails, mussels, and oysters are mollusks.

molt·en (mōl′tən) made fluid by heat: *a drop of molten lead.*

mom (mŏm) a fond word for "mother."

mo·ment (mō′mənt) **1** instant; a certain point in time: *I knew you the moment I saw you.* **2** present time: *Because of his victory the general is the hero of the moment.*

3 importance: *The decision to build a new gymnasium is of great moment to the school.*

mo·men·tar·y (mō′mən tĕr′ĭ) **1** lasting for a moment: *a momentary silence.* **2** happening at any moment: *A spy must expect momentary capture.* **mo·men·tar·i·ly.**

mo·men·tous (mō mĕn′təs) very important. **mo·men·tous·ly.**

mo·men·tum (mō mĕn′təm) **1** force of motion in a moving body: *the momentum of a bullet.* **2** tendency to continue moving forward; impetus: *The candidate's speech gave momentum to his campaign.* **mo·men·ta** or **mo·men·tums.**

Mon. Monday.

mon·arch (mŏn′ərk) ruler, such as a king, queen, emperor, etc.

mon·ar·chy (mŏn′ər kĭ) **1** system of government headed by a monarch. **2** country ruled by a monarch. **mon·ar·chies.**

mon·as·ter·y (mŏn′ə stĕr′ĭ) **1** the building or buildings occupied by a religious society of men. **2** a society of men who live together and devote themselves to a religious life. **mon·as·ter·ies.**

Mon·day (mŭn′dā or mŭn′dĭ) the second day of the week.

mon·ey (mŭn′ĭ) **1** metal coins and paper notes used to pay for things. **2** anything used as coins or paper money are used. Sea shells, pieces of iron, gold, and silver have all been used for money. **3** wealth.

money order an order for the payment of a stated sum of money, especially a government order sold at a post office that can be cashed at another post office by the person to whom it is made out.

mon·goose (mŏng′gōōs) a fierce, weasel-like animal of India, famous as a killer of rats, mice, and poisonous snakes.

mon·grel (mŏng′grəl or mŭng′grəl) **1** dog of no particular breed or of mixed breed. **2** of mixed breed or

Indian mongoose, about 16 in. long

kind: *The Indian trader spoke a mongrel language of English and Indian words.*

mon·i·tor (mŏn′ə tər) **1** pupil in school with special duties, such as keeping order, taking attendance, etc. **2** receiver or screen for checking radio or television transmissions. **3** to check (radio or television transmissions) by listening in with a receiver or watching in with a monitor screen. **4** large lizard of Africa, Asia, and Australia. **5** warship, carrying heavy guns and armor, built for coastal defense. **6 Monitor** name of the first vessel of this type, used in the Civil War.

monk (mŭngk) man who has taken religious vows and lives in a monastery with other men of the same religious order.

mon·key (mŭng′ki) **1** an animal of the group nearest to man in appearance and intelligence, especially one of the smaller, long-tailed members of this group. **2** a mischievous person. **3** to meddle; trifle; play carelessly: *Do not monkey with a gun.*

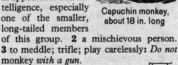
Capuchin monkey, about 18 in. long

mon·o·gram (mŏn′ə grăm′) a group of interlaced or fancifully combined letters, especially the initials of a name, used on stationery, clothing, etc.

Monogram of Albrecht Dürer

mon·o·plane (mŏn′ə plān′) airplane with one set of wings. Most modern airplanes are monoplanes.

mo·nop·o·ly (mə nŏp′ə li) **1** exclusive control of the use, sale, or distribution of a commodity or service by one person or one group of persons: *One bus company has a monopoly of our city's transportation.* **2** a thing controlled in this way: *Coinage is a government monopoly.* **3** organization exercising such control. **mo·nop·o·lies.**

mon·o·syl·la·ble (mŏn′ə sĭl′ə bəl) word of one syllable.

mo·not·o·nous (mə nŏt′ə nəs) always the same; tiresome because of sameness: *Her monotonous voice never changed expression while she read the story.* **mo·not·o·nous·ly.**

mo·not·o·ny (mə nŏt′ə ni) dull sameness; lack of variety: *The monotony of his stories bored me.*

mon·soon (mŏn sōōn′) **1** wind in the Indian Ocean and Southern Asia which blows from the southwest from April to October, and from the northeast from October to April. **2** rainy season that comes with the southwest monsoon.

mon·ster (mŏn′stər) **1** animal or plant that is ugly and misshapen or unnatural: *A dragon is an imaginary monster.* **2** very wicked or cruel person: *Only a monster would mistreat a child.*

mon·strous (mŏn′strəs) **1** not normal; differing from the natural shape: *a monstrous creature with two heads.* **2** huge; enormous; great: *He ate a monstrous helping of ice cream.* **3** shocking; horrible; causing disgust: *a monstrous act of cruelty.* **mon·strous·ly.**

Mont. Montana.

Mon·tan·a (mŏn tăn′ə) a State in northwestern United States.

month (mŭnth) **1** one of the twelve parts into which the year is divided. A calendar month is about four weeks. **2 lunar month** the 28 days from one new moon to the next new moon.

month·ly (mŭnth′li) **1** done, payable, published, or happening once a month: *a monthly cleaning; monthly bills; a monthly magazine.* **2** once a month; every month: *He collects for the paper monthly.* **3** continuing through a month: *a commuter's monthly ticket.* **4** magazine published once a month. **month·lies.**

mon·u·ment (mŏn′yŏŏ mənt) **1** something set up or built in memory of a person or event, such as a statue, column, tomb, etc. **2** work or achievement that is worthy to be remembered: *The discovery of radium was a monument of scientific research.*

mon·u·men·tal (mŏn′yŏŏ měn′təl) **1** of or serving as a monument: *a monumental inscription.* **2** lasting; important: *The Gettysburg Address is a monumental speech.* **3** very great; colossal; imposing: *Building a bridge is a monumental task.* **mon·u·men·tal·ly.**

moo (mōō) **1** the sound made by a cow. **2** to make the sound of a cow.

mood (mōōd) state of mind or feeling; humor; disposition: *in a merry mood; in the mood to work.*

---

fāte, făt, fâre, fär; bē, bĕt; bīte, bĭt; nō, nŏt, nôr; fūse, fŭn, fûr; tōō, tŏŏk; foil; foul; thin; ~~then~~; hw for wh as in *wh*at; zh for s as in u*s*ual; ə for a, e, i, o, u, as in *a*go, lin*e*n, per*i*l, at*o*m, min*u*s

mood·y (mōō′dĭ) **1** having changes in state of mind or temper: *a moody disposition.* **2** bad-tempered; gloomy; glum: *Everyone shuns him when he is moody and unfriendly.* **mood·i·er, mood·i·est; mood·i·ly.**

moon (mōōn) **1** the heavenly body that revolves around the earth 13 times a year. It reflects light from the sun. **2** any similar body revolving around a planet: *The planet Mars has two moons.* **3** in American Indian reckoning, a month. **4** a moon-shaped object, either round or crescent: *The flag of Turkey has a* moon *and star on it.* **5** to wander or look about in a dreamy or listless way.

FIRST QUARTER

FULL MOON   NEW MOON

LAST QUARTER

Phases of moon

moon·beam (mōōn′bēm′) ray of light from the moon.

moon·light (mōōn′līt′) **1** light of the moon. **2** taking place by moonlight: *a moonlight cruise.*

moon·lit (mōōn′lĭt′) lighted by the moon: *a moonlit landscape.*

moon·shine (mōōn′shīn′) **1** moonlight: *The moonshine made the night bright as day.* **2** foolish or idle talk; nonsense.

¹moor (mōōr) an area of open, waste land, especially one in England or Scotland covered with low plant growth such as heather. [**¹moor** is a form of an Old English word (mōr) meaning marshy land.]

²moor (mōōr) to fasten or secure a vessel in place with cables or anchors. [**²moor** is a word of Germanic origin.]

moor·ings (mōōr′ĭngz) **1** ropes, cables, or anchors used to fasten a vessel in place. **2** the place where a vessel is anchored or made fast.

moor·land (mōōr′lănd′) barren land covered with heather; moor.

moose (mōōs) the largest American deer. It is found in Canada and the northern United States. It frequently weighs 1,000 pounds. pl. **moose.**

Moose, about 6 ft. high at shoulder

mop (mŏp) **1** bundle of coarse yarn, cloth, etc., or a sponge, fastened to a handle and used for washing floors or dishes. **2** to clean or wipe (with a mop or cloth): *Larry mopped up the puddle of spilled milk.* **3** something like a mop: *a mop of hair.* **mopped, mop·ping.**

mope (mōp) **1** to be dull, quiet, and sad: *Instead of going out, he moped all day in his room.* **2** person who is dull, quiet, and sad. **moped, mop·ing.**

mor·al (môr′əl or mŏr′əl) **1** having to do with the difference between right and wrong: *a moral problem; one's moral standards.* **2** right; virtuous: *He made a very moral decision.* **3** able to understand the difference between right and wrong: *Man is a moral being.* **4** lesson taught by a story, fable, experience, etc.: *The moral was given in a sentence at the end of the fable.* **5 morals** standards of right and wrong. **6 moral sense** ability to distinguish between right and wrong. **7 moral support** encouragement, usually given by taking a person's side.

mo·rale (mə rǎl′) state of mind that helps a person keep up hope, courage, good spirits, etc., in the face of danger or discouragement: *The morale of the troops was high as they went into action that day.*

mo·ral·i·ty (mô rǎl′ə tĭ) **1** the rightness or wrongness of an action. **2** a standard of right and wrong in conduct. **3** virtue; uprightness; good morals. **mo·ral·i·ties.**

mor·al·ly (môr′ə lĭ or mŏr′ə lĭ) **1** in a good or virtuous manner: *Because he lived morally, he gained the respect of his neighbors.* **2** according to ideas of right and wrong: *Although he broke no law, his conduct was morally questionable.* **3** practically; almost: *I can't prove it, but I'm morally certain I've seen him before.*

mo·rass (mə rǎs′) piece of soft, swampy ground; bog; swamp.

mor·bid (môr′bĭd) **1** having too much to do with unpleasant and gloomy things; not healthy: *Reading a great many horror stories may show a morbid taste.* **2** caused by or having to do with disease: *A cancer is a morbid growth in the body.* **mor·bid·ly.**

more (môr) **1** greater in number, amount, degree, etc.: *Our catcher made more hits than any other player.* **2** a greater number, amount, degree, etc.: *We used a pint of paint on the fence, but the shed will take* more *than that.* **3** additional: *The third quarter of the game just ended, so there is only one* more *quarter to play.* **4** an additional amount or number: *Please buy* more *of that delicious cake.* **5** again: *He hasn't come yet, so call him once* more. **6** to a greater extent or degree: *This sofa is* more *comfortable than that bench.*

more·o·ver (môr ō′vər) besides; also; furthermore: *That basketball player is fast; moreover, he is tall.*

morn (môrn) morning. (Homonym: mourn)

morn·ing (môr′ning) **1** the first part of the day, from midnight until noon, or from dawn until noon. **2** having to do with the morning: *our* morning *exercises; the* morning *coffee.* (Homonym: mourning)

morn·ing-glo·ry (môr′ning glôr′ĭ) a climbing vine bearing heart-shaped leaves and trumpet-shaped blossoms that close in a twist in bright light. The blooms are purple, blue, pink, or white.

Morning-glory

mor·on (môr′ŏn) person whose mental ability does not develop beyond that of a child between 8 and 12 years old.

mo·rose (mō rōs′ or mə rōs′) gloomy; sullen: *Keep your spirits high and don't become* morose *over failure or disappointment.* **mo·rose·ly.**

mor·row (mŏr′ō or môr′ō) **1** the day after any particular day: *After a good rest the traveler felt better on the* morrow. **2** morning: *Good* morrow.

Morse code (môrs kōd) an alphabet of dots, dashes, and spaces used in transmitting messages.

mor·sel (môr′səl) small piece; bit; scrap: *He threw some* morsels *of bread to the birds.*

mor·tal (môr′təl) **1** subject to death: *All living things are* mortal. **2** human being: *No* mortal *could eat all that food at one*

time. **3** human: *We all have* mortal *weaknesses that we should try to overcome.* **4** causing death; fatal: *a* mortal *wound.* **5** extreme; great: *in* mortal *fear.* **6** causing spiritual death: *a* mortal *sin.* **7** lasting until death: *a* mortal *struggle; a* mortal *enemy.* **8** associated with death or dying: *The wounded shark thrashed about in* mortal *agony.* **mor·tal·ly.**

mor·tar (môr′tər) **1** a kind of building cement to hold stones or bricks together. **2** a kind of cannon for firing shells in a high curve. **3** a heavy bowl of glass, earthenware or other material in which drugs, spices, and the like are pounded or ground to powder with a pestle.

Mortar and pestle

mor·ti·fi·ca·tion (môr′tə fə kā′shən) **1** shame; humiliation: *The singer was overcome with* mortification *when her voice cracked.* **2** discipline of self by acts of self-denial such as fasting and the like. **3** a cause of shame or humiliation: *The soiled and worn rug was a* mortification *to the hostess.* **4** in medicine, death or decay of part of a human or animal body.

mor·ti·fy (môr′tə fī′) **1** to embarrass; cause shame or humiliation: *It* mortifies *me to forget the name of a person I am introducing.* **2** to discipline oneself, as by acts of self-denial such as fasting and the like. **mor·ti·fied, mor·ti·fy·ing.**

mo·sa·ic (mō zā′ĭk) **1** a picture or design made by fitting together bits of colored glass, stone, or tile. **2** made of or resembling mosaic: *Some public buildings have* mosaic *floors.*

Mosaic

Mos·cow (mŏs′kou or mŏs′kō) capital of the Soviet Union, in the central part of European Russia.

Mos·lem (mŏz′ləm or mŏs′ləm) **1** a believer in the religion founded by Mohammed. **2** having to do with the followers of

---

fāte, făt, fâre, fär; bē, bĕt; bite, bĭt; nō, nŏt, nôr; fūse, fŭn, fûr; tōō, tŏŏk; foil; foul; thin; ~~then~~; hw for wh as in *wh*at; zh for s as in u*s*ual; ə for a, e, i, o, u, as in *a*go, lin*e*n, per*i*l, at*o*m, min*u*s

Mohammed, their religion, or their customs: *a Moslem country*. Also spelled **Muslim.**

mosque (mŏsk) a Moslem church.

mos·qui·to (mə skē'- tō) a kind of slender, long-legged, gauze- winged, blood-suck- ing insect, the bite of which may cause swelling and itching. Some kinds carry yellow fever or malaria germs. **mos·qui·toes** or **mos·qui·tos.**

Mosque

Mosquito

moss (môs or mŏs) a small plant with tiny leaves. Moss grows in thick clusters which form a mat on damp ground, rocks, trees, etc.

moss·y (môs′ĭ or mŏs′ĭ) 1 covered with moss: *a mossy stone.* 2 like moss. **moss·i·er, moss·i·est.**

most (mōst) 1 greatest amount or number of: *The team that scores the most runs wins the game.* 2 the greatest amount, number, or degree: *What is the most you will pay?* 3 to the greatest extent or degree: *I like a lot of sports, but I like swimming most.* 4 the majority; the larger part: *I have read most of the book and can finish it tomorrow.*

most·ly (mōst′lĭ) for the most part; chiefly: *Our yard is mostly lawn, with a few shrubs.*

mote (mōt) tiny particle, especially of dust. (Homonym: moat)

mo·tel (mō tĕl′) roadside hotel or group of cottages for people traveling by car.

moth (môth or mŏth) any of a large num- ber of downy, four- winged insects of widely different size, resembling the but- terflies, usually most active at night. They are generally less bril- liantly colored than butterflies and may be told from them by their stouter bodies and pointed or feathered antennae. The larvae of many kinds are destructive of cloth, foliage, and fruit.

Moth

moth·er (mŭth′ər) 1 female parent: *Every child has a father and a mother.* 2 to care

for as a mother does; act as a mother toward: *The old hen mothered the ducklings as if they were her own chicks.* 3 source of something: *Necessity is the mother of inven- tion.* 4 as learned from one's mother; na- tive: *Juan speaks English well but Spanish is his mother tongue.* 5 **Mother Superior** head of a convent or religious community.

moth·er·hood (mŭth′ər hŏŏd′) 1 being a mother: *She took seriously the duties of* motherhood. 2 mothers in general: *On Mother's Day, we honor the motherhood of the country.*

moth·er·in·law (mŭth′ər ĭn lô′) mother of a person's husband or wife. **moth·ers- in-law.**

moth·er·ly (mŭth′ər lĭ) of or like that of a mother; maternal: *a motherly hug.*

moth·er·of·pearl (mŭth′ər əv pûrl′) 1 the glossy lining of some shells that shows rainbow colors in changing lights. 2 made of this material: *a mother-of-pearl card case.*

mo·tion (mō′shən) 1 action or movement; a changing from one place or position to another: *The motion of a boat on a rough sea makes some people ill.* 2 gesture: *He made a commanding motion for silence.* 3 to make a gesture or movement to express meaning: *The host motioned for the visitor to be seated.* 4 formal suggestion or pro- posal made at a meeting: *The secretary made a motion to select a program committee.*

mo·tion·less (mō′shən lĭs) not moving; still: *The hunting dog stood motionless when he saw the birds.* **mo·tion·less·ly.**

motion picture moving picture.

mo·tive (mō′tĭv) 1 inner reason which causes a person to act as he does under certain circumstances; purpose or incentive for acting in a certain way: *Her motive for taking the blame was to shield her brother.* 2 caus- ing motion: *The wind supplies the motive power for a sailboat.*

mot·ley (mŏt′lĭ) 1 mixed; varied; mottled; made up of different colors or things: *A motley crowd filled the street.* 2 garments made of different colors: *The clown was dressed in motley.*

Motley

mo·tor (mō′tər) 1 machine that turns elec- tric power into motion. An electric fan has

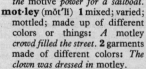

a motor. **2** any engine: *Our automobile motor broke down and delayed our trip.* **3** to travel by automobile: *We motored across the country.* **4** having to do with movement: *a motor muscle; motor nerves.*

mo·tor·boat (mō'tər bōt') boat run by a motor.

mo·tor·car (mō'tər-kär') automobile.

mo·tor·cy·cle (mō'-tər sī'kəl) **1** a heavy motor-propelled bicycle. **2** to travel by motorcycle: *We motorcycled to New York.* **mo·tor·cy·cled, mo·tor·cy·cling.**

Motorcycle

mo·tor·ist (mō'tər ist) person who drives or travels in an automobile.

mo·tor·ize (mō'tə rīz') **1** to equip with a motor. **2** to supply with motor vehicles: *We have motorized our army since World War I.* **mo·tor·ized, mo·tor·iz·ing.**

mo·tor·man (mō'tər mən) the operator of a streetcar or an electric train. **mo·tor·men.**

mot·tled (mŏt'əld) spotted or streaked with different colors: *The marble table top has a mottled pattern.*

mot·to (mŏt'ō) **1** sentence, phrase, or word used as a guiding rule or principle: *"Early to bed and early to rise" was his motto.* **2** sentence or phrase expressing a principle, slogan, or the like, inscribed on a coin, seal, flag, etc.: *In the United States, the coins all bear the* motto *"In God We Trust."* **mot·toes** or **mot·tos.**

mould (mōld) mold.

mould·er (mōl'dər) molder.

mould·y (mōl'dī) moldy. **mould·i·er, mould·i·est.**

mound (mound) **1** heap or bank of earth, stones, or sand. **2** small hill or knoll. **3** in baseball, a small, raised area from which the pitcher throws.

¹mount (mount) mountain. [**¹mount** comes through French from a form (montis) of a Latin word (mons) meaning "mountain."]

²mount (mount) **1** to go up; ascend: *He mounted to the top of the steps.* **2** to go up

or rise (in amount); increase: *Her bill kept mounting as she bought more items.* **3** to get up on: *The rider mounted his horse. The speaker mounted the platform.* **4** to furnish with a horse or horses: *The captain mounted his men on the captured horses.* **5** horse or other animal used for riding. **6** to put in position or set up for use: *Cannon were mounted on the hilltop overlooking enemy territory.* **7** to provide a setting, frame, or support for: *to mount a jewel; to mount a picture; to mount stamps in an album.* **8** thing used as a setting, frame, or support. [**²mount** is from a French word (monter) meaning "to climb." The French word comes from the Latin word (mons) for "mountain."]

moun·tain (moun'tən) **1** any part of a land mass that rises high above the surrounding area. **2** anything of great size or amount: *a mountain of potatoes; a mountain of work.* **3** coming from the mountains; found, born, or used in the mountains: *the mountain folk; a mountain hut.*

moun·tain·eer (moun'tə nir') **1** person who lives in the mountains. **2** mountain climber.

mountain goat an animal of the Rocky Mountains that looks like a goat but is related to the antelopes. It has shaggy white hair, black horns and hoofs, and is about three feet high at its humped shoulders.

mountain lion a large, tawny cat of western America. Also called puma, panther, and cougar.

Mountain lion, about 8 ft. long

moun·tain·ous (moun'tə nəs) **1** having many mountains: *Switzerland is a mountainous country.* **2** like a mountain; huge; enormous: *The waves were mountainous during the gale.* **moun·tain·ous·ly.**

mountain range row or connected series of mountains.

moun·tain·side (moun'tin sīd') slope of a mountain: *We camped on a mountainside during our vacation.*

---

fāte, făt, fâre, fär; bē, bĕt; bīte, bĭt; nō, nŏt, nôr; fūse, fŭn, fûr; tōō, tŏŏk; foil; foul; thin; ~~then~~; hw for wh as in *wh*at; zh for s as in u*s*ual; ə for a, e, i, o, u, as in *a*go, lin*e*n, per*i*l, at*o*m, min*u*s

mourn (môrn) to feel or show sorrow or grief (for); grieve (for): *Tommy* mourned *the loss of his pet dog.* (Homonym: morn)

mourn·er (môr'nər) person who grieves or is sorrowful.

mourn·ful (môrn'fəl) sorrowful; sad: *the* mournful *sound of a dove.* **mourn·ful·ly.**

mourn·ing (môr'ning) 1 a grieving. 2 outward expression of sorrow, such as the wearing of black clothes. 3 the clothes: *The* widow wore mourning *for a year.* (Homonym: morning)

mouse (mous) any of several small gnawing animals with soft gray or brown fur. The common house mouse is gray, has small beady eyes and a long tail, and is most active at night. White mice are sometimes kept as pets. **mice.**

House mouse, about 7 in. long

mouse·trap (mous'trăp') trap for catching mice.

mous·tache (mŭs'tăsh or məs tăsh') mustache.

¹mouth (mouth) 1 opening in the head of a person or animal through which he takes in food and drink. The mouth contains the teeth and tongue, and is also used to form sounds. 2 the lips: *The little girl has a very* pretty *mouth.* 3 a passage or opening like a mouth: *the mouth of a cave or of a pitcher.* 4 the place a river flows into another body of water: *The* mouth *of the Mississippi is near New Orleans.* 5 **with open mouth** amazed; dumbfounded: *I stood with open* mouth *watching the fireworks.* 6 **down at the mouth** downhearted; sad.

²mouth (mouth) to speak in a pompous way: *The mayor* mouthed *his Fourth of July* speech.

mouth·ful (mouth'fool') 1 as much as the mouth can usually take in at one time. 2 a small amount: *The sick boy could eat no more than a* mouthful.

mouth·piece (mouth'pēs') 1 the part of a pipe, musical instrument, etc., which a person places against the lips or in the mouth. 2 person, newspaper, etc., that expresses the opinions and feelings of others; a spokesman.

mov·a·ble (moo'və bəl) 1 capable of being moved or carried from one place to another; not fixed. 2 changing from one date

to another: *Easter is a* movable *holy day.* 3 **movables** furniture, goods, or any personal property which can be carried from one place to another. Also spelled **moveable. mov·a·bly.**

move (moov) 1 to change from one position or place to another. 2 a change of place or position. 3 to change homes, places of business, etc. 4 a change of home, etc. 5 to go forward; progress: *The work on the new gymnasium* moved *slowly.* 6 to cause to move or act: *The wind gently* moved *the leaves. His pride* moved *him to try the high dive.* 7 action done for a purpose; step: *What will your next* move *be?* 8 to arouse or stir up the feelings of: *The sad play* moved *the audience to tears.* 9 to act; do something: *The police* move *quickly whenever a crime is committed.* 10 a turn to move the pieces in games such as chess or checkers. 11 to make a formal request: *to* move *for a new trial.* 12 to propose (in a meeting): *I* move *that we take a vote on that next week.* 13 to be active; have interests and take part in: *This child* moves *in a world all his own.* 14 to be in motion; go: *When you press the button, the wheels of the machine begin to* move. 15 **on the move** moving about: *That energetic man is always* on the move.

move heaven and earth to make every effort.

moved, mov·ing.

move·ment (moov'mənt) 1 a moving; change of position or location: *the movement of the dancer's feet.* 2 action; activity: *The detectives watched every* movement *of the gang members.* 3 joint action and effort for a special purpose: *the antislavery* movement. 4 the moving parts of a watch, clock, etc. 5 rhythm: *the* movement *of the dance music.* 6 section of a piece of music: *the first* movement *of a symphony.* 7 progress: *the quick* movement *of the plot.* 8 an emptying of the bowels.

mov·er (moo'vər) person or thing that moves or causes to move, especially a person who hauls furniture from one house to another.

mov·ie (moo'vi) 1 a moving picture. 2 **the movies** motion pictures.

mov·ing (moo'ving) 1 that moves: *a moving* wheel. 2 that causes motion or action: *a* moving *force*. **3** stirring the emotions or feelings: *a* moving *story*. **mov·ing·ly.**

moving picture a series of pictures taken by a special camera. These are projected on a screen so quickly that what is shown seems to be moving; motion picture.

¹mow (mō) **1** to cut down (grass, grain, etc.) with a scythe or machine: *to* mow *grass*. **2** to cut grass or grain from: *The boys* mowed *the lawn*.

mow down to shoot or strike down in great numbers: *The machine gun* mowed down *the men in the enemy lines*.

mowed, mowed or **mown, mow·ing.** [¹**mow** is a form of an Old English word (māwan).]

²mow (mou) **1** heap of hay or sheaves of grain stored in a barn. **2** place in the barn where hay or sheaves of grain are stored. [²**mow** is a form of an Old English word (mūga).]

mow·er (mō′ər) person or machine that mows: *a lawn* mower.

mown (mōn) See **mow.** *The children played in the new-*mown *hay*. (Homonym: moan)

Mr. (mĭs′tər) Mister; title used before a man's name or the name of his position: *my father,* Mr. *Smith;* Mr. *President*. **Messrs.**

Mrs. (mĭs′ĭs, mĭs′ĭz, or mĭz′ĭz) Mistress; title used before a married woman's name.

Mt. or **mt. 1** mount: *the peak of* Mt. *Hood*. **2** mountain. **Mts., mts.**

much (mŭch) **1** a great deal; a large amount: *Did that cost* much? *There isn't* much *left*. **2** a great amount of: *They don't waste* much *time*. **3** something which is great, important, or worthy of notice: *The old building doesn't seem like* much, *but it has a famous history*. **4** to a great degree; greatly: *I'm* much *taller than you*. **5** nearly; almost: *They left the room* much *as they had found it*. **6 make much of** to make a fuss over: *The baby's grandparents* make much of *everything he does*. **7 not much of a** poor; not very good. **8 too much for** (1) more than a match for: *We lost the game because the other team was* too much for *us*. (2) more than (someone) can bear or stand: *The bad news was* too much for *her and she fainted*. **more, most.**

mu·ci·lage (mū′sə lĭj) thick, sticky substance used to stick things together.

muck (mŭk) mire or filth.

mu·cous mem·brane (mū′kəs mĕm′brān) layer of animal tissue that produces mucus. A mucous membrane lines the mouth, nose, throat, and other passages of the body that open to the air. It helps to protect the body against infection.

mu·cus (mū′kəs) slimy fluid produced by the mucous membrane of the nose, throat, etc.

mud (mŭd) soft, wet earth.

mud·dle (mŭd′əl) **1** to confuse: *His brain was* muddled *by too many questions*. **2** to make a mess of; bungle: *The stupid king* muddled *the country's affairs*. **3** a mess; state of being confused and in disorder: *All the papers in his desk were in a* muddle. **4** to blunder; act in a haphazard way: *to* muddle *along*. **mud·dled, mud·dling.**

mud·dy (mŭd′ĭ) **1** full of mud; covered with mud: *a* muddy *road;* muddy *feet*. **2** to soil with mud: *I only* muddied *the palms of my hands when I fell*. **3** not clear; dark or cloudy: *a* muddy *color; a* muddy *complexion*. **4** obscure; confused: *This composition is full of* muddy *ideas*. **mud·di·er, mud·di·est; mud·died, mud·dy·ing; mud·di·ly.**

muff (mŭf) **1** a tube of padded fur or cloth into which the hands may be placed for warmth. **2** in baseball, to fail to hold (a ball). **3** to handle clumsily: *By his laziness John* muffed *the chance to get good marks*.

Muff

muf·fin (mŭf′ĭn) small, round piece of cornbread or cakelike bread, usually served hot.

muf·fle (mŭf′əl) **1** to lessen or deaden (sound): *Closing the window* muffled *the noises from the street outside*. **2** to wrap or cover (to deaden the sound): *to* muffle *a bell*. **3** to dress or wrap (for protection against the cold): *Children* muffled *up to play in the snow*. **muf·fled, muf·fling.**

muf·fler (mŭf′lər) **1** scarf worn about the neck. **2** device that muffles noise: *A car has a* muffler *attached to the exhaust*.

---

fāte, făt, fâre, fär; bē, bĕt; bīte, bĭt; nō, nŏt, nôr; fūse, fŭn, fûr; tōō, tŏŏk; foil; foul; thin; ~~then~~; hw for wh as in *what*; zh for s as in u*s*ual; ə for a, e, i, o, u, as in *a*go, lin*e*n, per*i*l, at*o*m, min*u*s

mug (mŭg) **1** a large flat-bottomed cup with high straight sides and a large handle. **2** quantity a mug holds.

mug·gy (mŭg′ĭ) hot, damp, and stuffy: *the muggy days of August.* **mug·gi·er, mug·gi·est.**

Mug

mul·ber·ry (mŭl′bĕr′ĭ) **1** a tree with broad leaves and a sweet, edible, berrylike fruit. Some mulberries are dark purple and some are white. The white mulberry is grown for its leaves on which silkworms feed. **2** dark purplish red. **mul·ber·ries.**

mulch (mŭlch) **1** grass, leaves, straw, etc. spread over the ground around trees and plants. Mulch is used to protect roots from temperature changes, to hold moisture in the soil, and to keep strawberries, etc., clean. **2** to spread or cover with mulch.

mule (mūl) **1** a strong work animal, half horse and half donkey, noted for its stubbornness. **2** machine that spins cotton into yarn and then winds it on spools.

Mule, about 5 ft. high at shoulder

mu·le·teer (mū′lə tĭr′) driver of mules.

mul·ish (mū′lĭsh) like a mule; stubborn. **mul·ish·ly.**

mul·let (mŭl′ĭt) any one of several saltwater or fresh-water fish, some of which are used as food.

mul·ti·ple (mŭl′tə pəl) **1** a number that contains another number a certain number of times without a remainder: *12 is a multiple of 2, 3, 4, and 6.* **2** many times repeated: *We have received multiple requests for this book.* **3** of many parts; made up of many things: *his multiple interests.*

mul·ti·pli·cand (mŭl′tə plə kănd′) in multiplication, the number that is added a given number of times. In 3 × 4 = 12, 4 is the multiplicand.

mul·ti·pli·ca·tion (mŭl′tə plə kā′shən) **1** a quick way of finding the answer when the same number must be added several times. The sign used in multiplication is ×, usually read as "times." The answer in multiplication is called the product. **2** multiplying; increasing.

mul·ti·pli·er (mŭl′tə pli′ər) in multiplication, the number that tells how many times another number (the multiplicand) is added. In 3 × 4 = 12, the multiplier is 3.

mul·ti·ply (mŭl′tə pli′) **1** to add the same number a given number of times, to find the product. To multiply 4 by 3 (3 × 4) is the same as adding 4 + 4 + 4. **2** to increase: *Rabbits* multiply *at a rapid rate.* **mul·ti·plied, mul·ti·ply·ing.**

mul·ti·stage (mŭl′tĭ stāj′) having or marked by two or more steps or stages in the completion of an action, process, etc.: *a* multistage *booster rocket.*

mul·ti·tude (mŭl′tə tōōd′ or mŭl′tə tūd′) great number; crowd: *a multitude of stars.*

mum (mŭm) not saying anything; silent: *to keep* mum *about a surprise party.*

mum·ble (mŭm′bəl) **1** to speak low and not clearly; mutter: *The old woman mumbled something I couldn't understand.* **2** a low muttering sound: *She answered me with a mumble.* **mum·bled, mum·bling.**

mum·my (mŭm′ĭ) a body, especially the body of an ancient Egyptian, preserved from decay by being embalmed or dried. **mum·mies.**

Upper part of mummy case

mumps (mŭmps) contagious disease that causes the glands about the jaw to swell and makes chewing and swallowing difficult. It is a common disease of children.

munch (mŭnch) to chew noisily and with much working of the jaws: *He munched a carrot.*

mu·nic·i·pal (mū nĭs′ə pəl) of or having to do with a town or city, its government, etc.: *a municipal parking lot;* municipal *elections.* **mu·nic·i·pal·ly.**

mu·nic·i·pal·i·ty (mū nĭs′ə păl′ə tĭ) town, city, or district that has local self-government. **mu·nic·i·pal·i·ties.**

mu·ni·tions (mū nĭsh′ənz) ammunition, guns, and similar materials used in war.

mu·ral (mūr′əl) **1** having to do with a wall: *famous* mural *decorations.* **2** picture painted on a wall.

mur·der (mûr′dər) **1** the crime of killing a person. **2** to kill (a person) on purpose.

3 to spoil or ruin by lack of skill or experience: *to* murder *a song; to* murder *a foreign language.*

mur·der·er (mûr′dər ər) person guilty of murder.

mur·der·ous (mûr′dər əs) **1** having to do with murder: *a* murderous *plot.* **2** intending murder: *a* murderous *bandit.* **3** capable of murder: *a* murderous *stab in the back.* **mur·der·ous·ly.**

murk (mûrk) darkness; gloom.

murk·y (mûr′ki) dark; gloomy: *a dismal,* murky *room suited to ghost stories.* **murk·i·er, murk·i·est; murk·i·ly.**

mur·mur (mûr′mər) **1** a low sound that is not clear: *a* murmur *of voices through a heavy door.* **2** to speak in a low voice. **3** to complain or grumble in a low, muttering tone: *The students* murmured *about the homework.* **4 without a murmur** without complaint or grumbling: *He paid the fine without a murmur.*

mus·cle (mŭs′əl) **1** a bundle of body fibers which, by lengthening and shortening, causes motion in some part of a living body. **2** the flesh of such a bundle. **3** bodily strength. (Homonym: mussel)

Muscles of arm

mus·cu·lar (mŭs′kyŏŏ lər) **1** having to do with the muscles: *Massage sometimes relieves a* muscular *ache.* **2** having well-developed muscles; strong: *His legs were* muscular *from work on the track team.* **mus·cu·lar·ly.**

muse (mūz) to think deeply or dreamily; meditate: *He* mused *all the summer afternoon.* **mused, mus·ing.**

Mus·es (mū′ziz) in Greek myths, the nine goddesses who encouraged and protected the arts of poetry, history, dancing, etc.

mu·se·um (mū zē′əm) a building in which interesting objects are collected and displayed. Some museums show paintings and sculptures. Others have exhibits of plant and animal life or mechanical inventions and science.

mush (mŭsh) **1** corn meal boiled in water. **2** any soft, thick mass.

mush·room (mŭsh′rŏŏm) **1** any rapidly growing umbrella-shaped fungus, especially the kinds that are good to eat. **2** to grow rapidly: *Shopping centers seemed to* mushroom *overnight.*

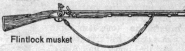
Mushrooms

mu·sic (mū′zĭk) **1** the art of combining and arranging pleasing sounds. Music is one of the fine arts. **2** the pleasing sounds made. We make music by singing and by playing musical instruments. **3** written or printed signs for the sounds: *I brought my trumpet but left my* music *at home. A composer writes* music. **4** a musical composition or the work of a composer: *the* music *of Mozart.* **5** any pleasing sounds: *the* music *of falling rain.* **6 set to music** to provide music for: *to set a poem to* music.

mu·si·cal (mū′zə kəl) **1** having to do with music: *a* musical *instrument; a* musical *program.* **2** melodious: *the* musical *song of a bird.* **3** fond of or skilled in music: *A* musical *family usually enjoys music together.* **4** musical comedy; a light, amusing play, with songs and dances. **mu·si·cal·ly.**

musical instrument a device for making music, such as a piano, violin, or trumpet.

mu·si·cian (mū zĭsh′ən) person skilled in music, especially one whose profession is playing music.

musk (mŭsk) strong-smelling, oily substance obtained from a special gland of one kind of deer. It is used for making perfumes.

Flintlock musket

mus·ket (mŭs′kĭt) an old-fashioned infantry gun, replaced by the rifle.

mus·ket·ry (mŭs′kĭt rĭ) **1** the firing of muskets. **2** muskets used by troops. **3** troops armed with muskets.

musk·mel·on (mŭsk′mĕl′ən) **1** a large, rounded fruit with sweet, juicy flesh. The outside is covered with a hard rind. **2** the vine it grows on.

---

fāte, făt, fâre, fär; bē, bĕt; bīte, bĭt; nō, nŏt, nôr; fūse, fŭn, fûr; tōō, tŏŏk; foil; foul; thin; ~~then~~;
hw for wh as in *wh*at; zh for s as in usual; ə for a, e, i, o, u, as in *a*go, lin*e*n, per*i*l, at*o*m, min*u*s

musk ox

musk ox long-haired animal of the arctic, between a sheep and an ox in appearance. It has a musklike odor. **musk ox·en.**

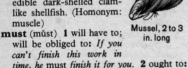

Musk ox, about 5 ft. high at shoulder   Muskrat, about 2 ft. long including tail

musk·rat (mŭsk′răt′) **1** a North American brown water rat with webbed hind feet. **2** the valuable glossy fur of this animal.

Mus·lim (mŭz′ləm) Moslem.

mus·lin (mŭz′lĭn) **1** a thin, soft, cotton cloth used for dresses, bedclothes, curtains, etc. **2** made of muslin: *a muslin gown.*

muss (mŭs) **1** to rumple; crease; make untidy: *Albert mussed the rug as he dragged the heavy chair across it.* **2** a mess; confusion; disorder: *a room left in a muss.*

mus·sel (mŭs′əl) **1** a freshwater clam with a thin greenish-black shell. **2** an edible dark-shelled clamlike shellfish. (Homonym: muscle)

Mussel, 2 to 3 in. long

must (mŭst) **1** will have to; will be obliged to: *If you can't finish this work in time, he must finish it for you.* **2** ought to: *I must try to go to see her very soon.* **3** to be almost certain to: *Her coat isn't here, so she must have gone.*

mus·tache (mŭs′tăsh or məs tăsh′) hair that grows on the upper lip. Also spelled **moustache.**

mus·tang (mŭs′tăng) small, sturdy, wild or half-wild horse of western North American plains.

mus·tard (mŭs′tərd) **1** a plant bearing small fourpetaled yellow flowers and long pods containing peppery seeds. **2** the powdered seeds of this plant or the ground seeds mixed with vinegar, used as seasoning.

Mustard

mutual

mus·ter (mŭs′tər) **1** to assemble troops for roll call, review, etc. **2** to call up; gather: *If you muster your courage, you will confess you broke the window.* **3** a gathering, especially of troops.

must·n't (mŭs′ənt) must not.

mus·ty (mŭs′tĭ) **1** having a stale moldy odor or taste: *Houses at the seashore often smell musty after being closed up for the winter.* **2** stale; out of date: *the musty ideas of the old professor.* **mus·ti·er, mus·ti·est.**

mu·tant (mū′tənt) new type of plant or animal produced as a result of mutation.

mu·ta·tion (mū tā′shən) **1** a change; alteration. **2** in plants and animals, sudden appearance of new characteristics which are not handed down from a parent.

mute (mūt) **1** making no sound; silent: *The puppy stared at our candy in* mute *appeal.* **2** without the power of speech; dumb: *The magician's tricks left us* mute *with amazement.* **3** person who cannot speak. **4** a device placed in or on a musical instrument, to soften its tone. **5** to soften or muffle the tone of. **mut·ed, mut·ing; mute·ly.**

mu·ti·late (mū′tə lāt′) to damage by tearing, cutting, soiling, or removing some part: *Never rip out pages, tear the cover, or otherwise mutilate a book.* **mu·ti·lat·ed, mu·ti·lat·ing.**

mu·ti·neer (mū′tə nîr′) person who takes part in a mutiny.

mu·ti·nous (mū′tə nəs) rebellious; defiant: *The mutinous crew refused to obey the captain's orders.* **mu·ti·nous·ly.**

mu·ti·ny (mū′tə nĭ) **1** uprising against lawful authority, especially by sailors against their commanding officers. **2** to rebel against authority; revolt. **mu·ti·nies; mu·ti·nied, mu·ti·ny·ing.**

mut·ter (mŭt′ər) **1** to speak in a low, mumbling tone: *The witch muttered a few magic words under her breath.* **2** to make low, rumbling sounds: *Thunder muttered in the distance.* **3** low, indistinct talk or sounds: *to speak in a mutter.*

mut·ton (mŭt′ən) flesh of a sheep, used for food.

mu·tu·al (mū′chŏŏ əl) **1** done or felt by each of two toward the other: *The horse and I looked at each other with mutual suspicion.* **2** shared by two or more persons; in com-

472

mon: *Sally and Sue have a* mutual *friend who lives in California.* **mu·tu·al·ly.**

muz·zle (mŭz′əl) **1** the nose and jaws of an animal; snout. **2** an arrangement of straps or wire mesh to be placed over an animal's snout to keep it from biting or eating. **3** the front end of a gun barrel. **4** to put a muzzle on an animal. **5** to prevent the telling or writing of something: *The dictator* muzzled *the press.* **muz·zled, muz·zling.**

Muzzle

my (mī) **1** of or belonging to me: *I want you to meet* my *mother. Where is* my *hat?* **2** made or done by me: *I have finished* my *homework.* **3** inhabited by me: *This is* my *country.* **4** an exclamation of wonder or surprise: *Oh* my! *What a big boy you've grown to be!*

myr·i·ad (mĭr′ĭ əd) **1** a vast number. **2** countless; innumerable: *The* myriad *stars blinked in the black night sky.*

myrrh (mûr) fragrant, gummy resin with a bitter taste, obtained from several shrubs growing in Arabia and eastern Africa. It is used in medicines, perfumes, and incense.

myr·tle (mûr′təl) **1** a sweet-smelling evergreen shrub with shiny leaves, white or pink flowers, and black berries. **2** a blue-flowered creeping vine.

my·self (mī sĕlf′) **1** my own self: *I burned* myself *on the stove. I am pleased with* myself. **2** word used with "I" for emphasis: *I* myself *know his story is true.* **3** my normal self; my true self: *Since I was sick I haven't been quite* myself. **4** by myself **(1)** alone: *I was sitting* by myself *in the car.* **(2)** without any help: *I hemmed this scarf* by myself.

mys·te·ri·ous (mĭs tîr′ĭ əs) puzzling; unknown or unexplained: *a* mysterious *light in the sky.* **mys·te·ri·ous·ly.**

mys·ter·y (mĭs′tə rĭ) **1** something that is secret, strange, or unexplained: *The name of the thief is a* mystery. **2** that which is beyond human understanding: *a religious* mystery. **3** secrecy; obscurity: *a stranger shrouded in* mystery. **mys·ter·ies.**

mys·tic (mĭs′tĭk) **1** having a hidden meaning; mysterious: *the* mystic *ceremonies; the* mystic *arts of magic.* **2** a student of the hidden meanings and symbolism of religion, philosophy, etc. **3** one who believes that in this life he will or has attained direct communication with God. **4** giving a feeling of awe and wonder: *the* mystic *beauty of the night.*

mys·ti·cal (mĭs′tə kəl) having a spiritual meaning not understood by everybody: *a* mystical *symbol.*

mys·ti·fy (mĭs′tə fī′) to puzzle; baffle; bewilder: *The magician* mystified *his audience by pulling a chicken out of his hat.* **mys·ti·fied, mys·ti·fy·ing.**

myth (mĭth) **1** an old story or legend told about imaginary persons and events to explain the early history and beliefs of a race or nation: *the* myths *of Greece and Rome.* **2** an imagined thing, story, or person: *Elves are only a* myth.

myth·i·cal (mĭth′ə kəl) **1** existing in myths: *Atlas was a* mythical *hero.* **2** imaginary; made-up: *The story takes place in a* mythical *kingdom.* **myth·i·cal·ly.**

my·thol·o·gy (mĭ thŏl′ə jĭ) **1** collection of myths: *Hercules is a character from the* mythology *of ancient Greece.* **2** the study of myths. **my·thol·o·gies.**

N

N, n (ĕn) 14th letter of the English alphabet.

N. 1 north. **2** northern.

¹nag (năg) horse, especially one that is old and worn out: *Nobody could win a race on a* nag *like that.* [¹nag is a form of an earlier English word (nagge).]

²nag (năg) to scold or find fault with continually: *Mother* nags *me about my table manners.* **nagged, nag·ging.** [²nag is a word of Scandinavian origin.]

nai·ad or **Nai·ad** (nā′ăd or nī′ăd) water maiden in ancient Greek stories.

fāte, făt, fâre, fär; bē, bĕt; bīte, bĭt; nō, nŏt, nôr; fūse, fŭn, fûr; tōō, tŏŏk; foil; foul; thin; then; hw for wh as in *what*; zh for s as in usual; ə for a, e, i, o, u, as in *ago*, linen, peril, atom, minus

nail (nāl) **1** slender, sharp-pointed, metal pin made to fasten together pieces of wood or the like by being driven through or into them. **2** the horny growth at the end of a finger or toe. **3** to fasten with nails: *Peter nailed the cover on the box.* **4** to make certain or secure: *to nail an order for goods.*

FINISHING

WIRE

FINGER   HORSESHOE

Nails

na·ïve or **na·ive** (nä ēv′) **1** childlike; artless; ingenuous; unsophisticated: *a naïve young woman;* naïve *remarks.* **2** foolishly simple: *It is naïve to suppose you won't have to pay for your mistakes.* **na·ïve·ly** or **na·ive·ly.**

na·ked (nā′kĭd) **1** wearing no clothes; undressed. **2** bare; without the usual covering: *The leafless trees stood almost* naked *in the snow.* **3** plain; unconcealed: *the* naked *truth.* **4 the naked eye** the eye unhelped by glasses, telescope, microscope, etc.: *Germs cannot be seen with the naked eye.* **na·ked·ly.**

na·ked·ness (nā′kĭd nĭs) **1** state of being unclothed. **2** lack of cover; bareness: *Stripped of their ivy, the walls stood in stark* nakedness.

name (nām) **1** word or title by which a person, place, or thing is known: *His* name *is James. What is the* name *of that book you're reading?* **2** to give a name to: *What did they* name *their baby?* **3** reputation; repute: *A good* name *is a precious possession.* **4** to choose; appoint: *The principal* named *a new third-grade teacher.* **5** to identify; call (something) by its right name: *Can you* name *the capital of Ohio?* **6** to choose for a special purpose: *We must* name *the day for our picnic.* **named, nam·ing.**

name·less (nām′lĭs) **1** unknown: *the* nameless *inventor of the wheel.* **2** impossible to describe or identify: *a* nameless *fear.* **3** unnamed; not marked with a name: *We saw a* nameless *grave alongside the road.* **name·less·ly.**

name·ly (nām′lĭ) specifically; that is to say: *Pennsylvania has given us only one President,* namely *James Buchanan.*

name·sake (nām′sāk′) a person who has been named after another, or has the same name as another.

¹nap (năp) **1** short sleep; daytime rest: *He took a* nap *in the afternoon.* **2** to rest during the day; take a short sleep. **napped, nap·ping.** [**¹nap** is probably a form of an Old English word (hnappian).]

²nap (năp) surface of short hairs or fibers on some fabrics, as velvet plush, etc.; pile. [**²nap** is probably taken from an Old English word (knoppian) meaning "to pluck."]

Nape

nape (nāp) the back of the neck.

naph·tha (năp′thə or năf′thə) a clear fluid that will burn easily, made from petroleum and used as fuel and for dissolving certain substances.

nap·kin (năp′kĭn) small square of cloth or paper used for wiping the fingers and lips and to protect the clothes.

nar·cis·sus (när sĭs′əs) **1** a spring-blooming plant, grown from a bulb, bearing slender leaves and flat six-petaled white flowers with white or orange centers. Jonquils and daffodils, which are sometimes yellow, are also narcissuses. **2** the blooms of these plants. **nar·cis·sus·es** or **nar·cis·si.**

Narcissus

nar·cot·ic (när kŏt′ĭk) **1** drug that can cause sleep or relieve pain. **2** having the power to cause sleep or relieve pain: *a* narcotic *effect.*

nar·rate (nă rāt′ or năr′āt) to tell or give an account of (a story): *The teacher* narrated *a story of an Indian boy.* **nar·rat·ed, nar·rat·ing.**

nar·ra·tive (năr′ə tĭv) **1** story; account of events: *The speech was a* narrative *of the speaker's childhood.* **2** relating; telling (events or a story): *Longfellow wrote a* narrative *poem about Hiawatha.* **nar·ra·tive·ly.**

nar·row (năr′ō) **1** not wide. **2** to make or become less wide: *This road* narrows *to one lane.* **3** limited in amount or size: *a* narrow *choice.* **4** to limit; confine: *We* narrowed *the possibilities to one answer.* **5** not tolerant; biased; limited: *a* narrow *mind.* **6** strict; exact: *a* narrow *examination of the facts.* **7** close; with little to spare: *Walter*

had a narrow *escape from drowning.* **8 nar-**
rows part of a river, lake, channel, etc.
that is narrow. **nar·row·ly.**

nar·row·ness (năr′ō nĭs) a being narrow
(in any sense).

na·sal (nā′zəl) **1** of or having to do with the
nose. **2** pronounced or coming through
the nose: *M and ng are* nasal *sounds.*
3 nasal sound or the letter which represents
it. M and n are nasals. **na·sal·ly.**

na·stur·tium (nă stûr′shəm) **1** a vine
bearing round leaves and funnel-shaped
orange, yellow, or
red flowers. The
spicy seeds are some-
times pickled. **2** the
flower of this vine.

Nasturtium

nas·ty (năs′tĭ) **1** unpleasant; very disa-
greeable: *We didn't*
go on a picnic because of the nasty *weather.*
Joe made a nasty *remark about his sister's*
low grades. **2** vicious; spiteful: *The watch*
dog has a nasty *growl.* **3** harmful; dangerous: *John had a* nasty *fall from the porch*
railing. **4** very dirty; filthy: *The yard was*
a nasty *mess with bits of garbage littered*
about. **5** indecent. **nas·ti·er, nas·ti·est;**
nas·ti·ly.

na·tion (nā′shən) **1** the people (as a whole)
of an independent country: *The whole*
nation *will vote in the next election.* **2** an
independent country. **3** people united by
the same religion, language, history, etc.,
but not necessarily living together in one,
independent country: *the gypsy* nation.

na·tion·al (năsh′ən əl) **1** of or having to do
with a nation. **2** citizen or subject of a
nation. **na·tion·al·ly.**

na·tion·al·ism (năsh′ən ə lĭz′əm) ardent
belief in the importance of one's nation,
its people, customs, and language, and its
right to independence. This belief is sometimes expressed without regard for the
rights of other countries.

na·tion·al·i·ty (năsh′ə năl′ə tĭ) **1** person's
connection with a particular nation by birth
or by citizenship. **2** independence as a
nation: *Many African states are obtaining*
nationality. **na·tion·al·i·ties.**

national park special area set aside and
preserved by a government for the enjoyment of all.

na·tive (nā′tĭv) **1** inherited from one's place
of birth: *one's* native *tongue; one's* native
land. **2** person born in a given country or
place: *I am a* native *of Ohio.* **3** animal or
plant that originated or was found in a
particular place. **4** born or originating in:
a native *Bostonian.* **5** natural; inborn: *The*
little boy's beautiful painting showed his
native *ability as an artist.* **6 native to**
originally found in: *Corn is a grain* native *to*
America. **na·tive·ly.**

na·tiv·i·ty (nā tĭv′ə tĭ) **1** birth. **2** the time,
place, etc., of birth. **3 Nativity (1)** the
birth of Christ. **(2)** a picture or sculpture
of the birth of Christ. **na·tiv·i·ties.**

NATO (nā′tō) North Atlantic Treaty Organization, an alliance of some of the
nations of North America and Europe for
mutual defense and economic co-operation.

nat·u·ral (năch′ə rəl) **1** belonging to by
nature; inborn; native: *Ellen has a* natural
skill on the piano. **2** formed or made by
nature; not artificial: *There is a famous*
natural *bridge in Virginia.* **3** according to
the usual way things happen; ordinary:
Fatigue is the natural *result of hard work.*
4 concerning nature and the things of
nature: *The study of plants and animals is*
called natural *history.* **5** true to life: *a very*
natural *portrait.* **6** simple; sincere; not
affected: *That movie star is always* natural
with other people. **7** in music, the note
which is neither a sharp nor a flat.

nat·u·ral·ist (năch′ə rəl ĭst) person who
makes a study of the things of nature,
especially plants and animals.

nat·u·ral·ize (năch′ə rə līz′) **1** to give
citizenship to; make (a foreigner) a citizen.
2 to adopt (a foreign plant, word, etc.):
The French word "garage" has become
naturalized *in America.* **nat·u·ral·ized,**
nat·u·ral·iz·ing.

nat·u·ral·ly (năch′ə rə lĭ) **1** by nature:
Rose's hair is naturally *curly.* **2** in a natural
manner: *He spoke on the radio as* naturally
as if he were chatting with us at home. **3** of
course: *Yes,* naturally, *I will thank Tom.*

---

fāte, făt, fâre, fär; bē, bĕt; bīte, bĭt; nō, nŏt, nôr; fūse, fŭn, fûr; tōō, tŏŏk; foil; foul; thin; ~~then~~;
hw for wh as in *wh*at; zh for s as in u*s*ual; ə for a, e, i, o, u, as in *a*go, linen, peril, at*o*m, min*u*s

natural resources anything in nature that man knows how to use, including water, soil, plants, minerals, etc.

na·ture (nā′chər) **1** the physical universe, including all things in it not created by man: *Gravitation is one of the forces of* nature. **2** natural scenery; trees, flowers, etc.: *the beauties of* nature. **3** mental and spiritual make-up (of a person); character: *He has a friendly* nature. **4** all the qualities of something that make it what it is: *Scientists are learning much about the* nature *of the atom.* **5** kind; sort; type: *I don't like mystery stories or any books of that* nature.

nature study a watching and learning about the things in nature.

naught (nôt) **1** in arithmetic, zero, written as 0; a cipher. **2** nothing: *The wicked shall come to* naught. Also spelled **nought.**

naugh·ti·ness (nô′ti nĭs) mischief; disobedience: *One's* naughtiness *usually brings punishment.*

naugh·ty (nô′tĭ) mischievous; disobedient. **naugh·ti·er, naugh·ti·est; naugh·ti·ly.**

nau·sea (nô′shə) **1** upset stomach; a desire to vomit. **2** great disgust.

nau·se·at·ed (nô′shĭ ā′təd) made sick by: *He was* nauseated *by the sight of blood.*

nau·seous (nô′shəs or nô′shĭ əs) **1** causing nausea; sickening: *a* nauseous *feeling on a rough sea.* **2** loathsome; disgusting: *the* nauseous *odor of rancid oil.* **nau·seous·ly.**

nau·ti·cal (nô′tə kəl) **1** having to do with ships, sailors, and navigation. **2 nautical mile** about 6,080 feet. **nau·ti·cal·ly.**

nau·ti·lus (nô′tə ləs) **1** any of several shellfish. Some kinds have a spiral shell and a pearly inside. **2 Nautilus** name of the first atomic submarine. **nau·ti·lus·es** or **nau·ti·li.**

na·val (nā′vəl) having to do with a navy or warships. (Homonym: navel)

nave (nāv) main part of a church between the side aisles. (Homonym: knave)

na·vel (nā′vəl) small pucker or hollow in the skin at the middle of the human abdomen. (Homonym: naval)

navel orange an orange, usually seedless, with a small pit opposite the stem.

nav·i·ga·ble (năv′ə gə bəl) **1** capable of being traveled by ship: *The Missouri River is not* navigable *by ocean liners.* **2** capable

of being steered: *We went up in a* navigable *balloon.* **nav·i·ga·bly.**

nav·i·gate (năv′ə gāt′) **1** of a ship, airplane, or space ship, or someone in such a vehicle, to travel over or through: *The boat can easily* navigate *the Atlantic. I can easily* navigate *the Atlantic in this boat.* **2** to steer, operate, or manage (a vehicle): *With the small crew he was barely able to* navigate *the ship.* **3** to determine or plot the course of (such a vehicle): *On the training flight, Adams piloted and Jones* navigated. **nav·i·gat·ed, nav·i·gat·ing.**

nav·i·ga·tion (năv′ə gā′shən) **1** the act of travel by ship, airplane, or spaceship: *That harbor will be open to* navigation *when the ice breaks up.* **2** science of figuring out the course for ships, airplanes, and spaceships. **3** science or art of steering or operating ships or aircraft.

nav·i·ga·tor (năv′ə gā′tər) **1** person skilled in the science of navigation. **2** person who determines or plots the course of a ship, airplane, or spaceship: *On the training flight, Adams was pilot and Jones was* navigator.

na·vy (nā′vĭ) **1** all of the warships of a nation used for sea defense and warfare. **2** a nation's government department and personnel responsible for defense and warfare at sea. **3 navy blue** dark shade of blue. **na·vies.**

nay (nā) **1** no. **2** negative answer or vote. **3** not only that, but also: *I feel,* nay *I'm positive, we'll win.* (Homonym: neigh)

N.B. take notice; note well.

N.C. North Carolina.

N.Dak. North Dakota.

NE or **N.E. 1** northeast. **2** northeastern.

near (nĭr) **1** not far from; close to: *Frogs are always found* near *water.* **2** not far off in time: *Spring is* near. **3** closely related; intimate; dear: *one's* near *relatives;* near *friends.* **4** barely missing: *a* near *hit; a* near *tragedy.* **5** closely resembling: *a* near *silk dress.* **6** almost: *a* near *perfect score.* **7** to approach; draw or come close to: *The ship* neared *land.*

near·by or **near·by** (nĭr′bī′) close; near at hand.

near·ly (nĭr′lĭ) **1** almost: *I tripped over the loose board and* nearly *fell.* **2** closely: *First cousins are* nearly *related.*

near·ness (nir'nĭs) a being near or close in time, distance, etc.

near-sight·ed (nir'sī'tĭd) able to see clearly at close distance only. **near-sight·ed·ly.**

neat (nēt) **1** clean and orderly; tidy: *The living room was* neat *after mother cleaned and straightened it.* **2** simple and pleasing in appearance: *The school girls' neat* blue *and white uniforms made a pretty picture.* **3** skillful; clever: *It was easy to understand the teacher's* neat *explanation.* **neat·ly.**

neat·ness (nēt'nĭs) a being neat.

Nebr. Nebraska.

Ne·bras·ka (nə brăs'kə) a middle western State of the United States.

nec·es·sar·i·ly (nĕs'ə sĕr'ə lĭ) as a matter of course or necessity: *Even though the weather report predicted rain, that does not* necessarily *mean it will rain.*

nec·es·sar·y (nĕs'ə sĕr'ĭ) **1** needed; required: *A license is* necessary *to drive a car.* **2** essential: *Good food is* necessary *to health.* **3** that cannot be avoided; inevitable: *His illness was the* necessary *result of overwork and little sleep.* **4** thing that cannot be done without: *Food, clothing, and shelter are* necessaries *of life.* **nec·es·sar·ies.**

nec·es·si·tate (nə sĕs'ə tāt') to make necessary; require; demand: *The threat of riot* necessitates *prompt action by the police.* **nec·es·si·tat·ed, nec·es·si·tat·ing.**

nec·es·si·ty (nə sĕs'ə tĭ) **1** something needed; something one cannot get along without: *Water is a* necessity *of life.* **2** situation or occasion that calls for help: *In case of* necessity, *you can call on me.* **3** extreme poverty; lack of things needed for life: *Cruel* necessity *forced him to beg.* **4** a compelling force or need: *the* necessity *of sleep.* **nec·es·si·ties.**

neck (nĕk) **1** part of the body between the head and the shoulders. **2** of a garment, the part worn at the neck. **3** narrow part of a bottle, vase, cruet, or other container. **4** point of land extending into water; an isthmus.

Neck

neck·er·chief (nĕk'ər chĭf) handkerchief or scarf worn around the neck.

neck·lace (nĕk'lĭs) string of beads or jewels, or an ornament of metalwork, worn about the neck.

neck·tie (nĕk'tī') narrow band of cloth worn around the neck under the collar and tied in front in a knot or bow.

nec·tar (nĕk'tər) **1** sweet liquid found in some flowers: *Bees use* nectar *to make honey.* **2** in Greek mythology, a drink of the gods. **3** any delicious or pleasant drink.

Necklace

need (nēd) **1** to require; must have: *Plants* need *sunlight and water to grow.* **2** necessity; a use: *There is a growing* need *for grade-school teachers.* **3** to be obliged (to): *You don't* need *to return the book until tomorrow.* **4** poverty; extreme want: *His empty pockets and shabby clothes showed he was in* need. **5** time of trouble: *A friend in* need *is a friend indeed.* **6 if need be** if necessary. (Homonym: knead)

need·ful (nēd'fəl) required; necessary: *Do whatever is* needful *to make the patient comfortable.* **need·ful·ly.**

nee·dle (nē'dəl) **1** sewing tool consisting of a slender, pointed steel wire pierced with a hole, or "eye," to hold a thread. **2** plain slender rod, or a rod with a small hook at the end, used in knitting or crocheting. **3** steel bar of a magnetic compass. **4** hollow, pointed wire with an opening at the tip, used by doctors to give injections. **5** any needle-shaped thing: *The ground was covered with brown pine* needles. **6** to tease; annoy. **nee·dled, nee·dling.**

Sewing needle
Compass needle
Crochet needle
Knitting needle

need·less (nēd'lĭs) unnecessary: *His* needless *grumbling annoys people.* **need·less·ly.**

nee·dle·work (nē'dəl wûrk') work done with a needle; sewing; embroidery.

need·n't (nē'dənt) need not.

need·y (nē'dĭ) not having sufficient food, clothing, or other basic wants; very poor. **need·i·er, need·i·est; need·i·ly.**

---

fāte, făt, fâre, fär; bē, bĕt; bīte, bĭt; nō, nŏt, nôr; fūse, fŭn, fûr; tōo, tŏok; foil; foul; thin; ~~then~~; hw for wh as in *what*; zh for s as in usual; ə for a, e, i, o, u, as in *a*go, lin*e*n, per*i*l, at*o*m, min*u*s

ne'er (nâr) never.

neg·a·tive (nĕg'ə tĭv) **1** saying no; expressing denial or refusal: *a negative answer.* **2** word expressing "no"; denial or refusal: *"Never," "nothing," and "nobody" are* negatives. **3** not positive or forceful: *a negative person; a negative attitude.* **4** plate or film that has been exposed and from which a photograph can be printed. The dark tones of the scene photographed appear light on the negative, and the light tones appear dark. **5** in debating, the side arguing against the statement. **6** in mathematics, naming a number or quantity to be subtracted; a minus. **7 negative charge** in electricity, the condition of having more electrons than protons. **neg·a·tive·ly.**

neg·lect (nĭ glekt') **1** failure to do what should be done; lack of care: *The garden, overgrown with weeds, showed* neglect. **2** to fail to do what should be done, through carelessness or on purpose: *Don't neglect your homework.* **3** to pay too little attention to; fail to care for properly: *He neglects his family.*

neg·li·gence (nĕg'lə jəns) carelessness; failure to pay attention; failure to take proper care or to do what should be done; neglect: *His negligence cost him his job at the airplane factory.*

neg·li·gent (nĕg'lə jənt) careless; not attentive; failing to take care or do what should be done. **neg·li·gent·ly.**

ne·go·ti·ate (nĭ gō'shĭ āt') **1** to discuss and make arrangements for, as for a business deal, treaty, loan, etc.: *to negotiate a treaty.* **2** to sell or make a fair exchange: *to negotiate a sale of property.* **3** to clear, pass, or surmount (something): *The old car could hardly negotiate the hill.* **ne·go·ti·at·ed, ne·go·ti·at·ing.**

ne·go·ti·a·tion (nĭ gō'shĭ ā'shən) act of negotiating; the talking over and settling the terms of a treaty, business agreement, etc.

Ne·gro (nē'grō) **1** a member of one of the main races of man, having brown or black skin. **2** of or having to do with Negroes: *a* Negro *spiritual.* **Ne·groes.**

neigh (nā) **1** the sound that a horse makes; a whinny. **2** to make this sound. (Homonym: nay)

neigh·bor (nā'bər) **1** person who lives near-by. **2** person, country, or thing that is near another: *Canada is our* neighbor *to the north.* **3** fellow man: *"Love thy* neighbor *as thyself."*

neigh·bor·hood (nā'bər hŏŏd') **1** area or district where a person lives: *Our* neighborhood *has a new shopping center.* **2** the people living near-by or near one another: *The* neighborhood *held a barbecue.* **3 in the neighborhood of** near; not far from: *The town is* in the neighborhood of *the Great Lakes. The price is* in the neighborhood of *$50.*

neigh·bor·ing (nā'bər ing) **1** near; nearby: *in a* neighboring *village.* **2** adjoining: *Henry and Edward just bought two* neighboring *lots of land.*

neigh·bor·ly (nā'bər lĭ) friendly; kindly; proper or suitable for neighbors: *The people here are very* neighborly.

nei·ther (nē'thər or nī'thər) **1** not the one and not the other: *No,* neither *one is right.* **2** not either: *I have* neither *time nor money.* **3** nor; nor yet: *Don't you want to go?* Neither *do I!*

ne·on (nē'ŏn) a chemical element. It is a gas similar to helium but heavier. Neon gives off a red glow when an electric current passes through it.

neph·ew (nĕf'ū) the son of one's brother or sister, or of one's brother-in-law or sister-in-law.

Nep·tune (nĕp'tōōn or nĕp'tūn) **1** planet, eighth in order of distance from the sun. **2** the Roman god of the sea.

nerve (nûrv) **1** any fiber or group of fibers that carries feeling or directions for action between the brain and spinal cord and other parts of the body. Nerves carry the feelings of touch, hearing, etc., and also the electrical impulses that cause muscles to act. **2** courage; bravery: *It took* nerve

Nerves of the upper back

to be cheerful in the leaking boat. **3** impudent boldness: *When it came to asking favors, Dick never lacked* nerve. **4** to arouse strength or courage in: *George had to* nerve *himself for danger.* **nerved, nerv·ing.**

ner·vous (nûr'vəs) **1** of the nerves: *the* nervous *system.* **2** easily excited; high-strung: *A* nervous *person gets upset often.* **3** fearful; tense; uneasy; restless: *You make me nervous by standing so close to the edge of the cliff.* **ner·vous·ly.**

ner·vous·ness (nûr'vəs nis) a being nervous, restless, tense, or uneasy.

-ness suffix used to change an adjective to a noun. It means "the condition or quality of being" (what the adjective says). The condition of being "hard" (adjective) is "hardness" (noun). The quality of being "good" (adjective) is "goodness" (noun): *a good man known for his good*ness.

Robin's nest

Oriole's nest   Wasp nest

nest (nĕst) **1** a place where a bird lays eggs and cares for its young. **2** a place for the same use made by wasps and some other insects. **3** den or burrow, especially the part of it used for sleeping and caring for young: *We found a squirrel's nest in the hollow tree.* **4** any warm and cozy place. **5** to build or use a nest: *Birds nested in the maple tree.* **6** to place in a nest. **7** a group of things fitting neatly into one another: *This nest of boxes came from Japan.* **8** to fit into one another: *The boys nested the cartons to save space.*

nest egg 1 a real or false egg left in a nest to encourage the hen to lay eggs there. **2** money put aside; savings.

nes·tle (nĕs'əl) **1** to settle comfortably; snuggle: *to nestle down in a warm bed.* **2** to press closely; cuddle: *The little girl nestled her doll in her arms.* **nes·tled, nes·tling.**

nest·ling (nĕst'ling or nĕs'ling) a bird too young to fly from the nest.

¹net (nĕt) **1** remaining after all necessary expenses have been paid: *The net profit is the actual gain.* **2** to earn as clear profit: *The rummage sale netted about $30.*

3 profit so gained. **4 net price** the price at which goods are actually sold, after discounts have been allowed. **5 net weight** weight of goods, not including the weight of the container. **net·ted, net·ting.** [¹**net** comes from an Old French word (net) which is from a Latin word (nitidus) meaning "bright."]

²net (nĕt) **1** fabric of knotted cords, used for catching fish; a seine. **2** bag of knotted cords with the open end attached to a ring with a handle. It is used to catch butterflies, land hooked fish, etc. **3** a small, circular piece of silk or hair mesh with a drawstring, to keep ladies' hair in place. **4** open-work fabric for veils. **5** a snare; an entanglement: *He was caught in a net of lies.* **6** to catch with or as with a net. **net·ted, net·ting.** [²**net** is the unchanged form of an Old English word.]

Butterfly net

Neth·er·lands (nĕth'ər ləndz) a country in northwestern Europe; Holland.

net·tle (nĕt'əl) **1** any of several plants which have stems and leaves with hairs or spines that irritate the skin on contact. **2** to annoy; vex: *Seth's continual questions nettled his father.* **net·tled, net·tling.**

net·work (nĕt'wûrk') **1** a net. **2** system or arrangement of lines that cross: *a network of roads; a network of telephone wires.* **3** a chain of radio or television stations which carry the same programs: *The President's speech was carried by all networks.*

Nettle

neu·rot·ic (nŏŏ rŏt'ĭk) **1** having to do with the nerves or a nervous condition. **2** person suffering from a nervous condition.

neu·tral (nŏŏ'trəl or nū'trəl) **1** not taking sides in a war or contest: *Switzerland was neutral during World War II. The referee of a game should be neutral.* **2** country, city, person, etc., that does not take sides, as in a war. **3** having no special mark or quality:

---

fāte, făt, fâre, fär; bē, bĕt; bite, bĭt; nō, nŏt, nôr; fūse, fŭn, fûr; tōō, tŏŏk; foil; foul; thin; ~~then~~; hw for wh as in *what*; zh for s as in u*s*ual; ə for a, e, i, o, u, as in ago, linen, peril, atom, minus

Gray is a neutral *color.* **4** in chemistry, neither acid nor alkali. **5** in electricity, having the same number of electrons as protons. **neu·tral·ly.**

neu·tral·i·ty (nōō trăl′ə tĭ or nū trăl′ə tĭ) state of being neutral or taking no side in a dispute or in war: *the traditional* neutrality *of Switzerland.*

neu·tral·ize (nōō′trə līz′ or nū′trə līz′) **1** to make inactive or without effect: *Our football team's alert defense* neutralized *their passing attack. His intelligence is* neutralized *by his laziness.* **2** to agree to keep a city or country out of war, or to take away its ability to make war: *Switzerland was* neutralized *during World War II.* **3** in chemistry, to destroy the active nature of a substance: *to* neutralize *an acid with baking soda.* **neu·tral·ized, neu·tral·iz·ing.**

neu·tron (nōō′trŏn or nū′trŏn) one of the basic particles in the nucleus or central core of an atom. The neutron has no electrical charge.

Nev. Nevada.

Ne·vad·a (nə vă′də or nə văd′ə) a State in the western part of the United States.

nev·er (nĕv′ər) **1** not ever; not at any time: *You should* never *swim alone.* **2** not at all; under no condition: *"This will* never *do,"* said Father *when the puppy dug holes in the lawn.* **3** not even: *He* never *so much as said "Hello."*

nev·er·more (nĕv′ər môr′) never again: *The banished prince would* nevermore *see his native land.*

nev·er·the·less (nĕv′ər ~~the~~ lĕs′) in spite of that; however; yet; still: *It may rain;* nevertheless, *we will start on our trip.*

new (nōō or nū) **1** recently made, built, or grown: *a* new *car;* new *corn.* **2** not known before; recently invented or discovered: *a* new *idea; a* new *kind of motor; a* new *land.* **3** recently come into a position or relationship: *a* new *principal; a* new *friend.* **4** unaccustomed: *He is still* new *to the job.* **5** following the previous one; beginning afresh: *a* new *year.* **6** not used or worn: *Is the bicycle* new *or second-hand?* **7** greatly improved in health, character, etc.: *After a rest I felt like a* new *man.* **8** modern; different from what went before; not like the old: *a* new *age.* **9** recently; newly:

While walking through the fields, we smelled new-*mown hay.* (Homonym: knew.)

new·born (nōō′bôrn′ or nū′bôrn′) **1** just born: *a* newborn *baby.* **2** renewed; born anew: *a* newborn *hope; a* newborn *courage.*

new·com·er (nōō′kŭm′ər or nū′kŭm′ər) someone who has arrived recently; a new arrival.

New England the six States in the northeastern United States, including Connecticut, Maine, Massachusetts, New Hampshire, Rhode Island, and Vermont.

new·fan·gled (nōō′făng′gəld or nū′făng′gəld) new; recent; different or novel: *a* newfangled *gadget;* newfangled *ideas.*

New Hamp·shire (nōō hămp′shĭr or nū hămp′shər) a State in the northeastern part of the United States.

New Jer·sey (nōō jûr′zĭ or nū jûr′zĭ) a State in the eastern part of the United States.

new·ly (nōō′lĭ or nū′lĭ) recently; lately: *a* newly *married couple.*

New Mexico a State in the southwestern part of the United States.

news (nōōz or nūz) **1** recent or fresh information: *Have you had any* news *from our old friend Tom?* **2** recent events or fresh information reported in the newspaper or over the radio or television: *The sports* news *is just beginning.*

news·cast (nōōz′kăst′ or nūz′kăst′) radio or television news report.

news·pa·per (nōōz′pā′pər or nūz′pā′pər) sheet of printed paper, or many sheets folded together (but not attached to each other), containing news, pictures, advertisements, etc.

news·reel (nōōz′rēl′ or nūz′rēl′) motion picture of current news events.

news·stand (nōōz′stănd′ or nūz′stănd′) a stand or store where newspapers and periodicals are sold.

newt (nōōt or nūt) one of several kinds of small, harmless, insect-eating salamanders, born in the water but spending part or all of its adult life on land, where it lives under stones and fallen logs.

Newt, about 4 in. long

New Testament (nōō tĕs′tə mənt or nū tĕs′tə mənt) one of the two main divisions of the Bible, containing accounts of the life and teachings of Jesus and writings of some of the early Christians.

New World North and South America; the Western Hemisphere.

new year 1 the coming year: *In the new year we hope to get out of debt.* 2 **New Year** the first day or days of a new year. 3 **New Year's Day** January first.

New York (nōō yôrk′ or nū yôrk′) 1 a State in the eastern part of the United States. 2 **New York City** city in New York State and the largest city in the United States.

next (někst) 1 coming immediately after; nearest in time, place, or rank: *the next bus; the* next *street; next month.* 2 in the time, place, or rank immediately following: *When* next *we meet, smile! My name comes* next *on the list. After Ken, John is the* next *oldest boy in the class.* 3 **next⁺ to** (1) beside: *Sit* next *to me.* (2) almost: *It's* next *to nothing. It's* next *to impossible.*

N. H. New Hampshire.

Ni·ag·a·ra Falls (ni ăg′ə rə fôlz) the falls on the Niagara River, located on the border of New York State and Ontario, Canada.

nib·ble (nib′əl) 1 to take a small bite; eat in small bites or a little at a time: *The rabbit* nibbled *the lettuce.* 2 small bite or piece: *She gave the baby a* nibble *of her cooky.* 3 small or cautious bite at the bait: *We fished all day and didn't have a* nibble. **nib·bled, nib·bling.**

Nic·a·ra·gua (nĭk′ə rä′gwə) country in Central America on the Caribbean Sea and the Pacific Ocean.

nice (nis) 1 pleasant; agreeable: *What* nice *weather for a picnic!* 2 refined; well-bred: *children of* nice *families.* 3 discriminating: *a* nice *taste in reading.* 4 precise; very fine: *Artists must make* nice *distinctions between shades of a color.* **nic·er, nic·est; nice·ly.**

niche (nĭch) 1 a place hollowed out of a wall to hold a statue, urn, or the like. 2 job or position for which one

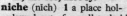

Niche

is best suited: *Miss Jones found her* niche *in teaching after she received her college degree.*

nick (nĭk) 1 a notch; small cut or break: *a* nick *in the rim of a glass.* 2 to make a notch, a small cut, or a break in: *The hunter's bullet* nicked *the tree trunk.*

nick·el (nĭk′əl) 1 hard, silver-white metal element, used chiefly in magnets and tough steel. 2 in the United States and Canada, a coin made of nickel and copper, worth five cents.

nick·name (nĭk′nām′) 1 shortened or familiar form of a person's name, such as "Ed" for "Edward" or "Johnny" for "John." 2 a substitute for a person's real name, sometimes given in fun, such as "Red" for someone with red hair. 3 to give a nickname to. **nick·named, nick·nam·ing.**

nic·o·tine (nĭk′ə tēn′) poison found in tobacco.

niece (nēs) the daughter of one's brother or sister; also, the daughter of one's brother-in-law or sister-in-law.

nig·gard·ly (nĭg′ərd li) 1 stingy; frugal to excess. 2 very small; scant: *to give* niggardly *aid.* 3 stingily.

nigh (nī) old word meaning "near."

night (nit) 1 the time from sunset to sunrise. 2 the coming of night; nightfall: *Before we were out of the woods,* night *caught us.* 3 darkness of night or like night. (Homonym: knight)

night·cap (nit′kăp′) 1 soft cap or head covering worn in bed. 2 a drink taken before going to bed.

night·fall (nit′fôl′) the ending of daylight and the coming of night; evening twilight: *At* nightfall *the stars begin to appear.*

night·gown (nit′- goun′) loose sleeping garment worn by women and girls.

night·in·gale (ni′tən gāl′ or ni′tĭng gāl′) 1 a small russet-brown bird (the European thrush), noted for the

Nightingale, about 6 in. long

sweetness of its song, heard mostly at night. 2 person with a fine singing voice.

---

fāte, făt, fâre, fär; bē, bĕt; bīte, bĭt; nō, nŏt, nôr; fūse, fŭn, fûr; tōō, tŏŏk; foil; foul; thin; ~~then~~; hw for wh as in *w*hat; zh for s as in usual; ə for a, e, i, o, u, as in ago, linen, peril, atom, minus

481

night·ly (nīt'lĭ) **1** every night: *The wolf howls* nightly *from the hill.* **2** happening every night: *the* nightly *howl of the wolf.* (Homonym: knightly)

night·mare (nīt'mâr') **1** very bad dream. **2** terrifying experience: *The train crash was a* nightmare *I shall never forget.*

night watch 1 guard kept for protection at night. **2** person or persons on guard at night. **3** period of time during which a night guard is on duty.

nim·ble (nĭm'bəl) **1** quick and active: *Squirrels are* nimble *in climbing trees.* **2** quick in thought or reply; clever and alert: *a* nimble *mind; a* nimble *answer.* **nim·bler, nim·blest; nim·bly.**

nine (nīn) amount or quantity that is one greater than eight; 9.

nine·teen (nīn'tēn') amount or quantity that is one greater than 18; 19.

nine·teenth (nīn'tēnth') **1** next after the 18th; 19th. **2** one of 19 equal parts.

nine·ti·eth (nīn'tĭ ĭth) **1** next after the 89th; 90th. **2** one of 90 equal parts.

nine·ty (nīn'tĭ) amount or quantity that is one greater than 89; 90. **nine·ties.**

ninth (nīnth) **1** next after the eighth; 9th. **2** one of nine equal parts.

¹nip (nĭp) **1** to bite, pinch, or squeeze: *My puppy* nips *my ankles playfully.* **2** to clip or pinch off: *to* nip *buds on a plant; to* nip *off a piece of wire.* **3** a bite or pinch: *A crab gave my toe a painful* nip. **4** to sting or hurt, as cold does: *The cold* nipped *her ears.* **5** sharp cold: *the* nip *of a fall morning.* **6** to stop the growth of; to blight; kill: *A late frost* nipped *the first flowers.* **7 nip and tuck** very close, as a race.

nip in the bud to stop in the beginning: *The mutiny was* nipped *in the bud.*

nipped, nip·ping. [**¹nip** seems to come from a Dutch word (nijpen).]

²nip (nĭp) a small drink; a swallow. [**²nip** is short for an earlier word "nipperkin" meaning "a half-pint measure."]

ni·trate (nī'trāt) one of a group of chemical compounds containing nitrogen. Certain nitrates, called saltpeter, are used as fertilizer.

ni·tro·gen (nī'trə jən) a chemical element. It is a colorless gas, and makes up four-fifths of the air around us. It is also a necessary element in all living matter.

nit·wit (nĭt'wĭt') stupid person.

N.J. New Jersey.

N. Mex. New Mexico.

no (nō) **1** not: *Please be at the game* no *later than 3 o'clock.* **2** not a or an; not any: *There was* no *desk in the room. There were* no *lights in the hall.* **3** opposite of yes: *Jane wouldn't take* no *for an answer. He said, "*No*, I can't see you now."* **4** negative vote or voter: *The* noes *were in the majority.* **noes.** (Homonym: know)

no·bil·i·ty (nō bĭl'ə tĭ) **1** greatness of character: *We did not agree with his methods, but admired the* nobility *of his aims.* **2** in some countries, high social position by reason of birth or title conferred by the ruler. **no·bil·i·ties.**

no·ble (nō'bəl) **1** having or showing very high character and great ideals: *a* noble *person; a* noble *life; a* noble *sacrifice.* **2** in some countries, of a high social position by birth or by title conferred by the ruler: *a* noble *family.* **3** person in such a position: *A duke and an earl are* nobles. **no·bler, no·blest; no·bly.**

no·ble·man (nō'bəl mən) man of noble birth or rank; a peer. **no·ble·men.**

no·bod·y (nō'bŏd'ĭ) **1** no one; no person. **2** person of no importance or influence: *He felt like a* nobody *in the presence of such famous people.* **no·bod·ies.**

noc·tur·nal (nŏk tûr'nəl) **1** of the night; happening or done at night: *a* nocturnal *sound; a* nocturnal *activity such as looking at the stars.* **2** active at night: *a* nocturnal *animal.* **3** of plants, having flowers that are open at night and closed in the daytime. **noc·tur·nal·ly.**

nod (nŏd) **1** to bow the head and raise it quickly as a greeting or as a sign of assent or agreement: *The boy* nodded *when asked if he had lost something.* **2** a bow with such a purpose: *He waited for a* nod *from the teacher before beginning his talk.* **3** to express or indicate by a nod: *to* nod *a greeting to a friend.* **4** to let the head droop forward from sleepiness. **5** a falling forward or nodding of the head due to sleepiness. **6** to bend or sway: *The lilies were* nodding *in the breeze.* **nod·ded, nod·ding.**

No·el (nō ĕl') **1** Christmas. **2 noel** a Christmas carol.

noise (noiz) **1** sound, especially if loud, harsh, or confused. **2** to spread by rumor: *A story that the doctor was leaving was noised about the town.* **noised, nois·ing.**

noise·less (noiz′lĭs) producing no noise, or much less noise than is usual; quiet; silent: *a noiseless breeze; a noiseless machine.* **noise·less·ly.**

nois·y (noi′zĭ) **1** full of loud, harsh sound: *a noisy room.* **2** making noise: *the noisy children.* **nois·i·er, nois·i·est; nois·i·ly.**

no·mad (nō′măd) member of a tribe, without a fixed home, that wanders from place to place in search of food for itself and its animals.

nom·i·nate (nŏm′ə nāt′) **1** to propose or select as a candidate for possible election to an office. **2** to appoint to an office: *The governor nominated Mr. Allen as Commissioner of Education.* **nom·i·nat·ed, nom·i·nat·ing.**

nom·i·na·tion (nŏm′ə nā′shən) **1** a proposing of a candidate for election: *We will now hear the nominations for club secretary.* **2** selection by a political party of a single candidate for a public office: *He sought the Republican nomination for president.*

nom·i·nee (nŏm′ə nē′) person named as a candidate for an office: *Which nominee was elected class president?*

non- prefix meaning "not" or "without": non*living;* non*stop.*

non·cha·lant (nŏn′shə lənt or nŏn′shə länt′) calmly unconcerned; indifferent: *John greeted the famous visitors with a nonchalant air.* **non·cha·lant·ly.**

non·con·duc·tor (nŏn′kən dŭk′tər) something that prevents passage of sound, heat, or electricity; an insulator: *Glass is a nonconductor of electricity.*

none (nŭn) **1** not any; no part or quantity: *He has done none of his work.* **2** no one; not one: *I'm afraid none of the boys will come.* **3 none the less** nevertheless. (Homonym: nun)

non·liv·ing (nŏn′lĭv′ĭng) not alive.

non·sense (nŏn′sĕns) **1** words or sentences that have no meaning: *"Fee-fi-fo-fum" is nonsense.* **2** foolishness: *Stop your nonsense and get to work!*

non·stop (nŏn′stŏp′) making no stops; express: *a nonstop flight.*

noo·dles (nōō′dəlz) food like macaroni but usually made with egg and cut in ribbon-like strips.

nook (nŏŏk) **1** small, out-of-the-way place: *a quiet nook for studying.* **2** corner.

noon (nōōn) midday; 12 o'clock in the middle of the day: *He went home at noon.*

noon·day (nōōn′dā′) at noon; occurring at midday: *a noonday meal; the noonday sun.*

no one (nō′wŭn′) nobody: *I saw no one. No one came.* Also spelled **no-one.**

noon·tide (nōōn′tīd′) noon.

noose (nōōs) loop of rope or cord which can be made smaller by pulling the loose end of the rope. A lasso is a noose.

nor (nôr) word used after "neither" to mean "and not": *I had time for neither breakfast nor lunch today.*

nor·mal (nôr′məl) **1** usual; regular; standard: *a normal condition; a normal temperature.* **2** usual condition: *During the flood the river rose five feet above normal.* **3** of average physical or mental development: *a normal child of 12 years.* **nor·mal·ly.**

Noose

Norse (nôrs) **1** of or having to do with the language, people, or countries of Scandinavia in olden times. **2** the people of ancient Scandinavia. **3** language of ancient Norway and Iceland.

north (nôrth) **1** the direction toward the North Pole; also, the point of the compass indicating this direction; opposite of south. **2** the part of the world, country, or continent in this direction: *the north of Europe.* **3 the North** (**1**) the northern part of the United States, especially the states north of Maryland, the Ohio River, and Arkansas. (**2**) in the Civil War, the states opposed to the Confederacy (the South); the Union. **4** in or to the north: *the north wall.* **5** of winds, from the north. **6** toward the north: *He walked north one block.*

North

---

fāte, făt, fâre, fär; bē, bĕt; bite, bĭt; nō, nŏt, nôr; fūse, fŭn, fûr; tōō, tŏŏk; foil; foul; thin; ~~then~~;
hw for wh as in *w*hat; zh for s as in u*s*ual; ə for a, e, i, o, u, as in ago, linen, peril, ato*m*, min*u*s

North America continent in which the United States is situated.

North American 1 of or relating to North America. 2 person who lives in North America or is of North American descent.

North Car·o·li·na (nôrth kăr′ə li′nə) a southeastern State of the United States on the Atlantic coast.

North Da·ko·ta (nôrth də kō′tə) a north central State of the United States.

north·east (nôrth′ēst′) 1 the direction halfway between north and east; also, the point of the compass indicating this direction. 2 the part of any area lying in this direction as seen from the center of the area. **3 the Northeast** the northeastern part of the United States, including New York, New Jersey, Pennsylvania, and New England. 4 in or to the northeast: *a northeast current.* 5 of winds, from the northeast. 6 toward the northeast: *The wagons moved* northeast.

north·east·ern (nôrth′ēs′tərn) located in or to the northeast: *the* northeastern *sky.*

north·er·ly (nôr′thər li) 1 northward: *They traveled in a* northerly *direction.* 2 of winds, coming from the north.

north·ern (nôr′thərn) 1 located in or to the north. 2 from the north.

northern lights glowing or flickering streamers of light seen at night in the northern sky; the aurora borealis.

north·ern·most (nôr′thərn mōst′) farthest north: *Alaska is the* northernmost *State.*

North Pole the northern end of the earth's axis.

North Star star which is very nearly over the North Pole. It is useful for finding direction at night.

north·ward (nôrth′wərd) toward the north.

north·west (nôrth′wĕst′) 1 the direction halfway between north and west; also, the point of the compass indicating this direction. 2 the part of any area lying in this direction as seen from the center of the area. 3 in or to the northwest: *a northwest current.* 4 of winds, from the northwest. 5 toward the northwest: *The wagons moved* northwest. **6 the Northwest** the northwestern part of the United States, especially Washington, Oregon, and Idaho and adjacent Canada.

north·west·ern (nôrth′wĕs′tərn) located in or to the northwest.

Nor·way (nôr′wā) country in northern Europe, occupying the western and northern part of the same peninsula as Sweden.

Nor·we·gian (nôr wē′jən) 1 of or pertaining to Norway, its people, or its language. 2 citizen of Norway or person of Norwegian descent. 3 language of the Norwegian people.

nose (nōz) 1 the organ through which people and animals breathe and with which they smell. 2 the snout of an animal. 3 anything that is like a nose because of its shape or position: *the* nose *of an airplane.* 4 ability to smell: *A dog has a keen* nose. 5 ability to find out, as if by scent: *a* nose *for news.* 6 to sniff, smell: *The foxhound* nosed *the grass in search of a trail.* 7 to fondle by rubbing with the nose. 8 to advance cautiously: *The ship* nosed *slowly through the fog.* **nosed, nos·ing.**

nose·bleed (nōz′blēd′) a bleeding from the nose.

nose cone the front end of a rocket.

nose dive 1 a nose-first plunge by an airplane. 2 any sudden drop, as of temperature.

Nose cone

nose-dive (nōz′dīv′) to take a sudden downward plunge. **nose-dived** or **nose-dove, nose-dived, nose-div·ing.**

nos·tril (nŏs′trəl) either of the two outer openings of the nose.

not (nŏt) word used to make negative statements: *He is* not *here at the moment.* (Homonym: knot)

no·ta·ble (nō′tə bəl) 1 worthy of notice or attention; memorable: *a* notable *event.* 2 important or distinguished person. **no·ta·bly.**

no·ta·ry (nō′tə ri) public official empowered to witness documents officially and, by his seal and signature, guarantee that the maker has sworn that they are true and correct. Usually called **notary public.** **no·ta·ries; no·ta·ries pub·lic.**

no·ta·tion (nō tā′shən) 1 set of signs, letters, or symbols used to represent notes, sounds, numbers, etc. Music, mathematics, and phonetics each has its own system of notation. 2 a putting down or use of any such symbols. 3 a note; written record.

notch

notch (nŏch) **1** a V-shaped cut; a nick. **2** a pass between hills: *Yesterday, during our horseback-riding trip, we drove through Smuggler's* Notch. **3** to make or cut notches in: *When the boys went hiking through the woods, they* notched *trees to mark a trail so they could find their way back.*

FULL   HALF   QUARTER   EIGHTH   SIXTEENTH
Musical notes

note (nōt) **1** short letter. **2** reminder: *The student took* notes *on the lecture.* **3** brief comment or explanation: *The* notes *in this book make its meaning clear.* **4** notice: *He took little* note *of what was going on.* **5** fame; importance: *Jones is a man of some* note. **6** written promise to pay. **7** musical tone or the symbol that stands for it. **8** to make a memorandum of: *Please* note *my phone number in your address book.* **9** to observe; notice: *Joe* noted *that the door was open.* **10** to mention: *He* noted *that fact in his lecture.* **11** a trace or hint: *a* note *of sadness in her voice.* **not·ed, not·ing.**

note·book (nōt′bŏŏk′) book in which to write notes, comments, or reminders.

not·ed (nō′tĭd) well-known; famous; celebrated: *This restaurant is* noted *for its good Italian food.*

note·wor·thy (nōt′wûr′thĭ) worthy of attention or notice: *The development of the airplane was a* noteworthy *contribution to travel.*

noth·ing (nŭth′ĭng) **1** not anything. **2** not at all; in no way: *But this picture looks* nothing *like her!* **3** thing or person of no use or importance: *He felt like a mere* nothing *in the presence of such a great man.*

no·tice (nō′tĭs) **1** to give or pay attention to: *I especially* noticed *Jane's new dress.* **2** to see; observe: *I* noticed *that Jane was wearing a new dress.* **3** attention: *He tiptoed quietly into the room to escape* notice. **4** statement or warning of what one intends to do: *We gave* notice *that we would move out of our apartment.* **5** written or printed announcement or descrip-

tion (of some special event or about some particular thing): *There are several new* notices *on the bulletin board.* **6** take notice of to pay attention to. **no·ticed, no·tic·ing.**

no·tice·a·ble (nō′tĭs ə bəl) easily seen or observed; likely to attract attention: *Mother mended my sweater so well that the torn place wasn't even* noticeable. **no·tice·a·bly.**

no·ti·fy (nō′tə fī′) to make known to; inform; give notice to: *He* notified *the post office of his change of address.* **no·ti·fied, no·ti·fy·ing.**

no·tion (nō′shən) **1** idea; understanding: *He had no* notion *of the meaning of the strange words.* **2** belief; view: *We sometimes have strange* notions *about other countries.* **3** fancy; whim: *We got a sudden* notion *to go fishing.* **4** notions small useful articles such as pins, needles, snaps, etc.

no·to·ri·ous (nō tôr′ĭ əs) widely known; noted, especially in a bad way: *Kidd was a* notorious *pirate.* **no·to·ri·ous·ly.**

not·with·stand·ing (nŏt′wĭth stăn′dĭng) **1** in spite of: *The property was finally sold,* notwithstanding *its high price.* **2** still; nevertheless; yet: *Tired as we were, we struggled on* notwithstanding.

nought (nôt) naught.

noun (noun) word that names or stands for a person, place, thing, condition, etc. "Boy," "seacoast," "table," "idea," etc. are nouns.

nour·ish (nûr′ĭsh) **1** to help to grow and develop or keep alive and well with food; feed: *Babies are* nourished *with milk.* **2** to build up; keep alive: *He* nourished *high hopes for his son's future.*

nour·ish·ment (nûr′ĭsh mənt) food; anything which helps to keep up or strengthen the body, promote growth, or improve quality.

Nov. November.

no·va (nō′və) star that suddenly explodes, becoming many times brighter, and then fades away in a few weeks or months.

nov·el (nŏv′əl) **1** long, narrative story written about imaginary characters, treated as if they were real: *"Little Women" is a* famous *novel about four sisters.* **2** new: *Studying French was a* novel *experience.*

fāte, făt, fâre, fär; bē, bĕt; bite, bĭt; nō, nŏt, nôr; fūse, fŭn, fûr; tŏŏ, tŏŏk; foil; foul; thin; then; hw for wh as in what; zh for s as in usual; ə for a, e, i, o, u, as in ago, linen, peril, atom, minus

485

nov·el·ist (nŏv′əl ĭst) person who writes novels.

nov·el·ty (nŏv′əl tĭ) **1** new or unusual idea or thing: *The camel ride at the zoo is a popular* novelty *for small children.* **2** freshness; newness; strangeness: *the* novelty *and excitement of a first plane trip.* **3 novelties** small, attractive, and unusual objects made and sold for a low price: *The department store sells paper hats, balloons, and other* novelties *for New Year's Eve.* **nov·el·ties.**

No·vem·ber (nō vĕm′bər) the eleventh month of the year. November has 30 days.

nov·ice (nŏv′ĭs) **1** beginner; person without experience: *Today's pitcher is only a* novice *in big-league baseball and still has a lot to learn.* **2** person in training before becoming a full member of a religious order.

now (nou) **1** at the present time; immediately: *I must do this* now. *I'm leaving* now. **2** the present time: *By* now *you should have finished all your homework.* **3** next (in a story or account); after this; then: *Cinderella* now *pulled the matching slipper out of her pocket.* **4** under these conditions; as things are: *We have lost the trail;* now *we will have to camp overnight.* **5** since: *We'd better start shoveling,* now *the snow has stopped.* **6** word used to express a warning, disbelief, surprise, etc.: *He exclaimed, "*Now, *what have you done!"* **7 just now** a moment ago: *The telegram came* just now. **8 now and then** or **now and again** occasionally; from time to time.

now·a·days (nou′ə dāz′) at the present time; these days: *We do things differently* nowadays.

no·where (nō′hwâr′) not in, to, or at any place: *My pen is* nowhere *to be found.*

no·wise (nō′wīz′) not at all; in no way.

nox·ious (nŏk′shəs) harmful; dangerous; poisonous: *Gasoline has* noxious *fumes.* **nox·ious·ly.**

noz·zle (nŏz′əl) the metal spout at the end of a hose, pipe, or bellows through which liquids and gases may be released.

Nozzle of hose

nu·cle·ar (nōō′klĭ ər or nū′klĭ ər) having to do with the nucleus of a cell, atom, etc.

nuclear fission the splitting apart of the nucleus of a very heavy atom into two lighter atoms by a neutron. When the atom

splits, some of its mass is changed to energy which is released in the form of heat.

nuclear fusion the combining of two lightweight atoms into a heavier atom. In the process, one or more of the neutrons in the original atoms are changed to energy in the form of heat.

nuclear physics branch of physics dealing with the nucleus of the atom.

nu·cle·us (nōō′klĭ əs or nū′klĭ əs) **1** the central part or core, especially of the atom or the living cell. **2** small number of people who begin an undertaking or who are the active center of a larger group. **nu·cle·us·es** or **nu·cle·i** (nōō′klĭ ī′ or nū′klĭ ī′).

nude (nōōd or nūd) **1** without clothes; naked; bare. **2** in art, a picture of an unclothed human figure: *The museum bought three* nudes *from a collector.*

nudge (nŭj) **1** to push or touch gently with the elbow: *Henry* nudged *me to go ahead.* **2** slight push with the elbow. **nudged, nudg·ing.**

nug·get (nŭg′ət) **1** lump of gold found in the earth. **2** a small, valuable bit of anything: *a* nugget *of wisdom.*

nui·sance (nōō′səns or nū′səns) person or thing that annoys or is troublesome.

numb (nŭm) **1** deprived of or without the power to feel or move: *The sound of footsteps on the stairs at midnight made us* numb *with fear.* **2** to cause to be without feeling; deaden: *The icy cold* numbed *our fingers.* **numb·ly.**

num·ber (nŭm′bər) **1** amount; quantity: *What is the* number *of persons present?* **2** word, figure, or numeral that stands for an amount or quantity. **3** figure or numeral which identifies a person or thing: *My locker* number *is 3214.* **4** to amount to: *The school's library* numbers *about 5,000 books.* **5** to give a number to: *We* numbered *the tickets 1 to 500.* **6** to count: *I* number *the people in the group to be 26.* **7** one of a series: *Give me the January* number *of the magazine.* **8** musical piece; song: *For her next* number *Jane will sing a folk song.* **9** to limit in number: *The days of his life are* numbered. **10** to include: *I* number *him among my closest friends.* **11** form of a word which shows whether it refers to the singular or plural: *"Man" is singular and* *"men" is plural in* number. **12 Numbers** the fourth book of the Old Testament. **13 a number of** any amount between few and many: *A tour of the ice cream factory was made by* a number of *children.*

num·ber·less (nŭm′bər lĭs) **1** too many to be counted: *The grains of sand on the seashore are* numberless. **2** not having a number: *a* numberless *page.*

numb·ness (nŭm′nĭs) a being numb; lack of feeling.

num·er·al (noo′mər əl or nū′mər əl) figure which stands for a number. The Arabic numerals are 1, 2, 3, etc. The Roman numerals are I, II, III, etc.

nu·mer·a·tor (noo′mər rā′tər or nū′mə-rā′tər) **1** the numeral above the line in a fraction. In the fraction ¾, 3 is the numerator. **2** the first of two numbers in a ratio.

nu·mer·i·cal (noo mĕr′ə kəl or nū mĕr′ə-kəl) expressed in, consisting of, or having to do with numbers: *Arrange the numbered sheets in* numerical *order before taking the examination.* **nu·mer·i·cal·ly.**

nu·mer·ous (noo′mər əs or nū′mər əs) **1** more than a few; many: *I had* numerous *telephone calls this morning.* **2** many in number: *a* numerous *collection of butter-flies.* **nu·mer·ous·ly.**

nun (nŭn) woman who has taken religious vows and lives in a convent. Many nuns do teaching, nursing, charitable work, etc. (Homonym: none)

nup·tial (nŭp′shəl) **1** of or having to do with marriage: *a* nuptial *ceremony.* **2 nuptials** a marriage or wedding.

nurse (nûrs) **1** one who takes care of the sick or infirm. **2** to care for in sickness: *She* nursed *soldiers wounded at the battle-front.* **3** one who cares for a young child or children. **4** to tend carefully; give special care to: *I* nursed *that plant along for a year before it bloomed.* **5** to give or take milk at the mother's breast. **nursed, nurs·ing.**

nurse·maid (nûrs′mād′) girl or woman who takes care of a child or children.

nurs·er·y (nûr′sə rĭ) **1** baby's or child's room. **2** a place where babies or young children are cared for and tended: *a day* nursery. **3** a place where young plants are raised. **4 nursery school** school for children too young for kindergarten. **nurs·er·ies.**

nur·ture (nûr′chər) **1** to feed; nourish and care for: *Baby chicks must be carefully* nurtured *when they are first hatched.* **2** nourishment and care; promotion of growth: *the* nurture *of baby chicks.* **3** to bring up; train; rear: *The music teacher carefully* nurtured *Alice's voice.* **4** up-bringing; training: *With careful* nurture, *Alice's voice developed a beautiful tone.* **nur·tured, nur·tur·ing.**

nut (nŭt) **1** the hard or corklike shell of certain trees, such as the almond, pecan, and chestnut, together with the seeds inside the shell. **2** seed or kernel of any nut when removed from the shell. **3** metal

Nut on a bolt

block with a threaded hole into which the threaded end of a bolt fits.

nut·crack·er (nŭt′krăk′ər) tool for cracking nuts.

nut·meg (nŭt′mĕg) **1** hard, nut-like kernel of the seed of an East Indian tree, which is grated and used as spice. **2** the tree itself.

nu·tri·ent (noo′trĭ ənt or nū′trĭ-ənt) **1** something that promotes growth and strength; food. **2** promoting growth and strength; nourishing: *Bacteria are grown in* nutrient *liquids.*

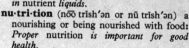
Nut cracker

nu·tri·tion (noo trĭsh′ən or nū trĭsh′ən) a nourishing or being nourished with food: *Proper* nutrition *is important for good health.*

nu·tri·tious (noo trĭsh′əs or nū trĭsh′əs) nourishing; promoting growth: *Foods rich in vitamins, minerals, and proteins form a* nutritious *diet.* **nu·tri·tious·ly.**

NW or **N.W. 1** northwest. **2** northwestern.

N.Y. New York.

ny·lon (nī′lŏn) **1** chemical plastic from which fibers, cloth, machine parts, etc. are manufactured. **2 nylons** stockings made of nylon fibers.

fāte, făt, fâre, fär; bē, bĕt; bīte, bĭt; nō, nŏt, nôr; fūse, fŭn, fûr; too, took; foil; foul; thin; ~~then~~; hw for wh as in *wh*at; zh for s as in u*s*ual; ə for a, e, i, o, u, as in *a*go, linen, peril, atom, minus

487

nymph (nĭmf) **1** in Greek and Roman mythology and in poetry, a minor goddess of nature, living in the mountains, woods, streams, etc.: *Robert dreamed of nymphs playing on the wooded mountainside.* **2** an insect in a certain stage of development.

O

¹O, o (ō) 15th letter of the English alphabet.

²O (ō) an exclamation used in speaking formally to someone: *We praise thee, O Lord.* (Homonyms: oh, owe)

oak (ōk) **1** any acorn-bearing tree; the most important of American hardwoods. There are nearly three hundred kinds. **2** the wood of these trees.

WHITE OAK

oak·en (ō′kən) made of oak.

oar (ôr) **1** wooden paddle with a flat or somewhat curved blade and a long handle, used to row or guide a boat. **2** rower: *Felix is the best oar of the crew.* (Homonyms: o'er, or, ore)

LIVE OAK
Oaks

oars·man (ôrz′mən) person who rows a boat. **oars·men.**

Oar

o·a·sis (ō ā′sĭs) **1** fertile spot in a desert. **2** place of refreshment. **o·a·ses** (ō ā′sēz).

Caravan leaving an oasis

oat (ōt) **1** a cereal plant, the seeds of which are ground for oatmeal or used as food for horses. **2 oats** the seed or grain of the oat plant.

oath (ōth) **1** solemn statement, made with God as a witness, that one will tell the truth or keep a promise: *He gave his oath that he would tell us exactly how the accident happened. The mayor took the oath of office.* **2** careless or profane use of the name of God or of anything sacred. **3** curse word: *to shout oaths in anger.*

oat·meal (ōt′mēl′) **1** rolled or ground oats. **2** a breakfast dish made of boiled rolled oats.

o·be·di·ence (ō bē′dĭ əns) a doing what one is told to do; willingness to obey: *If you are patient and kind, you can teach a dog obedience without making him fear you.*

o·be·di·ent (ō bē′dĭ ənt) willing to follow orders, rules, or the will of others: *An obedient child obeys promptly.* **o·be·di·ent·ly.**

ob·e·lisk (ŏb′ə lĭsk) a tapering four-sided column with a tip shaped like a pyramid.

o·bey (ō bā′) **1** to follow orders; do as one is told: *If you won't obey you'll be punished.* **2** to comply with; yield to the authority of: *Everyone should obey the law.*

Obelisk

¹ob·ject (ŏb′jĭkt) **1** thing that has shape and can be touched or seen: *The only object rescued from the fire was an old chair.* **2** purpose; goal; ambition: *Bill's one object in life is to become a famous surgeon.* **3** person or thing that arouses feeling or action: *an object of pity; an object of praise.*

²ob·ject (əb jĕkt′) **1** to protest; show disapproval: *Mother always objects when we leave the turtles in the bathtub.* **2** to oppose; give reasons for disliking: *The girls objected to our plans and gave us no help.* **3** to offer an argument against a proposal: *He objected that nobody would have time for so much extra work.*

ob·jec·tion (əb jĕk′shən) **1** feeling or expression of opposition or dislike; an objecting: *The cat showed his objection to the stray dog by arching his back.* **2** reason for opposing something: *My only objection to the trip is that it will cost too much.*

ob·jec·tion·a·ble (əb jĕk′shən ə bəl) undesirable; likely to be objected to: *A swamp* *would be an* objectionable *place for a picnic, because of the damp ground and insects.* **ob·jec·tion·a·bly.**

ob·jec·tive (əb jĕk′tĭv) **1** aim; goal: *Learning should be our first objective in school.* **2** unprejudiced; not influenced by feelings: *Is the news story objective or prejudiced?* **3** real; not imaginary. **4** the lens of a microscope or telescope nearest the thing being examined. The objective receives light from the subject and passes it to the eyepiece. **ob·jec·tive·ly.**

ob·li·gate (ŏb′lə gāt′) to bind by a promise, contract, or sense of duty: *Patriotism obligates us to serve our country.* **ob·li·gat·ed, ob·li·gat·ing.**

ob·li·ga·tion (ŏb′lə gā′shən) **1** duty: *Your first obligation is to learn all you can.* **2** debt of gratitude, loyalty, affection, etc.: *I feel an obligation to everyone who helps me.* **3** legal debt: *He is careful to meet his obligations promptly.*

o·blige (ə blīj′) **1** to place under a duty or necessity: *Most teachers are obliged to do as much homework as their pupils.* **2** to do (someone) a favor: *Will you oblige me by lending me your skates?* **o·bliged, o·blig·ing.**

o·blig·ing (ə blī′jĭng) helpful; willing to help; kindly: *The police in your city are most obliging to travelers.* **o·blig·ing·ly.**

ob·lique (ō blēk′) slanting; sloping; neither vertical nor horizontal; diagonal: *Wind drove the rain in oblique lines.* **ob·lique·ly.**

Oblique lines

ob·lit·er·ate (ə blĭt′ə rāt′) to wipe out; destroy completely: *The earthquake obliterated an entire city.* **ob·lit·er·at·ed, ob·lit·er·at·ing.**

ob·liv·i·on (ə blĭv′ĭ ən) **1** condition of being forgotten: *A single great novel has saved many a novelist from oblivion.* **2** forgetfulness; unawareness of what is going on: *Jim sat dreaming in utter oblivion of the activity around him.*

ob·liv·i·ous (ə blĭv′ĭ əs) unaware; inattentive: *He roared down Main Street in his car, oblivious of the traffic lights.* **ob·liv·i·ous·ly.**

ob·long (ŏb′lông) **1** a right-angled figure that is longer than it is wide. **2** having greater length than width: *This is an oblong picture.*

Oblongs

ob·nox·ious (əb nŏk′shəs) nasty; offensive; disagreeable: *an obnoxious odor; an obnoxious person.* **ob·nox·ious·ly.**

o·boe (ō′bō) a high-pitched wooden musical instrument, played by blowing into a mouthpiece made of two thin pieces of reed.

Man playing oboe

ob·scure (əb skūr′) **1** dim; dark; indistinct: *Increasing darkness made the road signs obscure.* **2** to hide; darken: *A heavy fog obscured the street lamps.* **3** not clear; hard to understand: *The meaning of that sentence is obscure.* **4** to make less clear: *All those long words obscure his meaning.* **5** remote; out of the way: *an obscure village.* **6** unknown: *an obscure country lawyer.* **ob·scur·er, ob·scur·est; ob·scured, ob·scur·ing; ob·scure·ly.**

ob·scu·ri·ty (əb skūr′ə tĭ) **1** lack of clear meaning: *The obscurity of the speaker's remarks confused his audience.* **2** condition of being unknown: *Many once famous names have now passed into obscurity.* **3** dimness; indistinctness: *the obscurity of the carving on the old monument.* **ob·scu·ri·ties.**

ob·serv·ance (əb zûr′vəns) **1** the keeping of a law or custom: *The banks will be closed Tuesday for the observance of Washington's birthday.* **2** ceremony; rite: *a religious observance.*

ob·serv·ant (əb zûr′vənt) quick to notice; watchful: *The teacher is very observant of everything that goes on.* **ob·serv·ant·ly.**

ob·ser·va·tion (ŏb′zər vā′shən) **1** act of watching, seeing, or noticing: *A half-hour's observation taught me the game.* **2** power or ability to see clearly and examine with

---

fāte, făt, fâre, fär; bē, bĕt; bīte, bĭt; nō, nŏt, nôr; fūse, fŭn, fûr; tōō, tŏŏk; foil; foul; thin; ~~then~~; hw for wh as in *wh*at; zh for s as in u*s*ual; ə for a, e, i, o, u, as in *a*go, lin*e*n, per*i*l, at*o*m, min*u*s

exactness: *A detective must develop his* observation. **3** thing noted by observing: *Write your* observations *of the experiment in your notebooks.* **4** notice; a being seen: *Certain birds often escape* observation *because of protective coloring.* **5** a remark or comment that results from observing: *My aunt made an* observation *about how much I had changed in the last year.*

ob·serv·a·to·ry (əb zûr′və tôr′ĭ) **1** building with a telescope and other equipment for studying the heavens. **2** tower or place designed for watching or studying a volcano, the sea, or other phenomena of nature. **ob·serv·a·to·ries.**

ob·serve (əb zûrv′) **1** to see; notice; watch carefully: *to* observe *a flash of lightning; to* observe *the growth of a flower.* **2** to say; remark: *"A good day for planting," the farmer* observed *one clear morning.* **3** to obey; follow: *Swimmers must* observe *the rules of the pool.* **4** to keep; celebrate: *The Fourth of July is* observed *as a patriotic holiday.* **ob·served, ob·serv·ing.**

ob·serv·er (əb zûr′vər) **1** one who watches: *He stood apart as an* observer *of the fight.* **2** one who follows or conforms to rules and customs: *a strict* observer *of the Sabbath.* **3** an official delegate at a meeting who takes note of the proceedings but has no part in them.

ob·serv·ing (əb zûr′vĭng) quick to notice; in the habit of noticing; observant. **ob·serv·ing·ly.**

ob·so·lete (ŏb′sə lēt′) out of date; no longer used: *The development of Diesel engines has made steam locomotives* obsolete *on most of our railroads.* **ob·so·lete·ly.**

ob·sta·cle (ŏb′stə kəl) thing that stands in the way or blocks; obstruction: *We had to climb over fallen rocks and other* obstacles *on the mountain path. Not knowing the language of another country is an* obstacle *to understanding its people.*

ob·sti·na·cy (ŏb′stə nə sĭ) stubbornness; determination not to yield: *Mules often show great* obstinacy *and refuse to budge even when forcibly urged.*

ob·sti·nate (ŏb′stə nĭt) unyielding; not giving in to pressure or reasoning; stubborn: *Once John got an idea, he was so* obstinate *that nobody could argue him out of it.* **ob·sti·nate·ly.**

ob·struct (əb strŭkt′) **1** to block; close: *A fallen tree* obstructed *the road and halted all traffic.* **2** to be or get in the way of; hinder: *Heavy frost on the windshield* obstructed *the driver's view.* **3** to prevent or slow down the progress of: *Stony ground and rain* obstructed *the building of the tennis court.*

ob·struc·tion (əb strŭk′shən) **1** something that blocks: *The water won't run out of the sink because there is an* obstruction *in the drain.* **2** a blocking: *Heavy snows caused* obstruction *of railroads and highways.*

ob·tain (əb tān′) **1** to get; acquire by effort, purchase, or request: *Practice long and hard, and you'll* obtain *results.* **2** to be in use or in fashion; prevail: *Shaking hands upon meeting is a custom that* obtains *in many countries.*

ob·tain·a·ble (ŏb tān′ə bəl) capable of being bought or acquired: *She pays high prices to get the best clothes* obtainable.

ob·tuse (əb tōōs′ or əb tūs′) **1** not sensitive; slow to understand; dull: *Sam was* obtuse *when it came to people's feelings.* **2** obtuse angle angle greater than a right angle. For picture, see **angle. ob·tuse·ly.**

ob·vi·ous (ŏb′vĭ əs) plain to see; clear; evident: *One runner was far ahead of the others, and it was* obvious *that he would win.* **ob·vi·ous·ly.**

oc·ca·sion (ə kā′zhən) **1** a particular time or event: *I remember the* occasion *of our first meeting.* **2** a time or event that is special or important: *A girl's first formal dance is a real* occasion. **3** opportunity; chance: *This is the first* occasion *I have had to congratulate him on his graduation.* **4** reason or cause: *The* occasion *of my call is our annual hospital drive.* **5** to bring about; cause: *The proposal to lengthen the school day* occasioned *many protests.* **6 on occasion** once in a while; as need or opportunity demands: *He can show great ability* on occasion.

oc·ca·sion·al (ə kā′zhən əl) **1** occurring once in a while: *an April day with* occasional *showers.* **2** created or used for a special event: *A poem written for graduation is an* occasional *poem.*

oc·ca·sion·al·ly (ə kā′zhən ə lĭ) once in a while; now and then: *At the lake we swim a lot and* occasionally *go fishing.*

oc·ci·dent (ŏk′sə dənt) **1** the west. **2 the Occident** countries of Europe and the Americas as distinguished from those of Asia.

oc·cu·pant (ŏk′yŏŏ pənt) person who occupies or makes use of a building, house, room, seat, etc.: *The firemen used ladders to rescue the* occupants *of the upper floors of the building.*

oc·cu·pa·tion (ŏk′yŏŏ pā′shən) **1** business, trade, or job: *Selling automobiles is his* occupation. **2** an occupying or being occupied: *Quick* occupation *of these new houses is expected.* **3** seizure and holding: *The* occupation *of an important city had cut off enemy troops from their supplies and forced them to surrender.*

oc·cu·py (ŏk′yŏŏ pī′) **1** to take up; fill up: *The dinner and entertainment* occupied *two hours.* **2** to settle in or live in: *My friend is waiting to* occupy *the new house he just bought.* **3** to take possession of; seize: *The army advanced and* occupied *ten square miles of enemy territory.* **4** to hold; have: *A student council* occupies *an important place in school affairs.* **5** to keep busy: *The naturalist* occupies *himself with studying plants and animals.* **oc·cu·pied, oc·cu·py·ing.**

oc·cur (ə kûr′) **1** to take place; happen: *Several accidents have* occurred *at that corner.* **2** to suggest itself (to someone's mind): *It just* occurred *to me that Monday is a holiday.* **3** to be found; exist: *How many times does the word "the"* occur *in the sentence you are reading?* **oc·curred, oc·cur·ring.**

oc·cur·rence (ə kûr′əns) **1** a happening; event: *An eclipse of the sun is a rare* occurrence. **2** a taking place; occurring: *Frequent* occurrence *of floods led to the building of levees along this river.*

o·cean (ō′shən) **1** the vast body of salt water covering three fourths of the earth's surface: *The old sailor has spent most of his life on the* ocean. **2** any of the four particular oceans into which the ocean as a whole is divided: *the Atlantic* Ocean, *the Pacific* Ocean, *the Indian* Ocean, *and the Arctic* Ocean.

o·ce·lot (ō′sə lŏt or ŏs′ə lŏt′) a spotted member of the cat family found in Central and South America.

Ocelot, about 4 ft. long

o'clock (ə klŏk′) according to the clock: *Let's meet at three* o'clock.

Oct. October.

oc·ta·gon (ŏk′tə gŏn′) a plane figure with eight sides and eight angles. When all the sides and all the angles are equal the figure is called **a regular octagon.**

oc·tag·o·nal (ŏk tăg′ə nəl) having eight sides. **oc·tag·o·nal·ly.**

Octagon

oc·tave (ŏk′tĭv or ŏk′tāv) **1** the difference in pitch between any musical note and the next note of the same name above or below it. **2** any note that is next above or below another note of the same name. In the drawing, the middle C is an octave of either the lower C or the higher C. The middle C has exactly twice as many vibrations per second as the lower C, and half as many as the upper C. **3** any note played with the next note of the same name above or below it. **4** two such notes and all the notes between them.

OCTAVE   OCTAVE

Octaves on piano

Oc·to·ber (ŏk tō′bər) tenth month of the year. October has 31 days.

oc·to·pus (ŏk′tə pəs) sea animal with a bulb-shaped body from which stretch eight long tentacles with sucking disks on the underside for grasping prey.

TENTACLES

Octopus, a few inches to 20 ft. spread

oc·u·list (ŏk′yŏŏ lĭst) doctor who specializes in treating diseases of the eye.

odd (ŏd) **1** unusual: *It's* odd *that he should be late; he's usually on time.* **2** queer; different; peculiar: *an* odd *old fellow who lived alone with six pet geese.* **3** without a mate; not paired: *I found several* odd *socks of*

fāte, făt, fâre, fär; bē, bĕt; bīte, bĭt; nō, nŏt, nôr; fūse, fŭn, fûr; tōō, tŏŏk; foil; foul; thin; ~~then~~;
hw for wh as in *wh*at; zh for s as in u*s*ual; ə for a, e, i, o, u, as in *a*go, lin*e*n, per*i*l, at*o*m, min*u*s

491

different colors in my drawer. **4** plus a few more: *I've 40 odd dollars in my pocket.* **5** extra: *The odd player can keep score or substitute.* **6** occasional: *John does odd jobs during vacation.* **7 odd number** number that has a remainder of 1 after being divided by 2. 1, 3, 17, and 239 are odd numbers. **odd·ly.**

odd·i·ty (ŏd′ə tĭ) **1** person or thing that is unusual, peculiar, or strange: *Our tame bear was an oddity in the neighborhood.* **2** strangeness; peculiarity: *The oddity of his behavior made us very curious.* **odd·i·ties.**

odds (ŏdz) **1** advantages; difference that favors one side against another: *In a tug of war the odds are with the heavier team.* **2** chances; probability: *If we have a red sunset, the odds are that tomorrow will be be fair.* **3 at odds** in disagreement: *Jack and Pete are always at odds as to who bats first.* **4 odds and ends** small articles of little value; things left over.

ode (ōd) poem which expresses noble feelings in a dignified style, usually in honor of a person or thing.

o·di·ous (ō′dĭ əs) hateful; disgusting: *The sight of food was odious to the seasick girl.* **o·di·ous·ly.**

o·dor (ō′dər) scent; smell: *The damp basement has a musty odor. Lilacs have a pleasant odor.*

o·dor·less (ō′dər lĭs) having no odor.

o'er (ôr) over. (Homonyms: oar, or, ore)

of (ŏv) **1** made with or from: *windows of glass; ornaments of silver; carvings of wood.* **2** containing: *a box of candy; a bag of oranges.* **3** belonging to: *the roof of a house; the color of violets.* **4** from: *Chicago is west of New York.* **5** about; concerning: *a book of science; news of the world; pictures of a trip.* **6** by: *poems of Robert L. Stevenson.* **7** with; having: *a man of wealth; a girl of beauty.* **8** named: *the city of Denver.* **9** to or before: *We leave at 20 minutes of six.*

off (ôf or ŏf) **1** away from (a place, thing, or position): *I just got off the bus. He dived off the pier. Take the dishes off the table.* **2** away (in time or distance): *The station is about a mile off. Vacation is just a week off.* **3** removed: *He worked with his coat off.* **4** not running; not in operation: *The refrigerator was off during our vacation.* **5** away from work: *He went swimming on*

his day off. **6** not busy: *It was an off season for fishing.* **7** on the way; started: *I must be off to the office early in the morning.* **8** canceled: *In case of rain, the trip will be off.* **9** less than: *The toys were sold at five percent off the usual price.* **10** wrong; incorrect: *My figuring of the bill was off by one dollar.* **11 off and on** now and then: *It rained off and on all day.*

of·fence (ə fĕns′) offense.

of·fend (ə fĕnd′) **1** to annoy; make angry; hurt the feelings of: *Such a personal question might offend some people.* **2** to be disagreeable to (the senses): *Colors that don't match offend the eyes.* **3** to do wrong; break a law or rule: *Those who offend are often punished.*

of·fend·er (ə fĕn′dər) person who breaks a law or rule.

of·fense (ə fĕns′) **1** the breaking of a law or rule: *Stealing is a criminal* offense. **2** act of offending: *an offense against good taste.* **3** something which annoys or displeases: *The loud discords were an offense to his sense of harmony.* **4** injury; insult: *Being left out of the game was an offense to his pride.* **5** (also ŏ′fĕns) attack; action against; assault: *The boxer's best offense was his left punch.* **6 give offense** to cause a feeling of hurt, annoyance, or displeasure. **7 take offense** to be annoyed, hurt, or displeased: *Jim took offense because he thought his friends were laughing at him.* Also spelled **offence.**

of·fen·sive (ə fĕn′sĭv) **1** annoying; disagreeable: *Susan's loud laughter was offensive to her quiet friend.* **2** unpleasant (to the senses): *Some people think that onions have a very offensive smell.* **3** having to do with attack: *to forbid the use of offensive weapons.* **4** an attack: *The troops hurled back the enemy's offensive.* **of·fen·sive·ly.**

of·fer (ôf′ər or ŏf′ər) **1** to express willingness; volunteer: *Many offered to help with the dishes.* **2** to put before (for acceptance or refusal): *The entertainment committee offered a plan for the party.* **3** to give: *This book offers several suggestions on decorating your room.* **4** something volunteered, presented, or proposed: *We appreciate your kind offer.* **5** to put up for sale: *The house was offered at a low price.* **6** a price bid: *The dealer accepted our offer of $500 for* *the old car.* **7** to attempt: *Will the enemy* offer *any resistance?* **8** to present itself; arise: *He will travel any time the opportunity* offers.

of·fer·ing (ôf′ər ĭng or ŏf′ər ing) **1** a giving; presenting: *the offering of help to those in need.* **2** something which is offered or given; gift, especially for religious use: *She placed her offering in the collection plate.*

off·hand (ôf′hănd′ or ŏf′hănd′) **1** without giving much thought or preparation: *Tell me offhand, how many beans are in this jar.* **2** said or done without preparation: *He made a few offhand remarks.*

of·fice (ôf′is or ŏf′is) **1** room or rooms where business or professional services are carried on or clerical work is done: *a doctor's office.* **2** position, especially a public position to which a person is elected: *the office of sheriff.* **3** duty or service: *She performs the office of hostess very graciously.* **4** in some countries, a branch or department of government: *The British Foreign Office corresponds to our Department of State.*

of·fi·cer (ôf′ə sər or ŏf′ə sər) **1** person who is given authority and trust, especially for public duties: *police officer.* **2** person elected or appointed to a position of responsibility: *Class officers; company officers.* **3** person who has rank or authority to command in the armed services, especially one who holds a commission or warrant. **4** persons in authority on commercial ships: *ship's officers.*

of·fi·cial (ə fish′əl) **1** person who holds a position of authority: *All the company's officials are in a meeting.* **2** having to do with a position of trust or authority: *The President has many official duties to perform.* **3** coming from the proper authority; approved: *Since the ambassador gave the report, it is considered official.* **of·fi·cial·ly.**

¹off·set (ôf sĕt′ or ŏf sĕt′) to make up for; take the place of; balance: *Skill may offset weakness.* **off′set, off′set·ting.**

²off·set (ôf′sĕt′ or ŏf′sĕt′) something that makes up for something else; a compensation: *Success is an offset for failure.*

off·shore (ôf′shôr′ or ŏf′shôr′) **1** off or away from the shore: *The ship anchored*

two miles offshore. **2** moving from the shore; toward the sea: *an offshore wind.*

off·spring (ôf′spring′ or ŏf′spring′) **1** child or children; descendant or descendants of a person or animal. **2** something created: *the offspring of a vivid imagination.*

oft (ôft or ŏft) often.

of·ten (ôf′ən or ŏf′ən) frequently.

of·ten·times (ôf′ən tīmz′ or ŏf′ən tīmz′) often.

o·gre (ō′gər) **1** a make-believe man-eating giant. **2** any vicious or cruel man.

oh (ō) **1** an exclamation of surprise, wonder, sorrow, etc.: *He said, "Oh! dear me! Oh, I didn't know that."* (Homonyms: O, owe)

O·hi·o (ō hī′ō) **1** a State in the north central part of the United States. **2** a large river which flows into the Mississippi.

ohm (ōm) unit of resistance to a current in an electric circuit.

oil (oil) **1** any one of many greasy or fatty substances, usually liquid, obtained from animals, plants, or minerals: *whale oil; olive oil.* **2** petroleum. **3** to put oil in or on; lubricate: *to oil a squeaky hinge.* **4** coloring matter or pigment mixed with oil: *to paint in oils.* **5** a painting in oils: *an exhibit of oils.*

oil·cloth (oil′klôth′ or oil′klŏth′) cloth waterproofed by a coating of paint and used for floor covering, shelf covering, etc.

oil well a well from which petroleum is taken.

oil·y (oi′lĭ) **1** of or like oil; smooth and slippery: *the oily feel of waxed paper.* **2** coated with oil; soaked in oil; greasy: *A fire may start in oily rags.* **oil·i·er, oil·i·est.**

oint·ment (oint′mənt) salve, often perfumed or medicated, used to soften the skin or to soothe rashes, burns, etc.

O.K. (ō′kā′) **1** all right; correct. **2** to write O.K. on; to approve. **O.K.'d, O.K.'ing.** Also spelled **okay.**

o·ka·pi (ō kä′pē) animal somewhat like a small giraffe, with short skin-covered

Okapi, about 4 ft. high at shoulder

---

fāte, făt, fâre, fär; bē, bĕt; bīte, bĭt; nō, nŏt, nôr; fūse, fŭn, fûr; tōō, tŏŏk; foil; foul; thin; then; hw for wh as in *wh*at; zh for s as in u*s*ual; ə for a, e, i, o, u, as in *a*go, lin*e*n, per*i*l, at*o*m, min*u*s

horns and with horizontal stripes on its legs. The okapi lives in central Africa.

o·kay (ō′kā′) O.K.

Okla. Oklahoma.

O·kla·ho·ma (ō′klə hō′mə) a State in the south central part of the United States.

o·kra (ō′krə) **1** tall plant with yellow blossoms and pointed, sticky seed pods. **2** its young, tender pod or pods, used in soups and eaten as a vegetable.

old (ōld) **1** having lived or existed a long time: *The old man talks of his distant boyhood. Twelve years is old for a dog. Sing us an old song.* **2** of (a certain) age: *I am nine years old.* **3** seeming old: *a young man with an old face.* **4** belonging to the past: *The man visited his old home, where he had lived as a boy.* **5** former times; the past: *in days of old.* **6** not new; used, worn, or owned for a long time: *We'll make our old car do for another year.* **7** known for a long time: *an old friend.* **8** of long experience: *The captain was an old hand at managing his ship in a storm.* **9** of long standing: *an old custom.* **old·er** or **eld·er, old·est** or **eld·est.**

old·en (ōl′dən) long ago; bygone: *In olden times, minstrels sang their poems.*

Old English language spoken in England from the 5th century until shortly after the Norman Conquest (1066). It is related to German.

old-fash·ioned (ōld′fāsh′ənd) **1** keeping to old ways; showing a liking for old ideas and customs: *the old-fashioned virtues of independence and self-reliance.* **2** done or made in the style of a past time: *an old-fashioned bouquet.* **3** out-of-date: *"Staff" is an old-fashioned word for "cane."*

Old French language, descended from Latin, which was spoken in France from the 9th century to the 14th century.

Old Norse language spoken in Norway, Denmark, and Iceland from the 8th century to the 14th century. It is related to Old English.

Old Testament (ōld tĕs′tə mənt) the first part of the Bible. The books of the Old Testament were written before the time of Jesus.

Old World the parts of Europe, Asia, and Africa known before the discovery of America.

o·le·o·mar·ga·rine (ō′li ō mär′jə rin) butterlike spread made of animal or vegetable fats; margarine.

ol·ive (ŏl′ĭv) **1** the small, oval fruit of an evergreen tree which grows in warm regions. Olives are pickled either green or ripe, or pressed for their fine oil. **2** the tree itself. **3** the fine cabinet wood of this tree. **4** greenish yellow, like olives that are not ripe: *an olive dress.*

Olives

olive branch branch from an olive tree, used as a symbol of peace.

olive oil oil pressed from ripe olives, used in cooking, for salads, in making soap, etc.

O·lym·pic games (ō lĭm′pĭk gāmz) **1** festival of ancient Greece, with contests in athletics, music, and poetry. **2** modern sports competition held every four years in a different country. Amateur athletes from many countries compete in the Olympic games.

om·e·let or **om·e·lette** (ŏm′ə lĭt) eggs beaten with milk, cooked, and folded over, often with chopped ham, cheese, jelly, etc., as a filler.

o·men (ō′mən) a sign or happening supposed to predict good or bad luck; an indication of coming events.

om·i·nous (ŏm′ə nəs) like an omen of bad luck; threatening evil: *Dark ominous clouds foretold a storm.* **om·i·nous·ly.**

o·mis·sion (ō mĭsh′ən) **1** an omitting; leaving out: *The omission of your signature will disqualify your entry in the contest.* **2** thing omitted or left out: *Several omissions made the list incomplete.*

o·mit (ō mĭt′) **1** to leave out; fail to include: *Copy the names of the group but omit your own.* **2** to fail to do; neglect; leave undone. **o·mit·ted, o·mit·ting.**

om·ni·bus (ŏm′nə bŭs′) **1** a collection of many different writings: *an omnibus of mystery stories.* **2** including many different items: *an omnibus bill in Congress.* **3** a bus.

om·nip·o·tent (ŏm nĭp′ə tənt) all-powerful: *God alone is omnipotent.* **om·nip·o·tent·ly.**

on (ŏn or ôn) **1** upon; supported by and touching: *Sit on this chair. I'll hang a picture on the wall.* **2** located upon: *blisters* on *my feet.* **3** along; situated near: *a house on the river; a town* on *the border.* **4** covering: *gloves* on *her hands; new paint* on *the ceiling.* **5** being worn: *She has no hat on.* **6** forward: *Go* on *to the bottom of the hill.* On *to victory!* **7** offered for: *popcorn* on *sale;* on *view.* **8** available at a: *a doctor* on *call; water* on *tap.* **9** for the purpose of; in order to carry out: *out of town* on *business;* on *an errand.* **10** following; keeping to: *pioneers* on *the trail;* on *course.* **11** toward: *Have pity* on *us. There's a door opening* on *the garden.* **12** a member of: *I'm* on *the committee.* **13** about; concerning: *a talk* on *Alaska; to agree* on *a plan.* **14** when it is or was: *Come* on *Monday.* **15** upon\the event of; at the time of: *He felt better* on *going ashore. I'll meet you* on *your arrival.* **16** not behind or ahead of: *to come* on *time;* on *schedule.* **17** in progress: *The game was already* on *when we arrived.* **18** in use or action: *The light is* on. *The brakes are* on. **19** using (something) as an instrument: *Play a piece* on *the piano.* **20** taking part in a: *to be* on *strike.* **21** subject to; getting a: *to be* on *trial.* **22** taking: *to be* on *a vacation.* **23** planned; taking place: *We have a party* on *tonight, so we can't come.* **24** by reason of; in accordance with: *news* on *the best authority;* on *my honor.* **25 on and on** for a long time without stopping; continuously: *The students became restless as the speaker talked* on and on.

once (wŭns) **1** at one time; formerly: *We* once *lived in Ohio.* **2** a single time: *Sing the song through just* once. *Once is enough.* **3** if ever; whenever: *I never wake before eight o'clock,* once *I get to sleep.* **4** at any time; ever: *If she* once *starts talking, she is hard to stop.* **5 at once** (1) immediately. (2) at the same time: *At the signal, all start* at once.

one (wŭn) **1** the first and smallest number. **2** a single: *Only* one *person should talk at a time.* **3** a single person or thing: *When two teams play a game, only* one *can win.* **4** a particular person or thing: *The black puppy is the* one *I want.* **5** a certain: *He came home* one *day last week.* **6** some: *I'll call you* one *day soon.* **7** only: *The* one

thing to do is to admit your mistake. **8** any person: *From here* one *can just see the school.* **9 all one** (1) united; without difference: *We are all* one *in wishing you great success.* (2) of no importance: *It is* all one *to me whether we go now or later.* **10 at one** in agreement: *We all are* at one *about the plan for the exhibit.* **11 one by one**, one after the other: *In roll call the names are called* one by one. **12 one another** of a group of three or more, each one (to) every other: *The committee members should keep* one another *informed as we go along.* (Homonym: won)

one·self (wŭn sĕlf′) a person's self; one's own self: *To listen to* oneself *on a tape recorder is sometimes fun.*

one-sid·ed (wŭn′sī′dĭd) **1** prejudiced; unfair because only one side (of a question or matter) is considered: *a* one-sided *account of an accident.* **2** unequal: *The* one-sided *baseball game ended with a score of 14 to 1.* **one-sid·ed·ly.**

on·ion (ŭn′yən) **1** plant of the lily family with a strong odor and biting taste. **2** the bulb of this plant used as food.

TOP
BULB
Onion

on·look·er (ŏn′lŏŏk′ər or ŏn′-lŏŏk′ər) spectator; one who watches but does not take part: *I enjoy the sport as an* onlooker *rather than as a player.*

on·ly (ŏn′lĭ) **1** sole; without others: *our* only *pet; our* only *worry.* **2** single one (of all): *the* only *person I would trust; the* only *person for the job.* **3** solely; merely; exclusively: *We play the game for pleasure* only. **4** but; except that: *I'd go,* only *I have another engagement.* **5 if only** I wish that: *Jack exclaimed, "If* only *I could go swimming!"* **6 only too** very: *I am* only too *glad to go.*

on·rush (ŏn′rŭsh′ or ôn′rŭsh′) strong forward flow or rush: *The* onrush *of the flood swept everything before it.*

on·set (ŏn′sĕt′ or ôn′sĕt′) **1** an attack; assault: *The enemy was driven back by the* onset *of our troops.* **2** beginning: *We put away our summer clothes at the* onset *of cold weather in the fall.*

---

fāte, făt, fâre, fär; bē, bĕt; bīte, bĭt; nō, nŏt, nôr; fūse, fŭn, fûr; tōō, tŏŏk; foil; foul; thin; ~~then~~; hw for wh as in *what*; zh for s as in u*su*al; ə for a, e, i, o, u, as in *ago, linen, peril, atom, minus*

on·slaught (ŏn′slôt′ or ŏn′slôt′) violent attack or onset: *the* onslaught *of enemy troops; the* onslaught *of a hurricane.*

on·to (ŏn′tōō or ŏn′tōō) on to; on: *Let's get onto the ferry before it leaves without us.*

on·ward (ŏn′wərd or ôn′wərd) forward; toward a farther point in time or distance: *to move* onward *into unknown territory; to continue the* onward *march.*

ooze (ōōz) **1** to flow slowly out or through; seep: *The mud* oozed *between the child's squeezing fingers.* **2** to give out little by little through a small opening or openings: *His pores were* oozing *perspiration.* **3** soft, slimy mud, especially at the bottom of the ocean or of a river. **oozed, ooz·ing.**

o·pal (ō′pəl) precious stone that displays soft color changes on its smooth surface as it is moved in the light.

o·paque (ō pāk′) not permitting light to pass through; not transparent: *An* opaque *window shade shuts out the sunlight.* **o·paque·ly.**

o·pen (ō′pən) **1** not shut, closed, covered, etc.: *an* open *window; an* open *book; an* open *well; a road* open *to traffic.* **2** to cause (something) to be no longer closed: *to* open *a door; to* open *a book to page nine; to* open *a road to traffic.* **3** to become no longer closed; to become ready for business: *The door suddenly* opened. *The market* opens *at nine.* **4** to place formally in use: *to* open *a store; to* open *a new bridge.* **5** to begin or cause to begin: *to* open *a meeting.* **6** not blocked or obstructed; not sealed, wrapped, or tied: *an* open *drain; an* open *letter.* **7** to remove the covering, wrapper, or seal to see what is inside: *to* open *a letter; to* open *an ancient tomb.* **8** exposed to the weather; bare of natural shelter: *an* open *plain, an* open *field.* **9** not filled, engaged, or scheduled: *We have a waiter's job* open. *I have an* open *evening next Tuesday.* **10** to expose or lay bare (one's thoughts): *to* open *one's mind.* **11** public; not restricted: *an* open *letter to a newspaper.* **12** subject to discussion and decision: *an* open *question.* **13** frank; straightforward: *an* open *face.* **14** not folded up; spread out: *an* open *umbrella.* **15** to spread out; extend to a larger size: *to* open *an umbrella;* open *a road map.* **16** to unfold: *This bud is just* opening. **17** to lead into; make available:

Books open *a world of enjoyment and knowledge.* **18** to appear (as a split): *During the earthquake cracks* opened *in the earth.* **19** open to **(1)** exposed to: *One side of the shed is* open *to the weather.* **(2)** subject or liable to: *He is* open *to criticism.* **(3)** ready to consider: *I am* open *to any offers for this bicycle.*

open a person's eyes: to surprise one; show unexpected things (to someone): *The science exhibit was wonderful and really* opened *my eyes.*

open into or onto to lead to: *The kitchen has one door that* opens *into the dining room and another that* opens *onto the patio.*

open up to make open; make available for use or trade: *The airplane is* opening *up many remote places.*

open air outdoors: *We spent the morning in the* open air.

o·pen-air (ō′pən âr′) outdoor: *an* open-air *rally.*

o·pen-hand·ed (ō′pən hăn′dĭd) generous.

open house party or hospitality for all who come: *We're keeping* open house *on New Year's Day.*

o·pen·ing (ō′pən ĭng) **1** a hole, gap, or space: *an* opening *in the wall; an* opening *in the clouds.* **2** a clearing or open land in woods: *Deer were grazing in an* opening *in the forest.* **3** the start or beginning: *The sound of the guns signalled the* opening *of the battle.* **4** introductory; beginning: *the* opening *speeches.* **5** job vacancy: *The Smith Company has an* opening *for an engineer.* **6** favorable opportunity: *He waited for an* opening *in the discussion to offer his plan.* **7** formal beginning: *the millinery department's spring* opening.

o·pen·ly (ō′pən lĭ) without secrecy; without trying to hide or conceal: *He* openly *rebelled against the king.*

open mind mind that is not prejudiced or made up: *I have an* open mind *concerning who should be captain of the team.*

open season period of the year during which hunting or fishing is permitted.

op·er·a (ŏp′ər ə) a play with most of the lines sung instead of spoken, while an orchestra accompanies the singers.

op·er·ate (ŏp′ə rāt′) **1** to go, work, or run; to function: *A jet engine should* operate *smoothly.* **2** to cause to work or run: *Can* *he* operate *that car?* **3** to do surgery on a human being or animal. **4** to be in charge of or manage (a business): *He operates a coal mine and a store.* **op·er·at·ed, op·er·at·ing.**

op·er·at·ic (ŏp′ə răt′ĭk) having to do with opera.

op·er·a·tion (ŏp′ə rā′shən) **1** action; way in which something goes, works, or runs: *Smooth* operation *makes an engine last longer.* **2** surgical treatment on the body: *Removal of the tonsils is usually a simple* operation. **3** move or moves made to carry out a plan of action: *The invasion of France in World War II was a huge* operation.

op·er·a·tor (ŏp′ə rā′tər) **1** someone who works or runs a machine, mechanism, etc.: *an X-ray* operator; *a telephone switchboard* operator. **2** person who manages a business or other enterprise: *He is a big mine* operator.

op·er·et·ta (ŏp′ə rĕt′ə) short musical play, like a little opera, usually gay or funny, with most lines sung, not spoken.

o·pin·ion (ə pĭn′yən) belief or statement based on one's own judgment rather than on certain knowledge: *Each member of the committee was asked to give his* opinion *of the new plan.*

o·pi·um (ō′pĭ əm) very strong drug, useful in relieving pain, made from seed pods of flowers called **opium poppies.**

o·pos·sum (ə pŏs′əm) nocturnal animal of the southern United States that lives in trees and carries its young in a fur-lined pouch. It falls into a deathlike trance when frightened.

Opossum, about 2½ ft. long

op·po·nent (ə pō′nənt) someone who is on the other side in any kind of game, sport, race, or even war: *Mudville has always been our* opponent *in baseball.*

op·por·tu·ni·ty (ŏp′ər tōō′nə tĭ or ŏp′ər-tū′nə tĭ) time and circumstances that are good for a purpose; a good chance: *an* opportunity *to be committee chairman; an* opportunity *to try the new ice skates.* **op·por·tu·ni·ties.**

op·pose (ə pōz′) **1** to be against or struggle against (somebody or something): *to* oppose *a tax;* oppose *a dictator in open rebellion.* **2** to contrast; set against: *to* oppose *sunlight and shadow in a picture.* **op·posed, op·pos·ing.**

op·pos·ing (ə pō′zĭng) on the opposite side; conflicting: *two* opposing *political parties.*

op·po·site (ŏp′ə zĭt) **1** facing, in front of, or across from: *Who lives in the house* opposite *yours?* **2** the reverse; person or thing in marked contrast to another: *Darkness and daylight are* opposites. **3** contrary: *The whaling ship met a merchant ship traveling in the* opposite *direction.* **op·po·site·ly.**

op·po·si·tion (ŏp′ə zĭsh′ən) **1** an opposing or being opposed: *Our governor won praise for his* opposition *to high taxes.* **2** opposing force; resistance: *The enemy attacks met with fierce* opposition. **3** a position opposed or opposite (to another): *In checkers the red men are placed in* opposition *to the black.* **4** person or persons opposing: *The* opposition *did not want our man to run for mayor of the town.*

op·press (ə prĕs′) **1** to treat harshly and unjustly; rule with a heavy hand: *The American colonists felt that England was* oppressing *them by unfair taxes.* **2** to weigh heavily or press upon (the mind or spirit): *Alan looks as if all the cares of the world* oppress *him.*

op·pres·sion (ə prĕsh′ən) **1** cruel, unjust treatment; crushing, despotic rule: *The king's* oppression *caused many people to leave the country.* **2** a sense of being overpowered; feeling of heavy discomfort and depression: *We felt the* oppression *that accompanies the moments of stillness before a storm.*

op·pres·sive (ə prĕs′ĭv) **1** crushing; cruel and unjust: *an* oppressive *law; an* oppressive *ruler.* **2** heavy and overpowering; burdening: *an* oppressive *worry;* oppressive *heat.* **op·pres·sive·ly.**

---

fāte, făt, fâre, fär; bē, bĕt; bīte, bĭt; nō, nŏt, nôr; fūse, fŭn, fûr; tōō, tŏŏk; foil; foul; thin; then; hw for wh as in *what*; zh for s as in usual; ə for a, e, i, o, u, as in *ago*, linen, peril, atom, minus

op·pres·sor (ə prĕs′ər) one who oppresses or uses those under his power in a harsh, unjust way.

op·tic (ŏp′tĭk) **1** relating to the eye or to sight. **2 optics** the branch of physics dealing with the behavior of light.

op·ti·cal (ŏp′tĭ kəl or ŏp′tĭ kəl) **1** having to do with light and sight. **2** made to assist sight: *A microscope is an optical instrument.* **3 optical illusion** something that appears different from what it really is. For picture, see **illusion. op·ti·cal·ly.**

op·ti·cian (ŏp tĭsh′ən) maker and seller of eyeglasses and other optical instruments.

op·ti·mis·tic (ŏp′tə mĭs′tĭk) hopeful; disposed to see the bright side; inclined to a cheerful outlook.

or (ôr) **1** a connecting word that is used to show choice: *You must either sink or swim! Do you prefer currant, or grape jelly?* **2** word used with "either" to show a choice: *Either you or I must go.* **3** else; otherwise: *You had better go or you will be sorry.* **4** in other words; namely: *The puma, or cougar, is found in both North and South America.* (Homonyms: oar, o'er, ore)

-or suffix meaning "one who" or "the thing that": *sail*or; *inspect*or.

or·a·cle (ŏr′ə kəl or ôr′ə kəl) **1** in ancient Greece and Rome, a person believed to receive messages from a god and give them to human beings. **2** message so given. **3** place where such messages were given. **4** person whose wisdom and statements are considered beyond question: *Uncle John is the village oracle.*

o·ral (ôr′əl) **1** spoken, not written: *This year's final examination was oral.* **2** of or having to do with the mouth: *Cleaning of the teeth is a part of oral hygiene.* **o·ral·ly.**

Orange

or·ange (ŏr′ĭnj or ôr′inj) **1** round, golden fruit having a juicy pulp. **2** an evergreen tree of warm climates which bears fragrant white blossoms and this fruit. **3** the color of the fruit, reddish yellow; golden. **4** having this color: *an* orange *ribbon.*

or·ange·ade (ŏr′ĭnj ād′ or ôr′ĭnj ād′) drink made by mixing orange juice, sugar, and water.

o·rang·u·tang (ō răng′ōō tăng′) long-armed, tree-dwelling ape of Borneo and Sumatra. Its color is a reddish brown.

o·ra·tion (ô rā′shən) formal public speech, usually given on a special occasion: *a funeral* oration.

or·a·tor (ôr′ə tər or ŏr′ə tər) public speaker, especially a skillful one.

Orangutang, 4 to 5 ft. tall

¹or·a·to·ry (ŏr′ə tôr′ĭ or ôr′ə tôr′ĭ) **1** the art of speaking in public. **2** skill and eloquence in public speaking: *Abraham Lincoln's Gettysburg Address is an example of great oratory.* [¹oratory is from a Latin phrase (ars oratoria) meaning "art of oratory."]

²or·a·to·ry (ôr′ə tôr′ĭ or ŏr′ə tôr′ĭ) chapel for private prayer. **or·a·to·ries.** [²oratory is from a Latin word (oratorium) meaning "a place of prayer."]

orb (ôrb) **1** globe; sphere. **2** the sun, moon, or any other heavenly body.

or·bit (ôr′bĭt) **1** the path in which a heavenly body moves about another. **2** the path of a man-made satellite. **3** to start or put (a satellite) in such a path. **4** circle of influence: *Poland is within the Communist orbit.*

Orbit of a satellite

or·chard (ôr′chərd) **1** area of land on which fruit trees are cultivated for their fruit. **2** group of fruit trees.

or·ches·tra (ôr′kĭs trə) **1** group of musicians who play together on various instruments, usually including stringed instruments. **2** all the string, woodwind, brass, and percussion instruments played by such a group. **3** sunken section below and in front of the stage of a theater or opera house where these musicians play. **4** main floor of a theater, especially the part near the stage.

or·chid (ôr′kĭd) **1** any of a large group of plants that have flowers with three petals. **2** the flower of this plant. **3** pinkish lavender.

or·dain (ôr dān′) **1** to appoint; order; decree; establish by law: *to* ordain *a day of Thanksgiving.* **2** to admit to the ministry of a church by means of an official ceremony.

or·deal (ôr dēl′) severe test or dreadful experience: *Keeping the ship on course during the hurricane was an* ordeal *for the captain.*

or·der (ôr′dər) **1** a command: *The captain gave the* order *to abandon ship.* **2** to command; to direct with authority: *The captain* ordered *the passengers to abandon ship.* **3** a request for goods or services: *The principal sent in the* order *for 200 dictionaries.* **4** to request goods or services: *We have already* ordered *our Christmas cards.* **5** a document directing the payment of money: *a money* order. **6** goods ordered: *Send this* order *to 21 Midland Avenue.* **7** portion of food for one person: *The chef prepared four* orders *of fried chicken.* **8** arrangement; sequence: *alphabetical* order. **9** condition; state: *My work is in good* order. **10** proper arrangement or condition: *to keep* order *in a closet.* **11** to cause to be in proper arrangement or condition: *I hope to* order *my affairs better next year.* **12** established practice or custom: *the* order *of church worship.* **13** condition in which rules are observed and people behave quietly and peacefully: *to keep* order *in the hallways or streets.* **14** class or degree: *His work is usually of a high* order. **15** a social, religious, or honorary organization: *Masonic* Order; *Dominican* Order; Order *of the Garter.* **16 orders** office of a priest or minister in some churches. **17 in order** (**1**) in the right position. (**2**) in good working condition: *The candy machine is* in order *now.* (**3**) suitable or appropriate; in keeping with the rules: *Nominations for secretary are now* in order. **18 in order to** for the purpose of (doing something): *A crowbar was needed* in order to *move the stone.* **19 in order that** so that. **20 on the order of** somewhat like. **21 out of order** not in order.

or·der·ly (ôr′dər lì) **1** well arranged and tidy: *Mother kept the house clean and* orderly. **2** well managing; systematic: *An* orderly *person plans his work.* **3** well conducted or managed: *an* orderly *meeting.* **4** well behaved: *an* orderly *crowd.* **5** soldier assigned to an officer to carry messages and otherwise assist him. **6** an attendant in a hospital. **or·der·lies.**

or·di·nal num·ber (ôr′də nəl nŭm′bər) any number, such as first, second, third, etc., that shows a position in a sequence, as distinguished from a cardinal number, such as 1, 2, 3, etc.

or·di·nance (ôr′də nəns) an official law, rule, or decree, especially one made by the authorities of a town or city.

or·di·nar·i·ly (ôr′də nĕr′ĭ lĭ) usually; normally; customarily: *Our dog* ordinarily *sleeps quietly, but he howled all last night.*

or·di·nar·y (ôr′də nĕr′ĭ) **1** usual; customary; normal. **2** commonplace; lacking in imagination or originality; mediocre: *an* ordinary *speech; an* ordinary *dress.*

ord·nance (ôrd′nəns) **1** the heavy guns used in warfare. **2** military weapons and ammunition in general.

ore (ôr) rock or other earth material having enough metal to make the mining of it profitable. (Homonyms: oar, o′er, or)

Oreg. Oregon.

Or·e·gon (ôr′ə gŏn′ or ŏr′ə gən) a north Pacific State of the United States.

Oregon grape **1** small dark blue berry of western United States. Its small yellow blossom is the state flower of Oregon. **2** the evergreen shrub on which it grows.

or·gan (ôr′gən) **1** part of the body or of a plant that has a special duty. The eyes, heart, and stomach are a few of the organs of men and animals. **2** musical instrument played by touching keys which release jets of air into pipes or over reeds. **3**

Pipe organ

newspaper or magazine that spreads information: *Our company publishes a house* organ *for its employees.*

---

fāte, făt, fâre, fär; bē, bĕt; bīte, bĭt; nō, nŏt, nôr; fūse, fŭn, fûr; tōo, tŏŏk; foil; foul; thin; ~~then~~;
hw for wh as in *wh*at; zh for s as in u*s*ual; ə for a, e, i, o, u, as in *a*go, lin*e*n, per*i*l, at*o*m, min*u*s

or·gan·dy or **or·gan·die** (ôr′gən dĭ) thin, light, stiff cloth used for making dresses, curtains, trimmings, etc. **or·gan·dies.**

or·gan·ic (ôr găn′ĭk) **1** having to do with the organs of an animal or plant: *an* organic *disease.* **2** about a chemical compound, containing carbon. **3** made up of related parts: *an* organic *whole.*

or·gan·ism (ôr′gə nĭz′əm) living plant or animal: *Many microscopic* organisms *are found in sea water.*

or·gan·ist (ôr′gən ĭst) person who plays the organ.

or·gan·i·za·tion (ôr′gən ə zā′shən) **1** a uniting and grouping so that people or things work well together; an organizing or being organized: *The good* organization *of the colonel's troops helped him win many battles.* **2** way in which parts of a whole are arranged: *The men who wrote our constitution planned the general* organization *of our government.* **3** group of people united to do certain work: *the Red Cross* organization.

or·ga·nize (ôr′gə nīz′) **1** to put or come together in working order; unite or group so that things or persons work well together: *The coach* organized *a good football team by much drilling and hard work.* **2** to plan and arrange: *A scientist must* organize *his work carefully.* **or·ga·nized, or·ga·niz·ing.**

o·ri·ent (ôr′ĭ ĕnt′) **1** to place (a person or oneself) in the right relation to the points of the compass: *At night I can* orient *myself if I find the North Star.* **2** to adjust to or acquaint (a person or oneself) with the surroundings: *It doesn't take very long to* orient *yourself when you move to a new city.* **3 the Orient** (also ôr′yənt) the countries of Asia, especially the Far East and the islands off the coast of Asia.

o·ri·en·tal (ôr′ĭ ĕn′tǝl) **1** eastern. **2** of or pertaining to the countries in the Orient or their people: *strange* oriental *music;* oriental *customs.* **3 Oriental** person belonging to or descended from one of the native peoples of the Orient.

or·i·fice (ôr′ə fĭs) a mouth or opening; vent: *The nostril is the nasal* orifice.

or·i·gin (ôr′ə jĭn or ŏr′ə jĭn) **1** a beginning; start; source: *Nobody knows the* origin *of that rumor.* **2** family; background: *He never concealed his humble* origin.

o·rig·i·nal (ə rĭj′ə nəl) **1** first; earliest: *The Indians were the* original *inhabitants of America.* **2** imaginative; able to produce new ideas: *Your story shows you have an* original *mind.* **3** not copied; new; done for the first time: *Our teacher wrote an* original *Easter pageant.* **4** first model from which something is copied: *This is a copy of our Constitution but the* original *is in Washington, D.C.* **5** language in which something is first written: *College students often read French books in the* original.

o·rig·i·nal·i·ty (ə rĭj′ə năl′ə tĭ) **1** novelty; freshness: *That idea has great* originality. **2** ability to create or invent: *Fred's* originality *is seen best in his posters.*

o·rig·i·nal·ly (ə rĭj′ə nə lĭ) **1** at first; in the beginning: *The capital of the United States was* originally *Philadelphia.* **2** in a new way: *The stage decorations were designed very* originally.

o·rig·i·nate (ə rĭj′ə nāt′) **1** to start; begin: *The fire* originated *in the engine room and soon spread throughout the ship.* **2** to invent; make up: *The Chinese* originated *fireworks.* **o·rig·i·nat·ed, o·rig·i·nat·ing.**

o·ri·ole (ôr′ĭ ōl′) either of two American songbirds, the black-and-orange Baltimore oriole and the black-and-chestnut orchard

Baltimore oriole, about 8 in. long

oriole, that build hanging nests.

O·ri·on (ō rī′ən) bright constellation named for a hunter in Greek mythology.

Or·lon (ôr′lŏn) trade name for a synthetic fiber used in making textiles.

¹or·na·ment (ôr′nə mənt) **1** object used to decorate or beautify: *The cat likes to play with the Christmas tree* ornaments. **2** decoration; adornment: *She wore a white dress with a blue sash as* ornament. **3** person who adds grace, dignity, or honor to a group: *She is an* ornament *to the teaching profession.*

²or·na·ment (ôr′nə mĕnt′) to adorn; decorate; beautify: *The hall was* ornamented *with banners and flags.*

or·na·men·tal (ôr′nə mĕn′tǝl) decorative: *The chest was covered with* ornamental *carvings.* **or·na·men·tal·ly.**

or·nate (ôr nāt′) elaborately decorated: *The flowered lamp was too* ornate *for her very simple furniture.* **or·nate·ly.**

or·phan (ôr′fən) **1** child who has lost one or, usually, both parents by death. **2** to make an orphan of: *Thousands of children were* orphaned *by the last war.*

or·phan·age (ôr′fən ij) home for the care of orphans.

or·tho·dox (ôr′thə dŏks′) **1** usual; approved; conventional: *Raising one's hand is an* orthodox *way of getting the teacher's attention.* **2** following accepted teachings or beliefs, especially in religion. **3 Orthodox Church** one group of Catholic churches that recognizes a head other than the Pope in Rome.

Osprey, about 2 ft. long

os·prey (ŏs′prĭ) a large fish-eating hawk. Also called **fish hawk.**

os·ten·ta·tious (ŏs′tĕn tā′shəs) showy; pretentious; done to impress people or to attract attention: *an* ostentatious *show of knowledge.* **os·ten·ta·tious·ly.**

os·trich (ôs′trĭch or ŏs′trĭch) the largest of birds. It can run swiftly but cannot fly. Its curly plumes are used for decoration and its skin for leather.

oth·er (ŭth′ər) **1** different: *I have* other *things to worry about.* **2** more; additional: *I can show you* other *suits if you don't like this one.* **3** opposite: *the* other *side of the street.* **4** reverse:

Ostrich, 6 to 8 ft. high

Write your answers on the other *side of the paper.* **5** the second of two: *One laughed, the* other *cried.* **6** alternate: *You have no* other *choice.* **7** differently: *We can do no* other *than defend ourselves against attack.* **8 others** additional persons or things:

When shall we tell the others? *I'll take the big suitcase if you'll carry the* others. **9 other than** (**1**) except for: *I see no reason for staying indoors* other than *the chance of rain.* (**2**) different from: *Would you want your best friend to be* other than *what he is?* **10 none other than** nobody else but: *Our guest tonight is* none other than *your favorite singer!* **11 someone or other** some unknown person: *Are you certain that* someone or other *will be there to meet you?* **12 on the other hand** in contrast to this: *I don't want to vote for Jack, but* on the other hand *I'd hate to hurt his feelings.* **13 each other** each the other: *They disliked* each other. **14 the other day** a few days ago: *I saw your father in town* the other day. **15 every other** every alternate: *We have art class* every other *day.*

oth·er·wise (ŭth′ər wīz′) **1** if not: *Stay home if you're sick, but* otherwise *we'll expect you early tomorrow.* **2** or else: *Keep your firewood dry,* otherwise *it won't burn.* **3** differently: *With no help how could we have done* otherwise? **4** in other respects: *He has a quick temper, but he's a good friend* otherwise. **5** different: *I thought the facts were* otherwise *until you explained them.*

ot·ter (ŏt′ər) **1** a playful, water-loving animal of the weasel family, valued for its rich brown fur. **2** the fur of this animal.

River otter, about 3½ ft. long

ought (ôt) **1** to have a duty; have an obligation: *You* ought *to be kind to your pets.* **2** to be almost certain; be expected: *The piano* ought *to sound better when it is tuned.* **3** to need: *We* ought *to leave now if we are not going to be late. This girl* ought *to have new shoes.*

ounce (ouns) **1** in ordinary weight, 1/16 of a pound. **2** in troy weight, for weighing drugs and precious metals, 1/12 of a pound. **3** in liquid measure, 1/16 of a pint or 1/8 of a standard half-pint kitchen measuring cup.

our (our) **1** of or belonging to us: *This is* our *first year at school.* **2** made or done by

fāte, făt, fâre, fär; bē, bĕt; bīte, bĭt; nō, nŏt, nôr; fūse, fŭn, fûr; tōō, tŏŏk; foil; foul; thin; then; hw for wh as in *wh*at; zh for s as in u*s*ual; ə for a, e, i, o, u, as in *a*go, lin*e*n, per*i*l, at*o*m, min*u*s

us: *We wrote* our *play in three days.*
3 inhabited by us: *This is* our *city.* **4** sometimes used for "my" in official writing or speaking. (Homonym: hour)

ours (ourz) the thing or things belonging to us: *Those books are* ours.

our·self (our sĕlf') formal and old-fashioned way of saying "I myself" usually used by kings and queens.

our·selves (our sĕlvz') **1** our own selves: *We dressed* ourselves. **2** word used with "we" for emphasis: *We* ourselves *will sew the costumes.* **3** our real selves; our true selves: *We haven't been quite* ourselves *in all this excitement.* **4 by ourselves** (**1**) alone: *Come to visit us when we are* by ourselves. (**2**) without any help: *We baked the cake* by ourselves.

oust (oust) to drive or force out: *The umpire* ousted *him from the game.*

out (out) **1** not in or confined: *The cat was* out *all night.* **2** in a direction away from the inside; toward the outside: *to look* out *of a window; to fall* out *of a car.* **3** outdoors; outside: *Go* out *and play.* **4** away from: *to go* out *of town.* **5** not at home, in an office, etc.; not receiving callers: *The doctor is* out. **6** to others: *to pass* out *books.* **7** into view; forth: *The flower's came* out. *The sun came* out. **8** on view; on sale; open to inspection: *The truth is* out. *The magazine is* out *today.* **9** from among others: *Pick* out *one of the marbles.* **10** aloud: *The child cried* out *in its sleep.* **11** completely: *Clean* out *the rubbish. Clean* out *the closet.* **12** finished; ended; extinct: *The fire is* out. **13** discarded; not to be considered: *That plan is* out. **14** to the end; to a state of uselessness: *Play the game* out. *My shoes are worn* out. **15** an explanation; evasion; excuse: *He is looking for an* out *for his mistake.* **16** in baseball, having lost the right to continue batting or running bases. **17 strike out** in baseball, to miss or pass three fair pitches. **18 out of** (**1**) beyond; outside: *She went* out *of bounds.* (**2**) lacking: *be* out *of practice;* out *of money.* **19 out of hand** wild; unruly: *The frightened horse was completely* out *of hand.* **20 speak out** to speak boldly, firmly, or defiantly: *Let all men* speak out *against this injustice.* **21 down and out** penniless and out of work.

out- prefix meaning (**1**) at a distance away from: *an* out*building,* out*post;* out*lying.* (**2**) forth; away: *an* out*cry;* out*burst;* out*cast.* (**3**) greater than; better than: *to* out*do;* out*distance;* out*run.* (**4**) more than; longer than: *to* out*live;* out*last.*

out-and-out (out'ənd out') complete: *That's an* out-and-out *lie!*

out·board mo·tor (out'bôrd' mō'tər) small engine and propeller that may be attached to the outside of the stern of a small boat.

Outboard motor

out·break (out'brāk') **1** outburst: *an* outbreak *of temper.* **2** riot; rebellion. **3** epidemic: *an* outbreak *of measles.*

out·build·ing (out'bil'dǐng) small building like a shed, separate from a main building.

out·burst (out'bûrst') sudden, violent gush; a bursting forth: *an* outburst *of anger; an* outburst *of lava from a volcano.*

out·cast (out'kăst') **1** person or animal driven out or rejected by others. **2** driven out; exiled: *an* outcast *wolf, driven from the pack.*

out·come (out'kŭm') result: *His speed made the* outcome *of the race certain.*

out·cry (out'krī') a crying out or shouting; clamor: *The crowd raised an* outcry *at the umpire's decision.* **out·cries.**

out·did (out dǐd') See **outdo.** *The cook* outdid *herself in preparing the dinner.*

out·dis·tance (out dǐs'təns) to leave something or someone behind by traveling faster: *to* outdistance *a hare.* **out·dis·tanced, out·dis·tanc·ing.**

out·do (out dōō') to do better than: *He can* outdo *me in every subject but science.* **out·did, out·done, out·do·ing.**

out·done (out dŭn') See **outdo.**

out·door (out'dôr') **1** in the open air: *Football is an* outdoor *game.* **2** fond of the open air: *an* outdoor *type.*

out·doors (out dôrz') **1** world outside of buildings; the open air: *Campers can enjoy the* outdoors. **2** in the open: *It's too nice a day not to be* outdoors.

out·er (ou'tər) **1** having to do with the outside: *the* outer *layer of skin.* **2** farther from the center or inside: *Uranus is one of the* outer *planets of our solar system.*

out·er·most (ou′tər mōst′) farthest from the center: *Midway is one of the* outermost *islands of the Hawaiian group.*

out·field (out′fēld′) **1** part of baseball field beyond the diamond or infield; opposite of infield. **2** baseball players who play in the outfield.

out·fit (out′fit′) **1** things needed for a special purpose: *Bait, rod, line and a creel completed my fishing* outfit. **2** to equip for a special purpose: *The Geographic Society will* outfit *an expedition to Antarctica.* **3** complete costume: *She wore a tweed sports* outfit. **4** group of men, such as a business firm, political group, etc.: *The Jones* outfit *sells good plywood.* **out·fit·ted, out·fit·ting.**

out·go·ing (out′gō′ing) **1** a going out. **2** leaving; retiring: *the* outgoing *chairman.*

out·grew (out grōō′) See **outgrow.** *The baby* outgrew *her shoes.*

out·grow (out grō′) **1** to grow too big for: *Those goldfish will* outgrow *that small tank.* **2** to give up or drop as one grows older: *He* outgrew *his shy habits.* **3** to grow larger or faster than: *If you leave your garden without care, weeds will soon* outgrow *the flowers.* **out·grew, out·grown, out·grow·ing.**

out·grown (out grōn′) See **outgrow.**

out·growth (out′grōth′) **1** anything that grows out of something else: *an* outgrowth *of new branches on the tree trunk; an* outgrowth *of hair.* **2** condition that grows out of or develops from something; a result: *Tom's interest in horses is an* outgrowth *of his visit to his uncle's ranch.*

out·ing (ou′ting) short trip taken for pleasure: *They had a good* outing *at the beach.*

out·last (out lăst′) **1** to keep on longer than: *On a long hike, he could always* outlast *me.* **2** to wear or remain usable longer than: *Leather shoes usually* outlast *those made of cloth.* **3** to live longer than: *The old man* outlasted *many of his friends.*

out·law (out′lô′) **1** person officially declared no. longer protected by law; an outcast: *Robin Hood was a famous* outlaw. **2** a criminal; a bandit: *Jesse James was a*

notorious outlaw. **3** to declare outside the law's protection; to make unlawful or ban: *The hope of the world is to* outlaw *war.*

out·lay (out′lā′) **1** a putting forth: *an* outlay *of energy.* **2** total amount expended: *The* outlay *on clothes was $20.*

out·let (out′lĕt′) **1** an opening or passage to the outside: *the* outlet *of the fish tank.* **2** way of expression for emotions, energy, etc.: *Painting is an* outlet *for emotion.*

out·line (out′līn′) **1** a drawing showing only the outer edge of an object: *Draw an* outline *of Cape Cod.* **2** line which forms such a drawing: *The* outline *of this drawing is scratchy and broken.* **3** short summary; list of main ideas in proper order: *Don wrote an* outline *of his history lesson.* **4** to draw the outer line of: *to* outline *the figures in a picture.* **5** to give a summary of: *to* outline *a plan or idea.* **out·lined, out·lin·ing.**

Outline target

out·live (out lĭv′) **1** to live or last longer than. **2** to live through; survive: *Robinson Crusoe alone* outlived *the shipwreck.* **out·lived, out·liv·ing.**

out·look (out′lŏōk′) **1** a view: *The* outlook *from the fire tower includes the lake and the mountains.* **2** point of view; way of thinking: *a narrow* outlook. **3** way things are expected to happen; prospect: *The business* outlook *for next year is favorable.*

out·ly·ing (out′lī′ing) located at a distance from the center or main part; remote: *There are still some farms in the* outlying *districts of the city.*

out·num·ber (out nŭm′bər) to be greater in number than; exceed in number.

out-of-date (out′əv dāt′) **1** old-fashioned: *The old gentleman wore* out-of-date *clothes.* **2** not suited to present conditions: *Gas street lights are* out-of-date *in a modern city.*

out·post (out′pōst′) **1** a place manned by soldiers at a distance from the main army and kept to warn of or delay an attack: *Fort Laramie was once an* outpost *of the United States Army.* **2** soldier or soldiers stationed in an outpost. **3** settlement on the frontier or in a distant place.

---

fāte, făt, fâre, fär; bē, bĕt; bīte, bĭt; nō, nŏt, nôr; fūse, fŭn, fûr; tōō, tŏŏk; foil; foul; thin; ~~then~~; hw for wh as in *wh*at; zh for s as in u*s*ual; ə for a, e, i, o, u, as in *a*go, lin*e*n, per*i*l, at*o*m, min*u*s

503

out·put (out′pŏŏt′) amount made or produced: *The coal mine's daily* output *is 1,000 tons.*

out·rage (out′rāj′) **1** violence committed against law and decency: *During a war many acts of* outrage *are committed.* **2** to do violence to (a person or thing). **3** any violent, shocking, or shameful act: *A lynching is an* outrage *in a democracy.* **4** to harm, insult, or shock: *The daring train robbery and murder* outraged *the people of the State.* **out·raged, out·rag·ing.**

out·ra·geous (out rā′jəs) shocking; beyond the limits of what is decent and just; atrocious: *Kidnaping is an* outrageous *crime.* **out·ra·geous·ly.**

out·ran (out răn′) See **outrun.** *The fox* outran *the hounds.*

¹out·right (out′rīt′) **1** openly; straightforwardly; frankly: *He always says* outright *just what he thinks.* **2** at once; immediately: *He responded* outright *to the appeal.* **3** completely; at one time, not in installments: *Father paid for the new car* outright *in cash.*

²out·right (out′rīt′) **1** direct; downright; thorough: *The teacher caught Johnny in an* outright *lie.* **2** complete; entire: *The ruined building was an* outright *loss.*

out·run (out rŭn′) **1** to go or run faster than. **2** to go beyond; exceed: *The scouts' enthusiasm for overnight trips* outran *their counselor's.* **out·ran, out·run, out·run·ing.**

out·set (out′sĕt′) a beginning; start: *It began to rain at the* outset *of our trip.*

out·side (out′sīd′) **1** outdoors; in the open air. **2** outer part or side; exterior. **3** of, on, or to the outside or outer part: *an* outside *room.* **4** coming from the outside: *Get* outside *help.* **5** beyond; past the limits of: *His trip took him* outside *the country.* **6** besides a person's regular activities: *Golf is one of my father's* outside *interests.* **7** greatest possible: *The* outside *figure given for the cost of the new school is $1,000,000.* **8 outside of** besides; except for. **9 at the outside** at the most: *There were only 25 people at the meeting at the* outside.

out·sid·er (out′sī′dər) person who does not belong to a particular group or place.

out·skirts (out′skûrts′) outer edges; outlying parts: *the* outskirts *of a city.*

out·spo·ken (out′spō′kən) frank. **out·spo·ken·ly.**

out·spread (out sprĕd′) spread out; stretched out; extended: *the housedog with his paws* outspread.

out·stand·ing (out′stăn′dĭng) **1** standing out; distinguished; well-known: *George Washington is among the* outstanding *men in American history.* **2** unpaid: *an* outstanding *debt of $2,000.* **out·stand·ing·ly.**

out·stretched (out strĕcht′) spread or stretched out.

out·strip (out strĭp′) **1** to go faster than. **2** to outdo. **out·stripped, out·strip·ping.**

out·ward (out′wərd) **1** of or on the outside; external: *The* outward *appearance of the house is very attractive. The girl's* outward *cheerfulness covered a deep sadness.* **2** away from a place: *The ship is leaving the wharf,* outward *bound for Europe.* **3** toward the outside: *This door opens* outward.

out·ward·ly (out′wərd lĭ) **1** in appearance: *to be* outwardly *calm.* **2** toward the outside: *Waves spread* outwardly *in the lake.*

out·wards (out′wərdz) toward the outside; outward.

out·wear (out wâr′) to wear longer than; outlast. **out·wore, out·worn, out·wear·ing.**

out·weigh (out wā′) **1** to be greater in importance, value, etc., than: *A mother's advice would* outweigh *a friend's.* **2** to be greater in weight than.

out·wit (out wĭt′) to get the better of by being more skillful or clever: *Jimmy can always* outwit *me at checkers.* **out·wit·ted, out·wit·ting.**

out·worn (out′wôrn′) **1** See **outwear.** *Tommy's skates have* outworn *yours because he takes better care of them.* **2** worn out: *an* outworn *pair of shoes.* **3** out-of-date: *an* outworn *point of view.*

o·val (ō′vəl) **1** egg-shaped; shaped like an ellipse: *A race track is usually* oval. **2** an egg-shaped plane figure; an ellipse: *The game was played at Alumni* Oval. **o·val·ly.**

Ellipse   Oval

o·va·ry (ō′və rĭ) **1** organ of the female body in which eggs are formed. **2** part of a plant in which the seeds are formed. **o·va·ries.**

o·va·tion (ō vā′shən) very enthusiastic applause or welcome.

ov·en (ŭv′ən) enclosed space for baking, heating, or drying.

o·ver (ō′vər) **1** above in position, authority, etc.: *a canopy over the sidewalk; a roof over our heads; a scout leader* over *the scouts.* **2** from one side to the other of: *to cross over a bridge; to jump* over *a fence.* **3** on top of: *Put a board* over *the hole.* **4** so that the under side will be up: *Turn the table cloth* over. **5** down from the top, edge, or brim: *Water filled the tub and ran* over. **6** ended: *Is the party* over *so soon?* **7** during: *We were away* over *the holidays.* **8** here and there in; throughout: *He has traveled* over *most of the country. The wreckage was scattered* over *a wide area.* **9** about; because of: *She cried* over *her lost doll.* **10** too; excessively: *The water is* over *hot.* **11** more than: *You may not spend* over *a dollar.* **12** in addition; remaining: *There are some sandwiches left* over. **13** again: *He said the same thing* over *and* over. **14** from an upright position; down: *to topple* over. **15** along: *to drive* over *a new road.* **16** from beginning to end: *Let me think it* over.

o·ver- prefix meaning (1) "too," "too much," "excessively": over*tired.* (2) "extra," "beyond the normal": over*time.* (3) above or across in position, direction, or rank: over*coat;* over*seas.* (4) causing to change to a lower position: over*throw;* over*turn.*

o·ver·all (ō′vər ôl′) including everything: *The overall cost of our vacation was $300.*

o·ver·alls (ō′vər ôlz′) loose garment like trousers with an attached chest piece. They are sometimes worn over other clothing to protect it.

o·ver·ate (ō′vər āt′) See **overeat.** *Because he overate Joe was sick all night.*

o·ver·bear·ing (ō′vər bâr′ing) showing scornful disregard for the rights or feelings of others; self-important; arrogant; insolent. **o·ver·bear·ing·ly.**

o·ver·board (ō′vər bôrd′) over the side of a ship or boat and into the water.

Overalls

o·ver·bold (ō′vər bōld′) too bold. **o·ver·bold·ly.**

o·ver·came (ō′vər kām′) See **overcome.** *Shyness overcame Jane as she faced her large audience.*

o·ver·cast (ō′vər kăst′) **1** dark; cloudy: *an overcast sky.* **2** to take long loose stitches over the edges of a seam to keep the material from raveling. **o·ver·cast, o·ver·cast·ing.**

¹o·ver·charge (ō′vər chärj′) **1** to charge too much: *The grocer overcharged me for the butter.* **2** to overload; put too great a strain on: *to overcharge a gun.* **o·ver·charged, o·ver·charg·ing.**

²o·ver·charge (ō′vər chärj′) **1** too great a charge: *There was an overcharge on my bill.* **2** excessive strain or burden on: *an overcharge on an electric circuit.*

o·ver·coat (ō′vər kōt′) outer coat worn for warmth.

o·ver·come (ō′vər kŭm′) to get the better of; conquer: *It took Jimmy a long time to overcome his fear of the dark.* **o·ver·came, o·ver·come, o·ver·com·ing.**

o·ver·crowd (ō′vər kroud′) to fill too full; put too many people or things into a space: *to overcrowd a bus.*

o·ver·did (ō′vər dĭd′) See **overdo.**

o·ver·do (ō′vər dōō′) **1** to carry too far; exaggerate: *You're overdoing the story by bringing in so many details.* **2** to wear oneself out by too much work or activity: *The doctor told him he must be careful of overdoing.* **3** to cook too long. **o·ver·did, o·ver·done, o·ver·do·ing.**

o·ver·done (ō′vər dŭn′) **1** cooked too much. **2** too profuse; too elaborate; exaggerated beyond good taste: *His compliments were so overdone that they sounded silly.* **3** See **overdo.**

¹o·ver·dose (ō′vər dōs′) too big a dose: *an overdose of medicine.*

²o·ver·dose (ō′vər dōs′) to give too big or too many doses to. **o·ver·dosed, o·ver·dos·ing.**

o·ver·due (ō′vər dōō′ or ō′vər dū′) **1** late; not happening at the usual or scheduled time: *The train is 30 minutes overdue.* **2** of a bill, unpaid when due.

---

fāte, făt, fâre, fär; bē, bĕt; bīte, bĭt; nō, nŏt, nôr; fūse, fŭn, fûr; tōō, tŏŏk; foil; foul; thin; ~~then~~;
hw for wh as in *wh*at; zh for s as in u*s*ual; ə for a, e, i, o, u, as in *a*go, lin*h*en, per*i*l, at*o*m, min*u*s

o·ver·eat (ō′vər ēt′) to eat too much. **o·ver·ate, o·ver·eat·en, o·ver·eat·ing.**

¹o·ver·es·ti·mate (ō′vər ĕs′tə māt′) to estimate at too high a number, force, value, etc.; overvalue: *Don't overestimate your strength in trying to swim across that wide river.* **o·ver·es·ti·mat·ed, o·ver·es·ti·mat·ing.**

²o·ver·es·ti·mate (ō′vər ĕs′tə mĭt) an estimate that is too high: *an overestimate on building costs.*

¹o·ver·flow (ō′vər flō′) to flow over or spread beyond the proper limits: *The river sometimes overflows its banks. The crowd overflowed into the halls.* **o·ver·flowed, o·ver·flown, o·ver·flow·ing.**

²o·ver·flow (ō′vər flō′) 1 a running over: *There was some overflow at the dam.* 2 the amount by which something runs over: *The overflow of the reservoir is now a million gallons a day.*

o·ver·grew (ō′vər grōō′) See **overgrow.**

o·ver·grow (ō′vər grō′) 1 to grow over; overspread with growth: *Every year we kill the weeds that overgrow the path.* 2 to outgrow: *The puppy overgrew his box in three months.* **o·ver·grew, o·ver·grown, o·ver·grow·ing.**

o·ver·grown (ō′vər grōn′) 1 See **overgrow.** 2 grown beyond fit size: *an overgrown puppy.*

o·ver·hand (ō′vər hănd′) 1 in sports, with the hand higher than the shoulder. 2 skill in delivering overhand strokes: *His overhand is better than his serve.*

¹o·ver·hang (ō′vər hăng′) a part that sticks out over a lower part, as the eaves of a house or the upper story of some old houses.

²o·ver·hang (ō′vər hăng′) to hang or stick out above: *Icicles on the roof overhang the doorway. Trees overhang the brook.* **o·ver·hung, o·ver·hang·ing.**

Overhang on a house

o·ver·haul (ō′vər hôl′) 1 to repair completely: *to overhaul a car's engine.* 2 to catch up with; to overtake.

¹o·ver·head (ō′vər hĕd′) up in the air or sky; above a person's head: *Clouds are threatening overhead.*

²o·ver·head (ō′vər hĕd′) 1 located or operating above a person's head: *Our room has overhead lighting.* 2 general expenses of running a business. Rent, light, heat, etc., are part of overhead.

o·ver·hear (ō′vər hir′) to hear something by accident or by listening to what is said to someone else: *I sometimes overhear strange conversations when I am riding on the bus.* **o·ver·heard, o·ver·hear·ing.**

o·ver·heard (ō′vər hŭrd′) See **overhear.**

o·ver·heat (ō′vər hēt′) to heat beyond a point of comfort, safety, or efficiency: *The climb up the steep hill overheated the engine in my car.*

o·ver·hung (ō′vər hŭng′) See **²overhang.** *Steep cliffs overhung the sandy shore.*

o·ver·joyed (ō′vər joid′) very pleased; made very happy: *Tim was overjoyed when he found his lost dog.*

o·ver·laid (ō′vər lād′) See **¹overlay.** *The top of the wooden chest was overlaid with silver.*

o·ver·land (ō′vər lănd′) across the land, not by sea: *Did you take the overland route, or did you go by sea?*

¹o·ver·lap (ō′vər lăp′) 1 to lay or place so that part of one thing covers part of another: *The carpenter overlapped one row of shingles with another.* 2 to lie so that part of one thing covers part of another: *Fish scales overlap.* 3 to be partly the same as: *The class treasurer's duties overlap those of the secretary.* 4 to occur partly at the same time, or at the same time as: *Our vacations overlap. Their birthdays overlap.* **o·ver·lapped, o·ver·lap·ping.**

²o·ver·lap (ō′vər lăp′) extension of part of one thing over part of another.

¹o·ver·lay (ō′vər lā′) to spread or cover with something: *The carpenter will overlay the pine table top with a mahogany veneer.* **o·ver·laid, o·ver·lay·ing.**

²o·ver·lay (ō′vər lā′) 1 something put or laid on as a covering: *a tissue-paper overlay on a drawing.* 2 layer of material, such as fine wood or precious metal, applied to a surface for decoration.

¹o·ver·load (ō′vər lōd′) 1 to load or burden too heavily: *to overload a car.* 2 to cause to have too much explosive or electric current: *to overload a gun; to overload an electric circuit.*

²o·ver·load (ō′vər lōd′) **1** too great a load or burden. **2** amount by which a load is too great.

o·ver·look (ō′vər lŏŏk′) **1** to fail to see or notice: *to overlook a name on a list.* **2** to pass over and excuse; ignore: *I'll overlook that mistake if you'll be more careful next time.* **3** to look down on from above; have or give a view over: *The house on the hill overlooks the harbor.*

o·ver·lord (ō′vər lôrd′) nobleman to whom others pledge allegiance.

o·ver·night (ō′vər nīt′) **1** during the night: *The weather changed overnight.* **2** lasting through a night: *an overnight trip on the train.* **3** used for, or remaining for, a night's stay: *an overnight bag; overnight guests.*

o·ver·pow·er (ō′vər pou′ər) to defeat or subdue with greater force or strength: *The police caught up with the thieves and quickly overpowered them.*

o·ver·ran (ō′vər răn′) See **overrun.** *Enemy soldiers quickly overran the defenseless city.*

o·ver·rate (ō′vər rāt′) to value or estimate too highly: *Merton had overrated his strength and had to give up.* **o·ver·rat·ed, o·ver·rat·ing.**

o·ver·rule (ō′vər rōōl′) **1** to set aside; declare of no effect: *The superior court overruled the judgment of the lower court.* **2** to decide against; veto: *The editor overruled his assistant's suggestion.* **o·ver·ruled, o·ver·rul·ing.**

o·ver·run (ō′vər rŭn′) **1** to spread over and cover, often in a harmful way: *Weeds overran the garden.* **2** to run or go beyond: *to overrun first base.* **o·ver·ran, o·ver·run, o·ver·run·ning.**

o·ver·saw (ō′vər sô′) See **oversee.**

o·ver·seas (ō′vər sēz′) **1** across or over the sea: *During the war, many soldiers were sent overseas.* **2** situated or lying on the other side of the ocean: *an overseas job.*

o·ver·see (ō′vər sē′) to keep watch over; direct; have charge of: *to oversee work done in a factory.* **o·ver·saw, o·ver·seen, o·ver·see·ing.**

o·ver·seen (ō′vər sēn′) See **oversee.** *Our work is overseen by the foreman, Mr. Weeks.*

o·ver·se·er (ō′vər sē′ər) one who is in charge of workers and inspects the work they do.

o·ver·shad·ow (ō′vər shăd′ō) **1** to cast a shadow on; to darken. **2** to cause to appear less important, as if in a shadow: *His quick temper overshadowed his real kindness.* **3** to tower above; to be more important than: *His later success overshadowed his early failure.*

o·ver·shoe (ō′vər shōō′) waterproof shoe to wear over one's usual footwear for warmth or dryness.

Overshoe

o·ver·sight (ō′vər sīt′) slip or mistake caused by carelessness or failure to notice something: *The omission of your name from the list was an oversight.*

o·ver·sleep (ō′vər slēp′) to sleep longer than intended; sleep past the usual time for rising. **o·ver·slept, o·ver·sleep·ing.**

o·ver·slept (ō′vər slĕpt′) See **oversleep.** *She overslept and was late for work.*

o·ver·spread (ō′vər sprĕd′) to spread or extend over; cover: *Clouds overspread the sky.* **o·ver·spread, o·ver·spread·ing.**

o·ver·step (ō′vər stĕp′) to go beyond; exceed: *to overstep one's authority.* **o·ver·stepped, o·ver·step·ping.**

o·ver·take (ō′vər tāk′) to catch up with: *With the head start he has, it will be hard to overtake him.* **o·ver·took, o·ver·tak·en, o·ver·tak·ing.**

o·ver·tak·en (ō′vər tā′kən) See **overtake.** *The speeding car was overtaken by the motorcycle police.*

o·ver·threw (ō′vər thrōō′) See ¹**overthrow.**

¹o·ver·throw (ō′vər thrō′) **1** to bring down; upset; overturn: *to overthrow a government.* **2** in sports, to throw beyond (where one is aiming): *He often overthrows first base.* **o·ver·threw, o·ver·thrown, o·ver·throw·ing.**

²o·ver·throw (ō′vər thrō′) **1** a bringing down; overthrowing; ruin; defeat: *The revolution ended in the overthrow of one dictator and the setting up of another.* **2** in sports, a throw above and beyond where it is aimed.

---

fāte, făt, fâre, fär; bē, bĕt; bīte, bĭt; nō, nŏt, nôr; fūse, fŭn, fûr; tōō, tŏŏk; foil; foul; thin; ~~then~~;
hw for wh as in *wh*at; zh for s as in u*s*ual; ə for a, e, i, o, u, as in *a*go, lin*e*n, per*i*l, at*o*m, min*u*s

o·ver·thrown (ō'vər thrōn') See **¹over-throw.**

o·ver·time (ō'vər tīm') **1** time worked in addition to regular hours: *Father put in ten hours of* overtime *this week.* **2** for or during that time: *to work* overtime; overtime *pay.*

o·ver·took (ō'vər tŏŏk') See **overtake.** *The storm* overtook *us a mile from camp.*

o·ver·ture (ō'vər chər) **1** piece of music played by the orchestra to introduce an opera, etc. **2** beginning suggestion; first offer: *to make* overtures *of peace.*

o·ver·turn (ō'vər tûrn') to turn over; upset: *Rough water rocked the canoe but didn't* overturn *it. The tractor* overturned.

¹o·ver·weight (ō'vər wāt') heavier than a person or thing should be: *This parcel is two pounds* overweight.

²o·ver·weight (ō'vər wāt') **1** the condition of being heavier than one should be: *a diet to reduce* overweight. **2** weight above a desirable, usual, or permitted amount: *to pay for the* overweight *of luggage.*

o·ver·whelm (ō'vər hwĕlm') **1** to flood and bury beneath; to overpower: *A high wave* overwhelmed *the boat. Your generosity* overwhelms *me.* **2** to overcome; sweep off one's feet: *A series of misfortunes* overwhelmed *him.*

o·ver·work (ō'vər wûrk') **1** to work or cause to work harder or longer than is good for one: *James overworked for several months.* **2** too much or too hard work: *James was sick from* overwork.

owe (ō) **1** to be in debt: *Aaron still* owes *for the book.* **2** to be in debt to: *He* owes *the book store.* **3** to be under obligation to pay or give: *to* owe *money; to* owe *loyalty.* **4** to be indebted for: *Peter* owes *his life to his doctor's skill.* **owed, ow·ing.** (Homonyms: O, oh.)

ow·ing (ō'ing) **1** not paid; due: *This money will pay all the bills that are* owing. **2 owing to** because of; resulting from; due to: *The crops are poor* owing to *the drought.*

owl (oul) any of a group of birds with flat faces, large eyes, and a short, hooked

Horned owl, 18 to 25 in. long

beak. Owls have a hooting or quavering call, a noiseless flight, and usually hunt at night.

own (ōn) **1** belonging to oneself: *This cat is my* own. *Working on Saturday is his* own *idea.* **2** to have; possess: *Do you* own *your house or do you rent it?* **3** to admit; confess; recognize: *to* own *a mistake.* **4 come into one's own** to get one's due; obtain the fame, wealth, etc., that a person deserves. **5 hold one's own** to take care of oneself; manage not to be defeated: *to hold one's* own *in a fight or argument.* **6 of one's own** belonging to oneself: *Do you have a room* of your own? **own up** to confess: *He* owned up *that he had taken the book from me without permission.*

own·er (ō'nər) person who owns; proprietor: *to return a wallet to the* owner.

own·er·ship (ō'nər ship') condition of being an owner; right of possession: *The* ownership *of land carries a great many responsibilities.*

ox (ŏks) **1** any of several animals related to domestic cattle. **2** fully-grown male animal of this kind, trained for hauling. **ox·en.**

ox·bow (ŏks'bō') **1** a U-shaped wooden collar under and around the neck of one of a team of oxen. Two oxbows and a crosspiece form a yoke. **2** a U-shaped bend in a river.

ox·cart (ŏks'kärt') cart drawn by oxen.

ox·en (ŏk'sən) more than one **ox.**

ox·ford (ŏks'fərd) low shoe that laces over the instep.

ox·i·dize (ŏk'sə dīz') to combine with oxygen; to rust, tarnish, etc., by exposure to the air; to burn: *Iron* oxidizes *quickly in damp air.* **ox·i·dized, ox·i·diz·ing.**

ox·y·gen (ŏk'sə jən) a chemical element. It is a gas without color, smell, or taste and makes up about one fifth of the air around us. All animals and most plants must have oxygen to live, and it is necessary for almost all burning.

oys·ter (ois'tər) a food shellfish enclosed in a rough, two-part shell, found in shallow sea water. Some kinds produce pearls.

Oyster

oz. ounce.

P

P, p (pē) 16th letter of the English alphabet.
Pa. Pennsylvania.
pace (pās) **1** a single step: *Walk ten paces to the north. The runner lengthened his* pace. **2** the length of a single step: *The military* pace *is about 2½ feet.* **3** to walk with slow or even steps. **4** to walk back and forth or across: *to* pace *the floor anxiously.* **5** rate of moving; the speed in running or walking: *a* pace *of three miles an hour.* **6** way of walking or running: *a strutting* pace; *the* pace *of a horse.* **7 keep pace with** to keep up with; run as fast as. **8 set the pace** to set the rate of speed for others to keep up with.
  pace off to measure by taking steps: *to* pace off *a plot of ground; to* pace off *50 feet.*
  paced, pac·ing.
Pa·cif·ic (pə sif′ik) **1** the ocean lying between Asia and Australia on the west and the American continents on the east. **2** of, on, or near the Pacific: *California is located on the* Pacific *coast.*
pa·cif·ic (pə sif′ik) **1** peaceable; not quarrelsome: *the* pacific *words at an international conference.* **2** peaceful; calm: *a quiet* pacific *people; the pleasure of rowing a boat on* pacific *waters.*
pac·i·fy (pas′ə fī′) to calm; quiet; soothe: *to* pacify *a crying baby with a bottle; to* pacify *an angry man with kind words.*
  pac·i·fied, pac·i·fy·ing.
pack (pak) **1** bundle of things tied together for carrying. **2** to fit compactly in a bag, box, etc.: *Have you* packed *your clothes for the trip? The dishes were* packed *in straw.* **3** to fill; cram: *People* packed *the theater.* **4** group of animals living together or hunting together: *a* pack *of wolves; a* pack *of hounds.* **5** group; mass: *a* pack *of nonsense; a* pack *of fools; an ice* pack. **6** complete set of playing cards; deck. **7 send packing** to send away.
  pack off to send away.
pack·age (pak′ij) **1** bundle of goods; parcel: *The books were mailed in a* package. **2** to

make into a bundle: *He* packaged *the groceries for me.* **pack·aged, pack·ag·ing.**
pack animal any animal that carries goods upon its back.

Pack animal

pack·et (pak′it) **1** small bundle or package: *a* packet *of seeds.* **2** a small ship that sails regularly on a fixed route, carrying mail, etc.
pact (pakt) any agreement between people or countries: *New settlers often broke* pacts *they had made with the near-by Indians.*
¹pad (pad) **1** cushion; small mattress. **2** small, often fitted, cushion used to fill out a hollow or to protect a surface: *shoulder* pads *of a dress; table* pads. **3** to put layers of materials in clothes, quilts, etc., for warmth or better fit: *My winter coat is* padded *heavily.* **4** to expand with extra material: *He* padded *the lecture to fill up the time.* **5** a writing or drawing tablet: *He took notes on a* pad. **6** ink-soaked cushion used with a marking stamp. **7** the floating leaf of a water plant: *The frog jumped from a lily* pad. **8** fleshy cushion on the foot of certain animals: *A cut* pad *made our dog limp.* **pad·ded, pad·ding.** [**¹pad** is of unknown origin.]
²pad (pad) to walk with dull, thudding steps like a pacing lion; walk softly as with bare feet. **pad·ded, pad·ding.** [**²pad** is formed from "path" which comes from a Germanic word.]
¹pad·dle (pad′əl) **1** short oar with a broad blade or blades, used in canoes. **2** to propel (a boat) with paddles: *to* paddle *a canoe.* **3** broad-bladed tool used to stir or mix: *She used a* paddle *to whip up cake batter.* **pad·dled, pad·dling.** [**¹paddle** is a word of uncertain origin.]
²pad·dle (pad′əl) **1** to splash in shallow water: *Children were* paddling *in the mud puddles.* **2** to swim slowly, like some ani-

fāte, făt, fâre, fär; bē, bĕt; bīte, bĭt; nō, nŏt, nôr; fūse, fŭn, fûr; tōō, tŏŏk; foil; foul; thin; then;
hw for wh as in *wh*at; zh for s as in u*s*ual; ə for a, e, i, o, u, as in *a*go, lin*e*n, per*i*l, at*o*m, min*u*s

509

paddle wheel

mals. **pad·dled, pad·dling.** [²**paddle** is probably related to ²**pad** meaning "to walk."]

paddle wheel wheel set with projecting paddles used in old water mills and on steamboats.

pad·dock (păd′ək) **1** small enclosed field used for exercising horses. **2** enclosure at a track to display horses about to be raced.

pad·dy (păd′ĭ) **1** rice in the husk, either growing or gathered. **2** rice field. **pad·dies.**

pad·lock (păd′lŏk′) **1** kind of lock like a small metal box with a movable curved bar which may be snapped tight by catches in the box. **2** to lock with, or as with, a padlock: *The sheriff* padlocked *the store.*

Padlock

pa·gan (pā′gən) **1** person who is not a Christian, Jew, or Moslem. The word has been applied to ancient Romans, Greeks, etc. **2** having to do with such persons or their customs. **3** not religious; heathen.

¹**page** (pāj) either side of a leaf of a book or the written or printed matter on it: *He checked* page 72 *for errors.* [¹**page** comes through French from a Latin word (pagina) of the same meaning.]

²**page** (pāj) **1** errand boy, as in a hotel: *A page called her name in the dining room.* **2** to call for a person by public announcement: *You were* paged *in the train station.* **3** in the Middle Ages, a boy in training to become a knight. **paged, pag·ing.** [²**page** comes through Old French from a Medieval Latin word (pagius) which may come from a Greek word (paidion) meaning "a small child."]

pag·eant (păj′ənt) play or procession to celebrate an event, usually a historical event.

pa·go·da (pə gō′də) in some Asiatic countries, a many-storied temple or memorial building. Since each story is narrower than the one below, a pagoda becomes a tapering tower.

Pagoda

paid (pād) See **pay.** *She was* paid *every week.*

pail (pāl) **1** bucket. **2** the amount a pail will hold: *It took several* pails *of water to fill the fish tank.* (Homonym: pale)

pail·ful (pāl′fŏol′) the quantity a pail will hold.

pain (pān) **1** sharp ache or soreness of body or mind: *a stomach* pain. **2** to cause hurt to the body: *My cut knee* pains *me.* **3** to make unhappy: *Her rudeness* pained *him.* **4** careful patient effort: *Jim took great* pains *to be neat.* **5** risk; threat: *under pain of death.* (Homonym: pane)

pain·ful (pān′fəl) **1** full of or causing a sharp ache or pain: *Bee stings can be very* painful. **2** trying; unpleasant: *Any task becomes* painful *if delayed too long.* **pain·ful·ly.**

pain·less (pān′lĭs) **1** without pain. **2** causing no pain. **pain·less·ly.**

pains·tak·ing (pānz′tā′kĭng) giving or needing great care and thought: *Embroidery takes* painstaking *skill.* **pains·tak·ing·ly.**

paint (pānt) **1** to make a picture with colors: *John* painted *a picture of his mother.* **2** coloring matter made of pigments and oil or water: *Painters often prepare their own* paints. **3** to coat or cover something with paint, lotion, medicine, etc.: *to* paint *the wall; to* paint *a cut with iodine.* **4** to tell a story vividly; to picture in words: *He* paints *quite a picture of his travels.*

¹**paint·er** (pān′tər) **1** someone who paints houses, furniture, etc., for a living: *The painters are doing the roof today.* **2** someone who paints pictures; artist: *a portrait* painter. [¹**painter** is a form of the word **paint.**]

²**paint·er** (pān′tər) rope used to tie the front of a boat to something. [²**painter** is from an Old French word (pentoir) that comes from a Latin word (pendere) meaning "to hang."]

paint·ing (pān′tĭng) **1** a picture in colors: *Many* paintings *hang in art museums.* **2** the work of a painter.

pair (pâr) **1** two of a kind made for the same purpose: *a* pair *of gloves.* **2** animals working together; a span: *a* pair *of horses.* **3** of animals, mates that live and raise their young together: *In our garden live a* pair *of robins.* **4** something with two similar parts: *a* pair *of scissors; a* pair *of pants.* **5** to match; form a pair.

pair off to come together in twos for some purpose: *They* paired off *for the dance.* (Homonyms: pare, pear)

510

pa·ja·mas (pə jä′məz or pə jăm′əz) sleeping suit, usually a loose coat and pants. Also spelled **pyjamas.**

pal (păl) close friend; companion; playmate.

pal·ace (păl′ĭs) **1** official home of a ruler. **2** large, splendid mansion.

pal·at·a·ble (păl′ət ə bəl) **1** having a pleasant taste. **2** agreeable; pleasant to the feelings: *I don't find his scolding words very palatable.* **pal·at·a·bly.**

pal·ate (păl′ĭt) **1** the roof of the mouth. The bony front part is the **hard palate;** the fleshy back part, the **soft palate. 2** sense of taste: *These grapes please my palate.* (Homonyms: palette, pallet)

Palate

¹**pale** (pāl) **1** without color; white. **2** light in color: *a pale pink.* **3** not bright: *a pale moon.* **4** to grow or become pale: *Mother paled as she heard the bad news.* **pal·er, pal·est; paled, pal·ing; pale·ly.** [¹**pale** is the unchanged form of an Old French word that comes from a Latin word (pallidus). As can be seen, it is related to **pallid.**] (Homonym: pail)

²**pale** (pāl) **1** picket in a fence. **2** fence or boundary: *His acts placed him beyond the pale of decent society.* [²**pale** comes from Old French (pal) from a Latin word (palus) meaning "a stake."] (Homonym: pail)

pale·ness (pāl′nĭs) a being pale; lack of color; pallor.

Pal·es·tine (păl′ə stīn′) land in western Asia on the eastern shore of the Mediterranean. Palestine, also known as the Holy Land, was the original home of the Jews.

pal·ette (păl′ĭt) thin board on which an artist mixes colors. (Homonyms: palate, pallet)

pal·frey (pôl′frĭ) word formerly used for a riding horse, especially a horse used by ladies.

Frontier palisade

pal·i·sade (păl′ə sād′) **1** protective fence of closely set, pointed stakes driven firmly into the ground. **2** line of steep cliffs which looks somewhat like such a fence.

¹**pall** (pôl) to become dull or tiresome: *The conversation palled as we ran out of things to discuss.*

pall on to have a tiresome effect on: *The holiday parties began to pall on him.* [¹**pall** is a short form of **appall.**]

²**pall** (pôl) **1** heavy covering, usually velvet, put over a coffin. **2** something that covers or overspreads with gloom or darkness: *A pall settled over the party as soon as the news was heard.* [²**pall** is a form of an Old English word (pæl) that comes from a Latin word (pallium) meaning "cover," "pall."]

pall·bear·er (pôl′bâr′ər) one of the people who carry the coffin at a funeral.

pal·let (păl′ĭt) small bed or mattress, usually of straw. (Homonyms: palate, palette)

pal·lid (păl′ĭd) lacking in color; pale.

pal·lor (păl′ər) lack of color; paleness.

¹**palm** (päm) **1** the inside of a person's hand from the wrist to the fingers. **2** to hide or conceal in the palm of the hand: *The magician palmed the coin after he had picked it out of the air.*

palm off to get rid of by trickery: *The peddler palmed off an imitation oriental rug on the tourist.* [¹**palm** comes through Old French (palme) from a Latin word (palma) meaning "the palm of the hand."]

²**palm** (päm) **1** any of a large group of trees that grow in or near the tropics. Palms usually have an undivided trunk topped with large leaves. **2** palm leaf or branch as a symbol of victory. **3** any prize or honor: *Jane's story wins the palm.* [²**palm** is the unchanged form of an Old English word that comes from Latin (palma). It was supposed that the leaf resembled a hand.]

Date palms

pal·met·to (păl mĕt′ō) any of several kinds of palm trees with fan-shaped leaves, grow-

fāte, făt, fâre, fär; bē, bĕt; bīte, bĭt; nō, nŏt, nôr; fūse, fŭn, fûr; tōō, tŏŏk; foil; foul; thin; ~~then~~;
hw for wh as in *wh*at; zh for s as in u*s*ual; ə for a, e, i, o, u, as in *a*go, lin*e*n, per*i*l, at*o*m, min*u*s

511

ing in the southern United States and the West Indies. **pal·met·tos** or **pal·met·toes.**

pal·o·min·o (păl'ə mē'nō) tan or cream-colored horse with a white mane and tail, bred chiefly in southwestern United States. **pal·o·min·os.**

pal·pi·tate (păl'pə tāt') to beat or throb rapidly; flutter; tremble: *The frightened puppy's heart* palpitated *with terror.* **pal·pi·tat·ed, pal·pi·tat·ing.**

pal·sied (pôl'zĭd) 1 having palsy. 2 shaking; tottering: *He was so excited that he moved about with a palsied gait.*

pal·sy (pôl'zĭ) loss of the power to control the movement of a part of the body; paralysis. **pal·sies.**

pal·try (pôl'trĭ) almost worthless; contemptible; petty: *Two dollars is a paltry donation for a millionaire to make.* **pal·tri·er, pal·tri·est.**

pam·pas (păm'pəz) grassy plains without trees in South America.

pam·per (păm'pər) to give way to; spoil; indulge: *The children* pamper *the puppy by giving it candy and cookies.*

pam·phlet (păm'flĭt) small book of a few pages with a paper cover: *a pamphlet of instructions.*

pan (păn) 1 glass or metal cooking dish, usually shallow. 2 any shallow container, such as the pans of a balance. 3 to cook in a pan. 4 to wash gold-bearing gravel.

Pans

pan out to result; turn out: *The venture* panned out *well.*

panned, pan·ning.

Pan·a·ma (păn'ə mä') 1 country in Central America, lying on either side of the Panama Canal Zone. 2 the capital of this country.

Panama Canal a canal connecting the Atlantic and Pacific oceans and separating North America and South America.

Panama Canal Zone ten-mile-wide strip of land through which the Panama Canal flows, governed by the United States.

pan·cake (păn'kāk') thin cake made of batter and fried in a pan or griddle.

pan·cre·as (păn'krĭ əs) large gland near the stomach, that produces digestive juices.

pan·da (păn'də) 1 a large black-and-white animal that looks somewhat like a bear but is related to the raccoons. It is found in Tibet. 2 a Himalayan raccoon. It is rusty in color and has a ringed tail.

Giant panda, about 6 ft. long

pane (pān) piece of glass in a window or door. (Homonym: pain)

pan·el (păn'əl) 1 part of a wall, ceiling, or door framed by the surrounding parts or a border. 2 to furnish or decorate with panels: *a room paneled in pine.* 3 part of a painting or the board on which it is made. 4 group of speakers in an organized discussion: *a panel of experts.* 5 list of persons called to serve on a jury.

pang (păng) 1 sudden, sharp pain: *the* pangs *of hunger.* 2 sudden, strong feeling: *He had a* pang *of sorrow when he remembered his lost dog.*

pan·ic (păn'ĭk) 1 fear so great as to cause loss of self-control: *The crowd was in a* panic. 2 to fill with or have such a fear: *At the sound of the explosion the crowd* panicked. **pan·icked, pan·ick·ing.**

pan·ick·y (păn'ĭk ĭ) wildly terrified; deprived of self-control by fear: *a* panicky *mob.*

pan·ic-strick·en (păn'ĭk strĭk'ən) frightened out of one's wits; filled with panic.

pan·o·ram·a (păn'ə răm'ə or păn'ə rä'mə) 1 wide picture or view of a scene or subject: *the* panorama *of a city as seen from a tall building.* 2 broad view or account of a subject showing its various stages: *a* panorama *of the development of transportation.*

pan·sy (păn'zĭ) 1 plant of the violet family that bears flowers with large velvety petals of many colors. 2 the flower of this plant. **pan·sies.**

Pansies

pant (pănt) 1 to breathe quickly and hard: *The dog lay* panting *after his long chase.* 2 short, quick gasp. 3 to speak in short gasps: *The scout* panted *an urgent message as he leaped from his horse.*

pan·ta·loon (păn′tə lōōn′) **1** clown or foolish character in pantomime: *We laughed merrily at the* pantaloon. **2 pantaloons** trousers.

pan·ther (păn′thər) **1** any large member of the cat family in size below the lion, tiger, or jaguar, especially the black form of leopard. **2** the American mountain lion, also called cougar or puma.

pan·to·mime (păn′tə mīm′) **1** actions, gestures, and facial expressions that show meaning without words: *We acted out the story in* pantomime. **2** a play without any talking: *We went to see a pantomime of Goldilocks.*

pan·try (păn′trī) room or closet where food, dishes, etc., are stored. **pan·tries.**

pants (pănts) trousers.

pap (păp) soft food for infants.

pa·pa (pä′pə) father.

pa·paw (pô′pô or pə pô′) **1** a greenish-yellow fruit with a bananalike flavor. **2** the small tree of the southern and central United States that bears this fruit. Also spelled **paw·paw.**

pa·per (pā′pər) **1** material made from wood pulp, rags, straw, etc., usually in the form of a thin sheet: *wrapping* paper; *writing* paper; *wall*paper. **2** sheet of this material: *Write your address on this* paper. **3** newspaper. **4** identification; record which gives information about the person carrying it: *We need to have certain papers to travel in foreign countries.* **5** written matter; document: *legal* papers; *official* papers. **6** written assignment; an essay or report: *Our history papers are due tomorrow.* **7** small paper package (of something): *a paper of pins.* **8** to cover with paper: *Our dining room is being* papered.

pa·per·back (pā′pər băk′) book bound in paper, usually to be sold more cheaply than those bound in leather, cardboard, etc.

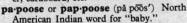
Papoose

pa·poose or **pap·poose** (pă pōōs′) North American Indian word for "baby."

pap·ri·ka (pă prē′kə or păp′rə kə) mild, red seasoning made from the pods of a cultivated pepper plant.

pa·py·rus (pə pi′rəs) **1** reedlike plant from which the ancient Egyptians made a kind of paper. **2** the paper made from this plant or a manuscript written on it. **pa·py·ri** (pə pi′ri)

par (pär) **1** normal, usual, or average condition: *With his injured knee, Joe's running is not up to* par. **2** number of strokes for a course or hole in golf. **3 on a par** equal; of equal value: *His work is not on a par with the fine work his father used to do.*

par·a·ble (păr′ə bəl) a short, simple story that teaches a moral lesson.

par·a·chute (păr′ə shōōt′) **1** umbrella-shaped device made to assure a gentle descent to a person or package suspended from it, when dropped from a great height. **2** to descend in a parachute: *to parachute from a plane.* **par·a·chut·ed, par·a·chut·ing.**

Parachute

pa·rade (pə rād′) **1** a march or procession for display: *a circus* parade; *a military* parade. **2** informal procession of many strollers: *the Easter* parade. **3** group composing such processions. **4** place where soldiers drill or people walk for pleasure: *The mall became a* parade *on Sunday afternoons.* **5** a formal military review or inspection: *evening* parade. **6** to show off: *Jim liked to* parade *his swimming skill.* **7** vulgar display or showing off: *a parade of wealth.* **8** to take part in a formal march. **pa·rad·ed, pa·rad·ing.**

par·a·dise (păr′ə dis′) **1** heaven. **2** place or condition of beauty or happiness: *Hawaii has been called an island* paradise. **3 Paradise** the Garden of Eden.

par·a·dox (păr′ə dŏks′) **1** statement that seems to contradict itself but expresses an element of truth: *"Make haste slowly" is a* paradox. **2** person or thing which seems to show contradictions: *It is a paradox that the germ which causes a disease may be used to prevent it.*

---

fāte, făt, fâre, fär; bē, bĕt; bīte, bĭt; nō, nŏt, nôr; fūse, fŭn, fûr; tōō, tŏŏk; foil; foul; thin; ~~then~~;
hw for wh as in *what*; zh for s as in *usual*; ə for a, e, i, o, u, as in *ago*, *linen*, *peril*, *atom*, *minus*

par·af·fin (păr′ə fĭn) white or colorless waxy substance made from petroleum. It is used to make candles, to seal preserves, to coat wax paper, etc.

par·a·graph (păr′ə grăf′) small section of a piece of writing, usually made up of a number of sentences on one idea or topic. The beginning of each paragraph is on a new line and is usually indented.

Par·a·guay (păr′ə gwā′ or păr′ə gwī′) an inland country of South America between Brazil and Argentina.

par·a·keet (păr′ə kēt′) small colorful parrot, usually slender-bodied and long-tailed. Parakeets are active, inquisitive, and affectionate pets.

Shell parakeet, about 7½ in. long

par·al·lel (păr′ə lĕl′) 1 everywhere the same distance apart: *The rails of a railroad track are parallel.* 2 similar; alike: *You and I have had parallel experiences.* 3 a comparison: *The January temperatures of this and of last year show an interesting parallel.* 4 to be parallel to: *The road parallels the river. Your experience parallels mine.* 5 **parallel (of latitude)** any of the east-west lines on a map or globe which mark degrees of latitude: *Philadelphia is on the 40° North parallel.*

Three sets of parallel lines

pa·ral·y·sis (pə răl′ə sĭs) 1 loss of ability to move or feel in a part of the body. 2 disease causing such paralysis: *infantile paralysis.* 3 a standstill; halting; movement or operation: *The blizzard caused paralysis of the railroads and bus lines.*

par·a·lyze or **par·a·lyse** (păr′ə līz′) 1 to cause loss of ability to move or feel: *Polio may paralyze those who get it.* 2 to stop movement in or of; make unable to do anything: *A flood can paralyze transportation lines. The rabbit was paralyzed by fright.* **par·a·lyzed** or **par·a·lysed, par·a·lyz·ing** or **par·a·lys·ing.**

par·a·mount (păr′ə mount′) supreme; above all others: *Her baby was her paramount concern.*

par·a·pet (păr′ə pĭt) 1 low wall around a roof or terrace or along a stairway or bridge to keep people from falling off. 2 protective wall on a fortification to shelter its defenders.

Parapet

par·a·site (păr′ə sīt′) 1 plant or animal that lives in or on another of a different species and gains nourishment from it: *Mistletoe growing on trees is a parasite.* 2 person who associates with another just to gain some advantage for himself.

par·a·sol (păr′ə sôl′) small, light umbrella used by women to keep off the sun.

par·a·troop·er (păr′ə trōō′pər) soldier trained to land from the air by parachute.

par·cel (păr′səl) 1 package; bundle. 2 group (of persons or things of one kind): *a parcel of thieves; a parcel of lies.* 3 a piece or section: *a parcel of land or ground.* 4 to divide (out) into parts; to distribute in portions: *The captain parceled out the remaining food among the survivors.*

parcel post 1 division of the postal service that carries packages. 2 by parcel post: *to send a package parcel post.* 3 of the parcel post: *a parcel post package.*

parch (pärch) to dry up: *The desert is parched by the burning sun.*

parch·ment (pärch′mənt) 1 writing material, prepared from the skin of sheep or goats. 2 a piece of writing on parchment, such as an old manuscript. 3 heavy paper resembling parchment.

par·don (pär′dən) 1 to forgive: *Please pardon me for bumping into you.* 2 forgiveness: *I beg your pardon for misspelling your name.* 3 to free or release from punishment: *The criminal has been pardoned and gets out of prison today.*

pare (pâr) 1 to cut off the skin or outer part of; peel (something) with a knife: *to pare an apple.* 2 to take off (an outer part) by cutting: *to pare rind from a melon.* 3 to reduce; cut down: *We must pare our expenses to the bone until we pay off our debt.* **pared, par·ing.** (Homonyms: pair, pear)

par·ent (pâr′ənt) 1 father or mother. 2 a plant or animal that reproduces its kind: *A Georgia peach tree was the parent of this* *orchard.* **3** a cause; origin; source: *Idleness and bad company are* parents *of mischief.*

par·ent·age (pâr′ən tĭj) **1** birth; family; origin: *of humble* parentage. **2** being a father or mother: *the joys and responsibilities of* parentage.

pa·ren·tal (pə rĕn′təl) of a father or mother; relating to a parent or parents: *a case of* parental *love;* parental *control.* **pa·ren·tal·ly.**

pa·ren·the·sis (pə rĕn′thə sĭs) **1** either or both of the small curving lines ( ) used as marks of punctuation to set off words, figures, etc. A figure is often put in parenthesis to make clear a price, for example, fifty cents ($.50). **2** an extra word, figure, or group of words put into a piece of writing, which interrupts the form of the sentence but does not affect it otherwise. **pa·ren·the·ses** (pə rĕn′thə sēz′).

pa·ri·ah (pə rī′ə) **1** person shunned by others; outcast. **2** member of one of the lowest classes of society in southern India.

Par·is (păr′ĭs) capital of France, in the northern part of the country.

par·ish (păr′ĭsh) **1** church district having its own church and clergyman. **2** the people or members of a parish: *The* parish *voted to enlarge the church.* **3** in Louisiana, a political division corresponding to a county in other States.

park (pärk) **1** area set aside for public recreation. **2** to put (an automobile or other vehicle) in a definite spot. **3** place where vehicles are or may be parked; parking lot: *an artillery* park. **4** extensive grounds surrounding a big country house. **5 amusement park** a permanent recreation center with a merry-go-round, rides, games of chance, etc. **6 ball park** a baseball field with grandstands.

par·ka (pär′kə) short coat with a hood.

park·way (pärk′wā′) wide, landscaped drive or road, often with a center strip of grass or trees.

par·ley (pär′lĭ) **1** to discuss terms with an enemy: *Both groups of soldiers wanted to* parley. **2** conference or discussion, especially a military conference between representatives of opposing forces.

par·lia·ment (pär′lə mənt) a body of persons appointed or elected as lawmakers of a country: *The House of Commons and the House of Lords together make up the English* Parliament.

par·lia·men·ta·ry (pär′lə mĕn′tə rĭ) having to do with the customs, rules, or members of a parliament or other public body: *to use* parliamentary *procedure.*

par·lor (pär′lər) sitting room in a house, hotel, etc., usually for entertaining guests or for other formal occasions.

parlor car railroad passenger car with reserved seats.

pa·ro·chi·al (pə rō′kĭ əl) narrow; local; having a limited viewpoint: *He has lived in one place so long that his ideas are all* parochial. **pa·ro·chi·al·ly.**

parochial school school run by a church parish, usually Roman Catholic.

pa·role (pə rōl′) **1** release, for good conduct, of a criminal from prison before he has finished his full sentence. A person who receives a parole is free, but is under the supervision of a parole officer until the end of the time he has been sentenced to serve. **2** to put on parole. **pa·roled, pa·rol·ing.**

par·rot (păr′ət) **1** tropical bird with a hooked beak and bright feathers, often kept as a pet. It may learn to repeat words and phrases. **2** person who repeats rather than originates. **3** to repeat from memory rather than understanding: *The lazy pupil* parroted *the sentences in his book.*

par·ry (păr′ĭ) **1** to turn aside or deflect: *The boy* parried *the question of his lateness by changing the subject.* **2** a turning aside: *the* parry *of a blow.* **par·ries; par·ried, par·ry·ing.**

pars·ley (pärs′lĭ) garden plant, the green leaves of which are used as a garnish and for flavoring.

Green parrot, about 17 in. long

---

fāte, făt, fâre, fär; bē, bĕt; bīte, bĭt; nō, nŏt, nôr; fūse, fŭn, fûr; tōō, tŏŏk; foil; foul; thin; then; hw for wh as in *wh*at; zh for s as in u*s*ual; ə for a, e, i, o, u, as in *a*go, lin*e*n, per*i*l, at*o*m, min*u*s

pars·nip (pärs'nĭp) **1** plant of the carrot family growing from a tapering, light-colored root. **2** the spicy root of this plant which is eaten as a vegetable.

par·son (pär'sən) **1** clergyman in charge of a parish. **2** any clergyman.

par·son·age (pär'sən ĭj) house provided by a parish for its minister: *The needy could always find help at the* parsonage.

TOP

ROOT
Parsnip

part (pärt) **1** anything less than the whole: *Only* part *of that statement is accurate.* **2** a share in some job or duty: *The bloodhound's* part *was to find the criminal.* **3** piece of something: *Her brother's auto* parts *are all over the cellar.* **4** to divide (the hair) in a line: *He should* part *his hair more carefully.* **5** to break or tear: *He* parted *the log with one blow of the axe.* **6** to separate or keep apart: *A fool and his money are soon* parted. **7** to go different ways; separate: *They* parted *at the crossroads.* **8** member of a group: *He felt himself to be a* part *of the gang.* **9** role of an actor or actress: *Bill had the villain's* part *in the play.* **10** melody or a melodious sequence sung by one of a group of singers. **11** side, in a contest or dispute: *She always takes her brother's* part *in an argument.* **12 part and parcel** an essential part: *The guarantee was* part and parcel *of the bargain.* **13 for one's part** as far as one is concerned: *I don't like candy of any kind, and* for my part, *you can take all of it.* **14 take part** to join: *Joan took* part *in every game that year.*

part company to bring a friendship, association, agreement, etc., to an end: *The friends* parted company *over politics.*

part with to let go of; release: *They refused to* part with *any money.*

par·take (pär tāk') to take part; participate: *to* partake *in the activities of the school.*

partake of **1** to take or share in: *to* partake of *a meal.* **2** to be like; resemble: *Your impatience* partakes of *rudeness.*

par·took, par·tak·en, par·tak·ing.

par·tak·en (pär tā'kən) See **partake.** *They had already* partaken *of dinner.*

par·tial (pär'shəl) **1** incomplete; in part: *I made a* partial *payment on a new icebox.* **2** biased: *I can't make a fair*

---

judgment because *I'm* partial. **3 partial to** fond of: *She is very* partial to *apple cake.* **par·tial·ly.**

par·tic·i·pate (pär tĭs'ə pāt') to take part (in); share (in): *He is sick, or he would* participate *in the game.* **par·tic·i·pat·ed, par·tic·i·pat·ing.**

par·ti·cle (pär'tə kəl) tiny or minute bit (of anything): *There's not a* particle *of truth in that story. I looked at a* particle *of dust under the microscope.*

par·tic·u·lar (pər tĭk'yə lər) **1** of or belonging to one person or thing: *His* particular *skill is for tennis.* **2** strict; demanding; fussy: *Edith is most* particular *about her clothes.* **3** special; noteworthy: *to receive a souvenir of* particular *interest.* **4** a detail; an item: *In what* particular *did he fail in the chemistry examination?* **5** distinct from others: *a* particular *day of the week.* **par·tic·u·lar·ly.**

part·ing (pär'tĭng) **1** a taking leave; saying good-by: *the* parting *of friends.* **2** farewell; done on leaving: *The Indian fired a* parting *shot at us.*

par·ti·san (pär'tə zən) **1** supporter of a person or idea: *He was a* partisan *of the king against the parliament.* **2** one-sided: *She takes a very* partisan *view of that quarrel.*

par·ti·tion (pär tĭsh'ən) **1** thin wall; dividing panel: *The desks in the office were separated by* partitions. **2** to divide; to split up into parts: *A weak country may be* partitioned *by its conquerors.* **3** the division or splitting up (of something): *The* partition *of our playground gave the younger children their own area.*

part·ly (pärt'lĭ) in part; not entirely: *That answer is only* partly *right.*

part·ner (pärt'nər) **1** associate in business or other enterprise: *We were* partners *in a paint concern.* **2** one who shares something with another: *to be* partners *in sorrow.* **3** one who dances with another: *She and her* partner *dance well enough to go on the stage.* **4** someone on whose side one plays a game: *I was his tennis* partner *once a week.* **5** husband and wife: *Grandpa and Grandma were lifelong* partners.

part·ner·ship (pärt'nər shĭp') **1** two or more people joined in a business or profession: *The automobile salesman and me-*

chanic formed a partnership *to sell used cars.* **2** association in which two or more share things.

par·took (pär tŏŏk´)
See **partake.** *Everybody* partook *in the victory celebration.*

par·tridge (pär´trij)
1 name given to various game birds, as the ruffed grouse, bobwhite, and other quails. **2** any of several European quails and pheasants.

Partridge (bobwhite), about 10 in. long

par·ty (pär´ti) **1** an entertainment or social gathering: *a birthday* party. **2** of, for, or having to do with an entertainment or social gathering: *a* party *dress;* party *decorations.* **3** group of people associated or acting together; group interested in some common purpose: *A search* party *set out to find the missing boy.* **4** person concerned or interested in some affair: *The injured* party *sued the driver.* **5** a political organization: *In an election, each* party *has a candidate.* **6** of, for, or having to do with political organizations: *a matter of* party *politics.* **par·ties.**

pasque·flow·er (pǎsk´flou´ər) plant of the anemone family with purple or white flowers that bloom in early spring. It is the state flower of South Dakota.

pass (pǎs) **1** to move from place to place, or change from one state to another: *to pass down the street; to pass from youth to age.* **2** to permit to go past or enter: *The sentry* passed *the returning soldiers.* **3** to go past; overtake: *The second runner* passed *the first at the turn.* **4** to go by: *Time* passes *quickly.* **5** to meet the requirements of; get by: *Tim* passed *the test.* **6** to hand along: *Please* pass *the bread.* **7** to approve or enact (a law): *Congress* passed *the bill without debate.* **8** gap in a mountain range permitting passage. **9** gesture; a motion: *The magician made* passes *over the hat.* **10** free ticket. **11** state; situation: *Things*

have come to a pretty pass. **12** to throw (a football, basketball, etc.) to another player. **13** a throw of the ball from one player to another. **14 come to pass** to happen; occur: *It* came to pass *that there was famine in the country.*

pass for to be accepted as; get by as: *Madge baked something that* passed for *cake.*

pass up to skip; let go by: *I* passed up *television to study my reading*

pas·sage (pǎs´ij) **1** a passing or moving from one place to another. **2** corridor, aisle, hallway, or the like. **3** trip; a journey, especially a voyage: *a calm* passage *across the Atlantic.* **4** permission or right to pass through, over, or into: *The government granted the consul* passage *across the country.* **5** verse, sentence, or the like from a book or speech: *a* passage *from a poem.* **6** approval (of a bill, law, etc.): *The* passage *of the bill was certain.*

pas·sage·way (pǎs´ij wā´) **1** any road, lane, or alley, over which people or vehicles may pass. **2** hall or corridor in a building or connecting buildings.

pas·sen·ger (pǎs´ən jər) person riding in a vehicle.

pass·er-by (pǎs´ər bī´) one who goes past or by. **pass·ers-by.**

pass·ing (pǎs´ing) **1** a going by: *The* passing *of the parade brought people to their windows.* **2** going by: *the* passing *years.* **3** enactment; the making into law: *The* passing *of the Nineteenth Amendment gave women the right to vote.* **4** death; ending: *Some people mourn the* passing *of "the good old times."* **5** brief; not lasting: *a* passing *glance; a* passing *fashion.* **6** equal to or better than a required standard: *a* passing *grade.*

pas·sion (pǎsh´ən) **1** any strong feeling, such as love, hate, etc. **2** enthusiasm; desire: *a* passion *for learning.* **3** an object of intense feeling or interest: *Antiques are Mrs. Oldham's* passion. **4** an outburst of violent wrath; great rage: *Philip flew into a* passion *when Bob broke his bat.* **5 Passion** the suffering of Christ on the cross, or from the Last Supper to His death.

---

fāte, făt, fâre, fär; bē, bĕt; bīte, bĭt; nō, nŏt, nôr; fūse, fŭn, fûr; tōō, tŏŏk; foil; foul; thin; ~~then~~;
hw for wh as in *wh*at; zh for s as in u*s*ual; ə for a, e, i, o, u, as in *a*go, lin*e*n, per*i*l, at*o*m, min*u*s

pas·sion·ate (păsh'ən it) **1** filled with strong feeling or eager desire. **2** hot-tempered; wrathful. **3** intense; overwhelming: *a passionate interest in politics.* **pas·sion·ate·ly.**

pas·sive (păs'ĭv) **1** not acting or taking part: *a passive interest in games.* **2** enduring without resistance: *The child listened to the scolding in* passive *silence.* **pas·sive·ly.**

Pass·o·ver (păs'ō'vər) yearly Jewish holiday in memory of the delivering of the Hebrews from slavery in Egypt.

pass·port (păs'pôrt) document or booklet showing citizenship and granting permission to travel in a foreign land.

pass·word (păs'wûrd) secret word or phrase used by members of a group to identify themselves, as in passing a guard.

past (păst) **1** time gone by: *The old men talked of the* past. **2** one's earlier life or history: *The explorer has a colorful* past. **3** gone by; completed: *a record of* past *events.* **4** just ended: *in the* past *week.* **5** former: *a* past *president.* **6** by: *We went* past *the post office.* **7** beyond: *It was far* past *Fred's bedtime. The harm done was* past *recall.*

paste (păst) **1** mixture of flour and water, or the like, used to stick things together. **2** to fasten with paste: *Harriet pasted the pictures in her scrapbook.* **3** kind of dough used to make light pie crust. **4** soft or finely ground preparation, such as some sandwich spreads or toothpaste. **5** a material used to make imitation jewels: *Her dazzling necklace was all* paste. **past·ed, past·ing.**

paste·board (păst'bôrd') stiff material made of pressed pulp or of layers of paper pasted together.

pas·tel (păs těl') **1** chalklike crayon used by artists. **2** picture made with such crayons. **3** light and soft in color: *dressed in* pastel *blue.*

pas·teur·ize (păs'chə rīz' or păs'tə rīz') to destroy certain harmful bacteria in milk or other foods by heating followed by rapid cooling. **pas·teur·ized, pas·teur·iz·ing.**

pas·time (păs'tīm') game, sport, amusement, or hobby which makes time pass happily.

pas·tor (păs'tər) a minister in charge of a Christian parish.

pas·tor·al (păs'tə rəl) **1** having to do with shepherds or country life: *a pastoral poem.* **2** having to do with a minister in charge of a church: *to have* pastoral *duties.* **pas·tor·al·ly.**

pas·try (păs'trĭ) **1** pies, tarts, or other foods made of or with a rich crust. **2** having to do with such food or its making: *a pastry cook; a* pastry *brush.* **pas·tries.**

pas·tur·age (păs'chər ĭj) **1** land used for grazing animals; pasture land. **2** grass and other plants that cattle eat: *The horses found rich* pasturage *along the river.*

pas·ture (păs'chər) **1** piece of land on which animals are put to graze. **2** grass and other plants that animals eat: *The rocky hillside had enough* pasture *for sheep.* **3** to put animals to graze: *Mr. Wilson* pastured *his cows in the north lot.* **pas·tured, pas·tur·ing.**

pat (păt) **1** light friendly tap. **2** tapping sound: *the pat of a child's bare feet.* **3** to stroke lightly or affectionately: *to pat a dog.* **4** small, molded portion: *a pat of butter.* **5** to shape by patting: *The child* patted *the mud into a cake.* **6** ready or memorized: *a pat answer.* **7 stand pat** to remain firm or unmoved. **8 have down pat** to have thoroughly mastered: *Hope has her spelling down* pat. **pat·ted, pat·ting.**

patch (păch) **1** small piece of cloth, metal, etc., used to cover a hole or worn spot. **2** piece of cloth, plaster, etc., used to cover an injury or wound: *an eye* patch. **3** to mend; cover; repair with a piece of some kind of material. **4** small area: *a vegetable* patch. **5** spot differing from the surrounding area: *a patch of brown on the black dog.* **6** to put together pieces to make something: *The girls patched* quilts *for their home.*

patch up 1 to settle; fix; smooth over: *The children* patched up *their quarrel.* **2** to repair; restore in a hasty, makeshift way: *I've* patched up *the leaky boat.*

patch·work (păch'wûrk') **1** work consisting of a collection of odds and ends roughly put together; a jumble. **2** hastily or carelessly thrown together: *a* patchwork *treaty that satisfied nobody.* **3** quilt made of irregular pieces of material sewn together at the edges. **4** act of making such a quilt: *Mother enjoys doing* patchwork.

pate (pāt) the top of the head: *the old man's bald* pate.

pat·ent (păt'ənt) **1** official paper, issued by the federal government, which protects the rights of an inventor. A patent gives him the right to be the only one to manufacture and sell his invention for a certain length of time. **2** to obtain the sole right to (something): *He is careful to* patent *each new invention so no one else can use it.* **3** protected by a patent, brand name, or trademark: *Harley's cough syrup is a* patent *medicine.* **4** (also pā'tənt) clear to all; obvious: *His claim that he worked all day is a* patent *lie.* **pat·ent·ly.**

patent leather leather, usually black, with a smooth, shiny surface.

pa·ter·nal (pə tûr'nəl) **1** of or like a father: *our* paternal *home;* paternal *advice.* **2** related through the father: *a* paternal *grandmother.* **pa·ter·nal·ly.**

path (păth) **1** narrow track worn by human or animal footsteps: *an Indian* path *through the forest.* **2** way made for walking: *a garden* path. **3** course; direction: *the earth's* path *around the sun.* **4** way of conduct: *the* path *of goodness.*

pa·thet·ic (pə thĕt'ĭk) arousing feelings of pity or sympathy; pitiful.

pa·thos (pā'thŏs) quality that arouses feelings of pity or sympathy.

path·way (păth'wā') **1** footpath. **2** any road or course.

pa·tience (pā'shəns) **1** capacity to go through any hardship, annoyance, delay, etc., without complaining: *Driving in heavy traffic takes much* patience. **2** perseverance: *It takes* patience *to sew well.*

pa·tient (pā'shənt) **1** showing patience of any kind: *Joe gave a* patient *shrug.* **2** person under medical care. **pa·tient·ly.**

pa·ti·o (păt'ĭ ō') **1** courtyard in the center of a building or surrounded by buildings. **2** porch or terrace. **pa·ti·os.**

Patio

pa·tri·arch (pā'trĭ ärk') **1** father and ruler of a family, tribe, etc.: *Abraham is one of*

the great *Jewish* patriarchs. **2** old man worthy of honor and respect. **3** bishop of the highest rank in the Roman Catholic and Orthodox Eastern churches.

pa·tri·ot (pā'trĭ ət or pā'trĭ ŏt') person who has great love for his country and supports it with enthusiasm.

pa·tri·ot·ic (pā'trĭ ŏt'ĭk) showing or having to do with patriotism: *The* patriotic *young man served his country in troubled times.*

pa·tri·ot·i·cal·ly (pā'trĭ ŏt'ĭ kəl ĭ) in a patriotic manner.

pa·tri·ot·ism (pā'trĭ ə tĭz'əm) love of one's country and great devotion to its welfare or interests.

pa·trol (pə trōl') **1** to go the rounds or the length (of a certain area) in order to guard: *The Coast Guard* patrols *the coast of the United States.* **2** act of doing this. **3** man or men engaged in such activity, such as policemen, soldiers, or guards: *The captain sent out a* patrol *of six men.* **4** group of eight boy scouts in a troop of Boy Scouts. **pa·trolled, pa·trol·ling.**

pa·trol·man (pə trōl'mən) man who patrols, especially a policeman assigned to keep order in a certain district. **pa·trol·men.**

pa·tron (pā'trən) **1** person who supports or aids a special cause, person, etc.: *Most of the orchestra's expenses are paid by* patrons. **2** regular customer, especially of a restaurant. **3 patron saint** saint looked upon as the special guardian of a person, place, or thing.

pa·tron·age (pā'trə nĭj or păt'rə nĭj) **1** protection; support; encouragement: *The food bazaar is under the* patronage *of the Mothers' Club.* **2** act of being a regular customer. **3** in politics, power to control appointments to office.

pa·tron·ess (pā'trə nĭs) woman patron.

pa·tron·ize (pā'trə nīz' or păt'rə nīz') **1** to act as a guardian, protector, or supporter (to someone or thing). **2** to treat with a superior air: *The opera star* patronized *the members of the chorus.* **3** to deal with regularly as a customer: *Mother* patronizes *the grocery store on the corner.* **pa·tron·ized, pa·tron·iz·ing.**

---

fāte, făt, fâre, fär; bē, bĕt; bīte, bĭt; nō, nŏt, nôr; fūse, fŭn, fûr; tōō, tŏŏk; foil; foul; thin; then; hw for wh as in *w*hat; zh for s as in u*s*ual; ə for a, e, i, o, u, as in *a*go, lin*e*n, per*i*l, at*o*m, min*u*s

¹pat·ter (păt′ər) **1** to move or strike with a quick series of light sounds: *The little girl pattered across the room to her father.* **2** quick series of light sounds: *the patter of raindrops on the window.* [¹**patter** is formed from **pat**.]

²pat·ter (păt′ər) **1** rapid, easy speech to fill the time or to hold the attention while something else is being done: *the magician's patter.* **2** to speak in such a way. **3** chatter; gabble: *the patter of the children in the nursery.* **4** to chatter; to gabble. [²**patter** is a form of "pater-" in the Latin word (paternoster) meaning "Lord's Prayer," "Our Father." The meaning arose from the habit of mumbling this prayer.]

pat·tern (păt′ərn) **1** model; example; thing meant to be copied: *The seamstress cut the dress according to a pattern. The soldier's brave deeds served as a pattern for others.* **2** to copy; make after a model: *He patterned his life after his father's. Mother patterned our new curtains after the ones she saw in the store.* **3** design; figure: *rugs with a rose pattern; the frost pattern on the window.*

pat·ty (păt′ĭ) **1** small, round, fried cake of fish, meat, or potatoes. **2** round, flat piece of candy: *mint patty.* **3 patty shell** a round shell of pastry to hold creamed meat, fish, etc. **pat·ties.**

paunch (pônch) abdomen or belly, especially a large belly: *His large paunch was the result of eating too much candy.*

pau·per (pô′pər) very poor person living on charity.

pau·per·ize (pô′pə rīz′) to bring to extreme poverty; make very poor: *The king's frequent wars pauperized his kingdom.* **pau·per·ized, pau·per·iz·ing.**

pause (pôz) **1** brief stop or rest: *Everyone welcomed the pause during the long test.* **2** to stop or rest for a short time: *The speaker paused, cleared his throat, and continued speaking.* **3** brief stop in speaking, shown in writing by a comma, period, etc. **paused, paus·ing.**

pave (pāv) to cover (a road, street, etc.) with concrete, asphalt, or the like.

pave the way to make smooth, easy, etc.: *Daniel Boone paved the way to the West for the settlers.*

paved, pav·ing.

pave·ment (pāv′mənt) surface of a road or street covered with concrete, asphalt, or the like.

pa·vil·ion (pə vĭl′yən) **1** large platform with a roof but open at the sides, used for dancing or entertainments. **2** small ornamental building, as in a garden or park. **3** large tent.

Pavilion

pav·ing (pā′vĭng) **1** the material used to cover a road, street, etc. **2** the paved surface of a street or road.

paw (pô) **1** foot of a four-footed animal with claws. Bears, cats, dogs, and tigers have paws. **2** to scrape or beat with the front foot: *The horse pawed the ground before starting the race.* **3** to handle or touch roughly or clumsily: *During the sale hundreds of women pawed the reduced coats.*

¹pawn (pôn) **1** to leave (something of value) with the lender as security for a loan: *He pawned his watch for $20.* **2** thing left to be security for a loan. **3 in pawn** in someone's possession as security for a loan. [¹**pawn** is from an Old French word (pan) meaning "pledge."]

²pawn (pôn) **1** the least valuable and the smallest piece in the game of chess. **2** person deliberately used by another: *The ambitious actress used her friends as pawns to get fame.* [²**pawn** is from an Old French word (paon, peon) meaning "foot soldier," which in turn is based on the form of a Latin word (pes) meaning "foot."]

paw·paw (pô′pô) papaw.

pay (pā) **1** to give money for services or for something bought: *I paid three dollars for the ball. He pays fifty cents to ride the bus.* **2** money given for work done; salary; wages: *The pay for this job is $60 a week.* **3** to make payment on; settle; take care of: *to pay the income tax; to pay bills.* **4** to suffer a penalty: *The thief paid for his crime with a heavy jail sentence.* **5** to offer or give freely: *to pay a visit; to pay attention; to pay a compliment.* **6** to be worthwhile; be profitable: *It pays to get homework done on time.* **7** to make up for; compensate: *Money will not pay for the loss of happiness.* **paid, pay·ing.**

pay·a·ble (pā′ə bəl) that must be paid; due.

pay·load (pā'lōd') **1** cargo transported for profit in a vehicle, as distinct from the weight of the vehicle. **2** the part of a rocket or missile which is not fuel or shell. The cargo in a space cabin of a rocket ship, and the nose cone of a missile containing explosives are both payloads. The weight of instruments in a satellite makes up the payload.

pay·ment (pā'mənt) **1** a giving of money to pay for something: *The doctor demanded prompt* payment *of the bills.* **2** that which is paid: *to make monthly* payments. **3** reward: *Her gratitude was sufficient* payment *for my trouble.*

pay·roll (pā'rōl') **1** list of employees and their salaries. **2** amount paid in salaries for a certain period. **3 meet the payroll** to pay the employees of a company the salaries due them at the time agreed upon.

pea (pē) **1** plant or vine bearing long, boat-shaped pods which hold several round seeds. **2** the seed, eaten as a vegetable.

peace (pēs) **1** calm; tranquillity: *After the noisy children had gone to bed there was* peace *and quiet in the house.* **2** freedom from war. **3** freedom from
Pea
disorder, lawlessness, or disturbance: *The strike was marked by riot and other breaches of the* peace. **4** agreement or treaty to end a war. **5** freedom from fear, anxiety, nervousness, etc.: *to have* peace *of mind.* **6 at peace** free from war; getting along together: *The tribes have stopped fighting and are* at peace. (Homonym: piece)

peace·a·ble (pē'sə bəl) **1** not quarrelsome: *The* peaceable *citizens got along together as neighbors.* **2** peaceful. **peace·a·bly.**

peace·ful (pēs'fəl) **1** calm; serene; undisturbed: *Nothing looks so* peaceful *as a country snow scene.* **2** not given to quarrels or violence; liking peace: *The* peaceful *tribe of Indians seldom went to war.* **peace·ful·ly.**

peace pipe pipe smoked by North American Indians as a rite sealing a peace treaty.

peach (pēch) **1** sweet, juicy fruit, usually round, having a large, rough stone in the center. It has white or yellow fuzzy skin tinged with red. **2** the tree it grows on. **3** yellow-pink color.

pea·cock (pē'kŏk') **1** male of a kind of pheasant about the size of a turkey. It is admired for the metallic bronze, blue, green, and gold feathers of its very long tail, which may be spread out like a huge fan. The female is called a **peahen.** **2** vain person.

Peacock, 7 to 8 ft., including tail

peak (pēk) **1** sharp tip or point: *There is a wasp nest in the* peak *of the gable.* **2** highest or greatest point: *a mountain* peak; *the* peak *of traffic.* **3** visor: *Mark's cap has a large brown leather* peak. (Homonyms: peek, pique)
Peak

peal (pēl) **1** a loud, rolling sound: *a* peal *of thunder; the* peal *of bells;* peals *of laughter.* **2** to ring out or sound loudly: *During the celebration the bells of the city* pealed *gaily.* **3** a set of tuned bells. **4** the sound of such bells ringing in certain orders. (Homonym: peel)

pea·nut (pē'nŭt') **1** the seed pod or the nutlike edible seed of a plant of the pea family. Peanuts are unusual in ripening underground. **2** the plant, bearing yellow flowers, which produces peanuts.

pear (pâr) **1** fleshy, juicy fruit of mild flavor, usually larger at the bottom than at the stem end. **2** the tree that bears this fruit. (Homonyms: pair, pare)

pearl (pûrl) **1** small, hard, smooth, lustrous white or gray gem formed in the shells of certain kinds of oysters. **2** something like a pearl in shape, color, or value: *leaves covered with* pearls *of dew.* **3** mother-of-pearl. **4** made with one or more pearls: *a beautiful* pearl *necklace.*
Pear

---

fāte, făt, fâre, fär; bē, bĕt; bīte, bĭt; nō, nŏt, nôr; fūse, fŭn, fûr; tōō, tŏŏk; foil; foul; thin; then; hw for wh as in *what*; zh for s as in usual; ə for a, e, i, o, u, as in *a*go, lin*e*n, per*i*l, at*o*m, min*u*s

pearl·y (pûr'lĭ) **1** like pearl or mother-of-pearl: *The comb is made of a pearly plastic.* **2** made of pearl. **pearl·i·er, pearl·i·est.**

peas·ant (pěz'ənt) **1** in Europe, a small farmer or farm laborer. **2** of peasants; rustic: *a peasant dance.*

peas·ant·ry (pěz'ən trĭ) peasants as a social class.

peat (pēt) spongy, decayed vegetable matter which is found in certain swampy places. In some countries it is used for fuel, but in the United States it is used chiefly as a top dressing for beds of shrubs and flowers.

peb·ble (pěb'əl) **1** small stone worn smooth by water. **2** to cover with small stones: *to pebble a path.* **peb·bled, peb·bling.**

peb·bly (pěb'lĭ) covered with or made up of pebbles: *a pebbly beach.* **peb·bli·er, peb·bli·est.**

pe·can (pĭ kän', pĭ kăn', or pē'kăn) **1** smooth, edible, thin-shelled nut grown in the southern United States. **2** the tree, of the hickory family, that produces pecans.

pec·car·y (pěk'ə rĭ) American wild pig found from Texas to the middle of South America. **pec·car·ies.**

Peccary, about 3 ft. long

¹peck (pěk) **1** unit of dry measure equal to eight quarts or one quarter of a bushel. **2** container holding just a peck. **3** a lot: *a peck of trouble.* [¹**peck** is from an Old French word (pek) meaning "a measure of oats for horses."]

²peck (pěk) **1** to strike with the beak, usually with quick jabs or strokes. **2** a jab or stroke with the beak or a pointed tool: *The woodpecker made a few pecks at the tree.* **3** light kiss: *She gave him a hasty peck, then left.* **4** to cut or chop (something) with the beak or a pointed tool: *To get out of its egg, an unborn chick must peck a hole in the shell.* **5** to pick up (grain, feed, etc.) bit by bit with the beak: *The chickens pecked the corn until it was gone.* **6** mark or dent made by pecking: *Some pecks in the tree showed that a woodpecker had been there.* [²**peck** is probably a changed form of **pick.**]

pe·cul·iar (pĭ kūl'yər) **1** odd; queer; strange: *a peculiar idea.* **2** special; particular: *This rare orchid will be of peculiar interest to a botanist.* **3 peculiar to** pos-

sessed exclusively by; characteristic of: *Each person's fingerprint is peculiar to himself and different from all others.* **pe·cul·iar·ly.**

pe·cu·li·ar·i·ty (pĭ kū'lĭ ăr'ə tĭ) **1** odd or queer trait or characteristic. **2** distinctive feature or quality: *A keen sense of smell is a peculiarity of the bloodhound.* **3** a being odd or unusual: *In New York peculiarity attracts less notice and comment than in most places.* **pe·cu·li·ar·i·ties.**

ped·al (pěd'əl) **1** something worked by the foot: *Father steps on the brake* pedal *to stop the car. Rick's bicycle leaps forward when he steps on the* pedals. **2** to work a pedal: *Charles pedaled his bicycle with one foot.* **3** of or worked by the foot or a pedal: *The mechanic straightened the* pedal *rod.* (Homonym: peddle)

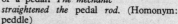
Pedal

ped·dle (pěd'əl) to sell (goods carried with one on the street or from house to house). **ped·dled, ped·dling.** (Homonym: pedal)

ped·dler (pěd'lər) person who sells small articles which he carries from place to place. Also spelled **pedlar.**

ped·es·tal (pěd'ĭs təl) **1** base or shaft for holding or displaying something: *The bust stood upon a pedestal.* **2** the attached base of a tall lamp or vase. **3** place of high honor: *Mary set her movie hero on a* pedestal.

Pedestal

pe·des·tri·an (pə děs'trĭ ən) **1** person who goes on foot, particularly where vehicles are present. **2** of or for people on foot: *crowded* pedestrian *traffic; a* pedestrian *bridge.* **3** not inspired; dull; plodding: *The lecture was so* pedestrian *that it put many in the audience to sleep.*

pe·di·a·tri·cian (pē'dĭ ə trĭsh'ən) physician who specializes in the care of children.

ped·i·gree (pěd'ə grē') **1** systematic list of ancestors; family tree: *This* pedigree *shows that my collie is a purebred animal.* **2** descent: *The duke is a man of noble* pedigree.

ped·lar (pěd'lər) peddler.

pe·dom·e·ter (pĭ dŏm'ə tər) instrument that counts one's steps and records the distance traveled.

peek (pēk) **1** to look in a cautious or sly way, often through a small or hidden opening; peep: *The hunter* peeked *through the bushes and saw a deer approaching.* **2** cautious or sly glance; a peep: *A* peek *from his hiding showed him that the pursuers were still near.* (Homonyms: peak, pique)

peel (pēl) **1** to remove the skin or outer covering from: *to* peel *an orange.* **2** to remove by peeling; strip off: *to* peel *the skin from a banana.* **3** skin or rind of certain fruits; a piece of such skin: *a lemon* peel. **4** to come off in a layer or in flakes: *Where the paint has* peeled *you can see the bare wood.* **5** to lose the outer layer of skin, bark, etc.: *My nose is* peeling *from sunburn.* (Homonym: peal)

¹peep (pēp) **1** to look through a crack or from a hiding place: *The naughty puppy* peeped *around the corner at me.* **2** quick look; a glimpse: *You can get a* peep *at the parade from this window.* **3** to appear as if peeping from a hiding place: *The moon* peeped *from behind a cloud.* [¹**peep** is probably a changed form of **peek**.]

²peep (pēp) **1** high chirping sound like that made by a young bird; a cheep. **2** to make such a sound. [²**peep** is probably an imitation of a sound.]

¹peer (pir) **1** person of the same or equal rank; an equal: *In tennis he is the champion and has no* peers. **2** member of the British nobility. [¹**peer** comes through Old French (per) from a Latin word (par) meaning "equal."] (Homonym: pier)

²peer (pir) **1** to look closely or out of curiosity: *Please stop* peering *over my shoulder to see what I'm doing.* **2** to peep out; come into sight: *The sun* peered *from behind a cloud.* [²**peer** is a changed form of **appear**.] (Homonym: pier)

peer·less (pir′lĭs) without equal; matchless: *a princess of* peerless *beauty.* **peer· less·ly.**

pee·vish (pē′vĭsh) fretful: *The spoiled child became* peevish *when she didn't get her way.* **pee·vish·ly.**

peg (pĕg) **1** short piece of wood or metal used to fasten something or to hang some-

thing on: *a tent* peg; *a clothes* peg. **2** to fasten with a peg; put a peg into. **3 take down a peg** to humble: *Your frank criticism really took him* down a peg.

peg away at to work steadily: *to* peg away at *one's homework for two hours.*

peg out to mark with pegs; stake: *to* peg out *a mining claim.*

pegged, peg·ging.

Pe·king (pē′kĭng′) or **Pei·ping** (pā′pĭng′) capital of Communist China, in northeast part of the country.

Pekingese, about 15 in. long

Pe·king·ese (pē′kĭn ēz′ or pē′kĭng ēz′) long-haired, flat-faced small dog, first raised in China. pl. **Pe·king· ese.**

pel·i·can (pĕl′ə kən) large water bird with a long bill, the lower part of which has a pouch for storing freshly caught fish.

pel·let (pĕl′ĭt) **1** little ball: *A pill is a* pellet *of medicine.* **2** small missile; bullet.

pell-mell (pĕl′mĕl′) in a disorderly or hurried manner: *The children rushed out onto the playground* pell-mell.

Pelican, about 5 ft. long

¹pelt (pĕlt) the furry, untanned skin of an animal. [¹**pelt** is perhaps from a Latin word (pellis) meaning "skin."]

²pelt (pĕlt) **1** to strike with a number of missiles in rapid succession: *to* pelt *a person with snowballs.* **2** to hurl: *to* pelt *pebbles at a window.* **3** to beat heavily: *The hail* pelted *down.* **4** a blow from something falling or thrown: *the* pelt *of a rain drop.* **5 full pelt** at top speed. [²**pelt** is a word of unknown origin.]

Pelt

¹pen (pĕn) **1** small enclosure, especially one in which animals are kept: *a pig* pen; *a*

fāte, făt, fâre, fär; bē, bĕt; bīte, bĭt; nō, nŏt, nôr; fūse, fŭn, fûr; tōō, tŏŏk; foil; foul; thin; ~~then~~; hw for wh as in *wh*at; zh for s as in u*s*ual; ə for a, e, i, o, u, as in *a*go, lin*e*n, per*i*l, at*o*m, min*u*s

523

play pen. **2** to shut up in, or as if in, an enclosure: *to* pen *in sheep*. **penned** or **pent, pen·ning.** [¹**pen** is a form of an Old English word (penn).]

²**pen** (pĕn) **1** instrument used for writing with ink. **2** to write with, or as with, a pen: *to* pen *a letter*. **penned, pen·ning.** [²**pen** is from a Latin word (penna) meaning "feather."]

pe·nal·ize (pē′nəl līz′) to impose a punishment or penalty on: *The referee* penalized *the team for unnecessary roughness*. **pe·nal·ized, pe·nal·iz·ing.**

pen·al·ty (pĕn′əl tĭ) **1** punishment for a crime or offense: *The* penalty *for treason is death*. **2** fine or forfeit imposed for breaking a law or rule. **pen·al·ties.**

pen·ance (pĕn′əns) **1** act to repair a wrong, imposed in the sacrament of forgiveness of sin in certain Christian churches. **2** any suffering or punishment accepted to show repentance for wrongdoing. **3 do penance** to perform an act of penance.

pence (pĕns) more than one British **penny.**

pen·cil (pĕn′səl) **1** stick of black graphite, colored chalk, etc., usually covered with wood, and used for writing, drawing, etc. **2** to write or sketch with a pencil: *to* pencil *in an outline for a painting*.

pend·ant (pĕn′dənt) hanging jewel or ornament: *The lady wore an emerald* pendant *on her necklace. Glass* pendants *decorated the candlestick*. Also spelled **pendent.**

Pendant

pend·ing (pĕn′dĭng) **1** not yet acted on or decided: *The lawsuit between the two companies is still* pending. **2** until; while awaiting: *We sat in the hotel lobby* pending *Father's return*.

pen·du·lum (pĕn′jə ləm or pĕn′də ləm) a freely swinging weight used to measure time or to regulate the timing of a clock.

Pendulum

pen·e·trate (pĕn′ə trāt′) **1** to enter into; go through; pierce: *The troops* penetrated *the enemy lines*. **2** to soak through; spread through: *The early morning dampness* penetrated *our clothes*. **3** to find out;

understand: *Scientists try to* penetrate *the mysteries of nature*. **pen·e·trat·ed, pen·e·trat·ing.**

pen·e·tra·tion (pĕn′ə trā′shən) **1** a going or entering into; a piercing: *The* penetration *of the jungle was slow and difficult*. **2** keenness of mind: *We admired his* penetration *in dealing with the problem*.

pen·guin (pĕn′gwĭn) sea bird found near the South Pole. It cannot fly but uses its wings like flippers in swimming.

Emperor penguin, about 3½ ft. long

pen·i·cil·lin (pĕn′ə sĭl′ĭn) powerful germ-killing drug used in treating infectious diseases. It is made from molds.

pen·in·su·la (pə nĭn′sə lə) area of land that is nearly surrounded by water: *Italy is a* peninsula *shaped like a boot*.

pen·i·tence (pĕn′ə təns) repentance; remorse; sorrow for wrongdoing.

pen·i·tent (pĕn′ə tənt) **1** sorrowful; repentant: *The* penitent *child was forgiven when he promised to behave*. **2** person who is sorry for wrongdoing. **pen·i·tent·ly.**

pen·i·ten·tia·ry (pĕn′ə tĕn′shə rĭ) a prison, especially a state or federal prison, for persons convicted of serious crimes. **pen·i·ten·tia·ries.**

pen·knife (pĕn′nīf′) small pocketknife. **pen·knives.**

pen·man (pĕn′mən) **1** person skilled in handwriting. **2** writer. **pen·men.**

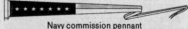

Navy commission pennant

pen·nant (pĕn′ənt) **1** long, narrow flag or streamer used on ships. **2** triangular flag used as a decoration or as a school or club flag. **3** mark of championship: *The hometown baseball team won the league* pennant *this year*.

pen·ni·less (pĕn′ĭ lĭs) without a penny; very poor.

Penn·syl·va·ni·a (pĕn′səl vā′nĭ ə) a State in the eastern part of the United States.

pen·ny (pĕn′ĭ) **1** cent. **2** British coin made of bronze. **pen·nies.**

pen·sion (pĕn′shən) **1** sum paid regularly by the government or other employer to a person after he has been injured and can no longer work or after he has worked for a long period and retired. **2** to give a pension to: *Grandfather's company* pensioned *him after 33 years of service at the office.*

pen·sive (pĕn′sĭv) **1** thoughtful; thinking seriously: *a pensive mood.* **2** expressing serious or sad thought: *a pensive poem.* **pen·sive·ly.**

pent (pĕnt) **1** See ¹**pen:** *He was pent in the city all summer.* **2** pent up shut in or up; held or kept in: *His rage was pent up.*

pent·house (pĕnt′hous′) a house or apartment on the roof of a building.

pe·on (pē′ən) in Spanish America, an unskilled laborer.

pe·o·ny (pē′ə nĭ) **1** garden plant bearing large, showy, many-petaled pink or white flowers. **2** blossom of this plant. **pe·o·nies.**

Peony

peo·ple (pē′pəl) **1** persons; men, women, and children: *There were a lot of* people *at the beach.* **2** persons belonging to a community, race, tribe, or nation: *all* the peoples *of the world.* **3** persons of a particular group or place: *The farm* people *have formed a club.* **4** relatives; family: *I want you to come home with me and meet my* people. **5** to fill with persons; inhabit: *to* people *a new colony.* **peo·pled, peo·pling.**

pep·per (pĕp′ər) **1** spice made of ground, hot-tasting berries. **2** plant bearing these berries. **3** garden plant bearing a somewhat hollow, spicy, green or red fruit. **4** this fruit, which is used as a vegetable or for pickles. **5** to sprinkle with, or as with, pepper: *Lois* peppered *her letter with commas.* **6** to spray with small missiles: *Fritz* peppered *the target with bird shot until it was torn to shreds.*

Sweet pepper

pep·per·mint (pĕp′ər mĭnt′) **1** strong-smelling, cool-tasting plant of the mint family. **2** oil from this plant, used in flavoring. **3** candy flavored with this oil.

per (pər) **1** at the rate of; for each: *$10 per day.* **2** by: *You will receive a note* per *special delivery.*

per an·num (pər ăn′əm) each year; annually: *He gets a pension of $1,000 per annum.*

per·cale (pər kāl′) closely woven cotton fabric.

per cap·i·ta (pər kăp′ə tə) to, for, or by each person: *a per capita tax;* per capita *output;* per capita *sugar supply; water used* per capita.

per·ceive (pər sēv′) **1** to become aware of through the senses; notice: *to perceive a dim light, a faint sound, a slight change in temperature, etc.* **2** to understand: *I* perceived *that he would refuse.* **per·ceived, per·ceiv·ing.**

per cent 1 one of a hundred parts: *Six per cent of a hundred apples is six apples.* **2** figured in parts of one hundred: *Six* per cent *interest on a loan of $100 is $6.*

per·cent·age (pər sĕn′tĭj) portion of something figured in parts of a hundred; a part: *A certain* percentage *of his wages is taken in taxes.*

per·cep·ti·ble (pər sĕp′tə bəl) noticeable; capable of being perceived: *There is a* perceptible *change in the weather.* **per·cep·ti·bly.**

per·cep·tion (pər sĕp′shən) **1** a becoming aware of something through sight, smell, or the other senses: *the* perception *of an odor in the room.* **2** ability to understand: *man of keen* perception.

¹**perch** (pûrch) **1** stout-bodied, sharp-finned, yellow-green, fresh-water food fish, growing to a foot in length. **2** salt-water fish somewhat like it. pl. **perch;** rarely, **perch·es.** [¹**perch** comes through French from a Latin word (perca).]

²**perch** (pûrch) **1** resting place, as for a bird on a limb, rod, etc. **2** any lofty resting place: *From her* perch *on the high stool, Molly watched the playful kittens.* **3** to rest or place as on a perch: *Dick* perched *in*

---

fāte, făt, fâre, fär; bē, bĕt; bīte, bĭt; nō, nŏt, nôr; fūse, fŭn, fûr; tōō, tŏŏk; foil; foul; thin; then; hw for wh as in *what*; zh for s as in u*s*ual; ə for a, e, i, o, u, as in *a*go, lin*e*n, per*i*l, at*o*m, min*u*s

his tree hut. [²**perch** is from a French word (perche) which comes from a Latin word (pertica) meaning "pole."]

per·chance (pər chăns′) perhaps.

per·co·late (pûr′kə lāt′) **1** to drip or seep through: *Water* percolates *through the soil to form springs.* **2** to cause a liquid to seep through: *to* percolate *coffee.* **per·co·lat·ed, per·co·lat·ing.**

per·co·la·tor (pûr′kə lā′tər) coffeepot in which boiling water seeps through ground coffee.

per·cus·sion (pər kŭsh′ən) **1** the striking of one thing against another: *the* percussion *of ball and bat.* **2** the vibration made by one thing striking against another: *the loud* percussion *of a drum.* **3** the striking of sound waves on the ear drum.

percussion instrument musical instrument that is played by striking it with a hand, stick, hammer, etc. Drums, cymbals, xylophones are percussion instruments.

per·en·ni·al (pə rĕn′ĭ əl) **1** lasting the whole year, as evergreen foliage. **2** growing or blooming year after year without replanting: *a* perennial *plant.* **3** a plant that lives for more than two years: *A rose is a* perennial. **4** continuous; unceasing: *a subject of* perennial *interest; a* perennial *candidate.* **per·en·ni·al·ly.**

¹**per·fect** (pûr′fĭkt) **1** flawless; without defects: *a* perfect *gem.* **2** faultless; excellent: *a* perfect *bit of writing;* perfect *weather.* **3** complete; whole: *a* perfect *set of china.* **4** exact: *a* perfect *circle.* **per·fect·ly.**

²**per·fect** (pər fĕkt′) **1** to remove all flaws from: *The pianist worked to* perfect *his technique.* **2** to improve as far as possible.

per·fec·tion (pər fĕk′shən) **1** state or condition of completeness, exactness, and freedom from faults. **2** a making (something) perfect: *to strive for* perfection.

per·fo·rate (pûr′fə rāt′) to make a hole or holes in; pierce, especially pierce with a line of small holes to make tearing easy. **per·fo·rat·ed, per·fo·rat·ing.**

per·force (pər fôrs′) of necessity: *Being a successful playwright he* perforce *knows a great deal about the theater.*

per·form (pər fôrm′) **1** to do; execute: *The surgeon* performed *an operation.* **2** to carry out; fulfill: *to* perform *a duty.* **3** to act, as in a play: *The players* performed *before a large audience.* **4** to give an exhibition of artistic or physical skill: *While the band played, the clowns* performed.

per·form·ance (pər fôr′məns) **1** a doing or carrying out: *The sheriff was wounded in the* performance *of his duty.* **2** that which is done; deed; feat: *The singer's* performance *was brilliant.* **3** a public exhibition, especially on a stage: *There are two* performances *of the play on Saturday.*

per·form·er (pər fôr′mər) person or animal that performs.

¹**per·fume** (pûr′fūm) **1** agreeable fragrance: *The breeze carried the* perfume *of lilacs.* **2** preparation that gives off such a scent: *a bottle of* perfume.

²**per·fume** (pər fūm′) to give a pleasant smell: *Apple blossoms* perfumed *the air.* **per·fumed, per·fum·ing.**

per·haps (pər hăps′) maybe; possibly.

per·i·gee (pĕr′ə jē′) the point nearest the earth in the orbit of the moon or a man-made satellite.

per·il (pĕr′əl) **1** very great danger: *The sailor adrift at sea was in great* peril. **2** a risk: *You cross a street between crossings at your own* peril. **3** something dangerous: *Icebergs are a* peril *to ships.*

per·il·ous (pĕr′ə ləs) dangerous; risky. **per·il·ous·ly.**

pe·rim·e·ter (pə rim′ə tər) **1** the line or edge around an area: *the* perimeter *of a circle; the* perimeter *of a wheel.* **2** distance around an area: *The* perimeter *of a one-inch square is four inches.*

pe·ri·od (pĭr′ĭ əd) **1** given length of time: *Our classes are in 30-minute* periods. **2** indefinite length of time; a spell: *a* period *of cold weather.* **3** portion of time in which something occurs regularly; part of a cycle: *A day is divided into* periods *of light and darkness.* **4** an era; a time name for some important person, event, etc.: *the Revolutionary* period; *the Spanish War* period. **5** in writing and printing, a dot marking the end of a statement.

pe·ri·od·ic (pĭr′ĭ ŏd′ĭk) occurring at regular intervals: *the* periodic *changes of the moon; the* periodic *drip of a leaking faucet.*

pe·ri·od·i·cal (pĭr′ĭ ŏd′ə kəl) **1** occurring or issued at regular intervals; periodic.

2 a publication appearing on regular dates, except a daily newspaper. **pe·ri·od·i·cal·ly.**

per·i·scope (pĕr'ə skōp') **1** arrangement of mirrors in a tube by which a person may look around a solid body. **2** upright tube fitted with mirrors by which a person in a submarine or trench can see what is going on above the surface without showing himself.

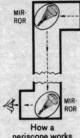

MIR-ROR

MIR-ROR

How a periscope works

per·ish (pĕr'ish) **1** to die: *Many explorers perished trying to reach the North Pole.* **2** to spoil; decay: *Some fruits perish quickly if not properly packed.* **3** to disappear; vanish; become extinct: *Dinosaurs perished long ago.*

per·ish·a·ble (pĕr'ish ə bəl) likely to spoil quickly: *Fresh fruits and vegetables are perishable foods.*

per·ju·ry (pûr'jə rĭ) the telling of a lie under oath: *The judge warned the prisoner that perjury was a serious offense.* **per·ju·ries.**

perk (pûrk) to lift in a saucy, brisk way: *The little bird perked its head.*

   perk up 1 to brighten; get back hope, courage, or enthusiasm: *She perked up after his compliment.* **2** to encourage: *His compliment perked her up.*

per·ma·nence (pûr'mə nəns) a being permanent; continued existence: *the permanence of the universe.*

per·ma·nent (pûr'mə nənt) **1** lasting forever or for a long time: *the permanent ice at the poles.* **2** lasting, as the opposite of temporary: *a permanent job.* **per·ma·nent·ly.**

per·me·ate (pûr'mĭ āt') to spread through: *The odor of onions permeated the kitchen.* **per·me·at·ed, per·me·at·ing.**

per·mis·si·ble (pər mĭs'ə bəl) that may be permitted; allowable: *Stealing bases is permissible in a baseball game.* **per·mis·si·bly.**

per·mis·sion (pər mĭsh'ən) a permitting; consent; leave: *Mother gave Priscilla permission to go to the movies.*

¹**per·mit** (pər mĭt') **1** to allow; give leave to: *Mother permitted Clyde to take the train alone.* **2** to allow; not to prevent or oppose: *to permit parking.* **per·mit·ted, per·mit·ting.**

²**per·mit** (pûr'mĭt) written proof of permission: *a hunting permit.*

per·ni·cious (pər nĭsh'əs) very destructive; harmful; ruinous: *the pernicious influence of bad companions.* **per·ni·cious·ly.**

per·pen·dic·u·lar (pûr'pən dĭk'yōō lər) **1** straight up and down; vertical: *Two perpendicular posts held up the porch roof.* **2** vertical line or position: *The Tower of Pisa leans from the perpendicular.* **3** at a right angle: *The arms of a cross are perpendicular to its upright.* **4** line or surface at right angles to another line or surface. **per·pen·dic·u·lar·ly.**

PERPENDICULAR POLE

PERPENDICULAR WALL

per·pe·trate (pûr'pə trāt') to do; perform; commit (usually a wrong): *Clive perpetrated a cruel joke on his little brother.* **per·pe·trat·ed, per·pe·trat·ing.**

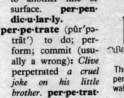

The flagpole is perpendicular to the wall of the building

per·pet·u·al (pər pĕch'ōō əl) **1** permanent; lasting forever: *A perpetual fire burns at the Tomb of the Unknown Soldier.* **2** continuous; without stopping: *to indulge in perpetual chatter.* **per·pet·u·al·ly.**

per·pet·u·ate (pər pĕch'ōō āt') to make permanent; cause to be remembered: *The Lincoln Memorial perpetuates the memory of a great American president.* **per·pet·u·at·ed, per·pet·u·at·ing.**

per·plex (pər plĕks') to puzzle; fill with uncertainty; bewilder: *His strange silence perplexes me.*

---

fāte, făt, fâre, fär; bē, bĕt; bīte, bĭt; nō, nŏt, nôr; fūse, fŭn, fûr; tōō, tŏŏk; foil; foul; thin; ~~then~~; hw for wh as in *what*; zh for s as in *usual*; ə for a, e, i, o, u, as in *ago, linen, peril, atom, minus*

per·plex·i·ty (pər plĕk′sə tĭ) **1** a feeling of being perplexed; confusion: *He explained each step so there would be no* perplexity *over what to do next.* **2** something that puzzles or confuses: *Our choice of a vacation spot is an annual* perplexity. **per·plex·i·ties.**

per·se·cute (pûr′sə kūt′) **1** to harass or abuse repeatedly or continuously: *to* persecute *a timid child with continuous faultfinding.* **2** to oppress or put to death on account of religion, politics, or race: *The early Christians were* persecuted *by the Roman emperors.* **per·se·cut·ed, per·se·cut·ing.**

per·se·cu·tion (pûr′sə kū′shən) **1** a being unjust or oppressive; persecuting. **2** a being treated with injustice or abuse; oppression: *The Pilgrims came to America to escape* persecution *for their religious beliefs.*

per·se·ver·ance (pûr′sə vîr′əns) continued effort in spite of difficulties; patience; steadfastness: *The scientist often makes his discoveries only after long years of study and* perseverance.

per·se·vere (pûr′sə vîr′) to keep at (something); continue; persist: *to* persevere *no matter how difficult the task.* **per·se·vered, per·se·ver·ing.**

per·sim·mon (pər sĭm′ən) **1** orange-colored, sweet, spicy fruit, fit for eating only when thoroughly ripe. **2** tree of the southeastern States which bears this fruit.

Persimmon

per·sist (pər sĭst′) **1** to continue steadily (in spite of opposition); keep on: *Jim* persists *in mispronouncing that word, although he's been corrected many times.* **2** to last; remain: *We hope the good weather* persists *for our holiday.*

per·sist·ence (pər sĭs′təns) a continuation, often in spite of difficulties or opposition: *to work with* persistence; *a* persistence *of good spirits.*

per·sist·ent (pər sĭs′tənt) **1** lasting; unceasing: *a month of* persistent *rain.* **2** untiring; undaunted; dogged: *a* persistent *salesman.* **per·sist·ent·ly.**

per·son (pûr′sən) **1** human being; man, woman, or child: *Everyone says Mr. Hale is a very kind* person. **2** body; bodily appearance: *We should keep our* persons

clean. **3 in person** bodily: *Please send a substitute if you can't come* in person.

per·son·age (pûr′sən ĭj) **1** person of importance or distinction: *There were many* personages *present at the coronation.* **2** character in a play or novel.

per·son·al (pûr′sən əl) **1** of or about a particular person; private: *He does not discuss his* personal *business with anyone.* **2** of a person's body or appearance: *her* personal *beauty.* **3** relating to a particular individual (often in an unpleasant way): *I meant nothing* personal, *so do not take it to heart.* **4** done in person, and not by an agent: *his* personal *signature; a* personal *telephone call.* **5** in law, having to do with movable belongings: *Books, clothes, and furniture are* personal *property.*

per·son·al·i·ty (pûr′sə năl′ə tĭ) **1** all the traits and qualities which make up an individual: *Every member of that family has a very different* personality. **2** person, especially an outstanding one; personage: *a leading* personality *of the stage.* **3 person·alities** offensive remarks about a person: *In their quarrel he would not stoop to* personalities. **per·son·al·i·ties.**

per·son·al·ly (pûr′sən ə lĭ) **1** by oneself; without help from another: *Mother attended to all the dinner preparations* personally. **2** as far as one is concerned: *I am* personally *opposed to this plan.* **3** as a person: *I admire his paintings, but he is* personally *unpleasant.*

per·son·nel (pûr′sə nĕl′) all the people who work in any company, factory, etc.: *The* personnel *of the office got together for a picnic.*

per·spec·tive (pər spĕk′tĭv) **1** in a picture, the impression of distance given by the relative size and distinctness of the objects or parts shown. **2** a picturing of distant things in their apparent size. **3** the understanding of things in their relative importance: *Looked at in* perspective, *yesterday's problems seem small.*

per·spi·ra·tion (pûr′spə rā′shən) **1** sweat: *Drops of* perspiration *covered his face.* **2** a perspiring: *Exercise causes heavy* perspiration.

per·spire (pər spīr′) to sweat: *He* perspired *heavily whenever he played basketball.* **per·spired, per·spir·ing.**

per·suade (pər swād′) to win over or convince by argument, urging, advice, etc.: *I'm glad you* persuaded *me to change my mind.* **per·suad·ed, per·suad·ing.**

per·sua·sion (pər swā′zhən) **1** tactful argument designed to lead a person to believe or do something; a persuading: *to use* persuasion *rather than force.* **2** belief, especially religious belief: *They go to different churches because they are of different* persuasions.

per·sua·sive (pər swā′siv) capable of influencing; convincing: *It took some* persuasive *arguments to win Barry over to our side.* **per·sua·sive·ly.**

pert (pûrt) saucy; bold; sprightly: *a* pert *little toss of the head.* **pert·ly.**

per·tain (pər tān′) **1** to refer (to); relate (to): *The farmers' long talk* pertained *to crops.* **2** pertaining *to* relating to; belonging to; forming a part of: *Botany is the study of plants and all things* pertaining *to them.*

per·ti·nent (pûr′tə nənt) having to do with; to the point: *not* pertinent *to the argument.* **per·ti·nent·ly.**

per·turb (pər tûrb′) to disturb, especially in the mind; to agitate: *Any change in her schedule greatly* perturbs *Aunt Mary.*

Pe·ru (pə rōō′) country on the west coast of South America.

pe·ruse (pə rōōz′) to read carefully; examine: *He* perused *the book, looking for information.* **pe·rused, pe·rus·ing.**

per·vade (pər vād′) to spread throughout; be in every part of: *The smell of fish* pervaded *the cannery. Cares and worries* pervaded *his mind.* **per·vad·ed, per·vad·ing.**

per·verse (pər vûrs′) **1** contrary; going against what is wanted: *A* perverse *wind blew the sailboat off its course.* **2** willfully naughty or wicked: *Tim took a* perverse *pleasure in annoying his brother.* **per·verse·ly.**

per·vert (pər vûrt′) **1** to turn (something) away from its proper purpose: *Students* pervert *their tastes when they read trash.* **2** to deliberately give a wrong meaning (to something): *He* perverted *the facts to support his argument.*

pe·so (pā′sō) a coin used in certain Spanish-American countries and the Philippines. Its value varies in different countries. **pe·sos.**

pes·si·mis·tic (pĕs′ə mis′tik) inclined to take a gloomy view of things or to believe there is more evil than good in the world.

pest (pĕst) **1** someone or something that annoys or causes trouble: *Flies are a* pest *in the summertime.* **2** a plague; pestilence.

pes·ter (pĕs′tər) to annoy, bother, or irritate: *Ticks* pester *many dogs in the summer.*

pes·ti·lence (pĕs′tə ləns) deadly, widespread disease: *The people of the Middle Ages lived in fear of* pestilence.

pes·tle (pĕs′əl or pĕs′təl) a pounding or mashing tool with a blunt end, used especially in the preparation of drugs.

Pestle

¹pet (pĕt) **1** animal of any kind, kept for company or affection: *Dogs, cats, and parrots all make good* pets. **2** favorite; beloved: *a* pet *dog; a* pet *idea.* **3** to stroke or smooth as one would a favorite animal: *Don't* pet *strange dogs that may be vicious.* **pet·ted, pet·ting.** [**¹pet** is a word of uncertain origin.]

²pet (pĕt) peevish state of mind; fit of ill humor: *Ellen was in a* pet *from not being allowed to play outside.* [**²pet** is a word of unknown origin.]

pet·al (pĕt′əl) one of the white or colored parts of a flower which surround the stamens and pistil.

Petals

pe·tite (pə tēt′) small or tiny: *Her doll has* petite *socks and shoes.*

pe·ti·tion (pə tish′ən) **1** formal request to a superior or to an official authority: *They got up a* petition *to the mayor for cleaner streets.* **2** to make such a request to: *Our club* petitioned *the city to build a pier on the lake.*

pet·rel (pĕt′rəl) small sea bird with pointed wings, often seen far from land.

Stormy petrel, about 6 in. long

pet·ri·fy (pĕt′rə fī′) **1** to replace animal or vegetable cells with minerals; to turn into

---

fāte, făt, fâre, fär; bē, bĕt; bīte, bĭt; nō, nŏt, nôr; fūse, fŭn, fûr; tōō, tŏŏk; foil; foul; thin; then; hw for wh as in what; zh for s as in usual; ə for a, e, i, o, u, as in ago, linen, peril, atom, minus

stone. **2** to render motionless as if turned
to stone: *Fear petrified me.* **pet·ri·fied,
pet·ri·fy·ing.**

pe·tro·le·um (pə trō′lĭ əm) natural oil
found in the earth. Many fuels come from
petroleum.

pet·ti·coat (pĕt′ĭ kōt′) underskirt worn by
girls and women.

pet·ty (pĕt′ĭ) **1** unimportant; trivial: *Many
quarrels have a petty beginning.* **2** narrow-
minded; not generous; mean: *Gossip is
petty.* **3 petty officer** a naval officer of
rank similar to that of a sergeant or
corporal in the army. **pet·ti·er, pet·ti·est;
pet·ti·ly.**

pet·u·lant (pĕch′ə lənt) irritable or impatient, especially over trifles; cross: *She was
petulant because she couldn't have a new
dress.* **pet·u·lant·ly.**

pe·tu·ni·a (pə tōō′nĭ ə or pə tū′nĭ ə) **1** a
garden plant with trumpetlike flowers of
various colors. **2** its flower.

pew (pū) any one of the
benches which make up
the seats of a church.

pe·wee (pē′wē) **1** any of
several small, insect-eating
birds that look somewhat
like a phoebe. The bird's
call suggests its name. **2** the phoebe.

Pews

pew·ter (pū′tər) alloy of tin and other
metals, used in making dishes, candlesticks,
and other utensils.

phan·ta·sy (făn′tə sĭ) fantasy. **phan·ta·
sies.**

phan·tom (făn′təm) **1** apparition; ghost;
specter: *We were scared by tales of a
phantom seen in the house.* **2** like a phantom; unreal: *The children saw phantom
horses in the clouds.*

Phar·aoh (fâr′ō) title of the kings of
ancient Egypt; the ancient Egyptian ruler:
The Pharaohs built the pyramids.

phar·ma·cist (fär′mə sĭst) person trained
in the preparation of medicines; druggist.

phar·ma·cy (fär′mə sĭ) **1** art or practice of
preparing medicines. **2** drugstore. **phar·
ma·cies.**

phase (fāz) **1** period or stage in the progress
or development of a thing: *an early phase
of airplane flight; the final phase of her
career.* **2** one side or view of a subject:
The admiral wrote about the naval phase of

the invasion. **3** particular stage of the moon
or a planet according to the amount of
surface which is shining. The full moon
and the new moon are the phases that
show the most and
the least surface.

pheas·ant (fĕz′ənt)
game bird of several
kinds, usually having
a long tail and hand-
some feathers. Pea-
cocks belong to the
pheasant family.

Ring-necked pheasant,
34 to 36 in. long

phe·nom·e·nal (fĭ nŏm′ə nəl) marvelous;
remarkable; extraordinary: *There has been
a phenomenal growth of shopping centers in
the past few years.* **phe·nom·e·nal·ly.**

phe·nom·e·non (fĭ nŏm′ə nŏn′) **1** thing,
fact, occurrence, etc., that can be observed:
The sunrise is a daily phenomenon. **2** person, thing, or happening that is extraordinary: *A man ten feet tall is a phenomenon.*
phe·nom·e·na (fĭ nŏm′ə nə).

phi·al (fī′əl) small glass bottle; vial.

phil·an·throp·ic (fĭl′ən thrŏp′ĭk) kindly
toward others and doing things for them,
especially for those in need; benevolent;
charitable: *Our new hospital building was
given by a philanthropic banker.*

phi·lan·thro·pist (fĭ lăn′thrə pĭst) person
who promotes human welfare, often by
giving money for hospitals, schools, charitable institutions, etc.

phi·lan·thro·py (fĭ lăn′thrə pĭ) **1** love of
mankind, especially as expressed by the
desire to help people: *The basis of much
public charity is* philanthropy. **2** action or
institution that benefits humanity, such as
works of charity, the Red Cross, Salvation
Army, or the like. **phi·lan·thro·pies.**

phi·lat·e·list (fĭ lăt′ə lĭst) person who collects and studies postage stamps.

Phil·ip·pine Is·lands (fĭl′ə pēn′ ī′ləndz)
country consisting of a group of islands in
the western Pacific Ocean.

phi·los·o·pher (fĭ lŏs′ə fər) **1** founder of a
system of philosophy. **2** person who studies
philosophy and seeks wisdom. **3** person
who calmly and intelligently makes the best
of life and events as they happen.

phil·o·soph·ic (fĭl′ə sŏf′ĭk) philosophical.

phil·o·soph·i·cal (fĭl′ə sŏf′ə kəl) **1** of or
about philosophy: *a philosophical argu-*

ment. **2** wise; calm: *Tom's* philosophical *attitude.* **phil·o·soph·i·cal·ly.**

phi·los·o·phy (fi lŏs′ə fĭ) **1** study that aims at understanding the basic principles of the universe, life, morals, etc. **2** system of beliefs about the universe and life: *the* philosophy *of the Plains Indians.* **3** guiding principles followed in a particular activity or field of knowledge: *a philosophy of education.* **phi·los·o·phies.**

phlox (flŏks) **1** American garden plant bearing clusters of red, white, or purple flowers on a tall stalk. **2** the flower of this plant.

phoe·be (fē′bĭ) small, insect-eating bird with a brown back and wings and a light breast, named for its two-note call.

Phoe·ni·ci·a (fə nĭsh′ə) an ancient country in western Asia, on the Mediterranean, noted for its sailors and merchants.

Phoe·ni·ci·an (fə nĭsh′ən) **1** of or having to do with Phoenicia. **2** inhabitant of Phoenicia.

phone (fōn) **1** telephone. **2** to telephone: *I phoned George.* **phoned, phon·ing.**

pho·net·ic (fō nĕt′ĭk) **1** indicating or having to do with speech sounds. The long mark (¯) and the short mark (ŭ) over vowels are phonetic symbols to show pronunciation. **2 phonetics** science of speech sounds and the symbols used to represent them.

pho·no·graph (fō′nə grăf′) **1** machine for reproducing sound from a disk with grooves in it; record player. **2** of or for a record player: *a phonograph needle.*

phos·phate (fŏs′fāt) one of a group of chemical compounds containing phosphorus. Phosphates are obtained from bones and certain rocks and are used chiefly in fertilizers.

phos·pho·rus (fŏs′fə rəs) yellowish, waxy solid element that glows in the dark and easily bursts into flame. It is a necessary element in bones, nerves, and other living matter.

pho·to (fō′tō) photograph. **pho·tos.**

pho·to·el·ec·tric cell (fō′tō ĭ lĕk′trĭk sĕl) device in which a certain metal gives off electrons when a beam of light strikes it, thus causing a weak electric current; electric eye.

pho·to·graph (fō′tə grăf′) **1** picture made with a camera containing a film or glass plate which is sensitive to light. **2** to take a picture of with a camera.

pho·tog·ra·pher (fə tŏg′rə fər) person who takes photographs.

pho·to·graph·ic (fō′tə grăf′ĭk) **1** having to do with photography: *a photographic lens.* **2** able to remember accurately: *a photographic mind.* **3** sharp; clear; distinct; very accurate: *to paint a picture in* photographic *detail.*

pho·tog·ra·phy (fə tŏg′rə fĭ) the art of taking pictures with a camera.

pho·to·syn·the·sis (fō′tō sĭn′thə sĭs) in living plants, the changing of water and carbon dioxide into sugar, by the action of light in the presence of chlorophyll.

phrase (frāz) **1** group of related words often found within a sentence. In "He was at home," "at home" is a phrase. **2** short and striking expression of a thought: *Bacon's clever phrases are often quoted.* **3** to put into words: *Cedric phrased his letter carefully.* **phrased, phras·ing.**

phys·ic (fĭz′ĭk) **1** medicine, often a laxative. **2** to give medicine to or treat with medicine.

phys·i·cal (fĭz′ə kəl) **1** having to do with the material objects and forces of the universe: *In science we deal with physical matters; in church with spiritual.* **2** having to do with the body: *great physical strength.* **3 physical education** education in the care and development of the body, and exercises promoting health and strength. **phys·i·cal·ly.**

phy·si·cian (fə zĭsh′ən) person licensed to treat sick people; medical doctor.

phys·i·cist (fĭz′ə sĭst) person who has a great knowledge of the science of physics and follows it as a profession.

phys·ics (fĭz′ĭks) the science that deals with matter and energy, and the transfer of energy from one place to another.

phys·i·ol·o·gy (fĭz′ĭ ŏl′ə jĭ) science dealing with the workings of living things or their parts.

phy·sique (fĭ zēk′) structure or appearance of the body: *Samson was famous for his* physique.

---

fāte, făt, fâre, fär; bē, bĕt; bīte, bĭt; nō, nŏt, nôr; fūse, fŭn, fûr; tōō, tŏŏk; foil; foul; thin; ~~then~~;
hw for wh as in *wh*at; zh for s as in u*s*ual; ə for a, e, i, o, u, as in *a*go, lin*e*n, per*i*l, at*o*m, min*u*s

pi·an·ist (pĭ ăn′ĭst or pē′ə nĭst) person who plays the piano.

pi·an·o (pĭ ăn′ō) large musical instrument played by key-operated hammers that strike tuned wires stretched across a sounding board. A grand piano has a horizontal sounding board; an upright piano a vertical sounding board. **pi·an·os.**

Pianos

pi·az·za (pĭ ăz′ə) **1** in the United States, a roofed porch. **2** in Italy, a public square.

pic·co·lo (pĭk′ə lō′) small, flutelike wind instrument with a sharp, high tone, played by blowing across the mouthpiece. **pic·co·los.**

pick (pĭk) **1** to choose: *to pick a good day for the picnic.* **2** choice: *Take your pick.* **3** very best: *the pick of*

Piazzas

the crop. **4** to pull off or take from: *to pick a peach from the tree.* **5** to remove feathers, etc., from: *to pick a chicken.* **6** to make a hole in with a picking motion: *to pick ice.* **7** a picking tool, such as a pickax or ice pick. **8** to start; bring about deliberately: *Why pick a quarrel?* **9** to tear; separate: *to pick apart; to pick to pieces.*

pick a lock to open a lock with a bit of wire or the like.

pick a pocket to remove by stealth from a person's pocket; steal from one's person.

pick at to eat daintily or listlessly: *Alice just picked at her dinner.*

pick flaws to find fault with; criticize.

pick off to remove by accurate shooting: *Enemy sharpshooters picked off our men as we advanced.*

pick up **1** to get unexpectedly: *All of us like to pick up a bargain.* **2** to learn or grasp: *Jean picked up knitting very quickly.* **3** to continue; carry on: *When Peter stopped for breath, Paul picked up the story.* **4** to meet and take along; give a ride to: *Frank picked up Ted on the way to school.*

pick·ax or **pick·axe** (pĭk′ăks′) digging tool having a slightly curved head with pointed ends, set at right angles to a wooden handle.

Pickax

pick·er·el (pĭk′ər əl) a slender, mottled, fresh-water food fish, with a pointed head and large mouth. pl. **pick·er·el.**

pick·et (pĭk′ət) **1** narrow, often pointed, stake used as an upright in a fence, to tie an animal to, etc. **2** to enclose an area with a fence made of such stakes. **3** to tie to a post or peg: *to picket a horse.* **4** military guard stationed to give warning of an enemy approach. **5** to station as a watcher; surround with guards: *to picket troops at the border.* **6** during a strike, person stationed outside a factory, shop, etc., to persuade workers or customers not to go in.

pick·le (pĭk′əl) **1** to soak in brine or vinegar to preserve or flavor food: *to pickle onions.* **2** vegetable, especially a cucumber, preserved by this method. **3** embarrassing situation: *The boys caught in the orchard were in a pretty pickle.* **pick·led, pick·ling.**

pick·pock·et (pĭk′pŏk′ĭt) thief who steals from pockets, handbags, etc.

pic·nic (pĭk′nĭk) **1** outdoor meal by a family or group, the diners often supplying the food for a common table: *The steamfitters' picnic will be held at Seaside Park.* **2** any good time: *We had a picnic at the school dance.* **3** to go on or take part in a picnic: *Our family picnics around our barbecue on pleasant Sunday afternoons.* **pic·nicked, pic·nick·ing.**

pic·nick·er (pĭk′nĭk ər) one who goes on or takes part in a picnic.

pic·to·ri·al (pĭk tôr′ĭ əl) **1** having to do with, shown by, or containing pictures: *A photograph album is a pictorial record of a family.* **2** suitable for or suggesting a picture: *a pictorial description of a battle.* **pic·to·ri·al·ly.**

pic·ture (pĭk′chər) **1** painting, drawing, or photograph. **2** to represent in a painting, drawing, etc.: *The artist pictured a country scene.* **3** something worth picturing: *In her new dress the baby is a picture.* **4** image on a television or movie screen. **5** likeness; image; representation: *She is the picture of her mother and the picture of health.* **6** clear or colorful description: *This book* *gives a good* picture *of life in colonial days.* **7** to describe vividly in words. **8** mental image: *I have a picture of the old swimming hole in my memory.* **9** to imagine: *Try to* picture *yourself in another person's place.* **10** movie: *Did you like the picture last night?* **pic·tured, pic·tur·ing.**

pic·tur·esque (pĭk'chə rĕsk') interesting, colorful, or charming, as a picture might be: *Quebec is a* picturesque *city.* **pic·tur·esque·ly.**

pid·gin (pĭj'ĭn) a mixed language using the words of more than one language and a simple grammar. (Homonym: pigeon)

pie (pī) **1** dish of meat, fruit, or custard baked with a single upper or lower crust, or between two crusts.
2 lower crust containing a separately prepared filling, such as banana cream pie. **3** two layers of cake with

Pie

custard or jelly between them, such as Boston cream pie and Washington pie. [¹**pie** is a word of uncertain origin.]

²**pie** (pī) magpie. [²**pie** is the unchanged form of an Old French word that comes from a Latin word (pica) meaning "magpie."]

piece (pēs) **1** part of a whole; bit; fragment: *to tear to* pieces. **2** small portion or quantity: *a piece of pie; a piece of cloth.* **3** quantity; section; unit: *a valuable* piece *of property.* **4** a separate instance or example; item: *a* piece *of news; a* piece *of advice; a* piece *of nonsense.* **5** musical or literary composition: *What is your favorite piano* piece? **6** single object of a group: *There are thirty-two* pieces *in a chess set.* **7** fixed amount or size in which goods or other articles are sold: *Muslin comes at twelve yards to the* piece. **8** coin: *a five-cent* piece. **9** to enlarge or mend by adding material: *to* piece *a skirt.* **10** to make by joining sections together: *to* piece *a patchwork quilt.* **11 of a piece** or **of one piece** alike; of the same sort: *You can't trust any of them; they are all* of a piece. **pieced, piec·ing.** (Homonym: peace)

piece·meal (pēs'mēl') in portions or parts; by degrees; gradually; bit by bit: *to do a job* piecemeal.

pied (pīd) **1** having two or more colors in patches: *Our black and white cat has a* pied *coat.* **2** wearing many-colored clothing: *the* Pied *Piper of Hamelin.*

pied·mont (pēd'mŏnt) **1** area at the base of a mountain. **2** lying at the base of a mountain: *a* piedmont *valley.* **3 Piedmont (1)** hilly section of the United States, east of the Appalachian Mountains. **(2)** region in northwestern Italy.

pier (pîr) **1** supporting pillar; partition between arches that supports the structure above it. **2** the part of a wall between openings. **3** a buttress. **4** wharf or promenade extending into or over water. (Homonym: peer)

Piers of arch

pierce (pîrs) **1** to puncture; run through or into: *The rose thorn* pierced *my finger.* **2** to make a hole in: *The cannon ball* pierced *the fortress wall.* **3** to affect deeply or strongly: *The loss of her kitten* pierced *Ada's heart.* **4** to force a way through; penetrate: *The tanks* pierced *the enemy defenses. The sun* pierced *the clouds.* **5** to see through; solve: *to* pierce *a mystery.* **pierced, pierc·ing.**

pierc·ing (pîr'sĭng) sharp; cutting; penetrating: *a shrill,* piercing *cry; the* piercing *cold.* **pierc·ing·ly.**

pi·e·ty (pī'ə tĭ) **1** reverence for God; devotion to religion: *the* piety *of a saint.* **2** loyal devotion to parents, family, a race, a country, etc. **3** act of reverence or devotion: *prayers and other* pieties. **pi·e·ties.**

pig (pĭg) **1** kind of farm animal raised for its meat (pork); hog; swine; especially a young animal of this kind. **2** dirty or greedy person. **3** small bar of metal, especially iron, ready to be reworked into useful articles.

Pig, about 3½ ft. long

pi·geon (pĭj'ən) plump, city-loving bird with sleek white or colored feathers, widely

---

fāte, făt, fâre, fär; bē, bĕt; bīte, bĭt; nō, nŏt, nôr; fūse, fŭn, fûr; tōō, tŏŏk; foil; foul; thin; then; hw for wh as in *wh*at; zh for s as in u*s*ual; ə for a, e, i, o, u, as in *a*go, lin*e*n, per*i*l, at*o*m, min*u*s

distributed throughout the world and sometimes bred for food, for racing, and for carrying messages. (Homonym: pidgin)

pi·geon-toed (pĭj′ən-tōd′) with the toes turned in: *to walk* pigeon-toed.

Pigeon, about 1 ft. long

pig·gy·back (pĭg′ĭ-băk′) **1** on the back or shoulders: *to ride* piggyback. **2** having to do with the transporting of loaded truck trailers on railroad flat cars, or an airplane carried aloft by a larger plane.

pig-head·ed (pĭg′hĕd′ĭd) obstinate; stubborn.

pig iron crude iron as it comes from the blast furnace. It is usually cast into rough molds called **pigs**.

pig·ment (pĭg′mənt) **1** any substance used to give color to something, especially paints. **2** material that gives color to living things: *the* pigment *in the skin; the* pigment *in plants.*

pig·my (pĭg′mĭ) pygmy. **pig·mies.**

pig·sty (pĭg′stī′) pen for pigs. **pig·sties.**

pig·tail (pĭg′tāl′) braid of hair at the back of the head; queue: *The little girl's* pigtails *came down to her waist.*

¹pike (pīk) weapon formerly carried by foot soldiers, consisting of a long wooden shaft with a metal spearhead. [¹**pike** is from a French word (pique) that is related to another French word (pic) meaning "pickax."]

²pike (pīk) slender, sharp-headed, green-and-white, greedy, fresh-water fish of the pickerel family. pl. **pike**; rarely, **pikes**. [²**pike** is ¹**pike** in a meaning that arose from the shape of the fish's pointed snout.]

Pike, 1 to 4½ ft. long

³pike (pīk) **1** road on which a charge is usually made for driving; a turnpike. **2** any main road. [³**pike** is a short form for **turnpike**.]

¹pile (pīl) **1** heap; stack; mass: *a pile of sand*. **2** to place or throw in a heap; arrange: *to pile bricks one on top of the other.* **3** large

amount. **4** to fill; load: *The wagon was* piled *high with hay.* **5** to press forward in a mass; to crowd: *The school children* piled *into the bus.*

pile up to accumulate: *He* piled up *a fortune. Don't let bills* pile up.

piled, pil·ing. [¹**pile** is from a Latin word (pila) meaning "pillar."]

²pile (pīl) a timber driven into the ground or a river bed, for a wharf, building foundation, or the like; also, metal or concrete columns used in this way. [²**pile** is a form of an Old English word (pil) meaning "stake," which comes from a Latin word (pilum) meaning "javelin."]

³pile (pīl) **1** nap of cloth, especially the furry or velvety surface of velvet, plush, carpets, etc.: *a carpet with a thick* pile. **2** short, soft hair; down. [³**pile** is from a Latin word (pilus) meaning "a hair."]

pil·fer (pĭl′fər) to steal in small amounts: *A rat had* pilfered *from the pantry all winter.*

pil·grim (pĭl′grĭm) **1** traveler to a holy place: *Many* pilgrims *still journey to the Holy Land every year.* **2** traveler; wanderer. **3 Pilgrim** one of the English settlers who founded the colony of Plymouth, Massachusetts, in 1620.

pil·grim·age (pĭl′grə mĭj) journey made because of reverence or affection, especially to a sacred place.

pill (pĭl) **1** medicine in the shape of a tiny ball or capsule: *Water helps in swallowing a* pill. **2 bitter pill** anything hard to bear or unpleasant: *Having our team lose was a* bitter pill.

pil·lage (pĭl′ĭj) **1** to rob or plunder: *Last month, bandits* pillaged *two villages in the west.* **2** a robbing or plundering. **3** whatever is taken as plunder: *A lot of* pillage *was recovered when the outlaws were captured.* **pil·laged, pil·lag·ing.**

pil·lar (pĭl′ər) **1** round, square, or ornamental column used to hold up a floor, roof, or the like, or as a monument or high pedestal. **2** a firm supporter: *Deacon Jones is a* pillar *of the church.*

Pillar

pil·lo·ry (pĭl′ə rĭ) **1** framework with opening for the neck and wrists of a person held up to public shame, used in olden times to punish minor lawbreakers. **2** to expose to public shame: *The newspapers pillory dishonest politicians.*

pil·lo·ries; pil·lo·ried, pil·lo·ry·ing.

pil·low (pĭl′ō) **1** support for the head in resting or sleeping; cushion. **2** to rest, as on a pillow; to cushion: *He pillowed his head on his arm.*

pil·low·case (pĭl′ō kās′) removable cloth cover, open at one end, to hold a pillow.

Pillory

pi·lot (pī′lǝt) **1** man who flies a plane: *Ruth's father was a bomber pilot in the war.* **2** man who guides a large ship, usually into or out of a harbor: *The river pilot left in a tug as we cleared the harbor.* **3** to fly a plane or guide a ship. **4** any guide and leader. **5** to guide and lead: *to pilot a nation.*

pim·ple (pĭm′pǝl) small, hard, inflamed swelling on the skin.

pin (pĭn) **1** short piece of wire with a sharp point at one end and a blunt head at the other, used to fasten things together. **2** piece of wood, metal, etc., resembling a pin or having a similar use, such as a hairpin, tiepin, clothespin. **3** ornament or badge, fitted with a pin and a clasp. **4** to hold firmly in one position: *The fallen tree pinned him to the earth.* **5** to fasten with a pin: *John tried to pin the tail on the donkey.* **6** in bowling, a wooden club used as a target for the ball.

pin down to get (a person) to stick to a course of action, a promise, an opinion, etc.: *I couldn't pin her down to a date.*
pinned, pin·ning.

pin·a·fore (pĭn′ǝ fôr) loose, sleeveless apron, or covering for a child's dress.

pin·cers (pĭn′sǝrz) **1** tool with jaws hinged like scissors, for holding, bending, twisting, or pulling. **2** the pinching claws of a crab or lobster.

Pincers

pinch (pĭnch) **1** to squeeze or nip between the thumb and a finger, or between two

edges: *She cried when her brother* pinched *her arm.* **2** nip or squeeze: *a playful* pinch. **3** to press on painfully: *Her shoes* pinch *her feet.* **4** painful pressure: *the* pinch *of new shoes.* **5** amount that can be picked up between the thumb and a finger: *This soup needs another* pinch *of salt.* **6** to cause to become cramped or drawn, as by pain, hunger, etc.: *The biting wind* pinched *the child's face.* **7** distress; hardship: *the* pinch *of poverty.* **8** to economize; be miserly or stingy: *When short of money we are forced to* pinch. **9 in a pinch** in an emergency: *You can count on Joe in a pinch.*

¹**pine** (pīn) **1** evergreen tree bearing cones and needle-shaped leaves and having a sticky sap. **2** the wood of this tree. [¹**pine** is a form of an Old English word (pin) which comes from a Latin word (pinus) that also means "pine, fir tree."]

White pine

²**pine** (pīn) to sicken slowly from sorrow or loneliness: *That dog* pined *away during his owner's long absence.*

pine for to long intensely; yearn: *The father* pined *for his lost son.*
pined, pin·ing. [²**pine** is the changed form of an Old English word (pīnian) meaning "to torture, afflict."]

pine·ap·ple (pīn′ăp′ǝl) **1** cone-shaped fruit with firm juicy pulp. **2** the spiny-leafed tropical plant which bears this fruit.

ping-pong (pĭng′pŏng′) game, somewhat like tennis, played with solid rackets and a light, plastic ball over a low net on a table.

pin·hole (pĭn′hōl′) **1** small hole made by a pin or as by a pin. **2** hole into which a pin or peg fits.

Pineapple

pin·ion (pĭn′yǝn) **1** to tie or fasten the arms firmly: *His arms were* pinioned *with a stout rope.* **2** the wing, or any of the stiff flying feathers, of a bird: *The swan had a* pinion *trimmed, so that he could not*

---

fāte, făt, fâre, fär; bē, bĕt; bīte, bĭt; nō, nŏt, nôr; fūse, fŭn, fûr; tōō, tŏŏk; foil; foul; thin; then; hw for wh as in *wh*at; zh for s as in u*s*ual; ǝ for a, e, i, o, u, as in *a*go, lin*e*n, per*i*l, at*o*m, min*u*s

fly. **3** the smaller wheel of a gear. For picture, see **gear.** (Homonym: piñon)

¹pink (pingk) **1** very pale red: *the pink and gold of the morning sky.* **2** of a very pale-red color: *Sunrise turned the sky pink in the east.* **3** the highest degree: *the pink of health.* **4** garden plant like the carnation with narrow grassy leaves and spicy smelling flowers that are pink, white, or red. [¹**pink** is from "pinkeye," an early English word meaning "small eye," which is a translation of the French name (oeillet) for the flower.]

²pink (pingk) **1** to cut the edge of cloth in a notched pattern; scallop the edge of a piece of cloth. **2** to prick or pierce with a pointed blade: *to be pinked in the arm during a duel.* [²**pink** is a form of an earlier English word (pynken) of the same meaning.]

pink·eye (pingk′ī′) contagious disease of the eye and eyelids, marked by pain, redness, and watering.

pin·nace (pin′is) **1** formerly, a small boat that attended a larger vessel and was used to transport messages, supplies, etc. **2** any boat carried by a ship.

pin·na·cle (pin′ə kəl) peak or highest point: *the pinnacle of a mountain; the pinnacle of fame.*

pi·ñon (pin′yən) pine tree of the western states, having edible seeds. (Homonym: pinion)

pint (pint) measure, either liquid or dry, of half a quart or ⅛ of a gallon: *Children should have at least a pint of milk a day.*

pin·to (pin′tō) **1** marked with spots of more than one color. **2** pinto horse or pony. **pin·tos.**

pi·o·neer (pī′ə nir′) **1** person who goes first to prepare the way for others: *The West was settled by pioneers. Benjamin Franklin was a pioneer in the study of electricity.* **2** to lead the way (in exploring or studying some idea, science, etc.): *Walter Reed pioneered in finding the cause of yellow fever.*

pi·ous (pī′əs) **1** devout; very religious: *a pious man.* **2** having to do with religious devotion: *to be put to pious uses.* **3** appearing to be religious when one is not: *a pious rascal.* **pi·ous·ly.**

pipe (pīp) **1** tube used to carry liquids, gases, etc., from one place to another. **2** to

carry by pipes: *Oil and gas can be piped from the Atlantic to the Pacific coast.* **3** to supply with pipes: *to pipe the house for water.* **4** small bowl with a hollow stem, used for smoking tobacco. **5** amount of tobacco used to fill a pipe: *Dad smokes two pipes of tobacco a day.* **6** any wooden, metal, or reed tube used to make musical sound, such as a flute or one of the pipes of an organ. **7** to blow or play on a musical pipe: *The band piped a merry dance.* **8** high, shrill voice or sound. **9** the call or sound of a bird or insect. **10** to sound, speak, or utter loudly and shrilly: *The little boy piped a tune in his squeaky voice.* **11 pipes** bagpipes. **piped, pip·ing.**

pipe·line (pīp′līn′) line of pipes for carrying oil, water, gas, etc.

pip·er (pī′pər) person who plays on a pipe, especially the bagpipes.

pip·ing (pī′ping) **1** amount of a pipe, or a system of pipes in a building, street, etc. **2** the music of a pipe, or a shrill sound, such as the song of birds. **3** shrill: *a piping voice.* **4 piping hot** very hot.

pique (pēk) **1** slight anger, resentment, especially because of wounded pride: *Joan was in a fit of pique because everyone was late for her party.* **2** to wound the pride of; displease: *Their rudeness piqued her.* **3** to arouse; stir up; excite: *to pique one's curiosity.* **4** to pride (oneself): *The actor piqued himself on his good looks.* **piqued, pi·quing.** (Homonyms: peak, peek)

pi·ra·cy (pī′rə sī) **1** armed robbery on the high seas. **2** the using of another's invention, literary work, or the like, without permission. **pi·ra·cies.**

pi·rate (pī′rət) **1** sea robber. **2** person who uses another's invention or creation without permission. **3** to use (another's invention or creation) without permission: *The company was fined for pirating the invention.* **pi·rat·ed, pi·rat·ing.**

pis·til (pis′til) the part of a flower that produces the seed.

pis·tol (pis′təl) short firearm to be held in and fired by one hand, especially feeding bullets from its handle.

Pistil

Pistol

piston

pis·ton (pĭs′tən) close-fitting disk or circular block that slides back and forth in a hollow cylinder.

¹pit (pĭt) **1** hole in the ground, either natural or artificial: *a gravel pit.* **2** hollow place on the body: *an arm* pit; *the pit of the stomach.* **3** scar caused by a disease, such as smallpox. **4** to mark with pits: *Smallpox had* pitted *the man's face.* **5** to set to oppose or fight; match: *to pit two wrestlers against each other.* **6** concealed section in front of the stage where the orchestra sits. **7** deep chasm; abyss; hell. **pit·ted, pit·ting.** [¹**pit** is a form of an Old English word (pytt).]

²pit (pĭt) **1** the seed or stone of certain fruits such as a cherry or plum. **2** to remove the pits of: *Sarah will* pit *the cherries for the pie.* **pit·ted, pit·ting.** [²**pit** is from a Dutch word of the same spelling.]

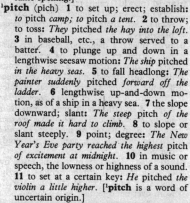

Pit

¹pitch (pĭch) **1** to set up; erect; establish: *to* pitch *camp; to* pitch *a tent.* **2** to throw; to toss: *They* pitched *the hay into the loft.* **3** in baseball, etc., a throw served to a batter. **4** to plunge up and down in a lengthwise seesaw motion: *The ship* pitched *in the heavy seas.* **5** to fall headlong: *The painter suddenly* pitched *forward off the ladder.* **6** lengthwise up-and-down motion, as of a ship in a heavy sea. **7** the slope downward; slant: *The steep* pitch *of the roof made it hard to climb.* **8** to slope or slant steeply. **9** point; degree: *The New Year's Eve party reached the highest* pitch *of excitement at midnight.* **10** in music or speech, the lowness or highness of a sound. **11** to set at a certain key: *He* pitched *the violin a little higher.* [¹**pitch** is a word of uncertain origin.]

²pitch (pĭch) **1** thick, sticky, dark-colored substance made from wood, coal, or petroleum. Pitch is used for varnish, roofing paper, street paving, etc. **2** resin from some evergreens. [²**pitch** is a form of an Old English word (pic) which comes from a Latin word (pix) of the same meaning.]

pituitary

pitch·blende (pĭch′blĕnd′) brown or black ore of uranium.

¹pitch·er (pĭch′ər) vessel with a handle on its side and a pouring lip opposite the handle, used to hold and serve liquids. [¹**pitcher** comes through Old French (pichier) from a Latin word (bicarium) that means "pitcher," "beaker."]

Pitcher

²pitch·er (pĭch′ər) person who throws or hurls, especially in baseball the player who throws the ball to the batter. [²**pitcher** is formed from ¹**pitch.**]

Pitchfork

pitch·fork (pĭch′fôrk′) tool with steel tines and a long wooden handle, used to move hay, straw, and the like.

pitch pipe small metal pipe that sounds a single tone. It is used in setting the pitch for a singer or in tuning an instrument.

pit·e·ous (pĭt′ĭ əs) arousing sorrow or pity; pitiful: *An injured animal is a* piteous *sight.* **pit·e·ous·ly.**

pit·fall (pĭt′fôl′) **1** hidden pit used as a trap for animals. **2** hidden danger or trap.

pith (pĭth) **1** soft, spongy tissue forming a central core, especially in the stem of certain plants. **2** important or essential part: *His notes summed up the* pith *of the lecture.*

pit·i·a·ble (pĭt′ĭ ə bəl) **1** arousing pity or sympathy: *The poor beggar was a* pitiable *sight.* **2** arousing contempt or scorn: *a* pitiable *alibi.* **pit·i·a·bly.**

pit·i·ful (pĭt′ĭ fəl) **1** arousing pity or sorrow. **2** worthy of contempt; pitiable: *The thief made a* pitiful *attempt to get out of his punishment by lying.* **pit·i·ful·ly.**

pit·i·less (pĭt′ĭ lĭs) without sympathy or pity; merciless: *Only a* pitiless *person would make a dog suffer.* **pit·i·less·ly.**

pi·tu·i·tar·y (pĭ tōō′ə tĕr′ĭ or pĭ tū′ə tĕr′ĭ) **1** small round gland at the base of the brain. It produces hormones that have an effect on rate of growth, building up and breaking down of tissues, etc. **2** having to do with this gland.

---

fāte, făt, fâre, fär; bē, bĕt; bīte, bĭt; nō, nŏt, nôr; fūse, fŭn, fûr; tōō, tŏŏk; foil; foul; thin; then;
hw for wh as in what; zh for s as in usual; ə for a, e, i, o, u, as in ago, linen, peril, atom, minus

pit·y (pĭt′ĭ) **1** feeling of sorrow over the suffering of others; mercy: *She was moved by* pity *to take in the homeless orphan.* **2** cause for regret or pity: *It is a* pity *that she can't come to our party.* **3** to feel sorry for; sympathize with: *I* pity *anybody who is in continual pain.* **4** have pity on or take pity on to show sympathy and mercy towards: *We took* pity on *the hungry cat and gave it some milk.* **pit·ies; pit·ied, pit·y·ing.**

piv·ot (pĭv′ət) **1** the point on which a thing turns. **2** the bar, pin, or other thing which forms such a point. **3** to turn or depend on: *The argument* pivots *on that one point.* **4** to turn as on a pivot: *Ivan* pivoted *on his toe and faced me.* **5** a turning movement made as if on a pivot. **6** to supply or mount on a pivot.

Pivot

pix·y or **pix·ie** (pĭk′sĭ) little fairy; elf. **pix·ies.**

piz·za (pēt′sə) Italian dish resembling a pie, made by baking tomatoes, cheese, spices, etc., on flat bread dough.

pk. **1** peck. **2** park. **3** peak.

pl. plural.

plac·ard (plăk′ärd) **1** piece of heavy paper with a public notice or advertisement on it; poster. **2** to post such notices on; advertise with such notices.

pla·cate (plā′kāt or plăk′āt) to soothe (someone who is angry); appease: *Nothing could* placate *Grandfather once he had lost his temper.* **pla·cat·ed, pla·cat·ing.**

place (plās) **1** particular location: *a* place *to hang a picture.* **2** to put in a particular spot or position: *to* place *dishes on the table; to* place *a person in a job.* **3** city, town, village, locality, or the like: *His family and mine come from the same* place. **4** building or area used for a special purpose: *a* place *of amusement; a* place *of business.* **5** a dwelling; house and its grounds: *They have a* place *in town and a* place *in the country.* **6** particular part or spot on the body or a surface: *a sore* place *on the back; a worn* place *in a coat.* **7** rank; position; standing: *to know one's* place; *Shakespeare's* place *in literature.* **8** space or seat, as at a table,

in a bus, etc. **9** job; position: *He lost his* place *at the bank.* **10** duty; responsibility: *It's your* place *to look after your guest.* **11** to identify by connecting with a place, time, circumstance, etc.: *I finally* placed *him as an old schoolfellow.* **12** in place (1) in customary, assigned, or proper place: *to put one's books* in place. (2) fitting; proper; timely: *Laughter is not* in place *in church.* **13** out of place (1) not in proper place. (2) not fitting. **14** take place to happen; occur: *The parade* takes place *tomorrow.* **15** take the place of to be a substitute for: *The nurse* takes the place of *the mother.* **16** in place of instead of: *margarine* in place of *butter.* **placed, plac·ing.**

plac·er min·ing (plăs′ər mī′nĭng) method of washing gold-bearing gravel or sand through troughs at high pressure. The gold particles sink from their weight and are caught, while the other material washes through.

plac·id (plăs′ĭd) calm; tranquil: *The lake is very* placid on still evenings. *The old lady sat reading her Bible in* placid *contentment.* **plac·id·ly.**

plague (plāg) **1** dangerous contagious disease carried by fleas that have bitten sick rats or other rodents. **2** any dangerous disease that spreads quickly; an epidemic. **3** thing causing misery or great trouble; affliction: *A* plague *of locusts devoured the crops.* **4** to afflict with great harm: *Dust storms have* plagued *some of our western states.* **5** to pester or annoy: *The child* plagued *his uncle with questions.* **plagued, pla·guing.**

plaid (plăd) **1** pattern of weaving made by crossing bands of different colors at right angles. **2** kind of shawl of such material, worn over one shoulder by a Scottish person. **3** woven in this pattern: *A dress of red and blue* plaid *wool.* **4** any material with such a pattern. *The girl wore a skirt of Stuart* plaid.

plain (plān) **1** easy to see or hear; distinct: *All the figures in the photograph are very* plain. *His voice was clear and* plain *over the telephone.* **2** easy to understand; clear: *He made his meaning quite* plain. **3** simple; not luxurious: *a* plain *meal;* plain *living.* **4** simple in manners; ordinary: *The poli-*

tician always said he came from plain *people.*
5 all of one color; without a pattern or design: *a plain* yellow *dress; a plain* wall-paper. **6** without ornament; not elaborate: *dressed in plain* clothes. **7** outspoken; frank: *a man of plain, blunt speech.* **8** homely: *Many plain* girls grow into beautiful women. **9** flat expanse of open land. **plain·ly.** (Homonym: plane)

plain-spo·ken (plān′spō′kən) frank and direct in speech.

plain·tive (plān′tĭv) sad; melancholy: *a* plaintive *song.* **plain·tive·ly.**

plait (plāt) **1** flat fold; pleat: *The skirt has plaits at the waist.* **2** to fold: *Mother* plaited *paper on the edge of the shelf.* **3** a braid: *The little girl wore her hair in a plait.* **4** to braid: *Grandmother* plaited *rags for a braided rug.* (Homonym: plate)

Plaits

plan (plăn) **1** course of action worked out beforehand; fixed design; scheme: *Paul made plans to visit Paris.* **2** arrangement of details: *Here is the plan of my story.* **3** drawing showing details of a proposed building, street map, machine, or the like. **4** to arrange; work out: *Ellen planned a big party.* **5** to lay out; design: *Engineers will plan the new suburb.* **6** to scheme; plot: *Big Nick planned to rob the bank.* **planned, plan·ning.**

STAGE

Theater seating plan

¹plane (plān) **1** smoothing tool used in woodworking. **2** to use such a tool: *The carpenter planed the board.* **planed, plan·ing.** [**¹plane** is from a Latin word (planare) "make flat."] (Homonym: plain)

Plane

²plane (plān) **1** smooth, flat surface, usually level. **2** airplane. **3** one of the flat supporting surfaces of an airplane wing. **4** level (of thought, morals, etc.): *on a high moral plane; the plane of the discussion.*

5 **plane geometry** subject dealing with lines and figures in two dimensions, such as triangles, circles, etc. [**²plane** is from a Latin word (planus) meaning "flat."] (Homonym: plain)

plan·et (plăn′ĭt) any of nine heavenly bodies, like the Earth and Mars, that go around the sun and shine by reflecting light.

plan·e·tar·i·um (plăn′ə târ′ĭ əm) a theater to show the movements of heavenly bodies. It consists of a room with a domed ceiling on which moving points of light show the heavenly bodies. **plan·e·tar·i·ums** or **plan·e·tar·i·a** (plăn′ə târ′ĭ ə).

plan·e·tar·y (plăn′ə tĕr′ĭ) having to do with a planet or planets.

plan·e·toid (plăn′ə toid′) small, solid natural body going around the sun; asteroid.

plank (plăngk) **1** long, broad piece of timber; thick board. **2** to cover or furnish with planks: *The new dock will be planked in a week and ready for use.* **3** statement of principle forming a part of the platform of a political party: *a civil rights* plank.

plank·ton (plăngk′tən) small, floating animals and plants near the surface of fresh or salt water, that are the food of many swimming animals.

plant (plănt) **1** any form of vegetable life, such as a tree, flower, grass, etc. **2** small plant, as opposed to a tree or shrub. **3** a sprout, young shoot, or seedling ready for transplanting: *We bought some tomato* plants *in little pots.* **4** to set in the ground in order to grow. **5** to provide (an area) with seeds or plants: *We had to plant a lawn and a flower garden at our new home.* **6** to fix in position; put: *He planted his feet and wouldn't move. He planted the stake in the ground.* **7** to introduce or instill (an idea, feeling, etc.): *The principle of honesty should be planted in all young minds.* **8** to settle; establish: *to plant a colony.* **9** the building and equipment of a factory, business, etc.: *This school has a fine plant but not enough teachers.* **10** equipment or apparatus for a mechanical process or operation: *The school's heating plant broke down.*

¹plan·tain (plăn′tĭn) **1** tropical plant bearing a kind of banana. **2** edible fruit of this

fāte, făt, fâre, fär; bē, bĕt; bīte, bĭt; nō, nŏt, nôr; fūse, fŭn, fûr; tōō, tŏŏk; foil; foul; thin; then; hw for wh as in what; zh for s as in usual; ə for a, e, i, o, u, as in ago, linen, peril, atom, minus

539

plantain

plant. [¹**plantain** is from a West Indian word (prattana), influenced by a Spanish word (plátano).]

²**plan·tain** (plăn'tĭn) common weed with large leaves that lie on or near the ground. Each plant has slender stalks that become solid spikes of tiny, greenish flowers. [²**plantain** is from an Old French word that comes from a Latin word (plantago).]

Plantain

plan·ta·tion (plăn tā'shən) 1 large estate in a southern or tropical region, where cotton, sugar cane, rubber, etc., are grown. 2 group of plants or trees that have been planted: *a rubber* plantation. 3 a settlement or colony: *Plymouth* Plantation.

plant·er (plăn'tər) 1 person or machine that sows or plants. 2 person who owns or manages a plantation.

plash (plăsh) 1 splash or splashing sound: *the plash of a fountain.* 2 to splash lightly.

plas·ma (plăz'mə) straw-colored liquid that remains after the blood cells have been removed from whole blood. Plasma contains proteins, salts, water, etc., and is much used in transfusions.

plas·ter (plăs'tər) 1 mixture of lime, sand, and water which hardens as it dries and is used to coat walls. 2 to cover with or as with plaster. 3 substance spread on a cloth which is applied to the body to relieve soreness, etc.: *a mustard* plaster.

plas·tic (plăs'tĭk) 1 having to do with or made by molding or modeling: *We made pottery and clay figures in* plastic *arts class.* 2 capable of being molded: *Soft wax is a* plastic *material.* 3 any of a large group of materials manufactured from chemicals and made into useful shapes by heat, pressure, or both. Rayon and cellophane are two types of plastics. 4 made of plastic: *a* plastic *toy.*

plate (plāt) 1 shallow, usually round, dish from which food is eaten. 2 the amount of food a plate will hold: *to eat a plate of spaghetti.* 3 food served to one person at

play

a meal: *The banquet cost $25.00 a* plate. 4 dishes and other utensils made of or plated with gold or silver: *She inherited the family* plate. 5 thin, flat piece or sheet of metal or other material. 6 to coat with metal; to cover with sheets of metal. 7 in baseball, the home base. **plat·ed, plat·ing.** (Homonym: plait)

pla·teau (plă tō') high area of flat land; tableland. **pla·teaus** or **pla·teaux.**

plat·form (plăt'fôrm) 1 structure raised above the surrounding ground or floor: *a railroad* platform; *a speaker's* platform. 2 statement of a group's beliefs and policies: *a political* platform.

plat·i·num (plăt'ə nəm) heavy, silver-white precious metal much used in chemists' equipment and jewelry. It is an element.

pla·toon (plə tōōn') body of soldiers, usually consisting of two to four squads.

plat·ter (plăt'ər) large, usually oval, flat dish from which meat, etc., is served at table.

Platter

plat·y·pus (plăt'ə pəs) small water animal of Australia, which lays eggs; the duckbill. For picture, see **duckbill.**

plau·si·ble (plô'zə bəl) seemingly true or reasonable: *His excuse for being late sounded* plausible *at the time, but later we found out the truth.* **plau·si·bly.**

play (plā) 1 to have fun; amuse oneself; take part in recreation. 2 recreation; fun; sport. 3 to take part in (a game): *to play baseball.* 4 to compete with (in a game): *to play another team.* 5 drama; performance of a drama. 6 to act the part of (a character) in a play: *Pat played Wendy in "Peter Pan."* 7 to act in a drama: *to play in summer theater.* 8 to perform (on a musical instrument): *to play the piano.* 9 to perform (music) on an instrument: *to play a waltz.* 10 to perform music: *to play in a band.* 11 to pretend or imitate in fun; make believe: *to play cowboy and Indians; to play a line of chairs is a train.* 12 any act or move in a game: *to score in the last play of a football game; a clever play in chess.* 13 one's turn in a game: *It's Hal's play next.* 14 action or use: *to bring all one's knowledge into play in solving a problem.* 15 to put (something) into action in

540

a game or contest: *to play a card.* **16** to act
or behave (in a certain way): *to play false
with a friend.* **17** conduct; dealings: *fair
play; foul play.* **18** lively or fitful movement: *the play of shadows on a wall.* **19** to
move lightly or quickly; flicker: *The moonlight played on the water.* **20** to put or be
in constant or repeated action: *to play a
hose on a lawn; fountains playing in the
sunshine.* **21** freedom or room for movement or action: *to give full play to the
imagination.*

play into (someone's) hands to give
(someone) an advantage without intending to.

play on or **upon** to make use of (a person's feelings, good nature, etc.) for one's
advantage: *He played on the teacher's
kindness when he was late for school.*

play with to trifle with; toy with: *to play
with the food on one's plate; to play with
the idea of going to the seashore.*

play·er (plā′ər) **1** one who plays, especially
in a game. **2** actor. **3** performer on a
musical instrument.

play·fel·low (plā′fel′ō) playmate.

play·ful (plā′fəl) **1** lively; frisky: *a playful
puppy.* **2** joking; merry: *a playful remark;
a playful tap on the back.* **play·ful·ly.**

play·ground (plā′ground′) ground used
for games, especially by children.

play·house (plā′hous′) **1** theater. **2** small
house for children to play in.

playing card one of the cards of a pack
used for playing games; especially one of
a pack of 52 cards divided into four suits
called diamonds, hearts, spades and clubs.

play·mate (plā′māt′) one who plays with
another person.

play·thing (plā′thing′) thing to play with;
toy.

play·wright (plā′rit′) person who writes
plays; dramatist.

pla·za (plā′zə or plăz′ə) public square or
open place in a city or town.

plea (plē) **1** an appeal; entreaty: *Mother did
not even listen to the children's pleas to keep
the kittens.* **2** explanation; excuse: *Freddy's
plea was that he had completely forgotten
about the time.* **3** an answer to charges in

a law court: *The lawyer entered a plea of
not guilty for his client.*

plead (plēd) **1** to beg earnestly; entreat:
*The frightened boy pleaded with the others
to stop tilting the canoe.* **2** to argue for or
against something: *The speakers on both
sides of the debate pleaded their cases well.*
3 to conduct a case in a court of law: *That
lawyer has pleaded before many judges.*
4 to answer to a charge in a law court. **5** to
offer as an excuse or as an apology: *The
tramp pleaded poverty when he was caught
stealing.* **plead·ed** or **pled, plead·ing.**

pleas·ant (plez′ənt) agreeable; delightful;
pleasing. **pleas·ant·ly.**

pleas·ant·ness (plez′ənt nis) a being pleasant; condition of being enjoyable: *the
pleasantness of the cool garden.*

pleas·ant·ry (plez′ən tri) humorous or
playful remark: *I enjoy your pleasantries,
but they're not an answer to my question.*
pleas·ant·ries.

please (plēz) **1** to give pleasure or happiness to; be agreeable to: *It always pleases
a teacher when her pupils are interested in
their work.* **2** to choose; prefer: *He does
as he pleases without thinking about other
people.* **3** "if you like" or "if you please," a
polite form used in asking: *Pass the butter,
please.* **4 be pleased to** to be glad or
happy to: *I shall be pleased to go with you.*
pleased, pleas·ing.

pleas·ing (plē′zing) agreeable; enjoyable;
delightful. **pleas·ing·ly.**

pleas·ur·a·ble (plezh′ər ə bəl) providing
pleasure; enjoyable. **pleas·ur·a·bly.**

pleas·ure (plezh′ər) **1** enjoyment; satisfaction: *Parents receive a great deal of pleasure
from the success of their children.* **2** something that gives enjoyment, satisfaction,
etc.: *the pleasure of your company.* **3** choice;
desire; will: *It is the king's pleasure to hunt
today.*

pleat (plēt) **1** a fold, ornamental
or to improve fit, in cloth, paper,
or the like. **2** to fold in pleats.

pled (plēd) See **plead.** *He pled
to make the trip with his father.*   Pleat

pledge (plej) **1** promise or agreement (to
do or not do something): *All the club*

fāte, făt, fâre, fär; bē, bĕt; bīte, bĭt; nō, nŏt, nôr; fūse, fŭn, fûr; tōō, tŏŏk; foil; foul; thin; ~~then~~;
hw for wh as in *what*; zh for s as in u*s*ual; ə for a, e, i, o, u, as in *a*go, lin*e*n, per*i*l, at*o*m, min*u*s

541

members signed a pledge *to keep their meetings secret.* **2** to promise (something) faithfully: *to* pledge *allegiance to the flag.* **3** something given or held as security or as a guarantee: *I'm holding his car as a* pledge *for the loan.* **4** to give as a security or guarantee. **5** a toast; a drink to the health of: *Let's have a* pledge *to the Queen.* **6** to drink to the health of; to toast. **7** sign of good will, friendship, love, etc.: *a* pledge *of friendship.* **pledged, pledg·ing.**

plen·te·ous (plĕn′tĭ əs) plentiful; abundant. **plen·te·ous·ly.**

plen·ti·ful (plĕn′tĭ fəl) abundant; fruitful: *a* plentiful *harvest.* **plen·ti·ful·ly.**

plen·ty (plĕn′tĭ) full supply; abundance. **plen·ties.**

pli·a·ble (plī′ə bəl) **1** easily bent; flexible: *a thin* pliable *wire.* **2** easily influenced; yielding: *He is so* pliable *he changes his mind whenever someone disagrees with him.* **pli·a·bly.**

pli·ant (plī′ənt) **1** easily bent; pliable. **2** easily influenced. **pli·ant·ly.**

plied (plīd) See ¹**ply.**

pli·ers (plī′ərz) tool of many shapes, with jaws hinged like scissors, for holding, bending, twisting, or pulling.

plies (plīz) **1** See ¹**ply.** *He* plies *his friends with favors.* **2** See ²**ply.** *a tire with three* plies *of rubber.*

Pliers

¹**plight** (plīt) state or condition, usually unfortunate or dangerous: *The knight heard of the maiden's* plight, *and rescued her from the dragon.* [¹**plight** is a form of an earlier English word (plit) meaning "a state," "a fold." It is related to **pleat.**]

²**plight** (plīt) to pledge or promise: *The young couple* plighted *their love for each other.* [²**plight** is a form of an Old English word (pliht) meaning "danger," "risk."]

plod (plŏd) **1** to walk slowly, heavily, and with effort: *The old horse* plodded *along pulling the heavy wagon.* **2** to work slowly, steadily, and with effort: *Ted* plodded *away at his school work until he was first in his class.* **plod·ded, plod·ding.**

plot (plŏt) **1** secret plan or scheme; conspiracy: *The rebels formed a* plot *against the government.* **2** to form a secret plan or

conspiracy: *The pirates* plotted *to rob the treasure ship.* **3** small area of ground: *The children planted a vegetable* plot *in the backyard.* **4** main story or plan of a play or novel: *The* plot *of "Swiss Family Robinson" is about a shipwrecked family.* **5** to mark or locate on a map or chart: *The navigator* plotted *the ship's course on the chart.* **plot·ted, plot·ting.**

plough (plou) plow.

plov·er (plŭv′ər or plō′vər) small shore bird with a short bill and tail, long legs, and pointed wings.

Plover (killdeer), about 10 in. long

plow (plou) **1** farm tool, either horse- or tractor-drawn, for turning up or breaking the ground. **2** device for clearing away snow. **3** to use a plow. **4** to advance through, or as through, obstructions: *The ship* plowed *through the rough sea. We* plowed *through our work.* Also spelled **plough.**

Plow

plow·man (plou′mən) **1** person who plows. **2** farmer. **plow·men.**

plow·share (plou′shâr′) sharp blade of a plow, which cuts the ground.

pluck (plŭk) **1** to pull off, up, or out; snatch: *to* pluck *weeds; to* pluck *a child from a fire.* **2** to pick or gather: *to* pluck *flowers.* **3** courage; bravery: *That boy showed* pluck *when he faced the angry crowd.* **4** to strip of feathers: *to* pluck *a chicken.*

pluck up (**courage**) to gather or gain courage: *At the tiger's growl, he* plucked up courage *and fired his gun.*

pluck·y (plŭk′ĭ) brave; courageous: *That* plucky *dog will face a wildcat.* **pluck·i·er, pluck·i·est; pluck·i·ly.**

plug (plŭg) **1** piece of wood, wad of paper, or other material used to fill a hole or crack, or stop a leak: *Ed filled the hole in the window with a* plug *of cloth.* **2** rubber or metal stopper for a sink or bathtub drain. **3** two-pronged or threaded electric connection for toasters, radios, and the like.

WASH BASIN
CASK
ELECTRIC
Plugs

4 piece of pressed tobacco. **5** small pointed piece cut from a melon to test its ripeness. **6** to cut a piece from, leaving a small hole: *You'd better plug that watermelon before you buy it.* **7** fire hydrant. **8** to fill with or insert a plug. **9** to make an electric connection: *Please plug in the toaster.* **10** to work steadily: *Rose plugged away at her spelling lesson.* **plugged, plug·ging.**

plum (plŭm) **1** small, soft, juicy fruit, often red or purple in color. **2** tree bearing this fruit. **3** something choice or desirable, especially a job: *Among the jobs available she got the plum.*

plum·age (ploo'mĭj) feathers of a bird: *The beautiful plumage of a peacock.*

plumb·er (plŭm'ər) workman who supplies, installs, or repairs bathroom fixtures, water and gas pipes, etc.

plumb·ing (plŭm'ĭng) **1** occupation of putting in or repairing pipes, drains, etc. **2** pipes, drains, and the like.

plume (ploom) **1** fluffy, curly feather or tuft of feathers. **2** fluffy decoration, like a tuft of ostrich feathers: *The horses had plumes in their bridles.* **3** to smooth with the beak: *The canary plumed its feathers.* **4** to show pride in: *Marie plumes herself on her singing.* **plumed, plum·ing.**

Plume

plum·met (plŭm'ĭt) **1** lead weight attached to the end of a line for measuring depths or for determining whether something is exactly vertical. **2** to fall or plunge straight downward.

¹plump (plŭmp) well rounded; well filled out: *She selected a plump chicken.* **plump·ly.** [**¹plump** is a word of uncertain origin.]

²plump (plŭmp) **1** to fall, sit, or drop heavily or suddenly: *She plumped the bundles on the table and plumped into a chair.* **2** heavily or suddenly: *The cow fell off the bridge plump into the water.* [**²plump** is from an earlier English word (plumpen) that is thought by some to be an imitation of a sound.]

plun·der (plŭn'dər) **1** to loot, rob, or pillage: *Indians plundered the wagon train.*

2 that which is robbed or stolen; loot: *The retreating army left its plunder behind.*

plunge (plŭnj) **1** to leap (into); throw oneself (into): *The swimmer plunged into the pool.* **2** to sink: *He has no money, and is plunged into debt. John was plunged deep in despair.* **3** a thrust or dive: *George took a plunge into the cool water.* **plunged, plung·ing.**

plu·ral (ploor'əl) **1** indicating more than one. **2** form of a word showing that more than one is meant. The plural of "cat" is "cats," of "child" is "children."

plu·ral·i·ty (ploo răl'ə tĭ) **1** large number of votes, though not necessarily a majority. **2** difference between the largest number of votes and those received by the candidate with the next to the largest. **plu·ral·i·ties.**

plus (plŭs) **1** extra; more: *An A plus is the highest mark at many schools.* **2** added to, or combined with; opposite of minus: *Good planning plus hard work make for success.*

plush (plŭsh) soft, heavy cloth, like velvet, but with a deeper and softer pile.

Plu·to (ploo'tō) **1** the outermost planet in the solar system, ninth in order of distance from the sun. **2** the Greek god of the underworld.

plu·to·ni·um (ploo tō'nĭ əm) radioactive metal element, made from uranium and used in atomic reactors and bombs.

¹ply (plī) **1** to keep supplying (someone with something) in a pressing way: *to ply with food; to ply with questions.* **2** to work with; use: *He plied his oars while she watched.* **3** to go back and forth according to a timetable: *This boat plies between Philadelphia and Wilmington.* **plies, plied, ply·ing.** [**¹ply** is a short form of **apply.**]

²ply (plī) **1** thickness or layer: *Two plies of cloth go into this collar. That collar is triple ply for strength.* **2** strand in a cord, rope, etc. **plies.** [**²ply** is from a French word (pli) that comes from a Latin word (plicare) meaning "to fold," "twist."]

ply·wood (plī'wood') thin layers of wood, glued and pressed together.

P.M. or **p.m.** between noon and midnight; after twelve noon.

---

fāte, făt, fâre, fär; bē, bĕt; bīte, bĭt; nō, nŏt, nôr; fūse, fŭn, fûr; tōō, tŏŏk; foil; foul; thin; ~~then~~; hw for wh as in *wh*at; zh for s as in u*s*ual; ə for a, e, i, o, u, as in *a*go, lin*e*n, per*i*l, at*o*m, min*u*s

pneumatic

pneu·mat·ic (nōō măt′ĭk or nū măt′ĭk) **1** having to do with air: *under pneumatic pressure.* **2** operated by air pressure: *a pneumatic drill.* **3** containing air: *a pneumatic cushion.*

pneu·mo·ni·a (nōō mōn′yə or nū mōn′yə) inflammation of the lungs. Some forms are contagious.

¹poach (pōch) to cook (an egg) by breaking (it) into boiling water. [**¹poach** is from an Old French word (pochier) meaning "to cook eggs in their pouch or pocket," the yolk having been conceived as being in a pocket.]

²poach (pōch) to hunt or fish illegally. [**²poach** comes through Old French (pochier) meaning "thrust one's finger into" from a Germanic word (poken) meaning "to poke."]

pock·et (pŏk′ĭt) **1** small bag sewn in a article of clothing to hold things. **2** to put in a pocket; wallet, etc.: *The customer pocketed his change.* **3** small: *a pocket edition of a book.* **4** in airplane travel, an area where a change in the density of air causes the plane to drop. **5** to suppress; hide: *The boy pocketed his pride and agreed to take his little sister with him.*

pock·et·book (pŏk′ĭt bŏŏk′) bag or case used to carry papers, money, etc.; purse.

pock·et·knife (pŏk′ĭt nĭf′) small knife with blades that fold into the handle. **pock·et·knives.**

pod (pŏd) the seed container of certain plants such as the pea and bean. For picture, see also **milkweed.**

po·em (pō′ĭm) composition in rhythmical language, often with rhyme.

Seedpod of violet

po·et (pō′ĭt) person who writes poetry.

po·et·ic (pō ĕt′ĭk) **1** having to do with poetry or a poet: *the poetic works of Shakespeare.* **2** having qualities fit for poetry or a poet: *a poetic landscape; a poetic story; a poetic appearance.* **3** imaginative; fanciful: *Jack Frost is a poetic image of winter or frost.*

po·et·i·cal (pō ĕt′ĭk əl) poetic. **po·et·i·cal·ly.**

po·et·ry (pō′ĭt rĭ) **1** act of composing poems: *He writes good prose but has no talent for poetry.* **2** poems: *a book of*

pointer

poetry. **3** something which has the nature of poetry: *the poetry of a mountain sunset.*

poin·set·ti·a (poin sĕt′ĭ ə) plant whose tiny flowers are surrounded by bright red leaves which look like petals.

point (point) **1** sharp or narrowed end of a thing; tip: *the point of a pin; a pencil point; a point of land.* **2** to sharpen: *to point a pencil; to point an argument with facts.* **3** to call attention to by extending the finger; show; indicate: *to point the way.* **4** to direct; aim: *The hunter pointed his rifle at the moose.* **5** to face: *The weather vane pointed north.* **6** to give force to; show the purpose of; illustrate: *All the teacher's stories point a moral.* **7** main or important part: *Keep to the point when you answer.* **8** detail: *The speaker carefully listed each point of his plan.* **9** feature; trait: *Everyone has both good and bad points.* **10** certain degree or stage: *The temperature dropped to the freezing point. He reached the point when he could no longer control his anger.* **11** certain position: *a point on the map; the point where two lines cross.* **12** written or printed dot: *a decimal point; an exclamation point.* **13** one of the 32 directions on the compass: *Northwest is a point of the compass.* **14** of hunting dogs, to point out where game is by facing in its direction. **15** unit of scoring or measuring: *Our team leads by two points.* **16 on the point of** ready to; just about to. **17 make a point of** to insist upon.

point off to separate with a decimal point.

point out to show; direct attention to: *The teacher pointed out our mistakes.*

point·ed (poin′tĭd) **1** having a sharp end. **2** direct; striking: *Joyce made a pointed remark about my bad grades.* **point·ed·ly.**

point·er (poin′tər) **1** thing that points to or toward something. **2** slender stick used to point with: *The teacher touched each word on the blackboard with her* point-er. **3** short-haired hunting dog trained to stand and point with its nose toward game.

Pointer, about 4 ft. long

poise (poiz) **1** manner of carrying the head and body; carriage: *the fine* poise *of a ballet dancer.* **2** self-possession: *Anyone who speaks in public must have* poise. **3** to balance: *The diver* poised *on the edge of the diving board.* **4** balance: *the* poise *of a tightrope walker.* **poised, pois·ing.**

poi·son (poi′zən) **1** substance that can injure or kill when it is taken in or absorbed by a living thing. **2** to injure or kill with such a substance. **3** to put a deadly substance into something: *to* poison *the king's food.* **4** to corrupt; ruin: *Envy* poisoned *their friendship.* **5** anything that can corrupt or injure a person's character: *the* poison *of envy.*

poison ivy plant or vine with three-part leaves which are often glossy. Touching any part of the plant usually causes a painful, spreading rash.

Poison ivy

poi·son·ous (poi′zən əs) **1** having properties that may injure or kill; venomous: *a* poisonous *snake.* **2** like a poison; harmful: *a* poisonous *rumor.* **poi·son·ous·ly.**

poke (pōk) **1** to push; prod: *to* poke *a fire.* **2** to thrust: *The little girl* poked *her head out the window.* **3** a thrust or push: *He gave me a* poke *with his elbow.* **4** to move lazily or slowly. **poked, pok·ing.**

¹pok·er (pō′kər) metal rod used to stir a fire. [**¹poker** is formed from **poke.**]

²pok·er (pō′kər) a kind of card game. [**²poker** is a word of unknown origin.]

pok·y or **pok·ey** (pō′kĭ) **1** slow; dull. **2** small; cramped in space: *a* poky *room.* **pok·i·er, pok·i·est.**

Po·land (pō′lənd) a country in north central Europe.

po·lar (pō′lər) of or near the earth's North or South Pole: *a* polar *exploration;* polar *ice.*

Polar bear, about 9½ ft. long

polar bear large white bear found in the far north.

Po·lar·is (pō lăr′ĭs) the North Star.

pol·der (pōl′dər) land that has been reclaimed from the sea or other body of water by means of dikes.

¹pole (pōl) **1** long, slender rod or piece of solid material: *a flag* pole; *fishing* pole. **2** to push or move with a pole: *to* pole *a boat upstream.* **poled, pol·ing.** [**¹pole** is a form of an Old English word (pāl) which comes from a Latin word (palus) meaning "stake." This word is related to **²pale.**] (Homonym: poll)

²pole (pōl) **1** point marking either of the two ends of the axis of a round body such as the earth. The earth's poles are called the North Pole and the South Pole. **2** either of the terminals of an electric battery or a magnet. [**²pole** is the unchanged form of an Old French word which comes from a Latin word (polus).] (Homonym: poll)

pole·cat (pōl′kăt′) **1** small European animal of the weasel family. **2** name for the North American skunk.

pole·star (pōl′stär′) the North Star. It is located almost directly above the North Pole, and has been widely used to determine direction.

po·lice (pə lēs′) **1** a department of government set up to keep order, enforce law, and deal with criminals. **2** the persons in such a force. **3** to patrol and keep order by means of police. **4** to keep neat, as a camp. **5** of or having to do with police: *a* police *escort; a* police *record.* **po·liced, po·lic·ing.**

police dog large, intelligent dog that looks like a wolf. Police dogs are trained to help the police and to guide the blind.

po·lice·man (pə lēs′mən) member of a police force. **po·lice·men.**

pol·i·cy (pŏl′ə sĭ) **1** way or principle of doing things: *The new librarian has changed the library* policy. **2** written contract between an insurance company and the person or persons insured. **pol·i·cies.**

po·li·o (pō′lĭ ō′) poliomyelitis.

po·li·o·my·e·li·tis (pō′lĭ ō mi′ə li′tĭs) contagious disease of the nervous system, sometimes causing paralysis; infantile paralysis; polio. The disease may attack at

fāte, făt, fâre, fär; bē, bĕt; bite, bĭt; nō, nŏt, nôr; fūse, fŭn, fûr; tōō, tŏŏk; foil; foul; thin; then; hw for wh as in what; zh for s as in usual; ə for a, e, i, o, u, as in ago, linen, peril, atom, minus

545

any age but is especially dangerous to children.

pol·ish (pŏl'ish) **1** paste, liquid, or preparation used to make something clean and shiny: *shoe* polish; *silver* polish. **2** to clean and shine by rubbing. **3** to become clean and bright: *This old metal is rusted and won't polish.* **4** smooth, glossy finish: *This table has a fine polish.* **5** refinement or culture: *He has acquired polish by years of study and travel.*

po·lite (pə līt') **1** having good manners; courteous: *a* polite *answer.* **2** refined; well-bred: *in* polite *society.* **po·lit·er, po·lit·est; po·lite·ly.**

po·lite·ness (pə līt'nĭs) courtesy; polite behavior.

pol·i·tic (pŏl'ə tĭk) prudent; shrewd: *The speaker soothed the angry audience by his politic answers.*

po·lit·i·cal (pə lĭt'ə kəl) of or having to do with government, the state, or politics: *The presidency is the highest political office in the United States.* **po·lit·i·cal·ly.**

pol·i·ti·cian (pŏl'ə tĭsh'ən) person who is active in politics, particularly in party politics.

pol·i·tics (pŏl'ə tĭks) **1** the science dealing with forms of government: *As a diplomat he had a wide knowledge of politics.* **2** political plans, ideas, and affairs: *He is active in local politics and is running for mayor.*

pol·ka (pōl'kə) **1** lively dance that originated in central Europe. **2** to dance the polka.

poll (pōl) **1** the voting and recording of votes in an election or survey: *The poll goes on all day Tuesday.* **2** total number of votes cast: *a large poll.* **3** the result of an election or survey: *The poll was 88 for Blake and 64 for Adams.* **4** to receive a certain number of votes: *He polled over 8,000 votes.* **5** a sampling and study of public opinion: *This magazine has the results of a poll on foreign aid.* **6** to take votes or opinions: *to poll the town on the building project; to poll housewives on their favorite brands.* **7 polls** place to vote: *to go to the polls on election day.* (Homonym: pole)

pol·len (pŏl'ən) grains which are the male cells produced by a flower to fertilize egg cells of the same or other flowers.

pol·li·na·tion (pŏl'ə nā'shən) the transferring of pollen for fertilizing a flower. Bees are the chief agents of pollination.

pol·li·wog (pŏl'ī wŏg') tadpole.

poll tax tax of so much per head. In some States it is paid by every person who wishes to vote.

pol·lute (pə lōōt' or pə lūt') **1** to make unclean or impure: *The stream was so polluted with garbage that the fish died.* **2** to destroy the purity of (the minds, morals, etc.): *Horror magazines should not be allowed to pollute the minds of children.* **pol·lut·ed, pol·lut·ing.**

pol·lu·tion (pə lōō'shən or pə lū'shən) a making or being unclean or impure; a contaminating: *the pollution of a stream by garbage.*

po·lo (pō'lō) game played on horseback with a wooden ball and long mallets.

pol·y·gon (pŏl'ī gŏn') a plane figure which has three or more sides.

pol·yp (pŏl'ĭp) small water animal without a backbone, and shaped like a flower. Most polyps build skeletons of lime around themselves: *the coral polyp.* For picture, see **coral.**

pome·gran·ate (pŏm'grăn'ĭt) **1** fruit with a thick red skin and a reddish pulp. It contains many seeds and has a pleasant sweet-sour taste. **2** the tree that bears this fruit.

pom·mel (pŭm'əl or pŏm'əl) **1** the raised front of a saddle. **2** knob on the handle of a sword. **3** to beat, especially with the fists.

pomp (pŏmp) solemn or showy display: *the pomp of a military parade.*

pom·pon (pŏm'pŏn) **1** ornamental ball-shaped tuft of fibers, feathers, or the like. **2** a kind of chrysanthemum.

pom·pous (pŏm'pəs) displaying pomp; self-important in a solemn manner; pretentious: *The governor listed all his accomplishments in a long and pompous speech.* **pom·pous·ly.**

pon·cho (pŏn'chō) blanket with a hole for the head, used as a coat. **pon·chos.**

pond (pŏnd) small lake; still, quiet pool of water.

pon·der (pŏn'dər) to think about; think over: *He pondered the advantages of joining our club.*

pon·der·ous (pŏn′dər əs) **1** heavy; weighty and massive: *The ponderous elephants moved nimbly from side to side.* **2** slow, clumsy, or labored: *a ponderous way of thinking.* **pon·der·ous·ly.**

pon·iard (pŏn′yərd) dagger or knife.

pon·toon (pŏn tōōn′) **1** flat-bottomed boat used in building a floating bridge. **2** one of a pair of pointed, air-filled cylinders attached to some airplanes to permit them to alight on water.

po·ny (pō′nĭ) **1** any one of a group of small or dwarf horses, such as a Shetland pony. **2** young horse; colt. **po·nies.**

Pontoons

pony express in the pioneer West, a type of postal service by relays of horseback riders.

poo·dle (pōō′dəl) pet dog, noted for intelligence, having thick, curly hair often trimmed in an elaborate manner.

¹pool (pōōl) **1** small body of still water, such as a pond or a wide place in a stream. **2** large outdoor or indoor tank for swimming. **3** puddle of any spilled liquid. [**¹pool** is a form of an Old English word (pōl).]

²pool (pōōl) **1** table game played with sticks called cues and many balls that are to be driven into pockets; pocket billiards. **2** to put to common use; share in common: *If they would* pool *their money, they could buy a boat.* [**²pool** is from a French word (poule) meaning "hen." This French word once had a slang meaning of "booty," "stakes in a game."]

poor (pōōr or pôr) **1** having little or no money: *He's been very* poor *since his business failed.* **2** not good: *Joe is a* poor *speller.* **3** people who are without money or resources: *The poor should be helped in every way possible.* **4** shiftless: *He tells lies because he's a* poor *worthless creature.* **5** badly made: *This is* poor *cloth.* **6** pathetic; needing sympathy: *The poor child mourns her lost pet.* (Homonyms: pour, pore)

poor·house (pōōr′hous′) a building where poor people are fed and housed at public expense.

poor·ly (pōōr′lĭ) **1** badly; in a clumsy manner: *She dislikes water and swims poorly.* **2** sickly: *Jane felt poorly in bad weather.*

pop (pŏp) **1** short, sharp noise: *His toy gun went off with a pop.* **2** to make any noise like a crack or pop: *A balloon pops when it bursts.* **3** to thrust, appear, or leave suddenly: *The rabbit popped out of his hole.* **4** any kind of sweet drink made with soda water. **popped, pop·ping.**

pop·corn (pŏp′kôrn′) a kind of corn which explodes into fluffy white masses when heated.

Pope or **pope** (pōp) bishop of Rome and the head of the Roman Catholic Church.

pop·lar (pŏp′lər) **1** any of a group of fast-growing trees of the willow family, which includes the aspens and cottonwood. **2** the soft wood of these trees.

Poplar leaves and catkins

pop·lin (pŏp′lĭn) finely ribbed cotton, rayon, silk, or woolen cloth.

pop·py (pŏp′ĭ) **1** plant with deeply notched leaves, hairy stems, and large-petaled flowers. Some kinds of poppy are a source of opium. **2** the flower of this plant. **pop·pies.**

pop·u·lace (pŏp′yōō lĭs) the common people; the masses.

pop·u·lar (pŏp′yōō lər) **1** well liked generally or by a group: *a* popular *classmate; a* popular *television program.* **2** widespread; common; prevalent; general: *a* popular *myth; a* popular *remedy.* **3** of, for, or representing the people: *Democracy is* popular *government.* **4** suited to the average understanding and taste: *a* popular *explanation;* popular *music.* **5** within the means of average persons: *goods at* popular *prices.* **6** springing from or created by the common people: *Folktales are of* popular *origin.* **pop·u·lar·ly.**

Poppy

fāte, făt, fâre, fär; bē, bĕt; bīte, bĭt; nō, nŏt, nôr; fūse, fŭn, fûr; tōō, tŏŏk; foil; foul; thin; ~~then~~; hw for wh as in *wh*at; zh for s as in u*s*ual; ə for a, e, i, o, u, as in a*g*o, lin*e*n, per*i*l, at*o*m, min*u*s

pop·u·lar·i·ty (pŏp′yŏŏ lăr′ə tĭ) a being well liked by many people.

pop·u·late (pŏp′yŏŏ lāt′) 1 to fill or supply with people: *Rhode Island is thickly* populated. 2 to inhabit: *Bands of gypsies once* populated *this area*. **pop·u·lat·ed, pop·u·lat·ing.**

pop·u·la·tion (pŏp′yŏŏ lā′shən) 1 the total number of people living in a city, country, etc. 2 the people themselves or any one group of the people: *the adult* population; *the farm* population.

pop·u·lous (pŏp′yŏŏ ləs) having many people; thickly populated: *This once* populous *community is a ghost town.* **pop·u·lous·ly.**

por·ce·lain (pôr′sə lin) 1 fine, white, glazed earthenware so thin that light can be seen through it. 2 dishes or ornaments made from this; china.

porch (pôrch) roofed entrance to a building; veranda; portico.

por·cu·pine (pôr′kyŏŏ pin′) animal of the beaver family. Its back and tail are covered with stiff, dark hairs with white, barbed tips which cause a painful wound to an attacking person or animal.

Porcupine, about 30 in. long

¹pore (pôr) tiny hole or opening through which water or air can pass: *the* pores *in the skin; the* pores *in a leaf.* [¹**pore** is the unchanged form of a French word which comes from a Latin word (porus) meaning "opening." It is related to the Latin word (porta) for "portal."] (Homonyms: pour, poor)

²pore (pôr) to read or think (over): *to* pore *over books; to* pore *over a problem.* **pored, por·ing.** [²**pore** is a word of uncertain origin.] (Homonyms: pour, poor)

pork (pôrk) the flesh of pigs or hogs used for food.

po·rous (pôr′əs) full of tiny holes, allowing liquids to pass through or soak in: *A sponge is* porous.

Porpoise, 4 to 6 ft. long

por·poise (pôr′pəs) sea animal of several kinds related to the whale. Porpoises gather in groups called schools.

por·ridge (pôr′ĭj or pŏr′ĭj) food made by boiling a cereal or vegetable in water or milk until it thickens: *oatmeal* porridge.

por·ring·er (pôr′ĭn jər or pŏr′ĭn jər) small shallow bowl for cereal or other food.

¹port (pôrt) 1 place where large ships come to load and unload; harbor. 2 town or city with a harbor. [¹**port** is the unchanged form of an Old English word that comes from a Latin word (portus) meaning "a haven."]

²port (pôrt) 1 round window or opening in the side of a ship; porthole. 2 an opening in a machine for letting in or out steam, water, etc. [²**port** comes through French from a Latin word (porta) meaning "door."]

³port (pôrt) 1 the left side of a ship when facing the bow. For picture, see **aft.** 2 on the left side of a ship: *a* port *cabin.* 3 to turn to the left side of a ship: *to* port *the helm.* [³**port** is a word of unknown origin.]

⁴port (pôrt) sweet, dark-red wine, originally from Portugal. [⁴**port** comes from the name of a Portuguese city, Oporto.]

port·a·ble (pôr′tə bəl) capable of being carried or moved: *a* portable *typewriter.*

por·tage (pôr′tĭj) 1 the carrying of boats and goods overland from one river or lake to another. 2 the route taken. 3 to carry (boats and goods) overland from one river or lake to another: *to* portage *a canoe.* **por·taged, por·tag·ing.**

por·tal (pôr′təl) gate; door; entrance: *The peasants awaited the arrival of their lord at the* portal *of the castle.*

port·cul·lis (pôrt kŭl′ĭs) heavy grating that can be lowered to close the entrance of a castle or fort.

Portcullis

por·tend (pôr tĕnd′) to give warning or sign of; foreshadow: *Ancient sailors believed that a certain bird following their ship would* portend *danger.*

por·tent (pôr′tĕnt) something that foretells or hints at a coming event; a warning, especially of trouble; omen of disaster: *Some people believe that breaking a mirror is a* portent *of seven years of bad luck.*

¹por·ter (pôr′tər) 1 person employed to carry baggage at a railroad station or hotel.

2 attendant in the parlor car or sleeping car of a train. [¹**porter** comes through Old French (porteous) from a Latin word (portare) meaning "to carry."]

²**por·ter** (pôr′tər) doorkeeper. [²**porter** comes through Old French (portier) from a Latin word (porta) meaning "gate," "door."]

port·hole (pôrt′hōl′) **1** opening or window, usually round, in a ship. **2** hole, as in a fort, through which to shoot.

por·ti·co (pôr′tə kō′) entrance porch having its roof supported by columns. **por·ti·coes** or **por·ti·cos.**

Portico

por·tion (pôr′shən) **1** piece or part (of something): *A portion of the money raised will go to the school library.* **2** to divide into shares: *Mary portioned the candy evenly among us.* **3** a serving of food; a helping. **4** share or part, especially of property, left an heir: *a widow's portion.*

port·ly (pôrt′lĭ) **1** fat; stout: *A portly passenger took up most of the seat on the bus.* **2** stately; dignified: *The portly old gentleman bowed graciously to each of the women.* **port·li·er, port·li·est.**

por·trait (pôr′trāt) **1** picture of a person. **2** picture in words: *The witness gave a clear portrait of the thief.*

por·tray (pôr trā′) **1** to make a picture, carving, etc., of: *The artist portrayed the sunny field in brilliant color.* **2** to describe: *The author portrayed the village as a delightful place.* **3** to play (a part) on the stage or screen.

Por·tu·gal (pôr′chə gəl) country on the western coast of the Spanish peninsula.

Por·tu·guese (pôr′chə gēz′) **1** of Portugal; its people, or language. **2** a citizen of Portugal; a person of Portuguese descent. **3** the language of the Portuguese people and of Brazil. pl. **Por·tu·guese.**

pose (pōz) **1** to take and hold a certain position of the body: *She posed for the photographer.* **2** to place in a certain posi-

tion: *The director posed all the characters around a fireplace for the scene.* **3** pretense; something done to impress or fool others: *His gaiety was a pose to hide his fear.* **4** to present; set forth: *An extra guest poses a problem because we haven't enough beds.*

pose as to pretend to be: *The poor man posed as a prince in the strange city.*

posed, pos·ing.

po·si·tion (pə zish′ən) **1** place where a thing or person stands or is: *I was in a good position to see the whole stage.* **2** correct or proper place: *The director told all the players to take their positions.* **3** posture: *It is very tiring to sit in an uncomfortable position.* **4** job; situation: *He has a good position at the bank.* **5** social standing or rank: *The Hardys occupy a high position in their community.* **6** way of looking at or thinking about (a subject): *What is your position on the question of a longer school year?*

pos·i·tive (pŏz′ə tĭv) **1** clearly stated; definite; leaving no doubt: *Father gave us positive directions to come home before dark.* **2** sure; certain; confident: *Are you positive that Fred will call?* **3** practical; constructive; not negative: *to give positive help; to make positive suggestions.* **4** photograph that shows light and dark in the same places as the object photographed. **5** showing agreement; affirmative: *a positive answer to our request.* **6** **positive charge** the condition of having more protons than electrons. **pos·i·tive·ly.**

pos·se (pŏs′ĭ) group of citizens authorized by a sheriff to assist in carrying out the law.

pos·sess (pə zĕs′) **1** to have; own: *King Midas possessed much gold.* **2** to occupy; control: *At one time the Spanish possessed Florida.* **3** to influence strongly: *I don't know what possesses the boy to act like that!*

pos·ses·sion (pə zĕsh′ən) **1** ownership: *The wily old pirate tried to get possession of the treasure map.* **2** something owned or possessed: *There were few possessions she prized as much as the old locket.* **3** control; occupancy: *The new cook came in and took full possession of our kitchen.*

fāte, făt, fâre, fär; bē, bĕt; bīte, bĭt; nō, nŏt, nôr; fūse, fŭn, fûr; tōō, tōŏk; foil; foul; thin; ~~then~~; hw for wh as in *wh*at; zh for s as in u*s*ual; ə for a, e, i, o, u, as in *a*go, linen, peril, atom, min*u*s

pos·ses·sive (pə zĕs′ĭv) **1** showing possession: *a possessive pronoun.* **2** a word that shows possession, as "his," "its," "ours," etc. **3** having a strong desire to own or keep: *Veronica's possessive habits kept her from sharing her toys.* **pos·ses·sive·ly.**

pos·ses·sor (pə zĕs′ər) person who owns or has something.

pos·si·bil·i·ty (pŏs′ə bĭl′ə tĭ) **1** chance; likelihood: *I don't think there is a possibility of his coming this late at night.* **2** something that might happen; possible result: *Ford could see great possibilities of profit in producing inexpensive automobiles.* **pos·si·bil·i·ties.**

pos·si·ble (pŏs′ə bəl) **1** capable of existing; capable of happening: *Specialized work is possible only if you have the right training. It is not possible to get to our cabin without a car.* **2** worth considering: *Your suggestion is a possible solution to our problem.*

pos·si·bly (pŏs′ə blĭ) **1** perhaps; maybe: *We may possibly move next April.* **2** by any means: *I cannot possibly finish this work without some help.*

pos·sum (pŏs′əm) opossum.

¹post (pōst) **1** upright piece of timber, metal, stone, etc., used as a marker or support for something: *a sign* post; *a lamp* post; *the starting* post. **2** to attach to a post or wall in public view: *The police posted a no-parking sign on our street.* **3** to publish by means of a sign or notice: *The honor roll will be posted today.* **4** to close (a place) to the public by means of signs or notices: *We were fined $25 for hunting on land that has been posted.* [**¹post** is the unchanged form of an Old English word that comes from a Latin word (postis) meaning "a prop."]

²post (pōst) **1** the mail or delivery of mail: *It came to me by* post. **2** to put (something) in the mail: *This letter was posted yesterday in Boston.* **3** in earlier times, one of a number of riders placed at regularly spaced stations along a road or route, each of whom carried mail to the next station or stage. **4** the place where horses were stabled for such riders. **5** to travel with speed: *to post through the countryside and warn of the enemy's advance.* **6 parcel post** the system of delivering packages by mail: *We sent your birthday present by*

parcel post. **7 keep posted** to keep fully informed: *Please keep me posted on your progress.* [**²post** is **³post** in a later meaning. The mail or post was once forwarded by riders "placed" at various points of a route.]

³post (pōst) **1** place where a person is stationed or assigned for duty: *A good soldier never deserts his* post. **2** to station or assign: *My cousin was posted to duty with the Air Force.* **3** military camp or station: *Most of the officers live off the* post. **4** position of trust: *His grandfather held a post in a large bank.* **5 trading post** store of settlement in undeveloped country where trading is done: *Many of the fur trappers were absent from the* trading post *for months at a time.* [**³post** comes through French from a form (positum) meaning "placed" of a Latin word (ponere) meaning "to place."]

post·age (pōs′tĭj) **1** the cost of sending something by mail: *The book costs $3.50 plus nine cents* postage. **2 postage stamp** an official mark or marked piece of paper attached to mail to show that postage has been paid.

post·al (pōs′təl) **1** relating to mail or the mail system: *The postal laws prohibit the mailing of firearms and explosives.* **2 postal card** card on which a government postage stamp is printed. **3** a post card.

post card mailing card, often with a picture on one side, to which a postage stamp must be attached; postal card.

post·er (pōs′tər) a placard, sign, etc., by which something is advertised or announced.

pos·ter·i·ty (pŏs tĕr′ə tĭ) **1** future generations: *If we act wisely,* posterity *will praise us.* **2** all the descendants of a person.

pos·tern (pŏs′tərn or pōs′tərn) back door or gate; entrance other than the main one: *The princess waited at the* postern *for the knight.*

post·man (pōst′mən) mailman; letter carrier. **post·men.**

post·mas·ter (pōst′măs′tər) **1** the director of the postal system of a city or town. **2 Postmaster General** the member of the President's cabinet who heads the United States Post Office Department.

post office 1 the government department responsible for the collection, sorting, and delivery of mail. **2** a local branch of this department.

post·paid (pōst′pād′) with postage prepaid: *a postpaid return envelope.*

post·pone (pōst pōn′) to delay; put off till a later time: *The school picnic has been postponed until next Friday.* **post·poned, post·pon·ing.**

post·script (pōst′skrĭpt′) **1** a message added to a letter after the signature: *Aunt Helen told me in a postscript that she's coming to visit next month.* **2** material added at the end of a book, article, etc.: *The author added a postscript telling why he wrote the book.*

pos·ture (pŏs′chər) **1** the way a person holds his body: *Be careful of your posture or you'll grow round-shouldered.* **2** a pose; position: *He tried to dance, but only leaped about in awkward postures.* **3** to take a position or pose: *He postured before the mirror rehearsing for the play.* **pos·tured, pos·tur·ing.**

po·sy (pō′zĭ) flower or bunch of flowers: *She wore a yellow posy on her hat.* **po·sies.**

pot (pŏt) **1** china or earthenware container: *a flower pot.* **2** metal or earthenware cooking vessel; kettle: *Betsy hung the stew pot over the fire and put the bean pot in the oven.* **3** the amount a pot will hold: *Belle made a pot of soup.* **4** to transplant into a pot: *Martha will pot the geraniums in the fall.* **5** to preserve meat in or as in a pot. **pot·ted, pot·ting.**

Flower pot

Coffee pot

pot·ash (pŏt′ăsh) chemical compound of potassium and oxygen, used in making soap, glass, fertilizers, etc. Its name came from the fact that it used to be obtained by soaking wood ashes in iron pots.

po·tas·si·um (pə tăs′ĭ əm) a soft, silver-white metal element. Its compounds are used in making explosives, soap, fertilizer, etc.

po·ta·to (pə tā′tō) **1** the rootlike bulb, or tuber, of a certain plant, widely used as a vegetable and to make flour and starch. **2** the plant that bears this bulb. **3** a sweet potato. **4** made of potatoes: *a sack of potato flour;* potato *cakes.* **po·ta·toes.**

potato chip thin slice of potato that has been fried crisp.

po·tent (pō′tənt) **1** strong; very effective: *This is a potent medicine and must be taken in small doses.* **2** having authority or power: *For centuries the emperor of China was the most potent ruler in Asia.*

po·ten·tate (pō′tən tāt′) powerful monarch or ruler.

po·ten·tial (pə tĕn′shəl) **1** capable of coming into existence or being developed; possible but not actual: *Our mineral deposits are a great source of potential wealth.* **2** qualities that can be developed; possibilities; capabilities: *A good student always tries to develop his potential.* **po·ten·tial·ly.**

Potato leaf, tuber, and flower

po·tion (pō′shən) a drink, especially one containing drugs or medicine: *When the prince swallowed the witch's potion he turned into a giant frog.*

pot·tage (pŏt′ĭj) thick soup or broth.

¹pot·ter (pŏt′ər) person who makes pots, dishes, etc., of clay. [¹**potter** is formed from the word **pot**.]

²pot·ter (pŏt′ər) to work lazily or without much purpose: *to potter around in the garden.* [²**potter** is formed from a dialect word (pote) meaning "to poke."]

pot·ter·y (pŏt′ə rĭ) **1** things made of baked clay, as pots, dishes, and ornaments. **2** place where such things are made. **3** the art of a potter. **pot·ter·ies.**

GREEK

INDIAN

CHINESE

Pottery

pouch (pouch) **1** bag or sack of any kind: *a mail pouch; a money pouch.* **2** any baglike part of certain animals: *The kangaroo carries its young in a pouch.*

---

fāte, făt, fâre, fär; bē, bĕt; bīte, bĭt; nō, nŏt, nôr; fūse, fŭn, fûr; tōō, tŏŏk; foil; foul; thin; ~~then~~;
hw for wh as in *wh*at; zh for s as in u*s*ual; ə for a, e, i, o, u, as in *a*go, lin*e*n, per*i*l, at*o*m, min*u*s

poul·try (pōl'trĭ) domestic fowls, such as chickens, turkeys, etc.

pounce (pouns) **1** to spring suddenly or unexpectedly: *The cat* pounced *on the rolling ball of yarn.* **2** sudden, swooping attack. **pounced, pounc·ing.**

¹pound (pound) **1** in ordinary weight, a measure equal to 16 ounces. **2** in troy weight, for weighing drugs and precious metals, a measure equal to 12 ounces. **3** the standard of money in Great Britain; 20 shillings. Also called the **pound sterling,** written £. [**¹pound** is a form of an Old English word (pund) that comes from a Latin word (pondo) meaning "by weight."]

²pound (pound) place where stray animals are kept: *a dog* pound. [**²pound** is a form of an Old English word (pund) meaning "an enclosure."]

³pound (pound) **1** to beat; strike (something) with force: *to* pound *a nail into the wall.* **2** heavy blow. **3** to crush into small pieces or powder: *to* pound *kernels of grain into meal.* **4** to deal blows; beat heavily or steadily: *Waves* pounded *against the seashore.* **5** to walk with heavy steps. [**³pound** is a form of an Old English word (pundian) meaning "to bruise."]

pour (pôr) **1** to cause to flow in a stream: *to* pour *milk from a pitcher.* **2** to stream: *Water* poured *from the broken pipe.* **3** to go in or out in large numbers: *The pupils* poured *out onto the playground.* **4** heavy rain; downpour.

    pour out to tell in detail freely: *The lost boy* poured out *his story to the policeman.* (Homonyms: pore, poor)

pout (pout) **1** to push out or pucker the lips in sullenness, displeasure, etc. **2** sullen or sulky expression made in such a way.

pov·er·ty (pŏv'ər tĭ) **1** state of being poor or needy. **2** lack of something needed or wanted; poorness: *None of the seeds grew because of the* poverty *of the soil.*

pow·der (pou'dər) **1** any dry material in fine particles; fine dust. **2** to make into powder: *Sugar is* powdered *by grinding and sifting.* **3** any substance made in powder form: *face* powder; *tooth* powder; *blasting* powder. **4** to cover or sprinkle with or as if with powder: *to* powder *toast with cinnamon.* **5** to use powder on the face.

powder horn cow's horn fashioned to carry gunpowder which was poured into old-fashioned guns from the small end.

pow·der·y (pou'də rĭ) **1** like powder; in the form of powder: *A* powdery *snow is good to ski on.* **2** covered or sprinkled with any kind of powder: *The bee's legs were* powdery *with pollen.*

Powder horn

pow·er (pou'ər) **1** strength; vigor: *The pitcher had plenty of* power *but little control. The* power *of his argument won many to his side.* **2** ability to act or do (something): *They did everything in their* power *to win the game.* **3** authority to do or have done: *the* powers *of Congress.* **4** control (of the government): *in* power; *out of* power. **5** an important or strong person, group, or nation: *At one time the Roman Empire was a world* power. **6** producing electricity, steam, etc., for useful purposes: *a* power *plant.* **7** run by engines or motors: *a* power *lawnmower.* **8** the magnifying capacity of a lens: *the* power *of a microscope.* **9** in physics, the rate of doing work (measured by the amount of work that can be done in a given time).

pow·er·ful (pou'ər fəl) having great power, strength, or influence: *a* powerful *ruler; a* powerful *engine; a* powerful *odor.* **pow·er·ful·ly.**

pow·er·house (pou'ər hous') place where electric power is generated.

pow·er·less (pou'ər lĭs) not having power or ability (to do something); weak; helpless: *The unarmed city was* powerless *in the face of the attack.* **pow·er·less·ly.**

pow·wow (pou'wou') **1** ceremonial feast or dance held by North American Indians to gain religious or magical aid for a hunt, war, etc. **2** any meeting or gathering in order to confer or discuss, especially a noisy one. **3** to hold a powwow.

pp. pages.

pr. pair.

prac·ti·ca·ble (prăk'tə kə bəl) capable of being done, practiced, or used: *a* practicable *plan.* **prac·ti·ca·bly.**

prac·ti·cal (prăk'tə kəl) **1** having to do with or gained through experience, action, or use: *The laboratory assistant had a* practical *knowledge of the apparatus.* **2** capable of being put to use; useful; sensible: *Mother thought of a practical arrangement for dividing the ice cream.* **3** preferring or tending to act or do things rather than to think or daydream about them: *Tom is the* practical *brother and Jerry is the one who has his head in the clouds.*

practical joke a trick played on someone in fun.

prac·ti·cal·ly (prăk′tĭk lĭ) **1** in a practical manner; through actual experience or practice: *Speaking* practically, *I think we'll need at least two days for our trip.* **2** in fact though not in name; virtually: *My grandfather founded our family business and still comes to the office, but my father is* practically *the head of the company now.* **3** almost: *He is* practically *impossible to please.*

prac·tice (prăk′tĭs) **1** to put into actual use: *Always* practice *what you preach.* **2** to do as a rule; do regularly: *He* practiced *charity toward all.* **3** to perform or do to get better (at something): *She* practiced *ceaselessly at swimming.* **4** to work at the profession of: *The old doctor no longer* practiced *medicine.* **5** training by doing: *Let's go to baseball* practice. *He was not in* practice *to play baseball.* **6** area where a profession is practiced or followed: *The doctor's* practice *lay in the northern part of town.* **7** custom; habit: *He has a bad* practice *of eating peas with a knife.* **8** act of doing what has been taught: *She finally mastered the* practice *of good spelling.* **prac·ticed, prac·tic·ing.**

prac·ticed or **prac·tised** (prăk′tĭst) highly experienced: *My opponent was a* practiced *master of the art of swordsmanship.*

prac·tise (prăk′tĭs) to practice. **prac·tised, prac·tis·ing.**

prai·rie (prâr′ĭ) level or rolling grassland without trees.

prairie dog burrowing animal like a small woodchuck, with a whistling bark. Prairie dogs live in large groups, or colonies.

Prairie dog, 15 to 17 in. long

prairie schooner large covered wagon in which pioneer families traveled to the West.

praise (prāz) **1** to speak or write favorably of: *Out of politeness I* praised *her singing.* **2** approval; applause: *She won great* praise *for her acting.* **3** to glorify and worship: *to sing,* "Praise *God from whom all blessings flow.*" **praised, prais·ing.**

Prairie schooner

praise·wor·thy (prāz′wûr′thĭ) deserving praise or approval: *Helping poor people is always* praiseworthy.

prance (prăns) **1** to advance with bounding leaps of the hind legs, as do spirited horses: *Three horses* pranced *around the circus ring.* **2** to caper or skip: *The little boy* pranced *about in his new clothes.* **3** to strut; swagger: *The band leader twirled her baton as she* pranced *at the head of her company.* **pranced, pranc·ing.**

prank (prăngk) piece of mischief; a trick: *Squirting water on me was a silly* prank.

prat·tle (prăt′əl) **1** childish talk; silly chatter; babble of small children: *We enjoyed hearing the* prattle *of the children on the beach.* **2** to talk like a child; to babble foolishly. **prat·tled, prat·tling.**

pray (prā) **1** to speak to God with love, thanks, appeal, etc.: *She* prays *every day for her son's safety.* **2** to request; beg; implore: *They* prayed *the king to free his prisoners.* **3** be good enough to; please: *If I am wrong,* pray *tell me.* (Homonym: prey)

pray·er (prâr) **1** a speaking to God with love, thanks, appeal, etc.: *a* prayer *for peace.* **2** an earnest request or appeal: *His entire speech was a* prayer *for justice.*

pre- prefix meaning "before": *a* prehistoric *animal; a* prepaid *package.*

preach (prēch) **1** to speak to a group about religion; give a sermon. **2** to urge publicly or persistently: *The mayor* preached *the need for new fire trucks.* **3** to bore with tedious advice: *It is hard to talk with him because he always* preaches.

fāte, făt, fâre, fär; bē, bĕt; bite, bĭt; nō, nŏt, nôr; fūse, fŭn, fûr; tōo, tŏŏk; foil; foul; thin; then; hw for wh as in *what*; zh for s as in usual; ə for a, e, i, o, u, as in *ago*, linen, peril, atom, minus

preach·er (prē'chər) **1** person who preaches. **2** in everyday speech, a clergyman.

pre·car·i·ous (prə kâr'i əs) uncertain; risky or perilous: *a precarious perch in a tree.* **pre·car·i·ous·ly.**

pre·cau·tion (pri kô'shən) care taken beforehand to prevent harm, loss, etc.: *to wrap up well as a* precaution *against cold; the* precautions *against fire.*

pre·cede (prē sēd') to go or happen before: *A lull generally* precedes *a storm. June* precedes *July.* **pre·ced·ed, pre·ced·ing.**

prec·e·dent (près'ə dənt) an act in the past used to justify one in the present: *There are several* precedents *for closing this meeting early.*

pre·ced·ing (prē sē'ding) going or happening before: *In the* preceding *chapter of the book, the reader met all the characters.*

pre·cept (prē'sĕpt) a rule of conduct; a guide or example: *The* precepts *of our forefathers tell us to guard our liberty.*

pre·cinct (prē'singkt) **1** area in a town or city marked off as a police or voting district: *Police from the 11th* precinct *chased the robbers.* **2** space enclosed by walls or boundaries, especially within a church: *The procession was held within the* precinct *of the cathedral.*

pre·cious (prĕsh'əs) **1** of great price; costly: *The crown was studded with* precious *stones.* **2** highly valued; much loved: *Human freedom is our most* precious *possession.* **pre·cious·ly.**

prec·i·pice (près'ə pis) steep face of a cliff: *The goat climbed down the* precipice.

¹pre·cip·i·tate (pri sip'ə tāt') **1** to bring about; hasten: *The employers' refusal to talk to the union* precipitated *the strike.* **2** to cast or hurl down from a height. **3** to condense from vapor into moisture and fall as rain, dew, sleet, etc. **4** to separate a solid from a liquid solution or suspension: *Silt is* precipitated *at the mouth of the Mississippi.* **pre·cip·i·tat·ed, pre·cip·i·tat·ing.**

²pre·cip·i·tate (pri sip'ə tit) **1** solid separated from a solution or suspension: *The crystals were a* precipitate *from the salt solution.* **2** headlong; hasty; rash: *After Helen upset the vase, she made a* precipitate *departure from the party.*

pre·cip·i·ta·tion (pri sip'ə tā'shən) **1** headlong rush, fall, or procedure: *At sight of the hunters, the birds flew away in great* precipitation. **2** rash haste: *She made the decision with* precipitation. **3** moisture, condensed from the air, that falls as rain, snow, or the like: *cold and cloudy with some* precipitation. **4** the measure of moisture that falls in a given time and place: *four inches of* precipitation. **5** process of causing solid matter to separate from a solution or suspension.

pre·cip·i·tous (pri sip'ə təs) **1** very steep: *The* precipitous *walls of the prison made escape impossible.* **2** rushing; very rapid: *the* precipitous *flow of water in a spring freshet.* **3** hasty; rash: *a* precipitous *action.* **pre·cip·i·tous·ly.**

pre·cise (pri sis') **1** exact; definite; accurate: *a* precise *explanation.* **2** overcareful; prim: *her* precise *manners.* **pre·cise·ly.**

pre·ci·sion (pri sizh'ən) exactness; accuracy: *The* precision *of a clock.*

pre·clude (pri klood') to make impossible; shut out: *Illness* precludes *my joining you at the dance.* **pre·clud·ed, pre·clud·ing.**

pre·co·cious (pri kō'shəs) showing skill or development unusual for his or her age: *My* precocious *little niece speaks German and French as well as English.* **pre·co·cious·ly.**

pred·a·tor·y (prĕd'ə tôr'i) living by plunder or by preying on others: *a* predatory *tribe;* predatory *animals.*

pred·e·ces·sor (prĕd'ə sĕs'ər) person or thing that comes before another: *My* predecessor *in this job left the records in a mess. The horse and buggy was the* predecessor *of the car.*

pre·dic·a·ment (pri dik'ə mənt) dangerous or unpleasant situation: *She was in a* predicament *when she lost her key because nobody was at home.*

pred·i·cate (prĕd'ə kit) the part of a sentence which tells something about the subject. "Is small" is the predicate of "Jack is small."

pre·dict (pri dikt') to foretell; to prophesy: *My almanac* predicts *a good harvest.*

pre·dic·tion (pri dik'shən) a foretelling; a prophecy.

pre·dom·i·nant (pri dŏm'ə nənt) greater in strength, power, number, etc.; prevailing: *a predominant influence; a predominant color*. **pre·dom·i·nant·ly**.

pre·dom·i·nate (pri dŏm'ə nāt') to be superior in numbers, power, influence, etc.: *Roses predominate in our garden*. **pre·dom·i·nat·ed, pre·dom·i·nat·ing**.

preen (prēn) 1 to clean and smooth (feathers) with the beak, as a bird does. 2 to dress or beautify (oneself) with care: *She spent hours preening for the dance*.

pre·fab·ri·cat·ed (prē fāb'rə kā'tĭd) manufactured in standardized parts that can be assembled quickly: *a prefabricated house*.

pref·ace (prĕf'ĭs) 1 introduction to a book, speech, etc. 2 to introduce (a book, speech, etc.) by some act or statement: *The teacher prefaced her lecture with a rap for silence*. **pref·aced, pref·ac·ing**.

pre·fer (pri fûr') 1 to like better: *to prefer tea to coffee*. 2 to present for consideration: *She preferred the charge against the thief*. **pre·ferred, pre·fer·ring**.

pref·er·a·ble (prĕf'ər ə bəl) more desirable: *I find summer preferable to winter*. **pref·er·a·bly**.

pref·er·ence (prĕf'ər əns) 1 the liking or favoring of one thing over another: *The employer's son was given preference*. 2 thing that is chosen or favored: *The purple dress is my preference*.

¹pre·fix (prē'fĭks) syllable or syllables placed at the beginning of a word or word root to qualify its meaning. "Un" is the prefix in the word "unknown."

²pre·fix (prē fĭks') to place before or at the beginning of: *He always prefixed "Baron" to his name*.

preg·nant (prĕg'nənt) 1 of a woman or a female animal, soon to become a mother. 2 full of significance or importance: *a pregnant statement*.

pre·his·tor·ic (prē'hĭs tôr'ĭk or prē'hĭs-tôr'ĭk) of or having to do with the period before written records: *Cave paintings have added to our knowledge of prehistoric man*.

prej·u·dice (prĕj'ə dĭs) 1 strong feeling for or against something, formed without any real knowledge or reason; bias: *It is foolish*

to have a prejudice *against ideas just because they are new*. 2 to influence or fill with a strong feeling for or against: *Some of the parents were prejudiced against the idea of building a new school until the principal explained its need*. 3 to injure or harm, especially in a law case: *The defendant's case was prejudiced by the new evidence*. **prej·u·diced, prej·u·dic·ing**.

prel·ate (prĕl'ĭt) priest or minister who is a high official of the church.

pre·lim·i·nar·y (pri lĭm'ə nĕr'ĭ) 1 coming before or preparing for the main thing: *the preliminary arrangements for a picnic*. 2 anything before or preparing for the main thing: *After the preliminaries of introductions, the men settled down to talk business*. **pre·lim·i·nar·ies; pre·lim·i·nar·i·ly**.

prel·ude (prĕl'ūd or prē'lūd) 1 something that goes before or introduces a more important thing: *The morning fog was a gloomy* prelude *to the rest of the day*. 2 an introductory part of a piece of music: *an organ prelude*.

pre·ma·ture (prē'mə chŏor' or prē'mə tūr' or prē'mə tŏor') happening or coming before the usual time; too early: *Alice's gray hair is premature*. **pre·ma·ture·ly**.

pre·med·i·tate (pri mĕd'ə tāt') to think over and plan beforehand: *to premeditate a crime*. **pre·med·i·tat·ed, pre·med·i·tat·ing**.

pre·mier (prē'mĭr) 1 principal; chief; first: *of premier importance*. 2 (also prĭ-mĭr') prime minister; chief minister of government.

pre·mi·um (prē'mĭ əm) 1 prize; reward: *The company offered a* premium *to the salesman with the highest sales for the month*. 2 sum or amount above the usual amount: *Fred had to pay a* premium *to get a seat for the hit play*. 3 payment made for an insurance policy.

pre·paid (prē pād') paid in advance.

prep·a·ra·tion (prĕp'ə rā'shən) 1 a making ready; preparing: *Joe spends an hour every day in* preparation *for the next day's classes*. 2 things or steps needed to get ready: *Ted took care of the tents, food, and all the other* preparations *for our camping trip*. 3 food,

---

fāte, făt, fâre, fär; bē, bĕt; bīte, bĭt; nō, nŏt, nôr; fūse, fŭn, fûr; tōō, tŏŏk; foil; foul; thin; ~~then~~;
hw for wh as in *wh*at; zh for s as in u*s*ual; ə for a, e, i, o, u, as in *a*go, lin*e*n, per*i*l, at*o*m, min*u*s

medicine, lotion, etc., made up for a special use: *Every spring Mother used to give the children a* preparation *of sulfur and molasses.*

pre·par·a·to·ry (pri pâr′ə tôr′ĭ) **1** serving to make ready for something: *A* preparatory *school fits a student for college.* **2 preparatory to** as a preparation for something: *The test pilot carefully checked his equipment* preparatory to *taking off.*

pre·pare (pri pâr′) **1** to make ready: *to* prepare *for bad news; to* prepare *for a trip.* **2** to make or put together out of ingredients: *to* prepare *a meal; to* prepare *medicine.* **pre·pared, pre·par·ing.**

prep·o·si·tion (prĕp′ə zĭsh′ən) word which shows a relation between a word naming a thing, place, or person, and another word. "To" in "go to the seashore," "of" in "the price of bread," and "about" in "reading about the Romans," are prepositions.

pre·pos·ter·ous (pri pŏs′tər əs) contrary to what is reasonable; very foolish or ridiculous: *People used to think it was a* preposterous *notion that man could reach the moon.* **pre·pos·ter·ous·ly.**

pre·scribe (pri skrib′) **1** to order as a remedy or cure: *The doctor* prescribed *plenty of fresh air and rest for the invalid.* **2** to order or direct officially: *The law* prescribes *the use of special forms for income tax returns.* **pre·scribed, pre·scrib·ing.**

pre·scrip·tion (pri skrip′shən) **1** doctor's written order for the making and use of a medicine. **2** the medicine ordered by a doctor.

pres·ence (prĕz′əns) **1** a being present (in a certain place): *The* presence *of the mayor at the ceremony added to its importance.* **2** company; nearness (of another person or thing): *He swore an oath in the* presence *of witnesses.* **3** appearance or behavior; bearing: *The young prince had a noble* presence. **4 presence of mind** ability to think and act quickly and calmly: *The students kept their* presence of mind *when the fire alarm sounded.*

¹pre·sent (pri zĕnt′) **1** to introduce: *The teacher* presented *the visitor to the class.* **2** to put before the public; show; exhibit: *This theater is* presenting *a new French star. In spite of her troubles, Helen managed to* present *a gay appearance at the party.* **3** to give as a gift. **4** (prĕz′ənt) a gift. **5** to offer

for consideration: *Taking a trip always* presents *the problem of what to do with the pets.* **6** to put (oneself) in another's presence: *He* presented *himself at the principal's office.* **7** to deliver; submit: *The grocer* presented *his monthly bill.* [¹present comes through French from a Latin word (praesentare) meaning "to place before."]

²pres·ent (prĕz′ənt) **1** existing or happening now: *Crowded schools are a* present *problem.* **2** the time now: *At* present *there is a great deal of interest in space travel.* **3** being on hand; not absent: *For the first time this year the whole class is* present. *You are always* present *in my thoughts.* [²present comes through French from a form of a Latin word (praesens) meaning "being in front of or at hand."]

pre·sent·a·ble (pri zĕn′tə bəl) **1** suitable to be presented or offered: *Your homework is not* presentable *until you have corrected it.* **2** fit to appear in public or company: *Until you have your hair cut you are not* presentable. **pre·sent·a·bly.**

pres·en·ta·tion (prĕz′ən tā′shən or prē′zĕn tā′shən) **1** a giving: *The* presentation *of the prizes will be at two o'clock.* **2** the showing or presenting before the public: *We held many rehearsals before the* presentation *of our school play.* **3** formal introduction: *a* presentation *to the queen.*

pres·ent·ly (prĕz′ənt lĭ) **1** soon; in a little while: *He will be home* presently. **2** at the present time; now: *He is* presently *staying with friends.*

pres·er·va·tion (prĕz′ər vā′shən) **1** a keeping from decay or injury: *The* preservation *of life is the doctor's aim.* **2** freedom from decay or injury; soundness: *The castle is in a good state of* preservation.

pre·serve (pri zûrv′) **1** to keep from injury or harm; save: *Careful driving helps to* preserve *lives.* **2** to maintain; keep from ruin: *The city took steps to* preserve *the bridge.* **3** to keep (food) for future use by canning, pickling, and the like. **4** fruit preserved with sugar: *Jerry likes strawberry* preserves *on toast.* **5** place where fish or animals are protected. **pre·served, pre·serv·ing.**

pre·serv·er (pri zûr′vər) person or thing that saves, protects, or defends.

pre·side (pri zīd′) **1** to act as chairman at a meeting. **2** to have direction or control:

Robin Hood presided *over his band of merry men.* **pre·sid·ed, pre·sid·ing.**

pres·i·den·cy (prĕz′ə dən sĭ) **1** office of president. **2** length of time a president holds office: *Eisenhower's presidency lasted eight years.* **pres·i·den·cies.**

pres·i·dent (prĕz′ə dənt) **1** the highest officer of a company, bank, college, club, etc. **2 President** the highest executive officer of a modern republic.

pres·i·den·tial (prĕz′ə dĕn′shəl) having to do with a president or his work.

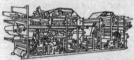

Printing press and fruit press

press (prĕs) **1** to thrust; push against: *to press a button.* **2** to squeeze together; crush: *The meat packer pressed the ham into tin cans.* **3** to smooth; iron: *to press a shirt.* **4** a pressing or pushing: *the press of the crowd.* **5** machine made to squeeze, force together, stamp, or crush something: *a cider press; a printing press.* **6** to clasp; grip: *Bob pressed his friend's hand.* **7** to bear down on: *to press the pedal of a car brake.* **8** to weigh heavily: *Worries pressed on his mind.* **9** pressure; urgency: *The press of work kept Father late at the office.* **10** to insist upon; urge in a forceful way: *The quarrelsome boy pressed an argument.* **11** to force or thrust upon: *He presses unwelcome gifts on me.* **12** to push forward: *The boy pressed through the line of guards to get a look at the celebrity.* **13** newspapers and magazines and those who work for them: *The press has great political influence.* **14 be pressed for** to have barely enough: *to be pressed for time or money.*

press on or **forward** to continue; keep going: *The tired hikers did not stop to rest but pressed on in order to reach the town before dark.*

press·ing (prĕs′ĭng) needing immediate attention; urgent: *a pressing appointment.*

pres·sure (prĕsh′ər) **1** a pressing force or weight: *the pressure of a clamp; the pressure of a roller on the road.* **2** force of air, steam, water, etc., against a unit of area: *The air pressure in the tire is twenty pounds per square inch.* **3** strong, forceful, and continued attempt to influence: *She gave up her trip because of the pressure of her parents.* **4** urgent and heavy demands: *the pressure of business.* **5** burden or stress (on a person): *the pressure of worries; the pressure of debts; the pressures of city life.* **6 pressure cooker** a closed, heavy container that cooks food under steam pressure.

pres·su·rize (prĕsh′ə rīz′) to keep a normal air pressure in the interior of a plane at any altitude. **pres·su·rized, pres·su·riz·ing.**

pres·tige (prĕs tēzh′ or prĕs tēj′) influence or reputation gained by achievement, position, etc.: *The old scientist enjoyed great prestige after many years of successful research.*

pres·to (prĕs′tō) **1** quickly; suddenly: *The sun was shining when,* presto, *it began to rain.* **2** exclamation used by a magician when performing a trick. **3** in music, rapidly.

pre·sum·a·ble (prĭ zōōm′ə bəl or prĭ zūm′ə bəl) that may be taken for granted or expected; probable: *a presumable, but not certain, result.* **pre·sum·a·bly.**

pre·sume (prĭ zōōm′ or prĭ zūm′) **1** to take for granted; suppose; assume: *I presume the children will like the homemade ice cream.* **2** to venture boldly; dare (to do something): *The young lawyer presumed to tell the judge he was wrong.* **3** to take as true without enough proof; jump to a conclusion: *Never presume that a man is guilty until he is proven so.*

presume on or **upon** make selfish use of; take advantage of: *The girl presumed on her friend's hospitality and wore out her welcome.*

pre·sumed, pre·sum·ing.

pre·sump·tion (prĭ zŭmp′shən) **1** a taking (of something) for granted: *He did his homework carelessly on the* presumption

---

fāte, făt, fâre, fär; bē, bĕt; bīte, bĭt; nō, nŏt, nôr; fūse, fŭn, fûr; tōō, tŏŏk; foil; foul; thin; ~~then~~; hw for wh as in *wh*at; zh for s as in usual; ə for a, e, i, o, u, as in ago, linen, peril, atom, minus

that the teacher would not collect it. **2** acceptance and belief of something not fully proved: *based on presumption and not on fact.* **3** extreme pride; overconfidence in a person's own worth or ability; arrogance: *His presumption led Steve to believe he could win without practice.*

pre·sump·tu·ous (prĭ zŭmp′chŏŏ əs) **1** overconfident; rash: *John is presumptuous to think he can get good grades without studying.* **2** overbearing: *presumptuous conduct.* **pre·sump·tu·ous·ly.**

pre·tend (prĭ tĕnd′) **1** to make believe: *The trapeze artist pretended to fall just to thrill the audience. The children put on Mother's old clothes and pretended they were grown-ups.* **2** to use (something) as an excuse: *She pretended sickness to get out of doing the dishes.* **3** to claim: *He pretends to know everything just because he reads the encyclopedia.*

pre·tense or **pre·tence** (prĭ tĕns′ or prē′tĕns) **1** false show: *a pretense of innocence.* **2** false reason; excuse; pretext: *The lazy boy used the slightest pretense to get out of doing any work.* **3** claim; pretension: *a pretense to knowledge.* **4** a display; show: *A simple and sincere man is free from pretense.* **5** a make-believe; deceit; fraud: *Don't believe his story because it's all pretense.*

pre·ten·sion (prĭ tĕn′shən) **1** a claim: *The princess had pretensions to the throne.* **2** showy display: *We were amused by the pretensions of her furs and jewels.*

pre·ten·tious (prĭ tĕn′shəs) showy; ostentatious: *a pretentious display of wealth.* **pre·ten·tious·ly.**

pre·text (prē′tĕkst) false reason which covers the real one; excuse; pretense: *A pretext for coming late to school is that the alarm did not go off.*

pret·ty (prĭt′ĭ) **1** pleasing in a graceful and dainty way: *a pretty girl; a pretty house.* **2** rather; fairly; moderately: *a pretty good report card.* **pret·ti·er, pret·ti·est; pret·ti·ly.**

pret·zel (prĕt′səl) narrow strip of dough bent into a knot, glazed, sprinkled with salt, and baked crisp.

Pretzel

pre·vail (prĭ vāl′) **1** to win; triumph: *Good will prevail over evil.* **2** to be widespread;

be found generally: *Superstition prevails among ignorant people.*

prevail on or **upon** to persuade: *We prevailed on the musician to play for us.*

pre·vail·ing (prĭ vā′lĭng) widespread; common; general: *It is a prevailing custom to hang stockings by the chimney the night before Christmas.* **pre·vail·ing·ly.**

prev·a·lence (prĕv′ə ləns) widespread occurrence: *a prevalence of colds this winter.*

prev·a·lent (prĕv′ə lənt) occurring often; widespread: *Colds are prevalent during the winter.* **prev·a·lent·ly.**

pre·vent (prĭ vĕnt′) to keep from doing or happening; hinder: *His quick thinking prevented an accident.*

pre·ven·tion (prĭ vĕn′shən) the stopping of something before it happens: *the prevention of fire; the prevention of crime.*

pre·ven·tive (prĭ vĕn′tĭv) **1** thing that stands in the way or hinders: *Keeping within speed limits is a preventive of traffic accidents.* **2** medicine that prevents a disease. **3** serving to prevent: *a preventive measure against crime.* **pre·ven·tive·ly.**

pre·vi·ous (prē′vĭ əs) earlier; preceding: *My nephew has grown much since my previous visit.* **pre·vi·ous·ly.**

prey (prā) **1** animal hunted or killed by another for food. **2** victim: *The banker turned out to be the swindler's easy prey.* **3 bird** or **beast of prey** animal that kills another for food: *An eagle is a bird of prey.*

prey on or **upon 1** to hunt or kill for food: *A tiger preys on antelope.* **2** to injure; wear down: *The lie preyed upon his conscience.* (Homonym: pray)

price (prĭs) **1** amount of money something costs: *The price of the ball is $2.00.* **2** to put a price on: *The rent was priced too high for our family.* **3** to ask the price of: *We priced several cars before buying.* **4** worth; value: *jewels of great price.* **5** the amount of effort, sacrifice, etc. needed to get something: *the price of fame; the price of victory.* **6** money offered for the capture of a criminal: *a price on a man's head.* **priced, pric·ing.**

price·less (prĭs′lĭs) worth a great deal; beyond what money can buy: *a priceless work of art.*

prick (prĭk) **1** to pierce or wound with a sharp point: *The thorn pricked my finger.*

prickle

2 small hole made by a sharp point: *The pin left pricks in the material.* **3** sharp point: *the pricks of a cactus.* **4** sharp pain: *He felt a prick when the bee stung him.* **5** to bother; sting: *His conscience pricked him.*

prick up the ears **1** to make the ears erect: *The dog pricked up his ears when he heard his master's voice.* **2** to become attentive: *She pricked up her ears when she heard her name.*

prick·le (prĭk′əl) **1** sharp point; thorn: *This vine is full of prickles.* **2** a stinging or tingling feeling: *I feel a prickle when I use this lotion on my face.* **3** to give a stinging or tingling feeling: *The ointment doesn't burn but it prickles.* **prick·led, prick·ling.**

prick·ly (prĭk′lĭ) **1** full of sharp points: *A cactus is a prickly plant.* **2** causing tingling or stinging: *a prickly feeling from a wool scarf.* **prick·li·er, prick·li·est.**

pride (prīd) **1** high opinion of a person's own ability or importance; conceit: *His pride was his downfall.* **2** self-respect; dignity: *His pride kept him from asking for money.* **3** a feeling of pleasure or satisfaction: *He takes pride in his work.* **4** thing or person giving others pleasure or satisfaction: *He was the pride of his family.*

pride oneself on to be proud of; be pleased and satisfied with: *He prides himself on always doing his best.*

prid·ed, prid·ing. (Homonym: pried)

pried (prīd) **1** See **¹pry.** *She pried into my affairs.* **2** See **²pry.** *He pried the jar open with a knife.* (Homonym: pride)

pries (prīz) **1** See **¹pry.** *She pries into his letters.* **2** See **²pry.** (Homonym: prize)

priest (prēst) man ordained to perform religious rites; clergyman.

priest·hood (prēst′hŏŏd′) **1** position or duties of a priest. **2** all priests: *The priesthood in America is exempt from military service.*

priest·ly (prēst′lĭ) having to do with or like a priest: *to carry out priestly duties.* **priest·li·er, priest·li·est.**

prim (prĭm) very proper and stiff in appearance and conduct; very neat or precise: *the prim old maid.* **prim·mer, prim·mest; prim·ly.**

primer

pri·ma·ry (prī′mĕr′ĭ or prī′mə rĭ) **1** major; chief; principal: *The primary ingredient of an omelet is eggs. Mr. Eaton's primary purpose in making the trip was business.* **2** first; basic: *The primary meaning of "flash" is a burst of light, not a piece of news.* **3** elementary: *the primary grades of school.* **4** election to decide the candidates for a main election: *States have primaries to decide upon candidates for the regular elections.* **pri·ma·ries; pri·ma·ri·ly.**

primary accent **1** the stress the voice puts on the strongest syllable of a word. In the word man·u·fac·tur·er the syllable "fac" has the primary accent. **2** the mark (′) used to show the strongest syllable.

primary color yellow, blue, or red. These colors are called primary colors because by mixing them together properly one can get any other color.

¹prime (prīm) **1** first in time; original: *The prime reason for the family feud was a disagreement over who owned this piece of land.* **2** chief; major; most important: *His prime concern is the welfare of his family.* **3** first in quality; best: *The prime ribs of beef are very expensive.* **4** the time of a person's life when he is his best in health, mind, beauty, etc. **5** prime number a number that can be divided evenly only by 1 or itself, as 1, 3, 43, etc. **prime·ly.** [**¹prime** is from a Latin word (primus) meaning "first."]

²prime (prīm) **1** to prepare a thing to work: *to prime a pump by pouring water into it.* **2** to prepare a person beforehand by telling him what to say; coach: *to prime students for an examination.* **3** to prepare a surface for painting. **primed, prim·ing.** [**²prime** is probably **¹prime** in a later and special meaning.]

prime minister head of an elected government in some countries; the premier: *Winston Churchill was one of England's prime ministers during this century.*

prim·er (prĭm′ər) **1** book used in giving the first lessons in reading. **2** the first instruction book in any subject: *That book is not only interesting, but a good primer in chemistry.*

---

fāte, făt, fâre, fär; bē, bĕt; bīte, bĭt; nō, nŏt, nôr; fūse, fŭn, fûr; tōō, tŏŏk; foil; foul; thin; ~~then~~;
hw for wh as in *wh*at; zh for s as in u*s*ual; ə for a, e, i, o, u, as in ago, linen, peril, atom, minus

pri·me·val (pri mē′vəl) belonging to the earliest times; primitive: *Indians were the* primeval *inhabitants of America.*

prim·i·tive (prim′ə tiv) **1** original; earliest; of the earliest times: *The museum showed us many relics of* primitive *man.* **2** simple and crude, as in early times: *The natives of that region still live in* primitive *straw huts.* **prim·i·tive·ly.**

prim·rose (prim′rōz′) **1** any of several wild or cultivated plants. Most American kinds spring from a rosette of leaves with a tall flower stalk and bloom in summer or fall. **2** the blossom of this plant, usually a shade of yellow. **3** pale-yellow color.

Evening primrose

prince (prins) **1** monarch; ruler: *The king appealed to his fellow* princes *for help in repelling the invasion.* **2** son of a king or queen. **3** in some countries, a nobleman of very high rank. **4** a distinguished member of a class of men: *a merchant* prince. **5 Prince of Wales** the oldest son of the king or queen of England. **6 prince consort** the husband of a reigning queen.

prince·ly (prins′li) **1** worthy of a prince; generous; lavish: *The town has received many* princely *benefits from its loyal citizens.* **2** having to do with a prince. **3** noble; high-ranking: *a* princely *family.*

prin·cess (prin′sis) **1** daughter of a reigning monarch. **2** wife or daughter of a prince: *The prince chose Cinderella as his* princess.

prin·ci·pal (prin′sə pəl) **1** main; chief; leading; most important: *Illness was the* principal *cause of absences during the school year.* **2** the chief person; leader; head: *My teacher sent me to see the school* principal. **3** person who takes a leading part in some activity: *Betty and Bob are* principals *in the play.* **4** sum of money used to earn income or interest; the original amount of a loan for investment. (Homonym: principle)

prin·ci·pal·i·ty (prin′sə păl′ə ti) the territory ruled by a prince: *the* Principality *of Monaco.* **prin·ci·pal·i·ties.**

prin·ci·pal·ly (prin′sə pə li) mainly; chiefly: *Paper is made* principally *of vegetable fibers.*

prin·ci·ple (prin′sə pəl) **1** a basic fact or rule; law by which something works: *the* principles *of multiplication and division; a* mechanical principle. **2** rule of conduct: *Sally's one* principle *is her determination to take good care of her family.* **3** honesty; integrity: *He shows great concern for* principle *in business affairs.* (Homonym: principal)

print (print) **1** letters or numerals stamped by type: *That* print *is too small to read.* **2** to mark or stamp with type, plates, or blocks: *On the map was* printed *the single word "treasure."* **3** to produce by marking with inked type: *This book was* printed *in the United States.* **4** a stamp; mark; impression: *In the sand Robinson Crusoe saw the* print *of a human foot.* **5** to cause to be printed or published: *Now that he's written his story he doesn't want to* print *it.* **6** picture or design reproduced by printing: *The walls were decorated with many colorful* prints. **7** cloth on which a pattern or design is stamped: *She chose a pretty cotton* print *for her new dress.* **8** to write letters that resemble those made by type: *Billy* prints *well for a child of his age.* **9** sign; indication; mark: *Her face bore the* print *of many hardships.* **10** a photograph reproduced from a negative: *We want six* prints *of that snapshot of Harry and the crocodile.* **11** to reproduce a photograph from a negative: *You used too much light when you* printed *that picture.*

print·er (prin′tər) person who, or company that, reproduces something in print: *We sent your essay to the* printer *this morning.*

print·ing (prin′ting) **1** the process of stamping letters, designs, or pictures on paper or other surfaces by means of type, plates, or blocks: *Before the invention of* printing *all books had to be copied by hand.* **2** letters that resemble print: *His handwriting is hard to read, but his* printing *is clear.* **3** the business of a printer: *He made a lot of money in* printing.

printing press machine for printing letters, pictures, or designs on paper or other materials by means of type, plates, or wooden blocks, etc.

¹pri·or (pri′ər) **1** earlier; previous: *I'd like to go to your party, but I've accepted a* prior *invitation.* **2** more important because it came sooner: *We must give the reward to Tony because he has* prior *claim to it.* **3 prior to** before: *Our present mayor practiced law* prior *to his election.* [**¹prior** is from a Latin word (prior) meaning "former," "previous."]

²pri·or (prī′ər) the head of a religious house for men, called a priory. [**²prior** is the unchanged form of an Old English word.]

pri·or·ess (prī′ə rĭs) the head of a religious house for women, called a priory.

pri·or·i·ty (prī ôr′ə tĭ) **1** precedence; coming or being first in time, place, or order: *There's a long line of people waiting, and those with* priority *will receive tickets first.* **2** the right to precede: *In wartime, production of weapons has* priority *over the manufacture of luxuries.*

pri·o·ry (prī′ə rĭ) a monastery ruled by a prior, or a convent ruled by a prioress. A priory ranks below an abbey and is often under its control. **pri·o·ries.**

prism (prĭz′əm) **1** a solid with any number of flat sides and with two flat ends that are parallel and exactly alike in size and shape. **2** transparent prism with triangular ends used to reflect light or separate it into its different colors.

Prisms

pris·mat·ic (prĭz măt′ĭk) **1** many-colored, like the band of rainbow colors produced by a prism. **2 prismatic colors** the colors produced when white light is passed through a prism.

pris·on (prĭz′ən) **1** place where lawbreakers are confined and punished: *He was sent to prison for ten years.* **2** any place where a person is held against his will: *His office was a prison to him on fine spring days.*

pris·on·er (prĭz′ə nər) **1** person who is held in prison. **2** one who is under arrest, or held for a crime: *The prisoner pleaded guilty to a charge of reckless driving.* **3** any person or thing held captive against his will: *He kept his dog a prisoner in his garage.* **4** a soldier captured by the enemy.

prith·ee (prĭ h′ĭ) old word for "I pray thee" or "please."

pri·va·cy (prī′və sĭ) **1** the being apart from other people; seclusion: *Hard study usually requires privacy.* **2** secrecy: *Jim and his friends studied the treasure map in privacy.* **3** the right to freedom from interference by others: *Governments should respect the privacy of citizens.*

pri·vate (prī′vĭt) **1** belonging to a particular person or group: *This lake is private, and no fishing is allowed.* **2** personal; individual: *I have private reasons for wanting to stay home.* **3** personal, not official: *The senator was a rancher in private life. A policeman may have to enforce laws of which he disapproves as a private citizen.* **4** secret; confidential: *We made private arrangements for the surprise party.* **5** closed to the public: *The actors gave a private performance last night.* **6** lowest ranking soldier in an army. **7 in private** secretly: *The committee met in private to discuss new club members.* **pri·vate·ly.**

pri·va·teer (prī′və tĭr′) **1** armed ship, privately owned but allowed by a government to attack and capture enemy ships. **2** commander or one of the crew members of such a ship. **3** to sail as a privateer.

pri·va·tion (prī vā′shən) lack of the necessities of life, especially food, clothing, and shelter; hardship: *The soldiers suffered great privation at Valley Forge during the winter.*

priv·i·lege (prĭv′ə lĭj) **1** special right or advantage granted or enjoyed by a person or group of persons: *the privilege of a college education; the privileges enjoyed from rank and wealth.* **2** to grant a special right or advantage (to): *I am privileged to know him.* **priv·i·leged, priv·i·leg·ing.**

priv·i·leged (prĭv′ə lĭjd) having been granted special rights or advantages: *A few privileged visitors met the President.*

priv·y (prĭv′ĭ) **1** for private, not public, use; personal: *A privy purse is money set aside for the English monarch's personal use.* **2** an enclosed outdoor toilet. **3 privy to** secretly informed about: *There were only six privy to the conspiracy.* **priv·ies.**

---

fāte, făt, fâre, fär; bē, bĕt; bīte, bĭt; nō, nŏt, nôr; fūse, fŭn, fûr; tōō, tŏŏk; foil; foul; thin; then; hw for wh as in *what*; zh for s as in u*s*ual; ə for a, e, i, o, u, as in *a*go, lin*e*n, per*i*l, at*o*m, min*u*s

prize

¹prize (prīz) **1** reward offered or won in a contest: *to win a prize for the best costume at a party.* **2** something of value; choice: *This puppy is the prize of the litter.* **3** to value highly; think highly of: *to prize someone's friendship.* **4** given or worthy of being given a prize: *the prize painting in the show.* **prized, priz·ing.** [¹**prize** is from an Old French word (prisier) meaning "to praise," which comes from a Latin word (pretiare) meaning "to put a value on." It is related to **price.**] (Homonym: pries)

²prize (prīz) **1** something captured in war, especially a ship or its cargo. **2** to force something by means of a lever; pry: *to prize a lid off a box.* **prized, priz·ing.** [²**prize** is from a form (prise) of an Old French word (prendre) based on a Latin word (prehendere) meaning "to seize, take hold."] (Homonym: pries)

pro (prō) **1** in favor of; for. **2** an argument, reason, etc. in favor of something. **3 pros and cons** arguments for and against (something): *to discuss the pros and cons of buying a new car.*

prob·a·bil·i·ty (prŏb'ə bĭl'ə tĭ) **1** likelihood; chance: *The probability of his making the trip in such a bad snowstorm is very small.* **2** something likely to happen: *His coming this weekend is a probability.* **prob·a·bil·i·ties.**

prob·a·ble (prŏb'ə bəl) very likely to happen or prove true: *When storm clouds gather, rain is probable. The rain is the probable cause of his lateness.* **prob·a·bly.**

pro·ba·tion (prō bā'shən) **1** trial or testing of a person's character, ability, etc. **2** period of trial or testing: *to hire a new employee on probation.* **3** legal system of permitting young law breakers or first offenders to go free under police supervision instead of being put in prison.

probe (prōb) **1** to examine or inquire into closely: *The police probed for clues to the crime.* **2** a searching inquiry or examination. **3** a slender surgical instrument for examining a wound, cavity, etc. **4** to examine with such an instrument. **probed, prob·ing.**

prob·lem (prŏb'ləm) **1** a question hard to understand; a matter difficult to settle or find a solution to: *The family solved the housing problem by buying a trailer.* **2** in

procure

mathematics, something to be worked out or solved.

pro·ce·dure (prə sē'jər or prō sē'jər) way or system of proceeding or of doing things: *What procedure should I follow in applying for a driver's license?*

pro·ceed (prə sēd') to go on or forward: *to proceed on a journey; to proceed with a speech.*

proceed from to result or issue from: *My criticism of your work proceeds from a wish to help you improve.*

pro·ceed·ing (prə sē'dĭng) **1** an action or course of action: *What a strange proceeding it all seemed!* **2 proceedings** record of the business accomplished during a meeting.

pro·ceeds (prō'sēdz) money got from a business transaction, especially from selling something: *We bought new curtains for our club with the proceeds of our candy sale.*

proc·ess (prŏs'ĕs) **1** action or series of actions which lead to a desired or expected result: *Training to become a doctor is a lengthy process. The process of growth is helped by proper nourishment.* **2** in industry, a special method of operation or treatment: *a new process for making steel.* **3** to give something a special treatment: *to process grain in making cereals.* **4** an outgrowth or projecting part (especially on a bone): *the spinelike process of a vertebra.* **5 in (the) process of** in the course of (being done or carried on): *a house still in process of construction; to be in the process of moving to a new neighborhood.*

pro·ces·sion (prə sĕsh'ən) **1** formal parade: *A military procession escorted the President to the White House.* **2** the persons composing such a parade.

pro·claim (prō klām') to announce publicly or officially; declare: *to proclaim a holiday; to proclaim one's ideas to anyone who will listen.*

proc·la·ma·tion (prŏk'lə mā'shən) formal or public announcement: *The king's page read the proclamation of the prince's marriage.*

pro·cure (prō kūr') **1** to get; obtain: *to procure the services of a good doctor.* **2** to cause; bring about: *The secret service procured the arrest of the spy.* **pro·cured, pro·cur·ing.**

prod (prŏd) **1** to punch or poke with a pointed instrument: *The trainer prodded the elephant into the ring.* **2** to urge; goad rouse: *to prod a lazy person into doing his work.* **3** a pointed implement for poking or pricking, such as a goad or pointed stick. **4** a poke or dig: *a prod in the ribs.* **prod·ded, prod·ding.**

prod·i·gal (prŏd'ə gəl) **1** reckless, especially with money; lavish; wasteful: *Jim was so prodigal with his allowance on Saturday that now he has no money left for lunch.* **2** a spendthrift. **prod·i·gal·ly.**

pro·di·gious (prə dĭj'əs) **1** huge; great: *The athlete ate a prodigious amount of food.* **2** marvelous; wonderful; amazing: *The Egyptian pyramids are prodigious monuments.* **pro·di·gious·ly.**

prod·i·gy (prŏd'ə jĭ) **1** highly gifted or talented person, especially a child. **2** a marvel; wonder: *The Grand Canyon is a prodigy of nature.* **prod·i·gies.**

¹pro·duce (prə dōōs' or prə dūs') **1** to create; put out; make: *Boiling water produces steam. This factory produces 700 machines a day. Charles Dickens produced many books.* **2** to yield; give forth; bear: *Poor soil produces a small crop.* **3** to present for inspection; exhibit; show: *Please produce your tickets at the gate. The lawyer produced the evidence during the trial. The magician reached in his hat and produced a rabbit.* **4** to present to the public: *to produce a play.* **pro·duced, pro·duc·ing.**

²pro·duce (prŏd'ūs, prŏd'ōōs, prō'dūs, prō'dōōs) anything which the garden or farm puts out or yields. Eggs, meat, and vegetables are produce.

pro·duc·er (prə dōō'sər or prə dū'sər) **1** a person or thing that makes or yields something: *Mr. Thompson is a great steel producer. This farm is the largest producer of corn in the area. This cow is a good producer of milk.* **2** a person who supervises the staging of a play, motion picture, etc.

prod·uct (prŏd'əkt or prŏd'ŭkt) **1** anything made or yielded: *farm products; factory products; a product of the imagination.* **2** result; outcome: *His failure was a product of laziness.* **3** in arithmetic, the result ob-

tained by multiplying two or more numbers: *The product of 4 × 3 is 12.*

pro·duc·tion (prə dŭk'shən) **1** a producing: *This factory specializes in the production of ball-point pens.* **2** the total amount that is made or produced: *A business that wants to expand must increase its production.* **3** the staging of a play, motion picture, etc.

pro·duc·tive (prə dŭk'tĭv) **1** having the ability to make or create; creative: *a productive inventor.* **2** fertile; rich: *This productive soil yields large crops.* **3** yielding a profit: *a productive oil well; productive mine; productive idea.* **pro·duc·tive·ly.**

pro·fane (prō fān') **1** abusing, or without respect for, sacred things; not reverent: *a profane speech.* **2** to treat a sacred thing or place with scorn, abuse, or lack of respect: *Visitors profaned the shrine by writing their names on the wall.* **pro·faned, pro·fan·ing; pro·fane·ly.**

pro·fan·i·ty (prō făn'ə tĭ) irreverent behavior or speech. **pro·fan·i·ties.**

pro·fess (prə fĕs') **1** to declare openly and freely: *to profess one's religion; to profess a dislike for playing cards.* **2** to claim; pretend: *He professes to know all about music because he took piano lessons.*

pro·fes·sion (prə fĕsh'ən) **1** occupation that requires special education. Medicine, law, and architecture are professions. **2** the group of persons engaged in an occupation: *the medical profession.* **3** open and free declaration: *a profession of faith.*

pro·fes·sion·al (prə fĕsh'ən əl) **1** having to do with a profession or career: *the professional duties of a lawyer.* **2** engaged for pay in a trade or occupation: *a professional musician; professional politician; professional tennis player.* **3** an expert in some sport or other activity, who engages in it as a business: *to take skiing lessons from a professional.* **pro·fes·sion·al·ly.**

pro·fes·sor (prə fĕs'ər) teacher of higher rank than instructor in a college or university.

prof·fer (prŏf'ər) **1** to offer for acceptance: *to proffer a gift; to proffer a suggestion.* **2** an offer.

---

fāte, făt, fâre, fär; bē, bĕt; bīte, bĭt; nō, nŏt, nôr; fūse, fŭn, fûr; tōō, tŏŏk; foil; foul; thin; then; hw for wh as in what; zh for s as in usual; ə for a, e, i, o, u, as in ago, linen, peril, atom, minus

proficient

pro·fi·cient (prə fish'ənt) highly skilled; expert: *a proficient* typist; *a proficient* nurse. **pro·fi·cient·ly.**

pro·file (prō'fīl) 1 side view or a picture of it. 2 sectional view, as an outline drawing of a landscape showing the hills and valleys.

Profile

prof·it (prŏf'ĭt) 1 the amount of money gained from a business venture after all the expenses have been paid; earnings: *After subtracting expenses of the dance from the $500.00 taken in, we had a profit of $200.00.* 2 to make money; gain: *Our school has profited $100.00 from the dance.* 3 a benefit; advantage: *Having such an excellent teacher is to your* profit. 4 to improve; benefit: *It would* profit *you to read better books.* (Homonym: prophet)

prof·it·a·ble (prŏf'ĭt ə bəl) 1 yielding gain or profit: *Selling ice is a* profitable *business in the summer.* 2 rewarding; beneficial; useful: *It is* profitable *to read good books.* **prof·it·a·bly.**

pro·found (prə found') 1 deep: *The* profound *depths of the ocean.* 2 deep in meaning: *the* profound *sayings of the Bible.* 3 complete; thorough; very great: *a* profound *silence;* profound *knowledge of science;* profound *interest in music.* 4 deeply felt: *a* profound *sorrow.* **pro·found·ly.**

pro·fuse (prə fūs') 1 plentiful; abundant: *a* profuse *apology;* profuse *kindness;* profuse *thanks.* 2 generous; extravagant; lavish: *Not all millionaires are* profuse *in their spending.* **pro·fuse·ly.**

pro·fu·sion (prə fū'zhən) 1 abundance; great quantity: *During spring there is a* profusion *of flowers in our garden.* 2 lavishness; extravagance: *She spent money in great* profusion.

prog·e·ny (prŏj'ə nĭ) children; descendants; offspring. **prog·e·nies.**

pro·gram (prō'grăm) 1 list of the features, participants, etc., of an entertainment, ceremony, etc.: *the* program *of a concert; a graduation* program. 2 the entertainment, ceremony, etc., itself: *Did you enjoy the* program *on the radio?* 3 a plan to be followed: *What's the* program *for today?* 4 to plan in a program: *A committee* programed *the activities for the May Day celebration.*

projector

¹prog·ress (prŏg'rĕs) 1 movement forward: *We made no* progress *through the heavy traffic.* 2 development: *the* progress *of medicine.* 3 improvement: *We can notice Billy's* progress *on the piano.*

²pro·gress (prə grĕs', prō grĕs') 1 to move forward: *to* progress *on a trip.* 2 to develop: *The new building is* progressing *rapidly.* 3 to improve: *She has* progressed *under doctor's care.*

pro·gres·sive (prə grĕs'ĭv) 1 in favor of new ideas and changes for the sake of improvement: *The* progressive *town council built a new recreation center.* 2 making progress; advancing: *Building a new recreation center in our town was a* progressive *step.* 3 moving forward steadily or step by step: *The* progressive *stages in growing up.* 4 marked by steady progress: *a* progressive *improvement in a child's penmanship during a school year.* 5 person who believes in reform, especially in political reform. **pro·gres·sive·ly.**

pro·hib·it (prō hĭb'ĭt) 1 to refuse to permit; forbid by law: *Parking is* prohibited *on Main Street.* 2 to hinder; prevent: *The expenses of the new house* prohibit *a vacation this year.*

pro·hi·bi·tion (prō'ə bĭsh'ən) 1 act of forbidding. 2 a law, order, or rule that forbids: *a* prohibition *against walking on the grass.* 3 the forbidding by law of the manufacture and sale of alcoholic liquors.

¹proj·ect (prŏj'ĕkt) plan; scheme: *a* project *to build a new gymnasium.*

²proj·ect (prə jĕkt') 1 to plan (something to be done, a course of action, etc.): *to* project *a new school building.* 2 to throw or shoot forward: *to* project *a missile.* 3 to cause (a beam of light, shadow, picture, etc.) to fall on a surface: *to* project *a movie on a screen.* 4 to jut out or extend: *A balcony* projects *over the sidewalk.*

pro·jec·tile (prō jĕk'tĭl) something thrown or shot forward, especially an explosive missile such as an artillery shell or rocket.

pro·jec·tion (prō jĕk'shən) 1 an extending or jutting out; a projecting. 2 something that extends or juts out: *He disappeared behind a* projection *of rock.*

pro·jec·tor (prō jĕk'tər) machine or apparatus for throwing light, sound, etc.: *a movie* projector; *a sound* projector.

564

pro·lif·ic (prō lif'ĭk) **1** producing many off-spring: *The rabbit is a prolific animal.* **2** very productive: *a prolific author.*

pro·long (prə lông') to lengthen; draw out; extend: *to prolong a visit; to prolong a conversation.*

prom·e·nade (prŏm'ə nād' or prŏm'ə näd') **1** a walk, especially one taken in public for pleasure, display, etc. **2** to take a prome-nade: *to promenade at the seashore.* **3** place for such a walk: *to walk down the promenade.* **4** a march that begins a dance or is part of a square dance. **prom·e·nad·ed, prom·e·nad·ing.**

prom·i·nence (prŏm'ə nəns) **1** a being dis-tinguished, noticeable, or conspicuous: *a place of prominence in history.* **2** some-thing that juts up or rises sharply: *Cliff dwellers once lived on this rocky prominence.*

prom·i·nent (prŏm'ə nənt) **1** important; well-known: *The mayor is a prominent citizen in the community.* **2** conspicuous; very noticeable: *a prominent place in the newspaper.* **3** standing or jutting out; pro-jecting: *The camel has a prominent hump.* **prom·i·nent·ly.**

prom·ise (prŏm'ĭs) **1** pledge that one will or will not do something: *Did you keep your promise not to eat candy before dinner?* **2** to pledge to do or not to do something: *Johnny promised to be at school on time today but he's late again.* **3** to make a promise of; agree to give or get (something) for someone: *Dad promised me a new bicycle for my birthday.* **4** cause or reason for hope or expectation: *Before the drought, the crops gave promise of a good harvest.* **5** to give reason to expect: *The thunder promised rain before the end of our picnic.* **prom·ised, prom·is·ing.**

prom·is·ing (prŏm'ə-sing) likely to be successful or satisfac-tory; likely to turn out well: *the most prom-ising pup in a litter.*

Promontory

prom·on·to·ry (prŏm'ən tôr'ĭ) high point of land jutting into water; lofty cape; head-land. **prom·on·to·ries.**

pro·mote (prə mōt') **1** to help the growth, development, or success of: *a sales cam-paign to promote a new product.* **2** to raise to a higher rank or class: *Mary was promoted to the sixth grade in June.* **3** to set in motion; aid in organizing: *to promote a new business undertaking.* **pro·mot·ed, pro·mot·ing.**

pro·mo·tion (prə mō'shən) **1** advancement to a better position or higher class or rank in school, business, etc.: *to win a promotion in the army.* **2** furthering of any cause or purpose: *The promotion of learning is the goal of our schools.*

prompt (prŏmpt) **1** without delay: *a prompt mail service.* **2** ready and quick: *Mother was prompt to show her disapproval of the child's rudeness.* **3** on time; not tardy: *to be prompt in arriving at school.* **4** to rouse to action; inspire: *Dick's cruel treatment of the dog prompted me to scold him. Mr. Smith's generosity prompted his large donation.* **5** to supply (someone, especially an actor) with forgotten words. **prompt·ly.**

prompt·ness (prŏmpt'nĭs) a being prompt; readiness; quickness: *a promptness in answering letters.*

prone (prōn) **1** naturally inclined or dis-posed: *She is prone to forget people's names.* **2** lying face downward: *a prone position on the floor.*

prong (prŏng or prông) **1** one of the pointed ends of a fork. **2** any sharp point or sharply pointed instrument.

pro·noun (prō'noun') word which refers to or is used in place of a noun or name. In "Who owns the car that is parked in front of hers?" "Who," "that," and "hers" are pronouns.

pro·nounce (prə nouns') **1** to utter or make the sounds of: *to pronounce a name cor-rectly.* **2** to declare or announce formally or with authority: *The minister pronounced them man and wife.* **pro·nounced, pro·nounc·ing.**

pro·nounced (prə nounst') marked; de-cided: *The cool winds from Canada caused a pronounced change in the weather.* **pro·counc·ed·ly.**

---

fāte, făt, fâre, fär; bē, bĕt; bīte, bĭt; nō, nŏt, nôr; fūse, fŭn, fûr; tōō, tŏŏk; foil; foul; thin; then; hw for wh as in *what*; zh for s as in usual; ə for a, e, i, o, u, as in *ago*, linen, peril, atom, minus

565

pro·nun·ci·a·tion (prǝ nŭn′sǐ ā′shǝn) **1** act or manner of uttering the sounds which form words: *American pronunciation is different from British* pronunciation. **2** the way a word is generally pronounced: *Some words have two* pronunciations.

proof (proof) **1** means by which something is shown to be true or correct: *The best* proof *of his innocence would be the discovery of the stolen wallet in someone else's possession.* **2** convincing evidence: *He was unable to offer* proof *of his whereabouts on the night of the robbery.* **3** establishment of the truth of something: *The* proof *of his client's innocence is up to the lawyer.* **4** in photography, a trial print from a negative. **5** in printing, an impression taken from set type for correction: *page* proofs. **6 to the proof** to the test; on trial: *to put a new invention to the* proof. **7 proof against** immune to: *Vaccination made him* proof against *smallpox.*

proof·read (proof′rēd′) to read proofs of type matter and mark errors to be corrected before it goes to press. **proof·read** (proof′rēd′), **proof·read·ing.**

prop (prŏp) **1** to hold a thing up by placing something under or against it. **2** to support; sustain: *We* propped *up his low spirits with a bit of good news.* **3** a support: *Mother used a block of wood as a* prop *for the short leg of the table.* **propped, prop·ping.**

prop·a·gan·da (prŏp′ǝ găn′dǝ) **1** an idea spread to influence opinion: *the* propaganda *against reckless driving.* **2** an organized plan or scheme for spreading an idea, opinion, etc.: *Advertising is a form of* propaganda.

prop·a·gate (prŏp′ǝ gāt′) **1** to produce offspring: *Rabbits* propagate *quickly.* **2** to cause to increase by production of young: *to* propagate *a breed of dogs.* **3** to spread from person to person: *to* propagate *an idea.* **prop·a·gat·ed, prop·a·gat·ing.**

pro·pel (prǒ pĕl′ or prǝ pĕl′) to move (something) by pushing or driving: *The paddle wheel* propels *a river boat.* **pro·pelled, pro·pel·ling.**

Propellers

BOAT   AIRPLANE

pro·pel·ler (prǒ pĕl′ǝr or prǝ pĕl′ǝr) device of whirling blades for propelling a ship or airplane.

pro·pen·si·ty (prǝ pĕn′sǝ tǐ) a leaning; tendency; inclination: *The sickly girl has a* propensity *to colds.* **pro·pen·si·ties.**

prop·er (prŏp′ǝr) **1** suitable; appropriate: *We wore the* proper *clothes for the sleigh ride and didn't feel the cold.* **2** correct; accurate; right: *In its* proper *sense "peculiar" does not mean "funny."* **3** in a narrow or exact sense: *A shark is not a* proper *fish.* **4** measuring up to standards of good conduct or manners; respectable: *It is never* proper *to wear gloves while eating.*

prop·er·ly (prŏp′ǝr lǐ) **1** correctly; suitably: *to be* properly *dressed for skiing.* **2** justifiably; with reason: *quite* properly *afraid of fire.*

prop·er·ty (prŏp′ǝr tǐ) **1** thing or things owned by someone; possessions: *These books are my* property. **2** land; real estate: *He bought some* property *near the river.* **3** quality that sets one thing apart from another: *Stickiness is a* property *of glue.* **4 properties** articles used on the stage, except costumes and scenery. **prop·er·ties.**

proph·e·cy (prŏf′ǝ sǐ) **1** a telling of what is to come; prediction: *In the Old Testament there is a* prophecy *of the coming of The Messiah.* **2** the power of prophesying: *the gift of* prophecy. **proph·e·cies.**

proph·e·sy (prŏf′ǝ sǐ′) to tell what is going to happen or come; predict; foretell: *It's impossible to* prophesy *the outcome of the election.* **proph·e·sied, proph·e·sy·ing.**

proph·et (prŏf′ǐt) **1** holy man who warns of or foretells the future. **2** person who foretells or predicts events: *I'm no weather* prophet. **3 the Prophets** the books in the Old Testament from Joel to Malachi. **4 the Prophet** Moslem term for Mohammed. (Homonym: profit)

pro·phet·ic (prǝ fĕt′ĭk) **1** of the nature of a prophecy: *a* prophetic *remark.* **2** like that of a prophet: *his* prophetic *wisdom.*

pro·pi·tious (prǝ pĭsh′ǝs) favorable: *We were lucky to have such* propitious *weather during our vacation. Let's choose a* propitious *time to ask Dad for a raise in our allowance.*

pro·por·tion (prǝ pôr′shǝn) **1** number, size, or amount of a thing or group as compared with another thing or group: *the* proportion *of men to women in a country; the* proportion *of sugar to flour in a cake.*

proposal   **prosperous**

2 share; part: *a* proportion *of the profits.*
3 to put (one thing) in a right relation (to
another): *He* proportions *his rent to his
salary.* **4 in proportion (to)** in proper or
pleasing relation; in balance or harmony
(with): *The design of the wallpaper was in
proportion to* the size *of the room.* **5 out of
proportion (to)** not in proper or pleasing
relation; not in balance or harmony
(with): *Her anger was out of proportion to
the offense.* **6 proportions** (1) size; dimensions: *a desert of vast proportions.*
(2) dimensions in relation to one another:
the beautiful proportions *of a room.*

pro·pos·al (prə pō′zəl) **1** a presenting or
suggesting of a plan: *Mother's proposal to
paint the house started a discussion.* **2** plan
or scheme: *The proposal for painting the
house was forgotten.* **3** an offer of marriage.

pro·pose (prə pōz′) **1** to offer for consideration or discussion; suggest: *to propose a
plan.* **2** to suggest or present someone's
name for office; nominate. **3** to intend;
plan: *I* propose *to get up early.* **4** to make
an offer of marriage. **pro·posed, pro·
pos·ing.**

prop·o·si·tion (prŏp′ə zĭsh′ən) **1** statement: *The* proposition *for debate was
"Resolved, that it is desirable to have a
school uniform."* **2** a plan; proposal. **3** an
undertaking: *It was a tough* proposition *to
start the lemonade stand.*

pro·pri·e·tor (prə prī′ə tər) person who
has a legal title to property; owner: *the*
proprietor *of a ranch.*

pro·pri·e·ty (prə prī′ə tĭ) **1** fitness; correctness: *We question the* propriety *of children's staying out alone after dark.* **2 pro-
prieties** proper attitudes and customs observed by polite and well-behaved people.
pro·pri·e·ties.

pro·pul·sion (prō pŭl′shən or prə pŭl′shən)
1 the act of giving or imparting forward
motion: *the* propulsion *of blood by the heart.*
2 something that propels; a driving force:
An outboard motor furnishes propulsion *for
our boat.*

pro·sa·ic (prō zā′ĭk) lacking in imagination
and originality; commonplace; dull: *The
host bored his guests with* prosaic *jokes.*

prose (prōz) ordinary spoken or written
language without the rhythm or meter of
poetry.

pros·e·cute (prŏs′ə kūt′) **1** to accuse (someone) before a court of law: *The city* prosecuted *the man for stealing.* **2** to bring or
conduct legal action in a court (against
someone): *The city* prosecuted *a claim
against the man for stealing.* **3** to carry on;
follow up; continue: *The detective* prosecuted *the investigation in spite of the difficulties.* **pros·e·cut·ed, pros·e·cut·ing.**

pros·e·cu·tion (prŏs′ə kū′shən) **1** bringing
or conducting of legal action in a court: *A*
prosecution *was begun against the three auto
thieves.* **2** the party who begins legal
accusation: *The district attorney represented
the* prosecution. **3** the following up; carrying on; pursuit: *The* prosecution *of the
doctor's duties never left him an idle moment.*

pros·pect (prŏs′pĕkt) **1** broad view or
scene: *Below us lay a* prospect *of green
hills, fertile valleys, and shining rivers.*
2 outlook for the future: *With more people
living in the town the* prospect *for business
is good.* **3** hope; expectation: *Sickness and
poverty gave him little* prospect *of staying in
school.* **4** possible customer: *Our salesmen
have found a number of new* prospects. **5** to
search or explore a region: *Many men have
spent their lives* prospecting *for gold.*
6 prospects chance for success: *Hard
work should improve your* prospects.

pro·spec·tive (prə spĕk′tĭv) expected;
probable; likely to be made or become: *We
discussed* prospective *changes in the sports
program for next year.* **pro·spec·tive·ly.**

pros·pec·tor (prŏs′pĕk tər) person who
searches or explores a place for gold or
other valuable minerals: *We heard the
legend of the lost mine from an old* prospector.

pros·per (prŏs′pər) to be successful; thrive;
flourish: *His business is* prospering *because
he works hard.*

pros·per·i·ty (prŏs pĕr′ə tĭ) success; good
fortune; well-being: *We wish you great
happiness and* prosperity *in your new job.*

pros·per·ous (prŏs′pər əs) successful;
thriving; flourishing: *His fine clothes made
him look* prosperous. **pros·per·ous·ly.**

---

fāte, făt, fâre, fär; bē, bĕt; bīte, bĭt; nō, nŏt, nôr; fūse, fŭn, fûr; tōō, tŏŏk; foil; foul; thin; then;
hw for wh as in *wh*at; zh for s as in u*s*ual; ə for a, e, i, o, u, as in *a*go, lin*e*n, per*i*l, at*o*m, min*u*s

567

pros·trate (prŏs'trāt') **1** lying flat and face downward: *We found him* prostrate *in the street.* **2** to throw (oneself) down in humility or reverence: *Let us* prostrate *ourselves before the altar of the Lord.* **3** to throw down; flatten: *The storm prostrated the birches.* **4** to weaken; make helpless: *An attack of fever completely* prostrated *me.* **5** worn out; exhausted: *to be* prostrate *with grief.* **6** helpless; conquered: *the* prostrate *victims of a war.* **pros·trat·ed, pros· trat·ing.**

pro·tect (prə tĕkt') to keep safe; guard; defend against danger or injury: *A tigress will fight savagely to* protect *her cubs. He wore a thick overcoat to* protect *him from the bitter cold.*

pro·tec·tion (prə tĕk'shən) **1** someone who or something that protects: *We bought new tires as a* protection *against blowouts.* **2** safekeeping: *The gold shipment arrived under the* protection *of the United States marshal.*

pro·tec·tive (prə tĕk'tĭv) giving protection or shelter: *The artist sprayed a* protective *coating over the drawing to keep it from smudging.* **pro·tec·tive·ly.**

pro·tec·tor (prə tĕk'tər) **1** guardian; defender: *It looks as if he has chosen me as his* protector *against the bigger boys.* **2** something that gives protection: *A welder must wear a glass shield as a* protector *for his eyes.*

pro·tec·tor·ate (prə tĕk'tər it) weak country under the control or protection of a strong country.

pro·te·in (prō'tē in or prō'tēn) any of a group of substances containing nitrogen, that make up the living parts of plant and animal cells. Proteins are necessary for the growth and repair of the body. Some foods rich in proteins are meat, fish, eggs, lima beans, and milk.

¹pro·test (prə tĕst') **1** to object to; express disapproval of: *We all* protested *the extra homework the teacher assigned.* **2** to state a formal objection: *The American colonies* protested *against taxes levied on them by the British Parliament.* **3** to assert strongly against opposition: *Harold* protested *that he never stole a penny in his life.*

²pro·test (prō'tĕst) **1** formal complaint or objection: *The President sent a* protest *to the Russian Ambassador.* **2** objection; re-

sistance: *The burglar went to jail without* protest. **3 under protest** unwillingly: *We paid the traffic fine* under protest.

Prot·es·tant (prŏt'ĭs tənt) **1** member of any Christian church other than the Roman Catholic Church and the Orthodox Eastern Church. **2** relating to such a church or its members.

pro·ton (prō'tŏn) tiny particle of matter having one unit of positive charge. The nucleus of any atom has at least one proton.

pro·to·plasm (prō'tə plăz'əm) the essential living substance in any animal or plant cell.

pro·to·zo·an (prō'tə zō'ən) any single-celled animal; one of a large group (Protozoa) making up the simplest form of animal life. Protozoans are all microscopic and most of them live in water.

pro·trude (prō trōōd') **1** to project; stick out: *A book* protruded *from the man's coat pocket.* **2** to cause to stick out: *The turtle* protruded *its head from its shell.* **pro·trud· ed, pro·trud·ing.**

proud (proud) **1** thinking oneself better than others; conceited; haughty: *He's too* proud *to play with the rest of us.* **2** dignified; self-respecting: *Tom's not a coward. He's just too* proud *to fight over unimportant things.* **3** giving pride and satisfaction: *It was a* proud *day for the school when the team returned undefeated.* **4** noble; magnificent: *The police force marched past us in* proud *formation.* **5 proud of** taking great pride in; pleased and satisfied with: *We're all* proud *of the way you stood up to that bully.* **proud·ly.**

prove (prōōv) **1** to show that something is true: *Her loyalty* proved *her friendship.* **2** to demonstrate by experiment: *Tests are used to* prove *things in laboratories.* **3** to show that something is genuine: *The stranger* proved *his claim to the silver mine by showing us a deed.* **4** to test the quality of: *The band of hungry children* proved *the pudding by eating it.* **5** to show one's own quality or condition: *By that single act John* proved *himself brave and loyal.* **6** to turn out: *After all our worry about the weather, Saturday* proved *to be warm and sunny.* **proved, proved** or **prov·en, prov·ing.**

prov·en (prōō'vən) See **prove.** *The man's innocence was clearly* proven *during the trial.*

prov·en·der (prŏv'ən dər) dry feed for livestock, such as corn, hay, or oats: *With fertile fields and ample water, there should be plenty of* provender *for your cattle.*

prov·erb (prŏv'ərb) **1** short saying, usually traditional, that states some truth or warning, or gives advice about human conduct; maxim; adage. "Half a loaf is better than none" and "Waste not, want not" are proverbs. **2 Proverbs** a book of the Old Testament containing wise sayings.

pro·vide (prə vīd') **1** to furnish; equip: *The police are* provided *with guns only for defense.* **2** to make advance preparations: *Squirrels gather nuts in the fall to* provide *for the winter.* **3** to state as a necessary condition: *Bill's contract* provides *that he must be allowed to choose his own helpers.*
provide for to supply with all necessities: *Father works hard to* provide for *his large family.*
pro·vid·ed, pro·vid·ing.

pro·vid·ed (prə vī'dĭd) on the condition that; if.

prov·i·dence (prŏv'ə dəns) **1** thrifty care for the future: *Because of my mother's* providence *we were all able to go to college.* **2** the care and protective guidance of God or nature: *A special* providence *seemed to watch over him.* **3 Providence** God, as guiding man and protecting him: *With prayers for the protection of* Providence, *the expedition set sail.*

prov·i·dent (prŏv'ə dənt) **1** showing or having care in planning for the future. **2** economical; thrifty: *a* provident *man who wasted nothing.* **prov·i·dent·ly.**

prov·ince (prŏv'ĭns) **1** division of a country or empire. **2** certain field of action, study, business, etc.: *All school activities fall in the* principal's province. **3 provinces** parts of the country away from the capital or cultural centers.

pro·vin·cial (prə vĭn'shəl) **1** having to do with a province: *the* provincial *government.* **2** interested only in local affairs: *A* provincial *person will not be concerned about the international news.* **3** crude; awkward; rustic: *He lost his* provincial *manners after living a year in New York.* **4** person who

lives in or comes from the provinces. **pro·vin·cial·ly.**

pro·vi·sion (prə vĭzh'ən) **1** preparation; care beforehand: *to make* provisions *for a journey.* **2** condition or clause (in a law, will, etc.): *There are severe* provisions *in the law for those breaking the speed limit.* **3 provisions** supply of food: *The prospector took three weeks'* provisions *with him.* **4** to supply with provisions: *to* provision *the camp.*

pro·vi·sion·al (prə vĭzh'ən əl) for the time being; temporary: *a* provisional *government; to make* provisional *arrangements.* **pro·vi·sion·al·ly.**

prov·o·ca·tion (prŏv'ə kā'shən) **1** a provoking: *Deliberate* provocation *of a quarrel is a serious matter.* **2** something which arouses or stirs up anger: *What* provocation *was there for you to hit him?*

pro·voke (prə vōk') **1** to irritate; annoy; incite to anger: *Her rude answer* provoked *John.* **2** to stir up; arouse; excite: *The article against jazz* provoked *much criticism.* **pro·voked, pro·vok·ing.**

prow (prou) the forward end of a boat or ship.

Prow

prow·ess (prou'ĭs) **1** great bravery; valor: *The Indian brave showed great* prowess *by fighting* the bear single-handed. **2** very great skill or ability: *Dan proved his* prowess *as a swimmer by swimming across the lake twice.*

prowl (proul) **1** to walk or move about secretly or slyly looking for food, plunder, etc.: *The thief* prowled *around the big house.* **2 on the prowl** roving and hunting: *The wolves are* on the prowl *for sheep.*

prox·y (prŏk'sĭ) **1** person given authority to act for another; agent: *My lawyer acted as my* proxy *in claiming the money.* **2** authority given to a person to act for another: *to marry by* proxy. **prox·ies.**

pru·dence (prōō'dəns) good sense; caution in practical matters, especially in a person's own affairs: *His* prudence *kept him from taking any wild chances.*

---

fāte, făt, fâre, fär; bē, bĕt; bīte, bĭt; nō, nŏt, nôr; fūse, fŭn, fûr; tōō, tŏŏk; foil; foul; thin; then; hw for wh as in what; zh for s as in usual; ə for a, e, i, o, u, as in ago, linen, peril, atom, minus

pru·dent (prōō′dənt) having or showing good judgment in practical affairs; careful: *A prudent housewife shops for bargains.* **pru·dent·ly.**

¹prune (prōōn) **1** kind of plum which dries without spoiling. **2** dried plum. [**¹prune** comes through French from a Latin word (prunum) meaning "a plum."]

²prune (prōōn) **1** to cut away branches, buds, roots, etc. from a plant in order to improve it. **2** to cut away unnecessary parts from anything to improve it: *By the time the teacher had pruned all the extra words from my composition it was good.* **pruned, prun·ing.** [**²prune** comes through Old French (proignier) from a Latin word (provineare) also meaning "to trim, prune." The Latin word is based on another Latin word (vinea) meaning "vine."]

¹pry (prī) to peer; investigate closely or curiously: *to pry into other people's affairs.* **pries, pried, pry·ing.** [**¹pry** is a word of unknown origin.]

²pry (prī) **1** to raise or open with a lever: *We pried up the top of the jar with a knife blade.* **2** to move (something) with difficulty. **pries, pried, pry·ing.** [**²pry** is a greatly changed form of an English word (prize) meaning "raise."]

P.S. postscript.

psalm (säm) **1** sacred poem or song. **2 Psalm** one of the sacred songs in the Book of Psalms in the Old Testament.

psy·chi·a·try (si kī′ə trī) the branch of medicine that studies and treats mental illness.

psy·chic (sī′kĭk) **1** having to do with the mind or soul. **2** having to do with forces outside or beyond known physical laws. **3** influenced by, or aware of, things which cannot be explained by information received through the five senses: *You must be psychic to know what I'm thinking!*

psy·chol·o·gist (si kŏl′ə jĭst) **1** person trained in psychology and engaged in it as a profession. **2** person without formal training in this subject but who understands human nature.

psy·chol·o·gy (si kŏl′ə jĭ) **1** science of the human mind and the way it acts. **2** science that deals with the way human beings and animals behave.

pt. 1 pint. **2** point. **3** port. **4** part.

pto·maine (tō′mān or tō mān′) any of a group of chemicals, often poisonous, produced by the actions of certain bacteria on proteins.

pub·lic (pŭb′lĭk) **1** of, for, or having to do with the people as a whole: *a public office; a public holiday.* **2** open to everyone; not private: *a public library.* **3** the people as a whole: *The museum is open to the public.* **4** a certain group of people: *the voting public; the music-loving public.* **5** generally known: *The President made the news of the treaty public.*

pub·li·ca·tion (pŭb′lə kā′shən) **1** a printed and published work, as a newspaper, magazine, book, etc.: *a recent publication about the American Indians.* **2** a printing and offering for sale: *The publication of school books is a growing business.*

pub·lic·i·ty (pŭb lĭs′ə tĭ) **1** state of being widely known; public attention: *The publicity given to a national hero.* **2** means by which someone or something becomes publicly known: *He is in charge of publicity for the school play.*

pub·lic·ly (pŭb′lĭk lĭ) in a public manner; openly.

public opinion opinion formed when an open question is discussed and decided on by the general public: *The reform was brought about by public opinion.*

public school school paid for out of taxes, and open to all.

public utility company or organization that supplies such services as electricity, gas, water, transportation, telephone, etc., to a whole community.

pub·lish (pŭb′lĭsh) **1** to print and distribute: *What year was this book published?* **2** to make known, especially make known formally, proclaim: *to publish a will.*

pub·lish·er (pŭb′lĭsh ər) person or company whose business is printing and distributing books, newspapers, magazines, etc.

puck (pŭk) **1** mischievous sprite; elf. **2** hard rubber disk used in playing ice hockey.

puck·er (pŭk′ər) **1** to draw together into folds or wrinkles: *Little brother puckered his lips to give me a kiss.* **2** small fold or wrinkle: *The hot iron made puckers in the piece of silk.*

pud·ding (pŏŏd′ĭng) **1** any of various cake-like or soft desserts, often served with a sauce, as plum pudding, bread pudding, Indian pudding, etc. **2 blood pudding** a kind of sausage. **3 hasty pudding** boiled corn meal, eaten as a cereal. **4 Yorkshire pudding** a kind of batter baked with a roast.

pud·dle (pŭd′əl) **1** small pool of dirty or muddy water, usually from rain or snow. **2** small pool of any liquid: *The kitten left a* puddle *of milk on the floor.*

pue·blo (pwĕb′lō) American Indian village of adobe or stone houses, especially one with many families living in houses resembling apartment houses. **pue·blos.**

Puer·to Ri·can (pwĕr′tō rē′kən) **1** having to do with Puerto Rico or its people. **2** citizen of Puerto Rico or person of Puerto Rican descent.

Puer·to Ri·co (pwĕr′tō rē′kō) island about 1,000 miles southeast of Florida. It is a commonwealth of the United States.

puff (pŭf) **1** short, quick blast: *A puff of wind caught my hat and blew it down the street.* **2** to blow out in puffs: *Smoke puffed from the chimney.* **3** to move or go with puffing: *The train puffed up the hill.* **4** the sound of a short blast of air: *the puff of a locomotive.* **5** to blow; swell: *to puff up one's cheeks.* **6** to breathe quickly and hard: *I was really puffing after that race.* **7** soft pad: *a powder puff.* **8** pastry shell with a filling: *a cream puff.*

puf·fin (pŭf′ĭn) stout-bodied, short-necked northern sea bird. Its large bill is marked with red and yellow stripes.

Puffin, about 13 in. long

puff·y (pŭf′ĭ) **1** puffed up; swollen: *to have* puffy *eyelids.* **2** coming in puffs; breathing hard. **puff·i·er, puff·i·est.**

pug·na·cious (pŭg nā′shəs) quick to fight; quarrelsome. **pug·na·cious·ly.**

pug nose (pŭg′nōz′) a turned-up nose, broad at the tip.

pull (pŏŏl) **1** to draw toward oneself: *to pull a wagon; to pull a nail.* **2** to draw out or tear away: *to pull a tooth; to pull weeds.* **3** to tug at with force: *to pull hair.* **4** to tear or rend: *They pulled the old sheet to pieces for rags.* **5** to move in any direction: *We pulled our chairs up to the fire. A strange car pulled into the driveway.* **6** a pulling; tug: *The puppy gave my trousers a* pull. **7** effort or force: *a long pull up the hill; the pull of the moon on the tides.*

pul·let (pŏŏl′ĭt) young hen.

pul·ley (pŏŏl′ĭ) **1** grooved wheel over which a rope may be pulled to raise weights or change the direction of a pull. **2** such a wheel and the frame in which it turns.

Pulley

Pull·man (pŏŏl′mən) railroad car with private sleeping rooms or seats that can be made up into berths, or one in which especially comfortable chairs may be reserved. Also called **Pullman car.**

pulp (pŭlp) **1** soft, fleshy part of a fruit or plant stem. **2** inner part of a tooth containing the nerves and blood vessels. **3** soft, moist mass: *The pulp for making paper is wood ground up and mixed with water.*

pul·pit (pŏŏl′pĭt) **1** in some churches a small elevated balcony from which the minister speaks. **2** the clergy as a group: *The pulpit is not very influential in this town.*

pulp·wood (pŭlp′wŏŏd′) wood prepared for making paper.

Pulpit

pul·sate (pŭl′sāt) **1** to throb or beat with a regular rhythm, as the heart. **2** to quiver; vibrate. **pul·sat·ed, pul·sat·ing.**

pulse (pŭls) **1** the throbbing or beating in an artery as blood is pumped through it by the heart. **2** any regular stroke or beat: *the pulse of the music.* **3** to beat; throb; vibrate: *Her heart pulsed faster with excitement.* **pulsed, puls·ing.**

---

fāte, făt, fâre, fär; bē, bĕt; bite, bĭt; nō, nŏt, nôr; fūse, fŭn, fûr; tōō, tŏŏk; foil; foul; thin; ~~then~~; hw for wh as in *wh*at; zh for s as in usual; ə for a, e, i, o, u, as in ago, linen, peril, atom, minus

pul·ver·ize (pŭl'və rīz') **1** to grind or pound into a powder or dust: *By stepping on a piece of chalk, you* pulverize *it.* **2** to become powder or dust: *Rocks* pulverize *through the action of frost, rain, and mud.* **pul·ver·ized, pul·ver·iz·ing.**

pu·ma (pū'mə) large American wildcat; mountain lion or cougar.

pum·ice (pŭm'ĭs) light, spongy, volcanic rock, used in polishing and cleaning.

¹pump (pŭmp) **1** machine for moving liquids or gases by pressure or suction. **2** to raise or draw by means of a pump: *Tony* pumped *a pail of water from the well.* **3** to act as a pump: *The heart* pumps *blood.* **4** to question closely: *The woman* pumped *the child about his father's business.* [¹**pump** is probably a word of Germanic origin.]

Pump

²pump (pŭmp) shoe that is cut low. It is without a lace, strap, or other fastening. [²**pump** seems to be from a French word (pompe) meaning "an ornament."]

pump·kin (pŭmp'kĭn or pŭng'kĭn) **1** a large, golden yellow, usually round fruit of a vine. It is used for pies and as cattle food. **2** the large-leafed vine which bears this fruit.

Pumpkin

pun (pŭn) **1** a play on words alike in sound but different in meaning, or on different meanings of the same word: *"He went and told the sexton and the sexton tolled the bell." is a* pun. **2** to make a pun. **punned, pun·ning.**

¹punch (pŭnch) **1** tool for making holes. **2** to make a hole with a punch: *The conductor* punched *the ticket.* **3** tool to stamp numbers, letters, and the like on metal: *The mechanic used a* punch *to stamp a number on the engine.* **4** a blow with the fist. **5** to strike a blow with the fist: *The boxer* punched *the punching bag.* [¹**punch** is short for an English word (puncheon) meaning "tool that stamps."]

Punches

²punch (pŭnch) a drink made by mixing various liquids: *a fruit* punch. [²**punch** is ultimately from a word meaning "five" from the five ingredients of the drink.]

punc·tu·al (pŭngk'chŏŏ əl) on time; not late; prompt: *He was as* punctual *as the striking of the clock.* **punc·tu·al·ly.**

punc·tu·ate (pŭngk'chŏŏ āt') **1** to use periods, commas, and other marks between written words to make the meaning clear. **2** to emphasize: *He* punctuated *his remarks with gestures.* **3** to interrupt from time to time: *a speech* punctuated *with cheering and booing.* **punc·tu·at·ed, punc·tu·at·ing.**

punc·tu·a·tion (pŭngk'chŏŏ ā'shən) **1** system of using certain marks such as commas and periods to make the meaning of a sentence clear. **2 punctuation mark** any of these marks, such as a comma (,), question mark (?), etc.

punc·ture (pŭngk'chər) **1** small hole or wound made by something pointed: *The nail made a* puncture *in our tire.* **2** to make a hole in; prick; pierce: *The mischievous boy* punctured *his sister's balloon with a needle.* **punc·tured, punc·tur·ing.**

pun·gent (pŭn'jənt) **1** sharp or biting: *Sulfur has a* pungent *smell. Mustard has a* pungent *taste.* **2** stinging; piercing; sarcastic: *a* pungent *remark.* **pun·gent·ly.**

pun·ish (pŭn'ĭsh) **1** to cause a person to pay a penalty for a fault or crime; chastise: *My mother* punished *me for going out without permission.* **2** to impose a penalty for (an offense against the law): *Crimes are* punished *by the law.*

pun·ish·a·ble (pŭn'ĭsh ə bəl) liable to or deserving punishment: *In wartime, treason is* punishable *by death.*

pun·ish·ment (pŭn'ĭsh mənt) **1** penalty imposed for a crime or fault: *Tom's* punishment *was that he had to stay at home on Saturday.* **2** a punishing or being punished: *Harsh* punishment *only made the stubborn child worse.*

punk (pŭngk) **1** a preparation that burns slowly without flame, often used in sticks to light fireworks. **2** decayed wood used as tinder.

punt (pŭnt) **1** shallow, flat-bottomed boat with square ends. **2** to drive (a boat) forward by pushing with a pole against a river or lake bottom: *He* punted *the boat* along the shallow river. **3** to drop a football from the hands and kick it before it touches the ground. **4** such a kick.

pu·ny (pū′nĭ) **1** undersized; weak: *a puny baby.* **2** half-hearted; feeble: *a puny effort.* **pu·ni·er, pu·ni·est.**

pup (pŭp) **1** young dog; puppy. **2** the young of foxes, wolves, seals, and several other mammals.

pu·pa (pū′pə) insect in the resting stage between a larva and an adult insect. **pu·pae** or **pu·pas.**

Pupa

pu·pil (pū′pəl) **1** person who is learning under the direction of a teacher; a schoolboy or schoolgirl. **2** the dark opening in the center of the eye through which one sees.

Pupil

pup·pet (pŭp′ĭt) **1** jointed doll that can be made to move by pulling strings or by movements of a hand inserted in it. **2** person who follows without question the orders of another: *The king was the dictator's puppet.*

pup·py (pŭp′ĭ) young dog. **pup·pies.**

pur·chase (pûr′chəs) **1** to buy. **2** a buying: *the purchase of Christmas presents.* **3** something bought: *I brought my purchase home to show you.* **pur·chased, pur·chas·ing.**

Puppet

pur·chas·er (pûr′chəs ər) person who buys something.

pure (pyŏŏr) **1** free of foreign matter; clean; clear; unmixed: *of pure silver; pure food.* **2** without guilt or sin; innocent. **3** mere; sheer; nothing but: *to meet by pure chance; to talk pure nonsense.* **pur·er, pur·est.**

pure·bred (pyŏŏr′brĕd′) of an animal, having ancestors of unmixed breed.

pu·rée (pyŏŏ rā′) **1** boiled or strained pulp of vegetables or fruit. **2** thick soup of such materials: *pea purée; tomato purée.*

pure·ly (pyŏŏr′lĭ) merely; only: *I am doing this work purely to please you.*

pure·ness (pyŏŏr′nĭs) a being pure; cleanliness: *the pureness of rain water.*

pur·ga·to·ry (pûr′gə tôr′ĭ) in the belief of some Christian churches, the state of the soul after death in which it is cleansed of sin before entering heaven.

purge (pûrj) **1** to cleanse; remove impurities or foreign matter from; purify. **2** to free from guilt or sin: *She purged herself by confessing what she had done.* **3** a cleansing; a freeing from mixture. **4** a removing of persons who are not desirable or loyal: *There was a purge when the new government took command.* **5** to clear or empty the bowels with a medicine. **6** a medicine used to empty the bowels. **purged, purg·ing.**

pu·ri·fi·ca·tion (pyŏŏr′ə fə kā′shən) **1** a cleansing from guilt or sin. **2** removal of impurities: *Chlorine is used for the purification of water in swimming pools.*

pu·ri·fy (pyŏŏr′ə fī) to make pure; cleanse. **pu·ri·fied, pu·ri·fy·ing.**

pu·ri·tan (pyŏŏr′ə tən) **1** person who is very strict in religion or morals. **2** Puritan member of a group of Protestants in England and the American colonies in the sixteenth and seventeenth centuries. The Puritans supported reforms in the Church of England and believed in a strict moral code and simplicity in religious worship.

pu·ri·ty (pyŏŏr′ə tĭ) **1** freedom from impurities or foreign matter: *Are you certain of the purity of this chemical?* **2** freedom from evil or sin; innocence.

pur·loin (pər loin′) to steal.

pur·ple (pûr′pəl) **1** color made by mixing red and blue. **2** of this color. **3** robe of this color worn by a king or other person of great power. **4** symbol of royal power, great wealth, or high rank: *born to the purple; to wear the purple.*

pur·plish (pûr′plĭsh) somewhat purple.

¹pur·port (pər pôrt′) to give or convey a meaning (often false, as a statement or action): *The message purported to come from the president.*

²pur·port (pûr′pôrt) meaning; significance: *to grasp the purport of the note.*

---

fāte, făt, fâre, fär; bē, bĕt; bīte, bĭt; nō, nŏt, nôr; fūse, fŭn, fûr; tōō, tŏŏk; foil; foul; thin; ~~then~~
hw for wh as in *wh*at; zh for s as in u*s*ual; ə for a, e, i, o, u, as in *a*go, lin*e*n, per*i*l, at*o*m, min*u*s

pur·pose (pûr′pəs) **1** aim; intention; desired result: *My* purpose *in criticizing you is to make you do better next time.* **2** to intend: *I* purpose *to have this book finished by the end of the week.* **3 on purpose** not by accident; intentionally. **pur·posed, pur·pos·ing.**

pur·pose·ful (pûr′pəs fəl) having a purpose; determined. **pur·pose·ful·ly.**

pur·pose·ly (pûr′pəs li) intentionally; on purpose: *She dropped her handkerchief* purposely *to see if he would pick it up.*

purr (pûr) **1** the low, murmuring sound made by a cat when it seems to be contented. **2** any similar sound: *the* purr *of a car's motor.* **3** to make such a sound. **4** to express with such a sound: *She* purred *her contentment.*

purse (pûrs) **1** small bag or case to carry money. **2** woman's handbag. **3** sum of money; funds: *The war was a great drain on the public* purse. **4** money offered as a prize, reward, or gift: *The pupils got up a* purse *for the teacher who was retiring.* **5** to wrinkle or pucker: *He* pursed *his lips to whistle.* **pursed, purs·ing.**

pur·sue (pər sōō′ or pər sū′) **1** to chase; follow in order to capture: *The police were called in to* pursue *the escaped convict.* **2** to follow; engage in: *He* pursued *law as a profession.* **3** to follow through; keep up; continue: *She* pursued *her struggle to gain fame.* **4** to seek: *She* pursues *pleasure but she does not seem happy.* **pur·sued, pur·su·ing.**

pur·su·er (pər sōō′ər or pər sū′ər) one who follows after; one who takes part in a chase or pursuit: *He fled his* pursuers.

pur·suit (pər sōōt′ or pər sūt′) **1** a chase: *the* pursuit *of a deer.* **2** a seeking; a quest: *the* pursuit *of fame.* **3** occupation or pastime: *Singing is one of her many* pursuits.

pus (pŭs) a yellow-white substance produced by sores, abscesses, etc.

push (pŏŏsh) **1** to press against in order to move: *We* pushed *the desk, but it was too heavy to move.* **2** to urge; press: *We* pushed *him to make a speech.* **3** to move forward with an effort: *The army* pushed *on through the snow.* **4** to make a great effort to sell: *The store is* pushing *toys because the Christmas rush is over.* **5** a shove; a thrust: *Joe gave Tom a playful* push.

push button a button which, when pushed, turns an electric current on or off: *Our garage door opens and closes by* push button.

push·cart (pŏŏsh′kärt′) small cart which is pushed by hand.

puss (pŏŏs) cat.

puss·y (pŏŏs′i) cat. **pus·sies.**

pussy willow small willow that bears furry, pearl-gray buds early in the spring.

put (pŏŏt) **1** to place; set; cause to be (in a certain place or condition): *to* put *the dishes on the table; to*

Pussy willow

put *someone in a bad temper.* **2** to express; set forth: *The speaker* puts *his case plainly.*

put away 1 to put in the proper place: *to* put away *the dishes.* **2** to save, or set aside, for later use: *to* put away *money for a trip.*

put down 1 to overcome with force; suppress: *to* put down *a rebellion.* **2** to write down; record: *to* put down *an address.*

put off to delay: *He* put off *his departure.*

put on 1 to get into: *He* put on *his clothes in a hurry.* **2** to apply: *The actor* put on *make-up.* **3** to assume: *The fighter* put on *a bold front.* **4** to stage: *to* put on *a play.*

put out 1 to extinguish: *to* put out *a light.* **2** to annoy: *I was* put out *by her rudeness.*

put through to carry out; accomplish: *to* put *through a deal.*

put up 1 to pack or preserve (fruit, etc.). **2** to build. **3** to offer (for sale): *They* put up *furniture at auction.* **4** to give or occupy lodging: *The tourists* put up *at a motel.* **5** to provide money or services (for). **6** to raise: *to* put up *a flag; to* put up *prices.*

put up to to get (someone) to do by suggestion: *Nobody* put *the boy* up to *that mischief, he thought it up by himself.*

put up with to tolerate; endure: *A pioneer must* put up with *hardship.*

put, put·ting.

pu·trid (pū′trid) rotten; foul: *The garbage had become* putrid.

put·ty (pŭt′i) **1** soft cement used for filling cracks, holding glass in a window frame, etc. It is usually made of powdered chalk and boiled linseed oil. **2** to apply putty to: *to putty a window frame.* **put·tied, put·ty·ing.**

puz·zle (pŭz′əl) **1** something difficult and confusing to understand: *How our team could play so poorly is a puzzle to me.* **2** to perplex; confuse; bewilder: *Not getting a letter from my parents puzzles me.* **3** toy or game presenting some problem or difficulty which is fun to solve: *a crossword puzzle; a jigsaw puzzle.*

puzzle out to find the meaning to something difficult by thinking carefully: *Bill puzzled out the meaning of the sentence.*

puzzle over to be perplexed; think about something difficult or confusing: *The class puzzled over the difficult problem.* **puz·zled, puz·zling.**

pyg·my (pĭg′mi) **1** undersized person; a dwarf. **2** Pygmy member of an African race of small people. **pyg·mies.**

py·ja·mas (pə jä′məz or pə jăm′əz) pajamas.

Pyramids

pyr·a·mid (pĭr′ə mĭd) **1** a solid with triangular sides meeting at a point, and a flat base. **2** any of the great, four-sided, stone pyramids built by the ancient Egyptians.

pyre (pīr) pile of wood on which corpses are burned.

py·ro·ma·ni·ac (pī′rō mā′nĭ ăk′) insane person who cannot keep from setting houses and other things on fire.

py·thon (pī′thŏn) a type of large snake which kills its prey by winding around an animal and crushing it.

Q

Q, q (kū) 17th letter of the English alphabet. **qt.** quart.

¹quack (kwăk) **1** the sound made by a duck. **2** to make a sound like a duck. [¹**quack** is the imitation of a duck's sound.]

²quack (kwăk) **1** person who dishonestly, or through ignorance, pretends to be skilled in medicine or other science. **2** not genuine; false; pretended: *a quack doctor; a quack medicine.* [²**quack** is short for "quacksalver" of the same meaning. The word "quacksalver" comes from a Dutch word (kwakzalver) meaning "one who quacks or boasts of his salves or secret remedies."]

quad·ru·ped (kwŏd′rŏŏ pĕd′) animal with four feet.

quad·ru·plet (kwŏd′rŏŏ plĭt′ or kwŏd rŏŏ′-plĭt) **1** any one of four children born at one birth. **2** group or combination of four things.

quaff (kwäf or kwăf) to drink in long, large swallows or gulps: *to quaff lemonade.*

¹quail (kwāl) small, plump game bird. Some kinds are called bobwhite or partridge. [¹**quail** is from an Old French word (quaille) of Germanic origin.]

²quail (kwāl) to lose courage; draw back in fear: *The dog quailed before his harsh master.* [²**quail** is probably from an Old French word (coaillier) meaning "to curdle." The French word comes from a Latin word (coagulare) meaning "to coagulate."]

California quail, 9½ to 11 in. long

quaint (kwānt) **1** pleasantly old-fashioned: *a quaint old lady.* **2** odd but attractive: *a quaint idea; a quaint song.* **quaint·ly.**

quake (kwāk) **1** to shake; shiver; tremble: *Tom quaked at the thought of his examination.* **2** a shaking or trembling, especially an earthquake. **quaked, quak·ing.**

---

fāte, făt, fâre, fär; bē, bĕt; bite, bĭt; nō, nŏt, nôr; fūse, fŭn, fûr; tōō, tŏŏk; foil; foul; thin; ~~then~~; hw for wh as in *what*; zh for s as in u*s*ual; ə for a, e, i, o, u, as in *a*go, lin*e*n, per*i*l, at*o*m, min*u*s

qual·i·fi·ca·tion (kwŏl'ə fə kā'shən)　**1** knowledge, strength, skill, or experience needed for a task or position: *He has excellent* qualifications *for team captain.* **2** limitation; modification; reservation: *The teacher praised his essay, but with* qualifications.

qual·i·fied (kwŏl'ə fīd')　**1** having done what is required: *a man* qualified *to vote.* **2** having the skills, experience, etc., that are required: *a man* qualified *for a job.* **3** with some reservations: *His daring plan had the* qualified *support of his teammates.*

qual·i·fy (kwŏl'ə fī')　**1** to gain or give the necessary skill, knowledge, etc. (for a purpose): *He* qualified *for the football team by hard training. His training* qualifies *him for the job.* **2** to make less strong or positive; modify: *The jury* qualified *the conviction with a recommendation of mercy.* **3** to describe; name: *The audience* qualified *the speaker as a bore.* **qual·i·fied, qual·i·fy·ing.**

qual·i·ty (kwŏl'ə tĭ)　**1** that which makes a person or thing different from another; characteristic: *Ability to think is man's outstanding* quality. **2** worth; value: *The shop sold goods of both high and low* quality. **3** excellence; high merit: *The restaurant earned its fine reputation by the* quality *of its food.* **4** an essential part of a person or thing: *the melodious* quality *of her voice; the acid* quality *of a lemon.* **qual·i·ties.**

qualm (kwäm or kwôm)　**1** misgiving; pang of doubt about one's behavior; twinge of conscience: *She felt* qualms *about repeating the gossip she had overheard.* **2** sudden feeling of faintness or nausea.

quan·ti·ty (kwŏn'tə tĭ)　**1** amount: *What* quantity *of flour was used in this cake?* **2** considerable amount: *We were dismayed to see the* quantity *of food wasted on the picnic.* **quan·ti·ties.**

quar·an·tine (kwŏr'ən tēn' or kwôr'ən-tēn')　**1** a keeping of a person away from other people because he has a contagious disease. **2** a place where such people are kept. **3** to keep (a person or thing) away from others. **4** time before a ship docks when passengers are examined for disease. **quar·an·tined, quar·an·tin·ing.**

quar·rel (kwŏr'əl or kwôr'əl)　**1** an angry dispute, argument, or disagreement. **2** to

have a dispute: *The ranchers* quarreled *over the use of the water hole.* **3** a cause for disagreement: *I have no* quarrel *with your arrangements for the trip.* **4** to find fault with: *to* quarrel *with a proposal.*

quar·rel·some (kwŏr'əl səm or kwôr'əl-səm)　inclined to quarrel. **quar·rel·some·ly.**

¹quar·ry (kwŏr'ĭ or kwôr'ĭ)　**1** open pit from which marble, slate, or other stone is obtained by cutting or blasting. **2** to dig or obtain from a quarry. **quar·ries; quar·ried, quar·ry·ing.** [¹quarry comes from the Old French (quarriere) from another Old French word (carre) meaning "squared stone."]

²quar·ry (kwŏr'ĭ or kwôr'ĭ)　object of pursuit or chase, especially in hunting: *The hounds followed their* quarry *to the foxhole.* **quar·ries.** [²quarry comes through Old French (cuiree) from a Latin word (corium) meaning "skin." In earlier times a portion of the flesh of a hunted animal was placed on its hide and given to the hounds as a reward.]

quart (kwôrt)　**1** measure, either liquid or dry, of two pints or one quarter of a gallon. **2** container which holds a quart.

quar·ter (kwôr'tər)　**1** one of the four equal parts of a thing; one fourth: *A* quart *is a* quarter *of a gallon.* **2** the fourth part of a dollar; twenty-five cents: *"Here's a* quarter," *said Hans, handing the clerk two dimes and a nickel.* **3** a twenty-five cent piece: *May I have five nickels for this* quarter? **4** the fourth part of an hour: *The clock just struck the* quarter. **5** fourth part of a year: *We showed a fine profit the second* quarter. **6** any one of the four monthly changes of the moon: *The moon was in its last* quarter. **7** person or group of persons who are part of a larger group: *The news came in from several* quarters *of the congregation.* **8** any one of the four main points of the compass: *People came from all* quarters *of the globe.* **9** district; area: *New Orleans has a quaint French* quarter. **10** any of the four legs of an animal with the parts near it: *a* quarter *of beef.* **11** to divide into fourths: *Dora* quartered *the apple.* **12** permission

Quarter

quarterback

to live; mercy: *The enemy showed no
quarter.* **13** to supply with a place to live:
*The colonel quartered his men in the town
hall.* **14 quarters** place to live; assigned
place: *The bugle called the men to* quarters.
15 close quarters narrow, crowded space.

quar·ter·back (kwôr′tər bäk′) one of four
players behind the front line on a football
team. He calls the signals.

quar·ter·ly (kwôr′tər li) **1** occurring once
every three months: *to make* quarterly
payments. **2** magazine published every
three months. **quar·ter·lies.**

quar·ter·mas·ter (kwôr′tər mäs′tər) **1** in
the army, officer in charge of stores,
equipment, etc. **2** in the navy, petty officer in charge of steering, signals, etc.

quar·ter·staff (kwôr′tər stäf′) stout wood-
en pole from six to eight feet long, formerly
used as a weapon.

quar·tet (kwôr tět′) **1** group of four persons or things. **2** musical composition for
four singers or instruments. **3** four singers
or players who perform together.

quartz (kwôrts) common hard mineral
found in crystals or masses. Pure quartz is
transparent and colorless, and is used in
special kinds of glass.

qua·sar (kwā′sär′) one of a small group of
heavenly bodies, recently discovered, that
give out very large amounts of light and
radio waves, and seem to be the most
distant bodies ever detected.

qua·ver (kwā′vər) **1** a shaking or trembling.
2 trembling or quiv-
ering sound. **3** to
tremble; shake.

Quay

quay (kē) wharf;
stone-built landing
place. (Homonym:
key)

queen (kwēn) **1** wife of a king. **2** woman
who rules over a country. **3** woman who
is a real or honorary leader in a certain
field or activity: *the* queen *of the cherry
blossom festival; a society* queen. **4** town,
ship, place, or thing spoken of as first in
honor, respect, or value: *The* queen *of the
fleet made her maiden voyage last year.*
5 ant or bee that lays eggs and is the head

questionable

of a colony. There is usually only one
queen ant or bee in a colony. **6** a playing
card with the picture of a queen on it.
7 in chess, the only piece which can move
across the board in any direction.

queen·ly (kwēn′li) like a queen or fit for
a queen: *a* queenly *woman; a* queenly
manner; queenly *robes.* **queen·li·er, queen·
li·est.**

queer (kwir) **1** different from what is
normal; odd; peculiar: *He has a* queer
sense of humor. **2** giddy; dizzy: *I had to
stop and sit down for a moment because
I felt* queer. **queer·ly.**

quell (kwěl) to subdue; put down; put an
end to: *The policemen* quelled *the riot.*

quench (kwěnch) **1** to put an end to; slake:
He quenched *his thirst at the fountain.*
2 to put out: *to* quench *a fire.*

quer·u·lous (kwěr′ə ləs) faultfinding; complaining; peevish: *to make a* querulous
answer. **quer·u·lous·ly.**

que·ry (kwir′i) **1** a question: *Does anyone
have a* query *concerning Bill's report on
Africa?* **2** to ask or question: *The reporters*
queried *the mayor about his decision to run
again.* **3** to question the truth of; feel
doubt about: *Allen* queried *my statement.*
que·ries, que·ried, que·ry·ing.

quest (kwěst) **1** a search: *a prospector's* quest
for valuable minerals. **2** in stories of the
Middle Ages, a mission; a dedicated
search: *Sir Lancelot's* quest *for the Grail.*

ques·tion (kwěs′chən) **1** something asked;
a request for information. "What is your
name?" is a question. **2** to ask (to get
information): *The pupils* questioned *the
teacher about the results of the test.* **3** objection; doubt: *The senator raised a* question
about the housing bill. **4** to doubt: *Some
customers* questioned *the truth of the advertisement.* **5** matter (or problem) to be
considered or discussed: *The city council
considered the* question *of repairing the
streets.* **6 out of the question** not to be
considered; impossible: *A trip to Europe is
out of the* question *this year.* **7 beyond
question** absolutely certain.

ques·tion·a·ble (kwěs′chən ə bəl) **1** open
to doubt; not certain: *It is* questionable

---

fāte, fǎt, fâre, fär; bē, bět; bīte, bǐt; nō, nǒt, nôr; fūse, fǔn, fûr; tōō, tŏŏk; foil; foul; thin; ~~then~~;
hw for wh as in *wh*at; zh for s as in u*s*ual; ə for a, e, i, o, u, as in *a*go, lin*e*n, per*i*l, at*o*m, min*u*s

whether Columbus was the first European to see America. **2** dubious; to be suspected: I think his actions are highly questionable. **ques·tion·a·bly.**

question mark a mark (?) at the end of a sentence to show that a question is being asked.

ques·tion·naire (kwĕs′chə när′) series of prepared questions on a particular subject, asked of certain people to find out opinions, facts, etc.

queue (kū) **1** a braid of hair hanging down the back. **2** a waiting line of people: A long queue stretched from the ticket office window. (Homonym: cue)

Queue

quick (kwĭk) **1** fast; rapid; done with speed. **2** fast to notice or understand; alert; lively: A person with a quick mind could have avoided the accident. **3** easily excited or aroused: She tried to control her quick temper by counting to 10 when annoyed. **4** sensitive flesh, especially the skin under the fingernail. **5 to the quick** very deeply: Our aunt was hurt to the quick when the family didn't visit her. **6 the quick and the dead** the living and the dead. **quick·ly.**

quick·en (kwĭk′ən) **1** to move or cause to move faster; hurry; hasten: Their pace quickened. They quickened their pace. **2** to become more lively or eager: Their interest in Jefferson quickened when they heard a story about his boyhood.

quick·ness (kwĭk′nĭs) **1** speediness. **2** liveliness; alertness.

quick·sand (kwĭk′sănd′) deep mass of very fine, wet sand which will not hold up a heavy weight.

quick·sil·ver (kwĭk′sĭl′vər) the silvery liquid metal, mercury.

quick-wit·ted (kwĭk′wĭt′ĭd) keen; alert; clever: The quick-witted debater had a ready answer for every question. **quick·wit·ted·ly.**

qui·et (kwī′ət) **1** silent; making little or no sound or disturbance: The baby was quiet all night. **2** still; without motion: The sea was quiet with hardly any waves. **3** peaceful; calm; without much activity or excitement: We spent a quiet evening at home reading. **4** to make or become calm, peace-

ful, still, or silent: His calm voice quieted the mob. The mob quieted down when the police arrived. **5** stillness; silence: There was a sudden quiet between claps of thunder. **6** calmness; peacefulness: in the quiet of the evening. **7** mild; gentle; calm: Rachel has a quiet disposition and seldom loses her temper. **8** not loud or bright; not showy: Pale blue is a quiet color. Mr. Temple favors quiet neckties. **qui·et·ly.**

qui·et·ness (kwī′ət nĭs) **1** stillness; silence. **2** peacefulness; calm.

quill (kwĭl) **1** long, stiff feather. **2** the stiff, hollow shaft of a feather. **3** pen made of a feather. **4** one of the stiff, barbed, spinelike hairs of a porcupine.
Quill

quilt (kwĭlt) **1** bed cover made of two layers of cloth with a layer of wool, down, etc., between them. The layers are held together and the filling kept in place by stitching or by tufting; comforter. **2** to make quilts, often by a group of people: The ladies of the sewing circle quilted as they chatted. **3** to sew together over padding: to quilt the lining of a jacket.

quince (kwĭns) **1** hard yellow fruit shaped like a pear, with an acid taste. Quinces are used chiefly in making jellies, preserves, etc. **2** the tree this fruit grows on.

qui·nine (kwī′nīn) bitter medicine made from the bark of a tropical tree. It is used in the treatment of malaria.

quin·tet (kwĭn tĕt′) **1** any group of five, especially a group of five musicians. **2** music written for five musical instruments.

quin·tup·let (kwĭn′tyoŏ plĭt or kwĭn tŭp′-lĭt) **1** any one of five children born at one birth. **2** group or combination of five things.

quit (kwĭt) **1** to stop; cease: I quit playing when mother called. **2** to leave; depart from: He quit the army. **3** to come to a stop: Let's quit and go home. **4** free: I'm glad to be quit of that debt. **quit** or **quit·ted, quit·ting.**

quite (kwĭt) **1** completely; entirely; wholly: You are quite right. **2** to a considerable degree: It is quite cold today.

quit·ter (kwĭt′ər) person who gives up, especially from laziness or cowardice.

578

¹quiv·er (kwĭv'ər) the case in which an archer carries his arrows. [**¹quiver** is from an Old French word (cuivre). The French word is of Germanic origin.]

Quiver

²quiv·er (kwĭv'ər) **1** to shake or tremble rapidly: *Rabbits* quiver *in the cold. Her voice* quivers *when she sings.* **2** a trembling motion or sound: *I see a* quiver *in the leaves.* [**²quiver** is probably a form of **quaver.**]

quiz (kwĭz) **1** an informal examination, sometimes in the form of a game: *She did very well on the history quiz.* **2** to question or examine informally: *I quizzed him on his studies.* **quiz·zes; quizzed, quiz·zing.**

quoit (kwoit) **1** in a game, a flat iron ring meant to be tossed over a peg driven into the ground. **2 quoits** the game played with such rings.

quo·ta (kwō'tə) portion (of a whole) that is due from or allotted to a person, group, or district; share; proportion: *We've brought our quota of food for the picnic.*

quo·ta·tion (kwō tā'shən) **1** a quoting of someone else's words. **2** the words thus quoted. **3** a passage repeated from a book, poem, etc. **4** statement of a market price: *stock* quotations *in the newspaper.* **5 quotation mark** either of a pair of marks (" ") placed at the beginning and end of a passage or word to show that it was said, asked, or written. Examples are: "Stop the car," said Mother. "Jackie lost his cap." We read in the Bible, "Thou shalt love thy neighbor as thyself."

quote (kwōt) **1** to repeat the words of another person or a passage from a book, poem, etc. **2** the words or passage thus repeated. **3** to enclose in quotation marks: *You should* quote *this passage in your composition.* **quot·ed, quot·ing.**

quoth (kwōth) said; spoke. This word is old-fashioned and seldom used except in poetry.

quo·tient (kwō'shənt) an answer to a problem in division; result obtained when one number is divided by another: *If 12 is divided by 2, the* quotient *is 6.*

R

R, r (är) 18th letter of the English alphabet.

rab·bi (răb'ī) **1** in the Jewish religion, a man authorized to teach and interpret law and ritual. **2** minister of a Jewish congregation. **rab·bis** or **rab·bies.**

rab·bit (răb'ĭt) small burrowing animal related to the hare but with shorter ears and less powerful hind legs. Some hares are called rabbits, as the jackrabbit.

Eastern cottontail, 11 to 17 in. long

rab·ble (răb'əl) **1** an unruly crowd; a mob. **2** a term of contempt for the common people: *The aristocrats' contempt for the* rabble *led to the French Revolution.*

ra·bies (rā'bēz) infectious disease of warm-blooded animals, often fatal; hydrophobia.

It is sometimes given to man by the bite of an infected animal.

rac·coon (ră kōon') **1** grayish-brown, tree-dwelling animal with a bushy, ringed tail and face markings like a black mask. **2** fur of this animal. Also spelled **racoon.**

Raccoon, about 2 ft. long

¹race (rās) **1** a contest of speed: *a boat* race. **2** a contest for a prize, office, etc.: *a race for the governorship.* **3** to try to outdo in speed: *I'll* race *you to the corner.* **4** to move with speed; hurry: *You'll have to* race *to catch the bus.* **5** to cause to speed: *He* raced *the motor of his car.* **6** a swift, rushing current: *a* race *of water in a stream.* **raced, rac·ing.** [**¹race** is from an Old Norse word (rās) meaning "a running."]

---

fāte, făt, fâre, fär; bē, bĕt; bīte, bĭt; nō, nŏt, nôr; fūse, fŭn, fûr; tōō, tŏŏk; foil; foul; thin; ~~then~~; hw for wh as in *wh*at; zh for s as in u*s*ual; ə for a, e, i, o, u, as in *a*go, lin*e*n, per*i*l, at*o*m, min*u*s

²**race** (rās) **1** group of people having similar characteristics and a common ancestry: *the Negro* race. **2** group of people with similar geographical and cultural backgrounds: *the Mediterranean* race. **3** a large division of living creatures: *the human* race. [²**race** comes through French from an Italian word (razza) of the same meaning.]

race·course (rās′kôrs′) track or route marked out for contests of speed, whether by land or water.

rac·er (rā′sər) **1** person or animal trained for or competing in a contest of speed: *That horse is a great* racer. **2** vehicle or boat used or suitable for use in a contest of speed: *His new car is a* racer. **3** a swift snake, usually the American black snake.

race track a field or course laid out for races.

ra·cial (rā′shəl) having to do with the races of man. **ra·cial·ly.**

Towel rack   Hay rack   Storage rack

rack (răk) **1** framework of shelves, bars, or hooks on or in which articles may be hung, stored, or displayed. **2** an old instrument of torture, which stretched and dislocated a victim's joints. **3** to exert severely; torment: *to* rack *one's brain for a solution.*

¹**rack·et** (răk′it) **1** disturbing noise; din; uproar: *The children were causing a* racket. **2** dishonest or irregular way of earning a living or making money. [¹**racket** is probably the imitation of a sound.]

²**rack·et** (răk′it) net-covered oval frame ending in a straight handle, used to bat a light ball in certain games. [²**racket** comes through French (raquette) from an Arabic word (rāhāt) meaning "the palms of the hands."]

Tennis racket

ra·coon (ră kōōn′) raccoon.

ra·dar (rā′där) device for finding the position and distance of unseen objects, such as airplanes or ships, by reflected radio waves.

ra·di·al (rā′dĭ əl) branching out from a central point; radiating like the spokes of a wheel. **ra·di·al·ly.**

ra·di·ance (rā′dĭ əns) **1** great brightness: *He would never forget the* radiance *of the August countryside.* **2** sparkling appearance of well-being, loveliness, or joy: *the* radiance *of her smile.*

ra·di·ant (rā′dĭ ənt) **1** shining; full of brightness: *It was a* radiant *sunset.* **2 radiant energy** energy that is given off by a source in the form of rays. **ra·di·ant·ly.**

ra·di·ate (rā′dĭ āt′) **1** to give out energy in the form of heat, light, X rays, or other kinds of rays. **2** to extend in several directions from a central point: *Spokes* radiate *from the center of a wheel.* **3** to spread: *to* radiate *a sense of happiness.* **ra·di·at·ed, ra·di·at·ing.**

ra·di·a·tion (rā′dĭ ā′shən) **1** the giving off of energy in the form of heat, light, or other rays: *the* radiation *of heat from the sun.* **2** the energy or rays sent out.

ra·di·a·tor (rā′dĭ ā′tər) **1** system of pipes through which hot water or steam is forced to heat a room or building. **2** a honeycomb tank in an automobile where water from the cooling system is cooled by the air.

AUTOMOBILE   HOUSE
Radiators

ra·di·cal (răd′ə kəl) **1** basic or fundamental: *This organization needs a* radical *change of policy.* **2** extreme: *I find his ideas very* radical. **3** person holding extreme opinions. **rad·i·cal·ly.**

ra·di·o (rā′dĭ ō′) **1** the sending and receiving of music, messages, etc., from place to place by means of electric waves traveling through space. **2** instrument for receiving such sounds: *I bought a new* radio *yesterday.* **3** to send messages through space by electric waves: *We must* radio *the ship that help is coming.* **4** having to do with such communication or instruments: *a* radio *broadcast; a* radio *tube.* **ra·di·os; ra·di·oed, ra·di·o·ing.**

ra·di·o·ac·tive (rā′dĭ ō ăk′tĭv) sending forth energy in the form of rays or particles by the breaking down of an atom such as radium, uranium, etc.: *the* radioactive *fallout from atomic bombs.*

ra·di·o·ac·tiv·i·ty (rā′dĭ ō′ăk tĭv′ə tĭ) the condition of being radioactive.

ra·di·o·sonde (rā′dĭ ō sŏnd′) device with a radio transmitter, which is sent into the upper atmosphere by balloon to record temperature, pressure, and humidity.

radio telescope device with a large surface that reflects radio waves from stars, planets, etc., and focuses them so that they can be picked up by a receiver.

rad·ish (răd′ĭsh) 1 garden plant with a spicy root. 2 its root, usually eaten raw.

ra·di·um (rā′dĭ əm) radioactive metal element, that gives off several kinds of very powerful rays, including X rays. It is used in the treatment of cancer.

ra·di·us (rā′dĭ əs) 1 distance from the center of a circle to its edge. 2 a straight line showing this distance. 3 area enclosed by a circle of a given radius: *All buildings within the* radius *of a mile will be inspected.* **ra·di·i** (rā′dĭ ī) or **ra·di·us·es.**

Radius

raf·fi·a (răf′ĭ ə) leaf fiber from an East Indian palm tree, used in weaving hats, baskets, etc.

raf·fle (răf′əl) 1 kind of contest or lottery in which people buy chances for a small sum to win a prize. 2 to offer as a prize in a raffle: *to raffle off a television set.* **raf·fled, raf·fling.**

raft (răft) 1 floating platform of logs fastened together. 2 to carry by means of such a platform: *Pioneers rafted their belongings across rivers.*

Raft

raft·er (răf′tər) one of the sloping beams that support a roof.

rag (răg) 1 piece of cloth cut or torn from a larger piece; remnant. 2 made of such pieces of cloth: *a rag doll; a* rag *rug.* 3 **rags** torn, frayed, worn-out clothing; shreds and tatters: *a beggar's rags.*

Rafters

rage (rāj) 1 intense or violent anger; fury: *When opposed, he often went into a fit of*

rage. 2 to express anger: *He never ceased raging against his enemy.* 3 uncontrolled violence: *the rage of the storm.* 4 to continue with great fury: *The storm raged all night.* 5 intense passion: *He was in a rage of grief.* 6 passing fashion: *Crew haircuts are the rage of this year.* **raged, rag·ing.**

rag·ged (răg′ĭd) 1 torn; tattered; worn out: *a ragged coat.* 2 dressed in tattered clothing. 3 shabby; neglected: *a ragged garden.* 4 rough; uneven; sharp: *a ragged cliff.* **rag·ged·ly.**

rag·weed (răg′wēd′) common weed with coarse, deeply notched leaves and yellow-green flowers. The pollen of ragweed is one cause of hayfever.

raid (rād) 1 sudden attack or invasion, followed by withdrawal after the mission has been completed: *an air raid; a police raid.* 2 to make such an attack or invasion: *The police raided the gangster's headquarters.*

¹rail (rāl) to scold violently; use bitter or angry language at someone. [**¹rail** is from a French word (railler).]

²rail (rāl) 1 metal or wooden bar. Rails are used in fences, railroad tracks, clothes hangers, and the like.
2 top bar to the banisters on a staircase.
3 railroad: *The mail was carried by* rail.
4 to enclose with or as with a rail or rails: *The football field was railed off by a rope.* [**²rail** comes through Old French (reille) from a Latin word (regula) meaning "a straight piece of wood," "a ruler."]

Rail fence

³rail (rāl) any of several kinds of birds living in grassy marshes and having short wings, narrow bodies, and long legs. [**³rail** is from an old French word (raille).]

¹rail·ing (rā′lĭng) 1 a fence: *There is a railing around the monument.* 2 a rail and its supports, placed to keep people from falling: *A handsome railing surrounds the balcony.* [**¹railing** is formed from **²rail.**]

Railing

---

fāte, făt, fâre, fär; bē, bĕt; bīte, bĭt; nō, nŏt, nôr; fūse, fŭn, fûr; tōō, tŏŏk; foil; foul; thin; ~~then~~;
hw for wh as in *wh*at; zh for s as in u*s*ual; ə for a, e, i, o, u, as in *a*go, lin*e*n, per*i*l, at*o*m, min*u*s

²rail·ing (rā′lĭng) scolding; loud and long complaining: *His wife's railing drove him out of the house.* [²**railing** is formed from ¹**rail.**]

rail·road (rāl′rōd′) **1** permanent road with tracks for trains, locomotives, etc. **2** an entire system of transportation, including tracks, trains, buildings, etc.: *The Q.E.D. System bought the B & Q Railroad.* **3** to push through rapidly so as to prevent full consideration: *to railroad a bill through Congress.*

rail·way (rāl′wā′) **1** railroad. **2** any system of tracks on which cars run.

rai·ment (rā′mənt) clothing.

rain (rān) **1** moisture condensed from the air and falling in drops. **2** to fall in drops of condensed moisture from the air. **3** a fall or shower of moisture in drops: *The heavy rains flooded the land.* **4** shower of anything: *a rain of blessings.* **5** to shower upon; give or offer abundantly: *Their friends rained presents on the bride and groom.* (Homonyms: reign, rein)

rain·bow (rān′bō′) arch of colored light that appears when the sun's rays are refracted by and reflected from raindrops, mist, or spray. A rainbow shows the colors red, orange, yellow, green, blue, indigo and violet.

rain·coat (rān′kōt′) waterproof outer coat.

rain·drop (rān′drŏp′) a drop of rain.

rain·fall (rān′fôl′) **1** a shower of rain. **2** quantity of water from rain, snow, etc., falling within a given time and area. Rainfall is measured by the height of a column collected in a rain gauge: *The yearly rainfall in Washington, D. C. is about 40 inches.*

rain·y (rā′nĭ) **1** marked by rain: *a rainy afternoon.* **2** having much rain: *a rainy climate.* **3** wet with rain: *a rainy umbrella.* **rain·i·er, rain·i·est.**

raise (rāz) **1** to lift up: *to raise a window.* **2** to rouse; bring back to life: *That noise is enough to raise the dead.* **3** to stir up; to bring about: *to raise dust; to raise trouble.* **4** to build; construct: *to raise a house.* **5** to gather; collect: *to raise an army; to raise money.* **6** to grow; breed; rear: *to raise wheat; to raise horses; to raise a family.* **7** to present for consideration; mention: *to raise an objection.* **8** to lift up in rank, or position; promote: *to raise to*

corporal. **9** to make higher; increase: *to raise prices; to raise the bet.* **10** an increase in amount, height, size: *a raise in pay.* **11** to make rise (with yeast): *to raise dough.* **12** to end; abandon: *to raise a siege.*

raise one's voice against to express opposition to; oppose: *He raised his voice against the corrupt conditions in his town.*

raise the roof to explode with anger: *Father raised the roof when he saw my report card.*

raised, rais·ing. (Homonym: raze)

rai·sin (rā′zən) dried sweet grape.

ra·jah (rä′jə) king, prince, or chief in some parts of Asia.

rake (rāk) **1** tool like a large comb with wide spaces between its teeth, joined to a long handle. It is used to collect leaves, sticks, and stones without hurting the grass and to smooth spaded ground. **2** to use a rake on: *Kenneth raked the lawn.* **3** to collect; gather: *The reporter raked up new evidence of fraud.* **4** to search carefully and tirelessly: *Bud raked the library for material for his story.* **5** to sweep with the eye; sweep with gunfire, etc.: *The gunners raked the trenches. The lookout's eyes raked the ocean for whales.* **raked, rak·ing.**

Garden rake

Leaf rake

¹ral·ly (răl′ĭ) **1** to bring into order again; assemble and reunite: *to rally troops after a battle.* **2** to recover from disorder: *The troops rallied after the retreat.* **3** to regain strength; recover: *to rally after a fever.* **4** a return of strength: *a rally in prices.* **5** to bring together for strength and support: *to rally one's supporters.* **6** to come together for strength and support. **7** a mass meeting in support of something: *a political rally.* **8** in tennis, to hit the ball back and forth a number of times before a point is won. **9** such an exchange of strokes. **ral·lies; ral·lied, ral·ly·ing.** [¹**rally** comes through French (rallier) from two Latin forms, one (re-) meaning "again" and the other (alligare) meaning "to tie."]

²ral·ly (răl′ĭ) to make fun of good-naturedly; tease. **ral·lied, ral·ly·ing.** [²**rally** is from a French word (railler) meaning "to tease," "rail." It is related to ¹**rail.**]

ram (răm) **1** a male sheep. **2** heavy, iron-tipped pole used to batter a wall or break down a door: *a battering* ram. **3** to strike head-on: *The car rammed the wall.* **4** to stuff; pack: *The workmen rammed earth into the hole in the dam.* **rammed, ramming.**

Mutton ram, about 2 ft. high at shoulder

ram·ble (răm′bəl) **1** to stroll without purpose or direction. **2** a stroll; aimless walk. **3** to flow or meander with many twists and turns: *The river rambled through the valley.* **4** to talk or write without thought or sequence. **ram·bled, ram·bling.**

ram·bling (răm′blĭng) **1** wandering; walking aimlessly. **2** spread out in an irregular way: *a rambling castle.* **3** lacking plan or unity: *Nobody could follow her rambling talk.*

ramp (rămp) sloping walk or roadway leading from one level to another.

Ramp

¹ram·page (răm′pāj) a violent rage.

²ram·page (răm pāj′) to run wildly about in a violent manner. **ram·paged, ram·pag·ing.**

ramp·ant (răm′pənt) **1** fierce; raging; furious. **2** uncontrolled; growing luxuriantly and unchecked: *After the owners left, the weeds grew* rampant *in the garden.*

ram·part (răm′pärt or răm′pərt) protective wall or bank of earth around a fort.

Rampart

ram·rod (răm′rŏd) rod used to load a gun through the muzzle.

ran (răn) See **run.** *He ran home.*

ranch (rănch) **1** in western United States and Canada, a farm with extensive grazing lands where livestock such as cattle, sheep, and horses are raised. **2** any large farm raising a specific crop: *a fruit ranch.* **3** to manage or live on a farm where cattle or other livestock are raised.

ranch·er (răn′chər) one who owns or runs a ranch.

ran·dom (răn′dəm) **1** aimless; haphazard; chance: *a random choice.* **2** **at random** in a haphazard way; aimlessly: *He wandered at random through the streets.* **ran·dom·ly.**

ra·nee (rä′nĭ) wife of a rajah; a reigning princess. Also spelled **rani.**

rang (răng) See **ring.** *I rang the bell for attention.*

range (rānj) **1** limits within which someone can do something or something can be done; extent; scope: *beyond the range of his vision; within the range of possibility.* **2** limits within which something varies: *a wide range of prices.* **3** to vary or extend within fixed limits: *The colors ranged from dark to pale.* **4** to put in a row or series: *He ranged the boys according to height.* **5** tract of land, especially for cattle grazing. **6** chain of mountains. **7** large cooking stove. **8** a place for target practice: *rifle range.* **9** to travel or wander over: *He ranged the coast of California.* **10** to ally with: *During the Revolutionary War, France ranged herself with the American Colonies.* **ranged, rang·ing.**

rang·er (rān′jər) **1** one who patrols an area, guarding wildlife or forest lands. **2** member of a body of mounted police patrolling a large area. **3** wanderer.

¹rank (răngk) **1** a line; row: *a rank of soldiers.* **2** to place in a line: *to rank men according to their height.* **3** position, grade, or classification in an organized body or in society: *the rank of colonel; the rank of bishop.* **4** to occupy a place or rank: *A major ranks above a captain. I rank low in my class.* **5** to place in a special group: *I ranked her with the better students.* **6** dignity, honor, or merit: *a churchman of high rank; an artist of the first rank.* **7 the ranks** the common people; the body of enlisted soldiers as distinguished from the officers: *The president of the firm had come up from the ranks. The general had risen from the ranks.* [**¹rank** is from an Old French word (ranc) of Germanic origin of the same meaning.]

fāte, făt, fâre, fär; bē, bĕt; bīte, bĭt; nō, nŏt, nôr; fūse, fŭn, fûr; tōō, tŏŏk; foil; foul; thin; ~~then~~; hw for wh as in *wh*at; zh for s as in u*s*ual; ə for a, e, i, o, u, as in *a*go, lin*e*n, per*i*l, at*o*m, min*u*s

583

²rank (răngk) **1** growing rapidly; luxuriant: *Vegetation is* rank *in the tropics.* **2** bad smelling or tasting: *Old bacon becomes* rank. **3** absolute; outright: *That's a* rank *insult.* **rank·ly.** [**²rank** is a form of an Old English word (ranc) meaning "strong, bold."]

ran·kle (răng′kəl) **1** to continue to be sore and painful: *His wound* rankled. **2** to be the source of persistent mental pain and irritation: *The insult* rankled *in his memory for years.* **ran·kled, ran·kling.**

ran·sack (răn′săk) **1** to search thoroughly. **2** to turn topsy-turvy, as in the case of robbers searching for valuables.

ran·som (răn′səm) **1** payment of a price for the release of a captive: *They kidnaped her and held her for* ransom. **2** price demanded for such release: *They demanded a* ransom *of ten thousand dollars.* **3** to set free by paying a demanded price; redeem: *Her father* ransomed *her.* **4** to release after such payment has been made: *The kidnapers* ransomed *her as soon as the money arrived.* **5** freedom obtained through payment of a price: *She knew her* ransom *would surely come.*

rap (răp) **1** quick, sharp blow; a tap: *a* rap *on the knuckles.* **2** the sound of a sharp blow: *I heard a* rap *on the window.* **3** to strike sharply, often noisily: *He* rapped *the desk to get attention.* **rapped, rap·ping.** (Homonym: wrap)

rap·id (răp′ĭd) **1** fast; quick: *We walked at a* rapid *pace.* **2 rapids** place in a river or stream where the water flows especially fast because of a steep slope in the river bed. **rap·id·ly.**

rap·id·i·ty (rə pĭd′ə tĭ) speed; swiftness.

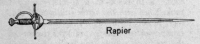

Rapier

ra·pi·er (rā′pĭ ər) a sword with a light hand guard and a straight, slender, double-edged blade, used for thrusting.

rapt (răpt) carried away by delight, awe, etc.; enchanted; absorbed: *We listened to the organ in* rapt *silence.* **rapt·ly.**

rap·ture (răp′chər) delight; blissful joy.

rap·tu·rous (răp′chə rəs) joyful; inspiring rapture. **rap·tu·rous·ly.**

¹rare (râr) **1** unusual; distinctive; uncommon: *A total eclipse of the sun is* rare. **2** not thick or dense; thin: *the* rare *atmosphere of high mountains.* **rar·er, rar·est.** [**¹rare** comes through French from a Latin word (rarus) meaning "thin," "scattered."]

²rare (râr) lightly cooked; underdone: *a* rare *steak.* **rar·er, rar·est.** [**²rare** is from an Old English word (hrēr) meaning "not thoroughly cooked."]

rare·ly (râr′lĭ) seldom; hardly ever: *Cats* rarely *neglect to clean themselves.*

rar·i·ty (râr′ə tĭ) **1** anything rare and unique. **2** uncommonness: *the* rarity *of true genius.* **3** of air, etc., thinness; lack of density: *the* rarity *of the atmosphere in high altitudes.* **rar·i·ties.**

ras·cal (răs′kəl) **1** scoundrel; rogue; scamp. **2** mischievous person, especially a playful child.

ras·cal·ly (răs′kə lĭ) mean; base; dishonest: *a* rascally *scheme.*

¹rash (răsh) a breaking out of the skin in red spots, often causing itching. [**¹rash** is from an Old French word (rasche) that probably comes from a Latin word (radere) meaning "to scratch."]

²rash (răsh) hasty; reckless: *She regretted her* rash *decision.* **rash·ly.** [**²rash** is a form of earlier English (rasch), which is probably of Dutch or German origin.]

rasp (răsp) **1** a kind of coarse file with raised teeth instead of ridges. **2** to use such a file: *The blacksmith* rasped *the horse's hoof.* **3** to make a harsh, grating, or scraping sound: *The boat* rasped *over the gravel as we pulled it ashore.* **4** rough, harsh sound: *Her voice has a* rasp. **5** to grate upon; irritate: *Her bossy manner* rasped *on the timid child.*

Rasp

rasp·ber·ry (răz′bĕr′ĭ) **1** a prickly-stemmed vinelike shrub having leaves grouped in threes. **2** the round, juicy fruit of this plant, composed of small, closely set globes, usually red, but in some kinds black, purple, or yellow. **rasp·ber·ries.**

Raspberry

rat (răt) a gnawing animal, usually gray, black, or brown, with small, beady eyes and a long, hairless tail. Rats look somewhat like large mice.

Brown rat, about 1½ ft. long

rate (rāt) **1** amount or degree of something measured in relation to something else: *Our* rate *of speed is ten miles per hour.* **2** a speed: *We're traveling at a fast* rate. **3** a set price or wage: *The* rate *for picking peaches has gone up.* **4** quality; class; rank: *first*-rate. **5** to put a value on: *He* rated *her low on reading skills.* **6** to be ranked or valued: *He* rated *high on the team.* **7 at any rate** in any case. **rat·ed, rat·ing.**

rath·er (răth′ər) **1** somewhat: *I'm* rather *tired after our trip.* **2** sooner; preferably: *I would* rather *go home now than later.* **3** more exactly: *Her dress is red, or* rather, *it's orange red.*

rat·i·fi·ca·tion (răt′ə fə kā′shən) confirmation; approval: *the* ratification *by Congress of a treaty.*

rat·i·fy (răt′ə fī′) to approve or confirm. **rat·i·fied, rat·i·fy·ing.**

ra·tio (rā′shi ō′ or rā′shō) **1** comparison between two numbers expressed by dividing the second into the first: *The* ratio *of eight to four is 8/4 or 2.* **2** a proportion: *There was a high* ratio *of boys to girls in the class.* **ra·tios.**

ra·tion (răsh′ən or rā′shən) **1** assigned portion; allowance: *He ate his daily* ration *of chocolate after lunch.* **2** to give out in fixed amounts: *The government* rations *gasoline in time of war.* **3 rations** food or supplies issued in fixed amounts.

ra·tion·al (răsh′ən əl) **1** able to reason: *Man is a* rational *being.* **2** guided by reason; logical: *His argument was* rational *until he lost his temper.* **ra·tion·al·ly.**

rat·tle (răt′əl) **1** to make a series of short, sharp sounds: *Stones* rattled *in the pail.* **2** to move with a clatter: *The cart* rattled *over the rough road.* **3** to talk quickly and idly: *She always* rattles *on for hours.* **4** to

cause to make a rattling noise: *to* rattle *a door to get attention.* **5** to utter quickly: *She can* rattle *off the multiplication table.* **6** series of short, sharp sounds; a clatter: *I hear a* rattle *in the attic.* **7** anything intended to make a clatter; a baby's toy that makes a clattering noise. **8** to confuse or cause to be nervous: *Applause* rattled *the speaker.* **rat·tled, rat·tling.**

rat·tler (răt′lər) **1** person or thing that makes a clattering sound, such as a freight train. **2** rattlesnake.

rat·tle·snake (răt′əl snāk′) any of various New World poisonous snakes with horny knoblike rings at the end of the tail. The rings make a rattling sound as the snake vibrates its tail when disturbed.

Diamond-back rattlesnake, 4 to 8 ft. long

rau·cous (rô′kəs) hoarse; harsh sounding: *the* raucous *voice of the crow.* **rau·cous·ly.**

rav·age (răv′ij) **1** to lay waste; plunder; despoil: *Locusts* ravaged *the fields.* **2** destruction; ruin; havoc: *the* ravage *of war.* **rav·aged, rav·ag·ing.**

rave (rāv) **1** to talk in a wild and disconnected manner: *The mental patient* raved *about his imaginary business.* **2** to talk with great enthusiasm: *She* raved *about her trip to Europe.* **raved, rav·ing.**

rav·el (răv′əl) **1** to fray, or separate the threads of, woven or knitted material. **2** to come apart or unwoven: *The shirt began to* ravel *at the sleeves.* **3** a thread loosened from woven or knitted material.

ra·ven (rā′vən) **1** crow-like bird with glossy black feathers. **2** shiny black.

Raven, about 2 ft. long

rav·en·ous (răv′ən əs) starving; mad for food; greedy. **rav·en·ous·ly.**

ra·vine (rə vēn′) long, deep gully or valley, usually worn by water.

---

fāte, făt, fâre, fär; bē, bĕt; bite, bit; nō, nŏt, nôr; fūse, fŭn, fûr; tōō, tŏŏk; foil; foul; thin; then; hw for wh as in what; zh for s as in usual; ə for a, e, i, o, u, as in ago, linen, peril, atom, minus

585

rav·ish (răv′ish) **1** to carry away by force. **2** to overcome with rapture: *He was* ravished *by the beauty of the music.*

rav·ish·ing (răv′ish ing) causing great joy or admiration; enchanting; captivating. **rav·ish·ing·ly.**

raw (rô) **1** in a natural state; unrefined; unprocessed: *One seldom uses raw* lumber *for building.* **2** uncooked. **3** painfully open or exposed: *a raw wound.* **4** harsh; crude: *His manners are raw.* **5** not experienced; not trained: *a raw beginner.* **6** cold; damp; chilly: *a raw November morning.* **raw·ly.**

raw-boned (rô′bŏnd′) with little flesh on the bones; thin; gaunt: *the raw-boned, weather-beaten faces of the cowboys.*

raw·hide (rô′hīd′) **1** hide or skin of cattle or other animals before it is tanned. **2** a whip or cord made of this hide.

raw material 1 petroleum, iron, metal ores, coal, wood, and other materials in their natural state, needed to make or manufacture finished products. **2** person having a natural ability or talent which needs training: *good raw material for the football team.*

¹ray (rā) **1** beam of light, heat, electrons, etc.: *The sun's* rays *warm the earth.* **2** one of several parts sticking out from a center: *starfish's* rays; *the* rays *of a daisy.* **3** a gleam; a slight or uncertain promise: *The news brought a* ray *of hope.* [¹**ray** is from an Old French word (rai) that comes from a Latin word (radius) meaning "a beam."]

Rays

²ray (rā) a kind of fish with a flat, fan-shaped body and a whiplike tail; a skate or torpedo. [²**ray** is from an Old French word (raie) that comes from a Latin word (raia).]

Devil ray, often 20 ft. across

ray·on (rā′ŏn) **1** fiber, made from wood pulp, used in making cloth or industrial products. **2** cloth resembling silk that is made from these fibers.

raze (rāz) to level to the ground; destroy completely: *The fire razed the building.* **razed, raz·ing.** (Homonym: raise)

ra·zor (rā′zər) **1** very sharp knife for shaving off hair. **2** close-cutting electric clipper used as a razor.

rd. road.

R.D. Rural Delivery; delivery of mail, in farm or suburban areas, by a postman in a vehicle.

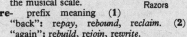

SAFETY

ELECTRIC

STRAIGHT

Razors

re (rā) the second note of the musical scale.

re- prefix meaning **(1)** "back": re*pay,* re*bound,* re*claim.* **(2)** "again": re*build,* re*join,* re*write.*

reach (rēch) **1** to arrive at; come to: *We* reached *the city before dusk. He finally* reached *a decision.* **2** to get to; communicate with: *You can* reach *him at this phone number.* **3** to stretch to; extend to: *This road* reaches *the river. The cost of that building has* reached *a million dollars.* **4** distance a person or thing can stretch: *He missed the catch because the ball was out of his* reach. **5** what the mind is able to grasp or imagine: *That arithmetic problem is beyond my* reach. **6** to stretch arms or hand to touch or grasp (something): *He* reached *out to greet me. Can you* reach *that hook for me?* **7** a stretching out to touch something: *It was a long* reach *from the bed to the light switch.*

re·act (rĭ ăkt′) **1** to respond: *The ear* reacts *to sound. The patient* reacted *favorably to the treatment.* **2** in chemistry, to change by the action of two or more substances on each other. **3** to have an effect upon the person who is acting: *John's bad manners will* react *against him in time.*

re·ac·tion (rĭ ăk′shən) **1** response: *the ear's* reaction *to sound; a patient's* reaction *to a new medicine; the* reaction *of an audience to a speaker.* **2** in chemistry, the action of two or more substances on each other to form new substances.

re·ac·tor (rĭ ăk′tər) large tank in which controlled nuclear fission takes place. Nuclear reactors are used for producing new nuclear fuel, steam for electric power, etc.

¹read (rēd) **1** to look at and understand the meaning of written or printed words or symbols: *to read a book; to read a thermometer.* **2** to say aloud (written or printed words): *He will read the report to the class.*

3 to understand; get the meaning of; acquire information by or as by reading: *to* read *riddles; to* read *a fortune; to* read *someone's intentions.* **4** to show; register: *The speedometer reads 45 miles an hour.*

read between the lines to find a special meaning in something not actually said or written: *From her letter I could* read between the lines *that she was homesick.*

read, read·ing. (Homonym: reed)

²**read** (rĕd) See ¹**read.** *I* read *that magazine last week.* (Homonym: red)

read·er (rē′dər) **1** person who reads. **2** textbook used for learning how to read.

read·i·ly (rĕd′ə lĭ) **1** willingly and quickly: *He* readily *came to my aid when I needed him.* **2** without difficulty; easily: *The baby* readily *learned to eat with a spoon.*

read·i·ness (rĕd′ĭ nĭs) **1** a prepared condition: *Everything is in* readiness *for the arrival of guests.* **2** willingness; desire: *He shows a* readiness *to co-operate.*

read·ing (rē′dĭng) **1** a getting of information or amusement from written or printed words. **2** public recital where something is read to the audience: *Our class gave a* reading *of Dickens' "A Christmas Carol."* **3** written or printed words to be read: *There is little* reading *in this picture magazine.* **4** record shown by an instrument: *The monthly* reading *of the electric meter.*

read·y (rĕd′ĭ) **1** prepared, fit, or equipped (to do something): *We're packed and* ready *to go on the trip.* **2** prepared for immediate use; finished; complete: *Your dress is* ready. *Dinner is* ready. **3** willing; inclined: *always* ready *to obey;* ready *to criticize.* **4** quick; prompt: *The students gave* ready *answers.* **5 ready cash** money on hand for immediate use. **read·i·er, read·i·est.**

read·y-made (rĕd′ĭ mād′) **1** already prepared; ready for immediate use: *a ready-made television dinner.* **2** of clothing, made in quantity from patterns before being bought; not made specially for a single person.

re·al (rē′əl or rēl) **1** true; genuine: *a real friend;* real *diamonds.* **2** actual; not imagined: *Was the figure you saw last night* real *or imaginary?*

real estate land and anything on it including the minerals, buildings, etc.

re·al·is·tic (rē′ə lĭs′tĭk) having to do with events and people as they really are.

re·al·i·ty (rĭ ăl′ə tĭ) **1** existence in fact, as contrasted to imaginary existence: *He doubted the* reality *of what he heard.* **2** something or someone real: *When the boat left the dock, the trip finally became a* reality. **3 in reality** actually; in fact: *I may seem younger, but* in reality *I am past twenty.* **re·al·i·ties.**

re·al·i·za·tion (rē′əl ə zā′shən) **1** a making something become real: *He spent years in the* realization *of his hopes for a hospital.* **2** full awareness of the truth or existence (of something): *Ann's* realization *of the problems in her new project made her hesitate to begin.*

re·al·ize (rē′ə līz′) **1** to become fully aware of; to understand fully; grasp: *She didn't* realize *her danger until it was too late to call for help.* **2** to make real; attain: *He* realized *his ambition to be a doctor.* **3** to get as profit: *Henry* realized *fifty dollars on the sale of the ring.* **re·al·ized, re·al·iz·ing.**

re·al·ly (rē′ə lĭ or rē′lĭ) actually; truly; in fact.

realm (rĕlm) **1** kingdom. **2** region or sphere: *the* realm *of fancy.* **3** special field or province: *the* realm *of science.*

ream (rēm) formerly 480 sheets of paper, now sometimes 500.

reap (rēp) **1** to harvest a crop, such as grain, by cutting it. **2** to receive or obtain (something) as by harvesting: *John did the work, so he should* reap *the benefits.*

reap·er (rē′pər) **1** person who cuts grain; a mower. **2** machine for mowing grain.

re·ap·pear (rē′ə pir′) to come in sight again.

Reaper

¹**rear** (rir) **1** the back part of anything: *the* rear *of the drawer.* **2** the space or position behind: *He was at the* rear *of the building.* **3** back part of an

---

fāte, făt, fâre, fär; bē, bĕt; bīte, bĭt; nō, nŏt, nôr; fūse, fŭn, fûr; tōō, tŏŏk; foil; foul; thin; ~~then~~; hw for wh as in *wh*at; zh for s as in u*s*ual; ə for a, e, i, o, u, as in *a*go, lin*e*n, per*i*l, at*o*m, min*u*s

army or fleet: *They engaged the enemy in the rear.* **4** at, in, or near the back: *the rear section of the car.* [¹**rear** is the short form of an English word (arrear) that means "that in which one has fallen behind." This word comes through Old French (ariere) from two Latin forms, one (ad-) meaning "to" and the other (retro-) meaning "backward."]

²**rear** (rir) **1** to bring up; raise: *to rear a child.* **2** to build; erect: *to rear a castle.* **3** to lift; raise up: *He reared his head.* **4** to rise on hind legs: *When the horse reared, he threw his rider.* [²**rear** is a form of an Old English word (ræran) meaning "to raise."]

rear admiral naval officer who ranks below a vice-admiral.

rear guard group of men guarding the rear of a body of troops.

re·ar·range (rē'ə rānj') to arrange again, usually in a different order: *The teacher rearranged the seating so the smallest children could be in front.* **re·ar·ranged, re·ar·rang·ing.**

rea·son (rē'zən) **1** motive or purpose (for an action): *John's reasons for leaving his post were never explained.* **2** fact or assumption leading someone to (a belief, thought, or conclusion): *We have reasons for believing that he is still in Mexico.* **3** ability to think: *Man has reason; animals do not.* **4** sanity: *He lost his reason.* **5** to think or argue logically: *Dr. Brown reasons so clearly that anyone can follow him.* **6** to try to use persuasion (with): *to reason with a child.* **7 stands to reason** is reasonable to believe: *Since I saw him ten minutes ago, it stands to reason that he is not far away.*

rea·son·a·ble (rē'zən ə bəl) **1** in keeping with reason or logic; just; fair; sensible: *a reasonable decision.* **2** within the limits of what is probable: *a reasonable assumption.* **3** not expensive: *Chicken is reasonable this week.* **rea·son·a·bly.**

rea·son·ing (rē'zən ing) the act or process of using thought to reach an answer, form judgments, or come to conclusions: *Jack solved the problem after long reasoning.*

re·as·sure (rē'ə shŏŏr') to restore confidence in; comfort: *He was worried about his health, but the doctor reassured him.* **re·as·sured, re·as·sur·ing.**

¹**reb·el** (rĕb'əl) **1** one who opposes or seeks to overthrow the government. **2** one who resists any authority. **3** resisting the government or any authority; rebellious: *the rebel army; his rebel spirit.*

²**re·bel** (ri bĕl') **1** to oppose or rise in arms against the government. **2** to oppose any authority: *He rebels as a matter of habit.* **re·belled, re·bel·ling.**

re·bel·lion (ri bĕl'yən) **1** a taking up of arms against the government; revolt. **2** defiance of or resistance to any form of authority.

re·bel·lious (ri bĕl'yəs) **1** defying and opposing lawful authority: *the rebellious officers.* **2** resisting; unruly: *a rebellious child.* **re·bel·lious·ly.**

re·birth (rē bûrth') return of activity, growth, or life; revival: *a rebirth of interest; the rebirth of flowers after a long winter.*

re·born (rē bôrn') born again; taking on new life; revived: *a reborn delight in music.*

¹**re·bound** (ri bound') to spring or bounce back.

²**re·bound** (rē'bound') a springing back: *to catch a ball on the rebound.*

re·buff (ri bŭf') **1** curt or unexpected denial, refusal, or snub: *I met with a rebuff when I asked for the car.* **2** to refuse curtly; repulse; snub: *He rebuffed me when I asked.*

re·build (rē bild') to make or build anew; reconstruct: *Please rebuild the broken steps.* **re·built, re·build·ing.**

re·built (rē bilt') See **rebuild.**

re·buke (ri būk') **1** to speak to in sharp disapproval: *The judge rebuked the driver for his carelessness.* **2** sharp criticism of one's behavior: *The driver listened to the rebuke in silence.* **re·buked, re·buk·ing.**

re·call (ri kôl') **1** to summon or call (somebody) back: *Senator Baines was recalled to Washington.* **2** to succeed in remembering: *He recalled the entire story.* **3** to relieve of duty; order back: *Captain Jasper was recalled from his post.* **4** to cancel: *to recall an order.*

re·cap·ture (rē kăp'chər) **1** to take back (after losing); capture again: *The marines recaptured the island yesterday.* **2** to find again (in feeling or memory): *to recapture one's youth.* **3** a taking back (after losing): *We just heard of the recapture of the island.* **re·cap·tured, re·cap·tur·ing.**

re·cede (ri sēd′) **1** to withdraw; move backward: *to watch the waves* recede *from the rocks.* **2** to slope gradually away from: *The beach* receded *from the base of the cliff.* **re·ced·ed, re·ced·ing.**

re·ceipt (ri sēt′) **1** a receiving: *the* receipt *of a letter.* **2** written statement acknowledging that money or goods have been received. **3** to sign a statement saying that money or goods have been received. **4** a recipe. **5** **receipts** money taken in: *the* receipts *of the football game.*

re·ceive (ri sēv′) **1** to get or gain (something given or sent): *to* receive *a gift; to* receive *a letter; to* receive *an education.* **2** to take in: *a barrel to* receive *rain water.* **3** to take up; support; sustain: *These pillars* receive *the full weight of the roof.* **4** to be subjected to; undergo; experience: *to* receive *a shock.* **5** to greet or accept: *The speech was* received *with wild applause.* **6** to admit into one's presence; accept; welcome: *to* receive *an ambassador.* **7** to be at home to visitors: *My grandmother always* received *on Wednesdays.* **8** to pick up radio or other waves and from them produce sound or light. **re·ceived, re·ceiv·ing.**

re·ceiv·er (ri sē′vər) **1** someone who holds, takes, or is given (something): *John was the* receiver *of the football award.* **2** receptacle; container: *an ash* receiver. **3** the part of a telephone instrument through which one speaks or listens. **4** the part of a radio that picks up the broadcast.

re·cent (rē′sənt) happening not long ago; occurring lately: *The recent storm caused all that damage.* **re·cent·ly.**

re·cep·ta·cle (ri sĕp′tə kəl) container; holder.

re·cep·tion (ri sĕp′shən) **1** act or process of receiving: *Radio* reception *from Mexico was good last night.* **2** greeting or welcome: *The team was given a warm* reception. **3** formal entertainment held to greet or introduce someone: *a* reception *for the new club president.*

re·cess (ri sĕs′ or rē′sĕs) **1** brief rest from work or activity: *Congress will be in* recess *until January.* **2** (ri sĕs′ only) to take a brief rest: *Congress* recessed *till January.* **3** a notch or hollow space as between cliffs, etc.: *a pool in a rocky* recess. **4** a space set back in a wall; a niche: *a bookcase built into the* recess *of a wall.*

rec·i·pe (rĕs′ə pē′) directions or formula for making anything: *Mother uses my* recipe *when she bakes a cake.*

re·cip·i·ent (ri sip′i ənt) receiver: *He was the* recipient *of the award.*

re·cit·al (ri sī′təl) **1** narration; telling: *They were interested in the* recital *of his adventures.* **2** musical performance: *There was a piano* recital *last night.*

rec·i·ta·tion (rĕs′ə tā′shən) **1** the act of repeating (a poem, etc.) from memory. **2** the poem, etc., as repeated. **3** oral presentation of a lesson: *a* recitation *in spelling.*

re·cite (ri sīt′) **1** to repeat from memory: *He* recited *the poem with good expression.* **2** to tell in detail, especially in school. **re·cit·ed, re·cit·ing.**

reck (rĕk) as used in older writings, to heed: *The hero* recked *not the danger.* (Homonym: wreck)

reck·less (rĕk′lis) careless; rash; heedless: *John's* reckless *courage;* reckless *driving.* **reck·less·ly.**

reck·on (rĕk′ən) **1** to count; add up: *The cashier* reckoned *my bill.* **2** to judge; consider: *It was* reckoned *a great play by the critics.*

reckon on to expect; provide for: *He didn't* reckon on *his opponent's strength.*

reckon with 1 to take into account: *He's a person to* reckon with. **2** to settle accounts with: *They will* reckon with *him later.*

reck·on·ing (rĕk′ən ing) **1** a settling of an account: *a day of* reckoning. **2** a counting or computing: *the* reckoning *of a ship's position.* **3** a bill for goods or services, especially at an inn.

re·claim (ri klām′) **1** to gain back; get back: *He* reclaimed *his pen at the lost-and-found office.* **2** to bring into use; obtain from waste: *to* reclaim *desert land by irrigation.*

rec·la·ma·tion (rĕk′lə mā′shən) a restoring to useful purpose: *the* reclamation *of land.*

fāte, făt, fâre, fär; bē, bĕt; bīte, bĭt; nō, nŏt, nôr; fūse, fŭn, fûr; tōō, tŏŏk; foil; foul; thin; ~~then~~; hw for wh as in *wh*at; zh for s as in usual; ə for a, e, i, o, u, as in *a*go, linen, peril, atom, minus

re·cline (ri klīn') to lie down; lean back in a restful manner: *She reclined on the sofa.* **re·clined, re·clin·ing.**

re·cluse (rĕk'loōs or ri kloōs') person who lives alone and shuns the company of others.

rec·og·ni·tion (rĕk'əg nish'ən) **1** a being aware of someone or something known before: *He gave no sign of recognition.* **2** approval: *His acting won early recognition from the critics.* **3** acknowledgment of a right or condition; formal acknowledgment of a country's independence or a government's sovereignty: *the United States' recognition of Israel.*

rec·og·nize (rĕk'əg nīz') **1** to become aware of or perceive something known before; to identify: *He recognized his old friend's voice.* **2** to perceive; realize: *The audience recognized the conductor's ability.* **3** to accept; admit: *He recognized the man's right to argue his point of view.* **4** to greet in an informal way: *She recognized him with a wave of the hand.* **5** to set up formal relations with a foreign government. *The United States recognized the new African states.* **rec·og·nized, rec·og·niz·ing.**

¹re·coil (ri koil') **1** to shrink back; show distaste or horror: *She recoiled at the sight of the accident.* **2** to spring back or rebound.

²re·coil (rē'koil) **1** a shrinking back. **2** a springing back or rebound, especially of a gun when it is fired.

rec·ol·lect (rĕk'ə lĕkt') to recall; call back to mind; remember: *He recollected the days of his childhood.*

rec·ol·lec·tion (rĕk'ə lĕk'shən) **1** the act of calling back to the mind or remembering. **2** person's memory or the period of time over which it extends: *The day you describe is not within my recollection.* **3** memory of something: *School days were among his happiest recollections.*

rec·om·mend (rĕk'ə mĕnd') **1** to speak or write favorably of: *to recommend a new book.* **2** to advise; counsel: *The doctor recommended a long rest.* **3** to make pleasing or worthy of acceptance: *His careful workmanship recommends him.* **4** to entrust (to someone's care): *The family doctor recommended the injured child to a bone specialist.*

rec·om·men·da·tion (rĕk'ə mĕn dā'shən) **1** the act of writing or speaking well of. **2** spoken or written praise: *My recommendation helped him to get the job.* **3** advice: *It was the doctor's recommendation that I should go to the hospital.* **4** qualities that make pleasing or worthy: *His good working habits were a fine recommendation.*

rec·om·pense (rĕk'əm pĕns') **1** to pay back: *The bank was recompensed for the loan.* **2** to reward: *He was recompensed for his good deeds.* **3** to make amends; give compensation for: *The company recompensed him for his leg injury.* **4** something given or done as a reward or atonement. **rec·om·pensed, rec·om·pens·ing.**

rec·on·cile (rĕk'ən sīl') **1** to bring together after a quarrel; make peace between: *After months of argument, the two were finally reconciled.* **2** to bring into harmony; settle: *They reconciled their differences of opinion.* **3** to bring into agreement with the facts; make consistent: *It is difficult to reconcile his promises with what he actually did.* **4** to make (oneself) content with; resign (oneself) to: *He reconciled himself to his recent bad luck.* **rec·on·ciled, rec·on·cil·ing.**

rec·on·cil·i·a·tion (rĕk'ən sĭl'ĭ ā'shən) **1** a coming or bringing together on a friendly basis after a quarrel. **2** an adjustment of differences of opinion.

rec·on·noi·ter or **rec·on·noi·tre** (rē'kə noi'tər or rĕk'ə noi'tər) to examine, explore, or survey, especially for military purposes: *to reconnoiter an enemy's position.*

re·con·sid·er (rē'kən sĭd'ər) to consider again; to think or talk about again: *to reconsider a decision.*

re·con·struct (rē'kən strŭkt') **1** to build again: *to reconstruct a steeple struck by lightning.* **2** to construct again in exactly the same way; restore to the original form: *Soldiers' huts used during the Revolutionary War have been reconstructed at Valley Forge.* **3** to trace from clues or suggestions: *to reconstruct the wanderings of the lost child.*

¹re·cord (ri kôrd') **1** to set down officially for the purpose of evidence or historical data: *to record the events as they occurred.* **2** to prepare for reproduction on a phono-

graph or the like: *to record the operetta.*
3 to register; tell: *Clocks record time.*

²**re·cord** (rĕk′ərd) **1** body of facts comprising what is known about a person or thing: *The student had an excellent* record. **2** official document telling of facts or events for future reference: *a congressional* record; *a court* record. **3** disk, cylinder, etc., for reproducing sound on a phonograph. **4** best or highest performance to date: *He holds the* record *in underwater swimming.* **5** never before reached or attained: *a* record *attendance.*

re·cord·er (rĭ kôr′dər) **1** any device for keeping a record of vibrations, temperatures, impulses, etc., by tracings, printed words, etc.; especially, a device for recording sound to be reproduced on a phonograph or the like. **2** town clerk, secretary, or the like, who makes and keeps records. **3** a kind of flute.

Boy playing
a recorder

¹**re·count** (rĭ kount′) to tell or repeat in detail: *He* recounted *his adventures.*
[¹**recount** is from an Old French word (reconter) meaning "relate."]

²**re·count** (rē kount′) **1** to count again: *He* recounted *his money.* **2** (also rē′kount′) a counting again: *The defeated candidate demanded a* recount *of the votes.* [²**recount** is formed from a prefix (re-) meaning "again" plus the word "¹count."]

re·course (rē′kôrs or rĭ kôrs′) **1** a turning to for help, comfort, etc.: *He had* recourse *to books in his loneliness.* **2** a source of aid or help: *In fact, books were his only* recourse.

re·cov·er (rĭ kŭv′ər) **1** to get back; regain: *He* recovered *his health. She* recovered *her lost purse.* **2** to make up: *to* recover *lost time.* **3** to return to a healthy or normal state: *Jack quickly* recovered *from his cold.* **4** to obtain by legal judgment: *to* recover *damages for an injury or wrong.*

re·cov·er (rē kŭv′ər) to put a new cover on: *to* re-cover *a chair.*

re·cov·er·y (rĭ kŭv′ə rĭ) **1** act of getting back: *the* recovery *of a lost coat.* **2** a return

to a healthy or normal state: *He made a rapid* recovery *from his losses.* **re·cov·er·ies.**

rec·re·a·tion (rĕk′rĭ ā′shən) any form of amusement, relaxation, or sport: *Baseball was his favorite* recreation.

re·cross (rē krôs′ or rē krŏs′) to cross again.

re·cruit (rĭ krōōt′) **1** person newly enlisted into military service. **2** new member of an organization or group. **3** to enlist: *to* recruit *young men for the navy.*

Rectangles

rec·tan·gle (rĕk′tăng′gəl) a figure with parallel sides and right-angled corners.

rec·tan·gu·lar (rĕk tăng′gyōō lər) shaped like a rectangle. **rec·tan·gu·lar·ly.**

rec·ti·fy (rĕk′tə fī′) **1** to correct; amend: *to* rectify *a mistake.* **2** in electricity, to change from alternating to direct current. **rec·ti·fied, rec·ti·fy·ing.**

rec·tor (rĕk′tər) **1** clergyman in the Protestant Episcopal Church who has charge of a parish. **2** priest in the Roman Catholic Church who is head of a religious house for men. **3** head of certain universities, colleges, and schools.

re·cur (rĭ kûr′) **1** to occur again: *His hay fever* recurs *each autumn.* **2** to return in thought or memory: *One memory often* recurred *to her.* **3** to go back to an earlier subject: *After dinner, we* recurred *to plans for our summer vacation.* **re·curred, re·cur·ring.**

red (rĕd) **1** primary color, or variations of it, shading from deep crimson to light pink; the color at the lower edge of a rainbow. Red has the longest wave length of all visible light. **2** having this color. **3 Red** (1) having to do with radical politics, especially Communism. (2) an extreme radical in politics, especially a Communist. **red·der, red·dest.** (Homonym: ²read)

red·bird (rĕd′bûrd′) any one of several kinds of birds having a red color, as the cardinal.

Red Cross organization devoted to caring for the sick and wounded in war and to giving relief in times of calamities such as floods, earthquakes, etc.

fāte, făt, fâre, fär; bē, bĕt; bīte, bĭt; nō, nŏt, nôr; fūse, fŭn, fûr; tōō, tŏŏk; foil; foul; thin; ~~then~~;
hw for wh as in *w*hat; zh for s as in u*s*ual; ə for a, e, i, o, u, as in *a*go, lin*e*n, per*i*l, at*o*m, min*u*s

591

red·den (rĕd′ən) 1 to become red. 2 to blush. 3 to make red.

red·dish (rĕd′ish) somewhat red.

re·deem (rĭ dēm′) 1 to buy back; regain possession (of something) by payment in money or action: *to redeem a mortgage; to redeem one's reputation by good actions.* 2 to fulfill; perform: *to redeem a promise.* 3 to make up for; compensate: *An apology redeemed his rudeness.* 4 to rescue; ransom; free: *to redeem from sin; redeem from captivity.*

re·demp·tion (rĭ dĕmp′shən) 1 act of redeeming or buying back. 2 deliverance from sin; salvation.

red·head (rĕd′hĕd′) person who has hair of a reddish color.

red-hot (rĕd′hŏt′) 1 red with heat; very hot. 2 inflamed with anger, enthusiasm, hatred, etc. 3 fresh from the source; up-to-the-minute: *a bit of red-hot news.*

re·dis·cov·er (rē′dĭs kŭv′ər) to find again; discover again.

re·dou·ble (rē dŭb′əl) 1 to double again. 2 to increase greatly: *As he neared the finish line, the runner redoubled his efforts.* **re·dou·bled, re·dou·bling.**

re·doubt·a·ble (rĭ dou′tə bəl) arousing fear or respect; valiant; brave: *a man redoubtable in the face of danger or hardship.* **re·doubt·a·bly.**

re·dress (rĭ drĕs′) 1 to set right; remedy. 2 (also rē′drĕs) compensation: *There is no redress for loss of honor.*

Red Sea a narrow sea, part of the Indian Ocean, separating Arabia from Africa. It is connected with the Mediterranean Sea by the Suez Canal.

re·duce (rĭ dōōs′ or rĭ dūs′) 1 to make less; decrease: *to reduce the price; to reduce the swelling.* 2 to lose weight by diet, exercise, etc. 3 to change numbers to a simpler form without changing the value: *to reduce a fraction.*

reduce to to bring to (a less favorable or happy condition): *to reduce to poverty; to reduce to tears; to reduce to the ranks.* **re·duced, re·duc·ing.**

re·duc·tion (rĭ dŭk′shən) 1 act of reducing or of being reduced. 2 amount by which something is reduced: *a reduction of ten dollars.* 3 a copy (of something) that is smaller than the original.

red·wood (rĕd′wŏŏd′) 1 kind of cone-bearing evergreen tree of the Pacific coast. These trees grow to giant size. 2 the wood of this tree.

Redwood

reed (rēd) 1 any of various firm-stemmed, jointed grasses growing in or near water. 2 musical wind instrument, such as a clarinet, in which the sound is produced by the vibration of one or more strips of reed. (Homonym: ¹read)

¹**reef** (rēf) sand bar or shelf of rock at, or just below, the surface of the water. [¹reef is a form of an earlier English word (riff) that comes from a Dutch word meaning "a sandbank or rift in the shoreline."]

²**reef** (rēf) 1 a fold or roll in a sail, used to make the sail smaller. 2 to make a sail smaller by tying such a fold or roll. [²reef is a form of an earlier English word (riff) that comes from a Scandinavian word meaning "rib", perhaps related to ¹reef.]

reek (rēk) 1 unpleasant smell: *the reek of burning rubber.* 2 to give off a disagreeable smell: *The kitchen reeked of gas because of a leak in the stove.* (Homonym: wreak)

¹**reel** (rēl) 1 spool or other device on which may be wound a length of hose, fishing line, picture film, etc. 2 amount wound on one reel of film. 3 to wind on or off a reel: *to reel in a line; to reel out a hose.*

reel in to pull in by use of a reel: *to reel in a fish.*

reel off to say or tell rapidly: *The speaker reeled off a long list of names.* [¹reel is a form of an Old English word (hrēol) meaning a device on which yarn is wound.]

Fishing reel

²**reel** (rēl) 1 to stagger or sway from a blow or shock; feel dizzy. 2 to seem to rock or whirl: *The room reeled before his eyes when he heard the great news.* 3 to walk unsteadily; stagger. [²reel is ¹reel in a very special use, arising from the fact that in staggering, people tend to move in a circle.]

³**reel** (rēl) 1 a lively folk dance. 2 the music for this dance. [³reel is ¹reel in a special use, arising from the circular movement of the dance.]

re·e·lect (rē′ə lĕkt′) to elect again, especially for the next term of office.

re·en·force (rē′in fôrs′) reinforce. **re·en·forced, re·en·forc·ing.**

re·en·ter (rē ĕn′tər) to go in again; enter again.

re·en·try (rē ĕn′trĭ) **1** a going in again or entering again. **2** the return of a space ship to the Earth's atmosphere after travel in space. **re·en·tries.**

re·es·tab·lish (rē′əs tăb′lĭsh) to set up again; establish again; restore: *After the revolution, the republic was re-established.*

re·fer (rĭ fûr′) **1** to direct (a person) for information or aid: *I refer you to the dictionary for the correct spelling.* **2** to seek information from: *to refer to a map.* **3** to call or direct attention (to): *He referred to my work.* **4** to turn over to for settlement or decision: *to refer a dispute to a referee.* **re·ferred, re·fer·ring.**

ref·er·ee (rĕf′ə rē′) **1** person who settles disputes and whose decision is final. **2** a judge in certain games, such as basketball, football; an umpire. **3** to act as umpire in (a settlement or contest): *to referee a football game.* **ref·er·eed, ref·er·ee·ing.**

ref·er·ence (rĕf′ər əns) **1** act of referring to an authority for information or confirmation: *a reference to a dictionary for the spelling of a word.* **2** source of information, as an encyclopedia, etc. **3** allusion; a mention: *This history contains many references to George Washington.* **4** person who may be asked about one's character or ability: *I gave Mr. Lawford as my reference when I applied for the job.* **5** written statement answering for someone's character or ability: *Alec's teacher gave him a good reference for a summer job.* **6** a passage or note in a book calling attention to some other book or passage. **7 in** or **with reference to** about; in regard to; concerning. **8 reference book** book used for looking up information rather than for continuous reading.

¹re·fill (rē fĭl′) to make full again; fill again: *The workmen refilled the trench.*

²re·fill (rē′fĭl′) replacement; a new duplicate of something used up: *a refill for a pen.*

re·fine (rĭ fīn′) **1** to make pure; rid of all unwanted matter: *to refine a metal.* **2** to improve; polish: *The tennis player refined his serve by practice.* **re·fined, re·fin·ing.**

re·fined (rĭ fīnd′) **1** freed from impurities or unwanted matter: *We use refined sugar.* **2** having good manners and taste; cultured; free from coarseness: *She was not expensively dressed, but her manner and speech were refined.*

re·fine·ment (rĭ fīn′mənt) **1** a freeing from impurities or unwanted matter: *the refinement of metal.* **2** good manners and taste; freedom from coarseness: *a lady of great refinement.* **3** improvement: *The inventor made many refinements on the machine before it was put into use.*

re·fin·er·y (rĭ fī′nə rĭ) factory where sugar, ore, oil, or the like is made pure or more usable. **re·fin·er·ies.**

re·fit (rē fĭt′) to make ready for use again; repair or equip with supplies again: *to refit a ship.* **re·fit·ted, re·fit·ting.**

re·flect (rĭ flĕkt′) **1** to throw back (rays of light, heat, sound, etc.) **2** to give back an image as does a mirror or clear water. **3** to give back as a result: *His act reflects honor upon him.* **4** to speak after careful thought. **reflect on** to cast discredit on; to cast doubt on: *Much of what he said reflected on his truthfulness.*

re·flec·tion (rĭ flĕk′shən) **1** image of anything in a mirror or in still water: *We could see the reflection of the mountains in the lake.* **2** a throwing back: *An echo is caused by the reflection of a sound.* **3** serious thought; meditation: *A week's reflection led to a new plan.*

Reflection

4 statement or observation resulting from serious thought: *Einstein's reflections on the universe.* **5 reflection on** a casting of discredit or reproach on: *Your remarks are a reflection on my truthfulness.*

re·flec·tor (rĭ flĕk′tər) **1** surface used to reflect light, heat, radio waves, etc. **2** curved mirror in a telescope, light, etc.

fāte, făt, fâre, fär; bē, bĕt; bīte, bĭt; nō, nŏt, nôr; fūse, fŭn, fûr; tōō, tŏŏk; foil; foul; thin; then; hw for wh as in what; zh for s as in usual; ə for a, e, i, o, u, as in ago, linen, peril, atom, minus

593

re·flex (rē′flĕks) automatic action of the body in response to some force or influence. Reflexes are controlled by nerve centers and are not conscious actions.

re·for·est (rē fôr′ĭst or rē fôr′ĭst) to replant with forest trees: *Progressive lumbering firms* reforest *cut-over land.*

re·for·est·a·tion (rē′fôr əs tā′shən or rē′-fôr əs tā′shən) the renewing of forest growth by planting seeds or young trees.

re·form (rĭ fôrm′) 1 to correct what is wrong by removing some evil or abuse: *The judge promised to* reform *the courts if elected.* 2 a change for the better; improvement: *The* reform *in the school system was long overdue.* 3 having to do with reform: *a* reform *bill; a* reform *movement.*

ref·or·ma·tion (rĕf′ər mā′shən) 1 a changing for the better; improvement in social, political, or religious affairs. 2 **Reformation** the religious movement in the 16th century which resulted in the establishment of various Protestant churches.

re·form·a·to·ry (rĭ fôr′mə tôr′ĭ) school or institution for the special training of young offenders against the law and for the betterment of their character and conduct. **re·form·a·to·ries.**

re·form·er (rĭ fôr′mər) person who speaks for, or attempts to carry out, improvements or reforms.

re·fract (rĭ frăkt′) to cause light or other radiation to bend as it passes in or out of a substance. Lenses refract light to cause larger or smaller images.

re·frac·tion (rĭ frăk′shən) the bending of light or other radiation in passing from one substance or medium into another.

¹re·frain (rĭ frān′) phrase or verse repeated at regular intervals in a poem or song; chorus. [**¹refrain** is from a French word of the same spelling.]

²re·frain (rĭ frān′) to hold oneself back; restrain oneself: *Please* refrain *from interrupting me.* [**²refrain** is from an Old French word (refrener) meaning "to bridle," which in turn comes from a Latin word (refrenare).]

re·fresh (rĭ frĕsh′) 1 to make fresh again; restore; renew after fatigue, usually with food or rest: *A nap will* refresh *you.* 2 to renew; quicken; stimulate: *His words re-freshed my memory.*

re·fresh·ing (rĭ frĕsh′ĭng) 1 reviving; invigorating; restoring; renewing: *a* refreshing *rain.* 2 unexpectedly pleasing: *her* refreshing *frankness.* **re·fresh·ing·ly.**

re·fresh·ment (rĭ frĕsh′mənt) 1 a refreshing or being refreshed: *the* refreshment *from a shower bath.* 2 something that refreshes or revives: *Her witty speech was a* refreshment *to the tired audience.* 3 **refreshments** food, drink, or both, served at a party, meeting, etc.

re·frig·er·ate (rĭ frĭj′ə rāt′) to make or keep cold. **re·frig·er·at·ed, re·frig·er·at·ing.**

re·frig·er·a·tor (rĭ frĭj′ə rā′tər) a box, cabinet, or room where food or other perishable things may be kept at a low temperature by means of ice or cold air.

re·fuge (rĕf′ūj) 1 shelter: *He sought* refuge *from the storm in a near-by barn.* 2 anyone or anything offering peace or rest: *Music was his* refuge *from his many cares.*

ref·u·gee (rĕf′ū jē′) person who flees from danger, especially one who is forced to leave his own country in time of war or because of political or religious persecution.

¹re·fund (rĭ fŭnd′) to give back (money previously paid): *Please* refund *my payment on the camera.*

²re·fund (rē′fŭnd) money paid back or to be paid back: *I'll expect a* refund *if you don't deliver the books.*

re·fus·al (rĭ fū′zəl) 1 act of refusing; denial; rejection: *His plans met with a* refusal. 2 the right to accept or reject something before others have the opportunity: *She was to have first* refusal *if the property was offered for sale.*

¹re·fuse (rĭ fūz′) 1 to decline to accept; reject: *to* refuse *an invitation; to* refuse *an offer; to* refuse *a bribe.* 2 to decline to give; deny: *to* refuse *permission; to* refuse *food.* 3 to decline (to do something); say one will not: *I asked him to leave but he* refused. **re·fused, re·fus·ing.**

²ref·use (rĕf′ūs) waste matter; garbage; rubbish.

re·fute (rĭ fūt′) to prove false: *It was easy to* refute *his argument.* **re·fut·ed, re·fut·ing.**

re·gain (rĭ gān′) 1 to get back; recover: *to* regain *leadership.* 2 to reach again; return to: *to* regain *the main road after a detour.*

re·gal (rē′gəl) **1** of or having to do with a king; royal: *the* regal *power;* regal *descent.* **2** fit for a king; splendid: *a* regal *feast.* **re·gal·ly.**

re·gale (ri gāl′) to entertain or amuse; delight: *They* regaled *their friends with music and a banquet.* **re·galed, re·gal·ing.**

re·gard (ri gärd′) **1** to look at closely; scrutinize: *Peter* regarded *the beggar suspiciously.* **2** to consider: *Do you* regard *him as fit for the job?* **3** to pay attention to; heed: *Now* regard *what I have to say.* **4** to concern: *My decision* regards *your happiness.* **5** to admire or esteem: *She* regards *scholarship highly.* **6** consideration; care: *to feel* regard *for one's safety.* **7** esteem; respect: *a high* regard *for truth.* **8** a look. **9 regards** best wishes: *Please give them my* regards.

re·gard·ing (ri gär′dĭng) concerning; about; in respect to.

re·gard·less (ri gärd′lĭs) **1** heedless; showing no care for; unmindful: *He continued to criticize,* regardless *of her feelings.* **2** anyway: *I'm going out tonight* regardless. **re·gard·less·ly.**

re·gat·ta (ri găt′ə) boat race or series of boat races.

re·gent (rē′jənt) **1** person appointed to govern when a ruler is under age or incapable. **2** member of the governing board in some state universities.

re·gime (ri zhēm′ or rā zhēm′) **1** system of government; method of ruling: *under the* regime *of Napoleon.* **2** orderly way of living to improve health, treat an illness, etc.

¹reg·i·ment (rĕj′ə mənt) the group of battalions under the command of a colonel.

²reg·i·ment (rĕj′ə mĕnt′) **1** to organize into a rigid pattern or system for the sake of discipline and control: *The dictator* regimented *even the children.* **2** to require the same rigid pattern of behavior from all: *That school is very strict and* regiments *all the boys.*

re·gion (rē′jən) **1** a part of the earth's surface; district: *the polar* regions; *tropical* regions. **2** area of the earth's surface with fairly uniform plant life, agriculture, mining, industry, etc.: *an industrial* region; *a*

dairy region. **3** area or sphere of thought or action: *the* region *of politics.*

reg·i·ster (rĕj′is tər) **1** official written book or list where facts are entered as a record: *the* register *of births, marriages, deaths, etc.* **2** to enter in such a record; to record or cause to be recorded: *to* register *a birth; to* register *a letter; to* register *for voting.* **3** mechanical device that records: *a cash* register. **4** to show a reading on a scale: *Yesterday the thermometer* registered *the heat as 97°.* **5** to show a response or reaction through movement of the face or body: *to* register *surprise.* **6** in a heating system, a device that regulates the passage of air.

reg·is·tra·tion (rĕj′is trā′shən) **1** act of registering. **2** entry in a register. **3** number of persons registered; total enrollment.

re·gret (ri grĕt′) **1** to be sorry about: *to* regret *a mistake.* **2** sorrow; disappointment; remorse: *a person's* regret *for a mistake.* **3** to remember with a sense of loss: *to* regret *the years gone by.* **4 regrets** courteous reply declining an invitation: *to send one's* regrets. **re·gret·ted, re·gret·ting.**

re·gret·ful (ri grĕt′fəl) feeling or showing regret; remembering with sorrow. **re·gret·ful·ly.**

re·gret·ta·ble (ri grĕt′ə bəl) to be regretted; lamentable. **re·gret·ta·bly.**

re·group (rē group′) **1** to come together or bring together in the original group; to reassemble: *After the play, the football teams* regrouped. **2** to form into new groups: *to* regroup *children into teams of equal ability.*

reg·u·lar (rĕg′yŏŏ lər) **1** usual; habitual; customary: *a* regular *seat in school.* **2** habitual or consistent in action; orderly: *a* regular *routine; a* regular *life.* **3** happening at even intervals of time: *the* regular *tick of a clock; the* regular *beating of the heart.* **4** happening again and again at fixed times: *the* regular *holiday of Thanksgiving;* regular *meals.* **5** even in form, arrangement, etc.; symmetrical: *Ann's features are very* regular. **6** thorough; complete: *a* regular *rascal.* **7** loyal and active member: *a* regular *in a*

---

fāte, făt, fâre, fär; bē, bĕt; bīte, bĭt; nō, nŏt, nôr; fūse, fŭn, fûr; tōō, tŏŏk; foil; foul; thin; ~~then~~;
hw for wh as in *wh*at; zh for s as in u*s*ual; ə for a, e, i, o, u, as in *a*go, lin*e*n, per*i*l, at*o*m, min*u*s

political party; a regular *at the club.* **8 regular army** army kept up in peace as well as in war; standing army. **reg·u·lar·ly.**

reg·u·lar·i·ty (rĕg′yo͞o lăr′ə tĭ) the state of being regular; evenness; balance.

reg·u·late (rĕg′yo͞o lāt′) **1** to govern or correct according to rule or custom: *to* regulate *a person's own habits.* **2** to put into working order; adjust: *The furnace smokes so much that it needs to be* regulated. **3** to make regular or even; control: *to* regulate *the temperature of a room.* **reg·u·lat·ed, reg·u·lat·ing.**

reg·u·la·tion (rĕg′yo͞o lā′shən) **1** a control or adjustment: *the* regulation *of one's behavior; the* regulation *of a furnace.* **2** rule; law; written order: *according to* regulations*; school* regulations. **3** made or done according to rule or custom: *a* regulation *uniform.*

re·hears·al (rĭ hûr′səl) **1** a practice performance (of a play, musical part, etc.) in preparation for a public performance. **2 dress rehearsal** rehearsal in which the actors are costumed as they will appear before an audience.

re·hearse (rĭ hûrs′) **1** to practice for a public performance. **2** to give an account of; tell: *to* rehearse *the story of one's life.* **re·hearsed, re·hears·ing.**

reign (rān) **1** period of rule, as of a king: *The American Revolution was fought during the* reign *of George III.* **2** to rule as a monarch. **3** to prevail: *Happiness* reigned *in every heart at the news of victory.* (Homonyms: rain, rein)

rein (rān) **1** one of the two long straps attached to the bit of a horse to guide and control it. **2** a control; something that holds in check: *Keep a tight* rein *on your temper.* **3** to check; to control. (Homonyms: rain, reign)

Reins

rein·deer (rān′dĭr′) a northern deer with large, branching antlers, related to the caribou. It is tamed, and is valued as a draft animal and for its milk, meat, and hide. pl. **rein·deer.** For picture, see next column.

re·in·force (rē′ĭn fôrs′) to add to in order to strengthen: *to* reinforce *an army platoon; to* reinforce *the elbow of a jacket with a*

leather patch. **re·in·forced, re·in·forc·ing.** Also spelled **re·enforce.**

re·in·force·ment (rē′ĭn fôrs′mənt) **1** a strengthening or a being strengthened by addition of (something). **2** person or thing added in order to strengthen.

re·in·state (rē′ĭn stāt′) to put back into a former position or condition: *When he returned from his travels they* reinstated *him as chairman of the committee.* **re·in·stat·ed, re·in·stat·ing.**

re·it·er·ate (rē ĭt′ə rāt′) to say or do again or several times: *to* reiterate *a complaint.* **re·it·er·at·ed, re·it·er·at·ing.**

re·ject (rĭ jĕkt′) to turn down; refuse to take, believe, use, etc.; discard as valueless: *to* reject *a suggestion.*

re·jec·tion (rĭ jĕk′shən) **1** a rejecting or throwing away; refusal to accept. **2** a being rejected: *The stranger was puzzled at his* rejection *by the villagers.*

re·joice (rĭ jois′) **1** to feel or express joy or happiness: *I* rejoice *to hear of your good luck.* **2** to gladden; delight: *The chairman was* rejoiced *by the vote of confidence.* **re·joiced, re·joic·ing.**

re·join (rĭ join′) **1** to return to: *Frank will* rejoin *us as soon as he finishes the phone call.* **2** to answer; reply (to): *"I don't need any help, thank you."* Mary rejoined *to her brother's offer.*

re·lapse (rĭ lăps′) **1** to return to a former condition or habit: *He ran a little way, then* relapsed *into his usual stride.* **2** a return to a former condition or habit after an improvement: *Last night Mary had a* relapse *and will have to stay in bed for another week.* **re·lapsed, re·laps·ing.**

re·late (rĭ lāt′) **1** to tell; narrate. **2** to connect; associate: *Many experts* relate *crime to slums.* **3** to be connected or associated: *Many experts think that crime* relates *to slums.* **re·lat·ed, re·lat·ing.**

re·lat·ed (rĭ lā′tĭd) **1** connected by blood or marriage. **2** connected (in some way): *Reading and writing are* related *subjects.*

Reindeer, about 6 ft. long

re·la·tion (rĭ lā'shən) **1** a telling; narration; story. **2** person who is connected by blood or marriage; a relative. **3** connection; link (between): *There is a relation between nutrition and growth.* **4 relations** dealings; affairs: *foreign* relations; *public* relations.

re·la·tion·ship (rĭ lā'shən shĭp') **1** connection. **2** tie of blood, marriage, or affection between people.

rel·a·tive (rĕl'ə tĭv) **1** person connected by blood or marriage. **2** comparative; measured by comparison: *the* relative *speeds of a car and a bicycle.* **3** having meaning only in connection with something else. *More, less, small,* and *large* are relative words. **4 relative to** having to do with or referring to; about: *a discussion* relative *to education.*

rel·a·tive·ly (rĕl'ə tĭv lĭ) in comparison with other persons or things: *In his town, Mr. Jackson was considered* relatively *rich.*

re·lax (rĭ lăks') **1** to make less tight or tense; slacken: *to relax one's grip.* **2** to make less strict, severe, or harsh: *to relax the rules.* **3** to become less tense; to rest in mind and body: *After work John relaxed with a mystery novel.* **4** to ease; set at rest: *Playing folk songs on the banjo relaxes me.*

re·lax·a·tion (rē'lăk sā'shən) **1** a lessening of tenseness. **2** an easing of strictness, discipline, or harshness: *a relaxation of the rules.* **3** a resting; a seeking of amusement: *He plays tennis for relaxation.* **4** that which provides amusement; recreation: *My relaxation these days is tennis.*

re·lay (rē'lā or rĭ lā') **1** fresh supply, as of horses or men, to relieve others in the same job; a shift: *The men worked on the tunnel in relays.* **2** in electricity, a switch operated by an electromagnet hooked up to a separate circuit. **3** to receive and pass along: *to relay a message.* **4 relay race** running race between teams, each teammate in succession running a part of the course.

re·lease (rĭ lēs') **1** to let go; unlock: *to release the brakes of a car.* **2** to set free: *to release a prisoner or a trapped animal.* **3** to free (from suffering, obligation, etc.): *to release from debt; to release from pain.* **4** device for unlocking or unfastening: *the*

trigger release *of a gun.* **5** freedom (from suffering, confinement, debt, etc.): *to apply for* release *from duty.* **6** a setting free or an order to set free: *The prisoner's* release *arrived today.* **7** to permit publication, use, etc.: *to release a news item or motion picture.* **8** publication; a making public: *We anxiously awaited the* release *of the new movie.* **9** the thing released: *Today's paper published a number of government press* releases. **re·leased, re·leas·ing.**

re·lent (rĭ lĕnt') to become less harsh, cruel, or severe; yield to pity or to earnest entreaty.

re·lent·less (rĭ lĕnt'lĭs) unyielding; without letup; without pity or mercy: *He let no one stand in his way in his* relentless *drive for power.* **re·lent·less·ly.**

rel·e·vance (rĕl'ə vəns) a being relevant; a having some bearing on; connection: *I can't see the* relevance *of your question in this discussion.*

rel·e·van·cy (rĕl'ə vən sĭ) relevance.

rel·e·vant (rĕl'ə vənt) having to do with; having some bearing on; related: *The judge ruled that the evidence was* relevant *to the case.* **rel·e·vant·ly.**

re·li·a·ble (rĭ lī'ə bəl) trustworthy; capable of being trusted or relied on: *a* reliable *source of information; a* reliable *person.* **re·li·a·bly.**

re·li·ance (rĭ lī'əns) **1** trust; confidence: *The little girl had complete* reliance *in her parents.* **2** dependence: *As she grew older, she had less* reliance *on her family and more on her friends.* **3** person or thing depended on, mainstay: *When she married, her husband became her chief* reliance.

rel·ic (rĕl'ĭk) **1** an object or idea (from the past) that no longer has a practical use: *The suit of armor is a* relic *from the days of knighthood.* **2** object held sacred for having belonged to a holy person.

re·lief (rĭ lēf') **1** a lessening of pain, worry, fear, or the like: *It is a* relief *to know that you are safe.* **2** anything that lessens worry, pain, tenseness, etc.: *The warm sun was a* relief *after days of rain.* **3** a release from a job or duty: *The rescuers worked in eight-hour shifts with two hours'*

---

fāte, făt, fâre, fär; bē, bĕt; bite, bĭt; nō, nŏt, nôr; fūse, fŭn, fûr; tōō, tŏŏk; foil; foul; thin; ~~then~~; hw for wh as in *wh*at; zh for s as in usual; ə for a, e, i, o, u, as in a*g*o, lin*e*n, per*i*l, at*o*m, min*u*s

relief. **4** one who takes over the duties of another: *The sentry awaited the coming of his* relief. **5** aid; alms; help; assistance: *The Red Cross sent* relief *to the flood victims.* **6** sculpture in which figures stand out from a flat surface. **7** the amount by which pieces of land differ in height; all the differences in height of land in a given area. **8 in relief** carved or molded so as to stand out from a flat surface.

Relief on Mount Rushmore

relief map a map that shows the physical features of the land such as mountains, valleys, plains, etc.

re·lieve (rĭ lēv′) **1** to free from pain, anxiety, distress. **2** to bring help or succor: *Red Cross nurses helped to* relieve *the town after the flood.* **3** to remove or lessen; alleviate: *to* relieve *the pressure.* **4** to replace or take the place of a person on duty. **5** to lessen the monotony of: *The brilliant mural* relieved *the severity of the white walls.* **re·lieved, re·liev·ing.**

re·li·gion (rĭ lĭj′ən) **1** belief in and worship of God or gods. **2** particular system of faith and worship: *the Christian* religion; *the Buddhist* religion. **3** a way of living based on moral beliefs; a philosophy. **4** something of great importance in a person's life: *The stage was her* religion.

re·li·gious (rĭ lĭj′əs) **1** of or having to do with religion: *a* religious *book.* **2** person who has taken the vows of a religious community. **3** devout; pious; god-fearing. **4** extremely careful; strict: *a* religious *attention to work.* **re·li·gious·ly.**

re·lin·quish (rĭ lĭng′kwish) to give up; surrender: *Paul* relinquished *his football practice to help his mother.*

rel·ish (rĕl′ĭsh) **1** pleasure; taste: *The stunt aviator had a* relish *for excitement.* **2** sauce; food eaten with other food to add flavor or make appetite sharper: *A spicy* relish *made the meat taste better.* **3** to enjoy: *He didn't* relish *the idea of losing his car. She* relished *her stay in Rome.*

re·load (rē lōd′) **1** to fill again: *Will you* reload *the wagon?* **2** to put ammunition in a gun again.

re·luc·tance (rĭ lŭk′təns) hesitation; unwillingness: *The students returned to school with* reluctance.

re·luc·tant (rĭ lŭk′tənt) unwilling: *I was* reluctant *to spend more money.* **re·luc·tant·ly.**

re·ly on or **upon** (rĭ lī′) to depend upon; trust: *You can always* rely upon *Jane to do her best.* **re·lied, re·ly·ing.**

re·main (rĭ mān′) **1** to stay behind after others go: *Will you* remain *after the dance and help clean up?* **2** to be left: *So much work* remains *to be done! One side of the house* remained *after the tornado.* **3** to continue to be as before: *He* remained *my friend.*

re·main·der (rĭ mān′dər) **1** portion left after part has been taken away, used, or destroyed. **2** in mathematics, (1) number left over after one number has been subtracted from another: *5 subtracted from 8 leaves a* remainder *of 3.* (2) number left over after one number has been divided by another: *5 divided by 2 gives 2 and a* remainder *of 1. 4 divided by 2 gives 2 and a* remainder *of 0.*

re·mains (rĭ mānz′) **1** part or parts left: *The* remains *of the dinner were getting cold.* **2** ancient ruins. **3** dead body.

re·mark (rĭ märk′) **1** brief comment: *Did he make a* remark *about my lateness?* **2** to make a brief comment: *He* remarked *about the mud on my shoes.* **3** to observe; notice: *We* remarked *his sad face.*

re·mark·a·ble (rĭ märk′kə bəl) worthy of notice; extraordinary: *He has a* remarkable *memory.* **re·mark·a·bly.**

re·med·i·al (rĭ mē′dĭ əl) for the purpose of correcting; providing a remedy: *After her accident she was given* remedial *exercises to help her walk.* **re·med·i·al·ly.**

rem·e·dy (rĕm′ə dĭ) **1** anything used to cure or relieve illness: *a headache* remedy. **2** action or method to right wrongs: *To collect your money your only* remedy *is to go to court.* **3** to correct or make better (a bad condition): *He* remedied *the rattle in the refrigerator.* **rem·e·dies; rem·e·died, rem·e·dy·ing.**

re·mem·ber (rĭ mĕm′bər) **1** to retain or keep in the mind; recall: *Do you* remember *your mother's birth date?* **2** to give a present to; tip: *Will you* remember *the elevator man* *at Christmas?* **3** to carry greetings for: *Please* remember *me to your family.*

re·mem·brance (rĭ měm′brəns) **1** a remembering; a recalling to mind. **2** a memory: *The remembrance of the party gave Jean pleasure.* **3** object or objects that call to mind persons or events: *The blue ribbon was a remembrance of Paul's first horse show.* **4** gift or token: *The pin was a remembrance from her father.*

re·mind (rĭ mīnd′) to bring to mind; cause to remember: *Please remind me to return that book tomorrow.*

re·mind·er (rĭ mīn′dər) anything that helps a person to remember.

re·mit (rĭ mĭt′) **1** to send in payment: *Please remit the money you owe for your new car.* **2** to forgive; cancel: *The jail sentence will be remitted if you pay a fine.* **3** to make less; relax: *to remit one's efforts.* **re·mit·ted, re·mit·ting.**

re·mit·tance (rĭ mĭt′əns) **1** a sending of money. **2** the money sent.

rem·nant (rĕm′nənt) **1** small piece or part left over; fragment; scrap: *the scattered remnants of an army.* **2** piece of fabric left over from a large piece and sold at a low price.

re·mod·el (rē mŏd′əl) to make over: *If you remodel that old suit it will look like new again.*

re·mon·strance (rĭ mŏn′strəns) strong protest: *My speech was a remonstrance against war.*

re·mon·strate (rĭ mŏn′strāt′) to plead strongly in protest: *to remonstrate against higher taxes; to remonstrate with a congressman about higher taxes.* **re·mon·strat·ed, re·mon·strat·ing.**

re·morse (rĭ môrs′) painful regret or anguish caused by a feeling of guilt: *We feel remorse when we have harmed someone.*

re·morse·less (rĭ môrs′lĭs) merciless; pitiless: *He was a remorseless driver of men.* **re·morse·less·ly.**

re·mote (rĭ mōt′) **1** far off; distant in time: *the remote past.* **2** far away; distant in space: *a remote land.* **3** set apart; secluded: *a house remote from the village.* **4** only distantly related or connected: *a*

remote *relative; a* remote *bearing on a question.* **5** slight: *I haven't a* remote *idea of what you mean.* **re·mot·er, re·mot·est; re·mote·ly.**

re·mov·al (rĭ mōō′vəl) **1** a moving or taking away. **2** a moving to a new place: *the removal of furniture to a new house.* **3** a dismissing from an official position.

re·move (rĭ mōōv′) **1** to take away: *to remove the dishes from the table.* **2** to get rid of; put an end to: *to remove a cause of worry by paying a debt.* **3** to dismiss from an official position. **4** to move from one place to another; change residence. **5** interval of distance; step: *many removes from his former way of life.* **re·moved, re·mov·ing.**

rend (rĕnd) **1** to tear apart violently: *We watched the wind rend the sails to tatters.* **2** to tear away: *The king threatened to rend the barons' power from them.* **rent, rend·ing.**

ren·der (rĕn′dər) **1** to make; cause to be or become: *Surprise rendered him speechless.* **2** to give; furnish; supply: *to render aid; render praise; render a bill.* **3** to perform: *to render a song.*

ren·dez·vous (rän′də vōō′) **1** a meeting by arrangement. **2** place of meeting. **3** to meet by arrangement: *We will rendezvous at the ranger's cabin.*

ren·e·gade (rĕn′ə gād′) one who deserts his own people, political party, etc.; traitor.

re·new (rĭ nōō′ or rĭ nū′) **1** to make new again; revive: *Encouragement renewed his enthusiasm.* **2** to take up again; resume: *to renew one's efforts; to renew a friendship.* **3** to extend: *to renew a loan, magazine subscription, etc.*

re·new·al (rĭ nōō′əl or rĭ nū′əl) a renewing or being renewed.

ren·net (rĕn′ĭt) substance prepared from the stomach lining of a calf, used in curdling milk, making cheese, etc.

re·nounce (rĭ nouns′) **1** to cast off; disown; refuse to have to do with: *to renounce an heir.* **2** to give up; abandon; surrender: *The princess renounced her right to the throne.* **re·nounced, re·nounc·ing.**

ren·o·vate (rĕn′ə vāt′) to make like new; restore: *The room was renovated with wall-*

---

fāte, făt, fâre, fär; bē, bĕt; bite, bĭt; nō, nŏt, nôr; fūse, fŭn, fûr; tōō, tōŏk; foil; foul; thin; ~~then~~; hw for wh as in *wh*at; zh for s as in u*s*ual; ə for a, e, i, o, u, as in *a*go, lin*e*n, per*i*l, at*o*m, min*u*s

paper and paint. **ren·o·vat·ed, ren·o·vat·ing.**

re·nown (rĭ noun′) fame; reputation: *a novelist of* renown.

re·nowned (rĭ nound′) famous.

¹rent (rĕnt) **1** to pay or charge a sum of money periodically for the use of something: *to rent a house by the month.* **2** sum paid or charged for something rented: *The rent for the automobile was ten dollars a day.* [**rent** comes from French (rente) from a Latin word (reddita, renditâ) meaning "something given back"; "something paid in."]

²rent (rĕnt) **1** torn place: *a rent in a dress.* **2** division; split: *a rent in a political party.* **3** See **rend.** *The country was rent by civil war.* [**²rent** is a form of **rend.**]

rent·al (rĕn′tǝl) amount paid or received as rent; income from rents.

re·o·pen (rē ō′pǝn) **1** to open again: *The shop reopened after the holiday.* **2** to begin again; renew: *I do not want to reopen the argument.*

re·or·gan·ize (rē ôr′gǝ nīz′) to organize anew; change a system: *The new owner completely reorganized the firm.* **re·or·gan·ized, re·or·gan·iz·ing.**

re·paid (rĭ pād′) See **repay.** *He finally repaid his debts.*

¹re·pair (rĭ pâr′) **1** to restore to good condition: *to repair a flat tire.* **2** act of repairing or renovating: *the repair of a flat tire.* **3** to make up for; to remedy: *to repair a wrong.* **4** condition of a thing with regard to its usefulness: *The plumbing is in bad* repair. **5 repairs** a piece of repairing or restoring: *This old house needs a lot of* repairs. [**repair** comes through French from a Latin word (reparare) meaning "prepare again."]

²re·pair (rĭ pâr′) to go (to): *to repair to the living room after dinner.* [**²repair** is from an Old French word (repairer) meaning "to return." The French word comes from a Latin word (repatriare) meaning "to return to one's country."]

rep·a·ra·tion (rĕp′ǝ rā′shǝn) **1** a making good for an injury or wrong; compensation: *I'll send a check in* reparation *for the damage I've done your car.* **2 reparations** money or goods paid in compensation, especially for war damages.

re·past (rĭ pǎst′) a meal; food.

re·pay (rĭ pā′) **1** to pay back: *to repay a debt.* **2** to make return for: *to repay a favor.* **re·paid, re·pay·ing.**

re·peal (rĭ pēl′) **1** to do away with; strike out; cancel: *to repeal a law.* **2** a doing away with: *the repeal of a law.*

re·peat (rĭ pēt′) **1** to do or say again: *He played the tune once and then repeated the first part.* **2** to tell what one has heard: *to repeat the news.* **3** to recite: *to repeat a poem from memory.* **4** to say exactly what someone else has just said: *Please repeat these words after me.* **5** a doing or saying again; a repetition: *a repeat of last week's show.* **6** done again: *a repeat performance.*

re·peat·ed (rĭ pē′tĭd) done, said, or sounded again or over and over. **re·peat·ed·ly.**

re·pel (rĭ pĕl′) **1** to drive back; force away; repulse: *They repelled the invaders and saved the town.* **2** to refuse to accept or consider; reject: *He repelled the offer of a bribe.* **3** to cause a feeling of dislike; disgust: *The violence of the scene repelled me.* **re·pelled, re·pel·ling.**

re·pel·lent (rĭ pĕl′ǝnt) **1** causing dislike or loathing; repulsive: *a repellent sight.* **2** driving or pushing back: *a repellent thrust by the army.* **3** something that serves to drive back or keep off: *a water repellent; an insect repellent.*

re·pent (rĭ pĕnt′) to feel regret and sorrow for (one's own act, word, or thought that was done or left undone); be penitent (for): *He repented his unkind remarks. After his unkind remarks, he repented.*

re·pent·ance (rĭ pĕn′tǝns) sorrow and regret for doing wrong.

re·pent·ant (rĭ pĕn′tǝnt) feeling or showing regret and sorrow (for something done or left undone); contrite: *She apologized and was truly repentant for her rudeness.* **re·pent·ant·ly.**

rep·er·toire (rĕp′ǝr twär′ or rĕp′ǝr twôr′) all the plays, operas, musical pieces, or parts that a company, musician, or actor is prepared to perform.

rep·e·ti·tion (rĕp′ǝ tish′ǝn) **1** a doing or saying (of something) over again or more than once; a repeating: *There was a great deal of unnecessary* repetition *in his letter.* **2** the thing that is said or done over again: *This lesson is a* repetition *of one we did.*

re·place (rĭ plās′) **1** to put or place back; restore to original position: *She* replaced *the book on the shelf.* **2** to take or fill the place of: *It will not be easy to find someone to* replace *him in that position.* **re·placed, re·plac·ing.**

re·place·ment (rĭ plās′mənt) person or thing that takes the exact place of another; a substitute.

re·plen·ish (rĭ plĕn′ĭsh) to fill up again; restock: *to* replenish *food supplies.*

rep·li·ca (rĕp′lə kə) exact copy; duplicate: *This portrait is a* replica *of the original that hangs in the National Gallery.*

re·ply (rĭ plī′) **1** answer: *His* reply *was both clear and exact.* **2** to make answer (to): *He* replied *to my question with great skill.* **re·plies; re·plied, re·ply·ing.**

re·port (rĭ pôrt′) **1** to give spoken or written account of: *He* reported *on yesterday's meeting at the United Nations.* **2** to complain about or denounce (a person): *to* report *someone to the police.* **3** written or spoken formal statement; presenting of facts: *the treasurer's* report; *a school* report. **4** to present oneself (for a purpose at a given time or place): *He always* reported *for work at exactly nine o'clock.* **5** general talk; rumor: *There was a* report *that the bridge was dangerous.* **6** sound of an explosion: *a rifle* report.

re·port·er (rĭ pôr′tər) **1** person who reports. **2** person employed to gather news.

¹re·pose (rĭ pōz′) **1** quiet rest; sleep: *to labor all day and earn a night's* repose. **2** to lie at rest; be asleep: *Jane* reposed *peacefully on the couch.* **3** calmness; peace and quiet; tranquillity (of manner). **re·posed, re·pos·ing.** [¹repose comes through French from a Latin word (repausare) meaning "rest, pause."]

²re·pose (rĭ pōz′) to place (trust and confidence in): *He* reposed *great trust in his son.* **re·posed, re·pos·ing.** [²repose is from a form (repositum) of a Latin word (re·ponere) meaning "replace."]

rep·re·sent (rĕp′rĭ zĕnt′) **1** to show; be a likeness of; portray (in art) or describe (in writing): *This statue* represents *Lincoln as a young man.* **2** to point out; set forth:

This book represents *very clearly the dangers facing the nation.* **3** to act for (another person or persons): *He will continue to* represent *us in Congress.* **4** to describe; characterize: *The candidate* represented *himself as a friend of the people.* **5** to take the place of; correspond to; stand for; be a symbol of: *The letters of the alphabet* represent *sounds.*

rep·re·sen·ta·tion (rĕp′rĭ zĕn tā′shən) **1** fact of being represented: *Each of our 50 states has* representation *in Congress.* **2** picture, statue, etc., that represents: *That statue is a good* representation *of a sleeping tiger.* **3** symbol; sign; emblem: *Red is often used as a* representation *of danger.* **4** word picture; account: *His* representation *of her part in the accident was untrue.*

rep·re·sent·a·tive (rĕp′rĭ zĕn′tə tĭv) **1** person given power and authority to act for others; a delegate: *For many years he served as our* representative *at the United Nations.* **2** typical or characteristic example (of): *The Indian boy was a fine* representative *of his race.* **3** typical; characteristic: *That was a* representative *sample of his idea of wit.* **4** acting or having power to act for others or another: *a* representative *government.* **5 House of Representatives** lower house of the Congress of the United States.

re·press (rĭ prĕs′) **1** to keep back or down; check; restrain: *He might have been a great actor had his family not* repressed *his talent.* **2** to put down; suppress: *The ship's captain sternly* repressed *the mutiny.*

re·pres·sion (rĭ prĕsh′ən) a keeping under or within; suppression: *His* repression *of his fears made him seem very courageous.*

re·proach (rĭ prōch′) **1** to scold; blame; rebuke: *The teacher* reproached *Tom for his lack of attention.* **2** a cause of shame or blame; disgrace: *The slums of this city are a* reproach *to every citizen.* **3** blame; censure: *John well deserved his mother's* reproach.

re·proach·ful (rĭ prōch′fəl) expressing blame or rebuke; full of reproach: *His team gave him a* reproachful *look when he fumbled the ball.* **re·proach·ful·ly.**

---

fāte, făt, fâre, fär; bē, bĕt; bīte, bĭt; nō, nŏt, nôr; fūse, fŭn, fûr; tōō, tŏŏk; foil; foul; thin; then; hw for wh as in *wh*at; zh for s as in u*s*ual; ə for a, e, i, o, u, as in *a*go, lin*e*n, per*i*l, at*o*m, min*u*s

re·pro·duce (rē′prə dōōs′ or rē′prə dūs′)
1 to cause to appear again; produce again:
This record almost exactly reproduces *the
sound of the orchestra.* **2** of animals, to
bear offspring: *Mules do not* reproduce.
3 of plants, to form new plants of the same
kind. **4** to make a copy; duplicate. **re·
pro·duced, re·pro·duc·ing.**

re·pro·duc·tion (rē′prə dŭk′shən) **1** a
causing to exist again in the original or
something like the original form: *the reproduction of sound.* **2** of animals, the
producing of offspring: *animal reproduction.* **3** of plants, the producing of new
plants of the same kind. **4** a copy (of a
work of art): *This is an excellent* reproduction *of the painting in the museum.*

re·proof (rĭ prōōf′) words of blame; rebuke; censure: *She deserves reproof for
her rudeness.*

re·prove (rĭ prōōv′) to speak to in blame
or disapproval; rebuke; censure: *She re-
proved me for letting her oversleep.* **re·
proved, re·prov·ing.**

rep·tile (rĕp′tĭl) any of a class of cold-
blooded animals that crawl or creep.
Snakes, lizards, turtles, and alligators are
all reptiles.

rep·til·i·an (rĕp tĭl′yən) of or having to do
with reptiles; like a reptile.

re·pub·lic (rĭ pŭb′lĭk) **1** a country in
which the supreme power of government
rests with the voters. The voters elect
representatives to govern the country. The
United States is a republic. **2** the form of
government in which those who govern
hold office through the vote of the people.

re·pub·li·can (rĭ pŭb′lə kən) **1** having to
do with a republic. **2** favoring a republic:
She had republican *sentiments.* **3** person
who favors a republic. **4 Republican
Party** one of two major political parties
in the United States. **5 Republican
(1)** belonging to or favoring the Republican Party. **(2)** member of the Republican Party.

re·pu·di·ate (rĭ pū′dĭ āt′) **1** to refuse to
accept or acknowledge; reject as unjust
or untrue: *to* repudiate *a statement.* **2** to refuse to have anything to do with; disown:
He repudiated *his family.* **3** to refuse to
pay: *to* repudiate *a debt.* **re·pu·di·at·ed,
re·pu·di·at·ing.**

re·pulse (rĭ pŭls′) **1** to drive back: *The
army* repulsed *the advance of the enemy.*
2 a driving back by force; a defeat; a check:
The navy met with a repulse *in the Mediterranean.* **3** flat refusal to accept; discourteous rejection: *Her kindness met with
a* repulse. **re·pulsed, re·puls·ing.**

re·pul·sive (rĭ pŭl′sĭv) causing a feeling of
strong dislike; very disgusting: *Rotten eggs
have a* repulsive *odor.* **re·pul·sive·ly.**

rep·u·ta·ble (rĕp′yōō tə bəl) having a good
name; of good reputation; respected: *It
pays to buy from a* reputable *firm.* **rep·u·
ta·bly.**

rep·u·ta·tion (rĕp′yōō tā′shən) **1** worth or
quality of a person or thing as judged by
others. *He had a poor* reputation *as a
lawyer.* **2** good name: *He lost his* reputation *when he started to gamble.*

re·pute (rĭ pūt′) **1** popular estimate of
worth or ability; reputation: *a man of good*
repute. **2** to regard; consider: *He is*
reputed *to be an able lawyer.* **re·put·ed,
re·put·ing.**

re·put·ed (rĭ pū′tĭd) supposed; generally
considered: *The* reputed *worth of the
property is $20,000.00.* **re·put·ed·ly.**

re·quest (rĭ kwĕst′) **1** to ask: *She* requested
me to leave her a book. She requested *that
I leave her a book.* **2** to ask for: *She* requested *a book.* **3** act of asking for something: *I heard a* request *for a book.* **4** something asked for: *I thought one book was a
small enough* request. **5 in request**
sought after or asked for; in demand. **6 by
request** in answer to a request.

re·quire (rĭ kwīr′) **1** to need: *I* require
seven hours sleep a night. **2** to demand:
Good taste requires *that he make an apology
immediately.* **re·quired, re·quir·ing.**

re·quire·ment (rĭ kwīr′mənt) **1** something
required; a demand; a necessary condition: *That school has several* requirements *for admission.* **2** a need; a necessity:
Among a pupil's first requirements *are a
book, pencil, and paper.*

req·ui·site (rĕk′wə zĭt) **1** a necessary thing;
an essential: *A library card is a* requisite
for taking out a book. **2** necessary; indispensable: *Proper breathing is a* requisite
skill for a good swimmer.

req·ui·si·tion (rĕk′wə zĭsh′ən) **1** to make
an official order or request (for supplies):

We can requisition *a toaster for the club-house.* **2** an official order or demand, especially in writing: *There has been a requisition for paper.*

res·cue (rĕs′kū) **1** to save from danger or harm: *to rescue someone from a burning building.* **2** a rescuing or being rescued: *We watched the rescue of the men from the flooded coal mine.* **res·cued, res·cu·ing.**

res·cu·er (rĕs′kū ər) someone or something that rescues.

re·search (rē′sûrch or rĭ sûrch′) careful search for accurate information: *Many scientists are engaged in research to discover the causes of the common cold.*

re·sem·blance (rĭ zĕm′bləns) likeness; similarity: *She shows a great resemblance to her father, both in appearance and character.*

re·sem·ble (rĭ zĕm′bəl) to be like or similar to in appearance or quality: *This speech resembles the one you made last year.* **re·sem·bled, re·sem·bling.**

re·sent (rĭ zĕnt′) to feel angry or indignant at: *I resent being made to do her share of the work.*

re·sent·ful (rĭ zĕnt′fəl) feeling angry or indignant: *I've been resentful since her rudeness.* **re·sent·ful·ly.**

re·sent·ment (rĭ zĕnt′mənt) a feeling of having been badly treated or insulted; anger; indignation; ill will: *It is hard not to feel resentment when you are treated unfairly.*

res·er·va·tion (rĕz′ər vā′shən) **1** arrangement by which something is reserved for a person: *It is a popular restaurant and you must have a reservation to eat there.* **2** limitation; exception; qualification: *I accept your plan with two small reservations.* **3** land set aside by the government for a particular purpose: *an Indian reservation.*

re·serve (rĭ zûrv′) **1** to keep back for later use: *to reserve some money for an emergency.* **2** to keep for the special use of: *The hotel reserved a room for us.* **3** to set apart for a special purpose: *We reserve Saturday evenings for entertaining friends.* **4** to keep as one's own; keep control of: *He reserves all rights in his inventions.* **5** to postpone; hold over until later: *The*

judge reserved *his decision. I will* reserve *judgment until I hear your side of the story.* **6** something stored or kept back for later use: *a reserve of food; bank reserves.* **7** the state of being reserved or kept for special use: *to have a little money in reserve.* **8** an area of land set aside for a special purpose: *a game reserve; a forest reserve.* **9** limitation; restriction; qualification: *to agree to something without reserve.* **10** a keeping one's thoughts and feelings to oneself; restraint: *It is difficult to break through Mary's reserve.* **11** **reserves** military troops not in active service. **re·served, re·serv·ing.**

re·served (rĭ zûrvd′) **1** set aside or arranged for in advance: *This seat is reserved.* **2** quiet in manner; self-restrained in speech and behavior; reticent: *She is reserved with strangers but very gay with her friends.*

res·er·voir (rĕz′ər vwär′ or rĕz′ər vôr′) **1** place where water is stored for present and future use: *The city had several reservoirs supplying its water.* **2** tank; part of a machine or any apparatus that holds liquid: *an ink reservoir in a fountain pen.* **3** a supply or store (of facts, knowledge, etc.).

re·side (rĭ zīd′) **1** to live in or at a place; have one's home in: *Our family has resided in this town for generations.* **2** to stay or rest (in): *In a democracy, it is with the people that the real power resides.* **re·sid·ed, re·sid·ing.**

res·i·dence (rĕz′ə dəns) **1** home; dwelling: *The White House is the residence of the President.* **2** the fact of living in a place; occupancy: *Proof of residence is required for voting.* **3** the period of time in which one lives in a place: *She studied during her three years' residence in Italy.*

res·i·dent (rĕz′ə dənt) **1** person who lives in a place: *She is a resident of New York.* **2** living in a place: *She is a resident member of the club.*

res·i·den·tial (rĕz′ə dĕn′shəl) **1** having to do with residence: *There are certain residential requirements for voting in this city.* **2** having private homes: *the residential section of a town or city.*

---

fāte, făt, fâre, fär; bē, bĕt; bīte, bĭt; nō, nŏt, nôr; fūse, fŭn, fûr; tōō, tŏŏk; foil; foul; thin; then; hw for wh as in what; zh for s as in usual; ə for a, e, i, o, u, as in ago, linen, peril, atom, minus

res·i·due (rĕz′ə dōō′ or rĕz′ə dū′) what remains after part has been taken away: *There was a residue of ash after the fire.*

re·sign (rǐ zǐn′) **1** to give up: *He resigned his position on the school board.* **2** to give up a position or office: *The president of the club has just resigned.*

resign oneself (to) to submit to; accept without complaint: *When you take a long trip, you have to resign yourself to occasional discomfort.*

res·ig·na·tion (rĕz′ĭg nā′shən) **1** the giving up of a job. **2** formal statement saying one is doing so: *He handed in his resignation as president of the club.* **3** a being resigned to conditions: *to accept one's fate with resignation.*

re·signed (rǐ zǐnd′) accepting calmly, and without complaint; submitting patiently: *to be resigned to one's fate; to grow resigned to old age.* **re·sign·ed·ly.**

re·sil·i·ence (rǐ zǐl′ĭ əns) **1** ability to spring back; elasticity: *Rubber bands lose their resilience when they are old.* **2** power of recovery, physical or mental: *the resilience of a patient after an operation;* resilience *after disappointment.*

re·sil·i·ent (rǐ zǐl′ĭ ənt) **1** springing back; returning to its original form: *Watch springs are made of a resilient metal.* **2** recovering strength or good humor quickly; buoyant; cheerful: *to have a resilient nature.* **re·sil·i·ent·ly.**

res·in (rĕz′ĭn) a sticky substance found in certain trees, especially firs and pines. It turns yellow or brown when hard and is used in making varnish and some medicines.

res·in·ous (rĕz′ĭn əs) made of or like resin.

re·sist (rǐ zǐst′) **1** to fight back against; oppose; prevent the advance of: *The regiment successfully resisted the attack.* **2** to withstand; try not to yield to: *to resist temptation.* **3** to keep from; refrain from: *I couldn't resist laughing.* **4** to be undamaged or unaffected by: *You can bake in this glass dish because it resists heat.*

re·sist·ance (rǐ zǐs′təns) **1** act of resisting; opposition: *His firm and stubborn resistance spoiled our plans.* **2** an opposing force: *The hull of the boat was designed to reduce the resistance of the water.* **3** in electricity, an opposition to the flow of an electric current through a substance. Rubber and glass have higher electrical resistance than copper. **4** ability or inclination to resist: *to feel a great resistance to new ideas; the resistance of the body to disease.* **5 have resistance to** to be able to withstand: *She was tired and had no resistance to colds.*

re·sist·ant (rǐ zǐs′tənt) **1** opposed; resisting: *a resistant nature.* **2 resistant to** able to withstand: *Some rose bushes are more resistant to disease than others.*

res·o·lute (rĕz′ə lōōt′ or rĕz′ə lūt′) determined; firm; steadfast: *a resolute effort to succeed.* **res·o·lute·ly.**

res·o·lu·tion (rĕz′ə lōō′shən or rĕz′ə lū′-shən) **1** quality of being resolute: *The president showed great resolution in the recent crisis.* **2** that which is determined; set purpose: *a New Year's resolution.* **3** formal statement of the sentiments of an official meeting. **4** solution; final explanation: *the resolution of a mystery.*

re·solve (rǐ zŏlv′) **1** to make up one's mind; decide; determine: *He resolved to work hard.* **2** something decided or determined on: *to keep one's resolve to work hard.* **3** firmness of character and purpose: *The office of the presidency calls for a man of great resolve.* **4** to decide by vote; pass a resolution: *Congress resolved to adjourn the first week in August.* **5** to make clear or explain: *The mystery was resolved when he told us the facts.* **6** to separate or break up: *In this experiment the compound resolves itself into three parts.* **re·solved, re·solv·ing.**

re·solved (rǐ zŏlvd′) decided; determined.

res·o·nant (rĕz′ə nənt) **1** echoing; resounding: *the resonant walls of the cave.* **2** having a full, rich sound: *a resonant voice.* **res·o·nant·ly.**

re·sort (rǐ zôrt′) **1** person to whom or a thing to which one goes for help: *A dictionary was her first resort when she was not sure of a spelling.* **2** place where many people go and stay for recreation: *a mountain resort.* **3** a turning to for help: *in the last resort.*

resort to to turn to for help; use: *He resorts to force when argument fails.*

re·sound (rǐ zound′) **1** to make a loud sound: *The trumpet resounded through the* *auditorium.* **2** to be full of sound; echo: *The hills* resounded *with their shouts.*

re·source (rǐ sôrs′ or rē′sôrs) **1** a stock or supply of anything useful: *Power is a necessary* resource *for industry.* **2** something a person turns to in emergency or desperation: *With his supplies gone, his only* resource *was his knowledge of the woods.* **3 resources** all the wealth of an individual, company, or country: *a country of unlimited* resources.

re·source·ful (rǐ sôrs′fəl) good at finding a way of doing things or getting out of difficulties: *He was very* resourceful *in emergencies.* **re·source·ful·ly.**

re·spect (rǐ spěkt′) **1** honor; esteem; high opinion; regard: *I have great* respect *for your work.* **2** to show esteem for; be polite to: *Children should* respect *their teachers.* **3** to pay attention to; show consideration for: *to* respect *someone's wishes.* **4** to be mindful of; avoid breaking or violating: *to* respect *the law.* **5** special feature; detail; point: *They resemble each other in all* respects. **6 respects** good wishes; greetings; regards: *Give them our best* respects. *We paid our* respects *to the hostess.* **7 with respect to,** or **in respect to** concerning; about; with reference to: *The company made its plans* with respect to *future needs.*

re·spect·a·ble (rǐ spěk′tə bəl) **1** deserving respect; having a good reputation: *a* respectable *man.* **2** of a kind considered right or good enough: *to wear* respectable *clothes;* respectable *behavior.* **3** fairly large or good: *a* respectable *number;* respectable *talents.* **re·spect·a·bly.**

re·spect·ful (rǐ spěkt′fəl) showing proper respect or courtesy; polite. **re·spect·ful·ly.**

re·spect·ing (rǐ spěk′tǐng) regarding; concerning; about: *an argument* respecting *the merits of the case.*

re·spec·tive (rǐ spěk′tǐv) belonging or proper to each; particular; individual: *The students were graded according to their* respective *efforts.*

re·spec·tive·ly (rǐ spěk′tǐv lǐ) each in the order named: *Andy, Helen, and Ralph won the first, second, and third prizes* respectively.

res·pi·ra·tion (rěs′pə rā′shən) the act or process of breathing.

res·pi·ra·to·ry (rěs′pə rə tôr′ǐ or rǐ spīr′ətôr′ǐ) having to do with breathing: *Asthma is a* respiratory *disease.*

res·pite (rěs′pǐt) **1** short period of rest or relief: *a* respite *from worry.* **2** a short postponement of a penalty, such as a sentence of death. **3** to grant a respite to (someone). **res·pit·ed, res·pit·ing.**

re·splend·ent (rǐ splěn′dənt) shining brilliantly; splendid; dazzling: *The birthday cake was* resplendent *with candles.* **re·splend·ent·ly.**

re·spond (rǐ spǒnd′) **1** to reply; answer: *to* respond *to a letter.* **2** to react; show the effects of: *to* respond *to kindness;* respond *to medical treatment.*

re·sponse (rǐ spǒns′) **1** answer; reply: *Her* response *to my question was very intelligent. My letter to her brought no* response. **2** reaction: *He was disappointed by the lack of* response *to his jokes.* **3** in church, the words spoken or sung by the people in reply to the priest or minister.

re·spon·si·bil·i·ty (rǐ spǒn′sə bǐl′ə tǐ) **1** state of being responsible: *He refuses to accept any* responsibility *for the accident.* **2** that for which one is responsible; a duty: *A family is a great* responsibility. *The president has many* responsibilities. **re·spon·si·bil·i·ties.**

re·spon·si·ble (rǐ spǒn′sə bəl) **1** able to assume or carry out a duty; reliable; trustworthy: *A* responsible *boy should be chosen to collect the club dues.* **2** in a position where one has something in his care and can be blamed for loss, damage, etc.; in a position where one can be held to blame; accountable: *The students are* responsible *for any books lent them. A bus driver is* responsible *for the safety of the passengers.* **3** deserving credit or blame for: *Hard work was* responsible *for his success.* **4** involving responsibility; requiring a person to take charge of important matters: *a* responsible *job.* **re·spon·si·bly.**

re·spon·sive (rǐ spǒn′sǐv) **1** answering: *He showed his support by a* responsive *wink.* **2** responding readily; sympathetic: *a*

---

fāte, făt, fâre, fär; bē, bět; bīte, bǐt; nō, nŏt, nôr; fūse, fŭn, fûr; tōō, tŏŏk; foil; foul; thin; ~~then~~; hw for wh as in *wh*at; zh for s as in usual; ə for a, e, i, o, u, as in *a*go, linen, peril, atom, minus

responsive *nature; a* responsive *audience.*
re·spon·sive·ly.

¹rest (rĕst) **1** freedom from activity, movement, disturbance, etc.; relaxation; quiet: *to need rest after a long journey.* **2** sleep: *to get a good night's* rest. **3** place of shelter or lodging: *a sailor's* rest. **4** lack of motion; a stopping: *The pendulum came to rest when the clock ran down.* **5** something that supports; a stand: *an arm* rest. **6** a pause in music or the symbol for it. **7** to be still; stop working; relax: *to rest a bit before continuing with one's work.* **8** to get rest by lying down; sleep. **9** to be dead: *to rest in peace;* rest *in the cemetery.* **10** to give rest to: *to rest one's horse;* rest *one's eyes.* **11** to pause: *His glance* rested *for a moment on her face.* **12** to stand, depend, or be based (on): *The statue* rests *on a pedestal. Success or failure* rests *on your efforts.* [¹**rest** is the unchanged form of an Old English word.] (Homonym: wrest)

Music rests

²rest (rĕst) whoever is left; whatever is left: *Some of us stayed; the* rest *went home. Eat as much as you want and put the* rest *in the refrigerator.* [²**rest** comes through French from a Latin word (restare) meaning "remain."] (Homonym: wrest)

res·tau·rant (rĕs'tə rənt or rĕs'tə ränt') place where meals are served to customers.

rest·ful (rĕst'fəl) **1** giving rest: *a restful sleep.* **2** giving a sense of peace or tranquility: *a restful scene.* **rest·ful·ly.**

rest·less (rĕst'lĭs) **1** continually active or in motion: *The* restless *boy fidgeted in his chair. We watched the tossing of the* restless *sea.* **2** giving no rest; uneasy: *a restless slumber.* **rest·less·ly.**

rest·less·ness (rĕst'lĭs nĭs) **1** a being restless; desire for change or action. **2** activity: *the mental* restlessness *of an inquiring mind.*

re·stock (rē stŏk') to supply again.

res·to·ra·tion (rĕs'tə rā'shən) **1** act of bringing back or being brought back to the way a thing was: *a* restoration *to health; the* restoration *of a painting.* **2** something brought back to its former condition or appearance; replica: *the* restoration *of a dinosaur in a museum.*

re·store (rĭ stôr') **1** to bring back (something) to the way it once was: *to restore an old building.* **2** to give or put back: *to restore stolen money; to restore a book to the shelf.* **re·stored, re·stor·ing.**

re·strain (rĭ strān') to check; hold back: *I could not restrain my enthusiasm.*

re·straint (rĭ strānt') **1** a holding back; a keeping in check: *It is necessary to keep dangerous animals under* restraint. **2** self-control: *Lee showed great* restraint *in not answering when his sister teased him.* **3** thing or condition that restrains or holds back: *The harsh laws were a* restraint *to freedom.*

re·strict (rĭ strĭkt') to keep within a certain limit; confine: *He restricted himself to one meal a day.*

re·stric·tion (rĭ strĭk'shən) **1** a restricting or being restricted: *We are permitted to use the library without* restriction. **2** something that restricts: *The police have placed a* restriction *on parking on the main street.*

re·sult (rĭ zŭlt') **1** that which follows a cause; consequence; outcome: *All this damage is the* result *of the wind storm.* **2** to happen or occur from a cause: *A flood* resulted *from the heavy rain.* **3** an answer to a problem in arithmetic: *The* result *of adding 9 and 5 is 14.*

result in to lead to; end in: *Your efforts should* result *in success.*

re·sume (rĭ zōōm' or rĭ zūm') **1** to begin again: *Class will* resume *work after the holiday.* **2** to occupy again: *Please resume your seats.* **re·sumed, re·sum·ing.**

re·sump·tion (rĭ zŭmp'shən) a beginning again (after an interruption): *There will be a* resumption *of the program after the intermission.*

res·ur·rect (rĕz'ə rĕkt') **1** to bring to life again; raise from the dead. **2** to bring back to attention or into use again: *to resurrect a forgotten opera.*

res·ur·rec·tion (rĕz'ə rĕk'shən) **1** a return to life after death. **2** a bringing back into use; revival: *the resurrection of a forgotten style.* **3 the Resurrection** Christ's rising from the dead, celebrated at Easter.

re·tail (rē'tāl) **1** direct sale to user of small quantities of goods (as opposed to wholesale): *Bread is sold at* retail *as are most other foods.* **2** having to do with retail selling:

Mr. Jones, a retail *merchant, owns a* retail *store and sells his clothing at* retail *prices.* **3** to be sold at retail: *That dress retails at $25.* **4** in a retail manner: *He buys wholesale and sells retail.*

re·tail·er (rē´tā lər) one who sells goods retail.

re·tain (ri tān´) **1** to keep; preserve; continue to have: *We should always try to retain our sense of humor. This paint retains its luster.* **2** to keep in a fixed place or condition: *We built a wall to retain the earth behind our house. Some metals retain heat for a long time.* **3** to remember: *to retain facts.* **4** to engage the services of (usually by payment of a fee): *to retain a lawyer.*

re·tain·er (ri tā´nər) **1** fee paid in advance, as to a lawyer. **2** formerly, the servant of a person of high rank. **3** a servant; dependent: *an old family retainer.*

re·tal·i·ate (ri tǎl´i āt´) to reply to an action or utterance by a similar one; to pay back an injury or insult; return like for like: *It is only natural to retaliate when you are injured or insulted. If you attack them they will be forced to retaliate.* **re·tal·i·at·ed, re·tal·i·at·ing.**

re·tard (ri tärd´) to hold back; hinder; delay: *Deep snowdrifts retarded our progress.*

ret·i·na (rĕt´ə nə) inner layer of the eyeball, made up of the expanded end of the optic nerve. The retina picks up the image from the lens and sends it to the brain through the optic nerve. For picture, see **eye.**

ret·i·nue (rĕt´ə nōō´ or rĕt´ə nū´) a group of persons accompanying a person of rank and performing various services for him.

re·tire (ri tīr´) **1** to give up one's work or position: *He will receive a pension when he retires.* **2** to cause to retire: *This company retires its employees at 65.* **3** to withdraw; go away: *He has retired to the country for a rest.* **4** to go to bed: *to retire at ten o'clock.* **5** of soldiers, to retreat: *Heavy attack caused the enemy to retire.* **6** to take (money, bonds, etc.) out of circulation. **7** in baseball, etc., to put out: *The batter was retired on his third strike.* **re·tired, re·tir·ing.**

re·tired (ri tīrd´) **1** withdrawn from activity; secluded: *Widow Brown lives a retired life.* **2** no longer working at one's job or profession: *The retired doctor spends much of his time fishing.*

re·tire·ment (ri tīr´mənt) a retiring or being retired.

re·tir·ing (ri tīr´ing) **1** avoiding society or publicity. **2** bashful; shy; modest: *He has a retiring nature.*

re·tort (ri tôrt´) **1** to answer back or reply sharply: *He retorted quickly when they made fun of him.* **2** quick, witty, sharp, or angry answer.

re·trace (ri trās´) to go back over: *You will have to retrace your steps if you hope to find the lost book.* **re·traced, re·trac·ing.**

re·tract (ri trǎkt´) **1** to take back a statement, opinion, or promise: *I will not retract what I said about him.* **2** to pull back or in: *Cats can retract their claws.*

re·treat (ri trēt´) **1** to fall back; withdraw from action: *The marines will have to retreat if they don't receive help from the navy.* **2** a falling back; withdrawal: *the army's retreat to the Potomac.* **3** to go for privacy or rest: *You can always retreat to the country on week ends.* **4** place for quiet, rest, or refuge: *He went to his mountain retreat every Saturday.* **5** a signal for withdrawal: *The trumpets sounded retreat.*

re·trieve (ri trēv´) **1** to get back; regain; recover: *He retrieved the ball from the river. You may retrieve your lost fortune.* **2** to make good; put right again; make amends for: *to retrieve a mistake.* **3** of animals, to find and bring back. **re·trieved, re·triev·ing.**

re·triev·er (ri trē´vər) a dog trained to go after and bring back game that a hunter has shot.

Retriever, about 4 ft. long

re·turn (ri tûrn´) **1** to come or go back to a person, place, or condition: *We will return home after the movie.* **2** a coming back: *the return home after the movie.* **3** to appear or happen again: *Summer returns.*

fāte, fǎt, fâre, fär; bē, bĕt; bīte, bĭt; nō, nŏt, nôr; fūse, fŭn, fûr; tōō, tŏŏk; foil; foul; thin; ~~then~~;
hw for wh as in *what*; zh for s as in usual; ə for a, e, i, o, u, as in *ago*, linen, peril, atom, minus

607

4 a coming again: *the return of the swallows year after year.* **5** to come or go back in thought: *Let's return to the statement you made five minutes ago.* **6** to bring, send, carry, or put back: *Please return my pen when you're through with it.* **7** a giving back: *the return of the books to the library.* **8** to give or send back in the same manner: *The army returned the enemy's fire immediately.* **9** to answer; reply: *"Impossible!" he returned angrily.* **10** having to do with a return: *a return trip; a return game.* **11** a profit: *a poor return on his investment.* **12** official report or account: *an election return; an income-tax return.* **13 in return** as repayment; in exchange: *Though we helped them, we received nothing in return.*

re·un·ion (rē ūn′yǝn) a bringing or coming together again of friends, relatives, or groups: *We held a family reunion on Thanksgiving Day.*

re·u·nite (rē′ū nit′) to bring or come together again; join after separation (persons or things): *The members of the family were reunited after a long separation.* **re·u·nit·ed, re·u·nit·ing.**

re·veal (ri vēl′) **1** to make known; disclose; divulge: *You must never reveal our club secrets.* **2** to show; expose; to display: *The fog cleared and revealed the distant hills.*

rev·eil·le (rĕv′ǝ lĭ) a signal, such as a drum beat, bugle call, etc., that wakes soldiers, sailors, etc., for the day's duties.

rev·el (rĕv′ǝl) **1** to make merry; be gay and noisy: *They reveled all night long.* **2** a merry celebration.
revel in to take pleasure in; take delight in; enjoy thoroughly: *They reveled in their good fortune.*

rev·e·la·tion (rĕv′ǝ lā′shǝn) **1** a making known of something secret or private. **2** that which is made known: *It was quite a revelation to hear the real explanation of the incident.* **3 Revelation** the last book of the New Testament.

rev·el·ry (rĕv′ǝl rĭ) boisterous, gay merry-making: *The sound of their revelry kept me from my work.* **rev·el·ries.**

re·venge (ri vĕnj′) **1** to pay back (a wrong or injury); do something to get satisfaction for a wrong or injury; avenge: *to revenge an insult.* **2** act of paying back a wrong or injury. **3** desire for revenge.

revenge oneself to inflict an injury, punishment, or the like in return for a wrong done to oneself: *The small boy saw his chance to revenge himself on the bully.* **re·venged, re·veng·ing.**

re·venge·ful (ri vĕnj′fǝl) showing or feeling a desire for revenge. **re·venge·ful·ly.**

rev·e·nue (rĕv′ǝ nōō′ or rĕv′ǝ nū′) money that comes in from any source, such as investments or tax collections.

re·ver·ber·ate (ri vûr′bǝ rāt′) to echo back; resound: *The thunder reverberated throughout the house.* **re·ver·ber·at·ed, re·ver·ber·at·ing.**

re·vere (ri vir′) to look up to; to respect and love: *The whole family revered Grandfather.* **re·vered, re·ver·ing.**

rev·er·ence (rĕv′ǝr ǝns) **1** deep respect mingled with wonder: *The artist was treated with reverence by his followers.* **2** love and respect for God. **3** to feel deep respect for. **rev·er·enced, rev·er·enc·ing.**

rev·er·end (rĕv′ǝr ǝnd) **1** worthy of deep respect or reverence. **2 Reverend** a title for clergymen: *the Reverend Mr. Jones.*

rev·er·ent (rĕv′ǝr ǝnt) **1** feeling and showing deep respect: *He was reverent toward the law.* **2** feeling and showing love and respect for God or sacred things: *A scout is reverent.* **rev·er·ent·ly.**

rev·er·ie or **rev·er·y** (rĕv′ǝ rĭ) deep musing or dreaminess; a daydream: *I was in a reverie when Miss Philips called me to the blackboard.* **rev·er·ies.**

re·verse (ri vûrs′) **1** turned the opposite way round; turned backward; having the opposite position or direction: *the reverse side of a page; a reverse movement; in reverse order.* **2** to turn the other way round; turn inside out; turn upside down: *If you reverse the two sentences, the paragraph makes more sense.* **3** the opposite; the contrary: *He did the reverse of what he was asked to do.* **4** machine or automobile gear which causes the machine to go backwards: *Bill put the car in reverse so he could back into the garage.* **5** the back of coins or medals. **6** to set aside; revoke: *The judge reversed the original sentence and pardoned the prisoner.* **7** a change from good to bad; loss or defeat: *He had a business reverse.* **re·versed, re·vers·ing; re·verse·ly.**

re·vert (rĭ vûrt′) to return or go back (to a former habit, condition, idea, belief, or practice): *Many tamed animals* revert *to a wild state when set free.*

re·view (rĭ vū′) **1** to go over again in one's mind; study or think about again: *They reviewed their lessons for the test. We* reviewed *the events of the past.* **2** a going over again (in one's mind); a looking back at: *a review of what one has learned; a review of past events.* **3** to inspect (troops, soldiers, etc.) officially: *The general reviewed the troops.* **4** official inspection. **5** to write an account of (new books, etc.): *He reviewed books for our local newspaper.* **6** an account of (new books, etc.). **7** a magazine which contains articles on current events, book reviews, etc.

re·vile (rĭ vil′) to swear at; call bad names: *He reviled his enemies.* **re·viled, re·vil·ing.**

re·vise (rĭ viz′) **1** to change; correct; alter: *to revise one's opinion of someone.* **2** to read carefully in order to correct or improve; examine and improve: *The poet revised his poems when a new edition was called for.* **re·vised, re·vis·ing.**

re·vi·sion (rĭ vĭzh′ən) **1** a revising or doing over to correct or improve: *He is working on the revision of his manuscript.* **2** a revised form; a work that has been gone over and corrected or improved: *This is the third revision of this poem.*

re·viv·al (rĭ vi′vəl) **1** a bringing back to life or consciousness: *the revival of a drowned man.* **2** a bringing back to use or knowledge again; making current again: *the revival of an old custom.* **3** a bringing back to public attention; a new presentation of a play, motion picture, etc., some time after its original performance or showing: *the revival of old movies on television.* **4** a meeting to arouse interest in religion.

re·vive (rĭ viv′) **1** to bring or come back to life or consciousness: *The lifeguard revived the man he rescued from drowning.* **2** to regain vigor: *Flowers revive in water.* **3** to give new strength or vigor to; refresh: *Coffee often revives a tired person.* **4** to bring back to use; restore; make current again: *to revive old customs.* **re·vived, re·viv·ing.**

re·voke (rĭ vōk′) to do away with; cancel; repeal: *to revoke a driver's license.* **re·voked, re·vok·ing.**

re·volt (rĭ vōlt′) **1** to rise up against; rebel: *Charlotte revolted against her family's discipline.* **2** rebellion. **3** to turn or be turned away in disgust: *Human nature revolts at the mistreatment of children.* **4** to disgust: *Cruelty revolts decent people.*

rev·o·lu·tion (rĕv′ə lōō′shən or rĕv′ə lū′shən) **1** the overthrow of a government or reign: *The revolution of 1789 in France dethroned King Louis XVI.* **2** complete change: *The steam engine brought about a revolution in manufacturing.* **3** a turning around a certain point; a revolving: *the revolution of the earth around the sun.* **4** one complete turn: *The motor runs at 2,000 revolutions per minute.*

rev·o·lu·tion·ar·y (rĕv′ə lōō′shə nĕr′ĭ or rĕv′ə lū′shə nĕr′ĭ) **1** causing a great change in ideas or affairs: *a revolutionary program in government.* **2** person who encourages the idea of, or helps cause, a revolution. **rev·o·lu·tion·ar·ies.**

Revolutionary War American Revolution.

rev·o·lu·tion·ist (rĕv′ə lōō′shən ĭst or rĕv′ə lū′shən ĭst) person who supports, or takes part in, a revolution.

rev·o·lu·tion·ize (rĕv′ə lōō′shə nīz′ or rĕv′ə lū′shə nīz′) to change completely: *to revolutionize a person's own way of life.* **rev·o·lu·tion·ized, rev·o·lu·tion·iz·ing.**

re·volve (rĭ vŏlv′) **1** to turn around; rotate: *Wheels revolve on their axles.* **2** to move in a curved path around a center: *The moon revolves around the earth.* **3** to consider something again and again: *Anne revolved the problem in her mind all night.* **re·volved, re·volv·ing.**

re·volv·er (rĭ vŏl′vər) pistol that carries a supply of bullets in a revolving cylinder.

Revolver

re·ward (rĭ wôrd′) **1** something given in return for service or performance: *The soldier got a medal as a reward for valor in battle.* **2** something given for the return of

---

fāte, făt, fâre, fär; bē, bĕt; bīte, bĭt; nō, nŏt, nôr; fūse, fŭn, fûr; tōō, tŏŏk; foil; foul; thin; ~~then~~; hw for wh as in *wh*at; zh for s as in u*s*ual; ə for a, e, i, o, u, as in *a*go, lin*e*n, per*i*l, at*o*m, min*u*s

a lost object: *He offered a* reward *for his missing wallet.* **3** money given for information or capture of a criminal: *There is a $1,000* reward *for the capture of the bank robber.* **4** to give a reward to or for.

R.F.D. properly called **R.D.**; Rural Free Delivery.

rhe·a (rē′ə) small South American three-toed ostrich.

rheu·mat·ic (rŏō mǎt′ĭk) **1** having to do with rheumatism. **2** person having rheumatism. **3 rheumatic fever** a serious disease, especially of the young, marked by fever, swelling of the joints, and often damage to the heart.

rheu·ma·tism (rŏō′mə tiz′əm) disease marked by inflammation, stiffness, and pain in the muscles and joints.

rhi·noc·er·os (rī nŏs′-ər əs) large, thick-skinned animal with one or two upright horns on its nose. It is found in African and Asian swamps.

African rhinoceros, up to 15 ft. long

Rhode Island (rōd ī′lənd) a State in the northeastern part of the United States.

rho·do·den·dron (rō′-də děn′drən) shrub with glossy evergreen leaves, and large clusters of brilliantly colored flowers.

rhu·barb (rŏō′bärb) **1** plant with large green leaves on reddish stems. **2** the leaf stems of this plant, used for sauce and for pie filling.

Rhododendron

rhyme (rīm) **1** similarity of sound in words or in the final syllable or syllables of words. "Bird" and "herd," "day" and "away," "never" and "clever" are rhymes. **2** to make words rhyme; make verses. **3** rhymed verse: *"Mary, Mary, Quite Contrary" is a nursery* rhyme. **4** to be a rhyme for each other: *"June" and "moon"* rhyme. **rhymed, rhym·ing.** Also spelled **rime.** (Homonym: rime)

rhythm (rĭth′əm) movement (especially in poetry, music, or the dance) in which

some one element (as a beat, accent, etc.) comes and goes, rises and falls, increases and lessens in a regular manner.

rhyth·mi·cal (rĭth′mə kəl) or **rhyth·mic** (rĭth′mĭk) of or having rhythm. **rhyth·mi·cal·ly.**

R.I. Rhode Island.

rib (rĭb) **1** one of the bones curving forward from the spine and enclosing the chest. **2** something that resembles a rib in appearance or function: *the ribs of an umbrella; ribs of a ship's frame; the rib of a leaf.*

rib·bon (rĭb′ən) **1** strip of fabric. **2 ribbons** shreds; tatters: *torn to ribbons.*

ri·bo·fla·vin (rī′bō flā′vən) vitamin found in milk, green vegetables, eggs, etc. Lack of riboflavin stunts one's growth and causes loss of hair.

rice (rīs) **1** a plant of the grass family, usually grown in flooded fields. It yields a grain which is a staple food in many parts of the world. **2** the grain of this plant. **3** made from this plant or its grain: *fine* rice *paper; rice cakes.*

rich (rĭch) **1** having much money or valuable possessions; wealthy. **2** luxurious; expensive: *a rich fabric; rich garments.* **3** abundant or rewarding: *The farmers had a rich harvest. The trip abroad was a rich experience.* **4** productive; fertile: *a rich soil.* **5** containing much fat or sugar: *a rich diet.* **6** of colors, deep and glowing. **7** of sound, full-toned; sonorous. **rich·ly.**

rich·es (rĭch′əs) **1** wealth; abundance. **2** valuable possessions or qualities: *The writings of the wise are* riches *open to all.*

rich·ness (rĭch′nĭs) state or quality of being rich.

rick·ets (rĭk′ĭts) children's disease marked by softening of the bones and, sometimes, crooked growth. It is caused by poor diet or lack of sunshine.

rick·et·y (rĭk′ĭt ĭ) **1** feeble; shaky: *The old table was so* rickety *that we had to throw it away.* **2** suffering from rickets.

rick·sha or **rick·shaw** (rĭk′shô) jinrikisha.

ric·o·chet (rĭk′ə shā′) **1** to bounce or skip away, as a bullet along the ground or a stone along the surface of the water; bounce off at a slant; rebound. **2** the skipping away or rebound of an object from a flat surface.

rid (rĭd) **1** to free (of something not wanted): *He wants to* rid *himself of debt.* **2 be** or **get rid of** to be freed of: *to* get rid of *a cold.* **rid** or **rid·ded, rid·ding.**

rid·dance (rĭd′əns) **1** the act of ridding or freeing; state of being freed from something unpleasant. **2 good riddance** an exclamation of relief that something or someone disagreeable has been removed.

rid·den (rĭd′ən) See **ride.** *Jim hasn't* ridden *his bicycle since the big snowfall.*

¹**rid·dle** (rĭd′əl) **1** puzzling question or problem: *The answer to the riddle, "What has an eye but cannot see?" is "a needle."* **2** person or thing difficult to understand; a mystery. **3 speak in riddles** to speak with doubtful meaning. [¹**riddle** is a form of an Old English word (rǣdels) that was formed from the same word (rǣdan) that gave us the word "read."]

²**rid·dle** (rĭd′əl) **1** to pierce with holes in many places: *They* riddled *the target with bullet holes.* **2** coarse sieve for separating chaff from corn or for sifting sand, coal, or the like. **3** to sift: *to* riddle *sand.* **rid·dled, rid·dling.** [²**riddle** is a form of an Old English word (hrĭddel) meaning "a coarse sieve."]

ride (rĭd) **1** to be carried on an animal, in a vehicle or a boat, etc.: *We* rode *in the car as Tom drove.* **2** to sit on and cause to move: *Do you prefer to* ride *a bicycle or a donkey?* **3** to sit on a horse and cause it to move: *Do you* ride *well?* **4** a journey on an animal or in a vehicle, boat, etc.: *Hester enjoyed her first airplane* ride. **5** to ride frequently on horseback, especially for pleasure: *Martin and Geraldine like to* ride *for pleasure.* **6** to cover a distance: *He* rode *60 miles before he found a gasoline station.* **7** to carry: *Father* rode *the baby on his back.* **8** to float or be carried on water or air: *The ship* rode *at anchor in the harbor.* **9** to move in a particular way: *The car* rides *smoothly over bumps in the road.* **rode, rid·den, rid·ing.**

rid·er (rĭd′ər) **1** person or thing that rides, especially a horseman. **2** an addition to a bill, document, etc., often having little or nothing to do with the main subject matter.

ridge (rĭj) **1** a range of hills or mountains. **2** raised line or strip: *A washboard contains* ridges. **3** the backbone of an animal. **4** raised part between furrows in a field. **5** top line where two sloping sides meet: *the* ridge *of a roof.* **6** to mark with raised lines or ridges: *I* ridged *the edge of the garden path with pebbles.* **ridged, ridg·ing.**

ridge·pole (rĭj′pōl′) the timber that runs along the top of a sloping roof. The upper ends of the rafters are fastened to it.

Ridgepole

rid·i·cule (rĭd′ə kūl′) **1** to laugh at; make fun of; cause (somebody or something) to appear foolish: *to* ridicule *an idea or suggestion.* **2** words or acts used to ridicule; derision: *to pour* ridicule *on someone; hold someone up to* ridicule. **rid·i·culed, rid·i·cul·ing.**

ri·dic·u·lous (rĭ dĭk′yo͞o ləs) deserving or causing scornful laughter; absurd: *Women's hats sometimes look* ridiculous *to men.* **ri·dic·u·lous·ly.**

rife (rīf) **1** common; widespread: *Reports of the bank's failure suddenly became* rife. **2 rife with** full of: *The village was* rife *with gossip about the arrival of the new neighbors.*

¹**ri·fle** (rī′fəl) **1** gun with spiral grooves inside the barrel to give the bullet spin for greater accuracy, especially such a gun that is fired from the shoulder. **2** to make such grooves in. **ri·fled, ri·fling.** [¹**rifle** is short for "rifled gun" meaning "a gun with a grooved bore."]

²**ri·fle** (rī′fəl) to plunder and strip bare of; to search in order to steal: *The thieves* rifled *the two safes in their search for the jewels.* **ri·fled, ri·fling.** [²**rifle** is from an Old French word (rifler) meaning "steal."]

ri·fle·man (rī′fəl mən) soldier or other person armed with, or skilled in the use of, a rifle. **ri·fle·men.**

rift (rĭft) an opening; split; cleft; division: *The* rift *in the rock was caused by an earthquake.*

fāte, făt, fâre, fär; bē, bĕt; bīte, bĭt; nō, nŏt, nôr; fūse, fŭn, fûr; to͞o, to͝ok; foil; foul; thin; ~~then~~; hw for wh as in *what*; zh for s as in u*s*ual; ə for a, e, i, o, u, as in ago, linen, peril, atom, minus

611

rig (rĭg) **1** to equip a ship with ropes, sails, spars, etc. **2** an arrangement of sails, masts, etc., on a ship. **3** to set up; fit out; erect: *The tent was rigged up next to the stream.* **4** to arrange by fraud: *They rigged the prices to keep them high.* **5** unusual clothes: *Ed was dressed in his clown's rig.* **rig out** to dress: *He was rigged out as a clown.* **rigged, rig·ging.**

rig·ging (rĭg′ĭng) **1** the ropes and cables that support a ship's masts and sails. **2** equipment used in drilling for oil or working on the outside of tall buildings. It includes tackle and raised scaffolds.

right (rīt) **1** just; good: *Telling the truth was the right thing to do.* **2** anything correct, just, or honorable; opposite of wrong: *to know the difference between right and wrong.* **3** suitable; proper: *Let us hope that the right man is chosen for the job.* **4** correct; true: *He was right in his opinions.* **5** correctly: *John guessed right.* **6** properly; in the correct manner: *to do a job right the first time.* **7** straight on; directly: *He looked right at the target. He looked him right in the eye.* **8** precisely; exactly: *My friend was standing right behind me.* **9** the side that is opposite to left: *The seat on my right is reserved.* **10** on the right side: *Most people write with the right hand.* **11** toward the right side: *We made a right turn at the corner.* **12** in good health or spirits: *Although Roy looked pale, he assured his mother that he was feeling all right.* **13** having the surface that is meant to be seen: *Place the tablecloth with the right side up.* **14** to set (something) in order: *After the storm we had to right the capsized boat.* **15** to make (something) good, just, or correct: *to right an injustice.* **16** something to which a person has a legal or moral claim: *the right to vote.* **17** **right of way** the right to move first, as in traffic. **18** **right away** immediately: *You must come right away.* **19** **by rights** in keeping with justice; if things had happened properly: *He said, "By rights I would have inherited the farm, but it had to be sold."* **right·ly.** (Homonyms: rite, wright, write)

right angle an angle like each of the four angles of a cross; a 90° angle.

Right angle

right·eous (rī′chəs) **1** doing what is right; virtuous; upright. **2** justified: *his righteous anger over the injustice done his friend.* **right·eous·ly.**

right·eous·ness (rī′chəs nĭs) a being and doing right; justice.

right·ful (rīt′fəl) **1** belonging to one legally: *The land behind his house was his rightful property.* **2** having a legal claim to: *The prince is the rightful heir to the throne.* **3** just; by rights: *his rightful position as leader of the team.* **right·ful·ly.**

right-hand (rīt′hănd′) **1** situated on the right: *He was advised to make a right-hand turn at the next traffic light.* **2** having to do with the right hand of a person. **3** **right-hand man** a valuable helper; a chief helper: *Henry is my right-hand man.*

right-hand·ed (rīt′hăn′dĭd) **1** using the right hand more skillfully than the left. **2** used or done with the right hand: *a right-handed pitch.* **3** made to be used by a right-handed person: *a right-handed golf club.* **4** turning from left to right like the hands of a clock: *a right-handed screw.*

rig·id (rĭj′ĭd) **1** not to be bent; stiff; hard: *He used a rigid stick to poke the fire.* **2** unyielding; not flexible: *He had very rigid opinions about tardiness.* **rig·id·ly.**

rig·or (rĭg′ər) **1** sternness; strictness: *The traffic laws were enforced with rigor.* **2** preciseness; exactness: *The scholar pursued his course of studies with rigor.* **3** hardship; severity: *Our forefathers experienced the rigors of pioneer life.*

rig·or·ous (rĭg′ər əs) **1** strict: *Discipline at the army training camp was very rigorous.* **2** exact; precise: *The scientist insisted on rigorous accuracy in his assistants.* **3** harsh; severe: *a rigorous climate.* **rig·or·ous·ly.**

rill (rĭl) small brook or stream.

rim (rĭm) **1** border; margin; edge: *the rim of the coffee cup.* **2** to put a rim around. **rimmed, rim·ming.**

¹rime (rīm) white, icy covering of frozen dew found on grass, leaves, etc.; hoarfrost. [**¹rime** is a form of an Old English word (hrim).] (Homonym: rhyme)

²rime (rīm) rhyme. **rimed, rim·ing.** [**²rime** is from an Old French word (rime) of the same meaning.]

rind (rīnd) **1** outer skin or covering: *the rind of a melon.* **2** the bark of a tree.

¹ring (rĭng) **1** a circle, especially a circle around something: *A ring of stones enclosed the flowerbed.* **2** any object of circular form: *John put a tag on his key* ring. **3** circular band of precious metal, often ornamented, for wearing on the finger. **4** a place for showing animals, holding exhibitions, conducting sporting events, and the like: *Bareback riders performed in the circus* ring. **5** group of people using underhand methods to gain a selfish end: *A small ring of insiders got control of the club.* **6** to put a ring around: *He ringed the horse in an enclosure.* **7** to toss a ring over: *Tony ringed the stake when he played quoits.* **8 the ring** boxing: *The sports writer took great interest in the* ring. [¹**ring** is a form of an Old English word (hring).] (Homonym: wring)

Finger ring

²ring (rĭng) **1** clear, resonant sound, such as results when metal hits a glass, a hollow place, etc. **2** to make a clear, resonant sound: *The blacksmith's hammer rang on the anvil.* **3** sound of a buzzer, telephone, any bell. **4** to cause (a bell or buzzer) to sound: *They rang but they got no answer.* **5** to echo or resound: *The schoolyard rang with the childrens' voices.* **6** particular quality or tone: *The general's voice had the ring of authority.* **7** to appear to be; seem: *His version of what happened rings true.* **8** to telephone: *I'll ring you in the morning.* **9** telephone call.

ring for to summon by a bell: *She rang for the maid.*

ring off to end a phone call.

ring up 1 to telephone. **2** to raise: *to ring up the curtain.*

rang, rung, ring·ing. [²**ring** is a form of an Old English word (hringan).] (Homonym: wring)

ring·lead·er (rĭng'lē'dər) person who leads others in a mutiny, riot, crime, etc.; leader in any sort of mischief: *He is always the ringleader when any mischief is afoot.*

ring·let (rĭng'lĭt) **1** lock of hair; curl. **2** small ring.

ring·side (rĭng'sīd') **1** space just surrounding the ring at a boxing match, circus, etc.

2 ringside seat a place or situation providing a close view of something.

ring·worm (rĭng'wûrm') a skin disease caused by various kinds of very tiny fungi, and marked by a red scaly ring on the skin.

rink (rĭngk) area of ice for skating or a floor used for roller skating.

rinse (rĭns) **1** to wash lightly. **2** to use clear water for removing soap after cleansing. **3** water used for removing soap after cleansing. **4** a light washing: *Since the blouse wasn't very dirty, it just needed a rinse.* **rinsed, rins·ing.**

ri·ot (rī'ət) **1** an outbreak of disorder by a group of persons: *Student riots were the first sign of political unrest.* **2** to join in a riot: *The prisoners rioted as a protest against conditions in the jail.* **3** disorderly conduct; noisy behavior. **4** to make merry in a noisy and wild way: *The students rioted all night after the football game.* **5** bright, luxuriant display: *the fields were a riot of color.* **6 run riot** (1) to act without restraint. (2) of plants, to grow wildly and luxuriantly.

ri·ot·ous (rī'ət əs) **1** marked by violent or noisy disturbance of the peace: *The police brought the riotous crowd to order.* **2** running wild; unrestrained: *He indulged in riotous living.* **ri·ot·ous·ly.**

rip (rĭp) **1** to tear; rend: *Pete ripped his coat on a nail.* **2** to cut or break stitches: *to rip at the seams; rip out a seam.* **3** a tear; a torn place; a burst seam: *to sew up a rip in a coat.* **ripped, rip·ping.**

ripe (rīp) **1** ready to be gathered; ready to use as food: *The apple was ripe enough to be picked. The tomatoes are ripe enough to eat.* **2** fully developed; mature: *My uncle has ripe experience in these matters.* **3** prepared; ready for action: *The infantry company was ripe for the assault.* **rip·er, rip·est; ripe·ly.**

rip·en (rī'pən) to grow to the stage of full development; to mature: *Grapes must ripen on the vine or you can't eat them.*

ripe·ness (rīp'nĭs) a being ripe; maturity: *the ripeness of a banana; the ripeness of age.*

rip·ple (rĭp'əl) **1** tiny wave on the surface of water. **2** slight curling; wavelike surface of any soft material. **3** sound similar

---

fāte, fǎt, fâre, fär; bē, bĕt; bīte, bĭt; nō, nŏt, nôr; fūse, fŭn, fûr; tōo, tŏok; foil; foul; thin; ~~then~~; hw for wh as in *what*; zh for s as in u*s*ual; ə for a, e, i, o, u, as in ago, linen, peril, atom, minus

to that of small waves: *A ripple of laughter went through the audience.* **4** to cause to flow in tiny waves: *The brook rippled over the stones.* **5** to make tiny waves on or in: *The wind rippled the surface of the pond.* **rip·pled, rip·pling.**

rip·tide (rĭp′tīd′) strong, narrow current flowing rapidly outward from a shore.

rise (rīz) **1** to get up from a sitting, lying, or kneeling position: *We all rose when the flag went by.* **2** to go from a lower to a higher place; mount. **3** to get out of bed: *Arlene rises late Saturday mornings.* **4** to revolt; rebel: *The slaves rose against their masters.* **5** to grow or spring up; be built up: *The new building rises higher each day.* **6** to come into view: *The mountain rose before us on the horizon.* **7** a going up from a lower to a higher position; ascent or climb: *a sudden rise to power; a rise in food prices.* **8** to swell; increase in size: *Bread dough rises.* **9** to achieve promotion or higher rank: *You will rise in your job if you have ability.* **10** to be equal to (a situation): *Ronald rises to the demands of his school work.* **11** small hill or incline. **12** to have its origin or source in: *The Nile rises near the equator and flows northward.* **13** source; origin: *The Nile has its rise near the equator.* **14** **give rise to** to be the cause of; to start: *His disappearance gave rise to many rumors.* **rose, ris·en, ris·ing.**

ris·en (rĭz′ən) See **rise.** *The sun has risen.*

ris·ing (rī′zĭng) **1** that rises: *The rising moon cast a glow over the yard.* **2** act of anyone or anything that rises: *an eight o'clock rising; the sun's rising.*

risk (rĭsk) **1** to take a chance on loss or danger: *Would you risk your job by being absent when you don't have to?* **2** a chance of loss; danger; peril: *The risk was great.*

risk·y (rĭs′kĭ) dangerous, hazardous: *It's too risky to go sailing without life preservers.* **risk·i·er, risk·i·est.**

rite (rīt) customary form used in a ceremony, especially a religious service: *They were baptized according to the rites of their religion.* (Homonyms: right, wright, write)

rit·u·al (rĭch′o͞o əl) **1** set form or way of conducting a ceremony, service, etc. **2** routine faithfully followed: *His daily game of tennis has become a ritual with him.* **rit·u·al·ly.**

ri·val (rī′vəl) **1** competitor; person trying to achieve the same particular goal as another: *John was my rival in the class elections.* **2** to try to do as well as or better than; compete with: *The department stores rival one another in special sales.* **3** competing; acting as a rival or rivals: *the rival stores.* **4** to be a match for: *She rivaled her sister in beauty.*

ri·val·ry (rī′vəl rĭ) an attempting to do as well or better; competition: *The rivalry between the two boys need not destroy their friendship.* **ri·val·ries.**

riv·er (rĭv′ər) **1** large stream of water that flows in a natural channel and empties into a lake, ocean, sea, or another river. **2** any great stream or flow: *a river of tears.*

riv·er·side (rĭv′ər sīd′) **1** bank of a river. **2** beside the river; on the bank of a river: *a riverside trail.*

riv·et (rĭv′ĭt) **1** a kind of bolt, one end of which is flattened after the rivet is in place, thus making a head on each end. **2** to fasten with or as with rivets: *Fear riveted his feet to the floor.*

Rivets

riv·u·let (rĭv′yo͞o lĭt) small or tiny stream.

road (rōd) **1** any route: *A line of notched trees marked the road through the dense forest.* **2** public way for foot or vehicle travel between two or more places. **3** means by which anything is reached: *There is no simple road to success.* (Homonym: rode)

road·bed (rōd′bĕd′) **1** bed or foundation for the rails and ties of a railroad. **2** stone and gravel base for a paved road. **3** sometimes, the surface of such a road.

road·block (rōd′blŏk′) arrangement of men or materials to block traffic on a road.

road·side (rōd′sīd′) **1** land along a road or highway. **2** located beside a road or highway: *a roadside store.*

road·way (rōd′wā′) **1** road. **2** the part of a street or highway used by vehicles.

roam (rōm) to ramble; wander without purpose: *I like to roam over the countryside on week ends.* (Homonym: Rome)

roan (rōn) **1** especially of horses, reddish-brown, black, or chestnut thickly sprinkled with gray or white: *I choose the roan horse.* **2** horse of this color. Red-roans have few white hairs, but blue-roans have many.

roar (rôr) **1** any loud, deep, hoarse sound or noise made by people, animals, waves, etc.: *The crowd uttered a* roar *of approval. The* roar *of the cannon and the* roar *of a lion are quite different.* **2** to make such a loud, deep, hoarse sound or noise: *The lion* roared.

roast (rōst) **1** to cook meat or other food before or over an open fire, coals, or embers, or in an oven: *We* roasted *corn when we went on the picnic.* **2** large piece of meat suitable for cooking over a fire or in an oven: *A* roast *of beef is a fine meal for Sundays.* **3** to become too warm: *We are* roasting *in this summer heat.*

rob (rŏb) **1** to take unlawfully from; steal from: *to* rob *a bank.* **2** to deprive in an unjust or wrong way: *Slander* robbed *him of his good name.* **robbed, rob·bing.**

rob·ber (rŏb′ər) person who steals; thief.

rob·ber·y (rŏb′ə rǐ) the unlawful taking of another's money or possessions; theft: *Our neighbor's house escaped* robbery *last night because his dog awoke and barked.* **rob·ber·ies.**

robe (rōb) **1** long, loose, outer garment worn on official or ceremonial occasions as mark of office or rank: *the judge's* robe; *the priests'* robes. **2** any long covering garment: *a lounging* robe; *a bath*robe. **3** to put on or wear official or ceremonial dress. **robed, rob·ing.**

rob·in (rŏb′ǐn) **1** American thrush with a dark back and a reddish breast. **2** a somewhat smaller but more colorful English bird.

Robin, about 10 in. long

ro·bot (rō′bət or rō′bŏt) **1** machine that acts and looks like a man. **2** person who behaves like a machine.

ro·bust (rō bŭst′) strong; vigorous; healthy: *Tom was so robust that he never caught cold.* **ro·bust·ly.**

¹rock (rŏk) **1** solid stone; hard mineral matter that lies under the soil and forms the earth's crust: *After drilling 30 feet, they hit*

rock *and had to abandon the well.* **2** stony mass rising steeply above the level of earth or sea to form a cliff or crag: *The* Rock *of Gibraltar stands at the entrance of the Mediterranean Sea.* **3** detached, single piece of stone; boulder: *The trail down the mountain was covered with* rocks. **4** firm foundation or support. [¹**rock** is from an Old French word (roque) of the same meaning.]

²**rock** (rŏk) **1** to move gently back and forth or from side to side: *the hand that* rocks *the cradle; branches* rocked *by the breeze.* **2** to shake; sway violently: *The earthquake* rocked *many buildings.* **3** rocking movement. [²**rock** is a form of an Old English word (roccian) meaning "pull" or "push."]

Rockers of a rocking chair

rock·er (rŏk′ər) **1** one of the curved wooden pieces on the legs of a chair or the bottom of a cradle which enables it to move with a swaying motion. **2** rocking chair. **3** in certain machines, a part with a rocking movement.

rock·et (rŏk′ǐt) **1** a kind of firework which bursts into a shower of sparks high in the air. It is driven by the burning of powder in its cardboard tube. **2** large missile driven in a similar manner with a nose cone containing explosives or scientific instruments. **3** to move very fast; to speed: *The last of the racing automobiles* rocketed *past us.*

rock·et·ry (rŏk′ǐt rǐ) branch of science which deals with the building and firing of rockets.

Rock·ies (rŏk′ǐz) the Rocky Mountains.

rocking chair a chair set on curved pieces of wood (rockers) on which it rocks.

Military rocket

rocking horse a wooden or plastic horse set on rockers or springs so that a child can rock back and forth.

---

fāte, făt, fâre, fär; bē, bĕt; bīte, bĭt; nō, nŏt, nôr; fūse, fŭn, fûr; tōō, tŏŏk; foil; foul; thin; ~~then~~;
hw for wh as in *wh*at; zh for s as in u*s*ual; ə for a, e, i, o, u, as in *a*go, lin*e*n, per*i*l, at*o*m, min*u*s

rock salt common salt found in solid rock-like state.

¹rock·y (rŏk′ĭ) **1** full of rocks: *The road to the village was very* rocky. **2** made of rocks. **3** like rock; hard; unyielding. **rock·i·er, rock·i·est.** [¹rocky is formed from ¹rock.]

²rock·y (rŏk′ĭ) not firm; shaky; wobbly. **rock·i·er, rock·i·est.** [²rocky is formed from ²rock.]

Rocky Mountains chief mountain range in North America. The Rocky Mountains extend from New Mexico to the arctic region of Alaska.

rod (rŏd) **1** thin, straight, circular stick made of wood, metal, etc.: *a fishing* rod; *a curtain* rod. **2** stick or switch used to punish or correct children: *Spare the* rod *and spoil the child.* **3** measurement of length that is equal to 5½ yards.

rode (rōd) See **ride.** *The cowboy* rode *home from the range.* (Homonym: road)

ro·dent (rō′dənt) **1** any animal that gnaws with its strong front teeth. Rats, mice, squirrels, and beavers are all rodents. **2** gnawing: *to have* rodent *teeth.*

ro·de·o (rō′dĭ ō′ or rō dā′ō) **1** a show or exhibition where cowboys display skills in horseback riding, roping cattle, etc. **2** a roundup of cattle. **ro·de·os.**

¹roe (rō) the eggs of fish. [¹roe is a form of an earlier English word (rown) that is probably of Germanic origin.] (Homonyms: ¹row, ²row)

²roe (rō) small deer found in Europe and western Asia. pl. **roe;** rarely, **roes.** [²roe is the greatly changed form of an Old English word (rā) meaning "striped," "spotted."] (Homonyms: ¹row, ²row)

roe·buck (rō′bŭk′) male roe deer.

rogue (rōg) **1** dishonest person; cheat. **2** one who plays pranks or teases; mischievous one. **3** any solitary, vicious animal living apart from the herd: *a* rogue *elephant.*

ro·guish (rō′gĭsh) **1** mischievous; playful: *a* roguish *smile.* **2** dishonest; rascally. **ro·guish·ly.**

roil (roil) **1** to stir up sediment in water or other liquids. **2** to irritate; vex.

role (rōl) **1** part or character taken in a play. **2** part or function played in life: *Helen liked playing the* role *of mother to children and friends alike.* Also spelled **rôle.** (Homonym: roll)

roll (rōl) **1** to move by turning over and over: *The ball* rolled *down the hill.* **2** to cause to move in this manner: *He* rolled *a ball down the hill.* **3** to move on wheels or rollers: *The carriage* rolled *down the street.* **4** to wind (something) to form a tube or ball: *to* roll *wool into a ball.* **5** anything wound to form a tube or ball: *a* roll *of paper.* **6** to turn around: *to* roll *the eyes.* **7** small cake of bread or pastry. **8** food prepared in a tube shape: *a meat* roll; *an egg* roll. **9** to make flat or even with a roller: *to* roll *a lawn; to* roll *dough for pastry.* **10** to extend or move in gentle rises and falls: *hills that* roll *to the sea; an ocean that* rolls *toward shore.* **11** gentle rising and falling: *the* roll *of hills; the* roll *of the ocean.* **12** to move from side to side: *The ship* rolled *on the stormy sea.* **13** this motion: *the* roll *of the ship on the stormy sea.* **14** to make a long echoing sound: *The thunder* rolled. **15** a long echoing sound: *the* roll *of thunder.* **16** to pronounce with a trill: *He* rolls *his r's.* **17** a list; catalogue: *the* roll *of officers.*

roll in to accumulate; arrive in large quantities: *Subscriptions are* rolling *in.*

roll out to unwind from a roll: *He* rolled out *the map.*

roll up 1 to wind into a tube or ball: *to* roll up *a carpet; to* roll up *wool.* **2** to accumulate; pile up in large quantities: *to* roll up *many debts.* (Homonym: role)

roll·er (rō′lər) **1** cylinder that rolls, smoothes, or crushes. **2** small wheel: *Walter oiled the* rollers *of his skates.* **3** rod on which something is rolled up: *Oliver tacked the window shade to its* roller. **4** one of the

Road roller

round bars placed under heavy objects to make pushing them easy: *Workmen moved the heavy box on* rollers. **5** large wave: *Heavy* rollers *make swimming difficult at this beach.*

roller skate 1 skate with small wheels instead of a blade. **2 roller-skate** to skate on roller skates. **rol·ler-skat·ed, rol·ler-skat·ing.**

Roller skate

rolling mill 1 factory where metal is rolled into sheets, bars, etc. 2 machine used for doing this.

rolling pin cylinder, with handles at each end, for rolling out dough.

Ro·man (rō'mən) 1 of ancient or modern Rome, its people, or language. 2 citizen or native of ancient or modern Rome. 3 pertaining to the Church of Rome. 4 **roman** (1) upright type used in ordinary print. (2) referring to upright type. 5 **Romans** in the New Testament, the epistle written by St. Paul to the Roman Christians.

ro·mance (rō'măns or rō măns') 1 story of unusual adventures or love in an exotic setting: *a romance of the South Seas.* 2 medieval tale of heroic adventure. The tales of King Arthur are a romance. 3 (rō mans' only) to invent adventures; exaggerate: *Susan is always* romancing. 4 love affair: *The* romance *of Romeo and Juliet was made into a play.* 5 love, excitement, adventure, etc., like that in old stories: *to travel in search of* romance; *to stay at a picturesque old inn with an air of* romance *about it.* **ro·manced, ro·manc·ing.**

Roman Empire ancient empire which at one time included much of Europe and parts of Africa and parts of Asia, all ruled from the city of Rome.

ERECTED
MCMXLVIII

I	V	X	L	C	D	M
1	5	10	50	100	500	1000

Roman numerals

Roman numeral any of the letters used instead of figures in ancient Rome. They are used today only in inscriptions and the like.

ro·man·tic (rō măn'tĭk) 1 having to do with high adventure, chivalry, courtly love, far-off places, etc.: *a romantic story of the Orient.* 2 affected by ideas of romance and adventure; impractical; unreal: *The very young often have a* romantic *view of life.* 3 picturesque; appealing to the imagination: *a romantic inn in the Alps.* 4 in the arts, imaginative and fanciful rather than

correct, restrained, or classical. 5 having to do with love: *a* romantic *attachment.*

Rome (rōm) 1 capital of Italy, in the central part of the country. It was the capital of the ancient Roman Empire. 2 the Roman Empire. (Homonym: roam)

romp (rŏmp) 1 to play or frolic in a lively or noisy way: *The children* romped *all over the house.* 2 lively or noisy play. 3 person, especially a girl, who plays in a lively and noisy manner. 4 to run quickly and easily: *The horse* romped *to the finish line.*

romp·ers (rŏm'pərz) one-piece outer garment worn by small children.

roof (rŏof) 1 top covering of a house or other building. 2 something which is like a roof: *the* roof *of a car; the* roof *of the mouth.* 3 to cover with a roof: *to* roof *a house.* 4 to cover or extend over something, as a roof does: *a path* roofed *with overhanging branches.*

roof·tree (rŏof'trē') large timber along the top of a roof, to which rafters are attached.

rook (rŏok) a mischievous European bird that looks like a small crow and lives in large flocks.

Rook, about 1½ ft. long

room (rŏom) 1 area separated by walls or partitions: *a dining room.* 2 space: *This table takes up too much* room. *Is there* room *for me in the back seat?* 3 space within which something may happen; scope; opportunity: *some* room *for improvement.* 4 people in a room: *The* room *became silent when Jack sat down at the piano.* 5 to lodge; occupy a room or rooms. 6 **rooms** lodgings; apartment: *The sign read:* "Rooms for Rent."

room·i·ness (rŏom'ĭ nĭs) spaciousness; ample area or space.

room·mate (rŏom'māt') one who shares a room with one or more persons.

room·y (rŏom'ĭ) having plenty of room; ample; large. **room·i·er, room·i·est.**

roost (rŏost) 1 branch or perch on which birds rest at night. 2 shelter in which

fāte, făt, fâre, fär; bē, bĕt; bīte, bĭt; nō, nŏt, nôr; fūse, fŭn, fûr; tōō, tŏŏk; foil; foul; thin; ~~then~~; hw for wh as in *what*; zh for s as in u*s*ual; ə for a, e, i, o, u, as in *a*go, lin*e*n, per*i*l, at*o*m, min*u*s

617

birds can stay the night. **3** to rest or stay for the night.

roost·er (rōōs′tər) a male barnyard fowl; cock.

¹root (rōōt) **1** that part of a plant (usually underground) which keeps it in place and takes in nourishment. **2** underground part of a plant; bulb; tuber. **3** to begin to grow; take root; become established. **4** anything looking

Plymouth Rock rooster, about 9½ pounds

like a root in use or position: *the* roots *of his hair.* **5** basic part: *to get to the* root *of the matter.* **6** source; origin; cause: *The* root *of Ellen's difficulties is her lack of money.* **7** word from which other words are formed; element of a language that cannot be further broken down and forms the basis of its vocabulary: *"Love" is the* root *of "lovable."* **8** of ideas, etc., to establish firmly: *His beliefs were* rooted *in prejudice.* **9** to be unable to move; become fixed: *Paul was* rooted *to the spot.* [**¹root** is a form of an Old English word (rote) of the same meaning.]

²root (rōōt) **1** to turn over or dig up soil with the snout. **2** to search through; rummage: *Dorothy* rooted *through the whole desk before she found her library card.*

root out or **up 1** to dig out; destroy: *The District Attorney's office was busy* rooting *out gambling.* **2** to discover by rummaging: *We* rooted *out their secret.* [**²root** is a form of an Old English word (wrōtan) meaning "root up." It is based on another Old English word (wrot) meaning "snout."]

³root (rōōt) to give support to or cheer for a team, contestant, etc. [**³root** is probably a form of a Scottish word (rout), meaning "to make a loud noise," which is in turn a form of an Old English word (wrūtan).]

rope (rōp) **1** large strong cord made of twisted smaller cords. **2** a string: *a* rope *of pearls.* **3** a festoon: *The* ropes *of laurel hung across the street.* **4** to bind with, or as with, a rope: *We* roped *and tied his*

Rope

feet so he couldn't escape.* **5** to use a rope as a fence: *Police* roped *off the street.* **6** to lasso: *to* rope *a calf.* **roped, rop·ing.**

ro·sa·ry (rō′zə rĭ) **1** string of beads for counting and reciting a series of prayers. **2** series of prayers thus recited. **ro·sa·ries.**

¹rose (rōz) **1** any of various thorny shrubs or plants bearing flowers of many colors. **2** the flower of this plant. **3** a delicate pink color. **4** something shaped like a rose such as certain cuts of gems. [**¹rose**

Wild and garden roses

comes from Old English (rose) from a Latin word (rosa) of the same meaning.]

²rose (rōz) See **rise.** *She* rose *early and went for a swim.* [**²rose** is a form of **rise.**]

rose·bud (rōz′bŭd′) bud of a rose.

ro·sette (rō zĕt′) **1** rose-shaped ornament made of loops of ribbon gathered at the center, or of a piece of cloth drawn in around a center: *The gift was tied with a green* rosette. **2** ornament of a similar shape made of glass, wood, metal, etc. **3** circle of lines, leaves, or the like, stretching from a central point: *This flower stalk springs from a* rosette *of flat leaves.*

Rosette

Rosh Ha·sha·na (rōsh′hə shä′nə) Jewish New Year, occurring in the early autumn.

ros·in (rŏz′ĭn) **1** solid substance that remains after distilling crude turpentine from certain resins. **2** to rub with rosin.

ros·y (rō′zĭ) **1** pinkish or reddish: *Their cheeks were* rosy *from the cold.* **2** hopeful; full of promise: *his* rosy *prospects.* **ros·i·er, ros·i·est; ros·i·ly.**

rot (rŏt) **1** to spoil; decay; make rotten: *Dampness* rots *wood.* **2** process of decaying: *Dry rot had set in in the old timbers.* **3** something that is decayed or decaying: *The fallen tree had become a mass of crumbling* rot. **4** certain diseases of plants or animals: *foot rot.* **rot·ted, rot·ting.**

ro·tate (rō′tāt or rō tāt′) **1** to turn around on a center point or line: *A wheel* rotates *on its axle. The earth* rotates *on its axis.* **2** to cause to turn around: *to* rotate *a wheel.*

3 to take turns: *The members of the club rotated in office.* **4** to cause to take turns: *to rotate men in office.* **ro·tat·ed, ro·tat· ing.**

ro·ta·tion (rō tā′shən) **1** a turning around on a center, point, or line: *the earth's rotation.* **2** a taking of turns: *the rotation of men in office.* **3** a system of varying the crops grown in the same field to keep up the fertility of the soil.

rote (rōt) **1** set, mechanical way of doing something. **2 by rote** by memory without understanding: *to learn the alphabet by rote.* (Homonym: wrote)

ro·tor (rō′tər) **1** part of a machine that revolves in or around a stationary part. **2** system of revolving blades: *the rotor of a helicopter.*

rot·ten (rŏt′ən) **1** decayed; spoiled: *a rotten egg.* **2** not sound; in danger of breaking: *a rotten beam.* **3** bad; disagreeable; contemptible: *That was a rotten thing to do.* **rot·ten·ly.**

rot·ten·ness (rŏt′ən nĭs) a being rotten; decay; corruption.

ro·tund (rō tŭnd′) **1** round; plump. **2** full-toned; deep: *a rotund phrase.* **ro·tund·ly.**

rouge (rōōzh) **1** pink or red preparation for coloring the cheeks or lips. **2** to use rouge. **rouged, roug·ing.**

rough (rŭf) **1** having an uneven surface; not smooth: *a rough road;* rough *cloth.* **2** violent; severe; harsh: *in rough games;* rough *weather.* **3** not polished: *a rough gem.* **4** incomplete; unfinished: *a rough sketch.* **5** vulgar; without refinement: *his* rough *manners.* **6** a coarse, violent person. **7** unpleasant; difficult: *a rough day.* **8** approximate; not thought out: *a rough guess.* **9** to treat roughly: *The boys were roughed up in the football game.* **10** on a golf course, area of grass and weeds not tended. **11 in the rough** in an unfinished condition.

rough in or **out** to sketch or outline in a general way: *to rough in a drawing; to rough out a plan.*

rough it to do without ordinary comforts, as on a camping trip.

rough·ly. (Homonym: ruff)

rough·age (rŭf′ĭj) material in a rough or crude state, especially coarse or bulky parts of food or fodder, such as bran or straw.

rough-and-tum·ble (rŭf′ən tŭm′bəl) **1** a violent fight or struggle with little regard for rules of fair play: *In the rough-and-tumble of battle, Marshall had no time to think.* **2** having to do with such a fight: *bruised in a* rough-and-tumble *fight.*

rough·en (rŭf′ən) to make or become rough: *hands* roughened *by the weather.*

rough·ness (rŭf′nĭs) harshness; coarseness.

round (round) **1** shaped like a ball; ball-shaped: *a round apple.* **2** shaped like a ring or circle: *a round mirror.* **3** curved; plump: *the baby's round cheeks.* **4** full; complete: *a round dozen.* **5** large; ample: *a good round sum.* **6** moving in a circle: *a round dance.* **7** full-toned: *a round voice.* **8** anything that is round in shape: *a round of beef.* **9** succession of duties, events, etc.: *my daily* round; *a round of parties.* **10** division of a sport or game; one complete game or set of games: *the sixth round of a fight; a round of golf.* **11** volley, as of shots, hand clapping, etc.: *a round of cannon shots; a round of applause.* **12** amount of ammunition needed for a volley of shots. **13** a portion of drink, etc., served to each of the members of a group: *a round of drinks.* **14** a dance in which the performers move in a circle. **15** song sung by two or more people, each one singing the same thing, starting at intervals one after another. **16** to make or become round: *to* round *the lips.* **17** to go around: *to round a curve or a corner.* **18** in a circle or half-circle: *A wheel goes* round. *We turned* round *for a last look.* **19** on all sides: *Gather* round! **20** in circumference; by measuring the outside surface (of a round object): *This globe is 12 inches* round. **21** from one to another: *Please hand these papers* round. **22** by a longer route: *If you can't climb over the fence, you'll have to go* round. *We came home the long way* round. **23** to or from a place where the speaker is or will be: *Come* round *to see me at eight tonight.* **24** in the neighborhood: *People*

---

fāte, făt, fâre, fär; bē, bĕt; bīte, bĭt; nō, nŏt, nôr; fūse, fŭn, fûr; tōō, tŏŏk; foil; foul; thin; ~~then~~;
hw for wh as in *w*hat; zh for s as in u*s*ual; ə for a, e, i, o, u, as in *a*go, lin*e*n, per*i*l, at*o*m, min*u*s

came from miles round *to see the fair.* **25** on every side of; in a circle: *a wall* round *a house.* **26** in a circular direction or manner: *to fly* round *the world.* **27 in round numbers** expressed in numbers without fractions or in tens or hundreds. **28 in the round** of sculpture, carved out or modeled fully on all sides; not done in relief.

round off 1 to make curved or round: *to* round off *edges of a table.* **2** to finish; bring to perfection: *He* rounded off *his story with a joke.*

round out 1 to make or become fuller or plumper. **2** to make complete: *Your visit* rounds out *my day.*

round up to gather together: *to* round up *cattle.*

round·a·bout (round′ə bout′) **1** not direct; not straightforward: *a* roundabout *route; a* roundabout *appeal for money.* **2** surrounding: *the country* roundabout.

round·ish (round′ish) more or less round; tending to be round.

round·ly (round′li) with vigor; bluntly; in plain language: *to scold* roundly; *to tell a person* roundly *that he isn't wanted.*

round-shoul·dered (round′shōl′dərd) having shoulders that bend forward; not erect.

round trip a journey to a place and then back again to the starting point.

round·up (round′ŭp′) **1** the herding together of cattle, horses, etc., for branding, inspection, etc. **2** men and horses that herd the animals together. **3** a gathering together of things or people: *The police made a* roundup *of all the tramps.*

rouse (rouz) **1** to awaken from sleep: *The fire alarm* roused *the household.* **2** to excite; stir up to anger or strong action: *The news of the Boston Tea Party* roused *all the American colonists.* **3** to set in motion: *Strong winds* roused *the sea.* **roused, rous·ing.**

¹rout (rout) **1** complete defeat followed by a disorderly flight: *When the enemy brought up the heavy cannon, our army's retreat turned into a* rout. **2** to defeat so completely that the enemy is in disorder. **3** disorderly mob. [**¹rout** comes through Old French (route) meaning "a throng"; "a defeat" from a Latin word (ruptum) meaning "broken"; "dispersed."]

²rout (rout) to awaken; turn out (by force): *Mother came up and* routed *the children from their beds.* [**²rout** is **¹rout** in a special meaning.]

route (rōōt or rout) **1** certain road, way, or course: *sea* routes; *U.S.* Route *1.* **2** to send *by* a route: *It is a complicated job to* route *freight cars across the country.* **3** job of supplying customers in a certain district with a particular thing: *a newspaper* route. **rout·ed, rout·ing.**

rou·tine (rōō tēn′) **1** usual or regular way of doing things: *the daily* routine *of classes and homework.* **2** regular; usual; ordinary; customary: *Purely* routine *work is often fatiguing.*

rove (rōv) to wander; go from place to place and not settle down: *to* rove *all over the world.* **roved, rov·ing.**

rov·er (rō′vər) person who wanders.

¹row (rō) series of persons or things in a line, especially a straight line. [**¹row** is a form of an Old English word (rāw) meaning "a line" or "series."] (Homonym: roe)

²row (rō) **1** to move a boat by pulling on oars. **2** to take or carry (someone or something) in a boat with oars: *The boatman* rowed *us up the river.* **3** a ride in a row-boat: *a* row *on the lake.* [**²row** is a form of an Old English word (rōwan) of the same meaning.] (Homonym: roe)

³row (rou) **1** noisy argument or quarrel: *to have a* row *with one's neighbors.* **2** loud noise; disturbance; uproar. [**³row** is a word of uncertain origin.]

row·boat (rō′bōt′) small boat moved in water by means of oars.

Rowboat

row·dy (rou′dī) **1** noisy, rough, and disorderly: *The audience became so* rowdy *that the speaker had to stop.* **2** a rowdy person. **row·dies; row·di·er, row·di·est; row·di·ly.**

roy·al (roi′əl) **1** of or having to do with kings, queens, etc.: *the* royal *family.* **2** like a king: *He behaved with* royal *dignity.* **3** of or having to do with the government of a king or queen: *the* royal *navy.* **4** fit for a king; splendid: *a* royal *welcome.*

roy·al·ly (roi′ə lī) in a way fitting for a king or queen.

roy·al·ty (roi′əl tĭ) **1** kings, queens, and their families: *a play performed before* royalty. **2** position, power, or duties of kings, queens, etc.: *Crowns and scepters are symbols of* royalty. **3** kingly nature or quality. **4** a payment made to the owner of a copyright or patent: *Publishers pay a* royalty *to an author on the copies of his books which they sell.* **roy·al·ties.**

R.R. 1 railroad. **2** rural route.

rub (rŭb) **1** to move (one thing) backwards and forwards on the surface of (another): *to rub one's hands with soap; to rub one's hands together; to rub suntan lotion on one's skin.* **2** to wipe thoroughly so as to make dry or clean: *Mother rubbed the baby with a towel.* **3** an act of rubbing: *to give something a good rub with a cloth.* **4** something that causes trouble; a difficulty: *"There's the rub" is an expression that means "There is the point at which the difficulty arises."*
rub down to massage.
rub elbows with to be friendly with; come into contact with: *The prince rubbed elbows with the common people.*
rub it in to keep on mentioning a failure, mistake, etc., in order to irritate someone.
rub off or **out** to remove; erase.
rub the wrong way to annoy; irritate. **rubbed, rub·bing.**

rub·ber (rŭb′ər) **1** hard, elastic material made from the sap of some trees or manufactured from a combination of chemicals. Rubber is used in making tires, balls, boots, etc. **2** made of this material: *a pair of* rubber *gloves.* **3** person or thing that rubs, polishes, erases, etc. **4** in bridge and certain other card games, a series of games, usually three, which is decided when one side wins two. **5** the decisive game in a series of this sort. **6 rubbers** overshoes.

rubber band elastic band made of rubber.

rub·bish (rŭb′ish) **1** waste; trash; worthless stuff. **2** nonsense: *Don't talk rubbish!*

ru·ble (rōō′bəl) **1** basic unit of money in Soviet Russia. **2** also, the silver coin or paper money representing it.

ru·by (rōō′bĭ) **1** red-colored precious stone. **2** deep red. **ru·bies.**

rud·der (rŭd′ər) **1** a hinged, flat, vertical piece of wood or metal that extends into the water at the stern of a boat or ship. By turning it the craft is steered. **2** a like piece on the tail of an airplane. For picture, see **airplane.**

Rudder

rud·dy (rŭd′ĭ) **1** rosy; red or reddish. **2** having the color of health: *Cold weather gave him a* ruddy *glow.* **rud·di·er, rud·di·est.**

rude (rōōd) **1** not polite; discourteous: *a* rude *manner; a* rude *reply; a* rude *person.* **2** roughly made; crude: *a* rude *mountain cabin;* rude *verses.* **3** primitive: *our* rude *forefathers.* **4** rough; violent; severe: *a* rude *shock.* **rud·er, rud·est; rude·ly.**

rude·ness (rōōd′nĭs) **1** bad manners; discourtesy. **2** roughness: *The* rudeness *of the work showed the maker's inexperience.*

ru·di·ment (rōō′də mənt) **1** a first or beginning step; one of the basic rules and principles (of any skill, art, or science): *My brother has already learned the* rudiments *of radio.* **2** in plant or animal life, a part or organ that has not fully grown or developed: *Some deer have only the* rudiments *of antlers.*

ru·di·men·ta·ry (rōō′də mĕn′tə rĭ) **1** beginning; elementary: *Alan had only a* rudimentary *knowledge of science.* **2** in biology, pertaining to an undeveloped part or organ: *a deer's* rudimentary *antlers.*

rue (rōō) to look back with shame and sorrow; regret: *He will* rue *his unkindness to the children.* **rued, ru·ing.**

rue·ful (rōō′fəl) **1** filled with regret; sadly disappointed; mournful; doleful: *Anne was* rueful *when she saw her poor report card.* **2** causing pity or grief: *She was a* rueful *sight after the rainstorm.* **rue·ful·ly.**

ruff (rŭf) **1** high collar formed by vertical folds of starched cloth, worn by men and women in olden times. **2** a ring or roll of feathers or fur which makes a standing collar around the neck of a bird or animal. (Homonym: **rough**)

Ruff

---

fāte, făt, fâre, fär; bē, bĕt; bīte, bĭt; nō, nŏt, nôr; fūse, fŭn, fûr; tōō, tŏŏk; foil; foul; thin; then; hw for wh as in *what*; zh for s as in u*s*ual; ə for a, e, i, o, u, as in *a*go, lin*e*n, per*i*l, at*o*m, min*u*s

ruf·fi·an (rŭf′ĭ ən) rough, brutal fellow; a bully.

ruf·fle (rŭf′əl) 1 to make rough; cause to lose the flatness or evenness of: *The frightened bird ruffled its feathers when it saw the cat.* 2 to disturb; annoy; disquiet: *Our late arrival ruffled our hostess.* 3 to draw into folds or pleats. 4 a frill: *Instead of a collar, her new dress has a ruffle of lace round the neck.* **ruf·fled, ruf·fling.**

rug (rŭg) 1 heavy woven, braided, or hooked mat used to cover part of a floor; a carpet woven in a single piece: *Mrs. Brown had the most beautiful Oriental rugs in her living room.* 2 thick, warm piece of cloth used as a blanket: *We had better take the rug along on the picnic in case we stay late.*

rug·ged (rŭg′ĭd) 1 rough and uneven; steep and rocky: *Our hike took us through very rugged country.* 2 strongly marked: *He has rugged features.* 3 harsh; severe: *a rugged winter.* 4 sturdy; robust; vigorous: *The pioneers had to be rugged men.* **rug·ged·ly.**

ru·in (rōō′ĭn) 1 destruction; severe damage: *the ruin of our hope; the ruin of property in a fire; to plan someone's ruin.* 2 the cause of destruction; the cause of someone's downfall: *Gambling was his ruin.* 3 something that has fallen into pieces or decay: *The old castle is now only a ruin.* 4 to damage or spoil entirely; destroy: *The last frost ruined the crops.* 5 **ruins** remains of a building, city, etc.: *the ruins of an Egyptian temple.*

ru·in·ous (rōō′ə nəs) leading to or being in a state of downfall or collapse. **ru·in·ous·ly.**

rule (rōōl) 1 principle made to guide and control action or behavior; a standard; regulation: *The Golden Rule of doing unto others as you wish they would do unto you.* 2 usual course; regular action: *It is Gerard's rule to take a walk before breakfast.* 3 reign; governing power: *Before the American Revolution we were under the rule of Britain.* 4 to have power over; govern; control: *The king ruled his country wisely.* 5 to order; direct; decide: *The court ruled that the information had nothing to do with the case.* 6 to make straight lines on, with a ruler, or a straight piece of wood or metal: *The boy ruled his paper very neatly, divid-*

ing it into four columns. 7 piece of wood, metal, etc., used as a ruler. 8 **as a rule** usually; in general: *Cats, as a rule, don't like water.* **ruled, rul·ing.**

rul·er (rōō′lər) 1 person who governs or reigns; a sovereign. 2 strip of wood, metal, etc., that is often marked with inches or the like, and used to draw and measure straight lines.

rul·ing (rōōl′ĭng) 1 decision made by an authority: *the ruling of the court.* 2 governing; having authority: *the ruling classes.* 3 most widely held: *The ruling sentiment of the town is in favor of the new mayor.*

rum (rŭm) alcoholic drink made from sugar cane, molasses, etc.

rum·ble (rŭm′bəl) 1 dull, heavy sound: *We knew that a storm was coming when we heard the rumble of thunder.* 2 to move with a heavy, rolling sound: *The truck rumbled down the street.* 3 to make a dull, heavy sound. **rum·bled, rum·bling.**

ru·mi·nant (rōō′mə nənt) 1 any animal that chews a cud or food that has been swallowed and then brought back to the mouth for further, more thorough chewing. Cows, sheep, goats, camels, and giraffes are all ruminants. 2 of animals, cud-chewing: *a ruminant animal.*

rum·mage (rŭm′ĭj) 1 to make a search; hunt (through or among in order to find some particular object): *She rummaged all through her desk before she found your letter.* 2 thorough search. 3 **rummage sale** a sale of odds and ends, such as old clothes, unwanted articles, etc., to raise money for charity, etc. **rum·maged, rum·mag·ing.**

rum·my (rŭm′ĭ) card game in which the object is to get groups of three or more cards that make a set.

ru·mor (rōō′mər) 1 talk, story, or report that is passed from person to person before the actual facts are known or without regard for its truthfulness; hearsay. 2 to report or spread by rumor.

rump (rŭmp) 1 hind quarters of an animal. 2 a cut of meat from this region.

rum·ple (rŭm′pəl) to wrinkle and crease; crumple; muss: *She rumpled her skirt by not hanging it properly.* **rum·pled, rum·pling.**

rum·pus (rŭm′pəs) 1 loud noise; uproar; a playful scuffle. 2 a brawl.

run (rŭn) **1** to move faster than at a walking speed. **2** a rapid pace. **3** to hurry; rush: *George ran carelessly through his homework.* **4** to make regular trips or follow a regular route: *This bus runs from the north to the south side of town.* **5** to move at a rate of speed: *to run at 50 miles an hour.* **6** to operate: *to run a business; to run a machine.* **7** to work; function: *This car won't run.* **8** to flow: *Tears ran down her cheeks.* **9** to cause to flow: *to run water into the sink.* **10** to discharge a fluid: *A nose runs.* **11** to cause to move in a certain direction or into a certain place: *to run one's fingers through one's hair; run one's fingers over the keys of a piano; run one's eyes over a page; to run a herd of cattle.* **12** free use: *to give guests the run of one's house.* **13** to move about freely: *Dogs were found running in the streets.* **14** school of fish moving together: *a run of tuna.* **15** to extend: *The story runs through four installments in the magazine. The road ran around the park.* **16** a losing of stitches; an unraveling: *a run in a stocking.* **17** to be a candidate; compete: *to run for office in an election.* **18** to climb or creep: *The ivy runs along the wall.* **19** to spread to parts where it does not belong: *Will the color run in this cloth?* **20** to pierce; to thrust: *The soldier ran a sword through his adversary.* **21** to expose oneself to: *to run a risk.* **22** to become; pass into a specified condition: *to run dry; run short of money.* **23** to occur: *The idea kept running through my mind.* **24** distance traveled: *The train's run from St. Louis to Chicago is over 300 miles.* **25** succession; repetition: *a run of good luck.* **26** number of performances: *The play had a short run.* **27** in baseball, etc., a unit of scoring: *The visiting team scored three runs.* **28** the average sort: *The run of people you meet believe in fair play.* **29** to do by running: *to run errands.* **30** to publish: *The newspaper ran the story of the game.* **31** to vary in price, size, etc.: *The tickets run from $1.50 to $5.00.* **32** an enclosed place for animals: *a chicken run.* **33 in the long run** eventually: *to win in the long run.*

run across to meet accidentally: *We ran across some old friends at the party.*

run down 1 of machinery, to stop operating: *My watch has run down.* **2** to knock down: *The bus ran down the old man.* **3** to speak against: *Don't run down the good name of your friend.*

run into 1 to meet accidentally: *I ran into a friend while shopping yesterday.* **2** to be likely to fall into: *He will run into debt if he is not careful about his spending.*

run out to come to an end: *His money has run out.*

run out of to have no more: *He ran out of time and couldn't finish his examination.*

run over 1 to overflow: *The water ran over the dam.* **2** to review; go over again: *Let's run over the script once more.* **3** to knock down with a vehicle: *We should cross the streets carefully to avoid being run over.*

run through 1 to spend: *Roger will run through his allowance before the week is up.* **2** to examine or rehearse quickly: *I only ran through the book. Let's run through that song again.*

ran, run, run·ning.

run·a·way (rŭn′ə wā′) **1** one who runs away; a fugitive: *a runaway from school.* **2** a horse out of control. **3** having run away or running away: *a runaway horse.*

run-down (rŭn′doun′) **1** weakened in health: *Joan has felt run-down ever since her operation.* **2** in a bad state of repair: *a run-down house.*

¹**rung** (rŭng) See ²**ring**. *The church bells were rung on Sunday morning.* [¹**rung** is a form of ²**ring**.] (Homonym: wrung)

²**rung** (rŭng) rodlike step of a ladder, or a rod joining the legs of a chair. [²**rung** is a form of an Old English word (hrung) meaning "a staff," "rod."] (Homonym: wrung)

Rungs

run·ner (rŭn′ər) **1** person, animal, etc., that runs: *A runner in a race.* **2** messenger: *The runner was sent from the bank with the money.* **3** one of the long narrow pieces on

fāte, făt, fâre, fär; bē, bĕt; bīte, bĭt; nō, nŏt, nôr; fūse, fŭn, fûr; tōō, tŏŏk; foil; foul; thin; ~~then~~; hw for wh as in *wh*at; zh for s as in u*s*ual; ə for a, e, i, o, u, as in *a*go, lin*e*n, per*i*l, at*o*m, min*u*s

which a sled moves; blade of a skate.
4 piece of long, narrow cloth used to cover
a table, chest of drawers, etc. **5** long, thin
rug. **6** a stem that runs along the ground,
putting down roots at intervals, or a plant
with this stem, such as the strawberry.

run·ning (rŭn′ĭng) **1** act of moving swiftly.
2 carried on while running: *a running fight;
a running jump.* **3** a managing: *the successful running of a business.* **4** one after
another; in succession: *It rained three days
running during our vacation.* **5** continuous;
uninterrupted: *a running fire of questions;
a running commentary.* **6** of a nose, wound,
etc., discharging; with a liquid coming out:
a running nose; a running sore.

runt (rŭnt) undersized animal or person:
the runt in a litter of puppies.

run·way (rŭn′wā′) **1** beaten path or way
along which animals pass. **2** a paved or
cleared strip where planes take off and
land. **3** fenced place: *a runway for dogs.*

rup·ture (rŭp′chər) **1** a bursting or breaking apart: *a rupture of the appendix.* **2** an
interruption of friendly relations. **3** to
break or burst apart. **rup·tured, rup·
tur·ing.**

ru·ral (rŏŏr′əl) having to do with the
country: *Most people in rural areas are
farmers.* **ru·ral·ly.**

ruse (rŏŏz) a trick; a deceitful way of doing
or getting something: *The army's pretended
retreat was a ruse to put the enemy off
guard.*

¹rush (rŭsh) **1** to move with speed; hurry:
*The doctor rushed to the scene of the acci-
dent.* **2** to cause to move or travel quickly:
*Please rush this package to the post office.
They rushed troops to the battlefield.* **3** to
act quickly and without enough thought:
*He is always rushing into things; he never
stops to think about the consequences.* **4** requiring haste: *a rush job.* **5** act or instance
of rushing: *a rush of wind; the rush of a
flood.* **6** hurry; bustle and excitement: *the
rush of life in a big city.* **7** sudden movement of people and a state of unusual
activity: *the gold rush to California in 1849;
the Christmas shopping rush.* **8 the rush
hours** the time when most people are
traveling to or from work. [**¹rush** goes
back to an old French word (rehusser)
meaning "push back."]

²rush (rŭsh) any of certain marsh plants
having hollow stems. The stems are often
dried and used for making baskets, hats,
chair seats, etc. [**²rush** is a form of an Old
English word (risc).]

rus·set (rŭs′ĭt) **1** reddish-brown color.
2 homespun cloth of that color: *The shepherds in the pageant were clad in russet.*
3 kind of apple with a rough, reddish-
brown skin.

Rus·sia (rŭsh′ə) country in eastern Europe
and western and northern Asia. It is also
known as the Soviet Union.

Rus·sian (rŭsh′ən) **1** of Russia, its people
or language. **2** citizen of Russia or person
of Russian descent. **3** language of the
Russian people.

rust (rŭst) **1** reddish-brown coating that
forms on iron or steel when exposed to air
or damp. **2** to become covered with rust:
*The spade rusted when it was left out in the
rain.* **3** to cause something to be covered
with rust: *Damp air rusts iron.* **4** of the
mind, memory, etc., to fail or weaken from
lack of use. **5** any of certain plant blights.
6 reddish brown.

rus·tic (rŭs′tĭk) relating to the country;
rural; the opposite of urban: *the rustic
charm of an old farmhouse; rustic speech or
manners.*

rus·tle (rŭs′əl) **1** to make a soft sound by
stirring or fluttering (something): *The
wind rustled the dry leaves.* **2** sound caused
by rustling. **3** to steal cattle, etc. **rus·tled,
rus·tling.**

rus·tler (rŭs′lər) person who steals cattle,
etc.

rus·ty (rŭs′tĭ) **1** covered with rust: *a rusty
tool.* **2** less perfect because of lack of
practice: *My Latin is rusty.* **3** faded; discolored: *a rusty gray.* **4** having the color
of rust. **rus·ti·er, rus·ti·est; rus·ti·ly.**

rut (rŭt) **1** track or groove made by a wheel.
2 fixed or mechanical way of acting or
thinking: *Some people get into a rut and
never change their ways.*

ruth·less (rŏŏth′lĭs) showing no mercy;
cruel: *a ruthless enemy.* **ruth·less·ly.**

rye (rī) **1** cereal plant closely related to
wheat and having a grain used as food.
2 the grain of this plant. **3** made from
this grain or plant: *a slice of rye bread.*
(Homonym: wry)

S

S, s (ĕs) 19th letter of the English alphabet.
S. South.

-s or **-es** word ending meaning (1) more than one: *two hats; nine dresses.* (2) that he, she, or it is doing an action at the present time: *He works. She fixes. It rings.*

Sab·bath (săb'əth) day of rest and religious worship. The Sabbath is Sunday for most Christians. It is Saturday for Jews and some groups of the Christian faith.

sa·ber or **sa·bre** (sā'bər) slightly curved cavalry sword.

sa·ble (sā'bəl) 1 small, dark-brown animal of the weasel family. 2 the American marten. 3 the valuable fur of these animals. 4 the color black. For picture, see **marten.**

sab·o·tage (săb'ə täzh') 1 deliberate destruction of an employer's property by workmen during labor troubles. 2 damage to a nation's property, such as bridges, railroads, etc., by enemy agents in time of war. 3 to damage or destroy by sabotage. **sab·o·taged, sab·o·tag·ing.**

sab·o·teur (săb'ə tûr') person who engages in sabotage.

sac (săk) in some plants and animals, a small baglike part usually filled with liquid. (Homonym: sack)

sa·chem (sā'chəm) American Indian chief.

¹sack (săk) 1 bag, especially a large one of rough cloth: *a potato sack.* 2 any cloth or paper bag. 3 the amount a bag can hold. 4 to put into a bag: *to sack wheat.* 5 loose jacket, especially for women or children: *a baby's sack.* [¹sack is a form of an Old English word (sacc) that comes through Latin (saccus) from a Greek word (sakkos) of the same meaning.] (Homonym: sac)

²sack (săk) 1 to break into and steal from; rob or plunder. 2 the robbing and looting of a town or city that has been taken by the enemy during a war. [²sack comes through French from a Medieval Latin word (saccare) meaning "put in a sack," "plunder." The meaning arose from the use of a sack in carrying off booty.] (Homonym: sac)

sac·ra·ment (săk'rə mənt) solemn religious act or ceremony held to be instituted by Jesus to give holiness: *Matrimony is one of the seven sacraments in the Catholic Church, and baptism is one of the two sacraments in many Protestant churches.*

sa·cred (sā'krĭd) 1 holy; belonging to God: *Jehovah is the sacred name in the Old Testament.* 2 set apart for religious use; having to do with religion: *a sacred book.* 3 worthy of great respect; deserving reverence: *a sacred promise.* **sa·cred·ly.**

sac·ri·fice (săk'rə fīs) 1 to offer something to a god as an act of worship, especially a human or animal life. 2 the act of making such an offering, or that which is offered in such an act of worship. 3 to give up something of value to help a person or a cause: *She sacrificed her leisure to work for the hospital.* 4 a giving up of something for someone else: *The parents made great sacrifices in order to keep their son in college.* 5 to sell at a loss: *I had to sacrifice my car.* 6 loss: *Her fur coat was sold at a sacrifice.* **sac·ri·ficed, sac·ri·fic·ing.**

sac·ri·lege (săk'rə lĭj) act of violence or disrespect toward sacred things or persons.

sac·ri·le·gious (săk'rə lĭj'əs) showing insult, violence, or disrespect to sacred persons or things. **sac·ri·le·gious·ly.**

sad (săd) 1 unhappy; sorrowful: *She was sad over the death of her dog.* 2 causing unhappiness or grief: *the sad news of the accident.* 3 pathetic; unsuccessful: *his sad attempt to be funny.* **sad·der, sad·dest; sad·ly.**

sad·den (săd'ən) to make sad: *Her troubles sadden me.*

sad·dle (săd'əl) 1 a seat strapped to an animal's back. 2 the seat of a bicycle, motorcycle, or the like. 3 to put a saddle on. 4 cut of meat from the back of an animal: *We were served roast saddle of mutton.* 5 ridge joining two hilltops. 6 to load; burden: *The*

Saber

Saddle

fāte, făt, fâre, fär; bē, bĕt; bīte, bĭt; nō, nŏt, nôr; fūse, fŭn, fûr; tōō, tŏŏk; foil; foul; thin; then; hw for wh as in what; zh for s as in usual; ə for a, e, i, o, u, as in ago, linen, peril, atom, minus

625

shopkeeper was saddled *with his dead partner's debts.* **sad·dled, sad·dling.**

sad·ness (săd′nĭs) unhappiness; sorrow; grief.

safe (sāf) **1** free from danger or harm; secure: *to be* safe *indoors in a storm.* **2** reliable; to be trusted: *That dog is* safe *around children.* **3** dependable; certain to be successful: *That's a* safe *bet.* **4** unable to do harm; securely held: *The thief is* safe *in prison.* **5** not injured: *He came home* safe *after the war.* **6** metal cabinet or chest to protect things of value, such as money and jewelry, from fire and theft. **saf·er, saf·est; safe·ly.**

safe·guard (sāf′gärd′) **1** to keep safe; keep from harm or danger; protect. **2** something that guards or protects; protection: *A dike is a* safeguard *against floods.*

safe·keep·ing (sāf′kē′pĭng) a keeping safe; protection: *I'll put these papers in the file for* safekeeping.

safe·ty (sāf′tĭ) **1** freedom from danger; protection: *She reached the* safety *of the house before the storm broke.* **2** so constructed as to prevent accident or injury: *a* safety *pin; a* safety *razor.*

saf·fron (săf′rən) **1** a variety of crocus that blooms in the fall. **2** bright orange-yellow dye or flavoring obtained from this flower. **3** orange yellow.

sag (săg) **1** to bend or sink downward in the middle from pressure, weight, or lack of tension: *The clothesline* sagged *with the weight of wet clothes.* **2** to become weak; lose firmness; droop: *His good spirits* sagged *when he thought of the work ahead.* **3** a drooping; a settling: *the* sag *of a broken chair seat.* **sagged, sag·ging.**

sa·ga (sä′gə) **1** medieval Norse legend or history of heroes or their families. **2** any tale or legend of heroic deeds.

sa·ga·cious (sə gā′shəs) of keen intelligence; shrewd; having sound judgment: *By his* sagacious *choice of personnel, the president saved the company from failure.* **sa·ga·cious·ly.**

sa·gac·i·ty (sə găs′ə tĭ) sound judgment; shrewdness.

¹**sage** (sāj) **1** wise; shrewd. **2** extremely wise man: *Confucius is considered one of the greatest* sages *of all time.* **sag·er, sag·est; sage·ly.** [¹sage comes through Old French

from a Latin word (sapiens) meaning "wise."]

²**sage** (sāj) plant of the mint family with gray-green leaves used for flavoring foods. [²sage comes through Old French (sauge) from a Latin word (salvia). This Latin word was formed from another Latin word (salvus) meaning "well," "healthy." The plant was once thought to have a healing effect.]

sage·brush (sāj′brŭsh′) low, woody shrub of the dry western plains.

said (sĕd) See **say.** *He* said *he would come.*

sail (sāl) **1** piece of canvas spread to catch the wind and make a ship move. **2** voyage in a ship: *We went for a* sail *in Uncle John's new sloop.* **3** to travel on a ship: *We* sailed *for England on the "Queen Mary."* **4** any sailing vessel or craft: *a fleet of 30* sail. **5** to pass over on or as on a ship: *They* sailed *the Pacific on a raft.* **6** to direct or navigate, especially a ship with sails: *to* sail *a ship through a storm.* **7** to move or glide smoothly: *to* sail *ahead.* **8** anything resembling a sail, such as an arm of a windmill. **9 set sail** to begin a voyage. **10 under sail** moving with sails spread. (Homonym: sale)

Sailboat

sail·boat (sāl′bōt′) boat with sails, intended to be driven by the wind.

sail·or (sāl′lər) **1** member of a vessel's crew; seaman. **2** straw hat with a flat brim and a low flat crown.

saint (sānt) **1** holy and godly person. **2** in some churches, an exceptionally godly person who after death is officially declared worthy of reverence.

Saint Ber·nard (sānt bər närd′) a large, intelligent dog. These dogs were originally trained and used for mountain rescue work in Switzerland.

Saint Bernard, about 2½ ft. at shoulder

saint·ly (sānt′lĭ) **1** like a saint; very good: *a* saintly *person.* **2** worthy of a saint: *a* saintly *work.* **saint·li·er, saint·li·est.**

saith (sĕth or sā'ǝth) old or poetic form of **says.**

sake (sāk) **1** purpose; motive; end: *for the sake of argument.* **2** benefit; welfare: *The soldier fights for his country's sake.* **3 for old time's sake** because of, or in memory of, former days or old friendship.

sa·laam (sǝ läm') **1** Oriental greeting which means "Peace." **2** low bow, with the palm of the hand placed on the forehead. **3** to make a low, formal bow or salaam. **4** to greet with such a bow.

sal·ad (săl'ǝd) cold preparation of lettuce or other vegetables, meat, fish, fruit, etc., usually served with a dressing.

sal·a·man·der (săl'ǝ măn'dǝr) animal with a smooth skin that looks much like a lizard and lives part or all of its life in water. Those on land hide in damp places.

Salamander (mud puppy), about 12 in. long

sal·a·ry (săl'ǝ rĭ) fixed sum of money paid at regular intervals for work. **sal·a·ries.**

sale (sāl) **1** an exchange (of goods or property) for money: *The sale of his car did not make him happy.* **2** an offering of goods at a reduced price: *This department store is having a big January sale.* **3** amount sold: *The daily sales of department stores before Christmas are much higher than usual.* **4** chance to sell; market: *There was almost no sale for ice skates last winter because of the warm weather.* (Homonym: sail)

sales·man (sālz'mǝn) man who sells goods or services. **sales·men.**

sales·wom·an (sālz'wŏŏm'ǝn) woman who sells goods or services. **sales·wom·en.**

sa·li·va (sǝ lī'vǝ) watery fluid produced by glands in the mouth. It keeps the mouth moist and helps in the digestion of food.

sal·i·var·y gland (săl'ǝ vĕr'ĭ glănd) organ that produces saliva.

sal·low (săl'ō) of a pale, sickly, yellow color or complexion: *Jane looked sallow after her long stay in bed.*

sal·ly (săl'ĭ) **1** to go (forth or out): *We sallied forth to have a look at the town.* **2** a sudden rushing forth: *The wolf pack*

made a sally *from the woods.* **3** a witty remark: *At the comedian's first sally there was a roar of laughter.* **sal·lies; sal·lied, sal·ly·ing.**

salm·on (săm'ǝn) **1** any of a number of kinds of fish whose flesh is a yellowish pink. The ocean salmon lay their eggs in fresh-water streams. **2** the color orange red. pl. **salm·on;** rarely, **salm·ons.**

Chinook salmon, 25 pounds or over

sa·loon (sǝ lŏŏn') **1** large room or hall, especially on a passenger ship, where people gather for some general purpose: *a dining saloon.* **2** place where alcoholic drinks are sold; bar; tavern.

salt (sôlt) **1** white substance (sodium chloride) found in sea water and mineral deposits and used to season and preserve food. **2** containing or preserved in salt: *a pan of* salt *water;* salt *pork.* **3** to use salt for seasoning or preserving: *Did you* salt *the potatoes?* **4** in chemistry, any of a large number of compounds, usually formed by the union of an acid and a base.

salt away to store or keep; to save.

salt down to preserve in brine: *to* salt down *meat.*

salt lick natural deposit of salt where animals go to lick.

salt·pe·ter (sôlt'pē'tǝr) salty, white powder used in making gunpowder and matches and in preserving food.

salt-wa·ter (sôlt'wô'tǝr) **1** living in, coming from, or having to do with the water of the ocean: *a* salt-water *fish.* **2** consisting of salt water: *a* salt-water *lake.*

salt·y (sôl'tĭ) **1** full of or tasting of salt. **2** witty; sharp. **salt·i·er, salt·i·est; salt·i·ly.**

sal·u·tar·y (săl'yŏŏ tĕr'ĭ) **1** good for the health: *the* salutary *mountain air.* **2** bringing a good effect; beneficial: *Her cheerfulness was* salutary *for all of us.*

sal·u·ta·tion (săl'yŏŏ tā'shǝn) **1** greeting: *He waved his hand in* salutation *as we passed him on the street.* **2** the opening words of a letter: *"Dear Sir" is the usual* salutation *in a business letter.*

fāte, făt, fâre, fär; bē, bĕt; bīte, bĭt; nō, nŏt, nôr; fūse, fŭn, fûr; tōō, tŏŏk; foil; foul; thin; ~~then~~;
hw for wh as in *wh*at; zh for s as in u*s*ual; ǝ for a, e, i, o, u, as in *a*go, lin*e*n, per*i*l, at*o*m, min*u*s

627

sa·lute (sə lo͞ot′ or sə lūt′) **1** act of respect or recognition; a greeting: *Julia waved a good-morning salute as she passed.* **2** formal act of respect done in a set way: *The private touched his cap in salute to the passing general.* **3** a discharge of guns as a mark of respect: *The presidential salute is 21 guns.* **4** to perform or honor with a salute; greet. **sa·lut·ed, sa·lut·ing.**

Salute

sal·vage (săl′vij) **1** the rescue of a ship or cargo from wreck, fire, etc.; the rescue of other property from destruction. **2** the saved ship or property. **3** payment made to those who rescued the property. **4** to save or rescue from destruction: *Although the ship sank they were able to salvage the cargo.* **sal·vaged, sal·vag·ing.**

sal·va·tion (săl vā′shən) **1** a saving; a rescue: *the salvation of passengers in a shipwreck.* **2** that which saves or rescues: *Her care was my salvation when I was sick.* **3** in religion, a soul's acceptance by God and the receiving of a soul into heaven; redemption.

salve (săv or säv) **1** soft greasy substance or ointment used on sores or wounds to heal or lessen pain. **2** something that calms and soothes: *Time is a salve for anger.* **3** to soothe: *Nothing could salve his grief.* **salved, salv·ing.**

same (sām) **1** not different; identical: *Let's leave at the same time he does.* **2** person or thing just spoken of or mentioned: *Whatever you do, I'll do the same.* **3** similar; generally alike (in quality, kind, or degree): *She has on the same dress as you.* **4** not different; unchanged: *He seemed much the same as five years ago.* **5** equal: *Although we took different roads we had to walk the same distance to get here.* **6** the identical person or thing: *Please give me more of the same.* **7** all the **same** nevertheless. **8** just the same (1) in the same way. (2) nevertheless.

Sa·mo·a (sə mō′ə) group of islands in the South Pacific, several of which belong to the United States.

samp (sămp) **1** coarsely ground corn. **2** coarse corn mush.

sam·pan (săm′păn) light, flat-bottomed boat with one sail, rowed from the stern, used mainly in China.

sam·ple (săm′pəl) **1** a part that shows what the whole is like; an example; a specimen: *I will need a sample of your work before I can hire you.* **2** to test or judge by taking a small piece or amount: *I sampled the stew before serving it.* **3** serving as an example: *A sample copy of his book is being mailed you.* **sam·pled, sam·pling.**

sam·pler (săm′plər) **1** person who judges what a whole is like from a small amount or sample: *Her father works as a tea sampler but he always drinks coffee at home.* **2** a piece of cloth embroidered in various designs and stitches made to show a person's skill with the needle.

sanc·ti·fy (săngk′tə fī′) **1** to make holy; set apart for sacred or religious use: *"God blessed the seventh day and sanctified it."* **2** to justify; cause to be loved and respected: *Giving thanks at Thanksgiving has been sanctified by custom.* **sanc·ti·fied, sanc·ti·fy·ing.**

sanc·tion (săngk′shən) **1** approval or permission from those in authority: *She had no sanction for leaving college in the middle of the year.* **2** to give permission for; to approve: *to sanction a marriage.*

sanc·ti·ty (săngk′tə tĭ) sacred or hallowed character: *the sanctity of a church; the sanctity of the home.* **sanc·ti·ties.**

sanc·tu·ar·y (săngk′cho͞o ĕr′ĭ) **1** holy place; temple; church. **2** the most sacred part of a church or temple: *In a Christian church the altar is in the* sanctuary. **3** a place of refuge and protection: *a bird* sanctuary. **sanc·tu·ar·ies.**

sand (sănd) **1** fine, tiny particles or grains of worn or crushed rock found on the seashore, along large bodies of water, in deserts, etc. **2** to smooth down or polish by rubbing with sand or sandpaper. **3** to sprinkle or cover with sand: *to sand a road after an ice storm.*

ANCIENT

san·dal (săn′dəl) **1** topless shoe held to the foot by leather cords or straps. **2** modern light shoe with an openwork top.

MODERN

Sandals

sandaled

san·daled (săn'dəld) wearing sandals.

sand·pa·per (sănd'pā'pər) **1** strong, heavy paper with a coating of sand on one side used in wearing down, smoothing, or polishing surfaces. **2** to use such a paper.

sand·pip·er (sănd'pi'pər) small shore bird with a sharp bill and rather long legs. It has an odd, mincing walk.

Spotted sandpiper, 7 to 9 in. long

sand·stone (sănd'stōn') kind of rock made chiefly of sand.

sand·storm (sănd'stôrm') storm of wind in which sand is blown about in clouds.

sand·wich (sănd'wĭch) **1** two or more slices of bread with a layer of meat, cheese, or other food placed between them. **2** to fit tightly or squeeze (between two others): *a small house* sandwiched *between two office buildings.*

sand·y (săn'dĭ) **1** made of, filled with, or like sand. **2** reddish yellow: *His* sandy *hair is too light to be called red.* **sand·i·er, sand·i·est.**

sane (sān) **1** sound and healthy in mind: *As he was able to tell the difference between right action and wrong action, the judge said he was sane.* **2** sensible; rational: *a sane approach to a problem.* **san·er, san·est; sane·ly.** (Homonym: seine)

sang (săng) See **sing.** *The chorus sang the words so clearly that we heard every syllable.*

san·guine (săng'gwĭn) **1** of the color of blood; ruddy: *a sanguine complexion.* **2** naturally cheerful; hopeful; optimistic: *He was sanguine about his chances of getting on the team.* **san·guine·ly.**

san·i·tar·i·um (săn'ə târ'ĭ əm) **1** home or establishment for the care and treatment of the sick and convalescent. **2** health resort.

san·i·tar·y (săn'ə tĕr'ĭ) **1** of or having to do with health. **2** free from dirt and disease: *That kitchen does not look very* sanitary *to me.* **san·i·tar·i·ly.**

san·i·ta·tion (săn'ə tā'shən) methods and practice of bringing about conditions that

satanic

protect health; hygiene: *The department of sanitation keeps the streets clean.*

san·i·ty (săn'ə tĭ) soundness of mind; mental balance: *From the way you've been acting lately, I question your sanity.*

sank (săngk) See **sink.** *The great ship sank.*

¹sap (săp) juice that circulates through the tissues of trees and plants and keeps them alive. [**¹sap** is a form of an Old English word (săp) which is related to a Latin word (sapor) meaning "flavor."]

²sap (săp) **1** to undermine; dig under: *Floods* sapped *the foundations of the cottage.* **2** to weaken gradually: *His brother's cruel teasing* sapped *his confidence in himself.* **sapped, sap·ping.** [**²sap** is from a French word (saper) meaning "to undermine."]

sap·ling (săp'lĭng) young tree.

sap·phire (săf'ir) **1** deep-blue, hard, transparent, precious stone. **2** bright, clear, deep blue: *the* sapphire *sea.*

sar·casm (sär'kăz əm) **1** bitter, taunting way of talking or writing (about a person, idea, or thing): *His* sarcasm *lost him many friends.* **2** a sneering, taunting remark.

sar·cas·tic (sär kăs'tĭk) bitterly scornful or sneering; mocking and contemptuous: *I am sick and tired of his* sarcastic *tongue.*

sar·dine (sär dēn') small fish belonging to the herring family. They are generally preserved in oil and packed in cans for use as food.

¹sash (săsh) broad band of cloth or ribbon worn around the waist as an ornament, or across one shoulder as part of a uniform or as a decoration. [**¹sash** comes from an Arabic word (shāsh) meaning "muslin."]

²sash (săsh) the framework which holds the glass in a window: *Most house windows have two* sashes *which slide up and down.* [**²sash** is a greatly changed form of "chassis."]

Sash

sat (săt) See **sit.** *When you got up he* sat *down in your chair.*

Sat. Saturday.

Sa·tan (sā'tən) the Devil.

sa·tan·ic (sā tăn'ĭk or sə tăn'ĭk) **1** of or like Satan. **2** devilish; evil; wicked.

fāte, făt, fâre, fär; bē, bĕt; bīte, bĭt; nō, nŏt, nôr; fūse, fŭn, fûr; tōō, tŏŏk; foil; foul; thin; then; hw for wh as in *what*; zh for s as in u*s*ual; ə for a, e, i, o, u, as in *ago, linen, peril, atom, minus*

629

satch·el (săch′əl) small bag for carrying personal belongings, papers, books, etc.

Satellites: moon (of earth); man-made Pioneer V, Earth, and Venus (of sun)

sat·el·lite (săt′ə līt′) **1** heavenly body that revolves about another: *The moon is a satellite of the earth.* **2** steady attendant: *The actress was usually surrounded by her many* satellites. **3** country whose acts are controlled by another: *Poland is a satellite of Russia.* **4** man-made body shot into orbit around the earth or sun.

sat·in (săt′ən) **1** closely woven silk or rayon material with glossy surface. **2** of or like satin; glossy; very smooth: *a satin dress; a satin skin.*

sat·is·fac·tion (săt′ĭs făk′shən) **1** a being pleased; contentment: *The cat purred with satisfaction over its bowl of milk.* **2** source of pleasure or contentment: *Bill's grades were a great satisfaction to his father last term.* **3** a paying back or getting even; reparation: *to receive satisfaction for an insult.*

sat·is·fac·to·ry (săt′ĭs făk′tə rĭ) meeting needs, hopes, or requirements; sufficient; adequate. **sat·is·fac·to·ri·ly.**

sat·is·fy (săt′ĭs fī′) **1** to meet a desire or need; to content; gratify: *That satisfied my hunger.* **2** to convince: *If you are satisfied of this man's guilt, you must bring in a verdict of "Guilty"* **3** to pay in full; make good: *to satisfy a claim.* **sat·is·fied, sat·is·fy·ing.**

sat·u·rate (săch′ə rāt′) to soak through and through: *The ground was saturated with dew. He saturated himself in ancient history.* **sat·u·rat·ed, sat·u·rat·ing.**

Sat·ur·day (săt′ər dĭ or săt′ər dā) seventh day of the week.

Sat·urn (săt′ərn) **1** second largest planet in the solar system, sixth in order of distance from the sun. **2** the Roman God of agriculture.

sat·yr (săt′ər or sā′tər) in ancient Greece, one of a group of woodland gods, pictured as part man and part goat, given to wild revels.

sauce (sôs) **1** liquid preparation served with food to add spice or flavor. **2** stewed fruit: *plum sauce.*

sauce·pan (sôs′păn′) pot with a handle, used for cooking food.

sau·cer (sô′sər) shallow dish to hold a cup.

Satyr

sau·cy (sô′sĭ) pert; rude; impudent: *a saucy answer.* **sau·ci·er, sau·ci·est; sau·ci·ly.**

saun·ter (sôn′tər) **1** to stroll idly: *to saunter in the park.* **2** a leisurely walk; a stroll.

sau·sage (sô′sĭj) ground, seasoned meat usually enclosed in a thin tubelike casing.

sav·age (săv′ĭj) **1** member of a primitive tribe. **2** uncultivated person. **3** fierce; vicious: *a savage animal; a savage reply.* **4** cruel, fierce person. **5** wild; uncivilized: *a savage country;* savage *rites.* **sav·age·ly.**

sav·age·ry (săv′ĭj rĭ) **1** uncivilized or uncultivated condition. **2** fierceness; cruelty: *the savagery of wolves.* **sav·age·ries.**

sa·van·na or **sa·van·nah** (sə văn′ə) flat, open grassland having scattered clusters of trees.

¹save (sāv) **1** to free from danger or disaster; rescue: *to save a life.* **2** to keep from wear or decay: *to save a dress by wearing an apron.* **3** to avoid the waste of: *to save time, labor, and trouble.* **4** to lay away; keep: *to save money.* **5** to preserve from sin. **saved, sav·ing.** [**¹save** is from an Old French word (salver) which comes from a Latin word (salvus) meaning "safe."]

²save (sāv) except; not including: *Jack attended every meeting save one.* [**²save** is from an Old French word (sauf) meaning "making exception of."]

sav·ing (sā′vĭng) **1** a rescue; delivery from danger: *a saving of lives.* **2** redeeming: *Her only saving trait was a sense of humor.* **3** frugal; economical: *her saving habits.* **4** an economical purchase or action: *If you buy now, you can get a saving of 10%.* **5 savings** money saved and put away. **6 savings bank** bank which specializes in receiving small deposits and paying interest on them.

sav·ior or **sav·iour** (sāv'yər) **1** person who rescues or saves. **2 Saviour** or **Savior** Jesus Christ.

sa·vor (sā'vər) **1** a taste or odor: *The salad had a savor of garlic.* **2** to taste or smell with pleasure; enjoy; relish: *to savor the odor of cooking when hungry; to savor revenge.* **3** suggestion; trace: *There was a savor of suspicion in his manner.* **4** to have a suggestion or trace (of): *His actions savored of treachery.*

¹**sa·vor·y** (sā'və rĭ) pleasing or agreeable, usually in taste or smell. [¹**savory** is formed from **savor**.]

²**sa·vor·y** (sā'və rĭ) herb of the mint family used in cooking. **sa·vor·ies.** [²**savory** is ¹**savory** in a special meaning. Nearly all plants of the mint family, including savories, have a strong flavor or savor.]

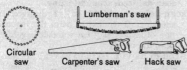

Circular saw
Lumberman's saw
Carpenter's saw
Hack saw

¹**saw** (sô) **1** a cutting tool with teeth along or around the edge of a thin, flat blade. **2** to cut or shape with a saw: *After Oscar sawed the firewood, he sawed out a weathervane.* **3** to use a saw: *He sawed steadily for an hour.* **4** to move the hands and arms as if sawing: *The excited orator sawed the air.* **sawed, sawed** or **sawn, saw·ing.** [¹**saw** is a form of an Old English word (saga) meaning "a cutter."]

²**saw** (sô) proverb; wise saying: *"Don't count your chickens before they are hatched" is an old* saw. [²**saw** is a form of an Old English word (sagu) meaning "a saying."]

³**saw** (sô) See ¹**see.** *I saw him fall from the roof.* [³**saw** is a form of ¹**see.**]

saw·dust (sô'dŭst') fine particles that fall when wood is sawed.

saw·horse (sô'hôrs') frame to hold wood while being sawed.

saw·mill (sô'mĭl') place where logs are sawed into lumber by machine.

sawn (sôn) See ¹**saw.** *The tree was sawn into planks.*

sax·o·phone (săk'sə fōn') musical wind instrument consisting of a sharply bent metal tube with keys, and a reed mouthpiece.

Saxophone

say (sā) **1** to utter in words; speak. **2** to assert; declare: *I say he must go.* **3** to repeat; recite: *Claire is saying her prayers.* **4** a chance to express an opinion: *to have a say in the matter.* **said, say·ing.**

say·ing (sā'ing) **1** something uttered; anything said. **2** proverb: *an old saying of my grandmother's.*

S.C. South Carolina.

scab (skăb) **1** crust that forms over a sore or wound while it heals. **2** worker who does not join a strike.

scab·bard (skăb'ərd) a sheath or case for the blade of a sword or dagger.
Scabbard

scaf·fold (skăf'əld or skăf'ōld) **1** temporary platform on which workmen may stand. **2** platform on which criminals are put to death.

scald (skôld) **1** to burn with hot liquid or steam. **2** to rinse or dip in boiling-hot water: *to scald dishes; to scald tomatoes before peeling them.* **3** to heat almost to the boiling point: *to scald milk.* **4** a burn from hot water or steam. **5 scalding tears** tears of bitter sorrow or regret.
Scaffold

¹**scale** (skāl) **1** any machine for weighing. **2** a balance, or one of its pans. [¹**scale** is from an Old Norse word (skāl) meaning "a bowl." The plural of "bowl" came to mean a weighing balance.]

Scales

²**scale** (skāl) **1** one of the thin, horny plates that form the covering of most fishes, reptiles, etc. **2** to scrape off scales, as from

fāte, făt, fâre, fär; bē, bĕt; bīte, bĭt; nō, nŏt, nôr; fūse, fŭn, fûr; tōō, tŏŏk; foil; foul; thin; then; hw for wh as in *wh*at; zh for s as in u*s*ual; ə for a, e, i, o, u, as in *a*go, lin*e*n, per*i*l, at*o*m, min*u*s

a fish. **3** to break or peel off in small bits: *The paint is* scaling *from the wall.* **scaled, scal·ing.** [²**scale** is from an Old French word (escale) meaning "a husk," "an eggshell."]

³**scale** (skāl) **1** series of marks made at regular distances along a line, used in measuring: *A tape measure has a* scale *in inches.* **2** basis for a system of numbering: *The decimal* scale *goes by tens.* **3** arrangement (of anything) in a series from low to high: *the* scale *of grades in a class; the social* scale; *wage* scale. **4** relation between the actual size of an object and its size in a drawing, painting, model, etc.: *The* scale *of the town map is one inch to three miles.* **5** in music, a series of tones in a regular order, up or down. **6** to control; regulate according to a standard: *He is wise to* scale *his spending to his income.* **7** to climb up by degrees or steps: *to* scale *a ladder.* **scaled, scal·ing.** [³**scale** comes through Italian from a Latin word (scala) meaning "a ladder." The spacing of the steps of a ladder suggested the regular intervals of various types of scales.]

scal·lop (skăl′əp *or* skŏl′əp) **1** one of a series of shell-shaped curves or semicircles used to ornament the edge of lace, shelf paper, and the like. **2** a shellfish with a roundish double shell marked with fanlike grooves and an indented edge. **3** the muscle of this shellfish used as food. **4** to bake (oysters, potatoes, etc.) in layers with milk, butter, flour or crumbs, and seasoning. **5** to make scallops in or on: *Lois* scalloped *the edge of her doily.*

Scallops

scalp (skălp) **1** the skin at the top of the head, usually covered by hair. **2** to cut off or tear off the scalp: *Indians* scalped *their victims to record the number they had killed.*

scal·y (skā′lĭ) **1** having thin, horny plates; covered with scales: *Snakes have a* scaly *skin.* **2** flaky; peeling: *It's so long since the house was painted that the walls are* scaly. **scal·i·er, scal·i·est.**

scamp (skămp) **1** rogue; rascal. **2** person who is playfully mischievous, especially a young person.

scam·per (skăm′pər) **1** to run quickly; hasten away: *The puppy* scampered *after John.* **2** to frolic or move around merrily: *The children were* scampering *about in the garden.*

scan (skăn) **1** to examine closely; scrutinize: *She* scanned *his face anxiously to see why he was angry.* **2** to look through quickly; glance at hastily: *I* scanned *the classified ads.* **3** to read or mark (a line of poetry) to show the number and kind of metrical feet used. **scanned, scan·ning.**

scan·dal (skăn′dəl) **1** something shameful: *The slums in this city are a* scandal. **2** malicious gossip: *Mother loves a bit of* scandal.

scan·dal·ize (skăn′də līz′) to shock or offend by misbehaving; jar someone by acting against his ideas of what is proper: *Max* scandalized *his aunt by his behavior.* **scan·dal·ized, scan·dal·iz·ing.**

scan·dal·ous (skăn′də ləs) **1** disgraceful; shocking. **2** tending to harm the reputation of someone: *What* scandalous *gossip!* **scan·dal·ous·ly.**

Scan·di·na·vi·a (skăn′də nā′vĭ ə) **1** Norway, Sweden, Denmark, and Iceland. **2** peninsula of Norway and Sweden.

Scan·di·na·vi·an (skăn′də nā′vĭ ən) **1** of a Scandinavian country, its people, or its language. **2** a citizen of a Scandinavian country or person of Scandinavian descent. **3** a group of Germanic languages which includes Norwegian, Swedish, and Danish.

scant (skănt) hardly enough; insufficient: *a* scant *supply of cookies.*

scant·y (skăn′tĭ) **1** not enough; narrow; too small: *a* scanty *little jacket.* **2** barely enough: *the* scanty *portions served in this restaurant.* **scant·i·er, scant·i·est; scant·i·ly.**

scar (skär) **1** mark or blemish left on the skin after the healing of a wound or burn. **2** any mark left on the mind by sorrow, grief, or suffering. **3** a damaging mark left on a car, furniture, landscape, etc. **4** to leave a damaging mark on: *The piano was badly* scarred *by a cigarette burn.* **scarred, scar·ring.**

scarce (skârs) not common or available in large quantity; scanty; hard to get: *Strawberries are very* scarce *this year.* **scarc·er, scarc·est.**

632

scarce·ly (skârs′lĭ) not quite; hardly: *There are* scarcely *any currants in this cake.*

scar·ci·ty (skâr′sə tĭ) too small a quantity; limited or insufficient supply: *a* scarcity *of fruit this summer.* **scar·ci·ties.**

scare (skâr) **1** to frighten; startle; fill with sudden fear: *The crowded street* scared *the timid old lady.* **2** to frighten away: *The dog* scared *off the stranger.* **3** panicky, often groundless, fear: *a war* scare. **scared, scar·ing.**

scare·crow (skâr′krō′) **1** a figure, usually made of sticks dressed in old clothes, set up in a field, to scare birds away from crops. **2** a thin and raggedly dressed person.

scarf (skärf) **1** long piece of material (silk, wool, etc.) worn about the shoulders or neck, or over the head, for warmth or decoration. **2** long strip of cloth used to cover tables, dressers, etc. **scarfs** or **scarves.**

scar·let (skär′lĭt) vivid red color.

scarlet fever contagious disease marked by a bright red rash, high fever, and sore throat.

scat (skăt) word used to drive away a cat.

scat·ter (skăt′ər) **1** to fling about in all directions; throw here and there: *to* scatter *rubbish all over a picnic ground.* **2** to go in different directions: *The crowd* scattered.

scav·en·ger (skăv′ĭn jər) **1** person who collects refuse and rubbish from houses and streets. **2** any of various birds, animals, or fish that eat waste matter and spoiled food.

scene (sēn) **1** place of an actual event: *Oxford was the* scene *of the boat race.* **2** time, place, and circumstances in which a play, novel, etc., takes place: *The* scene *of the story is New Orleans during the Civil War.* **3** a division of an act in a stage play: *the second* scene *of the third act.* **4** in the theater, the painted background, stage properties, etc., that show the place of action: *The opening* scene *in this opera is a garden.* **5** a view; landscape: *a beautiful* scene. **6** a display of bad temper or anger before others: *Peter made a* scene *because dinner was so late.* (Homonym: seen)

scen·er·y (sē′nə rĭ) **1** general view of a landscape: *The* scenery *in the Alps is beautiful.* **2** the background, hangings, painted screens, etc., used on the stage.

sce·nic (sē′nĭk or sĕn′ĭk) **1** having natural beauty; picturesque: *the* scenic *delights of the mountain trail.* **2** having to do with stage effects or stage scenery: *The* scenic *designs were the best part of the play.*

scent (sĕnt) **1** odor; smell: *These roses have a delightful* scent. **2** odor left by an animal: *The hounds picked up the* scent *of the fox.* **3** to smell; recognize by smelling: *The hounds* scented *a fox.* **4** sense of smell: *Hounds hunt by their keen* scent. **5** to get a hint of; to be aware of: *The reporter* scented *a story in the man's suspicious behavior.* **6** a hint or clue by which something is recognized or followed: *the* scent *of danger; on the* scent *of a criminal.* **7** perfume: *a bottle of* scent. **8** to fill with an odor; to perfume: *The lilacs* scented *the air.* (Homonyms: cent, sent)

scep·ter or **scep·tre** (sĕp′tər) **1** ornamental rod or staff held in ceremonies by a ruler as a sign of authority and power. **2** royal rank or power: *At the death of the old king the* scepter *passed to the prince.*

sched·ule (skĕj′ōol) **1** written or printed list of times for certain events: *The* schedule *for spring basketball practice was printed in the school newspaper.* **2** notice of arrivals or departures of planes, trains, buses, etc. **3** to make or plan an appointment, a meeting, or a timetable. **sched·uled, sched·ul·ing.**

scheme (skēm) **1** a plan, design, or system to be followed in doing something: *The* scheme *for building the new highway was presented to the town board.* **2** underhanded plot: *His* scheme *to overthrow the government was discovered in time.* **3** planned arrangement of color: *The* scheme *of our living room is restful to the eyes.* **4** mapped plans; diagrams: *The* scheme *of the attack was given to all the officers of the platoon.* **5** to plan; to plot: *The dictator* schemed *to get power.* **schemed, schem·ing.**

Schick test (shĭk tĕst) skin test that shows whether one is immune to diphtheria.

---

fāte, făt, fâre, fär; bē, bĕt; bīte, bĭt; nō, nŏt, nôr; fūse, fŭn, fûr; tōō, tŏŏk; foil; foul; thin; then; hw for wh as in *wh*at; zh for s as in u*s*ual; ə for a, e, i, o, u, as in *a*go, lin*e*n, per*i*l, at*o*m, min*u*s

schol·ar (skŏl'ər) **1** student; pupil: *The fourth-grade* scholars *studied their spelling.* **2** person having thorough and expert knowledge in one or more fields of learning; a learned person: *I was taught by the outstanding* scholars *of this university.*

schol·ar·ly (skŏl'ər li) **1** showing great and well-organized knowledge: *In his* scholarly *paper Frank clearly and carefully presented the history of Indian burial grounds.* **2** having the qualities of a learned man or scholar.

schol·ar·ship (skŏl'ər shĭp) **1** knowledge gained through long study. **2** money or aid given to a deserving student or scholar to allow him to continue his studies: *Joan was given a* scholarship *to college because of her superior grades in high school.*

schol·as·tic (skō lăs'tĭk or skə lăs'tĭk) of education; having to do with schools, teachers, studies, or students: *the high* scholastic *standing of our school.*

¹school (skōōl) **1** place of teaching and learning. **2** the total group of pupils and teachers (at one place of learning): *The entire* school *will go to the track meet.* **3** time when instruction is given: *to have no* school *because of the snowstorm.* **4** persons influenced by the same teacher or having ideas in common: *I am not of his* school *of thought.* **5** division of a university given over to one branch of learning: *Does your university have a law* school? [¹school is a form of an Old English word (scŏl) that comes from a Latin word (schola). The Latin word comes from a Greek word (scholē) meaning "leisure, employment of leisure."]

²school (skōōl) large group of fish that swim or feed together. [²school is from a Dutch word of the same spelling. The word is related to ¹school.]

school·book (skōōl'bŏok') book used in schools; textbook.

school·boy (skōōl'boi') boy who attends school.

school·fel·low (skōōl'fĕl'ō) schoolmate; a companion at school.

school·girl (skōōl'gûrl') girl who attends school.

school·house (skōōl'hous') building where school is held.

school·ing (skōō'lĭng) education; training and instruction in school.

school·mas·ter (skōōl'măs'tər) man who teaches in a school.

school·mate (skōōl'māt') companion or associate at school.

school·room (skōōl'rōōm') room where students are taught or instructed.

school·teach·er (skōōl'tē'chər) person who teaches pupils in school, particularly in the lower grades.

school·yard (skōōl'yärd') playground of a school.

schoon·er (skōō'nər) **1** a kind of sailing vessel with two or more masts fitted with booms to carry sails rigged fore and aft. **2** covered wagon used by pioneers on the western prairies of the United States.

Schooner

schwa (shwä) **1** a vowel sound which occurs in many unstressed syllables in English, as *a* in *about, e* in *spoken, i* in *pencil, o* in *atom, u* in *circus.* **2** phonetic symbol for the sound of a schwa (a reversed e): ə.

sci·ence (sī'əns) **1** study of all material things and how they behave under different conditions. Also, the knowledge gained from such study, consisting of facts and laws. Physics, chemistry, biology, etc., are branches of science. **2** organized study of a group of material things: *Botany is the* science *of plant life.* **3 biological science** science of living things. **4 physical science** science of nonliving things. **5 social science** science of man's behavior in society.

sci·en·tif·ic (sī'ən tĭf'ĭk) **1** having to do with science: *a* scientific *instrument.* **2** based on facts or logical ideas developed from facts; open-minded: *a* scientific *attitude.*

sci·en·tif·i·cal·ly (sī'ən tĭf'ĭk ə lĭ) in a scientific way.

sci·en·tist (sī'ən tĭst) **1** person having great knowledge of some branch of science which he follows as a profession. **2** person doing scientific research.

Scimitar

scim·i·tar (sĭm'ə tər) sword with a curved blade used by Arabs and other peoples of the Middle East.

scis·sors (sĭz'ərz) cutting tool with pivoted double blades that close against each other with a shearing action.

scoff (skôf or skŏf) **1** to make fun of (in order to show disbelief); scorn; mock: *They scoffed at his plan but later they found that he was right.* **2** a jeer; taunt: *the scoffs of an angry mob.*

scold (skōld) **1** to speak sharply to; find fault with; chide; reprove: *She scolded the class for talking when they should have been studying.* **2** woman who is accustomed to speaking sharply and abusively.

Scissors

scoop (skōop) **1** any of a variety of kitchen tools of various shapes which are used to take up flour, sugar, ice cream, etc.: *Reba took the scoop to fill the sugar bowl.* **2** deep shovel for moving coal, grain, or the like. **3** the bucket of a dredge or mechanical shovel. **4** a dipping movement: *Harvey caught the minnow with a scoop of the hand.* **5** the amount held by a scoop: *Dora helped herself to a scoop of ice cream.* **6** to dip up: *Otto scooped the fish into his net.*

Scoop

scoot (skōot) to run or walk swiftly; dart quickly: *He scooted around the corner when he saw the policeman.*

scoot·er (skōo'tər) toy consisting of a board slung between two aligned wheels and equipped with an upright steering bar. The rider stands on the board with one foot and drives the toy forward by pushing against the ground with the other foot.

Scooter

scope (skōp) **1** range of understanding; ability to understand: *Algebra is beyond the scope of such a small child.* **2** area covered; extent: *The scope of his travels includes Europe and America.* **3** freedom; room to move about: *He has been given enough scope in his work to do as he pleases.*

scorch (skôrch) **1** to burn the surface of; discolor by burning: *I scorched a shirt when I ironed it.* **2** to wither or dry up by heat: *We had a hot summer and the grass was badly scorched.* **3** a slight burn.

score (skôr) **1** line or notch cut or scratched in a surface, often used for keeping a record. **2** to mark down; record; keep account of by marking down: *He scored the points in the basketball game on a special card.* **3** a record of points won in a game: *What was the final score in the football game?* **4** to win (points in a game): *I scored five points over my opponent.* **5** to win a point in a game or in an argument; achieve a success: *He was winning the argument but I finally scored when I brought out some facts he didn't know.* **6** anything to be paid back or paid off; a debt; a grudge: *I have a score to settle with you.* **7** an excuse or reason: *She begged off going out to dinner on the score that she was too tired.* **8** twenty of anything. **9** a written copy of music; often, the music as distinguished from the words of an opera or musical comedy. **10** to make or cut lines or notches in: *We scored the chestnuts before roasting them.* **scored, scor·ing.**

scorn (skôrn) **1** feeling that a person or thing is mean or worthy of contempt; disdain: *to have scorn for a coward.* **2** to look down on; treat with contempt; disdain: *She scorned his underhanded attempt to blame her for what he had done.* **3** to turn down; to spurn; to reject: *I scorned his attempt to make friends with me.* **4** person who is looked down upon; an object of contempt: *He was the scorn of the neighborhood because he bragged so much.*

scorn·ful (skôrn'fəl) feeling or showing great disapproval, contempt, or disdain: *She was scornful of the silly way we acted.* **scorn·ful·ly.**

scor·pi·on (skôr'pĭ ən) animal related to the spiders, having a slender body, pincers, and a poisonous sting at the end of its tail.

Scorpion, 1 to 8 in. long

Scotch (skŏch) of Scotland, its people, or its language; Scottish.

Scot·land (skŏt'lənd) a part of Great Britain, north of England.

fāte, făt, fâre, fär; bē, bĕt; bīte, bĭt; nō, nŏt, nôr; fūse, fŭn, fûr; tōō, tŏŏk; foil; foul; thin; then; hw for wh as in what; zh for s as in usual; ə for a, e, i, o, u, as in ago, linen, peril, atom, minus

635

Scottish

Scot·tish (skŏt′ĭsh) **1** of Scotland, its people, or its language. **2** English as spoken by the people of Scotland. **3 the Scottish** the people of Scotland.

scoun·drel (skoun′drəl) person of bad character; rascal; rogue.

¹scour (skour) **1** to clean by rubbing hard with a rough material or with soap and water. **2** to wear away by rubbing: *The stream* scoured *out a new bed during the rains.* **3** a cleaning by hard rubbing: *I gave the kitchen floor a good* scour *before we moved into the house.* [**¹scour** comes through Dutch (schuren) from an Old French word (escurer) meaning "clean," "scour." The French word is from two Latin forms, one (ex-) meaning "out" and the other (curare) meaning "take care," "keep clean."]

²scour (skour) to look over inch by inch; search thoroughly; go over carefully looking for something: *to* scour *the woods for a lost child.* [**²scour** is a word of uncertain origin.]

scourge (skûrj) **1** a whip. **2** to whip; cause pain by, or as by, whipping; punish. **3** person or thing that causes pain, torment, or trouble. **4** to torment; trouble; drive with relentless force: *Necessity* scourged *him on.* **5** a torment; a punishment: *a* scourge *of locusts.* **scourged, scourg·ing.**

scout (skout) **1** person sent out to get information, especially during a war. **2** to go out to gather information, particularly about the enemy during a war: *Our planes* scouted *the front.* **3** member of the Boy Scouts or of the Girl Scouts. **4** to take part in the activities of a scout, particularly of a boy scout or a girl scout. **5** to go in search of something: *You'd better* scout *for wood before it gets dark.*

scout·ing (skou′tĭng) the activities of a scout, especially of a boy scout or a girl scout.

scout·mas·ter (skout′-măs′tər) man who leads a troop of Boy Scouts.

scow (skou) boat with a flat bottom and square ends, used for carrying garbage, gravel, or other heavy loads.

Scow

scrape

scowl (skoul) **1** a wrinkling of the forehead in anger, displeasure, or deep thought: *Nate's forehead was drawn into an angry* scowl. **2** to wrinkle the forehead: *Jesse* scowled *over the arithmetic problem.*

Scowl

scram·ble (skrăm′bəl) **1** to crawl over or force one's way by the use of hands, feet, knees, etc.: *to* scramble *up a rock; to* scramble *through the underbrush.* **2** to struggle or fight to get something: *They* scrambled *for pennies in the street.* **3** to mix (the whites and yolks of eggs) together and cook. **4** to mix up: *He* scrambled *the letters so that they were no longer in alphabetical order.* **5** a hard climb: *It was a* scramble *to reach the top of the hill.* **6** confused struggle: *There was a* scramble *at the store during the bargain day sale.* **scram·bled, scram·bling.**

scrap (skrăp) **1** small piece; a bit: *a* scrap *of lace; a* scrap *of evidence.* **2** discarded or rejected bit: *They fed the dog table* scraps. **3** to discard; throw away as useless: *to* scrap *worn-out machinery.* **4** broken, worn-out, or useless material; junk: *The foundry bought six carloads of* scrap. **5** no longer useful for its original purpose: *a load of* scrap *iron;* scrap *paper.* **scrapped, scrap·ping.**

scrap·book (skrăp′book′) book with blank pages in which clippings, photographs, pictures, etc., may be pasted.

scrape (skrăp) **1** to take off (something) by rubbing with a sharp tool: *to* scrape *paint from a floor.* **2** to remove paint or paper from: *to* scrape *walls.* **3** to scratch; to graze: *to* scrape *a fender.* **4** to accumulate or gather (up) in small amounts: *Ben* scraped *up old parts from the junk yard to rebuild his car.* **5** to pass or squeeze (by or through) with difficulty: *The two cars managed to* scrape *by without touching. He barely* scraped *through the examination.* **6** harsh or grating sound: *The* scrape *of her fingernail across the blackboard.* **7** difficult or embarrassing situation: *Jim's* scrape *with the policeman was because of his careless driving.*

scrape along to manage to live, but with difficulty. **scraped, scrap·ing.**

scrap·er (skrā′pər) **1** person who scrapes: *We hired* scrapers *to prepare the wall for papering.* **2** a tool, device, or machine for scraping: *The road* scraper *smoothed the bumpy road. He cleaned his shoes on the* scraper.

WALL

FLOOR

Scrapers

scratch (skrăch) **1** to mark or tear the surface of with something rough or pointed: *to scratch the polished table.* **2** the mark or scar left by such treatment: *The vase left* scratches *on the piano.* **3** to mark with scratches: *Bob scratched his name on the wall.* **4** to dig with claws or nails: *Rover scratched up the lawn to bury his bones.* **5** to scrape with claws or fingernails: *to scratch one's ear.* **6** to make a scraping sound: *Chalk scratches on the blackboard.* **7 from scratch** from the very beginning.

scrawl (skrôl) **1** to write hastily or carelessly in awkward or badly formed letters. **2** bad handwriting.

scraw·ny (skrô′nĭ) **1** lean; skinny. **2** stunted: *Those trees are too scrawny to use for lumber.* **scraw·ni·er, scraw·ni·est.**

scream (skrēm) **1** to give a loud, shrill, piercing cry (from fear or pain, etc.): *She screamed when she saw the mouse.* **2** high, sharp, piercing cry.

screech (skrēch) **1** harsh, piercing cry or sound: *I heard the* screech *of the brakes when the car pulled up.* **2** to utter a piercing cry or sound: *An owl screeched in the night.*

Window screen

Television screen

Japanese screen

screen (skrēn) **1** frame covered with fine net or mesh of wire or plastic, used in doors and windows to keep out insects. **2** something that hides or conceals: *a screen of trees; a* smoke screen. **3** a concealing or protective partition or frame of folding panels. **4** to shelter; shield: *to screen one's eyes with an eyeshade.* **5** a surface on which motion pictures, etc. are shown. **6** coarse wire mesh set in a frame used in sifting or grading. **7** to sift and classify: *Grower's* screen *oranges to keep the same sizes together.* **8** to interview or test in order to classify: *The manager* screened *the boys looking for the job.*

screw (skrōō) **1** a fastener, usually metal, having a spiral thread and a slotted head, which is forced into place by twisting. **2** anything that looks or works like a screw. **3** ship or airplane propeller. **4** to fasten and tighten with, or as with, a screw: *Malcom screwed down the lid.*

Screws

screw·driv·er (skrōō′drī′vər) tool with a blunt blade, the tip of which fits into the slot or head of a screw and is used to turn it.

scrib·ble (skrĭb′əl) **1** to write hastily and carelessly. **2** hasty, careless piece of writing. **scrib·bled, scrib·bling.**

scribe (skrīb) **1** person who copied manuscripts, etc., before the invention of printing presses. **2** teacher of the law among the Jews in olden times.

scrim·mage (skrĭm′ĭj) **1** a rough tussle; confused struggle: *There was a* scrimmage *over the ball.* **2** in football, the action of the forward line after the ball is put in play.

script (skrĭpt) **1** letters or figures written by hand. **2** style of writing: *old-fashioned* script. **3** printing type that resembles handwriting. **4** text of a play or movie.

Scrip·ture (skrĭp′chər) the Bible.

scroll (skrōl) **1** a book handwritten on a long strip of paper or parchment with rods at each end so that the reader rolls it up as he reads. **2** a curved or spiral ornament or flourish.

Scrolls

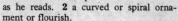

fāte, făt, fâre, fär; bē, bĕt; bīte, bĭt; nō, nŏt, nôr; fūse, fŭn, fûr; tōō, tŏŏk; foil; foul; thin; ~~then~~;
hw for wh as in *wh*at; zh for s as in u*s*ual; ə for a, e, i, o, u, as in *a*go, lin*e*n, per*i*l, at*o*m, min*u*s

¹scrub (skrŭb) to wash or clean by hard rubbing with a cloth, brush, or the like: *We* scrubbed *the dance floor before we waxed it.* **scrubbed, scrub·bing.** [¹scrub is a form of an earlier English word (scrobben) meaning "rub down a horse." The word is probably of Scandinavian origin.]

²scrub (skrŭb) **1** below normal size; stunted. **2** any person, animal, or plant that is undersized or inferior in growth or quality. **3** a player on a second or inferior team: *The varsity football team practiced against the* scrubs. **4** stunted shrubs, bushes, or trees. [²scrub is probably a changed form of **shrub.**]

scruff (skrŭf) back of the neck; loose skin at the back of the neck.

scru·ple (skrōō′pəl) **1** feeling of uneasiness, doubt, or uncertainty arising from one's conscience: *I had* scruples *about missing class.* **2** to hesitate or be stopped by conscience or unwillingness: *He did not* scruple *to take his sister's share of the money.* **scru·pled, scru·pling.**

scru·pu·lous (skrōō′pyŏŏ ləs) strict; conscientious: *He has a* scrupulous *regard for the truth.* **scru·pu·lous·ly.**

scru·ti·nize (skrōō′tə niz′) to examine closely or minutely: *The police* scrutinized *the fingerprints.* **scru·ti·nized, scru·ti·niz·ing.**

scru·ti·ny (skrōō′tə nĭ) close examination; detailed inspection: *The teacher gave his arithmetic homework a careful* scrutiny. **scru·ti·nies.**

scud (skŭd) **1** to run or move swiftly; skim along: *The boat* scudded *before the rising gale.* **2** a scudding. **scud·ded, scud·ding.**

scuff (skŭf) **1** to shuffle; walk without lifting the feet: *Tom* scuffed *along, kicking up the fallen leaves.* **2** to make rough or scratched by hard wear: *He* scuffed *his new shoes while playing ball.*

scuf·fle (skŭf′əl) **1** a confused, often playful, fight or struggle: *There was a* scuffle *over the football.* **2** to fight or struggle in a disorderly manner. **3** to walk with dragging feet; shuffle. **4** the sound of shuffling: *I heard the familiar* scuffle *of mother's slippers on the stair.* **scuf·fled, scuf·fling.**

scull (skŭl) **1** kind of short oar. **2** light racing boat. **3** to row with a scull or sculls, especially to row with a single oar at the stern of a boat. **4** to move oneself through water, usually lying on one's back, by moving the hands in figure eights. (Homonym: skull)

Scull

scul·lion (skŭl′yən) servant who does rough work in a kitchen.

sculp·tor (skŭlp′tər) artist who carves or models sculpture in wood, stone, clay, or metal.

sculp·tress (skŭlp′trĭs) woman sculptor.

sculp·ture (skŭlp′chər) **1** the art of carving, modeling, or casting figures or designs in various materials, such as stone, wood, or clay. **2** figure or design formed in this way. **3** to carve, model, or cast in stone, clay, wood, or metal. **sculp·tured, sculp·tur·ing.**

scum (skŭm) **1** thin layer of more or less solid matter on the surface of a liquid or body of water: *A green* scum *often forms on still ponds.* **2** worthless people: *the* scum *of the earth.*

scur·ry (skûr′ĭ) **1** to run quickly; to hurry: *The mice* scurried *back into the hole.* **2** a hasty running; a scamper. **scur·ries; scur·ried, scur·ry·ing.**

scur·vy (skûr′vĭ) **1** a sickness caused by not eating enough fresh fruit and vegetables. Some symptoms of scurvy are weakness, loss of weight, and bleeding gums. **2** mean; low; contemptible: *a* scurvy *trick; to receive* scurvy *treatment; a* scurvy *fellow.* **scur·vi·er, scur·vi·est; scur·vi·ly.**

¹scut·tle (skŭt′əl) to run with short, quick steps; hurry or hurry away. **scut·tled, scut·tling.** [¹scuttle is a form of an earlier English word (scuddle) that was formed from **scud.**]

²scut·tle (skŭt′əl) kind of pail with a projecting lip. It is used for carrying coal to a stove or fireplace; a hod. [²scuttle is a form of an Old English word (scutel) meaning "dish," "platter," which comes from a Latin word (scutella).]

Scuttle

³scut·tle (skŭt′əl) **1** small opening with a lid in the roof of a house or in the deck, side, or bottom of a ship. **2** the lid for such an opening. **3** to cut a hole in a ship's bottom so as to sink it. **scut·tled, scut·tling.** [³**scuttle** comes through French (escoutille) from a Spanish word (escotilla). The Spanish word is formed from another Spanish word (escotar) meaning "make a hole."]

scythe (sith) mowing tool consisting of a long, slightly curved blade on a handle so bent that the blade lies flat and close to the ground when in use.

Scythe

S. Dak. South Dakota.

SE or **S.E.** southeast.

sea (sē) **1** the body of salt water which covers most of the earth's surface, or any large part of this, smaller than an ocean, partly or entirely enclosed by land. **2** the surface condition of the ocean: *a calm* sea. **3** high wave; an ocean swell: *A great sea almost sank the ship.* **4** anything like the sea in vastness: *a sea of trouble.* **5** found on, in, or above the sea: *a sea animal; a sea bird.* **6 at sea (1)** sailing on the ocean. **(2)** confused; lost. **7 follow the sea** to earn a living by working as a sailor. **8 go to sea (1)** to become a sailor. **(2)** to leave for an ocean voyage. **9 put to sea** to sail from land. **10 the Seven Seas** all the oceans of the world. (Homonym: see)

sea·board (sē′bôrd′) land along a sea or ocean; coastline; shore: *the Atlantic* seaboard.

sea·coast (sē′kōst′) land bordering a sea or ocean; shore.

sea·far·ing (sē′fâr′ĭng) **1** traveling on the sea or ocean: *a seafaring ship.* **2** sea travel: *Do you enjoy* seafaring? **3** making a living on the ocean: *a seafaring man.* **4** the work of a sailor: *He knew all the skills of* seafaring.

sea gull large, graceful sea bird, usually white with gray or black markings.

sea horse kind of small fish with a head which in profile looks somewhat like that of a horse. For picture, see next column.

¹seal (sēl) **1** sea animal with a round head, long body, and flippers instead of feet. Some kinds are valuable for their fur. **2** the fur of these animals. [¹**seal** is a form of an Old English word (seolh) of the same meaning.]

Fur seal, 4 to 6 ft. long

²seal (sēl) **1** something that fastens firmly or closes completely. **2** to fasten tightly: *Anita sealed the letter.* **3** design or mark used in place of a signature or to guarantee a signature: *Given under my hand and seal.* **4** paper wafer, wax or embossed impression, or the circled word "seal" used to prove the genuineness of a document or prevent its alteration: *The notary put his seal upon the paper.* **5** an engraved stamp, ring, or die used to impress a seal in wax or emboss it on paper: *The seal on the king's ring left its impression in the wax.* **6** gummed stamp: *a Christmas seal.* **7** to attach a seal to: *to seal a deed.* **8** to decide finally; confirm: *to seal a criminal's fate.* [²**seal** comes through Old French (seel) from a Latin word (sigillum) meaning "a little image." This Latin word comes from another Latin word (signum) meaning "a mark," "a sign."]

United States seal

sea level position of the surface of the ocean when it is halfway between high tide and low tide. The positions of all other land on the earth, including the bottoms of seas, are measured above or below sea level.

Sea horse, 4 to 12 in. long

sealing wax substance used to seal letters and packages.

fāte, făt, fâre, fär; bē, bĕt; bite, bĭt; nō, nŏt, nôr; fūse, fŭn, fûr; tōō, tŏŏk; foil; foul; thin; ~~then~~; hw for wh as in *wh*at; zh for s as in u*s*ual; ə for a, e, i, o, u, as in *a*go, lin*e*n, per*i*l, at*o*m, min*u*s

sea lion large seal that lives in the Pacific Ocean.

seal·skin (sēl′skin′) **1** skin of a fur seal. **2** garment made from the skin of a fur seal.

seam (sēm) **1** line made when two pieces of material are sewn, welded, or otherwise joined together. **2** wrinkle, welt, scar, or furrow: *The seam of an old cut crossed his cheek.* **3** to join together, especially by sewing: *to seam up a dress.* **4** to mark with scars and furrows: *Wind and water had seamed the old seaman's face.* **5** layer of mineral in the earth: *A seam of quartz runs through the cliff.* (Homonym: seem)

sea·man (sē′mən) **1** sailor. **2** person enlisted in the navy who is below the rank of commissioned officer. **sea·men.**

seam·stress (sēm′strĭs) woman who sews, especially one who sews for a living.

sea·plane (sē′plān′) airplane designed to land on and take off from water.

sea·port (sē′pôrt′) **1** port or harbor for ocean vessels. **2** town or city containing such a port or harbor.

sear (sĭr) **1** to dry up; wither: *A hot summer has seared the crops this year.* **2** to burn the surface of; scorch: *to sear a steak.* **3** to make callous; harden: *The tragedy had seared his mind.* **4** withered; dried up. (Homonym: seer, sere)

search (sûrch) **1** to seek; try to find: *to search for a lost wallet.* **2** a seeking for something: *The policeman made a thorough search for the missing weapon.* **3** to examine with thoroughness: *He searched his heart many days before making a decision.* **4** in search of looking for; trying to find.

search·ing (sûr′chĭng) **1** sharply penetrating: *His friend gave him a searching look.* **2** thorough; probing: *The art critic's new book is a very searching work.* **search·ing·ly.**

search·light (sûrch′lĭt′) large, powerful electric light, the beam of which may be turned in any direction to light up or to detect something.

sea·shore (sē′shôr′) **1** land bordering on the sea. **2** a beach.

sea·sick (sē′sĭk′) suffering from illness or nausea caused by the motion of a ship.

sea·side (sē′sīd′) **1** land bordering the sea. **2** on or having to do with such a place: *a seaside cottage.*

sea·son (sē′zən) **1** any of the four divisions of the year (spring, summer, autumn, winter). **2** an appropriate or proper time: *There is a time and season for everything.* **3** period of the year associated with a special activity; time: *the harvest season; the football season; the opera season.* **4** to make tasty by adding spices. **5** to make ready for use; mature: *Timber is seasoned by exposure to the air. He was seasoned by his early experiences.* **6** to make agreeable; add interest to: *to season a lecture with pleasant anecdotes.* **7** to strengthen or harden by growing accustomed to: *The pioneers were seasoned by harsh weather and scarcity of food.*

sea·son·ing (sē′zən ĭng) ingredient or ingredients (salt, pepper, and the like) added to food to flavor it.

seat (sēt) **1** a place to sit, as a chair, stool, and the like. **2** the part of the body on which one sits, or the piece of clothing that covers it: *He had to have the seat of his trousers mended.* **3** to cause to sit; place in a seat: *The teacher seated the pupils at nine o'clock.* **4** a center where something flourishes or takes place: *Paris is the seat of intellectual life in France.* **5** the right to sit because of membership: *a seat in Congress; a seat on the stock exchange.* **6** to furnish with places to sit: *The theater seats two thousand persons.* **7 county seat** a town or city in which the county offices are located.

seat belt strap that fastens a person to the seat of an airplane, automobile, etc., to protect him from being tossed about by bumps, jolts, etc.

sea urchin round-shaped sea animal that has a thin shell covered with movable spines.

sea wall wall or embankment to break the force of the waves or to prevent erosion of the seashore.

sea·ward (sē′wərd) in the direction of the sea: *a seaward breeze; to travel seaward.*

sea·wards (sē′wərdz) seaward: *The river flowed seawards.*

sea·weed (sē′wēd′) any plant or plants growing in the sea or on the rocks washed by the tide.

sec. 1 second. **2** seconds. **3.** secretary. **4** section. **5** sections.

se·clude (si klōōd′) to withdraw from company or society; keep apart from others: *He* secluded *himself that summer in his small home in the mountains.* **se·clud·ed, se·clud·ing.**

se·clud·ed (si klōō′did) shut off from others; isolated: *The searching party at last found the* secluded *cabin. The hermit led a secluded life.*

se·clu·sion (si klōō′zhən) place or condition of privacy: *He sought seclusion in his home.*

¹sec·ond (sĕk′ənd) **1** one sixtieth part of a minute. **2** a very short time: *I'll be finished in just a second.* [¹**second** comes through French from a Latin phrase (secunda minuta) meaning "second minute," that is, a further division beyond a minute.]

²sec·ond (sĕk′ənd) **1** next after the first: *Our club meets the* second *day of every month.* **2** next to the first in value or importance: *The first prize was 50 dollars and the* second *prize 25 dollars.* **3** another; other; duplicate of the first: *We were so hungry that we all had* second *helpings.* **4** the one who is next after the first: *to be the* second *in command.* **5** to give support to (the motion or nomination of another): *Don* seconded *Tom's nomination of John as captain of the team.* **6** one who assists or helps another in a duel or prize fight. **7** to assist or help in such a contest. **sec·ond·ly.** [²**second** comes through Old French from a Latin word (secundus) meaning "following," "second." This Latin word is from another Latin word (sequi) meaning "to follow."]

sec·ond·ar·y (sĕk′ən dĕr′i) **1** next in order in place, time, importance, etc.: *His interest in music was* secondary *to his interest in the theater.* **2** higher than elementary: *High schools are* secondary *schools.* **sec·ond·ar·i·ly.**

sec·ond-hand (sĕk′ənd hănd′) **1** not new; having had a former owner. **2** dealing in used goods: *a second-hand furniture store.* **3** taken from someone else; not learned or told personally: *a second-hand piece of news.*

se·cre·cy (sē′krə si) **1** a keeping things from being known: *Everyone was sworn to secrecy about the surprise party.* **2** the ability to keep a secret: *I am relying on your secrecy in this matter.* **3 in secrecy** not openly; secretly.

se·cret (sē′krit) **1** kept from the knowledge or sight of others: *a secret pocket; a secret drawer.* **2** something hidden or concealed: *to keep a secret.* **3** working or acting without others' knowledge: *a secret agent; secret society.* **4** hidden cause or true explanation: *The secret of Bill's success was hard work.* **5 in secret** without the knowledge of others; not openly. **se·cret·ly.**

sec·re·tar·y (sĕk′rə tĕr′i) **1** someone who writes letters and keeps records for a person, company, etc. **2** government official in charge of a department: *the Secretary of Labor.* **3** a writing desk. **sec·re·tar·ies.**

se·crete (si krēt′) **1** of living things, to produce and give off a useful substance: *Glands* secrete *liquids inside the body. Spiders* secrete *a liquid that hardens into a web. Flowers* secrete *nectar.* **2** to hide; put in a secret place: *Squirrels* secrete *nuts and acorns.* **se·cret·ed, se·cret·ing.**

se·cre·tion (si krē′shən) **1** the producing and giving off of a substance by an animal, a plant, or a bodily organ. **2** the substance secreted: *Bile is a secretion of the liver.*

sect (sĕkt) group of people having the same principles, beliefs, or opinions: *a religious sect.*

sec·tion (sĕk′shən) **1** a part; division; one of a group of units: *New England is a section of the United States.* **2** a cutting, especially a cutting across the grain, or a view of such a cutting; a cross section: *This* section *of a tomato shows the seed arrangement.* **3** division of land measuring one mile square. **4** to cut or divide into sections.

Cross section of a tomato

sec·u·lar (sĕk′yōō lər) having to do with the world; not religious or spiritual: *a secular education in the public schools.* **sec·u·lar·ly.**

fāte, făt, fâre, fär; bē, bĕt; bite, bĭt; nō, nŏt, nôr; fūse, fŭn, fûr; tōō, tŏŏk; foil; foul; thin; ~~then~~; hw for wh as in *w*hat; zh for s as in u*s*ual; ə for a, e, i, o, u, as in ago, linen, peril, atom, minus

641

se·cure (si kūr') **1** safe; free from danger or fear; protected against attack, loss, etc.: *The little girl felt secure because her parents were home. All the animals in the zoo were secure in their cages.* **2** firmly fixed; sure and certain: *a secure knot; a secure foundation; a secure belief.* **3** fastened, closed, or shut tight: *windows and doors secure against a storm.* **4** to make certain; make sure: *The first Amendment to the Constitution secured our freedom of speech, press, and religion.* **5** to get; obtain: *We secured the reading list from our librarian.* **6** to fasten; tighten: *Before take-off, the airplane stewardess says; "Secure your seat belts!"* **7** to protect against many kinds of losses by insurance. **se·cured, se·cur·ing; se·cure·ly.**

se·cu·ri·ty (si kūr'ə tǐ) **1** a feeling of safety: *Grandmother enjoyed the cozy security of the bright fire and her cheerful room.* **2** protection: *The watchman was hired for security.* **3** something given as a pledge that a person will pay his debt: *When you borrow money you may be asked to give something as security.* **4 securities** bonds, stocks, and other titles to property: *Keep your securities in a safe place.* **se·cu·ri·ties.**

se·dan (si dǎn') **1** closed automobile with seats for four to six passengers. **2 sedan** or **sedan chair** enclosed traveling chair for one person, carried on poles by two men.

Sedan chair

se·date (si dāt') calm; composed; serious: *a sedate bishop.* **se·date·ly.**

Se·der (sā'dər) feast held in Jewish homes at Passover. The Seder is in memory of the exodus of the Jews from Egypt.

sedge (sěj) any of many grasslike herbs or plants with solid stems growing in wet places.

sed·i·ment (sěd'ə mənt) solid matter that settles to the bottom of a body of water or other liquid: *ocean sediment; the sediment in a cup of chocolate.*

sed·i·men·ta·ry (sěd'ə měn'tə rǐ) formed from a sediment: *Sandstone is a sedimentary rock.*

se·di·tion (sə dǐsh'ən) the stirring up of discontent or rebellion against a government.

se·duce (si doos' or si dūs') to persuade to do wrong; tempt; entice: *The basketball player was seduced by a bribe to lose the game.* **se·duced, se·duc·ing.**

¹see (sē) **1** to look at; perceive with the eyes: *Can you see that red sail way out there?* **2** to have the power of sight: *The old dog could hardly see.* **3** to find out: *Would you please see who is at the door?* **4** to make sure: *Please see that nothing is left behind when you gather the picnic things.* **5** to escort; accompany: *The whole family saw Grandmother to the station.* **6** to visit: *The senator tried to make an appointment to see the President.* **7** to know; experience: *That old man had seen better days.* **8** to understand; grasp: *Do you see what I mean? I see your point.*

see through 1 to understand the actual character or purpose of: *She saw through his scheme.* **2** to stay or continue with to the end: *to see a friend through a difficulty.*

see to to take care of: *Mother promised me that if I would see to dinner she would finish sewing my party dress.*

saw, seen, see·ing. [**¹see** is a form of an Old English word (sēon) of the same meaning.] (Homonym: sea)

²see (sē) **1** district in which a bishop has authority. **2 Holy See** the place from which the Pope exercises his authority; Rome. [**²see** comes through Old French (sie) from a Latin word (sedes) meaning "a seat."] (Homonym: sea)

seed (sēd) **1** small object produced by a flowering plant and containing an egg cell which can grow into a young plant. **2** offspring; descendants: *The Jewish people call themselves the seed of Abraham.* **3** the beginning or origin of anything: *The seeds of discontent grew rapidly into open revolt.* **4** to sow with seed: *I helped my next door neighbor seed his lawn.* **5** to remove seeds from: *Be sure to seed the grapefruit and the oranges before you make the fruit salad.* (Homonym: cede)

seed·case (sēd'kās') a hollow container, such as the pod of a pea or a milkweed pod, containing seeds.

seed·ling (sēd'ling) young plant or tree grown from seed.

seek (sēk) **1** to look or search for; try to find: *When gold was discovered in California, thousands rushed there to seek their fortunes.* **2** to attempt; aim at; greatly desire: *For years men* sought *to climb Mount Everest.* **sought, seek·ing.**

seem (sēm) to appear to be; look (as if); give the impression of being: *Things are not always as they* seem. (Homonym: seam)

seem·ing·ly (sē'ming li) in outward appearance; apparently: *He was seemingly her friend until she asked him to help her.*

seen (sēn) See **see**. *Have you* seen *Mary today?* (Homonym: scene)

seep (sēp) to leak slowly (in or out); ooze: *When it rains, water* seeps *into our cellar.*

seer (sir) person who looks into the future; prophet. (Homonyms: sear, sere)

see·saw (sē'sô') **1** a board balanced on a central support, the ends of which alternately rise and fall as riders on the ends shift their weight. **2** the pastime enjoyed on such a board. **3** any up-and-down or to-and-fro movement. **4** to ride a seesaw. **5** to move like a seesaw: *The game* seesawed *back and forth until the home team won.*

Seesaw

seethe (sēth) **1** to move with a boiling, bubbling motion; surge: *When the dam broke, a torrent of water* seethed *down on the town.* **2** to be violently moved or agitated: *I* seethed *with anger when she slapped the baby.* **seethed, seeth·ing.**

seg·ment (sĕg'mənt) **1** any one of the parts into which a thing is naturally divided: *I ate only one orange segment for breakfast.* **2** to divide into such parts. **3** in geometry, a part cut off from a circle by a chord.

Segment

se·go lil·y (sē'gō lil'ĭ) plant with trumpet-shaped flowers, common in southwestern United States.

seg·re·gate (sĕg'rə gāt') **1** to separate from others; isolate; set apart: *Children with measles have to be* segregated *from those who haven't yet had them.* **2** to set apart because of race or color. **seg·re·gat·ed, seg·re·gat·ing.**

seg·re·ga·tion (sĕg'rə gā'shən) **1** a separation from others; a setting apart: *The doctor ordered the* segregation *of all students who had not been vaccinated.* **2** a separation of one race from other races, especially in public places.

seine (sān) **1** hauling net used by fishermen. Weighted on one edge, it has floats on the other so that it hangs straight down in the water and fish are caught when the net is drawn in. **2** to use this net to catch fish. **seined, sein·ing.** (Homonym: sane)

seis·mo·graph (siz'mə grăf') instrument that detects and records vibrations of the earth, especially earthquakes.

seize (sēz) **1** to lay hold of violently; grip suddenly: *In her fright she* seized *his arm.* **2** to take possession of by force or legal authority: *The sheriff* seized *the outlaw's house and lands.* **3** to grasp with the mind: *He was quick to* seize *the suggestion that we should be friends again.* **seized, seiz·ing.**

sei·zure (sē'zhər) **1** sudden possession by force; capture: *the* seizure *of the town by the enemy.* **2** sudden attack (of illness): *a* seizure *of cramps.*

sel·dom (sĕl'dəm) hardly ever; rarely: *After March, one* seldom *sees snow in this locality.*

se·lect (sĭ lĕkt') **1** to pick out; choose: *I found the two books I* selected *from our reading list in the library.* **2** carefully or specially chosen; choice; exclusive: *a* select *brand of canned goods; a* select *group of friends.*

se·lec·tion (sĭ lĕk'shən) **1** choice: *Jack would be a fine* selection *for captain of the team.* **2** representative example: *a book of* selections *from Shakespeare.* **3** a choosing: *The* selection *of a house requires much thought.*

self (sĕlf) **1** the entire personality which makes one person different from another:

---

fāte, făt, fâre, fär; bē, bĕt; bīte, bĭt; nō, nŏt, nôr; fūse, fŭn, fûr; too, took; foil; foul; thin; ~~then~~; hw for wh as in *wh*at; zh for s as in u*s*ual; ə for a, e, i, o, u, as in *a*go, lin*e*n, per*i*l, at*o*m, min*u*s

*He was shy and only his friends knew his
real* self. **2** particular side or aspect of a
person's character: *I lost my temper and
showed my worse* self. **3** personal interest
and advantage: *You might almost call
him a saint for he has no thought of* self.
selves.

self-ad·dressed (sĕlf'ə drĕst') addressed
to oneself; bearing one's own name and
address, as an envelope enclosed with a
letter for the reply.

self-as·sur·ance (sĕlf'ə shŏŏr'əns) confidence in one's ability, talent, or the like;
self-confidence.

self-con·fi·dence (sĕlf'kŏn'fə dəns) trust
and belief in one's self and ability: *The
coach's harsh remarks made Frank lose his*
self-confidence.

self-con·scious (sĕlf'kŏn'shəs) apprehensive of one's appearance or actions in the
presence of others; embarrassed; shy: *He
was* self-conscious *at his first dance.* **self-
con·scious·ly.**

self-con·trol (sĕlf'kən trōl') command
over one's own actions and feelings: *Although angry he kept his* self-control.

self-de·fense or **self-de·fence** (sĕlf'dĭ-
fĕns') protection of one's own person,
property, or good name from attack or injury: *the manly art of* self-defense.

self-gov·ern·ment (sĕlf'gŭv'ərn mənt) **1**
government of a nation by its own people;
independence: *Many countries in Africa
which were once colonies have now achieved*
self-government. **2** government of any
group of persons by themselves, or of one
person by himself.

self-im·por·tant (sĕlf'ĭm pôr'tənt) having
a too great or exaggerated sense of one's
own value; pompous. **self-im·por·tant·ly.**

self·ish (sĕl'fĭsh) **1** putting one's own
wishes or needs ahead of other people's:
Claire is so selfish *that she will not share her
candy.* **2** coming from a person's interest
in himself: *a* selfish *deed; a* selfish *thought.*
self·ish·ly.

self·ish·ness (sĕl'fĭsh nĭs) great concern
with one's own needs and interests.

self-pit·y (sĕlf'pĭt'ĭ) pity for oneself; a
feeling sorry for oneself.

self-pos·ses·sion (sĕlf'pə zĕsh'ən) control
over one's feelings; composure; calmness;
poise.

self-re·li·ance (sĕlf'rĭ lī'əns) dependence
on or confidence in one's own resources:
enough self-reliance *not to call for help.*

self-re·spect (sĕlf'rĭ spĕkt') proper regard
for oneself: *He had too much* self-respect
to tell a lie.

self-re·straint (sĕlf'rĭ strānt') control of
one's impulses or desires by force of will:
It is easy to lose weight if you have self-
restraint.

self·same (sĕlf'sām') the very same; identical.

self-sat·is·fac·tion (sĕlf'săt'ĭs făk'shən) **1**
a being pleased with oneself, one's beliefs,
actions, position, etc. **2** smugness.

sell (sĕl) **1** to give in exchange for money:
She sells sea shells. **2** to deal in: *We sell
only shoes in this shop.* **3** to find purchasers
or a market: *Umbrellas sell best on a rainy
day.* **4** to betray for a reward: *He sold his
country for money.* **5** to convince; cause
acceptance of: *Jack sold me on the idea of
continuing school and now I'm grateful.*
sold, sell·ing. (Homonym: cell)

sell·er (sĕl'ər) **1** person who sells; salesman.
2 best seller item which sells faster than
other things of the same kind: *His first
book was a* best seller. (Homonym: cellar)

selves (sĕlvz) more than one **self.**

sem·a·phore (sĕm'ə fôr') **1** signaling system in which different positions of arms,
bars, or flags have
special meanings. By
these changes of posi-
tion, messages are
transmitted. **2** a post
with wooden arms
that swing up and
down. It is used
especially for railroad signals. **3** to signal
by semaphore. **sem·a·phored, sem·a·
phor·ing.**

Semaphore

sem·blance (sĕm'bləns) **1** outward appearance: *a* semblance *of wealth.* **2** appearance
that is false or put on: *Her* semblance *of
innocence got her out of punishment.*

se·mes·ter (sĭ mĕs'tər) one of the terms
that make up the school year in high school
or college.

sem·i- prefix meaning (1) "half": semi-
circle. (2) "partly": semi*skilled.* (3) "happening twice in a (given period)": semi-
annual.

sem·i·cir·cle (sĕm′ĭ sûr′kəl) **1** a half circle: *Doris put a semicircle of stones around her flower bed.* **2** a line roughly a half circle: *The family sat in a semicircle around the hearth.*

Semicircle

sem·i·co·lon (sĕm′ĭ-kō′lən) punctuation mark (;) that indicates a greater separation in a sentence than that shown by a comma.

sem·i·fi·nal (sĕm′ĭ fī′nəl) **1** game, contest, round, etc., before the final one in a match, tournament, or the like. **2** of or having to do with such a game, contest, round, etc.

sem·i·nar·y (sĕm′ə nĕr′ĭ) **1** private school, especially of high-school level. **2** school that prepares students for the ministry. **sem·i·nar·ies.**

sen·ate (sĕn′ĭt) **1** council or group which makes laws. **2 Senate** upper legislative body in some countries, as the United States, Canada, Australia, etc.

sen·a·tor (sĕn′ə tər) member of a senate.

send (sĕnd) **1** to cause, make, or order to go: *to send a messenger; to send a child to play.* **2** to cause to be carried or transmitted: *to send a telegram.* **3** to force to go; impel; throw: *The dog sent the chickens flying. He sent the ball into the bleachers.* **4** to transmit: *The telegraph operator sent the message.*

send away to order from a distance: *Beth sent away for every free sample in the magazine.*

send for 1 to request someone to come; summon. **2** to ask that something be sent; to place an order for.

send on to cause to go ahead: *We sent our furniture on to our new home a week before we left.*

send out to give off; emit: *The sun sends out heat and light.*

sent, send·ing.

sen·ior (sēn′yər) **1** older or oldest. It is used after the name of the father when the father and son have the same name, and is abbreviated to **Sr.: *Thomas Cox,* Sr. 2** higher in rank or position; longer in office: *the senior senator from Utah.* **3** person who

is older or higher in rank. **4** having to do with the final year in high school or college. **5** student in his last year at high school or college.

se·ñor (sĕn yôr′) **1** Spanish title or form of address, equivalent to Mr. or sir. **2** a Spanish gentleman.

se·ño·ra (sĕn yôr′ä) **1** Spanish title or form of address, equivalent to Mrs. or Madam. **2** a Spanish lady.

se·ño·ri·ta (sĕn′yô rē′tä) **1** Spanish title or form of address, equivalent to Miss. **2** a Spanish young lady.

sen·sa·tion (sĕn sā′shən) **1** a feeling through the senses: *a sensation of cold.* **2** a mental or emotional feeling: *a sensation of dread.* **3** an arousing or exciting of the senses or feelings: *It was quite a sensation to see the Queen at close hand.* **4** something that excites feelings and interest: *The scandal was a ten-day sensation.*

sen·sa·tion·al (sĕn sā′shən əl) **1** having to do with the senses. **2** thrilling; startling; extraordinary: *The last quarter of the football game was sensational.* **3** meant to cause intense feeling, to shock, thrill, etc.: *a sensational movie.* **sen·sa·tion·al·ly.**

sense (sĕns) **1** any one of the five physical powers through which a creature becomes aware of its surroundings. Our senses are sight, hearing, smell, touch, and taste. **2** a bodily feeling; sensation: *a sense of cold.* **3** understanding; judgment; practical wisdom or intelligence: *He shows a great deal of sense in going home early.* **4** keen awareness; appreciation: *a sense of humor.* **5** to feel or be conscious of: *The tiger sensed the approach of danger.* **6** meaning (of a word or statement): *I don't intend it in that sense.* **sensed, sens·ing.**

sense·less (sĕns′lĭs) **1** without the power of feeling; unconscious: *The ball hit him and knocked him senseless.* **2** without meaning or sense; stupid; foolish: *A senseless argument wastes time.* **sense·less·ly.**

sen·si·bil·i·ty (sĕn′sə bĭl′ə tĭ) **1** capacity to feel: *The sensibility of the body to cold and heat.* **2** sensitiveness or delicacy in feeling and perception: *an artistic sensibility.* **sen·si·bil·i·ties.**

---

fāte, făt, fâre, fär; bē, bĕt; bīte, bĭt; nō, nŏt, nôr; fūse, fŭn, fûr; tōō, tŏŏk; foil; foul; thin; ~~then~~; hw for wh as in *w*hat; zh for s as in u*s*ual; ə for a, e, i, o, u, as in *a*go, lin*e*n, per*i*l, at*o*m, min*u*s

sen·si·ble (sĕn′sə bəl) **1** full of good sense; reasonable: *You're a sensible person and I know you won't do anything foolish.* **2** large enough to be felt; considerable: *a sensible change in the weather.* **3** aware; conscious: *I am sensible of your feelings.* **sen·si·bly.**

sen·si·tive (sĕn′sə tiv) **1** quick to be affected by objects or conditions: *a sensitive skin.* **2** responding to or recording slight shades or changes of sound, light, touch, etc.: *a sensitive photographic film.* **3** readily affected or moved by the problems or work of others: *a sensitive teacher.* **sen·si·tive·ly.**

sen·so·ry (sĕn′sə ri) **1** having to do with the five senses or with sensation. **2 sensory nerves** the nerves which carry impressions from the sense organs to the brain.

sent (sĕnt) See **send.** *She sent a letter to Europe yesterday.* (Homonyms: cent, scent)

sen·tence (sĕn′təns) **1** group of words, or sometimes one word, that tells or expresses a complete thought by making a statement, asking a question, or giving a command: "*John ran home.*" *is a* sentence. **2** legal judgment; punishment: *His sentence was three years in prison.* **3** to give or pronounce a legal judgment or punishment: *The judge sentenced him to a fine.* **sen·tenced, sen·tenc·ing.**

sen·ti·ment (sĕn′tə mənt) **1** an opinion based on one's feelings rather than on reason: *Mrs. Black's political sentiments were due to the candidate's good looks, not his ability.* **2** feeling; emotion; the thought rather than the way it is expressed: *a good sentiment despite poor expression.*

sen·ti·men·tal (sĕn′tə mĕn′təl) **1** easily moved (by an emotion); tender in feeling: *She was so sentimental that she always cried at sad movies.* **2** appealing only to the emotions: *The play was far too sweet and sentimental.* **3** of or caused by sentiment: *Ellen treasured the locket for sentimental reasons.* **sen·ti·men·tal·ly.**

sen·ti·nel (sĕn′tə nəl) person who guards and keeps watch; sentry.

sen·try (sĕn′tri) person, especially in the armed forces, stationed to prevent illegal passing or to warn of approaching danger. **sen·tries.**

se·pal (sē′pəl) one of the pointed leaflike parts of the calyx, at the base of a flower.

Sepals

¹**sep·a·rate** (sĕp′ə rāt′) **1** to divide: *A river separates the two states.* **2** to branch; spread apart: *High Street separates into East Street and Elm Street at the monument.* **3** to set apart; place in, or as in, groups: *to separate good apples from bad; to separate truth from fiction.* **sep·a·rat·ed, sep·a·rat·ing.**

²**sep·a·rate** (sĕp′ə rit) **1** branching; different: *to go separate ways.* **2** taken one by one; individual: *Let's question each separate child.* **3** distinct; individual; apart; not joined: *Keep this separate from the rest. The children have separate rooms.* **sep·a·rate·ly.**

sep·a·ra·tion (sĕp′ə rā′shən) a separating or being separated: *There is a fort at the separation of the river. After a long separation they were reunited.*

sep·a·ra·tor (sĕp′ə rā′tər) **1** person or thing that divides or separates. **2** mechanical device used to separate or sort out (one thing from another): *a cream separator.*

Sept. September.

Sep·tem·ber (sĕp tĕm′bər) the ninth month of the year. September has 30 days.

sep·tic (sĕp′tik) **1** having to do with poisoning or decay of animal tissue because of germs. **2** infected by germs: *a septic sore throat.* **3 septic tank** a tank for sewage in which bacteria destroy the refuse and kill harmful germs.

sep·ul·cher or **sep·ul·chre** (sĕp′əl kər) tomb or grave.

se·quel (sē′kwəl) **1** that which follows or comes after: *Winter is the sequel of fall.* **2** result or consequence: *Anger followed as the sequel of their argument.* **3** continuation (of a book or poem): *She wrote a sequel to her first book but it was not as good.*

se·quence (sē′kwəns) **1** the coming of one thing after another; a succession. **2** a following after in some regular order; a series: *1, 2, 3, 4 is a number sequence; l, m, n, o, p is an alphabetical sequence.*

se·quoi·a (si kwoi′ə) giant evergreen trees growing in California. The redwood and the "big tree" are both sequoias and they grow to an immense height.

sere (sǐr) withered; dried up: *the* sere *leaves of autumn.* (Homonyms: sear, seer)

ser·e·nade (sĕr'ə nād') **1** music sung or played at night, usually beneath a lady's window and in her honor. **2** to sing or play a serenade to. **3** a singing or playing of such music. **ser·e·nad·ed, ser·e·nad·ing.**

se·rene (sə rēn') calm; peaceful: *a* serene *sea; a* serene *disposition.* **se·rene·ly.**

se·ren·i·ty (sə rĕn'ə tǐ) **1** clearness; brightness; peacefulness: *the* serenity *of the starlit sky.* **2** calmness; composure: *The noise and bustle in the room did not disturb her* serenity.

serf (sûrf) **1** in the Middle Ages, person who could not leave the land he worked on and who was usually sold with it. **2** a slave. (Homonym: surf)

serge (sûrj) woolen material woven with slanting ribs, used for clothing. (Homonym: surge)

ser·geant (sär'jənt) **1** minor officer in the army, ranking next above a corporal. **2** police officer of minor rank.

se·ri·al (sǐr'ǐ əl) **1** story, told in one installment after another, as in a magazine, on television, etc. **2 serial number** one of a series of numbers assigned to a group of similar things so that each item can be identified: *the* serial numbers *on tickets, paper money, etc.* **se·ri·al·ly.** (Homonym: cereal)

se·ries (sǐr'ǐz) a number of similar things following one another: *a* series *of pranks; a* series *of baseball games; a* series *of classrooms.* pl. **se·ries.**

se·ri·ous (sǐr'ǐ əs) **1** thoughtful; grave; solemn: *That young fellow has a* serious *manner for his age.* **2** not frivolous or trifling; in earnest: *A good worker is* serious *about his job.* **3** demanding thought and attention: *A* serious *book deserves* serious *reading.* **4** important because of possible danger: *a* serious *illness; a* serious *predicament.* **se·ri·ous·ly.**

se·ri·ous·ness (sǐr'ǐ əs nǐs) **1** earnestness: *a* seriousness *in his manner.* **2** importance: *the* seriousness *of a situation.*

ser·mon (sûr'mən) **1** public talk on religion or morals, usually given in church by a

priest or minister. **2** any serious talk on morals, behavior, duty, etc.: *When his report card arrived, the boy got a* sermon *from his father on the meaning of hard work.*

ser·pent (sûr'pənt) **1** snake. **2** sly, deceitful person.

ser·pen·tine (sûr'pən tēn' or sûr'pən tīn') **1** winding and twisting; like a serpent: *a* serpentine *path.* **2** crafty; cunning:

se·rum (sǐr'əm) **1** yellowish, clear liquid that remains after blood has clotted. **2** such a fluid, taken from the blood of an animal that has been given a certain disease. This fluid is used to fight the same disease in human beings.

ser·vant (sûr'vənt) **1** person who works in a household, hotel, club, etc., for wages. **2** person who dedicates himself or offers his services to a belief, cause, government, etc.: *a* servant *of God; a public* servant.

serve (sûrv) **1** to work for. **2** to wait upon (persons) at a table or in a shop. **3** to discharge a duty of office or position: *to serve as president; to serve on a committee; to serve as a bridesmaid.* **4** to assist; aid; help: *Discoveries in the cure of disease* serve *all mankind.* **5** to be useful to: *This old car has* served *me for years in all weathers.* **6** to promote; make a contribution to: *What purpose does this constant quarreling* serve? **7** to act as a substitute; be sufficient: *On our camping trip, sleeping bags* served *as beds and the trees* served *to shelter us from the rain.* **8** to undergo: *to serve a prison sentence.* **9** to deliver: *to serve a summons to appear in court.* **10** in games, such as tennis, to start the ball going by sending it to an opponent as the first stroke. **11** the act of serving the ball; the ball served; the turn for serving: *Whose* serve *is it?* **served, serv·ing.**

serv·er (sûr'vər) **1** person who serves. **2** tray for dishes.

serv·ice (sûr'vǐs) **1** employment: *in the* service *of a company.* **2** something done as a duty or favor: *The boy carried the parcels as a* service *to his grandmother.* **3** manner of serving: *The* service *in this restaurant is very poor.* **4** religious ceremony: *The family went to ten o'clock* service *at their*

fāte, făt, fâre, fär; bē, bĕt; bite, bit; nō, nŏt, nôr; fūse, fŭn, fûr; tōō, tŏŏk; foil; foul; thin; ~~then~~;
hw for wh as in *wh*at; zh for s as in u*s*ual; ə for a, e, i, o, u, as in *a*go, lin*e*n, per*i*l, at*o*m, min*u*s

647

church. **5** professional or official functions or duties, or the department in which these functions are performed: *legal* services; *military* service. **6** a benefit; advantage: *The library and the fire department perform* services *to the town.* **7** to put into, or maintain in, condition; put back into good shape: *That electrician* services *our television set.* **8** arrangement to meet public needs: *postal* service; *train* service; *telephone* service. **9** a serving of the ball in tennis, etc. **serv·iced, serv·ic·ing.**

serv·ice·a·ble (sûr′vĭs ə bəl) **1** useful. **2** capable of long use or wear: *an overcoat of* serviceable *material.* **serv·ice·a·bly.**

ser·vile (sûr′vĭl or sûr′vīl) **1** slavish; having to do with or consisting of slaves: *The dictator reduced the country to a* servile *state.* **2** behaving like a slave; lacking self-respect: *Flattery of one's superiors is the sign of a* servile *man.* **ser·vile·ly.**

ser·vi·tude (sûr′və tōōd′ or sûr′və tūd′) **1** lack of freedom; slavery; bondage. **2** service or labor enforced as a punishment.

ses·sion (sĕsh′ən) **1** a meeting of a court, council, lawmaking body, or the like. **2** series of such meetings, and the time covered by them: *a session of Congress; a court* session.

set (sĕt) **1** to place or fix in a position; put. **2** to put in order; make ready for use: *to* set *a table; to* set *a trap.* **3** to regulate: *to* set *a clock; to* set *a schedule.* **4** to put a broken bone into position to knit. **5** to adapt words to music. **6** fixed or established: *A dance is a* set *way of moving one's feet.* **7** immovable; obstinate: *to be* set *in one's ways.* **8** to sink below the horizon: *The moon* sets *early at this time of the month.* **9** to become firm or rigid: *The cement* set *overnight.* **10** a number of things of the same kind: *a* set *of golf clubs; a* set *of false teeth.* **11** equipment or apparatus: *a chemistry* set; *a carpenter* set. **12** series of games which count as a unit: *a* set *of tennis.* **13** group of people united by a common interest: *the jazz* set. **14** location or background of an action in a play, movie, etc.: *Felix designed the* set *for the school play.* **15** of a fowl, to sit upon a nest of eggs. **16** to put (a hen) upon a nest of eggs, or (eggs) under a hen. **17** posture; arrangement: *the* set *of her features.* **18** in math-

ematics, a group of objects, quantities, etc., that have something in common that makes them different from everything else in the universe.

set about to begin: *It is time we* set **about** *doing this work.*

set forth **1** to begin a journey. **2** to make known; declare: *The principles of the American government are* set forth *in the Declaration of Independence.*

set in to become established: *Cold weather* set in *early in December.*

set off **1** to explode: *to* set off *the fireworks.* **2** to make more striking by contrast; enhance. **3** to start.

set out to start a journey.

set up to build; establish: *to* set up *a business.*

set, set·ting.

set·back (sĕt′băk′) **1** a stop; check to progress or advancement: *Money troubles caused a temporary* setback *in his education.* **2** distance set back from anything: *The city requires a ten-foot* setback *for buildings on this street.*

set·tee (sĕ tē′) long seat or short sofa with a back and arms.

set·ter (sĕt′ər) kind of bird dog with long, silky black-and-white or red hair, that comes to a rigid stand and points with its muzzle when it scents game.

Irish setter, about 27 in. at shoulder

set·ting (sĕt′ĭng) **1** the surroundings, environment, and background of anything: *The* setting *of the story is in eighteenth century New York.* **2** framework in which a jewel is securely held: *Mother's diamond ring has a gold* setting. **3** music that is composed for a special story or poem. **4** the scenery, costumes, and background for a play or opera. **5** the eggs on which a brooding hen sets. **6** sinking: *the* setting *sun.*

¹**set·tle** (sĕt′əl) **1** to sink: *Dust* settled *on the piano. Tea leaves* settled *to the bottom of the pot.* **2** to become more firmly or evenly based: *A new house* settles *after a few years.* **3** to come to rest: *Our parakeet will often* settle *on my finger.* **4** to make one's home: *We* settled *in a distant town.* **5** to compose oneself; make oneself comfortable: *to*

settle *down in an easy chair*. **6** to calm; relieve discomfort or tension: *to* settle *jangled nerves*. **7** to adjust; bring to an end: *to* settle *a dispute*. **8** to fulfill; pay: *to* settle *an obligation; to* settle *a bill*. **9** to agree (upon): *to* settle *upon a plan*. **10** to put in order: *to* settle *one's affairs*. **11** to populate: *to* settle *a new country*. **set·tled, set·tling**. [¹**settle** is from an Old English word (setlan) formed from another Old English word (setlan) meaning "to fix."]

¹**set·tle** (sĕt′əl) an old-fashioned, long, wooden seat with arms and a high, straight back. [²**settle** is a form of an Old English word (setl) meaning "a seat."]

set·tle·ment (sĕt′əl mənt) **1** property or money given (to someone) as a legal gift: *Uncle Bob received a large* settlement *from Grandpa*. **2** location in a new country or place where a number of people have gone to live. **3** a settling a new region: *We are interested in the* settlement *of the Yukon*. **4** the deciding of an argument over debts, property, and the like: *Finally a* settlement *was made out of court*. **5** community center, often in the poorer section of a city, which provides instruction, amusement, and advice to people in that area.

set·tler (sĕt′lər) person who makes his home in a new, or newly developed, country; colonist.

sev·en (sĕv′ən) amount or quantity that is one greater than six; 7.

sev·en·teen (sĕv′ən tēn′) amount or quantity that is one greater than 16; 17.

sev·en·teenth (sĕv′ən tēnth′) **1** next after the 16th. **2** one of 17 equal parts.

sev·enth (sĕv′ənth) **1** next after the sixth. **2** one of seven equal parts.

sev·en·ti·eth (sĕv′ən tĭ ith) **1** next after 69th; 70th. **2** one of 70 equal parts.

sev·en·ty (sĕv′ən tĭ) amount or quantity that is one greater than 69; 70. **sev·en·ties**.

sev·er (sĕv′ər) **1** to cut off; divide; cut in two: *to* sever *the limb of a tree*. **2** to break off (relations with) or part from: *A quarrel can* sever *a close friendship*.

sev·er·al (sĕv′ər əl) some; three or more but not many: *Today* several *pupils were late for class*.

se·vere (sĭ vîr′) **1** strict; grave; stern: *a* severe *schoolmaster*. **2** simple; very plain: *a* severe *dress*. **3** sharp, extreme: *a* severe *pain; a* severe *cold*. **4** hard; difficult: *a* severe *exam*. **se·ver·er, se·ver·est; se·vere·ly**.

se·ver·i·ty (sĭ vĕr′ə tĭ) **1** sternness; strictness. **2** extreme plainness. **3** harshness (of the weather); intensity (of cold): *They didn't go skating because of the* severity *of the snowstorm*. **se·ver·i·ties**.

sew (sō) to make stitches with a needle and thread; make, fasten, or mend (something): *She* sewed *all morning. She* sewed *a dress*.

sew up to close with stitches: *The doctor* sewed up *the cut on the boy's forehead*. **sewed, sewed or sewn, sew·ing**. (Homonyms: so, ²sow)

sew·age (sōō′ĭj) waste matter carried off by sewers.

sew·er (sōō′ər) large underground pipes or drains that carry off waste matter and water from towns and cities.

sew·ing (sō′ĭng) **1** a making of stitches. **2** anything to be sewed; needlework. **3** work of someone who sews.

sewn (sōn) See **sew**. *Have you* sewn *the rip in your dress?* (Homonym: sown)

sex (sĕks) **1** one of two groups into which human beings and most animals are divided: *Men and boys belong to the male* sex. *Women and girls belong to the female* sex. **2** the characteristics which make the difference between male and female: *We know that* sex *has nothing to do with the ability to learn*.

sex·tant (sĕks′tənt) instrument used by a navigator to measure the angle between the horizon and the sun or a star. With these measurements he can find his position (latitude and longitude).

sex·ton (sĕks′tən) man employed by a parish to take care of the church and churchyard, attend to burials, etc.

shab·by (shăb′ĭ) **1** worn out; much used; frayed; old: *a shabby* coat. **2** poorly dressed; ragged: *a shabby* beggar. **3** mean; unfair: *a shabby* trick. **shab·bi·er, shab·bi·est; shab·bi·ly**.

---

fāte, făt, fâre, fär; bē, bĕt; bīte, bĭt; nō, nŏt, nôr; fūse, fŭn, fûr; tōō, tŏŏk; foil; foul; thin; ~~then~~; hw for wh as in *wh*at; zh for s as in u*s*ual; ə for a, e) i, o, u, as in *a*go, lin*e*n, per*i*l, at*o*m, min*u*s

shack (shăk) very poor, small house; hut; hovel; shanty.

shack·le (shăk′əl) **1** iron ring joined by a chain to another ring, used for fastening a prisoner's ankles or wrists; handcuff. **2** anything that prevents free action. **3** to fasten with shackles; fetter. **4** to hinder; restrain. **shack·led, shack·ling.**

shad (shăd) large salt-water fish that lays eggs in fresh water and is commonly found along the Atlantic coast of the United States. pl. **shad.**

shade (shād) **1** darkness; dimness; reduced light: *The* shades *of night were falling.* **2** cooling shadow: *In the* shade *of the trees.* **3** shady spot: *90° in the* shade. **4** thing that reduces light or brightness: *a* lamp shade; *a window* shade. **5** degree of darkness (of a color); a variation of color: *Lavender is a* shade *of purple.* **6** slight difference: *A word may have many* shades *of meaning.* **7** ghost. **8** to cast a shadow: *Trees* shade *the swimming hole.* **9** to darken; tint: *Joyce* shaded *her drawing.* **10** to change (color) little by little: *The sunset* shaded *from flame color to pale yellow.* **11** to protect or shield from glare: *Jessie* shaded *her eyes with her hand.* **shad·ed, shad·ing.**

Shades

shad·ing (shā′ding) **1** slight difference in color or tone: *The wallpaper samples have different* shadings *in the same pattern.* **2** act of coloring or toning.

shad·ow (shăd′ō) **1** dark figure or image which is cast by something that cuts off light: *a* shadow *cast by the statue.* **2** to cast a shade or shadow upon: *Evening* shadowed *the street.* **3** sadness; gloom: *The bad news cast a* shadow *over the party.* **4** slight trace: *a* shadow *of a doubt.* **5** inseparable companion: *Tom was his brother's* shadow. **6** poor likeness (of a former condition): *Maude is a* shadow *of her former self after her illness.* **7** protection: *"Hide me under the* shadow *of Thy wings."* **8** to protect; shelter. **9** to follow; watch closely: *The detective* shadowed *the suspect.*

shad·ow·y (shăd′ō ĭ) **1** shady; filled with shadows: *a* shadowy *lane.* **2** faint; dim; ghostly: *a* shadowy *figure in the mist.*

3 unreal; impossible to explain or account for: *a* shadowy *fear.*

shad·y (shā′dĭ) **1** sheltered from the sun; dusky: *a* shady *street; a place too* shady *for taking photographs.* **2** of doubtful or questionable character: *a* shady *stock transaction.* **shad·i·er, shad·i·est; shad·i·ly.**

shaft (shăft) **1** straight rod or bar; the handle or long, slender part of any of a number of tools, machine parts, or items of athletic equipment: *Lyle broke the* shaft *of his golf club.* **2** arrow, spear, or the like: *Robin Hood shot his* shaft *straight to the target.* **3** pit or well: *The mine* shaft *went down 500 feet.* **4** vertical well in a building: *an air* shaft; *an elevator* shaft. **5** a ray or beam: *A* shaft *of light came from the lighthouse.* **6** either of the two long bars by which a vehicle is drawn by a horse harnessed between them. **7** the part of a column between its base and its capital.

Shaft

shag·gy (shăg′ĭ) **1** having long, rough, and uneven hair: *After the shearing the sheep were no longer* shaggy. **2** having long hair or threads, as wool: *We bought a* shaggy *rug for the bedroom.* **shag·gi·er, shag·gi·est.**

shake (shāk) **1** to tremble or quiver (with cold, emotion, etc.): *My hand* shook *so badly that I almost dropped the cup.* **2** to dislodge with force; stir up; cast off: *Please* shake *the snow from your shoes before you come in.* **3** to cause to move, quiver, or tremble: *The wind* shook *the window panes.* **4** to weaken; unnerve (a person): *He was* shaken *by his father's harsh scolding.* **5** to wave; brandish: *He* shook *his fist at the retreating mob.* **6** to clasp (another person's hand) in greeting: *We* shook *hands with all the guests.* **7** a shaking: *a* shake *of the head.* **8** to get away from or get rid of: *He* shook *his pursuers from his trail.* **9** to rattle or mix (dice) before casting or throwing. **10** to blend; mix: *to* shake *milk before pouring it.* **shook, shak·en, shak·ing.**

shak·en (shā′kən) See **shake.**

shak·y (shā′kĭ) **1** not firm; not secure; ready to fall: *The table was too* shaky *to use.* **2** trembling; shaking; weak: *We were still* shaky *from the explosion.* **3** weak; not convincing: *a* shaky *excuse; a* shaky *argument.* **shak·ier, shak·i·est; shak·i·ly.**

shale (shāl) rock formed by the hardening of clay and found in layers that are easily split.

shall (shăl) **1** word used with *I* and *we* in talking about things that are still to happen: *I shall be leaving tomorrow. We shall eat soon.* **2** have to; must: *You shall do this, whether you want to or not.* **3** am, is, or are determined to: *When the Japanese forced him to leave the Philippines, General MacArthur said, "I shall return."* **should.**

shal·lop (shăl′əp) small, light boat with sails, oars, or both.

shal·low (shăl′ō) **1** not deep: *The stream was shallow and we could walk across it without difficulty.* **2** lacking in depth of thought, emotion, etc.; superficial: *His feelings were very shallow.* **3 shallows** place or places where the water is not deep: *The boat went aground in the shallows.* **shal·low·ly.**

shalt (shălt) an old form of **shall** used with *thou*: *Thou shalt not steal.*

sham (shăm) **1** to fake, deceive, or pretend: *She was shamming when she said she was sick.* **2** not real; pretended: *The troops conducted a sham battle for the visiting general.* **3** trick; fraud: *His actions were a sham to disguise his real motives.* **shammed, sham·ming.**

sha·man (shä′mən or shä′mən or shăm′ən) medicine man; tribal worker of magic; magic healer.

sham·ble (shăm′bəl) to walk awkwardly; shuffle: *He shambled across the stage.* **sham·bled, sham·bling.**

sham·bles (shăm′bəlz) scene of disorder or destruction: *The army left the town in a shambles.*

shame (shām) **1** painful feeling of having done something one shouldn't have; embarrassment caused by a feeling of awkwardness, wrongdoing, improper behavior, or the like: *He was filled with shame when caught in the lie.* **2** disgrace; dishonor: *David brought shame to his family when he stole the car.* **3** something to be ashamed of: *The poor condition of our streets is a shame and a disgrace.* **4** to force or drive by a feeling of shame or guilt: *We shamed

him into doing his share of the work. **5** a cause for being sorry; pity: *It's a shame you can't come home for Christmas.* **shamed, sham·ing.**

shame·faced (shām′fāst′) **1** bashful; shy. **2** showing embarrassment or shame. **shame·fac·ed·ly.**

shame·ful (shām′fəl) causing shame; disgraceful. **shame·ful·ly.**

shame·less (shām′lis) showing no sense of shame, decency, modesty, or the like: *a shameless lie.* **shame·less·ly.**

sham·poo (shăm pōō′) **1** to wash or clean (hair, etc.) with soap and water or detergent: *to shampoo the dog; to shampoo rugs.* **2** a washing or cleaning of the hair, etc. **3** preparation used in washing or cleaning hair.

sham·rock (shăm′rŏk) clover or sorrel plant with a leaf that has three lobes. There are several shamrocks, one of which is the Irish national emblem.

shank (shăngk) **1** leg, especially the part between ankle and knee in man and some animals. **2** the straight, slender part of an implement or tool: *the shank of a spoon; shank of a key; shank of a fishhook.* **3** in beef, a cut from the upper part of the foreleg.

Shamrocks

shan't (shănt) shall not.

shan·ty (shăn′tĭ) flimsy, poorly made, small house; shack; hovel. **shan·ties.**

shape (shāp) **1** outline of a person or thing; outward appearance or form; contour of the body; figure: *The tree took the shape of a ghost in the fog.* **2** to give form to: *to shape a reply.* **3** condition: *Swimming keeps a person in good shape.* **4** definite form; orderly arrangement: *Plans are taking shape for our summer vacation.* **shaped, shap·ing.**

shape·less (shāp′lis) without form or definite shape: *a shapeless dress; a shapeless lump of clay.* **shape·less·ly.**

shape·ly (shāp′lĭ) having a good, pleasing shape; well-formed: *a shapely swimmer.* **shape·li·er, shape·li·est.**

---

fāte, făt, fâre, fär; bē, bĕt; bite, bĭt; nō, nŏt, nôr; fūse, fŭn, fûr; tōō, tŏŏk; foil; foul; thin; then; hw for wh as in *wh*at; zh for s as in u*s*ual; ə for a, e, i, o, u, as in ag*o*, lin*e*n, per*i*l, at*o*m, min*u*s

share (shâr) **1** portion or part of something received, done, or enjoyed by one of a number of persons: *He took his* share *of the profits. She did more than her* share *of the work.* **2** to take part; join: *to* share *in a friend's joy;* share *in the expense.* **3** to use, enjoy, or endure with someone: *to* share *a burden;* share *the cost;* share *a room.* **4** each of the equal parts into which the capital of a business is divided: *There are 20,000* shares *in the company.* **5** to divide or portion (something with others): *Please* share *your lunch with your sister.* **shared, shar·ing.**

share·crop·per (shâr′krŏp′ər) tenant farmer who gives part of his crop to his landlord in return for the use of the land which he farms.

Hammerhead shark, 15 ft. long and blue shark, 22 ft. long

shark (shärk) **1** any of several kinds of fish, some of which are large and dangerous. **2** a grasping person; a swindler.

sharp (shärp) **1** having a thin, fine, cutting edge or point: *a* sharp *knife; a* sharp *needle.* **2** pointed: *a* sharp *nose;* sharp *features; a* sharp *ridge.* **3** of sound, piercing; shrill: *a* sharp *whistle; a* sharp *cry of distress.* **4** quickly aware of things; observant; keen: *a* sharp *eye;* sharp *ears;* sharp *wits.* **5** having a nipping or biting taste: *a* sharp *cheese.* **6** cutting; harsh: *a* sharp *remark; a* sharp *scolding.* **7** abrupt and sudden: *a* sharp *turn; a* sharp *curve in the road.* **8** of feeling, piercing; keen: *a* sharp *pain.* **9** clear; distinct: *a* sharp *outline.* **10** done or acting with a keen eye to one's advantage; unscrupulous: *a* sharp *bargain; a* sharp *gambler.* **11** the musical sign (♯) to show that a note is raised half a tone. **12** promptly; punctually: *The game begins at two o'clock* sharp. **sharp·ly.**

sharp·en (shär′pən) **1** to make or become sharp or sharper; give a sharp edge or point to: *to* sharpen *the pencils.* **2** to make quick and keen: *This puzzle should* sharpen *your wits.*

sharp·en·er (shär′pən ər) person or thing that puts a keen edge or point on: *a knife* sharpener; *a scissors* sharpener.

sharp·ness (shärp′nis) **1** condition of having a cutting edge or a keen point. **2** quickness of perception; ability to understand. **3** bitterness: *Violet answered with considerable* sharpness. **4** biting taste of a food. **5** piercing quality of sound: *the* sharpness *of the train whistle.*

sharp·shoot·er (shärp′shōō′tər) good marksman; person who shoots accurately.

shat·ter (shăt′ər) **1** to break or smash suddenly into small pieces as by a blow or fall. **2** to ruin; destroy: *to* shatter *someone's hopes, ideals, etc.* **3** to weaken; disable; completely disorder: *Her nerves were* shattered *after the plane crash.*

shat·ter·proof (shăt′ər prōōf′) made so as not to shatter: *a* shatterproof *glass.*

shave (shāv) **1** to cut off closely with a razor: *to* shave *one's beard.* **2** to remove hair with a razor: *He* shaves *twice a day.* **3** to cut thin slices (from): *to* shave *a slice from the ham.* **4** to pass very close to; almost touch; graze: *The two cars* shaved *each other on the highway.* **5** a cutting off of hair with a razor. **6 close shave** a narrow escape from some danger: *He did not run into the telegraph pole but it was a close* shave. **shaved, shaved** or **shav·en, shav·ing.**

shav·en (shā′vən) See **shave.**

shav·ing (shā′vĭng) **1** act of one who shaves. **2** very thin slice of wood, metal, etc., cut off by a plane or the like.

shawl (shôl) piece of cloth, usually square or oblong, worn over the shoulders or head, especially by women.

she (shē) woman, girl, or female animal that has already been mentioned: *Ann says* she *is ill.*

sheaf (shēf) **1** bundle of cut grain tied about the middle. **2** any of various groups tied in this way: *a* sheaf *of arrows; a* sheaf *of papers.* **sheaves.**

Sheaf

shear (shĭr) **1** to clip or cut off (wool, hair, etc.) with shears or large scissors: *to* shear *wool.* **2** to remove wool from sheep, etc., with shears or clippers: *to* shear *a lamb.* **sheared, sheared** or **shorn, shear·ing.** (Homonym: sheer)

shears (shirz) any of various kinds of large scissors for shearing sheep, cutting grass, cloth, sheet metal, etc.

sheath (shēth) **1** protective covering or envelope: *The caterpillar wound a silken sheath about itself.* **2** a close-fitting metal or leather case for a sword or dagger.

Sheath

sheathe (shēth) to put into a scabbard or case for protection: *to sheathe a knife or sword.* **sheathed, sheath·ing.**

sheaves (shēvz) more than one **sheaf.**

¹shed (shĕd) **1** to pour out; let fall: *The girl shed tears.* **2** to cause to flow: *The war shed the blood of thousands.* **3** to pour forth; spread about: *The moon shed its light on the garden. The Christmas tree shed joy among the children.* **4** to throw off; get rid of: *He shed his troubles as a duck sheds water.* **5** to cast away; let fall: *We shed our overcoats in the spring as a snake sheds its skin.* **shed, shed·ding.** [¹**shed** is a form of an Old English word (scēad) meaning "a protection."]

²shed (shĕd) small building, sometimes with open sides, used for storage, shelter, etc.: *a tool shed; a cow shed.* [²**shed** seems to be a changed form of **shade.** The meaning arises from the fact that shade was one of the things that a shed would afford.]

she'd (shēd) **1** she had. **2** she would.

sheen (shēn) brightness, especially from a surface that reflects light; luster; a shine: *the sheen of her hair; the sheen of silver.*

sheep (shēp) **1** timid, defenseless animal, related to the goat, with a thick coat of curly wool. It is raised for its flesh, its wool, and its hide **2** timid yielding person. **3 black sheep (of the family)** person who is different in a bad way. **4 separate the sheep from the goats** to distinguish between those who are good or able and those who are not. **5 as well be hanged for a sheep as a lamb** as well commit a big crime as a small one (since the punishment will be severe in any case). pl. **sheep.**

Wool sheep

sheep dog any one of several breeds of large dogs that have been trained to help shepherds tend their flocks.

sheep·herd·er (shēp′hûr′dər) person who tends large flocks of sheep in the western United States.

sheep·ish (shē′pish) bashful; embarrassed; somewhat silly: *a sheepish grin.* **sheep·ish·ly.**

sheep·skin (shēp′skin′) **1** skin of a sheep, usually with the wool left on, often used for making clothing. **2** leather or parchment made from the skin of sheep. **3** document written on parchment, such as a graduation diploma.

¹sheer (shir) **1** unmixed; utter; complete: *It was sheer madness to try to swim against that current.* **2** very thin or fine; transparent: *The sunlight streamed through the sheer curtains.* **3** straight up and down; perpendicular; straight: *a sheer drop of 1,000 feet to the valley below.* **sheer·ly.** [¹**sheer** is a form of earlier English (schere) meaning "pure," "bright." The word is probably from Old Norse.] (Homonym: shear)

²sheer (shir) to turn from a course; swerve: *The car sheered away from the animal in the road.* [²**sheer** seems to be **shear** in a later and special use. From the idea of dividing comes that of swerving.] (Homonym: shear)

¹sheet (shēt) **1** broad thin piece of anything, as cloth, glass, metal, etc. **2** piece of cloth used to cover a bed: *to cover the sheets with a blanket.* **3** single piece of paper: *The letter went on to a second sheet.* **4** newspaper. **5** broad expanse or surface: *a sheet of water or snow.* [¹**sheet** is a form of an Old English word (scēte, sciēte).]

²sheet (shēt) rope attached to the lower corner of a sail to hold and regulate it. [²**sheet** is a form of an Old English word (scēatline) meaning "a line or rope tied to the lower corner of a sail."]

sheet iron iron in sheets or thin plates.

sheik or **sheikh** (shēk) head of an Arab family, tribe, or clan.

---

fāte, făt, fâre, fär; bē, bĕt; bīte, bĭt; nō, nŏt, nôr; fūse, fŭn, fûr; tōō, tŏŏk; foil; foul; thin; then; hw for wh as in *wh*at; zh for s as in u*s*ual; ə for a, e, i, o, u, as in *a*go, lin*e*n, per*i*l, at*o*m, min*u*s

shelf (shĕlf) **1** flat narrow piece of wood, metal, etc., fastened to a wall or set into a bookcase or cupboard. **2** something resembling a shelf in appearance, as a slab of rock that sticks out. **shelves.**

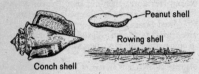

Peanut shell

Rowing shell

Conch shell

shell (shĕl) **1** the hard protective covering of a nut, seed, egg, crab, or the like. **2** hollow structure somewhat like a shell: *a pastry shell.* **3** the outer walls and roof only of a building: *After the fire the building was a mere shell.* **4** the horny covering of a tortoise. **5** an explosive missile fired from a gun or cannon. **6** cartridge for a rifle or shotgun. **7** light racing boat. **8** to bombard: *to shell a fort.* **9** to remove from a shell, husk, or cob: *to shell nuts; to shell peas; to shell corn.*

she'll (shĕl) she will.

shel·lac (shə lăk') **1** sticky substance used in making sealing wax, varnish, etc. **2** to coat with this substance. **shel·lacked, shel·lack·ing.**

shell·fire (shĕl'fīr') a firing or shooting of shells.

shell·fish (shĕl'fĭsh') water animal having a shell, such as oysters, lobsters, crabs, scallops, etc.

shel·ter (shĕl'tər) **1** anything that protects, covers, or shields: *We run for any shelter in a storm.* **2** to protect; defend: *The country church sheltered us from the rain.* **3** to find shelter.

¹shelve (shĕlv) **1** to put on a shelf. **2** to dismiss from the mind; to postpone indefinitely: *To shelve a problem is not to solve it.* **shelved, shelv·ing.** [**¹shelve** is formed from the word **shelf.**]

²shelve (shĕlv) to slope gradually. **shelved, shelv·ing.** [**²shelve** is probably a form of **shelf** though some take it back to an Old Norse word (shelgga) meaning "to twist," "become oblique."]

shelves (shĕlvz) more than one **shelf.**

shep·herd (shĕp'ərd) **1** person who takes care of sheep. **2** minister or priest. **3** to

take care of; guide; lead: *The students were shepherded through the museum.*

shep·herd·ess (shĕp'ər dĭs) woman who watches or cares for sheep.

sher·bet (shûr'bət) frozen dessert made of fruit juice with water, milk, gelatin, etc.

sher·iff (shĕr'ĭf) chief law-enforcing officer of a county.

sher·ry (shĕr'ĭ) strong wine, light yellow to brown in color, originally made in Spain. **sher·ries.**

she's (shēz) **1** she is: *Do you know if she's staying with us?* **2** she has: *I think she's been here for one hour.*

shied (shīd) **1** See **¹shy.** *The horse shied at the shadow and refused to go on.* **2** See **²shy.** *He shied some stones into the brook.*

shield (shēld) **1** leather- or metal-covered, protective piece of armor once carried on the arm by soldiers. **2** anything that, or anyone who, protects: *Vaccination is a shield against smallpox.* **3** to protect; guard: *This raincoat will shield you.*

GREEK

ROMAN

MIDDLE AGES

Shields

shies (shīz) **1** See **¹shy.** *The baby shies away from strangers.* **2** See **²shy.** *He shies flat stones across water to see them skip.*

shift (shĭft) **1** to move from one person, place, or position to another: *to shift the blame; to shift a bundle from one hand to the other.* **2** a move from one person, place, position, to another; a change: *a shift in jobs; a shift in ideas; a shift in the weather.* **3** to change gears (in a car). **4** group of people working at one time: *a night shift in a factory.* **5** work period: *The street cleaners worked in long shifts during the snowstorm.* **6** trick; indirect method; expedient: *Tom tried every shift he could think of to avoid work.* **7 make shift** to make do with what is available; get along with: *We must make shift with these old tools.*

shift for oneself to make one's own way; manage: *Helen had to shift for herself after her parents died.*

shift·less (shĭft'lĭs) lazy; worthless. **shift·less·ly.**

shil·ling (shĭl'ĭng) British silver coin equal to 12 pence.

shim·mer (shĭm'ər) **1** to shine with a wavering light; glimmer: *The moonlight* shimmers *on the lake.* **2** wavering light; sheen: *the shimmer of a satin gown.*

shin (shĭn) **1** the forepart of the leg between the ankle and the knee. **2** to climb with alternate grips of knees and hands: *Percy shinned up the tree.* **shinned, shin·ning.**

shine (shĭn) **1** to give off or reflect light or radiance; gleam: *The sun* shone. *His face* shone *with joy.* **2** to cause to give forth a glow or luster; to polish: *to* shine *silverware; to* shine *shoes.* **3** glow; radiance; luster: *the* shine *of new money.* **4** polish, as given to shoes, etc.: *Tony used his sleeve to give the apple a* shine. **5** to be best at; excel: *Jenny* shines *in foreign languages.* **6** sunshine: *come rain or come* shine. **shone** or **shined, shin·ing.**

¹shin·gle (shĭng′gəl) **1** one of the thin, wedge-shaped boards placed on buildings in overlapping rows to keep out rain. **2** any paper or slate substitute for a wooden shingle. **3** to lay, or put on, shingles. **4** small sign: *a doctor's* shingle. **shin·gled, shin·gling.** [**¹shingle** seems to go back to a Latin word (scindula) also meaning "shingle." This Latin word is formed from another Latin word (scindere) meaning "to split."]

Shingles

²shin·gle (shĭng′gəl) rounded seashore pebbles, coarser than ordinary gravel. [**²shingle** is a word of unknown origin.]

shin·y (shī′nĭ) bright; glossy. **shin·i·er, shin·i·est.**

ship (shĭp) **1** large vessel built for ocean travel. **2** entire company of a vessel: *The rumor raced through the* ship. **3** airplane. **4** vehicle for travel beyond the atmosphere: *a rocket* ship. **5** to send or transport by ship, rail, truck, etc. **6** to take a job on a vessel: *He* shipped *as a steward.* **7** to take (water) in over the sides of a vessel: *to* ship *water; to* ship *a wave.* **shipped, ship·ping.**

-ship suffix meaning **(1)** "state of," "condition of," or "quality of": *friend*ship;

*hard*ship. **(2)** "position of": *king*ship. **(3)** "the art or skill of": *horseman*ship; *leader*ship.

ship·board (shĭp′bôrd′) **1** a ship. **2 on shipboard** on or in a ship.

ship·load (shĭp′lōd′) full load of cargo or passengers on a ship.

ship·ment (shĭp′mənt) **1** transportation or sending of goods: *to prepare merchandise for* shipment. **2** goods sent at one time: *Your second* shipment *of books did not arrive in good condition.*

ship·per (shĭp′ər) person or company who sends goods by any means of transportation.

ship·ping (shĭp′ĭng) **1** act or business of sending goods from one place to another: *Jack's father wanted him to go into* shipping. **2** all of the ships of a port, nation, company, etc.

ship·shape (shĭp′shāp′) in good order; neat.

ship·wreck (shĭp′rĕk′) **1** destruction or loss of a ship: *Only a few were saved from the* shipwreck. **2** ship that has been wrecked. **3** to cause to suffer the loss or destruction of a ship: *They were* shipwrecked *on a small island.* **4** utter destruction; ruin: *I have seen the* shipwreck *of my plans.* **5** to ruin; destroy: *Jim's failure in the examination* shipwrecked *all hopes for his career.*

ship·yard (shĭp′yärd′) place where ships are built or repaired.

shirk (shûrk) to neglect or shun (work, duty, etc.) deliberately: *You shouldn't* shirk *your responsibilities.*

shirt (shûrt) **1** garment, usually with a collar and long or short sleeves, for the upper part of the body. **2** knitted, usually sleeveless, undergarment; an undershirt.

shirt·waist (shûrt′wāst′) woman's blouse or shirt with collar and cuffs. It has ends that are usually tucked in under a skirt or trousers.

¹shiv·er (shĭv′ər) **1** to tremble, shake or quiver (from cold, fear, etc.). **2** a quiver: *He was so frightened that* shivers *ran up and down his spine.* [**¹shiver** may be a blend of **shake** and **quiver.**]

---

fāte, făt, fâre, fär; bē, bĕt; bīte, bĭt; nō, nŏt, nôr; fūse, fŭn, fûr; tōō, tŏŏk; foil; foul; thin; ~~then~~; hw for wh as in *wh*at; zh for s as in u*s*ual; ə for a, e, i, o, u, as in *a*go, lin*e*n, per*i*l, at*o*m, min*u*s

²shiv·er (shĭv'ər) **1** to break or cause to break into small pieces or splinters; shatter: *He shivered the glass with a single blow.* **2** small piece or fragment; sliver. [**²shiver** is a word of uncertain origin.]

¹shoal (shōl) **1** shallow place in any body of water. **2** sand bank or sand bar that is exposed at low tide. [**¹shoal** is a form of an Old English word (sceald) meaning "shallow."]

²shoal (shōl) large group, number, or mass; school: *a shoal of fish.* [**²shoal** is a form of an Old English word (scolu) meaning "a crowd."]

¹shock (shŏk) **1** sudden or violent blow; impact, jar, or concussion: *The shock of the explosion was felt for miles around.* **2** violent upset of the mind or emotions as a result of fear, pain, grief, etc. **3** effect of electric current on the body: *You will receive a shock if you touch that live wire.* **4** sudden physical weakening or collapse caused by extreme fatigue, loss of blood, wounds, or pain. **5** to surprise, horrify, or disgust: *Our parents were shocked when they saw what had happened to the car.* [**¹shock** is from a French word (choquer) meaning "to collide."]

²shock (shŏk) thick, bushy mass of hair. [**²shock** may be a changed form of **shag** meaning "coarse or rough hair."]

³shock (shŏk) **1** sheaves of grain stacked upright in a field to dry. **2** to place in sheaves. [**³shock** is from an Old English word (schokke) which is probably from a word of Germanic origin meaning "corn shock."]

shock·ing (shŏk'ĭng) very disgusting; causing great horror or surprise: *The murder was a shocking incident.* **shock·ing·ly.**

shod (shŏd) See **shoe.** *The horses were shod last week.*

shod·dy (shŏd'ĭ) **1** woolen cloth of poor quality made by reweaving woolen waste, raveled rags, etc. **2** of poor quality: *a shoddy piece of work.* **shod·dies; shod·di·er, shod·di·est; shod·di·ly.**

shoe (shōō) **1** outer covering for the foot, made of cloth, leather, or the like. It generally consists of a stiff bottom layer or sole and a soft upper part. **2** horseshoe. **3** to fit with shoes: *to shoe a horse.* **shod, shoe·ing.** (Homonym: shoo)

shoe·lace (shōō'lās') length of string, cord, or leather used to fasten or lace a shoe.

shoe·mak·er (shōō'mā'kər) person who makes or repairs shoes; cobbler.

shoe·string (shōō'strĭng') **1** shoelace. **2** very small amount (of money or resources): *They started their business on a* shoestring.

shone (shōn) See **shine.** *The sun shone brightly.* (Homonym: shown)

shoo (shōō) **1** to scare or drive away (animals or birds): *Tod shooed the chickens out of the cornfield.* **2** word used to scare or drive away. (Homonym: shoe)

shook (shŏŏk) See **shake.** *The children shook the apples from the tree.*

shoot (shōōt) **1** to hit, wound, or kill with a bullet, arrow, or other missile. **2** to discharge or fire a gun, arrow, or the like. **3** to send forth like a bullet or arrow: *to shoot questions; to shoot a look.* **4** to streak with different colors: *The sky was shot with many colors.* **5** to move a bolt in or out of place: *He shot the bolt to lock the barn.* **6** to pass over or through quickly, rapidly: *to shoot the rapids.* **7** to grow or thrust upward or out: *The warm weather made the plants shoot up.* **8** to protrude; jut out: *The island shoots out into the sea.* **9** to photograph: *to shoot a picture.* **10** to throw, drive, or cast: *to shoot dice; to shoot marbles.* **11** to make a score or points: *He shot in the low 90's in the golf tournament.* **12** shooting match; hunt: *a turkey shoot.* **13** young and tender branch or stem of a plant: *Rabbits ate the first shoots in the garden.* **shot, shoot·ing.** (Homonym: chute)

shooting gallery enclosed place for target practice.

shooting star meteor. Also called **falling star.**

shop (shŏp) **1** a store; place where merchandise is sold. **2** to visit stores or shops to look at or purchase merchandise. **3** place where a particular kind of work is done: *a carpenter's shop.* **4 set up shop** to start a business. **5 shut up shop** (1) to close business. (2) to go out of business. **6 talk shop** to talk about one's business or profession. **shopped, shop·ping.**

shop·keep·er (shŏp'kē'pər) person who carries on business in a shop; retailer.

shop·ping (shŏp'ĭng) a looking at or purchasing of merchandise.

¹shore (shôr) land that borders on a body of water. [**¹shore** is from an Old English word (schōre) of the same meaning.]

²shore (shôr) **1** to prop, steady or hold up with timbers, etc.: *We shored up the walls of the barn to keep them from falling.* **2** a timber used as a prop or temporary support. **shored, shor·ing.** [**²shore** is from a Dutch word (schoor) meaning "a prop."]

shorn (shôrn) See **shear.** *The sheep were shorn yesterday.*

short (shôrt) **1** not tall or long: *a short man; a short journey.* **2** incomplete; insufficient: *a short supply.* **3** lacking the usual amount: *a short dozen.* **4** brief in time: *a short visit.* **5** lacking: *a dollar short of train fare.* **6** curt: *His answer was a short "No."* **7** suddenly; on an instant: *to stop short.* **8** of cake or pastry, crisp or crumbling. **9 cut short** to bring to an immediate close; stop: *The chairman cut the speaker short.* **10 fall short** to fail to come up to expectations, promise, etc.: *The play fell short of what we expected.* **11 in short** briefly; in a few words. **12 run short** (1) to use up: *I ran short of patience.* (2) to be used up: *The ice cream ran short at the picnic.* **13 short vowel** the ă of "hat," ĕ of "net," ĭ of "hit," ŏ of "not," ŭ of "nut," or o͞o of "took."

short·age (shôr'tij) **1** amount lacking to complete anything: *There is a shortage of $50 in his bank account.* **2** too small a quantity to satisfy a demand or need: *a sugar shortage.*

short·cake (shôrt'kāk') slightly sweetened biscuit or sponge cake, usually served with crushed berries as a dessert.

short circuit a bringing together of the two main wires of an electric circuit so that the current flows directly between them without passing through a lamp, heater, etc., that offers resistance to it. This allows a much larger current to flow, causing great heat in the wires and, often, fires.

short-cir·cuit (shôrt'sûr'kit) to cause or become a short circuit.

short·com·ing (shôrt'kŭm'ing) a falling short of a standard of conduct, duty, or perfection; fault.

short cut route or method shorter than the regular one: *Joe took a short cut across the field to meet the bus.*

short·en (shôr'tən) **1** to make shorter: *Mother shortened Mary's coat for Sue.* **2** to grow or become shorter: *The days shorten in the fall.* **3** to add butter, lard, etc., to cake or pastry dough.

short·en·ing (shôr'tən ing) **1** a making short: *the shortening of a skirt.* **2** butter, lard, etc., added to bread, cake, or pastry dough to make it crisp or crumbling.

short-haired (shôrt'hârd') having short hair or fur: *Horses, giraffes, and many breeds of dogs are short-haired.*

short·hand (shôrt'hănd') any system of rapid writing in which strokes, symbols, and abbreviations are used instead of letters, words, and phrases.

short·horn (shôrt'hôrn') **1** describing a kind of cattle raised for beef: *a shorthorn steer.* **2** an animal of this kind: *The cowboy rounded up his shorthorns.*

short·ly (shôrt'li) **1** very soon; presently: *The plane leaves shortly.* **2** briefly; in sharp, terse words: *Speak shortly and to the point.*

short·ness (shôrt'nis) **1** a being short; brevity. **2** curtness.

shorts (shôrts) short trousers.

short-sight·ed (shôrt'sī'tĭd) **1** considering only the present; not looking toward the future: *It is short-sighted to spend one's money as fast as one gets it.* **2** nearsighted; unable to see distant objects clearly. **short-sight·ed·ly.**

short·stop (shôrt'stŏp') in baseball, the player between second and third base.

short wave 1 radio wave with a much higher frequency and shorter length than standard (AM) waves. **2 short-wave** using such waves: *a short-wave radio.*

¹shot (shŏt) **1** discharge of a firearm or the sound made by it: *The shot echoed through the woods.* **2** bullet, especially one of the small bullets fired from a shotgun. **3** person who shoots; marksman: *Sylvia is a good shot.* **4** a throw; cast: *The basketball player made a long shot and scored for his team.* **5** injection (of medicine) into the body: *Have you had your polio shot?* **6** a

---

fāte, făt, fâre, fär; bē, bĕt; bīte, bĭt; nō, nŏt, nôr; fūse, fŭn, fûr; to͞o, to͝ok; foil; foul; thin; then; hw for wh as in *wh*at; zh for s as in u*s*ual; ə for a, e, i, o, u, as in *a*go, lin*e*n, per*i*l, at*o*m, min*u*s

try; attempt: *When Ignace finished school he took a* shot *at reporting.* [**¹shot** is a form of **shoot** in a changed meaning.]

²shot (shŏt) See **shoot.** *I* shot *an arrow into the air.* [**²shot** is a form of **shoot.**]

Shotgun

shot·gun (shŏt′gŭn′) firearm for shooting a spreading charge of shot at short range.

should (shŏŏd) **1** ought to; have a duty to; have an obligation to: *You really* should *study more.* **2** does or do (expressing possibility); happens or happen to: *If it* should *rain, close the windows.*

shoul·der (shōl′dər) **1** the part of the human body between the shoulder and the arm, or the part between the neck and the foreleg of most animals. **2** the part of a garment intended to cover this part. **3** the upper part of an animal's foreleg or the upper part of the foreleg and nearby parts prepared for food: *a pork* shoulder; *a* shoulder *of mutton.* **4** to push aside or force one's way through with the shoulder: *The policeman* shouldered *his way through the crowd.* **5** to place upon one's shoulder: *to* shoulder *a gun.* **6** to take on; assume: *to* shoulder *responsibilities.*

shoulder blade flat bone behind each shoulder that contains the socket of the shoulder joint.

should·n't (shŏŏd′ənt) should not.

shouldst (shŏŏdst) old form of **should** used with *thou.*

shout (shout) **1** to cry, call, or talk loudly: *The children* shouted *with joy.* **2** loud cry or call.

shove (shŭv) **1** to push: *Jack* shoved *the paper across the table to me.* **2** to push roughly; jostle: *The big, surly man* shoved *through the subway crowd.* **3** a push. **shoved, shov·ing.**

shov·el (shŭv′əl) **1** digging or scooping tool with a broad blade, used for handling things like coal, snow, or earth. **2** the amount a shovel holds: *Lloyd put a* shovel *of coal on the fire.* **3** to use a shovel; dig or throw with, or as if with, a shovel: *Omar* shoveled *the snow*

Shovels

from the steps. **4** to make with a shovel: *to* shovel *a path.*

show (shō) **1** to place in sight; display; exhibit: *to* show *goods in a shop.* **2** to reveal; make known: *to* show *one's feelings.* **3** to make clear: *to* show *the solution of a puzzle.* **4** to point out; guide; direct: *to* show *the way to the village.* **5** to give; grant; accord; bestow: *to* show *kindness.* **6** something for display or effect: *This china is only for* show *and not for use.* **7** to be visible or noticeable: *Her embarrassment* showed *when she blushed.* **8** any kind of public performance, exhibition, or display: *a horse* show; *an automobile* show. **9** appearance: *a* show *of health in her rosy cheeks.* **10** pretense; deceitful appearance: *His boasting was only a* show *of courage.* **show off** to make a display to impress. **show up 1** to reveal truth about; expose: *to* show up *an impostor.* **2** to appear: *He didn't* show up *for class.*

showed, shown or **showed, show·ing.**

show·case (shō′kās′) box with glass sides to display articles, as in a store or museum.

show·er (shou′ər) **1** short fall of rain. **2** bath in which water comes down from a spray. **3** to take such a bath. **4** to wet with a spray or drops: *Rain* showered *the crowd.* **5** something resembling a shower; an outburst: *a* shower *of abuse.* **6** to give generously (to a person): *The audience* showered *praise on the actress.* **7** party where gifts are to be given: *We are giving a* shower *for our friend who is going to be married.*

show·man (shō′mən) person who puts on shows or other entertainment. **show·men.**

shown (shōn) See **show.** *The trophies were* shown *on the mantel.* (Homonym: shone)

show·y (shō′i) **1** making a conspicuous display: *a* showy *corsage.* **2** flashy and not in good taste: *a* showy *display of wealth.* **show·i·er, show·i·est; show·i·ly.**

shrank (shrăngk) See **shrink.** *Joan's dress* shrank *in the wash.*

shrap·nel (shrăp′nəl) shell filled with bullets and powder designed to burst and shatter.

shred (shrĕd) **1** small piece cut or torn off (something); scrap; fragment: *to tear a letter into* shreds. **2** to cut or tear into strips or fragments: *to* shred *cabbage for a salad.* **shred·ded** or **shred, shred·ding.**

shrew (shrōō) **1** quarrelsome, scolding woman. **2** very small mouselike animal with a long pointed nose and tiny eyes. It is a fierce and ready fighter.

Short-tailed shrew, about 4½ in. long

shrewd (shrōōd) clever; keen in practical matters: *Ted made a* shrewd *move and won the game of checkers.* **shrewd·ly.**

shrewd·ness (shrōōd′nĭs) cleverness; sharpness in practical matters: *His shrewdness in business made him a rich man.*

shriek (shrēk) **1** loud, sharp sound; an outcry: *the shriek of sirens.* **2** to cry out in a sharp, shrill sound: *to shriek with laughter.*

shrill (shril) **1** having a high, sharp sound: *The shrill cry of a hyena pierced the silence.* **2** to make a high, piercing sound or cry: *Katydids shrilled in the tree outside my window.* **shril·ly.**

Shrimp, 2 to 3 in. long

shrimp (shrĭmp) **1** small sea creature that looks somewhat like a small lobster without claws. It is used for food. **2** small person or one of little importance.

shrine (shrīn) **1** holy place; sacred building or city: *Mecca is a Moslem shrine.* **2** place of prayer or meditation, often containing a sacred statue. **3** box containing sacred relics. **4** the tomb of a saint. **5** any place held in reverence for historic, or artistic reasons.

Roadside shrine

shrink (shringk) **1** to make or become smaller: *The sweater shrunk when it was washed in hot water.* **2** to withdraw or move away (from something dangerous or unpleasant); avoid: *to shrink from a hard task.* **shrank** or **shrunk, shrunk** or **shrunk·en, shrink·ing.**

shrink·age (shrĭngk′ĭj) **1** a shrinking; a reducing in size or quantity: *the shrinkage*

of woolen goods; shrinkage *of dollar value.* **2** amount anything shrinks: *allowance for shrinkage.*

shriv·el (shrĭv′əl) to dry or curl up; wither; wrinkle: *Leaves* shriveled *in the summer heat.*

¹shroud (shroud) **1** garment or covering in which a dead person is buried. **2** something that covers or conceals: *a shroud of mist; a* shroud *of mystery.* **3** to cover or veil; conceal. [**¹shroud** is a form of an Old English word (scrūd) meaning "a garment, clothing."]

²shroud (shroud) one of the set of ropes extending from the upper part of a mast to the side of a ship to steady the mast. [**²shroud** is **¹shroud** in a later and special meaning.]

Shrouds

shrub (shrŭb) woody plant smaller than a tree, usually with many separate stems starting from near the ground. A rosebush is a shrub.

shrub·ber·y (shrŭb′ə rĭ) **1** group of shrubs; bushes. **2** place planted with shrubs. **shrub·ber·ies.**

shrug (shrŭg) **1** to raise the shoulders to express doubt, indifference, impatience, or the like: *Tom* shrugged *when asked his opinion.* **2** a shrugging: *a shrug of the shoulders.* **shrugged, shrug·ging.**

shrunk (shrŭngk) See **shrink.** *These trousers have* shrunk *too much for me to wear them.*

shrunk·en (shrŭngk′ən) See **shrink.** *A person* shrunken *by age.*

shuck (shŭk) **1** outer covering; shell; husk. **2** to take off an outer covering; shell; husk. *He* shucked *a basket of corn for the picnic.*

shud·der (shŭd′ər) **1** to tremble; shake; quiver: *He* shuddered *in the chill wind.* **2** a sudden trembling: *He thought of the horror movie with a shudder.*

shuf·fle (shŭf′əl) **1** to walk with a scuffling or dragging step. **2** sliding or dragging step. **3** to pass or shift from one person or place to another: *We* shuffled *the book*

fāte, făt, fâre, fär; bē, bĕt; bīte, bĭt; nō, nŏt, nôr; fūse, fŭn, fûr; tōō, tŏŏk; foil; foul; thin; ~~then~~;
hw for wh as in *what*; zh for s as in u*s*ual; ə for a, e, i, o, u, as in *a*go, lin*e*n, per*i*l, at*o*m, min*u*s

659

back and forth between us because we had only one copy. **4** to mix up or rearrange: *to shuffle a deck of cards.* **5** a rearranging or mixing up. **shuf·fled, shuf·fling.**

shuf·fle·board (shŭf'əl bôrd') game where disks are slid with a stick along a flat surface, such as the deck of a ship, to numbered squares.

shun (shŭn) to avoid; keep away from: *He shunned the company of his classmates because he was shy.* **shunned, shun·ning.**

shut (shŭt) **1** to close: *Please shut the door.* **2** to fold up: *to shut a screen and put it away.* **3** to become closed: *The gate shut in the wind.* **4 shut-in** a person unable to leave the house, usually because of illness.

shut down to stop working: *The summer resort shut down during the winter.*

shut in to confine: *She shut the child in his room until he stopped crying.*

shut off to turn off; stop from working: *Please shut off the radio.*

shut out to prevent from entering: *to shut out sunlight.*

shut up 1 to confine; enclose: *to shut a puppy up in a pen.* **2** discontinue; close: *to shut up shop for the night.* **3** to stop talking. **4** to make (someone) stop talking. **shut, shut·ting.**

shut·ter (shŭt'ər) **1** door or panel of solid wood or overlapping slats to cover the outside of a window. **2** part of a camera that covers the lens.

shut·tle (shŭt'əl) **1** in weaving, an instrument in the shape of a cigar that carries the thread from side to side. **2** on a sewing machine, a device called a **bobbin** that holds thread and carries it back and forth to an upper thread to make a stitch. **3** anything that moves back and forth in a similar way. A train that makes short trips back and forth between two stations is called a shuttle. **4** to move back and forth between two places. **shut·tled, shut·tling.**

¹**shy** (shī) **1** timid; bashful; self-conscious; uneasy in the presence of other people: *He was shy when he first went to school.* **2** to jump; start; draw back quickly: *The horse shied at the passing car.* **shi·er, shi·est; shies, shied, shy·ing; shy·ly.**

[¹**shy** is from an Old English word (scēoh).]

²**shy** (shī) **1** to throw with a sudden movement; to fling: *He shied a stone into the water.* **2** a sudden throw; a fling. **shies; shies, shied, shy·ing.** [²**shy** is a word of uncertain origin.]

shy·ness (shī'nĭs) bashfulness; timidity.

sick (sĭk) **1** not well; ill; in poor health: *He is sick with measles.* **2** nauseated; vomiting or feeling as if one is going to vomit: *Bus rides make him sick.* **3** greatly troubled or annoyed: *It makes me sick to think of what he has done.* **4** tired (of something); bored by: *I'm sick of this weather.* **5** accompanied by nausea: *a sick headache.* **6 the sick** ill people in general: *She cares for the sick.*

sick·bed (sĭk'bĕd') bed to which a sick person is confined.

sick·en (sĭk'ən) **1** to become ill: *She sickened in the change of climate.* **2** to become tired and disgusted with: *She sickened of sweet things when she worked in the candy shop.* **3** to make ill; disgust: *The odor of the stagnant pool sickened me.*

sick·le (sĭk'əl) mowing tool consisting of a curved blade on a short handle, used for cutting grain, trimming lawns, etc.

Sickle

sick·ly (sĭk'lĭ) **1** weak; frail; unhealthy: *a sickly child.* **2** having to do with or caused by illness: *His face had a sickly color.* **3** likely to cause illness: *a sickly climate.* **4** weak; dim: *a sickly light.* **5** lacking spirit: *a sickly smile.* **6** sickening; cloying: *a sickly perfume.* **sick·li·er, sick·li·est.**

sick·ness (sĭk'nĭs) illness; poor health: *a sickness caused by spoiled food.*

side (sīd) **1** the edge of a surface; especially, one of the long edges of a rectangle rather than the ends. **2** one of the surfaces of a solid: *A box has six sides.* **3** one of the surfaces of a thin sheet of anything: *This paper has writing on one side but not on the other.* **4** the right or left part of a person, animal, or thing. **5** position right or left of a central point or line: *Please put the chair on that side of the room.* **6** a line of descent either from the mother or from the father: *He was my great-grandfather on my mother's side.* **7** one of two opposing posi-

tions: *There are always two* sides *to an argument. They divided into two* sides *to play the game.* **8** group of people holding opposing positions. **9** pertaining to or located on a side: *I have a side ache from running.* **10** not important; minor: *a side issue.* **11** directed to one side: *a side glance.* **12** aspect; quality; part: *to look on the bright* side; *the sunny* side *of her nature.*
     side with to take a position in an argument, game, etc.: *We each* sided *with our parents in the argument.*
     sid·ed, sid·ing.

side·board (sīd′bôrd′) piece of dining-room furniture with cupboards and drawers for storing table linen and silver.

side line 1 a line bordering and limiting an area: *The spectators sit behind the* side lines *at a tennis match.* **2** branch from a main line: *A* side line *of pipe runs from the house to the garage.* **3** second trade or occupation followed in addition to a main one: *The artist had a* side line *of cabinet making.* **4** goods carried by a merchant in addition to his main stock: *The florist carried a* side line *of candy.*

side·long (sīd′lông′) directed to or along the side: *a* sidelong *look.*

side show a minor show accompanying a main one: *the* side show *at a circus.*

side-step (sīd′stĕp′) to avoid by, or as by, stepping to the side; to evade: *She* side-stepped *all unpleasant issues. He* side-stepped *the puddle by walking around it.*
     side-stepped, side-step·ping.

side·track (sīd′trăk′) **1** to switch a train to a siding or off the main track. **2** to turn something from a main course; divert: *He* sidetracked *the argument from the real issues.* **3** a railroad spur.

side·walk (sīd′wôk′) a footpath or walk, usually paved, at the side of a road or street.

side·ways (sīd′wāz′) **1** on, to, or toward the side: *a* sideways *glance; a* sideways *movement.* **2** from or toward a side: *to look at a thing* sideways. **3** with the side or edge foremost: *to move* sideways; *to carry a table through a door* sideways.

side·wise (sīd′wīz′) sideways.

sid·ing (sī′dĭng) **1** short railroad track to which trains may be switched from the main track. **2** clapboards or the like on the outside wall of a building.

si·dle (sī′dəl) to move sideways, especially in a shy or stealthy manner: *The frightened child* sidled *up to his mother.* **si·dled, si·dling.**

siege (sēj) **1** the surrounding of a place, by an army or fleet, to cut off supplies and force its surrender. **2** long or persistent effort to get possession of something by overcoming resistance: *The knight laid* siege *to the lady's heart.* **3** long, distressing period: *a* siege *of illness.*

si·er·ra (sĭ ĕr′ə) chain of mountains rising in irregular peaks.

si·es·ta (sĭ ĕs′tə) a nap or rest at noon or after the midday meal.

sieve (sĭv) utensil with a perforated or screened bottom for drain-ing or sifting matter put in it.

Sieve

sift (sĭft) **1** to separate small-er pieces (of something) from larger, often with a sieve. **2** to examine close-ly: *Let us* sift *the facts before we make a decision.*

sigh (sī) **1** deep, audible breath expressing fatigue, sorrow, relief, etc. **2** to sound like a sigh: *The wind* sighed *in the trees.* **3** to draw a deep, audible breath: *Fritz* sighed *when he thought of his neglected oppor-tunities.*

sight (sīt) **1** power of seeing; vision: *His* sight *was restored by an operation on his eyes.* **2** a seeing, or thing seen: *The first* sight *of the sea was a thrill to the boy from the Middle West.* **3** something startling, fright-ening, or beautiful to be seen: *The car was a* sight *after the accident. She was a lovely* sight *in her wedding dress.* **4** device on a gun or optical instrument to help in guid-ing the aim or eye. **5** to aim: *to* sight *a gun or compass.* **6** to see for the first time on any occasion: *We* sighted *land at dawn.* **7 sights** things worth seeing; interesting places. (Homonyms: cite, site)

sight·less (sīt′lĭs) without sight; blind.

---

fāte, făt, fâre, fär; bē, bĕt; bīte, bĭt; nō, nŏt, nôr; fūse, fŭn, fûr; tōō, tŏŏk; foil; foul; thin; then; hw for wh as in *wh*at; zh for s as in u*s*ual; ə for a, e, i, o, u, as in *a*go, lin*e*n, per*i*l, at*o*m, min*u*s

sight·see·ing (sīt′sē′ing) **1** a visiting of places of interest: *They spent their holiday sightseeing in New York.* **2** having to do with sightseeing: *a sightseeing bus.*

sign (sīn) **1** a mark, character, or emblem that represents a thing or an idea: *The Cross is a sign of the Christian religion.* **2** that by which anything is made known; token; proof: *His trembling was a sign of fright.* **3** indication; omen: *Sunshine on Groundhog Day is a sign of six more weeks of winter.* **4** gesture or signal used instead of words to express some thought or command: *The policeman gave a sign to the driver to stop the car.* **5** lettered board or plate giving the name of a business, information, etc.: *the butcher's sign; a road sign.* **6** in arithmetic, a symbol for adding, subtracting, multiplying, etc., as $+$, $-$, $\times$. **7** to write one's name at the end of: *to sign a document; to sign a check.*

sig·nal (sĭg′nəl) **1** sign agreed upon for sending instructions, information, notice of danger, etc.: *The captain gave the signal for attack. The ship sent out a signal of distress.* **2** to make such a sign: *The driver signaled a left turn and then turned right.*

sig·na·ture (sĭg′nə chər) **1** name of a person in his own handwriting; autograph. **2** in music, a mark that is placed at the beginning of a staff to show the key.

sign·board (sīn′bôrd′) board having a sign, advertisement, notice, or the like, on it.

sig·net (sĭg′nĭt) a seal; official stamp.

sig·nif·i·cance (sĭg nĭf′ə kəns) **1** meaning; sense: *I don't understand the significance of your remark.* **2** importance: *an event of great significance in history.*

sig·nif·i·cant (sĭg nĭf′ə kənt) **1** important; notable: *The Boston Tea Party was a significant step towards American independence.* **2** having or giving a hidden or special meaning: *a significant tone of voice.* **sig·nif·i·cant·ly.**

sig·ni·fy (sĭg′nə fī′) **1** to make known; show by a sign: *By a laugh he signified that he was amused.* **2** to have importance; to matter or count: *Your opinion in this case doesn't signify.* **sig·ni·fied, sig·ni·fy·ing.**

si·gnor (sēn′yôr′) **1** Italian title or form of address, equivalent to Mr. or sir. **2** an Italian gentleman.

si·gno·ra (sēn yôr′ə) **1** Italian title or form of address, equivalent to Mrs. or Madam. **2** an Italian lady.

si·gno·ri·na (sēn′yə rē′nə) **1** Italian title or form of address, equivalent to Miss. **2** an Italian young lady.

sign·post (sīn′pōst′) post having a notice or direction on it.

si·lage (sī′lij) green fodder stored in a silo.

si·lence (sī′ləns) **1** absence of sound or noise; stillness. **2** to cause to be quiet: *to silence an audience.* **si·lenced, si·lenc·ing.**

si·lent (sī′lənt) **1** saying nothing; speechless; making no sound: *He remained silent through the entire movie.* **2** free from sound; quiet; still: *It was a silent evening.* **3** not expressed by sound; not spoken: *a silent approval; a silent command.* **4** written but not pronounced: *The "b" in dumb is silent.* **5** owning a share of business, but taking no active part in managing it: *a silent partner.* **si·lent·ly.**

sil·hou·ette (sĭl′ōō ĕt′) **1** picture of a profile in a solid color, usually black. **2** a shadow: *the cat's dark silhouette on the wall.* **3** to show in outline or silhouette. **sil·hou·et·ted, sil·hou·et·ting.**

sil·i·con (sĭl′ə kən) brown chemical element similar to carbon, found in sand, quartz, and most other rocks. It makes up about one fourth of the earth's crust.

Silhouette

sil·i·cone (sĭl′ə kōn′) any of a group of compounds in which part of the carbon has been replaced by silicon. Silicones resist extreme temperatures. They are used in lubricants, synthetic rubber, and other products.

silk (sĭlk) **1** soft, shiny fiber obtained from the cocoons of silkworms. **2** thread made from the cocoon fibers of silkworms. **3** material, used for clothing, etc., made from this thread. **4** anything having the softness or appearance of silk: *milkweed silk.* **5** of or like silk: *a silk curtain.*

silk·en (sĭl′kən) **1** made of silk. **2** smooth; soft: *the silken speech of the salesman.*

silk·worm (sĭlk′wûrm′) larva or caterpillar form of several kinds of moths. The silkworm spins a soft, fine fiber (silk) to form a cocoon.

silk·y (sĭl′kĭ) soft and smooth like silk: *the silky nose of a horse.* **silk·i·er, silk·i·est; silk·i·ly.**

sill (sĭl) piece or bar of wood, stone, etc., forming the bottom of a door or window opening, or the lowest beam in the frame of a building.

sil·ly (sĭl′ĭ) **1** having little judgment; stupid: *You are silly to believe such a liar.* **2** not sensible; absurd: *He gave a silly answer to a silly question.* **sil·li·er, sil·li·est.**

si·lo (sī′lō) airtight and waterproof cylindrical building for storing green fodder, cornstalks, or the like to be used as cattle feed. **si·los.**

silt (sĭlt) **1** fine particles of earth or sand suspended in or carried by water and left as sediment. **2** to fill or close up with silt.

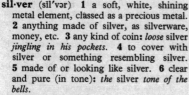

Silo

sil·van (sĭl′vən) sylvan.

sil·ver (sĭl′vər) **1** a soft, white, shining metal element, classed as a precious metal. **2** anything made of silver, as silverware, money, etc. **3** any kind of coin: *loose silver jingling in his pockets.* **4** to cover with silver or something resembling silver. **5** made of or looking like silver. **6** clear and pure (in tone): *the silver tone of the bells.*

sil·ver·smith (sĭl′vər smĭth′) person who makes articles of silver.

sil·ver·ware (sĭl′vər wâr′) articles made of silver or plated with silver, which are especially designed for table use. Knives, forks, bowls, pitchers, etc., are pieces of silverware.

sil·ver·y (sĭl′və rĭ) **1** silver in appearance: *the silvery moonlight.* **2** clear and sweetly ringing: *the silvery tone of a bell.*

sim·i·lar (sĭm′ə lər) alike without being the same: *Pink and rose are similar colors.* **sim·i·lar·ly.**

sim·i·lar·i·ty (sĭm′ə lăr′ə tĭ) likeness; resemblance: *There is a great similarity between John and his younger brother.* **sim·i·lar·i·ties.**

sim·mer (sĭm′ər) **1** to cook or boil gently. **2** to cook in liquid just below the boiling point: *Mother simmered the meat for three hours.* **3** to make a low, gentle, murmuring sound when boiling gently. **4** to be on the verge of breaking out with emotion: *He simmered with rage while the policeman gave him a summons.* **5** a gentle boiling: *to cook the soup at a simmer.*

sim·ple (sĭm′pəl) **1** easy to understand; not complicated: *The machine is so simple a child can run it.* **2** plain; unadorned; bare: *We ate a very simple meal. He told the simple truth.* **3** straightforward; not pretending: *The great man had a simple manner.* **4** lowly or humble; ordinary: *His neighbors are simple people working hard to make ends meet.* **5** foolish; unsophisticated: *You must think me very simple if you expect me to believe that.* **sim·pler, sim·plest.**

sim·ple·ton (sĭm′pəl tən) person who is easily fooled or silly.

sim·plic·i·ty (sĭm plĭs′ə tĭ) **1** the quality of being easily understood; lack of complexity: *the simplicity of language.* **2** naturalness; artlessness: *the charming simplicity of a child.* **3** lack of showiness: *the neat simplicity of her dress.* **4** freedom from guile; directness: *his simplicity of dealing.* **5** lack of common sense or shrewdness.

sim·pli·fy (sĭm′plə fī′) to make something clearer, plainer, or easier: *to simplify a question.* **sim·pli·fied, sim·pli·fy·ing.**

sim·ply (sĭm′plĭ) **1** in a clear and plain way: *Dr. Barnes presented his talk very simply.* **2** without show or adornment: *Dad always dresses simply when he goes to the office.* **3** just; merely; only: *His reply was simply one of ignorance.*

si·mul·ta·ne·ous (sī′məl tā′nĭ əs or sĭm′-əl tā′nĭ əs) occurring at the same time: *Their arrivals by sea and air were simultaneous.* **si·mul·ta·ne·ous·ly.**

sin (sĭn) **1** to break God's laws in thought or act. **2** any act of wrongdoing, such as stealing, telling a lie, or harming anyone on purpose. **sinned, sin·ning.**

since (sĭns) **1** from a certain date or time in the past until now: *Joan visited us at Easter and hasn't been back since.* **2** some

---

fāte, făt, fâre, fär; bē, bĕt; bīte, bĭt; nō, nŏt, nôr; fūse, fŭn, fûr; tōō, tŏŏk; foil; foul; thin; then; hw for wh as in *what*; zh for s as in u*su*al; ə for a, e, i, o, u, as in *a*go, lin*e*n, per*i*l, at*o*m, min*u*s

time after a past event and before now: *They did live here then but have since moved away.* **3** ago; before now: *Bonnets have long* since *been out of fashion.* **4** because: *I will feed the cattle* since *you are leaving.* **5** from and after a time when: *I have not seen him* since *that happened.* **6** from the time of; during the time after: *Fred has not visited us* since *Easter.*

sin·cere (sĭn sĭr′) really meaning what one says or does; honest; straightforward; truthful: *His praise was* sincere *and not mere flattery.* **sin·cer·er, sin·cer·est; sin·cere·ly.**

sin·cer·i·ty (sĭn sĕr′ə tĭ) freedom from pretense; truthfulness; genuineness of character; honesty: *Although I do not agree with you, I do not doubt your* sincerity.

sin·ew (sĭn′ū) **1** strong cord that joins a muscle to a bone. **2** a means of supplying strength or power: *Money, men, and materials are the* sinews *of war.*

sin·ew·y (sĭn′ū ĭ) **1** of meat, having many sinews; tough; stringy. **2** strong and vigorous; muscular.

sin·ful (sĭn′fəl) **1** guilty of many sins: *a* sinful *man.* **2** wicked; wrong: *Murder is* sinful. **sin·ful·ly.**

sing (sĭng) **1** to use the voice to make musical sounds: *Do you like to* sing? **2** to utter (words) with musical tones: *to sing a lullaby.* **3** to make a whistling, humming sound: *The kettle is* singing. **4** to talk about enthusiastically; extol: *He is always* singing *her praises.* **5** to intone; chant: *to* sing *the Mass.* **6** to lull by singing: *to sing a child to sleep.* **7** to tell in a song or poetry: *Homer sang of the Trojan war.*

sing out to call loudly; shout: *to* sing out *orders.*

sang, sung, sing·ing.

singe (sĭnj) **1** to burn slightly; scorch: *The hot iron* singed *my dress.* **2** to remove feathers, bristles, fluff, etc., by scorching: *to* singe *a duck before cooking it.* **3** a slight burn. **singed, singe·ing.**

sing·er (sĭng′ər) person or bird that sings.

sin·gle (sĭng′gəl) **1** only one; one and no more: *a* single *ticket to the theater.* **2** unmarried: *a* single *woman.* **3** for the use of one person only: *a* single *bed; a* single *room.* **4** performed by one person on each side: *in* single *combat.* **5** of flowers, having

one set of petals: *A wild rose has* single *petals.* **6 singles** a game, such as tennis, when it is played with only one player on each side: *They played* singles *at handball.*

single out to choose from among others: *The teacher* singled out *his work for special praise.*

sin·gled, sin·gling.

sin·gle-hand·ed (sĭng′gəl hăn′dĭd) without help from others; done by one person: *The policeman made a* single-handed *stand against the mob.* **sin·gle-hand·ed·ly.**

sin·gly (sĭng′glĭ) **1** one by one; one at a time; separately: *Let's take up the matters* singly. **2** in a single-handed manner; without help: *He was* singly *responsible for the success of the party.*

sin·gu·lar (sĭng′gyŏŏ lər) **1** rare; unusual; noteworthy; exceptional: *a* singular *example of courage.* **2** odd; eccentric; peculiar: *a person of* singular *habits.* **3** in grammar, relating to a single person or thing. **sin·gu·lar·ly.**

sin·is·ter (sĭn′ĭs tər) **1** showing ill will; expressing evil intentions: *a* sinister *glance.* **2** wicked; dishonest; corrupt: *A* sinister *gang of hoodlums terrorized the city.* **sin·is·ter·ly.**

sink (sĭngk) **1** to fall or become lower slowly and gradually; descend little by little: *The sun is* sinking *in the west.* **2** to become submerged in water: *The boat sank within sight of land.* **3** to cause to submerge: *The submarine sank the battleship.* **4** to excavate downward: *to* sink *a well; to* sink *a shaft.* **5** to lower; degrade in character: *to* sink *to the level of the gutter.* **6** to invest (money): *He* sank *everything in the stock market.* **7** to fail; become increasingly and dangerously ill: *The patient is* sinking *rapidly.* **8** a basin of porcelain, metal, etc., with a drain, used for washing dishes, etc. **sank** or **sunk, sunk, sink·ing.**

sin·ner (sĭn′ər) person who sins; offender or wrongdoer.

si·nus (sī′nəs) a hollow in a bone or soft tissue, especially one of several such hollows in the bones of the skull that connect with the nose.

sip (sĭp) **1** to drink a very little at a time; drink little by little: *to* sip *tea.* **2** small quantity of liquid; a little taste. **sipped, sip·ping.**

si·phon (sī′fən) **1** a bent tube or pipe which carries a liquid over a higher point. **2** bottle from which a stream of liquid may be forced by pressure of a gas. **3** to draw off with a siphon: *Oscar siphoned the gasoline out of the tank.*

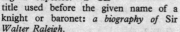

Siphon

sir (sûr) **1** polite form of address for a stranger, friend, or equal, or as a term of respect in addressing a superior. **2 Sir** title used before the given name of a knight or baronet: *a biography of* Sir *Walter Raleigh.*

sire (sīr) **1** father or male ancestor. **2** the male parent of animals. **3** to be the father of: *This stallion* sired *a champion race horse.* **4 Sire** title of respect used when addressing a king or ruler. **sired, sir·ing.**

si·ren (sī′rən) **1** device for making a loud or high sound that carries or penetrates: *an air raid* siren; *an ambulance* siren. **2** in Greek mythology, a creature who lured sailors to their destruction on the rocks by her singing. **3** bewitching or captivating woman. **4** dangerously fascinating; bewitching: *lured by siren voices.*

Sir·i·us (sīr′ĭ əs) the brightest star in the sky.

sir·up (sīr′əp or sûr′əp) syrup.

si·sal (sī′səl or sĭs′əl) **1** strong, white fiber of a cactuslike plant, used for making cord or rope. **2** plant from which this fiber comes.

sis·sy (sĭs′ĭ) shy, timid boy. **sis·sies.**

sis·ter (sĭs′tər) **1** girl or woman who has the same parents as another person. **2** woman or girl who is a very close friend: *She has been a* sister *to me.* **3** woman who is a member of a religious community. **4 sister ships** two ships having the same design.

sis·ter-in-law (sĭs′tər in lô′) **1** sister of one's husband or wife. **2** wife of one's brother. **sis·ters-in-law.**

sit (sĭt) **1** to rest one's weight on the lower part of the body; use a seat; be seated. **2** to be situated: *The island* sits *in the harbor.* **3** to press or weigh: *Your duties* sit *lightly on your shoulders.* **4** to pose or model: *to* sit *for a portrait.* **5** to have or keep a seat upon: *He* sits *his horse very badly.* **6** to perch or roost: *The robin is* sitting *on the branch.* **7** to cover eggs in order to hatch: *My old hen isn't* sitting *this year.* **8** to be in session: *The court will* sit *next week.* **9** to fit or suit: *Your jacket does not* sit *well in the shoulders.*

sit in to participate; take part in: *I'd like you to* sit in *on this conference.*

sit on 1 to meet in judgment on: *The board of directors is* sitting on *that issue at this moment.* **2** to be a member of in order to investigate and judge: *to* sit on *a jury.*

sit out 1 to remain seated during: *Betty* sat out *three dances with Frank.* **2** to endure; wait through: *We* sat out *the storm.* **3** to stay later than (another): *We* sat out *the other guests.*

sit up 1 to raise the body to an erect sitting position: *to* sit up *in bed; to* sit up *straight.* **2** to take notice; pay attention: *Janet's engagement made everyone* sit up. **3** to stay up past one's usual bedtime: *We let the children* sit up *on Christmas Eve.* **sat, sit·ting.**

site (sīt) **1** place where something is or was located: *the* site *of the battle.* **2** area set aside for a particular purpose: *the building* site. (Homonyms: cite, sight)

sit·ting (sĭt′ĭng) **1** session or meeting of a court, legislature, etc. **2** period of posing or act of posing: *The artist scheduled Helen's* sitting *for late afternoon.* **3** group of eggs for hatching. **4 at one sitting** at one time; without a break: *I finished writing this story at one* sitting.

sitting room living room; parlor.

sit·u·at·ed (sĭch′ōō ā′tĭd or sĭt′ū ā′tĭd) placed; located: *The chapel is* situated *on the hillside.*

sit·u·a·tion (sĭch′ōō ā′shən or sĭt′ū ā′shən) **1** place; location. **2** circumstances; state of affairs: *an amusing* situation; *an embarrassing* situation. **3** job; position.

six (sĭks) amount or quantity that is one greater than five; 6.

six·pence (sĭks′pəns) small silver coin worth six British pennies or half a shilling.

---

fāte, făt, fâre, fär; bē, bĕt; bīte, bĭt; nō, nŏt, nôr; fūse, fŭn, fûr; tōō, tŏŏk; foil; foul; thin; ~~then~~; hw for wh as in *wh*at; zh for s as in u*s*ual; ə for a, e, i, o, u, as in *a*go, linen, peril, atom, minus

six·teen (sĭks'tēn') amount or quantity that is one greater than 15; 16.

six·teenth (sĭks'tēnth') 1 next after 15th; 16th. 2 one of 16 equal parts.

sixth (sĭksth) 1 next after fifth; 6th. 2 one of six equal parts.

six·ti·eth (sĭks'tĭ ĭth) 1 next after 59th; 60th. 2 one of 60 equal parts.

six·ty (sĭks'tĭ) amount or quantity that is one greater than 59; 60. **six·ties.**

¹size (sīz) 1 amount of height, width, or thickness of a thing; measurements; dimensions: *the* size *of a room.* 2 largeness or smallness; bulk: *Notice the* size *of that spider.* 3 a measure showing how large something is: *Baby's shoe* size *changes quickly.* 4 to sort or arrange according to size.

size up to form an estimate or opinion of: *Janice sized up people as soon as she met them, often wrongly.*

sized, siz·ing. [¹size is a shortened form of the English word (assize) originally meaning "that which is fixed."]

²size (sīz) 1 any of various thin pastes or glues used to glaze paper, cloth, walls, etc., or make them heavier. 2 to cover or treat with this type of paste or glue. **sized, siz·ing.** [²size is from a French word (assise) meaning "a layer."]

siz·zle (sĭz'əl) 1 to make a hissing sound, as grease in a very hot frying pan. 2 a hissing sound. **siz·zled, siz·zling.**

¹skate (skāt) 1 flat-edged blade or runner fixed on or clamped to the sole of a shoe, for gliding over ice. 2 plate with wheels that is attached to the shoe for gliding over a surface: *a roller skate.* 3 to glide on skates. **skat·ed, skat·ing.** [¹skate is a form of the earlier word "skates" which comes through the Dutch (schaats) from an Old French word (esca-che) meaning "stilt."]

²skate (skāt) fish with a flat body in the shape of a fan; a ray. It has a whiplike tail. [²skate comes from an Old Norse word (skata) perhaps from Latin (squatus), "a flat fish."]

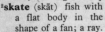

Barndoor skate, about 5 ft. long

skat·er (skā'tər) 1 person who skates. 2 a spiderlike water insect.

skein (skān) quantity of thread or yarn wound in a loose coil.

skel·e·ton (skĕl'ə tən) 1 the body framework of an animal, especially an animal with a backbone; the bones of a body fitted together after the flesh has decayed away or been removed: *a dinosaur* skeleton. 2 the supporting framework for a building or ship. 3 a very thin, lean person or animal: *Her illness reduced her to a mere* skeleton. 4 the first outline or idea for something: *a skeleton for a play.* For picture, see **spine.**

sketch (skĕch) 1 a drawing quickly made. 2 short, brief description or account of something. 3 to draw or describe quickly: *to sketch a kitten.* 4 to make sketches: *He sketched in the country all summer.*

sketch·y (skĕch'ĭ) done roughly and without care or detail; incomplete; inadequate: *a sketchy plan.* **sketch·i·er, sketch·i·est; sketch·i·ly.**

ski (skē) 1 one of a pair of long, narrow strips of wood, metal, or plastic, strapped to the boots, for moving over snow. 2 to move over snow on skis. **skis** or **ski; skied, ski·ing.**

skid (skĭd) 1 to slip or slide sideways while moving: *The car* skidded *in turning the corner.* 2 of a wheel, to slide without turning. 3 a wedge or drag used to check the motion of a wheel. 4 rail, often one of a pair, sometimes greased, on which heavy weights may be slid. 5 a slipping or sliding sideways: *a skid on the ice.* **skid·ded, skid·ding.**

skies (skīz) See **sky.**

skiff (skĭf) small light boat, usually for a single rower.

skill (skĭl) 1 ability to do something well and expertly as a result of training, practice, or experience: *his skill in fencing.* 2 an art; an accomplishment: *to teach arithmetic skills.*

skilled (skĭld) experienced; trained; expert; possessing or showing skill: *an example of skilled work.*

skil·let (skĭl'ĭt) frying pan; shallow cooking vessel with a projecting handle, used for frying.

Skillet

skill·ful or **skil·ful** (skĭl'fəl) having or showing the ability to do something well; adept. **skill·ful·ly** or **skil·ful·ly.**

skim (skĭm) **1** to remove from the surface of a liquid: *to skim the cream off milk.* **2** to remove something from the surface of: *to skim soup.* **3** to move swiftly and lightly (over a surface, barely touching): *A gull skims over the water.* **4** to read or look through quickly or carelessly; skip: *to skim a book.* **skimmed, skim·ming.**

skim milk milk from which the cream has been removed.

skimp·y (skĭm'pĭ) scanty; inadequate: *I had a very skimpy breakfast.* **skimp·i·er, skimp·i·est; skimp·i·ly.**

skin (skĭn) **1** outer covering of the body in man and animals. **2** pelt or hide of an animal after it is removed from the body: *a rug made of the skin of a tiger.* **3** rind of a fruit: *orange skin; banana skin.* **4** container made of skin for liquids such as wine or water. **5** to remove the complete covering of an animal or bird from the body: *to skin a rabbit.* **6** to scrape: *to skin one's knee in a fall.* **7 have a thick skin** to be insensitive; to be difficult to hurt by rebuke, criticism, or unkindness. **8 have a thin skin** to be sensitive; to be easily hurt by rebuke, unkindness, or criticism. **9 mere skin and bones** extremely thin or skinny. **10 save one's skin** to escape with one's life. **11 the skin of one's teeth** a narrow margin: *He escaped by the skin of his teeth.* **skinned, skin·ning.**

skin-deep (skĭn'dēp') **1** on the surface of the skin: *a skin-deep cut.* **2** shallow; superficial: *a beauty only skin-deep.*

skin diver a diver whose only equipment is an air tank carried on the back, connected to a protective mask.

skin·flint (skĭn'flĭnt') person who hates to part with his money; miser.

skin·ny (skĭn'ĭ) very thin; without much flesh. **skin·ni·er, skin·ni·est.**

skip (skĭp) **1** to jump or leap lightly and quickly; spring: *to skip out of the way of a car.* **2** to jump lightly over (a rope): *to skip rope.* **3** to leave out; pass over: *He always skips the preface to a book. Lucy* skipped *from the third to the fifth grade.* **4** to run away; escape. **5** gay, dancing walk with light hops on alternate feet: *The girls went down the street at a skip.* **6** to go along hopping on alternate feet. **skipped, skip·ping.**

skip·per (skĭp'ər) captain of a ship.

skir·mish (skûr'mĭsh) **1** a brief fight between small groups of persons, or small detachments of armies or fleets. **2** any slight struggle or encounter. **3** to take part in a brief fight or encounter.

skirt (skûrt) **1** girl's or woman's garment that hangs from the waist. **2** the lower part of a dress, coat, or other garment. **3** to move along the edge of a place or group of people: *to skirt the crowd.*

skit (skĭt) short piece of humorous writing, especially one for the stage.

skulk (skŭlk) **1** to hide or stay out of sight through cowardice or to avoid duties or dangers: *Tom skulked in the barn to avoid punishment.* **2** to move stealthily; to sneak about with an evil purpose: *The fox was skulking in the grass, not far from the hens.*

skull (skŭl) **1** bones of the head taken as a whole. **2 thick skull** stupidity; slowness in understanding. (Homonym: scull)

skull·cap (skŭl'kăp') a close-fitting cap without a brim.

skunk (skŭngk) **1** black and white striped animal with a bushy tail. A skunk protects itself with a spray of strong, choking scent. **2** the fur of this animal.

Skunk, about 3 ft. long

sky (skī) **1** the upper air or heavens; space above the earth; the arch that seems to be above the world: *a cloudy sky.* **2 out of a clear sky** suddenly; unexpectedly. **skies.**

sky·lark (skī'lärk') **1** small European bird, nesting on the ground, and noted for its sweet, continuous song as it flies up into the sky. **2** to frolic: *The children* skylarked *on Halloween.*

Skylight

sky·light (skī'līt') window in a roof or ceiling.

fāte, făt, fâre, fär; bē, bĕt; bīte, bĭt; nō, nŏt, nôr; fūse, fŭn, fûr; tōō, tŏŏk; foil; foul; thin; then; hw for wh as in what; zh for s as in usual; ə for a, e, i, o, u, as in ago, linen, peril, atom, minus

667

sky·line (skī'līn') **1** the line where the sky seems to meet land or water; horizon. **2** outline of buildings, trees, etc., against the sky: *From the ship they could see the skyline of the city.*

sky·rock·et (skī'rŏk'ĭt) **1** small rocket that explodes high in the air with a shower of colored sparks, stars, etc. **2** to rise with great speed: *She skyrocketed to fame.*

sky·scrap·er (skī'skrā'pər) very tall building.

sky·writ·ing (skī'rī'tĭng) **1** the tracing of words or messages in the sky by means of smoke or vapor released from an airplane. **2** message left in this way.

slab (slăb) thick, flat piece: *a slab of stone; a slab of bread.*

slack (slăk) **1** loose; relaxed; not tight: *a slack rope.* **2** slow: *a slack current in a stream.* **3** not busy; dull; inactive: *a slack time of day.* **4** careless; slipshod: *a slack student.* **5** that part of something that is not stretched tight: *the slack in a rope.* **slack off** to slacken. **slack·ly.**

slack·en (slăk'ən) **1** to make slower: *to slacken speed at a crossroads.* **2** to loosen: *to slacken a taut rope.* **3** to become loose; relax: *The wire slackened under its own weight.* **4** to lessen: *My energy slackens in the afternoon.*

slacks (slăks) trousers for casual wear.

slag (slăg) waste rock left over from the smelting of an ore. The slag is taken from the furnace as a liquid and allowed to cool and harden.

slain (slān) See **slay.** *Goliath was slain by David.*

slake (slāk) **1** to relieve; quench; satisfy: *Water will slake your thirst.* **2** to mix (lime) with water. **slaked, slak·ing.**

slam (slăm) **1** to shut with violence and noise: *to slam a door.* **2** to hit or throw with violence and noise: *He slammed the book down on the desk.* **3** to close with a bang: *The gate slammed in the wind.* **4** noisy blow; a bang: *I heard a slam and thought someone had come in the house.* **slammed, slam·ming.**

slan·der (slăn'dər) **1** false report made with malice to hurt a person's reputation: *The slander almost ruined the politician's career.* **2** to make a false report damaging

to a person's character or reputation: *They slandered him when they accused him wrongly of theft.*

slang (slăng) **1** words or phrases in common use but not yet accepted by the majority of people of good taste. **2** the special expressions used by a particular group of people: *Sailors have a colorful slang of their own.*

slant (slănt) **1** a turning from the level; an angle; a tilt; a slope: *The roof has a slight slant.* **2** to put on a slope or at an angle: *to slant a board to make a slide.* **3** to be on a slope, at an angle, or in a tilted position: *The land slants northward.* **4** attitude; point of view; bias: *We need a new slant on this problem.* **5** to present from a certain point of view; bias: *to slant the news.*

slap (slăp) **1** a blow, particularly with the open hand. **2** to hit with such a blow. **3** an insult. **4** to throw or place noisily or carelessly: *He slapped the books down on the desk. She slapped her papers together hurriedly.* **slapped, slap·ping.**

slap·stick (slăp'stĭk') **1** a form of comedy that uses exaggerated movements, pie-throwing, etc. **2** having to do with this kind of comedy: *a slapstick movie.*

slash (slăsh) **1** to cut with a sweeping motion: *He slashed the tall weeds with a scythe.* **2** a sweeping stroke. **3** to lash out wildly with, or as with, a sword or knife: *The pirates slashed at each other.* **4** a long cut; gash. **5** to reduce in a drastic manner: *The council slashed the mayor's budget.*

slat (slăt) thin, narrow strip of wood or metal: *the slat of a shutter.*

slate (slāt) **1** hard, blue-gray rock that splits into thin, smooth layers. **2** thin layer of this rock, used for roofing, blackboards, etc. **3** to cover with this rock: *to slate a roof.* **4** dark blue-gray color. **5** a list of candidates for election. **6** to choose; assign to a job: *She was slated to wash dishes tonight.* **7** **clean slate** report or record without marks against a person **slat·ed, slat·ing.**

slaugh·ter (slô'tər) **1** the killing of an animal for food. **2** to kill for food. **3** brutal, violent killing; massacre. **4** to kill brutally and violently, often in large numbers.

slaugh·ter·house (slô'tər hous') place where animals are butchered for the markets.

slave (slāv) **1** person who is owned by or completely under the control of someone else. **2** person who is under the control of some impelling influence: *a slave to fashion; a* slave *to a habit.* **3** a drudge; someone who works hard and long over his work: *a* slave *to his job.* **4** to work hard and long. **5** having to do with a slave: *a* slave *market.* **slaved, slav·ing.**

slav·er·y (slā′və rĭ) **1** a being a slave; bondage: *He was sold into* slavery. **2** the practice of buying, selling, and owning slaves: *Abraham Lincoln helped end* slavery *in America.* **3** long, hard work that is poorly paid. **4** state of being under some control or influence: *her* slavery *to fashion.*

slav·ish (slā′vĭsh) **1** befitting a slave; mean; base: *a* slavish *job.* **2** not original; imitating blindly: *a* slavish *repeating of what someone else has said.* **slav·ish·ly.**

slay (slā) to kill by violent means. **slew, slain, slay·ing.**
(Homonym: sleigh)

sled (slĕd) **1** vehicle on low runners, either for coasting or for moving heavy loads.
Sled
2 to travel or be carried on a sled. **sled·ded, sled·ding.**

¹sledge (slĕj) sled; sleigh. [¹sledge seems to come from an early Dutch word (sleedse) of the same meaning.]

²sledge (slĕj) hammer weighing four to sixteen pounds, used for driving posts, breaking up pavement, etc. Also called **sledge hammer.** [²sledge is a form of an Old English word (slĕcg) of the same meaning.]
Sledge

sleek (slēk) **1** smooth; glossy: *her* sleek *hair.* **2** well-fed; well-groomed: *a* sleek *cat.* **3** to make smooth or glossy. **sleek·ly.**

sleep (slēp) **1** rest of mind and body; state of not being awake. **2** to be or continue to be asleep; to have the ordinary activity of the mind and body at rest: *A baby* sleeps *most of the time.* **3** a state resembling sleep: *the* sleep *of death; the* sleep *of a hibernating*

bear. **4** to be in a state that resembles sleep; remain inactive: *The town* slept. **5** to provide with accommodation for sleeping: *This room can* sleep *four.*

sleep away to waste, pass, or spend in sleeping or in doing nothing: *On awaking that evening, Jane discovered she had* slept away *the whole day.*

sleep off to get rid of in sleep: *I can usually* sleep off *a headache.*

sleep on to postpone a decision to think about something: *Before you act on this scheme,* sleep on *it for a night or two.* **slept, sleep·ing.**

sleep·er (slē′pər) **1** person who sleeps: *I'm a light* sleeper. **2** railroad car with arrangements for sleeping: *to take the* sleeper *for Chicago.*

sleep·less (slēp′lĭs) **1** without sleep: *a* sleepless *night.* **2** constantly active; restless: *the* sleepless *sea.* **sleep·less·ly.**

sleep·y (slē′pĭ) **1** drowsy; ready for sleep. **2** inactive: *a* sleepy *village.* **sleep·i·er, sleep·i·est; sleep·i·ly.**

sleet (slēt) **1** frozen or partially frozen rain. **2** to fall from the air as frozen or partially frozen rain.

sleeve (slēv) **1** that part of a garment which covers the arm. **2 have (something) up one's sleeve** to have some decision, fact, or plan ready for use when needed: *He is looking so sly he must* have something up his sleeve. **3 laugh up one's sleeve** to be secretly amused.

sleeve·less (slēv′lĭs) without sleeves, as a vest.

sleigh (slā) **1** vehicle on runners, used on snow or ice. **2** to travel by or ride in a sleigh. (Homonym: slay)
Sleigh

slen·der (slĕn′dər) **1** slim; thin: *a* slender *figure; a* slender *vase.* **2** weak; meager; slight: *a* slender *possibility; a* slender *income.* **slen·der·ly.**

slept (slĕpt) See **sleep.** *After the examination, John* slept *for two days.*

sleuth (slōŏth) a detective.

---

fāte, făt, fâre, fär; bē, bĕt; bīte, bĭt; nō, nŏt, nôr; fūse, fŭn, fûr; tōō, tŏŏk; foil; foul; thin; ~~then~~; hw for wh as in *wh*at; zh for s as in u*s*ual; ə for a, e, i, o, u, as in *a*go, lin*e*n, per*i*l, at*o*m, min*u*s

669

¹slew (slōō) See **slay.** *David* slew *Goliath.*
[**¹slew** is a form of **slay.**]

²slew (slōō) a great number; a lot of: *Jimmy
has a* slew *of marbles.* [**²slew** seems to be
from an Irish, that is Celtic, word (sluagh)
meaning "a large crowd."]

slice (slīs) **1** flat section cut from something:
a slice *of bread.* **2** to cut in flat pieces: *to*
slice *a roast; to* slice *the watermelon.* **sliced,
slic·ing.**

slick (slik) **1** smooth; glossy. **2** to smooth
down; make glossy: *to* slick *down hair.*
3 smooth and silky in speech and manner;
tricky: *The salesman was so* slick *that I
bought twice as much as I wanted.* **4** slippery: *The streets were* slick *with ice.*
slick·ly.

slick·er (slik′ər) long, loose waterproof
coat made of oiled or varnished cloth.

slid (slid) See **slide.** *Jimmy* slid *down the
banister.*

slide (slīd) **1** to move smoothly along on a
surface. **2** to cause to move smoothly: *to*
slide *a drawer into a chest.* **3** a smooth
move; glide. **4** any smooth surface, either
flat or sloping, on which one may slide: *a*
slide *in a playground.* **5** to move quietly or
without being seen: *The cat* slid *back into
the room after it had been put out for the
night.* **6** to pass gradually: *The days* slid
by during vacation. **7** piece of glass on
which one puts objects to examine them
under a microscope. **8** transparent picture
that can be projected on a screen. **9** a mass
of earth, rock, snow, etc., that falls down a
steep slope; avalanche: *The rock* slide
blocked the highway. **10 let slide** to let go
by; postpone.
slide over to pass over quickly.
slid, slid·ing.

slight (slīt) **1** slender; thin: *a* slight *girl.*
2 not important; small: *a* slight *error.*
3 frail; not strong: *a* slight *hope.* **4** snub;
insolent indifference; a show of disrespect
or neglect: *Helen took her hostess' patroniz-
ing treatment before the guests as a studied*
slight. **5** to insult: *Dotty felt* slighted *when
she didn't get an invitation.* **6** to pay little
attention to: *Jack's football practice caused
him to* slight *his studies.*

slight·ly (slīt′lĭ) **1** to a small or unimportant degree: *I am* slightly *ill.* **2** slen-
derly: *She is very* slightly *built.*

slim (slim) **1** slender; thin: *a* slim *figure.*
2 scant; insufficient: *a* slim *excuse.* **slim·
mer, slim·mest; slim·ly.**

slime (slīm) **1** soft, slippery mud. **2** any
sticky, slippery, or unpleasant substance;
filth. **3** sticky substance given off by certain plants or animals such as snails.

slim·y (slī′mĭ) **1** sticky; slippery; covered
with or oozing slime. **2** unpleasant; foul.
slim·i·er, slim·i·est; slim·i·ly.

sling (sling) **1** device of ropes and hooks
for raising and lowering heavy objects.
2 strap for supporting
a gun. **3** a bandage
to support an injured
arm. **4** piece of
leather between two
thongs, from which a
stone may be thrown.
5 to throw with a
swinging motion of
the arm; hurl; fling: *Amos* slung *a stone
over the wall.* **6** to put or place with a
swinging motion: *Albert* slung *the rifle over
his shoulder.* **7** to hang or raise by means of
a sling. **slung, sling·ing.**

Slings

sling·shot (sling′shŏt′) a stick in the shape
of a "Y" with a rubber band tied to its
pointed ends, for shooting stones and
other small objects.

slink (slingk) to go furtively; sneak or steal
along, often in a guilty manner: *The tiger*
slinks *silently through the tall grass.* **slunk,
slink·ing.**

¹slip (slip) **1** to slide; glide: *The sleigh*
slipped *along over the snow.* **2** to lose one's
foothold: *He* slipped *on a banana peel.* *The
car* slipped *sidewise on the icy road.* **3** to
escape from control: *The ax* slipped *and cut
my foot.* **4** to pass unnoticed: *Days, weeks,
months* slipped *by.* **5** to escape one's
memory: *Your name has* slipped *my mind.*
6 to put in easily: *to* slip *a key into a lock.*
7 a place between wharves for a ship to
enter. **8** any involuntary small error: *a* slip
of the tongue; a slip *of the hand; a* slip *in a
person's plans.* **9** to put on or off easily: *to*
slip *on one's coat.* **10** a woman's dresslike
undergarment. **11 give the slip** to escape:
The thief gave *the police the* slip. **slipped,
slip·ping.** [**¹slip** comes from an earlier
English word (slippen) of the same
meaning.]

slip   slow

²**slip** (slĭp) **1** a small piece; strip: *a slip of paper.* **2** a printed form: *a sales* slip; *a laundry* slip. **3** a plant cutting intended to be planted. [²**slip** comes from a Medieval Dutch word (slippen) meaning "to cut on a slant."]

slip·per (slĭp′ər) **1** low, easy shoe for house wear. **2** girl's or woman's light party shoe: *Cinderella had glass slippers.*

slip·per·y (slĭp′ə rĭ) **1** difficult to hold or stand on because of smoothness, grease, or slime: *as slippery as an eel; a slippery sidewalk.* **2** tricky, not trustworthy; skillful at getting out of trouble: *Job is such a slippery fellow you never know whether to believe him or not.* **slip·per·i·er, slip·per·i·est.**

slip·shod (slĭp′shŏd′) careless; sloppy; slovenly: *a slipshod way of dressing;* slipshod *work;* slipshod *manners.*

slit (slĭt) **1** long, narrow cut or opening: *The pupil of the cat's eye narrowed into a slit when it came into the light.* **2** to make a straight, narrow cut or slot in: *to slit cloth to make a fringe; to slit a box cover so that coins may be dropped in.* **slit, slit·ting.**

sliv·er (slĭv′ər) **1** small, slender sharp-pointed piece of wood, glass, etc.; a splinter. **2** to split or be split into slender fragments: *Lightning slivered the sturdy old oak.*

sloe (slō) **1** a purplish, oval, plumlike fruit. **2** the plant that bears this fruit. **3** any of various wild plums. (Homonym: slow)

slo·gan (slō′gən) **1** motto, phrase, jingle, or the like, intended by frequent repetition to impress the hearer or reader: *"All the news that's fit to print," is a famous newspaper slogan.* **2** a battle cry.

sloop (slōōp) a kind of sailing ship with a single mast, and the mainsail on a boom pointed aft.

slop (slŏp) **1** to spill in splashes: *Milk slopped from Roy's pail as he walked*

Sloop

along. **2** to splash: *The baby slopped milk on the floor.* **3** to walk with splashes through water or mud: *We slopped through the rain.* **4** watery waste, garbage, etc. **slopped, slop·ping.**

slope (slōp) **1** any line or surface that slants upward or downward: *The village is on the eastern slope of the mountain.* **2** to slant: *The land slopes upward from the river.* **3** to cause to slant: *to slope a roof.* **4** amount of slant: *The land rises in a gentle slope.* **sloped, slop·ing.**

slop·py (slŏp′ĭ) **1** wet; rainy: *the sloppy weather this spring.* **2** muddy; filled with slush: *the sloppy sidewalks.* **3** careless; slovenly: *a piece of sloppy work;* sloppy *clothes.* **slop·pi·er, slop·pi·est; slop·pi·ly.**

slosh (slŏsh) to splash about; flounder; wallow: *We sloshed through the mud and slush of the country road.*

slot (slŏt) **1** straight, narrow groove: *The curtain rings slide back and forth in a slot.* **2** straight, narrow opening; slit: *a mail slot in a door; a coin slot in a vending machine.*

sloth (slŏth or slôth) **1** extreme laziness; dislike of effort. **2** a slow-moving South American animal that lives in trees, hanging upside down from a limb.

Two-toed sloth, about 2 ft. long

sloth·ful (slŏth′fəl or slôth′fəl) very lazy; slow to act. **sloth·ful·ly.**

slouch (slouch) **1** to act with slow, loose-jointed movements; shamble: *Leon slouched lazily to school. Marie slouched wearily into a chair.* **2** person who habitually acts in this manner. **3** a drooping, loose-jointed posture: *to walk with a slouch.*

slov·en·ly (slŭv′ən lĭ) slipshod; sloppy; untidy; not neat. **slov·en·li·er, slov·en·li·est.**

slow (slō) **1** not quick; moving, acting, or progressing with little speed; sluggish: *the slow passing of the hours; the slow progress of a snail.* **2** not up to normal speed: *a moving picture in* slow *motion.* **3** behind

---

fāte, făt, fâre, fär; bē, bĕt; bīte, bĭt; nō, nŏt, nôr; fūse, fŭn, fûr; tōō, tŏŏk; foil; foul; thin; ~~then~~; hw for wh as in *wh*at; zh for s as in u*s*ual; ə for a, e, i, o, u, as in *a*go, lin*e*n, per*i*l, at*o*m, min*u*s

time: *The clock is ten minutes* slow. **4** not quick to understand; dull-witted: *a* slow *pupil.* **5** slowly: *to go* slow. **6** to cause to move slowly or more slowly; hinder: *He* slowed *up work.*

slow down or **up** to reduce speed: *to* slow down *when driving near a school.*

slow·ly. (Homonym: sloe)

¹slug (slŭg) **1** a kind of snail that has no shell. **2** caterpillar that looks like this animal. **3** small lump or disk of metal. [**¹slug** comes from a Medieval English word (slugge) mean- Slug, 2 to 4 in. long ing "a slow or clumsy person, a sluggard."]

²slug (slŭg) to strike heavily with the fist or with a weapon: *The thief* slugged *his victim with his revolver butt.* **slugged, slug·ging.** [**²slug** is a word of uncertain origin.]

slug·gard (slŭg′ərd) person who is habitually lazy and listless; one who thinks or acts slowly and unwillingly; idler.

slug·gish (slŭg′ĭsh) **1** slow moving: *a* sluggish *river.* **2** slow thinking or acting; indolent: *a* sluggish *brain.* **3** not working with normal efficiency: *a* sluggish *motor; a* sluggish *sink.* **slug·gish·ly.**

sluice (slōōs) **1** channel or trough for directing the flow of water. **2** an overflow channel. **3** a dam and water gate, or the gate alone, for regulating the flow of water. **4** to draw off water with a sluice. **5** to throw water on: *Otis* sluiced *the campfire.* **6** to wash in or with running water. **sluiced, sluic·ing.**

Sluice and sluice gate of irrigation canal

slum (slŭm) poor or run-down section of a town, marked by bad living conditions.

slum·ber (slŭm′bər) **1** to sleep. **2** state of rest, calm, or inactivity: *His* slumber *was not disturbed by the noise.* **3** to be quiet, calm, or inactive: *His plans for the job* slumbered *during vacation.*

slump (slŭmp) **1** to sink or fall heavily: *Maude* slumped *to the floor in a faint.* **2** a falling, sagging, or dropping: *a* slump *to*

the floor. **3** heavy decline in sales or prices: *Business was in a* slump *during the depression.*

slung (slŭng) See **sling.** *They* slung *the packs on their backs and marched off.*

slunk (slŭngk) See **slink.** *The cat* slunk *slowly toward the bird.*

slur (slûr) **1** to pass over rapidly, quickly, or lightly: *The congressman* slurred *over the facts to make his point.* **2** to pronounce words or syllables so indistinctly as not to be understood: *He* slurred *his speech so badly that we could not understand him.* **3** indistinct pronunciation: *to speak with a* slur. **4** anything harmful to a person's reputation; discredit; insult: *His remark was a* slur *on my family name.* **slurred, slur·ring.**

slush (slŭsh) partly melted snow or ice.

sly (slī) **1** cunning; tricky; underhanded: *For all their* sly *tricks, pickpockets are often caught.* **2** mischievous in a playful way; roguish: *Dad gave me a* sly *wink about mother's hat.* **3 on the sly** in a secret way. **sli·er** or **sly·er, sli·est** or **sly·est; sly·ly.**

¹smack (smăk) **1** slight taste or flavor: *a* smack *of garlic in the meat.* **2** suggestion; trace: *a* smack *of the Orient; a* smack *of humor.*

smack of to suggest; have a trace of. [**¹smack** is a form of an Old English word (smæc) meaning "a taste."]

²smack (smăk) **1** quick, sharp noise made with the lips as a sign of pleasure. **2** to make this sound: *The pie was so good, I* smacked *my lips.* **3** loud, resounding kiss. **4** to kiss in this manner. **5** to slap or hit sharply and quickly with the flat of the hand: *Dad* smacked *Paul for talking back.* **6** a sharp slap of a hand. [**²smack** is probably the imitation of a sound.]

³smack (smăk) small sailing vessel or sloop with one sail. [**³smack** comes from a Dutch word (smak).]

small (smôl) **1** not big or large; little in size, amount, or degree: *An ounce is a* small *weight. The mouse is a* small *animal.* **2** unimportant; insignificant; petty: *Don't bother me with these* small *matters.* **3** mean; not generous: *It was* small *of him to take back what he had given.* **4 small hours** the few early hours after midnight. **5 small letter** any letter that is not capitalized.

6 small talk light conversation about everyday, ordinary things: *The travelers passed their time in* small talk *about the weather.* **7 small of the back** concave or narrowest part of the back.

small·pox (smôl′pŏks′) very contagious disease marked by fever and sores which often leave pitted scars.

smart (smärt) **1** to feel sharp, stinging pain: *The extreme cold made my face* smart. **2** to cause a sharp, stinging pain: *Ouch! That alcohol* smarts. **3** sharp, stinging pain: *I could still feel the* smart *from the bee sting the next day.* **4** to feel injury or distress: *He* smarted *from the rebuke.* **5** brisk; fresh: *They ran at a* smart *pace.* **6** bright; quick; clever: *He was very* smart *in mathematics.* **7** neat; trim: *The captain presented a very* smart *picture in his uniform.* **8** fashionable: *She is always* smart *in her Paris clothes.* **smart·ly.**

smart·ness (smärt′nĭs) **1** shrewdness; cleverness; quickness; alertness. **2** bold and saucy conduct. **3** trim or stylish appearance: *the* smartness *of cadets on parade.* **4** briskness: *the* smartness *of the breeze.*

smash (smăsh) **1** to break into pieces with violence: *He* smashed *the window with a rock.* **2** to be broken: *The glass* smashed *on the floor.* **3** to destroy; shatter: *His business was* smashed *by the depression.* **4** to rush into or crash violently: *The car* smashed *into the wall.* **5** sound of breaking or crashing: *The* smash *of glass startled me.* **6** violent collision: *the* smash *of two cars in an accident.*

smash·up (smăsh′ŭp′) violent collision; a wreck.

smear (smîr) **1** to cover, spread, or streak with anything dirty, greasy, or sticky: *The baby* smeared *the walls with jam.* **2** a stain; smudge; streak: *a* smear *of jam on the baby's face.* **3** to harm or injure a person's reputation by hints or accusations of wrongdoing, etc.: *The politician* smeared *his opponent.* **4** a harming or spoiling of a reputation; slander: *The newspaper published a* smear *against the opposing candidate.*

smell (smĕl) **1** sense that enables one to perceive and to identify odors: *A dog's*

smell *is keener than that of a human being.* **2** to recognize or determine something by inhaling its odor: *I* smell *burning rags.* **3** act of smelling: *With one* smell *the dog picked up the scent.* **4** to sniff: *The puppy* smelled *all the corners of his new home.* **5** odor; aroma. **6** to give off an odor: *The garden* smells *of lilacs.* **7** to give off an unpleasant odor; stink: *The garbage* smells. **smelled** or **smelt, smell·ing.**

¹smelt (smĕlt) **1** to melt ore in order to separate metal from rock. **2** to refine impure metal. [**¹smelt** is from an early Dutch word (smelten) meaning "to melt."]

²smelt (smĕlt) small silvery food fish found in northern waters. [**²smelt** is the unchanged form of an Old English word.]

³smelt (smĕlt) See **smell**. *The kitchen* smelt *of spice.* [**³smelt** is a form of **smell**.]

smelt·er (smĕl′tər) **1** person who smelts ore or refines impure metal. **2** furnace used for smelting ore, or refining impure metal.

smile (smīl) **1** upward movement of the corners of the mouth, showing pleasure, happiness, etc. **2** act of smiling: *a* smile *at a joke.* **3** to show a smile: *Let's* smile. **4** to present a happy, gay or cheerful attitude. **5** to look with favor or approval: *The gods* smiled *on him.* **smiled, smil·ing.**

smirk (smûrk) **1** a smile that indicates feelings of self-satisfaction or of knowing something unknown to others. **2** to smile in this manner.

smite (smīt) **1** to strike or hit with the hand or a weapon. **2** to affect with any strong feeling or emotion: *He was* smitten *with love for Mary.* **3** to come upon as a sudden blow: *The explosion* smote *the still night.* **smote, smit·ten** or **smit, smit·ing.**

smith (smith) person who shapes or makes things out of metal: *a* silver*smith; tin*smith; lock*smith.*

smith·y (smith′ĭ or smith′ĭ) workshop of a blacksmith; a forge. **smith·ies.**

smit·ten (smĭt′ən) See **smite**. *I am* smitten *by Lydia's charms.*

Smock

smock (smŏk) long, loose, shirt-like garment with sleeves gathered into cuffs, worn to protect the clothing.

---

fāte, făt, fâre, fär; bē, bĕt; bīte, bĭt; nō, nŏt, nôr; fūse, fŭn, fûr; tōō, tŏŏk; foil; foul; thin; then; hw for wh as in *what*; zh for s as in u*sual*; ə for a, e, i, o, u, as in *a*go, lin*e*n, per*i*l, at*o*m, min*u*s

673

smog (smŏg) a mixture of smoke and fog.

smoke (smōk) **1** cloud of gas and solid particles given off when something is burned. **2** anything like smoke. **3** to give off smoke, especially more smoke than wanted, or in the wrong place: *The chimney smokes. The fireplace smokes.* **4** to breathe the fumes of burning tobacco for pleasure. **5** the act of breathing smoke for pleasure. **6** to preserve or flavor food by exposing to wood smoke: *to* smoke *ham, bacon, fish, etc.*

smoke out to drive out by smoke: *They smoked the bees out of the tree to get at the honey.*

smoked, smok·ing.

smok·er (smō′kər) **1** person who smokes tobacco. **2** railway car, or section of one, where smoking is allowed.

smoke·stack (smōk′stăk′) **1** tall pipe used as a chimney on a factory, etc. **2** the flue of a steam locomotive.

smok·y (smō′kï) **1** giving off smoke: *The* smoky *fire made me cough.* **2** like smoke in taste, smell, or color: *the* smoky *flavor of ham; eyes of a* smoky *blue.* **3** filled with smoke: *The room was* smoky *so we opened the window.* **smok·i·er, smok·i·est; smok·i·ly.**

smol·der or **smoul·der** (smōl′dər) **1** to burn and smoke without flame: *The fire* smoldered *because the wood was damp.* **2** of anger, jealousy, and the like, to remain pent up: *His rage* smoldered *at the insult, but he did not say a word.*

smooth (smo͞oth) **1** not rough; even in texture or surface: *as* smooth *as silk; a* smooth *asphalt pavement.* **2** steady in motion; not jerky or jarring: *The airplane made a* smooth *landing.* **3** to make flat or even: *to* smooth *the sheets on the bed.* **4** to calm or soothe: *to* smooth *a bad temper.* **5** calm; pleasant; serene: *a* smooth *disposition.* **6** to polish; refine; soften: *The tomboy's manners were* smoothed *at boarding school.* **7** easy and flattering in speech or manner; ingratiating: *The salesman was a* smooth *talker.* **8** to make easy: *His friendship with the manager* smoothed *his way in the firm.* **smooth·ly.**

smote (smōt) See **smite.** *David* smote *the giant Goliath with a stone from a sling.*

smoth·er (smŭ**th**′ər) **1** to keep from breathing. **2** to die from lack of breath. **3** to suffocate; stifle: *to* smother *a fire.* **4** to keep back; suppress: *to* smother *a yawn.*

smudge (smŭj) **1** a stain; smear: *Bill had a* smudge *on his face.* **2** to mark with dirty streaks; blur: *to* smudge *a drawing.* **3** thick smoke. **smudged, smudg·ing.**

smug (smŭg) satisfied with oneself. **smug·ger, smug·gest; smug·ly.**

smug·gle (smŭg′əl) to bring something into or out of a country, prison, etc., secretly and illegally. **smug·gled, smug·gling.**

smug·gler (smŭg′lər) person who takes into or out of a country, prison, etc., something that is prohibited or for which the tax has not been paid.

snack (snăk) light meal.

snag (snăg) **1** sharp or jagged projecting part: *the* snags *in a bramble patch; the* snags *on barbed wire.* **2** a stump or branch held fast in a river or lake bed and dangerous to boats. **3** any unexpected difficulty or obstacle: *The railway strike caused a* snag *in our trip.* **4** to catch or tear on a sharp or rough projection: *I* snagged *my stocking on the edge of the chair.* **snagged, snag·ging.**

snail (snāl) crawling, slow-moving creature with a soft body, spiral shell, and eyes on long stalks.

Land snail, about 2 in. long

snake (snāk) **1** long, scaly, crawling animal without legs; serpent. **2** sly, deceitful person. **3** to crawl or twist like a snake: *The river* snaked *its way through the valley.* **snaked, snak·ing.**

snap (snăp) **1** to break suddenly; give way: *The branch* snapped *in the strong wind.* **2** to give way under strain: *After hours of waiting, his patience* snapped. **3** a sudden breaking off, as of something stiff or tense: *the* snap *of a twig.* **4** to make a sudden sharp sound: *The wood* snapped *and crackled in the fireplace.* **5** a sudden, sharp sound: *The twig broke with a* snap. **6** to seize suddenly or try to bite: *The dog* snapped *at the stranger's heels.* **7** a sudden snatch or bite: *The fish caught the bait with a* snap. **8** to seize eagerly: *to* snap *at an opportunity.* **9** to close with a sharp sound: *She* snapped *down the top of the trunk. The dog's jaws* snapped *on the meat.* **10** to speak quickly and sharply: *to* snap *a command.* **11** to move quickly and smartly: *to* snap *to attention.* **12** made quickly without much thought; impulsive: *a* snap *judgment.* **13** a kind of thin, crisp cooky: *a ginger* snap; *a lemon* snap. **14** clasp or fastening: *a* snap *on a dress.* **15 cold snap** a brief period of cold weather. **snapped, snap·ping.**

snap·drag·on (snăp′drăg′ən) flowering plant with bag-shaped flowers of white, purple, red, or yellow.

snapping turtle large turtle, of American rivers and lakes, with jaws which close with great force.

snap·pish (snăp′ĭsh) **1** apt to bite or snap. **2** impatient; curt and sharp in speech or manner: *My grandfather was* snappish *this morning, so I tried to stay out of his way.* **snap·pish·ly.**

snap·py (snăp′ĭ) **1** likely to bite or snap: *a* snappy *dog.* **2** quick, lively; brisk: *The soldiers marched with a* snappy *step.* **3** irritable; short-tempered: *She has been* snappy *since she lost her job.* **snap·pi·er, snap·pi·est; snap·pi·ly.**

snap·shot (snăp′shŏt′) small, informal photograph.

snare (snâr) **1** a kind of trap that catches game in a noose. **2** anything that entraps or entangles: *His flattery proved a* snare. **3** to catch with, or as if with, a snare; talk someone into something. **snared, snar·ing.**

Snare

snare·drum (snâr′drŭm′) small drum with catgut strings stretched across the lower head, that rattle when the upper head is struck.

¹snarl (snärl) **1** angry or vicious growl with the teeth exposed. **2** to show the teeth and make a growling noise. **3** angry, rough tone of voice. **4** to speak in a rough, angry tone of voice. **5** to utter in a rough, angry way; growl out: *He* snarled *commands.* [**¹snarl**

is a form of an earlier English word (snar) that is probably of Germanic origin.]

²snarl (snärl) **1** tangle; a knot: *She has a* snarl *in her hair.* **2** to tangle: *The kitten* snarled *the ball of wool.* **3** confusion: *Traffic was in a* snarl *this afternoon.* **4** to confuse; complicate: *Unexpected guests* snarled *our plans.* [**²snarl** is a word probably formed from **snare**.]

snatch (snăch) **1** to grab or try to grab suddenly or rudely: *to* snatch *a purse; to* snatch *at a chance to travel.* **2** quick, grabbing motion. **3** small piece; a bit: *We heard a* snatch *of music as we passed the park.* **4** brief period of time: *She sleeps only in* snatches.

sneak (snēk) **1** to move or go in a secret or sly way; slink: *She* sneaked *into the house after everyone was asleep.* **2** to act in a sly or furtive way: *Why do you* sneak *instead of acting openly?* **3** sly, underhanded, cowardly person. **4** to take in a furtive way; steal: *When nobody was looking he* sneaked *a piece of cake.*

sneer (snîr) **1** to show scorn by an expression on the face: *I saw him* sneer *at his sister behind their mother's back.* **2** look of contempt. **3** to speak with scorn; jeer at; ridicule. **4** words expressing scorn; ridicule: *I've had enough of your* sneers.

sneeze (snēz) **1** sudden, explosive burst of breath through the mouth and nostrils. **2** to expel the breath in this manner: *Cyril* sneezed *violently when he filled the pepper shaker.* **sneezed, sneez·ing.**

snick·er (snĭk′ər) **1** sly laugh indicating scorn, disrespect, or amusement at something improper. **2** to laugh in this manner.

sniff (snĭf) **1** to draw air through the nostrils in short breaths that can be heard. **2** to smell by taking sniffs: *to* sniff *perfume.* **3** intake of breath that can be heard. **4** to express contempt by, or as by, a sniff: *She* sniffed *at my attempt to be funny.*

snif·fle (snĭf′əl) **1** to sniff again and again: *She always* sniffles *when she cries.* **2** sound produced by this act; a whimper. **3 sniffles** a cold. **snif·fled, snif·fling.**

snip (snĭp) **1** to cut with short, quick clips. **2** a single, small cut; a clip. **3** small piece;

---

fāte, făt, fâre, fär; bē, bĕt; bīte, bĭt; nō, nŏt, nôr; fūse, fŭn, fûr; tōō, tŏŏk; foil; foul; thin; then; hw for wh as in *what*; zh for s as in u*s*ual; ə for a, e, i, o, u, as in *a*go, lin*e*n, per*i*l, at*o*m, min*u*s

675

a bit cut off something: *a snip of cloth.*
snipped, snip·ping.

snipe (snīp) **1** brown-and-white marsh bird with short legs and a long bill. **2** to shoot (at) from an ambush.
sniped, snip·ing.

snob (snŏb) **1** someone who looks up to people of wealth and social position and looks down on people he considers his inferiors. **2** someone who thinks himself better than others in some way: *an intellectual* snob.

Snipe, about 1 ft. long

snob·bish (snŏb'ish) haughty; feeling superior; like a snob or having the attitude of a snob. **snob·bish·ly.**

snoop (snoop) **1** to search in a sneaky way; pry: *He snooped through my desk when I wasn't home.* **2** person who pries.

snoop·ing (snoo'ping) a search carried out in a sneaky way; a prying.

snooze (snooz) **1** to doze; take a nap. **2** a nap; a doze. **snoozed, snooz·ing.**

snore (snôr) **1** to breathe with a hoarse noise while sleeping. **2** noisy, hoarse breathing of a sleeping person. **snored, snor·ing.**

snor·kel (snôr'kəl) **1** on submarines, a system of tubes to take air in and out. **2** a mask with tube, worn by swimmers to permit breathing under water.

snort (snôrt) **1** to make a harsh noise by forcing air out through the nostrils. **2** harsh noise made by forcing air out through the nostrils. **3** to express anger or contempt by a harsh nasal sound. **4** to utter with a harsh nasal sound: *He snorted his answer to me.*

snout (snout) **1** projecting nose, and sometimes mouth and jaws, of an animal; muzzle: *a pig's* snout. **2** anything that resembles this.

snow (snō) **1** soft white flakes of frozen water vapor that form in the sky and fall to earth. **2** to form into these white flakes and fall to earth. **3** something like these white flakes: *There was a snow of soap flakes on the floor.* **4** a fall of snow, or a shower resembling this: *the heavy snows last winter; a snow of confetti.* **5** to fall or shower like snow: *Streamers snowed down.*

snow in to shut in with snow: *During the blizzard they were snowed in for a week.*

snow·ball (snō'bôl') **1** snow packed together into a ball. **2** to grow rapidly, as a rolling ball of snow: *The rumor snowballed as it passed from person to person.* **3** shrub with large clusters of white flowers that look like balls of snow.

snow·drift (snō'drĭft') heap of snow piled up by the wind.

snow·fall (snō'fôl') **1** a falling of snow: *a heavy snowfall.* **2** amount of snow which falls during one period of time or in one area.

snow·flake (snō'flāk') the form in which snow falls; tiny, feathery, white snow crystal or small mass of crystals.

snow·man (snō'măn') figure of a man, made of snow. **snow·men.**

INDIAN   BEAR PAW

Snowshoes

snow·shoe (snō'shoo') one of two wood frames that are tied onto the feet and used for walking on deep snow. They are usually shaped like rackets and filled in with a network of rawhide cords.

snow·storm (snō'stôrm') heavy fall of snow, especially with strong winds.

snow·y (snō'i) **1** having snow, marked by snow, or covered with snow: *a snowy winter;* snowy *mountain peaks.* **2** white or clean, like fresh snow: *a snowy sheet.* **snow·i·er, snow·i·est; snow·i·ly.**

snub (snŭb) **1** to treat rudely or with deliberate show of indifference: *Mary snubbed some of the girls by not inviting them to her party.* **2** rude treatment or deliberate show of indifference: *It was a snub to the hostess not to answer the invitation.* **3 snub nose** a short nose which turns up at the tip. **snubbed, snub·bing.**

¹**snuff** (snŭf) **1** to smell; to sniff; to inhale. **2** fine tobacco powder which is sniffed in through the nose. **3 up to snuff** up to a usual standard: *I don't feel quite up to snuff today.* [¹**snuff** is from an early Dutch (snuffen) meaning "clear the nose." It is related to **sniff.**]

²**snuff** (snŭf) to put out (a candle), as by pinching the wick.

676

snuff out **1** to put out; extinguish: *We* snuffed out *the fire by putting sand over it.* **2** to put an end to; destroy: *The plane crash* snuffed out *his life.* [²**snuff** is a form of earlier English (snuffen) meaning "snuff a candle."]

snug (snŭg) **1** comfortable; cozy: *a* snug *corner by the hearth.* **2** tight (in fit): *This dress is a little too* snug. **3** small but enough for comfort: *a* snug *income.* **snug·ger, snug·gest; snug·ly.**

snug·gle (snŭg'əl) **1** to press close to; get comfortable in: *to* snuggle *in bed.* **2** to hold close: *Mother* snuggled *the baby in her arms.* **snug·gled, snug·gling.**

¹**so** (sō) **1** in the way or degree shown, stated, understood, etc.: *Now that I've shown you, make the bed just* so. **2** to such a degree; in such a way: *It was* so *hot we went swimming.* **3** as: *not* so *big as I.* **4** very: *That problem was* so *hard.* **5** very much: *My sprained ankle hurts* so. **6** what has already been said or named: *He was always a poor player and will always remain* so. **7** therefore: *They were bad* so *Mother wouldn't let them go to the movies.* **8** also: *The Smiths were present and* so *were the Farleys.* **9** an exclamation expressing surprise, doubt, etc.: *They exclaimed, "*So *you managed to come again after all!"* **10 or so** more or less: *five dollars* or so. **11 so as** or **so that** in order that; with the result that: *We all left* so that *he could rest.* **12 so-so** neither very good nor very bad: *Tim was feeling* so-so. [¹**so** is a form of an Old English word (swā) with the same meaning.] (Homonyms: sew, ²sow)

²**so** (sō) sol. [²**so** is not from any particular language but is a syllable that was made up, perhaps by an Italian, G. B. *Doni.*] (Homonyms: sew, ²sow)

soak (sōk) **1** to wet through and through: *The rain* soaked *the ground.* **2** to become wet throughout: *Mother let the clothes* soak *for two hours.* **3** to let lie in water, liquid, etc.: *to* soak *the beans in water before cooking.* **4** a thorough wetting: *a* soak *in the rain.*

soak up to absorb: *A sponge* soaked up *the water.*

soap (sōp) **1** cleansing substance used in washing. Soap is made of boiled fats and oils mixed with salts called alkalis. **2** to cover or wash with soap.

soap·box (sōp'bŏks') box used as a platform by street speakers.

soap·stone (sōp'stōn') soft, grayish stone with a smooth surface that feels like soap.

soap·suds (sōp'sŭdz') foam made with soap and water.

soap·y (sō'pĭ) **1** filled or covered with soap. **2** like soap. **soap·i·er, soap·i·est.**

soar (sôr) **1** to fly or glide high: *The eagle* soared *through the air.* **2** to rise rapidly: *The cost of living has* soared *in the last ten years.* (Homonym: sore)

sob (sŏb) **1** to weep with gasping, short breaths. **2** tearful gasp; choking sound: *the* sobs *of a lost child.*

sob out to tell while crying: *to* sob out *one's troubles.*

sobbed, sob·bing.

so·ber (sō'bər) **1** sedate; staid; not gay or frivolous: *The Pilgrims were noted for their* sober *lives.* **2** quiet; not showy: *Gray is a* sober *color.* **3** serious; solemn: *From his* sober *expression, I feared bad news.* **4** to make or become serious: *The news of the accident* sobered *the gay party.* **5** reasonable; serious: *Father gave us some* sober *advice about spending money.* **6** not drunk.

sober down to make or become calm or serious.

so·ber·ly.

so-called (sō'kôld') named so, but not truly so: *This* so-called *butter is really margarine.*

soc·cer (sŏk'ər) form of football in which the ball is hit with the feet, legs, body, or head. The arms and hands cannot be used for hitting the ball or stopping an opponent.

so·cia·ble (sō'shə bəl) **1** friendly; liking company. **2** giving or affording opportunity for conversation and companionship: *a pleasant,* sociable *evening with friends.* **3** informal party. **so·cia·bly.**

so·cial (sō'shəl) **1** of or having to do with human beings in a group: *Slums are an urgent* social *problem.* **2** inclined to live in

fāte, făt, fâre, fär; bē, bĕt; bīte, bĭt; nō, nŏt, nôr; fūse, fŭn, fûr; tōō, tŏŏk; foil; foul; thin; then; hw for wh as in *wh*at; zh for s as in u*s*ual; ə for a, e, i, o, u, as in *a*go, lin*e*n, per*i*l, at*o*m, min*u*s

677

association with others: *Human beings are* social *creatures*. **3** of or having to do with the activities of the rich and fashionable: *the* social *whirl; a* social *climber.* **4** of, for, or in the company of others: *a social club; a* social *evening.* **5** liking the company of others; sociable. **6** an informal gathering: *a church* social. **7** of animals, living together in colonies or communities. Ants, beavers, and bees are social animals. **so·cial·ly.**

so·cial·ism (sō′shə liz′əm) **1** doctrine according to which the means of producing and distributing food and goods, should be owned by the people as a whole and operated by the government. **2** political movement that seeks to bring about such a state of affairs.

so·cial·ist (sō′shə list) person who advocates socialism.

social studies the study of man in relation to society and his environment, including history, geography, etc.

social worker person working in an organization concerned with the welfare of the community, as in health, housing, recreation, etc.

so·ci·e·ty (sə si′ə ti) **1** a community of people living together at a particular time and place: *The police exist to protect* society. **2** persons joined together for a common aim or purpose: *a* society *to preserve historical monuments.* **3** class of people of wealth and fashion or their activities: *She reports on* society *for the newspaper.* **4** company; companionship: *We missed his* society *after he moved away.* **so·ci·e·ties.**

sock (sŏk) short stocking not reaching the knee.

sock·et (sŏk′it) a hollow into which something is fitted: *the* socket *of the eye; an electric light* socket.

sod (sŏd) **1** grass and the layer of soil just under it that contains the roots of the grass; turf: *Under the* sod *the boys found many Indian arrowheads.* **2** a piece of this, usually cut square. **3** to cover with sod or turf: *We plan to* sod *the path and make a lawn of the backyard.* **sod·ded, sod·ding.**

ELECTRIC LAMP

CURTAIN ROD

Sockets

so·da (sō′də) **1** any of several chemical compounds containing sodium and oxygen. The most common ones are baking soda, used in cooking and medicine, and washing soda, used for softening water. **2** water that contains carbon dioxide gas, so that it bubbles and fizzes. Also called **soda water.** **3** soft drink made with this water and flavoring.

soda fountain a counter, often in a drug store, where soda water, soft drinks, ice cream, sandwiches, etc., are sold.

soda water water charged with gas (carbon dioxide) so that it bubbles and fizzes.

sod·den (sŏd′ən) **1** very damp and heavy with moisture; soggy: *My shoes are still* sodden *from crossing the path.* **2** dull; heavy; stupid from fatigue, drunkenness, etc.: *He is too* sodden *to understand a word you say.* **sod·den·ly.**

so·di·um (sō′di əm) silver-white metal element obtained from common salt (sodium chloride).

so·fa (sō′fə) long, upholstered seat or couch made with a back and two arms.

soft (sôft or sŏft) **1** not hard; easily yielding to touch or pressure; readily shaped or worked: *a soft pillow;* soft *clay.* **2** quiet and gentle; low and mild: *a soft voice.* **3** smooth; pleasing to the touch: *a soft skin.* **4** weak; lacking strength; flabby: *His muscles were* soft *from lack of exercise.* **5** pronounced with the sound of **g** in "gentle" or **c** in "cease," not hard like the **g** in "got" or **c** in "cow." **6 soft coal** coal that burns with more smoke and leaves more ash than hard coal; bituminous coal. **7 soft drinks** drinks or beverages containing no alcohol. **8 soft water** water that is free from certain minerals, such as lime, and readily forms a lather with soap. **soft·ly.**

soft·ball (sôft′bôl′ or sŏft′bôl′) **1** game similar to baseball, but played on a smaller field, with a larger, softer ball and a lighter bat. There are ten men on a team. **2** ball used in this game.

soft·en (sôf′ən or sŏf′ən) to make or become less hard, loud, glaring, severe, etc.: *Butter* softens *in the heat. Awnings* soften *the light. The judge* softened *the punishment.*

soft·ness (sôft′nis or sŏft′nis) **1** a being soft. **2** gentleness; mildness.

soft·spo·ken (sôft'spō'kən or sŏft'spō'kən) speaking in a gentle or soft tone of voice; mild: *a soft-spoken young man.*

soft·wood (sôft'wŏŏd' or sŏft'wŏŏd') **1** any cone-bearing tree. **2** the wood of such a tree.

sog·gy (sŏg'ĭ) wet and heavy; soaked with moisture; dank: *Tom placed his soggy boots in front of the fire to dry.* **sog·gi·er, sog·gi·est; sog·gi·ly.**

¹soil (soil) **1** top layer of the earth's surface other than rock, water, or ice, especially the part in which plants will grow: *The soil here is so rich that almost any plant will thrive. Nothing grows in this sandy desert* soil. **2** land; country: *He longed to return once more to his native* soil. [**¹soil** is from an Old French word (soile) that was taken from a Latin word (solium) meaning "a seat." This Latin word was confused with another Latin word (solum) meaning "ground."]

²soil (soil) **1** to make dirty: *He soiled his hands working in the garden.* **2** to stain; tarnish: *One should never spread false rumors that will* soil *a reputation.* [**²soil** is from an Old French word (soillier) that comes from a Latin word (suillus) meaning "piglike."]

so·journ (sō'jûrn) **1** (also sō jûrn') to go and stay for a time; dwell: *This winter he plans to* sojourn *in Florida.* **2** short stay or outing: *We enjoyed our* sojourn *in the country. Our* sojourn *in Europe was unforgettable.*

Sol (sŏl) **1** the sun. **2** the sun god of the ancient Romans.

sol-(sōl) fifth note in the musical scale. Also spelled **so.**

sol·ace (sŏl'ĭs) **1** comfort; consolation: *the* solace *of a sympathetic friend.* **2** to give comfort or relief to; console; soothe: *One can always* solace *oneself with the thought that it might have been worse.* **sol·aced, sol·ac·ing.**

so·lar (sō'lər) of or having to do with the sun: *a solar eclipse;* solar *time;* solar *energy.*

solar battery device for producing an electric current directly from sunlight.

solar system the sun and all the planets and other heavenly bodies that revolve around it.

sold (sōld) See **sell.** *He* sold *his house for a very good price.*

sol·der (sŏd'ər) **1** melted metal, or metal alloy, that is used to join or mend other metal surfaces. **2** to join together or mend with this metal: *My brother* soldered *together my broken tin soldier and now it is as good as new.*

sol·dier (sōl'jər) **1** person enlisted in an army, especially a private. **2** man who is experienced and skilled in warfare: *Wellington was a great* soldier. **3 a soldier of fortune** adventurer; man who will serve in any army for money or adventure.

sol·dier·y (sōl'jər ĭ) **1** soldiers as a group; military troops: *The* soldiery *swarmed all over the village.* **2** military knowledge or training.

¹sole (sōl) **1** a kind of flatfish prized as food. **2** its flesh used as food. [**¹sole** comes through Old French from a Latin word (solea) meaning "sole of a shoe." The flatness of this fish brings to mind a shoe sole.] (Homonym: soul)

European sole,
1 to 1½ ft. long

²sole (sōl) **1** bottom part of the foot. **2** bottom of a shoe, boot, or slipper. **3** to put a sole on a shoe. **soled, sol·ing.** [**²sole** is the unchanged form of an Old English word that comes from a Latin word (solea).] (Homonym: soul)

³sole (sōl) **1** one and only; single: *the* sole *occupant of an apartment; the* sole *reason for going.* **2** belonging or pertaining to one group or individual: *He has the* sole *rights to the book.* **sole·ly.** [**³sole** comes through Old French (sol) from a Latin word (solus) meaning "alone." (Homonym: soul)

sol·emn (sŏl'əm) **1** carried out with sacred rites or ceremonies: *the* solemn *festivals of the church.* **2** causing awe: *Despite the crowd of tourists, the cathedral was a* solemn *place.* **3** earnest; serious; grave: *The judge has a* solemn *face.* **sol·emn·ly.**

so·lem·ni·ty (sə lĕm'nə tĭ) **1** great seriousness; gravity. **2** formal ceremony: *The queen was crowned with traditional* solemnity. **so·lem·ni·ties.**

---

fāte, făt, fâre, fär; bē, bĕt; bīte, bĭt; nō, nŏt, nôr; fūse, fŭn, fûr; tŏŏ, tŏŏk; foil; foul; thin; then; hw for wh as in what; zh for s as in usual; ə for a, e, i, o, u, as in ago, linen, peril, atom, minus

679

so·lic·it (sə lis′it) 1 to ask (for) earnestly or repeatedly; entreat or beg (for something): *to solicit a person for money.* 2 to seek orders, support, votes, etc.: *The cleaners on the corner were here to* solicit *our business.*

sol·id (sŏl′id) 1 one of the three main forms of matter (solid, liquid, gas). A solid has a definite size and its own definite shape. 2 hard; firm; able to support weight: *the* solid *ground.* 3 without space inside; not hollow: *a solid bar of iron.* 4 the same throughout: *of solid silver or gold; a solid color.* 5 firmly built; strong: *a solid building.* 6 of sound character; reliable; trustworthy: *a solid man.* 7 with a strong financial position: *a solid business.* 8 whole; uninterrupted; continuous: *We waited a* solid *week for their answer.* 9 showing firm agreement among a great majority: *a solid vote for the mayor.* 10 in mathematics, having to do with three dimensions (length, width, and thickness). **solid·ly.**

so·lid·i·fy (sə lid′ə fī′) 1 to make or become hard or firm; change from a fluid to a solid state: *Cold* solidifies *water into ice.* 2 to unite firmly: *to* solidify *a friendship.* **so·lid·i·fied, so·lid·i·fy·ing.**

so·lid·i·ty (sə lid′ə ti) 1 the property of occupying or filling space; density. 2 stability; firmness; hardness. **so·lid·i·ties.**

sol·i·tar·y (sŏl′ə těr′i) 1 alone; without companions; lonely: *a solitary monk; a* solitary *traveler.* 2 seldom visited; secluded: *a solitary village.* 3 spent or done alone: *a solitary walk.* 4 **solitary confinement** confinement of a prisoner apart from all others. **sol·i·tar·i·ly.**

sol·i·tude (sŏl′ə tōōd′ or sŏl′ə tūd′) 1 state of being or living alone. 2 a lonely and remote place: *the solitude of the mountains.*

so·lo (sō′lō) 1 piece of music to be played or sung by a single performer: *a violin* solo. 2 any performance by one person: *a dance* solo. 3 done without a partner, instructor, etc.: *his first solo flight.* **so·los.**

so·lo·ist (sō′lō ist) person who performs a solo.

sol·u·ble (sŏl′yə bəl) 1 capable of being dissolved (in a liquid): *Sugar is* soluble *in water.* 2 capable of being solved. **sol·u·bly.**

so·lu·tion (sə lōō′shən or sə lū′shən) 1 act of solving: *The* solution *of the problem took*

him ten minutes. 2 correct answer: *He found the* solution *of the problem in ten minutes.* 3 a mixing of a substance in another (usually liquid) so that the first one disappears; a dissolving: *The* solution *of sugar is faster in hot water than in cold.* 4 such a mixture: *a sugar-and-water* solution.

solve (sŏlv) 1 to find the answer to a problem or puzzle: *to solve a crossword puzzle; to solve the riddle of the crime.* 2 to find the way out of a difficulty: *We shall probably have to buy a house to solve the housing problem.* **solved, solv·ing.**

som·ber or **som·bre** (sŏm′bər) 1 dark; dull: *a somber sky.* 2 gloomy; dismal: *the* somber *expression of the mourners.* **som·ber·ly** or **som·bre·ly.**

som·brer·o (sŏm brâr′ō) hat with a broad brim and high crown, popular in Latin America and the southwestern part of the United States. **som·brer·os.**

Sombrero

some (sŭm) 1 a certain or particular, but not known or named: *It was* some *boy who did that. There were* some *children in the park.* 2 of an indefinite number or quantity; a few; a little: *You must get* some *new clothes. Will you have* some *coffee?* 3 about; approximately: *He said* some *20 persons were at his party.* 4 of a considerable amount, number, degree, or quantity: *It took* some *courage to break the bad news to John.* 5 indefinite number or quantity: *There were* some *who came very late. He spilled* some *of the water.* (Homonym: sum)

-some suffix meaning "tending to" or "apt to": *tiresome; troublesome.*

some·bod·y (sŭm′bŏd′i) 1 person unknown; someone: *I think* somebody *has borrowed my umbrella.* 2 an important person: *Having that new car makes her think she is somebody.* **some·bod·ies.**

some·day (sŭm′dā′) at some future time or day: *We will go to the zoo someday before long.*

some·how (sŭm′hou′) in one way or another; in some way: *We'll get home somehow.*

some·one (sŭm'wŭn') somebody; some person unknown: *Tomorrow someone will call for this parcel.*

som·er·sault (sŭm'ər sôlt') **1** to leap or dive in the air and turn head over heels. **2** such a leap or dive. Also **som·er·set.**

some·thing (sŭm'thĭng') **1** particular thing or things not specified: *The baby wants something to play with.* **2** thing not definitely known or understood: *There is something strange about that house.* **3** person or thing of importance: *He thinks he's something now that he has a car. It's something to own property.* **4** somewhat; rather: *You look something like your brother.*

some·time (sŭm'tīm') at a time or date not known or exactly indicated: *The trains stopped running sometime last year.*

some·times (sŭm'tīmz') now and then; from time to time; once in a while: *We go there sometimes.*

some·what (sŭm'hwŏt') to some extent; in some degree; rather: *She is somewhat lazy.*

some·where (sŭm'hwâr') **1** in, at, or to some place not known or named: *I've left my gloves somewhere.* **2** at some point in time: *It happened somewhere about a hundred years ago.*

son (sŭn) **1** male child in relation to his parent or parents: *the son of pioneer parents.* **2** descendant: *We are all sons of Adam.* **3** a man considered as the product of his native land, a school, cause, etc.: *a true son of France; the sons of the revolution.* **4** affectionate form of address to a boy or man by an older person. (Homonym: sun)

so·nar (sō'när) device that detects and locates objects under water by means of sound waves echoed back from them. Sonar is used in detecting submarines, schools of fish, etc.

so·na·ta (sə nä'tə) composition for one or two musical instruments, especially the piano, in three or four movements.

song (sông) **1** piece of music to be sung by a human voice. **2** musical sounds or notes produced by a bird: *the song of a canary.* **3** poetry; verse suitable for singing. **4** sing-

ing: *to break into* song. **5 Song of Solomon** the twenty-second book of the Old Testament. **6 for a song** for a small price; for a trifle: *This discontinued model is now going for a song.*

song·bird (sông'bûrd') bird that sings, such as a canary, thrush, etc.

song·ster (sông'stər) **1** singing bird. **2** person who sings. **3** writer of songs or poetry.

son-in-law (sŭn'ĭn lô') a daughter's husband. **sons-in-law.**

so·no·rous (sə nôr'əs) **1** having a full, deep, rich sound; richly resonant: *the sonorous voices of the chorus.* **2** having an impressive sound; claiming dignity or importance: *a sonorous but meaningless speech.* **so·no·rous·ly.**

soon (sōōn) **1** in a short time from now; before long: *We shall soon be having snow.* **2** shortly; quickly: *They left soon after five o'clock.* **3** willingly; readily: *I would as soon go with you as stay here.*

soot (sŏŏt or sōōt) black powder, mostly carbon, that forms when coal, wood, oil, etc., are burned.

soothe (sōōth) **1** to make (a person or animal) quiet and calm; to comfort: *to soothe a restless patient;* soothe *a nervous horse.* **2** to make less painful; relieve: *The salve soothed Eric's earache.* **soothed, soothing.**

so·phis·ti·cat·ed (sə fĭs'tə kā'tĭd) **1** formed by or showing worldly experience, cultivation, education, etc.: *a sophisticated taste in food; a sophisticated audience.* **2** artificial; not natural or simple: *Their conversation was only sophisticated chatter.* **so·phis·ti·cat·ed·ly.**

soph·o·more (sŏf'ə môr') student in the second year at an American university, college, or high school.

so·pra·no (sə prăn'ō) **1** highest singing voice: *to sing soprano in the choir.* **2** woman or boy with such a voice: *The boy sopranos in the choir sounded like angels.* **3** of, written for, or able to sing soprano: *a soprano role in an opera.* **so·pra·nos.**

sor·cer·er (sôr'sər ər) person believed to practice magic with the aid of evil spirits; magician.

---

fāte, făt, fâre, fär; bē, bĕt; bite, bĭt; nō, nŏt, nôr; fūse, fŭn, fûr; tōō, tŏŏk; foil; foul; thin; ~~then~~; hw for wh as in *wh*at; zh for s as in u*s*ual; ə for a, e, i, o, u, as in *a*go, lin*e*n, per*i*l, at*o*m, min*u*s

sor·cer·ess (sôr′sər ĭs) woman sorcerer; witch.

sor·cer·y (sôr′sə rĭ) magic; witchcraft; enchantment. **sor·cer·ies.**

sor·did (sôr′dĭd) **1** dirty; squalid: *the sordid houses of the slums.* **2** mean; low; contemptible: *a sordid quarrel.* **sor·did·ly.**

sore (sôr) **1** painful and tender; hurting when touched: *a sore knee.* **2** painfully infected or bruised place on the body. **3** sad; grieved; filled with sorrow: *Her heart was sore after the loss of her son.* **4** resentful; offended; annoyed: *He was sore about the insult he received.* **5** grievous; severe: *The Jones family are in sore need.* **sor·er, sor·est.** (Homonym: soar)

sore·ly (sôr′lĭ) **1** severely; in a grievous way: *The rude remark sorely hurt him.* **2** very much; to a great extent: *to be sorely tempted.*

sore·ness (sôr′nĭs) a being sore; painfulness: *a muscle soreness.*

sor·ghum (sôr′gəm) grain with a jointed stalk somewhat like Indian corn, from the sweet sap of which a molasses is made. Some kinds are used as fodder.

Sorghum

¹sor·rel (sŏr′əl or sôr′əl) any of several common edible plants with sour leaves and juice. [**¹sorrel** comes through the French from an Old German word (sūr) meaning "sour." The plant leaves have a pleasantly acid taste.]

²sor·rel (sŏr′əl or sôr′əl) **1** reddish brown. **2** reddish-brown horse: *I'm sorry I traded my black horse for a sorrel.* [**²sorrel** is from an Old French word (sorel) of the same meaning.]

sor·row (sŏr′ō or sôr′ō) **1** distress of mind caused by loss, suffering, disappointment, etc.; grief; deep sadness: *the sorrow caused by the death of a friend.* **2** to feel or express grief, sadness, etc.: *He sorrowed over a lost chance.* **3** cause of grief, sadness, etc.: *Bob's late hours were a sorrow to his parents.*

sor·row·ful (sŏr′ə fəl or sôr′ə fəl) **1** sad; unhappy; melancholy: *the sorrowful relatives at the funeral.* **2** expressing sadness or grief: *a sorrowful song.* **3** causing distress

or unhappiness: *The train wreck was a sorrowful sight.* **sor·row·ful·ly.**

sor·ry (sŏr′ĭ or sôr′ĭ) **1** feeling regret, repentance, or pity: *I'm sorry I can't meet you. I'm sorry I told a lie. Agnes was sorry for the sick cat.* **2** sad; miserable: *It was a sorry day when our team lost.* **3** poor; worthless: *This old wreck is a sorry excuse for a piano.* **sor·ri·er, sor·ri·est; sor·ri·ly.**

sort (sôrt) **1** kind; type: *Tom is the sort who is always late. This sort of weather is good for the farmer.* **2** to classify; put into groups: *to sort the laundry.* **3** thing bearing some, but very slight, resemblance (to something): *The cold war is a sort of peace.* **4 out of sorts** not oneself; not feeling well; ill-tempered: *Lily is out of sorts in the morning before she has her coffee.*

sort out to separate one kind from the others: *If you sort out your thoughts before you speak, you will be easier to understand.*

SOS a call for help, usually sent by radio on the high seas.

sought (sôt) See **seek.** *Henry sought success for years before he found it.*

soul (sōl) **1** spiritual part of a person, thought to leave the body at death. **2** moral or emotional nature of man: *a little man with a great soul.* **3** vital part (of anything); quality (of something) that gives life or energy: *The soul of the music was lost through careless playing.* **4** person who gives life and spirit (to something): *The leader was the soul of the expedition.* **5** person who is an example of some quality: *He is the soul of honesty.* **6** person: *There was not a soul in the house.* (Homonym: sole)

¹sound (sound) **1** that which is heard; sensation produced by vibrations in the surrounding air and picked up by the ear: *the sound of bells.* **2** to make a sound: *Running feet sounded through the halls.* **3** to cause to make a sound: *Please sound the bell.* **4** distance something can be heard: *within the sound of my voice.* **5** to give an impression; seem: *That explanation sounds flimsy.* [**¹sound** comes through French (son) from a Latin word (sonus) meaning "a sound."]

²sound (sound) **1** healthy; free from illness, injury, decay, or defect: *Athletes must have sound lungs.* **2** safe; prudent; dependable:

682

a sound *business;* sound *advice.* **3** in accord with accepted beliefs: *a* sound *political speech.* **4** legal; valid: *a* sound *title to property.* **5** thorough: *a* sound *whipping; a* sound *grounding in mathematics.* **6** deep: *a* sound *sleep.* **sound·ly.** [²**sound** is a form of an Old English word (gesund) meaning "strong," "healthy."]

³**sound** (sound) **1** to measure the depth of water by means of a weight attached to a line; to fathom. **2** to try to discover a person's opinions or feelings, usually in an indirect way. [³**sound** is from a French word (sonder) which is considered by some to be made up of two Latin words (sub) meaning "under," and (unda), "wave."]

⁴**sound** (sound) long, narrow body of water connecting two larger bodies of water or lying between an island and the mainland. [⁴**sound** is a form of an Old English word (sund) of the same meaning.]

sound·proof (sound'prŏŏf') **1** not letting sound in or out. **2** to insulate so that sound cannot pass through.

soup (sŏŏp) liquid food prepared by boiling meat, vegetables, or fish in a fluid.

sour (sour) **1** having an acid taste, like vinegar or green fruit. **2** fermented: *a dish of* sour *cream.* **3** to ferment; to cause to become acid: *Hot weather will* sour *milk quickly.* **4** unpleasant; disagreeable. **5** to make peevish or unpleasant: *Many years of hardship have* soured *her temper.* **sour·ly.**

source (sôrs) **1** beginning of a stream or river. **2** place or thing from which something comes or is obtained: *Brazil is a* source *of coffee.* **3** person, book, or article from which information is obtained.

south (south) **1** the direction toward the South Pole; also, the point of the compass indicating this direction; opposite of north. **2** the part of the world, country, or continent in this direction: *the* south *of France.* **3 the South** (1) the part of the United States lying generally south of the Ohio River and Pennsylvania. (2) in the Civil War, the states op-

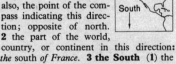

posed to the Union (the North); the Confederacy. **4** in or to the south: *the* south *gate.* **5** of winds, from the south. **6** toward the south: *He turned* south.

South Africa country at the southern tip of Africa, formerly called **Union of South Africa.**

South America continent southeast of North America.

South American 1 of South America or its people. **2** citizen of a country in South America; a person from South America.

South Car·o·li·na (south kăr'ə li'nə) a southeastern State of the United States on the Atlantic coast.

South Da·ko·ta (south də kō'tə) a north-central State of the United States.

southeast (south'ēst') **1** the direction halfway between south and east; also, the point of the compass indicating this direction. **2** the part of any area lying in this direction as seen from the center of the area. **3 the Southeast** the southeastern part of the United States. **4** in or to the southeast: *a* southeast *current.* **5** of winds, from the southeast. **6** toward the southeast: *The troops marched* southeast.

south·east·ern (south'ēs'tərn) located in or to the southeast: *a* southeastern *state.*

south·er·ly (sŭth'ər li) **1** southward: *a* southerly *flight of birds.* **2** of winds, coming from the south: *a* southerly *breeze.*

south·ern (sŭth'ərn) **1** located in or to the south. **2** from the south.

South Pole the southern end of the earth's axis.

south·ward (south'wərd) to or toward the south: *to sail* southward; *a* southward *cruise.* **south·ward·ly.**

south·wards (south'wərdz) southward.

south·west (south'wĕst') **1** the direction halfway between south and west; also, the point of the compass indicating this direction. **2** the part of any area lying in this direction as seen from the center of the area. **3 the Southwest** the southwestern part of the United States. **4** in or to the southwest: *a* southwest *current.* **5** of winds, from the southwest. **6** toward the southwest: *The car turned* southwest.

---

fāte, făt, fâre, fär; bē, bĕt; bite, bĭt; nō, nŏt, nôr; fūse, fŭn, fûr; tōō, tŏŏk; foil; foul; thin; ~~then~~;
hw for wh as in *wh*at; zh for s as in u*s*ual; ə for a, e, i, o, u, as in *a*go, lin*e*n, per*i*l, at*o*m, min*u*s

southwester

south·west·er (south′wĕs′tər) or **sou′-west·er** (sou′wĕs′tər) **1** a storm or strong wind from the southwest. **2** waterproof hat the brim of which is widest at the back.

south·west·ern (south′-wĕs′tərn) located in or to the southwest: *the* southwestern *part of the state.*

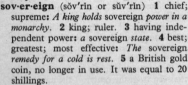
Southwester

sou·ve·nir (sōō′və nir′) something kept as a reminder of a person, place, or happening; keepsake.

sov·er·eign (sŏv′rĭn or sŭv′rĭn) **1** chief; supreme: *A king holds* sovereign *power in a monarchy.* **2** king; ruler. **3** having independent power: *a* sovereign *state.* **4** best; greatest; most effective: *The* sovereign *remedy for a cold is rest.* **5** a British gold coin, no longer in use. It was equal to 20 shillings.

sov·er·eign·ty (sŏv′rĭn tĭ or sŭv′rĭn tĭ) supreme power: *In a monarchy* sovereignty *rests with the king but in a democracy it rests with the people.* **sov·er·eign·ties.**

So·vi·et Un·ion (sō′vĭ ĭt ūn′yən) federation of communist states in eastern Europe and western and northern Asia. Also called **Union of Soviet Socialist Republics.**

¹sow (sou) full-grown female pig. [¹**sow** is a form of an Old English word (sū) of the same meaning.]

²sow (sō) **1** to spread or scatter (as seeds); to plant: *They* sowed *corn in the spring.* **2** to plant with seeds: *The lawn is already* sown. **3** to plant in the mind; spread: *She* sowed *hatred with her bitter words.* **sowed, sown** or **sowed, sow·ing.** [²**sow** is a form of an Old English word (sāwan) meaning "to scatter seed."] (Homonyms: sew, so)

sown (sōn) See **²sow.** (Homonym: sewn)

soy·bean (soi′bēn′) a plant which came originally from China and Japan. Its seed is used in making flour, oil, etc.: *to serve rice with* soybean *sauce.*

space (spās) **1** the expanse without limits in which the universe exists. **2** a definite distance or area: *the* space *between houses; the* space *for a desk.* **3** an interval of time: *She worked for the* space *of one hour.* **4** in written music, the open places between

Spaniard

the lines of the staff. **5** in writing or printing, the open places separating letters or words. **6** to arrange (letters, etc.) with open places in between: *She* spaced *the letters so that they were all even.* **7 outer space** all space outside the earth's atmosphere. **spaced, spac·ing.**

space ship or **space·ship** (spās′shĭp′) a rocket-driven vehicle for travel beyond the earth's atmosphere.

spa·cious (spā′shəs) **1** roomy: *She has a* spacious *house so she can have visitors over the week ends.* **2** broad; extensive: *There is a* spacious *view from this window.* **spa·cious·ly.**

spade (spād) **1** a kind of shovel. **2** to dig with a spade: *Horace* spaded *the flower bed.* **3** any one of a suit of playing cards marked with a black spade-shaped design. **spad·ed, spad·ing.**

spa·ghet·ti (spə gĕt′ĭ) food made of wheat paste shaped into long, stringlike pieces thinner than macaroni.

Spades

Spain (spān) a country in southwest Europe.

spake (spāk) old or poetic form of ¹**spoke.**

¹span (spăn) **1** distance measured from the outstretched thumb to the tip of the little finger; nine inches. **2** to measure with the outstretched thumb and little finger. **3** distance between two limits: *the* span *of a river.* **4** distance between the supports of an arch or of a bridge. **5** period (of time): *a* span *of years.* **6** to reach or extend over: *The bridge* spanned *the river.* **spanned, span·ning.** [¹**span** is a form of Old English (spann) meaning "a measure."]

²span (spăn) pair of horses or other draft animals driven together in harness: *Our driver brought his* span *of dappled grays to a sudden stop.* [²**span** is from a Dutch or German word (spannen) meaning "unite," "fasten."]

span·gle (spăng′gəl) **1** tiny disk of shining metal used for decoration. **2** any small, bright spot or object. **3** to decorate with or as with spangles: *The American flag is* spangled *with stars.* **span·gled, span·gling.**

Span·iard (spăn′yərd) citizen of Spain; person of Spanish descent.

span·iel (spăn′yəl) one of several kinds of small to medium-size hunting or pet dogs, all of which have long, silky hair, hanging ears, and short legs.

Span·ish (spăn′ĭsh) **1** of Spain, its people, or its language. **2** the language of the people of Spain, Mexico, Central America, and most of South America. **3 the Spanish** people of Spain.

English springer spaniel, 18 in. high

Spanish-American War war between the United States and Spain (1898).

spank (spăngk) to punish by slapping on the bottom with the open hand, a slipper, or the like; strike; smack.

spank·ing (spăngk′ĭng) **1** as punishment, a number of slaps with the open hand; a smacking: *He had a* spanking *for being so naughty.* **2** brisk; rapid; moving swiftly: *The horses went at a* spanking *pace.*

¹spar (spär) mast or one of the other poles used to support and stretch out a ship's sails. [**¹spar** is a form of an earlier English word (sparre) that seems to come from an Old Norse word (sparri) meaning "a beam."]

²spar (spär) **1** to box with skill and caution: *The boys love to* spar *with each other.* **2** to wrangle; dispute: *to* spar *about politics.* **sparred, spar·ring.** [**²spar** is from an Old French term used in cockfighting (esparer) meaning "to strike with the spurs." The French word comes from an Italian word (sparare) meaning "to kick, discharge."]

spare (spâr) **1** to avoid injuring, harming, or destroying; show mercy to: *The victors* spared *their prisoners.* **2** to show consideration for; deal gently with: *We must* spare *Dora's feelings and not criticize her.* **3** to do without: *We can't* spare *the car tonight.* **4** to free or save (someone) from: *I'll* spare *myself the trip and send a telegram instead.* **5** to afford to give: *I can* spare *the money. I have time to* spare. **6** saved for use at another time; extra: *a* spare *bit of cash;*

spare *tire.* **7** lean; thin; having little flesh: *a tall,* spare *man.* **spared, spar·ing.**

spare·ribs (spâr′rĭbz′) ends of pork ribs with the meat that joins them.

spar·ing (spâr′ĭng) **1** careful; frugal: *She has to be a* sparing *housewife as they have so little money.* **2** limited; scanty; stingy: *They were very* sparing *with the sugar in this cake.* **spar·ing·ly.**

spark (spärk) **1** hot, glowing bit thrown off from something burning or produced by striking hard stone and metal, etc.: *The* sparks *flew from the burning logs.* **2** one of the tiny flashes caused by an electric arc: *A shower of* sparks *flew from the broken toaster cord.* **3** to send out sparks: *The broken cord* sparked. **4** the electric device that lights the fuel of a gas engine. **5** a trace of something; small amount or sign: *There is a* spark *of life in the wounded bird.*

spar·kle (spär′kəl) **1** to send forth sparks of light; glitter; glisten: *Her eyes* sparkled *with fun.* **2** a gleam; flash; glitter: *the* sparkle *of diamonds.* **3** to be brilliant; to flash: *His wit* sparkled *at the party.* **4** brilliance; liveliness: *the* sparkle *of his wit.* **spar·kled, spar·kling.**

spar·row (spăr′ō) a small, brownish-gray bird found in most parts of the world, especially in cities.

sparse (spärs) not dense or thick; occurring here and there: *a* sparse *growth of trees.* **spars·er, spars·est; sparse·ly.**

Spar·ta (spär′tə) a country in the southern part of ancient Greece famous for the severe military training of its youth.

Spar·tan (spär′tən) **1** inhabitant of Sparta. **2** hardy and courageous, like the soldiers of Sparta.

spasm (spăz′əm) **1** sudden, involuntary, and unnatural drawing together of a muscle or muscles. **2** sudden violent seizure: *a* spasm *of pain;* spasm *of fear.* **3** sudden brief spell of activity or energy: *a* spasm *of work.*

¹spat (spăt) See **²spit.** *He* spat *out his chewing gum.* [**¹spat** is a form of **²spit.**]

²spat (spăt) slight or petty quarrel: *They had a* spat *about who should drive.* [**²spat** is probably the imitation of a sound.]

---

fāte, făt, fâre, fär; bē, bĕt; bite, bĭt; nō, nŏt, nôr; fūse, fŭn, fûr; tōō, tŏŏk; foil; foul; thin; ~~then~~; hw for wh as in *wh*at; zh for s as in u*s*ual; ə for a, e, i, o, u, as in *a*go, lin*e*n, per*i*l, at*o*m, min*u*s

³spat (spăt) cloth covering for the upper part of the shoe. [**³spat** is short for (spatter-dash) meaning "a gaiter, a covering for the leg."]

spat·ter (spăt'ər) **1** to let fall in drops; scatter in all directions: *Ruth* spattered *ink on the desk.* **2** a falling in drops; pattering: *a* spatter *of raindrops, hailstones, etc.* **3** to splash; soil by splashing: *A car* spattered *my coat with mud.*

spat·u·la (spăch'ə lə) flexible, broad-bladed, dull-edged, knifelike implement for use in cooking or for spreading pastes or the like.

spawn (spôn) **1** eggs, or the newly hatched young, of fishes, frogs, oysters, and other water creatures. **2** to deposit these eggs: *Salmon* spawn *in fresh water.* **3** to give birth to or bring forth in great numbers: *The author* spawned *forty novels, each worse than the last.* **4** offspring; a swarming brood: *the criminal* spawn *of the slums.*

speak (spēk) **1** to say words; talk: *The baby* speaks *very little.* **2** to make known; tell: *I must* speak *to Mother before I can go riding.* **3** to use (a particular language): *Jaqueline* speaks *Spanish too.* **4** to make a speech; address an audience: *Dr. Smith will* speak *to the music class tomorrow.*

speak for to represent; state the wishes, views, or opinions of another; act as spokesman for.

speak one's mind to say exactly what one thinks.

speak out or **up 1** to give one's opinions without fear. **2** to speak clearly and loudly.

speak volumes to say a lot; be significant: *His silence* spoke volumes.

speak well to be evidence in favor of; give a favorable idea of: *It* spoke well *for the boy that he owned up to his mistake.*
spoke, spo·ken, speak·ing.

speak·er (spē'kər) **1** person who speaks. **2** person who makes a public speech. **3** loudspeaker. **4** **Speaker** officer who presides over an assembly or lawmaking body: *the* Speaker *of the House of Representatives; the* Speaker *of the House of Commons.*

¹spear (spir) **1** weapon consisting of a long, slender rod or shaft with a sharp, pointed head. **2** to thrust or pierce with, or as if

with, a spear: *Alvin* speared *the potato with his fork.* [**¹spear** is a form of an Old English word (spēre) meaning "a hunting spear."]

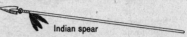
Indian spear

²spear (spir) blade or sprout of a plant: *a* spear *of grass.* [**²spear** is a changed form of **spire.** The spelling was influenced by **¹spear.**]

spear·head (spir'hĕd') **1** point of a spear. **2** leading person or group in an endeavor, especially in a military attack.

spear·mint (spir'mĭnt') common garden mint, used for flavoring.

spe·cial (spĕsh'əl) **1** belonging to a distinct person, class, or thing: *Gilbert's* special *talent was for solving puzzles.* **2** made for a particular purpose: *These* special *tires are for use on icy roads.* **3** out of the ordinary; not general: *a* special *holiday.* **4** highly esteemed; chief: *her* special *friend; a* special *interest in games.* **spe·cial·ly.**

spe·cial·ist (spĕsh'əl ist) person who devotes himself to a particular branch of study, business, etc.: *A pediatrician is a doctor who is a* specialist *in the care of children.*

spe·cial·ize (spĕsh'ə liz') **1** to follow a particular line of action or study: *The doctor* specialized *in surgery.* **2** to give special attention to: *This catering company* specializes *in weddings.* **spe·cial·ized, spe·cial·iz·ing.**

spe·cial·ty (spĕsh'əl tĭ) **1** line of study or work to which a person particularly devotes himself: *Mr. Jackson's* specialty *is raising pigeons.* **2** service, article, or line of goods mainly or exclusively dealt in: *The* specialty *of the shop is fine fishing tackle.* **spe·cial·ties.**

spe·cies (spē'shēz') **1** single kind of plant or animal: *All breeds of dogs belong to the same* species. **2** a kind; variety: *Teasing is often a* species *of cruelty.*

spe·cif·ic (spi sĭf'ik) **1** of a definite kind; particular; precise: *He had* specific *orders to wait after school.* **2** medicine that cures a particular disease: *Penicillin is a* specific *for pneumonia. Quinine is a* specific *for malaria.*

spec·i·fi·ca·tion (spĕs'ə fə kā'shən) **1** act of specifying; a laying down of details or particulars: *His* specification *is based on careful research.* **2 specifications** detailed description of requirements: *the architect's* specifications *for a house.*

spec·i·fy (spĕs'ə fī') to mention or name definitely; state fully and clearly: *Did Grandfather's will* specify *who was to inherit the farm?* **spec·i·fied, spec·i·fy·ing.**

spec·i·men (spĕs'ə mən) sample of something, or one of a group of things which can be studied as an example of the whole: *a* specimen *of iron ore; a* specimen *of deep sea life; a* specimen *of cowboy songs.*

speck (spĕk) **1** small spot or stain: *Wipe the* speck *off your cheek.* **2** tiny thing; particle: *There wasn't a* speck *of dust in the entire room. Is there a* speck *of truth in what he says?* **3** to mark with a speck.

speck·le (spĕk'əl) **1** small spot in or on something. **2** to mark with speckles. **speck·led, speck·ling.**

speck·led (spĕk'əld) marked or covered with small spots or speckles, as on the skin: *a* speckled *dog.*

spec·ta·cle (spĕk'tə kəl) public display; unusual or impressive sight: *The* spectacle *of the fireworks excited the children. Travelers are awed by the* spectacle *of the Alps.*

spec·ta·cles (spĕk'tə kəlz) pair of glasses to help or correct a person's vision, protect the eyes, etc.

spec·tac·u·lar (spĕk tăk'yŏŏ lər) making a great display: *The hero came home to a* spectacular *celebration.* **spec·tac·u·lar·ly.**

spec·ta·tor (spĕk'tā tər or spĕk tā'tər) one who looks on without taking part; observer: *I was only a* spectator *of the quarrel.*

spec·ter or **spec·tre** (spĕk'tər) ghost.

spec·tro·scope (spĕk'trə skōp') instrument for breaking up light into its parts and showing them as bands of different colors. It is used to tell what elements are present at the source of the light.

spec·trum (spĕk'trəm) band of colors formed when light is broken up into its parts, as in the rainbow or when light passes through a prism. **spec·tra** or **spec·trums.**

spec·u·late (spĕk'yŏŏ lāt') **1** to reflect on; form opinions without having complete knowledge: *to* speculate *on the existence of life on other planets.* **2** to buy or sell when there is a risk, with the hope of profiting from a change of prices: *He made his fortune* speculating *on the stock exchange.* **spec·u·lat·ed, spec·u·lat·ing.**

spec·u·la·tion (spĕk'yŏŏ lā'shən) **1** a thinking about; consideration of a subject: *There was much* speculation *about whether there is life on other planets.* **2** opinion or idea reached by speculating: *Early* speculations *about the causes of disease proved false.* **3** the buying or selling of shares of stock, goods, etc., with the hope of profiting from a change in prices.

sped (spĕd) See **speed.** *The arrow* sped *to its mark.*

speech (spēch) **1** power of uttering words. **2** act of speaking: *to burst into rapid* speech. **3** that which is spoken; words; remarks: *The sailor's* speech *was full of slang.* **4** manner of speaking: *His rapid* speech *suggests that he is nervous.* **5** language or dialect: *Italian is a musical* speech: **6** formal talk delivered in public: *a graduation* speech.

speech·less (spēch'lĭs) **1** not speaking; silent: *John remained* speechless *throughout the scolding.* **2** lacking ability to speak. **3** impossible to express in words: *a* speechless *rage.* **speech·less·ly.**

speed (spēd) **1** rapidity; swiftness: *He completed the errand with great* speed. **2** to move rapidly: *The plane* sped *through the air.* **3** to cause to move at a fast rate: *He* sped *his horse over the fields.* **4** rate of moving or doing; velocity: *He drove at a* speed *of twenty miles per hour. His* speed *in the test was two problems per minute.* **5** luck; success; good fortune: *He wished him all* speed. **6 speed limit** fastest speed permitted by law. **sped** or **speed·ed, speed·ing.**

speed·boat (spēd'bōt') motorboat meant to go at high speed.

speed·om·e·ter (spē dŏm'ə tər) device for measuring the speed at which a moving vehicle goes and the number of miles that it travels.

---

fāte, făt, fâre, fär; bē, bĕt; bīte, bĭt; nō, nŏt, nôr; fūse, fŭn, fûr; tōō, tŏŏk; foil; foul; thin; then; hw for wh as in *wh*at; zh for s as in u*s*ual; ə for a, e, i, o, u, as in *a*go, lin*e*n, per*i*l, at*o*m, min*u*s

speedway

speed·way (spēd'wā') **1** road or highway for travel at high speeds. **2** a track for automobile races.

speed·y (spē'dĭ) fast; quick; swift: *He did a speedy job of painting the kitchen.* **speed·i·er, speed·i·est; speed·i·ly.**

¹spell (spĕl) **1** to form words with letters: *to learn how to spell.* **2** to give in proper order the letters (of a word): *He asked me to spell "cat."* **3** to form (a word): *Does c, a, t spell "cat"?* **4** to mean; give warning of: *The dark sky spelled danger of a storm.* **spelled** or **spelt, spell·ing.** [¹**spell** is from an Old French word (espeller) that comes from a Germanic word.]

²spell (spĕl) **1** magic influence; fascination: *The beauty of the sea at evening cast a spell over him.* **2** word or words supposed to have magic power: *The witch pronounced a spell over her enemy.* [²**spell** is the unchanged form of an Old English word meaning "story, saying."]

³spell (spĕl) **1** any period of time: *a hot spell of weather.* **2** to take the place of (a person); alternate with: *He spelled him at painting the fence.* **3** a period of work: *He took a spell at the wheel.* **4** attack (of illness): *a fainting spell; a coughing spell.* [³**spell** is a form of an Old English word (spelian) meaning "to act for another."]

spell·bound (spĕl'bound') enchanted; intrigued; fascinated; held in awe: *They were spellbound by the beauty of the music.*

spell·er (spĕl'ər) **1** person who spells (words): *He was the poorest speller in his class.* **2** book for teaching students how to form words from letters.

spell·ing (spĕl'ĭng) **1** the act of forming words with letters. **2** the way in which a particular word is spelled: *The spelling of dog is d, o, g.*

spelling bee contest in spelling between persons or teams.

spelt (spĕlt) See ¹**spell.** *How is that word spelt?*

spend (spĕnd) **1** to pay out money: *He spends a great deal for clothes.* **2** to use up; exhaust: *to spend energy.* **3** to pass (time): *He spent a quiet day reading and listening to music.* **spent, spend·ing.**

spend·thrift (spĕnd'thrift') **1** person who spends money extravagantly. **2** extravagant; wasteful: *his spendthrift habits.*

spike

spent (spĕnt) See **spend.** *He spent his money foolishly.*

sperm whale (spûrm hwāl) large, square-headed, toothed whale valued for its oil.

sphere (sfir) **1** round object with a surface that is everywhere the same distance from a center point; ball; globe. **2** place, field, or extent of a person's knowledge, activity, etc.: *When he talks about music he is outside his sphere.*

spher·i·cal (sfĕr'ə kəl) in the shape of a sphere; round. **spher·i·cal·ly.**

sphinx (sfĭngks) **1** in Greek and Egyptian legend, a creature with a human, ram's, or hawk's head and a lion's body, sometimes winged. **2** statue of such a creature. **3** secretive, mysterious person.

Egyptian sphinx

spice (spīs) **1** vegetable substance, such as ginger, cinnamon, nutmeg, pepper, and the like, used to give flavor to food. **2** to give flavor to (food) with spice: *to spice a sauce.* **3** to give added interest or zest: *He spiced his conversation with humorous anecdotes.* **4** added interest or zest: *the spice of wit.* **spiced, spic·ing.**

spick-and-span (spĭk'ən spăn') neat and clean; fresh; tidy: *a spick-and-span kitchen.*

spic·y (spī'sĭ) **1** flavored with spice: *a spicy meal.* **2** bright; witty: *a bit of spicy talk.* **spic·i·er, spic·i·est; spic·i·ly.**

spi·der (spī'dər) **1** an eight-legged, round-bodied creature, some kinds of which build webs to catch insects. **2** a frying pan.

Garden spider, ½ to ¾ in. across

spied (spīd) See **spy.** *The guard spied him.*

spies (spīz) See **spy.** *Jack often spies on his neighbors.*

spig·ot (spĭg'ət) **1** small plug or peg used to stop up a hole or tube through which the contents of a barrel or cask are withdrawn. **2** faucet.

¹spike (spīk) **1** large metal nail. **2** to fasten with a spike: *He spiked the plank to the post.* **3** to stop; halt; put an end to: *She spiked the rumor that her family would* move. **4** sharp point on the sole of a shoe to prevent slipping. **5** to pierce or hurt with such a spike or spikes: *Ed spiked the catcher when he slid home.* **6** any point or slender, pointed object: *Ice hung from the eaves in long spikes.* **spiked, spik·ing.** ['**spike** is from an Old Norse word meaning "a nail."]

Spike of wheat

Railroad spike

²**spike** (spīk) **1** ear or head of grain. **2** slender, pointed spray: *a spike of gladioli.* [²**spike** is from a Latin word (spica) meaning "ear of grain."]

spill (spil) **1** to overflow; pour out: *He filled his glass of milk so full that it spilled over the top.* **2** to let, or cause to, run over or pour out: *He tripped and spilled his cup of coffee.* **3** a fall: *He ran down the hill carelessly and took a bad spill.* **4** to scatter; throw out: *She spilled the contents of her purse on the table.* **spilled** or **spilt, spill·ing.**

spill·way (spil'wā') channel for overflow water to escape from a reservoir, etc.

spilt (spilt) See **spill.** *When Cora upset her cup, the coffee spilt on the table.*

spin (spin) **1** to go round and round; whirl: *A top spins.* **2** to cause to go round and round: *to spin a top.* **3** a rapid whirling: *the spin of a wheel.* **4** to form and twist into a thread: *People used to spin wool on a spinning wheel.* **5** to produce a fine thread as do silkworms and spiders. **6** to make by spinning: *Spiders spin webs.* **7** to tell (a story), especially one that the teller makes up as he goes along: *The old sailor spun a tale of pirates.* **8** of a vehicle, to move swiftly: *The coach spins merrily down the road.* **9** to seem to whirl; be confused or dizzy: *All these orders make my head spin.* **spun, spin·ning.**

spin·ach (spin'ich or spin'ij) **1** a leafy garden plant. **2** leaves of this plant boiled and eaten as a vegetable.

spi·nal (spī'nəl) **1** having to do with the backbone. **2 spinal column** spine; backbone. **3 spinal cord** thick cord of nerve

tissue running from the brain down through the backbone.

spin·dle (spin'dəl) **1** slender rod, often cigar-shaped, that draws out and twists the thread in hand spinning. **2** slender rod upon which something turns. **3** spike for holding papers.

spine (spīn) **1** chain of small bones running down the back; backbone. **2** any connecting or strengthening part like a backbone. **3** stiff growth

SPINE

Spine of a cat

with a sharp point on a plant or animal. Rose thorns and porcupine quills are spines.

spine·less (spīn'lis) **1** having no backbone: *A snail is a spineless creature.* **2** without thorns: *a spineless cactus.* **3** lacking energy, spirit, or determination. **spine·less·ly.**

spin·et (spin'it) **1** an old-fashioned musical instrument with a keyboard like a piano. **2** small piano.

spinning wheel old-fashioned machine for twisting wool, flax, etc., into yarn or thread.

Spinning wheel

spin·ster (spin'stər) woman who has not married.

spi·ral (spī'rəl) **1** shape of a circular line drawn from a center and constantly expanding like a coil of rope, a line drawn around a cone from its tip to its base, or a line drawn around a cylinder from top to

Spirals

bottom: *The plane rose in a widening spiral. The tower stairway was built in a spiral.* **2** an object or course in any of these forms: *A snail shell is a spiral. The bird flew up in a spiral.* **3** like or in the shape of a spiral: *a spiral coffee cake; a spiral flight; a spiral staircase.* **4** to move in a spiral: *The aviator spiraled to earth.* **spi·ral·ly.**

---

fāte, făt, fâre, fär; bē, bĕt; bīte, bĭt; nō, nŏt, nôr; fūse, fŭn, fûr; tōō, tŏŏk; foil; foul; thin; then; hw for wh as in *what*; zh for s as in *usual*; ə for a, e, i, o, u, as in *ago, linen, peril, atom, minus*

spire (spir) **1** the topmost, pointed part of a steeple: *A church* spire *thrust its sharp point above the trees.* **2** anything that is slender and points upward: *Hemlocks stood in black* spires *against the red sunset.*

spir·it (spir′it) **1** force which gives life to the body; life principle. **2** a being which is not physical: *good and evil* spirits. **3** vigor, enthusiasm, courage, etc.: *a boy of* spirit; *to fight with* spirit. **4** person or idea thought of as being a driving force: *the* spirit *of the American Revolution.* **5** special quality; attitude; tendency: *the* spirit *of the times.* **6** real meaning or intent: *to obey the* spirit *as well as the letter of the law.* **7** to carry (off or away) suddenly and secretly: *His friends* spirited *him from the jail.* **8** spirits (1) frame of mind; mood; temper: *a boy of high* spirits. (2) distilled liquid, especially alcohol.

spir·it·ed (spir′it id) full of life or vigor; animated; lively: *a* spirited *horse; a* spirited *debate.* **spir·it·ed·ly.**

spir·i·tu·al (spir′i chōō əl) **1** having to do with the spirit or mind rather than with material things: *the* spiritual *growth of the poet.* **2** having to do with religion or the church: *the* spiritual *duties of a clergyman.* **3** hymn or sacred song, especially one created by the Negroes of the South. **spir·i·tu·al·ly.**

¹spit (spit) **1** a rod or bar on which meat is roasted over an open fire. **2** narrow cape or point of land extending into water. **3** to pierce with or as with a spit, as meat to be roasted. **spit·ted, spit·ting.** [¹spit is a form of an Old English word (spitu) meaning "a sharp-pointed stick."]

Spit

²spit (spit) **1** saliva; the liquid formed by glands in the mouth. **2** to throw or squirt saliva from the mouth. **3** to cast (something) out of the mouth: *to* spit *out grape seeds.* **4** to throw off: *The broken electric wire was* spitting *sparks.* **5** to hiss, as an angry cat. **spat** or **spit, spit·ting.** [²spit is a form of an Old English word (spittan) meaning "to spit."]

spite (spit) **1** malice; ill will; desire to injure: *Joe's reply showed his* spite *toward his rival.* **2** to show ill will or malice toward; seek to hurt or aggravate: *We'll* spite *them for not being asked to their party.* **3** in spite of notwithstanding; despite. **spit·ed, spit·ing.**

spite·ful (spit′fəl) showing or feeling spite; inclined to petty annoyance or continuous attempts to injure or offend: *His* spiteful *resentment showed in every belittling word.* **spite·ful·ly.**

splash (splash) **1** violent scattering and flying about of a liquid, caused by a stroke, plunge, or slop: *The diver made a great* splash *when he hit the water.* **2** to scatter a liquid and set it flying in this way. **3** to paddle vigorously or romp (in the water): *The children* splashed *about in the lake.* **4** to slop, toss, or throw (a liquid): *to* splash *water on a campfire.* **5** to soil by splashing: *Mud* splashed *our car.* **6** any blotch, spot, or the like: *That picture makes a* splash *of color on the drab wall.* **7** sound of a splash.

splash·y (splash′i) **1** making a splash. **2** making the sound of splashing: *the* splashy *raindrops on the windowsill.* **3** full of irregular marks or streaks: *a* splashy *print.* **4** showy; loud; attracting attention: *a* splashy *car.* **splash·i·er, splash·i·est.**

splat·ter (splat′ər) to spatter; splash.

spleen (splēn) **1** a gland near the stomach which makes certain changes in the blood. In former times, it was thought to be the seat of certain feelings, such as ill temper and spite. **2** bad temper or spite.

splen·did (splen′did) **1** magnificent; spectacular: *the* splendid *ceremonies of a coronation.* **2** excellent; fine; praiseworthy: *a* splendid *effort.* **splen·did·ly.**

splen·dor (splen′dər) **1** glory; richness; brilliance: *the* splendor *of a summer sunset.* **2** great show; pomp; magnificence: *the* splendor *of the royal court.*

splice (splis) **1** to join by weaving together, as the ends of rope; unite by overlapping, as timbers. **2** section of rope, timber, etc., joined in this way. **spliced, splic·ing.**

splint (splint) **1** device made of wood strips, plaster, or metal, used to hold broken bones in place. **2** thin strip of wood or cane used in making baskets, etc.

splin·ter (splin′tər) **1** thin, sharp, broken piece of wood, bone, glass, etc.; sliver: *The* splinter *in my hand caused me pain.* **2** to break into sharp, thin pieces, or slivers: *Lightning* splintered *the tree.*

split (splĭt) **1** to divide or cut lengthwise or in layers: *The farmer* split *the logs for firewood.* **2** to tear or burst apart: *The extreme cold made the rocks* split. **3** a tear; crack: *a* split *in the side of the drawer.* **4** to divide or separate into portions: *Please* split *the ice cream so there will be enough for everyone.* **5** division in a political party or group (of anything): *There was a* split *on the tax question.* **6** parted lengthwise; divided. **7 split ticket** ballot cast for candidates of more than one party. It is the opposite of **straight ticket. split, split·ting.**

splotch (splŏch) **1** an irregular spot; smear; stain. **2** to mark with splotches: *to* splotch *paint on a wall.* **splotched, splotch·ing.**

splut·ter (splŭt′ər) **1** to speak in a hasty or confused manner as in excitement or embarrassment: *Bob could only* splutter *when he was told he had won the car in the lottery.* **2** to make a hissing sound; sputter.

spoil (spoil) **1** to ruin; damage or injure. **2** to cause (someone) to become lazy, expect too much from others, etc., by pampering: *The mother* spoiled *the child by letting her have her own way.* **3** to become unfit for use: *The milk* spoiled *because I forgot to keep it cool.* **4 spoils** things won or taken by force. **spoiled** or **spoilt, spoil·ing.**

spoilt (spoilt) See **spoil.**

¹spoke (spōk) See **speak.** *He* spoke *to my father about me.* [**¹spoke** is a form of **speak.**]

²spoke (spōk) **1** bar connecting the hub of a wheel and its rim. **2** ladder rung. [**²spoke** is a form of an Old English word (spāca) of the same meaning.]

spo·ken (spō′kən) See **speak.** *We have* spoken *to them about the dance.*

Spoke

spokes·man (spōks′mən) person who speaks for another or others: *You will be our chief* spokesman. **spokes·men.**

sponge (spŭnj) **1** a type of sea animal having a framework with many openings or pores.

2 the light, dried framework of this animal. It absorbs great quantities of liquid and is used for bathing and cleaning. **3** any light substance with many pores like a sponge. **4** to bathe or clean with a sponge: *We* sponged *the dirt from our bodies.* **5** to absorb moisture or liquids: *to* sponge *up spilled milk with a towel.* **6** to live or get something by imposing on others: *to* sponge *on friends for meals.* **7** person who acts in this way. **sponged, spong·ing.**

sponge cake a light, spongy cake made of flour, eggs, sugar, etc., but no shortening.

spon·gy (spŭn′jĭ) full of small holes; absorbent. **spon·gi·er, spon·gi·est.**

spon·sor (spŏn′sər) **1** person who lends support to, or is responsible for, another person or thing: *He is a* sponsor *for my application to college.* **2** to support and approve: *I will* sponsor *your idea.* **3** business firm or other organization which pays the cost of radio or TV programs as an advertisement. **4** godfather; godmother.

spon·ta·ne·ous (spŏn tā′nĭ əs) arising or acting from a natural impulse: *a* spontaneous *burst of applause.* **spon·ta·ne·ous·ly.**

spook (spŏŏk) ghost; spirit; specter.

spool (spŏŏl) **1** cylindrical piece of wood with flaring ends on which thread may be wound. **2** any piece in the shape of a cylinder that is used in a like way; a reel: *a* spool *of motion picture film.*

Spool

spoon (spŏŏn) **1** small shallow bowl with a long handle, that is used in preparing, serving, or eating food. **2** to take up in a spoon: *to* spoon *the soup.*

spoon·ful (spŏŏn′fŏŏl′) as much as a spoon will hold.

spore (spôr) tiny cell given off by flowerless plants and some microscopic animals. It can grow into a new plant or animal. Molds, ferns, and mosses reproduce by spores.

sport (spôrt) **1** game or pastime: *Golf and tennis are* sports *you can enjoy until you are old.* **2** of or for sports: *a* sport *stadium;* sport *clothes.* **3** amusement; fun: *We often*

---

fāte, făt, fâre, fär; bē, bĕt; bīte, bĭt; nō, nŏt, nôr; fūse, fŭn, fûr; tōō, tŏŏk; foil; foul; thin; ~~then;~~
hw for wh as in *wh*at; zh for s as in u*s*ual; ə for a, e, i, o, u, as in a*g*o, lin*e*n, per*i*l, at*o*m, min*u*s

do things just for the sport *of it. Mother teased us in* sport. **4** to wear; show off in public: *Bob* sported *a new hat on Sunday.* **5** person who plays fair and is willing to take chances; lively companion: *Mark is a* sport *and always ready for a lark.* **6 good** or **bad sport** person who accepts defeat, teasing, etc., with good or bad humor. **7 make sport of** to make fun of; ridicule: *Don't* make sport of *that tall girl.*

sport·ing (spôr′ting) **1** engaged or interested in sports: *The athlete belonged to a* sporting *crowd.* **2** playing fair and willing to take a risk: *The children were taught to be* sporting *in their games.* **3** having to do with sports: *Horse racing is a* sporting *amusement.* **sport·ing·ly.**

sports·man (spôrts′mən) **1** person who takes part in sports, such as hunting and fishing, etc. **2** person who plays fair or is honorable. **sports·men.**

sports·man·ship (spôrts′mən ship′) **1** skill in or liking for sports. **2** behavior expected of a sportsman, such as fair play or good grace in defeat.

spot (spŏt) **1** a stain; mark; patch: *a grease* spot; *a spot of white on the black dog.* **2** a blemish: *a spot on the family name.* **3** to cause or make spots: *We* spotted *the tablecloth with gravy.* **4** to become spotted: *This material* spots *easily.* **5** place or area: *We can picnic in this* spot. **6** to pick out; locate: *Can you* spot *your father in the crowd?* **7 on the spot** at once; immediately: *We closed the bargain* on the spot. **spot·ted, spot·ting.**

spot·less (spŏt′lĭs) without a mark or stain; immaculate. **spot·less·ly.**

spot·light (spŏt′lit′) **1** in the theater, strong light focused on an object, person, or persons on the stage. **2** public attention: *He was in the* spotlight *after his victory at the Olympics.*

spot·ty (spŏt′ĭ) **1** marked with spots. **2** not steady; irregular: *His attendance in class was* spotty. **spot·ti·er, spot·ti·est; spot·ti·ly.**

spouse (spous or spouz) either one of a married couple; one's husband or wife.

spout (spout) **1** projection, such as a tube or nozzle, with an opening from which a liquid flows or is poured: *This teapot doesn't pour well because it has a broken* spout. **2** to spurt a jet ~~~~~~~~

spouts. *A whale* spouts. **3** to spurt (liquid): *The leaking pipe* spouted *oil.* **4** to come out in spurts: *Oil* spouted *from the pipe.* **5** a gush of liquid: *a spout of oil.* **6** to speak in a self-important, pompous way: *He* spouts *his opinions at every opportunity.*

sprain (sprān) **1** injury caused by a bad twist to the muscles or ligaments around a joint. **2** to twist the muscles or ligaments around a joint.

sprang (sprăng) See **spring.** *The leopard* sprang *from the tree and landed in front of the hunters.*

sprawl (sprôl) **1** to sit or lie in a careless or awkward position: *She* sprawled *on the sofa because she was tired.* **2** to move along awkwardly, using the arms and legs; scramble: *The baby* sprawled *across the floor to reach the rattle.* **3** to spread out in an irregular way: *The roses had not been cared for and their branches* sprawled *across the path.* **4** awkward or spreading movement or position: *We found him asleep in a* sprawl *across the bed.*

¹spray (sprā) small branch or shoot of a plant with its leaves and flowers or berries. [**¹spray** is a form of an Old English word (spræc) meaning "a sprig" or "spray."]

²spray (sprā) **1** to scatter a liquid in fine drops or a mist: *The hose* sprayed *gently across the lawn.* **2** fine drops or a mist of water driven by the wind, as from waves breaking on the shore or a boat cutting through water: *He stood on the deck and felt the ocean* spray. **3** anything like these fine drops: *a spray of pebbles.* **4** to apply in fine drops or mist: *She* sprayed *perfume on her handkerchief.* **5** to cover (something) with a fine mist (of anything): *He* sprayed *the walls with paint.* **6** a device that scatters a fine liquid mist: *a garden* spray. **7** a liquid used in any device that shoots out a fine mist: *a spray for mosquitoes.* [**¹spray** is probably from an early Dutch word (sprayen) of the same meaning.]

spread (sprĕd) **1** to put as a covering on: *to* spread *butter on toast.* **2** to cover the surface of: *to* spread *toast with butter.* **3** to unfold; unroll; open out: *to* spread *the blanket on the bed.* **4** to stretch out: *The eagle* spread *its wings.* **5** a stretching out or extension: *the* spread *of an eagle's wings.* **6** to distribute: *to* spread *the pamphlets* ~~~

through the town. **7** to make known; communicate: *to spread* news; *to spread* disease. **8** to extend over an area: *Fire spread* through the building. **9** the extent something stretches; width: *the* broad spread *of the lawn; the* spread *of a man's* hand. **10** growth or expansion: *the* spread *of knowledge.* **11** the covering on a bed, table, etc. **12** meal set out on a table; a feast. **13** food meant to be put on bread: *Apple butter is a* spread. **spread, spread·ing.**

spread-ea·gle (sprĕd′ē′gəl) **1** having the figure of an eagle with wings and legs spread out. **2** exaggerated or boastful, especially in a display of patriotism. **3** to spread out in the form of a spread eagle. **spread-ea·gled, spread-ea·gling.**

spree (sprē) **1** lively frolic; merry time. **2** bout of drinking.

sprig (sprĭg) small twig, shoot, or branch.

spright·ly (sprīt′lĭ) lively; gay. **spright·li·er, spright·li·est.**

spring (sprĭng) **1** metal spiral, set of clamped plates, or strip of elastic metal intended to move, drive, or cushion something: *a door spring; a watch spring; an automobile spring.* **2** natural well; a place where water comes to the surface of the ground. **3** a source or beginning. **4** to arise; grow: *Flowers* spring *from the soil.* **5** to arise suddenly; come into being: *A light breeze* sprang up. *New houses* sprang up *overnight.* **6** bounce; elasticity: *The spring of youth was in the old man's step.* **7** to rebound: *The bent branch* sprang *back suddenly.* **8** a leap; jump; bound: *The dog made a* spring *toward us.* **9** to leap; jump; bound: *The dog* sprang up. **10** the season between winter and summer. **11** to release; *to* spring *a joke; to* spring *a trap.* **12** to split or crack open, warp, etc.: *The roof has* sprung *a leak.* **sprang** or **sprung, sprung, spring·ing.**

spring·board (sprĭng′bôrd′) **1** a flexible board that gives added height or spring to

Leaf spring

Coil spring   Spiral spring

a jump; a diving board. **2** something that gives a good start: *His success as governor was the* springboard *for his Presidential campaign.*

spring·time (sprĭng′tīm′) season of spring.

spring·y (sprĭng′ĭ) able to spring back; elastic; flexible; full of spring. **spring·i·er, spring·i·est; spring·i·ly.**

sprin·kle (sprĭng′kəl) **1** to spray with small drops of water: *You'll have to* sprinkle *the garden today.* **2** to scatter in small drops or particles: *The child* sprinkled *sand on the floor.* **3** to rain lightly. **4** a light rain. **5** small amount of something: *A* sprinkle *of dew still remains on the ground.* **sprin·kled, sprin·kling.**

sprint (sprĭnt) **1** to run at full speed, as in a short race. **2** a short race at full speed.

sprite (sprīt) fairy, elf, or goblin.

sprock·et (sprŏk′ĭt) **1** any one of the teeth on a chain-driven cogwheel. **2** the wheel itself.

SPROCKETS
Sprocket wheel

sprout (sprout) **1** to start to grow; to put forth buds or shoots: *Cabbages are* sprouting *in the garden.* **2** to grow quickly; shoot up: *Gas stations* sprouted *like mushrooms along the new highway.* **3** a beginning growth; a bud; a shoot: *This* sprout *will soon be a plant.*

¹spruce (sprōōs) neat; tidy; trim: *Tommy looked very* spruce *for Sunday school.*

spruce up 1 to make neat and tidy: *She* spruced up *the room before her friends came.* **2** to make oneself neat: *She will* spruce up *before going home.*

spruc·er, spruc·est; spruced, spruc·ing; spruce·ly. [¹**spruce** was once the first word of a phrase, "spruce leather," which meant "Prussian leather," that is, an elegant leather from a large region of Germany.]

Red spruce

²spruce (sprōōs) **1** pointed evergreen tree that bears cones and short, thick needles. **2** the wood of

---

fāte, făt, fâre, fär; bē, bĕt; bīte, bĭt; nō, nŏt, nôr; fūse, fŭn, fûr; tōō, tŏŏk; foil; foul; thin; ~~then~~; hw for wh as in *what*; zh for s as in usual; ə for a, e, i, o, u, as in *a*go, lin*e*n, per*i*l, at*o*m, min*u*s

the spruce, used for lumber and paper pulp. [²**spruce** is short for an old word (sprucefir) which means "a fir from Spruce." "Spruce" was an early misspelling of an Old French word (Pruce) meaning "Prussia," a large state in Germany.]

sprung (sprŭng) See **spring.** *The boxer had sprung to his feet and was ready to fight.*

spry (sprī) active; nimble: *The old lady is very spry for her age.* **spry·er** or **spri·er, spry·est** or **spri·est; spry·ly.**

spume (spūm) foam; froth; scum.

spun (spŭn) See **spin.** *The top had spun a long time when it began to topple.*

spunk (spŭngk) courage; spirit: *He's a small boy but he has a lot of spunk.*

spur (spûr) **1** metal frame with pricking point or points, fitted to a rider's boot heel, with which to urge on his horse. **2** to urge; goad; drive: *Fear spurred him on.* **3** sharp, horny spine on a rooster's leg. **4** anything shaped or used like a rooster's spur: *the spur of a columbine blossom.* **5** a branch railroad track. **6** a ridge of hills at an angle with the main range. **spurred, spur·ring.**

spu·ri·ous (spyŏor′ĭ əs) not genuine; false: *a spurious antique.* **spu·ri·ous·ly.**

spurn (spûrn) **1** to push away, as with the foot. **2** to turn down with scorn.

spurt (spûrt) **1** sudden gush of liquid. **2** to gush forth suddenly in streams: *Blood spurted from the open wound.* **3** sudden increase: *a spurt of activity; a spurt of speed.* **4** to have a short burst of energy or activity; increase greatly: *Sales are expected to spurt before Christmas.*

sput·ter (spŭt′ər) **1** noise like spitting or spluttering: *The engine gave a final sputter and died.* **2** to make a noise like spitting or spluttering. **3** to throw off particles of saliva in excited speech. **4** to talk in a disconnected and explosive manner. **5** confused, rapid speech.

spy (spī) **1** secret agent employed to get information about another country. **2** person who watches others secretly: *Our landlady is a spy who listens at the door.* **3** to act as a spy; watch secretly. **4** to notice at a distance; catch sight of: *Jack spied the church steeple, and knew where he was.* **spies; spies, spied, spy·ing.**

spy·glass (spī′glăs′) small telescope.

squab (skwŏb) young pigeon.

squab·ble (skwŏb′əl) **1** noisy, petty quarrel. **2** to quarrel over unimportant things: *The children have been squabbling all morning.* **squab·bled, squab·bling.**

squad (skwŏd) **1** small number of soldiers brought together for drill, work, etc. **2** small group of people gathered together for a common enterprise: *a traffic squad.*

squad·ron (skwŏd′rən) **1** body of cavalry. **2** group of warships on a special mission. **3** group of armed planes flying or fighting together. **4** any group organized for work.

squal·id (skwŏl′ĭd) dirty; wretched; miserable: *a squalid existence.* **squal·id·ly.**

¹**squall** (skwôl) **1** harsh, loud cry or scream: *The baby's squalls could be heard all over the house.* **2** to cry or scream violently and harshly. [¹**squall** is from an Old Norse word (skvala) meaning "to squeal."]

²**squall** (skwôl) sudden, violent, brief wind storm. It may be accompanied by rain or snow. [²**squall** is ¹**squall** in a later meaning, which arose from the noise of the wind.]

squal·or (skwŏl′ər) wretched and filthy condition; poverty and dirt.

squan·der (skwŏn′dər) to spend in a wasteful manner; waste foolishly: *to squander money; to squander talents.*

square (skwâr) **1** figure having four equal straight sides and a right angle at each corner. **2** like a square: *a square box.* **3** having or making right angles and straight sides: *Is the end of the board square? He has square shoulders.* **4** to cut or shape to, or roughly to, a right angle: *He squared the ends of the board before nailing it in place.* He squared his shoulders. **5** tool shaped like an L or T for checking or marking right angles. **6** city block; area enclosed by two pairs of parallel streets. **7** the length of the side of a city block: *Go three squares east.* **8** public place, often a park, surrounded by streets. **9** place where several streets come together. **10** in arith-

Carpenter's square

metic, the product of a number multiplied by itself: *9 is the* square *of 3.* **11** to multiply a number by itself. **12** honest; fair: *We respect* square *dealing.* **13** full; complete; satisfying: *a* square *meal.* **14** to settle; adjust: *Mr. Smith and Mr. Jones* squared *their bills.* **15** settled; adjusted: *All accounts are* square. **16** to agree; fit in with: *This does not* square *with what you said last night.* **squar·er, squar·est; squared, squar·ing; square·ly.**

square dance old-fashioned dance consisting of a series of set steps for a number of couples arranged in a square.

square knot knot used for joining the ends of ropes, consisting of two loops in which one passes around, and tightens down on, the strands forming the other. For picture, see **knot.**

square-rigged (skwår′rĭgd′) having square or rectangular sails as the main sails. They are hung crosswise to the length of the ship, and not lengthwise as in vessels with fore-and-aft rigging.

square root number which when multiplied by itself will produce a given number: *6 is the* square root *of 36.*

¹**squash** (skwŏsh) **1** vine of the gourd family which bears a fleshy fruit. **2** the fruit of this plant used as a vegetable. [¹**squash** is from an American Indian word (askuta-squash) meaning "vegetables eaten green."]

Squashes

²**squash** (skwŏsh) **1** to crush; mash into a pulp: *Tim* squashed *the berries as he tramped through the bushes.* **2** to suppress; put an end to: *The uprising was promptly* squashed. **3** to make sounds by tramping through slush or soft mud: *If you must* squash *around in the mud, do it in your bare feet.* **4** game similar to tennis played with rackets and a soft ball in a walled court. [²**squash** is from an Old French word (esquasser) that comes from two Latin forms, one (ex-) meaning "very," and the other (quassus) meaning "shaken."]

squat (skwŏt) **1** to crouch on one's heels;

sit on the ground or floor with the legs drawn up closely to the body: *The boys* squatted *around the fire and told stories.* **2** a squatting position. **3** to settle on land without right. **4** to settle on government land in order to get title to it. **5** short and stocky: *a* squat *figure.* **squat·ted, squat·ting; squat·ter, squat·test.**

squat·ter (skwŏt′ər) **1** person who settles on land without legal right. **2** person who settles on public land in order to acquire ownership of it. **3** person or thing that squats or crouches.

squaw (skwô) American Indian woman or wife.

squawk (skwôk) **1** loud, harsh cry. **2** to utter a loud, harsh cry: *The ducks* squawked.

squeak (skwēk) **1** weak, thin, shrill noise, like that of a mouse. **2** to make such a noise: *Shoes* squeak. *Mice* squeak. **3** **narrow squeak** narrow escape.

squeak·y (skwē′kĭ) making weak, thin, shrill sounds. **squeak·i·er, squeak·i·est; squeak·i·ly.**

squeal (skwēl) **1** to utter a shrill prolonged cry: *The pig* squealed *in pain.* **2** such a cry. **3** to tattle on another.

squeeze (skwēz) **1** to put pressure on from the outside; press: *to* squeeze *a hand.* **2** a pressure: *Tom gave Bill's arm a* squeeze. **3** a hug or embrace. **4** to compress; cram: *Helen couldn't* squeeze *both dresses into the suitcase.* **5** to extract by, or as by, pressure: *to* squeeze *juice from a lemon; to* squeeze *a confession from the prisoner.* **6** to make one's way by force: *to* squeeze *through the crowd.* **7** to oppress: *to* squeeze *the poor with heavy taxes.* **8 tight, close,** or **narrow squeeze** predicament; situation from which escape is difficult: *He had a* tight squeeze *in passing the examination.* **squeezed, squeez·ing.**

squint (skwĭnt) **1** to partly close the eyes: *The sunshine made Percy* squint. **2** partial closing of the eyes. **3** sidelong glance: *The tramp eyed Rover with an angry* squint. **4** to look sideways. **5** to be cross-eyed. **6** a being cross-eyed: *Glasses corrected her* squint.

squire (skwīr) **1** man who attended a knight in olden times. **2** country gentle-

fāte, făt, fâre, fär; bē, bĕt; bīte, bĭt; nō, nŏt, nôr; fūse, fŭn, fûr; too, took; foil; foul; thin; then; hw for wh as in *w*hat; zh for s as in u*s*ual; ə for a, e, i, o, u, as in a*go, linen, peril, atom, minus*

695

man. **3** title used for a justice of the peace. **4** an escort. **5** to escort (a lady). **squired, squir·ing.**

squirm (skwûrm) **1** to twist about; writhe; wriggle: *The little boy* squirmed *in embarrassment.* **2** a twist; a wriggle.

squir·rel (skwûr′əl) **1** small, tree-loving animal, usually red or gray, with a bushy tail. **2** the fur of this animal.

Gray squirrel, about 18 in. long

squirt (skwûrt) **1** to force out in a fine jet or stream: *to* squirt *water from a water pistol.* **2** of a liquid, to spurt; spray: *The grapefruit juice* squirted *in my eye.* **3** amount squirted: *Isobel put a* squirt *of perfume on her handkerchief.* **4** a squirting: *Give your throat a good* squirt *with that medicine.*

Sr. 1 Senior. **2** Señor.

St. 1 Saint. **2** Street.

stab (stăb) **1** to pierce with a pointed weapon: *In the last act the villain* stabs *the hero with a dagger.* **2** piercing wound made by something pointed: *a* stab *in the arm.* **3** stabbing motion; jab; thrust. **4** to jab; stick or thrust something pointed into: *to* stab *a roast with a fork.* **5** to hurt the feelings by treachery, harsh words, or the like: *The children's jeers* stabbed *Tony to the heart.* **stabbed, stab·bing.**

sta·bil·i·ty (stə bĭl′ə tĭ) **1** firmness; the quality of being stable or steady: *the* stability *of a well-constructed bridge.* **2** the quality of being lasting and durable: *the* stability *of the pyramids.* **3** the quality of being reliable or dependable: *Everyone who knows his* stability *counts on John.*

sta·bi·lize (stā′bə līz′) to make or keep stable, steady, firm, or level. **sta·bi·lized, sta·bi·liz·ing.**

sta·bi·liz·er (stā′bə līz′ər) device used to steady the motion of a ship, aircraft, etc.

¹sta·ble (stā′bəl) **1** firm; solid: *a building of* stable *construction.* **2** durable; lasting: *a* stable *peace.* **3** steady; dependable: *a man of* stable *character.* **sta·bly.** [**¹stable** is from a Latin word (stabilis) meaning "firm, steady."]

²sta·ble (stā′bəl) **1** building in which animals, especially horses, are kept. **2** a group

of horses under a single ownership: *The Duke of Doodle has a large racing* stable. **3** to put or keep in a stable. **sta·bled, sta·bling.** [**²stable** comes through Old French (estable) from a Latin word (stabulum) meaning "a standing place for animals."]

stack (stăk) **1** a (rounded) pile: *Neat hay*stacks *dotted the field.* **2** tall chimney. **3** set of open bookshelves: *Go to the* stack *and choose your book.* **4** to pile neatly; heap up. **5** to arrange dishonestly: *The gambler* stacked *the cards.* **6** conical stand of rifles with their muzzles together.

Stack of guns

sta·di·um (stā′dĭ əm) field for athletic contests surrounded, or partially surrounded, by permanent tiers of seats. **sta·di·ums** or **sta·di·a.** For picture, see **bowl.**

staff (stăf) **1** a long cane, used for walking or defense. **2** a supporting pole: *flag* staff. **3** a rod as a sign of authority: *a bishop's* staff. **4** a prop; a support: *Bread is called the* staff *of life.* **5** group of persons working as a unit: *The museum* staff *is made up of the director and his assistants.* **6** group of assistants working under a head: *the editor and his* staff. **7** to provide with workers: *to* staff *an office.* **8** a set of five lines and the spaces between them on which music is written. **staves** or **staffs.**

Staff

stag (stăg) **1** the full-grown male of some kinds of deer. **2** for men only: *a* stag *party.* **3** without a lady: *John went* stag *to the dance.*

Stag, about 6 ft. high at shoulder

stage (stāj) **1** raised platform, especially the part of a theater on which a play is acted. **2** profession of acting: *Jean hoped to make the* stage *her life work.* **3** the theater: *Mr. Silver, the banker, is very fond of the* stage. **4** scene of

stagecoach

action: *Dunkirk was the* stage *for a spectacular troop withdrawal in World War II.* **5** to produce as a play: *The school will* stage *Little Red Ridinghood.* **6** step; phase; degree: *the caterpillar* stage *in the life of a butterfly.* **7** distance between stopping places in a journey. **8** stagecoach. **staged, stag·ing.**

Stagecoach

stage·coach (stāj′kōch′) closed vehicle, drawn by horses, with seats for passengers inside and outside on the top, which made regular trips between towns. Some stagecoaches carried mail and parcels as well as passengers.

stag·ger (stăg′ər) **1** to walk with swaying or uncertain steps; reel; totter: *The wounded man* staggered *across the street.* **2** an unsteady walk or gait: *He walked with a slight* stagger. **3** to cause to reel or sway: *The boxer was* staggered *by the blow.* **4** to cause to pause or hesitate: *The argument* staggered *him, but he quickly regained confidence.* **5** to overwhelm; shock: *He was* staggered *by the loss of his job.* **6** to arrange in zigzag fashion: *to* stagger *two rows of trees.* **7** to fix at different times: *Our typists* stagger *their lunch hours.*

stag·nant (stăg′nənt) **1** of water, sluggish; without motion; foul from standing still: *a* stagnant *pool covered with scum.* **2** of the mind, dull; torpid. **stag·nant·ly.**

staid (stād) quiet, dignified; sedate: *a* staid *talk;* staid *behavior.* **staid·ly.**

stain (stān) **1** to discolor; spot; soil: *Ruth* stained *her dress with jam. Weather had* stained *the shingles silver gray.* **2** a discolored spot. **3** to color with a penetrating pigment; dye: *We have* stained *the table walnut.* **4** a dye. **5** a blot (on one's character, reputation, etc.); a disgrace; stigma. **6** to cast a blot on someone's character.

stair (stâr) **1** a step in a flight of steps. **2** usually **stairs,** a flight of steps: *She passed me on the* stair. (Homonym: stare)

stair·case (stâr′kās′) flight of stairs with its stair rail.

stair·way (stâr′wā′) flight of stairs or steps.

¹stake (stāk) **1** post driven, or suitable for driving, into the ground. **2** to mark with stakes: *He* staked *out a plot of ground.* **3** to fasten to a stake: *to* stake *a horse; to* stake *tomato plants.* **4 pull up stakes** to move; leave permanently.

stake a claim to give notice of ownership by marking with a stake or by declaring one has a right (in): *The stepson* staked a claim *to an interest in the will.*

staked, stak·ing. [¹stake is a form of an Old English word (staca) of the same meaning.] (Homonym: steak)

²stake (stāk) **1** something of value risked or played for. **2** to risk: *to* stake *money on a race.* **3** an interest; share: *I have a* stake *in this business.* **staked, stak·ing.** [²stake is from both ¹stake in a special use and a Dutch word (staken) meaning "to fix, place."] (Homonym: steak)

sta·lac·tite (stə lăk′tīt) stone formation like an icicle, hanging from the roof of a cave.

sta·lag·mite (stə lăg′mīt) a cone-shaped stone formation on the floor of a cave, usually under a stalactite. Sometimes stalactites and stalagmites join to form a pillar.

Stalactites and stalagmites

stale (stāl) **1** not fresh; dried out (especially of food): *a piece of* stale *bread.* **2** no longer of interest; worn out by repetition or use: *a* stale *joke.* **3** out of condition; lacking in originality or freshness: *The pianist was* stale *from continually playing the same pieces.* **4** to lose freshness: *Even pleasures* stale *after a time.* **stal·er, stal·est; staled, stal·ing; stale·ly.**

stalemate

stale·mate (stāl′māt′) **1** in chess, a tie. **2** a deadlock: *The teams were at a stalemate.* **3** to bring to a standstill. **stale·mat·ed, stale·mat·ing.**

¹stalk (stôk) **1** slender rod that supports something. A flower's stem is a stalk. **2** slender group of leaves or stems: *a stalk of celery.* [**¹stalk** is formed from an Old English word (stela, stæla) of the same meaning, plus the ending (-ock) meaning "little."]

²stalk (stôk) **1** to pursue or approach cautiously and under cover: *The hunter stalked his game.* **2** to walk in a proud or haughty way: *The indignant man stalked from the room.* **3** to sweep silently through: *Fear stalked the city.* **4** act of stalking. [**²stalk** is a shortened form of an Old English word (bestealcian) meaning "to walk carefully."]

Stalks

stall (stôl) **1** room or enclosure for an animal in a stable. **2** booth or small enclosure from which things are sold: *The big market was divided into stalls.* **3** a seat in a church or theater; a pew. **4** to place in a stall: *Roger stalled his horse for the night.* **5** to cause to stop working without meaning to: *Joe stalled his car.* **6** to stop working: *The car stalled on the hill.* **7** to prevent or delay action: *The merchant stalled off his creditors until he could pay his debts.*

Stalls in a stable

stal·lion (stăl′yən) male horse.

stal·wart (stôl′wərt) **1** strong and muscular; robust. **2** brave; daring: *a stalwart soldier.* **3** brave, reliable person; firm partisan: *Patrick Henry was a stalwart in the cause of liberty.* **4** firm and reliable: *He was always my stalwart friend.* **stal·wart·ly.**

sta·men (stā′mən) one of the parts of a flower that bears pollen.

Stamens

stam·i·na (stăm′ə nə) physical strength; power of endurance: *It takes stamina to be a fine athlete.*

stand

stam·mer (stăm′ər) **1** to repeat the same sound several times before completing a word: *"I d-d-don't know," he* stammered. **2** to speak in a hesitating, confused way due to fear, anger, and the like: *He stammered out an apology.* **3** confused, halting speech; a stutter.

stamp (stămp) **1** small piece of paper sold by the government and put on letters, documents, packages, etc., to show that a fee or tax has been paid: *a postage* stamp; *a revenue* stamp. **2** to put a postage or other official stamp upon: *to stamp a letter.* **3** any special mark or imprint: *The documents bore the* stamp *of his initials.* **4** to make a special mark or imprint on: *He* stamped *the document with his initials.* **5** anything that makes a special mark or imprint: *a rubber* stamp. **6** to put the foot down heavily on: *to stamp the floor.* **7** to trample; tread: *to stamp out the fire.* **8** to indicate; show; reveal: *His manners* stamp *him as a man of breeding.* **9** impression; sign of: *His hands bore the* stamp *of long manual labor.* **10** special quality: *You seldom see plays of that stamp.*

stam·pede (stăm pēd′) **1** sudden wild running away, as of a herd of animals. **2** any sudden rush or movement on the part of a crowd: *a stampede for the exit.* **3** to move together in a general rush: *The fans* stampeded *over the football field when the game was over.* **4** to cause (a herd or crowd) to run wildly: *The rustlers* stampeded *the cattle.* **stam·ped·ed, stam·ped·ing.**

stanch (stônch or stănch) **1** to stop the flow of. **2** to stop the flow of blood from: *to stanch a wound.* Also spelled **staunch.**

stand (stănd) **1** to be erect upon the feet; rise to the feet: *The horses stand in the shade. Please stand.* **2** to rest upon: *The dock stands upon piles. The vase stands on the table.* **3** to place in an upright position: *to stand a book on end.* **4** to be situated: *Our house stood here years ago.* **5** to remain firm: *The rule stands.* **6** to occupy a place in a series of things: *to stand first.* **7** to endure: *Kitty cannot stand pain.* **8** a halt; stop: *The retreating army made a stand at the river.* **9** a defending or supporting position: *We take a stand for clean politics.* **10** to take a defending or supporting posi-

698

tion: *We* stand *behind our candidate.* **11** to be in a certain condition: *The men stood ready for action.* **12** place where one stands: *The guard took his stand at the gate.* **13** small table, pedestal, or frame to hold something: *a plant stand; a music stand.* **14** counter where something is sold: *a fruit stand on the corner.* **15** platform: *a band stand.* **16** group of trees: *Here is a fine stand of spruce.* **17 stands** set of sloping outdoor seats: *The stands were full for the parade.*

Plant stand

stand by 1 to support; aid. **2** to be ready: *Please stand by for an important announcement.*

stand for 1 to represent; take the place of: *"U.S." stands for "United States."* **2** to take the side of; uphold: *The new major stands for honest government.* **3** to put up with: *I won't stand for any more nonsense.*

stand out to be noticeable, conspicuous: *The charming girl stood out in the crowd.* **stood, stand·ing.**

stand·ard (stăn′dərd) **1** level of excellence used as a basis of comparison: *school work below standard; a high standard of living.* **2** authorized weight or measure. **3** of recognized excellence or authority: *a standard work on the subject; a standard author.* **4** emblem or flag: *The Stars and Stripes is the standard of America.* **5** upright support: *a standard for the lamp; a standard for a camera.*

stand·ard·ize (stăn′dər dīz′) to make according to an established size, weight, shape, or the like; make uniform: *to standardize automobile parts; to standardize the size of oranges.* **stand·ard·ized, stand·ard·iz·ing.**

standard time system of keeping time in 24 time zones, east and west, around the earth. All clocks in one time zone are set one hour ahead of the next time zone to the west. The four time zones in the continental United States are Eastern, Central, Mountain, and Pacific.

stand·ing (stăn′dĭng) **1** reputation; position: *He has a good standing at the club.* **2** duration: *a habit of long standing.* **3** permanent; operating continuously: *a standing invitation; a standing order; a standing army.* **4** in an erect position; upright. **5** stagnant; stationary; not flowing: *a standing pool of water.*

stand·point (stănd′point′) basis or standard from which things are considered or judged; point of view: *From the standpoint of honor, it was a cowardly thing to do.*

stand·still (stănd′stĭl′) a stop; halt.

stank (stăngk) See **stink.** *The pier stank of dead fish.*

stan·za (stăn′zə) group of lines forming a section of a poem or song.

¹sta·ple (stā′pəl) **1** chief or principle product of a place: *Wine is the staple of many provinces in France.* **2** very important or major element: *The election was the staple of conversation.* **3** a raw material for manufacture. **4** fiber of cotton, wool, and the like. [**¹staple** comes through Old French (estaple) from an early Dutch word (stapel) meaning "a post, support."]

²sta·ple (stā′pəl) **1** piece of metal shaped like a U, used to fasten wire, papers, etc. **2** to fasten with a staple: *Please staple these report sheets together.* **sta·pled, sta·pling.** [²**staple** is a form of an Old English word (stapel) meaning "post," or "pillar."]

for WOOD

for PAPER

Staples

star (stär) **1** any of the heavenly bodies, other than the moon or planets, seen on a clear night. **2** a five- or six-pointed figure that represents a star. **3** a mark (*) that looks somewhat like a star. **4** a leading actor or athlete. **5** to have a leading role in a play or other activity. **starred, star·ring.**

Stars

star·board (stär′bôrd′) **1** the right side of a ship when a person on deck faces towards the front part of it: *The passengers ran from port to starboard when somebody sighted a whale.* **2** on the right side of a ship: *We have a starboard cabin on the "America."* For picture, see **aft.**

fāte, făt, fâre, fär; bē, bĕt; bīte, bĭt; nō, nŏt, nôr; fūse, fŭn, fûr; tōo, tŏŏk; foil; foul; thin; ~~then~~; hw for wh as in *what;* zh for s as in u*s*ual; ə for a, e, i, o, u, as in *a*go, lin*e*n, per*i*l, at*o*m, min*u*s

starch (stärch) **1** white food substance without taste or odor found in most plants, especially in the seeds. **2** preparation of this substance in a powder form which is mixed with water and used to stiffen clothes and fabrics: *Mother uses* starch *to stiffen collars.* **3** to make stiff with starch: *The organdy curtains must be* starched.

starch·y (stär'chĭ) **1** containing starch: *Potatoes are a* starchy *food.* **2** stiffened with starch. **3** stiff in manner; not friendly: *The young prince was* starchy *with his inferiors.* **starch·i·er, starch·i·est.**

stare (stâr) **1** to look or gaze intently or fixedly, with eyes wide open: *To* stare *is very rude.* **2** long, fixed look with wide-open eyes: *the* stare *of a daydreamer.* **3** to look with surprise or shock: *That hat will make everyone* stare.

stare down or **out of countenance** to make (someone) nervous, confused, uneasy, or embarrassed by staring.

stare one in the face to be right in front of one's eyes; be perfectly plain and clear: *Your lost book is* staring *you in the face.*

stared, star·ing. (Homonym: stair)

star·fish (stär'fĭsh') sea animal with a star-shaped body.

stark (stärk) **1** bare; unadorned: *A* stark *description of the shipwreck is given in the papers.* **2** bleak; desolate; barren: *It is* stark *country up here in the winter.* **3** sheer; utter; absolute: *She was speechless with* stark *terror.* **stark·ly.**

Starfish, 3 to 5 in. across

star·light (stär'līt') light given by the stars: *It was a night made beautiful by* starlight.

star·ling (stär'lĭng) bird about the size of a robin, glossy black in summer, that lives in large flocks.

star·lit (stär'lĭt') lighted by the stars.

star·ry (stär'ĭ) **1** containing many stars: *a* starry *sky.* **2** shining like stars; bright: *to watch with* starry *eyes.* **3** shaped like a star. **star·ri·er, star·ri·est.**

Starling, about 8½ in. long

Stars and Stripes the flag of the United States, with a star representing each state, and a stripe representing each of the thirteen colonies at the time of the Revolutionary War.

start (stärt) **1** to begin to go somewhere or do something: *The train has just* started. *We* start *school at nine o'clock.* **2** to set going; bring into being; open up: *to* start *a fire; to* start *a discussion on politics.* **3** to cause or enable (a person) to accomplish something: *He* started *his son in a small business.* **4** a beginning: *the* start *of the race; a good* start *in life.* **5** to move suddenly and involuntarily: *to* start *with surprise.* **6** sudden, involuntary movement: *a* start *of surprise.* **7 to start with** in the first place: *We can't make the trip because,* to start with, *we don't have the time.* **8 by fits and starts** with frequent pauses; with interruptions: *Traffic moved* by fits and starts.

star·tle (stär'təl) **1** to frighten suddenly; surprise: *You* startled *me by coming in so quietly.* **2** to cause to move suddenly: *The dog* startled *the quail into flight.* **star·tled, star·tling.**

star·tling (stärt'lĭng) frightening; surprising; alarming: *a* startling *discovery.* **star·tling·ly.**

star·va·tion (stär vā'shən) condition of being starved; death or suffering caused by lack of food: *The deserted family faced the threat of* starvation.

starve (stärv) **1** to die or suffer from lack of food. **2** to suffer from great poverty or need: *In the midst of great wealth there are many who* starve. **3** to have great need of; long for; hunger: *to* starve *for companionship.* **4** to be very hungry: *I'm simply* starving. **5** to kill or make suffer from lack of food: *The severe winter* starved *the wildlife over a large part of the country.* **starved, starv·ing.**

state (stāt) **1** condition in which a person or thing is: *a* state *of good health; a* state *of disorder in the kitchen.* **2** government; nation. **3** one of the main political and geographical subdivisions of some nations: *the fifty* States *of the United* States. **4** rich, imposing display; dignity and pomp: *The President received the ambassador in* state. **5** to express in words: *to* state *an opinion.* **stat·ed, stat·ing.**

stat·ed (stā'tĭd) fixed; regular: *The doctor has* stated *office hours.*

state·ly (stāt'lĭ) having a grand manner or appearance; impressive; dignified; imposing: *a stately walk; a stately palace.* **state·li·er, state·li·est.**

state·ment (stāt'mənt) **1** an expressing in words; a stating: *Her* statement *was very hard to hear.* **2** expression in words; something stated: *to make a* statement *for the press.* **3** financial report: *a bank* statement.

states·man (stāts'mən) person skilled in, and taking important part in, the management of public affairs. **states·men.**

states·man·ship (stāts'mən shĭp') skill of a statesman in managing public affairs: *the Congressman showed real* statesmanship.

stat·ic (stăt'ĭk) **1** inactive; at rest; not moving. **2** in radio, blurred and noisy spitting sounds caused by thunderstorms or the operation of near-by electrical equipment.

static electricity 1 electric charge on an object resulting from adding or subtracting electrons. **2** sudden movement of electrons from one electric charge to another, often as a spark or a lightning flash.

sta·tion (stā'shən) **1** position held for a particular purpose or duty: *a military* station *abroad.* **2** an assigned location or place: *The gunners were in their battle* stations. **3** to place in a position: *A guard was* stationed *at the gate.* **4** building or place used as headquarters for an organization: *a police* station. **5** a regular stopping place, and the building there: *a railway* station; *a bus* station. **6** position of a person in society; standing: *a man of high* station *in the community.* **7** a place equipped for sending out radio or television programs.

sta·tion·ar·y (stā'shə nĕr'ĭ) **1** not moving: *The traffic was* stationary *during the parade.* **2** immovable; fixed: *a stationary bookcase.* **3** not changing in size, numbers, condition, etc.: *a stationary population.* (Homonym: stationery)

sta·tion·er·y (stā'shə nĕr'ĭ) paper, envelopes, and other writing materials. (Homonym: stationary)

sta·tis·ti·cal (stə tĭs'tə kəl) having to do with statistics. **sta·tis·ti·cal·ly.**

sta·tis·tics (stə tĭs'tĭks) **1** facts and figures gathered to give information about a particular subject: *Traffic* statistics *prove that careless driving is the main cause of accidents.* **2** science of gathering and interpreting facts and figures.

stat·u·ar·y (stăch'ōō ĕr'ĭ) **1** collection of statues. **2** art of sculpture.

stat·ue (stăch'ōō) representation of a person or animal, sculptured in marble, bronze, clay, or the like: *There is a* statue *of Washington in our town square.*

stat·ure (stăch'ər) **1** height (of a person): *Bob's* stature *is normal for a boy of his age.* **2** moral or intellectual worth: *George Washington was a man of* stature.

sta·tus (stā'təs *or* stăt'əs) **1** social or professional rank or standing: *His high* status *in the town was due to his wealth.* **2** position or condition: *What is the present* status *of the peace conference?*

stat·ute (stăch'ōōt) a law or rule: *a* statute *against speeding; the* statutes *of the club.*

staunch (stônch) **1** firm; strong; resolute: *The army put up a* staunch *defense.* **2** loyal; steadfast: *He is a* staunch *friend through thick and thin.* **staunch·ly.**

stave (stāv) **1** heavy stick; a staff; a cudgel. **2** one of the thin, curved pieces of wood that go into the making of a barrel, cask, or bucket. **3** stanza or verse.

Stave

stave in to break into; break up; puncture: *Joe* staved in *the side of the barrel with one blow of the axe.*

stave off to hold off: *to* stave off *defeat.* **staved** *or* **stove, stav·ing.**

staves (stāvz) **1** more than one **stave.** **2** more than one **staff.**

¹stay (stā) **1** to remain in one place; wait: *Please* stay *here until I return.* **2** to dwell or reside for a short time: *I will* stay *at mother's for the week end.* **3** a visit; sojourn: *a short* stay *in the country.* **4** to keep on being; continue (a condition): *The weather* stayed *cold for more than a week.* **5** to

---

satisfy for a time: *Joe* stayed *his hunger with a snack before dinner.* **6** to postpone; delay: *The judge* stayed *judgment until he could gather more facts.* **7** a postponement: *a* stay *of execution.* [¹**stay** comes through Old French (ester) from a Latin word (stare) meaning "to stand."]

²**stay** (stā) **1** thin strip of metal or plastic used for stiffening corsets, shirt collars, etc. **2** prop, brace, used to steady something: *We placed a* stay *against the sagging tree to keep it from falling.* [²**stay** is from an Old French word (estai) meaning "a prop."]

³**stay** (stā) rope or wire used as a support or brace for ship masts or spars. [³**stay** is a form of an Old English word (stæg) meaning "a rope for supporting the mast."]

stead (stĕd) **1** the place which another had or might have: *My sister went in my* stead. **2 stand (a person) in good stead** to be useful or of advantage: *Your new car will* stand you in good stead.

stead·fast (stĕd′făst′) **1** firmly fixed; not moving: *a steadfast gaze.* **2** constant; not fickle or changing: *a steadfast faith.* **stead·fast·ly.**

stead·i·ness (stĕd′ĭ nĭs) a being firm or steady: *He showed great* steadiness *during the excitement.*

stead·y (stĕd′ĭ) **1** firm; not shaky: *a steady foundation for a building.* **2** constant in feeling or faith: *His love for her has been very* steady *over the years.* **3** sure; not wavering: *His step is still* steady *in spite of his old age.* **4** habitual; regular: *They are* steady *TV watchers.* **5** reliable; having good habits: *She is a* steady *young woman.* **6** to make, become, or keep steady or firm: *to* steady *a ladder.* **stead·i·er, stead·i·est; stead·ied, stead·y·ing; stead·i·ly.**

steak (stāk) slice of meat or fish, cut for broiling or frying. (Homonym: stake)

steal (stēl) **1** to take by theft; to take without leave or right: *to* steal *a car; to* steal *time from a job.* **2** to gain or win by charm, surprise, etc.: *to* steal *a kiss; to* steal *attention.* **3** to move secretly or in a quiet way: *Let's* steal *out of the room on tiptoe.* **4** something bought at an extremely low price: *Mother's hat was a* steal *at $2.00.* **stole, stol·en, steal·ing.** (Homonym: steel)

stealth (stĕlth) secret or sly means or action: *He obtained the money by* stealth *while no one was home.*

stealth·y (stĕl′thĭ) done in a secret or sly manner: *the* stealthy *approach of a wolf.* **stealth·i·er, stealth·i·est; stealth·i·ly.**

steam (stēm) **1** the invisible gas that forms when water boils. **2** in popular use, cloud or mist of tiny water drops formed when water vapor is cooled: *The* steam *came out of the spout of the boiling teakettle.* **3** to give off vapor: *The tea was* steaming. **4** to move under the power of steam engines: *The ship* steamed *away.* **5 let off steam** to express strong feelings that have been pent up.

steam·boat (stēm′bōt′) boat driven by steam engines.

steam engine 1 engine driven by the pressure of hot steam on a piston that moves back and forth in a cylinder. **2** an engine in which the steam drives an enclosed wheel with fan blades mounted on it; a steam turbine.

steam·er (stē′mər) **1** steamship. **2** engine driven by steam. **3** container in which things are cooked by steam.

steam roller a heavy roller, driven by steam, used in road building.

steam·ship (stēm′shĭp′) ship driven by steam.

steed (stēd) horse, especially a spirited horse.

steel (stēl) **1** iron mixed with carbon and other elements. **2** any instrument or weapon made of steel. **3** piece of steel for striking fire from flint. **4** made of steel. **5** to make hard or strong: *The soldiers* steeled *their courage before the attack.* (Homonym: steal)

steel wool fine threads of steel, massed together, and used to clean and polish metal and other surfaces.

¹**steep** (stēp) **1** having a sharp slope or incline; almost straight up and down: *The hill was too* steep *to climb.* **2** very high, said of prices: *Isn't that pretty* steep *for a used car?* **steep·ly.** [¹**steep** is a form of an Old English word (stēap) meaning "tall," "prominent."]

²**steep** (stēp) to soak; immerse: *to let tea* steep *before pouring it; to* steep *oneself in mathematics; to be* steeped *in crime.* [²**steep**

is a form of an earlier English word (stēpen) that probably comes from an Old Norse word (steypa) meaning "to pour."]

stee·ple (stē'pəl) high tower, especially on a church. It generally has a spire.

Steeple

¹**steer** (stir) **1** to direct or guide by means of a wheel, rudder, or other device: *We'll* steer *the boat to shore.* **2** to direct or make one's way: *They* steered *home after the party.* **3** to be guided: *Your car doesn't* steer *easily.*

   steer clear of to avoid: *Better* steer clear of *him if you want to stay out of trouble.* [¹**steer** is a form of an Old English word (stēoran) of the same meaning.]

²**steer** (stir) **1** a male of beef cattle. **2** young ox. [²**steer** is a form of an Old English word (stēor) meaning "heavy" as applied to beasts.]

¹**stem** (stěm) **1** the trunk, or main stalk, of a plant from which other parts branch off. **2** anything like such a trunk, such as the main highway of a road system. **3** any slender connecting part: *the* stem *of a flower.* **4** the tube of a tobacco pipe or the like. **5** bow or front of a ship.

Stems

6 to branch (from); develop (from); spring (from): *Paths* stemmed *from the main road. The legends* stemmed *from fear of lightning.* **stemmed, stem·ming.** [¹**stem** is a form of an Old English word (stæfn) meaning "stem of a tree."]

²**stem** (stěm) **1** to stop; check; dam up: *He* stemmed *the flow of water.* **2** to make progress or headway against: *They* stemmed *the heavy gale.* **stemmed, stem·ming.** [²**stem** is probably from an Old Norse word (stemma) meaning "to stop."]

ste·nog·ra·pher (stə nŏg'rə fər) person who uses shorthand to record what is being said, to make notes, etc., especially a person who does this as an occupation.

step (stěp) **1** movement made by lifting the foot and placing it in a new position: *to take a* step. **2** to make such a movement or movements: *to* step *forward.* **3** distance covered by one such movement or any short distance: *Our house is only a few* steps *from the beach.* **4** to walk a short distance: *to* step *across the street.* **5** sound made by stepping: *We could hear his* steps *in the hall.* **6** to place the foot (on): *to* step *on a tack.* **7** footprint: *We followed his* steps *in the snow.* **8** gait; manner of walking: *His* step *was fast and light.* **9** degree in grade or rank: *A major is one* step *above a captain.* **10** stair; rung of a ladder. **11** an action or measure taken toward an end: *Collecting all the facts is the first* step *in making a decision.* **12** definite pattern of movements of the body and feet, as in a dance: *a waltz* step. **13** degree between two notes on a musical scale; a tone: *It is a half* step *between B and B flat.* **14 in step** (**1**) at the same pace with another person or thing. (**2**) in accord: *She is* in step *with today's fashions.* **15 keep step** to move at the same pace: *The marchers kept* step *with the band.* **16 out of step** (**1**) having a different pace. (**2**) not in accord with common custom: *The old man was* out of step *with the times.*

step down 1 to reduce (a current or the like). **2** to resign from (a position).

step into to enter; take possession of: *He* stepped into *a fortune.*

step off to measure by steps: *to* step off *ten feet.*

step up to speed up; make go faster: *to* step up *the output of a factory; to* step up *sales.*

stepped, step·ping. (Homonym: steppe)

step·broth·er (stěp'brŭth'ər) a son of one's stepfather or stepmother.

step·child (stěp'child') a child of one's husband or wife by a previous marriage. **step·chil·dren.**

step·daugh·ter (stěp'dô'tər) a daughter of one's husband or wife by a previous marriage.

step·fa·ther (stěp'fä'thər) man married to one's mother following the death or divorce of one's father.

fāte, făt, fâre, fär; bē, bĕt; bite, bĭt; nō, nŏt, nôr; fūse, fŭn, fûr; tōō, tŏŏk; foil; foul; thin; then; hw for wh as in what; zh for s as in usual; ə for a, e, i, o, u, as in ago, linen, peril, atom, minus

703

step·lad·der (stĕp'lăd'ər) ladder with flat steps instead of rungs, and often with folding legs.

step·moth·er (stĕp'mŭth'-ər) woman married to one's father following the death or divorce of one's mother.

steppe (stĕp) dry, level or rolling grassland without trees, but in the natural state having a cover of short grass. (Homonym: step)

Stepladder

step·sis·ter (stĕp'sis tər) a daughter of one's stepfather or stepmother.

step·son (stĕp'sŭn') a son of one's husband or wife by a previous marriage.

ster·e·o·phon·ic (stĕr'ĭ ə fŏn'ĭk or stŭr'ĭ ə-fŏn'ĭk) having to do with sound reproduction through two or more independent sets at the same time. If the microphones and speakers are carefully located, the listener has the feeling of being at the original performance.

ster·ile (stĕr'ĭl) 1 free from any living germs or microbes. 2 not fertile; unable to produce young; barren. **ster·ile·ly.**

ster·i·lize (stĕr'ə liz') to make sterile: *Doctors* sterilize *their instruments after each use.* **ster·i·lized, ster·i·liz·ing.**

ster·ling (stûr'lĭng) 1 of British coins, made of metal of standard purity. 2 having at least 92.5 per cent silver: *a piece of* sterling *silver.* 3 pure; of genuine worth: *His* sterling *character made us admire him.*

¹**stern** (stûrn) severe or strict: *Mr. Parnell gave us a* stern *talking to.* **stern·ly.** [¹**stern** is a form of the Old English word (steorne) of the same meaning.]

²**stern** (stûrn) aft end of a ship or boat. For picture, see **aft.** [²**stern** is probably from an Old Norse word (stjorn) meaning "a steering device" or "rudder." The stern, then, is the part of the ship to which the rudder which guides the ship is attached.]

stern·ness (stûrn'nĭs) a being stern; strictness; severity; harshness: *Tim saw by the* sternness *of his father's expression that something was wrong.*

steth·o·scope (stĕth'-ə skōp') doctor's instrument for listening to heartbeats and other sounds in the body.

Stethoscope

stew (stōō or stū) 1 dish made of small pieces of meat or fish and vegetables cooked in a liquid. 2 to cook slowly in a liquid: *to* stew *prunes, pears, etc.* 3 a state of worry: *I'm in a* stew *as to my future.* 4 to worry; fret.

stew·ard (stōō'ərd or stū'ərd) 1 man in charge of another's property. 2 man in charge of the food and table service in a ship, club, dining car, etc. 3 on passenger ships, an attendant.

stew·ard·ess (stōō'ər dĭs or stū'ər dĭs) woman who has charge of the needs of the passengers on a train, plane, ship, etc.

¹**stick** (stĭk) 1 a long, narrow piece of wood. 2 anything shaped like a stick: *a candy* stick; *a walking* stick. [¹**stick** is a form of an Old English word (sticca) meaning "stick," "peg."]

²**stick** (stĭk) 1 to push something sharp or pointed into; pierce: *The nurse* stuck *me with a needle.* 2 to attach; fasten: *to* stick *a notice on a bulletin board.* 3 to stay or hold together: *This glue will make anything* stick. 4 to have the point embedded: *The splinter* stuck *in his arm for a week.* 5 to put (something) in a place: *Please* stick *this book in the drawer. Don't* stick *your head out the window!* 6 to be caught so that it does not work; to be or become stuck: *The door* sticks *because it is warped.*

stick out to protrude: *to* stick out *one's tongue; a handkerchief* sticking out *of his pocket.*

stick to 1 to keep on with; continue with: *He* stuck to *the job until it was finished.* 2 to be faithful to; keep: *You must* stick to *your promise.*

stick up for to stand up for; take sides for: *You should always* stick up for *your rights.*

stuck, stick·ing. [²**stick** is from an Old English word (stician) meaning "to stab."]

stick·y (stĭk'ĭ) 1 tending to stay together or attached: *The glue left my fingers* sticky. 2 hot and humid: *the* sticky *weather of the tropics.* **stick·i·er, stick·i·est, stick·i·ly.**

stiff (stĭf) 1 not easily bent; firm: *a stiff collar; a stiff piece of cardboard.* 2 hard to move or operate: *a stiff lock; a stiff crank.* 3 not able to move with ease and freedom: *a stiff neck.* 4 formal: *The butler gave us a* stiff *bow.* 5 difficult; hard: *a stiff chemistry*

test; a stiff *climb.* **6** strong; severe: *A* stiff
wind blew down the branch. It was a stiff
punishment to stay in the house all day. **7** not
liquid or fluid: *to beat egg whites until* stiff.
stiff·ly.

stiff·en (stĭf′ən) to make or become stiff:
She stiffened *the shirt with starch. His
limbs* stiffened *with age.*

sti·fle (stī′fəl) **1** to make breathing more
difficult for; suffocate; smother: *The heat
in the room* stifled *us.* **2** to extinguish: *We*
stifled *the campfire with sand.* **3** to hold
back: *to* stifle *a yawn.* **4** to put an end to;
suppress: *to* stifle *a rebellion.* **sti·fled, sti·
fling.**

stig·ma (stĭg′mə) **1** mark of shame or dishonor: *the* stigma *of slavery.* **2** the upper
part of a flower pistil on which the pollen
falls.

stile (stīl) set of steps placed across a fence
or wall. (Homonym: style)

still (stĭl) **1** without movement; motionless:
Please stand still *while I comb your hair.*
2 quiet; silent: *a* still *night.* **3** to make
quiet; calm: *Mother* stilled *the baby by
giving him a rattle.* **4** in spite of that; nevertheless: *Tim's toothache grew worse;* still *he
didn't complain.* **5** even; yet: *You may be
tall but your brother is* still *taller.*

still·ness (stĭl′nĭs) absence of sound or motion; calm: *the* stillness *of the sea; the* stillness *of the night.*

stilt (stĭlt) one of a pair of long sticks with
a block on which a person may
stand and walk at a distance
above the ground.

stim·u·lant (stĭm′yə lənt) something that arouses, quickens, or
intensifies the senses or bodily
functions: *Since coffee is a
stimulant, I can't drink it before
going to bed.*

stim·u·late (stĭm′yōō lāt′) **1** to
quicken; arouse to greater activity: *Brisk walking* stimulates *the
circulation.* **2** to excite; stir up:
The rally stimulated *the hopes of
the team. This book has* stimulated *my
interest in science.* **stim·u·lat·ed, stim·u·
lat·ing.**

Stilts

stim·u·lus (stĭm′yōō ləs) **1** anything that
urges a person to action; incentive: *The
teacher's praise was a* stimulus *to better
work.* **2** anything that causes a reaction in
a plant or animal: *the* stimulus *of light on
the retina of the eye.* **stim·u·li.**

sting (stĭng) **1** to prick or wound with a
sharp point, as do bees, wasps, etc. **2** the
wound caused in this way: *My face swelled
with the* sting. **3** sharp, pointed organ of
bees, wasps, etc., which often contains
poison. **4** to cause a sharp pain or hurt:
Alcohol stings *when put on a wound. His
insults* stung *my pride.* **5** sharp, burning
pain: *The* sting *of the medicine made my
eyes water.* **stung, sting·ing.**

stin·gy (stĭn′jĭ) **1** reluctant to give, lend, or
spend: *The* stingy *boy refused to let anyone
play with his toys.* **2** scanty; skimpy: *a*
stingy *helping of food.* **stin·gi·er, stin·gi·
est; stin·gi·ly.**

stink (stĭngk) **1** to give off a disgusting odor:
Garbage stinks. **2** disgusting odor: *The*
stink *of the spoiled fish made me sick.* **stank**
or **stunk, stunk, stink·ing.**

stint (stĭnt) **1** to keep within a narrow
margin; limit: *to* stint *an allowance.* **2** to
be sparing, frugal, or skimpy: *Don't* stint
during your vacation. **3** a limit: *During
Christmas people gave without* stint *to
charity.* **4** chore; task assigned: *My daily*
stint *is to make my bed and clean my room.*

stir (stûr) **1** to move or shake: *The storm*
stirred *the sea to fury. A light breeze* stirred
the leaves. **2** a movement, often slight:
There was not a stir *during the entire performance.* **3** to give a circular motion (to
something): *to* stir *coffee with a spoon.* **4** a
stirring: *Give the gravy a* stir *so that it won't
stick to the pot.* **5** to arouse; excite: *to*
stir *one's interest.* **6** to become brisk;
lively: *During the Christmas holidays things
are really* stirring *at our house.* **7** commotion; excitement: *There was quite a* stir
when the actress entered the hotel. **stirred,
stir·ring.**

stir·ring (stûr′ĭng) **1** full of action; moving:
These are stirring *times.* **2** exciting; thrilling: *a* stirring *performance by the orchestra.*
stir·ring·ly.

fāte, făt, fâre, fär; bē, bĕt; bīte, bĭt; nō, nŏt, nôr; fūse, fŭn, fûr; tōō, tŏŏk; foil; foul; thin; then;
hw for wh as in *what;* zh for s as in u*s*ual; ə for a, e, i, o, u, as in *a*go, lin*e*n, per*i*l, at*o*m, min*u*s

stir·rup (stûr′əp or stĭr′əp) one of a pair of metal or wooden loops hung from the side of a saddle to hold a rider's foot.

stitch (stich) **1** a complete movement of a threaded needle in and out of material; similar movement of a knitting needle or crochet hook. **2** loop of thread or yarn made with such a movement of a needle or crochet hook. **3** to sew or decorate with stitches. **4** single bit: *I haven't had a* stitch *of new clothes for months.* **5** sudden sharp pain: *a* stitch *in the side.*

Stirrup

stock (stŏk) **1** a supply; store: *Jones' store has a large* stock *of goods.* **2** to lay in; store: *We* stocked *the freezer with frozen foods.* **3** to furnish with; supply: *The state* stocked *the lake with fish.* **4** animals; cattle. **5** raw or basic material: *A ham bone is* stock *for soup.* **6** liquid in which meat, and sometimes vegetables, has been cooked. It is often used as the basis for various soups. **7** trunk or stump of a tree; stem of a plant. **8** ancestry: *The Lodges come from Colonial* stock. **9** shares in a business: *Mr. White owns most of the company's* stock. **10** trust; belief: *I take little* stock *in his story.* **11** the shoulder piece of a firearm or crossbow. **12** theatrical company in which the same actors give a series of plays. **13** **stocks** a frame for holding a seated prisoner's ankles while he was held up to public scorn. **14 stock exchange** place where shares of stock are bought and sold. **15 stock market** business carried on at a stock exchange. **16 in stock** available for use or sale; on hand. **17 out of stock** not available for use or sale; lacking.

Stocks

stock·ade (stŏk ād′) **1** strong defensive fence made of tall, closely set posts with sharpened tops, much used about frontier forts and animal

Stockade

pens; palisade. **2** the area or buildings enclosed by such a fence.

stock·hold·er (stŏk′hōl′dər) person who owns stock or shares in a company or corporation.

stock·ing (stŏk′ĭng) a knit covering for the foot and leg, made of cotton, wool, nylon, or other material.

stock·y (stŏk′ĭ) short, solid, and sturdy in build: *He is a* stocky *youngster.* **stock·i·er, stock·i·est; stock·i·ly.**

stock·yards (stŏk′yärdz′) enclosure with pens and sheds where livestock is kept and slaughtered for food.

sto·ic (stō′ĭk) **1** person who can suffer without complaint: *Betty was a* stoic *through all her troubles.* **2** self-controlled; uncomplaining.

sto·i·cal (stō′ə kəl) like a stoic: *The Indian braves were* stoical *under torture.* **sto·i·cal·ly.**

¹stole (stōl) See **steal**. *He* stole *a car.* [¹stole is a form of **steal**.]

²stole (stōl) long scarf of cloth or fur worn over the shoulders with the ends hanging down in front. [²stole is the unchanged form of an Old English word that comes from a Latin word (stola) meaning "robe." The Latin word is from a Greek word (stolē) meaning "a garment."]

sto·len (stō′lən) See **steal**. *This horse has been* stolen *and will have to be returned.*

stom·ach (stŭm′ək) **1** part of the digestive tract; pouch where food goes after it is swallowed and where digestion takes place. For picture, see **intestine**. **2** a liking; an inclination: *I have no* stomach *for bullfights.* **3** to put up with; tolerate: *I can no longer* stomach *your rudeness.*

stone (stōn) **1** hard mineral body; small rock or pebble. **2** the mineral matter which makes up such bodies of any size. **3** precious stone; gem: *The diamond cutter had polished many* stones. **4** something like a stone in looks or hardness: *a cherry* stone. **5** to remove stones from: *Irma will* stone *the cherries.* **6** to throw stones at. **7** made of stoneware: *a stone jar.* **stoned, ston·ing.**

Stone

stone·ware (stōn′wâr′) coarse, glazed pottery containing sand and flint.

ston·y (stō′nĭ) **1** covered with stones: *a stony beach.* **2** cold; like stone; rigid: *a stony look.* **ston·i·er, ston·i·est; ston·i·ly.**

stood (stŏŏd) See **stand.** *I stood in line to see the movie.*

stool (stōōl) **1** seat on a long leg or legs, sometimes with a low back. **2** backless seat with short legs: *a milking stool.* **3** low rest for the feet.

Stools

¹stoop (stōōp) **1** to lean down with back and shoulders bent: *I had to stoop to pick up the box.* **2** to have a bent posture with the shoulders bent forward: *He stooped because he was tired.* **3** bent posture with head and shoulders forward: *He walked with a stoop.* **4** to condescend; lower oneself: *She would not stoop to gossip.* [**¹stoop** is a form of an Old English word (stupian) of the same meaning.]

²stoop (stōōp) porch or platform at the entrance of a house. [**²stoop** is from a Dutch word (stoep) meaning "a high step at the door."]

stop (stŏp) **1** to leave off; cease; desist from: *She stopped talking when I came into the room.* **2** to come to a halt; cease moving: *The car stopped suddenly for a red light.* **3** to check the motion of; bring to a halt: *You must stop the car at the red light.* **4** to block; obstruct; close (up): *Dead leaves have stopped the gutter.* **5** a plug; an obstruction: *There must be a stop in this pipe.* **6** to stay with; visit: *We are stopping at my sister's house overnight.* **7** short visit: *We made a stop at the museum.* **8** a halt: *He came to a stop when he saw me.* **9** place where something comes to a halt: *a subway stop.* **10** key or other device to change the pitch of an instrument, especially an organ. **stopped, stop·ping.**

stop·per (stŏp′ər) plug, cork, etc., used to close an opening, as in a bottle or a sink.

stop watch a watch with a hand that can be started or stopped instantly by pressing a button. This watch will record times down to a fraction of a second. It is used to time races and other contests.

stor·age (stôr′ĭj) **1** a keeping or reserving of goods in a safe place: *the storage of furniture in a warehouse.* **2** place for storing or state of being stored: *My piano is in storage.* **3** the cost of keeping goods in a warehouse or other place for storing: *Can you pay the storage on your piano?* **4** cold storage cool or refrigerated place to keep perishable goods.

storage battery battery containing certain chemicals that store energy from an electric current fed into it. It releases the energy as an electric current when needed.

store (stôr) **1** place where goods are kept and sold: *a grocery store; a department store.* **2** a reserve; a supply for future use: *Do we have a store of canned goods for winter?* **3** to put aside for future use or safekeeping: *I have stored my furniture in a warehouse. Squirrels store nuts for the winter.* **4** to fill with; furnish: *I stored my mind with information for future use.* **stored, stor·ing.**

store·house (stôr′hous′) place where goods are kept for future use; warehouse.

store·keep·er (stôr′kē′pər) person in charge of a store where goods are displayed and sold.

store·room (stôr′rōōm′) room in which things are stored.

stork (stôrk) long-legged, sharp-beaked bird. It often nests on roofs and chimneys.

Stork, about 3 ft. high

storm (stôrm) **1** violent disturbance of the weather, with gusts of wind, rain, snow, sand, etc. **2** to blow violently; to rain, hail, snow, etc. **3** to attack with force: *to storm a fort.* **4** to rage: *Helen stormed out of the room.* **5** violent outburst: *a storm of tears.* **6 a storm in a teacup** great excitement over something trivial. **7 take by storm** to capture or seize by violent attack.

storm·y (stôr′mĭ) **1** of or having to do with storms: *a season of stormy weather.* **2** of or having to do with violent emotions;

fāte, făt, fâre, fär; bē, bĕt; bīte, bĭt; nō, nŏt, nôr; fūse, fŭn, fûr; tōō, tŏŏk; foil; foul; thin; ~~then~~; hw for wh as in *wh*at; zh for s as in u*s*ual; ə for a, e, i, o, u, as in *a*go, lin*e*n, per*i*l, at*o*m, min*u*s

707

agitated: *a stormy meeting.* **storm·i·er, storm·i·est; storm·i·ly.**

¹sto·ry (stôr′i) **1** account, oral or written, of something that has happened: *a newspaper story of an accident.* **2** a tale of fiction: *the story of Gulliver's adventures.* **3** a lie: *I want the truth, not a story.* **sto·ries.** [**¹story** comes through Old French (estoire) from a Latin word (historia) meaning "a narrative."]

²sto·ry (stôr′i) any level of a building: *Dot lives on the third story.* **sto·ries.** [**²story** is **¹story** in a special use that grew out of its earlier meaning of "a row of painted windows that told or illustrated a story."]

stout (stout) **1** stocky; fat. **2** strong; firm: *His wrists were bound with stout cords.* **3** brave; courageous: *the stout self-confidence of the pioneers.* **stout·ly.**

Early American stove

Modern electric stove

¹stove (stōv) any of various heating or cooking devices which use coal, wood, oil, gas, or electricity as a fuel. [**¹stove** is a form of an Old English word (stofa) meaning "a room for a warm bath."]

²stove (stōv) See **stave.** *Bill's canoe was stove in by the hidden rock.* [**²stove** is a form of **stave.**]

stow (stō) to pack; put away; store: *The crew stowed the cargo quickly so that they could sail on the next tide.*

stow·a·way (stō′ə wā′) person who hides on a ship in order to get free passage.

strad·dle (străd′əl) to sit or stand with one leg on each side (of something): *to straddle a horse or a chair.* **strad·dled, strad·dling.**

strag·gle (străg′əl) **1** to wander in a rambling manner; stray: *The children straggled in, one by one.* **2** to spread or grow in a ragged, uneven fashion: *Untidy vines straggled over the fence.* **strag·gled, strag·gling.**

straight (strāt) **1** without bend or curve: *a straight line.* **2** level: *to put a hat on*

straight. **3** tidy; in good order: *to keep a room straight; to keep records straight.* **4** honest; sincere: *a straight answer.* **5** reliable: *a straight piece of information.* **6** in a direct line: *to shoot straight.* **7** by a direct route: *to go straight home.* **8** without delay: *I must go straight in because he's waiting.* **9** sequence of cards in games. **10 keep a straight face** to avoid laughing. **11 straight from the shoulder** directly; in an honest manner: *Dave gave him the facts straight from the shoulder.* **12 come straight to the point** to take up or explain clearly, directly, and without dallying. **13 straight ticket** ballot cast for candidates of only one party. It is the opposite of **split ticket. straight·ly.** (Homonym: strait)

straight·en (strāt′ən) **1** to make or become straight and even: *to straighten a path.* **2** to make neat or tidy: *to straighten a drawer.*

straighten out to make clear; put in order: *Have you straightened out the difficulty?*

straight·for·ward (strāt′fôr′wərd) honest; frank; direct: *a straightforward answer.* **straight·for·ward·ly.**

straight·way (strāt′wā′) at once; immediately.

¹strain (strān) **1** to stretch or pull with great force: *The weight of the piano strained the ropes almost to breaking.* **2** to exert to the utmost: *She strained her ears to overhear the conversation.* **3** extreme pressure, force, or pull: *The cable snapped under the strain.* **4** to weaken or injure by too much exertion: *Bill strained his back lifting the carton.* **5** injury due to too great exertion; a sprain. **6** effect of too much effort, pressure, etc.: *Ellen became ill under the strain of overwork.* **7** to separate liquid from solid matter by use of a strainer or sieve. **8** to stretch (the meaning): *Jack strained the truth to justify himself.* [**strain** comes through a French word (estreindre) from a Latin word (stringere) meaning "to draw tightly."]

²strain (strān) **1** race, stock, or breed: *a horse of Arabian strain.* **2** inherited trait or quality: *There was a strain of madness in that family.* **3** manner of expression; tone; style: *There was a strain of sadness in* her voice. **4** melody or tune. [²**strain** is probably a form of an Old English word (strēon) meaning "offspring."]

strain·er (strā′nər) **1** kitchen vessel with a wire-mesh or perforated bowl for draining away liquid or removing solids that are not wanted; colander. **2** any filter for removing dirt or impurities.

Strainer

strait (strāt) **1** narrow channel connecting two larger bodies of water. **2 straits** difficulties; desperate circumstances: *He is always in financial* straits *since he spends more than he earns.* **3 strait jacket** narrow, confining coat, made to prevent the use of the arms. (Homonym: straight)

¹**strand** (strănd) **1** one of several bundles of thread, hair, wire, etc., twisted together to form a rope. **2** a thread or rope: *a* strand *of hair; a* strand *of beads.* [¹**strand** is from an Old French word (estran) of the same meaning.]

Strand

²**strand** (strănd) **1** beach or shore. **2** to run aground: *The skiff was* stranded *on the reef.* **3** to place in a helpless position: *The actors were* stranded *in a strange town without work or money.* [²**strand** is a form of an Old English word of the same spelling.]

strange (strānj) **1** unusual; odd; peculiar: *That was a* strange *thing to say.* **2** not previously experienced, met, or seen; unfamiliar: *a* strange *country.* **3** out of place; uneasy: *Jo felt* strange *at school for the first week.* **strang·er, strang·est; strange·ly.**

strange·ness (strānj′nĭs) a being strange or unusual; unfamiliarity; peculiarity: *the* strangeness *of someone's behavior; the* strangeness *of a foreign country.*

stran·ger (strān′jər) **1** person one does not know. **2** somebody from another place: *There were many* strangers *in town over the holiday.*

stran·gle (străng′gəl) **1** to kill by squeezing the throat; choke. **2** to be choked: *to* strangle *on a fishbone.* **3** to suppress: *When the policeman scolded him, he* strangled *the impulse to answer back.* **stran·gled, strangling.**

strap (străp) **1** narrow strip of leather or other material used to hold things together or keep something in place: *a watch* strap. **2** to fasten with a strap: *to* strap *the luggage to the car.* **strapped, strap·ping.**

strap·ping (străp′ĭng) tall and robust: *a* strapping *boy.*

stra·ta (strā′tə or străt′ə) **1** layers, especially layers of rock and soil laid down by nature: *A cliff often shows* strata *of different colored rocks.* **2** levels of society, with respect to rank, cultural development, education, etc.

strat·a·gem (străt′ə jəm) a trick to deceive: *The general used the* stratagem *of retreat to draw the enemy out of the city.*

Rock strata

stra·te·gic (strə tē′jĭk) **1** having to do with strategy, especially with military strategy: *Gibraltar is of* strategic *importance in defending the Mediterranean.* **2** skillfully adapted to a purpose: *By several* strategic *moves he gained control of the business.*

strat·e·gy (străt′ə jĭ) **1** art or science of war. **2** skill in managing or planning any affair: *The team succeeded more by* strategy *than brute strength.* **strat·e·gies.**

strat·o·sphere (străt′ə sfîr′ or strā′tə sfîr′) layer of the atmosphere between about seven and twenty miles above sea level.

stra·tum (strā′təm or străt′əm) **1** a layer of material, as rock or earth: *There is a* stratum *of limestone below the creek bed.* **2** level or rank: *a low* stratum *of society.* **stra·ta** or **stra·tums.**

straw (strô) **1** stalk of grain after it has been cut and threshed. **2** hollow stalk or something resembling one: *Lenore sipped the drink through a* straw. **3** made of straw: *a* straw *basket.* **4** something worthless; a trifle: *not worth a* straw.

Strawberry

straw·ber·ry (strô′bĕr′ĭ) **1** red oval fruit with tiny, seedlike dots on its surface. **2** the plant that bears this fruit. **straw·ber·ries.**

fāte, făt, fâre, fär; bē, bĕt; bīte, bĭt; nō, nŏt, nôr; fūse, fŭn, fûr; tōō, tŏŏk; foil; foul; thin; then; hw for wh as in what; zh for s as in usual; ə for a, e, i, o, u, as in ago, linen, peril, atom, minus

709

stray (strā) **1** to lose one's way; go wrong; wander: *We* strayed *off our path in the dark woods.* **2** lost animal; wanderer: *The dog we picked up in the park was a stray.* **3** here and there; scattered: *There was only a stray taxi to be found at that time of night.* **4** casual; incidental: *Through a stray remark by a stranger I learned where you were.*

streak (strēk) **1** long mark or line; a stripe. **2** trait of character: *a streak of cruelty.* **3** to mark with streaks: *Clowns* streak *their faces with paint.*

stream (strēm) **1** a flow of water; creek; small river. **2** steady flow: *a stream of light; a* stream *of cars.* **3** to move or flow continuously: *The crowd* streamed *out of the stadium.* **4** to pour or flow: *The athlete* streamed *with perspiration.* **5** to float; wave: *Flags* streamed *in the wind.*

stream·er (strē′mər) **1** long narrow ribbon or flag. **2** newspaper headline that runs across the page.

stream·line (strēm′lin′) **1** shaped to offer the least resistance to air or water: *The car's* streamline *body was designed for speed.* **2** to make more modern or efficient: *The business was* streamlined *to increase profits.* **stream·lined, stream·lin·ing.**

street (strēt) road in a city or town, usually lined with buildings.

street·car (strēt′kär′) public passenger car that runs on rails; trolley car.

strength (strĕngth or strĕngkth) **1** the quality of being physically, mentally, or morally strong; power; force; vigor: *the strength of an athlete;* strength *of will.* **2** ability to resist strain; toughness: *the strength of a rope.* **3** effectiveness; intensity: *the strength of a drug.* **4** force in numbers: *The squadron is at full strength.* **5** source of power; support: *Knowledge is his* strength. **6 on the strength of** trusting in; relying on: *I bought this car on the strength of a one year guarantee.*

strength·en (strĕngk′thən or strĕng′thən) to make or become stronger.

stren·u·ous (strĕn′yŏo əs) **1** vigorous; energetic; zealous: *a strenuous campaigner.* **2** requiring great effort or exertion: *a strenuous schedule.* **stren·u·ous·ly.**

stress (strĕs) **1** pressure; strain: *in times of stress; the stress of wind on tall buildings.* **2** emphasis; importance: *This school puts*

a stress *on discipline.* **3** to insist upon; emphasize: *The mayor* stressed *the need for changes in the city government.* **4** extra emphasis given to a syllable in a word. In the word "bicycle" the stress is on the first syllable.

stretch (strĕch) **1** to draw out in length or width: *Jacob* stretched *the rubber band until it broke.* **2** to extend: *The road* stretched *as far as the eye could see.* **3** an unbroken expanse: *a stretch of water; a stretch of time.* **4** to exaggerate: *to* stretch *facts.* **5** an effort: *by a* stretch *of the imagination.* **6** a stretching or being stretched; an extending.

Stretcher

stretch·er (strĕch′ər) **1** a frame or expanding instrument by which something may be given shape or made larger: *a curtain* stretcher; *a glove* stretcher. **2** portable cot or mattress on which a sick or injured person may be carried lying at full length.

strew (strŏo) **1** to scatter or let fall in a careless way: *He* strewed *his clothes all over the room.* **2** to cover with something scattered: *The walk was* strewn *with leaves.* **strewed, strewed** or **strewn, strew·ing.**

strewn (strŏon) See **strew.** *The floor was* strewn *with the children's toys.*

strick·en (strĭk′ən) **1** See **strike.** **2** hit or attacked by sickness, troubles, etc., in a sudden manner: *Bill was* stricken *with chicken pox.*

strict (strĭkt) **1** severe; stern: *Father is* strict *but fair.* **2** rigid; not changing: *Our family has a* strict *rule about bedtime.* **3** absolute; entire: *in* strict *privacy; in* strict *confidence.* **strict·ly.**

strid·den (strĭd′ən) See **stride.**

stride (strīd) **1** to walk with long steps: *to* stride *along the beach.* **2** long step or steps: *The child could not keep up with his father's* strides. **3** to sit or stand with one leg on either side of something; straddle: *to* stride *a horse.* **4 take in one's stride** to do or deal with easily and without much effort. **strode, strid·den, strid·ing.**

strife (strīf) a conflict; struggle: *the* strife *of battle.*

strike (strīk) **1** to hit: *The car* struck *the wall.* **2** to deliver a blow against: *to strike the waters with a paddle.* **3** a blow: *a strike of the fist.* **4** to afflict or affect by disease, emotion, etc.: *An epidemic of measles* struck *the town. We were* struck *with horror when we saw the cars collide.* **5** to come to mind; impress: *The idea* struck *us as being absurd.* **6** to attack; come suddenly: *The storm* struck *at dawn.* **7** to proceed; advance: *If you* strike *through the woods you will come to the farm.* **8** to produce by stamping or printing: *The city* struck *a medal on the occasion of the President's visit.* **9** to make burn by friction: *to* strike *a match.* **10** to sound: *The clock is* striking *the hour.* **11** to discover luckily or in a sudden manner: *The miner* struck *gold.* **12** to reach; make; conclude: *The shopkeeper* struck *a bargain with the customer.* **13** to cross out; cancel: *His remarks were* struck *from the minutes of the meeting.* **14** in baseball, a fairly pitched ball missed or allowed to pass by the batter. **15** to stop work in order to gain more pay, better working conditions, etc.: *The union threatened to* strike *to get their demands.* **16** a stopping work for these reasons.

strike out 1 in baseball, of a batter, to fail to hit the ball between the base lines in three attempts. **2** of a baseball pitcher, to cause a batter to strike out.

strike up to begin: *We* struck up *a friendship.*

struck, struck or strick·en, strik·ing.

strik·ing (strī'king) very noticeable; claiming attention; attractive: *a striking example of efficiency; a striking dress.* **strik·ing·ly.**

string (string) **1** thin cord or twine. **2** anything used to tie something: *a shoe string, apron strings.* **3** set of things arranged on a cord: *a string of beads.* **4** to put on a cord: *to string beads for a necklace.* **5** series or line of something: *a string of lanterns; a string of cars.* **6** to furnish with strings: *to string a tennis racket.* **7** to remove strings or fibers from: *to string beans.* **8** wire or catgut cord for a musical instrument. **9** strings musical instruments such as violins, violas, etc. **strung, string·ing.**

stringed instrument musical instrument fitted with strings, as a guitar, violin, etc.

string·y (string'ĭ) **1** like string. **2** full of fibers: *a stringy piece of meat.* **string·i·er, string·i·est.**

¹**strip** (strip) **1** to remove (a covering); peel: *to strip wallpaper from a wall.* **2** to undress: *The boys* stripped *and went swimming.* **3** to rob: *The bandits plotted to strip the bank of all its money.* **stripped, strip·ping.** [¹**strip** is a form of an Old English word (strippan) of the same meaning.]

²**strip** (strip) **1** long, narrow, flat piece. **2** place for airplanes to land and take off. [²**strip** is probably a combination of ¹**strip** and the word **stripe.**]

stripe (strip) **1** long, narrow band or streak: *Tigers have* stripes *of yellow and black.* **2** band of color attached to a uniform to show rank, achievement, etc.: *His heroism earned him another* stripe. **3** to mark with stripes: *The barber's pole was* striped *with red and white.* **4** a stroke from a whip or a rod: *The criminal was sentenced to fifteen* stripes. **5** sort or kind: *They are persons of the same* stripe. **striped, strip·ing.**

striped (stript) marked with or made in stripes: *The candy cane was* striped *red and white.*

strip·ling (strip'ling) boy just passing from youth to manhood.

strive (strīv) **1** to try hard; make an effort: *You must* strive *for better marks.* **2** to struggle; battle: *The sailboat* strove *against the heavy wind.* **strove, striv·en, striv·ing.**

striv·en (striv'ən) See **strive.** *We had* striven *to reach our goal.*

strode (strōd) See **stride.** *Dad* strode *so quickly that I couldn't keep up with him.*

¹**stroke** (strōk) **1** to move the hand gently along a surface: *She* stroked *her kitten.* **2** a gentle, repeated movement of the hand, etc., in the same direction across something: *The sick child was comforted by the* stroke *of her mother's hand.* **stroked, strok·ing.** [¹**stroke** is the greatly changed form of an Old English word (strācian) of the same meaning.]

²**stroke** (strōk) **1** act of striking a blow, or the blow itself: *The lumberjack lopped off*

---

fāte, făt, fâre, fär; bē, bĕt; bite, bĭt; nō, nŏt, nôr; fūse, fŭn, fûr; tōō, tŏŏk; foil; foul; thin; then; hw for wh as in *wh*at; zh for s as in u*s*ual; ə for a, e, i, o, u, as in *a*go, lin*e*n, per*i*l, at*o*m, min*u*s

the branch with one stroke *of his ax.* **2** anything resembling a blow: *a* stroke *of lightning.* **3** one of a series of complete movements or actions: *a* stroke *of a swimmer; a* stroke *of an oar.* **4** the sound of a striking clock and the time marked: *on the* stroke *of midnight.* **5** movement, or mark made by a pen, pencil, brush, etc.: *The painter completed the picture with a few* strokes. **6** any sudden attack of illness: *sun*stroke, stroke *of paralysis.* **7** single effort, or its result: *We passed the summer without a* stroke *of work.* **8 stroke of luck** sudden good fortune. [²**stroke** is a form of an Old English word (strac) of the same meaning.]

stroll (strōl) **1** quiet, slow walk; a saunter: *We went for a* stroll *after dinner.* **2** to go for a slow, easy walk. **3** to wander on foot from place to place: *The musicians* strolled *from table to table.*

strong (strông) **1** physically powerful: *a* strong *wrestler; a* strong *horse.* **2** healthy; sound: *a* strong *constitution; to feel* strong *again.* **3** determined; firm: *a* strong *character; a* strong *will.* **4** hearty; ardent; passionate: *a man of* strong *affections and* strong *dislikes.* **5** intellectually powerful; vigorous: *a* strong *mind; the* strong *arguments in his favor.* **6** affecting one of the senses powerfully: *a* strong *light; a* strong *odor; a* strong *flavor.* **7** not easily broken or destroyed; durable: *a* strong *table; a* strong *fortress.* **8** firmly held and not easily changed: *a man of* strong *religious beliefs.* **strong·ly.**

strong·box (strông'bŏks') very strong box or chest equipped with a lock, used for storing money, jewelry, etc.; a safe: *Keep valuable papers in a* strongbox.

strong·hold (strông'hōld') **1** a place safe from attack or danger. **2** place where a certain idea or cause is especially strong: *Ancient Greece was a* stronghold *of democracy.*

stron·ti·um (strŏn'shĭ əm) **1** hard silver-white metal element similar to calcium. It is used in fireworks to give a red flame. **2 strontium 90** a radioactive form of strontium present in atomic fallout.

strove (strōv) See **strive.** *The swimmer* strove *against the high waves.*

struck (strŭk) See **strike.** *The tree was* struck *by lightning.*

---

struc·ture (strŭk'chər) **1** way or manner something is put together: *the* structure *of the human body; the* structure *of a sentence.* **2** thing built; construction: *The new bridge will be the largest* structure *of this type in the world.*

strug·gle (strŭg'əl) **1** to make a strong effort; strive: *The young African* struggled *to get an education. The fish* struggled *to get free from the hook.* **2** very great effort or attempt: *It was a* struggle *to learn the whole poem by heart.* **3** a contest; fight. **strug·gled, strug·gling.**

strung (strŭng) See **string.** *Japanese lanterns were* strung *through the trees of the garden.*

¹**strut** (strŭt) **1** to walk with vain, showy, self-important steps: *The peacock* strutted *and spread his tail.* **2** a proud, vain step. **strut·ted, strut·ting.** [¹**strut** is a form of an Old English word (strūtian) of the same meaning.]

²**strut** (strŭt) a piece of timber or metal placed at an angle to something for a support. [²**strut** is from a Germanic word (strutt) meaning "stiff," "rigid."]

Struts

stub (stŭb) **1** short remaining end of anything, such as a cigar, pencil, etc. **2** part of a check, bill, ticket, etc., kept and used as a record after the rest has been torn off. **stub one's toe** or **foot** to strike one's toe or foot against something. **stubbed, stub·bing.**

stub·ble (stŭb'əl) **1** short stalks of grain left standing in the field after the harvest. **2** anything looking like this, as a short growth of beard.

stub·born (stŭb'ərn) **1** fixed in an opinion, way, etc.; not willing to change; obstinate: *The* stubborn *child refused to wear mittens.* **2** done in a determined, persistent way: *The settlers made a* stubborn *effort to clear the forests.* **3** difficult or hard to manage, handle, or treat: *a* stubborn *cold in the head; a* stubborn *wood to carve.* **stub·born·ly.**

stub·by (stŭb'ĭ) **1** like a stub; short and thick: *a* stubby *beard;* stubby *fingers.* **2** covered with stubble: *a* stubby *field.*

stuc·co (stŭk′ō) **1** a kind of plaster or cement used to cover walls, moldings, etc. **2** to cover with stucco. **stuc·coes** or **stuc·cos.**

stuck (stŭk) See ²**stick.** *The paste stuck to his fingers.*

¹**stud** (stŭd) **1** small knob, button, etc., used as a fastener or for decoration: *Shirt studs are used to fasten collars. The horse's collar was decorated with brass studs.* **2** to set or decorate with projecting objects: *The jeweler studded the bracelet with diamonds.* **3** upright timber in a wall to which horizontal boards or laths may be nailed. **4** to be scattered over: *Stars studded the sky.* **stud·ded, stud·ding.** [¹**stud** is a form of an Old English word (studu) meaning "post."]

²**stud** (stŭd) **1** any male animal, especially a horse, kept for breeding purposes. **2** collection of horses for racing, hunting, or breeding, or the place where they are kept. [²**stud** is a form of an Old English word (stōd) meaning a "herd of horses."]

stu·dent (stōō′dənt or stū′dənt) **1** person who attends school. **2** person who is devoted to books and learning: *a student of history.*

stud·ied (stŭd′id) deliberate; showing thought and effort: *The courtier made a studied effort to praise the king.*

stu·di·o (stōō′di ō′ or stū′di ō′) **1** room where an artist works. **2** place set up to broadcast radio or TV programs or to film motion pictures. **stu·di·os.**

stu·di·ous (stōō′di əs or stū′di əs) **1** given to or fond of study. **2** thoughtful; painstaking: *a studious attention to detail.* **stu·di·ous·ly.**

stud·y (stŭd′i) **1** an effort to gain knowledge by using the mind: *to devote much time to study.* **2** to make such an effort: *Rob had to study for two hours every evening.* **3** to make a mental effort to learn: *to study arithmetic; to study to become a doctor.* **4** branch of learning: *Claude did better in science than in English studies.* **5** to think about carefully; examine: *to study a problem, a map, a puzzle, etc.* **6** to consider or examine carefully; investigate: *The presi-*

dent appointed a commission to study foreign trade. **7** investigation; report: *The city prepared a study on the slum problem.* **8** deep thought; reflection: *He was in deep study and didn't hear a thing.* **9** room in a house set aside for reading and writing. **10** sketch in preparation for a painting: *The artist made several studies of his subject before he began the portrait.* **stud·ies; stud·ied, stud·y·ing.**

stuff (stŭf) **1** to fill very full; pack closely; cram: *to stuff oneself at the table; to stuff a trunk.* **2** to fill the inside of (something): *Mother stuffed the turkey with bread and seasoning. The upholsterer stuffed the cushions with feathers.* **3** things; belongings: *Put all your stuff away.* **4** essential quality; element; material: *Courage and obedience are the very stuff of good soldiers.* **5** cloth. **6 stuff and nonsense** foolishness.

stuffed (stŭft) of an animal, bird, etc., that is not alive, with the skin filled inside so as to look lifelike or alive: *a stuffed bald eagle.*

stuff·ing (stŭf′ing) **1** material with which something is filled or packed: *mattress stuffing; the stuffing of a sofa.* **2** mixture of bread, chopped meat, seasonings, etc., used to fill a turkey, chicken, or the like.

stuff·y (stŭf′i) **1** without fresh air; close. **2** boring; dull: *a stuffy conversation.* **3** not open to new ideas: *a stuffy old codger who hated anything modern.* **stuff·i·er, stuff·i·est; stuff·i·ly.**

stum·ble (stŭm′bəl) **1** to fall or trip while walking: *I stumbled over a log in the path.* **2** a fall or trip while walking: *The baby made only one stumble as he crossed the room.* **3** to make a mistake; falter; blunder: *Everyone stumbled over his lines in the play.* **4** a mistake; error: *Joseph made several stumbles while reciting the poem.*

stumble on, across, etc. to come upon by chance: *The detective happened to stumble on a new clue.*

stum·bled, stum·bling.

stump (stŭmp) **1** the base of a tree or plant left after most of the trunk has been cut down. **2** what remains after the main part has been removed; stub: *That puppy has*

fāte, făt, fâre, fär; bē, bĕt; bīte, bit; nō, nŏt, nôr; fūse, fŭn, fûr; tōō, tŏŏk; foil; foul; thin; then; hw for wh as in *what*; zh for s as in usual; ə for a, e, i, o, u, as in *ago*, linen, peril, atom, minus

713

only a stump of tail. **3** to defeat; baffle: *Your question* stumps *me and I can't answer it.* **4** to travel over an area making political speeches: *He* stumped *the whole country before the election.* **5** a place or platform used by a political speaker. **6** to walk stiffly with noisy steps: *He* stumped *into the house in his heavy boots.*

stun (stŭn) **1** to make unconscious; daze: *He was* stunned *by a blow on the head.* **2** to shock; overwhelm: *He was* stunned *by the sudden news of war.* **stunned, stun·ning).**

stung (stŭng) See **sting.** *A bee* stung *her.*

stunk (stŭngk) See **stink.** *The dead fish* stunk.

stun·ning (stŭn'ing) striking; very handsome: *a* stunning *girl.* **stun·ning·ly.**

¹stunt (stŭnt) to check (the growth or development of); retard: *The tomato plants were* stunted *by the dry weather.* [**¹stunt** is the unchanged form of an Old English word meaning "dull," "foolish."]

²stunt (stŭnt) a show or display of skill or daring: *a stunt on a high trapeze.* [**²stunt** may be from a German word (stunde) meaning "lesson."]

stu·pe·fy (stoo'pə fī' or stū'pə fī') **1** to make stupid; dull the senses of: *The heat and noise* stupefied *us.* **2** to amaze; stun: *We were* stupefied *by the news of the tragedy.* **stu·pe·fied, stu·pe·fy·ing.**

stu·pen·dous (stoo pĕn'dəs or stū pĕn'dəs) amazing, particularly because of great size; tremendous; marvelous; immense: *The Grand Canyon is* stupendous. **stu·pen·dous·ly.**

stu·pid (stoo'pĭd or stū'pĭd) **1** not intelligent; dull: *a stupid person.* **2** boring; uninteresting: *a stupid conversation.* **3** foolish; silly. **stu·pid·ly.**

stu·pid·i·ty (stoo pĭd'ə tĭ or stū pĭd'ə tĭ) lack of intelligence; dullness.

stu·por (stoo'pər or stū'pər) a daze; state of apathy: *I had so little sleep that I was in a* stupor.

stur·dy (stûr'dĭ) **1** strong; robust. **2** firm; resolute: *a sturdy resolve to make better grades.* **stur·di·er, stur·di·est; stur·di·ly.**

stur·geon (stûr'jən) large food fish with bony plates along its sides. Its smoked roe is considered a great delicacy. For picture, see next column.

stut·ter (stŭt'ər) **1** to speak with pauses, repeating the beginning sounds of words; stammer: *She doesn't like to talk to strangers because she* stutters. **2** hesitant speech with a repetition of the beginning sounds of words; a stammer: *He no longer speaks with a* stutter.

¹sty (stī) **1** pen for pigs. **2** filthy place: *After the childrens' party the room was a* sty. **sties.** [**¹sty** is a form of an Old English word (stig) meaning "enclosure."]

²sty (stī) inflamed swelling on the eyelid or the rim of the eye. **sties.** [**²sty** is a form of an earlier English word (styan-eye) meaning "rising eye" but mistakenly understood as "sty on eye." The earlier form is based on two Old English words (stigan) meaning "to climb" and (ye) meaning "eye."]

style (stīl) **1** manner or method of doing or making something, such as writing, speaking, acting, building, etc.: *a graceful* style *of dancing; the Gothic* style *of architecture.* **2** distinction and polish: *The diplomat conducted himself with* style. **3** the fashion: *Her clothes are out of* style. **4** sort; kind: *What* style *of woman is she?* **5** to call; name: *George Washington was* styled *"the Father of our Country."* **6** pointed instrument used by the ancients to write in wax, or a similar instrument used in engraving, etching, etc. **7** to design according to some particular fashion: *to* style *hats.* **styled, styl·ing.** (Homonym: stile)

styl·ish (stī'lish) fashionable; up to date; elegant: *Her dress was* stylish *ten years ago but it is out of date now.* **styl·ish·ly.**

sub- prefix meaning "under": sub*marine;* sub*soil;* sub*way.*

sub·di·vide (sŭb'dĭ vīd') to divide or separate again into smaller parts: *The buyer* subdivided *the farm into acre lots. The*

Atlantic sturgeon, about 15 ft. long

second part of this book subdivides *into six short chapters.* **sub·di·vid·ed, sub·di·vid·ing.**

sub·di·vi·sion (sŭb′dĭ vĭzh′ən) **1** division of parts into smaller parts. **2** a smaller part produced by subdividing something larger. **3** a building site that has been produced by subdividing a larger tract of land: *The family built a house in the new* subdivision.

sub·due (səb dōō′ or səb dū′) **1** to conquer; overcome: *The army* subdued *the enemy and captured the town.* **2** to control; calm: *to* subdue *one's temper.* **3** to tone down or soften: *The heavy drapes* subdued *the noise from the street.* **sub·dued, sub·du·ing.**

sub·head (sŭb′hĕd′) **1** secondary title under a main title, covering a division of a book, newspaper, etc. **2** to give a title to (such a division).

¹sub·ject (sŭb′jĭkt) **1** topic treated in writing, conversation, painting, etc.; theme: *What* subject *is under discussion? The first Thanksgiving was the* subject *of the painting.* **2** person owing loyalty and obedience to a sovereign: *The English are* subjects *of Queen Elizabeth II.* **3** course of study: *History is one* subject *he is taking at school.* **4** in a sentence, the word or group of words about which something is said or asked. In the sentence "I like you." the subject is "I." **5 subject to** (1) under the control of: *He is* subject to *his father's will.* (2) liable to; likely to have: *He is* subject to *moods of depression.* (3) on the condition of; dependent on: *a plan* subject to *your approval.*

²sub·ject (səb jĕkt′) **1** to bring under control. **2** to expose; to make undergo: *The witness was* subjected *to close questioning.*

sub·lime (sə blīm′) **1** inspiring awe, reverence, wonder: *to hear* sublime *music.* **2** out of the ordinary; supreme: *a* sublime *conceit;* sublime *ignorance.* **3** something that is lofty or noble: *from the* sublime *to the ridiculous.* **sub·lime·ly.**

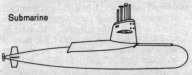

Submarine

sub·ma·rine (sŭb′mə rēn′) **1** being, living, or growing beneath the sea; undersea;

underwater: *The water was so clear we could see the* submarine *plants.* **2** boat that can travel on or beneath the surface of the water.

sub·merge (səb mûrj′) **1** to cover with water or liquid: *Water* submerges *the small island at high tide.* **2** to sink or plunge under water: *The submarine* submerged. **sub·merged, sub·merg·ing.**

sub·mis·sion (səb mish′ən) **1** a surrender; a giving in to the power and authority of another: *Lack of ammunition forced the gun crew into* submission. **2** obedience; meekness; humility: *In* submission *the shy little boy gave the school bully his apple.*

sub·mis·sive (səb mĭs′ĭv) obedient; humble; docile: *The* submissive *child obeyed without question.* **sub·mis·sive·ly.**

sub·mit (səb mĭt′) **1** to place oneself under the control of another; yield; surrender: *The team* submitted *to the umpire's decision.* **2** to refer or present to others for criticism or decision: *Ronald* submitted *his drawings to the teacher.* **sub·mit·ted, sub·mit·ting.**

¹sub·or·di·nate (sə bôr′də nĭt) **1** inferior to; below another in rank, etc.: *In the army, a captain is* subordinate *to a major.* **2** dependent upon; subject to: *The army's movements were* subordinate *to the plans of the general.* **3** one who is below another in rank, power, etc.: *The employer expected loyalty from his* subordinates.

²sub·or·di·nate (sə bôr′də nāt′) to make obedient or subject (to); make secondary (to): *The children* subordinated *their wishes to those of their parents.* **sub·or·di·nat·ed, sub·or·di·nat·ing.**

sub·scribe (səb skrīb′) **1** to contribute or promise to contribute to a cause: *Father always* subscribes *$20 to the local charities each year.* **2** to contract for a certain number of forthcoming magazines, newspapers, etc., or for a book or set of books to be delivered later. **3** to show agreement; give approval or consent by signing or assenting to something: *We cannot* subscribe *to such severe punishment for such a minor offense.* **sub·scribed, sub·scrib·ing.**

sub·scrib·er (səb skrī′bər) person who subscribes, especially one who gives money

fāte, făt, fâre, fär; bē, bĕt; bīte, bĭt; nō, nŏt, nôr; fūse, fŭn, fûr; tōō, tŏŏk; foil; foul; thin; then; hw for wh as in *wh*at; zh for s as in u*s*ual; ə for a, e, i, o, u, as in *a*go, lin*e*n, per*i*l, at*o*m, min*u*s

715

to a cause or agrees to take a magazine or newspaper regularly.

sub·scrip·tion (səb skrĭp′shən) **1** sum of money given for a cause: *a subscription to charity.* **2** an order for a certain number of issues of a magazine or newspaper.

sub·se·quent (sŭb′sə kwənt) coming after; following: *We made plans that subsequent developments changed.* **sub·se·quent·ly.**

sub·side (səb sīd′) **1** to sink to a lower level; fall: *The flood waters will subside when the rain stops.* **2** to become quiet, calm, or less violent; diminish; grow less: *The fury of the storm has subsided. Tom's fever subsided during the night.* **sub·sid·ed, sub·sid·ing.**

sub·sist (səb sĭst′) **1** to maintain life; live: *We cannot subsist without food and water. The widow subsists on her late husband's pension.* **2** to continue to be; exist: *Ancient festivals still subsist in many countries.*

sub·sist·ence (səb sĭs′təns) means of supporting life: *Eskimos used to depend on hunting and fishing for their subsistence.*

sub·soil (sŭb′soil′) layer of earth just below the surface soil.

sub·stance (sŭb′stəns) **1** matter; material: *Wood is a solid substance.* **2** stuff of which something is made: *A soft limestone is the substance of chalk.* **3** essential part or meaning; essence: *Tell me the substance of last night's speech.* **4** body: *A vegetable soup has more substance than a broth.* **5** property; material possessions; money: *a man of substance.*

sub·stan·tial (səb stăn′shəl) **1** made or built in a solid or strong manner: *a substantial bridge; a substantial house.* **2** ample: *a substantial sum of money; a substantial meal.* **3** wealthy; important; prosperous: *a substantial business.* **4** essential; reasonable: *The witnesses were in substantial agreement.* **sub·stan·tial·ly.**

sub·sti·tute (sŭb′stə tōot′ or sŭb′stə tūt′) **1** person replacing another; one acting instead of another. **2** thing that is used instead of something else. **3** to use in place of something: *Let's substitute strawberries for pineapple on the sundaes.* **sub·sti·tut·ed, sub·sti·tut·ing.**

sub·sti·tu·tion (sŭb′stə tōo′shən or sŭb′stə tū′shən) the putting of a person or thing in the place of another: *the substitution of honey for sugar in a recipe.*

sub·ter·ra·ne·an (sŭb′tə rā′nĭ ən) **1** below the surface of the earth; underground: *a subterranean river.* **2** hidden; out of sight; secret.

sub·tle (sŭt′əl) **1** delicate; fine: *to make a subtle distinction; the subtle difference in two shades of blue.* **2** difficult to understand the meaning of; elusive: *It was hard to tell from her subtle smile what she meant.* **3** able to understand or make fine differences of meaning; discerning: *a subtle mind; a subtle wit.* **4** underhanded; crafty; sly: *a subtle trick to outwit another.* **sub·tler, sub·tlest; sub·tly.**

sub·tle·ty (sŭt′əl tĭ) **1** quality of being subtle, especially acuteness; discernment; keenness or delicacy of mind. **2** something subtle, especially a finely drawn distinction: *I cannot follow the subtleties of your argument.* **sub·tle·ties.**

sub·top·ic (sŭb′tŏp′ĭk) a division of the subject under the main topic.

sub·tract (səb trăkt′) to deduct or take away: *If you subtract 3 from 6, you have 3.*

sub·trac·tion (səb trăk′shən) a taking away or subtracting: *the subtraction of a number.*

sub·tra·hend (sŭb′trə hĕnd′) in subtracting, the number or quantity that is taken away from another: *In 5 − 4 = 1, the subtrahend is 4.*

sub·trop·i·cal (sŭb trŏp′ə kəl) having to do with a region bordering on the tropical zone.

sub·urb (sŭb′ûrb) residential district that lies close to a large city: *to live in a suburb and work in town.*

sub·ur·ban (sə bûr′bən) having to do with a suburb.

sub·way (sŭb′wā′) **1** underground electric railway. **2** underground passage: *a subway under the street.*

suc·ceed (sək sēd′) **1** to gain or accomplish one's aim or purpose; to do extremely well: *Jim is a person who is bound to succeed in life.* **2** to come directly after: *The light of dawn succeeds the dark.* **3** to be the heir or follow next in line (to an office, title, or property): *Queen Elizabeth succeeded to the throne when her father died.*

suc·cess (sək sĕs′) **1** favorable result; good outcome; triumph: *Hard work is often the surest means to success.* **2** person or thing that succeeds. **3** degree of achievement (in

716

gaining a desired result): *What* success *did you have in persuading your father to let you go on the trip?*

suc·cess·ful (sək sĕs'fəl) **1** having or meeting with success; gaining what is desired or aimed at; turning out favorably. **2** fortunate and prosperous: *Dick's father is a highly* successful *lawyer*. **suc·cess·ful·ly**.

suc·ces·sion (sək sĕsh'ən) **1** the coming of one after another in unbroken order; series; sequence: *a long* succession *of happy days*. **2** the taking over of another's office, title, or property through legal right or inheritance: *the* succession *to the throne*.

suc·ces·sive (sək sĕs'ĭv) following one after the other without interruption; consecutive: *Last spring our baseball team won six* successive *games*. **suc·ces·sive·ly**.

suc·ces·sor (sək sĕs'ər) person or thing that succeeds another, especially a person who succeeds to an office, rank, property, etc.

suc·cor (sŭk'ər) **1** to give needed help; aid. **2** the aid or relief given. (Homonym: sucker)

suc·cu·lent (sŭk'yŏŏ lənt) delicious and juicy: *This is the most* succulent *pear I have ever tasted*. **suc·cu·lent·ly**.

suc·cumb (sə kŭm') **1** to give way; surrender after a struggle: *Fighting against overwhelming odds, he finally* succumbed *to debt*. **2** to die: *When she was 94, she quietly* succumbed.

such (sŭch) **1** of the same kind, quality, or degree: *Courage* such *as his is all too rare*. **2** of that sort or kind (already mentioned or meant): *My mother would never repeat* such *gossip*. **3** so much; so extreme: *He is* such *a fool*. **4** that, this, these, or those: *It was bad luck, but* such *is life*.

suck (sŭk) **1** to draw into the mouth by action of the lips and tongue: *The baby* sucked *the milk from his bottle*. **2** to draw or drain the liquid from: *to* suck *oranges*. **3** to take in; absorb: *Plants* suck *moisture from the ground*. **4** act of sucking; suction.

White sucker, about 20 in. long

suck·er (sŭk'ər) **1** young, nursing animal. **2** a kind of soft-lipped fish that sucks up its food. **3** one of the organs on the arm of an octopus by which it holds its prey, or a like organ on certain other animals. **4** a shoot from the root of a plant or tree. **5** a kind of hard candy; a lollipop. **6** a dupe; person easily deceived. (Homonym: succor)

suc·tion (sŭk'shən) **1** act or process of sucking. **2** the drawing of a gas, liquid, etc., into a space from which the air has been withdrawn. **3** force created by a vacuum. **4** suction pump pump that sucks up liquid, etc., by creating a vacuum.

sud·den (sŭd'ən) **1** unexpected; unforeseen; happening quickly and without warning: *The hunter made a* sudden *movement which gave the fox a chance to escape*. **2** all of a sudden in a sudden manner. **sud·den·ly**.

sud·den·ness (sŭd'ən nĭs) a being sudden: *the* suddenness *of a summer thunderstorm*.

suds (sŭdz) the froth, bubbles, and lather that are formed when a soap is dissolved in water; soapsuds.

sue (sŏŏ or sū) **1** to take legal action against: *Mr. Brown is going to* sue *Jack Green for damaging his property*. **2** to beg or plead (for): *The general was sent to* sue *for peace*. **sued, su·ing**.

suede (swād) **1** soft leather with a dull surface and a slightly raised nap. **2** made of suede: *a* suede *jacket*.

su·et (sŏŏ'ĭt or sū'ĭt) hard fat that comes from the loins and kidneys of sheep and beef. Suet is used in cooking and in making tallow.

suf·fer (sŭf'ər) **1** to bear physical or mental pain or distress: *He* suffers *during the hay-fever season*. **2** to have or endure (pain, hardship, grief, etc.) **3** to allow; permit; tolerate: *I will not* suffer *his nonsense*. **4** to be damaged, harmed, or injured: *His work* suffered *from his lack of attention in class*.

suf·fer·ing (sŭf'ər ĭng) physical or mental pain; distress: *The new medicine relieved her* suffering.

suf·fice (sə fīs') **1** to be enough, or sufficient: *This money will not* suffice *for my needs*. **2** to be sufficient for; satisfy: *The money* sufficed *him*. **suf·ficed, suf·fic·ing**.

---

fāte, făt, fâre, fär; bē, bĕt; bīte, bĭt; nō, nŏt, nôr; fūse, fŭn, fûr; tōō, tŏŏk; foil; foul; thin; ~~then~~;
hw for wh as in *wh*at; zh for s as in u*s*ual; ə for a, e, i, o, u, as in ago, linen, peril, atom, minus

suf·fi·cient (sə fish′ənt) enough: *This is not* sufficient *lumber to build the porch.* **suf·fi·cient·ly.**

suf·fix (sŭf′ĭks) syllable or syllables added to the end of a word to make a new word: *The suffix "ness" is added to "good" to form the word "goodness."*

suf·fo·cate (sŭf′ə kāt′) **1** to kill by stopping the breath of; stifle. **2** to be smothered or stifled: *I thought I would* suffocate *in the crowded theater.* **suf·fo·cat·ed, suf·fo·cat·ing.**

suf·frage (sŭf′rĭj) the right to vote: *Woman* suffrage *was granted in 1920.*

sug·ar (shŏog′ər) **1** sweet substance obtained from sugar beets, sugar cane, maple trees, fruits, etc. **2** to sweeten with sugar or sprinkle sugar on: *Do you want me to* sugar *your berries?* **3** to make pleasant; make less disagreeable: *He* sugared *his criticism with a few flattering words.*

sugar beet kind of beet with a white root and high sugar content. Sugar is obtained from the sugar beet.

sugar cane a plant somewhat like bamboo, the jointed stems of which yield a sweet juice which is made into syrup and sugar.

Sugar cane

sug·gest (səg jĕst′) **1** to offer (a plan, idea, etc.) for consideration: *She* suggests *that we meet at the station.* **2** to call to mind: *This weather* suggests *spring.* **3** to hint at; imply: *His look* suggests *that he would like us to leave.*

sug·ges·tion (səg jĕs′chən) **1** a suggesting: *We joined his party at his* suggestion. **2** thing suggested: *We accepted his* suggestion *and changed our route.* **3** a hint; trace: *There was a* suggestion *of a French accent in his speech.* **4** an idea brought to mind because of its association with something else: *The smell of burning leaves was a* suggestion *of autumn.*

sug·ges·tive (səg jĕs′tĭv) **1** tending to bring to mind ideas, images, etc.: *This painting is* suggestive *of the hills of upper New York.* **2** tending to bring some improper thought to mind. **sug·ges·tive·ly.**

su·i·cide (sōō′ə sīd′) **1** intentional killing of oneself; self-destruction. **2** person who intentionally takes his own life.

suit (sōōt or sūt) **1** set of clothes to be worn together, as a jacket and either trousers or a skirt. **2** a case in court; a legal action. **3** to be suitable for; fit: *These decorations* suit *the Christmas season.* **4** to look well on; become: *That dress* suits *you.* **5** to please; satisfy: *A television program cannot* suit *every taste.* **6** one of the four sets of cards into which a pack is divided: *The four* suits *are spades, hearts, clubs, and diamonds.* **7 follow suit (1)** to do as the person before has done: *If you contribute a dollar I will* follow suit. **(2)** to play a card of the same suit as has just been played.

suit oneself to follow one's own wishes.

suit·a·ble (sōō′tə bəl or sū′tə bəl) fitting; appropriate: *That dress is not* suitable *for the dance.* **suit·a·bly.**

suit·case (sōōt′kās′ or sūt′kās′) flat, rectangular, traveling bag.

suite (swēt) **1** number of things making up a set, series, etc.: *a* suite *of furniture; a* suite *of rooms.* **2** in music, a series of movements or pieces composed as a group. Originally a suite consisted of a series of dance movements. **3** group of servants; staff; retinue: *The king never traveled without his* suite. (Homonym: sweet)

suit·or (sōō′tər or sū′tər) **1** man who courts or woos a woman. **2** person who brings a case into a court of law. **3** someone who makes a request or petition.

sul·fa drug (sŭl′fə drŭg) any of a group of drugs containing sulfur and used in the treatment of germ diseases.

sul·fur or **sul·phur** (sŭl′fər) a light-yellow chemical element that burns with a blue flame, giving off a sharp, choking smell.

sulk (sŭlk) **1** to pout; show bad humor; be sullen. **2** fit of pouting; sullen mood: *She went into a* sulk *when she didn't get her way.*

Racing sulky

sulk·y (sŭl′kĭ) **1** very light two-wheeled vehicle used in harness racing. **2** in a bad or sullen humor: *The boy became* sulky *when he couldn't have the toy.* **sulk·ies; sulk·i·er, sul·ki·est; sulk·i·ly.**

sul·len (sŭl′ən) **1** showing bad humor; silent because of anger; sulky; glum: *a sullen look.* **2** gloomy; dismal; threatening: *the sullen winter skies.* **sul·len·ly.**

sul·phur (sŭl′fər) sulfur.

sul·tan (sŭl′tən) a ruler of certain Moslem countries.

sul·tan·a (sŭl tăn′ə) wife, daughter, mother, or sister of a sultan.

sul·try (sŭl′trĭ) hot, close, and moist: *The jungle has a sultry climate.* **sul·tri·er, sul·tri·est.**

sum (sŭm) **1** the total of two or more numbers or things: *The grocer adds the prices of items sold to find the sum the customer must pay.* **2** the result obtained by adding two or more numbers: *He added 2 and 3 and 4 to get the sum of 9.* **3** problem in arithmetic: *Arithmetic homework consisted of five sums.* **4** amount of money: *The sum of five dollars is due.* **5** all the main parts; the total expressed briefly: *That book contains the sum of 50 years of thought.*

  sum up 1 to state in a brief form; make a summary of: *The boss summed up the talk by asking everyone to make a greater effort.* **2** to add into one amount.

  summed, sum·ming. (Homonym: some)

su·mac or **su·mach** (shōō′măk or sōō′măk) **1** shrub with narrow leaves and a cone-shaped bunch of dark red fruit. **2** a very poisonous kind of this shrub with sprays of white berries. The leaves of both kinds are brilliant red in the fall.

sum·ma·rize (sŭm′ə rīz′) to sum up briefly the main points of a fuller statement: *Mary was asked to summarize the book she had read.* **sum·ma·rized, sum·ma·riz·ing.**

Staghorn sumac

sum·ma·ry (sŭm′ə rĭ) **1** brief statement giving only the main points: *He gave a five-point summary of the last session of Congress.* **2** brief; condensed: *a summary account of the accident on the radio program.* **3** done without delay or formality; prompt and direct: *The police were authorized to take summary action against all traffic violators.* **sum·ma·ries.**

sum·mer (sŭm′ər) **1** warmest season of the year. **2** to pass or spend this season: *The children always summer in the mountains.* **3** of or happening in summer: *sudden summer showers.*

sum·mer·time (sŭm′ər tim′) season of summer.

sum·mit (sŭm′ĭt) top; highest point: *The climb to the summit of the mountain was steep and slow. The summit of the boy's hopes was to become president of his class.*

sum·mon (sŭm′ən) **1** to call; send for: *We summoned the doctor in the middle of the night.* **2** to demand officially (the presence of): *The witness was summoned to appear in court.* **3** to rouse; stir to activity; gather together: *The diver had to summon all his courage to swim among the sharks.*

sum·mons (sŭm′ənz) **1** official order to appear in court on a certain day. **2** the document containing such an order. **3** a command to appear: *The navy officer received his summons for active duty.* **sum·mons·es.**

sump·tu·ous (sŭmp′chōō əs) rich; lavish; luxurious; magnificent: *Cinderella went from the kitchen to a sumptuous ball.* **sump·tu·ous·ly.**

sun (sŭn) **1** central body of our solar system around which the earth and other planets revolve. It is the source of light and heat. **2** sunshine: *Dragonflies flitted about in the sun.* **3** to expose to sunlight: *Alex sunned himself for two hours.* **4** any heavenly body like the sun. Stars are suns very far away. **5** something that shines like the sun or around which things revolve. **sunned, sun·ning.** (Homonym: son)

Sun. Sunday.

sun·beam (sŭn′bēm′) ray of sunlight: *The sunbeams streamed through the blinds.*

Sunbonnet

sun·bon·net (sŭn′bŏn′ĭt) light bonnet with a wide brim surrounding the face and a cover for the neck at the back.

---

fāte, făt, fâre, fär; bē, bĕt; bite, bĭt; nō, nŏt, nôr; fūse, fŭn, fûr; tōō, tōŏk; foil; foul; thin; ~~then~~; hw for wh as in *wh*at; zh for s as in u*s*ual; ə for a, e, i, o, u, as in *a*go, lin*e*n, per*i*l, at*o*m, min*u*s

sun·burn (sŭn′bûrn′) **1** a darkening of the skin by the rays of the sun; a tan. **2** reddening or blistering of the skin from too much sun. **3** to tan or burn the skin by the sun's rays: *She sunburns easily because of her fair skin.* **sun·burned** or **sun· burnt, sun·burn·ing.**

sun·burnt (sŭn′bûrnt′) **1** of skin, tanned or burned by the sun's rays. **2** See **sunburn.**

sun·dae (sŭn′dī) a serving of ice cream topped with syrup, crushed fruit, or nuts. (Homonym: Sunday)

Sun·day (sŭn′dā or sŭn′dī) first day of the week, among most Christian denominations, a day of rest and worship. (Homonym: sundae)

Sunday school classes held by churches on Sunday for study of religion and the Bible.

sun·der (sŭn′dər) to divide; separate; part.

sun·di·al (sŭn′dī′əl) a plate marked with the hours and having a projecting pointer, set flat on the top of a pedestal or vertically into a wall. The shadow of the pointer tells the time on sunny days.

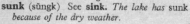

Sundial

sun·down (sŭn′doun′) sunset: *At sundown the valley suddenly became dark.*

sun·dry (sŭn′drī) **1** various; several: *Mother was stocking up on sundry things for the church bazaar.* **2 sundries** odds and ends; items too small or numerous to be mentioned: *The bill did not include the sundries we had bought at the notions counter.*

sun·flow·er (sŭn′flou′ər) **1** any of various tall plants that bear a flower like a daisy and have edible seeds that yield a useful oil. Some kinds are very big. **2** the flower of this plant. It has a brown center surrounded by yellow petals.

Garden sunflower

sung (sŭng) See **sing.** *Christmas carols were sung in church this morning.*

sunk (sŭngk) See **sink.** *The lake has sunk because of the dry weather.*

sunk·en (sŭngk′ən) **1** situated below the level around it: *to step down from the hall into the* sunken *den.* **2** below the surface of a body of water; submerged: *The* sunken *rocks were a danger to passing ships.* **3** fallen in; hollow: *the invalid's* sunken *cheeks.*

sun·light (sŭn′līt′) the light of the sun: *The sunlight made the room cheery.*

sun·lit (sŭn′lit′) lighted by the sun: *The sunlit garden was very pleasant.*

sun·ny (sŭn′ī) **1** having much sun: *a sunny afternoon.* **2** warmed or lighted by the sun: *a sunny balcony.* **3** cheerful; bright: *He has a sunny disposition.* **sun·ni·er, sun·ni·est; sun·ni·ly.**

sun·rise (sŭn′rīz′) **1** the morning rising of the sun from below the horizon. **2** the time when the sun rises. **3** appearance of the sky when the sun rises: *the colorful sunrises in the tropics.*

sun·set (sŭn′sĕt′) **1** disappearance of the sun below the horizon. **2** time at which the sun disappears below the horizon. **3** appearance of the sky when the sun sets: *The sunset was a brilliant orange.*

sun·shine (sŭn′shīn′) **1** light rays from the sun. **2** place where rays of the sun fall: *Stand in the* sunshine *and you will feel warmer.* **3** brightness; cheer: *His smile is always full of* sunshine.

sun·spot (sŭn′spŏt′) one of the dark patches seen from time to time on the surface of the sun.

sun·stroke (sŭn′strōk′) sudden, and often fatal, illness caused by too much exposure to the sun.

sun·up (sŭn′ŭp′) sunrise.

¹sup (sŭp) to eat the evening meal; have supper. **supped, sup·ping.** [¹sup is short for **supper.**]

²sup (sŭp) **1** to take liquid in small mouthfuls; sip: *I supped the hot soup from my spoon.* **2** small mouthful of liquid. **supped, sup·ping.** [²sup is a form of an Old English word (sūpan) of the same meaning.]

su·per- prefix meaning "above," "going beyond," or "greater than others": super*natural,* super*market.*

su·perb (sŏŏ pûrb′) **1** grand; majestic: *The view from the hill was superb.* **2** elegant; rich: *The bride's gown is superb.* **3** very fine; excellent: *The orchestra gave a superb performance.* **su·perb·ly.**

su·per·char·ger (soō'pər chär'jər or sū'-pər chär'jər) a blower that increases the power of an automobile or airplane engine by forcing extra air into the cylinders.

su·per·fi·cial (soō'pər fish'əl) **1** on the surface; not deep: *His wound was only* superficial *and healed quickly.* **2** slight; shallow; not thorough: *a superficial knowledge of history;* superficial *study of a lesson.* **su·per·fi·cial·ly.**

su·per·flu·ous (soō pûr'floō əs) beyond what is needed; excessive: *to cut out* superfluous *words in a composition.* **su·per·flu·ous·ly.**

su·per·in·tend (soō'pər in tĕnd' or sū'pər in tĕnd') to supervise, direct, or manage (work or workers).

su·per·in·tend·ent (soō'pər in tĕn'dənt or sū'pər in tĕn'dənt) person who supervises or directs: *the superintendent of schools; the superintendent of an apartment house.*

su·pe·ri·or (sə pir'i ər or soō pir'i ər) **1** above the average in quality or excellence; exceptional: *He has a* superior *mind.* **2** higher in rank, position, office, etc.: *a* superior *officer.* **3** one who is higher in rank or position: *Captain Jones is my* superior. **4** greater in quantity or number: *The* superior *strength of the opposing army caused our defeat.* **5** snobbish; disdainful: *Paul's* superior *attitude lost him friends.* **6 superior to** (1) above; not stooping or yielding to: *He is* superior to *petty jealousies.* (2) better or greater than: *His mind is* superior *to his brother's.*

su·pe·ri·or·i·ty (soō pir'i ôr'ə tĭ or soō pir'-i ôr'ə tĭ) superior state; superior quality: *the* superiority *of modern engineering.*

su·per·la·tive (sə pûr'lə tĭv or soō pûr'lə-tĭv) **1** best or greatest in degree, kind, etc.; supreme: *a woman of* superlative *beauty.* **2** of a word, denoting the greatest possible degree, extent, etc., as in "best" or "greatest." **su·per·la·tive·ly.**

su·per·man (soō'pər măn' or sū'pər măn') man of unusual strength, or ability; one who is more than human in power or ability: *He was called the* superman *of the boxing ring because of his skill and strength.* **su·per·men.**

su·per·mar·ket (soō'pər mär'kĭt or sū'pər-mär'kĭt) large store where food and other goods are displayed so that customers can wait on themselves.

su·per·nat·u·ral (soō'pər năch'ə rəl or sū'-pər năch'ə rəl) outside or beyond what is natural; not explained by the laws of nature; miraculous: *Many things that are now explained by science were once thought to be* supernatural. **su·per·nat·u·ral·ly.**

su·per·sede (soō'pər sēd' or sū'pər sēd') to take the place of; supplant: *Automobiles have* superseded *the horse and carriage.* **su·per·sed·ed, su·per·sed·ing.**

su·per·sti·tion (soō'pər stĭsh'ən or sū'pər-stĭsh'ən) **1** an unreasoning fear of the unknown; belief in magic, witchcraft, etc. **2** an instance of such belief: *A fear of the number thirteen is a* superstition.

su·per·sti·tious (soō'pər stĭsh'əs or sū'-pər stĭsh'əs) having to do with or caused by superstition; full of superstitions: *She was* superstitious *about black cats.* **su·per·sti·tious·ly.**

su·per·vise (soō'pər vīz' or sū'pər vīz') to watch over the work of; to direct; superintend; oversee: *She* supervised *the painters when they mixed the colors for the room.* **su·per·vised, su·per·vis·ing.**

su·per·vi·sion (soō'pər vĭzh'ən or sū'pər-vĭzh'ən) direction; management: *The playground is under my* supervision.

su·per·vi·sor (soō'pər vī'zər or sū'pər vī'-zər) person who directs or supervises.

sup·per (sŭp'ər) evening meal (when dinner is eaten at midday); last meal of the day.

sup·plant (sə plănt') **1** to take the place of; displace: *Machines have* supplanted *men in many jobs.* **2** to take the place of (another) by unfair means: *The prince tried to* supplant *his father on the throne.*

sup·ple (sŭp'əl) **1** bending without breaking; flexible; pliant: *The* supple *young trees withstood the storm.* **2** adaptable to other persons or changing circumstances; elastic: *a* supple *mind.* **sup·pler, sup·plest; sup·ple·ly.**

sup·ple·ment (sŭp'lə mənt) **1** something added to complete a thing or supply a deficiency: *She took vitamins as a* supple-

fāte, făt, fâre, fär; bē, bĕt; bīte, bĭt; nō, nŏt, nôr; fūse, fŭn, fûr; tōō, tŏok; foil; foul; thin; then; hw for wh as in what; zh for s as in usual; ə for a, e, i, o, u, as in ago, linen, peril, atom, minus

721

ment *to her diet.* **2** an extra section of a newspaper or an addition to a book. **3** to make additions to; complete.

sup·pli·cate (sŭp′lə kāt′) **1** to ask humbly; beg; entreat: *The condemned prisoner supplicated the governor for mercy.* **2** to pray humbly and earnestly. **sup·pli·cat·ed, sup·pli·cat·ing.**

sup·pli·ca·tion (sŭp′lə kā′shən) humble request; entreaty; prayer: *an earnest supplication for forgiveness.*

sup·ply (sə plī′) **1** to furnish; provide: *The farmer supplied shelter for the hikers.* **2** to fill; satisfy: *Can you supply the demand for coffee?* **3** quantity of something for use or sale; stock: *The store had a supply of canned goods.* **sup·plies; sup·plied, sup·ply·ing.**

sup·port (sə pôrt′) **1** to bear or hold up; to prop: *Buttresses support the walls of the church.* **2** thing that bears or holds up (something): *Cables are the support for a suspension bridge.* **3** to provide for; maintain: *The widow supported her three children.* **4** provision for food and shelter; subsistence: *He failed to provide support for his family.* **5** to aid; comfort: *Her kindness always supports me in time of trouble.* **6** to approve; uphold: *The mayor hopes the voters will support his plan to build a new school.* **7** approval; backing: *We must all give our support to the president's decision.* **8** to show the truth of; make valid; verify: *These papers support his claim to the property.* **9** something that helps to verify: *Your evidence is a support to my theory.* **10** to put up with; endure: *She could not support the children's rudeness.*

sup·port·er (sə pôr′tər) **1** person or thing that supports (something). **2** person who upholds or backs (something): *a supporter of town planning.*

sup·pose (sə pōz′) **1** to assume; expect; take for granted: *I suppose I'll see you at the party?* **2** to imagine; believe: *The girl liked to suppose that she was a princess in disguise.* **sup·posed, sup·pos·ing.**

sup·posed (sə pōzd′) thought to be; assumed: *He is the supposed author of the anonymous book.* **sup·pos·ed·ly.**

sup·pos·ing (sə pō′zĭng) assuming; if; in the event that: *Just supposing you could travel, where would you go first?*

sup·press (sə prĕs′) **1** to put down by force; crush; subdue: *The police suppressed the riot.* **2** to restrain; hold back: *He tried to suppress his laughter.* **3** to stop the publication of: *His book was suppressed.*

sup·pres·sion (sə prĕsh′ən) **1** a putting down by force: *the suppression of a revolt.* **2** a holding back; restraint: *the suppression of anger.*

su·prem·a·cy (sə prĕm′ə sĭ or sŏŏ prĕm′ə-sĭ) **1** the state of being supreme: *Shakespeare's supremacy among poets.* **2** highest authority or power: *the supremacy of a ruler; the supremacy of an air force.*

su·preme (sə prĕm′ or sŏŏ prĕm′) **1** most powerful; highest in authority. **2** of highest degree: *an act of supreme courage.* **3** greatest; most important: *This duet marks the supreme moment of the opera.* **su·preme·ly.**

Supreme Court 1 highest court in the United States. **2** similar court in some States and in other countries.

sure (shŏŏr) **1** confident: *I am sure you will succeed.* **2** certain: *You are sure to find what you are looking for in that book.* **3** safe; reliable; trustworthy: *a sure bet.* **4** firm; sound: *a sure foothold.* **5** surely; certainly. **sur·er, sur·est.**

sure-foot·ed (shŏŏr′fŏŏt′ĭd) not likely to fall or stumble: *Mountain goats need to be sure-footed to jump from rock to rock.* **sure-foot·ed·ly.**

sure·ly (shŏŏr′lĭ) **1** without fail: *Slowly but surely summer turns into autumn.* **2** with skill; in a deft manner; without a slip: *The expert skier glided surely down the slope.* **3** certainly; undoubtedly: *You surely can't be serious.*

sur·e·ty (shŏŏr′ə tĭ) **1** sureness; certainty. **2** guarantee against damage, loss, etc.: *The government gave the farmers surety for their crops.* **3** person who assumes responsibility for another: *He was surety for his friend's debt.* **sur·e·ties.**

surf (sûrf) the breaking of waves on a beach: *We have a high surf today.* (Homonym: serf)

Surf

sur·face (sûr′fĭs) **1** the outside of anything: *to restore the surface of the furniture; the surface of the lake.* **2** having to do with the surface or top of anything: *the underground and* surface *transportation of the city.* **3** outward appearance: *He was happy on the* surface, *but we knew he grieved in silence.* **4** insincere; superficial: *Garry showed only a* surface *interest in the subject.* **5** to give a surface to; to smooth: *I* surfaced *this table with three coats of varnish.* **6** to come to the surface from below: *The whale* surfaced *just ahead of the ship.* **sur·faced, sur·fac·ing.**

surge (sûrj) **1** large wave, swell, or billow of water. **2** to rush, sweep, or push forth like a rolling or swelling wave: *The crowd* surged *past the line of police.* **3** something like a wave: *His anger overcame him in one great* surge. **surged, surg·ing.** (Homonym: serge)

sur·geon (sûr′jən) doctor who practices surgery.

sur·ger·y (sûr′jə rĭ) **1** branch of medicine that deals with the treatment of illness by operation, such as removing diseased parts of the body, repairing injuries, correcting deformities, etc. **2** the work of a doctor who operates on people or animals. **3** room in which operations are performed. **sur·ger·ies.**

sur·gi·cal (sûr′jĭ kəl) having to do with or used in surgery: *The nurse laid out the* surgical *instruments.* **sur·gi·cal·ly.**

sur·ly (sûr′lĭ) bad-tempered; rude; sullen: *He was in a* surly *mood after their argument.* **sur·li·er, sur·li·est; sur·li·ly.**

sur·mise (sər mīz′) **1** to guess: *He* surmised *that our absence resulted from illness.* **2** (also sûr′mīz) a guess or conjecture based upon little evidence: *It was only a* surmise, *but it proved correct.* **sur·mised, sur·mis·ing.**

sur·mount (sər mount′) **1** to overcome; conquer: *He* surmounted *his difficulties by working harder.* **2** to be situated at the top of: *The castle* surmounts *the hill.* **3** to rise or tower above: *The mountain* surmounts *the village.*

sur·name (sûr′nām′) **1** last or family name: *"Dickens" is Charles Dickens'* surname. **2** in former times, name added to a first or given name to indicate some characteristic or trait; nickname, such as "Charles the

Fat." **3** to give an additional name to: *King Richard was* surnamed *"the Lion-Hearted."* **sur·named, sur·nam·ing.**

sur·pass (sər păs′) **1** to be better, stronger, etc., than (something); exceed: *The results have* surpassed *my highest hopes.* **2** to go beyond the reach, power, or limit of (something): *The difficulties the explorers met with* surpassed *their endurance.*

sur·plus (sûr′plŭs) **1** quantity over and above what is needed; excess: *After we used what we needed from our farm, we sold the* surplus. **2** over and above what is used or needed: *We sold our* surplus *vegetables by the roadside.*

sur·prise (sər prīz′) **1** to take (one) unawares; to come upon unexpectedly: *He* surprised *me by his visit. Our night raid* surprised *the enemy.* **2** a catching unawares: *to be caught by* surprise. **3** to cause to feel wonder or astonishment: *The mild old man's sudden fury* surprised *us.* **4** something sudden or unexpected: *The new car was a* surprise *for Mother.* **5** coming as a surprise: *a* surprise *party; a* surprise *attack.* **6** a feeling caused by the sudden or unexpected; astonishment: *Imagine Mother's* surprise *when she saw the new car!* **sur·prised, sur·pris·ing.**

sur·pris·ing (sər prī′zĭng) causing surprise, wonder, or astonishment: *His loss in weight was* surprising, *considering how much he ate.* **sur·pris·ing·ly.**

sur·ren·der (sə rĕn′dər) **1** to yield or give up: *The fisherman* surrendered *his catch to the game warden. The army* surrendered. **2** act of yielding or giving up.

sur·rey (sûr′ĭ) light carriage with four wheels and two seats.

sur·round (sə round′) to shut in on all sides; enclose; encircle: *The town is* surrounded *by farms.*

Surrey

sur·round·ings (sə roun′dĭngz) conditions, people, things, etc., that surround one; setting; environment: *He lived in poor* surroundings.

fāte, făt, fâre, fär; bē, bĕt; bīte, bĭt; nō, nŏt, nôr; fūse, fŭn, fûr; tōō, tŏŏk; foil; foul; thin; then; hw for wh as in *wh*at; zh for s as in u*s*ual; ə for a, e, i, o, u, as in *a*go, lin*e*n, per*i*l, at*o*m, min*u*s

723

¹**sur·vey** (sər vā′) **1** to examine generally; take a broad view of: *We surveyed the scene from the hill.* **2** to examine closely with regard to condition or value: *Dad surveyed the used car carefully before he bought it.* **3** to measure the boundaries of land: *The surveyor surveyed the farm before we bought it.*

²**sur·vey** (sûr′vā or sər vā′) **1** act of examining: *a survey of goods on sale.* **2** examination made by gathering information, such as statistics: *a survey of the drivers in the town.* **3** a measuring of the boundaries of land: *The surveyor made a survey of the construction site.*

sur·vey·ing (sər vā′ing) science or occupation of measuring the boundaries of land.

sur·vey·or (sər vā′ər) person who surveys: *The city surveyor laid out a park.*

sur·vi·val (sər vi′vəl) **1** act or fact of surviving: *the survival of the fittest.* **2** person or thing that has survived: *Superstitions are survivals of former times.*

sur·vive (sər viv′) **1** to continue to live or be: *The pyramids have survived through the centuries.* **2** to outlive; outlast: *Mr. Jones' wife survived him nine years.* **3** to last through; endure: *Of all the trees, only the great oak survived the hurricane.* **sur·vived, sur·viv·ing.**

sur·vi·vor (sər vi′vər) person or thing left after others have died or disappeared after a disaster: *Robinson Crusoe was the only survivor of the shipwreck.*

sus·cep·ti·ble (sə sĕp′tə bəl) **1** easily affected or influenced; very sensitive: *Arthur is a susceptible child, quick to respond to kindness.* **2 susceptible to** easily affected with; liable to: *to be susceptible to colds.* **3 susceptible of** capable of; allowing: *a message susceptible of several meanings.*

¹**sus·pect** (sə spĕkt′) **1** to believe in the guilt of, without proof: *I suspect him of cheating.* **2** to think likely: *I suspect you are correct.* **3** to view with suspicion; doubt; question: *I suspect his motives.*

²**sus·pect** (sŭs′pĕkt) **1** person under suspicion, especially of having committed a crime: *After the robbery, the police arrested several suspects.* **2** (also sə spĕkt′) viewed with suspicion; questionable; dubious: *The miser's sudden generosity was suspect.*

sus·pect·ing (sə spĕkt′ing) having to do with suspicion: *a suspecting nature.*

sus·pend (sə spĕnd′) **1** to cause to hang down: *We suspended a sprig of mistletoe from the ceiling.* **2** to hold, as if hanging: *The balloons appeared to be suspended in mid-air.* **3** to delay; withhold: *to suspend judgment.* **4** to keep out, for a while, from some privilege, office, or the like: *to suspend a pupil from school.*

sus·pend·ers (sə spĕn′dərz) straps designed to pass over the shoulders to hold up the trousers.

sus·pense (sə spĕns′) condition of doubt or uncertainty, accompanied by anxiety: *The closeness of the election kept us in suspense until the last vote was counted.*

sus·pen·sion (sə spĕn′shən) a suspending or being suspended: *a suspension of judgment; a suspension of work.*

suspension bridge bridge hung on cables stretched across a river, canyon, etc. For picture, see **bridge.**

sus·pi·cion (sə spĭsh′ən) **1** a believing that something is wrong with little or no evidence: *A suspicion of foul play made the police investigate.* **2** feeling or impression of one who suspects: *Robert had a suspicion that he was being followed.* **3** a trace; hint: *a suspicion of garlic in the salad.*

sus·pi·cious (sə spĭsh′əs) **1** distrustful: *I am suspicious of a politician's promise.* **2** inviting doubt or distrust: *His actions were suspicious enough to make the police watch him.* **3** expressing or showing suspicion: *a suspicious question; a suspicious glance.* **sus·pi·cious·ly.**

sus·tain (sə stān′) **1** to support: *There was barely enough air to sustain life.* **2** to bear up; hold up: *Stone arches sustain the weight of the dome.* **3** to uphold: *The Supreme Court sustained the decision of the lower courts.* **4** to endure; suffer: *to sustain a broken leg.* **5** to hold; continue; keep going: *to sustain a high note; to sustain a discussion.* **6** to bear out: *The outcome of the election sustained my prediction.*

sus·te·nance (sŭs′tə nəns) something that supports or sustains life, such as food and water.

SW or **S.W.** **1** southwest. **2** southwestern.

swab (swŏb) **1** a mop. **2** to clean with a mop: *to swab the deck.* **3** tuft of cotton or the like used to apply medicine to or clean a sore or infected part. **4** to use such a device: *The doctor swabbed Toni's throat with iodine.* **swabbed, swab·bing.**

swag·ger (swăg'ər) **1** to strut about and act in a showy or overbearing manner: *The fellow swaggered into the restaurant and demanded service.* **2** an overbearing walk or way of acting: *His swagger, as he entered the room, annoyed everyone.*

swain (swān) old word for a country youth; young man or lover: *a swain and his shepherdess.*

¹swal·low (swŏl'ō) slender, forked-tailed bird with pointed wings, admired for its swift, graceful flight. [¹**swallow** is a form of an Old Eng-

Barn swallow, about 5 in. long

lish word (swalwe) of the same meaning.]

²swal·low (swŏl'ō) **1** to transfer (food or drink) from the mouth to the stomach through the throat: *to swallow a piece of cake.* **2** act of swallowing: *He drained his glass at one swallow.* **3** the amount so transferred at one time: *George took a swallow of water.* **4** to believe easily: *Dick will swallow any story you tell him.* **5** to accept without protest: *to swallow insults.* **6** to refrain from expressing: *to swallow one's pride; to swallow anger.* **7** to engulf; destroy: *The stormy ocean swallowed the ship.* [²**swallow** is a form of an Old English word (swelgan) meaning "to swallow," "engulf."]

swam (swăm) See **swim**. *The little fishes swam right over the dam.*

swamp (swŏmp) **1** watery land; marsh; bog; fen. **2** to fill with water or cause to sink by flooding: *The big wave swamped the boat.* **3** to sink by being flooded: *The boat swamped and went to the bottom.* **4** to overwhelm: *Tom was swamped with homework.*

swamp·y (swŏm'pĭ) muddy; marshy; filled with swamps: *The river runs through swampy land. A swampy forest barred the footsore travelers' path.* **swamp·i·er, swamp·i·est.**

swan (swŏn) large, usually white, swimming bird with a long, curved neck, admired for its grace on the water. It resembles a huge goose.

Swan, about 5 ft. long

swap (swŏp) **1** to exchange for something other than money; trade; barter: *Stephen swapped his knife for a baseball.* **2** an exchange: *to make an even swap.* **swapped, swap·ping.**

sward (swôrd) a stretch of grassy ground; turf.

swarm (swôrm) **1** mass or large number of insects clustered closely in a group: *a swarm of ants; a swarm of mosquitoes.* **2** a mass of bees, led by a queen bee, which flies off from a hive to form a new colony: *A swarm of bees settled in the hollow apple tree.* **3** of bees, to leave a hive in a swarm to form a new colony. **4** a crowd; a large number of moving people, animals, etc.: *Great swarms of people streamed through the streets.* **5** to move in great numbers: *Europeans swarmed to America in the 19th century.* **6** to be crowded: *The beach swarmed with people on the weekend.*

swarth·y (swôr'thĭ) of a dusky color; having a dark skin: *The Indian's swarthy complexion was partly natural, partly due to exposure to the sun.* **swarth·i·er, swarth·i·est; swarth·i·ly.**

swat (swŏt) to strike or hit with a sharp, quick blow, usually with a flat object: *to swat a fly.* **swat·ted, swat·ting.**

sway (swā) **1** to cause to move steadily backward or forward, or from side to side: *The wind sways the branches.* **2** to move steadily backward and forward, or from side to side; swing: *The boat swayed with the movement of the waves.* **3** to move or influence: *His brilliant speeches swayed the masses in his favor.* **4** to make waver; weaken another's opinion or change another's mind: *She cannot be swayed from her beliefs.* **5** a rule; an influence: *under Queen Victoria's sway; under love's sway.* **6** a swaying: *the sway of the shutters during a wind storm.*

---

fāte, făt, fâre, fär; bē, bĕt; bīte, bĭt; nō, nŏt, nôr; fūse, fŭn, fûr; tōō, tŏŏk; foil; foul; thin; ~~then~~; hw for wh as in *what*; zh for s as in usual; ə for a, e, i, o, u, as in *ago*, linen, peril, atom, min*u*s

swear (swâr) **1** to declare solemnly on one's oath; vow: *He* swore *by the Bible to tell the truth. He* swore *eternal friendship.* **2** to bind by a solemn vow or promise; obtain a solemn promise from: *He* swore *me to secrecy.* **3** to use bad words, curses, or profane language.

swear by to have great confidence in; recommend highly: *Tom* swears by *his doctor.*

swear in to administer an oath of office to: *to* swear in *a jury.*

swear off to promise to renounce or give up: *to* swear off *smoking, etc.*

swear out to get or obtain by making a charge under oath: *to* swear out *a warrant.*

swore, sworn, swear·ing.

sweat (swĕt) **1** to give forth moisture through the pores of the skin; perspire. **2** to cause to perspire: *The hard gallop across the fields* sweated *Tony's pony.* **3** moisture given off through the pores of the skin: *The laborer wiped the* sweat *from his brow.* **4** to work hard: *They* sweated *to repair their boat in time for the yacht race.* **5** to become damp on the outside of (something): *A glass of ice water* sweats. **6** to employ at long hours of hard work for low wages. **7 in a sweat** covered with sweat; wet with perspiration. **8 by the sweat of one's brow** by hard work. **9 in a cold sweat** badly frightened and having a chilly feeling. **sweat·ed** or **sweat, sweat·ing.**

sweat·er (swĕt'ər) knitted or crocheted garment, with or without sleeves, for the upper part of the body.

Swede (swēd) native of Sweden or person of Swedish descent.

Swe·den (swē'dən) a country on the Scandinavian Peninsula in northern Europe.

Swed·ish (swē'dish) **1** of Sweden, its people, or its language. **2** language of the Swedish people.

sweep (swēp) **1** to clean or remove litter from (a rug, floor, steps, etc.) with a broom, brush, etc.: *It's Sophie's turn to* sweep *the porch today.* **2** to remove or clean away: *to* sweep *up dead leaves; to* sweep *off the snow.* **3** to move quickly on or over with great force: *A hurricane* swept *the Florida coast.* **4** to cause to disappear; remove by violent action: *The pier was*

swept *away by the flood. The waves* swept *me off the raft.* **5** to move or stretch over a long, curving course: *The current* sweeps *along the coast.* **6** wide expanse: *the* sweep *of land.* **7** to move in a swift but stately manner: *The bride* swept *up the aisle.* **8** to pass over or across with a swift, steady motion: *His eyes* swept *the faces in the room. The musician* swept *the strings of the harp.* **9** a swift, curving motion: *with a* sweep *of his arm.* **10** long, gradual curve or curving line: *the* sweep *of an arch or building; the* sweep *of his forehead.* **11** a single or steady stroke: *with one* sweep *of the oar.* **12** a long oar for moving or steering a boat. **13** a long pole, attached to a post, for raising or lowering a bucket in a well. **14** person whose work is sweeping: *a chimney* sweep. **15 make a clean sweep** to get rid of old things or old ways of doing things: *We* made a clean sweep *of everything in the attic.*

sweep all before one to have a tremendous success at anything.

sweep off one's feet to overcome or carry away by power of persuasion or fascination: *The dashing Spaniard* swept *her off her feet.*

swept, sweep·ing.

sweep·er (swē'pər) person or thing that sweeps: *a carpet* sweeper; *a crossing* sweeper.

sweep·ing (swē'ping) **1** a cleaning or brushing with broom, brush, etc. **2** of great scope or range; overwhelming: *a* sweeping *majority of votes.* **3 sweepings** rubbish, dust, or refuse swept together for disposal: *Put the* sweepings *in the dust can.* **sweep·ing·ly.**

sweet (swēt) **1** pleasant to the taste, as sugar or honey. **2** having a pleasant fragrance or aroma: *the* sweet *scent of violets;* sweet *herbs.* **3** of sounds, pleasant, soothing, or melodious: *a* sweet *voice.* **4** kind; tender; mild: *a* sweet *disposition.* **5** attractive in manner or appearance: *a* sweet *little girl.* **6** pie, pudding, or tart, etc.; dessert. **7** not stale, sour, or salty: *the taste of* sweet *milk;* sweet *butter.* **8 sweets** chocolate, candy, etc. **sweet·ly.** (Homonym: suite)

sweet corn a kind of corn with a sweetish flavor, usually eaten when it is young and tender.

sweet·en (swē'tən) **1** to make sweet to the taste with sugar, honey, etc.: *Please* sweeten *my tea.* **2** to make more endurable or pleasant: *A friend's kindness* sweetened *his lot.* **3** to become sweet; to become more tolerant or agreeable: *The old lady's disposition* sweetened *somewhat with her advancing years.*

sweet·en·ing (swē'tən ĭng) that which sweetens: *Some recipes call for honey instead of sugar as* sweetening.

sweet·heart (swēt'härt) person who is beloved; lover.

sweet·ish (swē'tĭsh) rather sweet.

sweet·meats (swēt'mēts') small pieces of fruit or nuts preserved in sugar; candy.

sweet·ness (swēt'nĭs) quality or condition of being sweet.

sweet pea 1 a kind of plant of the pea family, bearing fragrant blossoms of many colors. **2** the flower of this plant.

sweet potato 1 a trailing plant with a sweetish, starchy root. **2** this root cooked and eaten as a vegetable.

Sweet pea

swell (swĕl) **1** to increase in size, volume, etc.: *David's knee began to* swell *after his fall downstairs. In time, Ann's savings will* swell *into a substantial amount. The thaw will* swell *the river.* **2** to fill out; inflate: *Wind* swells *the sail.* **3** to puff up with strong feeling: *to* swell *with pride.* **4** an increase in size, volume, etc.: *the* swell *of the organ's tone.* **5** a long, slow continuous wave: *the* swell *of the ocean after a storm.* **swelled, swelled** or **swol·len, swell·ing.**

swell·ing (swĕl'ĭng) an increase in size; enlargement; swollen place or lump on the body.

swel·ter (swĕl'tər) to suffer from the heat; sweat a great deal: *We* sweltered *at the August picnic.*

swept (swĕpt) See **sweep.** *Alec* swept *the leaves off the lawn.*

swept-back (swĕpt'băk') spreading outward and backward, such as the wings of some airplanes.

swerve (swûrv) **1** to turn aside: *The car* swerved *on the icy pavement. Although there were many obstacles in his path, he never swerved from his duty.* **2** a sudden turning aside. **swerved, swerv·ing.**

swift (swift) **1** moving or able to move rapidly; fast: *the* swift *runner.* **2** coming, happening, or done quickly or without delay: *a* swift *reply to a letter.* **3** bird somewhat like a swallow, usually seen in groups in zigzag, batlike flight. **swift·ly.**

Chimney swift, about 5 in. long

swift·ness (swift'nĭs) quickness; speed: *Tommy's kite soared upwards with the* swiftness *of a bird.*

swig (swĭg) **1** to drink in deep drafts; gulp. **2** a deep gulp of a liquid: *He took a quick* swig *of the cold cider.* **swigged, swig·ging.**

swill (swĭl) **1** to drink or gulp greedily in large quantities: *The pirates* swilled *the brandy from the captured ship.* **2** a drink taken in large quantities. **3** food for animals, especially liquid garbage for swine. **4** garbage.

swim (swĭm) **1** to pass through water by moving legs, arms, fins, etc. **2** to cross by swimming: *His team* swam *the English Channel.* **3** act of swimming: *The boys were allowed an hour's* swim *before dinner.* **4** to float: *Apples dropped into the brook and* swam *downstream.* **5** to be immersed in or covered by a liquid: *Sad news caused the girl's eyes to* swim *with tears.* **6** to cause to swim or float: *He* swam *the cattle across the river. Masses of clouds were* swimming *across the mountain.* **7** to be dizzy: *Her head* swam *after the waltz.* **8 in the swim** taking part in what is current or fashionable. **swam, swum, swim·ming.**

swim·mer (swĭm'ər) person or animal that swims.

swin·dle (swĭn'dəl) **1** to get money or property from (someone) under false pretenses; cheat; defraud: *The gold-mine salesman* swindled *the old lady out of her fortune.* **2** a cheating; a dishonest scheme: *By the*

---

fāte, făt, fâre, fär; bē, bĕt; bīte, bĭt; nō, nŏt, nôr; fūse, fŭn, fûr; tōō, tŏŏk; foil; foul; thin; ~~then~~; hw for wh as in *wh*at; zh for s as in u*s*ual; ə for a, e, i, o, u, as in *a*go, lin*e*n, per*i*l, at*o*m, min*u*s

time the swindle *was discovered, Mr. Krook had left town.* **swin·dled, swin·dling.**

swin·dler (swind'lər) person who defrauds others by dishonest schemes.

swine (swīn) **1** animal of the hog family with bristly skin and a long snout; pig. **2** crude person. pl. **swine.**

swine·herd (swīn'hûrd') person who takes care of hogs or swine.

swing (swing) **1** to move back and forth in regular motion, as the pendulum of a clock. **2** a swaying motion or sweeping stroke: *The horses chased away the flies by a swing of their tails.* **3** to move in a sweeping curve: *The batter swung the bat at the ball and missed.* **4** to hoist, lift, or hang: *The woodcutter swung the heavy sack onto his back.* **5** apparatus for swinging, as a rope or ropes holding a seat. **6** to move back and forth on a swing. **7** to move with a loose, free motion: *The carefree children went* swinging *along singing a song.* **8** a strong, steady beat or rhythm as in poetry or music. **9** to manage or handle a matter successfully: *With a few more votes we can* swing *the election.* **10 swing music** a kind of jazz marked by its strong, insistent beat, while variations of the original melody are freely interpreted and improvised on by the individual players. **11 in full swing** at the height of activity: *After the first week, classes were* in full swing. **swung, swing· ing.**

swirl (swûrl) **1** to move with a twisting, whirling motion: *The snowflakes* swirled *through the air.* **2** a circular motion of water, falling snow, or the like, such as a whirlpool. **3** spiral twist: *a* swirl *of hair.*

swish (swish) **1** rustling or hissing sound: *the swish of the actress' petticoats as she came on stage.* **2** to make a rustling or hissing sound: *The snake* swished *through the dry leaves.* **3** to switch; lash; move (something) briskly back and forth: *He* swished *his cane to and fro. She* swished *the clothes up and down in the rinse water.*

Swiss (swis) **1** of Switzerland, or its people. **2** citizen of Switzerland or person of Swiss descent. **3** the people of Switzerland. pl. **Swiss.**

switch (swich) **1** slender, flexible shoot of a tree. **2** such a shoot, or something like it, used as a light whip. **3** a blow with, or as

with, a switch. **4** to whip lightly: *Francis* switched *the grass with a cattail.* **5** to brush with a whipping motion; flick; whisk: *The horse* switched *the flies with its tail.* **6** to make a whipping or lashing motion: *The horse* switched *its tail.* **7** a tress of long hair, to be added to a woman's own hair. **8** on a railroad, a set of movable

Electric switches

rails for connecting one track with another. **9** something used to make a connection: *an electric light* switch. **10** sudden change: *The news caused a* switch *in plans.* **11** to change: *The wind* switched *to the east.* **12** to exchange: *Peter and John* switched *seats at the movie.*

switch·back (swich'băk') a railway up a steep incline. The tracks are laid in a series of zigzag curves to offset the steepness of the grade.

switch·board (swich'bôrd') flat panel or panels with switches and plugs for connecting electrical lines: *a telephone* switchboard.

Switz·er·land (swit'sər lənd) country in west-central Europe.

swiv·el (swiv'əl) **1** pair of links, or a hook and line, connected by a bolt or rivet on which one of them can turn. **2** anything that consists of a part which turns on a fixed part: *The swivel of a revolving stool at the soda fountain.*

Swivel

3 to turn or swing with a circular motion: *Mr. Brown* swiveled *around and faced me.*

swol·len (swō'lən) See **swell.** *His ankle was so swollen he could barely walk.*

swoon (swōōn) **1** to faint: *The lady* swooned *when she saw a mouse run across the floor.* **2** a fainting spell.

swoop (swōōp) **1** to sweep down suddenly upon prey: *The hawk* swooped *down on the chicken yard.* **2** sudden downward plunge.

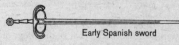

Early Spanish sword

sword (sôrd) **1** weapon like a long, slender knife with a handle at the end, used by soldiers, fencers, etc. **2** this weapon used

as an emblem of war or armed might:
"*The pen is mightier than the* sword."

sword·fish (sôrd′fĭsh′) large food fish the upper jaw of which ends in a long, slender, bony blade.

Swordfish, about 15 ft. long

sword·play (sôrd′plā′) the act or art of wielding a sword; fencing: *The two knights engaged in fancy* swordplay.

swords·man (sôrdz′mən) **1** person who fights with a sword. **2** person skilled in the use of a foil; fencer. **swords·men.**

swore (swôr) See **swear.** *Upon taking office, the President* swore *to uphold the Constitution of the United States.*

sworn (swôrn) See **swear.** *He made a* sworn *statement in court saying he knew nothing of the robbery.*

swum (swŭm) See **swim.** *Leander has* swum *this river often.*

swung (swŭng) See **swing.** *Omar* swung *his little sister in the swing.*

syc·a·more (sĭk′ə môr′) in America, a tree with smooth, ivory bark, leaves somewhat like those of the maple, and seeds in a round, hairy pod.

syl·lab·i·cate (sĭ lăb′ə kāt′) to separate into syllables. **syl·lab·i·cat·ed, syl·lab·i·cat·ing.**

syl·lab·i·ca·tion (sĭ lăb′ə kā′shən) the act or method of separating words into syllables.

syl·lab·i·fy (sĭ lăb′ə fī′) to syllabicate. **syl·lab·i·fied, syl·lab·i·fy·ing.**

syl·la·ble (sĭl′ə bəl) **1** one of the separate sounds made in pronouncing a word: "*Artichoke*" *has three* syllables. **2** letter or group of letters indicating one of the separate sounds which together make up a word. A syllable always contains a vowel sound and may contain one or more consonants.

syl·la·bus (sĭl′ə bəs) brief summary of a book, subject, course of study, etc.

sylph (sĭlf) **1** an imaginary being supposed to live in the air. **2** a slender, graceful young woman.

syl·van (sĭl′vən) having to do with woods; rustic: *a* sylvan *glen.* Also spelled **silvan.**

sym·bol (sĭm′bəl) **1** device that stands for something; anything used as a sign for something else: *Our flag is our nation's* symbol. **2** in writing and printing, a mark or letter that takes the place of or indicates a word, phrase, or thing: *O is the* symbol *of oxygen.* $ *is the* symbol *for a dollar or dollars. In music,* ♪ , ♫ , *and* ♩ *are* symbols *for different note lengths.* (Homonym: cymbal)

sym·bo·lism (sĭm′bə lĭz′əm) **1** the use of symbols to express ideas, especially in art and literature. **2** set or system of symbols standing for a particular idea: *Bible stories are rich in* symbolism.

sym·bol·ize (sĭm′bə lĭz′) **1** to stand for; represent: *The skull and crossbones* symbolize *piracy.* **2** to represent by a symbol: *The artist* symbolized *famine by a child with hollow cheeks.* **sym·bol·ized, sym·bol·iz·ing.**

sym·met·ri·cal (sĭ mĕt′rə kəl) balanced; having opposite parts alike in form but reversed: *The arrangement of a butterfly's wings is* symmetrical. *A sphere has* symmetrical *halves.* **sym·met·ri·cal·ly.**

Symmetrical figures and objects

sym·me·try (sĭm′ə trĭ) **1** correspondence of parts. There are two kinds of symmetry; one a balance of halves on opposite sides of a line, and the other a balance of parts around a central point. **2** balanced proportion; orderly arrangement of parts: *A face with regular features has* symmetry *but is not always interesting.* **sym·me·tries.**

fāte, făt, fâre, fär; bē, bĕt; bīte, bĭt; nō, nŏt, nôr; fūse, fŭn, fûr; tōō, tŏŏk; foil; foul; thin; ~~then~~; hw for wh as in *wh*at; zh for s as in usual; ə for a, e, i, o, u, as in *a*go, lin*e*n, per*i*l, at*o*m, min*u*s

729

sym·pa·thet·ic (sĭm′pə thĕt′ĭk) **1** feeling or showing sympathy. **2** inclined toward; in agreement with; favorable to: *I am sympathetic to your ideas for our vacation.* **3** understanding or sharing the same feelings; congenial: *Julia found Abigail a sympathetic companion and confided in her a great deal.*

sym·pa·thet·i·cal·ly (sĭm′pə thĕt′i kəl ĭ) **1** in a sympathetic manner; with compassion: *Hugo spoke sympathetically to his grieving friend.* **2** favorably: *We regard the matter sympathetically and will do our best to help make it succeed.*

sym·pa·thize (sĭm′pə thīz′) **1** to feel compassion for another's troubles. **2** to share in another's feelings; be in agreement with: *Many Englishmen sympathized with the Colonies' cause in the Revolution.* **sym·pa·thized, sym·pa·thiz·ing.**

sym·pa·thy (sĭm′pə thĭ) **1** a sharing of another's feelings, etc.: *Nell's sympathy soothed Joan in her grief.* **2** fellow feeling; harmony of interests: *The group of actors was united in a bond of sympathy.* **3** compassion: *We feel sympathy for the flood victims.* **4** general agreement (with): *I am in sympathy with your plan.* **sym·pa·thies.**

sym·pho·ny (sĭm′fə nĭ) **1** long and elaborate musical composition for an orchestra. **2** pleasing blend of sound, colors, or the like; harmony: *Her outfit was a symphony of different shades of blue.* **sym·pho·nies.**

symp·tom (sĭmp′təm) **1** sign of illness: *Chills and fever are symptoms of the flu.* **2** an indication of something: *Poor writing and poor spelling are symptoms of carelessness.*

syn·a·gogue (sĭn′ə gŏg′ or sĭn′ə gôg′) **1** a Jewish religious congregation. **2** Jewish house of worship.

syn·chron·ize (sĭng′krə nīz′) **1** to happen or move at the same time: *The music and action in the movie synchronized perfectly.* **2** to make agree in time: *We synchronized our watches so that we would all be there on time.* **syn·chron·ized, syn·chron·iz·ing.**

syn·di·cate (sĭn′də kĭt) a group or company of persons formed to carry out a particular enterprise, especially involving large sums of money: *A motion picture syndicate distributes the film.*

syn·o·nym (sĭn′ə nĭm) word having almost the same meaning as another word. "Short" and "brief" are synonyms. "Big" and "large" are synonyms.

syn·thet·ic (sĭn thĕt′ĭk) **1** made by a combination of chemicals similar to those of which a natural product is composed: *nylon, rayon, and other synthetic fibers.* **2** man-made substance formed by combining chemicals: *Nylon and rayon are synthetics.* **3** artificial; not spontaneous: *the synthetic applause.*

sy·rin·ga (sə rĭng′gə) a garden shrub with fragrant white flowers blooming in early summer. The syringa is sometimes called "mock orange" because its flowers resemble orange blossoms.

sy·ringe (sə rĭnj or sĭr′ĭnj) **1** a narrow tube with a bulb or plunger at one end for drawing in and discharging liquid. It is used for injecting fluid into the body, cleaning wounds, etc. **2** to cleanse by a syringe: *to syringe the ears.* **sy·ringed, sy·ring·ing.**

sy·rup or **sir·up** (sĭr′əp or sûr′əp) **1** thick, sticky, sweet liquid obtained by condensing the juices of certain plants: *corn syrup; maple syrup.* **2** sugar syrup flavored with fruit juices, etc.

sys·tem (sĭs′təm) **1** group of things which go together to make up a whole: *The trains, the tracks, the schedule, and the engineer are all parts of a railroad system.* **2** a combination of parts of the body that work together and are dependent on one another: *the circulatory system; the digestive system.* **3** set of facts, rules, laws, etc., organized so as to make up a body of knowledge or a way of doing something: *a system of government; a system of education.* **4** orderly method of doing things; routine: *Hugh has a system for his day's work.* **5** bodily and mental make-up: *One's system can stand just so much.*

sys·tem·at·ic (sĭs′tə măt′ĭk) **1** having to do with a system. **2** orderly; methodical: *He made a systematic check of the cashier's books.*

sys·tem·at·i·cal·ly (sĭs′tə măt′ĭ kəl ĭ) according to a definite plan; in a methodical manner: *He planned his day systematically, with a set time for everything from breakfast to bed.*

T

T, t (tē) 20th letter of the English alphabet.

T. **1** Tuesday. **2** Territory. **3** township.

tab (tăb) **1** small projection on a file card or on the edge of a page for indexing purposes. **2** little loop or tag on a garment for lifting or hanging it, or on a package for pulling it open or closing it.

tab·er·nac·le (tăb′ər năk′əl) **1** place of worship. **2** in some churches, a box resting on the altar and containing the sacred Host. **3 the Tabernacle** structure carried by the Jews on their journey from Egypt to Palestine for use as a place of worship.

ta·ble (tā′bəl) **1** piece of furniture having a flat top supported by legs. **2** people seated at table: *His conversation amused the whole table.* **3** food served at the table: *a hotel noted for its good table.* **4** level surface; tableland; plateau. **5** orderly arrangement of facts or figures, etc., used for reference; a list: *the multiplication* table; *the table of contents in a book.* **6** thin, flat piece of wood, stone, or metal used as a writing or carving surface; tablet: *Moses received the Ten Commandments on* tables *of stone.* **7** to postpone: *The school board* tabled *the recommendation for a new school.* **8 turn the tables** to reverse a situation: *After a bad beginning, Bill* turned the tables *on his opponent and won the game.* **ta·bled, ta·bling.**

ta·ble·cloth (tā′bəl klôth′ or tā′bəl klŏth′) cloth used to cover a table.

ta·ble·land (tā′bəl lănd′) high level plain; plateau.

ta·ble·spoon (tā′bəl spoon′) **1** large spoon used in preparing and serving food. It may hold as much as three teaspoons. **2** the amount such a spoon will hold: *The recipe calls for two* table-spoons *of butter.*

Tablets

tab·let (tăb′lĭt) **1** block or book of writing or drawing paper. **2** stone slab or metal plate bearing an inscription, set into a wall or monument as a memorial or the like. **3** thin sheet, or several joined sheets, of hard material, like ivory, for writing, drawing, etc. **4** flat pill: *a vitamin* tablet.

table tennis ping-pong.

tack (tăk) **1** small nail with a large, flat head. **2** to nail with tacks: *Claude tacked up the notice.* **3** change of direction in sailing a boat against the wind: *Take a starboard* tack. **4** to change course: *The yacht tacked around the buoy.* **5** to sail a zigzag course against the wind. **6** any change of course: *Harold's thoughts went off on a new* tack. **7** to sew in a loose fashion: *Katherine* tacked *the dress together for a fitting.*

Tacks

tack·le (tăk′əl) **1** pulley or series of pulleys and the ropes to work them, used for moving heavy weights, sails, etc. **2** gear; equipment: *Clarence put his fishing* tackle *in the boat.* **3** a football position between a guard and an end. **4** in football, to grasp and try to stop: *Victor downed the ball carrier with a smashing* tackle. **5** to undertake: *No job was too big or too hard for him to* tackle. **tack·led, tack·ling.**

Single and double tackles

tact (tăkt) sensitive understanding; sense of the right thing to do or say to avoid giving offense or to win good will in dealing with others, especially in difficult situations; diplomatic handling: *Teacher's* tact *saved the boy from embarrassment.*

tact·ful (tăkt′fəl) **1** having the ability to say or do the right thing: *a tactful person.* **2** showing the ability to say or do the right thing: *The* tactful *hostess pretended not to notice when I spilled my soup.* **tact·ful·ly.**

tac·tics (tăk′tĭks) **1** science or practice of managing military or naval forces to gain advantage against an enemy. **2** any (skillful) move or maneuver designed to gain an end: *The lawyer won his case with his clever* tactics *of flattering the jury.*

fāte, făt, fâre, fär; bē, bĕt; bīte, bĭt; nō, nŏt, nôr; fūse, fŭn, fûr; tōō, tŏŏk; foil; foul; thin; ~~then~~; hw for wh as in *what*; zh for s as in u*s*ual; ə for a, e, i, o, u, as in ag*o*, lin*e*n, per*i*l, at*o*m, min*u*s

731

tadpole

tad·pole (tăd'pōl') frog or toad in an immature stage of growth.

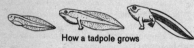

How a tadpole grows

taf·fe·ta (tăf'ə tə) fine, shiny, slightly stiff silk or rayon fabric.

¹tag (tăg) **1** a piece of paper, cardboard, leather, etc., tied to something in order to identify or label it: *a price* tag; *a luggage* tag. **2** to fix or attach a tag to: *Will you* tag *the lamps according to their price?* **3** to follow closely: *The kittens* tagged *after their mother.* **4** reinforcement made of plastic, leather, or metal at the end of a shoelace. **tagged, tag·ging.** [¹**tag** is probably a word of Scandinavian origin.]

²tag (tăg) **1** children's game in which the player called "it" runs after the other players until he touches (tags) someone who then becomes "it." **2** to tap or touch with the hand. **tagged, tag·ging.** [²**tag** is ¹**tag** in a special meaning.]

tail (tāl) **1** the extension of an animal's backbone beyond its body. **2** anything resembling an animal's tail: *the* tail *of a comet or kite.* **3** end or rear part of anything: *the* tail *of a parade.* **4** the side of a coin opposite the head. **5** to follow close behind: *We* tailed *him for five miles before we lost him.* (Homonym: tale)

tail·less (tāl'lĭs) without a tail.

tai·lor (tā'lər) **1** person whose business it is to make or repair clothes. **2** to make or repair (a garment) by sewing, fitting, etc.: *to* tailor *a suit.*

tail·spin (tāl'spĭn') downward spinning movement of an airplane in which the tail forms a wider circle than the nose.

tail wind a wind blowing from behind a ship or aircraft, thus helping to increase its speed.

taint (tānt) **1** a spot; stain; trace of something bad, impure, or corrupt: *The* taint *of a prison record clung to him despite his efforts to reform.* **2** to become spoiled: *Meat will* taint *if not refrigerated.* **3** to spoil; to cause to become tainted.

take (tāk) **1** to grasp; hold: *to* take *someone's hand.* **2** to capture; seize: *The Indians* took *the fort.* **3** to assume possession of:

take

We will take *the apartment if you paint it.* **4** to accept: *Please* take *this gift.* **5** to catch: *to* take *cold.* **6** to remove; subtract: *to* take *2 from 5.* **7** to steal: *The thief* took *the money.* **8** to choose: *You may* take *whichever candy you want.* **9** to eat, drink, or inhale: *to* take *breakfast; to* take *ether before an operation.* **10** to lead: *This road* takes *you to town.* **11** to carry: *I will* take *your trunk to the attic.* **12** to require; need: *It* takes *three eggs to make this cake.* **13** to please; attract: *Your hat* takes *my fancy.* **14** to travel on: *to* take *a plane to Boston.* **15** to make: *to* take *a photograph; to* take *a trip.* **16** to feel; have: *I* take *pride in my work.* **17** to react to; receive: *He* took *the bad news very calmly.* **18** to catch on; start: *The fire* took *with only one match.* **19** to be effective: *My vaccination didn't* take *the first time.* **20** amount or quantity taken: *I have a big* take *of fish.* **21** to perform, use, etc: *to* take *exercise; to* take *care; to* take *as an example.* **22** to conduct; escort: *to* take *someone to a party.* **23** to subscribe to: *to* take *the morning papers.* **24** to win: *to* take *the first prize.* **25** to write down: *to* take *notes; to* take *dictation.* **26** to consider; regard: *We* took *him to be intelligent.* **27** to understand (in a certain way): *How do you* take *that remark?*

take after to look or be like; resemble: *She* takes after *her mother in disposition.*

take in 1 to accept; admit: *She* takes in *boarders.* **2** to make smaller: *I am going to* take in *the waist of my skirt.* **3** to include: *The survey* takes in *all the schools in this district.* **4** to cheat; deceive: *You can't* take *me* in *with your impossible stories.* **5** to grasp with the mind: *At first he didn't* take in *the seriousness of the accident.*

take off 1 to remove: *to* take off *one's coat.* **2** to leave: *to* take off *for California.* **3** to leave the ground, as an airplane.

take on 1 to hire. **2** to undertake: *He* took on *more than he could handle.*

take to 1 to like or enjoy instinctively: *to* take to *a stranger at once;* take to *water like a duck.* **2** to go to; escape to: *We are* taking *to the woods for peace and quiet.*

take up 1 to begin; start: *She will* take up *knitting. I* took up *the story where I left off.* **2** to shorten: *to* take up *a hem.*

took, tak·en, tak·ing.

tak·en (tā′kən) See **take.** *My book was
taken from my desk.*

take-off (tāk′ôf′ or tāk′ŏf′) **1** a leaving the
ground by plane or rocket. **2** having to do
with leaving the ground: *The take-off time
for the plane was thirty seconds.*

talc (tălk) soft mineral, greasy to the touch,
used in making talcum powder, soap,
paper, and other products.

tal·cum pow·der (tăl′kəm pou′dər) fine
white powder made from talc, usually perfumed. It is used to powder the face and
body.

tale (tāl) **1** story: *This is a good tale to tell
by an open fire.* **2** falsehood; lie: *I know
that is only a tale you are telling to cover up
the truth.* **3 tell tales** to tattle: *Don't tell
tales about your friends.* (Homonym: tail)

tal·ent (tăl′ənt) **1** special ability: *He has a
talent for writing.* **2** people of special
ability: *The newspaper was proud of the
talent on its staff.*

tal·ent·ed (tăl′ən tĭd) having talent or
ability.

tal·is·man (tăl′ĭs mən or tăl′ĭz mən) ring,
stone, etc., engraved with figures, supposed
to bring good luck and to protect against
evil; a charm. **tal·is·mans.**

talk (tôk) **1** to utter words; to make thoughts
known through speech: *The baby can't talk
yet.* **2** speak; converse: *They are still
talking in the conference room.* **3** to speak,
or be able to speak, a language: *to talk
French.* **4** to express in words: *to talk
nonsense.* **5** to discuss: *to talk business.*
6 a speech; address: *He gave a talk to the
garden club.* **7** conversation: *We had a talk
about the weather.* **8** a rumor; gossip:
*There is talk that you are going to sell your
house.* **9** an object of gossip or discussion:
Her party is the talk of the town. **10** to influence, persuade, bring to, etc., by talk:
*They talked him over to their side. He can
talk me to sleep. I talked him into seeing a
movie with me.*

talk·a·tive (tô′kə tĭv) fond of talking: *He is
so talkative that no one else gets a chance to
say anything.* **talk·a·tive·ly.**

talk·er (tô′kər) person who talks, particularly one who talks a great deal.

tall (tôl) **1** of more than average height: *a
tall man; a tall building.* **2** high: *He is six
feet tall.* **3** exaggerated: *a tall story.*

tal·low (tăl′ō) the fat from certain animals,
used to make candles, soap, etc.

tal·ly (tăl′ĭ) **1** originally, a stick on which
notches were cut to keep an account; now, a
card on which a score is kept: *bridge
tallies.* **2** a score: *Please keep tally for this
game.* **3** to record; reckon up. **4** counterpart; duplicate. **5** to match:
Do these stories tally? **tallies; tal·lied, tal·ly·ing.**

Tal·mud (tăl′mŭd or tăl′-
mŏŏd) the collection of
Jewish civil and religious
law.

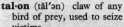
Talon

tal·on (tăl′ən) claw of any
bird of prey, used to seize
victims.

ta·mal·e (tə mä′lĭ) Mexican dish made of
rolled corn meal wrapped in corn husks,
and baked, boiled, or steamed. Sometimes
it is filled with finely chopped ingredients
such as red peppers and meat.

tam·bou·rine (tăm′bə rēn′) musical instrument consisting of a
drumhead stretched over
a shallow metal hoop in
which are set tinkling
metal disks.

Tambourine

tame (tām) **1** changed from a wild to an
obedient state: *Do you think that the circus
lion is really tame?* **2** harmless; gentle;
without fear: *This raccoon is very tame.*
3 to make docile; domesticate: *Henry
tamed the wild dog.* **4** to subdue; soften:
Long years of hardship tamed his courage.
5 dull: *a tame play; a tame book.* **tam·er,
tam·est; tamed, tam·ing; tame·ly.**

tam·per (tăm′pər) to meddle with so as to
injure or alter anything: *He tampered with
the car and now it won't run.*

tan (tăn) **1** to turn hide to leather by soaking
it in a liquid that preserves and toughens
it. **2** to be made into leather. **3** yellow-
brown color. **4** to make the skin brown by
exposing it to the sun. **5** to become brown
from exposure to the sun: *I tan easily.*
tanned, tan·ning.

fāte, făt, fâre, fär; bē, bĕt; bīte, bĭt; nō, nŏt, nôr; fūse, fŭn, fûr; tōō, tŏŏk; foil; foul; thin; then;
hw for wh as in *wh*at; zh for s as in u*s*ual; ə for a, e, i, o, u, as in *a*go, lin*e*n, per*i*l, at*o*m, min*u*s

733

tan·ge·rine (tăn′jə rēn′) **1** small, reddish-yellow, sweet orange with a loose skin somewhat thinner than that of an orange. **2** reddish-orange color.

tan·gi·ble (tăn′jə bəl) **1** capable of being touched or felt by the touch. **2** real; definite: *Tom's visit was* tangible *proof of his friendship.* **tan·gi·bly.**

tan·gle (tăng′gəl) **1** to twist and knot in a snarl: *to* tangle *yarn.* **2** a knot; snarl. **3** confusion; muddle: *a traffic* tangle. **tan·gled, tan·gling.**

Army tank with water tank in background

tank (tăngk) **1** any large container for liquids: *a household water-heater* tank; *a gasoline or fuel-oil* tank. **2** large cylindrical reservoir, often elevated. **3** swimming pool. **4** round, airtight structure to hold and distribute gas for heating and cooking. **5** large armored motor vehicle carrying guns and moving on caterpillar treads.

tank·ard (tăngk′ərd) tall mug with a hinged cover.

tank·er (tăng′kər) ship fitted with tanks for carrying oil or other liquids.

tan·ner (tăn′ər) person who makes leather by tanning hides.

tan·ner·y (tăn′ə rĭ) place where leather is made by tanning hides. **tan·ner·ies.**

tan·nic a·cid (tăn′ĭk ăs′ĭd) chemical found in tea, oak bark, and other plants and used in tanning leather, dyeing, etc.

Tankard

tan·ta·lize (tăn′tə līz′) **1** to tease or torment by promising or offering something and then withholding it. **2** to tease by being just out of reach: *The sight of all those cherries on the top branch* tantalized *me.* **tan·ta·lized, tan·ta·liz·ing.**

tan·trum (tăn′trəm) sudden outburst of bad temper: *The baby had a* tantrum *when his mother took away his bottle.*

¹tap (tăp) **1** wooden pipe with a plug stopper for drawing a liquid from a cask. **2** faucet. **3** to pierce (a cask or tree) to draw off liquid: *Farmers* tap *maple trees for their sap.* **4** to open up; draw upon: *To stay in business they'll have to* tap *new markets.* **tapped, tap·ping.** [**¹tap** is a form of an Old English word (tæppa) of the same meaning.]

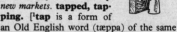

Tap

²tap (tăp) **1** to hit or touch lightly: *He* tapped *on the window to get our attention.* **2** to cause to hit or touch lightly: *We* tapped *our feet to the beat of the music.* **3** light blow or touch; a pat: *Give him a* tap *so he will wake up.* **4** to replace a sole of a shoe. **5** the sole of leather or other material used for this. **tapped, tap·ping.** [**²tap** is from an Old French word (taper) meaning "tap," "rap," "strike."]

tape (tāp) **1** long, narrow strip of metal, cloth, paper, plastic, etc., used to tie or bind something. **2** to fix, fasten, or bind with tape: *The doctor* taped *my arm.* **3** a line or rope stretched across a track to mark the finish of a race. **4** long, narrow magnetic strip wound on a reel and used in a tape recorder. **taped, tap·ing.**

tape measure long, narrow strip of cloth, paper, or metal marked off in inches, feet, etc., for measuring length.

ta·per (tā′pər) **1** to grow gradually smaller toward an end: *A sharpened pencil* tapers *to a point.* **2** long, slender candle. (Homonym: tapir.)

tape recorder machine used to record and play back sound by means of a magnetic tape.

tap·es·try (tăp′ĭs trĭ) fabric that is woven with pictures or designs and usually hung on walls. **tap·es·tries.**

tape·worm (tāp′wûrm′) any of several kinds of tapelike worms that live in the intestines. One may get a tapeworm from eating improperly cooked meat or fish.

tap·i·o·ca (tăp′ĭ ō′kə) starchy food obtained from the roots of the cassava plant and used for puddings, etc.

ta·pir (tā′pər) South and Central American hoofed animal somewhat like a pig with a long trunklike snout. (Homonym: taper)

tap·root (tăp′rōōt′) main root of a plant from which small roots spread out.

Tapir, 6 to 8 ft. long

taps (tăps) bugle or drum signal to order lights out at night.

¹tar (tär) 1 thick, black, sticky substance obtained from coal, wood, etc. 2 to cover with tar: *The workmen* tarred *the road.* **tarred, tar·ring.** [**¹tar** is a form of an Old English word (teru) originally meaning the resin of the fir tree.]

²tar (tär) sailor. [**²tar** is short for **tarpaulin.**]

ta·ran·tu·la (tə răn′chə lə) large tropical hairy spider with a poisonous bite.

tar·di·ness (tär′dĭ nĭs) a being tardy; lateness: *Sandra's tardiness was due to the fact that she didn't get up on time.*

tar·dy (tär′dĭ) 1 not on time; late: *We were all tardy because of the storm.* 2 slow: *a tardy growth of plants.* **tar·di·er, tar·di·est; tar·di·ly.**

Tarantula, body about 3½ in. long

tare (târ) 1 any of several trailing plants with small leaves, used as fodder. 2 the seed of any of these plants. 3 in the Bible, a nasty weed. (Homonym: ¹tear)

tar·get (tär′gĭt) 1 a mark to aim or shoot at, as a series of painted circles one within the other, the center circle marking the highest score. 2 something to work or strive for; goal; aim: *A teaching job was Olive's target.* 3 object of insult, ridicule, questioning, etc.: *A man in public life is always a target for criticism.*

Target

tar·iff (tăr′ĭf) 1 list of duties or taxes placed by a government on goods entering or leaving a country. 2 the tax or duty levied according to such a list or schedule: *There is a tariff on Swiss watches.* 3 any list, or schedule of rates, charges, etc.: *The tariff for ski rentals is posted in the lodge.*

tar·nish (tär′nĭsh) 1 to lose brightness; become dull: *Silver tarnishes rapidly in this atmosphere.* 2 to dull the brightness of; to stain; disgrace: *His good name was tarnished by rumors he had taken a bribe.* 3 loss of brightness; dullness: *a tarnish on silver.*

ta·ro (tär′ō) plant grown on many Pacific islands, where its starchy root is used for food. **ta·ros.**

tar·pau·lin (tär pô′lĭn) 1 heavy, waterproofed canvas or cloth used as a cover for protection from the weather: *workmen stretched a tarpaulin over the truck when it began to rain.* 2 sailor's hat or coat made of such material.

¹tar·ry (tăr′ĭ) 1 to stay or live in a place for a short time: *We tarried in Italy longer than we had planned.* 2 to linger or delay: *He is always late because he tarries on his way to work.* **tar·ried, tar·ry·ing.** [**¹tarry** is formed from two words, an Old English word (tergan) meaning "vex," "hinder," and a Latin word (tardare) meaning "to delay."]

²tar·ry (tär′ĭ) of, covered with, or like tar: *There were tarry footprints all over our new rug.* [**²tarry** is formed from "tar" and "-y," a word ending that means "like," "marked," "characterized by."]

¹tart (tärt) pastry shell filled with fruit or jam, without a top crust. [**¹tart** is from an Old French word (tarte) related to the Latin word "torta" meaning "twisted."]

²tart (tärt) 1 sour; acid: *These apples are too tart.* 2 sharp; somewhat biting: *"Do it yourself," was his tart reply.* **tart·ly.** [**²tart** is a form of an Old English word (teart) meaning "sharp," "rough."]

tar·tan (tär′tən) 1 woolen cloth woven with the plaid patterns which are the badges of the various Scottish clans. 2 the design of such a plaid, called by the name

fāte, făt, fâre, fär; bē, bĕt; bīte, bĭt; nō, nŏt, nôr; fūse, fŭn, fûr; tōō, tŏŏk; foil; foul; thin; ~~then~~; hw for wh as in *wh*at; zh for s as in u*s*ual; ə for a, e, i, o, u, as in *a*go, lin*e*n, per*i*l, at*o*m, min*u*s

of the clan it belongs to: *the Campbell tartan.* **3** made from, or in the pattern of, tartan.

tar·tar (tär'tər) **1** hard crust that collects on the teeth. **2** a scale deposited in wine barrels by fermenting wine.

Tartan

task (tăsk) **1** piece of work to be done; duty: *The boy's task was to clean up the yard.* **2** to burden; put a strain on: *to task one's memory; task one's power of endurance.* **3 take to task** to scold; find fault with: *The coach took the team to task for breaking curfew.*

tas·sel (tăs'əl) **1** tuft of threads, loose at one end and gathered into a ball at the other, used as a hanging ornament. **2** a hanging flower cluster like that of a birch or willow tree.

taste (tāst) **1** that sense by which one tells the flavor of anything: *Good cooks have a keen sense of taste.* **2** flavor: *the sweet taste of honey; the sour taste of vinegar.* **3** to perceive or test the flavor (of something) by taking some into the mouth: *Gwendolyn tasted the fried rice to see if it had enough seasoning.* **4** to have a certain flavor: *This butter tastes of fish.* **5** to sample: *Let me taste just a little of your fried chicken.* **6** a sample: *During our week at the farm, we had a taste of country life.* **7** ability to appreciate what is beautiful; trained judgment: *a cultivated taste in poetry.* **8** style or character showing the presence or lack of such ability: *His remarks were in the worst possible taste.* **9** a preference; liking: *There is no accounting for tastes.* **10** to experience: *a country that had tasted freedom.* **tast·ed, tast·ing.**

taste·ful (tāst'fəl) showing good judgment and appreciation of beauty: *The Japanese have a talent for tasteful flower decorations.* **taste·ful·ly.**

taste·less (tāst'lĭs) **1** without flavor; flat: *This cake looks good but is absolutely tasteless.* **2** dull; not attractive; lacking good taste; in poor taste: *The tasteless display of goods in the store did not attract customers.* **taste·less·ly.**

tast·y (tās'tĭ) having a good flavor; pleasing to the taste. **tast·i·er, tast·i·est; tast·i·ly.**

tat·ter (tăt'ər) **1** rag; torn and hanging part. **2** to tear or wear to pieces: *The boys tattered their clothes while climbing over the barbed wire.* **3 tatters** torn and ragged clothing: *The beggar was dressed in tatters.*

tat·tered (tăt'ərd) torn in shreds; ragged: *a tattered flag.*

tat·tle (tăt'əl) **1** to tell secrets; gossip; chatter: *If nobody tattles, the other team can't learn our plans.* **2** foolish, indiscreet talk; chatter. **tat·tled, tat·tling.**

¹tat·too (tă tōō') **1** picture or design pricked into the skin with colored inks. **2** to make such a design: *The man tattooed a ship on the sailor's chest.* [**¹tattoo** comes from a Tahitian (tä-hē'tĭ ən) word (tatu) meaning "mark." Tahitian is a language of the South Pacific.]

Tattoo

²tat·too (tă tōō') **1** drum or bugle signals calling soldiers or sailors to their quarters at night. **2** a continuous beating or tapping: *John annoyed his mother by beating a tattoo with his fingers against the window-pane.* [**²tattoo** is from a Dutch word (taptre) meaning "shut the tap," a cry that was the signal for the night closing of taverns.]

taught (tôt) See **teach.** *Jane was taught to read and write when she was five.* (Homonym: taut)

taunt (tônt) **1** to ridicule by naming faults, physical defects, etc.; jeer at: *The bully taunted him for refusing to fight.* **2** to provoke by taunting: *He was taunted into taking the dare.* **3** a stinging remark; gibe.

taut (tôt) **1** tightly stretched; tense: *a taut rope; the taut muscles of the athlete.* **2** in good condition; neat: *a taut ship.* **taut·ly.** (Homonym: taught)

tav·ern (tăv'ərn) **1** place where beer, wine, or other alcoholic beverages are sold and drunk. **2** inn; country hotel.

taw·ny (tô'nĭ) of a brownish-yellow color: *a tawny lion.* **taw·ni·er, taw·ni·est.**

tax (tăks) **1** money paid by citizens to the government for public purposes. **2** to put a tax on: *Property and people's earnings are* taxed *in order to pay for schools, police, and other services.* **3** to put a heavy burden on; strain: *Climbing the mountain in the heavy snowstorm* taxed *the strength of the rangers.* **4** a burden; strain: *a tax on the heart.* **5** to find fault with; accuse: *Dad taxed Jim with carelessness when the car ran out of gas.*

tax·a·tion (tăk sā′shən) **1** the act of taxing; the system of raising money by taxes: *Unjust taxation angered the American colonists.* **2** amount of money people pay in duties or taxes to the government.

tax·i (tăk′sĭ) **1** taxicab. **2** to ride in a taxi. **3** of an airplane, to move along the ground or on the surface of the water: *Before take-off the plane taxied down the runway.*

tax·i·cab (tăk′sĭ kăb′) automobile for public hire, usually for short distances. It often has a meter that registers the fare to be paid.

tea (tē) **1** shrub with pointed leaves and white flowers, grown in the Far East. **2** the leaves of this shrub, dried for use. **3** drink made from these leaves in hot water. **4** a similar drink made from leaves or meat extract: *sage* tea; *beef* tea. **5** an afternoon party at which tea is served. (Homonym: tee)

Tea

teach (tēch) **1** to instruct; educate: *to teach a pupil.* **2** to give instruction in: *Mr. Bean teaches history and sports.* **3** to give instruction: *She taught for many years in our local high school.* **taught, teach·ing.**

teach·er (tē′chər) person who teaches.

teach·ing (tē′chĭng) **1** work of one who teaches; profession of a teacher. **2** that which is taught: *the teachings of Christ.*

tea·cup (tē′kŭp′) **1** cup in which tea is served. **2** amount that such a cup holds: *a teacup of sugar.*

tea·ket·tle (tē′kĕt′əl) covered metal vessel with a spout and handle in which water is boiled.

teal (tēl) river duck that breeds in Canada and winters in the south.

team (tēm) **1** group of people working or playing together with a common purpose; one of the sides in a match or competition: *a baseball* team. **2** two or more horses, oxen, or other animals harnessed together to a plow, carriage, etc. **3** to join in a team: *Bill* teamed *up with his friends.* (Homonym: teem)

Blue-winged teal, about 16 in. long

team·mate (tēm′māt′) fellow member of a team.

team·ster (tēm′stər) **1** driver of a team of animals. **2** truck driver.

team·work (tēm′wûrk′) common effort of a group of people working together: *The game was won by* teamwork.

tea·pot (tē′pŏt′) covered vessel with a spout and handle, in which tea is brewed and from which it is served.

Teapot

¹tear (târ) **1** to pull or rend into pieces; rip: *The hungry dog* tore *the meat with its teeth.* **2** to cut deeply; gash: *The loose nail* tore *a jagged gash in his leg.* **3** to remove by force: *The wind* tore *the picture from the wall.* **4** to cause great pain or sadness: *It* tore *his heart to leave his children.* **5** to become torn: *Her dress* tore *on a nail.* **6** hole made by tearing; rent: *a tear in a coat.* **7** to rush; move at great speed: *The children* tore *out of school. The car* tore *up the road.* **tore, torn, tear·ing.** [¹**tear** is a form of an Old English word (teran) meaning "to destroy."] (Homonym: tare)

²tear (tĭr) drop of salty water that comes from the eye, especially when crying. [²**tear** is a form of an Old English word (tēar) of the same meaning.] (Homonym: tier)

tear·ful (tĭr′fəl) **1** shedding tears; weeping. **2** causing tears: *a tearful good-by.* **tear·ful·ly.**

tease (tēz) **1** to taunt or annoy in fun or with malicious intent: *Joe teased the dog*

fāte, făt, fâre, fär; bē, bĕt; bīte, bĭt; nō, nŏt, nôr; fūse, fŭn, fûr; tōō, tŏŏk; foil; foul; thin; then; hw for wh as in *wh*at; zh for s as in u*s*ual; ə for a, e, i, o, u, as in *a*go, lin*e*n, per*i*l, at*o*m, min*u*s

737

with a stick until it bit him. **2** person who teases: *Artie is such a tease that his sister is often in tears.* **3** to beg repeatedly; pester: *Rob teased Father to let him take the car.* **teased, teas·ing.**

tea·spoon (tē′spoon′) **1** small spoon for stirring tea or coffee or for general table use. **2** amount a teaspoon will hold; one third of a tablespoon.

tea·spoon·ful (tē′spoon fool′) as much as a teaspoon will hold.

tech·ni·cal (tĕk′nə kəl) **1** having to do with the industrial or mechanical arts and sciences: *An architect must have a long technical training.* **2** having to do with the methods of an occupation, art, or science: *A surgeon must have both knowledge and technical skill.* **tech·ni·cal·ly.**

tech·ni·cian (tĕk nĭsh′ən) person who is skilled in the technical methods of a particular subject or profession: *a laboratory technician.*

tech·nique (tĕk nēk′) method used in carrying out a mechanical, artistic, or scientific work; technical skill: *the technique of casting a statue in bronze; the technique of heart surgery; poor technique at the piano.*

tech·nol·o·gy (tĕk nŏl′ə jĭ) study of how to put scientific knowledge to practical use; applied science.

te·di·ous (tē′dĭ əs or tē′jəs) wearisome; tiresome; boring: *a tedious job; a tedious conversation.* **te·di·ous·ly.**

tee (tē) **1** in golf, the place at each hole from which the ball is first driven. **2** small mound of sand or small pin of wood, metal, or rubber with a slightly cupped head on which a golf ball is placed for driving off at the beginning of each hole.
tee off ′to drive a golf ball off the tee. **teed, tee·ing.** (Homonym: tea)

teem (tēm) **1** to be crowded to overflowing; swarm: *On holidays the beaches teem with bathers.* **2** to be full, productive, fertile, etc.: *a country teeming with wild game; a teeming brain.* (Homonym: team)

teen·ag·er (tēn′ā′jər) person between the ages of 13 and 19.

tee·pee (tē′pē) tepee.

tee·ter (tē′tər) to move unsteadily from side to side; to seesaw: *The boys teetered as they walked on top of the fence.*

teeth (tēth) **1** the hard, white, bony growths in the jaw with which a person or animal bites or chews. A child about 10 years old has 28 teeth. **2** any group of toothlike parts or things: *the teeth of a saw; teeth of a cogwheel; teeth of a rake or comb.*

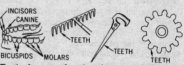

Teeth of a man, of a rake, of a saw, and of a gear

tel·e·cast (tĕl′ə kăst′) **1** to broadcast by television: *All stations plan to telecast the parade.* **2** television program.

tel·e·gram (tĕl′ə grăm′) message sent by telegraph.

tel·e·graph (tĕl′ə grăf′) **1** electric or radio device for sending and receiving messages. **2** to send (a message) by such a device: *Please telegraph the news to me, as soon as you can. Please telegraph me as soon as you can. Please telegraph.*

tel·e·me·ter (tə lĕm′ə tər) **1** automatic instrument or system of instruments used to measure conditions at a distance (such as in outer space) and to radio the measurements back to a receiver. **2** to measure or send by telemeter.

tel·ep·a·thy (tə lĕp′ə thĭ) communication of thought by some means other than by use of any of the five senses: *He seemed to read my thoughts by telepathy.*

tel·e·phone (tĕl′ə fōn′) **1** instrument or system for sending and receiving speech and other sounds over electric wires. **2** to use this instrument to speak to someone; call: *Please telephone tomorrow. Please telephone the news to me tomorrow.* **tel·e·phoned, tel·e·phon·ing.**

Simple telescope

tel·e·scope (tĕl′ə skōp′) **1** instrument for making distant things appear larger, especially a large instrument of this kind for studying heavenly bodies. **2** to fit a smaller into a larger similar object; nest: *Let us telescope these boxes to save space.* **3** to slide into one another; collapse like the sections of a field glass. **tel·e·scoped, tel·e·scop·ing.**

Tel·e·type (tĕl′ə tīp′) **1** a kind of teletypewriter. **2 teletype (1)** to send a message by this means. **(2)** the message itself. **tel·e·typed, tel·e·typ·ing.**

tel·e·type·writ·er (tĕl′ə tīp′rī′tər) a telegraph in which a typewriter at one end automatically reproduces a message typed at the other end.

tel·e·vise (tĕl′ə vīz′) to send a still or moving picture over a distance by television: *The boxing match will be televised.* **tel·e·vised, tel·e·vis·ing.**

tel·e·vi·sion (tĕl′ə vĭzh′ən) **1** the sending and receiving of moving pictures by shortwave radio. **2 television set** instrument for receiving such pictures.

tell (tĕl) **1** to relate; narrate: *to tell a story.* **2** to utter; say: *to tell the truth.* **3** to reveal; make known: *Your actions tell more than your words.* **4** to recognize: *I can't tell at this distance who it is.* **5** to order; command: *Don't tell me what to do.* **6** to be effective; have a result: *My scolding must have told because she has been good ever since.* **7** to count off: *to tell the beads on a rosary.* **8** to reveal a secret; act as telltale; tattle: *to kiss and tell.* **told, tell·ing.**

tell·er (tĕl′ər) **1** person who tells a story; narrator. **2** clerk in a bank who pays out and receives money.

tell·tale (tĕl′tāl′) **1** person who reveals secrets; someone who tattles: *She was a telltale and the other children didn't like her.* **2** giving information about something supposed to be secret; betraying: *a telltale blush.*

tem·per (tĕm′pər) **1** disposition; mood: *an even temper.* **2** tendency to anger quickly: *She has a violent temper.* **3** rage: *She flies into a temper when she's contradicted.* **4** control of anger: *Don't lose your temper.* **5** to make less extreme; to moderate by mixing with something else: *A wise man tempers his emotions with reason.* **6** to

change the quality of a substance by adding something to it or by treating it in some way: *Steel is tempered by heat.* **7** the degree of hardness, toughness, etc., in a substance: *the temper of the steel in a blade.*

tem·per·a·ment (tĕm′pər ə mənt) a person's disposition; mental and emotional makeup: *a calm temperament; an artistic temperament.*

tem·per·a·men·tal (tĕm′pər ə mĕn′təl) easily excited or upset; moody: *The temperamental actress flew into a rage and walked off the stage.* **tem·per·a·men·tal·ly.**

tem·per·ance (tĕm′pər əns) **1** a being moderate; self-restraint, especially in the use of alcoholic drink. **2** complete abstinence from alcoholic drink.

tem·per·ate (tĕm′pər it) **1** moderate; restrained; controlled: *a man of temperate habits.* **2** neither hot nor cold; moderate in temperature: *a temperate climate.* **3 Temperate Zone** old name for all the earth between the tropics and the polar regions. **tem·per·ate·ly.**

tem·per·a·ture (tĕm′pər ə chər) **1** hotness or coldness, usually measured with a thermometer: *The temperature outside is five below zero.* **2 normal temperature** body temperature of about 98.6 degrees, usually found in a well person. **3 run a temperature** or **have a temperature** to have a body temperature that is greater than normal; to have a fever.

tem·pest (tĕm′pĭst) **1** violent storm with high winds. **2** any violent outburst: *When the music ended there was a tempest of applause.*

tem·pes·tu·ous (tĕm pĕs′chŏŏ əs) **1** having to do with a tempest; stormy: *a tempestuous wind; a tempestuous night.* **2** violent: *a tempestuous display of anger.* **tem·pes·tu·ous·ly.**

¹tem·ple (tĕm′pəl) **1** building dedicated to the worship of a god or gods: *the temple of Apollo.* **2** place for worship; Christian church. **3 the Temple** any of the three temples built by the Jews at various times in ancient Jerusalem. [¹**temple** comes from a Latin word (templum) meaning "a sacred enclosure."]

---

fāte, făt, fâre, fär; bē, bĕt; bīte, bĭt; nō, nŏt, nôr; fūse, fŭn, fûr; tōō, tŏŏk; foil; foul; thin; ~~then~~;
hw for wh as in *what*; zh for s as in u*s*ual; ə for a, e, i, o, u, as in *ago, linen, peril, atom, minus*

²**tem·ple** (tĕm′pəl) the flat place on either side of the forehead above and behind the eye. [²**temple** comes through French from a Latin word (tempora) meaning "the temples of the head."]

Temple

tem·po (tĕm′pō) 1 the speed at which music is played. 2 the pace (of living, working, etc.): *the tempo of city life.* **tem·pos.**

tem·po·rar·y (tĕm′pə rĕr′ĭ) for a short time; not permanent: *a temporary job.* **tem·po·rar·i·ly.**

tempt (tĕmpt) 1 to persuade or try to persuade to do something, especially something wrong or evil: *Hunger tempts some to steal.* 2 to lure; entice: *She was tempted by the bargains at the sale.* 3 to provoke or defy: *to tempt fate.*

temp·ta·tion (tĕmp tā′shən) 1 a tempting; a persuading to do what is wrong: *the temptation of a weak person by bad companions.* 2 state of being tempted: *"Lead us not into temptation."* 3 something that tempts; attraction; enticement: *Spring fever is a temptation to laziness.*

ten (tĕn) amount or quantity that is one greater than nine; 10.

te·na·cious (tĭ nā′shəs) 1 holding fast or firmly: *He held his father's hand in a tenacious grip.* 2 stubborn; persistent: *Jack stuck to his job with tenacious energy.* 3 capable of retaining: *He had a tenacious memory for facts.* **te·na·cious·ly.**

te·nac·i·ty (tĭ năs′ə tĭ) 1 firmness or stubbornness in following one's purpose: *His tenacity overcame discouragements.* 2 quality of being adhesive: *the tenacity of glue.*

ten·ant (tĕn′ənt) 1 person who pays rent for the use of property. 2 any occupant or inhabitant: *The deer and the fox are tenants of the woods.* 3 to occupy; inhabit: *The country is mostly tenanted by farmers.*

Ten Commandments in the Bible, the ten laws given to Moses by God.

¹**tend** (tĕnd) 1 to lean toward or favor; be inclined in action or thought: *He tends to follow the ideas of his parents.* 2 to be likely to have a certain result: *Ill health tends to make some people grumpy.* 3 to move or take a direction toward: *Our course tends east-*

ward. [¹**tend** comes through French from a Latin word (tendere) meaning "to extend," "tend."]

²**tend** (tĕnd) 1 to care for; watch over: *The shepherd tends his flock.* 2 to take charge of; manage: *to tend a machine.* [²**tend** is a short form of **attend.**]

tend·en·cy (tĕn′dən sĭ) 1 a being inclined to move in a certain direction; trend: *All governments have a tendency to increase taxes.* 2 natural bent; inclination: *Her hobbies show artistic tendencies.* **tend·en·cies.**

¹**ten·der** (tĕn′dər) 1 not tough; soft: *a tender steak; a baby's tender skin.* 2 not hardy; delicate: *These tender plants must be protected against strong wind.* 3 very sensitive to touch; painful: *His leg was still tender in the place where he was kicked.* 4 of a delicate or painful nature: *The score was a tender subject to the defeated team.* 5 soft; gentle: *The tender touch of his hand calmed the sick animal.* 6 gentle; kind; loving: *a tender glance; a tender smile.* 7 young; immature: *a child's tender years.* **ten·der·ly.** [¹**tender** comes through French (tendre) from a Latin word (tener) meaning "soft," "delicate."]

²**ten·der** (tĕn′dər) 1 to offer for acceptance: *to tender a resignation.* 2 something that is offered for acceptance: *a tender of friendship.* 3 **legal tender** any form of money that must, by law, be accepted in payment of a debt: *The silver dollar is still legal tender.* [²**tender** comes through French from a Latin word (tendere) meaning "to extend."]

³**tend·er** (tĕn′dər) 1 person who takes charge of or attends to: *A nurse is a tender of children.* 2 small coal or water car attached to a locomotive. 3 small boat supplying a larger one with provisions, fuel, etc., or used to land passengers from a larger boat. [³**tender** is formed from ²**tend.**]

ten·der·foot (tĕn′dər fŏŏt′) 1 inexperienced person, especially one unused to hardships or rough living; novice: *He was a tenderfoot when it came to camping out.* 2 beginning rank of the Boy or Girl Scouts. 3 member of this group.

ten·der·ness (tĕn′dər nĭs) state or quality of being tender: *the tenderness of meat; the tenderness of her smile; a slight tenderness from a bruise.*

ten·don (tĕn′dən) tough cord or band of tissue that attaches a muscle to a bone, another muscle, or an organ of the body; sinew.

ten·dril (tĕn′drĭl) **1** slender stem of certain climbing plants which twines about any support. **2** a curling, threadlike part: *a tendril of hair.*

Tendril

ten·e·ment (tĕn′ə mənt) **1** dwelling house, especially a rented dwelling. **2** apartment or set of rooms, usually of inferior grade. **3 tenement house** building containing many sets of rooms, usually in the poorer parts of a city and occupied by persons of small means.

ten·fold (tĕn′fōld′) ten times as much or as many: *Fertilizer increased the crops tenfold.*

Tenn. Tennessee.

Ten·nes·see (tĕn′ə sē′) **1** south central State in the United States. **2** river flowing from Tennessee into the Ohio River.

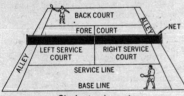

Singles tennis court

ten·nis (tĕn′ĭs) a game for two or two pairs of players in which a light ball is hit back and forth across a net in the middle of a marked area called a **tennis court.**

ten·or (tĕn′ər) **1** general settled course or direction: *the even tenor of a monk's life.* **2** general course, nature, or meaning: *the tenor of the talk.* **3** a man's highest natural singing voice. **4** singer with such a voice. **5** in music, song or part written for a tenor voice. **6** of an instrument, corresponding to the range of a tenor voice: *a tenor saxophone.*

¹tense (tĕns) the form that a word of action or verb takes to show the time of an action or when something takes place: *"Was" is the past tense of "is." "Will go" is the future tense of "go." "Ran" is the past tense of "run."* [¹**tense** comes through Old French (tens) from a Latin word (tempus) meaning "time."]

²**tense** (tĕns) **1** stretched taut; rigid: *His muscles were tense from exercise.* **2** having to do with or showing mental or emotional strain: *It was a tense moment when the car almost hit us.* **3** to make taut; tighten: *Andy proudly tensed the muscles of his arm.* **tens·er, tens·est; tensed, tens·ing; tense·ly.** [²**tense** is from a form (tensum) of a Latin word (tendere) meaning "to stretch."]

ten·sion (tĕn′shən) **1** a stretching, straining, or pulling taut. **2** condition of being stretched or pulled taut: *To tune a violin you increase or lessen the tension on the strings.* **3** mental or emotional strain: *He was in a state of extreme tension as a result of his financial worries.* **4** friction or ill will (between two people): *Since the quarrel over the car, there is tension between Ralph and his brother.*

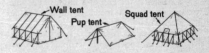

Wall tent   Pup tent   Squad tent

tent (tĕnt) **1** a shelter of canvas stretched on poles, used by soldiers and campers or for large outdoor gatherings, such as a circus. **2** to camp out in a tent.

ten·ta·cle (tĕn′tə kəl) **1** one of the slender, flexible organs growing from the heads of certain animals and used for feeling, holding, etc. The octopus has eight tentacles. For picture, see **octopus. 2** hairlike growth on the leaves of certain plants.

tenth (tĕnth) **1** next after ninth; 10th. **2** one of ten equal parts.

Tepee

te·pee (tē′pē) a cone-shaped tent of the Plains Indians. Also spelled **tee·pee.**

fate, tàt, fãre, fär; bē, bĕt; bīte, bĭt; nō, nŏt, nôr; fūse, fŭn, fûr; tōō, tŏŏk; foil; foul; thin; ~~then~~;
hw for wh as in *wh*at; zh for s as in u*s*ual; ə for a, e, i, o, u, as in *a*go, lin*e*n, per*i*l, at*o*m, min*u*s

tep·id (tĕp'ĭd) slightly warm; lukewarm: *a tepid bath.* **tep·id·ly.**

term (tûrm) **1** expression or word, especially one with a special meaning in some profession, science, art, etc.: *I don't understand the legal terms in this document.* **2** to name, call, or designate: *She has been termed the most beautiful woman in Washington.* **3** period of time set for a purpose; fixed, limited period of time: *spring term at school; the mayor's term of office; to sign a contract for a three-year term.* **4 terms** conditions offered for acceptance in an agreement: *the terms of surrender; the terms of a sale.* **5 come to terms** to arrive at an agreement. **6 not on speaking terms** not friendly with one another. **7 in terms of** with reference to; considered as: *Our vacation was expensive in terms of money but in terms of pleasure it was a bargain.* **8 be on good** or **bad terms** to be friendly or unfriendly.

ter·mi·nal (tûr'mə nəl) **1** forming the end, or being at the end of something: *a terminal examination at the close of school.* **2** station at the end of a railway, bus line, or air line. **3** metal connection on an electric wire, battery, etc.

ter·mi·nate (tûr'mə nāt') **1** to put an end to; finish; conclude: *to terminate a friendship.* **2** to come to an end: *Our lease terminates in June.* **3** to mark the end of; bound: *The river terminates our farm.* **ter·mi·nat·ed, ter·mi·nat·ing.**

ter·mi·na·tion (tûr'mə nā'shən) a bringing to an end; conclusion.

ter·mi·nus (tûr'mə nəs) **1** an end; limit. **2** station or town at the end of a railway line, bus line, etc. **ter·mi·ni** (tûr'mə nī) or **ter·mi·nus·es.**

ter·mite (tûr'mīt) a kind of ant-like insect living in very large groups. An American kind lives in and destroys the woodwork of houses.

Termite

ter·race (tĕr'ĭs) **1** raised platform of earth, either grassed or paved, or such platforms cut in wide steps on a hillside. Some terraces are used as gardens. **2** to make such platforms: *The Incas terraced the mountainsides in Peru.* **3** a balcony or porch, used for dancing, etc. **ter·raced, ter·rac·ing.**

ter·ra·pin (tĕr'ə pin) **1** web-footed turtle with a handsomely marked shell, found in streams along the South Atlantic and Gulf Coast. **2** the flesh of this turtle as a food delicacy.

Diamond-back terrapin, 7 to 8 in. long

ter·rar·i·um (tə râr'-i əm) an enclosure like a dry aquarium for growing plants indoors or keeping small land animals such as toads or lizards.

ter·res·tri·al (tə rĕs'trĭ əl) **1** of the planet Earth: *In his study of space science, he forgot terrestrial matters.* **2** consisting of land; not water or air: *the terrestrial surface of the earth.* **3** living on or in the ground: *Dogs are terrestrial animals. Fishes and most birds are not* terrestrial. **ter·res·tri·al·ly.**

ter·ri·ble .(tĕr'ə bəl) **1** causing terror; dreadful; awful: *a terrible hurricane.* **2** distressing; causing sorrow: *a terrible accident.* **3** severe; causing extreme discomfort: *The heat was terrible last week.* **4** very bad; unpleasant: *a terrible book; a terrible mess.* **ter·ri·bly.**

ter·ri·er (tĕr'ĭ ər) any of several kinds of small, active, intelligent dogs once used to hunt small game.

ter·ri·fic (tə rĭf'ĭk) **1** arousing great fear or dread; terrible; appalling; alarming: *A terrific tornado practically destroyed the town.* **2** excessive; great: *The Presidency places a man under a terrific strain.*

Airedale terrier, 23 in. high

ter·ri·fy (tĕr'ə fī') to cause great alarm to; frighten: *The thought of an airplane flight terrified her.* **ter·ri·fied, ter·ri·fy·ing.**

ter·ri·to·ry (tĕr'ə tôr'ĭ) **1** large area of land; district or region. **2** an extent of land and water under the jurisdiction of a government or sovereign state: *The Northwest Territories is a territory of Canada.* **3** district allotted to a salesman or agent: *Tom's territory is outside Boston.* **ter·ri·to·ries.**

ter·ror (tĕr'ər) **1** overwhelming fear; fright: *She has a terror of the dark.* **2** person or thing which terrifies, fills with fear or dread: *My cat is a* terror *to the dog next door.* **3** annoying or mischievous person: *Harry is very bright but he is the* terror *of his class.*

ter·ror·ist (tĕr′ər ĭst) person who governs or opposes a government by acts of violence that arouse terror.

ter·ror·ize (tĕr′ə rīz′) **1** to fill with terror by threats or acts of cruelty; terrify. **2** to govern by means of terror. **ter·ror·ized, ter·ror·iz·ing.**

terse (tûrs) short; brief, concise, and to the point: *In answer to Carl's request for a larger allowance, his father's letter was very terse.* **ters·er, ters·est; terse·ly.**

test (tĕst) **1** examination; trial: *an eye* test; *a driver's* test. **2** questions and exercises to judge the skill, knowledge, and intelligence of a student: *The chemistry* test *for the class is tomorrow morning.* **3** something which tries or measures a person or thing: *Misfortune is often a* test *of a man's character.* **4** to prove the quality or strength, etc., of a person or thing; try: *Misfortunes* test *a person's character.* **5** in chemistry, an experiment to identify a substance: *a* test *for copper in ore.*

test out to try out.

tes·ti·fy (tĕs′tə fī′) **1** to give testimony; swear under oath: *I will* testify *that you had no part in the robbery.* **2** to give evidence or proof of: *His work* testifies *to his ability.* **tes·ti·fied, tes·ti·fy·ing.**

tes·ti·mo·ny (tĕs′tə mō′nĭ) **1** statement made to establish a fact, especially one given under oath in a court of law: *The* testimony *of the witness convinced the jury.* **2** proof; evidence: *Her tears were* testimony *of her grief.* **tes·ti·mo·nies.**

test tube thin glass tube, closed at one end, used in chemical tests. For picture, see **tube.**

tes·ty (tĕs′tĭ) irritable; cross; touchy. **tes·ti·er, tes·ti·est; tes·ti·ly.**

tet·a·nus (tĕt′ə nəs) serious nerve disease causing contraction of the muscles until they are rigid. When it affects the lower jaw, it is called **lockjaw.** It is caused by a germ that gets into the body through an open wound.

teth·er (tĕth′ər) **1** rope or chain by which an animal is tied, as when grazing. **2** to tie an animal with a length of rope or chain. **3 at the end of one's tether** at the limit of one's abilities, endurance, etc.

Tex. Texas.

Tex·as (tĕk′səs) a State in the southwestern part of the United States.

text (tĕkst) **1** the main body of writing in a book, or on a printed page, as distinguished from the notes and illustrations. **2** a passage of the Bible taken as the theme of a sermon. **3** theme; subject: *the* text *of a speech.* **4** textbook.

text·book (tĕkst′bŏŏk′) book written for the teaching of a certain subject: *The children had* textbooks *in English.*

tex·tile (tĕks′tĭl or tĕks′tīl) **1** cloth; woven material. **2** woven: *a* textile *fabric.* **3** suitable or fit for weaving: *Cotton and wool are* textile *fibers.* **4** having to do with weaving: *the* textile *industry.*

tex·ture (tĕks′chər) **1** kind or quality of surface: *Tweed has a rough* texture. **2** structure or arrangement of parts; composition: *This cake has a very spongy* texture.

than (~~thăn~~ or ~~thən~~) **1** compared with: *You read faster* than *Helen.* **2 other than** with the exception of: *Children other* than *those accompanied by an adult are not admitted to the theater.*

thank (thăngk) **1** to say that one is grateful to; express or show gratitude to: *I will* thank *him myself for the book.* **2 to have oneself to thank** to be to blame: *You have yourself to* thank *for your bad marks.*

thank·ful (thăngk′fəl) feeling or showing gratitude or thanks; grateful: *I am* thankful *for this good weather.* **thank·ful·ly.**

thank·ful·ness (thăngk′fəl nĭs) a being thankful; gratitude.

thank·less (thăngk′lĭs) **1** not appreciated; unrewarding: *Washing dishes is a* thankless *task.* **2** showing no appreciation; ungrateful. **thank·less·ly.**

thanks (thăngks) **1** thank you. **2** gratitude or an expression of gratitude: *The Pilgrims gave* thanks *after the first harvest.* **3 thanks to** owing or due to; because of: *It was* thanks *to him that things went so well.*

---

fāte, făt, fâre, fär; bē, bĕt; bīte, bĭt; nō, nŏt, nôr; fūse, fŭn, fûr; tōō, tŏŏk; foil; foul; thin; ~~then~~;
hw for wh as in *wh*at; zh for s as in u*s*ual; ə for a, e, i, o, u, as in *a*go, lin*e*n, per*i*l, at*o*m, min*u*s

thanks·giv·ing (thăngks´gĭv´ĭng) expression of gratitude or thanks; a prayer expressing thanks.

Thanksgiving or **Thanksgiving Day** in the United States, a day set apart for giving thanks to God, usually the fourth Thursday in November. Thanksgiving was first celebrated by the Pilgrims at Plymouth in 1621.

that (th̄ăt) **1** thing or person at a distance: *This is the house I was talking about, not* that. **2** indicating a thing or person at a distance or already mentioned: *Give the papers to* that *boy over there.* **3** something already mentioned or pointed out: *Do I have to tell you* that *again?* **4** the other, as in contrast with **this**: *This is a nicer ring than* that. **5** who; whom; which: *the man that I saw; the book that I read.* **6** to such a degree; so: *She can walk that far.* **7** "That" is a word used to connect other words in sentences, in ways such as these: *I heard that you had gone home. The last time that you were here we had a picnic. His parents saved money that he might go to college. I am so hungry that I want dinner right away. Do you think that it will rain? Oh that I had money to buy a bicycle!* **8 in that** because: *She was sure he would come in that he said he would.* **those.**

thatch (thăch) **1** straw, reeds, or the like used to cover a roof. **2** roof of such material: *Mice made their nests in the thatch.* **3** something that looks like thatch, as thick, ragged hair: *Giles had a thatch of red hair.* **4** to put on thatch: *Joe thatched the roof.*

Thatched cottage

that's (th̄ăts) that is: *I think that's fine.*

thaw (thô) **1** to melt: *The ice thawed in the warm room.* **2** to cause to melt or bring to a temperature above the freezing point: *The sun will thaw the snow. You will have to thaw the turkey before you cook it.* **3** temperature above the freezing point; weather warm enough to melt ice: *The thaw came late this spring.* **4** to make or become friendlier or less formal: *The guests thawed when the birthday party got under way.*

the (th̄ə or th̄ĭ) **1** referring to a particular person or thing: *There's the man I told you about.* **2** any; every: *The rabbit is a quiet animal.* **3** (th̄ē) without equal; best, greatest, etc.: *Our Christmas ball turned out to be the dance this winter.* **4** by that much; to that extent: *The more I see him, the more I like him.*

the·a·ter or **the·a·tre** (th̄ē´ə tər) **1** place where plays are performed by live actors, puppets, or on film. **2** the drama; the writing and acting of plays: *He is writing a book on the modern American theater.* **3** striking scene or vivid, dramatic acting: *The chariot race in "Ben Hur" is good theater.* **4** area (of action): *General Eisenhower commanded the European theater in World War II.*

the·at·ri·cal (th̄ĭ ăt´rə kəl) **1** having to do with the theater or actors: *the theatrical profession; a theatrical tradition in the family.* **2** more appropriate for the theater than for real life; not natural; exaggerated; designed for effect: *She always does things in the most theatrical way.* **the·at·ri·cal·ly.**

thee (th̄ē) old, poetic, or religious form of "you": *With this ring I thee wed. My country 'tis of thee we sing.*

theft (thĕft) act of stealing; robbery: *The theft was committed sometime between two and three o'clock.*

their (th̄âr) of or belonging to them: *First prize was given to their class project.* (Homonyms: there, they're)

theirs (th̄ârz) that which belongs to them: *The book is theirs but you may borrow it.* (Homonym: there's)

them (th̄ĕm) persons, things, or animals spoken or written about as being the objects of an action or as being those acted upon: *I heard them singing. Put them on the shelf. Pass them the cookies. I waved to them. We went with them.*

theme (th̄ēm) **1** subject written or talked about; topic: *the theme of a discussion.* **2** short essay: *Students write themes at school.* **3** in music, a short tune or melody that occurs again and again in various forms in a composition.

them·selves (th̄əm sĕlvz´) **1** their own selves: *They have only themselves to blame.* **2** they (in an emphatic form): *Not even the* *parents* themselves *were allowed to see the sick child.* **3** their normal selves: *The children haven't been themselves since they heard the bad news.* **4 by themselves** (1) alone: *The two boys went hunting* by themselves. (2) without any help: *The children planned the party by themselves.*

then (thĕn) **1** at that time: *We were working then, but now we are resting.* **2** after that: *Eat dinner and then go to bed.* **3** therefore; in that case: *If you are sure you can swim the lake, then do it!* **4** of that time; existing at a time mentioned: *the then President, Woodrow Wilson.* **5** that time; a time mentioned: *By then I will be ready to go.* **6 then and there** at once; immediately: *They decided to leave then and there.*

thence (thĕns) from that place: *First she went to Paris, and thence to Rome.*

thence·forth (thĕns′fôrth′ or thĕns′fôrth′) from that time on; thereafter: *They quarreled and thenceforth never spoke to one another again.*

the·ol·o·gy (thē ŏl′ə jĭ) the systematic study of God or of the relation of man and the universe to God; the study of divinity: *Though very religious, my father had no interest in theology.*

the·o·ry (thē′ə rĭ) **1** the principles as opposed to the practice of an art or science: *Although he did not draw well, he had studied art theory.* **2** an opinion, based on careful observation and study, of how something works or has come about; an explanation that fits the known facts but has not yet been proved true: *The doctors had various theories on treating the disease.* **3** a guess based upon observation: *After the first chapter, I had a theory how the story would end.* **the·o·ries.**

there (thâr) **1** in or at that place: *Put it there, not here.* **2** to or toward that place; thither: *I can walk there in an hour.* **3** that place: *We came from there an hour ago.* **4** in that matter; on that point: *I disagree with you there.* **5** an exclamation of pleasure, defiance, sympathy, etc.: *I won't listen, so there!* There, there, *don't cry.* (Homonyms: their, they're)

there·a·bouts (thâr′ə bouts′) or **there·a·bout** (thâr′ə bout′) close to that time, place, degree, etc.: *We will come at six or thereabouts.* They lived in Boston or thereabouts. He earned five thousand a year *or* thereabouts.

there·af·ter (thâr ăf′tər) from that time on; after that; afterwards: *For the first few days they came on time but not* thereafter.

there·by (thâr bī′ or thâr′bī′) **1** by that means: *She gave the dog a bone, thereby stopping his barking.* **2** near there: *The knight stopped to drink at the well and met the wizard who lived thereby.*

there·for (thâr fôr′) for that, this, or it: *They gave money for a hospital and the equipment* therefor.

there·fore (thâr′fôr′) for that reason; on account of that: *He was sick and therefore missed three days of school.*

there·from (thâr frŏm′ or thâr frŭm′) from this; from that; from it: *He got a nail in his foot and a severe infection developed therefrom.*

there·in (thâr ĭn′) **1** in this or that place; in it: *The house and all the furniture therein are for sale.* **2** in that respect: *I thought the matter settled, but therein I was wrong.*

there·of (thâr ŏv′ or thâr ŭv′) **1** of this; of that: *When the princess saw the wine and drank thereof she fell into an enchanted sleep.* **2** from this or that cause: *Blackie gobbled up the poisoned meat and became sick thereof.*

there·on (thâr ŏn′ or thâr ŏn′) on that or this place or thing: *the table and all the silver thereon.*

there's (thârz) there is: *If you want more dessert, there's plenty here.* (Homonym: theirs)

there·to (thâr tōō′) **1** to it; to that: *He locked the box and lost the key thereto.* **2** moreover; also.

there·un·to (thâr ŭn′tōō) thereto; in addition: *She wrote a long letter, and added thereunto a yet longer postscript.*

there·up·on (thâr′ə pŏn′ or thâr′ə pŏn′) **1** upon that; at once; immediately after: *The teacher said, "Ready," and thereupon Matilda began to read.* **2** thereon.

---

fāte, făt, fâre, fär; bē, bĕt; bīte, bĭt; nō, nŏt, nôr; fūse, fŭn, fûr; tōō, tŏŏk; foil; foul; thin; then; hw for wh as in *what*; zh for s as in u*s*ual; ə for a, e, i, o, u, as in *a*go, lin*e*n, per*i*l, at*o*m, min*u*s

therewith

there·with (t͟hâr with′ or t͟hâr wit͟h′) **1** with it; with that; with this: *He received a diploma and all the privileges connected therewith.* **2** thereupon: *Our host said, "Good-by," and therewith we left.*

ther·mom·e·ter (thər mŏm′ə tər) instrument for indicating temperature; in common use, a tube containing mercury or colored alcohol set against a scale marked in degrees for Fahrenheit readings or for centigrade readings. The centigrade scale is divided into 100 degrees between the freezing and boiling points; in the Fahrenheit, freezing is at 32 degrees and boiling at 212 degrees.

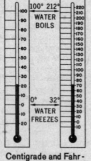

Centigrade and Fahrenheit thermometers

Ther·mos bot·tle (thûr′məs bŏt′əl) trade name for a vacuum bottle in which liquids remain hot or cold.

ther·mo·stat (thûr′mə stăt′) kind of thermometer that automatically controls furnaces, air conditioners, refrigerators, etc.

these (t͟hēz) plural of **this**, as in contrast with **those**: *I think these apples are riper than those. Those are different from these.*

they (t͟hā) **1** the people, animals, or things named before: *The boys and girls met and then they went to the art show. The dogs howled for an hour and then they slept.* **2** people in general: *What do they say?*

they'd (t͟hād) **1** they would: *I think they'd be better off at home.* **2** they had: *They thought they'd come too early.*

they'll (t͟hāl) **1** they will: *If they don't study, they'll regret it.* **2** they shall: *Even if I have to carry them, they'll be there.*

they're (t͟hâr) they are: *Do you think they're ready?* (Homonyms: their, there)

they've (t͟hāv) they have: *It seems that they've made their plans already.*

thick (thĭk) **1** large across or between sides: *a thick branch; a thick slice of bread.* **2** of a liquid, heavy; not watery: *a thick syrup; thick condensed milk.* **3** dense; close together: *the thick woods; thick hair.* **4** in

thine

distance through; in distance between opposite sides: *a board two inches thick.* **5** the thickest part; center of action: *the thick of the battle.* **6** foggy: *The weather was thick and drizzly.* **7** hoarse: *a thick voice.* **8** stupid. **9** extremely friendly or intimate. **10** through thick and thin through fortune and misfortune; under all conditions. **thick·ly.**

thick·en (thĭk′ən) to make or become thick or thicker: *Mother thickened the gravy with flour. The woods thickened as we pushed into them.*

thick·et (thĭk′ĭt) clump of dense and tangled underbrush.

thick·ness (thĭk′nĭs) **1** distance through or between opposite surfaces: *The thickness of that tree trunk is four feet. Bread is sliced in different thicknesses.* **2** density: *the thickness of the crowd.* **3** layer: *In cold weather, we sleep under several thicknesses of blanket.*

thief (thēf) one who steals, especially one who steals secretly rather than by force. **thieves.**

thieve (thēv) to steal or rob. **thieved, thiev·ing.**

thieves (thēvz) more than one **thief.**

thigh (thī) upper part of the leg.

thim·ble (thĭm′bəl) metal or plastic cap for the finger, used to push a needle in sewing.

Thimble

thin (thĭn) **1** not thick; of little distance between opposite sides: *a thin wall; thin paper.* **2** slender; lean; gaunt: *Rachel was very thin after her sickness.* **3** not dense: *a thin mist.* **4** widely spaced; sparse: *a thin population; thin hair.* **5** watery: *a thin soup.* **6** weak; not deep or strong: *Maizie has a thin voice.* **7** easy to see through; flimsy: *a thin excuse.* **8** to make thin or less dense: *These plants should be thinned every few years.* **9** to become less thick or dense: *The crowd thinned after the parade passed.* **thin·ner, thin·nest; thinned, thin·ning; thin·ly.**

thine (t͟hīn) **1** old, poetic, or religious form of "yours": *"My house is thine," said the monk to the traveler. We send greetings to thee and thine.* **2** your (used for "thy" before a vowel): *With thine ears thou shalt hear.*

746

thing (thĭng) **1** something which can be known through the senses, thought of, or imagined; whatever exists. A stone, an odor, a noise, an idea, and a fairy tale are all things. **2** act; affair: *What a thing to do! This thing is none of your business.* **3** person or animal (spoken of with affection, contempt, pity, etc.): *Uncle Horace is a sweet old thing. The poor thing broke its leg.* **4 things** (1) personal belongings: *I can get all my things into one suitcase.* (2) state of affairs; situation: *Are things getting better or worse?*

think (thĭngk) **1** to use the mind in order to come to decisions, form ideas, opinions, judgments, etc.: *You should think before you speak. Do dogs and cats think?* **2** to have in the mind (an idea, opinion, belief, etc.): *What do you think of this matter? I think you are wrong. He thinks the strangest thoughts.* **3** to anticipate; expect: *I think we shall be home for lunch. Do you think we shall have a good time?* **4** to call to mind; remember: *I can't think what I came out to buy. He thought of her always.* **5** to imagine: *I can't think where you get such ideas.* **thought, think·ing.**

think·er (thĭngk′ər) **1** person who thinks; sensible person who is capable of reasoning clearly. **2** philosopher.

third (thûrd) **1** next after second. **2** one of three equal parts: *He ate a third of the pie.* **third·ly.**

thirst (thûrst) **1** dry feeling in the mouth and throat caused by the need for something to drink. **2** to desire something to drink; to be thirsty. **3** a strong desire; craving: *a thirst for praise.* **4** to have a strong desire; crave: *to thirst for knowledge.*

thirst·y (thûrs′tĭ) **1** feeling thirst. **2** without moisture; parched: *the thirsty garden.* **thirst·i·er, thirst·i·est; thirst·i·ly.**

thir·teen (thûr′tēn′) amount or quantity that is one greater than 12; 13.

thir·teenth (thûr′tēnth′) **1** next after 12th. **2** one of 13 equal parts.

thir·ti·eth (thûr′tĭ ĭth) **1** next after 29th. **2** one of 30 equal parts.

thir·ty (thûr′tĭ) amount or quantity that is one greater than 29; 30. **thir·ties.**

this (thĭs) **1** thing or person near at hand or just mentioned: *I think this is the picture I wanted you to see.* **2** referring to a thing or person near at hand or just mentioned: *John, I want you to meet this man.* **3** fact or idea about to be mentioned or pointed out: *What I mean is this.* **4** thing or person contrasted with another thing or person: *You will agree that this is a better house than that.* **5** referring to a thing or person contrasted with another thing or person: *I can tell that this painting is finer than that one.* **6** to this extent; so: *He lost the race by this much.* **these.**

this·tle (thĭs′əl) **1** any of several plants with spiny, deeply cut leaves, a spiny stem, and handsome, usually purple, flowers. **2** flower of this plant. The purple thistle is the national flower of Scotland.

this·tle·down (thĭs′əl-doun′) the soft down on ripe thistle seeds.

Thistle

thith·er (thĭth′ər or thĭth′ər) toward that place; in that direction.

tho or **tho'** (thō) though.

thong (thŏng or thông) narrow strip of leather, especially one used as a fastening.

tho·rax (thôr′ăks) **1** the part of the body between the neck and the abdomen, consisting of chest, upper back, and everything between them. **2** the middle of three sections of an insect's body. For picture of insect's thorax, see **abdomen.**

thorn (thôrn) **1** sharp, slender spike growing on certain trees, shrubs, and vines, as the hawthorn and the rose. **2** tree or shrub that has thorns. **3** any annoyance or constant distress: *That fellow is a thorn in my side.*

Thorn

thorn·y (thôr′nĭ) **1** having thorns; full of thorns. **2** annoying; difficult: *a thorny problem.* **thorn·i·er, thorn·i·est.**

---

fāte, făt, fâre, fär; bē, bĕt; bīte, bĭt; nō, nŏt, nôr; fūse, fŭn, fûr; tōō, tŏŏk; foil; foul; thin; then; hw for wh as in *wh*at; zh for s as in u*s*ual; ə for a, e, i, o, u, as in *a*go, lin*e*n, per*i*l, at*o*m, min*u*s

thor·ough (thûr'ō) **1** complete; accurate; exact: *a thorough job of research.* **2** in every way; absolute: *a thorough rascal.* **thor·ough·ly.**

thor·ough·bred (thûr'ə brĕd') **1** of unmixed breed or stock: *a thoroughbred horse.* **2** a thoroughbred animal.

thor·ough·fare (thûr'ə fâr') street, road, or passage open at both ends.

those (thōz) plural of **that,** as in contrast with **these:** *Of all those islands, that one was the most beautiful. These people are my friends, but I don't care for those.*

thou (thou) old, poetic, or religious form of "you": *One of the Ten Commandments is* "Thou *shalt not kill.*"

though (thō) **1** in spite of the fact that; although: *He kept on working though it was very late.* **2** even if: *Start the job now* though *you may not be able to finish it.*

thought (thôt) **1** the working of the mind; thinking; reflection; meditation: *deep in thought.* **2** that which one thinks; a memory, idea, notion, etc.: *He put down his thoughts in a journal.* **3** power of reasoning and imagining; intellect: *Man is above the beasts because he has the gift of thought.* **4** care; consideration; concern: *We should give some thought to the future.* **5** opinion; belief: *What are your thoughts on the subject?* **6** a way of thinking characteristic of a particular period, group, etc.: *the thought of the Middle Ages; scientific thought.* **7** See **think.** *I thought he would never come.*

thought·ful (thôt'fəl) **1** full of thought; serious: *a thoughtful expression.* **2** kind; considerate of others: *It was very thoughtful of you to remember my birthday.* **thought·ful·ly.**

thought·ful·ness (thôt'fəl nis) a being thoughtful and considerate of others: *She had thoughtfulness for the needy.*

thought·less (thôt'lĭs) **1** not thinking; careless: *It was thoughtless of you to forget to lock the door.* **2** not considerate of others: *a thoughtless host.* **thought·less·ly.**

thou·sand (thou'zənd) amount or quantity that is one greater than 999; 1,000.

thou·sandth (thou'zəndth) **1** next after 999th; 1,000th. **2** one of 1,000 equal parts.

thrall (thrôl) **1** a slave; one who is in bondage or under some strong influence: *a* thrall *to television.* **2** slavery or bondage: *held in* thrall.

thrash (thrăsh) **1** to beat or flog: *The farmer thrashed the thief with his horsewhip.* **2** to beat out (grain) from the husk; thresh. **thrash about** to move or toss restlessly or violently: *to thrash about in one's sleep.* **thrash out** to discuss thoroughly: *to thrash out a problem.*

thrash·er (thrăsh'ər) **1** one who thrashes. **2** a long-tailed, North American thrush-like bird.

thread (thrĕd) **1** fine cord of twisted silk, cotton, wool, or similar fibers from which cloth is woven or with which things are sewed. **2** filament of rayon, metal, etc. **3** slender beam; fine ray: *A thread of light came through the keyhole.* **4** something running through and connecting the parts of anything: *the thread of a story.* **5** slight prospect; slender assurance: *With the news came a thread of hope.* **6** spiral ridge of a screw. **7** to put a thread through: *to thread a needle; thread beads.* **8** to make one's way among obstacles: *We threaded our way through the crowd.*

Thread

thread·bare (thrĕd'bâr') **1** worn down to the threads: *a threadbare carpet.* **2** wearing threadbare clothes; shabby: *a threadbare tramp.* **3** worn out; trite: *a threadbare joke; a threadbare excuse.*

threat (thrĕt) **1** expression of an intention to hurt or punish: *The sheriff received many threats on his life.* **2** a warning of unpleasantness or evil to come: *the threat of rain; the threat of war.*

threat·en (thrĕt'ən) **1** to make threats; express an intention to injure: *The enemy threatened war.* **2** to give warning of: *The dark skies threatened a bad storm.* **3** to be a source of danger or harm; to be a menace to: *The volcano threatened the villages on its slope.*

three (thrē) amount or quantity that is one greater than two; 3.

three·fold (thrē'fōld') **1** triple; having three parts: *Our trip served a threefold purpose.* **2** three times as much: *He increased his earnings threefold.*

three·score (thrē'skôr') three times twenty; sixty.

thresh (thrĕsh) **1** to beat out grain from its husk by use of a flail or machine. **2** to toss or move about wildly; thrash.

thresh·er (thrĕsh′ər) person or machine that threshes.

thresh·old (thrĕsh′ōld or thrĕsh′hōld) **1** the stone or piece of wood under a door; sill of a doorway. **2** point of entering; beginning point: *the threshold of a new era.*

threw (thrōō) See **throw**. *He threw the ball.* (Homonym: through)

thrice (thrīs) **1** three times. **2** in a three-fold manner or degree; greatly: *He was thrice blessed in his son, his wife, and his job.*

thrift (thrĭft) careful management; economy; habit of saving: *Their mother's thrift paid for the family vacation.*

thrift·y (thrĭf′tĭ) not extravagant; saving; economical: *a thrifty use of time;* thrifty *with money.* **thrift·i·er, thrift·i·est; thrift·i·ly.**

thrill (thrĭl) **1** sudden feeling or quiver of excitement: *He felt a thrill on first hearing the famous singer.* **2** to fill with a feeling of excitement: *He thrilled the audience by his daring trapeze stunts.* **3** to feel excitement: *She thrilled at the thought of her first ocean voyage.* **4** to quiver or vibrate: *The speaker's voice thrilled with emotion.*

thrive (thrīv) **1** to flourish; prosper; succeed: *The business thrived under new management.* **2** to grow vigorously: *The children thrived at camp that summer.* **thrived** or **throve, thrived** or **thriv·en, thriv·ing.**

thro' or **thro** (thrōō) through.

throat (thrōt) **1** passage running from the back of the mouth to the lungs and stomach: *a sore throat; a bone caught in the throat.* **2** front of the neck: *She wore a diamond pin at her throat.* **3** narrow entrance or passage: *the throat of a cave.*

throb (thrŏb) **1** to beat; vibrate: *The sound of drums throbbed in the small room. His heart throbbed with excitement.* **2** a beat; pulse; vibration: *the throb of drums.* **throbbed, throb·bing.**

throne (thrōn) **1** seat, usually raised and ornate, where a king or other person of great power sits on official occasions.

2 power or authority of a king, queen, etc.: *The* throne *commands obedience.* (Homonym: thrown)

throng (thrŏng or thróng) **1** large gathering of people; crowd: *A throng gathered to hear the president speak.* **2** to gather together in a crowd: *Pigeons thronged to get the bread crumbs.* **3** to crowd: *Music lovers thronged the concert hall.*

throt·tle (thrŏt′əl) **1** to choke by pressing on the windpipe; strangle. **2** valve to control the flow of fuel to an engine: *He opened the throttle and the car shot ahead.* **3** to stop the flow of fuel: *to throttle an engine.* **throt·tled, throt·tling.**

through (thrōō) **1** from one end to the other; from one side to the other: *to go through a tunnel; to read a book through.* **2** extending or going from one end to another: *a through street.* **3** going from one place to another without stopping: *a through train.* **4** thoroughly; entirely: *This shirt is soaked through.* **5** among: *Circulate these pamphlets through the crowd.* **6** by means of: *I reached her through your help.* **7** on account of: *I ran through fear of the bull.* **8** finished: *I'm through with this work.* (Homonym: threw)

through·out (thrōō out′) **1** in every part of: *There was smoke throughout the house. There is snow on that mountain throughout the year.* **2** in every part: *The building was cold throughout.*

throve (thrōv) See **thrive**. *The cattle throve in the new pasture.*

throw (thrō) **1** to fling with a motion of the arm; hurl: *to throw a ball.* **2** to cause to fall; cause to lose balance: *One wrestler threw the other. His horse threw him.* **3** to cast; project: *The lamp throws a shadow on the wall.* **4** to put in a particular position, state, or the like: *The party threw the household into a turmoil.* **5** a flinging; a casting: *a throw of dice.* **6 stone's throw** short distance.

throw cold water on to discourage: *He threw cold water on my enthusiasm by his lack of interest.*

throw in to add as an extra; include: *I will throw in my knife if you trade rifles.*

---

fāte, făt, fâre, fär; bē, bĕt; bīte, bĭt; nō, nŏt, nôr; fūse, fŭn, fûr; tōō, tŏŏk; foil; foul; thin; then; hw for wh as in what; zh for s as in usual; ə for a, e, i, o, u, as in ago, linen, peril, atom, minus

throw over to abandon; leave: *He threw over the study of Latin for engineering.*

throw up 1 to give up; relinquish: *to throw up a job.* **2** to vomit.

threw, thrown, throw·ing.

thrown (thrōn) See **throw.** (Homonym: throne)

thru (thrōō) through.

thrush (thrŭsh) song-bird of several kinds, some of which have a rusty-brown back and a brown-flecked breast. The American robin is a thrush.

Wood thrush, 7 to 8 in. long

thrust (thrŭst) **1** to push with force; shove: *He thrust through the crowd.* **2** a push or shove: *He braced himself against the thrust of the crowd.* **3** to extend (outward): *The tree thrust out many branches.* **4** to push (something into or through): *He thrust the needle through the cloth.* **5** to make a fast stabbing motion: *to thrust with a sword.* **6** a stabbing motion: *a sword thrust.* **7** a forward force, especially that produced by a propeller, a jet engine, or a rocket. **thrust, thrust·ing.**

thud (thŭd) **1** heavy, dull sound. **2** to fall or hit with a heavy, dull sound: *The sack of flour thudded to the ground.* **thud·ded, thud·ding.**

thumb (thŭm) **1** the short, thick finger of the hand. **2** to go (through) by turning the pages: *Would you thumb through this book and see if there's any information in it I need.* **3** to rub or soil with the thumb or by handling: *His new book is already thumbed.* **4** that part of a mitten or glove that covers the thumb. **5** to ask for or obtain (a ride) by signaling with the thumb. **6 all thumbs** clumsy.

thump (thŭmp) **1** to give a heavy blow to: *She thumped the pillows.* **2** a heavy blow. **3** the dull sound made by such a blow: *He lost his balance on the swing and fell to the ground with a thump.* **4** to pound or throb: *His heart thumped with excitement.*

thun·der (thŭn'dər) **1** rumbling or crashing sound caused by the passage of lightning through the air. **2** any noise resembling such a sound. **3** to make a loud, crashing noise: *First it thundered, then it started to rain. The cannon thundered.*

4 to shout with a roar: *He thundered commands from the deck of the ship.*

thun·der·bolt (thŭn'dər bōlt') **1** flash of lightning followed by a clap of thunder. **2** something sudden, unexpected, and terrible: *The news of the general's death came as a thunderbolt.*

thun·der·clap (thŭn'dər klăp') **1** loud crash of thunder. **2** something unexpected and startling: *The news of my sister's engagement came as a thunderclap.*

thun·der·cloud (thŭn'dər kloud') dark cloud charged with electricity and producing lightning and thunder.

thun·der·ous (thŭn'dər əs) full of or like thunder: *a thunderous applause.*

thun·der·storm (thŭn'dər stôrm') a storm of lightning and thunder, usually with a downpour of rain.

thun·der·struck (thŭn'dər strŭk') amazed; astonished: *I was thunderstruck when I heard that I had won the prize.*

Thurs. Thursday.

Thurs·day (thûrz'dā or thûrz'dĭ) fifth day of the week.

thus (thŭs) **1** in this or that way or manner: *You will follow my plan thus.* **2** to this degree or extent; so: *We have had no further news thus far.* **3** therefore; consequently: *The milk is spilt, and thus it is useless to cry over it.*

thwack (thwăk) **1** to strike or hit in a sharp manner with something flat: *Bill thwacked me with his ruler.* **2** sharp blow with something flat; a thump: *Give him a thwack if he doesn't behave.*

thwart (thwôrt) **1** to prevent (from doing something); oppose: *Dad thwarted my plan to go to the movie by making me study.* **2** seat reaching across a boat where a rower sits.

thy (thī) old, poetic, or religious form of **your:** *Thy will be done.*

thyme (tim) small herb with fragrant leaves, used for seasoning. (Homonym: time)

thy·roid (thī'roid) **1** gland in the neck which helps to regulate the body's growth. **2** medicine prepared from animal thyroid glands, used to help people whose own thyroids do not work properly.

thy·self (thī sĕlf') old, poetic, or religious form of **yourself:** *Know thyself.*

ti (tē) seventh note of the musical scale.

ti·ar·a (tī är′ə or tĭ är′ə) **1** head ornament like a small crown, worn by women. **2** the Pope's triple crown.

¹tick (tĭk) **1** to make a slight clicking or tapping sound which is regularly repeated: *The old clock ticked in the silence of the hall.* **2** light, regular clicking or tapping sound. **3** to mark or note with check marks, dots, etc.: *He ticked off each number as it was called.* **4** a mark like a check or dot. [¹**tick** is a word that imitates the sound of a watch.]

Woman wearing tiara

²tick (tĭk) **1** small creature, like a spider, that has eight legs and sucks blood. Ticks live on animals and many carry disease. **2** small insect related to flies that sucks blood and lives on the bodies of certain animals. [²**tick** is a form of an earlier English word (tike, teke) of the same meaning.]

Sheep tick

Dog tick

³tick (tĭk) or **tick·ing** (tĭk′ĭng) strong cloth used in making cases or coverings for pillows, mattresses, etc. [³**tick** comes through Latin (theca) from a Greek word (thēkē) meaning "a case," "cover."]

tick·et (tĭk′ĭt) **1** slip of paper or cardboard that gives the holder the right to certain privileges, such as train rides, entrance to amusements, etc. **2** small note on paper or cardboard, etc., stating the price, size, etc., of goods; tag; label. **3** list of candidates offered by a particular party, group, or faction to be voted upon by the public: *the Liberal ticket; the Democratic ticket.* **4** to mark or identify with a tag or label. **5** summons requiring a person to go to court, especially for a traffic violation: *a ticket for speeding.*

tick·le (tĭk′əl) **1** to touch in a light way, producing a tingling sensation and usually causing laughter. **2** to excite amusement in; delight: *The idea tickled me.* **3** to feel a tingling sensation: *My foot tickles.* **4** the sensation so produced: *an annoying throat tickle.* **tick·led, tick·ling.**

tick·lish (tĭk′lĭsh) **1** easily made to laugh or wriggle when tickled. **2** delicate or risky to handle: *How to break the bad news was a ticklish problem.* **3** risky; unsteady; unstable: *It was ticklish climbing down the cliff.* **4** of people, easily upset; difficult to deal with: *Mom is ticklish on the subject of waste.* **tick·lish·ly.**

tid·al (tī′dəl) pertaining to or affected by the tide: *a tidal river.*

tidal wave large, destructive ocean wave produced by an earthquake or heavy winds.

tid·bit (tĭd′bĭt′) small, choice bit of anything: *a tidbit of cake; a tidbit of gossip.* Also spelled **titbit.**

tide (tīd) **1** regular rise and fall of the ocean about every twelve hours, caused by the pull (attraction) of the moon and sun. **2** a flow of water caused by the rise and fall of the ocean: *He was rowing against the tide.* **3** season or period in a year, as Christmas, Easter, etc. **4** anything that increases or decreases: *the tide of business.*

tide (someone) over to enable (someone) to manage: *This money will tide him over the difficulty.*

tid·ed, tid·ing.

tide·wa·ter (tĭd′wô′tər or tĭd′wŏt′ər) **1** water covering land that is dry at low tide. **2** land bordered by such water.

ti·di·ness (tī′dĭ nĭs) state of being neat, orderly, trim: *The tidiness of his clothes always impressed me.*

ti·dings (tī′dĭngz) news; information; message: *He brought us tidings of our family.*

ti·dy (tī′dĭ) **1** neat; orderly; trim: *He keeps his room tidy.* **2** to put in order; make neat: *Will you tidy up the living room?* **3** considerable: *He saved a tidy sum for his old age.* **ti·di·er, ti·di·est; ti·died, ti·dy·ing; ti·di·ly.**

tie (tī) **1** to attach, fasten, or bind something with a string, rope, etc., by bringing the ends together and knotting: *to tie a tag to merchandise; to tie one's shoelaces.* **2** necktie. **3** to make a knot or bow in: *to tie a scarf.* **4** to form a bow or knot: *The sash ties at the back.* **5** string, cord, or rope that is used to fasten or secure. **6** to restrict; limit: *We were tied to home because*

---

fāte, făt, fâre, fär; bē, bĕt; bīte, bĭt; nō, nŏt, nôr; fūse, fŭn, fûr; tōō, tŏŏk; foil; foul; thin; then; hw for wh as in *what*; zh for s as in u*s*ual; ə for a, e, i, o, u, as in *a*go, lin*e*n, per*i*l, at*o*m, min*u*s

of the baby. **7** to equal an opponent in score: *That run tied the game.* **8** equality of points: *After the tie was broken, the score was 5 - 6.* **9** blood relationship or other connection that holds people together: *family, business, or political ties.* **10** plank or rod to which railroad tracks are fastened. **11** in music, a curved line joining two notes of the same pitch. **tied, ty·ing.**

tier (tir) a row or rank; any of a set of rows arranged one above the other: *We sat in the third tier of the theater.* (Homonym: ²tear).

ti·ger (tī'gər) large, fierce animal of the cat family. It has a tawny yellow back and sides, with narrow black stripes.

tight (tīt) **1** firm; not loose: *We made a tight knot in the rope.* **2** having so close a texture, weave, or fit that it will not allow the passage of water,

Tiger, about 10 ft. long

steam, air, etc., in or out: *a tight barrel; a tight pot cover; a tight faucet.* **3** fitting closely, or so closely that one feels uncomfortable. **4** stingy. **5 sit tight** to stick to one's position. **6 tight squeeze** (1) a close fit. (2) narrow margin: *He passed the test but it was by a tight squeeze.* (3) dangerous or embarrassing situation: *John was caught in the tight squeeze of many debts.* **tight·ly.**

tight·en (tī'tən) **1** to draw or make tight: *The baby tightened his grasp on his mother's thumb. He tightened his belt one more notch.* **2** to become tight.

tight·rope (tīt'rōp') a tightly stretched rope or cable on which acrobats walk and balance themselves while performing.

ti·gress (tī'gris) female tiger.

tile (tīl) **1** thin piece of baked clay used for roofs, floors, walls, in ornamental work, etc.: *There are blue tiles around our fireplace.* **2** linoleum, plastic, etc., square used to surface floors, etc. **3** to cover with tiles. **4** a number of tiles (used for something): *a roof of tile.* **5** earthenware pipe used as a drain. **tiled, til·ing.**

¹till (til) **1** until; up to the time when: *We can't leave till the guest of honor has gone.* **2** up to the time of: *Wait for me till seven o'clock.* [¹**till** is a form of an Old English word (til) meaning "to."]

²till (til) to plow and prepare land for raising crops; cultivate: *The Joneses tilled their land, but the Smiths raised cattle.* [²**till** is a form of an Old English word (tilian) meaning "to strive after," "to work for."]

³till (til) drawer, tray, etc., for keeping money, as in a shop. [³**till** is from an earlier English word (tillen) meaning "to draw," "pull."]

Tiller

till·er (til'ər) the handle of a rudder by which a boat is steered.

Knights tilting

tilt (tilt) **1** to slope; slant: *The land tilts toward the sea.* **2** to cause to slope or slant; tip: *Don't tilt the table. Harold tilted the rock over into the chasm.* **3** a sloping or slanting position: *Mac put a block under the short table leg to correct its tilt.* **4** in a knight's tournament, to fight with spears (often blunted) on horseback. **5** a duel with spears on horseback; a joust.

tim·ber (tim'bər) **1** wood suitable for carpentry, building of ships, etc. **2** trees large enough to be of commercial value for wood: *That estate has fifty acres of fine timber.* **3** large piece of wood prepared to form part of a structure: *The rafters and beams in old churches and houses are usually beautiful old timbers.* **4** to furnish or construct with timber.

timber line line on mountains and in arctic regions beyond which trees will not grow.

time (tim) **1** past, present, and future, taken separately or as a whole: *until the end of time.* **2** length of time: *How much time do you need?* **3** instant, minute, etc., when something happens: *At the time of the explosion nobody was around.* **4** regular, planned, or appropriate time for something to happen: *It is time to go home. It is time we took a vacation.* **5** to measure the speed of: *He* timed *the horse.* **6** time free (for something): *She has no* time *for bridge.* **7** hour, minutes, seconds (by the clock): *What* time *is it?* **8** period associated with certain historical happenings; epoch or age: *in Washington's* time. **9** part of the year associated with special activity; season: *harvest* time; *carnival* time. **10** to choose the moment for: *He* timed *his visit to suit my convenience.* **11** in music, the grouping of rhythmic beats; tempo: *waltz* time. **12 for the time being** for now, for the present: *We will stay here* for the time being. **13 in time** (1) early enough: *Will you be home in* time *for dinner?* (2) eventually: *I hope,* in time, *to learn Spanish.* **14 on time** not late: *He usually arrives* on time. **15 lose time** to go at too slow a rate: *The train* lost time *between Chicago and St. Louis.* **16 gain time** (1) to go at too fast a rate: *Our kitchen clock* gains time. (2) to save time: *to* gain time *by taking a short cut.* **17 behind the times** not up to date on current events, ideas, etc.; old-fashioned: *He was* behind the times *in his scientific views.* **18 time out of mind** longer than anyone can remember. **19 take time out** to set aside a period of time for some special purpose: *Let's take* time out *for lunch.* **timed, tim·ing.** (Homonym: thyme)

time·ly (tīm′lĭ) occurring at the right time: *Ralph's return home from abroad on his mother's birthday was most* timely. **time·li·er, time·li·est.**

time·piece (tīm′pēs′) any instrument that records time; watch or clock.

times (tīmz) **1** occasions; situations: *There were* times *when he proved to be a friend in need.* **2** period of time: *hard* times; *the* times *in which we live.* **3** multiplied by (indicated by the sign ×): *Four* times *five equals twenty* $4 \times 5 = 20$. **4** actions or occasions which recur, as in a series: *I telephoned a number of* times.

time·ta·ble (tīm′tā′bəl) list of dates and hours systematically arranged for events, particularly for trains, boats, buses, etc., giving the time of arrival and departure; time schedule.

tim·id (tĭm′ĭd) lacking in courage, nerve, etc.; shy; easily frightened: *Nancy was so* timid *at the party she refused to leave her corner.* **tim·id·ly.**

ti·mid·i·ty (tĭ mĭd′ə tĭ) shyness; lack of courage: *Peter's* timidity *prevents his taking part in many sports.*

tim·or·ous (tĭm′ər əs) very timid; fearful: *His* timorous *approach will never make him a good salesman.* **tim·or·ous·ly.**

tim·o·thy (tĭm′ə thĭ) a coarse grass with long spikes, grown for fodder.

tin (tĭn) **1** a soft, silver-white metal element. It is used to coat the inside of food containers made of other metals and also in many alloys. **2** thin plates of iron or steel covered with this metal; tin plate. **3** container made of this metal; a can: *a* tin *of sardines; a pie* tin. **4** to cover or coat with tin. **tinned, tin·ning.**

tin·der (tĭn′dər) **1** any dry substance that is easily inflammable. **2** material used to kindle a fire from a spark; flint and steel struck together to obtain fire.

tine (tīn) sharp projecting spike or prong: *the* tine *of a fork.*

tin·foil (tĭn′foil′) tin in very thin sheets, used for wrapping candies, cigarettes, etc.

tinge (tĭnj) **1** to tint or stain slightly with color: *The sunset* tinged *the sky with pink and gold.* **2** slight degree of some color; tint: *There was a* tinge *of red in her hair.* **3** to give a trace of some quality to: *A sadness* tinged *the joy of their reunion.* **4** a touch; trace: *a* tinge *of humor; a* tinge *of pride.* **tinged, ting·ing.**

tin·gle (tĭng′gəl) **1** to have a slight prickling or stinging feeling: *His toes* tingled *with the cold.* **2** to thrill; be roused; flutter: *The wild animals at the circus made Leonora* tingle *with excitement.* **3** physical or emotional sensation of tingling. **tin·gled, tin·gling.**

tin·ker (tĭng′kər) **1** a person who makes minor repairs in metal, as soldering leaks in pans, etc. **2** clumsy or unskillful workman. **3** to potter; busy oneself in a trifling way.

tin·kle (tĭng′kəl) **1** a high-pitched sound, as of a small bell. **2** to make or cause to make

fāte, făt, fâre, fär; bē, bĕt; bīte, bĭt; nō, nŏt, nôr; fūse, fŭn, fûr; tōō, tŏŏk; foil; foul; thin; then;
hw for wh as in *wh*at; zh for s as in u*s*ual; ə for a, e, i, o, u, as in ag*o*, lin*e*n, per*i*l, at*o*m, min*u*s

753

such a sound: *Ice* tinkled *in the glasses as Mother passed the lemonade.* **tin·kled, tin·kling.**

tin·sel (tĭn'səl) **1** threads, foil, or spangles of glittering metal used for decoration, especially on Christmas trees. **2** something showy or gaudy, but of little value; pretense: *Her flattering and friendly ways were mere tinsel.*

tin·smith (tĭn'smĭth') person who works with tin; one who makes tinware.

tint (tĭnt) **1** a shade, especially a paler shade, of a color: *Pink is a* tint *of red. The sunrise showed many tints of pink.* **2** to color, especially with pale colors.

tin·ware (tĭn'wâr') articles made of tin, such as cake pans, cooky sheets, etc.

ti·ny (tī'nĭ) very small. **ti·ni·er, ti·ni·est.**

¹tip (tĭp) **1** an end, especially a pointed end. **2** something placed on a tip: *a shoelace with a metal tip.* **3** to place on or at a tip: *to tip an arrow with steel.* **tipped, tip·ping.** [**¹tip** is probably from an early German word (tip) which is probably related to **²tap.**]

²tip (tĭp) **1** to lean or slant: *The table tips toward the wall.* **2** to cause to lean or slant: *He tipped the table toward him.*

tip over to upset; overturn; capsize: *The boat tipped over in the heavy surf.*

tipped, tip·ping. [**²tip** is probably **¹tip** in the original special sense of "pushing the tip over."]

³tip (tĭp) **1** small gift of money for services, as to a waiter, cab driver, or the like. **2** to make such a gift: *Mr. Brackett tipped the waiter.* **3** a hint; bit of private information: *a tip on the stock market.* **4** to give such information: *The customs officials were tipped that smugglers were on board.* **tipped, tip·ping.** [**³tip** is a word of unknown origin.]

tip·sy (tĭp'sĭ) slightly drunk. **tip·si·er, tip·si·est; tip·si·ly.**

tip·toe (tĭp'tō') **1** on the tips of one's toes: *The baby could reach the table when he stood* tiptoe. **2** to walk quietly on, or as on, one's toes: *Dennis* tiptoed *down the hall.* **tip·toed, tip·toe·ing.**

tip·top (tĭp'tŏp') **1** highest point: *At the* tiptop *of the crag was an eagle's nest.* **2** very fine; excellent; first-rate: *The snow was* tiptop *for skiing.*

¹tire (tīr) **1** to fatigue in body, mind, or spirit: *Studying had so tired Jane, she was ready for bed. That woman's endless talking* tires *me beyond measure.* **2** to become fatigued: *He* tires *easily.* **tired, tir·ing.** [**¹tire** is a form of an Old English word (teorian) of the same meaning.]

²tire (tīr) a band of metal or rubber, or a circular, air-filled rubber tube, around the rim of a wheel. [**²tire** is a short form of **attire.** A tire was regarded as the covering of a wheel.]

tired (tīrd) exhausted; weary; fatigued. **tired·ly.**

tire·less (tīr'lĭs) **1** not easily fatigued: *a* tireless *worker.* **2** unceasing; never lessening: *a* tireless *effort.* **tire·less·ly.**

tire·some (tīr'səm) **1** annoying; irritating: *Don't be* tiresome. **2** boring; wearying; tedious: *a* tiresome *argument.* **tire·some·ly.**

'tis (tĭz) it is: *They say* 'tis *better to give than to receive.*

tis·sue (tĭsh'ōō) **1** the cells and connecting parts that make up any part of an animal or plant: *muscle* tissue. **2** thin, gauzy cloth. **3** soft, thin paper, used for wrapping, handkerchiefs, etc.; tissue paper. **4** web or network: *a* tissue *of lies.*

tissue paper thin, gauzy, soft paper used for wrapping delicate articles.

tit·bit (tĭt'bĭt') tidbit.

tithe (tĭth) **1** one tenth of a person's income, given toward the support of his church or for charitable purposes. **2** to pay or take such an amount. **tithed, tith·ing.**

tith·ing (tī'thĭng) **1** a paying or taking of tithes. **2** amount which is taken or set apart as a tithe.

ti·tle (tī'təl) **1** name of a book, painting, or the like. **2** word showing the office, rank, status, etc., of a person, generally used before a person's name or as a mark of respect: *Judge, Lord, Mr., are* titles. **3** right of ownership: *Mr. White holds* title *to his house.* **4** championship: *He held the golf* title.

title page first printed page of a book, containing the title of the work, the names of the author and the publisher, and often the date of printing.

TNT a powerful explosive used in artillery shells, rock blasting, etc.

to (tŏŏ or tə) **1** toward; in the direction of: *on my way* to *school; from right* to *left.* **2** as far as: *going* to *Boston; generous* to *a fault.* **3** for the purpose of: *built* to *endure.* **4** for: *a key* to *the door; the door* to *the oven; a room* to *himself.* **5** for the benefit or enjoyment of; into the possession of: *open* to *the public; a present given* to *father.* **6** opposite: *face* to *face.* **7** on; upon; against: *Please fasten the notice* to *the bulletin board.* **8** until; till: *The play lasts* to *10:30.* **9** before: *five minutes* to *six.* **10** in agreement or harmony with: *words set* to *music;* to *my way of thinking.* **11** in: *12 eggs* to *a dozen.* **12** during: *15 beats* to *a minute.* **13** used with action words in various meanings: *She began* to *sing.* To *err is human.* **14 to and fro** back and forth. (Homonyms: too, two)

American toad,
2 to 4 in. long

toad (tŏd) a harmless, froglike, hopping animal with a rough skin. It is a valuable destroyer of insects.

toad·stool (tŏd'stŏŏl') any of several umbrella-shaped mushrooms, some of which are highly poisonous.

toast (tōst) **1** to brown by heating. **2** one or more slices of bread browned on both sides. **3** to warm or heat thoroughly: *We toasted our hands before the open fire.* **4** to drink in someone's honor: *We toasted the royal guests.* **5** a drinking to the health or success of someone or something: *a toast in his honor.*

Toadstools

toast·er (tōs'tər) device for toasting bread, rolls, or the like.

to·bac·co (tə băk'ō) **1** plant with pink or white blossoms and large leaves from which cigars and other tobacco products are made. **2** the dried and processed leaves of this plant. **to·bac·cos** or **to·bac·coes.**

Drying tobacco

to·bog·gan (tə bŏg'ən) **1** a sled without runners and with a curved end. It is used for sliding downhill. **2** to slide downhill on such a sled.

Toboggan

to·day or **to-day** (tə dā') **1** this present day. **2** on this day: *We will go to the movies* today. **3** present time; in this particular age: *the writers of* today; *today's fashion.*

tod·dle (tŏd'əl) to walk with short, uncertain steps: *The baby* toddled *across the room.* **tod·dled, tod·dling.**

toe (tō) **1** one of the five separate digits or divisions of the foot. **2** the fore part of the foot or of any foot covering: *He tore the toe of his shoe when he bumped his toe against the rock.* **3** to touch, strike, or point with the toe: *to toe the mark in a race; to toe in while walking.* **toed, toe·ing.** (Homonym: tow)

toe·nail (tō'nāl') nail growing on a toe.

tof·fee (tôf'ĭ or tŏf'ĭ) candy made of sugar and butter, boiled until it thickens, and then poured into a dish to cool and harden.

to·ga (tō'gə) formal outer garment worn by citizens of ancient Rome. It consisted of an elaborately draped piece of woolen cloth with the wearer's rank shown by the color of its border.

Toga

to·geth·er (tŏŏ gĕth'ər) **1** in one gathering, company, or association; with each other: *We live together in one house.* **2** without a break; continuously: *We marched for days together.* **3** at the same time; in a simultaneous way: *All the cannon went off together.*

¹**toil** (toil) **1** to work long or hard; labor: *The farmer toiled in the field.* **2** work or effort that exhausts the body or mind: *After years of toil, he owned the farm.* [¹**toil** comes through Old French (toillier) from a Latin word (tudiculare) meaning "to stir about." The latter is based on another Latin word (tudicula) meaning "a small machine for bruising olives."]

fāte, făt, fâre, fär; bē, bĕt; bīte, bĭt; nō, nŏt, nôr; fūse, fŭn, fûr; tŏŏ, tŏŏk; foil; foul; thin; ~~then~~;
hw for wh as in *w*hat; zh for s as in u*s*ual; ə for a, e, i, o, u, as in a*g*o, lin*e*n, per*i*l, at*o*m, min*u*s

755

²toil (toil) **1** old-fashioned word for net; trap. **2 toils** snare; grip: *caught in the toils of crime.* [**²toil** comes through Old French (toile) from a Latin word (tēla) meaning "woven material," "a web."]

toil·er (toi′lər) one who works hard and long.

toi·let (toi′lĭt) **1** bathroom. **2** a plumbing fixture in a bathroom used to flush away bodily waste. **3** having to do with dressing and grooming: *personal* toilet *articles;* toilet *water.* **4** washing; dressing and grooming oneself: *Tom's brief* toilet *consisted of brushing his hair and washing his hands.*

to·ken (tō′kən) **1** sign, mark, or symbol of some feeling, event, or fact: *A four-leaf clover is a* token *of good luck.* **2** keepsake; remembrance: *The pin was a* token *from my uncle.* **3** piece of metal used as money: *a bus* token; *a subway* token. **4 token payment** part payment of a debt to show that one is going to pay it all.

told (tōld) **1** See **tell**. *I told* them *I couldn't go.* **2 all told** counting all: *There were 26 people there* all told.

tol·er·a·ble (tŏl′ər ə bəl) **1** capable of being suffered or endured: *The pain was bad but it was* tolerable. **2** fairly good; not bad; acceptable: *His drawing was* tolerable *but Bob's was far better.* **tol·er·a·bly.**

tol·er·ance (tŏl′ər əns) willingness to allow other people to hold opinions or follow customs which differ from one's own: *The ministers showed great* tolerance *for one another's views when they met at the conference.*

tol·er·ant (tŏl′ər ənt) willing to allow others to think or act as they please even when one does not approve of their opinions or actions: *Uneducated people tend to be prejudiced against foreign nations; educated people, however, are inclined to be more* tolerant *in this respect.* **tol·er·ant·ly.**

tol·er·ate (tŏl′ə rāt′) to permit to exist without interference; put up with; endure: *Lateness will not be* tolerated. *We must* tolerate *other people's ideas.* **tol·er·at·ed, tol·er·at·ing.**

¹toll (tōl) **1** to cause (a bell) to sound with regular and continuous strokes: *The sexton* tolled *the bell to gather the townspeople together.* **2** to sound or strike in this way: *The bell* tolled *three.* **3** the sound made by

the regular striking of a bell. [**¹toll** is from an earlier English word (tollen). It was probably the imitation of the sound.]

²toll (tōl) **1** tax or fee paid for some special privilege, or for the right to use something: *We paid a* toll *to use the new highway.* **2** a charge for a telephone call. [**²toll** is the unchanged form of an Old English word that comes through Latin from a Greek word (telos) meaning "tax."]

tom·a·hawk (tŏm′ə hôk′) **1** American Indian battle-ax which was also used as a tool. **2** to use a tomahawk.

Tomahawk

to·ma·to (tə mā′tō or tə mä′tō) **1** red or yellow fruit with juicy pulp, used as a vegetable. **2** the plant it grows on. **to·ma·toes.**

tomb (tōōm) **1** grave or vault for the dead. **2** monumental stone coffin on the floor of a church, etc.

tom·boy (tŏm′boi′) a lively, noisy girl who behaves like a boy.

tomb·stone (tōōm′stōn′) stone placed over or at the head of a grave, usually bearing the dead person's name and dates of birth and death.

tom·cat (tŏm′kăt′) male cat.

to·mor·row (tə mŏr′ō or tə môr′ō) **1** the day after today: *Is* tomorrow *a holiday?* **2** on the day after today: *My mother will roast a turkey* tomorrow.

tom-tom (tŏm′tŏm′) a kind of drum, played by beating with the hands.

ton (tŭn) a measure of weight; 2,000 pounds (short ton) in the United States and Canada; 2,240 pounds (long ton) in Great Britain.

tone (tōn) **1** vocal or musical sound; its quality: *The quiet* tones *of the harp were* drowned out by the loud tones *of the voices from outside.* **2** one of the sounds or notes in a musical scale: *to sing the* tone *of G.* **3** style or manner of speaking or writing: *In a pleading* tone, *Tom's mother begged him to be careful with firecrackers.* **4** spirit; general character; quality: *The* tone *of the meeting was set by the president's friendly*

Tom-tom

welcoming speech. **5** normal, healthy condition of the body: *An athlete keeps his body in* tone. **6** general effect . of combined colors, as in a painting: *Most of Rembrandt's paintings are in a reddish-brown* tone. **7** tint or shade of a particular color.

tone down **1** to make (a color or sound) less harsh or vivid: *to tone down a voice; tone down a shade of blue.* **2** to soften; make less intense: *She toned down the angry words in the letter.*

tone up to make or become brighter or more intense.

toned, ton·ing.

tongs (tŏngz) tool of many sizes and shapes, usually with two arms hinged like scissors, used for lifting or carrying ice, embers, lump sugar, pickles, etc.

Ice tongs

Fire tongs

tongue (tŭng) **1** the muscular, movable organ in the mouth used in tasting and also, in human beings, for talking. **2** a language: *His native tongue is English.* **3** power of speech: *My mother asked me if I had lost my tongue.* **4** manner of speaking: *Our neighbor has a sharp tongue.* **5** anything like a tongue in shape or use, such as a leaping flame or the piece of leather under the laces of a shoe. **6** animal's tongue used as food.

tongue-tied (tŭng′tīd′) **1** unable to speak normally because of a defect of the tongue. **2** silent; unable to speak freely because of shyness, shock, surprise, or the like: *Alice was tongue-tied with wonder at the sight of the Christmas tree.*

ton·ic (tŏn′ĭk) **1** something that strengthens, especially medicine: *After Susan had been sick, the doctor recommended a tonic to build up her strength.* **2** bracing; stimulating: *the tonic effect of a cold shower.*

to·night or **to-night** (tə nīt′) **1** the night of this present day: *We are going out for dinner tonight.* **2** on or during this night: *The weather report predicts snow tonight.*

ton·nage (tŭn′ĭj) **1** the amount of weight a ship can carry. **2** total amount of shipping of a port or country, stated in tons: *Although Norway is a small country, it is an important shipping nation and has a large tonnage.* **3** total weight in tons.

ton·sil (tŏn′səl) one of a pair of oval lumps of spongy tissue on either side of the throat at the back of the mouth. They sometimes become infected and have to be removed.

ton·sil·li·tis (tŏn′sə lī′tĭs) inflammation of the tonsils.

too (tōō) **1** also; in addition; besides: *The school band was invited to the opera matinee, and the glee club too.* **2** more than enough: *There was far too much food for just the four of us. This dress is much too long for you.* **3** very: *We were only too glad to see the end of winter.* (Homonyms: to, two)

took (tŏŏk) See **take.** *Alex took his dog with him to school.*

tool (tōōl) **1** instrument used in doing work, especially with the hands, such as a chisel, hammer, knife, or saw. **2** anything used as a tool, such as books, money, etc. **3** person used as a tool: *The general was a tool of the dictator's scheme.* **4** to work on with a tool: *to tool leather.*

toot (tōōt) **1** of a whistle, horn, trumpet, etc., to give one or more short, sharp blasts. **2** short, sharp blast on a whistle, horn, trumpet, etc.

tooth (tōōth) **1** any of the hard, white, bonelike growths in the jaw, used for biting or chewing. **2** one of the points on the cutting edge of a saw. **3** cog on a cogwheel. **4** one of the long points on a rake or comb. **teeth.**

CROWN

NECK

ROOT

Tooth

tooth·ache (tōōth′āk′) pain in a tooth or in the teeth.

tooth·brush (tōōth′brŭsh′) small long-handled brush for cleaning the teeth.

tooth·pick (tōōth′pĭk′) small, pointed piece of wood, metal, plastic, etc., for removing bits of food from between the teeth.

¹top (tŏp) **1** highest part; summit; peak: *the top of a mountain; the top of a building.* **2** highest: *the top shelf.* **3** upper side or part of anything: *the top of a car; the top of a table.* **4** that part of anything that is first: *He was in the top half of his class.*

---

fāte, făt, fâre, fär; bē, bĕt; bīte, bĭt; nō, nŏt, nôr; fūse, fŭn, fûr; tōō, tŏŏk; foil; foul; thin; ~~then~~;
hw for wh as in *wh*at; zh for s as in u*s*ual; ə for a, e, i, o, u, as in *a*go, lin*e*n, per*i*l, at*o*m, min*u*s

5 cover or lid for a box, jar, etc. **6** to put a top or lid on a bottle, jar, etc. **7** the part of a plant above the ground, said of plants with edible roots, such as carrots or radishes. **8** to be first or at the head of: *He* tops *his history class.* **9** to surpass; exceed: *to* top *last year's record.* **10** highest step or degree: *the* top *of one's desires.* **11** greatest; foremost: *at* top *speed.* **12** to go over the top of; surmount: *We* topped *the hill.* **13** to cut off the upper part (of a plant). **topped, top·ping.** [¹**top** is from an Old English word of the same spelling. It is related to ¹**tip**.]

²**top** (tŏp) child's toy shaped like a cone and having a point on which it spins by means of a string or spring. [²**top** is a form of an Old English word of the same spelling.]

to·paz (tō′păz) mineral used as a gem, varying in color from yellow to blue or green.

top·ic (tŏp′ĭk) subject of a conversation, argument, composition, etc.: *Her wedding was the* topic *of the day. The teacher assigned several* topics *from the history book.*

top·knot (tŏp′nŏt′) tuft of hair on the top of the head, or a crest of feathers on the head of a bird.

top·mast (tŏp′măst′) second section of a mast above the deck of a ship.

top·most (tŏp′mōst′) at the very top; highest; uppermost.

top·ple (tŏp′əl) **1** to fall top first; tumble: *The trees* toppled *into the lake.* **2** to cause to fall in this manner: *The wind* toppled *the church tower.* **top·pled, top·pling.**

top·sail (tŏp′sāl′) second sail above the deck on the mast of a square-rigged vessel.

top·soil (tŏp′soil′) top or upper part of the soil, especially the fertile surface layer of soil.

top·sy-tur·vy (tŏp′sĭ tûr′vĭ) **1** upside down: *The car turned* topsy-turvy. **2** in confusion; in disorder: *After the party the house was* topsy-turvy.

tor·ah (tôr′ə) **1** the body of Jewish religious thought and literature. **2 Torah** among the Jews, the first five books of the Old Testament taken as a whole.

Torch of liberty

torch (tôrch) **1** stick of resinous wood, bundle of rushes, or the like, burning at one end with an open flame, used to give light: *Before the days of lighted streets, people hired boys to carry* torches *before them at night.* **2** any of various devices that give off a hot flame: *a plumber's* torch.

tore (tôr) See **tear.** *I* tore *my suit on the nail.*

¹**tor·ment** (tôr′mĕnt) **1** extreme mental or physical suffering; great pain: *suffering the* torments *of jealous rage.* **2** something that causes suffering or pain: *His reckless driving was the* torment *of his mother's life.*

²**tor·ment** (tôr mĕnt′) **1** to tease: *Joe* tormented *the puppy by pulling its tail.* **2** to torture: *Ann was* tormented *by pangs of conscience.*

tor·men·tor (tôr mĕn′tər) person or thing that torments; torturer: *The black flies were our* tormentors *during the whole vacation.*

torn (tôrn) See **tear.** *The sail was* torn *by the heavy wind.*

tor·na·do (tôr nā′dō) violent, whirling wind that travels rapidly in a narrow path. It is seen as a twisting, dark cloud shaped like a funnel. **tor·na·does** or **tor·na·dos.**

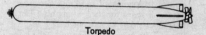

Torpedo

tor·pe·do (tôr pē′dō) **1** an underwater, self-driven explosive missile used to blow up enemy ships. **2** to blow up with a torpedo or submarine mine. **3** kind of firework. **4** a noise-making explosive charge placed on a railroad track as a signal. **tor·pe·does; tor·pe·doed, tor·pe·do·ing.**

tor·pid (tôr′pĭd) **1** inactive; sluggish; dull: *The heavy meal made me* torpid. **2** dormant: *Bears live in a* torpid *state during the winter.* **tor·pid·ly.**

tor·rent (tŏr′ənt or tôr′ənt) **1** violent, rapidly flowing stream or river. **2** any similar flow: *a* torrent *of rain.*

tor·rid (tôr′id or tŏr′id) **1** extremely hot or burning; dried by the sun's heat: *the* torrid *climate of the desert.* **2 Torrid Zone** old name for the tropics. **tor·rid·ly.**

tor·til·la (tôr tē′yä) thin, unleavened pancake made from corn meal and baked on a flat plate of iron or earthenware. It is a staple of diet in Latin American countries.

tor·toise (tôr′təs) turtle, especially a land turtle, often burrowing, that lives in arid regions.

tor·ture (tôr′chər) **1** to inflict severe pain upon (as punishment, revenge, or for persuasion): *The bandits tortured the prisoner to learn his secrets.* **2** method of inflicting such pain: *The rack used to be a form of* torture. **3** extreme pain of mind or body: *to suffer* torture *from a toothache.* **tor·tured, tor·tur·ing.**

Gopher tortoise, about 1 ft. long

toss (tôs or tŏs) **1** to throw up into the air or through the air; throw without using much force: *to toss a ball.* **2** to cause to roll back and forth; cause to pitch: *The waves tossed the small boat.* **3** to fling up; jerk up: *She tossed her head and walked away.* **4** to be restless; roll from side to side: *I couldn't sleep and I tossed all night.* **5** to be flung back and forth; be buffeted: *The balloons tossed about on their strings in the wind.* **6** a tossing; throw; fling: *a toss of a ball; a toss of the head.*

tot (tŏt) small child: *The kindergarten tots gathered around their teacher.*

to·tal (tō′təl) **1** whole; entire: *This is our total supply of books for the year.* **2** complete; absolute: *in total confusion.* **3** to add up: *Please total these numbers for me.* **4** sum; amount to which something adds up: *When you finish adding please give me the total.* **5** to amount to: *Our costs total ten dollars,* **to·tal·ly.**

to·tem (tō′təm) **1** animal or object believed by some primitive peoples to be closely related to their tribe or clan. **2 totem pole** a pole carved with symbolic figures, marking the descent of the clan or family displaying it, found among several American Indian tribes, especially those of the northern Pacific coast.

Totem pole

tot·ter (tŏt′ər) **1** to walk with weak, unsteady steps: *Small children* totter *before they walk well.* **2** to shake or wobble as if about to fall: *The cup tottered on the edge of the table.*

touch (tŭch) **1** to be in contact: *Their two heads touched as they whispered.* **2** to feel with the fingers: *She touched the wet paint.* **3** to cause to be in contact with: *He touched the stick to the ground.* **4** a contact: *at the touch of a hand; in touch with absent friends.* **5** to strike lightly; tap. **6** a tap: *He felt a soft touch on the arm.* **7** the sense of feeling: *the highly developed touch of the blind.* **8** way of touching with the fingers: *She plays the piano with a light touch.* **9** small amount: *A touch of color would improve this room.* **10** to eat; taste: *She didn't touch her breakfast.* **11** to mention: *I didn't dare touch the subject of a raise.* **12** to compare with; equal: *My skill at chess doesn't touch yours.* **13** to affect; concern: *Our conversation doesn't touch you.* **14** to move; affect the feelings or emotions; cause sympathy or gratitude: *Your kindness touches me.* **15** to affect slightly; harm a little: *This plant has been touched by frost.* **16** special way of doing something; style: *You can see his touch in all these paintings.*

touch up to improve (something) by making slight changes: *to touch up a drawing or photograph.*

touch upon to refer to: *He touched upon several subjects.*

touch·down (tŭch′doun′) **1** in football, a play in which the player carries the ball over the opponent's goal line. **2** score made in this way.

touch·ing (tŭch′ing) **1** causing feelings of sympathy or gratitude; moving: *Your concern for my happiness is* touching. **2** with regard to; concerning: *The teacher said nothing* touching *a holiday.* **touch·ing·ly.**

tough (tŭf) **1** strong but pliant: *a baseball glove of* tough *cowhide.* **2** not easily broken or cut: *Steak grows tough if it is cooked too long.* **3** strong; robust; hardy: *You have to be tough to camp out in the winter.* **4** rough; disorderly: *a tough*

---

fāte, făt, fâre, fär; bē, bĕt; bīte, bĭt; nō, nŏt, nôr; fūse, fŭn, fûr; tōō, tŏŏk; foil; foul; thin; ~~then~~; hw for wh as in *wh*at; zh for s as in u*s*ual; ə for a, e, i, o, u, as in *a*go, lin*e*n, per*i*l, at*o*m, min*u*s

neighborhood. **5** hard to change; stubborn: *a* tough *will*. **6** a hardened or rough person. **7** difficult: *a* tough *lesson*. **tough·ly**.

tough·en (tŭf′ən) to make or become tough: *He* toughened *himself by exercise. The young soldier* toughened *in service*.

tour (toŏr) **1** a journey in which a traveler makes a short stop at a number of places and returns to the place from which he started; a sightseeing trip: *We went on a long* tour *through Europe*. **2** to travel through: *to* tour *Europe*. **3** to make a tour: *Our family likes* touring.

tour·ist (toŏr′ĭst) **1** person who travels for pleasure. **2** of or for tourists: *a* tourist *agency*.

tour·na·ment (toŏr′nə mənt or tûr′nə-mənt) **1** a series of contests in skill between a number of players: *a golf* tournament; *a chess* tournament. **2** in the Middle Ages, a contest with blunt weapons by knights on horseback.

tour·ni·quet (toŏr′nə kĕt′ or toŏr′nə kā′ or tûr′nə kĕt′ or tûr′nə kā′) a tight bandage, capable of being twisted to stop bleeding by pressing on a blood vessel.

tou·sle (tou′zəl) to put into disorder (usually used of the hair); ruffle; muss: *to* tousle *a child's hair*. **tou·sled, tou·sling**.

Tourniquet

¹tow (tō) **1** to pull by a rope: *We* towed *the canoe up to the dock*. **2** a towing or a being towed: *a car in* tow. **3** something towed: *the tugboat couldn't manage its large* tow. **4** rope or chain used for towing. [**¹tow** is a form of an Old English word (togian) meaning "drag," "pull," "tug."] (Homonym: toe)

²tow (tō) short, coarse fibers of hemp or flax, ready for spinning. [**²tow** is the unchanged form of an Old English word.] (Homonym: toe)

to·ward (tôrd or tə wôrd′) or **to·wards** (tôrdz or tə wôrdz′) **1** in the direction of: *We sailed* toward *China*. **2** close upon; near: *We camped* toward *sundown*. **3** about; regarding: *What is your attitude* toward *the candidates?* **4** with a view to; for the purpose of: *to save* toward *one's old age*.

tow·el (tou′əl) piece of cloth or paper for drying something wet.

tow·er (tou′ər) **1** high structure, or part of a building rising higher than the rest of it. **2** stronghold; fortress. **3** thing superior to others: *a* tower *of strength; a* tower *of wisdom*. **4** to rise high: *The mountain* towers *to the sky. The cliff* towers *above the village*.

tow·er·ing (tou′ər ĭng) **1** very high; tall: *a* towering *mountain*. **2** intense; violent: *a* towering *rage*.

Bell tower

town (toun) **1** group of houses and buildings, larger than a village but smaller than a city. **2** the city as opposed to the country. **3** the people of a community: *The whole* town *is talking about it*.

town cri·er (toun krī′ər) person who formerly made public announcements in the streets of a town or village.

town hall building where public meetings are held and where town offices are located; municipal building.

town·ship (toun′shĭp) **1** subdivision of a county, consisting of a village or group of villages having certain powers of self-government. **2** in some states, a tract of land six miles square.

tox·ic (tŏk′sĭk) **1** poisonous: *a* toxic *drug*. **2** producing poisons or poisoning: *a* toxic *germ*.

tox·in (tŏk′sĭn) any poison produced by certain germs in plant or animal tissue: *diphtheria* toxin.

toy (toi) **1** child's plaything. **2** of or like a toy; made like a toy: *a* toy *radio*.

toy with 1 to handle carelessly in an absent-minded way: *He* toyed with *his pencil*. **2** to amuse oneself with; play with (an idea, etc.): *to* toy with *the idea of buying a new car*.

¹trace (trās) **1** a mark or sign left by something that has passed or happened: *We found* traces *of an old civilization. We saw* traces *of deer in the snow*. **2** slight evidence: *There was a* trace *of sorrow in his voice*. **3** small quantity or amount: *There were still* traces *of water in the dry river bed*. **4** to draw on transparent paper by following the lines of a picture underneath it. **5** to sketch; outline: *The commander traced the plan of attack.* **6** to follow the traces of: *to trace a deer through the forest; to trace a family back to the "Mayflower."* **traced, trac·ing.** [¹**trace** comes through Old French (tracier) from a form (tractus) of a Latin word (trahere) meaning "to draw."]

²**trace** (trās) either of the two straps of a harness by which a vehicle is pulled. [²**trace** comes through an Old French word (trais) meaning "traces" from a Latin word (tractus) meaning "a dragging."]

tra·che·a (trā'kĭ ə) air tube leading from the back of the mouth to the lungs; windpipe.

trac·ing (trā'sĭng) a copy of a picture, inscription, etc., made on transparent paper placed over the original.

track (trăk) **1** a print left by a foot, tire, etc. **2** to leave marks or footprints on or with: *Boys tracked the fresh cement. The crowd tracked mud all over the vestibule.* **3** trail of footprints, wheel marks, sparks, etc., left by a moving object: *The Indian scout followed the tracks of the wagon train.* **4** to follow by sight or scent: *The hounds tracked the fox to its den.* **5** path; road: *A wagon* track *leads across the field.* **6** a specially prepared course used for races: *a race* track; *a cinder* track. **7** having to do with the athletic sports which take place there: *a track man; track events.* **8** a rail, or rails, for directing the course of something: *railroad* tracks. **9 keep track of** to keep informed about: *He kept track of old school friends.*

track down to capture by tracking; find by tracking: *to track down an animal.*

¹**tract** (trăkt) **1** unbroken expanse or area: *a tract of land; a vast tract of ocean.* **2** a system of body organs: *the digestive tract.* [¹**tract** is from a form (tractus) meaning "a stretch of land" of a Latin word (trahere) meaning "to draw," "to stretch."]

²**tract** (trăkt) pamphlet, especially one upon a religious or political subject. [²**tract** is short for "tractate," meaning "a pamphlet," "an essay."]

trac·tor (trăk'tər) heavy motor vehicle for pulling plows, trucks, etc.

trade (trād) **1** a buying and selling; commerce: *All the ships in the harbor were engaged in foreign* trade. **2** to buy and sell. **3** a barter; exchange of goods for other goods: *A brisk* trade *of furs for knives sprang up between the Indians and the colonists.* **4** to exchange; swap: *Enoch* traded *his top for Tom's whistle.* **5** work one does for a living, especially skilled work done with the hands; craft: *the carpenter's* trade. **6** people in the same business considered as a group: *the building* trade. **7** customers: *The new clerk proved popular with the* trade. **trad·ed, trad·ing.**

Tractor

trade·mark (trād'märk') a mark, word, picture, etc., often registered with the government by a maker or manufacturer to identify his product from others.

trad·er (trā'dər) **1** person who trades; merchant: *The fur* trader *exchanged beaver skins for flour.* **2** ship used in trade.

trades·man (trādz'mən) retailer; shopkeeper. **trades·men.**

trade union organization of workers to protect their rights in matters of wages, hours, and working conditions; labor union.

trade wind either of two steady winds found to the north and south of the equator. North of the equator they blow from the northeast, and south of the equator from the southeast.

trading post frontier store, especially one that barters with hunters and trappers.

tra·di·tion (trə dĭsh'ən) **1** the handing down of tales, beliefs, customs, etc., from generation to generation: *Many legends are preserved by* tradition. **2** that which is handed down: *Exchanging gifts at Christmas is an old* tradition.

tra·di·tion·al (trə dĭsh'ən əl) **1** having to do with tales, beliefs, customs, etc., handed down from generation to generation. **2** established by long usage; customary: *a* traditional *family name.* **tra·di·tion·al·ly.**

fāte, făt, fâre, fär; bē, bĕt; bīte, bĭt; nō, nŏt, nôr; fūse, fŭn, fûr; tōō, tŏŏk; foil; foul; thin; ~~then~~; hw for wh as in *wh*at; zh for s as in u*s*ual; ə for a, e, i, o, u, as in a*g*o, lin*e*n, per*i*l, at*o*m, min*u*s

761

traf·fic (trăf'ĭk) **1** movement of people, goods, and vehicles from place to place: *The traffic on city streets is a serious problem.* **2** the transportation business done by a railway, steamship line, etc., carrying persons or goods. **3** trade; business: *the traffic in stolen goods.* **4** to trade or deal: *to traffic in cotton.* **traf·ficked, traf·fick·ing.**

trag·e·dy (trăj'ə dĭ) **1** a serious play with an unhappy ending. **2** sad event, especially one involving death; disaster: *Their mother's death was a tragedy for the children.* **trag·e·dies.**

trag·ic (trăj'ĭk) **1** of plays, having an unhappy ending: *"Hamlet" is perhaps the best-known example of the tragic drama.* **2** very sad; disastrous: *Both parents were killed in a tragic accident.*

trail (trāl) **1** path through woods or wild country: *It had snowed so hard we couldn't find the trail.* **2** a track; footprints; a scent which points the way: *The dog followed the trail of the rabbit.* **3** to follow the path or footprints of: *Some dogs can trail a man for many miles.* **4** a stream of people, dust, rubbish, etc., behind something moving: *The train left a trail of smoke.* **5** to drag behind (one); pull along the ground: *The boy trailed a wagon.* **6** to be dragged along behind: *Her coat trailed in the mud.* **7** to follow behind; straggle: *She was tired and she trailed behind the others.*

trail·er (trā'lər) **1** person, animal, or thing that follows behind. **2** van for carrying loads which is hooked to any vehicle. **3** vehicle with living quarters that can be hauled from place to place by a car. **4** a trailing plant or vine.

train (trān) **1** an engine with a line of cars attached to it. **2** a group of people or things traveling together: *The wagon train crossed the prairie.* **3** a series of ideas or events: *a train of thought.* **4** a group of attendants: *The ambassador and his train stayed at the Savoy.* **5** an extension of a lady's skirt that trails behind her. **6** to educate; bring up; rear: *to train children to bo good citizens.* **7** to teach so as to make skillful; instruct systematically: *to train*

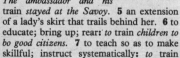

Train

radio operators; *to train a dog to do tricks.* **8** to prepare for by practice: *John trained for the race.* **9** to aim; point: *The officer trained his guns on the fort.* **10** to cause to grow in a certain way: *Marian trained the vines to climb up the wall.*

train·er (trā'nər) person who trains, especially one who trains athletes for sports contests, horses for racing, animals for the circus, etc.

train·ing (trā'nĭng) **1** instruction for some occupation: *Have you had training as a nurse?* **2** course of exercise, diet, etc., for an athlete. **3** good condition maintained by following such a course: *I am out of training.* **4** used for training: *a training bridle for a colt.*

train·man (trān'mən) person who works on a train and assists the conductor. **train·men.**

trait (trāt) feature or characteristic, especially of personality: *She has some very nice traits, but she is lazy.*

trai·tor (trā'tər) person who betrays his country, a cause, a friend, etc.: *He committed treason and was hanged as a traitor.*

trai·tor·ous (trā'tər əs) of or like a traitor; treacherous.

tramp (trămp) **1** to walk with heavy steps; trudge: *He tramped upstairs. He tramped home, tired after a day's hike.* **2** to step on heavily and repeatedly; tread: *The peasants tramp the grapes in making wine.* **3** the sound of heavy steps: *I hear the tramp of soldiers in the distance.* **4** to walk over: *We have tramped this whole area in search of the little boy.* **5** a walk or hike: *a tramp through the woods.* **6** a man who goes about on foot doing odd jobs or begging; a vagabond. **7** a freight steamer that has no regular schedule but picks up cargo wherever it can.

tram·ple (trăm'pəl) **1** to tramp on; stamp on; crush: *The cow got through the fence and trampled my flower bed.* **2** the sound of tramping or stamping.

trample on to treat cruelly or ruthlessly: *to trample on a person's feelings.* **tram·pled, tram·pling.**

trance (trăns) **1** an unconscious state like sleep: *She has been in a trance since the automobile accident.* **2** a daze; daydream: *The music put him in a trance.* **3** a state* produced by hypnotism in which the mind is powerless to act by itself and is governed by outside suggestion.

tran·quil (trăng′kwĭl) calm; quiet; serene: *a tranquil mind; a tranquil scene.* **tran·quil·ly.**

tran·quil·iz·er (trăng′kwə lī′zər) a drug that makes a person calm and relaxed without putting him to sleep.

tran·quil·li·ty or **tran·quil·i·ty** (trăng-kwĭl′ə tĭ) a being tranquil; calmness; peacefulness; serenity.

trans·act (trăn săkt′ or trăn zăkt′) to carry on; perform; complete (business, etc.): *to transact a deal.*

trans·ac·tion (trăn săk′shən or trăn zăk′-shən) **1** the management of any business or affair: *He is in charge of all* transactions *with the government.* **2** a business deal: *This* transaction *involves a lot of money.*

trans·con·ti·nen·tal (trăns′kŏn tə nĕn′-təl) **1** going across a continent: *a trans-continental flight from New York to Los Angeles.* **2** on the other side of a continent.

¹**trans·fer** (trăns fûr′ or trăns′fər) **1** to carry or remove from one person or place to another: *to transfer papers from one file to another.* **2** to change from one place, position, etc., to another: *to transfer from New York to the San Francisco office.* **3** to change from one streetcar, bus, etc., to another. **4** to imprint on one surface from another: *to transfer a design to an Easter egg.* **trans·ferred, trans·fer·ring.**

²**trans·fer** (trăns′fər) **1** a passing or carrying from one person or place to another: *A porter helped me in the transfer of my luggage from the cab to the baggage room.* **2** a ticket allowing passage from one public vehicle to another: *a bus transfer.*

trans·form (trăns fôrm′) **1** to change the nature or appearance of; change into something else: *Cinderella's fairy godmother transformed mice into coachmen.* **2** to change the character or personality of: *Loving care transformed the child.* **3** to change from one form of energy to another: *to transform water power into electric power.*

trans·for·ma·tion (trăns′fər mā′shən) a transforming or being transformed, in ap-

pearance, nature, or the like: *the transformation of a tadpole into a frog.*

trans·form·er (trăns fôr′mər) in electricity, a device that steps up or steps down the voltage in a circuit.

trans·fu·sion (trăns fū′zhən) a transfer, such as of blood from one person to another.

trans·gress (trăns grĕs′ or trănz grĕs′) **1** to break a law, rule, etc.; sin: *She transgressed but she is ready to accept her punishment.* **2** to go beyond (any limit or bounds): *He transgressed every legal and social code in his eagerness to get ahead.*

tran·sient (trăn′shənt) **1** not permanent; brief; passing: *Her joy was transient.* **2** stopping for a short time: *a transient guest at the hotel.* **3** a visitor or boarder who remains only for a short time: *a hotel for transients.*

tran·sis·tor (trăn zĭs′tər) tiny electronic device used to control the flow of current in portable radios, hearing aids, etc. It takes the place of a vacuum tube.

tran·sit (trăn′sĭt or trăn′zĭt) **1** a passing through or over; passage: *rapid transit.* **2** a carrying from one point to another: *The tomatoes were spoiled in transit.*

tran·si·tion (trăn zĭsh′ən) the passing from one place, period, state, subject, or the like, to another: *the transition from boyhood to manhood; the transition from one paragraph to the next.*

trans·late (trăns lāt′ or trănz lāt′) **1** to change from one language into another: *Hans Christian Andersen's fairy tales are translated from Danish.* **2** to put into different words: *The teacher translated the theory of atomic power into language the children could understand.* **3** to move from one place, condition, or position to another: *The prophet Elijah was translated to heaven by means of a burning chariot.* **trans·lat·ed, trans·lat·ing.**

trans·la·tion (trăns lā′shən or trănz lā′-shən) **1** the changing of something written or spoken from one language to another; a translating: *The United Nations has a large staff for the translation of documents.* **2** result of translating: *There are several different translations of the Bible in English.*

---

fāte, făt, fâre, fär; bē, bĕt; bīte, bĭt; nō, nŏt, nôr; fūse, fŭn, fûr; tōō, tŏŏk; foil; foul; thin; then; hw for wh as in what; zh for s as in usual; ə for a, e, i, o, u, as in ago, linen, peril, atom, minus

translucent

trans·lu·cent (trăns lōō'sənt or trăns lū'-sənt) letting light pass through, but not allowing images to be clearly seen on the other side. Frosted glass, some plastics, alabaster, and the like are all translucent. **trans·lu·cent·ly.**

trans·mis·sion (trăns mĭsh'ən) **1** a passing from one person or place to another; communication: *the transmission of orders, electric power, disease, etc.* **2** part of a vehicle that connects two drive shafts by means of gears, hydraulic devices, etc. **3** a passing of radio waves through the air.

trans·mit (trăns mĭt') **1** to cause or allow to pass along or through: *to transmit news; to transmit disease; to transmit sound, light, etc.* **2** to pass on from one person to another: *Certain traits are transmitted from parents to children. He transmitted joy to his friends.* **3** to conduct: *Copper wires transmit electricity.* **trans·mit·ted, trans·mit·ting.**

trans·mit·ter (trăns mĭt'ər) person by whom, or thing through which, something is sent or carried, especially the mouthpiece of a telephone, or a radio set that sends radio waves.

tran·som (trăn'səm) **1** hinged window above a door, or a movable section of a large window. **2** crosspiece to which such a window is hinged.

Transom

trans·par·ent (trăns pâr'ənt) **1** clear enough to be easily seen through; sheer: *a transparent window.* **2** easy to detect: *a transparent lie.* **trans·par·ent·ly.**

trans·plant (trăns plănt') **1** to remove and plant again in another place: *My father bought shrubs from the florist and transplanted them in our garden.* **2** to move to another place: *After the war whole populations were transplanted to other countries.*

¹trans·port (trăns pôrt') **1** to carry from one place to another: *Large vans transported the elephants from their winter quarters to the circus.* **2** to be carried away (by strong feeling): *The children were transported with delight by the circus.* **3** to deport or banish (criminals) from a country.

travel

²trans·port (trăns'pôrt) **1** a carrying, as of goods or soldiers; transportation. **2** ship, plane, or other vehicle that moves troops, supplies, passengers, mail, or the like. **3** sudden burst of emotion: *in a transport of fury.*

trans·por·ta·tion (trăns'pər tā'shən) **1** a carrying or being carried from one place to another: *All transportation came to a standstill during the blizzard.* **2** means of carrying or being transported: *The jet plane is our fastest form of transportation.* **3** cost of travel; ticket: *The transportation was included in the price of the tour.* **4** the banishing of a criminal to another country.

trap (trăp) **1** any device for catching and holding animals or persons; snare; pitfall; ambush. **2** to set traps for animals: *Jacques traps for a living.* **3** to catch in a trap: *The hunter trapped a mink.* **4** argument, question, or the like that leads to an admission or confession: *The lawyer's questions proved a trap for the witness.* **5** to gain an admission or confession by cunning questions: *The police trapped the prisoner into a confession.* **6** S-shaped or U-shaped pipe that prevents the escape of air or gas. **7** trap door. **8** machine for hurling clay disks as rifle targets. **trapped, trap·ping.**

trap door door in a floor or roof.

tra·peze (tră pēz') swinging horizontal bar hung by ropes, used by acrobats and for gymnastics.

trap·per (trăp'ər) one who traps animals for their furs.

trap·pings (trăp'ĭngz) **1** decorative covering or harness for a horse. **2** any ornamental dress; decorations.

trash (trăsh) worthless, useless things; rubbish; refuse.

trav·ail (trăv'āl' or trə vāl' or trăv'əl) **1** exhausting labor; toil. **2** physical or mental agony. **3** to toil; work hard and painfully.

trav·el (trăv'əl) **1** to go from place to place; take a trip: *Last summer we traveled around Europe.* **2** the going from place to place: *These photographs are a record of our travels.* **3** to journey from place to place on business: *That salesman travels for a paint firm.* **4** to move: *Light travels much faster than sound.*

trav·el·er or **trav·el·ler** (trăv′əl ər) one who travels.

trav·erse (trăv′ərs or trə vûrs′) **1** to pass over, across, or through: *The hunters* traversed *the jungle without mishap.* **2** to lie or extend across: *A bridge* traverses *the stream.* **3** something lying across something else, such as a crossbar, rung of a ladder, etc. **trav·ersed, trav·ers·ing.**

trawl (trôl) **1** large baglike net dragged behind a boat in catching fish. **2** long fishing line to which are attached many short lines with hooks. **3** to fish with such a net or line.

trawl·er (trô′lər) **1** person who fishes with a trawl. **2** boat used in trawling.

tray (trā) flat receptacle with a raised rim, used for carrying or holding articles: *The waiter dropped a tray full of dishes.*

treach·er·ous (trĕch′ər əs) **1** betraying a trust; traitorous; disloyal: *The treacherous servant spied on his employer.* **2** not to be trusted in spite of appearances: *a treacherous current in a quiet river.* **treach·er·ous·ly.**

treach·er·y (trĕch′ə rĭ) **1** a betrayal of faith or confidence; disloyal conduct: *It was* treachery *for little Armstrong to tell the secrets of the club.* **2** treason. **treach·er·ies.**

trea·cle (trē′kəl) molasses obtained during the refining of sugar.

tread (trĕd) **1** to walk on, over, or along: *He* trod *the moors all night.* **2** to oppress; crush; destroy: *to* tread *on an enemy.* **3** to press beneath the foot; trample: *In Europe, peasants still* tread *grapes to make wine.* **4** to make by walking or trampling: *to* tread *a path through the woods.* **5** way or manner of walking: *to walk with a light* tread. **6** a walking or marching, or the sound of this: *the* tread *of troops.* **7** horizontal part of a step or stair. **8** part of a wheel or tire that touches the road or rail. **tread water** to maintain one's head above water while in an upright position by moving the feet as if riding a bicycle. **trod, trod** or **trod·den, tread·ing.**

trea·dle (trĕd′əl) **1** lever or pedal worked by the foot to operate a lathe, sewing machine, and the like. **2** to work a treadle. **trea·dled, trea·dling.**

tread·mill (trĕd′mĭl′) **1** mill worked by having animals or persons walk on the moving steps of a wheel or tread an endless sloping belt. **2** monotonous or tiring activity in which one seems to get nowhere.

trea·son (trē′zən) betrayal of one's country; an attempt to overthrow the government of one's country; in a monarchy, an attempt to injure the sovereign.

trea·son·ous (trē′zən əs) having to do with treason. **trea·son·ous·ly.**

treas·ure (trĕzh′ər) **1** a hoard of money, precious stones, etc.: *The pirates buried their* treasure *deep in the sand.* **2** any valued thing or person: *The faded photographs were the old lady's* treasures. **3** to hoard or store away. **4** to value highly; cherish: *He* treasured *the memory of his school days.* **treas·ured, treas·ur·ing.**

treas·ur·er (trĕzh′ər ər) person in charge of the funds or finances of a business, government, club, or the like.

treas·ur·y (trĕzh′ə rĭ) **1** place where the public funds or the money of an organization are kept: *the club* treasury. **2** the funds or money of an organization. **3** department in charge of receiving and paying out public funds for a city, state, or government: *the* Treasury *of the United States.* **4** place where valuable objects are stored. **treas·ur·ies.**

treat (trēt) **1** to deal with; handle: *The lecturer* treated *his subject in great detail. This painter is famous for* treating *sporting scenes.* **2** to behave or act toward: *She* treated *her guests with the utmost courtesy.* **3** to help towards a cure: *Has a doctor* treated *your cold?* **4** to regard; consider: *He* treated *the matter far too seriously.* **5** to subject to some process for a particular result: *to* treat *a metal with acid.* **6** something which gives great pleasure: *The Halloween party was a great* treat *for the children.* **7** to entertain at one's own expense; give (something), especially as a friendly or sociable gesture: *His father* treated *him to the movies.*

treat·ment (trēt′mənt) **1** manner or way of dealing with someone or something: *the captain's excellent* treatment *of his crew; the*

---

fāte, făt, fâre, fär; bē, bĕt; bite, bĭt; nō, nŏt, nôr; fūse, fŭn, fûr; tōō, tŏŏk; foil; foul; thin; ~~then~~; hw for wh as in *w*hat; zh for s as in u*s*ual; ə for a, e, i, o, u, as in ag*o*, lin*e*n, per*i*l, at*o*m, min*u*s

writer's treatment *of his theme.* **2** medical or surgical care: *a new* treatment *for polio.*

trea·ty (trē′tĭ) a formal agreement between nations: *a peace* treaty. **trea·ties.**

tre·ble (trĕb′əl) **1** threefold; triple. **2** to make or become three times as great or many; triple. **3** in music, of or for the highest instrumental or vocal part. **4** the highest part in music. **5** instrument or voice playing or singing this part; soprano. **6** high-pitched; shrill: *the* treble *sounds of children's voices.* **tre·bled, tre·bling.**

tree (trē) **1** large plant with a woody trunk developing into branches bearing leaves. **2** shrub or bush resembling a tree: *a rose* tree. **3** to chase up a tree: *to* tree *an opossum.* **4** a piece of wood used for a particular purpose: *a shoe* tree; *a hat* tree. **5 family tree** outline or diagram, sometimes shaped like a tree, showing family descent and how the members are related.

trek (trĕk) **1** to make a journey, particularly by wagon. **2** a journey, especially by wagon; migration: *the* trek *to the West.* **trekked, trek·king.**

trel·lis (trĕl′ĭs) **1** ornamental framework on or over which vines may be trained. It is usually made of small wood strips, crossed and widely spaced.

Trellis

2 to train (vines) on a trellis: *to* trellis *a climbing rose.*

trem·ble (trĕm′bəl) **1** to shake or shiver, as from fear, cold, etc.; shudder. **2** an involuntary shaking; shudder. **trem·bled, trem·bling.**

tre·men·dous (trĭ mĕn′dəs) **1** awe inspiring; of great importance: *the* tremendous *results of this day's victory.* **2** huge; enormous: *the* tremendous *mountains;* tremendous *acclaim.* **tre·men·dous·ly.**

tre·mor (trĕm′ər or trē′mər) **1** a shaking, quivering, or trembling: *the* tremor *of an earthquake.* **2** a thrill of emotion, as of excitement or fear: *a* tremor *of anxiety.*

trem·u·lous (trĕm′yə ləs) **1** quivering, shaking, or trembling: *a voice* tremulous *with fear.* **2** showing nervousness or timidity: *The young actress was* tremulous *as the curtain went up.* **trem·u·lous·ly.**

trench (trĕnch) **1** long, narrow furrow in the earth. **2** long, deep ditch with earth thrown up in front of it as a protection for soldiers in warfare. **3** to dig a ditch in: *to* trench *a field for drainage.*

trench·er (trĕn′chər) in former times, a wooden plate or platter on which meat was carved or served.

trend (trĕnd) **1** a general tendency or course; drift: *the* trend *of business; a business* trend. **2** to take a direction or course: *The river* trends *eastward.* **3** to have a general tendency: *Prices are* trending *upward.*

trep·i·da·tion (trĕp′ə dā′shən) **1** state of nervous alarm; fear mingled with uncertainty: *He approached his new job with* trepidation. **2** a trembling or vibration.

tres·pass (trĕs′pəs) **1** to commit an offense; sin: *A thief* trespasses *against the laws of the state and of the church.* **2** an illegal act or a sin: *Forgive us our* trespasses. **3** to enter property in an illegal manner: *We* trespassed *in the neighboring woods.* **4** to intrude; encroach (on or upon): *Are we* trespassing *on your time?*

tress (trĕs) curl or lock of hair.

tres·tle (trĕs′əl) **1** metal or timber framework used as a bridge. **2** a frame, such as a carpenter's horse, used to support a platform, table top, etc.

Trestle

tri- prefix meaning **(1)** "having three": tri*color;* tri*angle.* **(2)** once in three; happening every third: tri*weekly.* **(3)** three times; into three parts: tri*sect.*

tri·al (trī′əl) **1** a testing or putting to a test: *The* trial *of the new car showed up its flaws.* **2** done or used for the purpose of testing: *a* trial *speech; a* trial *cake of soap.* **3** hardship, temptation, etc., that tries one's endurance: *The long winter was a* trial *for the pioneers.* **4** person or thing that tries one's patience, faith, love, etc.: *He was a* trial *to his family.* **5** the hearing and deciding of a case in a court of law: *His* trial *for theft started today.*

tri·an·gle (trī′ăng′gəl) **1** any closed figure formed by three straight lines. **2** anything shaped like a triangle. **3** musical instrument, consisting of a steel rod bent in the form of a triangle, open at one corner, and sounded with a light metal rod.

tri·an·gu·lar (trī ăng'-gyōō lər) **1** shaped like a triangle; having three sides and three corners or angles. **2** concerned with or made up of three persons, parts, or the like: *a triangular treaty.* **tri·an·gu·lar·ly.**

Triangles

trib·al (trī'bəl) having to do with a tribe: *a tribal dance; a tribal custom.* **tri·bal·ly.**

tribe (trīb) **1** a group of primitive people having a common ancestor and forming a community under a common leader: *Several Indian tribes once roamed these prairies.* **2** a group of people united by a common interest, occupation, etc.: *a tribe of thieves.* **3** a group or class of plants or animals.

tribes·man (trībz'mən) member of a tribe. **tribes·men.**

trib·u·la·tion (trĭb'yōō lā'shən) great distress or sorrow; affliction; trial: *the tribulation of war.*

tri·bu·nal (trĭ bū'nəl or trī bū'nəl) **1** court of justice. **2** any final authority: *the tribunal of conscience.*

trib·u·tar·y (trĭb'yōō tĕr'ĭ) **1** stream or river flowing into a larger stream, river, or lake. **2** flowing into another: *a tributary stream.* **3** state or government that pays taxes to or is under the control of a superior government. **4** paying tribute, such as taxes: *a tributary country.* **trib·u·tar·ies.**

trib·ute (trĭb'ūt) **1** stated sum of money or amount of goods paid by one government or ruler to another to obtain protection, insure peace, or fulfill the terms of a treaty. **2** any money exacted for safety or protection: *The gangsters collected tribute from the timid merchant.* **3** an acknowledgment of worth, service rendered, etc.; praise: *The country pays tribute to the memory of George Washington each February 22.*

trick (trĭk) **1** something done in order to deceive or cheat: *His illness was only a trick to avoid school.* **2** to deceive or cheat: *Paul was tricked into buying a worthless ring.* **3** prank; practical joke: *He played a trick on his mother.* **4** foolish or mean act: *the trick of putting salt in the sugar bowl.* **5** a show of skill in order to amuse: *a trick in balancing; a card trick.* **6** particular skill; knack: *The cook knew all the tricks of pleasing hungry boys.* **7** peculiarity of manner; habit: *He had an annoying trick of cracking his knuckles.* **8** the cards played in one round of a game: *She took the trick with her king.* **9** period of duty; shift: *It was Marion's trick at the wheel.* **10** that tricks: *a trick cigar.*

trick out (or **up**) to dress up; array: *all tricked out in Easter clothes.*

trick·er·y (trĭk'ə rĭ) the use of tricks; deception; fraud; cheating. **trick·er·ies.**

trick·le (trĭk'əl) **1** to flow slowly in a thin or broken stream: *Rain trickles from the trees.* **2** to cause to flow slowly: *He trickled sand through his fingers.* **3** thin flow or stream; a trickling: *a trickle of blood; a trickle of people.* **trick·led, trick·ling.**

trick·y (trĭk'ĭ) **1** likely to play tricks; deceitful: *a tricky card player.* **2** not reliable; unpredictable: *a tricky horse.* **trick·i·er, trick·i·est; trick·i·ly.**

tri·col·or (trī'kŭl'ər) **1** having three colors. **2** flag having three large areas of color, especially the flag of France, which is blue, white, and red.

tri·cy·cle (trī'sĭk əl) a three-wheeled vehicle usually worked by pedals, especially one for children.

tri·dent (trī'dənt) a spear with three prongs.

tried (trīd) See **try.** *I tried to phone you but your line was busy.*

Trident

tri·fle (trī'fəl) **1** anything of little value or importance: *He was so occupied with trifles that he didn't pass his examination.* **2** small amount of money: *The toys cost a mere trifle.* **3** a little bit: *a trifle costly.* **4** to spend or waste (time) on frivolous things: *He trifled whole months away.* **5** to talk or

---

fāte, făt, fâre, fär; bē, bĕt; bīte, bĭt; nō, nŏt, nôr; fūse, fŭn, fûr; tōō, tŏŏk; foil; foul; thin; ~~then~~; hw for wh as in *w*hat; zh for s as in u*s*ual; ə for a, e, i, o, u, as in *a*go, lin*e*n, per*i*l, at*o*m, min*u*s

act flippantly or lightly: *This work is not to be* trifled *with.* **6** to play or toy with: *The children only* trifled *with the food on their plates.* **tri·fled, tri·fling.**

tri·fler (trīf'lər) one who trifles and wastes his time on unimportant things; frivolous, superficial person.

tri·fling (trīf'ling) **1** of slight value or importance; trivial: *I cannot have my time taken up by such* trifling *nonsense.* **2** that trifles; shallow; frivolous: *a* trifling *character.* **tri·fling·ly.**

trig·ger (trĭg'ər) **1** on a firearm, a small lever the squeezing of which fires the gun. **2** a catch that springs a trap. **3** to set going; start: *The battle of Lexington* triggered *the American Revolution.*

Trigger

trill (trĭl) **1** quick changes back and forth between two musical tones: *Marie played the piece with many* trills. **2** a similar sound, such as the warble of a bird. **3** to sing, sound, speak, or play with a trill or trills: *The birds* trilled *in the shrubbery.*

trim (trĭm) **1** to make orderly, neat, and tidy by cutting, clipping, etc.: *to* trim *hair or a beard; to* trim *a hedge.* **2** order; condition: *to keep in* trim; *to be in poor* trim. **3** to decorate; adorn: *to* trim *a coat with fur; to* trim *the Christmas tree.* **4** to put into shape; make ready for use: *to* trim *the lumber; to* trim *the wick of a lamp.* **5** to balance (a vessel) by arranging cargo, etc.; to adjust (sails and yards) in position for sailing: *to* trim *the sails.* **6** to defeat: *We* trimmed *our opponents by a good score.* **7** neat; tidy: *a* trim *figure; a* trim *lawn; a* trim *room.* **trimmed, trim·ming; trim·mer, trim·mest; trim·ly.**

trim·ming (trĭm'ing) **1** decoration; ornament, especially on clothes: *the* trimming *on a hat.* **2** the act of one who decorates, arranges, trims, etc. **3 trimmings** (1) parts removed by cutting off the edges: *the* trimmings *of meat.* (2) the side dishes of a meal: *roast goose with all the* trimmings.

Tri·ni·ty (trĭn'ə tĭ) union of the Father, Son, and Holy Ghost in one Divine Being.

trin·ket (trĭng'kĭt) **1** small ornament or jewel. **2** trifle; toy.

tri·o (trē'ō) **1** in music, a composition for three voices or three instruments. **2** group

of three singers or musicians. **3** any group of three. **tri·os.**

trip (trĭp) **1** journey; voyage: *He took a flying* trip *to Brazil.* **2** to catch one's foot in something; stumble: *to* trip *over a footstool; to* trip *on the stairs.* **3** to cause to stumble and fall: *Bud* tripped *Sidney with his foot.* **4** a stumble: *a* trip *on the stairs.* **5** to make a mistake: *He* tripped *on the arithmetic problem.* **6** to cause to make an indiscreet or foolish mistake: *His vanity has* tripped *him up more than once.* **7** a slip; mistake: *There are several bad* trips *in this homework.* **tripped, trip·ping.**

tripe (trĭp) part of the stomach of an ox or cow, used for food.

tri·ple (trĭp'əl) **1** having three parts; threefold: *a* triple *picture frame.* **2** three times as much or as many: *to charge a* triple *price.* **3** an amount three times as much or as many: *In that shop you pay* triple *what you would pay elsewhere.* **4** to make or become three times as much or as many: *to* triple *the output of work; property that will* triple *in value.* **tri·pled, tri·pling; tri·ply.**

tri·plet (trĭp'lĭt) **1** any one of three children born at one birth. **2** set of three things.

tri·pod (trī'pŏd) **1** a support or stand with three legs, as for a camera or the like. **2** any article with three legs, such as a stool.

trite (trīt) worn out by too frequent use; commonplace; stale: *such a* trite *expression; his* trite *remarks.* **trite·ly.**

Tripod

tri·umph (trī'əmf) **1** victory; conquest; achievement; success: *the* triumph *of knowledge.* **2** to be victorious or successful: *to* triumph *over great odds.* **3** in ancient Rome, a spectacular parade and celebration in honor of a returning victorious general and his army. **4** joy over success, victory, etc.: *shouts of* triumph. **5** to rejoice in success, victory, etc.

tri·um·phal (trī ŭm'fəl) in celebration or memory of a victory or triumph: *a* triumphal *feast; a* triumphal *arch.*

tri·um·phant (trī ŭm'fənt) **1** victorious. **2** rejoicing or showing elation over having been successful or victorious: *a* triumphant *march.* **tri·um·phant·ly.**

triv·i·al (trĭv′ĭ əl) **1** insignificant; unimportant; of little value; paltry: *a trivial remark.* **2** ordinary; commonplace: *the trivial tasks of everyday life.* **triv·i·al·ly.**

trod (trŏd) See **tread.** *He trod wearily back to the farmhouse.*

trod·den (trŏd′ən) See **tread.** *The cattle have trodden down the new corn.*

¹troll (trōl) **1** to sing with a rolling tone, in a lighthearted way, the different parts for different voices in succession, until finally everyone is singing together: *They merrily trolled "Three Blind Mice."* **2** a round, or part song. **3** to fish by dragging the line through the water, as from a moving boat: *We trolled the river for pike.* **4** rod, line, etc., used in trolling. [¹troll is from an Old French word (troller) meaning "to ramble."]

²troll (trōl) in Scandinavian folklore, an ugly giant or, in later tales, an impish dwarf who was supposed to live in caves, hills, and such places. [²troll is probably from an Old Norse word of the same spelling.]

trol·ley (trŏl′ĭ) **1** an electric streetcar. Also called **trolley car.** **2** the grooved wheel, at the end of a pole on a streetcar, which makes contact with an overhead wire. **3** a wheeled carriage, basket, etc., that runs suspended from an overhead track.

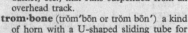

Electric trolley

trom·bone (trŏm′bōn or trŏm bōn′) a kind of horn with a U-shaped sliding tube for varying the tone.

Trombone

troop (trōōp) **1** large number, group, company, or collection of people or animals: *a troop of tourists.* **2** to flock together; move in large numbers: *Crowds trooped out of the skating rink when it closed.* **3** military group, usually of armored cavalry. **4** in the Boy Scouts and the Girl Scouts, a group consisting of from two to four patrols (from 16 to 32 scouts). **5 troops** soldiers. (Homonym: troupe)

troop·er (trōō′pər) member of a troop of mounted or motorized, police or soldiers: *State troopers directed traffic around the accident.*

tro·phy (trō′fĭ) **1** anything captured in battle and kept as a token of victory, such as a gun or flag. **2** token of achievement; prize: *a tennis trophy; a hunter's trophy.* **tro·phies.**

trop·i·cal (trŏp′ə kəl) of or like the tropics: *a tropical plant; a tropical climate.* **trop·i·cal·ly.**

Trop·ic of Can·cer (trŏp′ĭk ŏv kăn′sər) an imaginary circle around the earth, north of the equator and forming the northern limit of the tropics.

Trop·ic of Cap·ri·corn (trŏp′ĭk ŏv kăp′rə kôrn′) an imaginary circle around the earth, south of the equator and forming the southern limit of the tropics.

trop·ics (trŏp′ĭks) the region of the earth lying between the Tropic of Cancer and the Tropic of Capricorn, formerly called the "Torrid Zone." *The tropics are warm the year round except at high altitudes.*

trop·o·sphere (trŏp′ə sfîr′) the layer of the atmosphere next to the earth and below the stratosphere; the region of the air where clouds form.

trot (trŏt) **1** jogging gait of a horse when the right front foot and the left hind foot are raised first, and then the other two feet. A trot is faster than a walk but slower than a canter or gallop. **2** to cause a horse to move with this gait: *He trotted the horse to the starting line for the race.* **3** to move with such a gait: *The horses trotted to the fence.* **4** a jogging run: *The children came at a trot.* **5** to move with a jogging gait: *The little boy trotted to his mother's side.* **trot·ted, trot·ting.**

troth (trôth or trōth) **1** old-fashioned word for faith, loyalty, or truth: *I swear by my troth.* **2 plight one's troth** to pledge one's word to marry; become engaged.

trou·ble (trŭb′əl) **1** disturbance; commotion: *The police rushed to the scene of trouble.* **2** a distress; worry: *He is having money troubles.* **3** to worry or disturb: *He is troubled by debt.* **4** an inconvenience;

---

fāte, făt, fâre, fär; bē, bĕt; bīte, bĭt; nō, nŏt, nôr; fūse, fŭn, fûr; tōō, tŏŏk; foil; foul; thin; ~~then~~;
hw for wh as in *what*; zh for s as in u*s*ual; ə for a, e, i, o, u, as in *a*go, lin*e*n, per*i*l, at*o*m, min*u*s

effort; bother: *Please don't go to any* trouble *for me.* **5** to inconvenience; pester; bother: *May I* trouble *you for a match?* **6** difficulty: *the* trouble *with your plan; in* trouble *at home.* **7** ailment: *heart* trouble; *stomach* trouble. **trou·bled, trou·bling.**

trou·bled (trŭb′əld) distressed; worried; disturbed: *His* troubled *look told me that something was wrong.*

trou·ble·some (trŭb′əl səm) annoying; causing trouble; difficult: *a* troublesome *child; a* troublesome *problem.* **trou·ble·some·ly.**

trough (trôf or trŏf) **1** long, narrow container to hold water or food for animals. **2** similar container for kneading dough or washing ore. **3** uncovered gutter for draining water. **4** hollow (between waves): *He watched the gulls floating in the* troughs *of the sea.*

trounce (trouns) **1** to whip severely: *His father* trounced *him for lying.* **2** to beat thoroughly in a game or argument. **trounced, trounc·ing.**

troupe (trōōp) group of people, especially of performers. (Homonym: troop)

trou·sers (trou′zərz) two-legged outer garment worn from the waist to the ankles; long pants.

trous·seau (trōō sō′ or trōō′sō) the clothes, linens, etc., that a bride collects in preparation for her wedding. **trous·seaux** or **trous·seaus.**

trout (trout) any of several fresh-water food or game fishes of the salmon family, as the brook trout, the lake trout, the rainbow trout. pl. **trout;** rarely, **trouts.**

Brook trout, about 1 ft. long

trow (trō) old-fashioned word for "believe" or "suppose."

trow·el (trou′əl) a small, short-handled shovel of varying shape, used by masons, plasterers, and gardeners.

GARDEN

MASON'S
Trowels

Troy (troi) an ancient city in NW Turkey, site of the Trojan War.

troy weight (troi wāt) system of weights for precious metals and gems, in which twelve ounces equal one pound.

tru·ant (trōō′ənt) **1** child who stays away from school without permission. **2** person who shirks work. **3** idle; errant. **4 play tru·ant** to stay away from school, work, etc.

truce (trōōs) temporary peace or rest, especially during a war by mutual agreement.

¹truck (trŭk) **1** a large vehicle for carrying heavy loads: *We sent the machinery across the country by* truck. **2** a small vehicle operated by hand or motor and used for carrying boxes, baggage, etc., especially in a factory, on a wharf, or the like: *Pete wheeled the bale to the loading platform on a* truck. **3** the group of wheels and their frame at each end of a railroad car. **4** to move or carry by truck: *He* trucked *the goods to Chicago.* [**¹truck** is probably from a Greek word (trochos) meaning "wheel." This Greek word is formed from another Greek word (trechein) meaning "to run."]

Hand truck

²truck (trŭk) **1** to deal with; trade. **2** garden vegetables raised for market. **3** having to do with such gardening: *a* truck *farmer.* **4** dealings; traffic: *I will have no* truck *with him.* **5** trash; rubbish: *Let's get rid of the* truck *in the attic.* [**²truck** is from an Old French word (troquer) meaning "to barter."]

trudge (trŭj) **1** to walk steadily or doggedly, especially to walk wearily. **2** a long, tiring walk. **trudged, trudg·ing.**

true (trōō) **1** according to fact; not false: *She gives a* true *account of what happened.* **2** loyal; faithful: *to be* true *to one's word.* **3** real; genuine: *a* true *gentleman;* true *gold.* **4** corresponding to a standard, etc.; correct; exact: *a* true *color; a* true *copy; a* true *aim.* **5** rightful; legitimate: *the* true *heir to the throne.* **6** truthfully; accurately: *The arrow sped* true *to the mark.* **tru·er, tru·est.**

tru·ly (trōō′li) **1** in a true manner; honestly; faithfully: *Please answer all question.* truly. **2** really; indeed: *I am* truly *sorry about your misfortune.*

trum·pet (trŭm′pit) **1** a brass wind instrument with a looped tube, keys, and a flaring bell. **2** to sound a trumpet. **3** a

770

sound like that of a trumpet, especially the sound an elephant makes. **4** to make the sound an elephant does. **5** to spread widely and noisily, as news, rumor, etc.: *He trumpeted his woes to all who would listen.* **6** something like a trumpet or its sound: *the trumpet call of duty; a trumpet flower.*

Trumpet

trum·pet·er (trŭm′pit ər) person who plays a trumpet.

trun·dle (trŭn′dəl) **1** to make (something) roll along: *Hector trundled his wagon behind him wherever he went.* **2** to roll along: *The empty cart trundled down the hill with a clatter.* **3** a small wheel. **4** a low cart or truck on wheels. **5 trundle bed** low bed on wheels which can be wheeled under a larger bed when not in use. **trun·dled, trun·dling.**

trunk (trŭngk) **1** the main stem of a tree. **2** a box with a hinged cover for storing or moving goods. **3** all the body except the limbs and head. **4** the long nose of an elephant. **5** a main line of a railroad, highway system, nervous system, or the like. **6** like or belonging to a main line: *a trunk line of a railroad.*

Trunk

truss (trŭs) **1** in engineering, a supporting framework of joined triangles. **2** bundle. **3** kind of bandage or belt used to support a weakened part of the body. **4** bundle of hay or straw. **5** to tie securely: *The robbers trussed up their victim.*

TRUSSES

Bridge truss

trust (trŭst) **1** belief in the honesty, justice, or power of someone or something: *We place our trust in God.* **2** to have faith in; be convinced of someone's honesty, fairness, or ability; depend on: *Mother trusts the children's nurse.* **3** to confide in; rely on: *Can I trust you with a secret?* **4** to expect or hope: *I trust you found everything in order when you got home.*

5 confidence; reliance: *to put no trust in the future.* **6** something put into one's care or charge; responsibility: *The child's care was to her a sacred trust.* **7** to give into the care or charge of another: *to trust one's affairs to a lawyer.* **8** property held and managed by one person or concern for the benefit of another. **9** having to do with such property: *a trust fund.* **10** credit given by a business firm: *He got the car on trust.* **11 in trust** in custody or keeping for another: *The house is held in trust by my uncle.*

trus·tee (trŭs tē′) person or concern responsible for the property or affairs of another person, company, or institution.

trust·ful (trŭst′fəl) full of trust; ready to believe in others; trusting: *Jim was too trustful for his own good.* **trust·ful·ly.**

trust·ing (trŭs′tĭng) not suspicious; ready to believe in others: *What a trusting soul he is.* **trust·ing·ly.**

trust·wor·thy (trŭst′wûr′thĭ) reliable; dependable: *Jones is a trustworthy employee.*

trust·y (trŭs′tĭ) **1** reliable; faithful: *His trusty servant had been with him for 20 years.* **2** prisoner who has special privileges because of good behavior. **trust·ies; trust·i·er, trust·i·est; trust·i·ly.**

truth (trооth) **1** the quality of being according to fact; agreement with facts: *His story has the ring of truth.* **2** honesty or sincerity of speech and action: *There is no truth in him.* **3** a generally accepted or proved fact or principle: *the truths of science.* **4 in truth** actually; in fact.

truth·ful (trооth′fəl) **1** telling the truth; honest: *a truthful witness.* **2** true: *a truthful report.* **truth·ful·ly.**

try (trī) **1** to make an effort; to attempt: *Ed tried very hard not to sneeze during the concert.* **2** an effort; an attempt: *We all had a try at pinning the tail on the donkey.* **3** to strain; make demands on: *Noisy Alice tried her mother's patience.* **4** to find out about; test: *You may try this appliance before you buy it.* **5** to place on trial before a court of law; to conduct the trial of (a person or case): *The man was tried for theft and found guilty. Judge Brown will try that case.*

---

fāte, făt, fâre, fär; bē, bĕt; bite, bit; nō, nŏt, nôr; fūse, fŭn, fûr; tōо, tоŏk; foil; foul; thin; ~~then~~; hw for wh as in *what*; zh for s as in usual; ə for a, e, i, o, u, as in ago, linen, peril, atom, minus

try on to put on and test the appearance or fit of: *to* try on *new shoes.*

try out to test or be tested.

tries; tried, try·ing.

try·ing (trī′ĭng) annoying; tiresome; distressing: *a* trying *climate; a* trying *child.*

try·ing·ly.

try·out (trī′out′) a test of fitness (for something): *the* tryouts *for the glee club.*

tset·se fly (tsĕt′sĭ flī) any of several kinds of African biting flies, one of which is a carrier of the germs of sleeping sickness.

Tub

T-shirt (tē′shûrt′) a light, short-sleeved sport shirt or undershirt.

tub (tŭb) **1** large, round vessel of wood or metal used to hold water for washing clothes, bathing, etc. **2** bathtub. **3** a bath: *Alec takes a cold* tub *every morning.* **4** a wooden container like a large covered wooden pail for holding lard and the like. **5** the amount such a container holds: *a* tub *of butter.* **6** an unwieldy or run-down ship.

Tuba

tu·ba (tōō′bə or tū′bə) a large, deep-toned horn.

tube (tōōb or tūb) **1** a pipe or hose, especially one of small diameter. **2** something like a hose or pipe: *the bronchial* tubes. **3** metal or plastic cylinder with a screw cap for tooth paste and the like. **4** tunnel. **5** bulb used in X rays, radios, and television sets. **6** test tube.

Radio tube

Test tube

tu·ber (tōō′bər or tū′bər) thick, often edible part of an underground stem, as a potato.

tu·ber·cu·lo·sis (tōō bûr′kyōō lō′sĭs or tū-bûr′kyōō lō′sĭs) contagious disease affecting various parts of the body, especially the lungs.

tuck (tŭk) **1** to draw or gather into folds: *Your sleeves will get wet unless you* tuck *them up.* **2** to put the edges (of a sheet, shirt, etc.) into place: *The nurse taught us how to* tuck *a sheet firmly under a mattress.*

Before you go out, tuck *your shirt in.* **3** to cover or wrap snugly: *When we were little, Mother* tucked *us in every night.* **4** to fit into a small space: *Alice* tucked *her handkerchief into her pocket.* **5** a fold sewn into a garment. **6** to make or sew a fold or folds into something.

Tues. Tuesday.

Tues·day (tōōz′dā or tūz′dā or tōōz′dĭ or tūz′dĭ) third day of the week.

tuft (tŭft) **1** an erect bunch of feathers, grass, or the like: *The* tuft *of feathers on a bluejay's head makes a pretty topknot.* **2** a clump; tight cluster: *The swamps were filled with* tufts *of alder bushes.* **3** fringed threads or a button at the end of a cord drawn through a mattress, cushion, or the like, to hold the filling in place. **4** to decorate or supply with such tufts: *Grandma* tufted *the quilt with red wool yarn.*

tug (tŭg) **1** to pull hard or drag: *He* tugged *at the stuck drawer.* **2** a hard pull: *Molly gave her mother's hand a* tug *when she saw the doll.* **3** a tugboat. **4** one of the straps by which a horse pulls a vehicle; a trace of a harness. **tugged, tug·ging.**

tug·boat (tŭg′bōt′) small, powerful boat used to help large ships into or out of harbors, or to push or pull barges.

tug of war contest of strength in which two teams pull on the rope against each other in an attempt to draw one team across a central mark.

Tugboat

tu·i·tion (tōō ĭsh′ən or tū ĭsh′ən) **1** fee paid to a school for instruction, etc. **2** instruction; teaching.

tu·lip (tōō′lĭp or tū′lĭp) **1** a large, cup-shaped spring flower. **2** the bulb-grown plant which bears these flowers.

tum·ble (tŭm′bəl) **1** to fall suddenly and heavily: *The child* tumbled *down the stairs. The water* tumbled *over the dam.* **2** to roll about: *The children* tumbled *in the grass.* **3** to perform as an acrobat. **4** to cause to fall; throw down: *The*

Tulip

truck driver tumbled *the barrels out of the van.* **5** to move in an awkward, hasty manner: *to* tumble *out of bed.* **tum·bled, tum·bling.**

tum·ble-down (tŭm′bəl doun′) falling apart; in a ruined condition; dilapidated: *We took refuge from the storm in a leaking,* tumble-down *shack.*

tum·bler (tŭm′blər) **1** a stemless drinking glass. **2** the amount such a glass will hold. **3** acrobat who performs somersaults, feats of leaping, balancing, and the like. **4** part of a lock which must be turned to a certain point by a key before the lock will open.

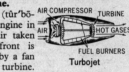
Tumbler

tu·mult (tōō′mŭlt or tū′mŭlt) great disorder; confused uproar; violent agitation: *The rally ended in noisy* tumult.

tu·mul·tu·ous (tōō mŭl′chōō əs or tū mŭl′chōō əs) **1** noisy; excited: *a* tumultuous *crowd.* **2** stormy; tempestuous: *a* tumultuous *sea.* **tu·mul·tu·ous·ly.**

tu·na (tōō′nə) a kind of large food fish found in warm seas. It sometimes grows to a length of 10 feet and a weight of 1,000 pounds. pl. **tu·na;** rarely, **tu·nas.**

tun·dra (tŭn′drə) area of grass, moss, flowering plants, and a few stunted trees, found mostly in high latitudes.

tune (tōōn or tūn) **1** a melody; air. **2** a simple musical composition: *a popular* tune. **3** to give the proper pitch to: *to* tune *a violin.* **4** the right or proper pitch: *to sing out of* tune. **5 in tune** in harmony: *to be* in tune *with the crowd.*

tune in to adjust a radio or television set to the station desired.

tune up to put in proper or good working condition: *to* tune up *an engine.* **tuned, tun·ing.**

tune·ful (tōōn′fəl or tūn′fəl) harmonious; full of tunes; melodious: *a* tuneful *opera.* **tune·ful·ly.**

tung·sten (tŭng′stən) a hard, heavy metal element used in making tool steel and for the filaments in electric lamps.

tu·nic (tōō′nĭk or tū′nĭk) **1** in ancient Greece and Rome, a shirtlike garment. **2** a woman's loose blouse reaching to the

hips. **3** in some military and police uniforms, a short coat.

tuning fork metal fork with two long prongs, that sounds a certain, fixed note when struck. It is used to find the right pitch in singing, etc.

Tuning fork

tun·nel (tŭn′əl) **1** an underground passageway, as for trains, cars, etc., or dug by a burrowing animal. **2** to make or dig such a passageway: *Moles have* tunneled *under our lawn.*

tun·ny (tŭn′ĭ) a kind of fish; the tuna. **tun·nies.**

tur·ban (tûr′bən) **1** an Eastern headdress for men consisting of a scarf wound about the head or about a cap in set folds. A turban is sometimes decorated with jewels. **2** a woman's brimless hat somewhat like this headdress.

Turban

tur·bine (tûr′bin or tûr′bīn) a kind of engine operated by the pressure of water, steam, or air on ridges or fins, called vanes, on the side of a rotating disk. For picture, see **jet engine.**

tur·bo·jet (tûr′bō-jĕt′) **1** jet engine in which the air taken in at the front is compressed by a fan driven by a turbine. The turbine is driven by hot gases passing through it at the rear of the engine. **2** airplane driven by such engines.

AIR COMPRESSOR TURBINE
AIR HOT GASES
FUEL BURNERS
Turbojet

tur·bo·prop (tûr′bō prŏp′) jet engine in which part of the power of the burning fuel drives a turbine hooked up to a propeller.

tur·bu·lent (tûr′byōō lənt) **1** disorderly; violent: *The mob was* turbulent *when the police arrived.* **2** disturbed; agitated; stormy, as of water, weather, etc. **tur·bu·lent·ly.**

tu·reen (tōō rēn′ or tū rēn′) large, deep, bowl-shaped or oval dish, with a lid, from which soup is served.

Tureen

---

fāte, făt, fâre, fär; bē, bĕt; bīte, bĭt; nō, nŏt, nôr; fūse, fŭn, fûr; tōō, tŏŏk; foil; foul; thin; ~~then~~; hw for wh as in *wh*at; zh for s as in u*s*ual; ə for a, e, i, o, u, as in *a*go, lin*e*n, per*i*l, at*o*m, min*u*s

turf

turf (tûrf) **1** a surface layer of earth and grass. **2** a track for horse racing.

tur·key (tûr′ki) **1** native American bird, now bred in large flocks for the market. Male turkeys may weigh over 30 pounds. **2** the flesh of this bird used as food.

Domestic turkey, about 4 ft. long

tur·moil (tûr′moil) disturbance; commotion; uproar; tumult: *the turmoil of a busy market.*

turn (tûrn) **1** to move round; rotate: *A wheel turns. The earth turns.* **2** to cause to move round or rotate: *to turn a wheel; to turn a key.* **3** act of rotating; single revolution: *The wheel made three turns and stopped.* **4** to do by a rotating motion: *to turn a somersault.* **5** to change direction or position: *The path turns into the wood. He turned to face me.* **6** a change of direction or position: *a turn in the road.* **7** to go around: *to turn a corner.* **8** to cause to go; send: *She turned the tramp from the door.* **9** to change in condition: *Leaves turn in the autumn. The milk turned sour. The girl turned pale. The dog turned friendly.* **10** a change in condition: *a turn for the worse; a turn in the weather; a turn of luck.* **11** to change one's attitude: *He turned against his friend.* **12** to spoil or sour: *The hot weather turned the cream.* **13** to change (something) into something else: *to turn cream into butter; to turn failure into success.* **14** to reverse (the sides of): *to turn a page; to turn the collar of a shirt.* **15** to unsettle or upset: *That smell turned my stomach.* **16** to seem to whirl or spin: *My head is turning.* **17** a shock: *The shriek in the night gave us quite a turn.* **18** time or opportunity to do something after someone else: *It's your turn to ride the pony.* **19** to depend; hinge: *Our business turns on the tourist trade.* **20** deed; act: *One good turn deserves another.* **21** short walk or ride, for exercise or pleasure: *a turn in the park.* **22 by turns** one after another. **23 in turn** in order: *You must get on the bus in turn.* **24 to a turn** just right; perfectly: *The roast was done to a turn.*

turpentine

turn down 1 to reject; refuse. **2** to fold back or over: *to turn down a card.*

turn in 1 to go to bed. **2** to return: *All library books must be turned in today.* **3** to exchange: *to turn in an old car for a new.*

turn off to cause to stop working; shut off: *Please turn off the radio.*

turn on 1 to start the flow of: *to turn on the water.* **2** to attack or oppose suddenly.

turn out 1 to put out or shut off: *Have you turned out the lights?* **2** to put outside: *We turned out the cat for the night.* **3** to come or go out; assemble: *Everyone turned out for the wedding.* **4** to produce: *This factory turns out shoes.* **5** to prove to be; result: *It turned out he was not the man for the job.* **6** to dress: *She was turned out in her best clothes.*

turn over 1 to hand over: *He turned over the money to me.* **2** to think about; ponder: *She turned it over in her mind.*

turn up to arrive: *to turn up late.*

tur·nip (tûr′nəp) **1** the rounded, edible root, white or yellow, of a certain plant, the leaves of which may also be cooked and eaten. **2** the plant.

turn·out (tûrn′out′) gathering of people (for some occasion or event): *There was a large turnout for the concert.*

Turnips

turn·o·ver (tûrn′ō′vər) **1** a turning over; an upset. **2** pie or tart made by turning half the crust back over the filling. **3** number or quantity of people or things gone and replaced: *the turnover of guests in a hotel; the fast turnover of goods in a store.*

turn·pike (tûrn′pik′) **1** road on which tolls were or are collected. **2** a station where tolls are collected. **3** a main highway.

turn·spit (tûrn′spit′) person or mechanical device that turns a spit.

turn·stile (tûrn′stil′) gate of bars crossed at right angles which turns on a central post, allowing one person to pass through at a time.

tur·pen·tine (tûr′pən tin′) **1** a light-yellow oil obtained from the sap of certain trees including the pine and fir, used in paints, varnish, and certain medicines. **2** the sap from which this oil is obtained.

Turnstile

tur·quoise (tûr′kwoiz or tûr′koiz) **1** a blue or blue-green stone used in jewelry. **2** the color of this stone; blue-green.

tur·ret (tûr′it) **1** small tower built into the corner of a building or larger tower. **2** low, round, rotating structure on a ship or in a fort, from which big guns are fired.

Turrets

tur·tle (tûr′təl) **1** an animal, the body of which is encased in a horny round or oval shell into which its head and legs may be drawn for protection. **2** especially such an animal living mostly in water.

Spotted turtle, about 5 in. long

tusk (tŭsk) a long tooth that sticks out of the mouth, as in an elephant or wild boar. The tusks of elephants furnish ivory.

tus·sle (tŭs′əl) **1** to struggle; wrestle: *The two children tussled over the rag doll.* **2** a struggle; a scuffle: *The boys got into a tussle over the football.* **tus·sled, tus·sling.**

tut (tŭt) an exclamation of annoyance, rebuke, or impatience.

Tusks

tu·tor (tōō′tər or tū′tər) **1** private teacher: *He had a tutor during the summer.* **2** to teach or instruct privately.

TV (tē′vē′) television.

twain (twān) old-fashioned word for **two**: *Naught shall come between us twain.*

twang (twăng) **1** to make or cause to make a sharp, ringing sound: *The string twanged as it broke.* **2** a sharp, ringing sound. **3** a nasal tone of voice: *He spoke with a twang.* **4** to speak with such a tone.

'twas (twŏz or twŭz) it was: *He quoted, "'Twas the night before Christmas."*

tweed (twēd) soft woolen cloth with a rough surface, usually woven from yarns of different colors.

twelfth (twĕlfth) **1** next after 11th; 12th. **2** one of 12 equal parts.

twelve (twĕlv) one more than 11; 12.

twelve·month (twĕlv′mŭnth′) a year.

twen·ti·eth (twĕn′tĭ ith) **1** next after 19th; 20th. **2** one of 20 equal parts.

twen·ty (twĕn′tĭ) one more than 19; 20. **twen·ties.**

'twere (twûr) it were.

twice (twis) **1** two times: *The doctor visited twice a day.* **2** two times over; doubly: *He made twice the money working overtime.*

twid·dle (twĭd′əl) to turn or twirl idly round and round: *I just sit and twiddle my thumbs,* **twid·dled, twid·dling.**

twig (twĭg) small branch or shoot of a tree or plant.

twi·light (twi′lit′) **1** the period of half-light just after sunset and before dusk. **2** period of time marking the dying out or end of something: *In the twilight of his life, he wrote his memoirs.* **3** done or happening during twilight: *a twilight baseball game.* **4** resembling twilight: *his twilight years.*

'twill (twĭl) it will.

twin (twĭn) **1** either of two children or animals born at one birth. **2** one of two persons or things that are very much alike: *This vase is the twin of that one.* **3** forming or being one of a closely connected pair: *a twin peak; twin beds.*

twine (twĭn) **1** strong, twisted thread or string made up of two or more strands. **2** to twist; wind: *The girls twined flowers into a garland. The snake twined around the tree trunk.* **twined, twin·ing.**

twinge (twĭnj) **1** sudden, sharp pain of mind or body: *a twinge of conscience; a muscular twinge.* **2** to have a sudden sharp pain. **twinged, twing·ing.**

twin·kle (twĭng′kəl) **1** to sparkle or flicker with light: *The stars twinkled dimly. Her eyes twinkled with merriment.* **2** to move quickly and lightly: *The dancer's feet twinkled to and fro.* **3** a flicker of light; sparkle; gleam: *a merry twinkle in his eye.* **twin·kled, twin·kling.**

twirl (twûrl) **1** to make rapid turns; rotate; spin: *Autumn leaves twirled in the wind.* **2** to cause to turn rapidly around: *The seal*

fāte, făt, fâre, fär; bē, bĕt; bīte, bĭt; nō, nŏt, nôr; fūse, fŭn, fûr; tōō, tŏŏk; foil; foul; thin; ~~then~~; hw for wh as in *wh*at; zh for s as in u*s*ual; ə for a, e, i, o, u, as in *a*go, lin*e*n, per*i*l, at*o*m, min*u*s

775

twirled *the ball on his nose.* **3** a twist, spin, or whirl: *She gave her baton a* twirl.

twist (twist) **1** a turn: *He gave the wheel a* twist *to avoid the car ahead.* **2** to twine or wind: *to* twist *a scarf around the neck.* **3** to wrench by turning: *He* twisted *his leg playing football.* **4** a wrench, as of a muscle: *a* twist *of the ankle.* **5** to wind or turn in a curve: *The road* twisted *to the right.* **6** to wind together: *Strands are* twisted *to make a rope.* **7** a sharp turn: *a twist in the road.* **8** to distort the meaning of: *You are* twisting *my words.* **9** to distort (the face, etc.): *His mouth was* twisted *in disgust* **10** unexpected turn (of action, speech, etc.): *a new twist to an old plot.* **11** mental tendency; bias: *a poetic twist of mind.*

twitch (twich) **1** to move in a quick, jerky manner: *He nervously* twitched *his fingers.* **2** to jerk; pull at suddenly: *Impatiently she* twitched *the cloth from the table.* **3** brief, involuntary spasm of a muscle: *a facial* twitch. **4** short pull or jerk.

twit·ter (twit′ər) **1** to make a series of short, sharp sounds; chirp: *The canary* twittered *in its cage.* **2** rapid series of short, sharp sounds; a chirping. **3** state of restless excitement; flutter: *She was in a* twitter.

two (too͞) one more than one; 2. (Homonyms: to, too)

two·fold (too͞′fōld′) **1** having two parts; double: *a twofold answer.* **2** two times as much; doubly: *He increased it* twofold.

two·pence (tŭp′əns) **1** in England, the sum of two pennies. **2** former British coin of this value.

'twould (twood͞) it would.

ty·ing (tī′ing) See **tie**. *He is* tying *his tie.*

type (tīp) **1** kind; sort: *A man of that type always likes children.* **2** to classify: *The actor was* typed *for comic parts.* **3** a group or division that share common characteristics: *boys of the athletic type.* **4** to write with a typewriter. **5** a piece of metal, etc., with a raised letter or figure on the end, used in printing. **6** the impression made from such pieces: *a line of italic type.* **7** a

ROMAN

ITALIC

BOLD FACE

Type and type faces

number or quantity of such pieces: *We bought 50 pounds of* type. **typed, typ·ing.**

type·writ·er (tīp′rī′tər) machine that prints letters upon a sheet of paper when keys marked with the same letters are struck by the operator's fingers.

ty·phoid (tī′foid′) serious, contagious disease carried by flies, impure water, etc. Also called **typhoid fever.**

ty·phoon (tī foon͞′) name for hurricane in the western Pacific area.

ty·phus (tī′fəs) serious disease carried by rat fleas and the body louse. Also called **typhus fever.**

typ·i·cal (tip′i kəl) **1** having the traits of its kind or type; representative: *a* typical *school library.* **2** characteristic of its type: *He gave one of his* typical *long-winded answers.* **typ·i·cal·ly.**

typ·i·fy (tip′ə fī′) **1** to be typical of; represent: *Kit Carson* typifies *the pioneer.* **2** to be a symbol of; symbolize: *The eagle* typifies *the United States.* **typ·i·fied, typ·i·fy·ing.**

typ·ist (tī′pist) person who operates a typewriter, especially a person employed to do this: *The company hired ten* typists.

ty·pog·ra·phy (tī pŏg′rə fī) **1** the art or work of printing. **2** the arrangement or appearance of printed matter.

ty·ran·ni·cal (tī răn′i kəl) of or like a tyrant; cruel and unjust: *a tyrannical dictator.* **ty·ran·ni·cal·ly.**

tyr·an·nize (tĭr′ə nīz′) to be or act like a tyrant: *He* tyrannizes *over his children.* **tyr·an·nized, tyr·an·niz·ing.**

ty·ran·no·sau·rus (tī răn′ə sôr′əs) a huge and fierce, meat-eating dinosaur that lived in North America millions of years ago. It had powerful hind legs and stood upright.

tyr·an·nous (tĭr′ə nəs) cruel and unjust; tyrannical. **tyr·an·nous·ly.**

tyr·an·ny (tĭr′ə nĭ) **1** cruel, unjust treatment; oppression: *To deny us the vote is* tyranny. **2** any harsh and unjust rule or government: *Nazi Germany was a* tyranny. **tyr·an·nies.**

ty·rant (tī′rənt) **1** cruel, unjust ruler or master. **2** absolute monarch; despot.

ty·ro (tī′rō) beginner at learning or doing something; novice: *Tom is a* tyro *at skiing.* **ty·ros.**

tzar (zär) czar.

U

U, u (ū) 21st letter of the English alphabet.

U-boat (ū'bōt') German submarine.

ud·der (ŭd'ər) large gland of a cow, sheep, goat, etc., which produces milk.

ugh (ōō and various other sounds) exclamation expressing horror, disgust, or the like.

ug·li·ness (ŭg'lĭ nĭs) a being ugly.

ugly (ŭg'lĭ) **1** very unpleasant to the sight: *an* ugly *face.* **2** disagreeable: *an* ugly *task;* ugly *news.* **3** threatening; dangerous: *an* ugly *sky; an* ugly *tone of voice.* **4** cross; quarrelsome: *an* ugly *temper.* **ug·li·er, ug·li·est; ug·li·ly.**

u·ku·le·le (ū'kə lā'lĭ) small guitar with four strings.

ul·ti·mate (ŭl'tə mĭt) **1** final; last: *his* ultimate *goal; the* ultimate *result of his actions.* **2** basic; fundamental: *some* ultimate *truths.* **ul·ti·mate·ly.**

ul·tra- prefix meaning (1) "beyond": ultraviolet. (2) "excessively"; "very": ultramodern.

ul·tra·mod·ern (ŭl'trə mŏd'ərn) extremely modern: *an* ultramodern *structure;* ultramodern *tastes.*

ul·tra·son·ic (ŭl'trə sŏn'ĭk) of sound, higher than can be heard by the human ear.

ul·tra·vi·o·let rays (ŭl'trə vī'ə lĭt rāz) **1** radiant energy that is somewhat similar to violet light but is invisible because of shorter wave lengths. **2** ultraviolet having to do with such rays.

um·brel·la (ŭm brĕl'ə) a circular waterproof cloth cover spread on metal ribs attached to the end of a sticklike handle, used as a protection against sun or rain.

u·mi·ak (ōō'mĭ ăk') a long, open, Eskimo boat made of skins stretched on a frame. It is propelled by a number of paddlers. Also written **umiack** and **oomiak.**

um·pire (ŭm'pīr') **1** person who acts as a judge in a dispute, especially in settling the rules and score of a game. **2** to act as an umpire. **um·pired, um·pir·ing.**

un- prefix meaning (1) "not," "the opposite," or "lack of": unlucky; unemployment. (2) "to do the opposite of": unlock.

un·a·ble (ŭn ā'bəl) not able.

un·ac·cent·ed (ŭn ăk'sĕn tĭd or ŭn'ăk sĕn'tĭd) not accented or stressed. The "-or" in "doctor" is unaccented.

un·ac·count·a·ble (ŭn'ə koun'tə bəl) **1** impossible to account for or explain; strange; odd: *an* unaccountable *delay; a man of* unaccountable *moods.* **2** not responsible: *The poor fellow is* unaccountable *for his actions.* **un·ac·count·a·bly.**

un·ac·cus·tomed (ŭn'ə kŭs'təmd) **1** not accustomed; unused (to): *He is* unaccustomed *to heavy work.* **2** not customary; unusual: *the boy's* unaccustomed *interest.*

un·aid·ed (ŭn ā'dĭd) not aided; without help: *Joel did the task* unaided.

u·nan·i·mous (ū năn'ə məs) **1** united in a single opinion; agreeing: *We were* unanimous *in our approval.* **2** with no dissent: *a* unanimous *vote.* **u·nan·i·mous·ly.**

un·armed (ŭn ärmd') not armed; lacking weapons; defenseless.

un·as·sum·ing (ŭn'ə sōō'mĭng or ŭn'ə sū'mĭng) modest; retiring; not given to pushing oneself forward. **un·as·sum·ing·ly.**

un·at·tend·ed (ŭn'ə tĕn'dĭd) **1** without an escort; alone: *Mrs. Roberts is going to the concert* unattended. **2** receiving no attention or care; without supervision: *The shop was left* unattended.

un·a·vail·ing (ŭn'ə vā'lĭng) without result or effect; useless: *Her calls for help were* unavailing. **un·a·vail·ing·ly.**

un·a·void·a·ble (ŭn'ə voi'də bəl) impossible to escape or overcome: *an* unavoidable *delay.* **un·a·void·a·bly.**

un·a·ware (ŭn'ə wâr') not conscious; ignorant: *I was* unaware *of your presence.*

un·a·wares (ŭn'ə wârz') **1** without being aware: *He walked into the surprise party*

Ukulele

Umbrella

fāte, făt, fâre, fär; bē, bĕt; bīte, bĭt; nō, nŏt, nôr; fūse, fŭn, fûr; tōō, tŏŏk; foil; foul; thin; ~~then~~; hw for wh as in *what*; zh for s as in u*s*ual; ə for a, e, i, o, u, as in *a*go, lin*e*n, per*i*l, at*o*m, min*u*s

unawares. 2 without being expected: *You came upon me* unawares.

un·bar (ŭn bär') to remove a bar or bars (from a gate or door); open; unlock: *The farmer* unbarred *the door to the corncrib.* **un·barred, un·bar·ring.**

un·bear·a·ble (ŭn bâr'ə bəl) not bearable; intolerable; impossible to endure: *an* unbearable *pain.* **un·bear·a·bly.**

un·be·com·ing (ŭn'bĭ kŭm'ĭng) 1 unsuitable; improper; unworthy: *her* unbecoming *conduct.* 2 inappropriate; not flattering: *an* unbecoming *hat.* **un·be·com·ing·ly.**

un·be·liev·ing (ŭn'bĭ lē'vĭng) 1 not believing; doubting; incredulous. 2 not accepting religious teachings. **un·be·liev·ing·ly.**

un·bend (ŭn běnd') 1 to straighten or become straight: *to* unbend *one's legs after a long ride.* 2 to relax; become less severe; be informal: *He* unbent *enough to say hello to everybody.* **un·bent, un·bend·ing.**

un·bi·ased or **un·bi·assed** (ŭn bī'əst) not biased; not taking sides; free from prejudice; impartial: *an* unbiased *opinion.*

un·bid·den (ŭn bĭd'ən) 1 not asked; not invited: *He came* unbidden *to our party.* 2 not ordered; not commanded.

un·bind (ŭn bīnd') to untie; unfasten; set free. **un·bound, un·bind·ing.**

un·bolt (ŭn bōlt') to withdraw a bolt (of a door); unlock.

un·born (ŭn bôrn') not yet born; future; still to come: *the* unborn *generation.*

un·bound (ŭn bound') 1 not tied; free: *The* unbound *pony galloped across the field.* 2 not confined or limited: *a man* unbound *by custom.* 3 of a book, having pages not fastened together or not bound between covers. 4 See **unbind.** *He* unbound *me.*

un·bound·ed (ŭn boun'dĭd) without limits; boundless.

un·bro·ken (ŭn brō'kən) 1 not broken; not damaged: *an* unbroken *toy.* 2 without interruption: *an* unbroken *dry spell.* 3 not tamed or trained: *an* unbroken *colt.*

un·buck·le (ŭn bŭk'əl) to undo or unfasten the buckle of: *to* unbuckle *a belt.* **un·buck·led, un·buck·ling.**

un·but·ton (ŭn bŭt'ən) to undo the button or buttons of; open: *to* unbutton *a coat.*

un·called-for (ŭn kôld'fôr') not necessary; out of place: *rude,* uncalled-for *remarks.*

un·can·ny (ŭn kăn'ĭ) 1 not to be explained by reason: *His knowledge of my past seemed* uncanny. 2 mysterious; strange; weird: *an* uncanny *silence.* **un·can·ni·ly.**

un·ceas·ing (ŭn sē'sĭng) without stop; continuous: *The noise of traffic in the city is* unceasing. **un·ceas·ing·ly.**

un·cer·tain (ŭn sûr'tən) 1 not certain; not sure; doubtful: *I am* uncertain *of the answer. This butter is of* uncertain *quality.* 2 not dependable; not predictable: *The weather is* uncertain. **un·cer·tain·ly.**

un·cer·tain·ty (ŭn sûr'tən tĭ) lack of certainty; doubt: *There was some* uncertainty *about the date.* **un·cer·tain·ties.**

un·chain (ŭn chān') to unfasten the chain of; set free: *to* unchain *a door;* unchain *a dog.*

un·change·a·ble (ŭn chān'jə bəl) impossible or unlikely to be changed: *His honesty is* unchangeable. **un·change·a·bly.**

un·changed (ŭn chānjd') not changed; the same: *My feelings are* unchanged.

un·civ·i·lized (ŭn sĭv'ə līzd') not civilized; barbaric; savage: *an* uncivilized *manner;* uncivilized *tribes.*

un·clasp (ŭn klăsp') 1 to undo the clasp of: *to* unclasp *a brooch.* 2 to let go of; release: *to* unclasp *one's grasp.* 3 to come open: *The buckle of my boot* unclasped.

un·cle (ŭng'kəl) 1 the brother of one's father or mother. 2 the husband of one's aunt.

un·clean (ŭn klēn') 1 not clean; dirty: *hands* unclean *from work.* 2 impure; sinful. **un·clean·ly.**

Uncle Sam 1 the United States of America represented as a tall, slender, old man dressed in the national colors. 2 the United States Government: *We trust* Uncle Sam *to safeguard ourselves and our property.*

Uncle Sam

un·coil (ŭn koil') 1 to unwind: *to* uncoil *a spool of wire.* 2 to become unwound: *The snake* uncoiled.

un·com·fort·a·ble (ŭn kŭm'fər tə bəl) 1 not comfortable: *Are you* uncomfortable *in that chair?* 2 causing discomfort: *Yes, this is an* uncomfortable *chair.* 3 unpleasant; uneasy: *There was an* uncomfortable *silence when he left.* **un·com·fort·a·bly.**

un·com·mon (ŭn kŏm′ən) unusual; rare; extraordinary. **un·com·mon·ly.**

un·com·pro·mis·ing (ŭn kŏm′prə mī′-zĭng) unyielding; firm: *Her honesty is uncompromising.* **un·com·pro·mis·ing·ly.**

un·con·cern (ŭn′kən sûrn′) **1** lack of worry or anxiety: *She showed an amazing uncon·cern when her purse was stolen.* **2** lack of interest; indifference: *He was worried over his son's unconcern about school.*

un·con·cerned (ŭn′kən sûrnd′) not con·cerned; indifferent: *I am unconcerned about your opinions.* **un·con·cern·ed·ly.**

un·con·di·tion·al (ŭn′kən dĭsh′ən əl) with·out any "ifs" or "buts"; without condi·tions; absolute: *an unconditional sur·render; unconditional guarantee.* **un·con·di·tion·al·ly.**

un·con·quer·a·ble (ŭn kŏng′kər ə bəl) not capable of being conquered: *an unconquer·able army; unconquerable courage.* **un·con·quer·a·bly.**

un·con·scious (ŭn kŏn′shəs) **1** not con·scious: *to be unconscious after a bad acci·dent.* **2** without realization; not aware: *to be unconscious of having said the wrong thing.* **3** not deliberate; accidental: *an unconscious insult.* **un·con·scious·ly.**

un·con·sti·tu·tion·al (ŭn′kŏn stə tōō′-shən əl or ŭn′kŏn stə tū′shən əl) not in keeping with the constitution of a country or state. **un·con·sti·tu·tion·al·ly.**

un·con·trol·la·ble (ŭn′kən trō′lə bəl) not capable of being controlled; impossible to check or restrain: *The broncos were uncon·trollable.* **un·con·trol·la·bly.**

un·couth (ŭn kōōth′) **1** ungainly; awk·ward; clumsy: *an uncouth backwoodsman.* **2** crude; vulgar: *to have uncouth manners.* **un·couth·ly.**

un·cov·er (ŭn kŭv′ər) **1** to remove the cover or covering from: *to uncover a dish of food.* **2** to disclose; reveal; lay bare; expose or make known: *The plot was un·covered by the police.* **3** to remove one's hat or cap, as a sign of respect or saluta·tion: *to uncover for a passing funeral.*

un·cul·ti·vat·ed (ŭn kŭl′tə vā′tĭd) **1** not tilled; not cultivated for production of food. **2** not developed; not practiced; neglected: *Jean's talent for art is completely uncultivated.* **3** uncivilized; not refined by education: *the uncultivated tribes.*

un·curl (ŭn kûrl′) **1** to straighten out; to remove the curl as from hair or feathers. **2** to become uncurled; come out of curl: *Betty's hair uncurled in the rain.*

un·daunt·ed (ŭn dôn′tĭd) unafraid; not made fearful; bold: *He was undaunted by the dangers he faced.* **un·daunt·ed·ly.**

un·de·cid·ed (ŭn′dĭ sī′dĭd) **1** not yet de·termined or settled; doubted: *The question of moving to the country is still undecided.* **2** not having made up one's mind; waver·ing: *We are undecided about what to give him for his birthday.* **un·de·cid·ed·ly.**

un·de·ni·a·ble (ŭn′dĭ nī′ə bəl) not to be denied; true or real beyond doubt; obvious: *His good looks are undeniable. Horace is a boy of undeniable talent.* **un·de·ni·a·bly.**

un·der (ŭn′dər) **1** below; beneath: *the cat under a chair; a boat going under a bridge; to stand under a porch.* **2** less than: *costing under $10; children under five years; under ten minutes.* **3** in conformity with; bound by: *to be under the law of the land; under oath; under the conditions of a contract; under obligation.* **4** subject to the action or effort of; in the course of: *to be under doctor's treatment; a road under repair; a plan under consideration.* **5** oppressed by; subjected to: *to labor under tyranny; to break down under grief or loss; under pres·sure or strain; under suspicion.* **6** during the time or rule of: *America under Wash·ington.* **7** in view of; because of: *I can't go under those conditions.* **8** so as to be hidden, covered, etc.: *The ball was sucked under by the current.* **9 go under** to fail; be ruined; fall to a lower position. **10 knuckle under** to submit; surrender. **11 under age** not of legal age. **12 speak under one's breath** to speak in a whisper. **13 under one's nose** clearly visible; right in front of one.

un·der- prefix meaning (1) "beneath," "below": under*ground;* under*water.* (2) "inadequately," "not sufficiently": under*valued;* under*cooked.* (3) "of a lower rank, grade, etc.": under*study;* under*secretary.*

---

fāte, făt, fâre, fär; bē, bĕt; bite, bĭt; nō, nŏt, nôr; fūse, fŭn, fûr; tōō, tŏŏk; foil; foul; thin; then; hw for wh as in *wh*at; zh for s as in u*s*ual; ə for ā, e, i, o, u, as in *a*go, lin*e*n, per*i*l, at*o*m, min*u*s

un·der·brush (ŭn'dər brŭsh') bushes, shrubs, small trees, etc., growing thickly under large trees in a wood or forest; undergrowth.

un·der·clothes (ŭn'dər klōz' or ŭn'dər-klōthz') clothes worn under outer clothing, especially garments worn next to the skin; underwear.

un·der·cur·rent (ŭn'dər kûr'ənt) **1** current flowing below the surface of a body of water. **2** hidden trend or tendency of opinion, feeling, etc.: *An undercurrent of jealousy ran through his apparent friendliness.*

un·der·dog (ŭn'dər dôg' or ŭn'dər dŏg') **1** the losing dog in a dogfight. **2** person or group expected to lose in a struggle.

¹**un·der·es·ti·mate** (ŭn'dər ĕs'tə māt') to estimate at too low a value, rate, amount, etc.; undervalue: *The team underestimated the strength of its opponents.* **un·der·es·ti·mat·ed, un·der·es·ti·mat·ing.**

²**un·der·es·ti·mate** (ŭn'dər ĕs'tə mĭt) an estimate that is too low.

un·der·fed (ŭn'dər fĕd') not properly nourished; given too little or inadequate food.

un·der·foot (ŭn'dər fŏŏt') **1** beneath the feet; on the ground: *It is muddy and slick underfoot.* **2** in the way; in danger of being stepped on: *The puppy is always underfoot.*

un·der·gar·ment (ŭn'dər gär'mənt) an article of underwear.

un·der·go (ŭn'dər gō') **1** to be subjected to; go through: *This country will undergo many changes during the next few years.* **2** to endure; suffer: *to undergo many hardships.* **un·der·went, un·der·gone, un·der·go·ing.**

un·der·gone (ŭn'dər gŏn' or ŭn'dər gôn') See **undergo.**

un·der·ground (ŭn'dər ground') **1** situated below the ground: *an underground passage.* **2** beneath the surface of the earth: *The miners were trapped underground.* **3** secret: *an underground movement or political party.* **4 the underground** a secret group working in a country against the established government.

un·der·growth (ŭn'dər grōth') small trees, shrubs, and vines growing beneath larger trees in a wood or forest, especially those growing in a tangled manner; underbrush.

un·der·hand (ŭn'dər hănd') **1** sly; deceitful; secret; not open or honest: *He used underhand methods to achieve his goal.* **2** with an upward swing of the hand, the palm turned up: *an underhand pitch; to throw underhand.*

un·der·hand·ed (ŭn'dər hăn'dĭd) dishonest; not open and straightforward; deceptive and unfair: *He tried to gain control of the company in an underhanded way.* **un·der·hand·ed·ly.**

un·der·line (ŭn'dər lin' or ŭn'dər lin') **1** to draw a line under. **2** to emphasize: *The tone of his voice underlined the importance of his words.* **un·der·lined, un·der·lin·ing.**

un·der·lin·ing (ŭn'dər li'nĭng) lines drawn under words, usually for emphasis.

un·der·mine (ŭn'dər mĭn' or ŭn'dər mĭn') **1** to dig a hollow or tunnel under; dig beneath. **2** to weaken by wearing away the base of: *The flood undermined our house.* **3** to work against secretly; injure by underhand methods: *to undermine a man's authority.* **4** to weaken; impair; destroy gradually: *Lack of sleep can undermine one's health.* **un·der·mined, un·der·min·ing.**

un·der·neath (ŭn'dər nēth') beneath; below: *a stream flowing underneath a bridge; to lie underneath a tree.*

un·der·pass (ŭn'dər păs') road or passage that goes under a highway, bridge, etc.

un·der·rate (ŭn'dər rāt') to place too low an estimate or value upon: *Don't underrate his ability* **un·der·rat·ed, un·der·rat·ing.**

un·der·sea (ŭn'dər sē') beneath the surface of the sea: *lovely undersea plants;* undersea *oil wells.*

un·der·sell (ŭn'dər sĕl') to sell things at a lower price than (a competitor). **un·der·sold, un·der·sell·ing.**

un·der·shirt (ŭn'dər shûrt') a close-fitting shirt worn next to the skin.

un·der·stand (ŭn'dər stănd') **1** to grasp the meaning of: *I don't understand this book.* **2** to be familiar with; know well: *to understand French; to understand children.* **3** to get the meaning; comprehend: *As often as I've explained, you still don't understand.* **4** to get as information; learn: *I understand that you are taking music lessons.* **5** to accept as a fact: *It is*

understood *you will pay me next week.*
6 to supply mentally something that has been left out: *In the sentence "If you can swim, why can't I?" "swim" is understood after "I."* **un·der·stood, un·der·stand·ing.**

un·der·stand·ing (ŭn′dər stăn′dĭng) **1** a grasping by the mind; knowledge; comprehension: *an understanding of a situation.* **2** ability to comprehend; intelligence: *Your words show that you have great understanding.* **3** knowledge and possible agreement about what each other wants and means: *We will have to come to an understanding over this property settlement.* **4** sympathetic in an intelligent way: *It is understanding of you to listen to my problems.* **un·der·stand·ing·ly.**

un·der·stood (ŭn′dər stŏŏd′) See **understand.** *He understood what I meant.*

un·der·stud·y (ŭn′dər stŭd′ĭ) **1** actor who is prepared to play a role if the actor who usually plays it cannot appear. **2** to learn a part as an understudy: *She understudied the lead in the play.* **3** to act as an understudy to (another actor): *Lucille is understudying a famous actress.* **un·der·stud·ies; un·der·stud·ied, un·der·stud·y·ing.**

un·der·take (ŭn′dər tāk′) **1** to take upon oneself; attempt: *The ambassador undertook the mission to make peace.* **2** to contract to do; promise: *Liza and Joan undertake to bring the food for the picnic.* **un·der·took, un·der·tak·en, un·der·tak·ing.**

un·der·tak·er (ŭn′dər tā′kər) person who makes a business of preparing the dead for burial and conducting funerals.

un·der·tak·ing (ŭn′dər tā′kĭng) something tried or taken up; task: *Weeding the garden is a big undertaking.*

un·der·tone (ŭn′dər tōn′) **1** low tone of voice: *We talked in an undertone so no one else could hear.* **2** undercurrent; emotions, thoughts, feelings that exist, but not openly: *There was an undertone of discontent among the sailors on the ship.* **3** color showing faintly through another color: *an undertone of brown in this pink.*

un·der·took (ŭn′dər tŏŏk′) See **undertake.** *We undertook to do the job ourselves.*

un·der·wa·ter (ŭn′dər wô′tər) happening, growing, or used beneath the surface of the water: *a record for* underwater *swimming; an* underwater *mask; an* underwater *plant.*

un·der·wear (ŭn′dər wâr′) clothing worn underneath outer clothes.

un·der·went (ŭn′dər wĕnt′) See **undergo.** *He* underwent *an operation.*

un·de·served (ŭn′də zûrvd′) not deserved; not merited: *an* undeserved *reward;* undeserved *punishment.* **un·de·serv·ed·ly.**

un·de·sir·a·ble (ŭn′dĭ zi′rə bəl) not desirable; disagreeable; objectionable. **un·de·sir·a·bly.**

un·did (ŭn dĭd′) See **undo.** *I* undid *the buckle of my belt.*

un·dig·ni·fied (ŭn dĭg′nə fīd′) lacking dignity: *He looked* undignified *in his wet clothes.* **un·dig·ni·fied·ly.**

un·dis·put·ed (ŭn′dĭs pū′tĭd) not questioned or doubted; not disputed; accepted: *Your right to the money is* undisputed. **un·dis·put·ed·ly.**

un·dis·turbed (ŭn′dĭs tûrbd′) not disturbed; peaceful; calm: *Let her rest* undisturbed.

un·di·vid·ed (ŭn′dĭ vī′dĭd) not divided; whole; continuous: *an* undivided *tract of land; your* undivided *attention.* **un·di·vid·ed·ly.**

un·do (ŭn dŏŏ′) **1** to loosen; unfasten; open: *Please* undo *this package.* **2** to ruin; bring to ruin: *He is already conceited and this sudden fame will* undo *him.* **3** to do away with; cancel out: *We can't* undo *the damage now.* **un·did, un·done, un·do·ing.**

un·do·ing (ŭn dŏŏ′ĭng) **1** a reversing or canceling out what has been done: *There is no* undoing *the injury done to him.* **2** a doing away with; spoiling: *This delay will cause the* undoing *of all our plans.* **3** cause of ruin: *The late hours he keeps will be his* undoing.

un·done (ŭn dŭn′) **1** not finished; not tied, closed, etc.: *He left the work* undone. *My shoelaces are* undone. **2** ruined: *Our cause is now* undone. **3** See **undo.** *Haven't you* undone *the package yet?*

---

fāte, făt, fâre, fär; bē, bĕt; bite, bĭt; nō, nŏt, nôr; fūse, fŭn, fûr; tōō, tŏŏk; foil; foul; thin; ~~then~~;
hw for wh as in *wh*at; zh for s as in u*s*ual; ə for a, e, i, o, u, as in *a*go, lin*e*n, per*i*l, at*o*m, min*u*s

un·doubt·ed (ŭn dou'tĭd) not questioned; certain: *The boy's* undoubted *ability made us put up with his laziness.* **un·doubt·ed·ly.**

un·dress (ŭn drĕs') **1** to remove one's clothes. **2** to remove the clothes from. **3** not formal: *in* undress *uniform.*

un·due (ŭn dōō' or ŭn dū') **1** more than necessary; excessive: *an* undue *worry.* **2** not right or proper: *Peter's* undue *criticism of his parents.* **un·du·ly.**

un·du·late (ŭn'də lāt' or ŭn'dyŏō lāt') **1** to move in waves, or in a wavelike, curving way: *The wheat field* undulated *under the breeze.* **2** to cause to move in waves, or in a wavelike, curving way: *Wind* undulated *the wheat.* **un·du·lat·ed, un·du·lat·ing.**

un·dy·ing (ŭn dī'ĭng) not dying; unending; eternal; immortal. **un·dy·ing·ly.**

un·earth (ŭn ûrth') **1** to dig out of the ground: *They* unearthed *the buried treasure.* **2** to discover: *to* unearth *important evidence.*

un·earth·ly (ŭn ûrth'lĭ) **1** not of this world; supernatural. **2** eerie: *an* unearthly *cry from inside the cave.*

un·eas·i·ness (ŭn ē'zĭ nĭs) **1** lack of ease or comfort, in mind or body. **2** worry; anxiety.

un·eas·y (ŭn ē'zĭ) **1** not easy in manner; awkward: *He felt* uneasy *in his new surroundings.* **2** anxious; restless; worried: *The violent storm made everyone* uneasy. **3** disturbing: *an* uneasy *suspicion.* **un·eas·i·er, un·eas·i·est; un·eas·i·ly.**

un·em·ployed (ŭn'ĭm ploid') **1** not being used; not in use. **2** out of work. **3** the **unemployed** people out of work.

un·em·ploy·ment (ŭn'ĭm ploi'mənt) a being out of a job; lack of employment.

un·end·ing (ŭn ĕn'dĭng) without end; unceasing: *an* unending *devotion to a cause.* **un·end·ing·ly.**

un·e·qual (ŭn ē'kwəl) **1** not of the same merit, rank, size, number, amount, etc. **2** unbalanced; uneven; unfair: *an* unequal *contest.* **3** not uniform; irregular. **4** **unequal to** not able enough or adequate for: *He was* unequal *to the task.* **un·e·qual·ly.**

un·e·qualed or **un·e·qualled** (ŭn ē'kwəld) not surpassed; supreme: *an* unequaled *achievement.*

un·err·ing (ŭn ûr'ĭng or ŭn ĕr'ĭng) without error; unfailing; correct: *a man* unerring *in his duties.* **un·err·ing·ly.**

un·e·ven (ŭn ē'vən) **1** not smooth or flat; not level: *an* uneven *floor.* **2** not of the same size; not uniform: *The legs of the table were* uneven. **3** not fair: *an* uneven *distribution of profits.* **4** of numbers, having a remainder of one when divided by 2; odd. Three, nine, and seventeen are uneven numbers. **un·e·ven·ly.**

un·e·vent·ful (ŭn'ĭ vĕnt'fəl) without anything important taking place; not eventful; monotonous: *an* uneventful *day.* **un·e·vent·ful·ly.**

un·ex·pect·ed (ŭn'ĕk spĕk'tĭd) not expected; unforeseen: *an* unexpected *thing to say; an* unexpected *pleasure.* **un·ex·pect·ed·ly.**

un·fail·ing (ŭn fā'lĭng) **1** not failing; never running short; inexhaustible: *an* unfailing *supply of food.* **2** faithful; reliable: *an* unfailing *friend.* **un·fail·ing·ly.**

un·fair (ŭn fâr') not fair; unjust: *an* unfair *wage; unfair treatment.* **un·fair·ly.**

un·faith·ful (ŭn fāth'fəl) **1** not faithful; false to a promise or duty; disloyal: *an* unfaithful *friend.* **2** not accurate or exact: *an* unfaithful *copy.* **un·faith·ful·ly.**

un·fa·mil·iar (ŭn'fə mĭl'yər) **1** not familiar; not well known: *an* unfamiliar *face.* **2** not acquainted: *to be* unfamiliar *with the customs of a country.* **un·fa·mil·iar·ly.**

un·fas·ten (ŭn fãs'ən) to undo the fastening of; untie; loosen.

un·fath·om·a·ble (ŭn fãth'əm ə bəl) **1** too deep to measure. **2** impossible to understand, explain, or account for: *an* unfathomable *mystery.*

un·fa·vor·a·ble (ŭn fā'vər ə bəl) **1** not favorable; not helpful; indicating poor results: *an* unfavorable *climate for cotton.* **2** opposing; adverse: *an* unfavorable *decision.* **un·fa·vor·a·bly.**

un·feel·ing (ŭn fē'lĭng) **1** pitiless; hardhearted; cruel: *an* unfeeling *person;* unfeeling *criticism.* **2** not able to feel. **un·feel·ing·ly.**

un·fin·ished (ŭn fĭn'ĭsht) **1** not completed: *some* unfinished *business.* **2** rough; lacking refinement; not polished or finished: *the boy's* unfinished *manners;* unfinished *furniture.*

un·fit (ŭn fĭt') **1** not suitable: *a house* unfit *for this climate.* **2** not worthy; not qualified: *a person* unfit *for high office.*

un·flinch·ing (ŭn flĭn′chĭng) unyielding in the face of danger, pain, or disagreeable duty; steadfast; resolute. **un·flinch·ing·ly.**

un·fold (ŭn fōld′) **1** to open the folds of; to spread out: *to unfold a towel.* **2** to become open, as the petals of a flower. **3** to develop so as to be seen or known: *As the enemy's plan unfolded, we knew he would be hard to stop.* **4** to reveal; tell by degrees: *The spy unfolded his plans.*

un·fore·seen (ŭn′fôr sēn′) not looked for; not expected; not counted on or provided for: *We were delayed by unforeseen interruptions.*

un·for·get·ta·ble (ŭn′fər gĕt′ə bəl) not to be forgotten: *the unforgettable meeting with the president.* **un·for·get·ta·bly.**

un·for·tu·nate (ŭn fôr′chə nĭt) **1** not fortunate; not lucky; having bad fortune: *He is most unfortunate in all his ventures.* **2** regrettable; not suitable: *an unfortunate remark.* **3** unlucky person. **un·for·tu·nate·ly.**

un·found·ed (ŭn foun′dĭd) without basis; not backed by facts: *an unfounded suspicion.*

un·friend·ly (un frĕnd′lĭ) **1** not friendly; hostile: *an unfriendly remark.* **2** not favorable; not pleasant: *an unfriendly climate.*

un·furl (ŭn fûrl′) to unroll; unwind; spread out: *to unfurl an umbrella, sails, a flag, etc.*

un·fur·nished (ŭn fûr′nĭsht) not furnished; without furniture: *an unfurnished apartment.*

un·gain·ly (ŭn gān′lĭ) awkward; clumsy.

un·god·ly (ŭn gŏd′lĭ) wicked; sinful; impious.

un·gra·cious (ŭn grā′shəs) discourteous; rude; unkind. **un·gra·cious·ly.**

un·grate·ful (ŭn grāt′fəl) not thankful; not appreciative: *The boy is ungrateful for all his father's kindness.* **un·grate·ful·ly.**

un·guard·ed (ŭn gär′dĭd) **1** not guarded: *an unguarded doorway.* **2** thoughtless; careless; lacking caution: *She revealed the secret in an unguarded moment.* **un·guard·ed·ly.**

un·guent (ŭng′gwənt) a soothing salve or ointment.

un·hand (ŭn hănd′) to let go of: *The hero shouted, "Unhand that girl!"*

un·hap·pi·ness (ŭn hăp′ĭ nĭs) a lack of pleasure or enjoyment; sadness.

un·hap·py (ŭn hăp′ĭ) **1** sad; sorrowful: *an unhappy child; an unhappy life.* **2** unlucky; unfortunate: *an unhappy meeting; an unhappy result.* **3** not suitable: *an unhappy remark; an unhappy name.* **un·hap·pi·er, un·hap·pi·est; un·hap·pi·ly.**

un·harmed (ŭn härmd′) not harmed; not hurt or injured in any way; safe; undamaged: *Ted escaped from the fire unharmed.*

un·har·ness (ŭn här′nĭs) **1** to remove a harness from. **2** to take off armor.

un·health·ful (ŭn hĕlth′fəl) harmful to health: *A swamp is an unhealthful place to build a house.* **un·health·ful·ly.**

un·health·y (ŭn hĕl′thĭ) **1** not in good physical or mental condition; sickly: *an unhealthy child.* **2** indicating poor health: *an unhealthy appearance.* **3** harmful to health: *an unhealthy climate.* **un·health·i·er, un·health·i·est; un·health·i·ly.**

un·heard (ŭn hûrd′) **1** not heard. **2** not noted or heeded: *Laura let her mother's advice pass unheard.* **3** without a hearing: *to condemn a person unheard.*

un·heard-of (ŭn hûrd′ŏv′ or ŭn hûrd′ŭv′) **1** not heard of before; unknown previously; brand-new: *an unheard-of improvement in transportation.* **2** strange; fantastic: *such unheard-of behavior.*

un·heed·ed (ŭn hē′dĭd) not heeded; not paid attention to; disregarded.

un·heed·ing (ŭn hē′dĭng) not paying attention; careless. **un·heed·ing·ly.**

un·hes·i·tat·ing·ly (ŭn hĕz′ə tā′tĭng lĭ) **1** without delay; at once: *Lawrence unhesitatingly took the dare.* **2** without doubt or reservation; in full confidence: *I unhesitatingly recommend this plan.*

un·hinge (ŭn hĭnj′) **1** to remove from hinges. **2** to put in a state of confusion; upset; unsettle: *The train crash unhinged the poor fellow's mind.* **un·hinged, un·hing·ing.**

un·hitch (ŭn hĭch′) to untie; set (something) free from being hitched; set loose: *to unhitch a horse from a wagon.*

---

fāte, făt, fâre, fär; bē, bĕt; bīte, bĭt; nō, nŏt, nôr; fūse, fŭn, fûr; tōō, tŏŏk; foil; foul; thin; then; hw for wh as in *wh*at; zh for s as in u*s*ual; ə for a, e, i, o, u, as in *a*go, lin*e*n, per*i*l, at*o*m, min*u*s

un·hook (ŭn hŏŏk′) to loosen by, or as by, freeing a hook from an eye, staple, etc.: *Please unhook the screen door.*

un·horse (ŭn hôrs′) to throw or force from the saddle; unseat (a rider). **un·horsed, un·hors·ing.**

un·hurt (ŭn hûrt′) not injured.

u·ni·corn (ū′nə kôrn′) imaginary animal somewhat like a horse but having one long horn on its forehead, the hind legs of an antelope, and the tail of a lion.

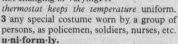

Unicorn

u·ni·form (ū′nə fôrm′) **1** all alike in appearance, quality, quantity, etc. **2** not changing or varying: *A thermostat keeps the temperature* uniform. **3** any special costume worn by a group of persons, as policemen, soldiers, nurses, etc. **u·ni·form·ly.**

u·ni·form·i·ty (ū′nə fôr′mə tĭ) **1** condition of being all the same or alike: *a* uniformity *in customs or ideas;* uniformity *in dress.* **2** continuous sameness: *the* uniformity *of a dull job.*

u·ni·fy (ū′nə fī′) to unite; make into one; cause to act as one: *Resistance to British taxes* unified *the American colonies.* **u·ni·fied, u·ni·fy·ing.**

un·im·por·tant (ŭn′ĭm pôr′tənt) not important; not significant; petty.

un·in·hab·it·ed (ŭn′ĭn hăb′ə tĭd) without inhabitants; not lived on or in: *an* uninhabited *house; an* uninhabited *plain.*

un·in·tel·li·gi·ble (ŭn′ĭn tĕl′ə jə bəl) impossible to understand: *The frightened man made* unintelligible *sounds and gestures.* **un·in·tel·li·gi·bly.**

un·ion (ūn′yən) **1** a joining together or uniting of two or more into one. **2** a joining together or uniting of separate political groups or states under a common government; federation: *the* union *of the American colonies.* **3** a whole thus united: "... *a perfect* union, *one and inseparable.*" **4** league or association formed to protect and promote a common interest: *a trade or labor* union. **5** marriage: *They had a long and happy* union. **6 the Union** the United States of America.

union jack 1 flag standing for a union of states. **2 Union Jack** (**1**) in the United

States, a blue flag with fifty white stars. (**2**) British national flag.

Union of Soviet Socialist Republics official name for the Soviet Union. It is often written U.S.S.R.

u·nique (ū nēk′) **1** alone of its kind; different from all others: *The platypus is* unique *among animals.* **2** odd; rare; unusual: *a* unique *bit of china.* **u·nique·ly.**

u·ni·son (ū′nĭ sən) **1** state of being united; agreement: *the* unison *of their appeal for justice.* **2** in music, sameness of pitch of two or more tones, voices, bells, etc. **3 in unison** all together; with everybody acting at the same time: *to recite a poem* in unison.

u·nit (ū′nĭt) **1** one (of anything). **2** group of people, ideas, or things thought of as being together in one whole: *A family is a* unit *of society.* **3** selected distance, amount, etc., used for measuring: *A degree is a* unit *of temperature. A yard is a* unit *of length. A ton is a* unit *of weight. A minute is a* unit *of time.*

u·nite (ū nīt′) **1** to join together; combine; make or become one: *The two nations were* united *by treaty.* **2** to agree to act together (for a purpose): *The quarreling groups* united *against the common enemy.* **u·nit·ed, u·nit·ing.**

United Kingdom island kingdom in northwest Europe made up of Great Britain and Northern Ireland.

United Nations world organization, founded after World War II, for nations to work together to settle disputes peacefully and to improve the living conditions of all peoples.

United States of America a country of fifty states, mainly located in North America and including the islands of Hawaii, the District of Columbia, and outlying possessions. Also called **United States.**

u·ni·ty (ū′nə tĭ) **1** oneness; the state of being a whole. **2** an arrangement of parts to form a complete whole: *A work of art should have* unity. **3** harmony; agreement: *to live together in* unity.

u·ni·ver·sal (ū′nə vûr′səl) applying to all; belonging to or done by everyone: *The need for food, shelter, and clothing is* universal, *but we have no* universal *language.* **u·ni·ver·sal·ly.**

un·i·verse (ū′nə vûrs′) all things considered as a whole; everything that exists: *The sun, moon, and stars are parts of the universe.*

u·ni·ver·si·ty (ū′nə vûr′sə tĭ) the highest institution of learning, usually divided into schools of law, medicine, language, art, music, etc. A university can give bachelor's, master's, and doctor's degrees. **u·ni·ver·si·ties.**

un·just (ŭn jŭst′) not just; unfair. **un·just·ly.**

un·kempt (ŭn kĕmpt′) 1 not combed: *to have unkempt hair.* 2 sloppy; untidy: *an unkempt appearance.*

un·kept (ŭn kĕpt′) not kept up; not cared for; neglected: *A boy was hired to mow the unkept lawn.*

un·kind (ŭn kīnd′) not kind or sympathetic; harsh; cruel: *The unkind words made the little girl cry.*

un·kind·ly (ŭn kīnd′lĭ) 1 without kindness or consideration: *His bitter words showed his unkindly mood.* 2 in a harsh or cruel manner: *to speak unkindly.*

un·kind·ness (ŭn kīnd′nĭs) 1 lack of kindness and affection; cruelty. 2 an unkind act: *Her latest unkindness was hiding her sister's toys.*

un·known (ŭn nōn′) 1 strange; unfamiliar; not in one's knowledge: *The book you speak of is* unknown *to me.* 2 not discovered: *Robinson Crusoe was shipwrecked on an unknown island.* 3 person or thing not known.

un·lace (ŭn lās′) to unfasten; loosen (something held together with laces). **un·laced, un·lac·ing.**

un·law·ful (ŭn lô′fəl) against the law; illegal: *Driving above the speed limit is unlawful.* **un·law·ful·ly.**

¹**un·learn·ed** (ŭn lûr′nĭd) not educated; ignorant; without schooling. **un·learn·ed·ly.**

²**un·learned** (ŭn lûrnd′ or ŭn lûrnt′) not learned: *an unlearned lesson.*

un·leav·ened (ŭn lĕv′ənd) not leavened or fermented. There is no yeast in unleavened bread.

un·less (ŭn lĕs′) if (something) does not or is not: *The snow will melt unless the weather gets colder.*

un·like (ŭn līk′) 1 different; not like: *They contributed* unlike *amounts.* 2 different from: *How unlike Jack to forget to lock up!* 3 in a manner different from; not becoming: *behavior* unlike *a soldier.*

un·like·ly (ŭn līk′lĭ) 1 not likely; not believable; not probable: *a most unlikely story; an unlikely event.* 2 not likely to succeed: *Jack is unlikely material for the team.* **un·like·li·er, un·like·li·est.**

un·like·ness (ŭn līk′nĭs) difference; lack of resemblance; quality of being unlike.

un·lim·it·ed (ŭn lĭm′ə tĭd) 1 without limits; having no bounds; vast: *the unlimited expanse of the sky.* 2 very great; unrestricted: *to have* unlimited *power.*

un·load (ŭn lōd′) 1 to remove (from): *to unload trunks from a car.* 2 to remove freight or cargo from: *They unloaded the truck.* 3 to discharge freight: *The ship unloaded at the dock.* 4 to remove bullets from: *to unload a gun.* 5 to rid oneself of; pass off: *He unloaded his troubles onto his father.*

un·lock (ŭn lŏk′) 1 to open by means of a key: *to unlock the door.* 2 to open (anything firmly closed): *to unlock the jaws.*

un·looked-for (ŭn lŏŏkt′fôr′) not expected; unforeseen: *an unlooked-for happiness.*

un·loose (ŭn lōōs′) 1 to let go; unfasten: *He unloosed his grip on the branch.* 2 to set free; release: *They unloosed the prisoner.* **un·loosed, un·loos·ing.**

un·love·ly (ŭn lŭv′lĭ) 1 not attractive or pleasing to the eye. 2 unpleasant; disagreeable: *an unlovely episode.*

un·luck·y (ŭn lŭk′ĭ) 1 not lucky; not fortunate: *an unlucky gambler; an unlucky choice.* 2 bringing bad luck: *Many people consider 13 an* unlucky *number.* **un·luck·i·er, un·luck·i·est; un·luck·i·ly.**

un·mar·ried (ŭn măr′ĭd) not married; single.

un·mask (ŭn măsk′) to remove a mask or disguise from; show the true character of: *to unmask a traitor; to unmask someone's true intentions.*

un·mer·ci·ful (ŭn mûr′sə fəl) without humane feeling or pity; showing no mercy; cruel. **un·mer·ci·ful·ly.**

---

fāte, făt, fâre, fär; bē, bĕt; bīte, bĭt; nō, nŏt, nôr; fūse, fŭn, fûr; tōō, tŏŏk; foil; foul; thin; ~~then~~; hw for wh as in *wh*at; zh for s as in u*s*ual; ə for a, e, i, o, u, as in *a*go, lin*e*n, per*i*l, at*o*m, min*u*s

un·mind·ful (ŭn mīnd′fəl) heedless; careless; forgetful: *We started out* unmindful *of the weather.* **un·mind·ful·ly.**

un·mis·tak·a·ble (ŭn′mĭs tā′kə bəl) clear; certain; obvious; not capable of being mistaken: *an* unmistakable *signature; an* unmistakable *symptom.* **un·mis·tak·a·bly.**

un·mixed (ŭn mĭkst′) not mixed with anything else; uniform in character throughout: *an* unmixed *blessing.*

un·mo·lest·ed (ŭn′mə lĕs′tĭd) not harmed or disturbed; left in peace.

un·moved (ŭn mōōvd′) **1** not moved; in the same place. **2** not swayed by feelings, thoughts, or ideas: *He was* unmoved *by his friend's argument.*

un·nat·u·ral (ŭn năch′ə rəl) **1** not considered natural or normal; inhuman; abnormal: *an* unnatural *taste for violence.* **2** artificial; assumed: *an* unnatural *way of speaking.* **un·nat·u·ral·ly.**

un·nec·es·sar·y (ŭn nĕs′ə sĕr′ĭ) not necessary; not needed; needless: *It was an* unnecessary *error.* **un·nec·es·sar·i·ly.**

un·nerve (ŭn nûrv′) to deprive of courage or self-control: *The sight of the disaster* unnerved *him.* **un·nerved, un·nerv·ing.**

un·no·ticed (ŭn nō′tĭst) **1** not observed; not seen or noticed: *The celebrity passed* unnoticed *through the crowd.* **2** without note or attention: *He let the matter pass* unnoticed.

un·num·bered (ŭn nŭm′bərd) **1** not counted. **2** without numbers: *a series of* unnumbered *paragraphs.* **3** numerous; countless: *The stadium was jammed with* unnumbered *fans.*

un·ob·served (ŭn′əb zûrvd′) not observed; not noticed; not seen.

un·oc·cu·pied (ŭn ŏk′yōō pīd′) **1** vacant; without an occupant: *an* unoccupied *house.* **2** not seized or possessed: *Part of France remained* unoccupied *during World War II.* **3** not at work or busy; idle: *I'm* unoccupied *for an hour if you wish to see me.*

un·of·fi·cial (ŭn′ə fĭsh′əl) not official; not approved by proper authority. **un·of·fi·cial·ly.**

un·o·pened (ŭn ō′pənd) not opened; closed; shut: *an* unopened *letter.*

un·pack (ŭn păk′) **1** to take out (something from where it was packed): *to* unpack *clothing; to* unpack *a trunk; to* unpack *after*

a trip. **2** to remove the load from a pack animal: *They* unpacked *the horses.*

un·paid (ŭn pād′) not paid or without pay: *to leave a bill* unpaid; *an* unpaid *volunteer.*

un·par·al·leled (ŭn păr′ə lĕld′) having no equal; unrivaled.

un·pin (ŭn pĭn′) to unfasten by removing pins. **un·pinned, un·pin·ning.**

un·pleas·ant (ŭn plĕz′ənt) not pleasant; disagreeable. **un·pleas·ant·ly.**

un·pop·u·lar (ŭn pŏp′yōō lər) not generally liked; disliked: *To be different is often to be* unpopular. **un·pop·u·lar·ly.**

un·prac·ticed or **un·prac·tised** (ŭn-prăk′tĭst) **1** not practiced; not put into practice. **2** unskilled; not expert.

un·prec·e·dent·ed (ŭn prĕs′ə dĕn′tĭd) not done before; having no precedent; exceptional: *an* unprecedented *amount of snow for this time of year.* **un·prec·e·dent·ed·ly.**

un·pre·dict·a·ble (ŭn′prĭ dĭk′tə bəl) **1** not to be foretold: *this* unpredictable *weather.* **2** not reliable; acting through whim: *an* unpredictable *person.* **un·pre·dict·a·bly.**

un·pre·pared (ŭn′prĭ pârd′) **1** done without preparation; not arranged beforehand: *an* unprepared *speech.* **2** not equipped; not ready: *He was* unprepared *for college.*

un·prin·ci·pled (ŭn prĭn′sə pəld) without good moral principles; unscrupulous.

un·prof·it·a·ble (ŭn prŏf′ə tə bəl) yielding no profit or advantage; useless. **un·prof·it·a·bly.**

un·ques·tion·a·ble (ŭn kwĕs′chən ə bəl) beyond question or doubt; certain. **un·ques·tion·a·bly.**

un·rav·el (ŭn răv′əl) **1** to undo something knitted or woven; separate a thread or threads from: *Mother* unraveled *the sweater and used the wool for something else.* **2** to untangle: *I* unraveled *the ball of yarn.* **3** to come apart, as something knitted or woven: *The sock* unraveled *at the heel.* **4** to make or become clear; solve: *to* unravel *a mystery.*

un·re·al (ŭn rē′əl) not real; imaginary; fantastic.

un·re·al·i·ty (ŭn′rē ăl′ə tĭ) **1** quality of being unreal or imaginary. **2** something that does not exist: *Ghosts and witches are* unrealities. **un·re·al·i·ties.**

un·rea·son·a·ble (ŭn rē′zən ə bəl) **1** not rational or reasonable; without good sense or sound judgment: *an* unreasonable *per-*

son; an unreasonable *request*. **2** excessive; exorbitant: *an* unreasonable *price*. **un·rea·son·a·bly.**

un·re·mit·ting (ŭn′rĭ mĭt′ĭng) without stopping; unceasing; persistent; not slackening or giving up: *to make* unremitting *efforts; to require* unremitting *toil*. **un·re·mit·ting·ly.**

un·rest (ŭn rĕst′) restlessness; state of disturbance; dissatisfaction: *Injustice and poverty cause social* unrest

un·re·strained (ŭn′rĭ strānd′) not restrained; not held back; unchecked: *Our joy was* unrestrained. **un·re·strain·ed·ly.**

un·ri·valed or **un·ri·valled** (ŭn rī′vəld) having no rival; matchless; unequaled: *This firm has an* unrivaled *reputation*.

un·roll (ŭn rōl′) **1** to unfold and spread out: *to* unroll *a carpet*. **2** to become unfolded: *The carpet* unrolled. **3** to make known; display; reveal: *The book* unrolled *the story of Captain Cook's voyages*. **4** to become known; reveal itself: *We listened in fascination as the story* unrolled.

un·ru·ly (ŭn rōō′lĭ) not obeying; difficult to control: *an* unruly *child*. **un·ru·li·er, un·ru·li·est.**

un·sad·dle (ŭn săd′əl) **1** to remove the saddle from (a horse, etc.). **2** to cause to fall out of a saddle; unhorse. **un·sad·dled, un·sad·dling.**

un·safe (ŭn sāf′) not safe; dangerous; insecure: *an* unsafe *bridge*.

un·said (ŭn sĕd′) not said or spoken; thought but not expressed: *Some things are better left* unsaid.

un·san·i·tar·y (ŭn săn′ə tĕr′ĭ) not sanitary; full of germs and dirt; unclean; unhealthy **un·san·i·tar·i·ly.**

un·sat·is·fac·to·ry (ŭn′săt ĭs făk′tə rĭ) not satisfactory; not satisfying or fulfilling a requirement; disappointing: *an* unsatisfactory *answer to a question; an* unsatisfactory *experience*. **un·sat·is·fac·to·ri·ly.**

un·sat·is·fied (ŭn săt′ĭs fīd′) not satisfied, fulfilled, or relieved: *an* unsatisfied *hunger*.

un·screw (ŭn skrōō′) **1** to take out or remove the screw or screws from: *to* unscrew *the hinges of a door*. **2** to remove by turning: *to* unscrew *the top of a jar*.

un·scru·pu·lous (ŭn skrōō′pyōō ləs) without moral principles; without conscience; unprincipled: *He is* unscrupulous *in money matters*. **un·scru·pu·lous·ly.**

un·seal (ŭn sēl′) **1** to remove or break the seal of. **2** to open something that has been tightly shut, as if sealed.

un·seat (ŭn sēt′) **1** to throw or remove (someone) from a seat: *The horse* unseated *his rider*. **2** to remove (someone) from an official position.

un·seem·ly (ŭn sēm′lĭ) not proper; unfitting: *It is* unseemly *to gossip about one's neighbors*.

un·seen (ŭn sēn′) **1** unnoticed: *The pickpocket passed* unseen *through the crowd*. **2** invisible: *He felt an* unseen *presence in the room*.

un·self·ish (ŭn sĕl′fĭsh) not selfish; not influenced solely by one's own interests; generous: *her* unselfish *attention ... the patients in the hospital*. **un·self·ish·ly.**

un·set·tle (ŭn sĕt′əl) to make confused or uncertain; disturb: *The shock of the accident* unsettled *him for some time*. **un·set·tled, un·set·tling.**

un·set·tled (ŭn sĕt′əld) **1** not decided or determined: *an* unsettled *question*. **2** without order or stability; disturbed: *The country was in an* unsettled *condition for many months after the revolution*. **3** not paid or disposed of: *an* unsettled *debt*. **4** not populated or inhabited: *an* unsettled *land*. **5** not certain; changeable: *an* unsettled *temper;* unsettled *weather*. **6** still suspended in the air or a liquid; not come to rest: *the* unsettled *silt in a muddy stream*.

un·shak·en (ŭn shā′kən) **1** firm; unyielding: *an* unshaken *belief*. **2** not confused; strong of mind or purpose while under stress: *He remained* unshaken *throughout the crisis*. **un·shak·en·ly.**

un·sheathe (ŭn shēth′) to remove from a sheath or scabbard: *to* unsheathe *a sword*. **un·sheathed, un·sheath·ing.**

un·shod (ŭn shŏd′) **1** without shoes; barefoot. **2** not shod, as a horse.

un·sight·ly (ŭn sīt′lĭ) not attractive or appealing to the eye; ugly: *The old witch was an* unsightly *creature*.

---

fāte, făt, fâre, fär; bē, bĕt; bīte, bĭt; nō, nŏt, nôr; fūse, fŭn, fûr; tōō, tŏŏk; foil; foul; thin; ~~then~~;
hw for wh as in *wh*at; zh for s as in u*s*ual; ə for a, e, i, o, u, as in *a*go, lin*e*n, per*i*l, at*o*m, min*u*s

un·skilled (ŭn skĭld′) without training or skill for a specific kind of work.

un·skill·ful or **un·skil·ful** (ŭn skĭl′fəl) without skill; awkward: *He was very unskillful at handicrafts.* **un·skill·ful·ly; un·skil·ful·ly.**

un·so·phis·ti·cat·ed (ŭn′sə fĭs′tə kā′tĭd) **1** not sophisticated; without knowledge or experience in the ways of the world. **2** simple; artless: *a piece of* unsophisticated *humor.* **un·so·phis·ti·cat·ed·ly.**

un·sound (ŭn sound′) **1** not firm in mind or body; unhealthy. **2** not strong or solid; unsafe: *the* unsound *foundations of a bridge.* **3** false or ill-founded: *an* unsound *argument.* **4** not dependable or reliable: *an* unsound *investment.* **5** not complete; broken: *a night of* unsound *sleep.* **un·sound·ly.**

un·speak·a·ble (ŭn spē′kə bəl) **1** not capable of being expressed in words; beyond description: *an* unspeakable *happiness.* **2** evil or bad beyond words: *his* unspeakable *treachery.* **un·speak·a·bly.**

un·sta·ble (ŭn stā′bəl) not fixed, secure, or steady: *an* unstable *friendship; an* unstable *ladder.* **un·sta·bly.**

un·stead·y (ŭn stěd′ĭ) not steady; unstable; not reliable: *an* unsteady *table; his* unsteady *habits.* **un·stead·i·ly.**

un·stressed (ŭn strěst′) not stressed or accented.

un·suc·cess·ful (ŭn′sək sěs′fəl) not successful; without success: *an* unsuccessful *attempt to win a race.* **un·suc·cess·ful·ly.**

un·suit·a·ble (ŭn sōō′tə bəl or ŭn sū′tə bəl) not suitable; not proper to the circumstances: *A bathing suit is* unsuitable *in a classroom.* **un·suit·a·bly.**

un·sung (ŭn sŭng′) **1** not sung. **2** not praised or celebrated, especially not praised in song or poetry: *the many* unsung *heroes who fought bravely for their country.*

un·sus·pect·ed (ŭn′sə spěk′tĭd) **1** not under suspicion: *It was an* unsuspected *man who stole the money.* **2** not believed to exist; not known about: *The hermit died leaving an* unsuspected *fortune.*

un·sus·pect·ing (ŭn′sə spěk′tĭng) not suspecting; having no suspicion: *The* unsuspecting *victim walked right into the trap.* **un·sus·pect·ing·ly.**

un·taught (ŭn tôt′) **1** not taught or educated; ignorant: *an* untaught *backwoods-*

man. **2** learned without a teacher's help; natural: *an* untaught *skill in drawing.*

un·think·a·ble (ŭn thĭngk′ə bəl) that cannot be thought, imagined, or considered: *It is* unthinkable *that we should have a tenth cat in this house!*

un·think·ing (ŭn thĭngk′ĭng) not thinking; careless; inconsiderate. **un·think·ing·ly.**

un·ti·dy (ŭn tī′dĭ) not tidy; sloppy; slovenly: *Mae left her room* untidy *this morning.* **un·ti·di·er, un·ti·di·est; un·ti·di·ly.**

un·tie (ŭn tī′) **1** to undo something that has been tied; open a knot or bow: *He* untied *his shoelaces and removed his shoes.* **2** to set loose (something that has been tied): *He* untied *the horse and let it wander.* **un·tied, un·ty·ing.**

un·til (ŭn tĭl′) **1** up to the time that: *We shall wait* until *you arrive.* **2** up to the time of: *We shall wait for you* until *ten o'clock.* **3** before: *He did not go* until *dawn.* **4** up to the place, degree, or condition that: *He talked* until *he was hoarse.*

un·time·ly (ŭn tīm′lĭ) **1** happening at an unsuitable time: *an* untimely *request for a favor.* **2** happening too soon or before the usual time: *An early snow put an* untimely *end to autumn.* **3** too soon.

un·tir·ing (ŭn tīr′ĭng) not growing tired; tireless: *her* untiring *efforts to help the sick.* **un·tir·ing·ly.**

un·to (ŭn′tōō) old-fashioned or poetic way of saying "to": *Give* unto *each man that which is due him.*

un·told (ŭn tōld′) **1** not told; not revealed: *We all wanted to know the* untold *story behind the events.* **2** countless; innumerable: *the* untold *stars in the sky.*

un·touched (ŭn tŭcht′) not having been touched or affected: *a sleepy old town* untouched *by modern life.*

un·to·ward (ŭn tôrd′) **1** hard to manage; wayward; unruly: *an* untoward *child.* **2** inconvenient; unfortunate: *an* untoward *meeting.* **3** unbecoming; not appropriate or suitable: *We disliked his* untoward *rudeness to the stranger.*

un·trained (ŭn trānd′) not trained; without discipline, education, or preparation: *an* untrained *horse; an* untrained *voice; an* untrained *mind.*

un·tried (ŭn trīd′) **1** not tried; not tested: *Mother has many* untried *recipes.* **2** without a court trial: *The sheriff refused to hang the man* untried.

un·true (ŭn trōō′) **1** not true; false: *All his stories about hunting elephants were* untrue. **2** not faithful; not loyal: *She was* untrue *to her promise.*

un·truth (ŭn trōōth′) **1** lack of truth; falseness: *We proved the* untruth *of all his claims.* **2** a lie; false statement: *She has told many* untruths *which people have believed.*

un·ty·ing (ŭn tī′ĭng) See **untie.** *He spent a full hour* untying *all the knots in the rope.*

un·used (ŭn ūzd′) **1** not having been used; not in use: *Lucie returned the* unused *dishes to the store.* **2** unused to (ŭn ūst′) not accustomed: *He was* unused to *city life.*

un·u·su·al (ŭn ū′zhōō əl) not usual; out of the ordinary; uncommon; rare: *It is* unusual *for him to be late.* **un·u·su·al·ly.**

un·ut·ter·a·ble (ŭn ŭt′ər ə bəl) that cannot be put into words; unspeakable: *our* unutterable *joy.* **un·ut·ter·a·bly.**

un·veil (ŭn vāl′) **1** to remove a veil or covering from: *The artist* unveiled *the monument for the whole town to see.* **2** to take off one's veil: *The mysterious stranger* unveiled. **3** to reveal: *The plot was* unveiled *and the conspirators arrested.*

un·war·y (ŭn wâr′ĭ) not cautious; careless; heedless: *He is* unwary *of the dangers around him.* **un·war·i·ly.**

un·wea·ried (ŭn wîr′ĭd) **1** not weary; not tired: *He was* unwearied *despite the trip.* **2** tireless; untiring: *his* unwearied *search for buried treasure.*

un·wel·come (ŭn wĕl′kəm) not welcome; not received with pleasure: *an* unwelcome *guest.*

un·well (ŭn wĕl′) not well; sick; ill: *He felt slightly* unwell *and decided to go home.*

un·whole·some (ŭn hōl′səm) **1** not good for the body; unhealthful: *an* unwholesome *food.* **2** morally harmful: *his* unwholesome *companions.* **3** appearing unhealthy: *an* unwholesome *complexion.* **un·whole·some·ly.**

un·wield·y (ŭn wēl′dĭ) hard to handle or manage; bulky; clumsy: *A grand piano is* unwieldy.

un·will·ing (ŭn wĭl′ĭng) not willing; not agreeing; reluctant: *The taxi driver was an* unwilling *accomplice in the bank robbery.* **un·will·ing·ly.**

un·will·ing·ness (ŭn wĭl′ĭng nĭs) a feeling of not wanting to do (something); reluctance: *They were surprised at his* unwillingness *to join in the game.*

un·wind (ŭn wīnd′) **1** to cause to unroll; wind off. **2** to uncoil; come unwound: *The snake* unwound *and slid away.* **un·wound, un·wind·ing.**

un·wise (ŭn wīz′) not wise; not sensible; foolish: *an* unwise *decision.* **un·wise·ly.**

un·wit·ting (ŭn wĭt′ĭng) not conscious or intentional: *an* unwitting *favor; an* unwitting *insult.* **un·wit·ting·ly.**

un·wont·ed (ŭn wŭn′tĭd) not usual; not customary: *His* unwonted *gaiety surprised us all.* **un·wont·ed·ly.**

un·wor·thy (ŭn wûr′thĭ) **1** not worthy (of); not deserving (of): *I am* unworthy *of your kindness.* **2** not deserving respect; not suitable: *his* unworthy *conduct.* **un·worth·i·er, un·worth·i·est; un·wor·thi·ly.**

un·wound (ŭn wound′) See **unwind.** *The kitten* unwound *the ball of wool.*

un·wrap (ŭn răp′) to take the covering or wrapper off: *to* unwrap *a package.* **un·wrapped, un·wrap·ping.**

un·yield·ing (ŭn yēl′dĭng) firm; resolute; not yielding or giving way: *an* unyielding *army;* unyielding *opinion.* **un·yield·ing·ly.**

up (ŭp) **1** in the direction away from the center of the earth. **2** from a lower to a higher position; into the air: *to throw a ball* up; *to look* up. **3** at a higher place: *put* up *on a shelf.* **4** from less to more; to a higher degree or to a higher position on a scale: *Prices go* up. **5** farther along: *She walked* up *the street.* **6** above the horizon: *The sun is* up. **7** in an erect position; on one's feet; out of bed: *to sit* up; *stand* up; *get* up *early in the morning.* **8** entirely; thoroughly: *Eat* up *your dinner.* **9** at an end: *Your time is* up. **10** together: *It all adds* up *to twenty-five.* **11** well informed: *She is* up *on all the latest gossip.* **12** near: *She came* up *and said hello.* **13** into notice or consideration: *Excuse me for bringing* up

---

fāte, făt, fâre, fär; bē, bĕt; bīte, bĭt; nō, nŏt, nôr; fūse, fŭn, fûr; tōō, tŏŏk; foil; foul; thin; ~~then~~;
hw for wh as in *wh*at; zh for s as in u*s*ual; ə for a, e, i, o, u, as in ago, linen, peril, atom, min*u*s

an unpleasant subject. **14** away; aside: *to lay* up *provisions.* **15** in baseball, at bat: *Who is* up *now?* **16** each: *The score is two* up. **17** to raise: *to* up *prices.* **18 up for** (**1**) running as a candidate for: *He is* up for *club treasurer.* (**2**) on trial for: *He is* up for *treason.* **19 up to** (**1**) ready to do or in process of doing: *He is* up to *no good.* (**2**) in the hands of: *The choice of restaurants is* up to *you.* (**3**) able to do: *Is he* up to *reading such difficult books?* (**4**) as far as: *We went* up to *the river and turned back.* **20 ups and downs** successes and misfortunes: *the* ups and downs *in life.* **upped, up·ping.**

up- prefix meaning "up": up*hill;* up*hold;* up*town.*

up·braid (ŭp brād′) to scold severely; blame: *She upbraided him for his rudeness.*

up·heav·al (ŭp hē′vəl) **1** a great pushing or heaving from beneath: *Mountains were formed by great upheavals of the earth's crust.* **2** a sudden great and violent change in circumstances: *The revolution caused a great upheaval in that country.*

up·held (ŭp hĕld′) See **uphold.**

up·hill (ŭp′hĭl′) **1** toward the top of a hill: *Walk* uphill. **2** going up a hill; slanting up: *a steep* uphill *road.* **3** difficult: *He found the job* uphill *work.*

up·hold (ŭp hōld′) **1** to give support to; back: *She* upheld *his opinions.* **2** to hold up; support: *Marble columns* uphold *the roof.* **3** to refuse to set aside; confirm: *The higher court* upheld *the lower court's decision.* **up·held, up·hold·ing.**

up·hol·ster (ŭp hōl′stər) to provide (furniture) with cushions, springs, covering, etc.: *The old chair we* upholstered *now looks new.*

up·hol·ster·y (ŭp hōl′stə rĭ) **1** material used to cover furniture; draperies, cushions, curtains, etc. **2** the business of upholstering.

up·keep (ŭp′kēp′) **1** the act of keeping in good order or repair; maintenance: *A hired man helps in the* upkeep *of the farm.* **2** the cost of looking after someone or something: *The* upkeep *of a zoo is high.*

up·land (ŭp′lənd or ŭp′lănd′) **1** high land: *a hilly* upland. **2** on or for use on high land: *an* upland *farm.*

¹up·lift (ŭp lĭft′) **1** to raise; elevate. **2** to improve the condition of (morally, socially,

or spiritually): *The minister worked hard to* uplift *his flock.*

²up·lift (ŭp′lĭft′) a lift or action of lifting to a higher physical, moral, or emotional state: *The concert gave her spirits quite an* uplift.

up·on (ə pŏn′ or ə pôn′) on.

up·per (ŭp′ər) higher in place or position: *the* upper *floor; the* upper *classes.*

up·per·most (ŭp′ər mōst′) **1** highest; most frequent or dominant: *a thing* uppermost *in his thoughts.* **2** at the top; first.

up·raise (ŭp rāz′) to lift up; raise. **up·raised, up·rais·ing.**

up·rear (ŭp rĭr′) **1** to rear; rise or raise to an erect position. **2** to bring up (children, animals, etc.).

up·right (ŭp′rīt′ or ŭp rīt′) **1** straight up; vertical; erect: *an* upright *posture.* **2** in an erect position: *The soldiers stood* upright *at attention.* **3** just; honorable: *an* upright *character.* **4** something set or standing straight up: *Four* uprights *supported the roof of the porch.* **up·right·ly.**

up·right·ness (ŭp′rīt′nĭs) honesty; integrity.

up·ris·ing (ŭp′rī′zĭng or ŭp rī′zĭng) rebellion; revolt.

up·roar (ŭp′rôr′) noisy, violent disturbance; tumult: *After the speech, the crowd broke into an* uproar.

up·root (ŭp rōōt′) **1** to tear out by the roots: *to* uproot *a plant.* **2** to remove completely and forcibly: *Most wars* uproot *many families.*

¹up·set (ŭp sĕt′) **1** to knock over; overturn: *The baby* upset *the teapot.* **2** to throw out of order; interfere with: *The holiday crowds* upset *the train schedule.* **3** to disturb mentally or physically: *The news of the shipwreck* upset *the captain's wife. Too much lobster* upset *Malcolm's stomach.* **up·set, up·set·ting.**

²up·set (ŭp′sĕt′) **1** the act of interfering with or disturbing; an overthrow; defeat: *the* upset *of our plans.* **2** physically or mentally disturbed: *an* upset *stomach.*

up·shot (ŭp′shŏt′) result; conclusion: *The* upshot *of all our planning was a trip to the mountains.*

up·side (ŭp′sīd′) upper side or top part.

upside down 1 with the top part at the bottom. **2 turn upside down** of a place, to throw into complete disorder: *Our room was* turned upside down *by the thieves*.

up·stairs (ŭp stârz′) **1** on an upper floor: *The attic is always* upstairs. **2** to or toward an upper floor: *The children climbed* upstairs *to bed.* **3** of or belonging to an upper floor: *an* upstairs *sitting room.* **4** upper floor or floors.

up·stand·ing (ŭp stăn′dĭng) upright; honorable: *He is a fine,* upstanding *member of the community.*

up·start (ŭp′stärt′) person who has suddenly risen to wealth or high position, especially one who takes liberties or is arrogant because of success.

up·stream (ŭp′strēm′) toward the source of a stream; against the current.

up-to-date (ŭp′tə dāt′) **1** up to the present time: *Are these records kept* up-to-date? **2** in the current fashion; keeping up with the times.

up·town (ŭp′toun′) **1** pertaining to the upper part of a town or city: *an* uptown *resident.* **2** in or toward that part of town: *Are you going* uptown? *I live* uptown *and work downtown.*

¹**up·turn** (ŭp′tûrn′) a change for the better: *an* upturn *in one's fortunes; an* upturn *in business.*

²**up·turn** (ŭp tûrn′) to turn over: *She* upturned *the queen of hearts.*

up·ward (ŭp′wərd) **1** toward a higher place or level: *to progress* upward. **2** moving up; directed up: *the* upward *march of progress.* **3** above; over: *from the age of five and* upward. **4 upward of** over the number of; more than: *There were* upward of *two dozen people in the crowd.*

up·wards (ŭp′wərdz) upward: *to climb* upwards.

u·ra·ni·um (yŏŏ rā′nĭ əm) very heavy, white, radioactive metal element. It is the chief fuel in atomic reactors, and one form of it is used in atomic bombs.

U·ra·nus (yŏŏr′ə nəs) **1** planet, seventh in order of distance from the sun. **2** early Greek god who was a symbol of heaven.

ur·ban (ûr′bən) having to do with or living in a city or town; not rural: *an urban resident.*

ur·chin (ûr′chĭn) **1** small, mischievous boy. **2** poor, neglected child; waif.

urge (ûrj) **1** to plead with; persuade: *His friends* urged *him to accept the job.* **2** to drive or force (ahead): *The jockey* urged *his horse forward with a whip.* *Tom* urged *himself to study harder.* **3** strong impulse: *Betty had an* urge *to eat something sweet.* **4** to speak earnestly for; recommend strongly: *He* urged *exercise to maintain good health.* **urged, urg·ing.**

ur·gent (ûr′jənt) calling for immediate action or attention; pressing: *There was an* urgent *message waiting for him at his office.* **ur·gent·ly.**

u·rine (yŏŏr′ĭn) fluid given off by the kidneys and discharged from the bladder as waste.

urn (ûrn) **1** vase, especially one with a foot or a pedestal. **2** large container in which a beverage, such as coffee, is kept hot and from which it is served. (Homonym: earn)

Decorative urn

U·ru·guay (yŏŏr′ə gwä′ or yŏŏr′ə gwī′) country in southern South America, on the Atlantic Ocean.

us (ŭs) form of "we" used when "we" is the object of some action, happening, etc.: *Kate amused* us *with stories of her trip.* *It doesn't matter to* us *if it rains where we are going.*

Coffee urn

U.S. United States.

U.S.A. United States of America.

u·sa·ble (ūz′ə bəl) that can be used; fit to be used.

us·age (ū′sĭj or ū′zĭj) **1** way of saying or writing something: *British and American* usage *often differ.* **2** way of using; treatment: *Our record player was ruined by rough* usage.

¹**use** (ūz) **1** to put into service; to employ: *We should* use *sharp tools very carefully.* **2** to make a habit of employing: *She uses a lot of garlic in her salads.* **3** to exploit for selfish ends): *She was always using her younger brother.* **4** to act or behave toward;

fāte, făt, fâre, fär; bē, bĕt; bīte, bĭt; nō, nŏt, nôr; fūse, fŭn, fûr; tōō, tŏŏk; foil; foul; thin; ~~then~~; hw for wh as in *wh*at; zh for s as in u*s*ual; ə for a, e, i, o, u, as in *a*go, lin*e*n, per*i*l, at*o*m, min*u*s

treat: *The foreman* used *his workers in an inconsiderate manner.* **5** to practice; exercise: *You should* use *your common sense.*

used to (ūst tōō) **1** accustomed to; familiar with: *We are* used to *sleeping in a cold room.* **2** formerly did: *Mary* used to *scream when she saw a mouse.*

use up to consume completely: *The eggs are all* used up. *My allowance is all* used up.

used, us·ing.

²**use** (ūs) **1** the act of using: *The* use *of fireworks is forbidden in the city.* **2** practical value: *A sled would be of no* use *to me in Florida.* **3** opportunity or ability to use: *I have the* use *of my brother's car whenever I need it.* **4** way of using: *He learned the proper* use *of woodworking equipment.*

use·ful (ūs′fəl) helpful; serviceable; of use: *To earn her allowance, Betty made herself* useful *around the house.* **use·ful·ly.**

use·ful·ness (ūs′fəl nĭs) a being useful: *The* usefulness *of fire extinguishers in the home has often been proved.*

use·less (ūs′lĭs) **1** worthless; of no use: *These old clothes may be* useless *to you but someone can use them.* **2** producing no results; vain: *It is* useless *to tell him to stop biting his nails.* **use·less·ly.**

us·er (ū′zər) person who puts something into service.

ush·er (ŭsh′ər) **1** person who directs people to their seats in a church, theater, or the like. **2** to escort; conduct; bring in: *The bride was* ushered *to the altar by her father.*

U.S.S.R. Union of Soviet Socialist Republics.

u·su·al (ū′zhōō əl) ordinary; customary: *It is* usual *for him to swim before breakfast.* **u·su·al·ly.**

u·su·rer (ū′zhə rər) a person who lends money at interest, especially a grasping lender of money.

u·surp (ū sûrp′ or ū zûrp′) to take possession of (power, position, authority) without right, or by force: *The crown prince tried to* usurp *his father's throne.*

u·su·ry (ū′zhə rĭ) **1** the practice of lending money at a rate of interest higher than the legal rate. **2** a very high rate of interest: *to charge* usury *for a loan.*

U·tah (ū′tä or ū′tô) a State in the western part of the United States.

u·ten·sil (ū tĕn′səl) implement, tool, dish, etc., used in making or doing something: *kitchen* utensils; *shaving* utensils.

u·til·i·ty (ū tĭl′ə tĭ) **1** usefulness. **2** a useful object: *A kitchen cabinet is a* utility. **3** public utility: *Gas, electricity, water, etc. are public* utilities. **u·til·i·ties.**

u·til·ize (ū′tə līz′) to put to profitable use; employ; take advantage of: *All available space was* utilized *for the overflow of guests.* **u·til·ized, u·til·iz·ing.**

ut·most (ŭt′mōst′) **1** greatest; extreme; farthest: *the* utmost *confidence;* utmost *poverty;* utmost *borders of the country.* **2** greatest possible effort or ability: *Herbert put his* utmost *into the work.*

¹**ut·ter** (ŭt′ər) **1** to say: *Muriel* uttered *the new word slowly.* **2** to sound: *Dolly* uttered *a scream of terror.* [¹**utter** is a form of an earlier English word (outren) which was formed from another word (out) meaning "to say," "speak out."]

²**ut·ter** (ŭt′ər) entire; absolute; complete: *This is* utter *nonsense.* **ut·ter·ly.** [²**utter** is a form of an Old English word (ūttra) meaning "farther out."]

ut·ter·ance (ŭt′ər əns) **1** something said: *It seemed a strange* utterance *coming from Casper.* **2** manner of speaking: *Her* utterance *was hoarse and thick.* **3** act of saying: *John Lei's continued* utterance *of Chinese proverbs became tiresome.*

ut·ter·most (ŭt′ər mōst′) utmost.

V

V, v (vē) **1** the 22nd letter of the English alphabet. **2** Roman numeral for five.

Va. Virginia.

va·can·cy (vā′kən sĭ) **1** unoccupied place or position: *a* vacancy *in the new office building; a* vacancy *in the teaching staff.* **2** an empty space; a void: *Vance gazed into* vacancy *as he daydreamed in the sun.* **3** condition of being empty or unoccupied: *The* vacancy *is only temporary.* **va·can·cies.**

va·cant (vā′kənt) **1** empty; unoccupied; without a tenant: *a* vacant *building lot; a* vacant *job; a* vacant *house.* **2** showing lack of understanding or unawareness of surroundings: *The* vacant *stare of a deaf or absent-minded man.* **va·cant·ly.**

va·cate (vā′kāt′) to make empty; move out of (a house, etc.). **va·cat·ed, va·cat·ing.**

va·ca·tion (vā kā′shən or və kā′shən) **1** an absence from work for rest and pleasure: *Our school* vacation *is from July to September.* **2** a holiday; a pleasure trip or visit: *Our* vacation *at the seashore gave me a good tan.* **3** to spend a period of rest and recreation: *We* vacationed *in the mountains.*

vac·ci·nate (văk′sə nāt′) to introduce vaccine into the body to prevent certain diseases, such as smallpox, typhoid, polio, etc. **vac·ci·nat·ed, vac·ci·nat·ing.**

vac·ci·na·tion (văk′sə nā′shən) **1** a vaccinating. **2** the sore or scar caused by a vaccination.

vac·cine (văk sēn′ or văk′sēn′) killed or weakened germs of a disease, introduced into the body to make it resistant to attacks of that disease.

vac·il·late (văs′ə lāt′) **1** to swing to and fro; waver. **2** to waver back and forth in forming an opinion or making a decision: *Daisy* vacillated *between the two houses, until it was too late to buy either.* **vac·il·lat·ed, vac·il·lat·ing.**

vac·u·um (văk′yōō əm) **1** an empty space. **2** the space inside a container from which the air has been removed.

vacuum bottle 1 glass container made of two bottles, one inside the other, with a vacuum between them. **2** such a container and a metal or plastic covering, used to keep substances hot or cold.

vacuum cleaner a cleaning device that sucks dust and dirt into a bag. A fan driven by a motor creates a vacuum.

vacuum tube device, somewhat like a light bulb, that contains wires and metal grids. It is used in radios and other electronic equipment to select and amplify electric signals.

vag·a·bond (văg′ə bŏnd′) **1** person who travels idly from place to place with no

settled home; a wanderer. **2** wandering: *to have* vagabond *fancies.*

va·grant (vā′grənt) **1** idle, homeless wanderer; a tramp. **2** wandering; unsettled: *a* vagrant *breeze.*

vague (vāg) **1** faint; dim: *the tree's* vague *outline in the fog.* **2** not clear; indistinct: *Some* vague *sounds came from the moonlit forest.* **3** unfounded; indefinite: *a* vague *rumor about sending rockets to the moon.* **va·guer, va·guest; vague·ly.**

vain (vān) **1** proud of oneself; self-satisfied; conceited. **2** useless; unavailing; futile: *a* vain *effort.* **3** worthless; idle; without force: *a* vain *threat.* **4 in vain** without success; to no purpose. (Homonym: vane, vein)

vain·ly (vān′lĭ) **1** in a conceited or self-satisfied manner: *The big-game hunter* vainly *paraded up and down before a large audience.* **2** without success: *The fox* vainly *tried to reach the grapes.*

vale (vāl) valley. (Homonym: veil)

val·en·tine (văl′ən tīn′) **1** a card, often fancy, or gift sent on St. Valentine's Day as a token of affection. **2** sweetheart.

val·et (văl′ĭt or văl′ā′) **1** man who acts as a personal servant to another, taking care of his clothes and other personal items. **2** hotel employee who cleans and presses clothes, shines shoes, etc. **3** to serve (someone) as a valet.

val·iant (văl′yənt) showing great bravery; courageous; heroic: *a* valiant *knight; a* valiant *act.* **val·iant·ly.**

val·id (văl′ĭd) **1** based on facts; legitimate; acceptable: *He had a* valid *excuse for missing the meeting.* **2** acceptable in a court of law; binding: *The judge said the rumor was not* valid *evidence. The court ruled the contract* valid. **val·id·ly.**

va·lise (və lēs′) a traveling case used for carrying clothes or other personal possessions; suitcase.

val·ley (văl′ĭ) **1** a low land area between mountains or hills. **2** all the land drained by a river system: *the Tennessee* Valley.

val·or (văl′ər) great courage, especially in battle; bravery and prowess: *His* valor *on the battlefield won him a medal.*

---

fāte, făt, fâre, fär; bē, bĕt; bīte, bĭt; nō, nŏt, nôr; fūse, fŭn, fûr; tōō, tŏŏk; foil; foul; thin; ~~then~~;
hw for wh as in *wh*at; zh for s as in u*s*ual; ə for a, e, i, o, u, as in ag*o*, lin*e*n, per*i*l, at*o*m, min*u*s

valuable

val·u·a·ble (văl′yo͞o ə bəl) **1** highly prized; held in high esteem; very useful: *Roger was a valuable member of the team.* **2** costing much money; worth a great deal: *Her diamonds were very valuable.* **3 valuables** possessions of value, especially small personal objects such as jewelry: *She kept her valuables in the bank for safety.*

val·u·a·tion (văl′yo͞o ā′shən) **1** a putting a price (on something); an estimating of the worth: *His valuation of the watch at $30 was too high.* **2** estimated worth or price: *They sold the land for twice its original valuation.*

val·ue (văl′ū) **1** quality that makes a thing worth having: *The ring has a sentimental value.* **2** amount (something) is worth in money or things; price: *The value of that necklace is $50.* **3** to put a price on; to consider (something) to cost a certain amount: *He valued the car at $300.* **4** importance; worth: *His report was of value to the governor.* **5** to consider to have worth or importance: *The cowboy values his horse.* **val·ued, val·u·ing.**

valve (vălv) **1** part of a bodily organ or other device which prevents the backward flow of a liquid or a gas. **2** a faucetlike part for admitting or shutting off the flow of a liquid or a gas: *Elmer turned the radiator valve on because he suddenly felt cold.* **3** either of the two shells of certain shellfish.

Valve closed

Valve open

¹van (văn) front part of an army, fleet, or other group; leading position: *The destroyers were in the van, with the aircraft carrier just behind them.* [¹van is short for **vanguard.**]

²van (văn) large, covered truck. [²van is short for **caravan.**]

van·dal (văn′dəl) person who, with malice, destroys property, especially beautiful or valuable property: *The police caught the vandal who broke the statues.*

vane (văn) **1** a weathercock. **2** one of the blades of an electric fan, windmill, etc. (Homonyms: vain, vein.)

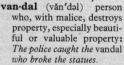

Vane

variation

van·guard (văn′gärd′) **1** leading section of a moving army or other organized march: *the vanguard of the parade.* **2** the leaders of a political or social movement or the leading position in such a movement.

va·nil·la (və nĭl′ə) **1** a food flavoring made from the beanlike seed pods of a tropical plant. **2** the plant that bears these pods.

van·ish (văn′ĭsh) **1** to be removed from sight; disappear from view: *The ship vanished in the fog as we watched.* **2** to cease to be; depart forever: *Both dinosaurs and dodoes have vanished from the face of the earth. Our hope for an early spring vanished when the snow fell.*

van·i·ty (văn′ə tĭ) **1** excessive pride in one's appearance or abilities; conceit: *She showed her vanity by always looking into the mirror.* **2** lack of usefulness, worth, or effect: *the vanity of trying to persuade him that he was wrong.* **3** a dressing table. **4 vanity case** small suitcase, containing a mirror, for carrying cosmetics, comb and brush, etc. **van·i·ties.**

van·quish (văng′kwĭsh) to defeat thoroughly; conquer.

van·tage (văn′tĭj) **1** old word meaning "advantage," still used in tennis to designate the first point won after deuce. **2 vantage ground** favorable position. **3 vantage point** or **point of vantage** position giving advantage.

va·por (vā′pər) **1** gaseous form of something that is usually a solid or liquid: *water vapor; mercury vapor.* **2** moisture that can be seen in the air as mist or steam.

var·i·a·ble (vâr′i ə bəl) changing; likely to change: *He has a variable nature, sometimes friendly and other times hostile.* **var·i·a·bly.**

var·i·ance (vâr′i əns) **1** disagreement; difference: *There is a large variance in our opinions of him.* **2** variation; change: *a variance in temperature.* **3 at variance** not agreeing; differing: *Our opinions of him are still at variance.*

var·i·a·tion (vâr′i ā′shən) **1** a varying or change (from what is usual or customary): *We can expect a variation in temperature tonight.* **2** amount of difference or change: *a variation of several dollars in price.* **3** form or version (of something) that differs from the original version: *a new variation of an old song.* **4** in music, the

varied

vegetable

repeating of a single tune or theme with changes that vary, and often elaborate it.

var·ied (vâr′id) **1** having different shapes, forms, colors, sizes, etc.: *The town has houses of* varied *appearance.* **2** of many sorts or kinds; full of variety: *a* varied *collection of pictures; a* varied *career.*

va·ri·e·ty (və rī′ə ti) **1** assortment of many different kinds: *The store had a large* variety *of candies.* **2** a kind: *a new* variety *of melon.* **3** change; lack of sameness or monotony: *He always said, "*Variety *is the spice of life."* **4 variety store** shop that sells many kinds of goods. **5 variety show** theatrical performance consisting of many different acts. **va·ri·e·ties.**

var·i·ous (vâr′i əs) **1** of different kinds: *Beverly received* various *gifts on her birthday.* **2** several; many and different: *Roses are of* various *colors.* **var·i·ous·ly.**

var·let (vär′lit) old-fashioned word for scoundrel.

var·nish (vär′nish) **1** liquid made from resins. It is transparent and can be spread like paint to give, when dry, a hard, smooth, glossy finish to wood, metal, plastics, etc. **2** surface made by varnish. **3** to cover with varnish. **4** outer show; superficial polish: *His fine manners are mere* varnish.

var·y (vâr′i) **1** to change; be or become different: *Weather* varies *from day to day.* **2** to cause to change; alter: *She* varies *the appearance of a room by rearranging the furniture.* **var·ied, var·y·ing.**

vase (vās or vāz or väz) ornamental container of glass, pottery, etc., often used as a flower holder.

Vase

vas·sal (văs′əl) in olden times, a person who owed certain duties to another in return for protection, land, etc.: *The nobles were* vassals *of the king. The peasants were* vassals *of the nobles.*

vast (văst) of great size or extent; huge; enormous: *the* vast *plains of the western United States.* **vast·ly.**

vast·ness (văst′nis) great size, extent, etc.: *One can see the* vastness *of the universe on a clear night.*

vat (văt) tub or tank for holding liquids.

Vat·i·can (văt′ə kən) **1** the headquarters in Rome of the Roman Catholic Church. **2** the home of the Pope.

Bank vault entrance

¹vault (vält or vôlt) **1** arched roof or ceiling. **2** something suggesting a vault, as the sky. **3** storage cellar. **4** room in a bank where valuables may be kept. **5** a tomb. **6** to put such an arched roof over; cover with a vault. [**¹vault** comes through Old French (volte, vaulte) from the form (volutus) of a Latin word (volvere) meaning "to turn about," "roll."]

²vault (vält or vôlt) **1** a leap over something, made with the aid of the hands or a pole. **2** to make such a jump: *Benton* vaulted *over the wall.* [**²vault** is **¹vault** in a special sense, arising from the fact that in leaping one moves in a curve that is like an arch.]

Boy vaulting a fence

vaunt (vônt) **1** to describe in glowing terms; brag about; boast of: *Travel advertisements* vaunt *the pleasures of a cruise.* **2** a boast or brag.

veal (vēl) flesh of a calf, used as food.

veer (vir) **1** to change direction: *The north wind* veered *to the east.* **2** to cause to change direction: *Bob* veered *the car to avoid the hole in the road.*

veg·e·ta·ble (vĕj′ə tə bəl) **1** a plant or part of a plant (root, blossom, leaves, etc.) used for food. Tomatoes, carrots, potatoes, cauliflower, and cabbage are vegetables. **2** made from plants or parts of plants: *Corn, peanuts, soybeans, etc., yield* vegetable *oils. We all like* vegetable *soup.* **3** having to do with plants: *Trees, grasses, weeds, etc., are all members of the* vegetable *kingdom.*

---

fāte, făt, fâre, fär; bē, bĕt; bīte, bĭt; nō, nŏt, nôr; fūse, fŭn, fûr; too͝, too͞k; foil; foul; thin; ~~then~~; hw for wh as in what; zh for s as in usual; ə for a, e, i, o, u, as in ago, linen, peril, atom, minus

veg·e·tar·i·an (vĕj′ə târ′ĭ ən) **1** person who eats only vegetables or vegetable products, or avoids eating animal flesh. **2** containing no meat: *a dish of* vegetarian *baked beans.*

veg·e·ta·tion (vĕj′ə tā′shən) plants of any kind: *The rocky hills have no trees, no grass, no* vegetation *at all.*

ve·he·mence (vē′ə məns) **1** great feeling; fervor; passion: *The orator spoke with fiery* vehemence. **2** violence; fury: *the* vehemence *of the storm.*

ve·he·ment (vē′ə mənt) **1** forceful; fiery; fervent: *a* vehement *demand for better housing.* **2** violent; wild; furious: *a* vehement *wind.* **ve·he·ment·ly.**

ve·hi·cle (vē′ə kəl) **1** any device for carrying passengers or goods, such as a car, sleigh, airplane, etc., especially one traveling on land. **2** a means of conveying thoughts, information, or the like: *Books and paintings are* vehicles *for authors' and artists' thoughts.* **3** liquid in which pigments and the like are dissolved: *Water is the* vehicle *for water colors.*

veil (vāl) **1** piece of cloth, often wide-meshed and transparent, used to hide or protect the face or for ornament. **2** the part of a nun's or bride's headdress that covers the head and falls over the shoulders, on each side of the face. **3** anything that hides like a curtain: *a* veil *of secrecy; a* veil *of mist.* **4** to hide or cover with a veil. **5** to hide partially as with a veil: *He did not trouble to* veil *his dislike.* **6 take the veil** to become a nun. (Homonym: vale.)

vein (vān) **1** a blood vessel in which blood flows toward the heart. **2** any blood vessel: *The red blood of youth was in his* veins. **3** one of the branching lines on a leaf or an insect's wing. **4** a strip of color or of ore in a rock. **5** a strain; streak: *A* vein *of humor ran through the book.* (Homonyms: vain, vane)

Veins of a leaf

vel·lum (vĕl′əm) **1** thin, smooth, tanned skin, usually of a calf, once used as writing paper, but now used for covers of expensive books; fine parchment. **2** writing paper imitating this material.

ve·loc·i·ty (və lŏs′ə tĭ) speed in a given direction. It is measured by the distance covered in each second, minute, hour, etc.: *the* velocity *of a rocket; the* velocity *of light.* **ve·loc·i·ties.**

vel·vet (vĕl′vĭt) **1** fine, closely woven fabric of silk or rayon with either a silk or cotton backing and a short, thick, soft nap or pile. **2** made of, or covered with, velvet. **3** pleasingly soft in appearance or to the touch: *the* velvet *darkness of a summer sky; the* velvet *skin of a peach.*

vel·vet·een (vĕl′və tēn′) imitation velvet made of cotton material.

vel·vet·y (vĕl′və tĭ) **1** of a texture like velvet to the touch. **2** soft and mellow to sight, hearing, or taste: *a strain of* velvety *music;* velvety *moonlight.*

vend (vĕnd) to sell, offer for sale; peddle.

ven·dor or **vend·er** (vĕn′dər) one who sells or offers for sale.

ve·neer (və nîr′) **1** thin layer of fine wood, etc., used to overlay the surface of furniture: *This chest has a beautiful walnut* veneer. **2** thin layer of tile or brick, covering a coarser building material: *a building with a brick* veneer. **3** to apply veneer to. **4** a camouflage for something coarse or inferior: *His cold nature showed through the thin* veneer *of genial behavior.*

ven·er·a·ble (vĕn′ər ə bəl) **1** deserving of respect and honor by reason of age, dignity, character, and high associations: *a* venerable *scholar.* **2** of buildings or places, sacred because of historic, religious, or ancient associations: *a* venerable *church.* **ven·er·a·bly.**

ven·er·ate (vĕn′ə rāt′) to regard with feelings of the highest respect and honor; to revere because of wisdom and age. **ven·er·at·ed, ven·er·at·ing.**

ven·er·a·tion (vĕn′ə rā′shən) **1** the act of venerating. **2** deep respect and reverence.

Ve·ne·tian blind (və nē′shən blĭnd) a shade of movable slats hung on tapes. The slats may be tilted or the shade raised by cords.

Venetian blind

Ven·e·zue·la (vĕn′ə zwē′lə or vĕn′ə zwā′lə) a country in northern South America.

venge·ance (vĕn′jəns) **1** act of causing harm to another in payment for harm suffered at his hands; revenge. **2 with a vengeance** with great force and energy: *He attacked the job with a vengeance.*

ven·i·son (vĕn′ə sən or vĕn′ə zən) the flesh of a deer, used as food.

ven·om (vĕn′əm) **1** the poisonous fluid injected by the bite of some snakes or by the sting or bite of scorpions and some insects. **2** spite; ill will; malice: *Her ill-tempered comment had a trace of venom.*

ven·om·ous (vĕn′əm əs) **1** poisonous; secreting venom: *the venomous sting of a scorpion.* **2** full of spite or malice: *a venomous tongue.* **ven·om·ous·ly.**

vent (vĕnt) **1** hole, opening, or outlet that serves as a passage for air, gas, liquid, etc.: *steam from the vent of a radiator; the vent of a chimney.* **2** an outlet; a means or opportunity of escape: *to give vent to anger; to find vent in tears.* **3** to give expression to; pour out: *to vent anger on a dog.*

ven·ti·late (vĕn′tə lāt′) **1** to bring fresh air into and drive stale air out of; to air: *Open the windows and ventilate the room.* **2** to bring out (a subject) for public examination and discussion: *The plans for the new park were ventilated in the newspapers.* **ven·ti·lat·ed, ven·ti·lat·ing.**

ven·ti·la·tion (vĕn′tə lā′shən) **1** the act of supplying with fresh air. **2** the supply of fresh air: *the ventilation in the schoolroom.*

Ventilators

ven·ti·la·tor (vĕn′tə lā′tər) any device for admitting or circulating fresh air, such as an opening, a fan, or an air-conditioning unit.

ven·tril·o·quist (vĕn trĭl′ə kwĭst) person skilled in the art of producing voice sounds which appear to come from some other person or from a distance.

ven·ture (vĕn′chər) **1** course of action or undertaking that contains some risk: *a venture into a wilderness; a mining venture; a new business venture.* **2** to hazard; dare

to say or do: *She ventured an opinion on the candidate.* **3** to risk; stake: *The explorer ventured his life in a trip through the jungle.* **ven·tured, ven·tur·ing.**

ven·ture·some (vĕn′chər səm) **1** daring; willing to take risks: *The venturesome boy was rescued from the mountain.* **2** involving risk, hazard, danger, etc.: *a venturesome experiment.* **ven·ture·some·ly.**

Ve·nus (vē′nəs) **1** the most brilliant of the nine planets, second in order of distance from the sun. **2** the Roman goddess of beauty, called Aphrodite by the Greeks.

ve·ran·da or **ve·ran·dah** (və răn′də) a porch, especially a covered one of some length.

Veranda

verb (vûrb) word that expresses doing, being, or happening. Verbs are sometimes called "action words" because most of them express some kind of action. "Kicked," "runs," "laughed," "is," and "became" are verbs in these sentences:

> *Robert kicked the ball.*
> *Jean runs to school.*
> *The audience laughed.*
> *The baby is one year old.*
> *The house became quiet.*

ver·bal (vûr′bəl) **1** having to do with or consisting of words: *a verbal picture.* **2** spoken; oral: *a verbal agreement between friends.* **3** word for word; literal: *This is a verbal translation of the Latin proverb.* **ver·bal·ly.**

ver·be·na (vər bē′nə) garden plant of spicy fragrance with flat clusters of flowers of various colors.

ver·dant (vûr′dənt) green with grass or leaves: *The trees are verdant in the spring.* **ver·dant·ly.**

ver·dict (vûr′dĭkt) decision or judgment, especially one made by a jury in a court trial.

ver·dure (vûr′jər) green vegetation; foliage.

verge (vûrj) edge; border; brink: *on the verge of the woods; on the verge of starvation.*

---

fāte, făt, fâre, fär; bē, bĕt; bīte, bĭt; nō, nŏt, nôr; fūse, fŭn, fûr; tōō, tŏŏk; foil; foul; thin; then; hw for wh as in what; zh for s as in usual; ə for a, e, i, o, u, as in ago, linen, peril, atom, minus

verge on to border on; adjoin; approach: *Our garden* verges on *woodland. Her remarks* verge on *rudeness.* **verged, verg·ing.**

ver·i·fy (vĕr′ə fī′) **1** to confirm the truth of; prove: *Science* verifies *its theories by experiments before accepting them as true.* **2** to check the truth of: *You can* verify *his statement by calling the library.* **ver·i·fied, ver·i·fy·ing.**

ver·i·ly (vĕr′ə lĭ) an old word meaning "truly"; "really"; "in fact."

ver·i·ta·ble (vĕr′ə tə bəl) true; actual; genuine: *a* veritable *genius.* **ver·i·ta·bly.**

ver·mil·ion (vər mil′yən) **1** a brilliant red coloring material. **2** bright red: *a* vermilion *sunset.*

ver·min (vûr′mĭn) unpleasant or harmful insects and small animals: *The house was overrun with mice, fleas, and other* vermin.

Ver·mont (vər mŏnt′) a State in the northeast part of the United States.

ver·sa·tile (vûr′sə tĭl) able to do many things; having many abilities: *The* versatile *actor could play any role.* **ver·sa·tile·ly.**

verse (vûrs) **1** poetry; poem; a rhythmic composition, usually in rhyme. **2** section of a poem or song; stanza. **3** short, numbered division of a chapter of the Bible. **4** single line of poetry.

versed (vûrst) experienced; informed; skilled: *He is* versed *in many subjects.*

ver·sion (vûr′zhən or vûr′shən) **1** account or description from one point of view: *This is his* version *of the accident.* **2** a particular translation or edition (of a written work): *the King James* version *of the Bible.*

ver·sus (vûr′səs) Latin word for "against." It is shortened in writing to vs.: *Harvard* vs. *Yale.* In legal writing, it is shortened to v.: *Jones* v. *Smith.*

ver·te·bra (vûr′tə brə) one of the bones that make up the backbone. **ver·te·brae** (vûr′tə brē′) or **ver·te·bras.**

ver·te·brate (vûr′tə brāt′ or vûr′tə brĭt) **1** animal with a backbone or spine. Men, dogs, snakes, fishes, and birds are vertebrates, but lobsters, worms, and bees are not. **2** having a spine or backbone: *a* vertebrate *animal.*

ver·ti·cal (vûr′tə kəl) **1** up-and-down; upright; erect: *There is a* vertical *wall around our school. The flagpole is* vertical, *too.* **2** something straight up-and-down: *Draw a* vertical *where the lines cross.* **ver·ti·cal·ly.**

ver·y (vĕr′ĭ) **1** to a high degree; extremely: *He is* very *angry.* **2** same: *This is the* very *man I was talking about.* **3** absolutely: *This is the* very *last thing I will do for you.* **4** mere: *The* very *thought of leaving the cozy fire made him shiver.*

Vertical

ves·pers or **Ves·pers** (vĕs′pərz) religious service held in the late afternoon or evening.

ves·sel (vĕs′əl) **1** hollow container for a liquid: *She set out several bowls as* vessels *for soup.* **2** a large boat or ship. **3** a tube in a creature's body through which a liquid flows: *a blood* vessel.

vest (vĕst) **1** sleeveless jacket worn over a shirt and under a coat. **2** undershirt. **3** to clothe or endow (with authority, power, or the like): *The church* vests *its bishops with certain powers.* **4** to put into the care of another: *The management of the company is* vested *in its officials.*

Vest

ves·ti·bule (vĕs′tə būl′) **1** small entrance hall to a building or room. **2** enclosed platform of a railway passenger car.

ves·tige (vĕs′tĭj) trace, sign, or mark left of something: *Not a* vestige *of the original paint was left on the wall. Vestiges of beauty remained in the old lady's face.*

vest·ment (vĕst′mənt) robe; gown; garment, especially one worn by a clergyman performing religious rites.

ves·try (vĕs′trĭ) **1** room in a church where the clergy put on their robes or vestments **2** room in a church used for Sunday school, business, or prayer meetings. **3** in the Episcopal Church, a committee that manages the affairs of a church. **ves·tries.**

vet·er·an (vĕt′ər ən) **1** person who has done active military service: *His father is a* veteran *of both World Wars.* **2** one who is experienced from long practice and service: *Ethel Barrymore was a* veteran *of the stage.* **3** long-trained or practiced, especially as a soldier: *the* veteran *troops; the* veteran *actor.*

Veteran's Day November 11th, originally a holiday to celebrate the Armistice of World War I, now a holiday in honor of the veterans of the Armed Forces.

vet·er·i·nar·i·an (vĕt′ər ə när′ĭ ən) doctor who treats sick or injured animals.

vet·er·i·nar·y (vĕt′ər ə nĕr′ĭ) **1** having to do with surgical or medical care of animals: *A farmer finds* veterinary *skills useful* **2** doctor who treats animals. **vet·er·i·nar·ies.**

ve·to (vē′tō) **1** right or power of a president, governor, etc., to prevent or delay bills from becoming law: *the Presidential* veto. **2** the exercise of such right: *The bill met with a* veto. **3** to forbid with authority; refuse to consent to: *The governor* vetoed *a bill to make gambling legal. John's father* vetoed *our plans to go camping.* **ve·toes; ve·toed, ve·to·ing.**

vex (vĕks) to annoy; make cross; disturb: *My friend* vexed *me by being late for an appointment.*

vex·a·tion (vĕk sā′shən) **1** annoyance; irritation: *The captain's face showed* vexation *at the delay.* **2** something that annoys or distresses: *That dull can opener is a* vexation.

vi·a (vī′ə) by way of: *We drive from New York to Mexico* via *New Orleans.*

Modern viaduct over turnpike intersection

vi·a·duct (vī′ə dŭkt′) a long bridge of many short spans, built to carry a road or railway over a valley, marsh, etc.; also, an elevated roadway over city traffic.

vi·al (vī′əl) a small glass or plastic bottle, sometimes ornamental, used for perfume, tablets, etc. (Homonym: viol)

vi·and (vī′ənd) article of food, especially a delicacy: *The banquet table was heaped with fine* viands.

vi·brant (vī′brənt) **1** vibrating, as with life, energy, enthusiasm, etc.: *a vibrant personality.* **2** rich in sound; resonant: *Her* vibrant *soprano voice thrilled the audience.* **vi·brant·ly.**

vi·brate (vī′brāt′) **1** to move back and forth very rapidly, often making a sound: *The windows* vibrated *with every passing truck.* **2** to thrill; be stirred; quiver: *to* vibrate *with happiness.* **vi·brat·ed, vi·brat·ing.**

vi·bra·tion (vī brā′shən) rapid motion back and forth; shaking: *the* vibration *of an engine; the* vibration *of a violin string.*

vic·ar (vĭk′ər) **1** person who acts in place of another, especially in church affairs. **2** in some churches, a parish priest.

vice (vīs) **1** bad habit or fault: *Drunkenness is a* vice. **2** wickedness, corruption. (Homonym: vise)

vice-pres·i·dent (vīs′prĕz′ə dənt) officer next in rank to a president, who takes the president's place when necessary.

vice·roy (vīs′roi) governor of a colony or province who rules as a deputy of a king or queen.

vi·ce ver·sa (vī′sə vûr′sə or vīs vûr′sə) the same action, thought, etc., but reversed in order: *Emily has great respect for Victor, and* vice versa.

vi·cin·i·ty (vĭ sin′ə tĭ) surrounding area; neighborhood: *There is no parking allowed in our* vicinity. **vi·cin·i·ties.**

vi·cious (vĭsh′əs) **1** wicked; bad; evil: *a* vicious *life.* **2** full of malice; spiteful; nasty: *a* vicious *retort;* vicious *gossip* **3** bad-tempered; unruly and dangerous; inclined to violence: *a* vicious *dog; a* vicious *criminal.* **4** severe; extremely unpleasant: *a* vicious *headache; a* vicious *snowstorm.* **vi·cious·ly.**

vi·cis·si·tudes (vĭ sis′ə tōōdz′ or vĭ sĭs′ə-tūdz′) changes of fortune, condition, circumstance, or the like; the ups and downs (of life)

vic·tim (vĭk′tim) **1** one who is injured or killed by another, by a disease, or by an act of nature: *the* victims *of an earth-*

fāte, făt, fâre, fär; bē, bĕt; bīte, bĭt; nō, nŏt, nôr; fūse, fŭn, fûr; tōō, tŏŏk; foil; foul; thin; ~~then~~; hw for wh as in *wh*at; zh for s as in u*s*ual; ə for a, e, i, o, u, as in *a*go, lin*e*n, per*i*l, at*o*m, min*u*s

799

quake. **2** one who is misused, cheated, or tormented by another: *the* victim *of a practical joke.* **3** an animal or a person chosen for sacrifice to a god.

vic·tor (vĭk'tər) winner; conqueror.

vic·to·ri·ous (vĭk tôr'ĭ əs) having conquered in battle or some kind of contest such as a game; triumphant. **vic·to·ri·ous·ly.**

vic·to·ry (vĭk'tə rĭ) **1** the defeat of an enemy. **2** any triumph. **vic·to·ries.**

vict·ual (vĭt'əl) **1** to supply with food: *We* victualed *the fort for a long siege.* **2** **vict·uals** food; provisions.

vie (vī) to try to show oneself as best; contend; compete; strive for superiority: *to* vie *for a spelling prize.* **vied, vy·ing.**

view (vū) **1** to look at: *to* view *pictures in an art gallery.* **2** the act of seeing: *Our first* view *of the ocean was in March.* **3** something seen: *The* view *from the tower is magnificent.* **4** picture of a scene, especially of a landscape. **5** distance and area one can see: *The ship was soon beyond* view. *The train came into* view *around the bend.* **6** to regard critically; form an opinion or judgment: *Mr. Warren* viewed *the plan from every angle.* **7** way of regarding (something); opinion; judgment: *We have different* views *on the matter.* **8** **in view** under consideration: *What we have in* view *is a book children will enjoy.* **9** **in view of** because of: *We shall postpone our visit in* view *of the hot weather.* **10** **on view** on display: *The goods will be on* view *next Thursday.* **11** **with a view to** with a hope or intention of: *We wish to learn more about the property,* with a view to *purchasing it.*

view·point (vū'point') **1** place from which something is looked at. **2** way of looking at things; standpoint: *From the* viewpoint *of your committee, the project is unwise.*

vig·il (vĭj'əl) **1** a keeping awake for the purpose of watching, especially at night: *to keep* vigil *over a sick person.* **2** the day and night before a religious festival.

vig·i·lance (vĭj'ə ləns) a being vigilant; watchfulness; alertness: *Through the scout's* vigilance *the wagon train avoided a trap.*

vigilance committee **1** in unorganized communities, a self-appointed group organized to prevent and punish crime where regular law enforcement is absent or

broken down. **2** any self-appointed group devoted to the suppression of real or fancied evil.

vig·i·lant (vĭj'ə lənt) watchful; alert. **vig·i·lant·ly.**

vig·i·lan·te (vĭj'ə lăn'tĭ) member of a vigilance committee.

vig·or (vĭg'ər) bodily or mental strength and energy; stamina; vitality.

vig·or·ous (vĭg'ər əs) full of life; strong; energetic. **vig·or·ous·ly.**

vi·king or **Vi·king** (vī'kĭng) one of the sea rovers from Norway, Sweden, and Denmark that terrorized the coast towns of Europe a thousand years ago.

vile (vīl) **1** wicked; contemptible: *a* vile *deed;* vile *language.* **2** disgusting; repulsive; loathsome: *a* vile *odor.* **vil·er, vil·est.**

vil·la (vĭl'ə) country house, especially one built for show and recreation.

vil·lage (vĭl'ĭj) **1** small town. **2** the people living in a village: *The whole* village *went to the band concert.*

vil·lag·er (vĭl'ə jər) person living in a village.

vil·lain (vĭl'ən) **1** wicked person; rascal. **2** in a play or novel, the character who opposes the hero.

vil·lain·ous (vĭl'ən əs) **1** wicked; rascally: *a* villainous *deed.* **2** very bad; highly unpleasant: *I have a* villainous *cold.* **vil·lain·ous·ly.**

vil·lain·y (vĭl'ən ĭ) **1** wickedness. **2** wicked deed; crime: *What* villainy *is he up to now?* **vil·lain·ies.**

vim (vĭm) vigor; energy; strength.

vin·di·cate (vĭn'də kāt') **1** to clear of suspected guilt or wrongdoing; absolve: *He claimed that he was innocent and that new evidence would be found to* vindicate *him.* **2** to uphold; prove and establish the truth of: *to* vindicate *a claim or cause.* **vin·di·cat·ed, vin·di·cat·ing.**

vin·di·ca·tion (vĭn'də kā'shən) a proving or proof of right or innocence after charges of wrong or guilt: *the* vindication *of a claim; the* vindication *of an accused prisoner.*

vin·dic·tive (vĭn dĭk'tĭv) filled with a desire for revenge; spiteful and malicious: *He is too* vindictive *to accept my apology.* **vin·dic·tive·ly.**

vine (vīn) any plant with a long stem that trails along the ground or climbs upward by fastening its tendrils to a support: *Grapes and melons grow on* vines.

vin·e·gar (vĭn′gər) sour liquid used to flavor or preserve food. Vinegar is a water solution of a mild acid produced by fermenting slightly alcoholic liquids, such as cider, wine, etc.

vine·yard (vĭn′yərd) land used for the cultivation of grapes.

vin·tage (vĭn′tĭj) **1** wine made from the grapes of some particular region in some particular year. **2** annual harvest of grapes **3** made from a specially good grape harvest; choice: *a vintage wine.* **4** group or crop of anything: *That's a play of old* vintage.

vi·ol (vī′əl) **1** any of a class of stringed instruments, played with a bow and used in the Middle Ages. From the viols came the modern violin family. **2** bass viol. (Homonym: vial)

vi·o·la (vĭ ō′lə or vĭ ō′lə) stringed instrument deeper in tone and slightly larger than a violin, and belonging to the same family.

vi·o·late (vī′ə lāt′) **1** to act against; break: *to* violate *a treaty; to* violate *a law.* **2** to disturb; interrupt: *to* violate *the silence.* **3** to treat (a holy place) with lack of reverence or respect: *to* violate *a shrine.* **vi·o·lat·ed, vi·o·lat·ing.**

vi·o·la·tion (vī′ə lā′shən) **1** the act of breaking (a law, treaty, promise, etc.). **2** interruption or disturbance: *a* violation *of privacy.* **3** action lacking respect or reverence: *Their noisy laughter was a* violation *of the dignity of the court.*

vi·o·la·tor (vī′ə lā′tər) one who commits a violation.

vi·o·lence (vī′ə ləns) **1** physical force, usually resulting in harm: *an act of* violence; *the* violence *of a storm.* **2** intensity; passion: *the* violence *of his rage.* **3** damage: *to do* violence *to a garden by tramping through it.*

vi·o·lent (vī′ə lənt) **1** physically forceful or resulting from physical force: *a* violent *blow on the head; a* violent *death.* **2** intense: *his* violent *anger.* **3** resulting from and showing intense feeling: *an outburst of* violent *speech;* violent *tears.* **vi·o·lent·ly.**

vi·o·let (vī′ə lĭt) **1** a small, low-growing spring plant with flowers of yellow, white, or purple. **2** the flower of this plant. **3** bluish purple. **4** the bluish-red color produced by the shortest rays of visible light.

Common violet

vi·o·lin (vī′ə lĭn′) the smallest and highest in tone of the four-stringed instruments played with a bow. It is rested against the shoulder while being played.

vi·o·lin·ist (vī′ə lin′-ist) person who plays a violin.

vi·o·lon·cel·lo (vī′ə-lən chĕl′ō or vē′ə lən-chĕl′ō) a bass violin. The violoncello has four strings and is larger and has a deeper tone than the violin or viola.

Girl playing violin

vi·per (vī′pər) **1** any of a group of poisonous snakes. **2** an evil, treacherous person.

vir·gin (vûr′jin) **1** a maiden; woman who has remained pure. **2** pure, as a maiden. **3** very clean; spotless: *white as* virgin *snow.* **4** not yet changed or used: *a* virgin *forest.* **5 Virgin Mary** the mother of Jesus.

Vir·gin·ia (vər jin′yə) a State in the southeastern part of the United States on the Atlantic coast.

Virgin Islands group of islands in the West Indies, some of which belong to the United States and some to the United Kingdom.

vir·tu·al (vûr′chōō əl) real in effect or for practical purposes, if not strictly in name or fact: *The expression on her face was a* virtual *admission of guilt.* **vir·tu·al·ly.**

vir·tue (vûr′chōō) **1** moral excellence; goodness; high character. **2** particular moral quality or good habit: *the* virtue *of charity.* **3** excellence; merit; value: *The* virtue *of this car is that it runs on very little fuel.* **4** power to produce a result; efficacy: *This medicine has very little* virtue *for curing headaches.* **5 by virtue of** because of: *He succeeded* by virtue of *hard work.*

---

fāte, făt, fâre, fär; bē, bĕt; bīte, bĭt; nō, nŏt, nôr; fūse, fŭn, fûr; tōō, tŏŏk; foil; foul; thin; then; hw for wh as in *wh*at; zh for s as in u*s*ual; ə for a, e, i, o, u, as in *a*go, lin*e*n, per*i*l, at*o*m, min*u*s

vir·tu·ous (vûr′chŏŏ əs) having moral excellence; good. **vir·tu·ous·ly.**

vi·rus (vī′rəs) **1** a form of living matter, much smaller than bacteria, that can multiply in plants and animals. Viruses cause mumps, measles, the common cold, and many other illnesses. **2** anything poisonous to the mind or character: *the* virus *of hate.*

vis·age (vĭz′ĭj) the face.

vis·count (vī′kount) nobleman of a rank just below an earl or count and just above a baron.

vise (vīs) a tool which holds things rigidly between two jaws which are tightened by turning a screw. (Homonym: vice)

Vises

vis·i·bil·i·ty (vĭz′ə bĭl′ə tĭ) **1** the capability of being seen; the condition of being visible. **2** the distance at which things can be seen under given weather conditions: *The* visibility *from this tower is forty miles on a clear day.*

vis·i·ble (vĭz′ə bəl) **1** capable of being seen; to be seen: *In the fog my hand was not* visible *before my face.* **2** clear; apparent; perceptible: *He has no* visible *income.* **vis·i·bly.**

vi·sion (vĭzh′ən) **1** sense of sight; ability to see: *His* vision *was affected by the heavy smoke.* **2** a sight: *She was a* vision *of beauty.* **3** foresight; imagination; broad understanding: *the* vision *of a great scientist; a statesman of* vision. **4** mental image; something imagined: *She had a* vision *of the way the new house would look.*

vi·sion·ar·y (vĭzh′ə nĕr′ĭ) **1** person of great imagination, especially one with impractical ideas or schemes; dreamer: *He was a poet and a* visionary. **2** of, or as seen in, a vision: *The* visionary *form beckoned her to follow.* **3** imaginary; unreal; impractical: *a* visionary *scheme.* **vi·sion·ar·ies.**

vis·it (vĭz′ĭt) **1** to come or go to: *We* visit *our grandparents every Christmas.* **2** to stay for a time: *to* visit *in New York.* **3** to be a guest of: *I am* visiting *Thelma for two weeks.* **4** a social or professional call: *a* visit *for tea; a doctor's* visit. **5** to afflict; come upon: *Many towns in the Middle Ages were* visited *by the plague.*

vis·i·tor (vĭz′ə tər) one who visits; guest.

vi·sor (vī′zər) **1** of a helmet, the movable front part that protects the face. **2** the brim of a cap. Also spelled **vizor.**

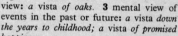

Visors

vis·ta (vĭs′tə) **1** a view, especially through a long, narrow passage: *There was a* vista *of the river at the end of the street.* **2** the passage that forms the view: *a* vista *of oaks.* **3** mental view of events in the past or future: *a* vista *down the years to childhood; a* vista *of promised happiness.*

vis·u·al (vĭzh′ŏŏ əl) using or having to do with the sense of sight: *Pictures are* visual *aids in learning to spell. Movies have a great* visual *appeal.* **vis·u·al·ly.**

vis·u·al·ize (vĭzh′ŏŏ əl īz′) to form a mental picture (of): *It is hard for me to* visualize *the house from these rough sketches.* **vis·u·al·ized, vis·u·al·iz·ing.**

vi·tal (vī′təl) **1** full of life and energy; lively. **2** needed for life: *The heart and lungs are* vital *organs.* **3** essential: *Your help is* vital *if we are to get this work done.* **4** causing death or ruin; fatal: *a* vital *wound; to strike a* vital *blow.* **5** of or having to do with life: *to keep* vital *statistics;* vital *energy.* **6 vitals** organs of the body essential for life, as the heart, liver, and lungs. **vi·tal·ly.**

vi·tal·i·ty (vī tăl′ə tĭ) **1** ability to keep on living: *Her* vitality *was weakened by illness.* **2** strength; liveliness; energy: *The children's* vitality *expressed itself in a glorious romp.*

vi·ta·min (vī′tə mĭn) any of a class of substances found in very small amounts in food and necessary for health.

vi·va·cious (vĭ vā′shəs or vī vā′shəs) lively; gay; high-spirited. **vi·va·cious·ly.**

vi·vac·i·ty (vĭ văs′ə tĭ or vī văs′ə tĭ) gaiety; liveliness; high spirits.

viv·id (vĭv′ĭd) **1** bright; intense: *a* vivid *red.* **2** lifelike; convincing: *a* vivid *description of a circus.* **3** lively; active: *a* vivid *imagination.* **viv·id·ly.**

vix·en (vĭk′sən) **1** a female fox. **2** a sharp-tempered, quarrelsome woman.

vi·zier or **vi·zir** (vĭ zĭr′) in Moslem countries, a high official, especially a state minister.

vi·zor (vī′zər) visor.

vo·cab·u·lar·y (vō kăb′yŏŏ lĕr′ĭ) **1** all the words in a language. **2** all the words used by a group or an individual: *He had a very limited* vocabulary. **3** alphabetical list of the words used in a book, often including their translations or definitions. **vo·cab·u·lar·ies.**

vo·cal (vō′kəl) **1** of or having to do with the voice; oral: *a vocal* selection. **2** uttered with the voice, especially in an insistent manner: *a vocal* protest. **3** inclined to speak freely: *a vocal person.* **vo·cal·ly.**

vocal cords two bands of tough, elastic tissue in the larynx that vibrate when air from the lungs is pushed between them, thus producing the sound of the voice.

vo·ca·tion (vō kā′shən) **1** person's occupation, trade, or profession: *At first he grew flowers for fun, then as a* vocation. **2** work which a person feels called to do; calling: *He was a good businessman but felt that teaching was his* vocation *in life.*

vo·cif·er·ous (vō sif′ər əs) **1** speaking out or shouting noisily: *a vociferous audience.* **2** clamorous; noisy because of shouting: *the* vociferous *applause.* **vo·cif·er·ous·ly.**

vogue (vōg) **1** fashion at the particular time: *Full skirts are in* vogue. **2** popularity: *His play had a great* vogue *that year.*

voice (vois) **1** sound coming from the mouth, especially the human mouth. **2** tone quality of vocal sounds: *She has a soft* voice. **3** power of making sounds: *The singer lost his* voice. **4** expression; utterance: *They gave* voice *to their indignation.* **5** to give expression to: *He* voiced *his feelings.* **6** anything resembling or likened to human speech or sound: *the* voices *of birds; the* voice *of the wind.* **7** opinion; choice; power to make or help make a decision: *He had no* voice *in the matter.* **voiced, voic·ing.**

void (void) **1** empty; vacant. **2** an empty space: *to fill a* void. **3** a feeling of emptiness or loss: *His death left a* void *in our hearts.* **4** to make empty; empty out (the contents of). **5** in law, to cancel or annul; to make not valid: *to* void *a contract.* **6** in law, not having any force; not valid: *The will was declared* void *by the court.* **7 void**

of entirely without; devoid of: *a man* void *of humor.* **8 the void** space beyond mortal knowledge: *within the* void *of heaven; to disappear into* the void.

vol. volume.

vol·a·tile (vŏl′ə tĭl) **1** easy or quick to evaporate; readily turning into vapor: *Gasoline is a* volatile *liquid.* **2** changeable; fickle; lively; lighthearted: *a* volatile *disposition.*

vol·can·ic (vŏl kăn′ĭk) **1** having to do with a volcano: *high* volcanic *peaks.* **2** like a volcano; violent; explosive: *a man of* volcanic *energy.*

vol·ca·no (vŏl kā′nō) **1** a break in the earth's crust which throws out melted rock, ashes, and steam. **2** hill or mountain formed by material thrown out of a break in the earth's crust. **vol·ca·noes** or **vol·ca·nos.**

Alaskan volcano

vol·ley (vŏl′ĭ) **1** flight of many bullets or other missiles at the same time: *a* volley *of arrows.* **2** a discharge of numerous firearms at the same time: *The platoon fired a* volley *in salute.* **3** to fly or be shot all at once: *Wild ducks* volleyed *into the air like rockets.* **4** sudden burst or shower (of something): *a* volley *of words; a* volley *of applause.* **5** in sports, to bat something back and forth as across a net. **6** a batting back and forth as across a net.

vol·ley·ball (vŏl′ĭ bôl′) **1** game in which two teams attempt to bat a large ball back and forth across a net with their hands without letting the ball touch the ground. **2** the ball used in this game.

volt (vōlt) unit for measuring the force that causes electrons to move in an electric circuit.

volt·age (vōl′tĭj) electric force measured in volts.

vol·u·ble (vŏl′yŏŏ bəl) speaking with an easy flow of words; talkative: *Some people are* voluble *without saying anything.*

vol·ume (vŏl′yəm) **1** bulk or space, measured by cubic inches, cubic feet, etc.: *the* volume *of a hollow sphere.* **2** quantity, meas-

---

fāte, făt, fâre, fär; bē, bĕt; bīte, bĭt; nō, nŏt, nôr; fūse, fŭn, fûr; tōō, tŏŏk; foil; foul; thin; ~~then~~; hw for wh as in *wh*at; zh for s as in u*s*ual; ə for a, e, i, o, u, as in *a*go, lin*e*n, per*i*l, at*o*m, min*u*s

voluminous

ured in quarts, gallons, barrels, etc.: *the* volume *of water in the tank.* **3** of sound, amount or loudness: *Please turn down the* volume *of the radio.* **4** book: *His library numbered three hundred* volumes. **5** any one of a set of books: *Please give me* volume *three of the encyclopedia.*

vo·lu·mi·nous (və lōō′mə nəs) **1** large in quantity or size: *He took voluminous notes for his essay.* **2** capable of filling a large volume or volumes: *a voluminous history; a voluminous author.* **vo·lu·mi·nous·ly.**

vol·un·tar·y (vŏl′ən těr′ĭ) **1** done of one's own free choice, without force or compulsion: *a voluntary confession.* **2** intentional; not accidental: *His crime was ruled a deliberate and voluntary act.* **3** partly supported by contributions from private persons: *a voluntary hospital.* **4** controlled by the will: *Muscles in the arm are voluntary, but the muscles in the heart are not.* **vol·un·tar·i·ly.**

vol·un·teer (vŏl′ən tîr′) **1** person who enters into any service, especially one of the armed services, without being compelled to do so by law. **2** person who offers to do something of his own free will, without being ordered to do so: *The sergeant called for* volunteers *for the dangerous patrol.* **3** to offer of one's own accord: *He* volunteered *to walk the dog.* **4** having to do with services given without pay or of one's own accord: *a* volunteer *nurse.*

vom·it (vŏm′ĭt) **1** to discharge the contents of the stomach through the mouth; throw up. **2** matter discharged in this way. **3** to pour forth violently: *He* vomited *abuse. The volcano* vomited *lava.*

vo·ra·cious (vôr ā′shəs) **1** greedy in eating; craving huge amounts of food; ravenous: *a* voracious *animal; a* voracious *appetite.* **2** eager in some pursuit; devouring; insatiable: *a* voracious *reader.* **vo·ra·cious·ly.**

vor·tex (vôr′těks) **1** a whirling mass of water or air that sucks anything near it into the vacuum at its center; a whirlpool or whirlwind. **2** any situation or state of affairs that seems to swallow up everything exposed to its violent whirl and activity: *the* vortex *of war.* **vor·tex·es** or **vor·ti·ces** (vôr′tə sēz′).

vote (vōt) **1** a choice or wish expressed by written ballot, voice, or show of hands, by

vulgar

one or more persons in favor of some particular person or thing, as in an election. **2** ballot: *The* votes *were still coming in at midnight.* **3** the right to express such a choice: *She is too young to have a* vote. **4** number of such expressions, taken as a whole: *The* vote *was unanimous.* **5** to express a choice in an election; to cast a ballot. **6** to decide, give, or establish by a vote: *The town council* voted *funds for a new library.* **vot·ed, vot·ing.**

vot·er (vō′tər) **1** person who has a legal right to vote in elections. **2** person who casts a ballot.

vouch (vouch) to guarantee.

vouch for to be a witness for: *I am ready to* vouch *for* him. *We can* vouch *for the truth of that statement.*

vouch·safe (vouch sāf′) to be kind or gracious enough to give or grant (something): *to* vouchsafe *someone a reply.* **vouch·safed, vouch·saf·ing.**

vow (vou) **1** a promise or pledge, especially one made to God and binding from a religious point of view: *a nun's* vows. **2** a pledge of love and fidelity: *their marriage* vows. **3** to promise in a solemn manner; to swear; to resolve: *to* vow *secrecy.* **4** to say emphatically or earnestly: *I* vow *that this is the best cake I've ever tasted.* **5 take vows** to become a member of a religious order.

vow·el (vou′əl) **1** a speech sound made by the vocal cords, with the mouth partly open to allow a clear passage of air. **2** a letter representing such a sound. A, E, I, O, U are vowels.

voy·age (voi′ĭj) **1** a journey by ship on the sea or along a river, usually to a distant place: *a voyage to the Philippine Islands; a voyage up the Amazon.* **2** a journey by air. **3** to travel by water or by air. **voy·aged, voy·ag·ing.**

voy·ag·er (voi′ĭj ər) person who travels or who makes a voyage.

vs. versus.

Vt. Vermont.

vul·gar (vŭl′gər) **1** showing bad taste; crude; coarse: *a vulgar person;* vulgar *habits; a vulgar display of wealth.* **2** of the common people; in common use: *the* vulgar *tongue;* vulgar *superstitions.* **vul·gar·ly.**

vul·gar·i·ty (vəl găr′ ə tĭ) behavior or speech showing a lack of refinement, delicacy, or good taste. **vul·gar·i·ties.**

vul·ner·a·ble (vŭl′nər ə bəl) **1** not protected against injury or attack; easily hurt or destroyed: *a vulnerable person; a vulnerable outpost.* **2 vulnerable to** easily

Vulture (California Condor), about 4 ft. long

hurt by; open to: *a person* vulnerable to *ridicule; an outpost* vulnerable to *surprise attack.* **vul·ner·a·bly.**

vul·ture (vŭl′chər) **1** any of numerous large birds of prey that eat meat left by other animals. Vultures resemble hawks and eagles but have bald heads. **2** a grasping, merciless person. For picture, see opposite column.

vy·ing (vī′ĭng) See **vie.** *Everybody is* vying *for the honor of greeting the President when he comes to town.*

W

W, w (dŭb′əl yōō) the 23rd letter of the English alphabet.

W. west.

wab·ble (wŏb′əl) wobble. **wab·bled, wab·bling.**

wad (wŏd) **1** small mass of soft material, used as padding or to stop up an opening: *a wad of cotton.* **2** to make into a wad: *to* wad *cotton.* **3** to stop up with a wad: *to* wad *one's ears with cotton.* **4** small compact mass (of something) squeezed together: *a wad of tobacco; a wad of paper.* **5** round piece of felt, cloth, or paper used to plug the powder and shot in position in a gun. **wad·ded, wad·ding.**

wad·dle (wŏd′əl) **1** to walk with short, clumsy steps in a rocking and swaying motion from side to side: *The duck waddled back to the pond.* **2** clumsy, rocking gait. **wad·dled, wad·dling.**

wade (wād) **1** to walk through water, snow, mud, tall grass, or anything else that hinders one's progress: *to wade in a brook.* **2** to cross by walking through water, mud, etc.: *to wade a shallow stream.* **3** to proceed slowly and with difficulty: *to wade through a tedious lesson.*

wade into to go at (something) with vigor: *to wade into a dispute.* **wad·ed, wad·ing.**

wa·fer (wā′fər) **1** very thin biscuit or cake. **2** small, round piece of unleavened bread used in the communion service in certain

churches. **3** small colored piece of sticky paper used for sealing documents, letters, etc.

waf·fle (wŏf′əl) kind of crisp pancake cooked between two hinged metal plates with studded surfaces, called a waffle iron. The studs leave deep impressions on the cake.

waft (wăft or wäft) **1** to carry lightly through the air or over water: *The breeze* wafted *the scent of roses in from the garden.* **2** to float or be carried along in a smooth manner: *A scent of roses* wafted *in the window.* **3** a gust or puff, as of wind: *a waft of smoke; a waft of cooking smells.*

wag (wăg) **1** to move, or cause to move, repeatedly and quickly, from side to side, up and down, or forwards and backwards: *The dog's tail* wagged. *He* wagged *his finger. Her tongue* wagged *in gossip all over town.* **2** a wagging movement: *the wag of a dog's tail; to show disagreement or doubt by a wag of the head.* **3** person fond of making jokes; a wit. **wagged, wag·ging.**

wage (wāj) **1** to engage in; carry on: *to* wage *a war; to* wage *a campaign against mosquitoes.* **2** payment made or received for work or services: *a weekly* wage; *summer* wages *earned by students.* **waged, wag·ing.**

wa·ger (wā′jər) **1** to agree to pay another if one's guess is proved wrong; to bet. **2** to be willing to bet: *I'll* wager *it will rain*

---

fāte, făt, fâre, fär; bē, bĕt; bīte, bĭt; nō, nŏt, nôr; fūse, fŭn, fûr; tōō, tŏŏk; foil; foul; thin; then; hw for wh as in *wh*at; zh for s as in u*s*ual; ə for a, e, i, o, u, as in *a*go, lin*e*n, per*i*l, at*o*m, min*u*s

tomorrow. **3** an agreement to pay another if one's guess is wrong; a bet. **4** the money that is bet: *a wager of $10.*

wag·gish (wăg′ĭsh) **1** fond of playing jokes; mischievous. **2** lightly humorous or jesting; roguish: *His waggish remarks used to set the class laughing.* **wag·gish·ly.**

wag·gle (wăg′əl) **1** to move back and forth; wag: *His tongue waggles all day with useless chatter.* **2** a wagging motion: *The dog welcomed us with a friendly waggle of his tail.* **wag·gled, wag·gling.**

wag·on (wăg′ən) **1** vehicle with four wheels that is drawn by a horse and used to carry loads. **2** light motor truck for house-to-house delivery: *a milk wagon; a bread wagon.* **3** hand cart for indoor use: *a tea wagon.* **4** a child's toy cart.

Wagon

wag·on·er (wăg′ən ər) one who drives a wagon or carries goods in a wagon.

waif (wāf) homeless wanderer; lost person or animal, especially a lost child.

wail (wāl) **1** to cry or moan in grief or pain: *The sick child wailed all day.* **2** a sound of pain or misery: *We could hear the wail of the mourning women.* **3** to make a mournful sound: *The wind wailed in the pine branches.*

waist (wāst) **1** narrow part of the body between the ribs and the hips. **2** blouse or shirt. **3** part of an object which is narrower than the rest of it: *the waist of a violin.* (Homonym: waste)

waist·coat (wāst′kōt′ or wĕs′kĭt) short, sleeveless jacket that is worn under a man's coat; vest.

waist·line (wāst′lin′) **1** the line of the waist between the ribs and the hips. **2** narrow part of a piece of clothing which falls at the waist, or above or below it, as the fashion changes: *This year waistlines are being worn higher.*

wait (wāt) **1** to stay or linger until someone comes or something happens: *We waited for the train. She waits for me every evening.* **2** length of time before something happens or someone appears: *It was a long wait before George found a taxi.* **3** to keep something ready; delay: *Mother waits supper until the whole family is home.* **4** to await;

wait for: *to wait one's turn.* **5 lie in wait** to remain in hiding to attack: *The Indians lay in wait for the wagon train.*

wait on or **upon 1** to serve people, especially in a restaurant or shop: *Ellen waited on our table.* **2** to call on formally: *Last week the duke waited on the king.* (Homonym: weight)

wait·er (wā′tər) **1** man who serves food or drinks to people at a table or counter. **2** person who waits. **3** a serving tray for dishes.

wait·ing (wā′tĭng) **1** a lingering until something happens or someone comes: *I hate waiting for people who are late.* **2** lingering: *The waiting crowd was impatient for the parade.* **3** attending; serving: *a waiting woman.* **4 in waiting** in attendance: *a lady in waiting.*

wait·ress (wā′trĭs) woman who serves food or drinks to people at a table or counter.

waive (wāv) **1** to give up a claim to; refrain from pressing as a charge; relinquish: *to waive legal rights to an inheritance; to waive a summons.* **2** to postpone; put aside: *to waive a question.* **waived, waiv·ing.** (Homonym: wave)

¹wake (wāk) **1** to stop sleeping: *I wake each morning at seven o'clock.* **2** to make (someone else) stop sleeping: *Don't wake John until dinner is ready.* **3** to become alert or awake: *They woke to the danger of the enemy's plot.* **4** vigil, especially a watch over a dead body before burial. **woke** or **waked, waked, wak·ing.** [¹wake is a form of an Old English word (wacan) meaning "to be awake."]

²wake (wāk) **1** track left behind a moving ship. **2 in the wake of** following close behind; after: *Rain came in the wake of the thunder.* [²wake is probably from an Old Norse word (vök) meaning "an opening in the ice."]

wake·ful (wāk′fəl) **1** unable to sleep; free from sleep: *The baby spent a wakeful night.* **2** alert; keen; watchful: *The wakeful scouts saw a column of troops in the distance.* **wake·ful·ly.**

wake·ful·ness (wāk′fəl nĭs) **1** condition of not being able to sleep. **2** alertness: *the wakefulness of the scouting party.*

wak·en (wā′kən) to wake: *He wakened to the smell of coffee. The noise wakened Kathy.*

Wales (wālz) a division of Great Britain, west of England.

walk (wôk) **1** to go on foot at a moderate pace; stroll: *I like to* walk *in the park.* **2** to go over on foot: *I've* walked *this path before.* **3** path along which people may go on foot: *From the house to the farm there is a* walk *shaded by apple trees.* **4** distance which may be covered on foot: *It is a long* walk *to the store.* **5** a going somewhere on foot; a stroll: *Did you have a pleasant* walk *through the woods?* **6** manner of walking: *She had a* walk *like a duck.* **7** to accompany a person or animal on foot: *Please* walk *Mr. Stone to the gate. I must* walk *the dog before bed.* **8** to cause (a horse, etc.) to go at the slowest gait: *to* walk *a horse uphill.* **9** in baseball, to move or cause to move to first base, after four balls have been pitched. **10 walk of life** occupation; calling; position in society: *He would have been happier in another* walk of life.

walk·ie-talk·ie (wô′ki tô′ki) a sending and receiving radio which is light enough to be carried by one person.

walk·o·ver (wôk′ō′vər) **1** in horse racing, the action of a lone horse going around the track and being called the winner of a race. **2** any unopposed or easily won victory.

wall (wôl) **1** solid upright structure that encloses an area, separates one space from another, or supports a roof. **2** to build a partition, fence, or barrier around (something): *They* walled *their town to protect it from attack.* **3** side; lining: *the* wall *of the stomach; the* walls *of a cave.* **4** anything that acts as a barrier as a wall does: *A* wall *of suspicion kept them from being friends.*

wal·let (wŏl′it) **1** small, flat, folding case, usually made of leather, to hold money and papers. **2** a pouch for keeping food or clothing one might take on a hike or journey; knapsack.

wal·lop (wŏl′əp) **1** to hit hard; beat; thrash: *The boxer* walloped *his opponent on the head.* **2** a very hard blow. **3** to defeat thoroughly as in a game: *Our team* walloped *the other side.*

wal·low (wŏl′ō) **1** to roll around (in something): *Pigs* wallow *in mud.* **2** act of wallowing: *a* wallow *in mud.* **3** muddy place where animals are used to rolling. **4** to live and revel in: *She* wallows *in luxury.*

wall·pa·per (wôl′pā′pər) **1** paper used to decorate or cover the inside walls of houses. **2** to cover with this paper.

wal·nut (wôl′nŭt) **1** hard-shelled nut the kernel of which may be eaten. **2** tree that produces this nut. **3** wood from this tree. **4** shade of brown similar to walnut wood. **5** made of or resembling the wood or the nut: *a* walnut *table; a* walnut *grain in linoleum;* walnut *ice cream.*

wal·rus (wôl′rəs or wŏl′rəs) large arctic sea animal related to the seal. It is valued for its blubber, its tusks, and its skin, which makes a tough leather.

Walrus, about 10½ ft. long

waltz (wôlts) **1** gliding dance in triple time. **2** to perform this dance. **3** music for this dance: *The orchestra played a* waltz.

wam·pum (wŏm′pəm) beads made of shells, used by early American Indians as money, ornaments, etc.

Wampum

wan (wŏn) **1** pale; pallid: *The sick child's face was drawn and* wan. **2** weak; sickly: *a* wan *smile.* **wan·ner, wan·nest; wan·ly.**

wand (wŏnd) a slender rod: *a magician's* wand; *an orchestra conductor's* wand.

wan·der (wŏn′dər) **1** to roam without a particular purpose: *I* wandered *through the old gardens, lost in thought.* **2** to get lost; stray: *A search party was sent after the child who had* wandered *from camp.* **3** to ramble (in speech or thought): *The speaker began to* wander *from the subject.*

wan·der·er (wŏn′dər ər) person or animal that wanders or roams, especially one with no fixed home.

wane (wān) **1** to grow less or smaller: *The moon* wanes *after it is full.* **2** to decrease; decline; grow weaker: *My energy* wanes *at the end of the day.* **3 on the wane** de-

---

fāte, făt, fâre, fär; bē, bĕt; bīte, bĭt; nō, nŏt, nôr; fūse, fŭn, fûr; tōō, tŏŏk; foil; foul; thin; ~~then~~;
hw for wh as in *wh*at; zh for s as in u*s*ual; ə for a, e, i, o, u, as in *a*go, lin*e*n, per*i*l, at*o*m, min*u*s

creasing; declining; growing less, weaker, etc.: *His power was on the wane.* **waned, wan·ing.**

want (wŏnt or wônt) **1** to wish for; desire: *All I want is privacy.* **2** to need; require: *This soup wants a little more salt.* **3** a need: *This tool fills a long-felt want.* **4** to lack: *Beryl sings well, but she wants confidence.* **5** a lack: *The grass is dying for want of rain.* **6** poverty: *There is want in even the richest cities.*

want·ing (wŏn′tĭng or wôn′tĭng) **1** lacking; missing; absent: *Directions for assembling this toy are wanting.* **2** not up to standard; without necessary qualifications: *tried and found wanting.*

wan·ton (wŏn′tən) **1** not controlled or regulated: *a gang of wanton boys.* **2** frisky; playful: *We watched the wanton antics of the kittens.* **3** useless; needless; thoughtless: *the wanton destruction of shade trees by careless builders.* **4** unfeeling; cruel: *a wanton abuse of power.* **5** immoral. **6** an immoral person, especially a woman. **wan·ton·ly.**

war (wôr or wär) **1** armed fight between nations, tribes, or parts of a nation. **2** any organized struggle: *a war on disease or crime.* **3** to fight: *The county warred against mosquitoes all summer.* **4** military science, art, or profession: *skilled in war.* **5 cold war** a kind of war between countries which is waged with propaganda, economic pressures, etc., instead of armed fighting. **warred, war·ring.**

War between the States the armed conflict between the northern and southern States of the United States (1861–1865).

war·ble (wôr′bəl or wär′bəl) **1** to trill; sing with trills: *The canary warbled in the sunny window.* **2** to sing (a song), especially with trills: *Abner warbled a song as he drove the cows to pasture.* **3** a bird's song or any warbling sound. **war·bled, war·bling.**

war·bler (wôr′blər or wär′blər) **1** person or bird that warbles. **2** any one of several kinds of small, brightly colored songbirds.

ward (wôrd) **1** section of a hospital containing a number of beds or devoted to the treatment of a special disease, condition, or group: *a children's ward.* **2** section of a prison. **3** one of the sections into which some cities are divided for purposes of

government. **4** person under the care of a guardian: *The orphan was a ward of the court.*

ward off to turn aside; avert: *to ward off danger.*

-ward or **-wards** suffix meaning "in the direction of"; "toward": *east*ward; *home*-wards.

ward·en (wôr′dən) **1** the governing officer of a prison. **2** watcher; keeper; officer empowered to enforce certain laws: *a game warden; an air-raid warden.*

ward·er (wôr′dər) watchman; guard: *the warder of the castle gate.*

ward·robe (wôrd′rōb′) **1** all of one's clothes: *The poor fellow's wardrobe consisted of one threadbare suit, a dirty shirt, and a pair of run-down shoes.* **2** closet or cabinet in which clothing is kept.

ware (wâr) **1** kind of article manufactured for sale: *glass*ware; *silver*ware. **2 wares** articles for sale: *The peddler sold his wares from house to house.* (Homonym: wear)

ware·house (wâr′hous′) building where goods are stored; storehouse: *The store has a warehouse near the railroad.*

war·fare (wôr′fâr′ or wär′fâr′) fighting, especially active combat of armed forces.

war·i·ness (wâr′ĭ nĭs) caution; distrust; suspicion: *The cat and dog eyed each other with wariness.*

war·like (wôr′līk′ or wär′līk′) **1** fond of fighting; quick to fight: *a warlike people.* **2** hostile; threatening war: *The chief sent a warlike challenge to the neighboring tribe.* **3** of or for war; military: *The camp bristled with warlike preparations.*

warm (wôrm) **1** having or giving off a moderate degree of heat; more hot than cold: *Hawaii has a warm climate. I drink warm milk at bedtime.* **2** keeping the heat in: *a warm blanket.* **3** affectionate; enthusiastic: *a warm greeting.* **4** excited; heated; brisk: *The debate aroused warm interest.* **5** of colors, suggesting warmth, as red, orange, or yellow: *Her dress was a warm shade of brown.* **6** to make or become warm: *Mother warmed the milk.* **7** to make or become eager, excited, etc.: *The thought of seeing the family again warmed my heart.* **8 warm front** the forward edge of a mass of warm air coming into a colder area.

warm to to become more sympathetic toward or interested in: *to* warm to *his work.*

warm up **1** to make warm or hot: *to* warm up *supper; to* warm up *an engine.* **2** to exercise or practice briefly before entering a game, contest, etc.: *The new pitcher is* warming up. **3** to make or become more friendly, interested, etc.: *The party began to* warm up *after he came.* **warm·ly.**

warm-blood·ed (wôrm′blŭd′ĭd) having warm blood and an unchanging body temperature: *Mammals are* warm-blooded *animals.*

warmth (wôrmth) **1** moderate heat; a being warm: *The* warmth *of the sun felt good on my face.* **2** enthusiasm; earnestness: *the* warmth *of a friend's greeting.*

warn (wôrn) **1** to put on guard against danger or evil; alert; caution: *The Coast Guard* warned *all ships of the hurricane.* **2** to notify; signal: *Her look* warned *us it was time to leave.*

warn·ing (wôr′nĭng) previous notice or cautioning; something that warns: *Let this mistake be a* warning *to you!*

War of 1812 the war between the United States and Great Britain (1812–1815).

warp (wôrp) **1** the lengthwise threads of a woven cloth through which woof threads are interlaced to form the pattern. **2** a bend; twist: *Dampness gave the board a bad* warp. **3** mental twist: *Worry had given his mind a strange* warp. **4** to twist or bend: *The hot sun had* warped *the shingles.* **5** to twist mentally: *Bias* warped *the man's thinking.* **6** to work, as a ship into its slip.

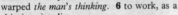

Warp / Woof

war·path (wôr′păth′ or wär′păth′) **1** route taken by American Indians on a warlike expedition. **2 on the warpath** **(1)** at war; ready for war. **(2)** angry; ready for a fight: *The theft of his peaches set the farmer on the* warpath.

war·rant (wŏr′ənt or wôr′ənt) **1** official paper that gives authority to do something, as to make an arrest, search or seize property, etc. **2** that which gives a right; justification: *What* warrant *have you to say such a thing?* **3** to justify; give sufficient grounds for: *The crime* warranted *a severe punishment.* **4** something which guarantees: *I left my ring as a* warrant *that I would pay the bill.* **5** to guarantee; promise: *"I'll* warrant *that this is the only dress of its kind," said the saleswoman.*

war·ran·ty (wŏr′ən tĭ or wôr′ən tĭ) guarantee. **war·ran·ties.**

war·ren (wŏr′ən or wôr′ən) a place in which rabbits breed or are numerous.

war·ri·or (wôr′ĭ ər or wär′ĭ ər) man experienced in fighting; soldier.

war·ship (wôr′shĭp′ or wär′shĭp′) ship that is built and armed for war.

wart (wôrt) a small, usually hard, lump on the skin or on a plant.

war·y (wâr′ĭ) **1** on one's guard; cautious: *a* wary *boxer.* **2** marked by caution; guarded: *a* wary *look; a* wary *reply.* **3 wary of** suspicious of: *The old farmer was* wary *of city folk.* **war·i·er, war·i·est; war·i·ly.**

was (wŏz or wŭz) See **be.** *I* was *ready on time. There* was *an old woman who lived in a shoe. The money was* stolen.

wash (wŏsh or wôsh) **1** to clean with a liquid, usually water: *to* wash *the dishes.* **2** to clean oneself with water: *to* wash *before dinner.* **3** to wash clothes, linens, etc.: *The laundress* washes *once a week.* **4** a washing or being washed: *That boy could stand a good* wash. **5** collection of things to be, or which have been, washed: *Mrs. McGinty hung the* wash *on the line.* **6** to remove or be removed by washing: *That stain will* wash *out.* **7** to undergo cleaning by water without damage: *This sweater* washes *beautifully.* **8** that can be washed without damage: *a* wash *dress.* **9** to move, carry, or wash away by the action of water: *The flood* washed *the bridge downstream.* **10** matter that is carried and deposited by water: *The channel was blocked by* wash *from the river.* **11** sound or movement of water: *the* wash *of the waves on the beach.*

---

fāte, făt, fâre, fär; bē, bĕt; bite, bĭt; nō, nŏt, nôr; fūse, fŭn, fûr; tōō, tŏŏk; foil; foul; thin; ~~then~~;
hw for wh as in *wh*at; zh for s as in usual; ə for a, e, i, o, u, as in *a*go, lin*e*n, per*i*l, at*o*m, min*u*s

Wash.

12 to beat or splash over or on: *The waves washed the raft.* **13** to make wet: *Her eyes were washed with tears.* **14** liquid with which anything is washed or tinted: *a mouth wash; white*wash, etc. **15** to cover with a thin coating of color or metal. **16** a thin overlay of metal or paint. **17** disturbed water behind the propellers, oars, etc., of a boat. **18** disturbed air behind a moving airplane.

Wash. Washington (State).

wash·board (wŏsh′bôrd′ or wôsh′bôrd′) a board covered with metal or glass ridges for scrubbing dirt out of clothes.

wash·bowl (wŏsh′bōl′ or wôsh′bōl′) bowl or basin for use in washing one's hands and face, etc.

wash·cloth (wŏsh′klŏth′ or wôsh′klôth′) small cloth used in washing the face or body.

wash·er (wŏsh′ər or wôsh′ər) **1** person who washes something: *a window washer; a car washer.* **2** washing machine. **3** disk of metal, leather, fiber, or rubber used to make a tight joint: *Put a washer in the faucet to stop the leak.*

METAL   FAUCET
Washers

wash·ing (wŏsh′ing or wôsh′ing) clothes washed or to be washed: *The washing was drying on the roof.*

Wash·ing·ton (wŏsh′ing tən or wôsh′ing-tən) **1** State in the northwestern part of the United States. **2 Washington, D.C.** capital of the United States, covering the same area as the District of Columbia. **3 George Washington** (1732–1799) first President of the United States.

wash·room (wŏsh′rōōm′ or wôsh′rōōm′) **1** a room with washstands or other washing facilities. **2** a public lavatory or rest room.

wash·stand (wŏsh′stănd′ or wôsh′stănd′) **1** a stand holding a basin and pitcher for washing hands and face. **2** bathroom sink.

wash·tub (wŏsh′tŭb′ or wôsh′tŭb′) tub for washing clothes, often with water faucets and a drain.

was·n't (wŏz′ənt or wŭz′ənt) was not: *It wasn't raining when I came in.*

wasp (wŏsp or wôsp) slender-waisted flying insect armed with a sting. Some wasps build paper or mud nests. For picture, see next column.

wast (wŏst) old form of **were** used with *thou.* "Thou wast" means "you were."

waste (wāst) **1** to squander; use without profit: *I am afraid that my brother wasted his allowance on useless things.* **2** useless expenditure; profitless use: *a waste of opportunity.* **3** discarded materials; refuse; something left over: *Factory waste sometimes pollutes our rivers.* **4** useless; worthless: *The waste matter was removed in big cartons.* **5** to destroy; spoil; ruin: *The forest was wasted by fire.* **6** wilderness; desert: *Nothing grows in those desolate wastes.* **7** desolate; bare: *the waste spaces of the moon.* **8** to wear away gradually: *His frame was wasted by a long illness.* **9** a wearing down gradually; slow decay: *the waste of disease.* **10 lay waste** to destroy; make desolate; ravage: *The army laid waste the whole countryside.* **wast·ed, wast·ing.**

waste·bas·ket (wāst′băs′kĭt) basket or box for wastepaper or other useless material.

waste·ful (wāst′fəl) using or spending more than is needed; extravagant: *He is wasteful with his parents' money. This is a wasteful process.* **waste·ful·ly.**

watch (wŏch or wôch) **1** to look carefully; be attentive; be on the lookout: *If you watch, you may see how I do this trick.* **2** close observation or a being attentive: *If you keep careful watch, you may see a falling star.* **3** to see; look at: *to watch a parade.* **4** to pay careful attention to: *Please watch what you're doing.* **5** to keep guard; attend: *We watched through the night, but all was quiet.* **6** wakefulness for the purpose of guarding or tending to: *a mother's watch over a sick child.* **7** period of time for guard duty; period of vigil: *The sailor's watch was from midnight to four o'clock.* **8** person or group on guard: *The watch reported a ship on the horizon.* **9** a small timepiece carried in a pocket or worn on the wrist.

watch for to look in order to see; wait for: *to watch for the mailman.*

watch out to be careful.

Mud wasp, about 1 in. long

watch·dog (wŏch′dôg′ or wôch′dôg′) dog kept or trained to guard property.

watch·er (wŏch'ər or wôch'ər) person who watches: *a bird* watcher.

watch·ful (wŏch'fəl or wôch'fəl) wide-awake; vigilant; on the watch: *The watchful detective guarded the building.* **watch·ful·ly.**

watch·man (wŏch'mən or wôch'mən) a person whose duty it is to watch and guard: *a night* watchman. **watch·men.**

watch·tow·er (wŏch'tou'ər or wôch'tou'ər) tower from which a guard or sentinel keeps watch.

watch·word (wŏch'wûrd' or wôch'wûrd') **1** secret word or phrase used to gain admission or prove one's identity; password. **2** a rallying cry; slogan: *The* watchword *is "Fight the good fight." "All the news that is fit to print" is a* watchword.

wa·ter (wô'tər or wŏt'ər) **1** colorless, tasteless, odorless liquid of which rivers, oceans, rain, etc., consist. Water is a compound of hydrogen and oxygen and freezes to form ice. **2** lake, river, ocean, or other body of this liquid: *We crossed the* water *by ferry.* **3** to sprinkle or provide with water: *to* water *flowers; to* water *the lawn.* **4** to provide with water for drinking: *One of your jobs will be to* water *the horses.* **5** to dilute with water: *to* water *milk.* **6** to flow with water or liquid similar to water: *His eyes* watered *in the smoke.* **7** having to do with water or meant for use on or in water: *to take part in* water *sports.* **8** any liquid containing or resembling water: *soda* water.

water bird bird that swims in or lives near water. Ducks and herons are water birds.

water buffalo a buffalo of Asia, the Philippine Islands, etc., used mainly for pulling loads. Also called **carabao.**

water chestnut **1** a water plant with an edible nutlike fruit. **2** the nutlike fruit of this plant.

water color **1** paint that is mixed with water instead of oil. **2** a painting done with this kind of paint or pigment. **3** art of painting with water colors. **4** having to do with water colors.

wa·ter·course (wô'tər kôrs' or wŏt'ər-kôrs') **1** stream of water, as a brook or river. **2** channel for water: *The plain was furrowed with dry* watercourses.

water cress a plant that grows in running water, or the sharp-tasting leaves of this plant, used as food.

wa·ter·fall (wô'tər fôl' or wŏt'ər fôl') stream of water falling over a cliff, etc.; cataract; cascade: *The brook plunged down the hillside in a series of* waterfalls.

wa·ter·fowl (wô'tər foul' or wŏt'ər foul') bird that lives in or near water.

water front land bordering on water, especially the wharf or dock section of a port city.

water hole place where water collects, as in a hollow or dry river bed; pool, especially one where animals come to drink.

water lily **1** water plant having round, flat, floating leaves. **2** flower of this plant. **water lilies.**

Water lily

water main a chief or main pipe for carrying a water supply.

wa·ter·man (wô'tər mən or wŏt'ər mən) **1** man who operates or works a boat for hire. **2** person skilled in rowing, etc.; oarsman. **wa·ter·men.**

wa·ter·mark (wô'tər märk' or wŏt'ər-märk') **1** a mark that shows the height of the rise of water. **2** a faintly visible marking or design in some kinds of paper, seen when the paper is held to the light. **3** to put a watermark on: *to* watermark *stationery.*

wa·ter·mel·on (wô'tər mĕl'ən or wŏt'ər-mĕl'ən) **1** large melon with sweet, juicy, pink or red pulp. **2** trailing vine on which this melon grows.

water power power produced by the flow or fall of water, used to generate electricity, run machinery, etc.

wa·ter·proof (wô'tər prŏŏf' or wŏt'ər-prŏŏf') **1** not capable of being penetrated by water: *a* waterproof *coat.* **2** raincoat. **3** to treat (something) to make it waterproof: *to have a raincoat* waterproofed.

wa·ter·shed (wô'tər shĕd' or wŏt'ər shĕd') land area from which water drains into a river, lake, or reservoir.

---

fāte, făt, fâre, fär; bē, bĕt; bīte, bĭt; nō, nŏt, nôr; fūse, fŭn, fûr; tōō, tŏŏk; foil; foul; thin; ~~then~~;
hw for wh as in *wh*at; zh for s as in u*s*ual; ə for a, e, i, o, u, as in *a*go, lin*e*n, per*i*l, at*o*m, min*u*s

water table

water table level below which the ground is saturated with water.

wa·ter·tight (wô′tər tīt′ or wŏt′ər tīt′) **1** made in such a way that water cannot enter; without a leak: *The ship's bottom was* watertight. **2** so clear and sound that it cannot be misunderstood or disturbed; without fault: *a* watertight *argument; a* watertight *alibi.*

wa·ter·way (wô′tər wā′ or wŏt′ər wā′) **1** body of water that can be navigated: *This state is rich in* waterways. **2** channel in which water flows.

wa·ter·y (wô′tə rĭ or wŏt′ə rĭ) **1** of or like water: *a* watery *soup.* **2** soggy: *the* watery *ground.* **3** full of or discharging water: *the* watery *skies;* watery *eyes.*

watt (wŏt) a unit of electric power.

wave (wāv) **1** a rise and swell on the surface of a body of water: *an ocean* wave. **2** anything that has the form of or resembles a wave of water: *the* wave *in his hair.* **3** to give a curved or wavy shape to: *Jane* waves *her hair.* **4** an increase or surge of a feeling, condition, etc.: *a* wave *of anger; a heat* wave. **5** to move up or down or back and forth: *He* waved *his stick at the little boy. The flag* waved *in the wind.* **6** to signal with a back-and-forth motion of the hand: *He* waved *good-by to me.* **7** a waving: *a* wave *of the hand.* **8** in physics, the wave-like motion of light, heat, sound, etc. **waved, wav·ing.** (Homonym: waive)

wave length distance from a point on one wave to the corresponding point of the next.

wa·ver (wā′vər) **1** to hesitate; be undecided: *She* wavered *over choosing the birthday present.* **2** to flicker: *The candle flame* wavered *in the open window.* **3** to sway back and forth: *He was so tired that he* wavered *as he stood.* **4** to fail or begin to give way: *The sick man's mind* wavered. **5** a wavering; a shaking: *a* waver *in the voice.*

wav·y (wā′vĭ) **1** of a line, marked by repeated rounded ups and downs: *In his picture, Otis showed the ocean by wavy lines.* **2** of motion, bobbing like the surface of a wind-blown field of grain. **wav·i·er, wav·i·est; wav·i·ly.**

Wavy lines

¹wax (wăks) **1** plastic, light-yellow substance of a honeycomb. **2** any of several mineral or vegetable substances somewhat resembling this: *a sealing* wax; *paraffin* wax. **3** a compound containing wax for giving a luster to floors, furniture, etc. **4** to polish or coat with wax. **5** of or like wax: *a bowl of* wax *fruit.* [**¹wax** is a form of an Old English word (weax) meaning "beeswax."]

²wax (wăks) **1** to increase in apparent size, as the moon before it is full. **2** to grow; become increasingly: *He* waxed *talkative after dinner.* [**²wax** is a form of an Old English word (weaxan) meaning "to grow."]

wax·en (wăk′sən) **1** made of wax. **2** like wax: *a* waxen *complexion.*

way (wā) **1** path, road, or any passage: *The* way *was muddy after the rain.* **2** the route (from one place to another): *the* way *to Boston; the* way *home.* **3** direction: *Everyone face this* way! **4** distance: *She lives a long* way *from here.* **5** away; far: *to be* way *behind in a race.* **6** room; space for action: *Make* way *for the parade.* **7** progress; advance; headway: *We pushed our* way *through the crowd. He made his* way *in business.* **8** manner: *The child has winning* ways. **9** means or method: *Sailors know many* ways *of tying a knot.* **10** habit; customary manner: *The* ways *of another country are different from our own.* **11** a wish; desire; will: *Little Cyril's mother always lets him have his* way. **12** characteristic; respect; feature: *In many* ways *she is like her father.* **13** condition: *The old dog is in a bad* way. **14 by way of** (**1**) by the route of; via: *She went to the West Coast by way of Chicago.* (**2**) as a means or method: *He gave me this check by way of payment for the car.* **15 give way** (**1**) to collapse: *The bridge gave way in the flood.* (**2**) to surrender: *She gave way to my persuasion.* **16 right of way** (**1**) the right to move first, as in traffic. (**2**) right of use in travel, or the path so used: *a right of way across private property.* **17 under way** in motion or progress: *The building of the new school is under way.* **18 ways and means** methods and resources for doing something, especially for raising money. (Homonym: weigh)

way·far·er (wā′fâr′ər) traveler, especially one who travels on foot.

way·far·ing (wā'fâr'ĭng) traveling, especially on foot.

way·laid (wā'lād' or wā'lād') See **waylay.**

way·lay (wā'lā' or wā'lā') **1** to lie in wait for and attack; ambush: *The thieves planned to* waylay *the truck in the middle of the night.* **2** to wait for and stop (a person) by surprise: *The fans waylaid the actress to ask for her autograph.* **way·laid, way·lay·ing.**

way·side (wā'sīd') **1** the edge of a road: *We stopped by the wayside to change a tire.* **2** on or along the side of a road: *a wayside fruit stand.*

way·ward (wā'wərd) **1** disobedient; willful: *a wayward child.* **2** not steady; unpredictable; irregular: *a wayward wind.* **way·ward·ly.**

we (wē) **1** another or others plus myself; group of people including the speaker or writer: *Yesterday we went to town.* **2** one person, such as a sovereign, author, judge, etc., speaking or writing in a formal or official way: *"We are not amused," said Queen Victoria.* (Homonym: wee)

weak (wēk) **1** lacking physical strength: *to be* weak *from hunger;* weak *eyes.* **2** liable to break, collapse, etc., under pressure or strain: *a weak bridge; a weak rope; a weak link in a chain.* **3** lacking in ability or strength (in something named): *He is weak in many subjects at school.* **4** lacking in mental power or intelligence: *He means well, but has weak judgment.* **5** lacking moral strength; easily influenced: *a weak will.* **6** lacking in force, power, or effectiveness: *a weak leader.* **7** lacking in sound, amount, volume, etc.: *a weak cry; a weak stream of water.* **8** thin and watery; diluted: *this weak coffee.* (Homonym: week)

weak·en (wē'kən) to make or become weak or weaker: *Sickness weakened her. His eyes weakened as he grew older.*

weak·ling (wēk'lĭng) **1** weak, thin, puny person: *He couldn't play games as a child because he was a weakling.* **2** person of weak character.

weak·ly (wēk'lĭ) **1** not robust; sickly; feeble: *a weakly child.* **2** in a weak or faint way: *She answered weakly.* **weak·li·er, weak·li·est.** (Homonym: weekly)

weak·ness (wēk'nĭs) **1** lack of strength: *He suffered weakness after the accident.* **2** weak point; fault: *the weakness in your argument; a weakness in character.* **3** a liking; special fondness: *That girl has a weakness for chocolates.*

wealth (wĕlth) **1** large amount of money or possessions; riches. **2** abundance: *a wealth of ideas; a wealth of words.*

wealth·y (wĕl'thĭ) rich: *a wealthy man; a country wealthy in natural resources.* **wealth·i·er, wealth·i·est.**

wean (wēn) **1** to accustom (a child or a young animal) to take food other than its mother's milk. **2** to draw (someone) away from a habit or interest.

weap·on (wĕp'ən) any implement used for fighting or defense: *Cave men made weapons of stone.*

wear (wâr) **1** to have on or about the body: *She wore furs, a corsage, and pearls.* **2** articles of clothing: *men's wear.* **3** to display: *to wear a broad grin.* **4** to bear: *The great man wore his honors with dignity and modesty.* **5** to last: *This cloth wears well.* **6** endurance; lasting quality: *This material is famous for long wear.* **7** to use up; injure or destroy by use or action: *The rough streets wore the soles of my shoes.* **8** result of use or action: *The machine showed signs of wear.* **9** a using or being used: *These shoes have seen a lot of wear.* **10** to diminish by friction; rub: *The swift stream wore the stones smooth.* **11** to exhaust: *Joan's constant pleading wore down her mother's opposition.* **12** to pass gradually: *Time wore on, day by day.* **13 wear and tear** loss or damage from time and use.

wear down 1 to damage by use or wear. **2** to reduce or overcome by constant effort; weaken.

wear off to gradually lose effect: *His headache wore off at last.*

wear out 1 to wear until it is no longer fit for use. **2** to tire out and weary; to make or become exhausted.

wore, worn, wear·ing. (Homonym: ware)

wear·er (wâr'ər) one who wears.

wea·ri·ness (wĭr'ĭ nĭs) the state of being weary; fatigue.

---

fāte, făt, fâre, fär; bē, bĕt; bīte, bĭt; nō, nŏt, nôr; fūse, fŭn, fûr; tōō, tŏŏk; foil; foul; thin; then; hw for wh as in *what*; zh for s as in u*s*ual; ə for a, e, i, o, u, as in *a*go, lin*e*n, per*i*l, at*o*m, min*u*s

wearisome

wea·ri·some (wîr′ĭ səm) wearying; fatiguing; tedious: *a wearisome lecture; a wearisome afternoon, pulling weeds.* **wea·ri·some·ly.**

wea·ry (wîr′ĭ) **1** tired; fatigued: *to be weary after work.* **2** tiring; fatiguing to mind or body: *a weary round of duties.* **3** lacking patience; bored: *I'm weary of that same old tune.* **4** to tire or become tired: *The long argument wearied me more than the walk home.* **wea·ri·er, wea·ri·est; wea·ried, wea·ry·ing; wea·ri·ly.**

wea·sel (wē′zəl) small, active animal of the same family as the mink and the skunk, with a pointed face and a long, thin body. It is destructive to poultry, mice, etc.

Weasel (ermine), about 11 in. long

weath·er (wĕth′ər) **1** the atmospheric conditions at any place at a particular time: *The weather in Chicago today is cool, dry, and sunny.* **2** a stormy condition: *We have just passed through a spell of weather.* **3** to come through safely or successfully: *to weather a storm; to weather a crisis.* **4** to become bleached, dried, etc., by the action of the sun, wind, rain, etc.: *The shingles of the old house had weathered to a beautiful silver gray.* **5 under the weather** not feeling well; sick; ill.

weath·er-beat·en (wĕth′ər bē′tĕn) **1** worn by the weather: *The weather-beaten shacks of fishermen line the beach.* **2** toughened by exposure to the weather: *the fisherman's weather-beaten face.*

Weather Bureau bureau of the United States Department of Commerce that gathers information in order to predict the weather, issue warnings of storms, floods, etc.

weath·er·cock (wĕth′ər-kŏk′) a pointer to show the direction of the wind; a weather vane, especially one shaped like a rooster.

weather map map showing various weather conditions at a particular time, usually over a wide area.

Weathercock

weather station place where observations of local weather conditions are made and

wedding

recorded. Weather stations also study reports of weather conditions over a large area and make forecasts.

weather strip a strip of metal, felt, etc., placed along the joints or edges of a window or door to keep out drafts, cold, etc.

weather vane weathercock, the pointer of which is made in various shapes, as a ship, horse, arrow, etc.

weave (wēv) **1** to interlace threads, wires, or the like, to make cloth, screens, etc.: *Polly wove a mat of rushes.* **2** to spin: *A spider weaves a silken web.* **3** to take an in-and-out path among obstacles: *Waldo wove his way through the crowd.* **4** to gather deeds, events, etc., into a story: *The author wove an exciting tale of pirates.* **5** a style or pattern of weaving: *The bedspread had a fancy weave.* **wove** or **weaved, wov·en** or **wove, weav·ing.**

Weave

weav·er (wē′vər) one who weaves or whose trade is weaving.

web (wĕb) **1** something woven from fibers or strips; a woven fabric. **2** a mesh; something that entangles: *a spider's web; caught in a web of difficulties.* **3** the skin which joins the toes of ducks, beavers, and certain other water dwellers.

Spider web
Web on duck's foot

webbed (wĕbd) **1** having a web: *the webbed seat of a chair.* **2** joined by a membrane, as the toes of a duck's foot.

wed (wĕd) **1** to marry; unite in wedlock: *With this ring, I thee wed.* **2** to unite; join: *to wed skill with hard work.* **wed·ded, wed·ded** or **wed, wed·ding.**

Wed. Wednesday.

we'd (wēd) **1** we had. **2** we would; we should. (Homonym: weed)

wed·ded (wĕd′ĭd) **1** united in marriage: *one's wedded wife.* **2 wedded to** firmly devoted to: *to be wedded to one's profession.*

wed·ding (wĕd′ĭng) **1** marriage ceremony. **2** anniversary of a marriage: *a silver wedding.*

wedge

wedge (wĕj) **1** triangular block of metal driven into a log to split it. **2** anything used like a wedge to force an entrance: *Jake used his father's permission as a wedge for greater demands.* **3** to split with a wedge. **4** anything used to hold something tight or keep it in place: *John put a wedge of newspaper between the window sashes so the window could neither rattle nor be opened.* **5** to fasten with a wedge. **6** to pack tightly; press or crowd in: *The guard wedged the passengers into the streetcar.* **7** anything shaped like a wedge. **wedged, wedg·ing.**

Wedge

wed·lock (wĕd′lŏk) the married state; matrimony.

Wed·nes·day (wĕnz′dā or wĕnz′dĭ) the fourth day of the week.

wee (wē) small; tiny; very little. **we·er, we·est.** (Homonym: we)

weed (wēd) **1** any wild, uncultivated, useless plant: *The weeds have ruined our lawn.* **2** to remove undesirable plants from the ground: *to weed the flower beds; to spend the afternoon weeding.*

   weed out to remove what is useless, harmful, inferior, and not wanted: *to weed out bad apples from a bushel.* (Homonym: we'd)

weeds (wēdz) mourning clothes: *Our neighbor still wears widow's weeds.*

weed·y (wē′dĭ) **1** overgrown with weeds: *a weedy path.* **2** of persons or animals, long or tall, thin and ungainly: *a weedy colt.* **weed·i·er, weed·i·est.**

week (wēk) **1** period of seven successive days, usually beginning with midnight on Saturday until midnight on the following Saturday. **2** the working days or working period of the week; the five school days of the week: *My father is in town all week but spends week ends in the country.* (Homonym: weak)

week·day (wēk′dā′) any day of the week except Sunday.

week end or **week·end** (wēk′ĕnd′) **1** the time from Friday night or Saturday to

weight

Monday morning, usually used for rest or recreation. **2** a visit, holiday, or house party during this period: *a week end at the beach.*

week·ly (wēk′lĭ) **1** of or for a week: *the student's weekly assignment.* **2** performed, happening, appearing, payable, etc., regularly each week, or once a week: *a weekly letter; a weekly wage.* **3** newspaper or magazine published once a week. **week·lies.** (Homonym: weakly)

weep (wēp) **1** to express sorrow, grief, anguish, or some other deep emotion by tears; cry: *Susan wept when the kitten was injured.* **2** to give forth moisture: *The skies wept.* **3** to mourn or lament. **wept, weep·ing.**

wee·vil (wē′vəl) any of several beetles with hard shells and long snouts. Weevils are very destructive to cotton, grain, and other crops.

Cotton-boll weevil

weft (wĕft) **1** in weaving, threads that are carried by the shuttle back and forth across the warp; the woof. **2** yarn used for the weft. **3** something woven.

weigh (wā) **1** to find out the heaviness (of something) by means of a scale or balance, or by balancing in the hand: *to weigh a parcel.* **2** to have a certain weight: *He weighs 90 pounds.* **3** to turn over in the mind; ponder: *to weigh the advantages of a scholarship.* **4** to be a burden: *His lie weighed on his conscience.* **5** to bend: *Fruit weighed down the plum tree.* **6** to have importance: *His opinion doesn't weigh with me at all.*

   weigh anchor to raise an anchor from the water; to start a voyage.

   weigh out to measure or dole out in set amounts: *to weigh out half a pound of currants.* (Homonym: way)

weight (wāt) **1** amount a thing weighs; quantity of heaviness: *the weight of a feather; the weight of a man.* **2** an object, usually metal, of specific heaviness used to balance a scale: *a set of weights from one ounce to five pounds.* **3** system of units used in determining weight, such as apothe-

---

fāte, făt, fâre, fär; bē, bĕt; bite, bĭt; nō, nŏt, nôr; fūse, fŭn, fûr; tōo, tŏok; foil; foul; thin; ~~then~~; hw for wh as in *what*; zh for s as in u*s*ual; ə for a, e, i, o, u, as in *a*go, lin*e*n, per*i*l, at*o*m, min*u*s

caries' weight. **4** something used for its heaviness: *a paper* weight; *the* weights *in a grandfather clock.* **5** to load down: *He sank the boat by* weighting *it with rocks.* **6** a burden: *Dennis found being club treasurer quite a* weight *on his mind.* **7** to burden: *The President was* weighted *with the cares of his country.* **8** importance; value; influence: *a man of potential* weight *in the future government.* **9 pull one's weight** to do one's part or share of anything. **10 put on weight** to grow fat; become heavier. (Homonym: wait)

weight·y (wā′tĭ) **1** heavy; of great weight: *too* weighty *to carry.* **2** crushing; burdensome: *his* weighty *responsibilities.* **3** influential; important: *a* weighty *argument.* **weight·i·er, weight·i·est; weight·i·ly.**

weird (wĭrd) **1** very strange; mysterious; eerie: *a* weird *noise in the attic.* **2** curious in appearance or nature; odd: *Women wear* weird *hats these days. He really is a* weird *character.* **weird·ly.**

wel·come (wĕl′kəm) **1** to greet kindly and gladly; receive with hospitality: *She* welcomed *her guests at the front door.* **2** hospitable greeting: *A hearty* welcome *to you!* **3** giving pleasure and joy: *a* welcome *change of weather; a* welcome *letter.* **4** given a right (to): *You are* welcome *to any book. You're* welcome *to come and go as you please.* **5** conventional response to thanks: *You are quite* welcome. **wel·comed, wel·com·ing.**

weld (wĕld) **1** to join (pieces of metal) by heating to the melting point and pressing or hammering together, or until the melted edges flow together: *The plumber* welded *the broken pipe.* **2** to become welded: *Iron* welds *easily.* **3** to unite closely: *a family* welded *together by deep affection and mutual interests.* **4** a welded joint.

wel·fare (wĕl′fâr′) **1** good health, happiness, and prosperity: *Parents look after their children's* welfare. **2 welfare work** organized effort to promote the health and well-being of a community or a group.

¹well (wĕl) **1** deep hole or shaft sunk into the earth, from which water, oil, gas, and the like are obtained. **2** natural spring or fountain of water. **3** to flow, spring, or gush forth: *water that* wells *from the ground; tears* welling *from the eyes.* **4** en-

closed space extending from the top to the bottom of a building, as a shaft for an elevator, air, and light, or inside a winding staircase. **5** a steady source of supply: *The encyclopedia is a* well *of information.* [¹well is a form of an Old English word (wielle) that was formed from another Old English word (weallan) meaning "to bubble up."]

²well (wĕl) **1** in a satisfactory, pleasing, or desirable manner: *to sleep* well; *to live* well. **2** in good health: *I'm perfectly* well *now.* **3** in a becoming or proper manner; skillfully: *to treat them* well; *to end it* well; *lessons* well *done.* **4** thoroughly: *He should be* well *spanked for this. The school is* well *established by now.* **5** to a considerable extent or degree: *He must be* well *over sixty.* **6** clearly; definitely: *You know* well *what I mean.* **7** with reason; justifiably: *You may* well *ask why I do this.* **8** good; fortunate: *It is* well *you remind me of the appointment.* **9** in a good way; fortunately: *That house is* well *situated in a large garden.* **10** an exclamation of surprise, agreement, relief, wonder, etc., or used merely before something further is said: Well, *that's over.* Well, *I'm ready.* Well, *they're here at last.* **11 as well as** also; in addition to. **12 well off** in a favorable condition; prosperous. **bet·ter, best.** [²well is a form of an Old English word (wel) originally meaning "according to one's will or desire."]

we'll (wĕl) we shall; we will.

well-be·ing (wĕl′bē′ĭng) general health and happiness; welfare.

well-born (wĕl′bôrn′) born into a good family.

well-bred (wĕl′brĕd′) **1** having or showing good breeding; of good family; having good manners. **2** of animals, bred of good stock: *a* well-bred *spaniel.*

well-known (wĕl′nōn′) generally recognized; widely known; famous: *a* well-known *actor.*

well-nigh (wĕl′nī′) very nearly; almost.

well-to-do (wĕl′tə dōō′) prosperous; moderately rich.

welt (wĕlt) **1** long, narrow swelling on the skin caused by, or as if by, a blow of a rod or whip. **2** a blow. **3** to beat soundly; flog. **4** narrow strip of leather joining the sole and upper part of a shoe.

wel·ter (wĕl′tər) **1** to tumble about, as in mud, slush, or the like; wallow. **2** a tumbling about. **3** turmoil; confusion: *a welter of Christmas shoppers.*

wen (wĕn) a harmless growth on the skin.

wench (wĕnch) **1** girl or young woman. **2** a serving maid: *a kitchen* wench. Both uses are old-fashioned.

wend (wĕnd) to go; travel; pursue (one's way, etc.): *The caravan* wended *its way across the desert.*

went (wĕnt) See **go.** *We* went *to bed early.*

wept (wĕpt) See **weep.** *Cynthia* wept *when the heroine died.*

were (wûr) See **be.** *Forty children* were *at the picnic.*

we're (wēr) we are: *I think* we're *going later, but* we're *not sure.*

were·n't (wûr′ənt) were not: *They* weren't *there yesterday.*

wert (wûrt) old form of **were** used with *thou.*

west (wĕst) **1** the direction halfway between north and south and generally toward the setting sun; also, the point of the compass indicating this direction; opposite of east. **2** the region or part of a country or continent in this direction: *the west of England.* **3 the West** **(1)** Europe and North and South America as distinct from Asia; the Occident. **(2)** the western part of the United States, especially the area west of the Mississippi River. **(3)** the United States and its allies, as distinct from the Soviet Union and its Allies. **4** in or to the west: *the* west *side of town.* **5** of winds, from the west. **6** toward the west.

west·er·ly (wĕs′tər li) **1** westward. **2** of winds, coming from the west.

west·ern (wĕs′tərn) **1** located in or toward the west: *the* western *part of the state.* **2** from the west: *a* western *accent.* **3** motion picture, television show, or the like, about cowboy or pioneer life in the western United States. **4 Western (1)** of or in the western part of the United States. **(2)** of or in Europe and the Americas.

West In·dies (wĕst in′dēz) group of islands in the Atlantic Ocean between the United States and South America.

West Virginia a State in the eastern part of the United States.

west·ward (wĕst′wərd) **1** to or toward the west: *The wagon train rolled* westward. **2** moving, facing, or situated toward the west: *the* westward *trek of pioneers.* **3** west; direction of the setting sun or a point in that direction: *Away to the* westward *rolled a range of mountains.*

wet (wĕt) **1** to moisten or soak: *to* wet *the lawn.* **2** covered or soaked with water or other liquid; moist; damp. **3** not yet dry. **4** moisture; rain: *Let's go in out of the* wet. **5** rainy; misty: *a* wet *season.* **6 wet blanket** person or thing that dampens enthusiasm or has a depressing effect. **wet** or **wet·ted, wet·ting; wet·ter, wet·test.**

wet cell electric battery in which the chemical between the two solid poles is a liquid.

wet·ness (wĕt′nis) a being wet; moistness.

we've (wēv) we have.

whack (hwăk) **1** noisy slap. **2** the sound made by, or as by, such a slap. **3** to give (someone or something) a resounding slap or blow.

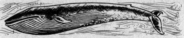

Blue whale, 80 to 100 ft. long

whale (hwāl) **1** any of several large air-breathing sea animals that live in herds. Some are hunted for their oil and bone. **2** to hunt whales. **whaled, whal·ing.**

whal·er (hwā′lər) **1** person who hunts whales. **2** whaling ship.

whal·ing (hwā′ling) the hunting of whales.

wharf (hwôrf) fixed platform to which a ship can be moored and loaded or unloaded. **wharves** (hwôrvz) or **wharfs** (hwôrfs).

what (hwŏt) **1** in questions, which thing or things: What *do you wish?* **2** the thing that; that which: *A good spanking is* what *he needs.* **3** which: *He asked* John what *color he preferred.* **4** how much: *If*

fāte, făt, fâre, fär; bē, bĕt; bīte, bĭt; nō, nŏt, nôr; fūse, fŭn, fûr; tōō, tŏŏk; foil; foul; thin; ~~then~~; hw for wh as in *wh*at; zh for s as in u*s*ual; ə for a, e, i, o, u, as in *a*go, lin*e*n, per*i*l, at*o*m, min*u*s

we share expenses, what *do I owe you?* **5** as much as; as many as: *Take* what *stamps you need.* **6** the kind of: *Take* what *measures you need to do the job.* **7** used as an exclamation to express surprise: *The campers said,* "What! *More rain?*" **8 what with** because of: *We were two hours late* what with *the heavy traffic.*

what·ev·er (hwŏt ĕv′ər) **1** any; any kind of: *Make* whatever *plans seem best.* **2** no matter what: *Don't give up,* whatever *you do.* **3** at all; of any kind: *Have we no voice* whatever *in the matter?* **4** forceful way of asking **what:** *Tell me,* whatever *did you do?*

what's (hwŏts) what is: *I know* what's *wrong.*

what·so·ev·er (hwŏt′sō ĕv′ər) stronger form of **whatever:** *I have no confidence* whatsoever *in that fellow's report.*

wheat (hwēt) **1** a kind of grasslike grain. For picture, see **spike. 2** the seeds of this plant, used especially to make flour. **3** having to do with or made of wheat: *a* wheat *field;* wheat *flour;* wheat *bread.*

whee·dle (hwē′dəl) **1** to influence by flattery or an ingratiating manner; coax: *Guy* wheedled *his father into giving him a bigger allowance.* **2** to get by coaxing: *Elvira* wheedled *a new dress from her mother.* **whee·dled, whee·dling.**

wheel (hwēl) **1** a round frame supported by spokes, or a disklike part, on which a vehicle rolls. **2** a round movable part of certain machines, as a steering wheel or cogwheel. **3** to make a cycle or complete revolution: *The seasons* wheeled *around and it was Christmas again.* **4** a revolving or turning movement: *a wheel* in the opposite direction. **5** to face about. **6** to move on a wheel or wheels: *Dan* wheeled *his bicycle up the hill.* **7** a machine of which a wheel is the main part: *a potter's* wheel. **8** the workings of something: *the* wheels *of government; the wheels* of fate.

Wheel

Wheelbarrow

wheel·bar·row (hwēl′băr′ō) vehicle with a wheel at one end and two straight handles at the other which is pushed by hand.

wheel·wright (hwēl′rīt′) person who makes or repairs wheels and wheeled vehicles.

wheeze (hwēz) **1** to breathe with a sighing, whistling sound. **2** to make such a sound: *The old tugboat* wheezed *and gasped as it pushed the heavy scow.* **3** the sound made by or as by such breathing: *We recognized the* wheeze *of Pete's old car.* **wheezed, wheez·ing.**

wheez·y (hwē′zĭ) **1** having difficulty in breathing. **2** making a sighing, whistling sound. **wheez·i·er, wheez·i·est.**

whelk (hwĕlk) a kind of edible sea snail with a cone-shaped spiral shell.

whelp (hwĕlp) **1** a young flesh-eating animal, such as a puppy, cub, etc. **2** of animals, to give birth (to whelps). **3** worthless boy or young man.

when (hwĕn) **1** at what time: *Tell me* when *I should phone.* **2** at or during a time; while: *We stay indoors* when *it rains.* **3** at a particular time: *Call me* when *you are ready.* **4** in the event of; at such time as: *Ask your teacher* when *in doubt.* **5** what or which time: *About* when *did this happen?* **6** though; although: *The waiter brought me oatmeal* when *I asked for corn flakes.*

whence (hwĕns) from where; from what place: *The king asked,* "Whence *come these messengers?*"

when·e'er (hwĕn âr′) whenever.

when·ev·er (hwĕn ĕv′ər) at whatever time; as often as: *He telephones* whenever *he's in town.*

where (hwâr) **1** at what place: *Say* where *I should meet you.* **2** at the place: *to plant a tree* where *it will get the sun.* **3** in or at which: *the place* where *the rivers meet.* **4** to what place: *I don't know* where *my money goes.* **5** in what way; in what respect: *Can you tell me* where *I was at fault?* **6** what place: *He asked me,* "Where *do you come from?*"

where·a·bouts (hwâr′ə bouts′) **1** where; near or at what place: *Can you tell me* whereabouts *the hotel in this town is?* **2** a place where a person or thing is: *The* whereabouts *of the missing child was unknown.*

where·as (hwâr ăz′) **1** considering that; since: *The judge said,* "Whereas *the court declares the defendant guilty, he is ordered to pay the fine.*" **2** while on the contrary:

Coffee may keep one awake whereas *warm milk is a good bedtime drink.*

where·at (hwâr ăt´) **1** where; at which: *The dog remained on the spot* whereat *his master had left him.* **2** whereupon: *The king came to the balcony,* whereat *the crowd cheered.*

where·by (hwâr bī´) by which; by means of which: *the stars* whereby *the ship is steered.*

where·fore (hwâr´fôr´) **1** why: *Now* wherefore *should we worry?* **2** for which reason; therefore.

where·in (hwâr ĭn´) **1** in which: *a government* wherein *we can put our trust.* **2** in what; in what way: *My friend,* wherein *have I deceived you?*

where·of (hwâr ŏv´ or hwâr ŭv´) of what; of which; of whom: *to know* whereof *one speaks.*

where·on (hwâr ŏn´ or hwâr ôn´) on which; on what: *The ground* whereon *the magician stood suddenly sprouted flowers.*

where·so·ev·er (hwâr´sō ĕv´ər) wherever.

where·un·to (hwâr ŭn´tōō) old form of **to which:** *a deed of land to the knight* whereunto *the king signed his name.*

where·up·on (hwâr´ə pŏn´ or hwâr´ə pôn´) **1** in questions, upon what; upon what grounds. **2** following which; upon which: *The child fell asleep,* whereupon *the mother went downstairs.*

wher·ev·er (hwâr ĕv´ər) at, to, or in whatever place: *He always wrote to me* wherever *I was.*

where·with (hwâr wĭth´ or hwâr wĭth´) with what; with which: *a song* wherewith *to serenade a lady.*

where·with·al (hwâr´wĭth ôl´) whatever is needed to accomplish or pay for something: *He didn't have the* wherewithal *to buy a new car.*

wher·ry (hwĕr´ī) light rowboat. **wher·ries.**

whet (hwĕt) **1** to put a keen edge on (tools) by rubbing on or with a whetstone; sharpen: *to whet a knife.* **2** to stimulate or excite; make eager: *What I have read of his book* whets *my appetite for more.* **whet·ted, whet·ting.**

wheth·er (hwĕth´ər) **1** if: *I do not know whether you are telling the truth or not.* **2** no matter if: *The race is beginning whether you are ready or not.*

whet·stone (hwĕt´stōn´) stone for sharpening tools such as knives, scissors, etc.

whew (hwū) exclamation of relief, surprise, disgust, dismay, etc.

whey (hwā) thin, watery part of milk that separates from the milk after it has curdled.

which (hwĭch) **1** what one or ones: *I don't know which of these roads to take. Which is longer, 2 feet or 1 yard?* **2** that: *the horse which I bought.* **3** the one that; any that; whichever: *Let them choose which they want.* **4** what: *Kevin,* which *car is yours?*

which·ev·er (hwĭch ĕv´ər) **1** any one or ones that: *Read* whichever *book looks most interesting. Buy* whichever *pleases you most.* **2** no matter which: *It's all the same to us* whichever *day you come.*

whiff (hwĭf) **1** light gust or puff; breath: *a whiff of smoke; a whiff of fresh air.* **2** a slight odor or smell: *the whiff of burning leaves.* **3** to inhale or exhale: *to whiff the sea breeze.*

while (hwīl) **1** during the time that; at the same time that: *John was busy studying* while *the other children played outside.* **2** period of time: *He came and stayed with us a little while.* **3** although: *Alex is tall,* while *his parents are short.* **4 worth one's while** worth one's time, effort, or consideration: *It will be worth your while to read this book.*

while away to spend or pass idly: *to while away the time fishing and swimming.* **whiled, whil·ing.**

whilst (hwīlst) while.

whim (hwĭm) sudden or passing fancy or notion; caprice: *Jack says he wants to travel, but it's only a whim.*

whim·per (hwĭm´pər) **1** to cry with feeble, whining, broken sounds: *The sick puppy whimpered.* **2** a cry made by whimpering: *The child gave a whimper of pain.*

whim·si·cal (hwĭm´zə kəl) **1** full of odd or fanciful notions; capricious. **2** odd; quaint: *His old hat gave him a* whimsical *appearance.* **whim·si·cal·ly.**

---

fāte, făt, fâre, fär; bē, bĕt; bīte, bĭt; nō, nŏt, nôr; fūse, fŭn, fûr; tōō, tŏŏk; foil; foul; thin; then; hw for wh as in *wh*at; zh for s as in u*s*ual; ə for a, e, i, o, u, as in *a*go, lin*e*n, per*i*l, at*o*m, min*u*s

whim·sy (hwim′zĭ) **1** an odd fancy or whim. **2** an odd or quaint humor: *"Alice in Wonderland" is full of* whimsy. **whim·sies.**

whine (hwīn) **1** to make a low, complaining cry or sound: *The dog* whines *when he is cold.* **2** a cry made by whining. **3** to say with a whine: *He is always* whining *complaints.* **4** to complain or coax in a peevish, childish way: *He* whined *to be taken to the movies.* **whined, whin·ing.**

whin·ny (hwĭn′ĭ) **1** the low neigh of a horse. **2** to neigh. **whin·nies; whin·nied, whin·ny·ing.**

whip (hwĭp) **1** rod with a lash; long lash with a short handle; slender, flexible switch. **2** to strike with, or as with, a whip; lash; switch: *to* whip *a horse;* whip *the grass with a cane.* **3** to punish or urge forward with a whip. **4** a person who or thing that drives or urges: *a Senate* whip; *the* whip *of conscience.* **5** to dart; move suddenly: *to* whip *around a corner.* **6** to flap: *The drying clothes* whipped *in the wind.* **7** to draw or pull suddenly: *to* whip *off a belt;* whip *out a gun.* **8** to beat to a froth as with a fork or egg beater: *to* whip *eggs for an omelet.* **9** a dessert made of whipped egg white, cream, fruit juices, or a combination of these: *a dish of prune* whip. **10** to defeat: *Our team* whipped *theirs.*

whip up 1 to prepare in a hurry: *She* whipped up *a dinner for the unexpected guests.* **2** to stir the emotions of; excite: *The angry speaker* whipped up *the crowd.* **whipped, whip·ping.**

whip·poor·will (hwĭp′ər wĭl′) brown mottled bird that hunts flying insects in the evening. Its whistling call gives it its name.

Whippoorwill, about 10 in. long

whir or **whirr** (hwûr) **1** to revolve or move rapidly with a whizzing or buzzing sound. **2** whizzing or buzzing sound caused by rapid motion: *the* whir *of wings.* **whirred, whir·ring.**

whirl (hwûrl) **1** to turn round and round rapidly; spin: *The dancers* whirled *to the music.* **2** to give a whirling or spinning motion to: *The wind* whirled *people's hats away.* **3** a spinning movement: *the* whirl

of a falling leaf. **4** bewilderment; confusion of mind: *My thoughts are in a* whirl. **5** confused and bustling activity: *the* whirl *of the holiday season.*

whirl·pool (hwûrl′pōōl′) water in rapid spinning motion; eddy.

whirl·wind (hwûrl′wĭnd′) **1** current of air with a violent spiral motion. **2** done with irresistible speed or vigor: *a* whirlwind *courtship.*

whisk (hwĭsk) **1** to brush with a quick, sweeping motion: *The horse* whisked *the flies away with his tail.* **2** to move or cause to move suddenly or rapidly: *The frightened deer* whisked *through the woods. The waiting car* whisked *the actress away from the crowd.* **3** sudden, light, quick movement: *The waitress gave the table a few* whisks *with her napkin.* **4** small broom or brush. Also called **whisk broom.** **5** to beat (eggs, cream, etc.) into a froth.

whis·ker (hwĭs′kər) **1** the long, bristly hair on either side of the mouth of some animals, such as a cat or rat. **2** whiskers hair growing on a man's face; beard: *My grandfather has white* whiskers.

whis·key or **whis·ky** (hwĭs′kĭ) strong alcoholic drink made from grain. **whis·keys; whis·kies.**

whis·per (hwĭs′pər) **1** to speak very softly: *Tim* whispered *in order not to disturb his mother.* **2** a murmuring; soft, low, spoken sound: *We spoke in* whispers *because it was late.* **3** to make a faint, rustling, hissing sound: *The wind* whispered *in the tall grass.* **4** a faint, rustling sound: *The wind died down to a* whisper. **5** to tell confidentially: *Susan* whispered *something to Ann.* **6** a hint; suggestion; rumor: *The* whispers *about him were merely empty gossip.*

whis·tle (hwĭs′əl) **1** sharp, shrill, piercing sound: *the* whistle *of a quail.* **2** such a sound made by forcing air through the puckered lips or between the teeth: *Tom heard Huck's low* whistle *beneath his window.* **3** similar sound made by forcing air or steam into a vibrating tube. **4** device used to make a whistle: *The traffic officer blew his* whistle. **5** to make a shrill, piercing sound: *The locomotive* whistled *as it neared the*

STEAM

POLICE Whistles

station. **6** to move with a whistling sound: *The bullet* whistled *past.* **whis·tled, whis·tling.**

whit (hwĭt) the least bit: *It doesn't make a* whit *of difference.*

white (hwĭt) **1** color of snow; opposite of black. **2** having this color: *a* white *wedding gown; a* white *polar bear.* **3** having a light-colored skin: *the* white *race.* **4** white person. **5** pale from fear or other strong emotion: *Alice turned* white *when she thought she saw a ghost.* **6** white clothing: *Nurses wear* white. **7** without stain or spot; pure; innocent. **8** silvery; gray; hoary: *My grandmother has* white *hair.* **9** white part of something such as an eye, an egg, or a target. **whit·er, whit·est.**

white ant termite that destroys wood and paper.

white·cap (hwĭt′kăp′) the crest or ridge of a wave as it breaks into foam; a white-topped wave.

white·fish (hwĭt′fĭsh′) an edible, fresh-water fish of the salmon family. pl. **white·fish;** rarely, **white·fish·es.**

white flag flag of truce or surrender.

White House official residence of the President of the United States, in Washington, D. C.

white lie fib or falsehood about a trivial matter, usually told to save someone's feelings.

whit·en (hwĭ′tən) to make or become white: *We* whiten *laundry with a bleach. The clothes* whitened *in the sunshine.*

white·ness (hwĭt′nĭs) a being white: *The* whiteness *of the snow dazzled our eyes.*

white·wash (hwĭt′wŏsh′ or hwĭt′wôsh′) **1** mixture of lime and water used to coat walls, fences, etc. **2** to cover with this liquid. **3** to cover up or hide the faults or mistakes of: *His gifts to charity could never* whitewash *the dishonest way he made his fortune.*

whith·er (hwĭth′ər) to what place; where.

whit·ish (hwĭ′tĭsh) somewhat white.

whit·tle (hwĭt′əl) **1** to trim or shape a piece of wood bit by bit with a knife. **2** to make or shape something in this way: *At camp the boys learned to* whittle *wooden spoons.*

3 to reduce bit by bit: *They* whittled *down their mother's objection to the party.* **whit·tled, whit·tling.**

whiz or **whizz** (hwĭz) **1** to speed with a buzzing or hissing sound: *The motorcycle* whizzed *by in a cloud of dust.* **2** a buzzing or hissing noise: *the* whiz *of the airplane overhead.* **whizzed, whiz·zing.**

who (hoō) **1** what person or persons; which person or persons: *I wonder* who *that man is.* Who *else was there with you?* **2** the one or ones that: *Mr. Smith,* who *owns this land, said we could play here.* **3** that: *The person* who *finds the treasure may keep it.*

whoa (hwō or wō) stop! stand still! (used especially in halting horses).

who'd (hoōd) who would.

who·ev·er (hoō ĕv′ər) **1** anyone or every-one who: *The coach said,* whoever *wants to play should be on the field.* **2** no matter who: *Don't open the door,* whoever *it may be.* **3** forceful way of asking who: *He wondered* whoever *on earth could have done it.*

whole (hōl) **1** not broken; in one piece: *Although I dropped the vase, it's still* whole. **2** not injured; sound: *All the survivors escaped the accident* whole. **3** with nothing removed; entire; complete: *a* whole *loaf of bread;* whole *milk.* **4** entire amount or sum: *The* whole *is equal to the sum of its parts. If you will give me the* whole, *I will divide it fairly between us.* **5** a complete system; unity: *The organs of the human body work as a* whole. (Homonym: hole)

whole·heart·ed (hōl′här′tĭd) sincere; hearty: *Your suggestion has my* whole-hearted *approval.* **whole·heart·ed·ly.**

whole number a number that is expressed without the use of a fraction, such as 5, 12, 23.

whole·sale (hōl′sāl′) **1** selling or buying in large quantity: *a* wholesale *grocer.* **2** to sell or buy in large quantity. **3** at or by wholesale: *He sells* wholesale *to shops.* **whole·saled, whole·sal·ing.**

whole·some (hōl′səm) **1** improving one's bodily or spiritual well-being: *a* wholesome *exercise;* wholesome *entertainment.* **2** having an appearance of good health: *a* whole-some *complexion.* **whole·some·ly.**

fāte, făt, fâre, fär; bē, bĕt; bīte, bĭt; nō, nŏt, nôr; fūse, fŭn, fûr; toō, tŏŏk; foil; foul; thin; then; hw for wh as in *wh*at; zh for s as in u*s*ual; ə for a, e, i, o, u, as in *a*go, lin*e*n, per*i*l, at*o*m, min*u*s

whole-wheat (hōl′hwēt′) made of entire wheat kernel: *bread made of* whole-wheat *flour.*

who'll (hōōl) who will; who shall: *I don't know* who'll *do it.*

whol·ly (hō′li) entirely; completely; thoroughly: *I am* wholly *satisfied with our new house.* (Homonym: holy)

whom (hōōm) **1** what person: *To* whom *am I speaking?* **2** that (person): *This is the man* whom *I mentioned yesterday.*

whoop (hōōp or hwōōp) **1** to give a loud shout or cry: *He* whooped *for joy when he got his bicycle.* **2** a loud shout or cry. **3** to gasp loudly, as in whooping cough. **4** loud gasp, as in whooping cough.

whooping cough a contagious disease marked by coughing and gasping for breath. Whooping cough usually occurs in childhood.

whooping crane a large, rare American crane with a peculiar call. Only about 20 are now living.

who's (hōōz) who is: *I don't know* who's *coming tonight.*

whose (hōōz) of whom; of which: *the woman whose purse was stolen.*

who·so·ev·er (hōō′sō ĕv′ər) old form of **whoever.**

why (hwī) **1** for what reason: *He wondered why you smiled.* **2** for which; on account of which: *the reason* why. **3** the cause; reason: *Men still puzzle over the* why *of the universe.* **4** exclamation showing surprise or pleasure: *She said, "*Why! *It couldn't be easier."*

wick (wĭk) loosely woven, absorbent fibers in a candle or lamp that draw up melted wax or oil to be burned.

wick·ed (wĭk′ĭd) **1** bad; evil; sinful: *a* wicked *deed; a* wicked *rascal.* **2** mischievous; naughty: *a* wicked *grin.* **3** severe; dangerous: *a* wicked *blow on the head; a* wicked *weapon.* **wick·ed·ly.**

wick·ed·ness (wĭk′ĭd nĭs) **1** a sinful state or quality: *a sermon on the* wickedness *of greed.* **2** a wicked act; sin: *Lying is a* wickedness.

wick·er (wĭk′ər) **1** flexible twigs, especially of willow, that can be woven to make baskets, etc. **2** made of these twigs woven together: *a* wicker *chair.*

Wick

wick·et (wĭk′ĭt) **1** small door or gate. **2** ticket window or the like. **3** a wire arch in croquet.

wide (wīd) **1** extending some distance from edge to edge or side to side; broad: *a* wide *road; a* wide *piece of cloth.* **2** in width: *This paper is eight inches* wide. **3** of great extent; immense: *a* wide *range of friends.* **4** to the full extent; fully: *to open the door* wide. **5** fully opened: *She gazed at him with* wide *eyes.* **6** to a distance: *Our land stretches far and* wide. **7** far from the mark aimed at: *to shoot* wide. **wid·er, wid·est; wide·ly.**

Croquet wicket

wide-a·wake (wīd′ə wāk′) **1** fully awake. **2** alert: *He's a* wide-awake *boy with many interests.*

wide-eyed (wīd′īd′) with eyes open wide, as in surprise, wonder, etc.: *The farmer was* wide-eyed *on his first trip to the city.*

wid·en (wī′dən) **1** to extend the width of; make wider; broaden: *Workmen are* widening *the road.* **2** to become wider: *The stream* widens *as it goes along.*

wide·spread (wīd′sprĕd′) **1** covering a wide area; extensive: *Measles has been* widespread *this spring.* **2** spread out; opened to full extent: *a bird's* widespread *wings.*

wid·ow (wĭd′ō) woman whose husband has died, and who has not remarried.

wid·ow·er (wĭd′ō ər) man whose wife has died, and who has not remarried.

width (wĭdth) the size of something across; the measurement from side to side; breadth: *The* width *of this is 54 inches. The porch runs the* width *of the house.*

wield (wēld) **1** to use with the hands: *to* wield *a brush; to* wield *a sword.* **2** to exercise, as power, influence, authority.

wie·ner (wē′nər) sausage of pork and beef, usually smaller than a frankfurter.

wife (wīf) married woman; spouse: *a man and* wife. **wives.**

Wig

wig (wĭg) a head covering of human or other hair used to hide baldness, for adornment, or as a part of an official uniform: *British judges wear* wigs.

wiggle

wig·gle (wĭg′əl) **1** to move or jerk about with short, quick, nervous movements; wriggle; squirm: *to wiggle one's toes; to wiggle about in a chair.* **2** movement of this kind. **wig·gled, wig·gling.**

wight (wīt) old word for "person," "human being," "creature": *a poor, luckless wight.*

wig·wag (wĭg′wăg′) **1** to signal by moving flags, flashing lights, etc., in a code. **2** a signaling with flags, lights, etc. **wig·wagged, wig·wag·ging.**

Wigwag

wig·wam (wĭg′wŏm or wĭg′wôm) dome-shaped hut made of poles tied together and covered with bark. The wigwam was used by some of the eastern American Indians.

wild (wīld) **1** not tamed; living in the natural state: *Indians used to catch and tame wild horses.* **2** growing in a natural state; uncultivated: *native wild flowers; wild fruit.* **3** primitive; not civilized; savage: *We found relics of wild Indians.* **4** with few or no inhabitants; remote: *the wild north woods.* **5** not controlled or disciplined; unruly: *a wild temper.* **6** not kept in order: *Bill's wild hair; everything in wild confusion.* **7** very eager; keen: *She's wild to start on the trip. We are wild to see them.* **8** rash; fantastic: *a wild scheme; wild dreams.* **9** violently agitated or disturbed: *to be wild with rage; wild with joy; a wild sea.* **10** wilds desert; wilderness; a region not cultivated or inhabited by men: *They explored the wilds of the jungle.* **wild·ly.**

Wigwam

American wildcat, about 3 ft. long

wild·cat (wīld′kăt′) **1** any of several of the smaller forest cats, especially the lynx.

will

2 involving chance; risky: *a wildcat mining venture.*

wil·der·ness (wĭl′dər nĭs) a wild, usually desolate and uninhabited, region: *a forest wilderness; an ocean wilderness.*

wild·fire (wīld′fīr′) fire that spreads rapidly and is difficult to extinguish.

wild flower 1 the flower of any uncultivated plant found in fields, woods, etc.: *Some wild flowers, such as the mountain laurel, are protected by State law.* **2** a plant that has such flowers: *to transplant wild flowers to the garden.*

wild fowl wild birds hunted as game, such as wild geese and ducks, partridges, pheasants, and quail.

wild·life (wīld′līf′) wild animals, trees, and plants of a region.

wild·ness (wīld′nĭs) a being wild, uncultivated, or untamed: *the wildness of the jungle.*

wile (wīl) **1** cunning trick or deception. **2** charming tricks for a particular purpose: *women's wiles.* **3** to obtain by trickery: *She wiled the secret from him.* **wiled, wil·ing.**

¹will (wĭl) **1** power of the mind to make decisions and carry them out: *I do this by my own free will.* **2** strong purpose; determination: *Where there's a will there's a way.* **3** a wish; choice; intention: *I was forced to do that against my will.* **4** to determine; decide; choose: *We shall do it as the king wills.* **5** to compel (oneself); bring the will to bear on: *Although he was sleepy, he willed himself to stay awake.* **6** disposition toward others: *A person of good will trusts his fellow men.* **7** a person's written instructions telling what is to be done with his belongings after he is dead. **8** to give by means of a will; bequeath: *to will money to charity.* [¹**will** is a form of an Old English word (willa) meaning "a wish," "a determination."]

²will (wĭl) **1** am, is, or are going to: *They will like this new game.* **2** am, is, or are determined to: *I will go out and play, even if I am punished for it.* **3** want or wants to; wish or wishes to: *Ask him if he will have some cake.* **4** am, is, or are bound or are able to: *This radio will receive only three*

---

fāte, făt, fâre, fär; bē, bĕt; bīte, bĭt; nō, nŏt, nôr; fūse, fŭn, fûr; tōō, tŏŏk; foil; foul; thin; then; hw for wh as in *wh*at; zh for s as in u*s*ual; ə for a, e, i, o, u, as in ago, linen, peril, atom, minus

stations. [²**will** is a form of an Old English word (willen) that comes from the same Latin word as ¹**will**.]

will·ful or **wil·ful** (wil'fəl) **1** determined to have one's own way; stubborn: *The willful boy will not obey.* **2** deliberate; intentional: *a willful waste of food; willful destruction of property.* **will·ful·ly** or **wil·ful·ly.**

will·ing (wil'ing) **1** ready (to oblige, comply, or accept): *I am willing to take the job.* **2** done or given without urging and in a cheerful spirit: *to give willing assistance.* **will·ing·ly.**

will·ing·ness (wil'ing nis) a being willing.

wil·low (wil'ō) **1** tree or shrub with slender leaves and tough, flexible branches, usually growing in watery ground. **2** the wood and branches of this tree used for making furniture, baskets, etc.

Weeping willow

wil·ly-nil·ly (wil'i nil'i) whether one likes it or not: *He must accept the decision, willy-nilly.*

¹**wilt** (wilt) **1** of a plant, to droop or fade: *The leaves wilted in the hot sun.* **2** of a person, to become weak, faint, and exhausted. **3** to cause to wilt: *The sun wilted the geraniums.* [¹**wilt** is a form of an obsolete word (welk) meaning "to wither."]

²**wilt** (wilt) old form of **will** used with *thou*. [²**wilt** was formed from ²**will**.]

wil·y (wi'li) sly; cunning; crafty: *a wily fox.* **wil·i·er, wil·i·est; wil·i·ly.**

win (win) **1** to come off best in: *to win a battle; to win a race.* **2** to gain a victory: *Our team won.* **3** to gain by effort, charm, or persuasion: *to win honors; to win friends; to win support.* **won, win·ning.**

wince (wins) **1** to shrink away; start back; flinch: *Luther winced when the doctor examined his bruised knee.* **2** a flinching. **winced, winc·ing.**

winch (winch) machine for lifting or pulling by a rope wound on a roller turned by a crank or an engine. For picture, see **windlass.**

¹**wind** (wind) **1** natural current of air, especially one of some force: *the wind from the*

north. **2** to cause to be out of breath: *The steep climb winded the mountaineers.* **3** breath; ability to breathe: *The horse was fairly old, but his wind was sound.* **4** to get or follow the scent of: *The hounds winded a fox.* **5** air-borne scent: *The deer caught our wind.* **6 winds** the wind instruments in an orchestra. **7 before the wind** with the wind: *to sail before the wind.* **8 down the wind** in the same direction as the wind is blowing. **9 up the wind** in a direction opposite to that of the wind. **10 in the wind** being discussed; about to happen: *Plans for a Christmas party were in the wind.* **11 get wind of** to know or hear about. [¹**wind** is the unchanged form of an Old English word.]

²**wind** (wind) **1** to twist; twine: *to wind a string about one's finger.* **2** to encircle or wrap: *to wind an electric wire with tape.* **3** to twist together: *to wind the strands of a rope.* **4** to turn or make tight a crank or propelling spring: *to wind a watch or a spring-driven toy.* **5** to follow a twisting course: *The road winds among the hills.*

wind up to bring to a close; put an end to: *to wind up a business.*

wound, wind·ing. [²**wind** is a form of an Old English word (windan) meaning "to wind," "to circle round."]

³**wind** (wind or wind) to blow (a horn). **wind·ed** or **wound, wind·ing.** [³**wind** is ¹**wind** in a special sense but influenced in its first pronunciation by ²**wind.**]

wind·break (wind'brāk') a shelter or protection from the wind, such as a wall or row of trees.

wind·fall (wind'fôl') **1** something blown down by the wind, such as fruit from a tree. **2** an unexpected stroke of good fortune.

wind instrument (wind in'strə mənt) musical instrument sounded by a current of air blown into it, such as a flute, a saxophone, or a trumpet.

Windlass or winch

wind·lass (wind'ləs) machine for lifting or pulling by a rope wound on a roller, turned by a crank; a simple form of winch.

wind·mill (wind′mil′) mill or machine operated by the wind turning its large sails or vanes, now used mostly as a water pump.

win·dow (win′dō) **1** an opening in a wall of a building, side of an automobile, etc., usually supplied with glass, to admit light and air. **2** the glass and its frame which fills such an opening.

win·dow·pane (win′dō pān′) pane or panel of glass in a window.

window sill shelf or ledge across the bottom of a window: *Pots of flowers stood on the* window sill.

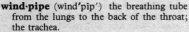

Windmill

wind·pipe (wind′pīp′) the breathing tube from the lungs to the back of the throat; the trachea.

wind·row (wind′rō′) hay or grain raked into a row to dry.

wind·shield (wind′shēld′) window at the front of a vehicle to protect its riders from wind, spray, dust, etc.

wind·storm (wind′stôrm′) gale, hurricane, tornado, or other violent movement of air, often without rain.

wind·ward (wind′wərd) **1** a side or direction from which the wind blows: *Off to* windward *we saw a small island.* **2** in the direction or on the side from which the wind blows: *The* windward *side of this building is too cold for comfort.*

wind·y (win′dī) **1** subject to or exposed to wind: *a* windy *seacoast; a* windy *hill.* **2** talkative; wordy: *a* windy *speaker.* **wind·i·er, wind·i·est; wind·i·ly.**

wine (win) **1** fermented juice of grapes. **2** similar product of other fruits or plants: *cherry* wine. **3** to serve wine to: *to* wine *and dine someone.* **wined, win·ing.**

wing (wing) **1** one of the organs or parts by means of which a bird, bat, insect, etc., flies. **2** to fly: *The crow* winged *over the cornfield.* **3** one of the main supporting surfaces of an airplane. **4** in the army or navy, a force at the left or right of the main force. **5** in a building, a part projecting at right angles from the main part: *in a* wing *of the palace.* **6** a part of a political party

or movement: *The right* wing *is more conservative than the left* wing. **7** the space on either side of a theater stage, or the scenery on either side. **8** to wound a bird on the wing; wound anyone or anything slightly. **9 on the wing** in flight; flying: *to shoot ducks* on the wing.

winged (wingd or wing′id) **1** having wings. **2** moving as if on wings; swift; rapid: *a* winged *message by telegram.*

wing·less (wing′lis) without wings.

wing·spread (wing′sprĕd′) distance from tip to tip across the wings of a plane or the widespread wings of a bird.

wink (wingk) **1** to close and open either eye or both eyes quickly; blink. **2** to close and open one eye quickly as a signal, hint, warning, etc., to another person: *Felix* winks *at all the girls.* **3** to move or remove by winking: *She* winked *her tears away.* **4** to blink, flash, or twinkle at intervals: *The lights of a passing ship* winked. **5** very short period of time: *I'll be back in half a* wink. *I didn't get a* wink *of sleep last night.* **6 forty winks** very short nap. **wink at** to deliberately overlook; pretend not to see: *to* wink at *a person's faults.*

win·ner (win′ər) person or thing that wins.

win·ning (win′ing) **1** in contests, successful; victorious: *the* winning *team.* **2** attractive; engaging; persuasive: *a* winning *manner;* winning *smile.* **3 winnings** something won or gained, especially money. **win·ning·ly.**

win·now (win′ō) **1** to blow or fan off the chaff and husks from grain by a stream of air: *to* winnow *wheat.* **2** to sift; separate: *to* winnow *good from bad.*

win·some (win′səm) attractive; charming: *a* winsome *personality.* **win·some·ly.**

win·ter (win′tər) **1** the coldest season of the year, between autumn and spring. In the Northern Hemisphere, it lasts from December 21 to March 21. **2** of or for winter: *a* winter *sport;* winter *clothes.* **3** to live during or pass the winter: *to* winter *in Florida.* **4** to keep during the winter: *to* winter *cattle.*

win·ter·green (win′tər grēn′) **1** low-growing, woody, evergreen plant with red

fāte, făt, fâre, fär; bē, bĕt; bīte, bĭt; nō, nŏt, nôr; fūse, fŭn, fûr; tōō, tŏŏk; foil; foul; thin; ~~then~~; hw for wh as in *wh*at; zh for s as in u*s*ual; ə for a, e, i, o, u, as in *a*go, lin*e*n, per*i*l, at*o*m, min*u*s

825

berries, white flowers, and leaves which yield an aromatic oil. **2** the oil of this plant used as a flavoring or in medicine. **3** the flavor of this oil.

win·ter·time (win'tər tim') season of winter.

win·try (win'tri) **1** of winter or like winter; cold, chilly, snowy, etc. **2** cold and unfriendly in manner or expression; lacking warmth: *a* wintry *smile.* **win·tri·er, win·tri·est.**

wipe (wip) **1** to pass a cloth or some soft material over (something) in order to dry or cleanse it: *to* wipe *the teacups; to* wipe *the windshield.* **2** to remove by rubbing: *to* wipe *away tears; to* wipe *off oil or mud.* **3** the act of wiping: *Give my glasses a* wipe.

wipe out to destroy completely; obliterate: *The failure of the crops* wiped out *the farmer's savings.*

wiped, wip·ing.

wire (wir) **1** metal drawn out into a thread of a given thickness. **2** such metal used for different purposes: *telephone and telegraph* wires; *barbed* wire. **3** made of wire: *a* wire *netting;* wire *rope.* **4** to furnish or provide with wire: *to* wire *for electric current.* **5** to bind with wire: *to* wire *bales of hay.* **6** a telegram: *to send a* wire *home.* **7** to send a message by telegraph: *Please* wire *me when to expect you.* **8 live wire** **(1)** a wire charged with electricity. **(2)** an energetic, efficient person. **9 pull wires** to use roundabout influence to gain some end or purpose. **wired, wir·ing.**

wire·less (wir'lis) **1** without wires or the use of wires; by radio. **2** message sent by radio instead of over wires: *a* wireless *telegram.*

wir·ing (wi'ring) a system of wires to provide electricity.

wir·y (wi'ri) **1** made of wire. **2** having the qualities of wire; stiff; tough: *a* wiry *head of hair.* **3** of persons or animals, lean but sinewy. **wir·i·er, wir·i·est; wir·i·ly.**

Wis. Wisconsin.

Wis·con·sin (wis kŏn'sən) State in the north central part of the United States.

wis·dom (wiz'dəm) **1** good judgment and knowledge of what is right and true. **2** scholarly knowledge; learning.

wisdom tooth the last back tooth on either wide of each human jaw.

¹wise (wiz) **1** possessing or showing knowledge and good judgment: *a piece of* wise *advice.* **2** having knowledge or information upon (some subject): *to be* wise *in the ways of men.* **wis·er, wis·est; wise·ly.** [**¹wise** is a form of an Old English word (wis) of the same meaning.]

²wise (wiz) way, manner, or mode: *in no* wise; *in such* wise. [**²wise** is a form of an Old English word (wise) of the same meaning.]

wish (wish) **1** to have or express a desire that: *to* wish *it were summer; to* wish *we lived by the sea.* **2** to crave; want: *You may have more cake, if you* wish. **3** to invoke (something) for another: *Please* wish *me good luck. I* wish *you a happy trip.* **4** a strong desire or longing: *her* wish *for peace and a quiet life.* **5** thing wished for: *You will get your* wish.

wish on (someone) to pass on to, or palm off on, another: *The dishwashing was* wished on *poor Bertha.*

wish·bone (wish'bōn') the forked bone in a fowl's breast.

wish·ful (wish'fəl) having a wish or wishes; full of longing.

wisp (wisp) **1** small bundle or bunch; tuft; something thin and sometimes twisted: *a* wisp *of straw; a* wisp *of hair.* **2** a small or slight bit (of): *a* wisp *of cotton; a* wisp *of a child.*

wis·tar·i·a or **wis·te·ri·a** (wis tir'i ə) a climbing shrub of the pea family, bearing drooping clusters of purple or white flowers.

wist·ful (wist'fəl) longing; wishful: *The child cast a* wistful *glance at the candy counter.* **wist·ful·ly.**

wit (wit) **1** power to see and express what is odd or amusing in a situation or idea: *Tod's* wit *kept us smiling in spite of our troubles.* **2** someone who has the ability to see and say what is odd or amusing: *Tod is a great* wit. **3** wisdom; intelligence: *He hadn't the* wit *to come in out of the rain.* **4 wits** mental ability: *Zachary kept his* wits *during the accident.* **5 at one's wits' end** at the end of one's mental powers; at a loss.

Wishbone

Wistaria

witch (wĭch) **1** woman believed to have supernatural evil powers. **2** an ugly old woman; crone; hag. **3** a fascinating young woman.

witch·craft (wĭch′krăft′) craft or power of a witch: *to cast a spell by* witchcraft.

witch·er·y (wĭch′ə rĭ) **1** great charm; fascination: *There was* witchery *in the moonlight.* **2** witchcraft; magic.

witch·ing (wĭch′ĭng) of supernatural events or practices; relating to witchcraft; eerie: *Midnight is called the* witching *hour.*

with (wĭth or wĭth) **1** in the company of; in the presence of: *Come* with *me to the barn.* **2** having; possessing: *I prefer the dress* with *the collar.* **3** on the side of: *Are you* with *me or against me?* **4** in spite of: *He still smiles,* with *all his troubles.* **5** against (in a situation that suggests opposition): *We argued* with *them.* **6** by means of; using: *to cure* with *drugs; to hear* with *one's ears.* **7** in the spirit of; in the condition of: *He said good-by* with *great sadness.* **8** at the same time as; during: *We rise* with *the sun every morning.* **9** in proportion to: *Many wines improve* with *age.* **10** as a result of; because of: *His hands froze* with *cold.* **11** from: *I hate to part* with *all this money.* **12** between (one's side and another's): *America makes pacts* with *foreign countries.* **13** in the care of: *He left the dog* with *his mother when he went away.* **14** in respect to; in regard to: *It is all the same* with *him whether he stays or leaves.*

with·al (wĭth ôl′ or wĭth ôl′) in addition; besides: *She had health and wealth, and beauty* withal.

with·draw (wĭth drô′ or wĭth drô′) **1** to draw back; pull away: *She* withdrew *her hand from the hot iron.* **2** to take back: *to* withdraw *unkind words.* **3** to take away; remove: *to* withdraw *money from the bank.* **4** to go away; retire: *The army* withdrew *under fire.* **with·drew, with·drawn, with·draw·ing.**

with·draw·al (wĭth drô′əl or wĭth′drô əl) a removing: *a* withdrawal *from the room; a* withdrawal *of money from the bank.*

with·drawn (wĭth drôn′ or wĭth drôn′) **1** apart: *He stood* withdrawn *from the*

crowd. **2** See **withdraw.** *He has* withdrawn *his support.*

with·drew (wĭth drōō′ or wĭth drōō′) See **withdraw.** *He* withdrew *from the club.*

with·er (wĭth′ər) **1** to dry out, wrinkle, and fade: *In autumn, leaves* wither *on the trees. The hot sun* withered *the flowers.* **2** to make (someone) feel uncomfortable or ashamed: *She* withered *him with an angry glance.*

with·held (wĭth hĕld′ or wĭth hĕld′) See **withhold.**

with·hold (wĭth hōld′ or wĭth hōld′) to keep or hold back: *to* withhold *permission; to* withhold *information.* **with·held, with·hold·ing.**

with·in (wĭth ĭn′ or wĭth ĭn′) **1** inside of: *boxes nested one* within *another.* **2** indoors; inside: *Although it is cold outside, it is warm* within. **3** inside the limits of: *I'll be there* within *the hour. Do anything* within *the law to help her.*

with·out (wĭth out′ or wĭth out′) **1** not with; not having; lacking: *Seth likes his cereal* without *sugar. You can bake this cake* without *any trouble.* **2** with neglect or avoidance of: *He walked by* without *speaking to me.* **3** outside; outdoors: *It was raining* without, *but dry and warm inside by the fire.* **4** on the outside of: *There is still real country* without *the city limits.* **5** beyond: *It is true* without *any doubt.*

with·stand (wĭth stănd′ or wĭth stănd′) to oppose; resist; endure: *to* withstand *the cold; to* withstand *a siege.* **with·stood, with·stand·ing.**

with·stood (wĭth stōōd′ or wĭth stōōd′) See **withstand.**

wit·less (wĭt′lĭs) without good sense or sound judgment; stupid: *Her* witless *remarks hurt many people's feelings.* **wit·less·ly.**

wit·ness (wĭt′nĭs) **1** to see something in person: *He* witnessed *many brave deeds in battle.* **2** someone who has first-hand knowledge of something: *Percy was a* witness *of the accident.* **3** person who gives a sworn statement in court about something: *Percy was asked to be a* witness *for the man who was injured.* **4** to give a statement sworn to be true: *Percy* witnessed

fāte, făt, fâre, fär; bē, bĕt; bīte, bĭt; nō, nŏt, nôr; fūse, fŭn, fûr; tōō, tŏŏk; foil; foul; thin; then; hw for wh as in what; zh for s as in usual; ə for a, e, i, o, u, as in ago, linen, peril, atom, minus

827

that it was the driver's fault. **5** to sign (a document) as a witness: *Josephine witnessed the signing of the will.* **6** a person who was present at the signing of a legal document: *Josephine was a witness of the will.* **7** evidence; testimony: *to give witness to the truth of a statement.* **8** to be or give proof or evidence of: *Her red face witnessed her embarrassment.*

wit·ty (wit′ĭ) amusing in a sharp and clever way. **wit·ti·er, wit·ti·est; wit·ti·ly.**

wives (wīvz) more than one **wife.**

wiz·ard (wiz′ərd) **1** man who has magic powers; magician. **2** very clever person.

wk. week.

wob·ble (wŏb′əl) **1** to move unsteadily from side to side; to waver. **2** to cause to waver or totter: *Stop wobbling the table.* **3** a wobbling motion. **wob·bled, wob·bling.**

wob·bly (wŏb′lĭ) teetering; unsteady.

woe (wō) **1** deep sorrow or grief. **2** cause of sorrow; affliction: *War, poverty, sickness, and death are common woes of life.*

woe·ful (wō′fəl) **1** full of woe; mournful: *He tells his woeful tale to anyone who will listen.* **2** regrettable: *a woeful neglect; woeful ignorance.* **woe·ful·ly.**

woke (wōk) See ¹**wake.** *The mother woke at dawn, but woke the children an hour later.*

wolf (wŏŏlf) a fierce, usually gray, animal, somewhat like a large dog with pointed ears and a bushy tail. Wolves often hunt in packs in the winter and sometimes kill sheep or other farm animals. **wolves.**

Timber wolf, about 5½ ft. long

wolf·hound (wŏŏlf′hound′) any of several breeds of large dogs formerly used for hunting wolves, as the Irish wolfhound or the Russian wolfhound.

wolf·ish (wŏŏl′fĭsh) **1** like a wolf; savage; fierce: *a wolfish cruelty.* **2** greedy; voracious: *a wolfish appetite.* **wolf·ish·ly.**

wol·ver·ine (wŏŏl′və-rēn′) a shaggy, stocky animal with short legs, that is related to the badger. It is noted for its cunning and supposed fierceness.

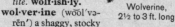

Wolverine, 2½ to 3 ft. long

wolves (wŏŏlvz) more than one **wolf.**

wom·an (wŏŏm′ən) **1** adult female human being. **2** female sex in general: *"Man works from sun to sun, woman's work is never done"* is an old saying. **3** female servant: *The old woman had been with the family for many years.* **wom·en.**

wom·an·hood (wŏŏm′ən hŏŏd′) condition of being a woman: *The little girl we knew has grown to womanhood.*

wom·an·kind (wŏŏm′ən kīnd′) women in general.

wom·an·ly (wŏŏm′ən lĭ) like, or suitable for, a woman; feminine: *a womanly interest in clothes; a womanly tenderness towards the sick.*

wo·men (wĭm′ən) more than one **woman.**

wom·en·folk (wĭm′ĭn fōk′) **1** women in general. **2** a particular group of women, as of a household: *The womenfolk prepared dinner while the men were plowing the field.*

won (wŭn) See **win.** *He won the game.* (Homonym: one).

won·der (wŭn′dər) **1** feeling or state of mind produced by something marvelous or unexpected: *to gaze in wonder at the shooting star.* **2** thing or event that causes surprise, astonishment, awe, etc.: *the seven wonders of the world.* **3** to feel surprise, amazement, etc.; to marvel: *They wondered with open mouths as the magician performed his tricks.* **4** to be doubtful and curious; speculate about; want to know: *The boys wondered what was in the Christmas packages.*

won·der·ful (wŭn′dər fŏŏl) causing wonder; extraordinary; remarkable: *a wonderful feat of strength; wonderful discoveries in outer space.* **won·der·ful·ly.**

won·der·ment (wŭn′dər mənt) state of wonder; amazement.

won·drous (wŭn′drəs) marvelous; astonishing. **won·drous·ly.**

wont (wŭnt or wōnt or wônt) **1** accustomed: *He is wont to have his own way.* **2** habit; custom: *It is her wont to go south in the winter.*

won't (wōnt) will not: *We won't be home for dinner.*

wont·ed (wŭn′tĭd or wōn′tĭd or wôn′tĭd) usual; customary: *He won every race with his wonted ease.*

woo (wōō) **1** to make love to; to court. **2** to strive for; seek to attain: *to woo fame and fortune.* **3** to try to persuade or win over.

wood (wŏŏd) **1** hard, fibrous material under the bark of trees and shrubs. **2** this material cut and treated, ready for use; lumber: *a house made of* wood. **3** used with or having to do with wood: *a wood screw; a wood merchant.* **4** thick growth of trees; grove; forest. **5 woods** thick growth of trees; forest; wood. **6 out of the woods** safe from danger or difficulty: *to be out of the woods after illness.* (Homonym: would)

wood·bine (wŏŏd′bīn′) any of several vines of the honeysuckle family.

wood·chuck (wŏŏd′chŭk′) chunky, russet-brown, vegetable-eating animal that digs a deep burrow in which it sleeps all winter; groundhog.

Woodchuck, about 2 ft. long

wood·cock (wŏŏd′kŏk′) small, brown game bird. It has a long bill, short legs, and a short, stubby tail.

wood·craft (wŏŏd′krăft′) **1** skill and knowledge in anything pertaining to the woods, such as camping, hunting, forestry, etc. **2** the carving of objects from wood.

wood·cut·ter (wŏŏd′kŭt′ər) one who cuts wood or fells trees.

wood·ed (wŏŏd′ĭd) having many trees; covered with trees.

wood·en (wŏŏd′ən) **1** made of wood: *a wooden bucket.* **2** stiff; clumsy: *a wooden movement.* **3** lifeless; dull: *a wooden smile.* **wood·en·ly.**

wood·land (wŏŏd′lănd′ or wŏŏd′lənd) **1** land covered with trees; forest. **2** of, in, or having to do with woods: *a woodland brook.*

wood·man (wŏŏd′mən) **1** woodcutter. **2** person who lives in the woods. **wood·men.**

wood·peck·er (wŏŏd′pĕk′ər) any of several birds with feet and tails adapted for climbing tree trunks. Their beaks can drill through the bark to get the insects and larvae on which they feed. For picture, see next column.

wood·shed (wŏŏd′shĕd′) shed for storing firewood.

woods·man (wŏŏdz′mən) **1** man familiar with life in the woods, especially a hunter, trapper, etc. **2** woodman. **woods·men.**

wood thrush migrant North American thrush with bell-like note.

wood wind (wŏŏd′wĭnd′) musical wind instrument, formerly made of wood but now often of metal, such as the oboe, bassoon, flute, etc.

wood·work (wŏŏd′wûrk′) interior wooden fittings of a house, such as stairs, doors, window frames, etc.

wood·y (wŏŏd′ĭ) **1** covered with trees. **2** consisting largely of wood: *a woody shrub.* **3** like or suggesting wood or woods: *a woody scent.* **wood·i·er, wood·i·est.**

woof (wŏŏf) **1** in weaving, the threads carried back and forth by the shuttle. For picture, see **warp.** **2** texture of a fabric.

wool (wŏŏl) **1** fleece of sheep and some other animals. **2** yarn made from this fleece. **3** cloth made from this yarn. **4** made of this cloth or yarn: *a wool dress; a wool sweater.* **5 pull the wool over one's eyes** to deceive: *Don't let that rascal pull the wool over your eyes.*

wool·en or **wool·len** (wŏŏl′ən) **1** made of wool. **2** of or having to do with wool: *the woolen trade.* **3 woolens** fabrics or garments made of wool: *Mother always stores the woolens during the summer.*

wool·ly or **wool·y** (wŏŏl′ĭ) consisting of or like wool: *the woolly feel of a fabric.* **wool·li·er** or **wool·i·er, wool·li·est** or **wool·i·est.**

word (wûrd) **1** a sound or a combination of sounds meaning a certain thing, feeling, idea, etc. **2** a written or printed representation of such a sound. **3** a brief expression: *a word of warning;* word *of greeting.*

Woodpecker, about 8 in. long

4 promise; guarantee: *He gave me his* word *not to tell.* **5** news; information: *Send me* word *when you know who won the game.*

---

fāte, făt, fâre, fär; bē, bĕt; bīte, bĭt; nō, nŏt, nôr; fūse, fŭn, fûr; tōō, tŏŏk; foil; foul; thin; ~~then~~; hw for wh as in *wh*at; zh for s as in u*s*ual; ə for a, e, i, o, u, as in *a*go, lin*e*n, per*i*l, at*o*m, min*u*s

6 to say or write with words: *This note should be* worded *differently.* **7** password; slogan: *Let the* word *be:* "*On they come.*"

word·ing (wûr′dĭng) way in which words are used to express a thought; choice of words: *The* wording *of his message is not clear.*

word·y (wûr′dĭ) expressed with too many words: *a long,* wordy *speech.* **word·i·er, word·i·est; word·i·ly.**

wore (wôr) See **wear.** *He* wore *his honors with dignity.*

work (wûrk) **1** physical or mental effort; labor: *He was too weak for hard* work. **2** piece of work; task: *Come, there's* work *to do.* **3** a thing done, made, or obtained by labor or effort: *This statue is a* work *of Rodin. This is vandal's* work. **4** employment: *Abner tramped the streets looking for* work. **5** to labor: *Joseph* worked *as a carpenter.* **6** to employ; use; cause to labor: *The farmer* worked *his horses hard.* **7** to operate: *Will this machine* work? **8** to run; cause to operate: *to* work *a pump.* **9** to do by degrees or with an effort: *to* work *a tight cork into a bottle.* **10** to fashion; shape: *Abel* worked *the clay into a pretty vase.* **11** to ferment: *Cider* works *and produces vinegar.* **12 works (1)** a place where industrial activity goes on: *down by the gas-works.* **(2)** operating parts: *the* works *of a watch.* **(3)** deeds; accomplishments: *a man famous for his good* works.

work up 1 to excite; stir up: *He* worked *himself up into a rage.* **2** to make one's way by degrees: *to* work *oneself up in a profession.* **3** to develop: *to* work *up a portrait from a sketch.*

work·bench (wûrk′bĕnch′) table or bench at which a mechanic, carpenter, etc., works.

work·book (wûrk′bŏŏk′) student's practice book containing problems to be solved or questions to be answered with space provided for his work.

work·er (wûr′kər) **1** person, animal, or thing that works. **2** a bee, ant, wasp, or termite which does the work in the colony.

work·ing (wûr′kĭng) **1** laboring: *The* working *crew includes the foreman and those under him.* **2** having to do with work: *a* working *day;* working *hours.* **3** the way something works; a functioning: *the* work-

ing *of a machine, plan, or mind.* **4** kept for work rather than as a pet: *Some* working *dogs are trained to herd sheep.*

work·ing·man (wûr′kĭng măn′) laborer; worker, especially a man who works with his hands. **work·ing·men.**

work·man (wûrk′mən) person who works, especially one skilled in his trade; craftsman. **work·men.**

work·man·like (wûrk′mən līk′) of a good workman; skilled: *a* workmanlike *piece of plumbing.*

work·man·ship (wûrk′mən shĭp′) **1** skill; artistic or technical ability: *His finished* workmanship *stamped him as a master.* **2** quality of something made or done: *the fine* workmanship *of an antique.*

work·out (wûrk′out′) **1** trial: *I'd like to give this car a* workout *before I decide to buy it.* **2** practice: *The basketball team had a* workout *before the game.*

work·room (wûrk′rŏŏm′) room in which work is done.

work·shop (wûrk′shŏp′) room or building where work is done, often by a number of workers: *a potter's* workshop.

world (wûrld) **1** the earth. **2** the universe: *Space travel will teach us more of the* world. **3** definite part of the earth or civilization: *the New* World; *Roman* world. **4** all people; everybody: *The* world *honors power. All the* world *came to the fair.* **5** any area of interest or activity: *the* world *of music.* **6** a group of people, animals, or things: *the plant* world. **7** great deal: *He gets a* world *of pleasure from music.* **8** social life and its interests and pleasures: *a man of the* world.

world·ly (wûrld′lĭ) having to do with the things of this world: *the* worldly *pleasures of eating and drinking.* **world·li·er, world·li·est.**

World War I the war from 1914 to 1918 in which the major nations were involved.

World War II the war from 1939 to 1945 in which the major nations were involved.

worm (wûrm) **1** a crawling or creeping creature with a long, slender body. **2** the larva of certain insects. **3** a despised or insignificant person. **4** to crawl or creep; work one's way in and out: *to* worm *through tall grass; to* worm *one's way through a crowd.* **5** to get or attain by slow and roundabout means: to worm *a secret from a friend;* to worm *oneself into someone's confidence.*

worm·y (wûr'mĭ) full of worms; infested with worms: *a wormy apple.* **worm·i·er, worm·i·est.**

worn (wôrn) **1** See **wear**. *He has worn that hat for years.* **2** showing signs of use: *His coat was worn and tattered.*

worn-out (wôrn'out') **1** useless or not working well because of long wear or use: *a worn-out pair of socks with holes in the toes;* worn-out *machinery.* **2** thoroughly tired; exhausted: *She was worn-out by all the excitement.*

wor·ry (wûr'ĭ) **1** to be anxious, troubled, or concerned. **2** to cause (someone) to be anxious or concerned: *His bad behavior at school worries his mother.* **3** a cause for anxiety or concern; a care: *The chance of fire in this wooden house is a worry to me.* **4** to bite or tear at with the teeth: *The puppy worried the edge of the carpet.* **wor·ries; wor·ried, wor·ry·ing.**

worse (wûrs) **1** more evil, bad, or worthless; more disagreeable: *I can't imagine a worse piece of news.* **2** more ill; less well: *She was worse before she took this medicine.* **3** in a more disagreeable or bad manner: *She sang worse tonight because she had a cold.* **4** condition that is more unpleasant or bad than another: *The patient took a turn for the worse.*

wor·ship (wûr'shĭp) **1** to show religious devotion to; perform acts of reverence to: *He belonged to a savage tribe that worshiped idols.* **2** act of religious devotion or reverence; prayer, etc.: *The whole family took part in Sunday worship.* **3** to take part in religious devotion: *We worship at the same church.* **4** to love intensely; admire and adore: *He worshiped his father.* **5** intense love. **6** title showing respect or honor: *He addressed the judge as "Your Worship."* **wor·shiped** or **wor·shipped, wor·ship·ing** or **wor·ship·ping.**

wor·ship·er or **wor·ship·per** (wûr'shĭp-ər) person who takes part in acts of religious devotion or who shows an intense love for someone or something.

wor·ship·ful (wûr'shĭp fŏŏl) **1** worthy of respect or honor, especially used as a formal title of respect. **2** worshiping: *the worshipful eyes of a dog watching his master.* **wor·ship·ful·ly.**

worst (wûrst) **1** bad to the greatest degree; most evil, unpleasant, etc.: *the worst boy in the class; the worst headache I've ever had.* **2** in the poorest way: *She sings worst when she is nervous.* **3** that which is worst: *I've had to deal with the worst in sickness and poverty.* **4** to defeat; overcome; get the better of: *He worsts me in every game of checkers.*

wor·sted (wŏŏs'tĭd) **1** yarn of long, closely twisted wool strands or the cloth made of this yarn. **2** of this yarn or cloth: *a worsted suit.*

worth (wûrth) **1** value; merit: *She has little worth as a student.* **2** money value: *My jewelry would have little worth if I tried to sell it.* **3** worthy or deserving of: *This book is worth reading.* **4** valued at; of a value equal to: *That boat is worth a great deal of money.* **5** virtue; excellence: *a man of worth.* **6** having possessions equal to: *He was worth millions when he died.*

wor·thi·ness (wûr'thĭ nĭs) merit; worth: *The man's good character and worthiness are well known.*

worth·less (wûrth'lĭs) worth nothing; useless; bad: *a worthless book; a worthless rascal.*

worth·while (wûrth'hwil') deserving the cost or effort: *a worthwhile charity;* worthwhile *work.*

wor·thy (wûr'thĭ) **1** meriting respect; admirable: *a worthy character.* **2** deserving (of): *a deed worthy of praise.* **3** person of merit or importance: *All the worthies agree, so it must be so.* **wor·thies; wor·thi·er, wor·thi·est; wor·thi·ly.**

would (wŏŏd) **1** was or were intending to: *She told us that she would return soon.* **2** was or were determined to: *They would play in the rain, no matter how cold it was.* **3** might be expected to: *You would do a thing like that.* **4** used to: *Every day last summer we would read a different book.* **5** to be willing or able to (used with polite

---

fāte, făt, fâre, fär; bē, bĕt; bīte, bĭt; nō, nŏt, nôr; fūse, fŭn, fûr; tōō, tŏŏk; foil; foul; thin; then; hw for wh as in *wh*at; zh for s as in u*s*ual; ə for a, e, i, o, u, as in *a*go, lin*e*n, per*i*l, at*o*m, min*u*s

requests): *Please,* would *you hand me that book?* **6** word used to say what might have been true: *He* would *have helped you if he had been there.* **7** word used to express a wish: *Oh,* would *that it were true!* (Homonym: wood)

would·n't (wŏŏd′ənt) would not.

wouldst (wŏŏdst) old-fashioned form of **would,** used with *thou.*

¹wound (wŏŏnd) **1** physical injury in which skin or tissue is cut, pierced, or torn. **2** injury to the feelings or emotions. **3** to hurt, either physically or emotionally: *He was* wounded *by a bullet. Her sharp words* wounded *me deeply.* [**¹wound** is a form of an Old English word (wund) of the same meaning.]

²wound (wound) See **wind.** *She* wound *the string several times around the package.* [**²wound** is formed from **²wind.**]

wove (wōv) See **weave.** *She* wove *a basket.*

wo·ven (wō′vən) See **weave.** *This rug is* woven *of many different colored wools.*

wraith (rāth) **1** apparition of a person supposed to appear just before or after that person's death. **2** ghost; specter.

wran·gle (răng′gəl) **1** to argue or quarrel noisily or violently. **2** noisy argument or dispute. **3** to herd cattle. **wran·gled, wran·gling.**

wrap (răp) **1** to cover or enfold: *to wrap a baby in a blanket; to* wrap *a package.* **2** to twine or wind: *She* wrapped *a scarf around her neck.* **3** to cover or hide: *Clouds* wrapped *the mountain's peak.* **4** a cover; concealment: *under the* wrap *of secrecy.* **5 wraps** outer garments: *She wore heavy* wraps *when she went out in the storm.* **6 wrapped up** deeply interested in; devoted to: *to be* wrapped up *in one's work.* **wrapped** or **wrapt, wrap·ping.** (Homonym: rap)

wrap·per (răp′ər) **1** a covering: *Take off the* wrapper *and see what's in the package.* **2** person who wraps. **3** housecoat or woman's dressing gown: *She had breakfast in her* wrapper *and slippers.*

wrath (răth) anger; rage; fury.

wrath·ful (răth′fəl) full of wrath; furious; very angry. **wrath·ful·ly.**

wreak (rēk) **1** to inflict (feelings of rage, malice, etc., on): *He* wreaked *his vicious temper on everyone around him.* **2** to cause

or carry out (punishment, revenge, or the like): *The army* wreaked *havoc as it went.* (Homonym: reek)

wreath (rēth) **1** a ring of leaves or flowers: *The winner in Greek games was crowned with a laurel* wreath. **2** something of ringlike shape: *A wreath of gnats circled the fisherman's head.*

Wreath

wreathe (rēth) **1** to weave or twist into a wreath: *Mary* wreathed *the flowers.* **2** to entwine; encircle: *Thick fog* wreathed *the ship.* **3** to hang or decorate with wreaths: *We* wreathed *the fireplace with Christmas greens.* **wreathed, wreath·ing.**

wreck (rĕk) **1** damage or destruction caused by wind, collision, etc.: *The icy roads caused many* wrecks. **2** remains of anything ruined or destroyed: *The* wreck *was hauled away.* **3** to damage or ruin: *a crop* wrecked *by frost; plans* wrecked *by bad luck.* **4** damage or destruction: *the* wreck *of one's health; the* wreck *of one's plans.* **5** to destroy; dismantle: *The building was* wrecked *because it was a fire hazard.* (Homonym: reck)

wreck·age (rĕk′ĭj) **1** a wrecking or being wrecked; destruction: *the* wreckage *caused by the earthquake.* **2** remains of anything that has been wrecked: *The street was littered with* wreckage *after the earthquake.*

wreck·er (rĕk′ər) **1** person or thing that wrecks. **2** person or vehicle that clears away a wreck: *The* wrecker *towed the car off the road.* **3** person or machine that tears down old buildings. **4** person or vessel employed to recover wrecked vessels or their cargoes.

wren (rĕn) small, pert songbird that builds its nest near houses. It has a slender bill, russet back feathers, and an upright tail.

House wren, about 5 in. long

wrench (rĕnch) **1** violent twist: *Bob loosened the board with a powerful* wrench. **2** tool for turning or holding a nut, pipe, etc. It usually consists of two jaws, one of them movable, on a

832

long handle. **3** a sprain: *I gave my back a wrench in lifting the heavy box.* **4** to twist or pull violently: *Bill* wrenched *himself loose.* **5** to sprain: *Ellen* wrenched *her ankle.* **6** sudden feeling of grief; pang: *the wrench of leaving one's old friends.*

Pipe wrench

Monkey wrench

wrest (rĕst) **1** to turn or twist violently; pull away by force: *The policeman skillfully wrested the gun from the gangster.* **2** to take away by force; usurp: *The prince tried to* wrest *the kingdom from his father.* (Homonym: rest)

wres·tle (rĕs′əl) **1** to struggle with an opponent in order to throw him to the ground. **2** wrestling match. **3** to struggle; strive: *Ann* wrestled *with her arithmetic problem for a whole afternoon.* **4** a hard struggle. **wres·tled, wres·tling.**

wrest·ler (rĕs′lər) one who wrestles, especially in wrestling matches.

wretch (rĕch) **1** unfortunate or miserable person. **2** bad, contemptible person.

wretch·ed (rĕch′ĭd) **1** miserable; unhappy: *The wretched man lost all his belongings in the fire.* **2** bad; wicked: *the* wretched *pirate.* **3** poor; unsatisfactory; inadequate: *a* wretched *piece of work.* **wretch·ed·ly.**

wretch·ed·ness (rĕch′ĭd nĭs) wretched condition; great misery or affliction: *The* wretchedness *of the flood victims.*

wrig·gle (rĭg′əl) **1** to twist and turn; writhe; squirm: *Jack kept* wriggling *in his seat at the concert.* **2** to move or cause to move by twisting and turning: *a worm* wriggling *along the ground; to* wriggle *one's toes.* **3** a squirming, twisting motion. **4** to gain an end by trickery or shifty means: *He* wriggled *out of his difficulty by telling a lie.* **wrig·gled, wrig·gling.**

wrig·gler (rĭg′lər) **1** person or thing that wriggles. **2** larva of the mosquito. For picture, see **larva.**

wright (rīt) person who makes something; workman: *a play*wright; *ship*wright; *wheel*wright. (Homonyms: right, rite, write)

wring (rĭng) **1** to squeeze or twist hard: *to* wring *wet sheets.* **2** to force out by or as by twisting or pressing: *to* wring *water out of wet sheets; to* wring *a confession from a thief.* **3** twisting, squeezing movement. **4** to cause pity or anguish in: *The account of the tragedy* wrung *our hearts.* **wrung, wring·ing.** (Homonym: ring)

wring·er (rĭng′ər) anything that wrings, especially a machine for pressing water from clothes after washing.

wrin·kle (rĭng′kəl) **1** ridge or fold on a surface; crease: *a dress full of* wrinkles; *the* wrinkles *in a face.* **2** to crease or become creased: *Be sure not to* wrinkle *this suit when you pack it. This suit* wrinkles *easily.* **wrin·kled, wrin·kling.**

wrist (rĭst) joint connecting the hand and forearm.

wrist·band (rĭst′bănd′) part of a sleeve that covers the wrist.

wrist·let (rĭst′lĭt) **1** a leather or knitted band worn about the wrist for support or warmth. **2** an ornamental bracelet.

writ (rĭt) **1** old form of **written.** **2** something written, usually said of the Bible: *Holy* Writ. **3** written official order of a law court.

write (rīt) **1** to make letters or words with a pen, pencil, chalk, or the like: *Lucy could* write *when she was five.* **2** to express in words or symbols with a pen, pencil, etc.: *The teacher is* writing *the answers on the blackboard.* **3** to tell in a letter: *Susan has* written *twice that she is having a wonderful time.* **4** to produce stories or compose music: *Grimm* wrote *fairy tales. Beethoven* wrote *nine symphonies.* **5** to show by leaving marks, traces, or signs: *Tim's guilt was* written *all over his face.* **6 write-in** a name not on a printed ballot but added to it by a voter.

write down to put into writing: *Don't try to remember it;* write *it down.*

write out to write in full: *The reporter* wrote *out his notes of the meeting for his paper.*

write up to describe in detail by writing: *For homework, you are to* write *up the experiment you saw today.*

---

fāte, făt, fâre, fär; bē, bĕt; bite, bĭt; nō, nŏt, nôr; fūse, fŭn, fûr; tōō, tŏŏk; foil; foul; thin; ~~then~~;
hw for wh as in *wh*at; zh for s as in u*s*ual; ə for a, e, i, o, u, as in *a*go, lin*e*n, per*i*l, at*o*m, min*u*s

wrote, writ·ten, writ·ing. (Homonyms: right, rite, wright)

writ·er (rī′tər) **1** person who writes. **2** person whose occupation is writing; author.

writhe (rith) **1** to twist or squirm, as from pain: *I* writhed *all night with a toothache.* **2** to suffer from emotional distress, such as embarrassment: *to* writhe *at an insult.* **writhed, writh·ing.**

writ·ing (rī′tīng) **1** act of one who writes. **2** anything that is written, such as a letter, document, manuscript, inscription, etc. **3** handwriting; penmanship: *I cannot read your* writing. **4** manner of expressing oneself in writing; literary style: *The student imitated the* writing *of his favorite author.* **5** occupation of a writer or author: *He chose* writing *as a career.* **6 writings** literary works: *His* writings *are famous the world over.*

writ·ten (rĭt′ən) See **write.** *He hasn't* written *me yet.*

wrong (rông or rŏng) **1** not right; bad; wicked: *It is* wrong *to steal or tell lies.* **2** incorrect; false: *The answer to this question is* wrong. **3** an injustice; an evil: *Two* wrongs *never make a right.* **4** to do wrong to another; injure, harm, or treat unjustly: *You* wronged *Phillip by thinking he took your bicycle.* **5** out of order; amiss: *There is something* wrong *with my watch.* **6** unsuitable; inappropriate: *to do or say the* wrong *thing.* **7** describing a part not intended to show; unfinished (side of cloth, wood, etc.): *This sweater is* wrong *side out.*

8 go wrong (1) to turn out badly: *Everything* went wrong *with the dinner.* (2) to go astray morally; go to the bad. **9 in the wrong** mistaken; guilty. **wrong·ly.**

wrong·do·ing (rông′dōō′ing or rŏng′dōō′-ing) the doing of wrong; evil behavior.

wrong·ful (rông′fəl or rŏng′fəl) evil; unjust; injurious. **wrong·ful·ly.**

wrong-head·ed (rông′hĕd′id or rŏng′-hĕd′id) obstinate in opinions; stubborn against persuasion or entreaty: *That mule is certainly a* wrong-headed *beast.*

wrote (rōt) See **write.** *They* wrote *me they were coming.* (Homonym: rote)

wroth (rôth) angry; indignant; wrathful.

wrought (rôt) **1** worked; fashioned; made: *jewelry* wrought *by hand.* **2** fashioned from the rough by beating with a hammer: *a candlestick of* wrought *iron;* wrought *silver.*

wrought iron iron with low carbon content, tough and easily drawn out into wire and hammered into shape.

wrought-up (rôt′ŭp′) greatly excited or disturbed: *George was* wrought-up *when he lost his job.*

wrung (rŭng) See **wring.** *She* wrung *her hands when the roast burned.* (Homonym: rung)

wry (rī) crooked; twisted; contorted: *a* wry *face; a* wry *grin.* **wri·er, wri·est; wry·ly.** (Homonym: rye)

W.Va. West Virginia.

Wyo. Wyoming.

Wy·o·ming (wī ō′mĭng) State in the northwestern part of the United States.

X

X, x (ĕks) **1** the 24th letter of the English alphabet. **2** Roman numeral for ten.

Xmas Christmas.

X ray (ĕks′rā′) **1** a ray, with much shorter wave length than light, that will go through or into matter, such as a human body, and cast shadows of hidden parts on a screen or photographic plate. **2** instrument that pro-

X ray of boy's foot kicking football

duces such rays. **3** photograph made by such rays.

X-ray (ĕks′rā′) **1** to use an X-ray instrument on: *The doctor* X-rayed *Mr. Jones in a tuberculosis checkup.* **2** having to do with X rays: *an* X-ray *photograph.*

xy·lo·phone (zī′lə-fōn′) a musical instrument made of strips of wood that give off different tones when struck with wooden hammers.

Xylophone

Y

Y, y (wī) the 25th letter of the English alphabet.

-y suffix meaning (**1**) "characterized by": *rainy*; *thorny*. (**2**) "small": *dolly*. It is also used in nicknames to show affection: *Billy*; *daddy*.

yacht (yŏt) **1** vessel for pleasure-cruising or racing, driven by sails or engines. **2** to sail or race in a yacht.

yacht·ing (yŏt′ing) the sport or practice of sailing or racing in a yacht.

yachts·man (yŏts′mən) person who owns or spends much time sailing a yacht. **yachts·men**.

yak (yăk) long-haired ox of Central Asia and Tibet, often domesticated and used as a beast of burden.

yam (yăm) **1** climbing tropical vine with fleshy, starchy, edible roots. **2** in the United States, a kind of sweet potato.

yank (yăngk) **1** to pull or jerk sharply: *Billy yanked Beth's pigtail.* **2** a quick, sharp pull or jerk.

Yan·kee (yăng′kē) **1** person who is a native of the New England States. **2** native of the United States, especially of a northern State.

yap (yăp) **1** to bark sharply, shrilly, snappishly; yelp: *Small dogs usually yap.* **2** a sharp, shrill bark. **yapped, yap·ping.**

¹yard (yärd) **1** standard unit of length; 3 feet; 36 inches: *a yard of velvet.* **2** spar; one of the crosspieces on a ship's mast from which a sail is hung. [**¹yard** is a form of an Old English word (gerd) meaning "rod."]

Yards

²yard (yärd) **1** an enclosed, or partially enclosed, space adjoining a house, stable, barn, school, or other building: *farm*yard; *school*yard. **2** a space, usually partly enclosed, used for some special work or occupation: *railway* yard, *ship*yard, etc. [**²yard** is a form of an Old English word (geard).]

yard·arm (yärd′ärm′) either end of a yard that supports a square sail.

yard·stick (yärd′stĭk′) **1** flat, wooden or metal stick a yard long, marked with subdivisions, used for measuring. **2** any set standard used for measuring, comparing, etc.: *Honesty is a* yardstick *of a man's worth.*

yarn (yärn) **1** a spun thread, especially a heavy woolen thread for knitting or crocheting. **2** exaggerated tale or story: *The children were spellbound by Grandpa's yarns of his years at sea.*

yawl (yôl) sailboat with the mainmast well forward and a smaller mast far aft.

yawn (yôn) **1** to open the mouth wide with a deep breath, because of sleepiness, boredom, etc.: *Betty yawned over her book,* for it was long past her bedtime. **2** the act of yawning. **3** to be wide open; gape: *They turned back when the chasm yawned below them.*

Yawl

yd. yard.

ye (yē) old form of **you:** *Thank ye kindly, my friend.*

yea (yā) **1** old form of **yes. 2** indeed; truly. **3** a vote favoring something.

year (yĭr) **1** length of time it takes the earth to revolve once around the sun, about 365¼ days. **2** period of 365 days or, in the case of leap year, 366 days, beginning January 1 and divided into twelve months: *In what year were you born?* **3** any period of 12 consecutive months: *I began work on August 14, two years ago today.* **4** period of time, usually less than a year, spent in some particular activity: *the school* year. **5 year in, year out** repeatedly, through the year or years.

year·book (yĭr′bŏŏk′) book published every year, giving information about the year before: *a school* yearbook.

---

fāte, făt, fâre, fär; bē, bĕt; bīte, bĭt; nō, nŏt, nôr; fūse, fŭn, fûr; tōō, tŏŏk; foil; foul; thin; ~~then~~; hw for wh as in *wh*at; zh for s as in u*s*ual; ə for a, e, i, o, u, as in *a*go, lin*e*n, per*i*l, at*o*m, min*u*s

835

year·ling (yîr′lĭng or yûr′lĭng) **1** animal between one and two years old. **2** one year old: *a yearling colt.*

year·ly (yîr′lĭ) **1** happening once a year or every year: *a yearly visit; a yearly vacation.* **2** for a year: *a yearly salary.*

yearn (yûrn) **1** to feel a strong desire; have a deep longing: *to yearn for home.* **2** to have tender feelings; be moved by compassion and sympathy: *to yearn over a frightened child.*

yearn·ing (yûr′nĭng) **1** strong desire; longing: *a yearning to be home again.* **2** showing or feeling strong desire: *a yearning look; a yearning heart.* **yearn·ing·ly.**

yeast (yēst) **1** small plants or cells that multiply rapidly in sweet or starchy liquids, giving off carbon dioxide. Yeast is used in making beer, raising bread, etc. **2 yeast cake** yeast mixed with starch and pressed into a small cake.

yell (yĕl) **1** to shout; to utter in a loud-pitched voice: *to yell with defiance; to yell out an order.* **2** loud, sharp, strong cry or shriek: *a yell of agony, terror, or excitement.* **3** a shout or cheer: *a college yell.*

yel·low (yĕl′ō) **1** color ranging from gold to the color of a ripe lemon. **2** of this color. **3** to make or become yellow: *The book had yellowed with age.* **4** yolk of an egg.

yellow fever tropical disease, often ending in death, spread by a variety of mosquito.

yel·low·ish (yĕl′ō ish) ʹhaving a yellow tinge.

yellow jacket any of several small American wasps marked with yellow.

Yel·low·stone Na·tion·al Park (yĕl′ō-stōn năsh′ə nəl pärk) largest national park of the United States, mainly in Wyoming but also covering parts of Montana and Idaho.

yelp (yĕlp) **1** to utter a short, sharp bark or cry, especially in pain or fright. **2** short, sharp bark or cry: *The fox terrier gave a loud yelp when the cat bit it.*

¹yen (yĕn) unit of money in Japan; gold or silver Japanese coin. [**¹yen** comes through Japanese from a Chinese word (yüan) meaning "round," "a dollar."]

²yen (yĕn) **1** a desire or longing for. **2** to desire or long for. **yenned, yen·ning.** [**²yen** is from a Chinese word (yen) meaning "opium."]

yeo·man (yō′mən) **1** in the navy, petty officer who does clerical duty. **2** in England, small farmer who owns his own land. **3 Yeoman of the Guard** member of the bodyguard of the British royal family. **yeo·men.**

yes (yĕs) **1** affirmative answer to a question; opposite of "no": *Why, yes, we will come to your party.* **2** more than that; even more: *It is very cold, yes, freezing.*

Ye·shi·vah (yə shē′vä) school of Jewish studies, especially a seminary for the training of rabbis.

yes·ter·day (yĕs′tər dĭ or yĕs′tər dā′) **1** day before today. **2** on the day before today: *We finished painting the house yesterday.* **3** recent past. **4** in the recent past: *Janey was in pigtails only yesterday.*

yet (yĕt) **1** up to this time; up to a particular time: *Nothing has happened yet. At noon, Agnes was not yet at work.* **2** even so; nevertheless: *Helen saw the rabbit vanish, yet she couldn't believe it.* **3** besides; in addition: *There is much yet to see at the fair.* **4** eventually; at some future time: *Henry may learn to ride a bicycle yet.* **5** still; as before: *We are living in the same house yet.*

yew (ū) **1** a kind of evergreen tree. **2** wood of the yew. It was once used for making bows. (Homonyms: ewe, you.)

English yew

yield (yēld) **1** to give in; submit: *to yield to persuasion.* **2** to give way; bend: *The willow yields to the wind.* **3** to produce: *This ground yields a good crop. Bank deposits yield interest.* **4** that which is produced: *a good yield from this farm.*

yield·ing (yēl′dĭng) giving in; submissive. **yield·ing·ly.**

yo·del (yō′dəl) **1** to sing or call with quick changes from a natural voice to one unusually high in pitch. **2** song or call made in this way.

Yoke

yoke (yōk) **1** wooden double collar for a pair of oxen, etc. **2** to harness, as with such a collar. **3** a pair, as of oxen. **4** wooden frame fitting a person's shoulders, from the ends of which buckets, etc., can be hung. **5** part of a garment fitting over the shoulders, to which the lower part and sleeves are attached. **6** fixed, curved frame under which prisoners of antiquity had to pass. **7** slavery; bondage: *under the* yoke *of a dictatorship.* **8** a tie; bond: *the* yoke *of friendship.* **yoked, yok·ing.** (Homonym: yolk)

yolk (yōk) yellow part of an egg. (Homonym: yoke)

Yom Kip·pur (yōm kip′ər) the chief religious holiday of the Jews, meaning "Day of Atonement." Yom Kippur occurs in the fall and is observed with prayer and fasting.

yon (yŏn) yonder.

yon·der (yŏn′dər) **1** distant, but in sight: *On* yonder *hill there stands a castle.* **2** over there: *You'll find Mr. Young* yonder.

yore (yôr) time long ago: *in days of* yore.

you (ū) **1** person or persons spoken to: *Are you* happy? **2** one; anyone: *If you* want *to be sure of a seat, you* should *get tickets in advance.* (Homonyms: ewe, yew)

you'd (ūd) **1** you had: *Mother said, "You'd* better come in before it rains." **2** you would: *I think* you'd *like it in Bermuda.*

you'll (ūl) you will; you shall: *I warn you* you'll *pay for this.* (Homonym: yule)

young (yŭng) **1** in the early part of life or growth: *Oh, to be* young *again?* **2** having the qualities or appearance of youth; youthful: *How do you stay so* young? **3** of or having to do with youth; vigorous; fresh: *a man of* young *ideas.* **4** immature; inexperienced: *Jeremy is* young *for his years.* **5** those who are in the early part of life: *This book is written for the* young. **6** offspring of animals: *the tiger's* young.

young·ster (yŭng′stər) **1** child. **2** young person.

your (yŏor) **1** of or belonging to you: *Be sure to bring* your *umbrella.* **2** made or done by you: *Tom,* your *book report was excellent.*

you're (yŏor) you are: *When* you're *away, will you remember me?*

yours (yŏorz) **1** belonging to you: *The shoes are* yours. **2** thing or things belonging to you: *I won't take my car if we take* yours.

your·self (yŏor sĕlf′) **1** your own person: *Did you wash* yourself *this morning?* **2** your true self: *You are not* yourself *when angered.* **3** word used to emphasize you: *You* yourself *should go to see him.* **your·selves.**

youth (ūth) **1** state of being young: *The old man still has the energy of* youth. **2** period between childhood and the time when one is grown up: *One's* youth *is the time of adventure and daring.* **3** young person, especially a boy. **4** young people: *the* youth *of a nation.* **5** early stage of anything: *Life was very different in our country's* youth.

youth·ful (ūth′fəl) **1** young. **2** pertaining or fitting to youth: *Playing marbles is a* youthful *pastime.* **youth·ful·ly.**

you've (yŏov) you have: *You shouldn't be hungry after you've eaten a large meal.*

yowl (youl) **1** long, loud, wailing sound. **2** to make such a sound: *The cat* yowled *all night on the back fence.*

yr. **1** year. **2** your.

yuc·ca (yŭk′ə) **1** a desert plant with a tall stalk of white flowers and stiff, sharp, pointed leaves. **2** the lilylike flower of this plant.

yule (ūl) **1** Christmas; Yuletide. **2** yule log a huge log brought indoors for an open fire on Christmas Eve. (Homonym: you'll)

yule·tide (ūl′tīd′) Christmas season; yule.

Yucca

Z

Z, z (zē) the 26th letter of the English alphabet.

zeal (zēl) eagerness; enthusiasm; earnestness: *His* zeal *for studying pleased his father.*

---

fāte, făt, fâre, fär; bē, bĕt; bīte, bĭt; nō, nŏt, nôr; fūse, fŭn, fûr; tōo, tŏŏk; foil; foul; thin; ~~then~~; hw for wh as in *wh*at; zh for s as in u*s*ual; ə for a, e, i, o, u, as in ag*o*, lin*e*n, per*i*l, at*o*m, min*u*s

zeal·ot (zĕl′ət) person of too great zeal; fanatic: *a zealot who can tolerate no religion but his own.*

zeal·ous (zĕl′əs) eager; enthusiastic: *Nathan Hale was a zealous patriot.* **zeal·ous·ly.**

ze·bra (zē′brə) African animal of the horse family, marked with black and white stripes.

Zebra, 4 to 5 ft. high at shoulder

ze·nith (zē′nĭth) 1 that point in the heavens directly over a person. 2 greatest height; summit: *He had at last reached the zenith of success.*

zeph·yr (zĕf′ər) 1 west wind. 2 soft, mild breeze: *A light zephyr rustled the leaves of the maples.*

ze·ro (zĭr′ō) 1 figure which stands for naught (0): *There are three zeros in 1,000.* 2 point on a scale from which readings begin in either direction: *The temperature was five degrees below zero.* 3 nothing. 4 a very low point: *Our hopes of getting a new car sank to zero.* **ze·ros** or **ze·roes.**

zest (zĕst) 1 relish; enthusiasm: *a zest for sports.* 2 something that gives flavor or enjoyment: *Your company will add zest to our trip.*

Zeus (zoos) in Greek mythology, the ruler of the gods, called Jupiter in Roman mythology.

zig·zag (zĭg′zăg′) 1 marked by repeated sharp Z-shaped turns: *a zigzag path.* 2 one of such turns: *A side path went off in a sharp zigzag.* 3 to follow or take a zigzag course: *The driver*

Zigzag path

Zigzag line

zigzagged *down the road.* **zig·zagged, zig·zag·ging.**

zinc (zĭngk) blue-white metal element used in alloys, paint, and medicine. Zinc is the covering metal on galvanized iron.

zin·ni·a (zĭn′ĭ ə) an annual plant bearing large, showy flowers.

Zi·on (zī′ən) 1 hill in Jerusalem, site of the royal palace and the temple. 2 the people of Israel. 3 heaven; the heavenly city.

Zi·on·ism (zī′ə nĭz′əm) plan or movement to establish and promote a Jewish nation in Palestine.

zip (zĭp) 1 short hissing sound, as of a bullet. 2 to make this sound. 3 energy; vigor: *full of zip.* 4 to move quickly: *to zip through homework.* 5 to fasten by closing a zipper. **zipped, zip·ping.**

zip·per (zĭp′ər) trademark name of a fastener, in which opposite rows of tiny teeth are interlocked when drawn together by a sliding tab.

zith·er (zĭth′ər) musical stringed instrument consisting of a shallow sounding box strung with 30 to 40 wire strings. It is played by plucking the strings with a horn or metal pick.

Zither

zo·di·ac (zō′dĭ ăk′) band of sky in which the sun, moon, and principal planets seem to move around the earth. The zodiac is divided into twelve signs, or sections, each named for a constellation within its area.

zone (zōn) 1 any district, division, or section set apart for a special purpose: *time zone; hospital zone.* 2 to divide or separate into zones, or establish zones: *The city council zoned this section commercial.* 3 one of the five temperature belts into which the earth is divided. 4 one of the areas into which the country about a post office is divided for parcel-post rates; postal zone. **zoned, zon·ing.**

zoo (zoo) place where living animals are kept for the public to see: *the antics of the monkeys at the zoo.* **zoos.**

zo·o·log·i·cal (zō′ə lŏj′ə kəl) having to do with zoology or animal life. **zo·o·log·i·cal·ly.**

zoological garden zoo.

zo·ol·o·gist (zō ŏl′ə jĭst) person trained in the science of animals and animal life.

zo·ol·o·gy (zō ŏl′ə jĭ) science that deals with animal life.

zoom (zoom) 1 to move with a humming or buzzing sound. 2 to drive an airplane in a sudden upward course. 3 to cause (an airplane) to zoom.

zwie·back (zwī′băk or swī′băk or tswē′băk) kind of sweetened bread that is sliced and toasted after baking.

Famous Persons

A

Ad·ams (ăd′əmz), **Henry** 1838-1918, U.S. historian and author. —**John** 1735-1826, second President of the United States (1797-1801). —**John Quincy** (kwĭn′sē) 1767-1848, sixth President of the United States (1825-29). —**Samuel** 1722-1803, a leader in the American Revolution.

Ad·dams (ăd′əmz), **Jane** 1860-1935, U.S. social worker.

Ade·nau·er (ä′də nou′ər), **Konrad** (kŏn′räd′) born 1876, chancellor of West Germany (1949-63).

Ae·sop (ē′sŏp′) ancient Greek writer of fables.

Ag·as·siz (ăg ə sē′), **J. Louis** 1807-73, U.S. naturalist, born in Switzerland.

A·gui·nal·do (äg′ē näl′dō), **Emilio** (ā mē′lē ō) 1869-1964, Filipino leader.

Ak·bar (ăk′bär′) 1542-1605, emperor of Northern India. Also **Ak′ber′.**

Al·ber·tus Mag·nus (ăl bûr′təs măg′nəs), **Saint** 1193?-1280, German philosopher, teacher of Thomas Aquinas.

Al·cott (ôl′kŏt′), **Louisa May** (lə wē′zə) 1832-88, U.S. novelist.

Al·den (ôl′dən), **John** 1599?-1687, Pilgrim settler at Plymouth, Massachusetts.

Al·drich (ôl′drĭch′), **Thomas Bailey** 1836-1907, U.S. poet and novelist.

Al·ex·an·der the Great (ăl′ĭg zăn′dər) 356-323 B.C., king of **Mac·e·don** (măs′ə dən), a kingdom in northern Greece (336-323), conquered the Persian Empire.

Al·fred the Great (ăl′frəd) 849-99, king of **Wes·sex** (wĕs′əks), a kingdom in southern England (871-99), united southern England by defeating the invading Danes.

Al·ger (ăl′jər), **Horatio** 1832-99, writer of books for boys, always telling how a poor, honest boy makes good in business, usually aided by marriage to the boss's daughter.

Al·len (ăl′ən), **Ethan** (ē′thən) 1738-89, soldier in the American Revolution.

A·ma·ti (ə mä′tē) family of Italian violin makers, especially **Nicolò** (nĭk′ə lō) 1596-1684.

Amerigo VesPucci See **Vespucci.**

Am·pére (ăm′pēr′), **Andrè** (än drā′) 1775-1836, French physicist, studied electricity.

A·mund·sen (ä′mŏŏn′sən), **Roald** (rō′äl′) 1872-1928, Norwegian explorer, discovered the South pole (1911).

An·der·sen (ăn′dər sən), **Hans Christian** (hänz krĭs′chən) 1805-75, Danish writer of fairy tales.

An·der·son (ăn′dər sən), **Marian** born 1902, U.S. contralto. —**Maxwell** 1889-1959, U.S. dramatist. —**Sherwood** 1876-1941, U.S. author.

An·drè (ăn′drē), **John** 1751-80, British major, hanged as a spy during the American Revolution.

An·gel·i·co, Fra (frä′än jĕl′ĭ kō) 1387-1455, Italian painter and monk.

Anne (ăn) 1665-1714, queen of Great Britain (1702-14), daughter of James II.

An·tho·ny (ăn′thə nē), **Susan B.** 1820-1906, one of the foremost promoters of woman suffrage in the United States.

An·to·ny, Mark See **Mark Antony.**

A·qui·nas (ə kwī′nəs), **Saint Thomas** 1225?-74, Italian monk, philosopher, especially in theology.

Arc, Jeanne d' (zhän′därk′) See **Joan of Arc.**

Ar·chi·me·des (är′kə mē′dēz) 287?-212 B.C., Greek mathematician, discovered the principle of the lever.

Ar·is·toph·a·nes (ăr′ĭs tŏf′ə nēz′) 450?-380? B.C., Greek comic dramatist.

Ar·is·tot·le (ăr′ĭs tŏt′əl) 384-322 B.C., Greek philosopher, pupil of Plato.

Ark·wright (ärk′rīt′) **Sir Richard** 1732-92, English inventor of the spinning jenny.

Arm·strong (ärm′strông′), **Louis** born 1900, U.S. band leader and jazz trumpeter.

Ar·nold (är′nəld), **Benedict** (bĕn′ə dĭkt′) 1741-1801, American general who turned traitor during the Revolution. —**Matthew** 1822-88, English poet and critic.

Ar·thur (är′thər), **Chester Alan** 1830-86, 21st President of the United States (1881-85).

As·tor (ăs′tər), **John Jacob** 1763-1848, U.S. fur trader and capitalist, born in Germany.

A·ta·hual·pa (ä′tä-wäl′pə) died 1533, last Inca emperor of Peru (1525-33).

At·ti·la (ăt′ə lə) 406-453, king of the Huns, known as the **Scourge of God.**

Au·du·bon (ô′də bŏn′), **John James** 1785-1851, U.S. painter who studied birds, born in Haiti.

Au·gus·tine (ô′gəs tēn′, ə gŭs′tən), **Saint** 354-430, philosopher and bishop of northern Africa, one of the early Church fathers.

Au·gus·tus Cae·sar (ə gŭs′təs sē′zər) 63-14 B.C., first Roman emperor (27-14).

B

Bach (bäk), **Johann Sebastian** (yō′hän′ sə bäs′chən) 1685-1750, one of the earliest and greatest German composers.

Ba·con (bā′kən), **Francis** 1561-1626, Baron Verulam, Viscount St. Albans, English philosopher and statesman.

Ba·den Pow·ell (bā′dən pou′əl), **Sir Robert** 1856-1941, British general, founder of the Boy Scouts (1908).

Bal·bo·a (băl bō′ə), **Vasco da** (väs′kō dä) 1475-1517, Spanish explorer, discovered the Pacific Ocean (1513).

Bar·num (bär′nəm), **Phineas T.** (fĭn′ē əs) 1810-91, U.S. showman and circus owner.

Bar·rie (băr′ē), **Sir James M.** 1860-1937, Scottish novelist and playwright.

Bar·thol·di (bär tŏl′dē), **Frédéric** (frä dā rēk′) 1834-1904, French sculptor, known especially for the Statue of Liberty.

Bar·ton (bär′tən), **Clara** 1821-1912, founder of the U.S. Red Cross.

Bau·douin (bō dwăn′) born 1930, king of Belgium (1951-).

Beard (bîrd), **Daniel Carter** 1850-1941, U.S. naturalist, founder of the Boy Scouts of America.

Beau·re·gard (bō′rĭ gärd′), **Pierre Gustave** (pyěr gŭs täv′) 1818-93, Confederate general in the Civil War.

Beech·er (bē′chər), **Henry Ward** 1813-87, U.S. clergyman, writer, and lecturer.

Bee·tho·ven (bā′tō vən), **Ludwig von** (lōōd′vĭg′ fŏn) 1770-1827, German composer.

---

fāte, făt, fâre, fär; bē, bĕt; bīte, bĭt; nō, nŏt, nôr; fūse, fŭn, fûr; tōō, tŏŏk; foil; foul; thin; ~~then~~; hw for wh as in *wh*at; zh for s as in u*s*ual; ə for a, e, i, o, u, as in *a*go, lin*e*n, per*i*l, at*o*m, min*u*s

Famous Persons

Bell (bĕl), **Alexander Graham** 1847-1922, U.S. scientist, born in Scotland, inventor of the telephone.

Bel·yay·ev (bĕl yi'yĕf), **Pavel** (pä'vəl) born 1925, Russian astronaut, first man to leave an orbiting space craft (May 18, 1964).

Ben·ton (bĕn'tĕn), **Thomas Hart** 1782-1858, U.S. poet and statesman who settled in Missouri, was elected senator, and became an abolitionist.

Ber·li·oz (bĕr'lē ōz'), **Hector** (hĕk'tər) 1803-69, French composer.

Bern·hardt (bûrn'härt'), **Sarah** 1844-1923, French actress.

Bern·stein (bûrn'stīn'), **Leonard** 1918- U.S. conductor and composer, active in concerts for young people.

Bes·se·mer (bĕs'ə mər), **Sir Henry** 1813-98, English inventor who developed a process for making steel.

Be·thune (bĕth'ūn'), **Mary McLeod** (mə kloud') 1875-1955, U.S. educator, famous for her work in improving the education of Negroes.

Bis·marck (bis'märk'), **Prince Otto von** (ŏt'ō fŏn) 1815-98, German statesman.

Bi·zet (bē zā'), **Georges** (zhôrzh) 1838-75, French composer.

Blaine (blān), **James G.** 1830-93, U.S. statesman, a defeated presidential nominee (1884).

Blake (blāk), **William** 1757-1827, English artist and poet.

Bohr (bôr), **Niels** (nēlz) 1885-1962, Danish physicist, studied the nature of the atom.

Bol·í·var (bŏ lē'vär), **Simón** (sē mōn') 1783-1830, general and statesman of Venezuela, liberated South America.

Bo·na·parte (bōn'ə pärt'), **Napoleon** See **Napoleon I.**

Boone (bōōn), **Daniel** 1734-1820, American pioneer, founded the first settlements in Kentucky.

Booth (bōōth), **John Wilkes** (wilks) 1838-65, actor who assassinated Abraham Lincoln. —**William** 1829-1912, English clergyman, founder of the Salvation Army.

Bor·glum (bôr'gləm), **Gutzon** (gŭt'zən) 1867-1941, U.S. sculptor.

Bot·ti·cel·li (bŏt'ə chĕl'ē), **Sandro** (sän'drō) 1444?-1510, Italian painter.

Boyle (boil), **Robert** 1627-91, English chemist and physicist, born in Ireland, studied the behavior of gases.

Brad·dock (brăd'ək), **Edward** 1695-1755, British general in the French and Indian War, a war between France and England in America (1754-63).

Brad·ford (brăd'fərd), **William** 1590?-1657, second governor of the Pilgrim colony at Plymouth, Massachusetts.

Brahms (brämz), **Johannes** (yō hä'nəs) 1833-97, German composer and pianist.

Braille (brāl), **Louis** (lwē) 1809-52, French educator and inventor of a system of printing for the blind.

Bran·deis (brăn'dīs), **Louis** 1856-1941, associate justice of the U.S. Supreme Court (1916-39).

Breck·in·ridge (brĕk'ən rij'), **John** 1821-75, U.S. vice-president (1857-61), Confederate general, a defeated presidential candidate (1860).

Brezh·nev (brĕzh'nĕv'), **Leonid** (lā'ə nid') born 1906, Russian politician; president of the U.S.S.R. (1960-64); first secretary of the Central Committee of the Communist Party (1964-).

Bridg·er (brij'ər), **James** 1804-81, U.S. frontiersman and fur trader in the West.

Brown (broun), **John** 1800-59, U.S. abolitionist, hanged after attacking a U.S. arsenal.

Brown·ing (broun'ing), **Elizabeth Barrett** (băr'ət) 1806-61, English poet, wife of Robert. —**Robert** 1812-89, English poet.

Bruce (brōōs), **Robert** 1274-1329, king of Scotland (1306-29).

Bru·tus (brōō'təs), **Marcus Junius** (mär'kəs jōō'nē əs) 85?-42 B.C., Roman politician and general, an assassin of Julius Caesar.

Bry·an (brī'ən), **William Jennings** 1860-1925, U.S. statesman and orator, a defeated presidential candidate (1896 and 1900).

Bry·ant (brī'ənt), **William Cullen** 1794-1878, U.S. poet.

Bu·chan·an (bū kăn'ən), **James** 1791-1868, 15th President of the United States (1857-61).

Bud·dha (bōōd'ə) 563?-483?, mystic of India, founder of Buddhism.

Buffalo Bill See **William Cody.**

Bunche (bŭnch), **Ralph** born 1904, U.S. educator and United Nations diplomat.

Bun·sen (bŭn'sən), **Robert** 1811-99, German chemist, inventor of the Bunsen burner.

Bur·bank (bûr'bank'), **Luther** 1849-1926, U.S. botanist, developed new and better fruits and vegetables.

Bur·goyne (bər goin', bûr'goin'), **John** 1722-92, British general in the American Revolution.

Burns (bûrnz), **Robert** 1759-96, Scottish poet.

Burr (bûr), **Aaron** 1756-1836, American politician, Vice-President of the United States (1801-05), killed Alexander Hamilton in a duel.

Byrd (bûrd), **Richard E.** 1888-1957, U.S. rear admiral, aviator, and polar explorer.

By·ron (bī'rən), **Lord** 1788-1824, [George Gordon Noel, 6th Baron Byron] English poet.

C

Cab·ot (kăb'ət), **John** 1451?-98, Italian navigator in the English service, reached North America (Labrador, 1497). —**Sebastian** (sə băs'chən) 1474?-1557, English seafarer, son of the proceeding.

Cae·sar (sē'zər), **Gaius Julius** (gī'əs jōōl'yəs) 100-44 B.C., Roman statesman, general, and historian.

Cal·houn (kăl hōōn'), **John Caldwell** (kôld'wĕl') 1782-1850, U.S. statesman, Vice-President of the United States (1825-32).

Cal·vert (kăl'vərt), **Sir George** 1580?-1632, first **Baron Baltimore,** English statesman, founder of Maryland.

Cal·vin (kăl'vən), **John** 1509-64, French Protestant reformer.

Car·lo·ta (kär lŏt'ə) 1840-1927, empress of Maximilian of Mexico. Also called **Car·lot'ta.**

Car·ne·gie (kär'nə gē, kär nä'gē), **Andrew** 1835-1919, U.S. industrial leader and philanthropist.

Car·roll (kăr'əl), **Lewis** Charles Lutwidge Dodgson, 1832-98, English mathematician and author of "Alice in Wonderland."

Car·son (kär'sən), **Kit** (**Christopher**) 1809-68, U.S. frontiersman and fur trader in the West.

Car·tier (kär tyä'), **Jacques** (zhäk) 1491-1557, French explorer, discovered the St. Lawrence River (1535).

840

Famous Persons

Cart·wright (kärt'rit'), **Edmund** 1743-1823, English clergyman, inventor of the power loom.

Ca·ru·so (kə rōō'sō), **Enrico** (ĕn rē'kō) 1873-1921, Italian operatic tenor.

Car·ver (kär'vər), **George Washington** 1864?-1943, U.S. Negro botanist and chemist. —**John** 1575-1621, first governor of the Pilgrim colony at Plymouth, Massachusetts.

Cas·ey Jones (kā'sē jōnz), [**John Luther Jones**] 1864-1900, U.S. locomotive engineer, who stayed in his cab after the brakes failed, and died in the wreck.

Cas·tro (käs'trō), **Fidel** (fē dĕl') born 1926, Cuban revolutionary leader; premier (1959-   ).

Cat·lin (kăt'lən), **George** 1796-1872, U.S. artist, painter of American Indians.

Cax·ton (kăks'tən), **William** 1422?-91, English printer who first introduced printing into England.

Cel·li·ni (chə lē'nē), **Benvenuto** (bĕn'və nōō'tō) 1500-71, Italian sculptor and goldsmith.

Cer·van·tes (sĕr văn'tās), **Miguel de** (mē gĕl'dā) 1547-1616, Spanish writer, author of "Don Quixote".

Cé·zanne (sā zăn'), **Paul** 1839-1906, French painter.

Cha·ka (chä'kə) 1773-1828, powerful king of the **Zulus** (zōō'lōōz'), who conquered most of southeastern Africa.

Cham·plain (shăm plān'), **Samuel de** (săm wĕl'də) 1567-1635, French explorer, founder of Quebec, Canada.

Char·le·magne (shär'lə mān') 742?-814, king of the **Franks**, a Germanic people that lived in France, Germany, and Italy; called **Charles the Great**.

Charles I (chärlz), [**Charles Stuart**] 1600-49, king of England (1625-49); was beheaded. —**Charles II** 1630-85, king of England (1660-85). —**Charles V** 1500-58, emperor of Germany (1519-56) and king of Spain (as **Charles I**, 1516-56).

Chau·cer (chô'sər), **Geoffrey** (jĕf'rē) 1340?-1400, English poet.

Che·ops (kē'ŏps) Egyptian king of the fourth dynasty (2900?-2877 B.C.), builder of the Great Pyramid.

Chiang Kai-shek (chăng'ki'shĕk') born 1886, Chinese general and statesman, president of the Republic of China.

Cho·pin (shō'păn', shō păn'), **Frédéric François** (frā dā rēk' frän swä') 1810-49, composer and pianist, active in France.

Chou En-lai (jō'ĕn'lī') born 1898, premier of the People's Republic of China (1949-   ).

Chris·to·pher (krĭs'tə fər), **Saint** died 250? A.D., Christian martyr, known as the patron saint of travelers.

Church·ill (chûr'chĭl'), **Sir Winston** 1874-1965, British statesman and historian, prime minister (1940-45, 1951-55).

Cic·e·ro (sĭs'ə rō'), **Marcus Tullius** (mär'kəs tŭl'ē əs) 106-43 B.C., Roman statesman and orator.

Cid, El (ĕl sēd'), 1044?-99, Spanish epic hero in the war against the Moslems of North Africa.

Clark (klärk), **George Rogers** 1752-1818, soldier and pioneer in the American Revolution. —**William** 1770-1838, brother of George Rogers, explorer with Meriwether Lewis. See **Lewis, Meriwether.**

Clay (klā), **Henry** 1775-1852, U.S. statesman and orator, a defeated presidential candidate (1824, 1832, 1844).

Clem·ens (klĕm'ənz), **Samuel Langhorne** (lăng'hôrn') See **Mark Twain.**

Cle·o·pat·ra (klē'ō pā'trə) 69-30 B.C., queen of Egypt (51-49, 48-30).

Cleve·land (klēv'lənd) (**Stephen**) **Grover** 1837-1908, 22nd and 24th President of the United States (1885-89, 1893-97).

Clin·ton (klĭn'tən), **De Witt** (də wĭt') 1769-1828, U.S. lawyer and statesman, governor of New York who promoted the building of the Erie Canal across New York State.

Cobb (kŏb), **Ty** (tī) 1886-1961, U.S. baseball player; full name **Tyrus Raymond Cobb.**

Co·dy (kō'dē), **William** 1846-1917, U.S. frontier scout and showman; called **Buffalo Bill.**

Cole·ridge (kōl'ər ĭj), **Samuel Taylor** 1772-1834, English poet and critic.

Co·lum·bus (kə lŭm'bəs), **Christopher** (krĭs'tə fər) 1446-1506, Italian explorer, discovered America for Spain (October 12, 1492). *Spanish* **Cristobal Colon** (krĭs tō'bäl kō lōn'). *Italian* **Cristoforo Colombo** (krĭs'tə fôr'ō kə lŭm'bō).

Con·fu·cius (kən fū'shəs) 551?-478? B.C., Chinese philosopher and teacher.

Con·stantine I (kŏn'stən tēn', -tĭn') 288?-337, first Christian emperor of Rome (306-37); called **Constantine the Great.**

Cook (kŏŏk), **Captain James** 1728-79, English explorer, discovered the Hawaiian Islands.

Coo·lidge (kōō'lĭj), (**John**) **Calvin** 1872-1933, 30th President of the United States (1923-29).

Coop·er (kōō'pər, kŏŏp'ər), **James Fenimore** (fĕn'ə môr') 1780-1851, U.S. novelist.

Co·per·ni·cus (kə pûr'nĭ kəs), **Nicholas** 1473-1543, Polish astronomer, who proved that the earth and other planets orbit the sun.

Cop·land (kō'plənd), **Aaron** born 1900, U.S. composer.

Corn·wal·lis (kôrn wäl'ĭs), **Charles** 1738-1805, first **Marquis Cornwallis**, English general and statesman.

Co·ro·na·do (kôr'ə nä'dō), **Francisco** (frän sĭs'kō) 1510-54, Spanish explorer.

Cor·tés (kôr tĕz'), **Hernando** (hĕr nän'dō) 1485-1547, Spanish conqueror of Mexico. Also **Cor·tez'.**

Crazy Horse 1849?-1877, a chief of the Sioux who helped defeat General Custer at the Little Big Horn, but was eventually forced to surrender.

Crock·ett (krŏk'ət), **David** 1786-1836, U.S. frontiersman and politician, died in the defense of the Alamo; called **Davy Crockett.**

Croe·sus (krē'səs) died in 546 B.C., king of Lydia (560-46), noted for his great wealth.

Crom·well (krŏm'wĕl'), **Oliver** 1599-1658, English general and statesman, lord protector of England (1653-58).

Cu·rie (kū rē'), **Marie** 1867-1934, born in Poland, and her husband **Pierre** 1859-1906, French physicists, discovered radium.

Cus·ter (kŭs'tər), **George Armstrong** 1839-76, Union lieutenant general in the Civil War. He was also an

---

fāte, făt, fâre, fär; bē, bĕt; bīte, bĭt; nō, nŏt, nôr; fūse, fŭn, fûr; tōō, tŏŏk; foil; foul; thin; ~~then~~;
hw for wh as in *wh*at; zh for s as in u*s*ual; ə for a, e, i, o, u, as in *a*go, lin*e*n, per*i*l, at*o*m, min*u*s

Famous Persons

Indian fighter and was killed at the Little Big Horn River in Montana.

D

da Ga·ma (də gäm′ə), **Vasco** (väs′kō) 1469-1524, Portuguese explorer, discovered the sea route from Portugal to India (1498).

Dal·ton (dôl′tən), **John** 1766-1844, English chemist and physicist, studied the behavior of gases and the nature of atoms.

Dan·te A·li·ghie·ri (dän′tā â lē′gyèr′ē, dän′tē) 1265-1321, Italian poet, author of the "Divine Comedy."

Da·ri·us I (də rī′us, dâr′ē əs) 558?-486? B.C., king of Persia, defeated at Marathon; called **Darius the Great**.

Dar·win (där′win), **Charles** 1809-82, English naturalist who originated the theory of evolution.

Da·vid (dā′vəd) 1040?-970? B.C., king of Judah and Israel (1010-970), succeeded Saul.

da Vin·ci (dä vin′chē), **Leonardo** (lā ə när′dō) 1452-1519, Italian sculptor, painter, architect, and engineer.

Da·vis (dā′vəs), **Jefferson** 1808-89, U.S. statesman, president of the Confederacy (1862-65).

Da·vy (dā′vē), **Sir Humphrey** 1778-1829, English chemist, developed a safety lamp for miners.

Debs (děbz), **Eugene** 1855-1926, U.S. labor leader, five times socialist candidate for the presidency between 1900 and 1920.

De·bus·sy (dā bū′sē′), **Claude** (klōd) 1862-1918, French composer.

De·ca·tur (dē kā′tər), **Stephen** 1779-1820, U.S. naval commander.

De·foe (də fō′), **Daniel** 1660?-1731, English journalist and novelist, author of "Robinson Crusoe."

De·gas (də gä′), **(Hilaire Germain) Edgar** (ē lèr′ zhèr măn′ēd gär′) 1834-1917, French impressionist painter and sculptor.

de Gaulle (də gōl′), **Charles André** (shärl än drā′) born 1890, French general, president of France (1944-45, 1959-).

de la Mare (də lä mâr′), **Walter** 1873-1956, English poet and novelist.

De·mos·the·nes (də mŏs′thə nēz′) 384?-322 B.C., Athenian orator and statesman.

De Soto (dī sō′tō), **Hernando** (hèr nän′dō) 1500?-42, Spanish explorer, discovered the Mississippi River (1541).

De Va·le·ra (děv′ə lâr′ə), **Eamon** (ā′mən) born 1882, Irish statesman and prime minister, born in the United States, president of Ireland (1959-).

De Vo·to (də vō′tō), **Bernard** (bər närd′) 1895-1955, U.S. literary critic and historian of exploration and discovery in North America.

Dew·ey (dōō′ē), **Thomas E.** born 1902, U.S. politician, defeated presidential candidate (1944 and 1948). **—George** 1837-1917, U.S. admiral in the Spanish-American War. **—John** 1859-1952, U.S. philosopher and educator.

Di·as (dē′äs, -äsh), **Bartholomeu** (bär′tōl ə mā′ōō) 1450?-1500, Portuguese explorer, discovered the Cape of Good Hope. Also **Di′az**.

Dick·ens (dik′ənz), **Charles** 1812-70, English novelist.

Dick·in·son (dik′in sən), **Emily** 1830-86, U.S. poet.

Di·og·e·nes (dī ŏj′ə nēz′) 412?-323 B.C., Greek philosopher, said to have wandered at midday with a lantern, searching for an honest man.

Do·bie (dō′bē), **James Frank** 1888-1964, U.S. author and professor of the history and folklore of Texas.

Dodg·son (dŏj′sən), **Charles Lutwidge** See **Carroll, Lewis.**

Doug·las (dŭg′ləs), **Stephen A.** 1813-61, U.S. senator, defeated presidential candidate (1860).

Doug·lass (dŭg′ləs), **Frederick** 1817?-95, U.S. Negro orator and abolitionist.

Doyle (doil), **Sir Arthur Conan** (kō′nən) 1859-1930, English physician and novelist, creator of Sherlock Holmes.

Drake (drāk), **Sir Francis** 1540?-96, first Englishman to circumnavigate the globe (1580).

Du·mas (dōō ma′), **Alexandre** (ăl ĕk sän′drə) 1802-70 [**Dumas pére** (pèr)] French novelist and dramatist who wrote "The Three Musketeers."—**Alexandre** 1824-95 [**Dumas fils** (fēs)] French novelist and dramatist.

Du·rer (dŏŏr′ər), **Albrecht** (äl′brēkt′) 1471-1528, German painter and engraver.

Dvor·ak (dvôr′zhäk′), **Anton** (än′tŏn) 1841-1904, Czech composer.

E

Earp (ûrp), **Wyatt** (wi′ət) 1848-1929, U.S. frontiersman, deputy marshal of Dodge City, Kansas, and later a deputy sheriff at Tombstone, Arizona.

Ed·dy (ĕd′ē), **Mary Baker** 1821-1910, born Mary Morse Baker, U.S. religious leader, founder of the Church of Christ, Scientist (Christian Science).

Ed·i·son (ĕd′ə sən), **Thomas** 1847-1931, U.S. inventor of the incandescent lamp, the phonograph, the dynamo, etc.

Ed·ward VII (ĕd′wərd) 1841-1910, king of England (1901-10), son of Queen Victoria. **—Edward VIII** born 1894, king of England (1936), abdicated the same year and became Duke of Windsor.

Ehr·lich (âr′lik), **Paul** 1854-1915, German biochemist and bacteriologist.

Ein·stein (in′stin′), **Albert** 1879-1955, U.S. physicist born in Germany, stated the relation between matter, energy, and the speed of light.

Ei·sen·how·er (i′zən hou′ər), **Dwight David** (dwit) born 1891, 34th President of the United States, Allied commander-in-chief in World War II (1943-45).

El Gre·co (ĕl grĕk′ō) 1548?-1614, Spanish painter born in Crete.

E·liz·a·beth I (ə liz′ə bĕth′, -bəth) 1533-1603, queen of England (1558-1603), daughter of Henry VIII and Anne Boleyn. **—Elizabeth II** born 1926, queen of England (1952-), daughter of George VI and wife of Prince Philip.

Em·er·son (ĕm′ər sən), **Ralph Waldo** (wôl′dō) 1803-82, U.S. essayist, philosopher, and poet.

Er·ic·son (ĕr′ək sən), **Lief** (lēf) Viking chieftain, son of Eric the Red, probably discovered North America around 1000 A.D.

Er·ics·son (ĕr′ər sən), **John** 1803-89, U.S. engineer and inventor born in Sweden, invented the screw propeller and built the *Monitor*.

Er·ic the Red (ĕr′ik) born 950? A.D., Scandinavian navigator; explored the coast of Greenland, an island off NE North America, around 982 A.D.

Eu·clid (ū′klid) Greek mathematician of the third century B.C., noted for his development of the basic principles of geometry.

Famous Persons

F

Far·a·day (făr′ə dā′), **Michael** 1791-1867, English physicist and chemist, made discoveries in electricity and magnetism.

Far·ra·gut (făr′ə gət), **David G.** 1801-70, Northern admiral in the Civil War.

Fawkes (fôks), **Guy** 1570-1606, English conspirator involved in the "Gunpowder Plot" (1604-05), a plot to assassinate King James I and the members of Parliament.

Fer·di·nand V of Castile (fûr′də nănd) 1452-1516, king of Spain, husband of Isabella I, founded the Spanish monarchy. Also called **Ferdinand the Catholic.**

Fer·mi (fĕr′mē), **Enrico** (ĕn rē′kō) 1901-54, Italian nuclear physicist, active in the United States.

Field (fēld), **Cyrus** (sī′rəs) 1819-92, U.S. merchant, planned the laying of the first cable across the Atlantic Ocean (1858). —**Eugene** 1850-95, U.S. poet and journalist.

Fill·more (fil′môr), **Millard** (mil′ərd) 1800-74, 13th President of the United States (1850-53), a defeated presidential candidate (1852).

Fitz·pa·trick (fits′păt′rik), **Thomas** 1799?-1854, U.S. fur trader, trapper, scout, and Indian agent, born in Ireland.

Flem·ing (flĕm′ing), **Sir Alexander** 1881-1955, Scottish physician, one of the discoverers of penicillin.

Foch (fôsh), **Ferdinand** (fĕr də nän′) 1851-1929, French general, Allied commander-in-chief (1918) in World War I.

Ford (fôrd), **Henry** 1863-1947, U.S. automobile manufacturer and philanthropist.

Fos·ter (fôs′tər, fŏs′tər), **Stephen** 1826-64, U.S. composer and song writer.

Fox (fŏks), **George** 1624-91, English religious leader, found the Society of Friends (Quakers).

France (frăns, French frăns), **Anatole** (än′ə tōl′) pseudonym of **Jacques Thibault** (zhăk tē bō′) 1844-1924, French novelist and critic.

Fran·co (frăng′kō), **Francisco** (frän sĭs′kō) born 1892, Spanish general, chief of state since 1939.

Frank·lin (frăngk′lin), **Benjamin** 1706-90, American patriot, inventor, and statesman, signer of the Declaration of Independence.

Fré·mont (frē′mŏnt′), **John Charles** 1813-90, U.S. soldier, explorer, and politician, a defeated presidential candidate (1856); called **the Pathfinder.**

Freud (froid), **Sigmund** (sĭg′mənd) 1856-1939, Austrain specialist in nervous disorders, founded a type of modern psychology.

Fro·bish·er (frō′bish′ər), **Sir Martin** 1535?-94, English navigator, sailed westward in search of a passage to India.

Fron·te·nac (frŏn′tə năk′, French frŏn′tə năk′), **Comte Louis de** (kônt lwē də) 1620-98, French governor of Canada (1672-82; 1689-98).

Frost (frôst), **Robert** 1875-1963, U.S. poet.

Ful·ton (fŏŏl′tən), **Robert** 1765-1815, U.S. inventor, developed first successful and practical steamboat (1803).

G

Ga·gar·in (gə gär′in), **Yuri** (yŏŏr′ē) born 1934, Russian astronaut, first man to orbit the earth (April 12, 1961).

Gains·bor·ough (gānz′bûr′ə), **Thomas** 1727-88, English painter.

Ga·len (gā′lən) 130?-200?, Greek physician and medical writer.

Gal·i·le·o (găl′ə lē′ō) 1564-1642, Italian astronomer and physicist who advanced proof that the earth travels around the sun. Full name **Galileo Galilei** (-le′ē).

Gan·dhi (gän′dē), **Mohandas Karamchand** (mō′hən-däs′ kûr′əm chŭnd′) 1869-1948, Hindu political, social, and spiritual leader. Also called **Ma·hat′ma Gandhi** (mə hät′mə).

Gar·field (gär′fēld′), **James Abram** 1831-81, 20th President of the United States, assassinated during his first year in office.

Gar·i·bal·di (găr′ə bôl′dē, gä′rə bäl′dē), **Giuseppe** (jə sĕp′ē, Italian jŏŏ zĕp′pä) 1807-82, Italian patriot and general, helped to unite Italy.

Gar·ri·son (găr′ə sən), **William Lloyd** 1805-79, U.S. editor and reformer who opposed slavery.

Gau·guin (gō găn′), **Paul** (pôl) 1848-1903, French painter.

Gen·ghis Khan (jĕn′gĭz kän′) 1167?-1227, Mongol conqueror of central Asia. Also **Jen′ghiz Khan.**

George (jôrj) name of six kings of England, notably: **George III** 1738-1820, king of England (1760-1820), reigned during the American Revolution; **George V** 1865-1936, king of England (1910-36); and **George VI** 1895-1952, king of England (1936-52).

George El·i·ot (ĕl′ē ət) name used in the writings of **Mary Ann Evans,** 1819-80, English novelist.

George, Saint died 303? Christian martyr, patron saint of England.

Ge·ron·i·mo (jə rŏn′ə mō′) 1829-1909, Apache Indian chief, active in SW United States and in Mexico.

Gersh·win (gûrsh′wən), **George** 1898-1937, U.S. composer.

Gil·bert (gil′bərt), **Sir Humphrey** 1539?-83, English navigator, founded a colony in Newfoundland.

Gilbert, Sir William S. 1836-1911 and **Sul·li·van** (sŭl′ə vən), **Arthur H.** 1842-1900, a team of English composers of comic operas. Gilbert wrote the words and Sullivan wrote the music.

Giot·to (jŏt′tō) 1266?-1337, Florentine painter and architect.

Glenn (glĕn), **John** born 1921, U.S. astronaut, first American to orbit the earth (Feb. 20, 1962).

Goe·thals (gō′thəlz), **George W.** 1858-1928, U.S. army engineer, builder of the Panama Canal.

Goe·the (gā′tə), **Johann Wolfgang von** (yō′hän′ vôlf′gäng′fôn) 1749-1832, German poet, dramatist, and novelist.

Gold·smith (gōld′smith′), **Oliver** 1728-74, British novelist and dramatist.

Gold·wa·ter (gōld′wô′tər), **Barry Morris** born 1909, U.S. senator, a defeated presidential candidate (1964).

Gom·pers (gŏm′pərz), **Samuel** 1850-1924, U.S. labor leader, founder and first president of the American Federation of Labor (1886).

---

fāte, făt, fâre, fär; bē, bĕt; bīte, bĭt; nō, nŏt, nôr; fūse, fŭn, fûr; tōō, tŏŏk; foil; foul; thin; then; hw for wh as in what; zh for s as in usual; ə for a, e, i, o, u, as in ago, linen, peril, atom, minus

843

Famous Persons

Good·year (good'yir'), **Charles** 1800-60, U.S. industrialist and originator of a process for strengthening rubber.

Go·ya (goi'ə), **Francisco de** (frän thĕs'kō dä) 1746-1828, Spanish painter and etcher.

Gra·ham (grā'əm), **Martha** born 1894, American creator of dances and dancer.

Grant (gränt), **Ulysses S(impson)** (ū lis'ēz simp'sən) 1822-85, U.S. general in the Civil War, 18th President of the United States (1869-77).

Gree·ley (grē'lē), **Horace** 1811-72, U.S. journalist, politician, and leader against slavery, a defeated presidential candidate (1872).

Greg·o·ry (grĕg'ə rē) name of 16 popes, notably: **Gregory I** 540?-604, pope (590-604), reformed church services and was called **Gregory the Great.** —**Gregory XIII** 1502-85, pope (1572-85), reformed the calendar.

Grieg (grēg, grig), **Edvard** (ĕd'värt') 1843-1907, Norwegian composer.

Grimm (grim), **Jacob** (yä'kōp') 1785-1863, and his brother **Wilhelm** (vil'hĕlm') 1786-1859, German language experts who collected folklore and fairy tales.

Guar·ne·ri (gwär'nä'rē) family of Italian violin makers in Cremona, especially **Giuseppe** 1687?-1745. Also **Guar·nie'ri.**

Gu·ten·berg (good'tən bûrg'), **Johann** (yō'hän') 1400?-68?, German printer who invented printing from movable type.

H

Hai·le Se·las·sie (hi'lē sə läs'ē) born 1891, emperor of Ethiopia (1930-36, 1941-   ).

Hale (hāl), **Nathan** 1755-76, patriot in the American Revolution, hanged as a spy by the British.

Ham·il·ton (hăm'əl tən), **Alexander** 1755-1804, American statesman, secretary of the treasury under Washington, was killed by Aaron Burr.

Ham·mar·skjöld (hăm'ər shŭld', -shōld', -shĕld'), **Dag** (däg) 1905-61, Swedish statesman, secretary-general of the United Nations (1953-61).

Ham·mu·ra·bi (hä'mə rä'bē) king of Babylonia, an ancient kingdom east of Palestine, around 2,000 B.C. The first humanitarian code of laws was made during his reign.

Han·cock (hăn'kŏk'), **John** 1737-93, statesman during the American Revolution, signer of the Declaration of Independence. —**Winfield Scott** 1824-86, Northern general of the Civil War, a defeated presidential candidate (1880).

Han·del (hăn'dəl), **George Frederick** 1685-1759, British composer, born in Germany.

Han·dy (hăn'dē), **W(illiam) C.** 1873-1958, U.S. composer; called the **Father of the Blues.**

Han·ni·bal (hăn'ə bəl) 247-183? B.C., general born in Carthage, a city in north Africa, invaded Italy by crossing to Spain and then crossing the Alps.

Har·ding (här'ding), **Warren Gamaliel** (wär'ən gə mā'lē əl) 1865-1923, 29th President of the United States (1921-23).

Har·ri·son (hăr'ə sən), **Benjamin** 1833-1901, 23rd President of the United States (1889-93), grandson of William Henry. —**William Henry** 1773-1841, ninth President of the United States (1841) for one month.

Harte (härt), **Bret** (brĕt) 1836-1902, U.S. novelist and short-story writer.

Ha·run al-Ra·shid (hä rōōn'äl rä shēd') 764?-809, famous caliph in the "Arabian Nights."

Har·vey (här'vē), **William** 1578-1657, English scientist in anatomy, discovered the circulation of the blood.

Haw·thorne (hô'thôrn'), **Nathaniel** (nə thăn'yəl) 1804-64, U.S. novelist and writer of short stories.

Hay·den (hi'dən), **Franz Joseph** (fränz'yō'səf) 1732-1809, Austrian composer.

Hayes (hāz), **Rutherford B.** (rŭth'ər fərd) 1822-93, 19th President of the United States (1877-81).

Hearst (hûrst), **William Randolph** (răn'dōlf') 1863-1951, U.S. newspaper publisher.

Hei·fetz (hi'fəts), **Jascha** (yä'shə) born 1901, U.S. violinist, born in Lithuania.

Hem·ing·way (hĕm'ing wā'), **Ernest** 1899-1961, U.S. novelist and short-story writer.

Hen·ry II (hĕn'rē) 1133-89, king of England (1154-89), called **Henry Plantagenet** (plăn'tăj'ə nət). —**Henry IV** 1367-1413, king of England (1399-1413), called **Bolingbroke** (bŏl'ing brook'). —**Henry VIII** 1491-1547, king of England (1509-47).

Henry IV 1553-1610, king of France (1589-1610). Also called **Henry of Navarre** (nə vär').

Henry, Joseph 1797-1878, U.S. physicist, made discoveries in electricity. —**Patrick** 1736-99, statesman and orator during the American Revolution.

Henry, O. See **O. Henry.**

Henry the Navigator 1394-1460, Portuguese prince, patron and promoter of sea exploration.

Her·bert (hûr'bərt), **Victor** 1859-1924, U.S. composer, born in Ireland.

Her·od (hĕr'əd) 73?-4 B.C., king of the southern part of ancient Palestine (37-4); called **Herod the Great.** —**Herod Antipas** (hĕr'əd ăn'ti päs'), died 39? A.D., governor of a region in northern Palestine (4 B.C.-39 A.D.), son of the above.

Her·schel (hûr'shəl), **Sir William** 1738-1822, English astronomer, born in Germany, discovered Uranus.

Hi·a·wath·a (hi'ə wô'thə, hē'ə wä'thə) Mohawk Indian chief, one of the organizers of the Five Nations Confederacy, an alliance of Iroquois Indians (1570).

Hick·ok (hik'ŏk), **James Butler** 1837-76, U.S. frontier scout and peace officer in the West; called **Wild Bill.**

Hin·den·burg (hin'dən bûrg'), **Paul von** (pôl fŏn) 1847-1934, German general, last president of Germany (1925-34) before Hitler.

Hip·poc·ra·tes (hi pŏk'rə tēz') 460?-377? B.C., Greek physician; called the **Father of Medicine.**

Hi·ro·hi·to (hē'rō hē'tō) born 1901, emperor of Japan (1926-   ).

Hit·ler (hit'lər), **Adolf** (ā'dŏlf) 1889-1945, German dictator, born in Austria, leader of the Nazi Party and chancellor (1933-45).

Ho Chi Minh (hō'chē'min') born 1892?, Vietnamese Communist leader, president of North Vietnam (1945-   ).

Holmes (hōlmz), **Oliver Wendell** (wĕn'dəl) 1809-94, physician and writer. —**Oliver Wendell** 1841-1935, associate justice of the U.S. Supreme Court (1902-32), son of the above.

Ho·mer (hō'mər) Greek epic poet of the ninth century B.C., wrote the "Iliad" and "Odyssey."

Ho·mer (hō'mər), **Winslow** (winz'lō) 1836-1910, U.S. painter.

Famous Persons

Hoo·ver (hōō′vər) **Herbert** 1876-1964, mining engineer and statesman, 31st President of the United States (1929-33).

Hor·ace (hôr′əs) 65-8 B.C., Roman poet.

Hous·ton (hū′stən), **Sam** 1793-1863, U.S. general, first president of the Republic of Texas (1836-38).

Howe (hou), **Elias** (ĭ lī′əs) 1819-67, U.S. inventor of the sewing machine. —**William** 1729-1814, fifth **Viscount Howe,** British general in the American Revolution.

Hud·son (hŭd′sən), **Henry** died 1611?, English navigator, discovered the Hudson River (1609) and Hudson Bay (1610).

Hughes (hūz), **Langston** (lăng′stən) born 1902, U.S. poet, playwright, and journalist, famous for his portrayals of Negroes in New York City.

Hum·boldt (hŭm′bōlt′), **Baron Alexander von** 1769-1859, German naturalist and explorer.

Hux·ley (hŭk′slē), **Thomas Henry** 1825-95, English biologist, promoted Darwin's theories.

I

ibn-Sa·ud (ē′bən sä ōōd′), **Abdul Azis** (äb′dōōl′ä zez′) 1880-1953, king of Saudi Arabia (1932-53).

Ig·na·tius of Lo·yo·la (ĭg nā′shəs əv loi ō′lə), **Saint** 1491-1556, Spanish soldier and priest, founder of the Society of Jesus (Jesuits).

Ir·ving (ûr′vĭng), **Washington** 1783-1859, U.S. short-story writer and historian.

Is·a·bel·la I (ĭz′ə bĕl′ə) 1451-1504, queen of Spain, wife of Ferdinand V, gave help to Columbus.

I·van III (ī′vən) 1440-1505, grand duke of ancient Russia (1462-1505), called **Ivan the Great.** —**Ivan IV** 1530-84, grandson of Ivan III, first czar of Russia (1547-84), called **Ivan the Terrible.**

J

Jack·son (jăk′sən), **Andrew** 1767-1845, U.S. general, seventh President of the United States (1829-37). —**Thomas** 1824-63, Confederate general in the Civil War; called **Stonewall Jackson.**

James I (jāmz) 1566-1625, king of England (1603-25). —**James II** 1633-1701, king of England (1685-88), deposed.

Jay (jā), **John** 1745-1829, first chief justice of the U.S. Supreme Court.

Jef·fer·son (jĕf′ər sən), **Thomas** 1743-1826, American statesman and diplomat, drafted the Declaration of Independence; third President of the United States (1801-09).

Jen·ner (jĕn′ər), **Edward** 1749-1823, English physician, discovered vaccination.

Joan of Arc (jōn′əv ärk′), **Saint** 1412?-31, French national heroine, made a saint in 1920. Also **Jeanne d'Arc** (zhän därk′).

John (jŏn) 1167?-1216, king of England, signed the Magna Carta, a document guaranteeing certain liberties (1215).

John (jŏn) name of 21 popes, especially **John XXIII** [**Angelo Giuseppe Roncalli** (än′jə lō jə sĕp′ē rōn-käl′ē)] 1881-1963, pope (1958-63).

John·son (jŏn′sən), **Andrew** 1807-75, 17th President of the United States (1865-69). —**Lyndon B.** born 1908, 36th President of the United States (1963-). —**Sam-**

uel 1709-84, English lexicographer, poet, and man of letters; called **Dr. Johnson.**

Jol·li·et (jŏ′lē ĕt′), **Louis** (lwē) 1645-1700, French-Canadian explorer of the Mississippi and the Great Lakes region. Also **Jo′li·et′.**

Jones, Casey See **Casey Jones.**

Jones (jōnz), **John Paul** 1747-92, American naval officer in the American Revolution, born in Scotland.

Jo·seph (jō′zəf), **Chief** 1840-1904, American Indian soldier and statesman, Nez Perce chief.

Jo·seph·ine (jō′zə fēn′), **Empress** 1763-1814, wife of Napoleon I.

Jua·rez (wä rĕz′), **Benito** (bə nē′tō) 1806-72, Mexican patriot and statesman, president of Mexico (1857-72).

K

Keats (kēts), **John** 1795-1821, English poet.

Kel·ler (kĕl′ər), **Helen Adams** born 1880, U.S. deaf and blind writer and lecturer.

Ke·mal A·ta·turk (kē mäl′ä tä tûrk′) 1881-1938, Turkish general and statesman, first president of Turkey (1923-38).

Kempis, Thomás a See **Thomás a Kempis.**

Ken·ne·dy (kĕn′ə dē), **John Fitzgerald** 1917-63, 35th President of the United States (1961-63); assassinated (November 22).

Kep·ler (kĕp′lər), **Johann** (yō′hän′) 1571-1630, German astronomer and mathematician, discovered three important laws of planetary motion.

Key (kē), **Francis Scott** 1779-1843, American lawyer, author of "The Star-Spangled Banner."

Khru·shchev (krōōsh′chĕv′, krōōsh′chôf′), **Nikita** (nĭ kē′tə) born 1894, Russian premier (1958-64).

Kidd (kĭd), **William** 1645?-1701, navigator and pirate; called **Captain Kidd.**

King (kĭng), **Martin Luther, Jr.** born 1929, U.S. clergyman, leader of the Negro civil rights movement, and winner of the Nobel Prize for Peace (1964).

Kip·ling (kĭp′lĭng), **Rudyard** (rŭd′yərd) 1865-1936, English author and poet.

Knox (nŏks), **John** 1505?-72, Scottish religious reformer and historian.

Koch (kôk), **Robert** 1843-1910, German physician, one of the founders of modern bacteriology.

Kos·ci·us·ko (kŏ′sē ŭs′kō, kŏ′sē ōōs′kō), **Thaddeus** (thăd′ē əs) 1746-1817, Polish patriot, born in Lithuania; fought in the American Revolution.

Ko·sy·gin (kŏ sē′gĭn), **Aleksei** (ä′lĕk sā′) born 1904, Soviet politician, premier of the U.S.S.R. (1964-).

Kreis·ler (krīs′lər), **Fritz** 1875-1962, U.S. violinist and composer, born in Austria.

Kub·la Khan (kōō′blə kän′) 1216?-94, founder of a great ruling family in China. Also **Ku′blai Khan** (kōō′blī kän).

L

La·fa·yette (lä′fē yĕt′), **Marquis de** (mär kē′də) 1757-1834, French general and revolutionist; fought in the American Revolution.

La Fol·lette (lə fŏl′ət), **Robert Marion** 1855-1925, U.S. political leader and reformer.

La Fon·taine (lä fŏn tĕn′), **Jean de** (zhän də) 1621-95, French writer of fables.

---

fāte, făt, fâre, fär; bē, bĕt; bite, bĭt; nō, nŏt, nôr; fūse, fŭn, fûr; tōō, tŏŏk; foil; foul; thin; ~~then~~; hw for wh as in _wh_at; zh for s as in u_s_ual; ə for a, e, i, o, u, as in _a_go, lin_e_n, per_i_l, at_o_m, min_u_s

Famous Persons

Lamb (lăm), **Charles** 1775-1834, English essay writer and critic.

La Salle (lă săl'), **Cavalier de** (kă vəl yä'də) 1643-87, French explorer of the Mississippi River valley.

La·voi·sier (lă vwä zyā'), **Antoine** (än twän') 1743-94, French chemist; discovered oxygen.

Law·rence (lô'rəns), **Ernest Orlando** (ôr lăn'dō) 1901-58, U.S. physicist. —**T(homas) E(dward)** 1885-1935, English soldier, writer, and student of ancient life and culture; called **Lawrence of Arabia.**

Lee (lē), **Henry** 1756-1818, general in the American Revolution; called **Light-Horse Harry.** —**Jason** 1803-45, U.S. missionary in Oregon from 1843, influential in establishing the government of the territory. —**Robert E.** 1807-70, U.S. general and statesman, commander-in-chief of Confederate forces in the Civil War.

Le·nin (lĕn'ĭn), **Nikolai** (nĭk'ə lī') 1870-1924, Russian revolutionist, leader of the Communist revolution, head of the U.S.S.R. (1917-24).

Le·o (lē'ō) name of 13 popes, especially **Leo XIII** [**Gioacchino Vincenzo Pecci** (jō'ä kē'nō vĕn chĕn'zō pĕch'ē)] 1810-1903, pope (1878-1903).

Leonardo da Vinci See **da Vinci, Leonardo.**

Lew·is (lōō'ĭs), **John L.** born 1880, U.S. labor leader. —**Meriwether** (mĕr'ə wĕth'ər) 1774-1809, U.S. explorer, together with William Clark led an expedition from St. Louis, Missouri, to the mouth of the Columbia River in Oregon (1804-6).

Lie (lē), **Trygve** (trĭg'vē) born 1896, Norwegian statesman, first secretary-general of the United Nations (1946-53).

Lin·coln (lĭng'kən), **Abraham** 1809-65, 16th President of the United States (1861-63), assassinated by John Wilkes Booth.

Lind·bergh (lĭnd'bûrg'), **Charles** born 1902, U.S. aviator, made the first nonstop flight across the Atlantic (1927).

Lin·nae·us (lĭ nē'əs), **Carolus** (kə rō'ləs) 1707-78, Swedish scientist in the field of botany.

Lis·ter (lĭs'tər), **Joseph** 1827-1912, English surgeon, founder of antiseptic surgery.

Liszt (lĭst), **Franz** 1811-86, composer and pianist, born in Hungary.

Liv·ing·stone (lĭv'ĭng stən), **David** 1813-73, Scottish explorer and missionary in Africa.

Locke (lŏk), **John** 1632-1704, English philosopher, whose ideas of liberty and human rights influenced Thomas Jefferson and the Declaration of Independence.

Lon·don (lŭn'dən), **Jack** 1876-1916, U.S. author.

Long·fel·low (lông'fĕl'ō), **Henry Wadsworth** (wŏdz'-wûrth') 1807-82 U.S. poet.

Louis XVI (lwē) 1754-93, king of France (1774-92), dethroned during the French Revolution, guillotined.

Low·ell (lō'əl), **James Russell** 1819-91, U.S. poet, essay writer, and diplomat.

Loyola See **Ignatius of Loyola, Saint.**

Lu·ther (lōō'thər), **Martin** 1483-1546, German monk and pioneer in theology, leader of the Reformation.

M

Mac·Ar·thur (mək är'thər), **Douglas** 1880-1964, U.S. general, commander in the Pacific in World War II.

Mac·Dow·ell (mək dou'əl), **Edward** 1861-1908, U.S. composer and pianist.

Mach·i·a·vel·li (măk'ē ə vĕl'ē), **Niccolo** (nĭk'ə lō) 1469-1527, Italian statesman and political philosopher.

Mad·i·son (măd'ə sən), **Dolly** 1768-1849, wife of James. —**James** 1751-1836, fourth President of the United States (1801-17); called the **Father of the Constitution.**

Ma·gel·lan (mə jĕl'ən), **Ferdinand** (fûr'də nănd) 1480?-1521, Portuguese navigator serving Spain, first to sail around the world.

Mahatma Gandhi See **Gandhi, Mohandas Karamchand.**

Ma·hom·et (mə hăm'ət) See **Mohammed.**

Mann (măn), **Horace** 1796-1859, U.S. educational pioneer.

Mao Tse-tung (mou dzŭ dōōng') born 1893, Chinese Communist leader, chairman of the People's Republic of China (1950-59).

Mar·co·ni (mär kō'nē), **Guglielmo** (gōō lyĕl'mō) 1874-1937, Italian engineer and inventor, developed the wireless telegraph.

Mar·co Po·lo (mär'kō pō'lō) 1254?-1324?, Italian traveler and author.

Ma·rie An·toi·nette (mə rē' än'twə nĕt') 1755-93, queen of France, wife of Louis XVI; guillotined.

Mark An·to·ny (märk än'tə nē) 83-30 B.C., Roman ruler and general.

Mark Twain (märk'twän') name used in the writings of Samuel Clemens, 1835-1910, U.S. humorist and author.

Mar·quette (mär kĕt'), **Jacques** (zhäk) 1637-75, French missionary and explorer in America, led an expedition with Louis Jolliet down the Mississippi River to the mouth of the Arkansas River in SE Arkansas (1673).

Mar·shall (mär'shəl), **George Catlett** 1880-1959, U.S. general and statesman. —**John** 1755-1835, U.S. statesman and judge, chief justice of the U.S. Supreme Court (1801-35).

Marx (märks), **Karl** (kärl) 1818-83, German political philosopher and socialist.

Mary Stu·art (stōō'ərt) 1542-87, queen of Scotland (1542-67); beheaded.

Mas·sa·soit (măs'ə soit', măs ə sō'ĭt) 1580?-1661, American Indian chief in Massachusetts, friend of the Pilgrims.

Max·i·mil·i·an (măk'sə mĭl'ē ən) 1832-67, emperor of Mexico (1864-67), sent by Napoleon III; executed by revolutionaries.

Max·well (măks'wĕl'), **James Clerk** (klärk) 1831-79, Scottish physicist and astronomer, made important discoveries in magnetism.

Mc·Clel·lan (mə klĕl'ən), **George** 1826-85, Union general in the Civil War, a defeated presidential candidate (1864).

Mc·Cor·mick (mə kôr'mĭk), **Cyrus** (sī'rəs) 1809-84, U.S. inventor of the reaping machine.

Mc·Kin·ley (mə kĭn'lē), **William** 1843-1901, 25th President of the United States (1897-1901); assassinated.

Meade (mēd), **George** 1815-72, Northern general in the Civil War.

Me·di·ci (mĕd'ə chē') famous Italian family: **Cosimo** (kō zē'mō) 1389-1464. —**Lorenzo** (lə rĕn'zō), called the **Magnificent,** 1395-1440. —**Giulio** (jōō'lē ō) 1478?-1534. **Catherine** 1519-89.

Men·del (mĕn'dəl), **Gregor** (grĕg'ôr') 1822-84, Austrian monk and scientist, discovered laws of heredity.

Famous Persons

Men·de·ley·ev (měn′də lā′əf), **Dmitri** (də mē′trē) 1834-1907, Russian chemist, classified chemical elements. Also **Men′de·le′ev.**

Men·dels·sohn (měn′dəl sən), **Felix** 1809-47, German composer.

Mi·chel·an·ge·lo (mī′kəl ǎn′jə lō) 1475-1564, Italian sculptor, painter, and architect. Full name **Michelangelo Buonarroti** (bwŏn′ä rŏt′ē).

Mil·lay (mə lā′), **Edna St. Vincent** 1892-1950, U.S. poet.

Mil·ler (mǐl′ər), **Alfred Jacob** 1810-74, U.S. artist, painted Indians and trappers of the Rocky Mountains.

Mil·let (mē lā′), **Jean Francois** (zhän frän swä′), 1814-75, French painter.

Mil·li·kan (mǐl′ǐ kən), **Robert** 1868-1953, U.S. physicist.

Milne (mǐln), **Alan Alexander** 1882-1956, English poet and playwright, known for his books about "Winnie-the-Pooh."

Mil·ton (mǐl′tən), **John** 1608-74, English poet and political writer.

Mo·ham·med (mō hǎm′id) 570-632, Arabian prophet, founder of the Moslem religion. Also **Mahomet, Muhammed.**

Mo·liere (mō lyěr′) 1622-73, French actor and playwright.

Mon·roe (mən rō′), **James** 1758-1831, fifth President of the United States (1817-25).

Mont·calm (mŏnt kǎm′, mōn kälm′), **Marquis Louis de** (mär kē′lwē də) 1712-57, French general, defeated by the English General Wolfe in Quebec, Canada.

Mon·te·zu·ma II (mŏn′tə zōō′mə) 1479?-1520, last Aztec emperor of Mexico.

Moore (mōōr), **Thomas** 1779-1852, Irish poet.

Mor·gan (môr′gən), **Sir Henry** 1635?-88, English buccaneer, raided the Spanish Main. —**John Pierpont** (per′pŏnt′) 1837-1913, U.S. financier, art collector, and philanthropist.

Mor·ris (môr′əs) **Gouverneur** (gŭv′ər nir′) 1752-1816, statesman and diplomat during the American Revolution.

Morse (môrs), **Samuel** 1791-1872, U.S. inventor and artist, made the first telegraph instrument.

Mo·zart (mō′tsärt′), **Wolfgang Amadeus** (vôlf′gäng′ ä′mə dā′əs) 1756-91, Austrian composer.

Mu·ham·med (mə hǎm′əd) See **Mohammed.**

Muir (myōōr), **John** 1838-1914, U.S. naturalist, born in Scotland.

Mus·so·li·ni (mōō′sə lē′nē, mũs′ə lē′nē), **Benito** (bə-nē′tō) 1883-1945, Italian dictator (1922-45); executed.

N

Nan·sen (nän′sən), **Fridtjof** (frit′yôf′) 1861-1930, Norwegian arctic explorer, zoologist, statesman, and humanitarian.

Na·po·le·on I (nə pō′lē ən) 1769-1821, military leader, emperor of France (1804-15). Also **Napoleon Bonaparte.** —**Napoleon III** 1808-73 [**Louis Napoleon** (lwē)], emperor of France (1852-70).

Nas·ser (nä′sər, nǎs′ər), **Gamal Abdel** (gä′mäl′äb′dəl) born 1918, Egyptian chief of state (1954-), president of the United Arab Republic (1958-).

Na·tion (nā′shən), **Carrie** 1846-1911, U.S. temperance leader.

Ne·fer·ti·ti (něf′ər tē′tē) 14th-century B.C. Egyptian queen.

Neh·ru (nâr′ōō), **Jawaharlal** (jə wä′hər läl′) 1889-1964, Indian leader and statesman, first prime minister (1947-64); called **Pan′dit Neh′ru** (pŭn′dit).

Nel·son (něl′sən), **Lord** 1758-1805, **Viscount Horatio,** British admiral, killed at the battle of Trafalgar, off the SW coast of Spain.

Ne·ro (nir′ō) 37-68 A.D., emperor of Rome (54-68), committed suicide. Original name, **Lucius Domitius Ahenobarbus** (ā ē′nō bâr′bəs).

New·man (nōō′mən, nū′mən), **John Henry** 1801-90, English cardinal, theologian, and writer.

New·ton (nōō′tən, nū′tən), **Sir Isaac** 1642-1727, English scientist and mathematician, discovered laws of motion and gravitation.

Nich·o·las II (nik′ə ləs) 1868-1918, czar of Russia (1894-1917), executed by the Communists.

Nich·o·las, Saint (nik′ə ləs) fourth-century Christian prelate, patron of Russia and of children. To many he is **Santa Claus.**

Night·in·gale (nī′ting gāl′), **Florence** 1820-1910, English nurse born in Italy, pioneer of modern nursing.

Ni·jin·sky (nə jin′skē), **Vaslav** (vä släf′) 1890-1950, Russian ballet dancer.

Nix·on (nik′sən), **Richard** born 1913, U.S. lawyer and Vice-President (1953-61), a defeated presidential candidate (1960).

No·bel (nō běl′), **Alfred** 1833-96, Swedish industrialist and inventor, founder of the **Nobel Prizes,** annual awards in physics, chemistry, medicine, literature, and the advancement of world peace.

O

Of·fen·bach (ôf′ən bäk′), **Jacques** (zhäk) 1819-80, French composer, born in Germany.

O·gle·thorpe (ō′gəl thôrp′), **James Edward** 1696-1785, English philanthropist, colonial founder of Georgia.

O. Hen·ry (ō hěn′rē) name used in the writings of **William Porter** (pôr′tər), 1862-1910, U.S. short-story writer.

Ohm (ōm), **Georg Simon** (gyôrg si mōn′) 1787-1854, German physicist, made important discoveries in the field of electricity. The ohm, a unit of electric resistance, is named in his honor.

O·mar Khay·yam (ō′mär′kä yäm′) died 1123?, Persian poet, mathematician, and astronomer, wrote the "Rubaiyat" (rōō′bī ät′).

Op·pen·hei·mer (ŏp′ən hī′mər), **J. Robert** born 1904, U.S. physicist.

Ov·id (ŏv′id) 43 B.C.-18 A.D., Roman poet.

P

Pa·de·rew·ski (pǎd′ə rŏōōski), **Ignace** 1860-1941, Polish pianist and statesman, premier of Poland (1919).

Pa·ga·ni·ni (pǎg′ə nē′nē), **Nicolo** (nik′ə lō) 1782-1840, Italian violinist and composer.

Paine (pān), **Thomas** 1737-1809, American patriot, signer of the Declaration of Independence, born in England.

Par·a·cel·sus (pâr′ə sěl′səs) 1493-1541, Swiss scientist.

---

fāte, fǎt, fâre, fär; bē, bět; bīte, bǐt; nō, nŏt, nôr; fūse, fǔn, fûr; tōō, tōŏk; foil; foul; thin; ~~then~~; hw for wh as in *wh*at; zh for s as in u*s*ual; ə for a, e, i, o, u, as in ag*o*, lin*e*n, peri*l*, at*o*m, min*u*s

Famous Persons

Park·man (pärk′mən), **Francis** 1823-93, U.S. historian, author of books on the West.

Pas·teur (păs tûr′), **Louis** (lwē) 1822-95, French chemist, founder of modern bacteriology.

Pat·rick (pă′trĭk), **Saint** 389?-461?, Christian missionary and patron saint of Ireland.

Paul (pôl) died 67? A.D., the great Christian missionary to the Gentiles and author of many New Testament epistles. Also **Saint Paul.**

Paul VI (pôl) [**Giovanni Battista Montini** (jɔ vä′nē bä tēs′tä mōn tē′nē)] born 1897, pope (1963-   ).

Pea·ry (pēr′ē), **Robert** 1856-1920, U.S. arctic explorer, first to reach the North Pole (1909).

Penn (pĕn), **William** 1644-1718, English Quaker, founded Pennsylvania.

Per·ry (pĕr′ē), **Matthew** 1794-1858, U.S. naval commander, opened Japan to American commerce. **—Oliver** 1785-1819, U.S. naval commander, defeated the British on Lake Erie (1813).

Persh·ing (pûr′shĭng), **John Joseph** 1860-1948, U.S. General of the Armies.

Pe·trarch (pē′trärk′), **Francesco** (frän chĕs′kō) 1304-74, Italian poet and scholar.

Philip II (fĭl′əp) 1527-98, king of Spain (1556-98), king of Portugal (1580-98).

Pi·cas·so (pĭ kä′sō), **Pablo** (pä′blō) born 1881, Spanish painter and sculptor, active in France.

Pierce (pîrs), **Franklin** 1804-69, 14th President of the United States (1853-57).

Pitt (pĭt) **William** 1708-78, English statesman, prime minister (1766-68); called the **Great Commoner.**

Pi·us X (pī′əs) [**Giuseppe Sarto** (jɔ sĕp′ē sär′tō)] 1835-1914, pope (1903-14), canonized (1954). **—Pius XII** [**Eugenio Pacelli** (ĕ ōō jā′nē ō pä chĕl′ē)] 1876-1958, pope (1939-58).

Pi·zar·ro (pĭ zä′rō), **Francisco** (frän sēs′kō) 1471?-1541, Spanish conquistador, conquered Peru.

Pla·to (plā′tō) 427?-347 B.C., Greek philosopher.

Plu·tarch (plōō′tärk′) 46?-120? A.D., Greek biographer of famous Greeks and Romans.

Po·ca·hon·tas (pō′kɔ hŏn′tɔs) 1595?-1617, American Indian princess, daughter of Powhatan.

Poe (pō), **Edgar Allan** 1809-49, U.S. poet and short-story writer, wrote horror tales.

Polk (pōk), **James Knox** (nŏks) 1795-1849, eleventh President of the United States (1845-49).

Pom·pey (pŏm′pē) 106-48 B.C., Roman general and statesman.

Pon·ce de Le·ón (pŏn′sä dä lā ōn′) 1460?-1521, Spanish explorer, discovered Florida (1513).

Pon·ti·ac (pŏn′tē ăk′) died 1769, Ottawa Indian chief.

Pow·ha·tan (pou′ɔ tăn′) 1550-1618, Algonquian Indian chief in Virginia, father of Pocahontas.

Pro·kof·iev (prō kô′fē ĕf′), **Sergei** (sĕr gā′) 1891-1953, Russian composer. Also **Pro·kof′ieff.**

Ptol·e·my (tŏl′ɔ mē), **Claudius** (klô′dē ɔs) second-century A.D. Greek mathematician and geographer.

Puc·ci·ni (pōō chē′nē), **Giacomo** (jä′kɔ mō) 1858-1924, Italian operatic composer.

Pu·las·ki (pɔ lăs′kē), **Casimir** (kăz′mîr′) 1748?-79, Polish general, fought in the American Revolution.

Q

Que·zon (kā sōn′), **Manuel** (măn wĕl′) 1878-1944, Philippine statesman, first president (1935-44).

R

Ra·cine (ră sēn′), **Jean Baptiste** (zhän băp tēst′) 1639-99, French dramatist.

Ra·leigh (rô′lē), **Sir Walter** 1552?-1618, English courtier, navigator, and poet, founded a colony in Virginia, which did not survive.

Raph·a·el (răf′ē ɔl, rä′fē ɔl) 1483-1520, Italian painter.

Ra·vel (rɔ vĕl′), **Maurice** (mō rēs′) 1875-1937, French composer.

Rem·brandt (rĕm′brănt′) 1606-69, Dutch painter and etcher.

Re·noir (rĕn wär′), **Pierre** 1841-1919, French impressionist painter.

Re·vere (rɔ vēr′), **Paul** 1735-1818, patriot and silversmith during the American Revolution.

Rhodes (rōdz), **Cecil** 1853-1902, British colonial statesman and philanthropist, active in South Africa.

Rich·ard I (rĭch′ɔrd) 1157-99, king of England (1189-99). Also called **Coeur de Lion. —Richard III** 1452-85, king of England (1483-85); usurped the crown.

Ri·che·lieu (rĭ′shɔ lōō′, *French* rē shɔ lyü′), **Duc de** 1585-1642, French cardinal and statesman, prime minister (1624-42).

Ri·ley (rī′lē), **James Whitcomb** (hwĭt′kɔm) 1849-1916, U.S. poet.

Rim·sky-Kor·sa·kov (rĭm′skē kôr′sɔ kôf′), **Nikolai** (nĭk′ɔ lī′) 1844-1908, Russian composer.

Robes·pierre (rōbz′pyĕr′), **Maximilian de** (măk sɔ mē lyän′dɔ) 1758-94, a leader of the French Revolution, guillotined.

Rob·in·son (rŏb′ɔn sɔn), **Edwin Arlington** (är′lĭng tɔn) 1869-1935, U.S. poet.

Ro·cham·beau (rō shăm bō′), **Comte de** (kônt dɔ) 1725-1807, French marshal during the American Revolution.

Rock·e·fel·ler (rŏk′ɔ fĕl′ɔr), **John D.** 1839-1937, U.S. capitalist, made a fortune in oil. **—Nelson A(ldrich)** born 1908, governor of New York, grandson of John D.

Ro·din (rō dăn′), **Auguste** (ō gōōst′) 1840-1917, French sculptor.

Roent·gen (rŭnt′jɔn, rĕnt′gɔn), **Wilhelm** (vĭl′hĕlm′) 1845-1923, German physicist, discovered X rays.

Ro·gers (rŏj′ɔrz), **Will** 1879-1935, U.S. actor and humorist.

Roo·se·velt (rōz′ɔ vĕlt), **(Anna) Eleanor** 1884-1962, U.S. lecturer, writer, and diplomat, wife of Franklin Delano Roosevelt. **—Franklin Delano** (dĕl′ɔ nō′) 1882-1945, 32nd President of the United States (1933-45). **—Theodore** 1858-1919, 26th President of the United States (1901-09).

Ross (rôs), **Betsy** 1752-1836, American patriot, legendary maker of the first American flag.

Ru·bin·stein (rōō′bɔn stīn′), **Anton** (ăn′tŏn′) 1829-94, Russian pianist and composer.

Ruth (rōōth), ~~George Herman~~ 1895-1948, U.S. baseball player; known as **Babe Ruth.**

Ruth·er·ford (rŭth′ɔr fɔrd), **Sir Ernest** 1871-1937, English physicist, first to propose that atoms consist of a nucleus and outer electrons.

S

Saint-Gau·dens (sānt gō′dɔnz), **Augustus** 1848-1907, U.S. sculptor, born in Ireland.

Sal·a·din (săl′ɔ dɔn) 1137?-93, sultan of Egypt and Syria (1174?-93), fought the Crusaders.

Famous Persons

Salk (sôlk), **Jonas** born 1914, U.S. scientist in bacteriology, developed the first vaccine for preventing poliomyelitis.

Sand·burg (săn′bûrg′), **Carl** born 1878, U.S. poet and writer of biographies.

San·ta A·na (săn′tə än′ə), **Antonio** (ăn tō′nē ō) 1795-1876, Mexican general and president (1833-35, 1841-47, 1853-55). Also **San′ta An′na.**

Sar·gent (sär′jənt), **John Singer** 1856-1925, U.S. painter, born in Italy.

Schil·ler (shil′ər), **Johann von** (yō′hän′ fôn) 1759-1805, German poet and dramatist.

Schu·bert (shōō′bərt), **Franz** (fränts) 1797-1828, composer, born in Austria.

Schu·mann (shōō′män′), **Robert** 1810-56, German composer.

Schwei·tzer (shwīt′sər), **Albert** 1875-1965, French clergyman, physician, missionary, and musician.

Scott (skŏt), **General Winfield** 1786-1866, U.S. general, highest commander in the Mexican War. —**Sir Walter** 1771-1832, Scottish novelist and poet.

Sew·ard (sōō′ərd), **William** 1801-72, U.S. statesman, secretary of state (1861-69), proposed and completed the purchase of Alaska.

Shake·speare (shāks′pir′), **William** 1564-1616, English poet and dramatist. Also **Shak′spere, Shak′-speare.**

Shel·ley (shĕl′ē), **Percy Bysshe** (bĭsh) 1792-1822, English poet. —**Mary Wollstonecraft** (wōōl′stən kräft′) 1797-1851, English novelist, wife of Percy Bysshe.

Sher·i·dan (shĕr′ə dən), **Philip** 1831-88, Northern general in the Civil War, later promoted the destruction of the buffalo, so as to starve the Indians into peace.

Sher·man (shûr′mən), **William** 1820-91, Northern general in the Civil War.

Si·be·li·us (sĭ bā′lē əs), **Jean** (yän) 1865-1957, Finnish composer.

Sitting Bull 1834?-90, Sioux Indian leader, defeated Custer at the battle of Little Big Horn (1876).

Smith (smith), **Alfred** 1873-1944, U.S. political leader. —**Bessie** born 1894, U.S. jazz singer and song writer. —**Joseph** 1805-44, U.S. founder of the **Church of Jesus Christ of Latter-day Saints [Mormon Church** (môr′mən)]. —**Captain John** 1580-1631, English colonist in America.

Soc·ra·tes (sŏ′krə tēz′) 469?-399 B.C., Greek philosopher.

So·lon (sō′lən) 638?-559? B.C., Athenian lawmaker.

Sou·sa (sōō′zə), **John Philip** 1854-1932, U.S. band leader and composer.

Sta·lin (stä′lĭn), **Joseph** 1879-1953, Soviet political leader, chief of state (1924-53).

Stan·dish (stăn′dĭsh), **Miles** (mīlz) 1584?-1656, English soldier who voyaged with the Pilgrims to Plymouth and helped found the colony.

Stan·ley (stăn′lē), **Sir Henry** 1841-1904, British journalist and explorer in Africa.

Steu·ben (stōō′bən), **Baron Friedrich** (frē′drĭk) 1730-94, German general, served under Washington, became an American citizen (1783).

Ste·ven·son (stē′vən sən), **Adlai** (ăd′lā) 1900-65, U.S. lawyer and statesman. —**Robert Louis** 1850-94, Scottish novelist; active in the United States and Samoa.

Stowe (stō), **Harriet Beecher** (bē′chər) 1811-96, U.S. novelist, author of "Uncle Tom's Cabin."

Stra·di·va·ri (strä′dē vä′rē) family of Italian violin makers, especially **Antonio** (ăn tō′nē ō), 1644-1737. Also **Stra·di·va′ri·us** (străd′ə vĕr′ē əs).

Strauss (strous), **Johann** (yō′hän′) 1825-99, Austrian composer, called the **Waltz King.** —**Richard** (rĭ′kärt′) 1864-1949, German composer.

Stra·vin·ski (strə vĭn′skē), **Igor** (ē′gôr′) born 1882, U.S. composer, born in Russia.

Stu·art (stōō′ərt), **Gilbert** 1755-1828, U.S. painter. —**James** 1688-1766, Prince of Wales; called the **Old Pretender.** —**Mary** See **Mary Stuart.**

Stuy·ve·sant (stī′vəs ənt), **Peter** 1592-1672, last Dutch governor in America.

Sul·li·van, Sir Arthur See **Gilbert, Sir William S.**

Sun Yat-sen (sŭn′yăt′sĕn′) 1866-1925, Chinese political leader.

Swift (swift), **Jonathan** 1667-1745, English writer and satirist, born in Ireland, author of "Gulliver's Travels."

T

Taft (tăft), **William Howard** 1857-1930, 27th President of the United States (1909-13).

Tam·er·lane (tăm′ər lān′) 1336?-1405, Mongol conqueror. Also **Tam′bur·laine.**

Tark·ing·ton (tär′kĭng tən), **Booth** 1869-1946, U.S. novelist, author of several books for boys.

Tay·lor (tā′lər), **Zachary** (zăk′ə rē) 1784-1850, U.S. general, twelfth President of the United States (1849-50).

Tchai·kov·sky (chə kou′skē, chĭ kŏv′skē), **Pëtr Ilich** (pyŏtr il′yĭch′) 1840-93, Russian composer.

Te·cum·seh (tə kŭm′sə) 1768?-1813, Shawnee Indian chief, soldier, and statesman.

Ten·ny·son (tĕn′ə sən), **Alfred** 1809-92, first **Baron Tennyson,** English poet.

Thack·er·ay (thăk′ə rē), **William Makepiece** (māk′-pēs′) 1811-63, British novelist, born in India.

Thant (thänt), **U** (ōō) born 1909, diplomat, secretary-general of the United Nations (1961-   ), born in Burma.

Thomas á Beck·et (tŏm′əs ə bĕk′ət), **Saint** 1118?-70, English prelate, archbishop of Canterbury (1162-70).

Thomas Aquinas (tŏm′əs ə kwī′nəs) See **Aquinas, Saint Thomas.**

Tho·reau (thə rō′), **Henry** 1817-62, U.S. writer.

Ti·be·ri·us (tī bîr′ē əs) 42 B.C.-37 A.D., Roman emperor (14-37 A.D.).

Ti·tian (tĭsh′ən) 1477?-1576, Italian painter.

Ti·to (tē′tō) [**Josip Broz** (yō′sĭp brōz)] born 1892, Yugoslav leader, prime minister (1945-53), president (1953-   ).

Tol·stoy (tŏl′stoi′, tōl stoi′), **Count Leo** 1828-1910, Russian novelist and social reformer. Also **Tol·stoi.**

Tos·ca·ni·ni (tŏs′kə nē′nē), **Arturo** (är tōōr′ō) 1867-1957, Italian operatic and symphonic conductor, active in the United States.

Tra·jan (trā′jən) 53?-117, Roman emperor (98-117).

Trot·sky (trŏt′skē), **Leon** (lā ŏn′) 1879-1940, Russian

---

fāte, făt, fâre, fär; bē, bĕt; bite, bĭt; nō, nŏt, nôr; fūse, fŭn, fûr; tōō, tōŏk; foil; foul; thin; ~~then~~; hw for wh as in *wh*at; zh for s as in u*s*ual; ə for a, e, i, o, u, as in *a*go, lin*e*n, per*i*l, at*o*m, min*u*s

Famous Persons

Communist revolutionary and leader, banished (1929), murdered in Mexico.

Tru·man (trōō'mən), **Harry S.** born 1884, 33rd President of the United States (1945-53).

Tur·ner (tûr'nər), **Joseph** 1775-1851, English painter.

Tut·ankh·a·men (tōōt'ängk'ä'mən) 14th century B.C. Egyptian king. Also **Tut·ankh·a'mon.** Also called **King Tut.**

Twain, Mark (twān) See **Mark Twain.**

Ty·ler (tī'lər), **John** 1790-1862, tenth President of the United States (1841-45).

U

Und·set (ōōn'sĕt'), **Sigrid** (sĭg'rĭd) 1882-1949, Norwegian novelist.

V

Van Bu·ren (văn byōōr'ən), **Martin** 1782-1862, eighth President of the United States (1837-41).

Van·der·bilt (văn'dər bĭlt'), **Cornelius** 1794-1877, U.S. capitalist, made a fortune in railroads.

Van Gogh (văn gŏ'), **Vincent** 1853-90, Dutch painter.

Ve·ga (vā'gä), **Lope de** (lō pā'dā) 1562-1635, Spanish poet and dramatist.

Ve·las·quez (və läs'kwiz, və läs'kəs), **Diego** (dē ā'gō) 1599-1660, Spanish painter.

Ver·di (vĕr'dē), **Giuseppe** (jə sĕp'ē) 1813-1901, Italian composer of operas and church music.

Ver·meer (vər mir'), **Jan** (jän) 1632-75, Dutch painter.

Verne (vûrn), **Jules** 1828-1905, French writer, author of "Twenty Thousand Leagues Under the Sea."

Ver·ra·za·no (vĕr'ə zä'nō), **Giovanni da** (jə vän'ē dä) 1480?-1527?, Italian seafarer, discovered New York Bay. Also **Ver·raz·za'no.**

Ves·puc·ci (vĕs pōō'chē), **Amerigo** (ä mĕr'ē gō) 1451-1512, Italian navigator for whom America was named.

Vic·to·ri·a (vĭk tôr'ē ə) 1819-1901, queen of England (1837-1901).

Vil·la (vĭl'ə, vē'ə), **Francisco** (frän sēs'kō) 1877-1923, Mexican revolutionary chieftain; called **Pancho Villa** (pän'chō).

Vin·ci (vĭn'chē), **Leonardo da** (lā'ə när'dō dä) 1452-1519, Italian painter, sculptor, architect, and engineer.

Vir·gil (vûr'jəl) 70-19 B.C., Roman epic poet, author of the "Aeneid" (ə nē'ĭd).

Vol·taire (vōl târ') [Francois Arouet (frän swä' är wä')] 1694-1778, French philosopher, poet, historian, and dramatist.

Wag·ner (väg'nər), **Richard** (rĭ'kärt') 1813-83, German composer and music dramatist.

Wal·lace (wä'ləs), **Henry** 1888-1965, agriculture expert and administrator, U.S. Vice-President (1941-45), a defeated presidential candidate (1948).

Wal·ton (wôl'tən), **Izaak** (ī'zək) 1593-1683, English author and fishing enthusiast.

War·ren (wär'ən, wôr'ən), **Earl** born 1891, chief justice of the U.S. Supreme Court (1953-).

Wash·ing·ton (wôsh'ĭng tən, wäsh'-), **Booker T.** (bōōk'ər) 1856-1915, U.S. educator. —**George** 1732-99, American general and statesman in the American Revolution, first President of the United States (1789-97). —**Martha** 1731-1802, wife of George Washington.

Watt (wät), **James** 1736-1819, Scottish engineer and inventor, developed steam engines. The watt, a unit of electric power, is named in his honor.

Wayne (wān), **Anthony** 1745-96, American general in the American Revolution; called **Mad Anthony.**

Web·ster (wĕb'stər), **Daniel** 1782-1852, U.S. statesman and orator. —**Noah** 1758-1843, U.S. lexicographer.

Wedge·wood (wĕj'wōōd'), **Josiah** (jō sī'ə) 1730-95, English potter.

Wel·ling·ton (wĕl'ĭng tən), **Duke of** 1769-1852, **Arthur Wellesley,** British general and statesman born in Ireland, defeated Napoleon at Waterloo, Belgium (1815).

Wells (wĕlz), **H(erbert) G(eorge)** 1866-1946, English novelist and historian, author of science fiction.

Wes·ley (wĕs'lē), **John** 1703-91, English founder of the Methodist Church.

Whis·tler (hwĭs'lər), **James Abbott** 1834-1903, U.S. painter active in Paris and London.

Whit·man (hwĭt'mən), **Marcus** 1802-47, and his wife **Narcissa** (när sĭs'ə) 1808-47, U.S. missionary pioneers among the Indians in Oregon and Washington. —**Walt** 1819-92, U.S. poet.

Whit·ney (hwĭt'nē), **Eli** (ē'lī) 1765-1825, U.S. inventor of the cotton gin (1793).

Whit·ti·er (hwĭt'ē ər), **John Greenleaf** (grēn'lēf') 1809-92, U.S. poet.

Wil·liam I (wĭl'yəm) 1027?-87, **Duke of Normandy** (nôr'mən dē), king of England (1066-87); called **William the Conqueror.**

Wil·liams (wĭl'yəmz), **Roger** 1603?-83, American clergyman, born in England, founder of the Rhode Island colony.

Will·kie (wĭl'kē), **Wendell** 1892-1944, U.S. lawyer and political leader, a defeated presidential candidate (1940).

Wil·son (wĭl'sən), **Woodrow** 1856-1924, U.S. educator and statesman, 28th President of the United States (1913-21).

Win·throp (wĭn'thrəp), **John** 1588-1649, English colonist in New England, first governor of Massachusetts.

Wolfe (wōōlf), **James** 1727-59, British general, defeated the French under Montcalm at Quebec, Canada (1759).

Words·worth (wûrdz'wûrth'), **William** 1770-1850, English poet.

Wright (rīt), **Frank Lloyd** 1869-1959, U.S. architect. —**Orville** 1871-1948, and his brother **Wilbur** 1867-1912, U.S. pioneers in aviation.

Wyc·liffe (wĭk'lĭf'), **John** 1320?-84, English reformer and churchman, first translator of the entire Bible into English.

X

Xan·thip·pe (zăn tĭp'ē) wife of Socrates.

Xen·o·phon (zĕn'ə fən) 434?-355? B.C., Greek historian and military leader.

Xer·xes (zûrk'sēz') 519?-465 B.C., king of Persia (486-465 B.C.); called **Xerxes the Great.**

Y

Yeats (yāts), **William Butler** 1865-1939, Irish poet and dramatist.

Z

Zo·ro·as·ter (zôr'ō ăs'tər) sixth-century B.C. Persian prophet, founder of a religion.

Zwing·li (zwĭng'lē), **Ulrich** (ōōl'rĭk') 1481-1531, Swiss religious reformer.

Persons and Places in Mythology and Folklore

A

A·chil·les (ə kil′ēz) in the story of Troy, the foremost Greek hero of the Trojan War.

A·don·is (ə dŏn′əs) in Greek mythology, a beautiful youth beloved by Aphrodite.

Ae·ne·as (ə nē′əs) in classical legend, son of Venus and Priam, and hero of Virgil's poem, the **"Ae·ne′id"** (ə nē′id).

Aes·cu·la·pi·us (ĕs′kū lā′pē əs) in Roman mythology, the god of medicine and healing. He is identified with the Greek **As·cle·pi·us** (ə sklē′pē əs).

Ag·a·mem·non (ăg′ə mĕm′nŏn) in Greek legend, a Greek king, brother of Menelaus, and leader of the Greeks in the Trojan War. On his return from Troy he was killed by his wife, Clytemnestra.

A·jax (ā′jăks′) a Greek hero in the Trojan War.

A·lad·din (ə lăd′ən) in the "Arabian Nights," a boy who by rubbing his magic lamp could summon a jinni to do his bidding.

A·li Ba·ba (ăl′ē bä′bə) in the "Arabian Nights," a poor woodcutter who became rich by outwitting a band of forty thieves.

Am·a·zon (ăm′ə zŏn) in Greek legend, one of a group of female warriors who aided the Trojans in the Trojan War.

Am·mon (ăm′ən) ancient Egyptian god of life. Also **A′men**.

An·dro·cles (ăn′drə klēz′) in Roman legend, a slave whose life was spared by a lion from whose foot he had once drawn a thorn. Also **An′dro·clus** (-kləs).

An·drom·a·che (ăn drŏm′ə kē) in the legend of Troy, the wife of Hector.

An·drom·e·da (ăn drŏm′ə də) in Greek mythology, the daughter of Cassiopeia. Andromeda was rescued from a sea monster by Perseus, who then married her.

An·tig·o·ne (ăn tĭg′ə nē) in Greek legend, a daughter of Oedipus. Antigone was sentenced to death by her uncle for illegally burying her brother.

Aph·ro·di·te (ăf rə dī′tē) in Greek mythology, the goddess of love and beauty, identified with the Roman Venus.

A·pol·lo (ə pŏl′ō) in Greek and Roman mythology, the god of music, poetry, prophecy, and medicine.

Ar·es (âr′ēz) in Greek mythology, the god of war. He is identified with the Roman Mars.

Ar·go·naut (är′gə nôt′) in Greek legend, any one of the men who sailed with Jason to find the Golden Fleece.

Ar·gus (är′gəs) in Greek mythology, a monster with a hundred eyes, who guarded the Golden Fleece.

Ar·i·ad·ne (ăr′ē ăd′nē) in Greek mythology, daughter of Minos, King of Crete. Ariadne gave Theseus a ball of thread to guide him out of the Labyrinth.

Ar·te·mis (är′tə məs) in Greek mythology, goddess of the moon and of the hunt, and twin sister of Apollo. She is identified with the Roman Diana.

Ar·thur (är′thər) legendary sixth-century king of the Britons; hero of the Round Table.

As·gard (ăs′gärd′) in Norse mythology, the home of the gods and the heros slain in battle.

As·tar·te (ə stär′tē) in Phoenician mythology, the goddess of love, identified with the Greek Aphrodite.

A·the·na (ə thē′nə) in Greek mythology, the goddess of wisdom and of women's arts and crafts, identified with the Roman Minerva. Also **A·the′ne** (-nē).

At·las (ăt′ləs) in Greek mythology, a Titan forced to bear the heavens on his shoulders.

Au·ro·ra (ô rôr′ə) Roman goddess of the dawn.

B

Bac·chus (băk′əs) in classical mythology, the god of wine, identified with the Greek Dionysus.

ban·shee (băn′shē′) in the folklore of Ireland and Scotland, a spirit whose wailing was believed to foretell death.

Bunyan, Paul See Paul Bunyan.

C

Cal·li·o·pe (kə lī′ə pē′) in Greek mythology, the Muse of eloquence and heroic poetry.

Ca·lyp·so (kə lĭp′sō) in Greek legend, a sea nymph who kept Ulysses on her island for seven years.

Cas·san·dra (kə săn′drə) in Greek legend, a daughter of King Priam of Troy. She was endowed with the gift of prophecy, but was never believed by anyone.

Cas·si·o·pe·ia (kăs′ē ō pē′ə) in Greek mythology, the mother of Andromeda.

Cas·tor and Pol·lux (kăs′tər ənd pŏl′əks) in Greek mythology, twin sons of Leda and Zeus.

cen·taur (sĕn′tôr′) in Greek mythology, a creature that is half man and half horse.

Cer·ber·us (sûr′bər əs) in classical mythology, the three-headed dog guarding the gates of Hades.

Ce·res (sĭr′ēz) in Roman mythology, the goddess of vegetation, identified with the Greek Demeter.

Char·on (kâr′ən) in Greek mythology, the boatman who ferried the souls of the dead over the river Styx to Hades.

Chi·ron (kī′rŏn′) in Greek mythology, a wise centaur, teacher of Achilles and other Greek heroes.

Cir·ce (sûr′sē) in the story of Ulysses, an enchantress who changed the companions of Ulysses into swine by means of a magic drink.

Cly·tem·nes·tra (klī′təm nĕs′trə) in Greek legend, the wife of Agamemnon. She killed her husband on his return from the Trojan War, and was later killed by her son, Orestes.

Cu·pid (kū′pĭd) in Roman mythology, the god of love and son of Venus. He is identified with the Greek Eros.

Cy·clops (sī′klŏps′) in the story of Ulysses, one of a group of one-eyed giants.

D

Daed·a·lus (dĕd′ə ləs) in Greek legend, a great creator and inventor who devised, among other things, the wings of Icarus.

Dam·o·cles (dăm′ə klēz) in Greek legend, a courtier who was made to sit at a banquet under a sword suspended by a single hair.

Daph·ne (dăf′nē) in Greek mythology, a nymph who escaped from Apollo by changing into a laurel tree.

De·me·ter (də mē′tər) in Greek mythology, the goddess of agriculture, fertility, and marriage. She is identified with the Roman Ceres.

Di·an·a (dī ăn′ə) in Roman mythology, the goddess of the moon and of the hunt. She is identified with the Greek Artemis.

---

fāte, făt, fâre, fär; bē, bĕt; bīte, bĭt; nō, nŏt, nôr; fūse, fŭn, fûr; tōō, tŏŏk; foil; foul; thin; ~~then~~;
hw for wh as in *wh*at; zh for s as in u*s*ual; ə for a, e, i, o, u, as in *a*go, lin*e*n, per*i*l, at*o*m, min*u*s

Persons and Places in Mythology and Folklore

Di·do (dī′dō) in Roman legend, a queen who fell in love with Aeneas and stabbed herself to death when he left her.

Di·o·ny·sus (dī′ə nī′səs) in Greek mythology, a son of Zeus and god of wine and fertility. He is identified with the Roman Bacchus.

E

Ech·o (ĕk′ō) in Greek mythology, a nymph who, because of her love for Narcissus, pined away until only her voice remained.

Elaine of Astolat (ē lān′ əv ăs′tə lät′) in the story of King Arthur, a young girl who died of a broken heart when Lancelot ignored her love.

E·lec·tra (ĭ lĕk′trə) in Greek legend, a daughter of Agamemnon and Clytemnestra. Electra induced her brother, Orestes, to kill her mother for murdering her father.

Er·os (ĭr′ŏs′, ĕr′ŏs′) in Greek mythology, god of love and son of Aphrodite. He is identified with the Roman Cupid.

Eu·men·i·des (yōō mĕn′ə dēz′) in Greek mythology, the avenging Furies.

Eu·ryd·i·ce (yōō rĭd′ə sē) wife of Orpheus.

F

Fates (fāts) in classical mythology, the three goddesses who controlled human destiny.

Frey·a (frā′ə) in Norse mythology, the goddess of love.

Fu·ries (fyōōr′ēz) in Greek and Roman mythology, the three goddesses who avenge crimes previously unpunished.

G

Gae·a (jē′ə) in Greek mythology, the wife of Uranus and mother of the Titans.

Gal·a·had (găl′ə hăd′) in a later story of King Arthur, the noblest and purest knight of the Round Table, who was successful in his quest of the Holy Grail.

Gal·a·te·a (găl′ə tē′ə) in Greek mythology, an ivory statue of a maiden brought to life by Aphrodite after the sculptor, Pygmalion, had fallen in love with it.

Gan·y·mede (găn′ə mēd′) in Greek mythology, a beautiful youth whom Zeus carried to Olympus to be his cupbearer.

Ga·wain (gə wān′, gä′wən) in Arthurian legend, a knight of the Round Table, nephew of King Arthur.

gob·lin (gŏb′lĭn) in fable or myth, an evil or mischievous spirit having the form of an ugly, grotesque dwarf.

Golden Fleece in Greek legend, a fleece of gold guarded by a sleepless dragon. It was carried away by Jason and the Argonauts with the help of Medea.

Gor·gon (gôr′gən) in Greek mythology, any one of three sisters, of whom Medusa is best known, whose appearance was so terrifying that any person who looked at them was turned to stone.

Grail (grāl) in medieval legend, the cup used by Christ at the Last Supper. Also **Holy Grail.**

grif·fin or **grif·fon** (grĭf′ĭn) mythical monster with the head and wings of an eagle and the body of a lion.

Guin·e·vere (gwĭn′ə vĭr′, -vər) in the story of King Arthur, wife of King Arthur. She fell in love with Lancelot.

H

Ha·des (hā′dēz) in Greek mythology, ruler of the world of the dead, and a brother of Zeus; Pluto; also, his realm.

Har·py (här′pĭ) in Greek mythology, one of several filthy, winged monsters who are part woman and part bird. **Har·pies.**

He·be (hē′bē) in Greek mythology, the goddess of youth and cupbearer to the gods.

Hec·a·te (hĕk′ə tē, *also* hĕk′ət) in Greek mythology, the goddess of the underworld. She was later associated with sorcery.

Hec·tor (hĕk′tər) in the story of Troy, a Trojan hero killed by Achilles. He was the son of Priam and Hecuba.

Hec·u·ba (hĕk′yə bə) in the story of Troy, the wife of Priam and mother of Hector, Paris, Cassandra, and others.

Hel·en of Troy (hĕl′ən əv troi′) in Greek mythology, the beautiful wife of Menelaus, a Greek king. Her elopement with Paris caused the Trojan War.

He·li·os (hē′lē ŏs′) in Greek mythology, the sun god who drove his chariot across the sky.

Hel·las (hĕl′əs) Greece.

Henry, John See **John Henry.**

He·ra (hĭr′ə) in Greek mythology, the queen of the gods, sister and wife of Zeus, and goddess of marriage. She is identified with the Roman Juno.

Her·a·cles (hĕr′ə klēz′) Hercules.

Her·cu·les (hûr′kyə lēz′) in Greek and Roman mythology, a son of Jupiter known for his great strength and for his performance of twelve gigantic tasks imposed on him by Juno.

Her·mes (hûr′mēz′) in Greek mythology, the messenger of the gods. He is identified with the Roman Mercury.

He·ro (hĭr′ō) in Greek legend, a priestess of Aphrodite, whose lover, Leander, nightly swam the strait between Turkey and Greece to join her.

Hes·per·i·des (hĕs pĕr′ə dēz) in Greek mythology, the nymphs who guarded the golden apples of Hera.

Holy Grail See **Grail.**

Hy·dra (hī′drə) in Greek mythology, a nine-headed sea serpent that grew two heads for each one cut off, but was finally subdued by Hercules with a firebrand.

Hy·ge·ia (hī jē′ə) in Greek mythology, the goddess of health. She is the daughter of Aesculapius.

Hy·men (hī′mən) in Greek mythology, the god of marriage.

Hy·per·i·on (hī pĭr′ē ən) **1** in Greek mythology, the son of Uranus and the father of Helios. **2** in the story of Troy, Helios himself. **3** in later times, Apollo.

Hyp·nos (hĭp′nŏs′) in Greek mythology, the god of sleep. He is identified with the Roman Somnus.

I

Ic·a·rus (ĭk′ə rəs) in Greek legend, the son of Daedalus, who escaped from Crete by flying with wings made by his father. He flew so near the sun that it melted the wax fastening his wings, and he fell into the sea and drowned.

Iph·i·ge·ni·a (ĭf′ə jə nī′ə) in Greek legend, the daughter of Agamemnon, who offered her as a sacrifice to Artemis. The goddess permitted her to live.

I·ris (ī′rĭs) in Greek mythology, the goddess of the rainbow, and in the story of Troy, the messenger of the gods.

I·seult (ē sōōlt′) in the story of King Arthur, wife of King Mark of Cornwall. She was beloved by Tristram.

I·sis (ī′sĭs) in Egyptian mythology, the goddess of love and fertility. She was sometimes identified with Astarte.

852

Persons and Places in Mythology and Folklore

Ith·a·ca (ĭth'ə kə) an island of Greece, and in Greek mythology the home of Odysseus.

J

Ja·nus (jā'nəs) in Roman mythology, the god of portals, able to look into the past and future. He is usually represented with two heads.

Ja·son (jā'sən) in Greek legend, the hero who led the Argonauts in search of the Golden Fleece.

John Hen·ry (jŏn' hĕn'rĭ) in American folklore, a Negro railroad worker of unusually great strength.

Jove (jōv) Jupiter.

Ju·no (jōō'nō') in Roman mythology, the goddess of marriage, wife of Jupiter, and queen of the gods, identified with the Greek Hera.

Ju·pi·ter (jōō'pə tər) in Roman mythology, the ruler of gods and men, identified with the Greek Zeus; Jove.

L

Lab·y·rinth (lăb'ə rĭnth') in Greek mythology, a maze in Crete inhabited by the Minotaur.

Lan·ce·lot (lăns'ə lŏt') in Arthurian legend, the bravest and ablest knight of the Round Table.

Le·an·der (lē ăn'dər) in Greek legend, the lover of Hero.

Le·da (lē'də) in Greek mythology, the beloved of Zeus and mother of Helen of Troy and Castor and Pollux.

lep·re·chaun (lĕp'rə kôn') in Irish folklore, an elf, usually in the form of a little old man, who knows of hidden treasure.

Lo·ki (lō'kĭ) in Norse mythology, a God who took delight in wickedness and mischief.

M

Mars (märz) in Roman mythology, the god of war. He is identified with the Greek Ares.

Me·du·sa (mə dōō'sə, mə dū'sə) in Greek mythology, one of the Gorgons killed by Perseus.

Mel·pom·e·ne (mĕl pŏm'ə nē) in Greek mythology, the Muse of tragedy.

Men·e·la·us (mĕn'ə lā'əs) in Greek legend, a king of Sparta, brother of Agamemnon and husband of Helen of Troy.

Mer·cu·ry (mûr'kyə rē) in Roman mythology, the messenger of the gods, who presided over commerce, skill of hand, or quickness of wit.

Mer·lin (mûr'lən) in medieval legends, especially those of King Arthur, a magician and prophet.

mer·maid (mûr'mād') imaginary creature with the head and upper body of a woman and the tail of a fish.

Mi·das (mī'dəs) in Greek legend, a king who had the power to turn anything he touched into gold.

Mi·ner·va (mĭ nûr'və) in Roman mythology, the goddess of wisdom who presided over useful and ornamental arts. She is identified with the Greek Athena.

Mi·nos (mī'nŏs') in Greek mythology, a king and lawgiver of Crete; a son of Zeus.

Min·o·taur (min'ə tôr') in Greek mythology, a monster, half man and half bull, confined by Minos to the Labyrinth.

Mne·mos·y·ne (nə mŏs'ə nē) in Greek mythology, the goddess of memory and mother of the Muses.

Mo·dred (mō'drəd) in Arthurian legend, the treacherous nephew of King Arthur, who was killed in a battle with Arthur, but left Arthur with a mortal wound. Also spelled **Mor·dred** (môr'drəd).

Mor·gan le Fay (môr'gən lə fā') in Arthurian legend, the king's half sister, an enchantress.

Mor·phe·us (môr'fē əs) in Greek mythology, the god of dreams.

Muse (mūz) in Greek mythology, any one of the nine goddesses who presided over music, poetry, history, astronomy, etc.

Myr·mi·don (mûr'mə dŏn') in Greek legend, one of a band of warriors who followed Achilles in the Trojan War.

N

nai·ad (nā'ăd', nī'ăd') [pl. **nai·ads** or **nai·a·des** (-ə dēz)] in classical mythology, one of the nymphs supposed to live in fountains, rivers, lakes, etc.

Nem·e·sis (nĕm'ə sis) in Greek mythology, the goddess of justice or vengeance.

Nep·tune (nĕp'tōōn', nĕp'tūn') in Roman mythology, the god of the sea. He is identified with the Greek Poseidon.

Ne·re·id (nir'ē ĭd) in Greek mythology, one of the fifty sea nymphs, daughters of the sea god, **Ne·re·us** (nir'ē əs), who attended Poseidon.

Ni·ke (nī'kē) in Greek mythology, the goddess of victory, usually represented as a winged figure bearing a wreath and palm branch.

O

O·din (ō'dən) in Germanic mythology, the supreme god and the ruler of all the other gods.

O·dys·seus (ō dis'ē əs) Greek name for Ulysses.

Oed·i·pus (ĕ'də pəs, ĕd'ə pəs) in Greek legend, a king who unknowingly killed his father and married his mother.

O·lym·pus (ō lim'pəs) the highest mountain in Greece, and in Greek mythology, the home of the most important gods.

O·res·tes (ōr ĕs'tēz) in Greek legend, the son of Agamemnon and Clytemnestra. Orestes, induced by his sister Electra, killed his mother for murdering his father.

Or·phe·us (ōr'fē əs) in Greek legend, a musician whose music charmed even rocks and trees. When he descended into Hades to seek release of his wife, Eurydice, Pluto permitted him to lead her back provided he would not look at her on the way. He did look, however, and she was forced to return.

P

Pan (păn) in Greek mythology, a god of forests, flocks, and shepherds, shown as having the legs, hoofs, and horns of a goat. He is identified with the Roman Faunus.

Par·is (păr'is, pâr'is) in Greek mythology, the son of Priam and Hecuba, who carried Helen off to Troy, thereby causing the Trojan War.

Par·nas·sus (pär năs'əs) mountain in ancient Greece sacred to Apollo and the Muses.

Paul Bun·yan (pôl' bŭn'yən) in American folklore, a lumberjack hero, noted for his superhuman size and strength.

Peg·a·sus (pĕg'ə səs) in Greek mythology, a winged horse, the steed of the Muses.

---

fāte, făt, fâre, fär; bē, bĕt; bīte, bit; nō, nŏt, nôr; fūse, fŭn, fûr; tōō, tŏŏk; foil; foul; thin; ᵗhen; hw for wh as in *wh*at; zh for s as in u*s*ual; ə for a, e, i, o, u, as in *a*go, lin*e*n, per*i*l, at*o*m, min*u*s

Persons and Places in Mythology and Folklore

Per·ci·val (pûr'sə vəl) in Arthurian legend, a knight of the Round Table, who together with Sir Galahad succeeded in the search for the Holy Grail.

Per·seph·o·ne (pər sĕf'ə nē) in Greek mythology, a daughter of Zeus and Demeter, who was abducted by Pluto and became queen of the Underworld. She is identified with the Roman Proserpina.

Per·seus (pûr'sē əs, pûr'sōōs') in Greek mythology, a son of Zeus and a mortal, who slew Medusa and saved Andromeda from a sea monster.

Phil·o·mel (fil'ə mĕl') in Greek mythology, an Athenian princess who was changed into a nightingale.

Phoe·be (fē'bē) in Greek mythology, one of the names for Artemis.

phoe·nix (fē'niks) in ancient legend, a beautiful bird said to live over 500 years and then, after setting fire to itself, to arise, young and beautiful, from its own ashes.

Ple·ia·des (plē'ə dēz') *pl.* [*sing.* **Ple·iad**] in Greek mythology, the seven daughters of Atlas who were transformed into a group of stars.

Plu·to (plōō'tō) in classical mythology, the god of the underworld.

Po·sei·don (pə si'dən) in Greek mythology, the god of the sea. He is identified with the Roman Neptune.

Pri·am (pri'əm) in Greek legend, the king of Troy during the Trojan War, husband of Hecuba, and father of Paris, Hector, Cassandra, and many other children.

Pro·me·the·us (prə mē'thē əs) in Greek mythology, a Titan who stole fire from heaven and taught man how to use it. Zeus punished him with eternal torture.

Pro·ser·pi·na (prō sûr'pə nə) or **Pros·er·pine** (prŏs'ər pin, prə sûr'pə nē) in Roman mythology, a daughter of Jupiter and Ceres, who was abducted by Pluto. She is identified with the Greek Persephone.

Pro·te·us (prō'tē əs) in Greek mythology, a sea god who had prophetic powers and could change his shape at will.

Psy·che (si'kē) in classical mythology, a beautiful maiden beloved by Cupid. She is a symbol for the human soul.

Pyg·ma·li·on (pig māl'ē ən) in Greek legend, a sculptor of ancient Cyprus who fell in love with the statue he carved of Galatea.

R

Ra (rä) in Egyptian mythology, the god of the sun; the supreme diety. Also **Re** (rä).

Re·mus (rē'məs) in Roman legend, the twin brother of Romulus, by whom he was slain.

Rom·u·lus (rŏm'yə ləs) in Roman mythology, the son of Mars and founder of Rome, who together with his twin brother Remus was reared by a she-wolf.

Round Table 1 in medieval legend, a table at which King Arthur and his knights sat. **2** King Arthur and his knights.

S

Sat·urn (săt'ərn) Roman god of agriculture.

Sieg·fried (sēg'frēd, sig'frēd') hero of several Germanic legends with many different versions, and a principal character in some of Richard Wagner's operas.

Som·nus (sŏm'nəs) in Roman mythology, the god of sleep, identified with the Greek Hypnos.

sphinx (sfingks) in Egyptian and Greek legend, a monster with a human head and a lion's body.

Styx (stĭks) in Greek mythology, the principal river of Hades and Tartarus.

T

Tar·ta·rus (tär'tər əs) in Greek mythology, the deep abyss below Hades into which Zeus hurled the Titans who had rebelled against his authority.

The·seus (thē'sē əs) in Greek mythology, a king of Athens, famous for his defeat of the Minotaur in the Labyrinth.

The·tis (thē'tis) in Greek mythology, a Nereid and the mother of Achilles.

Thor (thôr) in Norse mythology, the god of war, thunder, and strength, for whom Thursday was named.

Ti·tan (ti'tən) in Greek mythology, a race of giant gods such as Atlas and Jupiter. They were the children of Gaea and Uranus.

Tris·tram (tris'trəm) knight of King Mark of Cornwall, who had a tragic love affair with Mark's wife, Iseult, after taking a magic love potion.

Troi·lus (troi'ləs) in Greek mythology, a son of Priam, slain by Achilles.

Tro·jan (trō'jən) one of the people of Troy.

Trojan horse in the story of Troy, a huge wooden horse filled with Greek soldiers and taken inside Troy's walls by the Trojans, who thought the gods had sent it to help them. Once inside the walls, the Greeks destroyed the city.

Trojan War the ten-year war between the Greeks and the Trojans, caused by the elopement of Helen, the wife of Menelaus, with Paris, a son of King Priam of Troy.

troll (trōl) in Scandinavian folklore, an ugly giant or, in later tales, an impish dwarf who was supposed to live in caves, hills, and such places.

U

U·lys·ses (ū lis'ēz) in Greek legend, king of Ithaca and a Greek leader in the Trojan War. Also called **Odysseus.**

u·ni·corn (ū'nə kôrn') legendary animal somewhat resembling a horse, usually represented as having one long horn on its forehead, the hind legs of an antelope, and the tail of a lion.

U·ra·nus (yōōr ā'nəs) in Greek mythology, the father of the Titans and the Cyclopes.

V

Val·hal·la (văl hăl'ə) in Norse mythology, the great hall of Odin, into which heroes slain in battle were brought by the Valkyries.

Val·ky·rie (văl kir'ē) in Norse mythology, one of Odin's warlike maidens who chose the fallen heroes from the battlefield and carried them to Valhalla.

vam·pire (văm'pi'ər) corpse that is superstitiously believed to rise from its grave at night and suck the blood of sleeping persons.

W

were·wolf (wir'wŏŏlf', wâr'wŏŏlf') in folklore, a person who can assume the form of a wolf at will for murderous acts.

Y

Y·mir (ē'mir) in Norse mythology, a wicked giant, whose body was used by the gods to make the earth.

Z

Zeus (zōōs) in Greek mythology, the supreme deity; husband of Hera. He is identified with the Roman god Jupiter.

The Nations of the World

Name	Capital	Location	Joined United Nations
Afghanistan (ăf găn'ə stăn)	Kabul (kä bŏŏl')	Southwest Asia	1946
Albania (ăl bā'nǐ ə)	Tirana (tē rä'nə)	Southeastern Europe	1955
Algeria (ăl jǐr'ǐ ə)	Algiers (ăl jǐrz')	North Africa	1962
Andorra (ăn dôr'ə)	Andorra (ăn dôr'ə)	Europe between France and Spain	——
Angola (ăng gōl'ə)	Luanda (lŏŏ ăn'də)	Southwest Africa	
Argentina (är jĕn tē'nə)	Buenos Aires (bwā'nəs ī'rĭz)	Southeastern South America	†1945
Australia (ôs trāl'yə)	Canberra (kăn'bĕr ə)	South Pacific, southeast of Asia	†1945
Austria (ôs'trē ə)	Vienna (vē ĕn'ə)	Central Europe	1955
Belgium (bĕl'jəm)	Brussels (brŭs'əlz)	Western Europe	†1945
Bhutan (bŏŏ tän')	Punakha (pŏŏ nŭk'ə)	Asia between India and Tibet	——
Bolivia (bə lǐv'ǐ ə)	La Paz *and* Sucre (lä päz' *and* sŏŏ'krē)	West-central South America	†1945
Brazil (brə zǐl')	Brasilia (brə zǐl'ǐ ə)	Central and Northeast South America	†1945
Bulgaria (bŭl gâr'ǐ ə)	Sofia (sō'fǐ ə *or* sō fē'ə)	Eastern Europe	1955
Burma (bûr'mə)	Rangoon (răng gŏŏn')	Southeast Asia	1948
Burundi (bŏŏ rŏŏn'də)	Usumbura (ŏŏ'sŏŏm bŏŏr'ə)	Central Africa	1962
Cambodia (kăm bō'dǐ ə)	Phnom Penh (pnŏm' pĕn')	Southeast Asia	1955
Cameroun (kăm rŏŏn')	Yaoundé (yä'ŏŏn dā')	West Africa	1960
Canada (kăn'ə də)	Ottawa (ŏt'ə wə)	North America, north of United States	†1945
Central African Republic (sĕn'trəl ăf'rǐ kən rǐ pŭb'lǐk)	Bangui (bäng'gē)	Central Africa	1960
Ceylon (sǐ lŏn')	Colombo (kō lŏm'bō)	Indian Ocean, south of India	1955
Chad (chăd)	Fort Lamy (fôrt lä'mē)	North-central Africa	1960
Chile (chǐl'ē)	Santiago (săn tē ä'gō)	Western South America	†1945
China, People's Republic of (chǐ'nə)	Peking (Peiping) (pē'kǐng') (bā'pǐng')	Eastern Asia	——
China, Republic of (chǐ'nə)	Taipei, Taiwan (tī'pā, tī'wän)	Eastern Asia, China Sea	†1945
Colombia (kə lŭm'bǐ ə)	Bogota (bō'gə tä')	Northwestern South America	†1945
Congo Republic (kŏng'gō rǐ pŭb'lǐk)	Brazzaville (brăz'ə vǐl)	Central Africa	1960
Congo, Democratic Republic of the	Léopoldville (lā'ə pōld vǐl)	Central Africa	1960
Costa Rica (kŏs'tə rē'kə)	San José (săn'hō zā')	Central America	†1945
Cuba (kū'bə)	Havana (hə văn'ə)	Caribbean Sea	†1945
Cyprus (sī'prəs)	Nicosia (nǐ kō sē'ə)	Mediterranean Sea	1960
Czechoslovakia (chĕk'ə slō vä'kǐ ə)	Prague (präg)	Central Europe	†1945
Dahomey (də hō'mǐ)	Porto Novo (pôr'tō nō'vō)	West Africa	1960
Denmark (dĕn'märk)	Copenhagen (kō'pĕn hāg'ən)	Northern Europe	†1945
Dominican Republic (də mǐn'ǐ kən rǐ pŭb'lǐk)	Santo Domingo (săn'tō də ming'gō)	Caribbean Sea	†1945

†Charter Member of the United Nations

855

Name	Capital	Location	Joined United Nations
Ecuador (ek'wä dôr)	Quito (kētō)	Northwest South America	†1945
Egypt (see United Arab Republic)			
El Salvador (ĕl säl'vä dôr)	San Salvador (sän säl'vä dôr)	Central America	†1945
Ethiopia (ē thē ōp'ĭ ə)	Addis Ababa (ăd'ĭs äb'ə bə)	Eastern Africa	†1945
Finland (fĭn'lənd)	Helsinki (hĕl'sĭng kĭ)	Northeast Europe	1955
France (frăns)	Paris (păr'ĭs)	Western Europe	†1945
Gabon (gä bôn')	Libreville (lē'brə vēl')	West Africa	1960
Gambia (găm'bĭ ə)	Bathurst (băth'ûrst)	West Africa	1966
Germany (jûr'mə nĭ)		Northwest-central Europe	——
East Germany	East Berlin (ēst bûr lĭn')		
West Germany	Bonn (bŏn)		
Ghana (gä'nə)	Accra (ăk'rə)	West Africa	1957
Greece (grēs)	Athens (ăth'əns)	Southeast Europe	†1945
Guatemala (gwä'tə mä'lə)	Guatemala City (gwä'tə mä'lə sĭt'ĭ)	Central America	†1945
Guinea (gĭn'ĭ)	Conakry (kŏ'nä krē')	West Africa	1958
Guyana (gē ä'nə)	Georgetown (jôrj'toun)	Northeast South America	——
Haiti (hā'tĭ)	Port-au-Prince (pôrt'ō prĭns')	Caribbean Sea	†1945
Honduras (hŏn dōōr'əs)	Tegucigalpa (tā gōō'sē gäl'pä)	Central America	†1945
Hungary (hŭng'gə rĭ)	Budapest (bōō'də pĕst)	Central Europe	1955
Iceland (īs'lənd)	Reykjavik (rā'kyə vēk')	North Atlantic Ocean	1946
India (ĭn'dĭ ə)	New Delhi (nū dĕl'ĭ)	Southern Asia	†1945
Indonesia (ĭn'dō nē'zhə)	Jakarta (jə kär'tə)	Malay Archipelago, Southeast Asia	——
Iran (ĭ răn' *or* ĭ răn')	Tehran (tĕ'răn')	Southwest Asia, Middle East	†1945
Iraq (ĭ răk' *or* ē räk')	Baghdad (băg'dăd)	Southwest Asia, Middle East	†1945
Ireland (īr'lənd)	Dublin (dŭb'lĭn)	Western Europe, British Isles	1955
Israel (ĭz'rĭ əl)	Jerusalem (jə rōō'sə ləm)	Southwest Asia, Middle East	1949
Italy (ĭt'ə lĭ)	Rome (rōm)	Southern Europe	1955
Ivory Coast (ī'və rĭ kōst)	Abidjan (äb'ĭ jän')	West Africa	1960
Jamaica (jə mā'kə)	Kingston (kĭng' stŏn)	Caribbean Sea	1962
Japan (jə păn')	Tokyo (tō'kĭ ō)	North Pacific Ocean	1956
Jordan (jôr'dən)	Amman *and* Jerusalem (ăm măn' *and* jə rōō'sə ləm)	Southwest Asia, Middle East	1955
Kenya (kĕn'yə *or* kēn'yə)	Nairobi (nī rō'bĭ)	East Africa	1963
Korea, People's Democratic Republic of (North) (kô rē'ə)	Pyongyang (pyŭng'yäng')	Northeast Asia	——
Korea, Republic of (South) (kô rē'ə)	Seoul (sōl)	Northeast Asia	——
Kuwait (kōō wāt')	Kuwait (kōō wāt')	Southwest Asia, Arabian Peninsula	1963

†Charter Member of the United Nations

Name	Capital	Location	Joined United Nations
Laos (lä′ōs *or* louz)	Vientiane (vyän′tyän′)	Southeast Asia	1955
Lebanon (lĕb′ə nən)	Beirut (bā rōōt′)	Southwest Asia, Middle East	†1945
Liberia (lī bĭr′ĭ ə)	Monrovia (mŏn rō′vĭ ə)	West Africa	†1945
Libya (lĭb′ĭ ə)	Tripoli *and* Bengazi (trĭp′ə lĭ *and* bĕn gä′zē)	North Africa	1955
Luxembourg (lŭk′səm bûrg)	Luxembourg (lŭk′səm bûrg)	Europe between Germany and Belgium	†1945
Malagasy Republic (măl ə găs′ĭ rĭ pŭb′lĭk)	Tananarive (tä nä nä rēv′)	West Indian Ocean, east of Africa	1960
Malawi (mə lä′wē)	Zomba (zŏm′bə)	East Africa	1964
Malaysia (mə lā′zhə)	Kuala Lumpur (kwä′lä lōōm′pŏŏr)	Southeast Asia	1957
Maldive Islands (măl′ dīv)	Male (mä lā′)	Indian Ocean	1966
Mali (mä′lĭ)	Bamako (bä mä kō′)	Western Africa	1960
Malta (môl′tə)	Valletta (vä lĕt′ə)	Mediterranean Sea	1964
Mauritania (mô′rə tā′nĭ ə)	Nouakchott (nwŏk′shŏt)	West Africa	1961
Mexico (mĕk′sĭ kō)	Mexico City (mĕk′sĭ kō sĭt′ĭ)	North America	†1945
Mongolia (mŏng gō′lĭ ə)	Ulan Bator (ōō′län bä′tôr)	Central Asia	1961
Morocco (mə rŏk′ō)	Rabat (rə bät′)	North Africa	1956
Mozambique (mō′zəm bēk′)	Lourenço Marques (lō rĕn′sō mär′kəs)	East Africa	——
Muscat and Oman (mŭs′kăt and ō man′)	Muscat	Southwest Asia, Arabian Peninsula	——
Nepal (nə pôl′)	Katmandu (kät′män dōō′)	Asia between India and Tibet	1955
Netherlands (nĕth′ər ləndz)	Amsterdam (ăm′stər dăm)	Northwest Europe	†1945
New Zealand (nū zē′lənd)	Wellington (wĕl′ĭng tən)	South Pacific Ocean, east of Australia	†1945
Nicaragua (nĭk′ə rä′gwə)	Managua (mə nä′gwə)	Central America	†1945
Niger (nī′jər)	Niamey (nē′ä mā′)	Northwest-central Africa	1960
Nigeria (nī jĭr′ĭ ə)	Lagos (lä′gōs)	West Africa	1960
Norway (nôr′wā)	Oslo (ŏz′lō)	Northern Europe	†1945
Pakistan (păk′ə stăn)	Rawalpindi (rä′wŭl pĭn′dĭ)	Southern Asia	1947
Panama (păn′ə mä)	Panama (păn′ə mä)	Central America	†1945
Paraguay (păr′ə gwä *or* păr′ə gwī)	Asunción (ä sōōn syôn′)	East-central South America	†1945
Peru (pə rōō′)	Lima (lē′mə)	Western South America	†1945
Philippines (fĭl′ ə pēnz)	Quezon City (kā′sôn sĭt′ĭ)	Pacific Ocean, Malay Archipelago	†1945
Poland (pō′lənd)	Warsaw (wôr′sô)	East Europe	†1945
Portugal (pôr′chŏŏ′gəl)	Lisbon (lĭz′bən)	Western Europe	1955
Rhodesia (rō dē′zhə)	Salisbury (sôlz′ bĕr ē)	Southern Africa	——
Rumania (rōō mā′nĭ ə)	Bucharest (bōō′kə rĕst′)	East Europe	1955
Rwanda (rwän′ dä)	Kigali (kĭ găl′ĭ)	Central Africa	1962
Saudi Arabia (sä ōō′dĭ ə rä′bĭ ə)	Riyadh (rĭ yäd′)	Southwest Asia, Arabian Peninsula	†1945
Sénégal (sĕn′ə gôl′)	Dakar (dä kär′)	West Africa	1960
Sierra Leone (sĭ ĕr′ə lĭ ō′nĭ)	Freetown (frē′toun)	Northwest Africa	1961
Singapore (sĭng′ gə pōr)	Singapore (sĭng′ gə pōr)	Southeast Asia	1966

†Charter Member of the United Nations

Name	Capital	Location	Joined United Nations
Somalia (sō mä′lǐ ə)	Mogadishu (mŏg′ə dǐsh′ōō)	East Africa	1960
South Africa, Republic of (south ăf′ rǐ kə)	Pretoria *and* Capetown (prǐ tôr′ ǐ ə *and* kāp′ toun)	South Africa	†1945
Spain (spān)	Madrid (mə drǐd′)	Southwestern Europe	1955
Sudan (sōō dăn′)	Khartoum (kär tōōm′)	East Africa	1956
Sweden (swē′dən)	Stockholm (stŏk′hōlm)	Northern Europe	1946
Switzerland (swǐt′sər lənd)	Berne (bûrn)	West-central Europe	——
Syria (sǐr′ǐə)	Damascus (də măs′kəs)	Middle East	1961
Tanzania (tăn zä′nǐ ə)	Dar es Salaam (där′ĕs sə lăm′)	East Africa	1961
Thailand (tī′lănd)	Bangkok (băng′kŏk)	Southeast Asia	1946
Tibet (tǐ bĕt′)	Lhasa (lä′sə)	South-central Asia	——
Togo (tō′gō)	Lomé (lô′mä)	West Africa	1960
Trinidad & Tobago (trǐn′ ǐ dăd ; tō bā′ gō)	Port of Spain (pŏrt ŏv spän)	Caribbean Sea	1962
Tunisia (tōō nǐsh′ə)	Tunis (tōō′nǐs)	North Africa	1956
Turkey (tûr′kǐ)	Ankara (ăng′kə rə)	Asia and Europe	†1945
Uganda (ū găn′ də)	Entebbe (ĕn tĕb′ ə)	Central Africa	1962
Union of Soviet Socialist Republics (sō′vǐ ĕt sō′shə lǐst rǐ pŭb′lǐks)	Moscow (mŏs′kou *or* mŏs′kō)	Europe and Asia	†1945
Byelorussian S.S.R. (bəl′ə rŭsh′yən)	Minsk (mǐnsk)	Western Russia	†1945
Ukrainian S.S.R. (ū krān′ǐ ən)	Kiev (kē′ĕf)	Southwestern Russia	†1945
United Arab Republic (ū nī′tǐd ăr′əb rǐ pŭb′lǐk)	Cairo (kī′rō)	Northeast Africa and Middle East	1958
Egypt (ē′jǐpt)	Cairo (kī′rō)	Northeast Africa	(†1945)
United Kingdom of Great Britain and Northern Ireland (ū nī′tǐd kǐng′dəm)	London (lŭn′dən)	Western Europe, British Isles	†1945
United States of America (ū nī′tǐd stāts əv ə mĕr′ǐ kə)	Washington (wŏsh′ǐng tən)	Central North America	†1945
Upper Volta (ŭp′ər vôl′tə)	Ouagadougou (wä′gä dōō′gōō)	West Africa	1960
Uruguay (ūr′ə gwä *or* ūr′ə gwī)	Montevideo (mŏn′tə vǐ dā′ō)	Southeast South America	†1945
Vatican City (văt′ ǐ kən sǐt′ ǐ)	Vatican City (văt′ ǐ kən sǐt′ ǐ)	Southern Europe	——
Venezuela (vĕn′ə zwē′lə *or* vĕn′ə zwā′lə)	Caracas (kə răk′əs)	Northern South America	†1945
Vietnam, Democratic Republic of (North) (vē ĕt′näm′)	Hanoi (hä noi′)	Southeast Asia	——
Vietnam, Republic of (South)	Saigon (sī gŏn′)	Southeast Asia	——
Western Samoa (wĕs′ tərn sə mō′ ə)	Apia (ä pē′ ä)	Pacific Ocean	——
Yemen (yĕm′ən)	San'a (sŏn′ä)	Southwest Asia	1947
Yugoslavia (ū′gō slä′vǐ ə)	Belgrade (bĕl′grād′)	Central Europe	†1945
Zambia (zăm′bǐə)	Lusaka (lōō sä′kə)	Southern Africa	1964

†Charter Member of the United Nations

The States of the United States

Name	Abbr.	Capital	Became State DATE	Rank in Area	Rank in Population	State Flower
Alabama (ăl'ə băm'ə)	Ala.	Montgomery (mŏnt gŭm'ər ĭ)	1819	29	19	Goldenrod
Alaska (ə lăs'kə)	. . .	Juneau (jōō'nō)	1959	1	50	Forget-me-not
Arizona (ăr'ə zō'nə)	Ariz.	Phoenix (fē'nĭks)	1912	6	35	Cactus
Arkansas (är'kən sô)	Ark.	Little Rock (lĭt'əl rŏk)	1836	27	31	Apple Blossom
California (kăl'ə fôrn'yə)	Calif.	Sacramento (săk'rə měn'tō)	1850	3	2	Golden Poppy
Colorado (kŏl'ə răd'ō or kŏl'ə rä'dō)	Colo.	Denver (děn'vər)	1876	8	33	Columbine
Connecticut (kə nět'ə kət)	Conn.	Hartford (härt'fərd)	†1788	48	25	Mountain Laurel
Delaware (děl'ə wâr)	Del.	Dover (dō'vər)	†1787	49	46	Peach Blossom
Florida (flôr'ə də)	Fla.	Tallahassee (tăl'ə hăs'ĭ)	1845	22	10	Orange Blossom
Georgia (jôr'jə)	Ga.	Atlanta (ăt lăn'tə)	†1788	21	15	Cherokee Rose
Hawaii (hə wī'ĭ)	. . .	Honolulu (hŏn'ə lōō'lōō	1959	47	44	Red Hibiscus
Idaho (ī'də hō)	. . .	Boise (boi'zĭ)	1890	13	42	Syringa
Illinois (ĭl'ə noi' or ĭl'ə noiz')	Ill.	Springfield (sprĭng'fēld)	1818	24	4	Native Violet
Indiana (ĭn'dĭ ăn'ə)	Ind.	Indianapolis (ĭn'dĭ ən ăp'ə lĭs)	1816	38	11	Zinnia
Iowa (ī'ə wə)	. . .	Des Moines (də moin')	1846	25	24	Wild Rose
Kansas (kăn'zəs)	Kans.	Topeka (tə pē'kə)	1861	14	29	Sunflower
Kentucky (kən tŭk'ĭ)	Ky.	Frankfort (frängk'fərt)	1792	37	22	Goldenrod
Louisiana (lə wē'zē ăn'ə)	La.	Baton Rouge (băt'ən rōōzh')	1812	31	20	Magnolia
Maine (mān)	. . .	Augusta (ô gŭs'tə)	1820	39	36	White-pine Cone
Maryland (měr'ə lənd)	Md.	Annapolis (ə năp'ə lĭs)	†1788	42	21	Black-eyed Susan
Massachusetts (măs'ə chōō'sĭts)	Mass.	Boston (bôs'tən)	†1788	45	9	Arbutus (Trailing)
Michigan (mĭsh'ĭ gən)	Mich.	Lansing (lăn'sĭng)	1837	23	7	Apple Blossom
Minnesota (mĭn'ə sō'tə)	Minn.	St. Paul (sānt pôl')	1858	12	18	Showy Lady-slipper
Mississippi (mĭs'ə sĭp'ĭ)	Miss.	Jackson (jăk'sən)	1817	32	28	Magnolia
Missouri (mə zōōr'ĭ)	Mo.	Jefferson City (jěf'ər sən sĭt'ĭ)	1821	19	13	Hawthorn

†One of the Thirteen Original States.

Name	Abbr.	Capital	Became State DATE	Rank in Area	Rank in Population	State Flower
Montana (mŏn tăn'ə)	Mont.	Helena (hĕl'ə nə)	1889	4	41	Bitterroot
Nebraska (nə brăs'kə)	Nebr.	Lincoln (lĭng'kən)	1867	15	34	Goldenrod
Nevada (nə văd'ə *or* nə vä'də)	Nev.	Carson City (kär'sən sĭt'ĭ)	1864	7	49	Sagebrush
New Hampshire (nū hămp'shər)	N. H.	Concord (kŏng'kərd)	†1788	44	45	Purple Lilac
New Jersey (nū jûr'zĭ)	N. J.	Trenton (trĕn'tən)	†1787	46	8	Violet
New Mexico (nū mĕk'sə kō)	N. Mex.	Santa Fe (săn'tə fā')	1912	5	37	Yucca
New York (nū yôrk')	N. Y.	Albany (ôl'bə nĭ)	†1788	30	1	Rose
North Carolina (nôrth kăr'ə lī'nə)	N. C.	Raleigh (rô'lĭ)	†1789	28	12	Dogwood
North Dakota (nôrth də kō'tə)	N. Dak.	Bismarck (bĭz'märk)	1889	17	43	Prairie Rose
Ohio (ō hī'ō)	. . .	Columbus (kə lŭm'bəs)	1803	35	5	Scarlet Carnation
Oklahoma (ōk lə hō'mə)	Okla.	Oklahoma City (ōk lə hō'mə)	1907	18	27	Mistletoe
Oregon (ôr'ə gŏn *or* ôr'ə gən)	Ore.	Salem (sā'ləm)	1859	10	32	Oregon Grape
Pennsylvania (pĕn'səl vā'nĭ ə)	Pa.	Harrisburg (hăr'ĭs bûrg)	†1787	33	3	Mountain Laurel
Rhode Island (rōd ī'lənd)	R. I.	Providence (prŏv'ə dəns)	†1790	50	39	Violet (unofficial)
South Carolina (south kăr'ə lī'nə)	S. C.	Columbia (kə lŭm'bĭ ə)	†1788	40	26	Yellow Jasmine
South Dakota (də kō'tə)	S. Dak.	Pierre (pĭr)	1889	16	40	American Pasque-flower
Tennessee (tĕn'ə sē')	Tenn.	Nashville (năsh'vĭl)	1796	34	17	Iris
Texas (tĕk'səs)	Tex.	Austin (ôs'tən)	1845	2	6	Bluebonnet
Utah (ū'tô *or* ū'tä)	. . .	Salt Lake City (sôlt lāk sĭt'ĭ)	1896	11	38	Sego Lily
Vermont (vər mŏnt')	Vt.	Montpelier (mŏnt pēl'yər)	1791	43	47	Red Clover
Virginia (vər jĭn'yə)	Va.	Richmond (rĭch'mənd)	†1788	36	16	American Dogwood
Washington (wŏsh'ĭng tən)	Wash.	Olympia (ō lĭm'pĭ ə)	1889	20	23	Western Rhododendron
West Virginia (wĕst' vər jĭn'yə)	W. Va.	Charleston (chärlz'tən)	1863	41	30	Rhododendron
Wisconsin (wĭs kŏn'sən)	Wis.	Madison (măd'ə sən)	1848	26	14	Violet
Wyoming (wī ō'mĭng)	Wyo.	Cheyenne (shī ăn')	1890	9	38	Indian Paintbrush

†One of the Thirteen Original States.

The Presidents of the United States

Name	Term of Office	Party
1. George Washington	1789–1797	Federalist
2. John Adams	1797–1801	Federalist
3. Thomas Jefferson	1801–1809	Democratic-Republican†
4. James Madison	1809–1817	Democratic-Republican
5. James Monroe	1817–1825	Democratic-Republican
6. John Quincy Adams	1825–1829	Democratic-Republican
7. Andrew Jackson	1829–1837	Democrat
8. Martin Van Buren	1837–1841	Democrat
9. William Henry Harrison††	1841–1841	Whig†
10. John Tyler	1841–1845	Whig
11. James K. Polk	1845–1849	Democrat
12. Zachary Taylor††	1849–1850	Whig
13. Millard Fillmore	1850–1853	Whig
14. Franklin Pierce	1853–1857	Democrat
15. James Buchanan	1857–1861	Democrat
16. Abraham Lincoln††	1861–1865	Republican
17. Andrew Johnson	1865–1869	Republican
18. Ulysses S. Grant	1869–1877	Republican
19. Rutherford B. Hayes	1877–1881	Republican
20. James A. Garfield††	1881–1881	Republican
21. Chester A. Arthur	1881–1885	Republican
22. Grover Cleveland	1885–1889	Democrat
23. Benjamin Harrison	1889–1893	Republican
24. Grover Cleveland	1893–1897	Democrat
25. William McKinley††	1897–1901	Republican
26. Theodore Roosevelt	1901–1909	Republican
27. William Howard Taft	1909–1913	Republican
28. Woodrow Wilson	1913–1921	Democrat
29. Warren G. Harding††	1921–1923	Republican
30. Calvin Coolidge	1923–1929	Republican
31. Herbert C. Hoover	1929–1933	Republican
32. Franklin D. Roosevelt††	1933–1945	Democrat
33. Harry S. Truman	1945–1953	Democrat
34. Dwight D. Eisenhower	1953–1961	Republican
35. John F. Kennedy††	1961–1963	Democrat
36. Lyndon B. Johnson	1963–1969	Democrat
37. Richard M. Nixon	1969–	Republican

† This party, founded by Thomas Jefferson and named by him Republican, was later called Democratic-Republican; it became the Democratic party in 1828. The modern Republican party was established in 1854; the Whig party opposed the Democrats from about 1834–1856.

†† Died in Office.

The Provinces and Territories of Canada

Name	Capital	Name	Capital
Provinces			
Alberta	Edmonton	Prince Edward Island	Charlottetown
(ăl bûr'tə)	(ĕd'mən tən)	(prĭns ĕd'wərd ī'lənd)	(shär'lət toun)
British Columbia	Victoria	Quebec	Quebec
(brĭt'ĭsh kə lŭm'bĭ ə)	(vĭk tôr'ĭ ə)	(kwĭ bĕk')	(kwĭ bĕk')
Manitoba	Winnipeg	Saskatchewan	Regina
(măn'ə tō'bə)	(wĭn'ə pĕg')	(săs kăch'ə wŏn)	(rĭ jī'nə)
New Brunswick	Fredericton		
(nū' brŭns'wĭk)	(frĕd ər ĭk tən)		
Newfoundland	St. John's	**Territories**	
(nū'fənd lănd')	(sānt jŏnz')		
Nova Scotia	Halifax	Northwest Territories	
(nō'və skō'shə)	(hăl'ə făks)	(nôrth'wĕst' tĕr'ə tô'rĭz)	
Ontario	Toronto	Yukon	Whitehorse
(ŏn târ'ĭ ō)	(tə rŏn'tō)	(ū'kŏn)	(hwīt'hôrs')

Sixty Indian Tribes of North America

Name	Original Home
Algonquin (ăl gŏng'kĭn *or* äl gŏng'kwĭn)	Forest: Quebec
Apache (ə păch'ĭ)	Southwest: Arizona, New Mexico
Arapaho (ə răp'ə hō)	Plains: Colorado, Wyoming
Arikara (ə rĭk'ər ə)	Plains: North Dakota
Blackfeet (blăk'fēt)	Plains: Alberta, Saskatchewan, Montana
Caddo (kăd'ō)	Plains: Arkansas, Louisiana, Texas
Catawba (kə tô'bə)	Forest: North and South Carolina
Cayuse (kī ūs')	Mountains: Oregon
Cherokee (chĕr'ə kĭ)	Forest: North and South Carolina, Georgia
Cheyenne (shī ăn' *or* shī ĕn')	Plains: North and South Dakota
Chickasaw (chĭk'ə sô)	Forest: Mississippi
Chinook (chə nōōk')	Northwest Coast: Washington, Oregon
Chippewa (chĭp'ə wä *or* chĭp'ə wä)	Forest: Minnesota, North Dakota, Ontario
Choctaw (chŏk'tô)	Forest: Mississippi, Alabama
Comanche (kə măn'chĭ)	Plains: Oklahoma, Texas
Cree (krē)	Forest: Manitoba, Saskatchewan
Creek (krēk)	Forest: Georgia, Alabama
Crow (krō)	Plains: Montana, Wyoming
Delaware (dĕl'ə wâr)	Forest: New Jersey, Pennsylvania, Delaware
Flathead (flăt'hĕd)	Plains: Montana
Gros Ventre (grō văn'trə)	Plains: North and South Dakota
Haida (hī'də)	Northwest Coast: British Columbia
Hopi (hō'pĭ)	Southwest: Arizona
Huron (hūr'ən)	Forest: Ontario
Illinois (ĭl'ə noi' *or* ĭl'ə noiz')	Forest: Illinois, Iowa, Missouri

Sixty Indian Tribes of North America *(continued)*

Name	*Original Home*
Iroquois (ĭr′ə kwoi)	Forest : New York, Quebec
Cayuga (kī ū′gə *or* kā ū′gə)	
Mohawk (mō′hôk)	
Oneida (ō nī′də)	
Onondaga	
(ŏn′ən dô′gə *or* ŏn′ən dä′gə)	
Seneca (sĕn′ə kə)	
Kiowa (kī′ə wä)	Plains : South Dakota
Leni-Lenape (lĕn′ĭ lĕn′ə pē′)	
Delaware Indians	
Mandan (măn′dăn)	Plains : North Dakota
Massachuset (măs′ə chōō′sĕt)	Forest : Massachusetts
Miami (mī ăm′ĭ)	Forest : Wisconsin, Michigan, Illinois, Indiana, Ohio
Micmac (mĭk′măk)	Forest : Nova Scotia, New Brunswick
Modoc (mō′dŏk)	Northwest Coast : California, Oregon
Mohican (mō hē′kən)	Forest : New York
Narragansett (năr′ə găn′sĭt)	Forest : Rhode Island
Natchez (năch′ĭz)	Forest : Mississippi
Navaho (năv′ə hō)	Southwest : New Mexico, Arizona
Nez Perce (nĕz′pûrs′)	Mountains : Idaho
Ojibwa (ō jĭb′wä)	Forests : Ontario, Wisconsin, Minnesota
Osage (o′sāj)	Plains : Missouri, Kansas
Pawnee (pô nē′)	Plains : Nebraska, Kansas
Paiute (pī ōōt′)	Plains : Nevada, Utah
Pequot (pē′kwŏt)	Forest : Connecticut
Potawatomi (pŏt′ə wŏt′ō mĭ)	Forest : Michigan, Illinois
Powhatan (pou′ə tăn′)	Forest : Virginia
Pueblo (pwĕb′lō)	Southwest : Arizona, New Mexico
Sac or Sauk (săk *or* sôk)	Forest : Illinois, Iowa, Missouri
Seminole (sĕm′ə nōl)	Forest : Alabama, Georgia
Shawnee (shô nē′)	Forest : Kentucky, Georgia, Ohio, Pennsylvania
Shoshoni (shō shō′nĭ)	Mountains : Idaho, Nevada, Utah, Montana
Sioux (sōō)	Plains : Wisconsin, Minnesota, North and South Dakota
Tuscarora (tŭs′kə rôr′ə)	Forest : North Carolina
Ute (ūt)	Mountains : Colorado, Utah, Arizona, New Mexico
Winnebago (wĭn′ə bā′gō)	Forest : Wisconsin
Zuñi (zōōn′yĭ)	Southwest : New Mexico

Domestic Weights and Measures

Long Measure

1 foot	12 inches
1 yard	3 feet
1 rod or pole	5½ yards
1 furlong	40 rods
1 statute mile	8 furlongs (1,760 yards, or 5,280 feet)
1 league	3 miles

Mariners' Measure

1 fathom	6 feet
1 cable length	100 fathoms, or about 1/10 nautical mile
1 statute mile	5,280 feet
1 nautical mile	6,080.20 feet

Square Measure

1 square foot	144 square inches
1 square yard	9 square feet
1 square rod	30¼ square yards
1 acre	160 square rods or 43,560 square feet
1 square mile	640 acres
1 section	1 square mile

Cubic Measure

1 cubic foot	1,728 cubic inches
1 cubic yard	27 cubic feet
1 perch	24¾ cubic feet
1 cord	8 cord feet, or 128 cubic feet

(A pile 8' long, 4' wide, and 4' high contains 1 cord.)

Dry Measure

1 pint	33.60 cubic inches
1 quart	2 pints
1 peck	8 quarts
1 bushel	4 pecks, or 2,150.42 cubic inches

Liquid Measure

1 fluid dram	.2256 cubic inch
1 fluid ounce	8 fluid drams
1 gill	4 fluid ounces
1 pint	16 fluid ounces or 4 gills
1 quart	2 pints
1 gallon	4 quarts
1 barrel	31½ gallons
1 hogshead	2 barrels

(A standard U.S. gallon, the unit of liquid measure, is the same as the English wine gallon, and contains 231 cubic inches. A gallon of water weighs about 8⅓ pounds. A barrel contains about 4⅛ cubic feet.)

Avoirdupois Weight

1 pound	16 ounces
1 short hundredweight	100 pounds
1 long hundredweight	112 pounds
1 ton	20 hundredweight
1 short ton	2,000 pounds, or 20 short hundredweight
1 long ton	2,240 pounds, or 20 long hundredweight

The Metric System Simplified

The following tables of the metric system of weights and measures have been simplified as much as possible by omitting such denominations as are not in practical, everyday use in the countries where the system is used.

Tables of the System

Length

The denominations in practical use are the millimeter (mm.), centimeter (cm.), and kilometer (km.).

10 millimeters	1 centimeter
100 centimeters	1 meter
1,000 meters	1 kilometer

Weight

The denominations in use are the milligram (mg.), gram (g.), kilogram (kg.), and ton (metric ton).

1,000 milligrams	1 gram
1,000 grams	1 kilogram
1,000 kilograms	1 metric ton

Capacity

The denominations in use are the cubic centimeter (c.c.) and liter (l.).

1,000 cubic centimeters	1 liter

Relation of capacity and weight to length: 1,000 cubic centimeters is, approximately, a liter; and a liter of water weighs one kilogram.

Approximate Equivalents

A meter (39.37 inches) is about a yard.

A kilogram (2.2 pounds) is about two pounds.

A liter (0.91 dry qt. and 1.06 liquid qts.) is about a quart.

A centimeter (0.39 inch) is about 4/10 inch.

A metric ton (2204.6 pounds) is about a long ton.

A kilometer (0.62 mile, or 3280 feet) is about 5/8 mile.

A cubic centimeter is about a thimbleful.

A nickel weighs about five grams.

For postal purposes fifteen grams are considered the equivalent of one half ounce avoirdupois. At the mint a half dollar is considered to weigh 12.5 grams.